Writings

on American History

1960

Compiled by the

National Historical Publications Commission

James R. Masterson, Editor

Joyce E. Eberly, Assistant Editor

U.S. GOVERNMENT PRINTING OFFICE
WASHINGTON : 1972

For sale by the Superintendent of Documents, U.S. Government Printing Office
Washington, D.C. 20402 - Price $5.25 (cloth)
Stock No. 4702–0015

Writings on American History

1960

VOLUME II OF THE ANNUAL REPORT OF THE

AMERICAN HISTORICAL ASSOCIATION

FOR THE YEAR 1962

Foreword

This volume of the Writings on American History, a classified list of books and articles on United States History that were published during 1960, continues a series begun with the issuance of a volume that listed writings published in 1902. Including the present volume the series consists of 48 volumes, covering 50 years. Volumes for the years 1904-5 and 1941-47 have not been prepared.

In 1951 the National Historical Publications Commission assumed responsibility for the preparation of the Writings and for seeing the volumes through the press; it was agreed that they would continue to be published as parts of the Annual Reports of the American Historical Association.

Dr. James R. Masterson and Miss Joyce E. Eberly, members of the Commission's staff, compiled the entries. Mrs. Arney R. Childs, Columbia, South Carolina, prepared the index to this volume.

OLIVER W. HOLMES
Executive Director, National
Historical Publications Commission

JAMES B. RHOADS
Archivist of the United States

Preface

This volume is designed to cite every book and article published during 1960 that has any considerable value for study and research pertaining to the history of the United States from primitive times to the recent past.

The whole history, from the beginning, of the areas now within the United States or under its jurisdiction is here treated as belonging to the history of the United States. The history of Louisiana before 1803, of California before 1846, of Alaska before 1867, of Puerto Rico before 1898, and of other areas not within the original United States is considered to be as much within the scope of the Nation's history as that of the original thirteen States and the colonies from which they developed. The Philippine Islands are regarded as part of the United States from 1898 till the proclamation of their independence, July 4, 1946, and as foreign territory before and since that period.

The list of writings in this volume consists of three divisions, containing respectively (1) writings pertaining to the historical profession--its tasks and methods, its membership, the materials with which it works, and the collectors and custodians of these materials; (2) writings pertaining to the United States as a whole; and (3) writings pertaining to single regions, States, Territories, or dependencies of the United States.

The first and second divisions are subdivided by topic; the third is subdivided geographically. Writings pertaining to the historical profession are listed alphabetically (by author if known, or by title). In the rest of the volume, within each subdivision or part of a subdivision, writings cited with the dates of their subject matter are listed chronologically according to beginning date, and writings cited without such dates are listed alphabetically preceding the dated writings.

Titles that clearly indicate both the nature and the dates of their subject matter are cited without annotation. Titles that are adequate except for dates of subject matter are cited with bracketed dates. Other titles are provided with a minimum of annotation. The presence of bibliographies and bibliographic footnotes (the latter designating sources of facts and of quotations) is indicated by the words "bibliog." and "notes" respectively.

Certain publications are cited in this volume only for special reasons. Argumentative and expository works dealing mainly with current affairs are cited only when they incidentally present historical information that seems difficult to obtain from other sources or that may be useful as a clue to such sources. A few works of which the texts may have little value for historical purposes have been cited because they contain reproductions of maps, prints, or other illustrations of historical value. Also cited are books and articles inadvertently omitted from the volumes for 1948-59.

The main classes of publications deliberately excluded from citation are newspapers; book reviews; historical fiction (when its fictitious character is avowed or clearly recognizable);

juvenile and other elementary works (including textbooks for primary and secondary schools), except those treating somewhat limited subjects in detail; archeological reports on excavations of single prehistoric sites; articles on statutory law when these are purely argumentative and are organized topically; purely critical essays on literary compositions, containing no factual information; genealogical works that include neither documents nor biographical sketches; articles announced or recognized as extracts from forthcoming books; reports of the annual meetings, the membership, the officers, and the receipts and disbursements of learned organizations, public or private; bare lists (as distinguished from descriptive or annotated lists) of accessions of books, manuscripts, and other historical materials; works of general information, such as encyclopedias, dictionaries, and indexes, not dealing primarily or in large part with United States history; and writings concerned entirely with very recent events. The overwhelming quantity of such publications has precluded any effort to examine them systematically for purposes of citation in this volume.

Dates of publication of books are cited according to the practice of the Library of Congress. The date of publication of a single article or document that comprises the whole of an issue of a serial is cited in full, following the form of citation used for books. The year of publication of an article or document forming only a part of an issue of a serial is omitted if the year is 1960.

Articles published in installments continued beyond 1960 are omitted from this volume and will be cited under the year in which their publication was concluded.

Many works deserving citation in this volume may have been overlooked, either because their titles did not indicate that they contain historical subject matter or because they were not available for examination by the editor or were not referred to in the lists and bibliographies that he consulted. Many titles were obtained too late to be examined before the copy for this volume was sent to the printer. These works, and others of the same class issued in 1948-59, will be cited, so far as they become available to the editor, in the volume for 1961. He will welcome correspondence calling such works to his attention.

This volume was compiled mainly in the Library of Congress, which has provided the compilers with all facilities and privileges needed in their work. Certain books and serials were examined in the National Archives Library and the library of the Smithsonian Institution. The editor is grateful to these institutions for courteous and efficient services and also to Dr. H. Bartholomew Cox of the staff of the National Historical Publications Commission for extensive assistance.

JAMES R. MASTERSON

Contents

Page

Page

Page

The Historical Profession

HISTORIANS

THE AMERICAN GENEALOGIST. Evaluation of genealogical writers. Am. geneal., 36:12-15 (Jan). Contents.--V. Col. Charles Edward Banks, 1854-1931, by Walter Goodwin Davis.--VI. Gilbert Cope, 1840-1928, by Milton Rubincam. [1

AMERICAN HISTORICAL ASSOCIATION. Recent deaths. Am. hist. rev., 65:487-91, 778-81, 1047-8; 66:297-8 (Jan-Oct). Notices of deaths of historians, with brief unsigned biographical sketches of some of the deceased. [2

MAURICE WHITMAN ARMSTRONG. Charles A. Anderson--editor [of the Journal of the Presbyterian Historical Society, 1944-59]. Presbyt. Hist. Soc., Jour., 38:9-12 (Mar). [3

FREDERICK CLEVER BALD. Dr. Milo Milton Quaife, 1880-1959. Mich. hist., 44:36-8 (Mar). On his work as author and editor of historical publications, Superintendent of the State Historical Society of Wisconsin, Secretary of the Burton Historical Collection in the Detroit Public Library, and in other ways a promoter of historical studies till the day of his death in a highway accident. [4

HENRY C. BEZOU. Joseph Roger Baudier (1893-1960). La. hist., 1:350-53 (fall). Memorial to "a self-taught writer, researcher, and ecclesiologist," Catholic historian and journalist, author of The Catholic Church in Louisiana. [5

RAY ALLEN BILLINGTON. The American frontier thesis. Huntington Lib. quar., 23:201-16 (May). notes. Includes numerous quotations from the papers of Frederick Jackson Turner in the Huntington Library, and comments on his ideas and his working habits as exhibited in his correspondence and notes. [6

HORACE BAILEY CARROLL. [Dr. Claude Elliott, 1896-1958.] Southw. hist. quar., 63:600-602 (Apr). port., view. On his teaching of history, his historical writings, and his "outstanding library of Texas imprints and manuscripts." [7

ROBERT CRUDEN. The early historical writings of James Ford Rhodes, 1885-1886. Ohio hist. quar., 69:171-8 (Apr). notes. On an article and several reviews of historical works in the Magazine of Western history. [8

DONALD C. CUTTER. To the memory of Hubert Howe Bancroft, 1832-1918. Ariz. and the West, 2:105-6 (summer). port. [9

Sister RAPHAEL DIMOND. Francis Joseph Tschan [1881-1947]: a contemporary Catholic scholar. Am. Cath. Hist. Soc., Rec., 71:31-9 (Mar-Jun). notes. On his teaching and writing of Catholic history. [10

Dr. ARTHUR ADAMS (1881-1960). Natl. Geneal. Soc. quar., 48:161-4 (Sep). On his teaching of English and service as librarian at Trinity College, Hartford, his service as a priest of the Protestant Episcopal Church, and particularly his work in genealogy; with lists of his genealogical publications. [11

JEROME MELVIN EDELSTEIN. A Lincoln family gathering. Lib. Cong. quar. jour., 18:1-4 (Nov). On a gift to the Library of Congress from Lincoln Isham, great-grandson of Abraham Lincoln, of 24 historical biographies by Jacob Abbott or John Stevens Cabot Abbott, published 1854-58, received by Robert Todd Lincoln as gifts from a cousin and from his father, 1857-58; with evidence of Abraham Lincoln's high regard for the Abbott books as historical writing. [12

ESSAY PROOF SOCIETY. In memoriam: Clarence Wilson Brazer, D.Sc., 1880-1956. Essay proof jour., 13:131-58 (Jul 1956). facsim., ports., views. On his accomplishments as "philatelist, historian, antique authority and architect." Partial contents.--Clarence W. Brazer, architect and philatelist, by Julian Blanchard.--Professional tributes by members of the Society in memory of Dr. Clarence Wilson Brazer.--Clarence Wilson Brazer, D. Sc., at home ["Innerwick," Flushing, L.I.], by Edith M. Faulstich. [13

OSCAR JULIUS FALNES. Paul Christian Sinding [1813-87]: an early Scandinavian-American historian. Am.-Scandinavian rev., 48:53-8 (Mar). On his early life and Lutheran ministry in Denmark, his emigration to New York (ca. 1856), his A history of Scandinavia (New York, 1858, and several later editions till 1884), and the obscurity of his later years in New York. [14

BERNARD L. FONTANA. To the memory of Adolph F[rancis] A[lphonse] Bandelier, 1840-1914. Ariz. and the West, 2:1-5 (spring). port. On his standing as "anthropologist in the minds of historians and historian in the minds of anthropologists," who worked in New Mexico and Arizona from 1882 to 1892, and later in Latin America; with "A chronological list of the major works of Adolph F. A. Bandelier relative to the Southwest," 1877-1937. [15

CLINTON HARVEY GARDINER. Prescott ante el mundo. Estudios am., 19:126-40 (Mar-Apr). notes. On the world reputation of William Hickling's 3 major historical works, 1837-47, as shown by reprints, translations, and influence upon other historians. [16

CLINTON HARVEY GARDINER. Prescott's ties with Mexico. Jour. inter-Am. studies, 1:11-26 (Jan 1959). notes. On his acquisition of historical information from Mexico through the agency of Lucas Alamán, Angel Calderón de la Barca, the latter's wife Fanny, and Joaquín García Icazbalceta, 1838-56, and his assistance to Alemán and Icazbalceta in their historical publications. [17

RALPH LOUIS KETCHAM. William Cabell Rives, editor of the Letters and other writings of James Madison [1865]. Va. mag. hist. and biog., 68:131-6 (Apr). port. notes. On his work in preserving and editing the papers of James Madison, 1857-66. [18

HARRY WYNNE KIRWIN (1911-63). James J. Walsh [born 1865]--medical historian and pathfinder. Cath. hist. rev., 45:409-35 (Jan). notes. [19

FRANK JOSEPH KLINGBERG (born 1883). Memoirs of Frank J. Klingberg. P. E. Church, Hist. mag., 29:106-38 (Jun). On the author's early life and reading and his German Methodist upbringing in rural Dickinson County, Kan.; and his studies at the University of Kansas, the University of Wisconsin, and Yale, 1903-11, eventuating in a doctorate in history. [20

MADRID, UNIVERSIDAD DE. Seminario de Estudios Americanistas. En torno a la obra de Guillermo H. Prescott (en su centenario). Por R. Ferrando, L. Cabrero, y F. de P. Solano. Madrid, 1960. 108 p. port. notes. Four essays on his work between 1837 and 1847 as a historian of Mexico and Peru. [21

MARY GREENE NYE (1872-1956). Vt. Hist. Soc., News and notes, 7:61-2 (Apr 1956). On her "research in local and state history" in Vermont and her editing of documents found in "14 old tin trunks containing a mass of old state papers that had been stored in a lower vault in the Secretary of State's office," dated 1800-1840. [22

ARTHUR S. MAYNARD. Dr. Arthur Adams, 1881-1960. N.Y. geneal. and biog. rec., 91:193-4 (Oct). Deals particularly with his work as a genealogist. [23

MUNCY HISTORICAL SOCIETY AND MUSEUM OF HISTORY, Muncy, Pa. Dr. T[homas] Kenneth Wood [1877-1958], founder of the Muncy Historical Society, dies at the age of 81 years. Now and then, 12:129-31 (Jan 1959). On his life in Muncy as a physician, editor of Now and then (1929-57), and founder of the Society in 1936. See also "A portrait of Doctor Wood," by Eugene P. Bertin, President of the Society, containing a photograph and a tribute (12:59-61, Apr. 1958). [24

FRANCIS PARKMAN (1823-93). Letters of Francis Parkman. Edited and with an introduction by Wilbur R. Jacobs. Norman: Univ. of Oklahoma Press [1960]. 2 v. lxv, 204, [2]; xl, 286, [2] p. facsims., map, ports., views. notes. "Published in cooperation with the Massachusetts Historical Society." Letters to various persons, 1841-93, on family matters, his health, his arrangements for transcription of manuscripts (especially by Pierre Margry), his searches for information from individuals, his dealings with publishers, and his political opinions; with an extensive introduction on his life, writings, and ideas, and full notes on the letters. [25

WILLIAM JOHN PETERSEN. Dr. Mildred Throne (1902-1960). Ia. jour. hist., 58:287-8 (Jul). On her life in Iowa, her graduate studies of history, her brief experience as a teacher of history, and her service from 1948 to 1960 as Associate Editor of the Iowa journal of history. [26

HARVEY CARLYLE POLLOCK. Bernhard W[olf] Weinberger [1886-1960], dental historian. Am. jour. orthodontics, 46:595-9 (Aug). port. On his early life in Colorado, his studies at the University of Pennsylvania School of Dentistry and the Angle School of Orthodontics, his dental practice in Brooklyn, his teaching of dental history and literature at the New York University College of Dentistry, and his work in the history of dentistry; with a list of his "orthodontic papers" and his books, 1911-58. [27

MILTON RUBINCAM & KENN STRYKER-RODDA. Charles Carroll Gardner (1883-1960). Natl. Geneal. Soc. quar., 48:218-20 (Dec). Mainly on his work in the genealogy of New Jersey; with a list of his publications. [28

SAM E. SALEM. U[lrich] B[onnell] Phillips and the scientific tradition. Ga. hist. quar., 44:172-85 (Jun). notes. On the traces in his work of "pro-Southern feelings or social attitudes" in spite of his efforts, almost completely successful, "to write history in the scientific tradition of Leopold von Ranke." [29

BERNADOTTE EVERLY SCHMITT. Fifty years of exploring history. Bernadotte E. Schmitt, The fashion and future of history: historical studies and addresses (Cleveland: Press of Western Reserve Univ., 1960), p. 1-13. On the author's studies at Oxford University and the University of Wisconsin, his teaching of history at Western Reserve University and the University of Chicago, and his service from 1945 till 1952 in the historical program of the Department of State. [30

FLOYD CALVIN SHOEMAKER. Forty-five years as editor and author of Missouri history, 1915-1960. Mo. hist. rev., 54:225-30 (Apr). On the author's work as editor of The Missouri historical review and concurrently Secretary of the State Historical Society of Missouri; with a partial list of his publications on Missouri history. [31

WENDELL HOLMES STEPHENSON. Charles W[illiam] Ramsdell [1877-1942]: historian of the Confederacy. Jour. South. hist., 26:501-25 (Nov). notes. Review of his whole career as a historian. [32

TEXAS, UNIVERSITY OF. In memoriam: Rudolph L[eopold] Biesele [1886-1960]. Southw. hist. quar., 64:251-4 (Oct). On his life in Texas, his teaching of history in the University of Texas, and his 3 books and 6 articles on American and particularly Texas history. [33

FREDERICK JACKSON TURNER (1861-1932). The significance of the frontier in American history. ... With an introduction by John Alexander Carroll. El Paso, Tex.: Texas Western College Press for Academic Reprints, 1960. iv, 35, [1] p. notes. (The Academic reprint series.) Paper read 12 Jul. 1893. Appended: "A basic bibliography of the writings of Federick Jackson Turner" (p. 31-2) and "A chronological list of selected writings on Turner and his historical concepts--1921-1959" (p. 32-5). [34

VERMONT HISTORICAL SOCIETY. [Tributes to Arthur Wallace Peach (1886-1956).] Vt. Hist. Soc., News and notes, 7:89-93 (Aug 1956). port. On his life in Vermont as teacher, writer, lecturer, and editor, and from 1949 to 1956 Director and Editor of the Vermont Historical Society. [35

CHARLES VEVIER. "... simplicity, responsibility, honor, and service." John Arthur Garraty, ed., The unforgettable Americans (Great Neck, N.Y.: Channel Press [1960]), p. 281-5. On Brooks Adams as a "philosopher of history," 1894-1927. [36

HARVEY WISH. The American historian: a social-intellectual history of the writing of the American past [since 1630]. N.Y.: Oxford Univ. Press, 1960. viii, [2], 366 p. notes (p. 351-60). Chapters in chronological order on historians or groups of historians, including William Bradford, Thomas Hutchinson, Jared Sparks, Richard Hildreth, George Bancroft, Francis Parkman, John Bach McMaster, Henry Adams, Frederick Jackson Turner, Ulrich B. Phillips, Charles A. Beard, Vernon L. Parrington, and Allan Nevins. [37

HISTORICAL MATERIALS: INDEXES

AMERICAN history periodical index. Volume 3, Number 1[-8], January [-November] 1960. Chicago: Joseph A. Huebner, 1960. 284-384 leaves. Arranged by subject and author in a single alphabet, Frankfort, Kentucky - Giltner, James. [38

BIOGRAPHY index: a cumulative index to biographical material in books and magazines, September 1955-August 1958. Edited by Bea Joseph. Managing Editor: Rita Volmer Louis. N.Y.: H. W. Wilson Co., 1960. x, 1096 p. Vol. 4 in a series. [39

COLUMBIA HISTORICAL SOCIETY, Washington, D.C. Index to Volumes 1 to 48/49 (inclusive), Records of the Columbia Historical Society. By Maud Burr Morris and Laurence F. Schmeckebier. Wash. [1950?]. v, 49 p. Indexes to subjects, illustrations, and authors. [40

INDEX to American doctoral dissertations, 1959-1960. Compiled for the Association of Research Libraries. Ann Arbor: University Microfilms, 1960. 218 p. [41

JEFFERSON COUNTY [W.VA.] HISTORICAL SOCIETY. Index to the Magazine [of the Jefferson County Historical Society], Volumes I to XXV, 1935-1959. Jefferson Co. Hist. Soc., Mag., 25 (1959): 40-44. [42

KANSAS STATE HISTORICAL SOCIETY. Comprehensive index, 1875-1930, to Collections, Biennial reports, and Publications of the Kansas State Historical Society. Compiled by Louise Barry. Topeka, 1959. 514, [1] p. [43

HELEN MOULTON MEANWELL. Some notes on indexing and cataloging. Detroit Soc. Geneal. Research mag., 23:40 (fall 1959). On printed and manuscript indexes in Michigan that are useful to workers in Michigan genealogy. [44

MENNONITE CHURCH. General Conference. Historical Committee. Mennonite historical bulletin index. Volumes I-X (1940-49) [and XI-XX (1950-59). Compiled by] Nelson P. Springer. Mennonite hist. bul., 10(4):[5-8]; 20(4):1-8 (Oct 1949, Oct 1959). [45

ROBERT F. MUNN, comp. Index to West Virginiana. Charleston, W.Va.: Education Foundation [1960]. x, 154 p. Index to articles about West Virginia appearing in 12 West Virginia periodicals, 1871 ff., most of which survived only a few years. [46

SOCIETY OF AMERICAN ARCHIVISTS. General index to The American archivist, Volumes I-XX, January 1938 to October 1957. [Compiled by Dorothy R. Swift.] Cedar Rapids, Ia., 1960. 131 p. [47

SPEECH ASSOCIATION OF AMERICA. An index to Speech monographs, volumes I-XXVI (1934-1959). By Giles Wilkeson Gray. Speech monographs, 27:153-200. [48

U.S. Bureau of Labor Statistics. Subject index of bulletins published by the Bureau of Labor Statistics, 1915-59. [Prepared by M. Frances Marshall and Gladys B. Wash. Wash.: U.S. Govt. Print. Off., 1960.] iii, 102 p. (Its Bulletin 1281.) Includes "annotated listing of bulletins," 1895-1959. [49

U.S. Library of Congress. Manuscript Division. Index to the Abraham Lincoln Papers. Wash., 1960. x, 124 p. facsims., tables. bibliog. (p. vi-vii), notes. (Its Presidents' papers index series.) Index to names of writers and recipients in a body of papers (available also on microfilm) totaling 41 linear feet and ca. 40,000 items, 1833-1916. [50

U.S. Library of Congress. Manuscript Division. Index to the William H. Harrison Papers. Wash., 1960. viii, 10 p. facsim., tables. bibliog. (p. vi), notes. (Its Presidents' papers index series.) Index to names of writers and recipients in a body of papers (available also on microfilm) totaling 3 linear feet and 984 items, 1734-1939, mainly 1796-1841, consisting largely of fragmentary and miscellaneous items surviving the fire that destroyed the main body of the papers of William Henry Harrison in 1858. Includes materials relating to Indian affairs in the Middle West and to the War of 1812. [51

U.S. Library of Congress. Manuscript Division. Index to the Zachary Taylor Papers. Wash., 1960. viii, 9 p. facsims., tables. bibliog. (p. vi-vii). (Its Presidents' papers index series.) Index to names of writers and recipients in a body of papers (available also on microfilm) totaling 631 items, 1814-1931, including papers of Zachary Taylor's son, Richard Taylor (1826-79), Louisiana planter, and a few later materials. As explained in the introduction, the main body of the papers of Zachary Taylor was destroyed when Union soldiers pillaged Richard Taylor's plantation in 1862. [52

HISTORICAL MATERIALS: LISTS AND DESCRIPTIONS

AMERICAN LIBRARY ASSOCIATION. Association of College and Research Libraries. Acquisitions, gifts, collections. College and research lib., 21:93, 159-60, 229, 232, 299, 395-6, 477 (Jan-Nov). Brief accounts of recent acquisitions of books, manuscripts, and other scholarly materials by American college and research libraries. [53

AMERICAN MUSEUM OF FIRE FIGHTING, Hudson, N.Y. A guide to the collections. By Kenneth H[olcomb] Dunshee, Curator. [Hudson, 1960.] 28 p. facsims., flag, plan, ports. (1 col.), views. Account of equipment, photographs, and portraits, mainly from New York City. [54

ARCHIVES OF AMERICAN ART, Detroit. Report of acquisitions, October-December 1959 [through July-September 1960. By Miriam Lucker Lesley, Archivist.] Art quar., 23:69-70, 169-70, 375-7 (spring, summer, winter). On accessions of manuscripts, sketches, photographs, microfilms, tape recordings, and other materials relating to the history of American art and American artists. [55

CALIFORNIA, UNIVERSITY OF, Los Angeles. Library. Guide to special collections in the Library of the University of California at Los Angeles. Los Angeles, 1958. [8], 76, [10] p. (Its Occasional paper 7.) Topical list of manuscripts, pictorial materials, and photoreproductions. [56

COLUMBIA UNIVERSITY. Libraries. Our growing collections. [By] Roland Baughman. Columbia Lib. columns, 9(2):37-45; (3):33-41 (Feb, May). On recently acquired printed, manuscript, and museum materials of special rarity or other interest. [57

GEORGE JAMES FIRMAGE, comp. E. E. Cummings: a bibliography. Middletown, Conn.: Wesleyan Univ. Press [1960]. ix, 129, [1] p. Annotated list of the books, articles, and paintings of Edward Estlin Cummings (born 1894), 1911-59; with detailed formal descriptions of the books. [58

FREDERIC ALLEN WILLIAMS [born 1898], artist. Westerners brand book (N.Y.), 5:82, 94 (1959). port. On "the great collection of Indian, horse, cowboy and other Western material" bequeathed by him to the University of Texas as the Frederic Allen Williams Collection, including portrait heads, Indian sculptures, collections of Indian craftsmanship (textiles, baskets, pottery, utensils, etc.), and his Horse Museum ("several thousand items in which the horse appears as the chief decorative motif," to be expanded to "tell the saga of the horse ... its leading and final role in the process of civilization in the Western United States of America"). [59

ARRELL MORGAN GIBSON. Sources for research on the American Indian. Ethnohistory, 7:121-36 (spring). Annotated list of Federal and other agencies and organizations holding manuscript and pictorial sources, and list of "Published documents and other aids." [60

HENRY E. HUNTINGTON LIBRARY AND ART GALLERY. Acquisitions. [By Carey S. Bliss.] Huntington Lib. quar., 23:95-102, 194-7, 293-7, 395-8 (Nov 1959-Aug 1960). Description of recently acquired manuscripts, imprints, engravings, and paintings of American and European origin, including a high proportion of materials relating to English and American history and literature. [61

HISTORICAL SOCIETY OF WESTERN PENNSYLVANIA. Additions to collections. West. Pa. hist. mag., 43:397-411 (Dec). Annotated list of books, serials, maps, manuscripts, and a few museum articles, acquired Dec. 1959-Dec. 1960. [62

Mrs. HOWARD W. KENT, comp. A catalog of the Thoreau Collection in the Concord Antiquarian Society. Thoreau Soc. bul., 47:[1-4] (spring 1954). List of museum materials (e.g., "the last pen with which Henry D. Thoreau wrote," 4 nails from his cabin at Walden, a cologne bottle that belonged to his mother, a label for pencils made by J. Thoreau & Co.), photographs and lithographs, and a few manuscripts and books. [63

IRVIN KERLAN. The Bernard Meeks Collection: three hundred years of children's books, 1657-1957. Am. book collector, 10(8):6-11 (Apr). facsims. On a collection (in the Library of the University of California at Los Angeles) of "carefully selected books, drawings, manuscripts, peep-shows, games and related materials," ca. 2,000 items. [64

MISSOURI HISTORICAL SOCIETY. Among our new acquisitions. Mo. Hist. Soc., Bul., 16:186-91, 282-7, 363-6; 17:96-101 (Jan-Oct). Detailed descriptions of printed, manuscript, and museum materials. [65

NEW YORK. State Historian. Sights and sounds of New York State history. Compiled by William G. Tyrrell. N.Y. hist., 41:341-56 (Jul). A "listing of audiovisual materials, available as of December 31, 1959 ... 16mm sound motion pictures, 35mm silent filmstrips, and long-playing recordings, which may be used as teaching aids to supply realistic contacts with events and personalities in New York's past." [66

PRINCETON UNIVERSITY. Library. The literary career of William Faulkner: catalogue of an exhibition in the Princeton University Library. By James B. Meriwether. Princeton Univ. Lib. chron., 21:111-64 (spring). facsims., port. Annotated list of 335 manuscripts, typescripts, imprints, and photographs, 1919-57. [67

PRINCETON UNIVERSITY. Library. The world of John James Audubon: catalogue of an exhibition in the Princeton University Library, 15 May-30 September 1959. Compiled by Howard C. Rice, Jr. Princeton Univ. Lib. chron., 21:9-88 (autumn 1959-winter 1960). facsims., port., views. Heavily annotated chronological list of 173 manuscripts, maps, paintings, drawings, sketches, engravings, books and parts of books, etc., with quotations from Audubon and extensive bibliographical information. [68

STATE HISTORICAL SOCIETY OF WISCONSIN. Accessions. Wis. mag. hist., 43:232-5 (spring). Detailed account of manuscripts and museum materials recently acquired. [69

U.S. Library of Congress. Abraham Lincoln: an exhibition at the Library of Congress in honor of the 150th anniversary of his birth. Wash., 1959. iv, 94 p. cartoons, facsims., ports., views. Annotated catalogue of manuscripts, broadsides, pamphlets, books, prints, drawings, photographs, medals, and other materials, 235 entries. [70

U.S. Library of Congress. A catalog of the Alfred Whital Stern Collection of Lincolniana. Wash., 1960. xi, 498 p. port. Text in double columns. Introduction signed: Arthur G. Burton. Annotated topical list (5,201 entries) of books, broadsides, sheet music, prints, a few manuscripts, and medals, sculpture, and other museum materials. [71

VERMONT HISTORICAL SOCIETY. America's earliest press heads Society's exhibits. Vt. Hist. Soc., News & notes, 2(5):1-4 (Jan 1951). views. Brief account of "historical treasures" in the Vermont State Museum, including the press of Stephen Daye. [72

VIRGINIA, UNIVERSITY OF. Library. John Henry Ingram's Poe collection at the University of Virginia: a calendar of letters and other manuscripts, photographs, printed matter, and biographical source materials concerning Edgar Allan Poe assembled by John Henry Ingram. With a prefatory essay on Ingram as a Poe editor and biographer and as a collector of Poe materials, by John Carl Miller. Charlottesville: Univ. of Virginia Press, 1960. xlix, 397 p. Abstracts of materials dated 1817-1915, 1,044 entries. [73

HENRY WILLIS WELLS. Capturing the passing show: Columbia's resources for theatrical research. Columbia Lib. columns, 9(3):21-8 (May). facsim., port. [74

WHAT'S new in the restoration villages. Art in Am., 48(2):114-16, 118 (summer). views. On recent acquisitions by 8 museum villages. [75

YALE UNIVERSITY. Library. The Mexican War, 1846-1848: a collection of contemporary materials presented to the Yale University Library by Frederick W. Beinecke, 1909 S. [Compiled by Jerry E. Patterson.] Yale Univ. Lib. gaz., 34:94-123 p. facsim., view. Description of selected items from 975 groups--"manuscripts, maps, books, pamphlets, broadsides, prints, sheet music," including "materials in Spanish from the Mexican side of the war." [76

Bibliography: Current and Annual

ALABAMA. State Dept. of Archives and History. Some recent accessions of the Department of Archives and History. Compiled by Jessie E. Cobb, Librarian. Ala. hist. quar., 22:277-83 (winter). Annotated list of manuscript collections, maps, newspapers, microfilms, books, and other materials. [77

ALABAMA HISTORICAL ASSOCIATION. Articles on or related to Alabama appearing in current periodicals. Ala. rev., 13:287-90 (Oct). [78

BERTON WENDELL ALLRED, JEFFERSON CHENOWETH DYKES, & FREDERIC GORDON RENNER. Western book roundup. By the Old Bookaroos. Westerners brand book (Chicago), 16(1)-17(10): monthly installments (Mar 1959 - Dec 1960). Brief accounts of recent books about the early West. Also printed: Frontier times, 34(1-4): quarterly installments (winter-fall); True West, 7(3-6): monthly installments (Jan-Aug); Ariz. and the West, 2:198-201, 300-302, 395-8 (summer-winter); Am. book collector, 10(5-10): monthly installments (Jan-Jun). [79

AMERICAN EDUCATIONAL THEATRE ASSOCIATION. Graduate theses in theatre, 1958. [Compiled by] Franklin H. Knower. Educ. theatre jour., 12:128-38 (May). Annual list, nos. 2462-2731. Includes motion pictures, radio, and television. [80

AMERICAN JEWISH COMMITTEE and JEWISH PUBLICATION SOCIETY OF AMERICA. American Jewish bibliography. Compiled by Iva Cohen. Am. Jew. yr. bk., 60 (1959): 341-53; 61 (1960): 403-14. "Books of Jewish interest published in English in the United States," Jul. 1957-Jun. 1959. Annotated. [81

THE AMERICAN JOURNAL OF SOCIOLOGY. Higher degrees in sociology, 1958 [and 1959]. Am. jour. sociol., 65:77-90; 66:67-78 (Jul 1959, Jul 1960). List of master's and doctor's degrees granted by 67 departments of sociology in the United States and Canada. [82

AMERICAN NUMISMATIC SOCIETY. Numismatic literature. [Edited by Richard P. Breaden. Nos. 50-53.] N.Y., [Jan.-Oct.] 1960. 379, [1] p. Lists and abstracts of recent monographic and serial publications relating to coins, medals, tokens, seals, decorations, and paper money. Some of the abstracts are identified by initials of contributors. [83

AMERICAN POLITICAL SCIENCE ASSOCIATION. Doctoral dissertations in political science in universities of the United States and Canada. Compiled by William C. Seyler. Am. pol. science rev., 54:816-34 (Sep). Topical list of dissertations in progress or cently completed. [84

AMERICAN SPEECH. Bibliography. Am. speech, 35:60-72, 143-54, 220-35, 288-97 (Feb-Dec). Annotated lists of recent books and articles, compiled from reports made by a committee of readers. Contents.--Present-day English, by Eric W. Stockton.--General and historical studies, by Elliott V. K. Dobbie.--Phonetics, by Simon Belasco. [85

AMERICAN STUDIES ASSOCIATION OF METROPOLITAN NEW YORK. Committee on Bibliography. Articles in American studies. [Edited by Donald N. Koster.] Am. quar., 12:242-94 (summer). Annotated list (entries 1253-1791), arranged topically from "Art & architecture" to "Sociology & anthropology." [86

BIBLIOGRAPHICAL SOCIETY OF THE UNIVERSITY OF VIRGINIA. A selective check list of bibliographical scholarship for 1956[-58]. By Rudolf Hirsch ... [and] Howell J. Heaney. Studies in bibliog., 11 (1958): 269-90; 12 (1959): 234-54; 13 (1960): 262-83. List of books and articles that are lists or descriptions or that deal with the physical aspects of printed matter. The standards of selection are not stated. [87

JOHN WYATT BONNER, JR., comp. Bibliography of Georgia authors, 1959-1960. Ga. rev., 14:450-74 (winter). Eleventh of a series of annual annotated lists of books by authors born or living in Georgia. [88

KENNETH WALTER CAMERON, comp. Current bibliography on Ralph Waldo Emerson. Emerson Soc. quar., 19: leaves 97-8 (2d quar.). List of books, articles, and theses. [89

THE CANADIAN HISTORICAL REVIEW. Graduate theses in Canadian history and related subjects. Can. hist. rev., 40:260-68 (Sep). Annual list of doctors' and masters' theses. [90

THE CANADIAN HISTORICAL REVIEW. Recent publications relating to

Canada. Prepared in the editorial office of the University of Toronto Press by Marion Pope. Can. hist. rev., 40:87-92, 175-80, 269-72, 364-9 (Mar-Dec). [91

CIVIL WAR HISTORY. A bibliography of Civil War articles. Civil War hist., 6:180-86, 439-43 (Jun, Dec). Current list, arranged topically. [92

COLLEGE OF THE PACIFIC, Stockton, Calif. Library. Theses and dissertations accepted in partial fulfillment of the requirements for advanced degrees at the College of the Pacific, 1957-1960. Stockton, 1960. [3], 19 leaves. See "History and political science" (leaves 10-11) and titles pertinent to American history under other headings. Continues a list (1957) for the years 1913-56. [93

CORNELL UNIVERSITY. New York State School of Industrial and Labor Relations. Recent publications. [Compiled by] Curtis W. Stucki. Indus. and labor rel. rev., 13:96-114, 274-87, 420-36, 619-33 (Oct 1959-Jul 1960). Topical list of books, pamphlets, and articles on labor, particularly labor-management relations. [94

DEUTSCHE GESELISCHAFT FÜR AMERIKASTUDIEN. Deutsche amerikakundliche Veröffentlichungen, August 1957-Dezember 1959 (mit Nachträgen zu früheren Bibliographien). [Compiled by] Bernhard Fabian. Jahrbuch für Amerikastudien, 5:215-44. Topical list of books and articles, 673 entries. [95

WOOD GRAY, comp. United States. Am. hist. rev., 65:462-8, 723-8, 1029-34; 66:275-81 (Jan-Oct). List of recent articles and documents in periodicals, relating to the general and regional history of the United States. [96

HARVARD UNIVERSITY. Graduate School of Business Administration. Baker Library. Studies in enterprise, 1959: a selected bibliography. By Lorna M. Daniells. Bus. hist. rev., 33:217-39 (summer). Second annual supplement to the Library's Studies in enterprise (1957), listing "histories of industries, histories of specific corporate functions, episodes in the history of companies, and histories of trade associations and trade unions, as well as over-all histories of companies and biographies of businessmen." [97

HAWAII LIBRARY ASSOCIATION. Current Hawaiiana (quarterly bibliography). [Vol. 15, no 4-vol. 16, no. 4. Honolulu:] Issued ... through the cooperation of the Gregg M. Sinclair Library, Univ. of Hawaii, 1959-60. 5 issues. [8, 12, 8, 11, 16] leaves. [98

HISTORIA MEXICANA. Bibliografía histórica mexicana. [Compiled by] Susan Uribe de Fernández de Cordoba. Hist. mexicana, 9:620-60 (Apr-Jun). Topical list of recent books and articles, nos. 7406-8205, including works on Mexican relations with the United States. [99

HISTORICAL abstracts, 1775-1945: bibliography of the world's periodical literature. ... Eric H. Boehm, Editor. ... Vol. 5, no. 1[-4, and index number]. ... March[-December] 1959. N.Y.: [Historical Abstracts] 1959. [2], 90, [6], 91-219, [5], 221-319, [7], vi, 321-349, [1] p. Abstracts 1-3600, each with name or initial of abstracter, arranged in part topically, in part by period, in part by region; with "Bibliographical news," "Notes and news," and "World list of historical periodicals." [100

HISTORICAL SOCIETY OF DELAWARE. Recent publications of Delaware interest. Del. hist., 9:101-4 (Mar). Annotated list. [101

HOWARD UNIVERSITY. Bureau of Educational Research. Current literature bibliography. [Compiled by Dolores C. Leffall, Dorothy B. Porter, and Doris M. Hull.] Jour. Negro educ., 28:55-65, 154-62, 454-66; 29:59-69, 168-80, 479-89 (winter 1959-fall 1960). Lists of books, bulletins, pamphlets, "periodical references," and theses relating to Negroes and their education throughout the world. [102

INTERNATIONAL INSTITUTE FOR SOCIAL HISTORY. Bibliography. Internatl. rev. social hist., 4 (1959): 116-75, 285-360, 480-548; 5 (1960): 97-164, 291-360, 487-544. Abstracts of recent books relating to the social history of all parts of the world, arranged in 2 sections: "General issues" and "Continents and countries." [103

KANSAS STATE HISTORICAL SOCIETY. Kansas history as published in the press. Kan. hist. quar., 26: 104-8, 229-30, 341-2, 457-60 (spring-winter). References to articles on Kansas history in recent issues of Kansas newspapers. [104

FRANKLIN HAYWARD KNOWER, comp. Graduate theses and dissertations on broadcasting: 1956-1958.

Jour. broadcasting, 4:77-87 (winter). Continues a list compiled by Stuart W. Hyde (2:55-90, winter 1958). [105

THE LIBRARY QUARTERLY. Graduate theses accepted by library schools in the United States, 1959-60. [Compiled by] Howard W. Winger. Lib. quar., 30:274-9 (Oct). [106

MENNONITE LIFE. Mennonite bibliography, 1959. By John F. Schmidt and Nelson P. Springer. Mennonite life, 15:93-5 (Apr). List of books and articles (including a few titles in French or German). [107

MICHIGAN. Historical Commission. Michigan bibliography: 1959. [Compiled by] Donald R. Brown. Mich. hist., 44:147-87 (Jun). Annotated topical list of books, articles, and "unpublished materials" (theses, typescripts); with supplements to previous lists for the years 1950-58. [108

MISSISSIPPI. Dept. of Archives and History. Manuscript acquisitions of the Department of Archives and History [during 1959]. Jour. Miss. hist., 22:82-6 (Jan). [109

MISSISSIPPI HISTORICAL SOCIETY. A bibliography of theses and dissertations [completed and in progress] relating to Mississippi, 1959. Compiled by Willie D. Halsell. Jour. Miss. hist., 22:63-79 (Jan). [110

MISSISSIPPI VALLEY HISTORICAL ASSOCIATION. Recent articles of general interest. Miss. Valley hist. rev., 46:780-91; 47:190-200, 377-88, 566-75 (Mar-Dec). Quarterly lists of "articles of general interest" and articles concerning East, South, Middle West, or Far West. [111

MODERN LANGUAGE ASSOCIATION OF AMERICA. American Literature Group. Committee on Bibliography. Articles on American literature appearing in current periodicals. Am. lit., 31:516-38; 32:105-25, 235-52, 355-7 (Jan-Nov). Chairman of committee: C. Hugh Holman. Arranged in 4 periods, with a "General" section at the end. [112

MODERN LANGUAGE ASSOCIATION OF AMERICA. Anglo-German Literary Relations Group. Anglo-German literary bibliography for 1959. [Edited by] John R. Frey. Jour. Eng. and Germanic philol., 59:491-6 (Jul). Annual list of books and articles dealing with German studies and criticisms of English and American literature and with English and American studies of German literature. [113

MODERN LANGUAGE ASSOCIATION OF AMERICA. Anglo-German Literary Relations Group. Bibliography Americana Germanica. [Edited by Dieter Cunz.] Am.-German rev., 26(5):28-35 (Jun-Jul). Nineteenth annotated list of books, articles, and theses dealing with the Germans in America. [114

NATIONAL COUNCIL OF TEACHERS OF ENGLISH. Abstracts of English studies. [Boulder, Colo., 1958-60.] 3 v. 420; 480; 610 p. Abstracts, by signed contributors, of 6,652 articles and documents relating to the English language and literature in all parts of the world, published recently in serials in English or in foreign languages. Arranged in each volume alphabetically by title of serial. Each volume indexed. [115

NEW ENGLAND QUARTERLY. A bibliography of New England, 1959. [Compiled by] Mrs. Wendell Garrett. New Eng. quar., 33:128-42 (Mar). List of articles dealing with the history of New England. [116

NEW YORK PUBLIC LIBRARY. Reference Department acquisitions during 1958-59. N.Y. Pub. Lib., Bul., 64:88-94, 261-72 (Feb, May). Includes acquisitions of rare books, prints, music, maps, and manuscripts of American interest. [117

NEW YORK STATE HISTORICAL ASSOCIATION. Articles of interest to Yorkers. Selected by Dorothy C. Barck. N.Y. hist., 41:81-3, 232-4, 319-21, 448-50 (Jan-Oct). Current list of recent articles on the history of New York. [118

NEW YORK STATE HISTORICAL ASSOCIATION. Local history in the Library. [Compiled by] Dorothy C. Barck, Librarian and Editor. N.Y. hist., 41:84-8 (Jan). Discussion of books on New York local history published during 1959. [119

NEWBERRY LIBRARY. Notable accessions of the Library, 1959. Newberry Lib. bul., 5:130-56 (Apr). views. See particularly the section on the Ayer Collection. [120

OHIO HISTORICAL SOCIETY. A survey of publications in Ohio history and archaeology, August 1959-July 1960. Compiled by S. Winifred Smith. Ohio hist. quar., 69:379-93 (Oct). Annotated topical list of books, articles, and theses. [121

OREGON HISTORICAL SOCIETY. News notes. Ore. hist. quar., 61:85-93, 237-52, 360-67 (Mar-Sep). References to articles on Oregon history in recent periodicals and Oregon newspapers. [122

PAN AMERICAN INSTITUTE OF GEOGRAPHY AND HISTORY. Commission on History. Bibliografía de historia de America (1956-[1960]). Rev. hist. Am., 47-48:307-75, 703-55; 49-50:261-314, 591-683 (Jun 1959-Dec 1960). Edited by Agustín Millares Carlo (last installment by Susana Uribe de Fernández de Córdoba), with notes by several contributors including the editor. Abstracts of books and articles, arranged by topics, thereunder by periods, and thereunder by the regions and states of North and South America. Nos. 17968-19444, continuing previous installments. [123

PENNSYLVANIA, UNIVERSITY OF. Library. Gifts [of books and manuscripts] to the Rare Book Collection. Lib. chron., 26:37, 105-7 (winter, spring). Signed: N. M. W. Description of recent acquisitions. [124

DONALD M. POWELL, comp. Current Arizona bibliography. Ariz. quar., 16:79-82, 269-71 (spring, autumn). Annotated list of "separately published works about Arizona except those from official state and federal sources." [125

WILLIAM STEVENS POWELL, comp. North Carolina bibliography, 1958-1959. N.C. hist. rev., 37:271-8 (Apr). List of "books dealing with North Carolina or by North Carolinians published during the year ending June 30, 1959." [126

PRINCETON UNIVERSITY. Library. New & notable. Princeton Univ. Lib. chron., 21:172-82, 246-54; 22:42-6 (spring-autumn). On various accessions of manuscripts and imprints, including papers of F. Scott Fitzgerald and Gen. Adam Badeau. [127

RAILROAD MAGAZINE. Books of the rails. Railroad mag., 71(1-6): bimonthly installments (Dec 1959-Oct 1960). Annotated lists of recent books about railroads and their equipment. [128

JAMES IRVIN ROBERTSON, JR. The continuing war. Civil War hist., 6: 84-6, 187-91, 298-303, 444-7 (Mar-Dec). Commentary on recent books about the Civil War. [129

RUTGERS UNIVERSITY. Library. Gifts and acquisitions [mainly manuscripts and rare imprints]. Rutgers Univ. Lib., Jour., 23:58-62 (Jun). Annual list, signed: Herbert F. Smith. [130

ELSDON COLES SMITH, comp. Bibliography of personal names, 1959. Names, 8:172-9 (Sep). Annotated list of books and articles. [131

SOUTHERN FOLKLORE QUARTERLY. Folklore bibliography for 1959. By R[alph] S[teele] Boggs and Sarah Elizabeth Roberts. [Gainesville: Univ. of Florida in cooperation with the South Atlantic Modern Language Assoc., 1960.] 75 p. (Southern folklore quarterly, v. 24, no. 1.) World bibliography, arranged topically, 23d in an annual series of which the first 22 numbers were compiled by Boggs. Not annotated. [132

SOUTHERN HISTORICAL ASSOCIATION. Bibliographical. Jour. South. hist., 26:153-5, 277-95, 434-7, 577-93 (Feb-Nov). News notes about and lists of bibliographical publications, periodical articles, and manuscript and film collections of value for students of Southern history. [133

SOUTHERN SPEECH ASSOCIATION. A bibliography of speech and theatre in the South for the year 1959. Ralph T. Eubanks, V. L. Baker, and James Golden, editors. South. speech jour., 25:333-44 (summer). Annotated topical list of books, articles, and theses. [134

SPEECH ASSOCIATION OF AMERICA. A bibliography of rhetoric and public address for the year 1959. James W. Cleary, editor. Speech monographs, 27:201-38 (Aug). Annotated topical list of books and articles, mainly in English, relating to these subjects throughout the world. Consists of sections on ancient, medieval and Renaissance, and modern public address, pulpit address, radio and television, debate, and discussion. [135

SPEECH ASSOCIATION OF AMERICA. Graduate theses: an index of graduate work in speech, XXVII. [Compiled by] Franklin H. Knower. Speech monographs, 27:259-78, 328-39 (Aug, Nov). tables. List of master's and doctor's theses accepted, arranged by name of university, nos. 9695-10397, with a subject index. [136

THOREAU SOCIETY. Additions to the Thoreau bibliography. [Compiled by Walter Roy Harding.] Thoreau Soc.

bul., 22-57: quarterly installments (Jan 1948-fall 1956). Annotated list of books and articles. [137

TWENTIETH CENTURY LITERATURE. Bibliography Committee. Current bibliography. Twentieth cent. lit., 4:162-82 (Jan 1959). Abstracts of recent critical and historical articles on literature and authors of the 20th century. [138

U.S. Library of Congress. Manuscript Division. Manuscripts. [By Dorothy S. Eaton and the staff of the Manuscript Division.] Lib. Cong. quar. jour., 16:177-91 (May). notes. Annual report of acquisitions, including photoreproductions of manuscripts. [139

U.S. Library of Congress. Music Division. Music. [By Edward N. Waters, Assistant Chief.] Lib. Cong. quar. jour., 17:13-39 (Nov). facsims. Annual report of acquisitions, including printed and manuscript music, recordings, and related books and manuscripts. [140

U.S. Library of Congress. Rare Book Division. Rare Books. [By Frederick R. Goff, Chief.] Lib. Cong. quar. jour., 17:192-5 (May). facsims. Annual report of acquisitions. [141

UTAH HISTORICAL SOCIETY. [List of recent articles on Utah history.] Utah hist. quar., 28:90-91, 184-6, 416-19 (Jan, Apr, Oct). [142

INEZ RANEY WALDENMAIER, comp. Newly-published family histories and miscellaneous records. Geneal. newsletter, 6:63-86, 99-145 (fall, winter). List of books, articles, and recently organized manuscript records, arranged by name of family. [143

INEZ RANEY WALDENMAIER, comp. Where to find newly-published county histories. Geneal. newsletter, 6:7-8, 17-48 (spring, summer). List of books, pamphlets, items from serials, and newly organized manuscript records, arranged by name of State and thereunder by name of county. [144

CLYDE CAMERON WALTON. Recent Civil War writing. Midwest quar., 1:73-86 (Oct 1959). Bibliographical essay. [145

BRUCE E. WHEELER. Lincolniana in 1959. Hobbies, 64(12):27-30, 63-4, 84, 88 (Jan). ports., view. Extensively annotated list of writings about Lincoln, his family, and his contemporaries, printed in 1959. [146

WRITINGS on American history, 1952. Compiled for the National Historical Publications Commission. James R. Masterson, Editor. [Wash.: U.S. Govt. Print. Off., 1958.] xiii, 573 p. (American Historical Association. Annual report for 1954, v. 2.) Annotated topical list of books and articles, 7,919 entries. "Serials cited" (p. 423-43). [147

WRITINGS on American history, 1953. Compiled for the National Historical Publications Commission. James R. Masterson, Editor. [Wash.: U.S. Govt. Print. Off., 1960.] xiv, 705 p. (American Historical Association. Annual report for 1955, v. 2.) Annotated topical list of books and articles, 9,152 entries. "Serials cited" (p. 521-42). [148

YALE UNIVERSITY. Library. Recent acquisitions [mainly imprints and manuscripts]. Yale Univ. Lib. gaz., 34:134-5, 185-8; 35:48-9, 94-9 (Jan-Oct). [149

ZEITSCHRIFT FÜR ANGLISTIK UND AMERIKANISTIK. Bibliographie: aus dem Jahresverzeichnis der deutschen Hochschulschriften. [Compiled by Klaus Hansen.] Zeitschrift für Anglistik, 8:106-10, 220-22, 328-30, 442. List of doctoral dissertations accepted by German universities in the fields of English and American studies, particularly in language and literature, 1954-57 (nos. 3779-4003). [150

WORK IN PROGRESS

AMERICAN EDUCATIONAL THEATRE ASSOCIATION. Doctoral projects in progress in theatre arts, 1959. [Compiled by] Albert E. Johnson. Educ. theatre jour., 12:124-7 (May). Eighth annual survey, nos. 553-649. Includes motion pictures, radio, and television. [151

THE AMERICAN JOURNAL OF SOCIOLOGY. Doctoral dissertations in progress, 1958 [and 1959]. Am. jour. sociol., 65:91-9, 305; 66:79-86 (Jul, Nov 1959, Jul 1960). List of dissertations in progress in 41 departments of sociology in the United States and Canada. [152

AMERICAN LITERATURE. Research in progress. [Compiled by Daniel W. Patterson.] Am. lit., 31:510-15; 32: 103-4, 232-4, 351-4 (Jan-Nov). Current list of dissertations on individual authors, dissertations on topics of a general nature, and other research in progress, dissertation topics dropped, and dissertations completed. [153

AMERICAN STUDIES ASSOCIATION. American studies dissertations in progress. [Compiled by] Albert Van Nostrand. Am. quar., 12:295-304 (summer). [154

MENNONITE LIFE. Mennonite research in progress. By Melvin Gingerich and Cornelius Krahn. Mennonite life, 15:92-3 (Apr). List of doctor's and master's theses and "other projects." [155

NEW YORK. State Historian. New York State and local historical research in progress. Ninth annual listing--1959. N.Y. hist., 41:312-18 (Jul). Signed: Albert B. Corey, State Historian. [156

ZEITSCHRIFT FÜR ANGLISTIK UND AMERIKANISTIK. Bibliographie: in Arbeit befindliche Dissertationen. [Compiled by Hans Lange.] Zeitschrift für Anglistik, 8:102-5. List of doctoral dissertations in progress in 8 German and 2 Austrian universities in the fields of English and American studies, particularly in language and literature. [157

Bibliography: Noncurrent

RAY ALLEN BILLINGTON. A historian views the Everett D. Graff Collection. Newberry Lib. bul., 5:214-23 (Dec). On the collection of Western Americana presented by Graff to the Newberry Library. [158

BOSTON ATHENAEUM. A Boston Athenaeum miscellany: catalogue of an exhibition in honor of the visit of the Grolier Club on February 11, 1950. By Walter Muir Whitehill. Boston, 1950. ix, 17 p. facsims. (Robert Charles Billings Fund publications. Catalogue series, 1.) Detailed descriptions of several books, broadsides, manuscripts, and drawings, with an introduction on the library and its holdings. Includes items from the library of George Washington. [159

ELIZABETH FRENCH BOYD. The William A. Hughes Collection of Modern Literature [in the Rutgers University Library]. Rutgers Univ. Lib., Jour., 23:53-7 (Jun). [160

KENNETH WALTER CAMERON, comp. Harvard manuscript resources for students of Lowell. Emerson Soc. quar., 19: leaves 39-40 (2d quar.). List of manuscripts and a few pamphlets and other imprints relating to James Russell Lowell or written by him. [161

CORNELL UNIVERSITY. Labor Management Documentation Center. Guide to the records. Ithaca, N.Y. [1960. 1], 1, 1A, 2-61 leaves. Topical list of personal papers, papers of agencies and firms, court records, microfilms of serials and other materials, pamphlets and releases, reports, etc., assembled by an agency established in 1952 "to collect primary source material for research and study." [162

THOMAS EDWARD DRAKE. The Quaker Collection, Haverford College Library. Anna (Cox) Brinton, ed., Then and now: Quaker essays, historical and contemporary, by friends of Henry Joel Cadbury (Phila.: Univ. of Pennsylvania Press [1960]), p. 228-35. On a special collection of books and manuscripts, within a library founded in 1833. [163

WALTER ROY HARDING, comp. The Francis H. Allen Papers: a catalog. Thoreau Soc. bul., 34:[1-2]; 50:[1-2] (Jan 1951, winter 1955). List of papers of Francis Henry Allen (1866-1953) in the Concord Free Public Library, containing letters to Allen as editor of Thoreau's writings, typescripts of Thoreau-related materials, and newspaper clippings, pamphlets, and offprints of articles. On Allen's Thoreau publications, 1906-36, see no. 26 (Jan. 1949), including a portrait of Allen. [164

WILLARD ROUSE JILLSON, comp. A bibliography of the Cumberland River Valley in Kentucky and Tennessee: citations of printed and manuscript sources touching upon its history, geology, cartography, coal, iron, salt, fluorspar, phosphate, clays, oil and gas, with annotations. Frankfort, Ky.: Perry Pub. Co., 1960. [2], 46 p. map. Chronological list of 243 books, articles, maps, and manuscripts, 1674-1960. [165

LEWIS GASTON LEARY. Knickerbocker literature in the Benjamin Collections. Columbia Lib. columns, 9(2):22-7 (Feb). facsim. On literary New York City in the times of Washington Irving and James Fenimore Cooper as illustrated in a collection of books, periodicals, and manuscripts by or relating to Park Benjamin "from the mid-1830's to the mid-1860's," given to Columbia University by William Evarts Benjamin and augmented by members of his family. [166

MICHIGAN STATE MEDICAL SOCIETY. Bibliographic notes of Beaumont interest. Mich. State Med. Soc., Jour., 58:755-7 (May 1959). Annotated alphabetical list of materials relating to William Beaumont, M.D. (1785-1853). [167

NEW YORK PUBLIC LIBRARY. The Whitney Cookery Collection. By Lewis M. Stark. [Second edition.] N.Y., 1959. 27 p. Reprinted with corrections from the Library's Bulletin, Feb. 1946. Annotated list of manuscripts and "printed books," 218 entries, describing materials assembled by Helen (Hay) Whitney (1875-1944). [168

NEW YORK SCHOOL OF SOCIAL WORK. Library. Bibliography of the Charles Lionel Chute Collection, consisting largely of source material on child labor, 1899-1913. Arranged and annotated by Audrey S. Chute in consultation with the library staff. N.Y., 1959. 12 leaves. Lists of pamphlets, clippings, and manuscripts relating to child labor, industrial accidents, etc., collected by Chute (1882-1953) as special agent for the National Child Labor Committee and Executive Secretary of the Pennsylvania Child Labor Association. [169

M. HELEN PERKINS, comp. A preliminary checklist for a bibliography on Jane Addams [1860-1935]. Compiled ... under the direction of the Rockford Area Jane Addams Centennial Committee. Rockford, Ill., 1960. [2], 42, [1] p. Annotated topical list of books, articles, and manuscripts by and about Jane Addams. [170

PITTSBURGH, UNIVERSITY OF. Dept. of Music History and Literature. Library. Catalogue of the manuscripts and printed music of Adolph M. Foerster [1845-1927] in the Music Library, University of Pittsburgh. [Compiled] by S. Philip Kniseley. Pittsburgh: Univ. of Pittsburgh, 1960. [2], vi, 43 leaves. facsims. Includes an account of his early life in Pittsburgh, his musical education in Leipzig, his work as a composer, and his teaching at the Conservatory of Music, Fort Wayne, Ind., and Western Pennsylvania Female College, Pittsburgh. [171

THE POUND NEWSLETTER. The survey of library holdings. Pound newsletter, 1: leaves 10-13 (Jan 1954). List of "holdings of rare editions, manuscripts, letters, etc.," by or about Ezra Pound, in 89 libraries. [172

WILLIAM HENRY REICHERT, comp. Bibliography and index of the geology and mineral resources of Washington, 1937-1956. Olympia: State Print. Plant, 1960. iii, [3], 721 p. (Washington. Division of Mines and Geology. Bulletin 46.) Revision of thesis (M. L.)--Univ. of Washington. Continues a bibliography, 1814-1936, compiled by W. A. G. Bennett, published in 1939 as Bulletin 35 of the Division of Geology. List of books and articles in alphabetical order by name of author; with an index. Appended: "Bibliography and index of theses, student papers, and reports on geology and mineral resources of Washington, 1904-1956" (p. 601-76), and "List and index of unpublished reports and papers on geology and mineral resources of Washington, 1926-1956" (p. 677-721). [173

MARTIN SCHMIDT. History in a waterproof vault. Old Oregon, 38(5): 2-4 (Apr-May 1958). facsims. (1 double), port. On the Oregon Collection of the University of Oregon Library, consisting of manuscript and printed materials about Oregon or by Oregonians. [174

ROBERT ALAN SIGAFOOS, comp. Guide to public affairs research in Pennsylvania ... commentary on the status of research, with a selected bibliography of materials published from 1940 to 1959 on governmental, economic, social, and physical resource subjects. University Park: Pennsylvania State Univ., 1959. [3] leaves, A14, iv, 97 p. Topical list of books, pamphlets, articles, and unpublished theses. [175

THOMAS HUGH SPENCE, JR. The Historical Foundation [of the Presbyterian and Reformed Churches] and its treasures. Revised edition. Montreat, N.C.: Historical Foundation Publications, 1960. xii, [4], 171 p. ports., views. bibliog. (p. 159-60), notes. 1st ed. 1956. History of an organization founded in 1927; account of its holdings of personal papers and other manuscripts and of books and periodicals (p. 53-131); and catalogue of its records of Presbyterian and Reformed bodies of the United States (p. 147-55). [176

STANFORD UNIVERSITY. Libraries. The Papers of Bernard De Voto [1897-1955]: a description and a checklist of his works, with a tribute by Wallace Stegner. [Stanford? Calif., 1960. 2], 62 p. port. "Benny De Voto's America," a biographical and critical introduction by Wallace Stegner, on De Voto's accomplishments as "novelist, historian, critic, and editor" (p. 7-28); "A description of the Bernard De Voto Papers in the Stanford University Libraries," totaling more than 40,000 items, including much of his correspondence for almost 40 years and manuscripts and working papers of his major writings (p. 29-39); and "A checklist toward a bibliography of the writings of Bernard De Voto," based upon a thesis by Robert Edson Lee--Univ. of Iowa, 1957 (p. 40-62), including both his published and his unpublished writings. [177

COLTON EDWARDS STORM. The Everett D. Graff Collection in the Newberry Library. Newberry Lib. bul., 5:190-213 (Dec). facsims., map, port., views. On a collection of books, pamphlets, broadsides, maps, and manuscripts relating to the early history of the Ohio Valley and the Trans-Mississippi West. [178

KENN STRYKER-RODDA. That genealogical quagmire: New Jersey. Natl. Geneal. Soc. quar., 48:59-71 (Jun). notes. On sources of genealogical information in New Jersey or pertaining to it. [179

TEXAS, UNIVERSITY OF. Humanities Research Center. Sinclair Lewis [1885-1951]: an exhibition from the Grace Heger Lewis - Sinclair Lewis Collection. [Austin] 1960. 28 p. facsims., ports. Catalogue of manuscripts and imprints by or about Lewis, and of photographs. [180

JAMES R. TIGNER & DOUGLAS L. GILBERT, comps. A contribution toward a bibliography on the black bear. [Fort Collins? Colo.] 1960. [2] leaves, 42 p. (Colorado. Dept. of Game and Fish. Technical bulletin 5.) List of books, articles, and theses available in Colorado that contain information about Ursus americanus, including early references to its distribution and habits. [181

VIRGINIA, UNIVERSITY OF. Library. The Barrett Library, Charles Timothy Brooks [1813-83]: a checklist of printed and manuscript works of Charles Timothy Brooks in the Library of the University of Virginia. Compiled by Fannie Mae Elliott and Lucy Clark. Charlottesville: Univ. of Virginia Press, 1960. [8], 9 p. List of poems, translations from German, and sermons, totaling 16 titles, 1845-83. [182

VIRGINIA, UNIVERSITY OF. Library. Oliver Wendell Holmes [1809-94]: a checklist of printed and manuscript works of Oliver Wendell Holmes in the Library of the University of Virginia. Compiled by Anita Rutman and Lucy Clark, the manuscripts by Marjorie Carver. Charlottesville: Univ. of Virginia Press, 1960. [8], 109 p. port. Annotated topical list of materials in the Barrett Library. [183

VIRGINIA, UNIVERSITY OF. Library. Robinson Jeffers [born 1887]: a checklist of printed and manuscript works of Robinson Jeffers in the Library of the University of Virginia. Compiled by Anita Rutman and Lucy Clark, the manuscripts by Marjorie Carver. Charlottesville, Va.: Univ. of Virginia Press, 1960. [8], 41 p. Annotated topical list of materials in the Barrett Library. [184

ROBERT HANSON WOODWARD, comp. Harold Frederic [1856-98]: a bibliography. Studies in bibliog., 13:247-57. Annotated list of books and articles by and about Frederic, 1887 ff., and lists of his published and unpublished letters and of his manuscripts. [185

YALE UNIVERSITY. Library. Monroe, Wakeman, and Holman Collection. Catalogue of the Monroe, Wakeman, and Holman Collection of the Pequot Library, Southport, Connecticut. Deposited in the Yale University Library. New Haven, 1960. xi, [1], 522 p. facsims. On the Pequot Library Association, Southport, Conn., founded in 1887 by the Rev. William H. Holman (minister there from 1877 till ca. 1934), Virginia Marquand Monroe, and Mary Catherine Hull Wakeman, and the manuscripts and rare books collected for it by Holman, partly at the expense of the co-founders; with an annotated list of 855 early American imprints and 1,063 manuscripts, the latter including the papers of Joel Barlow. [186

BOOKS, PAMPHLETS, BROADSIDES, AND ARTICLES IN SERIALS

RICHARD DANIEL ALTICK & ANDREW H. WRIGHT, comps. Selective bibliography for the study of English and American literature. N.Y.: Macmillan [1960]. xii, 138 p. Alternate pages blank (p. 11-107). Annotated topical list. [187

AMERICAN COLLEGE OF SURGEONS. Library. A catalogue of the H. Winnett Orr Historical Collection, and other rare books in the Library of the American College of Surgeons. [Compiled by L. Marguerite Prime and Kathleen Worst, with an introduction by Sumner L. Koch.] Chicago, 1960. xxi, 198, [1] p. facsims., port. Catalogue (2,289 entries) of works relating to the history of surgery; with a biographical introduction on Hiram Winnett Orr (1877-1956) as a surgeon in Nebraska, his contributions to the progress of surgery, and his interest in its history. [188

AMERICAN STUDIES ASSOCIATION OF NEW YORK STATE. Writings on the theory and teaching of American studies. [Edited by Charles L. Sanford.] Am. quar., 12:305-9 (summer). Topical, annotated list of books and articles. [189

DEE ANDERSON. Reference material on American souvenir spoons. Antiques jour., 15(12):22-3, 25 (Dec). facsims. On books, advertisements, catalogues, and other sources of information, 1891 ff. [190

ARCTIC INSTITUTE OF NORTH AMERICA. Arctic bibliography. Prepared for and in cooperation with the Department of Defense. ... Edited by Marie Tremaine. Vol. IX. [Wash.:] Dept. of Defense, 1960. xiii, 1599 p. Abstracts of books and articles, entries 49087-56278, mainly recent, relating to the whole area within the Arctic Circle and various areas outside or partly outside it, including Alaska and the Aleutian Islands and much of Canada. Arranged in a single alphabet by name of author. [191

HERSCHEL CLAY BAKER, comp. Hyder Edward Rollins [1889-1958]: a bibliography. Cambridge: Harvard Univ. Press, 1960. [10], 51 p. port. Annotated chronological list of books and articles, 1914-58, mainly on English literature of the Elizabethan and Romantic periods, including editions of literary works; with a preliminary biographical sketch. Appended: "A list of doctoral dissertations written under the direction of Hyder Edward Rollins," at Harvard, 1930-58 (p. 33-41). [192

PHYLLIS BALL. The first hundred: foundations of a university library. Lawrence Clark Powell, ed., The Southwest of the bookman ([Los Angeles: Univ. of California at Los Angeles Library] 1959), leaves 4-9. From Arizona librarian, Jan. 1950. On the first 100 books acquired by the University of Arizona Library, 1891, now segregated as a collection; with a list of the books. [193

FRANCIS EARLE BARCUS, comp. A bibliography of studies of radio and television content, 1928-1958. Jour. broadcasting, 4:355-69 (fall). Based on thesis--Univ. of Illinois, 1959. List of books, articles, and theses. [194

WILLIAM PUSEY BARLOW, JR., comp. The Allen Press--a bibliography. Book Club Calif., Quar. news letter, 25:34-41 (spring). Detailed physical descriptions of the publications of the Press (originally the Press of Lewis & Dorothy Allen, later the L-D Press), printed at San Francisco and elsewhere, 1940-59. [195

DWIGHT WAYNE BATTEAU. Science fiction, prophet & critic: Harvard's collection of an esoteric genre. Harvard alumni bul., 60:209-11, 223 (30 Nov 1957). facsim., port. [196

HENRY PUTNEY BEERS, comp. Bibliographies in American history: guide to materials for research. [Paterson] N.J.: Pageant Books, 1959 [c1938. 2], xv, 487 p. Reprint of the second edition (1942) without change or addition. List, 7,806 entries, of books and articles that are bibliographies or that contain bibliographies of American history. [197

JOHN TERRY BENDER, comp. The publications of the Westgate Press, 1929-32: a check list for collectors ... with a prologue and an epilogue by Oscar Lewis. Book Club Calif., Quar. news letter, 25:54-9 (summer). Heavily annotated list of books and "minor pieces" (with Lewis as "Editor-Author" and Robert A. Grabhorn as "Typographer-Printer"), printed in San Francisco. [198

BIBLIOGRAPHICAL SOCIETY OF THE PHILIPPINES. Checklist of Philippine Government documents, 1917-1949. Compiled by Consolación B. Rebadavia ... Edited by Natividad P. Vergoza and Pacifíco M. Austria. Quezon City: Univ. of the Philippines Library, 1960. [2], xv, 817 p. Annotated list, 6,469 titles, of the publications "of all departments, bureaus, offices and other agencies of the Philippine government"; with an index including topical entries. [199

JACOB NATHANIEL BLANCK, comp. Bibliography of American literature. Compiled ... for the Bibliographical Society of America. Volume three: Edward Eggleston to Bret Harte. New Haven: Yale Univ. Press, 1959. xxi, 482 p. facsims., views. "Selective list" of "the native literature

America read in book form," i.e. "the many-faceted product called belles-lettres," exclusive of works published before the Revolution or written by authors who have died since 1930; with detailed physical descriptions of the books cited. This volume: entries 5088-7569, consisting of information about works of 34 authors. [200

T. Y. BOOTH, comp. The cliché: a working bibliography. Bul. bibliog., 23:61-3 (Sep-Dec). Selective list of books and articles, 1935-60. [201

CLARENCE WILSON BRAZER (1880-1956), comp. Bibliography of U.S. essays & proofs. Essay proof jour., 13:247-8 (Oct 1956). Chronological list of books and articles, 1888-1930. [202

JAMES BROWN IV. Child welfare classics. Social service rev., 34:195-202 (Jun). notes. Assessment of selected books deserving consideration in the history of child welfare, published 1824, 1872, 1902-46. [203

PENELOPE L. BULLOCK, comp. Michigan bibliographies and indexes. Ypsilanti: Eastern Michigan Univ. [1960]. vi, 30 p. Annotated alphabetical list, 96 entries, of "bibliographies and indexes that are devoted exclusively or primarily to the State of Michigan and were issued between 1921 and 1960." [204

HARVEY L. CARTER. The Far West in American history. Wash.: Service Center for Teachers of History [1960. 2]. 24 p. notes. (Service Center for Teachers of History. Publication 26.) Critical essay on the main books dealing with this subject. [205

A CHECKLIST of explications [of poems by Ezra Pound]. Pound newsletter, 5: leaves 20-21; 6: leaves 16-19 (Jan, Apr. 1955). Contents.--I: the pre-Canto poetry.--II: the Cantos. Signed: P.B. [206

THOMAS DIONYSIUS CLARK, ed. Travels in the Old South: a bibliography. Volume three. The ante bellum South, 1825-1860: cotton, slavery, and conflict. Norman: Univ. of Oklahoma Press [1959]. xviii, 406 p. Heavily annotated list of 506 books of description and travel by American and foreign observers. Contents.--I. The cotton South, 1826-1835, by James W. Patton.--II. A decade of nationalism, 1836-1845, by Charles S. Sydnor.--III. The slavery South at noontide, 1846-1852, by Robert G. Lunde.--IV. The South in sectional crisis, 1852-1860, by F. Garvin Davenport. [207

H. TREVOR COLBOURN, ed. The reading of Joseph Carrington Cabell: "A list of books on various subjects recommended to a young man . . ." Studies in bibliog., 13:179-88. notes. Reading lists prepared in 1800 by St. George Tucker, Thomas Jefferson, and Joseph Priestley for the "educational guidance" of young Cabell; with editorial remarks on the contents of the lists as a clue to reading in 1800, and some account of Cabell's later assistance to Jefferson in establishing the University of Virginia Library. [208

STUART M. COONEY, comp. Analysis of broadcast literature: periodical publications in law. Jour. broadcasting, 1:290-302 (summer 1957). Annotated list of articles in legal periodicals, 1920-55. [209

STUART M. COONEY, comp. Analysis of broadcasting literature: periodical publications of economics [1920-55]. Jour. broadcasting, 1:181-5 (spring 1957). Annotated list of articles. [210

STUART M. COONEY, comp. Analysis of broadcast literature: the Quarterly journal of speech. An annotated bibliography of articles on broadcasting and related subjects published in the QJS from 1915 to 1955. Jour. broadcasting, 1:91-6 (winter 1957). [211

FREDERICA DE LAGUNA, comp. Selected bibliography on the history of anthropology in America. Selected papers from the American anthropologist, 1888-1920, ed. Frederica De Laguna (Evanston, Ill.: Row, Peterson [1960]), p. 888-915. Annotated list of books and articles. Contents.--1. The history of the discipline.--2. Anthropological personnel and personalities.--3. Anthropological organizations.--4. Yearly survey of anthropological activities.--5. Anthropology as an academic discipline. [212

GERTRUDE EVELYN DOLE & ROBERT LEONARD CARNEIRO, comps. Bibliography of the published writings of Leslie A. White. Gertrude E. Dole & Robert L. Carneiro, eds., Essays in the science of culture: in honor of Leslie A. White (N.Y.: Crowell [1960]), p. 486-97. Annotated list of books, articles, and reviews, 1921-59, dealing mainly with cultural anthropology. [213

NADINE DONY, comp. Tennessee Williams: a selected bibliography. Mod. drama, 1:181-91 (Dec 1958). List of books and articles by and about him, 1945-58. See also addenda, compiled by Charles A. Carpenter, Jr., and Elizabeth Cook, 2:220-23 (Dec 1959). [214

JEFFERSON CHENOWETH DYKES, comp. A bibliographical check list of the writing of Samuel Stone Hall. Am. book collector, 10(7):15-18 (Mar). List of his novels and short stories, published 1877-1903, mainly in Beadle's New York Dime Library, Beadle's Half Dime Library, Beadle's Pocket Library, and Beadle's weekly. [215

JOHN EDMUNDS & GORDON BOELZNER, comps. Some twentieth century American composers: a selective bibliography. ... With introductory essay by Nicholas Slonimsky. Volume II. N.Y.: New York Public Library, 1960. 55 p. ports. Reprinted with additions and corrections from the Bulletin of the New York Public Library, Jul. and Aug. 1959. Vol. I published in 1959. Annotated list of writings by and about 17 composers. Not a list of their compositions. For Part III see the Bulletin, 64:361-76 (Jul.), adding 16 composers. [216

ELZA IVAN EDWARDS, comp. Desert treasure: a catalog-bibliography. Los Angeles: Edwards and Williams, 1948. [3], C-1 through C-30, [3], 42 p. Briefly annotated catalogue of 226 books in alphabetical order by title (including many that have no bearing upon California); and "Desert treasure: a bibliography," listing in order of publication, 1874-1945, books that describe California deserts. [217

ELZA IVAN EDWARDS, comp. Desert voices: a descriptive bibliography. Los Angeles: Westernlore Press, 1958. xxviii, 215, [2] p. facsims., views. Heavily annotated list of books and selected articles relating to the Mojave Desert, the Colorado Desert, and the High Desert. Includes "Appendix B: Partial record of journals, diaries, narratives, accounts, reports, notes, etc. of pioneers crossing the California deserts" (p. 185-92), and "Appendix C: Check-list of scientific and technical items relating to California deserts" (p. 193-203). [218

ERNEST M. ESPELIE, comp. Abraham Lincoln, 1860-1960: books and pamphlets in the Augustana College Library. O. Fritiof Ander, ed., Lincoln images: Augustana College centennial essays (Rock Island, Ill.: Augustana College Library, 1960), p. 137-51. Annotated list, 265 titles, arranged topically, of "Lincoln literature." [219

CLARA EVELYN (HALLARD) FAWCETT, comp. Bibliography--dolls. Hobbies, 65(3):36, 40 (May). List of books useful to collectors. [220

RAYMOND FIELDING, comp. Broadcast literature in motion picture periodicals: a bibliography. Jour. broadcasting, 3:172-92 (spring 1959). List of 627 articles from 19 journals, 1922-57. [221

CAROLYN FOREMAN. An analysis of publications issued by the American Library Association, 1907-57. Rochester, N.Y.: Univ. of Rochester Press for the Assoc. of College and Research Libraries, 1960. Micro-opaque copy of typescript. vii, 199 leaves reproduced on 3 cards (7.5 x 12.5 cm.). Thesis (M.L.S.)--Univ. of Texas. [222

ADA GIACCARI, comp. La fortuna di E. A. Poe in Italia: nota bibliografica. Studi americani, 5:91-118. Annotated lists of translations (1858-1958), Italian editions of English texts and of translations into languages other than Italian (1918-57), Italian criticism (1870-1958), and foreign criticism in Italy (1922-58). [223

GORDON D. GIBSON, comp. A bibliography of anthropological bibliographies: the Americas. Current anthropol., 1:61-75 (Jan). [224

VEDDER M. GILBERT, comp. The career of Maxwell Anderson: a check list of books and articles [by and about him, 1918-58]. Mod. drama, 2:386-94 (Feb). [225

GORDON GREB, comp. Analysis of broadcast literature: the Journalism quarterly, 1948-1958. Jour. broadcasting, 3:244-51 (summer 1959). List of articles. [226

STEPHEN GREENE, comp. An annotated list of 50 bridge books relating primarily to covered bridges. Brattleboro, Vt.: Book Cellar, 1960. 7 p. 11 x 23 cm. [227

LENNOX BOUTON GREY. Cultivating literary audiences. National Council of Teachers of English, Perspectives on English: essays to honor W. Wilbur Hatfield (N.Y.: Appleton-Century-Crofts [1960]), p. 69-88. notes. Bibliographical essay on writings,

1909-60, about American attitudes toward literature. [228

GROLIER CLUB, New York. Catalogue of an exhibition of historical and literary Americana, from the collections of Thomas W. Streeter and C. Waller Barrett, together with additions from the American Antiquarian Society and the Yale University Library, held in the exhibition hall of the Grolier Club, September 1959. N.Y., 1960. 47 p. Annotated list (104 items) of imprints, 1493-1854. [229

EDWARD ROBERT HAGEMANN & PHILIP C. DURHAM, comps. James M[allahan] Cain, 1922-1958: a selected checklist. Bul. bibliog., 23:57-61 (Sep-Dec). List of his articles, plays, stories, and novels, and their translations. [230

GEORGE LABAN HARDING, comp. The published writings of Carl Irving Wheat [born 1892]. ... With an appreciation by George P. Hammond. San Francisco, 1960. [2], ix, 20, [3] p. Annotated list of publications, 1912-60, on legal subjects, California history, fine printing in California, and the cartography of the West, including editions of documents of Western history; with a biographical sketch of Wheat as "the historian, cartographer, essayist, humorist, and bon vivant." [231

WALTER ROY HARDING, comp. A preliminary checklist of the editions of Walden [1854-1951]. Thoreau Soc. bul., 39:[2-3] (spring 1952). [232

LORENE ANDERSON HAWLEY & ALAN W. FARLEY, comps. Kansas imprints, 1854-1876: a supplement. Topeka: Kansas State Historical Soc., 1958. 89, [1] p. Supplement to Check list of Kansas imprints, 1854-1876, published in 1939 by the Historical Records Survey as no. 10 of the American Imprints Inventory. Contains 405 numbered addenda. [233

JAMES HAYDOCK, comp. Jack London: a bibliography of criticism. Bul. bibliog., 23:42-6 (May-Aug). List of "books, pamphlets, articles and some newspaper references about Jack London published between the years 1900 and 1955," and a few before and after that period. [234

FREDERICK G. KILGOUR. The Library of the Medical Institution of Yale College and its Catalogue of 1865. [New Haven:] Printed for the Yale Medical Library at the Carl Purington Rollins Printing-Office of the Yale Univ. Press, 1960. 74 p. facsims., tables. notes. Account of the Library, 1814-65, and catalogue of its contents (p. 23-68), based upon a manuscript catalogue prepared by Courtney Smith Kitchel (died 1931), a Yale senior. [235

BERTRAM WALLACE KORN. A proposal to the membership of the American Jewish Historical Society for a new American Jewish bibliography. Am. Jew. Hist. Soc., Pub., 50:68-72 (Sep). [236

JOE WALKER KRAUS. Book collections of five colonial libraries: a subject analysis. Ann Arbor: University Microfilms, 1960. Positive microfilm of typescript. [312] leaves. Thesis--Univ. of Illinois. Abstracted: Dissert. abstracts, 20:4666-7 (Jun). Analysis of catalogues and lists of books at Harvard, College of William and Mary, Yale, College of New Jersey (Princeton), and College of Rhode Island (Brown), 1638-1793. [237

DAN H. LAURENCE, comp. Robert Nathan [born 1894): a bibliography. New Haven: Yale Univ. Library, 1960. xi, 97 p. port. List mainly of novels and poems, 1916-59, with annotations. [238

HENRY GODDARD LEACH. The publications of the American-Scandinavian Foundation. Am.-Scandinavian rev., 48:237-40 (Sep). On The American-Scandinavian review, founded in 1913, and the books published by the Foundation. [239

ROBERT EDSON LEE, comp. The Easy Chair essays of Bernard De Voto: a finding list. Bul. bibliog., 23:64-9 (Sep-Dec). Annotated list of the 243 essays in Harper's magazine, 1935-56. [240

LITERARY history of the United States . . . Bibliography supplement. Edited by Richard M. Ludwig. N.Y.: Macmillan Co., 1959. xix, 268 p. Selective bibliography for publications issued in the decade 1948-58, supplementing vol. 3 of Literary history of the United States. [241

LIVINGSTONE COLLEGE, Salisbury, N.C. Carnegie Library. An annotated bibliography on Joseph Charles Price (1882-1893), founder of Livingstone College. Compiled at Livingstone College, 1956, by Louise M. Rountree, assistant librarian. [Salisbury, N.C.] c1960. [2], 10 leaves. Refers briefly to the life of Price (1854-93), Negro

Methodist minister, orator, and college president. [242

LIVINGSTONE COLLEGE, Salisbury, N.C. Carnegie Library. An index to biographical sketches and publications of the bishops of the A.M.E. Zion Church. Compiled by Louise M. Rountree, ass't librarian. Salisbury, 1960. [2], 18, [7] leaves. List of books and articles by and about the bishops of the African Methodist Episcopal Zion Church serving between 1822 and 1956. [243

ADELAIDE B. LOCKHART, comp. The H. M. Marvin Bruce Rogers Collection. Yale Univ. Lib. gaz., 35:53-60 (Oct). Annotated list of 20 books designed by Rogers (selected from more than 450 volumes, more than a hundred broadsides, leaflets, and other ephemera, and a number of autograph letters, all in the collection). [244

CHARLES GRANT LOOMIS, comp. Bibliography of the writings of Archer Taylor. Wayland Debs Hand & Gustave Otto Arlt, eds., Humaniora: essays in literature, folklore, bibliography, honoring Archer Taylor on his seventieth birthday (Locust Valley, N.Y.: J. J. Augustin, 1960), p. 356-74. Chronological annotated list, 1916-60, of books, articles, and reviews relating to German literature, to folklore in many parts of the world (including riddles and proverbs), and to the history of bibliography. [245

ROBERT HARRY LOWIE (1883-1957). Appendix: Syllabus of a seminar on work of Robert H. Lowie. Lowie's selected papers in anthropology, ed. Cora Du Bois (Berkeley: Univ. of California Press, 1960), p. 495-509. Annotated topical bibliography of writings by and about Lowie, compiled by him as the basis for an imaginary "seminar on his own work." [246

JANE MADDOX. Another fifty: Children's catalog. Wilson lib. bul., 34:145, 148 (Oct 1959). On the H. W. Wilson Company's Children's catalog, an annotated catalog of juvenile literature," 1909-59, "the best seller of all the Company's serial publications." [247

WILLIAM MATTHEWS, comp. American diaries: an annotated bibliography of American diaries written prior to the year 1861. Compiled by William Matthews with the assistance of Roy Harvey Pearce. Boston: J. S. Canner, 1959. xiv, 383 p. 1st ed. 1945. Annotated list of printed diaries in English, arranged chronologically by date of diary, 1629-1860. [248

JEROME MAZZARO, comp. The achievement of Robert Lowell [born 1917], 1939-1959. Detroit: Univ. of Detroit Press, 1960. [8], 41 p. Contemporary poets series, 2.) List of writings by Lowell, mainly poems, and writings about him. [249

AMELIA MELNIK, comp. The writings of Ruth Strang. Teachers College rec., 61:464-76 (May). Annotated list of writings on guidance and student personnel, reading and communication, health education, psychology and mental health, general education, gifted children, group work, and testing, 1923-60. [250

JACK D. MEZIROW & DOROTHEA BERRY, comps. The Literature of liberal adult education, 1945-1957. Compiled ... for the Center for the Study of Liberal Education for Adults. N.Y.: Scarecrow Press, 1960. x, 308 p. Abstracts of books and articles. [251

MIDDLE STATES COUNCIL FOR THE SOCIAL STUDIES. Bibliography Committee. Bibliography of historical fiction and biography of the Middle Atlantic States [New York, New Jersey, Pennsylvania, Delaware, Maryland]. N.Y. [1958]. ii, 26 p. (Middle States Council for the Social Studies. Resource bulletin 1.) Annotated list. [252

ROBERT W. MILLER, comp. Die amerikanische Deutschlandpolitik, 1945-1955: amtliche amerikanische Publikationen über Deutschland. United States policy towards Germany, 1945-1955: U.S. Government documents on Germany. Frankfurt/Main: Forschungs-institut der Deutschen Gesellschaft für Auswärtige Politik, 1956. 40 p. (Aktuelle Bibliographien des Europa-Archivs, 12.) [253

MINNESOTA. Statehood Centennial Commission. Centennial Literature Group. A selected bio-bibliography: Minnesota authors [living and deceased]. St. Paul, 1958. v, 79, [2] p. Biographical dictionary of about 700 authors of books published between 1830 and 1958 (particularly "fiction, poetry, history, essays, criticism, and the humanities in general"), who were born in Minnesota, lived there at least 6 years, or now are living there. [254

NATIONAL COUNCIL FOR THE SOCIAL STUDIES. World History Bibliography Committee. World history book list for high schools: a selection for supplementary reading. Alice W. Spieseke, Chairman. Wash. [1959]. viii, 119 p. (National Council for the Social Studies. Bulletin 31.) Heavily annotated list. [255

EARL NEHRING, comp. Selected bibliography of periodical literature on American politics, 1940-1958. . . . Revised by Ray Nichols, Jr., [and] Ed Graham. [Lawrence:] Kansas Citizenship Clearing House, Dept. of Political Science, Univ. of Kansas, 1958. [2], 62 leaves. On cover: Governmental Research Center, University of Kansas. [256

NEW YORK PUBLIC LIBRARY. Rare Book Division. Checklist of additions to Evans' American bibliography in the Rare Book Division of the New York Public Library. Compiled by Lewis M[orgrage] Stark and Maud D. Cole. N.Y.: New York Public Library, 1960. xii, 110 p. List of American imprints issued before 1801 that are not listed by Charles Evans in his chronological list of such publications. [257

NEW YORK STATE LIBRARY, Albany. Checklist of books and pamphlets in American history. Albany, 1960. [8], 82 p. forms. 39 cm. Text in 2 columns. Alphabetical list printed from punched cards, indicating name of author, short title, date, and "class mark." Does not include the Library's "uncataloged government documents" and its "considerable pamphlet and rare book material that has not been cataloged." [258

FREDERICK ABBOTT NORWOOD. Methodist historical studies, 1930-1959. Church hist., 28:391-417; 29:74-88 (Dec 1959, Mar 1960). Commentary on and survey of 336 books and articles, arranged topically; with a list of the titles. [259

OREGON STATE LIBRARY, Salem. Oregon: frontier of the future. [Salem, 1959.] ii, 66 p. Preface signed: Hazel E. Mills, Oregonia Librarian. Annotated topical list of books and pamphlets, "designed primarily for the adult general reader interested in learning more about Oregon, of the romance of the State's history and the promise of its future." [260

J. CARLYLE PARKER, comp. An annotated bibliography [sic] of the history of Del Norte and Humboldt Counties. Based on a preliminary study by R. Dean Galloway. [Arcata, Calif.:] Humboldt State College Library, 1960. [2], v, 87, [2] p. Annotated topical list of books and articles, 519 entries, with an index. [261

PENNSYLVANIA, UNIVERSITY OF. Edgar Fahs Smith Memorial Library. Catalog of the Edgar Fahs Smith Memorial Collection in the History of Chemistry. Boston: G. K. Hall, 1960. [6], 524 p. 37 cm. Text in triple columns. Facsimile reproduction of the "author-title card catalogue." [262

CLARENCE STEWART PETERSON, comp. 1955 supplement to bibliography of county histories of the counties in the 48 States. [n. p., 1955. 3], 11 leaves. Addenda to a list issued in 1935 and supplemented in 1944, 1946, and 1950. [263

GEORGE EWALD PETTENGILL, comp. Contributions to a bibliography of Arlington County. Arlington hist. mag., 1(3):3-6, 60; (4):39-42, 49 (Oct 1959, Oct 1960). Alphabetical lists of books and articles. [264

BERNARD H. PORTER, comp. The first publications of F. Scott Fitzgerald [1896-1940]. Denver: A. Swallow [1960]. 11 p. Annotated list of his published books, short stories, articles, and verses, including those published after his death. [265

THE POUND NEWSLETTER. Bibliography. Pound newsletter, 1-10: quarterly installments (Jan 1954 - Apr 1956). List of publications by Ezra Pound issued since Jan. 1951, of recent writings about him, and of additions to John Hamilton Edwards, A preliminary checklist of the writings of Ezra Pound (1953). [266

DONALD M. POWELL, comp. An Arizona gathering: a bibliography of Arizoniana, 1950-1959. Tucson: Arizona Pioneers' Historical Soc. [1960. 10], 77, [1] p. (Arizona Pioneers' Historical Society. Pamphlet series, 2.) Annotated list of 681 "separately published items of non-fiction." [267

W. D. QUESENBERY, JR., comp. Ellen Glasgow: a critical bibliography. Bul. bibliog., 22:201-6, 230-36 (May-Dec 1959). List of writings by and about her, 1897-1958, and of portraits. [268

JACK DE VERE RITTENHOUSE, comp. New Mexico Civil War bibliography, 1861-1865: an annotated checklist of [28] books & pamphlets. Houston: Stagecoach Press, 1960. [2], 19, [5] p. [269

PAULINE AUGUSTA SEELY & RICHARD BURL SEALOCK, comps. Place name literature, United States and Alaska, 1946-1951. Names, 6:26-50 (Mar 1958). Annotated list of books and articles, forming a second supplement to Sealock and Seely, Bibliography of place name literature (1948). [270

EUGENE PAUL SHEEHY & KENNETH A. LOHF, comps. Sherwood Anderson [1876-1941]: a bibliography. Los Gatos, Calif.: Talisman Press, 1960. 125 p. facsims., port. Annotated list of writings by and about Anderson. [271

CHARLES SHETLER, comp. Guide to the study of West Virginia history. Morgantown: West Virginia Univ. Library, 1960. vii, 151 p. Bibliography. Contents.--1. Town, county, and regional history [arranged alphabetically by name of county].--2. Topical studies. [272

ALICE WINIFRED SPIESEKE, comp. Social studies curriculum and methods: a bibliography of National Council for the Social Studies publications. Wash.: National Council for the Social Studies, 1955. v [i. e. vi], 56 p. Topical list of the contents of the Council's yearbooks, bulletins, curriculum bulletins, resource bulletins, etc., and of Social education, 1927-54. [273

DAVID H. STAM, comp. A bibliography of the published writings of Harry Miller Lydenberg, 1942-1960. N.Y. Pub. Lib., Bul., 64:298-302 (Jun). List of books and articles on libraries and librarianship and various subjects in American history and literature. Continues a list published in 1943. [274

DORA STEINGLASS, comp. A bibliography of the writings of Joshua Bloch. Abraham Berger, Lawrence Marwick, & Isidore S. Meyer, eds., The Joshua Bloch memorial volume: studies in booklore and history (N.Y.: New York Public Library, 1960), p. 180-219. Annotated lists of books, articles, and book reviews, 1918-58, in Hebrew, Yiddish, and English, mainly on Jewish subjects, particularly Jewish literature and authors; with an index. [275

RUTH M. STEMPLE, comp. Kenneth Roberts: a supplementary check-list. Bul. bibliog., 22:228-30 (Sep-Dec (1959). Addenda to a list compiled by George Albert, 1942-43. [276

STANLEY STEWART, comp. Carson McCullers, 1940-1956: a selected checklist. Bul. bibliog., 22:182-5 (Jan-Apr 1959). List of writings by and about her. [277

RAYMOND TOOLE STOTT, comp. Circus and allied arts: a world bibliography, 1500-1957. ... Volume one[-two]. Derby, Eng.: Harpur & Sons [1958-60]. 2 v. 185; 291 p. facsims., views. Heavily annotated list (4402 entries) of books and pamphlets, including sections on history, biography (Philip Astley, Phineas Taylor Barnum, Buffalo Bill, and Adah Isaacs Menken), "Technical" (acrobatics, equitation, juggling, animal training, etc.), "Phénomènes" (the "Hottentot Venus," the Siamese Twins, etc.), the circus in literature and art, fiction about the circus, etc. To be completed by a third volume. On the title page of vol. 1 the author's name appears as R. Toole Stott; on that of vol. 2, as R. Toole-Stott; and in the foreword to vol. 2, by D. L. Murray, as "R. Toole Stott." [278

THOMAS WINTHROP STREETER, comp. Bibliography of Texas, 1795-1845. ... Part II. Mexican imprints relating to Texas, 1803-1845. Cambridge: Harvard Univ. Press, 1956. xxiv, 283 p. bibliog. (p. xvii-xxi). Forms vol. 3 (Entries 671-1026) of a series of volumes begun in 1955, consisting of full transcriptions of titles, full physical descriptions, and extensive notes, with locations. Appended (p. 261-5): "Official government periodicals of Coahuila and Texas." [279

THOMAS WINTHROP STREETER, comp. Bibliography of Texas, 1795-1845. ... Part III. United States and European imprints relating to Texas. Volume I, 1795-1837 [and Volume II, 1838-1845]. Cambridge: Harvard Univ. Press, 1960. 2 v. xlii, 278; [6], 281-677 p. bibliog. (p. xxix-xxxviii). Entries 1027-1661 of a series of 5 volumes, 1955-60. Appended: "Speeches on Texas in the Congress of the United States, 1836-1845, printed in the appendix to the Congressional globe" (nos. A 1 - A 99); and "New entries for Parts I, II, and III, and corrections or changes in present entries" (entries 1632-1661 and other information). [280

EDWARD BENJAMIN SWANSON, comp. A century of oil and gas in

books: a descriptive bibliography. N.Y.: Appleton-Century-Crofts [1960]. xiii, [3], 214 p. Text in double columns. Sponsored by the American Petroleum Institute. Annotated topical list of books relating to the petroleum industry and trade throughout the world. [281

THOMAS TORRANS, comp. General works on the American Indian: a descriptive bibliography. Ariz. and the West, 2:79-103 (spring). Detailed commentary on 45 books, published 1841-1959. [282

RICHARD TUBER, comp. Broadcast rights: a bibliography. An annotated bibliography of articles published in legal literature from 1920 to 1955. Jour. broadcasting, 2:263-72 (fall 1958). [283

UNION UNIVERSITY, Schenectady. Library. Catalog of that portion of John Bigelow's library not represented by cards in the Library of Congress author catalog. Cataloged by Frances Shaver Smith. Schenectady: Union College Library, 1959. [10], 212 p. facsim. bibliog. (p. [9-10]). Reproductions of some of the cards for a collection of "some 8,000 volumes," bequeathed to Union College in 1952, relating to Emanuel Swedenborg and other mystics, the history of France, and a variety of other subjects. [284

U.S. Bureau of American Ethnology. River Basin Surveys. Lists of reports, articles, and notes relating to the salvage program published in other series. (As of April 1, 1959.) U.S., Bureau of American Ethnology, River Basin Surveys, River Basin Surveys papers, nos. 15-20, ed. Frank H. H. Roberts, Jr. (Wash.: U.S. Govt. Print. Off., 1960 [U.S., Bureau of American Ethnology, Bulletin 176]), p. 307-21. Alphabetical list of publications resulting from work of the Inter-Agency Archeological Salvage Program, dealing with sites doomed to be flooded behind dams, published 1947-59. [285

U.S. Bureau of Commercial Fisheries. Annotated bibliography on biology of American menhaden. By John W. Reintjes, James Y. Christmas, Jr., and Richard A. Collins. Wash.: U.S. Govt. Print. Off., 1960. iv, 297-322 p. (U.S. Fish and Wildlife Service. Fishery bulletin 170.) "Deals chiefly with the American menhaden, Brevoortia tyrannus (Latrobe), and the gulf menhaden, B. patronus Goode." Includes titles published as early as 1709, and many published before 1900. [286

U.S. Dept. of Health, Education, and Welfare. Library. References to the origin and development of social security in the United States [1935-60]. Social security bul., 23:71-4 (Aug). Annotated list of publications of Congress, the Social Security Administration, and a few private publishers. [287

U.S. Library of Congress. General Reference and Bibliography Division. The American Civil War: a selected reading list. Compiled by Donald H[enry] Mugridge. [Wash., 1960.] 24 p. Annotated topical list of books. [288

U.S. Office of Education. 1937-1959: publications [of the Office of Education]. Compiled by Beryl Parke and Zelma E. McIlvain. [Wash.: U.S. Govt. Print. Off., 1960.] v, 157 p. Lists, with author, subject, and title indexes. [289

U.S. Office of Military History. Reader's guide II. Compiled by the Chief Historian [Stetson Conn]. Wash., 1960. viii, 145 p. (United States Army in World War II: Master index.) "Descriptive sketches" of the volumes composing the series entitled United States Army in World War II, authorized in 1946 (53 volumes published or in press, about 25 more in preparation). Supersedes Reader's guide I (1955). [290

CLYDE CAMERON WALTON. An agonizing reappraisal: "Has the Lincoln theme been exhausted?" O. Fritiof Ander, ed., Lincoln images: Augustana College Centennial essays (Rock Island, Ill.: Augustana College Library, 1960), p. 99-135. Topical bibliography of writings about Lincoln; with an introductory essay. [291

RICHARD WERBNER, comp. A bibliography of writings by Paul Radin. Stanley Diamond, ed., Culture in history: essays in honor of Paul Radin (N.Y.: Columbia Univ. Press for Brandeis Univ., 1960), p. 1001-10. Chronological annotated list of publications, 1906-59, mainly concerning the languages and customs of primitive peoples, especially the Winnebago Indians. [292

WILLIAM WHITE, comp. Frank Norris: bibliographical addenda. Bul. bibliog., 22:227-8 (Sep-Dec 1959). Addenda to Kenneth A. Lohf and

Eugene P. Sheehy, Frank Norris: a bibliography (1959). [293

WILLIAM WHITE, comp. Nathanael West: a bibliography. Studies in bibliog., 11 (1958): 207-14. notes. Annotated topical list of books and articles by and about West. [294

EUGENE PAUL WILLGING & HERTA HATZFELD, comps. Catholic serials of the nineteenth century in the United States: a descriptive bibliography and union list. Second series: part two. Wisconsin. Wash.: Catholic Univ. of America Press, 1960. [8], 125 p. table. bibliogs. (p. 1-2, 107-18). Detailed histories of the Catholic serials established in Wisconsin before 1901, following each till its discontinuance or till 1958. [295

MANUSCRIPTS

GROVER C. BATTS. The James McKeen Cattell Papers. Lib. Cong. quar. jour., 17:170-74 (May). Papers of Cattell (1860-1944) in the Library of Congress, ca. 15,000 pieces, relating mainly to his work as Professor of Psychology at Columbia University, experimental psychologist, publisher and editor of Science, the Psychological review, Popular science monthly, and American men of science, and organizer of the Psychological Corporation. [296

RAY ALLEN BILLINGTON & WILBUR R. JACOBS. The Frederick Jackson Turner Papers in the Huntington Library. Ariz. and the West, 2:73-7 (spring). notes. [297

ROBERT ROOD BUELL. Public records of Wisconsin. Am. geneal., 36:79-83 (Apr). Annotated list of State records and vital records of special interest to genealogists. [298

KENNETH WALTER CAMERON, comp. Thoreau in the papers of Nathan Brooks and Abel Moore. Emerson Soc. quar., 19: leaves 42-5 (2d quar.). facism. List of 84 bundles of papers "in a large trunk in the basement of Concord Free Public Library," containing papers dated between 1790 and 1861. [299

HARRY JAMES CARMAN & ARTHUR WILLIAM THOMPSON. A guide to the principal sources for American civilization ["that of the United States"], 1800-1900, in the City of New York: manuscripts. N.Y.: Columbia Univ. Press, 1960. xlviii, [2], 453 p. Organized in 30 topical chapters. "Chronological successor" to A guide to the principal sources for early American history (1600-1800) in the City of New York, by Evarts Boutell Greene and Richard B. Morris (1929, rev. 1953). "Directory of the principal libraries and other depositories of New York City" (p. xxxiii-xlvi). [300

ELIZABETH WILLIAMS COSGROVE. The Grant Foreman Papers: Indian and pioneer history. Chron, Okla., 37:507-10 (winter). On the Indian-Pioneer History Project, set up by the W. P. A. in Oklahoma and directed by Dr. Grant Foreman, to obtain reports and interviews of "as many men and women, Indian, white, Negro, mixed-blood or foreign born, as possible, who had lived in the Indian Territory during or prior to the year 1900," edited, typed, and bound in 112 volumes as the Grant Foreman Papers (more than 45,000 pages and 11,000 interviews); with a few quotations from them. [301

FRANCIS B. DEDMOND, comp. A check list of manuscripts relating to Thoreau in the Huntington Library, the Houghton Library of Harvard University, and the Berg Collection of the New York Public Library. Thoreau Soc. bul., 43:[2-4] (spring 1953). For further information about the Harvard manuscripts, by Alexander Kern, see 53:[1-2] (fall 1955). [302

ERIC W. FLEISHER, comp. Swedish American diplomatic history: some sources in the Swedish National Archives [Sveriges Riksarkiv, Stockholm]. Swed. pioneer hist. quar., 11:116-23 (Jul). [303

WILLIAM B. GRIFFEN. The Stetson Collection. Fla. anthropol., 13:33-6 (Sep). bibliog. On a collection of photostats of manuscripts in the Archivo General de Indias, sevilla, and of typescripts of manuscripts in the Public Record Office, with related correspondence, dealing with early Florida, assembled at the expense of John B. Stetson, Jr., between 1924 and 1927 and now in the University of Florida. [304

DORS H. HAMILTON. Appletons' for Americana. Hobbies, 65(8):110-11 (Oct). On Appletons' cyclopaedia of American biography (6 v., 1887-89) as a source of autograph signatures and of information about their signers. [305

DORIS H. HAMILTON. An autographic souvenir. Hobbies, 65(2): 110-11

(Apr). facsims. Examples of replies to requests for autographs, 1861-1913. [306

DORIS H. HAMILTON. Autographs. Conducted by Doris Hamilton. Hobbies, 64(11)-65(10): monthly installments (Jan-Dec). facisms., views. Includes accounts of autograph auctions, seals and sealing wax, "Christmas autographs," and other subjects. [307

DORIS H. HAMILTON. Collecting checks of the Presidents. Hobbies, 65(9):111, 115 (Nov). On the collection of Edward Stern, sold in 1955, and the prices received for its contents. [308

DORIS H. HAMILTON. Early autograph catalogs. Hobbies, 64(12):110-11 (Feb). facism. Information from 5 catalogues, 1853-90, on offerings and prices of manuscripts. [309

KENNETH GARDINER HAMILTON. The resources of the Moravian Church archives. Pa. hist., 27:263-72 (Jul). view. [310

JAMES DAVID HART. Search and research: the librarian and the scholar. Book Club Calif., Quar. news letter, 24:27-34 (spring 1959). On the adventures of the author and an unnamed graduate student in search of manuscripts of Frank Norris. [311

HARVARD UNIVERSITY. Graduate School of Business Administration. Baker Library. Business manuscripts at Baker Library. ... By Robert W. Lovett. Bus. hist. rev., 34:345-51 (autumn). facism. [312

ARTHUR HECHT, comp. Confederate States postal records: the National Archives, the Library of Congress. Am. philatelist, 73:655-6, 687 (Jun). Annotated list of "the extant Confederate postal records." [313

J. STUART HEDGES. Inventory of records in the Saint Joseph County, Michigan, Courthouse [beginning in 1830]. Mich. heritage, 1:167 (summer). [314

ELIZABETH CLARKE KIEFFER, comp. Genealogical resources of the Historical Society of the Evangelical and Reformed Church, Fackenthal Library, Franklin and Marshall College, Lancaster, Pennsylvania. Natl. Geneal. Soc. quar., 48:113-26 (Sep). List of microfilmed church records from Pennsylvania, Maryland, and Virginia and of a few printed records. [315

E. KAY KIRKHAM. A survey of American church records. Volume II. Minor denominations. Including a special treatise on the Huguenots of France in America and religious migrations and immigrations in the United States. Salt Lake City, Utah: Deseret Book Co., 1960. xii, 106 p. Deals particularly with records having genealogical value. [316

LOUISE E. KOIER. Vermont remembers: Admiral George Dewey's letters revive stirring memories. Vt. Hist. Soc., News and notes, 5:65-7 (May 1954). view. On Dewey papers and memorabilia loaned to the Vermont Historical Society; with excerpts from a letter from Dewey to his brother Charles, dated Hong Kong, 2 Apr. 1898. [317

LOUISIANA STATE UNIVERSITY AND AGRICULTURAL AND MECHANICAL COLLEGE. Dept. of Archives and Manuscripts. Collections in the Department of Archives and Manuscripts, Louisiana State University. By V. L. Bedsole [Archivist]. La. hist., 1:328-34 (fall). [318

VAN DYK MacBRIDE, comp. The autographed field letters of R. E. Lee, Genl. Am. philatelist, 73:245-9 (Jan). facsims. Census of the 20 known letters owned by private collectors, dated 1862-65; with an introduction. [319

MICHIGAN STATE LIBRARY. Inventory of microfilms in Michigan State Library. By Mrs. Ruth Blystone, Michigan Section. Mich. heritage, 1:46-7, 125, 173-4 (winter 1959 - summer 1960). Account of census, land, marriage, and church records on microfilm, and their value to genealogists. [320

RUTH MONTEITH, comp. Inventory of records in the Allegan County, Michigan, courthouse [beginning 1834 or earlier). Mich. heritage, 2:45-6 (autumn). [321

RICHARD BRANDON MORRIS. Putting the John Jay Papers to work. Columbia Lib. columns, 9(3):3-7 (May). On a collection of papers (including photoreproductions) now being assembled and organized by Columbia University. [322

MARY OGILVIE. Department of Records, Arch Street, Philadelphia. Anna (Cox) Brinton, ed., Then and now: Quaker essays, historical and contemporary, by friends of Henry Joel Cadbury (Phila.: Univ. of Pennsylvania

Press [1960]), p. 212-15. On the records of the Philadelphia Yearly meeting since 1681, organized in a Department of Records established in 1912. [323

OKLAHOMA, UNIVERSITY OF. Library. Division of Manuscripts. A guide to regional manuscript collections in the Division of Manuscripts, University of Oklahoma Library. By A[rrell] M[organ] Gibson. Norman: Univ. of Oklahoma Press, 1960. vii, 222 p. Account of 694 manuscripts or groups of manuscripts. [324

CHARLES PERCY POWELL. Lincoln in the archives. Ralph G. Newman, ed., Lincoln for the ages (Garden City, N.Y.: Doubleday, 1960), p. 432-6. On collections of papers by or relating to Lincoln in the National Archives and the Library of Congress. [325

NATHAN REINGOLD. Manuscript resources for the history of science and technology in the Library of Congress. Lib. Cong. quar. jour., 17:161-9 (May). facsims. [326

MARGARET ROWLEY, comp. Inventory of records in the Keny County Courthouse [beginning with records of 1833]. Mich. heritage, 1:101-3 (spring). [327

ROBERT SEAGER 2d. The Samuel S. Wood Papers. Yale Univ. Lib. gaz., 34:166-77 (Apr). Personal and business papers of Samuel Smith Wood (1799-1881), Peekskill, N.Y., "merchant and minor Democratic politician," including some 500 items recording his activities as "an American entrepreneur in Nicaragua during the chaotic period, 1851-61." [328

SOUTHERN ILLINOIS UNIVERSITY, Carbondale. University Libraries. "The President of the United States": an exhibition of manuscripts, letters, and documents of the Presidents of the United States, from the collection of Elsie O. and Philip D. Sang ... Edited by John Clifford and Ralph E. McCoy. Carbondale: Morris Library, Southern Illinois Univ. [1960]. vi, 17, [1] p. facisms. Catalogue, 67 entries. [329

NELSON PAUL SPRINGER, comp. General catalogue of the archives of the Mennonite Church. Mennonite hist. bul., 10(1):1, 3-4 (Jan 1949). Account of church records and family and personal papers deposited in the Goshen College Memorial Library, Goshen, Ind. [330

STATE HISTORICAL SOCIETY OF WISCONSIN. Guide to the manuscripts of the State Historical Society of Wisconsin. Supplement number one. By Josephine L. Harper and Sharon C. Smith. Madison, 1957. xii, 222 p. Entries 803-1593, describing accessions from 1941 through May 1956 and continuing Guide to manuscripts of the Wisconsin Historical Society (listing acquisitions through 1940). [331

KATE MacLEAN STEWART. The Daniel Scott Lamont Papers. Lib. Cong. quar. jour., 17:63-83 (Feb). On papers of Lamont (1851-1905) in the Library of Congress, 1867-1905, relating mainly to his service as Grover Cleveland's private secretary (1885-89) and Secretary of War (1893-97), his earlier and later political activities, his work as a financier, and his domestic life. Includes many communications from and to Cleveland. [322

MERIWETHER STUART. The Record of Virginia Forces: a study in the compilation of Civil War records. Va. mag. hist. and biog., 68:3-57 (Jan). fold. facsim. notes. On Virginia legislation, 1861 ff., "to have complete and accurate lists of all the forces in the field made out and deposited in the state department," the work of Joseph Jackson, Jr., as "Record-Agent of the State of Virginia" or "Recorder of Virginia Forces," the destruction of most of the records in the Richmond fire of 1865, and the extent to which they may be reconstructed from surviving sources; with some account of similar undertakings by North Carolina, South Carolina, and Alabama. [333

EVELYN M. TAUBER. Land Office records as genealogical aids. Natl. Geneal. Soc. quar., 48:19-20 (Mar). [334

TENNESSEE STATE LIBRARY AND ARCHIVES, Nashville. Archives Division. Manuscript Section. Register, Henry Shelton Sanford Papers. Nashville, 1960. [4], 73 p. geneal. tables. Register of papers of Henry Shelton Sanford (1823-91), property of the City of Sanford, Fla., and to be housed there in the Henry Shelton Sanford Memorial Library (a microfilmed copy being retained in Tennessee), totaling 60 linear feet (50,000 items, 1769-1901) and consisting mainly of "correspondence, diaries, biographical and genealogical data, legal documents, briefs, speeches, articles, accounts, and business memoranda," originating in his work as Secretary of Legation at

St. Petersburg, Frankfort, and Paris, Minister to Belgium in the Civil War, business agent in Latin America, owner of plantations in Louisiana and Florida, and lawyer interested in railroads, Western lands, Florida real estate, and African and European trade. [335

TULANE UNIVERSITY. Howard-Tilton Memorial Library. Collections in the manuscript sections of Howard-Tilton Memorial Library, Tulane University. By Connie G. Griffith [Manuscript Librarian]. La. hist., 1:320-27 (fall). [336

U.S. Library of Congress. Manuscript Division. Douglas Southall Freeman [1886-1953]: a register of his papers in the Library of Congress. Wash., 1960. [2] p., [1], 14 leaves. On a collection (70,000 items) of his correspondence (especially with historians), diaries, working papers (including maps, photostats, and transcripts), and manuscripts of many of his speeches, articles, and books, 1902-54, mainly after 1934. [337

U.S. Library of Congress. Manuscript Division. Judson King [1872-1958]: a register of his papers in the Library of Congress. Wash., 1960. [2] p., [1], 10 leaves. On a body of papers, 20,000 items, 1900-1958, consisting of general correspondence (1912-58), "unpublished manuscripts of King's writings pertaining to the struggle for the control of the Tennessee River and electric power" (1898-1933), and "numerous scrapbooks, photographs, newspaper clippings and printed material." [338

U.S. Library of Congress. Manuscript Division. Morrison R[emick] Waite [1816-88]: a register of his papers in the Library of Congress. Wash., 1959. [4], 8 leaves. On a body of manuscripts (ca. 20,000 items), 1818-88, relating mainly to his service from 1874 to 1888 as Chief Justice of the United States. [339

U.S. Library of Congress. Manuscript Division. Robert W[ickliffe] Woolley [1871-1958]: a register of his papers in the Library of Congress. Wash., 1960. [2] p., [1], 21 leaves. On a body of papers, ca. 17,000 items, 1842-1958, mainly 1912-21, of which about a third deals with the Democratic national campaigns of 1912, 1916, and 1920 and about a third with Woolley's work in the Interstate Commerce Commission, 1917-21, and which contains also "the draft of an unpublished autobiography," family papers, and other matter. [340

U.S. Library of Congress. Manuscript Division. Wallace H[umphrey] White [1877-1952]: a register of his papers in the Library of Congress. Wash., 1959. [4], 23 p. On a body of manuscripts and clippings (ca. 24,000 items), 1916-49, relating mainly to his work as Representative and Senator from Main, 1917-49. [341

U.S. Library of Congress. Manscript Division. Walter L[owrie] Fisher [1862-1935]: a register of his papers in the Library of Congress. Wash., 1960. [2] p., [1], 9 leaves. On a body of papers, 14,000 items, 1879-1936, relating largely to Fisher's work as a lawyer and his activities in Chicago and national politics. [342

U.S. National Archives. Preliminary inventory of the records of inaugural committees (Record Group 274). Compiled by Hardee Allen. Wash., 1960. vi, 45 p. (Its Publication 61-8. Preliminary inventories, 131.) On records of committees, variously appointed by citizens, parties, presidents elect, etc., to stage "the traditional public ceremonies in the inauguration of a President and Vice President of the United States" in the District of Columbia, 1933-57. [343

U.S. National Archives. Preliminary inventory of the records of the Bureau of Insular Affairs (Record Group 350). Compiled by Richard S. Maxwell. Wash., 1960. v, 32 p. (Its Publication 61-7. Preliminary inventories, 130.) List of records, 1898-1935 (and a few of earlier and later date), relating mainly to the Philippines, Cuba, Puerto Rico, and the Dominican Republic. [344

U.S. National Archives. Preliminary inventory of the records of the Bureau of Naval Personnel (Record Group 24). Compiled by Virgil E. Baugh. Wash., 1960. vi, 135 p. (Its Publication 60-14. Preliminary inventories, 123.) List of records, 1789-1956, of an agency established in 1862, which maintained records of its activities and received custody of most of the earlier personnel records of the U.S. Navy and the U.S. Navy Department. [345

U.S. National Archives. Preliminary inventory of the records of the Collector of Customs, Puget Sound District, in the Federal Records Center, Seattle, Washington (Record Groups

36 and 41) [1851-1913]. Compiled by Elmer W. Lindgard. Wash., 1960. v, 18 p. (Its Publication 60-13. Preliminary inventories, 122.) [346

U.S. National Archives. Preliminary inventory of the records of the Committee for Congested Production Areas (Record Group 212) [1943-44]. Compiled by Leo [T.] Pascal and Jeanne [V.] McDonald. Wash., 1960. v, 16 p. (Its Publication 61-3. Preliminary inventories, 128.) [347

U.S. National Archives. Preliminary inventory of the general records of the Economic Stabilization Agency (Record Group 296) [1951-53]. Complied by Charles Zaid. Wash., 1960. v, 28 p. (Its Publication 61-6. Preliminary inventories, 129.) [348

U.S. National Archives. Preliminary inventory of the records of the Government of the Virgin Islands of the United States (Record Group 55) [1917-50]. Compiled by H. Donn Hooker. Wash., 1960. v, 31 p. (Its Publication 61-1. Preliminary inventories, 126.) [349

U.S. National Archives. Preliminary inventory of the records of the Headquarters, United Nations Command (Record Group 333) [1950-57]. Compiled by Paul [L.] Taborn and Andrew [A.] Putignano. Wash., 1960. v, 7 p. (Its Publication 61-2. Preliminary inventories, 127.) [350

U.S. National Archives. Preliminary inventory of the records of the Office of Community War Services (Record Group 215) [1940-47]. Compiled by Estelle Rebec. Wash., 1960. v, 28 p. (Its Publication 61-9. Preliminary inventories, 132.) Includes the records of the predecessor agencies: Office of the Coordinator of Health, Welfare, and Related Defense Activities and the Office of Defense Health and Welfare Services. [351

U.S. National Archives. Preliminary inventory of the records of the Public Works Administration (Record Group 135) [1933-43]. Compiled by L. Evans Walker. Wash., 1960. v, 32 p. (Its Publication 60-16. Preliminary inventories, 125.) [352

U.S. National Archives. Preliminary inventory of the records of the United States District Court for the Eastern District of Pennsylvania (Record Group 21). Compiled by Marion M. Johnson, Mary Jo Grotenrath, and Henry T. Ulasek. Wash., 1960. v, 44 p. (Its Publication 60-15. Preliminary inventories, 124.) List of records of the U.S. District Court for the Eastern District of Pennsylvania (1789-1911, and a few records of later date), the U.S. Circuit Court for the Eastern District of Pennsylvania (1790-1911, and a few records of earlier date), and the U.S. Circuit Court for the Western District of Pennsylvania (1801-2). [353

U.S. National Archives. Preliminary inventory of the records of the United States House of Representatives, 1789-1946 (Record Group 233). Compiled by Buford Rowland, Handy B. Fant, and Harold E. Hufford. Wash., 1959. 2 v. vi, 292; [4], 293-587 p. bibliog. (2: 470-78), notes. (Its Publication 59-12. Preliminary inventories, 113.) [354

The VIRGINIA and Richard Ehrlich Collection. Boston Pub. Lib. quar., 12:103-9 (Apr). On a collection of American and European manuscripts received by the Library from an anonymous donor in 1949 and expanded by subsequent acquisitions. [355

WYLMA ANNE WATES. The South Carolina public records as sources for revisionist interpretation of the American Revolution. S.C. Hist. Assoc., Proc., 1959, p. 18-24. notes. Describes "the principal collections relating to the years between 1763 and 1790," noting that the records of this period have survived in much greater quantity than was formerly believed. [356

EDWARD H. WEST. Ship documents. Natl. Geneal. Soc. quar., 48:183-4 (Dec). On the genealogical value of the "series of Custom House records ... started in 1784." [357

MARCIA WRIGHT. The growth of the Abraham Lincoln Papers. Lib. Cong. quar. jour., 18:5-9 (Nov). notes. Mainly on Lincoln papers received by the Library of Congress since 1947. [358

MAPS

BRUNO NETTL. Musical cartography and the distribution of music. Southw. jour. anthropol., 16:338-47 (autumn). map. notes. On projects for "mapping the distribution of music in the world," and some of their possible applications to music of the North American Indians. [359

THE OLD PRINT SHOP, INC., New York. Old American maps. [N.Y.: Harry Shaw Newman, 1959.] 24 p. maps, view. (The Old Print Shop portfolio, v. 19, no. 1, Aug.-Sep. 1959.) Annotated list of 24 maps or atlases and a view, 1606-1801. [360

JAY W. SHARP, comp. A collection of printed maps of Texas, 1835-1951, in the Eugene C. Barker Texas History Center. Southw. hist. quar., 64:96-123 (Jul). Annotated list. [361

U.S. Library of Congress. Map Division. Facsimiles of rare historical maps available for sale. Compiled by Walter W. Ristow, Map Division. [Wash.] 1960. 6 p. Annotated list of facsimile maps, mainly of America, 1424-1880, arranged by name of their present "publishers or distributors" (and not for sale by the Library of Congress). Dates of reproductions are not indicated. [362

MUSICAL COMPOSITIONS

BOB COLTON & LEN KUNSTADT, comps. Race Artists Vocalion Red Records. Record research, 31:8-9, 20 (Nov). ports. Discography of recordings "by blues-vocalistes who recorded for the Vocalion label from May 1923 through September 1924 just before the Brunswick company took over the reins." [363

COLUMBIA NEW PROCESS RECORDS. The golden age of blues recording, excerpts from the Columbia 1927 race catalogue: The latest blues by Columbia race stars. Record research, 31:10-11 (Nov). Reproduces 7 pages, each containing a portrait of a Negro singer and a list of recordings by the singer. [364

FRANK PIERCE DONOVAN, JR., comp. Hi-fi railroad recordings. Railroad mag., 71(6):50-51 (Oct). List of phonograph records with "exclusively railroad themes" or including such themes, especially "railroad ballads" and "the haunting sounds of steam power." [365

EDISON jazz survey. Record research, 19:12-15 (Sep-Oct 1958). List of recordings by Thomas A. Edison, Inc., 1917-29. [366

RICHARD HADLOCK. Morton's Library of Congress albums. Jazz, 2:133-7 (spring 1959). On 12 volumes of long-playing recordings by and about the jass pianist and composer Jelly Roll Morton, originally recorded by Allan Lomax in 1938 as interviews with Morton and illustrations by him on the piano. [367

HOBBIES: THE MAGAZINE FOR COLLECTORS. Historical records. Conducted by Aida Favia-Artsay. Hobbies, 64(11)-65(10): monthly installments (Jan-Dec). facsims., ports., views. Information for collectors of early recordings, European and American. [368

ALFRED WENDELL HUMPHREYS, comp. Index to Montana songs by title. Mont. Inst. Arts quar., 10(3):39, 56 (spring 1958). List, alphabetical by title, of songs dated 1894-1957. [369

JOHN KIRKPATRICK, comp. A temporary mimeographed catalogue of the music manuscripts and related materials of Charles Edward Ives, 1874-1954, given by Mrs. Ives to the Library of the Yale School of Music, September 1955. [n. p., 1960.] xxxv, 279 leaves. Topical list of compositions composed or published between 1887 and 1958. [370

IRVING LOWENS, comp. The American songster before 1821: a list of incomplete and unlocated titles. Bibliog. Soc. Am., Papers, 53:61-9 (1st quar.). List of 113 titles, 1750-1820, conforming to the definition of songster as "a collection of three or more secular poems intended to be sung ... issued in book of pamphlet form," including "works containing a separate section of songs." Cites locations of known copies and authority for the existence or former existence of works not located. [371

ANTHONY ROTANTE & PAUL SHEATSLEY, comps. The records of John Lee Hooker [born 1917]. Record research, 31:3-5, 20 (Nov 1960). port. Discography of "country blues" played by Hooker on an "amplified electric guitar," 1949-60; with an account of his early life in Mississippi and his work as a guitarist, mainly in Detroit. [372

HENRY SCHULTZ, comp. Some American Indian music on records. Am. record guide, 15:259-62, 291-6, 329-34; 16:7-10 (May-Sep 1949). views. Detailed description of 38 recordings of mainly traditional and ceremonial music in the Laguna, San Juan, Taos, and Hopi pueblos and among the Apache, Navajo, and Sioux Indians. [373

THESES

WALTER CROSBY EELLS, comp. American dissertations on foreign education: doctor's dissertations and master's theses written at American universities and colleges concerning education or educators in foreign countries and education of groups of foreign birth or ancestry in the United States, 1884-1958. Wash.: Committee on International Relations, National Education Assoc. of the United States, 1959. xxxix, 300 p. diagrs., tables. bibliog. (p. xxxvi-xxxix). Arranged by country, 5,698 items. "United States" (entries 4860-5698). [374

WALTER CROSBY EELLS, comp. American doctoral dissertations on English written by women in the nineteenth century. CLA jour. 2:25-33 (Sep 1958). Annotated list of 48 dissertations, 1885-1900. [375

STUART WALLACE HYDE, comp. Graduate theses and dissertations on broadcasting: a topical index. Compiled ... from research studies conducted by Raymond Cheydleur (1950) and Robert J. Golter (1956). Jour. broadcasting, 2:55-90 (winter 1958). List, 1920-56. [376

LAWRENCE CALVIN LITTLE, comp. Bibliography of doctoral dissertations in character and religious education ["accepted by American universities and theological seminaries"]. Pittsburgh: Dept. of Religious Education, Univ. of Pittsburgh, ©1960. [2] leaves, 273 p. A "preliminary edition." [377

LAWRENCE MYERS, JR., comp. Doctoral dissertations in radio and television [1925-56]. Jour. broadcasting, 1:377-83 (fall 1957). [378

OREGON STATE COLLEGE, Corvallis. Library. Theses and dissertations, 1943-1959. Compiled by Rodney K. Waldron with the assistance of Virginia Followell. Corvallis, 1960. 139 p. (Oregon State College, Corvallis. Bibliographic series, 6.) [379

FRANKLIN PARKER, comp. Doctoral dissertations pertaining to the history of teacher education. Austin, Tex. [1959?]. 3 leaves. Author list of 26 titles, 1912-59. [380

WILLIAM R. SHUNK & FRANKLIN PARKER, comps. History of education, philosophy of education, and comparative education: annotated bibliography of doctoral dissertations at the University of Texas, 1923-1958. [Austin:] Dept. of History and Philosophy of Education, Univ. of Texas, 1959. [66] leaves. List of chapters and indication of purpose, sources, and findings of each of 81 theses. [381

Iconography

ANTIQUES. In the museums. Antiques, 77(1)-78(6): monthly installments (Jan-Dec). ports., views. On recent acquisitions by American museums, especially in American decorative arts and painting. [382

THE ART QUARTERLY. Accessions of American and Canadian museums, October-December 1959 [through July-September 1960]. Art quar., 23:89-102, 182-94, 301-10, 398-407 (spring-winter). ports., views. List of recently acquired paintings, drawings, sculpture, engravings, and "decorative arts." [383

ARTS COUNCIL OF GREAT BRITAIN and ENGLISH-SPEAKING UNION OF THE UNITED STATES. James McNeill Whistler [1834-1903]: an exhibition of paintings and other works. [London] 1960. 127, [1] p. ports. (1 col.), views (1 col.). bibliog. (p. 111-25). Catalogue of paintings, drawings, and engravings, 155 entries; with an introductory biographical sketch. [384

BEN BLUMENTHAL, ed. The American commemorative stamp album, 1893-1959. N.Y.: Minkus Publications, ©1960. 80 leaves. facsims. [385

BOSTON MUSEUM OF FINE ARTS. New England miniatures, 1750 to 1850. [Exhibition, April 24 to May 28, 1957, sponsored by the National Society of Colonial Dames.] Boston, 1957. 18, [36], xxiv, [3] p. ports. (part col.). Catalogue, 211 entries, of small portraits "in water color on ivory with a few exceptions"; with an introduction ("The art of miniature painting in New England," by Barbara Neville Parker, p. 8-18), a list of other miniatures of New Englanders which are in private ownership, and a list of 14 "public institutions in New England containing collections of miniatures." [386

CLARENCE WILSON BRAZER (1880-1956), comp. The collection of the late William Alexander Smith, Jr. Essay proof jour., 13:237-9 (Oct 1956). Selective list of items sold at auction in New York, 26 Oct. 1903, from "perhaps the most complete lot of U.S. Essays and Proofs sold at auction up until that time." [387

CLARENCE WILSON BRAZER (1880-1956). Historical catalogue of U.S. stamp essays & proofs. Essay proof jour., 13:115-17 (Apr 1956). Introduction to a book published in preliminary serial form (in installments beginning as early as 1939) to receive the benefit of corrections and additions by readers and to facilitate a final revision. [388

CINCINNATI MUSEUM ASSOCIATION. Paintings by the Peale family. [Cincinnati, 1954.] 28 p. ports., views. Exhibition catalogue of 111 paintings (not here dated) by Charles Willson Peale, his brother James, Charles's sons Raphaelle, Rembrandt, and Rubens, and James's 4 children; with an introduction by Edward H. Dwight. [389

CINCINNATI MUSEUM ASSOCIATION. Walt Kuhn, 1877-1949. [Cincinnati] 1960. [76] p. cartoon, ports. (part col.), views (part col.). Foreword signed: Philip Rhys Adams. Catalogue (155 entries) of a memorial exhibition of his paintings; with a biographical sketch. [390

RICHARD J. CODA, comp. The standard catalog of New Hampshire precancels [1894-1954]. Editor: Crandall R. Wallenstein. N.J., c1960. [6], 20, [2] p. map, port. [391

COLONIAL WILLIAMSBURG, INC. The Abby Aldrich Rockefeller Folk Art Collection: a descriptive catalogue by Nina Fletcher Little. Williamsburg, Va.: Colonial Williamsburg; distributed by Little, Brown, Boston [1957]. xvi, 402, [2] p. 165 col. illus. bibliogs. Catalogue of "424 objects"--paintings in oil, watercolor, and pastel, needlework and painted textiles, paintings on glass, "fracturs, calligraphic drawings, and engravings," and sculpture in wood and metal, 1752 to ca. 1900. [392

COLORADO SPRINGS FINE ARTS CENTER. Taylor Museum. Navaho sandpainting: the Huckel Collection. [Text by] Leland C[lifton] Wyman. [Colorado Springs] 1960. 88 p. ports., table, views. bibliog. (p. 87-8), notes (p. 85-6). Annotated list of 111 paintings by Navajo artists, "water color reproductions" of Navajo sandpaintings, collected by John Frederick Huckel between 1922 and 1936. [393

DALLAS MUSEUM OF FINE ARTS. Famous families in American art. [Dallas, 1960. 44] p. ports., tables, views. Catalogue of an exhibition of paintings by Americans who were members of families of painters (e.g., the Peale family), 1729-1956. [394

DALLAS MUSEUM OF FINE ARTS. Retrospective exhibition, H[arold] O[sman] Kelly (1884-1955). [Dallas, 1960. 16] p. ports., views (1 col.). Catalogue (55 entries) of paintings, mainly Texas ranch and small-town scenes; with reminiscences of Kelly by William Weber Johnson and a sketch of Kelly's early life in Ohio, his work as a cowboy and in other occupations in the Southwest, and his settlement near Blanket, Tex. [395

FINE ARTS GALLERY, San Diego, Calif. Catalogue: a selective listing of all the collections of the Fine Arts Society [of San Diego]. San Diego, 1960. xx, 141 p. cartoon, ports. (part col.), views (part col.). 31 cm. Includes "American arts" (painting, engraving, sculpture), 1870-1945 (p. 1-21). [396

FINE ARTS GALLERY, San Diego, Calif. War, peace, and union. [San Diego, 1960.] 20 p. port., views. Catalogue of 51 paintings (most undated, one dated 1842) of scenes "of the last half of the 19th century," particularly scenes of the Civil War. [397

FRANKLIN D. ROOSEVELT LIBRARY, Hyde Park, N.Y. A preliminary list of Civil War paintings, drawings, and prints in the naval collection of Franklin D. Roosevelt. Compiled by Raymond H. Corry. Hyde Park, N.Y., 1960. [2], 17 p. List (103 entries) of paintings, drawings, prints, and sheet-music covers showing "actions and events," arranged chronologically, and vessels, arranged alphabetically. [398

NATHAN GOLD, comp. Unredeemed large size notes. Numismatist, 73: 419-26 (Apr). facsims., tables. A "complete record of all old series issues of paper currency and the amount still outstanding," issued 1861-1929 and outstanding in 1959. [399

An ICONOGRAPHICAL checklist of Ezra Pound. Pound newsletter, 9: leaves 5-7 (Jan 1956). List of paintings, sketches, sculpture, and photographs with Ezra Pound as subject. [400

BELLA CLARA LANDAUER, comp. Business, the new Maecenas. [N.Y.:] New-York Historical Soc., 1956. [15] p. 7 col. views (1 fold.) besides 20 views in pocket. 40 x 54 cm. Lists of paintings commissioned or reproduced by the Standard Oil Company of New Jersey (since 1943) and several other firms for use in advertising; with "A history of pharmacy in pictures: reproductions of a series of original oil paintings presented by Parke, Davis, & Company," painted by Robert A. Thom (prints c1952-53, in pocket). [401

BENJAMIN MORGAN LEWIS, comp. A guide to engravings in American magazines, 1741-1810. N.Y.: New York Public Library, 1959. iv, [2], 60, [1] p. views. bibliog. List arranged alphabetically by title of magazine. [402

LYMAN ALLYN MUSEUM, New London, Conn. Complete list of American and European drawings, paintings, and watercolors in the collection of the Lyman Allyn Museum. New London, 1960. 63 p. ports., views. [403

METROPOLITAN MUSEUM OF ART, New York. H. O. Havemeyer Collection. The H. O. Havemeyer Collection. Second edition. N.Y., 1958. x, [4], 125 p. ports., views. 1st ed. 1930. Annotated catalogue of paintings, drawings, prints, sculpture, ceramics, glass, textiles, etc., 1,972 entries, including a few American items (nos. 1-10, 194-233); with an account of the bequest of Louisine W. Havemeyer, widow of Henry O. Havemeyer, to the Museum in 1929. [404

EMILY WINTHROP MILES. An exhibition of paintings and drawings [1948-60] by Kenneth Callahan [born 1906], from the collection of Emily Winthrop Miles and lent by her for an extended tour of American museums, 1961-1964. [N.Y. ? 1960. 43] p. views (1 mount. col.). [405

MILWAUKEE ART CENTER. American painting, 1760-1960: a selection of 125 paintings from the collection of Mr. and Mrs. Lawrence A. Fleischman, Detroit. [By Edward H. Dwight, Director. Milwaukee, 1960.] 145 p. ports., views (1 col.). [406

MISSOURI HISTORICAL SOCIETY. The D. C. Humphreys Collection of Glass Negatives. By Miss Ruth Ferris, Curator of River Collections. Mo. Hist. Soc., Bul., 17:57-60 (Oct). Collection of 167 negatives taken by David Carlisle Humphreys (1855-1921), C. E., while "assistant engineer in a survey of the Missouri River" under Maj. Charles R. Suter, President of the Missouri River Commission, 1882, 1885, showing "mostly ... the Upper Missouri River country, steamboats, and Western characters, but including some views of Missouri and St. Louis"; with 13 prints on a folder following p. 60. [407

MUSEUM OF PRIMITIVE ART, New York. The Raymond Wielgus Collection. Foreword by Robert Goldwater; introduction by Raymond Wielgus. N.Y.: Distributed by University Publishers, 1960. [32] p. views. bibliog. (p. 32). Catalogue of a collection of primitive sculpture (105 entries), including work of American Indians. [408

NEW YORK STATE HISTORICAL ASSOCIATION. New-found art of the young republic. [Compiled by] Agnes Halsey Jones and Louis C. Jones. N.Y. hist., 41:117-231 (Apr). 80 ports. and views. Annotated preliminary catalogue in chronological order, 1784 to ca. 1875, of 81 primitive paintings acquired in 1958 for the Farmers' Museum at Cooperstown from the collection of Mr. and Mrs. William J. Gunn; with some account of their habits as collectors of paintings in New England and New York, and an introduction on "American folk art." [409

OLD photos depict Oregon. Old Oregon, 38(12):5-9 (Apr-May 1959). views. On a collection of Oregon, especially Portland, photographs made by the Angelus Photo Studios of Portland, 1870 to ca. 1940, purchased in 1955 by the University of Oregon Library. [410

THE OLD PRINT SHOP, INC., New York. [Currier & Ives lithographs. N.Y.: Harry Shaw Newman, 1960.] 169-192 p. ports., views. (The Old Print Shop portfolio, v. 19, no. 8, Apr. 1960) Annotated list of 32 prints, 1845-92. [411

THE OLD PRINT SHOP, INC., New York. [Currier & Ives lithographs collected by H. H. Kynett of Philadelphia. N.Y.: Harry Shaw Newman, 1959.] 25-48 p. views. (The Old Print Shop portfolio, v. 19, no. 2, Oct. 1959.) Annotated list, including entries for 14 yacht prints. [412

THE OLD PRINT SHOP, INC., New York. Marine issue. N.Y.: Harry Shaw Newman, 1960. 219-240 p. facsims., views. (The Old Print Shop portfolio, v. 19, no. 10, Jun.-Jul. 1960.) Annotated list of engravings, mainly of sailing ships. [413

THE OLD PRINT SHOP, INC., New York. Rare Philadelphia views. N.Y.: Harry Shaw Newman, 1959. 49-72 p. maps, views. (The Old Print Shop portfolio, v. 19, no. 3, Nov. 1959.) Annotated list of 32 maps and views, 1687-1875, collected by H. H. Kynett. [414

ELIZABETH H. PAYNE. Pitts family portraits of the eighteenth century. Antiques, 77:87-9 (Jan). ports. On "a recent acquisition of portraits and other memorabilia of the Pitts family" by the Detroit Museum of Arts, ranging "from seventeenth-century New England to twentieth-century Detroit"; with reproductions of 7 18th-century Boston portraits. [415

PAUL N. PERROT. American pictorial flasks at the Corning Museum of Glass. Antiques, 78:244-8 (Sep). views (1 col.). Illustrates and describes 43 pieces, 1820s-50s, and refers to other pieces from the McKearin Collection. [416

JACQUES SCHURRE, comp. A checklist of previously unrecorded Currier & Ives prints. Spinning wheel, 16(9): 18-19, 26 (Sep). port. Review of previous lists (published 1925-49), which cite 6,879 titles, and list of 106 prints now first recorded, 1840-88 (and many undated). [417

AUSTIN M. SHEEHAN, JR., comp. South Carolina obsolete notes: the first comprehensive listing of State, broken bank, town, city, railroad, and miscellaneous other notes. Numismatic scrapbook, 26(1-12): monthly installments (Jan-Dec 1960). facsims. Descriptive catalogue, 1789-1933, 413 entries. [418

U.S. Library of Congress. Prints and Photographs Division. Prints and Photographs. [By Alice Lee Parker and Milton Kaplan.] Lib. Cong. quar. jour., 18:40-52 (Nov). Annual report of acquisitions of prints, posters, original drawings, and photographs. Includes a topical list of "Historical prints" (p. 45-9), illustrating the "variety of subject matter" of American 19th-century engravings by publishers other than Currier & Ives. [419

YALE UNIVERSITY. Art Gallery. Prints and drawings from the Yale collections. Published for the Associates in Fine Arts at Yale University. [New Haven] 1957. 20 p. 14 plates (in pocket). bibliog. (p. 20). Catalogue, including "Americana" (p. 16-17). [420

Other Lists and Descriptions

ANTIQUES JOURNAL. The Ohio Historical Society issue. [Westfield, N.Y.: Guide Pub. Co., 1960] 66 p. views. (The antiques journal, v. 15, no. 6, Jun. 1960.) On the Society's holdings of early American ceramics and glass, pewter, iron and tin, coverlets, household utensils, toys, tools, firearms, paper money, paintings, etc. [421

THEODORE VERN BUTTREY. The Yale Numismatic Collection. Yale Univ. Lib. gaz., 35:42-5 (Jul). [422

CORNING MUSEUM OF GLASS, Corning, N.Y. Glass from the Corning Museum of Glass: a guide to the collections. Corning: Corning Glass Center, 1958. 96 p. map, views (part col.). bibliog. (p. 91-6). Includes antique American glass (p. 78-85). 1st ed. 1955. [423

JACQUES DEL MONTE. Coins: a complete guide to collecting. [Los Angeles: Trend Books, 1959.] 128 p. facsims., views. (Trend book 180.) Includes references to tokens, medals, and other "numismatic sidelines." [424

MALCOLM RAY DOUBLES. Pattern glass checklist. Richmond, 1959. [4], 100 p. Alphabetical list, 2,465 items, 1840-1930, incorporating lists of 4 previous writers. [425

GEORGE FULD & MELVIN FULD. Patriotic Civil War tokens ... a descriptive and price catalogue of the die varieties of patriotic type tokens used as a substitute for money during the American Civil War. Racine, Wis.: Whitman Pub. Co. [1960]. 77 p. tokens. Includes an introduction on previous studies and catalogues of these tokens. [426

HELEN McKEARIN. American glass from the McKearin Collection at the

Henry Ford Museum. Antiques, 77: 581-5 (Jun). views. On glass collected by the author's father, George S. McKearin; with illustrations and detailed descriptions of 15 pieces or groups, 18th and 19th centuries. [427

The MEDICAL arts apothecarians that Howard W. Mordue built. Hobbies, 64(11):58-9 (Jan). port., view. On a collection of American apothecary utensils, tools, etc., assembled by a Detroit pharmacist. [428

PHILBROOK ART CENTER, Tulsa, Okla. Indian pottery of the Southwest, post Spanish period [since 1540. Tulsa, 1960. 59] p. diagrs., views. On a collection of pottery assembled by Clark Field since 1935. [429

THELMA SHULL. Philip Norman's match book covers. Hobbies, 65(1): 114-15 (Mar). port. Account of a collection. [430

ELLA N. WADE, comp. Supplemental catalogue of medical medals, badges, and coins in the College of Physicians of Philadelphia. College Phys. Phila., Trans. & studies, 27:161-87 (Apr). Annotated topical list, supplementing a catalogue prepared by the same compiler in 1944. [431

HAROLD WARP. A history of man's progress--from 1830 to the present--a complete and historical description in chronological order, of every item on display at the Harold Warp Pioneer Village, Minden, Nebraska. [Minden, Neb., 1960.] 367 p. diagrs. (1 double), facsims., ports., table, views. "More than 1,000 illustrations" and text describing "20,000 historical items in 20 buildings," including home appliances, agricultural equipment, musical instruments, vehicles and boats, toy banks, Rogers groups, fire-fighting equipment, office equipment, etc. [432

HISTORICAL MATERIALS: REPOSITORIES AND CUSTODIANS

Archival Establishments

FREDERICK CLEVER BALD. The Historical Collections of the University of Michigan [established in 1935]. Mich. heritage, 2:81-2 (winter). On its purpose "to serve as the archives of the University" (1817 to the present) and "to gather manuscript and printed matter relating to all phases of Michigan history." [433

SPAIN. Archivo General de Indias, Seville. Archivo General de Indias de Sevilla: guía del visitante. Por José María de la Peña y Cámara, Director del Archivo. [Madrid] 1958. 206, [1] p. diagr., facsims., map, plan, views. bibliog. (p. 149-63). (Spain. Junta Técnica de Archivos, Bibliotecas, y Museos. Ediciones conmemorativas del centenario del Cuerpo Facultativo, 1858-1958, 13.) Includes information about records relating to the United States. [434

U.S. National Archives and Records Service. The Harry S. Truman Library, Independence, Missouri [1957-60. Wash.: U.S. Govt. Print. Off., 1960.] folder ([8] p.). facsim., plan, views. [435

DORMAN H. WINFREY. The Texas State Archives. West Tex. Hist. Assoc. yr. bk., 36:41-50. [436

Collectors and Dealers

ALBERT CARLOS BATES (1865-1954). Adventures of a collector. Conn. Hist. Soc. bul., 23:65-77 (Jul 1958). Paper read "a number of years ago" on the author's experiences in collecting manuscripts and rare books, particularly those of Connecticut interest. [437

MARTIN BIRNBAUM (born 1878). The last romantic: the story of more than a half-century in the world of art. N.Y.: Twayne, 1960. 262 p. port. On the author's emigration from Hungary (ca. 1890), his life in New York City, his studies at the College of the City of New York and the Columbia University Law School, his practice of law, and his activities from ca. 1910 to 1942 as an art dealer and collector, proprietor of a gallery in New York. [438

HARRIETTE M. CLUXTON. Gold in optometric attics. Am. jour. optometry, 36:450-53 (Aug 1959). notes. On rare regional and State optometric periodicals, and other rare materials sought by optometric libraries. [439

HARRIETTE M. CLUXTON. Specs 'n' stamps. Am. jour. optometry, 37:320-24 (Jun). On the collecting of "interesting portrait stamps illustrating the use of spectacles." [440

JOSEPH L. EISENDRATH, JR. The Civil War letters of Sgt. Robert Ardrey. Manuscripts, 12(2):43-7 (summer). facsims. On the author's acquisition of letters of a sergeant in the 111th Illinois Infantry and his search among persons still living for information about him. [441

HORATIO Alger, inspiration of a collector. Hobbies, 64(12): 108-9 (Feb). facsims., ports. On a collection of Horatio Alger boys' novels, 1850s-90s, assembled by Ralph D. Gardner of New York City. [442

LEON HOWARD. The case of the missing whaler. Manuscripts, 12(4): 3-9 (fall). On the author's "exciting, heartbreaking and ultimately lucky search for the document which filled a mysterious gap in the biography of Herman Melville." [443

VICTOR JACOBS. Mist'uh Speak'uh! Manuscripts, 12(2):27-31 (summer). On "the enjoyment and economics of collecting autographs of Speakers of the U.S. House of Representatives"; with a list of the 47 speakers, 1789-1960. [444

IRVIN KERLAN (1912-63). Collecting children's books: a rewarding pasttime. Pediatrics, 26:684-8 (Oct). facsim. bibliog. [445

MANUSCRIPT SOCIETY. What every collector should know--V. Signers of Declaration of Independence: a well-defined collecting area. Manuscripts, 12(1):20-25 (winter). Includes information about scarcity and prices, in alphabetical order under the names of the 56 Signers. [446

ALINE (BERNSTEIN) LOUCHHEIM SAARINEN. The proud possessors: the lives, times, and tastes of some adventurous American art collectors [since 1893]. N.Y.: Random House [1958]. xxiv, 423 p. ports., views. bibliog. (p. 397-414). Biographical sketches of Mrs. Potter Palmer (Berthe Honoré Palmer, 1850-1918), Mrs. Jack Gardner (Isabella Stewart Gardner, 1840-1924), J. Pierpont Morgan (1837-1913), John Graver Johnson (1841-1917), Charles Lang Freer (1856-1919), Henry Osborne Havemeyer (1847-1907) and Louisine Waldron (Elder) Havemeyer (1855-1925), Leo, Gertrude, Sarah, and Michael Stein, John Quinn (1870-1924), Katherine Sophie Drier (1877-1952), Edward Wales Root (1884-1956), Joseph H. Hirshhorn, Mrs. J. Watson Webb (Electra Havemeyer Webb), Thomas Gilcrease, Peggy Guggenheim, John D. Rockefeller, Jr., and Abby (Aldrich) Rockefeller, their sons John D. III, Nelson Aldrich, and David R. Rockefeller, Dr. Albert C. Barnes, Mary Cassatt, Henry Clay Frick, William Randolph Hearst, P. A. B. Widner, and Andrew Mellon; with some account of Luman Reed, Thomas Jefferson Bryan, and James Jackson Jarves, active 1832-70. [447

PAUL GINSBURG SIFTON. Pierre Eugene du Simitiere (1737-1784): collector in Revolutionary America. Ann Arbor: University Microfilms, 1960. Positive microfilm of typescript. [623] leaves. Thesis--Univ. of Pennsylvania. Abstracted: Dissert. abstracts, 21:868-9 (Oct). On his life in America, 1757-84, and his collections of pamphlets, broadsides, manuscripts, paintings, coins, engravings, etc., in the fields of politics, natural history, the Indians, the arts, and literature; with a comparison of his collections with those of some of his American predecessors and contemporaries. [448

ARTHUR SWANN. Arthur Swann-two experiences. [Edited by] Justin G. Turner. Manuscripts, 12(2):23-6 (summer). Recollections (1958) by a book dealer, of his unsuccessful bid for a Jefferson letter to Dr. Benjamin Rush, 23 Sep. 1800 (at an auction in 1943), and his acquisition of the James Lorimer Graham Collection (in private possession in Florence, Italy, and about "to be consigned to a furnance"). [449

FRANK WHEELER. The cartridge collector. Gun rep., 5(1-12): monthly installments (Jun 1959 - May 1960). Information useful to collectors. [450

Historic Buildings and Sites Maintained as Museums, Parks, or Villages

GERTRUDE SPRAGUE CARRAWAY. Tryon Palace restoration. D. A. R. mag., 94:4-6 (Jan). views. [451

FOUR Poe houses. Hist. preservation, 11 (1959): 60-63. views. On houses once occupied by Edgar Allan Poe in Baltimore, Richmond, Philadelphia, and New York City, 1831-49, all now maintained as museums. [452

PAUL LEROY GRIGAUT. The furnishings of the Beaumont Memorial [Mackinac Island, Mich.]. Mich State Med. Soc., Jour., 58:763 (May 1959). views. [453

BARBARA D. HOFFSTOT. America's national trust. Carnegie mag., 34: 281-4 (Oct). views. On the National Trust for Historic Preservation, 1949-60. [454

RICHARD HUBBARD HOWLAND. How a local community can survey, mark, and preserve its historic sites. Mo. hist. rev., 54:132-4 (Jan). port. [455

EDWARD JOHN LONG. America's national monuments and historic sites: a guide in pictures and text to our magnificent natural and historic treasures. Garden City, N.Y.: Doubleday [1960. 4], 256 p. facsims., col. maps, ports., views (part col., part double). [456

NATIONAL TRUST FOR HISTORIC PRESERVATION. Historic preservation: quarterly of the National Trust for Historic Preservation, "guarding America's heritage." [Vol. 11, nos. 1-4; vol. 12, nos. 1-4. Wash., 1959-60.] 2 v. 159; 158 p. facsims., views. Accounts of buildings and sites proposed for preservation, threatened with destruction, or recently destroyed. [457

NEW YORK. Division of Archives and History. Historic sites of New York State. [Albany, 1960.] 56, [1] p. facsims., map, ports., views. [458

NORMAN HOLMES PEARSON. New resources for American studies. II. The Mark Twain Memorial in Hartford, Connecticut. Cent. Miss. Valley Am. Studies Assoc., Jour., 1(2):11-16 (fall). On his house in Hartford, finished in 1874 and occupied by him till the 1890s, now preserved as a museum and library with a growing collection of Mark Twain papers of Hartford interest. [459

"WHAT good is a poet's house?" Hist. preservation, 12:44-50. port., views. On houses of eminent American authors which have been preserved as museums. [460

HISTORICAL MARKERS

JAMES ROBERT MILLS, comp. Historical landmarks of San Diego County. San Diego, Calif.: San Diego Historical Soc., c1960. [2], 27 p. map, views. Annotated list of historical markers, commemorating historical events since 1769. [461

NORTH CAROLINA. State Dept. of Archives and History. [Recently placed historical markers.] N.C. hist. rev., 37:129-36 (Jan). Annotated list of 51 markers, placed in 1959. [462

OKLAHOMA HISTORICAL SOCIETY. Oklahoma historical markers and monuments, 1959-1960. Chron. Okla., 38:208-17 (summer). ports. [463

STATE HISTORICAL SOCIETY OF MISSOURI. Missouri's program for highway historic markings, 1959. Directed by Floyd C. Shoemaker. Inscriptions by Ruby M. Robins. Mo. hist. rev., 54:254-61, 348-55 (Apr, Jul). ports., views. [464

Historical and Antiquarian Organizations

AMERICAN ASSOCIATION FOR STATE AND LOCAL HISTORY. Directory of historical societies and agencies in the United States and Canada, 1959. Compiled by Clement M. Silvestro [and] Ardelle J. Hough. [Madison, Wis., 1959.] 63 p. Arranged by State, thereunder by name of society. Supersedes a directory issued in 1956. [465

JOHN J. APPEL. Immigrant historical societies in the United States, 1880-1950. Ann Arbor: University Microfilms, 1960. Positive microfilm of typescript. [448] leaves. Thesis--Univ. of Pennsylvania. Abstracted: Dissert. abstracts, 21:859 (Oct). [466

JOHN J. APPEL. The New England origins of the American Irish Historical Society [1889-98]. New Eng. quar., 33:462-75 (Dec). notes. [467

HISTORICAL SOCIETY. In memoriam. Calif. Hist. Soc. quar., 39:74-9, 175-8, 355-7 (Mar, Jun, Dec). port. Memorial sketches, by various contributors, of Pierre Alexander Bergerot (1867-1959), Aubrey Drury (1891-1959), Milton D. Eisner (1886-1959), Marco Newmark (1878-1959), William Watkin Winn (1874-1959), Henry Carl Maier (1898-1960), and Hans Barkan (1882-1960)--members of the Society. [468

HENRY ALLEN CASTLE. Henry Allen Castle, sixty-five years a member. Conn. Hist. Soc. bul., 24:72-3 (Jul 1959). Letter to the editor, dated Plainville, Con., 4 Apr. 1959, containing reminiscences of the Society since 1894. [469

DIRECTORY of New Jersey historical societies. N.J. genesis, 8:294-9 (Oct). [470

RUSSELL W. FRIDLEY. The Minnesota Historical Society, the oldest institution in the State [1849-1960]. Lawrence Martin Brings, ed., Minnesota heritage (Minneapolis: T. S. Denison [1960]), p. 241-3. views. [471

GEORGIA. Civil War Centennial Commission. The Civil War centennial: to commemorate the War between the States, to honor our Confederate heroes, to tell the true story of Georgia's role in the conflict, to dramatize the great ideals that are the basis of our freedom and tradition. [Atlanta, 1960?] 35, [1] p. forms, ports. Manual for Georgians. [472

ARCH GRAHN. The local historical society and its problems. Mo. hist. rev., 54:135-42 (Jan). port. [473

TINA C. JEFFREY. George C. Marshall Research Foundation. Commonwealth (Va.), 27(6):27-9 (Jun). ports. On an organization established in 1953 to collect, make available, study, and publish documents and records relating to the life and public service of George Catlett Marshall. [474

ARTHUR MENZIES JOHNSON & BARRY E. SUPPLE. The businessman speaks to historians. Bus. hist. rev., 34:241-7 (summer). tables. Analysis of responses from 93 firms to a circular letter from the Harvard Graduate School of Business Administration regarding its program in business history. [475

LANCASTER COUNTY HISTORICAL SOCIETY. Obituaries of former members. Compiled by M. Luther Heisey. Lancaster Co. Hist. Soc., Jour., 61:42-4; 62:61-3; 63:53-5; 64:74-8 (annual installments, Jan 1957-Jan 1960). [476

LANCASTER COUNTY HISTORICAL SOCIETY. A survey of county historical societies in Pennsylvania. [Signed:] Jack W. Willson Loose, Secretary. Lancaster Co. Hist. Soc., Jour., 61:121-8 (Jul 1957). map, tables. [477

IRA DAVID LANDIS. Lancaster Mennonite Conference Historical Society begins its work. Mennonite hist. bul., 20(2): 1-2 (Apr 1959). From the Pastoral messenger, Jan. 1959. On a society organized in 1958, and its plans for assembling a library of books, manuscripts, and other historical materials and for establishing card inventories and indexes. [478

BERTRAM K. LITTLE. Retrospect: fifty years of historic preservation. Antiques, 77:466-75 (May). port., views. On the work of the Society for the Preservation of New England Antiquities, 1910-60, in preserving early buildings and their furnishings and in collecting photographs, plans, and other information and materials as to their original construction and contents. [479

CLIFFORD LEE LORD. Importance of the work of local historical societies. Mo. hist. rev., 54:107-15 (Jan). port. [480

MISSOURI HISTORICAL SOCIETY. In memoriam. Mo. Hist. Soc., Bul., 16:194, 291-6, 369-75; 17:104-12 (Jan-Oct). Memorial biographics of recently decreased members. [481

RUBY J. MONTGOMERY, ed. History of the Montana Institute of the Arts. Mont. Inst. Arts quar., 10(3-4), 11(2-3), 12(2): irregular installments (spring 1958-winter 1960). On an organization founded in 1948 "to preserve the heritage of the state as found in its history and folklore, to stimulate creative work in the several arts, and to make cultural resources available for the benefit and enjoyment of the people of Montana." The history consists of reminiscences or reports by its former presidents, H. G. Merriam, Paul A. Grieder, Verne Dusenberry, Robert A. Athearn, and Cyril Conrad, 1848-58, each dealing with his own term in office. [482

MUNCY HISTORICAL SOCIETY AND MUSEUM OF HISTORY, Muncy, Pa. Local history is our line, by Eugene P. Bertin: the annual report of the

President of the Muncy Historical Society and Museum of History. Now and then, 12:61-8, 157-65 (Apr 1958, Apr 1959). Reports dated 17 Jan. 1958 and 16 Jan. 1959, on "local history--its many phases, its content, its significance, its values, and the obligations it implies for all of us"; with numerous illustrations from Muncy, lists of facts useful for further studies in the history of Muncy, and a tribute to Dr. T. Kenneth Wood, "the Father of our Society." [483

OREGON. Centennial Commission. Oregon Centennial Commission, 1859-1959: fiscal report. [Salem? 1960. 4], 125, [4] p. ports., tables, views. Review of its activities, Jul. 1955 - May 1960. [484

WILLIAM JOHN PETERSEN. The State Historical Society of Iowa [1857-1960]. Iowa City, 1960. 357-404 p. facsims., ports., views (part col.). (The palimpsest, v. 41, no. 8.) Appended (p. 403-4): "some publications of the Society." [485

ERNEST H. RANKIN. Historical fact vs. fancy in a county historical society. Detroit Soc. Geneal. Research mag., 23:1-4 (fall 1959). Presents "a few examples of that which the Marquette County Historical Society has found in its research," relating mainly to early settlers in the Upper Peninsula of Michigan. [486

MARY ELLEN THOMSEN. Trolley museum. Harvard alumni bul., 59: 694-5 (8 Jun 1957). ports., views. On the New England Electric Railway Historical Society, Kennebunkport, Me., 1939-56. [487

U.S. Lincoln Sesquicentennial Commission. Abraham Lincoln sesquicentennial, 1959-1960: final report of the Lincoln Sesquicentennial Commission. Wash. [1960]. xvi, 193 p. facsims., ports., views. "New books on Lincoln" (p. 152-3). [488

KENNETH TRIST URQUHART. Seventy years of the Louisiana Historical Association [1889-1959]. La. hist., 1:5-23 (winter). port., views. notes. [489

VIRGINIA HISTORICAL AND PHILOSOPHICAL SOCIETY. Early records of the Virginia Historical Society, 1831[-1838]. Edited by William M. E. Rachal. Va. mag. hist. and biog., 67: 3-29, 186-206, 332-60, 450-69; 68: 92-103 (Jan 1959-Jan 1960). ports. notes. Letters received and sent, minutes, and other records of the ancestor of the Virginia Historical Society, 29 Dec. 1831 - 2 Apr. 1838. [490

WALTER MUIR WHITEHILL. Cerebration versus celebration. Va mag. hist. and biog., 68:259-70 (Jul). view. notes. Remarks on the proper work of historical societies, the proper observance of historic anniversaries, and the precautions needing to be taken against "the present-day horde of those that vulgarize and pervert history--riggers of television quizzes, promotional types who manufacture pseudohistoric monuments to catch the tourist dollar, eager 'salesmen of history' who pander rather than elevate the public taste by emphasizing what is trivial in the past, publishers who regard four-color illustrations on slick paper as acceptable substitutes for thought or style, and their kindred." [491

Libraries

AMERICAN LIBRARY ASSOCIATION. Association of College and Research Libraries. Necrology. College and research lib., 21:240, 308-10, 401 (May, Jul, Sep). Memorial sketches, by various contributors, of Charles Harvey Brown, Harry Miller Lydenberg, and Carleton B. Joeckel. [492

AMERICAN LIBRARY ASSOCIATION. Library Administration Division. Copyright problems. College and research lib., 21:212-22, 246 (May). notes. Contents.--Introduction: copyright law revision and libraries, by Richard E. Chapin.--Copyright, libraries, the public interest [since 1909], by Benjamin Kaplan.--Photocopying and fair use, by Edward G. Freehafer.--Copyright notice, by Joseph W. Rogers.--Deposit of copies of copyright works in the Library of Congress [since 1909], by Rutherford D. Rogers. [493

MARGARET (CULKIN) BANNING. The restricted shelf: censorship's last stand. Robert B. Downs, ed., The first freedom: liberty and justice in the world of books and reading (Chicago: American Library Assoc., 1960), p. 320-23. From Saturday review, 29 Oct. 1938. On "restricted shelves" in American libraries as a means of controlling access by children or other disqualified readers to materials deemed unsuitable for their perusal or likely to suffer physical damage in their hands. [494

ESTELLE BRODMAN & MARIE HARVIN. Medical libraries in the Washington area [1836-1960]. D.C. lib., 31:25-9 (Apr). [495

ADELIA BROWNELL. The birth of the Wyoming [Ohio] Library--1880. Hist. and Philos. Soc. Ohio, Bul., 18:137-41 (Apr). port., views. notes. Includes some account of the later history of the Library. [496

BULLETIN OF BIBLIOGRAPHY [Tributes to living librarians.] Bul. bibliog., 22:169-71, 193-4, 217-19; 23:1-3, 27-9, 49-51 (Jan 1959 - Dec 1960). ports. Contents.--Kenneth R. Shaffer, by Laurence J. Kipp and Rae C. Kipp.--John Stewart Richards, by Willard O. Youngs.--Rose L. Vormelker, by Jean K. Taylor.--John Taylor Eastlick, by Eulalia Dougherty Chapman.--Robert Bingham Downs, by Richard Harwell.--Ralph Theodore Esterquest, by Douglas W. Bryant. [497

HAROLD L. BURSTYN. The Salem Philosophical Library: its history and importance for American science [1781-1810]. Essex Inst. hist. col., 96:169-206 (Jul). notes. On a collection of scientific books and serials assembled by Richard Kirwan (1733-1812) of London, seized in transit from Ireland by an American privateer, sold to a group of Essex County citizens, augmented from time to time by new acquisitions, and acquired in 1810 by the Boston Athenaeum; with remarks on its uniqueness as "the only significant private collection of books primarily scientific" in the United States in the late 18th century, and accounts of the subscribers and their "importance ... in American and world science." [498

HERBERT CAHOON. A brief account of the Clifton Waller Barrett Library [of the University of Virginia Library]. Charlottesville: Univ. of Virginia, 1960. 35, [2] p. view. On a collection of imprints and manuscripts containing, "so far as it has been possible to assemble them, all fiction, poetry, drama, and essays published by an American in book form" from 1775 "up to and including the year 1875," as well as "a very nearly complete collection of the works of every major American writer" and of American writers "whose achievement were not of first rank but who ... occupy a place in the literary history of the Republic" since 1875. [499

CALIFORNIA, UNIVERSITY OF. Bureau of Public Administration. Public library law and administration in California: a review of selected problems [1850-1958]. By F. Patrick Henry. Berkeley, 1958. [8], iii, 88 p. tables. (Its Legislative problems, 1959, no. 3.) [500

TOMMIE JOE COLE. The origin and development of school libraries [1835-1959]. Peabody jour. educ., 37:87-92 (Sep 1959). bibliog. [501

PETER THOMAS CONMY. James Louis Gillis [1857-1917], Westerner and librarian. Wilson lib. bul., 34: 272-80, 283 (Dec 1959). notes. On his service as State Librarian of California, 1899-1917, and the growth of the California library system in his time; with some account of his earlier career in California business and politics. [502

LEO T. CRISMON. The Southern Baptist Theological Seminary Library making an ideal live. Rev. and expositor, 57:219-38 (Apr). notes. On the financial support, buildings, furnishings, equipment, staff, and holdings of the Library, 1859-1959. [503

JOHN D. CUSHING. The Lancaster [Mass.] Circulating Library [1790-1850]. N.Y. Pub. Lib., Bul., 64:432-6 (Aug). facsim. Includes a transcript of its manuscript catalogue of 1791, with added information concerning authors' names and titles of books. [504

JEROME CUSHMAN. Night-thoughts of a librarian. Midwest quar., 1:227-38 (Apr). On the "historical development of the public library movement" since 1876. [505

SUE DICKINSON. George Freedley is librarian of theatrical world. Commonwealth (Va.), 27(6):23-5, 72 (Jun). cartoon, ports. On the Theatre Collection of the New York Public Library (founded in 1931), and its "founder and curator," George Reynolds Freedley; with some account of his other services to the theatrical profession. [506

EDWARD GEIER FREEHAFER. Harry Miller Lydenberg, 1874-1960. N.Y. Pub. Lib., Bul., 64:295-7 (Jun). port. On his career as a librarian, particularly his services to the New York Public Library. [507

GENEALOGICAL SOCIETY OF UTAH. The Genealogical Library in Salt Lake City. By Archibald F. Bennett--Secretary and Librarian. Mich. heritage, 2:35-7 (autumn). Includes statistics of the quantity of "Microfilms of the Genealogical Society as of July 1, 1960," compiled by James M. Black, Microfilm Editor (totaling 250,984 100-ft. rolls of reproductions of American and foreign records). [508

DOROTHY G. HARRIS. Friends Historical Library, Swarthmore College [established 1871]. Anna (Cox) Brinton, ed., Then and now: Quaker essays, historical and contemporary, by friends of Henry Joel Cadbury (Phila.: Univ. of Pennsylvania Press [1960]), p. 215-18. notes. On its holdings of "meeting records, books, periodicals, paintings," and particularly manuscript diaries and letters. [509

CARL WILLIAM EDMUND HINTZ. Home for a half-million books. Old Oregon, 38(1):2-5 (Aug-Sep 1957). port., views. On the University of Oregon Library, 1872-1957. [510

E. J. JOSEY. The Savannah State College Library: in retrospect and prospect [1891-1960]. Savannah State College, Faculty research edition, 14(2):40-51 (Dec). notes. [511

AUGUSTUS FREDERICK KUHLMAN. Two ARL approaches to counting holdings of research libraries. College and research lib., 21:207-11 (May). notes. On efforts of the Association of College and Research Libraries to promote uniformity in counting either number of volumes or number of "bibliographical units," 1945-60. [512

PHILIP D. LAGERQUIST. New resources for American studies. I. The Harry S. Truman Library--a new research center for the Middle West. Cent. Miss. Valley Am. Studies Assoc., Jour., 1(1):1-9 (spring). [513

GLENN M. LEWIS. Minnesota's first public libraries [1849-1960]. Lawrence Martin Brings, ed., Minnesota heritage (Minneapolis: T. S. Denison [1960]), p. 244-9. facsim., port., table, views. [514

MARY EDMUND LINCOLN. Cultural significance of the Minneapolis Public Library [opened in 1889] in its origins and development: a study in the relations of the public library and American society. Ann Arbor: University Microfilms, 1958 [i. e. 1960]. Positive microfilm of typescript. vi, 381 leaves. diagrs., tables. bibliog. (leaves 361-81). Thesis--Univ. of Minnesota. Abstracted: Dissert. abstracts, 20:4118 (Apr). Includes some account of the Minneapolis Athenaeum, 1859-89. [515

CHARLES FLETCHER LUMMIS. Books in harness. Lawrence Clark Powell, ed., The Southwest of the bookman ([Los Angeles: Univ. of California Library] 1959), leaves 1-3. From Out West, Sep. 1906. On American public libraries, library associations, and library schools. [516

HARRY MILLER LYDENBERG (1874-1960). Two bookmen [Joshua Bloch and Wilberforce Eames (1855-1937)]. Abraham Berger, Lawrence Marwick, & Isidore S. Meyer, eds., The Joshua Bloch memorial volume: studies in booklore and history (N.Y.: New York Public Library, 1960), p. 1-9. On the early life of Eames in Maine, his work as a book clerk in New York City, later as Librarian of the Lenox Library and a staff member of the New York Public Library, and his activities as a collector of rare books and a bibliographer. [517

MARCUS ALLEN McCORISON. Harold Goddard Rugg, January 21, 1883 - February 13, 1957. Vt. Hist. Soc., News and notes, 8:42-3 (Mar 1957). port. On his work as a bibliographer of Vermont, a collector of Vermontiana, and developer of "the rare books collection and College Archives" of the Dartmouth College Library. For some account of his Vermont collections see 8:67, 85-6. [518

SYDNEY BANCROFT MITCHELL (1878-1951). Mitchell of California: the memoirs of Sydney B. Mitchell, librarian--teacher--gardener. With a preface by Lawrence Clark Powell. Berkeley: California Library Assoc., 1960. 263 p. ports. On the author's early life in Canada, his studies at the New York State Library School (Albany), his work as a cataloguer in the McGill University Library, and his service from 1908 to 1911 on the staff of Stanford University Library. Appended: reminiscent article by Mitchell (from the California library bulletin, Jun. 1950) on his career in librarianship at Stanford University and the University of California (Berkeley); "Sydney B. Mitchell, dean of horticulture in California," by Cora R. Brandt (from Journal of the California Horticultural Society, 1950); and "Sydney B. Mitchell bibliography," by Betty Rosenberg, listing his publications on library subjects, 1924-50, and gardening, 1918-50. [519

ISADORE GILBERT MUDGE (1875-1957). "A spot of brightness." Columbia Lib. columns, 9(3):14-20 (May). port. Anecdotes from a reminiscent chapter of Miss Mudge's manuscript, "Development of the Reference Department of the Columbia University Libraries," 1911-41. [520

STANLEY McCRORY PARGELLIS. AT--friend of libraries. Wayland Debs Hand & Gustave Arlt, eds., Humaniora: essays in literature, folklore, bibliography, honoring Archer Taylor on his seventieth birthday (Locust Valley, N.Y.: J. J. Augustin, 1960), p. 97-101. On the work of Archer Taylor as a Fellow of the Newberry Library, Chicago (1945), his "hundreds" of letters to the Librarian offering suggestions and advice as to acquisitions to be made, and his many-sided distinction as a humanistic scholar. [521

STANLEY McCRORY PARGELLIS. Everett D. Graff. Newberry Lib. bul., 5:187-9 (Dec). port. On his service as President of the Newberry Library and of the Art Insitutte of Chicago, his lifelong interest in Western Americana, and his gift of his collection to the Library. [522

PATRICIA PAYLORE. Inside Oklahoma. Lawrence Clark Powell, ed., The Southwest of the bookman ([Los Angeles: Univ. of California Library] 1959), leaves 34-9. From the Oklahoma librarian, Jul. 1956. On the author's early life in Clarkdale, Ariz., a copper town owned by Sen. William Andrews Clark, the development of her interest in reading and books, her "lifelong dedication to Southwestern Americana," her career as a librarian (though "I never read a book or set foot in a library till I was past fifteen"), and her visit in 1953 to the William Andrews Clark Memorial Library. [523

ERNEST H. RANKIN. The J. M. Longyear Research Library of the Marquette Historical Society. Inland seas, 16:326-30 (winter). On the expanding interest in the history of the Upper Peninsula of Michigan, the collection of books and periodicals relating to the Upper Peninsula assembled by John Munro Longyear (1850-1922) of Marquette, and the bequest of the library to the Marquette Historical Society by his widow with funds to maintain and expand it. [524

JAMES RANZ. The history of the printed book catalogue in the United States [1630s to ca. 1900]. Ann Arbor: University Microfilms, 1960. Positive microfilm of typescript. [332] leaves. Thesis--Univ. of Illinois. Abstracted: Dissert. abstracts, 21:1574 (Dec). On catalogues printed as books, gradually superseded after 1850 by card catalogues. [525

JEANNE ROSE. A brief history of the Arlington County libraries [1892-1960]. Arlington hist. mag., 1(4):28-38 (Oct). bibliog. [526

BERTHA M. ROTHE. Law library facilities in the District of Columbia. D.C. lib., 31:41-5 (Oct). [527

WAYNE SHIRLEY. Josephine Adams Rathbone [1864-1941]. Wilson lib. bul., 34:199-204 (Nov 1959). ports. On her work as "chief instructor" and vice-director of the Pratt Institute Library School, 1893-1938; with a detailed account of the school and of her teaching methods and mention of some of her eccentricities. [528

ANN ALLEN SHOCKLEY. A history of public library services to Negroes in the South, 1900-1955. Dover: Delaware State College [1959?]. 24 leaves. bibliog. (leaves 23-4), notes (leaves 21-2). [529

FLORENCE E. TURNER. The Library of the School of Medicine [Boston University, 1942-53]. Boston Univ. graduate jour., 2:118-20 (Apr 1954). From the Boston medical quarterly, Dec. 1953. [530

JAMES D. VAN TRUMP. A garden of books. Carnegie mag., 34:167-70, 177 (May). views. On a collection of early botanical publications assembled by Rachel McMasters Miller Hunt of Pittsburgh and organized as the Hunt Botanical Library. [531

LOUIS ROUND WILSON. The library of the first State university. Chapel Hill: Univ. of North Carolina Library, 1960. iv, 40 p. facsims., table, views. notes. On the Library of the University of North Carolina, 1795-1960. [532

Museums

EDWARD PORTER ALEXANDER. History museums: from curio cabinets to cultural centers. Wis. mag. hist., 43:173-80 (spring). ports. notes. On the historical museums of today as "an amalgam of at least three important cultural movements"--historical societies, public museums, and historic houses, 1791-1960; with an account of the "picture gallery" and the "cabinet" of the State Historical Society of Wisconsin since 1853. [533

HOMER G. BENTON, comp. Streetcars on display. Railroad mag., 71(3):50-53 (Apr). List of places in the United States and Canada where trolleys, interurban cars, and horsecars are preserved in "trolley museums" or other suitable quarters. [534

DANIEL JOSEPH BOORSTIN. An American style in historical monuments. Daniel J. Boorstin, America and the image of Europe: reflections on American thought (N. Y.: Meridian Books [1960]), p. 79-96. Revision of "Past and present in America: a historian visits Colonial Williamsburg," Commentary, Jan. 1958. [535

GEORGE R. CLAY. The lightbulb angel. N.Y. folklore quar., 16:163-73 (autumn). On "the related trio of indoor and outdoor folk museums of the New York State Historical Association at Cooperstown, New York"--the Farmers' Museum, the Village Crossroads, and Fenimore House; with a comparison of these with Old Sturbridge Village and Mystic Seaport. [536

CLEVELAND MUSEUM OF ART. The Cleveland Museum of Art. Text by William M[athewson] Milliken, Director. N.Y.: H. N. Abrams [1958]. 62 p. ports and views (part mount., col.). 39 cm. (Great museums of the world.) Brief account of the Museum, founded in 1913, and annotated reproductions of paintings and statuary, mainly European, in its collections. [537

ALEXANDER B. COOK. The Great Lakes Historical Society Museum [Vermilion, Ohio]. Inland seas, 16:75, 160-61, 244-5, 322-3 (spring-winter). double map. On holdings, acquisitions, services, and programs of the Museum. [538

DATY HEALY. A history of the Whitney Museum of American Art, 1930-1954. Ann Arbor: University Microfilms, 1960. Positive microfilm of typescript. [355] leaves. Thesis--New York Univ. Abstracted: Dissert. abstracts, 21:1161-2 (Nov). [539

RALPH NADING HILL & LILIAN BAKER CARLISLE. The story of the Shelburne Museum [1947-60]. ... Second edition. Shelburne, Vt.: Shelburne Museum, 1960. [7], 113, [2] p. facsims., maps, ports., views (part col., part double). 1st ed. 1955. Mainly a description of buildings and exhibits. [540

LUCETTA A. JOHNSON. The cabin in the wildflower woods. Hobbies, 65(8): 60-61; (9):57, 60 (Oct, Nov). views. On the Gene Stratton Porter Memorial, Geneva, Ind. [541

CARL LIVINGSTON. Ca' d' Zan: the House of John. Fla. handbook, 1949-50, p. 332-3. On the John and Mable Ringling Museum of Art, opened in 1931 at Sarasota, and the associated John and Mable Ringling Residence and Museum of the American Circus. [542

JOHN FRANCIS McDERMOTT. William Clark's museum once more. Mo. Hist. Soc., Bul., 16:130-33 (Jan). notes. Evidence that "part or all of Clark's Indian curiosities" were in possession of Albert Koch, proprietor of the St. Louis Museum, in 1837-38; and question concerning the fate of portraits of Indian chiefs painted at Clark's order in St. Louis as early as 1826. [543

JOHN ALDEN MASON. Observations on the function of the museum in anthropology. Stanley Diamond, ed., Culture in history: essays in honor of Paul Radin (N.Y.: Columbia Univ. Press for Brandeis Univ., 1960), p. 341-8. [544

MISSOURI HISTORICAL SOCIETY. The Heritage Rooms. By George Raithel Brooks, Curator. Mo. Hist. Soc., Bul., 16:260-64 (Apr). views. notes. On the newly refinished museum galleries of the Society, and some of the exhibits there. [545

MARIAN MURRAY. The three Ringling museums. Fla. handbook, 1951-52, p. 71-3. view. On the John and Mable Ringling Museum of Art (opened in 1931), the John and Mable Ringling Residence, and the Museum of the American Circus, Sarasota, Fla., established by John Ringling (who settled in Sarasota in 1911) and bequeathed by him to the State of Florida. Repeated in later biennial editions. [546

NEWARK MUSEUM ASSOCIATION. A survey: 50 years of the Newark Museum [1909-59]. Newark, N.J., 1959. 136 p. ports., tables, views. (The museum, v. 11, 1959.) History of the Museum by Katherine Coffey, Director, and accounts, by staff members, of its collections of painting, sculpture, decorative arts, coins, and ethnological and scientific materials. [547

NORTH CAROLINA MUSEUM OF ART. Raleigh. Supplement to the W. R. Valentiner memorial exhibition. [Raleigh] 1959. 52 p. ports., views. notes. (The North Carolina Museum of Art bulletin, 3.) Six tributes to William Reinhold Valentiner (1880-1958) and 7 brief articles in his memory, by various contributors, on his services as an executive of the Metropolitan Museum (1908-14), the Detroit Museum of Arts (1921-45), the Los Angeles County Museum (1945-54), and the North Carolina Museum of Art (1954-58); with text of a manuscript by him, "Two busts by Cellini." [548

ROBERT O'BRIEN. Ghost town. True West, 7(4):22-7 (Mar-Apr). port., views. From Reader's digest, Oct. 1957, with photographs added. On Knott's Berry Farm and Ghost Town, Buena Park, Calif., 1941-57. [549

OLD STURBRIDGE VILLAGE, Sturbridge, Mass. Old Sturbridge Village: a guidebook. [Third edition revised.] Sturbridge [1960. 4], 64, [4] p. views. (Old Sturbridge Village booklet series, 6.) On a "recreation of an imaginary representative New England community of the period 1790 to 1840." [550

JESSIE J. POESCH. A precise view of Peale's Museum [Philadelphia]. Antiques, 78:343-5 (Oct). ports., views. On a watercolor by Titian Ramsay Peale, Peale's Museum, 1822, done in meticulous detail by request of his father, Charles Willson Peale, to show "the minutia of objects" in "the Long Room." Shows a long, narrow room seen from one end, with paintings on the walls and cases of exhibits along the left wall and projecting at right angles from the right wall, and busts resting on some of the cases. [551

HELEN R. PURTLE. Armed Forces Institute of Pathology Medical Museum [1862-1960]. U.S. Armed Forces med. jour., 11:579-83 (May). views. [552

BARBARA SNOW. American art at Shelburne. Antiques, 78:448-51 (Nov). ports., views. On the recently established Webb Gallery of American Art at the Shelburne Museum and some of its holdings. [553

ELOISE SPAETH. American art museums and galleries: an introduction to looking. N.Y.: Harper [1960]. xii, 282, [1] p. ports., views. bibliog. (p. 265-6). Description and history of each museum (beginning with the Charleston Museum, 1773), arranged by regions; and brief listing of "Selected galleries," understood to be places where art is exhibited for sale. [554

TRAVELING in Missouri? Hobbies, 65(5):80, 86 (Jul). views. On the Million Dollar Museum of Musical Automation at the edge of Sikeston, Mo., which "houses the world's largest collection of restored nickelodeons," assembled and repaired since 1953 by Paul R. Eakins. [555

U.S. Post Office Dept. [The Postal History Museum in the Post Office Department Building, opened 23 Feb. 1960.] Southw. hist. quar., 64:144-6 (Jul). [556

JOHN A. WINKLER. Making a Missouri historical center of international fame. Mo. hist. rev., 54:148-57 (Jan). port., views (1 on cover). On the work of the Mark Twain Commission in preserving memorials to Mark Twain in Hannibal, Mo., 1935-59. [557

HISTORIOGRAPHY

EUGENE CAMPBELL BARKER (1874-1956). [Letter to Alex Dienst, dated Austin, 21 Dec. 1902.] Southw. hist. quar., 63: facsim. on [4] p. following p. 600 (Apr). port. Reproduction of a manuscript on the author's study, in progress, of events in the history of Texas and Mexico, ca. 1832, referring to Dienst's comments on a draft of a publication by Barker. [558

CHARLES AUSTIN BEARD (1874-1948). Written history as an act of faith. ... With an introduction by John P. Bloom. El Paso: Texas Western College Press for Academic Reprints, 1960. 19, [1] p. notes. (The Academic reprints series.) Presidential address, American Historical Association, 28 Dec. 1933. Appended (p. 17-19): "A selected bibliography of Charles Beard's writings." Includes Italian text and English translation of a letter to Beard from Benedetto Croce, 24 Jun. 1933. [559

CARL LOTUS BECKER (1873-1945). Detachment and the writing of history. Carl L. Becker, Detachment and the writing of history: essays and letters of Carl L. Becker, ed. Phil L. Snyder (Ithaca: Cornell Univ. Press [1958]), p. 3-28. First published in 1910. [560

CARL LOTUS BECKER (1873-1945). Everyman his own historian. ... With an introduction by Jack L. Cross. El Paso: Texas Western College Press for Academic Reprints, 1960 [c1959]. iv, 19, [1] p. notes. (The academic reprint series.) Presidential address, American Historical Association, 29 Dec. 1931. Appended: "A selected bibliography of Carl Becker's writings" (p. 19). [561

CARL LOTUS BECKER (1873-1945). On writing history. Carl L. Becker, Detachment and the writing of history: essays and letters of Carl L. Becker, ed. Phil L. Snyder (Ithaca: Cornell Univ. Press [1958]), p. 35-40. First published in 1925. [562

CARL LOTUS BECKER (1873-1945). What are historical facts? Carl L. Becker, Detachment and the writing of history: essays and letters of Carl L. Becker, ed. Phil L. Snyderk (Ithaca: Cornell Univ. Press [1958]), p. 41-64. Written in 1926; first printed in 1955. [563

CARL LOTUS BECKER (1873-1945). What is historiography? Carl L. Becker, Detachment and the writing of history: essays and letters of Carl L. Becker, ed. Phil L. Snyder (Ithaca: Cornell Univ. Press [1958]), p. 65-78. First published in 1938. [564

JOSEPH LEON BLAU. John Dewey's theory of history. Jour. philos., 57:89-100 (4 Feb). notes. Review of his whole intellectual career after ca. 1890 to find concepts bearing on historiography, and collection of his more or less explicit assertions on that subject in his Reconstruction in philosophy (1920) and Logic: the theory of inquiry (1938). [565

JAMES CALVIN BONNER. The writing of history. Ga. rev., 14:334-45 (autumn). [566

BRUCE CATTON. Michigan's past and the nation's future. [Edited by Alexander Brede.] Detroit: Wayne State Univ. Press for the Detroit Historical Soc., 1960. [8], 19 p. (The Lewis Cass lectures, 1959.) On "the immense revival of interest in history which has developed in this country during the last decade," and "the human story which our audience is demanding." Contains 4 paragraphs on Michigan (p. 8-10). [567

JOHN HOPE FRANKLIN. "As for our history ..." Charles Grier Sellers, Jr., ed., The Southerner as American (Chapel Hill: Univ. of North Carolina Press [1960]), p. 3-18. notes. On Southern historical writing and "historical consciousness," 1789-1956. [568

BRAY HAMMOND. A look at "historical truth": what was so and what was not. Dartmouth alumni mag., 52(6):6-7 (Mar). port. [569

ANNA HESSE. How to write and produce a historical pageant. Mo. hist. rev., 54:158-60 (Jan). port. [570

HENRY STUART HUGHES. The historian and the social scientist. Am. hist. rev., 66:20-46 (Oct). notes. On the need for "some clear concept of law and cause in history" and the indications that "a certain amount of social science theory can profitably be exploited for the purposes of historical explanation." [571

PHILIP DILLON JORDAN. The usefulness of useless knowledge. Historian, 22:237-49 (May). notes. Refers particularly to historical knowledge. [572

ROBERT HARRY LOWIE (1883-1957). Oral tradition and history. Lowie's selected papers in anthropology, ed. Cora Du Bois (Berkeley: Univ. of California Press, 1960), p. 202-10. notes. From Journal of American folk-lore, Apr.-Jun. 1917. Argument that "Indian tradition is historically worthless." [573

JAMES MADISON (1751-1836). A presidential comment on handwriting. [Edited by] Ralph [Louis] Ketcham. Manuscripts, 12(4):64-7 (fall). facsim. Letter to John Andrew Graham

(1764-1841), dated 15 Aug. 1828, acknowledging receipt of Graham's Memoirs of John Horne Tooke, expressing skepticism toward Graham's reliance upon handwriting in his attribution of the letters of Junius to Tooke, and noting that different samples of an individual's handwriting may show great variations; with an excerpt from a letter of Madison 4 years later, on the effect of rheumatism upon his writing. [574

THOMAS PATRICK NEILL. Dewey's ambivalent attitude toward history [1893-1951]. John Blewett, ed., John Dewey: his thought and influence (N.Y.: Fordham Univ. Press [1960]), p. 145-60. notes. [575

ALLAN NEVINS. Not Capulets, not Montagus. Am. hist. rev., 65:253-70 (Jan). Presidential address, American Historical Association, 29 Dec. 1959. On the reasons for the abandonment of "the proud pretensions which historians once made to the instruction of a whole nation," the present wide gap "between popular history and academic history," and the need, if "the appetite of 175,000,000 Americans for history" is to be satisfied, of a "distinct broadening of effort, and in particular a greater attention to a humanized and attractive presentation of the past." [576

The PULITZER Prizes in history, 1917-1959. Wis. mag. hist., 43:106-7 (winter). ports. List of annual prize-winning volumes. [577

MAX SAVELLE. The functions of history in the age of science. Historian, 22:347-60 (Aug). notes. [578

EDWARD NORMAN SAVETH. Scientific history in America: eclipse of an idea [1849-1959]. Donald Sheehan & Harold C. Syrett, eds., Essays in American historiography: papers presented in honor of Allan Nevins (N.Y.: Columbia Univ. Press, 1960), p. 1-19. notes. [579

BERNADOTTE EVERLY SCHMITT. The fashion and future of history. Bernadotte E. Schmitt, The fashion and future of history: historical studies and addresses (Cleveland: Press of Western Reserve Univ., 1960), p. 15-27. notes. Address, Feb. 1933. [580

BOYD CARLISLE SHAFER. History, not art, not science, but history: meanings and uses of history. Pac. hist. rev., 29: 159-70 (May). [581

MARIAN WESLEY SMITH (1907-61). Mandan "history" as reflected in Butterfly's winter count. Ethnohistory, 7:199-205 (summer). notes. Comment "on the events reflected in Plains calendrical records and in the Mandan concept of history," and on such records as a form of native historiography. [582

WILLIAM F. STEUBER, JR. Using history for fiction. Wis. mag. hist., 43:245-52 (summer). Advice to writers of historical fiction. [583

EARL E. THORPE. The frontier theory of Walter Prescott Webb [1932-59]. Quar. rev. higher educ. among Negroes, 28:34-41 (Jan). notes. [584

DAVID DIRCK VAN TASSEL. Recording America's past: an interpretation of the development of historical studies in America, 1607-1884. [Chicago:] Univ. of Chicago Press [1960]. xii, 222, [1] p. bibliog. (p. 191-212), notes. Based on thesis--Univ. of Wisconsin, 1955. Topical study of the motives, methods, and products of the teaching and writing of history in the United States. Appended: "American historical societies, 1790-1890" (p. 181-90). [585

R. RICHARD WOHL & A. THEODORE BROWN. The usable past: a study of historical traditions in Kansas City. Huntington Lib. quar., 23:237-59 (May). notes. On the "philosophy of local history" of Kansas City as "embodied in ten published books and many reminiscent articles," 1854-1950; with remarks upon the extent to which "what people believe about the history of their locale may shape their notions of how they ought to live in it and of the values they may hope to realize in their community." [586

COMER VANN WOODWARD. The age of reinterpretation. Am. hist. rev., 66:1-19 (Oct). notes. On "three fields for historical reinterpretation" since 1945: (1) "the end of the era of free security," i. e., "physical security from hostile attack and invasion," a change comparable to the end of the age of mass warfare"; (3) "the end of the age of European hegemony," of "an agelong European dominance," of "Europocentric" history--with general remarks on the perpetual desirability of reinterpretation as a process. [587

Examples of Methodology

ARIZONA: its people and resources [since prehistoric times]. Edited by Jack L[ee] Cross, Elizabeth H. Shaw, [and] Kathleen Scheifele. Tucson: Univ. of Arizona Press, 1960. [4], iii, [3], 385, [1] p. diagrs., facsims., maps, seals, tables, views. bibliog. (p. 377-85). Historical information is scattered through the volume, particularly in the section "Its people and their past" (p. 1-74). According to the editors, "Sixty-four separate essays were provided, and these form the basis for the text of this volume, and from this point of view the authors of the essays are the authors of this book. In order to attain uniformity of style and a flowing narrative, the editorial staff of the University of Arizona Press reworked some of the original contributions and therefore accepts responsibility for this volume." The "contributing authors and editors" are listed (p. iv-v), but their contributions are not identified. [588

LEE BENSON. Turner and Beard: American historical writing reconsidered. Glencoe, Ill.: Free Press [1960]. xiii, 241 p. notes. Contents.--Achille Loria's influence on American economic thought: including his contributions to the frontier hypothesis [from Agricultural history, Oct. 1950].--The historical background of Turner's frontier essay [from Agricultural history, Apr. 1951].--A critique of Beard and his critics. [Here first printed. Defense of Beard against recent attack by Robert E. Brown and Forrest McDonald, who "misread Beard" and fail to distinguish between "economic interpretation" and "economic determinism"; with an appendix on McDonald's "use of data."] [589

PETER J. COLEMAN. Beard, McDonald, and economic determinism in American historiography: a review article. Bus. hist. rev., 34:113-21 (spring). On Charles A. Beard's An economic interpretation of the Constitution of the United States, Robert E. Brown's Charles A. Beard and the Constitution (1956), and Forrest McDonald's We the people (1958); with general remarks on "the engaging but spurious generalizations which result from premature and irresponsible synthesis." [590

MATTHEW HODGSON. Bampson of Bampson's Legion: an informal study of Confederate command. Civil War hist., 6:157-9 (Jun). cartoon. notes. Illustration of Civil War scholarship in the form of a biography of Alpheus Tuesday Bampson, born 1822, organizer of the 9th Texas Partisan Rangers, a victim of the Battle of the Crater, 2 years after "the Battle of Yuma Gulch, or 'Bampson's Fiasco'"; with a panoply of footnotes. [591

WILLIAM STULL HOLT. What Wilson sent and what House received: or scholars need to check carefully. Am. hist. rev., 65:569-71 (Apr). notes. On differences between the message that Wilson wrote and the decoded message received by House in a cable of 29 Oct. 1918. [592

WILBUR R. JACOBS. The making of an American community: a case study of democracy in a frontier county. By Merle Curti ... Stanford: Stanford University Press, 1959. ... A review essay, Ariz. and the West, 2:294-9 (autumn). Evidence from the Turner Papers "that this is the kind of book Turner would have praised" because it demonstrates "that social science research techniques, largely neglected by historians, can be used with great effectiveness in the writing of history." [593

HERBERT LE ROY KAUFFMAN. Form and meaning in Henry Adams' History. Ann Arbor: University Microfilms, 1960. Positive microfilm of typescript. [175] leaves. Thesis--Stanford Univ. Abstracted: Dissert. abstracts, 21:874 (Oct). On his History of the United States of America during the administrations of Jefferson and Madison (1889-91) and its relation to his Life of Albert Gallatin (1879). [594

GEORGE FROST KENNAN. Soviet historiography and America's role in the intervention. Am. hist. rev., 65:302-22 (Jan). notes. On the "attitude toward the rules of historical evidence" exhibited in an account by S. F. Naida of American intervention in Russia, 1917-19 (O nekotorykh vosprosakh istorii grazhdanskoi voiny v S. S. S. R., Moscow, 1958). [595

IOSIF ROMUAL DOVICH LAVRETSKII. A survey of the Hispanic American review, 1956-1958. [Translated from Voprosy istorii, Dec. 1959, by J. Gregory Oswald.] Hisp. Am. hist. rev., 40:340-60 (Aug). notes. Concludes that in this periodical "the official Latin Americanists of the US falsify and distort the historical truth in order to benefit imperialism." [596

VIRGIL V. McNITT. Chain of error, and the Mecklenburg declarations of independence: a new study of manuscripts, their use, abuse, and neglect [1775-1917]. Palmer, Mass.: Hampden Hills Press, 1960 [label: all distribution by Heritage Printers, Charlotte, N.C. 2], 134 p. facsims., ports. (1 mount.). bibliog. (p. 129-31). [597

JACKSON TURNER MAIN & FORREST McDONALD. Charles A. Beard and the Constitution: a critical review of Forrest McDonald's We the people [1958]. ... With a rebuttal by Forrest McDonald. Wm. and Mary quar., 17:86-110 (Jan). notes. Debate on Beard's An economic interpretation of the Constitution of the United States (1913). [598

ROBERT DOUTHAT MEADE & DOUGLASS ADAIR. Letters to the Editor. Wm. and Mary quar., 17:283-7 (Apr). Protest by Meade against a review of the first volume of his work on Patrick Henry by Douglass Adair, and particularly against Adair's assertion "that I lack material for my book"; with Adair's comment on the protest. [599

ELTING ELMORE MORISON. The uneasy chair: selecting and editing the letters of Theodore Roosevelt. Harvard alumni bul., 60:598-601 (3 May 1958). facsim., view. On the task of the author and his staff of selecting about 6,500 letters of Theodore Roosevelt from a total of 100,000 letters, undertaken in 1948 and ending with publication of the letters, 1951-54. [600

LEE NATHANIEL NEWCOMER. Manasseh Cutler's writings: a note on editorial practice. Miss. Valley hist. rev., 47:88-101 (Jun). notes. On the editing of the Life, journals, and correspondence of Rev. Manasseh Cutler, LL.D. (Cincinnati, 1888) by William Parker Cutler and Julia Perkins Cutler, "septuagenarian grandchildren" of Manasseh Cutler; with evidence from his manuscripts, especially his diary, that they were inattentive to his interests and activities other than those connected with the Ohio Company and with Congress. [601

NORMAN POLLACK. Hofstadter on Populism: a critique of "The age of reform" [by Richard Hofstadter, 1955]. Jour. South. hist., 26:478-500 (Nov). notes. On his "preoccupation with present values" and the tendency of his "methodological assumptions" toward "the denial that protest ever existed in American society," so that "Radicalism ... becomes wholly discredited as a rational alternative while the present-day society is uncritically accepted." [602

JACK S. RADABAUGH. Charles A. Beard's economic interpretations of the Constitution [1913]: a consensus. Social studies, 51:243-50 (Dec). notes. Summary of varyingly favorable and unfavorable views and understandings of Beard's position or supposed position, 1932-56. [603

MAURICE D. SCHMAIER. Conrad Richter's The light in the forest [1953]: an ethnohistorical approach to fiction. Ethnohistory, 7:327-98 (fall). bibliog., notes. On his treatment of "Indian-White relations along the mid-18th century Pennsylvania frontier" in this novel, dealing with a white boy captured and reared by Delaware Indians, forcibly returned to a white community, and alienated from both the whites and the Indians; with an account of his use, in writing the novel, of "published ethnological and historical information" and of "advice from several recognized ethnological and historical scholars," a detailed confirmation of the factual accuracy of the book and its fidelity to the beliefs, feelings, and habits of the Indians and the whites, and general remarks on "Fiction and the living ethnohistorical past." [604

ANDREW MacKAY SCOTT. The Progressive Era in perspective. Jour. politics, 21:685-701 (Nov 1959). notes. On the misunderstanding of the Progressives shown by Richard Hofstadter in his The Age of Reform (1955), the falsity of "his thesis regarding the conservative nature of Progressivism" and his forced effort "to attribute all significant innovation to the New Deal," and his abuse of his "talent in the art of suggestion" as a substitute for "explicit argument and supporting fact"; with a condensed, schematic statement of "the leading features of Progressivism" as conceived by the author. [605

WARREN IRVING SMITH. How microscopic is regional history? Miss. quar., 13:6-12 (winter). bibliog. Based on thesis--univ. of Alabama. On sources and methods of the author's "microscopic study" of Montgomery County, Ala., 1817-60. [606

ALBERT KLECKNER STEIGERWALT, JR. The NAM and the Congressional investigations of 1913: a case study in the suppression of evidence. Bus. hist. rev., 34:335-44 (autumn). view, notes. On charges that the National Association of Manufacturers was an "invisible government," the sensational accusations by its former employee, M. M. Mulhall, in letters sold to newspapers, the investigation of the charges by a subcommittee of the Senate Committee on the Judiciary, the proof that most of them were false, the concealment by Sen. Lee S. Overman of a record of the dismissal of Mulhall from the Secret Service in 1893 on several grounds of misconduct, the failure of the Committee to publish its report and apparently to make its records, including the information about Mulhall, available to a House committee conducting a similar investigation, and the reliance upon the House report by historians to whom the Senate records have been available in the National Archives since 1935 and the Secret Service hearings on Mullhall since 1948. [607

FRANK THISTHETHWAITE. Reflections on Boorstin's America. Jour. mod. hist., 32:371-5 (Dec). On The Americans: the colonial experience, by Daniel Boorstin, as "the first major re-interpretation of American history since Turner, Parrington and Beard (I would say since Turner)." [608

Fields of Historical Research

HARRY WILLIAM BAEHR. A cycle of revisionism between two wars. Donald Sheehan & Harold C. Syrett, eds., Essays in American historiography: papers in honor of Allan Nevins (N.Y.: Columbia Univ. Press, 1960), p. 271-86. notes. On political and historical writings about the causes of World War I, 1917-55. [609

THOMAS DAY SEYMOUR BASSETT. Research in town history. Vt. hist., 28:288-92 (Oct). notes. On problems of purpose and method. [610

ARCHIBALD F. BENNETT. Advanced genealogical research. Salt Lake City: Bookcraft [1959]. xi, 256 p. diagr., facsims., ports., views. Twenty chapters on methods and problems. [611

ROWLAND TAPPAN BERTHOFF. The American social order: a conservative hypothesis. Am. hist. rev., 65:495-514 (Apr). notes. Observes that "In nearly eighty years of discussion since the time of McMaster and Eggleston we have not even managed to agree upon the proper subject matter of social history," nor have we found "an adequately 'dynamic principle,' or any 'great synthetic principle,' around which to organize this still amorphous material." Proposes "mobility" (geographic, and "occupational and social") as such a principle in American society. [612

CATHERINE (DRINKER) BOWEN. Adventures of a biographer. Boston: Little, Brown [1959]. xi, [3], 235 p. On the author's experience as a biographer of Peter Ilich Tchaikovsky, Anton Rubenstein, Oliver Wendell Holmes II, John Adams, and Sir Edward Coke, and her beliefs regarding biography as a literary form and a scholarly procedure. [613

RAYMOND BRANDES. Opportunities for research in Arizona history. Historian, 22:414-24 (Aug). On the abundance of hitherto unused historical materials in and concerning Arizona, and the many neglected or entirely ignored topics available for investigation in the history of Arizona. [614

HENRY W. BROUDE. The significance of regional studies for the elaboration of national economic history. Jour. econ. hist., 20:588-96 (Dec). notes. [615

ELIZABETH CASE. Statistics in stones. Detroit Soc. Geneal. Research mag., 24:27 (winter). Instructors to collectors of cemeterial inscriptions. [616

ANDREW HILL CLARK. Geographical change: a theme for economic history. Jour. econ. hist., 20:607-13 (Dec). notes. [617

JOHN BATES CLARK (1847-1938). General introduction [to A documentary history of American industrial society, 1909]. A documentary history of American industrial society (N.Y.: Russell & Russell, 1958), 1:33-53. On A documentary history as a contribution to "what is possibly the richest of all comparatively unworked fields of history," the value of sources of economic history for both the historian and the economist, the evidence "that a key to the understanding of American history and of all history is furnished by a knowledge of economic events," and some of the possible applications of this doctrine. [618

JOHN BOYD COATS, JR. On the utilization of medicomilitary history. Am. jour. surgery, 97:687-9 (Jun 1959). On the volumes published (14) or in progress in a history of the U.S. Army Medical Department in World War II. [619

RICHARD NELSON CURRENT. The Lincoln theme--unexhausted and inexhaustible. U.S., Lincoln Sesquicentennial Commission, Abraham Lincoln sesquicentennial, 1959-1960: final report (Wash. [1960]), p. 175-82. On the accomplishments and motives of "Lincoln scholarship" and the tasks awaiting it. [620

LANCE EDWIN DAVIS, JONATHAN R. T. HUGHES, & STANLEY REITER. Aspects of quantitative research in economic history. Jour. econ. hist., 20:539-47 (Dec). notes. On the value of statistical inference as a part of the study of economic history. [621

JOSEPH L. DRUSE. "My life in genealogy." Detroit Soc. Geneal. Research mag., 23:47-50 (winter 1959). On the author's devotion to this study even before his 10th year in spite of complete lack of encouragement from his family and associates, and the many reasons why he has continued to pursue it and why, in his opinion, it ought to be more widely pursued as a serious enterprise. [622

ABRAHAM GORDON DUKER. An evaluation of achievement in American local historical writing. Am. Jew. Hist. Soc., Pub., 49:215-64 (Jun). Summary and criticism of local histories of the Jews in the United States, arranged by name of State, and general remarks on the shortcomings of the works mentioned; with discussion by Selig Adler and Hyman Berman. [623

W. T. EASTERBROOK. Problems in the relationship of communication and economic history. Jour. econ. hist., 20:559-65 (Dec). notes. [624

OTTO EISENSCHIML. Too many Civil War books? Civil War hist., 6:250-57 (Sep). An effort to establish standards to be met by persons undertaking to write about the Civil War. [625

STANLEY M. ELKINS. Slavery: a problem in American institutional and intellectual life. [Chicago:] Univ. of Chicago Press [1959]. viii, 247, [1] p. notes. Review of the historiography of American slavery, 1893-1956, and of ideas expressed concerning "Institutions and the law of slavery," "Slavery and personality," "Slavery and the intellectual," and "The 'profitability' of slavery." [626

FRANK NELSON ELLIOTT. Genealogy and local history. Mich. heritage, 1:74-9 (spring). Defense of these forms of historical investigation and writing; with advice to genealogists, an expression of regret "that a higher proportion of genealogists do not write family histories," and some account of resources of the Museum of Michigan State University for promoting these studies. [627

RICHARD THEODORE ELY (1854-1943). Preface [to A documentary history of American industrial society, 1909]. A documentary history of American industrial society (N.Y.: Russell & Russell, 1958), 1:19-32. On the author's search since 1886 for manuscript and printed primary sources of information relating to the history of labor, the founding of the American Bureau of Industrial Research in 1904 "for the purpose of preparing a full and complete history of American industrial society," the work of the Bureau in collecting sources, "the general movement throughout western civilization which is diverting the interest of students and historians from wars, politics, and various forms of government to the economic life of the people," and the compilation of A documentary history as a contribution to this movement. [628

LOUIS FILLER. Slavery and antislavery: subjects in search of authors. Ohio hist. quar., 69:179-82 (Apr). On the need for further and continuing studies of the antislavery movement. [629

CARTER LYMAN GOODRICH. Economic history: one field or two? Jour. econ. hist., 20:531-8 (Dec). notes. On the question: "What, if anything, have the students of Economic Growth contributed to the understanding of economic change that economic historians of the more conventional sort had failed to supply? What contributions toward such understanding, if any, can be made only by economic historians using qualitative as well as quantitative methods?" [630

WILLIAM B. GRIFFEN. Suggestions for research in the culture and society of Spanish Florida. Fla. hist. quar., 38:226-38 (Jan). notes. On archival and manuscript materials in Florida relating to the years 1512-1765, and the many kinds of sociological and anthropological studies that could be based upon them. [631

EVA MURRELL HARMISON. How to arrange your family history. Detroit Soc. Geneal. Research mag., 24:36-8 (fall). [632

WILLIAM BEST HESSELTINE. Sectionalism and regionalism in American history. Jour. South. hist., 26: 25-34 (Feb). notes. Analysis of historiographic efforts to define and apply these concepts. [633

MARK DAVID HIRSCH. Reflections on urban history and urban reform, 1865-1915. Donald Sheehan & Harold C. Syrett, eds., Essays in American historiography: papers presented in honor of Allan Nevins (N.Y.: Columbia Univ. Press, 1960), p. 109-37. notes. On the historiography of this subject. [634

ANDREW H. HORN. Yesterday--today--tomorrow. Lawrence Clark Powell, ed., The Southwest of the bookman ([Los Angeles: Univ. of California Library] 1959), leaves 10-19. From Arizona librarian, winter 1959. On the growing interest in library history among librarians of the Southwest; with a sketch of the 5 periods of American library history, 1850-1950s, and 6 suggestions regarding the future of librarianship in the Southwest. [635

HAROLD MELVIN HYMAN. A man out of manuscripts: Edward [i. e. Edwin] M[cMasters] Stanton at the McCormick Reaper trial. Manuscripts, 12(2):35-9 (summer). notes. On the thorough reinterpretation of Stanton justified by available manuscript sources as illustrated by his supposed meeting with Abraham Lincoln at Cincinnati in 1855. [636

WALTER ISARD. Notes on the use of regional science methods in economic history. Jour. econ. hist., 20:597-600 (Dec). notes. [637

EDWARD CHASE KIRKLAND. The Robber Barons revisited. Am. hist. rev., 66:68-73 (Oct). notes. On the historiographic needs of this subject. [638

ERIC EDWIN LAMPARD. The price system and economic change: a commentary on theory and history. Jour. econ. hist., 20: 617-37 (Dec). notes. Argument that "There is a place for the sociologist and economist in the writing of economic history and also for the historian." [639

LEWIS GASTON LEARY. Bibliographical and textual studies and American literary history. Tex. quar., 3(2): 160-66 (summer). On the contributions of the first two to the study of the third, especially since 1948. [640

SEYMOUR MARTIN LIPSET. A sociologist looks at history. Pac. sociol. rev., 1:13-17 (spring 1958). notes. On the relations between history and sociology, and the contributions that each discipline can make to the other. [641

JOHN BERNARD McGLOIN. California Catholicism's neglected gold mine: a report on research and writing, 1850-1960. Church hist., 29:344-52 (Sep). notes. [642

GEORGE SMITH MAY. Michigan history and the graduate student. Mich. hist., 44:247-55 (Jun). On the subject matter of 345 masters' and 287 doctoral theses "which appear to have some relation to a phase of Michigan's history," the phases now in particular need of further study, and the desirability of encouraging greater number of graduate students to undertake theses in Michigan history. [643

HELEN MOULTON MEANWELL. Beginners' guides [in genealogy]. Detroit Soc. Geneal. Research mag., 24:86-7 (winter). Bibliographical essay. [644

MARVIN W. MIKESELL. Comparative studies in frontier theory. Assoc. Am. Geographers, Ann., 50:62-74 (Mar). notes. On efforts "to compare the westward movement in American history with the advance of settlement in other parts of the world," especially Canada, Australia, and South Africa. [645

EARL SPENCER POMEROY. Old lamps for new: the cultural lag in Pacific coast historiography. Ariz. and the West, 2:107-26 (summer). notes. On the activities of historians in the States of the Pacific coast, and the history curricula there, as compared with those of the East; and the themes and methods of the writings of the Pacific historians about the West. [646

WALLACE EVERETT PRATT. The value of business history in the search for oil [1859-1959]. Centennial Seminar on the History of the Petroleum Industry, Harvard University, 1959, Oil's first century: papers ([Cambridge:] Harvard Graduate School of Business Administration [1960]), p. 57-69. views. notes. [647

JAMES A RAWLEY. American historians and national politics from the Civil War to the First War [1865-1917]. Donald Sheehan & Harold C. Syrett, eds., Essays in American historiography: papers presented in honor of Allan Nevins (N.Y.: Columbia Univ. Press, 1960), p. 81-108. notes. On politics of this period as a theme of historical treatment. [648

WILLIAM WILCOX ROBINSON. Writing local history. Calif. Hist. Soc. quar., 39:209-17 (Sep). On the author's procedures in collecting information, maps, and pictures, using printed, manuscript, and oral sources, and writing about localities in sourthern California. [649

JOHN THOMAS SCHLEBECKER. The world metropolis and the history of American agriculture. Jour. econ. hist., 20:187-208 (Jun). notes. On the influence of "relative economic location" (distance of farm from metropolis) upon "the development of American agriculture," and the influence of "the people of the metropolis" upon "the activities of the people on the farms," as a proposed central theme of agricultural history; with illustrations from the United States. [650

BERNADOTTE EVERLY SCHMITT. Modern European history in the United States. Bernodotte E. Schmitt, The fashion and future of history: historical studies and addresses (Cleveland: Press of Western Reserve Univ., 1960), p. 65-73. Paper read in 1928, mainly a bibliographical essay on American studies in the field of modern European history. [651

FRANKLIN DANIEL SCOTT. The study of the effects of emigration. Scandinavian econ. hist. rev., 8:160-74. diagr. notes. Includes Illustrations from Scandinavian emigration to America. [652

PAGE SMITH. David Ramsay and the causes of the American Revolution. Wm. and Mary quar., 17:51-77 (Jan). notes. On his treatment of the subject in his History of the American Revolution (Philadelphia, 1789; London, 1793) as compared with the later treatments by George Bancroft, Sydney George Fisher, Arthur M. Schlesinger, Sr., Claude Van Tyne, Charles McLean Andrews, Lawrence Henry Gipson, and Edmund and Helen Morgan, supporting the conclusion: "There is, or has been so far, no panacea (like scientific method) which can perform for the historian the functions of judgment and analysis." [653

BARRY EMANUEL SUPPLE. Economic history and economic growth. Jour. econ. hist., 20:548-56 (Dec). notes. On the latter as only one of the themes, not the unique theme, of the former. [654

OWSEI TEMKIN. The study of the history of medicine. Johns Hopkins Hospital, Bul., 104:99-106 (Feb 1959). notes. [655

STITH THOMPSON. The historian and the genealogist. Filson Club hist. quar., 34:160-65 (Apr). Illustrations, from the author's experience, of the moral "that the genealogist would immensely enrich his own work if he studied more history, and that the historian can often make use of the more detailed work of the person who compiles family history." [656

FREDERICK BARNES TOLLES. 1652 in history: changing perspectives on the founding of Quakerism. Anna (Cox) Brinton, ed., Then and now: Quaker essays, historical and contemporary, by friends of Henry Joel Cadbury (Phila.: Univ. of Pennsylvania Press [1960]), p. 73-94. notes. On histories and interpretations of the founding of Quakerism and its early expansion in Great Britain and America, 1694-1957. [657

LUCILE MORRIS UPTON. Writing historical articles for local newspapers. Mo. hist. rev., 54:143-7 (Jan). port. [658

EVERETT WALTERS. Populism: its significance in American history [1892-1916]. Donald Sheehan & Harold C. Syrett, eds., Essays in American historiography: papers presented in honor of Allan Nevins (N.Y.: Columbia Univ. Press, 1960), p. 217-30. notes. On historical studies and treatments of Populism, 1896-1955. [659

RENE WELLEK. The concept of evolution in literary history. Morris Halle & others, ed., For Roman Jakobson: essays on the occasion of his sixtieth birthday (The Hague: Mouton, 1956), p. 653-61. bibliog., notes. On "evolutionism" as a guide to or principle of the history of literature. [660

THOMAS HARRY WILLIAMS. Lincoln and the causes of the Civil War. O. Fritiof Ander, ed., Lincoln images: Augustana College centennial essays (Rock Island, Ill.: Augustana College Library, 1960), p. 23-39. Reviews "the literature on the war's causation" published since the 1890s, and proposes the author's own interpretation. [661

KURT H. WOLFF. Sociology and history: theory and practice. Am. jour. sociol., 65:32-8 (Jul 1959). notes. [662

WALLACE F. WORKMASTER & ROBERT W. IVERSEN. Everyone his own historian: a guide for studying the history around you. University Park, Pa.: Center for Continuing Liberal Education, Pennsylvania State Univ. [1960. 4], 83 leaves. notes. Mainly a guide for the study of Pennsylvania history, particularly local history. [663

The Publication of Historical Works

MELVILLE JAMES BOYER. Montgomery's school history of Berks County: his account book of sales. Lehigh Co. Hist. Soc., Proc., 23:87-90. Information from an account book of Dr. Morton L. Montgomery recording sales and gifts of his School history of Berks County (Phila.: J. B. Rogers Print. Co., 1889), published at a cost of $1,030.87 and sold at a profit of some $2,600. [664

LYLE GLAZIER. American originals. Am. quar., 12:520-24 (winter). On recent publications of the letters of Henry James, Stephen Crane, Herman Melville, and Francis Parkman, the letters and journals of James Fenimore Cooper, the early lectures of Ralph Waldo Emerson, and his journals and miscellaneous notebooks; with remarks on general characteristics of this "golden harvest" of documentary publication. [665

LOWELL HAYES HARRISON. The Filson Club history quarterly: the first third of a century [1926-59]. Filson Club hist. quar., 34:166-74 (Apr). Analysis of vols. 1-33. [666

HISTORICAL SOCIETY OF BERKS COUNTY. Our silver anniversary: history of the Review as told by all its editors. Hist. rev. Berks Co., 25: 106-13, 133 (fall). facsims., ports. On the Historical review of Berks County, 1935-60; with recollections by Hanns Gramm, Mary Dives Impink, Milton W. Hamilton, J. Sherwood Weber, and Donald R. Shenton, and tributes from other persons interested in this publication. [667

RUBY J. MONTGOMERY. A running commentary of the M. I. A. bulletin and quarterly. Mont. Inst. Arts quar., 12(1):22-7 (autumn 1959). On The quarterly bulletin of the Montana Institute of the Arts, continued as The Montana Institute of the Arts quarterly, 1948-59. [668

COLTON EDWARDS STORM, ed. Hot lights and cold tea: an un-casual correspondence. Manuscripts, 12(1):26-33 (winter). ports. Correspondence of Forest H. Sweet, Clifford L. Lord, William B. Hesseltine, and Donald R. McNeil, 1958, on the various methods of Hesseltine and the State Historical Society of Wisconsin to promote the sale of Hesseltine's Pioneer's mission: the story of Lyman C. Draper, published by the Society in 1954 (including "no less than twenty-five articles" written or edited by Hesseltine "for the precise purpose of calling the attention of prospective buyers to the book"; 8,600 "direct mail pieces" sent to "3,200 American history faculty members," all University of Wisconsin history majors, many Wisconsin newspapers, numerous book reviewers and book dealers, etc.; and "radio and television appearances, teas and autograph parties"); with remarks on this case of a general phenomenon, attributable to "a non-book-buying history profession," burdening the Society with a large stock of unsold copies. [669

U.S. National Historical Publications Commission. A national program for the publication of the papers of American leaders: a preliminary report to the President of the United States. [By Philip M. Hamer, Executive Director.] Wash., 1951. vi, 47 p. "Lists of papers to be considered for publication" (p. 17-47). [670

WALTER MUIR WHITEHILL. The Adams Papers: the records of two centuries of a Harvard family. Harvard alumni bul., 57:117-19, 123-4 (23 Oct 1954). ports. On the planned publication, by the Massachusetts Historical Society, of the papers of John Adams and several of his descendants, to be edited by Lyman Henry Butterfield. [671

THE STUDY AND TEACHING OF HISTORY

ALBERT ALEXANDER. The gray flannel cover on the American history textbook. Social educ., 24:11-14 (Jan). notes. On changing characteristics of high-school textbooks of American history, and associated problems of their authors, publishers, and readers. [672

THOMAS ANDREW BAILEY. Revitalizing American history. Social educ., 24:371-4 (Dec). notes. On ways to "arouse the active interest and participation of the student" in "college-level American history." [673

CARL LOTUS BECKER (1873-1945). Carl Becker to James W. Gleed [20 Nov. 1916]. Carl L. Becker, Detachment and the writing of history: essays and letters of Carl L. Becker, ed. Phil L. Snyder (Ithaca: Cornell Univ. Press [1958]), p. 145-54. On conditions in the University of Kansas which had caused Becker, formerly a member of its department of history, to go elsewhere. [674

ALEX BERMAN. Some notes on teaching history of pharmacy in the extended curricula. Am. jour. pharmaceutical educ., 24:282-4 (summer). table. notes. [675

MELVIN H. BERNSTEIN. Emerson's sea shells. Am. quar., 12:231-6 (summer). notes. On "the method and content of American Studies" as a discipline which "actively seeks--not accidentally finds--relation of each to all." [676

C. MABEL CLAPP. Houston challenges the gifted history student. School rev., 67:106-9 (spring 1959). On courses in "advanced history" offered to "gifted students" in high schools of Houston. [677

JAMES BRYANT CONANT. History in the education of scientists. Am. scientists, 48:528-43 (Dec). notes. Includes memories of Prof. George Sarton of Harvard. Also printed: Harv. Lib. bul., 14:315-33 (autumn). [678

MARGARET PACE FARMER. History as a hobby. Ala. rev., 13:163-76 (Jul). Nine reasons for the amateur study of history. [679

JOSEPH FINKELSTEIN. Freshman history: the neglected course. Liberal educ., 46:267-72 (May). notes. [680

JEAN DRESDEN GRAMBS. The challenge to the social studies. Natl. Council Social Studies, Yr. bk., 30:273-89. bibliog., notes. On "the teacher of the social studies--1980 model." Predicts that "Certification requirements will be drastically altered because, despite the lure of history, the social studies of 1980 will be oriented toward the contemporary world"; that "The separate-track, separate-subject kind of instruction will yield to the need for interdisciplinary understanding"; and that "the concern will be to use history to throw a revealing light upon the predicaments of the present and the probable future." [681

SAMUEL P. HAYS. History as human behavior. Ia. jour. hist., 58:193-206 (Jul). On the "lack of emphasis on the vital human quality of the past" in the high-school and college teaching of history, and the need for "not simply ways of enhancing the 'human interest' factor in history, but ways of systematically studying human experience and behavior so that solid and concrete generalizations emerge." Includes suggestions as to how such a study could be made in Iowa. [682

ANTHONY HILLBRUNER. American studies and public address. West. speech, 24:49-51 (winter). On the absence of "the history and criticism of American Public Address" from "interdisciplinary programs in American Studies." [683

CHRISTA HOFMANN. Die Anglistik-Amerikanistik in der Deutschen Demokratischen Republik. Zeitschrift für Anglistik, 8:171-85. notes. On English studies and American studies in Germany since 1945, particularly in language and literature. [684

ERLING MESSER HUNT. Historians and the teaching of history: a study in leadership and responsibility [of the American Historical Association, 1884-1960]. Teachers College rec., 61:290-300 (Mar). notes. [685

ALFRED PROCTER JAMES. History as analysis and guidance. West. Pa. hist. mag., 43:43-5 (Mar). Mainly on "the extent to which history and the historical method are used in the varied and numerous fields of education and learning," considered in alphabetical order from agriculture to zoology. [686

JAMES HAMILTON KING. A critical analysis of experimental doctoral research in teaching secondary school social studies, 1941-1957. Ann Arbor: University Microfilms, 1959 [i. e. 1960]. Positive microfilm of typescript. [207] leaves. Thesis (Ed. D.)--Univ. of Colorado. Abstracted: Dissert. abstracts, 20:4052 (Apr). [687

WILLIAM THOMAS LAPRADE. Obstacles in studying history. South Atl. quar., 59:204-14 (spring). [688

LAWRENCE Kinnaird retires. Ariz. and the West, 2:185-7 (summer). port. On his teaching of history in the University of California; with a list of doctoral dissertations prepared at Berkeley under his supervision, 1947-59. [689

WALTER EVAN McPHIE. Factors in the use and value of dissertations in social studies education, 1934-1957. Ann Arbor: University Microfilms, 1959 [i. e. 1960]. Positive microfilm of typescript. [252] leaves. Thesis (Ed. D.)--Stanford Univ. Abstracted: Dissert. abstracts, 20:3207 (Feb). Includes "a comprehensive bibliographic guide to dissertations in social studies education, 1934-1957." [690

THOMAS A. MALLOY, JR. A historical study of the development of social science programs of elementary-school teacher-training curricula in Massachusetts State normal schools and teachers colleges [1839-1955]. Ann Arbor: University Microfilms, 1959 [i. e. 1960]. Positive microfilm of typescript. [250] leaves. Thesis (Ed. D.)--Univ. of Virginia. Abstracted: Dissert. abstracts, 20:3178 (Feb). [691

JOHN T. MARCUS. The sense of history and the education of scientists. Liberal educ., 46:305-13 (Oct). [692

HENRY A. MILLON. History of architecture: how useful? A. I. A. jour., 34(6):23-5 (Dec). [693

JOHN LEE MORRISON. Employing morality factor in teaching history [in Catholic colleges and universities]. Cath. educ. rev., 57:162-8 (Mar 1959). notes. [694

NATIONAL COUNCIL OF TEACHERS OF ENGLISH. Committee on the College Study of American Literature and Culture. American literature in the college curriculum. ... William G. Crane, Chairman. Chicago, 1948. v, 55 p. History of college teaching of the subject, 1827-1939, by John S. Lewis; study of "American literature in the college curriculum at the present time"; and "The growth of American civilization programs in the college curriculum." [695

DEXTER PERKINS. The satisfactions of a teacher of history. Educ. rec., 41:16-24 (Jan). [696

ARNOLD ROTHSTEIN. An experiment in developing critical thinking through teaching of American history [in an unnamed secondary school]. Ann Arbor: University Microfilms, 1960. Positive microfilm of typescript. [555] leaves. Thesis--New York Univ. Abstracted: Dissert. abstracts, 21:1141 (Nov). [697

LOUIS BERNARD SCHMIDT. To the memory of Louis Pelzer, 1879-1946. Ariz. and the West, 2:303-6 (winter). port. On his teaching of history in the University of Iowa; with "A chronological list of the major works of Louis Pelzer relative to the West," 1906-43. [698

HENRY ERNEST SIGERIST (1891-1957). Medical history in the United States: past--present--future: a valedictory address. Henry E. Sigerist, Henry E. Sigerist on the history of medicine, ed. Felix Marti-Ibañez (N.Y.: MD Publications [1960]), p. 233-50. notes. Paper read in 1947. On the teaching of the history of medicine in the United States, mainly since 1876, particularly in Johns Hopkins University. [699

HENRY ERNEST SIGERIST (1891-1957). University education. Henry E. Sigerist, Henry E. Sigerist on the history of medicine, ed. Felix Marti-Ibañez (N.Y.: MD Publications [1960]), p. 251-68. Address, 1939. On the author's study and teaching of the history of medicine during his earlier years in Germany and, after 1931, in the Johns Hopkins University. [700

HENRY NASH SMITH. Can "American Studies" develop a method? Joseph J. Kwiat & Mary C. Turpie, eds., Studies in American culture: dominant ideas and images (Minneapolis: Univ. of Minnesota Press [1960]), p. 3-15. On "American Studies as a collaboration among men working from within existing academic disciplines but attempting to widen the boundaries imposed by conventional methods of inquiry" and "to resolve the dilemma which separates social facts from aesthetic values." [701

ROBERT ERNEST SPILLER. American studies, past, present, and future [1927-60]. Joseph J. Kwiat & Mary C.

Turpie, eds., Studies in American culture: dominant ideas and images (Minneapolis: Univ. of Minnesota Press [1960]), p. 207-20. notes. [702

U.S. Office of Education. Social science requirements for bachelor's degrees: a study of anthropology, economics, history, political science, and sociology in general graduation requirements. By Jennings B. Sanders. [Wash.: U.S. Govt. Print. Off., 1959.] vi, 68 p. tables. [703

WILLIAM VERHAGE. History in general education: its use in the social-science curriculum. Jour. higher educ., 30:383-90 (Oct 1959). notes. [704

ELIZABETH WISNER. The uses of historical material in the social work curriculum. Social service rev., 34: 265-72 (Sep). notes. Includes an outline of "A course in American social welfare history." [705

National History

BOL'SHAIA SOVETSKAIA ENTSIKLOPEDIIA. A Soviet view of the American past: an annotated translation of the section on American history in the Great Soviet Encyclopedia. [Translated by Ann E. Yanko & Peter A. Kersten. Annotated by Warren L. Wittry, Merrill Jensen, Leon F. Litwack, O. Lawrence Burnette, Jr., and Fred Harvey Harrington. Preface by Adlai E. Stevenson.] Wis. mag. hist., 43:2-55 (autumn 1959). views. notes. Sketch of American history from prehistoric times to 1956, with footnote corrections of some of the more egregious distortions in the text. [706

JOHN COLEMAN. Authors of liberty. N.Y.: Vantage Press [1958]. 244 p. On the American traditions symbolized in "our shrines and monuments and memorials," with illustrative quotations identifying the traditions. [707

FIDELITY-BALTIMORE NATIONAL BANK. The flags of the United States, Federal, State, and Territorial. Baltimore [1958]. 31, [1] p. Colored view of the flag of the United States without other information, and colored views of the flags of 48 States with historical information about each. [708

CORRADO GINI. The location of Vinland. [Bergen] 1960. [1], 115 leaves. notes (leaves 67-115). (Institute of Economics, Norwegian School of Economics and Business Administration, Bergen. Papers, 13.) Documentary, anthropological, geographical, and botanical evidence that the Greenland Scandinavians ascended the St. Lawrence River, that Vinland was on the Gaspe Peninsula and the north shore of Lake Ontario, and that Scandinavian settlers left descendants in the form of "white Indians," radiating from Vinland to points as distant as Narragansett Bay and North Dakota. [709

ROBERT L. HEILBRONER. The/ the historic currents of our time/ future/ and the direction/ as/ in which they are taking America/ history. [Odd-numbered lines in large type.] N.Y.: Harper [1960]. 217, [2] p. notes. Contains few specific and dated references to events in the United States. [710

ROBERT GUSTAV ADOLF, FREIHERR VON HEINE-GELDERN. Theoretical considerations concerning the problem of pre-Columbian contacts between the Old World and the New. International Congress of Anthropological and Ethnological Sciences, 5th, 1956, Men and cultures: selected papers, ed. Anthony F. C. Wallace (Phila.: Univ. of Pennsylvania Press [1960]), p. 277-81. On "the reality of pre-Columbian trans-Pacific contacts," and "that terrific fear of the Pacific Ocean--one might almost say that kind of hydrophobia--from which many anthropologists and archaeologists seem to suffer." [711

GORDON RANDOLPH WILLEY. New World prehistory. Science, 131:73-86 (8 Jan). chron. charts, views. notes. [712

DAVID EGGENBERGER. Flags of the U.S.A. [ca. 1000 to 1959]. N.Y.: Crowell [1960, ©1959. 6], 206 p. facsims. flags (part col.), tables. Begins with "the banner of the Vikings--a black raven with outspread wings on a white field--carried across the Atlantic by the daring Leif Ericson about A. D. 1000." [713

AKADEMIIA NAUK SSSR. Institut istorii. Ocherki novoi i noveishei isitorii SShA. [Otvetstvennyi redaktor G. N. Sevost'ianov.] Moskva: Izd-vo Akademii Nauk SSSR, 1960. 2 v. [4], 630, [2]; 725, [2] p. fold. maps. bibliog. (1:608-15; 2:687-704), notes. History of the United States, vols. 1 (1492-1918) and 2 (1918-59). [714

HARRY CRANBROOK ALLEN. Bush and backwoods: a comparison of the frontier in Australia [since 1788] and the United States [since 1607. East Lansing:] Michigan State Univ. Press, 1959. xv, 153 p. notes (p. 119-41). On "the history of man in the environment of two untamed lands of continental extent" as compared with respect to the frontier traits listed by F. J. Turner. [715

CARL LOTUS BECKER (1873-1945). Beginnings of the American people

[1492-1782]. Ithaca, N.Y.: Great Seal Books [1960]. vi, [6], 293, xviii p. map. bibliog. (p. 277-93), notes. 1st ed. 1915. "Prefatory note" signed: Curtis P. Nettels. [716

ALFRED LE ROY BURT. If Turner had looked at Canada, Australia, and New Zealand when he wrote about the West. Walker D. Wyman & Clifton B. Kroeber, eds., The frontier in perspective (Madison: Univ. of Wisconsin Press, 1957), p. 59-77. bibliog. [717

HARRY JAMES CARMAN, HAROLD C. SYRETT, & BERNARD W. WISHY. A history of the American people. Volume I. [1492] to 1877. N.Y.: Knopf, 1960. xx, 860, xxvii, 1 p. cartoons, maps, ports., tables, views. bibliog. (p. 797-860), notes. 1st ed. 1952. [718

HENRY STEELE COMMAGER, ed. Documents of American history [1492-1957]. ... Sixth edition. N.Y.: Appleton-Century-Crofts [1958]. 2 v. in 1. xxiv, [2], 450; [2], 842 p. (Crofts American history series.) 1st ed. 1934. Limited mainly to "documents of an official and quasi-official character," dealing almost entirely with political, legal, and diplomatic matters. [719

RICHARD HOFSTADTER, WILLIAM MILLER, & DANIEL AARON. The American Republic [1492-1958]. Englewood Cliffs, N.J.: Prentice-Hall, 1959. 2 v. xiv, 722; xii, 723 p. cartoons, maps, ports., views. bibliogs. On the period before 1783 see 1:3-196. Volume 1 ends with 1865. [720

DUMAS MALONE & BASIL RAUCH. Empire for liberty: the genesis and growth of the United States of America [1492-1960]. N.Y.: Appleton-Century-Crofts [1960]. 2 v. xviii, [4], 882, xxxv; xviii, [4], 901, liv p. cartoons, diagrs., facsims., maps (part double), ports., tables, views (1 double). bibliogs. (1:797-844; 2:855-918). Attempt "to do justice to all the important aspects of American history--political, economic, constitutional, diplomatic, social, religious, artistic, and intellectual," with special emphasis on international relations and on "ideology and movements of thought." Volume I closes with 1865. [721

NATIONAL HISTORICAL WAX MUSEUM, Washington, D.C. Catalogue of the National Historical Wax Museum: great moments and famous personalities in American history. Wash.: National Historical Souvenir Center, 1959. 64 p. ports. (1 col.), views (1 col.). Images (specially made for the Museum according to "a secret plastic formula") representing events and individuals in American history, 1492-1945. [722

WALTER PRESCOTT WEBB (1888-1963). The western world frontier. Walker D. Wyman & Clifton B. Kroeber, eds., The frontier in perspective (Madison: Univ. of Wisconsin Press, 1957), p. 111-26. bibliog. Restatement of the thesis of the author's The Great Frontier (1952). [723

HOWARD LAWRENCE HURWITZ. Review-survey of American history [1565-1958]. ... Revised edition. N.Y.: Keystone Educ. Press, 1959. vii, 300, [34], ix-xvi p. cartoons, diagrs., maps. 1st ed. 1955. [724

HENRY BAMFORD PARKES. The United States of America: a history [1584-1958]. Second edition, revised. N.Y.: Knopf, 1959. xviii, [2], 783, xxiv, [2] p. cartoons, maps, ports., tables, views. bibliog. (p. 779-83). 1st ed. 1953. [725

THOMAS HARRY WILLIAMS, RICHARD N. CURRENT, & FRANK FREIDEL. A history of the United States [1584-1958]. N.Y.: Knopf, 1959. 2 v. xx, [2], 707, xxiv, [1]; xx, [2], 739, xxvi, [1] p. cartoons, diagrs., maps, ports., tables, views. bibliogs. (1:701-7; 2:733-9). [726

LIFE (Chicago). America's arts and skills. By the editors of Life. With an introduction by Charles F. Montgomery. N.Y.: Dutton, 1957. 172 p. diagrs., ports., and views (part col.). "Picture sources" (p. 165-8). 36 cm. Reprinted from Life, 1955-56. Information about buildings, tools, utensils, furniture, firearms, engravings, fabrics, vehicles, jewelry, and machines, in 9 periods, 17th-20th centuries. [727

RICHARD WARNER VAN ALSTYNE. The American empire: its historical pattern and evolution [1713-1945. London: Routledge and Paul for the Historical Assoc.] 1960. 28 p. bibliog. (inside of back cover). (Historical Association. General series, 43.) Based upon a lecture, "American conceptions of empire" (1953). On the territorial expansion of the British colonies and the United States into Indian, French, and Spanish areas in America and later abroad. [728

THOMAS DIONYSIUS CLARK. Frontier America: the story of the westward movement [1740s-1890s]. N.Y.: Scribner [1959]. xi, [3], 832 p. facsims., maps, port., views. bibliog. (p. 765-97). [729

JOHN RODERIGO DOS PASSOS. Prospects of a golden age. Englewood Cliffs, N.J.: Prentice-Hall [1959]. xvi, 271 p. facsims., map, plans, ports. (part col.), views (part col.). "Picture credits" (p. xv-xvi). "An effort to illustrate some snatches and samples of the lives of some of the great generation of 1776 and of the generations that followed immediately after," dealing with the "Age of the American Revolution," ca. 1749 to ca. 1810. Includes chapters on George Washington, surveyors, seafarers, limners, lawyers and litigants, the pen and the press, travelers and explorers, craftsmen, and mechanics and builders. [730

BERNHARD KNOLLENBERG. Origin of the American Revolution: 1759-1766. N.Y.: Macmillan, 1960. viii, [2], 486 p. tables. bibliog. (p. 397-452), notes (p. 283-396). On legislative and administrative action of the British Government, and activities of the Church of England, which departed from previous policy and increasingly angered the colonists. Includes "Epilogue to 1775." [731

HERBERT APTHEKER. The American Revolution, 1763-1783. N.Y.: International Publishers [1960]. 304 p. bibliog. (p. 284-97), notes (p. 279-83). (His A history of the American people: an interpretation, [2].) Marxist version of the political, military, diplomatic, social, and economic history of the period; with a chapter on "The Negro in the Revolution." [732

WILLIAM RANULF BROCK. The character of American history. London, Macmillan; N.Y.: St. Martin's Press, 1960. xii, 294, [1] p. maps. bibliog. (p. 273-88), notes. A history of American "politics in their broadest sense," 1763-1948, "intended primarily for those with no previous knowledge of the United States"; with an initial chapter on "The features of American history." [733

RICHARD WARNER VAN ALSTYNE. The rising American empire. N.Y.: Oxford Univ. Press, 1960. ix, [3], 215 p. fold. maps. notes. Lectures delivered at University College, London, 1956, on the "origins and the emergence of the United States as a national state," its territorial expansion, and its self-imposed "mission" for "making over the nations in the graven image of America," 1775-1919. [734

NOLAN FOWLER. The anti-expansionistic argument in the United States prior to the Civil War [1784-1861]. Ann Arbor: University Microfilms, 1955 [i.e. 1960]. Positive microfilm of typescript. viii, 747 leaves. bibliog. (leaves 735-47). Thesis--Univ. of Kentucky. Abstracted: Dissert. abstracts, 20:3700-3701 (Mar). On arguments that territorial expansion was unconstitutional, that it would create severe economic and governmental problems, that it would damage older sections, and that it was unethical. [735

JOSEPH SCOTT. Atlas of the United States, 1795-1800, featuring maps produced by Joseph Scott. Cleveland: Bloch [1960. 25] leaves. 20 maps. Maps of each state then in the Union and of "N. W. Territory," "S. W. Territory," and "The United States of America," reproduced from Scott's The United States gazetteer (1795) and The new and universal gazetteer (1800). [736

ADAM SZÁSZDI. Governor Folch and the Burr Conspiracy. Fla. hist. quar., 38:239-51 (Jan). notes. On references in the correspondence of Col. Vicente Folch y Juan, Governor of West Florida, 1806-7, to plans of Burr and his confederates for promoting a separation of the Mississippi Valley from the United States and for attacking the Spanish government of Mexico. [737

ALTON HARRINGTON KETCHUM. The man who was Uncle Sam: how meat-packer Samuel Wilson [1766-1854] of Troy, New York, gave his name to the nation [in 1813]. Am. rev., 1(1):73-84 (autumn). cartoon. [738

HENRY HARRISON SIMMS. Emotions at high tide: abolition as a controversial factor, 1830-1845. [Baltimore?] 1960. vi, [2], 243 p. notes. On abolitionism as a divisive influence in politics, among the States, in the churches, and in foreign relations; with a chapter on "The abolitionists and the Texas question, 1836-1845." [739

RAYMOND GUILLIEN. Océan Pacifique et politique extérieure des U.S.A. [since the 1840s]. Les fondements de la politique extérieur des États-Unis (Paris: Armand Colin, 1949 [Cahiers de la Fondation Nationale des Sciences

Politiques, 8]), p. 85-164. notes. Interpretation of American political and military expansion in the Pacific in terms of frontier theory, arguing that the frontier of the United States was not closed by 1890 but remained open till the westward movement of the world frontier was forever completed by its encirclement of the earth and arrival at its Eurasian starting-point, an event symbolized by the establishment of the Marshall Plan in 1947. [740

FREDERICK MERK. Presidential fevers. Miss. Valley hist. rev., 47: 3-33 (Jun). notes. On the attitudes of the Whigs and the Democrats in Congress toward the Oregon policies of President James K. Polk, 1845-46. [741

OTIS A. SINGLETARY. The Mexican War [1845-48. Chicago:] Univ. of Chicago Press [1960]. vii, [3], 181 p. maps, ports., views. bibliog. (p. 166-8). (The Chicago history of American civilization.) On interrelated military, diplomatic, and political events during these years. [742

CHARLES VEVIER. American continentalism: an idea of expansion, 1845-1910. Am. hist. rev., 65:323-35 (Jan). notes. On the effects of the "doctrine of geopolitical centralism" deduced from the geographic position of the United States between Europe and Asia. [743

RAYMOND WILLIAM POSTGATE. Story of a year: 1848. London: Jonathan Cape [1955]. 286 p. cartoons, facsims., maps, ports., views. notes (p. 271-9). Sketch of British events during the 12 months of 1848, including many references to America ("Emerson's report on England," "The beauties of New York," the Election of 1848, the Gold Rush, etc., as they affected England). [744

ROBERT F. DALZELL, JR. American participation in the Great Exhibition [of the Works of Industry of All Nations] of 1851. Amherst, Mass.: Amherst College Press, 1960. 64 p. notes. (Amherst College honors thesis 1.) Mainly on "American response to the things the British were saying about the United States display" at what was commonly called the Crystal Palace Exhibition in London. [745

ARI ARTHUR HOOGENBOOM. What really caused the Civil War? Wis. mag. hist., 44:3-5 (autumn). ports. Argument that "War is caused by the aggressive spirit in men and nations," that beards impart aggressiveness to hitherto beardless individuals, that the aggressiveness resulting from the sudden fashionableness of beards among American men in the late 1850s was inhibited by American moral ideas from expressing itself by seduction of "their friends' wives," and that the aggressiveness found alternative expression in killing "their neighbors beyond the Potomac"; with evidence for each step of the argument, a reply to possible counterarguments, and the conclusion that "The repressible conflict became irrepressible when men forsook their razors." [746

NATHAN N. EGLIT. Uncle Sam in numismatics. Numismatist, 73: 1779-86 (Dec). coins, facsims. bibliog. On the appearance of Brother Jonathan and Uncle Sam on tokens, medals, campaign buttons, scrip, etc., 1859-1945. [747

COURTLANDT CANBY, ed. Lincoln and the Civil War: a profile and a history. N.Y.: G. Braziller, 1960. 416 p. notes (p. 401-10). 1st ed. 1958. Excerpts from various printed works, 1868-1956, mainly secondary, intended "to present a tightly organized picture of Lincoln's presidency through selections from the more important titles already published in the field, the selections tied into each other by my own bridging passages." [748

ALLAN NEVINS. The War for the Union. Volume I [and Volume II]. N.Y.: Scribner, 1959[-60]. 2 v. x, [2], 436; xiv, [2], 557 p. maps, ports., views. bibliog. (1:417-24; 2:553-40), notes. Devoted in part to military history but "primarily to political, administrative, economic, and social history," particularly the transformation of "an inchoate nation, individualistic in temper and wedded to improvisation, into a shaped and disciplined nation, increasingly aware of the importance of plan and control." Contents.--1. The improvised war [Mar. 1861-Dec. 1861].--2. War becomes revolution [Jan. 1862-Jun. 1863]. To be continued. Includes judgments of the competence, wisdom, and integrity of Union and Confederate military and civilian leaders. [749

JOHN S. BLAY. After the Civil War: a pictorial profile of America from 1865 to 1900. N.Y.: Crowell [1960. 8], 312 p. cartoons, facsims., ports., views (part double). bibliog. (p. 304), "Picture credits" (p. 305-7). [750

JOHN ALLEN KROUT. United States since 1865. ... Fourteenth edition. N.Y.: Barnes & Noble [1960]. xvii, [3], 278 p. diagr., maps (1 double), tables, view. bibliog. (p. 257-66). (College outline series, 30.) 1st ed. 1933. [751

GERTRUDE ALMY SLICHTER. European backgrounds of American reform, 1880-1915. Ann Arbor: University Microfilms, 1960. Positive microfilm of typescript. [310] leaves. Thesis--Univ. of Illinois. Abstracted: Dissert. abstracts, 20:4646 (Jun). Includes chapters on "hours laws, minimum wage laws, workmen's compensation, forest conservation, municipal reform, and political reform." [752

GEORGE HARMON KNOLES. The new United States: a history since 1896. N.Y.: Holt [1959]. xvi, 650 p. diagrs., maps, tables, views. bibliog. (p. 620-27). [753

FRANK BURT FREIDEL. America in the twentieth century [1900-1960]. N.Y.: Knopf, 1960. xxii, 593, xxiii, [1] p. cartoons, diagrs., maps (part double), ports., views. bibliog. (p. 573-93). [754

WALTER LORD. The good years: from 1900 to the First World War. N.Y.: Harper [1960]. ix, [3], 369 p. cartoons, facsims., map, ports., views. bibliog. (p. 348-54). On the assassination of McKinley, the San Francisco earthquake, the Panic of 1907, the discovery of the North Pole, the progress of woman suffrage, and other selected topics, 1900-1914. [755

A. L. BENNETT. Profile of a year: 1910. Am. forests. 66(9):30-33, 40-45 (Sep). cartoons, ports. On all the newsworthy events of the year, including the discharge of Chief Forester Gifford Pinchot by President Taft and the pursuit of large foreign fauna by ex-President Roosevelt. [756

WILLIAM EDWARD LEUCHTENBURG. The perils of prosperity, 1914-32. [Chicago:] Univ. of Chicago Press [1958]. ix, 313 p. bibliog. (p. 277-97). (The Chicago history of American civilization.) Mainly on the economic history of these years. [757

PIERCE G. FREDERICKS. The great adventure: America in the First World War [1917-18]. N.Y.: Dutton, 1960. [2], 253 p. cartoons, facsim., maps, ports., views (part double). notes (p. 243-7). [758

JOHN DONALD HICKS. Normalcy and reaction, 1921-1933; and age of disillusionment. Wash.: Service Center for Teachers of History [1960. 2], 21 p. (Service Center for Teachers of History. Publication 32.) Bibliographical essay. [759

JOE ALEX MORRIS. What a year! Harper [1956]. xii, [2], 338 p. facsims., ports., views. Month-by-month narrative of the events of 1929, with glances before and after. [760

DAVID ALLEN SHANNON, ed. The great depression. [Englewood Cliffs, N.J.:] Prentice-Hall [1960]. xiii, [3], 171, [2] p. tables. (A Spectrum book, S-10.) Reprinted accounts, mainly magazine articles. Includes chapters on relief, nomads, bank failures, unemployment, education, fear of revolution, and "Some case histories," 1929-39, and a chapter on the agricultural depression of the 1920s. [761

CULTURAL HISTORY

GEORGE FREDERICK FRICK. Mark Catesby [1683-1749]: the discovery of a naturalist. Bibliog. Soc. Am., Papers, 54:163-75 (3d quar.). notes. New information from a copy of his Natural history of Carolina, Florida, and the Bahama Islands (1729-47), formerly in possession of Thomas Pennant (1726-98), interleaved by him and by his son David (died 1841) with "additional water-color drawings, prints, and manuscripts by many hands," including manuscripts and 3 drawings by Catesby and a long letter from George Edwards to Thomas Pennant, 5 Dec. 1761. [762

ADOLPH BURNETT BENSON, comp. Swedish members of the American Philosophical Society [founded 1743]. Am. Swed. Hist. Found., Yr. bk., 1959, p. 33-9. Annotated alphabetical list. [763

RUSSEL BLAINE NYE. The cultural life of the new nation, 1776-1830. N.Y.: Harper [1960]. xii, 324 p. facsims., music, ports., views. bibliog. (p. 295-310), notes. (The new American nation series.) Sections on ideas, science, social life, education, the churches, literature, music, theater, and art. [764

ROBERT CANTWELL. "... transformed a science into an art." John Arthur Garraty, ed., The unforgettable Americans (Great Neck, N.Y.: Channel Press [1960]), p. 104-9. On Alexander Wilson (1766-1813), emigrant from Scotland to Pennsylvania in 1794, author of books about American birds illustrated with prints from his own paintings. [765

MABEL RAYNOR BARTLETT. Washington Allston [1779-1843] as critic [of art and literature, early 19th century]. Ann Arbor: University Microfilms, 1960. Positive microfilm of typescript. [244] leaves. Thesis--Boston Univ. Abstracted: Dissert. abstracts, 21:1161 (Nov). [766

FRANCIS JAMES DALLETT, ed. Citizen Audubon: a documentary discovery. Princeton Univ. Lib. chron., 21:89-93 (autumn 1959 - winter 1960). notes. Three documents (1806, 1812, 1830) proving that John James Audubon was a naturalized citizen of the United States and containing other information about him. [767

WALDEMAR H. FRIES. John James Audubon: some remarks on his writings [1807-47]. Princeton Univ. Lib. chron., 21:1-7 (autumn 1959 - winter 1960). Includes reference to his engravings. [768

DONALD CULROSS PEATTIE (1898-1964). "... the bright wings he followed." John Arthur Garraty, ed., The unforgettable Americans (Great Neck, N.Y.: Channel Press [1960]), p. 109-13. On the work of John James Audubon, hunter and painter of birds, 1807 ff. [769

DARWIN SHRELL. Nationalism and aesthetics in the North American review: 1815-1850. Waldo McNeir & Leo B. Levy, eds., Studies in American literature (Baton Rouge: Louisiana State Univ. Press, 1960 [Louisiana State University studies, Humanities series, 8]), p. 11-21. notes. On disagreement among its contributors regarding the justification for "the use of natural American scenes in literature and art." [770

WADE CLAYTON THOMPSON. The aesthetic theory of Henry David Thoreau [1817-62]. Ann Arbor: University Microfilms, 1959 [i. e. 1960]. Positive microfilm of typescript. 165 leaves. bibliog. (leaves 161-5). Thesis--Columbia Univ. Abstracted: Dissert. abstracts, 20:3756 (Mar). [771

JOHN JAMES AUDUBON (1785-1851). Audubon and his journals. [Edited] by Maria R[ebecca] Audubon [his granddaughter]. With zoölogical and other notes by Elliott Coues. N.Y.: Dover Publications [1960]. 2 v. xiv, 532, [19]; viii, 554, [16] p. facsims., ports., views. notes. 1st ed. 1897. "Myself," an account addressed by Audubon to his sons, on his life to 1820 (1:7-38); biographical sketch by the editor; "The European journals, 1826-1829," recording his search for subscribers to his Birds of America and his work in London and Paris to prepare his drawings and paintings for its publishers (1:79-342); "The Labrador journal, 1833," on his voyage to collect birds (1:343-445); "The Missouri River journals, 1843," recording his journey from New York via the Ohio River to St. Louis and thence on a vessel of the American Fur Company to Fort Union and back, with excerpts copied by him from journals of John G. Bell and Alexander Culbertson, and his copy of Edwin T. Denig's "Description of Fort Union" (1:447-532; 2:1-195); and "Episodes," consisting of 58 prose sketches of travel, mainly from his "Ornithological biographies," 1808-33 (2:197-527). [772

PAUL RAMSEY, JR. Poe and modern art. College art jour., 18:210-15 (spring 1959). Symbolical interpretation of references to painting in "The fall of the House of Usher" (1839), suggesting "that the first modern nonobjective paintings were done by Roderick Usher." [773

HOWARD H. SCHLESS. Flaxman, Dante, and Melville's Pierre. N.Y. Pub. Lib., Bul., 64:65-82 (Feb). views. notes. Evidence that Melville owned pamphlets containing 110 engravings by John Flaxman illustrating the Divine comedy and forming part of the Oeuvre complet de Flaxman: receuil de ses compositions gravées au trait (Paris, 1833), probably acquired by Melville in 1849 and probably a source of "certain central images in Mardi, Moby Dick, and Pierre." [774

DONALD A. RINGE. Painting as poem in the Hudson River aesthetic. Am. quar., 12:71-83 (spring). view. notes. On expressions of this idea in and before the 1850s by William Cullen Bryant, James Fenimore Cooper, Washington Allston, Thomas Cole, and Asher Durand. [775

NEW YORK TIMES. America's taste, 1851-1959, [edited by] Marjorie Longley, Louis Silverstein, [and] Samuel A. Tower: the cultural events of a century reported by contemporary observers in the pages of the New York times. N.Y.: Simon and Schuster [1960. 8], 332 p. cartoons, facsims., plan, ports., views (part double). "Picture credits" (p. 328-32). Facsimile reproductions of front pages, obituaries, reviews of books, concerts, plays, and exhibitions, illustrations, etc., arranged in 10 periods. [776

ELDON CLEON HILL. Shaw's "biographer-in-chief." Mod. drama, 2:164-72 (Sep 1959). On Archibald Henderson (born 1877), his life in North Carolina, his service as a professor of mathematics at the University of North Carolina, and his numerous writings on mathematics, American history, European drama, and particularly Bernard Shaw. [777

THE AMERICAN RECORD GUIDE. [Carl Van Vechten (born 1880), "music critic, drama critic, dance critic, novelist, essayist, book reviewer, master of the photographic arts, founder and nurterer of libraries."] Am. record guide, 26:773-805 (Jun). ports. Appreciation by Edward Jablonski; Van Vechten's "Why music is unpopular" (1 Mar. 1917), on the music criticism of that time; and "A gallery of documentary photographs by Carl Van Vechten" (photographs of 20 musicians, 1932-56). [778

BENJAMIN ROWLAND, JR. Chandler Rathfon Post, 1881-1959. Art quar., 23:180-81 (summer). On his teaching of classical languages and fine arts at Harvard and his books on the history of sculpture and of Spanish painting. [779

JOSEPH J. KWIAT. Robert Henri and the Emerson-Whitman tradition. Joseph J. Kwiat & Mary C. Turpie, eds., Studies in American culture: dominant ideas and images (Minneapolis: Univ. of Minnesota Press [1960]), p. 153-70. notes. On the influence of the Transcendentalism of Emerson and Whitman on the paintings and the theories of art of Henri, 1886-1929. [780

CHARLES ANDREWS FENTON. A note on American expatriation. West. humanities rev., 14:323-9 (summer). On "American literary and artistic expatriation," its extent at different times, its motives, and its effects, especially in the years from ca. 1890 to ca. 1910. [781

JOHN GREENWAY. R. D. Jameson (1895-1959). West. folklore, 19:153-4 (Jul). port. On his accomplishments as "folklorist, Sinologist, litterateur, administrator, writer, and teacher." [782

OSCAR HANDLIN. Comments on mass and popular culture [1900-1960]. Daedalus, 89:325-32 (spring). [783

JOHN MacEACHEN. The humanities in Columbia College, 1900-1960: an analysis of trends in humanistic studies in the undergraduate curriculum of Columbia College. Ann Arbor: University Microfilms, 1960. Positive microfilm of typescript. [222] leaves. Thesis--New York Univ. Abstracted: Dissert. abstracts, 21:1101 (Nov). [784

MARGARET L. HARTLEY. The courageous idiosyncrasy of Albert Guérard. Southw. rev., 45:312-17 (autumn). On his teaching of comparative literature in Stanford University and several other colleges, 1906-59, and his more than 20 books of history and biography. [785

MARTHA M. MILLER. The discovery of me: E. E. Cummings reflects on a year at Harvard as Norton Professor [1952-53]. Harvard alumni bul., 55:610-14, 633 (9 May 1953). port. Includes reference to his early studies at Harvard and his work as a novelist, a poet, and a painter, 1911 ff. [786

GUSTAVE OTTO ARLT. Archer Taylor [born 1890]. Wayland Debs Hand & Gustave Otto Arlt, eds., Humaniora: essays in literature, folklore, bibliography, honoring Archer Taylor on his seventieth birthday (Locust Valley, N.Y.: J. J. Augustin, 1960), p. 1-7. On his teaching of Germanic languages and literatures in Washington University (1915-25), the University of Chicago (1925-39), and the University of California (since 1940), and his work in folklore ("the major interest of his life"), riddles, proverbs, and the history of bibliography. [787

HAROLD BAKER DUNKEL. Dewey and the fine arts. School rev., 67: 229-45 (summer 1959). notes. On the "mutual relations between Dewey's philosophic doctrine and the fine arts," 1916-38. [788

EMANIE LOUISE (NAHM) SACHS ARLING. A pot with feeling: flower paintings, with a short autobiography. N.Y.: Eriksson-Taplinger Co., 1960. 46 p. col. views. Views of extremely bright-colored flowers in very colorful vases and pots, and account of the author's persistent experiments in painting still life in spite of lack of encouragement; with some account of her early life in Bowling Green, Ky., her study of painting there, her marriage in 1917, her work as a novelist (1927-30), and her life in New York City and in Darien, Conn. [789

EDWARD ALBERT SHILS. Mass society and its culture [in America, 1920-60, and abroad]. Daedalus, 89: 288-314 (spring). For comment see Ernest Van den Haag, "A dissent from the consensual society" (89:315-24). [790

STANLEY EDGAR HYMAN. Ideals, dangers, and limitations of mass culture [1926-60]. Daedalus, 89:377-87 (spring). [791

BLISS PERRY (1860-1954). [Interview, reported by Prof. A. P. Savides, on literary and philosophical matters.] Harvard alumni bul., 55:272 (6 Dec 1952). First printed in 1934. [792

LASZLO KRAUSZ. Two loves have I. Am. artist, 24(1):49-53, 68-70 (Jan). ports., views. On the experience of the author, violinist in the Cleveland Orchestra, in making rapid drawings of musicians at work and of scenes noted by him while on tour in the United States and abroad, 1947-59. [793

FRANK STANTON. Parallel paths. Daedalus, 89:347-53 (spring). notes. On the "same general goal" of intellectuals and the mass media, 1948-60. [794

Art

WILLIAM HENRY HOLMES (1846-1933). On the evolution of ornament--an American lesson. Selected papers from the American anthropologist, 1888-1920, ed. Frederica de Laguna (Evanston, Ill.: Row, Peterson [1960]), p. 523-32. diagrs. First printed 1890. On geometric and "delineative or nature-derived elements" in prehistoric Indian art, and the tendency to transform the latter into the former. [795

WALDRON PHOENIX BELKNAP, JR. (1899-1949). Painters and craftsmen. Waldron Phoenix Belknap, Jr., American colonial painting: materials for a history, ed. Charles Coleman Sellers (Cambridge: Belknap Press of Harvard Univ. Press, 1959), p. 207-25. ports. Notes on New York limners, 4 17th-century glaziers in New York, "Paintings in New York wills," Thomas Smith (fl. 1680) of Boston, John Greenwood (fl. 1745-52), and a few other colonial artists. [796

BALTIMORE MUSEUM OF ART. Age of elegance: the rococo and its effect--an exhibition. [Baltimore, 1959.] 91 p. ports., views (1 col.). Catalogue (p. 27-91), including "The American colonies" (painting, silver, furniture, pottery, 1746?-1772, p. 85-90); with introductory essays on "Intellectual currents of the eighteenth century," by George Boas, and "The rococo and its effect," by James D. Breckenridge. [797

EUGENE MATTHEW BECKER. Whistler and the aesthetic movement. Ann Arbor: University Microfilms, 1959 [i.e. 1960]. Positive microfilm of typescript. [341] leaves. Thesis--Princeton Univ. Abstracted: Dissert. abstracts, 20:2744 (Jan). On the support given by James Abbott McNeill Whistler (1834-1903), both as a painter and as a critic, to the art-for-art's-sake school in Paris and London. [798

JAMES JACKSON JARVES (1818-88). The art-idea. ... Edited by Benjamin Rowland, Jr. Cambridge, Mass.: Belknap Press, 1960. xxix, 313, [2] p. notes (p. 295-306). (The John Harvard library.) Text of the first edition, 1864, including chapters on the history and present state of American art in general, American painting, sculpture, and architecture, American needs and duties with respect to art, and "Art-institutions and art-education in Europe and America"; with a biographical and critical introduction by the editor. [799

DETROIT INSTITUTE OF ARTS. Treasures from the Detroit Institute of Arts. [Edited by Paul L. Grigaut.] Detroit, 1960. [4], 286 p. ports., views. Reproductions of paintings and sculpture (p. 13-283), including "American art" (p. 233-81); with an introduction on the history of art museums in Detroit since 1883. [800

WILLIAM GEORGE HAAG. The artist as a reflection of his culture [20th century]. Gertrude E. Dole & Robert L. Carneiro, eds., Essays in the science of culture, in honor of Leslie A. White (N.Y.: Crowell [1960]), p. 216-30. bibliog. Argument that "all art is a reflection of the cultural milieu" and that "artists are relentlessly grasped by the strongest but subtlest force that moves the world, that is, cultural determinism." [801

JOHN IRELAND HOWE BAUR. Beauty or the beast? the machine and American art. Art in Am., 48(1):82-7 (spring). views. On painting and sculpture representing or inspired by machines since 1913, and the various ideas governing at various times the introduction of machinery into art. [802

Mrs. TALBOT J. ALBERT. The art of Kate Lord. Garden Club Am., Bul., 48(6):41-3 (Nov). view. On her work as a landscape architect and as an illustrator of country and farming scenes since ca. 1920. [803

FREDERIC WHITAKER. Emily Francis: a lady with a mission. Am. artist, 24(7):64-5 (Sep). port. On her work as "founder and president of Contemporary Arts, Inc., a New York organization whose purpose is to launch worthy young artists with one-man shows and other appropriate support," 1929-60, and of Collectors of American Art, founded in 1937. [804

LLOYD GOODRICH. American painting and sculpture, 1930-1959: the Moscow Exhibition. College art, 18: 289-301 (summer 1959). port., views. On the exhibition as "a survey of American painting and sculpture of the past quarter-century," undertaking "to present a balanced picture of the leading tendencies of the period as represented by about fifty painters and twenty-five sculptors." [805

ARCHITECTURE

WAYNE ANDREWS. Architecture in America: a photographic history from the colonial period to the present. N.Y.: Atheneum Publishers, 1960. [8], 179, [4] p. views. Mainly photographs (taken by the author) of structures built between 1642 and 1956. [806

DOROTHY PRATT & RICHARD PRATT. A guide to early American homes [ca. 1650 to ca. 1850]. N.Y.: McGraw-Hill [1956]. 2 v. viii, 251, [1]; viii, 227, [4] p. views. Guide to the location and history of early houses open to the public on payment of a fee or by appointment, totaling "well over nine hundred" in the North and "nearly seven hundred" in the South, arranged by State from New England to Delaware and as far west as Wisconsin (vol. 1) and from Maryland and Virginia to Florida and as far west as Missouri and Louisiana (vol. 2). [807

RICHARD PRATT & DOROTHY PRATT. The treasury of early American homes. New, revised, and enlarged edition. N.Y.: Hawthorn Books [1959]. 144 p. ports., col. views. 36 cm. 1st ed., by Richard Pratt, 1949; in present edition the name of Dorothy Pratt precedes that of Richard Pratt on title page. Consists of "color-illustrated articles" from the Ladies' home journal, showing views of exteriors and interiors of dwellings built between ca. 1650 and ca. 1850 in States along the Atlantic coast and a few dwellings in Natchez, New Orleans, and Monterey, Calif. In this edition about a third of the materials of the first edition is replaced by newer materials, published in the Ladies' home journal in recent years. [808

RICHARD PRATT & DOROTHY PRATT. The second treasury of early American homes. N.Y.: Hawthorn Books [1954]. 144 p. col. views. 35 cm. Consists of "color-illustrated articles" contributed by the authors to the Ladies' home journal since 1946, containing descriptions and color photographs of exteriors and interiors of 57 dwellings built between ca. 1650 and ca. 1850 in the States fronting on the Atlantic coast from Maine to Georgia (not including New Jersey) and in Tennessee. Continues A treasury of early American homes, by Richard Pratt (1949). [809

BARBARA SNOW. Preservation for use. Antiques, 77:370-77 (Apr). views. On several examples, from Massachusetts to Alabama and Oregon, of early dwellings and shops, 1670 ff., still in use or recently restored to usefulness. [810

VINCENT JOSEPH SCULLY, JR. The Precisionist strain in American architecture [1683-1959]. Art in Am., 48(3):46-53. views. [811

CARL BRIDENBAUGH. "...greatest of the colonial architects." John Arthur

Garraty, ed., The unforgettable Americans (Great Neck, N.Y.: Channel Press [1960]), p. 42-5. On Peter Harrison (1716-75), emigrant from England in 1739, architect in Charleston, Newport, and Boston. [812

ALAN GOWANS. Freemasonry and the neoclassic style in America. Antiques, 77:172-5 (Feb). views. On the Masonic attitude toward "the classical orders, arches, or geometric proportions" as "a symbolic language which set forth social ideals and universal moral principles that every enlightened person ought to hold," and the possible influence of the attitude upon neoclassic architecture and antiques, 1775-1825. [813

EDWARD DEMING ANDREWS. The Shaker manner of building [1792-1875]. Art in Am., 48(3):38-45. views. [814

BENJAMIN HENRY BONEVAL LATROBE (1764-1820). Latrobe on architects' fees, 1798. Soc. Architectural Historians, Jour., 19:115-17 (Sep). plan. notes. Letter to an unnamed person (evidently employed by the State of Virginia), dated Richmond, 14 Feb. 1798, submitting the author's bill for services in designing the Penitentiary House and commenting on the general subject of fees. [814a

OSMUND R. OVERBY. Ammi B[urnham] Young [1798-1874] in the Connecticut Valley. Soc. Architectural Historians, Jour., 19:119-23 (Sep). facsim., plans, views. notes. On his work as an architect in New England, 1827 (or earlier) to 1854, and in Washington as Supervising Architect of the Office of Construction of the Treasury Department, 1852-62. Includes accounts of buildings designed by him for Dartmouth College and of the U.S. Post Office at Windsor, Conn., which he designed as a Federal official. [814b

CARL W. CONDIT. American building art: the nineteenth century. N.Y.: Oxford Univ. Press, 1960. xvii, 371 p. diagrs., views. bibliog. (p. 345-51), notes (p. 275-344). Chapters.--1. Wood framing.--2. Iron framing.--3. The wooden bridge truss.--4. The iron bridge truss.--5. The suspension bridge.--6. The iron arch bridge.--7. The railway trainshed.--8. Concrete construction.--9. Architectural appraisal. [815

HAROLD N. COOLEDGE, JR., comp. A Sloan check list, 1849-1884. Soc. Architectural Historians, Jour., 19:34-8 (Mar). views. List of public buildings, civic buildings, schools and colleges, hospitals, orphanages, churches and church buildings, commercial buildings, and residential buildings designed by Samuel Sloan (1815-84) and erected in and near Philadelphia and in places as distant as Natchez and Kalamazoo. [815a

KENNETH MEYER SETTON. Aesthetics and the American democracy [in civic architecture since 1854]. Lib. chron., 26:45-60 (spring). [816

ALBERT BUSH-BROWN. Louis [Henry] Sullivan [1856-1924]. N.Y.: G. Braziller, 1960. 128 p. ports., views. bibliog. (p. 120-22), notes (p. 114-16). "Sources of illustrations" (p. 128). (The masters of world architecture series.) On his life in Chicago, 1873-1924, and his career as an architect. [817

WILLARD CONNELY. Louis [Henry] Sullivan [1856-1924] as he lived: the shaping of American architecture, a biography. N.Y.: Horizon Press, 1960. 322 p. plan, ports., views. bibliog. (p. 311-16). On his life in Chicago, 1873-1924, his work as an architect, and the reasons for his loss of business and reputation after 1895; with some account of his early life in Boston, his studies at the Massachusetts Institute of Technology, his unorthodox domestic arrangements, and his apparently excessive fondness for alcohol. [818

PETER BLAKE. The master builders. N.Y.: Knopf, 1960. xii, [4], ix, [4], 399 p. plans, ports., views. On Charles Édouard Jeanneret-Gris (born 1887), known as Le Corbusier, French painter and architect, designer in 1946 of the United Nations Headquarters in New York City; Ludwig Mies van der Rohe (born 1887), emigrant to America in 1937, architect, Director of Architecture at the Illinois Institute of Technology; and Frank Lloyd Wright (1869-1959), American architect. [819

ALISTAIR COOKE. Memories of Frank Lloyd Wright [1869-1959]. A.I.A. jour., 32(4):42-4 (Oct 1959). From The Manchester guardian weekly, 16 Apr. 1959. [820

VINCENT JOSEPH SCULLY, JR. Frank Lloyd Wright [1869-1959]. N.Y.: G. Braziller, 1960. 125 p. plans, port., table, views. bibliog. (p. 117-18), notes (p. 113-15). (The masters of world architecture series.) [821

SADAYOSHI OMOTO. Some aspects of the so-called "Queen Anne" revival style of architecture. Ann Arbor: University Microfilms, 1954 [i.e. 1960]. Positive microfilm of typescript. [330] leaves. Thesis--Ohio State Univ. Abstracted: Dissert. abstracts, 20: 3255-7 (Feb). Includes some account of the revival in America, 1870s-90s, especially in Ohio. [822

Mrs. LINCOLN CROMWELL. The lifework of Beatrix Farrand, 1872-1959. Garden Club Am., Bul., 48(6): 26-7 (Nov). On Beatrix Cadwalader (Jones) Farrand, landscape architect, founder of the Reef Point Landscape Art Library, Bar Harbor, Me. [823

STANLEY PETER ANDERSEN. American ikon: response to the skyscraper, 1875-1934. Ann Arbor: University Microfilms, 1960. Positive microfilm of typescript. [365] leaves. Thesis--Univ. of Minnesota. Abstracted: Dissert. abstracts, 21:841 (Oct). [824

CLAY LANCASTER. The Philadelphia Centennial towers [1876]. Soc. Architectural Historians, Jour., 19:11-15 (Mar). diagrs., views. notes. On the Sawyer Observatory (an invention of Lemuel B. Sawyer), "a tapering tube supporting an overhanging wire viewing cage on top," 185 or 200 feet high, ascended by an elevator, and apparently demolished soon after the close of the fair; and the Iron Tower, "a rectangular structure contracting slightly towards the top, consisting of an open framework of slender iron members," reported to be 300 feet high, with an elevator and 3 platforms (2 for serving refreshments, 1 for observation), moved after the fair to Coney Island, N.Y., where it continued in service till destroyed by a fire in 1911. [824a

OLIVER W. LARKIN. "... a new way of thinking about architecture." John Arthur Garraty, ed., The unforgettable Americans (Great Neck, N.Y.: Channel Press [1960]), p. 303-6. On the work of Louis Henry Sullivan as an architect, 1876-1924, and the influence of his architectural doctrines. [825

LEE H. NELSON. White, Furness, McNally, and the Capital National Bank of Salem, Oregon. Soc. Architectural Historians, Jour., 19:57-62 (Jun). views. notes. On a building front attributed by "local tradition" to Stanford White but actually designed by Cornelius Sarsfield McNally (1858?-1938), 1892-93, and copied by him from Frank Furness's design for the National Bank of the Republic (Philadelphia, 1884). [825a

VOORHEES, WALKER, SMITH, SMITH, & HAINES, New York. 75th anniversary. [N.Y., 1960. 8], 80, [1] p. facsims., medals, ports., views. On an architectural firm founded by Cyrus L. W. Eidlitz, 1885-1960. [826

AMERICAN INSTITUTE OF ARCHITECTS. Hurricanes. A.I.A. jour., 32(4):75-86 (Oct 1959). diagr., maps, tables, views. (Its AIA technical reference guide 13-1.) Statistics of American hurricanes, 1886-1957, with special reference to their destruction of buildings and the means for reducing damage by better construction and other methods; with a list (41 entries) of "Source material and additional references." [827

HAROLD ALLEN BROOKS, JR. The early work of the prairie architects. Soc. Architectural Historians, Jour., 19:2-10 (Mar). plans, views. notes. On houses designed by George W. Maher (1864-1926), Robert C. Spencer, Jr. (1864-1953), and Walter Burley Griffin (1876-1937), all of Chicago, 1887-1902, and their relation to work of Louis Sullivan and Frank Lloyd Wright. [827a

DAVID GEBHARD. Louis Sullivan and George Grant Elmslie [1871-1953]. Soc. Architectural Historians, Jour., 19:62-8 (Jun). plan, views. notes. On architectural designs done by Elmslie while employed by the firm of Adler and Sullivan (1887-95) and by Louis Sullivan (1895-1909) and as a partner of William Gray Purcell (firm name: Purcell and Elmslie, 1909-20). [827b

JAMES CARSON WEBSTER. "Skyscraper," etc. Am. speech, 35:307-8 (Dec). notes. Evidence that the word was used in Chicago in 1888 as a noun meaning "tall building." [828

MARK L. PEISCH. The Chicago School and Walter Burley Griffin, 1893-1914: growth and dissemination of an architectural movement and a representative figure. Ann Arbor: University Microfilms, 1959 [i.e. 1960]. Positive microfilm of typescript. [270] leaves. Thesis--Columbia Univ. Abstracted: Dissert. abstracts, 20:4070-71 (Apr). Includes some account of the domination of the movement by Frank Lloyd Wright, its wide diffusion, its relation to the Progressive Movement in politics, and its "sudden decline after 1914." [829

ROBERT SPENCE. Daniel H[udson] Burnham [1846-1912] and the "Renaissance" in American architecture. Wis. Acad. Sciences, Trans., 49: 295-309. notes. On his achievement as Director of Works at the World's Columbian Exposition, Chicago, 1893, the architectural influence of the structures erected there, the criticism of them by Louis Sullivan and Frank Lloyd Wright, and his later work in popularizing and perpetuating "classicism" in architecture. [830

FRANK LLOYD WRIGHT (1869-1959). Frank Lloyd Wright: writings and buildings. Selected by Edgar Kaufmann and Ben Raeburn. N.Y.: Meridian Books [1960]. 346 p. double map, plans (part double), port., views. (Meridian books, MG22.) Reprinted excerpts from his writings on architecture and illustrations of buildings designed by him. Appended (p. 331-46): "Frank Lloyd Wright's executed works, 1893-1959, a list of structures standing--1960--arranged geographically." [831

GEORGE M. WHITE. Corporate practice of architecture. West. Reserve law rev., 11:616-30 (Sep). notes. On associated legal problems, 1901-60. [832

GROPIUS in America. Harvard alumni bul., 53:71-4 (14 Oct 1950). views. On the service of Walter Gropius as a professor of architecture at Harvard and as the founder of the Architects Collaborative, 1937-50. [833

JAMES MARSTON FITCH. Walter Gropius [born 1883]. N.Y.: G. Braziller, 1960. 128 p. map, plans, views. bibliog. (p. 122-3), notes (p. 113-14). (The masters of world architecture series.) On his emigration to America (ca. 1937), his work as an architect in Germany and America, and his service as Chairman, Department of Architecture, Harvard University; with a select list of his books and articles, 1910-60. [834

ARTHUR DREXLER. Ludwig Mies van der Rohe [born 1886]. N.Y.: G. Braziller, 1960. 127 p. plans, port., views. bibliog. (p. 119-21). (The masters of world architecture series.) On his emigration from Germany to America in 1938, his work as an architect in Germany and America, and his service as Director of Architecture, Illinois Institute of Technology; with a list of articles written by him. [835

STAMO PAPADAKI. Oscar Niemeyer. N.Y.: G. Braziller, 1960. 127 p. plans, views. bibliog. (p. 121), notes (p. 113-16). (The masters of world architecture series.) On the life of Oscar Niemeyer Soares (born 1907) in Brazil and his career as a Brazilian architect; with an account of his design of the Brazilian Pavilion at the New York World's Fair (1939) and his service as a member of the advisory committee on the design of the United Nations Headquarters, New York. [836

WOLF VON ECKHARDT. Eric Mendelsohn [1887-1953]. N.Y.: G. Braziller, 1960. 128 p. facsim., views. bibliog. (p. 119, 121), notes (p. 113-14). (The masters of world architecture series.) On his early life, education, and work as an architect in Germany, his emigration to America in 1941, and his work in America as an architect and a lecturer and writer on architecture. [837

MINOR ARTS

JEREMIAH F. EPSTEIN. Note on burins. Ohio archaeol., 10:50-51 (Apr). views. bibliog. [838

CLAIRE (WALLIS) CALLAHAN. The beginning antique collector's handbook and guide to 1,000 items to collect. By Ann Kilborn Cole [pseud.]. N.Y.: D. McKay Co. [1959]. xiv, 232 p. views. [839

HELEN COMSTOCK. 100 most beautiful rooms in America [representing various styles prevalent from the 1640s to ca. 1850]. N.Y.: Studio Publications [1958]. 210 p. views (part col.). On the furnishings and decorations of the rooms. [840

EARLY American fire brigade accessories [1686-1886]. Spinning wheel, 16(7):16-17 (Jul). port., views. On fire buckets, brass speaking trumpets, metal hat fronts, color prints of fires, etc. [841

EDITH GAINES. Quillwork: American paper filigree. Antiques, 78:562-5 (Dec). On American "rolled-paper work," with "Check list of American quillwork," describing 21 examples of sconces, hatchments, and pictures, ca. 1725 to ca. 1750. [842

SUSANNA SHORT. An American vogue in French bibelots. Antiques, 78: 249-51 (Sep). views. On the great popularity of American themes as decorative motifs of French fans, linens, candelabra, plates, screens, etc., 1776-1800. [843

SUSANNA SHORT. An American vogue in French fashion. Antiques, 77:273-5 (Mar). views. On bonnets, men's hats, dresses, and other articles symbolizing American events or at least bearing American names (e.g., bonnets à la Boston, skirts à l'Anglo-Américaine, etc.), 1777-78 [844

LILIAN BAKER CARLISLE. Aunt Hannah, the most famous bandbox maker. Antiques jour., 15(10):12-17, 36 (Oct). views. On "hat boxes or bandboxes," made of pastboard or thin wood and covered with wallpaper or other paper printed in color, in which "ladies" carried bonnets, ribbons, dresses, hair pieces and artificial flowers, "and the thousand and one bagatelles so dear to the feminine heart"; with an account of Hannah Davis (1784-1863), of Jaffrey, N.H., who manufactured bandboxes at home and delivered them from her wagon to girl mill workers and other customers. Also printed, in condensed form: Aunt Hannah Davis--bandbox maker. Spinning wheel, 16(2):16-17 (Feb). facsims., port., views. Includes a paragraph on the trade cards pasted inside her wooden bandboxes and reproduces 4 of the cards. [845

CLARA EVELYN (HALLARD) FAWCETT. Rural history re-enacted in Steele's Tiny Old New England. Hobbies, 64(12):126-7 (Feb). views. On an exhibition of miniature rooms furnished with miniature articles and populated by miniature individuals, assembled or made by Mr. and Mrs. F. D. Steele, West Cummington, Mass., representing New England life from 1800 to 1900. [846

SHELBURNE MUSEUM. Hat boxes and bandboxes at Shelburne Museum. By Lilian Baker Carlisle. Shelburne, Vt.: Shelburne Museum [1960]. xiii, 195, [2] p. facsims., ports., views (part col.). (Its Museum pamphlet series, 4.) A study of the designs painted on the boxes or printed on their paper coverings, mainly in the 19th century. [847

JOSEPH T. BUTLER. A case study in nineteenth-century color: redecoration at Sunnyside. Antiques, 78:54-6 (Jul). views. Review of information in English and American printed sources, 1826-57, concerning "wall colors and their relationship to painted furniture," and the redecoration of several bedrooms in Sunnyside according to "the dictates of taste of the first half of the nineteenth century." [848

ADA W. DARLING. A Victorian Thanksgiving. Antiques jour., 15(11): 16-17, 39 (Nov). views. On dishes and utensils to be found on the Thanksgiving dinner table (ca. 1900?), especially "the six-bottle caster." [849

OTIS TUFTON MASON (1838-1908). The technic of aboriginal American basketry. Selected papers from the American anthropologist, 1888-1920, ed. Frederica De Laguna (Evanston, Ill.: Row, Peterson [1960]), p. 559-78. views. First printed in 1901. [850

LILLIAN F. BEVELACQUA. The story of Bucks County Provincial. [Rockville, Md.: Bucks County Provincial, Inc., 1960.] 76 p. diagrs., facsims., plans, ports., views (part col.). 31 cm. On furniture, fabrics, clocks, and pewter and brass articles in early Pennsylvania Dutch designs, manufactured by Bucks County Provincial since 1947. [851

BERNEICE GRISWOLD. Milan Historical Museum, Milan, Ohio. Antiques jour., 15(11):14-15, 36 (Nov). views. On the collection of glass and of dolls in this museum, established in 1954. [852

Ceramics and Glass

HOBBIES: THE MAGAZINE FOR COLLECTORS. Old glass and china. Hobbies, 64(11)-65(1): monthly installments (Jan-Dec). diagrs., ports., views. Articles, some by B. H. Leffingwell and Albert Christian Revi, on glass paperweights, china cats, American poison bottles, the "Carrie Nation bottle," the "Bob Fitzsimmons bottle," the Ta Tsing bitters bottle (patented 1868), etc. [853

WILLIAM HENRY HOLMES (1846-1933). Form and ornament in ceramic art [of prehistoric America]. Margaret Mead & Ruth L. Bunzell, eds., The golden age of American anthropology (N.Y.: George Braziller, 1960), p. 191-202. diagrs., views. First printed in 1886. [854

ROBERT E. GREENGO. Rocker-stamped pottery in the Old and New World. International Congress of Anthropological and Ethnological Sciences, 5th, 1956, Men and cultures: selected papers, ed. Anthony F. C. Wallace (Phila.: Univ. of Pennsylvania Press [1960]), p. 553-65. chron. charts. notes. Cites evidences that such pottery designs were made in the United States as early as ca. 2500 B.C. and as late as ca. 1000 A.D. [855

RHEA (MANSFIELD) KNITTLE. Early American glass. Garden City, N.Y.: Garden City Pub. Co. [1948]. xxii, 496 p. views. bibliog. (p. 449-53). 1st ed. 1927. On the manufacture of glassware in the United States, the manufacturers, and the styles, forms, and materials of the ware, 1608-10, 1621-24, 1641-43, 1654-1875. [856

JOHN SPARGO. Early American pottery and china [1657 to ca. 1900]. Garden City, N.Y.: Garden City Pub. Co. [1948]. xvii, 393 p. diagrs., tables, views. bibliog. (p. 373-6). 1st ed. 1926. [857

IVOR NOËL HUME. Rouen faïence in eighteenth-century America. Antiques, 78:559-61 (Dec). views. On examples of imported Rouen ovenware found in Williamsburg excavations in contexts of the 1770s, and mention of such ware in a Maryland newspaper in 1778 and a Philadelphia newspaper in 1784, with a reference to an undated example from Massachusetts. [858

JOHN ALDEN LLOYD HYDE. Oriental Lowestoft, Chinese export porcelain, porcelaine de la Cie des Indes. With special reference to the trade with China and the porcelain decorated for the American market. [Second edition.] Newport, Monmouthsire: Ceramic Book Co. [1954]. viii, 166, [2] p. facsims., views (part col.). 1st ed. 1936. On "American Marine Lowestoft," "American Decoration pieces of special importance," and pieces "decorated with the arms of the United States, the arms of the states of New York, New Jersey, and Pennsylvania, the emblems of the Society of the Cincinnati, etc.," imported through Europe into the United States before 1784 and directly into the United States from China after the first voyage thither from the United States in 1784 and until the discontinuance of the trade, ca. 1830. [859

JOHN GOLDSMITH PHILLIPS. China-trade porcelain: an account of its historical background, manufacture, and decoration and a study of the Helena Woolworth McCann Collection. Published for the Winfield Foundation and the Metropolitan Museum of Art. Cambridge: Harvard Univ. Press, 1956. xxi, 234 p. facsims., map, views (part col.). bibliog. (p. 222-7). On porcelain made in China as early as 1557 for export to Europe and after 1784 also to America, manufactured till ca. 1820, often copying designs of European and American origin. [860

MARY L. JACKSON. If dishes could talk. Boston: Meador Pub. Co. [1959]. 240 p. views. bibliog. (p. 229-33). Forty-seven chapters on American, English, and other antique earthenware, mainly of the 19th century. [861

ARTHUR GOODWIN PETERSON. Salt and salt shakers: hobbies for young and old. Wash.: Washington College Press [1960. 2], 148 p. diagrs., tables, views (part col.). notes. History of the manufacture of salt shakers in America, ca. 1800 to 1960, and abroad; "Pictures of 550 glass salt shakers" (p. 17-44); "List of 830 salt shakers in pattern and art glass" (p. 115-42); and advice to collectors. [862

MILLARD F. ROGERS, JR. Stylistic influences on nineteenth-century American glass. Antiques, 78:57-9 (Jul). views. Study of 10 illustrated pieces in the Toledo Museum of Art. [863

ETHEL BROENDEL. American historical scenes on Staffordshire china [manufactured 1818-68]: some of its borders and marks. Hobbies, 64(11): 80-82, 88 (Jan). views. bibliog. [864

ALICE HULETT METZ. Early American pattern glass [1829 to early 20th century]: identification and valuation of about 1500 patterns, clear photos, authoritative reproduction information, uses, terminology, rarities, bargain patterns, plate numbers from standard texts, and accurate indexing. [Westfield, N.Y.: Guide Pub. Co., 1958.] 243 p. views. [865

GERALD G. GIBSON. Marked American porcelain [1826-1904]. Antiques jour., 15(2):8-10 (Feb). facsims., views. [866

MARVIN D. SCHWARTZ. Fine American ceramics of the Victorian period. Antiques, 77:386-9 (Apr). views. On examples in "the Brooklyn Museum's spring exhibition of the arts and crafts of the Victorian era," 1848-90. [867

ETHEL HALL BJERKOE. Parian. Hobbies, 64(11):86 (Jan). On the characteristics of a type of porcelain made in England and as early as 1853 in America, used in "ceramic sculptures" and later for pitchers and vases. [868

ARTHUR GOODWIN PETERSON. Salt shaker agitators. Spinning wheel, 16(12):18 (Dec). plans. On mechanical devices to keep salt in shakers from caking or to pulverize it when caked, 1863-1960. [869

LILLIAN BAKER CARLISLE. Westward-Ho pattern glass at Shelburne Museum. Antiques jour., 15(7):12-14, 35 (Jul). views. On "one of the acid-frosted and clear patterns issued by Gillinder (sometimes spelled Gillender) & Sons of Philadelphia," known at the time when it was made (ca. 1878 or 1879) as the Pioneer pattern. [870

NANCY R. FitzPATRICK. America's first art pottery: Rookwood. Spinning wheel, 16(10):16-17; (11):14, 16 (Oct, Nov). port., views. On the Rookwood Pottery, Cincinnati, founded by Maria (Longworth) Nichols in 1880, still in operation in 1960, and its products. [871

SAMUEL FARBER. Durand glass. Antiques jour., 15(8):12-16 (Aug). facsim., views. On Victor Durand (1870-1931), French emigrant in 1884, glassblower, who established in 1897 the Vineland Flint Glass Works, Vineland, N.J., merged in 1932 with the Kimble Glass Company, maker of Durand Art Glass till shortly after the merger. [872

TRYON MASON SHEPHERD. Ulysses Simpson Grant plates. Hobbies, 65(7): 70-71 (Sep). views. On 10 china or glass plates honoring or commemorating Grant, ca. 1885 to ca. 1904. [873

GRAYDON LA VERNE FREEMAN. Iridescent glass. [By] Larry Freeman. Watkins Glen, N.Y.: Century House [1956]. 128 p. diagrs., facsims., views. Examination of "all lustred glass made in America from around the turn of the century [i. e. 1893] until 1930, when clear glass again became the vogue." [874

Clocks and Watches

HOBBIES: THE MAGAZINE FOR COLLECTORS. On time. Hobbies, 64(11)-65(10): monthly installments (Jan-Dec). views. Articles on antique clocks and related apparatus by L. W. Slaughter and Silvio A. Bedini. [875

DAVID R. PROPER. "Grandfather's clock" revisited. Natl. Assoc. Watch and Clock Collectors, Bul., 9:246-7 (Apr). On the term as an Americanism designating "a tall-case hall clock," possibly or probably originating with Henry Clay Work's song, "My grandfather's clock" (1876), about a clock (probably made ca. 1778) that had belonged to his wife's grandfather, Deacon Otis Parker (died 1855 aged 80), and is still in possession of the Parker family and still running. [876

ARTHUR WILDER. Levi and Abel, the Hutchins brothers. Natl. Assoc. Watch and Clock Collectors, Bul., 9:289-91 (Aug). view. On Levi Hutchins (born 1761) and his brother Abel (born 1763), apprenticed to Simon Willard of Roxbury, Mass., in 1783, later proprietors of a clockmaking shop in Concord, N.H.; with anecdotes from Levi's autobiography. [877

VICTOR GILBERT. Time and taverns. Natl. Assoc. Watch and Clock Collectors, Bul., 9:148-52 (Feb). views. On a "clock jack" or roaster governed by clockwork, patented in Massachusetts in 1784, and the clocks in inns and taverns, especially the Waldorf-Astoria clock made in 1893. [878

GEORGE HENRY ECKHARDT, comp. United States clock and watch patents, 1790-1890: the record of a century of American horology and enterprise. N.Y., 1960. xii, 231 p. diagrs., facsims., tables. [879

WILLIAM L. WADLEIGH, JR. Grandmother clocks. Natl. Assoc. Watch and Clock Collectors, Bul., 9:380-84 (Oct). views. On clocks between 40 and 50 inches high made by Joshua Wilder and a few other clockmakers in Massachusetts and New Hampshire, ca. 1800 to ca. 1850. [880

WESLEY G. HARDING. A Silas Burnham Terry regulator. Natl. Assoc. Watch and Clock Collectors, Bul., 9: 153-4 (Feb). views. On a clock made by Terry at Plymouth, Conn., sometime between 1824 and 1876. [881

L. W. SLAUGHTER. Calendar clocks & watches [manufactured ca. 1850 to ca. 1900]. Hobbies, 65(3):43-4; (4):44-5 (May, Jun). views. [882

JAMES W. GIBBS. The life and death of the Ithaca Calendar Clock Company [1865-1920. n. p., 1960. 2], 80, [2] p. diagrs., views. (Supplement to the Bulletin of the National Association of Watch and Clock Collectors, Inc.) Appended (p. 7-80): reproductions of various patent applications for calendar clocks and improvements therein, 1853-73, and copies of documents relating to the bankruptcy and liquidation of the company, 1917-18. [883

WESLEY R. HAUPTMAN. Swiss imitations of early American watches [1857 to ca. 1880]. Natl. Assoc. Watch and Clock Collectors, Bul., 9:270-76 (Aug). views. [884

JAMES W. GIBBS. Still more perpetual calendar clocks. Natl. Assoc. Watch and Clock Collectors, Bul., 9:319-23 (Aug). views. Describes and illustrates 6 American clocks made between 1861 or later and some date between 1875 and 1889, and 4 European clocks. [885

HARRISON F. BABCOCK & MARY E. BABCOCK. The railroad watch. Natl. Assoc. Watch and Clock Collectors, Bul., 9:385-7 (Oct). views. On watches made by various companies for Ball & Co. (afterward the Ball Watch Co.), 1893-1922, organized by Webb C. Ball of Cleveland after a study of timekeeping mechanisms used by railroads. [886

Fabrics and Buttons

DOROTHY FOSTER BROWN. Buttons. Hobbies, 64(11)-65(10): monthly installments (Jan-Dec). ports., views. Information for collectors. [887

EMILY-MAE THOMAS. Quilts, counterpanes, and coverlets [18th and 19th centuries]. Vt. Hist. Soc., News and notes, 7:44-7, 52 (Feb, Mar 1956). views. Includes a description of an exhibit by the Vermont Historical Society. [888

AMELIA E. (MacSWIGGAN) RAWDING. Bundle handkerchiefs and printed cotton. Hobbies, 65(1):28-9, 62-3 (Mar). facsims., ports., views. On a cloth carrier "made to hold one's bundles which were placed in the center of a colored cotton square, and the four corners drawn and knotted together, forming a handle," made in Salem and elsewhere, 1774 ff.; with some account of imported cotton fabrics printed with portraits and landscapes. [889

EDWARD H. DAVIS. Lafayette's presentation buttons of 1824 make a return visit to Waterbury. Natl. button bul., 18:103-7 (May 1959). views. On a set of solid gold buttons presented to Lafayette in 1825 "by the early partners of the present Scovill Manufacturing Company"; with a report on an examination of 2 of the buttons in 1958. [890

LUCILE FARNSWORTH REALS. Antique American quilts [1830-1915]. Hobbies, 65(10):28-9 (Dec). views. [891

EMORY STRONG. Phoenix buttons. Am. antiq., 25:418-19 (Jan). views. On "metal buttons bearing the Phoenix bird, a motto in French ['Je renais de mes cendres'], and a number ... found in quantity in historic sites along the lower Columbia River, and less commonly throughout western North America," made by an unidentified English firm "in the early 1800's" for King Henri Christophe of Haiti (but apparently not delivered to him) and brought to the Columbia River before 1835, perhaps brought in 1832-33 by Nathaniel Wyeth as Indian trade goods. [891a

MARGARET E. WHITE. Those Victorian parlor ornaments--remember them? N.J. Hist. Soc., Proc., 78:38-41 (Jan). views. On "feather flowers," antimacassars, "heavy draperies held back with tasseled cords," "woolwork," jewelry and wreaths made of human hair, etc., 1840s-80s. [891b

RAYMOND B. CLARK, JR. Historical handkerchiefs. D. A. R. mag., 94:15, 54 (Jan). views. On cotton handkerchiefs printed with American historical scenes, mainly imported from Great Britain and France "until after 1850." [892

LILLIAN (SMITH) ALBERT. Collecting uniform buttons an active hobby sixty years ago. Antiques jour., 15(2): 26-7 (Feb). On the American Buttonists Society, founded in 1901, and some of its members, and in recent years the growing interest of the National Button Society in buttons from uniforms. [893

Furniture and Furnishings

WILLIAM G. HENNESSY. It's time for antiques. N.H. profiles, 9(1-12): monthly installments (Jan-Dec). views. Advice and anecdotes for collectors of antique furniture. [894

HAROLD SACK. Authenticity in American furniture. Art in America, 48(2): 72-5 (summer). views. On means of detecting restorations and "the complete fake." [895

MARION DAY IVERSON. The American chair, 1630-1890. Illustrated by Ernest Donnelly. N.Y.: Hastings House [1957]. xiii, 241 p. views. bibliog. (p. 231-2), notes. Includes "Chairs and other furniture owned by George Washington" (p. 201-26). [896

WILLIAM G. HENNESSY. A look at wing chairs [1700-1830]. N.H. profiles, 9(8):48-52; (9):45-9 (Aug, Sep). diagrs., views. [897

HISTORICAL SOCIETY OF EARLY AMERICAN DECORATION. Esther Stevens Brazer Guild. The ornamented chair: its development in America (1700-1890). Edited by Zilla Rider Lea. Rutland, Vt.: C. E. Tuttle Co.

[1960]. 173 p. views (part col.). bibliog. (p. 165-7). Partial contents.--Our English heritage, by Shirley Spaulding De Voe.--Our fancy chairs adopt Sheraton details, by Emilie Rich Underhill.--Sheraton influences the Windsor chair, by Bernice M. Drury.--The Empire period produces the golden age of stencilling, by Florence E. Wright.--The rocking chair brings comfort to simple homes, by Helen Warren Chivers.--Other types vary in scattered localities, by Viola A. Burrows. [898

CELIA JACKSON OTTO. The secretary with the tambour cartonnier. Antiques, 77:378-81 (Apr). views. On a type of small, compact secretary or desk, 1790-1800. [899

Metal Articles

F. H. GRIFFITH. Old mechanical banks. Hobbies, 64(11)-65(10): monthly installments (Jan-Dec). views. On toy banks. [900

LOIS ELSIE SPRINGER. Bells. Hobbies, 64(11)-65(10): monthly installments (Jan-Dec). port., views. Information for collectors. [901

KATHRYN C. BUHLER. Harvard College plate. Harvard alumni bul., 57: 470-73 (26 Mar 1955). views. On the collection of pre-1800 silver plate in the Fogg Museum of Art, Harvard University, 1644-1913. [902

MARY EARLE GOULD. Antique tin & tole ware: its history and romance [1700 to ca. 1900]. Rutland, Vt.: C. E. Tuttle Co. [1958]. xvi, 136 p. facsims., views. On the manufacture of tin plate (sheet iron dipped in tin) and of utensils made from it--ovens, roasters, fire pans, foot stoves, graters and strainers, sausage guns, churns, pans, molds, scales, tubs, pitchers, "slop pails," trays, lamps and lanterns, candleholders and candle molds, etc.; with chapters on decorated tinware (tole ware) and "The tin peddler & his world." [903

ROBERT T. TRUMP. Early brass-cased rim locks. Soc. Architectural Historians, Jour., 19:117-19 (Sep). views. notes. On the characteristics of these locks, made in England and forming a main source of "door hardware" used in the United States in the 18th century "and well into the nineteenth century." [903a

[THREE Philip Syngs.] Phila. Mus. bul., 54:38, 50 (winter 1959). view. On Philip Syng, Irish emigrant to Philadelphia, from which he removed to Annapolis in 1721, and his son Philip, who remained in Philadelphia, both silversmiths; and the latter's nephew Philip, who in 1759 was a brassfounder in Annapolis. [904

JOHN DANIEL MEYER. Old penny banks [since ca. 1793]. Watkins Glen, N.Y.: Century House [1960]. 95, [49] p. diagrs., facsims., tables, views. Reissue of Meyer's A handbook of old mechanical penny banks (1948), to which is now appended an unpaged section, "Stills," by Graydon La Verne Freeman. Includes "List of old catalogues by courtesy of Mr. W. F. Ferguson," 1860-1940 (p. 16). [905

DEE ANDERSON. American souvenir spoons presenting the extraordinary. Antiques jour., 15(2):20-23 (Feb). views. Describes 30 spoons (1890s ff.) in the collection of Miss Jerry Garrett, Houston, Tex. [906

CHARLES M. ECKMAN. Metallurgical industries of Virginia: non-ferrous ornamental castings. Mineral industries jour., 5(2):4-5 (Jun 1958). views. On Virginia Metalcrafters, Inc. (formerly the Loth Stove Company), Waynesboro, Va., maker of brass castings duplicating the color and other qualities of 18th-century brass, and its affiliation with Colonial Williamsburg "in the development of souvenirs and reproductions of antiques to be sold at Williamsburg and throughout the country," 1938-58. [906a

DEE ANDERSON. Souvenir spoons of intriguing design. Hobbies, 64(12): 52-3, 57 (Feb). view. On a collection of American spoons assembled by Miss Jerry Garrett of Houston, Tex. [907

PICTORIAL ARTS

WALDRON PHOENIX BELKNAP, JR. (1899-1949). The discovery of the English prototype of American colonial portraiture. Waldron Phoenix Belknap, Jr., American colonial painting: materials for a history, ed. Charles Coleman Sellers (Cambridge: Belknap Press of Harvard Univ. Press, 1959), p. 271-329. ports. Catalogue consisting of 63 double entries, the first item in each entry being an English mezzotint and the second an American portrait copied from it or influenced by it, 1681 to ca. 1770, supporting the thesis, which Belknap did not live to develop fully, "that engravings, and particularly British portrait mezzotints, had either served as exact models to the painters of the entire Colonial period, or had otherwise exerted a pervasive, continuous influence upon them." [908

ALAN R. FERNALD. William Edgar Marshall [1837-1906]: painter and engraver. Essay proof jour., 13:20-22 (Jan 1956). facsims., port. Deals particularly with his engravings from portraits painted by himself, including those of Washington (1862), Lincoln (1866), Grant (1868), and other "notables that might be produced in quantity to meet a popular demand." [909

NICHOLAS BIDDLE WAINWRIGHT. Augustus [Theodore Frederick Adam] Kollner [1812-1906], artist. Pa. mag. hist. and biog., 84:325-51 (Jul). facsims., ports., views. notes. On his emigration from Germany in 1838, his work as an engraver and illustrator in Washington (1839-40) and Philadelphia, his expertness in engraving on stone, copper, and steel, his trade cards, labels, billheads, etc., his watercolors and other paintings (sketches of the American countryside made on long trips in the summer, views of American cities), and the preservation of "a remarkably large corpus of his work" in his files. [910

LESTER U. BEITZ. Frederick [W.] Halpin [1805-80]: master engraver. Essay proof jour., 13:109-11 (Apr 1956). facsims. On his work as an engraver and painter, especially of portraits, in New York, Cincinnati, Richmond (1863-65), and New York again, 1842-80. [911

GEORGE M. CRAVEN. Sheeler at seventy-five. College art jour., 18: 136-43 (winter 1959). views. On "the unhurried, steadily productive career" of Charles Sheeler (born 1883), photographer and painter, especially of industrial buildings, and his present views of the relation between photography and painting. [912

RUDOLPH PICKETT BLESH. Stuart Davis [born 1894]. By Rudi Blesh. N.Y.: Grove Press [1960]. 64 p. ports., views (part col.). notes. (Evergreen gallery book 11-E-199.) On his early life in Philadelphia and East Orange, his study of painting under Robert Henri in New York City, and his work as a commercial artist, magazine illustrator, and painter. [913

NORMAN ROCKWELL (born 1894). Norman Rockwell, my adventures as an illustrator. As told to Thomas Rockwell. Garden City, N.Y.: Doubleday, 1960. [12], 436 p. cartoons, ports. (1 col.), views (part col.). On the author's early life in New York City, his studies at the Art Students League there, and his work as a painter and a magazine illustrator (including his covers for the Saturday evening post). [914

DEREK ROMMEL HUDSON. Arthur Rackham [1867-1939]: his life and work. N.Y.: Scribner [1960]. 181 p. ports. (part mount., part col.), views (part mount., part col.). bibliog. (p. 159-60). On his life in England and his work as an illustrator of magazines and books; with some account of exhibitions of his paintings and drawings in America as early as 1904, and of his illustrations of books by Washington Irving, Nathaniel Hawthorne, and other Americans. [915

AMERICAN FEDERATION OF ARTS. Karl Schrag [born 1912]. By John Gordon. N.Y. [1960]. 28 p. ports., views (part col.). bibliog. (p. 20-22). On his emigration to America in 1938 and his work as an illustrator and painter. [916

NORMAN KENT. Two new Cornwell murals. Am. artist, 24(6):59-63, 87-8, 90-91 (Jun). port., views. On Dean Cornwell (born 1892), magazine illustrator since 1915, muralist since 1927. [917

ROBERT TAYLOR. Etchings and drawings of Arthur W. Heintzelman [since 1917]. Boston Pub. Lib. quar., 12:115-19 (Apr). [918

CARL BEETZ. The drawings & lithographs of Carl Beetz. [Reported by] Janice Lovoos. Am. artist, 24(1): 17-20, 66-8 (Jan). cartoons, views. Interview on his art studies in San Francisco, New York City, and Los Angeles, 1930-35, his teaching of drawing in Los Angeles and San Francisco, and his engravings and watercolors (including cartoons) of characters and scenes in "the sporting world." [919

ERNEST WILLIAM WATSON. Marshall Davis. Am. artist, 24(8):40-45, 68 (Oct). port., views (1 col.). On his work as a "repertorial" illustrator and painter since the 1930s. [920

Engraving

HOBBIES: THE MAGAZINE FOR COLLECTORS. The picture post card. Conducted by Louise Collins [and] Bob Finnegan. Hobbies, 64(11)-65(10): monthly installments (Jan-Dec). facsims., ports., views. [921

DICK MARTIN. Early American educational issues [of playing cards, 1744-1960]. Hobbies, 64(12):120 (Feb). views. [922

LEWIS MILES RAISIG. The Continental currency makers. Numismatic scrapbook, 26:2825-8 (Oct). facsims. bibliog. On the makers of paper money for the Continental Congress, 1775-76. [923

ROBERT D. CROMPTON. James Trenchard [born 1746? disappeared after 1797 or 1807] of the "Columbian" and "Columbianum." Art quar., 23:378-97 (winter). facsim., ports., views. On his work in Philadelphia as an engraver on copper, 1777-95, as "the co-owner and engraving master of the Columbian Magazine of Philadelphia between 1786 and 1790," and as a founder of the short-lived Columbianum or Association of Artists in America for the Protection and Encouragement of the Fine Arts. [924

NATHAN N. EGLIT. Indian peace medals and the Presidential Series [1789-1889]. Numismatic scrapbook, 26:929-50 (Apr). medals, tables. bibliog., notes. Includes some account of restrikes from original dies and of more recent smaller medals and medalets of some of the Presidents. [925

JEROME IRVING SMITH. Love for sale. Art in Am., 48(4):60-63. facsims. On valentines, including those made in America as early as 1806. [926

GEORGIA S. CHAMBERLAIN. Wright and the Scott and Taylor medals. Numismatist, 73:691-700 (Jun). facsim., medals, port. bibliog., notes. On the engraving by Charles Cushing Wright of the dies for striking medals presented to Major Generals Zachary Taylor and Winfield Scott, 1849; with a report from R. M. Patterson, Director of the Mint, to the Secretary of the Treasury, 23 Nov. 1850, on "the methods used in producing medals at the Mint," and references to the poor quality of the work of the Chief Engraver, James B. Longacre, and to Patterson's abortive efforts to replace him by Wright. [927

GRANT T. REYNARD. The prints of Childe Hassam, 1859-1935. Am. artist, 24(9):42-7 (Nov). views. [928

CHARLES MEADE PATTERSON. Envelopes that advertised firearms ["early 1860's" to 1898]. Gun rep., 5(1):8-12 (Jun 1959). facsims. notes. Mainly reproductions and detailed descriptions of 14 examples. [929

ARTHUR WILLIAM HEINTZELMAN. Modern wood-engraving in America [since the 1920s]. Boston Pub. Lib. quar., 12:57-63 (Jan). view. [930

DON E. NESKE (born 1929). Don E. Neske, illustrator: an interview by the editors. Am. artist, 24(6):24-9, 76-7 (Jun). ports., views. On his life in Milwaukee and his work as an illustrator of books, magazines, and advertising publications. [931

BARBARA R. MUELLER. The art of the postage stamp: definition, recognition, and promotion. Am. Philatelic Cong., Congress book, 26:41-9. facsims. Abstracts of 15 publications, 1940-60, dealing with "the art and aesthetic of the postage stamp," and 7-point outline for "systematic investigation" of the subject. [932

AMERICAN FEDERATION OF ARTS. Mauricio Lasansky [born 1914]. By Carl Zigrosser. N.Y. [1960]. 19 p. ports. (1 col.), views (1 col.). bibliog. (p. 15, 17-18). On his early life and work as an engraver in Argentina, his emigration to the United States in 1943, and his teaching of graphic arts in the University of Iowa. [933

Painting

WALDRON PHOENIX BELKNAP, JR. (1899-1949). Notes on colonial portraits. Waldron Phoenix Belknap, Jr., American colonial painting: materials for a history, ed. Charles Coleman Sellers (Cambridge: Belknap Press of Harvard Univ. Press, 1959), p. 227-70. 102 ports. Notes from an unfinished card file, arranged alphabetically by name of subject of portrait, listing "unattributed portraits, particularly of New York." [934

KENNETH JAMES LABUDDE. American Romanticism and European painting. Am. quar., 12:95-101 (spring). views. Commentary on the American paintings listed and discussed in an exhibition catalogue, The Romantic Movement (London: Arts Council of Great Britain, 1959). [935

WALDRON PHOENIX BELKNAP, JR. (1899-1949). The identity of Robert Feke. Waldron Phoenix Belknap, Jr., American colonial painting: materials for a history, ed. Charles Coleman Sellers (Cambridge: Belknap Press of Harvard Univ. Press, 1959), p. 3-34. facsims., ports. notes. From the

Art bulletin, Sep. 1947, with additions. On the evidence for the identification of Robert Feke (1705?-1750), the painter, with Robert Feke, Jr. (born 1705?), of Oyster Bay. [936

JOHN GALT (1779-1839). The life of Benjamin West (1816-1820). ... A facsimile reproduction with an introduction by Nathalia Wright. Gainesville, Fla., 1960. ix p., facsim. (iv, 160, 251 p.). ports., views. (Scholars' facsimiles & reprints.) Reproduction of a work published in 2 volumes in London. On Benjamin West (1738-1820), his early life in Philadelphia and New York, his travels and studies in Italy and elsewhere in Europe from 1759 to 1763, and his career as a painter in London, "Composed from materials furnished by himself." [937

JOHN WALKER. Paintings from America. Harmsworth, Middlesex: Penguin Books [1951]. 45, [1] p. 49 ports. and views (1 col.). Historical and analytical sketch of American painting, 1740s-1940s, and catalogue of the illustrations, 1760-1932. [938

YVON BIZARDEL. American painters in Paris [1760-1889]. ... Translated by Richard Howard. N.Y.: Macmillan, 1960. viii, [4], 177 p. ports., views. Deals largely with their personal and family lives. [939

GROSE EVANS. Benjamin West [1738-1820] and the taste of his times. Carbondale: Southern Illinois Univ. Press, 1959. [12], 144 p. 73 ports. (1 col.) and views. bibliog. (p. 129-38), notes (p. 109-27). On "West's paintings in relation to eighteenth-century critical expectations" and the extent to which "he realized the esthetic aims of his age." Deals mainly with his work in England, after he left America in 1760. [940

JAMES CAREY THOMAS FLEXNER. The light of distant skies, 1760-1835. N.Y.: Harcourt, Brace [1954]. xiii, 306 p. 102 ports. and views. bibliog. (p. 253-69), notes (p. 271-83). "Catalogue of illustrations" (p. 285-93). (His American painting, 2.) Part of "a projected many-volume history of American painting as an expression of American life." [941

WILLIAM G. HENNESSY. Portraits in profile. N.H. profiles, 9(4):37-40; (5):42-5 (Apr, May). ports. On painted, hollowcut, and mounted paper shadowgraphs (silhouettes), and painted ivory miniatures, 1760s-1830s. [942

JOHN SINGLETON COPLEY (1737-1815). John Singleton Copley to his wife. Boston Pub. Lib. quar., 12: 67-78 (Apr). notes. Letters to Susannah Farnum (Clarke) Copley, dated Rome, 5 Nov. 1774, and "Cologn," 23 Nov. 1775, on the writer's travels in Europe to inspect architecture and paintings, and part of a letter to him from his son, John Singleton Copley, Jr. (Boston? 1796?). [943

LAURENCE B. GOODRICH. Ralph Earl's debt to Gainsborough and other English portraitists [ca. 1777 to 1791]. Antiques, 78:464-5 (Nov). ports. [944

WILLIAM H. GUTHMAN. The Louis Warrington flask. Gun rep., 5(2):16 (Jul 1959). view. On a horn powder flask, undated, bearing a miniature oil portrait of Capt. Lewis Warrington (1782-1851), USN. [945

BARBARA HOLDRIDGE & LARRY HOLDRIDGE. Ammi Phillips [1788-1865]. Art in Am., 48(2):98-103 (summer). facsim., ports. On his life in Connecticut and eastern New York, his work as an itinerant painter of oil portraits, and the characteristics of his work that have enabled the authors to identify more than 120 of his paintings. [946

MARILOU ALSTON RUDULPH. George Cooke [1793-1849] and his paintings. Ga. hist. quar., 44:117-53 (Jun). ports., views. notes. On his early life and mercantile experience in Maryland and Washington, D.C., his sojourn in Europe as a painter, his industriousness and almost incredible output as an itinerant painter of portraits, landscapes, and interiors in most of the area between New York City and New Orleans, and his magazine articles; with a particular account of his work in Georgia, 1840-41, 1845. [947

THOMAS W. LEAVITT. Washington Allston [1779-1843] at Harvard. Harvard alumni bul., 58:550-53 (21 Apr 1956). facsim., ports., views. notes. On his studies there, 1796-1800, and his career as a painter. [948

The INVISIBLE portrait. University, 6:32 (fall). port. On the discovery of a portrait of Thomas Jefferson, painted by Rembrandt Peale in 1800, now in the Peabody Institute. [949

JAMES B. BYRNES. Thomas Sully [1783-1872]. N. C. Mus. Art bul., 1(1):17-21 (spring 1957). notes. On his more than 2,600 paintings, 1801-72, his life in Philadelphia after 1808, and particularly his group portrait of 5 of his children (1822-24); with biographical sketches of the children. [950

RITA SUSSWEIN GOTTESMAN. Copley versus West. Antiques, 78:478-9 (Nov). ports. On a controversy between John Singleton Copley and Benjamin West involving a painting exhibited by West in the Royal Academy, 1803. [951

IRMA (SIMONTON) BLACK. Children's art a century ago. Art in Am., 48(1): 98-9 (spring). Reproductions of 5 paintings by children, 1806-34, with commentary. [952

JOHN FRANCIS McDERMOTT. The art of Seth Eastman [1808-75] ... a traveling exhibition of paintings and drawings circulated by the Smithsonian Institution, 1959-1960. [Wash., 1960? 8], 34 p. views. bibliog. (p. 33-4), notes (p. 27). On his early life in Brunswick, Me., his studies at the U.S. Military Academy, his service as an Army officer, and his paintings (1829-70), chiefly of landscapes and Indians in the Sioux country; with a catalogue of 68 paintings. [953

LLOYD W. FOWLES. A forgotten Connecticut painter: Osbert Burr Loomis, 1813-1886. Conn. Hist. Soc. bul., 24: 65-71 (Jul 1959). views. On his life in Connecticut, South Carolina, and Cuba, and his paintings of Connecticut scenes. [954

JAMES B. BYRNES. Sully's copy of the "Lansdowne" Washington. N.C. Mus. Art bul., 1(3):17-20 (autumn 1957). port., view. notes. On a copy of Gilbert Stuart's portrait of Washington, painted by Thomas Sully in Philadelphia by order of the State of North Carolina, 1816, and now hanging in the North Carolina State Capitol. [955

HELEN BURR SMITH. Nicholas Biddle Kittell (1822-1894): a forgotten New York State artist. N.Y. Hist. Soc. quar., 44:394-412 (Oct). ports. notes. On his portraits and other paintings, done in Athens, Pa., New York City, and North Conway, N.Y.; with "Chronological checklist of works by or attributed to Nicholas Biddle Kittell," 1840/41-1894. [955a

ANN (HAWKES) HUTTON. Portrait of patriotism: Washington crossing the Delaware. Phila.: Chilton Co. [1959]. xi, 190 p. views. bibliog. (p. 178-81). Biography of Emanuel Gottlieb Leutze (1816-68), German emigrant to Philadelphia in 1825, "the most successful painter of his generation," painter of historical scenes; with some account of his descendants, his reputation, the Battle of Trenton (1776), Leutze's painting of the crossing of the Delaware by Washington's army (1851), and its exhibition since 1952 at Washington Crossing, Pa., on permanent loan from the Metropolitan Museum of Art. The biography is based mainly upon "many old family letters." [956

KENDALL BENARD TAFT. Adam and Eve in America. Art quar., 23:171-9 (summer). facsims., views. On 2 paintings by Claude Marie Dubufe (1790-1864), French artist, The temptation of Adam and Eve and The explusion from Paradise, painted in 1828, their exhibition in the United States in several cities from Boston to New Orleans, 1832-35, and the controversy about the moral effect of their portrayal of nudity. [957

JOSEPH EARL ARRINGTON. Otis A[llen] Bullard's moving panorama of New York City. N.Y. Hist. Soc. quar., 44:308-35 (Jul). facsims., map, port. notes. On the work of Bullard (1816-53) as a portraitist and genre painter in New York and Connecticut, 1838-53; his series of panoramic paintings of New York City, 1846-53; and its exhibition on rollers, with accompanying broadsides and lectures, in New York, in New England, and as far west as Wisconsin, 1850-67; with some account of earlier and later panoramas of New York City. [957a

PETER POLLACK. Fifteen self-portraits by American artists [ca. 1840 to 1959]. With an introduction and commentaries. Am. artist, 24(6): 30-34, 92-7 (Jun). ports. Reproductions, with biographical sketches of the painters. [958

CHARLES COLEMAN SELLERS. Rubens Peale [1784-1865]: a painters' decade. Art quar., 23:139-51 (summer). ports., views. On his activities between 1855 and 1865 at "Woodland Farm," Schuylkill County, and in Philadelphia, as recorded in his diary, particularly his new occupation of painting (which he began at the age of 71 with lessons from his daughter, Mary Jane, and other relatives); with an annotated catalogue of 131 paintings by him, mainly landscapes and flower pictures. [959

BARTLETT H. HAYES, JR. The American line: 100 years of drawing.

Andover, Mass.: Addison Gallery of American Art, Phillips Academy [1959. 114] p. cartoons, ports., views. 13x21 cm. Reproductions of 100 undated drawings, with editorial commentary on their technique, materials, and "function, or intent." [960

W. ARTHUR BUTCHER. First important West Virginia artist painted the Old West. W. Va. hist., 21:269-74 (Jul). port. On William Robinson Leigh (1866-1955), painter, native of West Virginia, resident in New York City. [961

ALFRED WERNER. A painter of space and dimension--Lyonel Feinsinger, 1871-1956. Am. artist, 24(8):26-31, 62-3 (Oct). views (1 col.). [962

REGINA SORIA. Some background notes for Elihu Vedder's "Cumean Sibyl" and "Young Marsyas" [both 1878]. Art quar., 23:71-87 (spring). facsim., ports., views. notes. On the circumstances under which these compositions were painted, and their reception, as shown in his correspondence. [963

HENRI DORRA. Ryder and Romantic painting. Art in Am., 48(4):22-33. port., views (part col.). On the various American and European influences acting upon Albert Pinkham Ryder as shown in his paintings during the 1880s and 1890s. [964

JAMES SCHUYLER. Edwin Dickinson [born 1891]. Portfolio, 2:88-103. ports. (1 col.), views (1 col.). On his work as a painter. [965

AMERICAN FEDERATION OF ARTS. Milton Avery [born 1893]. By Adelyn [Dohme] Breeskin. N.Y. [1960]. 26 p. ports., views (part col.). bibliog. (p. 16-25), notes. On his work as a painter. [966

WILLIAM CAXTON, JR. John C. Wenrich [born 1894]: recorder of locomotives in watercolor. Am. artist, 24(6):35-9 (Jun). port., views (1 col.). [967

AMERICAN FEDERATION OF ARTS. Abraham Rattner [born 1895]. By Frank Getlein. N.Y., c1960. 28 p. facsims., ports. (1 col.), views (1 col.). bibliog. (p. 13-14, 17-23). On his paintings and his teaching of art; with a catalogue of a retrospective exhibition. [968

CHARLES WEBSTER HAWTHORNE (1872-1930). Hawthorne on painting, from students' notes collected by Mrs. Charles W. Hawthorne. With an introduction by Edwin Dickinson, and an appreciation by Hans Hofmann. N.Y.: Dover Publications [1960. 4], 91 p. 1st ed. 1938. Notes taken by students in Hawthorne's classes in painting at the Cape Cod School of Art, ca. 1899 to ca. 1930; with an account by his son, Joseph Hawthorne, of his early life in Maine and his work as a painter. [969

KIM-GAUL KWAN (born 1899). Art's golden thread from west to east. By the painter himself and his critics. Text in English and French. Rutland, Vt.: C. E. Tuttle Co. [1958, c1957. 2], 49 p. 41 ports. and views (part col.). "Autobiography" (p. 14-25), "Kwan Kim-Gaul and the call of the Far East," by Barnett D. Conlon (p. 34-49), and other information about a native of China who came to the United States "when still a child," studied art there, and settled in France to pursue his career in painting. [970

JOHN IRELAND HOWE BAUR. Philip Evergood [born Philip Blashki, 1901]. N.Y.: Published for the Whitney Museum of American Art by Praeger [1960]. 116, [9] p. ports., 91 views (part col.). 24 x 29 cm. bibliog. (p. 121-2). (Books that matter.) On his life in New York City and in England and his work as a painter; with a catalogue of a retrospective exhibition of his paintings. [971

AMERICAN FEDERATION OF ARTS. Lee Gatch [born 1902]. By Perry T[ownsend] Rathbone. N.Y. [1960]. 28 p. ports., views (part col.). bibliog. (p. 22-4). On his work as a painter, with reproductions of 45 of his paintings. [972

AMERICAN FEDERATION OF ARTS. Walter Quirt [born 1902]. By Robert M. Coates. N.Y. [1960]. 28 p. port., views (part col.). bibliog. (p. 20-23). On his work as a painter. [973

NORMAN KENT. Herbert Barnett [born 1910], draughtsman & painter. Am. artist, 24(2):24-31, 63-4 (Feb). ports., views (1 col.). [974

VINCENT PRICE (born 1911). I like what I know: a visual autobiography. Garden City, N.Y.: Doubleday, 1959. 313 p. views. On the author's keen interest in paintings and museums since childhood, his almost lifelong activities as a collector of paintings, and his travels abroad to see and acquire paintings; with some account of his early life in St. Louis, his studies at Yale and London University, and his life in New York and Hollywood as an actor. [975

MARTIN L. FRIEDMAN. The Precisionist view. Art in Am., 48(3):30-37. views. On "a pioneer direction" in American painting since ca. 1917, represented particularly by Georgia O'Keefe, Charles Sheeler, Charles Demuth, Niles Spencer, Ralston Crawford, Louis Guglielmi, Preston Dickinson, and George Ault. [976

DORE ASHTON. Philip Guston [born 1913]. N.Y.: Grove Press [1960]. 63 p. views (part col.). bibliog. (p. 61). (Evergreen gallery book 10-E-196.) On his early life in Canada, his emigration to California in 1919, and his work as a painter in America and abroad. [977

EDWARD HOPPER. Edward Hopper. Interviewed by John Morse. Art in Am., 48(1):60-63 (spring). views (part col.). On some of his paintings since 1923. [978

DIEGO RIVERA (1886-1957). My art, my life: an autobiography. [By] Diego Rivera, with Gladys March. N.Y.: Citadel Press [1960]. 318 p. ports., views. Includes accounts of his work in the United States at intervals between 1926 and 1945, and the controversies aroused by his murals in Detroit, New York, and San Francisco. [979

KENNETH B. SAWYER. Clyfford Still [born 1904]. Portfolio, 2:74-87. port., views (1 col. double). On his paintings and his teaching of art since 1935. [980

ERNEST WILLIAM WATSON. The art of Ralston Crawford. Am. artist, 24(4): 47-51, 64-6 (Apr). port., views. On his representational and abstract paintings since 1938. [981

AMERICAN FEDERATION OF ARTS. William Pachner [born 1915. By] Kenneth Donahue. N.Y. [c1959]. 28, [24] p. illus. (part col.), port. bibliog. (p. 24-5). Catalogue of a retrospective exhibition; with an account of his work as a painter since his arrival in the United States as a refugee from Moravia in 1939. [982

GERDA WITH. The art of Gerda With. [Reported] by Janice Lovoos. Am. artist, 24(5):20-25, 64-7 (May). ports., views. Interview on her work as a painter in the United States since her emigration from Germany in 1939. [983

JANICE LOVOOS. Ruth Osgood: decorative painter [since 1945]. Am. artist, 24(6):40-45, 84-5 (Jun). port., views. [984

HENRY CLARENCE PITZ. The paintings of Paul [Warren] Zimmerman. Am. artist, 24(1):36-41, 72-3 (Jan). ports., views (1 col.). On his work as a painter, mainly of landscapes and buildings, and his teaching of art in Hartford, Conn., 1945-59. [985

Photography

JOHN FABER. Great moments in news photography [in America, 1860-1960, and abroad]. From the historical files of the National Press Photographers Association. N.Y.: T. Nelson [1960]. 126, [1] p. facsims., ports., views. "Credits" (p. 126-7). [986

FRITZ WENTZEL (born 1877). Memoirs of a photochemist. ... Edited by Louis Walton Sipley. Phila.: American Museum of Photography [1960]. xi, [1], 146, [1] p. facsims., ports., views. notes (p. 121-36). On the author's photographic researches in Germany (chaps. 1-10) and his work in America with ANSCO and AGFA, 1926-46 (chap. 11); with some account of the development of photographic chemistry and the technology of photosensitized paper. [987

LOU JACOBS, JR. School for magazine photographers. Infinity, 9(2):9 (Feb). view. On the Art Center School, Los Angeles, developed by Will Connell, 1931-60. [987a

ROBERT CATO. With an eye for clarity: Leslie Gill, 1908-1958, 25 years of his work. Infinity, 7(8):5-15 (Oct 1958). facsims., port., views. Mainly reproductions of his work as a commercial photographer, 1933-58. [987b

JACK Breed, cameraman: the story of a top photographer. Harvard alumni bul., 53:409-10 (24 Feb 1951). port. On John B. Breed, Harvard graduate of 1940, photographic intelligence officer in the Navy, professional photographer since World War II. [988

SCULPTURE

CLARA EVELYN (HALLARD) FAWCETT. Dollology. Hobbies, 64(11)-65(10): monthly installments (Jan-Dec). ports., views. Includes articles on doll clubs, doll carriages, doll houses, "friendship dolls," and "china-headed dolls." [989

ELSIE B. CHATTERTON. A Vermont sculptor. Vt. Hist. Soc., News and notes, 7:10-14 (Sep 1955). views. On Margaret F. Foley (1815/25?-1877), early resident of Vermont, schoolteacher, mill worker, cameo cutter in Boston, for 17 years a sculptor in Rome. [990

THOMAS BRENDLE BRUMBAUGH. On Horatio and Richard Greenough: a defence of neoclassicism in America [1820s ff.]. Am. quar., 12:414-17 (fall). notes. [991

MARGARET (FARRAND) THORP. Literary sculptors in the Caffé Greco. Am. quar., 12:160-74 (summer). On the "little band" of American sculptors who migrated to Rome, 1825-69, "the kind of life they could live there, even when their resources were small," and the advantage to each one of them of belonging there to "a respected and accepted profession," in which he was "no longer an eccentric, admired occasionally, more often smiled at." [992

ROBERT LEE GALE. Thomas Crawford, dear Lou, and the horse. Va. mag. hist. and biog., 68:171-92 (Apr). ports., views. notes. On his planning and execution of an "equestrian group" as a monument to George Washington to be installed in Richmond, and his letters on this subject to his wife, Louisa Ward Crawford, dated in America and Europe, 1845-57; with excerpts from the letters. [993

ELIZABETH CLEMENTINE (DODGE) KINNEY (1810-89). A minor poet meets Hiram Powers. [Edited by] Everard M[iller] Upjohn. Art bul., 42:63-6 (Mar). notes. Excerpts from a manuscript diary kept by his neighbor in Florence, "a minor American poet ... puritanical hypochondriac and blue stocking," 1854-56. [994

FRANCIS RUSSELL. Rogers and his groups. New-Eng. galaxy, 1(4):16-24 (spring). views. On small plaster groups or tableaux ("Rogers Groups") of figurines, manufactured between 1859 and 1892 by John Rogers (1829-1904). [995

AMERICAN FEDERATION OF ARTS. Hugo Robus [born 1885]. By Lincoln Rothschild. N.Y. [1960]. 36 p. ports., views. bibliog. (p. 30-34). On his work as a sculptor; with a catalogue of a retrospective exhibition. [996

H. H. ARNASON. John [Bernard] Flannagan [1895-1942] reappraised. Art in Am., 48(1):64-9 (spring). views. On his work as a sculptor. [997

VIVIEN (BULLOCH) KEATLEY. Tex Wheeler, the cowboy sculptor. Quarter horse jour., 3(1):6-7, 29 (Oct 1950). ports. (1 double), views. On Hughlette Wheeler (born 1901), his early life and work as a cowboy in Florida, his studies in the Cleveland School of Art and abroad, and his career in Alhambra, Calif., as a sculptor of miniature horses in bronze. [998

FREDERIC WHITAKER. The sculpture of Aristide B[erto] Cianfarani [died 1960]. Am. artist, 24(4):22-7, 60-63 (Apr). ports., views. On his emigration from Italy some years before World War I, his life in Providence, R.I., and Meriden, Conn., and his professional work "in both the commercial and aesthetic departments" of sculpture. [999

DIDI CASTLE THOMPSON. One thousand wooden horses. West. horseman, 25(6):42-3, 93-4 (Jun). ports., views. On a collection of miniature wooden horses and equipages, begun "40 years ago" by M. B. Mervis of Barrington, Ill. [1000

THE STUDY AND TEACHING OF ART

THOMAS MUNRO. Art education, its philosophy and psychology: selected essays. N.Y.: Liberal Arts Press, 1956. xvi, 387 p. Twenty-five essays on the visual arts in general education, the educational fostering of creative ability in art and of "powers of art appreciation and evaluation," art tests, "children's art abilities," "adolescence and art education," college art, education in aesthetics, the work of art museums, etc., reprinted from books and periodicals, 1925-53. [1001

Folklore

OSCAR BRAND, comp. Bawdy songs and backroom ballads ... as sung in Audio Fidelity's "Bawdy songs" LP series. With a foreword by Louis Untermeyer. Arranged for piano, guitar, and voice by Robert M. Abramson. N.Y.: Dorchester Press [1960]. 93, [3] p. cartoons, music. Forty-one songs (words and music), anonymous and presumably traditional, some of which (e. g., "The E-r-i-e was rising") are evidently of American origin; with a list of the contents of the 6 record albums from which these selections are taken. [1002

THOMAS E. CHENEY. Mormon folk song and the Fife Collection [at Brigham Young University]. Brigham Young Univ. studies, 3:57-63 (autumn). notes. Severe criticism of a collection assembled by Austin and Alta Fife from oral sources and "sent out on tapes by the Library of Congress." [1003

MIMI CLAR. Folk belief and custom in the blues. West. folklore, 19:173-89 (Jul). notes. [1004

JOHN GREENWAY. Folk songs as socio-historical documents. West. folklore, 19:1-9 (Jan). notes. States or implies disagreement with former restrictive concepts of folk literature in terms of communal origin, oral transmission, etc. [1005

BURL ICLE IVANHOE IVES. What is a folk song? Music jour., 18(2):10, 44 (Feb). port. [1006

PHIL ROWLAND JACK & RICHARD MERCER DORSON. Questions on "A theory for American folklore" [by Dorson]. Jour. Am. folklore, 72: 325-30 (Oct-Dec). Forty-four questions by Jack, and Dorson's replies to some of them. [1007

RAY McKINLEY LAWLESS. Folksingers and folksongs in America: a handbook of biography, bibliography, and discography. N.Y.: Duell, Sloan, and Pearce [1960]. xviii, 662 p. facsim., ports., views. notes. Definitions and problems of "folksong" and its relation to the fine arts, "An alphabetical presentation of singers of ballads and folksongs" (biographical sketches of "about 225 singers," p. 23-244), "Folk-music instruments" (p. 245-67), "Collections of ballads and folksongs" (heavily annotated list, p. 269-430), "Folklore societies and folk festivals" (p. 431-47), and "Folksong titles and discography" (p. 449-630, lists). [1008

KATIE LEE. The cowboys taught me. Ariz. highways, 36(2):34-9 (Feb). music, port. Remarks on cowboy songs, by a professional singer; with several texts and tunes. [1009

ALAN LOMAX, ed. The folk songs of North America in the English language. ... Melodies and guitar chords transcribed by Peggy Seeger, with one hundred piano arrangements by Matyas Seiber and Don Banks. Garden City, N.Y.: Doubleday [1960]. xxx, [2], 623 p. diagrs., col. maps, music. bibliog. (p. 597-600), discog. (p. 608-15). Collection of 317 songs or anecdotes, most with tunes, each with a headnote. Contents.--1. The North.--2. The Southern mountains and backwoods.--3. The West.--4. The Negro South. [1010

MARGARET MEAD. A new framework for studies of folklore and survivals. International Congress of Anthropological and Ethnological Sciences, 5th, 1956, Men and cultures: selected papers, ed. Anthony F. C. Wallace (Phila.: Univ. of Pennsylvania Press [1960]), p. 168-74. bibliog., notes. Effort "to present a theoretical framework within which the work of modern folklorists can be integrated with ongoing and developing theories of human evolution and cultural change." [1011

CLEMENT WOODWARD MEIGHAN. More on folk traditions. Jour. Am. folklore, 72:59-60 (Jan-Mar). On their relation to historical fact among "primitives." [1012

BRUNO NETTL. An introduction to folk music in the United States. Detroit: Wayne State Univ. Press, 1960. v, [3], 122, [1] p. music. bibliog. (p. 118-22), notes (p. 115-17). (Wayne State University studies. Humanities, 7.) Includes "Musical examples," 32 songs with music and words (p. 92-114). [1013

MARJORIE TALLMAN. Dictionary of American folklore. N.Y.: Philosophical Library [1960, c1959. 4], 324 p. A single alphabet, absentmindedness to Zeotrope, lacking reference to sources or statement of methods and standards. [1014

RICHARD T. WAGNER. The relations of folklore to the traditional academic disciplines. La. folklore misc., 1(4): 33-42 (Jan). notes. [1015

THELMA GOODWIN. The Devil in American folklore [since ca. 1692]. Tenn. Folklore Soc. bul., 26:36-45 (Jun). bibliog., notes. [1016

RICHARD MERCER DORSON. "... the American mock hero." John Arthur Garraty, ed., The unforgettable Americans (Great Neck, N.Y.: Channel Press [1960]), p. 183-9. On Sam Patch (born "before 1807," died 1829) as a jumper over waterfalls and as an "authentic folk hero." [1017

GEORGE MONTEIRO. Histoire de Montferrand: l'athlete canadien and Joe Mufraw. Jour. Am. folklore, 72: 24-34 (Jan-Mar). notes. On an account by Benjamin Sulte (published in 1883) of "the best known French-Canadian strong man of the age," who at the time of his death in 1864 was already the subject of legends intertwined with fact; the currency of the legends among French Canadians in New England, upper New York, Michigan, Wisconsin, and Minnesota; and the incorporation (probably literary only) of some of them into the myths or legends of Paul Bunyan. [1018

LAWRENCE SIDNEY THOMPSON. Mr. Beadle and the folklorists: popular elements in the dime novel. Wayland Debs Hand & Gustave Otto Arlt, eds., Humaniora: essays in literature, folklore, bibliography, honoring Archer Taylor on his seventieth birthday (Locust Valley, N.Y.: J. J. Augustin, 1960), p. 342-7. notes. On dime novels after 1878 as perpetuators of the "traditions of the frontier hero and the tall tales he and his companions told. They added almost nothing to already recorded folk tradition in these fields; but they preserved it, sometimes in corrupt forms and always in massive editions, for the late nineteenth and early twentieth century." [1019

CHARLES GUITEAU (ballad). Charles Guiteau. [Edited by] F[rancis] W[right] Bradley. South. folklore quar., 24: 282-3 (Dec). The versions of a ballad about the murder of James A. Garfield (1881), "sung fifty and sixty years ago," collected by the editor in South Carolina. [1020

DANIEL G. HOFFMAN. Jim's magic: black or white? Am. lit., 32:47-54 (Mar). notes. On the "superstitious lore" of "Jim, the Negro slave," in Huckleberry Finn (1884). [1021

ED KAHN. Josiah H. Combs, 1886-1960. Ky. folklore rec., 6:101-3. port. On his studies of "dialect, folklore and folksong," especially his early contributions to the study of Kentucky folklore. [1022

WAYLAND DEBS HAND. American folklore after seventy years [1888-1958]: survey and prospects. Jour. Am. folklore, 72:1-11 (Jan-Mar). notes. [1023

ARCHIE GREEN. John Neuhaus [1904-58]: Wobbly folklorist. Jour. Am. folklore, 72:189-217 (Jul-Sep). notes. On his membership in the International Association of Machinists and the Industrial Workers of the World and his collection of oral and printed versions of texts and tunes of labor songs and "radical songs"; with "A glossary of labor language in the John Neuhaus essay," "The John Neuhaus Collection in the library of Archie Green" (list), and several texts. [1024

JOHN QUINCY ANDERSON. "The Waco Girl"--another variant of a British broadside ballad. West. folklore, 19: 107-18 (Apr). diagrs. notes. Two texts of an American variant (one current as early as 1906) of "The Berkshire tragedy, or the Wittam miller," a London broadside inspired by a murder in "a town called Wittam in Berkshire County" in 1744; comparison with other American variants ("The Lexington Girl," "The Wexford Girl," "The Knoxville Girl," "The Oxford Girl," and others); and examination of the possible origins of its connection with Waco, Tex. [1025

STITH THOMPSON. Fifty years of folktale indexing. Wayland Debs Hand & Gustave Otto Arlt, eds., Humaniora: essays in literature, folklore, bibliography, honoring Archer Taylor on his seventieth birthday (Locust Valley, N.Y.: J. J. Augustin, 1960), p. 49-57. notes. On Antti Aarne's Verzeichnis der Märchentypen (Helsinki, 1910) and its revision and expansion by him and Thompson, The types of the folk-tale (Helsinki, 1928), the many published collections of national folklores (in many languages) that are arranged according to a system of types, Thompson's current work on a second revision of the Aarne-Thompson system, and Thompson's related Motif-index of folk-literature (Copenhagen and Bloomington, Ind., 1955-58). [1026

DANIEL G. HOFFMAN. Thoreau's "old settler" and Frost's Paul Bunyan. Jour. Am. folklore, 72:236-8 (Jul-Sep). notes. On possible sources of Frost's "Paul's wife" (1920). [1027

ARCHIE GREEN. The death of Mother Jones. Labor hist., 1:68-80 (winter). notes. On the death of Mary (Harris) Jones (1830-1930), the unknown origin of the anonymous ballad about her (in existence by 25 Feb. 1931), its transmission by recordings and by oral tradition till and since the printing of the lyric and the melody in the 1940s, the existence of variant forms of both lyric and melody, and the weight of these facts as evidence that it is a "folk song." [1027a

AMÉRICO PAREDES. "Tag, you're it." Jour. Am. folklore, 72:157-8 (Apr-Jun). On "Texas-Mexican" forms of an anecdote reported also from Maine, Kentucky, and California, 1935-56. [1028

GO tell Aunt Nabby. Vt. Hist. Soc., News and notes, 4:70-71 (May 1953). music. A version of "Go tell Aunt Nabby/ Her old grey goose is dead"; and description of 12 versions sent to the editor "from near and far states" in letters "adding many reminiscences of the days when it was sung, by whom, and under what conditions." See also 4:22, 29-30 (Nov, Dec 1952). [1029

ROSCOE CARLYLE BULEY. Water(?) witching can be fun. Ind. mag. hist., 56:65-77 (Mar). notes. Facetious commentary on Water witching, U.S.A., by Evon Z. Vogt and Ray Wyman (1959), with an account of the reviewer's "some twenty-five years experience with 'witching.'" [1030

ELLI KAIJA KONGAS. Immigrant folklore: survival or living tradition? Midw. folklore, 10:117-23 (fall). notes. Texts collected from Mrs. Fannie Jurva, native of Finland, in St. Albans, Vt., 1959, and questions suggested by them. [1031

VANDY, Vandy. [Edited by Ed Cray.] Jour. Am. folklore, 72:154-6 (Apr-Jun). music. notes. Text of a fragmentary version of a "disguised lover's return" ballad learned by the editor in Los Angeles; with reference to a version from North Carolina. [1032

MARIE WALTER. The fable of the folklorist. Midw. folklore, 10:33-9 (Mar). notes. On the present bad reputation of folklorists in "the popular press and other communication media" and the uncertainty as to what they do and why. [1033

Literature

CLEANTH BROOKS. Regionalism in American literature [with particular reference to the South]. Jour. South. hist., 26:35-43 (Feb). notes. [1034

GRAHAM GOULDEN HOUGH. Reflections on a literary revolution. Wash.: Catholic Univ. of America Press, 1960. vi, 127 p. notes (p. 126-7). Contents.--1. Imagism and its consequences [1914 ff.].--2. Imagist poetry and the tradition.--3. The nature of a revolution ["on the emergence of a second literature in the English language ... socially and experientially unrelated to much of the English tradition"--i. e. American literature]. [1035

WALTER BLAIR, THEODORE HORNBERGER, & RANDALL STEWART, eds. The literature of the United States: an anthology and a history. ... Revised single volume edition. Chicago: Scott, Foresman [1957]. xiii, 1378 p. notes. 1st ed. 1949. Six chronological divisions, 1588-1946, each preceded by a "historical interchapter" (dealing with "intellectual currents and literary trends") and including introductions to single authors and selections. [1036

LOUIS UNTERMEYER, ed. The Britannica library of great American writing. ... Edited, with historical notes and a running commentary, by Louis Untermeyer. Chicago. Britannica Press; and distributed in association with Lippincott, Philadelphia [1960]. 2 v. xvii, 877; ix, 879-1764 p. Selected poems, tales, letters, and essays, and excerpts from diaries and other longer compositions, in roughly chronological order, 1590-1958. [1037

LEON HOWARD. Literature and the American tradition [1608-1956]. Garden City, N.Y.: Doubleday, 1960. 354 p. A history of American literature attempting to answer the question: "Does the literary history of America reveal the existence of an attitude of mind consistent and durable enough to be called an aspect of the national character?" [1038

GORDON NORTON RAY, ed. Masters of American literature. ... [Under the general editorship of Gordon N. Ray.] Editors: Leon Edel ... Thomas H. Johnson ... Sherman Paul ... Claude Simpson. [Boston: Houghton Mifflin Co., 1959.] 2 v. xv, [3], 901; xvii, [3], 945 p. bibliog. (1:891-6; 2:933-9). Selections from "eighteen master authors of our native tradition," 1682-1954 (Edward Taylor, Jonathan Edwards, Franklin, Poe, Emerson, Thoreau, Hawthorne, Melville,

Whitman, Emily Dickinson, Mark Twain, Henry Adams, Henry James, Stephen Crane, Eugene O'Neill, Robert Frost, T. S. Eliot, and William Faulkner), each author with a biographical and critical introduction by one of the 4 editors. [1039

LEWIS P. SIMPSON. The city and the symbolism of literary community in the United States. Tex. quar., 3(3): 97-111 (autumn). On the reasons why the United States has no "literary capital," no "national locus of letters," the short-lived successive aspirations of Philadelphia, New York, and Boston to this distinction, their position as successive exemplars of "the decaying symbolism of literary order in the United States," and the coincidence of "the rise of the Republic of the United States" and the decline of "the Republic of Letters," 1770s to ca. 1900. [1040

HOWARD MUMFORD JONES. "... magnificent and haunting phrases." John Arthur Garraty, ed., The unforgettable Americans (Great Neck, N.Y.: Channel Press [1960]), p. 141-5. On the contributions of Edgar Allan Poe (1809-49) "to the development of literature in America and in the world at large." [1041

MARIANNE CRAIG MOORE. Abraham Lincoln and the art of the word. Ralph G. Newman, ed., Lincoln for the ages (Garden City, N.Y.: Doubleday, 1960), p. 378-83. [1042

LIONEL DARCY WYLD. The enigma of Poe: reality vs. l'art pour l'art [1830s-40s]. Lock Haven bul., 2:34-8. notes. [1043

OLIVER WENDELL EVANS. Infernal illumination in Poe. Mod. lang. notes, 75:295-7 (Apr). On "light from the lurid sea," the "ghastly light ... from a pestilential atmosphere," a "wild, sulphurous lustre," "the faint phosphoric radiance of decay," "a faintly luminous and distinctly visible ghastly exhalation," and other references to unnatural light, 1831-44, as "an obsessive interest" of Poe and "a dramatic device to heighten the atmosphere of horror and supernaturalism." [1044

WARNER B. BERTHOFF. American literature: traditions and talents [since 1835]. Oberlin, Ohio: Press of the Times [1960]. 23, [1] p. notes. [1045

LEO MARX. The vernacular tradition in American literature. Joseph J. Kwiat & Mary C. Turpie, eds., Studies in American culture: dominant ideas and images (Minneapolis: Univ. of Minnesota Press [1960]), p. 109-22. On "a vernacular mode or, if you will, a national style" in Whitman and Mark Twain, 1850s-80s, as "a distinctive achievement of American culture." [1046

RAYMOND WILLIAM ADAMS. Witnessing Walden [1854]. Thoreau Soc. bul., 48:[1-4] (summer 1954). On books published in 1854 that "seemed important in 1854" and are forgotten now, and the failure of Walden to seem "important" in the year of its publication. [1047

SEVERN PARKER COSTIN DUVALL. Robert Frost's "Directive" [1946] out of Walden [1854]. Am. lit., 31:482-8 (Jan). notes. Evidence of indebtedness. [1048

RAYMOND J. WALKER. Allibone's dictionary of authors. Hobbies, 65(9): 124 (Nov). On A critical dictionary of English literature and British and American authors living and deceased (Philadelphia, 1859-71), by Samuel Austin Allibone. [1049

GLAUCO CAMBON. La parola come emanazione (note marginali sullo stile di Whitman). Studi americani, 5:141-60. On the style of his verse and prose. [1050

WERNER HÜLLEN, WILHEIM ROSSI, & WALTER CHRISTOPEIT, eds. Zeitgenössische amerikanische Dichtung: eine Einführung in die amerikanische Literaturbetrachtung mit Texten und Interpretationen. Frankfurt am Main: Hirschgraben, 1960. 275 p. bibliog. (p. 260-66), notes. Texts in English or summaries in German of 6 short stories or novels, 6 plays, and 8 poems; with "Literaturbetrachtung in Amerika, 1900-1950: Überblick und Entwicklung," by Rudolf Sühnel (p. 7-21), and introduction by the editors of the 3 sections of fiction, drama, and poetry. [1051

MALCOLM COWLEY. The generation that wasn't lost. College Eng., 22:93-8 (Nov). From College English, 1944. On the literature, especially fiction, produced by "the generation that came of age during or shortly after the first World War." [1052

CHARLES ANDREWS FENTON (1919-60). A literary fracture of World

Mariner before writing Benito Cereno in late 1855 or early 1856." [1080

ROBERT BAIRD SHUMAN. A note on George Boker's Francesca da Rimini. Am. lit., 31:480-82 (Jan). notes. Includes a letter from Boker to a Mrs. Johnson, 7 Sep. 1882, recalling that in writing this play of Paolo and Francesca (published in Boston, 1856) he had obtained the "particulars" of their story from Boccaccio's commentary on the Divine Comedy. [1081

EDWARD HOFFMAN ROSENBERRY. Melville's ship of fools. PMLA, 75: 604-8 (Dec). notes. On the concept of "the ship-microcosm" in his novels, and the possible indebtedness of The confidence-man [1857] to Sebastian Brant's Das Narrenschiff [1494]. [1082

AGOSTINO LOMBARDO. La critica italiana sulla letteratura americana [since 1860]. Studi americani, 5 (1959): 9-49. notes. Identification of the critics, their writings on American literature, and the subjects of their writings. [1083

SERGIO ROSSI. E. A. Poe e la scapigliatura lombardo. Studi americani, 5:119-39. notes. On the popularity of his horror themes among Bohemian poets and artists in Milan, 1863 ff., mainly as known to them through Baudelaire's translations. [1084

DONALD CONGER EMERSON. Henry James and the limitations of realism [1865-1910]. College Eng., 22:161-6 (Dec). Includes references to his comments on French novelists. [1085

SOPHIA AMELIA (PEABODY) HAWTHORNE (1811-71). Mrs. Hawthorne on Dickens. [Edited by Edward Wagenknecht.] Boston Pub. Lib. jour., 12:120-21 (Apr). Letter to Annie Fields, dated probably 4 Dec. 1867, and part of a letter to her dated 24 May 1868. [1086

WILLIAM WHITE. Sir Edmund Gosse on Walt Whitman. Victorian studies, 1:180-82 (Dec 1957). Quotes a letter from Gosse to Whitman (London, 12 Dec. 1873), expressing the writer's "homage and love" and requesting forgiveness of the "importunity of your sincere disciple," a second letter (New York, 29 Dec. 1884) announcing that "I am very anxious not to leave this country without paying my respects to you" and requesting permission to "call upon you in Camden," Whitman's favorable reply (Camden, 31 Dec. 1884), and Gosse's statement in his Critical kit-kats (1896) that his account of his visit to Whitman is not like those of "disciples who approached the shrine adoring and ready to be dazzled," that he made the visit under "the disadvantage of being very unwilling to go," and that upon meeting Whitman he experienced "the peculiar magic of the old man, acting, not on a disciple, but on a stiff-necked and forward unbeliever." [1087

LOUIS GONZALEZ. Whitman's Hispanic fame [since 1881]. Ann Arbor: University Microfilms, 1960. Positive microfilm of typescript. [303] leaves. Thesis--Columbia Univ. Abstracted: Dissert. abstracts, 21:195-6 (Jul). [1088

DORIS M. ALEXANDER. Oedipus in Victorian New York. Am. quar., 12: 417-21 (fall). notes. On the reviews of the production of this play of Sophocles in New York City, Jan.-Feb. 1882, condemning it as "not actable as we understand acting," "highly immoral," "ghastly," a "theatrical curiosity," etc. [1089

ADA GIACCARI. Poe nella critica italiana [1885-1958]. Studi americani, 5:51-89. notes. Part of thesis--Univ. di Bari. [1090

EDWIN J. WEBBER. Alois Richard Nykl (1885-1958). Hispanic rev., 28: 96-8 (Jan). On his work in "the field of Arabic-Romance literary relations" as student, researcher, teacher, and author. [1091

GEORGE HENDRICK. Whitman and Sir Edwin Arnold. West. humanities rev., 14:83-9 (winter). notes. On Arnold's visit to Whitman at Camden in 1889 and again in 1891, his effusive tributes to Whitman, and the inconsistencies in the accounts of what occurred at the meetings. [1092

COLEMAN O. PARSONS. The background of The mysterious stranger [by Mark Twain, 4 versions, 1898-1906]. Am. lit., 32:55-74 (Mar). notes. On the sources, chiefly foreign, of this novelette or extended parable. [1093

KENNETH COX LYMAN. Critical reaction to Irish drama on the New York stage: 1900-1958. Ann Arbor: University Microfilms, 1960. Positive microfilm of typescript. [844] leaves.

Thesis--Univ. of Wisconsin. Abstracted: Dissert. abstracts, 21:699 (Sep). [1094

CHARLOTTE WEISS MANGOLD. Herman Melville in German criticism from 1900 to 1955. Ann Arbor: University Microfilms, 1959 [i. e. 1960]. Positive microfilm of typescript. [417] leaves. Thesis--Univ. of Maryland. Abstracted: Dissert. abstracts, 20:4114 (Apr). [1095

FRANZ KARL SCHNEIDER. The concept of realism in the novel: a reexamination. Ann Arbor: University Microfilms, 1959 [i. e. 1960]. Positive microfilm of typescript. [397] leaves. Thesis--Univ. of Washington. Abstracted: Dissert. abstracts, 20:2785-6 (Jan). Study of Theodore Dreiser's Sister Carrie (1900) and 4 European novels. [1096

JOS VAN DER STEEN. Amerikaanse romanciers van heden [1901-52]. Leuven: Davidsfonds [1955]. 220, [1] p. ports. Essays on Sinclair Lewis, Ernest Hemingway, William Faulkner, John Steinbeck, Thomas Wolfe, John Dos Passos, James T. Farrell, Erskine Caldwell, and John P. Marquand; with chapters on "Amerika en zijn literature" and on characteristics of the American novel. [1097

ALAIN BOSQUET, ed. Trente-cinq jeunes poètes américains. Traduction, préface, et choix par Alain Bosquet. Paris: Gallimard [1960]. 460, [1] p. (NRF, 35.) English texts and translations of poems by Americans born between 1903 and 1930; with "Notices biobibliographiques" (p. 439-55) and a critical introduction. [1098

JAMES WILLIAM GARGANO. The ambassadors [by Henry James, 1903] and Louis Lambert [by Honoré de Balzac]. Mod. lang. notes, 75:211-13 (Mar). On James's references to and implied criticism of the Balzac novel. [1099

ARCHIBALD HENDERSON. Shaw and America: the end of a century. Mod. drama, 2:173-7 (Sep 1959). Condensation of a paper in the Manchester guardian, 26 Jul. 1956. On the continuing popularity of the plays of Bernard Shaw in the United States, where he was already well known as early as 1904. [1100

STANLEY ARNOLD WEINTRAUB. Apostate apostle: H. L. Mencken as Shavophile and Shavophobe. Educ. theatre jour., 12:184-90 (Oct). notes. On his utterances about the plays of Bernard Shaw, 1904-45. [1101

DANIEL J. MURPHY. The reception of Synge's Playboy in Ireland and America: 1907-1912. N.Y. Pub. Lib., Bul., 64:515-33 (Oct). notes. On John Millington Synge's The playboy of the western world, received with hostility by Irish Nationalists in Ireland and the United States and condemned as "a most malignant travesty of Irish life and religion." [1102

RENATO LO SCHIAVO. Poesi minori di T. S. Eliot [1915 ff.]. Studi americani, 5:191-217. notes. [1103

KARL JAY SHAPIRO. W. B. Yeats: trial by culture. Karl Shapiro, In defense of ignorance (N.Y.: Random House [1960]), p. 87-113. On his part in the metamorphosis of "modern poetry ... into a religion," 1915-25, and its relation to the work of Ezra Pound, T. S. Eliot, and Wallace Stevens. [1104

JAY KENNETH KOCH. The reception and influence of modern American poetry in France, 1918-1950. Ann Arbor: University Microfilms, 1959 [i. e. 1960]. Positive microfilm of typescript. [319] leaves. Thesis--Columbia Univ. Abstracted: Dissert. abstracts, 20:4660 (Jun). [1105

JOHN NEWTON ALLEY. English and American criticism of Marcel Proust [since 1919]. Ann Arbor: University Microfilms, 1959 [i. e. 1960]. Positive microfilm of typescript. [480] leaves. Thesis--Univ. of North Carolina. Abstracted: Dissert. abstracts, 20: 2794 (Jan). [1106

LOUIS CLARK KEATING. French plays in New York, 1919-1944: the New York Times view. Mod. lang. quar., 43:122-6 (Mar 1959). Judgments from the criticisms of Alexander Woollcott, Jean Corbin, Stark Young, and Brooks Atkinson. [1107

ANNE MARIE SPRINGER. The American novel in Germany: a study of the critical reception of eight American novelists between the two world wars. Hamburg: Cram, De Gruyter, 1960. 116, [3] p. bibliog. (p. 99-112), notes. (Britannica et Americana, 7.) On the German vogue of Jack London, Upton Sinclair, Sinclair Lewis, Theodore Dreiser, John Dos Passos, Ernest Hemingway, William Faulkner, and Thomas Wolfe. [1108

ROBERT M. JORDAN. The limits of illusion: Faulkner, Fielding, and

Chaucer. Criticism, 2:278-305 (summer). notes. Comparison of fictional methods of William Faulkner, 1920s-50s, with those of Chaucer and Fielding. [1109

MARIE NICOLAAS JOSEPH POULSSEN. Onirische taal: Gaston Bachelard's theorieën over de "dromende" literaire verbeelding, getoest aan het oeuvre van William Faulkner [1920s-50s]. Nijmegen: Janssen, 1959. xxxviii, [2], 496 p. bibliog. (p. 449-53, 459-71), notes. Summaries in French and English. Academisch proefschrift-Nijmegen. On illustrations in Faulkner's work of the applicability of Bachelard's theory of "the 'dreaming' imagination" in literary creation. [1110

SANDRO SERPIERI. Il significato di Gerontion [1920] nella poesia eliotiana. Studi americani, 5:219-32. Part of thesis--Univ. di Firenze. [1111

KERSTIN BIRGITTA STEENE. The American drama and the Swedish theater, 1920-1958. Ann Arbor: University Microfilms, 1960. Positive microfilm of typescript. [524] leaves. Thesis--Univ. of Washington. Abstracted: Dissert. abstracts, 21: 268-9 (Jul). [1112

LILLIAN FEDER. Allen Tate's use of classical literature [in his poetry, 1922-47]. Centennial rev. arts & science, 4:89-114 (winter). notes. [1113

SAMUEL TAYLOR COLERIDGE (1772-1834). Eugene O'Neill's "The ancient mariner." [Edited by Donald Gallup.] Yale Univ. Lib. gaz., 35: 61-86 (Oct). Adaptation by O'Neill, "made presumably in 1923," presented in the Provincetown Playhouse in 1924, unfavorably reviewed and never revived, now printed from the manuscript. [1114

MATTHEW T. CONLIN. The tragic effect in Autumn fire [by Thomas Cornelius Murray in Ireland] and Desire under the elms [by Eugene O'Neill]. Mod. drama, 1:228-35 (Feb 1959). notes. On the similarity of these plays (1924) in theme and design. [1115

HORST FRENZ. Notes on Eugene O'Neill in Japan. Mod. drama, 3: 306-13 (Dec). Review of Japanese translations, performances, and criticisms of his plays, 1924-58. [1116

TRISTRAM P. COFFIN. Gatsby's fairy lover. Midw. folklore, 10:79-85 (summer). notes. On F. Scott Fitzgerald's The great Gatsby (1925) as "an odd mixture of the old Celtic fairy story that forms the basis of Keats' La belle dame sans merci and a Märchen that is classified as Aarne-Thompson 561." [1117

GEORGE O. MARSHALL, JR. Hardy's Tess [of the D'Urbervilles, 1891] and Ellen Glasgow's Barren ground [1925]. Tex. studies in lit. and lang., 1:517-21 (winter). notes. [1118

ANGELA GIANNITRAPANI. Wistaria: le immagini in Faulkner. Studi americani, 5:243-80. notes. On Faulkner's color words, color images, and color symbols, 1926 ff. [1119

CYRUS DAY. Amor fati: O'Neill's Lazarus as superman and savior. Mod. drama, 3:297-305 (Dec). notes. On "some of the ways in which the influence of Nietzsche's philosophy is revealed in Lazarus Laughed [1927]." [1120

HORST FRENZ. The reception of Thornton Wilder's plays in Germany [1929-58]. Mod. drama, 3:123-37 (Sep). notes. [1121

GIUSEPPE PREZZOLINI (born 1882). L'Italiano inutile: memorie litterarie di Francia, Italia, e America. Milano: Longanesi & C. [1954, c1953]. 409, [2] p. ports. ("Il cammeo," 44.) On the author's life in Italy till 1925 as a journalist, editor, and author, his service in Paris as a member of the staff of the Institut de Coopération Intellectuelle of the League of Nations, his work in America as director of the Casa Italiana of Columbia University from 1929 to 1940, his defense against charges that under his administration the Casa Italiana was an organ of "propaganda fascista, e non di liberi studi," his dealings with Italian intellectuals in the United States, and the bitter attacks made upon him as late as 1952 by Gaetano Salvemini. [1122

HILDEGARD SCHUMANN. Zum Problem des kritischen Realismus bei John Steinbeck. Halle: Max Niemeyer, 1958. 348 p. port. bibliog. (p. 336-45), notes. Habilitationsschrift--Humboldt-Universität, Berlin, 1954. Examination of his fiction and social criticism, 1929-52. [1123

PERCY G. ADAMS. The Franco-American Faulkner. Tenn. studies in lit., 5:1-13. notes. On French criticism of William Faulkner since 1931, and the great differences between French and American Faulkner criticism. [1124

STANLEY D. WOODWORTH. William Faulkner en France, 1931-1952. Paris: Lettres Modernes, 1959. 156, [3] p. bibliog. (p. 131-49). (Collection "Situation," 2.) "Panorama critique" of translations, reviews, and criticisms of his works and evidences of their influence upon French authors. [1125

GERHARD H. W. ZUTHER. Problems in translation: modern American dramas in German. Ann Arbor: University Microfilms, 1959 [i. e. 1960]. Positive microfilm of typescript. v, 211 leaves. bibliog. (leaves 206-11). Thesis--Indiana Univ. Abstracted: Dissert. abstracts, 20:4117 (Apr). Study of 7 plays (by Eugene O'Neill, Arthur Miller, Thornton Wilder, and Tennessee Williams, 1931-53) as rendered in German, and the omissions, additions, errors, and "successes" of the translations; with generalizations concerning translation. [1126

JOHN KILLINGER. Hemingway and the dead gods: a study in existentialism. [Lexington:] Univ. of Kentucky Press [1960]. viii, [2], 114, [3] p. notes (p. 103-9). On "the fictional world of Ernest Hemingway as it is related to the world view of existentialism," 1932-57. [1127

ELÉMIRE ZOLLA. Djuna Barnes. Studi americani, 5:301-13. On her novel Nightwood (1932) and her verse drama Antiphon (1958). Text in Italian. [1128

MARC L. RATNER. "Anywhere out of this world": Baudelaire and Nathanael West. Am. lit., 31:456-63 (Jan). notes. On the indebtedness of West's Miss Lonelyhearts (1933) to Charles Baudelaire's "prose poem 'Anywhere Out of This World (N'importe Où Hors Du Monde).'" [1129

MAURICE EDGAR COINDREAU. William Faulkner: translated from the English. University, 4:25-6 (spring). view. On the author's translations of Faulkner's fiction into French since 1934. [1130

WILLIAM M. JONES. Eudora Welty's use of myth in "Death of a traveling salesman" [1936]. Jour. Am. folklore, 72:18-23 (Jan-Mar). notes. Observes hidden classical parallels throughout the tale, to which the names of the characters are found to provide clues. [1131

D. S. BLAND. T. S. Eliot's case-book. Mod. lang. notes, 75:23-6 (Jan). notes. On his play The family reunion (1939) and the evidences of its indebtedness to novels of Ivy Compton-Burnett. [1132

LORENZA GALLI. La narrativa di Eudora Welty. Studi americani, 5:281-300. notes. Part of thesis--Univ. di Bologna. On her short stories, 1941-55. [1133

MARJORIE RYAN. Dubliners and the stories of Katherine Anne Porter. Am. lit., 31:464-73 (Jan). notes. On resemblances and differences between James Joyce's work and several stories by Miss Porter, 1944-56. [1134

RICHARD B. VOWLES. Tennessee Williams and Strindberg. Mod. drama, 1:166-71 (Dec 1958). On the relation between August Strindberg and Williams as "an affinity" rather than an influence, 1947-55. [1135

THOMAS A. HANZO. Eliot and Kierkegaard: "the meaning of happening" in The cocktail party [1950]. Mod. drama, 3:52-9 (May). [1136

CHARLES NEIDER & YAN BEREZNITSKY. Mark Twain and the Russians: an exchange of views. N.Y.: Hill and Wang [1960]. 32 p. notes. Review by Bereznitsky, translated from Literaturnaya gazeta, 18 Aug. 1959, of Neider's edition of Mark Twain's autobiography; Neider's protest against the review, and Bereznitsky's reply, both published 12 Dec. 1959; and Neider's rejoinder (publication declined). [1137

LITERARY BIOGRAPHY

MAX HALL. Hoax upon hoax: too many inventions for Ben. Emory Univ. quar., 16:221-8 (winter). notes. On Benjamin Franklin's unacknowledged authorship of "The speech of Polly Baker" (1747 and many later versions), and the false attribution to him, by Honoré de Balzac, of the tale of Inkle and Yarico. [1138

WILLIAM STEWART OSBORNE. John Pendleton Kennedy [1795-1870]: a study of his literary career. Ann Arbor: University Microfilms, 1960. Positive microfilm of typescript. [475] leaves. Thesis--Columbia Univ. Abstracted: Dissert. abstracts, 21:190 (Jul). On his travel sketches, essays, historical novels, satires, and political writings, 1816-65. [1139

RALPH WALDO EMERSON (1803-82). Emerson on Bronson Alcott [born

1799], conversationalist. [Edited] by Kenneth Walter Cameron. Emerson Soc. quar., 18: leaf 50 (1st quar.). notes. Contribution by Emerson to The new American cyclopaedia, ed. George Ripley and Charles A. Dana, 1 (1858): 301-2. [1140

JAMES FENIMORE COOPER (1789-1851). The letters and journals of James Fenimore Cooper. Edited by James Franklin Beard. Volume I[-II]. Cambridge: Belknap Press of Harvard Univ. Press, 1960. 2 v. xlv, 444; viii, 420 p. facsims., ports. (1 col. mount.), views. notes. "Biographical and critical sketch," account of the journals and papers and of the editorial plan, and text of letters 1-333 (1800-1833) and journals 1-25 (1828-33), written by Cooper as schoolboy in New York and naval officer (1800-1810), "gentleman farmer, entrepreneur" in New York (1811-22), resident of New York City (1822-26), and traveler in England and on the Continent (1828-33). [1141

WILLARD THORP. Thoreau's huckleberry party. Thoreau Soc. bul., 40: [1-4] (summer 1952). On resemblances and differences between Thoreau and Emerson. [1142

RALPH M. ADERMAN. James Kirke Paulding's literary income [1807-55]. N.Y. Pub. Lib., Bul., 64:117-29 (Mar). table. notes. [1143

JACQUES MARTIN BARZUN. Lincoln, the literary genius. Evanston, Ill.: Schori Private Press, 1960 [c1959. 4], 49, [2] p. port. On Lincoln as "the maker of a style that is unique in English prose and doubly astonishing in the history of American literature, for nothing led up to it." [1144

WARREN GRAHAM FRENCH. T. S. Arthur: an unexpected champion of Poe. Tenn. studies in lit., 5:35-41. notes. On parallels between the literary careers of Timothy Shay Arthur (1809-85) and Poe, 1830s-40s, Poe's low opinion of Arthur, and Arthur's qualified expressions of respect and occasionally of admiration for Poe's poetry, 1856-82. [1145

JOHN PENDLETON KENNEDY (1795-1870). Kennedy on Poe: an unpublished letter. [Edited by William S. Osborne.] Mod. lang. notes, 75:17-18 (Jan). notes. Part of a reminiscent letter to George Wolff Fahnestock, 13 Apr. 1869. [1146

ALVARO NOCETI. Edgard [sic] Allan Poe [1809-49]: análisis critico de El cuervo y otros ensayos. Montevideo [1955]. 133, [6] p. bibliog. (p. 127-33). "Poe y el psicoanálisis," and essays on "The raven," "The bells," "The fall of the House of Usher," "The gold-bug," and "The adventures of Arthur Gordon Pym." [1147

DAVID M. REIN. Edgar A. Poe [1809-49]: the inner pattern. N.Y.: Philosophical Library [1960. 8], 134 p. notes. Psychological interpretation of his dreams and horror stories, his relations with Virginia Clemm and "Elmira," and his "maternal deprivation." [1148

MADELEINE BETTINA STERN. Ann S. Stephens: author of the first Beadle dime novel, 1860. N.Y. Pub. Lib., Bul., 64:303-22 (Jun). facsim. On Ann Sophia (Winterbotham) Stephens (1810-86), "chatelaine of New York's literary society ... puller of political wires in Washington ... author of serials for popular consumption," inexhaustibly fertile writer of fiction and poetry from 1834 till her death, ranked with Poe and Longfellow during her lifetime, author of Malaeska (1839), the story of a white husband (killed by Indians) and his Indian wife and the suicide of their half-breed son, "grown to proud and wealthy manhood," when he discovered the facts of his "sable birthright" as the product of "an unnatural marriage," reprinted in 1860 with title Malaeska: the Indian wife of the white hunter (No. 1 of Beadle's Dime Novels), an "orange-colored pamphlet," reprinted several times in later series, a work of which eventually "perhaps as many as half a million copies" were sold. [1149

CLAUDE GERNADE BOWERS (1879-1958). "... and a national asset." John Arthur Garraty, ed., The unforgettable Americans (Great Neck, N.Y.: Channel Press [1960]), p. 137-41. On Washington Irving, traveler in Europe, U.S. Minister to Spain, the "first American writer to gain European recognition," 1815-59. [1150

RAYMOND WILLIAM ADAMS. Thoreau, imitator plus. Thoreau Soc. bul., 41:[1-2] (fall 1952). Argument that "doing little or nothing original, he did everything originally." [1151

VINCENT BURANELLI. The verdict on Thoreau. Ethics, 70:64-5 (Oct 1959). Reply to criticism by Ralph Louis Ketcham directed against the author's "The case against Thoreau." [1152

DAVID KALMAN. A study of Thoreau. Thoreau Soc. bul., 22:[1-3] (Jan 1948). port. "A digest of a much longer study done for a course in biographical psychology" at the University of Minnesota. Finds "marked repression of aggressive impulses," "guilt and feelings of inferiority," "seclusion," "a harsh superego," "regressive behavior," "masochism," "narcism," "latent homosexuality," "autism and mutism," "an obsessive-compulsive neurosis," "psychasthenia," "rationalization," etc. [1153

ROGER ASSELINEAU. The evolution of Walt Whitman [1819-92]: the creation of a personality. Cambridge, Mass.: Belknap Press of Harvard Univ. Press, 1960. x, [4], 376 p. notes (p. 271-376). French original published 1954; now translated by the author and Richard P. Adams, with minor revisions. [1154

RALPH WALDO EMERSON (1803-82). The journals and miscellaneous notebooks of Ralph Waldo Emerson. Edited by William H. Gilman, George P. Clark, Alfred R. Ferguson, [and] Merrell R. Davis. [Volume 1.] Cambridge: Belknap Press of Harvard Univ. Press, 1960. L, 430 p. facsims., view. notes. Part of an edition "planned in approximately sixteen volumes"; with an extensive introduction on the manuscripts, their editorial problems, and the procedures applied to them by previous editors. This volume contains journals, 25 Jan. 1820 - 10 Jul. 1822, and "miscellaneous notebooks" (college theme book, "Catalogue of books read, 1819-1824," and 3 others). [1155

MERLIN BOWEN. The long encounter: self and experience in the writings of Herman Melville [1819-91. Chicago:] Univ. of Chicago Press [1960]. vii, 282 p. notes. Based on thesis--Univ. of Chicago, 1957. [1156

EMORY HOLLOWAY. Free and lonesome heart: the secret of Walt Whitman [1819-92]. N.Y.: Vantage Press [1960. 4], 232 p. facsim., port., view. notes (p. 187-218). On "Whitman's nature, his knowledge and poetic treatment of sex and friendship, and the influence such treatment had in turn on his own life," attempting to present "a consistent, positive conception of Whitman's psychological makeup" and "the whole problem of his sexual classification," under study by the author as early as 1921; with a chapter of new information, suggesting that Walt Whitman was the father of John Whitman Wilder (1868?-1911), who sent flowers to his funeral. Appended (p. 219-21): "List of the author's publications concerning Whitman." [1157

PHILIP RAHV. Melville and his critics. Philip Rahv, Image and idea (Norfolk, Conn.: J. Laughlin, 1957), p. 182-7. Mainly on Newton Arvin's Herman Melville (1950). [1158

EDUARD FRIEDRICH FERDINAND CASTLE. Der grosse Unbekannte: das leben von Charles Sealsfield (Karl Postl). Wien: Manutiuspresse [1952]. 726, [2] p. facsim., fold. geneal. chart, ports., views. On the early life of Charles Sealsfield (1793-1864) in Moravia, his brief career as a monk, his settlement in the United States as a journalist and a novelist (1823-32), his successive residences in Louisiana, near Pittsburgh, and in New York City, his retirement to Switzerland in 1832, his later visits to America (1837, 1850, 1853), and his various activities in European politics and journalism. Offers evidence that after his flight from Austria he never used his original name (Carl Magnus Postl) and that he signed his will with his assumed name: Charles Sealsfield. [1159

PATRICK FRANCIS QUINN. Four views of Edgar Poe [1829 to 1849]. Jahrbuch für Amerikastudien, 5:138-46. [1160

JOHN SHEPHARD KEYES (1821-1910). John Shepard Keyes' reminiscences of Emerson. [Edited] by Kenneth Walter Cameron. Emerson Soc. quar., 19: leaves 15-16 (2d quar.). notes. Manuscript (1903), recalling the author's association with Emerson as early as 1835. [1161

LEWIS GASTON LEARY. Mark Twain [1835-1910]. Minneapolis: Univ. of Minnesota Press [1960]. 48 p. bibliog. (p. 46-8). (University of Minnesota. Pamphlets on American writers, 5.) [1162

MILTON MELTZER. Mark Twain himself [1835-1910]: a pictorial biography. N.Y.: Crowell [1960]. xii, [2], 303 p. facsims., maps, plan, ports., seal, views (1 double). bibliog. (p. 291). "Picture sources" (p. 295-7). [1163

ARTHUR LINCOLN SCOTT. Mark Twain today. Cent. Miss. Valley Am. Studies Assoc., Jour., 1(2):2-10 (fall).

On the multiplicity of recent publications by and about him, the heavy demand for his books, his showings on television, the prosperity of the Mark Twain Estate, and the growing collections of his books and manuscripts. [1164

CARL JULIUS BODE. "... practiced what he preached." John Arthur Garraty, ed., The unforgettable Americans (Great Neck, N.Y.: Channel Press [1960]), p. 145-8. On Henry David Thoreau (1817-62) as a "representative of the artist's dedication to his work and his rejection of everything that interferes with his self-expression," 1837-62. [1165

WILLIAM DEAN HOWELLS (1837-1920). An early autobiographical letter by William Dean Howells. [Edited by] James B. Stronks. New Eng. quar., 33:240-42 (Jun). notes. Letter to Edward Eggleston, editor of Hearth and home, dated Boston, 11 Mar. 1872, written at his request, reviewing the author's life to date. [1166

JEFFERSON CHENOWETH DYKES. Buckskin Sam, ranger and writer; or, The life and sub-literary labors of Samuel Stone Hall [1838-86]. Am. book collector, 10(7):8-18 (Mar). cartoon, facsim., ports. On his early life in Massachusetts, his service in the Texas Rangers, the C. S. Army, and the U.S. Army, his work as a hotel clerk in New York City, his voluminous output of dime novels between 1877 and 1886, the extent to which they embodied his own experience in the West and the characters he had known there, and the extreme rarity of the novels today. [1167

MARTIN ERNST HILLGER. Albion W[inegar] Tourgée [1838-1905]: critic of society. Ann Arbor: University Microfilms, 1959 [i. e. 1960]. Positive microfilm of typescript. xvii, 314 leaves. bibliog. (leaves 303-14). Thesis--Indiana Univ. Abstracted: Dissert. abstracts, 20:2802 (Jan). On his fictional treatment of differences between North and South, his advocacy of reforms, and his concept of the good society, particularly in the Reconstruction years. [1168

MARY PEABODY. A note on Hawthorne's juveniles. [Edited by Alexander C. Kern.] Philol. quar., 39:242-6 (Apr). notes. Letter to Horace Mann (the writer's future husband), 3 Mar. 1838, referring in part to the good qualities of Nathaniel Hawthorne, his very small income from his writing, and his plans to write for children. [1169

WILLIAM BYSSHE STEIN. Melville and the creative eros. Lock Haven bul., 2:13-26. Symbolical and psychoanalytic speculations on Melville's sexual psychology, 1840s-90s. [1170

LEON EDEL. Henry James [1843-1916]. Minneapolis: Univ. of Minnesota Press [1960]. 47 p. bibliog. (p. 42-7). (University of Minnesota. Pamphlets on American writers, 4.) [1171

JOHN G. BLAIR & AUGUSTUS TROWBRIDGE. Thoreau on Katahdin [1846]. Am quar., 12:508-17 (winter). notes. On "the philosophic distance between his experience with nature on the mountain and on the plain," and "the persistently disturbing effects of Katahdin on Thoreau's convictions." [1172

JOHN ELDRIDGE FROST. Sarah Orne Jewett [1849-1909]. Kittery Point, Me.: Gundalow Club [1960. 14], 174 p. ports., views. notes (p. 157-66). On her life in South Berwick, Me, and in Boston, and her work in fiction; with extensive quotations from her letters. [1173

GEORGE L. McMICHAEL. Minor figure: a biography of Octave Thanet. Ann Arbor: University Microfilms, 1959 [i. e. 1960]. Positive microfilm of typescript. vii, 336 leaves. bibliog. (leaves 305-35). Thesis--Northwestern Univ. Abstracted: Dissert. abstracts, 20:3747-8 (Mar). On the life of Alice French (1850-1934) in Massachusetts, Iowa, and Arkansas, and her articles and tales about the West and the South (published under her pseudonym, Octave Thanet, 1878-1913). [1174

RAYMOND WILLIAM ADAMS. Thoreau's year after Walden. Thoreau Soc. bul., 52:[1-2] (summer 1955). On his lecturing, writing, and other activities in the 12 months after the publication of the book, 1854-55. [1175

JEAN HOLLOWAY. Hamlin Garland [1860-1940]: a biography. Austin: Univ. of Texas Press [1960]. xii, [4], 346 p. ports., views. bibliog. (p. 332-4), notes. On his early life in Iowa and South Dakota, his studies at Boston University, his activities as a lecturer, his work in poetry, criticism, and fiction, his books on psychical research, and his 12 autobiographical volumes. [1176

MAX PUTZEL. Masters's "Maltravers": Ernest McGaffey [born 1861]. Am. lit., 31:491-3 (Jan). notes. On the friendship between McGaffey and Edgar Lee Masters in Chicago and elsewhere, 1891 till sometime after 1905, and the introduction of Masters to William Marion Reedy by McGaffey; with some account of McGaffey's obscure career as a poet. [1177

LILLIAN BARNARD GILKES. Cora Crane: a biography of Mrs. Stephen Crane. Bloomington: Indiana Univ. Press, 1960. 416 p. facsims., ports., tables, views. bibliog. (p. 388-404), notes. On Cora Howorth (1865-1910), her obscure early life in Boston and New York, her marriages to Thomas Vinton Murphy and Donald William Stewart (an Englishman), the first ending in divorce, the second apparently in permanent separation, her establishment of the Hotel de Dream at Jacksonville, Fla. (where a resident staff of girls entertained male callers or roomers), her meeting with Stephen Crane in 1898 (then a reporter of the War with Spain, 6 years younger than she), her life and travels with him in England and on the Continent as Mrs. Stephen Crane, her involvement after his death in 1900 in litigation over his estate, her return to Jacksonville and establishment of the Court (described as "a sporting-house" and "a disorderly house"), her marriage to Hammond P. McNeil (alcoholic saloonkeeper, aged 25), his quarrel with her concerning her alleged attentions to Harry Parker (19-year-old railroad conductor), his killing of Parker and divorce from her, her affair with Ernest Budd (alcoholic patron whose wife refused him a divorce), her bequest of her property to him and appointment of him as her executor, her death after a stroke, and her reputation as "a byword and a subject for indecent jokes"; with remarks on and quotations from her diary, letters, and other writings. [1178

THEODORA VAN WAGENEN WARD. The finest secret: emotional currents in the life of Emily Dickinson after 1865. Harv. Lib. bul., 14:82-106 (winter). [1179

ALFRED CROFTS. "... bridge between East and West." John Arthur Garraty, ed., The unforgettable Americans (Great Neck, N.Y.: Channel Press [1960]), p. 287-90. On Lafcadio Hearn (1850-1904), emigrant to America in 1869, journalist in Cincinnati and New Orleans till 1890, later a resident of Japan, writer about Japan, and lecturer there on American literature. [1180

VINCENT BROME. Frank Harris [1855-1931]. N.Y.: Thomas Yoseloff [1959]. ix, 246 p. cartoons, ports., views. bibliog. (p. 234-40). Includes reference to his 3 periods of residence in the United States (1871-76, 1915-23, 1928), with evidence that his account of his years in New York and Kansas (in My life and loves), 1871-76, was largely fiction. [1181

WARREN IRVING TITUS. Winston Churchill [1871-1947], American: a critical biography. Ann Arbor: University Microfilms, 1957 [i. e. 1960]. Positive microfilm of typescript. iii, 527 leaves. bibliog. (leaves 517-27). Thesis--New York Univ. Abstracted: Dissert. abstracts, 20:3475 (Mar). On his work as "novelist, playwright, politician, and lay preacher," with particular attention to his 10 novels and their historical, political, and social-reform themes. [1182

LEON EDEL. Willa Cather [1873-1947]: the paradox of success. Wash.: Reference Dept., Library of Congress, 1960. 17 p. Lecture delivered in the Library of Congress, 12 Oct. 1959. [1183

THORNTON WALDO BURGESS (born 1874). Now I remember: autobiography of an amateur naturalist. Boston: Little, Brown [1960]. viii, 338 p. port. On the author's early life in Sandwich, Mass., and his work as a writer of advertising copy in Boston, a contributor to Country life in America, an editor of Good housekeeping, "an amateur naturalist on the air waves," and author of a syndicated nature-study newspaper column and of animal stories for children. [1184

CAROLINE THOMAS HARNSBERGER. Mark Twain, family man. N.Y.: Citadel Press [1960]. 296 p. diagr., facsims., ports. bibliog. (p. 291-2), notes (p. 271-90). On his life with his wife, Olivia Langdon, and his 3 daughters--Susan, Clara, and Jean, 1874-1910. Deals mainly with Clara. [1185

ELIZABETH SHEPLEY SERGEANT (1881-1965). Robert Frost [1874-1963]: the trial by existence. N.Y.: Holt, Rinehart, and Winston [1960]. xxvii, 451 p. facsim., ports., views.

Biography, with extensive quotations from his poems and "hitherto unpublished letters." [1186

SHERWOOD ANDERSON (1876-1941). A story teller's story. N.Y.: Grove Press [1958. 6], 442 p. 1st ed. 1919. On the author's early life in "a money-saving prosperous corn-shipping, cabbage-raising Ohio village" (Clyde), and the growth of his imagination and powers of fancy; with incidental references to his years as a manufacturer in Ohio, an advertising man in Chicago, and "a writer, a word fellow." Another edition: Winesburg, Ohio. Introduction by Malcolm Cowley. N.Y.: Viking Press, 1960. [8], 247 p. [1187

MARGARET HALEY CARPENTER. Sara Teasdale [1884-1933]: a biography. N.Y.: Schulte Pub. Co., 1960. xix, 377, [1] p. facsims., ports., view. bibliog. (p. 349-52), notes. On her early life in St. Louis, her travels in Europe, her work as a poet, her marriage to and divorce from Ernst B. Filsinger (1880-1937, expert on international trade), and her friendships, especially with Vachel Lindsay (her rejected suitor) and later Elizabeth (Conner) Lindsay, his wife; with extensive quotations from letters received by her, especially those from Lindsay, 1913-31, and his wife, 1925 ff. Based in part upon "material that will never be available again" (not identified). Includes very little reference to letters written by Sara Teasdale. [1188

DONALD PIZER. Hamlin Garland's early work and career. Berkeley: Univ. of California Press, 1960. ix, [3], 220 p. bibliog. (p. 197-210), notes (p. 173-96). (University of California publications. English studies, 22.) On his "initial period of reform activity and Middle-border fiction," 1884-95, and his interests in the single tax, Populism, the commercial theatre, "reforming the arts," and literary criticism. [1189

CHARLES NORMAN. Ezra [Loomis] Pound [born 1885]. N.Y.: Macmillan, 1960. xvi, [2], 493 p. facsim., ports., views. bibliog. (p. 478-80), notes (p. 469-77). Includes a full account of his studies at the University of Pennsylvania and Hamilton College, in which he was registered as Ezra Weston Pound. [1190

WOODBRIDGE SPEARS. Elizabeth Madox Roberts [1886-1941]: a biographical and critical study. Ann Arbor: University Microfilms, 1953 [i. e. 1960]. Positive microfilm of typescript. xxiii, 254 leaves. bibliog. (leaves xv-xxi). Thesis--Univ. of Kentucky. Abstracted: Dissert. abstracts, 20:3753-4 (Mar). On her life in Kentucky and her writings, mainly novels. [1191

EDNA FERBER (born 1887). A peculiar treasure. Garden City, N.Y.: Doubleday, 1960. 383 p. cartoon, ports., views. 1st ed. 1938. On the author's early life in Kalamazoo, Mich., and Appleton, Wis., her Jewish upbringing, her work as a reporter for newspapers in Appleton and Milwaukee, and her work in fiction and drama to 1938. [1192

COLIN CHANDLER CAMPBELL. The poet as artist and citizen: a study of the life and writings of Archibald MacLeish [from 1892] through 1958. Ann Arbor: University Microfilms, 1960. Positive microfilm of typescript. [383] leaves. Thesis--Univ. of Pennsylvania. Abstracted: Dissert. abstracts, 21:888 (Oct). On "his public life, the central concepts in his prose, and the interpretive comments upon human experience offered in his plays and major poems." [1193

SAXE COMMINS (1892?-1958). Confessions of a ghost. Princeton Univ. Lib. chron., 22:26-35 (autumn). On the author's experiences since his college days as the writer, for persons professing to be the writers, of love letters, college themes, the reminiscences of an actress, a Ph. D. thesis, "the life and times of a dazzling courtesan," the adventures of a world traveler, a "glowing biography" of a politician, etc. [1194

PHILIP BUTCHER. Mutual appreciation: Dunbar and Cable. CLA jour., 1:101-2 (Mar 1958). On George W. Cable's aid to Paul Laurence Dunbar in publishing his work, ca. 1894 and 1896. [1195

WILLIAM DEAN HOWELLS (1837-1920). An edition of William Dean Howells' Literary friends and acquaintance, with an introduction treating literary reminiscence as a genre. [Edited by David Franklin Hiatt.] Ann Arbor: University Microfilms, 1960. Positive microfilm of typescript. [555] leaves. Hiatt's thesis--Univ. of New Mexico. Abstracted: Dissert. abstracts, 20: 4391-2 (May). Heavily annotated edition of a reminiscent work published in installments, 1894, 1895, 1900, and as a book in 1900. Includes a study of the magazine and the book versions and of the surviving fragments of the manuscript. [1196

MERCEDES DE ACOSTA (born 1898). Here lies the heart. N.Y.: Reynal [1960. 12], 372 p. facsim., ports. On the author's early life in New York, her travels in Europe, her work in fiction, poetry, and drama, her marriage to Abram Poole, and the living quarters, domestic lives, and personal habits of her many friends and associates. [1197

EDWARD HOWARD DODD, JR. Of nature, time, and Teale: a biographical sketch of Edwin Way Teale [born 1899]. N.Y.: Dodd, Mead, 1960. 63. [1] p. facsims., ports., views. On his early life in Joliet, his studies at Earlham College, his service on the staff of Popular science magazine, and his books and articles about nature in America; with "Notes about Teale's books," 1930-60 (p. 55-63). [1198

CLARENCE HUGH HOLMAN. Thomas Wolfe [1900-1958]. Minneapolis: Univ. of Minnesota Press [1960]. 47 p. bibliog. (p. 44-7). (University of Minnesota. Pamphlets on American writers, 6.) [1199

ELIZABETH NOWELL (died 1958). Thomas Wolfe [1900-1938]: a biography. Garden City, N.Y.: Doubleday, 1960. 456 p. port. Account by his former literary agent, containing all obtainable biographical information from his family, his friends and associates, and his correspondence, and dealing extensively with his personal habits, his friendships, his methods of writing, and his relations with editors and publishers. [1200

FANNIE HURST. Zora [Neale] Hurston [born 1901 or 1903, died 1960]: a personality sketch. Yale Univ. Lib. gaz., 35:17-22 (Jul). On her short service as "my live-in secretary," sometime not long before 1931. Appended: list of her books, letters, and other manuscripts, 1931-48, in the James Weldon Johnson Memorial Collection of Negro Arts and Letters founded by Carl Van Vechten. [1201

LEONARD RALPH CASPER. Robert Penn Warren [born 1905]: the dark and bloody ground. Seattle: Univ. of Washington Press, 1960. xix, 212 p. bibliog. (p. 201-8), notes (p. 183-9). On his teaching of literature in several universities and his work in fiction, biography, poetry, and literary criticism; with "The works of Robert Penn Warren: a chronological checklist," 1922-60 (p. 191-9). [1202

JAMES F. LIGHT. Genius on campus: Nathanael West at Brown. Contact, 3 (1959): 97-111. On his ideas, habits, and personal appearance during his undergraduate years at Brown University, 1922 ff. (where he was known by his real name, Nathan Weinstein), as recalled by some of his classmates and teachers. [1203

EDWARD NEHLS, ed. D. H. Lawrence: a composite biography. Gathered, arranged, and edited by Edward Nehls. Madison: Univ. of Wisconsin Press, 1957-59. 3 v. xxv, 614; xxi, 537; xxxi, 767 p. facsims., ports., views. bibliogs., notes. Reminiscences and criticisms concerning David Herbert Lawrence (1885-1930), and autobiographical selections from his writings, arranged in chronological order according to the time with which they deal. Includes documents relating to his stay in New Mexico (at Taos) and Mexico, Sep. 1922 - Nov. 1923 (2:163-282). [1204

EUGENE GLADSTONE O'NEILL (1888-1953). Inscriptions: Eugene O'Neill to Carlotta Monterey O'Neill. New Haven, 1960. [160] p. facsims., ports. Facsimile reproductions and printed texts of inscriptions on printed and manuscript copies of his plays given by him to his wife, 1926-52. Some of the inscriptions are long messages. [1205

JAMES GROVER THURBER. "Scott in thorns." The reporter, Our times: the best from The reporter, ed. Max Ascoli (N.Y.: Farrar, Straus, and Cudahy [1960]), p. 427-35. First published in 1951. Essay inspired by Arthur Mizener's The far side of Paradise; with recollections of a meeting with F. Scott Fitzgerald in 1934. [1206

LITERARY TYPES

ROBERT W. MANN. Afterthoughts on opera and The scarlet letter [1850]. Studi americani, 5:339-50. On operatic qualities discerned by Mann in the novel when he undertook to convert it into an opera. Appended (p. 351-81): "The scarlet letter: libretto in four acts and nine scenes. By Robert W. Mann." [1207

WALTER J. MESERVE. Colonel Sellers as a scientist: a play by S. L. Clemens and W. D. Howells. Mod.

drama, 1:151-6 (Dec 1958). notes. On a dramatization of The Gilded Age, undertaken by Howells at Clemens's request and with his collaboration, written in 1883, produced briefly after revision by Clemens as The American claimant (1887), but never printed in its earlier form. [1208

STEPHEN FOSTER ELLISTON. Dramatic and narrative art: studies of dramatizations on the New York stage, 1919-1958. Ann Arbor: University Microfilms, 1959 [i. e. 1960]. Positive microfilm of typescript. xi, 375 leaves. bibliog. (leaves 337-44). Thesis--Univ. of Illinois. Abstracted: Dissert. abstracts, 20:3290-91 (Feb). [1209

Children's Literature

ELLEN BARTLETT BALLOU. As the twig is bent. New-Eng. galaxy, 2(2): 13-21 (fall). facsims., views. On "juvenile literature" in America, 1826 to ca. 1860, particularly the work of Lydia Maria (Francis) Child. [1210

ELLEN BARTLETT BALLOU. Horace Elisha Scudder [1838-1902] and the Riverside magazine. Harv. Lib. bul., 14:426-52 (autumn). facsims. notes. On the Riverside magazine for young people (Boston, 1867-70), with special reference to Scudder's editorial policies and his critical commentaries on publications for children. [1211

Drama

DORE SCHARY. Lincoln as a dramatic subject. Ralph G. Newman, ed., Lincoln for the ages (Garden City, N.Y.: Doubleday, 1960), p. 349-54. On plays about Lincoln since ca. 1863. [1212

PAUL T. NOLAN. Williams' Dante: the death of nineteenth-century heroic drama.. South. speech jour., 25: 255-63 (summer). notes. On a play by Espy Williams, Dante and Beatrice, copyrighted in 1893, "never published nor produced," written for Lawrence Barrett, who died in 1891 without having seen the manuscript. [1213

BEVERLY ELISE CANNING. Henry Taylor Parker [1867-1934], drama critic. Ann Arbor: University Microfilms, 1960. Positive microfilm of typescript. [615] leaves. Thesis--Univ. of Michigan. Abstracted: Dissert. abstracts, 20:4752-3 (Jun). On his service as drama critic for 2 New York newspapers and the Boston evening transcript, 1900-1934. [1214

ROBERT F. WHITMAN. O'Neill's search for a "language of the theatre" [ca. 1912 to ca. 1946]. Quar. jour. speech, 46:153-70 (Apr). notes. [1215

EUGENE GLADSTONE O'NEILL (1888-1953). Lost plays of Eugene O'Neill. N.Y.: Citadel Press [1958]. 156 p. Introduction signed: Lawrence Gellert. Texts, now first printed, of "Abortion" (1914), "The movie man" (1914), "The sniper" (1915), "Servitude" (1914), and "A wife for life" (1913). [1216

NORMAN C. CHAITIN. O'Neill: the power of daring [1914-46]. Mod. drama, 3:231-41 (Dec). [1217

JANIS KLAVSONS. O'Neill's dreamer: success and failure. Mod. drama, 3: 268-72 (Dec). notes. On "the premise that the life of the sensitive man is aimless and ridiculous" as embodied in plays of O'Neill from 1914 to 1940. [1218

DREW B. PALLETTE. O'Neill and the comic spirit [1914-41]. Mod. drama, 3:273-9 (Dec). notes. [1219

THOMAS L. CAHALAN & PAUL A. DOYLE. Modern American drama. Boston: Student Outlines Co. [1960. 6], 169 p. bibliogs., notes. (Hymarx outline series, 122.) Biographical sketches and criticisms and summaries of plays of 20 American playwrights active since 1916. [1220

EDWIN ALEXANDER ENGEL. O'Neill, 1960. Mod. drama, 3:219-23 (Dec). Interpretation of plays of Eugene O'Neill, 1916-40. [1221

SIGNI LENEA FALK. Dialogue in the plays of Eugene O'Neill [1916-46]. Mod. drama, 3:314-25 (Dec). notes. [1222

EDD WINFIELD PARKS. Eugene O'Neill's quest. Tulane drama rev., 4(3):99-107 (Mar). Symbolical interpretation of his plays, especially the autobiographical ones, after 1919. [1223

JAMES T. NARDIN. Green grow the lyrics. Tulane drama rev., 3(2):21-9 (Dec 1958). On changes in American musical comedy since the 1920s, with Oklahoma (1943) as a turning-point, showing "the development of a twentieth century dramatic poetry, a lyricism which appeals to sophisticated and unsophisticated alike" and is "made acceptable by the use of music, which tends to reduce the sense of strict realism." [1224

WEBSTER LEROY CROXDALE SMALLEY. The characterization of the male protagonist in serious American drama from 1920 to 1940. Ann Arbor: University Microfilms, 1960. Positive microfilm of typescript. [625] leaves. Thesis--Stanford Univ. Abstracted: Dissert. abstracts, 21:1292 (Nov). [1225

WINIFRED LOESCH DUSENBURY. The theme of loneliness in modern American drama [1921-50]. Gainesville: Univ. of Florida Press, 1960. vi, 231 p. bibliog. (p. 219-23), notes (p. 213-18). Based on thesis--Univ. of Florida, 1956. [1226

EUGENE GLADSTONE O'NEILL (1888-1953) & JOHN S. MAYFIELD. Eugene O'Neill and the Senator from Texas. Yale Univ. Lib. gaz., 35:87-93 (Oct). Correspondence between Mayfield (son of Earle B. Mayfield, Senator from Texas) and O'Neill, 1924-28, concerning O'Neill's recently published All God's chillum got wings and Welded (texts issued together), concerning criticism of the plays by Col. Billy Mayfield (not a relative of Senator Mayfield), friend of the Ku Klux Klan, and a defense of O'Neill by Stark Young. [1227

SOPHUS KEITH WINTHER. Desire under the elms [by Eugene O'Neill, 1924]: a modern tragedy. Mod. drama, 3:326-32 (Dec). notes [1228

DAVID EDWARDS JONES. The plays of T. S. Eliot [1926 to 1958], London: Routledge & K. Paul [1960]. xiv, 242 p. bibliog. (p. 221-38), notes. Also published in Toronto: Univ. of Toronto Press, 1960. [1229

CARL ENOCH WILLIAM LEONARD DAHLSTROM. Dynamo [1929] and Lazarus laughed [1927, both by Eugene O'Neill]: some limitations. Mod. drama, 3:224-30 (Dec). [1230

PAUL CHARLES HARRIS, JR. The relation of dramatic structure to the ideas in Robert E[mmet] Sherwood's dramatic works [1927-40]. Ann Arbor: University Microfilms, 1960. Positive microfilm of typescript. [327] leaves. Thesis--Stanford Univ. Abstracted: Dissert. abstracts, 20: 4458 (May). [1231

RICHARD DANA SKINNER (1893-1941). Review of Eugene O'Neill's "Strange interlude." Pierre Albert Duhamel, ed., Essays in the American Catholic tradition (N.Y.: Rinehart [1960]), p. 120-24. From The commonweal, 22 Feb. 1928. [1232

ROGER ASSELINEAU. Mourning becomes Electra [by Eugene O'Neill, 1929] as a tragedy. Mod. drama, 1:143-50 (Dec 1958). notes. [1233

GEORGE R. SIDNEY. Faulkner in Hollywood: a study of his career as a scenarist. Ann Arbor: University Microfilms, 1959 [i. e. 1960]. Positive microfilm of typescript. [384] leaves. Thesis--Univ. of New Mexico. Abstracted: Dissert. abstracts, 20: 2810 (Jan). Study of the 34 "screenplays and treatments" written by William Faulkner, alone or in collaboration, for 3 Hollywood studios and an independent producer, 1932-55. [1234

JACOB H. ADLER. The worth of Ah, wilderness [by Eugene O'Neill, 1933]. Mod. drama, 3:280-88 (Dec). notes. [1235

JOHN CALELY WENTZ. Anderson's Winesburg and the Hedgerow Theatre. Mod. drama, 3:42-51 (May). notes. On a dramatization of Sherwood Anderson's Winesburg, Ohio (collection of short stories, 1919), considered by Anderson as early as that year, done by Arthur Barton (by Jan. 1933), revised by Anderson, produced in the Hedgerow Theatre of Rose Valley, a suburb of Philadelphia, as a play in 9 scenes by Jasper Deeter in 1934-36, and published in 1937. [1236

JILL C. RADCLIFFE. Those Boston critics! Harvard alumni bul., 62:434-5 (5 Mar). port. On the work of Daniel Taradash (Harvard, 1933) as a screenwriter and playwright since ca. 1935. [1237

BARNARD WOLCOTT HEWITT. Thornton Wilder says "Yes." Tulane drama rev., 4(2):110-20 (Dec 1959). On the quality of his Our town (1938), The skin of our teeth (1942), and The matchmaker (1954). [1238

GEORGE DARWIN STEPHENS. Our town [by Thornton Wilder, 1938]--great American tragedy? Mod. drama, 1:258-64 (Feb 1959). [1239

FRANCIS WILLIAM STURCKEN. An historical analysis of live network television drama from 1938 to 1958. Ann Arbor: University Microfilms, 1960. Positive microfilm of typescript. [366] leaves. Thesis-- Univ. of Minnesota. Abstracted: Dissert. abstracts, 21:269 (Jul). [1240

TOM FAW DRIVER. On the late plays of Eugene O''Neill [died 1953]. Tulane drama rev., 3(2):8-20 (Dec 1958). notes. On Long day's journey into night (written 1940, published 1955), The iceman cometh (produced 1946), and A touch of the poet (published 1957), here assessed as tragedies. [1241

TOM FAW DRIVER. Strength and weakness in Arthur Miller [1940s-50s]. Tulane drama rev., 4(4):45-52 (May). [1242

SIGNI LENEA FALK. The profitable world of Tennessee Williams [1940s-50s]. Mod. drama, 1:172-80 (Dec 1958). On the lucrative qualities of his plays, resting, "to a large degree, on his repudiation of values and attitudes which most intelligent and genuinely sensitive Americans care about." [1243

HENRY POPKIN. The plays of Tennessee Williams [1940s-50s]. Tulane drama rev., 4(3):45-64 (Mar). On the themes of the plays and the symbolism of their expression. [1244

RICHARD B. VOWLES. Tennessee Williams: the world of his imagery. Tulane drama rev., 3(2):51-6 (Dec 1958). On his "concern with images of liquid and water" in his plays and short stories, and his related dedication to "a principle of flow," 1940s-50s. [1245

HENRY HEWES, ed. Famous American plays of the 1940s. [N.Y.: Dell Pub. Co., 1960.] 447, [1] p. (The Laurel drama series, LX119.) Texts of The skin of our teeth (1942), by Thornton Wilder, Home of the brave (1946), by Arthur Laurents, All my sons (1947), by Arthur Miller, Lost in the stars (1949), by Maxwell Anderson, and Member of the wedding (1949), by Carson McCullers; with an introduction. [1246

WILLIAM ROBERT IRWIN. The unity of Frost's masques. Am. lit., 32: 302-12 (Nov). notes. On A masque of reason (1945) and A masque of mercy (1947). [1247

MORRIS PHILIP WOLF. Casanova's portmanteau: a study of Camino Real in relation to the other plays and stories of Tennessee Williams, 1945-1955. Ann Arbor: University Microfilms, 1959 [i. e. 1960]. Positive microfilm of typescript. [209] leaves. Thesis--Univ. of Georgia. Abstracted: Dissert. abstracts, 20:2817 (Jan). [1248

CYRUS DAY. The iceman and the bridegroom: some observations on the death of O'Neill's salesman. Mod. drama, 1:3-9 (May 1958). On his The iceman cometh (1946) as "a play about the death of a salesman," dealing with "the relationship between men's illusions and their will to live," with an interpretation suggested by the Biblical connotation of "-eth." [1249

WILLIAM B. DILLINGHAM. Arthur Miller and the loss of conscience. Emory Univ. quar., 16:40-50 (spring). On the "major theme of his ... four tragedies," 1947-55, as "man's obligation to assume his rightful place in a world unified by love and a sense of responsibility." [1250

M. W. STEINBERG. Arthur Miller and the idea of modern tragedy [1947-60]. Dalhousie rev., 40:329-40 (autumn). [1251

DEATH of a salesman [by Arthur Miller, 1949]: a symposium. Tulane drama rev., 2(3):63-9 (May 1958). Colloquy of a panel composed of Arthur Miller and 5 others, with Phillip Gelb as moderator. Revised from the radio series, Ideas and the theatre, produced by the University of Minnesota radio station KUOM. [1252

GEORGE DE SCHWEINITZ. Death of a salesman [by Tennessee Williams, 1949]: a note on epic and tragedy. West. humanities rev., 14:91-6 (winter). [1253

MARVIN FELHEIM. The autumn garden [by Lillian Hellman, 1950]: mechanics and dialectics. Mod. drama, 3:191-5 (Sep). [1254

Essays

PAUL BAENDER. The basis of Franklin's duplicative satires. Am. lit., 32:267-79 (Nov). notes. On his "Exporting of felons to the colonies" (1751), "An edict of the King of Prussia" (1773), and "On the slave trade" (1790), asking in effect: "How would you feel ... if the shoe was on the other foot?" [1255

HARRISON TALBOT MESEROLE. The American familiar essay, 1815-1835. Ann Arbor: University Microfilms, 1960. Positive microfilm of typescript. [405] leaves. Thesis--Univ. of Maryland. Abstracted: Dissert. abstracts, 21:624-5 (Sep). [1256

DON W. KLEINE. Civil disobedience [1849]: the way to Walden [1854]. Mod. lang. notes, 75:297-304 (Apr). Argument that "Walden encompasses Civil Disobedience. There is nothing 'in' the latter that is not in the former ... though a great deal of Walden is not in the earlier essay." [1257

The RECEPTION of Thoreau's first book. Thoreau Soc. bul., 27, 29, 35: irregular installments (Apr, Oct 1949, Apr 1951). Reviews of A week on the Concord and Merrimac Rivers (1849) by George Ripley (in the New York tribune), James Russell Lowell (in the Massachusetts quarterly review), and 3 anonymous critics. [1258

HENRY DAVID THOREAU (1817-62). Thoreau's passage on the "frozen-thawed" apple. [Edited] by R. Baird Shuman. Emerson Soc. quar., 18: leaves 34-9 (1st quar.). Facsimile reproduction of a 4-page manuscript fragment (undated) of his essay "Wild apples" in his Excursions; with a list of the differences between the manuscript and the printed version. [1259

WALTER ROY HARDING, ed. Some forgotten reviews of Walden [1854]. Thoreau Soc. bul., 38:[2-3]; 46:[2-3] (winter 1952, winter 1954). Texts, including a reproduction of an anonymous review in the National anti-slavery standard, 16 Dec. 1854. [1260

LAURIAT LANE, JR. On the organic structure of Walden [1854]. College Eng., 21:195-202 (Jan). notes. [1261

J. STEPHEN SHERWIN & RICHARD C. REYNOLDS, comps. A word index to Walden [1854], with textual notes. Charlottesville: Univ. of Virginia Press, 1960. viii, 165 p. Prepared from the Modern Library edition published in 1950 with title: Walden and other writings of Henry David Thoreau. Appended: list of differences between the 1950 text and the first edition (1854), and list of the 10 changes or queries made by Thoreau in manuscript in a copy of the first edition. [1262

WILLIAM BYSSHE STEIN. The motif of the Wise Old Man in Walden [1854]. Mod. lang. notes, 75:201-4 (Mar). notes. [1263

HENRY DAVID THOREAU (1817-62). Walden [1854] and Civil disobedience [1849]. ... Edited with an introduction and notes by Sherman Paul. Boston: Houghton Mifflin [1960]. xlvi, [2], 266, [1] p. bibliog. (p. xlv-xlvi). (Riverside editions, A14.) Appended (p. 257-66): "Life in the woods," by Charles Lane, an English reformer, associate of A. Bronson Alcott, from The dial, Apr. 1844. [1264

JACOB NATHANIEL BLANCK. Artemus Ward his book, 1862. Bibliog. Soc. Am., Papers, 54:121-5 (2d quar.). Addenda to the information about the signature marks of this volume in the compiler's Bibliography of American literature. [1265

Sister ANN CAROL VAUGHN. Agnes Repplier: social critic. Ann Arbor: University Microfilms, 1957 [i. e. 1960]. Positive microfilm of typescript. [121] leaves. Thesis--Michigan State Univ. Abstracted: Dissert. abstracts, 20: 3285 (Feb). Study of about 200 essays contributed by her to Life, "the former satirical weekly" (1883-1936), between 1893 and 1925, dealing with social and political matters, education, woman's sphere," and "the color of life." [1266

Fiction

TERENCE JOHN MARTIN. The emergence of the novel in America: a study in the cultural history of an art form [1789-1850]. Ann Arbor: University Microfilms, 1954 [i. e. 1960]. Positive microfilm of typescript. [340] leaves. Thesis--Ohio State Univ. Abstracted: Dissert. abstracts, 20:3299-3301 (Feb). [1267

ALBERT D. VAN NOSTRAND. The denatured novel. Indianapolis: Bobbs-Merrill [1960]. 224 p. Review of the business of publishing American novels, 1791-1958, and evidence, particularly for very recent years, that "The book trade denatures novels in an effort to sell more of them." [1268

JAMES FENIMORE COPPER (1789-1851). The pioneers [1823]. ... Introduction by Leon Howard. N.Y.: Rinehart [1959]. xxvii, 476, [2] p. bibliog. (p. xix). (Rinehart editions, 99.) [1269

JAMES FENIMORE COOPER (1789-1851). Tales for fifteen (1823) ... a facsimile reproduction with an introduction by (James Franklin Beard. Gainesville, Fla.: Scholars' Facsimiles & Reprints, 1959. xii p., facsim. (iv, 223 p.). Reproduction of Tales for fifteen: or, Imagination and heart, by James Morgan (N.Y.: C. Wiley, 1823), consisting of "Imagination" and "Heart," two "stories for adolescent girls," imitating "Mrs. Amelia Opie's popular moral tales." [1270

WARREN STANLEY WALKER. The frontiersman as recluse and redeemer. N.Y. folklore quar., 16:110-22 (summer). On Natty Bumppo, "the mythic hero of the Leather-Stocking Tales" (published 1823-41)--his traits and principles. [1271

ROBERT H. ZOELLNER. Conceptual ambivalence in Cooper's Leather-stocking [1823-41]. Am. lit., 31:397-420 (Jan). notes. [1272

JAMES FENIMORE COOPER (1789-1851). The last of the Mohicans [1826]. ... Edited with an introduction and notes by William Charvat. Boston: Houghton Mifflin [1958]. xxii, [4], 372, [2] p. map. bibliog. (p. xix (Riverside editions, A29.) [1273

WILLIAM WASSERSTROM. Cooper, Freud, and the origins of culture. Am. imago, 17:423-57 (winter). notes. Psychoanalytic interpretation of The prairie (1827), regarded as an illustration of Cooper's belief "that social conditions on the frontier recalled a situation 'as near barbarity' as that under which men lived in the prehistoric past," with "the tribe of Ishmael Bush" as an exemplar of "the patriarchal stage." [1274

RICHARD JOSEPH COANDA. Hawthorne on the imagination [1830s-50s]. Ann Arbor: University Microfilms, 1960. Positive microfilm of typescript. [274] leaves. Thesis--Univ. of Wisconsin. Abstracted: Dissert. abstracts, 21:562-3 (Dec). [1275

EDWARD MARION HOLMES. Hawthorne and Romanticism [1830s-50s]. New Eng. quar., 33:476-88 (Dec). notes. An essay in definition, suggesting that Hawthorne is not properly to be classified as a romanticist. [1276

EDGAR ALLAN POE (1809-49). The narrative of Arthur Gordon Pym of Nantucket [published serially in 1836, separately in 1838]. ... Introduction [by] Sidney Kaplan. N.Y.: Hill and Wong [1960]. xxv, 198 p. (American century series, AC29.) Introduction on the narrative as "the only long piece of fiction he ever wrote," summarizing previous critical and symbolic interpretations, and advancing the thesis that the work is a defense of "pigmentocracy" and slavery. [1277

KINGSLEY AMIS. New maps of hell: a survey of science fiction. N.Y.: Harcourt, Brace [1960]. 161 p. notes. Includes some account of American science fiction since 1837. [1278

WALTER E. BEZANSON. The troubled sleep of Arthur Gordon Pym. Rudolf Kirk & Charles Frederick Main, eds., Essays in literary history, presented to J. Milton French (New Brunswick, N.J.: Rutgers Univ. Press [1960]), p. 49-75. notes. On a tale by Edgar Allen Poe, "The narrative of Arthur Gordon Pym of Nantucket" (1837-38). [1279

STUART GEORGE LEVINE. Poe's Julius Rodman: Judaism, plagiarism, and the Wild West. Midw. quar., 1:245-9 (Apr). On an unfinished work printed as "The journal of Julius Rodman" in Burton's gentlemen's magazine, Jan.-Jun. 1840, pretending to be the "day-by-day account of a trip through the unsettled American west compiled by the leader of the expedition, a restless, energetic and artistic Jew"; with evidence that much of the work is plagiarized from travel books, and an explanation of the choice of a Jew as the main character. [1280

ELLERY QUEEN, pseud. Queen's quorum: a history of the detective-crime short story as revealed by the 106 most important books published in this field since 1845. Boston: Little, Brown, 1951. ix, 132 p. facsims. Critical commentary on each of the 106 books, 1845-1950. [1281

GEORGE R. CREEGER. The symbolism of whiteness in Melville's prose fiction [1846-90]. Jahrbuch für Amerikastudien, 5:147-63. notes. [1282

JAMES EDWIN MILLER, JR. The achievement of Melville. Univ. Kan. City rev., 26:59-67 (Oct 1959). Indications that his "moral imagination sought a synthesis of qualities which in isolation tended toward monstrosity, but which in union created the conditions for survival and endurance," 1846-90. [1283

ALLEN BALES. A study of point of view in the novels of Nathaniel Hawthorne [1850 to 1860]. Ann Arbor: University Microfilms, 1959 [i. e. 1960]. Positive microfilm of typescript. [207] leaves. Thesis--Northwestern Univ. Abstracted: Dissert. abstracts, 20:3724 (Mar). [1284

RICHARD HARTER FOGLE. Melville's shorter tales. Norman: Univ. of Oklahoma Press [1960]. ix, 150 p. port. notes. Accomplishes a study of the tales without citing their dates or the circumstances immediately attending their composition and publication. [1285

NATHANIEL HAWTHORNE (1804-64). The scarlet letter [1850]. Edited with an introduction and notes by Harry Levin. Boston: Houghton Mifflin [1960]. xxvii, 262 p. facsims., view. bibliog. (p. xxiii-xxvi), notes. (Riverside editions, A45.) Includes a critical introduction (p. vii-xxi). [1286

CHARLES ROBERT O'DONNELL. Hawthorne and Dimmesdale: the search for the realm of quiet [in The scarlet letter, 1850]. Nineteenth-cent. fiction, 14:317-32 (Mar). [1287

WILLIAM VAN O'CONNOR. The novel and the "truth" about America. Joseph J. Kwiat & Mary C. Turpie, eds., Studies in American culture: dominant ideas and images (Minneapolis: Univ. of Minnesota Press [1960]), p. 74-83. notes. On the "problem of the fictional representation of life," 1850s-1950s. [1288

JOHN D. SEELYE. The golden navel: the cabalism of Ahab's doubloon [in Moby-Dick, 1851]. Nineteenth-cent. fiction, 14:350-55 (Mar). notes. [1289

WILLIE T. WEATHERS. Moby Dick and the nineteenth-century scene. Tex. studies in lit. and language, 1:477-501 (winter). notes. On the "striking parallelism" between the "fictional events of Moby Dick and the actual events of the period" 1787-1851. [1290

WILLIAM L. HEDGES. Hawthorne's Blithedale: the function of the narrator. Nineteenth-cent. fiction, 14:303-16 (Mar). notes. On The Blithedale romance (1852). [1291

PETER B. MURRAY. Mythopoesis in The Blithedale romance [1852]. PMLA, 75:591-6 (Dec). notes. Symbolical interpretation. [1292

JOSEPH VINCENT RIDGELY. Woodcraft: Simms's first answer to Uncle Tom's cabin. Am. lit., 31:421-33 (Jan). notes. On The sword and the distaff; or, "Fair, fat, and forty," a story of the South, at the close of the Revolution (Charleston, 1852), by William Gilmore Simms, republished as Woodcraft; or, Hawks about the dovecote (1854). [1293

NICHOLAS CANADAY, JR. A new reading of Melville's "Benito Cereno" [1855]. Waldo McNeir & Leo B. Levy, eds., Studies in American literature (Baton Rouge: Louisiana State Univ. Press, 1960 [Louisiana State University studies, Humanities series, 8]), p. 49-57. notes. [1294

FRANKLIN R. ROGERS. Mark Twain's burlesque patterns, as seen in the novels and narratives, 1855-1885. Dallas: Southern Methodist Univ. Press, 1960. ix, 189 p. bibliog. (p. 179-83), notes (p. 163-77). Begun "as a doctoral dissertation at the University of California, Berkeley." [1295

WILLIAM BYSSHE STEIN. Melville's comedy of faith. ELH, 27:315-33 (Dec). notes. Symbolical interpretation of his "The piazza," in Piazza tales (1856). [1296

CLAUDE MITCHELL SIMPSON, ed. The local colorists: American short stories, 1857-1900. N.Y.: Harper [1960]. vi, [2], 340 p. bibliog. (p. 17-20), notes. Twenty-three stories by 18 authors, with a headnote for each author and a general introduction. [1297

JOHN S. MAYFIELD. Lanier in the florae; or, What would you have done? Am. book collector, 10(6):7-10 (Feb). view. Detailed physical description of Sidney Lanier's Tiger-lilies (1867) in its 3 "states." [1298

JOHN S. MAYFIELD. Sidney Lanier's Tiger-lilies [1867]: a bibliographical mystery. Bibliog. Soc. Am., Papers, 54:265-72 (4th quar.). [1299

MUNRO BEATTIE. Henry James, novelist [1870s-1910]. Dalhousie rev., 39:455-63 (winter). [1300

JOHN PATERSON. The language of "adventure" in Henry James [1870s-1910]. Am. lit., 32:291-301 (Nov). notes. [1301

LOUIS GEORGE PECEK. The Beadle story papers, 1870-1897: a study of popular fiction. Ann Arbor: University Microfilms, 1959 [i. e. 1960]. Positive microfilm of typescripts. [233] leaves. Thesis--Ohio State Univ. Abstracted: Dissert. abstracts, 20:3749 (Mar). On the Saturday journal (1870-82), Beadle's weekly (1882-85), and the Banner weekly (1885-97), issued by the firm of Beadle and Adams, and the 607 serialized novels published in them, of which 410 were contributed by Prentiss Ingraham, Albert W. Aiken, Joseph E. Badger, Frederick Whittaker, Oll Coomes, Anthony P. Morris, Jr., Charles Morris, Mary Reed Crowell, Metta V. Victor, and William F. Cody. [1302

JAMES ROBERT VITELLI. The innocence of Mark Twain. Bucknell rev.,

9:187-98 (Dec). On "his concern with the theme of Innocence," 1870s-90s. [1303

CARL LEROY MARSHALL. American critical attitudes toward the fiction of William Dean Howells [since 1872]. Ann Arbor: University Microfilms, 1954 [i. e. 1960]. Positive microfilm of typescript. [279] leaves. Thesis--Ohio State Univ. Abstracted: Dissert. abstracts, 20:3296-8 (Feb). [1304

BRYANT MOREY FRENCH. The Gilded Age manuscript [1873]. Yale Univ. Lib. gaz., 35:35-41 (Jul). notes. Examination of "Yale's total holdings of the manuscript" (amounting to more than 200 pages of the 284 "known extant pages" but less than a fifth of the entire manuscript), noting the division of labor between its joint authors (Mark Twain and Charles Dudley Warner) and the great difference in their habits and methods of composition. [1305

WALTER BLAIR. Mark Twain & Huck Finn. Berkeley: Univ. of California Press, 1960. xvi, [2], 436 p. cartoon, facsims., port., tables, views. bibliog. (p. 423-7), notes (p. 389-422). On the "forces which gave Adventures of Huckleberry Finn its substance and form," 1874-84. [1306

HENRY JAMES (1843-1916). Roderick Hudson [1875]. ... Introduction by Leon Edel. N.Y.: Harper [1960]. xvii, 334 p. (Harper torchbooks, TB1016. The Academy library.) Includes "the revisions first published in 1909." [1307

RICHARD POIRIER. The comic sense of Henry James: a study of the early novels. N.Y.: Oxford Univ. Press, 1960, 260 p. notes. On Roderick Hudson (1875), The American (1877), The Europeans (1878), Confidence (1879), Washington Square (1880), and The portrait of a lady (1882). London edition (Chatto & Windus) issued same year with same pagination and title. [1308

ESTHER JANE CARRIER. Fiction in public libraries of the United States, 1876-1900. Ann Arbor: University Microfilms, 1960. Positive microfilm of typescript. [592] leaves. Thesis--Univ. of Michigan. Abstracted: Dissert. abstracts, 21:346-7 (Aug). [1309

ALEX HOLDER. On the structure of Henry James's metaphors. Eng. studies, 41:289-97 (Oct). notes. Study of examples in 6 novels, 1876-1904. [1310

ELSA NETTELS. The drama of consciousness: the role of the central intelligence in selected novels of Henry James [from 1876 to 1904]. Ann Arbor: University Microfilms, 1960. Positive microfilm of typescript. [282] leaves. Thesis--Univ. of Wisconsin. Abstracted: Dissert. abstracts, 21:615-16 (Sep). [1311

HOWELL DANIELS. Henry James and "An international episode" [1878]. Brit. Assoc. Am. Studies, Bul., n. s., 1:3-35 (Sep). notes. On his treatment of the theme of Americans in Europe. [1312

JAMES WILLIAM GARGANO. Daisy Miller [by Henry James, 1879]: an abortive quest for innocence. South Atl. quar., 59:114-20 (winter). [1313

JOHN ROLAND DOVE. Tragic consciousness in Isabel Archer [in The portrait of a lady, by Henry James, 1881]. Waldo McNeir & Leo B. Levy, eds., Studies in American literature (Baton Rouge: Louisiana State Univ. Press, 1960 [Louisiana State University studies, Humanities series, 8]), p. 78-94. notes. [1314

H. G. FLINN & HOWARD C. KEY. Henry James and gestation. College Eng., 21:173-5 (Dec 1959). On an apparent inconsistency in the chronology of The portrait of a lady (1881), and the possibility that it may have been international. For comment by Jack E. Wallace and John C. Broderick and a reply to them by Howard C. Key, see 21:497-500 (May). [1315

MARY ELIZABETH GRENANDER, BEVERLY J. RAHN, & FRANCIS VALVO. The time-scheme in The portrait of a lady [by Henry James, 1881]. Am. lit., 32:127-35 (May). notes. [1316

MARION MONTGOMERY. The flaw in the portrait: Henry James vs. Isabel Archer [in The portrait of a lady, 1881]. Univ. Kan. City rev., 26:215-20 (Mar). [1317

RUDOLF KIRK & CLARA M. KIRK. Niagara revisited, by W. D. Howells: the story of its publication and suppresion. Rudolf Kirk & Charles Frederick Main, eds., Essays in literary history, presented to J. Milton French (New Brunswick, N.J.: Rutgers Univ. Press [1960]), p. 177-95. notes. On a short story printed in the Atlantic monthly, May 1883, its unauthorized publication by D. Dalziel of

Chicago as a pamphlet, Niagara revisited twelve years after their wedding journey by the Hoosac Tunnel route (1883?), issued for the Fitchburg Railroad Company to advertise its route to Niagara, the suppression of the pamphlet by Howells, and its later publication as part of a new edition of Their wedding journey (1887). [1318

JAMES WILLIAM GARGANO. Disguises in Huckleberry Finn [1884]. Univ. Kan. City rev., 26:175-8 (Mar). [1319

DONNA LORINE GERSTENBERGER. Huckleberry Finn [1884] and the world's illusions. West. humanities rev., 14:401-6 (autumn). [1320

CARSON GIBB. The best authorities. College Eng., 22:178-83 (Dec). notes. On the last 9 chapters of The adventures of Huckleberry Finn (1884). [1321

FRANKLIN JULIUS MEINE. Some notes on the first editions of "Huck Finn" [1884-85]. Am. book collector, 10(10):31-4 (Jun). facsims. Includes information about an "indecent" plate, promptly corrected. [1322

E. ARTHUR ROBINSON. The two "voices" in Huckleberry Finn [1884]. Mod. lang. notes, 75:204-8 (Mar). On "the voice of Mark Twain intruding upon Huckleberry Finn's." [1323

ERIC SOLOMON. Huckleberry Finn [1884] once more. College Eng., 22: 172-8 (Dec). notes. On the ending of the novel. [1324

ARVIN R. WELLS. Huck Finn and Holden Caulfield: the situation of the hero. Ohio Univ. rev., 2:31-42. notes. On a "difference in point of view, in underlying assumptions, that ultimately amounts to a difference in kind," between Huckleberry Finn (1884) and The catcher in the rye (by J. D. Salinger). [1325

NORRIS WILSON YATES. The "counter-conversion" of Huckleberry Finn [1884]. Am. lit., 32:1-10 (Mar). notes. [1326

AMHERST COLLEGE. Dept. of American Studies. Mark Twain's Huckleberry Finn [1885]. Edited with an introduction by Barry A. Marks. Boston: Heath [1959]. vii, [5], 108 p. bibliog. (p. 107-8), notes. (Problems in American civilization: readings selected in cooperation with the Department of American Studies, Amherst College.) Ten reprinted articles or chapters by various critics, first published 1920-55. [1327

STEPHEN CRANE (1871-1900). Stephen Crane's first story. [Edited] by Daniel G. Hoffman. N.Y. Pub. Lib., Bul., 64:273-8 (May). notes. "Sketches from life, by Stephen Crane. Uncle Jake and the bell-handle," printed from a manuscript (1885) "written in his large, open, clearly readable hand on lined tablet paper," now first published. [1328

DONALD PIZER. The ethical unity of The rise of Silas Lapham [by William Dean Howells, 1885]. Am. lit., 32: 322-7 (Nov). notes. [1329

DAVID L. FRAZIER. Time and the theme of Indian summer [by William Dean Howells, 1886]. Ariz. quar., 16: 260-67 (autumn). [1330

PAUL J. CARTER, JR. The influence of William Dean Howells upon Mark Twain's social satire [1887 ff.]. Univ. Colo. studies, lang. and lit., 4 (1953): 93-100. notes. Evidence that "Howells went beyond Twain in his social criticism to an extent which should have proved a stimulus rather than a hindrance," and that "there is no factual basis for the charge that he was responsible for Twain's failure to become a great social satirist, an American Swift." [1331

W. ARTHUR BOGGS. Looking backward at the Utopian novel, 1888-1900. N.Y. Pub. Lib., Bul., 64:329-36 (Jun). notes. Study of 69 works of fiction (several in German) "influenced by Edward Bellamy's Looking backward," most of which advocate or attack his socialism or his industrialism, though a few are examples of "the religious Utopia, the fantastic romance, the proletarian novel, and the quasi-fictional economic novel." [1332

JAMES MELVILLE COX. A Connecticut Yankee in King Arthur's court [by Mark Twain, 1889]: the machinery of self-preservation. Yale rev., 50: 89-102 (autumn). [1333

WARNER B. BERTHOFF. "Certain phenomenal men": the example of Billy Budd [by Herman Melville, 1890-91). ELH, 27:334-51 (Dec). notes. [1334

CHARLES BERNARD HANDS. Harold Frederic [1856-98]: a critical study of the American works [1890-96]. Ann Arbor: University Microfilms, 1959 [i. e. 1960]. Positive microfilm of typescript. viii, 272 leaves. bibliog.

(leaves 263-71). Thesis--Univ. of Notre Dame. Abstracted: Dissert. abstracts, 20:2801-2 (Jan). [1335

ELBERT LEROY HARRIS. Hamlin Garland's use of the American scene in his fiction [especially in the 1890s]. Ann Arbor: University Microfilms, 1959 [i. e. 1960]. Positive microfilm of typescript. [283] leaves. Thesis--Univ. of Pennsylvania. Abstracted: Dissert. abstracts, 20:3742-3 (Mar). [1336

HELEN HORNE. Basic ideas of James' aesthteics [sic] as expressed in the short stories concerning artists and writers [mainly 1890s]. Marburg, 1960. 175 p. bibliog. (p. 171-4), notes. Inaug.-Diss.--Philipps-Universität, Marburg. [1337

WILLIAM BYSSHE STEIN. The motif of the Wise Old Man in Billy Budd [1890-91]. West, humanities rev., 14: 99-101 (winter). On the fact that "The Dansker, while recognizing Billy's vulnerable innocence, refuses to guide him around the pitfalls of evil." [1338

WALTER SUTTON. Melville and the Great God Budd. Prairie schooner, 34:128-33 (summer). On affinities between his "beautifully-constructed novella" (written 1890-91) and Buddhism. [1339

EDITH NEWBOLD (JONES) WHARTON (1862-1937). The best short stories of Edith Wharton. Edited with an introduction by Wayne Andrews. N.Y.: Scribner [1958]. xxvii, 292 p. Undated texts (1890s-1920s?); with "The world of Edith Wharton: fragment of a biography in progress," by Andrews. [1340

LOTUS SNOW. Some stray fragrance of an ideal: Henry James's imagery for youth's discovery of evil [1892-99]. Harv. Lib. bul., 14:107-25 (winter). [1341

MARGARET O'BRIEN STEWART. A critical study of Ruth Suckow's fiction. Ann Arbor: University Microfilms, 1960. Positive microfilm of typescript. [280] leaves. Thesis--Univ. of Illinois. Abstracted: Dissert. abstracts, 21:1195-6 (Nov). On the novels and short stories of Ruth Suckow (1892-1960), dealing mainly with rural Iowa. [1342

ROBERT BERKELMAN. Henry James and "The real thing" [1893]. Univ. Kan. City rev., 26:93-5 (Dec). notes. [1343

GEORGE W. JOHNSON. Romance and realism in the novels of Frank Norris [1893 to 1903]. Ann Arbor: University Microfilms, 1960. Positive microfilm of typescript. [335] leaves. Thesis--Columbia Univ. Abstracted: Dissert. abstracts, 21:896-7 (Oct). [1344

JOHN HERMAN RANDALL III. Willa Cather's search for value: a critical and historical study of her fiction [1894-1940]. Ann Arbor: University Microfilms, 1957 [i. e. 1960]. Positive microfilm of typescript. [649] leaves. Thesis--Univ. of Minnesota. Abstracted: Dissert. abstracts, 20:4115 (Apr). [1345

DON DE VERE WALKER. Wister, Roosevelt, and James: a note on the Western. Am. quar., 12:358-66 (fall). notes. On Owen Wister's manuscript diary account of his association with a rancher who beat and kicked a tired horse (foaming red at the mouth) and finally gouged out one of its eyes, his fictionized treatment of the incident in his story "Balaam and Pedro" (1894), the insistence of Theodore Roosevelt that the gouging be left "to the reader's imagination," the inclusion of the incident in The Virginian (1902) with the gouging unmentioned, a laudatory letter from Henry James about the novel, and the relation of the Roosevelt and James comments to the "failure" of Wister and to the extent of his responsibility for "the flood of cheap Westerns that followed him." [1346

MARK KANZER. The figure in the carpet [by Henry James, 1896]. Am. imago, 17:339-48 (winter). bibliog. Psychoanalytic effort to identify the "figure" in the artistic motives of Henry James. [1347

GEORGE ADE (1866-1944). The America of George Ade (1866-1944): fables, short stories, essays. Edited with an introduction by Jean Shepherd. N.Y.: Putnam [1960. 2], 284 p. cartoons. Collection of syndicated newspaper pieces, 1897 till the early 1930s, not singly dated by the editor and apparently selected by her from his numerous volumes of collected reprints. [1348

JOHN STANLEY HILL. Frank Norris's heroines [1897-1902]. Ann Arbor: University Microfilms, 1960. Positive microfilm of typescript. [316] leaves. Thesis--Univ. of Wisconsin. Abstracted: Dissert. abstracts, 20:4397 (May). [1349

ERNEST HARRISON HOFER. The realization of conscience in the later Henry James [in his novels written after 1897]. Ann Arbor: University Microfilms, 1960. Positive microfilm of typescript. [153] leaves. Thesis--Cornell Univ. Abstracted: Dissert. abstracts, 21:197 (Jul). [1350

FREDERICK P. W. McDOWELL. Ellen Glasgow and the ironic art of fiction. Madison: Univ. of Wisconsin Press, 1960. xi, 292 p. bibliog. (p. 268-80). Mainly a critical study of each of her novels, 1897 ff.; with a list of "Ellen Glasgow's published work" (p. 265-7). [1351

ALAN H. ROPER. The moral and metaphorical meaning of The spoils of Poynton [1897, by Henry James]. Am. lit., 32:182-6 (May). notes. [1352

ERIC SOLOMON. A gloss on The red badge of courage. Mod. lang. notes, 75:111-13 (Feb). notes. On "The veteran," in Stephen Crane's The little regiment (1897), as an explanation of Henry Fleming in The red badge of courage. [1353

EDWARD WASIOLEK. Maisie: pure or corrupt? College Eng., 22:167-72 (Dec). On Henry James's What Maisie knew (1897). [1354

DONALD P. COSTELLO. The structure of The turn of the screw [by Henry James, 1898]. Mod. lang. notes, 75:312-21 (Apr). notes. [1355

GERALD WILLEN, ed. A casebook on Henry James's The turn of the screw [1898]. N.Y.: Crowell [1960]. vi, [2], 325 p. bibliog. (p. 319-22). (Crowell literary casebooks.) Text of the tale and of James's remarks on it; and 15 reprinted essays, 1924-59, by various critics. [1356

SÉAMUS COONEY. Awkward ages in The awkward age [1899, by Henry James]. Mod. lang. notes, 75:208-11 (Mar). notes. [1357

KENNETH ANDERSON BERNARD. The flight of Theodore Dreiser. Univ. Kan. City rev., 26:251-9 (Jun). An interpretation of his fiction, 1900-1947, as an effort to reconcile the images of his father and his mother. [1358

DANIEL G. HOFFMAN. Stephen Crane's last novel. N.Y. Pub. Lib., Bul., 64:337-43 (Jun). notes. On his plan to write "an historical novel on the fortunes of his own New Jersey forebears during the American Revolution," with texts of 2 brief outlines of it (1900?), found in his manuscripts. [1359

JOSEPH ANTHONY WARD. Social disintegration in "The wings of the dove" [by Henry James, 1902]. Criticism, 2:190-203 (spring). notes. [1360

OSCAR CARGILL. The ambassadors [by Henry James, 1903]: a new view. PMLA, 75:439-52 (Sep). notes. On Louis Lambert Strether as the central character of the novel. [1361

LEON EDEL. The text of The ambassadors [by Henry James, 1903-9, 1957-60]. Harv. Lib. bul., 14:453-60 (autumn). notes. [1362

MARY KYLE MICHAEL. Henry James's use of the word wonderful in The ambassadors [1903]. Mod. lang. notes, 75:114-17 (Feb). [1363

FREDERICK P. W. McDOWELL. "The old pagan scorn of everlasting mercy"--Ellen Glasgow's The deliverance [1904]. Twentieth cent. lit., 4:135-42 (Jan 1959). [1364

EDWARD ALAN BLOOM & LILLIAN D. BLOOM. Willa Cather's Troll garden. Books at Brown, 18:181-6 (Oct). notes. On a collection of 7 short stories (1905) dealing with "the artistic spirit--its strength and its weakness, its truth and its imposture." [1365

WILLA SIBERT CATHER (1873-1947). Five stories. With an article by George N. Kates on Miss Cather's last, unfinished, and unpublished Avignon story. N.Y.: Vintage Books, 1956. [6], 214, [2] p. Reprinted tales, 1905-48. Appended: "Willa Cather's unfinished Avignon story" (p. 175-214), by Kates, on a manuscript entitled "Hard punishments," on which she worked from 1942 to 1944 and which was destroyed after her death in obedience to her order. [1366

PRISCILLA GIBSON HICKS. "The story in it": the design of Henry James's "New York edition" [of his novels and tales, 24 vols., 1907-9]. Ann Arbor: University Microfilms, 1960. Positive microfilm of typescript. [662] leaves. Thesis--Boston Univ. Abstracted: Dissert. abstracts, 21:895-6 (Oct). [1367

MARCIA E. ALLENTUCK. Polyanna [1912-13], by Eleanor H. Porter. Ga. rev., 14:447-9 (winter). [1368

DAVID DANIEL ANDERSON. Sherwood Anderson and the meaning of the American experience [1912-40]. Ann

Arbor: University Microfilms, 1960. Positive microfilm of typescript. [448] leaves. Thesis--Michigan State Univ. Abstracted: Dissert. abstracts, 21:1189 (Nov). [1369

HOWARD WILLIAM WEBB, JR. The development of a style: the Lardner idiom. Am. quar., 12:482-92 (winter). notes. Based on thesis--State Univ. of Iowa. On Ring Lardner's "skillful blending of malapropisms, slang, confused pronouns and verb forms, mispronunciations, misspellings and rhetorical effects that describes socially and psychologically the characters who use it," 1913-16. [1370

HOWARD WILLIAM WEBB, JR. The meaning of Ring Lardner's fiction [1914-34]: a re-evaluation. Am. lit., 31:434-45 (Jan). notes. [1371

WILLIAM JOSEPH STUCKEY. A critical history of the Pulitzer prize novels, 1917-1947. Ann Arbor: University Microfilms, 1959 [i. e. 1960]. Positive microfilm of typescript. ix, 252 leaves. bibliog. (leaves 240-50). Thesis--Washington Univ. Abstracted: Dissert. abstracts, 20:3755 (Mar). [1372

JOSEPH WARREN BEACH (1880-1957). American fiction, 1920-1940. N.Y.: Russell & Russell, 1960. x, 371 p. 1st ed. 1941. On "American fiction between wars" as illustrated by John Dos Passos, Ernest Hemingway, William Faulkner, Thomas Wolfe, Erskine Caldwell, James T. Farrell, John P. Marquand, and John Steinbeck; with a "list of novels and main collections of short stories" (p. 365-7). [1373

MARTIN LIGHT. A study of characterization in Sinclair Lewis's fiction [1920s]. Ann Arbor: University Microfilms, 1960. Positive microfilm of typescript. [334] leaves. Thesis--Univ. of Illinois. Abstracted: Dissert. abstracts, 21:567 (Dec). [1374

IRVING MALIN. William Faulkner: an interpretation. Stanford, Calif.: Stanford Univ. Press [1957]. viii, [2], 99 p. notes. Analysis of Faulkner and his fiction, 1920s-50s, according to the theories of Freud and Jung; with chapters on "The theme of rigidity," "The father-son myth," "The women," Light in August, and "Faulkner and the Bible." [1375

KENNETH SPRAGUE ROTHWELL. From society to Babbittry: Lewis' debt to Edith Wharton. Cent. Miss. Valley Am. Studies Assoc., Jour., 1(1):32-7 (spring). notes. On The age of innocence (1920), by Wharton, as "the master blue print" for Babbitt (1922), by Sinclair Lewis. [1376

MATTHEW JOSEPH BRUCCOLI. Bibliographical notes on F. Scott Fitzgerald's The beautiful and the damned [1922]. Studies in bibliog., 13:258-61. notes. On the states of and differences between the first and the second impression (both 1922); and a republication in 1959. [1377

MATTHEW JOSEPH BRUCCOLI. Textual variants in Sinclair Lewis's Babbitt [1922]. Studies in bibliog., 11 (1958): 263-8. table. notes. [1378

ROBERT E. SCHOLES. The commitment of James Gould Cozzens. Ariz. quar., 16:129-44 (summer). Examination of his novels, 1924-57. [1379

ROBERT E. SCHOLES. The modern American novel and the Mason-Dixon Line. Ga. rev., 14:193-204 (summer). Comparison of Faulkner's Absalom, Absalom! (1936) and Fitzgerald's The great Gatsby (1925) as "studies of the so-called 'innocent' young man from the provinces attempting to rise in a more complex society," and of Hemingway's A farewell to arms (1929), Faulkner's The wild palms (1939), and Cozzens's Men and brethren (1936) as "representative treatments of illicit love and abortion in modern society," and analysis of the 5 novels as illustrations of the "cultural division" between North and South. [1380

J. S. WESTBROOK. Nature and optics in The great Gatsby [by F. Scott Fitzgerald, 1925]. Am. lit., 32:78-84 (Mar). notes. [1381

EARL HERBERT ROVIT. Herald to chaos: the novels of Elizabeth Madox Roberts [1926 to 1941. Lexington:] Univ. of Kentucky Press [1960]. ix, [3], 180 p. bibliog. (p. 165-9), notes (p. 171-9). [1382

CHARLES ALBERT ALLEN. William Faulkner: comedy and the purpose of humor [1929-40s]. Ariz. quar., 16: 59-68 (spring). [1383

MELVIN ABRAHAM BACKMAN. The pilgrimage of William Faulkner: a study of Faulkner's fiction, 1929-1942. Ann Arbor: University Microfilms, 1960. Positive microfilm of typescript. [281] leaves. Thesis--Columbia Univ. Abstracted: Dissert. abstracts, 21:193-4 (Jul). [1384

JOSEPH M. BACKUS. Names of characters in Faulkner's The sound and the fury [1929]. Names, 6:226-33 (Dec 1958). notes. [1385

BARBARA M. CROSS. The sound and the fury [by William Faulkner, 1929]: the pattern of sacrifice. Ariz. quar., 16:5-16 (spring). notes. [1386

ALLEN GUTTMANN. Collisions and confrontations [in the novels of William Faulkner, 1929 ff.]. Ariz. quar., 16:46-52 (spring). [1387

ELMO HOWELL. Faulkner's Jumblies: the nonsense world of As I lay dying [1929]. Ariz. quar., 16:70-78 (spring). notes. [1388

PASCHAL REEVES. The humor of Thomas Wolfe. South. folklore quar., 24:109-20 (Jun). notes. On a collection of passages from Wolfe, 1929-40, in which the author detects humorous qualities or an intent to be humorous. [1389

JAMES LAMAR ROBERTS. The individual and the family: Faulkner's As I lay dying [1929]. Ariz. quar., 16:26-38 (spring). notes. [1390

ERNEST WARNOCK TEDLOCK, JR., & CECIL VIVIAN WICKER, eds. Steinbeck and his critics, a record of twenty-five years: an anthology with introduction and notes. Albuquerque: Univ. of New Mexico Press [1957]. xli, 310 p. notes. Reprinted essays, chapters, and book reviews, 1929-56, and 3 previously unpublished contributions by Peter Lisca; with an extensive introduction. [1391

FLOYD C. WATKINS & WILLIAM B. DILLINGHAM. The mind of Vardaman Bundren [in William Faulkner's As I lay dying (1929)]. Philol. quar., 39: 247-51 (Apr). notes. Argument that he is not, as often alleged, an idiot. [1392

JAMES DEAN YOUNG. Quentin's Maundy Thursday [in Faulkner's The sound and the fury, 1929]. Tulane studies in Eng., 10:143-51. notes. [1393

RICHARD COLBERT BEDFORD. The apocatastasis of Henry Miller [1930 to 1959]. Ann Arbor: University Microfilms, 1960. Positive microfilm of typescript. [786] leaves. Thesis--State Univ. of Iowa. Abstracted: Dissert. abstracts, 21:1560-61 (Dec). On the "continuous changes" in his "ideational development." [1394

DOUGLAS COLE. Faulkner's Sanctuary [1931]: retreat from responsibility. West. humanities rev., 14: 291-8 (summer). [1395

A. M. TIBBETTS. The strange half-world of Nathanael West. Prairie schooner, 34:8-14 (spring). Comment on his novels, 1931-39. [1396

ROBERT LESLIE BERNER. The theme of responsibility in the later fiction of William Faulkner [after 1932]. Ann Arbor: University Microfilms, 1960. Positive microfilm of typescript. [231] leaves. Abstracted: Dissert. abstracts, 21:1561 (Dec). Thesis--Univ. of Washington. [1397

FREDERICK JOHN HOFFMAN & OLGA W. VICKERY, eds. William Faulkner: three decades of criticism [1932-60. Second edition. East Lansing:] Michigan State Univ. Press, 1960. xi, 428 p. bibliog. (p. 393-428), notes. 1st ed. 1951. Reviews and other criticism, with an introduction (p. 1-50) by Hoffman. [1398

FREDERICK P. W. McDOWELL. Theme and artistry in Ellen Glasgow's The sheltered life [1932]. Tex. studies in lit. & lang., 1:502-16 (winter). notes. [1399

JAMES LAMAR ROBERTS. The individual and the community: Faulkner's Light in August [1932]. Waldo McNeir & Leo B. Levy, eds., Studies in American literature (Baton Rouge: Louisiana State Univ. Press, 1960 [Louisiana State University studies, Humanities series, 8]), p. 132-55. notes. [1400

MONTGOMERY MORTON CULVER, JR. Hervey Allen, historical novelist. Ann Arbor: University Microfilms, 1959 [i. e. 1960]. Positive microfilm of typescript. [223] leaves. Thesis--Univ. of Illinois. Abstracted: Dissert. abstracts, 20:3289-90 (Feb). On his historical novels, published 1933-48; with "the fullest extant biographical sketch of Hervey Allen." [1401

ROBERT EUSTIS MORSBERGER. The world of Walter Mitty. Utah Acad. Sciences, Proc., 37:37-43. On the symbolism of "The secret life of Walter Mitty," a tale by James Thurber, and of several of his other writings, 1933-50. [1402

ROBERT EMANS. Treasure Island: the classic and the classic comic. Element. school jour., 60:253-7 (Feb). notes. On comic books in America, 1934-60, particularly the "classic-comic version" of Robert Louis Stevenson's Treasure Island (1949). [1403

KARL JAY SHAPIRO. The greatest living author. Karl Shapiro, In defense of ignorance (N.Y.: Random House [1960]), p. 313-38. On the fiction of Henry Miller since 1934. [1404

LESLIE A. FIEDLER. Henry Roth's neglected masterpiece. Commentary, 30:102-7 (Aug). On his "first and only novel," Call it sleep (1935), after which he "retired completely from the literary scene" until 1959. Appended (p. 107-9): "The dun Dakotas," by Roth. [1405

MADEMOISELLE. 40 best stories from Mademoiselle, 1935-1960. Edited by Cyrilly Abels and Margarita G. Smith. N.Y.: Harper [1960. 10], 479 p. Includes headnotes by the editors. The single stories are undated. [1406

THE MAGAZINE OF FANTASY AND SCIENCE FICTION. A decade of Fantasy and science fiction. Selected by Robert P. Mills. Garden City, N.Y.: Doubleday, 1960. 406 p. Twenty-five tales, by American and British authors, that appeared in the magazine at unstated times, from unstated sources. One tale was copyrighted in 1935. [1407

ROBERT OREN STEPHENS. Hemingway's riddle of Kilimanjaro: idea and image. Am. lit., 32:84-7 (Mar). notes. On his "The snows of Kilimanjaro" (1936). [1408

JAMES F. LIGHT. Nathanael West [1902-40] and the ravaging locust. Am. quar., 12:44-53 (spring). notes. On his The day of the locust (1939), dealing "indirectly" with "the approaching fascism that West ... felt closing in upon America because of the frustration of man's basic emotional needs." [1409

GORDON RAYMOND FOLSOM. Form and substance in Eudora Welty. Ann Arbor: University Microfilms, 1960. Positive microfilm of typescript. [213] leaves. Thesis--Univ. of Wisconsin. Abstracted: Dissert. abstracts, 21:621 (Sep). Study of her fiction "in relation to its Southern background and to the methods of selected Southern writers," 1940s-50s. [1410

FREDERICK LANDIS GWYNN & JOSEPH LEO BLOTNER. The fiction of J[erome] D[avid] Salinger [1940 to 1957. Pittsburgh:] Univ. of Pittsburgh Press [1958]. viii, 59 p. bibliog. (p. 57-9), notes (p. 55-6). (Critical essays in English and American literature, 4.) [1411

WARREN BECK. Faulkner's point of view. College Eng., 22:86-93 (Nov). Reprinted from College English, 1941. [1412

ROBERT Y. DRAKE, JR. Comments on two Eudora Welty stories [in her A curtain of green (1914)]. Miss. quar., 13:123-31 (summer). [1413

DAVID MADDEN. The hero and the witness in Wright Morris' Field of vision [1956]. Prairie schooner, 34: 263-78 (fall). Refers in part to his other fiction, 1942-58. [1414

LESLIE A. FIELD. Wolfe's use of folklore. N.Y. folklore quar., 16:203-15 (autumn). notes. On The hills beyond (1943), planned by Thomas Wolfe as "a book that will try to tell through the hundreds of members of one family the whole story of America," left unfinished at his death with only 10 chapters completed, and its account of William Joyner (strong man, hunter, shrewd trader, Yankee "with a wry sense of humor," teller of tall tales) and 8 of his children. [1415

CHARLES KAPLAN. Jack Burden: modern Ishmael. College Eng., 22: 19-24 (Oct). Interpretation of Robert Penn Warren's All the king's men (1946). [1416

CLINTON S. BURHANS, JR. The old man and the sea: Hemingway's tragic vision of man [1952]. Am. lit., 31: 446-55 (Jan). notes. [1417

Literary Correspondence

HENRY DAVID THOREAU (1817-62). Three unpublished Thoreau letters. New Eng. quar., 33:373-4. Letter to Thoreau from Margaret Fuller (25 Sep. 1843) and letters from him to George William Curtis (13 Apr. and 8 Aug. 1855). [1418

RALPH WALDO EMERSON (1803-82). Two unpublished Emerson letters. [Edited by] Vivian C[onstance] Hopkins. New Eng. quar., 33:502-6 (Dec). notes. Letter to George Putnam (19 Oct. 1855), recommending publication of an article by Delia Bacon; and letter to Caroline Healey Dall (10 Dec. 1857) on Miss Bacon's book on Shakespeare. [1419

SOPHIA E. THOREAU (1819-76). The correspondence of Sophia Thoreau and Marianne Dunbar. [Edited and abstracted by Walter Harding.] Thoreau Soc. bul., 33:[1-3] (Oct 1950). facsims. Annotated abstracts (with many quotations) of 32 letters from Sophia Thoreau to her second cousin, dated in Concord and in Bangor, Me., 1857-76, containing local and family news, including accounts of the illness and death of her father, her brother Henry, and her mother, of her work in editing Henry's papers for publication, and of the onset of her own final illness. [1420

WALT WHITMAN (1819-92). New letters of Walt Whitman. [Edited] by Edwin Haviland Miller. Mo. Hist. Soc., Bul., 16:99-113 (Jan). notes. Seventeen letters to his brother Thomas Jefferson Whitman (in St. Louis) and other members of the family, 1864-90, on family matters, Whitman's health, his travels (including a journey to Colorado and a stay in St. Louis), and other subjects. [1421

SAMUEL LANGHORNE CLEMENS (1835-1910) & WILLIAM DEAN HOWELLS (1837-1920). Mark Twain - Howells letters: the correspondence of Samuel L. Clemens and William D. Howells, 1872-1910. Edited by Henry Nash Smith and William M. Gibson with the assistance of Frederick Anderson. Cambridge: Belknap Press of Harvard Univ. Press, 1960. 2 v. xxv, 454; [8], 455-948 p. facsims., ports., geneal. tables, views. notes. Texts of "every written communication between Clemens and Howells known to the editors," 7 Jan. 1872 - 11 Feb. 1910, dealing with the family life and travels of the writers, literary matters, public affairs, etc.; with "Calendar of letters" (2:883-903) and account of the manuscripts. [1422

AMBROSE BIERCE (1842-1914?) & CHARLES WARREN STODDARD (1843-1909). Ambrose Bierce and Charles Warren Stoddard: some unpublished correspondence. [Edited] by M. E. Grenander. Huntington Lib. quar., 23:261-92 (May). notes. Letters exchanged between them, 1874-75, about their literary and journalistic activities in Europe, their meetings with Americans, and Stoddard's travels on the Continent; with excerpts from earlier letters and newspaper dispatches by Bierce about his sight-seeing and his domestic life in London, 1872-74, and excerpts from Bierce's correspondence with George Sterling, 1905-9, about Stoddard and his increasingly apparent homosexuality. [1423

WILLIAM WHITE. Walt Whitman to U.S. Grant: an unknown exchange. Prairie schooner, 34:120-22 (summer). Includes what appears to be part of a draft of a letter from Whitman (Feb. or Mar. 1874), Grant's letter of acknowledgment, and Whitman's eulogy of Grant (28 Sep. 1879). [1424

DAVID WATT BOWSER (1868?-1935) & SAMUEL LANGHORNE CLEMENS (1835-1910). Dear Master Wattie: the Mark Twain - David Watt Bowser letters. Edited and annotated by Pascal Covici, Jr. Southw. rev., 45:105-21 (spring). facsims., notes. Four letters from young Bowser at Dallas to Mark Twain and 5 from Mark Twain at Hartford to Bowser, 16 Mar. 1880 - 10 Jan. 1882, on Bowser's life and reading, his admiration for Mark Twain and his books for boys, and Mark Twain's sentiments regarding boyhood and English style. [1425

CHARLES E. FEINBERG. Percy Ives, Detroit, and Walt Whitman. Detroit Hist. Soc., Bul., 16(5):4-11 (Feb). facsims., ports. Includes correspondence between Whitman and Mrs. Elisa Seaman Leggett of Detroit, between her and her grandson Percy Ives (painter), and between Ives and Whitman, 1880-89 and Whitman reminiscences by Ives in the Detroit Sunday news tribune, 5 Apr. 1896, and reproductions of a painting and 2 sketches of Whitman by Ives. [1425a

GEORGE WASHINGTON CABLE (1844-1925). Mark Twain [and] G. W. Cable: the record of a literary friendship. [Edited by] Arlin Turner. [East Lansing:] Michigan State Univ. Press, 1960. xi, 141 p. port. notes (p. 137-41). Letters from Cable to his wife and to James Burton Pond (agent or manager of the "reading tour" of Cable and Mark Twain), 2 Apr. 1883 - 2 Mar. 1885; reminiscent sketches of Mark Twain by Cable, 1896 and 1910; and a few letters, not previously published, from Mark Twain to Pond written during the joint tour. [1426

FRANCIS MARION CRAWFORD (1854-1909). "My dear uncle"--three letters from Francis Marion Crawford to Samuel Ward. Edited by Robert L. Gale. Studi americani, 5:325-38. notes. Letters dated in Boston, 3 Jan. and 16 Apr. 1883, and Constantinople, 14 Mar. 1884, dealing mainly with the writer's literary plans and activities. [1427

FRANCIS HODGINS, JR. The Dreiser letters. Jour. Eng. and Germanic philol., 59:714-20 (Oct). On letters of Theodore Dreiser, 1897-1945, published in 2 collections in 1959, as a source of information about "Dreiser the writer." [1428

STEPHEN VINCENT BENÉT (1898-1943). Selected letters of Stephen Vincent Benet. Edited by Charles A. Fenton. New Haven: Yale Univ. Press, 1960. xxv, 436 p. Letters to various persons, 1908-43, selected to "reveal his character and illuminate his profession"; with an introduction on his letter-writing habits. [1429

JACK LONDON (1876-1916). Two unpublished letters of Jack London. Edited, with an introduction, by Warren I. Titus. Calif. Hist. Soc. quar., 39:309-10 (Dec). port. Letters to Winston Churchill, American novelist, dated Glenn Ellen, "Sanoma County," Calif., 23 Mar. and 20 Apr. 1913, on "royalty rates and magazine serialization fees Churchill was receiving." [1430

THEODORE DREISER (1871-1945). Letters to Louise: Theodore Dreiser's letters to Louise Campbell. Edited, with commentary, by Louise Campbell. Phila.: Univ. of Pennsylvania Press [1959]. 123 p. Letters, 1917-45, interspersed with the editor's reminiscences of Dreiser and her dealings with him, including her service as an editor of his work. [1431

Literary Criticism

HENRY DAVID THOREAU (1817-62). Thoreau's Of books and their titles: a new edition. [Edited] by R. Baird Shuman. Emerson Soc. quar., 18: leaves 26-34 (1st quar.). Essay written by Thoreau while a Harvard student, Mar. 1837, printed inaccurately in 1917, now printed from the recently discovered manuscript in his hand; with a facsimile reproduction of the manuscript. [1432

RAYMOND WILLIAM ADAMS. An early and overlooked defense of Thoreau. Thoreau Soc. bul., 32:[1-3] (Jul 1950). On Eugene Benson (1839-1908), painter and literary critic, and his article in the Galaxy, Sep. 1866, entitled "Literary frondeurs," defining a frondeur as "one who slings truths--unwelcome and often destructive truths--at some giant sham or honored Mumbo-Jumbo of society," and replying vigorously to James Russell Lowell's "bitter attack" on Thoreau's memory in the North American review, Oct. 1865. [1433

JACK EARL BENDER. Brander Matthews [1852-1929]: critic of the theatre [1873 to 1929]. Educ. theatre jour., 12:169-76 (Oct). notes. [1434

HERSHEL DALE ROWE. Basic elements in the criticism of Ezra Pound [born 1885]. Ann Arbor: University Microfilms, 1959 [i. e. 1960]. Positive microfilm of typescript. v, 253 leaves. bibliog. (leaves 246-52). Thesis--Univ. of Florida. Abstracted: Dissert. abstracts, 20:2807-8 (Jan). On his primary interest in "the production (as opposed to the consumption) of literature," and his advice to and judgments of writers as "a homiletic projection of his personal preferences." [1435

SCOTT COMPTON OSBORN. Richard Harding Davis: critical battleground. Am. quar., 12:84-92 (spring). notes. On the critical reception of his novels, 1891-1916, as illustrative of "the artifacts of something very near cultural anthropology." [1436

ILA JACUITH BLUE. A study of literary criticism by some Negro writers, 1900-1955. Ann Arbor: University Microfilms, 1960. Positive microfilm of typescript. [251] leaves. Thesis (Ed. D.)--Univ. of Michigan. Abstracted: Dissert. abstracts, 21:342 (Aug). [1437

DOROTHY NYREN, ed. A library of literary criticism: modern American literature. N.Y.: F. Ungar Pub. Co. [1960]. viii, 552 p. "Periodicals represented" (p. vii-viii). Continuation of Charles Wells Moulton's Library of literary criticism of English and American authors (completed in 8 vols. in 1905). Brief excerpts from "the critical accompaniment to the major literary performances of the last half century and more ... as it appeared in the scholarly journals and books," relating to 170 American authors "who wrote or became prominent after 1904." Arranged alphabetically by name of author criticized: Adams, Henry - Wright, Richard. [1438

STANLEY EDGAR HYMAN. The armed vision: a study in the methods of modern literary criticism [1912-40s]. N.Y.: Knopf, 1948. xv, 417, xxii, [1] p. bibliog. (p. 409-17), notes. Introduction on the nature and ancestry of modern literary criticism; essays on Edmund Wilson, Yvor Winters, T. S. Eliot, Van Wyck Brooks, Constance Rourke, R. P. Blackmur, Kenneth Burke, and other critics, each representing a type or style of criticism; and "Conclusion: attempts at an integration." [1439

JUSTIN BROOKS ATKINSON. Yankee on Broadway: in an extraordinary interview Brooks Atkinson tells his own story. [Reported] by Dom Bonafede. Nieman reports, 14(4):10-13 (Oct). Interview in 1960 on the author's life in journalism since 1917 and his career as a dramatic critic. [1440

ERNEST PHILIP BOLLIER. T. S. Eliot and The sacred wood [1920]. Colo. quar., 8:308-17 (spring). On a volume of "essays on poetry and criticism." [1441

ALLEN TATE. Collected essays. Denver: A. Swallow [1959]. xviii, 578 p. Forty-three critical essays, 1928-53, including "The present function of criticism," "Understanding poetry," "The profession of letters in the South," "The new provincialism," "What is a traditional society?" "Religion and the Old South," "The man of letters in the modern world," "A Southern mode of the imagination," and other essays on critical topics, and essays on Emily Dickinson, Hart Crane, John Peale Bishop, T. S. Eliot, Ezra Pound, Edwin Arlington Robinson, Archibald MacLeish, and Edgar Allan Poe. [1442

WILBUR MERRILL FROHOCK. Lionel Trilling and the American reality. Southw. rev., 45:224-32 (summer). Commentary on his critical writings (1930s-50s) concerning American, British, and continental cultures, particularly literature, and his inadequate knowledge of American culture outside New York City; with an analysis of his one novel, The middle of the journey (1947). [1443

RICHARD CROWDER. Robinson's Talifer [1933]: the figurative texture. Boston Univ. studies in Eng., 4:241-7 (winter). notes. On characteristics of this poem by Edward Arlington Robinson that were not noted by Allen Tate, R. P. Blackmur, Emery Neff, and Yvor Winters and that suggest "what may be a tendency among scholars and critics to ignore the real qualities of a relatively straightforward narrative poem." [1444

Poetry

NORMAN S. GRABO. Catholic tradition, Puritan literature, and Edward Taylor. Mich. Acad. Science, Papers, 45:395-402. notes. On the Catholic inspiration of his poetry, 1662-1725. [1445

EDWARD TAYLOR (1642-1729). The earliest poems of Edward Taylor. [Edited by] Donald E. Stanford. Am. lit., 32:136-51 (May). notes. Five hitherto unpublished poems, of which the first is dated 1662 and the last 1666. [1446

EDWARD TAYLOR (1642-1729). The poems of Edward Taylor. Edited by Donald E. Stanford. With a foreword by Louis L. Martz. New Haven: Yale Univ. Press, 1960. lxii, 543 p. facsim. bibliog. (p. 499-521), notes. Based upon Stanford's thesis--Stanford Univ., 1954. "Preparatory meditations before my approach to the Lords Supper." 217 poems, 1682-1725, called Sacramental meditations by Taylor's grandson, Ezra Stiles (p. 3-384); "God's determinations touching His elect," undated (p. 385-459); and "Miscellaneous poems" (p. 461-98); with a biographical sketch and an account of the manuscripts and their previous printings (by the editor), a study of the sources and the quality of the poems and the ideas that they convey (by Martz, p. xiii-xxxvii), and a description of Taylor's sermons and other prose works. [1447

PHILIP MORIN FRENEAU (1752-1832). Poems of Freneau. Edited with a critical introduction by Harry Hayden Clark. N.Y.: Hafner Pub. Co. [1960, c1929]. lxiii, 425 p. bibliog. (p. lxi-lxiii). (The Hafner library of classics, 19.) Poems, separately printed at various times after the 1770s, many of which were collected in a volume published in 1809, first issued in the Clark edition in 1929, with full notes and an extensive biographical and critical introduction. [1448

GORDON E. BIGELOW. Rhetoric and American poetry of the early national period [1775-1815]. Gainesville: Univ. of Florida Press, 1960. [8], 77, [1] p. bibliog. (p. 76-7), notes. (University of Florida monographs. Humanities, 4.) On the poetry and oratory of Philip Freneau, Joel Barlow, David Humphreys, Timothy Dwight, John Trumbull, Francis Hopkinson, Robert Treat Paine, and some of their contemporaries. [1449

JOHN GREENLEAF WHITTIER (1807-92.) Whittier. Selected with an introduction and notes, by Donald Hall. [N.Y.: Dell Pub. Co., 1960.] 159 p.

port. notes (p. 157-9). (The laurel poetry series, LB148.) Biographical and critical introduction and undated texts. [1450

NORMAN FERDINAND CHRISTENSEN. The imagery of William Cullen Bryant [1811 ff.]. Ann Arbor: University Microfilms, 1960. Positive microfilm of typescript. [219] leaves. Thesis--Univ. of Wisconsin. Abstracted: Dissert. abstracts, 21:195 (Jul). [1451

ALBERT F. McLEAN, JR. Bryant's "Thanatopsis" [1817, 1821]: a sermon in stone. Am. lit., 31:474-9 (Jan). notes. On the resemblance of the form of the poem to that of a sermon. [1452

EDGAR ALLAN POE (1809-49). Poe: complete poems [1827-49]. With an introduction and notes by the general editor [Richard Wilbur. N.Y.: Dell Pub. Co., 1959.] 159, [1] p. bibliog. (p. 39-40), notes (p. 118-52). (The Laurel poetry series, LB120.) [1453

AMHERST COLLEGE. Emily Dickinson [1830-86]: three views. ... Papers delivered at Amherst College as part of its observance of the bicentennial celebration of the town of Amherst, Massachusetts, on October 23, 1959. Amherst: Amherst College Press [1960]. 46 p. Contents.--Introduction, by Reginald F. French.--The private world, by Archibald MacLeish.--A mystical poet, by Louise Bogan.--Sumptuous destitution, by Richard Wilbur. [1454

DONALD ANDREW HALL. Whittier. Tex. quar., 3(3):165-74 (autumn). Review and critique of his poetry, 1830s-80s, and the ideas expressed in it. [1455

JOHN STEWART WHEATCROFT. Emily Dickinson [1830-86] and the orthodox tradition. Ann Arbor: University Microfilms, 1960. Positive microfilm of typescript. [390] leaves. Thesis--Rutgers Univ. Abstracted: Dissert. abstracts, 21:1186-7 (Nov). [1456

HARRY OSTER. Whittier's use of the sage in his ballads. Waldo McNeir & Leo B. Levy, eds., Studies in American literature (Baton Rouge: Louisiana State Univ. Press, 1960 [Louisiana State University studies, Humanities series, 8]), p. 58-77. notes. On his poetic development of a type of folk tale that "purports to be an account of an extraordinary happening believed to have actually occurred," 1831-90, illustrated in several of his New England poems and in "Barbara Frietchie." [1457

JOHN BENEDICT PICKARD. Whitter's ballads: the maturing of an artist [1831-77]. Essex Inst. hist. col., 96: 56-72 (Jan). notes. Based on thesis--Univ. of Wisconsin. [1458

SUSAN B. RILEY. Albert Pike as an American Don Juan. Ark. hist. quar., 19:207-24 (autumn). notes. On his "Los tiempos," a "long autobiographical poem in which he set down, Don-Juan like, his experiences and dreams and his comments on society, institutions, and government," consisting of 12 cantos in ottava rima, published in the Arkansas advocate (Little Rock), 1833-36, never reprinted as a whole though parts were later published as separate poems; with an introductory account of his indebtedness to Byron and other English Romantic poets. [1459

HENRY DAVID THOREAU (1817-62). A new Thoreau poem--"To Edith." [Edited] by Kenneth Walter Cameron. Emerson Soc. quar., 18: leaves 40-41 (1st quar.). Facsimile reproduction of a manuscript, apparently a copy in Emerson's hand, of a poem addressed to Emerson's infant daughter Edith, born 22 Nov. 1841. [1460

RALPH S. GRABER. New light on the dedication of Richard Henry Wilde's Hesperia. Ga. hist. quar., 44:97-9 (Mar). notes. Evidence confirming previous indications that the Marchesa Manfredina di Cosenza, to whom this undated poem (published after his death, which occurred in 1847) was dedicated, was Ellen (Adair) White-Beatty (1801-84). [1461

EDGAR ALLAN POE (1809-49). A note on Pliny Earle and Edgar Allan Poe. [Edited by] Jerome M. Schneck. Am. jour. psychiatry, 116:73 (Jul 1959). bibliog. Letter to H. S. Root, dated New York, 28 Jun. 1849, on the poetry of Dr. Earle (psychiatrist, a founder of the American Psychiatric Association). [1462

ADOLPH BURNETT BENSON. Jenny Lind in English and American verse. Am. Swed. Hist. Found., Yr. bk., 1957, p. 40-56. notes. Includes reference to American verse inspired by her tour of America, 1850-53; with several texts. [1463

HENRY HARBAUGH (1817-67). Heemweh. Mennonite hist. bul.,

17(2):2-3 (Apr 1956). port. Text in Pennsylvania Dutch and translation by author of an undated poem (1850?), expressing nostalgic memories of his childhood and his dead parents and the consolations offered by religion. [1464

ROWENA REVIS JONES. Emily Dickinson's "flood subject": immortality [1850s-80s]. Ann Arbor: University Microfilms, 1960. Positive microfilm of typescript. [285] leaves. Thesis--Northwestern Univ. Abstracted: Dissert. abstracts, 21: 1554-5 (Dec). [1465

ALFREDO RIZZARDI. La condizione americana: studi su poeti nordamericani. [n. p.:] F. Cappelli [1959]. 283 p. ports. notes. (Saggi e monografie di letteratura.) Essays on the poetry of Herman Melville, 1850s-70s, and of Wallace Stevens, Ezra Pound, E. E. Cummings, and Robert Lowell, 20th century, and on "La poesia americana nel secondo dopoguerra." [1466

FREDERICK GODDARD TUCKERMAN (1821-73). The cricket. [Edited by Mordecai Marcus.] Mass. rev., 2:33-8 (winter). Undated poem (1850?), "taken literally from the draft penciled in Tuckerman's notebook." Previously published in 1950. [1467

WILLIAM CULLEN BRYANT (1794-1878). Bryant's Crystal Palace choral. [Edited by Earle E. Coleman and David V. Erdman.] N.Y. Pub. Lib., Bul., 64:476-7 (Sep). facsims. Two manuscript texts and reprinted anonymous newspaper text of a poem consisting ultimately of 3 quatrains, 1852. [1468

LOREN K. DAVIDSON. Whitman's "Song of myself" [1855]. Ann Arbor: University Microfilms, 1959 [i. e. 1960]. Positive microfilm of typescript. [590] leaves. Thesis--Duke Univ. Abstracted: Dissert. abstracts, 20:4097-8 (Apr). Includes an account of revisions, 1856-82. [1469

JOHN R. DOYLE, JR. The poetry of Walt Whitman [1855 ff.]. Eng. studies in Africa, 3:35-47 (Mar). notes. [1470

KARL JAY SHAPIRO. The first white aboriginal. Karl Shapiro, In defense of ignorance (N.Y.: Random House [1960]), p. 187-204. On the poetry of Walt Whitman, 1855-90s; with some account of the Whitman criticism of D. H. Lawrence. [1471

SUZANNE MARIE WILSON. Structure and imagery patterns in the poetry of Emily Dickinson [1858 to [886]. Ann Arbor: University Microfilms, 1959 [i. e. 1960]. Positive microfilm of typescript. [196] leaves. Thesis--Univ. of Southern California. Abstracted: Dissert. abstracts, 20:3286-7 (Feb). [1472

WILLIAM CARLOS WILLIAMS (1883-1963). Measure--a loosely assembled essay on poetic measure. Spectrum, 3:131-57 (fall 1959). Includes comments on Sidney Lanier, The science of English poetry (1868), and on "The American idiom." [1473

JOHN LOVELL, JR. Appreciating Whitman: "Passage to India." Mod. lang. quar., 21: 131-41 (Jun). notes. On the qualities of a poem written in 1869 and included in Leaves of grass in the edition of 1881. [1474

KARL JAY SHAPIRO. Poets of the cosmic consciousness. Karl Shapiro, In defense of ignorance (N.Y.: Random House [1960]), p. 287-312. Evidence from American poetry since the late 19th century "of the capacity of the individual consciousness to experience a sense of total unity with all Nature, or the universe, or some degree of that experience," and argument that the idea of "a deep and irreconcilable division between Science and Art, between Reason and Imagination ... is perpetuated and restated from time to time, not by artists or scientists but by theoreticians, literary critics, and cultural opportunists." [1475

NELSON A. AULT. The sea-imagery in Melville's Clarel [1876]. State College Wash., Research studies, 27: 72-84 Jun 1959). notes. [1476

DANIEL FUCHS. The comic spirit of Wallace Stevens [1879-1955]: an aspect of the poet's mind. Ann Arbor: University Microfilms, 1960. Positive microfilm of typescript. [289] leaves. Thesis--Columbia Univ. Abstracted: Dissert. abstracts, 21:891-2 (Oct). [1477

ALAN B. OSTROM. The poetic world of William Carlos Williams [1883-1963]. Ann Arbor: University Microfilms, 1959 [i. e. 1960]. Positive microfilm of typescript. viii, 220 leaves. bibliog. (leaves 219-20). Thesis--Columbia Univ. Abstracted: Dissert. abstracts, 20:3748-9 (Mar). [1478

WALT WHITMAN (1819-92). Last words. [N.Y.: Kindle Press, 1959. 4]p.

Undated, previously unpublished manuscript poem, 5 lines; with an account of the poem (written in 1889 or early 1890 in successive drafts) by Harold W. Blodgett. [1479

JOHN F. LYNEN. The pastoral art of Robert Frost. New Haven: Yale Univ. Press, 1960. xii, [2], 208, [2] p. bibliog. (p. 191-202), notes. (Yale studies in English, 147.) Based on thesis--Yale Univ. On his poetry about country life and rural scenes, 1890-1959, regarded as a form of composition. [1480

FREDERICK WILLIS ECKMAN. The language of American poetry, 1900-1910. Ann Arbor: University Microfilms, 1954 [i. e. 1960]. Positive microfilm of typescript. [338] leaves. Thesis--Ohio State Univ. Abstracted: Dissert. abstracts, 20:2798-800 (Jan). [1481

LOUISE IMOGEN GUINEY (1861-1920). Louise I. Guiney on American women poets. [Edited by William L. Lucey.] Boston Pub. Lib. quar., 12:110-14 (Apr). notes. Letters to the Rev. William Garrett Horder, dated Oxford, 4 Feb. and 21 Apr. 1902. [1482

LUCY DICKINSON FRYXELL. Edwin Arlington Robinson as dramatist and dramatic poet. Ann Arbor: University Microfilms, 1955 [i. e. 1960]. Positive microfilm of typescript. vi, 153 leaves. bibliog. (leaves 144-53). Thesis--Univ. of Kentucky. Abstracted: Dissert. abstracts, 20: 4110-11 (Apr). Mainly on the dramatic structure of his narrative poems after 1904. [1483

KARL JAY SHAPIRO. Ezra Pound: the scapegoat of modern poetry. Karl Shapiro, In defense of ignorance (N.Y.: Random House [1960]), p. 61-85. On the "style" of his poetry, 1905-60, and his relationship with T. S. Eliot. [1484

NICLAS CHRISTOPH JOHN DE NAGY. The poetry of Ezra Pound: the pre-imagist stage [1908-12]. Bern: Francke [1960]. 183 p. bibliog. (p. 179-83), notes (p. 149-75). (The Cooper monographs on English and American language and literature, 4.) [1485

JOHN R. DOYLE, JR. Experiment in early twentieth-century American poetry. Eng. studies in Africa, 3:131-45 (Sep). Remarks on verses of T. S. Eliot, Ezra Pound, E. E. Cummings, Wallace Stevens, and Hart Crane, all undated. [1486

KARL JAY SHAPIRO. T. S. Eliot: the death of literary judgment. Karl Shapiro, In defense of ignorance (N.Y.: Random House [1960]), p. 35-60. Severe criticism of his poetry, 1910 ff. [1487

HENRY HIRSCH WASSER. A note on Eliot and Santayana. Boston Univ. studies in Eng., 4:125-6 (summer). notes. On the phrase "not with a bang" in Santayana's Three philosophical poets (1910) as a possible source of Eliot's "Not with a bang but a whimper" in "The hollow men." [1488

VIVIAN CONSTANCE HOPKINS. Robert Frost: out far and in deep [1912-57]. West. humanities rev., 14:247-63 (summer). notes. [1489

HAMMETT W. SMITH. Karl Jay Shapiro [born 1913]: a poet of human relations. CLA jour., 1:97-100 (Mar 1958). Deals particularly with his reference to Negroes. [1490

RICHARD M. GOLLIN. Wallace Stevens: the poet in society [1914-55]. Colo. quar., 9:47-58 (summer). [1491

RICHARD G. LANDINI. Vorticism and The cantos of Ezra Pound [1914 ff.]. West. humanities rev., 14:173-81 (spring). notes. [1492

A GUIDE to Ezra Pound's Cantos [I-X, 1917-48]. Analyst, 1-8, 11: irregular installments (Mar 1953 - Jul 1956). Contributions by E. M. Glenn, Donald H. Tritschler, Thelma Balagot, Robert Schneideman, Robert Mayo, Sybil Wuletich, and Anthony Manganaris-Decavalles, identifying persons, places, and things named in the poems, referring to sources, explaining allusions, correcting factual errors, translating passages in foreign languages, noting solecisms in Pound's Latin and other foreign languages, and divining his intentions. [1493

FRANCIS OTTO MATTHIESSEN (1902-50). The achievement of T. S. Eliot: an essay on the nature of poetry [1917 ff.]. ... With a chapter on Eliot's later work by C. L. Barber. Third edition. N.Y.: Oxford Univ. Press, 1959 [c1958]. xxiii, 248, [1] p. notes. (A Galaxy book, GB22.) 1st ed. 1935. [1494

ALLEN AUSTIN. T. S. Eliot's objective correlative. Univ. Kan. City rev., 26:133-40 (Dec). notes. Effort "to determine what Eliot means by the term," used by him in 1919, "and to relate it both to Eliot's poetic theory and to contemporary poetic theory." [1495

FRANK DOGGETT. Abstraction and Wallace Stevens. Criticism, 2:23-37 (winter). notes. On the "character of the abstract and the specific in Stevens' poems," 1920s-50s. [1496

GORDON KAY GRIGSBY. The modern long poem: studies in thematic form. Ann Arbor: University Microfilms, 1960. Positive microfilm of typescript. [492] leaves. Thesis--Univ. of Wisconsin. Abstracted: Dissert. abstracts, 21:622-3 (Sep). Examination of T. S. Eliot's The waste land and Four quartets, Ezra Pound's Cantos, Hart Crane's The bridge, and William Carlos Williams's Paterson, 1920-40s. [1497

JAY HERBERT MARTIN. Conrad Aiken: a life of his art [1920s-50s]. Ann Arbor: University Microfilms, 1960. Positive microfilm of typescript. [281] leaves. Thesis--Ohio State Univ. Abstracted: Dissert. abstracts, 21:900-901 (Oct). [1498

PAUL A. OLSON. Pound and the poetry of perception [1920-56]. Thought, 35:331-48 (autumn). notes. [1499

JOSEPH NEILL RIDDEL. The never-ending meditation: a study of myth metaphor and the poetry of order in the works of Wallace Stevens [1920s-50s]. Ann Arbor: University Microfilms, 1960. Positive microfilm of typescript. [564] leaves. Thesis--Univ. of Wisconsin. Abstracted: Dissert. abstracts, 21:627-8 (Sep). [1500

JAMES GRANVILLE SOUTHWORTH. The poetry of Richard Wilbur [born 1921]. College Eng., 22:24-9 (Oct). [1501

FRANCIS W. WARLOW. Marianne Moore: unfalsifying sun and solid gilded star. Ann Arbor: University Microfilms, 1959 [i. e. 1960]. Positive microfilm of typescript. [442] leaves. Thesis--Univ. of Pennsylvania. Abstracted: Dissert. abstracts, 20:2814 (Jan). Study of her poetry, mainly since 1921. [1502

BERNARD BENSTOCK. All the world a stage: the elements of drama in the poetry of E. E. Cummings [1923 to 1950]. Waldo McNeir & Leo B. Levy, eds., Studies in American literature (Baton Rouge: Louisiana State Univ. Press, 1960 [Louisiana State University studies, Humanities series, 8]), p. 104-31. notes. [1503

LAURENCE SANFORD DEMBO. Hart Crane and Samuel Greenberg: what is plagiarism? Am. lit., 32:319-21 (Nov). notes. Evidence that Crane's "Emblems of conduct" (1924) is more than "a composite of lines adapted from three sonnets by Samuel Greenberg, a then unknown poet who had died of tuberculosis in 1923." [1504

KARL F. KNIGHT. Love as symbol in the poetry of [John Crowe] Ransom [1924-47]. Miss. quar., 13:132-40 (summer). notes. [1505

JOSEPH WARREN BEACH (1880-1957). Obsessive images: symbolism in poetry of the 1930's and 1940's. ... Edited by William Van O'Connor. Minneapolis: Univ. of Minnesota Press [1960]. xii, [4], 396 p. bibliog. (p. 379-82). Described by the editor as "clearly an unfinished book." [1506

RAYMOND ALLEN COOK. Robert Frost: poetic astronomer. Emory Univ. quar. 16:32-9 (spring). On poems by Frost that reveal "his abiding interest in the motions and meanings of the heavenly bodies," 1930-49. [1507

LAWRENCE SANFORD DEMBO. Hart Crane's Sanskrit charge: a study of The bridge [1930]. Ithaca, N.Y.: Cornell Univ. Press [1960]. xii, 137 p. notes. Based on thesis--Cornell Univ., 1955. [1508

DONALD BURTON KUSPIT. Some images and themes in Hart Crane's The bridge [1930]. Jahrbuch für Amerikastudien, 5:164-74. notes. [1509

KARL JAY SHAPIRO. What is not poetry? Karl Shapiro, In defense of ignorance (N.Y.: Random House [1960]), p. 263-85. On the author's experience as a critic of poetry since ca. 1935, including service as editor of Poetry magazine; with "remarks ... not consecutive or logical" which "will attempt to point the way back to a poetry which is not restrained or informed by Modern Criticism or the poetry that has been written out of this criticism." [1510

FELIX CLOWDER. The bestiary of T. S. Eliot. Prairie schooner, 34:30-37 (spring). Explication of his Old Possum's book of practical cats (1939) as a more recondite poetical communication than ailurophiles have realized. [1511

ROBERT STUART FITZGERALD. Notes on American poetry after 1945. Am. rev., 1(1):127-35 (autumn). [1512

HARVEY SEYMOUR GROSS. Pound's Cantos [1948 ff.] and the idea of history. Bucknell rev., 9:14-31 (Mar). notes. [1513

WALTER SUTTON. Dr. Williams' "Paterson" and the quest for form. Criticism, 2:242-59 (summer). notes. On a poem by William Carlos Williams (1951, 1958). [1514

THE STUDY AND TEACHING OF LITERATURE

RICHARD MOTT GUMMERE. Some classical side lights on colonial education. Classical jour., 55:223-32 (Feb). notes. On classical languages and literatures in college curricula and their influence upon college men, 1636-1789. [1515

PORTER GALE PERRIN. Freshman composition and the tradition of rhetoric. National Council of Teachers of English, Perspectives on English: essays to honor W. Wilbur Hatfield, ed. Robert C. Pooley (N.Y.: Appleton-Century-Crofts [1960]), p. 119-32. notes. On the "background of rhetoric" in the "historical pattern of college instruction in composition," 1776-1960. [1516

PAUL EUGENE RIED. The Boylston Chair of Rhetoric and Oratory [Harvard, 1806-1959]. West. speech, 24:83-8 (spring). notes. On the gradual shift of emphasis, under successive incumbents in the Chair, from classical oratory to philology, grammar, oral interpretation, and ultimately poetics, and "from speech to writing, invention to grammar and style, classical rhetoric to modern poetics, and finally, to the attitude that speech is not a part of rhetoric, or if it is, that it is of secondary importance." [1517

PAUL EUGENE RIED. The philosophy of American rhetoric as it developed in the Boylston Chair of Rhetoric and Oratory at Harvard University [1806-1959]. Ann Arbor: University Microfilms, 1959 [i. e. 1960]. Positive microfilm of typescript. viii, 326 leaves. facsims. bibliog. (leaves 188-96). Thesis--Ohio State Univ. Abstracted: Dissert. abstracts, 20: 2961-2 (Jan). [1518

PAUL EUGENE RIED. Joseph McKean [1776-1818]: the second Boylston Professor of Rhetoric and Oratory [Harvard, 1809-18]. Quar. jour. speech, 46:419-24 (Dec). notes. Information from the 500-page manuscript of his lectures, with a list of the 41 lectures. [1519

EMERSON SOCIETY. [Essays on the teaching of Thoreau to college students.] Emerson Soc. quar., 18: leaves 2-26 (1st quar.). Brief contributions by Raymond Adams, John C. Broderick, Robert P. Cobb, Reginald L. Cook, Frank Davidson, Walter Harding, Alexander Kern, Kenneth Kurtz, Leo Marx, Andrew Schiller, Ethel Seybold, Carl F. Strauch, and Odell Shepard. [1520

DONALD EDGAR STAHL. The development of the English curriculum in the Chicago Public High Schools from 1856 to 1958. Ann Arbor: University Microfilms, 1960. Positive microfilm of typescript. [309] leaves. Thesis (Ed. D.)--Northwestern Univ. Abstracted: Dissert. abstracts, 21: 1121-2 (Nov). [1521

JOSEPH E. MERSAND. The teaching of literature in American high schools, 1865-1900. National Council of Teachers of English, Perspectives on English: essays to honor W. Wilbur Hatfield, ed. Robert C. Pooley (N.Y.: Appleton-Century-Crofts [1960]), p. 269-302. notes. [1522

ROBERT CECIL POOLEY. Introduction: W[alter] Wilbur Hatfield [born 1882]. National Council of Teachers of English, Perspectives on English: essays to honor W. Wilbur Hatfield (N.Y.: Appleton-Century-Crofts [1960]), p. 1-8. On his early life in Pittsfield, Ill., his studies at Illinois College, Jacksonville, his teaching of English in Chicago high schools and at Chicago Teachers College, and his services to the National Council of Teachers of English. [1523

HERSCHEL CLAY BAKER. Hyder Edward Rollins [1889-1958]. Harv. Lib. bul., 14:5-11 (winter). On his studies of the literature of the English Renaissance and the poetry of John Keats and his service as Gurney Professor of English at Harvard. [1524

JAMES DONALD ADAMS. Copey of Harvard: a biography of Charles Townsend Copeland [1860-1952]. Boston: Houghton Mifflin, 1960. [12], 306 p. cartoon, ports., views. bibliog. (p. 287-90). On his service in the Department of English of Harvard University, mainly in conducting courses in composition,

1893-1928, a period in which he "left his imprint upon more lives in their budding period than any other American teacher of his time"; with some account of his early life in Calais, Me., his studies at Harvard and the Harvard Law School, his brief career as a dramatic critic for Boston newspapers, and his eccentric personal habits and classroom mannerisms, the subject of many anecdotes. [1525

A COPELAND anthology. Harvard alumni bul., 55:19-23 (27 Sep 1952). cartoon, ports. Anecdotes and tributes by 6 persons (5 reprinted from various sources, 1914-36) celebrating Charles Townsend Copeland (1860-1952) as a teacher of English at Harvard, 1893-1928. [1526

DON MARION WOLFE. J[oseph] Milton French [born 1895]. Rudolf Kirk & Charles Frederick Main, eds., Essays in literary history, presented to J. Milton French (New Brunswick, N.J.: Rutgers Univ. Press [1960]), p. 3-12. On his early life in Randolph, Mass., his studies at Harvard, and his teaching of English at several colleges and universities, eventually as head of the Department of English in Rutgers University; with particular notice of his studies of John Milton. [1527

REMEDIOS O. CABEL. A study of the development of the English curriculum in the Philippines public secondary schools since 1900. Centro Escolar Univ., Graduate and faculty studies, 10 (1959): 1-17. notes. [1528

PATRICK S. COLLINS. The classics in translation. Cath. educ. rev., 58: 374-81 (Sep). On the teaching of Greek and Latin classics in English translations in American colleges and universities, 1909-59. [1529

NATIONAL COUNCIL OF TEACHERS OF ENGLISH. Golden anniversary. [Champaign? Ill.] ©1960. 64 p. facsims., ports., views. Essays by various contributors on the work of the National Council of Teachers of English, 1910-60, and on the teaching of English in American schools. [1530

WILLIAM SMITH WARD. A short history of the NCTE College Section. College Eng., 22:71-6 (Nov). On the interest of the National Council of Teachers of English in college teaching, 1911-60. [1531

HENRY ROBINSON SHIPHERD. Spring comes to Gerry's Landing. Harvard alumni bul., 52:442, 467 (11 Mar). Memories of the gathering held in the house of Prof. Kenneth Webster in the spring of 1914 for "men coming up that year for the doctorate in modern languages" and "the men under whose guidance they had been working for years past," and the "burlesque oral examination" of Prof. William Henry Schofield conducted on that occasion by Prof. George Lyman Kittredge. [1532

CHARLES W. FERGUSON. McGinnis: portrait of an individual. Southw. rev., 45:197-203 (summer). port. Memories of John Hathaway McGinnis (1884?-1960), teacher of English at Southern Methodist University (1915 ff.), "a legend and an inspiration to generations of students," editor of the Southwest review (1927-43), promoter of the establishment of the Southern Methodist University Press; with anecdotes of his eccentricities and his "strength of individuality." [1533

JOHN NASH DOUGLAS BUSH. Bliss Perry. Harvard alumni bul., 53:194-6 (25 Nov 1950). port. Memories of his teaching of American and English literature in the early 1920s. [1534

CHARLES CARPENTER FRIES. Linguistic science and the teaching of English [1920-60]. National Council of Teachers of English, Perspectives on English: essays to honor W. Wilbur Hatfield, ed. Robert C. Pooley (N.Y.: Appleton-Century-Crofts [1960]), p. 133-55. table. notes. [1535

HELEN KATHERINE MACKINTOSH. Let them all read. National Council of Teachers of English, Perspectives on English: essays to honor W. Wilbur Hatfield, ed. Robert C. Pooley (N.Y.: Appleton-Century-Crofts [1960]), p. 13-24. notes. On principles of teaching literature to children in elementary schools, 1922-59. [1536

LORENA E. KEMP. Dr. Bertram L. Woodruff [died 1957]. CLA jour., 1:93-6 (Mar 1958). On his teaching of English at West Virginia State College, 1942-49, 1952-57. [1537

Music

ALAN P. MERRIAM. Ethnomusicology: discussion and definition of the field. Ethnomusicol., 4:107-14 (Sep). bibliog. [1538

BRUNO NETTL. Music in primitive culture. Cambridge: Harvard Univ. Press, 1956. xviii, [2], 182, [18] p. music. bibliog. (p. 145-66), notes (p. 167-74). See "American primitive music north of Mexico" (p. 105-19), "African and New World Negro music" (p. 120-33), and "Examples of primitive music." [1539

TALMAGE WHITMAN DEAN. The organ in eighteenth century English colonial America. Ann Arbor: University Microfilms, 1960. Positive microfilm of typescript. [276] leaves. Thesis--Univ. of Southern California. Abstracted: Dissert. abstracts, 21:1583 (Dec). [1540

BRADFORD HARRISON III. A chronology of jazz [1700-1956]. Music jour., 18(1):62, 102 (Jan). [1541

GEORGE ROBINSON RICKS. Some aspects of the religious music of the United States Negro: an ethnomusicological study with special emphasis on the Gospel tradition [since ca. 1700]. Ann Arbor: University Microfilms, 1960. Positive microfilm of typescript. [428] leaves. Thesis--Northwestern Univ. Abstracted: Dissert. abstracts, 21:1020-21 (Nov). [1542

RUTH G. FROST. Concerning Moravian music [in America since 1740]. Music jour., 18(8):34, 76-7 (Nov-Dec). port. [1543

DONALD MACOMBER McCORKLE. The Moravian contribution to American music [1740-1956]. Winston-Salem: Moravian Music Foundation, 1956. 10 p. (Moravian Music Foundation. Publications, 1.) From the Music Library Association's Notes, Sep. 1956. [1544

HORACE ERVIN. Mr. Franklin and Mr. Mozart. Am. record guide, 25: 308-11, 349-50 (Jan 1959). port., views. On Franklin's invention of the armonica ("the celebrated glassychord invented by Mr. B. Franklin of Philadelphia") in 1762, its great popularity during his years in Europe, and a composition for it by Wolfgang Mozart in 1791. [1545

IRVING LOWENS. Andrew Law and the pirates. Am. Musicol. Soc., Jour., 13:206-23. facsims. notes. On a copyright granted by the Connecticut legislature to Law protecting his musical publications for a period of 5 years, Oct. 1781, and the publications by him and others involved in "his long and acrimonious personal war with a succession of real and imagined literary pirates," 1774-1816. [1546

C. A. BROWNE. The story of our national ballads. ... Revised by Willard A. Heaps. N.Y.: Crowell [1960. 6], 314 p. bibliog. (p. 285-96). 1st ed. 1919. Separate chapters on 15 songs from Yankee Doodle to God bless America, and chapters on Civil War, Spanish-American War, World War I, and World War II songs, ca. 1775 to 1945. [1547

MARY ELIZABETH KENT. Our musical Presidents. Music jour., 18(8):26, 75 (Nov-Dec). port. On American Presidents who composed music, performed on music instruments, sang, or merely showed an interest in music, 1778-1957. [1548

DOROTHY D. HORN. Tune detecting in 19th century hymnals. Tenn. Folklore Soc. bul., 26:99-109 (Dec). On "the melodic origins and antecedants [sic] of the hymns and tunes" in The Southern harmony (1854), The original sacred harp, and The new harp of Columbia (1867), involving an examination of 21 hymnals and songbooks, 1793-1864; with "List of alternative titles" of tunes. [1549

ERIC J. HOBSBAWM. The jazz scene. By Francis Newton [pseud.]. N.Y.: Monthly Review Press, 1960. 303 p. ports., tables, views. bibliog. (p. 296-8), discog. (p. 32-5), notes (p. 278-83). British account, written in 1958, of the development (mainly in America) of the music since ca. 1800, the musicians, the audience, and the business; with an appendix on "Jazz language." [1550

HENDRIK ROELOF ROOKMAAKER. Jazz, blues, spirituals [since ca. 1800]. Wageningen: Gebr. Zomer & Keuning [1960]. 219 p. facsims., ports., views. bibliog. (p. 203-4), notes (p. 205-12). On Negro music, particularly in the United States. Text in Dutch. [1551

ABRAHAM WOLD BINDER. The Jewish music movement in America [1818-1954] ... an informal lecture published in celebration of the American Jewish tercentenary. N.Y.: National Jewish Music Council, 1954. [2], 12 p. [1552

ARTHUR H. SANDERS. The banjo story. Hobbies, 65(1):33, 47 (Mar). On "the five-string banjo, America's only native instrument," invented by Ben and Joe Sweeney of South Carolina, brothers and wandering minstrels, ca. 1820, and long known as "Ben 'n Joe." [1553

KENNETH ANDERSON BERNARD. Lincoln and music. Ralph G. Newman, ed., Lincoln for the ages (Garden City, N.Y.: Doubleday, 1960), p. 338-43. On his fondness for music, exhibited as early as ca. 1830. [1554

WILLIAM HENRY GRATTAN FLOOD (1859-1928). Fair Harvard. Harvard alumni bul., 52:146-50, 180-81 (5 Nov 1949). music. From the Musical quarterly, Oct. 1919. On "My lodging it is on the cold ground," a tune presumed to be of Irish origin (published as early as 1775), "set to words" as a Harvard song by the Rev. Samuel Gilman in 1836. [1555

HENRI HERZ (1803/6-1888). Henri Herz's comments on musical taste in nineteenth century America. [Translated and edited by] Henry Bertram Hill and Larry Gara. Cent. Miss. Valley Am. Studies Assoc., Jour., 1(1): 17-22 (spring). notes. From his Mes voyages en Amérique (1866), on his 5-year tour of America as a concert pianist in the 1840s. [1556

WILLARD NILE RHODES. The Christian hymnology of the North American Indians [1845-1954]. International Congress of Anthropological and Ethnological Sciences, 5th, 1956, Men and cultures: selected papers, ed. Anthony F. C. Wallace (Phila.: Univ. of Pennsylvania Press [1960]), p. 324-31. music. notes. Appended: "Discography for the musical examples." [1557

JAN LA RUE. Melville and musicology. Ethnomusicol., 4:64-6 (May). Three excerpts from Typee (1846), describing musical instruments of a South Pacific island, and commentary on musicological information to be found in the work of travelers and others not specially concerned with music. [1558

ADOLF EDUARD ZUCKER. One hundred and ten years of German song. Am.-German rev., 26(6):10-11, 18 (Aug-Sep). port. On the Washington Sängerband, founded in 1851, and the Northeastern Sängerband, founded in 1850. [1559

PETER TAMONY. Jazz, the word. Jazz, 1:33-42 (Oct 1958). double facsim. notes. On its etymology, 1860-1958; with evidence that it may have been first recorded in its present use in 1913. [1560

CLAUDE TRIMBLE MARTIN. Parodies are compliments. By Deac Martin. Music jour., 18(6):28, 101 (Sep). On parodies of popular songs and folksongs since the Civil War. [1561

NOLBERT HUNT QUAYLE. American brass supreme. Music jour., 18(8): 50-51, 63 (Nov-Dec). On American brass instrumentalists, 1867?-1944? [1562

RUDOLPH PICKETT BLESH. Shining trumpets: a history of jazz [ca. 1870 to 1958]. By Rudi Blesh. Second edition, revised and enlarged. N.Y.: Knopf, 1958. xiv, 410, [24], xviii, [2] p. facsim., music, ports., views. notes. "List of records cited in the text" (p. 402-8). "Musical examples referred to in the text" ([24] p.). 1st ed. 1946. Includes a postscript (p. 342-81) on jazz since 1946. [1563

JAMES HENRY LYONS. A prophet passes. Am. record guide, 20:312-15, 343 (Jun 1954). port. On Charles Edward Ives, 1874-1954, and the problems of recording his compositions. [1564

ANGUS JOSS. Edison and the diamond disc. Am. record guide, 14:99-103, 139-44 (Dec 1947, Jan 1948). Reprinted: Record research, 19:3-8 (Sep-Oct 1958). ports., views. On his early experiments with a disc record in 1877 and his development of such a record (not long before he discontinued the cylinder record), 1910-29, ending with discontinuance of the Diamond Disc in competition with radio. [1565

ULYSSES WALSH. The phonograph 75 years ago [1877-1952]. Am. record guide, 18:359-64 (Aug 1952). port. [1566

MARGARET BRADFORD BONI, ed. Songs of the Gilded Age. ... Arranged for voice, piano, and guitar by Norman Lloyd. N.Y.: Golden Press [1960]. 156 p. col. cartoons (part double), music. Texts and tunes of 48 songs, 1883-1905 (and some undated), with historical headnotes by the editor and cartoons by Lucille Corcos. [1567

ADDISON FOSTER. Early methods of record manufacturing [1887 to ca. 1920].

Am. record guide, 19:35-40 (Oct 1952). diagrs. [1568

DUANE D. DEAKINS. Cylinder records: a description of the numbering systems, physical appearance, and other aspects of cylinder records made by the major American companies, with brief remarks about the earliest American companies and the foreign record manufacturers [1890-1913. Second edition.] Stockton, Calif. [1958. 2], 35, [1] p. facsims., tables. 1st ed. 1956. [1569

LEONARD G. FEATHER. The book of jazz: a guide to the field [1890s to 1957]. N.Y.: Horizon Press [1957]. viii, 280 p. music. discog. (p. 265-6), notes (p. 263-4). Reprinted with same title and collation, N.Y.: Meridian Books [1960]. (Meridian books, M67.) Includes a historical sketch, which denies the priority of New Orleans; 12 chapters on instruments and their master performers; and a chapter on "The anatomy of improvisation." [1570

NOLBERT HUNT QUAYLE. The old touring bands [1892-1932]. Music jour., 18(7):26 (Oct). On "the professional travelling concert band," which "became extinct" with the death of John Philip Sousa in 1932. [1571

ULYSSES WALSH. The funny side of the phonograph world. Am. record guide, 18:230-35, 262-5 (Apr, May 1952). Presents "a string of amusing anecdotes, arranged in no particular order," including anecdotes of President Taft (1912), "Mr. Edison's idiosyncrasies," "The big Victor fire" (Camden, N.J., 1904), and other subjects. [1572

COUNT BASIE [real name: William Basie]. The story of jazz ["from the New Orleans age to the present"]. Music jour., 18(8):16, 62 (Nov-Dec). port. Mainly reminiscences since ca. 1910. [1573

THOMAS ALVA EDISON (1847-1931). The Thomas A. Edison talent file. Record research, 19:9-10 (Sep-Oct 1958). Selected entries from Edison's "talent audition file," containing his personal comments on artists who recorded for him, 1914-29--e.g., "Awful," "Singer will be OK. If she can get rid cats on high (tremolo insignificant)," "Good if all tunes are as melodious like this." [1574

HARRY O. BRUNN. The story of the Original Dixieland Jazz Band. [Baton Rouge:] Louisiana State Univ. Press [1960]. xx, 268 p. facsims., ports., tables (part double), views. notes. On a band formed by Dominic James La Rocca (born 1889) in New Orleans in 1915, moved to Chicago in 1916 and to New York in 1917, disbanded in 1925, revived in 1936, and again disbanded, as a result of "internal friction," in 1938, when La Rocca returned to his business in New Orleans. Deals mainly with the personal relations among the members of the band (La Rocca, Edwin B. Edwards, Larry Shields, Anthony Sbarbaro, J. Russell Robinson, and others of shorter service). [1575

GEORGE GERSHWIN (1898-1937) & IRA GERSHWIN (born 1896). The George and Ira Gershwin song book. Foreword by Ira Gershwin. ... Arrangements by Albert Sirmay. [N.Y.:] Simon and Schuster [1960]. xiv, 178 p. col. facsims., music, ports. Forty songs (music and words), 1919-38. Appended (p. 171-7): "List of songs [1916-38] by George Gershwin with lyrics by Ira Gershwin and others, together with facts about the shows and motion pictures in which these songs were used, compiled by Alfred Simon." [1576

HUGUES PANASSIÉ. The real jazz [1920-60]. Revised and enlarged edition. N.Y.: Barnes [1960]. 284 p. bibliog. (p. 263-84), notes. 1st ed. 1942 (translation of a manuscript sent there in 1941 from France). Appended (p. 263-84): "Selection of the best jazz lp's available." [1577

MISCHA ELMAN. Chamber music as a hobby. Music jour., 18(4):10, 53 (Apr-May). port. On the author's establishment of and performance in a string quartet in New York City and on tour, "about 1924 or 1925" and for some time afterward. [1578

AARON COPLAND. The younger generation of American composers: 1926-59. Aaron Copland, Copland on music (Garden City, N.Y.: Doubleday, 1960), p. 141-78. "America's young men of promise" (from Modern Music, Mar.-Apr. 1926), "America's young men--ten years later" (from Modern music, May 1936), "The new 'school' of American composers" (from the New York Times magazine, 14 Mar. 1948), and "Postscript for the generation of the fifties," all undertaking "to discover the important composers of tomorrow among the young men of today." [1579

WILLIAM JAMES HENDERSON (1855-1937). Revisiting the "Golden(?) Age" with W. J. Henderson--an appreciation. By Philip L. Miller. Am. record guide, 25:566-9, 662-6 (May 1959). port. "Male singers put in their places" and "Female song birds duly noted," from Singing, Jan. and Feb. 1926, commenting on singers popular at that time; with editorial remarks on Henderson as a critic of music. [1580

ERNIE SMITH, ed. "Hot filmography": a limited listing. Record research, 29:6, 11 (Aug). Contemporary reviews (some from early issues of Variety) of 10 Vitaphone musical films, 1928-33. [1581

PETER TAMONY. Bop: the word. Jazz, 2:114-19 (spring 1959). notes. On the jazz terms rebop, bebop, and bop, 1928-58. [1582

VITTORIO FRANCHINI. L'era dello swing. Milano: G. Ricordi, 1960. 149, [6] p. bibliog. (p. 143), discog. (p. 139-41). notes. (Piccola biblioteca Ricordi, 13.) On mainly American developments, 1929-59, here studied largely from Italian recordings and Italian translations of American works. [1583

FRANKLIN S. DRIGGS. Washboard Rhythm Kings research. Record research, 29:7 (Aug). On recordings made by the Washboard Rhythm Kings in 1932 and by other "washboard groups": with oral recollections (recorded in 1957) by Ben Smith (born in Memphis ca. 1905) concerning Philadelphia and Camden jazz musicians, 1931-34. [1584

DUKE ELLINGTON [real name: Edward Kennedy Ellington]. A royal view of jazz. Jazz, 2:83-7 (spring 1959). On American jazz musicians and their popularity abroad as early as 1933; with reminiscences of the author's career in jazz. [1585

LEOPOLD ANTON STANISLAW STOKOWSKI. Leopold Stokowski talks on music and its reproduction with the editor. Am. record guide, 19: 137-42, 170-74 (Feb, Mar 1953). ports., view. Includes some account of efforts of Dr. Stokowski as early as 1934 to improve the quality of recording apparatus. [1586

HERBERT KUPFERBERG. Recordings of American operas [since 1935]. Music jour., 18(4):20-21, 71 (Apr-May). port. [1587

STANLEY DANCE. All too soon. Jazz rev., 1(2):16-17 (Dec 1958). ports. On the "deterioration of jazz" since 1937 as shown by "the number and duration of opportunities open to jazzmen to work as jazzmen," "the collapse of the big bands and increasing disinterest in their idiom," and "the virtual demise of the old-style jam session." [1588

GEORGE FRAZIER. Old tricks for new critics. Jazz, 1:3-8 (Oct 1958). On several jazz critics since 1937. [1589

JAMES HENRY LYONS. Riverdale Project: the story of Walter Toscanini and his father's recordings. Am. record guide, 22:127-9 (Apr 1956). ports. On his project to record permanently and with fidelity the performances of "the late NBC Symphony" conducted by Arturo Toscanini, 1937-53. [1590

EDWIN HUGHES. The National Music Council, 1940-1960. Natl. Music Council bul., 20(3):1-4 (spring). [1591

ROBERT B. CARNEAL. The reproduction of cylinder recordings at the Library of Congress [1941-60]. Folklore and folk music archivist, 3(3):[1, 4] (fall). [1592

ROBERT CROWLEY. Black, brown, and beige after 16 years. Jazz, 2:98-104 (spring 1959). On a composition advertised as "Duke Ellington's first symphony" and understood to be an "extensive work relating to Negro history," performed in Carnegie Hall, New York City, 23 Jan. 1943, and recorded in 1945. [1593

MICHAEL JAMES. Ten modern jazzmen: an appraisal of the recorded work of ten modern jazzmen. London: Cassell, 1960. xix, [3], 145 p. ports. Reprinted from Jazz monthly. Impressions formed by the critic from recordings made between 1945 and 1956. Includes comments on 8 Americans: Miles Davis (trumpeter), Stan Getz (tenor saxophonist), Dizzy Gillespie (trumpeter), Wardell Gray (alto saxophonist), John Lewis (pianist and arranger), Gerry Mulligan (baritone saxophonist and arranger), Charlie Parker (alto saxophonist), and Bud Powell (pianist). [1594

MUSICAL BIOGRAPHY

RICHARD ADDISON MONTAGUE. Charles Edward Horn: his life and works (1786-1849). Ann Arbor:

University Microfilms, 1959 [i.e. 1960]. Positive microfilm of typescript [212] leaves. Thesis (Ed.D.)--Florida State Univ. Abstracted: Dissert. abstracts, 20:3325 (Feb). On his work in America as "actor-singer, impresario, pianist, organist, teacher, conductor and publisher," adapter of foreign opera, composer of popular songs, collector of folk tunes and member of musical societies. [1595

NELSON LANSDALE. Memorials to Stephen Foster [1826-64]. Music jour., 18(1):48, 90 (Jan). views. On articles that he owned or used and places where he lived or which he visited, and the places where Foster memorabilia are now exhibited. [1596

FRANCES CAVANAH. A husband for the prima donna. Am. Swed. Hist. Found., Yr. bk., 1959, p. 7-13. On the marriage of Jenny Lind, at the age of 31, to her accompanist, Otto Goldschmidt, aged 23, at Boston, Feb. 1852; with a letter from "Jenny Goldschmidt" to Stephen Hopkins, Northampton bookseller, dated Dresden, 19 May 1858, thanking him for a gift of "maple-sap-sugar" and referring to the 2 Goldschmidt children. [1597

COLERIDGE ALEXANDER BRAITHWAITE. The life and creative activities of James Allen Bland (1854-1911). Savannah State College, Faculty research edition, 14(2):15-20 (Dec). bibliog., notes. On his early life in Flushing, N.Y., and Washington, his studies in Howard University, his work as an entertainer with minstrel shows, and his 700 songs; with a list of some of the songs, 1878-92. [1598

ALLEN G. DEBUS. The career and recordings of Frederick V. Bowers [born 1874]. Hobbies, 65(6):36, 84; (7): 37, 45 (Aug, Sep). ports. On his early life in Boston, his work as a singer in vaudeville and musical comedy, and his phonograph recordings (1910 ff.). [1599

BEN STINCHFIELD. Lillian Nordica [born Lillian Norton, 1858-1914]. Hobbies, 64(12):31-3; 65(1):32 (Feb, Mar). ports. On her career as a singer, 1876-1914. Appended: "Nordica records," by Randolph Gregory, on her 13 known recordings; and letters to Aida Favia-Artsay from R. B. Stone, denying that Nordica's voice deteriorated in her later years. [1600

ULYSSES WALSH. George Wilton Ballard [1877-1950]. Hobbies, 65(2): 34-5, 45, 53, 84 (Apr). ports. On his phonograph recordings, 1912-26; with an account of his early life in Syracuse, N.Y., and his work as a concert tenor. [1601

THERESE S. JOSE. The great Richard Jose. By Therese S. Jose as told to H. Hamlin. Pony Express, 24(6):3-6; (8):6 (Nov 1957, Jan 1958). facsims., ports. On Richard Juan Jose (1869-1941), emigrant from Cornwall in 1878, blacksmith in Reno, Nev., and his career from 1886 to 1932 as "America's foremost Contra-tenor, who was a sensation on three Continents, and perhaps the greatest the world has ever known." [1602

PAUL OLIVER. Blind Lemon Jefferson [1883?-1930]. Jazz rev., 2(7):9-12 (Aug 1959). On his life in Dallas and Chicago, originally as a "blues-singing beggar" and guitarist, maker of many recordings. [1603

Sir THOMAS BEECHAM, Bart. (1879-1961). Frederick Delius [1862-1934]. London: Hutchinson [1959]. 227, [1] p. map, ports., views. notes. Reprinted with same title and collation, N.Y.: Knopf, 1960. Includes a brief account of his journey from England to America, his establishment of a tobacco farm in Florida, his teaching of piano at Danville, Va., and at the Roanoke Female Seminary, and his return to England, 1884-86. [1604

RAY ELLSWORTH. In memory of a forgotten America. Am. record guide, 24:8-9 (Sep 1957). music, port. Tribute to Charles Tomlinson Griffes (1884-1920), composer. [1605

DAVID EWEN. The world of Jerome Kern: a biography. N.Y.: Holt [1960]. xii, [2], 178 p. cartoon, music, ports., views. On Jerome David Kern (1885-1945), his early life in New York City and Newark, his studies at the New York College of Music, and his work as a composer of musical comedy; with lists of his scores for Broadway stage productions, scores for motion pictures, instrumental music, "greatest songs," and "Selected recordings." [1606

MARTIN T. WILLIAMS. King Oliver. London: Cassell [1960. 6], 89, [1] p. ports. notes. discog. (p. 89-90). (Kings of jazz, 8.) On Joseph Oliver (1885-1938), native of New Orleans, jazz trumpeter, leader of King Oliver's Creole Jazz Band. [1607

EUGENE MATTHEW BECKER. John J[oseph] Becker [1886-1961], American composer. [Princeton, N.J., 1958. 1], 13 leaves. On his early life in Henderson, Ky., his studies at the Wisconsin Conservatory of Music, his teaching of music in 4 colleges, his service as Director of Music Projects of the State of Minnesota, and his work as a composer; with a selective list of his compositions (leaves 11-12) and publications (leaves 12-13). [1608

HORST HEINZ LANGE. Nick La Rocca: ein Porträt. Wetzlar: Pegasus Verlag [1960]. 48 p. ports. discog. (p. 43-8). (Jazz Bücherei, 8.) On Dominic James La Rocca (born 1889), of New Orleans, jazz cornettist, leader of the Original Dixieland Jazz Band in New Orleans, Chicago, and New York City. [1609

WILLIAM LEE CONLEY BROONZY (1893-1958). Big Bill's last session. [Recorded by] Studs Terkel. Jazz, 1:9-18 (Oct 1958). Tape-recorded interview with "Big Bill Broonzy," conducted in Cleveland shortly before his death, on his life as a jazz musician and composer. [1610

STANLEY GREEN. The world of musical comedy: the story of the American musical stage as told through the careers of its foremost composers and lyricists. N.Y.: Ziff-Davis Pub. Co. [1960]. xvi, [2], 391 p. Biographical sketches of 29 lyricists and composers, active from 1893 to 1960; with the author's reminiscences. Appended (p. 318-76): "Musical productions and discography." [1611

WARREN DODDS (1894-1959). The Baby Dodds story, as told to Larry Gara. Los Angeles: Contemporary Press, 1959. xiii, [3], 109 p. ports. notes. Edited from a tape recording of interviews concerning the author's early life as a New Orleans Negro and his career as a jazz drummer, terminated by his first stroke in 1949. [1612

VINCENT LOPEZ (born 1894). Lopez speaking: an autobiography. N.Y.: Citadel Press [1960]. 351 p. facsims., music, ports. On the author's early life in Brooklyn and his work as a professional pianist and leader of a dance band in America and abroad. [1613

JUDY BOUNDS COLEMAN. Charles [Edward] Ives [born 1874]: the man and his songs. Midwest quar., 1:295-320 (Jul). music. bibliog. On his work as a composer, 1898-1922. [1614

ALFRED VICTOR FRANKENSTEIN. "... a musical transcendentalism." John Arthur Garraty, ed., The unforgettable Americans (Great Neck, N.Y.: Channel Press [1960]), p. 323-6. On the work of Charles Ives as a composer, 1910-50. [1615

BURNETT JAMES. Bix Beiderbecke. London: Cassell [1959. 4], 90 p. music, ports. discog. (p. 80-90), notes. (Kings of jazz, 4.) On Leon Bismark Beiderbecke (1903-31), his early life in Davenport, Ia., and Chicago, and his work as a jazz pianist and cornettist; with a study of "just what he did and what he did not do as a practising jazz musician." [1616

CHARLES FOX. Fats Waller. London: Cassell [1960. 4], 89, [1] p. ports. notes. discog. (p. 84-90). (Kings of jazz, 7.) On Thomas Wright Waller (1904-43), jazz pianist, "comedian at the piano," Negro band leader. [1617

ULYSSES WALSH. Geoffrey O'Hara [born 1882]. Hobbies, 64(12):34-7, 47, 84 (Feb). ports. On his emigration from Canada to the United States in 1904 and his work as a singer, a composer of popular songs and operettas, and a staff member of the Department of the Interior in recording Indian music; with an account of his recordings, 1905-18. [1618

ULYSSES WALSH. Geoffrey O'Hara [born 1882]: singer and song writer. By Jim Walsh. Record research, 29:8 (Aug). On his early life in Canada, his removal to the United States in 1904, his work as a vaudeville entertainer, his service for the Department of the Interior in recording Navajo music in Arizona and for the Army as a "military song leader" during World War I, and his activities as a singer, composer of popular songs, and recording artist. [1619

HOWARD J. WATERS, JR. Jack Teagarden's music: his career and recordings. Stanhope, N.J.: W. C. Allen, c1960. [2], ix, 222 p. facsim., port. (Jazz monographs, 3.) On Weldon Leo Teagarden (born 1905), his early life in Texas and Nebraska, and his work as a jazz trombonist; with lists of his recordings (p. 42-210). [1620

RUTH BERGES. Mahler in America. Am.-German rev., 26(4):12-13 (Apr-May). On Gustav Mahler as an orchestral conductor and operatic conductor in New York and Boston and on tour, 1907-11. [1621

PETER HUGH REED. The Toscanini question. Am. record guide, 16: 319-23, 353-5 (Jun, Jul 1950). port. On his career as an orchestral conductor in the United States since 1908, and the poor quality of most of the recordings of his performances since 1929. [1622

WILBUR DE PARIS. Jazz and its audience. Music jour., 18(3):46, 105-6 (Mar). port. Observations on "the 50 years I've spent playing jazz." [1623

PETER HUGH REED & CHARLES A. JAHANT. The end of an era and one of its most memorable protagonists. Am. record guide, 17:77-80 (Nov 1950). port. On Giuseppe De Luca (1876-1950), native of Italy, singer, in the Metropolitan Opera, 1915-35, 1940, 1946. [1624

WALTER PAGE. About my life in music. ... As told to Frank Driggs. Jazz rev., 1(1):12-15 (Nov 1958). ports. On the author's early life and musical studies in Kansas City, ca. 1914 ff., his work as a jazz musician since 1923, and his organization and leadership of the Blue Devils band. [1625

JAMES P. JOHNSON. Conversations with James P. Johnson. [Recorded 2 years before he died, in the 1950s] by Tom Davin. Jazz rev., 2(5-7): monthly installments (Jun-Aug 1959). ports. On his life in Jersey City and New York City, his memories of early ragtime pianists, his distinction "from 1916 to 1930" as "the outstanding ragtime pianist and composer for piano in New York," and "the influence of his player-piano rolls" upon younger "cabaret ans sporting-house players." [1626

MILES KREUGER. From fortune to fame: the nonconventional Cole Porter--his life and works. Am. record guide, 25:584-7, 666 (May 1959). port., views. On his work as a composer for musical comedy since 1916; with "The complete Cole Porter discography," 1928-34. [1627

ULYSSES WALSH. Marguerite Farrell [1888-1951]. Hobbies, 65(1):34-5 (Mar). ports. On her phonograph recordings, 1916-22; with an account of her work as a singer in vaudeville and musical comedy. [1628

WERNER GÖTZE. Dizzy Gillespie: ein Porträt. Wetzlar: Pegasus Verlag [1960]. 48 p. ports. bibliog. (p. 48), discog. (p. 43-7). (Jazz Bücherei, 7.) On John Birks Gillespie (born 1917), his early life in South Carolina, and his career as a Negro jazz trumpeter. [1629

MARY JANE MATZ. Opera stars in the sun: intimate glimpses of Metropolitan personalities. N.Y.: Farrar, Straus, & Cudahy [1955]. xiv, 349 p. ports. (1 double). Brief sketches of 96 performers at the Metropolitan Opera House, New York City, 1917-55. [1630

GARVIN BUSHELL. Garvin Bushell and New York jazz in the 1930's. [Reported] by Nat Hentoff. Jazz rev., 2(1-3): monthly installments (Jan, Feb, Apr 1959). ports. Interview on Bushell's life in New York City as a professional jazz musician, 1919-23, and his adventures while on tour with jazz bands in the South and West. [1631

CONSTANTINE CALLINOCOS. The Mario Lanza story. By Constantine Callinicos with Ray Robinson. N.Y.: Coward-McCann [1960]. 256 p. ports. discog. (p. 251-6). On Mario Lanza, born Alfredo Arnold Cocozza (1921-59), his early life in Philadelphia, his work as a singer (with Callinicos as accompanist) in motion pictures and television in America and Italy, and the egregious self-indulgences that ended with his early death. [1632

AARON COPLAND. The conductor: Serge Koussevitzky. Aaron Copland, Copland on music (Garden City, N.Y.: Doubleday, 1960), p. 73-83. From Musical quarterly, Jul. 1944. On his work as conductor of the Boston Symphony Orchestra, 1922-44. [1633

EVANGELIA CALLAS [full name: Elmina Evangelia (Dimitroadis) Kalogeropoulos, born 1898]. My daughter Maria Callas [born 1923]. By Evangelia Callas in collaboration with Lawrence G. Blochman. N. Y.: Fleet Pub. Corp. [1960]. 186 p. ports., view. On the author's early life in Greece, her emigration to New York City with her husband in 1923, her return to Greece in 1938 in company with her daughter in order to promote the musical education of the latter, the return of Maria to New

York in 1945 and of her mother in 1946, the second return of the mother to Greece in 1949, her divorce by her husband (who had never returned to Greece) for desertion, her alienation from her daughter (an opera singer who developed "the 'prima donna disease'"), who after 1950 refused to see, support, or write to the mother, and the reasons "why Maria has turned against me." Apparently intended to publicize the undesirable traits and objectionable behavior of the father and the daughter and the blamelessness of the mother. [1634

RAY ELLSWORTH. The weird, wonderful world of Harry Partch. Am. record guide, 25:110-12 (Sep 1958). view. On a composer for very large "instruments of his own invention," in "a forty-three-tones-to-the-octave system of acoustic (not equal) intonation," 1923-58. [1635

GEORGE JELLINEK. Callas: portrait of a prima donna. N.Y.: Ziff-Davis Pub. Co. [1960]. xii, [2], 354 p. ports., tables (part double), view. On Maria Callas (name originally: Maria Anna Cecilia Sophia Kalogeropoulos), born in New York City of Greek emigrant parents in 1923, educated in Greece (1937-45), her marriage to and divorce from Giovanni Battista Meneghini, her career as an operatic singer in America and Europe, and the controversies about the quality of her voice and about her "temperamental" behavior; with lists of her repertoire (1944-57) and her recordings (1949-59). [1636

SIDNEY WALTER FINKELSTEIN. The music of Aaron Copland. Am. record guide, 17:290-94, 329-33 (May, Jun 1951). port. On his work as a composer since 1924 and as a musical theorist. [1637

VERNON DUKE (born Vladimir Dukelsky, 1903). Passport to Paris. Boston: Little, Brown [1955. 10], 502 p. ports. On the author's early life and musical education in Russia and France, his emigration to America in 1926, his work as a composer of musical comedies, and his very wide association with lyricists and producers. [1638

KATHRYN ELIZABETH SMITH (born 1910). Upon my lips a song. By Kate Smith. N.Y.: Funk & Wagnalls [1960. 8], 213 p. ports. On the author's work as a singer in musical comedy, radio, and television since 1926; with some account of her business manager, Ted Collins, formerly Recording Manager of the Columbia Phonograph Company, to whose judgment she attributes the great prosperity of her career. [1639

WOODY BACKENSTO. The Cass Hagen band of the 20's. Record research, 29:3-5 (Aug). port. On the work of Cass Hagen (born 1904) as a professional musician and dance-band leader, 1927-37. [1640

BUDDY TATE. My story. ... As told to Frank Driggs. Jazz rev., 1(2):18-20, 27 (Dec 1958). ports. On the author's early life in Texas and his work since 1927 as a jazz musician, especially in Dallas, Little Rock, and Omaha. [1641

SAMUEL BARCLAY CHARTERS. Abbe Niles, a pioneer jazz critic of the '20s. Jazz rev., 2(4):25-6 (May 1959). On his column in the Bookman, "Ballads, songs, and snatches," Feb. 1928 - Jan. 1929. [1642

ANDY KIRK. My story. ... As told to Frank Driggs. Jazz rev., 2(2):12-17 (Feb 1959). ports. On the author's work as a jazz musician since some time before 1929, especially in Texas and Oklahoma, and his Twelve Clouds of Joy band with headquarters at Kansas City, later at New York, conducted by him since 1929. [1643

GENE KRUPA. It's the rhythm that stays with 'em. Music jour., 18(7):12, 72-3 (Oct). port. On the author's work as a jazz drummer since 1929. [1644

MIKE ZACCAGNINO. "Swinging with Zacc"--Jake Koven [born 1910]. Record research, 29:13 (Aug). On the work of Koven as a trumpeter with burlesque, dance, and musical-comedy bands and orchestras, 1929-60. [1645

JILL C. RADCLIFFE. A way of life. Harvard alumni bul., 61:610 (1 May 1959). On the work of Peter Seeger (Harvard, 1940) as a folk singer, 1937-59. [1646

SIDNEY WALTER FINKELSTEIN. Bela Bartok (1881-1945): his music and the recordings. AM. record guide, 17:3-8, 39-43 (Sep, Oct 1950). ports. Includes some account of his life and work in the United States, 1940-45. [1647

THE STUDY AND TEACHING OF MUSIC

WILLIAM H. RICHARDS. How old is class piano? Music jour., 18(7):42, 85

(Oct). On classroom instruction in piano in America (since 1865) and abroad, as distinguished from separate teaching of individual pupils. [1648

FRANCIS HILL BAXTER. A history of music education in the Los Angeles City Schools [since 1885]. Ann Arbor: University Microfilms, 1960. Positive microfilm of typescript. [442] leaves. Thesis--Univ. of Southern California. Abstracted: Dissert. abstracts, 21:204 (Jul). [1649

THEODORE KRATT. Music--a growing force in American life. Old Oregon, 37(5):2-4 (Apr-May 1957). ports., views. On the University of Oregon School of Music, 1886-1957. [1650

ALICE BARTELS. A history of class piano instruction [in America since 1900, and abroad]. Music jour., 18(6):42, 96-7 (Sep). port. On classroom teaching of piano. [1651

PAUL BARTON GROVER. A history of string class instruction in American schools and its relationship to school orchestras [1911-60]. Ann Arbor: University Microfilms, 1960. Positive microfilm of typescript. [238] leaves. Thesis (Ed. D.)--Univ. of Illinois. Abstracted: Dissert. abstracts, 21:1585 (Dec). [1652

SALLY ALICIA MONSOUR. The establishment and early development of beginning piano classes in the public schools, 1915-1930. Ann Arbor: University Microfilms, 1960. Positive microfilm of typescript. [197] leaves. Thesis [Ed. D.)--Univ. of Michigan. Abstracted: Dissert. abstracts, 20:4680-81 (Jun). [1653

C. J. McNASPY. Loyola College of Music. Jesuit educ. quar., 22:193-5 (Mar). On the College of Music, Loyola University, New Orleans, 1919-60. [1654

MAURINE TIMMERMAN. A history of the Western Division of the Music Educators National Conference [since 1920]. Ann Arbor: University Microfilms, 1960. Positive microfilm of typescript. [476] leaves. Thesis (Ed. D.)--Univ. of Southern California. Abstracted: Dissert. abstracts, 41:119 (Jul). [1655

WILBUR DALE FULLBRIGHT. The history and development of the master's degree in music in the United States [since 1929]. Ann Arbor: University Microfilms, 1960. Positive microfilm of typescript. [266] leaves. Thesis--Boston Univ. Abstracted: Dissert. abstracts, 21:921-2 (Oct). [1656

WILTON MASON. The University of North Carolina Institute of Folk Music [1931-60]. Folklore and folk music archivist, 3(2):[1, 4] (summer). [1657

Philosophy

WALTER GEORGE MUELDER, LAURENCE SEARS, & ANNE V. SCHLABACH, eds. The development of American philosophy: a book of readings. Second edition. [Boston:] Houghton Mifflin [1960]. xi, 643 p. bibliogs., notes. 1st ed. 1940. Excerpts from writings of 45 "outstanding thinkers," from Jonathan Edwards to Morris R. Cohen, 18th-20th centuries, with introductory essays by the editors. [1658

HENDRIKUS BOEVE VAN WESEP. Seven sages: the story of American philosophy [1706-1952]. N.Y.: Longmans, Green, 1960. xiii, 450 p. bibliog. (p. v). Contents.--Benjamin Franklin: statesman-philosopher.--Ralph Waldo Emerson: gentle iconoclast.--William James: primitive pragmatist.--John Dewey: Promethean instrumentalist.--George Santayana: spiritual materialist.--Charles Sanders Peirce: trail-blazing logician.--Alfred North Whitehead: inspired metaphysician. [1659

PAUL LAUTER. Truth and nature: Emerson's use of two complex words. ELH, 27:66-85 (Mar). notes. Undated "representative examples of what we might call Emersonian semantics" (1830s ff.?), distinguishing senses A-C of truth and senses E-G of nature (but not accounting for D, whatever it may be). [1660

MILTON RIDVAS KONVITZ & GAIL KENNEDY, eds. The American pragmatists: selected writings. N.Y.: Meridian Books [1960]. 413 p. bibliog. (p. 405-8). (Meridian books, M105.) Selections from writings of Ralph Waldo Emerson, William James, Charles S. Peirce, Oliver Wendell Holmes, Jr., John Dewey, George

Herbert Mead, Percy W. Bridgman, C. I. Lewis, Horace M. Kallen, and Sidney Hook, 1836-1959. [1661

WILLIAM JOHN HAGGERTY, JR. Realism in the philosophy of Orestes A. Brownson [1840s-60s]. Ann Arbor: University Microfilms, 1960. Positive microfilm of typescript. [253] leaves. Thesis--Boston Univ. Abstracted: Dissert. abstracts, 21:927 (Oct). [1662

LEWIS WHITE BECK. Six secular philosophers. N.Y.: Harper [1960. 2], 126 p. bibliogs., notes (p. 119-24). Includes chapters on William James (1842-1910) and George Santayana (1863-1952). [1663

PETER ANTHONY BERTOCCI. Borden Parker Bowne [1847-1910]: philosophical theologian and personalist. Religion in life, 29:587-97 (autumn). notes. [1664

CHARLES SANTIAGO SANDERS PEIRCE (1839-1914). Collected papers of Charles Sanders Peirce. ... Edited by Charles Hartshorne and Paul Weiss. Cambridge: Belknap Press of Harvard Univ. Press, 1960. 6 v. in 3. xvi, 393; [12], 535; [2], xiv, 433; x, 601, [2], xii, 455; x, 461, [1] p. diagrs. notes. 1st ed. 1931-35, here "reproduced by offset lithography." Includes "the more important" of Peirce's manuscripts (largely undated, mainly 1860s to ca. 1910), organized topically instead of chronologically, "as well as his published papers." Contents.--I. Principles of philosophy.--II. Elements of logic.--III. Exact logic (published papers).--IV. The simplest mathematics.--V. Pragmatism and pragmaticism.--VI. Scientific metaphysics. [1665

CHARLES SANTIAGO SANDERS PEIRCE (1839-1914). Collected papers of Charles Sanders Peirce. Volume VII. Science and philosophy. [And Volume VIII. Reviews, correspondence, and bibliography.] Edited by Arthur W. Burks. Cambridge: Harvard Univ. Press, 1958. 2 v. xiv, 415; xii, 352 p. diagrs. Sections entitled "Experimental science," "Scientific method," "Philosophy of mind," "Reviews," and "Correspondence" (letters by Peirce), printed mainly from his manuscripts; and "Bibliography of the works of Charles Sanders Peirce," dated 1860-1908 (8:249-321). Includes sections on "The logic of drawing history from ancient documents" (7:89-164), "The study of great men" (7:165-74), and "The history of science" (7:175-80). Completes a series of which vols. 1-6 were published 1931-35. [1666

IVAN EUGENE FRICK. A study of the objective and subjective aspects of selfhood in the thought of Alfred North Whitehead [1861-1947]. Ann Arbor: University Microfilms, 1959 [i.e. 1960]. Positive microfilm of typescript. 253 leaves. bibliog. (leaves 246-53). Thesis--Columbia Univ. Abstracted: Dissert. abstracts, 20:3777 (Mar). [1667

RICHARD E. BUTLER. The life and world of George Santayana [1863-1952]. Chicago: H. Regnery Co. [1960]. xii, 205 p. notes. Includes details of the author's interviews with Santayana in his last years. [1668

CHARLES FRANKEL, ed. The golden age of American philosophy. N.Y.: G. Braziller, 1960. viii, 534, [1] p. bibliog. (p. 533-4). Excerpts from writings of Chauncey Wright, Charles Peirce, William James, Josiah Royce, George Santayana, John Dewey, Ralph Barton Perry, Clarence Irving Lewis, and Morris Raphael Cohen, 1865-1939; with an introduction on the characteristics of the "age." [1669

W. E. SCHLARETZKI. Scientific reasoning and the summum bonum. Philos. of science, 27:48-57 (Jan). notes. Commentary on C. S. Peirce's "Grounds of validity of the laws of logic" (1868) and "The doctrine of chances" (1878), dealing particularly with induction and probability. [1670

MAURICE F. BROWN, JR. Santayana's American roots. New Eng. quar., 33:147-63 (Jun). notes. Biographical analysis, ca. 1871 to 1912, indicating that "Santayana at twenty was a young Yankee," that he was "even less a true Catholic than a true Spaniard," and that he was an exemplar of a "Harvard aestheticism" which "persisted for only ten years." [1671

SIDNEY RATNER. Pragmatism in America. Donald Sheehan & Harold C. Syrett, eds., Essays in American historiography (N.Y.: Columbia Univ. Press, 1960), p. 193-216. bibliog., notes. On the pragmatic theories and methods of Charles Sanders Peirce, William James, and John Dewey, 1877-1952. [1672

RALPH BARTON PERRY (1876-1957). Santayana: impressions of an international figure in philosophy and letters. Harvard alumni bul., 55:72-4 (11 Oct 1952). port. On his studies and teaching of philosophy at Harvard and "his place in philosophy," 1880s-1950s; with a biographical sketch (from the Boston Globe, 29 Sep. 1952). [1673

MORTON GABRIEL WHITE. Harvard's philosophical heritage: the evolution of the discipline of James, Royce, & Santayana [since the 1880s]. Harvard alumni bul., 60:161-4, 172 (9 Nov 1957). ports. On the founders of the Department of Philosophy at Harvard--William James, Josiah Royce, and George Santayana. [1674

JOHN EDWARD BLEWETT. The origins and early mutations of John Dewey's ethical theory (1884-1904). Ann Arbor: University Microfilms, 1959 [i.e. 1960]. Positive microfilm of typescript. vii, 381 leaves. bibliog. (leaves 367-79). Thesis--St. Louis Univ. Abstracted: Dissert. abstracts, 20:3616-17 (Mar). [1675

JAMES DANIEL COLLINS. The genesis of Dewey's naturalism [1884-1909]. John Blewett, ed., John Dewey: his thought and influence (N.Y.: Fordham Univ. Press [1960]), p. 1-32. notes. A Catholic critique. [1676

BEATRICE HOPE ZEDLER. Dewey's theory of knowledge [1884-1952]. John Blewett, ed., John Dewey: his thought and influence (N.Y.: Fordham Univ. Press [1960]), p. 59-84. notes. [1677

EDWIN ARTHUR BURTT. The core of Dewey's way of thinking [as exhibited in his publications, 1886-1952]. Jour. philos., 57:401-19 (23 Jun). notes. [1678

KAI NIELSEN. Dewey's conception of philosophy [1890s-1950s]. Mass. rev., 2:110-34 (winter). notes. [1679

ROY WOOD SELLARS. Panpsychism or evolutionary materialism. Philos. of science, 27:329-50 (Oct). notes. Includes discussion of concepts expounded by C. S. Peirce, George Santayana, and John Dewey, 1890s ff. [1680

KARL ADALBERT PREUSCHEN. Das Problem der "Unity" und "Multiplicity" in seiner literarischen Gestaltung bei Henry Adams [1893 to 1918]. Frankfurt am Main [1954. 6], 133 p. bibliog. (p. 130-32), notes. Inaugural dissertation--Johann Wolfgang Goethe-Universität, Frankfurt am Main. [1681

MORRIS GROSSMAN. Santayana as dramatist and dialectician: a critical estimate made with the help of unpublished manuscripts. Ann Arbor: University Microfilms, 1960. Positive microfilm of typescript. [293] leaves. Thesis--Columbia Univ. Abstracted: Dissert. abstracts, 21:925-6 (Oct). Based upon undated manuscripts (copied in the appendix), apparently written in the early 20th century. [1682

WILLIAM JAMES (1842-1910). [Letter to Reginald C. Robbins, Chairman, Overseers' Committee to Visit the Department of Philosophy, Harvard, dated 3 Aug. 1908.] Harvard alumni bul., 52:194-6 (19 Nov 1949). On the "value of philosophy as a study and on teaching methods at Harvard." [1683

ROBERT C. POLLOCK. Process and experience. John Blewett, ed., John Dewey: his thought and influence (N.Y.: Fordham Univ. Press [1960]), p. 161-97. notes. On Dewey's doctrine of the "embodiment of values in experience," 1908-52. [1684

MARTIN LEVITT. The context of a contextualist philosophy. School rev., 67:247-57 (summer 1959). notes. On John Dewey's concept of "transaction," developed to describe the "conjoined content and methodological aspects of his philosophy," 1910-59. [1685

RALPH WILLIAM SLEEPER. Dewey's metaphysical perspective: a note on White, Geiger, and the problem of obligation. Jour. philos., 57:110-115 (4 Feb). notes. On "John Dewey's 'program' for the application of scientific method to values" as expressed in The quest for certainty and other writings as early as 1910, and the comments upon it by Morton G. White and George R. Geiger. [1686

JUDE P. DOUGHERTY. Recent American naturalism [1917-59]: an exposition and critique. Wash.: Catholic Univ. of America Press, 1960. xi, 75, [5] p. bibliog. (p. 71-5), notes. (Catholic University of America. Philosophical series, 197. Abstract 47.) Abstract of thesis--Catholic Univ. of America. [1687

CORINNE CHESHOLM FROST. John Dewey's letters to Corinne Chesholm Frost [1930 to 1950]. Columbia Lib. columns, 9(2):34-6 (Feb). Describes a body of correspondence between Dewey and his former student in philosophy. [1688

ERNEST NAGEL. The debt we owe to G[eorge] E[rnest] Moore [1873-1958].

Jour. philos., 57:810-16 (22 Dec). notes. On "some of our debts to Moore whether as an important writer on philosophic subjects, as a gifted teacher, or as a remarkable human character," particularly during his stay at Columbia University, 1942-44. [1689

MORTON GABRIEL WHITE. Memories of G. E. Moore. Jour. philos., 57: 805-10 (22 Dec). On the teaching and thinking of George Edward Moore in the Department of Philosophy, Columbia University, 1942 ff. [1690

RICHARD ISHMAEL McKINNEY. Some aspects of the teaching of philosophy [in American colleges, 1943-60]. Liberal educ., 46:366-79 (Oct). tables. notes. [1691

Religion

CLIFTON E. OLMSTEAD. History of religion in the United States [1526-1960]. Englewood Cliffs, N.J.: Prentice-Hall, 1960. xii, 628 p. col. maps. bibliog. (p. 595-611), notes. [1692

HILRIE SHELTON SMITH, ROBERT T. HANDY, & LEFFERTS A. LOETSCHER. American Christianity: an historical interpretation, with representative documents. ... Volume I. 1607-1820. N.Y.: Scribner, 1960. xv, [3], 615 p. facsims., ports., views. bibliogs., notes. Organized in 3 periods (1607-90, 1690-1765, 1765-1820) and thereunder in 11 topical chapters of text and documents. [1693

DAVID HENRY BRADLEY, SR. Beginnings of organized religion among Negroes [1619-1809]. A. M. E. Zion quar. rev., 58(3):3-9 (summer 1948). [1694

DANIEL J. FOLEY. The Christmas tree: an evergreen garland filled with history, folklore, symbolism, traditions, legends, and stories. Phila.: Chilton Co., Book Division [1960]. 159 p. diagr., facsim., ports., views (part col.). bibliog. (p. 154-6). On a custom, apparently of German origin, for which no documented reference to observance in America has been found for a date earlier than 1816. Includes reference to Protestant nonobservance of Christmas, regarded as a "popish holiday," as early as 1621. [1695

ROBERT WALTER ROOT. The religious ideas of some major early writers of America [1630s-1820s]. Ann Arbor: University Microfilms, 1959 [i. e. 1960]. Positive microfilm of typescript. vii, 989 leaves. bibliog. (leaves 968-88). Thesis--Syracuse Univ. Abstracted: Dissert. abstracts, 20:4378 (May). [1696

GUSTAVE A. WEIGEL. The college and the dimensions of reality. Liberal educ., 45:44-53 (Mar 1959). On the "theological function" of secular universities in America, 1636-1959. [1697

PAUL W. SCHMIDTCHEN. Important American Bibles. Hobbies, 65(5): 108-9; (6):106-7 (Jul, Aug). facsims. On Bibles and parts of Bibles printed in the United States, 1640 to ca. 1815. [1698

MARCUS WILSON JERNEGAN (1872-1949). Religious instruction and conversion of Negro slaves [1664-1776]. Marcus W. Jernegan, Laboring and dependent classes in colonial America, 1607-1783 (N.Y.: Ungar [1960]), p. 24-44. notes. From American historical review, 1915. [1699

MORRIS MONTFORT MORRIS. Deism in eighteenth century America [1713-1805]. N.Y.: Russell & Russell, 1960. 203 p. bibliog. (p. 179-93), notes. 1st ed. 1934. [1700

JOHN LORD O'BRIAN. What future for our Divinity School? Harvard alumni bul., 54:383-6 (9 Feb 1952). views. On Harvard facilities for the teaching and study of divinity, 1721-1952. [1701

HORACE CHRISTOPHER SAVAGE. Some aspects of a psychological study of the conversion process. Quar. rev. higher educ. among Negroes, 28: 185-96 (Jul). On religious conversion, 1737-1959. [1702

HENRY WILDER FOOTE. The religion of Thomas Jefferson [1743-1826]. Boston: Beacon Press [1960, c1947]. ix, 86 p. table. notes. (Beacon series in liberal religion, LR1.) 1st ed. 1947. [1703

RALPH LOUIS KETCHAM. James Madison and religion [1760s-1820s]--a new hypothesis. Presbyt. Hist. Soc., Jour., 38:65-90 (Jun). notes. [1704

TIMOTHY LAWRENCE SMITH. Historic waves of religious interest in

America [1790s, 1850s, 1895-1905, 1950s]. Am. Acad. Pol. and Social Science, Ann., 332:9-19 (Nov). notes. [1705

RICHARD PAUL GRAEBEL. The faith of Abraham Lincoln. Ralph G. Newman, ed., Lincoln for the ages (Garden City, N.Y.: Doubleday, 1960), p. 410-14. On his "religious attitudes." [1706

CONRAD WRIGHT. Early years of the Divinity School: foundations of non-sectarian theological education in American [1816-42]. Harvard alumni bul., 56:469-72 (20 Mar 1954). ports., view. [1707

WILLIAM HAROLD COWLEY. The role of anthropocentrism. Liberal educ., 46:46-7 (Mar). On the "secular point of view" in the "religious tradition in American education," 1825-1960. [1708

HARRY MODEAN CAMPBELL. Emerson and Whitehead. PMLA, 75: 577-82 (Dec). notes. On resemblances of the thinking of Alfred North Whitehead, 1926-41, to that of Emerson in and after the 1830s, and the place of both "in the history of religion." [1709

BARRY ALAN MARKS. The origins of original sin in Hawthorne's fiction [1830s-60s]. Nineteenth-cent. fiction, 14:359-62 (Mar). notes. [1710

RICHARD R. MATHISON. Faiths, cults, and sects of America: from atheism to Zen [mainly since 1830]. Indianapolis: Bobbs-Merrill [1960]. 384 p. Includes sections on "California: Mecca for cultists," "Cults of sex and violence," "Racial cultism," Baha'i, Psychiana, the Rosicrucians, the Mighty I Am, the Self-Realization Fellowship, the Satanic Mass, the Living Flame, the House of David, Holy City, the Penitentes, "vegetable, sun, and health worship," etc., and the better known Swedenborgians, Seventh-Day Adventists, Jehovah's Witnesses, Mormons, and other older groups. [1711

JOHN ENGLAND (1786-1842). Letter to the candid and unprejudiced people of America. Pierre Albert Duhamel, ed., Essays in the American Catholic tradition (N.Y.: Rinehart [1960]), p. 37-44. Letter from the Bishop of Charleston, dated Charleston, S.C., 3 Oct. 1831, on religious prejudice in America. [1712

PETER GORDON GOWING. Newman Smyth [1843-1925]--New England ecumenist. Ann Arbor: University Microfilms, 1960. Positive microfilm of typescript. [292] leaves. Thesis (D. Th.)--Boston Univ. Abstracted: Dissert. abstracts, 21:432 (Sep). On his work as a minister in New Haven and as "a pioneer of the Faith and Order Movement" and his conviction that the Protestant Episcopal Church ought to be the nucleus of a world union of Christian churches. [1713

CLIFTON HERMAN JOHNSON. The American Missionary Association, 1846-1861: a study of Christian abolitionism. Ann Arbor: University Microfilms, 1959 [i. e. 1960]. Positive microfilm of typescript. [595] leaves. Thesis--Univ. of North Carolina. Abstracted: Dissert. abstracts, 20: 2774-5 (Jan). [1714

JOSEPH THOMAS WARD. Herman Melville: the forms and forces of evil. Ann Arbor: University Microfilms, 1959 [i. e. 1960]. Positive microfilm of typescript. iv, 327 leaves. bibliog. (leaves 319-27). Thesis--Univ. of Notre Dame. Abstracted: Dissert. abstracts, 20:2786-7 (Jan). Deals particularly with the sources and expressions of "the many and varied elements of diabolism throughout his writings," 1846-90. [1715

FRANCIS XAVIER CURRAN. The religious revival and organized religion [ca. 1860 to 1960]. Thomas T. McAvoy, ed., Roman Catholicism and the American way of life ([Notre Dame, Ind.:] Univ. of Notre Dame Press, 1960), p. 28-38. notes. Argues that "Jews can be Puritans ... Protestants can be Puritans ... Nothing is more fundamentally opposed to Catholicism than Puritanism. ... Even Communism is essentially Puritan," etc. [1716

IRA VERNON BROWN. The higher criticism comes to America, 1880-1900. Presbyt. Hist. Soc., Jour., 38: 193-212 (Dec). notes. [1717

BERNARD R. DE REMER. Moody Bible Institute: a pictorial history [1886-1959]. Chicago: Moody Press [1960]. 128 p. facisms., ports., tables, views. On a school founded by Dwight L. Moody (1837-99) as the Chicago Evangelization Society, incorporated in 1887. [1718

WAYLAND DEBS HAND. A North Carolina Himmelsbrief. Middle Ages, Reformation, Volkskunde: Festschrift for John G. Kunstmann (Chapel Hill: Univ. of North Carolina Press, 1959), p. 201-7. notes. On "A copy of a letter written by Jesus Christ" (with text of the letter), supposed to have been found by a child more than a thousand years ago, cherished by his descendants, left by the last member of the family to a Mrs. Thompson, published by her in a Georgia newspaper in 1891, and preserved as a clipping; with some account of such letters in Europe and America as missives containing moral, hygienic, and religious advice and having power to ward off misfortune. [1719

LEO PFEFFER. Creeds in competition: a creative force in American culture [especially since 1900. N.Y.:] Harper [1958]. x, [2], 176 p. On disagreements and competition of Catholicism, Protestantism, and Judaism with respect to church and state, schools, "morals, censorship, and Blue Sunday," the family and the child, and "issues domestic and foreign." [1720

ROBERT ROLLIN HUDDLESTON. The relatedness of Goodwill Industries and the Christian church. Denver [1959?] viii, 375 leaves. mount. ports., mount. views. bibliog. (leaves 342-51), notes. Thesis (Th. D.)--Iliff School of Theology. On the Morgan Memorial Cooperative Industries and Stores, founded in 1905 to promote or provide employment for the unfortunate in collecting discarded household materials and restoring them to usefulness, a responsibility of the Board of Home Missions and Church Extension of the Methodist Church, later a nondenominational organization, renamed the Goodwill Industries of America, Inc.; with some account of the Rev. Henry Morgan (1825-84) and the Rev. Edgar James Helms (1863-1942) and a list of Helms's writings (leaves 355-7). [1721

NATHAN MARSH PUSEY. Harvard and religious faith: Mr. Pusey's Divinity School Address. Harvard alumni bul., 56:71, 78-80 (10 Oct 1953). On Charles W. Eliot's Divinity School address, "The religion of the future" (1909), expressing a religion "that placed its greatest reliance on increased knowledge and good works," the present "almost idolatrous preoccupation" with these goals, and the need for "a new effort of the human mind and heart and will." [1722

WILL HERBERG. Religion and culture in present-day America [1927-60]. Thomas T. McAvoy, ed., Roman Catholicism and the American way of life ([Notre Dame, Ind.:] Univ. of Notre Dame Press, 1960), p. 4-19. notes. [1723

BENSON YOUNG LANDIS. Trends in church membership in the United States [1936-60]. Am. Acad. Pol. and Social Science, Ann., 332:1-8 (Nov). [1724

ROYDEN KEITH YERKES. The beginnings of the Graduate School of Theology of the University of the South [1936-47]. ... Introduction by Arthur Ben Chitty. P. E. Church, Hist. mag., 23:315-24 (Dec). notes. Reminiscent letter to Chitty, 19 Apr. 1960. [1725

JOHN FOSTER DULLES (1888-1959). The spiritual legacy of John Foster Dulles: selections from his articles and addresses. Edited, with an introduction, by Henry P. Van Dusen. Phila.: Westminster Press [1960]. xxii, 232 p. notes. Twenty-two articles and speeches, 1937-58, some now first printed, on the Christian life, church and state, and Christianity in international affairs. [1726

CATHOLICISM

ANTHONY I. MARINO. The Catholics in America [1513-1960]. N.Y.: Vantage Press [1960. 4], 300 p. notes. [1727

HERBERT EUGENE BOLTON (1870-1953). The mission as a frontier institution in the Spanish American colonies [including Florida and the Southwest, 1570-1834]. ... With an introduction by John Alexander Carroll. El Paso: Texas Western College Press for Academic Reprints, 1960. iv, 24 p. (The academic reprints series.) First printed in 1917. Appended (p. 24): "A chronological list of the major works of Herbert E. Bolton." [1728

JUVENAL MARCHISIO. The Italian Catholic immigrant [1571-1960]. Thomas Timothy McAvoy, ed., Roman Catholicism and the American way of life ([Notre Dame, Ind."] Univ. of Notre Dame Press, 1960), p. 172-8. [1729

JOHN PERRY PRITCHETT. Black robe and buckskin: the story of Catholic pioneering in northern North America [Canada and the States of the United States adjoining the Canadian border, 1603 to ca. 1840]. N.Y.: College and University Press Services [1960]. 128 p. maps. bibliog. (p. 119-22). [1730

ALOYSIUS J. WYCISLO. The Polish Catholic immigrant [1608-1960].

Thomas Timothy McAvoy, ed., Roman Catholicism and the American way of life ([Notre Dame, Ind.:] Univ. of Notre Dame Press, 1960), p. 179-87. [1731

THOMAS TIMOTHY McAVOY. American Catholics: tradition and controversy. Thought, 35:583-600 (autumn). notes. On the Catholics as a minority in the United States since 1634. [1732

FRANCIS BORGIA STECK. Marquette legends. ... Edited by August Reyling. N.Y.: Pageant Press [1960]. xix, [3], 350 p. facsims., maps (part double), tables (1 double). bibliog. (p. 297-313), notes (p. 245-96). Outgrowth of the author's thesis--Catholic Univ. of America, 1927. On the service of Jacques Marquette, S. J., in Canada and the United States, 1666-75. Argues that "(1) Marquette's participation in the 1673 Jolliet expedition, (2) his subsequent sojourn at Saint Francis Xavier Mission near Green Bay from September, 1673, to Novermber, 1674, (3) his journey to the Illinois country in the fall and winter of 1674, (4) his stay among the Illinois Indians at Kaskaskia during Holy Week of 1675 and his founding of the Kaskaskia Mission, (5) the manner of his death and burial on the eastern shore of Lake Michigan in May 1675, (6) the removal of his mortal remains, two years later, to Saint Ignace Mission and their interment there in the mission chapel--all these traditionally accepted beliefs regarding the last years of Marquette lack convincing historical evidence and must be regarded as more or less legendary." Accuses Father Felix Martin, S. J., of having fabricated 4 documents upon which these beliefs mainly rest, and which Father John Gilmary Shea, historian of the Catholic Church in the United States, evidently first accepted as authentic and later rejected. [1733

THOMAS TIMOTHY McAVOY. Introductory essay. Thomas Timothy McAvoy, ed., Roman Catholicism and the American way of life ([Notre Dame, Ind.:] Univ. of Notre Dame Press, 1960), p. 131-9. On the relation between immigration and Catholicism in America, 1704-1960. [1734

JOHN TRACY ELLIS. American Catholicism in 1960: an historical perspective. Am. Benedictine rev., 11:1-20 (Mar-Jun). notes. On "a few general features of the past that have helped to make us American Catholics what we are today," 1784-1960. [1735

JOSEPH HENRY FICHTER. The Americanization of Catholicism [1784-1960]. Thomas Timothy McAvoy, ed., Roman Catholicism and the American way of life ([Notre Dame, Ind.:] Univ. of Notre Dame Press, 1960), p. 113-27. notes. [1736

DAVID SPALDING. The mystery of Mother Catherine Spalding's parents. Am. Cath. Hist. Soc., Rec., 71:118-24 (Sep-Dec). notes. On her birth in Charles County, Md., in 1793, and the "substantial evidence" that her parents were Edward Spalding (died 1808/9) and Juliet (Boarman) Spalding (died 1798?), that they removed to Kentucky in 1797, and that the father deserted his family and fled from payment of his debts in 1803 or 1804. [1737

ELIZABETH ANN (BAYLEY) SETON (1774-1821). Letters of Mother Seton to Mrs. Julianna Scott. [Edited by] the Rt. Rev. Mgr. Joseph B[ernard] Code. [Second edition.] N.Y.: Father Salvator M. Burgio Memorial Foundation in Honor of Mother Seton [1960. 2], 294 p. port., table. notes. 1st ed. 1935. Letters to Mrs. Scott of Philadelphia, the writer's lifelong friend, dated mainly in New York City (1798-1808), Baltimore (1808-9), and the house of the American Sisters of Charity at Emmitsburg, Md. (1809-20), on her 5 children, the failing health and early death of her husband (William Magee Seton), and later her founding and administration of the Sisters of Charity. [1738

THOMAS FRANCIS CASEY. The Sacred Congregation de Propaganda Fide and the revision of the First Provincial Council of Baltimore (1829-1830). Rome: Apud Aedes Universitatis Gregorianae, 1957. xv, [1], 233, [6] p. bibliog. (p. 227-33), notes. [1739

WILLARD EUGENE WIGHT. The native American Catholic, the immigrant, and immigration [1830-1924]. Thomas Timothy McAvoy, ed., Roman Catholicism and the American way of life ([Notre Dame, Ind.:] Univ. of Notre Dame, 1960), p. 211-24. notes. [1740

DONALD C. MacKINNON. An important bishop who was a Negro. Cath. school jour., 59(9):25 (Nov 1959). port. notes. On James Augustine Healy (1830-1900), probably a mulatto, his early life near Macon, Ga., his studies for the priesthood in Massachusetts, Canada, and France, and his service as a priest, eventually Bishop of Portland, Me. [1741

JOHN J. COSGROVE. Most Reverend John Lancaster Spalding [1840-1916], first Bishop of Peoria. Mendota, Ill.: Wayside Press, ©1960. 160 p. facsims., ports., views. notes. On his early life in Lebanon, Ky., his studies for the priesthood in America and abroad, his service as a priest in Louisville and New York, and his service from 1877 to 1908 as Bishop of Peoria. [1742

JOHN BERNARD McGLOIN. California's first archbishop: a visit to Vich. Am. eccles. rev., 143:112-16 (Aug). On the service of Joseph Sadoc Alemany (1814-88), native of Vich in Catalonia and buried there, as a Catholic priest in Ohio and Kentucky, 1840-50, and as Bishop of Monterey and Archbishop of San Francisco, 1850-85, and his return to Spain to pass his last days. [1743

THOMAS PATRICK JONES. The development of the office of prefect of religion at the University of Notre Dame, from 1842 to 1952. Wash.: Catholic Univ. of America Press, 1960. xviii, 314 p. fold. map, tables. bibliog. (p. 297-304), notes. Thesis--Catholic Univ. of America. [1744

EVA (KELLY) BETZ. Yankee at Molokai. Paterson, N.J.: St. Anthony Guild Press [1960]. vii, 150 p. On the early life of Ira Dutton (1843-1931) in Janesville, Wis., his early interest in gymnastics, his service in the Civil War, his business activities in Memphis, his conversion to Catholicism in 1883, his brief experience as a Trappist brother (name in religion: Joseph), and his service (as Brother Joseph) in the leper colony on the island of Molokai, Hawaiian Islands, from 1886 till his death. Fictional in form. [1745

JEROME W. RAUSCH. The Crosier story: a history of the Crosier Fathers in the United States [1850-1960]. Onamia, Minn.: Crosier Press, 1960. [8], 384 p. coat of arms, map, ports., tables, views. notes (p. 367-78). On the establishments of this Belgian order at and near Green Bay, Wis., and later at Onamia, Minn., Hastings, Neb., Fort Wayne, Ind., and elsewhere. Includes recollections of Crosier College, 1922-23, by Father Lawrence J. Kerich (p. 267-89). [1746

JAMES F. CONNELLY. The visit of Archbishop Gaetano Bedini [1806-64] to the United States of America (June 1853 - February 1854). Roma: Università Gregoriana, 1960. xiii, [3], 307 p. (Analecta Gregoriana, v. 109. Series Facultatis Historiae Ecclesiasticae. Sectio B, no. 20.) bibliog. (p. 298-304), notes. On his voyage to America (after making arrangements with the Department of State) as unaccredited Envoy Extraordinary from the Papal States to visit Catholic churches in the United States and study the "possibility of establishing an Apostolic Nunciature in Washington," the coldness of his reception by many American Catholics (including a number of bishops), the bitter newspaper criticisms of him and the Catholic Church, the anti-Catholic riots and the threats to his person in several cities, and the failure of the Government to welcome him to Washington by special honors or ceremonies; with text of his report on his journey, Rome, 12 Jul. 1854 (p. 193-287), including his itinerary to most of the larger cities from New York to Montreal, Milwaukee, and New Orleans. [1747

JOSEPH MATT. The Central Bureau: fifty years of achievement. Social justice rev., 51:390-92; 52:33-5, 70-71, 106-7 (Mar-Jun 1959). On the Catholic Central Verein, 1855-1958, founded "to provide leadership as well as protection for German Catholic immigrants." [1748

JOHN C. MURRETT. The Mary of Saint Martin's: the life of Mother Demetrias, foundress of the Mission Helpers of the Sacred Heart. Westminster, Md." Newman Press, 1960. 187 p. ports., views. On Mary Cunningham (1859-1940), her early life in Washington and Baltimore, her Catholic upbringing, her work as a bookkeeper in Baltimore, and her founding of the Mission Helpers of the Sacred Heart; with some account of the order since her death. [1749

COLEMAN JAMES BARRY. The German Catholic immigrant [1865-1960]. Thomas Timothy McAvoy, ed., Roman Catholicism and the American way of life ([Notre Dame, Ind.:] Univ. of Notre Dame Press, 1960), p. 188-203. notes. [1750

ROLLINS E. LAMBERT. The Negro and the Catholic Church [1865-1960]. Thomas Timothy McAvoy, ed., Roman Catholicism and the American way of life ([Notre Dame, Ind.:] Univ. of Notre Dame Press, 1960), p. 156-63. [1751

AURELE ADELARD DUROCHER. Mark Twain and the Roman Catholic Church [1867-1910]. Cent. Miss. Valley Am. Studies Assoc., Jour., 1(2):32-43 (fall). notes. [1752

JAMES PASTON. Our Roman Catholic brethren. Pierre Albert Duhamel, ed., Essays in the American Catholic tradition (N.Y.: Rinehart [1960]), p. 66-78. From The Atlantic monthly, Apr. 1868. On Protestant impressions of Catholic religious practices. [1753

HENRY H. REGNET. The Buffalo Mission [of the German Province of the Society of Jesus, 1869-1907]. Social justice rev., 52:384-6 (Mar). On a headquarters responsible for missions and schools as remote as South Dakota, Wyoming, and British Honduras. [1754

WALTER WAGNER. Peter Cahensly and Cahenslyism: his name has been misapplied. Social justice rev., 52: 10-12 (Apr 1959). notes. On his activities in founding the St. Raphaelsverein, to improve facilities for the physical, moral, and spiritual welfare of German Catholic emigrants en route to America or recently arrived there, 1871, and the ill-advised proposal of this organization for "German parishes with German pastors, German Bishops, parochial schools, equal rights for foreign and native priests, and the promotion of Catholic Societies" in America. [1755

JAMES P. SHANNON. The Irish Catholic immigration [1880-1960]. Thomas Timothy McAvoy, ed., Roman Catholicism and the American way of life ([Notre Dame, Ind.:] Univ. of Notre Dame Press, 1960), p. 204-10. [1756

FRANCIS JEREMIAH CONNELL. Is the Baltimore Catechism outmoded? Am. eccles. rev., 142:1-9 (Jan). notes. On a catechism first printed in 1885 by a committee of bishops deputed by the Third Plenary Council of Baltimore "to draw up a catechism for use in elementary religious instruction throughout the United States," revised in 1935 and following years, and published in revised and approved form in 1941; and the unsoundness of criticisms of it made by Fr. Johannes Hofinger, S. J., of Manila. [1757

JOSEPH SWASTEK. The Polish Seminary: Father Dabrowski's lasting contribution to American Catholicism. Poles in Michigan Associated, Poles in Michigan (Detroit, 1953 [i. e. 1955]), 1:54-63. On "the Polish Seminary, known presently by its three separate departments as St. Mary's Prep., St. Mary's College, and SS. Cyril and Methodius Seminary," opened in Detroit in 1886 by Father Joseph Dabrowski, moved to Orchard Lake, Mich., in 1909. [1758

ROGER LANE. James Jeffrey Roche and the Boston Pilot. New Eng. quar., 33:341-63 (Sep). notes. On his editorship of the "oldest and largest Catholic journal in America," serving as "spokesman for the Irish in America," Boston, 1890-1905. [1759

K. GERALD MARSDEN. Father Marquette and the A. P. A.: an incident in American Nativism. Cath. hist. rev., 46:1-21 (Apr). notes. On the ineffectual opposition of the American Protective Association to the placing of a statue of Father Jacques Marquette in the Statuary Hall of the U.S. Capitol as voted by the Wisconsin Legislature, 1894-98, the debates on this subject in Wisconsin newspapers, the Wisconsin legislature, and the U.S. Congress, and the final installation of the statue in 1904, 8 years after its delivery in Washington, in 1896. [1760

FREDERICK JAMES ZWIERLEIN. Americanism: some roots of a controversy [1897-99]. Social justice rev., 52:47-9 (May 1959). From the author's Documentary history of the Catholic Church in the United States, preface to vol. 5. [1761

JOHN PHILIP GLEASON. The Central-Verein, 1900-1917: a chapter in the history of the German-American Catholics. Ann Arbor: University Microfilms, 1960. Positive microfilm of typescript. [422] leaves. Thesis--Univ. of Notre Dame. Abstracted: Dissert. abstracts, 21:1540-41 (Dec). [1762

GERARD McGINLEY [secular name: John Bernard McGinley] (1906-55). A Trappist writes home: letters of Abbot Gerard McGinley, O. C. S. O., to his family. Introduction by Father Raymond. Milwaukee: Bruce Pub. Co. [1960]. ix, 175 p. ports., views. Letters written during the author's stay in the monastery of Our Lady of Gethsemani at Trappist, Ky., 1926-53, and the years of his service as Abbot of the monastery of Our Lady of the Genesee, Piffard, N.Y., 1953-55; with "Letters relating to the death of Abbot

Gerard," from various religious orders (p. 165-75). [1763

FAN STYLIAN NOLI. Fiftieth anniversary book of the Albanian Orthodox Church in America, 1908-1958. Boston: Albanian Orthodox Church in America, 1960. xx, 265 p. facsims., ports., views. Includes an autobiographical sketch of the author (born 1882), his early life in Albania and Greece, his emigration to America in 1906, and his service as a priest and eventually as Archbishop of the Albanian Orthodox Church in America (p. 34-129); with a list of his writings in Albanian and English (p. 129-34). [1764

KARL JOSEPH ALTER. The mind of an archbishop: a study of man's essential relationship to God, church, country, and fellow man, as expressed in the writings of the Most Rev. Karl J. Alter [from 1910 to 1960]. ... Editor: The Rev. Maurice E. Reardon. [Cincinnati: Archdiocese of Cincinnati; distributed by St. Anthony's Guild, Paterson, N.J., 1960.] xix, [1], 406 p. port. [1765

DAVID J. HASSELL. The sodalities of the future. Jesuit educ. quar., 21:236-51 (Mar 1959). notes. Includes some account of American sodalities, 1913-59. [1766

JAMES GIBBONS (1834-1921). Notations of Cardinal Gibbons on the Conclave of 1914. [Edited] by John Quentin Feller, Jr. Cath. hist. rev., 46:184-9 (Jul). notes. Excerpts from notes on the author's voyage to Rome in 1914 and a second voyage in 1915, including references to American affairs. [1767

JOHN ANTHONY O'BRIEN. Significant developments in the convert apostolate. Am. eccles. rev., 142:330-43 (May). On "techniques of instructing prospective converts or of recruiting them" to the Catholic Church since 1916. [1768

DOROTHY DAY. New life. Pierre Albert Duhamel, ed., Essays in the American Catholic tradition (N.Y.: Rinehart [1960]), p. 169-79. From the author's Union Square to Rome (1940). On her conversion to Catholicism, 1927, and her decision to rear her child as a Catholic. [1769

GERALD ELLARD. The "new" liturgy: its function and its challenge. Pierre Albert Duhamel, ed., Essays in the American Catholic tradition (N.Y.: Rinehart [1960]), p. 159-69. From The Catholic mind, Jan. 1937. On the "socialization of public worship" as "a teacher of Mystic Body consciousness." [1770

EDWARD ERNEST SWANSTROM. The newer Catholic immigration. Thomas Timothy McAvoy, ed., Roman Catholicism and the American way of life ([Notre Dame, Ind.:] Univ. of Notre Dame Press, 1960), p. 49-56. Based upon the author's experience since 1943 as Assistant Director and Director of the Catholic Relief Services of the National Catholic Welfare Conference. [1771

DONALD C. GEIST. Sister Marie Suzanne. Am. Cath. Hist. Soc., Rec., 71:112-17 (Sep-Dec). On Alice Novial (1889-1957), native of Paris, her entry into the Missionary Sisters of the Society of Mary, her laboratory studies in the Fiji Islands and in France and Italy to find the cause of leprosy, and her tour of America in 1954 to lecture on her work. [1772

HELEN (LINENBERGER) HALL. These are our religions: a genealogy. [Hutchinson? Kan.] 1959. [2], 316 p. ports. 22 x 29 cm. On 186 members of Catholic religious orders related to the author or to her husband, Edwin Boniface Hall. [1773

CHURCH AND STATE

WILLIAM FIFE TROUTMAN, JR. Respecting the establishment of religion in colonial America. Ann Arbor: University Microfilms, 1959 [i. e. 1960]. Positive microfilm of typescript. [593] leaves. Thesis--Duke Univ. Abstracted: Dissert. abstracts, 20: 3811-12 (Mar). On "establishment" as understood by the Anglican and Congregational colonies, and the sentiments of Presbyterians, Baptists, and Quakers regarding the issue, 1607-1775. [1774

JOSEPH MOSS IVES (1876-1939). Religious liberty in Catholic Maryland. Pierre Albert Duhamel, ed., Essays in the American Catholic tradition (N.Y.: Rinehart [1960]), p. 25-33. From the author's The ark and the dove (1936). Comparison of Maryland laws concerning religion with those of Massachusetts, Connecticut, New York, Pennsylvania, and Virginia, 1619-49. [1775

WILLIAM JOHN PETERSEN. Thanksgiving in Iowa. Iowa City, 1960. 405-436 p. cartoons, views (part col.). (The palimpsest, v. 41, no. 9.)

On Thanksgiving as a holiday in New England since 1621, as a national holiday since 1777, and as an Iowa holiday since 1844. [1776

RONALD R. HAUS. Sunday blue laws: a new battle on an old front [1656-1959]. Syracuse law rev., 11:254-63 (spring). notes. [1777

STATE Sunday laws and the religious guarantees of the Federal Constitution [1700-1959]. Harv. law rev., 73:729-46 (Feb). notes. [1778

MAURICE WHITMAN ARMSTRONG. The Dissenting Deputies and the American colonies. Church hist., 29: 298-320 (Sep). notes. On the Protestant Dissenting Deputies, an organization of representatives of Baptist, Congregational, and Presbyterian churches near London, formed to "keep in constant touch with legal and parliamentary affairs affecting the religious liberties of Dissenters," 1732-1828, and their correspondence relating to the Connecticut Separatists (1744-57), the licensing of Dissenting meeting-houses in Virginia (1751-56), and the prevention of the establishment of a colonial episcopate (1749-74). [1779

PAUL F. BOLLER, JR. George Washington and religious liberty [1751-99]. Wm. and Mary quar., 17:486-506 (Oct). notes. On his views of separatin of church and state, and his repeated expression of a belief in complete "religious liberty and freedom of conscience" as part of "the American tradition." [1780

HARRY P. KERR. Politics and religion in colonial fast and thanksgiving sermons, 1763-1783. Quar. jour. speech, 46:372-82 (Dec). notes. [1781

WILLIAM KAILER DUNN. What happened to religious education? the decline of religious teaching in the public elementary school, 1776-1861. Baltimore: Johns Hopkins Press, 1958. xv, 346 p. tables. bibliog. (p. 313-38), notes. Based on thesis--Johns Hopkins Univ., 1956. [1782

S. GERALD SANDLER. Lockean ideas in Thomas Jefferson's Bill for establishing religious freedom [Virginia House of Delegates, 1779]. Jour. hist. ideas, 21:110-16 (Jan-Mar). notes. Presents excerpts in parallel columns from (1) John Locke's A letter concerning religious toleration, (2) notes and comments by Jefferson on the letter, and (3) the bill of 1779, illustrating "five ideas concerning religious toleration which I have selected for comparison." [1783

F. WILLIAM O'BRIEN. Has government an interest in religion? Villanova law rev., 5:335-74 (spring). notes. Evidence from "the New England establishments," 1780-1854, from "aid to religion" in the Northeast, the South, the Middle West, and the Far West, and from Federal courts, 1815-1934, that such an interest exists. [1784

ARTHUR HERTZBERG. The Protestant "establishment," Catholic dogma, & the Presidency [1791-1960]. Commentary, 30:277-85 (Oct). [1785

HERBERT H. BROWN & JOSEPH J. MAHON, JR. Church and state--taxation of religious organizations--benefits granted by Federal and State governments. Villanova law rev., 5: 255-80 (winter). notes. On "the tax exempt status of certain property of religious organizations" as "compared with exemptions given other charitable and educational organizations" under State laws, 1810, 1877-1959, particularly those of Pennsylvania and Connecticut. [1786

JAMES KEITH MELVILLE. Theory and practice of church and state during the Brigham Young era [1843-71, particularly in Utah after 1847]. Brigham Young Univ. studies, 3:33-55 (autumn). notes. [1787

FREDRIC MITCHELL. The Supreme Court of the United States on religion and education [1844-1948]. Ann Arbor: University Microfilms, 1959 [i.e. 1960]. Positive microfilm of typescript. [326] leaves. Thesis--Columbia Univ. Abstracted: Dissert. abstracts, 20: 4001-2 [1788

THOMAS MEALEY HARRIS (1817-1906). Rome's responsibility for the assassination of Abraham Lincoln. [Los Angeles: Heritage Manor, 1960. 4]. 40 p. 1st ed. 1897. [1789

EDWARD AUGUSTUS FITZPATRICK (1884-1960). What Catholic pastors should know about the Federal Government and the schools [1867-1959]. Cath. school jour., 59(3):67-9 (Mar 1959). [1790

MYRON LUEHRS TRIPP. Some legal aspects of church-state relations in education [1869-1949]. Mont. Acad. Sciences, Proc., 9 (1951): 61-4. notes. [1791

JOHN WHITNEY EVANS. Catholics and the Blair Education Bill. Cath.

hist. rev., 46:273-98 (Oct). notes. On the debates on a bill "for the federal support of education" introduced by Senator Henry William Blair in 1881 and for the fourth and last time in 1890, involving Protestant objections to Federal support of Catholic schools and Catholic objections to public schools and secular education, the expected domination of the public schools by "militant Protestantism," and the questionable "right of the State to intervene in education." [1792

RAYMOND FRANCIS COUR. Catholics and church-state relations in America [1885-1960]. Thomas Timothy McAvoy, ed., Roman Catholicism and the American way of life ([Notre Dame, Ind.:] Univ. of Notre Dame Press, 1960), p. 99-112. notes. [1793

JAMES H. SMYLIE. The Roman Catholic Church, the state, and Al Smith [1928]. Church hist., 29:321-43 (Sep). notes. "An attempt to examine Roman Catholic teaching in America during the thirty years preceding the Al Smith campaign which was the provocation of a discussion of this basic issue among Smith's contemporaries," 1895-1928. [1794

STANLEY M. LIPNICK. A new trend in civil rights legislation? Sunday laws, released time, and Bible reading in the public schools as affected by the First Amendment [1896-1960]. Geo. Wash. law rev., 28:579-612 (Mar). notes. [1795

PERRY OSWIN CHRISMAN. The released time program in the public schools. Baylor law rev., 11:292-305 (summer 1959). notes. On efforts to accomplish "the divorce of church and state" in public education, 1917-52. [1796

ALFRED EMANUEL SMITH (1873-1944). Catholic and patriot. Pierre Albert Duhamel, ed., Essays in the American Catholic tradition (N.Y.: Rinehart [1960]), p. 133-43. From The Atlantic monthly, May 1927. "Open letter" to Charles C. Marshall, on the relation between the author's religion and his qualifications for public office. [1797

AARON RALPH MILLER. An analysis of the statutes and court decisions affecting school transportation in the United States, 1943-1957. Ann Arbor: University Microfilms, 1960. Positive microfilm of typescript. [240] leaves. Thesis (Ed. D.)--Temple Univ. Abstracted: Dissert. abstracts, 20: 4573-4 (Jun). [1798

FOREIGN MISSIONS

BYRON SAMUEL LAMSON. Venture! the frontiers of Free Methodism. Winona Lake, Ind.: Light and Life Press [1960]. 287 p. col. map, ports., views. notes (p. 265-74). On missions of the Free Methodist Church, 1860-1960. [1799

EUNICE GRIFFIN. The rise of American missions: the African Methodist Episcopal Church [since 1820. N.Y.?] Coker Press Books, c1960. 99, [6] p. Even numbers on recto. [1800

CARL C. BECK. George Jay Lapp [born 1879], disciple. Mennonite hist. bul., 14(3):1-4 (Jul 1953). port. On his early life in rural Nebraska and his service (in partnership with his wife, Esther (Ebersole) Lapp) as a Mennonite missionary in India, 1905-45. [1801

GUSTAV CARLBERG. The changing China scene: the story of the Lutheran Theological Seminary in its church and political setting over a period of forty-five years, 1913-1958. Hong Kong [introd. 1959. 2], 261, [2] p. diagrs., maps (1 double), ports., tables, views. bibliog. (p. 245-6). Includes some account of American and European missionary Lutheranism in the Hong Kong area since 1890. [1802

MARTIN P. DAVIS. A l-o-n-g honeymoon among lepers, outcastes, and aborigines. [Cincinnati?] c1960. [4], viii, 212 p. ports., views. On the service of the author and his wife as missionaries to the lepers at the Chandkuri Asylum, India, 1912-50; with some account of the author's service as a minister of an unnamed denomination in Indiana and Kentucky. Appended (p. 211): list of his writings. [1803

FRANCIS A. COX. The Cross and the Dragon: experiences and observations of a Protestant missionary in the Far East (1921-1942). N.Y.: Exposition Press [1960]. 120 p. ports., views. Does not identify the mission or missions or the denomination served by the author, or offer details of his religious activities. Consists mainly of anecdotes illustrating the national characteristics of the Chinese and the Japanese. [1804

MARTHA WALL. Splinters from an African log. Chicago: Moody Press

[1960]. 319 p. maps, ports., views. On the author's service as a medical missionary in the Sudan Interior Mission of an unnamed denomination at several stations in French West Africa and adjoining Nigeria since 1938; with some accounts of her training in California as a nurse. [1805

FRANK WILLARD PATTERSON. Caribbean quest. Nashville: Convention Press [1960]. viii, 136 p. double map, port., views. (Foreign mission graded series, 1960.) "A publication of the Foreign Mission Board." On the author's service as a missionary of the Foreign Mission Board of the Southern Baptist Convention in Caribbean countries since 1946. [1806

JUDAISM

ABRAHAM J. KARP. Simon Tuska [1835-71] becomes a rabbi. Am. Jew. Hist. Soc., Pub., 50:79-97 (Dec). notes. On his studies at the University of Rochester, his contributions to The Israelite (serial of Isaac M. Wise), his book The Stranger in the synagogue (Rochester, 1854), his studies in the Jewish Theological Seminary in Breslau (as "the first American Jew to take the rabbinate seriously enough to go to Europe to study for it"), and his service as a rabbi in Memphis, Tenn. [1807

JUDAH DAVID EISENSTEIN (1854-1956). Between two opinions. ... Translated by Robert L. Samuels. Am. Jew. arch., 12:123-42 (Oct). port., view. Translated article from New-Yorker jüdische Zeitung, 1886. Severe criticism, by an Orthodox Jew, of "the Reform and Conservative movements." [1808

NON-CHRISTIAN RELIGIONS OTHER THAN JUDAISM

DAVID BIDNEY. Paul Radin and the problem of primitive monotheism. Stanley Diamond, ed., Culture in history: essays in honor of Paul Radin (N.Y.: Columbia Univ. Press for Brandeis Univ., 1960), p. 363-79. bibliog. On his theories about the "problem of primitive monotheism against the background of evolutionary cultural anthropology," 1915-56. [1809

ELLI KAIJA KÖNGÄS. The Earth-Diver (Th. A 812). Ethnohistory, 7:151-80 (spring). bibliog., notes. On the almost worldwide distribution of this creation myth, particularly its occurrence in most parts of North America. [1810

JOHN GOTTLIEB ERNESTUS HECKEWELDER (1743-1823). Indian preachers and prophets. Margaret Mead & Ruth L. Bunzel, eds., The golden age of American anthropology (N.Y.: George Braziller, 1960), p. 89-94. notes. First printed in 1819. On 3 heathen prophets: an unnamed Delaware of Cayahaga, the Delaware Wangemond, and the Shawnee Tecumseh, 1762-1813, founders of native religious movements opposed to white men. [1811

JOHN QUINCY ANDERSON. The New Orleans voodoo ritual dance and its twentieth-century survivals. South. folklore quar., 24:135-43 (Jun). notes. On a part of "the ceremony of devil-worship which centered in the god Zombi, symbolized in the sacred snake, which the dance emulated," a cult introduced into the Caribbean ca. 1724 and into Louisiana as early as 1782, and the secular traces of its steps and patterns in ragtime and jazz dancing "all over the world." [1812

JOHN SYMONDS. The lady with the magic eyes: Madame Blavatsky--medium and magician. N.Y.: T. Yoseloff [1960, ©1959]. 254 p. facsims., plans, ports., views. notes. 1st ed. 1959. On Helene Petrovna (Hahn-Hahn) Blavatsky (1831-91), native of Russia, student of occult phenomena, spiritualist, Theosophist, and the evidences of spuriousness in her revelations. Includes some account of her stay in America, 1874-78, and her association with Col. Henry Steel Olcott in founding the Theosophical Society; and refers to American interest in spiritualism since ca. 1840. [1813

ARTHUR HOBART NETHERCOT. The first five lives of Annie Besant. [Chicago:] Univ. of Chicago Press [1960]. xii, 418, [1] p. facsims., ports., views. notes. On the multitudinous activities and interests of Annie (Wood) Besant (1847-1933) in England before she embraced Theosophy in 1888 or 1889 and her service as ultimately head of the Theosophical Society. Includes brief reference to her lecture tours in the United States, 1891-93. [1814

JOHN NAPOLEON BRINTON HEWITT (1859-1937). Orenda and a definition of religion. Selected papers from the American anthropologist, 1888-1920, ed. Frederica De Laguna (Evanston, Ill.: Row, Peterson [1960]), p. 671-84. notes. First printed in 1902. On "a subsumed mystic potence" attributed by Iroquois and other Indians to "all bodies," human and non-human, animate and inanimate; or perhaps the possession of the potence, as distinguished from the potence itself. [1815

KURT FRIEDRICH LEIDECKER. History of the Washington Friends of Buddhism [1952-60. Wash.:] Distributed by the United States Information Service, c1960. 61 leaves. Contains a "brief autobiography" of the Venerable Robert Stuart Clifton (born 1902/3), native of Alabama, who had adopted Buddhism by 1923, was ordained a Buddhist priest in San Francisco in 1933, and removed to the Orient in 1954 (leaves 2-4). [1816

JOSEPH CAMPBELL. Primitive man as metaphysician. Stanley Diamond, ed., Culture in history: essays in honor of Paul Radin (N.Y.: Columbia Univ. Press for Brandeis Univ., 1960), p. 380-92. notes. On studies of the origins of "myths, rituals, and symbols" in primitive societies, including those of the Jicarilla Apache and Oglala Sioux Indians, 1907-56. [1817

ALLAN LUCIUS WARD. An historical study of the North American speaking tour of 'Abdu'l-Baha ["leader of the Baha'i World Faith"] and a rhetorical analysis of his addresses [1912]. Ann Arbor: University Microfilms, 1960. Positive microfilm of typescript. [271] leaves. Thesis--Ohio Univ. Abstracted: Dissert. abstracts, 21:1667-8 (Dec). [1818

DANIEL PRATT MANNIX. The Beast. N.Y.: Ballantine Books [1959]. 139, [5] p. port. "The Scandalous Life of Aleister Crowley" (1875-1947), reporting that he practised "sex-magic," worshiped Satan, founded a religion based on drugs and debauchery, branded his "wives" and drove them insane," etc. Includes some account of the process by which he has become a hero of picaresque romance, and scanty details of his stay in the United States from 1914 to 1919. [1819

JOHN SYMONDS. The Great Beast: the life of Aleister Crowley [1875-1947]. ... Second impression. London: Rider and Co. [1951]. 316 p. diagrs., ports., views. notes. 1st ed. 1952. On the career of The Beast 666, "the Wickedest Man in the World," organizer of Ordo Templi Orientis and associated "sex-magic rituals," poet, painter, author of occult and mystical treatises; with a list of his publications (p. 301-10), compiled by Gerald Yorke. The account of his stay in the United States, 1914-19, lacks detail. [1820

DORIS M. ALEXANDER. Eugene O'Neill and Light on the path. Mod. drama, 3:260-67 (Dec). notes. On an undated book issued by the Theosophical Society, written by Mabel Collins, purporting to be a record of information written down by her in 1884 as received from "two gentlemen who had died many centuries ago," one of whom transmitted to her "the original rules in Atlantean script from the lost continent of Atlantis, which, theosophists believed, had sunk into the sea in 9654 B.C."; O'Neill's reading of the book in the winter of 1915-16; and its probably "profound influence on the structure" of his "aesthetic creed." [1821

ALEXANDER A. GOLDENWEISER (1880-1940). Review of Les formes élémentaires de la vie religieuse: le système totémique en Australie, by Émile Durkheim, 1912. Selected papers from the American anthropologist, 1888-1920, ed. Frederica De Laguna (Evanston, Ill.: Row, Peterson [1960]), p. 717-33. First published in 1915. Includes reference to comparable religious ceremonies and artifacts of American Indians. [1822

TOM DAVIS. J. D. Salinger: "Some crazy cliff" indeed. West. humanities rev., 14:97-9 (winter). On his interest in Zen Buddhism since ca. 1946, the appearance of "certain buddhist doctrines" in his short stories (1953-59), and the probability that "the central image" of The catcher in the rye is "the bodhisattva figure of Mahayana Buddhism." [1823

PROTESTANTISM

JOHN A. HARDON. The Protestant churches of America. [Revised edition.] Westminster, Md.: Newman Press, 1958. xxiii, 365, [2] p. 1st ed. 1956. Handbook, by a Jesuit, of information (including historical data) about 14 "major Protestant denominations" and several "minor Protestant denominations." [1824

LESLIE CONRAD, JR. The importance of preaching in the Great Awakening [1739-45]. Luth. quar., 12:111-20 (May). notes. Includes some account of earlier revivals since 1679. [1825

IRA DAVID LANDIS. The origin of the Brethren in Christ Church and its later divisions. Mennonite quar., rev.,

39:290-309 (Oct). notes. On its origin in Lancaster County, Pa., 1754 to ca. 1776, its various schisms, and the present dispersion of its 7,591 members from the Atlantic to the Pacific. [1826

JAMES E. JOHNSON. The life of Charles Grandison Finney [1792-1875]. Ann Arbor: University Microfilms, 1959 [i. e. 1960]. Positive microfilm of typescript. [445] leaves. Thesis--Syracuse Univ. Abstracted: Dissert. abstracts, 20:2763-4 (Jan). On his work as a Presbyterian, later a Congregational, evangelist and minister (originally in northern New York), 1823-75, and as Professor of Theology, Oberlin College, and later President of the College. [1827

CLIFFORD STEPHEN GRIFFIN. Their brothers' keepers: moral stewardship in the United States, 1800-1865. New Brunswick, N.J.: Rutgers Univ. Press [1960]. xv, 332 p. bibliog. (p. 306-21), notes (p. 265-305). On the various organized activities, for "moral suasion" and "political action," of those Protestants who "believed themselves the stewards of heavenly commands and the trustees of the Lord" and "claimed the right and alleged their duty to tell other men how to behave," forming the American Education Society, the American Home Missionary Society, the American Tract Society, the American Peace Society, the American Society for the Promotion of Temperance, the American Sunday School Union, the American Bible Society, and the American Antislavery Society. [1828

WALTER RALSTON MARTIN. The Christian and the cults: answering the cultist from the Bible. Grand Rapids, Mich.: Zondervan Pub. House [1956. 2], 152 p. bibliog. (p. 149-52). A "historical and theological" study of "the origins, theologies and methods of some of the most subtle and deceptive of non-Christian cults extant in America today," mainly products of the 19th century, including Unitarianism, Mormonism, Spiritualism, Christian Science, Jehovah's Witnesses, Bahaism, Theosophy, the Unity School of Christianity, the New Thought Movement, and the Peace Mission Movement; with efforts to demonstrate their non-Christian nature, and arguments and advice for the use of Christians in dealing with cults. [1829

HAZEL SPENCER PHILLIPS, comp. Shaker records. Hist. and Philos. Soc. Ohio, Bul., 18:53-63 (Jan). view. List of names of Shakers in communities in Ohio, Indiana, and Kentucky, with dates of birth and death and community of residence, 1805-1920. Compiled from "the Shaker journals and publications, newspapers of that day, court and census records and family Bibles"; with remarks on the Shaker custom of burial in unmarked graves. [1830

STEPHEN JACKSON ENGLAND. Alexander Campbell's views on baptism in the light of the ecumenical movement [1812-66]. Perry Epler Gresham, ed., The sage of Bethany: a pioneer in broadcloth (St. Louis: Bethany Press [1960]), p. 95-116. notes. [1831

LIONEL GEORGE CROCKER. Henry Ward Beecher [1813-87]. Speech Association of America, A history and criticism of American public address, ed. William Norwood Brigance, 2d ed. (N.Y.: Russell & Russell, 1960), 1: 265-93. bibliog., notes. On the oratorical and rhetorical characteristics of his Congregational and Presbyterian sermons and other public speaking in Indiana, Brooklyn, and elsewhere. [1832

ROLAND HERBERT BAINTON. Alexander Campbell and church unity. Perry Epler Gresham, ed., The sage of Bethany: a pioneer in broadcloth (St. Louis: Bethany Press [1960]), p. 81-94. On his attempt to "unite all of the evangelical churches" in America, 1820s-1866. [1833

VICTOR RAYMOND EDMAN. They found the secret: twenty transformed lives that reveal a touch of eternity. Grand Rapids: Zondervan Pub. House [1960]. 159 p. bibliog. (p. 156-9). On Protestants of various denominations who experienced conversion in the form of a crisis. Includes, in addition to Europeans, the Americans Samuel Logan Brengle, Charles Grandison Finney (converted 1821), Adoniram Judson Gordon, Richard C. Halverson, Dwight Lyman Moody, Robert E. Nicholas, William P. Nicholson, Charles G. Trumbull, Walter L. Wilson, and John Allan Wood. [1834

WILLIAM GERALD McLOUGHLIN, JR. Modern revivalism: Charles Grandison Finney to Billy Graham [1821-1958]. N.Y.: Ronald Press Co. [1959]. vii, 551 p. bibliog. (p. 531-5), notes. [1835

CLIFFORD STEPHEN GRIFFIN. Cooperation and conflict: the schism in the American Home Missionary Society, 1837-1861. Presbyt. Hist. Soc., Jour., 38:213-33 (Dec). notes. On growing disharmony between the Congregational and Presbyterian components of the Society, ending in the withdrawal of the Presbyterians. [1836

DONALD PAUL BRICKLEY. Man of the morning: the life and work of Phineas F[ranklin] Bresee [1838-1915]. Kansas City, Mo.: Nazarene Pub. House [1960]. 297 p. view. bibliog. (p. 289-94), notes. Based on thesis--Univ. of Pittsburgh, 1957. On his early life in Delaware County, N.Y., and Iowa, his service as a Methodist minister in Iowa and California, his founding of the Church of the Nazarene as a separate denomination 1895 and of its Pacific Bible College (now Pasadena College), his success in uniting the Church of the Nazarene and the Association of Pentecostal Churches of America to form the Pentecostal Church of the Nazarene (1907), and his incorporation into this church (without changing its name) of the Holiness Church of Christ (1908), the Eastern Conference of the Holiness Christian Church (1908), the Pentecostal Mission (1915), and the Pentecostal Church of Scotland (1915). [1837

CONRAD JOHN IMMANUEL BERGENDOFF. Ecumenical experiences [of the Augustana Lutheran Church, 1841-1960]. Augustana Evangelical Lutheran Church, Centennial Publication Committee, Centennial essays, Augustana Lutheran Church, 1860-1960, ed. Emmer Engborg, Conrad Bergendoff, & Edgar M. Carlson (Rock Island, Ill.: Augustana Press [1960]), p. 89-106. [1838

ARLO D. DUBA. The principles of theological language in the writings of Horace Bushnell [1802-76] and Paul Tillich [born 1886], and their implications for Christian education theory. [n. p.] 1960. xiv, 416 leaves. bibliog. (leaves 406-16), notes. Examination of writings of Bushnell, 1847-88, and Tillich, 1930-59. [1839

ELMER EDWIN BURTNER. The use of Biblical materials in the sermons of Harry Emerson Fosdick [born 1878]. Ann Arbor: University Microfilms [1960]. Positive microfilm of typescript. vii, 264 leaves. tables. bibliog. (leaves 253-6). Thesis (Th.D.)--Boston Univ. Abstracted: Dissert. abstracts, 20:2930 (Jan). [1840

WALTER RALSTON MARTIN & NORMAN H. KLANN. Jehovah of the Watchtower: a thorough expose of the important anti-Biblical teachings of Jehovah's Witnesses. N.Y.: Biblical Truth Pub. Soc. [1953]. 125 p. cartoon, facsim., ports., views. bibliog. (p. 118-25), notes. On "the doctrines of the International Bible Students Association, or 'Jehovah's Witnesses,'" and the Watch Tower Bible and Tract Society, 1879-1950s, and their founder, Charles Taze Russell (1852-1916). [1841

WINTHROP STILL HUDSON. Protestantism in post-Protestant America. Thomas Timothy McAvoy, ed., Roman Catholicism and the American way of life ([Notre Dame, Ind.:] Univ. of Notre Dame Press, 1960), p. 20-27. Evidence that as a result partly of Jewish and Catholic immigration since ca. 1880 and partly of "theological erosion," the United States "has become a pluralistic society in which Protestantism has ceased to enjoy its old predominance and near monopoly in the religious life of the nation." [1842

KLAUDE KENDRICK. The history of the modern Pentecostal movement [1901-58]. Ann Arbor: University Microfilms, 1959 [i. e. 1960]. Positive microfilm of typescript. [388] leaves. Thesis--Univ. of Texas. Abstracted: Dissert. abstracts, 20:2776 (Jan). Includes accounts of the Assemblies of God, the Pentecostal Church of God, the International Church of the Foursquare Gospel, the Open Bible Standard Church, the United Pentecostal Church, the Church of God in Christ, and various other Churches of God and Holiness organizations. [1843

ROBERT LEE. The social sources of church unity: an interpretation of unitive movements in American Protestantism [1911-59]. N.Y.: Abingdon Press [1960]. 238 p. bibliog. (p. 225-31), notes. [1844

KENDIG BRUBAKER CULLY. Along an ecumenical way: a religious autobiography. P. E. Church, Hist. mag., 29:153-9 (Jun). On the author's attendance in childhood at the Evangelical Church in Myerstown, Pa., 1913 ff., his studies at Hartford Theological Seminary, his experience as a Congregationalist minister in

New England and a Methodist minister in Evanston, Ill., and his ultimate entry into the Episcopal ministry. [1845

GEORGE SWEETING. The Jack Wyrtzen story: the personal story of the man, his message, and his ministry. Grand Rapids: Zondervan Pub. House [1960]. 151 p. ports., views. On Casper John Von Wyrtzen (born 1913), his early life in Brooklyn, his religious conversion, his work as an evangelist of an unnamed denomination (including tours in South America and Asia), his Word of Life Hour radio program, and his establishment of Word of Life Camp and Inn, Schroon Lake, N.Y., and Word of Life Ranch, Pottersville, N.Y. [1846

WILLIAM GERALD McLOUGHLIN, JR. Billy Graham, revivalist in a secular age. N.Y.: Ronald Press Co. [1960]. xi, 269, [2] p. bibliog. (p. 232-5), notes (p. 236-59). On William Franklin Graham (born 1918), his early life in Charlotte, N.C., his upbringing as a Presbyterian, his studies at Bob Jones College and the Florida Bible Institute, his ordination as a Baptist minister, his Fundamentalist doctrines, and his activities since 1947 as a "professional revivalist" in "America's fourth great awakening"; with a critical analysis of his methods. [1847

ROBERT T. HANDY. The American religious depression, 1925-1935. Church hist., 29:3-16 (Mar). notes. On "Protestantism's overall decline" during these years, and its distinguishability from the economic depression beginning in 1929. [1848

SYDNEY ECKMAN AHLSTROM. Theology and the present-day revival [1928-60]. Am. Acad. Pol. and Social Science, Ann., 332:20-36 (Nov). notes. [1849

ROBERT LEE. The social sources of ecumenicity: an interpretation of the social history of the church unity movement in American Protestantism [since 1929]. Ann Arbor: University Microfilms, 1958 [i. e. 1960]. Positive microfilm of typescript. [419] leaves. Thesis--Columbia Univ. Abstracted: Dissert. abstracts, 20:4735-6 (Jun). [1850

MARGARET FRAKES. Bridges to understanding: the "academy movement" in Europe and North America. Phila.: Muhlenberg Press [1960]. ix, 134 p. views. bibliog. (p. 130-31), notes. On "evangelical academies" and their efforts "to discover means of achieving renewal within the churches and of establishing communication between church and secular world," 1945-60. [1851

ARMENIAN MISSIONARY ASSOCIATION OF AMERICA. To the memory of Puzant H. Kalfayan, 1913-1959. N.Y., 1960. 55, [1] p. ports. On his life in the United States, 1946-59, as Executive Secretary of the Armenian Missionary Association; with some account of his early years in Turkey, Syria, and Lebanon and his work as Executive Secretary of the Armenian Evangelical Churches and the Christian Endeavor Union of Syria and Lebanon. Appended: eulogies, tributes, and a number of excerpts from his sermons. [1852

LOUIS WILLIAM BLOEDE. Development of new congregations in the United States and Canada by the Evangelical United Brethren Church [1946-58]. Ann Arbor: University Microfilms, 1960. Positive microfilm of typescript. [376] leaves. Thesis (Th. D.)--Boston Univ. Abstracted: Dissert. abstracts, 21:686-7 (Sep). [1853

Adventists

VIRGIL E. ROBINSON. Cabin boy to Advent crusader. Nashville: Southern Pub. Assoc. [1960]. 190 p. ports., views. bibliog. (p. 189-90). On Joseph Bates (1792-1872) of Massachusetts, cabin boy, sailor, and captain of American merchant ships, prisoner of the British during the War of 1812, member of New England temperance societies, convert to Seventh-Day Adventism, Adventist missionary in New England and the Middle West. [1854

BOOTON HERNDON. The seventh day: the story of the Seventh-Day Adventists [1810-1960]. N.Y.: McGraw-Hill [1960. 6], 267, [2] p. Deals particularly with medical missions. [1855

WALTER RALSTON MARTIN. The truth about Seventh-Day Adventism [1818-1960]. Grand Rapids: Zondervan Pub. House [1960]. 248, [6] p. bibliog. (p. 241-8), notes. [1856

DAVID DRAKE MITCHELL. Seventh-Day Adventists [1840-1957]: faith in action. N.Y.: Vantage Press [1958. 2], 334 p. ports., views. Includes some account of their medical missions. [1857

FREDERICK E. J. HARDER. Revelation, a source of knowledge, as conceived by Ellen G. White [1856 to 1915]. Ann Arbor: University Microfilms, 1960. Positive microfilm of typescript. [526] leaves. Thesis--New York Univ. Abstracted: Dissert. abstracts, 20:4735 (Jun). [1858

CARL DICMANN ANDERSON. The history and evolution of Seventh-Day Adventist Church organization [1863-1959]. Ann Arbor: University Microfilms, 1960. Positive microfilm of typescript. [635] leaves. Thesis--American Univ. Abstracted: Dissert. abstracts, 21:599 (Sep). [1859

Baptists

LEO T. CRISMON. The Lincoln family and the Baptists. Rev. and expositor, 57:69-73 (Jan). notes. On the Baptist church membership of Abraham Lincoln (1744-86), his son Thomas and the latter's wife, Nancy Hanks, and their daughter, Sarah (1807-28), in Virginia, Kentucky, and Indiana, 1780s-1820s, and the evidence that the future President of the United States passed his "formative years" in "a religious atmosphere which was predominantly Baptist," though he never joined a church. [1860

WILLIAM WRIGHT BARNES. Missions, antimissions, and methods among Baptists [1771-1929]. Quar. rev. (Bapt.), 20(1):60-68 (Jan-Mar). notes. [1861

OWEN D. PELT & RALPH LEE SMITH. The story of the National Baptists. N.Y.: Vantage Press [1960]. 272 p. ports., views. bibliog. (p. 264-7). On the National Baptist Convention of the United States of America, Inc., founded in 1895 by the union of 3 groups founded in and after 1880; with some account of Negro Baptist churches as early as 1773/75. [1862

JULIETTA HAYNES. A history of the Primitive Baptists [since ca. 1800]. Ann Arbor: University Microfilms, 1959 [i. e. 1960]. Positive microfilm of typescript. [410] leaves. Thesis--Univ. of Texas. Abstracted: Dissert. abstracts, 20:3868 (Mar). [1863

JAMES E. TULL. A study of Southern Baptist Landmarkism [since ca. 1850] in the light of historical Baptist ecclesiology. Ann Arbor: University Microfilms, 1960. Positive microfilm of typescript. [727] leaves. Thesis--Columbia Univ. Abstracted: Dissert. abstracts, 21:1273-4 (Nov). [1864

JOHN JETER HURT (born 1873). My fifty favorite stories. Atlanta [1960]. ix, 196 p. Reminiscences and anecdotes by a Southern Baptist minister, with religious applications. [1865

JOHN LEE EIGHMY. The social conscience of Southern Baptists from 1900 to the present as reflected in their organized life. Ann Arbor: University Microfilms, 1959 [i. e. 1960]. Positive microfilm of typescript. [276] leaves. Thesis--Univ. of Missouri. Abstracted: Dissert. abstracts, 20:2770-71 (Jan). [1866

KENNETH LEE SMITH. Shailer Mathews: theologian of social process. Ann Arbor: University Microfilms, 1959 [i. e. 1960]. Positive microfilm of typescript. [333] leaves. Thesis--Duke Univ. Abstracted: Dissert. abstracts, 20:3870-71 (Mar). Study of "the religious thought of the Baptist theologian, Shailer Mathews, Professor of Historical Theology (1906-1933) and Dean of the Divinity School of the University of Chicago (1908-1933)," with particular reference to his "Modernism." [1867

BRUCE LEON SHELLEY. Conservative Baptists: a story of twentieth-century dissent. Denver: Conservative Baptist Theological Seminary, 1960. [8], 164 p. notes (p. 157-62). On the Conservative Baptist Association of America, formed in 1947 as an association (not a "convention") of Baptist churches, mainly in the Northern Baptist Convention; with some account of its antecedents since 1907. [1868

Christian Scientists

JOHN B. STARR. Mary Baker Eddy and Dartmouth. Dartmouth alumni bul., 53(3):13-14 (Dec 1959). port. On Nathaniel Bouton, pastor of the First Congregational Church, Concord, N.H., and Albert Baker, brother of Mary Baker Eddy, Dartmouth graduates, and their influence upon her between 1825 and 1834. [1869

Church of the Brethren

DONALD FLOYD DURNBAUGH. Brethren beginnings: the origins of the Church of the Brethren in the early eighteenth century. Church hist., 29:353-4 (Sep). Abstract of thesis--Univ. of Pennsylvania. Includes some account of the migration of most of the Brethren to Pennsylvania between 1719 and 1735, and their reasons for not merging with the Mennonites. [1870

VERNON FRANKLIN SCHWALM. Arthur Cassel Wieand [1871-1954]. Elgin, Ill.: Brethren Press [1960]. 155 p. ports., table, views. notes. On his early life near Wadsworth, Ohio, his studies at Juniata College, MacPherson College, the University of Chicago, and the University of Chicago Divinity School, and his service from 1908 till 1946 in Bethany Bible School, Chicago, a "Bible training school for the Church of the Brethren" (of which he was President from its founding in 1908 till 1932). [1871

HERBERT WARD HOGAN. The intellectual impact of the twentieth century on the Church of the Brethren [1890-1950s]. Ann Arbor: University Microfilms, 1958 [i. e. 1960]. Positive microfilm of typescript. [461] leaves. Thesis--Claremont Graduate School. Abstracted: Dissert. abstracts, 21: 1173-4 (Nov). [1872

ROGER EDWIN SAPPINGTON. The development of social policy in the Church of the Brethren, 1908-1958. Ann Arbor: University Microfilms, 1959 [i. e. 1960]. Positive microfilm of typescript. x, 474 leaves. bibliog. (leaves 470-74). Thesis--Duke Univ. Abstracted: Dissert. abstracts, 20: 3715-16 (Mar). [1873

Congregationalists

WILLISTON WALKER (1860-1922), ed. The creeds and platforms of Congregationalism. With an introduction by Douglas Horton. Boston: Pilgrim Press [1960]. xvi, [2], 604 p. bibliogs., notes. 1st ed. 1893. Documents in 20 chronological chapters, 1582-1883, connected by "historic notes and comments" by the editor. Includes American documents, 1620-1883. [1874

ROBERT HENSON. Form and content of the Puritan funeral elegy [1647-1717]. Am. lit., 32:11-27 (Mar). notes. [1875

NORMAN S. GRABO. Edward Taylor on the Lord's Supper. Boston Pub. Lib. quar., 12:22-36 (Jan). notes. On his expression, in his manuscript sermons and commonplace books, of disagreement with the doctrine of the Rev. Solomon Stoddard that "no man could know he was saved with absolute certainty" and that therefore the churches should "admit all well-behaved Christians to the Sacrament," 1679-94. [1876

EDWARD TAYLOR (1642-1729). The poet to the pope: Edward Taylor to Solomon Stoddard [13 Feb. 1687/88. Edited by] Norman S. Grabo. Am. lit., 32:197-201 (May). notes. Letter from one Congregational minister to another, presenting 11 arguments against Stoddard's proposals "to bring all above 14 years of age, that live morally, and having Catechisticall knowledge of the Principalls of Religion, to the Lords Supper," without requiring "a public confession of conversion prior to gaining full church admission" or other evidence of regeneration. Appended: a short reply from Stoddard. [1877

DONALD ELWIN STANFORD. The Puritan poet as preacher--an Edward Taylor sermon. Waldo McNeir & Leo B. Levy, eds., Studies in American literature (Baton Rouge: Louisiana State Univ. Press, 1960 [Louisiana State University studies, Humanities series, 8]), p. 1-10. notes. Analysis of a sermon by Taylor forming part of a manuscript volume of his sermons, 1701-3, delivered in Westfield, Mass.; with remarks on the value of his 15 known sermons "as contributory to a fuller understanding of the poetry" of "our most important colonial poet." [1878

DOUGLAS J. ELWOOD. The Philosophical theology of Jonathan Edwards [1703-58]. N.Y.: Columbia Univ. Press, 1960. xii, [4], 220 p. port. bibliog. (p. 199-214), notes (p. 163-97). [1879

ORVILLE A. HITCHCOCK. Jonathan Edwards [1703-58]. Speech Association of America, A history and criticism of American public address, ed. William Norwood Brigance, 2d ed. (N.Y.: Russell & Russell, 1960), 1:213-37. bibliog., notes. On the oratorical and rhetorical characteristics of his Congregational sermons, delivered in Northampton and Stockbridge, Mass., and elsewhere, 1722-58. [1880

CHARLES EDWARD JEFFERSON (1860-1937). The best of Charles E. Jefferson. Selected and with an introduction by Frederick Keller Stamm. N.Y.: Crowell [1960]. ix, [3], 268 p. Collection of 14 sermons and 17 "conversations" by a Congregational minister at Chelsea, Mass., and the Broadway Tabernacle, New York City, 1905-34. [1881

LEILA W. ANDERSON. Pilgrim circuit rider. [By] Leila W. Anderson in collaboration with Harriet Harmon Dexter. N.Y.: Harper [1960]. xi, 200, [1] p. ports., views. On the author's studies in the University of Chicago Divinity School (1937-40), her ordination as a minister, her work in Christian education in South Dakota (especially among the Indians), and her employment since 1946 as a traveling visitor of rural churches of the Congregational Christian Churches throughout the United States and in parts of Europe and Asia to develop programs of Christian education; with some account of her early life in rural Illinois, her recovery from tuberculosis, her studies in Monmouth College, and her teaching from 1929 to 1937 in Iberia Junior College in the Ozarks. [1882

Disciples of Christ, Christian Churches, and Churches of Christ

ARTHUR MEIER SCHLESINGER, JR. The age of Alexander Campbell [1788-1866]. Perry Epler Gresham, ed., The sage of Bethany: a pioneer in broadcloth (St. Louis: Bethany Press [1960]), p. 25-44. notes. On "the contrasts between the old Calvinism and the new democratic individualism," ca. 1800 to 1866. [1883

KENNETH V. LOTTICK. Indigenous religions in the United States. V. The Disciples of Christ [since 1804]. Social studies, 51:20-26 (Jan). notes. [1884

LOUIS COCHRAN. The drama of Alexander Campbell [1788-1866]. Perry Epler Gresham, ed., The sage of Bethany: a pioneer in broadcloth (St. Louis: Bethany Press [1960]), p. 67-80. On the "epic quality" of his life after his immigration to America in 1809, as seen by the author, who has written a novel about Campbell. [1885

PERRY EPLER GRESHAM. Alexander Campbell [1788-1866]--schoolmaster. Perry Epler Gresham, ed., The sage of Bethany: a pioneer in broadcloth (St. Louis: Bethany Press [1960]), p. 9-23. On his emigration from Scotland in 1809, his religious, political, and economic activities in Washington County, Pa., and the adjacent part of future West Virginia, his share in founding Christian churches (each, apparently, having as its title either the Christian Church or the Church of Christ of a named place), his founding of Bethany College, and his publication of religious magazines. [1886

ROLAND HERBERT BAINTON. Alexander Campbell and the social order. Perry Epler Gresham, ed., The sage of Bethany: a pioneer in broadcloth (St. Louis: Bethany Press [1960]), p. 117-29. notes. On Campbell as a "highly representative American of the first half of the nineteenth century" in his attitudes toward social problems, 1815-66. [1887

JOHN WILLIAM McGARVEY (1829-1911). The autobiography of J. W. McGarvey (1829-1911). [Foreword by De Loris Stevenson and Dwight E. Stevenson.] Lexington, Ky.: College of the Bible, 1960. [2], 93 p. Reminiscences (finished in 1906) of the author's early life in Hopkinsville, Ky., his studies at Bethany College, and his service as a minister of the Disciples of Christ at Dover, Mo., and Lexington, Ky., and as Professor of Sacred History at the College of the Bible, Lexington; with references to his many theological publications. [1888

WARREN SAUNDERS JONES. G[rover] C[leveland] Brewer [1884-1956]: lecturer, debater, and preacher [of the Churches of Christ, mainly in Tennessee and Texas]. Ann Arbor: University Microfilms, 1960. Positive microfilm of typescript. [191] leaves. Thesis--Wayne State Univ. Abstracted: Dissert. abstracts, 21:265 (Jul). [1889

Episcopalians

GEORGE MacLAREN BRYDON. Concerning the financial support of the Church, 1066-1960. P. E. Church, Hist. mag., 29:302-14 (Dec). notes. Mainly on sources of funds for the Church of England in Virginia, 1607-1789, and for the Protestant Episcopal Church in the United States since 1789. [1890

GEORGE W. PILCHER. Virginia newspapers and the dispute over the proposed colonial episcopate, 1771-1772. Historian, 23:98-113 (Nov). [1891

JOHN FREDERICK WOOLVERTON. William Augustus Muhlenberg [1796-1877] and the founding of St. Paul's College. P. E. Church, Hist. mag., 29:192-218 (Sep). notes. Evidence that "during his childhood and the formative years of his youth" he "knew and was a part of the Episcopal Church and that alone" (and was not, as often alleged, influenced by his "Lutheran heritage"), and that his schools, the Flushing Institute (opened in 1828 at Flushing, L.I.) and St. Paul's College (opened in 1836), were clearly of "Episcopal character," but that he tended to see "Churches and Word and Sacrament as mere tools for the achievement of some other end." [1892

WILLIAM K. HUBBELL. Henry Caswall (1810-1870) and the backwoods church. P. E. Church, Hist. mag., 29:219-39 (Sep). notes. On his service as an Episcopal minister in Ohio, Kentucky, Indiana, and Missouri, 1831-42, and thereafter in his native England; and his America and the Catholic Church (1839 and later editions). [1893

MARIE KATHRYN HOCHMUTH & NORMAN W. MATTIS. Phillips Brooks [1835-93]. Speech Association of America, A history and criticism of American public address, ed. William Norwood Brigance, 2d ed. (N.Y.: Russell & Russell, 1960), 1:294-328. bibliog., notes. On the oratorical and rhetorical characteristics of his Episcopalian sermons in Philadelphia and Boston, 1859-93. [1894

IN memoriam: Edward Lambe Parsons, May 18, 1868 - July 18, 1960, bishop and doctor, member of the Joint Commission of the General Convention on Historical magazine, 1937-1955, Associate Editor of Historical magazine, 1947-1960. P. E. Church, Hist. mag., 29:182-4 (Sep). [1895

FRANCIS J. BLOODGOOD. Profile of Frank Gavin (1890-1938), priest and scholar. P. E. Church, Hist. mag., 29:51-5 (Mar). Reminiscences by a friend. [1896

ARTHUR WILSON (born 1888). Thy will be done: the autobiography of an Episcopal minister. N.Y.: Dial Press, 1960. [6], 213 p. On his early life and studies for the priesthood in England, his emigration to America in 1908, his ordination as an Episcopal priest after completion of his studies in the seminary at Nashotah, Wis., his ministry in Wisconsin, "a succession of small towns in Illinois" (including 7 years at Danville), Chattanooga, and Lockland (a Negro anti-white suburb of Cincinnati, to which he was assigned in 1930), the refusal of his wife to live in Lockland, her consent to a divorce, his excommunication for 7 years, his removal to Los Angeles (where he sold insurance and real estate), his second marriage (to Villette Stoddard), the death of his former wife in Illinois 12 years after his removal to Los Angeles, the resulting recognition of his right to remarry under Episcopal church law, his reinstatement as a priest, his assignment to St. Mary's Church near Los Angeles, and his gratification, when he revisited Lockland, to find great improvements attributable to his former work there. [1897

Lutherans

WILLARD DOW ALLBECK. John Stough [Johannes Stauch, 1762-1845], founder of Ohio Lutheranism. Luth. quar., 12:25-43 (Feb). notes. On his life as a farmer, miller, etc., in Pennsylvania, Maryland, West Virginia, and after 1806 in Columbiana and Crawford Counties, Ohio; his work as a "catechist," a "candidate," and after 1804 an ordained pastor; his organization of Lutheran churches in these States and Kentucky, of the Ohio Synod (later known as the Joint Synod of Ohio) in 1818, and of the English Lutheran Synod in 1840; and his favorable attitude toward revivalism and the use of English-language services. [1898

HENRY MELCHIOR MUHLENBERG (1711-87). The journals of Henry Melchior Muhlenberg. In three volumes. Translated by Theodore G. Tappert and John W. Doberstein. Volume III. Phila.: Evangelical Lutheran Ministerium of Pennsylvania and Adjacent States and the Muhlenberg Press, 1958. [10], 797 p. maps. Vol. I published in 1942. Very detailed record of the author's domestic and ministerial activities, religious travels, and receipts and expenditures, of Lutheran affairs in eastern Pennsylvania and elsewhere, and of many public events, 1 Jan. 1777 - 29 Sep. 1787; with an index to the 3 volumes (p. 755-97). [1899

SYDNEY ECKMAN AHLSTROM. Facing the New World: Augustana and the American challenge [1800-1906]. Augustana Evangelical Lutheran Church, Centennial Publication Committee, Centennial essays, Augustana Lutheran Church, 1860-1960, ed. Emmer Engberg, Conrad Bergendoff, & Edgar M. Carlson (Rock Island, Ill.: Augustana Press [1960]), p. 1-26. notes. [1900

FRANK H. SEILHAMER. The New Measure movement among Lutherans. Luth. quar., 12:121-43 (May). notes. On measures that involved "'protracted meetings,' animated, fiery 'heart-searching' preaching, calling out of 'sinners' for private prayer, 'anxious' or 'inquiry' meetings, and the 'mourner's bench,'" 1804-59 (especially in the early 1840s), the vehement differences of opinion among Lutherans and regarding the Christian validity of the "measures," and the gradual victory of their opponents. [1901

JOEL SWARTZ (1827-1914). A short story of a long life: an autobiography. Written for the family, 1904. Edited and published by Philip Allen Swartz. Poughkeepsie, N.Y. [1960? 2], xii, 224, [4] p. ports. On the author's early life in Lebanon, Va., his studies at Monongalia Academy (Morgantown, W. Va.), New Market Academy, and Capitol University in Columbus, Ohio, his teaching at Clover Hill Seminary (Friedens) and Strasburg Academy (Strasburg, Va.), his service as a Lutheran minister in a circuit of several churches in the Shenandoah Valley and later in Baltimore, Carlisle (Pa.), Philadelphia, Gettysburg, and elsewhere, his teaching at Wittenberg Seminary (Springfield, Ohio), and his change from the Lutheran ministry to the Congregational in his 67th year. The narrative of events after the Civil War is cursory. [1902

KARL E. MATTSON. The theology of the Augustana Lutheran Church [1849-1960]. Augustana Evangelical Lutheran Church, Centennial Publication Committee, Centennial essays, Augustana Lutheran Church, 1860-1960, ed. Emmer Engberg, Conrad Bergendoff, & Edgar M. Carlson (Rock Island, Ill.: Augustana Press [1960]), p. 28-50. notes. [1903

FREDERICK SHEELY WEISER. Serving love: chapters in the early history of the diaconate in American Lutheranism. [Gettysburg] 1960. [7] leaves, 228 p. tables. bibliog. (p. 223-8), notes. Thesis (B.D.)--Lutheran Theological Seminary. On organizations and "motherhouses" of deaconesses in the Lutheran churches, 1849-1916. [1904

EMMET E. EKLUND. Faith and education. Augustana Evangelical Lutheran Church, Centennial Publication Committee, Centennial essays, Augustana Lutheran Church, 1860-1960, ed. Emmer Engberg, Conrad Bergendoff, & Edgar M. Carlson (Rock Island, Ill.: Augustana Press [1960]), p. 70-88. notes. On "faith in its concrete relation to education within the history of the Augustana Lutheran Church," 1850-1960. [1905

CLIFFORD ANSGAR NELSON. Pulpit and altar. Augustana Evangelical Lutheran Church, Centennial Publication Committee, Centennial essays, Augustana Lutheran Church, 1860-1960, ed. Emmer Engberg, Conrad Bergendoff, & Edgar M. Carlson (Rock Island, Ill.: Augustana Press [1960]), p. 169-99. notes. On the development of the "structure of the worship life" of the Augustana Lutheran Church since the 1850s. [1906

GERHARD L. BELGUM. The Old Norwegian Synod in America, 1853-1890. Church hist., 29:93-4 (Mar). Abstract of thesis--Yale Univ., 1957. [1907

BURNICE FJELLMAN. Women in the Church [1853-1960]. Augustana Evangelical Lutheran Church, Centennial Publication Committee, Centennial essays, Augustana Lutheran Church, 1860-1960, ed. Emmer Engberg, Conrad Bergendoff, & Edgar M. Carlson (Rock Island, Ill.: Augustana Press [1960]), p. 200-226. notes. [1908

MARTIN E. CARLSON. Stewardship: Christianity lived responsibly. Augustana Evangelical Lutheran Church, Centennial Publication Committee, Centennial essays, Augustana Lutheran Church, 1860-1960, ed. Emmer Engberg, Conrad Bergendoff, & Edgar M. Carlson (Rock Island, Ill.: Augustana Press [1960]), p. 247-67. On the development of "the concept and program of Christian stewardship within the Augustana Lutheran Church," 1854-1960. [1909

EMMER E. ENGBERG. Augustana and code morality. Augustana Evangelical Lutheran Church, Centennial Publication Committee, Centennial essays, Augustana Lutheran Church, 1860-1960, ed. Emmer Engberg, Conrad Bergendoff, & Edgar M. Carlson (Rock Island, Ill.: Augustana Press [1960]), p. 122-49. notes. On the rules of moral conduct in the successive constitutions of the Augustana Evangelical Lutheran Church, 1857-1939, and in its other publications, relating to church discipline, athletic sports, the theater, cards, dancing, secret societies, birth control, and liquor, and the gradual weakening or disappearance of its opposition to all of these except the last. [1910

EVALD BENJAMIN LAWSON. The ministry. Augustana Evangelical Lutheran Church, Centennial Publication Committee, Centennial essays, Augustana Lutheran Church, 1860-1960, ed. Emmer Engberg, Conrad Bergendoff, & Edgar M. Carlson (Rock Island, Ill.: Augustana Press [1960]), p. 150-68. notes. On the "concept of the ministry held in the Augustana Lutheran Church," 1860-1960, with particular reference to "our pioneer pastors," many of whom were from Sweden. [1911

ERIC HERBERT WAHLSTROM. The means of grace. Augustana Evangelical Lutheran Church, Centennial Publication Committee, Centennial essays, Augustana Lutheran Church, 1860-1960, ed. Emmer Engberg, Conrad Bergendoff, & Edgar M. Carlson (Rock Island, Ill.: Augustana Press [1960]), p. 51-69. notes. On the development of doctrines of grace in the Church, 1860-1960. [1912

CARL WILLIAM SEGERHAMMER. Developing patterns of evangelism [in the Augustana Lutheran Church, 1870-1960]. Augustana Evangelical Lutheran Church, Centennial Publication Committee, Centennial essays, Augustana Lutheran Church, 1860-1960, ed. Emmer Engberg, Conrad Bergendoff, & Edgar M. Carlson (Rock Island, Ill.: Augustana Press [1960]), p. 107-21. notes. [1913

ROBERT W. HOLMEN. The ministry of mercy. Augustana Evangelical Lutheran Church, Centennial Publication Committee, Centennial essays, Augustana Lutheran Church, 1860-1960, ed. Emmer Engberg, Conrad Bergendoff, & Edgar M. Carlson (Rock Island, Ill.: Augustana Press [1960]), p. 227-46. On the deaconess sisterhoods of the Church and their hospitals, and the Augustana Lutheran homes for invalids, the aged, and orphan children, 1887-1960. [1914

Mennonites

WILLIAM ILDEPHONSE SCHREIBER. Amish wedding days. Jour. Am. folklore, 72:12-17 (Jan-Mar). notes. On the reasons in "cult practices of ancient, pre-Christian times" why Amish weddings are held only on Tuesday and Thursday. [1915

JOHN CHRISTIAN WENGER. Glimpses of Mennonite history and doctrine. [Third edition.] Scottdale, Pa.: Herald Press [1959. 10], 258 p. facsim., ports., views. bibliog. (p. 233-8). 1st ed. 1940. Includes some account of the Mennonites in the United States since 1644. [1916

ABRAHAM PETER TOEWS. American Mennonite worship: its roots, development, and application [1683-1958]. N.Y.: Exposition Press [1960]. 193 p. double table. bibliog. (p. 186-93), notes. (An Exposition-university book.) Thesis (M. S. T.)--Concordia Theological Seminary, 1958. On the forms of Mennonite worship. [1917

GT. BRIT. Exchequer. England invited Mennonites to America in 1717. [Edited by] Ira D. Landis. Mennonite hist. bul., 15(3):5-6 (Jul 1954). "Declaration of Johannes Rudolf Ochs, Secretary of the British Exchequer, April 11, 1717," here translated by Irvin B. Horst from a document evidently circulated on the Continent, stating terms on which Mennonites may settle in the British colonies in America, describing an unnamed area between 39° N and 43° N running west 200 miles, and giving information about money and equipment to take to America. [1918

WILLARD D. RUTH. The early life [and later years] of John F. Funk [1835-1930]. Mennonite hist. bul., 14(1):2-3;(2):1-3 (Jan, Apr 1953). On his life in eastern Pennsylvania, Chicago, and Elkhart, Ind., as a Mennonite, a schoolteacher, editor and publisher of the Herald of truth (Mennonite newspaper established in 1864), printer and publisher of Mennonite books, Mennonite minister, and patron of Menonite charities. [1919

MELVIN GINGERICH. The term "Old Mennonite" [in Pennsylvania and Kansas since 1847]. Mennonite hist. bul., 9(1):1, 3 (Jan 1948). For added information see "A communication" from Amos K. Stauffer, 10(1):4. [1920

CLAYTON SWARTZENTRUBER. John S. Coffman [1848-99]: pioneer Mennonite evangelist. Mennonite hist. bul., 11(2):1-3; (3):1-4 (Apr, May 1950). On his life in the Shenandoah Valley and at Elkhart, Ind., his service as a teacher and a minister, and his travels as a revivalist. [1921

REUBEN J. HEATWOLE (1847-1921). A Civil War story, written in 1919. Mennonite hist. bul., 9(1):3-4 (Jan 1948). On the success of the author, Henry G. Brunk (1836-73), and others in evading military service in Rockingham, Va., and escaping through the woods and by night travel to West Virginia, Maryland, Pennsylvania, and Illinois, 1861 ff. [1922

JOHN ANDREW HOSTETLER, comp. Titles printed (not published) by John F. Funk and the Mennonite Publishing Company, Mennonite hist. bul., 19(1):3, 5 (Jan 1958). Chronological list, 1864-1920, of titles in German or, in later years, often in English. [1923

HERMAN E. ROPP. Did our forefathers smoke? Mennonite hist. bul., 13(1):5-6 (Jan 1952). notes. Evidence that at the beginning of the 19th century "both European and American Mennonites smoked freely" (though Mennonite objections to tobacco had been expressed as early as 1639), that no American objection has been found before 1864, and that the use of tobacco has been increasingly criticized and discouraged since that time. [1924

TIMOTHY BRENNEMAN. Reminiscences of J. F. Funk. Mennonite hist. bul., 9(3):1-2 (Jul 1948). Undated recollections of Funk's stay in Elkhart as headquarters of his Mennonite Publishing Company, and of his opposition to "progressive" methods in the church, 1866-74. [1925

JOHN CHRISTIAN WENGER. Biography of Amos Daniel Wenger [1867-1935] until 1933. Mennonite hist. bul., 19(3):1-2, 6-8; (4):5-8 (Jul, Oct 1958). port. On his life in Virginia, Ohio, Missouri, and Pennsylvania, his work in America and abroad as a Mennonite evangelist, and his service (beginning in 1922) as principal of the Eastern Mennonite School, Harrisonburg, Va. [1926

JOHN MAURICE HOHLFELD. Historian, teacher, pastor, friend: Elmer Schultz Johnson [1872-1959]. Mennonite life, 15:118-23 (Jul). port. On his early life in Berks County, Pa., his studies at Perkiomen Academy, Princeton University, and Hartford Theological Seminary, his service as a Schwenkfelder minister in Philadelphia, his collection of the writings of Caspar Schwenkfeld in Europe, his teaching of medieval and Reformation history at Hartford, and his other scholarly and religious interests. [1927

FRANK H. EPP. Mennonitische Rundschau (1878-1956). Mennonite hist. bul., 17(4):1-3 (Oct 1956). notes. On the Nebraska Ansiedler (Lincoln, 1878-80) and its successor, Mennonitische Rundschau (Elkhart, Ind., 1880-1908; Scottdale, Pa., 1908-23; Winnipeg, Manitoba, 1923-56), "an inter-Mennonite paper." [1928

J. R. SHANK. Memories of John S. Coffman. Mennonite hist. bul., 17(1): 7-8 (Jan 1956). On missionary visits by him to the author's community or family in Missouri (1883, 1890) and Florida (1894). [1929

RAY BAIR. The merger of the Mennonite and the Amish Mennonite Conference from 1911 to 1928. Mennonite hist. bul., 13(4):2-4 (Oct 1952). notes. [1930

Methodists

DAVID C. SHIPLEY. The ministry in Methodism in the eighteenth century [1730s-1800]. Convocation of Methodist Theological Faculties, 1st, 1959, The ministry in the Methodist heritage, ed. Gerald O. McCulloh (Nashville: Dept. of Ministerial Education, Division of Educational Institutions, Board of Education, Methodist Church, 1960), p. 11-31. notes. [1931

RICHARD ALLEN (1760-1831). The life experience and Gospel labors of the Rt. Rev. Richard Allen, to which is annexed the rise and progress of the African Methodist Episcopal Church in the United States of America. Containing a narrative of the yellow fever in the year of Our Lord 1793. With an address to the people of color in the United States. ... With an introduction by George A. Singleton. N.Y.: Abingdon Press [1960]. 93 p. port., views. On the author's early life as a slave in Philadelphia and Delaware, his conversion to Methodism, his service as a Methodist circuit rider in the Middle Atlantic States, and his founding of the African Methodist Episcopal Church. The first edition was probably that of 1833. [1932

LESLIE RAY MARSTON. From age to age a living witness: a historical interpretation of Free Methodism's first century. Winona Lake, Ind.: Light and Life Press [1960]. 608 p. tables, col. double map. bibliog. (p. 591-6), notes. Includes an introductory account of Methodism from its origin to 1852, including its development in America since the 1760s. [1933

FRANCIS ASBURY (1745-1816). The journal and letters of Francis Asbury. ... Elmer E. Clark, editor-in-chief, J. Manning Potts, [and] Jacob S.

Payton. London: Epworth Press; Nashville: Abingdon Press [1958]. 3 v. xxiv, 778; [4], 871; xviii, 603 p. facsims., maps, ports., views. bibliog. (2:809-15), notes. Journal, 7 Aug. 1771 - 7 Dec. 1815, recording the author's voyage from England and his work in America as an itinerant minister, later Bishop of the Methodist Episcopal Church, involving travels in every State east of the Appalachians and also in Kentucky and Ohio, with notes identifying the places and persons mentioned in the text (printed from the edition of 1821 and earlier partial printings, the manuscript having been lost by fire in 1836); letters, 26 Oct. 1768 - [4 Mar. 1816?]; and sermons. [1934

FREDERICK ABBOTT NORWOOD. The Americanization of the Wesleyan itinerant [1783-1900]. Convocation of Methodist Theological Faculties, 1st, 1959, The ministry in the Methodist heritage, ed. Gerald O. McCulloh (Nashville: Dept. of Ministerial Education, Methodist Church, 1960), p. 33-65. notes. [1935

FRANZ HILDEBRANDT. The meaning of ordination in Methodism [1784-1959]. Convocation of Methodist Theological Faculties, 1st, 1959, The ministry in the Methodist heritage, ed. Gerald O. McCulloh (Nashville: Dept. of Ministerial Education, Division of Educational Institutions, Board of Education, Methodist Church, 1960), p. 67-100. notes. [1936

ARTHUR BRUCE MOSES. Asbury's first years as a bishop [1784-89]. A. M. E. Zion quar. rev., 64:99-102 (spring 1953). [1937

WILLIAM J. POWELL. A brief history of the African Methodist Episcopal Zion Church [1799-1947]. A. M. E. Zion quar. rev., 59:73-83 (spring 1949). bibliog., notes. [1938

JOHN OWEN GROSS. The Methodist Church and theological education [1800-1959]. Convocation of Methodist Theological Faculties, 1st, 1959, The ministry in the Methodist heritage, ed. Gerald O. McCulloh (Nashville: Dept. of Ministerial Education, Division of Educational Institutions, Board of Education, Methodist Church, 1960), p. 129-43. [1939

CARL FREDERICK WITTKE. William Nast [1807-99], patriarch of German Methodism. Detroit: Wayne State Univ. Press, 1959 [c1960]. vii, 248, [1] p. port. notes (p. 229-40). On his early life in Germany, his education for the Lutheran ministry, his emigration to America in 1828, his work as a tutor in Pennsylvania and New York, his teaching at Kenyon College, his conversion to Methodism, his service in the Ohio Methodist Conference as "missionary to the Germans of Cincinnati," his editorship of a newspaper, Der christliche Apologete, his service as president of Wallace College, Berea, Ohio, and his missionary activities in Germany. [1940

DAVID HENRY BRADLEY, SR. The Discipline of 1852 and 1856. A. M. E. Zion quar. rev., 67:45-50 (winter 1956). On The doctrine and discipline of the African Methodist Episcopal Zion Church in America (1858), a revision made in 1856 of a revision in 1852; with excerpts from its text. [1941

RICHARD R. BLEWS. Master workmen ... biographies of the late bishops of the Free Methodist Church during her first century, 1860-1960 [i. e. 1947]. Winona Lake, Ind.: Light and Life Press [1960]. 303 p. ports. Fourteen biographical sketches: Benjamin Titus Roberts, Edward Payson Hart, George Whitefield Coleman, Burton Rensselaer Jones, William Thomas Hogue, Walter Ashbel Sellew, John Samuel MacGeary, David Snethen Warner, William Henry Clark, Arthur de France Zahniser, George William Griffith, Burton Jones Vincent, Robert Hopkins Warren, and William Pearce. [1942

ALMER PENNEWELL. A voice in the wilderness: Jesse Walker, "the Daniel Boone of Methodism." Nashville: Parthenon Press, for Almer Pennewell, Niles, Ill. [195-?]. 192 p. facsim., table. bibliog. (p. 191-2). On the early life of Jesse Walker (1766-1835) in Virginia and North Carolina, his work as a Methodist circuit rider in Tennessee, Kentucky, Illinois, and Missouri, his establishment of an Indian school in Peoria and a church in Chicago, and his retirement and death in Des Plaines, Ill. Consists largely of anecdotes. [1943

CONGREGATIONAL METHODIST CHURCH. General Conference. Minutes of the General Conference, the first through the twentieth sessions, 1869-1945. Tehuacana, Tex.: Westminster College Print Shop [1960. 6], 130 p. tables (part fold.). Preface signed: Wilton Fowler, Jr. [1944

SAM H. FRANK. Samuel E[ugene] Hager [born 1869]: Kentucky missionary to Japan. Ky. Hist. Soc., Reg., 58:194-223 (Jul). notes. On his early life in Breathitt County, his teaching there in a rural school, his studies at Central College, Kentucky Wesleyan College, and the Theological Department of Vanderbilt University, his work as a Methodist minister in Kentucky, Missouri, Oklahoma, and Montana, and his departure from the United States in 1893 to serve in Japan. [1944a

DAVID HENRY BRADLEY, SR. The great Negro (Methodist) churches. A. M. E. Zion quar. rev., 67:19-33 (winter 1956). On the African Methodist Episcopal Church, the African Methodist Episcopal Zion Church, and the Colored Methodist Episcopal Church, 1880-1956. [1945

DAVID HENRY BRADLEY, SR. [A historical chart of the Church Extension Society of the African Methodist Episcopal Church, ca. 1905.] A. M. E. Zion quar. rev., 58(4):61-2 (fall 1948). Information from a broadside showing portraits of ministers and views of churches, with textual information about the Society, begun in 1896 and incorporated in 1905. [1946

WILLIAM J. McCUTCHEON. Theology of the Methodist Episcopal Church during the inter-war period (1919-1939). Church hist., 29:353 (Sep). Abstract of thesis--Yale Univ. [1947

CHARLES VICTOR FAIRBAIRN (born 1890). I call to remembrance. Winona Lake, Ind.: Light and Life Press, 1960. 185, [2] p. ports. On the author's work as a minister and bishop of the Free Methodist Church of North America in Kansas and throughout the United States since 1927, and his earlier life and ministerial work in Ontario. [1948

JOHN H. SATTERWRITE. An evaluation of Hood Theological Seminary in the light of its history [1943-53]. A. M. E. Zion quar. rev., 67:212-15 (autumn 1957). Abstract of thesis (D. Th.)--Boston Univ. [1949

Mormons

CLAIRE AUGUSTA (WILCOX) NOALL. Intimate disciple: a portrait of Willard Richards [1804-54], apostle to Joseph Smith--cousin of Brigham Young. [Salt Lake City:] Univ. of Utah Press, 1957. xi, 630 p. facsims., maps, ports., views. bibliog. (p. 621-30), notes (p. 585-620). On his early life in Massachusetts, his conversion to Mormonism, his emigration to Ohio, Illinois, and eventually Utah, his establishment of Mormon worship in England, and his work as an official of the Church of Jesus Christ of Latter-Day Saints; with some account of his several widows. Fictional in form. [1950

NORMA J. FISCHER. Portrait of a prophet. Salt Lake City: Bookcraft, 1960. 224, [4] p. bibliog. (p. 228), notes (p. 225-7). On Joseph Smith (1805-44). [1951

JOHN J. STEWART. Joseph Smith [1805-44], democracy's unknown prophet. Salt Lake City: Mercury Pub. Co. [1960]. 119 p. map, ports., views. [1952

HYRUM LESLIE ANDRUS. The second American revolution. Brigham Young Univ. studies, 2:71-100 (autumn-winter 1959-60). notes. On the "social, religious, and economic as well as political" changes between 1820 and ca. 1845, and their relations to Mormonism. [1953

CARTER ELDREDGE GRANT. Along the Susquehanna River. Improvement era, 63:306-9, 336, 338-44 (May). map, views. On the several movements of Joseph Smith from New York State to Harmony, Susquehanna County, Pa., and back, Oct. 1825 - Aug. 1830, his marriage there to Emma Hale, their 3-room house (sold in 1833), his dictation there of the text of the Book of Mormon (read from the plates with the aid of the Urim and Thummim), and his reception in the river of "the priesthood and the proper order of baptism." [1954

GEORGE BARTHOLOMEW ARBAUGH. Gods, sex, and saints: the Mormon story [1830-1956]. Rock Island, Ill.: Augustana Press [1957]. 61 p. bibliog. (p. 61), notes (p. 59-60). On Mormonism as "a new religion which in fundamental respects is more alien to Christianity than is Islam." [1955

ALMA PEXTON BURTON & CLEA M. BURTON. Stories from Mormon history [1830-1948]. Salt Lake City: Deseret Book Co. [1960. 6], 310 p. Mainly brief excerpts from printed sources. [1956

ROBERT KENT FIELDING. Historical perspectives for a liberal Mormonism [since 1830]. West. humanities rev., 14:69-82 (winter). notes. [1957

ELMER CECIL McGAVIN. How we got the Book of Mormon. Salt Lake City: Deseret Book Co. [1960]. vii, [3], 128 p. diagrs., facsims., tables. notes. On the circumstances of its composition in pre-Columbian times, its discovery and transcription by Joseph Smith, its publication in 1830, and its editions and sales in America and abroad. [1958

RUSSELL F. RALSTON. Fundamental differences between the Reorganized Church and the Church in Utah. [Independence, Mo.:] Herald House, 1960. 244 p. bibliog, (p. 236-9), notes. On differences between the Reorganized Church of Jesus Christ of Latter-Day Saints and the Church of Jesus Christ of Latter-Day Saints with respect to plurality of gods, polygamy, baptism for the dead, and other issues, 1830-1959. [1959

GEORGE REYNOLDS (1842-1909). Holiness to the Lord: a complete concordance of the Book of Mormon [1830]. ... Edited and arranged by Philip C. Reynolds. Salt Lake City: Deseret Book Co. [1957]. iv, 852 p. port. Reproduction of the first edition, 1899. [1960

ALBERT L. ZOBELL, JR. Where are the original manuscripts? *Improvement era*, 63:802-3, 826, 828 (Nov). facsims. On the printer's copy of the Book of Mormon, "mostly in Oliver Cowdery's handwriting," of which about 125 leaves, "some of which are worn and crumbled," survived the "irreparable damage" suffered by the manuscript after it was deposited in the cornerstone of the Nauvoo House by Joseph Smith in 1841 and before it was received in 2 installments (the latter in 1946) by the Church Historian's Office in Salt Lake City and photographed; and a copy retained by Cowdery for security purposes, which came into possession of the Reorganized Church of Jesus Christ of Latter Day Saints and in 1949 was "still in good condition." [1961

WILLIAM EDWIN BERRETT & ALMA PEXTON BURTON, *eds*. Readings in L. D. S. church history from original manuscripts. Volume II. A selection of and extracts from letters, editorials, private journals, records, periodicals, histories, biographies, and other original writings contemporary with and casting light upon early events in the Church of Jesus Christ of Latter-Day Saints. Salt Lake City, Utah: Deseret Book Co., 1955. xxviii, 617 p. bibliog. (p. 597-9), notes. This volume: from the death of Joseph Smith to the death of Brigham Young, 1844-77. Largely from printed sources. Vol. I published in 1953. [1962

KLAUS HANSEN. The political Kingdom of God as a cause for Mormon-Gentile conflict. *Brigham Young Univ. studies*, 2:241-60 (spring-summer). notes. On the Council of Fifty as a body having temporal as well as spiritual authority, 1844-90. [1963

CHURCH OF JESUS CHRIST OF LATTER-DAY SAINTS. Mormon economic organization: a sheaf of illustrative documents. [Edited] by Leonard J[ames] Arrington and Ralph W. Hansen. *Utah hist. quar.*, 28:40-55 (Jan). facsim., views. Broadside letters and circulars (with manuscript signatures) sent from Church headquarters in Salt Lake City to local Church authorities in Mormon communities throughout the West, on "The conservation of food" (1863), "Agricultural price control" (1864), "Constructing a telegraph line" (1865), "Church immigration teams" (1868), "Wool tithing" (1869), and "Temple construction" (1874). [1964

Presbyterians

ELWYN ALLEN SMITH. The doctrine of imputation and the Presbyterian schism of 1837-1838. Presbyt. Hist. Soc., *Jour.*, 38:129-51 (Sep). notes. On "the development of Calvinism from the pre-Edwardean period to the point at which debate broke out in Presbyterian circles, with particular reference to ... the imputation of Adam's sin to his descendants," 1741-1868. [1965

WILLIAM W. WOODSIDE. Presbyterian communion tokens. *Carnegie mag.*, 34:17-19 (Jan). views. On a collection (1748-1900) in the Coin Section of the Carnegie Museum, Pittsburgh. [1966

CARROLL W. PURSELL, JR. The fortunes of a religious newspaper: the *Christian repository* and the *Circular*, 1821-1825. Presbyt. Hist. Soc., *Jour.*, 38:91-102 (Jun). notes. On a newspaper published and edited at Wilmington, Del., by Robert Porter, printer, stationer, and Presbyterian elder. [1967

ELWYN ALLEN SMITH. The role of the South in the Presbyterian schism of 1837-38. Church hist., 29:44-63 (Mar). notes. On the relation of disagreement between the Old School and the New School and the disagreement concerning slavery. [1968

WILLIAM JUNIUS WADE. The origins and establishment of the Presbyterian Church in the United States. Ann Arbor: University Microfilms, 1959 [i. e. 1960]. Positive microfilm of typescript. 513 leaves. bibliog. (leaves 504-13). Thesis--Univ. of North Carolina. Abstracted: Dissert. abstracts, 20:2779 (Jan). On the secession of the Church from the Presbyterian Church in the U.S.A. as the Presbyterian Church in the Confederate States of America, and its persistence as a separate body after the war, 1861-70. [1969

ALVIN DUANE SMITH. Tribute to Dr. Charles A. Anderson [born 1889]. Presbyt. Hist. Soc., Jour., 38:1-8 (Mar). port. On his services as a Presbyterian minister in Watertown, N.Y., Maplewood, N.J., and the University of Pennsylvania (1916-31), as President of Tusculum College and Coe College (1931-44), and especially as Manager of the Department of History of the General Assembly of the United Presbyterian Church in the U.S.A. and Executive Secretary of the Presbyterian Historical Society (1944-59). [1970

Quakers

ROBERT OAKES BYRD. Quaker ways in foreign policy [1647-1950s. Toronto:] Univ. of Toronto Press [1960]. xxi, 230 p. Deals largely with the Quaker condemnation of war. [1971

FREDERICK BARNES TOLLES. Quakerism and politics [in America, 1672-1938, and abroad]. Frederick B. Tolles, Quakers and the Atlantic culture (N.Y.: Macmillan, 1960), p. 36-54. notes. First delivered as the 1956 Ward Lecture at Guilford College, and "separately printed by the College." [1972

FREDERICK BARNES TOLLES. The Quaker ethic and the spirit of capitalism [1717-91]. Frederick B. Tolles, Quakers and the Atlantic culture (N.Y.: Macmillan, 1960), p. 55-65. notes. From the William and Mary quarterly, 1947. [1973

KENNETH L. CARROLL. The influence of John Woolman on Joseph Nichols [1730?-1773/74] and the Nicholites. Anna (Cox) Brinton, ed., Then and now: Quaker essays, historical and contemporary, by friends of Henry Joel Cadbury (Phila.: Univ. of Pennsylvania Press [1960]), p. 168-79. notes. On a farmer in the Delmarva Peninsula (which Woolman visited in 1766), described by Woolman as "a Preacher, who I understand is not in outward Fellowship with any Religious Society of People, but who professeth nearly the same Principles as our Society doth"; the uncertainty whether Nichols ever met Woolman or was influenced by him in advocating pacifism, the wearing of undyed clothing, and the freeing of slaves; and the merger of the Nicholites with the Quakers at the end of the century. [1974

HOWARD HAINES BRINTON. Quakers and animals. Anna (Cox) Brinton, ed., Then and now: Quaker essays, historical and contemporary, by friends of Henry Joel Cadbury (Phila.: Univ. of Pennsylvania Press [1960]), p. 188-99. notes. On the Quaker attitude toward the treatment of animals since 1779. [1975

JAMES FLOYD MOORE. The ethical thought of Rufus Mattew Jones [1863-1948], with special reference to Biblical influences. Ann Arbor: University Microfilms, 1960. Positive microfilm of typescript. [381] leaves. Thesis--Boston Univ. Abstracted: Dissert. abstracts, 21:977-8 (Oct). Includes an effort "to contribute toward an evaluation of his position in relation to Quakerism and to the ecumenical church." [1976

MARY HOXIE JONES. Henry Joel Cadbury [born 1883]: a biographical sketch. Anna (Cox) Brinton, ed., Then and now: Quaker essays, historical and contemporary, by friends of Henry Joel Cadbury (Phila.: Univ. of Pennsylvania Press [1960]). p. 11-70. cartoon. notes. On his early life in Philadelphia, his studies at Harvard and at Haverford College, his teaching of Greek and Biblical literature at Haverford, Andover Theological Seminary, and Bryn Mawr, his service as Director of the Andover-Harvard Theological Library of Harvard University and as an official of the American Friends Service Committee, his life as a Quaker, and his contributions to Quaker history. [1977

Science

D. C. MARTIN. The tercentenary of the Royal Society. Science, 131: 1785-90 (17 Jun). ports., views. Includes some account of American membership in the Royal Society of London since 1660. [1978

RALPH SAMUEL BATES. Scientific societies in the United States. ... Second edition. N.Y.: Columbia Univ. Press, 1958. ix, [5], 297 p. bibliog. (p. 225-68), notes. 1st ed. 1945. Organized in 5 chronological chapters, 1683-1958. [1979

ROLAND LAMONTAGNE. La contribution scientifique de La Galissonière au Canada. Rev. hist. Am. française, 13:509-24 (Mar). notes. On Roland-Michel Barrin, Comte de la Galissonière, Governor ad interim of New France, as a promoter of scientific studies there, 1739-49. Refers to his instructions to commanders of forts to make an inventory of the natural history of areas under their jurisdiction (including Lake Champlain and the Niagara River), and his outline of scientific observations to be made by Gaspard-Joseph Chaussegros de Léry in a voyage to Detroit and by Michel Chartier, Marquis de Lotbinière, in a voyage to Michilimackinac, 1749. [1980

EMMET FIELD HORINE. Biographical sketch and guide to the writings of Charles Caldwell, M.D. (1772-1853), with sections on phrenology and on hypnotism. Brooks, Ky.: High Acres Press, 1960. [2], viii, [2], 155, [2] p. diagrs., facsims., ports. (part mount.). notes. Partial contents.--1. Biographical sketch of Charles Caldwell.--2. Guide to the published writings of Charles Caldwell [1795 to 1851; abstracts].--3. Phrenology [abstracts of publications by various authors, 1815-1956].--4. Hypnotism [abstracts of publications by various authors, 1885-1949].--5. Previous biographical sketches of Charles Caldwell [1853-1935].--6. Manuscripts [1832-49].--Appendix [Catalogue of the published writings and translations of Charles Caldwell, M.D., &c. &c. from the year 1794 until the year 1851 (by himself)]. The abstracts total 293 entries. The biographical sketch deals with his early life in Orange County, N.C., his medical studies and teaching of geology and natural history at the University of Pennsylvania, his service as "Physician General of the Volunteers and Militia Troops of Pennsylvania" in the War of 1812, his work as editor of The port folio (Philadelphia, 1814-16), his activities in the establishment and administration of the Medical Department of Transylvania University (1819-37) and the Medical Institute of the City of Louisville (1837-49), and his special interest in hypnotism and phrenology. [1981

DIRK JAN STRUIK. American science between 1780 and 1830. Science, 129: 1100-1106 (24 Apr 1959). diagrs., port., views. bibliog., notes. [1982

ILEEN E. STEWART & VINCENT W. McGURL. Dues and membership in scientific societies [in the United States, 1799-1960]. Science, 132: 939-42 (7 Oct). diagr., tables. notes. [1983

FOREST GARRETT HILL. Formative relations of American enterprise, government, and science [1802-65]. Pol. science quar., 75:400-419 (Sep). notes. On activities of the War and Navy Departments, the Smithsonian Institution, and other Federal agencies in promoting "the early advancement of science, and thereby of private enterprise as well." [1984

JEANNETTE E. GRAUSTEIN. Harvard's only Massachusetts Professor of Natural History: establishing Harvard's Botanic Garden and equipping it with a director. Harvard alumni bul., 61:242-3, 257-8 (13 Nov 1958). port., views. On the service of William Dandridge Peck (1763-1822) in this capacity, 1805-22. [1985

HARRY HAYDEN CLARK. Fenimore Cooper and science. Wis. Acad. Sciences, Trans., 48 (1959):179-204; 49 (1960:249-82. notes. On James Fenimore Cooper's references to science and the parallels between his "general attitudes" and the "ideas associated with the science of his day," 1820s-50s. [1986

JAMES FLETCHER DOSTER. A century and a quarter of science at the University of Alabama [1831-1959]. Ala. Acad. Science, Jour., 30(4):18-24 (Apr 1959). bibliog. [1987

BONNIE S. STADELMAN. Elias Loomis [1811-89] and the Loomis Observatory. Ohio hist. quar., 69: 157-70 (Apr). notes. On his service in Western Reserve College, Hudson, Ohio, as Professor of Mathematics and Natural Philosophy, 1836-44, and the observatory (still standing) and astronomical equipment provided for his department. [1988

ALFRED LOUIS KROEBER (1876-1960). Frederic Ward Putnam [1839-1915]. Selected papers from the American anthropologist, 1888-1920, ed. Frederica De Laguna (Evanston, Ill.: Row, Peterson [1960]), p. 138-44. First printed in 1915. On his early life in Salem, Mass., his studies at Harvard, and his work as a "natural historian" (ichthyologist, zoologist, geologist, archeologist) and as an assistant in geological surveys, a curator of museums, Secretary and later President of the American Museum for the Advancement of Science (1873-1903), and Professor of Anthropology and Director of the Anthropological Museum, University of California (1903-9). [1989

FRANCIS EAGAN REILLY. The method of the sciences according to Charles Sanders Peirce [1839-1914]. Ann Arbor: University Microfilms, 1959 [i. e. 1960]. Positive microfilm of typescript. iii, 310 leaves. bibliog. (leaves 305-9). Thesis--St. Louis Univ. Abstracted: Dissert. abstracts, 20:3781 (Mar). [1990

EDWARD LURIE. Louis Agassiz [1807-73]: a life in science. [Chicago:] Univ. of Chicago Press [1960]. xiv, 449 p. cartoon, diagr., facsims., ports., views. bibliog. (p. 421-30), notes (p. 391-419). On his life as "a student of nature," his early years and work as a naturalist in Switzerland, his emigration to Boston in 1846, his teaching of zoology and geology at Harvard, his work as Director of the Museum of Comparative Zoology there and as editor of the American journal of science, his scientific explorations in Brazil and elsewhere, his diversion in later years to speechmaking and popular writing, and his "public involvement at the expense of intellectual activity." [1991

LOUISE (HALL) THARP. Adventurous alliance: the story of the Agassiz family of Boston. Boston: Little, Brown [1959]. xiii, 354 p. ports., views. notes (p. 325-9). On Louis Agassiz (Jean Louis Rodolphe Agassiz, 1807-73), Swiss biologist and geologist who arrived in Boston in 1846, Professor of Zoology and Geology in Lawrence Scientific School, Harvard, Curator of the Harvard Museum of Comparative Zoology, organizer of scientific expeditions to the Great Lakes and the Amazon, lecturer, and some of his students (especially Nathaniel Southgate Shaler and William James); his wife, Cecile (Braun) Agassiz, who remained in Germany and died in 1848; his second wife, Elizabeth Cabot (Cary) Agassiz (1822-1907), whom he married in 1850, organizer of a school for girls, and from 1882 till 1903 President of the Society for the Collegiate Instruction of Women (later Radcliffe College); and his 3 children (all by his first wife)--Alexander (who married Anna Russell), Ida (Mrs. Henry Lee Higginson), and Pauline (Mrs. Quincy Adams Shaw). [1992

SIDNEY STEVENS NEGUS (1892-1963). Edgar Calvin Leroy Miller, M.D., 1867-1954. Va. jour. science, 6:1-4 (Jan 1955). port. On his work as a medical missionary in the 1890s, a biochemist, a pharmacologist, a bacteriologist, a teacher in the Medical College of Virginia, and an organizer of scientific enterprises. [1993

BERNHARD JOSEPH STERN (1894-1956). The scientist as product and agent of change [1876-1956]. Historical sociology: the selected papers of Bernhard J. Stern (N.Y.: Citadel Press [1960]), p. 36-44. notes. Address, 21 Apr. 1956. [1994

NATIONAL ASSOCIATION FOR RESEARCH IN SCIENCE TEACHING. [Recipients of the Science Education Recognition Award. By Clarence M. Pruitt.] Science educ., 44:3-6, 67-70, 157-62, 245-7, 329-31 (Feb-Dec). ports. Biographical sketches, statements of the educational principles, and lists of the publications of Harry Allen Cunningham (born 1891), Charles Edgar Montgomery (1884-1961), Kenneth Eugene Anderson (born 1910), William Ray Teeters (born 1887), and John Adam Hollinger (born 1877). [1995

WALLACE REED BRODE. Development of a science policy [by the U.S. Government, 1884-1959]. Science, 131: 9-15 (1 Jan). On proposals for "either a Department of Science, a National Science Institute, or some other coordinated structure." [1996

F. DOW SMITH. Education and physical science [1890-1954]. Boston Univ. graduate jour., 4:127-30 (Apr 1956). [1997

KENNETH EUGENE ANDERSON & CLARENCE M. PRUITT. Palmer Oliver Johnson, statistician and science educator, 1891-1960. Science educ., 44:168-70 (Apr). port. [1998

BERNHARD JOSEPH STERN (1894-1956). Freedom of research in American science. Historical sociology: the selected papers of Bernhard J. Stern (N.Y.: Citadel Press [1960]), p. 133-59. From Science and society, spring 1954. On the pressures placed upon universities by industries and by government to undertake projects of applied science, the efforts of government to ascertain the ideological soundness of scientists, the curtailment of the free communication and publication of research, and the frequency of "military infringement on university autonomy," 1894-1954. [1999

I. BERNARD COHEN. Science, servant of man: a layman's primer for the age of science. Boston: Little, Brown, 1948. xiv, [2], 362 p. views. bibliog. and notes (p. 315-48). On applied science, mainly in the 20th century. Includes chapters on plant hormones, weed-killing chemicals, electric current and radio, synthetic rubber and nylon, trace elements in plants, blood groups and blood transfusion, hybrid corn, micropaleontology and oil prospecting, synthetic chemical compounds, the ionosphere and radio communication, and other applications; with evidence that "planning in science must always be limited, and ... the future scientific discoveries will remain unpredictable." [2000

SPECIAL LIBRARIES ASSOCIATION. Science-Technology Division. Handbook of scientific and technical awards in the United States and Canada, 1900-1952. ... Edited by Margaret A. Firth. N.Y. [1956]. xxiv, [2], 491 p. "List of periodicals and abbreviations" (p. xi-xix). [2001

HENRY HERMAN BARSCHALL. Is the United States falling behind in science? Discourse, 3:203-14 (Oct). On scientific education in America since 1901. [2002

ELLSWORTH S. OBURN. Distinguished service in science education. Science educ., 44:7-10 (Feb). facsim. On the National Association for Research in Science Teaching, 1928-59. See also, by the same author, "The crisis in science education research" (p. 19-22), on the present "seeming lethargy" of the Association and the unmet needs of the profession of science education. [2003

BENTLEY GLASS. The academic scientist, 1940-1960. Science, 132: 598-603 (2 Sep). notes. [2004

CLARENCE MARTIN PRUITT. For the record. Science educ., 44:238-42, 244 (Apr). On the author's service as an official of the National Association for Research in Science Teaching and as editor of Science education since 1945. [2005

HAROLD ELMER JOHNSON. The nature and content of science courses in selected public senior high schools in the United States in the school year 1953-54. Ann Arbor: University Microfilms, 1960. Positive microfilm of typescript. [234] leaves. Thesis (Ed. D.)--Temple Univ. Abstracted: Dissert. abstracts, 20:4568-9 (Jun). [2006

ASTRONOMY

JOSEPH MILES CHAMBERLAIN. The sky in replica. Natural hist., 69(2): 9-15 (Feb). views (part double). On planetaria in America (late 1790s to 1960) and abroad. [2007

C. D. SHANE. William Hammond Wright (1871-1959) [astronomer]. Am. Philos. Soc., Yr. bk., 1959, p. 150-53. [2008

WILLIAM JACOB LUYTEN. White dwarfs and stellar evolution. Am. scientist, 48:30-39 (Mar). table. Mainly on the author's observations (at the Harvard Observatory) of the "spectra of stars of low luminosity," since 1921. [2009

SIMONE DARO GOSSNER. Sky reporter. Natural hist., 69(1):61-2 (Jan). views. On the discovery of Pluto, "our ninth planet," by Clyde W. Tombaugh at the Lowell Observatory, Flagstaff, Ariz., 18 Feb. 1930. [2010

MALCOLM D. ROSS. Plastic balloons for planetary research [1935-57]. Jour. astronautical sciences, 5:5-10 (spring 1958). diagr., views. notes. [2011

CHARLES POLLARD OLIVIER. The great fireball of 26 July 1938. Science, 131:86-8 (8 Jan). table. On a "great bolide or exploded fireball" observed in the skies by watchers in the area between Pennsylvania and Vermont. [2012

BIOLOGY

FRIEDA (COBB) BLANCHARD. Nathan A[ugustus] Cobb [1859-1932], botanist and zoologist, a pioneer scientist in

Australia. Asa Gray bul., 3:205-72 (spring 1957). ports. views. On his early life on a farm in Spencer, Mass.; his studies in the Worcester Polytechnic Institute (then Worcester Free Institute); his teaching of chemistry and drawing at Williston Seminary (Easthampton, Mass.); his studies in Germany; his work in Australia, 1889-1905, eventually as senior scientist of the New South Wales Department of Agriculture, especially concerned with plant pathology; and his work in Hawaii, 1905-7, and Washington, D.C., 1907-32, in the U.S. Bureau of Plant Industry as an agricultural technologist and eventually "the world's authority" as a nematologist; with the author's memories of his domestic life and working habits, and a list of his publications, "complete for the period of his botanical activity, 1885 through 1916," mainly on plant pathology and on mycology. [2013

ESMOND RAY LONG. Frederick G[eorge] Novy [1864-1957] and some origins of American bacteriology. College Phys. Phila., Trans. & studies, 26:34-9 (Jun 1958). bibliog. On his early life in Chicago, his studies of chemistry and medicine at the University of Michigan, his work as a microbiologist, and his service as head of the Department of Bacteriology and Dean of the Medical School of the University of Michigan. [2014

CHARLES A. FLESCHNER. Biological control of insect pests [in America, 1873-1958, and abroad]. Science, 129: 537-44 (Feb 1959). views. notes. [2015

ELMER GRIMSHAW BUTLER. Edmund Newton Harvey (1887-1959) [physiologist, researcher in bioluminescence and cellular biology]. Am. Philos. Soc., Yr. bk., 1959, p. 127-30. [2016

BERNHARD JOSEPH STERN (1894-1956). Genetics teaching and Lysenko. Historical sociology: the selected papers of Bernhard J. Stern (N.Y.: Citadel Press [1960]), p. 328-42. notes. From Science and society, spring 1949. Mainly on the American influence of the doctrines of T. Lysenko, Russian biologist, with regard to environment and heredity, 1894-1948. [2017

PAUL FRANKLIN CLARK. Hideyo Noguchi, 1876-1928. Bul. hist. med., 33:1-20 (Jan-Feb 1959). port. notes. On his life in the United States as a research bacteriologist, 1899-1928, and his studies of snake venoms, antibodies, "complement fixation," spirochaetes, syphilis, yellow fever, trachoma, poliomyelitis, and other subjects, published in 212 papers; with memories of his personal habits and traits, particularly his unwillingness to work with a team. [2017a

VICTOR A. McKUSICK. Walter S[tanborough] Sutton [1877-1916] and the physical basis of Mendelism. Bul. hist. med., 34:487-97 (Nov-Dec). port., view. Biographical sketch, dealing particularly with his studies of chromosomes, 1899-1903, and more briefly with his contributions to medicine and surgery during his later medical practice in Kansas. [2017b

RUBEN WILLIAM ENGEL. Nutrition, a young science [1908-54]. Va. jour. science, 5:53-9 (Apr 1954). bibliog. [2018

RICHARD BENEDICT GOLDSCHMIDT (1878-1958). In and out of the ivory tower: the autobiography of Richard B. Goldschmidt. Seattle: Univ. of Washington Press, 1960. xiii, 352 p. port. Reminiscences completed in 1958 but written for the most part 30 years earlier, dealing mainly with his life in Germany and his zoological and genetic researches there. Includes an account of his emigration to America in 1914, teaching at Yale, researches in the marine biological laboratory at Woods Hole, Mass., internment at Governor's Island during World War I, and return to Germany in 1920; a brief account of his re-emigration to America, teaching at the University of California, and continued researches, 1936-58; an appendix on his work in genetics; and a topical list of his publications, 1900-1960 (p. 327-42). [2019

HONOR B. FELL. Fashion in cell biology [1922-60]. Science, 132: 1625-7 (2 Dec). [2020

BRENTON REID LUTZ. Pioneering with the motion picture in biological research [Boston University, 1940-53]. Boston Univ. graduate jour., 2:89-90 (Feb 1954). [2021

HUDSON HOAGLAND. The Worcester Foundation for Experimental Biology [Shrewsbury, Mass., 1944-52]. Boston Univ. graduate jour., 1:67-8 (Oct 1952). [2022

Botany

CHRISTINE CHAPMAN ROBBINS. David Hosack's herbarium and its

Linnaean specimens. Am. Philos. Soc., Proc., 104:293-313 (15 Jun). facsim., ports., view. bibliog., notes. On the journey of David Hosack (1769-1835) to England and his botanical studies there (1792-94), his acquisition of specimens from the Linnaean Herbarium in England, his founding of the Elgin Botanic Garden in New York City (1796), the eventual ownership of the herbarium by the Lyceum of Natural History of New York, the lack of reference to the Linnaean specimens after 1830, the probability that the herbarium was destroyed by fire in 1866, and the possibility that the Linnaean specimens still exist. [2023

RICHARD G. BEIDLEMAN. Some biographical sidelights on Thomas Nuttall, 1786-1859. Am. Philos. Soc., Proc., 104:86-100 (15 Feb). facsim., port. notes. Collection of documented biographical facts, relating particularly to his work in the United States between 1810 and 1848 as a botanical traveler and collector, author, lecturer, curator, and editor, who returned to England for the last time in 1848 and remained there till his death. [2024

HARLEY HARRIS BARTLETT. History of the Gray Memorial Botanical Association and the Asa Gray bulletin. Asa Gray bul., 1:3-22 (Jan 1952). notes. On the inauguration of the study of botany in the University of Michigan by Asa Gray in 1837, the Gray Memorial Botanical Association (founded in 1887 as the Gray Memorial Chapter of the Agassiz Association), the Asa Gray bulletin (1893-1901), the Bulletin of the Gray Memorial Botanical Association (1934-39), the Journal of the same association (1939-43), the Michigan Botanical Gardens Association (founded 1925), and the revival of the Asa Gray bulletin (1952). See also reminiscent letters (1952-53) from Cornelius Lott Shear, born 1865, former editor and founder of the Asa Gray bulletin (1:28-9, 344-5), and the editor's account of Shear (1:346-8). [2025

WILLIAM HENRY HARVEY (1811-66). William H. Harvey's report on the marine algae of the United States North Pacific Exploring Expedition [under Capt. John Rogers], 1853-1856. Edited by E. Yale Dawson. Solvang, Calif.: Beaudette Foundation for Biological Research, 1959. 40 p. views on 10 plates. (Pacific naturalist, v. 1, no. 5, 19 Mar. 1959.) Manuscript catalogue, annotated, 231 entries, of algae collected by Charles Wright, mainly from Japan, "Loo Choo," Australia, and the Cape of Good Hope (a few from Bering Strait, one from Chilifornia). Prepared in 1859 by Harvey (not a member of the expedition) at Trinity College, Dublin, from preserved specimens sent to him by Asa Gray; now first printed. [2026

DOUGLAS HOUGHTON CAMPBELL (1859-1953). An autobiographical fragment and letters addressed to Dr. H[arry] B[aker] Humphrey. Asa Gray bul., 2:103-6 (spring 1953). facsim. Very short account (1949) of the author's work as a student and teacher of botany; with 2 letters, 3 May and 23 Jul. 1949. [2027

BRADLEY MOORE DAVIS. A memorial to Douglas Houghton Campbell [1859-1953]. Asa Gray bul., 2:131-6 (spring 1953). On his personal life and his career as a botanist, a teacher of botany, and a botanical traveler and author. [2028

HENRY ALLAN GLEASON. The scientific work of Nathaniel Lord Britton [1859-1934]. Am. Philos. Soc., Proc, 104:205-26 (Apr). On his work as a botanist, particularly in taxonomy and cataloguing, his mainly victorious participation in controversies regarding nomenclature, his organization and direction of the New York Botanical Garden, and his manuals of the flora of Staten Island (1879), the northern United States, Canada, "and the British possessions" (1896-98), Bermuda (1918), Puerto Rico and the Virgin Islands (1923-26), Cuba (unfinished), and northern South America (unfinished). [2029

MARY (CAMPBELL) HAYS. Douglas Houghton Campbell [1859-1953]: family, boyhood, youth, and travels. Asa Gray bul., 2:107-20 (spring 1953). ports. On his early life in Detroit, his early interest in natural history, the beginnings of his library, his studies at the University of Michigan and in Germany, his teaching of botany at Indiana University and Stanford University, and his botanical travels in many parts of the world. [2030

HARLEY HARRIS BARTLETT. Walter Tennyson Swingle [1871-1952]: botanist and exponent of Chinese civilization. Asa Gray bul., 1:107-28 (Apr 1952). ports. On his early life in Kansas, his studies at the Kansas Agricultural College, his work as a botanist with the U.S. Department of Agriculture, his particular concern with the history of Chinese botany and other sciences, his service as Honorary Consultant in the development of the Orientalia Collection of the Library of Congress, his studies of citrus diseases and citrus hybrids, and his introduction of date culture into America. [2031

HELEN MARGARET GILKEY. Morton Eaton Peck [1871-1959]. Torrey Bot. Club, Bul., 87:280-82 (Jul). port. On his teaching of biology at Willamette University, 1908-41, and his very large collections of Oregon plants (contributed to the Peck Herbarium); with a list of his botanical publications, 1905-56. [2032

ELMER DREW MERRILL (1876-1956). Autobiographical: early years, the Philippines, California. Asa Gray bul., 2:335-70 (autumn 1953). facsim., ports., view. Reminiscences (1930 ff.) of the author's early life in East Auburn, Me., his studies at Maine State College (Orono), his work as an agrostologist in the U.S. Department of Agriculture in Washington and as a botanist in the Philippine Bureau of Agriculture, and his service as Dean of Agriculture, University of California, Director of the Los Angeles Botanical Garden, and Director-in-Chief, New York Botanical Garden. [2033

JAMES PLUMMER POOLE. Professor Jesup's herbarium. Dartmouth alumni mag., 52(6):31-3, 40-41 (Mar). ports. On Henry Griswold Jesup (1826-1903), Congregational minister at Stanwich, Conn., Professor of Botany and Natural History at Dartmouth from 1876 to 1899, and the herbarium that he established there; with accounts of other herbaria founded there by Charles H. Hitchcock (Professor of Geology and Mineralogy, 1874-1908) and George Richard Lyman (Professor of Botany, 1901-15). [2034

W. REI ROBBINS. John Wesley Shive [1877-1960]. Torrey Bot. Club, Bul., 87:417-19 (Nov). port. On his teaching of botany, particularly plant physiology, in the College of Agriculture, Rutgers University, 1915-46, and his botanical studies, particularly in plant nutrition. [2035

WILLIAM CAMPBELL STEERE. Douglas Houghton Campbell, and especially his work on bryophytes. Asa Gray bul., 2:137-48 (spring). A "reasonably complete" list of his botanical publications, 1881-1947; with a biographical and reminiscent introduction. [2036

HORTON HOLCOMBE HOBBS, JR., & B. F. D. RUNK. Edwin Morris Betts, 1892-1958. Va. jour. science, 10:1-2 (Jan 1959). On his work as a botanist, his teaching of biology in the University of Virginia, and his studies of Thomas Jefferson as a farmer and a gardener. [2037

MASON E. HALE, JR. Alexander William Evans [1868-1959]. Torrey Bot. Club, Bul., 87:354-6 (Sep). port. On his teaching of botany at Yale, 1895-1936, and his studies and collections of hepaticae and lichens. [2038

GEORGE WILBER SELLECK. The climax concept. Botanical rev., 26: 534-45 (Oct-Dec). notes. On the meanings of the term climax in plant ecology in America, 1899-1960, and abroad. [2039

EARL MARTIN HILDEBRAND. Micrurgy and the plant cell. Botanical rev., 26:277-330 (Jul-Sep). notes. On studies of "micromanipulation in the study of plant cells" in America, 1904-58, and abroad. [2040

AMOS GEER AVERY, SOPHIE SATINA, & JACOB RIETSEMA. Blakeslee: the genus Datura. N.Y.: Ronald Press Co. [1959]. xli, 289 p. diagrs., ports., tables, views. (Chronica botanica, 20.) "Albert Francis Blakeslee [1874-1954]: a biographical sketch," by Edmund W. Sinnott; list of publications by Blakeslee and his associates relating to their studies of Datura, 1910-56; historical review of its narcotic uses by the American Indians, "early breeding experiments" (1760-1890), and the work of Blakeslee and associates on its genetics under the auspices of the Carnegie Institution of Washington at Cold Spring Harbor, L. I., and the Smith College Genetics Experiment Station, Northampton, Mass. (1915-55), by Avery; "A review of the taxonomic history of Datura," 1753-1958, by Satina and Avery; and chapters by various contributors on the experiments and discoveries made in the course of Blakeslee's studies. [2041

ELMER DREW MERRILL (1876-1956). Real values. Asa Gray bul., 3:27-32 (spring 1955). Reminiscences of a botanical expedition to China, Aug. 1917. [2042

FAY KENOYER DAILY. Botanists of the Butler University faculty [Indianapolis, 1920-55]. Ind. Acad. Science, Proc., 69:237-42. notes. [2043

MAX EDWIN BRITTON. A tribute to Lewis Hanford Tiffany. Am. Micros. Soc., Trans., 79:1-4 (Jan). port. On his teaching of botany in Ohio State University and Northwestern University, 1923-59, his studies of freshwater algae, and his botanical publications. [2044

IRA LOREN WIGGINS. Twenty-eight years with Douglas Houghton Campbell. Asa Gray bul., 2:121-8 (spring 1953). ports. Memories of his teaching of botany at Stanford University, 1924-25, and his continued botanical activities and interests there from his retirement in 1925 till his death in 1953. See also "A tribute to Professor Douglas Houghton Campbell," by Albert Wilson (p. 129-30). [2045

HARLEY HARRIS BARTLETT. "Farwelliana" [by Rogers McVaugh, Stanley A. Cain, and Dale J. Hagenah]: a review. Asa Gray bul., 2:315-21 (summer 1953). Includes the reviewer's recollections of the retirement of Oliver Atkins Farwell as Botanist for Parke, Davis, and Company, Detroit, 1933, and the gift of the herbarium and the associated botanical library of the Company, assembled by Farwell, to the University of Michigan. [2046

Human Biology

WALTER GOODWIN DAVIS. Multiple descents from John[1] Libby. Am. geneal., 36:182-4 (Jul). geneal. chart. On the extraordinary proportion of marriages of cousins among the descendants of John Libby, Cornish emigrant to Maine in 1636/37, without known bad genetic consequences. [2047

F. GUERRA. Harvey and the circulation of the blood in America during the colonial period. Bul. hist. med., 33:212-29 (May-Jun 1959). facsims. bibliog. On printed and manuscript evidence that the doctrines of William Harvey were known in the United States, 1687-1787, and in the French and Spanish colonies. [2047a

WILLIAM RAGAN STANTON. The leopard's spots: scientific attitudes toward race in America, 1815-59. [Chicago:] Univ. of Chicago Press [1960]. ix, 244, [1] p. table. notes (p. 197-238). Review of studies and publications in the United States concerning the nature of race, the relation of its physical elements to heredity and environment, and the common or diverse origin of mankind. [2048

ALEŠ HRDLIČKA (1869-1943). Physical anthropology in America: an historical sketch [1822-1914]. Selected papers from the American anthropologist, 1888-1920, ed. Frederica De Laguna (Evanston, Ill.: Row, Peterson [1960]), p. 310-56. notes. First printed in 1914. Biographical sketches of anthropologists and lists of their works. [2049

JOHN BACHMAN (1790-1897). The doctrine of the unity of the human race examined on the principles of pure science. Margaret Mead & Ruth L. Bunzel, eds., The golden age of American anthropology (N.Y.: George Braziller, 1960), p. 85-8. From the author's book of the same title (Charleston, 1850), defending the thesis "That there is but one true species in the genus Homo" and attacking "the advocates of a plurality." [2050

JAMES N. SPUHLER. Recent developments in the field of genetics. International Congress of Anthropological and Ethnological Sciences, 5th, 1956, Men and cultures: selected papers, ed. Anthony F. C. Wallace (Phila.: Univ. of Pennsylvania Press [1960]), p. 74-83. bibliog. On "developments in human genetics that are of interest to the biological side of anthropology," 1905-56, with particular attention to population genetics. [2051

PAUL F. CRANEFIELD. Microscopic physiology since 1908 [in the United States and abroad]. Bul. hist. med., 33:263-75 (May-Jun 1959). notes. [2051a

CHANDLER McC. BROOKS. The development of physiology in the last fifty years [in America and abroad]. Bul. hist. med., 33:249-62 (May-Jun 1959). notes. [2051b

C. W. WEIANT. Bruno Oetteking, 1871-1960. Am. anthropol., 62:675-80 (Aug). port. On his work in America in the Department of Anthropology at the American Museum of Natural History, the Columbia University Department of Anthropology, the Museum of the American Indian, and the Chiropractic Institute of New York, 1913-59; with a list of his publications, 1907-57, mainly on prehistoric craniology. [2051c

JACOB FINE. A teacher remembered. Harvard alumni bul., 60:558-9 (19 Apr 1958). port. On the author's study of anthropology at Harvard under Earnest Hooton, ca. 1919-20. [2052

JOHN BUETTNER-JANUSCH. The study of natural selection and the ABO(H) blood group system in man. Gertrude E. Dole & Robert L. Carneiro, eds., Essays in the science of culture, in honor of Leslie A. White (N.Y.: Crowell [1960]), p. 79-110. tables. bibliog., notes. On the stages by which "the concept of maternal-fetal incompability" has led to "the idea that the frequencies of the various blood groups in different human populations are due to selection," 1921-58. [2053

FRANZ BOAS (1858-1942). Report on an anthropometric investigation of the population of the United States. Margaret Mead & Ruth L. Bunzel, eds., The golden age of American anthropology (N.Y.: George Braziller, 1960), p. 412-31. notes. First printed in 1922. [2054

HOWARD W. STOUDT. ALBERT DAMON, & ROSS A. McFARLAND. Heights and weights of white Americans. Human biol., 32:331-41 (Dec). tables. bibliog. Based upon available data published since ca. 1935 or still unpublished. [2055

Zoology

MAURICE E. PHILLIPS. The first hundred years [of the American Entomological Society, 1859-1959]. Entomol. news, 70:1-6 (Jan 1959). [2056

JAMES LEE O'LEARY & G. H. BISHOP. C[harles] J[udson] Herrick [1869-1960] and the founding of comparative neurology. Arch. neurol., 3:725-31 (Dec). port. notes. On his teaching of zoology at Denison College and of neurology at the University of Chicago and his experimental studies of the neural anatomy of man and other animals during his years of service at the Marine Biological Laboratory, Woods Hole, Mass.; with some account of his earlier life and of his publications. [2057

ERNESTINE HOGAN BASHAM THURMAN. Robert Evans Snodgrass [born 1875], insect anatomist and morphologist. Smithsonian Institution, Studies in invertebrate morphology published in honor of Dr. Robert Evans Snodgrass (Wash., 1959), p. 1-22. cartoons, ports., views. Includes illustrations from his unpublished drawings and anecdotes derived from interviews with him. Appended (p. 19-22): "Bibliography of R. E. Snodgrass between the years 1896 and 1958" (79 titles). [2058

JOHN SPANGLER NICHOLAS. Samuel Randall Detwiler (1890-1957) [neuroembryologist, student of the comparative morphology and physiology of the eye]. Am. Philos. Soc., Yr. bk., 1959, p. 116-22. [2059

LAFE R. EDMUNDS. Mosquito control: its growth and importance in the United States [1913-54]. Miss. Acad. Sciences, Jour., 6:83-6. notes. [2060

ROGER PETERSON. The era of Ludlow Griscom [1890-1959]. Audubon mag., 62:102-3, 131, 146, 148 (May-Jun). On his work as an ornithologist in the American Museum of Natural History, New York, and the Museum of Comparative Zoology, Cambridge, Mass., 1925-59. [2061

CALTECH'S marine laboratory. Engineering and science, 23(1):32 (Oct 1959). view. On the Kerckhoff Marine Laboratory, Corona del Mar, Calif., about 50 miles from Pasadena, established for researches in "marine zoology, embryology and physiology," 1929-59. [2062

KIRBY LEE HAYS. Ecological observations on the imported fire ant, Solenopsis saevissima Richteri Forel, in Alabama. Ala. Acad. Science, Jour., 30(4):14-18 (Apr 1959). On a pest imported from South America sometime before 1930, now widely distributed. [2063

CHEMISTRY

MANUFACTURING CHEMISTS ASSOCIATION. The chemical industry [since 1635]. By Malcolm J. Harkins and Charles E. Wallace. John G. Glover & Rudolph L. Lagai, eds., The development of American industries: their economic significance, 4th ed. (N.Y.: Simmons-Boardman [1959]), p. 297-331. [2064

PAUL J. STAGEMAN. Early development of biochemistry in America [1760-1913]. Neb. Acad. Sciences, Proc., 68 (1958): 22-6. [2065

PETER WILLIAM MANGERY. An analysis of chemistry textbooks used in the American secondary schools before 1890 [published 1784-1890]. Ann Arbor: University Microfilms,

1959 [i.e. 1960]. Positive microfilm of typescript. [302] leaves. Thesis (Ed. D.)--Univ. of Pittsburgh. Abstracted: Dissert. abstracts, 20:4256 (May). [2066

HAROLD J. ABRAHAMS. The chemical library of Thomas Jefferson. Jour. chem. educ., 37:357-60 (Jul). bibliog., notes. Includes an annotated list of the 30 books on chemistry owned by him (acquired by the Library of Congress in 1815); with remarks on his amateur interest in the sciences. [2067

MELVILLE LAWRENCE WOLFROM. John Ulric Nef, June 14, 1862 - August 13, 1915. Natl. Acad. Sciences, Biog. memoirs, 34:204-27. diagrs., port. On his early life in Switzerland and (after emigration in 1864) in Massachusetts, his studies at Harvard and in Germany, his teaching of chemistry at Purdue University (1887-89), Clark University (1889-92), and the University of Chicago (1892-1915), and his researches in sugar chemistry; with a list of his publications, 1884-1918. [2068

EUGENE CORNELIUS SULLIVAN. George Augustus Hulett, July 15, 1867 - September 6, 1955. Natl. Acad. Sciences, Biog. memoirs, 34:83-105. port. On his early life in Indiana, his studies at Oberlin College and Princeton and abroad, his teaching of physical chemistry at the University of Michigan (1899-1905) and Princeton (1905-35), and his service as Chief Chemist of the U.S. Bureau of Mines (1912 ff.); with a list of his publications, 1894-1937. [2069

HENRY ALBERT LEPPER. A bit of AOAC history. Food drug cosmetic law jour., 15:407-12 (Jun). On the Association of Official Agricultural Chemists, Inc., 1884-1960, consisting of chemists of the U.S. Department of Agriculture, the agricultural experiment stations, and the State boards and departments of agriculture. [2070

RUSSELL MORSE WILDER. Calorimetry, the basis of the science of nutrition [1891-1957]. Arch. internal med., 103:146-54 (Jan 1959). diagrs., view. notes. [2071

LEWIS HASTINGS SARATT. The hormones. Jour. chem. educ., 37: 185-9 (Apr). diagrs., view. On the isolation of the 28 "currently accepted mammalian hormones" (i.e., "chemical messengers") by European and American research, 1900-1951, and the discovery of some of their effects. Includes reference to the author's synthesis of cortisone from desoxycholic acid. [2072

ROBERT COOLEY ELDERFIELD. Werner Emmanuel Bachmann, November 13, 1901 - March 22, 1951. Natl. Acad. Sciences, Biog. memoirs, 34:1-30. port. On his teaching of chemistry at the University of Michigan (1929-51), his work in the development of naval explosives in World War II, and his synthesization of hormones, carcinogens, and penicillin; with a list of his publications, mainly relating to organic chemistry, 1924-54. [2073

MAX TISHLER. Impact of research on the growth of medicinal chemistry [1905-59]. Jour. chem. educ., 37: 195-201 (Apr). diagrs. notes. [2074

FRANK H. WESTHEIMER. Morris Selig Kharasch, August 24, 1895 - October 9, 1957. Natl. Acad. Sciences, Biog. memoirs, 34:123-52. port. On his early life in the Ukraine, his emigration to America in 1908, his studies at the University of Chicago, his service there as Professor of Chemistry (1928-57), and his researches in free radicals; with a list of his publications, 1918-59. [2075

HAROLD S. KING. Pioneering research on isotopes at Harvard [by Theodore W. Richards and his coworkers, 1913-58]. Jour. chem. educ., 36:225-7 (May 1959). port. [2076

HARRY LINN FISHER. New horizons in elastic polymers [in America, 1929-60, and abroad]. Jour. chem. educ., 37:369-77 (Jul). diagrs., view. notes. [2077

IRVING HARRY ISENBERG. The Institute of Paper Chemistry [Appleton, Wis., 1929-58]. Jour. forestry, 56:566-9 (Aug 1958). views. [2078

ROGER ELDON BEYLER. Some recent advances in the field of steroids [1930-59]. Jour. chem. educ., 37:491-4 (Sep). diagrs. notes. [2079

B. R. SIEBRING. A comparison of institutions in the undergraduate training of Ph. D. chemists by occupational specialization [1932-48]. Science educ., 44:289-94 (Oct). tables. notes. [2080

DAVID NACHMANSOHN, SEVERO OCHOA, & FRITZ A. LIPMANN. Otto Meyerhof, April 12, 1884 - October 6, 1951. Natl. Acad. Science, Biog.

memoirs, 34:153-82. port. From Science, Apr. 1951, with additions. On his early life and medical practice in Germany, his emigration to America in 1940, and his service as research professor of physiological chemistry at the School of Medicine, University of Pennsylvania; with a list of his publications, 1910-53. [2081

J. C. WALLMAN. The first isolations of the transuranium elements: a historical survey. Jour. chem. educ., 36:340-43 (Jul 1959). bibliog. On the isolation of plutonium (1942), neptunium (1944), americum (1945), curium (1947), berkelium (1958), and californium (1958). [2082

L. REED BRANTLEY. History of the Pacific Southwest Association of Chemistry Teachers [1949-58]. Jour. chem. educ., 36:92-4 (Feb). [2083

ENGINEERING

SOCIETY FOR THE HISTORY OF TECHNOLOGY. Controversy. Technol. and culture, 1:201-234 (summer). notes. Contents.--An attempt to measure the rise of American inventing and the decline of patenting, by S. C. Gilfillan.--An economist takes issue, by Jacob Schmookler.--A patent attorney takes issue, by I. Jordan Kunik.--Dr. Gilfillan's reply. [2084

ROGER BURLINGAME. March of the iron men: a social history of union through invention. N.Y.: Grosset & Dunlap [1960. 2], xvi, 500 p. diagrs., facsims., map, ports., views. bibliog. (p. 445-67), notes. (The universal library, UL-74.) 1st ed. 1938. On "the history of the evolution of that social pattern which produced a nation from the United States ... told in terms of ... the factor of technological invention," 1606-1865. [2084a

JOHN BELL RAE. The "know-how" tradition: technology in American history [since the 1640s]. Technol. and culture, 1:139-50 (spring). notes. [2084b

ROBERT M. WEIDENHAMMER & IRVING H. SIEGEL. Patent and other factors in the future organization of the steel industry. Patent, trademark, and copyright jour., 1:112-18; 2:278-85 (Jun 1957, Jun 1958). notes. On "the attitude of the steel industry toward research, patents, and innovation" since its beginning in America in 1644. [2085

PASQUALE JOSEPH FEDERICO. Records of Eli Whitney's cotton gin patent [application submitted 1793, patent issued 1794]. Technol. and culture, 1:168-76 (spring). view. notes. [2085a

HAROLD BELL HANCOCK. An American papermaker in Europe--1795-1801. Paper maker, 28(2):11-15 (Sep 1959). facsims. On the English and European travels of Joshua Gilpin, who examined paper mills and noted procedures and equipment that might improve the operations of his own mills on Brandywine Creek, Del. [2085b

ROBERT S. WOODBURY. The legend of Eli Whitney and interchangeable parts [1798 ff.]. Technol. and culture, 1:235-53 (summer). notes. Concludes that "one is led to find the origins of the 'American system of manufacturing' in the culmination of a number of economic, social, and technical forces brought to bear on manufacture by several men of genius, of whom Whitney can only be said to have been perhaps one." [2085c

DANIEL HOVEY CALHOUN. The American civil engineer: origins and conflict. Cambridge: Technology Press, Massachusetts Institute of Technology; distributed by Harvard Univ. Press, 1960. xiv, [2], 295 p. fold. map, tables. bibliog. (p. 219-37), notes (p. 239-83). On the profession of civil engineering in the United States, 1812-46. Includes sections on the New York canal system, the Army Engineers, Loammi Baldwin the younger, John Langdon Sullivan, Benjamin Wright, "The B & O engineers," and the education, publications, and organizations of engineers. [2086

J. H. HARLOW. The ASME Boiler and Pressure Vessel Code: how the Code originated [1817-1959]. Mech. engineering, 81(7):56-8 (Jul 1959). [2087

CHARLES VAN RAVENSWAAY. "... victories over ignorance and selfishness." John Arthur Garraty, ed., The unforgettable Americans (Great Neck, N.Y.: Channel Press [1960]), p. 243-7. On James B. Eads (born 1820), designer and manufacturer of salvage boats, underwater diving equipment, and armored warships for the Union Navy, and his design of a bridge over the Mississippi at St. Louis, the headquarters of his business. [2088

WYNN LAURENCE LE PAGE. History of the Franklin Institute [Philadelphia, 1824-1959]. Franklin Inst., Jour., 269: 126-30 (Feb). On an organization founded "for the lay study of mechanical science," through which the members, not professional scientists, could collect apparatus and a library and establish a program of instruction for themselves and other interested persons. [2089

WALDEMAR BERNHARD KAEMPFFERT (1877-1956). "... industrial evolution of the United States." John Arthur Garraty, ed., The unforgettable Americans (Great Neck, N.Y.: Channel Press [1960]), p. 237-41. On Thaddeus S. C. Lowe (1832-1913), who made his first balloon ascent in 1858, made an ascent for the Union Army in 1861, served as a Union spy, and later invented methods and equipment for making artificial ice, cold-storage plants, "water gas," and coke. [2090

SAMUEL BICKNELL LINCOLN. Lockwood Greene: the history of an engineering business, 1832-1958. Brattleboro, Vt.: Stephen Greene Press, 1960. xii, [2], 861 p. ports., tables (part double), views. On New England enterprises of David Whitman (1799-1858), "millwright" and milling consultant, 1820-58, and Amos D. Lockwood (1811-84), operator and eventually owner of textile mills in New England and later the South, organizer of A. D. Lockwood and Company (1843-82) and Lockwood, Greene, & Company, Mill Engineers, Providence, later Boston (1882-1926), reorganized as Lockwood Greene Engineers, Inc., New York City (1928-60), consultants in structural design for all kinds of business building and public buildings and in the management of "large industrial projects"; with some account of Stephen Greene (1851-1901) and Edwin Farnham Greene (1879-1953), and excerpts from "Random reminiscenses [sic] by William P. Snow," 1890-1914 (p. 786-99). [2091

WILLIAM T. KING. History of the American steam fire-engine [1840-91]. Chicago: O. Davies, 1960. x, 150 p. diagrs., views. 1st ed. 1896. [2092

JACOB SCHMOOKLER. Technological progress and the modern American corporation [1840-1960]. Edward Sagendorph Mason, ed., The corporation in modern society (Cambridge: Harvard Univ. Press, 1959), p. 141-65, 309-10. On the differences among firms in the extent to which they engage in RD (research and development). [2093

ARTHUR MUMFORD SMITH. A. Lincoln, inventor. Fed. Bar jour., 20:274-80 (summer). notes. On his invention and patenting of a process for "Buoying Vessels over Shoals" (1848-49), his address on "Discoveries and inventions" (1859), and his encouragement and promotion of inventions of military equipment during the Civil War. [2094

DAVID OAKES WOODBURY. Elihu Thomson, beloved scientist, 1853-1937: inventive genius--engineer--educator, pioneer of the electrical age ... With appreciations by James R. Killian, Jr., and Owen D. Young. Boston: Museum of Science, 1960. xv, 358 p. ports., views. bibliog. (p. 349-50). 1st ed. 1944. On his emigration from England in 1858, his life in Philadelphia, and his work as an electrical engineer and inventor, holder of 692 patents granted between 1876 and 1935, mainly for electrical and electromagnetic equipment. [2095

KENNETH HAMILTON CONDIT. Lewis Buckley Stillwell, March 12, 1863 - January 19, 1941. Natl. Acad. Sciences, Biog. memoirs, 34:320-28. port. On his early life in Scranton, Pa., his studies at Lehigh University, and his work as a consulting electrical engineer; with a selective list of his publications, 1890-1934, and patents, 1889-1917, in the field of electrical engineering. [2096

GUY SUITS. Willis Rodney Whitney, August 22, 1868 - January 9, 1958. Natl. Acad. Sciences, Biog. memoirs, 34:350-67. port. On his early life in Jamestown, N.Y., his studies in the Massachusetts Institute of Technology and abroad, his work in electrochemistry at the Massachusetts Institute of Technology (1896-1900), his service as head of the General Electric Research Laboratory at Schenectady (1900-1932), and his distinction as "the 'father of basic research in industry' "; with a list of his publications, 1897-1944. [2097

VANNEVAR BUSH. Charles F. Kettering (1876-1958) [technologist, inventor, electrical engineer]. Am. Philos. Soc., Yr. bk., 1959, p. 130-33. [2098

GEORGE WASHINGTON UNIVERSITY. Patent, Trademark, and Copyright

Foundation. The Charles F[ranklin] Kettering commemorative issue. Patent, trademark, and copyright jour., 3:ii-vi, 103-58 (summer 1959). port. A "tribute to Dr. Kettering, inventor, researcher, research director, teacher, entrepreneur, and leader of men." Contents.--My father, Charles F. Kettering [1876-1958], by Eugene W. Kettering.--Man of the "tomorrow mind": his place in research and education, by T. A. Boyd.--An objective look at Boss Kettering, by J. Ralph Fehr.--Exponent of explanation, by Allen Orth.--Charles F. Kettering, the inventor's inventor, by John C. Green.--Memories of forty years of association with Charles F. Kettering, by Frank A. Howard.--Kettering bibliography and patents [list of writings by and about him, portraits of him, and patents granted to him, 1909-59]. [2099

ZAY JEFFRIES. Charles Franklin Kettering, August 29, 1876 - November 25, 1958. Natl. Acad. Sciences, Biog. memoirs, 34:106-22. port. On his early life in Ashland County, Ohio, his studies at Wooster College and Ohio State University, his early employment by the National Cash Register Company, his establishment of the Dayton Engineering Laboratories (Dayton, Ohio), his development of ignition systems for the General Motors Corporation and of many other improvements in automotive engineering, his inventions in many other fields, and his accomplishments as a lecturer and a "practical philosopher"; with a list of his publications, 1918-58, and selected patents, 1909-51. [2100

SIGMUND A. LAVINE. Kettering: master inventor. N.Y.: Dodd, Mead, 1960. xii, [2], 173, [2] p. ports., views. On Charles Franklin Kettering (1876-1958), reared on an Ohio farm, educated at Wooster College and Ohio State University, inventor of various automobile electrical systems and other automotive improvements, executive of the Ethyl Gasoline Corporation, Director of the General Motors Research Corporation, Dayton, Ohio, innovator in engineering, contributor to engineering in medicine. [2101

CARL COVALT CHAMBERS. Harold Pender (1879-1959) [electrical engineer, developer of electronic computers]. Am. Philos. Soc., Yr. bk., 1959, p. 141-3. [2102

JOHN E. ALMAN. Machines and research. Boston Univ. graduate jour., 1:5-8 (Apr 1952). On the use of "automatic computing and tabulating equipment" as a "necessary tool for the research worker," 1880-1952. [2103

The BRADFORD engine: its story and its inventor. Vt. Hist. Soc., News and notes, 5:67-8 (May 1954). view. On a small "rotary expansion steam engine" invented ca. 1883 by Fred W. R. Bradford (born 1865). [2104

JOHN W. DONOHUE. Dewey and the problem of technology. John Blewett, ed., John Dewey: his thought and influence (N.Y.: Fordham Univ. Press [1960]), p. 117-44. notes. On "his case for technology," 1884-1952. Does not define the "problem" mentioned in the title. [2105

GEORGE L. SCHERMERHORN (born 1868). Letters of an engineering student in the 1880s. Edited by Earle D. Ross. Ann. Ia., 35:434-53 (fall). notes. Letters from a student in the Iowa State Agricultural College, Ames, Ia., to his father, Dr. Winfield S. Schermerhorn, 28 Feb. 1884 - 3 Nov. 1887. [2106

WILBUR CROSS. An enduring heritage: seventy-five years of distinguished service in engineering. N.Y.: Parsons, Brinckerhoff, Quade, & Douglas, 1960. 64 p. facsims., maps (1 col.), ports. (1 double), views. On a firm of consulting engineers founded by William Barclay Parsons (1859-1932) and Henry de Berkeley Parsons in New York City in 1885, and its activities in planning and supervising the construction of subways, bridges, highways, dams, canals, tunnels, dry docks, airports, and other large engineering projects in many parts of the world. [2107

GEORGE W. PATTERSON. The first electric computer: a magnetological analysis. Franklin Inst., Jour., 270: 130-37 (Aug). diagrs. notes. On "a cardboard schematic diagram" of a machine not known to have been actually constructed, prepared ca. 1885 by Allan Marquand (1853-1942), Professor of Archeology and the History of the Arts, Princeton University, and its relation to "an earlier mechanical logic machine" invented by him. [2108

ROBERT GILMOUR LE TOURNEAU (born 1888). Mover of men and mountains: the autobiography of R. L. Le Tourneau. Englewood Cliffs, N.J.: Prentice-Hall [1960. 6], 282 p. ports., views. On the author's early life in Duluth, his work as an iron molder in San Francisco and proprietor of a garage in Stockton, Calif., and his business since 1918 as an earth-moving contractor and manufacturer of earth-moving equipment, employed in many parts of the United States and abroad, and his constant sense of divine guidance in his decisions. [2109

DAVID E. DONLEY. Memorial to Gerard Hendrik Matthes (1874-1959). [n. p.:] Mrs. G. H. Matthes, 1960. [2], 28 p. port. On his emigration from Holland in 1891, his studies at the Massachusetts Institute of Technology, his work as a hydraulic engineer with the U.S. Geological Survey and the Mississippi River Commission, his presidency of the Rocky Mountain Hydraulic Laboratory at Allensport, Colo., and his many public services as a hydraulic consultant. Appended: select list of his writings, 1887-1957. [2110

ROBERT W. MARKS. The Dymaxion world of Buckminster Fuller. N.Y.: Reinhold Pub. Corp. [1960]. 232 p. diagrs., facsims., maps, plans, ports., views. On Richard Buckminster Fuller, Jr. (born 1895), his early life in Milton, Mass., his studies at Harvard, his Navy service in World War I, and his achievements as "architect, engineer, inventor-designer, cartographer, and mathematician," founder of a "comprehensive, anticipatory design science" or "energetic-synergetic geometry," expressed in an esoteric vocabulary and embodied in "Dymaxion" constructions--houses, vehicles, bathroom assemblies, "geodetic structures," etc.--designed by the Stockade Building System, Chicago. [2111

BERNHARD JOSEPH STERN (1894-1956). The frustration of technology. Historical sociology: the selected papers of Bernhard J. Stern (N.Y.: Citadel Press [1960]), p. 47-74. notes. From Science and society, winter 1937. On the "suppression" of "technological invention" by acquisition and non-use of patents, 1896-1937, as a consequence of capitalism, inconsistent with "the very organization of socialist economy." [2112

BERNHARD JOSEPH STERN (1894-1956). Restraints upon the utilization of inventions [1897-1938]. Historical sociology: the selected papers of Bernhard J. Stern (N.Y.: Citadel Press [1960]), p. 75-101. notes. First printed in 1938. On "opposition to technological innovation by vested interests seeking to retain or gain control over a limited market," expressed by the suppression or non-use of patents and by proposals to prohibit the use of labor-saving devices. [2113

FREDERICK ANDREW WHITE. Significant contributions of American industrial research laboratories in the development of analytical instruments for the physical sciences, 1900-1950. Ann Arbor: University Microfilms, 1959 [i. e. 1960]. Positive microfilm of typescript. xv, 318 leaves. bibliog. (leaves 313-18). Thesis--Univ. of Wisconsin. Abstracted: Dissert. abstracts, 20:4095 (Apr). [2114

CHARLES EISLER. The million-dollar bend: the autobiography of the benefactor of the radio tube and lamp industry. N.Y.: William-Frederick Press, 1960. [4], 306, [8] p. diagrs., facsims., ports., views. On the author's emigration from Hungary in 1904, his work as an engineer with the Westinghouse Electric Company, his establishment of the Eisler Engineering Company, Newark, N.J., and his patents and manufacture of radio tubes and incandescent lamps. [2115

WILLIAM KERNS LE BOLD, EDWARD C. THOMA, JOHN W. GILLIS, & GEORGE A HAWKINS. A study of the Purdue University engineering graduate [1911-56. Lafayette, Ind.:] Purdue Univ. [1960]. vi, 300 p. diagrs., tables. notes. (Purdue University. Engineering extension series, 99. Engineering bulletin, v. 44, no. 1.) Based in part on theses of Thoma (Univ. of Illinois, 1958) and Gillis (Purdue Univ., 1958). Largely a statistical analysis of questionnaires. [2116

IRWIN L. TUNIS. The engineer and the law. Mech. engineering, 82(7):28-9 (Jul). notes. On the legal obligations of licensed engineers, 1915-60. [2117

IOWA, UNIVERSITY OF. Iowa Institute of Hydraulic Research. Fourth decade of hydraulics at the State University of Iowa. Edited by Lucien M. Brush, Jr., and Lawrence R[iedling] Mack, research engineers, Iowa Institute of Hydraulic Research. Iowa City: The University, 1960. 101 p. diagrs., views. (University of Iowa. Studies in engineering, bull. 40.) On research in hydraulics at the State

University of Iowa since 1918, especially since the founding of the Iowa Institute of Hydraulic Research; with a list of the publications relating to hydraulics issued by the University or written by its staff. [2118

SOCORRO CONCIO CRUZ. The role of Mapua Institue of Technology in the development of technological education in the Philippines [1925-58]. Centro Escolar Univ., Graduate and faculty studies, 10:18-33 (1959). notes. [2119

JAMES S. WORLEY. Industrial research and development and the new competition--a study of the leading employers of research and development personnel by industry group and by size of firm [1927-55]. Ann Arbor: University Microfilms, 1958 [i.e. 1960]. Positive microfilm of typescript. [179] leaves. Thesis--Princeton Univ. Abstracted: Dissert. abstracts, 20:2612. [2120

CERAMIC engineering at VPI [Virginia Polytechnic Institute, 1928-55]. Mineral industries jour., 2(1):7-8 (Mar 1955). view. [2121

BERNHARD JOSEPH STERN (1894-1956). Science and war production [1930-43]. Historical sociology: the selected papers of Bernhard J. Stern (N.Y.: Citadel Press [1960]), p. 102-21. notes. From Science and society, spring 1943. On the use of patents to limit production, to fix prices, and to obviate the danger or overproduction after the war. [2122

GILL ROBB WILSON. The sensational growth of Northrop Institute. Flying, 66(1):42-3, 77-81 (Jan). port., double view. On Northrop Institute of Technology, Los Angeles, 1942-59. [2122a

EDGAR WEINBERG & IRVING H. SIEGEL. Development and implications of the first transistor patents [by the Bell Telephone Laboratories, 1948-59]. Patent, trademark, and copyright jour., 3:392-7 (winter 1959). notes. [2123

GEOGRAPHY AND ALLIED SCIENCES

LYLE E. JONES. Cadastral surveys--the rectangular system surveys and protractions. Surveying and mapping, 20:459-68 (Dec). On the "cadastral survey activity" of the Bureau of Land Management and predecessor agencies, 1784-1960; with details of such activity in Alaska. [2124

RICHARD JAQUITH FOWLE. James Wilson's globes: an anniversary report and appeal. Vt. hist., 28:244-9 (Oct). facsims. notes. Includes a list of "Known editions of Wilson globes," 1809-35. [2125

CHARLES CARLYLE COLBY. Wellington Downing Jones, 1886-1957. Assoc. Am. Geographers, Ann., 50: 51-4 (Mar). port. On his study and teaching of geography at the University of Chicago, 1908-45, and his geographic field studies in several parts of the world; with a selected list of his publications, 1914-44. [2126

ARTHUR MELVIN GROVE. A study of the geography course offerings in a selected number of American colleges and universities for the college year 1949-50. Ann Arbor: University Microfilms, 1952 [i.e. 1960]. Positive microfilm of typescript. 201 leaves. tables. bibliog. (leaves 116-19). Thesis--Univ. of Kentucky. Abstracted: Dissert. abstracts, 20:3688-9 (Mar). [2127

LLOYD E. MARSDEN. How the National Map Accuracy Standards were developed [1912-60]. Surveying and mapping, 20:427-39 (Dec). [2128

RUSSELL C. BRINKER. The status of education in surveying [1936-60]. Surveying and mapping, 20:55-66 (Mar). tables (1 double). notes. [2129

Geology

ALEXANDER M. OSPOVAT. Werner's influence on American geology. Okla. Acad. Science, Proc., 40:98-103. bibliog. On the influence of the teaching and writings of Abraham Gottlob Werner (1749-1817), of the Bergakademie in Freiberg, Saxony. [2130

KIRTLEY FLETCHER MATHER. Geology, geologists, and the AAAS [1838-1958]. Science, 129:1106-11 (24 Apr 1959). facsim., ports. On the American Association for the Advancement of Science, originally the Association of American Geologists. [2131

FRANCES LYMAN PARKER. Robert Thomas Hill, Jr. [1858-1941], geologist. Southw. hist. quar., 64:140-42 (Jul). Abstract of thesis (M.A.)--Univ. of Texas. On his studies in Cornell University, his teaching of geology in Texas and elsewhere, and his voluminous writings on geology, particularly that of Texas; with some account of his early life in Tennessee and Texas. [2132

ADOLPH KNOPF. Louis Valentine Pirsson, November 3, 1860 - December 8, 1919. Natl. Acad. Sciences, Biog. memoirs, 34:228-48. port. On his early life in New York City, his studies at Sheffield Scientific School, his teaching of chemistry at Brooklyn Polytechnic Institute and physical geology at Sheffield Scientific School, and his work as a petrologist and a mineralogist; with a list of his publications, 1890-1921. [2133

FRANCIS BIRCH. Reginald Aldworth Daly (1871-1957) [geologist and geophysicist, "writer, teacher, and natural philosopher"]. Am. Philos. Soc., Yr. bk., 1959, p. 106-16. [2134

FRANCIS BIRCH. Reginald Aldworth Daly, May 19, 1871 - September 19, 1957. Natl. Acad. Sciences, Biog. memoirs, 34:31-64. port. On his work as physical geologist, petrologist, seismologist, and geophysicist, professor of geology at the Massachusetts Institute of Technology and at Harvard, and "natural philosopher"; with a list of his publications, 1896-1957. Also printed, without the list: Am. Philos. Soc., Yr. bk., 1959, p. 106-16. [2135

MARLAND PRATT BILLINGS. Diastrophism and mountain building. Geol. Soc. Am., Bul., 71:363-98 (Apr). diagrs., maps, tables. bibliog. On studies in America, 1890-1959, and abroad. [2136

BYRON NELSON COOPER. Marcellus Henry Stow, 1902-1957. Va. jour. science, 9:1-2 (Jan 1958). port. On his study and teaching of geology. [2137

LELAND HORBERG (1910-55). Current trends in geology and their relations to geological education [1939-54]. Jour. geol. educ., 3:1-6 (spring 1955). bibliog. [2138

Meteorology

IVAN RAY TANNEHILL. Hurricanes, their nature and history, particularly those of the West Indies and the southern coasts of the United States [1494-1955]. Princeton: Princeton Univ. Press, 1956. x, 308 p. diagrs., maps, tables, views. bibliog. (p. 295-303). 1st ed. 1938. Includes "List of tropical storms of the North Atlantic, including the Gulf of Mexico and Caribbean Sea, from 1494 to 1900" (p. 241-3), and chapters on "Early history of West Indian hurricanes," "Memorable hurricanes of the nineteenth century," and "Chronological account of hurricanes of the twentieth century." [2139

HORACE S. CARTER. Josiah Meigs [1757-1822], pioneer weatherman. Weatherwise, 13:166-7, 181 (Aug). port., view. On weather records kept by him at Athens, Ga., 1803-5 (perhaps 1801-10), and his efforts as Commissioner of the General Land Office, 1814-22, to induce regional offices to maintain such records. [2140

DAVID M. LUDLUM. The big snow of 1836 [in the States from Vermont to Pennsylvania]. Weatherwise, 13: 248-52 (Dec). map, table. [2141

GEORGE CASS DE LONG. Temperature changes in Northeastern United States, 1906-1955. Jour. geog., 59: 171-5 (Apr). diagrs., maps. On changes in the area "bounded on the west by the right-bank cities of the Mississippi River, plus Duluth, and on the south by the southern borders of Kentucky and Virginia." [2142

HORACE ROBERT BYERS. Carl-Gustaf Arvid Rossby, December 28, 1898 - August 19, 1957. Natl. Acad. Sciences, Biog. memoirs, 34:249-70. port. On his work in the United States as a meteorologist with the Weather Bureau and a professor of meteorology at the Massachusetts Institute of Technology and the University of Chicago, 1926-48, and his earlier and later years in Sweden; with a list of his publications, 1928-59. [2143

EARL G. DROESSLER. The present status and the promise of weather modification [1946-59]. Am. Geophysical Union, Trans., 41:26-34 (Mar). bibliog. [2144

MATHEMATICS

RAYMOND LOUIS WILDER. Mathematics: a cultural phenomenon. Gertrude E. Dole & Robert L. Carneiro, eds., Essays in the science of culture, in honor of Leslie A. White (N.Y.: Crowell [1960]), p. 471-85. bibliog. On the development of the concept of mathematics as a "cultural phenomenon which is in a constant state of evolution," 1919-53. [2145

JOHN ABRAHAM SCHUMAKER. Trends in the education of mathematics teachers: a study of the education of senior high school mathematics teachers in selected teacher education institutions in the United States in the period 1920-1958. Ann Arbor: University Microfilms, 1959 [i.e. 1960]. Positive microfilm of typescript. 3, x, 294 leaves. tables. bibliog. (leaves 254-64). Thesis--New York Univ. Abstracted: Dissert. abstracts, 20:4044-5 (Apr). [2146

MEDICINE

ELIZABETH BASS. These were the first. Am. Med. Women's Assoc., Jour., 14:67, 157, 248, 439, 615, 828, 1018; 15:72, 289, 517, 694, 900 (Jan 1959 - Sep 1960). On women physicians who were chronologically first in some respect in their profession. [2147

ELINOR BLUEMEL. Statuary Hall [in the U.S. Capitol]--its women and its doctors. Jour. med. educ., 34: 1038-41 (Oct 1959). [2148

RICHARD HARRISON SHRYOCK. Medicine and society in America, 1660-1860. [N.Y.:] New York Univ. Press, 1960. viii, [2], 182 p. notes. (The Anson G. Phelps lectures, 1959.) Contents.--Origins of a medical profession.--Medical thought and practice: 1660-1820.--Health and disease: 1660-1820.--Medicine and society in transition, 1820-1860. [2149

EDWARD A. MALLON. Documents ... (from the Random notes on early Catholic physicians and surgeons in America ... by Edward A. Mallon, M.D.). Collated by Therese F. Rider. Am. Cath. Hist. Soc., Rec., 71:59-61 (Mar-Jun). Selections on fathers and sons who practised medicine in America, 1687-1863, and on "Physicians-statesmen," 1749-1847. [2150

HENRY ERNEST SIGERIST (1891-1957). The history of medical licensure [1760-1935]. Henry E. Sigerist on the sociology of medicine, ed. Milton I. Roemer (N.Y.: MD Publications [1960]), p. 308-18. From Journal of the American Medical Association, 30 Mar. 1935. [2151

ANTONIO PACE. Postscriptum on John Morgan and Giovan Battisti Morgagni. Bul. hist. med., 33:75-7 (Jan-Feb 1959). notes. On "the margin of probability" that Benjamin Rush was correct when he asserted in 1789 that Morgagni (in 1746) claimed relationship with Morgan "from the similarity of their names" and that "on the blank leaf of a copy of his works, which he presented to him, he inscribed with his own hand the following words, 'Affini suo, medico praeclarissimo, Johanni Morgan, donat auctor.'" [2151a

WILLIAM J. FITZGERALD. The life of Dr. John Stearns [1770-1848]. N.Y. State jour. med., 59:2041-3 (15 May 1959). On his early life in Wilbraham, Mass., his studies at Yale, his practice of medicine in Waterford, N.Y., and his discovery of the value of ergot in obstetrics. [2152

WILLIAM SHAINLINE MIDDLETON. Charles Caldwell [1772-1853]: a biographic sketch. Jour. med. educ., 34:965-85 (Oct 1959). ports. bibliog., notes. First printed 1921. On his early life in Caswell County, N.C., his medical studies at the University of Pennsylvania, his service as surgeon in the Army expedition to quell the Whiskey Rebellion, his medical practice in Philadelphia, his service as Chairman, Institute of Medicine and Clinical Practice, Transylvania University, and his chronic involvement in controversy. [2153

OWSEI TEMKIN. A postscript to "Merrem's youthful dream." Bul. hist. med., 34:74-5 (Jan-Feb). notes. Proof that Dr. Christian Friedrich Michaelis (1754-1814), "physician with the Hessian troops during the Revolutionary War and eventually professor of surgery at the University of Marburg," attended Dr. Peter Middleton, New York Tory, in his final illness (1780) and visited Dr. John Morgan of Philadelphia in 1783. [2153a

ALFRED H. WHITTAKER. Centers of Beaumont interest. Mich. State Med. Soc., Jour., 58:742-50 (May 1959). facsims., medals, ports (1 col.), views. On "historic collections, societies, hospitals, and army medical facilities" in the United States and Canada named for William Beaumont (1785-1853), M.D., in honor of his studies of the physiology of digestion, and the locations of collections containing materials about him regardless of title. [2154

GENEVIEVE MILLER. Dr. John Delamater [1787-1867], "true physician." Jour. med. educ., 34:24-31 (Jan 1959). port. notes. On his early life and study and practice of medicine in Chatham, N.Y., his medical practice in Florida, Massachusetts, and Albany, N.Y., his teaching of medicine in medical schools in Massachusetts, New York, and Illinois, his settlement in Cleveland in 1842, and his founding of the Cleveland Medical College, where he served as Professor of Gynecology. [2155

JOSEPH BEN-DAVID. Scientific productivity and academic organization in nineteenth century medicine. Am. sociol. rev., 25:828-43 (Dec). diagr., tables. notes. Comparative study of "discoveries in the medical sciences" in the United States, England, France, Germany, and elsewhere, 1800-1926. [2156

ARTHUR LEONARD BLOOMFIELD, comp. A bibliography of internal medicine: selected diseases. [Chicago:] Univ. of Chicago Press [1960]. viii, 312 p. Abstracts of the books and articles (some published before 1800) that have most heavily contributed to the progress of knowledge concerning auricular fibrillation, coronary occlusion, Stokes-Adams disease, subacute bacterial endocarditis, periarteritis nodosa, pernicious anemia, chlorosis, leukemia, Hodgkin's disease, diabetes mellitus, diabetes insipidus, Addison's disease, Graves' disease, myxedema, tetany, hyperparathyroidism, gout, Bright's disease, bronchial asthma, scurvy, and trichinosis. Sequel to the compiler's A bibliography of internal medicine: communicable diseases (1958). [2157

ALFRED H. WHITTAKER. Observations of some physiologists who preceded Beaumont. Mich. State Med. Soc., Jour., 58:751-3 (May 1959). Includes reference to studies by Oliver H. Spencer (Philadelphia, 1802) relating to the physiology of digestion and probably useful to William Beaumont, M.D., in his later studies. [2158

JOSEPH V. KLAUDER. Historical remarks on the interrelation of human and veterinary medicine [1808-1958]. College Phys. Phila., Trans. & studies, 26:27-33 (Jun 1958). notes. [2159

LELA DUFF. Ann Arbor's best seller--Dr. Chase's recipe book. Washtenaw impressions, 14(3):14-20 (Jun). On Alvin Wood Chase (1817-85), originally a peddler of groceries and drugs, settler in Ann Arbor in 1856, M.D. from the Eclectic Medical Institute of Cincinnati (degree earned by 16 weeks of study), proprietor of Dr. Chase's Steam Printing Plant, author of a book of miscellaneous recipes and formulas "for Everybody, for Business and Professional Men, Mechanics, Artists, Farmers, and for Families Generally" (6th edition 1859, before which date 7,000 copies had been sold), of which the 10th edition (1864) was reprinted "practically unchanged" in ever higher edition numbers, still in print in 1931, with estimated total sales of more than 4 million copies. Quotes some of the medical folklore perpetuated even in late editions. [2159a

J. F. SMITHCORS. Medical men and the beginnings of veterinary medicine in America. Bul. hist. med., 33:330-41 (Jul-Aug). notes. Based upon an examination of American agricultural periodicals, 1819-70. [2159b

CHARLES L. LOSACCO. The Philadelphia journal of the medical and physical sciences, 1820-1827. Bul. hist. med., 34:75-9 (Jan-Feb). notes. [2159c

EDWARD HORTON BENSLEY. Alexis St. Martin [1794-1880]. Mich. State Med. Soc., Jour., 58:738-41, 765 (May 1959). facsim., views. notes. On his life in Canada and the United States, and particularly his association with Dr. William Beaumont (during the years 1822-25, 1829-34) as a patient for treatment of a gunshot wound, later as a subject for observation and experiment whose permanent gastric fistula permitted visual inspection of the interior of his stomach and of its contents in process of digestion. [2160

ALLAN JACOBS. Pernicious anemia, 1822-1929. Arch. internal med., 103: 329-33 (Feb 1959). notes. Includes some account of American studies, 1860-1929. [2161

CHARLES MAURICE WILTSE. "... to reach and treat the fallen." John Arthur Garraty, ed., The unforgettable Americans (Great Neck, N.Y.: Channel Press [1960]), p. 233-6. On Jonathan Letterman (1824-72), his early life in Pennsylvania, his studies at Jefferson Medical College, Philadelphia, his service as medical director of the Army of the Potomac in the Civil War, and his medical practice in Pennsylvania and California. [2162

CHARLES S. CAMERON. Homeopathy in retrospect [1825-1900]. College Phys. Phila., Trans. & studies, 27: 28-33 (Jul 1959). [2163

THOMAS JEFFERSON (1743-1826). The Jefferson-Dunglison letters. Edited by John M[orris] Dorsey. Charlottesville: Univ. of Virginia Press [1960]. 120 p. port. bibliog. (p. 107-10), notes. Letters exchanged between Jefferson and his physician, Dr. Robley Dunglison (1798-1869), Professor of Medicine at the University of Virginia, and between Jefferson and Dr. Robert Greenhow of New York City, May 1825-Apr. 1826, on Jefferson's health and his plans for the library and the medical school of the University of Virginia. [2164

DANA W. ATCHLEY. The uses of elegance. Ann. internal med., 52: 881-9 (Apr). On the style and form of medical writing, 1834-1960. [2165

LAWRENCE WILLSON. Thoreau's medical vagaries. Jour. hist. med., 15:64-74 (Jan). notes. On his attitudes toward "health and the preservation of it" and "medicine and the practitioners of it," and his reading about these subjects, 1836-62. [2166

JOSEPH EDWARD MAYNARD. Healing hands: the story of the Palmer family, discoverers and developers of chiropractic. Freeport, N.Y.: Jonorm Pub. Co. [1959]. xiii, [3], 365 p. ports. Account, fictional in form, of Daniel David Palmer (1842-1913), who opened a "magnetic cure and infirmary" in Davenport, Ia., sometime after 1881, and made the "Chiropractic discovery" ca. 1895, and his son, Bartlett Joshua Palmer (born 1881), who practised independently, established the Palmer School of Chiropractic in Iowa in 1905, and purchased the father's facilities and practice. Appended (p. 157-365): "The philosophy and science of chiropractic," by Joseph E. Maynard, Dr. of Chiropractory. [2167

AMERICAN MEDICAL ASSOCIATION. 1846-1958: digest of official actions, American Medical Association. [Chicago, 1959.] 779 p. [2168

EARL W. HAYTER. Livestock doctors, 1850-1890: the development of veterinary surgery. Wis. mag. hist., 43: 159-72 (spring). views. notes. Deals mainly with the continued application of folk medicines and quack surgery to unfortunate farm animals. [2169

NOAH DANIEL FABRICANT. 13 famous patients: Franklin D. Roosevelt [and others]. Phila.: Chilton Co., Book Division [1960]. ix, [7], 231 p. ports. bibliog. (p. 213-21). Includes "medical profiles" of Franklin Delano Roosevelt (1882-1945), Woodrow Wilson (1856-1924), F. Scott Fitzgerald (1896-1940), Clarence S. Darrow (1857-1938), George Gershwin (1898-1937), and Enrico Caruso (1873-1921), with special attention to their fatal illnesses. [2170

CATHARINE MACFARLANE. Women physicians and the medical societies [1870-1958]. College Phys. Phila., Trans. & studies, 26:80-83 (Aug 1958). [2171

JOHN F. SHRONTS. Industrial medicine--the changing scene, 1870-1960. Jour. lancet, 80:245-51 (May). notes. [2172

PHILIP DURYEE McMASTER & MICHAEL HEIDELBERGER. Florence Rena Sabin, November 9, 1871 - October 3, 1953. Natl. Acad. Sciences, Biog. memoirs, 34:271-319. port. On her early life in Central City, Colo., her studies at Smith College and the Johns Hopkins School of Medicine, her teaching of anatomy in the latter (1902-25), her researches in tuberculosis in the Rockefeller Institue for Medical Research (1925-38), her retirement to Denver, and her strenuous support of several programs in public health for the State of Colorado. [2173

THOMAS J. SULLIVAN. Osler's contributions to dermatology. Arch. dermatol., 82:487-94 (Oct). facsim., ports., view. notes. On the more than 100 articles and other publications of William Osler that deal "with subjects essentially dermatologic," 1873-1914. [2174

BURNS CHAFFEE (born 1880). My first eighty years ... the life story of a California surgeon. Los Angeles: Westernlore Press, 1960. xv, 264 p. facsim., ports., views. On the author's early life on a farm at Garden Grove, Calif., his studies at Stanford University and the Johns Hopkins Medical School, his medical practice in Pittsburgh, his service as an Army medical officer in World War I, and his work since 1919 as a surgeon in Long Beach, Calif. Deals almost entirely with his life before 1919. [2175

SAUL JARCHO. Some hoaxes in the medical literature. Bul. hist. med., 33:342-7 (Jul-Aug 1959). notes. Cites William Henry Welch, Sir William Osler, Appleton's cyclopaedia of American biography, and H. L. Mencken as American perpetrators of hoaxes, 1880s-1930s. [2175a

ALEXANDER FORBES. Eugene Floyd Du Bois (1882-1959) [physiologist, medical educator, researcher in metabolism and in aviation and submarine medicine]. Am. Philos. Soc., Yr. bk., 1959, p. 122-7. [2176

GERALD HEWES CARSON. The roguish world of Doctor Brinkley. N.Y.: Rinehart [1960. 8], 280 p. cartoons, facsims. (part double), ports., views (1 double). bibliog. (p. 259-62). On John Richard Brinkley (born John Romulus Brinkley, 1885-1942), native of North Carolina, itinerant healer in the South, briefly a student at Bennett Medical College, Chicago, recipient of a fraudulent medical diploma from the National University of Arts and Sciences, St. Louis, ca. 1918 (but back-dated to 1913), medical practitioner at Milford, Kan., operator of a hospital there, specialist in "goat-gland transplantation" surgery and other procedures to restore declining virility, newspaper columnist and "radio medicine man," defeated candidate for Governor of Kansas, later a medical practitioner and hospital owner in Del Rio, Tex., in repeated difficulties as "the medical maverick of Kansas and Texas," eminent in "the crowded field of pseudo-medicine," who died while under indictment for use of the mails to defraud. [2177

WILLIAM A. TAYLOR. What constitutes the practice of medicine in Wyoming [and other States, 1889-1954]. Wyo. law jour., 13:259-67 (spring 1959). [2178

WALTER G. ELMER. Some personal recollections of Dr. S. Weir Mitchell, College Phys. Phila., Trans. & studies, 26:40-50 (Jun 1958). port. On the author's association with Mitchell in Philadelphia and Bar Harbor, 1893-1913; with texts of conversations, "set down from memory," about Mitchell's travels in Europe and his studies of thought transference, wine-age assessment, rattlesnakes, and medical history. [2179

The DESIRABILITY of State licensing of medical technologists [1895-1959]. Minn. law rev., 44:1125-47 (May). notes. [2180

WINFRED OVERHOLSER. Note on Benjamin Rush. Am. jour. psychiatry, 116:937 (Apr). port. On a statue and monument to Rush, erected by the American Medical Association in Washington, 1896-1904. [2181

MAX RITVO. The role of diagnostic roentgenology in medicine 1896-1960]. New Eng. jour. med., 262:1201-9 (16 Jun). views. notes. [2182

ARTHUR CHRISTIAN DE GRAFF. Trends in therapeutic research [1899-1958]. Am. Geriatrics Soc., Jour., 7:93-9 (Feb 1959). [2183

CHAUNCEY DEPEW LEAKE. John Farquhar Fulton, 1899-1960. Isis, 51:560-62 (Dec). port. On his work as a physiologist, a teacher of physiology, a neurologist, a historian of medicine, and a collector of medical and surgical works of historical interest. [2184

JOSEPH CASTRO EDWARDS. Why some men became doctors. Phi Chi quar., 56:137-41 (Mar 1959). bibliog. On their reasons for choosing medicine as a career, 20th century. [2185

PHYLLIS E. LUFKIN. Dietary use of liver through the ages [in America, 1900-1960, and abroad]. Am. Dietetic Assoc., Jour., 36:326-36 (Apr). notes. [2186

MILFORD O. ROUSE. Spiritual allies in medicine. Phi Chi quar., 57:61-5 (Jan). On the interrelationships of medicine and religion in American medical thought, 20th century. [2187

DIABETES FOUNDATION, Boston. Diabetes Foundation, Inc., and the three trusts: the Diabetic Fund, the Permanent Diabetic Fund, the Diabetes Camp, Home, and Hospital Fund [1902-60]. Boston Safe Deposit and Trust Company, Trustee. [Boston] 1960. 50 p. medals, tables (1 double), views. Includes a reminiscent introduction by Elliott P. Joslin. [2188

RAYMOND RAY LANIER. Precautions in medical radiology. Ark. Med. Soc., Jour., 55:143-50 (Sep 1958). tables, views. notes. On the "hazards in medical radiology," 1902-58. [2189

THOMAS D. MOORE. For the good of the order. Jour. urol., 67:1-18 (Jan 1952). diagrs., map, tables. On the American Urological Association, 1902-51. [2190

RODERICK MURRAY. Current use of immunizing agents [1902-58]. N.Y. State jour. med., 59:1507-14 (15 Apr 1959). table. notes. [2191

BURR B. MARKHAM. A medical legal problem. Minn. med., 42:251-8 (Mar 1959). On "lawsuits against physicians" in America, 1905-55. [2192

HENRY N. WAGNER, JR. An outline of the use of iodine in endemic goiter [1907-58]. Arch. internal med., 103: 484-8 (Mar 1959). view. notes. [2193

JAMES L. DOENGES. "Third party" interference, the practice of medicine, and the market economy. Ind. State Med. Assoc., Jour., 52:547-62 (Apr 1959). On intervention by the U.S. Government between physician and patient, mainly since 1910. Issued also, according to the editor, as a pamphlet by the Association of American Physicians and Surgeons, Chicago. [2194

LEONARD J. GOLDWATER. A brief historical sketch of occupational medicine [1910-56]. Jour. chronic diseases, 9:85-8 (Feb 1959). notes. [2195

NEW YORK ALLERGY SOCIETY. Dinner in honor of Robert A. Cooke, M.D. N.Y. State med. jour., 59: 289-302 (15 Jan 1959). Proceedings, 27 Feb. 1958, consisting of reminiscent addresses by Dr. Robert Anderson Cooke (Director of the Institute of Allergy, founder of the Association for the Study of Asthma and Allied Conditions) and other physicians, on the progress of studies in allergy since 1910. [2196

HAROLD H. LOUCKS. China Medical Board of New York, Inc. [1914-59]. Jour. med. educ., 34:845-6 (Aug 1959). [2197

PAUL KLEMPERER. The knowledge of the connective tissue in historical perspective [in America, 1915-59, and abroad]. Joseph Berberich, Henry Lax, & Rudolf Stern, eds., Jubilee volume, 100th anniversary, Festschrift ... Rudolf Virchow Medical Society in the City of New York, N.Y. (Basel, N.Y.: S. Karger, 1960), p. 258-73. notes. [2198

LEO P. KRALL & ROBERT F. BRADLEY. Clinical evaluation of formamidinyliminourea, a new biguanide oral blood sugar lowering compound: comparison with other hypoglycemic agents [1918-58]. Ann. internal med., 50:586-613 (Mar 1959). diagrs., tables. notes. [2199

ALBERT WEINSTEIN. Radioactive iodine in the treatment of hyperthyroidism [1921-59]. Ark. Med. Soc., Jour., 56:225-9 (Nov 1959). notes. [2200

EUGENE CONSTANTINE DE SAVITSCH (1903-59). In search of complications: an autobiography. [London:] Andre Deutsch Ltd. [1958]. 352 p. 1st ed. 1940. On the author's early life in Russia and Japan; his migration to San Francisco in 1923; his recovery from tuberculosis at the Weimar Joint Sanatorium in the Sierra Nevadas; his work as a laboratory technician in the National Jewish Hospital, Denver; his studies in the University of Colorado School of Medicine and the University of Chicago School of Medicine; his stay abroad, 1936-38, to study leprosy and sleeping sickness in the Congo and Belgium and to visit the laboratories of Paris and Vienna; his practice of medicine in Washington, D.C.; and his medical travels abroad. [2201

CHARLES LYMAN SHORT. Rheumatoid arthritis: historical aspects [1924-58]. Jour. chronic diseases, 10:367-87 (Nov 1959). tables. notes. [2202

HENRY ERNEST SIGERIST (1891-1957). An introduction to the economics of medicine [in America, 1925-39, and abroad]. Henry E. Sigerist on the sociology of medicine, ed. Milton I. Roemer (N.Y.: MD Publications [1960]), p. 54-64. Manuscript (1940-41?), here first printed. [2203

JULIUS KLEEBERG. Etiology of gallstone formation in human beings. Joseph Berberich, Henry Lax, & Rudolf Stern, eds., Jubilee volume, 100th anniversary, Festschrift ... Rudolf Virchow Medical Society in the City of New York, N.Y. (Basel, N.Y.: S. Karger, 1960), p. 224-57. diagrs., tables, views. notes. On gallstone research in America, 1926-60, and abroad. [2204

AMERICAN COLLEGE OF PHYSICIANS. Committee for the Study of Hospital Standards in Medicine. Standards of practice of internal medicine: methods of judging its quality in hospitals [1928-58. Reported] by Arthur R. Colwell, Sr., and George Karl Fenn. Ann. internal med., 51:821-32 (Oct 1959). form, map, tables. notes. [2205

RALPH M. KNISELEY. Important non-biological contributions to radioisotopic diagnosis [1928-59]. Ia. State

Med. Soc., Jour., 49:619-24 (Oct 1959). diagr., tables. notes. [2206

WESLEY C. THOMAS. Sluder's headache and allied neuralgias [1928-58]. Med. Assoc. Ga., Jour., 48:64-8 (Feb 1959). notes. [2207

ROBERT GRAHAM. The evolution of corneal contact lenses [1929-54]. Am. jour. optometry, 36:55-72 (Feb 1959). diagrs., facsims., tables. notes. [2208

LAWRENCE FITCH. Notes on optometric manpower [1930-59]. Am. jour. optometry, 36:500-505 (Aug 1959). tables. [2209

ROBERT RAY McGEE, RICHARD L. WHITTAKER, & I. FRANK TULLIS. Apathetic thyroidism: review of the literature [1930-57] and report of four cases [John Gaston Hospital, Memphis, 1952-57]. Ann. internal med., 50: 1418-32 (Jun 1959). notes. [2210

G. A. GRANT PETERKIN. The changing pattern of dermatology [1931-57]. Arch. dermatol., 80:1-14 (Jul 1959). diagrs., tables. notes. [2211

WILLIAM NILES WISHARD, JR. Your American Board of Urology, Incorporated [1932-59]. Jour. urol., 82: 178-83 (Jul 1959). tables. [2212

ARTHUR P. LONG. Development and use of immunizing agents and procedures since 1934. Ia. State Med. Soc., Jour., 49:754-7 (Dec 1959). notes. [2213

JOSEPH WILLIAM GARBARINO. Price behavior and productivity in the medical market [1935-59]. Indus. and labor rel. rev., 13:3-15 (Oct 1959). tables. notes. On "the behavior of the fees of physicians." [2214

J. GARROTT ALLEN. Serum hepatitis: a study in retrospect [1937-59]. Stanford med. bul., 18:40-46 (Feb). [2215

JACK MASUR. Clinical research at National Institute of Health [1937-60]. Med. ann. Dist. Col., 29:199-201, 254-5 (Apr). [2216

THEODORE R. VAN DELLEN. The history of blood ["as a scientific medicinal tool," 1938-59]. Hospital management, 88(2):40, 116 (Aug 1959). facsim., view. [2217

HARRIET LOUISE HARDY. Delayed chemical pneumonitis in workers exposed to beryllium compounds [1941-46]. Am. rev. tuberculosis, 57:547-56 (Jun 1948). [2218

MONROE J. HIRSCH. A review of Darrell Boyd Harmon's experimental results. Am. jour. optometry, 37: 121-37 (Mar). notes. Critique of his writings on "vision and visual defects," prepared mainly during the years of his service as Director of the Division of School Health Services of the Texas State Department of Health, 1942-49, and based upon examination of 160,000 children. [2219

WILMA T. DONAHUE. Professional development in gerontology [since ca. 1945]. Am. Geriatrics Soc., Jour., 8:345-52 (May). notes. [2220

RICHARD K. LANSCHE. Corneal contact lenses: practice and complications [1945-60]. U.S. Armed Forces med. jour., 11:767-73 (Jul). notes. [2221

LEO GELFAND & REUBEN MERLISS. Trauma and rheumatism. Ann. internal med., 50:999-1009 (Apr 1959). notes. On studies of the "relationship between a specific injury and the subsequent appearance of arthritis, or the aggravation of a preexisting arthritis," 1946-55. [2222

LOUIS FAUGÈRES BISHOP. History of the American Therapeutic Society, 1947-1957. Am. Geriatrics Soc., Jour., 7:100-104 (Feb 1959). notes. [2223

HERBERT RICHARD AXELROD. The use of statistical techniques in medical and dental papers: a critique. Ann Arbor: University Microfilms, 1960. Positive microfilm of typescript. [408] leaves. Thesis--New York Univ. Abstracted: Dissert. abstracts, 21:1199-1200 (Nov). Study of 40 papers from 2 periodicals, 1949-54. [2224

ASSOCIATION OF AMERICAN PHYSICIANS. [In memoriam.] Assoc. Am. Physicians, Trans., 72 (1959): 12-32; 73 (1960): 8-50. Obituaries of John F. Anderson (1871-1958), Giuseppe Bastianelli (1862-1959), Frank Hartsuff Bethell (1903-59), Charles Sumner Bond (1856-1958), Eugene Floyd Du Bois (1882-1959), Ernest Edward Irons (1877-1959), Bernard Sutro Oppenheimer (1876-1958), George Draper (1880-1959), Channing Frothingham (1881-1959), James L. Gamble (1883-1959), Harold Walter Jones (1891-1959), Leo Loeb (1869-1959), Jonathan C. Meakins (1882-1959), Cornelius Packard

Rhoads (1898-1959), Leonard George Rowntree (1883-1959), Albert M. Snell (1896-1950), Tom Douglas Spies (1902-60), William Christopher Stadie (1886-1959), William Daniel Stroud (1891-1959), Edward Lewis Turner (1900-1960), and Russell M. Wilder (1885-1959). [2225

COLLEGE OF PHYSICIANS OF PHILADELPHIA. Memoirs. College Phys. Phila., Trans. & studies, 26: 51-8, 153-64, 189-200; 27:45-9, 107, 138-46, 159-60, 188-99 (June 1958 - Apr 1960). Obituary sketches, by various contributors, of Ralph Shepard Bromer (1886-1957), George Wagoner (1896-1957), William Egbert Robertson (1869-1956), John Allan Bertolet (1889-1956), Everett Pusey Barnard (1875-1957), William Zentmayer (1864-1958), Williams Biddle Cadwalader (1876-1957), John Stewart Rodman (1883-1958), Elliston Joseph Morris (1862-1958), Walter Roberts (1870-1958), Gabriel Tucker (1880-1958), Norris Wistar Vaux (1881-1958), Albert E. Bothe (1891-1955), Winifred Bayard Stewart (1899-1957), Daniel J. McCarthy (1874-1958), James William McConnell (1869-1958), Leon Jonas (1883-1958), Thomas C. Kelly (1882-1958), Arthur Parker Hitchens (died 1949), Frederick De Forest Weidman (1881-1956), Horatio C. Wood, Jr. (1874-1958), Donald Guthrie (1880-1958), Stirling Walker Moorhead (1882-1959), De Forest Porter Willard (1884-1957), Chevalier Jackson (1865-1958), Adolph J. Creskoff (1908-59), George Wilson (1888-1959), Isaac Sharpless (1911-59), and Joseph J. Toland, Jr. (1887-1959). [2226

Angiology and Cardiology

L. WHITING FARINHOLT, JR. Legal aspects. Md. State med. jour., 9:382-9 (Jul). On the attributability of heart disease and its sequelae to injuries, 1910-35. [2227

JEREMIAH STAMLER. The problem of elevated blood cholesterol [in the pathogenesis of atherosclerosis, 1920s ff.]. Am. jour. pub. health, 50 (3, pt. 2): 14-19 (Mar). notes. [2228

PAUL DUDLEY WHITE. Medical aspects [of the relation between injuries and heart disease as a problem in forensic medicine, 1921-60]. Md. State med. jour., 9:389-95 (Jul). [2229

EDWIN COWLES ANDRUS. A cardiologist looks at rehabilitation. Stanford med. bul., 18:5-9 (Feb). On progress since 1930 in the rehabilitation of patients with heart disease. [2230

WILLIAM E. DE MUTH, JR., WILLIAM T. FITTS, JR., & LEWIS T. PATTERSON. Collective review: mesenteric vascular occlusion. Internatl. abstracts surgery, 108: 209-23 (Mar 1959). tables. notes. Digest of the literature on this subject, and review of cases in the University of Pennsylvania Hospital and the Carlisle Hospital, 1930-56. [2231

HENRY ERNEST SIGERIST (1891-1957). Living under the shadow. Henry E. Sigerist, Henry E. Sigerist on the history of medicine, ed. Felix Martí-Ibañez (N.Y.: MD Publications [1960]), p. 269-81. First published in 1952. On the experience of the author, a physician, as a victim of chronic rhinitis and chronic hypertension since his arrival in America in 1931; with general remarks on the latter condition and the adjustments that can be made to it. [2232

PAUL WISWELL CLOUGH. Unilateral renal ischemia as a cause of hypertension [studies between 1937 and 1958]. Ann. internal med., 50:232-8 (Jan). notes. [2233

Communicable Diseases

SAMUEL X. RADBILL & GLORIA R. HAMILTON. Measles in fact and fancy [in America since ca. 1700, and abroad]. Bul. hist. med., 34:430-42 (Sep-Oct). notes. [2234

SIGISMUND PELLER. Walter Reed, C. Finlay, and their predecessors around 1800. Bul. hist. med., 33: 195-211 (May-Jun 1959). notes. On American studies of mosquitoes as the vectors of yellow fever, 1807, 1848, 1882, 1900-1901, and studies indicating that the disease is not transmitted directly from person to person, 1799, 1802-3. [2234a

CHARLES ROSENBERG. The cause of cholera: aspects of etiological thought in nineteenth century America [1832-73]. Bul. hist. med., 34:331-54 (Jul-Aug). notes. [2234b

PHYLLIS Q. EDWARDS & LYDIA B. EDWARDS. Story of the tuberculin test from an epidemiologic viewpoint [1892-1960. Baltimore: National Tuberculosis Assoc., 1960. 2], iii, 17 p.

tables. notes. (American review of respiratory diseases, v. 81, no. 1, pt. 2, Jan. 1960.) [2234c

JAY ARTHUR MYERS. The natural history of tuberculosis in the human body. II. Longitudinal observations imperative. Am. rev. resp. dis., 80:100-107 (Jul 1959). notes. On "long-term follow-up observation of patients" treated for tuberculosis, 1893-1959. [2235

CARL J. MARIENFELD & 3 others. Rheumatism: studies on the occurrence of bacteremia in rheumatic fever [1894-1958]. Jour. chronic diseases, 9:334-52 (Apr 1959). diagrs., tables. notes. [2236

DAVID W. WEISS. Vaccination against tuberculosis with nonliving vaccines. I. The problem and its historical background [1894-1959]. Am. rev. resp. dis., 80:340-58, 495-509, 676-88 (Sep-Nov 1959). notes. [2237

LESLIE L. ELLIS. Sylvatic plague in Oklahoma, with notes on its distribution in the United States [1900-1950]. Miss. Acad. Sciences, Jour., 6:80-82. notes. On a disease of wild rodents, found in Oklahoma on grasshopper mice in 1945 and 1950 in 2 counties of the Panhandle. [2238

SARAH REGAL RIEDMAN. Shots without guns: the story of vaccination. Chicago: Rand McNally [1960]. 232 p. diagrs., facsim., ports., views. Includes accounts of research in vaccines for scarlet fever and poliomyelitis in America, 1910-59. [2239

SARA ELIZABETH BRANHAM (1888-1962). A defense of Epimetheus: development of knowledge concerning the meningococcus [1913-60]. Am. Med. Women's Assoc., Jour., 15:571-5 (Jun). table. notes. [2240

HOBART ANSTETH REIMANN. Spectrums of infectious disease: a review, with special reference to inapparent and mild infections [1918-59]. Arch. internal med., 105: 779-815 (May). diagrs., table. notes. [2241

ROBERT W. PRITCHARD. The death of Enrico Caruso [1921]. Surgery, gynecol., & obstet., 109:117-20 (Jul 1959). cartoon. notes. On his respiratory illness and the details of his medical treatment in America and Italy, 1920-21. Includes information from his widow. [2242

JEAN GOULD. A good fight: the story of F. D. R.'s conquest of polio. N.Y.: Dodd, Mead, 1960. ix, [3], 308 p. On the experience of Franklin D. Roosevelt as a victim of poliomyelitis and the patron of a foundation to combat it, 1921-45. [2243

H. McLEOD RIGGINS & ROBERT P. GEARHART. Antibiotic and chemotherapy of tuberculosis [1931-47]. Am. rev. tuberculosis, 57:35-52 (Jan 1958). notes. [2244

MAXWELL FINLAND, WILFRED F. JONES, JR., & MILDRED W. BARNES. Changes in the occurrence of serious bacterial infections since the introduction of antibacterial agents [1935-57]. Assoc. Am. Physicians, Trans., 72 (1959): 305-22. diagrs., tables. [2245

EVERETT L. SCHILLER. Echinococcosis in North America [1935-59]. Ann. internal med., 52:464-76 (Feb). notes. [2246

HENRY WELCH & FÉLIX MARTÍ-IBÁÑEZ. The antibiotic saga [in America, 1951-60, and abroad]. N.Y.: Medical Encyclopedia, 1960. [8], 150, [2] p. [2247

ROBERT S. CARTWRIGHT & 3 others. The solitary pulmonary nodule: a critical evaluation [of treatments, 1944-59]. Postgraduate med., 26:836-40 (Dec 1959). ports., tables. notes. [2248

VIDA H. GORDON. The use of gamma globulin in infectious disease [1944-58]. Ark. Med. Soc., Jour., 55:299-303 (Jan 1959). notes. [2249

LOUIS WEINSTEIN, MORTON A. MADOFF, & CHARLES M. SAMET. The sulfonamides [1945-60]. New Eng. jour. med., 263:793-800, 842-9, 900-907, 952-7 (20 Oct - 10 Nov). notes. [2250

V. J. CABASSO. Oral poliomyelitis vaccine, Lederle--thirteen years of laboratory and field investigation. New Eng. jour. med., 263:1321-30 (29 Dec). tables. notes. On studies by the Lederle Laboratories of the American Cyanimid Company, 1947-60. [2251

AMERICAN TRUDEAU SOCIETY. Obituaries. Am. rev. tuberculosis, 57:308-10, 534-42 (Mar, May 1948). ports. Contents.--George Herbert Evans, 1869-1947, by Harold Guyon Trimble.--Max Pinner, 1891-1948, by Bruce H. Douglas.--Wm. Charles White, 1874-1947, by Esmond R. Long. [2252

Dentistry

EARLY American dentistry. New Eng. jour. med., 259:403-4 (21 Aug 1958). On A treatise on the human teeth (1794? 1796? 1801), by Richard Courtland Skinner of New York, and A treatise on dentistry (1802), by B. T. Longbotham of Baltimore. [2253

GEORGE BION DENTON. Some interrelations between German and American dentistry, 1800-1914. Am. Dental Assoc., Jour., 61:587-98 (Nov). notes. [2254

GEORGE BION DENTON. The craftsman and the dentist: from cutler to dental manufacturer [1820-1959]. Am. College Dentists, Jour., 27:195-200 (Sep). [2255

ALFRED JOHN ASGIS. Oral medicine: foundation of dental science and practice [1840-1959]. Ann. dentistry, 19: 1-5 (Mar). diagr. notes. [2256

ARTHUR L. ROBERTS. Present-day concepts in complete denture service [1840-1959]. Jour. prosthetic dentistry, 9:900-913 (Nov-Dec 1959). notes. [2257

N. C. HUDSON. Process patent litigation. Am. Dental Assoc., Jour., 58(7): 162-73 (Jun 1959). facsim. notes. On "dentistry's struggle against process patents" (processes of making plates, crowns, bridges, and casts), 1858-1948. [2258

BERNHARD WOLF WEINBERGER. From "irregularities of the teeth" to orthodontics as a specialty of dentistry [1858-1956]. Am. jour. orthodontics, 42:209-25 (Mar 1956). notes. [2259

AMERICAN DENTAL ASSOCIATION. American Dental Association: structure and function [1859-1959]. Am. Dental Assoc., Jour., 58(5):23-9, 15 (Apr (1959). views. [2260

AMERICAN DENTAL ASSOCIATION. A synoptic history of the American Dental Association. Am. Dental Assoc., Jour., 58(7): 19-76 (Jun 1959). facsims., ports., views. notes. Contents.--1859-1897, by J. Ben Robinson.--1898-1922, by Harold L. Faggart.--1923-1959 by Lon W. Morrey. [2261

EDGAR DAVID COOLIDGE. Past and present concepts in endodontics. Am. Dental Assoc., Jour., 61:676-88 (Dec). notes. On the treatment of pulpless teeth, 1870-1960. [2262

J. BEN ROBINSON. The American Association of Dental Examiners [and its predecessor, the National Association of Dental Examiners, 1883-1959]. Am. Dental Assoc., Jour., 58(7): 150-57 (Jun 1959). table. notes. [2263

GORDON L. TEALL. National Board of Dental Examiners [and its predecessor, the National Association of Dental Examiners, 1883-1958]. Am. Dental Assoc., Jour., 58(7):144-9 (Jun 1959). notes. [2264

NEW YORK ACADEMY OF DENTISTRY. Tribute to Dr. Davenport. Ann. dent., 18:1-13 (Mar 1959). port. On the work of S. Ellsworth Davenport, Jr. (1888-1958), as a dentist in New York City, and his contributions to the progress of dentistry; with 2 speeches by him on dental subjects (1940, 1956). [2265

JOSEPH D. EBY. Days of achievement [in American dentistry, particularly orthodontics, 1896-1957]. Am. jour. orthodontics, 43:610-21 (Aug 1957). port. [2266

WILLIAM W. PADEN. A survey of radiation hazards in orthodontics [1896-1960]. Am. jour. orthodontics, 46:575-87 (Aug). notes. [2267

VICTOR HUGO SEARS. Developments in the denture field during the past half century [1902-56]. Jour. prosthetic dentistry, 8:61-7 (Jan 1958). [2268

LOUIS M. CRUTTENDEN. The Relief Fund. Am. Dental Assoc., Jour., 58(7): 158-62 (Jun 1959). facsims., tables. On a fund established by the Association for the relief of dentists in distress, 1906-59. [2269

AMERICAN DENTAL ASSOCIATION. The Association and dental science. Am. Dental Assoc., Jour., 58(7):93-122 (Jun 1959). facsims., views. notes. Accounts, by 6 contributors, of physical, biological, therapeutic, and economic research, 1908-59. [2270

JACOB AMOS SALZMANN. Specialization and specialty boards in dentistry. Am. jour. orthodontics, 45: 861-5 (Nov 1959). notes. On the American Board of Orthodontics, 1928-59. [2271

OREN AUSTIN OLIVER. History of the American Board of Orthodontics [1929-57]. Am. jour. orthodontics, 43: 454-9 (Jun 1957). [2272

NOEL KAHO. Problems in unifying the administration of dental services in State institutions [1932-58]. Am. Dental Assoc., Jour., 60:29-34 (Jan). [2273

T. F. McBRIDE & O. W. BRANDHORST. A survey of current dental periodicals [1932-59]. Am. College Dentists, Jour., 26:51-64, 329-43 (Mar, Dec 1959). tables (part double). notes. Tabulation. [2274

OREN AUSTIN OLIVER. History of the Albert H. Ketcham Award [contributions to the science and art of orthodontics, 1937-57]. Am. jour. orthodontics, 43:606-8 (Aug 1957). [2275

AMERICAN ASSOCIATION OF ORTHODONTISTS. Orthodontic profiles. Am. jour. orthodontics, 42:858-66, 927-8; 43:46-51, 132-4, 210-18, 372-81, 460-62, 537-43, 688-95, 778-81, 869-72; 44:59-60, 141-4, 295-8, 382-4, 603-10, 699-706, 792-5, 864-6, 940-42; 45:289-92, 371-6, 536-8, 689-91; 46:695-9, 905-9 (Nov 1956 - Dec 1960). ports. notes. Biographical sketches of Milo Hellman (1872-1947), Marguerite Stadelhofer (1896-1956), Albin Oppenheim (1875-1945), Edward H. Angle, Calvin Suveril Case (1847-1923), Martin Dewey (born 1881), Allen Holman Suggett (1867-1946?), Norman Williams Kingsley (1829-1913), Victor Hugh Jackson (1850-1929), George Wellington Grieve (1870-1950), Simon Hayden Guilford (born 1841), Robert Dunn (1872-1937), Paul W. Simon (1883-1957), Harry Estes Kelsey (died 1946), Edmund H. Wuerpel (1866-1958), Rodrigues Ottolengui (born 1861), John Valentine Mershon (1867-1953), Albert H. Ketcham (1870-1935), Herbert A. Pullen (1873-1934?), Henry Albert Baker (1848-1934), Clinton C. Howard (1884-1955), William G. Law (1876-1920), Earl Wildes Swinehart (1875-1958), Lloyd Steel Lourie, Sr. (1877-1958), Frederick Sumner McKay (1874-1959), and Oliver W. White (born 1876). By various contributors. [2276

Gynecology and Obstetrics

J. L. McKELVEY Ninety years of obstetrics and gynecology [1870-1960]. Jour. lancet, 80:242-4 (May). [2277

JOE VINCENT MEIGS. An interest in endometriosis and its consequences [1899-1958]. Am. jour. obstet. and gynecol., 79:625-35 (Apr). facsims., tables. notes. [2278

Medical Education

HERBERT THOMS. The doctors of Yale College, 1702-1815, and the founding of the Medical Institution. Hamden, Conn.: Shoe String Press, 1960. xxi, 199 p. facsims., ports., views. bibliog. (p. 189-92), notes (p. 183-8). (Yale University. School of Medicine. Dept. of the History of Medicine. Publication 39.) On the 43 future physicians in the Yale classes of 1704 to 1815, with biographical sketches of 26 of them and shorter notices of the others, and an account of the 6 members of "the first medical faculty" at Yale. [2279

HENRY ERNEST SIGERIST (1891-1957). Boerhaave's influence upon American medicine. Henry E. Sigerist, Henry E. Sigerist on the history of medicine, ed. Felix Marti-Ibañez (N.Y.: MD Publications [1960]), p. 202-8. notes. On Americans who studied at Leiden under Herman Boerhaave or elsewhere under his pupils, the American prestige of his books, and the teaching of some of his doctrines in American medical education, 1729 to ca. 1775. [2280

JEAN ALONZO CURRAN. Internships and residencies: historical backgrounds and current trends [1751-1959]. Jour. med. educ., 34:873-84 (Sep 1959). table. notes. [2281

FRED B. ROGERS. Nicholas Romayne, 1756-1817: stormy petrel of American medical education. Jour. med. educ., 35:258-63 (Mar). facsims., port. notes. On his early life in New York City, his studies at the Medical School of King's College and at the University of Edinburgh, and his service as Professor of Physic at King's College and as President of the College of Physicians and Surgeons of New York. [2282

ROBERT I. CARLSON. The historical development of medical education in the United States [1760-1960]. Surgery, 47:695-702 (Apr). notes. [2283

OLIVER S. HAYWARD. Dr. Nathan Smith (1762-1829). New Eng. jour. med., 261:489-94: 263:1235-43, 1288-91 (3 Sep 1959, 15, 22 Dec. 1960). Also printed: A search for the real Nathan Smith. Jour. hist. med., 15: 268-81 (Jul 1960). facsims., ports., views. notes. On his early life in Rehoboth, Mass., and Chester, Vt., his studies at the Harvard Medical School, his medical practice in New Hampshire, his establishment of the Medical School of Dartmouth College and the Medical Institution of Yale College, and his activities in politics. [2284

RICHARD H. YOUNG. Medical education in the United States [1765-1959]. Jour. med. educ., 34:802-13 (Aug 1959). notes. [2285

DAVID MELVIN DAVIS. The history of the resident system [1791-1959]. College Phys. Phila., Trans. & studies, 27:76-81 (Oct 1959). bibliog. [2286

JOSEPH IOOR WARING. Samuel Henry Dickson (1798-1872). Jour. med. educ., 35:421-8 (May). facsim., ports., views. notes. On his life in Charleston, his studies at the College of Charleston, Yale, and the University of Pennsylvania, his medical practice in Charleston, and his teaching in the Medical College of the States of South Carolina and the Jefferson Medical College, Philadelphia. [2287

CHARLES T. OLCOTT. Pathology at the New York Hospital, 1810-1932. Bul. hist. med., 34:137-47 (Mar-Apr). port. On autopsies, the museum preservation of autopsy materials, and accompanying instruction in the hospital or by members of its staff in affiliated medical schools. [2287a

NORMAN SHAFTEL. Austin Fling, Sr. (1812-1886): educator of physicians. Jour. med. educ., 35:1111-35 (Dec). facsims., ports., view. notes. On his early life in Massachusetts, his studies at Amherst College and the Harvard Medical School, his practice of medicine in Northampton, Boston, and Buffalo, and his teaching of medicine at Rush Medical College (Chicago), the University of Buffalo, the Charity Hospital of Louisiana (New Orleans), the University of Louisville, and Bellevue Medical School and Hospital (New York City). [2288

OTTO FREDERIC KAMPMEIER. Nathan Smith Davis, 1817-1904: a biographical essay. Jour. med. educ., 34: 496-508 (May 1959). port. notes. On his early life in Chenango County, N.Y., his studies in the College of Physicians and Surgeons of the Western District of New York at Fairfield, his work as a physician, his services to the New York State Medical Society and as a founder of the American Medical Association, and his teaching in Chicago at Rush Medical College, Lind University, and Chicago Medical College. [2289

SAMUEL X. RADBILL. Robley Dunglison, M.D., 1798-1869, American medical educator. Jour. Med. educ., 34:84-94 (Feb 1959). ports. bibliog. On his early life and medical studies in England, his emigration to America in 1824, and his teaching of medicine at the University of Virginia, the University of Maryland (in Baltimore), and Jefferson Medical College (Philadelphia). Reprinted in part: Dr. Robley Dunglison and Jefferson. College Phys. Phila., Trans. & studies, 37:40-44 (Jul 1959). [2290

JOHN LOUIS PARKS. The George Washington University School of Medicine [1825-1960]. Med. ann. Dist. Col., 29:135-8 (Mar). [2291

MARTIN E. BLUTINGER. Influences of the first faculty of the Medical College of Georgia upon the American medical curriculum and the origin of the American Medical Association [1828-48]. Med. Assoc. Ga., Jour., 48:31-5 (Jan 1959). notes. [2292

ROBERT THOMAS DIVETT. The Medical College of Utah at Morgan [1880-82]. Med. Lib. Assoc., Bul., 48:1-10 (Jan). notes. Includes an account of Dr. Frederick S. Kohler (1836-1908). [2293

AMERICAN DENTAL ASSOCIATION. The Association and dental education. Am. Dental Assoc., Jour., 58(7): 123-43 (Jun 1959). map, port. notes. Contents.--1840-1938, by Harlan H. Horner.--1938-1950, by Gerald D. Timmons.--1951-1959, by Philip E. Blackerby. [2294

CHARLES HOOVER RUSSELL. Liberal education and dentistry. Educ. rev., 41:40-66 (Jan). table. notes. On college work as a prerequisite to admission to dental schools, 1840-1960. [2295

GEORGE FRANCIS CAHILL. Medical education and training in urology [1846-1953]. Jour. urol., 70:807-12 (Dec 1953). [2296

WALTER S. WIGGINS & GLEN R. SHEPHERD. The role of the Council on Medical Education and Hospitals of the American Medical Association [1847-1959]. Jour. med. educ., 34: 819-25 (Aug 1959). notes. [2297

GEORGE BORN MANHART. The Indiana Central Medical College [Indianapolis], 1849-1852. Ind. mag. hist., 56:105-22 (Mar). notes. [2298

STELLA GOOSTRAY. Mary Adelaide Nutting [1858-1948]. Am. jour. nursing, 58:1524-9 (Nov 1958). facsim., ports., view. notes. On her early life in Canada, her studies in the Johns Hopkins School of Nursing, her service there as superintendent of nurses, and her establishment of a department of household and institution administration, Teachers College, Columbia University. [2299

NEW YORK. DOWNSTATE MEDICAL CENTER, New York. Medical education in Brooklyn: the first hundred years, 1860-1960. [By Evelyn Goodwin, Public Relations Director.] Brooklyn [1960]. 61, [7] p. facsims., map, ports., views. On the Long Island College of Medicine, the Long Island College Hospital, and the State University of New York Downstate Medical Center. [2300

JOHN SPANGLER NICHOLAS. Ross Granville Harrison, 1870-1959. Yale jour. biol. and med., 32:407-12 (Jun). port. On his early life in Germantown, Pa., his medical education at Johns Hopkins University, and his service as professor of anatomy at Johns Hopkins University and as professor of comparative anatomy at Yale. [2301

WARD DARLEY. The Association of American Medical Colleges: its objectives and program [1876-1959]. Jour. med. educ., 34:814-18 (Aug 1959). notes. [2302

LEE POWERS. The Association of American Medical Colleges [1876-1959]. Am. jour. pharm. educ., 24: 149-55 (spring). notes. [2303

FREDERICK H. SHILLITO. Postgraduate training in occupational medicine at the University of Michigan Medical Center. Postgraduate med., 27:46-50 (Jan). port., table. Includes some account of instruction in occupational medicine in the Medical School as early as 1876. [2304

ISABEL MAITLAND STEWART. Elizabeth Chamberlain Burgess [1877-1949]. Am. jour. nursing, 58:1101-5 (Aug 1958). ports. On her early life in Maine, her studies at the Roosevelt Hospital School of Nursing and Teachers College, Columbia University, her service as superintendent of nurses at Michael Reese Hospital, Chicago, and as State Inspector of Nurses' Training Schools, New York State Department of Education, her conduct of a national survey of nursing in military hospitals during World War I, her establishment of the Army School of Nurses, and her service as Professor of Nursing, Teachers College, Columbia University. [2305

AVERILL A. LIEBOW & LEVIN L. WATERS. Milton Charles Winternitz, February 19, 1885 - October 3, 1959. Yale jour. biol. and med., 32:143-72 (Dec 1959). cartoon, ports., views. On his early life in Baltimore, his medical studies at Johns Hopkins University, his service as chairman of the Department of Pathology and Dean of the School of Medicine of Yale University, and the development of the school during the years of his service as Dean (1920-50); with a list of his writings, 1905-57. [2306

OWEN HARDING WANGENSTEEN. The Minnesota experience in surgical graduate education. Surgery, 48:985-93 (Nov). On the Medical School of the University of Minnesota, 1889-1960. Includes the author's reminiscences since 1930. [2307

RALPH WARREN EDWARDS. A history of the Western Dental College [Kansas City, Mo., 1890-1919]. Bul. hist. med., 33:137-44 (Mar-Apr 1959). facsim. notes. [2307a

KARL H. MARTZLOFF. Thomas Stephen Cullen [1868-1953]. Am. jour. obstet. and gynecol., 80:833-43 (Nov). port. bibliog., notes. On his study and teaching of gynecology in Johns Hopkins University, 1891 ff.; with some account of his early life and medical studies in Canada and his service on the Maryland Board of Health. [2308

ALAN MASON CHESNEY. The Johns Hopkins Hospital and the Johns Hopkins University School of Medicine: a chronicle. Volume II: 1893-1905. Baltimore: Johns Hopkins Press, 1958. xiv, 499 p. plans, ports., views. Twelve chronological chapters. Vol. I published in 1943. [2309

WILLIAM HENRY WELCH (1850-1934). The Johns Hopkins Hospital with especial reference to its relations to medical education and the promotion of medical knowledge [1893-1904]. ... With an explanatory note by Alan M. Chesney. Johns Hopkins Hospital, Bul., 104:1-10 (Jan 1959). facsim. Statement submitted by the author, "Pathologist to the Hospital and Professor of Pathology in the School of Medicine," to Starr J. Murphy, legal counsel to John D. Rockefeller, Sr., after the destruction by fire of several buildings endowed by Rockefeller, 1904. [2310

MELVIN R. GIBSON. President Henry Matthew Burlage [born 1897]: a biographical sketch. Am. jour. pharm. educ., 24:389-92 (fall). port. notes. On his early life in Indiana and his study and teaching of pharmacy, eventually as Dean of the College of Pharmacy, University of Texas. [2311

MELVIN WILLIAM GREEN. Graduate education in schools of pharmacy [1902-60]. Am. jour. pharm. educ., 24:492-508 (fall). [2312

EDWARD JERALD VAN LIERE & GIDEON S. DODDS. Women in medicine at West Virginia University [1902-58]. Jour. med. educ., 34:911-15 (Sep 1959). Also printed: Am. Med. Women's Assoc., Jour., 15:166-9 (Feb 1960). table. [2313

T. H. HARWOOD. History of the University of North Dakota School of Medicine [1905-60]. Jour. lancet, 80:252-6 (May). view. [2314

PHI CHI MEDICAL FRATERNITY. XI Chapter. The history of XI of Phi Chi [Fort Worth, 1907-59]. Phi Chi quar., 57:38-42 (Jan). views. [2315

JAMES GRAY. Education for nursing: a history of the University of Minnesota School [of Nursing, 1908-60]. Minneapolis: Univ. of Minnesota Press [1960. 10], 239 p. ports., views. notes. [2316

W. E. WILSON. Neil S. Dungay [1882-1958], M.D. Jour. lancet, 80:599-601 (Dec). port. On his teaching of biology and of hygiene and public health in Carleton College, Northfield, Minn., 1907-54. [2317

WILLARD C. RAPPLEYE. Major changes in medical education during the past fifty years [1909-59]. Jour. med. educ., 34:683-9 (Jun 1959). [2318

JOHN Z. BOWERS. The study of medical education in the United States [1910-59]. Jour. med. educ., 34: 1134-8 (Dec 1959). notes. [2319

CHARLES E. GOSHEN. Psychiatric training and its relation to medical education [1910-60]. Jour. med. educ., 35:360-68 (Apr). [2320

SAUL JARCHO. Medical education in the United States--1910-1956. Mt. Sinai Hospital, Jour., 26:339-85 (Jul-Aug 1959). cartoon. notes. [2321

MARION BALDUR SULZBERGER. Education for dermatology in the United States [1910-60]. Arch. dermatol., 82:311-24 (Sep). cartoons. notes. [2322

PHILIP D. HERRICK. Experiences in graduate medical education in a community teaching hospital [Beverly Hospital, Beverly, Mass., 1914-60]. New Eng. jour. med., 262:1269-72 (23 Jun). notes. [2323

HERMAN GATES WEISKOTTEN & others. Trends in medical practice: an analysis of the distribution and characteristics of medical college graduates, 1915-1950. Jour. med. educ., 35:1071-1121 (Dec). diagrs., form, tables. notes. [2324

JOHN McK. MITCHELL. Medical education and American specialty boards [1917-58]. Jour. med. educ., 34:555-60 (Jun 1959). notes. [2325

ROBERT ALLAN MOORE. Problems and trends in medical education [1918-58]. College Phys. Phila., Trans. & studies, 26:20-26 (Jun 1958). [2326

ROBERT ALLAN MOORE. The challenge to medical education in the nineteen sixties. Mt. Sinai Hospital, Jour., 27:322-39 (May-Jun). tables. Refers in part to development since 1920. [2327

Sir ALDO CASTELLANI (born 1874/77). A doctor in many lands: the autobiography of Aldo Castellani. Garden City, N.Y.: Doubleday, 1960. 359 p. London edition (Gollancz, 1960) has title: Microbes, men, and monarchs. On the author's early life and medical education in Italy and his medical practice and observations in several parts of Europe and Africa. Includes an account of his service as Chairman of Tropical Medicine, Tulane University Medical School, 1925-29. [2328

JAMES D. RIVES. The impact of the American Board of Surgery upon surgical education in the United States [1926-58]. Ann. surgery, 149:609-16 (May 1959). [2329

SOLOMON JACOB AXELROD & W. R. MILLS. Medical manpower in Michigan: applicants to medical school [1926-57]. Jour. med. educ., 34:916-26 (Sep 1959). diagrs., tables. notes. [2330

PRESTON T. BROWN. E[verett] D[udley] Plass and J[ohn] H. Randall, and obstetrics and gynecology at the State University of Iowa, 1926-1955. Ia. State Med. Soc., Jour., 50:229-33 (Apr). port. [2331

ROBERT C. PARKIN & OSLER L. PETERSON. The role of the preceptorship in medical education. Jour. med. educ., 34:644-8 (Jul 1959). tables. notes. On the University of Wisconsin Medical School Preceptorial Program of teaching in medicine, 1926-59. [2332

JOHN M. SHELDON, C. THOMAS FLOTTE, & MABEL F. KELLY. Postgraduate medical education at the University of Michigan Medical Center [1926-59]. Postgraduate med., 27: 94-8 (Jan). port., tables, view. notes. [2333

ARTHUR EBBERT, JR. A retrospective evaluation of research in the medical curriculum [Yale School of Medicine, 1928-52]. Jour. med. educ., 35:637-43 (Jul). tables. notes. [2334

CARROLL FRANKLIN SHUKERS. Paul L[ouis] Day [born 1899]--persistent investigator. Ark. Med. Soc., Jour., 56:258-60 (Dec 1959). On his service as Professor and Head of the Department of Biochemistry, Medical School, University of Arkansas, 1928-59. [2335

GLEN R. SHEPHERD. History of continuation medical education in the United States since 1930. Jour. med. educ., 35:740-58 (Aug). table. notes. On the growth of postgraduate study in medicine. [2336

GUNNAR GUNDERSEN. The American Medical Association - medical school partnership [1840-1958]. Jour. med. educ., 34:8-13 (Jan 1959). [2337

DAVID SCHULTZ PANKRATZ & JULIA C. DAVIS. A review of Mississippi's medical education program [1940-59]. Jour. med. educ., 35:352-6 (Apr). diagrs., table. notes. [2338

STANLEY WILLIAM OLSON & J. R. SCHOFIELD. Medical schools in wartime [1941-60]. Jour. med. educ., 35: 388-97 (May). notes. [2339

JOHN R. SAMPEY. Collegiate training of doctors of medicine [1942-57]. Jour. med. educ., 34:601-2 (Jun 1959). table. [2340

PHI CHI MEDICAL FRATERNITY. XI Chapter. University of Texas Southwestern Medical School [Dallas, 1944-59]. Phi Chi quar., 57:32-5 (Jan). views. [2341

FRANCIS J. CONLEY. Objectives of dental education in light of present day needs and trends [1945-59]. Am. College Dentists, Jour., 26:150-54 (Jun 1959). [2342

JOHN C. NUNEMAKER. The Veterans Administration - medical school relationship [1945-59]. Jour. med. educ., 34:77-83 (Feb 1959). [2343

Nursing

ANNE L. AUSTIN, ed. History of nursing source book. N.Y.: Putnam [1957]. 480 p. bibliog. (p. 453-70), notes (p. 433-52). Includes documents relating to nursing in the United States, 1620-1871 (p. 324-432), especially nursing during the Revolution and the Civil War. [2344

MARY M. ROBERTS (1876/77-1959). Stella Goostray. Am. jour. nursing, 58:352-5 (Mar 1958). ports. On her early life in Boston, her studies at Boston Children's Hospital School of Nursing and at Teachers College, Columbia University, her textbooks for nurses (1924 ff.), and her service as director of the nursing service of Boston Children's Hospital till her retirement in 1948. [2345

MARY M. Roberts, January 31, 1877 - January 11, 1959. Nursing outlook, 7:72-4 (Feb 1959). port. On her early life in Michigan, her studies at the Jewish Hospital School of Nursing in Cincinnati, and her work as a nurse, as Director of the Army School of Nursing in World War I, as editor of the American journal of nursing, as an official of the American Nurses' Association, and as a historian of nursing. [2346

VIRGINIA B. ELLIMAN. American Red Cross nursing services ... 50th anniversary [1888-1959]. Nursing outlook, 7:148-51 (Mar 1959). port., views. [2347

STELLA GOOSTRAY. Sophie [Caroline] Nelson. Am. jour. nursing, 60:1268-9 (Sep). port. On her early life in Massachusetts after emigration (in the 1890s?) from Denmark, her studies in the Waltham Training School for Nurses, and her work in public-health nursing, particularly in establishing a nursing service for policyholders of the John Hancock Mutual Life Insurance Company. [2348

GRETCHEN GERDS. Making ideals tangible. Am. jour. nursing, 60:672-6 (May). On "The Code for Professional Nurses" of the American Nurses' Association, 1897-1960. [2349

Mrs. HAROLD N. MARSH. The Visiting Nurse Association celebrates 60 years [1900-1960]. Med. ann. Dist. Col., 29:239-41 (Apr). port., view. [2350

JOHN J. PORTERFIELD. The practical nurse--her place in the sun [1900-1959]. Nursing outlook, 7:656-9 (Nov 1959). views. notes. [2351

GRETCHEN GERDS. Public and professional interests meet. Am. jour. nursing, 60:210-14 (Feb). On the activities of the American Nurses' Association Special Committee of State Boards of Nursing, 1914-60. [2352

HELEN L. BUNGE. Research is every professional nurse's business. Am. jour. nursing, 58:816-19 (Jun 1958). port. notes. On research in nursing, 1923-58. [2353

RUTH G. TAYLOR. Some significant developments in maternal and child health nursing [1930s-1960]. Nursing outlook, 8:442-7 (Aug). [2354

NEVA M. STEVENSON. Perspective on developments in practical nursing [1940-59]. Nursing outlook, 8:34-7 (Jan). notes. [2355

Oncology

HAROLD SHEELY DIEHL & WILLIAM H. STONER. Ninety years of cancer progress. Jour. lancet, 80:226-33 (May). On the progress of therapy, 1870-1960. [2356

DAVID A. KAMOFSKY. In memoriam: Cornelius Packard Rhoads (1898-1959). N.Y. Acad. Sciences, Trans., 22:2-6 (Nov 1959). port. On his work as a pathologist, Director of Memorial Hospital in New York City, and organizer of cancer research. [2357

CLARENCE COOK LITTLE. James Bumgardner Murphy, August 4, 1884 - August 24, 1950. Natl. Acad. Sciences, Biog. memoirs, 34:183-203. port. On his early life in North Carolina, his studies at the University of North Carolina and the Johns Hopkins Medical School, his service as a medical officer in World War I, and his work at Rockefeller Institute in the whole field of cancer research, with special attention to viruses; with a list of his publications, 1907-50. [2358

CORNELIUS PACKARD RHOADS. Cancer control [1911-58]--present and future. Am. jour. nursing, 58:516-19 (Apr 1958). views. [2359

JAMES F. McINTOSH & GORDON WORLEY, JR. Adenocarcinoma arising in extrophy of the bladder: report of two cases and review of the literature. Jour. urol., 73:820-29 (May 1955). views. bibliog. Includes an analysis of 25 cases at the University Hospitals, Madison, Wis., 1925-54. [2360

C. F. LIST. Brain tumor: the crucible of neurosurgery in the past thrity years [1930-60]. Jour. nervous and mental diseases, 130:542-6 (Jun). notes. [2361

WILLIAM L. PALMER. Cancer of the stomach [1930-56]. Rocky Mt. med. jour., 57(7):40-44 (Jul). diagrs., tables. [2362

ARCHIE L. DEAN & J. E. ASH. Study of the bladder tumors in the registry of the American Urological Association [1934-49]. Jour. urol., 63:618-21 (Apr 1950). tables. [2363

JOHN RODERICK HELLER. Research on cancer viruses [1934-60]. Pub. health reports, 75:501-6 (Jun). views. bibliog. [2364

THOMAS E. STARZL & VICTOR M. BERNHARD. Collective review: leiomyosarcoma of the duodenum. Internatl. abstracts surgery, 110: 313-22 (Apr). tables. notes. Digest of publications in America, 1934-60, and abroad. [2365

RALPH C. WILLIAMS, JR. Dermatomyositis and malignancy: a review of the literature [including American writings, 1934-58]. Ann. internal med., 50:1174-81 (May 1959). diagrs., tables. notes. [2366

BENJAMIN S. ABESHOUSE. The management of Wilms' tumor as determined by national survey and review of the literature [1936-56]. Jour. urol., 77:792-813 (Jun 1957). tables. bibliog. [2367

JOHN E. SKANDALAKIS, STEPHEN W. GRAY, & DUNCAN SHEPARD. Collective review, smooth muscle tumors of the stomach. Internatl. abstracts surgery, 110:209-26 (Mar). diagrs., tables, notes. Digest of publications, 1938-58. [2368

RICHARD C. PUTNAM. The chemotherapy of genitourinary cancer [1939-59]. Jour. urol., 83:1-6 (Jan). notes. [2369

CHARLES HUGGINS. On hormone dependence in cancer. Joseph Berberich, Henry Lax, & Rudolf Stern, eds., Jubilee volume, 100th anniversary, Festschrift ... Rudolf Virchow Medical Society in the City of New York, N.Y. (Basel, N.Y.: S. Karger, 1960), p. 192-8. notes. On the "control of cancer by physiologic means," 1940-60. [2370

C. GORDON ZUBROD. Useful drugs in the treatment of cancer [1943-60]. Arch. internal med., 106:663-78 (Nov). tables. notes. [2371

Pediatrics

BENJAMIN KRAMER & ABRAM KANOF. Diarrhea in children: a historical review [1777-1956]. Jour. pediatrics, 57:769-83 (Nov). tables. notes. [2372

LYTT IRVINE GARDNER. Abraham Jacobi: pediatric pioneer. Pediatrics, 24:282-7 (Aug 1959). port., view. notes. On his early life and medical studies in Germany, his settlement in New York City in 1853, his establishment of a pediatric clinic in the New York Infirmary for Women and Children, his service as Professor of Infantile Pathology and Therapeutics at the New York Medical College and as Clinical Professor of the Diseases of Infancy and Childhood at the College of Physicians and Surgeons of Columbia University, and his writings on pediatrics. [2373

LAURENCE G. PRAY. Pediatrics since 1870. Jour. lancet, 80:221-5 (May). [2374

ABRAHAM B. SCHWARTZ. Henry F. Helmholz (1882-1958). Jour. pediatrics, 56:562-70 (Apr). ports. On his medical studies at the Johns Hopkins University and abroad and his service as a pediatrician in Chicago, Head of the Section of Pediatrics of the Mayo Clinic, and official in various pediatric organizations. [2375

CHARLES A. JANEWAY. James Lawder Gamble (1883-1959). Jour. pediatrics, 56:701-8 (May). port. notes. On his early life in Kentucky, his medical education at Harvard and in Europe, and his teaching of pediatrics at Johns Hopkins University and at Harvard; with a list of his publications, 1914-58. [2376

PARK J. WHITE. Borden S. Veeder [born 1883]. Jour. pediatrics, 56: 139-46 (Feb). ports. notes. On his early life in Fonda, N.Y., his medical studies at the University of Pennsylvania and in Germany, and his service as an Army physician in World War I, head of the Department of Pediatrics, Washington University, and an official of the American Academy of Pediatrics. [2377

CLIFFORD GROCELLE GRULEE, JR. Pre- and postnatal irradiation hazards for infants and children [1897-1957]. Rocky Mt. med. jour., 57(4):35-41 (Apr). notes. [2378

ROY GERRARD SHORTER. Primary carcinoma of the liver in infancy and childhood: report of 11 cases [Mayo Clinic, 1905-58] and review of the literature. Pediatrics, 25:191-203 (Feb). tables, views. notes. [2379

HARRIS L. SMITH. Historical notes on parenteral fluid therapy of diarrhea in infants [1913-52]. Jour. pediatrics, 57:611-16 (Oct). notes. [2380

WILLIAM M. WALLACE. An account of the origins of the investigations of James L[awder] Gamble and an analysis of his contributions to physiology and medicine. Pediatrics, 26: 898-902 (Dec). port. notes. On his researches in children's diseases at Johns Hopkins University, Harvard, and Boston Children's Hospital since 1914. [2381

CHARLES D. COOK & others. Systemic lupus erythematosus: description of 37 cases in children and a discussion of endocrine therapy in 32 of the cases [Children's Hospital, Boston, and Children's Hospital, Cleveland, 1916-59]. Pediatrics, 26: 570-85 (Oct). diagrs., tables, views. notes. [2382

WALDO EMERSON NELSON. On the role of infections in neonatal mortality [1915-55]. Jour. pediatrics, 56: 274-84 (Feb). notes. [2383

JAMES LAWDER GAMBLE, G. S. ROSS, & F. F. TISDALL. A pediatric classic: facsimile excerpts from the first major paper from the laboratory of James L. Gamble. [Edited by Charles D. May.] Pediatrics, 26:903-6 (Dec). facsim. "The metabolism of fixed base during fasting," from The journal of biological chemistry, 1923. [2384

SYDNEY S. GELLIS. The Society for Pediatric Research [1929-59]. Am. jour. diseases of children, 98:545-52 (Nov 1959). facsims., maps, ports., tables. [2385

JULIUS B. RICHMOND. Some observations on the sociology of pediatric education and practice [1934-59]. Pediatrics, 23:1175-8 (Jun 1959). notes. [2386

JOHN PERRY HUBBARD. Practices and pitfalls in the early detection and control of heart disease in children [1938-55]. Jour. pediatrics, 56:544-50 (Apr). diagr., tables. notes. [2387

Pharmacy and Pharmacology

E. H. LUCAS. Folklore and plant drugs. Mich. Acad. Science, Papers, 45:127-36. On "(1) the drugs which have been tried in modern times but were found to be ineffective and therefore discarded, (2) the drugs which apparently have been overlooked, and (3) the folklore referring to plants which has never been recorded." [2388

SCHERING CORPORATION. The pharmaceutical industry [since Indian times. By Francis C. Brown.] John G. Glover & Rudolph L. Lagai, eds., The development of American industries: their economic significance, 4th ed. (N.Y.: Simmons-Boardman [1959]), p. 332-55. [2389

JO ANN CARRIGAN. Some medical remedies of the early nineteenth century. Historian, 22:64-88 (Nov 1959). notes. Based upon numerous contemporary and later printed sources and an anonymous "North Carolina manuscript," probably by Samuel Moore of Caswell County, N.C. [2390

HOWARD W. MORDUE. The druggists' show bottles. Hobbies, 64(3):28-9 (May). facsims. On bottles or globes of colored waters for exhibition in windows, ca. 1850 to 1930. [2391

RAYMOND NICHOLAS BIETER. Drug therapy: 1870. Jour. lancet, 80: 198-200 (May). notes. Information mainly from selected editions of The pharmacopoeia of the United States, 1875-1955. [2392

GEORGE F. ARCHAMBAULT. The legal responsibility of the hospital pharmacist in the United States [1876-1959]. Hospital management, 87(4): 44-5, 138-9; (5):108, 112, 138 (Apr, May 1959). notes. [2393

OTTO EMIL RUHMER & ARTHUR G. ZUPKO. Some contributions by Jews to pharmacy [in America, 1879-1960, and abroad]: a historical survey. [N.Y.:] Jewish Pharmaceutical Soc. of America in cooperation with the American Institute of the History of Pharmacy, Madison, Wis., 1960. [2], 25 p. notes. (p. 21-2). [2394

EDWARD T. PRICE. Root digging in the Appalachians: the geography of botanical drugs. Geog. rev., 50:1-20 (Jan). map, views. notes. Study of "148 medicinal plants that have had commercial value within the present century," distributed in most of the United States (especially the mountains of West Virginia, Virginia, North Carolina, and Tennessee and Kentucky), their native or exotic origin, their botanical classifications, their common and local names, the collectors and the buyers and sellers of the plants, and the medicinal properties of some of the plants, particularly ginseng. [2395

FRANCIS C. BROWN. Industry's skill and mankind's benefit. Mich. State Med. Soc., Jour., 58:229-34 (Feb). On the cooperation of American pharmaceutical manufacturers with physicians and pharmacists "for the purpose of providing the medical profession better instruments to use in conquering or managing disease," 1908-58. [2396

JACKSON P. ENGLISH. The chemotherapy of infectious disease, 1909-1959. Jour. chem. educ., 37:172-7 (Apr). views. notes. [2397

FREDERICK FRANCIS YONKMAN. New drugs for old uses and new uses for old drugs [1910-58]. Mich. State Med. Soc., Jour., 58:913-18 (Jun 1959). notes. [2398

JEROME BOONSHOFT & ROBERT KIRSCHNER. 40 years of AZO: a complete and factual history of the events and activities of the Alpha Zeta Omega pharmaceutical fraternity from its inception, December 19, 1919, until the present day. [N.Y.?] 1960. [6], 353, [1] p. facsims., ports., tables, views (1 double). [2399

Surgery

DE LOU PERRIN HALL. Our surgical heritage. Am. jour. surgery, 97:807-8; 98:128-9, 646-7, 779-80; 99:127, 257-8, 386-7, 974-5; 100:505-6, 653-4 (Jun 1959 - Oct 1960). ports. Biographical sketches of Philip Syng Physick (1768-1837), Valentine Mott (1785-1865), Ephraim McDowell (1771-1830), John Collins Warren (1778-1856), John Syng Dorsey (1783-1818), William Beaumont (1785-1853), Benjamin Winslow Dudley (1785-1870), Samuel

David Gross (1805-84), Paul Fitzsimmons Eve (1806-77), and John Morgan (born 1735), surgeons and teachers of surgery. [2400

MARK M. RAVITCH. The story of pyloric stenosis [1788-1960]. Surgery, 48:1117-43 (Dec). facsims., ports., table. notes. [2401

ELI IVES (1779-1861). Eli Ives and the medical use of ether prior to 1846. [Edited by Nicholas M. Greene.] Jour. hist. med., 15:297-9 (Jul). Notes taken by a student, Elijah M. Carpenter, on lectures of Ives, Professor of Materia Medica and Botany, Medical Institution of Yale College, 1813-14, mentioning various effects of ether but showing no knowledge of its analgesic and anesthetic effects. [2402

EDWARD WALDO FORBES. He found the use of ether. Harvard alumni bul., 55:392-3 (7 Feb 1953). port. On Charles Thomas Jackson's discovery of the anesthetic properties of ether, 1842; with an account of a crayon portrait of him by Seth Wells Cheney. [2403

ALMA DEA MORANI. The evolution of plastic surgery [ca. 1850 to 1958]. College Phys. Phila., Trans. & studies, 26:84-8 (Aug 1958). diagrs., port., view. [2404

JOHN B. HARTZELL & CARLOS MOTA. Advances in knowledge of the physiology of wound healing [1856-1956]. Mich. State Med. Soc., Jour., 58:223-8 (Feb 1959). notes. [2405

IRA S. GOLDENBERG. Catgut, silk, and silver--the story of surgical sutures [in America, 1857-1959, and abroad]. Surgery, 46:908-12 (Nov 1959). notes. [2406

HENRY KNOWLES UNANGST BEECHER & CHARLOTTE FORD. Nathan P[ayson] Rice's Trials of a public benefactor [N.Y., 1859]: a commentary. Jour. hist. med., 15: 170-83 (Apr). facsims. notes. Analysis of a book on the work of Dr. William T. G. Morton in the development and use of anesthetic "etherization." [2407

HELEN R. PURTLE. Claude Bernard's operating table. U.S. Armed Forces med. jour., 11:810-12 (Jul). port., view. On a table used by Bernard in the physiological laboratory of the Collège de France, given to Dr. Austin Flint, Jr., of New York in 1861, now owned by the Medical Museum of the Armed Forces Institute of Pathology. [2408

EMERY ANDREW ROVENSTINE. Nerve blocking [to diagnose or treat pain, 1884-1960]. Postgraduate med., 26:583-7 (Nov 1959). port. notes. [2409

GIOVANNI GALLETTI & ROSWELL K. BROWN. Halsted's operation for inguinal hernia: exactly what is it? Surgery, 47:633-5 (Apr). diagr. notes. On surgical techniques for inguinal hernia developed at the Johns Hopkins Hospital by W. S. Halsted, 1889-1903. [2410

J. C. ROSENBERG & C. WALTON LILLEHEI. The emergence of cardiac surgery [1893-1960]. Jour. lancet, 80:201-14 (May). diagrs., facsim., port., views. notes. [2411

GEORGE H. A. CLOWES, JR. The historical development of the surgical treatment of heart disease [in the United States and abroad, mainly on the 20th century]. Bul. hist. med., 33:29-51 (Jan-Feb). notes. [2411a

ALLEN OLDFATHER WHIPPLE (1881-1963). The continuing history of the Society of Clinical Surgery [1900-1959]. Ann. surgery, 150:783-9 (Nov 1959). [2412

OSWALD SWINNEY LOWSLEY & ALEJANDRO PEREZ VENERO. Persistent anterior lobe of the prostate gland [St. Clare's Hospital, New York City, and Clinica San Fernando, Panama, 1909-53]. Jour. urol., 71: 469-74 (Apr 1954). diagrs. [2413

CHARLES CLAUDE GUTHRIE. Blood vessel surgery and its applications. [Pittsburgh:] Univ. of Pittsburgh Press [1959]. xii, [iii]-xv, 360, 83 p. illus. 1st ed. 1912. Introduction, by Samuel P. Harbison and Bernard Fisher, on "The contributions of Dr. C. C. Guthrie to vascular surgery"; photofacsimile reproduction of his book ([iii]-xv, 360 p.), from which certain chapters and sections have been omitted; "Fifty years of vascular surgery," by Bernard Fisher; bibliography (last pagination, p. 41-65); biographical note on Guthrie; and list (p. 71-83) of his publications, 1903-48. [2414

HERMAN SHANN. Collective review: the complete prolapse or procidentia of the rectum, an unsolved surgical problem. Internatl. abstracts surgery, 109:521-31 (Dec 1959). notes. Digest of the literature relating to this problem, including American contributions, 1912-58. [2415

CHARLES A. ROCKWOOD, JR., & DON H. O'DONOGHUE. The surgical mask: its development, usage, and efficiency [1918-60]. Arch. surgery, 80:963-71 (Jun). diagrs., tables. notes. [2416

HERBERT R. KOBES & SAMUEL PRUZANSKY. The cleft palate team--a historical review. Am. jour. pub. health, 50:200-205 (Feb). notes. On the development of treatment for cleft palate, 1930-60. [2417

GEORGE O. EATON. The changing picture of orthopedic practice. Ind. State Med. Assoc., Jour., 52:374-86 (Mar 1959). From The journal of bone and joint surgery, 1958. Review of general changes in "the relationship between the physician and his patient" since the author "entered private practice 25 years ago." [2418

THOMAS B. BOULTON & ROBERT S. SWEET. The place of trichlorethylene in modern anesthesia [1934-58]. Mich. State Med. Soc., Jour., 59:270-73 (Feb. diagr., tables. notes. [2419

BURDICK GREEN CLARKE & W. F. LEADBETTER. Ureterosigmoidostomy: collective review of results in 2897 cases [treated by various urologists, 1936-54]. Jour. urol., 73: 999-1008 (Jun 1955). diagrs., tables. bibliog. [2420

PHYSICS

HAROLD WORTHINGTON WEBB. Bergen Davis, March 31, 1869-June 30, 1958. Natl. Acad. Sciences, Biog. memoirs, 34:65-82. port. On his early life in New Jersey, his studies at Rutgers College and Columbia University and abroad, and his teaching of physics at Columbia University from 1903 to 1939; with a list of his publications, 1900-1938. [2421

HAROLD ALFRED SONN. First high school course in "physics" began in Newark, New Jersey [taught by George C. Sonn, 1880 or 1881, and continued to 1906 with aid from Thomas A. Edison]. N.J. genesis, 6:215-16 (Jan 1959). [2422

JAMES BURKE FISHER. Dr. Irving G. Wolff, '16: a pioneer in electronics. Dartmouth alumni mag., 52(5):33-5 (Feb). port. On his work as a physicist and an administrator of research. [2423

The RETIRING Dean. Engineering and science, 23(3):19-21 (Dec 1959). ports., view. On Earnest C. Watson (born 1892), Professor of Physics and Dean of the Faculty of the California Institute of Technology, 1919-59, military physicist in World Wars I and II. [2424

MARY CLAPP. Nobel Prize winner. Dartmouth alumni mag., 52(3):29-30 (Dec 1959). port. On Owen Chamberlain (born 1920), Dartmouth student, physicist, winner of the Nobel Prize in physics in 1959. [2425

RUSSELL SPURGEON POOR. The impact of atomic energy on education. Va. jour. science, 1:177-90 (Jul 1950). notes. On "the impact of radiation on subject matter fields," and the facilities for atomic study and research, 1939-50. [2426

ISIDOR ISAAC RABI. My life and times as a physicist. Claremont, Calif.: Claremont College, 1960. vi, [2], 55 p. Two lectures: "The scientist and the statesman" and "Science and the humanities." Includes reminiscences of the author's part in establishing a laboratory at the Massachusetts Institute of Technology to "work on microwave radar," his work as a member of the United Nations Conference on the Peaceful Uses of Atomic Energy, and his service in various Government agencies, 1940-58. [2427

Theater

JOSEPH EARL ARRINGTON. John [Nepomuk] Maelzel [1772-1838], master showman of automata and panoramas. Pa. mag. hist. and biog., 84:56-92 (Jan). views. notes. On his inventions and exhibitions of musical and mechanisms (including the Chess Player, the Philharmonicon, and the Conflagration of Moscow) in Europe and (1826-37) in America, and the continued exhibition of some of them as late as 1863. [2428

LETTIE JO COTTON. The Negro in the American theatre [as an actor and as an object of caricature, 1826-1950s]. Negro hist. bul., 23:173-8 (May). [2429

HAROLD CLURMAN. Actors--the image of their era. Tulane drama rev.,

4(3):38-44 (Mar). From the New York Times magazine, 17 May 1953. American examples of the fact "that an actor's popularity is intimately related to the social complexion of an era," 1852-1952. [2430

DANIEL C. BLUM. A pictorial history of the American theatre: 100 years, 1860-1960. Phila.: Chilton Co., Book Division [1960]. 384 p. ports., views. 32 cm. 1st ed. 1950. [2431

WILLIE GEORGE (born ca. 1886). Running Bear--Indian cowboy. By Willie George, as told to Jack F. Contor. West. horseman, 25(9):32-3, 46-7 (Sep). facsims., ports., views. On the early life of the author, a Shoshone-Bannock Indian, on the Fort Hall Indian Reservation, Idaho, and his career from 1907 to ca. 1932 as a circus rider, rodeo performer, and motion-picture actor in California under the name Running Bear. [2432

GEORGE JEAN NATHAN (1882-1958). The magic mirror: selected writings on the theatre by George Jean Nathan. Edited, together with an introduction, by Thomas Quinn Curtiss. N.Y.: Knopf, 1960 p. xviii, 262, [2], xiii, [2] p. port. Reviews and other writings on plays, actors, playwrights, and theaters, 1917-49; with a biographical introduction on Nathan as a dramatic critic, 1908-56. [2433

THE CIRCUS

DANA W. STEVENS. Circusiana. Hobbies, 64(11)-65(10): monthly installments (Jan-Dec). Questions and answers. [2434

ESSE (FORRESTER) O'BRIEN. Circus: cinders to sawdust [1793-1952]. San Antonio: Naylor Co. [1959]. xxii, 268, [1] p. facsims., ports., views. [2435

CHYLENE JAENECKE. Mollie Bailey. Jr. historian (Tex.), 21(2):23-5 (Nov). view. On Mary Arline (Kirkland) Bailey (1842-1918) and her husband, Gus Bailey (died 1896), proprietors of a road show, and eventually of a circus with headquarters in Dallas and Houston, 1857-1918. [2436

RICHARD GARNER THOMAS. John Ringling [1866-1936]: circus magnate and art patron, a biography. B. Y.: Pageant Press [1960]. 268 p. On his early life in McGregor, Ia., and Baraboo, Wis., his career in partnership with his brothers in the formation and management of the Ringling Brothers Circus, his marriage to Mable Burton (1875-1929), his headquarters in Sarasota, Fla., his activities as a collector of art, his involvement in Ringling family litigation, and his bequests for 3 Ringling museums in Sarasota. [2437

WILLARD H. PORTER. Ike Rude and Buster. Quarter horse jour., 3(11):6-7, 38 (Aug 1951). ports., views. On Ike Rude (born 1894), cowboy and rodeo performer, and his quarter-horse gelding Buster (foaled 1940). [2438

HENRY RINGLING NORTH & ALDEN HATCH. The circus kings: our Ringling family story. Garden City, N.Y.: Doubleday, 1960. 383 p. ports., geneal, tables, views. On the author's "big, lusty, gusty uncles," the 7 Ringling Brothers, his early life in Baraboo, Wis., his activities from 1912 to 1958 in the Ringling Brothers--Barnum & Bailey Combined Shows, his eventual management of the family firm, and the family dissensions and litigations. [2439

BOB LLOYD. Rodeo bug. West. horseman, 25(4):56-7, 100-103 (Apr). ports., views. On rodeo performers, 1920-60; with illustrations from the careers of Eddie Yaklich (since 1954) and others. [2440

WILLARD H. PORTER. Bad bull business. Quarter horse jour., 6(7): 92-6 (Apr 1954). On John Lindsey as a rodeo clown, 1926-54. [2441

JO ROBERTS. From rodeo to rodeo equipment. West. horseman, 26(7): 44-5, 92 (Jul). facsim., ports. On Gerald Roberts, professional rodeo performer and motion-picture stunt man, and his establishment of the Roberts Rodeo Equipment Company, Hoyt, Kan., 1938-60; with a facsimile reproduction of his "Bull riding tips." [2442

MANUELITA MITCHELL. The great Little Joe. West. horseman, 25(1):13, 58 (Jan). ports. Memorial biography of a barrel-racing horse (1944-59), foaled in Texas, last owned by La Tonne Sewalt (born 1939), and his performance in rodeos with her as jockey. [2443

THE DANCE

GERTRUDE PROKOSCH KURATH. Dance and mythology [among the Indians] in North America. Midw. folklore, 10:207-12 (winter). notes. [2444

GERTRUDE PROKOSCH KURATH. Dance, music, and the daily bread. Ethnomusicol., 4:1-9 (Jan). bibliog. Includes dated references to dances of North American Indians, 1861-1959. [2445

GERTRUDE PROKOSCH KURATH & NADIA CHILKOVSKY. Jazz choreology. International Congress of Anthropological and Ethnological Sciences, 5th, 1956, Men and cultures: selected papers, ed. Anthony F. C. Wallace (Phila.: Univ. of Pennsylvania Press [1960]), p. 152-60. diagrs. bibliog., notes. On 13 "fundamental, recurrent qualities" of jazz dancing, beginning with "the ballroom two-step of 1890-1910." Illustrated by diagrams in "Labanotation" (Rudolf Laban's alphabet of "movement notation"). [2446

KATHRYN (KOHNFELDER) MURRAY. My husband, Arthur Murray [name originally: Murray Teichman, born 1895]. By Kathryn Murray with Betty Hannah Hoffman. N.Y.: Simon and Schuster, 1960. vii, 152 p. ports. (part double). On his early life in New York City, his studies of dancing (begun in 1912), his work as a dancing instructor, his establishment of a chain of dancing studios, and his marriage to the author in 1925. [2447

CHRISTENA LINDBORG SCHLUNDT. The role of Ruth St. Denis in the history of American dance, 1906-1922. Ann Arbor: University Microfilms, 1959 [i. e. 1960]. Positive microfilm of typescript. [218] leaves. Thesis--Claremont Graduate School. Abstracted: Dissert. abstracts, 20: 2778 (Jan). [2448

CHRISTENA LINDBORG SCHLUNDT. An account of Ruth St. Denis [American dancer] in Europe, 1906-1909. Am. Assoc. Health, Phys. Educ., and Recr., Research quar., 31:82-91 (Mar). notes. Information mainly from English, German, and Austrian newspapers. [2449

MOTION PICTURES

MARTIN QUIGLEY, JR. Magic shadows: the story of the origin of motion pictures. N.Y.: Quigley Pub. Co., 1960. 191 p. diagrs., ports., views. bibliog. (p. 177-84). 1st ed. 1948. Includes experiments and inventions in the United States, 1850-96, and traces "the scientific study of magic shadows and devices for creating them" to Roger Bacon, ca. 1267. [2450

JOHN DENNIS McCALLUM. Scooper: authorized story of Scoop Conlon's motion picture world. Seattle: Wood & Reber, 1960. [18], 274 p. cartoons, facsim., ports., views. On Paul Hubert Conlon (born 1892), his early life in Sharon, Pa., his studies at the University of Missouri, his work as a newspaper reporter and editor in Los Angeles, and his service as manager and publicity director for various actors and motion-picture companies. [2451

MOTION PICTURE ASSOCIATION OF AMERICA. The motion picture industry [since 1894. By Eric Johnston and Michael Linden.] John G. Glover & Rudolph L. Lagai, eds., The development of American industries: their economic significance, 4th ed. (N.Y.: Simmons-Boardman [1959]), p. 756-67. [2452

JAMES LANDON WILKINSON. An introduction to the career and films of John Ford [born 1895. Los Angeles] 1960. Positive microfilm of typescript. viii, 378 leaves. ports. bibliog. (leaves 286-94). Thesis (M.A.)--Univ. of Southern California. [2453

JOE FRANKLIN. Classics of the silent screen: a pictorial treasury. N.Y.: Citadel Press [1960, c1959]. 255 p. facsims., ports., views. Partial contents.--Part one: Fifty great films [1903, 1914-31].--Part two: Seventy-five great stars. [2454

JAY LEYDA. "... meaning and artistic courage." John Arthur Garraty, ed., The unforgettable Americans (Great Neck, N.Y.: Channel Press [1960]), p. 326-30. On David Wark Griffith as a producer and director of motion pictures, 1907 ff. [2455

CHARLES CHAPLIN, JR. (born 1925). My father, Charlie Chaplin. By Charles Chaplin, Jr., with N. and M. Rau. N.Y.: Random House [1960. 10], 369, [2] p. ports., view. On Charles Chaplin (born 1889), his youth in England as the "ragged, cold, hungry" son of an alcoholic actor, his employment there in "small comic and dancing parts in vaudeville skits," his life in the United States from 1910 to 1952 as a comedian and motion-picture actor, his marriages to Lita Grey (born Lillita McMurray), Paulette Goddard, and Oona O'Neill, and his removal to Europe in 1952; with the author's memories of a

Hollywood youth and a warm defense of his father's integrity in the conduct of his domestic affairs. [2456

JAMES RUFUS AGEE (1909-55). Comedy's greatest era. James Rufus Agee, Agee on film ([N.Y.:] McDowell, Obolensky [1958-60]), 1:1-19. On film comedy "in its glory in the years from 1912 to 1930, as practiced by the employees of Mack Sennett, the father of American screen comedy, and by the four most eminent masters: Charlie Chaplin, Harold Lloyd, the late Harry Langdon and Buster Keaton." [2457

EVERETT S. CARTER. Cultural history written with lightning: the significance of The birth of a nation [1915]. Am. quar., 12:347-57 (fall). notes. On the motion picture made by David Wark Griffin from Thomas Dixon's novel, The clansman, as a distortion of history, "an epic manqué," an achievement in "superb technique," "an enormous commercial success," and the event with which "significant motion picture history begins." [2458

BETH (FEAGLES) DAY. This was Hollywood: an affectionate history of filmland's golden years [1915 ff.]. Garden City, N.Y.: Doubleday, 1960. 287 p. ports., views. [2459

GEORGE E. FROST & S. CHESTERFIELD OPPENHEIM. A study of the professional color motion picture antitrust decrees and their effects [1947-58]. Patent, trademark, and copyright jour., 4:1-39, 108-45 (spring, summer). tables. notes. Includes some account of the technical development of color motion pictures by Technicolor, Inc., the Eastman Kodak Company, and other firms, 1915-58. [2460

ROBERT ARDREY. Hollywood: the tell of the frenzied forties. The reporter, Our times: the best from The reporter, ed. Max Ascoli (N.Y.: Farrar, Straus, and Cudahy [1960]), p. 453-62. On changes in the motion-picture industry resulting from the anti-Communist campaign and the competition of television, 1920s-50s. First published in 1957. [2461

DAVID HANNA. Ava, a portrait of a star. N.Y.: Putnam [1960]. 256 p. ports. On Ava Gardner (born 1922), her early life in North Carolina, her work as a motion-picture actress in America and Europe, her life in Spain, and her marriages to Artie Shaw and Frank Sinatra. Based upon the author's observations during 7 years as "publicist on her pictures, friend and personal managers." [2462

MUSEUM OF MODERN ART, New York. Film Library. Marlene Dietrich: image and legend. [Exhibition.] By Richard Griffith. Garden City, N.Y.: Doubleday [1959]. 32 p. ports. On the career of Maria Marlene Dietrich (born 1904) as an actress, 1923-59, and her removal from Germany to the United States in 1930; with a catalogue of films of motion pictures in which she acted. [2463

KING WALLIS VIDOR. Movies are not all harmony. Music jour., 18(5):7, 54-5 (Jun-Jul). cartoon, port. On the author's life as a motion-picture director and producer since 1925. [2464

MAURICE ZOLOTOW. Marilyn Monroe. N.Y.: Harcourt, Brace [1960]. xii, 340 p. ports. On Norma Jeane Mortensen (name on birth certificate) or Norma Jean Baker (1926-62), her early life in Los Angeles, her career as a motion-picture actress, and her marriages to James Dougherty, Jo Di Maggio, and Arthur Miller. [2465

DANIEL C. BLUM. A pictorical history of the talkies. N.Y.: Putnam [1958]. 318 p. ports., views. On motion pictures mechanically combined with accompanying sound, 1929-58. [2466

GEORGE SANDERS (born 1906). Memoirs of a professional cad. N.Y.: Putnam [1960]. 192 p. ports., views. On the author's early life in Russia and England, his emigration to America (ca. 1935?), and his work as an actor in motion pictures in America and Europe. [2467

BUTTERMILK and Trigger. West. horseman, 25(9):16-17, 91, 94 (Sep). ports., views. On the motion-picture performances of Trigger, "the most valuable piece of horseflesh in history," a palamino owned by Roy Rogers, wearing a $50,000-dollar saddle of leather, silver, and gold, studded with 1,500 rubies and further embellished with bas-reliefs showing 31 Western scenes, 1938 ff., and of Buttermilk (foaled 1948), a gold-colored quarter-horse gelding owned by Dale (Evans) Rogers. [2468

JAMES RUFUS AGEE (1909-55). Agee on film. [N.Y.:] McDowell, Obolensky [1958-60]. 2 v. [8], 432, [2]; x, [4], 488, [1] p. ports. Reviews of and comments on motion pictures, reprinted from the Nation and Time, 1941-50; and 5 film scripts, 1948-55. [2469

ZSA ZSA GABOR. Zsa Zsa Gabor, my story. Written for me by Gerold Frank. Cleveland: World Pub. Co. [1960]. 308, [3] p. ports. On the early life of the author (born Sari Gabor) in Hungary, her emigration to America in 1941, her work in motion pictures and television, and her 3 marriages. [2470

THE STAGE

VAN CARL KUSSROW, JR. On with the show: a study of public arguments in favor of theatre in America during the eighteenth century, designed to show the relevance of the arguments to the philosophies and beliefs directing American life during that century, the variety and emphases of the arguments offered, and the quantity of material set forth by the advocates of theatrical performances. Ann Arbor: University Microfilms, 1959 [i. e. 1960]. Positive microfilm of typescript. [405] leaves. Thesis--Indiana Univ. Abstracted: Dissert. abstracts, 20: 4217 (Apr). [2471

MARIE J. ROBINSON. Revivals on the New York stage, 1930-1950 with a statistical survey of their performances from 1750-1950. Ann Arbor: University Microfilms, 1960. Positive microfilm of typescript. [1290] leaves. Thesis--Northwestern Univ. Abstracted: Dissert. abstracts, 21:1291 (Nov). [2472

CHARLES CLIFFORD RITTER. The Hallam females. South. speech jour., 25:167-71 (spring). notes. On women belonging to the professional company of actors led to America by Lewis Hallam I, and the confusion and uncertainty as to their names and relationships, 1752-74. [2473

DONALD A. SEARS. The biographical muddle of Mrs. Snelling Powell. New Eng. quar., 33:368-71 (Sep). notes. On the confusion (originating with William Clapp, A record of the Boston stage, 1853) between Elizabeth (Harrison) Powell (born 1774), who married Snelling Powell in 1794, and an English Mrs. Powell, known also as Mrs. Farmer and Mrs. Renaud (1761?-1831), who married "a Mr. Powell, prompter," in 1789. [2474

RICHARD ANSELM MOODY. Edwin Forrest [1806-72], first star of the American stage. N.Y.: Knopf, 1960. xi, [1], 415, [1], xi, [4] p. facsims., ports., views. bibliog. (p. 408-16). On his early life in Philadelphia and his career from 1820 to 1872 as an actor. [2475

JERRY BLUNT. America's amazing lord. Theatre annual, 16:60-69. notes. On Lord Dundreary, in Tom Taylor's Our American cousin, originally a minor character with only 47 lines, first played in 1858, developed by his actor, Edward A. Sothern, into one of the best-known comic figures in the theaters of America and Great Britain. [2476

EDWARD CHARLES WAGENKNECHT. Julia Marlowe [born Sarah Frances Frost, 1865-1950]: portrait of an actress. Mod. drama, 1:244-55 (Feb 1959). On her stage career, 1876-1924. [2477

CHARLES CLIFFORD RITTER. Helena Modjeska: the story of a journey. West. speech, 24:155-9 (summer). notes. On her travels in the United States with her husband, Count Karol Bozenta Chlapowski, to improve her health, the failure of their efforts to support themselves and their son on a California farm, her resumption in America of her interrupted career as an actress, and the "great success" of her tour of 11 cities in the United States and Canada, 1876-78. [2478

PIERRE SICHEL. The Jersey Lily: the story of the fabulous Mrs. Langtry. Englewood Cliffs, N.J.: Prentice-Hall [1958. 8], 456 p. ports., views. bibliog. (p. 446-9). On Emilie Charlotte (Le Breton) Langtry (1852-1929), English actress, who made numerous tours of the United States (including the mining camps) between 1882 and 1917 and for a time lived on her ranch in California. Fictional in form. [2479

THERESA HELBURN (1887-1959). A wayward quest: the autobiography of Theresa Helburn. [With assistance from Elinore Denniston.] Boston: Little, Brown [1960]. vi, [2], 344 p. cartoon, ports. On the author's early life in New York City, her studies at Bryn Mawr and Radcliffe, her work as a playwright and dramatic critic in New York City and as an executive of the Theatre Guild, and her marriage to John Baker Opdyke. [2480

DORIS H. HAMILTON. Richard Mansfield, actor and writer. Hobbies, 65(3):110-11 (May). facsim. On 3 letters from him to E. A. Dithmar, drama reviewer, 1892, 1894, 1900, on theatrical matters; with excerpts. See also reminiscences of Mansfield in a letter to the editor from Dr. J. Darwin Nagel, (7):111 (Sep). [2481

MONROE LIPPMAN. Battle for bookings: independents challenge the trust. Tulane drama rev., 2(2):38-45 (Feb 1958). notes. On the establishment of "the Theatrical Syndicate" in 1896 to make bookings with "theatre managers and managers of attractions" who would "grant exclusive booking rights" to the Syndicate, the resentment aroused by its monopolistic efforts, the establishment of the Independent Booking Agency in 1902, and the battle between the agencies, ending with victory for the former in 1904. [2482

KEN MURRAY [real name: Kenneth Doncourt]. Life on a pogo stick: autobiography of a comedian. Phila.: Winston [1960]. xii, 180 p. ports., views. On the early life of the author (born 1903) in New York City, and his work as a performer in vaudeville and musical comedy. [2483

JOHN WALDHORN GASSNER. Theatre at the crossroads: plays and playwrights of the mid-century American stage [1915-60]. N.Y.: Holt, Rinehart, and Winston [1960]. xix, [3], 327 p. bibliog. (p. 313-14), notes. "New York chronicle: 1950-60" (p. 127-312). [2484

FRITIOF BILLQUIST. Garbo: a biography. ... Translated by Maurice Michael. N.Y.: Putnam [1960]. 255 p. ports. On Greta Garbo (born 1905), her early life in Sweden, her emigration to America in 1925, and her work as an actress in motion pictures; with lists of her films in Europe and America (p. 241-9). Also issued in London: A Barker [1960]. xii, 180 p. ports. [2485

PEOPLE should enjoy themselves! What happened when Richard Aldrich, '25, gave up banking for the theater. Harvard alumni bul., 55:225-6 (22 Nov 1952). port. On his work since 1927 as a theatrical producer. [2486

ALBERT BERMEL. The Phoenix has two heads. Tulane drama rev., 4(1): 60-89 (Sep 1959). notes. On the Phoenix Theatre, New York City, 1953-59; with some account of the previous theatrical experience of its managing directors, Charles Norris Houghton and T. Edward Hambleton, since 1927, and "Table of principal Phoenix productions." [2487

CLAY C. CURRAN. The Black Hills Passion Play. Mildred Fielder, ed., Lawrence County ([Lead? S. D., 1960]), p. 124-33. ports. On the emigration of Josef Meier from Germany to America in 1932, his presentation of the Luenen Passion Play in tours of the United States, and its presentation since 1939 at Spearfish, S.D., as the Black Hills Passion Play of America. [2488

Acting and Stagecraft

DAVID GEORGE SCHAAL. The English background of American rehearsal-direction practices in the eighteenth century [1752-1810]. Educ. theatre jour., 12:262-9 (Dec). notes. [2489

CHARLES McCORKLE STATHAM. The application of prevailing principles of elocution to theatrical criticism of American acting: 1815-1840. Ann Arbor: University Microfilms, 1959 [i. e. 1960]. Positive microfilm of typescript. [183] leaves. Thesis--Univ. of Florida. Abstracted: Dissert. abstracts, 20:2964-5 (Jan). [2490

NORMAN BEL GEDDES (1893-1958). Miracle in the evening: an autobiography. ... Edited by William Kelley. Garden City, N.Y.: Doubleday, 1960. 352 p. On the author's early life at Adrian, Mich., and in Chicago, his many visits to Newcomerstown, Ohio, his work as a vaudeville performer, his studies at the Cleveland Art Institute (1911) and the Chicago Art Institute, his 3 months on the Blackfoot Reservation in Montana, and his career as a theatrical and industrial designer; with "A Norman Bel Geddes chronology," 1913-57 (p. 341-52), listing theaters, stages, and settings designed by him, his many designs of commercial and industrial equipment (automobiles, jukeboxes, soap dispensers, etc.), and his theatrical scripts. [2491

JOHN HENRY JENNINGS. Winthrop Ames's notes for the perfect theatre. Educ. theatre jour., 12:9-15 (Mar). notes. Information from an 85-page notebook recording Ames's examination of 64 theaters and attendance at 53 "plays and shows" in Europe in 1907, summarizing "the features of theatre architecture, house management, stage mechanics, and scenic techniques which an artistically ambitious Boston producer thought suitable for introduction into America fifty years ago," and for incorporation in "an exemplary theatre of his own." [2492

CHARLES LEO METTEN. The development in America of theories of directing as found in American writings, 1914-1930. Ann Arbor: University Microfilms, 1960. Positive microfilm of typescript. [307] leaves. Thesis--State Univ. of Iowa. Abstracted: Dissert. abstracts, 20: 4459-60 (May). [2493

SETTINGS for the actors: three Harvard designers for the theatre [since 1915]. Harvard alumni bul., 53:116-25 (28 Oct 1950). ports., views. On the work of Robert Edmond Jones, Lee Simonson, and Donald Oenslager, Harvard graduates, as designers of stage settings. [2494

WENDELL GORDON COLE. The theatre projects of Frank Lloyd Wright [1916 to 1959]. Educ. theatre jour., 12:86-93 (May). [2495

CHARLES BROOKS. The multiple set in American drama. Tulane drama rev., 3(2):30-41 (Dec 1958). On "a set which is not changed during the play but allows the action to occur in more than one place--as several rooms or an entire house or several houses," and its growingly frequent use since the 1920s. [2496

ANNE DANIEL. The frozen countenance. South. speech jour., 25:190-98 (spring). notes. On O'Neill's use of masks on the stage, 1924-34, and his arguments in their defense. [2497

TEXAS, UNIVERSITY OF. Humanities Research Center. An exhibition of designs for the theatre by Eugene Berman [born 1899. Austin] 1960. [31] p. views. On his early life and education in Russia, his work as a painter in Europe, his emigration to America in 1935, and his work as a designer of theatrical scenery. [2498

JACK BROOKING. Directing Summer and smoke [by Tennessee Williams, 1948]: an existentialist approach. Mod. drama, 2:377-85 (Feb). notes. [2499

Dramatic Education

LEE SIMONSON. The university theater: its historical significance and its importance today [1900-1956]. Harvard alumni bul., 58:681-4 (9 Jun 1956). views. [2500

FLOYD LESLIE SANDLE. A history of the development of the educational theatre in Negro colleges and universities from 1911 to 1959. Ann Arbor: University Microfilms, 1959 [i. e. 1960]. Positive microfilm of typescript. [310] leaves. Thesis--Louisiana State Univ. Abstracted: Dissert. abstracts, 20: 2963 (Jan). [2501

CECIL ELLSWORTH HINKEL. An analysis and evaluation of the 47 Workshop of George Pierce Baker [at Harvard and Yale, 1912-33]. Ann Arbor: University Microfilms, 1959 [i. e. 1960]. Positive microfilm of typescript. [646] leaves. Thesis--Ohio State Univ. Abstracted: Dissert. abstracts, 20:4215 (Apr). [2502

ECONOMIC HISTORY

LOUIS MORTON HACKER. American capitalism its promise and accomplishment. Princeton, N.J.: Van Nostrand [1957]. 192. p. bibliog. (p. 196-7). (An Anvil original, 20.) Appended (p. 96-185): 30 documents, 1586-1956. [2503

GILBERT COURTLAND FITE & JIM EANES REESE. An economic history of the United States [1606-1957]. Boston: Houghton Mifflin [1959]. ix, 714 p. cartoons, diagrs., maps, tables, views. bibliog. (p. 673-701). [2504

CORNELIUS P. COTTER. Government and private enterprise [1791-1959]. N.Y.: Holt, Rinehart, and Winston [1960]. xiv, 527 p. cartoon, diagrs., facsim., tables. bibliogs., notes. Chapters or sections on the currency; the antitrust laws; the administrative regulation of trade, agricultural marketing, securities, public utilities, and natural-gas rates, transportation, communications, and atomic energy; and "maintaining a prosperous economy," with full employment. [2505

RESOURCES FOR THE FUTURE. Energy in the American economy, 1850-1975: an economic study of its history and prospects. By Sam H. Schurr and Bruce C[arlton] Netschert. Baltimore: Johns Hopkins Press [1960]. xxii, [2], 774 p. diagrs., tables (part double). notes. On the sources of energy (wood, coal, oil, natural gas), 1850-1955; "the future of energy supply" (coal, oil and natural gas, "hydropower"); and "the future of energy consumption." [2506

SIMON SMITH KUZNETS. Six lectures on economic growth. Glencoe, Ill.: Free Press [1960, c1959]. 122 p. tables (part double). notes. Lectures delivered at the Centro de Estudios Monetarios Latinoamericanos (CEMLA), Mexico City, Jul. 1958, on definition of growth, rates of growth, necessary conditions of growth, labor force, capital formation, and foreign trade, of the United States and other countries, 1869-1958. [2507

SIMON SMITH KUZNETS. The changing distribution and structure of economic activity [1880-1950]. Simon Smith Kuznets, Ann Rather Miller, & Richard A. Easterlin, Population redistribution and economic growth, 1870-1950 (Phila.: American Philosophical Soc.), 2 (1960): 205-87. tables. notes. Sections on "Changes in distribution of economic activity among states and geographic regions: total shift," "Changes in distribution of economic activity among states and regions: pattern of shift by subperiods," "Shifts in structure--intrastate compared with countrywide," and "The convergence of per capita income." [2508

YOSHIMITU IDE. The significance of Richard Hathaway Edmonds [1857-1930] and his Manufacturers' record [Baltimore weekly, 1882 till after 1930] in the New South. Ann Arbor: University Microfilms, 1959 [i.e. 1960]. Positive microfilm of typescript. [364] leaves. Thesis--Univ. of Florida. Abstracted: Dissert. abstracts, 20:2773-4 (Jan). Study of utterances on iron, cotton, the tariff, transportation, banking, and white, Negro, and immigrant labor. [2509

WALT WHITMAN ROSTOW. The problem of achieving and maintaining a high rate of economic growth ["since about 1910"]: a historian's view. Am. econ. rev., 50:106-18 (May). notes. [2510

WALLACE EVAN DAVIES, ed. The New Deal and business recovery [1929-42]. ... Revised by William Goetzmann. N.Y.: Holt [1960]. x, 70 p. notes (p. 70). (Select problems in historical interpretation, 6.) Contemporary documents, dealing mainly with the National Recovery Administration and the agricultural adjustment program. [2511

EUGENE VICTOR ROSTOW. Planning for freedom: the public law of American capitalism. New Haven: Yale Univ. Press, 1959. [2], x, [2], 437 p. diagr., tables. (University of Michigan. William W. Cook Foundation. Lectures, 9.) On "the legal control of the economy," 1929-58, including fiscal and monetary policy and "free and regulated markets"; with concluding remarks on "the debate between Socialism and Liberty." [2512

WALT WHITMAN ROSTOW. The dynamics of American society. Ralph Evans Freeman, ed., Postwar economic trends in the United States (N.Y.: Harper [1960]), p. 1-29. diagrs., tables. notes. On the changes in American society that affected economic behavior, 1930-58. [2513

JOSEPH EDWIN REEVE & others. Government component in the national wealth [1939-47]. Conference on Research in Income and Wealth, Studies in income and wealth, 12 (1950): 461-526. tables. [2514

KARL SCHRIFTGIESSER. Business comes of age: the story of the Committee for Economic Development and its impact upon the economic policies of the United States, 1942-1960. N.Y.: Harper [1960]. viii, 248 p. bibliog. (p. 230-36), notes. [2515

Consumption

LYMAN RAY PATTERSON. Manufacturer's statutory warranty: tort or contract? Mercer law rev., 10:272-321 (spring 1959). notes. On "the manufacturer's liability to the consumer based on negligence," 1870-1956, and the exceptions for dangerous articles and for privity. [2516

SIDNEY GOLDSTEIN. Consumption patterns of the aged [1880-1959. Phila.:] Univ. of Pennsylvania, 1960. xix, [3], 304 p. tables. notes. (Study of consumer expenditures, incomes, and savings.) Study of persons "65 years old and over." [2517

T. ALBERT WITCHER. Common law liability of liquor vendors [for injuries suffered by their customers, 1883-1959]. Baylor law rev., 12:388-400 (fall). notes. [2518

U.S. Bureau of Labor Statistics. How American buying habits change. Wash. [1959]. xiv, 253 p. diagrs., tables, views. bibliog. (p. 243-53), notes. On "the improvements in living standards which Americans have achieved since 1888" as shown in "changes in the consumption habits of the American people," particularly "the middle group of consumers--the families of the millions of blue-collar and white-collar workers who make up the vast bulk of our predominantly city life." [2519

RICHARD F. MUTH. The demand for non-farm housing. Arnold C. Harberger, ed., The demand for durable goods (Chicago: Univ. of Chicago Press [1960]), p. 27-96. diagrs., tables. notes. Econometric study of "the responsiveness of housing demand to changes in income and the price of housing," 1896-1953. [2520

ELIZABETH NEIGE TODHUNTER. A history of "Bulletin 28": food composition tables in the U.S.A. Am. Dietetic Assoc., Jour., 37:209-14 (Sep). notes. On The chemical composition of American food materials (1896), by W. O. Atwater, published as Bulletin 28 of the U.S. Department of Agriculture, and continued government research and publication concerning the composition of foods, 1896-1959. [2521

ROSCOE POUND (1870-1964). The problem of the exploding bottle. Boston Univ. law rev., 40:167-86 (spring). notes. On litigation involving personal injuries from the explosion of bottled goods, 1903-59. [2522

NEW-YORK HISTORICAL SOCIETY. Historical background of the stamp to mark the Pure Food and Drug Act [of 1906]. Essay proof jour., 13: 227-30 (Oct 1956). facsim. Account of an exhibition, "Eat, Drink and Be Wary--a backward glance at foods, drugs and cosmetics before the protective acts of 50 years ago," showing "an old grocery store and apothecary shop, as well as containers, posters, advertisements and labels illustrating the methods of manufacture and sale of foods and drugs before 1906," and books as early as 1731. [2523

PAUL B. DUNBAR. Memories of early days of Federal food and drug law enforcement. Food drug cosmetic law jour., 14:87-138 (Feb 1959). port. bibliog. On the Bureau of Chemistry and the Food and Drugs Administration during the years of the author's service in Washington, 1907-51. [2524

WILLIAM LLOYD PROSSER. The assault upon the citadel (strict liability to the consumer). Yale law jour., 69: 1099-1148 (Jun). notes. On cases in which "the seller of chattels defends against the ultimate consumer, with whom he stands in no privity of contract," and more generally the law of products liability since 1916. [2525

I. IRVING HOLLAND. An explanation of changing lumber consumption and price [1922-58]. Forest science, 6:171-92 (Jun). diagrs., tables. bibliog. [2526

JOSHUA J. KANCELBAUM. The manufacturer's duty to warn--a higher order of enterprise responsibility. West. Reserve law rev., 11:602-15 (Sep). notes. On warning labels intended to protect the consumer of manufactured products, 1933-59. [2527

IRVIN KERLAN (1912-63). Cosmetics and the Federal Food, Drug, and Cosmetic Act: current trends in cosmetic legislation [1938-60]. N.Y. State jour. med., 60:1930-34 (15 Jun). [2528

U.S. Agricultural Research Service. Farm family spending in the United States: some changes as indicated by recent U.S. Department of Agriculture Expenditure Surveys [mainly for 1941 and 1955]. Wash., 1958. [6], 49, [1] p. 30 diagrs., 19 tables. notes. (U.S. Dept. of Agriculture. Agriculture information bulletin 192.) [2529

JANET AUSTRIAN FISHER. Income, spending, and saving patterns of consumer units in different age groups [mainly in 1946]. Conference on Research in Income and Wealth, Studies in income and wealth, 15 (1952): 75-102. tables. notes. [2530

HOME ECONOMICS

DORIS H. HAMILTON. Household remedies & recipes. Hobbies, 65(4): 110-11 (Jun). On a "casual and a bit battered 19th century household book," anonymous and undated; with excerpts from the manuscript recipes and formulas written in it. [2531

KATHLEEN R. STITT. Nutritive values of diets today and fifty years ago [1895-1910, 1955]. Am. Dietetic Assoc., Jour., 36:433-40 (May). diagrs., tables. notes. [2532

RUTH TOWNSEND LEHMAN. The next fifty years in home economics education research. Jour. home econ., 52:23-6 (Jan). notes. Includes a historical sketch of research, 1906-59. [2533

PEARL SWANSON. During the past half-century: nutrition research in home economics [1910-60]. Jour.

home econ., 52:737-42 (Nov). notes. [2534

RUTH HIGHBERGER. Nursery education in home economics [1934-59]. Jour. home econ., 52:437-40 (Jun). notes. [2535

HELEN LORENA HOLLANDSWORTH. Factors influencing Montana State College home economics graduates for the years 1935 through 1955 to enter, to leave, or to remain in the teaching profession. Ann Arbor: University Microfilms, 1959 [i.e. 1960]. Positive microfilm of typescript. [178] leaves. Thesis (Ed. D.)--Michigan State Univ. Abstracted: Dissert. abstracts, 20:3649 (Mar). [2536

HELEN LORENA HOLLANDSWORTH. Why graduates stay in teaching. Jour. home econ., 52:443-4 (Jun). On a study of "factors which seemed to influence home economics graduates from Montana State College to enter, to leave, or to remain in the teaching profession," 1935-55. [2537

U.S. Office of Education. Division of Vocational Education. Enrollment in home economics education and placement of graduates from institutions reimbursed from Federal vocational funds: a 10-year summary, 1947-48 to 1956-57. [Wash., 1959.] v, 13 p. tables. (Its Misc[ellany] 3571.) [2538

Distribution

THOMAS A. GILLIAM. The scope of the phrase "interstate commerce" [1824-1954]--shall it be redefined? Dicta, 32:373-86 (Sep-Oct 1955). notes. [2539

AMERICAN ASSEMBLY. Wages, prices, profits, and [labor] productivity [1889-1959]: background papers and the final report of the Fifteenth American Assembly ... Final edition. [N.Y.:] American Assembly, Columbia Univ., 1959. ix, 193 p. diagrs., tables. notes. Papers by Albert Rees, John W. Kendrick, James S. Duesenberry, Clark Kerr, Lloyd G. Reynolds, John T. Dunbar, James P. Mitchell, and Sumner H. Slichter. [2540

BUSINESS CYCLES

RENDIGS FELS. American business cycles, 1865-1897. Chapel Hill: Univ. of North Carolina Press [1959. 12], 244 p. diagrs., tables. notes. [2541

OSKAR MORGENSTERN. International financial transactions and business cycles. Princeton: Princeton Univ. Press, 1959. xxvi, 591, [7] p. diagrs. (part fold.), tables. notes. (National Bureau of Economic Research. Studies in business cycles, [8].) Analysis of data from the United States, Great Britain, France, and Germany, 1876-1913, 1919-39. [2542

CURTIS HOOVER BRASCHLER. An investigation of the effects of varying rates of inflation and deflation on agricultural prices and incomes [1913-59]. Ann Arbor: University Microfilms, 1960. Positive microfilm of typescript. [159] leaves. Thesis--Purdue Univ. Abstracted: Dissert. abstracts, 21:1087-8 (Nov). [2543

GEORGE J. MALANOS & HENRY THOMASSEN. An econometric model of the American minor cycle [1947-57]. Atlanta, 1960. [4], 47 p. diagrs., tables. notes (p. 30-34). (Georgia State College of Business Administration. Bureau of Business and Economic Research. Studies in business and economics, bulletin 9.) [2544

FOREIGN TRADE

RICHARD B. SHERIDAN. The British credit crisis of 1772 and the American colonies. Jour. econ. hist., 20:161-86 (Jun). tables. notes. Deals particularly with debt in Virginia, 1772-76. [2545

ROBERT R. LIVINGSTON (1746-1813). Robert R. Livingston and the non-exportation policy: notes for a speech in the Continental Congress, October 27, 1775. [Edited] by Bernard Mason. N.-Y. Hist. Soc. quar., 44:296-307 (Jul). ports. notes. Outline of objections to the policy and argument "for re-opening exportation to Britain." [2546

REZIN FENTON DUVALL. Philadelphia's maritime commerce with the British Empire, 1783-1789. Ann Arbor: University Microfilms, 1960. Positive microfilm of typescript. [516] leaves. Thesis--Univ. of Pennsylvania. Abstracted: Dissert. abstracts, 21:861-2 (Oct). [2547

DOUGLASS CECIL NORTH. The United States balance of payments, 1790-1860. Conference on Research in Income and Wealth, Trends in the American economy in the nineteenth century, ed. William N. Parker (Princeton: Princeton Univ. Press, 1960 [Studies in income and wealth,

24]), p. 573-627. diagrs., tables. notes. [2548

JOSEPH COLLINS. A letter from Joseph Collins, master of the vessel Mountain Leader, to Colonel Christian Febinger, co-owner with James O'Hara, written from Portsmouth, Virginia, February the 22nd, 1796. West. Pa. hist. mag., 43:90-93 (Mar). Report on the author's difficulties in trading on a voyage from Philadelphia to Baltimore and Norfolk, his purchase of the Mountain Leader near Smithfield, and his plans for trade in the West Indies; with an appended affidavit (Philadelphia, 10 Aug. 1796) by Collins and others reporting the plundering of this vessel, en route from Curaçao to Philadelphia, by "a French Republican Privateer Schooner Vessel and Masters name unknown," somewhere near Haiti. [2549

EARL C. TANNER. Early 19th century Providence exports to Brazil [1800-1830]. R. I. hist., 19:89-94 (Oct). notes. Based on thesis--Harvard Univ., 1951. [2550

EARL C. TANNER. EARLY 19th century Providence exports to the Caribbean [1800-1830]. R. I. hist., 19:42-9 (Apr). notes. Based on thesis--Harvard Univ., 1951. [2551

WILLIAM B. ARDIFF. The ship Putnam. Essex Inst. hist. col., 96: 105-30 (Apr). notes. On a vessel built for Samuel Page, Abel Lawrence, Nathan Robinson, and Nathaniel Bowditch at Danversport, Mass., 1801-2, employed in a voyage under Captain Bowditch in a voyage to Sumatra for pepper and to Isle de France for coffee, 1802-3, in a voyage to Copenhagen, 1804, and in a voyage to the Straits of Singapore, 1804-5, where it was seized by Malay pirates who killed 7 men of the crew. [2552

JOE G. TAYLOR. The foreign salve trade in Louisiana after 1808. La. hist., 1:36-43 (winter). notes. [2553

RALPH A. SMITH. Mexican and Anglo-Saxon traffic in scalps, slaves, and livestock, 1835-1841. West Tex. Hist. Assoc. yr. bk., 36:98-115. notes. On the almost continual raids of the Comanche, Kiowa, and Apache Indians from American territory into Mexico, especially Chihuahua and Coahuila, and also into Texas, to steal horses, obtain captives, and kill Mexicans, the offer of bounties by Mexican states for the heads and scalps of the invaders, the entry of several Americans into the lucrative scalp-hunting business, and the special accomplishments of "a Scotch-Irishman named don Santiago Kirker" and his Old Apache Company, "professional hair dressers," mainly American riflemen. [2554

JOHN KING FAIRBANK. Trade and diplomacy on the China coast: the opening of the Treaty Ports. Cambridge: Harvard Univ. Press, 1953. 2 v. xiii, 489, [4]; [8], 88 p. maps, port., tables. bibliog. (2:62-80), notes (2:1-96). (Harvard historical studies, 62.) Study, mainly from Chinese sources, of Chinese policy with respect to foreign trade, particularly with Great Britain and the United States, 1842-54. [2555

ARCHIBALD WILLIAM CURRIE. British attitudes toward investment in North American railroads [ca. 1850 to 1945]. Bus. hist. rev., 34:194-215 (summer). views. notes. [2556

KEIJI O'HARA, ed. Japanese trade & industry in the Meijo-Taisho era. Compiled and edited by Ohara Keishi. Translated and adapted by Okata Tamotsu. Tokyo: Obunsha [1957. 4], 6, 566, [2] p. port., tables, views. notes. (The Centenary Culture Council, Tokyo. A history of Japanese-American culture relations (1853-1926), 1.) "An historical survey of economic relations between Japan and the United States," 1853-1926. Consists of sections on the opening of Japanese ports, the tea, silk, and cotton trades, "Japanese-American financial relations," and "Introduction of American technical know-how in Japanese industry." [2557

MORTON ROTHSTEIN. America in the international rivalry for the British wheat market, 1860-1914. Miss. Valley hist. rev., 47:401-18 (Dec). notes. [2558

MATTHEW SIMON. The United States balance of payments, 1861-1900. Conference on Research in Income and Wealth, Trends in the American economy in the nineteenth century, ed. William N. Parker (Princeton: Princeton Univ. Press, 1960 [Studies in income and wealth, 24]), p. 629-715. tables. notes. Based on thesis--Columbia Univ., 1955. [2559

GRANT L. REUBER. The growth and changing composition of trade between Canada and the United States [1867-1958. Wash.?] Canadian-American Committee [1960]. xii, 87 p. diagrs., tables. notes. (Reports on Canada - United States relations.) [2560

CHARLES POOR KINDLEBERGER. International trade and United States experience: 1870-1955. Ralph Evans Freeman, ed., Postwar economic trends in the United States (N.Y.: Harper [1960]), p. 337-73. diagrs., tables. notes. [2561

CHARLES G. JACKSON. The Manoa Company. Inter-Am. econ. affairs, 13(4):12-45 (spring). notes. Condensation of thesis (M.A.)--Univ. of North Carolina. On the tangled financial history of a corporation formed by Cyrenius C. Fitzgerald in Brooklyn, N.Y., to develop the resources of a large grant of land in the Orinoco Delta of Venezuela, 1883-99. [2562

JOHN FAIRFIELD THOMPSON & NORMAN BEASLEY. For the years to come: a story of International Nickel of Canada. N.Y.: Putnam [1960]. x, 374 p. col. maps. notes. Includes some account of the participation of American capital in the development of the International Nickel Company of Canada, Ltd., since 1889. [2563

MATTHEW SIMON. The hot money movement and the private exchange pool proposal of 1896. Jour. econ. hist., 20:31-50 (Mar). diagr., table. notes. On the "major disequilibrating outflow of short-term funds" resulting from the nomination of William Jennings Bryan on a free-silver platform, and the countermeasures taken by a group of bankers organized by J. Pierpont Morgan. [2564

IRVING BRECHER. The flow of United States investment funds into Canada since World War II. Duke University, Commonwealth-Studies Center, The American economic impact on Canada (Durham, N.C.: Duke Univ. Press, 1959), p. 100-126. notes. Includes some account of the process since 1900. [2565

Y. C. WANG. Free enterprise in China: the case of a cigarette concern, 1905-1953. Pac. hist. rev., 29:395-414 (Nov). notes. On the Nanyang Brothers Tobacco Company, 1909-37, and its rivalry with the British-American Tobacco Company. [2566

JOHN SENECA McGEE. Ocean freight rate conferences and the American merchant marine [1913-59]. Univ. Chicago law rev., 27:191-314 (winter). notes. On American policy toward and participation in "shipping cartels" in relation to antitrust laws and to subsidization of American ocean shipping. [2567

HUGH G. J. AITKEN. The changing structure of the Canadian economy, with particular reference to the influence of the United States. Duke University, Commonwealth-Studies Center, The American economic impact on Canada (Durham, N.C.: Duke Univ. Press, 1959), p. 3-35. tables. notes. On the displacement of Great Britain by the United States in the years since 1914 as the main buyer from, importer into, and foreign investor in Canada, and its effect upon the Canadian pulpwood, nickel, petroleum, and natural-gas industries. [2568

LADISLAS F. REITZER. United States - Russian economic relations, 1917-1920. U.S., Dept. of State, Office of Intelligence Research, Abstracts of completed doctoral dissertations, 1950-51 ([Wash.] 1952), p. 294-301. Abstract of thesis--Univ. of Chicago. [2569

ROBERT FREEMAN SMITH. Export trade ideology of American business and its relationship to foreign policy, 1919-1933. Discourse, 3:189-200 (Jul). notes. [2570

WILLIAM E. GORDON. Economic growth and foreign trade of Asia [1920-56]. Conference on American trade with Asia and the Far East, Marquette University, 1958, American trade with Asia and the Far East, ed. Robert J. Barr (Milwaukee: Marquette Univ. Press, 1959), p. 247-89. tables. notes. [2571

MAURICE LAMONTAGNE. The American economic impact on Quebec. Duke University, Commonwealth-Studies Center, The American economic impact on Canada (Durham, N.C.: Duke Univ. Press, 1959), p. 88-99. On American investments, imports, and tourists in the Province of Quebec since 1920. [2572

ROBERT SHAPLEN. Kreuger: genius and swindler. ... With an introduction by John Kenneth Galbraith. N.Y.: Knopf, 1960. xiv, [2], 251, xi, [2] p. diagr., port. On Ivar Kreuger (1880-1932), Swedish financier, prepetrator of huge frauds beginning in the 1920s which involved many individual and institutional investors in the United States. [2573

FOUAD ABDELAZIZ TAWFIK. Development and influence of the United States raw cotton policy on its economy [since the 1920s]. Ann Arbor: University Microfilms, 1959 [i.e. 1960]. Positive microfilm of typescript.

[361] leaves. Thesis--Univ. of Texas. Abstracted: Dissert. abstracts, 20: 2623 (Jan). [2574

STEPHEN D. MAGUIRE. The railway that chocolate bars built. Railroad mag., 71(6):16-20 (Oct). map, port., views. On the Hershey Cuban Railway, a steam and electric interurban system connecting Havana Harbor and Matanzas and serving the sugar refineries and plantations of the Hershey Chocolate Corporation (with headquarters at Hershey, Cuba), established in 1922, sold to Cuban interests in 1945, and still in operation in 1960. [2575

THOMAS A. PETIT. The impact of imports and tariffs on the American tuna industry [1924-58]. Am. jour. econ. and sociol., 19:275-88 (Apr). notes. [2576

J. HERBERT FURTH. International relations and the Federal Reserve System [1925-58]. Herbert V. Prochnow, ed., The Federal Reserve System (N.Y.: Harper [1960]), p. 273-94. bibliog., notes. [2577

BENJAMIN BARG. A study of United States economic control in Canadian secondary industry [1926-60. N.Y.] 1960. ix, [1], 392 leaves. tables. bibliog. (leaves 378-92), notes. Thesis--Columbia Univ. On capital from the United States as an agency of control of Canadian business. [2578

JOSEPH WILLIAM WALT. Saudi Arabia and the Americans: 1928-1951. Ann Arbor: University Microfilms, 1960. Positive microfilm of typescript. [516] leaves. Thesis--Northwestern Univ. Abstracted: Dissert. abstracts, 21:1548-9 (Dec). Deals largely with American interest in Arabian oil and with the Arabian American Oil Company. [2579

CLARENCE L. BARBER. The impact of United States farm policy on Canadian agriculture. Duke University, Commonwealth-Studies Center, The American economic impact on Canada (Durham, N.C.: Duke Univ. Press, 1959), p. 69-87. diagr. notes. On the effect of American price supports and creation of surpluses upon the Canadian market, especially the wheat market, since 1929. [2580

ROBERT LEE SAMMONS. Foreign investment aspects of measuring national wealth. Conference on Research in Income and Wealth, Studies in income and wealth, 12 (1950): 549-67. tables. bibliog. On "United States assets abroad and foreign assets in the United States," 1929-46. [2581

LAWRENCE WILLIAM WITT. Trade and agriculture policy [since 1931]. Am. Acad. Pol. and Social Science, Ann., 331:1-7 (Sep). notes. [2582

LLOYD CALVIN GARDNER. American foreign policy in a closed world: 1933-1945. Ann Arbor: University Microfilms, 1960. Positive microfilm of typescript. [385] leaves. Thesis--Univ. of Wisconsin. Abstracted: Dissert. abstracts, 21:604-5 (Sep). On changing policy toward foreign trade. [2583

JOHN R. STEVENSON. Legal aspects of the public offering of foreign securities in the United States market [1933-59]. Geo. Wash. law rev., 28: 194-213 (Oct 1959). notes. [2584

JOHN FOSTER DULLES (1888-1959). Vital importance of the extension of the Trade Agreements Act. Harold Karan Jacobson ed., America's foreign policy (N.Y.: Random House [1960]), p. 642-7. From the Department of State bulletin, 7 Jul. 1958. On the "trade agreements program" of the United States, 1934-58. [2585

EDWARD RENSHAW. Reclamation and the American sugar policy: a case of compounding resource misallocation [1934-54]. West. pol. quar., 11: 858-63 (Dec 1957). tables. notes. On the sugar-beet industry in the United States as a use of land and capital that might provide higher returns from other uses and as an unnecessary burden upon consumers in the form of high prices made possible by the sugar tariff; and the aggravation of the evil by plans to devote large areas of irrigated land in the Missouri Basin to sugar beets. [2586

C. C. LIANG. Trade relations of the United States with China (Taiwan), Japan, and Korea (South) [1937-57]. Conference on American Trade with Asia and the Far East, Marquette University, 1958, American trade with Asia and the Far East, ed. Robert J. Barr (Milwaukee: Marquette Univ. Press, 1959), p. 99-113. tables. [2587

E. G. CAMPBELL. Mahan's message on the merchant marine. U.S.N. Inst. proc., 86(5):92-5 (May). view. On Alfred Thayer Mahan's lectures and books on sea power, 1886 ff., as lessons to be studied in relation to the deterioration of the U.S. merchant marine since 1939, and the need for very heavy subsidy to restore it to a strong competitive position. [2588

ROBERT E. ASHER. Economic cooperation under U.N. auspices [1942-58]. Harold Karan Jacobson, ed., America's foreign policy (N.Y.: Random House [1960]), p. 709-30. notes. From International organization, summer 1958. [2589

V. S. DE BEAUSSET. Changing trade patterns as underdeveloped areas become developed. Conference on American Trade with Asia and the Far East, Marquette University, 1958, American trade with Asia and the Far East, ed. Robert J. Barr (Milwaukee: Marquette Univ. Press, 1959), p. 79-89. On American trade with and aid to Taiwan (Formosa), 1945-57, where the author was stationed for several years. [2590

JOHN J. DEUTSCH. Recent American influence in Canada, with particular reference to economic factors and Canadian reaction [since 1945]. Duke University, Commonwealth-Studies Center, The American economic impact on Canada (Durham, N.C.: Duke Univ. Press, 1959), p. 36-50. table. notes. [2591

RAYMOND VERNON. The American corporation in underdeveloped areas [abroad, 1945-59]. Edward Sagendorph Mason, ed., The corporation in modern society (Cambridge: Harvard Univ. Press, 1959), p. 237-59, 322. notes. [2592

ROBERT B. ANDERSON. The balance of payments problem [1946-59]. For. affairs, 38:419-32 (Apr). [2593

RANDALL WESTON HINSHAW. Implications of the shift in the U.S. balance of payments [1946-59]. Am. econ. rev., 49:274-83 (May 1959). [2594

HARRY BAYARD PRICE. The Marshall Plan and its meaning. ... Published under the auspices of the Governmental Affairs Institute, Washington, D.C. Ithaca: Cornell Univ. Press [1955]. xvi, 424 p. diagrs., views. notes. On the European Recovery Program and related programs for economic aid to China and other Asiatic countries, administered by the Economic Cooperation Administration, 1948-52. [2595

WALTER KRAUSE. American agricultural surpluses and foreign economic development. Iowa City, 1960. [8], 36 p. diagrs. (State University of Iowa. Bureau of Business and Economic Research. Studies in business & economics, n. s., 8.) On "the generation of agricultural surpluses" by price supports, the disposal of the surpluses abroad "as an instrument of the United States foreign economic policy," and the foreign responses to the disposal program, 1949-60. [2596

FREEDOM OF TRADE

L. JAMES HARRIS & IRVING H. SIEGEL. Positive competition and the patent system [since 1787]. Patent, trademark, and copyright jour., 3:21-32 (spring 1959). notes. [2597

HARLAN M. BLAKE. Employee agreements not to compete. Harv. law rev., 73:625-91 (Feb). notes. On "covenants in which an employee agrees not to compete with his employer after termination of employment," 1851-1957. [2598

THOMAS G. MANNING, ed. The Standard Oil Company: the rise of a national monopoly [1863-1958]. ... Revised by E. David Cronon ... and Howard R. Lamar. N.Y.: Holt [1960]. xii, 66 p. maps, tables. notes (p. 65-6). (Select problems in historical interpretation, 3.) Excerpts from primary sources and secondary works, with introductions by the editor. [2599

ARTHUR MENZIES JOHNSON. Public policy and concentration in the petroleum industry, 1870-1911. Centennial Seminar on the History of the Petroleum Industry, Harvard University, 1959, Oil's first century: papers ([Cambridge:] Harvard Graduate School of Business Administration [1960]), p. 43-56. view. notes. [2600

HAROLD FRANCIS WILLIAMSON & RALPH L. ANDREANO. Competitive structure of the American petroleum industry, 1880-1911: a reappraisal. Centennial Seminar on the History of the Oil Industry, Harvard University, 1959, Oil's first century: papers ([Boston:] Harvard Graduate School of Business Administration [1960]), p. 71-84. tables, views. notes. [2601

GEORGE SMITH WOLBERT, JR. The recurring spectre of pipeline divorcement. Centennial Seminar on the History of the Petroleum Industry, Harvard University, 1959, Oil's first century: papers ([Boston:] Harvard Graduate School of Business Administration [1960]), p. 105-40. tables, views. notes. On government regulation of oil pipelines, 1887-1959. [2602

ROBERT M. AGUE, JR. Resale price maintenance--a threat to free competition [1889-1958]. Dickinson law rev., 63:107-17 (Jan). notes. [2603

WALTER LESLEY DAYKIN. The status of unions under our antitrust laws [1890-1959]. Labor law jour., 11: 216-26, 256 (Mar). notes. [2604

MARY LUCETTA DOOLEY. Antitrust legislation and labor unions [1890-1960]. Labor law jour., 11:911-44 (Oct). [2605

VICTOR R. HANSEN. The antitrust laws in a changing economy [1890-1958]. U. C. L. A. law rev., 6:183-204 (Mar 1959). notes. [2606

ALAN D. NEALE. The antitrust laws of the United States of America: a study of competition enforced by law. Cambridge [Eng.]: University Press, 1960. xvi, 516, [3] p. bibliog. (p. 504-7), notes, "table of cases" (p. 508-16). (National Institute of Economic and Social Research. Economic and social studies, 19.) British view of the Sherman Act (1890), the Clayton Act (1914), and the Federal Trade Commission Act (1914), and of legislation exempting certain classes of monopolies (e.g., patents) from prohibition. [2607

EARL T. THOMAS. Federal anti-trust laws and the Mississippi lawyer. Miss. law jour., 30:117-34 (Dec 1958). notes. Outline of Federal statutes and decisions, 1890-1958. [2608

JOSEPH E. McDOWELL. Labor and antitrust [1893-1959]: collective bargaining or restraint of trade? Fed. Bar jour., 20:18-29 (winter). notes. [2609

MILTON A. KALLIS. Local conduct and the Sherman Act. Duke law jour., 1959:236-57 (spring 1959). notes. On "intrastate commerce affecting interstate commerce," 1895-1958. [2610

WILLIAM R. WARD. The agricultural cooperative and anti-trust law [1901-45]. Dicta, 30:245-52 (Jul 1953). notes. [2611

CARL KAYSEN. The corporation: how much power? what scope? Edward Sagendorph Mason, ed., The corporation in modern society (Cambridge: Harvard Univ. Press, 1959), p. 85-105, 307-8. table. notes. On social, political, and economic aspects of the "concentration of power in a small number of large corporate enterprises," 1907-58. [2612

MILTON C. DENBO. Labor exemption--an anti view. Fed. Bar jour., 20:30-34 (winter). notes. On the status of labor unions under Federal antitrust laws since 1908. [2613

JOHN LAWRENCE ENOS. Competition in technological innovation: the cracking processes and patents [1911-44]. Centennial Seminar on the History of the Petroleum Industry, Harvard University, 1959, Oil's first century: papers ([Boston:] Harvard Graduate School of Business Administration [1960]), p. 93-104. view. notes. [2614

SIMON NEWCOMB WHITNEY. Changes under law: the Sherman Act and the oil industry [1911-59]. Centennial Seminar on the History of the Petroleum Industry, Harvard University, 1959, Oil's first century: papers ([Cambridge:] Harvard Graduate School of Business Administration [1960]), p. 141-7. notes. [2615

RICHARD W. ERGO. ASCAP and the antitrust laws: the story of a reasonable compromise. Duke law jour., 1959:258-77 (spring 1959). notes. On the American Society of Composers, Authors, and Publishers as "an organization dealing exclusively in the licensing of copyright performing rights," 1913-58. [2616

GEORGE F. BARBARY. An enquiry into the social ideal of free competition in anti-trust law [1914-49]. Dicta, 30:253-63 (Jul 1953). notes. [2617

DANIEL J. McCAULEY, JR. Trade regulation--the Wilsonian concepts in a regulatory climate. Food drug cosmetic law jour., 15:93-8 (Feb). notes. On recommendations of Woodrow Wilson that the Government proceed not against businesses but against individual businessmen (including officers of corporations) in cases of misconduct in the interstate commerce, 1914-54. [2618

WILLIAM L. McGOVERN. Antitrust exemptions for regulated industries. Fed. Bar jour., 20:10-17 (winter). notes. On the extent to which the industries regulated by administrative agencies have been exempted from the application of the antitrust statutes, 1914-59. [2619

DONALD RANDALL RICHBERG. Labor union monopoly, a clear and

present danger. Chicago: H. Regnery Co., 1957. x, [4], 175 p. On the exemption of labor unions from prosecution as conspiracies in restraint of trade by the Clayton Anti-Trust Act (1914) and the active encouragement of labor monopolies by the U.S. Government since 1926. [2620

JOSEPH J. SAUNDERS. The status of agricultural cooperatives under the antitrust laws [1914-59]. Fed. Bar jour., 20:35-55 (winter). notes. [2621

MICHAEL CONANT. Antitrust in the motion picture industry: economic and legal analysis [1915-59]. Berkeley: Univ. of California Press, 1960. [2], xvii, [1], 240 p. facsim., tables. bibliog. (p. 221-6), index of cases (p. 227-31), notes. (University of California. Bureau of Business and Economic Research. Publications.) [2622

PETER BARTON HUTT. Restrictions on the free movement of fluid milk under Federal milk marketing orders [1935-60]. Univ. Detroit law jour., 37:525-604 (Apr). notes. [2623

JOHN ROBERT DAVIDSON. A study of the effect of the Robinson-Patman Act upon cooperative advertising policies and practices [1936-58]. Ann Arbor: University Microfilms, 1959 [i.e. 1960]. Positive microfilm of typescript. [372] leaves. Thesis--Ohio State Univ. Abstracted: Dissert. abstracts, 20:4300-4301 (May). [2624

JOHN EDWARD MURRAY, JR. Cost justification under the Robinson-Patman Act: impossibility revisited [1936-59]. Wis. law rev., 1960:227-64 (Mar). notes. [2625

JOHN C. STEDMAN. Twenty-four years of the Robinson-Patman Act [1936-59]. Wis. law rev., 1960:197-226 (Mar). notes. [2626

ROBERT ELLIOT FREER (1896-1962). The basing point pricing system. Dicta, 26:7-16 (Jan 1949). Address by the retiring Chairman of the Federal Trade Commission, 1948, reviewing evidence, 1937-47, to sustain the Commission's view that the system is a conspiracy in restraint of trade. For a reply see S. Arthur Henry, "Another view of the basing point controversy," 26:37-48 (Feb 1949). [2627

GEORGE E. FROST, S. CHESTERFIELD OPPENHEIM, & NEIL F. TWOMEY. Compulsory licensing and patent dedication provisions of antitrust decrees [1938-1956]--a foundation for detailed factual case studies. Patent, trademark, and copyright jour., 1:127-44 (Jun 1957). notes. [2628

VICTOR HORSLEY KRAMER. Criminal prosecutions for violations of the Sherman Act: in search of a policy [1938-60]. Georgetown law jour., 48: 530-42 (spring). notes. [2629

DALE G. BRICKNER. Labor and antitrust action [1941-59]. Indus. and labor rel. rev., 13:245-53 (Jan). notes. [2630

JAMES B. DONOVAN. Insurance--the case in favor of existing exemptions from the antitrust laws [1944-59]. Fed. Bar jour., 20:56-66 (winter). notes. [2631

LOUIS A. DOW. The Supreme Court, the "new competition," and "reasonable behavior." Okla. law rev., 13: 174-92 (May). notes. Evidence that "the courts have tended to breed the growth and emergence of oligopoly" and have labeled it "competition," 1945-56. [2632

EUGENE KOZIK. Oligopoly and the concept of workable or effective competition: an economic analysis of recent antitrust cases [1945-59]. Univ. Pittsburgh law rev., 21:621-45 (Jun). notes. Based on thesis--Univ. of Pittsburgh. [2633

FRANKLIN P. MICHELS. Insurance--the case against broad exemptions from the antitrust laws [1945-59]. Fed. Bar jour., 20:66-73 (winter). notes. [2634

INCOME AND WEALTH

HARRY I. GREENFIELD. Sliding wage scales: a theoretical and historical evaluation [ca. 1650 to 1950]. Ann Arbor: University Microfilms, 1959 [i.e. 1960]. Positive microfilm of typescript. [273] leaves. Thesis--Columbia Univ. Abstracted: Dissert. abstracts, 20:2636 (Jan). [2635

THEODORE FRANCIS MARBURG. Income originating in trade, 1799-1869. Conference on Research in Income and Wealth, Trends in the American economy, ed. William N. Parker (Princeton: Princeton Univ. Press, 1960 [Studies in income and wealth, 24]), p. 317-26. notes. [2636

STANLEY LEBERGOTT. Wage trends, 1800-1900. Conference on Research in Income and Wealth, Trends in the American economy in the nineteenth century, ed. William N. Parker (Princeton: Princeton Univ. Press, 1960 [Studies in income and wealth, 24]), p. 449-99. tables. notes. [2637

ANNA (JACOBSON) SCHWARTZ. Gross dividend and interest payments by corporations at selected dates in the 19th century [1835, 1859, 1863-71, 1890]. Conference on Research in Income and Wealth, Trends in the American economy in the nineteenth century, ed. William N. Parker (Princeton: Princeton Univ. Press, 1960 [Studies in income and wealth, 24]), p. 407-48. tables. notes. [2638

RICHARD ANILEY EASTERLIN. Interregional differences in per capita income, population, and total income, 1840-1950. Conference on Research in Income and Wealth, Trends in the American economy in the nineteenth century, ed. William N. Parker (Princeton: Princeton Univ. Press, 1960 [Studies in income and wealth, 24]), p. 73-140. diagrs., tables. notes. Based on thesis--Univ. of Pennsylvania. [2639

EDWARD C. BUDD. Factor shares, 1850-1910. Conference on Research in Income and Wealth, Trends in the American economy in the nineteenth century, ed. William N. Parker (Princeton: Princeton Univ. Press, 1960 [Studies in income and wealth, 24]), p. 365-406. diagrs., tables. notes. On 2 classes of shares: "wages and salaries representing the contractual income of hired workers, and the income of self-employed workers and property owners." [2640

ROLAND McMILLAN HARPER. Racial contrasts in income. Ala. lawyer, 21: 257-68 (Jul). tables. On incomes of Negroes and white persons, 1850-1958, especially in Alabama. [2641

REUBEN A. KESSEL & ARMEN A. ALCHIAN. Real wages in the North during the Civil War [1860-65]: Mitchell's data reinterpreted. Jour. law & econ., 2:95-113 (Oct 1959). diagrs., tables. notes. [2642

CLARENCE DICKINSON LONG. Wages and earnings in the United States, 1860-1890. Princeton: Princeton Univ. Press, 1960. xvii, [1], 169 p. diagrs., tables (part double). notes. (National Bureau of Economic Research. General series, 67.) [2643

HAROLD BARGER. Income originating in trade, 1869-1929. Conference on Research in Income and Wealth, Trends in the American economy in the nineteenth century, ed. William N. Parker [Studies in income and wealth, 24]), p. 327-36. tables. notes. [2644

RICHARD AINLEY EASTERLIN. Regional growth of income: long term tendencies [1880-1951]. Simon Smith Kuznets, Ann Ratner Miller, & Richard A. Easterlin, Population redistribution and economic growth, 1870-1950 (Phila.: American Philosophical Soc.), 2 (1960): 141-203. diagrs., tables. notes. Sections on "Regional patterns of income growth," "Interrelations among regional patterns of income growth," and "Factors in the convergence of per capita income." [2645

DOROTHY (STAHL) BRADY. Family savings in relation to changes in the level and distribution of income [1888-1948]. Conference on Research in Income and Wealth, Studies in income and wealth, 15 (1952): 103-30. diagrs., tables. notes. [2646

FRANK ALLAN HANNA. Analysis of interstate income differentials: theory and practice [1919-53]. Conference on Research in Income and Wealth, Regional income (Princeton: Princeton Univ. Press, 1957 [Studies in income and wealth, 21]), p. 113-93. diagrs., tables. notes. Includes comment by Edward F. Denison and others. [2647

DOROTHY (STAHL) BRADY. Research on the size distribution of income. Conference on Research in Income and Wealth, Studies in income and wealth, 13 (1951): 2-60. notes. On the lack of progress in the analysis of available data relevant to this subject, 1920-50, and the need for clearer definition of the concepts employed in analysis; with comment by Milton Friedman. [2648

ROBERT M. SOLOW. Income inequality since the war [1928-56]. Ralph Evans Freeman, ed., Postwar economic trends in the United States (N.Y.: Harper [1960]), p. 91-138. tables. notes. [2649

ABNER HURWITZ & CARLYLE P. STALLINGS. Interregional differentials in per capita real income change [1929-53]. Conference on Research in Income and Wealth, Regional income (Princeton: Princeton Univ. Press, 1957 [Studies in income and wealth, 21]), p. 195-270. diagrs., tables. notes. [2650

GEOFFREY SEDDON SHEPHERD. Farm programs for farm incomes [1930-58]. Jour. farm econ., 42: 639-50 (Aug). diagr., map, table. notes. On problems in defining farm and income, in ascertaining the size of farm income in relation to other income, and in establishing "programs, area by area, to cure the causes of the low incomes rather than alleviate the symptoms." [2651

DAVID GALE JOHNSON. Some effects of region, community size, color, and occupation on family and individual income [1935-46]. Conference on Research in Income and Wealth, Studies in income and wealth, 15 (1952): 49-74. tables. notes. [2652

MARGARET GILPIN REID. Distribution of nonmoney income. Conference on Research in Income and Wealth, Studies in income and wealth, 13 (1951): 124-85. tables. notes. On problems in the measurement and definition of "income in kind," and the sources of data for the study of these problems, 1938-46; with comment by Edward F. Denison. [2653

NEWMAN ARNOLD TOLLES. The purpose and results of U.S. minimum wage laws [since 1938]. Monthly labor rev., 83:238-42 (Mar). [2654

NATHAN M. KOFFSKY. Farm and urban purchasing power [1941]. Conference on Research in Income and Wealth, Studies in income and wealth, 11 (1949): 151-78. tables. notes. Statistical analysis. For comments by Margaret G. Reid (dealing particularly with the definition of parity) and E. W. Grove, and the author's reply, see p. 179-219. [2655

JOSEPH A. PECHMAN. Distribution of income before and after Federal income tax, 1941 and 1947. Conference on Research in Income and Wealth, Studies in income and wealth, 13 (1951): 186-218. diagrs., tables. Includes comment by George Garvy. [2656

MAURICE LIEBENBERG & HYMAN KAITZ. An income size distribution from income tax and survey data, 1944. Conference on Research in Income and Wealth, Studies in income and wealth, 13 (1951): 378-462. diagrs., tables. [2657

NATHAN M. KOFFSKY & JEANNE E. LEAR. Size distribution of farm operators' income in 1946. Conference on Research in Income and Wealth, Studies in income and wealth, 13 (1951): 220-64. diagrs., tables. notes. [2658

JAMES DOUGLAS BROWN, JR. Changes in inter-industry wage levels and cost-push inflation: the experience in manufacturing during the post-war period [1947-57]. Ann Arbor: University microfilms, 1960. Positive microfilm of typescript. [283] leaves. Thesis--Univ. of Wisconsin. Abstracted: Dissert. abstracts, 21:1397 (Dec). [2659

ALFRED H. CONRAD. The share of wages and salaries in manufacturing incomes, 1947-56. Materials prepared in connection with the study of employment, growth, and price levels for consideration by the Joint Economic Committee, Congress of the United States (Wash.: U.S. Govt. Print. Off., 1959), p. 137-53. diagrs., tables. notes. (Study paper 9.) [2660

WILLIAM FIELDING OGBURN (1886-1959) & FRANCIS R. ALLEN. Technological development and per capita income [1947-55]. Am. jour. sociol., 65:127-31 (Sep 1959). notes. For comment by George R. Wilson and reply by Francis R. Allen see 65: 505-7. [2661

GARNET DALE OLIVE. An analysis of the dividend policies of selected American corporations [1947-56]. Ann Arbor: University Microfilms, 1960. Positive microfilm of typescript. [434] leaves. Thesis--State Univ. of Iowa. Abstracted: Dissert. abstracts, 21:1407 (Dec). [2662

IRVING STERN & HERMAN TRAVIS. Trends in earnings of factory workers, 1947 to 1960. Monthly labor rev., 83: 809-21 (Aug). diagrs., tables. notes. [2663

U.S. Bureau of the Budget. Office of Statistical Standards. Revisions of first estimates of quarter-to-quarter movement in selected national income series, 1947-1958: seasonally adjusted data. [By Raymond Nassimbene and Benjamin Theodore Teeter.] Wash., 1960. iii, 40 p. fold. diagrs., tables. (Its Statistical evaluation reports, 2.) [2664

EDWIN MANSFIELD. City size and income, 1949. Conference on Research in Income and Wealth, Regional income (Princeton: Princeton Univ. Press, 1957 [Studies in income and wealth, 21]), p. 271-317. diagrs., tables. notes. [2665

WILLIAM G. BOWEN, DAVID G. BROWN, & LOUIS A. SIMPSON, comps. Sources of wage and salary data. Indus. and labor rel. rev., 13:411-19 (Apr). Table listing 35 types of wage data, their frequency and their classification by occupation, industry, or area, and their printed sources, 1950-60. [2666

CONFERENCE ON RESEARCH IN INCOME AND WEALTH. An appraisal of the 1950 Census income data. ... A report of the National Bureau of Economic Research, New York. Princeton: Princeton Univ. Press, 1958. x, 450 p. diagrs., tables. notes. (Its Studies in income and wealth, 23.) Thirteen sections, by various contributors, originally papers of the Conference at Princeton, 1956, edited by George Garvy. Includes "An appraisal of the data for farm families," by D. Gale Johnson; "The size distribution of farm income," by Ernest W. Grove; "A method of identifying chronic low-income groups from cross-section survey data," by Eleanor M. Snyder; "Changes in the industrial distribution of wages in the United States, 1939-1949," by Herman P. Miller; and "The effect of multi-industry employment on the industrial distribution of wages," by Lazare Teper. [2667

MARKETING

WANAMAKER (JOHN), INC. The retailing industry [since ca. 1700. By Richard C. Bond.] John G. Glover & Rudolph L. Lagai, eds., The development of American industries: their economic significance, 4th ed. (N.Y.: Simmons-Boardman [1959]), p. 802-9. [2668

HENRY HARRISON BAKKEN. Historical evaluation, theory and legal status of futures trading in American agricultural commodities [1752-1959]. Futures Trading Seminar, Chicago, 1959, Futures Trading Seminar, history and development (Madison, Wis.: Mimir Publishers, 1960), 1:1-28. tables. notes. Appended (p. 29-60): Discussion by James S. Schonberg, John W. Sharp, and John D. Black. [2669

JAMES HARVEY YOUNG. Patent medicines: an early example of competitive marketing [1790s-1860s]. Jour. econ. hist., 20:648-58. [2670

ETHEL DALLMEYER HOOVER. Retail prices after 1850 [till 1880]. Conference on Research in Income and Wealth, Trends in the American economy in the nineteenth century, ed. William N. Parker (Princeton: Princeton Univ. Press, 1960 [Studies in income and wealth, 24]), p. 141-90. diagr., tables. notes. [2671

JOSEPH MARK ZAREMBA. The trend of lumber prices [1860-1955]. Jour. forestry, 56:179-81 (Mar 1958). diagr., table. bibliog. [2672

JOHN WILLIAM FERRY. A history of the department store [in America, 1862-1960, and the British Commonwealth]. N.Y.: Macmillan, 1960, xii, 387 p. diagrs., map, views. bibliog. (p. 377-9). [2673

ROBERT C. KIRKWOOD. The Woolworth story at home and abroad. N.Y.: Newcomen Soc. in North America, 1960. 24 p. ports., views. On the F. W. Woolworth Company, 1879-1960, founded by Woolworth (1852-1919) in Lancaster, Pa., as a single department store, now forming a chain of stores throughout the United States and in several foreign countries. [2674

AL J. HANTEN. Life of a salesman. [La Jolla, Calif.:] La Jolla Print. & Pub. Co., 1960. [3], 160 p. (even numbers on recto). cartoons, facsims., ports., tables. On the author's early life on a farm near Dubuque, Ia., early 20th century, and his work as a traveling salesman. Inspired by Arthur Miller's Death of a salesman ("merely a sordid story about a second rate salesman"). [2675

FREDERIC J. MEYSTRE, JR. The salesman in the American novel of the twentieth century [1900-1958]. Ann Arbor: University Microfilms, 1959 [i.e. 1960]. Positive microfilm of typescript. [368] leaves. Thesis--New York Univ. Abstracted: Dissert. abstracts, 20:3982 (Apr). [2676

JOHN SHERMAN WRIGHT. The development of policies affecting the marketing operations of the Jewel Tea Company, Inc., 1901-1951. Ann Arbor: University Microfilms, 1954 [i.e. 1960]. Positive microfilm of typescript. [253] leaves. Thesis--Ohio State Univ. Abstracted: Dissert. abstracts, 20:2626-9 (Jan). Study of "a New York corporation with home offices located in Barrington, Illinois," retailing "food, household, and general merchandise products" in 42 States. [2677

JAMES CASH PENNEY (born 1875). View from the ninth decade: jottings from a merchant's daybook. N.Y.: T.

Nelson [1960]. 222 p. On the author's early life in Missouri, his establishment of a department store in Kemmerer, Wyo., in 1902, its expansion to a chain of J. C. Penney Company department stores, and the author's "Christian principles" in business; with advice to the reader on the attainment of success, the conduct of life, retirement, etc. [2678

U.S. Crop Reporting Board. Prices received by farmers for beef cattle, United States and by States, monthly and annual average, 1909-59. [Prepared by Ronald E. Johnson.] Wash., 1960. 74 p. tables. (U.S. Dept. of Agriculture. Statistical bulletin 265.) [2679

ABRAHAM DAVID HANNATH KAPLAN, JOEL B. DIRLAM, & ROBERT F. LANZILLOTTI. Pricing in big business [1914-56]: a case approach. Wash.: Brookings Institution [1958]. xiv, 344 p. diagrs., tables. notes. [2680

ROGER W. GRAY. The importance of hedging on futures trading, and the effectiveness of futures trading for hedging [ca. 1917 to 1958]. Futures Trading Seminar, Chicago, 1959, Futures Trading Seminar: history and development (Madison, Wis.: Mimir Publishers, 1960), 1:61-82. diagrs., tables (1 double). notes. Appended (p. 83-120): discussion by James P. Reichmann, C. Peairs Wilson, and Richard Phillips. [2681

GEORGE WELLS LADD. A statistical analysis of certain institutional variables in the butter and margarine market. Ames: Iowa State Univ. of Science and Technology, 1960. [2], 640-664 p. diagrs., tables. bibliog. (p. 655-6), notes. (Iowa. Agricultural and Home Economics Experiment Station, Ames. Research bulletin 474.) Includes "Historical summary of selected State and Federal oleomargarine laws, 1919-56," by George W. Ladd and J. D. Jenkins. [2682

U.S. Crop Reporting Board. Prices received by farmers for hogs, United States and by States, monthly and annual average prices, 1919-1958. [Prepared by Ronald E. Johnson.] Wash., 1960. 63 p. tables. (U.S. Dept. of Agriculture. Statistical bulletin 257.) [2683

GREGORY C. CHOW. Statistical demand functions for automobiles and their use for forecasting [1920-58]. Arnold C. Harberger, ed., The demand for durable goods (Chicago: Univ. of Chicago Press [1960]), p. 147-78. diagrs., tables. notes. Based on thesis--Univ. of Chicago, 1955. Econometric study. [2684

JOSEPH GRANT KNAPP. Seeds that grew: a history of the Cooperative Grange League Federation Exchange. Hinsdale, N.Y.: Anderson House, 1960. xvi, 535 p. diagrs., maps, ports., tables, views. notes. On an organization for cooperative buying, processing, and selling, 1920-60. [2685

WILLIAM F. SAALBACH. United States bituminous coal markets: trends since 1920 and prospects to 1975. [Pittsburgh:] Three Rivers Press [1960. 8], 44 p. diagrs., map, tables, views. bibliog. (p. 40-44), notes. Condensation of thesis--Univ. of Pittsburgh. [2686

U.S. Agricultural Marketing Service. Marketing costs and margins for livestock and meats [1920-60. By Dalton L. Wilson, Betty Sue Pence, and Victor B. Phillips. Wash., 1960.] vi, 65 p. diagrs., tables. bibliog. (p. 52-3). (U.S. Dept. of Agriculture. Marketing research report 418.) [2687

U.S. Agricultural Marketing Service. Cash receipts from major farm commodities by States, as percentages of State totals, 1924-59. [Prepared under the direction of Ernest W. Grove.] Wash., 1960. [2], 72 p. diagrs., tables. (U.S. Dept. of Agriculture. Statistical bulletin 262.) [2688

G. ROBINSON GREGORY. A statistical investigation of factors affecting the market for hardwood flooring [1927-58]. Forest science, 6:123-34 (Jun). diagrs., table. bibliog. [2689

EUNICE KITCHELL. Statistical investigation in the elasticities of demand for motor fuel, United States, 1929-57. Ann Arbor, Mich.: University Microfilms, 1959 [i.e. 1960]. Positive microfilm of typescript. vi, 66 leaves. diagrs., tables. bibliog. (leaves 63-6). Thesis--Univ. of Texas. Abstracted: Dissert. abstracts, 20: 2622 (Jan). [2690

DONALD DAVID PARKER. The marketing of consumer services [1929-58. Seattle] 1960. [3], vi, 142 leaves. tables. bibliog. (leaves 4-8), notes. (University of Washington. College of Business Administration. Business studies series, 1.) Issued on microfilm as thesis--Univ. of Washington, 1958. Includes a classification of "Significant services for which consumers make expenditures" (10 categories). [2691

MEYER LOUIS BURSTEIN. The demand for household refrigeration in the United States. Arnold C. Harberger, ed., The demand for durable goods (Chicago: Univ. of Chicago Press [1960]), p. 97-145. diagrs., tables. notes. Econometric study of the "price and income elasticity of demand for household refrigeration," 1931-55. [2692

THOMAS APPLEGATE HIERONYMUS. Effects of futures trading on prices [1931-58]. Futures Trading Seminar, Chicago, 1959, Futures trading seminar: history and development (Madison, Wis.: Mimir Publishers, 1960), 1: 121-61. diagrs., tables. notes. Appended (p. 163-201): discussion by Richard M. Withrow, Reynold P. Dahl, and Geoffrey S. Shepherd. [2693

ALLEN B. PAUL & WILLIAM T. WESSON. The future of futures trading in our changing agriculture. Futures Trading Seminar, Chicago, 1959, Futures trading seminar: history and development (Madison, Wis.: Mimir Publishers, 1960), 1:203-44. tables. notes. Appended (p. 245-71): Discussion by Walter M. Goldschmidt, Leonard W. Schruben, and Adlowe L. Larson. Includes some account of "relevant tendencies in market organization," 1931-58. [2694

JOHN H. WIKSTROM. The market outlook for lodgepole pine [1938-56]. Jour. forestry, 56:643-6 (Sep 1958). tables. notes. [2695

MARGARET GILPIN REID. Increase in rent of dwelling units from 1940 to 1950. Am. Statistical Assoc., Jour., 54:358-76 (Jun 1959). diagrs., tables. notes. [2696

JAMES DOWELL TAYLOR. A description, analysis, and partial explanation of changes in areal distribution of retail sales for selected store groups in the central cities of ninety-five standard metropolitan areas from 1948 through 1954. Ann Arbor: University Microfilms, 1960. Positive microfilm of typescript. [401] leaves. Thesis--State Univ. of Iowa. Abstracted: Dissert. abstracts, 21:1410 (Dec). [2697

U.S. Congress. House. Select Committee on Small Business. Status of small business in retail trade (1948-1958). Staff report. Wash.: U.S. Govt. Print. Off., 1960. vii, 183 p. diagrs., tables (p. 34-183). notes. (At head of title: 86th Cong., 2d sess. Committee print.) [2698

MONEY AND CREDIT

HAROLD GLENN MOULTON. Can inflation be controlled? Wash.: Anderson Kramer Associates, 1958. xii, [2], 302 p. diagrs. notes. Includes chapters on "War-time price phenomena" in the Revolution, the Civil War, World War I, and World War II, an "Appraisal of traditional theories," and an argument that "Unless the ratio of wage rates to productive output is held stable, prices will inevitably rise." [2699

JOSEPH HARRY DORFMAN & REXFORD GUY TUGWELL. The Reverend John McVickar [1787-1868]: Christian teacher and economist. Joseph Dorfman & R. G. Tugwell, Early American policy: six Columbia contributors (N.Y.: Columbia Univ. Press, 1960), p. 99-154. facsim., port. notes. From the Columbia University quarterly "in the 1930s." On his life in New York City, his studies at Columbia College, his service as an Episcopal minister in Hyde Park and as professor of moral philosophy, rhetoric, and belles-lettres at Columbia, and his activities as a "leader in the promotion of monetary and banking reform"; with text of an essay by him (1829). [2700

GERALD T. DUNNE. Monetary decisions of the Supreme Court. New Brunswick, N.J.: Rutgers Univ. Press [1960. 10], 112 p. bibliog. (p. 109-12). (The Rutgers banking series.) A study of cases, 1819-1937. [2701

E. R. WICKER. Railroad investment before the Civil War [1830-60]. Conference on Research in Income and Wealth, Trends in the American economy in the nineteenth century, ed. William N. Parker (Princeton: Princeton Univ. Press, 1960 [Studies in income and wealth, 24]), p. 503-45. tables. notes. [2702

GEORGE MACESICH. Sources of monetary disturbances in the United States, 1834-1845. Jour. econ. hist., 20:407-26 (Sep). diagrs., table. notes. [2703

GERALD T. DUNNE. President Grant and Chief Justice Chase. St. Louis Univ. law jour., 5:539-53 (fall 1959). notes. On their disagreements concerning paper currency as legal tender, 1862-70, culminating in 2 appointments by Grant to the Supreme Court. [2704

WESLEY CLAIR MITCHELL (1874-1948). A history of the greenbacks, with special reference to the economic consequences of their issue, 1862-65. [Chicago:] Univ. of Chicago Press [1960. 12], 577 p. diagrs., tables. notes. (Chicago reprint series.) 1st ed. 1903. [2705

DANIELL BARNETT CREAMER, SERGEI P. DOBROVOLSKY, & ISRAEL BORENSTEIN. Capital in manufacturing and mining: its formation and financing [1869-1953]. Princeton: Princeton Univ. Press, 1960. liv, 344 p. diagrs., tables (part double). notes. (National Bureau of Economic Research. Studies in capital formation and financing, 6.) Includes an extensive introduction by Simon Smith Kuznets. [2706

MELVILLE JACK ULMER. Capital in transportation, communications, and public utilities: its formation and financing [1870-1950]. Princeton: Princeton Univ. Press, 1960. xxxviii, [2], 548 p. diagrs., tables (part double). notes. (National Bureau of Economic Research. Studies in capital formation and financing, 4.) [2707

GEORGE W. BISHOP, JR. Charles H[enry] Dow [1851-1902] and the Dow Theory. N.Y.: Appleton-Century-Crofts [1960]. x, [2], 359 p. port., tables. notes. Based on thesis--New York Univ. On his early life in Sterling, Conn., his work on Springfield and Providence newspapers, his settlement in New York City in 1880 as a financial reporter, his partnership with Edward D. Jones to form Dow, Jones, & Company (founded 1882), his founding of the Wall Street journal (1889), and his service as its editor till his death; with an analysis of his editorials as expressions of a system of views, and a study of interpretations and developments of "the Dow Theory" by Samuel Armstrong Nelson (in The A B C of stock speculation, 1902) and by Dow's successors as editor, William Peter Hamilton (1908 to 1929) and Report Rhea (1932 to 1939). [2708

JOHN VIRGIL LINTNER. The financing of corporations [1900-1958]. Edward Sagendorph Mason, ed., The corporation in modern society (Cambridge: Harvard Univ. Press, 1959), p. 166-201, 310-18. notes. Largely on the "problem of pension funds and institutional investors in common stocks." [2709

U.S. Business and Defense Services Administration. Water and Sewerage Industry and Utilities Division. Water resources developments capital investment values, 1900-1975. Wash.: U.S. Govt. Print. Off., 1959. 12 p. diagrs., tables. bibliog. (p. 10-11). [2710

SEYMOUR EDWIN HARRIS. The incidence of inflation: or, Who gets hurt? [1902-59]. Materials prepared in connection with the study of employment, growth, and price levels for consideration by the Joint Economic Committee, Congress of the United States (Wash.: U.S. Govt. Print. Off., 1959), p. 1-113. tables. notes. [2711

SIDNEY RHEINSTEIN. Trade whims: my fifty years on the New York Stock Exchange [1909-60. N.Y.:] Priv. print., Ronald Press Co. [1960. 6], 211 p. cartoons, ports., views. Mainly anecdotes and characterizations of individuals. Refers briefly to the author's early life in Wilmington, Del., and New York City and his studies at Princeton University. [2712

HAROLD CLAYTON M'CASE. Farm debt adjustment during the early 1930s. Agric. hist., 34:173-81 (Oct). notes. On the ever-increasing distress of farmers and their creditors, 1920-33, the Farm Credit Act of 1933, and the work of the Farm Credit Administration through 1934. [2713

GARFIELD ALBEE DREW. Drew odd lot indexes: daily, 1936-1958 inclusive; monthly, 1920-1958 inclusive. Boston: Drew Investment Associates, c1959. [28] leaves. 30x42 cm. Introduction and 27 charts recording measurements of "Trend of buying sentiment" and "Trend of selling sentiment." [2714

H. S. HOUTHAKKER. Protection against inflation [1925-55]. Materials prepared in connection with the study of employment, growth, and price levels for consideration by the Joint Economic Committee, Congress of the United States (Wash.: U.S. Govt. Print. Off., 1959), p. 115-35. tables. notes. (Study paper 8.) [2715

DAVID L. GROVE. Selective credit controls [in America, 1929-58, and abroad]. Herbert V. Prochnow, ed., The Federal Reserve System (N.Y.:

Harper [1960]), p. 141-76. tables (1 double). bibliog., notes. [2716

CHARLES EDWARD WALKER. Monetary policy and economic stability [1929-58]. Herbert V. Prochnow, ed., The Federal Reserve System (N.Y.: Harper [1960]), p. 54-74. tables. bibliog., notes. [2717

ANDREW BARR & ELMER C. KOCH. Accounting and the S. E. C. [1933-58]. Geo. Wash. law rev., 28:176-98 (Oct 1959). notes. On procedures acceptable to the Securities and Exchange Commission. [2718

MANUEL FREDERICK COHEN. Federal legislation affecting the public offering of securities [1933-58]. Geo. Wash. law rev., 28:119-75 (Oct 1959). notes. [2719

WILLIAM ORVILLE DOUGLAS. Foreword [to a symposium on the Securities and Exchange Commission]. Geo. Wash. law rev., 28:1-5 (Oct 1959). History and reminiscences of the Securities and Exchange Commission, 1933-59. [2720

RALPH EVANS FREEMAN. Postwar monetary policy [1933-58]. Ralph Evans Freeman, ed., Postwar economic trends in the United States (N.Y.: Harper [1960]), p. 51-90. tables. notes. [2721

THOMAS A. HALLERAN & JOHN N. CALDERWOOD. Effect of Federal regulation on distribution of and trading in securities [1933-58]. Geo. Wash. law rev., 28:86-118 (Oct 1959). notes. [2722

JAMES McCAULEY LANDIS. The legislative history of the Securities Act of 1933. Geo. Wash. law rev., 28:29-49 (Oct 1959). notes. Reminiscences. [2723

THOMAS G. MEEKER. Current proposals to amend the Federal securities laws. Univ. Detroit law jour., 37:335-54 (Feb). notes. On the Securities Act of 1933, the Securities Exchange Act of 1934, the Public Utility Holding Company Act of 1935, the Trust Indenture Act of 1939, the Investment Company Act of 1940, and the Investment Advisers Act of 1940. [2724

FRANZ PICK. The United States dollar [1933-60]: deflate or devalue? N.Y.: Pick Pub. Corp. [1960. 4] p., 37 leaves. col. diagrs., facsims., tables. [2725

EDWARD N. GADSBY. Historical development of the S. E. C.--the Government view [1934-59]. Geo. Wash. law rev., 28:6-17 (Oct 1959). notes. [2726

PHILIP A. LOOMIS, JR. The Securities Exchange Act of 1934 and the Investment Advisers Act of 1940. Geo. Wash. law rev., 28:214-49 (Oct 1959). notes. [2727

LOUIS LOSS. The SEC proxy rules in the courts [1934-59]. Harv. law rev., 73:1041-85, 1249-97 (Apr, May). notes. Second installment entitled: The SEC proxy rules and State law. [2728

CHARLES F. MEEHLING. Federal credit unions in the United States [since 1934]: an analysis. Ann Arbor: University Microfilms, 1957 [i.e. 1960]. Positive microfilm of typescript. [187] leaves. Thesis--New York Univ. Abstracted: Dissert. abstracts, 21:795-6 (Oct). [2729

AVERY BERLOW COHAN. The price of underwriting services on corporate debt, 1935-1952. Ann Arbor, Mich.: University Microfilms, 1959 [i.e. 1960]. Positive microfilm of typescript. xii, 329 leaves. diagrs., tables. bibliog. (leaves 326-9). Thesis--Columbia Univ. Abstracted: Dissert. abstracts, 20:3557 (Mar). [2730

YEHUDA GRUNFELD (1930-60). The determinants of corporate investment. Arnold C. Harberger, ed., The demand for durable goods (Chicago: Univ. of Chicago Press [1960]), p. 209-66. diagrs., tables. notes. Econometric study of "year-to-year variations in investment expenditures" by Atlantic Refining Company, United States Steel Corporation, Union Oil Company of California, Goodyear Tire and Rubber Company, Diamond Match Company, American Steel Foundries, General Motors Corporation, and General Electric Company, 1935-54. [2731

MELVILLE PETERSON. A comparative study in debenture and mortgage bond financing [1937-39, 1946-54]. Ann Arbor: University Microfilms, 1959 [i.e. 1960]. Positive microfilm of typescript. [193] leaves. Thesis--Univ. of Illinois. Abstracted: Dissert. abstracts, 20:3113-14 (Feb). [2732

ALAN R. WEINER. The NASD--an unique experiment in cooperative regulation. Va. law rev., 46:1586-1600 (Dec). notes. On the National Association of Securities Dealers, Inc.,

1939-60, as an organization for self-regulation. [2733

MARC A. WHITE. National Association of Securities Dealers, Inc. [1939-59]. Geo. Wash. law rev., 28: 250-65 (Oct 1959). notes. [2734

LAWRENCE M. GREENE. The uniform offering price of mutual fund shares under the Investment Company Act of 1940. Univ. Detroit law jour., 37:369-89 (Feb). notes. [2735

FRANZ PICK. The United States dollar: requiem for a dead half. N.Y.: Pick Pub. Corp. [1958. 2], 22, [4] leaves. diagrs. On the "shrinkage of the Dollar" to less than 49 percent of its former purchasing power, 1940-57, and the probability that the Government will be forced to devaluate it. [2736

BEN MAJOR ALVORD. A study of the financing of the U.S. trunk airlines, 1946-55. Ann Arbor: University Microfilms, 1960. Positive microfilm of typescript. [399] leaves. Thesis--Univ. of Illinois. Abstracted: Dissert. abstracts, 21:1411 (Dec). [2737

ELI SHAPIRO & MORRIS MENDELSON. A decade of corporate capital investment: 1946-1955. Ralph Evans Freeman, ed., Postwar economic trends in the United States (N.Y.: Harper [1960]), p. 309-36. diagrs., table. notes. [2738

WALTER J. BLUM. The Interstate Commerce Commission as lawmaker: the development of standards for modification of railroad securities [1948-58]. Univ. Chicago law rev., 27: 603-60 (summer). notes. [2739

Banking

HERMAN EDWARD KROOSS. The historical background of the American banking system [1782-1913]. Herbert V. Prochnow, ed., The Federal Reserve System (N.Y.: Harper [1960]), p. 1 - 18. bibliog., notes. [2740

RALPH CHARLES HENRY CATTERALL (1866-1914). The Second Bank of the United States [1816-40. Chicago:] Univ. of Chicago Press [1960. 6], 538 p. diagrs., map, tables. bibliog. (p. 513-26), notes. (Chicago reprint series.) 1st ed. 1902. On events leading to its establishment, 1812-16, its activities under its successive presidents (William Jones, Langdon Cheves, Nicholas Biddle), its dissolution in 1836, and the discharge of its final obligations, 1836-40. [2741

CARTER HARRY GOLEMBE. The deposit insurance legislation of 1933: an examination of its antecedents and its purposes. Pol. science quar. 75: 181-200 (Jun). notes. On "bank-obligation insurance systems" and proposals between 1829 and 1933. [2742

JAMES L. CROUTHAMEL. Three Philadelphians in the Bank War: a neglected chapter in American lobbying. Pa. hist., 27:361-78 (Oct). notes. On activities of Thomas Cadwalader, John Sergeant, and Horace Binney, 1831-32. [2743

GEORGE W. COLEMAN Legal reserve requirements [1837-1959]. Herbert V. Prochnow, ed., The Federal Reserve System (N.Y.: Harper [1960]), p. 75-89. table. bibliog., notes. [2744

ALLAN NEVINS. "... largeness of action ... largeness of idea." John Arthur Garraty, ed., The unforgettable Americans (Great Neck, N.Y.: Channel Press [1960]), p. 275-9. On J. Pierpont Morgan (1837-1913) as a banker. [2745

GILBERT THOMAS STEPHENSON (born 1884). Reflections of a trustman. N.Y.: Trust Division, American Bankers Assoc. [1960. 10], 297 p. port. notes. From The trust bulletin, Dec. 1956-May 1960. On the author's early life in North Carolina, his studies at Wake Forest College and the Harvard Law School, his work as a lawyer in Winston-Salem, and his service as an official of the Wachovia Bank and Trust Company, Raleigh (1919-29), and the Equitable Trust Company, Wilmington, Del. (1929-36), and as Director of the Trust Research Department of the Stonier Graduate School of Banking of the American Bankers Association (1937-50). [2746

GORDON WELLS McKINLEY. Effects of Federal Reserve policy on nonmonetary financial institutions [1900-1958]. Herbert V. Prochnow, ed., The Federal Reserve System (N.Y.: Harper [1960]), p. 204-25. diagr. bibliog., notes. [2747

JAMES N. LAND. The Federal Reserve Act [1913-59]. Robert V. Prochow, ed., The Federal Reserve System (N.Y.: Harper [1960]), p. 19-32. maps, table. bibliog. [2748

LESTER VERNON CHANDLER. Benjamin Strong [1872-1928], central banker. Wash.: Brookings

Institution, 1958. x, [2], 495 p. port. On his work as Governor of the Federal Reserve Bank of New York from its founding in 1914 till his death. [2749

DAVID H. McKINLEY. The discount rate and rediscount policy [1914-59]. Herbert V. Prochnow, ed., The Federal Reserve System (N.Y.: Harper [1960]), p. 90-112. diagrs., table. bibliog., notes. [2750

THOMAS O. WAAGE. Service and supervisory functions of the Federal Reserve System [1914-58]. Herbert V. Prochnow, ed., The Federal Reserve System (N.Y.: Harper [1960]), p. 226-50. bibliog., notes. [2751

BENJAMIN HAGGOTT BECKHART, ed. Business loans of American commercial banks. N.Y.: Ronald Press Co. [1959]. vi, 453 p. diagrs., forms, tables. bibliog. (p. 431-7), notes. Fourteen chapters, by various members of the banking profession, on current practices; with "Introduction" and "Business loans: economic growth and stability," by the editor, reviewing the history of business loans from 1919 to 1957. [2752

C. RICHARD YOUNGDAHL. Open-market operations [by Federal Reserve Banks, 1922-57]. Herbert V. Prochnow, ed., The Federal Reserve System (N.Y.: Harper [1960]) p. 113-40. bibliog., notes. [2753

MABLE T. WALLICH & HENRY CHRISTOPHER WALLICH. The Federal Reserve System during the 1930's [1929-37]. Herbert V. Prochnow, ed., The Federal Reserve System (N.Y.: Harper [1960]), p. 317-37. bibliog. [2754

HOWARD RALPH NEVILLE. The Detroit banking collapse of 1933. East Lansing, 1960. [6], 67, [2] p. diagrs., tables. notes (p. 63-7). (Michigan State University. Bureau of Business and Economic Research. Occasional paper 2.) On 5 abuses in the practices of the Guardian Detroit Union Group, Inc., and the Detroit Bankers Company, and the shares of responsibility of these groups, the State of Michigan, the U.S. Government, Senator James Couzens, and Henry Ford for precipitating the collapse, which initiated the national banking holiday. [2755

CHRISTOPHER W. WILSON. Regulations of the Board of Governors [of the Federal Reserve System, 1934-59]. Herbert V. Prochnow, ed., The Federal Reserve System (N.Y.: Harper [1960]), p. 251-72. tables. bibliog., notes. [2756

JULES IRWIN BOGEN. The Federal Reserve System since 1940. Herbert V. Prochnow, ed., The Federal Reserve System (N.Y.: Harper [1960]), p. 338-54. bibliog., notes. [2757

ALBERT MURRAY LEVENSON. Differentials in interest rate and the cost of commercial bank lending [1942, 1946, 1955, 1957]. Ann Arbor: University Microfilms, 1959 [i.e. 1960]. Positive microfilm of typescript. 96 leaves. mount. diagr., tables (1 fold.). bibliog. (leaves 83-96). Thesis--Columbia Univ. Abstracted: Dissert. abstracts, 20:3559-60 (Mar). [2758

Insurance

The FIRST life insurance company in America. Insurance law jour., 1959: 2-4 (Jan 1959). On the Presbyterian Ministers' Fund, 1759-1959, established in Philadelphia as the Corporation for the Relief of Poor & Distressed Presbyterian Ministers and for the Poor & Distressed Widows & Children of Presbyterian Ministers. [2759

INSTITUTE OF LIFE INSURANCE, New York. Division of Statistics and Research. The historical statistics of life insurance in the United States, 1759 to 1958. N.Y. [1960]. 23 p. tables. bibliog. (p. 23), notes. Tables showing number of life-insurance companies (1759-1958), life-insurance sales by the companies (1854-1958), life insurance in force in U.S. life-insurance companies (1815-1958), life insurance in force in the United States (1815-1958), assets, earning rate, liabilities, capital, and surplus of U.S. life-insurance companies (1854-1958), income of the companies (1854-1958), and disbursements of the companies (1854-1958); and other information. [2760

HAWTHORNE DANIEL. The Hartford of Hartford: an insurance company's part in a century and a half of American history. N.Y.: Random House [1960]. viii, 312 p. facsims., ports., tables, views. notes. On the Hartford Fire Insurance Company, 1810-1960. [2761

O. KELLEY ANDERSON. New England Life: 125 years of mutual life insurance in America. N.Y.: Newcomen Soc. in North America, 1960. 24 p. ports., views. On the New England Mutual

Life Insurance Company, Boston, 1835-1960. [2762

HOME LIFE INSURANCE COMPANY, New York. The story of the Home Life Insurance Company, 1860-1960. [N.Y., 1960.] 48 p. diagr., facsims., ports., views. 21x24 cm. [2763

J. M. KESSLINGER. Guardian of a century, 1860-1960. N.Y.: Guardian Life Insurance Co. of America [1960. 6], 125, [6] p. ports., tables, views. On the Guardian Life Insurance Company of America, with headquarters in New York City. [2764

MILDRED FAIRBANKS STONE. The teacher who changed an industry: a biography of Dr. Solomon S[tephen] Huebner [born 1882], of the University of Pennsylvania. Homewood, Ill.: R. D. Irwin, 1960. ix, 393 p. maps, ports., views. bibliog. (p. 375-9), notes (p. 381-4). On his early life in Wisconsin, his studies at the University of Wisconsin, his graduate studies of economics at the University of Pennsylvania, his service as Chairman of the Insurance Department, University of Pennsylvania and as an executive of the American College of Life Underwriters, and his work as a consultant on insurance to various companies and government organizations; with a list (p. 357-73) of publications by and about him. [2765

HALSEY D. JOSEPHSON. Discrimination: a study of recent developments in American life insurance. N.Y.: Wesley Press [1960]. 216 p. On legislation in New York and the United States that "prohibits a life insurance company from making or permitting any discrimination between individuals of the same class or of equal expectation of life, in the amount or payment or return of premiums or rates charged for policies of insurance," 1889-1959, and methods of evading the law. [2766

GEORGE EMANUEL MANNERS, SR. History of Life Insurance Company of Georgia, 1891-1955. Ann Arbor: University Microfilms, 1959 [i.e. 1960]. Positive microfilm of typescript. xx, 462 leaves. diagrs., tables. bibliog. (leaves 448-62). Thesis--Emory Univ. Abstracted: Dissert. abstracts, 20: 3272 (Feb). [2767

DAVIS WEINERT GREGG. An analysis of group life insurance [1910-48]. Phila.: Univ. of Pennsylvania Press, 1950. xvii, [3], 268 p. tables. bibliog. (p. 251-8), notes. Based on thesis--Univ. of Pennsylvania. [2768

EASO JOHN. Investment experiences of twenty-five selected fire insurance companies, 1927 to 1955. Ann Arbor: University Microfilms, 1959 [i.e. 1960]. Positive microfilm of typescript. [412] leaves. Thesis--Northwestern Univ. Abstracted: Dissert. abstracts, 20:2621 (Jan). [2769

ALFRED M. SKOLNIK. Income-loss protection against short-term sickness: 1948-58. Social security bul., 23(1):3-10 (Jan). tables. notes. [2770

Numismatics

CHARLES FRENCH. Numismatics. Hobbies, 64(11)-65(10): monthly installments (Jan-Dec). Information for and advice to collectors of coins. [2771

HUGH McCOWN KNIGHT. A simplified guide to collecting American coins. ... Illustrated by the author. Garden City, N.Y.: Hanover House, 1959. 157 p. coins. [2772

TED N. WEISSBUCH. Eagles, jackasses, and other animals [represented on American coins]. Numismatic scrapbook, 26:2204-7 (Aug). coins. bibliog. [2773

RINALDO ALEXANDER WILSON, SR. The twenty-sixth edition of the American coin book and standard retail premium list of all United States coins. Los Angeles: American Numismatic Co. [1958]. 109 p. coins. 1st ed. 1933. List of values (fair, good, very good, fine, very fine, uncirculated) of U.S. coins, 1793-1957, arranged by denomination from half cents to double eagles; with information about colonial coins, 1652-1776, State coins, and paper money. [2774

U.S. Library of Congress. Legislative Reference Service. The American dollar bill [1861 ff.]. Numismatist, 73:1186-90 (Aug). facsims. From the Congressional record, 14 Jan. 1960. Includes an account of the Great Seal of the United States, 1776-82, and its use on all American dollar bills. [2775

ERIC P. NEWMAN. The source of the Nova Constellatio copper coinage [1786]. Numismatic scrapbook, 26:6-8 (Jan). coins. notes. Concludes that these coins were struck in Birmingham from dies made there by Thomas Wyon, that they were imported for American circulation as a private business venture of Gouverneur

Morris of New York, and that they had no relationship to the coinage of the Mint of North America other than being a copy of the design of its silver patterns. [2776

WALTER E. THOMPSON. The half dime of 1792. Numismatic scrapbook, 26:299-305 (Feb). coin, ports. On the lack of evidence for the legends that George and Martha Washington contributed their silver plate for use by the Mint and that Martha Washington is represented by the female head on the obverse. [2777

LEROY BURNETTE. Famous symbols on coins: thirteen stars! [1793-1945]. Numismatic scrapbook, 26:1569-72 (Jun). [2778

LYNN GLASER. Some undiscovered coins. Numismatic scrapbook, 26: 2513-17 (Sep). coin. bibliog. On reasons why various American coins officially reported to have been struck are not now known to exist, 1799-1877. [2779

LYNN GLASER. The time we nearly lost the Mint. Numismatic scrapbook, 26:3445-49 (Nov). On a bill to abolish the Mint and to contract with a private concern for providing coins, 1802; with letters from Elias Boudinot, Director of the Mint, and Robert Scott, Chief Engraver of the Mint, to the Secretary of the Treasury, 27 Feb.-22 Mar. 1802. [2780

TED N. WEISSBUCH. Notes on The confidence-man's counterfeit detector. Emerson Soc. quar., 19: leaves 16-18 (2d quar.). On small serial publications listing "locally uncurrent bank notes" and counterfeit, spurious, and altered bank notes, 1805-63, and the reference to these in Melville's novel (1857). [2781

LYNN GLASER. History of United States proof sets [of coins, 1817-1953]. Numismatic scrapbook, 26:3133-42 (Oct). tables. [2782

WALTER E. THOMPSON. The trouble at New Orleans Mint--1839. Numismatic scrapbook, 26:629-34 (Mar). view. On evidence suggesting collusion between political appointees to the Mint for the purpose of defrauding the Government. [2783

ARLIE R. SLABAUGH. Advertising money. Numismatic scrapbook, 26: 1890-1903, 2503-5 (Jul, Sep). coins, facsims. On "coins and paper money which are either genuine specimens bearing impressions of advertising or reproductions of actual coins and paper money (or similar to) which bear advertising." Includes lists of examples as early as 1848 and as late as the 1950s. [2784

WALTER E. THOMPSON. Our coinage, 1848-1849. Numismatic scrapbook, 26:3156-62 (Nov). coins, views. On the numismatic effects of the discovery of gold in California. [2785

FRED R. MARCKHOFF. Obsolete notes with interesting histories. Numismatic scrapbook, 26:256-7, 951-4, 2455-7 (Jan, Apr, Aug). facsims., map. On a note of the Kansas Valley Bank of Atchison with portraits of William B. Waddell and William H. Russell (1859?), currency of the Confederate mail packets (1861-62), and notes of banks at De Soto, Neb. (settled in 1854, abandoned ca. 1870, once a rival of Omaha for river trade). [2786

WALTER E. THOMPSON. The copper nickel cent. Numismatic scrapbook, 26:2489-92 (Sep). coins. On the flying eagle cent of 1857, designed to eliminate the Spanish dollar and its fractional parts from circulation. [2787

CHARLES FRENCH. U.S. paper money [1861-91]. Hobbies, 65(7):102-3 (Sep). [2788

PHILIP HARTLEY CHASE. Confederate Treasury notes: the chemicograph backs. Numismatist, 73:403-11 (Apr). facsims. bibliog. Reproduces the agreement between S. Straker & Sons, London, and Joseph Walker, Confederate agent, for the production of plates for printing the backs of 5-, 10-, 50-, 100-, and 500-dollar notes, 1 Sept. 1863, describes a set of the plates with their designs, explains why they were never used, reproduces a print made of each plate by the author, and accounts for the coined word "chemicographed." [2789

HARRY X. BOOSEL. 1873-1873 [2 styles of "3"] ... open and closed 3's [on gold and silver coins]. Numismatic scrapbook, 26:326-7 (Feb). table. [2790

STEPHEN GOTTHEIL RICH. Features of the 15 cent bank note issues. S. P. A. jour., 20:397 (May 1958). Evidence that all copies of the 1873 plate "which served for the 1873 and 1879 15 cent stamps, in use until 1890," except possibly some copies before 1874, show "a line, area, or spot in color" incised into the die in "the lower lip of the C" in "Cents";

and conjecture that the mark is not "the actual 'secret mark' by which the 15 cent stamp of 1873 and 1879 was to be demarcated from that of 1870" but is produced by a loose sliver of metal on the dye. [2791

CHARLES M. JOHNSON. Collecting small size paper money. Numismatist, 73:1619-31 (Nov). facsims. tables. On "small size paper currency," 1928-59; with lists of types and varieties, denominations, and series. [2792

NUMISMATIC SCRAPBOOK MAGAZINE. Twenty-five years. Numismatic scrapbook, 26:1-5 (Jan). History of Numismatic scrapbook magazine; with a reduced facsimile of vol. 1, no. 1, Jan. 1935. [2793

WALTER H. BREEN. The 1943 bronze cents. Numismatic scrapbook, 26: 306-10 (Feb). coins. Evidence that a few such coins were issued by error in the Mint and that they can be distinguished from counterfeits. [2794

CHARLES FRENCH. Numismatists! and the 1943 copper cent. Hobbies, 65(10):102-3, 123 (Dec). [2795

Economics

HENRY WILLIAM SPIEGEL, ed. The rise of American economic thought. Phila.: Chilton Co., Book Division [1960]. ix, [3], 202 p. tables. bibliog. (p. 187-96), notes. Collection of reprinted original writings on economic doctrine, 1639-1885. [2796

JOSEPH HARRY DORFMAN & REXFORD GUY TUGWELL. Henry Vethake [1792-1866]: Jacksonian Ricardian. Joseph Dorfman & Rexford Guy Tugwell, Early American policy: six Columbia contributors (N.Y.: Columbia Univ. Press, 1960), p. 155-204. port. notes. From the Columbia University quarterly, "1930s." On his emigration as a child from British Guiana with his family, his studies at Columbia College, his teaching of mathematics at the College of New Jersey, of economics at Dickinson College, and of mathematics at the University of the City of New York, and his service as President of Washington College (now Washington and Lee University) and as Provost of the University of Pennsylvania; with some account of his economic doctrines. [2797

JAMES LEIBY. Carroll [Davidson] Wright [1840-1909] and labor reform: the origin of labor statistics. Cambridge: Harvard Univ. Press, 1960. ix, 242, [2] p. bibliog. (p. 218-21), notes. (Harvard historical monographs, 46.) On his early life in Dunbarton, N.H., his Civil War service as commanding officer of the 14th Regiment of New Hampshire Volunteers, his legal practice in Reading, Mass., his service as head of the Massachusetts Bureau of Statistics of Labor (1873-88) and U.S. Commissioner of Labor (1885-1905) and as President of Clark College (1902 ff.) and a trustee of the Carnegie Institution of Washington (1902-8), his special concern with statistical investigation and "skepticism about theory," and his utterances on "labor reforms and industrial disputes." [2798

LAFAYETTE GEORGE HARTER, JR. John R[ogers] Commons [1862-1945], institutional economist. Ann Arbor: University Microfilms, 1960. Positive microfilm of typescript. [363] leaves. Thesis--Stanford Univ. Abstracted: Dissert. abstracts, 20:4295-6 (May). On his teaching in the University of Wisconsin, his studies of labor, his drafting of labor legislation for the State of Wisconsin, and his promotion of "progress away from laissez-faire individualism along the road to the welfare state." [2799

HERBERT RICHARD RUNYON. The economics of Irving Fisher [1867-1947]: the theory of value and the capitalistic processes. Ann Arbor: University Microfilms, 1960. Positive microfilm of typescript. [425] leaves. Thesis--Univ. of Michigan. Abstracted: Dissert. abstracts, 20: 4564-5 (Jun). [2800

PAUL ANTHONY SAMUELSON. American economics. Ralph Evans Freeman, ed., Postwar economic trends in the United States (N.Y.: Harper [1960]), p. 31-50. notes. On the American characteristics of economic study and theory in America, 1881-1960. [2801

JAMES P. CAVIN & RONALD L. MIGHELL. John Donald Black, 1883-1960. Jour. farm econ., 42:223-4 (May). On his contributions to and teaching of agricultural economics. [2802

ABRAM LINCOLN HARRIS (1899-1963). Economics and social reform. N.Y.: Harper [1958]. xvi, [2], 357 p. notes. Includes critical chapters on Thorstein Veblen and John R. Commons, 1899-1920s. [2803

EDWIN EMIL WITTE. Selig Perlman [1888-1959]. Indus. and labor rel. rev., 13:335-7 (Apr). port. On his study and teaching of economics at the University of Wisconsin, 1908-59, and his contributions to the theory and the history of the labor movement. [2804

JOSEPH HARRY DORFMAN. The economic mind in American civilization [1606-1933]. Volumes four and five, 1918-1933. N.Y.: Viking Press, 1959. 2 v. x, 398, xxxiv; [4], xxxixxli, [3], 401-776, [2], xlv-lxxxviii p. notes (p. xi-xxxiv, xlv-lxiv). Twenty-five topical chapters arranged in 2 periods: "The era of adjustment and progress, 1918-1929," and "The Great Depression, 1929-1933." Concludes a series of 5 volumes, 1946-59. [2805

VERITAS FOUNDATION, New York. Keynes at Harvard: economic deception as a political credo. N.Y. [1960. 2], 114 p. bibliog. (p. 107-8), notes. Argument that the "obscurity" of John Maynard Keynes "is deliberate ... that Keynesism is not an economic theory" but "a weapon of political conspiracy" to accomplish "the intertwining of socialist and Soviet interests in the United States"; and that since the 1920s the Keynsians (including Professors Joseph Alois Schumpeter, Alvin Hansen, Seymour E. Harris, Sumner H. Slichter, and John Kenneth Galbraith) have taken "advantage of the traditional tolerance of Harvard ... to infiltrate the faculty with their supporters and preach their socialist doctrine" and have "purged the Economics Department at least of all vestiges of free economic theories, advocates and text-books." [2806

DANIEL BELL. The prospects of American capitalism: on Keynes, Schumpeter, and Galbraith. Daniel Bell, The end of ideology: on the exhaustion of political ideas in the fifties (Glencoe, Ill.: Free Press [1960]), p. 68-85. notes. On the effect of John Maynard Keynes's doctrines in America, and the confirmatory and rebutting publications that they have inspired since the 1930s. [2807

THEODORE CHRISTIAN HOEPFNER. Economics of Agrarianism. Miss. quar., 13:61-8 (winter). notes. On the "Fugitive-Agrarian position" as stated in I'll take my stand (1930), Who owns America? (1936), and Fugitives' reunion (1959). [2808

TIPTON RAY SNAVELY. Notes on the founding of the Southern Economic Association. South. econ. jour., 26: 263-72 (Apr). notes. Based upon the author's recollections and correspondence, 1930-36. [2809

Elements of Production

ENTERPRISE

STUART WEEMS BRUCHEY. The inadequacy of profit maximization as a model of business behavior. Bus. hist. rev., 34:495-7 (winter). Historical evidence "that businessmen have often been unwilling to seek maximum profits at the cost of security" and that "If they have sought to maximize profits they have also sought to minimize risks"; and call for "a careful examination of particular investment decisions in the light of their relevant internal and external contexts as a prelude to the fashioning of a model more suited to historical actuality than the concept of profit maximization." [2810

ETNA MARIE KELLEY. The business founding date directory.... Alphabetical and chronological sections. Scarsdale, N.Y.: Morgan & Morgan [1954]. x, 228 p. List of "more than 9,000 business organizations in the United States founded between the years 1687 and 1915, inclusive, all in existence when the manuscript was delivered to the typesetter. Separately published: Supplement to the business founding date directory. ... Including founding dates for years 1916, 1917, 1918, 1931, 1932, and 1933. N.Y.: Morgan & Morgan [1956]. 16 p. [2811

CHARLES W. KAPPES, JR. The Second American Revolution: free enterprise under the Bill of Rights. Am. Bar Assoc. jour., 46:597-602 (Jun). port. bibliog., notes. On "governmental regulation of business in what is considered the national interest," 1789-1959. [2812

IRENE D. NEU. Erastus Corning, merchant and financier, 1794-1872. Ithaca, N.Y.: Cornell Univ. Press [1960]. xi, 212 p. port. bibliog. (p. 195-205), notes. On his early life in Norwich, Conn., and Chatham, N.Y., and his work as a merchant in Troy, a merchant, banker, and political leader in Albany, owner of New York iron works, organizer of the New York Central Railroad and other railroads, and speculator in lands in Michigan, Wisconsin, and other Middle Western States. [2813

RAYMOND W. SETTLE & MARY ANNA (LUND) SETTLE. Napoleon of the West. Ann. Wyo., 32:4-47 (Apr). facsims., ports., view. notes. On William Hepburn Russell (1812-72), native of Vermont who removed to Lexington, Mo., in 1830, clerk in J. & R. Aull's store there, partner in 2 other stores (one bankrupt in 1845), Postmaster of Lexington, partner in a freighting enterprise to deliver supplies to Santa Fe and to Fort Hall, Idaho, partner with Alexander Majors and William B. Waddell in obtaining a monopoly of military freighting west from Leavenworth (1855-57), organizer with them of the Leavenworth & Pike's Peak Express Company (1859) and the Central Overland California & Pike's Peak Express Company (1859-62, including the Pony Express, 1860-61), his appropriation "to his own use" of $830,000 in bonds of the Indian Trust Fund of the Interior Department (1861), the bankruptcy of all his enterprises, the failure of his mining and other ventures in Colorado during the Civil War and of his brokerage house in New York in 1866, his last bankruptcy (1868), and his death in Missouri. [2814

MONROE LIPPMAN. The American playwright looks at business. Educ. theatre jour., 12:98-106 (May). On American plays "whose main theme was Business," 1819-1936, most of which are satirical or denunciatory. [2815

MORRIS ALBERT ADELMAN. Some aspects of corporate enterprise [1820-1958]. Ralph Evans Freeman, ed., Postwar economic trends in the United States (N.Y.: Harper [1960]), p. 289-307. notes. [2816

KENNETH R. MILLISOR. State immunity from tort liability as affected by competitive business activity. Ohio State law jour., 21:648-66 (autumn). notes. On the extent of "a state's immunity when it engages in active competition with private enterprise," 1824-1960. [2817

JAMES HIGH. William Andrews Clark [1839-1925], Westerner: an interpretative vignette. Ariz. and the West, 2: 245-64 (autumn). port. notes. On his life in Montana as a merchant, a banker, and an organizer of mining enterprises, 1862-1901, his service as Senator from Montana, and his widespread and profitable investments in East and West. [2818

MORRIS ALLISON BEALLE. House of Rockefeller: how a shoestring was run into 200 billion dollars in two generations. Wash.: All America House [1959]. 287, [1] p. On the business enterprises of William Avery Rockefeller, his son John Davison Rockefeller, and the latter's descendants, 1853-1958, and the ventures of some of them into politics. [2819

RICHARD GARRETT SHERMAN. Charles G[ates] Dawes: an entrepreneurial biography, 1865-1951. Ann Arbor: University Microfilms, 1960. Positive microfilm of typescript. [384] leaves. Thesis--State Univ. of Iowa. Abstracted: Dissert. abstracts, 21:1408-9 (Dec). On his work as founder of a system of gas plants in the Middle West and president of a Chicago bank, as an Allied purchasing agent in World War I, as Chairman of the German Reparations Commission, and as Director of the Budget. [2820

HAL BRIDGES. The idea of the robber barons in American history [1865-1900]. Donald Sheehan & Harold C. Syrett, eds., Essays in American historiography: papers presented in honor of Allan Nevins (N.Y.: Columbia Univ. Press, 1960), p. 138-52. notes. [2821

FRANK ROCKWELL BARNETT. Management's role in national survival [in America, 1870-1959, and abroad]. Karl M. Ruppenthal, ed., Revolution in transportation (Stanford, Calif.: Graduate School of Business, Stanford Univ. [1960]), p. 1-11. [2822

MICHAEL MILLGATE. The novelist and the businessman: Henry James, Edith Wharton, Frank Norris. Studi americani, 5:161-89. On their novels about businessmen, 1879-1913, their delineation of a supposed antinomy between "money values" and "human relationships" (especially with women) as a characteristic of businessmen, and their lack of success in dealing with the business activities of businessmen as a theme of fiction. [2823

EUGENE VICTOR ROSTOW. To whom and for what ends is corporate management responsible? Edward Sagendorph Mason, ed., The corporation in modern society (Cambridge: Harvard

Univ. Press, 1959), p. 46-71, 302-5. notes. On the legal aspects of the development of "endocratic business enterprises" in America, ca. 1880 to 1958. [2824

KINGMAN BREWSTER, JR. The corporation and economic federalism. Edward Sagendorph Mason, ed., The corporation in modern society (Cambridge: Harvard Univ. Press, 1959), p. 72-84, 305-7. notes. On the "political and social consequences of the 'sovereignty' of the modern corporation," 1890-1958. [2825

WALTER HENRY EDWARD JAEGER. Joint ventures: origin, nature, and development [since ca. 1890]. Am. Univ. law rev., 9:1-23 (Jan). notes. [2826

JOHN ARTHUR GARRATY. "... a truly public-spirited citizen." John Arthur Garraty, ed., The unforgettable Americans (Great Neck, N.Y.: Channel Press [1960]), p. 298-301. On the work of George W. Perkins as an executive of the New York Life Insurance Company, the United States Steel Corporation, and the International Harvester Company, and his activities in national politics, 1892-1920. [2827

RALPH HEWINS. The richest American: J[ay] Paul Getty [born 1892]. N.Y.: Dutton, 1960. 404 p. ports., views. On his early life in Minneapolis and San Diego, his studies at Oxford University, his activities in finance and in land and oil speculation, and his 5 marriages and other incidents of his private life; with excerpts from his diary. [2828

LOREN BARITZ. The servants of power: a history of the use of social science in American industry [1895-1957]. Middletown Conn.: Wesleyan Univ. Press [1960]. xii, 273 p. notes (p. 211-60). Based on thesis--Univ. of Wisconsin, 1956. On the employment of social scientists, particularly psychologists and sociologists, by industries as tools "for the purpose of human control" in management and marketing; with an account of the professional development of industrial psychology and industrial sociology. [2829

SOL ALEXANDER RIPPA. Dissemination of the free-enterprise creed to American schools. School jour., 67: 409-21 (winter 1959). notes. On the distribution of materials to American schools as part of the public-relations program of the National Association of Manufacturers, 1895-1959. [2830

ROY E. LARSEN. The new managers of business: the tycoon is dead. Harvard alumni bul., 54:625-9 (10 May 1952). cartoons. On the "new American business manager," late 1890s to 1952, and the differences between him and his predecessors. [2831

RALPH L. COLLINS. The School of Business [Indiana University, 1902-60]: a little history and some suggestions. [Bloomington: School of Business, Indiana Univ., 1960.] 22 p. (Indiana business report 32.) [2832

JOHN THOMAS MAHONEY. The story of George [Wilcken] Romney [born 1907]: builder, salesman, crusader. By Tom Mahoney. N.Y.: Harper [1960]. ix, [3], 275 p. ports., tables, views. notes (p. 248-54). On his early life in a Mormon settlement in Chihuahua (disbanded in 1912 as a result of the Mexican Revolution) and in El Paso, Oakley (Idaho), and Salt Lake City, his studies at the University of Utah, his Mormon mission to Scotland and England (1927-28), his work in Washington on the staff of Sen. David Walsh of Massachusetts and later for the Aluminum Company of America (1929-40), his work in Detroit as manager of an office of the Automobile Manufacturers Association (1940-48), executive of Nash-Kelvinator (1948-54), and chief executive of American Motors Corporation (formed in 1954 by merger of Nash-Kelvinator and the Hudson Motor Company), his discontinuance of the Nash and the Hudson, his development of the Rambler, and his presentation of "the case for the compact car." [2833

DONALD COURTNEY STREEVER. Capacity utilization and business investment. [Urbana, Ill., 1960. 8], 76 p. diagrs., tables. bibliog. (p. 73-6), notes. (University of Illinois. Bureau of Economic and Business Research. Bulletin series, 86.) Based on thesis--Univ. of Illinois, 1957. An "analysis of the relationship of business capital expenditures to variations in the rate of utilization of productive capacity," 1920-55. [2834

WILLIAM LLOYD WARNER. The corporation man. Edward Sagendorph Mason, ed., The corporation in modern society (Cambridge: Harvard Univ. Press, 1959), p. 106-21, 309. notes. On the educational, "economic and social backgrounds" of American "business leaders," 1928-58. [2835

RALPH GENT WELLS. Bureau of Business Research [Collge of Business Administration, Boston University, 1928-52]. Boston Univ. graduate jour., 1:21-2 (May 1952). [2836

DAVID T. BAZELON. Portrait of a business generalist. Commentary, 29: 277-94 (Apr). Definition of "generalist" and illustration by the career of Arnold M. Grant since 1929, lawyer in New York and Los Angeles, "general expert" in "the merchandising of corporate values," and middleman in the assignment of corporate legal problems to law firms. [2837

CHARLES SIDNEY COTTLE & WILLIAM TATE WHITMAN. Corporate earning power and market valuation, 1935-1955. [By] Sidney Cottle [and] Tate Whitman. Durham: Duke Univ. Press, 1959. [12], 201 p. diagrs. (part col., part fold.), tables. 23x31 cm. Analysis of data for 150 companies. [2838

STEWART H. BENEDICT. The business novel [1945-59]. Mich. Acad. Science, Papers, 45:447-53. notes. [2839

LABOR

SANFORD COHEN. Labor in the United States [1619-1960]. Columbus, Ohio: C. E. Merrill Books [1960]. xii, 676 p. tables. bibliogs., notes. Topical study drawing "heavily from the fields of history, sociology, and political science" as well as economics. [2840

FOSTER RHEA DULLES. Labor in America: a history [1630-1960]. Second revised edition. N.Y.: Crowell, 1960. [12], 435 p. bibliog. (p. 414-22). 1st ed. 1949. [2841

MARCUS WILSON JERNEGAN (1872-1949). Economic and social influence of the indentured servant [1635-1777]. Marcus W. Jernegan, Laboring and dependent classes in colonial America, 1607-1783 (N.Y.: Ungar [1960]), p. 45-56. notes. From Harper's monthly magazine, Oct. 1913. [2842

FRANK KABELA, JR. The labor press: its history, nature, and influence [1828-1960]. Labor law jour., 11: 407-14 (May). notes. [2843

J. KENNETH DAVIES. A study of the labor philosophy developed within the Church of Jesus Christ of Latter-Day Saints [since 1830]. Ann Arbor: University Microfilms, 1960. Positive microfilm of typescript. [455] leaves. Thesis--Univ. of Southern California. Abstracted: Dissert. abstracts, 20: 3975 (Apr). [2844

ABRAHAM J. SIEGEL & CHARLES A. MYERS. Continuity and change in American labor problems [1840-1958]. Ralph Evans Freeman, ed., Postwar economic trends in the United States (N.Y.: Harper [1960]), p. 189-234. notes. [2845

DAVID BRODY. Steelworkers in America: the nonunion era [1866-1929]. Cambridge: Harvard Univ. Press, 1960. viii, [4], 303, [3] p. bibliog. (p. 281-90), notes. (Harvard historical monographs, 45.) Revision of thesis--Harvard Univ. [2846

RICHARD ALLEN LESTER. Where is labor going in the '60's? University, 3:9-11 (winter). cartoons. Includes historical information, 1896-1960. [2847

GERALD D. NASH. Franklin D. Roosevelt and labor: the World War I origins of early New Deal policy. Labor hist., 1:39-52 (winter). notes. On his experience with labor problems while serving as Assistant Secretary of the Navy and in other official capacities, 1917-18. [2848

OTEY M. SCRUGGS. The first Mexican farm labor program. Ariz. and the West, 2:319-26 (winter). notes. On the importation of farm laborers under contract in World War I and later, 1917-23. [2849

IRVING BERNSTEIN. A history of the American worker, 1920-1933: the lean years. Boston: Houghton Mifflin, 1960. xi, [3], 577 p. cartoons, ports., tables, views. notes (p. 517-59). [2850

U.S. Agricultural Marketing Service. The hired farm working force of 1958. [By James Daniel Cowhig and Sheridan Tacy Maitland. Wash., 1959.] 29 p. form, 19 tables. notes. (U.S. Dept. of Agriculture. Agriculture information bulletin 219.) Includes comparative figures for 1945 and later years. [2851

U.S. Agricultural Marketing Service. An analysis of the experienced hired farm working force, 1948-1957. [By] James D[aniel] Cowhig and Sheridan T[racy] Maitland. Wash. [1960]. 19 p. 11 tables. notes. (U.S. Dept. of Agriculture. Agriculture information bulletin 225.) [2852

Employment

SOLOMON FABRICANT. The changing industrial distribution of gainful workers: comments on the decennial statistics, 1820-1940. Conference on Research in Income and Wealth, Studies in income and wealth, 11 (1949): 1-45. tables. notes. Includes an evaluation of the census statistics as a source of relevant information. For comment by Daniel Carson see p. 144-50. [2853

DANIEL CARSON. Changes in the industrial composition of manpower since the Civil War [1870-1940, especially after 1910]. Conference on Research in Income and Wealth, Studies in income and wealth, 11 (1949): 46-134. tables. notes. Statistical study based upon decennial censuses. For comment on this paper, and the author's reply, see p. 134-50. [2854

ANN RATNER MILLER. Labor force trends and differentials [1870-1950]. Simon Smith Kuznets, Ann Ratner Miller, & Richard A. Easterlin, Population redistribution and economic growth, 1870-1950 (Phila.: American Philosophical Soc.), 2 (1960): 7-101. diagrs., tables. notes. Sections on "The age and sex composition of the labor force," "The shift away from agriculture," and "The changing industrial pattern." [2855

DANIEL F. O'KEEFE, JR. Due process and the "right" to a job. Va. law rev., 46:323-36 (Mar). notes. On "the nature and application of a person's constitutional rights to his job in public and private employment," 1889-1959. [2856

C. W. KROHL & J. R. WOLFE. Work-life expectancy, with tables. Mo. Bar, Jour., 15:369-79, 396-415 (Aug, Sep 1959). tables. On the use of life-expectancy tables in personal-injury and death cases since 1865, the need expressed as early as 1893 for tables of probable "duration of ability to earn money," and the admission of work-life expectancy tables as evidence in railroad cases since 1949; with copies of "Smith-Griffin, Railroad employees work life expectancy table." [2857

JOSEPH HENRY FOEGEN. Labor turnover: an historical survey [since 1897], with special reference to current practice in small and medium-size companies. Ann Arbor: University Microfilms, 1959 [i.e. 1960]. Positive microfilm of typescript. vii, 488 leaves. bibliog. (leaves 461-88). Thesis--Univ. of Wisconsin. Abstracted: Dissert. abstracts, 20:2620 (Jan). [2858

U.S. Bureau of Labor Statistics. Union wages and hours: building trades, July 1, 1959, and trend, 1907-59. [By Thomas C. Mobley.] Wash.: U.S. Govt. Print. Off., 1960. v, 39 p. tables. notes. (Its Bulletin 1269.) [2859

U.S. Bureau of Labor Statistics. Union wages and hours: printing industry, July 1, 1959, and trend, 1907-59. [By Thomas C. Mobley.] Wash.: U.S. Govt. Print. Off., 1960. v, 45 p. tables. notes. (Its Bulletin 1271.) [2860

DALE E. HATHAWAY. Migration from agriculture: the historical record and its meaning. Am. econ. rev., 50:379-91 (May). tables. notes. On "movements of labor out of agriculture" since 1920. Previously printed in more condensed form: Migration from farms and its meaning. Monthly labor rev., 83:136-40 (Feb). notes. [2861

MORRIS LEONARD STEVENS. Is full employment possible without inflation? Midwest quar., 1:163-82 (Jan). bibliog. On theories of the realtion between employment and inflation, 1929-59, especially since 1945. [2862

U.S. Bureau of Labor Statistics. Union wages and hours: local-transit operating employees, July 1, 1959, and trend, 1929-59. [By Thomas C. Mobley.] Wash.: U.S. Govt. Print. Off., 1960. v, 10 p. tables. notes. (Its Bulletin 1268.) [2863

DAVID MORRIS POTTER & WILLIAM H. GOETZMANN, eds. The New Deal and employment [1933-42]. N.Y.: Holt [1960]. x, 85 p. notes (p. 85). (Select problems in historical interpretation, 7.) Documents and secondary accounts, concerned mainly with the National Labor Relations Act and the Works Progress Administration. [2864

JOSEPH M. BECKER. Twenty-five years of unemployment insurance: an experiment in competitive collectivism [1935-60]. Pol. science quar., 75:481-99 (Dec). notes. [2865

THOMAS F. BRODEN, JR. General rules determining the employment relationship under Social Security laws: after twenty years an unsolved problem. Temple law quar., 33:307-30, 381-402 (spring, summer). notes. On the persistent inability of the Social Security Administration, the Internal Revenue Service, Congress, and the courts to discover an umambiguous definition of the word employee, 1935-57. [2866

PHILIP EDEN. The case against experience rating in unemployment insurance [1935-59]. Labor law jour., 11:347-66, 423-4 (May). notes. [2867

R. GORDON WAGNET. Twenty-five years of unemployment insurance in the United States [since 1935]. Social security bul., 23(8):50-59 (Aug). [2868

U.S. Bureau of Labor Statistics. Union wages and hours: motortruck drivers and helpers, July 1, 1959, and trend, 1936-59. [By Thomas C. Mobley.] Wash.: U.S. Govt. Print. Off., 1960. v, 32 p. tables. notes. (Its Bulletin 1270.) [2869

ELLA JOAN POLINSKY. Some implications of the employment pattern of women under social security [1937-57]. Ann Arbor: University Microfilms, 1959 [i.e. 1960]. Positive microfilm of typescript. [304] leaves. Thesis--American Univ. Abstracted: Dissert. abstracts, 20:2609 (Jan). [2870

U.S. Bureau of Labor Statistics. Area guide to industry employment statistics: industry by area, 1939-58. [Wash.] 1960. i, 90 p. tables. notes. Tabulation. [2871

STUART H. GARFINKLE. Tables of working life for women. [Wash., 1957.] vi, 33 p. diagrs., tables. (U.S. Bureau of Labor Statistics. Bulletin 1204.) Based on thesis--American Univ. Includes comparative information from 1940. [2872

DAVID GALE JOHNSON. Policies to improve the labor transfer process. Am. econ. rev., 50:403-12 (May). tables. notes. On migration of labor out of agriculture, particularly in the South, 1940-50. [2873

OTEY M. SCRUGGS. Evolution of the Mexican Farm Labor Agreement of 1942. Agric. hist., 34:140-49 (Jul). notes. On arrangements "under which braceros, contract laborers from Mexico, were to be imported to work on American farms," and the discussions leading to the agreement, 1940-42. [2874

JOSEPH P. FITZPATRICK. Trend toward a white-collar society [1947-58]. Thought, 35:269-89 (summer). bibliog. [2875

CLARENCE DICKINSON LONG. Prosperity unemployment and its relation to economic growth and inflation [since 1947]. Am. econ. rev., 50:145-61 (May). diagrs., tables. notes. On unemployment in a time of prosperity. [2876

JAMES ROY OTT, JR. Employment trends in the textile industry, 1947-1957. Ann Arbor: University Microfilms, 1959 [i.e. 1960]. Positive microfilm of typescript. [324] leaves. Thesis--Vanderbilt Univ. Abstracted: Dissert. abstracts, 20:2607-8 (Jan). [2877

RICHARD ALLEN LESTER. The economic significance of unemployment compensation, 1948-1959. Rev. econ. and statistics, 42:350-72 (Nov). diagr., tables. notes. [2878

Labor-Management Relations

G. R. BLAKEY & MATHEW T. HOGAN [and 3 others]. Student analysis: the legal framework of public intervention in industrial disputes [1806-1960]. Notre Dame lawyer, 35:654-90. notes. [2879

JOHN ROGERS COMMONS (1862-1945) & EUGENE A. GILMORE, eds. Labor conspiracy cases, 1806-1842. Selected, collated, and edited by John R. Commons ... and Eugene A. Gilmore. [N.Y.: Russell & Russell, 1958.] 2. v. [10], xii, 11-385; 341, [5], 15-136 p. facsims., table. (A documentary history of American industrial society, 3-4.) 1st ed. 1909. Records of 15 cases tried in Maryland, Pennsylvania, New York, and Connecticut, including Commonwealth v. Pullis (Philadelphia cordwainers, 1806), People v. Melvin (New York cordwainers, 1810), Commonwealth v. Morrow (Pittsburgh cordwainers, 1815), Commonwealth v. Moore (Philadelphia journeyman tailors, 1827), and 2 cases involving carpet weavers in Thompsonville, Conn., 1834-36; with an introduction by Commons on "Industrial stages, classes, and organizations" (1:19-58) and a new preface by Richard B. Morris. [2880

FREDERICK WINSLOW TAYLOR (1856-1915). The principles of scientific management [in America and England, ca. 1840 to 1911]. Harwood Ferry Merrill, ed., Classics in management (N.Y.: American Management Assoc. [1960]), p. 82-113. notes. Paper delivered Oct. 1911 and printed in 1912. [2881

DANIEL BELL. Interest and ideology: on the role of public opinion in industrial disputes [1877-1954]. Daniel Bell, The end of ideology: on the exhaustion of political ideas in the fifties (Glencoe, Ill.: Free Press [1960]), p. 191-207. notes. First printed in 1954. [2882

FREDERICK WINSLOW TAYLOR (1856-1915). Time study, piece work, and the first-class man. Harwood Ferry Merrill, ed., Classics in management (N.Y.: American Management Assoc. [1960]), p. 67-76. tables. Paper presented in Jun. 1903. On the author's application of the methods of "scientific management" in plants of the Bethlehem Steel Company, 1889-1901. [2883

ALEXANDER HAMILTON CHURCH & LEON PRATT ALFORD (1877-1942). The principles of management ... with special reference to the shop and factory [1892-1912]. Harwood Ferry Merrill, ed., Classics in management (N.Y.: American Management Assoc. [1960]), p. 197-214. notes. From American machinist, 30 May 1912. [2884

HENRY LAURENCE GANTT (1861-1919). A bonus system of rewarding labor, being a system of task work, with instruction cards and a bonus [Bethlehem Steel Company, 1900-1901]. Harwood Ferry Merrill, ed., Classics in management (N.Y.: American Management Assoc. [1960]), p. 117-35. form, tables. notes. Paper presented in Dec. 1901. [2885

ARTHUR MAX ROSS & PAUL T. HARTMAN. Changing patterns of industrial conflict [1900-1956]. N.Y.: Wiley [1960]. x, 220 p. diagrs., tables (part double). notes. "One of a series of books from the research program of the Institute of Industrial Relations, University of California." Condensed, with same title, by Ross: Monthly labor rev., 83:229-37 (Mar). [2886

S. HERBERT UNTERBERGER. The evolution of wage incentive systems [since ca. 1900]. Ann Arbor: University Microfilms, 1960. Positive microfilm of typescript. [163] leaves. Thesis--Univ. of Pennsylvania. Abstracted: Dissert. abstracts, 21:784-5 (Oct). [2887

NORMAN JEWEL WOOD. Industrial relations policies of American management, 1900-1933. Bus. hist. rev., 34:403-20 (winter). views. notes. On "the extent to which improvements in labor relations were undertaken because of management's internally generated drive for increased production efficiency." [2888

HENRY LAURENCE GANTT (1861-1919). Training workmen in habits of industry and cooperation [Bethelhem Steel Company, 1901-8]. Harwood Ferry Merrill, ed., Classics in management (N.Y.: American Management Assoc. [1960]), p. 136-50. Paper presented in Dec. 1908. [2889

JOHN ARTHUR GARRATY. The United States Steel Corporation versus labor: the early years [1901-19]. Labor hist., 1:3-38 (winter). notes. [2890

ROBERT H. GORSKE. Burden of proof in grievance arbitration [1901-57]. Marquette law rev., 43:135-79 (fall 1959). notes. [2891

MORTON GITELMAN. The evolution of labor arbitration [1903-59]. De Paul law rev., 9:181-95 (spring-summer). notes. [2892

HUGH G. J. AITKEN. Taylorism at Watertown Arsenal: scientific management in action, 1908-1915. Cambridge: Harvard Univ. Press, 1960. viii, [2], 269 p. tables. bibliog. (p. 243-4), notes (p. 245-64). On the application of methods advocated by Frederick Winslow Taylor, management consultant, to the U.S. Arsenal at Watertown, Mass. [2893

DANIEL BELL. Work and its discontents: the cult of efficiency in America [1910-56]. Daniel Bell, The end of ideology: on the exhaustion of political ideas in the fifties (Glencoe, Ill.: Free Press [1960]), p. 222-62. notes. Printed as a book in 1956. [2894

OSCAR KRAINES. Brandeis' philsophy of scientific management. West. pol. quar., 13:191-201 (Mar). notes. On the sudden publicity given to the concept by Louis Dembitz Brandeis in hearings conducted by the Interstate Commerce Commission on proposed railroad rate increases, the more or less favorable response of the railroads to proposals expected to reduce their expenses of operation by a million dollars a day, and the adverse response of most labor organizations, 1910-11. [2895

AMERICAN SOCIETY OF MECHANICAL ENGINEERS. Management Division. 50 years progress in management, 1910-1960: the development of the art and science of management as reflected in the cumulative "Ten years' progress in management" reports sponsored by the Management Division of ASME and published in the Transactions of the Society. N.Y. [1960. 8], 329 p. diagrs., port., views. bibliogs. "The present state of the art of management," 1912 (containing the majority and minority reports of a Sub-Committee on

Administration of the ASMS, and discussion of these at an annual meeting); "The status of industrial relations," by Leon P. Alford, 1919; and "Ten years progress in management," 1922 and 1932 (by Alford), 1942, 1952, and 1960 (by various contributors). [2896

FREDERICK WINSLOW TAYLOR (1856-1915). What is scientific management? Harwood Ferry Merrill, ed., Classics in management (N.Y.: American Management Assoc. [1960]), p. 77-81. Statement before the Special Committee of the House of Representatives to Investigate the Taylor and Other Systems of Shop Management, 25 Jan. 1912. [2897

SUMNER HUBER SLICHTER (1892-1959). The impact of collective bargaining on management [1932-59]. By Sumner H. Slichter, James J. Healy, [and] E. Robert Livernash. Wash.: Bookings Institution [1960]. xv, 982 p. notes. Thorough revision of Slichter's Union policies and industrial management (1941), amounting to "a wholly new treatment." [2898

NATHAN PAUL FEINSINGER. Trends in labor arbitration [1935-59]. Southw. law jour., 14:61-70 (winter). notes. [2899

JEROME D. FENTON. The Taft-Hartley Act and union control of hiring--a critical examination. Villanova law rev., 4:339-65 (spring 1959). notes. On union hiring halls, 1935-58. [2900

SYLVIA D. GARLAND. Comment--labor law--the National Labor Relations Act--collective bargaining [1936-58]. N.Y. law forum, 5:196-203 (Apr 1959). notes. [2901

MORRIS AARON HOROWITZ. The Diesel firemen issue on the railroads [since 1935]. Indus. and labor rel. rev., 13:550-58 (Jul). notes. [2902

J. WOODWARD HOWARD, JR. Frank Murphy and the sit-down strikes of 1937. Labor hist., 1:103-40 (spring). notes. On the conduct of Murphy, as Governor of Michigan, in this and later labor-management crises, 1937-39, his refusal to enforce an injunction against the strikers by a Michigan court, and his later revelation, when questioned in Congress as a nominee for the Supreme Court, that he had merely "suspended" the effective date of the injunction in return for a promise (faithfully observed) from John L. Lewis to end the strike before a date set by Murphy. [2903

NEIL W. CAMBERLAIN, FRANK C. PIERSON, & THERESA WOLFSON, eds. A decade of industrial relations research, 1946-1956. N.Y.: Harper [1958]. viii, [2], 205 p. notes. (Industrial Relations Research Association. Publication 19.) Topical digest of publications. Contents.--1. Union government and union leadership, by Joel Seidman and Daisy L. Tagliacozzo.--2. Collective bargaining, by Joseph Shister.--3. Wage determination in theory and practice, by Melvin Reder.--4. The economic effects of unionism.--5. Employee benefit plans, by Robert Tilove.--6. The labor movement abroad, by Adolf Sturmthal. [2904

DAVID B. JOHNSON. Dispute settlement in atomic energy plants [since 1946]. Indus. and labor rel. rev., 13:38-53 (Oct 1959). tables. notes. [2905

JAMES A. HART. Right-to-work laws and freedom of collective bargaining [1947-60]. Rev. social econ., 18:20-26 (Mar). [2906

DONALD A. MEYER. "Ally" or "neutral"--the secondary boycott dilemma [1947-59]. Tulane law rev., 34:343-52 (Feb). notes. [2907

JOHN A. MORGAN, JR. Supreme Court interpretation vs. Congressional intent: the non-Communist affidavit and collective bargaining requirements of the Taft-Hartley Act [1947]. Univ. Pittsburgh law rev., 21:507-21 (Mar). notes. Examination of the legislative history of the act and of court decisions under it. [2908

MELVIN JAMES SEGAL. Differences among secondary boycotts and the Taft-Hartley Act [1947-58]. Wayne law rev., 5:195-208 (spring 1959). notes. [2909

JAMES ELMER YOUNG. Unfair labor practices under the Labor-Management Relations Act, 1947-57: a study of NLRB cases pertaining to the unfair labor practices of unions under Section 8(b) of the Act. Ann Arbor: University Microfilms, 1959 [i.e. 1960]. Positive microfilm of typescipt. [356] leaves. Thesis--Ohio State Univ. Abstracted: Dissert. abstracts, 20:3977 (Apr). [2910

Labor Organizations

HARRY H. CRAIG. A short history of the labor injunction [1806-1958]. Mo. Bar jour., 15:128-37 (Mar 1959). port. notes. [2912

JOHN ROGERS COMMONS (1862-1945) & HELEN L. SUMNER, eds. Labor movement, 1820-1840. Selected, collated, and edited by John R. Commons ... and Helen L. Sumner. [N.Y.: Russell & Russell, 1958.] 2 v. [8], 9-392; 353 p. diagr., facsims., ports. bibliog. (1:39), notes. (A documentary history of American industrial society, 5-6.) 1st ed. 1910. Primary sources (mainly reprinted) relating to "Economic and social conditions," the Mechanics' Union of Trade Associations and the Philadelphia political movement, the Working Men's Party of New York, the New England Association of Farmers, Mechanics, and Other Workmen, the General Trades' Union of New York City and Vicinity, the General Trades' Union of the City and County of Philadelphia, other city central organizations, the National Trades' Union, and 5 other national unions; with a general introduction and introductions to the sections by the editors, and a new preface by George Rogers Taylor, correcting errors of fact and interpretation in the first edition. [2913

JOHN ROGERS COMMONS (1862-1945), ed. Labor movement, 1840-1860. Selected, collated, and edited by John R. Commons. [N.Y.: Russell & Russell, 1958.] 2 v. [6], 364; 346 p. facsims., ports. (A documentary history of American industrial society, 7-8.) 1st ed. 1910. Primary sources (mainly reprinted) relating to "Economic and social conditions," "Owenism and association" (Robert Owen and others), "Land reform," "Hours of labor," and "Labor organizations"; with a general introduction and introductions to the sections by the editor, and a new preface by Joseph Dorfman, correcting errors of interpretation in the first edition. [2914

DANIEL BELL. The capitalism of the proletariat: a theory of American trade-unionism [1860-1958]. Daniel Bell, The end of ideology: on the exhaustion of political ideas in the fifties (Glencoe, Ill.: Free Press [1960]), p. 208-21. notes. From Encounter, 1958. [2915

JOHN ROGERS COMMONS (1862-1945) & JOHN B. ANDREWS, eds. Labor movement, 1860-1880. Selected, collated, and edited by John R. Commons ... and John B. Andrews. [N.Y.: Russell & Russell, 1958.] 2 v. [8], 378; 370 p. facsims., ports. (A documentary history of American industrial society, 9-10.) 1st ed. 1910. Primary sources (mainly reprinted) relating to "Labor conditions," national labor unions, "Ira Steward and the hours of labor," "International attempts," the Knights of Labor, and farmers' organizations; with a general introduction and introductions to the sections by the editors, a new preface by Henry David (correcting errors in the first edition), "Finding list of sources quoted" in the 10 volumes of A documentary history (2:137-55), and index to the 10 volumes (2:157-370). [2916

HOWARD MARTIN GITELMAN. Attempts to unify the American labor movement, 1865-1900. Ann Arbor: University Microfilms, 1960. Positive microfilm of typescript. [565] leaves. Thesis--Univ. of Wisconsin. Abstracted: Dissert. abstracts, 21:490 (Sep). [2917

GERALD N. GROB. Organized labor and the Negro worker, 1865-1900. Labor hist., 1:164-76 (spring). notes. [2918

MARK PERLMAN. Labor union theories in America: background and development. Evanston, Ill.: Row, Peterson [1958]. xv, 313 p. bibliogs., notes. On theories of unionism "as a moral institution" (Richard Ely, John Ryan), "as a revolutionary institution" (Marxist, I. W. W., and Socialist writers, Norman Ware), "as a psychological reaction" (Thorstein Veblen, Carleton Parker, Robert Hoxie, Frank Tannenbaum), "as a welfare institution" (George E. Barnett), and "as part of the democratic process" (Henry Adams, John R. Commons, Selig Perlman), 1884-1945; with some account of early movements to promote the collection of labor statistics, 1867 ff., and of 4 Congressional investigations of unionism, 1878-1915. [2919

DANIEL BELL. The racket-ridden Longshoremen: the web of economics and polities. Daniel Bell, The end of ideology: on the exhaustion of political ideas in the fifties (Glencoe, Ill.: Free Press [1960]), p. 159-90. notes. On the International Longshoremen's Association and its predecessors, 1870s-1951. [2920

AUGUST CONSTANTINO BOLINO. Sequential growth and the development of American unionism. Jour. econ. hist., 20:314-17 (Jun). notes. On reasons for the slowness of growth of unionism between 1873 and 1899. [2921

WALTER BYRON EMERY. Samuel Gompers [1850-1924]. Speech Association of America, A history and criticism of American public address, ed. William Norwood Brigance, 2d ed. (N.Y.: Russell & Russell, 1960), 2: 557-79. bibliog., notes. On the oratorical and rhetorical characteristics of his public speaking as "a spokesman for labor," 1874-1924. [2922

DAVID RHOADS WEIMER. The man with the hoe and the good machine. Joseph J. Kwiat & Mary C. Turpie, eds., Studies in American culture: dominant ideas and images (Minneapolis: Univ. of Minnesota Press [1960]), p. 63-73. notes. On the American Federation of Labor, 1881-1917. [2923

VAL ROGIN LORWIN. Labor unions and political action [1886-1960]. Am. rev., 1(1):103-26 (autumn). views. [2924

GEORGE GLENN DAWSON. A study of the treatment of labor unions and labor union activities in selected American novels published between 1891 and 1910. Ann Arbor: University Microfilms, 1959 [i. e. 1960]. Positive microfilm of typescript. [325] leaves. Thesis--New York Univ. Abstracted: Dissert. abstracts, 20:3989-90 (Apr). [2925

MARK PERLMAN. Labor movement theories: past, present, and future. Indus. and labor rel. rev., 13:338-48 (Apr). notes. Includes an account of American theory, beginning with John R. Commons ca. 1900. [2926

ROBERT L. TYLER. The I. W. W. and the West. Am. quar., 12:175-87 (summer). notes. Sketch of the International Workers of the World, founded in 1905, "moribund" by 1924, active in many parts of the United States, and the development of the idea of "its peculiarly 'Western' character," with the result that "the I. W. W. has been incorporated into the corpus of Western folklore." [2927

EUGENE ALFRED FORSEY. The influence of American labor organizations and policies on Canadian labor [since 1910]. Duke University, Commonwealth-Studies Center, The American economic impact on Canada (Durham, N.C.: Duke Univ. Press, 1959), p. 127-47. notes. [2928

JACOB BENJAMIN SALUTSKY HARDMAN. The needle-trades unions: a labor movement at fifty. Social research, 27:321-58 (autumn). On the Amalgamated Clothing Workers of America, the International Ladies Garment Workers of America, and the United Hatters, Cap, and Millinery Workers International Union, 1910-60. [2929

HOWARD D. SAMUEL. Amalgamated panorama. [N.Y.: Amalgamated Clothing Workers of America, AFL-CIO, 1960.] 106, [2] p. diagrs., facsims., ports., double table, views. On the United Garment Workers of America, 1910-14, and the Amalgamated Clothing Workers of America, 1914-59. [2930

ARCHIBALD COX. The uses and abuses of union power [1914-60]. Notre Dame lawyer, 35:624-39. notes. [2931

ALBERT EVERETT REES. Do unions cause inflation? Jour. law & econ., 2:84-94 (Oct 1959). table. notes. Evidence, 1914-57, indicating the probable correctness of a negative answer. [2932

PHILIP TAFT. The I. W. W. in the Grain Belt. Labor hist., 1:53-67 (winter). notes. On the Agricultural Workers Organization 400, its largely successful efforts to organize the migratory grain-harvest workers, its use of force for this purpose in defiance of state laws, and the frustration of its plans to organize other migratory workers when the United States entered World War II, 1914-17. [2933

JOHN HUTCHINSON. Captain of a mighty host: a note on the retirement of John L. Lewis. Yale rev., 50:42-52 (autumn). On his service as President of the United Mine Workers of America, 1920-60, and founder and first President of the CIO; with a critical analysis of his decisions and his ideas. [2934

STANLEY IRA KUTLER. The judicial philosophy of Chief Justice Taft and organized labor, 1921-1930. Ann Arbor: University Microfilms, 1960. Positive microfilm of typescript. [265] leaves. Thesis--Ohio State Univ. Abstracted: Dissert. abstracts, 21:1174 (Nov). [2935

OMER STANISLAUS HOEBRECKX. Federal courts under Section 301 [of the Labor-Management Relations Act of 1947]. Marquette law rev., 43: 417-43 (spring). notes. On the jurisdiction of Federal courts "over suits brought by or against labor organizations for violation of contracts" and the liability of unions for "the payment of money damages," 1922-59. [2936

FRANK J. MURPHY. Agreement on the railroads--the Joint Railway Conference of 1926. Labor law jour., 11: 823-36, 864 (Sep). notes. [2937

RONALD M. LOEB. Accommodation of the Norris - La Guardia Act to other Federal statutes [1932-60]. Labor law jour., 11:473-92, 548 (Jun). notes. [2938

SYLVESTER PETRO. The sources and extent of union power. Notre Dame lawyer, 35:603-14. notes. Mainly on "special privileges and immunities--all condoning or authorizing compulsion" as "the most significant of the immediate sources of union power," 1932-60. [2939

GEORGE ROSE. The legal protection of voluntary union membership [1932-60]. Labor law jour., 11:385-406, 414 (May). notes. [2940

WALTER GALENSON. The CIO challenge to the AFL: a history of the American labor movement, 1935-1941. Cambridge: Harvard Univ. Press, 1960. xix, 732 p. ports., tables (1 double), views. notes (p. 647-714). (Wertheim publications in industrial relations. Studies in labor-management history.) [2941

BEVARS DU PRE MABRY. An analysis of State labor laws regulating trade union activities [since 1935]. Ann Arbor: University Microfilms, 1959 [i. e. 1960]. Positive microfilm of typescript. [567] leaves. Thesis--Tulane Univ. Abstracted: Dissert. abstracts, 20:3543 (Mar). [2942

PROTECTION and assistance for the union organizer [1935-58]. Duke law jour., 1959: 78-92 (winter 1959). notes. [2943

PIERRE WALINE. Les syndicats aux États-Unis: leur force et leur originalité. Paris: Armand Colin, 1951. [6], 191, [1] p. bibliog. (p. 189-91), notes. On labor unions, their organization and leaders, their ideologies, their relation of free enterprise, their political activities, their dealings with organizations of businessmen, their collective bargaining, their campaign for a closed shop, and the intervention of the U.S. Government in their affairs, particularly since 1935. [2944

ARNOLD ROBERT WEBER. Competitive unionism in the chemical industry [since 1936]. Indus. and labor rel. rev., 13:17-37 (Oct 1959). notes. On the relation of competition to "significant innovations in trade union policy and practice" and to "union democracy." [2945

GRANT B. HERING. Craft severance: the doctrine of American Potash. Va. law rev., 46:756-74 (May). notes. On petitions of groups of employees in a craft or department "where the existing bargaining unit is a plantwide, employer, or other such large, industrial unit," to be severed from the larger unit and recognized as an independent unit, 1937-60. [2946

DALLAS LEE JONES. Self-determination vs. stability of labor relations. Mich. law rev., 58:313-46 (Jan). tables. notes. On the right of units of craft workers to refuse absorption into larger units of production workers or to withdraw from such larger units after involuntary incorporation into them, 1939-60. [2947

JOSEPH KRISLOV. Organizational rivalry among American unions [1940-58]. Indus. and labor rel. rev., 13:216-26 (Jan). notes. [2948

GOETZ ANTONY BRIEFS. Compulsory unionism [1941-60]. Rev. social econ., 18:60-77 (Mar). [2949

J. T. CUTLER. Union security and right-to-work laws [1944-58]: is coexistence possible? Wm. and Mary law rev., 2 (1959): 16-39. notes. [2950

RICHARD A. GIVENS. Federal protection of employee rights within trade unions [1944-59]. Fordham law rev., 29:259-312 (Dec). notes. [2951

STANLEY WHITAKER THOMAS. The image of labor organization in church and trade union, 1945-1955. Ann Arbor: University Microfilms, 1960. Positive microfilm of typescript. [273] leaves. Thesis--Boston Univ. Abstracted: Dissert. abstracts, 21: 979-80 (Oct). On "the images ... held by the American Federation of Labor, the Congress of Industrial Organizations, the National Catholic Welfare Conference, the Federal Council of Churches, and the National Council of Churches." [2952

APPLYING the "contracts between labor organizations" clause of Taft-Hartley, section 301: a plea for restraint. Yale law jour., 69:299-320 (Dec 1959). notes. On the scope of applicability, 1947-58, particularly the question whether the section is applicable to a dispute between a branch or local union and its parent international union. [2953

JEROME H. KERN. The Taft-Hartley welfare and pension trust--an emerging legal entity [1947-60]. N.Y. Univ. law rev., 35:1181-9 (Jun). notes. [2954

KENNETH THOMSON STRAND. Jurisdictional disputes among the building trades unions [mainly since 1947]. Ann Arbor: University Microfilms, 1959 [i. e. 1960]. Positive microfilm of typescript. xiv, 522 leaves. bibliog. (leaves 510-22). Thesis--Univ. of Wisconsin. Abstracted: Dissert. abstracts, 20:2611-12 (Jan). [2955

JEROME LORRAINE TONER. Right-to-work laws and the common good [1947-60]. Rev. social econ., 18:1-19 (Mar). notes. [2956

NATURAL RESOURCES

PAUL BIGELOW SEARS. Deserts on the march. [Third edition, revised.] Norman: Univ. of Oklahoma Press [1959]. xiii, 178 p. 1st ed. 1935. On waste of natural resources in North America since the arrival of white men in 1492, and the progress of measures for conservation. [2957

ORSON W. ISRAELSEN. The historical background of reclamation [in America, 1835-1950, and abroad]. Agric. engineering, 32:321-4 (Jun 1951). diagrs., table. notes. [2958

HENRY EDWARD CLEPPER. Women in conservation [1875-1956]. Am. forests, 62(12):20-22, 52-3 (Dec 1956). ports. [2959

H. BOWMAN HAWKES. The paradoxes of the conservation movement. Salt Lake City: Extension Division, Univ. of Utah, 1960. 35 p. table. notes (p. 33-5). (Annual Frederick William Reynolds lecture, 24.) On the ebb and flow of conflict between the "concept of harmony and balance" and the "concept of use," 1901-60. [2960

HOWARD L. COOK. River basin planning as a fundamental concept [1909-59]. Agric. engineering, 40: 145-7, 151 (Mar 1959). [2961

SIEGFRIED V. CIRIACY-WANTRUP. Conceptual problems in projecting the demand for land and water [1910-58]. Land Economics Institute, University of Illinois, 1958, Modern land policy: papers (Urbana: Univ. of Illinois Press, 1960), p. 41-67. diagrs. notes. [2962

THEODORE S. PETTIT. A half-century of service to conservation. Pa. game news, 21(2):2-4 (Feb). facsim. On the conservation activities of the Boy Scouts of America, 1910-60. [2963

EARL GERARD DUNFORD. Watershed management research in the Lake States, intermountain, and Pacific Northwest regions [1912-59]. Jour. forestry, 58:288-90 (Apr). [2964

NICHOLAS V. OLDS. Public rights in conservation--their protection and preservation [1920-51]. Mich. conservation, 21(3):3-4, 23-5 (May-Jun 1952). [2965

ROBERT E. DILS. Educational programs in watershed management [1932-60]. Jour. forestry, 58:307-11 (Apr). tables. On curricula offered by several universities. [2966

CARL BARRIER BROWN. Flood prevention through watershed planning [1935-52]. Agric. engineering, 34: 159-62, 167 (Mar 1953). views. [2967

JOHN A. ALLIS. Runoff from conservation and non-conservation watersheds [near Coshocton, Ohio, Waco, Tex., and Hastings, Neb., 1937-52]. Agric. engineering, 34:766-8 (Nov 1953). diagrs., table. notes. [2968

CLARENCE EDWARD BUSBY. Water rights and administration with respect to soil and water conservation [1938-53]. Agric. engineering, 34:769-80 (Nov 1953). notes. [2969

EUGENE C. BUIE. Watershed planning [1944-60]. Agric. engineering, 41: 104-5, 108-9 (Feb). maps. [2970

SAM EDWARD CLAGG. The status of conservation education in selected institutions of higher learning in the Southeastern United States [11 States], 1954. Ann Arbor: University Microfilms, 1955 [i. e. 1960]. Positive microfilm of typescript. x, 374 leaves. maps, tables. bibliog. (leaves 371-4). Thesis (Ed. D.)--Univ. of Kentucky. Abstracted: Dissert. abstracts, 20: 4024-5 (Apr). [2971

Air

LESTER MACHTA. Meteorological aspects of large scale air pollution [1936-56]. Pub. health reports, 75: 307-12 (Apr). diagr., maps. notes. [2972

Land

U.S. Bureau of Land Management. The public lands: a brief sketch in United States history [1780-1960. Wash.? 1960? 2], ii, 98 p. diagr., maps, tables. notes (p. 84-98). [2973

LESLIE E. DECKER. The railroads and the Land Office: administrative policy and the land patent controversy, 1864-1896. Miss. Valley hist. rev., 46:679-99 (Mar). tables. notes. On the administration of railroad land grants by the General Land Office. [2974

THEODORE WILLIAM SCHULTZ. Land in economic growth [1869-1956]. Land Economic Institute, University of Illinois, 1958, Modern land policy: papers (Urbana: Univ. of Illinois Press, 1960), p. 17-39. tables. notes. [2975

FRANK C. MOCKLER. The open range: a vanishing concept. Wyo. law jour., 13:136-9 (winter 1959). notes. On its conflict with fence laws and trespass laws, 1876-1957, especially in the West and in application to reserved lands of the U.S. Government. [2976

MARK LOVEL NICHOLS & D. D. SMITH. Progress in erosion control over the past 50 years [1886-1957]. Agric. engineering, 38:422-5, 460 (Jun 1957). views. [2977

MARION CLAWSON. Land use and demand for land in the United States [1900-1958]. Land Economics Institute, University of Illinois, 1958, Modern land policy: papers (Urbana: Univ. of Illinois Press, 1960), p. 1-16. tables (1 double). notes. [2978

PETER FARB. Hugh Bennett [born 1881]: messiah of the soil. Am. forest, 66(1):18-19, 40-42 (Jan). port. On his service in the U.S. Soil Conservation Service, 1903-51; with some account of his early life in North Carolina. [2979

PAUL N. CARLIN. The aesthetic as a factor considered in zoning [1905-59]. Wyo. law jour., 15:77-84 (fall). notes. [2980

JAMES LEONARD BATES. The Midwest decision, 1915: a landmark in conservation history. Pac. Northw. quar., 51:26-34 (Jan). map, views. notes. On United States v. Midwest Oil Company, in which the Supreme Court "upheld the executive power to withdraw and protect public lands of the United States," prohibiting the patenting to private parties of the lands thus withdrawn, a power first exercised by President Taft in withdrawing from public entry more than a million acres of public land in California and Wyoming in 1909; and ensuing efforts of oilmen to obtain legislation modifying the impact of this decision. [2981

HAROLD WINFORD HANNAH & N. P. G. KRAUSZ. The role of law in the development of land resources. Land Economics Institute, University of Illinois, 1958, Modern land policy: papers (Urbana: Univ. of Illinois Press, 1960), p. 325-36. notes. On State and Federal laws concerning "conservation, water, landlord-tenant, credit, nuisance, prescription, inheritance, zoning, taxation, and titles," 1909-58. [2982

ELI GOLDSTON & JAMES H. SCHEUER. Zoning of planned residential developments. Harv. law rev., 73:241-67 (Dec 1959). notes. On the growing body of law governing these developments, 1910-59. [2983

EDWIN RUSSELL JACKMAN. More meat from the public lands. Am. forests, 62(3):10-11, 40, 42, 44 (Mar 1956). views. On the remaining public domain, mainly in "the eleven western states" and mainly desert, much of which was grassland as recently as 1917, was denuded by overgrazing, and could be restored to grassland by proper management. [2984

LOUIS F. BARTELT, JR. Shopping centers and land controls [1925-59]. Notre Dame lawyer, 35:184-210 (Mar). notes. [2985

LAWRENCE ADKINS REUSS. Land utilization data as background information for the national balance sheet and approximations of the value of forest lands [1929-46]. Conference on Research in Income and Wealth, Studies in income and wealth, 12 (1950): 219-33. tables. [2986

R. L. ADAMS. Our shrinking farm lands. Agric. engineering, 35:414-16 (Jan 1954). tables, views. On withdrawal of arable land from agricultural to other uses (e. g., highways, industrial or residential sites, parks, airports), 1930-53, with illustrative statistics from California. [2987

LOUIS BEMIS WETMORE. Trends in urban and urban-related land uses [1938-58]. Land Economics Institute, University of Illinois, 1958, Modern land policy: papers (Urbana: Univ. of Illinois Press, 1960), p. 143-55. notes. [2988

PAUL C. JOHNSON. The changing rural community [1939-58] and the need for modern land policy. Land Economics Institute, Univ. of Illinois, 1958, Modern land policy: papers (Urbana: Univ. of Illinois Press, 1960), p. 163-9. On the need for transferring land from agricultural to other uses under "the authority of government." [2989

C. P. BARNES. Land resource potentials of the United States [1947-58] and world regions. Land Economics Institute, University of Illinois, 1958, Modern land policy: papers (Urbana: Univ. of Illinois Press, 1960), p. 69-85. notes. [2990

Water

AMERICAN WATER WORKS ASSOCIATION. Experience with main breaks in four large cities: panel discussion. Am. Water Works Assoc., Jour., 52:1041-58 (Aug). diagrs., tables. Contents.--Philadelphia [since 1799], by Gerald E. Arnold.--New York, by Edward J. Clark.--Detroit [1920-60], by Gerald J. Remus.--Indianapolis [1925-59], by Howard J. Niemeyer. [2991

DAVID TEMPLE. Our evolving national water policy [1824-1956]. Am. forests, 62(9):34-41, 59 (Sep 1956). port., views. [2992

DONALD E. CHANEY. Constitutional validity of a Federal reforestation program for upper tributaries of navigable rivers. Mo. law rev., 25: 317-23 (Jun). notes. On the whole application of "the commerce clause of the federal constitution" to streams and waterways, 1829-1960. [2993

V. M. EHLERS. Seventy-five years of progress in public water supply [in America, 1829-1955, especially since ca. 1880]. Southwest water works jour., 37(10):11-20 (Jan 1956). table. [2993a

U.S. Geological Survey. Reservoirs in the United States [1870-1953]. By Nathan O. Thomas and G. Earl Harbeck, Jr. Wash.: U.S. Govt. Print. Off., 1956. v, 97 p. diagrs., maps (part fold. in pocket), tables. bibliog. (p. 98). (Its Water-supply paper 1360-A.) Revises and supersedes Geological Survey circular 23, Reservoirs in the United States (1948), by G. Earl Harbeck, Jr. [2994

ERNEST W. WHITLOCK. Concrete pressure pipe in today's water industry [1870-1960]. Am. Water Works Assoc., Jour., 52:1244-50 (Oct). diagrs. notes. [2995

SYRACUSE UNIVERSITY. Delaware Valley Project. River basin administration and the Delaware. [By] Roscoe C[oleman] Martin, Guthrie S. Birkhead, Jesse Birkhead, [and] Frank J. Munger. [Syracuse:] Syracuse Univ. Press [1960]. xii, 390 p. diagr., maps, tables. notes. Largely an argument for the establishment of a Delaware River Agency for Water (DRAW), a Federal agency to control the river. Includes some account of the use of the river water by Philadelphia, Port Jervis, and New York City, 1921-60, and a more general account of the "politics, economics, and administration of water" in American river basins since 1879. [2996

U.S. Geological Survey. Compilation of records of surface waters of the United States [from 1884] through September 1950. ... Prepared under the direction of J. V. B. Wells, Chief, Surface Water Branch. Wash.: U.S. Govt. Print. Off., 1954-60. 20 v. maps (part fold.), tables. (Its Water-supply paper, nos. 1301-1315, 1315A, 1316-1318, 1372.) Summary of "records of discharge of streams and contents of reservoirs summarized on a monthly and yearly basis," condensed from previous publications of the Geological Survey. [2997

HARRY A. FABER. Research in the United States [in the improvement of water supply, 1887-1960]. Am. Water Works Assoc., Jour., 52:1102-18 (Sep). diagrs., tables. [2998

KENNETH J. CARL. Municipal fire protection surveys as indicators of water system status. Am. Water Works Assoc., Jour., 52:413-20 (Apr). cartoon. On surveys conducted by the American Water Works Association, 1889-1959. [2999

MARK D. HOLLIS. Pollution and national water resources [1890s-1960]. Am. Water Works Assoc., Jour., 52:959-64 (Aug). [3000

JUDSON KING (1872-1958). The conservation fight, from Theodore Roosevelt to the Tennessee Valley Authority. Wash.: Public Affairs Press [1959]. xix, 316 p. notes (p. 297-304). On movements for the control of water power by the U.S. Government, 1897-1933, culminating in the establishment of the TVA. [3001

CLYDE OLLEN MARTZ. Water for mushrooming populations. W. Va. law rev., 60:1-67 (Dec 1959). notes. On laws concerning the ownership, control, and use of water, 1900-1959. [3002

EDWARD F. RENSHAW. Appraisal of Federal investment in water resources [1900-1957]. Land Economics Institute, University of Illinois, 1958, Modern land policy: papers (Urbana: Univ. of Illinois Press, 1960), p. 235-47. tables. notes. [3003

U.S. Public Health Service. Clean water: a chart book of America's water needs, 1900-1980. [Wash., 1960.] 48 p. of illus. (col. diagrs., col. maps, view). 16x24 cm. [3004

FRANK J. TRELEASE. Reclamation water rights. Rocky Mt. law rev., 32:464-501 (Jun). notes. On water rights and "vested interests therein" under the Reclamation Act of 1902, particularly in the West. [3005

A. A. KALINSKE. Advances in water supply technology [in the past "50 years or more"]. Am. Water Works Assoc., Jour., 52:199-204 (Feb). diagr. notes. [3006

SAMUEL S. BAXTER. Principles of rate making for publicly owned utilities. Am. Water Works Assoc., Jour., 52:1225-38 (Oct). notes. On water rates, 1917-59. [3007

FRANK C. ROE. Experiences in the use of porous-plate filter bottoms [1934-59]. Am. Water Works Assoc., Jour., 52:653-9 (May). [3008

JOHN J. CLOSNER. Use of prestressed concrete for storage facilities [for water supplies, 1936-59]. Am. Water Works Assoc., Jour., 52:373-7 (Mar). views. [3009

LAUREN W. GRAYSON. Water supply--America's greatest challenge [1940-59]. Am. Water Works Assoc., Jour., 52:1-5 (Jan). notes. [3010

JUANITA MAHAFFEY. Pollution, the worst poacher. Pa. game news, 21(3): 17-21 (Mar). cartoon, facsim., views. On water pollution in America, 1944-59, the "accompanying shrinkage of hunting and fishing areas," the threat to human health and water supplies, and the imperativeness of preventive measures. [3011

HUGH L. HAMILTON. Effects of soil corrosion on cast-iron pipe [1945-60]. Am. Water Works Assoc., Jour., 52: 638-50 (May). diagrs., map, tables. notes. [3012

Wildlife

OUTDOOR LIFE. The story of American hunting and firearms. By the editors of Outdoor life. N.Y.: McGraw-Hill [1959]. 172 p. views. Chapters on Indian hunters and their arms, wolves, the Kentucky rifle, grizzly bears, "the slaughter of the buffalo," waterfowling, "market hunters," and other subjects. [3013

MANLY S. MUMFORD. The skull of a buffalo. Westerners brand book (Chicago), 17:1-3, 5-8 (Mar). On "numbers, uses, and habits of the bison and the destruction of the tremendous herds," mentioned in the New World as early as 1521, originally found in all parts of the United States except New England and the Pacific Coast, used by the Indians of the Great Plains as a source of food, clothing, and fuel, and exterminated by wholesale commercial hunting between 1870 and 1875 except for a few survivors in isolated places. [3014

WINSTON E. BANKO. The trumpeter swan [Olor fuccinator]: its history, habits, and population in the United States. [Wash.: U.S. Fish and Wildlife Service, 1960.] x, 214 p. diagrs., maps, tables, views. bibliog. (p. 189-97). (U.S. Fish and Wildlife Service. North American fauna, 63.) Includes a review of historical references to the species in the United States and Canada (formerly approaching extinction but now increasing), 1632-1957, particularly in Montana and Wyoming. [3015

JAMES B. TREFETHEN. Another vanishing American. Am. forests, 65(1):17, 48-9 (Jan 1959). On wolves in North America, 1634-1958. [3016

IVAH GREEN. Wildlife in danger. N.Y.: Coward-McCann [1960]. 128 p. views. bibliog. (p. 125-6). On 20 species of extinct or "endangered birds and mammals" in America, 1714-1960. [3017

RUSSELL McKEE. Michigan's outdoor inventor. Mich. conservation, 29(6): 54-7 (Nov-Dec). ports., views. On Webster L. Marble (1865-1939) and the Marble Arms Corporation, Gladstone, Mich., maker of outdoor equipment, particularly "the Basic Four" (pocket safety ax, waterproof match case, woodsman compass, hunting knife). [3018

LEON LEONWOOD BEAN (born 1872). My story: the autobiography of a Down-East merchant. Freeport, Me., 1960. [4], 163 p. facsims., ports., tables, views. On the author's early life in Milton Plantation, Me., his great interest in hunting and fishing, the small beginnings of his manufacture of "the Maine Hunting Shoe," and the expansion of the business to form the L. L. Bean Company, Freeport, Me., maker of hunting and fishing equipment. [3019

NICHOLAS V. OLDS & HAROLD W. GLASSEN. Do States still own their game and fish? Mich. conservation, 20(4):9-12 (Jul-Aug 1951). notes. On litigation in Federal courts about "state ownership of game and fish," 1877-1951. [3020

DAVID LAMBERT LACK. The influence of weather on passerine migration: a review. Auk, 77:171-209 (Apr). bibliog. On migration in the North Temperate Zone, 1888-1958. [3021

DOUG DEMAREST. Pronghorns on postage stamps. Am. forests, 62(3): 24-5, 53-5 (Mar 1956). views. On postage stamps representing wildlife, 1898-1956. [3022

WALTER F. VAN DIEN. Bird banding [1909-49]. Mich. conservation, 19(1): 11-14 (Jan-Feb 1950). col. maps. [3023

WILL BARKER. Our vanishing species. Am. forests, 62(3):14-16 (Mar 1956). views. On nearly extinct species of North American mammals, birds, and fishes that have increased in numbers as a result of planned conservation since 1911. [3024

DAVID A. ARNOLD. The fox bounty [in Pennsylvania and Michigan, 1915-52]. Mich. conservation, 21(4):28-31 (Jul-Aug 1952). view. Evidence that it has not reduced the fox population or prevented its increase and "has not been responsible for the increases in small game." [3025

Mrs. LAIRD ARCHER. "Yours. Jerry Stillwell." Audubon mag., 62:76-9, 82 (Mar-Apr). port., views. On the work of Jerry Stillwell (died 1959) and his wife, Norma, in recording bird songs and calls in various parts of America and in organizing and editing the recordings, ca. 1925 to 1959. [3026

JOHN O'REILLY. Bob Allen--man with a mission. Audubon mag., 62: 164-6 (Jul-Aug). ports. On the work of Robert Porter Allen (born 1905) for the National Audubon Society, 1930-60. [3027

BRUCE S. WRIGHT. The return of the cougar. Audubon mag., 62:262-5, 292, 294-6 (Nov-Dec). map, port., views (1 double). Evidence that the panther was approaching extinction by 1930 and that its numbers may have increased in recent years to as many as about 100 in the Northeast, in addition to specimens along the Minnesota-Manitoba border. [3028

ROBERT PORTER ALLEN. Do we want to save the whooping crane? Audubon mag., 62:122-5, 134-5 (May-Jun). maps, views. notes. On efforts of the United States and Canada to prevent extinction of this bird, which breeds only in Wood Buffalo Park, Alberta and Northwest Territory, and winters only in Aransas National Wildlife Refuge, Tex., both of which areas are increasingly threatened by commercial or military encroachment, 1937-60. [3029

PROPERTY

MANUEL SERVIN. The act of sovereignty in the Age of Discovery [1492 to ca. 1900]. Ann Arbor: University Microfilms, 1959 [i. e. 1960]. Positive microfilm of typescript. [350] leaves. Thesis--Univ. of Southern California. Abstracted: Dissert. abstracts, 20: 4379 (May). On the "possession-taking activities by which the intrepid European navigators and explorers sought to acquire juridical ownership of terra nullius for their respective nations" and the conflict between the concepts of possession-taking and "effective occupation." [3030

LOUISE E. KOIER & ARTHUR W. PEACH. The first U.S. patentee, potash, and a puzzle: Who was Samuel Hopkins? Vt. Hist. Soc., News and notes, 7:2-4, 17-20 (Sep, Nov 1955). views. Text of the patent (for an apparatus for making potash and pearl ash) issued to Samuel Hopkins of Philadelphia, 31 Jul. 1790, "the first patent issued by the U.S." (printed from the original in the collections of the Chicago Historical Society);

with an account of Hopkins (1765-1840), for many years a resident of Pittsford, Vt., and some of his descendants, and remarks on the type of "the Vermont inventor." [3031

JAMES DON EDWARDS. History of public accounting in the United States [1766-1960]. East Lansing: Bureau of Business and Economic Research, Michigan State Univ. [1960]. xiv, 368 p. map, tables. bibliog. (p. 308-27), notes. (MSU business studies, 1960.) [3032

ROLLO GABRIEL SILVER. Prologue to copyright in America, 1772. Studies in bibliog., 11 (1958): 259-62. notes. [3033

KARL B. LUTZ. Can ornamental designs for useful articles be protected by copyright? Patent, trademark, and copyright jour., 2:289-302 (Jun 1958). notes. Evidence, 1787-1957. [3034

GILES S. RICH. Principles of patentability [1787-1959]. Geo. Wash. law rev., 28:393-407 (Jan). notes. [3035

AUBERT J. CLARK. The movement for international copyright in nineteenth century America [1790-1891]. Wash.: Catholic Univ. of America Press, 1960. ix, 215 p. bibliog. (p. 200-210), notes. Thesis--Catholic Univ. of America. [3036

ROY J. SAMPSON. American accounting education, textbooks, and public practice prior to 1900 [1796-1900]. Bus. hist. rev., 34:459-66 (winter). view. notes. [3037

RICHARD ROY BELDEN POWELL. Perpetuities in Arizona. Ariz. law rev., 1:225-52 (fall 1959). notes. On the law of perpetuities in New York since 1830, Michigan since 1837, Wisconsin since 1839, and Arizona since 1851. Includes comment by William H. Messinger, James Powers, Ozell M. Trask, and Gerald Jones. [3038

IRVING M. FREEDMAN. Certain aspects of the non-use of patented inventions [1832-1956]. Patent, trademark, and copyright jour., 2:159-67 (Mar 1958). notes. [3039

JOHN RITTENHOUSE, JR. Section 24 [of the Copyright Act of 1958]--renewal rights, survivors, and confusion. Dicta, 37:368-83 (Nov-Dec). notes. On the right, and the transfer or inheritance of the right, to renew a copyright, 1834-1958. [3040

HAROLD FRIEDMAN. The bankruptcy preference challenge to after-acquired property clauses under the Code [1843-1959]. Univ. Pa. law rev., 108: 194-224 (Dec 1959). notes. [3041

JERRY M. MURRAY. Easements of necessity to reach public lands. Wyo. law jour., 13:51-6 (fall 1958). notes. On legal problems concerning access to "public land that cannot be reached without crossing private lands," 1848-1958, with special notice of "the checkerboard pattern of ownership created in the railroad grants" in situations when the U.S. Government "has granted to private landowners all of the land surrounding a tract of land retained by the Government." [3042

MARJORIE DICK ROMBAUER. Easements by way of necessity across Federal lands [1848-1959]. Wash. law rev., 35:105-20 (spring). notes. On "the rights of owners deprived of free access to their properties by ever-changing federal land policies," particularly in the West. [3043

H. R. MAYERS. The United States patent system in historical perspective. Patent, trademark, and copyright jour., 3:33-52 (spring 1959). diagrs., tables. notes. On "Patent validity adjudications from 1850 to 1958." [3044

NEILL H. ALFORD, JR. The influence of the American Civil War upon the growth of the law of decedents' estates and trusts. Am. jour. legal hist., 4: 299-354 (Oct). notes. On the effects of emancipation, "a reduction in the efficiency of local government and a consequent breakdown in law enforcement," population movements, and "the inflation and ultimate loss of Confederate and state currency and the destruction of Confederate and state credit," 1861 to ca. 1890. [3045

JAMES E. DENNY. Eminent domain aspects of 28 USC 1498 [1863]. Patent, trademark, and copyright jour., 4: 257-75 (fall). notes. On the legality of patent infringement by the U.S. Government, 1863-1960. [3046

U.S. Bureau of Mines. Index of selected gasification patents (in three parts). I. United States patents. Compiled by Simon Klosky. Wash.: U.S. Govt. Print. Off., 1960. [2], 265 p. diagrs. notes. (Its Bulletin 581.) On patents for processes and apparatuses for converting coal to gas, 1867-1954. [3047

JOEL LARUS. The origin and development of the 1891 international copyright law of the United States. Ann Arbor: University Microfilms, 1960. Positive microfilm of typescript. [248] leaves. Thesis--Columbia Univ. Abstracted: Dissert. abstracts, 21: 1241-2 (Nov). [3048

WILLIAM N. HOGG. Patent misuse before and after Section 271 [1896-1958]. West. Reserve law quar., 11: 101-9 (Dec 1959). notes. [3049

JAMES ANGELL MacLACHLAN. The impact of bankruptcy on secured transactions. Columbia law rev., 60: 593-609 (May). notes. On several problems of bankruptcy law since 1898. [3050

SOLOMON FABRICANT. Government-owned nonmilitary capital assets since 1900. Conference on Research in Income and Wealth, Studies in income and wealth, 12 (1950): 527-47. tables. notes. [3051

PETER H. MORRISON. Copyright publication and phonograph records [1908-59]. Georgetown law jour., 48: 683-708 (summer). notes. [3052

LLOYD C. OWNBEY, JR. The civil remedies for disklegging. South. Calif. law quar., 33:190-207 (winter). notes. On "the unauthorized duplication of phonograph records" as a subject of litigation, 1909-55. [3053

KENNETH ROBERTS. The Luttes case--locating the boundary of the seashore. Baylor law rev., 12:141-74 (spring). notes. On California and Texas litigation concerning the location of the seashore in terms of tides, 1910-58, particularly in areas formerly included in Spanish and Mexican grants. [3054

JAMES R. GAFFEY. Certain aspects of the Armstrong regeneration, superregeneration, and superheterodyne controversies. Patent, trademark, and copyright jour., 4:173-87 (summer). diagrs. notes. On patents granted to Edwin Howard Armstrong, 1914-43, and suits for infringement filed by or against him. [3055

ALLAN TREZEVANT STEELE. A history of auditing in the United States, 1914 to 1957. Ann Arbor: University Microfilms, 1960. Positive microfilm of typescript. [245] leaves. Thesis--Univ. of Texas. Abstracted: Dissert. abstracts, 20:4557-8 (Jun). [3056

WILLIAM J. GEEN & HENRY K. SCHWARTZ. "Copyright" protection for uncopyrightables: the common-law doctrines. Univ. Pa. law rev., 108:699-734 (Mar). notes. On theories of common-law copyright, unfair competition, the right of privacy, and equitable servitude applied by State courts to the protection of "a creator's right in literary and artistic works," 1918-58. [3057

LENORE ALICE EPSTEIN. Consumers' tangible assets [1922-46]. Conference on Research in Income and Wealth, Studies in income and wealth, 12 (1950): 409-60. tables. notes. A study in measurement. [3058

EDWIN BURK COX. Trends in the distribution of stock ownership [since 1926 or earlier]. Ann Arbor: University Microfilms, 1960. Positive microfilm of typescript. [301] leaves. Thesis--Univ. of Pennsylvania. Abstracted: Dissert. abstracts, 21:793 (Oct). [3059

S. LAURENCE SHAIMAN. Bankruptcy--Section 14c(7), another milestone on the historical road toward protecting the creditor against dishonest petitions. Temple law quar., 33:210-18 (winter 1959). notes. On an amendment (1926) to the Bankruptcy Act of 1898. [3060

EDWARD ROSS ARANOW & HERBERT A. EINHORN. Proxy regulation [1934-59]: suggested improvements. Geo. Wash. law rev., 28:306-18 (Oct 1959). notes. [3061

MANUEL FREDERICK COHEN. The SEC and proxy contests. Fed. Bar jour., 20:91-110 (spring). notes. On rules developed by the Securities and Exchange Commission since 1935. [3062

BARKEV SAKAH SANDERS, JOSEPH ROSSMAN, & L. JAMES HARRIS. Patent acquisition by corporations [1936-55]. Patent, trademark, and copyright jour., 3:217-61 (fall 1959). tables. notes. [3063

DAVID FERBER, ARTHUR BLASBERG, JR., & MELVIN KATZ. Conflicts of interest in reorganization proceedings under the Public Utility Holding Company Act of 1935 and Chapter X of the Bankruptcy Act [1938]. Geo. Wash. law rev., 28:319-91 (Oct 1959). notes. On the responsibilities of the Securities and Exchange Commission in such proceedings. [3064

BARKEV SAKAH SANDERS, JOSEPH ROSSMAN, & L. JAMES HARRIS. The economic impact of patents. Patent, trademark, and copyright jour., 2:340-62 (Sep 1958). tables. notes. Analysis of replies to questionnaires addressed in 1957 to holders of patents issued in 1938, 1948, and 1952. [3065

BARKEV SAKAH SANDERS, JOSEPH ROSSMAN, & L. JAMES HARRIS. The non-use of patented inventions. Patent, trademark, and copyright jour., 2:1-60 (Mar 1958). tables. notes. Analysis of replies to questionnaires addressed in 1957 to holders of patents issued in 1938, 1948, and 1952. [3066

HENRY P. CHANDLER. The beginning of a new era in bankruptcy administration, 1939-1947. Natl. Assoc. Referees in Bankruptcy, Jour., 34:3-6, 44-53 (Jan, Apr). port. notes. [3067

LAWRENCE M. GREENE. Fiduciary standards of conduct under the Investment Company Act of 1940. Geo. Wash. law rev., 28:266-86 (Oct 1959). notes. [3068

EMANUEL ROBERT POSNACK. Inventions, patents, and society: an evaluation and re-evaluation. Fed. Bar jour., 20:263-73 (summer). On "judicial erosion of the patent system" by requirements of "creative imagination," "the advancement of science," a "flash of genius," etc., 1941-60. [3069

LESTER EDWIN NELSON. Sovereign immunity and Federal liens. Brooklyn law rev., 26:18-40 (Dec 1959). notes. On the authority of courts "to prescribe any legal or equitable remedy appropriate to quiet title to property subject to a claim of the Government" of the United States, 1942-59. [3070

FRANKLIN J. REISS. Land ownership and tenure in the United States [1945-54]. Land Economics Institute, University of Illinois, 1958, Modern land policy: papers (Urbana: Univ. of Illinois Press, 1960), p. 347-57. tables. notes. [3071

DONALD L. GUNNELS. Copyright protection for writers employed by the Federal Government [1947-59]. Wash. Univ. law quar., 1960:182-7 (Apr). notes. [3072

Industry

WILLIAM NELSON PARKER & FRANKLEE WHARTENBY. The growth of output before 1840 [1799-1839]. Conference on Research in Income and Wealth, Trends in the American economy in the nineteenth century, ed. William N. Parker (Princeton: Princeton Univ. Press, 1960 [Studies in income and wealth, 24]), p. 191-216. tables. notes. [3073

ROBERT EMIL GALLMAN. Commodity output, 1839-1899. Conference on Research in Income and Wealth, Trends in the American economy in the nineteenth century, ed. William N. Parker (Princeton: Princeton Univ. Press, 1960 [Studies in income and wealth, 24]), p. 13-71. tables. notes. On "the sum of value added by agriculture, mining, manufacturing, and construction," value added being "the value of output, at producers' prices, less the value of materials and fuels directly consumed in production, at delivered prices." [3074

JANET MONTGOMERY HOOKS. The contribution of household production to the national income. Ann Arbor: University Microfilms, 1960. Positive microfilm of typescript. [242] leaves. Thesis--Univ. of Illinois. Abstracted: Dissert. abstracts, 21:1397-8 (Dec). On "the value of production by housewives for the period from 1860 to 1950," measured in units of quantity determined by "one woman devoting her time primarily to housework in her own home." [3075

GILBERT WARREN NUTTER. The structure and growth of Soviet industry: a comparison with the United States [1870-1955]. Jour. law & econ., 2:147-74 (Oct 1959). diagrs., tables. notes. [3076

U.S. Bureau of Labor Statistics. Indexes of output per man-hour for selected industries, 1919 to 1958. [Wash.] 1959. 6 p. tables. notes. [3077

C. S. BAKER. Productivity potentials of new technologies related to land. Land Economics Institute, University of Illinois, 1958, Modern land policy: papers (Urbana: Univ. of Illinois Press, 1960), p. 103-12. diagrs. notes. On the "relation of technological change to production" in agricultural and nonagricultural production, 1930-58. [3078

AGRICULTURE AND RELATED INDUSTRIES

FRANK WILLIAM MOORE. The foundations of New World agriculture. Ann Arbor: University Microfilms, 1960. Positive microfilm of typescript. [243] leaves. Thesis--Columbia Univ. Abstracted: Dissert. abstracts, 21: 725-6 (Oct). Evidence that "agriculture originated in several areas of the New World under a variety of ecological conditions and it developed from a variety of plants," probably before 3000 B.C. [3079

U.S. Dept. of Agriculture. The agricultural industry. John G. Glover & Rudolph L. Lagai, eds., The development of American industries: their economic significance, 4th ed. (N.Y.: Simmons-Boardman [1959]), p. 1-29. On farming as a form of production since Indian times, and the activities and agencies of the U.S. Government established for the promotion and improvement of agriculture. [3080

JOHN HERBERT DAVIS & KENNETH HINSHAW. Farmer in a business suit. N.Y.: Simon and Schuster [1957]. x, 241, [2] p. On "all those factors both on and off the farm which are involved in the production, processing and distribution of food and fiber," i. e., "the modern combination of agriculture and business," and the changes leading to it since the 1630s. [3081

MARVIN W. TOWNE & WAYNE D. RASMUSSEN. Farm gross product and gross investment in the nineteenth century. Conference on Research in Income and Wealth, Trends in the American economy in the nineteenth century, ed. William N. Parker (Princeton: Princeton Univ. Press, 1960 [Studies in income and wealth, 24]), p. 255-315. tables. notes. [3082

AMY CHAMBLISS. The mulberry craze. Ga. rev., 14:156-64 (summer). On the reasons for the sudden interest in "this miracle tree" and in "silk-raising," and the accompanying "speculative flurry," 1837-44; with some account of American efforts since 1778 to encourage the silk industry, beginning with Ezra Stiles at Yale. [3083

W. G. KAISER. A century of progress in farm housing and storage structures [1852-1952]. Agric. engineering, 34: 34-6, 46 (Jan 1953). views. [3084

CHARLES MEYER HARDIN. Political planning: possibilities, limitations, and aberrations [1870s-1958]. Land Economics Institute, University of Illinois, 1958, Modern land policy: papers (Urbana: Univ. of Illinois Press, 1960), p. 251-67. notes. On "American agricultural policy as a major example of such planning in a modern constitutional democracy." [3085

U.S. Dept. of Agriculture. The tenure status of farmworkers [sic] in the United States [1880-1950]. By Frank H[erman] Maier, Sheridan T. Maitland, [and] Gladys K. Bowles. Wash.: Agricultural Research Service and Agricultural Marketing Service, U.S. Dept. of Agriculture, 1960. [4], 91 p. 33 diagrs., maps, 23 tables. bibliog. (p. 76-80). (Its Technical bulletin 1217.) On the changing ratio of owner-operators to tenants, sharecroppers, and farm laborers. [3086

WALLACE ASHBY. Fifty years of development in farm buildings [1900-1957]. Agric. engineering, 38:426-32, 459 (Jun 1957). plans, table. views. [3087

JAMES L. STALLINGS. Weather indexes. Jour. farm econ., 42:180-86 (Feb). tables. notes. Based on thesis--Michigan State Univ. On "indexes of the influence of weather" on various agricultural productions, 1900-1957. [3088

DEANE G. CARTER. Farm building trends [1907-57]. Agric. engineering, 38:433-5 (Jun 1957). views. On changes in materials, size, equipment, and types of farm structures other than dwellings. [3089

ZVI GRILICHES. Estimates of the aggregate U.S. farm supply function. Jour. farm econ., 42:282-93 (May). tables. bibliog., notes. On "the supply of farm products" as "a function of relative prices, weather, the state of technology, and other variables," 1920-57. [3090

FRANK ALOYSIUS BARRETT (1892-1962). The legal aspects of major programs administered by the United States Department of Agriculture. Wyo. law jour., 14:175-97 (spring). notes. Review of activities under the Packers and Stockyards Act (1921), the Sugar Act (1948), and the National Wool Act (1954). [3091

VERNON W. RUTTAN & THOMAS T. STOUT. Regional differences in factor shares in American agriculture: 1925-1957. Jour. farm econ., 42:52-68

(Feb). tables. notes. On the shares represented by labor, land, "nonland capital," and "current operating expenses and taxes." [3092

MERLE L. ESMAY & HENRY GIESE. Wind damage to farm buildings. Agric. engineering, 32:275-7 (May 1951). diagrs. On a study of farm losses from wind and fire, 1930-48, conducted by the Iowa Agricultural Experiment Station. [3093

CHRISTIANA McFADYEN CAMPBELL. The Farm Bureau and the New Deal, 1933-1940: a study in agricultural sectionalism. Chicago: [Dept. of Photoduplication, Univ. of Chicago Library] 1960. Positive microfilm of typescript. 273 leaves. bibliog. Thesis--Univ. of Chicago. [3094

U.S. Agricultural Research Service. Index numbers of agricultural production by regions, 1939-1958. [By Donald Douglas Durost. Wash., 1960.] 37 p. diagrs., tables. notes. (U.S. Dept. of Agriculture. Statistical bulletin 273.) [3095

WILL BARKER. World of words. Am. forests, 64(4):19, 58-61 (Apr 1958). ports., views. On The yearbook of agriculture as edited since 1945 by Alfred Stefferud. [3096

RALPH WESLEY PHILLIPS. Food and Agriculture Organization completes 15 years. Science, 132:871-81 (30 Sep). views. notes. On the participation of the United States in the Food and Agriculture Organization of the United Nations, 1945-60. [3097

DALE E. HATHAWAY & JOHN F. STOLLSTEIMER. The impact of price support programs upon the available supplies of farm products, 1948-56. East Lansing: Dept. of Agricultural Economics, Michigan State Univ., 1960. 55 p. tables. (Michigan. Agricultural Experiment Station, East Lansing. Technical bulletin 277.) [3098

Agricultural Education

VERNON ROSCO CARSTENSEN. The genesis of an agricultural experiment station. Agric. hist., 34:13-20 (Jan). notes. On the Wisconsin Agricultural Experiment Station, established in 1883; with some account of the development of agricultural education in Wisconsin since 1849. [3099

EARLE DUDLEY ROSS. Contributions of land-grant education to history and the social sciences [ca. 1865 to ca. 1900]. Agric. hist., 34:51-61 (Apr). notes. On these studies in the curricula of agricultural and mechanical colleges, and some of the scholars and administrators who promoted the studies. [3100

ROY VERNON SCOTT. Pioneering in agricultural education: Oren C. Gregg [1845-1926] and farmers' institutes. Minn. hist., 37:19-29 (Mar). port., views. notes. On his life in Minnesota, 1865-1926, as a lay minister, a prosperous dairyman in Lyon County, and an organizer of lectures for farmers at county fairs and other gatherings, and the support of the lecture program by the State (with Gregg as superintendent, 1887-1907). [3101

PAUL KEITH CONKIN. The vision of Elwood Mead [1858-1936]. Agric. hist., 34:88-97 (Apr). notes. On the contributions of "America's greatest irrigationist" to "a policy of aided and directed land settlement," "a new, planned agriculture in the United States," and the concept of planned agricultural communities, 1914-35. [3102

Agricultural Technology

NATIONAL CANNERS ASSOCIATION. The canning industry: its history, importance, organization, methods, and the public service value of its products [since 1819]. Second edition. Wash.: Information Division, National Canners Assoc., 1954. 36 p. diagrs., tables, views. bibliog. (p. 34-6). 1st ed. 1939. [3103

CHRIS NYBERG. High lights in the development of the combine [1828-1957]. Agric. engineering, 38:528-9, 535 (Jul 1957). facsim., views. [3104

B. H. SLICHER VAN BATH. The influence of economic conditions on the development of agricultural tools and machines in history. Jacob Louis Meij, ed., Mechanization in agriculture (Amsterdam: North-Holland Pub. Co., 1960), p. 1-36. tables. notes. Includes some account of mechanization in American agriculture, 1830-1930. [3105

JOHN WILLIS WEAVER, JR., NORMAN C. TETER, & SIDNEY H. USRY. The development of a farm crop drier [1830-1949]. Agric. engineering, 30:475-6, 478, 488 (Oct 1949). table, views. notes. [3106

EUGENE GEORGE McKIBBEN. The evolution of farm implements and machines [1831-1952]. Agric. engineering, 34:91-3 (Feb 1953). views. [3107

LEWIS ALLEN JONES. Drainage as a tool for increased crop production [1835-1952]. Agric. engineering, 34: 239-42, 250 (Apr 1953). views. [3108

JERALD EMMETT CHRISTIANSEN. Irrigation in relation to food production [1847-1952]. Agric. engineering, 34:400-406, 410 (Jun 1953). diagrs., tables. notes. [3109

HARRY BRUCE WALKER. Engineering appraisal of farm mechanization [1852-1952]. Agric. engineering, 33: 698-701, 704 (Nov 1952). diagr., views. notes. [3110

ARTHUR J. SCHWANTES. Agricultural engineering--past and present [1870-1949]. Agric. engineering, 30: 327-9 (Jul 1949). diagr., port. [3111

IVAN D. WOOD. The engineering revolution in agriculture [1870-1952]. Agric. engineering, 33:613-16, 626 (Oct 1952). port., views. [3112

EARL D. ANDERSON. Engineering developments and challenges in chemical weed control [1890-1952]. Agric. engineering, 33:482-4, 486 (Aug 1952). views. notes. [3113

HOMER D. WITZEL & BERNARD F. VOGELAAR. Engineering the hillside combine. Agric. engineering, 36: 522-5, 528 (Aug 1955). views. On harvesters for use on sloping land, 1890-1954. [3114

ROY BURTON GRAY & E. M. DIEFFENBACH. Fifty years of tractor development in the U.S.A. [1892-1957]. Agric. engineering, 38:388-97 (Jun 1957). views. [3115

DALE E. WOLF. Progress in chemical weed control [1896-1948]. Agric. engineering, 30:78-80 (Feb 1949). [3116

TRUMAN EDWARD HIENTON. Trends in rural electrification [1898-1956]. Agric. engineering, 38:453-9 (Jun 1957). diagr., tables, views. notes. [3117

GEORGE B. NUTT. Agricultural engineering in a changing economy [1898-1955]. Agric. engineering, 36: 477-8, 482 (Jul 1955). port. [3118

JOSEPH PETER SCHAENZER. Rural electrification since the turn of the century [1898-1955]. Agric. engineering, 38:442-52, 459 (Jun 1957). cartoons, diagrs., facsims., tables, views. notes. [3119

RUTH J. HEFFELFINGER. Experiment in concrete: a pioneer venture in grain storage. Minn. hist., 37:14-18 (Mar). views. notes. On the travels of Frank T. Heffelfinger (died 1959) in Europe in 1900 to examine concrete bins and other concrete structures for storing grain and to study the European market for American grain, and the work of Frank H. Peavey (his father-in-law) and Charles F. Haglin in constructing concrete buildings in Minnesota (including a "tubular concrete grain elevator" built in Minneapolis in 1899, still standing in 1960). [3120

FRANK J. ZINK. Administrative status of agricultural engineering in the USDA [1899-1949]. Agric. engineering, 31:283-4 (Jun 1950). diagr. [3121

JOHN GUICE SUTTON. Drainage developments during the past 50 years. Agric. engineering, 38:405-13 (Jun 1957). map, table, views. notes. On organized agricultural drainage enterprises, 1905-57. [3122

CARL W. HALL. Agricultural processing--past, present, and future [1906-56]. Agric. engineering, 38: 436-41 (Jun 1957). ports., table, views. notes. [3123

ROY BAINER. The engineer's place in agriculture [1907-57]. Agric. engineering, 38:377, 387 (Jun 1957). port. [3124

HENRY GIESE. ASAE--its founding and first fifty years. Agric. engineering, 38:378-87 (Jun 1957). ports., tables, views. notes. On the American Society of Agricultural Engineers, 1907-57. [3125

HOWARD FRANKLIN McCOLLY. Fifty years of farm machinery [1907-57]. Agric. engineering, 38:398-404 (Jun 1957). views. notes. [3126

U.S. Agricultural Marketing Service. Output of factories processing farm food products in the United States, 1909-1958. [By William Harold Waldorf. Wash., 1960.] vi, 43 p. 10 diagrs., 17 tables. bibliog. (p. 43), notes. (U.S. Dept. of Agriculture. Technical bulletin 1223.) [3127

EARL OREL HEADY. Extent and conditions of agricultural mechanization in the United States [1910-55]. Jacob Louis Meij, ed., Mechanization in agriculture (Amsterdam: North-Holland Pub. Co., 1960), p. 63-97. tables. notes. [3128

W. J. RIDOUT, JR. Farm electrification research by electric operating companies [1910-50]. Agric. engineering, 31:403-8 (Aug 1950). [3129

GEORGE H. SEFEROVICH. Handling materials on farms. Agric. engineering, 39:518-23, 537 (Sep 1958). diagrs., tables. notes. On changes in the "materials handling aspects of the post-harvesting operations" on American farms, 1910-57. [3130

U.S. Dept. of Agriculture. Numbers of selected machines and equipment on farms, with related data [1910-55. By Paul E. Strickler and Charles A. Hines.] Wash., 1960. 30 p. tables. notes. (Its Statistical bulletin 258.) A joint study by the Agricultural Research Service and the Agricultural Marketing Service. [3131

JOHN ROBERT HASWELL. Some tile drainage experiences. Agric. engineering, 30:81-3, 85 (Feb 1959). diagr., views. notes. On the author's work as a "drainage engineer" for the Pennsylvania Agricultural Extension Service and the U.S. Department of Agriculture, ca. 1917 to 1948. [3132

WALTER MONROE CARLETON. Progress in research methods and techniques [in agricultural technology, 1920-24, 1949-54]. Agric. engineering, 36:256-60 (Apr 1955). table. notes. [3133

ZVI GRILICHES. The demand for a durable input: farm tractors in the United States, 1921-57. Arnold C. Harberger, ed., The demand for durable goods (Chicago: Univ. of Chicago Press [1960]), p. 179-207. diagrs., tables. notes. Econometric study. [3134

ELIOT TOZER. Farmer's air force: industry survey and forecast. Flying, 67(2):22-5, 58 (Aug). views. On the insecticidal spraying and dusting of crops by airplanes, 1921-60. [3134a

C. R. HAGEN. Twenty-five years of cotton picker development [1922-51]. Agric. engineering, 32:593-6, 599 (Nov 1951). views. [3135

ROY BAINER. College-industry cooperative research [in agricultural technology, 1928-54]. Agric. engineering, 36:385-8 (Jun 1955). views. notes. [3136

JOHN R. BRAKE. Fertilizer demand in the South Atlantic and East North Central regions [1930-58]. Jour. farm econ., 42:676-86 (Aug). diagrs., tables. notes. [3137

E. C. EASTER. Engineered farm electric service [1927-52]. Agric. engineering, 34:155-6, 158 (Mar 1953). view. [3138

H. D. BRUHN. Status of hay crusher development. Agric. engineering, 36: 165-70 (Mar 1955). diagrs., views. notes. On equipment and procedures in relation to rate of drying, 1930-53. [3139

CLIFFORD LESLIE HAMILTON. Progress toward greater safety in agriculture [1930-51]. Agric. engineering, 33:419-20 (Jul 1952). diagrs. [3140

WILBUR MAGRUDER HURST. Industrial applications of agricultural engineering [1930-50]. Agric. engineering, 31:441-2, 444 (Sep 1950). views. notes. [3141

P. J. FORREST. Progress in tractor tire development [1932-54]. Agric. engineering, 35:853-4 (Dec 1954). [3142

FRED HAWTHORNE. Handling chopped forages on the farm [1932-48]. Agric. engineering, 30:125-8 (Mar 1949). views. [3143

ROBERT MUNDHENK SALTER. The engineer's job in developing America's agricultural capacity to produce. Agric. engineering, 34:83-7 (Feb 1953). views. On the contributions of agricultural engineering to the "advancement of soil and water technology," 1933-53. [3144

D. B. KRIMGOLD. Economic feasibility of supplemental irrigation. Agric. engineering, 35:22-7 (Jan 1954). diagr., tables. notes. On studies of the development of methods to determine times and amounts of irrigation in ordinarily rainy areas, 1934-53. Based in part on rainfall records of Seabrook and Bridgeton, N.J., 1883-1952. [3145

H. S. PRINGLE. Electrification changed the face of agriculture [1935-52]. Agric. engineering, 34:330-31 (May 1953). [3146

JOE FRANK DAVIS. Economic studies of farm electrification. Agric. engineering, 31:565-8 (Nov 1950). diagrs., table. On consumption of electric power on farms in northwestern Washington, eastern Iowa, and the upper Piedmont of Georgia, 1938-48. [3147

A. T. HENDRIX. Equipment and labor requirements for storing and feeding silage [1939-55]. Agric. engineering, 41:162-7 (Mar). diagrs., tables. notes. [3148

S. A. WITZEL & D. W. DERBER. Engineering phases of dairy barn research, 1941-1951. Agric. engineering, 33:635-43 (Oct 1952). plans, tables, views. notes. [3149

E. F. BLACKWELDER. Development of the Marbeet Sugar Beet Harvester [1943-48]. Agric. engineering, 29:481 (Nov 1948). [3150

SAMUEL A. GOLDBLITH. The teaching of food technology at Massachusetts Institute of Technology [1944-59]. Jour. chem. educ., 37:214-15 (Apr). [3151

E. W. TANQUARY. Standardization of farm equipment [1944-57]. Agric. engineering, 38:606-9 (Aug 1957). [3152

SILAS MILTON HENDERSON. Agricultural processing engineering [1945-54]. Agric. engineering, 35:333-6 (May 1954). diagrs. On processes applied on or near the farm to agricultural products to maintain or raise their quality or to change their form or characteristics (e. g., sorting and grading fruits, curing tobacco, treating seed, canning vegetables, dressing poultry, freezing meat). [3153

THEODORE CARROLL BYERLY. Goals of engineering research on poultry housing [1946-60]. Agric. engineering, 41:566-7 (Sep). diagr. bibliog. [3154

NORMAN CARROLL TETER. Peanut curing as related to mechanization [1946-53]. Agric. engineering, 35: 568-9, 573 (Aug 1954). tables. notes. [3155

Animal Industries

ROBERT MOORMAN DENHARDT. Bloodlines of the modern quarter horse. By Bob Denhardt. West. horseman, 25(4):32-3, 174-80 (Apr). views. Horse genealogies. [3156

TANNERS' COUNCIL OF AMERICA. The leather industry [since Indian times]. John G. Glover & Rudolph L. Lagai, eds., The development of American industries: their economic significance, 4th ed. (N.Y.: Simmons-Boardman [1959]), p. 117-36. [3157

ORVILLE HOWARD. Longhorns. Quarter horse jour., 12(10):20-21, 52, 64 (Jul). ports., view. On "mounted ornamental horns" of longhorn cattle, collected and sold by Paul Ansley of Amarillo, Tex., 1945-60; with some account of the history of longhorn cattle in America since 1521. [3158

AMERICAN MEAT INSTITUTE. The meat processing industry [since 1645. Prepared by Lawrence N. Eldred and Robert West Howard.] John G. Glover & Rudolph L. Lagai, eds., The development of American industries: their economic significance, 4th ed. (N.Y.: Simmons-Boardman [1959]), p. 30-44. [3159

FRANKLIN REYNOLDS. A history of quarter racing [1677-1950]. Quarter horse jour., 3(2-4): monthly installments (Nov 1950 - Jan 1951). Mainly information from John Hervey, Racing in America, 1665-1865 (1944), written for the Jockey Club, about "American Quarter Running Horses" in Virginia as early as 1674; with slight mention of the diffusion of racing and quarter horses in the South and the West. [3160

MARY WILLIS SHUEY. Early quarter horses. Quarter horse jour., 12(7):74, 132-3 (Apr). Pedigrees of American quarter horses, 1766-1824. [3161

H. D. SMILEY. The Cherokee side of the quarter horse. Quarter horse jour., 7(3):18-20 (Dec 1954). port. Argument that "the 'Cherokee horse,' or 'Chickasaw horse,' which I believe to be one and the same," was developed in the East as "a breed or strain that was distinctive and bred true to type" through the efforts of the Cherokees to cross Spanish horses from "the Florida stud ranches" and horses stolen or strayed from the Carolina colonists, that some of the Cherokees arrived in Arkansas as early as 1785 and must have taken horses with them, that the Indian horses in that region were descended from horses seized from the Spaniards in and after the 17th century (especially in the uprising of 1680 in New Mexico), that the Cherokee horses were interbred with the Indian horses, and that early white settlers in the Southwest bred the Cherokee mares to Thoroughbred stallions. [3162

BEN A. GREEN. Biography of the Tennessee walking horse. Nashville: Parthenon Press [1960]. 236 p. facsims., ports., views (part col., 1 double). On Bald Stockings, foaled in Kentucky in 1837, the first horse ever to show "the peculiar gait" known as the "running walk," and the breed of walking horses developed from him, particularly in Tennessee. [3163

AL LOUAILLIER. Story of the saddle. Quarter horse jour., 7(3):78-9 (Dec 1954). On Mexican saddles and their descendants in the United States since the 1840s or later. [3164

MAURICE SHELDON PRESCOTT. Holstein-Friesian history. Lacona, N.Y.: Holstein-Friesian World, Inc., 1960. vii, 557 p. ports., tables, views. notes. 31 cm. 1st ed. 1929. On "the first permanent establishment of Dutch cattle in this country" in 1852, commonly called Holstein cattle (though neither Holstein nor Friesian), the Holstein-Friesian Association of America (founded in 1885), auction records, shows and awards, "Families of the breed," and the breed in Canada. Includes chapters by Henry Hiram Wing and William A. Prescott. [3165

THE QUARTER HORSE. [Biographies of living breeders, raisers, and trainers of quarter horses, based upon interviews with the subjects.] Quarter horse, 2(11)-5(3): irregular installments (Feb 1948 - Jun 1949). Accounts of George Clegg (born 1872) of Alice, Tex., Everett Colborn (born 1892) of Dublin, Tex., G. B. Mathis (fl. 1898 ff.) of Texas, Lou Kirk (fl. 1900 ff.) of New Mexico, Ott Adams (born 1868) of Texas, Chester Cooper (fl. 1900 ff.) of Arizona, Ed Fields (born 1888) of Texas, John Wesley House (born 1873) of Texas, S. Coke Blake (born 1862) of Oklahoma, and Coy Herman Mansfield (born 1914), native of Bandera, Tex., rodeo performer. By various contributors. [3166

TOM BURRIER. Hoof beats 'round the world. West. horseman, 25(1):26, 67-9 (Jan). facsims. On horses in postage-stamp designs in America, 1870-1960, and abroad. [3167

ED BATEMAN, SR. The Traveler story. Quarter horse jour., 12(3):22, 66, 235 (Dec 1959). view. From The quarter horse, Jul. 1946. On a "light sorrel" horse foaled in northern New York (date and ancestry unknown), brought as a work horse to Texas "in the early eighties," where his racing potentialities were discovered and he was used as a stud as late as 1904, becoming the ancestor of "more than one-half of all registered Quarter Horses" and deserving recognition as "the greatest example of Quarter Horse pre-potency in this nation's history." [3168

DORYS CROW GROVER. Fur covered horses. West. horseman, 25(6):36-7, 70 (Jun). views. On horses with "about an inch of tightly curled hair all over the body," seen by C. A. Wolf running wild in the mountains of Oregon and later raised by him on his ranch at Pendleton; with 5 earlier references to such horses in Nevada and elsewhere as early as the 1880s, and speculations about their origin. See also "More on the curly horses," by Peter J. Damele, 25(8):5, on the breeding and raising of curly horses by him and his father, Peter L. Damele, on their ranch near Eureka, Nev., descended from wild horses caught ca. 1898. [3169

THEODORE R. GAMBLE. 75 years of Pet Milk Company (1885-1960): the company that founded an industry. N.Y.: Newcomen Soc. in North America, 1960. 28 p. port. On a firm founded by Louis Latzer in 1885 as the Helvetia Milk Condensing Company, Highland, Ill., later moved to St. Louis, and its later expansion into related fields, including dry milk and frozen desserts. [3170

HERBERT K. WEBB. To those who follow. Phila.: C. J. Webb Sons Co. [1960]. vii, 118 p. cartoons, facsims., double geneal. table, ports. (1 double), views. On Charles J. Webb (1858-1930) and his early life in Wilmington, Del.; Charles J. Webb & Company (1885-1921), Philadelphia and Boston, "wool merchants," wholesale dealers in wool and cotton yarn, later also in cloth; and Charles J. Webb Sons Company, Inc. (founded in 1921), organized by his sons Charles Edwin (1883-1950), Andrew Spangler (1886-1930), and Herbert K. (born 1791), dealers in various textile products. [3171

THE QUARTER HORSE. [Biographies of eminent quarter horses, mainly Texas racers and stallions.] Quarter horse, 2(10)-5(4): monthly installments (Jan 1948 - Jul 1949). Accounts of Rialto (1923-44), Ace of Hearts (died ca. 1918), Midnight (1916-36, by Nelson C. Nye), Diamond Jim (1941-45, of Kentucky, Texas, and Arizona, by E. L. Cowey), Jack Dempsey (1921-36, of New Mexico), Little Dick (1911-42, by Claude Mullins), Karnes City Jim (1900?-1922?), Zantanon (1917-41, of Texas and Mexico), Martin's Cananea 6600 (foaled 1930, Mexico and Arizona brood mare, by Doris Seibold), Peter McCue (1894-1923), My Texas Dandy (foaled 1926), Uncle Jimmie Gray (1906-32, of Oklahoma and Texas), Lone Star (foaled ca. 1920), El Lemon del Sur (1938-44), Joe Hancock (1923?-1944), Lucky Boots (foaled 1940), Ariel (foaled 1925), Ace of Diamonds (1920-43), and Dan Tucker (1887-1912, of Illinois). [3172

C. J. CRONAN, FR. American Saddle Horse Breeders Association, Incorporated [1891-1960]. West. horseman, 25(10):9, 101-2 (Oct). [3173

ROBERT MOORMAN DENHARDT. These were the greatest. By Bob Denhardt. Quarter horse jour., 8(3): 11 (Dec 1955). port. On the "15 greatest Quarter Horses that ever lived," 1900-1940. [3174

CARLE HODGE. Bucking horses. Ariz. highways, 36(2):16-29 (Feb). views (part col.). On the capricious conduct of these horses, the value to the rodeo industry of their unwillingness to be ridden and their willingness to test the talents of "bronc riders," and the growing scarcity of such horses and of horses in general, 1900-1960. [3175

JOE W. KOUDELE & EDWIN C. HEINSOHN. The egg products industry of the United States. Part I. Historical highlights [1900-1959]. Manhattan: Kansas State Univ. of Agriculture and Applied Science, 1960. 47, [1] p. tables (1 double), views. bibliog. (p. 47), notes. (Kansas, Agricultural Experiment Station, Manhattan. Bulletin 423. North Central regional publication 108.) On products for use by bakers and confectioners, including liquid eggs, dried eggs, frozen eggs (whites only, yolks only, mixed whites and yolks), and egg powder. [3176

ROBERT MOORMAN DENHARDT. Call me Joe. Quarter horse jour., 4(7):26-7, 70-71 (Apr 1952). ports., views. On the descendants, mainly in the West, of Little Joe (foaled ca. 1905), Old Joe Bailey of Weatherford (1907-34), Joe Bailey of Gonzales (foaled 1919; grandson of the preceding), Joe Blair (fl. 1916-19), Joe Reed, and Joe Hancock--Texas stallions. [3177

U.S. Agricultural Research Service. Animal units of livestock fed annually, 1909 to 1959. [By Earl F. Hodges. Wash.: U.S. Govt. Print. Off.] 1960. 12 p. diagrs., tables. (U.S. Dept. of Agriculture. Statistical bulletin 271.) [3178

U.S. Agricultural Research Service. Livestock-production units, 1910-1958, and consumption of feed by livestock, 1955-1958. [By Earl F. Hodges. Wash., 1960.] 31 p. diagrs., tables. (U.S. Dept. of Agriculture. Statistical bulletin 275.) [3179

JERRY ARMSTRONG. Leo Moomaw and Badger Mountain. West. horseman, 25(1):30-31, 74-6 (Jan). ports. On Moomaw as a rodeo performer and (in partnership with Tim Bernard) a contractor and producer of rodeo animals, 1917-60; with an account of his famous bucking horse, Badger Mountain (1926?-1954), celebrated "all over the country." [3180

GEORGIA McKINLEY. Michigan horseman. Quarter horse jour., 8(7): 85, 88 (Apr 1955). On Andy Quirie (born 1890), emigrant from Scotland to Canada in 1912 and to Kentucky in 1917, horse-breeder at Camden Farm near Versailles, Ky., later a breeder of Percheron and Belgian horses at Michigan State College. [3181

GEORGE LOWELL BAKER, JR. The structure of the U.S. meat industry [1920-60]. Ann Arbor: University Microfilms, 1960. Positive microfilm of typescript. [254] leaves. Thesis--Purdue Univ. Abstracted: Dissert. abstracts, 21:1087 (Nov). [3182

NED HOLLOWAY. Kentucky Derby winner from the Osage country. West. horseman, 25(8):45, 82-3 (Aug). port. On Black Gold (1921?-1928), a Thoroughbred racer in America and England, bred in Oklahoma by Al Hoots (who died before the colt was foaled), trained and attended throughout life by Hanley Webb (an Indian), and shot by Webb in New Orleans after breaking a leg in a race. [3183

FRANKLIN REYNOLDS. The history of Joe Reed [foaled 1921, living 1938]. Quarter horse jour., 12(3-5): monthly installments (Dec 1959 - Feb 1960). ports., tables, views. On a "sorrel, or chestnut" quarter horse stallion, owned and trained in Texas, who "in over-all appearance ... probably came nearer being exactly like the original Colonial American Quarter Running Horse than any other individual of the Twentieth Century"; with a detailed account of his distinguished ancestry and his many eminent descendants in the South and the West. [3184

U.S. Agricultural Research Service. Breeding experiments with Holstein-Friesian cattle: result of 35 years' research at Beltsville [since 1925. By Milton Henry Fohrman. Wash., 1960.] ii, 65 p. 5 diagrs., 31 tables. (U.S. Dept. of Agriculture. Technical bulletin 1220.) [3185

POODLE CLUB OF AMERICA. Poodles in America: a comprehensive record from 1929 to 1959. ... Compiled and edited by William H. Ivens, Jr., Chairman, Publicity and Information. [Doylestown? Pa.] c1960. 519 p. diagr., ports., seal, tables, views. Includes "The poodle in America before 1929" (1911-29), by Flora M. Bonney. [3186

ALBERT EDWARD DARLOW. The changing beef-producing industry [1930-58]. Agric. engineering, 41: 611-12 (Sep). [3187

ROBERT MOORMAN DENHARDT. Helen Michaelis, second Secretary AQHA. By Bob Denhardt. Quarter horse jour., 12(12):16-17, 136-8 (Sep). ports. Reminiscences of Helen Mary (Hall) Michaelis, rancher and rancher's wife in Texas, Secretary of the American Quarter Horse Association (1942-46), stringent enforcer of the rule that horses could not be registered without proof of "bloodlines"; with note of the excellent effect of this stringency upon the quality of the quarter horse breed today. [3188

Plant Industries

ROBERT K. HEIMANN. Tobacco and Americans [1492-1960]. N.Y.: McGraw-Hill [1960. 2], 265, [13] p. col. diagrs., facsims., ports., views. bibliog. (p. 269-70). On the use of tobacco by the Indians of the Americas, its later consumption in all parts of the world, its planting for sale and export, the first American factories ("small snuff mills" in Virginia, 1730), the enormous growth of the industry, and the successive vogues of snuff, chewing tobacco, pipe tobacco, cigars, and cigarettes. [3189

PARLEY M. PRATT. Rice: domestic consumption in the United States [1935-59]. Austin, 1960. xxi, [1], 217 p. diagrs., form, maps, tables. bibliog. (p. 211-17), notes. (University of Texas. Bureau of Business Research. Research monograph 21 [i. e. 22].) Based on thesis--Ohio State Univ. Includes a short introductory chapter on the history of the rice industry in the United States since 1609. [3190

AMERICAN SUGAR REFINING COMPANY. The sugar refining industry [since 1730. By William F. Oliver.] John G. Glover & Rudolph L. Lagai, eds., The development of American industries: their economic significance, 4th ed. (N.Y.: Simmons-Boardman [1959]), p. 355-75. [3191

VIRGINIA LONG BAILEY. Historical review of Ptelea trifoliata in botanical and medical literature [1753-1959]. Econ. botany, 14:180-88 (Jul-Sep). views. notes. Based on thesis--Univ. of Michigan. On a trifoliate garden shrub ("hop-tree, wafer-ash") with aromatic and bitter root bark and foliage, formerly used in medicine. [3192

NATHAN KENT ELLIS. Peppermint and spearmint production [in America, ca. 1812 to 1960, and abroad]. Econ. botany, 14:280-85 (Oct-Dec). [3193

HENRY ERNEST SIGERIST (1891-1957). American truffles: a Thanksgiving fantasia. Henry E. Sigerist, Henry E. Sigerist on the history of medicine, ed. Felix Marti-Ibañez (N.Y.: MD Publications [1960]), p. 282-90. First published in 1944. On the superiority of European to American truffles, and the reasons for the lack of popularity of truffles in America; with letters by Samuel L. Mitchill (1812) and E. Scheffer (1877) on the fungus called tuckahoe. [3194

RUBBER MANUFACTURERS ASSOCIATION. The rubber industry [since 1832. By Ross R. Ormsby.] John G. Glover & Rudolph L. Lagai, eds., The development of American industries: their economic significance, 4th ed. (N.Y.: Simmons-Boardman [1959]), p. 394-416. [3195

GORDON M. PHILPOTT. Daring venture: the life story of William H[enry] Danforth [1870-1955]. N.Y.: Random House [1960]. xvi, 174, [1] p. diagrs., facsims., ports., views. On his life in St. Louis, his studies in Washington University, his establishment of a feed business, the Robinson-Danforth

Commission Company, in 1894, and its development as the Ralston Purina Company; with some account of his childhood in Charleston, Mo., and his service in France during World War I in the Y. M. C. A. [3196

DONALD LE ROY VAN HORN. Production and uses of castor beans [1870-1952]. Agric. engineering, 33: 711-12 (Nov 1952). [3197

HUBERT EDSON (born 1868). Sugar from scarcity to surplus. ... Arranged for publication by Alfred E. Lewis. N.Y.: Chemical Pub. Co., 1958. 224 p. ports., views. On the author's early life in rural Indiana and his work from 1888 to 1950 as a sugar chemist, a manager of sugar properties and builder of sugar factories, and a consultant in the planning and modernization of sugar businesses. [3198

QUENTIN JONES & IVAN A. WOLFF. The search for new industrial crops. Econ. botany, 14:56-68 (Jan-Mar). diagr., views. notes. On "federal participation in plant introduction and new crops research," 1898-1958. [3199

MARC WILLIAMS. Flowers-by-wire: the story of the Florists' Telegraph Delivery Association [1909-60]. Detroit: Mercury House [1960. 2], 430 p. diagrs., facsims., ports., tables, views. [3200

U.S. Agricultural Research Service. Distribution of the varieties and classes of wheat in the United States in 1959. [By L. P. Reitz and L. W. Briggle. Wash.] 1960. [2], 83 p. maps, tables. (U.S. Dept. of Agriculture. Statistical bulletin 272.) Includes comparative statistics since 1919. [3201

LLOYD S. RIFORD. 40 years of progress: a brief history of the Beacon Milling Company Division, Spencer Kellogg and Sons, Inc., Cayuga, N.Y. [1920-60. n. p.] c1960. 63 p. ports., tables, views. On the Beacon Feed Company, processor of feeds for livestock and poultry, founded in 1920 and marged in 1956 with Spencer Kellogg and Sons, "leading processor of vegetable oil seeds"; with the author's recollections as an executive of the company since its beginning. [3202

Mrs. WILLIAM C. HENCKEN. The incomparable editor of the Bulletin (1921-1945), Mrs. T. H. B. McKnight: an appreciation by one of her subeditors. Garden Club Am., Bul., 48(6): 39-40 (Nov). [3203

U.S. Crop Reporting Board. Cotton and cottonseed: planted and harvested acres, yield per acre production, disposition, price, value, by States, 1944-58. [Prepared by Charles C. Burkhead, John J. Morgan, and Ella Sue Minor.] Wash., 1960. 20 p. diagrs., map, tables. notes. (U.S. Dept. of Agriculture. Statistical bulletin 264.) [3204

FISHERIES

U.S. Bureau of Commercial Fisheries. The fishing industry [since 1920, especially in recent years]. John G. Glover & Rudolph L. Lagai, The development of American industries: their economic significance, 4th ed. (N.Y.: Simmons-Boardman [1959]), p. 45-70. [3205

WILLIAM P. PALMER. Early American whaling. Historian, 22:1-8 (Nov 1959). notes. On the origin of the industry as a continuation of Indian whaling on Long Island, 1643-1719, and its transplantation to Nantucket in 1672. [3206

ROBERT WESTLAND MURCH. Black Jack and the whales: a Civil War whaling ship makes philatelic history. Am. Philatelic Cong., Congress book, 26:81-6. facsims. On an account book of the whaling bark Globe of New Bedford, particularly the information in it regarding the revenue stamps used when the crew was paid in New Bedford after return from a Pacific voyage, 1862-64. [3207

U.S. Fish and Wildlife Service. Annotated bibliography on the cutthroat trout [Salmo clarki]. By Oliver B. Cope. Wash.: U.S. Govt. Print. Off., 1958. ii, 417-442 p. (Its Fishery bulletin 140.) Very full abstracts of publications issued between 1874 and 1957. [3208

FRED BRUEMMER. Survival of American whaling terms in the Azores. Am. speech, 35:20-23 (Feb). On the early employment of Portuguese whalemen by New Bedford whalers visiting the Azores, the establishment of a whaling company there in 1876 (manned chiefly by men from New Bedford), the continuance of an Azores-based whale fishery "in small open boats with primitive hand harpoons," and the still current Portuguese adaptations of New England whaling terms (e. g., arpõa, from harpoon); with a 3-page list of such adaptations. [3209

JOSEPH GOMES (born 1894). Captain Joe, whaleman from New Bedford. By Captain Joseph Gomes as told to Don Sevrens. N.Y.: Vantage Press [1960]. 273 p. views. On his early life in the Azores and his work for several years after 1910 on whaling ships cruising between Spain, the West Indies, and New Bedford. Apparently ends before World War I. [3210

TOM GIFFORD. Anglers and muscleheads. N.Y.: Dutton, 1960. [2], 186 p. ports., views. On the author's work as an "offshore guide" to deep-sea fishermen, a "charter-boat skipper with my own boat," accommodating parties of fishermen along the Atlantic coast from Florida and the Bahamas to Nova Scotia, 1920-60; with some account of his early life in New Jersey and Oregon and his Navy service in World War I. [3211

FORESTRY AND RELATED INDUSTRIES

NATIONAL LUMBER MANUFACTURERS ASSOCIATION. The lumber industry [since 1607]. John G. Glover & Rudolph L. Lagai, eds., The development of American industries: their economic significance, 4th ed. (N.Y.: Simmons-Boardman [1959]), p. 71-82. [3212

AMERICAN PAPER AND PULP ASSOCIATION. The pulp and paper industry [since 1690. By John H. Vogel.] John G. Glover & Rudolph L. Lagai, eds., The development of American industries: their economic significance, 4th ed. (N.Y.: Simmons-Boardman [1959]), p. 376-93. [3213

ROBERT L. KENNEDY. The oak: tree beloved. Am. forests, 66(7):30-31, 92-4 (Jul). double view. Lore and history about American oak trees, 1758-1960. [3214

ALICELIA HOSKINS FRANKLIN. Ginkgo biloba L: historical summary and bibliography. Va. jour. science, 10:131-76 (Jul 1959). bibliog. (p. 140-76). On a tree of nearly worldwide distribution, native to eastern China, introduced into the United States in 1784. [3215

ANDREW JACKSON DADISMAN. Lumbering in the north woods [Michigan, Minnesota, Wisconsin, Idaho, Washington, and California, 1830s to ca. 1910]. W. Va. Acad. Science, Proc., 31:110-13. bibliog. [3216

CREIGHTON PEET. 12 billion dollar jackpot? Am. forests, 66(10):12-15, 42 (Oct). views. On the development of industrial uses of lignin since ca. 1869. [3217

AMERICAN FORESTRY ASSOCIATION. A capsule history of AFA [1875-1960]. Am. forests, 66(8):2, 70-76 (Aug). port. [3218

SAMUEL TRASK DANA. The first eighty years. Am. forests, 62(4):13-19, 42-8 (Apr 1956). ports., views. On the American Forestry Association, 1875-1956. [3219

MARTHA MEELIG. Theodore Roosevelt, forester. Jour. forestry, 56:387-92 (Jun 1958). cartoon, port. On his activities in conserving forests (especially by political action) and his encouragement of the young profession of forestry, 1881-1919. [3220

LEIGH JARVIS YOUNG. Pioneering in forestry at Michigan. Washtenaw impressions, 14(3):6-13 (Jun). On the teaching of forestry at the University of Michigan, 1881-1960. Includes the author's reminiscences. [3220a

I. F. AHLGREN & C. E. AHLGREN. Ecological effects of forest fires [in America, 1884-1959, and abroad]. Botanical rev., 26:483-533 (Oct-Dec). notes. [3221

JAMES B. CRAIG. Forestry's ambassador without portfolio. Am forests, 66(5):20-21, 41-2 (May). port. On Thomas Harvey Gill (born 1891), his studies at the Yale School of Forestry, his work in the U.S. Forest Service (1915-25), his service as Secretary, later Executive Director, of the Lathrop Pack Forestry Fund since 1926, his travels "in many out-of-the-way places" from the Equator to the Arctic Circle, and his other activities to promote "forestry and conservation education." [3222

BERNARD FRANK. Our national forests. Norman: Univ. of Oklahoma Press [1955]. xx, 238, [2] p. diagr., double map, views. On the administration of forests by the U.S. Government since the establishment of the first national forest reserves under legislation of 1891. [3223

FRED WILSON BESLEY (1872-1960). Maryland's first State Forester. Am. forests, 62(10):38, 77-8, 80, 82, 84 (Oct 1956). port. Interview dealing with Besley's career in forestry since 1900, his assignments in Kentucky, Texas, Nebraska, and Colorado, his service as State Forester of Maryland

(1906-42), his later management of his own woodlands, and his The forests of Maryland (1916). [3224

RALPH SHELDON HOSMER & HENRY CLEPPER. The Society of American Foresters: an historical summary [1900-1960]. Jour. forestry, 58:765-79 (Oct). [3225

RAYMOND JOSLYN HOYLE. Developments, trends, and problems in education and research in forest utilization [1900-1958]. Jour. forestry, 56:578-83 (Aug 1958). diagrs., views. [3226

MURRELL WILLIAMS TALBOT. Buffalo Bill's top hand. Am. forests, 66(5):37, 61 (May). port. On Jesse W. Nelson, early in life "the top rider for Buffalo Bill's Wild West Show," who from 1900 to ca. 1944 was employed by the U.S. Forest Service, mainly in the Far West. [3227

INMAN FOWLER ELDREDGE. Ride the white horse--memories of a Southern forester. [Recorded] by Elwood R. Maunder. Forest hist., 3(3-4):[3-14]; 4(1):[3-12] (winter, spring). port. Interview, Feb. 1959, on the author's attendance at the Biltmore Forest School, 1904-5, his employment as forester-manager of the Superior Pine Products Company in Georgia, his career in the U.S. Forest Service in the South and the Far West, and his work as a forest consultant. [3227a

INMAN FOWLER ELDREDGE. Ride the white horse ... an interview with "Mr. Southern Forestry." By Elwood R. Maunder. Am. forests, 66(10): 16-19, 60, 62, 64, 66, 68, 70, 72-89 (Oct). port. On the author's studies in the forest school at Biltmore, N.C., and his career in the Forest Service and in private forestry, 1904-56. [3228

I. IRVING HOLLAND. A suggested technique for estimating the future price of eastern white pine stumpage. Forest science, 6:369-96 (Dec). diagrs., tables. bibliog., notes. Largely an analysis of statistics of the production and use of whitepine lumber in America, 1905-57. [3229

OVID Butler [1881-1960], pioneer in forest education. Am. forests, 66(3): 27, 61 (Mar). port. On his service as a member of the staff of the U.S. Forest Service, 1907-22, and as Executive Director and Editor of the American Forestry Association. [3230

JOHN CAMPBELL GOODLETT. The development of site concepts at the Harvard Forest and their impact upon management policy. Petersham, Mass.: Harvard Forest, 1960. 128 p. tables. bibliog. (p. 124-8). (Harvard Forest. Bulletin 28.) On the management of "an area of woodland in central Massachusetts" in "the white pine era," 1908-38, and "the hardwood era," since 1938. [3231

JOHN NELSON SPAETH. Forest land resources and projected timber needs [1910-58]. Land Economics Institute, University of Illinois, 1958, Modern land policy: papers (Urbana: Univ. of Illinois Press, 1960), p. 215-22. diagrs., table. [3232

JAMES FLOYD STEVENS. "The business of life is to go forward." Am. forests, 62(1):18-19, 46-8 (Jan 1956). ports. On the service of William Buckhout Greeley as an official of the West Coast Lumbermen's Association in Oregon, 1937-55, and his more general contributions to the science of forestry, 1910-55. [3233

HENRY EDWARD CLEPPER. The cooperative role of the Society of American Foresters. Jour. forestry, 56:666-70, 674-6 (Sep 1958). On the cordial relations of the Society with other professional organizations and with schools, governmental agencies, and international agencies, 1913-58. [3234

WILSON MARTINDALE COMPTON. Forestry under a free enterprise system [1920-60]. Am. forests, 66(8): 26-7, 50-54 (Aug). port. On "industrial forestry" and "the forest management concept." [3235

PETER FARB. Money can grow on trees. Am. forests, 66(3):10-11, 48-52 (Mar). ports., view. On tree farming in America since ca. 1920. [3236

HAROLD OLSON. Penta comes of age. Am. forests, 62(11):34-5, 46 (Nov 1956). port., views. On the use of pentachlorophenol as a preservative of wood, 1936-56. [3237

ED KERR. Tree farming sweeps the country [1941-60]. Am. forests, 66(5): 28-30, 52-5 (May). ports. (1 double). [3238

AMERICAN FORESTRY ASSOCIATION. Report on American big trees. Am. forests, 61(9):32-40; 62(4):33-40 (Sep 1955, Apr 1956). views. List of "the largest living specimens of American trees," with circumference, height, spread, and location of each. [3239

MANUFACTURES

NATIONAL PAINT, VARNISH, AND LACQUER ASSOCIATION. The paint, varnish, and lacquer industry [since Indian times. By John F. Battley.] John G. Glover & Rudolph L. Lagai, eds., The development of American industries: their economic significance, 4th ed. (N.Y.: Simmons-Boardman [1959]), p. 462-71. [3240

BORIS PARL. An analysis of the shoe manufacturing industry with special emphasis on changes and trends in the use of various distribution channels by shoe manufacturers [1630-1957]. Ann Arbor: University Microfilms, 1960. Positive microfilm of typescript. [668] leaves. Thesis--Northwestern Univ. Abstracted: Dissert. abstracts, 21:1093-4 (Nov). [3241

MORRIS DE CAMP CRAWFORD. The early textile industry [1790 to ca. 1900]. John G. Glover & Rudolph L. Lagai, eds., The development of American industries: their economic significance, 4th ed. (N.Y.: Simmons-Boardman [1959]), p. 83-109. [3242

RICHARD AINLEY EASTERLIN. Redistribution of manufacturing [1869-1947]. Simon Smith Kuznets, Ann Ratner Miller, & Richard A. Easterlin, Population redistribution and economic growth, 1870-1950 (Phila.: American Philosophical Soc.), 2 (1960): 103-39. tables. notes. Sections on "Location of manufacturing production" and "Interstate differences in selected production characteristics." [3243

ROBERT F. SEVERSON, JR. The American manufacturing frontier, 1870-1940. Bus. hist. rev., 34:356-72 (autumn). maps, tables. notes. On changes in the geographic distribution of manufacturing. [3244

EDMUND F. BALL. From fruit jars to satellites: the story of Ball Brothers Company, Incorporated. N.Y.: Newcomen Soc. in North America, 1960. 24 p. port., views. On the Wood Jacket Can Company, founded by William C. Ball and his brothers, Frank C., Lucius L., Edmund B., and George A. Ball, makers of wood-jacketed oil cans and later of glass jars for home canning, Buffalo, 1880-86, removed to Muncie, Ind., in 1886 as Ball Brothers Glass Company, Inc., makers of Ball Mason fruit jars and later also of zinc cans and other zinc products, plastic containers, corrugated boxes, rubber goods, etc. [3245

RAYMOND SCHUESSLER. The story of the match. Am. forests, 62(1):24-6, 52-3 (Jan 1956). views (1 double). On the Diamond Match Company, Spokane, Wash., 1882-1955. [3246

ELY JACQUES KAHN, JR. The big drink: the story of Coca-Cola. N.Y.: Random House [1960]. xiii, 174, [1] p. facsim. Based on articles by the author in The New Yorker. On the Coca-Cola Company, 1886-1959. [3247

ALFRED BENJAMIN CARLIP. The slide fastener industry: a study of market structure and innovation [1893-1955]. Ann Arbor: University Microfilms, 1960. Positive microfilm of typescript. [228] leaves. Thesis--Columbia Univ. Abstracted: Dissert. abstracts, 21:478-9 (Sep). [3248

NESTOR E. TERLECKYJ. Sources of productivity advance: a pilot study of manufacturing industries, 1899-1953. Ann Arbor: University Microfilms, 1960. Positive microfilm of typescript. [174] leaves. Thesis--Columbia Univ. Abstracted: Dissert. abstracts, 21:784 (Oct). [3249

WILLIAM C. STOLK. American Can Company: revolution in containers [1901-60]. N.Y.: Newcomen Soc. in North America, 1960. 28 p. views. On a firm founded in 1901 by consolidation of smaller companies with 123 plants, and its manufacture of metal ("tin") cans, can-closing machines, and paper containers. [3250

ALFRED CARL FULLER (born 1885). A foot in the door: the life appraisal of the original Fuller brush man. ... As told to Hartzell Spence. N.Y.: McGraw-Hill [1960. 8], 250, [1] p. cartoons, ports., views. On the author's early life in rural Nova Scotia, his removal to Somerville, Mass., in 1903, his employment by a manufacturer of brushes in "direct selling" from door to door, his innovations in methods of manufacture, his establishment of his own factory in 1906 as the Capitol Brush Company, Hartford, Conn. (renamed the Fuller Brush Company in 1913), and his particular attention to the further development of "direct selling." [3251

MARK HUNTER. The Finn Magnus story. N.Y.: Odin Press [1960]. ix, 485 p. ports., tables, views. On Finn Haakon Magnus (born 1907), emigrant from Denmark in 1925, executive of the Button Corporation of America and the Orange Manufacturing Company, both in Newark, N.J., inventor and manufacturer of harmonicas, founder of the Magnus Harmonica Corporation, Newark, author of "The Magnus charts for success, happiness, peace of mind" (text, p. 463-75), etc. Presented as a series of explicit lessons in the achievement of business success by an individual who "can be anything he wants to be." [3252

MARTIN REUBEN GAINSBRUGH & LUCIE KRASSA. Compiled balance sheet of manufacturing enterprises [1929-46]. Conference on Research in Income and Wealth, Studies in income and wealth, 12 (1950): 275-324. tables. notes. A study in measurement. [3253

M. L. GERHART. Measurement of asphalt tile quality. Miss. Acad. Sciences, Jour., 6:164-7. On the manufacture of asphalt tile by the Armstrong Cork Company at Jackson, Miss., 1932-56, and elsewhere in the United States and abroad. [3254

The Arms Industry

HARRY WANDRUS. Firearms. Hobbies, 64(11)-65(10): monthly installments (Jan-Dec). diagrs., port., views. Information for collectors. [3255

FRED THEODORE DEXTER, comp. Half century scrapbook of vari-type firearms, based on the pictorial and descriptive catalog of the Frank E. Bivens, Jr., inspirational collection of varitype [sic] firearms and accessories. [Santa Monica? Calif., 1960. 4], 202 p. port., views. Catalogue (496 entries) representing "the true story of talented gunsmithy from 1350 to 1850," including many entries for American firearms. [3256

IRVING BROWNING. When the Indians got guns. Westerners brand book (N.Y.), 6:86-8 views. On the sale and trading of guns to Indians, begun by the Dutch in New York in 1614; with descriptions of 10 guns known to have been used by Indians, ca. 1720 to ca. 1862, and some account of other Indian weapons, including axes and tomahawks sold by traders. [3257

WALTER HAROLD BLACK SMITH (1901-59). The book of pistols & revolvers [in America, ca. 1677 to 1960, and abroad]: an encyclopedic reference work. [Fourth edition.] Harrisburg, Pa.: Military Service Division, Stackpole Co. [1960]. xvi, 718 p. tables, views. Revision of The N. R. A. book of small arms, v. 1, Pistols and revolvers (1946). A descriptive work, organized by size of caliber from smallest to largest; with "Supplement: post-war developments, by Kent Bellah" (p. 627-709). [3258

JOE KINDIG, JR. Thoughts on the Kentucky rifle in its golden age. ... Mary Ann Cresswell, editor; Samuel E. Dyke [and] Henry J. Kauffman, research; Bluford W. Muir, photographer. [Wilmington, Del.:] G. N. Hyatt, 1960. xii, [2], 561 p. diagrs., maps, views. 31 cm. On the Kentucky rifle as "the most artistic product of eighteenth century America" and its makers as "the finest artisans in eighteenth century America"; its origin by gradual modification of "the rifle brought to America by the first German settlers about 1710"; and the work of 90 identified gunmakers (besides several gunmaking families and unidentified craftsmen) in 10 Pennsylvania and 3 northern Maryland counties; with full-page illustrations by Patterson (who had contributed some of the information in the first printing). On John Harris Hall description of each, ca. 1783 to ca. 1815. [3259

HENRY J. KAUFFMAN. The Pennsylvania-Kentucky rifle [1729-1906]. Harrisburg, Pa.: Stackpole Co. [1960. 12], 376 p. diagrs., maps (1 double), plan, port., tables, views. bibliog. (p. 373-4), notes. On rifles made in Pennsylvania and "nearby Maryland"; with "Biographies" (p. 169-367) of gunmakers. [3260

HAROLD LESLIE PETERSON. The development of firearms [in America, 1750-1866, and abroad]. Am. rifleman, 108(3-6): monthly installments (Mar-Jun). diagrs., views. bibliog. [3261

JAMES EDSALL SERVEN. Powder horns with a message. Am. rifleman, 108(12):33-5 (Dec). views. On engravings cut on American powder horns, 1755 ff. [3262

CHARLOTTE (JUDD) FAIRBAIRN & CHARLES MEADE PATTERSON. Captain Hall, inventor. Gun rep., 5(5): 6-11; (6):14-21, 25-6 (Oct, Nov 1959). maps, plans, geneal. table, views. notes. First published as written by Mrs. Fairbairn in The Jefferson Republican, Charles Town, W. Va., 20 Sep. 1951; now reissued with additions by Patterson (who had contributed some of the information in the first printing). On John Harris Hall

(1778-1841), boat-builder in Portland, Me., who patented his first rifle invention ("the first breech-loader to be accepted by the United States ... for military use") in 1811, devised "interchangeable gunmaking machinery," and removed to Harpers Ferry in 1819, where his enlarged manufactory of guns for the United States was continued till 1841. [3263

JAMES FRITH & RONALD ANDREWS. Antique pistol collecting (1400-1860). N.Y.: Arco Pub. Co. [1960]. 122 p. diagrs., views. Includes some account of American pistols, ca. 1780 to 1830. [3264

ROGER BURLINGAME. "... five times without reloadings." John Arthur Garraty, ed., The unforgettable Americans (Great Neck, N.Y.: Channel Press [1960]), p. 160-63. On Samuel Colt as an inventer and manufacturer of guns, ca. 1830 to 1862. [3265

HERSCHEL C. LOGAN. Underhammer guns [in America, ca. 1835 to ca. 1860, and abroad]. Harrisburg, Pa.: Stackpole Co. [1960]. xiii, 249, [1] p. diagrs., facsims., map, ports., table, views. [3266

MARTIN RYWELL. Colt guns. Harriman, Tenn.: Pioneer Press [1957]. 134, [1] p. diagrs., port., tables, views. notes. 1st ed. 1953. On guns invented and manufactured by Samuel Colt, 1836-62; with proceedings of the London Institution of Civil Engineers on "rotating chambered-breech firearms," 25 Nov. 1851 (including an address by Colt), and other documents. [3267

JAMES L. MITCHELL, ed. Colt: a collection of letters about the man, the arms, the company. Harrisburg, Pa.: Stackpole Co. [1959. 12], 265, [4] p. facsims., plans, views. bibliog. (p. 267-9). Documents, 1846-62, concerning Samuel Colt and Colt's Patent Fire Arms Manufacturing Company, and connecting text. [3268

ADOLPH BURNETT BENSON. Swedish leaders in the American industry of explosives [1850-1919]. Am. Swed. Hist. Found., Yr. bk., 1955, p. 51-8. [3269

ALBERT W. LINDERT. John Brown's revolvers. Gun rep., 5(8):6-7, 29 (Jan). facsims., views. notes. On the 200 revolvers collected by Brown at Iowa City, Ia., for use in Kansas (but never taken there) and later at Harper's Ferry--their types and what became of them, 1857-59. [3270

CHARLES MEADE PATTERSON. More light on Starrs. Gun rep., 5(4): 12-13, 15-18 (Sep 1959). plans, views. notes. On "self-cocking .36 and .44 caliber percussion revolvers" made by Starr Arms Company, New York City, 1858-64. [3271

CHARLES R. SUYDAM. The American cartridge: an illustrated study of the rim-fire cartridge in the United States [1858-1959]. Santa Ana, Calif.: G. R. Lawrence [1960]. 184, [1] p. facsims., tables, views. bibliog. (p. 183-4). [3272

SHARPS RIFLE COMPANY, Bridgeport. Conn. Sharps' patent improved breech-loading and self-priming rifle, carbine, and shotgun, manufactured only by the Sharps' Rifle Manufacturing Company, at Hartford, Connecticut. [Phila.: R. Riling, 1960.] 14, [3] p. views. Facsimile reproductions of a prospectus dated 1 Nov. 1859 and of Manual of arms for the Sharps' rifle (undated, before 1864). [3273

JAMES ERNEST HICKS. Boynton magazine pistol [patented by Paul Boynton 3 Jan. 1860]. Gun rep., 5(9): 12-13 (Feb). plan, views. [3274

HERSCHEL C. LOGAN. E[dwin] A. Prescott [fl. 1846-74] and his revolvers. Am. rifleman, 108(9):46-8 (Sep). facsims., views. On his manufacture of revolvers in Worcester, Mass., 1860-62. [3275

GRAHAM BURNSIDE. Anton Spellerberg, Philadelphia. Gun rep., 5(7):25, 33 (Dec 1959). plan, views. On a breech-loader patented 30 Jul. 1861 by a maker otherwise unknown. [3276

RAY M. SMITH. The story of Pope's barrels, Harrisburg, Pa.: Stackpole Co. [1960. 12], 203, [8] p. diagrs., facsims., ports., tables, views. bibliog. (p. 197). On Harry Melville Pope (1861-1956), his early life in Walpole, N.H., and Boston and Brookline, Mass., his studies at the Massachusetts Institute of Technology, and his work as an independent maker of rifle barrels and accessories in Jersey City, San Francisco (1906-8), and again in Jersey City; with several of his letters. [3277

CHARLES MEADE PATTERSON. Aaron Vaughan's double-barreled percussion revolver [patented 27 May 1862; apparently very few produced]. Gun rep., 5(7):10-13 (Dec 1959). plan, views. notes. [3278

WILLIAM BENNETT EDWARDS. The West's greatest gun inventor. Westerners brand book (Chicago), 16:65-7 (Nov). On James Paris Lee (died) 1904) as an inventor and manufacturer of guns, 1864-1904. [3279

MARTIN E. ALGER. Remington rolling-block arms [1866-1902]. Am. rifleman, 108(7):29-32 (Jul). views. [3280

JAMES M. TRIGGS. Springfield Model 1873 .45-70 rifle. Am. rifleman, 108(6):22-3 (Jun). diagrs., view. Instructions for disassembling and reassembling. [3281

RICHARD ARNOLD. Automatic and repeating shotguns [early 1880s to 1960]. N.Y.: A. S. Barnes [1960]. 173 p. diagrs., tables, views. 1st ed. 1958. [3282

HENRY B. STOWERS. The game of trapshooting [1885-1960]. Am. rifleman, 108(4):27-30 (Apr). diagrs., views. [3283

CARL KOUNTZ. S&W single shot target pistols [made by Smith and Wesson, 1893-1936]. Gun rep., 5(10): 6-8 (Mar). views. bibliog. [3284

CHARLES MEADE PATTERSON. The McKinley assassination. Gun rep., 5(8):20-26 (Jan). port., views. notes. On the gun and the ammunition with which Leon F. Czolgosz shot William McKinley, Buffalo, 6 Sep. 1901. [3285

TOWNSEND WHELEN. Days of the Springfield. Gun digest, 15:103-9. port., views. notes. Memories of testing and using the U.S. Springfield, Model 1903 and Model 1906 (the latter popularly known as the 30-06 from its cartridge) and various later models, 1903-31. [3286

EDITH TILTON PENROSE. The growth of the firm, a case study: the Hercules Powder Company [1912-54]. Bus. hist. rev., 34:1-23 (spring). diagr. notes. On a firm detached from E. I. Dupont de Nemours by antitrust action, originally manufacturing black powder and dynamite, later also nitrogen products and nitrogen, agricultural chemicals, papermaking chemicals, resins, and cellulose and petrochemical plastics. [3287

JAMES M. TRIGGS. U.S. Model 1917 rifle. Am. rifleman, 108(8):20-21 (Aug). diagrs., view. Instructions for disassembling and assembling. [3288

The Chemical Industry

JOHN ALANSON PERKINS & ROBESON BAILEY. Harry Fletcher Brown [1867-1944]: an essay in appreciation. [Newark:] Univ. of Delaware Press, 1960. x, [2], 128 p. port. On his work as chief chemist for "all the smokeless powder plants" of the Du Pont International Powder Company, Wilmington, and later as President and Director of the E. I. du Pont de Nemours Company, 1904-44, and his benefactions to the University of Delaware; with some account of his early life in Natick, Mass., his Harvard studies in chemistry, and his early experience as a chemist and an administrator of chemical enterprises. [3289

The Construction Industry

NOBLE HOGGSON. A biography of Horace Chapin Henry, 1844-1928. Seattle, 1960. [1], vii, 3-185, [2] p. facsim., fold. geneal. table, ports., tables, views. On his early life in North Bennington, Vt., his service in the Union Army, his studies at Williams College, and his work as a builder and construction contractor, especially of railroads, with headquarters in Minneapolis (1866-90) and Seattle, to which he removed in 1890; with some account of his many philanthropic enterprises. [3290

ESMOND SHAW. Peter Cooper [1791-1883] & the wrought iron beam. [N.Y.: Cooper Union Art School, 1960. 2], 36, [3] p. facsims., plans, port. notes (p. 32). (CUAS, 7.) On his ironworks in Baltimore, New York City, and Trenton, 1828-60, and his manufacture of beams (for the construction of fireproof buildings) in his Trenton Iron Works, beginning in 1854. [3291

ROY LUBOVE. Homes and "a few well placed fruit trees": an object in Federal housing. Social research, 27: 469-86 (winter). notes. On the construction of housing for war workers by the Emergency Fleet Corporation (of the U.S. Shipping Board) and the U.S. Housing Corporation (of the Bureau of Industrial Housing, U.S. Dept. of Labor), 1918-19, the quality of the housing, the hopes of reformers and social planners that it would serve as a precedent for governmental responsibility for housing, and the prompt discontinuance of the program by Congress, unwilling to tolerate "socialism." [3292

DOROTHY (KRALL) NEWMAN. Housing in Britain and America [1948-58]. Monthly labor rev., 83:449-59, 561-8 (May, Jun). diagrs., tables. notes. [3293

JOSEPH QUINCY MITCHELL. The Mohawks in high steel. Edmund Wilson, Apologies to the Iroquois (N.Y.: Farrar, Straus, and Cudahy [1960]), p. 1-36. First published in 1949. On Mohawks from the Caughnawaga Reservation (near Montreal) and from a Mohawk colony in Brooklyn as migratory laborers employed in the United States to rivet the frames of high steel buildings and bridges, an occupation in which they work in gangs, intermittently from job to job, and in which their lack of fear of heights and noise is to their advantage. [3294

The Electrical Industry

EDISON ELECTRIC INSTITUTE. The electric power industry [since 1875. By Edwin Vennard.] John G. Glover & Rudolph L. Lagai, eds., The development of American industries: their economic significance, 4th ed. (N.Y.: Simmons-Boardman [1959]), p. 515-43. views. [3295

SIDNEY ALEXANDER MITCHELL. S[idney] Z[ollicoffer] Mitchell [1862-1944] and the electrical industry. N.Y.: Farrar, Straus, & Cudahy [1960. 14], 178 p. diagrs., ports., tables, views. bibliog. (p. 175), notes. On his work in Seattle (1885-1905) as an administrator of Edison companies in the Pacific Northwest and in New York (1905-33) as an organizer and administrator of the Electric Bond and Share Company and other electrical holding companies; with some account of his early life in Alabama and his studies in the U.S. Naval Academy. [3296

WESTINGHOUSE ELECTRIC CORPORATION. The electrical industry [since 1886]. John G. Glover & Rudolph L. Lagai, eds., The development of American industries: their economic significance, 4th ed. (N.Y.: Simmons-Boardman [1959]), p. 488-514. views. [3297

GLENN MARTZ. Ellis in wonderland: the amazing story of a million-dollar-a-year lobby, and the man who runs it. ... Part 1. [Wash.: Washington News Syndicate, 1959. 2], 42, [1] p. On the National Rural Electric Cooperative Association, founded in 1942, and Clyde Taylor Ellis, its General Manager since 1943; with quotations from his statements to Congress urging the extension of public power projects. [3298

The Machinery Industry

ROBERT S. WOODBURY. History of the milling machine: a study in technical development [ca. 1820 to 1956]. Cambridge: Technology Press, Massachusetts Institute of Technology [1960]. 107 p. diagrs., views. bibliog. (p. 103-4), notes. (Massachusetts Institute of Technology. Technology monographs: historical series, 3.) Three chapters on inventors and developers of the machine, from Eli Whitney to Joseph R. Brown, and 2 chapters analyzing "the progress of the technical features." [3299

NATIONAL MACHINE TOOL BUILDERS ASSOCIATION. The machine tool industry [since ca. 1825. By Alfred V. Bodine.] John G. Glover & Rudolph L. Lagai, eds., The development of American industries: their economic significance, 4th ed. (N.Y.: Simmons-Boardman [1959]), p. 472-87. views. [3300

WILLIAM CHARLES OURSLER. From ox carts to jets: Roy [C.] Ingersoll [born 1884] and the Borg-Warner story, a biography. By Will Oursler. Englewood Cliffs, N.J.: Prentice-Hall [1959]. vi, 346 p. facsims., ports., views. On his early life in Illinois and his many business interests in the manufacture of farm machinery and automobile transmisssions, other parts of automobiles, air-conditioning equipment, oil tools, refrigerators, etc., centered in the Borg-Warner Corporation, founded in 1928. [3301

ROGER N. PERRY, JR. From crude clay to diamonds. Am. Swed. monthly, 54(5):12-13 (May). port., views. On the Norton Company, Worcester, Mass., "the world's largest manufacturer of abrasive products," founded as the Norton Emery Wheel Company in 1885, and the contributions of George N. Jeppson (born 1873) and other Swedes to its development. [3302

DAVID A. MEEKER. Better eating, from start to finish ... the story of the Hobart Manufacturing Company. N.Y.: Newcomen Soc. in North America, 1960. 32 p. facsim., port., views. On a firm founded at Troy, Ohio, in 1897 as the Hobart Electric Manufacturing

Company, maker of electrical machines, particularly mixers, dishwashers, computing scales, slicers, waste disposers, and other kitchen and food-store equipment. [3303

GEORGE BERNARD SAUNDERS. Economics of the air conditioning industry [1902-56]. Ann Arbor: University Microfilms, 1959 [i. e. 1960]. Positive microfilm of typescript. [405] leaves. Thesis--Syracuse Univ. Abstracted: Dissert. abstracts, 20: 4303 (May). [3304

GEORGE E. FROST, S. CHESTERFIELD OPPENHEIM, & NEIL F. TWOMEY. The concrete block making machine industry. Patent, trademark, and copyright jour., 2:61-133 (Mar 1958). tables, views. notes. On the competition of Besser Manufacturing Company, Stearns Manufacturing Company, and other firms since 1942, and antitrust proceedings against them on charges of refusal to license patents; with accounts of all the firms in the industry, and an appendix on "The technological and patent history of the concrete block making machine industry," 1904-57. [3305

GEORGE E. FROST, S. CHESTERFIELD OPPENHEIM, & NEIL F. TWOMEY. The parking meter industry [1935-57]. Patent, trademark, and copyright jour., 2:376-407 (Sep 1958). tables. notes. Deals particularly with antitrust action connected with the licensing of patents. Includes histories of 6 companies. [3306

MURRAY BROWN & NATHAN ROSENBERG. Prologue to a study of patent and other factors in the machine tool industry [1939-55]. Patent, trademark, and copyright jour., 4:39-48 (spring). tables. notes. [3307

MINING AND RELATED INDUSTRIES

LIBBY-OWENS-FORD GLASS COMPANY. The non-plate glass industries [since 1607. By Wilfrid Hibbert.] John G. Glover & Rudolph L. Lagai, eds., The development of American industries: their economic significance, 4th ed. (N.Y.: Simmons-Boardman [1959]), p. 417-34. [3308

ARMCO STEEL CORPORATION. The iron and steel industry [since 1640]. John G. Glover & Rudolph L. Lagai, eds., The development of American industries: their economic significance, 4th ed. (N.Y.: Simmons-Boardman [1959]), p. 213-31. [3309

NATIONAL COAL ASSOCIATION. The bituminous coal industry [since 1750. Prepared by M. Edmund Spears.] John G. Glover & Rudolph L. Lagai, eds., The development of American industries: their economic significance, 4th ed. (N.Y.: Simmons-Boardman [1959]), p. 175-205. [3310

SAM H. SCHURR, comp. Historical statistics of minerals in the United States [1792-1956. Wash.:] Resources for the Future [1960?]. v, 42p. Tables (p. 1-24) and notes on the tables (p. 25-42). [3311

LEE E. PRESTON. Exploration for non-ferrous metals [1807-1956]: an economic analysis. [Wash.:] Resources for the Future [1960]. x, 198 p. diagrs., tables. bibliog. (p. 194-8), notes. Based on thesis--Harvard Univ. [3312

U.S. Bureau of Mines. Historical summary of coal-mine explosions in the United States, 1810-1958. By H[iram] B[rown] Humphrey. Wash.: U.S. Govt. Print. Off., 1960. viii, 280 p. maps, tables, views. bibliog. (p. 279-80). (Its Bulletin 586.) 1st ed. 1959. [3313

E. WILLIAM FAIRFIELD. Fire & sand ... the history of the Libbey-Owens Sheet Glass Company. Cleveland: Lezius-Hiles Co., 1960. [6], 128, [1] p. facsims., ports., tables, views. notes. Second volume in a trilogy, of which the first volume, by William Earl Aiken, deals with the Edward Ford Plate Glass Company. On the New England Glass Company, East Cambridge, Mass. (1818-88), and Toledo (1888-92), renamed as the Libbey Glass Company, Toledo (1892-1915), and the Libbey-Owens Sheet Glass Company, Toledo (1915-30), which merged in 1930 with the Edward Ford Plate Glass Company as the Libby-Owens-Ford Glass Company. Includes accounts of related corporations (Toledo Glass Company, Owens Bottle Company, Owens-Illinois Glass Company, and others) and of Edward Drummond Libbey (1854-1925), Michael Joseph Owens (1859-1923), and Irving Wright Colburn (1861-1917). [3314

LONE STAR CEMENT CORPORATION. The cement industry [since 1818]. John G. Glover & Rudolph L. Lagai, eds., The development of American industries: their economic significance, 4th ed. (N.Y.: Simmons-Boardman [1959]), p. 446-61. diagr.

Mainly on the manufacture of Portland cement since ca. 1875. [3315

AMERICAN BAR ASSOCIATION. Section of Mineral Law. Commitee on Special Publications. Conservation of oil & gas: a legal history, 1948. Edited by Blakely M. Murphy. [Chicago, 1949.] xvii, 754 p. notes. By numerous contributors. Consists mainly of histories of oil and gas conservation in each of 36 States, 1819-1948 (p. 17-541); with accounts of the Oil States Advisory Committee (1931-33), the Interstate Compact to Conserve Oil and Gas and its "central unit," the Interstate Oil Compact Commission (1935-48), and "The national government and the conservation of oil and gas." [3316

KENDALL BEATON. Founders' incentives: the pre-Drake refining industry. Centennial Seminar on the History of the Petroleum Industry, Harvard University, 1959, Oil's first century: papers ([Boston:] Harvard Graduate School of Business Administration [1960]), p. 5-19. facsim., view. notes. On the search for substitutes for the increasingly expensive whale oil, especially the development of "the coal-oil industry" (producer of "kerosene" from bituminous coal), 1840-61. [3317

COPPER & BRASS RESEARCH ASSOCIATION. The copper industry [since 1844. Prepared by T. E. Veltfort and Carl H. Pihl.] John G. Glover & Rudolph L. Lagai, eds., The development of American industries: their economic significance, 4th ed. (N.Y.: Simmons-Boardman [1959]), p. 249-61. diagr. [3318

AMERICAN ZINC INSTITUTE. The zinc industry [since ca. 1850]. John G. Glover & Rudolph L. Lagai, eds., The development of American industries: their economic significance, 4th ed. (N.Y.: Simmons-Boardman [1959]), p. 277-96. [3319

UNITED STATES STEEL CORPORATION. Tennessee Coal & Iron Division. Biography of a business. [n. p., 1960. 8], 72, [3] p. maps, ports., views. On the Sewanee Mining Company (1852-60), the Tennessee Coal and Railroad Company (1860-81), the Tennessee Coal, Iron, and Railroad Company (1881-1952), the acquisition by the last-mentioned of interests in Birmingham iron and steel, its acquisition by the U.S. Steel Company in 1907, and its change of name to the Tennessee Coal & Iron Division of the U.S. Steel Company in 1952 and of the U.S. Steel Corporation in 1953. [3320

AMERICAN PETROLEUM INSTITUTE. The petroleum industry [since 1859]. John G. Glover & Rudolph L. Lagai, eds., The development of American industries: their economic significance, 4th ed. (N.Y.: Simmons-Boardman [1959]), p. 137-74. [3321

HENRIETTA MELIA LARSON. The rise of big business in the oil industry. Centennial Seminar on the History of the Petroleum Industry, Harvard University, 1959, Oil's first century: papers ([Cambridge:] Harvard Graduate School of Business Administration [1960]), p. 27-42. views. notes. Mainly on the Standard Oil Company of Ohio and its predecessors, 1863-1911. [3322

HELEN E. (LEIGHTON) CANNON. Botanical prospecting for ore deposits. Science, 132:591-8 (2 Sep). tables, views. notes. On the recognition of plants as indicators of the presence of mineral deposits in America (since ca. 1880) and abroad. [3323

PITTSBURGH PLATE GLASS COMPANY. The plate glass industry [since ca. 1880. By E. C. Miles.] John G. Glover & Rudolph L. Lagai, eds., The development of American industries: their economic significance, 4th ed. (N.Y.: Simmons-Boardman [1959]), p. 434-45. [3324

W. E. BOSWELL. Metallurgical industries of Virginia: centrifugally cast pressure pipe. Mineral industries jour., 5(1):6-8 (Mar 1958). diagr., view. On the Glamorgan Pipe and Foundry Company, Lynchburg, Va., 1882-1958. [3325

MILDRED McCLARY TYMESON. The Wyman-Gordon way ... 1883-1958. Worcester, Mass. [1959]. x, [2], 136 p. facsims., maps, ports., views. On the Worcester Drop Forging Works (for iron and steel), founded by Lyman Francis Gordon and Horace Winfield Lyman, Worcester machinists, later expanded as the Wyman-Gordon Company, with branches in several States; with some account of other industries in Worcester. [3326

ALUMINUM COMPANY OF AMERICA. The aluminum industry [since 1886]. John G. Glover & Rudolph L. Lagai, eds., The development of American industries: their economic significance, 4th ed. (N.Y.: Simmons-Boardman [1959]), p. 232-48 diagr. [3327

FRED A. DEERING, JR. The labyrinth of royalty and mineral interests [in gas and oil, 1886-1956]. Dicta, 34:195-206, 319-34 (Jul-Oct 1957). port. notes. [3328

DWIGHT D. MURPHEY. Oil and gas leases--the habendum clause--sufficiency of shut in wells for extension beyond the primary term [1894-1955]. Dicta, 34:253-66 (Jul-Aug 1957). port. notes. [3329

EARL A. BROWN. The implied covenant for additional development [of gas and oil leases, 1897-1958]. Southw. law jour., 13:149-76 (spring 1959). notes. [3330

R.O. KELLAM. A century of correlative rights. Baylor law rev., 12:1-42 (winter). notes. On rights in underground reservoirs of oil and gas underlying the lands of more than one owner, 1897-1959. [3331

HENRIETTA MELIA LARSON & KENNETH WIGGINS PORTER. History of Humble Oil & Refining Company: a study in industrial growth [1897-1948]. N.Y.: Harper [1959]. xxiv, [2], 769 p. diagrs., maps, ports., tables, views. notes (p. 699-743). Result "of an independent study undertaken by the Business History Foundation under an arrangement with Humble." On an organization formed in 1917 by men who had been engaged in Texas oil production since 1897, with more than half of the stock owned by the Standard Oil Company of New Jersey. To be continued by a second volume. [3332

WALLACE GORDON MALONE. The evolution of shut-in royalty law. Baylor law rev., 11:19-83 (winter 1959). notes. On "a covenant of reasonable development" in gas leases, and the effect of "failure to market gas" upon the rights of lessor and lessee, 1904-56. [3333

PERCY C. SPENCER. Oil--and independence! The story of the Sinclair Oil Corporation. N.Y.: Newcomen Soc. in North America, 1957. 28 p. On Harry Sinclair (1876-1956), who entered the oil business in 1905 and founded the Sinclair Oil & Refining Corporation in 1916 and later other oil corporations. [3334

U.S. Bureau of Mines. Loss of Life among wearers of oxygen breathing apparatus [in mines, 1908-55]. By Alexander E. Morrow. [Wash.] 1959. iv, 28 p. table. (Its Information circular 7943.) [3335

DOW CHEMICAL COMPANY. The magnesium industry [since ca. 1914]. John G. Glover & Rudolph L. Lagai, eds., The development of American industries: their economic significance, 4th ed. (N.Y.: Simmons-Boardman [1959]), p. 271-6. [3336

JOSEPH L. MASSIE. Blazer and Ashland Oil: a study in management. [Lexington?] Univ. of Kentucky Press [1960]. xiv, [2], 253 p. diagrs., facsim., maps (1 double), ports., tables, views. "Study undertaken initially for a doctoral dissertation"--Univ. of Chicago. On the Ashland Refining Company, Ashland, Ky., and its reorganization as the Ashland Oil & Refining Company, 1918-57, its growth by acquisition of 21 other companies (engaged in production, refining, transportation, and marketing of oil), and its management from 1924 to 1957 by Paul G. Blazer (born 1890). [3337

JOHN W. WHITTEMORE. The Virginia Experiment Station and mineral industries research [Blacksburg, 1921-54]. Mineral industries jour., 1(4):1 (Dec 1954). port. bibliog. [3338

H. A. WILHELM. Development of uranium metal production in America [1922-59]. Jour. chemical educ., 37: 56-68 (Feb). diagrs., view. notes. [3339

LEAD INDUSTRIES ASSOCIATION. The lead industry [since 1925. Prepared by Robert L. Ziegfeld.] John G. Glover & Rudolph L. Lagai, eds., The development of American industries: their economic significance, 4th ed. (N.Y.: Simmons-Boardman [1959]), p. 262-70. [3340

DEAN RICHMOND. Design for growth: the story of National Gypsum Company in commemoration of its 35th anniversary. Buffalo, N.Y.: Baker, Jones, Hausauer [1960]. ix, 142 p. diagrs. (1 fold.), fold. map, fold. table. On a firm founded in 1925, manufacturer of wallboard, cement, ceramic tiles, and other wall materials. [3341

HARRY FOSTER BAIN & others. Subsoil wealth. Conference on Research in Income and Wealth, Studies in income and wealth, 12 (1950): 235-73. tables. notes. On estimates of "the amounts of the various minerals known to exist in the ground" and of their value, 1929-47. [3342

F. L. EICHNER. Metallurgical industries of Virginia: aluminum foil rolling at Reynolds Richmond plant. Mineral industries jour., 5(3):4-5 (Sep 1958). views. On work of the Reynolds Metals Company, 1930-59. [3343

M. L. BURGENER & DEANE C. CARTER. Protective coatings for weathered galvanized sheets. Agric. engineering, 31:67-70 (Feb 1950). diagrs., tables, views. notes. On tests of protective paints for galvanized metal, conducted by the American Zinc Institute, 1932-48. [3344

CHARLES O. GALVIN. Meyers v. Brown--jurisprudence in action. U. C. L. A. law rev., 7:589-616 (Jul). notes. On cases cited by Charles J. Meyers and Earl A. Brown in "a recent exchange of differences of opinion ... on the subject of implied covenants in oil and gas leases," 1934-59. [3345

CHARLES T. HOLLAND. Some aspects of roof control in coal mines [1935-54]. Mineral industries jour., 1(1):1-5 (Mar 1954). diagrs., tables, views. notes. [3346

FRED WARREN BULL. Hydrogenation studies on Midlothian coal. Va. jour. science, 1:63-73 (Jan 1950). bibliog. On the development of the "synthetic fuel industry" in America, 1937-50, and abroad, producing oils and tars; with a report on studies of coal in the Richmond Basin. [3347

LESLIE MOSES. Recent problems in connection with shut-in gas royalty provisions in oil and gas leases [1937-58]. Loyola law rev., 10:1-10. notes. On the right of the lessor to receive rental from the lessee for gas "produced" but stored underground ("shut in") and not marketed. [3348

ROGER JOHN WILLIAMS, JR. The premium price plan for copper, lead, and zinc [during World War II]. Ann Arbor: University Microfilms, 1959 [i. e. 1960]. Positive microfilm of typescript. [224] leaves. Thesis--Columbia Univ. Abstracted: Dissert. abstracts, 20:3546 (Mar). [3349

PAULINE NELSON. Oil and gas rights in railroad rights of way--the Union Pacific case. Dicta, 34:267-75 (Jul-Aug 1957). notes. On the question of the ownership of the mineral estate in lands granted to railroads under an act of 1 Jul. 1862 as litigated between 1942 and 1957. [3350

GARY L. LEARY. Compulsory unitization [1945-59]--the answer to oil and gas conservation? U. C. L. A. law rev., 7:312-27 (Mar). notes. [3351

U.S. Atomic Energy Commission. The atomic energy industry [since 1946]. John G. Glover & Rudolph L. Lagai, eds., The development of American industries: their economic significance, 4th ed. (N.Y.: Simmons-Boardman [1959]), p. 554-8. [3352

AMERICAN BAR ASSOCIATION. Section of Mineral and Natural Resources Law. Conservation of oil & gas: a legal history. 1958. Edited by Robert E[dwin] Sullivan. [Chicago, 1960.] xi, 351 p. notes. "Table of cases" (p. 347-8). Supplement, 1948-58, to a work of the same title and organization published in 1948 (cited above, no. 3316). Consists mainly of histories of oil and gas conservation in each of 38 States (p. 13-275). [3353

Transportation

NATIONAL SOCIETY FOR THE PRESERVATION OF COVERED BRIDGES. World guide to covered bridges. ... Edited by Betsy and Philip Clough. [Beverly? Mass., 1959.] xv, 141 p. tables, views. 14 x 22 cm. Includes a list of "Covered bridges of the United States," arranged by State and county (p. 1-85). [3354

CLARENCE PEARSON HORNUNG. Wheels across America: a pictorial cavalcade illustrating the early development of vehicular transportation [ca. 1700 to ca. 1925]. N.Y.: A.S. Barnes [1959]. 341 p. cartoons, diagrs., facsims., ports., views (part col.). "Picture credits (p. 337-41). Reproductions, mainly of prints and photographs dated mainly between the 1850s and the 1930s, showing horse-drawn vehicles (carriages, stage coaches, covered wagons, drays, etc.), railroad cars, horse-drawn and electrified cars on rails, bicycles and tricycles, automobiles, and associated roads, rails, freight yards, etc.; with explanatory text. Many of the illustrations show scenes in New York City. [3355

JOHN T. STARR. Covered bridges: links with the past [1805-1960]. Am. forests, 66(4):26-7, 48-51 (Apr). views (1 double). [3356

JULIUS RUBIN. Imitation by canal or innovation by railroad: a comparative study of the response to the Erie Canal in Boston, Philadelphia, and Baltimore [1825-35]. Ann Arbor: University Microfilms, 1959 [i. e. [1960]. Positive microfilm of typescript. 422 leaves. fold. diagrs., map, fold. table. bibliog. (leaves 402-22). Thesis--Columbia Univ. Abstracted: Dissert. abstracts, 20:3563 (Mar). [3357

JOHN ANDERSON MILLER. Fares, please! A popular history of trolleys, horse-cars, street-cars, buses, elevateds, and subways [1831-1940. N.Y.:] Dover Publications [1960]. ix, [3], 204, [19] p. diagrs., facsims, views. bibliog. (p. 195-6). 1st ed. 1941, reprinted unabridged with "a new preface and a selection of photographs." [3358

DAVID PAGE MORGAN. What price piggy back? Trains, 20(7):30-42; (8): 36-45 (May, Jun). views. On TOFC ("trailer-on-flat-car") transportation, its antecedents as early as 1858, its first commercial use in 1885, its rapidly increasing adoption since 1953, and the equipment that it requires. [3359

HOWARD FREAS. Aspects of transportation based on regulatory experience in the United States [1887-1958]. I. C. C. Practitioners' jour., 26:273-91, 385-423 (Dec 1958, Jan 1959). notes. [3360

A. P. HEINER. The transport revolution and regulation [mainly by the Interstate Commerce Commission, 1887-1959]. Karl M. Ruppenthal, ed., Revolution in transportation (Stanford, Calif.: Graduate School of Business, Stanford Univ. [1960]), p. 115-22. [3361

RUPERT L. MURPHY. Problems in transportation ratemaking [1887-1959]. I. C. C. Practitioners' jour., 26: 1138-45 (Sep 1959). [3362

JOHN GUANDOLO. The Elkins Act [1903]. I. C. C. Practitioners' jour., 26:994-1012 (Jun 1959). notes. On legislation, still in effect, to prohibit "any rebate, concession, or discrimination in respect to the transportation of any property in interstate or foreign commerce by any common carrier." [3363

LEONARD S. GOODMAN. The history and scope of Federal power to delay changes in transportation rates [1910-59]. I. C. C. Practitioners' jour., 27: 245-56 (Dec 1959). notes. For comment see Robert D. Brooks & John A. Daily, "The Commission's power of suspension and judicial review thereof," 27:589-606 (Mar 1960). [3364

ROBERT ALFRED NELSON. Ratemaking in transportation--Congressional intent. Duke law jour., 1960: 221-38 (spring). notes. On the transportation acts of 1920, 1940, and 1958. [3365

MORRIS FORGASH. Transport revolution at the last frontier--the thought barrier. Karl M. Ruppenthal, ed., Revolution in transportation (Stanford, Calif.: Graduate School of Business, Stanford Univ. [1960]), p. 55-70. On problems of standardization of "equipment that can ride on steel rails, on the highways, on the inland and coastal waterways and the high seas, and in the air, with facility of interchange," 1928-59. [3366

ROBERT W. MINOR. Coordinated or integrated transportation [1932-58]. I. C. C. Practitioners' jour., 26:16-28 (Oct 1958). port. [3367

PAUL F. YOUNT. The revolution and the motor truck. Karl M. Ruppenthal, ed., Revolution in transportation (Stanford, Calif.: Graduate School of Business, Stanford Univ. [1960]), p. 43-50. On the use of motor trucks during World War II and the Korean War and the operation of trucks by railroad companies, 1941-59. [3368

AIR TRANSPORTATION

HERBERT DAVIS DEIN. Cujus est solum ejus ets ... quousque tandem? Jour. air law and commerce, 26: 237-54 (summer 1959). notes. On the ownership and control of air space above private land, 1836-1946, and litigation concerning aviation space, 1930-58. [3369

JACK R. HUNT. Greatest air voyage ever made. Flying, 64(5):31-2, 88-9 (May 1958). On John Wise (1808-79) and his voyage in a balloon, the Atlantic, from St. Louis to New York, Jul. 1859. [3369a

AIRCRAFT INDUSTRIES ASSOCIATION OF AMERICA. The aeronautical industry [since 1895]. John G. Glover & Rudolph L. Lagai, eds., The development of American industries: their economic significance, 4th ed. (N.Y.: Simmons-Boardman [1959]), p. 669-91. On production of aeronautical equipment for military and commercial use. [3370

PAUL L. BRIAND, JR. Daughter of the sky: the story of Amelia Earhart. N.Y.: Duell, Sloan, and Pearce [1960]. xvii, 230 p. facsims., ports., views. bibliog. (p. 223-30). On Amelia M. Earhart (1898-1937), her early life in Kansas, her work as a magazine editor in New York, her marriage to George Palmer Putnam II, and her activities as an aviatrix from 1928 till her disappearance and presumed death in the Pacific. [3371

BARBARA CRAIG. The Wright brothers and their development of the airplane [1899-1903]. Raleigh: State Dept. of Archives and History, 1960. 23 p. ports., views. bibliog. (p. 23). [3372

CHARLES A. ROBERTS. Outer space and national sovereignty. Air Univ. quar. rev., 12(1):53-65 (spring). notes. On the development of "international air law" in America and abroad, 1900-1960. [3373

KENNETH SYDNEY DAVIS. The hero: Charles A[ugustus] Lindbergh [born 1902] and the American dream. Garden City, N.Y.: Doubleday, 1959. 527 p. bibliog. (p. 434-515). On his early life in Minnesota, his career as a flier, his contributions to aeronautics, his dislike of publicity and the New Deal, and his voluntary obscurity after the 1930s. [3374

NORMAN MACMILLAN. Great aircraft [in American, 1903-60, and abroad]. N.Y.: St. Martin's Press [1960]. 304 p. diagrs., views. [3375

HENRY ROBINSON PALMER, JR. This was air travel. Seattle: Superior Pub. Co. [1960]. 190 p. facsims., map, ports., views. Account, largely pictorial, of aeronautical developments in America, 1903-60, and abroad. [3376

GENE ROGER SIMONSON. The demand for aircraft and the aircraft industry, 1907-1958. Jour. econ. hist., 20: 361-82 (Sep). tables. notes. [3377

GROVER CLEVELAND LOENING. Lessons from the history of flight. Smithsonian Inst., Ann. rep., 1959, p. 347-59. views. notes. On "the historical achievements" and the "mistaken trends ... the jungle of misfits, false starts, and abandoned hopes" in the technology of aircraft and aeronautics, 1908-58. [3378

DAVID COXE COOKE. Racing planes that made history [in America, 1909-48, and abroad]. N.Y.: Putnam [1960]. 70 p. ports., views. 19 x 24 cm. [3379

GILL ROBB WILSON. Lockheed, industrial giant of the air age. Flying, 66(3-5): monthly installments (Mar-May). ports., views (1 double). On the Lockheed Aircraft Corporation, 1913-60. 3379a

EDWARD VERNON RICKENBACKER. Notes of a pioneer in aviation medicine. By Eddie Rickenbacker. Mil. med., 125:313-17 (May). On the development of "physical and mental requirements" for military and civilian fliers, 1917-60, particularly the experience of Eastern Air Lines, which in 1936, at the author's recommendation, established a Medical Department to maintain men as carefully as machines and to keep surveillance over the health of pilots. [3380

GILL ROBB WILSON. Convair, industrial giant of the age. Flying, 67(1-4): monthly installments (Jul-Oct). ports., views (part double). On Convair and predecessor organizations manufacturing airplanes since 1917, now a division of General Dynamics and diversified by extension into the manufacture of "nuclear-powered submarines," telecommunications and electronic equipment, "industrial and medical gases," etc. [3380a

ALEX DAWYDOFF. How Atlantic Aviation serves business flying. Flying, 65(4):54-6, 109-11 (Oct 1959). col. map, views. On an aircraft sale and maintenance service for businessmen, originating in Henry B. Du Pont's Du Pont Airport outside Wilmington in 1927 for the convenience of Du Pont employees and expanded in 1929 to form Atlantic Aviation Service. [3380b

ALBERT W. STOFFEL. American bilateral air transport agreements on the threshold of the jet transport age [1927-59]. Jour. air law and commerce, 26:119-36 (spring 1959). notes. [3381

JOHN WILLIAM WARD. The meaning of [Charles A.] Lindbergh's flight [from Long Island to Paris, 20 May 1927]. Joseph J. Kwiat & Mary C. Turpie, eds., Studies in American culture: dominant ideas and images (Minneapolis: Univ. of Minnesota Press [1960]), p. 27-40. [3382

ARTHUR D. LEWIS. Hawaiian Airlines, America's pioneer carrier in the Pacific [1929-60]. N.Y.: Newcomen Soc. in North America, 1960. 24 p. port., views. On a service founded by Stanley C. Kennedy as Inter-Island Airways, which later established air connections with the Pacific Coast and an office in New York City and which in 1948 superseded the last surviving water communication among the islands. [3383

DONALD WILLIE DOUGLAS. Of men and planes. By Donald W. Douglas as told to Douglas J. Ingells. Flying, (65(3):40-47, 54-64 (Sep 1959). ports., views. On the Douglas Commercial series of airplanes, DC-1, DC-2, and DC-3, manufactured by the author's company, the Douglas Aircraft Company, 1930-59. [3383a

JAMES G. RAY. Is the autogiro making a comeback? Flying, 66(1):34-5, 91-2 (Jan) views. On "rotary wing aircraft" or "flying windmills," 1931-59, and their present use for applying insecticidal dust to crop land. [3383b

LESTON FANEUF. Lawrence D[ale] Bell [1894-1956]: a man and his company, Bell Aircraft. N.Y.: Newcomen Soc. in North America, 1958. 36 p. On the Bell Aircraft Corporation, formed in 1935. [3384

ERNEST L. MARX. Governmental tort liability for operation of airports [1936-57]. Jour. air law and commerce, 26:173-81 (spring 1959). notes. [3385

EUGENE EDWARD WILSON. Kitty Hawk to Sputnik to Polaris ... a contemporary account of the struggle over military and commercial air policy in the United States. [Barre, Mass.: Barre Gazette, 1960.] xviii, 231 p. bibliog. (p. 223-5). Account, partly reminiscent, of the aircraft manufacturing industry and its relations with the U.S. Government since 1943; with suggestions concerning "world peace through world law." [3386

ELIOT TOZER. Revolution in air cargo. Flying, 66(1):24-5, 70-72 (Jan). diagrs., view. On the "air freight business," 1945-59. [3386a

RICHARD HAMMER. The Ayer story. Flying, 65(4):58-9, 118 (Oct 1959). port. On Frederick B. Ayer as a dealer in airplanes in New Jersey, 1946-58, and his organization of Frederick B. Ayer & Associates, "the world's largest aircraft dealer," New York City, 1958. [3386b

LOU DAVIS. Butler Aviation. Flying, 66(5):48-9, 74-8 (May). views (1 double). On an organization for airplane servicing and repair, established by Paul Butler in 1947. [3386c

HIGHWAY TRANSPORTATION

ERNEST R. ARCHAMBEAU, JR. Unavoidable automobile accidents [as a defense in suits for damages, 1898-1958]. Dicta, 36:426-42 (Sep-Oct 1959). notes. [3387

CORNELIUS J. PECK. Comparative negligence and automobile liability insurance [in 7 States, 1910-60]. Mich. law rev, 58:689-728 (Mar). tables. notes. [3388

PETER WARD. New York's Motor Vehicle Accident Indemnification Corporation: past, present, and future. Buffalo law rev., 8:215-41 (winter 1959). notes. On "financial responsibility legislation" in Connecticut, Massachusetts, and elsewhere, 1926-59, particularly in New York since 1929. [3389

PETER WARD. The uninsured motorist: national and international protection presently available and comparative problems in substantial similarity (1926-59]. Buffalo law rev., 9:283-320 (winter). notes. [3390

The DRIVER's license "display" statute: problems arising from its application [1927-59]. Wash. Univ. law quar., 1960: 279-91 (Dec). notes. [3391

THEODORE M. KRANITZ. The nature of truck reciprocity agreements. Mo. Bar, Jour., 15:140-47 (Mar 1959). port. notes. On interstate agreements since 1930 concerning regulation and taxation of trucks as "part of municipal or private international law" and, "for all practical purposes, treaties." [3392

ROBERT J. BERNARD. Tacking or combining of interstate operating rights [of motor carriers, 1935-58]. I. C. C. Practitioner's jour., 26:521-36 (Feb 1959). notes. [3393

CLEM CHARLES LINNENBERG, JR. The agriculatural exemptions in interstate trucking [1935-59]: mend them or end them? Law and contemp. problems, 25:139-83 (winter). notes. [3394

WILLIAM J. MONHEIM. An analysis of the question of reparation involving motor carriers. I. C. C. Practitioners' jour., 27:257-66 (Dec 1959). notes. On the question whether the Interstate Commerce Commission, under the Motor Carrier Act of 1935, had authority to award damages to shippers complaining that past rates paid by them to motor carriers had been "unjust and unreasonable," settled in the negative by the Supreme Court in 1959. [3395

JOHN HENRY O'BRIEN. Twenty-five years of Federal motor carrier licensing--the private versus for-hire vehicle carrier [1935-60]. N.Y. Univ. law rev., 35:1150-79 (Jun). notes. [3396

WILLIAM E. KNEPPER. The automobile in court. Wash. and Lee law rev., 17:213-28 (fall). notes. On "automobile accident litigation," 1946-60. [3397

RICHARD F. SEIBERT. When is operation of motor vehicles activity "within the scope of employment" under the Federal Tort Claims Act [of 1946]? Fed. Bar jour., 20:416-24 (fall). notes. [3398

Trails, Roads, and Highways

CHARLES OWEN MEIBERG. The "free" public road and government highway policy decisions [19th and 20th centuries]. Ann Arbor: University Microfilms, 1960. Positive microfilm of typescript. [183] leaves. Thesis--Univ. of Virginia. Abstracted: Dissert. abstracts, 21:1085-6 (Nov). [3399

THOMAS A. GILLIAM. The case for billboard control [1916-59]: precedent and prediction. Dicta, 36:461-74 (Nov-Dec 1959). port. notes. See also Joseph E. Little, "Colorado needs a constitutional and effective roadside sign law," 36:475-88 (Nov-Dec 1959). [3400

ERIC SCHENKER. Economic and social effects of highway improvements [1929-56]: an inventory of the economic factors influenced by a highway development program. East Lansing, Mich., 1960. vi, 32 leaves. tables. Joint enterprise of Michigan State University, the Michigan State Highway Department, and the U.S. Bureau of Public Roads. [3401

Vehicles

CHRISTY BORTH. 10 great men of Detroit. True, Automobile yearbook, 9:28-55. ports., views. Biographical sketches of Detroiters in the automobile industry: Ransom Eli Olds (1864-1950), Henry Martyn Leland (1843-1932), Roy Dikeman Chapin (1880-1936), William Crapo Durant (1861-1947), Charles Warren Nash (1864-1948), Henry Ford (1864-1947), Charles Franklin Kettering (1876-1958), Alfred Pritchard Sloan (born 1875), Walter Percy Chrysler (1875-1940), and George Wilcken Romney, several of whom worked only briefly in Detroit and had their headquarters elsewhere. [3402

THOMAS CHILDS COCHRAN. "... personality and good practical judgment." John Arthur Garraty, ed., The unforgettable Americans (Great Neck, N.Y.: Channel Press [1960]), p. 318-21. On Walter Chrysler (1875-1940), automobile manufacturer. [3403

JOHN THEODORE FLANAGAN. Four-wheeled ghosts. Southw. rev., 45:174-7 (spring). On "the folklore of the automobile industry" since the 1890s. [3404

GENERAL MOTORS CORPORATION. Story of General Motors [and its predecessors and components since 1890]. Detroit: Public Relations Staff, General Motors, ©1957. 84 p. facsims., views. 1st ed. 1942. [3405

L. SCOTT BAILEY. 1891 Lambert: a new claim for America's first gasoline automobile. Antique automobile, 24:341-9 (Oct). diagr., facsims., ports., views. On automobiles designed and manufactured by John William Lambert, Ohio City, Ohio, 1891-1911; with several documents supporting the belief that a vehicle designed by him in 1891 was "America's first gasoline automobile." [3406

AUTOMOBILE MANUFACTURERS ASSOCIATION. The automobile industry [since 1893]. John G. Glover & Rudolph L. Lagai, eds., The development of American industries: their economic significance, 4th ed. (N.Y.: Simmons-Boardman [1959]), p. 642-68. views. [3407

FIRST California automobile found. Antique automobile. 24:37, 65-7 (Feb). views. On the Pioneer automobile, designed and built by J. A. Meyer in San Francisco, 1893-96; with an account of the only surviving example. [3408

The SMITHSONIAN restores America's most famous antique automobile, the 1893 Duryea. Antique automobile, 24: 452, 484-5 (Dec). views. [3409

JOHN BELL RAE. The Electric Vehicle Company. Antique automobile, 24: 256-63, 310-12, 321 (Aug). facsim., view. On a New York firm founded as the Electric Carriage and Wagon Company, maker of electric taxicabs and other electric (and eventually gasoline-powered) vehicles, 1897-1910. Includes an account of inventions and a patent of George Baldwin Selden for a gasoline-driven vehicle, 1876-96, the purchase of the patent by the Electric Vehicle Company, and resulting litigation till 1912, ending with the decision that other mechanisms then in use for transmitting gasoline power to vehicles were not infringements of the Selden Patent. [3410

J. S. FOLEY III. Florida AACA early automotive pioneer. Antique automobile, 24:393-4 (Oct). ports. On Charles Birchwood as an automobile mechanic, driver, inventor, and manufacturer, 1898-1920s. [3411

A PORTFOLIO of electrics. Antique automobile, 24:269-79 (Aug). views. Photographs of 22 electric passenger automobiles, built between 1898 and 1922. [3412

L. SCOTT BAILEY. The great Barney Oldfield. Antique automobile, 24:182-6 (Jun). ports. On his career as a driver of racing cars (originally for Henry Ford), 1902-10. [3413

J. GEORGE JANES. The track Indy drivers fear. True, Automobile yearbook, 8 (1959): 44-9, 75-7. ports., views (1 double). On automobile races at Daytona Beach, Fla., 1902-59, and the dangers of the new International Speedway there for drivers accustomed to the Indianapolis Speedway. [3414

BOB KNEEDLER. 1902 Winton challenges Olds at Ormond Beach [Florida, 1902]. Antique automobile, 24:200-201 (Jun). ports. [3415

A RACING Duryea at Ormond. Antique automobile, 24:202, 207 (Jun). view. On races at Ormond Beach, Fla., 1902-6. [3416

ROBERT THEODORUS. Oldfield's famous 999. Antique automobile, 24: 187-8 (Jun). views. On a specially constructed racing car manufactured by Henry Ford and driven by Barney Oldfield (once by Ford himself), 1902-4, now preserved in the museum at Dearborn. [3417

DAVID COXE COOKE. Racing cars that made history [1903-58]. N.Y.: Putnam [1960]. 70, [2] p. ports., views. 19 x 24 cm. [3418

WALDEMAR G. HANSEN. Recalling the day Barney [Oldfield] broke his world's record, Nov. 20, 1903 [in Agricultural Park, Los Angeles]. As told to Scott Bailey. Antique automobile, 24:189-90, 207 (Jun). Eyewitness account. [3419

BERT JAY NORTH. I remember Ormond Beach [Fla.] and the Vanderbilt Cup [1903-6]. Antique automobile, 24:203-4 (Jun). [3420

CHARLES T. PEARSON. The indomitable Tin Goose: the true story of Preston Tucker [1903-56] and his car. N.Y.: Abelard-Schuman [1960]. 285 p. ports., views. On the early life of Preston Thomas Tucker in Capac, Mich., his work as an automobile salesman in Detroit, his efforts to design a new automobile independently of the established companies, his organization of the Tucker Corporation (Chicago) to construct a "rear-engined automobile," his indictment on 25 counts of mail fraud, 1 of conspiracy to defraud, and 5 of violations of Securities and Exchange regulations, the verdict of "Not guilty" on all charges, and the destruction of his business by the delays and costs of the litigation initiated by the Securities and Exchange Commission. [3421

ROLLS-ROYCE, the living legend, as reflected by half a century of contemporary British and American sales and institutional literature. Arcadia, Calif.: Post Motor Books, 1958. 384 p. facsims., ports., views. Originally published as separate volumes, British (1951) and American (1953). Reproductions of advertisements, catalogues, and other publications of or about Rolls-Royce, Ltd., and Rolls-Royce of America, Inc., 1907-58. [3422

BILL DAWN. The E-M-F story. Antique automobile, 24:10-12, 58-71 (Feb). views. On automobiles made by the E-M-F Company, Detroit, established by Barney R. Everitt, William E. Metzger, and Walter E. Flanders, 1908-11; with a full description of an E-M-F touring car acquired by the author. [3423

FREDERICK EUGENE MELDER. The "Tin Lizzie's" golden anniversary. Am. quar., 12:466-81 (winter). diagr.

notes. On the Model T Ford, 1908-27, and its "revolutionary influence on America's social and economic life." [3424

MARVIN F. STUDEBAKER. The first Plymouth was not a Chrysler. Antique automobile, 24:106-7 (Apr). facsim., views. On vehicles manufactured at Plymouth, Ohio, by the Commercial Motor Truck Company and its successor, the Plymouth Motor Truck Company, 1908 to 1914 or 1915. [3425

BROCK W. YATES. Famous Indianapolis cars and drivers. ... Illustrated with official Speedway photos. N.Y.: Harper [1960]. xii, [2], 219, [2] p. ports., views. On the Indianapolis Speedway Races, 1909-59. [3425a

The INVINCIBLE electric trucks of the Curtis Publishing Co. Antique automobile, 24:266-8 (Aug), views. On a fleet of 22 trucks manufactured between 1910 and 1927 by the Walker Vehicle Company, Chicago, Ill., and still in use by the Curtis Publishing Company in Philadelphia. [3426

MARY ELLEN REINERT. Father of power steering. Harvard alumni bul., 57:444-6 (12 Mar 1955). diagr., port., view. On the work of Francis W. Davis (Harvard, 1910) in automotive design and engineering since 1910. [3427

FRANKLIN MERING RECK. A car-traveling people: how the automobile has changed the life of Americans--a study of social effects [1912-60. New edition. Detroit: Automobile Manufacturers Assoc.] 1960. 48 p. maps, table, views (1 double). bibliog. (p. 48). 1st ed. 1945. [3428

KARL LUDVIGSEN. Detroit's future: front drive--or rear engine. True, Automobile yearbook, 9:82-7, 95-6. diagrs., ports., views. On rear-engine automobiles in the United States, 1919-60. [3429

RUSS CATLIN. The toothpick saucers. True, Automobile yearbook, 8 (1959): 38-9, 79-80. col. double view. On automobile races on "vulnerable and dangerous" board tracks in various parts of the United States, 1920-30. [3430

CHARLES L. BETTS, JR. A Paige from the past ... the story of America's most beautiful speedster. Antique automobile, 24:350-51, 395-7 (Oct). views. On the Paige Daytona, 1921-23. [3431

HENRY AUSTIN CLARK, JR. 1922, the first air cooled Chevrolet. Antique automobile, 24:112-13, 154-5 (Apr). views. [3432

EARL C. BUTON, JR. The Plymouth story. Antique automobile, 24:100-106, 108-9, 153 (Apr). facsim., tables, views. On the Plymouth automobiles manufactured in Detroit (a few in Los Angeles) by Walter P. Chrysler between 1928 and 1934; with a detailed account of their designs, materials, and types. [3433

LINDLEY F. Bothwell's collection of racing cars [assembled since 1929]. Antique automobile, 24:192-5, 210 (Jun). views. [3434

ROBERT ANGUS BANDEEN. State per capita automobile expenditures and income, 1930, 1940, and 1950. Ann Arbor: University Microfilms, 1959 [i. e. 1960]. Positive microfilm of typescript. [139] leaves. Thesis--Duke Univ. Abstracted: Dissert. abstracts, 20:3541-2 (Mar). [3435

ROBERT LEE BEHME. The crazy quest that never ends. True, Automobile yearbook, 8 (1959): 32-5, 94. diagr., views (part double). On "flying cars" invented by Waldo Waterman, Stephen Fulton, Molt Taylor, Leland Bryan, and "Skeets" Coleman, 1932-59. [3436

MR. Electric. Antique automobile, 24: 264-5 (Aug). port., view. On a collection of electric automobiles assembled by George De Laplaine during the past 26 years and exhibited in his Electric Museum, New Brunswick, N.J. [3437

HENRY L. FEINSINGER. 25 years of AACA history. Antique automobile, 24:419-29 (Dec). facsim., ports., views. On the Antique Automobile Club of America, 1935-60. [3438

CURTIS D. NORRIS. Reflections on selling a car. Antique automobile, 24: 21, 62-3 (Feb). On "a 1938 Cadillac '60' four-door sedan," acquired by the author sometime after 1951, and his present regrets that he did not keep it. [3439

KENDALL WILLIAMS. Dreams that cars are made of. True, Automobile yearbook, 8 (1959): 8-13, 77-8. views. On American experimental automobiles, 1940-59. [3440

ALAN D. HAAS. America's top test driver. True, Automobile yearbook, 8 (1959): 5-7, 70-71. ports., view. On

Curt Ferris (born 1920) as a test driver for the Ford Motor Company, 1944-59. [3441

RAIL TRANSPORTATION

MARION BEATTY. Railroad regulation from 533 A. D. to 1958. Bar Assoc. State Kan., Jour., 27:186-93 (Nov 1958). [3442

ROBERT E. CARLSON. British railroads and engineers and the beginnings of American railroad development [1824-30]. Bus. hist. rev., 34:137-49 (summer). views. notes. [3443

NEW YORK CENTRAL RAILROAD. The railroad industry [since 1825]. John G. Glover & Rudolph L. Lagai, eds., The development of American industries: their economic significance, 4th ed. (N.Y.: Simmons-Boardman [1959]), p. 613-41. [3444

JOHN ROBERT DAY. More unusual railways [in America, 1826-1960, and abroad]. N.Y.: Macmillan [1960]. 214 p. diagrs., views. Supplement to the author's Unusual railways. Chapters on "Horse and sail on railways," monorails, "Guide-rail systems," "Moving platforms," "Railways on gradients," and other systems. [3445

ROBERT SELPH HENRY. "... when two locomotives touched." John Arthur Garraty, ed., The unforgettable Americans (Great Neck, N.Y.: Channel Press [1960]), p. 247-50. On Grenville Mellen Dodge (1831-1916), builder of the Union Pacific Railroad. [3446

ROBERT WILLIAM FOGEL. The Union Pacific Railroad: a case in premature enterprise. Baltimore: Johns Hopkins Press, 1960. 129 p. tables. bibliog. (p. 120-23), notes. (The Johns Hopkins University studies in historical and political science, ser. 78, no. 2.) An application of economic theory to the measurement of the risks of the enterprise and the errors in the form of aid extended to it by the U.S. Government, 1862-80. [3447

DAVID MORRIS POTTER, ed. The railroads [1862-1960]. ... Revised by E. David Cronon and Howard R. Lamar. N.Y.: Holt [1960]. xii, 66 p. notes (p. 66). (Select problems in historical interpretation, 2.) Excerpts from printed primary sources and a few secondary works, on railroad corporations in relation to public grants, investors, monopoly and discrimination, and government regulation. [3448

D. T. GILCHRIST. Albert Fink [1827-97] and the pooling system. Bus. hist. rev., 34:24-49 (spring). port., view. notes. On his innovations in "railroad rate-making policies," 1870-87. [3449

GEORGE WOODMAN HILTON & JOHN FITZGERALD DUE. The electric interurban railways in America [1887-1960]. Stanford, Calif.: Stanford Univ. Press, 1960. ix, [3], 463 p. diagrs., maps, plans, tables, views. notes (p. 427-37). On the technology, finance, and government regulation of the industry, the rise and decline of the passenger and freight traffic, and "the decision to abandon" (p. 1-251); with histories of "The individual interurbans," arranged by State (p. 253-423). [3450

JOHN WALKER BARRIGER. Why consolidation? Karl M. Ruppenthal, ed., Revolution in transportation (Stanford, Calif.: Graduate School of Business, Stanford Univ. [1960]), p. 12-42. bibliog. On railroad consolidation, 1890-1959. [3451

DAVID PAGE MORGAN. The railroad image. Trains, 20(2):22-6 (Dec 1959). cartoon. On the bad "public relations" of the railroad industry in the 20th century, and the failure of "the orthodox railroad mentality" to realize that "the railroad problem is at least 80 per cent political instead of technical." [3452

J. PLOMER. "Sir Henry": some notes on the life of Sir Henry Thornton. Railway & Locomotive Hist. Soc., Bul., 103:7-20 (Oct). port. On his career as an executive of the Pennsylvania Railroad (1901-11), the Long Island Railroad (1911-14), the Great Eastern Railway in England (1914-19), and the Canadian National Railways (1919-32). [3453

JAMES CECIL NELSON. Effects of public regulation on railroad performance [since 1920]. Am. econ. rev., 50: 495-505 (May). notes. [3454

W. T. RICE. Railroads in the missile age [1941-59]. Karl M. Ruppenthal, ed., Revolution in transportation (Stanford, Calif.: Graduate School of Business, Stanford Univ. [1960]), p. 133-7. [3455

The RAILROAD on canvas. Trains, 20(7):48-57 (May). Black-and-white reproductions of 13 recent paintings, by various artists, showing railroad scenes, workers, and equipment. [3456

Railway Equipment

RAILROAD MAGAZINE. [Rosters of steam and Diesel locomotives. Compiled by Sy Reich.] Railroad mag., 1(1-6): bimonthly installments (Dec 1959 - Oct 1960). views. Tables of the locomotives now or formerly in use by Florida East Coast Railway, Chicago, Rock Island, & Pacific, Lehigh Valley Railroad, the Monon Railroad, St. Louis - San Francisco Railway, Grand Trunk (by John Davis), "shortlines of Ohio," Missouri Pacific Lines, Long Island Rail Road (by Savas Stavropoulos), St. Louis - Southwestern Railway, and Milwaukee Road. [3457

PAUL THEODORE WARNER. Locomotives of the Pennsylvania Railroad, 1834-1924. Chicago: O. Davies [1959]. 79, [1] p. diagrs., tables, views. From Baldwin locomotives, Apr.-Oct. 1924. [3458

DAVID MARSHALL. 135,000 reefers. Railroad mag., 71(2):22-7 (Feb). views. On refrigerator cars since 1842, the sources of ice for them, and their use in marketing. [3459

WILLIAM F. KNAPKE. True stories and legends of woodburning engines [1850s-1910]. By Bill Knapke. Railroad mag., 71(2):16-21 (Feb). views. [3460

H. L. KELSO. Consolidation type engines. Railroad mag., 71(3):23-7 (Apr). diagr., views. On 2-8-0 locomotives, 1864-1957. [3461

LUCIUS MORRIS BEEBE. Private varnish on shortlines. Railroad mag., 71(1):18-23 (Dec 1959). views. On private cars, usually "remarkably opulent," elegant, and luxurious, built as early as 1868, some in use as late as 1938. [3462

WALTER F. BECKER. Locomotive builders not mentioned in Bulletin no. 58, May 1942. Railway & Locomotive Hist. Soc., Bul., 103:61-5 (Oct). Historical sketches of 15 firms, 1871-92. [3463

HERMANN S. D. BOTZOW, JR. Monorails [in America, 1876-1960, and abroad]. N.Y.: Simmons-Boardman Pub. Corp., 1960. vii, 104 p. diagrs., views. bibliog. (p. 75-102). [3464

ARTHUR D. DUBIN. Some classic cars. Trains, 20(3):16-26 (Jan). port., views. Twenty-seven photographs of passenger cars, 1888-1938, with descriptive text. [3465

THOMAS T. TABER III & WALTER CASLER. Climax--an unusual steam locomotive. [Rahway? N.J.: Railroadians of America, 1960. 10], 97, [5] p. diagrs., port., tables, views (part col.). On logging locomotives made by the Climax Manufacturing Company, Corry, Pa., 1888-1928; with lists of the locomotives by construction number (nos. 1-1694) and by name of owner. [3466

H. L. KELSO. Mikados. Railroad mag., 71(1):24-8 (Dec 1959). views. On 2-8-2 locomotives, 1893-1957. [3467

FRED JUKES. Early Northern Pacific Consolidations. Railway & Locomotive Hist. Soc., Bul., 102:35-41 (Apr). diagrs., views. On Consolidation locomotives manufactured by the Baldwin Locomotive Works for use by the Northern Pacific Rail Road in Montana and Washington, 1896-1947. [3468

WILLIAM W. KRATVILLE & HAROLD E. RANKS. Union Pacific locomotives. [Omaha:] Barnhart Press, 1960. 2 v. [144]; 166 p. diagrs., facsims., port., seal, tables, views. Mainly "a collection of mechanical charts and specifications from the Archives of the Motive Power & Machinery Department of the Union Pacific," 1897, 1938, 1959, on the design and construction of steam, electric, diesel, and turbine locomotives of the Union Pacific Railroad Company and some of its subsidiaries (Oregon-Washington Railroad & Navigation Company, Oregon Short Line, Los Angeles & Salt Lake, St. Joseph and Great Island, and Laramie, North Park, & Western); with several chapters on locomotive parts (frames, fireboxes, stokers, etc.). Supplement to the authors' Motive power of the Union Pacific (1958). [3469

WAKE HOAGLAND. Fireman. Trains, 20(1):36-9 (Nov 1959). views. On the hardships and satisfactions of railroad firemen, early 20th century. [3470

WILLIAM W. KRATVILLE. Knife-noses and portholes. Trains, 20(9): 30-39 (Jul). facsims., views. On the "Mechanical Transmission Gasoline Motor Car," a railroad car powered by a gasoline engine, designed by William R. McKeen and manufactured by the McKeen Motor Car Company, Omaha, in cooperation with the shops of the Union Pacific Railroad there, 1905-20. [3471

DAVID PAGE MORGAN. Steam's finest hour. Milwaukee: Kalmbach Pub. Co., c1959. 126, [2] p. views. 29 x 42 cm. Photographic atlas of steam locomotives built between 1925 and 1958, with specifications, descriptive text, and introduction. [3472

H. L. KELSO. Ten driving wheels. Railroad mag., 71(5):16-23; (6):21-9 (Aug, Oct). views. On 2-10-2 locomotives, 1903-58, and 2-10-4 locomotives, 1926-49. [3473

DAVID PAGE MORGAN. Duplex-drives. Trains, 20(1):16-25 (Nov 1959). diagrs., tables, views. On experimental 4-cylinder steam locomotives of the Baldwin Locomotive Works, 1932-47. [3474

DAVID PAGE MORGAN. The diesel that did it. Trains, 20(4):18-25 (Feb). map, views. On "Electro-Motive No. 103, the 193-foot, 900,000-pound, 5400-horsepower machine" designed by Richard M. Dilworth that in 1938 "broke steam's century-old grip on the freight train" and was "the prototype for the world's first standardized, mass-produced line of diesel freight locomotives." [3475

JOE G. COLLIAS. The last of steam: a billowing pictorial pageant of the waning years of steam railroading in the United States [1939-58, mainly "steam from 1950 on"]. Berkeley, Calif.: Howell-North, 1960. 269 p. tables. views. [3476

WATER TRANSPORTATION

HARRY MILLER LYDENBERG (1874-1960), comp. Crossing the line: tales of the ceremony during four centuries. N.Y.: New York Public Library, 1957. [8], 239 p. views. From Bulletin of the New York Public Library, 1955-57, "with revisions and additions." Heavily annotated excerpts from dated descriptions in several languages, 1529-1958, including descriptions by voyagers to America of ceremonies at which the crew of a ship, when crossing the Equator, collected gratuities from the passengers or hazed those who were recalcitrant. [3477

SHIPBUILDERS COUNCIL OF AMERICA. The shipbuilding, ship repair, and shipping industries [since 1607. By Leigh R. Sanford.] John G. Glover & Rudolph L. Lagai, eds., The development of American industries: their economic significance, 4th ed. (N.Y.: Simmons-Boardman [1959]), p. 559-612. [3478

HEINZ W. FRIESE. Die Bedeutung der Binnenwasserwege für die Besiedlung und Erschliessung der USA. Jahrbuch für Amerikastudien, 5:185-214. maps, tables. bibliog. On canals in the United States since 1652, including the few that continue in use. [3479

AMERICAN PILOTS' ASSOCIATION. State pilotage in America: historical outline with European background. [By W. Hilton Lowe. Wash., 1960.] xi, 137 p. tables. bibliog. (p. 133-7), notes. On State and Federal legislation for the regulation of pilots in the United States, and the formation of associations by pilots to establish and enforce standards in their profession, 1669-1959. [3480

GEORGE CHANDLER. Liverpool shipping: a short history. London: Phoenix House [1960]. 256 p. facsim., flags, maps, tables, views. On "Liverpool's shipping companies and their part in world trade." On the trade to North America see p. 103-36, dealing with various lines since 1693, particularly the Cunard Steam-Ship Company, Ltd. [3481

MacEDWARD LEACH. Notes on American shipping based on records of the Court of the Vice-Admiralty of Jamaica, 1776-1812. Am. Neptune, 20: 44-8 (Jan). Illustrations of the value of these records, including papers of captured ships. [3482

WILLIAM EDWARD BENNETT. The Collins story. By Warren Armstrong [pseud.]. London: Robert Hale [1957]. 192 p. ports., views. On Edward Knight Collins (1802-78), founder of the Collins Line, native of Cape Cod. Consists largely of quoted dialogue and attributions of states of mind. [3483

HORACE JEROME CRANMER. Canal investment, 1815-1860. Conference on Research in Income and Wealth, Trends in the American economy in the nineteenth century, ed. William N. Parker (Princeton: Princeton Univ. Press, 1960 [Studies in income and wealth, 24], p. 547-70. diagrs., tables. bibliog. (p. 561-2), notes. [3484

ROBERT FRANCIS LUCID. Two years before the mast as propaganda. Am. quar., 12:392-403 (fall). notes. Evidence of the falsity of the interpretation of Richard Henry Dana's volume (1840) as "a trenchant, searing indictment of the world of the forecastle" and particularly of flogging, and as an influence that led to the abolition of flogging in 1850. [3485

EDWIN SEYMOUR-BELL. The Cunard tradition--a proud heritage. N.Y.: Newcomen Soc. in North America, 1960. 24 p. port., seal, views. On the Cunard Steam-Ship Company, Ltd., 1840-1960, founded by Samuel Cunard, "Nova Scotia businessman," particularly its passenger service between England and the United States. [3486

JOHN F. CAMPBELL. Marine intelligence from the Panama star [1849-53] and the Star & herald [1853-1957]. Am. Neptune, 20:118-33 (Apr). notes. Samples of information and documents in these Panama newspapers relating to American shipping and travel to and from Panama and elsewhere in Latin America, especially in the years 1850-57. Includes a communication from Allen McLane to H. H. Munro on the disabling of the Pacific Mail steamship Golden Age between the islands of Quibo and Quicara, 29 Apr. 1855, and the success of her captain, J. T. Watkins, in beaching her in a sheltered cove. [3487

Ships and Boats

U.S. Museum of History and Technology. The national watercraft collection. By Howard I[rving] Chapelle, Curator of Transportation. [Wash.: Smithsonian Institution, 1960.] xi, 327 p. plans, views. bibliog. (p. 305-10). (U.S. National Museum. Bulletin 219.) Catalogues of models of "merchant sail" and "merchant steam," each with a detailed introduction and each model described in full. Lists a few materials other than models. [3488

JOHN G. KUENZEL & HAROLD E. WORTH. The use of wood in ships and boats [in America since ca. 960, and abroad]. Jour. forestry, 56:549-55 (Aug 1958). views. notes. [3489

WILLIAM E. SCHEVILL. The weight of a whaleboat [1726-1958]. Am. Neptune, 20:63-4 (Jan). Computations from available data. [3490

FRANK OSBORN BRAYNARD. Voices from the past. Steamboat bill, 17: 38-40, 46 (summer). view. On the American steamship Savannah, 1818-21, and the contemporary accounts of it. [3491

HAROLD S. COLTON. Charles Dickens and the American steamboat. Steamboat bill, 17:103-5 (winter). view. On his references in American notes to the 11 steamboats on which he traveled in the United States, 1842. [3492

ROLLIN GERMAIN. One hundred years ago: Germain's steam ship. Inland seas, 16:152-3 (summer). Announcement (undated) of 4 lectures to be given by the author in Cleveland to demonstrate the possibility of steamers that run more than 100 miles an hour, are not endangered by "the greatest oceanic forces," will cost less than a fifth as much to operate as present steamers, will not draw more than 22 feet when heavily loaded, and in war "would be an overmatch for all existing navies"; with a summary of one of the lectures from the Cleveland tri-weekly plain dealer, 10 Mar. 1860. [3493

WILLIAM DU BARRY THOMAS. Collision at Sandy Hook. Steamboat bill, 17:77 (fall). view. On a collision between the steamboat City of Brockton and the tugboat J. C. Hartt in the open sea off Sandy Hook, 29 Sep. 1887, and ensuing litigation for damages, in which the tugboat owners were victorious. [3494

FRED B. DUNCAN. Coal smoke and oily steam. Steamboat bill, 17:3-7 (spring). views. Boyhood memories of tugboats and their masters in New York Harbor and San Francisco Bay, 1890s. [3495

GEORGE ATHAN BILLIAS. Nathaniel T. Palmer's fleet of great schooners. Am. Neptune, 20:237-42 (Oct). notes. On vessels built by him at Bath, Me., 1893-98. [3496

LLOYD M. STADUM, comp. Matson Navigation Company fleet list, 1901 to 1958 [amended to 1960]. Steamboat bill, 17:22-3, 78, 117-18 (spring, fall, winter). Table showing dimensions, year of building, years of service, type, and disposition. [3497

The BOWDOIN story. Log Mystic Seaport, 11(1):1-4 (winter 1959). port., view. On a schooner built for Donald B. MacMillan in 1921, used by him in various Arctic services and in voyages to Labrador and Greenland, and purchased for Mystic Seaport in 1959. [3498

VIRGINIA LOUISE SNIDER EIFERT. Delta Queen: the story of a steamboat. N.Y.: Dodd, Mead, 1960. xi, 242, [1] p. views. On a steamer built in parts in Scotland and Germany, assembled in California under the direction of James Burns, commissioned in 1925 by the California Transportation Company, used on the San Joaquin and Sacramento Rivers and in World War II by the Navy, navigated from San Francisco through the Panama Canal to the

Mississippi in 1947, and still in service as the "last of the overnight, sternwheel, passenger steamboats on Mark Twain's tremendous river." [3499

EDWIN ARNOLD PATT. [Excerpts from "some autobiographical notes ... in the form of memoirs" written in 1946.] Steamboat bill, 17:34, 46-8 (summer). On the author's very early interest in steamboats and in pictures of them and books about them, his own publications about steamboats (beginning in 1925), and his part in founding the Steamship Historical Society of America in 1935 and Steamboat bill of facts (now Steamboat bill) in 1940. [3500

LITTLE Toot. Log Mystic Seaport, 11(4):1-4 (fall 1959). view. On the 32-ft. tugboat Weir, built in 1931, employed in the Chesapeake and Delaware Canal, at Stonington, and on the Connecticut River and Long Island Sound, and recently acquired for Mystic Seaport. [3501

JAY ALLEN. Memo from the founder. Steamboat bill, 17:35-6 (summer). view. On the launching of Steamboat bill of facts in 1940. [3502

GORDON P. McGOWAN. The skipper and the Eagle. Princeton, N.J.: Van Nostrand [1960]. ix, 214 p. ports., views. On the author's service from 1946 to 1959 as commanding officer of the U.S. Coast Guard "three-masted bark" Eagle, used as a training ship (formerly the German naval ship Horst Wessel). [3503

STEAMSHIP HISTORICAL SOCIETY OF AMERICA. Ten year review. Steamboat bill, 17:49-55 (summer). views. On steamboats and steamships destroyed, converted to diesel power, retired from service, etc., 1950-60. Contents.--Duluth to Niagara, by Edward J. Dowling.--Niagara to the sea, by Daniel C. McCormick.--New York and Philadelphia area, by Harry Cotterell, Jr.--New England and eastern Canada, by Doris V. Green.--Chesapeake Bay and South, by John L. Lochhead.--West coast, by Robert W. Parkinson. [3504

ERNEST KIRKWOOD. From salt to fresh water, or, The story of Cliffs Victory. Inland seas, 16:203-5 (fall). views (1 double). On the purchase of the 454-ft. SS Notre Dame Victory from the U.S. Maritime Administration by the Cleveland-Cliffs Iron Company, her conversion at Baltimore to a 619-ft. ore boat, renamed Cliffs Victory, and her voyage to the Mississippi, the Illinois River, the Chicago River, and Lake Michigan, 1951. [3505

FAMILY HISTORY

HAZEL KRAFT EILERS. "At the sign of the crest." Hobbies, 64(11)-65(10): monthly installments (Jan-Dec). coats of arms. Brief accounts of 12 American families and their coats of arms. Contents.--Orr.--Tyler.--Pepperrell.--Lewis.--Lord.--Edgecombe.--Rainsborough.--Lawrence.--Oxenbridge.--Heyman.--Mason.--Hooker. [3506

DONALD LINES JACOBUS. Additions to The Bulkeley genealogy [1933]. Am. geneal., 36:100-105, 149-57 (Apr, Jul). Miscellany. [3507

DONALD LINES JACOBUS. Changes in English surnames. Am. geneal., 36: 219-22, 228 (Oct). On "the instability of surnames" in early America as a result of the slurring of unaccented syllables, the substitution of consonants, and the shifting of vowels; with advice to users of indexes to look for "every possible spelling." [3508

LENORE KIMBROUGH McLEAN (born 1942). Hite, McLean. [n. p.] ©1960. [124] leaves. 30 cm. Information, in alphabetical order, about 42 families of the author's American ancestry, including information about her Mississippi grandparents, Helen Ruth Hite (born 1880) and her husband, Lee Davidson McLean (1887-1928). [3509

JAMES BIRTLEY McNAIR. McNair, McNear, and McNeir genealogies. Supplement, 1955. Los Angeles [1955]. xviii, 457, [1] p. coat of arms, ports., view. notes.--[Same title.] Supplement, 1960. Los Angeles [1960]. xi, 314 p. coats of arms (1 col.), double map, ports., view. notes. Addenda, including detailed biographical sketches, to a work published in 1923. [3510

GEORGE ANDREWS MORIARTY. Additions and corrections to [John Osborne] Austin's Genealogical dictionary of Rhode Island [Albany, 1887]. Am. geneal., 36:54-6 (Jan). [3511

ZELMA (WELLS) PRICE. Of whom I came: from whence I came--Wells-wise, Rish-wise, and otherwise: a compilation of the genealogies of the families of Bolling, Colquitt, Gable, Norman, Rish, Robertson, Weatherbee, Wells, Wofford, with numerous related and connecting families. Greenville, Miss. [1959]. 4 v. xx, 490; xx, 175; xx, 193; xx, 234 p. coats of arms. 36 x 22 cm. bibliog. (1:vii-xiv). [3512

MILTON RUBINCAM. The noble ancestry of the Revercomb family. Va. mag. hist. and biog., 68:448-55 (Oct). view. notes. Evidence "that the Rubincams and Rubicams of Pennsylvania, Ohio, and elsewhere, and their kinsmen, the Revercombs of Virginia, West Virginia, Canada, and other places are derived in the female line from one of the most ancient families in the former Hessian principalities," here traced to Jost von Boyneburg genannt Hohenstein (died 1589), descended from the marriage of "Bodo von Boimeneburg (the original form of Boyneburg) and Countess Adelheid von Hohenstein" in the 13th century. [3513

DONALD LINES JACOBUS. George Steele of Hartford [married in England in 1608, died 1664?] and his son James [baptized 1622, living in 1698, father of James[3] and grandfather of James[4]]. Am. geneal., 36:186-90 (Jul). [3514

HOWARD FLEMING NEWMAN. The Newman story, 1618-1958. San Francisco: McDougall Press, 1959. [4], 85 p. On Robert Newman (1599? - living in 1640), English emigrant to the James River in 1618, and the direct line of descent from him to the author. [3515

HUGH MEGLONE MILTON II. The Milton genealogy, 1636-1960. [Wash.? 1960. 6], 98, [5], 13 leaves. col. coat of arms, maps, views. bibliog. (leaf [6]). On the descendants of William Milton, John Milton (1759-1818), Elijah Milton (1755-1833), and Moses Milton (born 1740), sons of Richard Milton III (1715-1800), of Virginia and Kentucky, and his descent from Richard Milton, emigrant from England to Virginia in 1620, still living in 1643. [3516

ROY BROWN SEWELL, SR. (born 1898). One Sewell family. [Atlanta, 1960.] xiv, [2], 94 p. coats of arms. (1 col.), facsims., maps, ports., views. On the author, an Atlanta clothing manufacturer, and his American Sewell ancestors, beginning with Henry Sewell (died 1644), emigrant from England to Virginia ca. 1620, settler at Elizabeth City. [3517

SOCIETY OF MAYFLOWER DESCENDANTS. General Society. Mayflower index. Revised edition of the two volumes of the Mayflower index which was compiled by the late William Alexander McAuslan and published by the General Society of Mayflower Descendants [in 1932]. Revised by Lewis Edwin Neff. [Tulsa, Okla.] 1960. 3 v. in 2. x, [2], 847; xiv, [2], 851, A-110 p. List of descendants of some of the 104 Pilgrims who are known to have left descendants. Apparently confined to descendants who were members of the Society of Mayflower Descendants before 10 Feb. 1931 (vols. 1-2) or who have become members subsequently (vol. 3) and to their ancestors since 1620. Vols. 1 and 2 are evidently a reproduction of the first edition with typed additions on many of the pages. Some of the materials in the first edition are apparently omitted from the new edition. Standards of inclusion and the scheme of arrangement are not clearly defined. [3518

HENRY CRUSE MURPHY (1810-82). Origin of some Dutch family names. N.J. genesis, 6:201-3 (Oct 1958). From the Brooklyn daily eagle, 1859. On names brought to the New World mainly between 1624 and 1664. [3519

TOLVA (ROBERTS) WHITEHEAD. Roberts and allied families. Atlanta [1960. 20], 653 p. coats of arms, facsims. (part double), double geneal. charts, maps (part double), ports. notes (p. 590-604). On the descendants of Elias Roberts, who emigrated from England to Virginia in 1624. [3520

HELEN KLINE, M. P. WHITENIGHT, & Mrs. HENRY STOLL. The Kline klan. Wauseon, Ohio: Gilson Lithographing Co., 1960. [2], 173 p. ports. On the descendants of Hieronymus Kline, who removed from New York to New Jersey ca. 1710, and his possible descent from Jan Cornelisson Klyn, emigrant from Holland to New Amsterdam ca. 1625. [3521

GEORGE ENGLERT McCRACKEN. A Hartford miscellany: Howard, Stone, Adsit-Edgett. Am. geneal., 36:29-38 (Jan). Includes lists of the children (first born ca. 1649, last before 1671) of Henry Howard (1626?-1709) and his wife, Sarah Stone (born 1625? living in 1716), and of those of John Stone (children born in England, 1600-1629) and Stephen and Ann (Reynolds) Edgitt of New York State (children born 1761-81). [3522

WALTER HENRY GRAY. Genealogy of the Right Reverned Walter Henry Gray, eighth Bishop, Diocese of Connecticut. Protestant Episcopal Church in the U.S.A. [Hartford? Conn.] 1960. [4], 30, [1] p. diagr. bibliog. (p-29-30). On the author's direct ancestors in America since 1630, including Henry Gray, settled in Hanover County, Va., by 1733, who probably died before 1798. [3523

JOHN DISMUKES GREEN. The union of the Green and Dismukes families: a genealogical sketch. [n. p.] 1960. [62] leaves. geneal. charts. bibliog. (leaf [62]). 30 cm. On the descendants of the author's parents, Thomas Dunbar Green (1870-1954) and Julia Alice (Dismukes) Green (born 1875), of New York, and all their American ancestors, including Thomas Green or Greene (1606-67) of Malden Mass., and William Des Meaux I (born in France ca. 1672), Huguenot, apparently an emigrant to Virginia. [3524

MILES MERWIN (1623-1697) ASSOCIATION. Miles Merwin (1623-1697) Association [1903-60. Milford? Conn.] 1960. 16 p. ports., views. On the descendants of an English emigrant of 1630 who settled eventually in Milford, Conn. [3525

WALTER PRICHARD. The Prichard-Pritchard genealogy of the New England (or Northern) family branch from the first known settler of that name, Roger Prichard (1600-1671), to 1960. [Takoma Park, Md., 1960.] vi, 22 leaves. On descendants of an English emigrant who arrived in Massachusetts between 1630 and 1636 and later settled in Milford, Conn. [3526

EDYTHE JOHNS (RUCKER) WHITLEY. Some of the descendants of Rev. Richard Denton. McMinville, Tenn.: Womack Print. Co., 1959. 94 [2] p. fold. map, port., views. On the Rev. Richard Denton (1586-1662), English immigrant in 1630, minister in Massachusetts, Connecticut, and Long Island, who returned to England in 1659; his son Samuel (died 1714), remained in America; and Samuel's descendants, particularly those in Tennessee. Includes long excerpts from family letters from Holland Denton (born 1818), dated 1895 (p. 42-9). [3527

FRANKLIN RUDOLPH ALDRIDGE. Aldridge family genealogy and history. Nashville: Printed by Commercial Letter Shop, 1960. [4] leaves, v, [3], 95, [2] p. diagr., ports. bibliog. (p. v). On Jesse Alldridge (married Rachel Cobb in 1813, died 1825/26) of Amite County, Miss., and adjacent Louisiana, his 5 children, his widow's marriage to Andrew Saltzgiver, her 3 children by this second marriage, the removal of the family to Kentucky, and the settlement of many descendants in Texas; with some account of the descent of the Allridge (Aldridge, Alldredge, Aldredge) family from George Aldrich, English emigrant in 1631, settler in Mendon, Mass. [3528

BUEL AMOS LANGDON. The genealogy of Daniel P. Brewer. [Wilmette? Ill.] 1950. 137 p. ports., tables. On descendants of Daniel Brewer (1596?-1646), emigrant from England in 1632, settler in Roxbury, Mass., particularly his descendant Daniel Porter Brewer (1809-1902), native of Massachusetts, who removed to Portland, Ill., in 1837. [3529

MORGAN HEWITT STAFFORD (1873-1940). Descendants of John Thorndike of Essex County, Massachusetts [emigrant from England, settled in Salem by 1632, died 1668. Ann Arbor? Mich.] 1960. [6], 349 p. [3530

W. RAYMOND CHEEK. The story of an American pioneer family: the frontier trail. N.Y.: Exposition Press [1960]. 124 p. On John Horton (1780-1861/65), Indian trader, worker on river steamboats, settler in Tipton County, Ind., in 1836; his descendants and related families to ca. 1905; and the removal of some of the descendants to Kansas in 1883 and later to the Indian Territory: with some account of Thomas and Jeremiah Horton, emigrants to Massachusetts in 1633, of Jeremy Horton, emigrant to New Haven in 1640, settler on Long Island, and of some of their descendants. [3531

WALDO CAMBERLAIN SPRAGUE. The Pigg or Pidge family in England and America. Am. geneal., 36: 110-17 (Apr). On Thomas Pigg (native of Essex in England, married to Mary or Merey Sothy in 1619, settled in Roxbury, Mass., in 1633, died 1643), his 9 children, and some of their descendants born before 1800. [3532

JESSIE IRENE (BEAL) BAKER. The American ancestors of Ray Stannard Baker [1870-1946]. Mich. heritage, 2:21-9, 75-80 (autumn, winter). On his descent from Alexander Baker (1603-85), emigrant from London to Massachusetts in 1635, father of 12 children; with an "Ahnentafel" in reverse chronological order from Ray Stannard Baker through the 8th generation. [3533

WALTER VANCION BALL. The Butterworth family of Maryland and Virginia: a genealogy and history of the Butterworth family for more than three hundred years, including allied families of Bond, Clark, Clement, Gilbert, Webster, Wheeler, and many others ... Edited by Helen Hutchinson Dickinson. Silver Spring, Md.: Westland Print. Co., 1960. [8], 141, [22] p. coat of arms, tables. On the descendants of Henry Butterworth (died 1635/45) of Weymouth, Mass. [3534

DOROTHY CHENEY. The descent of the founders of the Cheney silk industry. [n. p., 1960.] 33, [2] p. ports., view. On the author's memories of her 7 Cheney granduncles, sons of George Cheney (born 1771) and Electra (Woodbridge) Cheney (died 1853), and the descent of George from John Cheney (died 1666), English emigrant in 1635, settler in Newbury, Mass. Contains no account of the business activities of the Cheney Brothers. [3535

MABEL OLETTA (OLSEN) CONNELL. Connell family record. [Aberdeen, S. D., 1960?] 8 leaves. On descendants of John Gore (died 1657), English emigrant in 1635, settler in Roxbury, Mass., and particularly the descendants of his descendant Elizabeth Wison (1862-1911), who married John Philip Cornell (1860-1928) and had 9 children. [3536

WAYNE DUNHAM STOUT (born 1894). Genealogy of the Sagers, Fisk, and Stout families. Salt Lake City, 1960. 583 p. geneal. tables, ports. On Phineas Fiske (1610-73), emigrant from England in 1635, settler in Wrentham, Mass., and his descendants, particularly Hezekiah Fisk (1775-1839), Mormon convert, father of 14 children, and his descendants, mainly in Utah. Includes the author's memoirs (p. 482-513) and many biographical and autobiographical sketches. [3537

CARLTON D. PEPPER. Genealogy of the Pepper family in America. Richmond, 1960. viii, 119 leaves. coat of arms, geneal. charts, ports., view. On the descendants of Robert Pepper (1634-84), immigrant to Roxbury, Mass., with his parents from England in the year of his birth; with some account of other Peppers in Delaware, Pennsylvania, Maryland, and Virginia. [3538

CHARLES RAYMOND DILLON. Pruitt-Prewitt ancestors. [Los Angeles? 1960. 2], 209 p. (even numbers on recto), 211-242 leaves. geneal. tables. Data concerning persons named Pruitt, Prewitt, Prewit, Prewett, Pruett, Pruit, etc., in 15 States (particularly Virginia and Kentucky), and their descent from Thomas Prewitt (settler in Charles River County, Va., in 1636), Henry Pruet or Pruett (settler in Henrico County, Va., recorded 1679-87), John Pruet or Pruett (settled in Henrico County by 1690), and Roger Pruit (Huguenot settlers at Manakintown, Va., in 1699), all of whom are believed to have been emigrants (the first 3 from England). [3539

HESTER ELIZABETH GARRETT. Some Pucketts and their kin. [Lansing? Mich., 1960. 4, i, 285 p. ports. On John Puckett (died ca. 1677), probably an English emigrant in 1637, settler in Henrico County, Va., and his descendants, particularly numerous in Virginia and Kentucky. [3540

LOUIS AUSTIN WARREN. The ancestry of Abraham Lincoln. Ralph G. Newman, ed., Lincoln for the ages (Garden City, N.Y.: Doubleday, 1960), p. 38-42. On his descent from Samuel Lincoln, English emigrant in 1637, settler in Hingham, Mass. [3541

ROSALLIE FELLOWS BAILEY. New England heritage of Rousmaniere, Ayer, Farwell, and Bourne families. [Volume I.] N.Y., 1960. xviii, 118, [1] p. facsims., geneal. tables, maps, ports., tables (part double), views. notes (p. 56-62, 106-18). On John Easton Rousmaniere (1877-1944), "textile executive in New York City," and his wife, Mary Farwell (Ayer) Rousmaniere (1878-1954), and other descendants of Louis Rousmaniere (French emigrant in 1780, settler at Newport, R.I., died 1783/84) and John Ayer (English emigrant in 1638/39, settler at Haverhill, Mass., died 1657); with biographical sketches of 5 Rousmanieres and 6 Ayers and a sketch of Mary Farwell (Ayer) Rousmaniere by her sister, Elizabeth (Ayer) Inches. [3542

CHARLES EDWIN LAMBDIN (born 1903). Geneology [sic] of the Georgia branch of the Lambdin family and its Maryland forebears. [Hobart? Ind., 1960. 5], 44 leaves. ports. On the direct Lambdin ancestors of the author, beginning with Robert Lambdin (or Lambden), who emigrated from England to Virginia in 1638, removed to Maryland in 1663, and died ca. 1684; with the autobiography of the author (leaves 23-6), an accountant. [3543

ROBERT DEANE HARRIS. The story of the Bloods, including an account of the early generations of the family in America in genealogical lines from Robert Blood of Concord [1626?-1701) and Richard Blood of Groton. [Boston? 1960. 4], iv, 202, [1] p. facsims., maps, tables. notes. On the activities rather than the family relationships of a great many persons named Blood in the United States, beginning with James Blood (1605/6?-1683), who had settled in Concord by 1639. [3544

LOTTYE FRANCES (GRAY) VAN NESS. The Van Ness heritage and allied genealogies, 1546-1960. [Elizabeth? N.J., 1960.] vi, 2-88 leaves. coats of arms. bibliogs. On the descendants of Cornelis Hendrickse Van Ness (1604?-1684?), emigrant from Holland ca. 1640 or 1641, settler in Schenectady. [3545

MILTON RUBINCAM. American families of Hessian descent. Natl. Geneal. Soc. quar., 48:8-11, 75-80 (Mar, Jun). notes. On descendants of emigrants from the former principality of Hesse to New York and Pennsylvania, 1641 till the Revolution, and of auxiliary soldiers from Hesse in the service of Great Britain in America during the Revolution; with warnings against misuse of the term "Hessian" and false assumptions concerning Hessian soldiers. [3546

ANNA CATHERINE (SMITH) PABST. The John Beach & John Wade families. Delaware, Ohio, ©1960. [6], 227, [12] leaves. maps, plans. On descendants of Joseph Wade (1715?-1777) of New Jersey and John Beach (1623-77) of New Haven, the latter an emigrant from England before 1643. The John Wade named in the title is not clearly identified. Deals mainly with Ohio descendants of New Jersey Beaches and Wades. [3547

FRANCES (DAVIS) McTEER & FREDERICK C. WARNER. The Willis family of Sudbury, Massachusetts. New Eng. hist. and geneal. reg., 114: 23-43, 96-113, 193-207, 268-82 (Jan-Oct). On Roger Willis, settler in Sudbury, married to Ruth Hill (1644-1736) in 1664, died 1690/1700, his 8 children, and some of his further descendants. [3548

RUTH VESTA (POPE) WERNER ROSENGARTEN (1891-1957). Ezra Perry [1625-89; settled in Massachusetts by 1644 after emigration from England] of Sandwich, Massachusetts, and some of his descendants in Saratoga County, New York. Wash., 1955 [i. e. 1960. 169] p. [3549

THORN DICKINSON. John Okeson [1645-1696?] of Hempstead, Long Island, progenitor of the Okeson and Kissam families, and some of his descendants. N.Y. geneal, and biog. rec., 91:65-76, 130-38 (Apr, Jul). On descendants of Okeson and his wife, Susannah Thorne (1645?-1695/96?), "who either retained the name Okeson, or used that of Lokerson," as distinguished from those "who adopted the name Kissam." [3550

NATHAN GRIER PARKE II. The ancestry of Lorenzo Ackley [1826-94] & his wife Emma Arabella Bosworth [1830-1927] ... Edited by Donald Lines Jacobus Woodstock, Vt., 1960. xi. 325 p. geneal. tables, ports., view. notes. On Ackley's descent from Nicholas Ackley (died 1695), probably settled in Connecticut by 1649. [3551

FRANCIS STUART HARMON. A good inheritance ... a genealogical record of descendants of John Harmon [1650?-1742?] of Scarboro, Maine. N.Y.: Printed by P & D Press, ©1960. [10], x, 255 p. facsims. (part double), fold. geneal. table, map, ports., views. bibliog. (p. 243-55). Deals mainly with John Wesley Harmon (1820-1902), Methodist minister, his wife, Frances Eveline Stuart (1832-1904), and their descendants, especially those in Mississippi. Includes long biographical sketches. 3552

DAVID ANDREW STURGILL. The Sturgill family in America: a preliminary history. College Park, Md. ©1960. [6], 116, 61, 8, [3] p. or leaves. On John Stogdell (1625?-1705?). emigrant from England, settler in Virginia in 1650, and his descendants (named Stogdell, Stodghill, Stogill,

Stogel, Sturgill), mainly in western Virginia, North Carolina, and eastern Kentucky. [3553

ADELE ANDREWS [full name: Rheuella Adele Andrews]. The ancestors and descendants of Elijah Gleason [1778/79-1863] and his first wife, Cynthia Johnson [178-?-1838?], and his second wife, Betsey Davis [1817/18-1881. Norwalk? Ohio] 1960. [2], 115 leaves. ports. On his descent from Thomas Gleason (1607?-1686), English emigrant settled in Watertown, Mass., by 1652, his life as a farmer in Massachusetts and near Harpersfield, Ohio, his numerous children (13 by the first wife, 4 or 5 by the second), and some of their descendants. [3554

HOWARD MARSHALL LEMASTER. Lemaster family, U.S.A., 1960. By many interested members of the family as listed herein. Carlinville, Ill., 1960. [2], 117 p. port. On descendants of Claude Le Maistre (emigrant from Holland to New Amsterdam in 1652), Francis Le Maistre (settled in New Jersey by 1670), Abraham Lemaistre (settled in St. Mary's County, Md., by 1662), and Richard Lemaster (settled in St. Mary's County, Md., before 1675). [3555

MACLEAN W. McLEAN. Robert Parker [settled in Massachusetts by 1655, died 1684/85] of Barnstable. New Eng. hist. and geneal. reg., 112: 190-200, 257-65; 113:15-24, 104-23, 166-84, 249-62; 114:5-14 (Jul 1958 - Jan 1960). On his descendants through the 6th generation. [3556

GEORGE ENGLERT McCRACKEN. Mr. Thomas Denham [1621?-1689?], Puritan parson. Am. geneal., 36:229-42 (Oct). Evidence that a person of this name was serving as a minister in Maine as early as 1659, later as minister at Rye and Bedford (then in Connecticut, now in New York); with text of his will and inventory of his estate, and an account of his 6 children and some of their descendants till ca. 1750. [3557

DOROTHY FORDYCE LUCAS. More about the Pierre Billiou family of Staten Island, N.Y.; with references to Osborne, Pitney of New Jersey, et al. [Haddonfield, N.J.:] E. G. Van Name, 1960. 16 p. bibliog. (p. 15-16). On descendants of Pierre Billilou, alias Balou, Billon Bilyou (1632?-1699?), emigrant from Normandy in 1661, settler on Staten Island. [3558

ISAAC CLIFFORD ROLL. The Abraham Roll family from New Jersey, pioneers in Hamilton County, Ohio. By I. Clifford Roll with Marie Dickoré. Hist. and Philos. Soc. Ohio, Bul., 18:284-95 (Oct). port. views. On John Roll (1733-1808), who settled in Hamilton County at an unstated time (ca. 1800?), his descendants there (including Abraham Roll, 1759-1827), and his descent from John Mangels Roll (or Rool), Dutch emigrant "in the late 1600's or early 1700's A. D.," settler near Springfield, N.J., who died in 1782, and was probably a descendant of Jan Mangelse (settled in Albany as early as 1661, died ca. 1704). [3559

CHARLES EDWARD ACKERMAN, JR. Genealogical record of a branch of the family of the Dutch settler David Ackerman [1615?-1662/63], whose family settled in New Amsterdam in 1662. [Silver Spring, Md.] c1960. 57, iii leaves. col. mount. coats of arms, geneal. tables. [3560

RICHARD WILSON COOK. The Van Wickelen family. Geneal. mag. N.J., 35:49-53 (May). On Evert Jansen Van Wickelen, "b. prob. ca. 166-, d. ----," who probably came to America ca. 1664, and his descendants in Long Island and New Jersey to ca. 1750. [3561

LEONARD WEBSTER ELLINWOOD. The Magoon family. Wash., 1960. [1], 17 leaves. tables. notes. On descendants of Henry Magoon, a resident of Exeter, N.H., by 1664. [3562

CHRISTINE (SOUTH) GEE. The roots and some of the branches of the Puckett family tree. [Columbia, S.C.: State Commercial Print. Co. for the author, Greenwood, S.C., 1958.] vi, [2], 136 p. coat of arms, geneal. chart, view. On descendants of John Puckett and his wife, Anne (settled in Henrico County, Va., by 1665), especially those in Virginia, the Carolinas, Tennessee, and Alabama. [3563

GEORGE HARRISON SANFORD KING. The family of Parson Henry Goodloe (1730-1820). Ky. geneal., 1:3-14 (Apr-Jun 1959). On his life in Caroline and Spotsylvania Counties, Va., as a farmer and a Baptist preacher, his 17 children and some of their descendants, and his descent from George Goodloe (1639-1710), who had settled in Middlesex County, Va., before 1666. [3564

JOHN SAMUEL STATON. Staton history: every Staton we could find in the world. Charlotte, N.C.: Print. priv. for Staton families by Brooks Litho, 1960. [2], xix, 406 p. col. coat of arms, facsim., ports. On the descendants of John Staton, emigrant from England in 1666, settler near Milford, Del. [3565

LULU IRENE (WATERS) HARE. Genealogy of one branch of the family of Clayton in England and America, 1066 to 1960. [Wash.? 1960?] 59 leaves. 23 x 30 cm. On the descendants of William Clayton (died 1689), English emigrant to America in 1671, later a settler in Pennsylvania. [3566

RHEA EDNA (DURYEA) JOHNSON. Our Duryea and Turner lines. [Cornwall? Pa., 1959. 1], 102 leaves. coats of arms, facsims., ports., views. notes (leaves 21-86). On descendants of Joost Du Rieu (fl. 1672 to ca. 1727), French Huguenot emigrant to New York ca. 1675 (including Charles Edgar Duryea, 1861-1938, the author's father, "the inventor and builder of America's first gasoline automobile"); and of William Turner of New Market, Frederick County, Md. (fl. 1753); with full texts of several wills. Cites 49 spellings of the name "Duryea" (perhaps originally Durier). [3567

CHARLES EVANS WOLVERTON. Wolverton family history (of Wolvertons of West Virginia) from the year of 1660 to 1960. [Clarksburg? W. Va., 1960. 79] leaves. On the descendants of Charles Wolverton (born 1660), emigrant from England to New Jersey in 1682. [3568

ATHLYN LUCILLE (PERRIGO) LUZIER. As the Conard family tree grows. Section one. Abner Alexander Conard and Ann Susanna Neer's descendants. Colorado Springs: Rose Print. Co. [1960. 18], 345 p. col. coat of arms, facsims., ports., views. On Abner Alexander Conard (1821-98) and his wife, Ann Susanna Neer (1827-1913), their 14 children (born 1846-73), and later generations; with some account of his descent from Thomas Kunders (or Dennis Cunreds, apparently the same person, 1648?-1729), German emigrant in 1683, settler in Pennsylvania. [3569

ELIZABETH HARRIET (KELLY) ALLISON. Early southwest Virginia families of Kelly, Smyth, Buchanan, Clark, and related families of Edmondson, Keys, Beattie, Ryburn, McDonald. Auburn, Ala., 1960. ix, [3], 135 p. cost of arms, facsims., double geneal, table, tables, view. notes (p. 115-18). On Virginia descendants of John Kelly (1740?-1822, emigrant from Ireland ca. 1750), Tobias Smith (fl. 1750?-1760/70?), Samuel Buchanan (Irish emigrant to Pennsylvania in 1702, settled in Virginia by 1772), James Clark (1754?-1818, emigrant from Scotland ca. 1775), William Edmiston, Sr. (settled in Virginia by ca. 1750, died 1789), Benjamin Keys (settled in Virginia by 1782, died 1808), John Beattie (settled in Virginia by ca. 1747), and Brian McDonald (1645-1707, emigrant from Ireland in 1685, settler in Delaware). [3570

BENJAMIN HUGH BENNETT. A history of the Richard Bennett family of Westmoreland County, Virginia, and Iredell County, N.C. [Wash.?] 1960. [2], 21 leaves. On Thomas Bennett, Sr. (1685-1763), who may have been an English emigrant; his wife, Elizabeth, probably a native of Virginia; their 7 children; and the descendants of his son Thomas, Jr. (1725-89), mainly in North Carolina. [3571

MARJORIE F. WATERMAN. Genealogical department. Conn. Hist. Soc. bul., 23:11-16; 24:88-96 (Jan 1958, Jul 1959). On Capt. Ebenezer Brown (1685-1761) of Lebanon, Conn., his son Daniel (1728-75), Daniel's son Ebenezer (1772-1847), and Ebenezer's son Daniel Ebenezer Brown (1794-1873), Episcopal minister and missionary, who settled in Michigan in 1839. [3572

ALICE (CANTINE) HUNTINGTON. The Cantine family, descendants of Moses Cantine. West Hartford, Conn.: Chedwato Service, 1957. [4], 82 p. On Moyse Quantain, alias Kantyn, Huguenot emigrant to New York in 1686, who died in 1744, and his descendants. [3573

ANNA E. SHADDINGER. The Micheners in America. Rutland, Vt.: Charles E. Tuttle Co. [1958]. 627 p. geneal. chart, map. On descendants of John Michener (died 1765) and his wife, Sarah (Moore) Michener (died 1757), English Quaker settlers in Philadelphia in 1686 or 1687. [3574

CLAUDE W. BARLOW. The Titus family of Douglas, Mass., and Vershire, Vt. New Eng. hist. and geneal. reg., 114:169-77 (Jul). On descendants of Joseph Titus (1688-1756) and his brother Benjamin (1693-1756), natives of Reheboth, Mass. [3575

CHARLES ALBERT EARP. The genealogy of Amos Earp, Senior, of Howard County, Maryland (1798-1893): his ancestors and his descendants. [Baltimore?] 1956. [4], 28, [1] p. geneal. tables, port. notes. On the 8 children and the further descendants of Amos Earp, and his descent from Thomas Earp, Sr., who was living in the Baltimore area in the late 1690s. [3576

GEORGE ENGLERT McCRACKEN. Thomas Pursell and his earlier descendants. Am. geneal., 36:139-48, 204-13 (Jul, Oct). On references, apparently to the same individual, in New York, New Jersey, Pennsylvania, and Delaware records, 1697-1738; his 5 children (oldest born before 1698, youngest in 1708); and some of their descendants to ca. 1800. [3577

NORA DENIZA (NIMMONS) FIELD. Genealogy and history: Bowen-Field-Nimmons and kindred families. [Greenville? S.C.] 1960. xiii, 351 p. maps, ports. On Moses Bowen, English emigrant to Chester County, Pa., ca. 1698, and his descendants, particularly those of his son John (died ca. 1760), who removed to Augusta County, Va., ca. 1730. [3578

PAUL SELENE CHALFANT. The Chalfants. ... Chalfant genealogy, Ramey genealogy, Pryor genealogy, Benningfield genealogy. [Colorado Springs] 1959. 1 v. (various pagings). geneal. tables, ports. 30 cm. On some of the descendants of John Chalfont (1660-1725) and his wife, Ruth Chandler, English emigrants to Pennsylvania in 1699. The Library of Congress copy of this volume includes interleaved or inserted carbon copies, negative photostats, handwritten notes, and a number of holograph manuscripts, some dated as late as 1964. [3579

MARY McGREGOR MILLER. The Warder family: a short history. [n. p.] 1957. [35] p. geneal. chart, maps, ports., views. bibliog. (p. [29]), notes. On descendants of Willoughby Warder, English emigrant to Pennsylvania in 1699, particularly Jeremiah Warder (1780-1849), who settled in Springfield, Ohio, in 1830, and his 7 children. Appended: letters from Jeremiah Warder to F. B. Swaby in Pennsylvania, dated Springfield, Ohio, 21 Sep. 1830 and 3 May 1833, on lands, prices, farming, roads, etc. [3580

CHARLES W. FARNHAM. Rhodes family of Newport, R.I. Am. geneal., 36:199-200 (Oct). On William Rhodes (fl. 1700), John Rhodes (1670?-1745, probably his son), and others. [3581

JOHN CURRY HAGERTY. An history of the noble O Hegerty family, ancient lords of Magherabeg and Clainsullagh, in the County of Donegal and the Province of Ulster in Ireland, from Adam to this present time. Charleston, S.C., 1959. [1], x, [2], 156, [52] leaves. illus. bibliogs. Refers briefly (leaves 151-6) to O'Hegertys, Hegertys, Haggertys, Hagertys, Hagartys, etc., in the United States since ca. 1700. [3582

HARRY LA VIRD CRAIG. Descendants of Jane Taliaferro Craig, emigrant ancestress; with records of allied families, Hawkins, Johnson, Wright, Cave, Barger, Whitcomb, Benschoter, and many others. [Twin Falls? Idaho, 1960.] 177 p. On John Craig (1650-1704; died in Scotland), Jane Taliaferro (born 1670, married John Craig in 1703, emigrated to Virginia probably in 1704), Taliaferro Craig (born to Jane Taliaferro Craig at sea or after arrival in Virginia, died in Kentucky in 1799), his marriage in Virginia to Mary Hawkins, their 11 or 12 children (particularly Taliaferro Craig, Jr., alias Toliver Craig, died 1819), and some of their further descendants; with long biographical sketches of some of them. [3583

JOHN GRIFFITHS HUNT. An Ellis family of Mendon and Uxbridge, Mass. Am. geneal., 36:57-8 (Jan). On descendants of Stephen Ellis (died 1748?) and his wife, Ruth Turner (born 1706), of Rochester and Mendon, Mass. [3584

HENRY DOWNS JAMISON, JR. The Jamison family, 1647-1960: genealogical records and memoranda. Nashville, 1960. [7], 113, [1], 29 leaves. ports. On the descendants of Henry Jamison, who emigrated from Ireland ca. 1708 and settled in Pennsylvania. Includes correspondence between Robert David Jamison (1832-1912), Confederate soldier from Tennessee, and his wife, Camilla P. Jamison, 1862-64 (p. 75-84). [3585

JOHN CONRAD WEISER FAMILY ASSOCIATION. The Weiser family: a genealogy of the family of John Conrad Weiser, the Elder (d. 1746). ... Frederick S[heeley] Weiser, editor. [Manheim, Pa.] 1960. ix, 882 p. maps, ports. notes. On his emigration from Germany to New York in 1709, his 16 children, and his further descendants in New York and Pennsylvania. Deals mainly with John Conrad Weiser, Jr. (1696-1760), who removed to Pennsylvania, his 13 children (born 1722-44), and their descendants. [3586

WALTER HAMLIN KNISKERN. Some of the descendants of Johann Peter Kniskern of Schoharie County, New York, born circa 1685, died November 11, 1759 [who emigrated from Holland to New York in 1709]. Petersburg, Va.: Plummer Print. Co., 1960. x, 470 p. tables (part double). Includes church, Bible, cemetery, probate, and census records (p. 195-347). [3587

ANN McKINNEY (TODD) RUBEY, FLORENCE ISABELLE STACY, & HERBERT RIDGEWAY COLLINS. Speaking of families: the Tod(d)s of Caroline County, Virginia, and their kin. Columbia, Mo.; Artcraft Press, 1960. xx, [4], 628 p. ports., tables, views. notes (p. 557-603). On the descendants of Dr. George Tod (1711-90) of Caroline County, who may have been an imigrant from Scotland. Includes many biographical sketches. [3588

NEWMAN WARD ADSIT (1878-1949). Descendants of John Adsit [English settler in Connecticut before ca. 1716, died 1735] of Lyme, Connecticut. [n. p., 195-. 2], 226 p. On bearers of a name that appears in the founder's will as Ageet but in all later records, apparently, as Adsit. [3589

WINFRED BRYAN COLE. The Bryans of Ballyroney. Mo. Hist. Soc., Bul., 16:230-36 (Apr). notes. On William Bryan (1685-1789) and his brother Morgan (born 1671, living in 1748), emigrants from northern Ireland to Pennsylvania in 1718, later residents of Virginia and North Carolina, and some of their descendants, particularly in Missouri. [3590

GEAN WESLEY ADEE. Family tree of Adee. [n. p.] 1960. 1 loose-leaf v. ([4], 12, 3, 11, 19, 4, 2, 8, 7, 2, 6 leaves). coat of arms, geneal, charts. 30 cm. On descendants of John Adee (died 1784), English emigrant, settled in Providence, R.I., by 1720, later a settler in Rye, N.Y. [3591

MARCUS STULTS WRIGHT, JR. Our family ties: some ancestral lines of Marcus S. Wright, Jr., and Alice Olden Wright [his wife]. South River, N.J., 1960. 107 p. facsims., geneal. tables, ports., views. Ancestral lines traced to William Wright (1810-89, settled in New Jersey by 1859), William Olden (English emigrant, settler in Middlesex County, N.J., died 1720), and John Chambers (1677-1747), emigrant from Ireland in 1729, settler in Trenton, N.J.). [3592

FRANCIS CORWIN MILLSPAUGH. Millspaugh-Milspaw. [Swampscott, Mass., 1959.] A-I, 312 p. col. coat of arms. On the descendants of Matthias, Phillip, and Nicolas Melsbach (possibly brothers), German emigrants to Orange County, N.Y., "about 1725-1727," and the 36 or more spellings of the family name. [3539

JOHN WILLIAM HEISEY. Isaac T. Heisey [1868-1938; farmer and railroad worker in Cumberland County, Pa.] and his family. [York Springs? Pa.] 1960. [4], 28 leaves. On his descent from John Heisey, Sr. (Hans Hisy? John Heise?), German emigrant to Pennsylvania in 1727 his marriage to Adella Cora Evans (1872-1936), and their 5 children and further descendants. [3594

HELEN VIRGINIA (HESTER) KING, ERWIN MILES KING, & D. WALTER HAWKS. Descendants of John Gerradt Luckenbach [1690?-1758? emigrant from Germany in 1740, settler in York County, Pa.] & Conrad Hawk [descendant of John Jacob Houck, emigrant from Germany in 1729, settler in Lancaster County. Pa]. Warren, Ohio: Manufactured by Riffle Photography [1958. 5], 100, [13] p. (even numbers on recto). facsims., ports., views. bibliog. (p. 71-2). [3595

Mrs. ROYCE E. LORD. Isaac Clewley, father and son. New Eng. hist. and geneal. reg., 114:297-304 (Oct). notes. On Isaac Clewley or Cluly (1729-1800) of Malden, Mass., and Stockton Springs, Me., and his son Isaac (1755-1839) of Holden, Me.; with lists of the other children and the grandchildren of Isaac Sr. and the children and grandchildren of Isaac Jr. [3596

EULA MAE PRISCILLA (STUDIVANT) FAIRBANK. History of the Mallard family (an account of their ancestors and descendants); with the allied families of Sturdivant, McWatty, Fairbank, and Poe, also Holland, Rees, McGhee, and Crawford. [Richmond?] 1960. [4], 28, xi p. On the descrendants of George Mallard, French (possibly Swiss) emigrant in 1730, settler in Trenton, N.C. [3597

BURGES JOHNSON. Two plaintive ghosts. Vt. Hist. Soc., News and notes, 3:5-7, 11-22 (Sep, Oct 1951). facsim., view. On the Rev. Jeremiah Johnson (1763-1847), of Reading, Vt., and his wife, Thomazin (Blanchard) Johnson (1761?-1824, the only grandchild of James Gibson of Boston, fl. 1730-45), and some of their descendants. [3598

ROSE OWEN (McDAVID) MUNGER. Patton and allied families. [n. p., 1958.] 85 p. coat of arms, facsim., view. On the author's descent from 4 immigrants: Matthew Locke (1730-1801; settled in Rowan County, N.C., by 1771), James Weakley (settled in Cumberland County, Pa., by 1730), John Brahan (settled in Fauquier County, Va., in 1774, died 1777), and Robert Patton (1753-1823, settled in Monroe County, W. Va., by ca. 1790). [3599

TILDEN H. KERN (1876-1956). Kern family history, descendants of Abraham Kern, Wurtemberg to United States, 1731; complete genealogy of Lt. William Kern, Jr., and Catharine Hoover Kern and their descendants. [Completed and edited by Fern M. Colborn. Normalville? Pa.] 1960. 75 p. facsims., ports., views. On the descendants of William Kern (born 1703), emigrant from Holland in 1731, settler in Fayette County, Pa. [3600

RAYMOND MARTIN BELL & MABEL ARMSTRONG (GHERING) GRANQUIST. The Vautrin-Wotring-Woodring family: Lorraine-Alsace-Pennsylvania. Washington, Pa., revised 1958. 12 p. map. 1st ed. 1953. On Abraham Wotring (1700-1752, emigrant in 1733), his brother Samuel (1714?-1766, emigrant in 1749), their cousin John (1711-86, emigrant in 1739)--settlers in Pennsylvania, and the first 3 generations of their descendants. [3601

NORMAN RAY BURNS. The Bigler family: descendants of Mark Bigler [died 1787], who immigrated to America [from Germany] in 1733. [Bradford? Ohio, 1960. 4], 138 p. facsims., maps, ports., tables, views. notes. On his life in Frederick County, Md., his 3 sons (Mark II, 1747-1826; Jacob, 1752/53?-1829; Israel, 1757-1838), and their descendants, mainly in Ohio, Indiana, and Utah; with a biographical sketch of Cyrus M. Bigler (1844-1927; farmer in Darke County, Ohio), letters from Nicodemus C. Bigler (1829-1900) of Elkhart County, Ind., to his daughter Jane, 1875-99, and the author's memories of rural life in Darke County, 1905 ff. [3602

EDGAR PAUL ROTHROCK. Some descendants of Johann Georg Rothrock, 1721-1806. Vermillion, S. D., 1960. [4], 49 leaves. ports. notes. 30 cm. On Johannes Rothrock (born 1684), emigrant from Germany in 1736, settler at York, Pa.; his sons Philip Jacob (1713-1803) and Johann Georg (1721-1806), emigrants in 1733, settlers in Pennsylvania; and their descendants, particularly Edgar Sylvanus Rothrock (1862-1931), Congregational minister in Ohio. [3603

ANNA (RUSSELL) DES COGNETS. William Russell [1685?-1757; English emigrant to Virginia in 1735, settler in Orange County] and his descendants. [Princeton? N.J., 1960. 12], 319, [4] p. double facsim., geneal. table. notes. Facsimile reproduction of the original edition (Lexington, Ky., 1884). Appended (p. 153-317): "The Russell family in Virginia," by Louis Des Cognets, Jr., grandson of Anna (Russell) Des Cognets, continuing her work. Both works include accounts of Maryland and Kentucky Russells. [3604

MARY ELISABETH FEEMSTER. That moving clan. Boston: Christopher Pub. House [1960]. 81 p. ports. On descendants of John Feemster, Scottish emigrant to Georgia in 1736, especially those in the Carolinas, Mississippi, Illinois, and Missouri, and their affiliations with the Independent Presbyterian churches. Includes the author's memoirs of her life in Missouri and Kansas since some time before 1879. [3605

RICHARD MILTON JEINNINGS. The Jeinnings family: containing history and genealogy. [Eddington? Pa.] 1960. [41], 7-36 leaves. col. coat of arms, facsims., maps, port. 30 cm. On the descendants, mainly in Pennsylvania, of Solomon Jinnings, "of North Ireland origin," born "in the early 1700's," settled in Lehigh County by 1736, died 1757. The form "Jeinnings" was first used by John Jinnings (1796-1890), who signed "Jinnings" in 1832 and "Jeinnings" in 1835. [3606

MARSHALL R. ANSPACH, ed. The Wood family saga. Now and then, 12:29-37, 53-8, 87-90, 189-98, 211-14 (Jan 1958 - Oct 1959). "Statement of the ancestry of Thomas Wood [farmer, 1810-84], of Muncy, Lycoming County, Pa., son of William Wood, grandson of George Wood, and great-grandson of James Wood [born in Ireland ca. 1710, emigrant to Pennsylvania in 1737, died 1751], of East Pennsborough Township, Cumberland County, Pa."; letter from Robina (Allen) Dunlap to her mother in Ireland, Grezel (Orr) Allen, dated Cumberland County, Pa., 18 Nov. 1791, defending her Methodist faith against attack from her Presbyterian mother; and other letters from members of the family in the western United States, Ireland, and Australia, answering genealogical questions and adding lists of names of relatives--the whole copied in "a small cloth-bound notebook" in the handwriting of Maggie Wood Hill, apparently with additions by the editor or by his father-in-law, Dr. Thomas Kenneth Wood. [3607

HUGH NORMAN NICCUM. The Niccum-Nickum family in America: data. Tecumseh, Kan., ©1960. [1], 18 leaves. 34 cm. On descendants of Peter Nickum (born ca. 1715, emigrated from Germany in 1739, settled in Frederick County, Md.), especially those of his son Michael (1740-1800), who removed to Kentucky ca. 1796. Notes that the family name has been spelled "at least 47 different ways." [3608

ELEANOR (STELTZ) KEBLER. Weedon genealogy. [Wash.? 1960. 1], ii, 73 leaves. bibliog. (leaf 73). Supplement to a work by John Horatio Nelson (1908). On John Weedon, Sr., English emigrant (died in Westmoreland County, Va., 1740), and his descendants, particularly his grandson Augustine Weedon (1751-1833), Virginian, father of 6 children. [3609

MARY (LEWIS) STEVENSON (1865-1949). William Lewis [1740-1811; native of Virginia] of Horry County, South Carolina. Columbia, S.C.: Printed by R. L. Bryan Co., ©1960. viii, 181 p. port. On his removal to South Carolina in or before 1785, his 11 children, and his later descendants. [3610

LEONA R. WEIR. Reading Blunt [1740s?-1792/93] of Virginia and Kentucky and some of his Blunt-Blount descendants. Detroit Soc. Geneal. Research mag., 23:51-6, 103-9, 147-52 (winter 1959 - summer 1960). bibliogs. [3611

NANCY REBA ROY. The Phelps family of Virginia and Kentucky and allied families. La Mesa, Calif. [1960? 3], 166 leaves. On the descendants of Thomas Phelps (died 1751], who may have been a resident of Albermarle County, Va., by 1746. [3612

WALTER WESTON FOLGER. Folger Bible records and cemetery inscriptions. New Eng. hist. and geneal. reg., 114:14-21 (Jan). Records of Latham Folger (1749-1833) and his wife, Matilda Folger (1753-1843), natives of Nantucket, Quaker settlers in North Carolina, their 14 or 16 children, and some of their further descendants, mainly in the Carolinas. [3613

PINCKNEY GLASGOW McELWEE. Geneology [sic] of William McElwee II [1718-1807], of Clarks Fork of Bullocks Creek of York County, South Carolina. Wash., 1959. [37], 212, [5], 213-227 p. On his emigration from northern Ireland to Pennsylvania in 1750, his later settlement in Virginia, his removal in 1765 to South Carolina, his 8 children, and their descendants. [3614

HENRY OLIVER REA. Samuel Rea, 1725-1811: heritage and descendants. Dungannon, Northern Ireland: Printed by the Tryone Print. Co., 1960. [2], 70, [1] p. facsims., fold. geneal. tables, ports., views. On descendants of Samuel Rhea or Rea, who emigrated from Ireland between 1752 and 1754 and settled in Franklin County, Pa. [3615

H. HAROLD SHAMEL. A history of the Gabriel family of southern Pennsylvania and their descendants. Parsons, Kan.: Commercial Publishers [1960]. 296 p. ports., views. On the descendants of Richard Gabriel (died 1796), who had settled in Franklin County, Pa., by 1752. Includes "Sixty years of Gospel song," reminiscences by Charles Hutchinson Gabriel (1856-1932), composer of 8,000 hyms (p. 97-111), letters from Elias Gabriel (1789-1865) in Athens County, Ohio, 1852-58 (p. 66-9), and other family papers. [3616

RICHARD SHUE. The Kings of York County: pioneers, patriots, and papermakers. [York? Pa., 1959-60.] 4 v. [1], 26; [1], 28; 37; [1], 17 leaves. Biographical sketches of Nicholas King (Nicklaus Konig), emigrant from Germany to Pennsylvania in 1752, settled in York County by 1760, died 1776; Philip Jacob King the Elder, his son, born in Germany, died 1791-92; Philip Jacob King the Younger (1764-1829), son of the preceding; and George King (1794-1860), son of Philip Jacob the Younger. [3617

HUGH MILBURN ADDINGTON. Addington volume II, U.S.A. and England ... including a multitude of related families. Kingsport, Tenn.: Franklin print. Co., 1960. [8], 59 p. facsims., ports., views. Continuation of the author's History of the Addington family in United States and England. On descendants of Henry Addington (1727-1787?), English emigrant, who settled in South Carolina in 1755. [3618

ROBERT E. REID. Reid family: Jeremiah Reid [1755?-1822] of Timber Ridge, Hampshire Count, Virginia [now West Virginia, where he settled as early as 1777], and some descendants and affiliations. [n. p., 1960? 1], 278 p. mount. ports., mount. views. [3619

AIMEE (JACKSON) SHORT. Jackson-Taylor and related families. Dallas: Royal Pub. Co. [1960]. 184 p. ports., views. notes. On the descendants of Philip Jackson, probably and emigrant from Ireland, who had settled in Carlisle, Pa., by 1755. [3620

GENEVIEVE BEALL NICHOLS PORTER. Archibald Beall [1756-1840] of Bourbon County and some descendants. Ky. geneal., 2:43-8 (Apr-Jun). notes. On his early life in Maryland and Virginia, his service in the Revolution, his marriage in Kentucky to Mildred Crews, their 11 children (born 1786-1808), and later descendants. [3621

RICHARD AMIDON KLUMPH. Klumph genealogy and early Klumph history. Second and revised edition. [Kalamazoo, Mich.] 1960. 68 p. geneal, tables. 1st ed. 1957. On the descendants of John Thomas (or Gustavus) Klumph (1729-1818), emigrant from Germany to England ca. 1755 and to America ca. 1758, soldier in the British Army, settler in Albany. [3622

LORENA (MARTIN) SPILLERS. The Arnold-Martin family history: William Arnold, 1759-1825, Revolutionary soldier, N.C., and his son, James Arnold, 1780-1825, whose daughter, Martha Anne Arnold, 1817-1862, was married in 1834 to Henry Anderson Martin, 1811-1897, in Washington County, Georgia; and their descendants. Tulsa, Okla., 1960. [2], 94 p. [3623

DONNA HARPER DE VIEW. Benjamin Cave, 1760-1842. [Knoxville? Tenn., 1960. 1], 8, [5] leaves. fold. geneal. tables. notes (leaves [9-11]). On his early life in Culpeper County, Va., his service as an officer in the Revolution, his removal to Guilford County, N.C. (1781), and thence to Kentucky, and his descendants. [3624

ROBERT L. STEENROD. A genealogical study of the Steenrod family. Belvidere, Ill., 1960. 21, [9] leaves. notes (leaves 22-8). On the descendants of Edward Stenrod (settled in Westchester County, N.Y., by 1760), Cornelius Stenrod (settled there by 1757, died in Virginia ca. 1796), and Ebenezer Steenrod (1744-1836; removed from Westchester County to Delaware County, N.Y.). [3625

MABEL JOANNA (LOGUE) HOPKINS. The Crittenden-Tucker and related families. [Hayward? Calif., 1960. 5], 112, [16] leaves. On the descendants, most numerous in Indiana, Kentucky, and Missouri, of Richard Hazelwood Crittenden (1761-1841) and his wife, Sally (Tanner) Crittenden (1773-1850/52), and of James W. McClellan (1795-1873) and his wife, Louisiana (Tucker) McClellan (1805-77). Mainly a collection of documents, with a name index. [3626

HENRY MERCER SHANK III. Genealogy of John Shank, Ariaen Degoede, Elijah Teague, and Thomas Swann. [Denver, 1960. 4], iv, 82, [12] p. facsims., port. On the descent of the author's grandson Joel David Shank (born 1960) from John Shank (1761-1835, of Pennsylvania and Georgia), Lubertus Degoede (born 1896, emigrant from Holland, settled in Idaho by 1923), Elijah Teague (1718?-1790? settled in South Carolina by 1771), and Thomas Swann (1740?-1795? emigrant from Ireland ca. 1765, settler in North Carolina). [3627

CHARLES ROBERT PIETY & JAMES CATON PIETY (1869-1952). An early history of the Piety family and kinsmen, 1654-1956. [n. p., 1956?] xii, 182 p. facsims., ports., views. On Austin Piety (born 1740), British officer stationed at Forth Pitt from 1762 to 1774, who married Sarah Polke there in 1762 and returned to England in 1774, leaving his wife and 3 children, including a son Thomas (1770-1835), who lived in Kentucky and Indiana and had 13 children; account of the descendants of Thomas and of the Wilson and Yeager families of southern Indiana; reminiscences of Middletown, Ind.; and verses. [3628

SYLVESTER WILLIAM BAKER. A genealogy of the Enders family, 1740-1959. [Rutland, Vt.: Tuttle Pub. Co., 1960.] x, [6], 460 p. coat of arms, geneal. table, ports., views. On the descendants of Johann Philip Enders (born 1740), known also as Philip Christian Enders, emigrant from Germany in 1763, settler in Dauphin County, Pa. [3629

HUBERT WESLEY LACEY. The Goodner family, a genealogical history; with a brief history of the family of Jacob Daniel Scherrer [1730?-1795] and notes on other allied families. Dayton, Ohio, 1960. xii, 511, [5] p. facsims., geneal. tables, maps, ports., tables, views. bibliog. (p. 460). On the descendants of John Goodner, Sr. [Johannes Güttener] (1720?-1783/84?), emigrant from Germany at some time between 1763 and 1776, settler in Guilford County, N.C.; with detailed biographical sketches and numerous documents, including letters from William J. Goodner, 1850, and from Benjamin Franklin Goodner (died 1852) and Joseph Benson Goodner, 1852, Gold Rush travelers to California, to the Rev. Benjamin Goodner, father of the 3 boys, in St. Clair County, Ill., and Civil War letters from George Washington Goodner (another son of Benjamin Goodner), 1863. Deals particularly with Goodners in Illinois. [3630

FRANK STEWART KINSEY. Our Paddleford descendants: William and Hannah (Hoit) Paddleford and their children. [Chula Vista? Calif.] 1960. [5], 33 p. (even numbers on recto), ports. On Jonathan Paddleford (1704-83, settled in Enfield, N.H., by 1765), his descendant William Paddleford (1787-1858; farmer in New Hampshire and Illinois), the latter's wife, Hannah (Hoit) Paddleford (1790-1881), their son and 5 daughters, and the later generations of their descendants. [3631

LESLIE AULLS BRYAN. William Aulls [1748-1816, Irish emigrant in 1767, merchant in New Jersey and Pennsylvania, settler in 1793 in western New York], pioneer of Pleasant Valley, N.Y. New Eng. hist. and geneal. reg., 114:58-68 (Jan). notes. On the marriage to Elizabeth Morris (1746-1823, widow) in 1772, their 9 children, and several generations of further descendants. [3632

JOSEPH M. GLICK FAMILY HISTORICAL COMMITTEE. Across the years: a story of and a stream through the Glick family in the Shenandoah Valley of Virginia. Charlotte, N.C.: Delmar Print. Co., 1959. x, 221 p. col. coat of arms, facsims., ports., views. On descendants of Johannes Glück, Sr. (John Glick, Sr., alias Click, 1720/25?-1814), German emigrant to the Shenandoah Valley in 1767 or 1768. [3633

DAVID TRACY JONES. Some pioneer Jones families of Adams County, Ohio. Kankakee, Ill.: Mimeographed at Olivet Nazarene College, 1960. 24 leaves. On descendants of Andrew Jones (1768-1841) from Virginia, Matthew Jones (settled in Adams County in 1835), and Ephraim Jones (1793-1850; settled there by 1824). Andrew may have arrived in Adams County as early as ca. 1815. [3634

WILLIAM EDWARD DUNN. The James McMurry Dunn family of Texas and Kentucky: the migration of their ancestors from County Derry, Northern Ireland, to Pennsylvania, thence to the Province of Maryland, and their further migration to Kentucky and Texas. Wash., 1960. vi leaves, [2], 124 p., [5] leaves. facsims., maps, ports., tables. notes. On the descendants of James McMurry Dunn (1850-1928), native of Kentucky, school-teacher and Methodist minister, who removed to Texas probably in 1871 or 1872; and his descent from William Dunn, Sr., who was settled in Anne Arundel County, Md., by 1769 and who later removed to Kentucky. Includes long biographical sketches. [3635

ELLEN (KIRKPATRICK) KORBITZ & NORMAN DELBERT KORBITZ. John Whisler, 1770, German immigrant to Cumberland County, Pennsylvania: a roster of descendants. [Burlington? Ia., 1957. 2], iv, 29 p. geneal. chart, port. On John Whisler (1770-1848), German emigrant to Pennsylvania in infancy, settler in Indiana ca. 1831, and his descendants; with reminiscences by Jacob E. Whisler (1808-98) of Tipton County, Ind. [3636

WILLIAM WALLACE COCHRAN (born 1889). Histories of the John and Rosanna Cochran family and the Richard and Susan Jeffress family ... and recollections by the author. [Wash.? 1960.] iii, 55 p. On descendants of John Cochran (1790-1858) and Rosanna (Acton) Cochran (1792-1877), Irish emigrants to Missouri ca. 1842, of Richard Jeffress (1802-57) and Susan (Bruce) Jeffress (1804-71), natives of Virginia, later residents of

Missouri, and of Catherine Laurie (1771-1866), of Virginia and Missouri; with the author's recollections (p. 27-55) of his early life near and in Boonville, Mo., and his later years in Washington, D.C., and elsewhere. [3637

MABEL VAN DYKE BAER. The Vandeveers of North Carolina, Kentucky, and Indiana. Richmond: Whittet & Shepperson, 1960. xi, 180 p. coat of arms. On John Vandeveer, Sr. (recorded in Rowan County, N.C., in 1773, in Kentucky in 1803, in Indiana soon after 1810, still living in 1820, dead by 1835), and his descendants. [3638

MARY ANNA (GAMBILL) BOWLES. Bowles history and related families. [Ann Arbor: Edwards Bros.] 1959 [c1960. 4], 242, [2] p. facsims., map, ports., views. On various Bowles families in the British Isles and the United States, especially the descendants of John Bowles (born 1774; son of Lt. Thomas Philip Bowles I, a veteran of the Revolution), native of Virginia who settled in Missouri ca. 1821. Includes biographical sketches, copies of the author's genealogical correspondence, and narratives of her genealogical travels. [3639

JOHN D. BALDWIN III. Andrews families of western Connecticut. III. Addenda, the Farmington tribe. Am. geneal., 36:42-3 (Jan). Information from pension papers of Joseph[5] Andrus (died 1832), Massachusetts soldier in the Revolution, and other sources. [3640

SUSIE (BRUNSON) STELL. A tree is planted: the family tree and a bit of history of the Stells. [Plainview? Tex., 1960?] 224 p. ports. On John Stelle (probably a Hessian soldier in the Revolution, perhaps an English emigrant to America before the Revolution, later a settler near Cape Fear, N.C.) and his descendants, particularly Dennis Quimby Stell (1807-73; born in South Carolina, removed to Arkansas in 1835 and later to Texas), his son Albert Jerome Stell (1838-78, of Arkansas and Texas), and the latter's 7 children (including Thomas Dennis Quimby Stell, born 1866, living in 1956) and further descendants, mainly in Texas. Consists largely of biographical sketches. [3641

CONSTANCE (DUTTON) HEACOX MIKISKA. The Heacox family, with Hickock, Heacock, Hickok, Hickox Revolutionary and census lists. [Eureka Springs, Ark., 1960. 3], 34, [1] p. (even numbers on recto). facsim., map, ports. bibliog. (p. 34). On the descendants of Benjamin Heacox (1776-1880), centenarian, of Connecticut, later of Brazil, Ind. [3642

HENRY S. ROBINSON. Descendants of Daniel and Hannah Bruce, Negro hist. bul., 24:37-41 (Nov). ports. On Daniel Bruce (1779-1853) and his wife Hannah (1783-1850), Negro natives of Dumfries, Va., their 10 children (born in the District of Columbia), and some of their grandchildren, widely scattered in the United States. [3643

COLIN JAMES. John Hamill Poston (1786-1848) [of Clarksville, Tenn.], his ancestors and descendants: a Poston family genealogy. Denver, 1959. [20], 73, [7] p. geneal. charts, ports., views. [3644

ELIJAH DAVIS (born 1787?). The family of Elijah Davis of Nelson County, Kentucky. Contributed by Mrs. Edythe C. Newton. Ky. geneal., 2:148-9 (Oct-Dec). Very short account, written in 1870, of the author's ancestry. [3645

THELMA NICHOLS (KEITH) BEVAN, OWEN HABNER MEREDITH, & ROBERT M. McBRIDE. The Nichols family of north Georgia and the related Cansler, Black, Puett, Coffey, and Boone families: outline for a family history. Nashville, 1960. [2], 139 p. geneal. tables. bibliog. (p. 132-3). On Adam Amaziah Nichols (1798-1863), of South Carolina and Georgia, and his descendants; with some account of his descent from James Thadeus Nichols, who was a resident of Lancaster County, S.C., in 1790. [3646

JOHN FREDERICK DORMAN. John Slaughter [died 1812] of Knox County [Ky.] and some of his descendants. Ky. geneal., 1(1):4-10 (Jan-Mar 1959). notes. On his life in Knox County, Ky., and Madison County, Ala., 1790s-1812, his 8 children, and some of their descendants. [3647

EDWIN SCOTT MALONE III. The Malone genealogy. [n. p., 1959. 15] leaves. col. coat of arms, map. On Wynn Malone (recorded in Virginia in 1790, removed to Kentucky in 1795, "died in 1841 in [sic] 1847 (no definite date known)") and his descendants, especially Isaac Malone (1821?-1894) of Barren County, Ky., who removed in later years to Texas with his family, and the 8 children of Isaac Maline. [3648

GEORGE HARRISON SANFORD KING. The family of Michael Harrison [1796-1863] of Virginia, Tennessee, Kentucky, Ohio, and Illinois. Ky. geneal., 2:83-9 (Jul-Sep). notes. On his service in the War of 1812 under the name Micajah Harris, his marriage to Rachel Rupert in 1822, and their 11 children (born 1819-45, the first out of wedlock). [3649

CHARLES W. FARNHAM. Holden Rhodes (1797-1857): a Vermonter who became a Southerner [settled in Richmond]. Am. geneal., 36:84-7 (Apr). Includes a list of his brothers and sisters and an account of his descent from Zachariah Rhodes (1603-65) of Rhode Island. [3650

LOUISE EMILY (HANES) GALLAGHER. The David Hanes family. [Des Moines? 1960. 4] leaves, 138, [1] p., 10 leaves. geneal. charts. On David Hanes (1813-1900), his early life in Frederick County, Md., his removal to Wayne County, Ind. (1825), and Dallas County, Ia. (1855), his marriage to Hannah Cranor (1819-1901), and their 11 children and many further descendants. Includes biographical sketches. [3651

ROY HUTTON BALL. Pioneer heritage: geneology [sic] of one branch of the Hutton family. [Oklahoma City?] 1960. [3], 33 p. (even numbers on recto). ports., views. On John Hutton, resident of Washington County, Va., as early as 1817, who removed to Missouri in 1837; his sons Edward (born 1817/18, living in 1880), Amon (1820-1903), and John Milton (1822-1910), natives of Virginia and later residents of Missouri; and the descendants of the sons. [3652

RICHARD STEPHEN UHRBOCK. The Stephen J. Redden family of Worcester County, Maryland. [Athens? Ohio] ©1960. [1], 20 leaves. On Stephen John Redden [1817-1901], his marriages to Elizabeth Paradise, by whom he had 4 children, and to Ellen Pilchard (1837-1928), by whom he had 8 children; and some of his descendants in later generations. [3653

WARD JAY ROYLANCE. Remingtons of Utah with their ancestors and descendants. Salt Lake City, 1960, [7] leaves, 455 p. facsim., ports. bibliog. (p. 427-38). On Jerome Napoleon Remington (1819-77), native of western New York, and his wife, Lydia Ripley Badger (1831-1906), native of Vermont, Mormons, married in 1848, settlers in Utah in 1849; their descent from John Remington (1600?-1667, emigrant from England to Massachusetts in 1637) and Giles Badger (1611?-1647, settled in Massachusetts by 1635); their 12 children (born 1848-67); and the descendants of 8 of the children. Includes biographical sketches; autobiographies of Agnes May (Campbell) Remington (born 1893), Jerome Jackson Remington (1878-1957), William Jackson Remington (1883-1955), Ward Jay Roylance (born 1920), Rodney Badger Remington (1856-1940), and others; and many letters and other documents. [3654

LOLA WILKEY LUFOY. Some descendants of Jonathan Jackson Wilkey [1820-99] of Hopkins County, Kentucky. Ky. geneal., 2:12-18 (Jan-Mar). notes. On his life in Kentucky as a Baptist minister, his marriages to Sarah Jane McCulley and Elizabeth Jane Sisk, his 8 children by his first wife, and some of their descendants; with a list of his 7 children by his second wife. [3655

BARBER NELL HOOVER. The Barton-Barber family of Hays Co., Texas. [Doylestown? Pa., 1960? 2], 12 leaves. 30 cm. On the descendants of William James Barber (1805-1848?), emigrant from Scotland in 1825, settler in Bastrop County, Tex. Leaves 2 and 10-12 of this volume are carbon copies containing information compiled as late as 1964. [3656

MARJORIE (HUEY) CARRICK. The descendants of Erastus and Susan (Dale) Huey. Albuquerque, N.M.: Service Enterprises, 1959. [25] leaves. 36 cm. fold. geneal. chart, map, tables. On Erastus Huey (1830-1913), Illinois farmer, his wife, Susan (1836-91), their 6 children, and the numerous further descendants. [3657

JOHN SANDERSON DU MONT. Du Mont de Soumagne and allied families: being a genealogical and biographical history of the Du Mont de Soumagne family, including Du Mont von Moten and Du Mont in Köln. With collateral lines of [18 families], together with their armorial bearings and patriotic society references. Greenfield, Mass. 1960. [2], 166, [1] p. coats of arms, fold. geneal. table, ports., views. bibliog. (p. 151-7). Includes some account of Bernhard Julius Wilhelm Hermann du Mont (1807-53), German emigrant to Baltimore in 1830, who married Eliza Donovan in Baltimore, removed to Lancaster, Ohio, in 1832 and to Mobile, Ala., in 1842, and had 6 children and many further descendants. [3658

WILLIAM ALFRED HERRON (1861-1935) & WILLIAM HERRON HEZLEP. Our Herron family of Allegheny County, Pennsylvania. [Pittsburgh?] 1960. 80 leaves. bibliog. (leaves 68-9). Expansion of a mimeographed genealogy by the senior author. On the descendants of John Heron (1773-1856), emigrant from Ireland to Allegheny County in 1830, and his wife, Ann Bell (1789-1876). Includes biographical sketches. [3659

DELORIS HAMPTON (PITKIN) BENNETT. Descendants of John and Mary Scharnagel in the families of Willenborg, Eischeid, and Testroet. [West Covina? Calif.] 1960. vii, 81 p. ports., views. On John Scharnagel (1823-1907), German emigrant ca. 1836, settler in Clayton County, Ia.; his wife, Mary Kundiga (Hermann) Scharnagel; and their 8 children, of whom 4 married and had children: Mary (1861-1909, married John Willenborg), Theresa (1862-1933), married John Eischeid), Wilhelmina or Minnie (1864-1961, married Johann Heinrich or Henry Willenborg), and Sophia (1868-1949, married Theodore Testroet). [3660

The LINEAGE and the descendants of Tarpley Early Taylor [1837-1904, of Iowa]. Prepared by his children and grandchildren. [n. p., 1959?] 15 p. [3661

WILLIAM RAYMOND MANCHESTER. A Rockefeller family portrait, from John D. to Nelson. Boston: Little, Brown [1959]. xv, [3], 184 p. ports., views. Biographical sketches of John Davison Rockefeller (1839-1937) and his son and 5 grandsons. [3662

THOMAS JOHN CLAGETT. A genealogy of the Park family, 1860-1960. [Wayne? Pa., 1960? 2], 19, [1] p. On the descendants of Alexander Park [1836-1916), English emigrant living in Philadelphia by 1860. [3663

MILTON RUBINCAM. A brief record of the Heurich family. [Wash.? 1957?] 6 leaves. bibliog. (leaf 6). On Elizabeth Adelipa Heurich (Mrs. Hermann Jacobsen) and Christian Heurich (1842-1945), children of Kaspar and Anna Marguerite (Fuchs) Heurich in Germany; the settlement of the Jacobsens in Baltimore before 1860; the emigration of Christian Heurich in 1868, his work as a brewer in Chicago and Kansas, and his settlement in 1872 in Washington, where he founded the Christian Heurich Brewing Company and operated it till his death; and the descendants of Elizabeth and Christian. [3664

NELL (WOODS) BLACK. The Blacks, seven generations: a feature history of the John Black - Catherine Baxter family in North America from 1840 to 1960. Cedar Falls, Ia., 1960. [8], 53, [3] leaves. ports. On John Black (1799-1867) and his wife, Catherine Baxter (1797-1849), emigrants from Scotland to Ontario in 1840; their 9 children, particularly Malcolm (1826-73), who married Nancy Agnes McLellan (1824-1909) and in 1865 removed with his wife and children to a farm near Fort Dodge, Ia.; the children of Malcolm and Nancy, particularly Donald (1851-1933); and the descendants of Donald. [3665

THOMAS CARSON McCORMICK (1892-1954). Carson-McCormick family memorials. [Madison, Wis., 195-? 5], xix, 158 leaves. notes (leaves 145-58). On the ancestors and descendants of the author's parents, William Thomas McCormick (1867-1944) and Virginia Marr (Carson) McCormick (1866-1943), natives of Georgia and Alabama respectively. Includes references to the Horry, Jeter, Marr. Perkins, and Tooke families. [3666

PAUL M. HESTON. The descendants of George Lewis Heston [1867-1925] and Roseanna Jane Schnebly [born 1870. Haddonfield, N.J.] 1960. 23, v leaves. On their life in Ohio and Iowa, their 11 children (born 1891-1913), and later generations, mainly in Iowa. [3667

HELEN (LINENBERGER) HALL. The Hall genealogy. [Ann Arbor? Mich.] 1960. [2], 294 p. col. coat of arms, ports. On the descendants of Karl Hall (1829-71) in Germany and the United States, of whom 6 were emigrants to the United States: Joseph (1854-95, emigrant in 1870, settler in Kansas), Franz Karl Holland Matthias (1856-1921, emigrant in 1883, settler in Detroit), John (1860-1937, emigrant to St. Louis in 1876), Matthew (1864-1949, emigrant to Buffalo, N.Y., in 1882), Mathias (1866-1937, emigrant in 1883, settler in Kansas), and Mary Ann (1867-1946, emigrant to Kansas with her husband, Anton Durler, in 1902). Consists of biographical sketches of every descendant of Karl Hall, including also the author's autobiography (p. 283-91), dealing with her life in Kansas. [3668

FERDINAND HENRY STEINMETZ. Genealogy and family history of Johann Herman Steinmetz, born in Etzel, Germany, 9 November 1848, resided at Edwardsville, Illinois, 1870-1940. [Union Springs? N.Y.] 1960. [3] leaves, [6], ii, 55, [3], 4, 3 p. facsims., geneal. charts, port., views. notes. [3669

MARICHA (BALZER) VOTH. The Heinrich Balzer genealogy, 1775-1959. North Newton, Kan. [1960]. 180 p. facsims., maps, ports., tables. On Heinrich Balzer II (1810-85), Mennonite from Russia, his 8 children, their settlement in Kansas in and after 1874, his own emigration to Goessel, Kan., in 1878, and the later generations of the family, mainly in Kansas. [3670

HILMA MATILDA (JOHNSON) PEARSON. The John I. Johnson family, the Ola I. Levin family, and related families, Long Prairie, Minn.: Hart Press, 1960. 128, [4] p. facsims., geneal. chart, maps, ports., views. On descendants of 2 brothers from Sweden: Jöns Ingemansson (1846-1929; took the name John Ingeman Johnson), settler near Walnut Grove, Minn., in 1896, and Ola Ingemansson (1849-1922; took the name Ola Ingeman Levin), settler in Rock Springs, Wyo., in 1876 or 1877, later in Crystal Falls, Mich. Includes the author's account of her life in Minnesota, Texas, and Nebraska (p. 35-43). [3671

HILMA MATILDA (JOHNSON) PEARSON. John Nyman [1854-1924], Emma [Christina] J[ohnson] Nyman [1862-1939], and their known ancestors, kinsmen, descendants. Svea, Minn.: Family Pub. Co., c1960. 179, [1] leaves. facsims., geneal. tables, maps, ports., views. On their emigration from Sweden (John in 1879, Emma in 1881) and eventual settlement at Bancroft, Ia., their 12 children, and their many descendants in later generations. Includes several autobiographies. [3672

HILMA MATILDA (JOHNSON) PEARSON. Nordstrom and related families: a genealogical and biographical study. Long Prairie, Minn.: Hart Press, 1960. [2], 205, [9] p. cartoon, diagrs., facsims., geneal. tables, maps, music, ports., views. On Nils Nillson Nordström (1834-1900) and his wife, Anna Persdotter Nordström (1836-1913), who emigrated from Sweden to Walnut Grove, Minn., in 1897; their 10 children, of whom 3 accompanied them to America and 5 had preceded them between 1887 and 1892; and their descendants in later generations. [3673

JOSEPH FRANCIS DINNEEN. The Kennedy family. Boston: Little, Brown [1960, c1959. 12], 238 p. ports. On Joseph Patrick Kennedy (born 1888), his wife, Rose (Fitzgerald) Kennedy, and their children, particularly Joseph P. Kennedy, Jr. (1915-44), and John Fitzgerald Kennedy (born 1917), Senator from Massachusetts since 1947; and the eminence of the family in finance and in Boston, Massachusetts, and national politics. [3674

NATHAN ZUMOFF. Our family: a history of five generations in pictures & script, 1831-1956. Originated and designed by Abraham Zumoff. Edited by Nathan Zumoff, assisted by Barnett Zumoff [N.Y.:] Printed by Academy Photo-Of[s]set [1956 or 1957-]. 1 v., loose-leaf ([152] leaves, perhaps including leaves added to the original). ports. (part fold.). 43 cm. On Dov Ber Zumsky (1831-1909?) and his wife, Chaya-Riva (Ginsburg) Zumsky (1827?-1918?), and all of their known descendants (many in Russia), including Benzion Zumsky (1865?-1938, "known in America as Benjamin Zumoff"), his sisters Sophie and Luba, and his brother Mendel (1867-1946? "known in America as Max Zumoff"), emigrants to America between 1904 and the early 1920s, and their many descendants. [3675

ANCESTRY of Governor G[erhard] Mennen Williams [born 1911]. Mich. heritage, 1:93-4, 153 (spring, summer). bibliog. [3676

THE HISTORY OF IDEAS

DANIEL JOSEPH BOORSTIN. The place of thought in American life [since the 1600s]. Daniel J. Boorstin, America and the image of Europe: reflections on American thought (N.Y.: Meridian Books [1960]), p. 41-61. First printed in 1956. On the "unity or homogeneity, and ... diffuseness" of American "intellectual life." [3677

ANDREW DICKSON WHITE (1832-1918). A history of the warfare of science with theology in Christendom. N.Y.: Dover Publications [1960]. 2 v.

xxiii, [3], 415, [5], 15; [2], xiii, [3], 474, [4], 15 p. notes. Reproduction of 1st ed., 1896. Includes American aspects of the "warfare" as early as 1664. [3678

MAX SAVELLE. Prolegomena to a history of liberalism in eighteenth-century Anglo-America. Bucknell rev., 9:224-46 (Dec). notes. Argument that "there was a recognizable corpus of ideas and attitudes in Anglo-America in the eighteenth century that may be identified as liberalism ... about politics, economic and social life, religion, the press, education, and intellectual life generally." [3679

DANIEL JOSEPH BOORSTIN. The myth of an American enlightenment. Daniel J. Boorstin, America and the image of Europe: reflections on American thought (N.Y.: Meridian Books [1960]), p. 63-78. On the "notion of an American Enlightenment" in the 1760s, 1770s, and 1780s as the product of "a set of highly sophisticated oversimplifications" by American historians. [3680

FRED GLADSTONE BRATTON. The legacy of the liberal spirit: men and movements in the making of modern thought. Boston: Beacon Press [1960]. x, [4], 319 p. bibliog. (p. 294-311), notes. (Beacon series in liberal religion, LR3.) 1st ed. 1943. On the "course of the liberal tradition in its critical phases," with emphasis on the "connection between religious liberalism and political democracy" in America and abroad. Includes chapters on Thomas Paine, "American Deism," Theodore Parker, "New England Unitarianism," and John Dewey, 1770s-1940s. [3681

ALFRED OWEN ALDRIDGE. Man of reason: the life of Thomas Paine [1737-1809]. Phila.: Lippincott [1959]. 348 p. port. notes (p. 325-41). Summarized by author: "... luminous writings." John Arthur Garraty, ed., The unforgettable Americans (Great Neck, N.Y.: Channel Press [1960]), p. 61-5. On his life in America (1774 ff.), England, and France, his writings on political theory and religious dogma, and his experiments in engineering. [3682

CHARLES HOWELL FOSTER. The "theonomous analysis" of American culture. Joseph J. Kwiat & Mary C. Turpie, eds., Studies in American culture: dominant ideas and images (Minneapolis: Univ. of Minnesota Press [1960]), p. 189-206. notes. On a "common dissatisfaction with materialism and secularity" in American literary, social, and religious movements since 1782. [3683

WALTER WILLIAM STEVENS. The scholarship of Lewis Cass [1782-1866]. Mich. hist., 44:59-66 (Mar). notes. On his manuscripts, books, and articles on history, anthropology, geography, and a variety of other subjects, "his unremitting insistence upon the collection and preservation of documents, papers, and primary data relating to American history," his promotion of the work of Henry R. Schoolcraft and other scholars, and his services to learned societies. [3684

HARRY CRANBROOK ALLEN. Conflict and concord: the Anglo-American relationship since 1783. N.Y.: St. Martins Press [1960, c1959]. 247 p. double map, tables. notes. Revised and enlarged edition of Part I of the author's Great Britain and the United States (1954). British view of their economic, social, political, diplomatic, and cultural relations and their images of each other. [3685

LEWIS P. SIMPSON. Federalism and the crisis of literary order. Am. lit., 32:253-66 (Nov). notes. On an analogy expressed by Federalist men of letters "between the threat of democracy to political order and the danger of democracy to the organization and control of literature," 1800-1810, and the related concept of a Republic of Letters, assumed to be undermined by political faction, "the pernicious notion of equality," and "the secret influence of public opinion." [3686

CARL F. STRAUCH. Emerson as literary middleman. Emerson Soc. quar., 19: leaves 2-9 (2d quar.). An effort, in a single lecture, "to show something of Emerson's specific quality as it informed ideas." [3687

WINFRED ERNEST GARRISON. Pioneer in broadcloth. Perry Epler Gresham, ed., The sage of Bethany: a pioneer in broadcloth (St. Louis: Bethany Press [1960]), p. 45-65. On the "pioneer characteristics" in the political and religious thought of Alexander Campbell, 1809-66. [3688

MERRILL D. PETERSON. The Jefferson image in the American mind. N.Y.: Oxford Univ. Press, 1960. x, 548 p. bibliog. (p. 459-522), notes.

On "Jefferson's course in American thought and imagination," 1826-1960. [3689

JOSEPH HARRY DORFMAN & REXFORD GUY DORFMAN. Francis Lieber [1800-1872]: German scholar in America. Joseph Dorfman & Rexford Guy Tugwell, Early American policy: six Columbia contributors (N.Y.: Columbia Univ. Press, 1960), p. 249-311. port. notes. From the Columbia University quarterly, "1930s." On his emigration from Germany (ca. 1827?), his work as editor of the Encyclopaedia Americana (1829-33), his lectures, his service as Professor of History and Political Economy at Columbia University and the University of South Carolina, and his activities in national politics; with appended "Specimens of Francis Lieber's examinations," 1855-63. [3690

PERRY EPLER GRESHAM. Alexander Campbell against socialism. Perry Epler Gresham, ed., The sage of Bethany: pioneer in broadcloth (St. Louis: Bethany Press [1960]), p. 131-45. notes. On his stand as "an exponent of free enterprise and an ardent foe of socialism," 1828-66; with a detailed account of his debate with Robert Owen at Cincinnati, 13-21 Apr. 1829 ("with time out for the Lord's Day"), where Owen defended his "political and social views of determinism, irresponsibility, and religious skepticism ... the doctrine of environmental determinism ... and ... the derived doctrine of no responsibility." [3691

ROBERT D. JACOBS. Poe's earthly paradise [1829-47]. Am. quar., 12: 404-13 (fall). notes. On his theme of "the distortion in the physical universe that attended man's fall from a state of innocence and earthly immortality," and the power of the poetic imagination to form "a terrestrial paradise" from the materials of the physical and the moral universe. [3692

JAMES FENIMORE COOPER (1789-1851). A letter to his countrymen, by J. Fenimore-Cooper. New-York: John Wiley ... 1834. Jahrbuch für Amerikastudien, 5:245-307. (Page numbers of original indicated in margins of reprint.) Largely a reply to criticism, especially in Europe, of Cooper's The bravo, and to pejorative references to his political views and personal character; and complaint that Americans, particularly those in Europe, are unduly deferential to foreign opinion. [3693

GEORGE BERNARD DE HUSZAR, ed. The intellectuals: a controversial portrait. Glencoe, Ill.: Free Press [1960]. viii, 543 p. notes. Reprinted texts concerning "intellectuals" and their functions and characteristics, with an introduction. Includes American texts from Emerson's "The American scholar" (1837) to 1958. [3694

CHARLES ROBERT CROWE. Fourierism and the founding of Brook Farm. Boston Pub. Lib. quar., 12:79-88 (Apr). notes. On the shares of Fourierism and Transcendentalism in the socialistic thinking of George Ripley and in the establishment of Brook Farm, 1840-44. [3695

DAVID SPRAGUE HERRESHOFF. Americanizers of Marx. Ann Arbor: University Microfilms, 1959 [i.e. 1960]. Positive microfilm of typescript. [392] leaves. Thesis--Univ. of Minnesota. Abstracted: Dissert. abstracts, 20:4212 (Apr). Study of Orestes Brownson, Joseph Weydemeyer, Friedrich A. Sorge, and Daniel De Leon, 1840s to ca. 1910. [3696

RICHARD AUSTIN THOMPSON. Francis Parkman on the nature of man [1840s-80s]. Mid-America, 42:3-17 (Jan). notes. On his view of "human nature," including his ideas regarding heredity and environment, education, social class, race (particularly the Indians), male and female, war, politics, and greatness. [3697

ELEANOR MARGUERITE TILTON. Science and sentiment: a study of Oliver Wendell Holmes. College Phys. Phila., Trans. & studies, 26:89-98 (Aug 1958). notes. On his attitudes toward "reform," religion, and psychology, and his dislike of romanticism, 1840-84. [3698

DONALD A. RINGE. Cooper's Littlepage novels: change and stability in American society. Am. lit., 32:280-90 (Nov). notes. On Satanstoe (1845), The chainbearer (1845), and The redskins (1846) as a trilogy dealing with "the social function of an aristocracy" in a New York setting. [3699

DONALD A. RINGE. Cooper's last novels, 1847-1850. PMLA, 75:583-90 (Dec). notes. On The crater (1847), Jack Tier (1848), The oak openings (1848), The sea lions (1849), and The ways of the hour (1850), forming a set of metaphorical expressions of a system of ideas centered in "an ideal of Christian humility and self-control by which" his readers "should guide their lives and their society." [3700

JULIUS FROEBEL (1805-93). William Gilpin [1813-94], Sinophile and eccentric, as seen by the German scientist, journalist, and traveler Julius Froebel. [Edited] by Kenneth W. Porter. Colo. mag., 37:245-53 (Oct). notes. Observations made at Independence, Mo., 1852, ridiculing Gilpin's ideas about "a railroad to the Pacific," the purity of Chinese civilization, the prospective introduction of "the patriarchal democracy of the Celestial Empire" into the United States as an antidote to "European influences there," etc. [3701

PAUL F. BOLLER, JR. Darwin's American champion. Southw. rev., 45:156-64 (spring). On Asa Gray (1810-88), Harvard botanist, as a correspondent of Charles Darwin, 1854-82, "one of three men ... to have advance knowledge of the Darwinian theory" (from a confidential letter, 7 Sep. 1857), advocate of Darwin's doctrine of evolution (with reservations); and his arguments for "a designed Cosmos" as distinguished from the "fortuitous Cosmos" that Darwin seemed to imply. [3702

WILLIAM PIERCE RANDEL. Walt Whitman and American myths. South Atl. quar., 59:103-13 (winter). On his belief "that conception and content are more important than execution," that "an oligarchy of wealth and power exists to thwart or limit" the development of "the masses," that "the common people with their comradely love and mutual altruism needed to be eternally vigilant lest a selfish minority gain unfair advantage," and that "the chief requisite for success is to start from scratch," his part in creating "the Lincoln myth," and his identification of "the pervasive effect of the sex drive in all positive activity." [3703

AUGUST LYNN ALTENBERND. The influence of European travel on the political and social outlook of Henry Adams, William Dean Howells, and Mark Twain [1858-79]. Ann Arbor: University Microfilms, 1954 [i.e. 1960]. Positive microfilm of typescript. [290] leaves. Thesis--Ohio State Univ. Abstracted: Dissert. abstracts, 20:3737-9 (Mar). [3704

JOSEPH E. ILLICK III. The reception of Darwinism at the Theological Seminary and the College at Princeton, New Jersey [1859-83]. Presbyt. Hist. Soc., Jour., 38:152-65, 234-54 (Sep, Dec). notes. Mainly on utterances of Charles Hodge and James McCosh. [3705

FREDERIC LILGE. John Dewey, 1859-1959: reflections on his educational and social thought. Educ. forum, 24:351-61 (Mar). [3706

EDWARD LURIE. Louis Agassiz and the idea of evolution [1859-73]. Victorian studies, 3:87-108 (Sep 1959). notes. On the reasons in the intellectual history of Agassiz that led him to describe Darwin's Origin of species as "a scientific mistake, untrue in its facts, unscientific in its method, and mischievous in its tendency." [3707

SHERMAN PAUL. The identities of John Jay Chapman [1862-1933]. Jour. Eng. and Germanic philol., 59:255-62 (Apr). Review of his intellectual history as exhibited in his writings. [3708

ARTHUR HAZARD DAKIN. Paul Elmer More [1864-1937]. Princeton, N.J.: Princeton Univ. Press, 1960. xvii, 416 p. ports., view. bibliog. (p. 388), notes. An effort to "chart the main course of his inner life against a rough chronicle of his daily doings," and the stages by which, starting with "Calvinistic piety," he came to "a blend of Anglicanism, Buddhism, and Platonism"; with extensive quotations from his letters, references to his friendship with Irving Babbitt ("the closest friendship of my life"), and some account of his early life in St. Louis, his studies in Washington University and Harvard, his teaching of classics at Bryn Mawr, his service as literary editor of The independent and The nation, his teaching of classical languages and literatures at Princeton, and his articles and books on a variety of literary, philosophical, and religious subjects. [3709

JOSEPH JAMES CHAMBLISS. Natural selection and utilitarian ethics in Chauncey Wright. Am. quar., 12:144-59 (summer). notes. On opinions found in some of his letters and essays, 1866-75. [3710

SHERWOOD PRESTON CUMMINGS. Mark Twain and the sirens of progress. Cent. Miss. Valley Am. Studies Assoc., Jour., 1(2):17-24 (fall).

notes. On his glorification of "technological progress," especially inventions and "the inventive geniuses of his time," and his own efforts as an inventor and an investor in inventions, 1870s-90s; and his loss of "his brave faith in progress" in 1898. [3711

HESTER HASTINGS. William Ellery Channing [1780-1842] and l'Académie des Sciences Morales et Politiques, 1870: "L'étude sur Channing" and the "lost" prize essay. Providence: Brown Univ. Press, 1959 [i.e. 1960]. vi, 61 p. port. notes. Summary of 2 essays submitted for the Prix Stassart of the Academy, "William Channing, philanthrope chrétien," by Félix Cadet (manuscript), and Channing, sa vie et sa doctrine (1876), by René Lavallée, taking opposite views of Channing, Rhode Island Unitarian minister, with respect to his social and political doctrines; with remarks on his reputation in France, 1852-83. [3712

JACOB CLAVER LEVENSON. Henry Adams and the culture of science. Joseph J. Kwiat & Mary C. Turpie, eds., Studies in American culture: dominant ideas and images (Minneapolis: Univ. of Minnesota Press [1960]), p. 123-38. notes. On his efforts to point "the way to a culture of science that might redress a technological civilization," 1870s-1918. [3713

MELVIN ERNEST LYON. Symbol and idea in the major works of Henry Adams [1870s-1918]. Ann Arbor: University Microfilms, 1960. Positive microfilm of typescript. [612] leaves. Thesis--Univ. of Wisconsin. Abstracted: Dissert. abstracts, 21:623-4 (Sep). [3714

JOHN D. MOLLOY. [Herbert] Spencer's impact on American conservatism, 1870-1912. Ann Arbor: University Microfilms, 1959 [i.e. 1960]. Positive microfilm of typescript. [258] leaves. Thesis--Univ. of Cincinnati. Abstracted: Dissert. abstracts, 20:4430 (May). On his "impact on American business, the Republican party, organs of American government itself, leading conservative intellectuals, and the American clergy." [3715

RICHARD HARTER FOGLE. Melville's Clarel: doubt and belief. Tulane studies in Eng., 10:101-16. On Clarel: a poem and pilgrimage in the Holy Land (1876), based upon Melville's travels in 1856-57 and upon his reading and reflection, as an example of "the impact of the Holy Land upon men of the West" and as "a major treatment of the late-nineteenth century battle of faith and reason, more especially as it became the war between religion and science." [3716

COMER VANN WOODWARD. The Populist heritage and the intellectual. Comer Vann Woodward, The burden of Southern history (Baton Rouge: Louisiana State Univ. Press [1960]), p. 141-66. From The American scholar, 1959. On Populism and the New Deal in relation to American intellectual history, 1880-1940s. [3717

ELBERT LEROY HARRIS. Hamlin Garland [1860-1940]: examiner of the American scene. Quar. rev. higher educ. among Negroes, 28:219-25 (Jul). notes. Review of his opinions as a social and literary critic, 1885-1939. [3718

ALLEN GUTTMANN. Mark Twain's Connecticut Yankee [1889]: affirmation of the vernacular tradition? New Eng. quar., 33:232-7 (Jun). notes. Argument that he was "skeptical of precipitant civilizing" and had "serious doubts about technology itself," and that his Hank Morgan "is representative of something other than unmitigated good." [3719

H. R. DIETERICH. Revivalist as reformer--implications of George D. Herron's speaking. Quar. jour. speech, 46:391-9 (Dec). notes. On 2 speeches by a Congregational "evangelist-turned-reformer": "The message of Jesus to men of wealth," a sermon preached in 1890, and "Why I am a Socialist," delivered at the opening of the Social Democratic Party's national campaign in 1900. [3720

ARTHUR EDWARD MURPHY. John Dewey and American liberalism [1890s-1950s]. Jour. philos., 57:420-36 (23 Jun). [3721

PAUL ROSENBLATT. The image of civilization in the novels of Henry Blake Fuller [1890 to 1929]. Ann Arbor: University Microfilms, 1960. Positive microfilm of typescript. [215] leaves. Thesis--Columbia Univ. Abstracted: Dissert. abstracts, 91:902-3 (Oct). Examination of all his novels, and of the contrast between those about Europe and those about Chicago. [3722

WILLIAM B. DILLINGHAM. Frank Norris and the genteel tradition [1892-1902]. Tenn. studies in lit., 5:15-24. notes. On his "deviation from acceptable subject matter of fiction, his treatment of unpleasant details, and his Darwinism" as facts concealing his "kinship with the genteel tradition," and the evidence of the tradition in his "treatment of sex, in his characterization of woman as man's moral support, in his emphasis upon self-control, and in his frequent indulgence in sentimentality." [3723

HARRY GORDON HARLAND. Love and justice in the thought of Reinhold Niebuhr [born 1892]. Ann Arbor: University Microfilms, 1959 [i.e. 1960]. Positive microfilm of typescript. [397] leaves. Thesis--Drew Univ. Abstracted: Dissert. abstracts, 20:2932 (Jan). Printed with revisions: The thought of Reinhold Niebuhr. N.Y.: Oxford Univ. Press, 1960. xvii, 298 p. notes (p. 275-94). On his "theological ethic" and his "views on a number of issues, movements, and events pertaining to politics, economics, war, and race." [3724

JOSEPH LEON BLAU. John Dewey and American social thought [1894-1958]. Teachers College rec., 61: 121-7 (Dec 1959). notes. [3725

HARRY TUCHMAN LEVIN. Irving Babbitt and his New Humanism [1895-1933]. Harvard alumni bul., 63:209-11 (26 Nov). [3726

DAVID WATSON NOBLE. Dreiser and Veblen and the literature of cultural change [1899-1920s]. Joseph J. Kwiat & Mary C. Turpie, eds., Studies in American culture: dominant ideas and images (Minneapolis: Univ. of Minnesota Press [1960]), p. 139-52. notes. [3727

SAMUEL JOHN SACKETT. The Utopia of Oz. Ga. rev., 14:275-91 (fall). On the Oz books of L. Frank Baum, 1899-1916, as "Utopian fiction," inculcating "certain attitudes toward government and society." [3728

DANIEL JOSEPH BOORSTIN. Some American discontents. Daniel J. Boorstin, America and the image of Europe: reflections on American thought (N.Y.: Meridian Books [1960]), p. 119-38. First printed in 1954. On the "declining sense of American uniqueness" in the 20th century as the "great trauma of the American mind." [3729

RICHARD TRACY LA PIERE. The Freudian ethic. N.Y.: Duell, Sloan, and Pearce [1959]. x, 299 p. notes. On the distinction between "the Protestant ethic" and "the Freudian doctrine of man"; the propagation of the latter by "the permissive home," "the progressive school," "the adjustment motif," and the "condonation of crime"; and the exhibition of the Freudian doctrine by "the new bourgeoisie," "modern guildism," "political maternalism," and "the security goal"--especially in the United States in the 20th century. [3730

FRANCIS XAVIER DUGGAN. Paul Elmer More [1864-1937] and the American tradition. Ann Arbor: University Microfilms, 1960. Positive microfilm of typescript. [479] leaves. Thesis--Univ. of Pennsylvania. Abstracted: Dissert. abstracts, 21:889 (Oct). On the views presented in his Shelburne essays (1904-21), New Shelburne essays (1928-36), and The Greek tradition (1921-31). [3731

HORACE BANCROFT DAVIS. Schumpeter as sociologist. Science & soc., 24:13-35 (winter). notes. Marxist commentary on the work of Joseph Alois Schumpeter as "sociology, political science, history, and economics, jointly and by turns," in relation to his ideas concerning "imperialism, social classes and the theory of the state," 1906-50. [3732

GORDON HADDON CLARK. Dewey. Phila.: Presbyterian and Reformed Pub. Co., 1960. 69 p. notes. (International library of philosophy and theology. Modern thinkers series.) On the instrumental science, ethics, and logic of John Dewey as expounded in 10 of his books, 1916-46. [3733

THOMAS MARY BERRY. Dewey's influence in China. John Blewett, ed., John Dewey: his thought and influence (N.Y.: Fordham Univ. Press [1960]), p. 199-232. notes. On his lectures on philosophy in Chinese universities, and his influence upon the "political, philosophical and educational" areas of Chinese life, 1919-52. [3734

CARL LOTUS BECKER (1873-1945). Review of Henry Adams' The degradation of the democratic dogma. Carl L. Becker, Detachment and the writing of history: essays and letters of Carl L. Becker, ed. Phil L. Snyder (Ithaca: Cornell Univ. Press [1958]), p. 29-34.

First published in 1920. On a volume consisting of 2 reprinted letters and a previously unpublished essay ("The rule of phase applied to history"), with an introduction (125 p.) by the editor, Brooks Adams, dealing with the history of ideas in the Adams family since the time of John Adams. [3735

EDITH OPAL STONE. Democratic values in modern narrative poems. Ann Arbor: University Microfilms, 1960. Positive microfilm of typescript. [288] leaves. Thesis--Univ. of Michigan. Abstracted: Dissert. abstracts, 21:345 (Aug). Study of 10 poems, by John G. Neihardt, Stephen Vincent Benet, Theda Kenyon, and Robert Penn Warren, 1919-53. [3736

KENNETH MURCHISON ENGLAND. They came home again: Fugitives' return. Ga. rev., 14:80-89 (spring). Commentary on the Fugitives of the 1920s and the reunion of 10 of them at Nashville in 1956. [3737

KARL H. HERTZ. An evaluation of Reinhold Niebuhr's ethics [1920s-50s]. Luth. quar., 12:3-24 (Feb). notes. On the applications of his concepts of love, sin, and justice. [3738

RANDALL STEWART. The relation between Fugitives and Agrarians [1922-25, 1930]. Miss. quar., 13:55-60 (winter). [3739

JAMES ARTHUR KEHL. Defender of the faith: Orphan Annie and the conservative tradition. South Atl. quar., 59:192-203 (spring). On her service since 1924 as "an outlet for the expression of the political and economic philosophy of her creator and legal guardian, Harold Gray," as a "relentless antagonist" of the New Deal, and as "a firm believer in the Protestant ethic, in the pursuit of individual salvation through thrift and hard work, and in the competitive struggle." [3740

HERMAN CLARENCE NIXON. A thirty years' personal view. Miss. quar., 13:76-9 (winter). On the development of the author's "agrarian philosophy ... as inspired by the Fugitive movement," 1925-59. [3741

VIRGINIA ROCK. Dualisms in Agrarian thought [1927-59]. Miss. quar., 13:80-89 (winter). notes. [3742

PHILLIP C. CHAPMAN. The new conservatism: cultural criticism v. political philosophy [1949-56]. Pol. science quar., 75:17-34 (Mar). notes. [3743

American Concepts of Foreign Civilizations

PHILIP RAHV, ed. Discovery of Europe: the story of American experience in the Old World. Edited with a new introduction and comments. Garden City, N.Y.: Doubleday, 1960. xvi, 464 p. (Anchor books, A208.) 1st ed. 1947. Reprinted observations of 20 Americans, from Benjamin Franklin to Randolph Bourne, 1772-1914. [3744

H. WAYNE MORGAN. The Founding Fathers and the Middle Ages. Mid-America, 42:30-43 (Jan). notes. On the belief of John Adams, Jefferson, Madison, Hamilton, and others that the Middle Ages, as distinguished from Greek and Latin antiquity, were "a complete eclipse of the human mind continuing for centuries," "a thousand years of barons' wars, causing universal darkness, ignorance, and barbarity," "a rickety bridge spanning the chasm from ancient to modern times," the creator of "the canon and the feudal law," "a time of clerical domination" and of "cooperation between king and priest," "an era during which the arts and sciences languished," "an arid waste." [3745

THOMAS O'BRIEN HANLEY. Archbishop Carroll and the French Revolution. Am. Cath. Hist. Soc., Rec., 71:67-72 (Sep-Dec). notes. On Abp. John Carroll's "sympathy with the Francophobe Federalists," his identification of "the Republicans with the dangerous spirit of the French Revolution," the "dominantly religious aspect" of his "criticism of the French Revolution and its background," and the sharp distinction that he drew between the American Revolution and the French, 1782-1800. [3746

THOMAS FRANCIS McGANN. Latin America and Harvard: early ties, present relationships, & prospects for the future [1784-1956]. Harvard alumni bul., 59:588-91 (4 May 1957). cartoons. [3747

KURT BEERMANN. The reception of the French Revolution in the New York State press: 1788-1791. Ann Arbor: University Microfilms, 1960. Positive microfilm of typescript. [746] leaves. Thesis--New York Univ. Abstracted: Dissert. abstracts, 21:1170 (Nov). [3748

BEATRICE FRY HYSLOP. The American press and the French Revolution of 1789. Am. Philos. Soc., Proc., 104:54-85 (15 Feb). notes. [3749

EDWARD GEORGE EVERETT. Some aspects of pro-French sentiment in Pennsylvania, 1790-1800. West. Pa. hist. mag., 43:23-41 (Mar). notes. On the popularity of "the symbols and ideas of Revolutionary France" and its conversion into "the rabid patriotism that flourished between the years of 1798 and 1800." [3750

CHARLES H. NICHOLS. The image of the European father in American writing. Jahrbuch für Amerikastudien, 5:26-33. On analogues between the attitude of son toward father and that of Americans toward Europe, particularly the disposition to learn from the father's mistakes, as expressed by Jefferson, Emerson, Whitman, Hawthorne, Melville, Henry James, and others, 1808-1950s. [3751

HARVEY LEROY JOHNSON. A backward glance at Portuguese and Brazilian studies in the United States [since 1816]. Jour. inter-Am. studies, 1:477-88 (Oct 1959). [3752

EARLE E. COLEMAN. The exhibition in the Palace: a bibliographical essay. N.Y. Pub. Lib., Bul., 64:458-75 (Sep). views. notes. On the Exhibition of Works of Industry of All Nations, in the Crystal Palace, New York City, organized by the Association for the Exhibition of the Industry of All Nations, 1852-54, and the books, pamphlets, broadsides, and serial contributions to which it gave rise; with a checklist. [3753

PHILIP LOVELESS NICOLOFF. Emerson's thought in English traits [1856]. Ann Arbor: University Microfilms, 1959 [i.e. 1960]. Positive microfilm of typescript. 381 leaves. bibliog. (leaves 375-81). Thesis--Columbia Univ. Abstracted: Dissert. abstracts, 20:3748 (Mar). [3754

GEORGE ALBERT KNOX. Dissonance abroad: Julian Hawthorne's Saxon studies [1876]. Essex Inst. hist. col., 96:131-9 (Apr). notes. On his stay in Dresden, 1868-69, 1871-73, his "reminiscences of Dresden life," the extremely unfavorable reviews of his book, and "its place in the American-abroad genre of jaundiced realism." [3755

EDMUND ORDON. Polish studies at Wayne University [since 1947]. Poles in Michigan Associated, Poles in Michigan (Detroit, 1953 [i.e. 1955]), 1:116-19. Refers briefly to the teaching of the Polish language in Michigan since 1885. [3756

HELMUT SÜNDERMANN. Die Pioniere und die Ahnungslosen: Skizzen amerikanischer Vergangenheit und Gegenwart [1620-1960]. Leoni am Starnberger See: Druffel-Verlag [1960]. 240 p. maps, ports., views. notes. On American attitudes toward and relations with Europe and to some extent the rest of the world, mainly since 1898. [3757

HENRY CORD MEYER. Five images of Germany: half a century of American views on German history. Wash.: Service Center for Teachers of History [1960. 4], 56 p. bibliog. (p. 55-6), notes. (Service Center for Teachers of History. Publication 27.) Bibliographical essay. [3758

DANIEL JOSEPH BOORSTIN. America and the image of Europe [1914-45]. Daniel J. Boorstin, America and the image of Europe: reflections on American thought (N.Y.: Meridian Books [1960]), p. 17-39. First printed in 1956. Deals particularly with politics and literary criticism. [3759

SUSANNE UTA (EMMERLING) EISELE. Das Deutschlandbild in der amerikanischen Literatur des zweiten Weltkrieges. Erlangen [1959. 4], 177, [2] p. bibliog. (p. 160-68), notes (p. 134-59). Inaugural-Dissertation--Erlangen. On treatments of Germany and the German character in American fiction and drama, 1926-45. [3760

ROBERT JOSEPH HORGAN. Some American opinion of the Soviet Union, 1933-1939. Ann Arbor: University Microfilms, 1959 [i.e. 1960]. Positive microfilm of typescript. xxiii, 353 leaves. bibliog. (leaves 302-52). Thesis--Univ. of Notre Dame. Abstracted: Dissert. abstracts, 20:4152-3 (Apr). [3761

JOHN MARTIN MUSTE. The Spanish Civil War [1936-39] in the literature of the United States and Great Britain.

Ann Arbor: University Microfilms, 1960. Positive microfilm of typescript. [390] leaves. Thesis--Univ. of Wisconsin. Abstracted: Dissert. abstracts,21:1568-9 (Dec). [3762

CYRIL EDWIN BLACK & JOHN M. THOMPSON. Graduate education in Russian studies: a progress report [1946-58]. Jour. higher educ., 30: 246-54 (May 1959). notes. [3763

WILLIAM THEODORE DE BARY. Asian studies for undergraduates: the Oriental Studies Program at Columbia College [1946-58]. Jour. higher educ., 30:1-7 (Jan 1959). [3764

WILLIAM LEONARD LANGER. The Russian Research Center [at Harvard, 1948-55]. Harvard alumni bul., 57: 395-6 (26 Feb 1955). cartoon. [3765

LEONARD MILTON KENNEDY. The treatment of Moslem nations, India, and Israel in social studies textbooks used in elementary and junior high schools of the United States [published since 1956]. Ann Arbor: University Microfilms, 1960. Positive microfilm of typescript. [170] leaves. Thesis (Ed. D.)--Univ. of Washington. Abstracted: Dissert. abstracts, 21:498-9 (Sep). Study of textbooks that include "both geographical and historical material." [3766

Concepts of American Civilization

ANDRÉ ALLIX. Les conditions naturelles de l'occupation humaine. Les fondements de la politique extérieur des États-Unis (Paris: Armand Colin, 1949 [Cahiers de la Fondation Nationale des Sciences Politiques, 8], p. 9-18. Historical and geographic arguments supporting the thesis that in many respects the United States is still "une colonie d'Europe" and "une civilisation de colonisateurs." [3767

ROBERT N. BECK. America and the hand of history. Social educ., 24: 197-9, 206 (May). On America's "belief in transhistorical truths coupled with dynamism, messianism, exceptionalism, and moralism--'historical puritanism,'" and their conflict, increasingly apparent in recent years, with "the power relations among peoples which are the stuff of history," indicating "that we can no longer live with our original Enlightenment inheritance, and that we may be in mortal danger in continuing to believe that we can." [3768

GUSTAV H. BLANKE. Der Amerikaner: eine sozio-linguistische Studie. Meisenheim am Glan: Anton Hain, 1957 [©1956. 4], 336 p. notes. On words and phrases current in the United States as evidence of American national character, grouped in chapters designating the American as activist, moralist, optimist, pragmatist, and democrat since colonial times and particularly in recent years. [3769

LEO MARX. Shakespeare's American fable. Mass. rev., 2:40-71 (winter). On "Elizabethan ideas of America" embodied in The tempest (1611-12). [3770

WHITFIELD JENKS BELL, JR. "... sense of wonder and exultation." John Arthur Garraty, ed., The unforgettable Americans (Great Neck, N.Y.: Channel Press [1960]), p. 71-4. On Michel Guillaume de Crevecoeur (1735-1813), settler in Canada ca. 1755 and in New York ca. 1760, and his observations on American life in Letters from an American farmer (London, 1782). [3771

DENIS WILLIAM BROGAN. America in the modern world [1776-1959]. New Brunswick, N.J.: Rutgers Univ. Press [1960. 10], 117 p. Sections on the "hopefulness of the American view of life," the conflict of American democracy with "communism and authoritarian nationalism," "the character of American life," "American education," and "the character of American culture." [3772

ROBERT LEE WHITE. Some passionate pilgrims: The image of Italy in American romanticism [in art and literature, 1820s-60s]. Ann Arbor: Univerisity Microfilms, 1959 [i.e. 1960]. Positive microfilm of typescript. [483] leaves. Thesis--Univ. of Minnesota. Abstracted: Dissert. abstracts, 20:4101-2 (Apr). [3773

HENRY UNWIN ADDINGTON (d. 1870). Youthful America: selections from Henry Unwin Addington's Residence in the United States of America, 1822, 23, 24, 25. Edited, with an introduction and notes, by Bradford Perkins. Berkeley: Univ. of California Press, 1960. [2], v, [3], 115 p.

notes. (University of California publications in history, 65.) Selections from a previously unpublished diary kept by the British chargé d'affaires in Washington. [3774

GOLO MANN [name originally: Angelus Mann]. Tocqueville und das Amerika von heute. Jahrbuch für Amerikastudien, 5:11-25. On confirmations, especially since 1900, of predictions published by Alexis de Tocqueville after his travels in the United States in 1831 and 1832. [3775

GEORGE WILSON PIERSON. Le "second voyage" de Tocqueville en Amérique. France, Centre National de la Recherche Scientifique, Alexis de Tocqueville, livre du centenaire, 1859-1959 (Paris, 1960), p. 71-85. notes. On the process of composition of his De la démocratie en Amérique, 1833 ff., as indicated in his manuscripts. [3776

RENÉ RÉMOND. Tocqueville et La démocratie en Amérique. France, Centre National de la Recherche Scientifique, Alexis de Tocqueville, livre du centenaire, 1859-1959 (Paris, 1960), p. 181-90. On the "originalite" of this work, composed 1833 ff. [3777

CARL LOTUS BECKER (1873-1945). Why [Alexis] de Tocqueville wrote Democracy in America [1835-40]. Carl L. Becker, Detachment and the writing of history: essays and letters of Carl L. Becker, ed. Phil L. Snyder (Ithaca: Cornell Univ. Press [1958]), p. 167-76. Now first published. [3778

RALPH GEOFFREY NEWMAN. Lincoln and the family of man. Ralph Geoffrey Newman, ed., Lincoln for the ages (Garden City, N.Y.: Doubleday, 1960), p. 415-20. On his "conception of the mission of America," 1858-65. [3779

JOSEPH ANTHONY WARD. Henry James's America: versions of oppression. Miss. quar., 13:30-44 (winter). notes. On "James's vision of evil in America," 1870s-1916. [3780

RONALD F. HOWELL. Book classic: James Bryce's "The American Commonwealth" [1888 and later editions]. Jour. pub. law, 9:191-213 (spring). notes. Concludes that Bryce "was almost invariably correct in his appraisal of American government and life at the time he wrote" and that "the extent to which he is no longer correct is thus a reliable indicator of the monumental changes in American society since his edition of 1914." [3781

MARTÍN GARCÍA MÉROU. Estudios americanos. Con una introducción de Eugenio Díaz Romero. Nueva edición. [Buenos Aires?] Rosso [1955?]. 252, [1] p. (Colección grandes obras nacionales: la cultura popular.) 1st ed. 1900. Essays by a member of the Argentine Legation, on Boston, Chicago, St. Louis, Amherst College, John Hay, David Ames Wells, Henry Cabot Lodge, the U.S. Congress, American municipal government, and other subjects. [3782

EZRA LOOMIS POUND. Impact: essays on ignorance and the decline of American civilization. ... Edited with an introduction by Noel Stock. Chicago: H. Regnery Co., 1960. xviii, 285 p. bibliog. (p. 284-5), notes. Reprinted from various sources, 1918-44. [3783

HERBERT CHARLES MORTON. William Bolitho [1890-1930] today. Nieman reports, 13(2):17-19 (Apr 1959). On the ideas and observations expressed in Camera obscura, a reprint of 50 columns written by this British journalist while in New York as published in the New York World, 1928-29. [3784

RUEL NICHOLAS DENNY. How Americans see themselves. Joseph J. Kwiat & Mary C. Turpie, eds., Studies in American culture: dominant ideas and images (Minneapolis: Univ. of Minnesota Press [1960]), p. 16-26. notes. On writings by American "observers of the American national character," 1934-54. [3785

ROBERT FRANCIS McDONNELL & WILLIAM E. MORRIS, eds. Modern America through foreign eyes: selected source materials for college research papers. Boston: Heath [1959]. ix, 117 p. bibliog. (p. 116-17). Excerpts from 12 books by foreign observers of civilization in the United States, published 1938-58. [3786

MARY MAYFLOWER BENYAMIN. Fluctuations in the prestige of the United States in France: a description of French attitudes toward the United States and its policies, 1945-1955. Ann Arbor: University Microfilms, 1959 [i.e. 1960]. Positive microfilm of typescript. x, 456 leaves. tables. bibliog. (leaves 435-56). Thesis--Columbia Univ. Abstracted: Dissert. abstracts, 20:4157-8 (Apr). [3787

DENNIS HUME WRONG. The united States in comparative perspective: Max Lerner's America as a civilization [1957]. Am. jour. sociol., 65:499-504 (Mar). notes. Questions whether "America is a genuinely new civilization," as maintained by Lerner, and expresses dissatisfaction with his uses of the terms "civilization" and "America." [3788

MILITARY HISTORY

WILLIAM H. NELSON & FRANK EVERSON VANDIVER. Fields of glory: an illustrated narrative of American land warfare [from King Philip's War to the Korean War, 1675-1953]. N.Y.: Dutton [1960]. 316 p. cartoons, facsims., maps, plan, ports., views. Pictorial history; sources of illustrations not fully identified. Contains 19 pages (p. 16-34) on the Revolution. [3789

HOWARD HENRY PECKHAM. Speculations on the colonial wars [1689-1760]. Wm. and Mary quar., 17: 463-72 (Oct). notes. On the reasons for the ultimate defeat of France in North America and the ultimate victory of England and her American colonies. [3790

HOWARD HENRY PECKHAM. The War for Independence: a military history. [Chicago:] Univ. of Chicago Press [1958]. ix, 226 p. maps. bibliog. (p. 210-17). (The Chicago history of American civilization.) [3791

THOMAS HARRY WILLIAMS. Americans at war: the development of the American military system [1775-1918. Baton Rouge:] Louisiana State Univ. Press [1960]. xi, 138, [1] p. ports. bibliog. (p. 127-34), notes. [3792

JARED C. LOBDELL. Paramus in the War of the Revolution [New Jersey, 1776-82]. N.J. Hist. Soc., Proc., 78:162-77 (Jul). notes. Mainly on military operations in and near Paramus. [3792a

ALBERT W. HAARMANN. The Spanish conquest of British West Florida, 1779-1781. Fla. hist. quar., 39:107-34 (Oct). notes. [3793

WILLIAM WELLS. William Wells and the Indian council of 1793. Edited by Dwight L. Smith. Ind. mag. hist., 56:217-26 (Sep). port. notes. Deposition made to Anthony Wayne, 16 Sep. 1793, reporting the deponent's attendance as Wayne's representative at "the private council of the Hostile Indians lately held at the Rapids of the Miami of the Lake." [3794

FREDERICK COYNE HAMIL. Michigan in the War of 1812. Mich. hist., 44:257-91 (Sep). Separately printed: Michigan in the War of 1812. Lansing: Michigan Historical Commission, 1960. vii, 44, [1] p. cartoon, facsim., map, medals, ports., views. bibliog. (p. 44). (John M. Munson Michigan History Fund pamphlet 4.) On military activities in Michigan and the activities of Michigan armed forces, 1812-15. [3795

EUGENE T. NEWHALL. The military history of Minnesota [1812-1960]. Lawrence Martin Brings, ed., Minnesota heritage (Minneapolis: T. S. Denison [1960]), p. 337-43. ports., views. [3796

OHIO. Anthony Wayne Parkway Board. A short chronology: the War of 1812 in the Northwest [29 Apr. 1812 - 10 Oct. 1815]. By Richard C. Knopf. Columbia: Ohio State Museum, 1960. ii, 23 leaves.--Printed with additions: OHIO. Governor's Committee for Commemorating the Sesquicentennial of the War of 1812. Program suggestions for commemorating the sesquicentennial of the War of 1812, 1962-1963. [Columbus] 1960. [8], 23, [12] p. maps, port. For the chronology see p. 1-23. [3797

DONALD A. McPHERON. Soldiers of the frontier: a tribute. Chron. Okla., 38:108-9 (spring). On the U.S. Army in Oklahoma, 1817-84, and its neutrality "in all the gyrations of Oklahoma's fabulous history." [3798

LEWIS FRY RICHARDSON (1881-1953). Statistics of deadly quarrels. ... Edited by Quincy Wright and C. C. Lienau. Pittsburgh: Boxwood Press [1960]. xlvi, 373 p. diagrs. (part fold.), port., tables (1 fold.). bibliog. (p. 315-28), notes. Dialogue on the "application of statistical methods" to the determination of the causes of the 89 (or 102) wars in the world between 1820 and 1945. [3799

RICHARD KEITH McMASTER. The Ninth Military District (Territory of New Mexico), 1848-1862. Password, 5: 105-10 (Jul). notes. Includes a list of the engagements of each military unit in the district. [3800

BELLE BECKER SIDEMAN & LILLIAN FRIEDMAN, eds. Europe looks at the Civil War: an anthology. N.Y.: Orion Press [1960]. xx, 323, [4] p. bibliog. (p. 309-23). Reprinted excerpts from writings by contemporary British, French, German, Russian, Belgian, Spanish, Swedish, and Italian commentators, in roughly chronological order, 1859-65. [3801

AMERICAN HERITAGE. American heritage Civil War chronology, with notes on the leading participants. N.Y.: American Heritage Pub. Co., c1960. [39] p. Chronology (23 Apr. 1860 - 26 May 1865), index to the chronology, and biographical dictionary. [3802

PAUL McCLELLAND ANGLE & EARL SCHENCK MIERS, eds. Tragic years, 1860-1865 ... a documentary history of the American Civil War. N.Y.: Simon and Schuster, 1960. 2 v. x. 562; [8], 563-1097, [1] p. maps. notes (p. 1052-66). Excerpts from printed sources. [3803

THOMAS SCHOONOVER. Manpower, North and South, in 1860. Civil War hist., 6:170-73 (Jun). table. notes. [3804

EPHRAIM DOUGLASS ADAMS (1865-1930). Great Britain and the American Civil War. N.Y.: Russell & Russell [1958]. 2 v. in 1. xi, 307; v-vii, 340 p. cartoons, ports. notes. 1st ed. 1925. On "what the American Civil War meant to Great Britain; how she regarded it and how she reacted to it." Based largely upon British records and personal papers. [3805

AMERICAN HERITAGE. The American heritage picture history of the Civil War [1861-65]. By the editors of American heritage. Editor in charge: Richard M. Ketchum. Narrative by Bruce Catton. N.Y.: American Heritage Pub. Co.; book trade distribution by Doubleday [1960]. 630 p. cartoons, facsims., maps (part col.), ports. (part col.), views (part col., part double). Some of the illustrations are from unnamed sources. [3806

JOHN GILCHRIST BARRETT. North Carolina as a Civil War battleground, 1861-1865. Raleigh, N.C.: State Dept. of Archives and History, 1960. viii, 99, [2] p. fold. map, ports., views. bibliog. (p. 101). [3807

MARK MAYO BOATNER III. The Civil War dictionary. Maps and diagrams by Allen C. Northrop and Lowell I. Miller. N.Y.: D. McKay Co. [1959]. xvi, [2], 974 p. maps, plans. bibliog. (p. 970-74). A single alphabet of individuals, operations, organizations, weapons, tactics and strategy, "political issues," terminology, etc. [3808

BRUCE CATTON. Glory road began in the West. Civil War hist., 6:229-37 (Sep). Argument that Northern success in the Civil War began in Missouri and that "The final doom of the Confederacy was written in the west rather than in the east." [3809

BRUCE CATTON. The tragic structure of the Civil War. Thought, 35: 5-15 (spring). [3810

RAY CHARLES COLTON. The Civil War in the Western Territories: Arizona, Colorado, New Mexico, and Utah. Norman: Univ. of Oklahoma Press [1959. ix, 230 p. facsims., maps, ports., views. bibliog. (p. 210-16), notes. Includes accounts of associated political developments and Indian campaigns. [3811

RICHARD ERNEST DUPUY & TREVOR NEVITT DUPUY. The compact history of the Civil War. N.Y.: Hawthorn Books [1960]. 445 p. maps. bibliog. (p. 427-9). Account "of land and sea power in combination and opposition; of economic and political pressures; and of the interplay between civil and military power." [3812

ROBERT SELPH HENRY. Chattanooga and the War [1861-65]. Tenn. hist. quar., 19:222-30 (Sep). On Chattanooga, "the solar plexus of transportation in the western South," as "a veritable military magnet, attracting to and toward itself major movements of the armies of both North and South." [3813

INDIANA. Adjutant General's Office. Indiana in the War of the Rebellion: report of the Adjutant General. A reprint of volume 1 of the eight-volume report prepared by W[illiam] H. H. Terrell [1827-84] and published in 1869. [Indianapolis:] Indiana Historical Bureau, 1960. xii, 603 p. notes. (Indiana historical collections, 41.) Summary of the participation of Indiana in the Civil War. Vols. 2-8 were rosters of Indiana officers and soldiers. [3814

ALLEN W. JONES, comp. Military events in Florida during the Civil War, 1861-1865. Fla. hist. quar., 39:42-5 (Jul). Alphabetical list of 84 places where military events occurred, with dates and identification of events. [3815

ALLEN W. JONES, comp. Military events in Texas during the Civil War, 1861-1865. Southw. hist. quar., 64: 64-70 (Jul). Chronological list, indicating date, place, and "type of event." [3816

ALLEN W. JONES, comp. Military events in West Virginia during the Civil War, 1861-1865. W. Va. hist., 21:186-96 (Apr). List of events at 255 places, indicating type and date of each event. [3817

ROBERT HUHN JONES. The Civil War in the Northwest: Nebraska, Wisconsin, Iowa, Minnesota, and the Dakotas. Norman: Univ. of Oklahoma Press [1960]. xvi, 216 p. maps, ports., views. bibliog. (p. 202-9), notes. [3818

HERBERT KAHLER. The commemoration of the Civil War. Vt. hist., 28: 281-7 (Oct). Mainly on work of the Federal Civil War Centennial Commission and the National Park Service. [3819

JOE KLASSEN. The Civil War in Kansas City [1861-65]. Mo. Hist. Soc., Bul., 16:134-50 (Jan). notes. [3820

FRANCIS ALFRED LORD. They fought for the Union. Harrisburg, Pa.: Stackpole Co. [1960. 14], 375 p. diagrs., facsims., col. flags, insignia, map, ports., tables, views (part col.). bibliog. (p. 353-65), notes. Mainly "a description of the Federal soldier, sailor, and marine, and the material things which were furnished for life in camp, in the field, and at sea." Includes a list of "Manuals and training literature" (p. 39-52). [3821

JAY LUVAAS. The military legacy of the Civil War: the European inheritance. [Chicago:] Univ. of Chicago Press [1959]. xi, 252 p. ports., views. notes. On "the reasons why European soldiers have studied and written about the Civil War and what military lessons they have learned--or thought they could learn--from it"; with particular reference to English observers (1861-86), German observers (1861-1914), and French observers (1861-1914), a chapter on Capt. George Francis Robert Henderson, and a chapter on studies since World War I. [3822

JOHN G. MOORE. Mobility and strategy in the Civil War. Mil. affairs, 24:68-77 (summer). tables. notes. [3823

RALPH GEOFFREY NEWMAN & EVERETTE B. LONG, eds. The Civil War digest. N.Y.: Grosset & Dunlap [1960]. xiii, [1], 274 p. facsims., maps, ports., views (part double). bibliog. (p. 255-70). 1st ed. 1956. "Day by day, month to month, year to year" chronology of the Civil War" (p. 1-52); maps and views (p. 53-161); biographical sketches of officers (p. 174-238); reproductions of documents (p. 243-54); and "The war in books" (p. 255-70). [3824

ROBERT LOVE PARTIN. The sustaining faith of an Alabama soldier. Civil War hist., 6:425-38 (Dec). Notes. On references to religion in the letters of Hiram Talbert Holt, "a praying soldier" in Alabama Confederate forces, 1861-64. [3825

ESTELLE (SMITH) RIZK. No more muffled hoofbeats. Phila.: Dorrance [1960]. vii, [5], 80 p. map. On the Civil War in Carter County, Ky., 1861-65. [3826

ELEANOR LEE (READING) TEMPLEMAN. In the beginning. Arlington hist. mag., 1(4):43-9. port., views. On early Civil War events in and near Arlington County, May-Jun. 1861. [3827

TENNESSEE. Civil War Centennial Commission. Guide to the Civil War in Tennessee. Nashville: Division of Information, Dept. of Conservation, 1960. 32 p. col. fold. map, views (part col.). Includes a list of "Highway markers, monuments, monuments, and descriptive plaques dealing with the Civil War in Tennessee" and "Chronological synopsis of events of the Civil War in Tennessee," 9 Feb. 1861 - 28 Dec. 1864. [3828

U.S. War Dept. The official atlas of the Civil War. Introduction by Henry Steele Commager. N.Y.: T. Yoseloff [1958. 8] p., facsim. (29 p., 175 plates incl. col. flags, maps (part col.), plans, views (part col.)). 45 cm. Reproduction, slightly reduced, of Atlas to accompany the official records of the Union and Confederate Armies ... compiled by Capt. Calvin D. Cowles (Wash.: U.S. Govt. Print. Off., 3 v., 1891-95). [3829

IRVING WERSTEIN. 1861-1865: the adventure of the Civil War told with pictures. Paterson, N.J.: Pageant Books, 1960. 128 p. diagrs., facsims., maps, ports., views (part double).

Reproductions of contemporary prints and photographs. [3830

FREDERICK DE FORREST WILLIAMS. Michigan soldiers in the Civil War. Mich. hist., 44:1-35 (Mar). map. Printed separately: Michigan soldiers in the Civil War. Lansing: Michigan Historical Commission, 1960. vii, 43, [1] p. map, ports., views. bibliog. (p. 42-3). (John M. Munson Michigan History Fund. Pamphlet 2.) On their activities in combat and their life and state of mind in camp. [3831

THOMAS HARRY WILLIAMS. The military leadership of the North and the South [1861-65]. Colorado: U.S. Air Force Academy, 1960. [6], 23 p. port. (The Harmon memorial lectures in military history, 2.) Also printed: David Donald, ed., Why the North won the Civil War ([Baton Rouge:] Louisiana State Univ. Press [1960]), p. 23-47. [3832

WALTER BIRKBECK WOOD & SIR JAMES EDWARD EDMONDS. Military history of the Civil War, with special reference to the campaigns of 1864 and 1865. N.Y.: Putnam [1960]. xix, 328, [3] p. maps (part double). (Capricorn books, CAP29.) 1st ed. 1905; here reprinted from 1937 ed. A British study of the War. [3833

CHESTER M. OEHLER. The great Sioux uprising [1862]. N.Y.: Oxford Univ. Press, 1959. xvi, 272 p. maps, ports., views. bibliog. (p. 243-6), notes (p. 247-67). [3834

FELIPE MARTÍNEZ ARANGO. Cronología crítica de la guerra hispano-cubanoamericana [1898. Segunda edición.] Santiago de Cuba: Departamento de Extensión y Relaciones Culturales, Univ. de Oriente [1960]. 203, [7] p. map, port., views. bibliog. (p. 197-9), notes. (Publicaciones de la Universidad de Oriente. Libros, 13.) 1st ed. 1950. Appended (p. 137-95): documents relating to the war in Cuba. [3835

MORRIS JANOWITZ. The professional soldier: a social and political portrait. Glencoe, Ill.: Free Press [1960]. xiv, 464 p. tables. notes. On "the professional life, organizational setting, and leadership of the American military as they have evolved during the first half of this century." [3836

WILLIAM WILMON NEWCOMB, JR. Toward an understanding of war. Gertrude E. Dole & Robert L. Carneiro, eds., Essays in the science of culture, in honor of Leslie A. White (N.Y.: Crowell [1960]), p. 317-36. bibliog., notes. On reasons why in the 20th century "anthropologists have contributed so little to the understanding of warfare." [3837

U.S. Military Academy, West Point. Dept. of Military Art and Engineering. The West Point atlas of American wars. Volume II. 1900-1953. Chief Editor: Colonel Vincent J. Esposito. N.Y.: Praeger [1959]. xi, [517] p. incl. 254 maps. bibliog. (p. [507-17]). Contains 71 maps of World War I, 168 of World War II, and 15 of the Korean War, with text facing each map. [3838

EUGENE MORLOCK EMME. Technical change and Western military thought--1914-1945. Mil. affairs, 24:6-19 (spring). notes. [3839

LEWIS FRY RICHARDSON (1881-1953). Arms and insecurity ... a mathematical study of the causes and origins of war [1914-39]. Edited by Nicolas Rashevsky and Ernesto Trucco. Pittsburgh: Boxwood Press [1960]. xxv, 307 p. diagrs., port., tables. bibliogs., notes. A British study, with attention centered on Europe but many references to the United States, in the form of a dialogue with demonstrations from calculus. [3840

BERNADOTTE EVERLY SCHMITT. The War: twenty years after, 1914-1934. Bernadotte E. Schmitt, The fashion and future of history: historical studies and addresses (Cleveland: Press of Western Reserve Univ., 1960), p. 129-50. Address (1 Aug. 1934) on "the origins of the war and its lessons." [3841

BERNADOTTE EVERLY SCHMITT. The United States on the verge of World War II. Bernadotte E. Schmitt, The fashion and future of history: historical studies and addresses (Cleveland: Press of Western Reserve Univ., 1960), p. 165-82. Address (29 Apr. 1941) on the causes of World War II since 1919. [3842

STETSON CONN & BYRON FAIRCHILD. The Western Hemisphere: the framework of hemisphere defense. Wash.: Office of the Chief of Military History, Dept. of the Army, 1960. xv, 470 p. fold. col. map (in pocket). bibliog. (p. 425-30), notes. (United States Army in World War II: The Western Hemisphere.) On "the plans made and measures taken by the Army to protect the United States and the rest of the Western Hemisphere against military attack by the Axis Powers before and during World War II," 1939-45, with particular reference to military relations with Canada and Latin America. [3843

KENT ROBERTS GREENFIELD. Introductory essay. Kent Roberts Greenfield, ed., Command decisions (Wash.: Office of the Chief of Military History, Dept. of the Army, 1960), p. 1-9. col. fold. maps. notes. Introduces a volume of "studies ... extracted from the work of authors writing the history of World War II" and representing "the historical approach to the subject of decision in war." [3844

ROBERT C. RICHARDSON III. The stalemate in concepts. Air Univ. quar. rev., 12(2):2-13 (summer). double diagr. On changes in "security planning" for American military forces since ca. 1939. [3845

MARY H. WILLIAMS, comp. Chronology, 1941-1945. Wash.: Office of the Chief of Military History, Dept. of the Army, 1960. [12], 660 p. (United States Army in World War II: Special studies.) Chronological list of events in which the U.S. Army was concerned, 7 Dec. 1941 - 2 Sep. 1945. [3846

CARL H. COGGINS. Bacterial and chemical warfare: the current status [1943-60]. Calif. med., 93:82-5 (Aug). notes. [3847

RILEY SUNDERLAND. The secret embargo. Pac. hist. rev., 29:75-80 (Feb). notes. On an order from Chiang Kai-shek prohibiting shipment of arms to the Chinese forces trying to defend airfields in east China used by the planes of Maj. Gen. Claire L. Chennault, 1944, and the reason why Gen. Joseph W. Stilwell concealed the order from his superiors and why "he went silent to the grave." [3848

ARTHUR C. AGAN, JR. Aerospace defense [in America, 1945-60]. Air Univ. quar. rev., 12(3-4):89-103 (winter-spring). diagrs. (1 double), map, tables, views. [3849

FREDERIC H. SMITH, JR. Nuclear weapons and limited war. Air Univ. quar. rev., 12(1):3-27 (spring). diagrs. (1 double). On "historical situations favoring nuclear firepower" by American forces in World War II and the Korean War, 1945-51, and situations in which it might now be used in a rain forest, a deep valley, a mangrove forest, a "karst redoubt area," and a "mountain defile." [3850

NOEL F. PARRISH. Effective aerospace power. 1. Deterrence: the hard questions. Air Univ. quar. rev., 12(3-4):148-52 (winter-spring). On the development of the concept of military deterrence in America, 1946-60. [3851

Military Biography

CHARLES WILLIAM HEATHCOTE. General James Potter [1729-89]--a resolute Pennsylvania officer and friend of Washington. Picket post, 68:13-18 (May). [3852

LOUISE E. KOIER. "Long Tom" joins a comrade. Vt. Hist. Soc., News and notes, 5:9-11 (Oct 1953). On Remember Baker (1740?-1775), his service in Connecticut and Vermont forces, 1756-75, his death in action, and the recent acquisition of his gun by the Vermont Historical Society. [3853

CHARLES WILLIAM HEATHCOTE. General John Cadwallader [1742-86]--a sturdy Pennsylvania military officer and devoted to General Washington. Picket post, 70:4-9, 28 (Nov). port. [3854

THEODORE GEORGE THAYER. Nathanael Greene [1742-86]: strategist of the American Revolution. N.Y.: Twayne Publishers, 1960. 500 p. maps. bibliog. (p. 477-86), notes (p. 447-76. On his early life and business activities in Rhode Island, his service as an officer in the American Revolution (mainly in the South), and his life as a planter in South Carolina and Georgia. [3855

CHARLES WILLIAM HEATHCOTE. General Edward Hand [1744-1802]--a capable Pennsylvania military officer and colleague of Washington. Picket post, 69:14-22 (Jul). port., views. [3856

CHARLES WILLIAM HEATHCOTE. General William Irvine [1744-1804]--a trusted Pennsylvania officer and friend of Washington. Picket post, 67;6-14 (Feb). port., views. [3857

EDWARD ELLSBERG. "... just what this country needed." John Arthur Garraty, ed., The unforgettable Americans (Great Neck, N.Y.: Channel

Press [1960]), p. 81-5. On John Paul Jones (1747-92) as an officer in the U.S. Navy, 1775 ff. [3858

ROBERT DE LA CROIX. Paul Jones, le loup des océans. Paris: A. Fayard [1960]. 220, [3] p. (En flèche.) On the maritime and naval career of John Paul Jones (1747-92), with particular attention to his adventures in Europe. [3859

H. NORTH CALLAHAN. Henry Knox [1750-1806]: General Washington's general. N.Y. Hist. Soc. quar., 44: 150-65 (Apr). ports., views. On his Army career, 1775-83, and his service in Washington's cabinet as Secretary of War. [3860

H. NORTH CALLAHAN. Henry Knox [1750-1806]--his part in the American Revolution, 1775 to 1784. Ann Arbor: University Microfilms, 1956 [i.e. 1960]. Positive microfilm of typescript. [455] leaves. Thesis--New York Univ. Abstracted: Dissert. abstracts, 21:28 (Jul). [3861

CHARLES MALCOLM BROOKFIELD GILMAN. Mary Ludwig (Capt. Molly Pitcher), Huguenot, heroine of the American Revolution. D. A. R. mag., 94:425-6, 468 (Jun-Jul). On Mary (Ludwig) Hays McKolly (1754-1822), often confused with Margaret (Cochran) Corbin (1751-1800?), both called Captain Molly, both of whom distinguished themselves in the Battle of Monmouth. [3862

WALTER EDWIN HAVIGHURST. "... a man in buckskin." John Arthur Garraty, ed., The unforgettable Americans (Great Neck, N.Y.: Channel Press [1960]), p. 87-90. On the life of George Rogers Clark (1753-1818) in Virginia, western Maryland, West Virginia, and Kentucky, and his service, poorly rewarded, during the Revolution. [3863

KEMP MALONE. "... the greatest Indian fighter of them all." John Arthur Garraty, ed., The unforgettable Americans (Great Neck, N.Y.: Channel Press [1960]), p. 47-50. On Henry Bouquet (1719-65), native of Switzerland, colonel and general in the British Army, and his services against the French and the Indians in Pennsylvania, 1758-64. [3864

GEORGE ATHAN BILLIAS. General John Glover [1732-97] and his Marblehead mariners. N.Y.: Holt [1960. 2], xii, 243 p. maps, ports., views. notes (p. 202-36). On his command of "a regiment of Marblehead fishermen," a "soldier-sailor contingent" or "amphibious regiment" (the 21st Regiment in the Continental Army, redesignated as the 14th), his service in ferrying Washington's forces across the ice-strewn Delaware, and his later command of the 2d Massachusetts Brigade and other units in Rhode Island, Apr. 1775 - Jul. 1782; with some account of his early life in Salem, Mass., his work as a shoemaker and later a shipowner and merchant in Marblehead, and the service of his firm in outfitting ships for the American Navy during the Revolution. [3865

AMANDUS JOHNSON. Swedish officers in the American Revolution. Am. Swed. Hist. Found., Yr. bk., 1957, p. 33-9. [3866

PERRY EUGENE LE ROY. Sir Guy Carleton as a military leader during the American invasion and repulse in Canada, 1775-1776. Ann Arbor: University Microfilms, 1960. Positive microfilm of typescript. [687] leaves. Thesis--Ohio State Univ. Abstracted: Dissert. abstracts, 21:1176-7 (Nov). [3867

ALBERT W. HAARMANN. General Armand and his Partisan Corps, 1777-1783. Mil. collector & historian, 12:97-102 (winter). port. notes. On Brig. Gen. Charles Tuffin Armand, Marquis de la Rouerie (born 1756), French officer in the American Army under the name Charles Armand, 1777-84. [3868

CORNEL ADAM LENGYEL. I, Benedict Arnold [1741-1801]: the anatomy of treason. Garden City, N.Y.: Doubleday, 1960. 236 p. maps, ports. bibliog. (p. 220-22), notes (p. 223-31). On his ambiguous conduct in the American Army and his defection to the British Army, May 1778 - Sep. 1781, and his unprosperous later years in England. [3869

JOSEPH A. WYRTWAL. Memorials to General Casimir Pulaski [1748-79] in the United States. Ga. hist. quar., 44: 245-62 (Sep). notes. On his death in action at Savannah, and the "fortresses, statues, parks, schools, counties, and streets," highways, paintings, plaques and tablets, towns, and "hundreds of sports, social, civic and veteran groups throughout the country" that bear and commemorate his name, a symbol of the Polish people. [3870

LOUISE E. KOIER. A November journey: Vermont's debt to Capt. Justus Sherwood. Vt. Hist. Soc., News and notes, 6:17-20 (Nov 1954). views. On his service as a Loyalist agent from Canada in "secret conversations with Ethan and Ira Allen" (whom he had known before his expulsion from Vermont), 1780, and his erection of a blockhouse on North Hero Island in Lake Champlain in 1781. [3871

AMANDUS JOHNSON. John Paul Jones and the Swedes [1788-89]. Am. Swed. Hist. Found., Yr. bk., 1959, p. 40-46. [3872

ROBERT EDWARD LEE, JR. (1843-1914). My father, General Lee: a new edition of Recollections and letters of General Robert E. Lee [1807-70], by his son Robert E. Lee, Jr. With a new introduction and Lee chronology by Philip Van Doren Stern. Garden City, N.Y.: Doubleday, 1960. xxv, 453, [22] p. facsims., ports., views. 1st ed. 1904. [3873

THOMAS CHALMERS McCORVEY (1851-1932). Raphael Semmes [1809-77] and the Confederate Navy. T. C. McCorvey, Alabama historical sketches, ed. George Burke Johnston (Charlottesville: Univ. of Virginia Press, 1960), p. 117-35. notes. Unpublished lecture, 16 Jun. 1913. On his service in the U.S. Navy and the C.S. Navy, 1826-65; with some account of his earlier and later life. [3874

TOM HENDERSON WELLS. Commodore Moore and the Texas Navy. Austin: Univ. of Texas Press [1960. 14], 218 p. facsims., flags., medals, port., tables, views. bibliog. (p. 193-203), notes. On the service of Edwin Ward Moore (1811-65) as "the commanding officer of the Texas Navy," 1839-45, ending with his court-martial and discharge from the Navy at the instance of Sam Houston, President of the Texas Republic; with some account of his early life in Alexandria, Va., his studies at the U.S. Naval Academy, his service in the U.S. Navy, and his later years as a businessman in Washington, D.C. [3875

HARWOOD PERRY HINTON. The military career of John Ellis Wool [in the War of 1812, the Mexican War, and the Civil War, and in peacetime Army duties], 1812-1863. Ann Arbor: University Microfilms, 1960. Positive microfilm of typescript. [471] leaves. Thesis--Univ. of Wisconsin. Abstracted: Dissert. abstracts, 21: 1536-7 (Dec). [3876

FREEMAN CLEAVES. Meade of Gettysburg. Norman: Univ. of Oklahoma Press [1960]. xi, 384, [1] p. facsims., maps, ports., views. bibliog. (p. 359-68), notes. On the service of George Gordon Meade (1815-72) as an officer of the U.S. Army, 1835-72; with some account of his early life in Spain and Baltimore. [3877

RICHARD KEITH McMASTER. Washington slept here. Password, 5:148-9 (Oct). On Col. John Macrae Washington (died 1853), son of a second cousin of George Washington, commissioned in the Army in 1817, Artillery officer, who passed through El Paso in 1848 and was appointed Governor of New Mexico. [3878

THOMAS HARRY WILLIAMS. "... the South's first hero." John Arthur Garraty, ed., The unforgettable Americans (Great Neck, N.Y.: Channel Press [1960]), p. 213-17. On Pierre Gustave Toutant Beauregard (1818-93), native of Louisiana, graduate of the U.S. Military Academy, officer in the U.S. Army during the Mexican War, Confederate general, later a railroad executive and an agent of the Louisiana Lottery. [3879

EDWARD JAY NICHOLS. The military record of General John F[ulton] Reynolds [1820-63]. Lancaster Co. Hist. Soc., Jour., 63:113-27 (Jul 1959). port., views. notes. [3880

ANDREW NELSON LYTLE. Bedford Forrest and his critter company. ... Revised edition with an introduction by the author. N.Y.: McDowell, Obolensky [1960]. xvii, 402 p. port. bibliog. (p. 393-6). 1st ed. 1931. On the life of Nathan Bedford Forrest (1821-77) in Mississippi and as a planter in Tennessee, his service as an officer of the C.S. Army, and his activities after the Civil War as a leader of the Ku Klux Klan. [3881

JOHN ALLAN WYETH (1845-1922). That devil Forrest: life of General Nathan Bedford Forrest [1821-77]. Foreword by Henry Steele Commager. N.Y.: Harper [1959]. xxvi, 614 p. maps (1 fold. col.), ports., views. 1st ed. 1899. On his activities in the C.S. Army, 1861-65; with a brief account of his earlier and later life. [3882

HAVILAND HARRIS ABBOT. General John D[aniel] Imboden [1823-95]. W. Va. hist, 21:88-122 (Jan). port. notes. On his service in the C.S. Army, 1861-65; with some account of early years as a lawyer in Staunton and of his activity after the Civil War in developing a coal industry in southwestern Virginia and adjacent West Virginia. [3883

GLENN TUCKER. Hancock the Superb. Indianapolis: Bobbs-Merrill [1960]. 368 p. facsim., maps, ports. bibliog. (p. 343-53), notes (p. 315-41). On Winfield Scott Hancock (1824-86), his early life in Norristown, Pa., his studies at the U.S. Military Academy, his service as an Army officer, especially during the Mexican War and the Civil War, and his activities in national politics. [3884

MELVILLE JAMES BOYER. "Swords and cannon balls don't all." Lehigh Co. Hist. Soc., Proc., 23:60-67. view. On Col. Tilghman H. Good (1830-87) and Maj. Thomas Yeager (1825-62), "both Allentonians and heroes of the Civil War." [3885

LORINE LETCHER BUTLER. John Morgan and his men. Phila.: Dorrance [1960]. 357 p. port., views. bibliog. (p. 338-41). On the service of John Hunt Morgan (1825-64) as an officer in the C.S. Army, 1861-64; with some account of his early life in Lexington, Ky., his studies in Transylvania University, and his service in the U.S. Army in the Mexican War. [3886

JACOB MOGELEVER. Death to traitors: the story of General Lafayette C[harles] Baker [1826-68], Lincoln's forgotten Secret Service chief. Garden City, N.Y.: Doubleday, 1960. 429 p. facsim., ports. bibliog. (p. 421-9). On his early life in Stafford, N.Y., his voyage from New York to San Francisco and membership in the vigilante organization there, his work in Washington as a Union detective and in the South as a Union spy, and his establishment and administration of the Secret Service. [3887

FRANK HARRISON CUNNINGHAM. Knight of the Confederacy, Gen. Turner Ashby [1828-62]. San Antonio: Naylor [1960]. xvi, 225 p. facsims., col. flags, ports., views. bibliog. (p. 195-202). On his life as a planter in Fauquier County, Va., and his command of the Seventh Virginia Cavalry, C.S.A. [3888

ROBERT GERALD McMURTRY. Confederate General Ben Hardin Helm: Kentucky brother-in-law of Abraham Lincoln. A condensation of the original study. [Madison, Wis.] 1959. 18, [1] p. ports. (Lincoln Fellowship of Wisconsin. Historical bulletin 17.) Original published 1943. On the career of Benjamin Hardin Helm (1830-63), Kentuckian, as an officer of the U.S. and C.S. Armies; with some account of his wife, Emilie Paret (Todd) Helm (died 1930), sister of Mary (Todd) Lincoln. [3889

RUTH ELAINE (PAINTER) RANDALL. Colonel Elmer Ellsworth: a biography of Lincoln's friend and first hero of the Civil War. Boston: Little, Brown [1960]. xviii, [2], 295 p. facsim., flag, ports., views. bibliog. (p. 277-86). On Ephraim Elmer Ellsworth (1837-61), his early life in Malta and Mechanicsville, N.Y., his removal to Chicago in 1854, his work as a copier of documents while studying law, his volunteer labors as a gymnastic trainer of the Chicago Cadets and the Rockford City Grays, his command of Lincoln's escort to Washington in 1861 and of the Zouave Cadets (redesignated as the 11th New York Regiment), and his death in Alexandria while tearing down a Confederate flag, "the first conspicuous death" of the Civil War. Based largely upon his diary and upon about a hundred of his letters to his fiancée (Carrie Spofford). [3890

REYNOLD M. WIK. Captain Nathaniel Wyche Hunter [1810-49] and the Florida Indian campaigns, 1837-1841. Fla. hist. quar., 39:62-75 (Jul). notes. Topical summary of information in his diary and letters. [3891

WILLIAM WOODS HASSLER. Colonel John Pelham [1838-63]: Lee's boy artillerist. Richmond: Garrett & Massie [1960]. 185, [1] p. diagrs., maps, ports., views. bibliog. (p. 179). On his early life in Alabama, his studies at the U.S. Military Academy, his service as an officer of the C.S. Army, and his death in action. [3892

MERRILL J. MATTES. Indians, infants, and infantry: Andrew and Elizabeth Burt on the frontier. Denver: Old West Pub. Co., 1960. [8], 304 p. facsim., maps, ports., table, views. notes (p. 275-301). On Andrew Sheridan Burt (1839-1915) and his wife, Elizabeth Johnston (Reynolds) Burt (born 1839), and his service as an Army major at Fort Bridger, Fort C.F. Smith, Fort Russell, Fort Sanders, Omaha, and Fort Laramie, in Nebraska, Wyoming, and Montana, and in Indian campaigns in thse States and in Colorado, Utah, and Nevada, 1866-76; with some account of his service as a Union officer in the Civil War, a chapter on his Army career from 1876 till his retirement as a brigadier general in

1902, and long excerpts from the manuscript reminiscences (1912) of his wife. [3893

SYLVIA G. L. DANNETT. She rode with the generals: the true and incredible story of Sarah Emma Seelye, alias Franklin Thompson. N.Y.: T. Nelson [1960]. 326 p. ports. bibliog. (p. 308-16), notes (p. 301-7). On Sarah Emma Evelyn (Edmonson or Edmundson) Seelye (1841-98), her early life in rural New Brunswick as a "boyish girl," her flight from home "to gain independence from her father," her wanderings in New England and Michigan as a Bible salesman disguised as a young man named Edmonds, her enlistment in the 2d Michigan Volunteer Infantry as "Franklin Thompson," her desertion to serve as a Union spy, her service (as a woman) in nursing in Army hospitals, her Nurse and spy of the Union Army--comprising the adventures and experiences of a woman in hospitals, camps, and battlefields (Hartford, 1864), her marriage after the war to Linus Seelye, their life in La Porte, Tex., and her clearance from the charge of desertion by act of Congress in 1886. [3894

BOYCE HOUSE (1896-1961). Confederate Navy hero put the flag back in place! Tenn. hist. quar., 19:172-5 (Jun). On Capt. Dabney M. Scales (1842-1920) of the C.S. Navy and his daring conduct while a midshipman on the CSS Arkansas at the siege of Vicksburg, 15 Jul. 1862. [3895

PAUL JOSEPH SCHEIPS. Private Lane's gold medal. Mil. affairs, 24: 87-91 (summer). notes. Biographical sketch of Morgan D. Lane (born "sometime in the mid-1840's," died 1892), Army private from 1862 to 1865, ultimately in the Signal Corps, granted the Medal of Honor in 1866. [3896

DANIEL JACKSON. Henry Wirz (1822-65). New Eng. jour. med., 262: 31-3 (7 Jan). port. notes. On his early life and medical studies in Switzerland, France, and Germany, his emigration in 1849, his work as a physician in Massachusetts, Kentucky, and Louisiana, his service as a Confederate officer, his command of Camp Sumter (Andersonville, Ga., prison camp), and his execution after trial and conviction by a military court which held him responsible for the atrocities of Andersonville. [3897

DARRETT BRUCE RUTMAN. The war crimes and trial of Henry Wirz [1822-65]. Civil War hist., 6:117-33 (Jun). ports., views. notes. On his command (as a captain in the C.S. Army) of Camp Sumner, the prison camp at Andersonville, Ga., and his trial and execution by a Federal military court, 1864-65; with some account of his early life in Switzerland, his emigration in 1849, and his medical practice in Kentucky and Louisiana, and a detailed demonstration of the unfairness of his trial. [3898

DONALD BERT RUSSELL. Buffalo Bill's greatest show. Westerners brand book (Chicago), 17:57-9, 63-4 (Oct). On the military service with which William F. Cody is credited in official records, 1857-76, 1891, and the quite different careers attributed to him in some 1,700 novels between 1869 and 1932; and the stages of development of the quite erroneous belief, expressed as early as 1928, that he is mainly a creation of Ned Buntline. [3899

ARMY TIMES, Washington, D.C. The Yanks are coming: the story of General John J[oseph] Pershing [1860-1948]. N.Y.: Putnam [1960]. 182 p. facsims., insignia, ports., views (part double). bibliog. (p. 177-82). [3900

R. SHEPARD BROWN. Stringfellow of the Fourth. N.Y.: Crown Publishers [1960. 10], 307 p. map, ports., views. notes (p. 294-9). On the service of Benjamin Franklin Stringfellow (1840-1913), commonly known as Frank Stringfellow, in the 4th Virginia Cavalry, C.S. Army, 1861-65. Fictional in form. [3901

BRUCE CATTON. Grant moves south [1861-63]. Boston: Little, Brown [1960]. x, [2], 564 p. maps, port. bibliog. (p. 539-47), notes (p. 491-538). On his movements from the beginning of the Civil War to the end of the Vicksburg campaign. Continues Lloyd Lewis's Captain Sam Grant. [3902

HOLMAN D. JORDAN. The military career of Henry D[e Lamar] Clayton [officer in the C.S. Army, 1861-65]. Ala. rev., 13:127-34 (Apr). notes. [3903

EDWARD JAMES STACKPOLE. Generalship in the Civil War. Mil. affairs, 24:57-67 (summer). Evaluation of 7 generals in terms of 9 "principles of war." [3904

EZRA J. WARNER. Generals in gray: lives of the Confederate commanders [Baton Rouge:] Louisiana State Univ. Press [1959]. xxvii, 420 p. ports. bibliog. (p. 401-20), notes (p. 361-400). Biographical dictionary of the 425 general officers of the C.S. Army, with a portrait of each. [3905

ALFRED NEWTON WOLVERTON. Dr. Newton Wolverton [1846-1932]: an intimate anecdotal biography of one of the most colorful characters in Canadian history. [n. p., 195-. 2], 96 p. geneal. chart, ports. Includes some account of the Union Army service of Alfred, Jasper, Alonzo, and Newton Wolverton, brothers, 1861-63. [3906

J. GARNAND HAMILTON. The saga of Major Charles G. Chandler. Gun rep., 5(1):22-6 (Jun 1959). views. On his service in the 10th Vermont Volunteer Infantry, 1862-64, ending with dismissal after a court martial; with evidence that its verdict was not justified by the findings. [3907

SUZANNE (COLTON) WILSON. Column south: with the Fifteenth Pennsylvania Cavalry from Antietam to the capture of Jefferson Davis. ... Edited by J. Ferrell Colton and Antoinette G. Smith. Flagstaff [Ariz.]: J. F. Colton, 1960. [6], xxi, 389, 25 p. facsim., maps (part fold.), medal, ports., views. bibliog. (p. 388-9), notes (p. 372-87). On the service of Matthias Baldwin Colton (1839-1915) and William Francis Colton (1841-1921), brothers, 1862-65; with excerpts from their diaries, their letters to their family, and the letters received by them. [3908

JAMES M. FRY. The death of John Hunt Morgan [4 Sep. 1864]: a memoir of James M. Fry. Edited by W. A. Smith and Wallace Milam. Tenn. hist. quar., 19:54-63 (Mar). notes. Excerpts from the author's pamphlet, The death of General John H. Morgan and what led up to it, by an East Tennessee Confederate scout (Wills Point, Tex.: Chronicle Office [1905?], on the mystery of how the Federals learned the location of the Confederates before the action in which Morgan was shot and the question whether he was killed after surrendering. [3909

WILBUR G. KURTZ. The death of Major General W. H. T. Walker [at the beginning of the Battle of Atlanta], July 22, 1864. Civil War hist., 6:174-9 (Jun). map, views. [3910

MARTHA SUMMERHAYES (1846-1911). Vanished Arizona: recollections of the Army life of a New England woman. ... Historical introduction, glossary, and bibliographical notes by Ray Brandes. Fourth edition. Tucson: Arizona Silhouettes, 1960. [4], xvi, [2], 273 p. cartoons, col. maps, ports., views. notes (p. 240-73). 1st ed. 1908. On the author's life at Army posts in Arizona with her husband, Maj. John Summerhayes (1835-1911), 1874-78, and later in Nebraska, New Mexico, and Texas till his retirement in 1899; with a brief account of her early years in Nantucket, her education in Germany, and their life after 1899 in New York State. [3911

PEGGY (HASKELL) BENJAMIN. The last of Captain Jack. Montana, 10(2): 22-30 (Apr). ports., views. On a "subchief" of the Utes, leader in their protests against the despotic regime of Indian Agent Nathan Cook Meeker in the White River Reservation in Colorado and, when the protests were ignored, in a sanguinary rebellion in 1879, and his death in Wyoming as a fugitive in 1880. [3912

FORREST C. POGUE. A tribute to General George C[atlett] Marshall [1880-1959]. Pa. hist., 27:136-43 (Apr). ports. [3913

WILLIAM W. CHAFFIN. John Warwick Daniel's speech honoring Robert E. Lee, Lexington, Virginia, 1883. South. speech jour., 25:305-13 (summer). [3914

D. HARPER SIMMS. The Apache scouts who won a war. The Westerners, Potomac Corral, Great Western Indian fights (Garden City, N.Y.: Doubleday, 1960), p. 257-65. map, port., views. bibliog. On the service of Kayitah and Martine, Chiricahua Apache Indian scouts, with the Fourth Cavalry under Gen. George Crook in action against the Apache Indian uprisings in New Mexico and Arizona and in negotiating the surrender of Geronimo, May-Sep. 1885. [3915

MABEL EVELYN DEUTRICH. Fred C. Ainsworth: Army surgeon and administrator. Ann Arbor: University Microfilms, 1960. Positive microfilm of typescript. [368] leaves. Thesis--American Univ. Abstracted: Dissert. abstracts, 21:667 (Sep). On his activities in Washington in reorganizing the medical and military records of soldiers, and his other administrative accomplishments as chief of the Record and Pension Office and as Adjutant General, 1886-1912. [3916

JOHN D. HAYES. Dudley W. Knox, 1887-1960: an appreciation. Mil. affairs, 24:150-51 (fall). Also printed: U.S.N. Inst. proc., 86(11):103-5 (Nov). On his career as an officer of the U.S. Navy. [3917

[CHARLES Morgan, 1866-1959.] West Tenn. Hist. Soc. papers, 14:133-5. On "Gunner" Morgan, "the first enlisted man ever to receive a commission in the United States Navy," who enlisted in 1882 and was promoted to Chief Gunner (a commissioned rank) in 1901 in spite of the firm disapproval of Rear Adm. W. T. Sampson, and later promoted to Lieutenant Commander. [3918

CHARLES WEST. Colonel Harry C. Larter, Jr. [1902-60]. Mil. collector & historian, 12:86-7 (fall). On his service in the U.S. Army, 1925-50, and his contributions to military painting and museum management. [3919

HE educates air cadets. Old Oregon, 36(18):7, 28 (Nov-Dec 1955). port. On Brig. Gen. Don Z. Zimmerman (born 1903), his early life in Eugene, Ore., his studies at the University of Oregon and the U.S. Military Academy, and his service as an officer in the U.S. Army and the U.S. Air Force. [3920

EDITH A. AYNES. Colonel Florence A. Blanchfield. Nursing outlook, 7:78-81 (Feb 1959). ports. On her work as a nurse in Pittsburgh and the Canal Zone, 1908-20, and in the Army Nurse Corps (of which she was eventually the commander), 1920-47; with some account of her early life in West Virginia and her studies in Southside Hospital, Pittsburgh, and in Johns Hopkins Hospital. [3921

GEORGE CHURCHILL KENNEY. Dick Bong, ace of aces. N.Y.: Duell, Sloan, and Pearce [1960. 12], 116 p. facsim., ports., view. On Richard Ira Bong (1920-45) and his service under the author's command in the U.S. Army Air Forces, mainly in the Pacific, 1942-45. [3922

IRVING McKEE. Captain Edward Howe Watson [1874-1942] and the Honda disaster. Pac. hist. rev., 29:287-305 (Aug). notes. On the extent of his responsibility for the stranding of 7 destroyers of the U.S. Navy at Pedernales Point, Calif., "locally known as Point Honda," 8 Sep. 1923. Includes new information from the Watson Papers. [3923

PERSONAL NARRATIVES

DANIEL MORISON. The doctor's secret journal. By Daniel Morison, surgeon's mate. Edited by George S[mith] May. Mackinac Island: Fort Mackinac Division Press, 1960. 47 p. facsims. Diary kept during the author's service with the 2d Battalion, Royal American Regiment, at Fort Michilimackinac, 7 Nov. 1769 - 2 Jul. 1772. Mainly a record and catalogue of the villainous actions of Ensign Robert Johnson (or Johnstone) and Capt. George Turnbull. [3924

ROBERT McCREADY (1752-1846). A Revolutionary journal and orderly book of General Lachlan McIntosh's expedition, 1778. Edited by Edward G. Williams. West. Pa. hist. mag., 43: 1-17, 157-77, 267-88 (Mar-Sep). facsim., map. notes. Diary, 4-20 Nov. 1778, and orderly book, 17 Oct. - 8 Dec. 1778, kept by the adjutant of Col. John Stephenson's Regiment in movements from Fort Pitt to Fort McIntosh (at Beaver, Pa.) and Fort Laurens (site of Bolivar, Ohio). Heavily annotated. Introduction includes new biographical information about McIntosh. [3925

HANS CHRISTOPH FRIEDRICH IGNATZ LUDWIG, BARON VON CLOSEN HAYDENBURG (1752?-1830). The Revolutionary journal of Baron Ludwig von Closen, 1780-1783. Translated and edited with an introduction by Evelyn M. Acomb. Chapel Hill: Univ. of North Carolina Press for the Institute of Early American History and Culture, Williamsburg, Va. [1958]. xxxvi, [4], 392 p. map, ports., views. bibliog. (p. 366-82), notes. Memoirs (ca. 1823) and journal of services and observations of an aide-de-camp to Gen. Jean Baptiste Donatien de Vimeur, Comte de Rochambeau, in Rhode Island, New York, Virginia, and the West Indies, 4 Apr. 1780 - 30 Jun. 1783, illustrated with his drawings and a map by him and including much description of the country and its people. Appended: "Biographical directory" of persons named in the text (p. 339-65). Printed from some of his surviving manuscripts and from a manuscript transcript of an original later lost in a fire. [3926

JOHN CHARLES HUDEN, ed. Frontier dangers, 1781-1784. Part II[-III]. Vt. hist., 28:88-91, 148-51 (Jan, Apr). map. notes. Examination and deposition of Abel Davis of Peacham, Loyalist farmer, by British authorities, 19 Jun. and 14 Jul. 1782, after his capture by Indians; and "A journal of a scout sent from St. John's by order of Colonal [sic] Leger," 8-20 Aug. 1782, by Sgt. Augustus Ilgers, British Army, somewhere in northwestern Vermont. [3927

JUBAL ANDERSON EARLY (1816-94). War memoirs: autobiographical sketch and narrative of the War between the States. ... Edited with an introduction by Frank E. Vandiver. Bloomington: Indiana Univ. Press [1960]. xlviii, 496 p. ports., views. notes. (Civil War centennial series.) 1st ed. 1912. On the author's service in the C.S. Army, 1861-65; with some account of his early life in Franklin County, Va., his studies at the U.S. Military Academy, his service in the U.S. Army in the Seminole War and the Mexican War, his work as a lawyer in Virginia, and his activities in Virginia and national politics. [3928

JAMES LONGSTREET (1821-1904). From Manassas to Appomattox: memoirs of the Civil War in America. ... Edited with an introduction and notes by James I. Robertson, Jr. Bloomington: Indiana Univ. Press [1960]. xxix, [1], 13-692 p. facsims., maps, ports., tables, views. (Civil War centennial series.) 1st ed. 1895. Includes some account of the author's early life in South Carolina, his studies at the U.S. Military Academy, and his service during the Mexican War. Appended (p. 639-58): "Letters of General Robert E. Lee and General Longstreet," 1864-66. [3929

JAMES IREDELL WADDELL (1824-86). C.S.S. Shenandoah: the memoirs of Lieutenant Commanding James I. Waddell. Edited by James D[avid] Horan. N.Y.: Crown Publishers [1960. 6], 200 p. cartoon, facsims., maps, ports., views. bibliog. (p. 199-200), notes. Manuscript reminiscences of the author's early life in North Carolina, his service as an officer of the U.S. and C.S. Navies, and particularly his command of the Confederate cruiser Shenandoah (originally Sea King, built by Stevens and Sons in Glasgow); with an extensive editorial introduction ("A prefatory note about the C.S.S. Shenandoah and other Confederate cruisers," p. 1-51). [3930

GEORGE CROOK (1828-90). General George Crook: his autobiography. Edited and annotated by Martin F. Schmitt. [New edition.] Norman: Univ. of Oklahoma Press [1960]. xx, 326, [1] p. maps, ports., views. bibliog. (p. 310-17), notes. 1st ed. 1946. Unfinished recollections (1885-90), ending in 1876, with a continuation by the editor, of Crook's Army service in northern California, Oregon, and Washington (1848-61, including service in the Rogue River War); as commanding officer of the 36th Ohio Volunteer Infantry in the Civil War; and as commanding officer of the Department of the Columbia (1866-70), the Department of Arizona (1870-75, 1882-86), the Department of the Platte (1875-82, 1886-88), and the Division of the Missouri (1888-90); with excerpts from his letters, reports, and diaries. [3931

CHARLES EDWARD BRIGGS (1833-94). Civil War surgeon in a colored regiment. [Edited by his grandson, Walter De Blois Briggs. Berkeley, Calif., 1960. 14], 166, [1] p. port., table. notes. Letters, notes, and diaries written by Briggs during his studies at Harvard, his service as a physician on the merchant ship Newsboy, his service as assistant surgeon in the 27th and later the 24th Massachusetts Volunteer Infantry (1861-65), and his early years as a physician in St. Louis (1865-69), interspersed with biographical information provided by the editor, including an account of his early life in Boston and his studies in the Harvard Medical School. [3932

ALEXANDER BEAUFORT MEEK (1814-65). The journal of A. B. Meek and the Second Seminole War. 1836. Edited by John K. Mahon. Fla. hist. quar., 38:302-18 (Apr). notes. Record kept by an ensign in the Battalion of Volunteers from Tuscaloosa, 21 Feb.-19 Apr. 1836. [3933

VALERY HAVARD (1846-1927). Personal recollections and military record of Colonel Valery Havard, Medical Corps, U.S. Army. Asa Gray bul., 3:177-92 (spring 1957). port., table. notes. Letter to the Librarian, Army Medical Library, dated Fairfield, Conn., 15 Oct. 1924, on the author's early life in France, his emigration in 1865, his studies in the University Medical College of New York, his medical practice in San Francisco, and his service in the Army Medical Corps in Arizona, North Dakota, Texas, Wyoming, and elsewhere. Appended: accounts by Rogers McVaugh of Havard's botanical collections from the West (where he served 1871-94) and of his activities in an expedition under Maj. W. R. Livermore in western Texas (1878-83); with references to his botanical publications. [3934

ZACHARY TAYLOR (1784-1850). Old Rough and Ready speaks his mind: Zachary Taylor on the conduct of war, a letter to T. Butler, Matamoros, June 19, 1846. [Hartford:] Printed for F. W. Beinecke, 1960. [2], 13, [1] p. facsim. notes (p. 13). Letter to Thomas Butler, Louisiana judge and sugar planter, from "Headquarters, Army of Occupation of Invasion," on the military situation in Mexico and the inept administration of military affairs in Washington. [3935

BLACKSTON McDANNEL (1811-88). Blackston McDannel to Andrew Johnson: an East Tennesseean in the Mexican War. Edited by Le Roy P. Graf and Ralph W. Haskins. East Tenn. Hist. Soc. pub., 32:106-17. maps. notes. Letter dated Jalapa, 28 Jan. 1848, on activities of "the 'army of occupation'" and "the exciting events of the American march into the interior of Mexico" in 1847. [3936

CHARLES A. SCOTT (1830-1907). Charles A. Scott's diary of the Utah expedition, 1857-1861. Edited by Robert E. Stowers and John M. Ellis. Utah hist. quar., 28:154-76, 388-402 (Apr, Oct). ports., views. notes. Record kept intermittently by an Army private, 28 Mar. 1857 - 22 Oct. 1861, on his arrival in New York City from Nicaragua (where he had served in William Walker's filibustering forces), his enlistment in the Army, his journey by train and boat to Kansas, his march to southwestern Wyoming and winter there, his 3 years of service in Utah, and his return journey to the East. [3937

LUCIUS BELLINGER NORTHROP (1811-94). Some letters of Lucius Bellinger Northrop, 1860-1865. Edited by Willard E. Wight. Va. mag. hist. and biog., 68:456-77 (Oct). notes. Letters from the Commissary General of the C.S. Army, "probably the most unpopular appointee of President Jefferson Davis." [3938

JOHN DAVIS BILLINGS (born 1842). Hardtack and coffee: the unwritten story of Army life. ... Edited by Richard Harwell. Chicago: R. R. Donnelley, 1960. xxxii, 483 p. diagrs., facsim., music, port., views. notes. (The Lakeside classics, 58.) 1st ed. 1887. On the author's service as a private in the 10th Massachusetts Battery of Light Artillery, 1861-65. Includes "chapters on enlisting, life in tents and log huts, jonahs and beats, offences and punishments, raw recruits, foraging, corps and corps badges, the wagon trains, the Army mule, the Engineer Corps, the Signal Corps, etc.," as well as (in the original) "six elegant color plates; and over two hundred original sketches by Charles W. Reed." [3939

JOHN LOGAN BLACK (1830-1902). Crumbling defenses; or, Memoirs and reminiscences of John Logan Black, Colonel, C.S.A. Edited and published by Eleanor D. McSwain. Macon, Ga. [1960]. 133 p. facsims. (1 fold.), port. notes. Written ca. 1882 (see p. 64); apparently never finished. On the author's service in the 1st South Carolina Cavalry, 1861-65. [3940

JUNIUS NEWPORT BRAGG (born 1838). Letters of a Confederate surgeon, 1861-1865. [Edited] by Mrs. T. J. Gaughan. [Camden? Ark., 1960. 8], 276 p. facsim., ports., view. Letters to relatives, on the author's service with Arkansas forces in Arkansas, Louisiana, and Texas. [3941

W. B. C. COKER. [Letters to the writer's brother, F. M. Coker. Edited] by Sylvia Head. Ga. rev., 14:355-60 (winter). Dated Camp Cutts (1 mile from Manassas), 28 Jul. 1861, and Camp, Mercer's Brigade, Army of Tennessee, 15 Sep. 1864. On the writer's Confederate military experiences in Virginia and Georgia. [3942

ROBERT H. GASTON (died 1862) & WILLIAM H. GASTON (1840-1927). "Tyler to Sharpsburg": Robert H. and William H. Gaston (their war letters, 1861-62). Edited by Robert W. Glover. Waco, Tex.: W. M. Morrison, 1960. [4], 22 p. fold. mount. facsim., port., table. notes. Sixteen letters from 2 brothers (some written jointly) to their family, Jul. 1861 - Nov. 1862, all but one dated in Virginia, on their service in Company H, 1st Texas Infantry Regiment, C.S.A. [3943

JOHN CHEVES HASKELL (1841-1906). The Haskell memoirs. ... Edited by Gilbert E. Govan and James W. Livingood. N.Y.: Putnam [1960]. xiv,

[2], 176 p. port. bibliog. (p. 170-72), notes (p. 121-69). Reminiscences (ca. 1901) of the author's service as an officer of the Artillery Corps of the Army of Northern Virginia, C.S.A., 1861-65. [3944

FRANK HUME. A scouting expedition during the Civil War. Arlington hist. mag., 1(4):50-53 (Oct). Undated recollections, apparently fragmentary, of the author's movements as a Confederate spy from some point in Virginia across the Potomac and as far as Marlborough. [3945

JOSEPH EGGLESTON JOHNSTON (1807-91. Narrative of military operations directed during the late War between the States by Joseph E. Johnston, General, C.S.A. Introduction by Frank E. Vandiver. Bloomington: Indiana Univ. Press, 1959. xxxi, 621, [1] p. maps, ports., tables. notes. (Civil War centennial series.) 1st ed. 1874. Appended (p. 467-602): letters, orders, and reports. [3946

WILLIAM McKINLEY (1843-1901). A Civil War diary of William McKinley. Edited by H. Wayne Morgan. Ohio hist. quar., 69:272-90 (Jul). notes. Record of service as a private in Company E, 23d Ohio Volunteer Infantry Regiment, at Camp Jackson (renamed Camp Chase) near Columbus, and in present West Virginia, 15 Jun.-3 Nov. 1861. [3947

BARTLETT YANCEY MALONE (1838-90). Whipt 'em everytime: the diary of Bartlett Yancey Malone. Edited by William Whatley Pierson, Jr. Jackson, Tenn.: McCowat-Mercer Press, 1960. 131 p. facsims., ports., double view. Record of service as a private in the 6th North Carolina Infantry, Army of Northern Virginia, capture by Union forces, and imprisonment and release at Point Lookout, Md., 1861-65. [3948

JAMES WESLEY RILEY. Civil War diary of James Wesley Riley who served with the Union Army in the War between the States, April 22, 1861 - June 18, 1865. [Wash.? Stamped: C. W. Denslinger, c1960.] 108 leaves. Record of service of a Michigan private in an Illinois regiment, mainly in Tennessee and Georgia. [3949

LANGDON LESLIE RUMPH (1844-61). Letters of a teenage Confederate. Edited by Henry Eugene Sterkx and Brooks Thompson. Fla. hist. quar., 38:339-46 (Apr). notes. Letters from a private in the 1st Regiment of Alabama Volunteers to his father, Dr. James David Rumph, dated in Warrenton [i.e. Warrington Navy Yard] at Fort Barrancas, Fla., 10 Mar.-25 Jul. 1861, giving news of "this hot climate, fleas flies & mosquitos," sickness, and routine occupations in the camp; and letter to Dr. Rumph from M. B. Locke, 14 Aug. 1861, announcing the death of the son at Warrington, from either measles or typhoid fever, and the necessity of burying him there because of the extraordinarily rapid decomposition of his body in a zinc casket that proved to be not airtight. [3950

JOHN SHARP (1819-1901) & HELEN MARIA SHARP (died 1905). The Sharp family Civil War letters. Edited by George Mills. Ann. Ia., 34: 481-532 (Jan 1959). port. notes. Letters exchanged between husband and wife, 3 Dec. 1861 - 16 Oct. 1862, 2 Apr.-5 Aug. 1865, on his service in the 2d Regiment, Iowa Volunteer Infantry, in Tennessee and Mississippi, and later in the 10th Regiment, Iowa Volunteer Infantry, in the Carolinas, Virginia, and Arkansas, and her difficulties in providing food and shelter for their 5 children on their farm in Polk County and later in Dallas County, Ia. [3951

JAMES A. WALDEN (1843-86). The journals of James A. Walden. Part I--Confederate soldier. W[alter] J. Lemke, editor. Fayetteville, Ark., 1954. [87] p. (Washington County Historical Society. Bulletin series, 4.) Diary kept by the author as a soldier in the 16th Arkansas Regiment and a prisoner on Johnson's Island, 1 Jul. 1861 - 12 Feb. 1864. [3952

CHARLES W. CARR. Civil War letters of Charles W. Carr of the 21st Wisconsin Volunteers. Edited by Leo M. Kaiser. Wis. mag. hist., 43:264-72 (summer). views. notes. Letters to his wife, Sarah M. Carr in Appleton, dated in Kentucky, on his life in camp there, his loss of a toe in the Battle of Perrysville, his stay in General Hospital 11 at Louisville, and his work as a hospital steward, and 4 letters to him, 11 Aug. 1862-26 Jan. 1865. [3953

WILLIAM WALLER CARSON. Joseph Carson [1843-1902], Louisiana Confederate soldier. [Edited by] John Q. Anderson. La. hist., 1:44-69 (winter). notes. Reminiscences (1917) of the service of the author and his brother Joseph, the latter in the 28th Mississippi Cavalry and both in the 4th

Louisiana Cavalry, 1862-65; with some account of Joseph's later life in Louisiana and Mississippi as a cotton planter. [3954

JEFFERSON COLUMBUS DAVIS. The Yankees' Jeff Davis in Tennessee. Edited by James P. Jones. Tenn. hist. quar., 19:166-71 (Jun). notes. Part of a 47-page letter to Gen. John M. Palmer, 4 Jan. 1866, reviewing the author's services in Tennessee as a brigadier general, 26 Dec. 1862-1 May 1864. [3955

THEODORE DIMON (1816-89). A Federal surgeon at Sharpsburg. Edited by James I. Robertson, Jr. Civil War hist., 6:134-51 (Jun). notes. Excerpt from a diary, 15-18 Sep. 1862, and letter to the author's wife, dated "Field hospital for wounded, near Keedysville, Md.," 25 Sep. 1862. [3956

CORYDON EDWARD FOOTE (1849-1944). With Sherman to the sea: a drummer's story of the Civil War. As related by Corydon Edward Foote to Olive Deane Hormel. N.Y.: John Day Co. [1960]. 255 p. maps, ports. On his service as a "musician" in the 10th Michigan Infantry in Kentucky, Tennessee, Alabama, and Georgia, 1862-65. Reported in the third person from interviews with him when past the age of 90. [3957

HORACE NEWTON FISHER (1836-1916). A staff officer's story: the personal experiences of Colonel Horace Newton Fisher in the Civil War [1862-63. Edited] by Horace Cecil Fisher [his son]. Boston, 1960. [10], 134, [2] p. facsims., maps (part double col.), ports. notes. Six reminiscent manuscripts (undated), excerpts from letters to his parents, and insertions (by the editor) of "incidents he told me." [3958

JAMES GREENALCH (1837?-1892). Letters of James Greenalch. Edited with an introduction by Knox Mellon, Jr. Mich. hist., 44:188-240 (Jun). notes. Letters from a private in Company B, 1st Michigan Engineers and Mechanics, to his wife, Fidelia, and other relatives, 28 Sep. 1862 - 28 Apr. 1865, reporting his service in Kentucky, Tennessee, Georgia, and the Carolinas. [3959

ISAAC JACKSON (1842-1903). "Some of the boys ..." The Civil war letters of Isaac Jackson, 1862-1865. Edited by Joseph Orville Jackson. With a foreword by Bell Irvin Wiley. Carbondale: Southern Illinois Univ. Press [1960]. xx, [4], 264 p. facsims., ports. notes (p. 251-64). Letters from a private in the 83d Ohio Volunteer Infantry to his family, dated in Tennessee, Louisiana, Mississippi, and Alabama. [3960

EDWARD HASTINGS RIPLEY (1839-1915). Vermont general: the unusual war experiences of Edward Hastings Ripley, 1862-1865. Edited by Otto Eisenschiml. N.Y.: Devin-Adair, 1960. N.Y.: Devin-Adair, 1960. viii, [4], 340 p. maps, ports., views. Letters of Ripley to and from his family during his last year of study at Union College and his service in the Union Army. [3961

LIVINGSTON SCOTT (1839-1909). A soldier writes to his Congressman: the Civil War letters of Livingston Scott to Thomas A. Jenckes. [Edited] by Frank F. White, Jr. R. I. hist., 18: 97-114; 19:13-25 (Oct 1959, Jan 1960). notes. Letters from Rhode Island, 8 Jun. 1862-15 Jan. 1864, and Louisiana, 29 Apr. 1864 - 28 Sep. 1865, largely on rivalries and animosities among the officers of the Rhode Island forces. [3962

JAMES B. SHEERAN (1819-81). Confederate chaplain: a war journal of Rev. James B. Sheeran, C.SS.R., 14th Louisiana, C.S.A. Edited by Rev. Joseph T. Durkin, S. J. With a preface by Bruce Catton. Milwaukee: Bruce Pub. Co. [1960]. xiii, [3], 168 p. facsims., map, port., view. notes. Record of services in the Army of Northern Virginia, 2 Aug. 1862 - 7 May 1865. [3963

SENECA BROWN THRALL (1832-88). An Iowa doctor in blue: the letters of Seneca B. Thrall, 1862-1864. Edited by Mildred Throne. Ia. jour. hist., 58:97-188 (Apr). notes. On his medical service in the 13th Iowa Infantry in Mississippi, Tennessee, and Louisiana, reported in letters to his wife, 19 Sep. 1862-5 May 1864; with a letter to him from Dr. Moses W. Thomas, same regiment, dated Savannah, 20 Dec. 1864, on the activities of the regiment since May 1864. [3964

JOHN F. BROBST (1838/39-1917). Well, Mary: Civil War letters of a Wisconsin volunteer. Edited by Margaret Brobst Roth. Madison: Univ. of Wisconsin Press, 1960. ix, 165 p. maps. bibliog. (p. 157-8), notes. Letters from a private in the 25th Wisconsin Regiment, serving mainly in Tennessee, Mississippi, and Georgia, to Mary Englesby, his future wife, Mar. 1863-Jun. 1864. [3965

MICHAEL DOUGHERTY. Diary of a Civil War hero. N.Y.: Pyramid Books [1960]. 128 p. views (part double). (Pyramid books, R572.) 1st ed. 1908. Record of the author's service in the 13th Pennsylvania Cavalry, his capture by Confederates, and his confinement in Libby Prison, Richmond, 10 Oct. 1863-27 Jun. 1865. Inserted (p. 48-80): "A special illustrated account of the war," by James Boylan. [3966

HENRY WADSWORTH LONGFELLOW (1807-82) & CHARLES LONGFELLOW (1844?-1893). Charley Longfellow goes to war. [Edited by Andrew Hilen.] Harv. Lib. bul., 14:59-81, 283-303 (winter, spring). facsim., ports., view. notes. Mainly letters exchanged between father and son and from the father to other persons, 14 Mar. 1863-15 Feb. 1864, on the son's entry into the army against the father's wishes, and the father's repeated efforts to obtain promotion and special consideration for the son through Senator Charles Sumner and other influential persons. [3967

JOSEPH B. O'HAGAN (1826-78). The diary of Joseph B. O'Hagan, S. J., Chaplain of the Excelsior Brigade [commanded by Gen. Daniel Sickles]. Edited by the Rev. William L. Lucey. Civil War hist., 6:402-9 (Dec). notes. Record kept at Falmouth, Va., and on leave at Georgetown, 1-19 Feb. 1863. [3968

EUGENE FITCH WARE (1841-1911). The Indian War of 1864. ... With an introduction and notes by Clyde C. Walton. N.Y.: St. Martin's Press [1960]. xix, [3], 483 p. facsims., maps, plan. bibliog. (p. 429-30), notes (p. 431-74). 1st ed. 1911. On the author's service as an officer in Company F, 7th Iowa Cavalry, in Nebraska, Kansas, Colorado, and Wyoming, Sep. 1863-Mar. 1865; with a biographical sketch by the editor, of his early life in Hartford, Conn., his life as a homesteader near Fort Scott, Kan., his study of law and work there as a lawyer and newspaper writer, and his activities in Kansas and national politics. [3969

JOHN A. CURTIS. Squib versus Minnesota. [Edited] by Captain John C. Spencer. U.S.N. Inst. proc., 86(5): 154-5 (May). port. "My personal experience of an expedition on board of the Spar Torpedo Boat 'Squib,'" an undated account of the voyage of this Confederate wooden vessel from Richmond to Newport News, her success in torpedoing the frigate Minnesota, and her safe return to Richmond, Mar. 1864. [3970

GEORGE ST. LEGER OMMANCY GRENFELL (1808-1868?). Colonel George St. Leger Grenfell. ... [Edited] by Mabel Clare Weaks. Filson Club hist. quar., 34:5-23 (Jan). facsim. notes. Letters from an English volunteer officer in the C.S. Army to his daughters in England and other individuals there, dated in Richmond, Montreal, Chicago, and Fort Jefferson (in the Dry Tortugas, Fla.), 18 Mar. 1864 - 26 Feb. 1868; with a letter from his grandson, Anthony Horatio Packe, about a silk U.S. flag presented to the Kentucky Guards by the ladies of Leesburg in 1860. [3971

JACOB HAYES. With Sherman in Georgia. Password, 5:39-40 (Jan). Letter from a Union soldier to his wife, Isabella, dated Camp near Savannah, 17 Dec. 1864, on Sherman's march. [3972

FRANK MALCOLM (1834-84). "Such is war": the letters of an orderly in the 7th Iowa Infantry. Edited by James I. Robertson, Jr. Ia. jour. hist., 58:321-56 (Oct). notes. Letters to the author's wife, Eliza Ewing (Sample) Malcolm (in Fort Madison), dated in Tennessee, Georgia, North Carolina, camp near Washington, and Kentucky, 10 Mar. 1864 - 14 Jun. 1865. [3973

DAVID HUNTER STROTHER (1816-88). With Sigel at New Market: the diary of Colonel D. H. Strother. Edited by Cecil D. Eby, Jr. Civil War hist., 6:73-83 (Mar). notes. Record kept by an aide to Gen. Franz Sigel on a march from Martinsburg to New Market, 1-16 May 1864, detailing repeated instances of Sigel's incompetence. [3974

THOMAS MASON BRUMBY (1855-99). The fall of Manila, August 13, 1898. ... Edited by Willard E. Wight. U.S.N. Inst. proc., 86(8):88-93 (Aug). view. Letter from the flag lieutenant of Dewey's flagship to the writer's sister, dated Manila, 17 Aug. 1898. [3975

CHARLES JOHNSON POST (1873-1956). The little war of Private Post. With illustrations by the author. Boston: Little, Brown [1960]. xii, 340 p. ports., views (part col.). On the author's service in the Fifth Army Corps in the War of 1898. [3976

CONSUELO ANDREW SEOANE. Beyond the ranges. By Col. Consuelo Andrew Seoane (U.S.A. Ret.) as told to Robert L. Niemann. N.Y.: R. Speller, 1960. 256 p. map, port. Reminiscences of the author's service as an enlisted man and an officer in the U.S. Army, 1898-1940, and severe criticism of American military policy since World War I. [3977

ELEANOR (MATHEWS) SLINEY (born 1896). Forward ho! N.Y.: Vantage Press [1960. 2], 332 p. ports., views. On the author's marriage in 1915 to George W. Sliney, Army officer, and their life in Mexico, West Point, the Philippines, Hawaii, Washington (D.C.), San Francisco, and elsewhere. [3978

CLAUDE EDWARD DUNCAN. The real Italian Detachment: transcription of a tape recorded interview with Brigadier General Claude E. Duncan, U.S.A.F. (retired). Edited and assembled by John Sloan and George Hocutt. Cross & cockade jour., 1(2):42-52 (summer). ports. On the author's air service in the United States, Italy, France, and Germany, 1917-19. [3979

LIVINGSTON G. IRVING. The war experiences of Livingston G. Irving, USAS. From a tape recorded interview on 2 Oct. 1960. Cross & cockade jour., 1(4):75-84 (winter). port., views. On his experience in the U.S. Air Service in the United States and France, 1917-18. [3980

DONALD S. POLER. One of the "Warbirds." ... Prepared by John Sloan and George D. Hocutt. Cross & cockade jour., 1(1):20-29 (spring). Interview (1959) concerning the author's service in the No. 40 Squadron, Royal Air Force, and the 25th Aero Squadron, U.S. Air Service, in England and France, Sep. 1917 - Jun. 1919. [3981

CHARLES R. D'OLIVE. An interview [1959] with Charles R. D'Olive. Cross & cockade jour., 1(1):3-15 (spring). ports., view. On his service as a pilot in the 93d Pursuit Squadron, U.S. Army Air Service, in France, Aug.-Oct. 1918. [3982

HORACE P. WELLS. An interview with Horace P. Wells. From a tape recording made during autumn 1960. Transcribed by R. T. "Doc" Hood. Cross & cockade jour., 1(4):85-92 (winter). On his experience in the U.S. Air Service in England and France and as a prisoner of war in Germany, 1918. [3983

WILLIAM HENRY RANKIN (born 1920). The man who rode the thunder. Englewood Cliffs, N.J.: Prentice-Hall [1960. 12], 208 p. ports., views. On the author's early life in Pittsburgh and his service in the Marine Corps since 1940 as an enlisted man, "a Marine officer and a professional military aviator." [3984

DOROTHY STERLING, ed. I have seen war: 25 stories from World War II. N.Y.: Hill and Wang [1960]. xiii, 273 p. Chapters from books and articles from periodicals, mainly eyewitness accounts. [3985

EDGAR GABLE (died 1945). Edgar Gable's prison camp diary. Edited by Robert Ryal Miller. S. D. report and hist. col., 30:317-48. ports., view. Diary kept in Cabanatuan Prison Camp No. 1, Luzon, by an Army lieutenant, 22 Aug. 1942 - 11 Oct. 1944, written on scraps of paper and buried in a glass jar. [3986

FOREST J. STERLING. Wake of the Wahoo. Phila.: Chilton Co., Book Division [1960]. ix, [3], 210 p. ports., views. On the author's service as an enlisted man in Pacific operations of the submarine USS Wahoo, Oct. 1942 - Sep. 1943. [3987

JOSEPH BRYAN III. The sword over the mantel: the Civil War and I. N.Y.: McGraw-Hill [1960. 8], 123, [1] p. Facetious reminiscences of the author's service in the Army during World War II, 1943-45, intermingled with his early memories of Civil War veterans in Richmond, Va. [3988

HANS JOACHIM DECKER. 404 days! the war patrol life of the German U-505. U.S.N. Inst. proc., 86(3):33-45 (Mar). map, views. Recollections by an officer of service on this submarine, 1941-43, her many sinkings of American and other shipping in the Atlantic, and her capture by the USS Guadalcanal off the Cape Verde Islands, 4 Jun. 1943. [3989

JESSE GLENN GRAY. The warriors: reflections on men in battle. N.Y.: Harcourt, Brace [1959]. x, [2], 242 p. Observations based upon the author's work in the Counter Intelligence Corps in Europe, 1943-45, and upon the diary and letters written by him at that time, concerning the roots of war in human nature and the possible changes in human nature that might eliminate war. [3990

NORMA CATHERINE FURTOS. The Navy is my career. Am. Med. Women's Assoc., Jour., 14:516-17 (Jun 1959). On the author's service as a physician of the U.S. Navy in California and on the hospital ship USS Consolation, 1944-59. [3991

Military Costume

U.S. Quartermaster's Dept. Uniforms of the United States Army. N.Y.: T. Yoseloff [1959]. 51 p. (p. [5], 9-51 reprint). 44 col. plates. 44 cm. 1st ed. (1888) has title: The Army of the United States. Illustrated by 44 fac-simile plates from water color drawings by H[enry] A[lexander] Ogden. Text by Henry Loomis Nelson. Prepared and executed by the Quartermaster General of the United States, under authority of the Secretary of War. Text is a history of the Army uniform. Plates show uniforms worn by models, representing uniforms in use between 1774 and 1888. The models are usually grouped as several figures on horseback or afoot, with some typical Army landscape as a background. The earlier plates are evidently not derived from surviving samples or contemporary drawings of early uniforms. [3992

U.S. War Dept. Army uniform of 1822. [Edited] by Alfred H. Wittaker. Mich. State Med. Soc., Jour., 58:761-2 (May 1959). Excerpt from "General Regulations for the Army dated 2 March 1821, dealing with uniform." [3993

WILLIAM G. GAVIN. Accoutrement plates of the Federal forces, 1861-1865. Mil. collector & historian, 12:65-71 (fall). views. notes. On designs and devices on belt plates and cartridge-box plates, their Federal and State antecedents as early as 1834, and their manufacturers. [3994

U.S. Navy Dept. A reproduction of the 1841 naval uniform regulations. [Submitted] by Edgar A. Wischnowski. Mil. collector & historian, 11:15-18 (spring 1959). views. Regulations for the uniform and dress of the Navy of the United States (1841). [3995

CARROLL H. WALKER. Colonel Walter H. Taylor [1838-1916], C.S.A. Mil. collector & historian, 12:39-41 (summer). ports. notes. Information from 2 photographs, 1855(?) and 1861, about the uniforms worn by him as a cadet in the Virginia Military Institute and as first lieutenant of the Southern Guard, Norfolk (Company F, 54th Regiment of Virginia Militia). [3996

GEORGE E. GORMAN. Confederate accouterments. Gun rep., 5(11):6-8, 49 (Apr). views. On belts and buckles, cartridge boxes, holsters, cannisters, cap boxes, etc. [3997

STANLEY KERKSIS. Confederate States buttons [of Army and Navy, 1861-65]. Mil. collector & historian, 12:103-6 (winter). facsim., views. notes. [3998

RICHARD DENNIS STEUART. Confederate buttons. Natl. button bul., 19:22-7, 54-5, 131-3 (Jan-May). views. From Essex Institute historical collections, Jul. 1943. On the types and the manufacturers of C.S. military buttons. [3999

FRANK E. COMPARATO. The types militaires of Draner. Mil. collector & historian, 11:65-9 (fall 1959). cartoons. notes. On Types militaires: galerie militaire de toutes les nations, engraved by Draner (real name: Jules Renard, 1833-1926), consisting of 136 colored lithographs, 1862-71, "caricatures" that "dwell on the oddity and awkwardness of anatomical shapes, the minute and gross absurdities of military hierarchy, and the comical predicaments in which any soldier might find himself." Includes plates of 10 American uniforms. [4000

J. DUNCAN CAMPBELL. Badges for early birdmen. Mil. collector and historian, 12:33-8 (summer). views. On badges for U.S. military airmen, 1913-21. [4001

Military Education

ORON P. SOUTH. New dimensions in leadership. Air Univ. quar. rev., 12(2):33-44 (summer). On the development of concepts of "education and training" for leadership in the U.S. Army and the U.S. Air Force, 1776-1960. [4002

NORMAN B. WILKINSON. The forgotten "founder" of West Point. Mil.

affairs, 24:177-88 (winter). port. notes. On Louis de Tousard (1748?-1817), "who first conceived the idea of a national military school with a comprehensive curriculum and a prescribed training," proposed such a school in 1798 in a memorandum to the Secretary of War, and was detailed to organize and inaugurate the U.S. Military Academy in 1801-2. [4003

SOUTH Carolinians at the Partridge Military Academy [Norwich, Vt.], 1826. S.C. hist. mag., 61:11-12 (Jan). List. [4004

LEONARD TURLEY. K. M. I. covers. S. P. A. jour., 21:13-16 (Sep 1958). facsims., view. On the postal markings of the outgoing mail of the Kentucky Military Institute, 1851-1958. [4005

GENE MARTIN LYONS & JOHN WESLEY MASLAND. Education and military leadership ... a study of the R. O. T. C. Princeton: Princeton Univ. Press, 1959. xvii, 283 p. diagrs., tables. notes. On the history of the Reserve Officers Training Corps, 1917-57, its current problems, and its future; with some account of its background since 1862 and of the differences between Army, Navy, and Air Force R. O. T. C. programs. [4006

LAWRENCE C. LANDIS. The story of the U.S. Air Force Academy [authorized in 1954]. N.Y.: Rinehart [1960, c1959]. 224 p. ports., views. Includes some account of the growth of aviation in the Army, 1907-47, the separation of the Air Force from the Army in 1947, and the resulting need for a separate Air Force academy. [4007

OTIS OTTO BENSON, JR. From Hazelhurst to Brooks: a saga of aeromedical pioneering. U.S. Armed Forces med. jour., 10: 1273-86 (Nov 1959). views. notes. On the U.S. Air Force School of Aviation Medicine, Brooks Air Force Base, Tex., and predecessor organizations, 1912-59. [4008

RAYMOND M. DUKE. The Army Medical Service School: its history and mission [Carlisle, Pa., 1920-60]. U.S. Armed Forces med. jour., 11: 621-40 (Jun). coat of arms, diagr., tables, views. notes. [4009

JOHN M. SWOMLEY, JR. A study of the universal military training campaign, 1944-1952. Ann Arbor: University Microfilms, 1959 [i.e. 1960]. Positive microfilm of typescript. [481] leaves. Thesis--Univ. of Colorado. Abstracted: Dissert. abstracts, 20: 4156 (Apr). 4010

ROBERT O. BARNEY. Allied officer training at the U.S. Army Medical Service School [Brooke Army Medical Center, Fort Sam Houston, Tex., 1946-60]. Mil. med., 125:617-19 (Sep). table. notes. [4011

RAY HAWK. A new dimension in higher education: a program of the United States Air Force [1947-60]. Educ. rec., 41: 67-73 (Jan). table. notes. On the Air Force Institute of Technology. [4012

The Military Establishment

BRANCHES

LOUIS MORTON. The long road to unity of command [1905-41]. Mil. rev., 39(10):3-12 (Jan). [4013

ALLAN N. GLENNON. The perennial fallacy. U.S.N. Inst. proc., 86(12):55-61 (Dec). port. On proposals since 1921 for a "single service" (as distinguished from unification of the services, in which each keeps its identity). [4014

MURRAY GREEN. Stuart Symington and the B-36. Ann Arbor: University Microfilms, 1960. Positive microfilm of typescript. [358] leaves. Thesis--American Univ. Abstracted: Dissert. abstracts, 21:1541 (Dec). On his service as Assistant Secretary of War for Air in procuring Congressional approval of the unification of the armed forces, his decision as first Secretary of the Air Force to continue and accelerate the procurement of the B-36 bomber as a method "to maintain the combat integrity of the Strategic Air Command at the expense of all other missions, if necessary," the bitter opposition of the Navy Department to this policy, the decision of Louis Johnson, Secretary of Defense, "to retain a smaller Air Force despite the 'dramatic corrective' in the strategic picture caused by the Soviet A-device explosion," and the resignation of Symington, 1946-50. [4015

Air Forces

RUSSELL J. PARKINSON. United States Signal Corps balloons, 1871-1902. Mil. affairs, 24:189-202 (winter). notes. [4016

U.S. Office of Naval Operations. United States naval aviation, 1910-60. [By Adrian O. Van Wyen and Lee M. Pearson. Wash.] 1960. v, 239 p. ports., tables, views. notes. [4017

ELDON WILSON DOWNS. Contributions of U.S. Army aviation to uses and operation of aircraft. Ann Arbor: University Microfilms, 1959 [i.e. 1960]. Positive microfilm of typescript. ix, 488 leaves. bibliog. (leaves 457-88). Thesis--Univ. of Wisconsin. Abstracted: Dissert. abstracts, 20:2769-70 (Jan). On the work of Army fliers "in furthering commercial aviation while carrying out their own missions," 1918-1930s. Includes references to aerial photography, aerial patrol of timberlands, airmail, aerial crop dusting, night flying, blind flying, etc. [4018

ROBERT J. FRIEDMAN. Budgeting for the aerospace force [1930-60]. Air Univ. quar. rev., 12(3-4):222-6 (winter-spring). diagr. [4019

SAMUEL E. ANDERSON. Aerospace logistics. Air Univ. quar. rev., 12(3-4):161-75 (winter-spring). diagrs., maps, views. On the logistic system of the U.S. Air Force, 1941-60, including that of its predecessor, the U.S. Army Air Force. [4020

WALTER ERNEST TODD. Evolution of aerospace power [in America, 1941-60]. Air Univ. quar. rev., 12(3-4):9-24 (winter-spring). [4021

WILLIAM JONES WALLRICH. Superstition and the Air Force. West. folklore, 19:11-16 (Jan). Examples collected by an Air Force sergeant during and since World War II. [4022

STANLEY J. DONOVAN. Tactical aerospace forces [of the U.S. Air Force, 1945-60]. Air Univ. quar. rev., 12(3-4):74-88 (winter-spring). diagrs., tables, views. [4023

Amphibious Forces

LYNN MONTROSS (1895-1961). The United States Marines: a pictorial history [1775-1959]. ... Photographic research by David E. Schwulst. N.Y.: Rinehart [1959. 12], 242 p. ports., views. "Credits for photographs and quotations" (p. 240-42). [4024

PHILIP N. PIERCE & FRANK OLNEY HOUGH (1899-1958). The compact history of the United States Marine Corps [1775-1959]. N.Y.: Hawthorn Books [1960]. 326, [2] p. bibliog. (p. 309-12). [4025

Land Forces

JAMES MOONEY (1861-1921). [Review of Skalpieren und ähnliche Kriegsgebräuche in Amerika (1906), doctoral dissertation submitted to the University of Leipzig by Capt. Georg Friederici of the German Army.] Selected papers from the American anthropologist, 1888-1920, ed. Frederica De Laguna (Evanston, Ill.: Row, Peterson, 1960), p. 665-7. First printed in 1907. On scalping and similar military practices of American Indians, 1535-1863. [4026

MARK MAYO BOATNER III. Military customs and traditions. N.Y.: David McKay Co. [1956]. xiii, [3], 176 p. views. bibliog. (p. 171-6). Includes chapters on "Military Americana," "Soldier slang and jargon," "Significant dates in the forming of U.S. military tradition," and "'Customs of the service,'" 1636-1956. [4027

JAMES EDWARD OGLETHORPE (1696-1785). The mutiny at St. Andrews, 1738--a letter. Contributed by Robert G. McPherson. Ga. hist. quar., 44:456-60 (Dec). notes. Account enclosed in a letter to the accountant for the Trustees of Georgia, Nov. 1738, now first printed, on disaffection of forces stationed at Fort St. Andrews at the south end of Cumberland Island. [4028

JAMES J. CURTO. Sutlers and their tokens. Selections from The numismatist: United States paper money, tokens, medals, and miscellaneous (Racine, Wis.: Whitman Pub. Co., 1960), p. 109-21. views. First printed Aug. 1946. On the work of sutlers in the U.S. Army, 1756-1893, and the tokens issued by them. [4029

The ARMY almanac: a book of facts concerning the United States Army. [Second edition. Edited by Brig. Gen. Gordon R. Young.] Harrisburg, Pa.: Stackpole Co. [1959]. x, 797 p. diagrs., maps, tables. notes. Text in double columns. One-volume encyclopedia of the history and present condition of the U.S. Army, 1775-1958. Includes "An Army chronology," 1774-1958 (p. 494-507), an account of the wars of the United States since 1775 (p. 508-631, 696-710), records of combat units of World Wars I and II and the Korean War (p. 632-96, with lists of unit histories), lists of general officers (p. 329-50), and historical sections on the combat arms, the services, awards and decorations, and other topics. [4030

W. D. SMITHERS. The U.S. Cavalry. West. horseman, 25(11): 22-4, 79-80; (12):50-53, 97-9 (Nov, Dec). port., views. On the selection, training, accouterments, and uses of Cavalry horses, 1775-1942. [4031

JOHN FREDERICK REED. The naked and starving. Manuscripts, 12(1):9-11 (winter). Information from the papers of Anthony Wayne about the troops at Valley Forge, 1777-78. [4032

ORANGE COUNTY, Va. CITIZENS. Legislative petition, Orange Co., Va., March 14, 1781. Submitted by Anita Howard for the Henry Clay Chapter, Va. D. A. R. mag., 94:390 (May). Requests repeal of an act extending the term of militia duty from 3 to 18 months of continuous service. Includes list of signers so far as decipherable. [4033

JOHN K. MAHON. The American militia, decade of decision, 1789-1800. Gainesville: Univ. of Florida Press, 1960. [8], 69, [1] p. notes. (University of Florida monographs. Social sciences, 6.) [4034

ROBERT HARRY LOWIE (1883-1957). Property rights and coercive powers of Plains Indian military societies [mainly in the 19th century]. Lowie's selected papers in anthropology, ed. Cora Du Bois (Berkeley: Univ. of California Press, 1960), p. 247-61. notes. From Journal of legal and political sociology, 5 Apr. 1943. [4035

HAROLD W. RYAN. Matthew Arbuckle comes to Fort Smith. Ark. hist. quar., 19:287-92 (winter). notes. On the many difficulties and inept War Department administration of the transfer of troops commanded by Colonel Arbuckle from Fort Scott, Ga., to Arkansas, 1821. [4036

HENRY W. BARTON. The United States Cavalry and the Texas Rangers. Southw. hist. quar., 63:495-510 (Apr). notes. On the Texas Rangers, established in 1835, the slow and partial stages by which the U.S. Cavalry was created after 1828, the contact between the two during the Mexican War, and the question "what influence the Texas Rangers may have had on the cavalry of the United States." [4037

JAMES D. LUNT. Charge to glory! N.Y.: Harcourt, Brace [1960]. 248 p. maps. notes. World history of cavalry, including some account of that of the U.S. Army, 1833-76 (p. 110-31, 158-84). [4038

BYRON STINSON. The Yankee saddle. West. horseman, 25(2): 12, 71-3 (Dec). views. On saddles of the U.S. Cavalry, 1846-1906. [4039

DAVID HERBERT DONALD. The Southerner as a fighting man. Charles Grier Sellers, Jr., ed., The Southerner as American (Chapel Hill: Univ. of North Carolina Press [1960]), p. 72-88. notes. On the C.S. Army as an "extraordinarily democratic military organization and an extraordinarily aristocratic one," and the Southerner as "an admirable fighting man but a poor soldier." [4040

HIRST DILLON MILHOLLEN. Horsemen, blue and gray: a pictorial history. ... Text by James Ralph Johnson and Alfred Hoyt Bill. N.Y.: Oxford Univ. Press, 1960. vii, 236 p. facsims., maps, music, ports., views. bibliog. (p. 221-3). "Picture sources" (p. 225-30). Reproductions of prints and photographs showing Union and Confederate cavalry, 1861-65; with connected text. 4041

JEN-HWA LEE. The organization and administration of the Army of the Potomac under General George B. McClellan [1861-62]. Ann Arbor: University Microfilms, 1960. Positive microfilm of typescript. [179] leaves. Thesis--Univ. of Maryland. Abstracted: Dissert. abstracts, 21:608 (Apr). [4042

DONALD BERT RUSSELL. Some thoughts on brevet commissions--and Custer. Westerners brand book (Chicago), 16:49-50 (Sep 1959). On the meaning of brevet rank in the Civil War and until 1930. [4043

JOHN W. KILLIGREW. The impact of the Great Depression on the Army, 1929-1936. [Bloomington, Ind.] 1960. 1 v. (various pagings). tables. bibliog. (12 leaves at end), notes. Thesis--Indiana Univ. Chapters on budgets, reorganization, participation in relief projects, "the bonus incident," the Civilian Conservation Corps, and "mobilization planning and research and development." [4044

Sea Forces

ROBERT P. BEEBE. Guardians of sea power. U.S.N. Inst. proc., 86(6): 26-33 (Jun). views. On American realization of "the importance of sea power" in colonial, Revolutionary, and Federal times, "the neglect of the Navy" by Jefferson and many of his successors, the high appreciation of it by Albert Thayer Mahan, the present neglect of his works in naval education, the need for naval officers with intellectual and scholarly capabilities comparable to his, and the means by which "these men can be found and educated" to produce "a rigorous work of scholarship, able to stand the most partisan scrutiny, containing no element of propaganda." [4045

GEORGE M. BROOKE. The Virginia Navy in the American Revolution. D. A. R. mag., 94:187-91 (Mar). map, view. [4046

WILLIAM BELL CLARK. George Washington's Navy: being an account of His Excellency's fleet in New England waters [1775-84]. Baton Rouge: Louisiana State Univ. Press [1960]. xi, 275 p. facsims., map, ports., double table, views. bibliog. (p. 237-42), notes (p. 243-60). [4047

L. K. POMEROY. The Navy and national policy [1775-1960]. U.S.N. Inst. proc., 86(4):90-97 (Apr). notes. [4048

REGINALD HARGREAVES. "Sweethearts and wives"--a tribute. U.S.N. Inst. proc., 86(2):63-9 (Feb). view. On the low income and frequent unemployment of Navy men, the resulting difficulties (added to long periods of separation) of the wives of those who married, the special problems of captains' wives who accompanied their husbands to sea, and the employment of sailors' wives as "domestics" on board, in the U.S. Navy, 1776-1945, and the Royal Navy. [4049

MARSHALL SMELSER. The Congress founds the Navy, 1787-1798. [Notre Dame, Ind.:] Univ. of Notre Dame Press, 1959. ix, 229 p. bibliog. (p. 214-17), notes. [4050

H. O. WERNER. The beginnings of the United States Navy [1794-1804]. Elmer Belmont Potter, ed., Sea power: a naval history (Englewood Cliffs, N.J.: Prentice-Hall, 1960), p. 187-206. maps. notes. On the building of ships, the recruitment of officers and enlisted men, and the operations of the Navy in the Quasi-War with France and the War with Tripoli. [4051

HAROLD DAVID LANGLEY. The humanitarians and the United States Navy, 1798-1862. Ann Arbor: University Microfilms, 1960. Positive microfilm of typescript. [380] leaves. Thesis--Univ. of Pennsylvania. Abstracted: Dissert. abstracts, 21: 1174-5 (Nov). Deals particularly with "the movements to abolish the traditional spirit ration and punishment by flogging." [4052

LOUIS J. GULLIVER. Dear John. U.S.N. Inst. proc., 86(1):57 (Jan). On the language of the letters in which officers of the Navy were notified in 1801 that they had been discharged. [4053

EDWIN MALBURN HALL. Cooper and the Navy. Ann Arbor: University Microfilms, 1959 [i.e. 1960]. Positive microfilm of typescript. [557] leaves. Thesis--Pennsylvania State Univ. Abstracted: Dissert. abstracts, 20:4098-9 (Apr). On the naval service of James Fenimore Cooper, his references to the Navy in his novels, "his role as a leading spokesman for the navy," and his History of the Navy, ca. 1810 to ca. 1850. [4054

ELLERY H. CLARK, JR., & EDWIN M. HALL. Navies in transition, 1815-1860. Elmer Belmont Potter, ed., Sea power: a naval history (Englewood Cliffs, N.J.: Prentice-Hall, 1960), p. 225-43. maps. notes. On operations and technological developments of the American, British, and French navies. Includes a brief account of naval operations in the Mexican War, 1846-48. [4055

HISTORY of the Texas Navy. Edited by George F. Haugh. Southw. hist. quar., 63:572-9 (Apr). notes. Anonymous document published in the Texas almanac for 1860. Text apparently an excerpt from some longer account) deals with the years 1836-37. Appended: list of "Officers of the Texas Navy from 1835 to 1838." [4056

TOM HENSERSON WELLS. An evaluation of the Texas Navy [1837-43]. Southw. hist. quar., 63:567-71 (Apr). map. notes. [4057

PAOLO ENRICO COLETTA. Oceanography: Maury to MOHOLE [1838-1960]. U.S.N. Inst. proc., 86(4): 98-107 (Apr). diagrs., views. Deals largely with the participation of the U.S. Navy in the development of this science. [4058

NEVILLE T. KIRK. The rise of Japanese naval power [1853-1905]. Elmer Belmont Potter, ed., Sea power: a naval history (Englewood Cliffs, N.J.: Prentice-Hall, 1960), p. 346-65. maps. notes. Mainly on activities of the U.S. Navy in forcing Japan to open its ports to American trade, the resulting rapid growth of the Japanese navy, and the demonstration of its strength in the Russo-Japanese War. [4059

JOSEPH THOMAS DURKIN. Lincoln and the Navy. Ralph G. Newman, ed., Lincoln for the ages (Garden City, N.Y.: Doubleday, 1960), p. 258-62. On the tactical use of the Union Navy as an "aid to the ground troops" and its use as "an independent striking force," 1861-65. [4060

HYMAN R. KAPLAN. The U.S. Coast Guard and the Civil War. U.S.N. Inst. proc., 86(8):40-50 (Aug). views. [4060a

JAMES A. ARNOLD. Naval developments in the late 19th century. Elmer Belmont Potter, ed., Sea power: a naval history (Englewood Cliffs, N.J.: Prentice-Hall, 1960), p. 328-45. diagrs., maps. notes. Includes some account of technological developments in the navies of the world, 1865-98, "The decline of the United States Navy," its slow revival after 1881, and the "intellectual progress" exemplified by the sea-power doctrines of Capt. Alfred Thayer Mahan. [4061

TOSHIYUKI YOKOI. Thoughts on Japan's naval defeat. U.S.N. Inst. proc., 86(10):68-75 (Oct). views. On the Japanese Navy since 1868, with particular reference to naval strategy between 1941 and 1945. [4062

JOHN ROGER FREDLAND. The United States becomes a naval power [1898-1914]. Elmer Belmont Potter, ed., Sea power: a naval history (Englewood Cliffs, N.J.: Prentice-Hall, 1960), p. 378-93. notes. [4063

ALBERT CHARLES STILLSON. The development and maintenance of the American naval establishment, 1901-1909. Ann Arbor: University Microfilms, 1959 [i.e. 1960]. Positive microfilm of typescript. [445] leaves. Thesis--Columbia Univ. Abstracted: Dissert. abstracts, 20:3813-14 (Mar). [4064

RAYMOND H. SWARTZ. Navy men in the Olympic Games. U.S.N. Inst. proc., 86(8):56-67 (Aug). ports., view. Includes a list of all participants from the U.S. Navy, 1912-56. [4065

HENRY H. ADAMS, ELMER BLEMONT POTTER, & W. H. RUSSELL. Problems of the Pacific. Elmer Belmont Potter, ed., Sea power: a naval history (Englewood Cliffs, N.J.: Prentice-Hall, 1960), p. 628-45. diagrs., map. note. On the development of American "amphibious assault doctrine," "carrier doctrine," and "logistic doctrine," 1916-45. [4066

ALFRED EDWIN JARRELL. Lessons learned from the hump. U.S.N. Inst. proc., 86(8):79-86 (Aug). port., view. On policies and problems in the promotion and retirement of naval officers since 1934. [4067

RAY C. NEEDHAM. Officer evaluation and promotion. U.S.N. Inst. proc., 86(3):60-69 (Mar). diagrs., view. On the fitness reports and the promotions of officers of the U.S. Navy, 1938-60. [4068

JULIUS AUGUSTUS FURER. Administration of the Navy Department in World War II. Wash.: [U.S. Govt. Print. Off.] 1959 [i.e. 1960]. xxxvi, 1042, [1] p. diagrs., ports., tables, views. bibliog. (p. 953-67), notes. Chapters on the Naval Establishment, the Secretary of the Navy, the Chief of Naval Operations, fleet organization, the 7 bureaus of the Navy Department, the Shore Establishment, the Marine Corps, the Coast Guard, the Judge Advocate General, and various functions (external relations, logistics, research and development, industrial mobilization and material procurement, and civilian personnel), 1939-45; with brief accounts of earlier developments since 1798 (some as early as the Revolution). [4069

HENRY H. ADAMS & EDWIN M. HALL. Submarines in the Pacific [1941-45]. Elmer Belmont Potter, ed., Sea power: a naval history (Englewood Cliffs, N.J.: Prentice-Hall, 1960), p. 796-812. diagr. notes. Reprinted with revisions: E. B. Potter & Chester William Nimitz, eds., The great sea war: the story of naval action in World War II (Englewood Cliffs, N.J.: Prentice-Hall [1960]), p. 401-24. diagr. notes. [4070

INSTALLATIONS

L. A. VIGNERAS. Fortificaciones de la Florida. Anuario estudios am., 16 (1959): 533-52. plans. notes. Undertakes "una descripción completa de las fortificaciones españolas en Florida desde 1565 hasta 1586." [4071

JOHN CHARLES HUDEN. Some comments on Chimney Point. Vt. hist., 28:235-6 (Jul). Evidence, 1685-1759, bearing upon the question whether a fort was ever located at this point on the Vermont shore of Lake Champlain. [4072

DANIEL H. THOMAS. Fort Toulouse--in tradition and fact [1714-60]. Ala. rev., 13:243-57 (Oct). notes. Expanded: Fort Toulouse, the French outpost at the Alibamos on theCoosa [1717-64. n. p.: Alabama State Dept. of Archives and History, 1960.] 133-230 p. coin, maps (1 fold.), port. notes (p. 210-30). (The Alabama historical quarterly, v. 22, no. 3, fall 1960.) Based on thesis (M. A.)--Univ. of Alabama, 1929. Includes some account of the site in later years. [4073

ALBERT BICKMORE COREY. Arms, a fort, and a frontier. D. A. R. mag., 94:72-3, 174 (Feb). On Fort Ontario, Oswego, N.Y., built in 1755, burned in 1756, rebuilt 1759-62, destroyed in 1777, rebuilt in 1782, and turned over to New York State in 1946. [4074

WILLIAM ALBERT HUNTER. Forts on the Pennsylvania frontier, 1753-1758. Harrisburg, Pa.: Pennsylvania Historical and Museum Commission, 1960. xi, 596 p. facsims., maps, plans, view. bibliog. (p. 565-72), notes. History and description of each fort existing during these years; with abundant excerpts from contemporary sources. [4075

LOUISE E. KOIER. But these stayed on! the story of Moses Pierson's blockhouse. Vt. Hist. Soc., News and notes, 6:49-51 (Mar 1955). view. On his farm in Shelburne, Vt., his repulse of a British and Indian force attacking his blockhouse in 1778, the capture and escape of his 2 sons, and the abandonment and burning of his buildings, which he rebuilt after the return of the family from Orwell in 1783. [4076

C. RUSSELL IRWIN. Fort Slongo [Smithtown, L.I., 1781]. Long Island forum, 23:151-2, 154-5 (Jul). plan. Includes a report from Maj. Benjamin Tallmage, 3 Oct. 1781, on the capture of the fort by American forces. [4077

The BOSTON Naval Shipyear [1800-1960]. U.S.N. Inst. proc., 86(10): 88-101 (Oct). views. [4078

JOSEPH SAMUEL WHITING & RICHARD J. WHITING. Forts of the State of California [1809-1960. Seattle] 1960. [6], xxiv, 90 p. maps, tables, views. Very brief histories in alphabetical order. [4079

A CRITIC views Iowa's first military post. [Edited] by Donald Jackson. Ia. jour. hist., 58:31-6 (Jan). notes. Anonymous communication to an unnamed addressee, probably the Secretary of War, undated, received 8 Nov. 1811, signed: A Democrat, on the corrupt and inefficient administration of Fort Madison under the command of Capt. Horatio Stark. [4080

FLORIDA'S "Fort Sumter." Fla. handbook, 1951-52, p. 10-13. On Fort Pickens, at the western tip of Santa Rosa Island, Pensacola Harbor, built 1829-34 and transferred to the State of Florida in 1949. Repeated in later biennial editions. [4081

A. L. FLANNERY. Little known facts about Fort Laramie [Wyo., 1834-98]. Ann. Wyo., 32:104-8 (Apr). view. [4082

BILL JUDGE. The Echo Canyon War. Frontier times, 34(4):10-12, 56 (fall). ports., view. On the conflict between the Mormons and Jim Bridger for possession of Fort Bridger, founded by Bridger in 1843 as a trading post on Mexican territory, and the taking over of the post as an installation of the U.S. Army in 1857; with indications that the contumacy of the Mormons may have been the reason why the surrounding area was detached from Utah Territory and made part of Wyoming Territory. [4083

FRONTIER forts of New Mexico. N.M., 38(2):28-30, 40 (Feb). Includes a map showing all the forts, with their dates of occupancy, 1846-1910, and photographs of 12 forts. [4084

RAYMOND BRANDES. Frontier military posts of Arizona. Globe, Ariz.: D. S. King [1960]. xviii, 94 p. insignia, maps, plans, ports., views. bibliogs. Accounts of 46 Army camps and forts, established between 1849 and 1886, of which only 1 is still maintained by the Army. [4085

GEORGE RUHLEN. Fort Thorn--an historical vignette. Password, 5:126-37 (Oct). map, view. notes. On a post on the Rio Grande in southern New Mexico, occupied by Army forces 1853-59, 1862, of which the last buildings were washed away in a flood in 1884. [4086

GEORGE RUHLEN. Quitman's owners: a sidelight on frontier realty. Password, 5:54-64 (Apr). notes. On the disputed ownership of the land occupied by Fort Quitman, 75 miles down the Rio Grande below El Paso, 1858-84. [4087

LAIRD SAVAGE. Fort Wingate. N.M., 38(8):32-3, 37-8 (Aug). map, col. port. On military installations at Bear Spring since 1860, originally for control of the Navajo Indians, more recently for an Ordnance depot, and an Indian school and a station of the U.S. Forest Service at the same location. [4088

JOSEPH L. EISENDRATH, JR. Chicago's Camp Douglas, 1861-1865. Ill. State Hist. Soc., Jour., 53:37-63 (spring). port., table, views. notes. On a camp used mainly for the confinement of prisoners of war. [4089

CORNELIA BRUÈRE ROSE, JR. Civil War forts in Arlington. Arlington hist. mag., 1(4):14-27 (Oct). map. [4090

GIDEON WELLES (1802-78). Mr. Welles in answer to Mr. [Thurlow] Weed: the facts of the abandonment of the Gosport Navy Yard [Norfolk, Va., 20 Apr. 1861]. Selected essays by Gideon Welles: Civil War and Reconstruction, ed. Albert Mordell (N.Y.: Twayne Publishers, 1959), p. 15-35. From The galaxy, Jul. 1870. [4091

JAMES MONROE FOSTER, JR. Fort Bascom, New Mexico. N.M. hist. rev., 35:30-62 (Jan). notes. On a military post established on the Canadian River in New Mexico in 1863 and abandoned in 1870, and the operations from this base against the Indians in northeastern New Mexico and northwestern Texas. [4092

CHARLES B. McCORMACK. Contemporary description of Camp McClellan and vicinity [Davenport, Ia.]. Ann. Ia., 35:308-9 (spring). From the manuscript journal of the author, a soldier in Company D, 3d Iowa Cavalry, Feb. 1863. [4093

HOWARD M. SMITH. Hunters' Point Drydock [San Francisco Bay, 1865-1945]. U.S.N. Inst. proc., 86(3):152-5 (Mar). views. On a facility acquired by the U.S. Navy in World War II and designated in Dec. 1945 as the San Francisco Naval Shipyard. [4094

WILLIAM ALLEN WARD. Historic Fort Concho. Cattleman, 46(9):26, 28 (Feb). On a post at San Angelo, Tex., occupied by the Army from 1866 to 1889, now a museum. [4095

CHARLES RITTER. The early history of Fort Fetterman [Wyo., 1867-86]. Ann. Wyo., 32:220-24 (Oct). view. [4096

THERONNE THOMPSON. Fort Buffalo Springs, Texas border post [in Clay County, 1867-68]. West Tex. Hist. Assoc. yr. bk., 36:156-75. map, view. notes. [4097

G. HUBERT SMITH. Archeological investigations at the site of Fort Stevenson (32ML1), Garrison Reservoir, North Dakota. U.S. Bureau of American Ethnology, River Basin Surveys, River Basin Surveys papers, nos. 15-20, ed. Frank H. H. Roberts, Jr. (Wash.: U.S. Govt. Print. Off., 1960 [U.S., Bureau of American Ethnology, Bulletin 176], p. 159-238. fold. maps, plans, views. bibliog. (p. 236-8). On a fort in present McLean County occupied by the Army from 1867 to 1883, later used as an Indian school till 1894, excavated in 1951; with an inventory of building remains and military, civilian, and Indian artifacts recovered, including a list of "Cartridges and bullets." [4098

SUSAN MILES. A Fort Concho wedding. West Tex. Hist. Assoc. yr. bk., 36: 63-79. On the marriage of Miss Allie V. Bullock to Maj. George Wheeler Schofield, 10th U.S. Cavalry, 9 Nov. 1875; with some account of the later years of all the persons concerned in the wedding. [4099

SETH THOMAS BAILEY. Ft. Lincoln's phantom forger. By Tom Bailey. Frontier times, 34(4):6-7, 46-50 (fall). On forgeries perpetrated at Ft. Abraham Lincoln, D. T., by Charlie Riddell (died 1899), agent of a group of unnamed individuals who "made a fortune siphoning off army supplies from government warehouses and selling the goods back to the army," including a forged order to Gen. George A. Custer to postpone his departure for the Little Big Horn, fabricated by persons who expected his forces to be defeated there, an outcome that would reduce the volume of supplies available for pilfering,

1876; with some account of Custer's efforts to elicit corrective action from an indifferent War Department and an unconcerned President. [4100

U.S. Army. 35th Infantry. An incident at Fort Keogh. [Edited] by Edgar I. Stewart. Montana, 10(2):42-3 (Apr). view. Text of "Proceedings of a Board of Survey convened per S. O. 35 Hdqrs. Fort Keogh M. T., February 13, 1880," to "examine into, report upon, and fix the responsibility for a deficiency of twenty-four (24) cakes of 'Cashmere Bouquet' Soap, found in a box of Toilet Soap." [4101

ANNE HORNEY. Indiantown Gap: Pennsylvania's military post no. 1. Internal Affairs monthly bul., 28(7): 10-13, 26 (Jul). port., view. On Indian Town Gap Military Reservation, an installation of 26 square miles east of Harrisburg, purchased by the Commonwealth of Pennsylvania in 1931, leased to the U.S. Army. [4102

PHILIP T. FLAXMAN. Guide to Bunker Hill Air Force Base, Indiana, home of the 305th Bombardment Wing (M), Strategic Air Command. [Colorado Springs] 1960. 82 p. col. coat of arms, diagr., col. flag, col. insignia, map, ports. (part col.), views (part col.). On an installation at Bunker Hill, Ind., constructed by the U.S. Navy in 1942, used as a naval air station, 1943-46, deactivated in 1946, taken over by the Air Force in 1951, and formally activated as an Air Force base in 1954. [4103

EDWARD F. DISSETTE. Overseas bases--how long for this world? U.S.N. Insert. proc., 86(7):22-30 (Jul). view. On "our military bases scattered throughout the free world" since 1947. [4104

HOWARD R. TALKINGTON. NOTS, San Clemente Island. U.S.N. Inst. proc., 86(6):92-101 (Jun). diagr., maps, views. On the Naval Ordnance Test Station on San Clemente Island as "a base for development testing and evaluation of underwater ordnance," 1949-60. [4105

DAVID KUHNER. Florida in the space age. Fla. handbook, the U.S. Government at Cape Canaveral since 1950, with some account of the area since 1513. [4106

EDITH T. CARPER. The defense appropriations rider. University, Ala.: Univ. of Alabama Press for the ICP [1960]. 28 p. (Inter-University Case Program. ICP case series, 59.) On debates in Congress regarding the proposed discontinuance of the "ropewalk at the Boston Navy Yard" in the interests of economy, 1955-56. [4107

SERVICES

The Military Chaplaincy

HOWARD LEWIS APPLEGATE. Organization and development of the American chaplaincy during the Revolutionary War [1775-82]. Picket post, 68:19-21, 37-41 (May). notes. [4108

HERMAN ALBERT NORTON. Revivalism in the Confederate armies [1861-65]. Civil War hist., 6:410-24 (Oct). notes. Based on thesis--Vanderbilt Univ., 1956. [4109

Military Communications

DON EASTER. Stumpy John, flying ace. Flying, 64(6):55 (Jun 1959). view. On a carrier pigeon, Stumpy John Silver (1918-35), employed by American forces in France during World War I, severely wounded in line of duty, later assigned to the 11th Signal Company, U.S. Signal Corps, Honolulu, now mounted and preserved in the Air Force Museum. [4110

ISADORE WILLINGER. U.S. Army post offices of South American countries during WW-II, with particular reference to Chile [1941-43]. S. P. A. jour., 22:544-5 (Aug). diagr., facsim. [4110a

Military Disposal of the Dead

U.S. American Battle Monuments Commission. Netherlands American Cemetery and memorial [at Margraten; established in 1944 by the U.S. Ninth Army. Wash.] 1960. 22, [2] p. maps (1 double), tables, views. [4111

U.S. American Battle Monuments Commission. North Africa American Cemetery and memorial [established at Carthage in 1948. Wash.] 1960. 22, [2] p. maps (1 double), tables, views.

U.S. American Battle Monuments Commission. Florence [Italy] American Cemetery and memorial [established 1949. Wash.] 1960. 22, [2] p. maps (1 double), plans, tables, views. [4113

Military Engineering

HUBERTIS MAURICE CUMMINGS. Draughts by two of George Washington's French engineers. Internal Affairs monthly bul., 28(1-2):24-8 (Jan-Feb). On a Brouillon ou plan du camp de Vallée Forge (Dec. 1777 or Jan. 1778), by Col. Louis le Beque Duportail, and 3 "beautiful drawings" of fortifications near Philadelphia done by him in collaboration with Jean Louis Ambroise de Genton, Chevalier de Villefranche (1779). [4114

HUBERTIS MAURICE CUMMINGS. The Villefranche map for the defense of the Delaware. Pa. mag. hist. and biog., 84:424-34 (Oct). notes. On Maj. Jean Louis Ambroise de Genton, Chevalier de Villefranche, military engineer, French cartographer in Philadelphia, and his manuscript map, 44 x 67 in., prepared for the Supreme Executive Council of Pennsylvania, 1779, showing about 10 miles of the Delaware River and some of its shores at Philadelphia and the adjoining part of New Jersey. [4115

Military Intelligence

JOHN EDWIN BAKELESS. Turncoats, traitors, and heroes. Phila.: Lippincott [1960, c1959. 2], 406 p. bibliog. (p. 367-71), notes (p. 373-94). On "the espionage, counter-espionage, and other military intelligence services in the Continental and British armies in the main theatre of war" in America, 1775-82. [4116

RUFUS L. TAYLOR. Command and the intelligence process [1861-1960]. U.S.N. Inst. proc., 86(8):26-39 (Aug). port., views. [4117

HARRY HOWE RANSOM. Central intelligence and national security. Cambridge: Harvard Univ. Press, 1958. xiv, [2], 287 p. diagr. bibliog. (p. 233-56), notes (p. 257-73). On the military and civilian agencies of the U.S. Government concerned with the collection and interpretation of information about foreign countries, mainly since 1941, with special reference to the Central Intelligence Agency and the National Security Council. [4118

TAKEO YOSHIKAWA. Top secret assignment. ... With Lieutenant Colonel Norman Stanford. U.S.N. Inst. proc., 86(12):26-39 (Dec). views. On the author's service "in sole charge of espionage for the Imperial Japanese Navy at Pearl Harbor," Apr.-Dec. 1941. [4119

Military Justice

WILLIAM FRANKLIN FRATCHER. History of the Judge Advocate General's Corps, United States Army [1775-1956]. Mil. law rev., 4:89-122 (Apr 1959). notes. [4120

JAMES A. HAGAN. The general article--elemental confusion. Mil. law rev., 10:63-114 (Oct). notes. Based on thesis--Judge Advocate General's School, U.S. Army. On the authority of military courts to punish "all disorders and neglects to the prejudice of good order and military discipline in the armed forces, all conduct of a nature to bring discredit upon the armed forces, and crimes and offenses not capital" when such disorders, neglects, conduct, crimes, and offenses are "not specifically mentioned" in the articles, codes, or statutes governing the armed forces, 1775-1957. [4121

F. W. SCHWEIKHARDT. Non-judical punishment under the Uniform Code of Military Justice. N.Y. law forum, 5:45-72 (Jan 1959). notes. Includes a review of such punishment between 1775 and the adoption of the Code in 1950. [4122

U.S. Army. Courts Martial. Lieut. Colonel Joseph Barton's court martial in 1781. [Edited by] George E. McCracken. N.J. Hist. Soc., Proc., 78:33-5 (Jan). Record of the trial at New York, 24 Jun. 1781, of an officer of the 1st Battalion, New Jersey Volunteers, charged with "Disobedience of Orders, Neglect of duty and an un gentleman like behaviour." [4122a

ROBERT EMMETT QUINN. The United States Court of Military Appeals and individual rights in the military service. Notre Dame lawyer, 35:491-507 (Aug). notes. On the extent of the constitutional rights of Americans in the armed forces, 1787-1960, especially since the establishment of the Court of Military Appeals, with particular reference to the right of privacy in military quarters, freedom of speech, freedom of action, the right to be silent, and "justice and fair play." [4123

MARTIN MENTER. Codification of laws relating to the armed forces [1789-1958]. Air Univ. quar. rev. 12(2):45-51 (summer). [4124

RECENT limitations in court-martial jurisdiction over civilians. De Paul law rev., 9:197-210 (spring-summer). notes. Review of claims to such jurisdiction, 1806-1959. [4125

EBERHARD PAUL DEUTSCH. The United States versus Major General Andrew Jackson. Am. Bar Assoc., jour., 46:966-72 (Sep). ports. notes. On a newspaper article by Louis Louallier, naturalized American citizen and member of the Louisiana legislature, denying the authority of Jackson to issue an order requiring all French subjects to leave New Orleans, the arrest of Louallier by Jackson under the Second Article of War, the issuance of a writ of habeas corpus by U.S. District Judge Dominick Augustine Hall, the arrest of Hall by Jackson, the trial and acquittal of Louallier by a general court martial, the refusal of Jackson to release him, Jackson's release and temporary exile of Hall, an order from Hall for Jackson to show cause why process of attachment should not issue against him for contempt of court, the answer of Jackson prepared by Edward Livingston, the issuance of the attachment, the finding that Jackson was guilty of contempt of court, and his sentence to pay a fine of $1,000, 1815; and the reimbursement of the fine by act of Congress in 1844. [4126

MELVIN E. PEARL. The applicability of the Bill of Rights to a court-martial proceeding [1857-1959]. jour. crim. law, 50:559-65 (Mar-Apr). notes. [4127

ALFRED AVINS. The duty of military defense counsel to an accused [1864-1958]. Mich. law rev., 58:347-404 (Jan). notes. [4128

W. LINCOLN SIMON. Jeremiah S. Black: lawyer and statesman. Am. Bar Assoc. jour., 46:1313-14 (Dec). port. On "his classic defense of the right to trial by jury in Ex parte Milligan," 1866. [4129

ROBERT D. DUKE & HOWARD S. VOGEL. The Constitution and the standing army: another problem of court-martial jurisdiction. Vanderbilt law rev., 13:435-60 (Mar). notes. On the authority of courts martial in time of peace to try a capital or noncapital crime committed by a serviceman within the United States when the crime is "exclusively 'civil' in the sense that its commission does not have any substantial effect upon the maintenance of military discipline," 1878-1958. [4130

HENRY B. CABELL. Damnosa hereditas--special courts-martial. Mil. law rev., 7:145-53 (Jan). notes. On "the practical and administrative difficulties incident to the use of special courts-martial by battle groups and separate battalions," 1913-58. [4131

JAMES A. GEORGE. Elimination of peacetime court-martial jurisdiction over military dependants and employees in foreign countries (1916-60]. La. law rev., 20:714-31 (Jun). notes. [4132

JOHN RITTENHOUSE, JR. Courts-martial jurisdiction over civilians stationed overseas with United States troops [1917-60]. Dicta, 37:164-83 (May-Jun). table. notes. [4133

MAURER MAURER. The Korean conflict was a war. Mil. affairs, 24: 137-45 (fall). notes. On "the legal status of the fighting in Korea," 1950-53, especially as considered by the Court of Military Appeals. [4134

Military Medicine

HOWARD LEWIS APPLEGATE. The Pennsylvania military medical department of the American Revolution [1775-82]. Picket post, 70:20-23, 39-41 (Nov). views. notes. Includes a list of the Pennsylvanians in the Continental and State medical services. [4135

CHARLES MALCOLM BROOKFIELD GILMAN. Military surgery in the American Revolution [1775-83]. Med. Soc. N.J., Jour., 57:491-6 (Aug). table, view. notes. [4136

WILLIAM SHAINLINE MIDDLETON. Medicine in the Veterans Administration [1811-1959]. Mil. med., 125:21-5 (Jan). notes. [4137

ALBERT GALLATIN LOVE, EUGENE L. HAMILTON, & IDA LEVIN HELLMAN. Tabulating equipment and Army medical statistics. Wash.: Office of the Surgeon General, Dept. of the Army, 1958. x, 202 p. diagrs., forms, views. bibliogs., notes. On "the development of medical records of the Army in their individual service function, in their compilation as medical statistics, and in their analysis leading to new knowledge," 1818-1957, and particularly the Army medical use of "electrical tabulating equipment" since 1889 to record and analyze statistics. [4138

JOHN CHRISTIAN KRANTZ, JR. The implications of the medical history of General [Robert E.] Lee [from 1839 to 1870]. U.S. Armed Forces med. jour., 11:329-37 (Mar). ports. From the Virginia medical monthly, Jun. 1959. [4139

AMOS R. KOONTZ. Nicholas Senn [1844-1908], surgeon and soldier: a happy combination in military medicine. Mil. med., 125:203-6 (Mar). notes. On his medical studies and practice, his teaching of medicine in Chicago, and his many contributions to military medicine. [4140

R. W. TAYLOR. History of naval dentistry [ca. 1845 to 1958]. Am. College Dentists, Jour., 26:195-208 (Sep 1959). notes. [4141

JACOB MENDEZ DA COSTA (1833-1900). Functional heart disease in the Civil War (Da Costa, 1871). [Edited by] Saul Jarcho. Am. jour. cardiol., 4:809-17 (Dec 1959). "On irritable heart: a clinical study of a form of functional cardiac disorder and its consequences," from American journal of the medical sciences, 61 (1871). [4142

NORMAN W. HOOVER & JOHN C. IVINS. Wound débridement. Arch. surgery, 79:701-10 (Nov 1959). notes. On wound surgery in American wars, 1861-1945. [4143

CLARA RAVEN. Achievements of women in medicine, past and present--women in the Medical Corps of the Army [1861-1958]. Mil. med., 125: 105-11 (Feb). bibliog. [4144

NORAH ANTOINETTE SMARIDGE. Hands of mercy: the story of sister-nurses in the Civil War. N.Y.: Benziger Bros. [1960. 6], 180 p. (A Banner book, [13].) On the Sisters of Charity, caring without distinction for both Union and Confederate patients. [4145

RICHARD BOLES STARK & JANET C. STARK. Surgical care of the Confederate States Army [1861-65]. U.S. Armed Forces med. jour., 10: 50-68 (Jan 1959). diagr., facsim., ports., views. notes. From Bulletin of the New York Academy of Medicine, Jun. 1958. [4146

MORSE K. TAYLOR (1823-89). Morse K. Taylor on heart disease in the Civil War (1867). [Edited by] Saul Jarcho. Am. jour. cardiol., 4:240-45 (Aug 1959). Reprinted "Remarks on heart diseases as observed in the military service from 1861 to 1865 inclusive." [4147

LOUISA MAY ALCOTT (1832-88). Hospital sketches. Introduction by Earl Schenck Miers. N.Y.: sagamore Press, 1957. 157, [2] p. (American century series, S-15.) For contents see following entry. [4148

LOUISA MAY ALCOTT (1832-88). Hospital sketches. ... Edited by Bessie Z. Jones. Cambridge: Belknap Press of Harvard Univ. Press, 1960. xliv, [2], 91, [2] p. Signed: Tribulation Periwinkle. Based upon letters to her family. On her sightseeing in Washington and her efforts, as a volunteer nurse in Hurly-Burly House (Union Hotel Hospital, Georgetown, Dec. 1862 and Jan. 1863), to wash and feed wounded soldiers, assist in dressing their wounds, write letters for them, receive their visitors, comfort the dying, and cope with rats, alcoholic attendants, thievish messengers, and callous surgeons; with details of her journey by railroad and boat from Boston to Washington and her return home after recovery from typhoid fever. Includes an extensive introduction on her earlier life, her stay in Washington, and the Army hospitals and nurses there. [4149

HERBERT P. RAMSEY. Walter Reed Army Medical Center [1898-1959]. Med. ann. Dist. Col., 28:225-31 (Apr 1959). map, ports., views. bibliog. [4150

W. LEONA JACKSON. We've reached the golden years. Am. jour. nursing, 58:671-3 (May 1958). port., views. On the Navy Nurse Corps, 1908-58. [4151

LEONARD D. HEATON. Army medicine: past, present, future [1917-59]. U.S. Armed Forces med. jour., 11: 4-14 (Jan). diagr., port., views. [4152

JOSEPH ISRAELOFF. The emerging role of the Medical Service Corps officer in the evolution of the Army Medical Service [1917-60]. Mil. med., 125:267-74 (Apr). table. notes. [4153

OLIVER K. NIESS. Medicine in the aerospace age [1917-59]. U.S. Armed Forces med. jour., 11:27-37 (Jan). diagr., ports., views. [4154

ROBERT HENRY IVY. The influenza epidemic of 1918: personal experience of a medical officer in World War I. Mil. med., 125:620-22 (Sep). Report from the author, surgeon of troops aboard the USS Wilhelmina, to the Surgeon, Port of Embarkation, Hoboken, N.J., on influenza during a voyage from Hoboken to France, 22 Sep. - 6 Oct. 1918. [4155

LEO J. GEPPERT. Evolution of pediatric service in the U.S. Army [1920-58]. U.S. Armed Forces med. jour., 11:373-80 (Apr). tables. notes. [4156

CHARLES M. BELTING. Integration of the dental service with the general health program in the Veterans Administration [1921-58]. Am. Dental Assoc., Jour., 60:22-9 (Jan). forms. notes. [4157

HELEN COVEY MILIUS. Seagoing surgeon from Virginia. Commonwealth (Va.), 27(2):22-4, 39 (Feb). ports. On the early life of Herbert Lamont Pugh (born 1895) in Albermarle County, and his service as a surgeon in the U.S. Navy, 1923-56, eventually as Surgeon General of the Navy. [4158

LEONARD D. HEATON. Progress in Army medicine: medical progress in World War II [1940-60]. Md. State med. jour., 9:432-8 (Aug). [4159

JOHN RIZZOLO. The Armed Forces Epidemiological Board [and predecessor organizations, 1940-60]. Mil. med., 125:809-21 (Dec). notes. [4160

LEONARD D. HEATON. The practice of military medicine--broadening concepts [1941-59]. Mil. med., 125: 7-11 (Jan). [4161

WILLIAM S. JORDAN, JR. Activities of the Commission on Acute Respiratory Diseases [of the Armed Forces Epidemiological Board, Washington, D.C., "since its organization during World War II"]. U.S. Armed Forces med. jour., 11:1226-9 (Oct). notes. [4162

U.S. Army Medical Service. Preventive medicine in World War II. Volume V. Communicable diseases transmitted through contact or by unknown means. ... Editor for preventive medicine: Ebbe Curtis Hoff. Wash.: Office of the Surgeon General, Dept. of the Army, 1960. xxiii, 530 p. diagrs., maps, tables, views. (Its The Medical Department of the United States Army [in World War II].) Chapters, by various contributors, on schistosomiasis, skin infections, venereal diseases (p. 139-324), viral hepatitis, poliomyelitis, and maladies of less frequent occurrence. [4163

U.S. Army Medical Service. Surgery in World War II: hand surgery. Edited by Sterling Bunnell, M.D. Washington: Office of the Surgeon General, Dept. of the Army, 1955. ix, 447 p. diagrs., map, tables, views. notes. (Its Medical Department, United States Army in World War II.) Chapters by numerous contributors. On hand surgery in Zone of Interior, the European Theater of Operations, and the Mediterranean Theater of Operations. [4164

U.S. Army Medical Service. Surgery in World War II: neurosurgery. ... Editors for neurosurgery: R. Glen Spurling, M.D., [and] Barnes Woodhall, M.D. Wash.: Office of the Surgeon General, Dept. of the Army, 1958-59. 2 v. xix, 466; xxvi, 705 p. diagrs., forms, tables, views (part col.). notes. (Its Medical Department, United States Army in World War II.) Chapters by numerous contributors. [4165

U.S. Army Medical Service. Surgery in World War II: ophthalmology and otolaryngology. ... Editor for ophthalmology: M. Elliott Randolph, M.D. Editor for otolaryngology: Norton Canfield, M.D. Wash.: Office of the Surgeon General, Dept. of the Army, 1957. xxiii, [3], 605 p. diagrs., forms, ports. (part col.), tables, views. notes. (Its Medical Department, United States Army in World War II.) Chapters by numerous contributors. [4166

GILBERT WHEELER BEEBE & JOHN WILBERFORCE APPEL. Variation in psychological tolerance to ground combat in World War II. [Wash.: Follow-Up Agency, Division of Medical Sciences, National Academy of Sciences, National Research Council] 1958. iv leaves, v-xiii, 278 p., [1], 79-80 leaves. diagrs., forms, tables. bibliog. (leaves 279-80). Study made under contract with the Department of the Army, 1951-53. Analysis of records of 100 ETO rifle companies (Jun.-Dec. 1944) and 50 MTO rifle companies (Nov. 1942 - Sep. 1943) to find "a measure of the average psychologic strength and endurance of human beings in the combat environment of World War II" as indicated by Army records of "psychiatric breakdown"; with suggestions regarding "morale," "battle fatigue," and the desirability of a definite policy of "combat rotation." [4167

U.S. Army Medical Service. Cold injury, ground type, [By Tom French Whayne and Michael E. De Bakey.] Wash.: Office of the Surgeon General, Dept. of the Army, 1958. xxi, 570 p. diagrs., tables, views (part col.). notes. (Its Medical Department, United States Army in World War II.)

On frostbite and trenchfoot, their incidence, etiology, prevention, and treatment, in the theaters and in Zone of Interior, 1942-45. [4168

U.S. Army Medical Service. Surgery in World War II: orthopedic surgery in the European Theater of Operations [Jul. 1942 - May 1945]. ... Editor for orthopedic surgery: Mather Cleveland, M.D. Wash.: Office of the Surgeon General, Dept. of the Army, 1956. xv, 397 p. diagrs., forms, tables, views. notes. (Its Medical Department, United States Army in World War II.) [4169

U.S. Army Medical Service. Surgery in World War II: orthopedic surgery in the Mediterranean Theater of Operations [Nov. 1942-May 1945]. ... Editor for orthopedic surgery: Mather Cleveland, M.D. [Author: Oscar P. Hampton, Jr., M.D.] Wash.: Office of the Surgeon General, Dept. of the Army, 1957. xx, 368 p. diagrs., tables, views. notes. (Its Medical Department, United States Army in World War II.) [4170

WOLFGANG W. KLEMPERER. Spinal cord injuries in World War II. U.S. Armed Forces med. jour., 10:532-52, 701-14 (May-Jun 1959). diagrs., tables, views. notes. On the "treatment of 201 patients with spinal cord injuries sustained during the North African and European campaigns," by neurosurgeons of the Second Auxiliary Surgical Group, 1943. [4171

U.S. Army Medical Service. Surgery in World War II. Volume II. General surgery. ... Editor for general surgery: Michael E. De Bakey, M.D. Wash.: Office of the Surgeon General, Dept. of the Army, 1955. xxiv, 417 p. diagrs., tables, views. notes. (Its Medical Department, United States Army in World War II.) Chapters by numerous contributors. Analysis of data collected in the Mediterranean Theater of Operations by the 2d Auxiliary Surgical Group, 1943-44. Contents.--Part I. Resusciation, control of pain, and anesthesia.--Part II. Abdominal injuries and the initial surgery of abdominal wounds.--Part III. Colostomy. [4172

ROBERT E. ESCHBACH. Development of the Army's occupational vision program [1944-58]. Am. jour. optometry, 36:493-500 (Aug 1959). notes. On a program for civilian employees. [4173

U.S. Army. Mediterranean Theater of Operations. Board for the Study of the Severely Wounded. Surgery in World War II: the physiologic effects of wounds. [Edited by Henry K. Beecher.] Wash.: Office of the Surgeon General, Dept. of the Army, 1952. xi, [3], 376 p. diagrs., port., tables, views (part col.). (Medical Department, United States Army in World War II.) Report of a board appointed in Sep. 1944 to collect and study, in the field, data concerning men severely wounded and exhibiting traumatic shock. Prepared by the Historical Division, Army Medical Library, under the direction of Col. Joseph H. McNinch, Editor in Chief. [4174

WAYNE L. ERDBRINK. Vision in the U.S. Armed Forces. U.S. Armed Forces med. jour., 11:641-55 (Jun). diagr., tables. notes. On military ophthalmology, 1945-60. [4175

SILAS B. HAYS. The Society of Medical Consultants to the Armed Forces [1946-59]. U.S. Armed Forces med. jour., 11:38-48 (Jan). ports. [4176

ROBERT S. HIGDON. The present status of military dermatology [1946-58]. Arch. dermatol., 80:327-31 (Sep 1959). tables. [4177

GEORGE STRENGER & DAVID SCHWARTZ. Late effects of retained missile fragments [New York Regional Office of the Veterans Administration, 1946-59]. N.Y. State med. jour., 59:3967-70 (1 Nov 1959). tables. notes. [4178

J. W. HOLLINGSWORTH. Delayed radiation effects in survivors of the atomic bombings: a summary of the findings of the Atomic Bomb Casualty Commission, 1947-1959. New Eng. jour. med., 263:481-7 (3 Sept). table. notes. [4179

KRYDER VAN BUSKIRK & JAMES C. KIMBROUGH. Urological surgery in combat [8076th Mobile Army Surgical Hospital, Korea, 1950-51]. Jour. urol., 71:639-46 (May 1954). notes. [4180

PETER B. WALLACE & ARNOLD M. MEIROWSKY. The repair of dural defects by graft: an analysis of 540 penetrating wounds of the brain incurred in the Korean War [1950-52]. Ann. surgery, 151:174-80 (Aug). tables, views. notes. [4181

Ordnance

JAMES ERNEST HICKS. U.S. firearms, 1776-1956: notes on U.S. ordnance, vol. I. Beverly Hills, Calif.: Fadco Pub. Co., 1957. 128 p. facsims., table, views. 1st ed. 1940. Texts of

War Department records, 1777-1905, relating to specifications for and procurement and performance of Army ordnance; with connecting text. Appended: pen-and-ink drawings by Andre Jandot on 88 plates. Includes a table of "United States small arms data, 1795 to 1956" (p. 126-7). [4182

R. G. CARPENTER. The Citadel gun. Mil. collector & historian, 11:1-4 (spring 1959). seals, view. notes. On "a 4-pounder brass cannon" probably made by Louis Ansart de Marasquelle and Hugh Orr at Titicut, Mass., probably in 1777, probably captured by the British on Penobscot Bay in 1779, now exhibited in Quebec with an incorrect inscription. [4183

MARTIN RYWELL. United States military muskets, rifles, carbines, and their current prices. ... Firearms in American history. Harriman, Tenn.: Pioneer Press, ©1959. 50 p. facsims., tables, views. (Books of lasting interest.) "Lists, describes, and gives up-to-date prices of all U.S. martial shoulder arms (muskets, rifles, carbines) from 1795 through World War II." 1st ed. 1951. [4184

LOUISE E. KOIER. The story of a sword and a pistol. Vt. Hist. Soc., News and notes, 5:41-3 (Feb 1954). port., view. On the sword of Lord George Gordon Byron and the pistol of Col. Jonathan P. Miller (1797-1847) of Vermont, both used "valiantly in the Greek Revolution" in 1824, and the means by which they came into possession of the Vermont Historical Society. [4185

CHARLES MEADE PATTERSON. Firearms on the Wilkes Expedition [the United States South Sea Exploring Expedition, 1838-42]. Gun rep., 5(3):10-11, 13 (Aug 1959). port., views. [4186

CHARLES MEADE PATTERSON. Martial percussion revolver inspectors. Gun rep., 5(10:10-15, 43: (11): 11-17 (Mar, Apr). port., tables, view. On the names and procedures of U.S. Ordnance inspectors as identified by their initials stamped on stocks and grips of guns inspected, 1845-65. [4187

E. F. DONNELLY. "The Minié Rifle." Gun digest, 15:152-7. diagrs., table, views. On the Springfield 58-caliber rifle-musket, models of 1855 and following years, "the principal shoulder arm used by the Civil War soldiers," and the extraordinary lethality of "the Minié ball used in it." [4188

HERSCHEL C. LOGAN. The Confederate Le Mat revolver. Am. rifleman, 108(11):35-6 (Nov). diagrs., table, view. On a weapon patented by Dr. Jean Alexandre Francois Le Mat, of New Orleans, in 1856, and manufactured in France for the Confederate States, 1861-64. [4189

WILLIAM A. ALBAUGH III. Confederate edged weapons. N.Y.: Harper [1960]. xxiv, 198 p. diagrs., facsim., views. On the makers and the characteristics of Confederate swords, pikes and lances, bayonets, and knives. [4190

ROBERT VANCE BRUCE. President Lincoln and weapons policy. Ralph G. Newman, ed., Lincoln for the ages (Garden City, N.Y.: Doubleday, 1960), p. 252-7. On his efforts to stimulate the development of new weapons for Union forces, 1861-65. [4191

F. W. HACKLEY. A report on Civil War explosive ordnance. Indian Head, Md.: U.S. Naval Propellant Plant [1960? 1]. iv, 44 leaves. diagrs., views. At head of title: U.S. Naval School, Explosive Ordnance Disposal. Manual of information and photographs for the identification of land ordnance: shells, grenades, land mines, and fuzes. [4192

RICHARD KEITH McMASTER & GEORGE RUHLEN. The guns of Valverde. Password, 5:20-34 (Jan). map, ports., view. notes. On the guns used by Union and Confederate forces in the Battle of Valverde, N. M., Feb. 1862, and the later uses of some of the guns. For comment by Martin H. Hall see p. 79-80. [4193

JOHN SHIVERS. Dance Brothers Confederate revolvers. Jr. historian (Tex.), 19(2):1-3, 30 (Nov 1958). views. On weapons produced by James Henry Dance, George Perry Dance, and David Dance, blacksmiths and farm-implement manufacturers, at Marion, Tex., 1862-63, probably totaling at least 324 pieces, of which only 20 are known to survive. [4194

U.S. War Dept. Rules for the management and cleaning of the rifle musket, model 1863, for the use of soldiers. With descriptive plates. Springfield Armory, Apr. 28, 1863. Adopted by the War Department for the government of U.S. troops. Wash.: Govt. Print. Off., 1863. [Phila.: R. Riling, 1960.] facsim. (25, [1] p.) diagrs. [4195

ANDREW FRANKLYN LUSTYIK. The Warner carbine [made by James Warner, Springfield, and Greene Rifle Works, Worcester, 1864-65, for the U.S. Army]. Gun rep., 5(12):6-9, 39 (May). views. notes. [4196

JAMES A. SHUTT & JOSEPH THATCHER. The Courtenay coal torpedo. Mil. collector & historian, 11:7-8 (spring 1959). diagr. On iron castings filled with powder and disguised with a covering of tar and coal dust, secreted in the coal bunkers of Union ships and exploding when the coal was shoveled into the fire box--an invention of Capt. Thomas Edgeworth Courtenay, Confederate Secret Service, 1864. [4197

U.S. War Dept. Description and rules for the management of the Springfield rifle, carbine, and army revolvers. Calibre .45. [By James Gilchrist Benton, commanding the National Armory.] Springfield, Mass.: National Armory, 1874. [Phila.: R. Riling, 1960.] facsim. (51, [1] p.). diagrs. (1 fold.), tables, views. Includes additions by Col. Berkeley R. Lewis. [4198

STAN NELSON. The Merwin Hulbert pocket Army. Gun rep., 5(9):16-19 (Feb). views. On the Pocket Army model "short-barreled, 44-40 caliber double action revolver" (not an Army gun) made by Merwin Hulbert and Company and later by Hopkins and Allen, 1884-87. [4199

NATIONAL RIFLE ASSOCIATION OF AMERICA. Surplus military rifles. Part 1 of 4: United States [1898-1957] and Norway. Am. rifleman, 108(12): 21-5 (Dec). views. [4200

PHILIP M. SHOCKLEY. Forerunners of the 30-06. Gun rep., 5(7):18-22, 37 (Dec 1959). views. notes. On the lethality of the Spanish Mauser rifles in Cuba in 1898, and the incorporation of some of their characteristics into the "United States magazine rifle, caliber .30, Model of 1903"; with some account of earlier study of the Mauser system by the Ordnance Department since 1871. [4201

SAMUEL PIERPONT LANGLEY (1834-1906). Doctor Langley's paradox: two letters suggesting the development of rockets. [Edited] by Russell J. Parkinson. Wash., 1960. 4 p. port., views. (Smithsonian miscellaneous collections, v. 140, no. 3.) Letters to Charles M. Manly, 9 Mar. and 25 Sep. 1902, on "the possibility of wingless aircraft." [4202

ARTHUR GEORGE JOSEPH WHITEHOUSE. Tank: the story of their battles and the men who drove them from their first use in World War I to Korea [1917-53]. By Arch Whitehouse. Garden City, N.Y.: Doubleday, 1960. 383 p. maps, views. bibliog. (p. 368-71). [4203

DOROTHEA MAGDALENE FOX. Dr. Goddard. N.M., 38(9):4-7, 34 (Sep). ports. On the experiments of Robert Hutchings Goddard near Roswell, N.M., in the propulsion of rockets, 1930-41, the indifference of the U.S. Government to the experiments at this time and the keen interest taken by the Germans, who applied them in World War II, and the posthumous recognition of Goddard in the United States. [4204

E. H. HARRISON. The Ballistics Research Laboratories [Aberdeen Proving Ground, Md., U.S. Army, 1938-60]. Am. rifleman, 108(10):39-42 (Oct). diagrs., ports., views. [4205

HARRY C. THOMSON & LIDA MAYO. The Ordnance Department: procurement and supply [1940-45]. Wash.: Office of the Chief of Military History, Dept. of the Army, 1960. xix, [3], 504 p. diagrs., ports., tables, views. bibliog. (p. 477-8), notes. (United States Army in World War II: The Technical Services.) Chapters on requirements, ammunition, artillery and small arms, tanks and other fighting vehicles, motor transport vehicles, inspection and statistical quality control, contract termination and settlement, the depot system, "the language of supply," stock control, maintenance, and related subjects. [4206

JOHN B. MEDARIS. Transportation of missiles [1941-59]. Karl M. Ruppenthal, ed., Revolution in transportation (Stanford, Calif.: Graduate School of Business, Stanford Univ. [1960]), p. 71-8. [4207

BIRTH of the Atomic age ... date: July 16, 1945 ... time: 4:59 A. M. ... place: New Mexico. N.M., 38(7):5-7, 36-7 (Jul). views. [4208

UNITS

U.S. Army. 104th Infantry. History of a combat regiment, 1639-1945: 104th Infantry Regiment. [Baton Rouge, La.: Army and Navy Pub. Co., 1960. 126] p. coats of arms, maps, ports., views. 1st ed. 1945 (published in Austria, written by Henry Parrott, edited by Max Gissen), now expanded. History of a unit that originated as the Springfield Train Band, Springfield, Mass., served in the Civil War as the 10th Massachusetts Volunteer Infantry Regiment, and assumed its present designation in 1917. [4209

JOHN ROBERT ELTING. Further light on the beginnings of Gorham's Rangers [1744-51]. Mil. collector & historian, 12:74-7 (fall). On the military activities of John Gorham (1709-51) and his Massachusetts rangers in Nova Scotia, 1742-51. [4210

JOHN R. CUNEO. Factors behind the raising of the 80th Foot in America. Mil. collector & historian, 11:97-103 (winter 1959). ports., view. notes. On the growth of independent ranger companies under general command of Maj. Robert Rogers, 1756-58, and the establishment of a regiment of light infantry under Col. Thomas Gage in 1758; with an account of its uniforms and equipment. [4211

BERKELEY R. LEWIS. Power horn of the 77th Highlanders. Mil. collector & historian, 11:19-22 (spring 1959). map, view. notes. On the service of this regiment (Montgomerie's Highlanders, under Col. Archibald Montgomerie) in Pennsylvania, the Carolinas, and the West Indies, 1757-63; with a description of a power horn of an unknown private, incised with his map of the campaign against the Cherokees in 1760 and accompanied by a wampum carrying strap. [4212

CONNECTICUT INFANTRY. Sherburn's Regiment. Blackman's Company. Return of recruits raised by Captain Elijah Blackman for Colonel Sherburn's Regiment (Connecticut) in the Continental Army for three years and during the war years 1777 and 1778. (Contributed by Mrs. Waldon McBride ....) D. A. R. mag., 94: 26-7 (Jan). [4213

JAMES B. JACKSON. Our forgotten regiment: the Second Delaware Militia, 1780. Del. hist., 9:3-50 (Mar). tables. notes. Includes a roster. [4214

W. S. MURPHY. The Irish Brigade of Spain at the capture of Pensacola, 1781. Fla. hist. quar., 38:216-25 (Jan). notes. On the activities of the Bridgade's Regimiento de Hibernia (580 officers and men) in the seige; with biographical data concerning the officers. [4215

NEW JERSEY INFANTRY. 1st Regiment. Capt. Aaron Ogden's Company. Size roll, Captain Aaron Ogden's Company: First Regiment of Jersey (Colonel Matthias Ogden). [Edited] by William H. Dumont. Natl. Geneal. Soc. quar., 48:138-41 (Sep). List for the year 1782, including information as to age, height, color of hair, color of complexion, occupation, birthplace, and residence. [4216

U.S. Army. 5th Infantry. History of the Fifth United States Infantry [1798-1960. n. p., 1960. 4], 58, [2], 43, [1] p. map, tables. bibliog. (p. 44 at end). On services in the War of 1812, the Old Northwest, the Mexican War, the Southwest, the Civil War, the later Indian wars, the Philippines, Panama, Germany in World War I, Europe in World War II, and the Korean War. Includes a letter from Lt. Frank D. Baldwin to his wife, dated Fort Dodge, Kan., 17 Sep. 1874 (from the Pampa, Tex., News), his Montana diary (6 Nov. - 21 Dec. 1876), and other documents. [4217

GEORGE GLENN WOOD. Old milita days: my father's military life. Now and then, 12:273-4 (Jul). port. On Thomas Wood as an officer of the Muncy Guards, ca. 1834 to ca. 1850. [4218

JEWEL (DAVIS) SCARBOROUGH. The Georgia Battalion in the Texas Revolution: a critical study. Southw. hist. quar., 63:511-32 (Apr). notes. On the formation of the Battalion in Georgia and its service in Texas, 1835-36, its capitulation to the Mexicans, the shooting of many of its members in violation of the terms of capitulation, and the efforts of the State of Georgia in the 1850s to obtain some form of compensation from Texas; with biographical sketches of the officers and some of the privates of the Battalion. [4219

PHILIP CHARLES BLAKER. The Lancaster Fencibles. Lancaster Co. Hist. Soc., Jour., 64:165-93 (summer). view. notes. On a militia unit commanded by Capt. John H. Duchman, later by Capt. Emlen Franklin, 1855-62, absorbed in the latter year by the Lancaster County Regiment, which entered national service as the 122d Pennsylvania Volunteers. [4220

DOROTHY C. LA ROSE. U.S. Army camel bells. Hobbies, 64(12):54 (Feb). On bells worn by camels of the U.S. Army Camel Corps in the Southwest, 1856-58. [4221

CARROLL H. WALKER. The Woodes Rifles--1858-1861. Mil. collector & historian, 11:5-6 (spring 1959). port. On a Norfolk company of the 3d Battalion, 54th Regiment of Virginia Militia, which fought throughout the Civil War as Company C, 6th Virginia Regiment, C.S. Army. [4222

WARD BAKER. Mishawaka and its volunteers, Fort Sumter through 1861. Ind. mag. hist., 56:123-52 (Jun). notes. On the volunteers forming Company I of the 9th Indiana Regiment, and the war-related activities in Mishawaka, Apr.-Dec. 1861. [4223

EARL S. DANIEL. Lauderdale County [Ala.] soldiers in the Confederate Army. North Ala. Hist. Assoc., Bul., 5:13-18. On the units and their officers, 1861-65. [4224

BASIL WILSON DUKE. A history of Morgan's Cavalry. ... Edited with an introduction and notes by Cecil Fletcher Holland. Bloomington: Indiana Univ. Press [1960]. xvii, [3], 9-595 p. maps, port. notes (p. 579-81). (Civil War centennial series.) 1st ed. 1867. On Morgan's Cavalry Division, C.S.A., 1861-64, under command of John Hunt Morgan (1825-64), and its raids in Kentucky and Ohio. By Morgan's former second in command. [4225

EDWIN A. GLOVER. Bucktailed Wildcats, a regiment of Civil War volunteers. N.Y.: T. Yoseloff [1960]. 328 p. facsims., maps, ports., table, views. bibliog. (p. 275-9), notes (p. 280-308). On the First Pennsylvania Rifles, Pennsylvania Volunteer Reserve Corps, mustered into Federal service as the 42d Regiment, Pennsylvania Infantry, 1861-65, known as the Bucktail Regiment, composed largely of lumbermen and hunters from the Wildcat District (9 counties of north-central and northwestern Pennsylvania). [4226

LOUIS VAN LOAN NAISAWALD. Grape and canister: the story of the field artillery of the Army of the Potomac, 1861-1865. N.Y.: Oxford Univ. Press, 1960. xiv, 593 p. diagrs., maps. notes (p. 557-82). [4227

JAMES IRVIN ROBERTSON, JR. Jackson's stone wall: a history of the Stonewall Brigade. Ann Arbor: University Microfilms, 1959 [i. e. 1960]. Positive microfilm of typescript. [364] leaves. Thesis--Emory Univ. Abstracted: Dissert. abstracts, 20: 3274-5 (Feb). On the forces serving under Lt. Gen. Thomas Jonathan Jackson (1824-63). [4228

HOWARD THOMAS. Boys in Blue from the Adirondack foothills. Prospect, N.Y.: Prospect Books, 1960. xiv, 297 p. facsims., flag, maps, ports., views. bibliog. (p. 289-90), notes (p. 285-8). On "New York volunteer regiments containing large numbers of foothills men" (from Oneida and Herkimer Counties), 1861-65, particularly the 14th, 26th, 34th, 27th, 117th, 121st, 146th, and 152d Infantry. [4229

JACK C. VAUGHAN. Brigadier General Alfred Jefferson Vaughan's Brigade (Army of Tennessee, Confederate States of America). [Grand Prairie? Tex., 1959-60.] 6 v. (1171 leaves). facsims., maps, ports., tables, views. notes. (His American histories, 11-16.) On the 13th Tennessee Regiment and later also the 154th Tennessee Regiment under his command as Colonel and later as Brigadier General, Jun. 1861 - Dec. 1863; with a brief account of his early life in Virginia, work as a civil engineer in Missouri and California, and after 1856 a cotton planter in Marshall County, Miss. Consists mainly of voluminous excerpts from contemporary sources, in chronological order, with commentary by the author. [4230

The VERMONT Brigade. By one who did not belong to it, and who never was in Vermont. Vt. Hist. Soc., News and notes, 7:66-7 (May 1956). Anonymous contribution to the Troy times, Troy, N.Y., 1874. On a Civil War unit whose members "knew perfectly well they were the best fighters in the known world." [4231

WILLIAM STANLEY HOOLE. Alabama Tories: the First Alabama Cavalry, U.S.A., 1862-1865. Tuscaloosa, Ala.: Confederate Pub. Co., 1960. 141 p. tables. notes. (Confederate centennial studies, 16.) "Roster of the regiments" (p. 53-135). [4232

TENNESSEE INFANTRY (C.S.A.). 154th Regiment. Camp 154th of Tennessee Regiment: near Dalton, Georgia, January 14th, 1864. [Edited by] Buford C. Utley. West Tenn. Hist. Soc. papers, 14:124-5. Minutes of a meeting of all "the officers and men of this Regiment," containing a resolution, passed unanimously, offering to continue the services of the regiment without regard to dates of expiration of enlistment, and requesting that if the C.S. Congress reorganizes the Army it will "preserve to us our respective organizations so essential to the preservation of whatever historic character it may have been our fortune to have earned." [4233

MELBOURNE C. CHANDLER. Of GarryOwen in glory: the history of the Seventh United States Cavalry Regiment [1866-1957. Annandale? Va., 1960.] xv, 458, [5] p. cartoon, coats of arms, diagrs., flags (part col.), maps (1 fold.), ports., tables (part double), views. notes. Text in double columns. Detailed chronological narrative with numerous embedded orders and other documents, and 7 appendices. The first section deals with the service of the Regiment in the Indian wars in the West. [4234

JOHN BARSNESS & WILLIAM DICKINSON. Minutemen of Montana. Montana, 10(1):2-9 (Apr). facsim., ports. notes. On the Montana Militia, and some of its engagements with the Indians, 1867-77. [4235

U.S. Marine Corps. Hold high the torch: a history of the 4th Marines [since 1911]. By Kenneth W. Condit [and] Edwin T. Turnbladh. Wash.: Historical Branch, G-3 Division, Headquarters, U.S. Marine Corps, 1960. xii, 458 p. maps, ports., tables, views. bibliog. (p. 423-9), notes. Mainly on their service in the Dominican Republic (1916-24), China, the Philippines, Guam, Okinawa, and Japan. [4236

RAYMOND C. DICKIESON. From horses to missiles: the story of the 11th Field Artillery, 1916-1959. [n. p.:] 11th Field Artillery Veterans' Assoc. [1960?]. 40 p. coat of arms, map, views. On the services of this unit in Europe in World War I, in Hawaii between the wars, and in the Pacific in World War II. [4237

ROBERT D. BURHANS. History and heraldry of the 80th Division [1917-60], covering participation in World War I & World War II, including a section on customs of the service and the combat arms regimental system, U.S. Army. Richmond, 1960. [4], 53 p. mount. col. coats of arms. table. bibliog. (p. 53). Includes lineages of the 317th, 318th, 319th, and 320th Regiments. [4238

ALEXANDER MACLAREN WITHERSPOON. A history of the 325th Field Artillery of the 84th Division, A. E. F., 1917-1919. [n. p.] 1960. [3], iii leaves, 201 p. tables. On a unit formed in Aug. 1917 and disbanded in Mar. 1919. [4239

H. HUGH WYNNE. A brief history of the 27th Aero Squadron, Frist Pursuit Group, A. E. F. [1917-19]. Cross & cockade jour., 1(2): 10-41 (summer). insignia, ports., views. Includes flight reports and other documents. [4240

DANIEL B. CULLINANE. The last Indian scouts. Password, 5:101-4 (Jul). views. On a detachment of Apache scouts stationed at Fort Huachuca, Ariz., with the 7th Cavalry, 1927-29, under the author's command in 1928. [4241

RICHARD CROPP. A history of the 147th Field Artillery Regiment, 1939-1942. S. D. report and hist. col., 30:437-567. Thesis--State Univ. of South Dakota. On a unit of the South Dakota National Guard (in which the author commanded B Battery), mobilized at Mitchell, trained at Fort Ord, Calif., shipped to Australia, and assigned to the defense of Darwin; with brief reference to its later activities in Australia and New Guinea. [4242

U.S. Air Force. 1st Missile Division. History of the 1st Missile Division [1941-60]. By Carl Berger [Headquarters Historian]. California: Vandenberg Air Force Base [1960]. vi, [1] leaves, 99 p. diagr., map. ports., tables, views. bibliog. (p. 92-6), notes (p. 97-9). [4243

VESSELS

PHILLIPS MELVILLE. Lexington--brigantine-of-war, 1776-1777. U.S.N. Inst. proc., 86(4):51-9 (Apr). view. [4244

CHARLES GIEBELHAUS. East River treasure ship. Long Island forum, 23:37-9, 44, 48, 57-60, 70 (Feb, Mar). map. On the sinking of the British pay ship Hussar at Pot Rock, in the East River, 3 Nov. 1780, and the many efforts (the last in 1937) to find the ship and salvage its contents. [4245

M. LUTHER HEISEY. Local names on American ships. Lancaster Co. Hist. Soc., Jour., 63:17-36 (Jan 1959). views. On the USS Lancaster (1858-1933) and 4 other U.S. ships of the same name, the Revenue Cutter Harriet Lane (1858-84), the USS Fulton (1940-) and 4 earlier vessels of the same name (1814-1934), and U.S. ships named Conestoga, Susquehanna, and Octorara. [4246

MARSHALL SMELSER. Clinton Roosevelt's "invulnerable steam battery," 1835. Am. Neptune, 20: 167-73 (Jul). views. notes. On a scheme for an armored vessel that "was never seriously considered." [4247

RUTH (MORRIS) WHITE. Yankee from Sweden: the dream and the reality in the days of John Ericsson [1803-89]. N.Y.: Holt [1960]. xix, 299 p. ports., views. bibliog. (p. 281-5). On his early life in Sweden, his emigration in 1839, and his work as a naval architect and engineer. [4248

HENRY H. PARKER. John Ericsson and the Princeton. Am. philatelist, 73:417-20, 423 (Mar). diagr., facsim., view. On his work as a naval engineer in Sweden, England, and the United States, 1817-60s, and his planning of the hull, engines, boilers, armament, and "all of the details" of the 600-ton USS Princeton by request of Capt. Robert F. Stockton in 1841, the satisfactory performance of the ship till it was broken up in the 1850s, and the failure of all efforts of Ericsson and his heirs to obtain compensation for his work. [4249

EDMUND SCHACKELFORD DE LONG. Five Princetons in the nation's service. University, 6:28-31 (fall). views. On U.S. ships named Princeton, 1843-1960. [4250

HERBERT R. SPENCER. Explosion on the USS Michigan. Inland seas, 16:32-5 (spring). view. On the visit of President Zachary Taylor and Vice-President Millard Fillmore to Erie, and the accidental death of 2 men on the Michigan while firing a salute, Aug. 1849. [4251

ROBERT ERWIN JOHNSON. The stranding and salving of Hetzel. Steamboat bill, 17:71-4 (fall). port., view. On a steamer of the U.S. Coast Survey commanded by Lt. John Rodgers, driven ashore on Cape Canaveral in a storm, refloated by the extraordinarily hard work of commander and crew, sailed 60 miles to Indian River Inlet, beached there for repairs, refloated again, and sailed to New Orleans for completion of repairs, Feb.-Jun. 1850. [4252

JOHN ROGER FREDLAND. The new technology: ironclads in action [1861-64]. Elmer Belmont Potter, ed., Sea power: a naval history (Englewood Cliffs, N.J.: Prentice-Hall, 1960), p. 262-74. diagr., maps. notes. On the USS Monitor and the CSS Virginia (ex-USS Merrimack), other ironclads, and the use of mines and submarines. [4253

R. A. REDMOND. The Revenue Steamer E. A. Stevens in the Civil War. Am. Neptune, 20:155-66 (Jul). diagr. On the iron-hulled coastal steamer Naugatuck, refitted by Edwin Stevens of Hoboken as an armored vessel, 1861-90. [4254

SYDNEY W. JACKMAN. The Federal Navy's missing raft. U.S.N. Inst. proc., 86(7):154-5 (Sep). view. On a raft that drifted away from the vicinity of Cape Hatteras in a storm in 1862 and was beached in Bermuda in 1868. [4255

JAMES M. MERRILL. USS Weehawken--gallant iron ship [1862-63]. U.S.N. Inst. proc., 86(10):162-3 (Oct). view. [4256

ROBERT H. RANKIN. USS Dunderberg--old Thundering Mountain. U.S.N. Inst. proc., 86(11):158-9 (Nov). view. On a vessel ordered in 1862, launched 1865, sold to France, and renamed the Rochambeau. [4257

ROBERT H. RANKIN. The story of the first Idaho [1866-74]. U.S.N. Inst. proc., 86(6):173-4 (Jun). [4258

LLOYD M. HARMON. USS Thetis at San Diego, October 1887. U.S.N. Inst. proc., 86(7):150, 152 (Jul). view. [4259

ROBERT H. RANKIN. USS Iowa--alpha and omega [battleship, 1896-1957]. U.S.N. Inst. proc., 86(2):153-4 (Feb). view. [4260

ROBERT C. FOX. Before the Nautilus. Am. Neptune, 20:174-6 (Jul). On Frank R. Stockton's novel The great stone of Sardis (1897), about an imaginary voyage of the submarine Dipsey under Arctic ice to the North Pole in 1947, and the extraordinary resemblance of the submarine and the navigation to the USS Nautilus, which made such a voyage in 1958. [4261

RICHARD KNOWLES MORRIS. The story of the Holland submarine. U.S.N. Inst. proc., 86(1):78-89 (Jan). diagrs. (1 double), port., views. On SS-1 Holland, "the first submarine of the United States Navy," invented by John Philip Holland (1842-1914), tested by the Navy in 1897-1900, commissioned in 1900, exhibited in the Bronx International Exhibition in 1917, and "dismantled for junk" in 1930. [4262

R. WAYNE ANDERSON. USS Kearsarge--fifty-six years and three careers. U.S.N. Inst. proc., 86(1): 102-5 (Jan). views. On her service as a battleship, a training ship, and a crane ship, 1898-1956. [4263

WAYNE E. HOMAN. Is the Maine anchor authentic? Hist. rev. Berks Co., 25:114-19, 135-40 (fall). facsim., views. Evidence that the anchor exhibited in the City Park of Reading is a part of the vessel sunk in Havana Harbor in 1898 and that the controversy concerning it was inspired by the Democratic opponent of the Republican Congressman who obtained the anchor for Reading in 1914. [4264

JOHN HOOD (1859-1919). A personal reminiscense [sic] of 1905. Ala. hist. quar., 22:77-87. Eyewitness account of the sinking of the Maine, 15 Feb. 1898. [4265

FRANCIS E. CLARK. The last years of the sail navy. Am. Neptune, 20: 134-45 (Apr). On the continued uses of sailing vessels by the U.S. Navy after the general adoption of steam; with brief histories of all such vessels that were in the service of the Navy in 1900, and of a few constructed later--of all of which only the Constellation and the Constitution survive in 1960. [4266

CARL O. HOLMQUIST & RUSSELL S. GREENBAUM. The development of nuclear propulsion in the Navy [1939-60]. U.S.N. Inst. proc., 86(9):65-71 (Sep). view. [4267

VERNON J. MILLER. Major fleet units lost during World War II. U.S.N. Inst. proc., 86(1):90-101; (7): 96-7 (Jan, Jul). views. Annotated list of battleships, aircraft carriers, escort aircraft carries, and heavy and light cruisers (of all the navies participating in the War) that were sunk, scuttled, irreparably damaged, or surrendered, 1939-45. [4268

PHILIP A. CHAPLIN. The reincarnation of the four-stackers. U.S.N. Inst. proc., 86(3):94-103 (Mar). badge, port., views. On the 50 "overage destroyers" acquired from the U.S. Navy by the Royal Navy or the Royal Canadian Navy in the fall of 1940 and there designated as "'Town' class destroyers," of which 44 were named "for British towns with namesakes in the United States," and their service in waters of Canada and the United States and elsewhere till 1945. [4269

JOHN BUNKER. Tribute to the Liberties. U.S.N. Inst. proc., 86(3): 55-9 (Mar). views. On one of the "types of emergency ships" manufactured for the U.S. Maritime Commission, 1941-45. [4270

H. W. BLAKESLEE. The Minelayer Terror [1942-45]. U.S.N. Inst. proc., 86(1):112-13 (Jan). view. [4271

JOHN L. DETTBARN. Gold ballast: war patrol of USS Trent. U.S.N. Inst. proc., 86(1):51-7 (Jan). view. On the voyage of this submarine from Corregidor to Pearl Harbor with 24 tons of gold, silver, and securities, property of the Philippine Commonwealth, Jan.-Mar. 1942. See also recollections by Capt. E. W. Russell, 86(7):94-5. [4272

D. M. TOLLAKSEN. Last chapter for U-853. U.S.N. Inst. proc., 86(12):83-9 (Dec). map, port., views. On the destruction of this submarine and all its crew in 20 fathoms of water "a few miles south of Newport" by vessels of the U.S. Coast Guard (one of which was commanded by the author's father), May 1945. [4273

USS "Saint Paul" [heavy cruiser, 1945-60]. U.S.N. Inst. proc., 86(5): 159-61 (May). port., view. [4274

Military Operations

ROBERT C. JOHNSON. The Indian Massacre of 1622. Va. mag. hist. and biog., 68:107-8 (Jan). Quotes contemporary letters of John Chamberlain and William Wynn and a diary of Simonds D'Ewes. [4275

DAVID P. FRENCH. James Fenimore Cooper and Fort William Henry. Am. lit., 32:28-38 (Mar). notes. On the capitulation of the fort to a French and Indian force, and the ensuing massacre by Indians, 1757, and the extent to which Cooper's The last of the Mohicans is faithful to historical fact. [4276

THOMAS MARIE CHARLAND. The Lake Champlain army and the fall of Montreal [1759]. Vt. hist., 28:292-301 (Oct). notes. [4277

GT. BRIT. Army. King's Royal Rifle Corps. The orderly book of Colonel Henry Bouquet's expedition against the Ohio Indians, 1764. From the original in the William L. Clements Library. Edited by Edward G. Williams, with introduction and explanatory notes. Pittsburgh: Privately printed for the author [i.e. the editor] by Mayer Press, 1960. [6], 74 p. facsims., maps (1 double). notes (p. 51-74). From The western Pennsylvania historical magazine, 1959. Record of the march of British forces under Col. Henry Bouquet from Pittsburgh to approximately the site of Coshocton, 2 Oct. - 9 Nov. 1764, with extensive notes on the route and the persons involved. [4278

JOHN A. BARTON. Lexington [1775]: the end of a myth. History today, 9:382-91 (Jun 1959). ports., views. [4279

FANNY COCHRAN (born 1788?). Letter in original spelling and punctuation. Lebanon Hist. Soc., Ann. report, 2, leaves [7-9]. Letter to the writer's nephew Charles, dated Pembroke, N.H., 22 Jun. 1861, containing family news and her childhood recollections of information from elderly survivors of the campaigns of Bunker Hill, Ticonderoga, Crown Point, and Valley Forge. [4280

ROBERT GRANT CRIST. Captain William Hendricks and the march to Quebec (1775). Carlisle, Pa.: Hamilton Library and Historical Assoc. of Cumberland County, 1960. 32 p. facsim., maps (1 double). On his command of the Hendricks Riflemen, a company of the 1st Regiment of the Pennsylvania Line in the Continental Service, in a march from Carlisle to Maine and Quebec, where this and the other units under general command of Benedict Arnold were defeated by the British, 1775. [4281

THOMAS J. FLEMING. Now we are enemies: the story of Bunker Hill [16-17 Jun. 1775]. N.Y.: St. Martin's Press [1960. 8], 366 p. maps. bibliog. (p. 351-9), notes (p. 345-50). [4282

WINSTON B. LEWIS. The War of the American Revolution [1775-82]. Elmer Belmont Potter, ed., Sea power: a naval history (Englewood Cliffs, N.J.: Prentice-Hall, 1960), p. 66-107. maps. notes. On operations of the Continental Navy, the Royal Navy, and the French Navy in American and European waters and of the Royal and French Navies in the Far East, with special reference to strategy. [4283

JAC WELLER. The irregular war in the South [1775-81]. Mil. affairs, 24:124-36 (fall). notes. On the activities of guerrilla forces. [4284

STOCKBRIDGE H. BARKER. Washington's Christmas gamble. Mil. rev., 40(1):38-44 (Apr). maps. On the Battle of Trenton, 1776. [4285

JOHN A. BARTON. The Battle of Valcour Island [Lake Champlain, 11 Oct. 1776]. History today, 9:791-9 (Dec 1959). map, ports., views. [4286

RICHARD ERNEST DUPUY. The Battle of Hubbardton: a critical analysis. Prepared for the State of Vermont Historic Sites Commission. [Cornwall, N.Y.] 1960. [1], 39 leaves. bibliog. (leaves 37-9). On an engagement at Hubbardton, Vt., between American forces under Col. Seth Warner and British forces under Brig. Gen. Simon Fraser, 1777, "the only action fought on Vermont soil during the American Revolution." [4287

THOMAS HARTLEY (1748-1800). Col. Thomas Hartley's expedition of 1778. [Edited] by Dr. Richmond D. Williams. Now and then, 12:258-60 (Apr). notes. Letter to Thomas McKean, dated Sunbury, 2 Sep. 1778, on an expedition to protect Muncy, Pa., against Indians; with enclosed remarks (1 Sep. 1778, apparently from a newspaper) about the character of the Indians. [4288

GEORGE W. KYTE. Victory in the South: an appraisal of General [Nathanael] Greene's strategy in the Carolinas [1780-82]. N.C. hist. rev., 37:321-47 (Jul). notes. On the brilliant success of the strategy in spite of the frequent failure of the tactics. [4289

HENRY C. McMULLEN. "The Battle of Springfield, N.J.," June 23, 1780: skirmish(?) or decisive battle(?). N.J. genesis, 5:175 bis, 181-3 (Apr 1958). [4290

GEORGE W. KYTE. Strategic blunder: Lord Cornwallis abandons the Carolinas, 1781. Historian, 22:129-44 (Feb). notes. [4291

H. O. WERNER. The War of 1812. Elmer Belmont Potter, ed., Sea power: a naval history (Englewood Cliffs, N.J.: Prentice-Hall, 1960), p. 207-24. maps. notes. On the operations of the U.S. Navy, 1807-15. [4292

JEMIMA (TERRY) LATHAM (born 1803). The British at Orient in 1812. [Edited by] Melita Hofmann. Long Island forum, 23:221-2, 238 (Oct). view. Interview published in the Brooklyn daily eagle in 1896, recalling events off Orient Point in 1813 and 1814, when 3 English ships were anchored there, particularly the foraging parties of the English on shore. [4293

TED N. WEISSBUCH. A James Fenimore Cooper medal: the real Battle of Lake Erie. Numismatic scrapbook, 26:289-98 (Feb). On the parts taken by Capt. Oliver Hazard Perry and Capt. Jesse Duncan Elliott in the battle, 10 Sep. 1813, Cooper's account of the battle in his The history of the Navy (1839), the bitter partisan criticism of Cooper for not denouncing the conduct of Elliott, a scathing review of Cooper's account by William A. Duer, Cooper's successful litigation against Duer's publisher for libel, and the medal struck in Cooper's honor by the grateful Elliott. [4294

THOMAS WESLEY MARTIN. The story of Horseshoe Bend National Military Park. N.Y.: Newcomen Soc. in North America, 1960. 32 p. facsim., ports. On the battle in "the 'loop' of the Tallapoosa River" between Creek Indians allied with Great Britain and U.S. forces under Gen. Andrew Jackson, 27 Mar. 1814, and the national military park established at the site in 1956. [4295

BOYCE HOUSE (1896-1961). An incident at Velasco, 1832. Southw. hist. quar., 64:92-5 (Jul). notes. On the capture of the fort at the mouth of the Brazos River by Texas forces transported on the trading schooner Brazoria. [4296

GENE FALLWELL. The Comanche trail of thunder and the massacre at Parker's Fort. [n. p.] c1960. 26 p. map, ports., views. (Historic Trails Society. Bulletin 1.) On the settlement established at Fort Parker, Tex., by the Rev. Daniel Parker and emigrants from Crawford County, Ill., in 1833; the massacre of most of the settlers by Comanche and Kiowa Indians, 18 May 1836; the captivity of Rachel Plummer and her son James, ransomed by the Army in 1843, and of Cynthia Ann Parker (1827?-1864), discovered by Texas Rangers in 1860; and her half-Indian son, Quanah Parker (1854-1911), Comanche chief, rancher near Cache, Okla. [4297

GEORGE M. DOLSON (1812?-1842). Did David Crockett surrender at the Alamo? a contemporary letter. Edited by Thomas Lawrence Connelly. Jour. South. hist., 26:368-76 (Aug). notes. Reprinted from the Detroit Democratic press. Letter to the author's brother in Michigan, dated Camp Travis, Galveston Island, 19 Jul. 1836, on military affairs in Texas, the author's plans to settle there, and his information from eyewitness testimony of a Mexican officer (---- Almonte) that Crockett was one of 6 men who surrendered after the fall of the Alamo and were shot by order of Antonio López de Santa Anna and in his presence. [4298

JOE SPOTTED HORSE. Cannibal ally. By Wm. C. Hancock as told by Joe Spotted Horse. True West, 7(3): 18-20, 43-6 (Jan-Feb). port. On the defeat of a very large force of Comanche raiders by Texas forces under Gen. Edward Burleson assisted by Tonkawa warriors under their chief Placido, Aug. 1840, near the site of Lockhart at Big Prairie, the continued depredations of the Comanches, and their success in virtually exterminating the Tonkawas in 1862. [4299

OVIE CLARK FISHER. Battle of Bandera Pass. The Westerners, Potomac Corral, Great Western fights (Garden City, N.Y.: Doubleday, 1960), p. 41-5. bibliog. On an engagement some 50 miles west of San Antonio between a force of Comanche Indians and a body of Texas Rangers under Capt. John Coffee Hays, 1841. [4300

WALTER FLAVIUS McCALEB. The Mier Expedition. San Antonio: Naylor Co. [1959]. 122 p. On an expedition of Texas forces to Mier, on the Mexican bank of the Rio Grande, the order from their commanding general to return home, the refusal of 304 of the men to do so, their capture by the Mexicans, their imprisonment in Mexico City, and their eventual release, 1842-44. [4301

ANDREW ARMSTRONG. The Brazito battlefield. N. M. hist. rev., 35:63-74 (Jan). map. notes. On the location of the site of "the battle of Brazito," 23 Dec. 1846, near the Rio Grande in the Mesilla Valley of southern New Mexico. [4302

WITH Harney through the Bad Lands. [Pierre: South Dakota Historical Soc., 1960.] 3, [1] p. map. (The wi-iyohi, v. 14, no. 6, Sep. 1960.) On an expedition under Gen. William S. Harney from Ft. Laramie, Wyo., to Ft. Pierre, S.D., to quell "the refractory elements among the northern Sioux ... who roamed between the Missouri River and the Black Hills," 29 Sep. - 19 Oct. 1855; with information from manuscript diaries of Lt. G. K. Warren and Capt. J. B. S. Todd. [4303

JACK DODD. [Military actions in eastern Washington, 1858.] The Westerners, Potomac Corral, Great Western Indian fights (Garden City, N.Y.: Doubleday, 1960), p. 50-72. On a march of forces under Maj. William Jenner Steptoe from Fort Walla Walla to Colville "to try to develop an understanding between the miner-settlers there and the Indians," an unexpected attack by Spokane, Coeur D'Alene, and Yakima Indians, the retreat of Steptoe's forces to Fort Walla Walla, and a retaliatory campaign under Col. George Wright. [4304

ARTHUR W. EMERSON. The Battle of Pyramid Lake. The Westerners, Potomac Corral, Great Western Indian fights (Garden City, N.Y.: Doubleday, 1960), p. 73-81. bibliog. On "the final real stand of the Paiute Indians as a nation in Nevada," in an engagement between them and volunteer military forces from Genoa, Carson City, Silver City, and Virginia City, near the site of Wadsworth, Nev., 1860. [4305

JOHN ROGER FREDLAND. The American Civil War: the blockade and the cruisers [1861-65]. Elmer Belmont Potter, ed., Sea power: a naval history (Englewood Cliffs, N.J.: Prentice-Hall, 1960), p. 244-61. maps. notes. [4306

MARTIN HARDWICK HALL. Sibley's New Mexico campaign. Austin: Univ. of Texas Press [1960]. xv, 366 p. facsims. (part double), maps, ports., views. bibliog. (p. 331-43), notes. On the unsuccessful campaign of Confederate forces under Brig. Gen. Henry Hastings Sibley (1811-91) to "drive the Federal forces from New Mexico," 1861-62. Appended: "The muster rolls of the Army of New Mexico" (p. 227-329). [4307

BARNES F. LATHROP. The Lafourche District in 1861-1862: a problem in local defense. La. hist., 1:99-129 (spring). map. On the war in the swampy area bounded by the Mississippi, the Gulf of Mexico, and the Atchefalaya. [4308

JARED C. LOBDELL. Nathaniel Lyon and the Battle of Wilson's Creek [Missouri, 1861]. Mo. Hist. Soc., Bul., 17:3-15 (Oct). notes. [4309

ARTHUR SHOEMAKER. The Battle of Chustenahlah. Chron. Okla., 38:180-84 (summer). map, views. notes. On an engagement in Osage County, Okla., between Confederate troops under Col. James McIntosh and Union Indian forces under the Creek leader Opothyleyohola, 26 Dec. 1861, ending with victory for the former. [4310

WILLIAM ANDREW SWANBERG. Fort Sumter and war. Ralph G. Newman, ed., Lincoln for the ages (Garden City, N.Y.: Doubleday, 1960), p. 182-6. On the Confederate seige of Fort Sumter, Charleston Harbor, Mar.-Apr. 1861. [4311

GIDEON WELLES (1802-78). Admiral Farragut and New Orleans: with an account of the origin and command of the first three naval expeditions of the war [1861-62]. Selected essays by Gideon Welles: Civil War and Reconstruction, ed. Albert Mordell (N.Y.: Twayne Publishers, 1959), p. 114-79. From The galaxy, Nov. and Dec. 1871. Recollections by Lincoln's Secretary of the Navy. [4312

WINCHESTER - FREDERICK COUNTY CIVIL WAR CENTENNIAL COMMISSION. Civil War battles in Winchester and Frederick County, Virginia, 1861-1865. [Winchester? Va., 1960? 24] p. maps (1 double). Foreword signed: James E. Frew. On the Battle of Kernstown (23 Mar. 1862), the first, second, and third battles of Winchester (25 May 1862, 14 Jun. 1863, 19 Sep. 1864, the last known also as Battle of the Opequon), and the Battle of Cedar Creek (19 Oct. 1864). [4313

H. O. WERNER. The Mississippi Valley campaign [1861-64]. Elmer Belmont Potter, ed., Sea power: a naval history (Englewood Cliffs, N.J.: Prentice-Hall, 1960), p. 275-311. maps. notes. On naval operations on the Cumberland, Tennessee, Mississippi, and Red Rivers. [4314

STEPHEN E. AMBROSE. Henry Halleck and the second Bull Run campaign. Civil War hist., 6:238-49 (Sep). notes. Based on thesis (M.A.)--Louisiana State Univ. Argument that the General-in-Chief of the Armies of the United States was disastrously dominated in July and August 1862 by strategic doctrines held by Baron Henri Jomini, Swiss military theorist, and expressed in Halleck's own Elements of military art and science (1846). [4315

STEPHEN E. AMBROSE. The Union command system and the Donelson campaign. Mil. affairs, 24:78-86 (summer). map. notes. On the campaign against Forts Donelson and Henry, Feb. 1862, with special reference to the difficult position of Maj. Gen. Henry Wager Halleck. [4316

EDWIN C. BEARSS. Cavalry operations in the Battle of Stones River [Tenn., Dec. 1862 - Jan. 1863]. Tenn. hist. quar., 19:23-53, 110-44 (Mar, Jun). notes. [4317

EDWIN C. BEARSS. From Rolla to Fayetteville with General Curtis. Ark. hist. quar., 19:225-59 (autumn). maps. notes. On movements commanded by Brig. Gen. Sanuel Ryan Curtis, USA, commander of the Southwestern District of Missouri, Jan.-Feb. 1862. [4318

BARRON DEADERICK. Shiloh, Memphis, and Vicksburg [1862-63]. Memphis: West Tennessee Historical Soc. [1960. 8], 32 p. view. notes. [4319

CHARLES L. DUFOUR. The night the war was lost. Garden City, N.Y.: Doubleday, 1960. 427 p. maps (part col.), ports., views. bibliog. (p. 355-68), notes (p. 369-409). On the Battle of New Orleans, 1862. [4320

BARNES F. LATHROP. The Lafourche District in 1862: Confederate revival. La. hist., 1:300-319 (fall). notes. [4321

BARNES F. LATHROP. The Lafourche District in 1862: militia and partisan rangers. La. hist., 1:230-44 (summer). notes. Includes excerpts from Confederate correspondence. 4322

NOEL M. LOOMIS. The Battle of Wood Lake. The Westerners, Potomac Corral, Great Western Indian fights (Garden City, N.Y.: Doubleday, 1960), p. 86-93. bibliog. On a massacre of white settlers in Minnesota, Iowa, and South Dakota by Sioux Indians led by Little Crow, and their defeat at Wood Lake, Minn., by Army forces under Col. H. H. Sibley, 1862. [4323

GRADY McWHINEY. Controversy in Kentucky: Braxton Bragg's campaign of 1862. Civil War hist., 6:5-42 (Mar). notes. On the value, if any, of the campaign for Confederate purposes. [4324

STEPHEN B. OATES. The Prairie Grove campaign, 1862. Ark. hist. quar., 19:119-41 (summer). maps. notes. On military operations in northwestern Arkansas. [4325

JOHN W. SCHILDT. September echoes: the Maryland Campaign of 1862 [under Robert E. Lee]--the places, the battles, the results. [Middletown, Md.: Valley Register, 1960.] viii, 140 p. maps, ports., tables, views. bibliog. (p. 139-40), notes. [4326

JOSEPH S. STERN, JR. The siege of Cincinnati. Hist. and Philos. Soc. Ohio, Bul., 18:162-86 (Jul). views. notes. On the indications that the Confederates would attack Cincinnati, and the preparations to repel attack in Cincinnati, Covington, and Newport, in collaboration with Union forces under Maj. Gen. Lew Wallace and with assistance from the Governors of Ohio and Indiana and from volunteer forces ("the Squirrel Hunters") from the surrounding county, 2-13 Sep. 1862. [4327

U.S. National Park Service. Antietam National Battlefield Site, Maryland. By Frederick Tilberg. Wash., 1960. [4], 60 p. facsim., maps (1 double), ports., views. bibliog. (p. 56). (Its Historical handbook series, 31.) Includes an account of Lee's invasion of Maryland and the Battle of Antietam, 15 Sep. 1862, and of the National Cemetery at the site. [4328

Mrs. JOHN WAKEMAN. The Sioux uprising, by Mr. and Mrs. Harry Lawrence. Edited by Eugene T. Newhall. Lawrence Martin Brings, ed., Minnesota heritage (Minneapolis: T.S. Denison [1960]), p. 80-82. port. Text of a tape recording (1958) by Mrs. Wakeman for her daughter and her son-in-law, Harry Lawrence (Scarlet Boy) and Mrs. Harry Lawrence (Morning Star), containing her reminiscences of the Sioux uprising led by her brother-in-law, Chief Little Crow, Aug. 1862. [4329

CLINTON PRESBA ANDERSON. Canyon de Chelly. The Westerners, Potomac Corral, Great Western Indian fights (Garden City, N.Y.: Doubleday, 1960), p. 94-101. bibliog. On Navajo warfare against Army forces and white settlers in New Mexico and Arizona, and the engagement between the Navajos and the 1st Regiment of New Mexico Volunteers under Col. Kit Carson in Canyon de Chelly, Ariz., Apr. 1863 - Feb. 1864. [4330

MARTHA MITCHELL BIGELOW. The significance of Milliken's Bend in the Civil War. Jour. Negro hist., 45:156-63 (Jul). notes. On a river battle 15 miles above Vicksburg, 7 Jun. 1863, which "helped shatter the myth that the Negro would not fight." [4331

FRANK G. CLARK. Major Frank G. Clark's address at Loyal Legion, Thursday, October 27, 1910. Vt. Hist. Soc., News and notes, 8:58-9 (May 1957). Reminiscences by an officer of the former Vermont Brigade in the Battle of Gettysburg. [4332

FAIRFAX DAVIS DOWNEY. Storming of the gateway: Chattanooga, 1863. N.Y.: D. McKay Co. [1960]. xiv, 303 p. diagrs., maps, music, ports., tables, views. bibliog. (p. 289-95), notes (p. 275-88). On the Battle of Chattanooga and the Battle of Chickamauga and the campaign of which they were part. Includes a collection of contemporary verses (p. 233-67). [4333

JOHN ROGER FREDLAND & H. O. WERNER. Closing the Confederate ports [Charleston, Mobile, Wilmington, 1863-65]. Elmer Belmont Potter, ed., Sea power: a naval history (Englewood Cliffs, N.J.: Prentice-Hall, 1960), p. 312-27. maps. notes. [4334

WARREN W. HASSLER, JR. The first day's Battle of Gettysburg [1 Jul. 1863]. Civil War hist., 6:259-76 (Sep). notes. [4335

JACOB HOKE (1825-93). The great invasion. N.Y.: T. Yoseloff [1960. 2] p., reprint ([22], 33-613 p.; map, ports., views). notes. Account of the Battle of Gettysburg, by a civilian resident of Chambersburg, Pa., first published in 1887. Includes "a large number of illustrations of the battlefield" and "an appendix [p. 553-600] containing an account of the burning of Chambersburg, Pennsylvania, a statement of the General Sickles controversy, and other valuable historic papers." [4336

ARCHER JONES. The Gettysburg decision. Va. mag. hist. and biog., 68:331-43 (Jul). notes. On the locus of the decision-making process in Confederate strategy, Feb.-May 1863, involving Jefferson Davis, James A. Seddon (Secretary of War), and Robert E. Lee. [4337

J. T. ZELLER. Darius at the bridge. Lancaster Co. Hist. Soc., Jour., 64: 81-4 (winter). ports., view. On the burning of a covered bridge across the Susquehanna by order of Maj. Gen. Darius Nash Couch, Jun. 1863, to prevent the invasion of Lancaster County by Confederate forces. [4338

JAMES HARRIS ATKINSON. The action at Prairie De Ann [near Prescott, Ark., 10-13 Apr. 1864]. Ark. hist. quar., 19:40-50 (spring). map. notes. [4339

EDWIN C. BEARSS. Asboth's expedition up the Alabama and Florida Railroad. Fla. hist. quar., 39:159-66 (Oct). notes. On a movement under Brig. Gen. Alexander Asboth, USA, commanding at Pensacola, 21-25 Jul. 1864. [4340

EDWIN C. BEARSS. Grierson's winter raid on the Mobile and Ohio Railroad. Mil. affairs, 24:20-37 (spring). maps. notes. On movements of forces under Brig. Gen. Benjamin H. Grierson from Memphis into eastern Mississippi, Dec. 1864 - Jan. 1865. [4341

EDWARD CARRINGTON BOYKIN. Beefsteak Raid. N.Y.: Funk & Wagnalls [1960. 10], 305 p. map, ports., views (part double). bibliog. (p. 295-7), notes (p. 289-93). On the seizure of a herd of cattle (assembled by the Union Army on the James River near Petersburg) by Confederate forces led by Gen. Wade Hampton, Sep. 1864. Fictional in form. [4342

FRED E. BROWN. The Battle of Allatoona. Civil War hist., 6:277-97 (Sep). maps, port., view. notes. On the defense of Allatoona Pass, Ga., occupied by Union forces under Maj. Gen. John M. Corse, against Confederate forces under Maj. Gen. Samuel G. French, 5 Oct. 1864. [4343

LAWRENCE VERLYN COMPTON. The first Battle of Adobe Walls, Tex. [between Army forces under Col. Christopher Carson and a band of Comanche and Kiowa Indians, Oct.- Nov. 1864]. The Westerners, Potomac Corral, Great Western Indian fights

(Garden City, N.Y.: Doubleday, 1960), p. 102-7. bibliog. [4344

CLIFFORD SHIRLEY DOWDEY, JR. Lee's last campaign: the story of Lee and his men against Grant [in Virginia]--1864. Boston: Little, Brown [1960. 12], 415 p. maps (part col.). bibliog. (p. 377-400). [4345

WILLIAM LINDSEY McDONALD. Colonel James Jackson's raid in Lauderdale County, April 11, 1864. North Ala. Hist. Assoc., Bul., 5:10-13. port. bibliog. [4346

RAYMOND O. MILLER. A stupendous failure. Mil. rev., 40(4): 31-44 (Jul). maps, views. On the Battle of the Crater, Petersburg, Va., 27 Jul. 1864. [4347

IRA DON RICHARDS. The engagement at Marks' Mills [between Camden and Pine Bluff, Ark., 25 Apr. 1864]. Ark. hist. quar., 19:51-60 (spring). map. notes. [4348

EDWARD STEERE. The Wilderness Campaign. Harrisburg, Pa.: Stackpole Co. [1960. 14], 522 p. maps (part double). notes (p. 477-511). (Civil War campaigns.) On a series of movements and engagements, commonly called the Battle of the Wilderness, between Confederate forces under Lee and Union forces under Grant, Virginia, 5 May - 18 Jun. 1864. [4349

FRANK EVERSON VANDIVER. Jubal's Raid: General [Jubal Anderson] Early's famous attack on Washington in [July] 1864. N.Y.: McGraw-Hill [1960]. xiii, 198 p. maps, ports., double views. bibliog. (p. 189-92), notes (p. 181-8). On the Battle of Fort Stevens, D.C., and the Maryland campaign of which it was a part, Jun.-Aug. 1864. [4350

JOHN GILCHRIST BARRETT. Sherman and total war in the Carolinas. N.C. hist. rev., 37:367-81 (Jul). notes. On William Tecumseh Sherman's "philosophy of total war" and its application in the Carolinas, Jan.-Apr. 1865. [4351

BILL JUDGE. "I am no coward!" Frontier times, 34(2):28-9, 46-8 (spring). On Lt. Caspar Collins (1844-65), killed by Indians in Wyoming as a result of a taunt from a General Connor and an illegal order from Maj. Martin Anderson, combined with lack of judgment and apparently cowardice on the part of Connor, Anderson, and others; and the preservation of Collins's memory in the name of Casper [not Caspar], Wyo. [4352

THOMAS CHALMERS McCORVEY (1851-1932). A one-sided naval battle on Alabama waters. T. C. McCorvey, Alabama historical sketches, ed. George Burke Johnston (Charlottesville: Univ. of Virginia Press, 1960), p. 136-42. notes. From the Montgomery, Ala., Advertiser, 3 Apr. 1910. On an attack by vessels of the U.S. Navy on a flatboat of Joseph B. Packer in the Alabama River near Monroeville, in the belief that Packer was Jefferson Davis, 26 Apr. 1865. [4353

THOMAS CHALMERS McCORVEY (1851-1932). An unheralded battle. T. C. McCorvey, Alabama historical sketches, ed. George Burke Johnston (Charlottesville: Univ. of Virginia Press, 1960), p. 143-56. From the Montgomery, Ala., Advertiser, 10 Sep. 1911. On an engagement between the 15th Confederate Regiment (Mounted) under Lt. Col. Thomas J. Myers and the Separate Cavalry Brigade under Gen. T. J. Lucas, near Mount Pleasant, Monroe County, Ala., 11 Apr. 1865. Includes recollections by the author. [4354

LOUIS J. SCHULER. The last battle in the War between the States, May 13, 1865: Confederate force of 300 defeats 1,700 Federals near Brownsville, Texas [in the Battle of Palmetto Ranch. Brownsville? 1960.] v, [1], 30 p. facsim., col. flag., map, port., views. bibliog. (p. 29). [4355

JESSE WENDELL VAUGHN. Sergeant Custard's wagon train fight. Ann. Wyo., 32:227-34 (Oct). On an engagement between a detachment of 22 soldiers and 3 teamsters under Commissary Sergeant Amos J. Custard, Co. H, 11th Kansas Cavalry, and a party of Sioux, Cheyenne, and Arapaho Indians, at Platt Bridge, on the Platte River in southeastern Wyoming, Jul. 1865, ending with the torture (with hot iron), mutilation, killing, and scalping of the Custard party; with an account of the author's examination of the site in 1958. [4356

ROY EDGAR APPLEMAN. The Fetterman fight. The Westerners, Potomac Corral, Great Western Indian fights (Garden City, N.Y.: Doubleday, 1960), p. 117-31. map, view. bibliog. On the defeat of Company A, 18th Infantry (stationed at Fort Phil Kearny), led by Capt. William J. Fetterman, by a force of Sioux and Cheyenne Indians at Peno Creek in northern Wyoming, Dec. 1866. [4357

FRANKLIN and the Fenian "Battle of Richards' Farm" (May 25, 1870). Vt. Hist. Soc., News and notes, 4:41-3 (Feb 1953). views. On 2 attempts to invade Canada by American Irishmen who assembled in Franklin, Vt., 1866, 1870, and were repelled with a loss of 2 lives. Includes 2 contemporary photographs. [4358

SAMUEL STANLEY. The Valley of Death. True West, 7(4): 28-9, 53-4 (Mar-Apr). On the killing of Bvt. Lt. Col. William Fetterman and all the men under his command by Cheyenne and Sioux Indians taking advantage of his disobedience to orders of Col. Henry B. Carrington, near Fort Phil Kearny, Wyo., 21 Dec. 1866. [4359

MICHAEL WHITNEY STRAIGHT. The strange testimony of Major [James] Powell in the Fetterman Massacre inquiry. Westerners brand book (N.Y.), 7:4-8. ports. On an inquiry into the responsibility for the massacre of Bvt. Lt. Col. William Judd Fetterman and 81 of his men by Indians in Kansas, 1866, the inquiry conducted by a special commission, and the effort of Powell and John F. Kinney to place the blame upon Fetterman's superior officer, Col. Henry Carrington; with evidence that the false testimony given by Powell may have been due to insanity. [4360

ROY EDGAR APPLEMAN. The Hayfield Fight. The Westerners, Potomac Corral, Great Western Indian fights (Garden City, N.Y.: Doubleday, 1960), p. 132-47. map, view. bibliog. On the establishment of Fort C. F. Smith by Capt. N.C. Kinney, an attack by Sioux Indians led by Red Cloud on a "civilian haymaking party" in southern Montana, and the repulse of the Indians by the civilians and their military escort, Aug. 1866 - Aug. 1867. [4361

ROY EDGAR APPLEMAN. The Wagon Box Fight. The Westerners, Potomac Corral, Great Western Indian fights (Garden City, N.Y.: Doubleday, 1960), p. 148-62. view. bibliog. On an attack by Sioux Indians led by Red Cloud on a civilian woodcutting party and its military escort (led by Capt. James W. Powell, from Fort Phil Kearny, Wyo.) at Piney Island in the Piney River, northern Wyoming, Jul. 1867. [4362

WINFIELD FREEMAN (1848-1926). The Battle of the Arickaree. Everett Rich, ed., The heritage of Kansas (Lawrence: Univ. of Kansas Press, 1960), p. 141-9. From the Salina Journal, 14 Mar. 1934. On a raid of white settlements in the Saline and Solomon River valleys by "a body of Indians called renegades, composed of parts of several tribes," and their defeat at the Arickaree River by Army forces under Col. George A. Forsythe, 1868. [4363

JAMES S. HUTCHINS. The fight at Beecher Island. The Westerners, Potomac Corral, Great Western Indian fights (Garden City, N.Y.: Doubleday, 1960), p. 165-74. map, port., view. bibliog. On an engagement between Cheyenne Indians under Roman Nose and Army forces under Maj. "Sandy" Forsyth at an island in the Arickaree Fork of the Republican River in northeastern Colorado, Sep. 1868. [4364

JAMES T. KING. The Republican River expedition, June-July 1869. Neb. hist., 41:165-99, 281-97 (Sep, Dec). map, ports., view. notes. On an expedition of the 5th Cavalry under Bvt. Maj. Gen. Eugene Asa Carr, accompanied by Pawnee scouts, "in the area of the Republican River Valley in Kansas, Nebraska and Colorado ... with the duty of driving the Indian out of this last stronghold on the central plains," culminating in defeat of the Cheyennes at the Battle of Summit Springs, Colorado Territory. [4365

JUAN DE DIOS (born 1842?), Navajo Indian. The Medio Dia Massacre. [Reported from memory by] Frank C. Hibben. Southw. rev., 45:318-28 (autumn). Third-person narrative (from oral recollections of Juan de Dios, 1933 or later, as recalled by Hibben) of an Apache and Ute attack near Vermejo Creek, west of Raton Pass, upon a wagon train, "about 1870." [4366

VIRGIL L. KELLOGG. Massacre on the Marias. True West, 7(3):15, 58 (Jan-Feb). port. On the killing of "some 173" old men, women, and children of an unnamed Indian tribe, sick with smallpox, on the Marias River near present Shelby, Mont., by drunken forces of an unnamed cavalry unit commanded by the alcoholic Bvt. Col. Eugene M. Baker, 23 Jan. 1870. [4367

DONALD V. RATTAN. Antiguerrilla operations: a case study from history. Mil. rev., 40(2):23-7 (May). map. On operations against the

Apache Indians in New Mexico and Arizona by Army forces under Gen. George Crook, 1871-72. [4368

FREDERIC GORDON RENNER. Blood on the lava. The Westerners, Potomac Corral, Great Western Indian fights (Garden City, N.Y.: Doubleday, 1960), p. 192-9. view. bibliog. On conflicts between the Modoc Indians and U.S. Army detachments from Fort Klamath and Fort Vancouver, 1872-73. [4369

EDDIE JOE GLOVER. Packsaddle Mountain fight. Jr. historian (Tex.), 19(6):21-2, 30 (May 1959). On an engagement between a posse of 8 men and a band of Indians in Llano County, Tex., Aug. 1873, ending about 15 years of Indian depredations there. [4370

RAY H. MATTISON. The Battle of Massacre Canyon [near Trenton, Neb., 5 Aug. 1873]. The Westerners, Potomac Corral, Great Western Indian fights (Garden City, N.Y.: Doubleday, 1960), p. 185-8. bibliog. [4371

JEFFERSON CHENOWETH DYKES. The Battle of Palo Duro Canyon. The Westerners, Potomac Corral, Great Western Indian fights (Garden City, N.Y.: Doubleday, 1960), p. 214-20. bibliog. On the destruction of winter quarters of the Comanche, Kiowa, Cheyenne, and Arapaho Indians in Palo Duro Canyon, in the Texas Panhandle, by the 4th Cavalry under Col. Ranald Mackenzie, 28 Sep. 1874. [4372

JEFFERSON CHENOWETH DYKES. The second Battle of Adobe Walls. The Westerners, Potomac Corral, Great Western Indian fights (Garden City, N.Y.: Doubleday, 1960), p. 203-13. bibliog. On the reestablishment of a buffalo-hide trading post at Adobe Walls or Adobe Fort, Tex., by A. C. Myers (Charlie Myers), the attacks on buffalo hunters in the area by Comanche, Kiowa, and Cheyenne Indians, and their unsuccessful attack on Adobe Walls, 1874. [4373

JACK LAFFERTY. 6 medals of honor. True West, 7(5):26-7, 64 (May-Jun). views. On "the Buffalo Wallow Fight of 1874" in the Oklahoma Panhandle. [4374

FRED S. SNOW (1842-1924). Fred Snow's account of the Custer expedition of 1874. [Edited] by Ernest J. Moyne. N. D. hist., 27:143-51 (summer-fall). notes. Manuscript reminiscences (undated) of an expedition of the 7th Cavalry into the Black Hills, which "no team or white man had ever penetrated" before, and the discovery of gold there on 27 Jul. 1874. [4375

HARRY H. ANDERSON. Nelson A. Miles and the Sioux War of 1876-77 ["the campaign that followed Custer's defeat on the Little Big Horn"]. Westerners brand book (Chicago), 16:25-7, 32 (Jun 1959). [4376

JOHN BARSNESS & WILLIAM DICKINSON. Fight or die! Frontier times, 34(3):26-7, 52, 54-5 (summer). port., views. On the campaign of forces of the 3d Cavalry under Capt. Anson Mills to catch Crazy Horse in western South Dakota, and their engagements with the Sioux Indians in the Slim Buttes country and the Black Hills, Sep. 1876. Fictional in form. [4377

JOHN A. LEERMAKERS. The Battle of the Rosebud. The Westerners, Potomac Corral, Great Western Indian fights (Garden City, N.Y.: Doubleday, 1960), p. 225-34. bibliog. On an engagement between Army forces under Gen. George Crook and Sioux and Cheyenne Indians believed to have been led by Crazy Horse, 16 miles north of Decker, Mont., 17 Jun. 1876. [4378

EDGAR IRVING STEWART & EDWARD S. LUCE. The Reno scout. Montana, 10(3):22-8 (Jul). ports. On the extent to which Maj. Marcus A. Reno disobeyed his orders while leading a reconnaissance of "the upper reaches of the Powder River," 9-19 Jun. 1876, shortly before the Battle of the Little Big Horn. [4379

ROBERT MARSHALL UTLEY. The Battle of the Little Bighorn. The Westerners, Potomac Corral, Great Western Indian fights (Garden City, N.Y.: Doubleday, 1960), p. 235-53. maps. bibliog. On an engagement between the Seventh Cavalry under Gen. George Armstrong Custer and Sioux and Cheyenne Indians led by Sitting Bull and Crazy Horse, in southern Montana, 25-26 Jun. 1876. [4380

GEORGE D. WOLFE. Which Indian killed Custer [1876]? Frontier times, 34(1):22-3, 39-41 (winter). ports. [4381

BERTON WENDELL ALLRED. Massacre of the Dull Knife band. The Westerners, Potomac Corral, Great Western Indian fights (Garden City, N.Y.: Doubleday, 1960), p. 295-302.

port. bibliog. On the defeat of a band of Cheyenne Indians led by Dull Knife (Morningstar) by forces of the Third Cavalry, and their confinement at Fort Robinson, Neb., and Pine Ridge, S.D., 1877. [4382

FREDERICK A. MARK. The Bannack Indian War of 1878 [in Washington, Oregon, Idaho, Montana, and Wyoming]. The Westerners, Potomac Corral, Great Western Indian fights (Garden City, N.Y.: Doubleday, 1960), p. 270-80. map, views. bibliog. [4383

JACK P. RIDDLE. Besieged on Milk Creek. The Westerners, Potomac Corral, Great Western fights (Garden City, N.Y.: Doubleday, 1960), p. 281-91. facsim. bibliog. On the actions of Nathan C. Meeker as Indian agent at the White River Agency, Colo., and the resulting revolt of the Ute Indians, who ambushed a force of the Fifth Cavalry under Maj. T. T. Thornburg at Milk Creek, killed Meeker and some other whites at the Agency, took captives, and were overcome only by vigorous military action, 1878-79. [4384

BRADLEY H. PATTERSON, JR. The Pierre's Hole fight. The Westerners, Potomac Corral, Great Western Indian fights (Garden City, N.Y.: Doubleday, 1960), p. 30-40. view. bibliog. On dealings between the Rocky Mountain Fur Company (led by Bill Sublette) and the Nez Perce and Flathead Indians, and an attack by a band of Gros Ventre Indians at Pierre's Hole in the Teton Mountains of Wyoming, Jul. 1882. [4385

GEORGE METCALF. Tragedy at Wounded Knee. The Westerners, Potomac Corral, Great Western Indian fights (Garden City, N.Y.: Doubleday, 1960), p. 307-17. map, view. bibliog. On the massacre of a band of Sioux Indians by forces of the Seventh Cavalry at Wounded Knee Creek, S.D., 29 Dec. 1890. [4386

ELLERY H. CLARK, JR. The Spanish-American War. Elmer Belmont Potter, ed., Sea power: a naval history (Englewood Cliffs, N.J.: Prentice-Hall, 1960), p. 366-77. maps. notes. On U.S. naval operations in the Philippines and the Caribbean, 1898. [4387

EUGENE F. GANLEY. Mountain chase. Mil. affairs, 24:203-10 (winter). map. notes. On "the pursuit and capture of General Vicente Lukban, a famed leader of the Philippine Insurrection," by forces under Lt. Alphonse Strebler, Feb. 1902. [4388

ERNEST M. RICHARDSON. Battle of Lightning Creek [1903]. Montana, 10(3):42-52 (Jul). ports., views. On "the last Indian-white blood-letting in Wyoming," resulting from "illicit hunting trips" by the Sioux from Pine Ridge, S.D., into Weston County, Wyo., where they killed not only game but livestock until quelled in an engagement with a posse in which Sheriff William H. Miller and another white and 4 Indians were killed. [4389

TED C. HINCKLEY. Wilson, Huerta, and the twenty-one gun salute [Tampico, 9 Apr. 1914]. Historian, 22:197-206 (Feb). notes. [4390

C. D. WOOD. The Glen Springs raid. True West, 7(3):28-9, 50 (Jan-Feb). views. Recollections of the Mexican raid into Glen Springs, in the Big Bend country of Texas, 130 miles downriver from Presidio, 5 May 1916. [4391

ERNEST MILTON HALLIDAY. The ignorant armies. N.Y.: Harper [1960]. xvii, [3], 232 p. maps (1 double), ports., views. bibliog. (p. 225-6), notes (p. 219-24). On the program and the activities of the "American Expeditionary Force in North Russia," 1918-19. [4392

THE STARS AND STRIPES: THE OFFICIAL NEWSPAPER OF THE A. E. F. [News of American air activities in Europe as reported in the issues of 1 and 22 Mar., 19 Apr., and 10 May 1918.] Cross & cockade jour., 1(1):30-33; (2):53-5 (spring, summer). [4393

LOUIS MORTON. Germany first: the basic concept of allied strategy in World War II. Kent Roberts Greenfield, ed., Command decisions (Wash.: Office of the Chief of Military History, Dept. of the Army, 1960), p. 11-47. col. fold. maps. notes. On the development by American strategists, 1921-41, of "the war plan known as Rainbow 5," providing that "the main effort of the United States in a war with the Axis Powers of Europe and Asia should be made in the European theater and that Germany must be defeated first." [4394

TRUMBULL HIGGINS. The problem of a second front: an interpretation of coalition strategy before and during the turning point of the Second World War [1940-43]. U.S., Dept. of State, Office of Intelligence Research, Abstracts of completed doctoral dissertations, 1950-51 ([Wash.] 1952), p. 139-40. Abstract of thesis--Princeton Univ. [4395

ALBERT NORMAN. The Allied invasion of northwestern Europe: design and reality, 1940-1944. U.S., Dept. of State, Office of Intelligence Research, Abstracts of completed doctoral dissertations, 1950-51 ([Wash.] 1952), p. 141-2. Abstract of thesis--Clark Univ. [4396

BYRON FAIRCHILD. Decision to land United States forces in Iceland, 1941. Kent Roberts Greenfield, ed., Command decisions (Wash.: Office of the Chief of Military History, Dept. of the Army, 1960), p. 73-97. col. fold. maps. notes. [4397

WINSTON B. LEWIS & ELMER BELMONT POTTER. [Surface operations in the Pacific, 1941-44.] Elmer Belmont Potter, ed., Sea power: a naval history (Englewood Cliffs, N.J.: Prentice-Hall, 1960), p. 646-795. maps. notes. Contents (the first 2 chapters by Lewis, the others by Potter).--The period of Japanese expansion.--Midway and the Aleutians.--Guadalcanal.--The limited offensive.--Beginning the Central Pacific drive.--The dual advance to the Philippines.--The battle for Leyte Gulf. Reprinted with revisions: E. B. Potter & Chester William Nimitz, eds., The great sea war: the story of naval action in World War II (Englewood Cliffs, N.J.: Prentice-Hall [1960]), p. 189-400. maps. notes. [4398

LOUIS MORTON. The decision [of Gen. Douglas MacArthur] to withdraw to Bataan [Dec. 1941]. Kent Roberts Greenfield, ed., Command decisions (Wash.: Office of the Chief of Military History, Dept. of the Army, 1960), p. 151-72. maps (part col. fold.). notes. [4399

JOHN FRAYN TURNER. Battle stations: the U.S. Navy's war. N.Y.: Putnam [1960]. 192 p. maps, ports., views. On American naval operations during World War II. [4400

WILLIAM M. BELOTE & H. O. WERNER. The Allied [British and American] offensive against North Africa [Operation TORCH, 1942-43]. Elmer Belmont Potter, ed., Sea power: a naval history (Englewood Cliffs, N.J.: Prentice-Hall, 1960), p. 565-83. maps. notes. On operations against Morocco, Algeria, and Tunisia. Reprinted with revisions: E. B. Potter & Chester William Nimitz, eds., The great sea war: the story of naval action in World War II (Englewood Cliffs, N.J.: Prentice-Hall [1960]), p. 102-29; Chester W. Nimitz, Henry H. Adams, & E. B. Potter, eds., Triumph in the Atlantic: the naval struggle against the Axis (Englewood Cliffs, N.J.: Prentice-Hall [1960]), p. 102-29. maps. notes. [4401

LEO F. MEYER. The decision [by Roosevelt and Churchill] to invade North Africa (TORCH) [Nov. 1942]. Kent Roberts Greenfield, ed., Command decisions (Wash.: Office of the Chief of Military History, Dept. of the Army, 1960), p. 173-98. col. fold. maps. notes. [4402

WILLIAM F. PRICKETT. The Naval Battalion on Bataan. U.S.N. Inst. proc., 86(11):72-81 (Nov). maps, port. On land operations directed by Commander Francis J. Bridget, Jan. 1942. [4403

THADDEUS V. TULEJA. Climax at Midway. N.Y.: W. W. Norton [1960]. 248 p. diagrs., maps, ports., tables, views. bibliog. (p. 229-32), notes (p. 233-8). On the Battle of Midway, 26 May - 7 Jun. 1942. [4404

WILLIAM M. BELOTE & H. O. WERNER. Operations [British and American] against Sicily and Italy [1943-44]. Elmer Belmont Potter, ed., Sea power: a naval history (Englewood Cliffs, N.J.: Prentice-Hall, 1960), p. 584-604. maps. notes. Reprinted with revisions: E. B. Potter & Chester William Nimitz, eds., The great sea war: the story of naval action in World War II (Englewood Cliffs, N.J.: Prentice-Hall [1960]), p. 130-58; Chester W. Nimitz, Henry H. Adams, & E. B. Potter, eds., Triumph in the Atlantic: the naval struggle against the Axis (Englewood Cliffs, N.J.: Prentice-Hall [1960]), p. 130-58. maps. notes. [4405

ROBERT WALTER COAKLEY. The Persian corridor as a route for aid to the USSR [by the U.S. Army, 1943]. Kent Roberts Greenfield, ed., Command decisions (Wash.: Office of the Chief of Military History, 1960), p. 225-53. maps (part col. fold.). notes. [4406

RICHARD M. LEIGHTON. OVERLORD versus the Mediterranean at the Cairo-Tehran Conference. Kent Roberts Greenfield, ed., Command decisions (Wash.: Office of the Chief of Military History, Dept. of the Army, 1960), p. 255-85. maps (part col. fold.). notes. On "the decision of the Big Three--Roosevelt, Stalin, and Churchill--to make OVERLORD and its southern France complement, ANVIL, the supreme effort of the Western Allies against Germany," 1943-44. [4407

MAURICE MATLOFF. The ANVIL decision: crossroads of strategy. Kent Roberts Greenfield, ed., Command decisions (Wash.: Office of the Chief of Military History, Dept. of the Army, 1960), p. 383-400. col. fold. maps. notes. On the decision to send Allied forces into southern France, 1943-44. [4408

JOHN MILLER, JR. MacArthur and the Admiralties. Kent Roberts Greenfield, ed., Command decisions (Wash.: Office of the Chief of Military History, Dept. of the Army, 1960), p. 287-302. maps (part col. fold.). notes. On the development of plans for the capture of a group of islands in the Bismarck Archipelago by American forces, 1943-44. [4409

HENRY H. ADAMS & ELMER BELMONT POTTER. The defeat of Germany [1944-45]. Elmer Belmont Potter, ed., Sea power: a naval history (Englewood Cliffs, N.J.: Prentice-Hall, 1960), p. 605-27. maps. notes. Includes some account of American naval contributions to the landings in France. Reprinted with revisions: E. B. Potter & Chester William Nimitz, eds., The great sea war: the story of naval action in World War II (Englewood Cliffs, N.J.: Prentice-Hall [1960]), p. 159-88; Chester W. Nimitz, Henry H. Adams, & E. B. Potter, eds., Triumph in the Atlantic: the naval struggle against the Axis (Englewood Cliffs, N.J.: Prentice-Hall [1960]), p. 159-88. maps. notes. [4410

MARTIN BLUMENSON. General Bradley's decision at Argentan (13 August 1944). Kent Roberts Greenfield, ed., Command decisions (Wash.: Office of the Chief of Military History, Dept. of the Army, 1960), p. 401-17. col. fold. maps. notes. On the decision of Lt. Gen. Omar N. Bradley, commanding the 12th U.S. Army Group, to halt the advance of the XV Corps, commanded by Lt. Gen. George S. Patton. [4411

MARTIN BLUMENSON. General Lucas at Anzio. Kent Roberts Greenfield, ed., Command decisions (Wash.: Office of the Chief of Military History, Dept. of the Army, 1960), p. 323-50. col. fold. maps. notes. On the command of the VI Corps in Italy by Maj. Gen. John P. Lucas, 1944. [4412

PHILIP AXTELL CROWL. Campaign in the Marianas. Wash.: Office of the Chief of Military History, Dept. of the Army, 1960 [c1959]. xix, [3], 505 p. diagrs., maps (part fold. col. in pocket), ports., views. bibliog. (p. 459-64), notes. (United States Army in World War II: The war in the Pacific.) On operations of the U.S. Army in Saipan, Tinian, and Guam, Jun.-Aug. 1944. [4413

ANDREW HAMILTON. "Where is Task Force Thirty-Four?" U.S.N. Inst. proc., 86(10):76-80 (Oct). port. On a message garbled in transmission from Adm. Chester W. Nimitz to Adm. William F. Halsey, Jr., 25 Oct. 1944, and Halsey's resulting loss of the opportunity to fight what would have been "one of the biggest battles of the war." [4414

DAVID ARMINE HOWARTH. D Day, the sixth of June 1944. N.Y.: McGraw-Hill Book Co. [1959]. v, [3], 251 p. ports., views. Narrative by a British author. [4415

DOUGLAS LIVERSIDGE. The third front: the strange story of the secret war in the Arctic. London: Souvenir Press [1960]. 219 p. views. Includes some account of American military operations in the Arctic, 1944-45. [4416

CHARLES BROWN MacDONALD. The decision to launch Operation MARKET-GARDEN. Kent Roberts Greenfield, ed., Command decisions (Wash.: Office of the Chief of Military History, Dept. of the Army, 1960), p. 429-42. maps (part col. fold.). notes. On the decision of Eisenhower to launch an "airborne attack deep in the enemy's rear areas ... in conjunction with a ground attack by the British Second Army" from Einhoven to Arnhem in the Netherlands, 1944. [4417

SIDNEY T. MATHEWS. General Clark's decision to drive on Rome. Kent Roberts Greenfield, ed., Command decisions (Wash.: Office of the Chief of Military History, Dept. of the Army, 1960), p. 351-63. maps (part col. fold.). notes. On the decision of Gen. Mark W. Clark to move the VI Corps of the U.S. Fifth Army against Rome, 1944. [4418

MAURICE MATLOFF. The 90-division gamble. Kent Roberts Greenfield, ed., Command decisions (Wash.: Office of the Chief of Military History, Dept. of the Army, 1960), p. 365-81. col. fold. maps. notes. On the decision by Gen. George C. Marshall to "maintain the U.S. Army's ground combat strength at ninety divisions," 1944. [4419

SAMUEL ELIOT MORISON. Victory in the Pacific, 1945. Boston: Little, Brown, and Co., 1960. xxv, 407 p. maps (1 fold.), ports., tables, views. notes. (History of United States naval operations in World War II, v. 14.) Narrative of activities of the U.S. Navy in the Pacific, Oct. 1944 - Sep. 1945, particularly the conquest of Iwo Jima and Okinawa. Completes a series of volumes, 1947-60, prepared by the author at the request of and with assistance from the Navy but not forming an "official history." To be followed by vol. 15, an index to the series. [4420

ELMER BELMONT POTTER. The defeat of Japan. Elmer Belmont Potter, ed., Sea power: a naval history (Englewood Cliffs, N.J.: Prentice-Hall, 1960), p. 813-41. maps. notes. Deals particularly with naval operations in the western Pacific, 20 Oct. 1944 - Aug 1945. Reprinted with revisions: E. B. Potter & Chester Nimitz, eds., The great sea war: the story of naval action in World War II (Englewood Cliffs, N.J.: Prentice-Hall [1960]), p. 425-58. maps. notes. [4421

ROLAND G. RUPPENTHAL. Logistics and the broad-front strategy. Kent Roberts Greenfield, ed., Command decisions (Wash.: Office of the Chief of Military History, Dept. of the Army, 1960). p. 419-27. maps (part col. fold.). notes. On the decision of General Eisenhower to "build up his forces along the Rhine through the whole length of the Western Front, from the North Sea to Switzerland, before launching a final drive into the heart of Germany," 1944. [4422

ROBERT ROSS SMITH. Luzon versus Formosa. Kent Roberts Greenfield, ed., Command decisions (Wash.: Office of the Chief of Military History, Dept. of the Army, 1960), p. 461-77. col. fold. maps. notes. On the decision by the U.S. Joint Chiefs of Staff that the "principal objective of drives that had brought the Allies into the western Pacific should be Luzon." 1944. [4423

CHARLES V. P. VON LUTTICHAU. The German counter offensive in the Ardennes. Kent Roberts Greenfield, ed., Command decisions (Wash.: Office of the Chief of Military History, Dept. of the Army, 1960), p. 443-59. maps (part col. fold.). notes. On the counteroffensive (the Battle of the Bulge) by German forces against the U.S. 12th Army Group, 1944. [4424

LOUIS MORTON. The decision to use the atomic bomb [1945]. Kent Roberts Greenfield, ed., Command decisions (Wash.: Office of the Chief of Mititary History, Dept. of the Army, 1960), p. 493-518. col. fold. maps. notes. [4425

FORREST C. POGUE. The decision to halt at the Elbe. Kent Roberts Greenfield, ed., Command decisions (Wash.: Office of the Chief of Military History, Dept. of the Army, 1960), p. 479-92. col. fold. maps. notes. Evidence that the decision of General Eisenhower to halt his forces at the Elbe, 1945, was dictated by "military reasons only." [4426

HENRY H. ADAMS. The Korean War [1950-53]. Elmer Belmont Potter, ed., Sea power: a naval history (Englewood Cliffs, N.J.: Prentice-Hall, 1960), p. 858-73. maps. Deals particularly with naval operations in "the third largest war in American history." [4427

Military Prisoners

---- CORDINER. American prisoners of the French privateers, 1707. [Edited] by M[argaret] A. and C[arson] I. A. Ritchie. Am. Neptune, 20:112-17 (Apr). Excerpts from and summaries of a journal kept by a missionary of the Society for the Propagation of the Gospel in Foreign Parts, en route with 7 members of his family to his parish in Cecil County, Md., captured with other passengers in the English Channel by the privateer Duguay Trouin and brutally treated in France as prisoners of war. [4428

DON NEAL. The Girty brothers. Pa. game news, 21(10):20-25 (Oct). On Simon, George, and James Girty, born in Cumberland County, Pa., between 1744 and 1750, captured by Indians near Kittanning ca. 1755, their adoption by the Indians (Simon by the Senecas, George and James by the Shawnees), their disloyalty to both the Americans and the British, and their lifelong loyalty to their Indians. [4429

RICHARD H. AMERMAN. Treatment of American prisoners [by the

British] during the Revolution. N.J. Hist. Soc., Proc., 78:257-75 (Oct). notes. A collection of iniquities and atrocities. [4429a

ARTHUR DUNDORE GRAEFF. Regina, the Indian captive. Hist. rev. Berks Co., 25:54-7 (spring). facsim. On Regina Leininger, daughter of Sebastian Leininger, born ca. 1746, captive of the Indians in western Pennsylvania from 1755 to 1763, buried at an undetermined date near Stouchsburg, Pa, Pa. [4430

HUGH PAYNE GREELEY. Doctors afield and afloat. New Eng. jour. med., 259:84-5 (10 Jul 1958). notes. On a Massachusetts surgeon known as "Babcock," his voyage on an American privateer, his capture and imprisonment in Halifax, N.S., and England, and his return to Boston, 1813-16, as recorded in his anonymous A journal of a young man of Massachusetts (1816), edited and published anonymously by Benjamin Waterhouse. [4431

HUGH P. WILLIAMSON. Military prisons in the Civil War [North and South]. Mo. Hist. Soc., Bul., 16:329-32 (Jul). Mainly on the Federal prison at Alton, Ill., 1862-65, and 2 prisons in St. Louis. [4432

OVID LEON FUTCH. History of Andersonville Prison [1863-65]. Ann Arbor: University Microfilms, 1959 [i.e. 1960]. Positive microfilm of typescript. [245] leaves. Thesis--Emory Univ. Abstracted: Dissert. abstracts, 20:3706 (Mar). [4433

VAN DYK MacBRIDE. Clara Barton and the Civil War Parole Camp at Annapolis, Md. Am. philatelist, 73:817-19 (Aug). facsims. On the handling of mail from and about paroled Union prisoners exchanged by the Confederates and received at the camp, 1863-65, particularly a printed form, "Correspondence with friends of paroled prisoners," and the accompanying printed envelope, used by a Bureau of Records organized by Miss Barton for replying to inquiries about missing soldiers. [4434

MURRAY BURNS. Frank M. Buckelew [born 1852]--Indian captive. Jr. historian, 20(2):12-16 (Nov 1959). port. On his captivity in the hands of the Lipan Indians in western Texas and in Mexico, 1866-67. [4435

STETSON CONN. The decision to evacuate the Japanese from the Pacific coast [by the U.S. Army and the Department of Justice, 1941-42]. Kent Roberts Greenfield, ed., Command decisions (Wash.: Office of the Chief of Military History, 1960), p. 125-49. notes. Concludes that "the only responsible commander who backed the War Department's plan as a measure required by military necessity was the President himself, as Commander in Chief." [4436

ALBERT L. COX. The saboteur story. Columbia Hist. Soc., Rec., 57-59:16-25. Recollections of the military trial of the 8 "intended German saboteurs" caught in June 1942, their imprisonment, the electrocution of 6 men, and the condemnation of the others to life imprisonment. By the wartime Provost Marshal General of the District of Columbia. [4437

DONALD L. MANES, JR. Barbed wire command: the legal nature of the command responsibilities of the senior prisoner in a prisoner of war camp [1942-53]. Mil. law rev., 10:1-45 (Oct). notes. Based on thesis--Judge Advocate General's School, U.S. Army. [4438

HAROLD GEORGE WOLFF (1898-1962). Every man has his breaking point--(?): the conduct of prisoners of war [during the Korean War, 1950-53]. Mil. med., 125:85-104 (Feb). notes. Study of 6,654 "captured American servicemen," who suffered a 38% mortality. [4439

FREDERICK A. ZEHRER. Psychological indoctrination efforts among prisoners of war in Korea [1950-53]. Ind. State Med. Assoc., Jour., 52: 1798-1838 (Oct 1959). [4440

EDWARD HUNTER. Brainwashing, from Pavlov to Powers. N.Y.: Bookmailer [1960]- v, [1], 329 p. bibliog. (p. 329). 1st ed. 1956. Information from interviews with former prisoners in North Korea in 1953 concerning methods (including physical torture) of inducing mental surrender, traced back to Pavlov's studies of conditioned reflexes; with "The clinical analysis," by Dr. Leon Freedom, who writes of "corticovisceral psychiatry." [4441

Military Relations with Civil Life

ZERAH BROWN. A Loyalist's petition. Contributed by Mrs. L. Mortimer Lewis. Detroit Soc. Geneal. Research mag., 23:127-8 (spring). Petition to "President of Canada &&," undated (probably after ca. 1808), on the losses of the author, his father (Hezekiah Brown), his grandfather (Hezekiah Brown, Sr.), and his father-in-law (James Doolittle), in Connecticut, on Long Island, and elsewhere, during the Revolution. [4442

HAROLD BELL HANCOCK. John Ferdinand Dalziel Smyth: Loyalist. Md. hist. mag., 55:346-58 (Dec). notes. On his activities in Maryland, Pennsylvania, and Delaware, 1775-77, his efforts in England to obtain full compensation for his losses in America, 1780-1808, and the abundantly documented untruthfullness of his oral and written statements about his activities and property in America. [4443

Mrs. FORREST A. YEAGER. Another Punk's Hole story. Long Island forum, 23:50, 67-8 (Mar). Family tradition about the author's ancestor Isaac Raynor of the place now called Manorville, L.I., who sometime during the Revolution killed 4 British soldiers who tried to enter his house and seize him; with mention of the location of their graves and their guns. [4444

HUGH COLEMAN BAILEY. Reaction in the Tennessee Valley [of Alabama] to Federal invasion. North Ala. Hist. Assoc., Bul., 5:3-9. notes. On "cooperationist" (not antisecessionist) sentiment in the area, "the relative absence of overt Unionism," and the abuse of civilians by the forces under Gen. Lovell H. Rousseau, 1860-62. [4445

WILLARD EUGENE WIGHT. The churches and the Confederate cause [1860-65]. Civil War hist., 6:361-73 (Dec). notes. [4446

RICHARD NELSON CURRENT. God and the strongest battalions. David Donald, ed., Why the North won the Civil War ([Baton Rouge:] Louisiana State Univ. Press [1960]), p. 3-22. On the "chief errors" of Confederate "economic policy," 1861-65. [4447

BLANTON E. BLACK. Sherman, Savannah, and the Negro. Savannah State College, Faculty research edition, 14(2):52-6 (Dec). On the treatment of Negroes by Gen. W. T. Sherman, 1864-65, and his proposal to establish "the freed Negroes in self-sufficient reservations" in South Carolina, Georgia, and northern Florida. [4448

ANN JENKINS. The day in St. Albans. New Eng. teacher, 5(4):12, 14-15, 18 (Apr 1958). On the robbery of the Franklin County Bank, St. Albans, Vt., by Confederate soldiers, 19 Oct. 1864. [4449

ANN MOORE. The Fiesta de San Jacinto. Jr. historian (Tex.), 19(6): 5-8 (May 1959). views. On the Battle of Flowers, an annual affair in San Antonio, "inaugurated in 1891 as a special tribute to the Texans' victory at San Jacinto." [4450

Mrs. JAMES C. BONNER. Founding of the D. A. R. in Alabama [General Sumter Chapter, the first chapter in the State, since 1895]. D. A. R. mag., 94:220, 253 (Mar). [4451

ANNA CATHERINE (SMITH) PABST. Delaware City Chapter, Daughters of the American Revolution, Delaware, Ohio, organized March 10, 1909. ... "To cherish and maintain the traditions of American freedom." Delaware, 1960. [3], 37 leaves. tables. [4452

HENRY H. ADAMS & ELLERY H. CLARK, JR. The war against shipping [1914-18]. Elmer Belmont Potter, ed., Sea power: a naval history (Englewood Cliffs, N.J.: Prentice-Hall, 1960), p. 455-75. diagr., maps. notes. Includes some account of the entry of the United States into World War I after the adoption of unrestricted U-boat warfare by Germany. [4453

ROBERT DAVID WARD. The origin and activities of the National Security League, 1914-1919. Miss. Valley hist. rev., 47:51-65 (Jun). notes. On its work "for preparedness," including compulsory military training and later "the achievement of complete national unity of thought and action" and "100 per cent Americanism." [4454

MALACHY FRANCIS CAULFIELD. A night of terror: the story of the Athenia affair. By Max Caulfield. London: Frederick Muller Ltd. [1958]. 222 p. ports., views. American edition: Tomorrow never came: the story of the S.S. Athenia. N.Y.: Norton [1959]. 223 p. ports., views. On the sinking of the Athenia," the last passenger ship out of Europe before war began," overloaded with 1,147 passengers (Americans and Canadians), by a German submarine, 3 Sep. 1939 (immediately after the British declaration of war), with a loss of 112 lives. [4455

EDWARD N. BARNHART. The individual exclusion of Japanese Americans in World War II [1944-45]. Pac. hist. rev., 29: 111-30 (May). notes. On the exclusion of Japanese Americans from California and parts of Oregon and Washington, "an ineffective measure based on indefensible and arbitrary grounds, which continued for nine months to deprive a large number of American citizens of many of their rights and liberties." [4456

CIVILIAN CONTROL OF ARMED FORCES

WILLIAM GABRIEL CARRAS. The analysis and interpretation of the use of Presidential authority to order United States armed forces into military action in foreign territories without a formal declaration of war [1789-1956]. Ann Arbor: University Microfilms, 1959 [i.e. 1960]. Positive microfilm of typescript. ii, 425 (i.e. 420) leaves. bibliog. (leaves 416-20). Thesis--New York Univ. Abstracted: Dissert, abstracts, 20:4328 (May). [4457

ANTHONY WAYNE (1745-96). Anthony Wayne, a name in arms: soldier, diplomat, defender of expansion westward of a nation--the Wayne-Knox-Pickering-McHenry correspondence. Transcribed and edited by Richard C. Knopf. [Pittsburgh:] Univ. of Pittsburgh Press [1959, c1960. 8], 566 p. maps, plans, ports, views. notes. bibliog. (p. 547-52), notes. 1st ed. 1955. Instructions from Henry Knox, Secretary of War, and his successors, Timothy Pickering and James McHenry, to Major General Wayne, commanding "the frontier north and west of the Ohio," and his reports to them (enclosures not printed), Apr. 1792 - Nov. 1796. [4458

WERNER H. MARTI. Messenger of destiny: the California adventures, 1846-1847, of Archibald H. Gillespie [1812-73], U.S. Marine Corps. [San Francisco:] J. Howell--Books, 1960. viii, [4], 147 p. map, views. (The John Howell series on the U.S. Navy in old California.) On his service as a "secret agent of President Polk and ... his part in the military conquest and early occupation of California." [4459

JOHN HOPE FRANKLIN. Lincoln and the politics of war. Ralph G. Newman, ed., Lincoln for the ages (Garden City, N.Y.: Doubleday, 1960), p. 226-30. On his realization of the "political role of the President" and the "relationship between military and political victories," 1860-64. [4460

BRUCE CATTON. President Lincoln and General McClellan. Ralph G. Newman, ed., Lincoln for the ages (Garden City, N.Y.: Doubleday, 1960), p. 197-202. On Lincoln's relations with Gen. George B. McClellan as commander-in-chief and political rival, 1861-64. [4461

ULYSSES SIMPSON GRANT III. Lincoln: commander-in-chief. Ralph G. Newman, ed., Lincoln for the ages (Garden City, N.Y.: Doubleday, 1960), p. 242-7. On the "skill with which he was able to guide the resources and patriotic efforts of the North," 1861-65. [4462

EVERETTE BEACH LONG. President Lincoln and General Grant. Ralph G. Newman, ed., Lincoln for the ages (Garden City, N.Y.: Doubleday, 1960), p. 268-70. On the "similarity ... of character that enabled Lincoln and Grant, together, to win the war for the Union," 1861-65. [4463

DAVID MORRIS POTTER. Jefferson Davis and the political factors in Confederate defeat [1861-65]. David Donald, ed., Why the North won the Civil War ([Baton Rouge:] Louisiana State Univ. Press [1960]), p. 91-114. [4464

THOMAS HARRY WILLIAMS. Lincoln and the Committee on the Conduct of the War. Ralph G. Newman, ed., Lincoln for the ages (Garden City, N.Y.: Doubleday, 1960), p. 191-6. On his dealings with a joint committee of Congress and its chairman, Senator Ben Wade, 1861-65. [4465

PHILIP G. CARLETON. The eyes of the Union. Harvard alumni bul., 54: 113-15, 122-4 (27 Oct 1951). port., views. On the service of Charles Anderson Dana (1819-97) as "special commissioner of the War Department to investigate and report upon the condition of the pay service of the Western armies" and as Second Assistant Secretary of War, 1862-65. [4466

ARCHER JONES. Some aspects of George W[ythe] Randolph's service as Confederate Secretary of War [Mar.-Nov. 1862]. Jour. South. hist., 26:299-314 (Aug). notes. [4467

CLIFFORD SHIRLEY DOWDEY, JR. Lincoln in Richmond. Ralph G. Newman, ed., Lincoln for the ages (Garden City, N.Y.: Double-day, 1960), p. 355-61. On his visit to Richmond after the Confederate withdrawal, Apr. 1865. [4468

OTTO EISENSCHIML. Lincoln and the advent of peace. Ralph G. Newman, ed., Lincoln for the ages (Garden City, N.Y.: Doubleday, 1960), p. 344-8. On his visit to the Union front lines in Virginia and his statements about reconstruction in the South, 23 Mar.-14 Apr. 1865. [4469

HAROLD MELVIN HYMAN. Johnson, Stanton, and Grant: a reconsideration of the Army's role in the events leading to impeachment. Am. hist. rev., 66:85-100 (Oct). notes. On "civil-military relations," 1865-68. [4470

DAVID DIXON PORTER (1813-91). Lincoln and the miracles-at-sea. Ill. State Hist. Soc., Jour., 53:283-7 (autumn). Account (from the author's Incidents and anecdotes of the Civil War, 1885) of Lincoln's stay on Porter's flagship, the Malvern, Mar. 1865, where he was insulated, by his own request, from officeseekers, his cabinet, and his vice-president. [4471

WALTER MILLIS, HARVEY C. MANSFIELD, & HAROLD STEIN. Arms and the state: civil-military elements in national policy [1930-57]. N.Y.: Twentieth Century Fund, 1958. [12], 436 p. bibliog. (p. 415-20), notes [4472

MICHAEL HOWARD. Civil-military relations in Great Britain and the United States, 1945-1958. Pol. science quar., 75:35-46 (Mar). notes. [4473

ARCHIE J. KNIGHT & ALLEN F. HERZBERG. A proposal for the next step in defense reorganization. Air Univ. quar. rev., 12(2):53-90 (summer). diagrs. (part double). Includes an account of the organizational structure of the U.S. Department of Defense, 1947-60. [4474

TRUMBULL HIGGINS. Korea and the fall of MacArthur: a précis in limited war [1950-53]. N.Y.: Oxford Univ. Press, 1960. ix, [3], 229 p. map. bibliog. (p. 213-21), notes (p. 187-212). [4475

JOHN W. SPANIER. The Truman-MacArthur controversy and the Korean War. Cambridge, Mass.: Belknap Press, 1959. xii, 311 p. cartoons, map. bibliog. (p. 298-306), notes (p. 281-97). On MacArthur's command of American forces in Korea, Jun. 1950 - Apr. 1951, his removal by President Truman from "all his commands," the hearings in the Senate, and the unsettled question of the proper relation between civil and military authority. [4476

THE JOURNALISM OF WAR

SOLOMON LUTNICK. The American Revolution and the British press [1775-82]. Ann Arbor: University Microfilms, 1960. Positive microfilm of typescript. [373] leaves. Thesis--Columbia Univ. Abstracted: Dissert. abstracts, 21:864 (Oct). [4477

OSCAR EDWARD MAURER. "Punch" on slavery and civil war in America, 1841-1865. Victorian studies, 1:5-28 (Sep 1957). cartoons. notes. On satirical comments by Douglas Jerrold, satirical verses by Shirley Brooks, and cartoons by Sir John Tenniel, expressing the prevailingly pro-Southern and anti-Lincoln attitude of Punch, suddenly reversed after the death of Lincoln. [4478

C. RICHARD KING. The true blue. West Tex. Hist. Assoc. yr. bk., 36: 176-86. bibliog. On a handwritten newspaper (6 numbers) issued by members of the Texan Santa Fe Expedition imprisoned in Castle Santiago, Mexico City, Apr.-May 1842. [4479

JOHN O. WALLER. Charles Dickens and the American Civil War. Studies in philol., 57:535-48 (Jul). notes. On articles about America in Dickens's weekly magazine, All the year round, 1861-64, and the reasons for its pro-Southern stand. [4480

OLIVER HOLMES KNIGHT, JR. Following the Indian wars: the story of the newspaper correspondents among the Indian campaigners. Norman: Univ. of Oklahoma Press [1960]. xv, 348, [1] p. ports., views. bibliog. (p. 331-8), notes. Issued also in microfilm form as thesis--Univ. of Wisconsin, 1959. Abstracted: Dissert. abstracts, 20:4384-5 (May). On "the twenty identifiable accredited correspondents who reported the Western War during its important campaigns, from 1867 through 1881"--H. Wallace Atwell, Robert D. Bogart, William Mitchell Bunker, Reuben Briggs Davenport, Charles Sanford Diehl, John F. Finerty, Edward Fox, James William Howard, De Benneville

Randolph Keim, William F. Kellogg (Mark Kellogg), Barbour Lathrop, Alex McKay, T. C. MacMillan, James J. O'Kelly, Jerry Roche, Henry Morton Stanley, Jerome Stillson, Robert E. Strahorn, Thomas A. Sutherland, and Joe Wasson. [4481

THE STARS AND STRIPES. The Stars and stripes story of World War II. Edited by Robert [Eugene] Meyer, Jr. Foreword by Omar N. Bradley. N.Y.: D. McKay Co. [1960]. viii, 504 p. cartoons, port., views. bibliog. (p. 498-500). Excerpts from the "soldiers' newspaper," issued in many "editions" in various theaters of the war, Apr. 1942 - Sep. 1945. [4482

HANS-JOACHIM NETZER. Die neue Zeitung. Gazette, 2 (1956): 13-26. facsim. On Die neue Zeitung: eine amerikanische Zeitung für die deutsche Bevölkerung, Oct. 1945 - Jan. 1955, issued as "the organ of American Military Government." [4483

MILITARY GOVERNMENT

U.S. Provost Marshal General's School, Camp Gordon, Ga. Military government: an historical approach. [Camp Gordon? 1951.] iii, 117 p. notes. (Its Training packet 9.) Prepared by the Military Government Department for ORC units. On military government under authority of the United States in Mexico, the former Confederate States, Cuba, the Philippines, and Germany, 1847-1923. [4484

ELISABETH JOAN DOYLE. New Orleans courts under military occupation, 1861-1865. Mid-America, 42: 185-92 (Jul). notes. [4485

NONA W. BARRICK & MARY HELEN TAYLOR. Murder in Mesilla. N. M., 38(11):3-5, 34 (Nov). port. On a murderous assault upon Robert P. Kelley, C. S. Surveyor General of the Territory of Arizona, editor of the Mesilla times, by Col. John R. Baylor, C.S.A., 12 Dec. 1861, resulting in his death on 1 Jan. 1862, an indictment for murder against Baylor in Jun. 1863, and its failure to come to trial. [4486

MARTIN HARDWICK HALL. The Baylor-Kelley fight: a Civil War incident in old Mesilla. Password, 5:83-90 (Jul). notes. On the establishment of the C.S. Territory of Arizona (present New Mexico and Arizona south of the 34th parallel) by Lt. Col. John R. Baylor, with himself as military governor, the caustic criticism of his actions and denunciation of his character by Robert P. Kelley, editor of the Mesilla, N. M., Times, the resulting assault by Baylor, the death of Kelley, and the failure of a grand jury to return a true bill against Baylor, 1861. [4487

ELISABETH JOAN DOYLE. Nurseries of treason: schools in occupied New Orleans [1862-65]. Jour. South. hist., 26:161-79 (May). notes. On the efforts of the military government to control both public and private schools and to prescribe the political sentiments of their teachers and pupils. [4488

HASKELL MONROE. Men without law: Federal raiding in Liberty County, Georgia [Dec. 1864, Jan. 1865]. Ga. hist. quar., 44:154-71 (Jun). notes. Notes the contrast between the situation there and in Savannah, where Sherman "kept incidents of theft and pillage at a low level." [4489

SPENCER BIDWELL KING, JR. April in Macon. Ga. rev., 14:143-55 (summer). On the occupation of Macon by Union forces under Bvt. Maj. Gen. James Harrison Wilson, 20 Apr. - 11 May 1865, and his incompletely successful efforts to prevent looting and debauchery. [4490

EMILIO ROIG DE LEUCHSENRING. El Presidente McKinley y el Governador Wood, máximos enemigos de Cuba libre. [Habana:] Oficina del Historiador de la Ciudad de la Habana, 1960. 51, [4] p. notes. On "Las abominables actividades de McKinley para lograr la anexion de Cuba a los Estados Unidos" and La nefasta labor anticubana y anexionista de Leonardo Wood como Governador de Cuba," 1898-1901. [4491

HAROLD DON ALLEN. Military money: some guesses and conclusions. Numismatic scrapbook, 26:3497-3501 (Dec). facsims. On the 17 "Allied Occupation and United States Military Payment releases of and since World War II," 1943 ff. [4492

WILLIAM J. GANE. Foreign affairs of South Korea, August 1945 to August 1950. U.S., Dept of State, Office of Intelligence Research, Abstracts of completed doctoral dissertations, 1950-51 ([Wash.] 1952), p. 363-6. Abstract of thesis--Northwestern Univ. Deals largely with the U.S. Army Military Government in Korea. [4493

KAZUO KAWAI. Japan's American interlude. [Chicago:] Univ. of Chicago Press [1960]. vii, 257 p. bibliog. (p. 249-54), notes. On the occupation of Japan by American military forces, 1945-54. [4494

THEODORE McNELLY. The Japanese constitution: child of the Cold War [1945-58]. Pol. science quar., 74:176-95 (Jun 1959). notes. [4495

HAROLD SCOTT QUIGLEY. Revising the Japanese constitution. For. affairs, 38:140-45 (Oct 1959). notes. On the formation of a constitution in Japan by direction of the Supreme Commander for the Allied Powers in 1945, the subsequent proposals for its revision, and a recent visit of a Study Group headed by Prof. Kenzo Takayanagi to the United States to interview former members of the SCAP staff who had taken part in drafting the original constitution. [4496

MILITARY PROCUREMENT

DONALD B. WEBSTER, JR. Arms smuggling from Boston--1775. Gun rep., 5(10):24-5, 34 (Mar). notes. [4497

RICHARD K. MURDOCH. Benedict Arnold and the owners of the Charming Nancy. Pa. mag. hist. and biog., 84:22-55 (Jan). notes. On his reasons for issuing a "pass or safe-conduct" to permit this small schooner "to leave enemy-occupied Philadelphia and proceed to any port under American control." [4498

GEORGE H. GIBSON. Twenty-seven tickets. N.C. hist. rev., 37:477-87 (Oct). notes. On 27 tickets issued by forces of Gen. Cornwallis to Moravian residents of Bethania, Bethabara, and Salem who under compulsion had provided supplies for the British, Feb. 1781, stipulating payments totaling about 500 lb., and the unsuccessful efforts of their holders and of the North Carolina and U.S. governments to collect the sums due, 1781-1805. [4499

JAMES SPRUNT (1846-1924). Tales of the Cape Fear blockade, being a turn of the century account of blockade-running, told by the Hon. James Sprunt, formerly purser of the Confederate States Steamer "Lilian." ... Edited by Cornelious M.D. Thomas. Wilmington, N.C.: J. E. Hicks for the Charles Towne Preservation Trust, 1960. xii, [2], 134 p. fold. map, views. bibliog. (p. 127-30). (Clarendon imprint 4.) Includes "an editorial map showing the lower Cape Fear and coast of Brunswick County with plantations, places, fortifications, and wrecks of blockade-runners, 1861-1865." [4500

GEORGE COOPER REINHARDT & WILLIAM ROSCOE KINTNER. The haphazard years: how America has gone to war. Garden City, N.Y.: Doubleday, 1960. 242 p. notes. On the "role of America's industrial technology in shaping our national military policy" and "the interaction of civil-military technologies," 1898-1960. [4501

J. R. BRYANT. Food and health. Am. Dietetic Assoc., Jour., 36:226-31 (Mar). views. notes. On the work of the U.S. Army Veterinary Corps in inspecting meat and other animal products as food for military use, 1916-60. [4502

EDWIN HENRY RUTKOWSKY. The politics of military aviation procurement, 1926-1934: a study in the political assertion of consensual values. Ann Arbor: University Microfilms, 1960. Positive microfilm of typescript. [372] leaves. Thesis--Columbia Univ. Abstracted: Dissert. abstracts, 21:950 (Oct). [4503

RICHARD M. LEIGHTON. U.S. merchant shipping and the British import crisis [1943]. Kent Roberts Greenfield, ed., Command decisions (Wash.: Office of the Chief of Military History, Dept. of the Army, 1960), p. 199-223. col. fold. maps. notes. [4504

WILLIAM CHARLES TRUPPNER. The Defense Materials System. Construction rev., 6(2):4-9 (Feb). On the Controlled Materials Plan (1943 ff.) and the Defense Materials System as "means of directing the flow of materials and products to the Nation's military, space and atomic energy production and construction programs." [4505

U.S. Office of the Quartermaster General. Historical Branch. Special rations for the armed forces. By Franz A. Koehler. Wash., 1958. xvii, 377 p. tables, views. bibliog. (p. 357), notes. (Its QMC historical studies, series 2, no. 6.) On "the development of special or, more precisely, packed operational rations that took place at the Quartermaster Food and Container Institute between 1945 and 1952-53." [4506

MILITARY RECRUITMENT

GLENN WEAVER. The Mennonites during the French and Indian War. Mennonite hist. bul., 16(2):2-3 (Apr 1955). notes. On their pacifism and their charity to victims of war, 1755 ff. [4507

J. STEWART. The press-gangs of the Royal Navy. U.S.N. Inst. proc., 86(10): 81-7 (Oct). views. On the reasons for the growth of this method of recruitment (rooted in feudal law that has never been repealed), particularly in the late 17th century and the 18th century, and its part in bringing on the War of 1812. [4508

BILL G. REID. Confederate opponents of arming the slaves, 1861-1865. Jour. Miss. hist., 22:249-70 (Oct). notes. [4509

JOHN TORREY. An eyewitness account of the New York draft riots, July 1863. Edited by A. Hunter Dupree and Leslie H. Fishel, Jr. Miss. Valley hist. rev., 47:472-9 (Dec). notes. [4510

FREDERIC S. BERMAN. Selective Service and the courts--why a registrant must first exhaust his administrative remedies [1917-58]. N.Y. law forum, 5:179-90 (Apr 1959). notes. [4511

ALBERT ALEXANDER BLUM. The Army and student deferments during the second World War [1942-45]. Jour. higher educ., 31:41-5 (Jan). notes. [4512

BERNARD D. KARPINOS. Fitness of American youth for military service. Milbank Memorial Fund quar., 38: 213-47 (Jul). diagrs., tables, notes. Analysis of statistics of men examined for Army service during the Korean War, 1950-53. [4513

THE POLITICS AND DIPLOMACY OF WAR AND PEACE

L. A. BOITEUX. Un mémoire prophétique de Turgot sur la Révolution d'Amérique (1776). Rev. hist. dipl., 72:231-9 (Jul-Sep 1958). notes. On the difference of opinion between Charles Gravier, Comte de Vergennes, and Anne Robert Jacques Turgot, Baron de l'Aune, as to whether France should engage in active military participation in the Revolutionary War. [4514

RICHARD HOWE, EARL HOWE (1726-99). An unaccepted letter to George Washington from the original in the William L. Clements Library. Ann Arbor: [Printed for the Clements Library Associates at Sequoia Press, Kalamazoo] 1959. [12] p. notes (p. [11]). Facsimile reproduction of a letter from Vice-Admiral Howe, dated Eagle, off Staten Island, 13 Jul. 1776, to "George Washington Esq &c--&c," requesting an interview regarding Howe's commission to "grant pardons and declare peace if the rebellious Americans would lay down their arms and acknowledge the authority of Parliament"; and account of Washington's reasons for declining to receive it. [4515

LOWELL M. LIMPUS (1897-1957). Disarm! N.Y.: Freedom Press [1960]. 302 p. facsims., tables. bibliog. (p. 299-302). On American military disarmament plans, 1784-1948, and in recent years "the sinister relationship between pacifism, communism, and disarmament." [4516

WALTER MILLIS. The Constitution and the common defense [1787-1958]. N.Y.: Fund for the Republic [1959]. 48 p. [4517

RICHARD K. MURDOCH. The case of the Spanish deserters, 1791-93. Ga. hist. quar., 44:278-305 (Sep). notes. On political and diplomatic complications resulting from efforts of Capt. Henry Burbeck (1754-1848), commanding the U.S. post at St. Tammany, on the Georgia side of the St. Marys River, to effect exchange of American and Spanish deserters and fugitives. [4518

RICHARD K. MURDOCH, ed. Documents pertaining to the Georgia-Florida frontier, 1791-1793. Fla. hist. quar., 38:319-38 (Apr). notes. Correspondence of Luis de las Casas y Arogorri (Governor and Captain-General of Cuba), Juan Nepomuceno de Quesada (Governor of East Florida), Capt. Henry Burbeck (commanding the U.S. post at St. Mary's), Capt. Sebastian Creagh (commanding the Spanish post of San Vicente Ferrer on the St. John's River), Richard Long (Commissioner of the St. Mary's River), James Seagrove (Commissioner of the United States), José Moniño, Conde de Floridablanca (First Secretary of State of Spain), Josef de Jaudenes and Josef Ignacio de Viar (Agents of Spain to the United States), Thomas Jefferson (Secretary of State), and Henry Knox (Secretary of War), 16 Jun. 1790 - 5 Jul. 1793, relating to reciprocal return of military deserters who crossed the Florida-Georgia border. [4519

JACOB RADER MARCUS. The Valenzin affair. Abraham Berger, Lawrence Marwick, & Isidore S. Meyer, eds., The Joshua Bloch memorial volume: studies in booklore and history (N.Y.: New York Public Library, 1960), p. 140-50. notes. On the illegal seizure of David Valenzin, Jewish merchant, and his vessel (the Paulina) and cargo in the mediterranean by Commodore Richard V. Morris, commanding the USS Enterprize, the illegal imprisonment of Valentin in the United States, his release after action by Congress, his suicide, and the return to his family of what was left of his estate, 1803-4. [4520

EDWIN METCALF GAINES. Outrageous encounter! the Chesapeake-Leopard affair of 1807. Ann Arbor: University Microfilms, 1960. Positive microfilm of typescript. [174] leaves. Thesis--Univ. of Virginia. Abstracted: Dissert. abstracts, 21:1171-2 (Nov.) A study based mainly upon Admiralty and Foreign Office records and upon private correspondence of Englishmen. [4521

HORATIO NEWHALL. [Letter to Lucy Newhall in Lynn, dated Cambridge, 3 Mar. 1815.] Harvard alumni bul., 54:409 (23 Feb 1951). On the celebration of the signing of the Treaty of Ghent between the United States and Great Britain, ending the War of 1812. [4522

GEORGE M. BROOKE, JR. The voyage of the Kanrin Maru, 1860: an episode in American naval diplomacy. Am. Neptune, 20:198-208 (Jul). notes. On the stranding of Lt. John Mercer Brooke and his crew in Japan after the wreck of their U.S. surveying vessel, the plans of the Japanese Government to send a vessel of the Japanese Navy on a cruise to San Francisco, the acceptance of Brooke's offer of his services and his crew to assist in the navigation of the Japanese vessel (manned by inexperienced Japanese officers and crew), his efforts to teach to the Japanese the rudiments of navigation and to overcome their reluctance to exert themselves, the triumphant arrival of the vessel in San Francisco, and the demonstration of Brooke's success as a teacher when the Japanese completed their voyage to Japan without mishap. [4523

JAMES J. HESLIN. "Peaceful compromise" in New York City, 1860-1861. N.-Y. Hist. Soc. quar., 44:348-62 (Oct). ports., views. notes. On political sentiment regarding means of avoiding war. [4524

NORMAN ARTHUR GRAEBNER. Northern diplomacy and European neutrality [1861-65]. David Donald, ed., Why the North won the Civil War ([Baton Rouge:] Louisiana State Univ. Press [1960]), p. 49-75. [4525

LUDWELL H. JOHNSON. Fort Sumter and Confederate diplomacy. Jour. South. hist., 26:441-77 (Nov). notes. On the negotiations of a 3-man commission of the C.S. Government with officials of the U.S. Government in Washington, especially William H. Seward, concerning possession of Forts Sumter and Pickens, Feb.-Apr. 1861. [4526

GIDEON WELLES (1802-78). Fort Pickens: facts in relation to the reinforcement of Fort Pickens in the spring [April] of 1861. Selected essays by Gideon Welles: Civil War and Reconstruction, ed. Albert Mordell (N.Y.: Twayne Publishers, 1959), p. 83-113. From The galaxy, Jan. 1871. On the action and motive of William Henry Seward, Secretary of State, in ordering the USS Powhatan, en route to the relief of Fort Sumter, to be diverted to Fort Pickens without the authorization or knowledge of Welles, Secretary of the Navy. [4527

GIDEON WELLES (1802-78). Fort Sumter: facts in relation to the expedition ordered by the administration of President Lincoln for the relief of the garrison in Fort Sumter [Mar.-Apr. 1861]. Selected essays by Gideon Welles: Civil War and Reconstruction, ed. Albert Mordell (N.Y.: Twayne Publishers, 1959), p. 36-82. From The galaxy, Nov. 1870. [4528

HENRY ADAMS (1838-1918). Henry Adams silenced by the cotton famine. [Edited by] Joseph A. Borome. New Eng. quar., 33:237-40 (Jun). notes. "Private & confidential" letter to Henry J. Raymond, editor of the New York Times, London, 24 Jan. 1862, on the danger of British intervention in favor of the Confederate States. [4529

JOSEPH BURNS KELLY. Gas warfare in international law. Mil. law rev., 9: 1-67 (Jul). notes. Thesis (M. S.)--Georgetown Univ., 1960. On the concern of the United States in the antipersonnel use of gas in combat, 1862-64, 1915-18, later consideration of its use, and the international efforts since 1899 to limit use. [4530

GIDEON WELLES (1802-78). The capture and release of Mason and Slidell. Selected essays by Gideon Welles: Civil War and Reconstruction, ed. Albert Mordell (N.Y.: Twayne Publishers, 1959), p. 256-79. From The galaxy, May 1873. On the unauthorized action of Capt. Charles Wilkes, commanding a vessel of the U.S. Navy, in seizing John Slidell and James Murray Mason, Confederate emissaries en route to England, and the resulting embarrassment of Welles, Secretary of the Navy. [4531

ROBIN D. S. HIGHAM. The Russian fleet on the eastern seaboard, 1863-1864: a maritime chronology. Am. Neptune, 20:49-61 (Jan). notes. Includes some account of the reasons why the fleet visited America. [4532

WILLIAM JOHN ULRICH. The Northern military mind in regard to Reconstruction, 1865-1872: the attitudes of ten leading Union generals. Ann Arbor: University Microfilms, 1959 [i. e. 1960]. Positive microfilm of typescript. iii, 392 leaves. bibliog. (leaves 375-91). Thesis--Ohio State Univ. Abstracted: Dissert. abstracts, 20:3721-2 (Mar). [4533

H. M. BRENT. A little night music. Am. Neptune, 20:62 (Jan). Despatch from the U.S. Minister to Peru, 14 Nov. 1869, reporting that "for the purpose of testing the efficiency of the discipline on board," Captain Thornton and Captain Eastman, commanding respectively the U.S. men-of-war Kearsarge and Nyack, had discharged "some of their heavy ordnance" at about 2 A. M., 3 Nov 1869, in the Bay of Callao without the permission or foreknowledge of the local authorities or of the minister, and thereby had thoughtlessly created great alarm and indignation. [4534

STEPHAN A. THERNSTROM. Oswald Garrison Villard and the politics of pacifism [1897-1941]. Harv. Lib. bul., 14:126-52 (winter). notes. [4535

MARTIN DAVID DUBIN. The development of the concept of collective security in the American peace movement, 1899-1917. Ann Arbor: University Microfilms, 1960. Positive microfilm of typescript. [424] leaves. Thesis--Indiana Univ. Abstracted: Dissert. abstracts, 21:664 (Sep). [4536

ROBERT PAUL LISENSKY. Methodism as an initiator of social thought and action in the area of world peace (1900-1956). Ann Arbor: University Microfilms, 1960. Positive microfilm of typescript. [357] leaves. Thesis--Boston Univ. Abstracted: Dissert. abstracts, 21:1272 (Nov). [4537

LOUIS MORTON. Army and Marines on the China Station: a study in military and political rivalry. Pac. hist. rev., 29:51-73 (Feb). notes. On the American garrison in China, consisting of Marines and soldiers as 2 commands independent of each other, neither able to act without the consent of the Secretary of State, 1900-1938. [4538

RAYMOND JOHN TONER. We are all Americans. U.S.N. Inst. proc., 86(1): 23-37 (Jan). views. On relations of the United States with Latin America, particularly in diplomatic and military phases of hemispheric defense, 20th century. [4539

THOMAS C. WILSON. The Peace of Portsmouth [1905]. N.H. profiles, 9(9):41-4 (Sep). ports. [4540

EUGENE MORLOCK EMME, ed. The impact of air power: national security and world politics. Princeton, N.J.: D. Van Nostrand Co. [1959]. xiv, 914 p. diagrs., maps. bibliogs., notes. Contains 118 reprinted speeches, articles, chapters, etc., 1914-58, grouped in 12 chapters, which are collected in 3 parts: "The nature of air power," "The revolution in warfare," and "Air policy in national security and world politics," each chapter and part preceded by a detailed editorial introduction and each part followed by a bibliography. [4541

LAURENCE W. MARTIN. Woodrow Wilson's appeal to the people of Europe: British radical influence on the President's strategy [1914-18]. Pol. science quar., 74:498-516 (Dec 1959). notes. [4542

JAMES WEINSTEIN. Anti-war sentiment and the Socialist Party, 1917-1918. Pol. science quar., 74:215-39 (Jun 1959). notes. [4543

RAY STANNARD BAKER (1870-1946). Woodrow Wilson and world settlement: written from his unpublished and personal material. Gloucester, Mass.: P. Smith, 1960 [c1922]. 3 v. xxxv, [3], 432; xii, [2], 561; xv, [3], 508 p. cartoons, diagr., facsims., maps, ports. notes. Narrative of "what happened at Paris" in the Peace Conference, 1919 (vols. 1-2), and supporting documents (vol. 3). [4544

JOHN ROGER FREDLAND. Disarmament and rearmament [1919-38]. Elmer Belmont Potter, ed., Sea power: a naval history (Englewood Cliffs, N.J.: Prentice-Hall, 1960), p. 476-90. notes. [4545

BERNADOTTE EVERLY SCHMITT. After Munich. Bernadotte E. Schmidt, The fashion and future of history: historical studies and addresses (Cleveland: Press of Western Reserve Univ., 1960), p. 151-64. Address (Feb. 1939) on the uncertainty of Great Britain, France, and the United States about the "best course to pursue" toward the maintenance of peace after World War I, 1919 ff. [4546

BERNADOTTE EVERLY SCHMITT. The peace treaties of 1919-1920. Am. Philos. Soc., Proc., 104:101-10 (15 Feb). [4547

ROBERT W. TUCKER. The just war: a study in contemporary American doctrine [since 1932]. Baltimore: Johns Hopkins Press [1960]. vii, [5], 207 p. notes. Partial contents.--The American doctrine of the just war.--On the justice of defensive wars.--On banishing force from history. [4548

WAYNE STANLEY COLE. Senator Key Pittman and American neutrality policies, 1933-1940. Miss. Valley hist. rev., 46:644-62 (Mar). notes. [4549

DAVID KUN-HSI LU. From the Marco Polo Bridge to Pearl Harbor: Japan's entry into the Second World War [1937-41]. Ann Arbor: University Microfilms, 1960. Positive microfilm of typescript. [503] leaves. Thesis--Columbia Univ. Abstracted: Dissert. abstracts, 21:949-50 (Oct). [4550

JOHN McVICKAR HAIGHT. France, the United States, and the Munich crisis [1938]. Jour. mod. hist., 32: 340-58 (Dec). notes. [4551

KENNETH EWART BOULDING. The domestic implications of arms control [1939-59]. Daedalus, 89:846-59 (fall). tables. bibliog. On the illusory "association of disarmament with depression and with extensive economic dislocation." [4552

ANDREW J. SCHWARTZ. America and the Russo-Finnish War. Wash.: Public Affairs Press [1960]. vi, [2], 103 p. notes (p. 93-100). On "the course, the nature, and the objectives of American foreign policy toward Finland and the Soviet Union," 1939-44. [4553

ROBERT SOBEL. The origins of interventionism: the United States and the Russo-Finnish War. N.Y.: Bookman Associates [1960]. 204 p. bibliog. (p. 189-99), notes. Chapters on isolationism and neutrality, 1932-39, the effort to aid the Finns in repelling Russian attempts at annexation, and the change of orientation when German invasion of Russia shifted American approval to Russia and in effect aligned Finland with the Axis powers, 1939-40. [4554

ROBERT SOBEL. The United States and the Russo-Finnish War of 1939-1940. Ann Arbor: University Microfilms, 1957 [i. e. 1960]. Positive microfilm of typescript. [388] leaves. Thesis--New York Univ. Abstracted: Dissert. abstracts, 20:3717-18 (Mar). [4555

WALT WHITMAN ROSTOW. The United States in the world arena: an essay in recent history [1940-58]. N.Y.: Harper [1960]. xxii, 568 p. diagrs., tables. bibliog. (p. 551-2), notes. (Massachusetts Institute of Technology. Center for International Studies. American project series). Includes sections (p. 41-471) on "The Second World War," "The Truman-Stalin duel," and "The Eisenhower Administration and its crisis." [4556

ROBERT JOSEPH CHARLES BUTOW. The Hull-Nomura conversations: a fundamental misconception. Am. hist. rev., 65:822-36 (Jul). notes. On diplomatic talks between Secretary of State Cordell Hull and Ambassador Kichisaburō Nomura, Mar.-May 1941, and the latter's failure "to report fully and accurately" to the Japanese Government. [4557

LOUIS MORTON. Japan's decision for war [1941]. Kent Roberts Greenfield, ed., Command decisions (Wash.: Office of the Chief of Military History, Dept. of the Army, 1960), p. 99-124. maps (part col. fold.). notes. [4558

JAMES JAQUESS ROBINSON. Surprise attack: crime at Pearl Harbor and now. Am. Bar Assoc. jour., 46:973-80, 1085-91 (Sep, Oct). ports., views. notes. On "the crime of surprise attack, as codified, defined, and prohibited by the Third Hague Convention of 1907," the violation of the convention at Pearl Harbor in 1941, the Tokyo War Crimes Trial of 1948 (conducted by the International Military Tribunal for the Far East), and "the present public interest in preventing surprise attack." [4559

RUSSIA (1923- U.S.S.R.). Komissiia po Izdaniiu Diplomaticheskikh Documentov. Correspondence between the Chairman of the Council of Ministers of the U.S.S.R. and the Presidents of the U.S.A. and the Prime Ministers of Great Britain during the Great Patriotic War of 1941-1945. Moscow: Foreign Languages Pub. House, 1957. 2 v. 400, [4], 301, [3] p. notes (1:381-401; 2:283-302). Contains "the correspondence exchanged by J. V. Stalin, Chairman of the Council of Ministers of the U.S.S.R., with Franklin D. Roosevelt, President of the U.S.A., Harry S. Truman, President of the U.S.A., Winston S. Churchill, Prime Minister of Great Britain, and Clement R. Attlee, Prime Minister of Great Britain," 8 Jul. 1941-23 Dec. 1945. The communications received in English are printed as received; communications in Russian are translated. A Russian edition was published in 1957 (2 v.) with Russian originals printed as written and English texts in Russian translation. [4560

U.S. Dept. of State. Foreign relations of the United States: diplomatic papers. 1942 (in seven volumes). Volume I. General, the British Commonwealth, the Far East. Wash.: U.S. Govt. Print. Off., 1960. xi, 963 p. notes. Includes papers relating to the United Nations, a United Nations Commission for the Investigation of War Crimes, a United Nations Relief and Rehabilitation Administration, "postwar economic and financial arrangements," "the welfare and repatriation of American citizens in enemy and enemy-occupied countries," "agreements with enemy countries for the exchange of officials and non-officials," "governmental assistance to persons forced to emigrate for political or racial reasons," and other war-connected subjects. [4561

SOON SUNG CHO. United States policy toward the unification of Korea: 1943-1950. Ann Arbor: University Microfilms, 1960. Positive microfilm of typescript. [384] leaves. Thesis--Univ. of Michigan. Abstracted: Dissert. abstracts, 20:4702-3 (Jun). [4562

CLAUDE S. PHILLIPS, JR. The international legal status of Formosa [1944-56, particularly since 1950]. West. pol. quar., 11:276-89 (Jun 1957). notes. [4563

AMHERST COLLEGE. Dept. of American Studies. The Yalta Conference [1945]. Edited with an introduction by Richard F. Fenno, Jr. Boston: Heath [1955]. viii, [4], 112 p. bibliog. (p. 110-12). (Its Problems in American civilization: readings selected by the Department of American Studies, Amherst College.) Twelve articles and chapters from books. [4564

HENRY H. ADAMS. The uneasy peace. Elmer Belmont Potter, ed., Sea power: a naval history (Englewood Cliffs, N.J.: Prentice-Hall, 1960), p. 842-57. maps. notes. On interservice disagreements, the "unification" of the armed forces, and the war-related strategic and diplomatic problems developing in several parts of the world, 1945-50. [4565

ALLEN WELSH DULLES. The challenge of Soviet power [to the United States, 1945-59]. Harold Karan Jacobson, ed., America's foreign policy (N.Y.: Random House [1960]), p. 275-68. From the Department of State bulletin, 27 Apr. 1959. [4566

HERBERT FEIS. The secret that traveled to Potsdam. For. affairs, 38:300-317 (Jan). notes. On the knowledge possessed by the American delegation (and shared by them with Churchill) that the atomic bomb had been tested and would soon be available for use against Japan, the decision of Truman to inform Stalin, and the apparent failure of the information to influence "the Russian attitude toward the situations that were being talked about at the conference," 1945. Includes "Memorandum for the Secretary of War," by L. R. Groves, 18 Jul. 1945, reporting the test of the bomb at the Alamogordo Air Base, N. M., 16 Jul. 1945. [4567

WILLIAM R. FRYE. Characteristics of recent arms-control proposals and agreements [1945-60]. Daedalus, 89: 723-43 (fall). [4568

STAUGHTON LYND. How the Cold War began [1945-60]. Commentary, 30:379-89 (Nov). notes. [4569

BERNADOTTE EVERLY SCHMITT. The United States, Germany, and Europe [1945-49]. Bernadotte E. Schmitt, The fashion and future of history: historical studies and addresses (Cleveland: Press of Western Reserve Univ., 1960), p. 183-205. Address, Mar. 1949. [4570

MAX CHARLES. Berlin blockade [1948-49]. London: A. Wingate [1959]. 175 p. bibliog. (p. 174-5). [4571

FRANCIS JOSEPH THOMPSON. Destination Washington. London: R. Hale [1960]. 222 p. On the author's experience as a British police and security officer, 1928-53. Includes an account of his service as "Senior Security Officer at Her Majesty's Embassy, Washington," with "primary responsibility for the Security of the Embassy and downtown Missions, and for the supervision and checking of their Security arrangements," 1948-53. Accuses his superiors of lackadaisical indifference to the penetration of Communists into the service. [4572

WALTER SPENCER ROBERTSON. U.S. China policy [1949-59]. Harold Karan Jacobson, ed., America's foreign policy (N.Y.: Random House [1960]), p. 460-70. notes. From the Department of State bulletin, 6 Apr. 1959. [4573

OLIVER EDMUND CLUBB. Formosa and the offshore islands in American policy, 1950-1955. Pol. science quar., 74:517-31 (Dec 1959). notes. [4574

WILLIAM BROTHERS DUNN. American policy and Vietnamese nationalism: 1950-1954. Chicago: [Dept. of Photoduplication, Univ. of Chicago Library] 1960. Positive microfilm of typescript. 317 leaves. bibliog. Thesis--Univ. of Chicago. [4575

VETERANS

ANNIE (WALKER) BURNS [name formerly: Annie (Walker) Burns Bell]. Horn military records. Wash.: L. H. Walker [1960?]. 54 leaves. Abstracts of service and pension records of soldiers named Horn in the Revolution and the War of 1812. [4576

ANNIE (WALKER) BURNS [name formerly: Annie (Walker) Burns Bell]. Boyd military records and notes. Wash.: L. H. Walker [1960? 2], 44 leaves. Abstracts of pension records of soldiers named Boyd who served in the Revolution or the War of 1812. [4577

JOHN CARLYLE CURRY, comp. Michigan Revolutionary War pension payments. Mich. heritage, 1:95-100, 149-52; 2:50-54, 105-13 (spring-winter). List of "almost 2,000 names of persons who received Revolutionary War Pensions from the United States Government, and who lived in Michigan between the years 1818-1873," serving as a Michigan index to an unnamed series of manuscript volumes in the National Archives. [4578

ROSS B. JOHNSTON. West Virginians in the American Revolution. Parkersburg, W. Va.: West Augusta Historical and Genealogical Soc., 1959. 308, [7] p. (West Virginia Historical Society. Publication 1.) Reprinted from 33 issues of West Virginia history, Oct. 1939-Oct. 1947. Biographical dictionary. Appended: "Check lists of Revolutionary War soldiers from miscellaneous published records" (p. 309-14). [4579

KENTUCKY Agency rolls of Revolutionary pensioners. Ky. geneal., 1(1): 11-14; 1:15-18, 89-91, 128-31; 2:8-11, 49-52 (Jan 1959-Jun 1960). Alphabetical list of pensioners, with rank, date of last payment or of death, and information about transfer from other States to Kentucky or from Kentucky to other States, as authorized under an act of 1818 and other acts prior to 1832. The records from which the list is compiled are not clearly identified. [4580

[SOLDIERS of the American Revolution buried in New Jersey.] N.J. genesis, 6:198-200, 216; 7:259 (Oct 1958, Jan 1959, Jan 1960). Lists of soldiers buried in the Old Burying Ground of the Presbyterian Church, Morristown, in New Providence, and in the cemetery of Old Greenwich Presbyterian Church near Bloomsbury, N.J. [4581

U.S. General Land Office. Some Revolutionary soldiers and their heirs. [Abstracted] by William H. Dumont. New Eng. hist. and geneal. reg., 114: 117-93 (Jul). Names from a volume in the National Archives labeled: "Bounty land scrip--Act of 1833," containing entries dated 1833-70. The names listed are for the original 13 States except Virginia. [4582

BRADFORD MORSE. The veteran and his education. Higher educ., 16(7):3-6, 16-19 (Mar). port., table. On educational and rehabilitative benefits provided by the U.S. Government for military veterans, 1776-1960. [4583

KATIE-PRINCE WARD ESKER, ed. War of 1812 pensions at National Archives, Washington, D.C. Jour. Miss. hist., 22:128-37, 192-96, 271-88 (Apr-Oct). Abstracts of pension records of veterans and of veterans' widows living in Mississippi. [4584

AWARDS of the Congressional Medal of Honor to Irishmen, 1861-1890. Irish sword, 4:201-3 (summer). Signed: J. L. G. Names of "soldiers of Irish birth or apparent Irish descent who were awarded the Medal of Honor for services during the Indian Wars," selected from The Medal of Honor of the United States Army (1948) and arranged by name of action. [4585

MICHIGAN'S Civil War heroes. Mich. heritage, 1:9-12, 54-6, 111-12 (autumn 1959 - spring 1960). bibliog. Records of the 69 "Michigan Men to whom the Medal of Honor was awarded for service in the Civil War." [4586

IRIS GIBBS & ALONZO GIBBS. "Sermons in stones." Long Island forum, 23:77 (Apr). view. On the grave of Alfred S. Walters, Union soldier, who died in Nashville, Tenn., in 1865, aged 20, and was buried in the cemetery of the German Methodist Church, Plainedge, L.I.; with mention of 12 other young men from Plainedge who enlisted 21 Aug. 1862. [4587

ALFRED JACKSON HANNA & KATHRYN TRIMMER (ABBEY) HANNA. Confederate exiles in Venezuela [1866-1901]. Tuscaloosa, Ala.: Confederate Pub. Co., 1960. 149 p. bibliog. (p. 139-45), notes. (Confederate centennial studies, 15.) [4588

IOWAN suggested Memorial Day. Ann. Ia., 35:64-6 (Jul 1959). On its inauguration by Gen. Norton Parker Chipman (1834-1924), Adjutant General of the Grand Army of the Republic, in 1868. [4589

GEORGE J. WARNKE. So that people may know. [Denver? 1954.] 92 p. Reminiscences, by "the sickest veteran in the world," of his failures to obtain compensation for injuries sustained by him in military service in World War I, the brutality of the physicians who examined him, and the dishonesty and venality of the officials of the Veterans Administration who refused to act upon his claims. [4590

U.S. Dept. of Defense. Alabama's losses in the Korean conflict. Edited by James B. Sellers. Ala. rev., 13: 210-35, 258-79 (Jul, Oct). notes. List of the 558 men from Alabama who died in the Korean War. Obtained by the editor through correspondence with the Department of Defense. [4591

WAR AS A THEME OF ART, LITERATURE, AND MUSIC

LOIS VON VOIGTLANDER. "Strike up the band!" Music jour., 18(7):50, 85-6 (Oct). port. On military bands in the United States since 1773. [4592

CHARLES THOMAS BRUCE. Major literary concepts of the soldier as illustrated in certain American war novels [dealing with wars from the Revolution of World War II]. Ann Arbor: University Microfilm, 1960. Positive microfilm of typescript. [280] leaves. Thesis--Texas Technological College. Abstracted: Dissert. abstracts, 21:614-15 (Sep). [4593

CHOSEN songs of the Civil War: the sweet sixteen. Edited by students in "Oklahoma history, 162," Oklahoma State University ... Foreword by Charles Evans. [n. p.: Oklahoma Historical Soc., 1960.] 56 p. music. Texts and tunes of 16 Union and Confederate songs, with a brief account of each, 1856-64. [4594

CECIL DE GROTTE EBY, JR. Whittier's "Brown of Ossawatomie." New Eng. quar., 33:452-61 (Dec). notes. On "the genesis and influence" of this poem about John Brown, 1859, indicating that "Inadvertently the Quaker poet assisted in making a martyr of the man whose course he had always deplored." [4595

ERNEST K. EMURIAN. Stories of Civil War songs. Natick, Mass.: W. A. Wilde Co. [1960]. 96 p. On 12 songs, 1859-65, with information about the writers of the lyrics and the composers of the music and about their other works. [4596

RICHARD BARKSDALE HARWELL, ed. The war they fought. N.Y.: Longmans, Green, 1960. xxix, 389, ix, 362 p. Combined reprint of the editor's The Confederate reader (1957) and The Union reader (1958), consisting of texts and excerpts of "books and pamphlets, poems and sermons, songs and laws" produced by the Civil War, 1860-65. [4597

ROY PRENTICE BASLER. Lincoln as a man of letters [during the Civil War]. Ralph G. Newman, ed., Lincoln for the ages (Garden City, N.Y.: Doubleday, 1960), p. 367-71. [4598

BATTLES of the Civil War, 1861-1865: a pictorial presentation. [Little Rock? Ark., 1960.] 1 v. (unpaged). col. plates (flags and views) 48 x 64 cm. Reproductions of 36 prints published by Kurz & Allison, Chicago, as lithographs, later as chromolithographs, 1884-94, probably based on sketches done by Louis Kurz in the field. [4599

BENJAMIN ALBERT BOTKIN, ed. A Civil War treasury of tales, legends, and folklore. N.Y.: Random House

[1960]. xx, 625 p. ports., views. bibliog. (p. v-vi), notes (p. 577-607). Collection of "Civil War folk history and story history based on ... contemporary sources," arranged in groups by year, 1861-65. [4600

CURTIS PAPER COMPANY, Newark, Del. The Blue and the Grey, 1861. Newark [1960]. 4 plates (in portfolio). 34 x 49 cm. Copies (not reproductions) of 4 prints selected from "approximately 160 wood-cuts of the Civil War ... discovered by The Franklin Printing Company upon the acquisition of the George S. Ferguson Company." Each bears the words: "From an authentic Civil War wood engraving"; the engravings are not identified by the descriptive text on their backs. [4601

BURKE DAVIS. Our incredible Civil War. N.Y.: Holt, Rinehart, and Winston [1960]. 249 p. bibliog. (p. 247-9). "... a sampler of some of my favorite tales, facts, coincidences, and oddities of the strange, romantic, brutal conflict from which the modern United States emerged." [4602

CECIL DE GROTTE EBY, JR. The source of Crane's metaphor "Red badge of courage." Am. lit., 32:204-7 (May). notes. On the "red badge," "red diamond," or "red patch" of Gen. Philip Kearny's division in the Army of the Potomac as the source of the title of Crane's novel (1895). [4603

WILLARD ALLISON HEAPS & PORTER WARRINGTON HEAPS. The singing sixties: the spirit of Civil War days drawn from the music of the times. Norman: Univ. of Oklahoma Press [1960]. xiv, 423 p. col. facsims., music. bibliog. (p. 399-401), notes. Based on a thesis by P. W. Heaps--Northwestern Univ. Includes 23 "musical examples," 1861 ff., and numerous texts without melody. [4604

THOMAS CHALMERS McCORVEY (1851-1932). The war poetry of the South [1861-65]. T. C. McCorvey, Alabama historical sketches, ed. George Burke Johnston (Charlottesville: Univ. of Virginia Press, 1960), p. 223-45. From the New Orleans Times-Democrat, 28 Dec. 1884. [4605

NORTH CAROLINA. State Dept. of Archives and History. Pictures of the Civil War period in North Carolina. By D[avid] L[eroy] Corbitt. Raleigh, 1958. 8 p., [36] leaves, [1] p. facsims., ports., and views on 36 plates. fold. map. bibliog. Illustrations from Harper's weekly and Leslie's illustrated weekly, reproductions of separate prints, and photographs of objects in the Hall of History. [4606

MARVIN H. PAKULA. Centennial album of the Civil War. By Marvin H. Pakula in collaboration with William J. Ryan and David K. Rothstein. N.Y.: T. Yoseloff [1960]. 299 p. col. flags, col. insignia, ports., tables, views. bibliog. (p. 295-7). 37 cm. Charcoal-drawn portraits with a profile on each leader and a "selection of Army Corps insignia, uniforms, and various kinds of arms," with accompanying text. [4607

LEE STEINMETZ, ed. The poetry of the American Civil War. [East Lansing:] Michigan State Univ. Press [1960]. xii, [2], 264 p. bibliog. (p. 257-64). Poems written and published during the Civil War, each with an introductory essay. Includes, besides numerous short poems, texts or excerpts of long compositions in verse by George S. Rutherford, Henry Howard Brownell, Mary Hunt McCaleb Odom, John M. Dagnall, P. J. Randolph, Mary Sophie Shaw Homes, Kane O'Donnel, T. A. R. Nelson, F. O. Sayles, R. H. Stoddard, Elizabeth Otis Marshall Dannelly, and B. H. Barnes. [4608

The WAR in St. Louis. Mo. Hist. Soc., Bul., 16: folder bound following p. 348 (Jul). Thirteen portraits, views, and cartoons of the Civil War, reproduced from contemporary prints and patriotic envelopes. [4609

WALT WHITMAN (1819-92). Walt Whitman's Civil War. Compiled & edited from published & unpublished sources, by Walter Lowenfels, N.Y.: Knopf, 1960. xvi, 333, [3] p. views. bibliog. (p. 297-302), notes (p. 303-22). Showing "his varied responses to the war ... dispersed through dozens of notebooks, newspaper dispatches, letters, published and unpublished works." The sources of the single pieces are not identified in full detail. [4610

PAUL McCLELLAND ANGLE. "... the part played by music." John Arthur Garraty, ed., The unforgettable Americans (Great Neck, N.Y.: Channel Press [1960]), p. 230-33. On George Frederick Root (1820-95) as a composer of Civil War songs, 1862-64. [4611

ANDREW BENJAMIN BOWERING (died 1923). He didn't like "Dixie"! ... [Edited] by Chester Goolrick. Va. cavalcade, 9(4):4-10 (spring). facsims., ports. (1 col.), views. Undated reminiscences by the bugler and band leader of the 30th Virginia Infantry, C.S. Army, 1863-65. [4612

WALT WHITMAN (1819-92). Drum-taps (1865) and Sequel to Drum-taps (1865-6): a facsimile reproduction. Edited with an introduction by F. De Wolfe Miller. Gainesville, Fla.: Scholars' Facsimiles & Reprints, 1959. lx p., facsims. (72, 24 p.). Includes an extensive introduction on Whitman's activities during the Civil War and the manuscripts and the circumstances of publication of the 2 volumes, "A census of copies" (p. liv-lvi), and "Reviews of Drum-taps" (p. lvi-lix). [4613

EDWIN B. CODDINGTON. Rothermel's paintings of the Battle of Gettysburg. Pa. hist., 27:1-27 (Jan). view. notes. On a large painting and 5 smaller ones, by Peter Frederick Rothermel, 1866-70, intended to be seen together as delineations of incidents in or parts of the battle; with an account of his sources of information, his "judicious mixture of fact and artistic license," and the political controversies aroused by exhibitions of the paintings in Pennsylvania. [4614

HERMAN MELVILLE (1819-91). Battle-pieces and aspects of the war [1866] ... a facsimile reproduction with an introduction by Sidney Kaplan. Gainesville, Fla.: Scholars' Facsimiles & Reprints, 1960. xxviii p., facsim. (272 p.). notes (p. 247-55). "Supplement" (p. 259-72). Introduction deals with the text and all its known revisions. [4615

AMERIKA (ballad). A Swedish ballad of the American Civil War. [Edited and translated by] Robert L. Wright. Swed. pioneer hist. quar., 11:139-44 (Oct). notes. Text and translation of anonymous verses published in 1867 at Stockholm as "a four-page leaflet." The text is confused and occasionally unintelligible. [4616

BROOKE NIHART. American soldiers on cigarette cards: the Kinney military series--an evaluation and a checklist. Mil. collector & historian, 11:104-8 (winter 1959). views. notes. On a series of 622 numbered cards issued by the Kinney Tobacco Company, 1888, showing American and foreign military subjects, especially uniforms; with a list of the 253 American cards, showing subjects of the Army (18 cards, 1777-1847), Army and Navy (51 cards, 1886), and State militias (184 cards, 1886-87). [4617

DAVID RHOADS WEIMER. Ambrose Bierce and the art of war. Rudolf Kirk & Charles Frederick Main, eds., Essays in literary history, presented to J. Milton French (New Brunswick, N.J.: Rutgers Univ. Press [1960]), p. 229-39. On the Civil War stories reprinted in his Tales of soldiers and civilians (1891). [4618

WILLIAM GARDNER BELL. Old Bill: symbol of the cavalryman. Mil. collector & historian, 12:72-4 (fall). views. notes. On 2 drawings of a cavalryman by Frederic Remington, 1898-1902, inspired by the artist's observation of John Lannen, 3d Cavalry, and used on the covers of the Cavalry journal till the 1940s and later on the "masthead page" of Armor. [4619

WORLD'S child: the "family album" of the late photographer David Seymour [1912-56]. Infinity, 7(9):16-23 (Nov 1958). views. On his wandering life in Europe and America and his work as a photographer of war scenes and actions. [4620

JOSEPH JOHN WALDMEIR. Ideological aspects of the American novels of World War II. Ann Arbor: University Microfilms, 1959 [i. e. 1960]. Positive microfilm of typescript. Thesis--Michigan State Univ. Abstracted: Dissert. abstracts, 21:345-6 (Aug). [4621

JOHN T. ALGEO. Korean bamboo English. Am. speech, 35:117-23 (May). On "the special vocabulary of the American GI in Korea," 1950-53. See also "Korean bamboo English once more," by Grant Webster (35:261-5, Dec.), based upon his observations in Korea, 1955-56, and an anonymous document found by him, "The story of Cinderella-san." [4622

WAR-RELATED CHARITIES

JAMES O. HENRY. History of the United States Christian Commission. Ann Arbor: University Microfilms, 1959 [i. e. 1960]. Positive microfilm of typescript. [338] leaves. Thesis--Univ. of Maryland. Abstracted: Dissert. abstracts, 21:178-9 (Jul). On an organization founded to distribute religious literature to Union soldiers and sailors, conduct prayer meetings among them, deliver gifts of clothing and food, and assist surgeons on the battlefield and in the hospitals, 1861-66. [4623

JAMES O. HENRY. The United States Christian Commission in the Civil War [1861-65]. Civil War hist., 6: 374-88 (Oct). notes. On an organization supported by private gifts, whose members distributed Bibles, hymnbooks, and tracts, dispensed gifts to soldiers, wrote letters for them, visited hospitals, assisted the surgeons and the chaplains, sat with the sick, "gave Christian burial whenever possible," and marked graves. [4624

HERBERT CLARK HOOVER (1874-1964). An American epic: famine in forty-five nations; organization behind the front, 1914-1923. Volume II. Chicago: Henry Regnery Co., 1960. xiii, [3], 489 p. bibliog. (p. 469-73). On "the provision of supplies to 170,000,000 people in the Allied and Neutral nations by the United States Government" (Apr. 1917 - Nov. 1918), "the support by the American charitable organizations" (to Nov. 1918), American food shipments before and after the Armistice, "the organization of the United States governmental agencies behind the famine front," and "some of the great co-ordinated activities of the United States with the Allies 'behind the front.'" [4625

POLITICAL HISTORY

CROMWELL GIBBONS. Republic U.S.A. New Haven: Country Press [1960]. 228 p. facsims., col. flags, col. double map, ports. Historical sketches of the 50 States and Puerto Rico and biographical sketches of the Presidents. [4626

PAUL W. POLLOCK. The capital cities of the United States. Phoenix, Ariz., c1960. 206, [2] p. views. "Photo credits" (p. 208). History and description of 50 State capitals and of Washington, D.C. [4627

ROBERT HARRY LOWIE (1883-1957). Some aspects of political organization among the American aborigines [1607-1948]. Lowie's selected papers in anthropology, ed. Cora Du Bois (Berkeley: Univ. of California Press, 1960), p. 262-90. From Journal of the Royal Anthropological Institute of Great Britain and Ireland, 1948. [4628

ERNEST W. LEFEVER & WALTER V. HOHENSTEIN, eds. Profiles of American politics: readings in American government. Boston: Houghton Mifflin [1960]. xi, 367 p. cartoons, tables. notes. Collection of 99 reprinted documents, 1620-1958, grouped in 27 topical chapters. [4629

JOSEPH NATHAN KANE. The American counties: a record of the origin of the names of the 3,067 counties, date of creation and organization, area, population, historical data, etc. [1634-1949]. N.Y.: Scarecrow Press, 1960. 500 p. tables (1 double). [4630

MARTIN BLADEN (1680-1746). Martin Bladen's blueprint for a colonial union. [Edited by] Jack P. Greene. Wm. and Mary quar., 17:516-30 (Oct). notes. Presented to Sir Robert Walpole 27 Dec. 1739, proposing a federal government for the British colonies, with strong central powers and "a Plantation Parliament" subordinate to the British Parliament. [4631

VERNER WINSLOW CRANE & LAWRENCE HENRY GIPSON. On the drafting of the Albany Plan of Union [1754]. Pa. hist., 27:126-36 (Jan). Criticism by Crane of assumptions made by Gipson with respect to the manuscripts of the plan, and reply by Gipson. [4632

ALISON GILBERT OLSON. The British Government and colonial union, 1754. Wm. and Mary quar., 17:22-34 (Jan). notes. On the Albany Plan in relation to a plan of the Board of Trade and the political composition of Parliament. [4633

ROGER R. TRASK. Pennsylvania and the Albany Congress, 1754. Pa. hist., 27:273-90 (Jul). notes. On the rejection of the Plan of Union by the Pennsylvania Assembly. [4634

LEE ELMER OLM. The Chatham ministry and the American colonies, 1766-1768. Ann Arbor: University Microfilms, 1960. Positive microfilm of typescript. [274] leaves. Thesis--Univ. of Michigan. Abstracted: Dissert. abstracts, 21:334 (Aug). [4635

OLIVER MORTON DICKERSON. "... the fatal day had come." John Arthur Garraty, ed., The unforgettable Americans (Great Neck, N.Y.: Channel Press [1960]), p. 76-9. On the activities of Paul Revere in establishing the Sons of Liberty with a secret messenger service between Boston and Philadelphia and a system of communication by which minute-men companies in Massachusetts could be informed of "aggression from the British army under Gage" at Boston, early 1770s. [4636

EDMUND BURKE (1729?-1797). The correspondence of Edmund Burke. Volume I. April 1744-June 1768. [And Volume II. July 1768-June 1774.] Cambridge: At the University Press, 1958[-60]. 2 v. xxv, [3], 376, [1]; xxiii, [3], 566, [1] p. ports. Vol. I edited by Thomas W. Copeland; Vol. II, by Lucy S. Sutherland. Includes correspondence relating to America, particularly letters from Burke as Agent to the General Assembly of the Province of New York, 9 Jun. 1771-30 May 1774, and references to Parliamentary proceedings concerned with the American colonies. [4637

GEORGE SIMSON. Legal sources for Franklin's "Edict." Am. lit., 32:152-7 (May). notes. On Benjamin Franklin's "An edict of the King of Prussia" (1773). [4638

WILLIAM BREWSTER. The fourteenth commonwealths: Vermont and the States that failed. Phila.: G. S. MacManus Co., 1960. xiv, [2], 268 p. maps. bibliog. (p. 256-8), notes. On "four movements, for the establishment of states and their admission as the fourteenth member of the Confederated United States": Vermont, Westmoreland (now part of Pennsylvania), Franklin (now part of Tennessee), and Transylvania (now part of Kentucky), 1776-90. [4639

BERNADOTTE EVERLY SCHMITT. Some reflections on a revolutionary age. Bernadotte E. Schmitt, The fashion and future of history: historical studies and addresses (Cleveland: Press of Western Reserve Univ., 1960), p. 75-93. Address (Jun. 1927) on revolutions in America and Europe since 1776. [4640

LIBERTY Bell replica presented to Zion's Church. Lehigh Co. Hist. Soc., Proc., 23:33-5. Refers briefly to the concealment of the original Liberty Bell in Zion's Reformed Church, Allentown, during the winter of 1777 to protect it from seizure by the British, and to the survival of the iron brake-handle of the wagon that brought the bell to Allentown in 1777. [4641

LILLIAN (SMITH) ALBERT. Political, patriotic, and historical buttons from the Lydecker Collection. Antiques jour., 15(10-12): monthly installments (Oct-Dec). views. Reduced photographs of 20 9"-x-12" frames of buttons that "pertain to the President or Presidents depicted and to important incidents which took place during their administrations," 1789-1960. [4642

JOHN CHESTER MILLER. The Federalist era, 1789-1801. N.Y.: Harper [1960]. xv, 304 p. cartoons, maps, ports., views. bibliog. (p. 279-98), notes. (The new American nation series.) A political history. [4643

RICHARD L. GROSSMAN, ed. Bold voices: great debaters and dissenters speak out in Congress at crucial moments in American history. Edited, and with introductions, by Richard L. Grossman. Garden City, N.Y.: Doubleday, 1960. 474 p. bibliog. (p. 470-74), notes. Speeches delivered in the Senate or the House of Representatives by John Randolph (10 Dec. 1811), Henry Clay (13 Jan. 1824), Daniel Webster (26 and 27 Jan. 1830 and 7 Mar. 1850), Thomas Corwin (15 Feb. 1847), Clement L. Vallandingham (14 Jan. 1863), Andrew Johnson (20 Mar. 1875), Robert M. La Follette (22 Apr. 1886), Bourke Cockran (15 Jan. 1894 and 12 Apr. 1906), and William E. Borah (11 Feb. 1930). [4644

ARNOLD WHITRIDGE. No compromise! The story of the fanatics who paved the way to the Civil War [1820-65]. N.Y.: Farrar, Straus, and Cudahy [1960]. 212 p. bibliog. (p. 197-206). On "the handful of men North and South who fostered hatred between the two sections of the country, who magnified everything that might lead to misunderstanding, blocked every effort at compromise, and finally drove a reluctant people into a war they did not want to fight." Contents.--The Southern fanatics.--The abolitionists.--The search for the middle way. [4645

LOUIS FILLER. The crusade against slavery, 1830-1860. N.Y.: Harper [1960]. xvii, 318 p. cartoon, facsims., maps, ports., views. bibliog. (p. 281-303), notes. (The new American nation series.) On the activities of the Abolitionists. [4646

JOSEPH CHAMBERLAIN FURNAS. The road to Harpers Ferry. N.Y.: W. Sloane Associates, 1959. [12], 477 p. ports., views. bibliog. (p. 437-57), notes (p. 393-435). On John Brown as a chosen tool of the "Secret Six"--Theodore Parker, Dr. Samuel Gridley Howe, Gerrit Smith, Thomas Wentworth Higginson, George Luther Stearns, and Franklin Benjamin Sanborn--and their relation to the whole movement of Abolitionism, 1830s-1859. [4647

LARRY GARA. The Underground Railroad [1830s-50s]: a re-evaluation. Ohio hist. quar., 69:217-30 (Jul). notes. [4648

STATE HISTORICAL SOCIETY OF IOWA. John Brown among the Quakers. Iowa City, 1960. 80 p. map, ports., views. (The palimpsest, v. 41, no. 1, Jan. 1960.) Contributions (some reprinted) by William J. Petersen, John E. Briggs, Louis T. Jones, Irving B. Richman, Pauline Graham, and Thomas Teakle, on the Quaker settlement of Springdale, Ia., the stay of John Brown and his "band" at Springdale (1857-58), and the 14"-x-20" engraving of the executions at Charles Town issued by Leslie's illustrated newspaper. [4649

CARL G. BRANDT & EDWARD MERL SHAFTER, JR., eds. Selected American speeches on basic issues (1850-1950). Boston: Houghton Mifflin [1960]. iv, 426 p. bibliog. (p. 421-6), notes. Nineteen speeches on political issues, in chronological order from Henry Clay, John C. Calhoun, and Daniel Webster in 1850 to Franklin D. Roosevelt in 1941. [4650

L. WESLEY NORTON. The religious press and the Compromise of 1850: a study of the relationship of the Methodist, Baptist, and Presbyterian press to the slavery controversy, 1846-1851. Ann Arbor: University Microfilms, 1959 [i.e. 1960]. Positive microfilm of typescript. [314] leaves. Thesis--Univ. of Illinois. Abstracted: Dissert. abstracts, 20:3272-3 (Feb). [4651

SAMUEL LANGHORNE CLEMENS (1835-1910). Mark Twain and the Government. Selected and arranged by Svend Petersen. Caldwell, Idaho: Caxton Printers, 1960. 146 p. bibliog. (p. 141-4). Very brief excerpts from his writings, 1856-1910, expressing his views on "government and politics," arranged alphabetically under key word of topic. [4652

PHILIP SHRIVER KLEIN. The inauguration of President James Buchanan. Lancaster Co. Hist. Soc., Jour., 61: 145-68 (Oct 1957). ports., views. notes. Review of "the decisions he made between November 4, 1856 and March 4, 1857," and "the inauguration of his fundamental program in terms of his advisors and the trial of policy." [4653

HOMER T. ROSENBERGER. Inauguration of President Buchanan a century ago [4 Mar. 1857]. Columbia Hist. Soc., Rec., 57-59:96-122 ports., views. [4654

MARTYRDOM of John Brown. Exercises at the Town Hall, in Concord, on Friday, December 2nd 1859, at 2 o'clock, P.M. Thoreau Soc. bul., 54:[3] (winter 1956). Reproduction of a broadside, probably distributed 30 Nov. 1859. [4655

RICHARD NELSON CURRENT. Lincoln organizes the government. Ralph G. Newman, ed., Lincoln for the ages (Garden City, N.Y.: Doubleday, 1960), p. 171-5. On his formation of a cabinet, Nov. 1860-Mar. 1861. [4656

WALTER RAY FISHER. An analysis of the arguments in the Senate debate on the Crittenden Compromise Resolutions, 1860-61. Ann Arbor: University Microfilms, 1960. Positive microfilm of typescript. [204] leaves. Thesis--State Univ. of Iowa. Abstracted: Dissert. abstracts, 21:1661-2 (Dec). [4657

WILLIAM BEST HESSELTINE. Lincoln's plan of reconstruction. Tuscaloosa, Ala.: Confederate Pub. Co., 1960. 154 p. bibliog. (p. 142-7), notes. (Confederate centennial studies, 13.) Summarized by author, with same title: Ralph G. Newman, ed., Lincoln for the ages (Garden City, N.Y.: Doubleday, 1960), p. 372-7. On "the various plans that Lincoln instituted, operated, and abandoned; and ... the evolution of the rival programs of the Radical Republicans in Congress," 1860-65. Describes as a "legend" the "belief that, if Lincoln had lived, the years of reconstruction that followed would have been different." [4658

RICHARD REALF (1834-78). [Communication from Washington.] Southw. hist. quar., 64:146-7 (Jul). From Leslie's illustrated newspaper, 4 Feb. 1860. On the reasons why the author, a Texan, is no longer an abolitionist, and why, with reference to John Brown, "I repudiate his foray" but "I bow myself reverently before his otherwise high nature." [4659

JOHN ZANES. "This treasonable doctrine." N.H. profiles, 9(10):25-7 (Oct). facsim., port. On Abraham Lincoln's speeches in New Hampshire, 1860. [4660

JONATHAN TRUMAN DORRIS. The treatment of Confederates by Lincoln, Johnson, and Congress, 1861-1898. ... Edited by Wayne C. Temple. [Richmond? Ky., 1960.] 32 p. [4661

DAVID MORRIS POTTER. The six most fateful weeks in American history. Ralph G. Newman, ed., Lincoln for the ages (Garden City, N.Y.: Doubleday, 1960), p. 176-81. On the first 6 weeks of Lincoln's administration, 4 Mar.-12 Apr. 1861. [4662

JAMES MONAGHAN, JR. The Emancipation Proclamation [22 Sep 1862]. By Jay Monaghan. Ralph G. Newman, ed., Lincoln for the ages (Garden City, N.Y.: Doubleday, 1960), p. 231-5. [4663

GIDEON WELLES (1802-78). The history of emancipation. Selected essays by Gideon Welles: Civil War and Reconstruction, ed. Albert Mordell (N.Y.: Twayne Publishers, 1959), p. 228-55. From The galaxy, Dec. 1872. Recollections of the steps by which Lincoln came to the decision to proclaim emancipation, 1863. [4664

HOWARD KENNEDY BEALE. The critical year: a study of Andrew Johnson and Reconstruction [1865-66]. N.Y.: F. Ungar Pub. Co. [1958]. xv, [5], 454 p. cartoons. bibliog. (p. 407-35), notes. (American classics.) 1st ed. 1930. Includes a new foreword by the author. [4665

ERIC L. McKITRICK. Andrew Johnson and Reconstruction. [Chicago:] Univ. of Chicago Press [1960]. ix, 535, [1] p. bibliog. (p. 511-21), notes. On his policies with respect to the former Confederate States and their inhabitants, 1865-69. [4666

GRADY McWHINEY. Reconstruction: index of Americanism [1865-77]. Charlies Grier Sellers, Jr., ed., The Southerner as American (Chapel Hill: Univ. of North Carolina Press [1960]), p. 89-103. notes. [4667

DONALD HENRY SHEEHAN. Radical Reconstruction [1865-90]. Donald Sheehan & Harold C. Syrett, eds., Essays in American historiography: papers presented in honor of Allan Nevins (N.Y.: Columbia Univ. Press, 1960), p. 37-49. notes. [4668

GIDEON WELLES (1802-78). Lincoln and Johnson: their plan of reconstruction and the resumption of national authority [1865]. Selected essays by Gideon Welles: Civil War and Reconstruction, ed. Albert Mordell (N.Y.: Twayne Publishers, 1959), p. 180-227. From The galaxy, Apr. and May 1872. [4669

COMER VANN WOODWARD. The political legacy of Reconstruction [1865-77]. Comer Vann Woodward, The burden of Southern history (Baton Rouge: Louisiana State Univ. Press [1960]), p. 89-107. From The journal of Negro education, 1957. [4670

JOHN S. GOFF. President Arthur's domestic legislative program. N.Y. Hist. Soc. quar., 44:166-7 (Apr). port. notes. On the contents of the 4 annual messages of Chester Alan Arthur to Congress, 1881-84, indicating that he may have been "underrated by historians." [4671

H. WAYNE MORGAN. Western silver and the tariff of 1890. N.M. hist. rev., 35:118-28 (Apr). notes. On the activities of the "Silver Republicans" in the Senate. [4672

BISSELL BROOKE. "What America celebrates on Independence Day": a significant interpretation of our two early declarations by a distinguished statesman during a "calamity" in 1897. Hobbies, 65(5):28-9, 60 (Jul). On a Fourth of July editorial by Thomas Brackett Reed (1839-1902), Congressman from Maine, printed in the New York times, 1897; with excerpts from the editorial. [4673

LAURIN L. HENRY. Presidential transitions. Wash.: Brookings Institution [1960]. xviii, 755 p. notes. On the Taft-Wilson, Wilson-Harding, Hoover-Roosevelt, and Truman-Eisenhower transitions. Summarized by author: Transferring the Presidency: variations, trends, and patterns. Pub. admin. rev., 20:187-95 (autumn). [4674

THOMAS RICHARD GORMAN. Words and deeds: a study of the political attitudes of John Dos Passos [1920s-50s]. Ann Arbor: University Microfilms, 1960. Positive microfilm of typescript. [285] leaves. Thesis--Univ. of Pennsylvania. Abstracted: Dissert. abstracts, 21:893-4 (Oct). [4675

JOHN DONALD HICKS. Republican ascendency, 1921-1933. N.Y.: Harper [1960]. xvi, [2], 318 p. facsims., ports., table, views. bibliog. (p. 281-301), notes. (The new American nation series.) Political history of the United States. [4676

WALDEMAR BESSON. Franklin D. Roosevelt, der New Deal, und die neuen Leitbilder der amerikanischen Politik [1932-45]: zum politischen Selbstverständnis der Amerikaner im 20. Jahrhundert. Jahrbuch für Amerikastudien, 5:121-37. notes. [4677

MARIO EINAUDI. The Roosevelt revolution. N.Y.: Harcourt, Brace [1959]. x, [2], 372 p. Argumentative review of the political and legal changes in the United States, 1932-52. [4678

GLADYS MARIE KAMMERER. Opportunities missed: the "Little Hoover Commission" reports. Pub. personnel rev., 21:235-42 (Oct). On the disappointing quality of the reports of State commissions appointed since 1947 to recommend reorganization of State governments. [4679

JAMES ARTHUR WECHSLER. Reflections of an angry middle-aged editor. N.Y.: Random House [1960. 10], 245, [1] p. On American political ideas and action as observed by the author during his service as an editor of the New York Post, 1948-58. [4680

Elections and Parties

WILLIAM GOODMAN. The two-party system in the United States [1644-1960]. ... Second edition. Princeton, N.J.: Van Nostrand [1960]. xiv, 681 p. cartoons, facsims., map, tables. bibliogs., notes. (Van Nostrand political science series.) 1st ed. 1956. [4681

LAWRENCE H. LEDER. The politics of upheaval in New York, 1689-1709. N.-Y. Hist. Soc. quar., 44:413-27 (Oct). ports. notes. Mainly on relations between Robert Livingston (1654-1728) and the successive governors of the colony. [4682

NICHOLAS VARGA. Election procedures and practices in colonial New York. N.Y. hist., 41:249-77 (Jul). notes. Analysis of the votes "in about thirty-one General Assembly elections," 1691-1775. Based on thesis--Fordham Univ. [4683

ALEXANDER ATHANASIOU PALAMIOTIS. The citizen and alien in American constitutional law [1750s-1950s]. Ann Arbor: University Microfilms, 1959 [i.e. 1960]. Positive microfilm of typescript. [262] leaves. Thesis--Univ. of Utah. Abstracted: Dissert. abstracts, 20:3362-3 (Feb). On naturalization and expatriation. [4684

JOHN JOSEPH ZIMMERMAN. Benjamin Franklin and the Quaker party [in Pennsylvania], 1755-1756. Wm. and Mary quar., 17:291-313 (Jul). notes. Based on thesis--Univ. of Michigan. [4685

LESLIE JOSEPH THOMAS. Partisan politics in Massachusetts during Governor [Sir Francis] Bernard's administration, 1760-1770. Ann Arbor: University Microfilms, 1960. Positive microfilm of typescript. xi, 866 leaves. bibliog. (leaves 856-66). Thesis--Univ. of Wisconsin. Abstracted: Dissert. abstracts, 20: 4093-4 (Apr). [4686

CHILTON WILLIAMSON. American suffrage: from property to democracy, 1760-1860. Princeton: Princeton Univ. Press, 1960. x, [2], 306 p. bibliog. (p. ix-x), notes. [4687

BRUCE INGHAM GRANGER. Political satire in the American Revolution, 1763-1783. Ithaca, N.Y.: Cornell Univ. Press [1960]. xi, [3], 314 p. bibliog. (p. 306-8), notes. [4688

C. ASHLEY ELLEFSON. James Habersham and Georgia Loyalism, 1764-1775. Ga. hist. quar., 44:359-80 (Dec). notes. [4689

ROGER JAMES CHAMPAGNE. The Sons of Liberty and the aristocracy in New York politics, 1765-1790. Ann Arbor: University Microfilms, 1960. Positive microfilm of typescript. [528] leaves. Thesis--Univ. of Wisconsin. Abstracted: Dissert. abstracts, 21:1537-8 (Dec). [4690

HUGH DOUGLAS PRICE. How the American voter makes up his mind [1788-1960]. Am. rev., 1(1):85-102 (autumn). map. [4691

CHARLES GANO TALBERT. Kentuckians in the Virginia Convention of 1788. Ky. Hist. Soc., Reg., 58:187-93 (Jul). notes. On the reasons for their vote of 10 to 3 against ratification of the Federal Constitution. [4692

"AMERICA goes to the polls." Hobbies, 65(9):28-9 (Nov). cartoons, port., views. On a collection of "items recalling every U.S. presidential election ... political cartoons, campaign gadgets, buttons, banners, slogans, songs, hats, kerosene torches used in torchlight parades, etc.," 1789-1960, assembled by J. Doyle De Witt and exhibited by the Travelers Insurance Companies, Hartford, Conn. [4693

JOSEPH G. BROWN. Presidential campaign items [buttons, medals, etc.], 1789-1956. Hobbies, 65(6):28-9 (Aug). facsims., medals, ports. [4694

DENYS HARRISON HERBERT SMITH. Polls apart: background to the American Presidential election [1789-1956]. London: Cohen & West [1960]. 160 p. A British view, for British readers, of the whole subject of American elections, parties, and patronage. Based in part upon the author's observations "for over thirty years from the front-row seat of Washington Correspondent." [4695

JACK RICHON POLE. Constitutional reform and election statistics in Maryland, 1790-1812. Md. hist. mag., 55:275-92 (Dec). tables. notes. [4696

GEORGE LEITH ROTH. Verse satire on "faction," 1790-1815. Wm. and Mary quar., 17:473-85 (Oct). notes. On Federalist and anti-Federalist satire. [4697

DOROTHY (GANFIELD) FOWLER. Precursors of the Hatch Act. Miss. Valley hist. rev., 47:247-62 (Sep). notes. On "recurrent attempts ... to limit the influence of federal office-holders in party politics," 1791-1939, and the debated question of their "political rights." [4698

JOHN G. CARNEY. Highlights of Erie politics [1800-1960]. Erie, Pa. [1960]. 380, [4] p. ports., tables, views. Narrative of political activities; biographical dictionary of living and deceased officeholders in Erie County, the City of Erie, and other political units within the county (p. 94-181); and voting statistics for the years 1950-59 (p. 196-380). [4699

SIDNEY FINE. The history of the two-party system in the United States [since 1800]. Institute in Practical Partisan Politics, University of Michigan, 1959, Selected papers, ed. Sybil L. Stokes & Lynn W. Eley (Ann Arbor, 1960 [University of Michigan, Institute of Public Administration, Papers in public administration, 38]), leaves 16-23. [4700

NORMAN KURT RISJORD. The Old Republicans: Southern conservatives in Congress, 1806-1824. Ann Arbor: University Microfilms, 1960. Positive microfilm of typescript. [524] leaves. Thesis--Univ. of Virginia. Abstracted: Dissert. abstracts, 21:1179-80 (Nov). [4701

ABE CARL RAVITZ. John Pierpont and the Federalist muse in Essex County. Essex Inst. hist. col., 96: 140-48 (Apr). notes. On his stay in Newburyport, 1810-14, as a lawyer, a dabbler in verse and an aggressive... Federalist," and his poetic oration titled "The Portrait" [1812]. [4702

INDIANA. Indiana election returns, 1816-1851. Compiled by Dorothy [Lois] Riker and Gayle Thornbrough. [Indianapolis:] Indiana Historical Bureau, 1960. xxv, 493 p. (chiefly tables). notes. (Indiana historical collections, 40.) Compiled from records in the Archives Division of the Indiana State Library and from newspapers. [4703

ROBERT BENDINER. White House fever: an innocent's guide to principles and practices, respectable and otherwise, behind the election of American Presidents. N.Y.: Harcourt, Brace [1960]. ix, [3], 180 p. cartoons. notes. Includes incidental historical references, 1824-1960. [4704

WILLIAM BURLIE BROWN. The people's choice: the Presidential image in the campaign biography. Baton Rouge: Louisiana State Univ. Press [1960]. xiv, 177 p. cartoons, facsim., ports. bibliog. (p. 159-72), notes. On forms and symbols in these publications. Appended (p. 147-58): "A selected list of campaign biographies," 1824-1960. [4705

RICHARD PATRICK McCORMICK. New perspectives on Jacksonian politics. Am. hist. rev., 65:288-301 (Jan). tables. notes. Evidence that "None of the Jackson elections [1824-36] involved a 'mighty democratic uprising' in the sense that voters were drawn to the polls in unprecedented proportions," as they were in 1840, and that "the image of a 'mighty democratic uprising'" needs revision. [4706

EDWIN ARTHUR MILES. Jacksonian Democracy in Mississippi [1824-39]. Chapel Hill: Univ. of North Carolina

Press, 1960. [8], 192 p. bibliog. (p. 172-86), notes. (The James Sprunt studies in history and political science, 42.) [4707

PAUL CHESTER NAGEL. The Election of 1824: a reconsideration based on newspaper opinion. Jour. South. hist., 26:315-29 (Aug). notes. [4708

PAUL GEORGE GILMORE. Third party movements and independent political figures in Lycoming County [Pa., 1829-1936]. Now and then, 12: 42-9 (Jan 1958) [4709

WALTER EDWARD HUGINS. Jacksonian Democracy and the working class: a study of the New York Workingmen's movement, 1829-1837. Stanford: Stanford Univ. Press, 1960. vi, [2], 286 p. tables. bibliog. (p. 267-77), notes (p. 225-65). (Stanford studies in history, economics, and political science, 19.) Thesis--Columbia Univ., 1955, now somewhat revised. [4710

ABIGAIL CLEVELAND. Eighth of January 1830. Lebanon Hist. Soc., Ann. report, 1 (1959), leaves [11-13]. Verses ridiculing a celebration of the Battle of New Orleans by supporters of Andrew Jackson in Lebanon, N.H. [4711

WILLIAM HARRISON ADAMS III. The Louisiana Whig Party [1834-52]. Ann Arbor: University Microfilms, 1960. Positive microfilm of typescript. [379] leaves. Thesis--Louisiana State Univ. Abstracted: Dissert. abstracts, 20:4382 (May). [4712

DOROTHY DODD. Party politics in Florida [since 1838]. Fla. handbook, 1955-56, p. 160-62. view. Reprinted in later biennial editions. [4713

MELVILLE JAMES BOYER. Allentown publisher sued by Governor Porter. Lehigh Co. Hist. Soc., Proc., 23:101-7. On charges by G. Adolph Sage, publisher of Der Patriot und Demokrat, Allentown, that David Rittenhouse Porter (born 1788), Governor of Pennsylvania, had committed perjury to escape payment of his debts; Porter's suit for libel, ending with a verdict for the plaintiff; and Sage's appeal. [4714

HOW they used to vote. Harvard alumni bul., 55:132 (25 Oct 1952). facsims. On the form of ballots used in American political elections, 1840 ff., with illustrations from a collection of ballots assembled by William B. Munro. [4715

LUCILE FARNSWORTH REALS. Two Presidential campaign cottons. Hobbies, 65(8):29, 32 (Oct). view. On "cotton 'yarn goods'" manufactured to honor William Henry Harrison (1840) and James A. Garfield and Chester A. Arthur (1880). [4716

JUDICIAL attitude toward political question doctrine: the gerrymander and civil rights [1841-1959]. Wash. Univ. law quar., 1960:292-301 (Dec). notes. [4717

CENTRAL CLAY CLUB OF SHELBY COUNTY. Minutes of a Clay Club, Shelby County, Indiana, 1843-1844. Edited by Donald F. Carmony. Ind. mag. hist., 56:153-71 (Jun). notes. Constitution and proceedings of a Whig organization, 12 Dec. 1843-4 Oct. 1844. Appended (p. 169-77): Constitution of "the Shelbyville Central rough and ready Club, of Shelby County," and minutes of meetings of 15 and 18 Jul. 1848. [4718

MALCOLM COOK McMILLAN. Taylor's Presidential campaign in Alabama, 1847-1848. Ala. rev., 13: 83-108 (Apr). notes. On the agency of Alabama in procuring the Whig nomination for Taylor, and his contest against Lewis Cass, Democrat. [4719

HOWARD ROBERTS LAMAR. Political patterns in New Mexico and Utah Territories, 1850-1900. Utah hist. quar., 28:362-87 (Oct). ports., view. notes. [4720

JOHN MEADOR. Florida and the Compromise of 1850. Fla. hist. quar., 39: 16-33 (Jul). notes. Review of Whig and Democratic politics in Florida, 1850-54. [4721

THOMAS HENRY O'CONNOR. Cotton Whigs in Kansas. Kan. hist. quar., 26:34-58 (spring). notes. Based on thesis--Boston Univ., 1958. On the reasons why the New England Whigs condemned the Kansas-Nebraska Act of 1854 and intervened in the civil war in Kansas. [4722

ABE CARL RAVITZ. Harold Frederic's venerable Copperhead. N.Y. hist., 41:35-48 (Jan). notes. On his Seth's brother's wife: a study of life in the greater New York (1887), The Lawton girl (1890), and The Copperhead (1893), novels of the Mohawk Valley, as a defense of the political principles and actions of Horatio Seymour in the 1850s and 1860s. [4723

CLINTON LAWRENCE ROSSITER. Marxism: the view from America [1851-1958]. N.Y.: Harcourt, Brace [1960]. viii, [2], 338 p. notes

(p. 289-330). On Marxists in America, American opinions of Marxism, and the reasons why it "has had less success in this country than in any other in the world." [4724

INDIANA. Indiana votes: election returns for Governor, 1852-1956, and Senator, 1914-1958. Compiled and edited by Robert J. Pitchell. Bloomington: Bureau of Government Research, Indiana Univ., 1960. 103 p. maps, tables. notes. Tabulation. [4725

ANDREW WALLACE CRANDALL. The early history of the Republican Party, 1854-1856. Gloucester, Mass.: P. Smith, 1960. [2], 313 p. bibliog. (p. 289-305), notes. Reprint of thesis--Univ. of Pennsylvania, 1930. [4726

LAWRENCE VAN HORN. The Old Buck Cannon. Lancaster Co. Hist. Soc., Jour., 64:209-22 (autumn). diagrs., views. notes. On a cannon made by John Griffen in the Phoenix Iron Works, presented by him to "the Democratic party of the City of Lancaster" in celebration of the victory of James Buchanan in the Election of 1856, and apparently lost when the Confederates invaded Pennsylvania in 1863. Includes text of the patent (25 Dec. 1855) issued to Griffen for "Improved Manufacture of Wrought-Iron Cannon," with diagrams of his "Muzzle-Loading Fire-Arm." [4727

DON EDWARD FEHRENBACHER. The origins and purpose of Lincoln's "House-divided" speech [16 Jun. 1858]. Miss. Valley hist. rev., 46:615-43 (Mar). notes. [4728

RICHARD ALLEN HECKMAN. The Douglas-Lincoln campaign of 1858. Ann Arbor: University Microfilms, 1960. Positive microfilm of typescript. [345] leaves. Thesis--Indiana Univ. Abstracted: Dissert. abstracts, 21:606 (Sep). [4729

ABRAHAM LINCOLN (1809-65) & STEPHEN ARNOLD DOUGLAS (1813-61). The Illinois political campaign of 1858 [Wash.:] Library of Congress [1958. 2], 212 p. (p. 25-212, facsim.). "Notes and references" (p. 21-4). Stenographic texts of debates in Illinois, 21 Aug.-15 Oct. 1858, reproduced from the Chicago Press and tribune and the Chicago Times as assembled by Lincoln in mounted clippings in a scrapbook, marked by him for the printer, and published (1860) by Follett, Foster, and Co., Columbus; with an introduction by David C. Mearns. [4730

G. THEODORE MITAU. Politics in Minnesota [1858-1960]. Minneapolis: Univ. of Minnesota Press [1960. 8], 140 p. diagrs., map, tables (1 double). bibliog. (p. 129-31). [4731

ALLAN NEVINS. Lincoln re-enters politics. Ralph G. Newman, ed., Lincoln for the ages (Garden City, N.Y.: Doubleday, 1960), p. 107-12. On the contest in Illinois between Lincoln and Douglass, 1858. [4732

IRA RIDGWAY DAVIS. A century of voting in three Ohio counties [Ross, Pike, and Scioto, 1859-1959]. Ohio hist. quar., 69:121-56 (Apr). tables. notes. [4733

FLETCHER MELVIN GREEN. Lincoln: "the taste [of the Presidency] is in my mouth a little." South Atl. quar. 59:510-20 (autumn). notes. On his efforts to obtain favorable publicity, his search for the political support of powerful individuals, and his encouragement of campaign biographies, 1859-60. [4734

OREGON. Laws, statutes, etc. Legislative folklore. [Edited by] David C. Duniway. Ore. hist. quar., 61:457-9 (Dec). "An act for the relief of Cynthia A. Moon," introduced in the Oregon Legislature in May 1859, ridiculing by slight indirection the Democratic nomination of Lansing Stout as representative to the U.S. Congress. [4735

ALAN SCOULER BROWN. Southwestern Michigan in the Campaign of 1860. Mich. heritage, 2:67-74 (winter). bibliog. [4736

The CAMPAIGN of 1860: prelude to the Civil War. Hobbies, 65(8):48-9 (Oct). cartoon, ports., view. On an exhibition of various articles by the New-York Historical Society, Oct.-Nov. 1960. [4737

THE CHICAGO TRIBUNE. Why Lincoln won [1860]. Chicago hist., 5:340-45 (spring). Editorial from the issue of 18 May 1910. [4738

JOHNSON EDDY FAIRCHILD. Lincoln at the Cooper Union. Ralph G. Newman, ed., Lincoln for the ages (Garden City, N.Y.: Doubleday, 1960), p. 135-9. On his speech in Brooklyn, 27 Feb. 1860. [4739

ANDREW A. FREEMAN. Abraham Lincoln goes to New York. N.Y.: Coward-McCann [1960]. 160 p. facsim., ports., views (1 double). notes (p. 145-53). On 2 visits to New York, 24-27 Feb. 1860 and 19-21 Feb. 1861, during the first of which Lincoln delivered a speech at the Cooper Union. [4740

MURAT HALSTEAD (1829-1908). Three against Lincoln: Murat Halstead reports the caucuses of 1860. Edited with an introduction by William B[est] Hesseltine. Baton Rouge: Louisiana State Univ. Press, 1960. xxi, 321 p. tables. notes (p. 303-8). Dispatches to the Cincinnati Commercial reporting the proceedings of the Democratic, Constitutional Democratic, National Constitutional Union, and Republican national conventions, 23 Apr.-23 Jun. 1860. [4741

BERTHA LION HEILBRON. Manifest destiny in Minnesota's Republican campaign of 1860. Minn. hist., 37:52-7 (Jun). ports., view. notes. On issues of territorial expansion. [4742

WILLIAM BEST HESSELTINE. Abraham Lincoln and the politicians [1860-65]. Civil War hist., 6:43-55 (Mar). notes. [4743

ERLING THEODORE JORSTAD. Minnesota's role in the Democratic rift of 1860. Minn. hist., 37:45-51 (Jun). cartoon, view. notes. [4744

The NOMINATION of Lincoln, Chicago, May 16, 1860. N.J. Hist. Soc., Proc., 78:188-98 (Jul). Excerpts from printed and manuscript sources. [4745

The REPUBLICAN Convention of 1860. Chicago hist., 5:321-40 (spring). views. Information from newspapers. [4746

ALVIN P. STAUFFER. Douglas in Vermont [in the Campaign of 1860]. Vt. hist., 28:257-67 (Oct). notes. [4747

ADLAI EWING STEVENSON. The Election of 1860. Ralph G. Newman, ed., Lincoln for the ages (N.Y.: Doubleday, 1960), p. 145-9. [4748

MILDRED THRONE (1902-60), ed. Iowa newspapers report the 1860 nomination of Lincoln. Ia. jour. hist., 58: 228-80 (Jul). notes. [4749

WALTER TROHAN. The Republican Party chooses a candidate. Ralph G. Newman, ed., Lincoln for the ages (Garden City, N.Y.: Doubleday, 1960), p. 140-44. On the nomination in Chicago of Lincoln as Republican candidate for President, 18 May 1860. [4750

GIDEON WELLES (1802-78). Nomination and election of Abraham Lincoln. Selected essays by Gideon Welles: Lincoln's administration, ed. Albert Mordell (N.Y.: Twayne Publishers, 1960), p. 13-46. From The galaxy, Sep. and Oct. 1876. On the Election of 1860, Lincoln's formation of a cabinet, and his other activities till 20 Mar. 1861. [4751

QUINCY WRIGHT. Stephen A. Douglas and the Campaign of 1860. Vt. hist., 28:250-55 (Oct). [4752

WOOD GRAY. Lincoln and the Copperheads. Ralph G. Newman, ed., Lincoln for the ages (Garden City, N.Y.: Doubleday, 1960), p. 289-94. On "silent protests against the policies of conscription and the suspension of habeas corpus adopted by the Federal Government" by Northern opponents of the Civil War, 1861-65. [4753

MARVIN ANDREW HARDER. Some aspects of Republican and Democratic party factionalism in Kansas [1861-1958]. Ann Arbor: University Microfilms, 1959 [i. e. 1960]. Positive microfilm of typescript. [267] leaves. Thesis--Columbia Univ. Abstracted: Dissert. abstracts, 20:4151-2 (Apr). [4754

FRANK L. KLEMENT. The Copperheads in the Middle West. [Chicago:] Univ. of Chicago Press [1960]. xiii, 341 p. facsims., ports., cartoons. bibliog. (p. 327-31), notes (p. 269-325). On Northern Democratic opponents and critics of the Civil War and of the Lincoln administration, 1861-65, including the Knights of the Golden Circle and the Sons of Liberty. [4755

HOWARD KENNEDY BEALE. The Election of 1864. Ralph G. Newman, ed., Lincoln for the ages (Garden City, N.Y.: Doubleday, 1960), p. 307-11. On the campaigns of Lincoln and Gen. George B. McClellan. [4756

JAMES P. JONES. John A. Logan and the Election of 1864 in Illinois. Mid-Am., 42:219-30 (Oct). notes. [4757

MILTON LOMASK. A tantalizing query: Who offered Hannibal Hamlin the 1864 Republican Presidential nomination? Manuscripts, 12(2):40-42 (summer). [4758

GIDEON WELLES (1802-78). Lincoln's triumph in 1864. Selected essays by

Gideon Welles: Lincoln's administration, ed. Albert Mordell (N.Y.: Twayne Publishers, 1960), p. 198-223. From the Atlantic monthly, Apr. 1878. [4759

GIDEON WELLES (1802-78). The opposition to Lincoln in 1864. Selected essays by Gideon Welles: Lincoln's administration, ed. Albert Mordell (N.Y.: Twayne Publishers, 1960), p. 178-97. From the Atlantic monthly, Mar. 1878. Deals largely with the activities of U.S. Grant at this time. [4760

WARREN D. CUMMINGS. Sussex County campaigners in 1865. N.J. Hist. Soc., Proc., 78:22-32 (Jan). notes. On the New Jersey State election of 1865 in Sussex County, where Copperhead sentiment was strong. [4761

VINCENT P. DE SANTIS. Catholicism and Presidential elections, 1865-1900. Mid-America, 42:67-79 (Apr). notes. [4762

KEVIN EMMETT KEARNEY. Speaking in Florida on the issues of Presidential Reconstruction, 1865-1867: a rhetoric of reunion. Ann Arbor: University Microfilms, 1960. Positive microfilm of typescript. [308] leaves. Abstracted: Dissert. abstracts, 20:4755 (Jun). [4763

REINHARD HENRY LUTHIN. Waving the bloody shirt: Northern political tactics in post-Civil War times [1865-88]. Ga. rev., 14:64-71 (spring). [4764

WILLIAM DUNCAN MALLAM. Butlerism in Massachusetts. New Eng. quar., 33:186-206 (Jun). notes. On an organization devoted to the "political advancement of its leader and the economic advancement of its members," centered in Gen. Benjamin Franklin Butler, 1866-77. [4765

MARTIN LINTON ABBOTT, ed. Reconstruction in Louisiana: three letters. La. hist., 1:153-7 (spring). notes. Letters to the Commissioner of the Freedmen's Bureau from Thomas W. Conway (5 Jan. 1868) and Charles H. Fox (26 Mar. and 9 May 1868), on Louisiana politics. [4766

VAL BJORNSON. The Republican Party in Minnesota [1868-1960]. Lawrence Martin Brings, ed., Minnesota heritage (Minneapolis: T. S. Denison [1960]), p. 329-31. ports. [4767

HANS LOUIS TREFOUSSE. Ben Wade and the failure of the impeachment of Johnson. Hist. and Philos. Soc. Ohio, Bul., 18:240-52 (Oct). port. notes. On the reasons why many Republicans preferred Johnson to Benjamin F. Wade of Ohio, President pro temp. of the Senate, 1868, who believed "that Negroes should vote in Ohio as well as in South Carolina" and that "the maldistribution of wealth called for relief." [4768

WILFRED ANDERSON FERRELL. Portrait of the politician in the American novel: 1870-1910. Ann Arbor: University Microfilms, 1959 [i.e. 1960]. Positive microfilm of typescript. [186] leaves. Thesis--Univ. of Texas. Abstracted: Dissert. abstracts, 20:2783 (Jan). [4769

CHARLES W. HAVENS III. Federal legislation to safeguard voting rights: the Civil Rights Act of 1960. Va. law rev., 46:945-75 (Jun). notes. Includes a section on "some developments in voting rights since the Civil War," 1870-1960. [4770

JAMES W. HESS. John D[avis] Long and reform issues in Massachusetts politics, 1870-1889. New Eng. quar., 33:57-73 (Mar). notes. [4771

HAMBLETON TAPP. Three decades of Kentucky politics, 1870-1900. Ann Arbor: University Microfilms, 1950 [i.e. 1960]. Positive microfilm of typescript. 471 leaves. bibliog. (leaves 466-71). Thesis--Univ. of Kentucky. Abstracted: Dissert. abstracts, 20:4093 (Apr). [4772

LORENE ANDERSON HAWLEY. Kansas Congressmen and reapportionment [1872-1960]. Kan. hist. quar., 26:345-54 (winter). notes. Includes a table of "Kansas Congressmen, 1861-1960," at large and for each of the 8 districts in Kansas. [4773

JAMES CLAUDE MALIN. Eugene Ware and Dr. [Increase Sumner] Sanger: the code of political ethics, 1872-1892. Kan. hist. quar., 26:255-66 (autumn). notes. On the political oratory, poetry, and party symbols of these years in Kansas, especially "the quadrennial parade up Salt river." [4774

JAMES A. RAWLEY. The General Amnesty Act of 1872: a note. Miss. Valley hist. rev., 47:480-84 (Dec). notes. Reminder that the Act "removed the disqualification from officeholding on Confederate leaders, with certain exceptions," and that "at this time there existed no federal restriction on the suffrage of former Confederate adherents." [4775

JOHN A. MAYNE. L. Q. C. Lamar's "Eulogy" of Charles Sumner: a reinterpretation. Historian, 22:296-311 (May). notes. Manuscript evidence that the speech (occasioned by Sumner's death in 1874), by a Senator from Mississippi, "was a masterpiece of wirewalking," and that "Sumner was merely being used as a means to a desired end." [4776

WILLIAM W. WHITE. Mississippi Confederate veterans seek political appointments, 1876-1900. Miss. quar., 13:1-5 (winter). notes. [4777

VINCENT P. DE SANTIS. The Republican Party and the Southern Negro, 1877-1897. Jour. Negro hist., 45:71-87 (Apr). notes. [4778

CHARLES WYATT LOMAS. The agitator in American politics. West. speech, 24:76-83 (spring). notes. On the activities and methods of Dennis Kearney, Joseph Buchanan, Ben Butler, and Henry George, 1877-86, as illustrations of "traits common to all spokesmen of protest," and the results of the methods. [4779

DAVID MORRIS POTTER, ed. Party politics and public action, 1877-1917. ... Revised by Howard R. Lamar. N.Y.: Holt [1960]. xii, 84 p. notes (p. 84). (Select problems in historical interpretation, 5.) Excerpts from books and articles, with introductions by the editors. Contents.--1. The party system as a democratic instrument.--2. The Populist Party and national issues.--3. The Progressive Movement.--4. The reform movement in retrospect. [4780

FRANK BOWEN EVANS. Wharton Barker and the Republican National Convention of 1880. Pa. hist., 27:28-43 (Jan). notes. On his success in procuring the nomination of James A. Garfield. [4781

ALBERT VIRGIL HOUSE. Internal conflict in key States in the Democratic Convention of 1880. Pa. hist., 27:188-216 (Apr). notes. [4782

MARIAN DORIS IRISH. Political thought and political behavior in the South [1882-1959]. West. pol. quar., 13:406-20 (Jun). notes. [4783

GORDON S. WOOD. The Massachusetts Mugwumps [1884-92]. New Eng. quar., 33:435-51 (Dec). notes. [4784

THOMAS J. CONDON. Politics, reform, and the New York City election of 1886. N.-Y. Hist. Soc. quar., 44: 363-93 (Oct). cartoons, ports. notes. On the campaign for the mayoralty of Henry George, Abram S. Hewett, and Theodore Roosevelt and the involvement in national issues of "the play of politics, the meaning of reform, and the role of organized labor." [4785

VALDIMER ORLANDO KEY, JR. Secular realignment and the party system. Jour. politics, 21:198-210 (May 1959). diagrs. notes. On "a movement of the members of a population category from party to party that extends over several presidential elections and appears to be independent of the peculiar factors influencing the vote at individual elections," 1888-1952. [4786

DUNCAN MacRAE, JR., & JAMES A. MELDRUM. Critical elections in Illinois: 1888-1958. Am. pol. science rev., 54:669-83 (Sep). diagrs., map, tables. Statistical analysis. [4787

PAOLO ENRICO COLETTA. Bryan, Cleveland, and the disputed Democracy, 1890-1896. Neb. hist., 41:1-27 (Mar). notes. Deals largely with the conflict between the "free silverites," headed by William Jennings Bryan, and "the followers of Grover Cleveland, who demanded the gold standard." [4788

CASPAR HAROLD NANNES. Politics in the American drama [1890-1959]. Wash.: Catholic Univ. of America Press, 1960. xv, 256 p. bibliog. (p. 241-6), notes (p. 235-40). Appended (p. 226-34): "Plays on politics produced on the New York state from 1890 to 1960." [4789

HERBERT J. BASS. David B[ennett] Hill and the "Steal of the Senate," 1891. N.Y. hist., 41:299-311 (Jul). On apparently illegal and fraudulent activities of the Democratic Party in New York, particularly Dutchess County. [4790

STANLEY P. HIRSHON. James S. Clarkson versus Benjamin Harrison, 1891-1893: a political saga. Ia. jour. hist., 58:219-27 (Jul). notes. On the efforts of Clarkson, First Assistant Postmaster General and Chairman of the Republican National Committee, and others to obtain the Republican nomination in 1892 for James G. Blaine, and their attacks upon Harrison before and after his renomination and after the victory of Grover Cleveland. [4791

BERNARD H. BLOOM. Yiddish-speaking Socialists in America: 1892-1905. Am. Jew. arch., 12:34-68 (Apr). ports., views. notes. [4792

JOHN H. MOORE. James Gaven Field [born 1826]: Virginia's Populist spokesman. Va. cavalcade, 9(4): 35-41 (spring). ports., views (1 col.). On the campaign of a Virginia farmer and lawyer as Populist candidate for Vice-President, 1892; with an account of the Populist campaign in Virginia. [4793

JOSEPH ROGERS HOLLINGSWORTH. A study in party division: the Democratic Party, 1893-1900. Chicago: [Dept. of Photoduplication, Univ. of Chicago Library] 1960. Positive microfilm of typescript. 282 leaves. bibliog. Thesis--Univ. of Chicago. [4794

ELMER E. CORNWELL, JR. A note on Providence politics in the age of Bryan. R.I. hist., 19:33-40 (Apr). tables. notes. On "voting patterns in Providence around the landmark election of 1896." [4795

CHARLES WILLIAM FREDERICK DICK (1858-1945). Suggestions for a plan of county organization: Charles Dick lays the groundwork for the Campaign of 1896. Edited by Thomas E. Felt. Ohio hist. quar., 69:367-78 (Oct). notes. Reprint of Suggestions for plan of county organization (1896), by the Assistant Secretary of the Republican National Committee. [4796

GILBERT COURTLAND FITE. Republican strategy and the farm vote in the Presidential Campaign of 1896. Am. hist. rev., 65:787-806 (Jul). notes. [4797

EDWIN ARTHUR MILES. The keynote speech at national nominating conventions [1896-1956]. Quar. jour. speech. 46:26-31 (Feb). notes. [4798

ROBERT WAYNE SMITH (born 1926). Comedy at St. Louis: a footnote to nineteenth century political oratory. South. speech jour., 25:122-33 (winter 1959). notes. On the Democratic National Convention at St. Louis, 22-25 Jul. 1896, as reported in contemporary newspapers. [4799

CALVIN BREWSTER COULTER. John L. Wilson, Erastus Brainerd, and the Republican Party of Washington [1898-1911]. Idaho yesterdays, 4(2):11-15, 18-23 (summer). cartoons. notes. Includes comment by George A. Fryckman. [4800

FRED WHITESIDE. Three hundred grand! Edited by Dorothy M. Johnson. Montana, 10(1):40-50 (Jan). facsims., ports., view. Excerpts "from the unpublished journals of Fred Whiteside" a State Senator, on his success in exposing the attempted bribery by William Andrews Clark of members of the Montana legislature to gain their support of his designation as U.S. Senator from Montana, 1898-99; with excerpts from contemporary newspapers. [4801

AMY ELEANOR SMITH. The election of Thomas R. Bard to the United States Senate [California, 1900]. Ventura Co. Hist. Soc. quar., 5(2):11-20 (Feb). views. bibliog. [4802

WARREN IRVING TITUS. The Progressivism of the muckrakers: a myth reexamined through fiction. Cent. Miss. Valley Am. Studies Assoc., Jour., 1(1):10-16 (spring). notes. Distinguishes between the Progressivism from ca. 1900 to ca. 1908, "exemplified in the muckrakers," recommending "a return to the old values of Jeffersonian America," and the Progressivism from ca. 1908 to ca. 1917, turning "to direct government intervention and regulation to effect changes in the system itself"; with illustrations from novels of David Graham Phillips and Winston Churchill. [4803

D. JEROME TWETON. North Dakota editors and the Presidential candidates of 1900. N.D. hist., 27:35-42 (winter). notes. On their comments on McKinley and Roosevelt, Bryan and Charles Towne, and minor-party candidates. [4804

MERLE W. WELLS. Fred T. Dubois and the Idaho Progressives, 1900-1914. Idaho yesterdays, 4(2):24-31 (summer). port. notes. Includes comment by Robert E. Burke. [4805

SHEILA HART. Cowboy brigade. Frontier times, 34(2):22-3, 48-9 (spring). ports., view. On "Captain Seth Bullock's Cowboys," a group of friends and admirers of Theodore Roosevelt in the western Dakotas who traveled to Washington (accompanied by the author) to witness his inauguration in 1905, their attention-provoking conduct on that occasion, and a reunion of some of the survivors in 1926. [4806

MARY MARGARET ROBERTS. The New York legislative campaign speaking of Governor Charles Evans Hughes, 1907-1910. Ann Arbor: University Microfilms, 1959 [i.e. 1960]. Positive microfilm of typescript. [365] leaves. Thesis--Louisiana State Univ. Abstracted: Dissert. abstracts, 20: 2962-3 (Jan). [4807

JEAN HEIDER. Presidential campaign post cards [mainly of 1908 and 1912]. Hobbies, 65(8):116-17; (9):116-17 (Oct, Nov). cartoons, ports. [4808

ALFRED DONALD SUMBERG. A history of the Presidential Election of 1908. Ann Arbor: University Microfilms, 1960. Positive microfilm of typescript. [571] leaves. Thesis--Univ. of Wisconsin. Abstracted: Dissert. abstracts, 21:610-11 (Sep). [4809

FRANKLIN HICHBORN. The party, the machine, and the vote: the story of cross-filing in California politics [1909-17]. ... With an introduction by Senator Herbert C. Jones. Calif. Hist. Soc. quar., 38:349-57; 39:19-34 (Dec 1959, Mar 1960). [4810

STANLEY COBEN. A. Mitchell Palmer and the reorganization of the Democratic Party in Pennsylvania, 1910-1912. Pa. mag. hist. and biog., 84: 175-93 (Apr). notes. [4811

RICHARD H. HANSEN. Performance and potential of Presidential primary laws [1911-60]. Neb. law rev., 39: 473-527 (May). tables. notes. [4812

FRANCIS M. CARNEY. The rise of the Democratic clubs in California. [N.Y.:] Holt [1958]. 16 p. (Case studies in practical politics.) On the Democratic Party in California, 1912-58. [4813

BOYCE HOUSE (1896-1961). Bryan at Baltimore: the Democratic National Convention of 1912. Neb. hist., 41: 29-51 (Mar). cartoons, ports. notes. [4814

RICHARD B. SHERMAN. Charles Sumner Bird [1855-1927] and the Progressive Party in Massachusetts [1912-16]. New Eng. quar., 33:325-40 (Sep). notes. [4815

ROBERT HOLT SALISBURY, JR. St. Louis politics: relationships among interests, parties, and governmental structure [since 1914]. West. pol. quar., 13:498-507 (Dec). [4816

ARNOLD SANFORD RICE. The Southern wing of the Ku Klux Klan in American politics, 1915-1928. Ann Arbor: University Microfilms, 1959 [i.e. 1960]. Positive microfilm of typescript. [205] leaves. Thesis--Indiana Univ. Abstracted: Dissert. abstracts, 20:4090 (Apr). [4817

DAVID JOSEPH SAPOSS. Communism in American politics [1917-57]. Wash.: Public Affairs Press [1960]. viii, [2], 259 p. notes (p. 230-55). Includes sections on Communist activities in Washington State, California, and Minnesota, the American Labor Party, the Progressive Party, and the "Metamorphosis of Henry A. Wallace." [4818

BERNHARD JOSEPH STERN (1894-1956). Alternative proposals to democracy: the pattern of fascism. Historical sociology: the selected papers of Bernhard J. Stern (N.Y.: Citadel Press [1960]), p. 242-59. notes. From the Journal of Negro education, Jul. 1941. On "fascism in the United States," 1917-41. [4819

KARL F. ROLVAAG. The Democratic Farmer-Labor Party in Minnesota's history [1918-60]. Lawrence Martin Brings, ed., Minnesota heritage (Minneapolis: T. S. Denison [1960]), p. 332-6. ports. [4820

PAUL F. BOLLER, JR. An American irrelevance: CP, USA. Southw. rev., 45:293-301 (autumn). notes. On the Communist Party in the United States since 1919, its "tortuously twisting and turning party line," and "the way in which so many right-wingers (who today damn the New Dealers for having been 'beguiled' by the Russian war-time line) were praising Communist Russia during the war." [4821

J. JOSEPH HUTHMACHER. Massachusetts people and politics, 1919-1933. Cambridge: Belknap Press of Harvard Univ. Press, 1959. x, [6], 328 p. map, port., tables. bibliog. (p. 281-5), notes (p. 287-318). [4822

RAYMOND JUSTUS HANKS. The Democratic Party in 1920: the rupture of the Wilsonian synthesis. Chicago: [Dept. of Photoduplication, Univ. of Chicago Library] 1960. Positive microfilm of typescript. 487 leaves. bibliog. Thesis--Univ. of Chicago. [4823

GLEASON LEONARD ARCHER. Conventions, campaigns, and kilocycles in 1924: the first political broadcasts. Jour. broadcasting, 4:110-18 (spring). [4824

ERNEST M. COLLINS. The political behavior of the Negroes in Cincinnati, Ohio, and Louisville, Kentucky [1928-48]. Ann Arbor: University Microfilms, 1950 [i.e. 1960]. Positive microfilm of typescript. 226 leaves. bibliog. (leaves 216-22). Thesis--Univ. of Kentucky. Abstracted: Dissert. abstracts, 20:4150 (Apr). [4825

PAT CRANSTON. Political convention broadcasts: their history and influence [1924-56]. Journalism quar., 37:186-94 (spring). notes. [4826

CHARLES E. HERSHBERGER. Presidential Campaign of 1928 in El Paso County. Password, 5:5-19 (Jan). notes. [4827

NEVIN EMIL NEAL. The Smith-Robinson Arkansas campaign [sic] of 1928. Ark. hist. quar., 19:3-11 (spring). notes. Based on thesis--Univ. of Oklahoma. On the campaign of Alfred E. Smith and Joe T. Robinson, Democratic nominees for President and Vice President, and particularly the response of Robinson to those who objected to the Catholicism and the Tammany affiliations of Smith and to his enmity toward prohibition. [4828

RICHARD L. WATSON, JR. A political leader bolts--F[urnifold] M. Simmons in the Presidential Election of 1928. N.C. hist. rev., 37:516-43 (Oct). notes. On the efforts of a Senator from North Carolina to prevent the nomination of Alfred E. Smith, his refusal to support Smith when nominated, and his support of the State Democratic ticket. [4829

FRANK H. JONAS. The art of political dynamiting. West. pol. quar., 11:374-91 (Jun 1957). notes. On the career of Walter E. Quigley (born 1890) as "a master craftsman in the art of political publicity," "a professional political writer," "an expert in attacking a candidate, in dynamiting him out of office," 1930-57; with excerpts from his letters to the author and from his unpublished autobiography. [4830

ROBERT JAY ALPERIN. Organization in the Communist Party, U.S.A., 1931-1938. Ann Arbor: University Microfilms, 1959 [i.e. 1960]. Positive microfilm of typescript. xi, 517 leaves. bibliog. (leaves 485-517). Thesis--Northwestern Univ. Abstracted: Dissert. abstracts, 20:3808 (Mar). [4831

RUSSELL M. POSNER. California's role in the nomination of Franklin D. Roosevelt [1932]. Calif. Hist. Soc. quar., 39:121-39 (Jun). port. Attributes the nomination of Roosevelt at Chicago to support from William G. McAdoo, William Randolph Hearst, and John Nance Garner. [4832

HARRY WESLEY MORRIS. The Republicans in a minority role, 1933-1938. Ann Arbor: University Microfilms, 1960. Positive microfilm of typescript. [341] leaves. Thesis--Univ. of Iowa. Abstracted: Dissert. abstracts, 21:609 (Sep). [4833

EDWIN BLAINE BRONNER. The New Deal comes to Pennsylvania: the gubernatorial election of 1934. Pa. hist., 27:44-68 (Jan). ports. notes. On the defeat of William A. Schnader, Republican, by George H. Earle III, "recent convert from the Republican party." [4834

JAMES ARTHUR ROBINSON & WILLIAM H. STANDING. Some correlates of voter participation: the case of Indiana [1934-44, 1946-56]. Jour. politics, 22:96-111 (Feb). tables. notes. [4835

ROSS B. TALBOT. The North Dakota Farmers Union and North Dakota politics [1934-56]. West. pol. quar., 11:875-901 (Dec 1957). table. notes. [4836

ABRAHAM HOLTZMAN. Campaign politics: a new role for women [1936-58]. Southw. social science quar., 40:314-20 (Mar). notes. [4837

KARL A. LAMB. John Hamilton and the revitalization of the Republican Party, 1936-40. Mich. Acad. Science, Papers, 45:233-50. notes. On his work as "the first full-time, salaried, Republican Chairman." [4838

DONALD R. McCOY. Alfred M. Landon and the Presidential Campaign of 1936. Mid-America, 42:195-218 (Oct). notes. [4839

W. CAMERON MYERS. The Chicago newspaper hoax in the '36 election campaign. Journalism quar., 37:356-64 (summer). notes. On a charge "that the Communist party in Russia had instructed American Communists to support the candidacy of Roosevelt and to defeat Landon" and the resulting warfare between the Chicago Daily times (pro-Roosevelt) and the Tribune. [4840

EDGAR LITT. Status, ethnicity, and patterns of Jewish voting behavior in Baltimore [1940-56]. Jew. social studies, 22:159-64 (Jul). tables. notes. Based on thesis--Yale Univ. [4841

JOSEPH L. BERND. Grass roots politics in Georgia: the county unit system and the importance of the individual voting community in bi-factional elections, 1942-1954. Atlanta: Emory Univ. Research Committee, 1960. [2], iii, 172, [3] p. maps, tables. notes. Based on thesis--Duke Univ. Contents.--1. Bi-factionalism and the county unit system.--2. Election returns [p. 57-172; tabulations, with an introduction on sources and discrepancies]. [4842

EDWARD FRANCIS COOKE. Patterns of voting in Pennsylvania counties, 1944-1958. Pa. hist., 27:69-87 (Jan). maps, tables. notes. [4843

OSCAR GLANTZ. Recent Negro ballots in Philadelphia [1944-56]. Jour. Negro educ., 28:430-38 (fall 1959). tables. notes. [4844

MARTHE LEE SAENGER. Labor political action at mid-twentieth century: a case study of the CIOPAC campaign of 1944 and the Textile Workers Union of America. Ann Arbor: University Microfilms, 1959 [i.e. 1960]. Positive microfilm of typescript. ix, 643 leaves. tables. bibliog. (leaves 631-40). Thesis--Ohio State Univ. Abstracted: Dissert. abstracts, 20:3810-11 (Mar). On the CIO Political Action Committee. [4845

THADEAUS HENRY HOBBS. The dynamics of Negroes in politics in the Los Angeles Metropolitan Area, 1945-1956. [Los Angeles:] Univ. of Southern California, 1960. Positive microfilm of typescript. vii, 189 leaves. maps (part fold.), tables. bibliog. (leaves 179-89). Thesis (M. A.)--Univ. of Southern California. [4846

DAVID ALLEN SHANNON. The decline of American Communism: a history of the Communist Party of the United States since 1945. N.Y.: Harcourt, Brace [1959]. xiii, 425 p. bibliog. (p. 375-8), notes (p. 379-411). Communism in American life.) [4847

JOSEPH L. BERND & LYNWOOD M. HOLLAND. Recent restrictions upon Negro suffrage: the case of Georgia [1946-57]. Jour. politics, 21:487-513 (Aug 1959). notes. [4848

JEAN PIERRE LASSALE. La Cour Suprême et le problème communiste aux États-Unis [1947-55]. Paris: A. Colin, 1960. xiii, 275 p. bibliog. (p. 249-72), notes. (Cahiers de la Fondation Nationale des Sciences Politiques, 108.) Sections on Court action with respect to anti-Communist activities of Congress, the States, and the executive. [4849

ROBERT LEE SAWYER, JR. The Democratic State Central Committee in Michigan, 1949-1959: the rise of the new politics and the new political leadership. Ann Arbor, 1960. vii, 280 p. tables. notes. (University of Michigan. Bureau of Government. Michigan governmental studies, 40.) Revision of thesis--Univ. of Michigan. Includes some account of the Democratic Party in Michigan since 1932. [4850

ROBERT E. AGGER. Independents and party identifiers: characteristics and behavior in 1952. Eugene Burdick & Arthur J. Brodbeck, eds., American voting behavior (Glencoe, Ill.: Free Press [1959]), p. 308-29. tables. notes. [4851

VALDIMER ORLANDO KEY, JR., & FRANK MUNGER. Social determinism and electoral decision: the case of Indiana [in the Election of 1952]. Eugene Burdick & Arthur J. Brodbeck, eds., American voting behavior (Glencoe, Ill.: Free Press [1959]), p. 281-99. diagrs., maps, table. [4852

Federal-State Relations

ROALD FAY CAMPBELL. The folklore of local school control. School rev., 67:1-16 (spring 1959). notes. On the extent of the control of schools by State governments and the U.S. Government, 1642-1959. [4853

KENNETH WILLIAM TREACY. The Olmstead case, 1778-1809. West. pol. quar., 11:675-91 (Sep). notes. On the claims of Gideon Olmstead, Capt. Thomas Houston, and Capt. James Josiah to the British sloop Active and ensuing litigation raising questions of the respective authority of Pennsylvania and the United States. [4854

LEANDER L. BOYKIN. Why all this fuss about Federal aid to education? Social studies, 51:83-8 (Mar). bibliog. Review of such aid since 1785. [4855

WILLIAM L. MARBURY. Why should we limit Federal diversity jurisdiction? Am. Bar Assoc. jour., 46: 379-82 (Apr). port. Argument that constitutional provisions for this jurisdiction should not be changed. [4856

WILLIAM P. MURPHY. State sovereignty and the Founding Fathers [1787]. Miss. law jour., 30:135-64, 261-92; 31:50-82 (Dec 1958, May, Dec 1959). notes. Examination of the position of each delegate to the Constitutional Convention with respect to this subject, concluding that "only a handful of delegates ... believed in the perpetuation of a system which has been described as a compact of sovereign states" and that the others were "committed to the nationalist philosophy of a strong central government, supreme over the states." [4857

PAUL OBERST. The Supreme Court and States rights [1787-1959]. Ky. law jour., 48:63-102 (fall 1959). Includes comments by Anthony Lewis, Judge John R. Brown, and Clement Eaton. [4858

ORIE L. PHILLIPS & A. SHERMAN CHRISTENSON. The historical and legal background of the diversity jurisdiction [1787-1960]. Am. Bar Assoc. jour., 46:959-65 (Sep). ports. notes. [4859

JOHN WELLING SMURR. Territorial constitutions: a legal history of the frontier governments erected by Congress in the American West, 1787-1900. Ann Arbor: University Microfilms, 1960. Positive microfilm of typescript. [1005] leaves. Thesis--Indiana Univ. Abstracted: Dissert. abstracts, 21: 610 (Sep). [4860

A. A. WHITE. The Supreme Court's avenues of escape from the Constitution [1787-1959]. South Tex. law jour., 4:129-47 (spring 1959). notes. Evidence that the Court "has been controlled by considerations that have enhanced the power of the Federal government and minimized the power of the states." [4861

JOHN D. O'REILLY, JR. The Spencer Roanes of 1958. Villanova law rev., 4:92-116 (fall 1958). notes. Text of "Resolution adopted by the Conference of State Supreme Court Justices at Pasadena, California," 23 Aug. 1958, and commentary on the function of the U.S. Supreme Court since 1789. [4862

U.S. Congress. House. Committee on Agriculture. Government subsidy historical review: a summary of the use of subsidies to advance the aims and purposes of Government since the First Congress to the present time [1789-1960]. ... Revised. Wash.: U.S. Govt. Print. Off., 1960. iii, 12 p. 1st ed. 1954. (At head of title: 86th Cong., 2d sess. Committee print.) [4863

A STUDY of the conflict of Federal pre-emption and State sovereignty: disparate labor and jurisdiction policies [1790-1959]. St. John's law rev., 34:220-36 (May). notes. [4864

ROBERT CARTER PITTMAN. Due process of law: yesterday, today, and tomorrow. Ga. Bar jour., 21: 193-207 (Nov 1958). notes. On the scope of "due process of law" in the 5th and 14th Amendments (1791, 1866); with an argument that the latter does not make the first 10 amendments applicable to the States. [4865

DAVID WHITTINGHAM. The Bill of Rights [1791]: a limitation on the several States or the Federal Government? Wm. and Mary law rev., 2:437-59. notes. Dissent from views expressed by William W. Crosskey that the first 8 amendments formed a "constitutional limitation on State authority" and that the limitation suffered "destruction" in the Supreme Court. [4866

FRANCIS P. KELLY. The Supreme Court: some interpretations of Congressional, executive, and State power [1803-1957]. St. John's law rev., 34:22-41 (Dec 1959). notes. [4867

PARKER J. STONE & 5 others. Controversy over the Supreme Court [1803-1958]. Syracuse law rev., 10: 242-70 (spring 1959). notes. Consists mainly of sections on "The doctrine of preemption applied to subversion," "Federal preemption in the field of labor relations," "The Fourteenth Amendment and State employment controls," and "The Fourteenth Amendment and State criminal procedure." [4868

WILLIAM S. KOHN. Constitutional law--double jeopardy--a historical perspective--successive conviction for a crime by two sovereignties [1814-1959]. N.Y. law forum, 5:393-402 (Oct 1959). notes. [4869

ROGER C. CRAMPTON. The Supreme Court and the decline of State power [1816-59]. Jour. law & econ., 2:175-89 (Oct 1959). notes. [4870

ANTHONY GEORGE HALKIAS. Federal and State prosecutions for same offense [1820-1959]. W. Va. law rev., 60:164-70 (Feb). notes. [4871

FRANCIS J. DEMET. A trilogy of massive resistance. Am. Bar Assoc. jour., 46:294-6 (Mar). port. notes. On "past refusals by three states to obey mandates of the United States Supreme Court," 1830 and 1832 (Georgia), 1860 (Wisconsin, Virginia), 1956 (Virginia). [4872

JOHN CALDWELL CALHOUN (1782-1850). The Fort Hill address, July 26, 1831. [Richmond, 1960. 4], 20 p. notes. (Virginia Commission on Constitutional Government. Historic statements expounding the role of the States in their relation to the central government, 4.) Written statement (not an address), dated at Fort Hill. [4873

ROBERT WALTER JOHANNSEN. Stephen A. Douglas, popular sovereignty, and the Territories [1848-59]. Historian, 22:378-95 (Aug). notes. [4874

GORDON BARLOW DODDS. Arizona, Oregon, and the nation. West. pol. quar., 11:398-404 (Jun 1957). notes. Examination of the political ideas in the legislative messages of the governors of the 2 Territories, later States, 1849-1956, as a clue to "the attitudes of westerners toward the role of the national government in their affairs." [4875

EUGENE ROBERT HINKSTON. California's assertion of States' rights: a history of jurisdictional controversies with the Federal Government [since 1850]. Ann Arbor: University Microfilms, 1960. Positive microfilm of typescript. [469] leaves. Thesis--Univ. of Southern California. Abstracted: Dissert. abstracts, 21:1543-4 (Dec). [4876

JOHN AMASA MAY & JOAN REYNOLDS FAUNT. South Carolina secedes [1860]. ... With biographical sketches of members of South Carolina's Secession Convention, compiled by Joan Reynolds Faunt. Columbia: Univ. of South Carolina Press, 1960. xv, 231 p. facsims., ports., tables (1 double). notes. (A publication of the South Carolina Confederate War Centennial Commission.) [4877

HASKELL MONROE. Southern Presbyterians and the secession crisis [1860-61]. Civil War hist., 6:351-60 (Dec). notes. Synopsis of a thesis in progress--Rice Institute. [4878

HENRY STEELE COMMAGER. Lincoln and the whole nation. Ralph G. Newman, ed., Lincoln for the ages (Garden City, N.Y.: Doubleday, 1960), p. 362-6. On his "sense of the integrity of the Union, and of the interdependence of all its sections and peoples," 1861-65. [4879

WILFRED BUCK YEARNS. The Confederate Congress [1861-65]. Athens: Univ. of Georgia Press [1960]. viii, 293 p. bibliog. (p. 270-79), notes (p. 245-69). "Biographical notes on Confederate Congressmen" (p. 236-44). [4880

ISAIAH ALFONSO WOODWARD, ed. Opinions of President Lincoln and his cabinet on Statehood for Western Virginia, 1862-1863. W. Va. hist., 21:157-85 (Apr). facsim., port. notes. Request from Lincoln to his cabinet asking their opinions on the constitutionality and expediency of a bill for the admission of West Virginia into the Union, 23 Dec. 1862, their replies, and draft of an opinion by Lincoln, 31 Dec. 1862. [4881

DOMINIC B. KING. Federal-State relations in the control of water resources [1866-1959]. Univ. Detroit law jour., 37:1-27 (Oct 1959). notes. [4882

NATIONAL power to control State discrimination against foreign goods and persons: a study in federalism. Stanford law rev., 12:355-87 (Mar). notes. On "the means employed by states in discriminating against alien goods and persons, and the effect of such means upon the conduct of American foreign relations," 1876-1959. [4883

HAROLD E. MEIER. A review of present law on the admission of illegally obtained evidence in our State and Federal courts [1877-1956]. Wyo. law jour., 13:166-77 (winter 1959). notes. [4884

WALTER R. McDONALD. Federal usurpation of State regulatory authority [over transportation, 1886-1958]. I. C. C. Practitioners' jour., 26:985-93 (Jun 1959). notes. [4885

JOSHUA J. KANCELBAUM. Immunity from prosecution in the American federal system. West. Reserve law rev., 11:264-77 (Mar). notes. On the privilege against self-incrimination in the U.S. Constitution and the States in relation to compulsory testimony joined with immunity from prosecution, 1892-1958; and the belief that State immunity does not bind the Federal courts nor does Federal immunity bind the State courts. [4886

EDWARD G. DUCKWORTH. The "tidelands" problem. Dicta, 30:217-31 (Jun 1953). notes. On Federal or State title to, jurisdiction over, and property rights in, the lands underlying the Continental Shelf more than 3 miles from shore, 1898-1952. [4887

JULIUS BERMAN & PAUL OBERST. Admissibility of evidence obtained by an unconstitutional search and seizure--Federal problems [1914-60]. Northw. Univ. law rev., 55:525-40. notes. On the admissibility of such evidence in State but not in Federal courts. [4888

JAMES A. EICHNER. The "silver platter"--no longer used for serving evidence in Federal courts. Univ. Fla. law rev., 13:311-33 (fall). table. notes. On the doctrine "under which unlawfully obtained evidence, inadmissible if gathered by federal agents, could be received in federal trials if obtained by state or local officers," 1914-60. [4889

REED LUND FRISCHKNECHT. State extension services and the administration of farm price and income support programs: a case study in Federal-State relations [1914-56]. West. pol. quar., 11:416-41 (Jun 1957). notes. [4890

LOUIS H. YARRUT. Conflict in State-Federal jurisdiction in maritime matters [1917-60]. Fed. Bar jour., 20:202-6 (spring). notes. [4891

RALPH SARGENT, JR. Regulation of natural gas--Federal v. State [1918-49]. Dicta, 27:216-24 (Jun 1950). notes. [4892

WILLIAM T. PLUMB, JR. The priorities of Federal taxes over State and local taxes [1920-59, especially since 1954]. Natl. tax jour., 12:204-15 (Sep 1959). notes. [4893

EARL HERBERT ROVIT. The regions versus the nation: critical battle of the thirties [1921-41]. Miss. quar., 13:90-98 (winter). notes. [4894

THOMAS A. GILLIAM. The impact of Federal subsidies on State functions [1923-1960]. Neb. law rev., 39:528-46 (May). notes. [4895

RICHARD A. WATSON. Federalism v. individual rights: the legal squeeze on self-incrimination. Am. pol. science rev., 54:887-98 (Dec). notes. On the effect of Federal immunity statutes upon later State prosecutions, and of State immunity statutes upon later Federal prosecutions, of persons obliged by such statutes to testify, 1931-60. [4896

FRANCIS A. ALLEN. The Supreme Court, federalism, and State systems of criminal justice. De Paul law rev., 8:213-55 (spring-summer 1959). notes. On "the role of the Supreme Court of the United States in the development of federal power as it relates to the criminal law and its administration," 1932-58. [4897

EDWARD M. COWETT. Federal-State relationships in securities regulation [1933-59]. Geo. Wash. law rev., 28:287-305 (Oct 1959). notes. [4898

SUCCESSIVE prosecutions by State and Federal governments for offenses arising out of same act [1933-59]. Minn. law rev., 44:534-46 (Jan). notes. [4899

CHARLES OSCAR GREGORY. Federal or State control of concerted union activities [1935-60]. Va. law rev., 46:539-62 (Apr). notes. [4900

TERENCE G. ISON. Conflicts of State and Federal jurisdiction in the regulation of natural gas [since 1938] and electricity [since 1935]. Mercer law rev., 10:226-62 (spring 1959). notes. Evidence "that federal control is expanding at the expense of state autonomy" and "that the courts are forcing the pace further and faster than Congress is prepared to go." [4901

ALTON F. CURRY. The power of the State to enjoin picketing in light of Federal pre-emption [1937-1959]. Baylor law rev., 11:451-69 (fall 1959). notes. [4902

JOHN R. DETHMERS. On the report of the Conference of Chief Justices. Tenn. law rev., 27:1-12 (fall 1959). Defense by the Chief Justice of Michigan, Chairman of the Conference of State Supreme Court Justices at Pasadena, Calif., of the Conference's report, Federal-State relationships as affected by judicial decisions (1958), citing a series of decisions of the U.S. Supreme Court since 1938. [4903

FREDERIC PUTNAM STORKE. Conflicts Erie cases. Rocky Mt. law rev., 32:20-36 (Dec 1959). notes. On Erie Railroad Co. v. Tompkins (1938), "which requires a federal court to apply state law in diversity cases," Klaxon Co. v. Stentor Elec. Co. (1941), "which compels a federal court to apply the conflict-of-laws rules of state courts," and the resulting judicial difficulties and disagreements. [4904

WILLIAM JOSEPH BLOCK. The separation of the Farm Bureau and the Extension Service: political issue in a Federal system. Urbana: Univ. of Illinois Press, 1960. vii, 304 p. bibliog. (p. 278-88), notes. (Illinois studies in the social sciences, 47.) Published in 1956 in microfilm form as thesis--Univ. of Illinois. On the controversy over "separation of the county farm bureau units and the county offices of the Extension Service," 1939-59; with some account of related developments since the organization of the American Farm Bureau Federation in 1919. [4905

ISAAC G. IREY. Abstention: an exercise in federalism. Univ. Pa. law rev., 108:226-51 (Dec 1959). notes. On a doctrine "judicially constructed to avoid the premature determination of federal constitutional issues and to minimize federal interference with state domestic policy and state action," announced by Justice Felix Frankfurter, "speaking for a unanimous court," in Railroad Comm'n v. Pullman Co. in 1941; and the applications of the doctrine till 1959. [4906

LOUISIANA Power & Light v. Thibodaux [1959]: the abstention doctrine expanded. Yale Law jour., 69:643-62 (Mar). notes. On "the area in which federal courts, in deference to initial adjudication by the state judiciary, are to abstain from deciding cases," 1941-59. [4907

DAVID LEHMAN. The legal status of the Continental Shelf [1945-58]. La. law rev., 20:648-56 (Jun). notes. [4908

EDWARD FRANCIS CARTER. Federal-State court conflict. Fed. Bar jour., 20:409-15 (fall). notes. On "plain usurpations and encroachmens by federal courts upon the exclusive jurisdiction and powers of state courts," 1946-60. [4909

SELMA J. MUSHKIN. Barriers to a system of Federal grants-in-aid [since 1949]. Natl. tax jour., 13: 193-218 (Sep). tables. notes. [4910

KENNETH G. AINSWORTH. The differential impact of grants-in-aid upon the industry of the States [1954]. Am. jour. econ. and sociol., 19:27-44 (Oct 1959). tables. notes. [4911

Foreign Relations

DOROTHY JANE VAN HOOGSTRATE. American foreign policy: realists and idealists--a Catholic interpretation. St. Louis: B. Herder [1960]. xiii, 332 p. bibliog. (p. 308-22), notes. Based on thesis--St. Louis Univ., 1959. On the "degree of harmony or variance" between Catholic and other "philosophy and social doctrine" as they relate to American foreign policy. Includes chapters on "American history according to the realists" (Charles A. Beard, George K. Kennan, Hans J. Morgenthau) and "American history evaluated by the idealists" (Dexter Perkins, Robert E. Osgood, Frank Tannenbaum), and discusses the thinking of 33 other recent American authors on this subject. [4912

ROBERT A. DIVINE, ed. American foreign policy. N.Y.: Meridian Books [1960]. 318 p. bibliog. (p. 298-309), notes (p. 287-95). (Meridian documents of American history.) Texts, reprinted from various sources, of the "most relevant documents bearing on the evolution of American foreign policy," 1775-1959. [4913

NELSON MANFRED BLAKE & OSCAR THEODORE BARCK, JR. The United States in its world relations [1776-1960]. N.Y.: McGraw-Hill, 1960. viii, 840 p. maps. bibliog. (p. 789-812), notes. (McGraw-Hill series in American history.) On diplomatic relations of the United States. [4914

JACQUES LAMBERT. La formation des attitudes américaines en matière de politique extérieur. Les fondements de la politique extérieur des États-Unis (Paris: Armand Colin,

1949 [Cahiers de la Fondation Nationale des Sciences Politiques, 8]), p. 19-83. Explanation of the foreign policy of the United States since 1776 in terms of 9 elements. [4915

MAURICE WATERS. The ad hoc diplomat: a legal and historical analysis. Wayne law rev., 6:380-92 (summer). notes. Based on thesis--Univ. of Chicago. On special agents sent abroad by the President of the United States and responsible only to him, 1789-1958. [4916

HENRY MERRITT WRISTON. The special envoy. For. affairs, 38:219-37 (Jan). notes. On personal representatives of the President of the United States, serving by his appointment only, without the status of officers of the government and without the advice and consent, or necessarily the knowledge, of the Senate, employed by "every administration in our history," 1789-1959. [4917

ROY L. CAMERON. Passport control in the national interest and freedom to travel [1790-1959]. Temple law quar., 33:332-45 (spring). notes. [4918

ROBERT A. GOLDWIN, RALPH LERNER, & GERALD STOURZH, eds. Readings in American foreign policy. N.Y.: Oxford Univ. Press, 1959. x, 709 p. maps. Reprinted articles and primary sources, 1793-1958, grouped in 10 topical chapters. [4919

RICHARD A. FALK. The United States and the doctrine of nonintervention in the internal affairs of independent states [1797-1958]. Howard law jour., 5:163-89 (Jun 1959). notes. [4920

BILL L. HOISINGTON. Unanswered questions in the recent passport cases. Hastings law jour., 10:290-305 (Feb 1959). notes. On the extent of the authority of the U.S. Government, particularly the Secretary of State, to deny a passport to a citizen of the United States, 1803-1958. [4921

JOEL LARUS. Pell-mell along the Potomac. Wm. and Mary quar., 17:349-57 (Jul). notes. On President Jefferson's decree that "The diplomatic corps were not to be accorded social precedence" and that in executive receptions the members of the executive would adhere "to the ancient usage of the country, of gentlemen in mass giving precedence to the ladies in mass, in passing from one apartment ... into another"; the resultant anger of the Minister from Great Britain, and his request for instructions as to whether he should make a formal protest. [4922

NORMAN ARTHUR GRAEBNER. Lincoln and the national interest. O. Fritiof Ander, ed., Lincoln images: Augustana College centennial essays (Rock Island, Ill.: Augustana College Library, 1960), p. 83-98. On his foreign policy, 1861-65. [4923

WAYNE CALHOUN TEMPLE. Lincoln and American foreign affairs [1861-65]. Ralph G. Newman, ed., Lincoln for the ages (Garden City, N.Y.: Doubleday, 1960), p. 219-25. [4924

KENNETH M. MacKENZIE. American Methodism and imperialism [1865-1900]. Ann Arbor: University Microfilms, 1957 [i.e. 1960]. Positive microfilm of typescript. [284] leaves. Thesis--New York Univ. Abstracted: Dissert. abstracts, 21:180-81 (Jul). [4925

JAMES MARTIN MAHONEY. The influence of the Irish-Americans upon the foreign policy of the United States: 1865-1872. Ann Arbor: University Microfilms, 1959 [i.e. 1960]. Positive microfilm of typescript. [431] leaves. Thesis--Clark Univ. Abstracted: Dissert, abstracts, 20:2879 (Jan). [4926

LAWRENCE H. FUCHS. Minority groups and foreign policy. Pol. science quar., 74:161-75 (Jun 1959). notes. On "the persistence of chronic German- and Irish-American Anglophobia," and Jewish and other "other-nation loyalties," as influences, good or bad, upon American political action, 1876-1959. [4927

MILTON PLESUR. America looking outward: the years from Hayes to Harrison [1877-89]. Historian, 22: 280-95 (May). notes. Evidence that during these years "Interest in foreign policy was ... quiescent rather than dead." [4928

MANUEL R. GARCIA-MORA. International responsibility for subversive activities and hostile propaganda by private persons against foreign states. Ind. law jour., 35:306-35 (spring). notes. Includes criticism of the policy of the United States in this respect since 1885. [4929

KATHERINE ELIZABETH CRANE. Mr. Carr of State: forty-seven years in the Department of State. N.Y.: St. Martin's Press [1960]. xv, 365 p.

ports., views. On the service of Wilbur John Carr (1870-1942) in the Department of State, 1892-1939, including assignments as Assistant Secretary of State and Minister to Czechoslovakia. [4930

ROBERT JOHN FRYE. Deportation of aliens: a study in civil liberties [1892-1950s]. Ann Arbor: University Microfilms, 1959 [i.e. 1960]. Positive microfilm of typescript. [552] leaves. Thesis--Univ. of Florida. Abstracted: Dissert. abstracts, 20:2876-7 (Jan). [4931

ROBERT JOHN FRYE. Deportation of aliens: an exercise in judicial restraint [since 1893]. Ala. law rev., 12:324-40 (spring). notes. [4932

JAMES PATRICK SHENTON. Imperialism and racism [1898-1904]. Donald Sheehan & Harold C. Syrett, eds., Essays in American historiography: papers presented in honor of Allan Nevins (N.Y.: Columbia Univ. Press, 1960), p. 231-50. notes. [4933

PADRAIC COLUM KENNEDY. La Follette's imperialist flirtation. Pac. hist. rev., 29:131-44 (May). notes. On his support of the Spanish-American War and the occupation of former Spanish territory in his speeches in Wisconsin in the Election of 1900, and the question whether his opinion of imperialism changed in his later career. [4934

WILLIAM APPLEMAN WILLIAMS. Empire, new style. Monthly rev., 11: 83-93 (Jul-Aug 1959). On American foreign policy in the 20th century, and the differing rates at which the available courses of diplomatic action will eventuate in socialism. [4935

LEONARD BOUDIANOFF BOUDIN. Involuntary loss of American nationality [1907-58]. Harv. law rev., 73: 1510-31 (Jan). notes. [4936

JEAN-BAPTISTE DUROSELLE. De Wilson à Roosevelt: politique extérieure des États-Unis, 1913-1945. Paris: A. Colin, 1960. 494, [1] p. ports. bibliog. (p. 455-81), notes. (Sciences politiques. Relations internationales, 2.) [4937

C. DAVID TOMPKINS. Senator Arthur Hendrick Vandenberg: Middle Western isolationist. Mich. hist., 44:39-58 (Mar). notes. On his views of American foreign policy while editor of the Grand Rapids, Mich., Herald, and later Senator from Michigan, 1916-41. [4938

SIEGFRIED HESSE. The constitutional status of the lawfully admitted permanent resident alien: the inherent limits of the power to expel [1917-58]. Yale law jour., 69:262-97 (Dec 1959). notes. [4939

WALDO WARDER BRADEN. The Senate debate on the League of Nations, 1918-1920: an overview. South. speech jour., 25:273-81 (summer) [4940

RUSSELL H. BASTERT. The two American diplomacies [since 1940]. Yale rev., 49:518-38 (summer 1959). [4941

WILLIAM HENDERSON. United States policy and colonialism [1945-57]. Harold Karan Jacobson, ed., America's foreign policy (N.Y.: Random House [1960]), p. 528-37. notes. First printed in 1957. [4942

JOHN W. SPANIER. American foreign policy since World War II [1945-60]. N.Y.: Praeger [1960]. viii, [2], 234 p. bibliog. (p. 221-8). (Books that matter.) [4943

U.S. Congress. Senate. Republican Policy Committee. ABC's of U.S. foreign policy, 1945-1960: a factual survey by the Republican Policy Committee staff conducted under the direction of Styles Bridges, chairman. [Wash.] 1960. iv, [1], 143 leaves. tables. notes. [4944

MALCOLM EDWIN JEWELL. Evaluating the decline of Southern internationalism through Senatorial roll call votes [1947-58]. Jour. politics, 21:624-46 (Nov 1959). notes. [4945

BEATRICE RUSSELL. Living in state. N.Y.: D. McKay Co. [1959]. xiv, 272 p. On the author's marriage to Earle Russell, Jr., his work as a Foreign Service officer in Addis Ababa, Tunis, and Beirut, and her solutions of some of the difficulties inherent in their way of life, 1947-59. [4946

THE AMERICAS

ARTHUR PRESTON WHITAKER. The Western Hemisphere idea: its rise and decline. Ithaca: Cornell Univ. Press [1954]. x, [2], 194 p. bibliog. (p. 178-87), notes. On expressions of "the proposition that the peoples of this Hemisphere stand in a special relationship to one another which sets them apart from the rest of the world," 1776-1951, manifested in "the American System," Pan-Americanism, and the "Drago Doctrine," and weakened by "Yankeephobia," at its climax in 1928. [4947

Canada

FRANCIS NICHOLSON (1655-1728). The New England - Acadia fishery dispute and the Nicholson mission of August 1687. [Edited] by Bruce T[iebout] McCully. Essex Inst. hist. col., 96:277-90 (Oct). notes. Report from Colonel Nicholson to "the Plantations Office in London," dated Boston, 5 Sep. 1687, on his journey along the Maine coast and to Port Royal (now Annapolis, N.S.) and back; with a long historical introduction. [4948

JOHN A. SCHUTZ. Imperialism in Massachusetts during the governorship of William Shirley, 1741-1756. Huntington Lib. quar., 23:217-36 (May). notes. On his eagerness to expand Massachusetts to include Nova Scotia, his efforts to promote the expulsion of the French from Canada, the Great Lakes, and the Ohio Valley, and his tacit rejection of "the British containment policy." [4949

PAUL PHELPS HUTCHISON. "Friendly neighbours": some thoughts on Canadian-American relations [1775-1959]. Midwest quar., 1:113-27 (Jan). [4950

HERMAN JULIUS DEUTSCH. The evolution of the international boundary in the Inland Empire of the Pacific Northwest [1795-1846]. Pac. Northw. quar., 51:63-79 (Apr). maps, view. notes. Includes some account of proposals to annex British Columbia, 1850s-1871. [4951

FREDERICK COYNE HAMIL. American recruits for the invasion of Windsor. Detroit Hist. Soc., Bul., 15(6):7-14 (Mar 1959). views. notes. On the participation of citizens of the United States, especially Detroiters, in the Patriot War, and the means by which they were induced to join the rebel forces, 1837-38. [4952

JAMES O. McCABE. Arbitration and the Oregon question. Can. hist. rev., 40:308-27 (Dec). notes. On the reasons why the British were inclined toward arbitration of this issue and the Americans were firmly opposed to it, 1844-45. [4953

DONALD FREDERICK WARNER. The idea of continental union: agitation for the annexation of Canada to the United States, 1849-1893. [Lexington:] Univ. of Kentucky Press for the Mississippi Valley Historical Assoc. [1960]. ix, [3], 276 p. maps. bibliog. (p. 257-64), notes. [4954

ROBIN W. WINKS. Canada and the United States: the Civil War years [1861-65]. Baltimore: Johns Hopkins Press [1960]. xviii, [4], 430 p. bibliog. (p. 382-97), notes. Based on thesis--Johns Hopkins Univ. [4955

WILLIAM L. GRIFFIN. A history of the Canadian - United States Boundary Waters Treaty of 1909. Univ. Detroit law jour., 37:76-95 (Oct 1959). notes. [4956

JAMES PATRICK MANION (1907-59). A Canadian errant: twenty-five years in the Canadian Foreign Service. Edited by Guy Sylvestre. [Toronto:] Ryerson Press [1960]. ix, 196 p. port. Includes an account of the author's service in the Canadian Government Trade Commission in New York, Jul. 1940 - Dec. 1941. [4957

Latin America

ERNESTO DE LA TORRE VILLAR. Dos proyectos para la independencia de Hispanoamérica: James Workman y Aaron Burr. Rev. hist. Am., 49:1-83 (Jun). bibliogs., notes. On the discontent of the French people of Louisiana under American administration, the trials of James Workman and Lewis Kerr for organizing "an expedition for the conquest and emancipation of Mexico," Workman's earlier project for seizing the lower La Plata River with British and Irish aid, Burr's part in the Louisiana scheme and his efforts to induce the French Government to intervene in the affairs of Mexico, Florida, Jamaica, and Canada, 1800-1810; with Spanish translations of supporting documents. [4958

WILLIAM HOWARD DUSENBERRY. Halsey's claim against the government of Buenos Aires, 1818-1859. Inter-Am. econ. affairs, 13(4):95-107 (spring). notes. On a loan by Thomas Lloyd Halsey to the revolutionary government at Buenos Aires sometime before 1818, collected in 10 installments between 1851 and 1859 with assistance from the U.S. Department of State. [4959

CARLET R. AUGUSTE. Haiti dans le cadre de la Doctrine de Monroe et du Panaméricanisme [1823-1939]. Port-au-Prince, Haïti: Imprimerie de l'État, 1948 [cover: 1949]. 19 p. Written apparently in 1939. Largely a plea for more importation of Haitian products into the United States. [4960

ISIDRO FABELA. Buena y mala vecindad. México: Editorial América Nueva, 1958. 330, [5] p. On relations of the United States with the nations of Latin America since 1823, particularly with Guatemala. [4961

WILLIAM HOWARD DUSENBERRY. The service of William A. Harris [as chargé d'affaires] at Buenos Aires, 1846-1851. Americas, 16:251-69 (Jan). notes. [4962

JOSEPH R. BARAGER. Sarmiento and the United States. U.S., Dept. of State, Office of Intelligence Research, Abstracts of completed doctoral dissertations, 1950-51 ([Wash.] 1952), p. 53. Abstract of thesis--Univ. of Pennsylvania. Includes an account of the visit of Domingo F. Sarmiento, "Argentine educator, author and statesman," to the United States, 1847, and his stay there, 1865-68, his observations on the United States, and the influence of the United States upon his political, economic, and educational policies in the Argentine Republic. [4963

GENARO FERNÁNDEZ MAC-GREGOR. En la era de la mala vecindad. México: Ediciones Botas, 1960. 434, [1] p. Narrative of dealings between the United States and Mexico, 1848-70 (p. 7-304); and essays (p. 305-434) which appear to be revised book reviews, on Columbus, the supposed cruelty of the Spaniards toward the Indians, the revolution against Spain supported by the United States, Lorenzo de Zavala, Mariano Otero, Luis de la Rosa, Melchor Ocampo, Juan Antonio de la Fuente, the Louisiana Purchase, the volume of William Jay on the Mexican War, and the diary of James K. Polk. [4964

MANUEL VILLANOVA FERNÁNDEZ (1845-1901). Humboldt y Thrasher. Notas y prólogo por José L. Franco. Habana: Oficina del Historiador de la Ciudad de La Habana, 1960. 52, [3] p. port. bibliog. (p. 26-7). (Cuadernos de historia habanera, 69.) From the Havana La semana, 5 Sep. - 3 Oct. 1887. On Alexander Humboldt's Essai politique sur l'île de Cuba (1826), translated by John S. Thrasher as The island of Cuba (1856), from which the translator silently omitted a chapter of the original dealing with slavery; with details of Thrasher's activities to promote the annexation of Cuba by the United States. [4965

MATÍAS ROMERO (1837-98). Diario personal [1855-65]. Edición, prólogo, y notas de Emma Cosío Villegas. [México:] Colegio de México, 1960. xx, 656, [1] p. Includes a daily record of the author's life in Washington as Secretary of the Mexican Legation there, Dec. 1859-Jan. 1865. [4966

EDWARD FONTAINE (1814-84). Edward Fontaine and the Emperor Dom Pedro II [of Brazil], 1876. Edited by Joseph O. Baylen and Glover Moore. Jour. Miss. hist., 22:239-48 (Oct). notes. Excerpt from the author's diary, 26 May 1876, and letter to his daughter Susan, 2-3 Jun. 1876, on his meeting with the Emperor and the Empress in New Orleans, recording their conversations on scientific and other matters, and describing the Emperor's physique. [4967

WALTER FREDRICK LA FEBER. The American business community and Cleveland's Venezuela message. Bus. hist. rev., 34:393-402 (winter). port. notes. Based on thesis--Univ. of Wisconsin, 1959. On his message concerning "the boundary dispute between Venezuela and Great Britain," 17 Dec. 1895, with evidence "that influential businessmen in New York, Boston, and the Midwest approved Cleveland's policy and commended his creation of a vigorous, expansionistic Monroe Doctrine." [4968

BOYD CARTER. William Jennings Bryan in Mexico. Neb. hist., 41:53-64 (Mar). ports. notes. On his visits to Mexico, 1897, 1900, 1908, as reported in Nebraska and Mexico City newspapers, with particular reference to his praises of Porfirio Díaz, his visit to a brewery, and attendance at a champagne luncheon. Includes a long report translated from El mundo ilustrado, 6 Dec. 1908, containing text of Bryan's speech at the luncheon. [4969

DAVID FRANK HEALY. The formation of America's Cuban policy, 1898-1902. Ann Arbor: University Microfilms, 1960. Positive microfilm of typescript. [318] leaves. Thesis--Univ. of Wisconsin. Abstracted: Dissert. abstracts, 21:1542-3 (Dec). [4970

THEODORE PAUL WRIGHT, JR. Free elections in the Latin American policy of the United States. Pol. science quar., 74:89-112 (Mar 1959). notes. Based on thesis--Yale Univ., 1957. On interferences by the United States "in the electoral processes of Cuba, Panama, Nicaragua, Mexico, the Dominican Republic, Haiti, Costa Rica, Honduras, Guatemala and El Salvador," 1898-1933. [4971

THEODORE PAUL WRIGHT, JR. United States electoral intervention in Cuba [1898-1902, 1906-9, 1916-21]. Inter-Am. econ. affairs, 13(3):50-71 (winter 1959). notes. Indications "that the impartial support of free elections in countries where democracy has not already been firmly planted is to no avail," and that the abrogation of the Platt Amendment in 1934 was justified. [4972

I. E. CADENHEAD, JR. Will Rogers: good neighbor. Chron. Okla., 38:2-7 (spring). notes. On his interest in and published references to Latin America, 1902-34, showing a conflict between "his mid-western brand of isolationism" and "his instinctive humanitarianism." [4973

LAWRENCE O. EALY. The Republic of Panama in international cooperation, 1903-1950. U.S., Dept. of State, Office of Intelligence Research, Abstracts of completed doctoral dissertations, 1950-51 ([Wash.] 1952), p. 108-9 Abstract of thesis--Univ. of Pennsylvania. [4974

THEODORE PAUL WRIGHT, JR. Honduras: a case study of United States support of free elections in Central America [1911-24]. Hisp. Am. hist. rev., 40:212-23 (May). notes. Evidence that "the policy of supporting free elections was ineffective either for creating stability or as an end in itself where the prerequisites for democracy were missing." [4975

GEORGE JAY RAUSCH, JR. Victoriano Huerta [1854-1916]: a political biography. Ann Arbor: University Microfilms, 1960. Positive microfilm of typescript. [297] leaves. Thesis--Univ. of Illinois. Abstracted: Dissert. abstracts, 21:1546-7 (Dec). On his part in the overthrow of President Madero of Mexico and perhaps in Madero's murder, his service as interim President of Mexico, the intervention of the U.S. Government and the seizure of Vera Cruz, Huerta's flight to Europe, his later efforts to organize a new revolutionary movement from the United States, his arrest by the U.S. Government on charges of "conspiracy to violate United States neutrality," and his death while in United States custody, 1913-16. [4976

JEAN WALKER. Plan de San Diego. Jr. historian (Tex.), 21(1):5-6, 29 (Sep). port. On a plot concocted by Basilio Ramos, apparently with German encouragement, to raise the "Liberating Army for Races and Peoples" and take over Texas, New Mexico, Colorado, Arizona, and California as an independent republic, which would seek annexation by Mexico, 1915. [4977

EDMUND DAVID CRONON. Josephus Daniels [1862-1948] in Mexico. Madison: Univ. of Wisconsin Press, 1960. xiii, 369 p. facsims., ports., views. bibliog. (p. 293-303), notes (p. 304-353). On his service as U.S. Ambassador to Mexico, 1933-41. [4978

ALEX P. ZEIDENFELT. Anglo-American cooperation in the British and American non-self governing possessions in the Caribbean [since 1940]. U.S., Dept. of State, Office of Intelligence Research, Abstracts of completed doctoral dissertations, 1950-51 ([Wash.] 1952), p. 82-4. Abstract of thesis--New York Univ. Mainly on the Anglo-American Caribbean Commission, established in 1942, renamed the Caribbean Commission in 1945. [4979

NEW MEXICO, UNIVERSITY OF. School of Inter-American Affairs. United States-Latin American relations: post World War II developments in Latin America [1943-59]. Wash.: U.S. Govt. Print. Off., 1959. vii, 72 p. notes. Prepared at the request of the Subcommittee on American Republics Affairs, Committee on Foreign Relations, U.S. Senate. [4980

JAMES FRED RIPPY. U.S. aid to Latin America [1945-57]. Jour. inter-Am. studies, 1:83-96 (Jan 1959). tables. [4981

JAMES FRED RIPPY. United States role in Caribbean development [1945-58]. University of Florida, School of Inter-American Studies, The Caribbean: natural resources, ed. A. Curtis Wilgus (Gainesville: Univ. of Florida Press, 1959), p. 286-98. tables. notes. Deals particularly with economic development. [4982

ATLANTIC POWERS

JOSÉ MARTÍNEZ ÓRTIZ. Un Valenciano en la independencia de los Estados Unidos. Rev. hist. Am., 50:488-95 (Dec). notes. On the little-recognized aid given by Spain to the

United States in the Revolution, and the unofficial aid of Juan Miralles y Troillón to the United States, 1778-80. [4983

SAMUEL FLAGG BEMIS. Pinckney's treaty: America's advantage from Europe's distress, 1783-1800. [Revised edition.] New Haven: Yale Univ. Press, 1960. xvi, 372 p. maps. bibliog. (p. 317-24), notes. 1st ed. 1926. On the San Lorenzo Treaty between the United States and Spain negotiated by Thomas Pinckney in 1795, and the spoliation of American neutral ships, the free navigation of the Mississippi, and the southern boundary of the United States as problems before and after the treaty. [4984

H. PHILLIP LEVY. John Adams presents his credentials [to King George III as "America's first envoy to the Court of St. James's," 1785]. History today, 9:59-63 (Jan 1959). ports., views. [4985

ALEXANDER DE CONDE. A time for candor and a time for tact. Wm. and Mary quar., 17:341-5 (Jul). notes. On the nomination and appointment of Gouverneur Morris by President Washington as Minister Plenipotentiary to France, Morris's imprudent conduct in France, his recall by request of the French Government, and the less than frank communications from Washington to Morris, 1791-94. [4986

CHARLES STEVENSON. A British reaction to the Treaty of San Ildefonso. [Edited by] Hugh C. Bailey and Bernard C. Weber. Wm. and Mary quar., 17:242-6 (Apr). notes. Letter to William Windham, M. P., 8 May 1802, arguing that the retrocession of Louisiana by Spain to France would prove to be "highly injurious to the Interests" of Great Britain. [4987

WILLIAM PINKNEY (1764-1822). Excerpts from two Pinkney letter books. Edited by Dorothy Brown. Md. hist. mag., 55:360-70 (Dec). notes. Four private letters from the U.S. Minister to Great Britain to James Madison, Secretary of State, dated London, 17 Nov., 7 and 31 Dec. 1807, and 7 Sep. 1808. [4988

IRVING NEWTON BRANT. "... hatred of despotism." John Arthur Garraty, ed., The unforgettable Americans (Great Neck, N.Y.: Channel Press [1960]), p. 92-6. On the service of Joel Barlow as American Minister to France, 1811-12. [4989

ARNOLD WHITRIDGE. Joseph Bonaparte [1768-1844] in America. History today, 9:308-18 (May 1959). ports., views. On the older brother of Napoleon as a refugee in the United States and a resident of Bordentown, N.J., 1815-32, and his refusal while in America to cooperate in schemes of French expatriates to free Napolean from exile and to seize Mexico. [4990

ANDRÉ ARTONNE. Les débuts d'un diplomate: la mission de M. de Bourqueney aux États-Unis (1816). Rev. hist. dipl., 69:61-82 (Jan-Mar 1955). On the extraordinary range and variety of the services of ---- de Bourqueney to Jean Guillaume, Baron Hyde de Neuville, French Ambassador to the United States, 1816-17, and his commendable discharge of delicate functions rarely entrusted to a man aged 19. [4991

STEPHEN J. CAMPBELL. Footnote to an old treaty. For. Service jour., 37(3):40-42 (Mar). On the treaty between the United States and the Sultan of Muscat and Oman negotiated by Edmund Roberts and the Sultan in 1833. [4992

GEORGE P. McDONOUGH. American relations with Turkey, 1893-1901. U.S., Dept. of State, Office of Intelligence Research, Abstracts of completed doctoral dissertations, 1950-51 ([Wash.] 1952), p. 430-33. Abstract of thesis--Georgetown Univ., 1951. [4993

LOUIS PAUL LOCHNER. Herbert Hoover and Germany. N.Y.: Macmillan, 1960. vii, [3], 244 p. On the "exact relation of Mr. Hoover to imperial, republican, national-socialist, and postwar federal Germany and her people," 1914-54. [4994

KLAUS FERDINAND SCHOENTHAL. American attitudes toward Germany, 1918-1932. Ann Arbor: University Microfilms, 1959 [i.e. 1960]. Positive microfilm of typescript. [288] leaves. Thesis--Ohio State Univ. Abstracted: Dissert. abstracts, 20:3716-17 (Mar). Investigation of "the impact of American public attitudes on the foreign policy toward the German Republic." [4995

BARBARA ANN WELTER. The United States and Weimar Germany, 1919-1929. Ann Arbor: University

Microfilms, 1960. Positive microfilm of typescript. [354] leaves. Thesis--Univ. of Wisconsin. Abstracted: Dissert. abstracts, 21: 1537 (Dec). [4996

ROGER REED TRASK. The relations of the United States and Turkey, 1927-1939. Ann Arbor: University Microfilms, 1959 [i.e. 1960]. Positive microfilm of typescript. [419] leaves. Thesis--Pennsylvania State Univ. Abstracted: Dissert. abstracts, 20: 3720-21 (Mar). [4997

GORDON JUSTIN WRIGHT. Ambassador Bullitt and the fall of France. World politics, 10:63-90 (Oct 1959). notes. On the observations and activities of William Christian Bullitt as U.S. Ambassador to France, 1936-40, and the extreme differences of opinion among historians regarding his performance in this office. [4998

U.S. Dept. of State. Foreign relations of the United States: diplomatic papers. 1940 (in five volumes). Volume III. The British Commonwealth, the Soviet Union, the Near East and Africa. Wash.: U.S. Govt. Print. Off., 1958. vi, 1028 p. notes. [4999

DION JAMES JOHN ARCHON. The United States and the eastern Mediterranean [mainly since 1945]. U.S., Dept. of State, Office of Intelligence Research, Abstracts of completed doctoral dissertations, 1950-51 ([Wash.] 1952), p. 413-15. Abstract of thesis--Harvard Univ., 1951. [5000

WILLIAM CARL SPIELMAN. The United States in the Middle East [especially since 1945]: a study of American foreign policy. N.Y.: Pageant Press [1959]. 63 p. bibliog. (p. 59-61). [5001

FRED DIXON. U.S. - Israeli relations during the decade 1948-1958. Ann Arbor: University Microfilms, 1960. Positive microfilm of typescript. [308] leaves. Thesis--Univ. of Virginia. Abstracted: Dissert. abstracts, 21: 1240-41 (Nov). [5002

PACIFIC POWERS

LAWRENCE HENRY BATTISTINI. The rise of American influence in Asia and the Pacific [1776-1945. East Lansing:] Michigan State Univ. Press, 1960. [6], 241 p. bibliog. (p. 226-32), notes (p. 214-25). [5003

NIBONDH SASIDHORN. The United States and extraterriorality in Thailand: some unique aspects of American-Thai relations [1833-1925]. Ann Arbor: University Microfilms, 1960. Positive microfilm of typescript. [332] leaves. Thesis--Indiana Univ. Abstracted: Dissert. abstracts, 21:665-6 (Sep). [5004

W. D. McINTYRE. Anglo-American rivalry in the Pacific: the British annexation of the Fiji Islands in 1874. Pac. hist. rev., 29:361-80 (Nov). notes. Includes evidence that this result was in part the outcome of arbitrary and unauthorized action by a Commander Boutwell (full name not divulged), USS John Adams, in 1855. [5005

E. TAYLOR PARKS. The first Japanese diplomatic mission to the United States--1860. [Wash.: Office of Public Services, Bureau of Public Affairs, 1960. 2], 9, [1] p. port., views. notes (p. 9-10). (Department of State publication 7028. Far Eastern series, 96.) From the Department of State bulletin, 9 May 1960. Deals largely with the reception and entertainment of the visitors and with their impressions of the United States. [5006

DAVID F. ANTHONY. The administration of Hokkaido under Kuroda Kiyotaka, 1870-1882: an early example of Japanese-American cooperation. U.S., Dept. of State, Office of Intelligence Research, Abstracts of completed doctoral dissertations, 1950-51 ([Wash.] 1952), p. 360-62. Abstract of thesis--Yale Univ. On his use of American advisers. [5007

THOMAS JOSEPH McCORMICK. "A fair field and no favor": American China policy during the McKinley administrations, 1897-1901. Ann Arbor: University Microfilms, 1960. Positive microfilm of typescript. [426] leaves. Thesis--Univ. of Wisconsin. Abstracted: Dissert. abstracts, 21: 1545-6 (Dec). [5008

PAVEL PETROVICH SEVOST'IANOV. Ekspansionistskaia politika SShA na Dal'nem Vostoke (v Kitae i Koree v 1905-1911 GG.). Moskva: Gos. Izd-vo Polit. Lit-ry, 1958. 310, [2] p. bibliog. (p. 299-309), notes. On the "expansionist policy" of the United States toward China, Japan, and Korea. [5009

MANUAL FRANCIS TORREGROSA, JR. U.S. dollar diplomacy in China, 1909-1913. U.S., Dept. of State, Office of Intelligence Research, Abstracts of completed doctoral dissertations,

1950-51 ([Wash.] 1952), p. 335-9. Abstract of thesis--Georgetown Univ. [5010

JOHN KING FAIRBANK. Rethinking Asian policy. Harvard alumni bul., 53:678-81 (26 May 1951). Mainly on American policy toward China, 1911-51, and the causes of its "failure." [5011

ELIZABETH CECIL WILSON. The problem of value in technical assistance in education: the case of Korea, 1945-1955. Ann Arbor: University Microfilms, 1959 [i.e. 1960]. Positive microfilm of typescript. [349] leaves. Thesis (Ed. D.)--Univ. of Maryland. Abstracted: Dissert. abstracts, 20: 4006 (Apr). [5012

RUSSIA

JEROME BLUM. A Yankee at the court of the Tsars. For. Service jour., 37(6):24-6 (Jun). On the extremely expensive duties imposed upon John Quincy Adams as U.S. Minister Plenipotentiary to Russia, and the financial sacrifices required to continue his service there, 1809-14. [5013

EDWARD W. ELLSWORTH. Sea birds of Muscovy in Massachusetts. New Eng. quar., 33:3-18 (Mar). notes. On the reception and entertainment of the officers and seamen of the Russian fleet visiting Boston, May-Jun. 1864. [5014

EUGENE HAYWARD BACON. Russian-American relations, 1917-1921. U.S., Dept. of State, Office of Intelligence Research, Abstracts of completed doctoral dissertations, 1950-51 ([Wash.] 1952), p. 262-5. Abstract of thesis--Georgetown Univ., 1951. [5015

PIERRE FONTAINE. U.R.S.S. - U.S.A. Paris: Les Sept Couleurs [1960]. 245, [3] p. notes. On relations between the United States and Russia, 1917-60, and the position of France with respect to both. [5016

MONTHLY REVIEW: AN INDEPEPENDENT SOCIALIST MAGAZINE. A note on Foster Dulles. By the editors. Monthly rev., 11:407-9 (Mar). On the "War Trade Board of the United States Russian Bureau, Inc.," 1918-19. Retracts an earlier reference by the editors to "a scheme of the early 1920s, of which Dulles was the principal author, to carve up Russia into a number of protectorates of the Western imperialist powers," and attributes the erroneous reference to John Foster Dulles to a misreading of "certain passages in the Congressional Record for 1919." [5017

ROBERT PAUL BROWDER. The establishment of Soviet-American relations [1929-33]. U.S., Dept. of State, Office of Intelligence Research, Abstracts of completed doctoral dissertations, 1950-51 ([Wash.] 1952), p. 266-9. Abstract of thesis--Harvard Univ. [5018

Law

JOHN B. RENGIER. The law in Judge Jasper Yeates's library. Lancaster Co. Hist. Soc., Jour., 62:96-108 (Apr 1958). port. notes. On the contents of the library (1,043 volumes as catalogued by him in 1816) and the use that he made of it; with "a comparison of trial by jury in England as it existed in Colonial times and the trial by jury as it has been fashioned in our commonwealth," especially since 1776. [5019

CARL A. AUERBACH. Law and social change in the United States [1789-1959]. U.C.L.A. law rev., 6:516-32 (Jul 1959). notes. [5020

WILLARD HURST. Law and the limits of individuality [19th and 20th centuries]. Robert Ernest Spiller, ed., Social control in a free society (Phila.: Univ. of Pennsylvania Press [1960]), p. 97-136. notes. [5021

JOHN P. MAGNUSON. The private person's duty to assist the police in arrest. Wyo. law jour., 13:72-6 (fall 1958). notes. On the "obligation of citizens to respond when summoned" by a policeman "to assist in making an arrest," 1833-1953, and the liability of persons obeying such a summons to legal action when the arrest is determined to have been illegal. [5022

HAROLD SCHWARTZ. The controversial Dred Scott decision [1857]. Mo. hist. rev., 54:262-72 (Apr). ports. notes. [5023

RALPH M. CARSON. The prospect of liberty; or, The view from Saint-Remy. Mich. law rev., 58:1185-1216

(Jun). notes. On problems of American law and government since the founding of the University of Michigan Law School, 1859-1959. [5024

A. J. GUSTIN PRIEST. Major public utility decisions in perspective [1877-1959]. Va. law rev., 46:1327-44 (Nov). notes. [5025

ARNOLD M. PAUL. Conservative crisis and the rule of law: attitudes of bar and bench, 1887-1895. Ithaca, N.Y.: Cornell Univ. Press for the American Historical Assoc. [1960]. viii, [4], 256, [1] p. bibliog. (p. 238-47), notes, table of cases (p. 248-52). "A study of the relationship among the doctrines and decisions of the courts, the social tensions of the time, and the changing attitudes of lawyers and judges" in relation to the issues of freedom of contract, "judicial invalidation of state regulation," "corporate monopoly," the organization of labor unions, the right to strike and labor injunctions, the extent of the police power, progressive taxation of income, and lesser problems. [5026

JEROME HALL. The progress of American jurisprudence, 1906-1956. Arthur L. Harding, ed., The administration of justice in retrospect (Dallas: Southern Methodist Univ., 1957), p. 24-41. notes. Reprinted: Jerome Hall, Studies in jurisprudence and criminal theory (N.Y.: Oceana Publications [1958]), p. 131-42. notes. [5027

JEROME HALL. American tendencies in legal philosophy and the definition of "law" [1907-56]. Jerome Hall, Studies in jurisprudence and criminal theory (N.Y.: Oceana Publications [1958]), p. 119-30. From Comparative law review of Japan, 1956. [5028

ALVIN THALER. "With all deliberate speed." Tenn. law rev., 27:510-17 (summer). notes. Proof that the phrase was used by Oliver Wendell Holmes II in a letter to Sir Frederick Pollock, 7 Mar. 1909, and by Lord Byron in a letter to his publisher, 6 Apr. 1819, but has not been found "in any of the legal phrase books nor in any specific Chancery record." Notes occurrences of "with all convenient speed" in authors from Shakespeare to Browning and in both English and American phrase books and decisions. [5029

CLAUDIUS OSBORNE JOHNSON. Strain and restraint: the impact of subversive control on personal freedom [1915-58]. State College Wash., Research studies, 27:1-18 (Mar 1959). notes. [5030

JOE H. FOY. Cost adjustment in utility rate schedules [1917-59]. Vanderbilt law rev., 13:663-74 (Jun). notes. [5031

JAMES E. RUOFF. Robert Penn Warren's pursuit of justice from briar patch to cosmos. State College Wash., Research studies, 27:19-38 (Mar 1959). notes. On ideas of justice expressed in his poems and fiction, 1929-56. [5032

ANDREW J. RECK. The philosophical context of F. S. C. Northrop's legal theory [1931-59]. Tulane law rev., 34:505-22 (Apr). notes. [5033

EDGAR BODENHEIMER. A decade of jurisprudence in the United States of America: 1946-1956. Natural law forum, 3 (1958): 44-67. notes. Includes references to earlier developments. [5034

ADMIRALTY LAW

FRANKLYN CHRISTOPHER SETARO. The formative era of American admiralty law [1629-1789]. N.Y. law forum, 5:9-44 (Jan 1959). notes. [5035

JOHN V. LOVITT. Things are seldom what they seem: the jolly little wards of the admiralty. Am. Bar Assoc. jour., 46:171-4 (Feb). port. notes. On "seamen" (an ever more comprehensive term) as wards of courts of admiralty, 1823-1959, and the "judicial nonsense" of applying the concept today. For a reply see William L. Standard, "Are the admiralty's 'jolly little wards' really so privileged?" (46:1323-6, Dec.). [5036

WILLIAM ALPER. The maritime definition of an unsafe place to work. Univ. Miami law rev., 14:22-9 (fall 1959). notes. On litigation concerning "the shipowner's duty to provide seamen a safe place to work," 1902-59. [5037

WALTER D. O'HEARN, JR. The longshoreman and the Harborworker's Act--an exclusive remedy "full of sound and fury, signifying nothing". N.Y. law forum, 6:168-86 (Apr). notes. On remedies available to "the injured longshoreman," 1914-60. [5038

HERBERT R. BAER. At sea with the United States Supreme Court. N.C. law rev., 38:307-78 (Apr). notes. Topical review of its decisions in the field of admiralty law, 1917-59, in "the far greater number" of which "the division of the Court emphasizes the lack of a reasonable degree of certainty in our present law of the sea." [5039

EDMOND L. COHN. Death resulting from air crashes at sea--a survey of the law [1920-58]. Jour. air law and commerce, 26:344-52 (autumn 1959). notes. [5040

WILLIAM J. JUNKERMAN. Admiralty and the ocean air lines. N.Y. State Bar bul., 31:268-76 (Jul 1959). port. notes. On the interpretation of the Death on the High Seas Act, 1920. [5041

DAVID L. CAMPBELL. Seamen and the warranty of seaworthiness in maritime injuries--Sieracki today. Tulane law rev., 34:572-85 (Apr). notes. On the shipowner's duty to seamen "to provide a seaworthy vessel," and the extension since 1947 of the seaworthiness warranty "to others than traditional mariners" and to maritime structures other than ships. [5042

CONSTITUTIONAL LAW

PI SIGMA ALPHA. Committee on Publications. Major problems in State constitutional revision [1776-1960]. Edited by W[illiam] Brooke Graves. Chicago: Public Administration Service [1960]. xiv, 306 p. bibliog. (p. 283-98), notes. By various contributors. Includes an introductory chapter, "Myth and reality in State constitutional development," by Harvey Walker, and chapters on constitutional change and "The content of State constitutions". [5043

IRVING NEWTON BRANT. The Madison heritage. N.Y. Univ. law rev., 35:882-902 (Apr). notes. On the contributions of James Madison to the formation and early development of constitutional government in the United States, 1787-1817. [5044

JOSEPH L. CALL. Federalism and the Ninth Amendment. Dickinson law rev., 63:121-31 (Jan). notes. On the meaning of the amendment as illustrated in correspondence of James Madison and James Wilson, 1787-89. [5045

JACOB E. COOKE. Alexander Hamilton's authorship of the "Caesar" letters. Wm. and Mary quar., 17: 78-85 (Jan). notes. Argument that Hamilton was probably not the author of 2 letters in the New York Daily advertiser, 1 and 15 Oct. 1787, relating to the proposed Federal Constitution. [5046

WALTER GELLHORN. American rights: the Constitution in action. N.Y.: Macmillan, 1960. vi, [2], 232 p. notes (p. 203-27). Chapters on habeas corpus, the right to counsel, involuntary confessions, search and seizure, free speech, "legislative investigations," "the freedom of movement," school desegregation, and "'private government' and the Constitution," 1787-1960, especially in very recent years. [5047

STUART R. HAYS. The right to bear arms: a study in judical misinterpretation [1787-1939]. Wm. and Mary law rev., 2:381-406. notes. [5048

HUGO LAFAYETTE BLACK. The Bill of Rights [1791]. N.Y. law rev., 35:865-81 (Apr). notes. Argument that "one of the primary purposes of the Constitution with its amendments was to withdraw from the Government all power to act in certain areas" and "that Congress, in exercising its general powers, is expressly forbidden to use means prohibited by the Bill of Rights." [5049

OETJE JOHN ROGGE. The first and the fifth, with some excursions into others. N.Y.: T. Nelson [1960. 10], 358 p. notes (p. 307-50). On freedom of speech, due process, "Federal police power," "Sedition and obscenity," picketing, "The shrinking tenth amendment," "The right of silence," "Compulsory testimony acts," and "Unenumerated rights," all involving questions under the Bill of Rights. [5050

CHARLES B. HOCHMAN. The Supreme Court and the constitutionality of retroactive legislation [1798-1958]. Harv. law rev., 73:692-727 (Feb). notes. [5051

WALTER FRED BERNS. Freedom, virtue, & the First Amendment. Baton Rouge: Louisiana State Univ. Press [1957]. xiii, 264 p. notes, table of cases (p. 259-61). Chapters on censorship, "The danger test," "Preferred position," "Freedom and loyalty," and related legal problems as involved in court decisions, 1803-1954. [5052

LAWRENCE N. PARK. Admission of States and the Declaration of Independence. Temple law quar., 33:403-18 (summer). notes. On enabling acts that have admitted States into the Union, 1791-1959, and the requirement in the enabling acts for Nevada (1864), Nebraska (1864), Colorado (1875), and the 7 subsequently admitted States that their constitutions must not be "repugnant to the principles of the Declaration of Independence", concluding that the Declaration "is not binding on the original thirteen states, or any state admitted subsequently." [5053

SHERRILL HALBERT. Lincoln and the Fourteenth Amendment. Ralph G. Newman, ed., Lincoln for the ages (Garden City, N.Y.: Doubleday, 1960), p. 390-94. On the opposition of Lincoln and Andrew Johnson to the amendment, 1865-68. 5054

OSMOND KESSLER FRAENKEL. The Supreme Court and civil liberties: how the Court has protected the Bill of Rights. ... Published for the American Civil Liberties Union in its 40th anniversary year. N.Y.: Oceana Publications [1960. 2], 173 p. "Table of cases" (p. 149-68). Topical analysis of Supreme Court decisions relating to civil rights, 1866-1959. [5055

ROBERT JENNINGS HARRIS. The quest for equality: the Constitution, Congress, and the Supreme Court. Baton Rouge: Louisiana State Univ. Press [1960]. xiv, [2], 172, [1] p. notes. Table of cases (p. 159-66). On "the equal protection of the laws" (14th Amendment, section 1) and its judicial interpretation, 1868-1959; with some account of the origin of the concept. [5056

MILTON RIDVAS KONVITZ, ed. Bill of Rights reader: leading constitutional cases. ... Second edition, revised and enlarged. Ithaca, N.Y.: Cornell Univ. Press [1960]. xx, [2], 849 p. Table of cases (p. xvii-xx). (Cornell studies in civil liberty.) 1st ed. 1954. Annotated excerpts from court decisions relating to freedoms of religion, of assembly, petition, and association, of speech and press, and of labor, "freedom from race discrimination," and "personal security," 1872-1958. [5057

HARROP ARTHUR FREEMAN. Civil liberties and you--the 1959 test of American democracy. Syracuse law rev., 10:1-20 (fall 1958). notes. Includes a review of relevant Supreme Court decisions, 1873-1958. [5058

DAVID D. UCHNER. The constitutionality of curfew ordinances [1898-1957]. Wyo. law jour., 13:67-71 (fall 1958). notes. [5059

SID M. KRESSES & E. SHERWYN SYNA. The application of the Constitution outside the continental limits of the United States [1901-55]. Ga. Bar jour., 21:246-60 (Nov 1958). notes. Argument that the Constitution follows the flag. [5060

NICHOLAS H. MAGILL. Toward a more liberal construction of the Fourth [and the Fifth] Amendment. Dicta, 27:13-26 (Jan 1950). notes. On "the law of searches and seizures" as judicially interpreted, 1914-49. [5061

HERBERT WECHSLER. Toward neutral principles of constitutional law. Harv. law rev., 73:1-35 (Nov 1959). notes. Argument that judicial decisions ought to "rest on reasons with respect to all the issues in the case, reasons that in their generality and their neutrality transcend any immediate result that is involved"; with illustrations from the U.S. Supreme Court, 1914-59. [5062

JOHN WINCHESTER MacDONALD. The significance of the "Index-digest of State constitutions" [1915, 2d ed. 1959]. N.Y. State Bar jour., 32:408-13 (Dec). notes. [5063

DAVID ROGER MANWARING. The flag salute litigation. Ann Arbor: University Microfilms, 1959 [i.e. 1960]. Positive microfilm of typescript. ix, 747 leaves. bibliog. (leaves 711-47). Thesis--Univ. of Wisconsin. Abstracted: Dissert. abstracts, 20:2878-9 (Jan). On the opposition of Jehovah's Witnesses to the salute as "a sort of idolatry forbidden by the Bible," the decision of the U.S. Supreme Court that public-school children could be required "to salute and pledge allegiance to the United States flag," and its later decision "that no civilian citizen could constitutionally be required to salute a flag or participate in a pledge of allegiance, however worded," 1935-43. [5064

DANIEL MARVIN BERMAN. Freedom and Mr. Justice Black: the record after twenty years. Mo. law rev., 25:155-74 (Apr). notes. On the undeviating adherence of Hugo L. Black, as an Associate Justice of the Supreme Court, to the position that "the freedoms of speech, press and religion" and the privilege against self-incrimination are absolute and unqualified, protected by the Constitution against any effort of the Government to curb or suppress them, that the 14th Amendment applies all provisions of the Bill of Rights to the States, and that "in wartime the Constitution, if not completely silent, at least does not speak above a whisper," 1939-59. [5065

HENRY WHITE EDGERTON. Freedom in the balance: opinions relating to civil liberties. Edited by Eleanor Bontecou. [With a biographical sketch by Robert E. Cushman]. Ithaca, N.Y.: Cornell Univ. Press [1960]. xvii, [3], 278 p. port. Excerpts from opinions delivered by Edgerton as "an Associate Justice ... of the United States Court of Appeals for the District of Columbia ...," 1939-59, grouped in 6 chapters: "Freedom of religion, speech, and the press," "The 'informing function' of Congress," "Loyalty and the safety of the nation," "'Civilized standards of procedure,'" "Aliens and outcasts," and "Separate is not equal." [5066

JAMES P. HOLDEN. Constitutional shadows and security clearances--the right to confrontation [1946-59, especially since 1953]. Georgetown law jour., 48:576-93 (spring). notes. [5067

ROBERT F. ALLNUTT & GERALD J. MOSSINGHOFF. Housing and health inspection: a survey and suggestions in light of recent case law. Geo. Wash. law rev., 28:421-53 (Jan). notes. On "the right of entry of private dwellings for the purpose of health and housing inspections," 1949-59; with references to earlier cases. [5068

JOHN MICHENER. Health inspection of private homes. Md. law rev., 20: 345-52 (fall). notes. On the applicability of the Fourth Amendment to health inspections not authorized by a search warrant, 1949-60. [5069

STATE health inspections and "unreasonable search": the Frank exclusion of civil searches. Minn. law rev., 44:513-33 (Jan). notes. On the unrestricted right claimed by health inspectors to enter dwellings without a search warrant, 1949-59. [5070

CORPORATION LAW

EARL LATHAM. The body politic of the corporation. Edward Sagendorph Mason, ed., The corporation in modern society (Cambridge: Harvard Univ. Press, 1959), p. 218-36, 321-2. notes. On the development of American corporations as "systems of private government" and their rivalry with the "sovereignty of the state itself," 1606-1959. [5071

ABRAM CHAYES. The modern corporation and the rule of law [in America, since 1789, and abroad]. Edward Sagendorph Mason, ed., The corporation in modern society (Cambridge: Harvard Univ. Press, 1959), p. 25-45,301-2. notes. [5072

EDWARD R. HAYES. Extent of the legislature's reserve power to change common law attributes of corporations [1819-1959]. Vanderbilt law rev., 13:261-86 (Dec 1959). notes. [5073

ROBERT A. KESSLER. The statutory requirement of a board of directors: a corporate anachronism [1910-60]. Univ. Chicago law rev., 27:696-736 (summer). notes. [5074

TOKUSUKE KITAGAWA. Some reflections on the corporate theory--including a Japanese perspective. Duke law jour., 1960: 535-56 (fall). notes. On doctrines of "corporate personality" and of corporations as "legal entities," 1911-56. [5075

MIGUEL ANGEL DE CAPRILES. Fifteen-year survey of corporate developments, 1944-1959. Vanderbilt law rev., 13:1-19 (Dec 1959). notes. On legal developments. [5076

INTERNATIONAL LAW

DANIEL P. O'CONNELL. The relationship between international law and municipal law. Georgetown law jour., 48:431-85 (spring). notes. On cases in the law of the United States (including the Philippines), 1784-1955, see p. 462-7. [5077

EDWIN L. SMITH. The end of the consular courts. For. Service jour., 37(1):44-9 (Jan). On courts established in the American consulates in Morocco with jurisdiction over all disputes, both civil and criminal, in which American nationals were involved in Morocco, 1787-1957. [5078

HARRY FRANCIS MULLALY. United States refugee policy, 1789-1956: a study of the traditional policy of asylum for political, racial, or religious refugees. Ann Arbor: University Microfilms, 1959 [i.e. 1960]. Positive microfilm of typescript. iii, 363 leaves. facsims., forms. bibliog. (leaves 346-52). Thesis--New York Univ. Abstracted: Dissert. abstracts, 20:4158-9. [5079

WALTER HENRY EDWARD JAEGER. John Marshall: the man, the judge, and the law of nations. Am. Univ. law rev., 8:28-33 (Jan 1959). notes. [5080

RICHARD B. LILLICH. The Geneva Conference on the Law of the Sea [1958] and the immunity of foreign state-owned commercial vessels. Geo. Wash. law rev., 28:408-20 (Jan). notes. Includes reference to decisions of American courts involving such vessels, 1926-57. [5081

ALAN H. SCHECHTER. Towards a world rule of law--customary international law in American courts [State and Federal, 1945-60]. Fordham law rev., 29:313-56 (Dec). notes. [5082

JOHN D. ARNDT. International Court of Justice--legal effect, constitutional and international, of the Connally Reservation [1946-60]. Univ. Kan. City law rev., 28:1-34 (fall 1959). notes. [5083

ROBERT LAYTON. The dilemma of the World Court: the United States reconsiders compulsory jurisdiction. Stanford law rev., 12:323-54 (Mar). notes. On the Connally Amendment of 1946 and the events leading to its reconsideration in 1959. [5084

JACK E. LEVIN & GERALD A. TALLMAN. International law--world court--need for re-evaluation of the Connally Reservation [and the Morse Resolution, 1946-59]. Villanova law rev., 5:450-64 (spring). notes. [5085

EDWARD J. CARNEY, JR. Constitutional law--treaties--effect of the United Nations charter upon inconsistent State laws [1947-59]. Villanova law rev., 5:100-107 (fall 1959). notes. [5086

INTERSTATE RELATIONS

DANIEL L. ROTENBERG. Extraterritorial legislative jurisdiction and the State criminal law [1670-1959]. Tex. law rev., 38:763-87 (Jun). notes. [5087

DEVELOPMENT of the doctrine of forum non conveniens [1823-1958]. De Paul law rev., 8:350-62 (spring-summer 1959). notes. [5088

PAUL JAMES HARTMAN. State taxation of interstate commerce: a survey and an appraisal [1827-1959]. Va. law rev., 46:1051-1120 (Oct). notes. [5089

LOUIS C. JAMES. The effect of the autonomy of the parties on the validity of conflict of laws "illegal contracts"--Sunday, gambling, lottery, and other agreements. Am. Univ. law rev., 8:67-86 (Jun 1959). notes. On the validity of contracts illegal under the laws of the State in which they are made but containing stipulations by the contracting parties that they are made under the laws of another State, under which the contracts are permissible, 1835-1956. [5090

PAUL F. MICKEY & GEORGE B. MICKUM III. Congressional regulation of State taxation of interstate commerce [1869-1959]. N.C. law rev., 38:119-53 (Feb). notes. [5091

HUGH W. GIBERT. Congress muddies the water--some thoughts inspired by Public Law No. 86-272. Ala. law rev., 12:66-97 (fall 1959). notes. On efforts of the U.S. Government "to regulate state taxation of interstate commerce" since 1872. [5092

BOB R. BULLOCK. The expanding State judicial power over non-residents [1878-1957]. Wyo. law jour., 13:155-61 (winter 1959). notes. [5093

RUDOLF H. HEIMANSON. Federalism and the uniform law movement [since 1892]. N.Y. law forum, 6:161-7 (Apr). notes. [5094

BRAINERD CURRIE. The constitution and the "transitory" cause of action. Harv. law rev., 73:36-82, 268-303 (Nov, Dec 1959). notes. Argument "that, in the absence of congressional action, the full-faith-and-credit clause does not require a state to provide a forum for causes of action predicated on the law of a sister state when the refusal to do so is grounded in good faith upon a policy of promoting the efficiency of the local courts and protecting them against abuse"; with references to cases between 1914 and 1951. [5095

JESS N. ROSENBERG. State taxation of interstate motor carriers [1915-59]. Va. law rev., 46:1221-40 (Oct). notes. [5096

FLOYD E. BRITTON. Taxation without representation modernized. Am. Bar Assoc. jour., 46:369-74, 526-33 (Apr, May). port. notes. On "state taxation of non-resident businesses with respect to extraterritorial value and transactions," 1919-60. [5097

FLOYD E. BRITTON. State taxation of extraterritorial value: allocation of sales to destination [1920-59]. Va. law rev., 46:1160-71 (Oct). notes. [5098

MICHAEL B. SOLOMON. Nonresident personal income tax: a comparative study in eight States [1920-60]. Fordham law rev., 29:105-42 (Oct). [5099

GERALD R. GIBBONS. A survey of the modern nonresident motorist statutes [1927-60]. Univ. Fla. law rev., 13:257-310 (fall). notes. [5100

JAMES R. WILLARD. Missouri use tax--liability of out of State vendors. Mo. law rev., 25:188-94 (Apr). notes. Review of liability of such vendors under the laws of several States, 1937-59. [5101

DIXWELL LLOYD PIERCE. Form versus substance. Va. law rev., 46:1150-59 (Oct). notes. On State taxation of interstate commerce, 1938-60. [5102

WILFRED J. RITZ. Migratory alimony: a constitutional dilemma in the exercise of in personam jurisdiction. Fordham law rev., 29:83-104 (Oct). notes. On a State's jurisdiction over nonresident payers of alimony owed to residents, 1940-57. [5103

ARTHUR TAYLOR VON MEHREN. The validity of foreign divorces. Mass. law quar., 45(1):23-35 (Mar). notes. On "sister-state divorces" in relation to "the full-faith-and-credit" clause, 1942-59. [5104

LEONARD E. KUST & GRAHAM SALE, JR. State taxation of interstate sales [1944-59]. Va. law rev., 46:1290-1326 (Oct). notes. [5105

EMORY UNIVERSITY. Law School. Transient jurisdiction--remnant of Pennoyer v. Neff [1877]: a round table. Jour. pub. law, 9:281-337 (fall). notes. On the jurisdiction of States over nonresidents as a problem in the conflict of laws, mainly in the years 1945-60. Contents.--The converging limits of State jurisdictional powers, by Robert A. Leflar.--The length of the long arm, by Edward W. Cleary.--A British view, by Zelman Cowen.--Methods of progress in conflict of laws, by Rudolf B. Schlesinger.--Ehrenzweig in reply, by Albert A. Ehrenzweig. [5106

LAW GOVERNING COMPENSATION FOR DAMAGE, INJURY, OR LOSS

ROBERT B. YEGGE. Dog's bill of rights. Dicta, 34:178-81 (May-Jun 1957). port. notes. On the "vicious propensity test" of "dog bite liability," 1878-1955. [5107

GILBERT S. SOLOMON. Moving expenses in condemnation proceedings. Univ. Pittsburgh law rev., 21:97-106 (Oct 1959). notes. On moving costs as "consequential damages," 1893-1959. [5108

RICHARD J. SMITH. The use of deadly force by a peace officer in the apprehension of a person in flight [1904-54]. Univ. Pittsburgh law rev., 21:132-41 (Oct 1959). notes. [5109

WARREN LEONARD HANNA. Federal remedies for employee injuries. Albany, Calif.: Hanna Legal Publications [1955]. vi, 290 p. notes. On compensation claims against the U.S. Government and against private employers under the Employers' Liability Act (1906), the Federal Employers' Liability Act (1908), the Federal Employees' Compensation Act (1916), the Jones Act (1920), the Longshoremen's and Harbor Workers' Compensation Act (1927), the Federal Tort Claims Act (1946), and other Federal statutes. [5110

WILLIAM R. BAIRD. FELA, negligence, and jury trials--speculation upon a scintilla. West. Reserve law rev., 11:123-36 (Dec 1959). notes. On jury trials under the Federal Employers' Liability Act, covering railroad employees, 1908-59. [5111

STANLEY K. LAUGHLIN, JR. The FELA and trial by jury. Ohio State law jour., 21:422-37 (summer). notes. On provisions for jury trial in personal-injury cases of railroad employees under the Federal Employers Liability Act, 1908-60. [5112

FRANCIS K. RISKO & MAXIM E. EHRLICH. Negligence and responsibility in rescue cases. Dicta, 28:391-6 (Oct 1951). notes. On the doctrine that "the wrong that imperils life is a wrong to the imperiled victim" and "a wrong also to his rescuer"--i.e., "that in any situation where a human life is in a perilous position due to the negligence of the defendant, the party who is injured while attempting to rescue the one imperiled may recover for his injuries," 1910-44. [5113

EARL R. JONES. Workmen's compensation problems [in the United States, 1911-59]. Ia. State Med. Soc., Jour., 49:383-6 (Jul 1959). [5114

THOMAS A. CLEMONS. Workmen's compensation: the personal comfort doctrine. Wis. law rev., 1960:91-109 (Jan). notes. On "the situation where an employee is injured while taking a brief pause from his labors to minister to the various necessities of life," 1915-59, especially in Wisconsin and New York, and the distinction between injuries suffered on the employer's premises and off the premises. [5115

LE ROY E. ENDRES. Reparations procedure under the Perishable Agricultural Commodities Act of 1930. Geo. Wash. law rev., 28:719-57 (Apr). notes. [5116

GERALD REMUS. Changes in judicial concepts of utility liability [1933-59]. Am. Water Works Assoc., Jour., 52: 19-24 (Jan). notes. On "liability for damages or bodily injury resulting from broken mains or services." [5117

DAVID J. McCARTHY, JR., & EDWARD M. KOVACH. Sovereign consent to suit: third-party practice and the right to jury trial. Georgetown law jour., 48:737-61 (summer). notes. On the doctrine that "liability of a third party to the defendant upon the latter's liability to the plaintiff should be determined in the same proceeding" as applied to "suits in which the United States is a defendant," 1941-59. [5118

JAMES W. RINER. Just and reasonable compensation. Mo. law rev., 25: 324-54 (Jun). fold. table. notes. On awards in "cases involving the loss of legs, arms and fingers," 1943-58, and the legal standards governing size of awards. [5119

JAMES W. HUNT. The Federal Tort Claims Act: sovereign liability today [1946-58]. Mil. law rev., 8:1-34 (Apr). notes. Based on thesis--Judge Advocate General's School, U.S. Army. [5120

LAWYERS AND JUDGES

JOHN S. GOFF. Mr. Justice Trimble of the United States Supreme Court. Ky. Hist. Soc., Reg., 58:6-28 (Jan). notes. On Robert Trimble (1776-1828), born probably in present West Virginia, resident of Kentucky (1779-1828), lawyer at Paris, Ky., U.S. District Judge for Kentucky (1817-26), and Associate Justice of the U.S. Supreme Court (1826-28). [5121

ANTON-HERMANN CHROUST. The dilemma of the American lawyer in the post-Revolutionary era. Notre Dame lawyer, 35:48-76 (Dec 1959). notes. On the low standards of admission to the bar and eligibility for the bench, the "general condemnation" of lawyers and courts, the "strong and lasting sentiment" against the common law of England, and the lack of published legal records and treatises, especially in the 1780s, and the improvements in these respects by 1835. [5122

LAWRENCE B. CUSTER. Bushrod Washington and John Marshall: a preliminary inquiry. Am. jour. legal hist., 4:34-48 (Jan). notes. On their brief studies under George Wythe, their legal practice in Virginia, their political experience, their appointment to the Supreme Court, and their close agreement on nearly all cases before the Court; with 2 letters from Washington (to George Washington, 19 Oct. 1798, and Jedidiah Morse, 18 Feb. 1800). [5123

KATHRYN TURNER. The appointment of Chief Justice Marshall [1800-1801]. Wm. and Mary quar., 17:143-63 (Apr). notes. [5124

JOHN S. GOFF. Old age and the Supreme Court. Am. jour. legal hist., 4:95-106 (Apr). notes. Chronological account of "aged justices, suffering from various degrees of senility," beginning with William Cushing and ending with the retirement of Oliver Wendell Holmes in 1932. [5125

ALFONS JOSEPH BEITZINGER. Edward G[eorge] Ryan [1810-80]: lion of the law. Madison: State Historical Soc. of Wisconsin, 1960. vi, [2], 214, [1] p. ports., view. bibliog. (p. 202-8), notes (p. 173-201). (State Street books, 2.) On his emigration from Ireland in 1830, his study of law, his legal practice and violent political activities, his "political fanaticism" and "choleric" disposition, and his service as Chief Justice of Wisconsin (1875-80). [5126

WILLIAM NORWOOD BRIGANCE. Jeremiah S. Black [1810-83]. Speech Association of America, A history and criticism of American public address, ed. William Norwood Brigance, 2d ed. (N.Y.: Russell & Russell, 1960), 1: 459-82. bibliog., notes. On the oratorical and rhetorical characteristics of his public speaking in his practice of law in Pennsylvania and in Washington, D.C., "as a defender of the constitutional Bill of Rights against encroachment in time of stress," 1830-83. [5127

GERALD GORDON EGGERT. Richard Olney, corporation lawyer and Attorney General of the United States,

1835-1895. Ann Arbor: University Microfilms, 1960. Positive microfilm of typescript. [498] leaves. Thesis--Univ. of Michigan. Abstracted: Dissert. abstracts, 21:335-6 (Aug). [5128

GEORGE ANTHONY DONDERO. Lincoln the lawyer [1837-61]. Mich. State Bar jour., 38(2):22-30 (Feb 1959). port. [5129

IRVING DILLIARD. Lincoln remakes the Supreme Court. Ralph G. Newman, ed., Lincoln for the ages (Garden City, N.Y.: Doubleday, 1960), p. 301-6. On his appointments of Noah Haynes Swayne, Samuel Freeman Miller, David Davis, Stephen Johnson Field, and Salmon Porter Chase to the U.S. Supreme Court, 1862-64. [5130

THOMAS REED POWELL (1880-1955). Augustus Noble Hand [1869-1954]. Harvard alumni bul., 57:290-92 (15 Jan 1955). port. On his early life in Elizabethtown, N.Y., his studies at Harvard College and Harvard Law School, and his work as a lawyer and Federal judge. [5131

FELIX FRANKFURTER (1882-1965). Felix Frankfurter reminisces. Recorded in talks with Harlan B[uddington] Phillips. N.Y.: Reynal [1960]. ix, 310 p. Recordings begun in 1953, including Phillips's questions. Deals with Frankfurter's boyhood, his schooling, his legal studies and practice, his teaching in the Harvard Law School, and his service as an Associate Justice of the U.S. Supreme Court. Includes memories and appraisals of many persons of his acquaintance. [5132

HAROLD RAYMOND MEDINA. John Johnston Parker, 1885-1958. N.C. law rev., 38:299-306 (Apr). On his service as a U.S. Circuit Judge on the Court of Appeals for the Fourth Circuit (Maryland, Virginia, West Virginia, and the Carolinas), 1927 ff., and the rejection of his nomination in 1930 to the Supreme Court. [5133

DANIEL MARVIN BERMAN. Hugo L. Black [born 1886]: the early years. Cath. Univ. Am. law rev., 8:103-16 (May 1959). On his early life in Alabama, his work as a lawyer and judge in Birmingham and as Senator from Alabama, and his membership in the Ku Klux Klan. [5134

BERYL HAROLD LEVY. Cardozo twenty years later. Assoc. Bar City N.Y., Rec., 13:461-4 (Oct 1958). Commentary on the legal thinking of Benjamin N. Cardozo, 1889-1938. [5135

REGINALD HEBER SMITH. Joseph Nye Welch--1890-1960. Am. Bar Assoc. jour., 46:1196-7 (Nov). port. Recollections and anecdotes of his career as a lawyer. [5136

PHILIP MECHEM. In memoriam: Thomas Edgar Atkinson [1895-1960]. N.Y. Univ. law rev., 35:1233-5 (Nov). port. On his teaching of law in several universities. [5137

NATHAN GREENE. Mr. Justice Holmes and the age of man. Wayne law rev., 6:394-412 (summer). notes. On the reputation and the ideas of Oliver Wendell Holmes, Jr., 1896-1935, the arguments of "his supporters and detractors," and the influence of his doctrines upon later decisions of the Supreme Court. [5138

CHARLES HENRY KING. Edson R. Sunderland and the teaching of procedure [in the University of Michigan Law School, 1901-44]. Mich. law rev., 58:19-26 (Nov 1959). notes. Includes reference to his casebooks in this field. [5139

MICHIGAN, UNIVERSITY OF. Law School. Resolution of the Michigan law faculty on the death of Edson Read Sunderland [1874-1959]. Mich. law rev., 58:1-5 (Nov 1959). port. On his teaching in the Law School, 1901-44, and his numerous contributions to legal scholarship and to reform of legal procedure. [5140

DICTA. W. Gordon Johnston [1903-58]--the good life. Dicta, 35:155-61 (May-Jun 1958). Tributes from students and associates of the late Dean of the University of Denver College of Law; with a poem by him, apparently written immediately before his sudden death. [5141

HARVARD UNIVERSITY. HARVARD LAW SCHOOL ASSOCIATION. Council. Proceedings in honor of Mr. Justice Frankfurter and distinguished alumni at the meeting of the Council ... in Cambridge, April 30, 1960. Cambridge, 1960. [6], 69 p. facsims., port. (Harvard Law School. Occasional pamphlet, 3.) Includes 2 reminiscent addresses by Felix Frankfurter about his legal studies and legal and judicial experience since 1903. [5142

DANIEL J. FLOOD. Eulogy delivered by Hon. Daniel J. Flood. Dickinson law rev., 63:1-6 (Oct 1959). On Walter Harrison Hitchler, member of the faculty and eventually Dean of the Dickinson School of Law, 1906-54. [5143

HENRY JACOB FRIENDLY. Mr. Justice Brandeis: the quest for reason. Univ. Pa. law rev., 108:983-99 (May). notes. On the "general legal philosophy" of Louis D. Brandeis as an Associate Justice of the U.S. Supreme Court, 1909-39. [5144

HELEN SHIRLEY THOMAS. Felix Frankfurter, scholar on the bench. Baltimore: Johns Hopkins Press [1960]. xiv., 381 p. notes. Topical analysis and criticism of the ideas expressed in his articles, books, and Supreme Court opinions, 1913-59. [5145

NEVILLE MILLER. Justice Brandeis and the University of Louisville School of Law. Filson Club hist. quar., 34: 156-9 (Apr). Reminiscences by the former Dean of the School, of benefactions from Louis Dembitz Brandeis, 1920 ff. [5146

CHARLES J. DRIEBE. Incorporation of the bar. Ga. Bar jour., 21:527-39 (May 1959). tables. On proposals for incorporation of "all persons who enjoy the privilege of practicing law" in Georgia, 1925-58; with some account of the adoption of such incorporations in 17 other States, 1921-56. [5147

EDWARD ALLAN FARNSWORTH. John Hanna [born 1891]--an appreciation. Columbia law rev., 60:587-92 (May). notes. On his teaching in the Columbia School of Law, 1927-59; with a list of his legal publications. [5148

FELIX SOLOMON COHEN (1907-53). The legal conscience: selected papers. Edited by Lucy Kramer Cohen. ... Introduction by Eugene V. Rostow. New Haven: Yale Univ. Press, 1960. xvii, 505 p. port. notes. Twenty-seven articles and 17 reviews, grouped under the headings "Logic, law, and ethics," "The Indian's quest for justice," and "The philosophy of American democracy"; with a list of Cohen's writings, 1929-53, including unpublished writings. [5149

JOHN W. HOPKIRK. William O. Douglas--individualist: a study in the development and application of a judge's attitudes [since the 1930s]. Ann Arbor: University Microfilms, 1958 [i.e. 1960]. Positive microfilm of typescript. [588] leaves. Thesis--Princeton Univ. Abstracted: Dissert. abstracts, 20:4428-9 (May). [5150

MICHIGAN, UNIVERSITY OF. Law School. John Evarts Tracy [1880-1959]. Mich. law rev., 58:813-18 (Apr). port. On his teaching in the University of Michigan Law School, 1930-49, and his legal writings; with excerpts from his autobiography. [5151

JULIUS PAUL. The legal thinking of Jerome Frank: a study in contemporary American legal realism [1930-1950s]. Ann Arbor: University Microfilms, 1954 [i.e. 1960]. Positive microfilm of typescript. [259] leaves. Thesis--Ohio State Univ. Abstracted: Dissert. abstracts, 20:3356-8 (Feb). On his views of legal rules, "the role of the judge," the jury system, and legal education. [5152

WILLIAM ORVILLE DOUGLAS. Mr. Justice Cardozo. Mich. law rev., 58: 549-56 (Feb). notes. Recollections and evaluation of the work of Benjamin N. Cardozo, 1931-42. [5153

CHARLES WILLIAM TAYLOR, JR. Eminent law firms of the United States: Histories, 1958. Palo Alto, Calif. [1958. 2], 531 p. Histories of existing firms, including biographical sketches of some of their former and present members; with "Geographical index" and "General index." [5154

LEGAL EDUCATION

FRED B. DEVITT, JR. William and Mary: America's first law school. Wm. and Mary law rev., 2:424-36. port., view. notes. On the priorities of the chair of law at the College of William and Mary (1779), the Litchfield Law School (lectures ca. 1782, separate building 1784), and the professorship of law in the University of Pennsylvania (1790). [5155

ALBERT JAMES HARNO. American legal education [1779-1960]. Am. Bar Assoc. jour., 46:845-51 (Aug). port. notes. [5156

RONALD L. COLEMAN. Learning the law at Litchfield. Conn. Bar jour., 34:270-76 (Sep). notes. On the Litchfield Law School, Litchfield, Conn., 1784-1835, "the nation's first school of law ... the country's first national law school." [5157

CHARLES HOOVER RUSSELL. Liberal education and the law [1800-1956]. Jour. legal educ., 11 (1958-59): 6-23. notes. [5158

ELIZABETH GASPAR BROWN. The Law School of the University of Michigan: 1859-1959. Mich. State Bar jour., 38(7):16-28 (Aug 1959). ports., view. notes. [5159

JAMES A. RAHL & KURT SCHWERIN. Northwestern University School of Law: a short history, to commemorate its centennial, 1859-1959. Chicago, 1960. 89 p. ports., tables, views. notes. Also printed: Northw. Univ. law rev., 55:127-215 (May-Jun). ports., tables, views. notes. [5160

EDWARD McWHINNEY. Methodology and values in American legal education: some interactions and reciprocal influences [since the Civil War]. Natural law forum, 4 (1959): 119-28. notes. Deals particularly with "the case system of legal education," the law journal, and the "all-exclusive preoccupation with method," and "the need for a value or policy-oriented jurisprudence (whether natural law or otherwise)." [5161

HAROLD E. HURST. A history of legal education in Denver. Dicta, 36: 147-54 (Mar-Apr 1959). port. On a "Blackstone class" (1888 and probably following years), the University of Denver College of Law (founded in 1892), and the Westminster College of Law (founded in 1912, merged with the University of Denver College of Law in 1957). [5162

HOMER D. CROTTY. The accreditation of law schools [by the American Bar Association, 1890s-1960]. Jour. higher educ., 31:322-7 (Jun). [5163

EDWARD CALDWELL KING. A history of the University of Colorado School of Law [1892-1959]. Dicta, 36: 139-46 (Mar-Apr 1959). port. [5164

CHARLES LIEBERT CRUM. The history of the University of North Dakota School of Law [1899-1958]. N.D. law rev., 35:5-35 (Jan 1959). ports. [5165

JOHN E. CRIBBET. The evolving curriculum--a decade of curriculum change at the University of Illinois [1948-58]. Jour. legal educ., 11 (1958-59): 227-360. notes. [5166

Leaders in Public Life

MICHAEL GARIBALDI HALL. Edward Randolph [1632?-1703] and the American colonies, 1676-1703. Chapel Hill: Univ. of North Carolina Press for the Institute of Early American History and Culture [1960]. xi, [3], 241 p. maps. bibliog. (p. 224-30), notes. On his service as an agent of Charles II and James II in attempts to convert the proprietary colonies to royal colonies, later as Surveyor General of H. M. Customs in America (1690-95, 1698-1700), holder of various minor offices, and "free-lance informer." [5167

JOHN CHESTER MILLER. Sam Adams [1722-1803]: pioneer in propaganda. Stanford, Calif.: Stanford Univ. Press [1960. 10], 437 p. facsims., ports., views. bibliog. (p. 401), notes. 1st ed. 1936. Biography, dealing with his life in Boston, his studies at Harvard, and his activities in Boston, Massachusetts, and national politics. [5168

BERNARD BAILYN. "... the voice of the colonists' conscience." John Arthur Garraty, ed., The unforgettable Americans (Great Neck, N.Y.: Channel Press [1960]), p. 53-7. On John Dickinson (1732-1808), his early life in Delaware and work as a lawyer in Philadelphia, and his activities in Pennsylvania and national politics. [5169

JOHN D. CUSHING. A Revolutionary conservative: the public life of William Cushing, 1732-1810 [attorney in Maine, justice of the Superior Court of Judicature of Massachusetts, Chief Justice of Massachusetts, Associate Justice of the U.S. Supreme Court]. Ann Arbor: University Microfilms, 1959 [i.e. 1960]. Positive microfilm of typescript. viii, 347 leaves. bibliog. (leaves 337-47). Thesis--Clark Univ. Abstracted: Dissert. abstracts, 20: 2768 (Jan). [5170

JOSEPH NATHAN KANE. Facts about the Presidents: a compilation of biographical and historical data [from Washington to Eisenhower, 1732-1959]. N.Y.: H. W. Wilson Co., 1959 [printed 1960]. x, 348, [1] p. ports., seal. notes. [5171

THOMAS JEFFERSON WERTENBAKER. "... a fire alarm in the night." John Arthur Garraty, ed., The unforgettable Americans (Great Neck, N.Y.: Channel Press [1960]), p. 57-61. On

Patrick Henry (1736-99), Virginia lawyer, leader in Virginia and national politics. [5172

THOMAS JEFFERSON (1743-1826). Autobiography of Thomas Jefferson. With an introduction by Dumas Malone. N.Y.: Capricorn Books [1959. 2], 119, [3] p. (A Putnam Capricorn book, Cap 8.) Recollections dated at the beginning 6 Jan. 1821, dealing mainly with the author's activities in Virginia and national politics till 1790. [5173

GEORGE BUBB DANGERFIELD. Chancellor Robert R. Livingston of New York, 1746-1813. N.Y.: Harcourt, Brace [1960]. viii, [2], 532 p. port., fold. geneal. table. bibliog. (p. 441-50), notes (p. 451-516). On his early life in New York City, his studies in King's College, his activities in New York and national politics, his land speculations, and his effort to establish a monopoly of steam navigation on the Hudson. [5174

JOSEPH EDWARD FIELDS. A Signer and his signatures: or, The library of Thomas Lynch, Jr. [1749-79]. Harv. Lib. bul., 14:210-52 (spring). facsims. notes. Biographical sketch, and account of all his known signatures, totaling 81. [5175

MAX M. MINTZ. Gouverneur Morris, 1752-1779: the emergence of a nationalist. Ann Arbor: University Microfilms, 1957 [i.e. 1960]. Positive microfilm of typescript. [210] leaves. Thesis--New York Univ. Abstracted: Dissert. abstracts, 20:3711-12 (Mar). On his early life and legal practice in New York and his activities in the New York Provincial Congress and the Continental Congress. [5176

WALTER N. EASTBURN. John Morton [1724-77], changeable Signer. Manuscripts, 12(1):12-19 (winter). facsims., table. Examination of his handwriting in several documents, 1761-76. [5177

LOUIS A. MALLORY. Patrick Henry [1736-99]. Speech Association of America, A history and criticism of American public address, ed. William Norwood Brigance, 2d ed. (N.Y.: Russell & Russell, 1960), 2:580-602. bibliog., notes. On the oratorical and rhetorical characteristics of his public speaking as a Virginia lawyer and political leader, 1763-99. [5178

WARREN HASTY CARROLL. John Adams, Puritan revolutionist: a study of his part in making the American Revolution, 1764-1776. Ann Arbor: University Microfilms, 1959 [i.e. 1960]. Positive microfilm of typescript. 3, v, 449 leaves. bibliog. (leaves 394-449). Thesis--Columbia Univ. Abstracted: Dissert. abstracts, 20:2767-8 (Jan). Argument that he "was primarily motivated ... by his admiration of the Puritan revolutionaries of the previous century and their concept of a special mission and destiny for America." [5179

RICHARD E. WELCH, JR. Rufus King of Newburyport [born 1755]: the formative years (1767-1788). Essex Inst. hist. col., 96:241-76 (Oct). notes. On his studies in Dummer Academy and Harvard; his study and practice of law in Newburyport; and his activities in Massachusetts politics, in the Continental Congress, and the Convention of 1787. [5180

THOMAS CHALMERS McCORVEY (1851-1932). Thomas Jefferson and his political philosophy [as expressed during his career in politics, 1769-1809, and later]. T. C. McCorvey, Alabama historical sketches, ed. George Burke Johnston (Charlottesville: Univ. of Virginia Press, 1960), p. 185-207. bibliog., notes. Lecture, 18 Jun. 1909. [5181

JOSEPH HARRY DORFMAN & REXFORD GUY TUGWELL. Alexander Hamilton: nation-maker. Joseph Dorfman & R. G. Tugwell, Early American policy: six Columbia contributors (N.Y.: Columbia Univ. Press, 1960), p. 7-42. port. notes. From the Columbia University quarterly "in the 1930s." On his studies at King's College, his service in the Continental Army and later as Secretary of the Treasury, and his philosophy of a "natural fiscal policy," 1772-95. [5182

WILLIAM OMER FOSTER, SR. James Jackson [1757-1806], duelist and militant statesman. Athens: Univ. of Georgia Press [1960]. viii, 220 p. port. bibliog. (p. 202-12), notes (p. 193-201). On his emigration from England in 1772, his life in Savannah, his service in the Revolution, and his activities as Governor of Georgia and as Representative and Senator from Georgia. [5183

LOIS HOBART. Patriot's lady: the life of Sarah Livingston Jay. N.Y.: Funk & Wagnalls Co. [1960. 14], 274 p. view. On the courtship and marriage of Sarah Van Brugh Livingston and John Jay, 1773-74, and their married life till 1800. Deals almost entirely with the activities of John Jay during these years in New York and national politics. Contains no account of her early life and does not divulge the date and place of her birth. Fictional in form. [5184

BERNHARD KNOLLENBERG. Did Samuel Adams provoke the Boston Tea Party [1773] and the clash at Lexington [1775]? Am. Antiq. Soc., Proc., 70:493-503 (Oct). notes. Concludes that evidence supporting an affirmative answer is completely lacking. [5185

JOSEPH HARRY DORFMAN & REXFORD GUY TUGWELL. John Jay: revolutionary conservative. Joseph Dorfman & R. G. Tugwell, Early American policy: six Columbia contributors (N.Y.: Columbia Univ. Press, 1960), p. 43-98. port. notes. From the Columbia University quarterly "in the 1930s." On his career in New York and national politics, 1774-1801, and his political and legal ideas so far as he expressed them; with some account of his early life. [5186

V. B. REED & JAMES DAVID WILLIAMS, eds. The case of Aaron Burr [1756-1836]. Boston: Houghton Mifflin [1960]. xi, 204 p. map, tables. (Houghton Mifflin research series, 2.) Reprinted contemporary documents relating to his military and political activities, 1775-1807, culminating in the records of his trial for treason. [5187

HENRY LAURENS (1724-92). Henry Laurens on the Olympic Games. S.C. hist. mag., 61:146-7 (Jul). Note on proceedings in Congress, 2 Jul. 1779, expressing disagreement with William Henry Drayton's remarks proposing that Congress approve an application from a French officer "to exhibit certain grand fire works on the 5th Inst." [5188

ANNE WARD AMACHER. Myths and consequences: Calhoun and some Nashville Agrarians. South Atl. quar., 59:251-64 (spring). On the "somewhat romantic and rather inaccurate ... image" of John C. Calhoun (1782-1850) and his doctrines of slavery and the concurrent majority as presented in writings of Allen Tate and Andrew Nelson Lytle, 1928-56. [5189

GERALD MORTIMER CAPERS. John C[aldwell] Calhoun [1782-1850], opportunist: a reappraisal. Gainesville: Univ. of Florida Press, 1960. viii, 275 p. port. bibliog. (p. 267-8), notes (p. 257-66). Interpretation of his career in South Carolina and national politics. [5190

ARTHUR MEIER SCHLESINGER, JR. "... a consistent faith in the people." John Arthur Garraty, ed., The unforgettable Americans (Great Neck, N.Y.: Channel Press [1960]), p. 132-5. On Martin Van Buren (1782-1862) in New York and national politics. [5191

CHARLES G. MULLER. The proudest day: Macdonough on Lake Champlain. N.Y.: John Day Co. [1960]. ix, 373 p. map, port. bibliog. (p. 350-61), notes (p. 335-49). On the service of Thomas Macdonough (1783-1825) as an officer of the U.S. Navy, 1800-1825, particularly his command of the American fleet on Lake Champlain, 1812-14; with some account of his early life in Delaware. Fictional in form. [5192

GEORGE BUBB DANGERFIELD. "... dedication to civil liberties." John Arthur Garraty, ed., The unforgettable Americans (Great Neck, N.Y.: Channel Press [1960]), p. 65-9. On the activities of James Madison in Virginia and national politics, 1784-1815. [5193

S. SIDNEY ULMER. The role of Pierce Butler [delegate from South Carolina] in the Constitutional Convention [1787]. Rev. politics, 22:361-74 (Jul). notes. [5194

DAVID CUSHMAN COYLE. Ordeal of the Presidency. Wash.: Public Affairs Press [1960]. v, [3], 408 p. cartoons, facsims., music. Biographical sketches of "our most maligned Presidents": Washington, John Adams, Jefferson, John Quincy Adams, Jackson, Lincoln, Andrew Johnson, Theodore Roosevelt, Wilson, and Franklin D. Roosevelt, 1789-1945. [5195

MICHAEL A. LA CARRUBA. Presidents and wives: portraits, facts [1789-1959]. Wash.: Historic Publications [1959]. 47 p. ports., seal, views. [5196

GLORIA JAHODA. John Beckley: Jefferson's campaign manager. N.Y. Pub. Lib., Bul., 64:247-60 (May). notes. On his service as a political manager, press agent, pamphleteer, and purveyor of politically useful information for the Republican Party and Thomas Jefferson, 1792-1807; with excerpts from his letters to James Madison and James Monroe. [5197

LUCIUS WILMERDING, JR. James Monroe, public claimant. New Brunswick, N.J.: Rutgers Univ. Press

[1960]. viii, 144 p. facsim., port., views. notes (p. 133-44). On "his character for integrity in the manage- of public money," the claims presented by him in 1825 against the United States for alleged uncompensated services since 1794, and the reluctance of Congress to recognize the full validity of the claims. [5198

ERNEST J. WRAGE. Henry Clay [1777-1852]. Speech Association of America, A history and criticism of American public address, ed. William Norwood Brigance, 2d ed. (N.Y.: Russell & Russell, 1960), 2:603-38. bibliog., notes. On the oratorical and rhetorical characteristics of his public speaking as a Kentucky lawyer and a national political leader, 1798-1852. [5199

WILBUR SAMUEL HOWELL & HOYT HOPEWELL HUDSON. Daniel Webster [1782-1852]. Speech Association of America, A history and criticism of American public address, ed. William Norwood Brigance, 2d ed. (N.Y.: Russell & Russell, 1960), 2:665-733. bibliog., notes. On the oratorical and rhetorical characteristics of his public speaking as a New Hampshire and Massachusetts lawyer and a national political leader, 1800-1852. [5200

GEORGE MILLS. The crusade of John Brown [1800-1859]. Ann. Ia., 35: 101-11 (fall 1959). notes. Deals particularly with his movements in Iowa. [5201

EARL CONRAD. The Governor and his lady: the story of William Henry Seward [1801-73] and his wife Frances. N.Y.: Putnam [1960. 4], 433 p. On his early life in New York, his work as a lawyer in Auburn, N.Y., his married life with Frances Adeline (Miller) Seward, and his activities in New York and national politics. Consists mainly of dialogue. Gives little information about Mrs. Seward. [5202

JOHN EDMOND GONZALES. Henry Stuart Foote [1804-80]: a Republican appointee in Louisiana. La. hist., 1:137-46 (spring). notes. On his shift from the Democratic to the Republican Party, his support of the latter in the Election of 1876, and his reward with appointment as Superintendent of the U.S. Mint at New Orleans; with some account of his earlier activities in Mississippi, Tennessee, Confederate, and Federal politics since ca. 1830. [5203

NATHANIEL PEFFER. "... the basis for friendship and trust." John Arthur Garraty, ed., The unforgettable Americans (Great Neck, N.Y.: Channel Press [1960]), p. 175-8. On Townsend Harris (1804-78), his early life in New York City, his activities in New York politics, his travels across the Pacific and the Indian Ocean as a merchant, and his service as the first American consul in Japan. [5204

HAROLD COFFIN SYRETT & JEAN G. COOKE, eds. Interview in Weehawken: the Burr-Hamilton duel, as told in the original documents. ... With an introduction and conclusion by Willard M. Wallace. Middletown, Conn.: Wesleyan Univ. Press [1960. 10], 178, [2] p. facsims., pots., tables. notes. Documents relating to the mortal wounding of Alexander Hamilton by Aaron Burr in a duel at Weehawken, N.J., 11 Jul. 1804. [5205

HOLMES MOSS ALEXANDER. The famous five. N.Y.: The Bookmailer [1958]. xiii, 208, [1] p. bibliog. (p. 209). On the Senate service of Henry Clay, Daniel Webster, John Caldwell Calhoun, Robert Marion La Follette, and Robert Alphonso Taft, "the Senate's great men." 1806-1953. [5206

JOHN A. FORMAN. Lewis Charles Levin [1808-60]: portrait of an American demagogue. Am. Jew. arch., 12: 150-94 (Oct). port., view. bibliog., notes. On his Jewish birth in South Carolina, his 2 Philadelphia newspapers, his bitter attacks upon liquor, the stage, and Roman Catholics, his activities in the Native American Party, his service in Congress, and his "war against the immigrants." [5207

JOHN CORNELIUS STENNIS. The image of Jefferson Davis [1808-89]. Jour. Miss. hist., 22:123-7 (Apr). [5208

AMERICAN STORY (Radio program). The Abraham Lincoln story, 1809-1959, written by 70 distinguished Lincoln and Civil War scholars. N.Y.: Broadcast Music [c1959-60]. 72 separately paged pieces in 4 portfolios. ports. Scripts "distributed as a public service ... to radio stations and to local boards of education, public libraries and educational institutions to be used in connection with broadcasting." [5209

NORMAN ARTHUR GRAEBNER Lincoln's humility. Ralph G. Newman, ed., Lincoln for the ages (Garden City, N.Y.: Doubleday, 1960), p. 384-9. Instances, 1839-65. [5210

JEAN DRESDEN GRAMBS, ed. Abraham Lincoln through the eyes of high school youth. Wash.: National Education Assoc. [and] the Lincoln Sesquicentennial Commission of the United States, 1959. v, 73 p. bibliog. (p. 71-3). Poems, essays, editorials, short stories, short plays, speeches, etc., all laudatory, written by high-school students "all over the country" by request of their teachers. [5211

WILLIAM DEAN HOWELLS (1837-1920). Life of Abraham Lincoln. Bloomington: Indiana Univ. Press, 1960. xxxii p., facsim. (xi-xii, 17-94 p.; port.), [5] p. notes. Introduction signed: Clyde C. Walton. Reproduction of part of Lives and speeches of Abraham Lincoln and Hannibal Hamlin (Columbus, Ohio, 1860), from a copy containing manuscript corrections in Lincoln's handwriting. [5212

ROBERT LEE KINCAID (1893-1960). The self-education of Abraham Lincoln. Ralph G. Newman, ed., Lincoln for the ages (Garden City, N.Y.: Doubleday, 1960), p. 150-54. [5213

REINHARD HENRY LUTHIN. The real Abraham Lincoln [1809-65]: a complete one volume history of his life and times. Englewood Cliffs, N.J.: Prentice-Hall [1960]. xviii, [2], 778 p. bibliog. (p. 677-82), notes (p. 682-753). [5214

ALLAN NEVINS. Lincoln and democracy. U.S., Lincoln Sesquicentennial Commission, Abraham Lincoln sesquicentennial, 1950-1960: final report (Wash. [1960]), p. 182-92. [5215

CARL SANDBURG. Carl Sandburg on Abraham Lincoln: Carl Sandburg's speech before the Congress of the United States, February the eighteenth [i. e. twelfth], 1959. Followed by an introduction [by J. Christian Bay]. Cedar Rapids, Ia.: Privately printed for the friends of the Torch Press, 1959. 30 p. port. General commentary on Lincoln, 1809-65. [5216

STATE HISTORICAL SOCIETY OF IOWA. Abraham Lincoln. Iowa City, 1960. 81-144 p. facsims., ports., views. (The palimpsest, v. 41, no. 2, Feb. 1960.) Contributions by William J. Petersen, Harry J. Lytle, and Ray Murray, including some account of "Lincoln and Iowa" and other information about him. [5217

PHILIP VAN DOREN STERN. Abraham Lincoln: a biography in pictures. [N.Y.: Birk, 1960.] 14, [1] p. facsims., map, ports., views. [5218

U.S. Information Service, London. Abraham Lincoln, 12 February 1809 - 15 April 1865: interpretations on the one hundred and fiftieth anniversary of his birth. [London, 1959. 4], 56, [1] p. Contents.--He belongs to the ages: the story of Abraham Lincoln, by Paul M. Angle.--An immortal sign: Lincoln as a world figure, by Roy P. Basler.--Lincoln as politician, by David Donald.--Lincoln, the military strategist, by T. Harry Williams.--Lincoln and the meaning of the American union, by David M. Potter.--Lincoln and democracy, by Thomas Vernor Smith.--Lincoln the emancipator, by Kenneth A. Bernard.--Lincoln and human rights, by Harvey Wish.--Abraham Lincoln as a man of letters, by Earl Schenck Miers. [5219

U.S. Lincoln Sesquicentennial Commission. Lincoln day by day: a chronology, 1809-1865. Earl Schenck Miers, editor-in-chief. Volume I: 1809-1848. [Edited by] William E. Baringer. Wash., 1960. xx, 327, [1] p. [5220

HENRY BARTLETT VAN HOESEN (1885-1965). Lincoln and John Hay. Books at Brown, 18:141-80 (Oct). notes. Comparison and contrast of the lives and circumstances of Lincoln and Hay before 1861 and of their personalities throughout life, analysis of the "Lincoln-Hay relationship in 1861-65"; with comment on Hay's diary and letters, account of his life after 1865, and appraisal of John George Nicolay and John Hay's Abraham Lincoln: a history (1890). [5221

HERBERT L. CURRY. John C. Calhoun [1782-1850]. Speech Association of America, A history and criticism of American public address, ed. William Norwood Brigance, 2d ed. (N.Y.: Russell & Russell, 1960), 2:639-64. bibliog., notes. On the oratorical and rhetorical characteristics of his public speaking as a South Carolina and national political leader, 1810-50. [5222

ANNE McCAIN. Charles Edward Stuart [1810-87] of Kalamazoo. Mich. hist., 44:324-35 (Sep). notes. On his early years in New York and his legal studies there, his life in Kalamazoo, his practice of law, and his service in the U.S. House of Representatives and Senate. [5223

GAYLE ANDERSON BRADEN. The public career of Edward Dickinson Baker [1811-61]. Ann Arbor: University Microfilms, 1960. Positive microfilm of typescript. [303] leaves. Thesis--Vanderbilt Univ. Abstracted: Dissert. abstracts, 21:601-2 (Sep). On his practice of law, his political activities in Illinois, California, and Oregon, and in national politics, and his death in battle. [5224

DAVID HERBERT DONALD. Charles Sumner [1811-74] and the coming of the Civil War. N.Y.: Knopf, 1960. [2], xxii, 392, xxiv, [3] p. cartoons, ports. bibliog. (389-92), notes. On his early life in Boston, his studies at Harvard College and the Harvard Law School, and his activities in Massachusetts and national politics till 1861. [5225

BENJAMIN PLATT THOMAS (1902-56). "... often devious, sometimes downright deceitful." John Arthur Garraty, ed., The unforgettable Amercians (Great Neck, N.Y.: Channel Press [1960]), p. 207-10. On Edwin McMasters Stanton (1814-69), his early life in Steubenville, Ohio, his legal practice in Pittsburgh, and his service as Secretary of War. [5226

FRANCIS WORCESTER DOUGHTY. Medallic history of Andrew Jackson. Numismatist, 73:1459-60 (Oct). Condensed by Homer C. Platt from Leslie's popular monthly, May 1898. On medals, campaign medalets, "hard times tokens," store cards, and "copperheads" honoring Jackson, 1815 ff. [5227

WILLARD LEROY KING. Lincoln's manager, David Davis [1815-86]. Cambridge: Harvard Univ. Press, 1960. xiii, 383 p. facsims., map, ports., views. bibliog. (p. 319-25), notes (p. 327-71). On his early life and studies, his work as a lawyer in Illinois, and his activities in Illinois and national politics, particularly his service from 1862 to 1877 as an Associate Justice of the U.S. Supreme Court. [5228

MAC SWINFORD. Mr. Justice Samuel Freeman Miller (1816-1873[i.e. 1890]). Filson Club hist. quar., 34:35-44 (Jan). On his early years in Kentucky and Iowa and his service from 1862 to 1890 as an Associate Justice of the U.S. Supreme Court. [5229

HARRY C. BLAIR & REBECCA TARSHIS. The life of Colonel Edward D[ickinson] Baker [1811-61], Lincoln's constant ally. Together with four of his great orations. [Portland, Ore.: Oregon Historical Soc.] 1960. xiii, 233 p. facsims., maps, ports., views. notes (p. 211-23). On his emigration from England in 1816, service in the Black Hawk, Mexican and Civil wars, political speaker, criminal lawyer, "militant expansionist and Congressional filibusterer, ... life-long friend and confidant of Abraham Lincoln ... Illinois Congressman, Panama railroad promoter and whirlwind Oregon senator," killed in the Civil War. [5230

JOSEPH B. CUMMING. The Cumming-McDuffie duels. Ga. hist. quar., 44: 18-40 (Mar). notes. On disagreements between William Cumming and George McDuffie concerning State rights and national power, the printed insults exchanged between the two, and the concern of President Monroe, John C. Calhoun, John Quincy Adams, and others over the "public attention" given to their 7 meetings and 2 actual duels, 1821-22. [5231

JOSEPH GEORGE TREGLE, JR. The political apprenticeship of John Slidell. Jour. South. hist., 26:57-70 (Feb). notes. On his activities as "lawyer and politician" in Louisiana, "student and victim of Edward Livingston and Martin Gordon," and their defeated competitor for the favors of Andrew Jackson, 1821-33. [5232

CLARK C. SPENCE & ROBIN W. WINKS. William "Colorado" Jewett of the Niagara Falls Conference. Historian, 23:23-53 (Nov). notes. On William Cornell Jewett (1823-93), obscurely and uncertainly involved in thefts, Colorado mines, attempted mediation during the Civil War, efforts to procure foreign intervention in the war, writing unsolicited letters of advice to Lincoln and others, activity in both Republican and Democratic politics, etc. [5233

ELIZABETH LAWSON. The gentleman from Mississippi: our first Negro Congressman, Hiram R[hoades] Revels [1827?-1901. N.Y., 1960.] 63 p. cartoon, port. notes (p. 54-63). On his service as Senator from Mississippi, 1870-71; with some account of his early life in North Carolina, his studies in a Quaker seminary in Union County, Ind., and his abolitionist activities. [5234

ALEXANDRIA LEE LEVIN. Two Jackson supporters: Roger Brooke Taney and William Murdock Beall of Frederick. Md. hist. mag., 55:221-9 (Sep). notes. On their political and personal activities, 1827-37. [5235

VERMONT remembers President Arthur. Vt. Hist. Soc., News and notes, 6:9-12 (Oct 1954). port., view.

On the Chester A. Arthur Memorial House and Monument, North Fairfield, Vt., marking the site of Arthur's birth in 1830; with an editorial from the Burlington free press on "Vermont elements in Arthur's career." [5236

JOHN DONALD HICKS. "... an apostle of reform" John Arthur Garraty, ed., The unforgettable Americans (Great Neck, N.Y.: Channel Press [1960]), p. 265-9. On Ignatius Donnelly (1831-1901) in Minnesota and national politics. [5237

JOHN W. DELEHANT. Judah P. Benjamin [1811-84], lawyer and statesman. Dicta, 25:51-63 (Mar 1948). On his career in Louisiana, national, and Confederate law and politics, 1832-65. [5238

ROY FRANKLIN NICHOLS. Abraham Lincoln: master politician [1832-65]. Ralph G. Newman, ed., Lincoln for the ages (Garden City, N.Y.: Doubleday, 1960), p. 236-41. [5239

PAUL HOWARD DOUGLAS. Lincoln and Douglas. Ralph G. Newman, ed., Lincoln for the ages (Garden City, N.Y.: Doubleday, 1960), p. 124-9. On Stephen Arnold Douglas (1813-61) in Illinois and national politics, 1833-61. [5240

MILDRED FREBURG BERRY. Abraham Lincoln: his development in the skills of the platform [1834-65]. Speech Association of America, A history and criticism of American public address, ed. William Norwood Brigance, 2d ed. (N.Y.: Russell & Russell, 1960), 2: 828-58. notes. [5241

CLYDE CAMERON WALTON. Abraham Lincoln: Illinois legislator [1834-54]. Ralph G. Newman, ed., Lincoln for the ages (Garden City, N.Y.: Doubleday, 1960), p. 74-8. [5242

FOREST LIVINGS WHAN. Stephen A. Douglas [1813-61]. Speech Association of America, A history and criticism of American public address, ed. William Norwood Brigance, 2d ed. (N.Y.: Russell & Russell, 1960), 2: 777-827. bibliog., notes. On the oratorical and rhetorical characteristics of his public speaking as an Illinois and national leader, 1834-61, particularly in his debates with Lincoln in 1858. [5243

H. LE ROY JACKSON. Concerning the financial affairs of Abraham Lincoln, Esquire. Conn. Bar jour., 34:240-48 (Sep). tables. notes. On his income from his practice of law and during his service as President, 1836-65. [5244

THOMAS EDWARD FELT. The rise of Mark Hanna. [East Lansing? Mich.] 1960. [1], xv, 384 leaves. bibliog. (leaves 373-84), notes. Thesis--Michigan State Univ. On the activities of Marcus Alonzo Hanna (1837-1904) in Republican politics, 1863 through 1896; with some account of his early life and service in the Civil War, and his business enterprises in Cleveland. [5245

RALPH JOSEPH ROSKE. Lincoln and Lyman Trumbull. O. Fritiof Ander, ed., Lincoln images: Augustana College centennial essays (Rock Island, Ill.: Augustana College Library, 1960), p. 61-81. On their practice of law in Illinois and their activities and associations in Illinois and national politics, 1837-61. [5246

CHARLES ALLAN McCOY. Polk and the Presidency. Austin: Univ. of Texas Press [1960]. xiii, 238 p. cartoons, facsims., ports., view. bibliog. (p. 227-34), notes. On the activities of James Knox Polk (1795-1849) in Tennessee and national politics particularly the powers exercised by him while President. [5247

REXFORD S. MITCHELL. William L[owndes] Yancey [1814-63]. Speech Association of America, A history and criticism of American public address, ed. William Norwood Brigance, 2d ed. (N.Y.: Russell & Russell, 1960), 2: 734-50. bibliog., notes. On the oratorical and rhetorical characteristics of his public speaking as an Alabama lawyer and a national political leader, 1839-63. [5248

LESTER THONSSEN. William M[axwell] Evarts [1818-1901]. Speech Association of America, A history and criticism of American public address, ed. William Norwood Brigance, 2d ed. (N.Y.: Russell & Russell, 1960), 1:483-500. bibliog., notes. On the oratorical and rhetorical characteristics of his public speaking, especially as a lawyer and political leader, 1841.91. [5249

LE ROY P. GRAF. Andrew Johnson and the coming of the war. Tenn. hist. quar., 19:208-21 (Sep). notes. Review of his activities in Tennessee and national politics, 1843-61, with special attention to his political ideas and his position as "Southerner, Unionist, and Democrat." [5250

WILLIAM ALEXANDER GRAHAM (1804-75). The papers of William Alexander Graham. Edited by J. G. de Roulhac Hamilton. Volume three: 1845-1850. Raleigh: State Dept. of Archives and History, 1960. xvi, 541 p. notes. Letters and other papers written by or addressed to Graham, relating to his service as Governor of North Carolina, 1845-50, and as Secretary of the Navy, 1850, and his political and other activities. [5251

R. ELAINE PAGEL & CARL DALLINGER. Charles Sumner [1811-74]. Speech Association of America, A history and criticism of American public address, ed. William Norwood Brigance, 2d ed. (N.Y.: Russell & Russell, 1960), 2:751-76. bibliog., notes. On the oratorical and rhetorical characteristics of his public speaking as a Boston lawyer and a national political leader, 1845-71. [5252

DONALD WAYNE RIDDLE. Congressman Abraham Lincoln [from Illinois, 1846-48]. Ralph G. Newman, ed., Lincoln for the ages (Garden City, N.Y.: Doubleday, 1960), p. 96-100. [5253

STANLEY FITZGERALD HORN. Isham G[reen] Hariss (1818-97) in the pre-war years. Tenn. hist. quar., 19: 195-207 (Sep). On his activities in Tennessee and national politics, 1847-61, especially as Governor of Tennessee (1857-61). [5254

ROBERT DOUTHAT MEADE. Lincoln and the statesmen of rebellion. Ralph G. Newman, ed., Lincoln for the ages (Garden City, N.Y.: Doubleday, 1960), p. 295-300. On his political relationship with the leaders of the Confederacy, 1848-61. [5255

JOHN EDMOND GONZALES. Reminiscences of a Mississippian. Jour. Miss. hist., 22:101-9 (Apr). notes. On Henry Stuart Foote's Casket of reminiscences (1874), reprinted (with omissions) from 44 articles by him in the Washington Daily morning chronicle, Jul.-Oct. 1873, on Mississippi and national politics in the 1850s. [5256

BOYD BLYNN STUTLER. "... it was the curtain-raiser." John Arthur Garraty, ed., The unforgettable Americans (Great Neck, N.Y.: Channel Press [1960]), p. 197-202. On John Brown in the antislavery movement, 1850-59. [5257

BENJAMIN HARRISON (1833-1901). Letters of Benjamin Harrison. Edited by William B. Miller. Presbyt. Hist. Soc., Jour., 37:143-54 (Sep 1959). notes. Letters to John Alexander Anderson, a college friend, dated in Cincinnati and elsewhere; the early letters dealing mainly with the writer's legal studies, love affairs, and other interests; the later ones mainly with law and politics. [5258

PAUL A. VARG. "... carving of the Chinese melon." John Arthur Garraty, ed., The unforgettable Americans (Great Neck, N.Y.: Channel Press [1960]), p. 179-82. On William Woodville Rockhill (1853-1914), his early life and his service in the Department of State, eventually as U.S. Minister to China. [5259

CARL HAVERLIN. Lincoln and his hope for a just and lasting peace [1854-65]. Ralph G. Newman, ed., Lincoln for the ages (Garden City, N.Y.: Doubleday, 1860), p. 325-31. [5260

FRANKLIN RAY SHIRLEY. The rhetoric of Zebulon B[aird] Vance [1830-94]: Tarheel spokesman. Ann Arbor: University Microfilms, 1959 [i. e. 1960]. Positive microfilm of typescript. [411] leave. Thesis--Univ. of Florida. Abstracted: Dissert. abstracts, 20:2963 (Jan). On his speechmaking in North Carolina and national politics, 1854-94. [5261

EARL WELLINGTON WILEY. Abraham Lincoln: his emergence as the voice of the people [1854-65]. Speech Association of America, A history and criticism of American public address, ed. William Norwood Brigance, 2d ed. (N.Y.: Russell & Russell, 1960), 2:859-77. bibliog., notes. [5262

OSCAR FRITIOF ANDER. Lincoln and the founders of Augustana College. O. Fritiof Ander, ed., Lincoln images: Augustana College centennial essays (Rock Island, Ill.: Augustana College Library, 1960), p. 1-22. ports., views. On his associations with Swedes in Illinois, and their political support of him and the Republican Party, 1855-60. Reprinted (with notes added): Swed. pioneer hist. quar., 11:45-72 (Apr). ports., views. notes. [5263

REGINALD WRIGHT KAUFFMAN. Pine trees and pistols. New Eng. teacher, 1(1):13, 16-17, 21 (Oct 1953). On the national political activities of Sargeant S. Prentiss and Jonathan Cilley, emigrants from Maine to Mississippi and Georgia, middle 1850s. [5264

ARTHUR WALLACE PEACH. Justin Smith Morrill [1810-98]. Vt. Hist. Soc., News and notes, 7:74-8 (Jun 1956). port., view. On his service to Vermont and the nation in the U.S. House of Representatives, 1855-67, and the U.S. Senate, 1867-98. [5265

WALLACE F. WORKMASTER. Grover Cleveland: American Victorian. Historian, 22:185-96 (Feb). notes. On the "Victorian" quality of his personal habits and ethical standards, 1855-93. [5266

HENRY G. ROBERTS. James G. Blaine [1830-93]. Speech Association of America, A history and criticism of American public address, ed. William Norwood Brigance, 2d ed. (N.Y.: Russell & Russell, 1960), 2:878-90. bibliog., notes. On the oratorical and rhetorical characteristics of his public speaking as a national political leader, 1856-84. [5267

REX W. STRICKLAND. P[hilemon] T[homas] Herbert [1825-64]: antebellum resident of El Paso. Password, 5:43-53 (Apr). notes. On his involvement, while a Representative from California, in the killing of a waiter in a Washington hotel, his acquittal of a charge of murder, his political ostracism by former California supporters, his removal to Texas to practice law in El Paso and Mesilla, and his service in the C.S. Army, 1856-64. [5268

LAURA A. WHITE. Was Charles Sumner shamming, 1856-1859? New Eng. quar., 33:291-324 (Sep). notes. On the belief that, when assaulted by Preston Brooks, Sumner was "both a coward in meeting the attack and a hypocrite in feigning illness for three years after a complete recovery from wounds which were never serious." [5269

DAVID LINDSEY. "Sunset" Cox, irrepressible Democrat. Detroit: Wayne State Univ. Press, 1959. xx, 323, [2] p. port. bibliog. (p. 302-13), notes (p. 269-301). On Samuel Sullivan Cox as Representative from Ohio, 1857-65, and from New York, 1868-89. [5270

MORT REIS LEWIS. Abraham Lincoln: storyteller. Ralph G. Newman, ed., Lincoln for the ages (Garden City, N.Y.: Doubleday, 1960), p. 130-34. On his humor as one of the "strongest weapons" in his politics, 1858-65. [5271

RALPH WEBSTER YARBOROUGH. Lincoln as a liberal statesman [1858-65]. Ralph G. Newman, ed., Lincoln for the ages (Garden City, N.Y.: Doubleday, 1960), p. 279-83. [5272

DOROTHY ROSE BLUMBERG. Florence Kelley [1859-1932]: revolutionary reformer. Monthly rev., 11: 234-42 (Nov 1959). notes. On her various activities as a social worker, a reformer, and a Socialist. [5273

MARY EMILY ROBERTSON CAMPBELL. Tennessee's Congressional delegation in the sectional crisis of 1859-1860. Tenn. hist. quar., 19:348-71 (Dec). notes. On the 2 Senators and 10 Representatives from Tennessee in the 36th Congress, 1st session. [5274

VICTOR HICKEN. John A. McClernand and the House speakership struggle of 1859. Ill. State Hist. Soc., Jour., 53: 162-78 (summer). ports., views. notes. [5275

BOYD BLYNN STUTLER. Alexander R[obinson] Boteler's sketches of John Brown. Jefferson Co. Hist. Soc., Mag., 25 (1959): 32-8. ports. notes. On 4 sketches made in 1859 by a resident of Shepherdstown, with a brief biography of the artist (1815-92). [5276

AVARD TENNYSON FAIRBANKS. The face of Abraham Lincoln. Ralph G. Newman, ed., Lincoln for the ages (Garden City, N.Y.: Doubleday, 1960), p. 160-65. On descriptions and portraits of Lincoln, 1860-65. [5277

RICHARD BARKSDALE HARWELL. Lincoln and the South. Ralph G. Newman, ed., Lincoln for the ages (Garden City, N.Y.: Doubleday, 1960), p. 203-7. On Southern "scorn and hate" for Lincoln, 1860-65. [5278

KATHERINE (McCOOK) KNOX. "Healy's Lincoln no. 1." [Enlarged version. Wash., 1959. 12] p. ports. 23 x 11 cm. 1st ed. 1956. Portrait painted by George Peter Alexander Healey at Springfield in Nov. 1860, and the author's successful efforts to prove its authenticity, to disseminate colored prints of it, and to have it engraved on a stamp. [5279

DAVID LINDSEY. A. Lincoln/Jefferson Davis: the house divided. Cleveland: H. Allen [1960. 12], 186, [1] p. ports. bibliog. (p. 185-6), notes (p. 181-4). (Men and issues in American history.) Comparison of the 2 men with respect to their ideas and beliefs concerning society and government and their treatment of 11 "problems and issues," 1860-65. [5280

EDWARD JOHN MUZIK. Victor L[ouis] Berger [1860-1929]: a biography. Ann Arbor: University Microfilms, 1960. Positive microfilm of typescript. [486] leaves. Thesis--Northwestern Univ. Abstracted: Dissert. abstracts, 21:1027-8 (Nov). On his life in Milwaukee, 1881-1929, his membership in the Socialist Party of America and in labor organizations, his enmity toward the I. W. W. and the Communists, his terms in Congress, and his newspapers. [5281

SHELBY FOOTE. Lincoln goes to Washington. Ralph G. Newman, ed., Lincoln for the ages (Garden City, N.Y.: Doubleday, 1960), p. 166-70. On his journey from Springfield to Washington, 11-23 Feb. 1861. [5282

ROBERT STORY HARPER. The unpopular Mr. Lincoln [during the Civil War]. Ralph G. Newman, ed., Lincoln for the ages (Garden City, N.Y.: Doubleday, 1960), p. 307-11. [5283

VICTOR SEARCHER. Lincoln's journey to greatness: a factual account of the twelve-day inaugural trip [Springfield to Washington, 11-23 Feb. 1861]. Phila.: Winston [1960]. viii, 279 p. facsims., maps, ports., table, views. notes. [5284

FRANK EVERSON VANDIVER. Abraham Lincoln and Jefferson Davis [1861-65]. Ralph G. Newman, ed., Lincoln for the ages (Garden City, N.Y.: Doubleday, 1960), p. 284-8. [5285

JOHN WALTON. Character and politics: a portrait of Joseph L[ittle] Bristow [1861-1944], native of Kentucky. Filson Club hist. quar., 34: 256-63 (Jul). notes. On his life in Kansas as farmer and journalist, his service as Fourth Assistant Postmaster General and later as Senator from Kansas (1897-1918), and his austere life as a farmer in Fairfax County, Va. [5286

GIDEON WELLES (1802-78). Administration of Abraham Lincoln [1861-64]. Selected essays by Gideon Welles: Lincoln's administration, ed. Albert Mordell (N.Y.: Twayne Publishers, 1960), p. 47-177. From The galaxy, Jan., Feb., Oct.-Dec. 1877. Reminiscences by his Secretary of the Navy, mainly of political and military personalities in Washington from the beginning of Lincoln's first administration till the Election of 1864. [5287

ROY MEREDITH. The photogenic Mr. Lincoln. Ralph G. Newman, ed., Lincoln for the ages (Garden City, N.Y.: Doubleday, 1960), p. 319-24. On photographs of Lincoln, 1862-65. [5288

MILTON REES MERRILL. Reed Smoot [1862-1941], Apostle-Senator. Utah hist. quar., 28:342-9 (Oct). ports. On his dual career as an official of the Church of Christ of Latter-Day Saints and a leader in Utah and national Republican politics. [5289

WAYLAND MAXFIELD PARRISH & ALFRED DWIGHT HUSTON. Robert G. Ingersoll [1833-99]. Speech Association of America, A history and criticism of American public address, ed. William Norwood Brigance, 2d ed. (N.Y.: Russell & Russell, 1960), 1:363-86. bibliog., notes. On his position "in the top rank of American speakers as lecturer, lawyer, political campaigner, and speaker of occasional addresses," 1863-99, particularly as "no respecter of parsons." [5290

MILTON LOMASK. Andrew Johnson: President on trial. N.Y.: Farrar, Straus [1960]. viii, 376 p. views. bibliog. (p. 349-66), notes. On Andrew Johnson (1808-75) as Vice President and President of the United States, 1864-69; with some account of his earlier career in Tennessee politics, particularly as Governor of Tennessee, and his later service as Senator from Tennessee. [5291

HARRY X. BOOSEL. Abraham Lincoln and 1873. Numismatic scrapbook, 26:3457-60 (Nov). medal. On the bronze medal voted by Congress in 1871 and executed by A. C. Paquet for George F. Robinson, who had saved the life of William H. Seward in 1865 by interfering, with injuries to himself, in a murderous assault by Lewis Paine, a confederate of John Wilkes Booth. [5292

ARNOLD FRANCIS GATES. The nation mourns. Ralph G. Newman, ed., Lincoln for the ages (Garden City, N.Y.: Doubleday, 1960), p. 405-9. On funeral services for Lincoln held in Washington and Springfield, 15 Apr. - 4 May 1865. [5293

SARAH PORTER JOYNER. The last chapter of the Confederacy. [Jacksonville, Fla.: Evergreen Press, 1959.] 20 p. ports., views. On the life of Jefferson Davis from the fall of Richmond till his death, 1865-99, and some of the monuments to him. [5294

MARTIN NELSON McGEARY. Gifford Pinchot [1865-1946], forester-politician. Princeton, N.J.: Princeton Univ. Press,

1960. xi, [1], 481 p. bibliog. (p. 467-71), notes (p. 437-65). On his early life and schooling, his study of forestry and work as a forester, his service as Chief of the Division of Forestry of the Department of the Interior from 1898 till his dismissal by President Taft in 1910, his activities in the Republican and Progressive Parties, and his service as Governor of Pennsylvania (1923-27, 1931-35). [5295

RANDLE BOND TRUETT. Mr. Lincoln goes to the theatre. Ralph G. Newman, ed., Lincoln for the ages (Garden City, N.Y.: Doubleday, 1960), p. 400-404. On his attendance at a performance of Our American cousin at Ford's Theater and his assassination by John Wilkes Booth, 14 Apr. 1865. [5296

MARK ALBERT VAN DOREN. A playwright looks at Lincoln. Ralph G. Newman, ed., Lincoln for the ages (Garden City, N.Y.: Doubleday, 1960), p. 395-9. On the author's play, The last days of Lincoln (1959). [5297

RANDLE BOND TRUETT. Lincoln in philately. Wash., 1959. [4], 35 p. facsims., ports., table. On "all philatelic material, both U.S. and foreign, that bear the likeness of Abraham Lincoln," 1866-1959. [5298

ELTING ELMORE MORISON. Turmoil and tradition: a study of the life and times of Henry L[ewis] Stimson [1867-1950]. Boston: Houghton, Mifflin, 1960. xii, 686 p. ports., views. bibliog. (p. 657-62), notes. On his early life and schooling, his legal practice in New York, and his activities in New York and national politics. [5299

HOWARD WILSON ALLEN. Miles Poindexter [1868-1946]: a political biography. Ann Arbor: University Microfilms, 1959 [i. e. 1960]. Positive microfilm of typescript. [662] leaves. Thesis--Univ. of Washington. Abstracted: Dissert. abstracts, 20: 4639-40 (Jun). On his activities in Washington State and national politics, 1892-1928. [5300

MELVIN L. HAYES. Mr. Lincoln runs for President. N.Y.: Citadel Press [1960]. 352 p. cartoons, facsims., ports., views. bibliog. (p. 333-45). On his campaign for the Presidency and his activities before taking office, as reported in contemporary newspapers, Oct. 1859-Mar. 1861. [5301

J. H. MOSELEY. Sixty years in Congress and twenty-eight out. N.Y.: Vantage Press [1960. 4], 99 p. ports., double table. Biographical sketches of the 28 Negroes who since 1870 have served in the U.S. Senate or the U.S. House of Representatives. [5302

GAYLON LORAY CALDWELL. Utah's first Presidential candidate. Utah hist. quar., 28:326-41 (Oct). ports. notes. On Parley Packer Christensen (1872-1954), nominee of the Farmer-Labor Party in its convention of 1920. [5303

FRED L. ISRAEL. Nevada's Key Pittman [1872-1960]. Ann Arbor: University Microfilms, 1959 [i. e. 1960]. Positive microfilm of typescript. [355] leaves. Thesis--Columbia Univ. Abstracted: Dissert. abstracts, 20:3927 (Apr). On his legal practice in Seattle, Nome, and Tonopah, 1892-1912, and his service as Senator from Nevada, 1912-40. [5304

RONALD SCHAFFER. Jeannette Rankin [born 1880], Progressive-isolationist. Ann Arbor: University Microfilms, 1959 [i. e. 1960]. Positive microfilm of typescript. 2, 272 leaves. bibliog. (leaves 262-72. Thesis--Princeton Univ. Abstracted: Dissert. abstracts, 20:4386-7 (May). On her career as social settlement worker, suffragist, U.S. Representative from Montana, agent "for pro-labor and for anti-war organizations," and supporter of the Townsend Plan. [5305

ROBERT MARION LA FOLLETTE (1855-1925). A personal narrative of political experience: La Follett's autobiography. With a foreword by Allan Nevins. Madison: Univ. of Wisconsin Press, 1960. x, [2], 349 p. port. 1st ed. 1912. On the author's activities in Wisconsin and national politics, 1881-1912. [5306

CARROLL POLLOCK LAHMAN. Robert M. La Follette [1855-1925]. Speech Association of America, A history and criticism of American public address, ed. William Norwood Brigance, 2d ed. (N.Y.: Russell & Russell, 1960), 2:942-67. bibliog., notes. On the oratorical and rhetorical characteristics of his speeches in Wisconsin and national politics, 1881-1925. [5307

ROBERT M. ANCELL, JR., & WILLIAM W. STANHOPE. Patrick Jay Hurley [1883-1963]: soldier, statesman, diplomat. N. M., 38(9):12-17, 35-7 (Sep). ports., view. On his early life and legal studies, his practice of law and work as National Attorney for the Choctaw Nation, his Army record in World War I and service as Secretary of War from 1929 to 1933, his diplomatic career in and after World War II, and his removal to New Mexico. [5308

JOSEPH WILLIAM MARTIN, JR. (born 1884). My first fifty years in politics. As told to Robert J. Donovan. N.Y.: McGraw-Hill [1960. 8], 261, [2] p. cartoon, ports. (1 double), views (1 double). On the author's early life in North Attleboro, Mass., his activities in Massachusetts politics, and his service since 1925 as a Representative from Massachusetts. [5309

HEROLD TRUSLOW ROSS. Albert J. Beveridge [1862-1927]. Speech Association of America, A history and criticism of American public address, ed. William Norwood Brigance, 2d ed. (N.Y.: Russell & Russell, 1960), 2:919-41. bibliog., notes. On the oratorical and rhetorical characteristics of his public speaking, mainly political, 1884-1926. [5310

ELEANOR BUTLER (ALEXANDER) ROOSEVELT. Day before yesterday: the reminiscences of Mrs. Theodore Roosevelt, Jr. Garden City, N.Y.: Doubleday [1959]. 478 p. facsims., ports., views. Mainly on the activities of Theodore Roosevelt, Jr. (1887-1944), whom she married in 1910, bond salesman, Army officer in World War I, member of the New York Assembly, Assistant Secretary of the Navy, Governor of Puerto Rico, Governor General of the Philippines, commanding officer of the 26th Infantry in World War II; with some account of his early life in New York and of the author's early years there and in Paris. [5311

WOODROW WILSON (1856-1924). A young professor in search of a job. [Edited by] Lionel H. Laing. University of Michigan, Dept. of Political Science, The status and prospects of political science as a discipline (Ann Arbor [1960]), p. 50-54. Two letters to James B. Angell, President of the University of Michigan, 7 and 15 Nov. 1887, requesting Angell's aid in obtaining employment by the U.S. Government in Washington, preferably in the Department of State. [5312

MILDRED HOUGHTON COMFORT. John Foster Dulles [1888-1959], peacemaker: a biographical sketch of the former Secretary of State. Minneapolis: T. S. Denison [1960]. 202 p. port. Mainly on his service as Secretary of State, 1953-59. [5313

DEANE HELLER & DAVID HELLER. John Foster Dulles [1888-1959], soldier for peace. N.Y.: Holt, Rinehart, and Winston [1960. 8], 328 p. port. On his career as "the world's highest paid lawyer" and as Secretary of State. [5314

MYRON G. PHILLIPS. William Jennings Bryan [1860-1925]. Speech Association of America, A history and criticism of American public address, ed. William Norwood Brigance, 2d ed. (N.Y.: Russell & Russell, 1960), 2:891-918. bibliog., notes. On the oratorical and rhetorical characteristics of his public speaking as a Nebraska lawyer and a national political leader, 1888-1925. [5315

JOHN PETER ALTGELD (1847-1902). The mind and spirit of John Peter Altgeld: selected writings and addresses. Edited by Henry M. Christman. Urbana: Univ. of Illinois Press, 1960. [6], 183 p. Ten speeches and other documents, 1889-97, on the administration of justice in Chicago, crime there, labor, the gold standard, the Pullman strike, and other subjects; with an appended memorial address by Clarence Darrow (Chicago, 20 Apr. 1902) and a biographical sketch by the editor. [5316

JOHN K. MAHON. Benjamin Franklin Tracy [1830-1915], Secretary of the Navy, 1889-1893. N.-Y. Hist. Soc. quar., 44:178-201 (Apr). ports., views. notes. [5317

THOMAS MARTIN. Dynasty: the Longs of Louisiana. N.Y.: Putnam [1960]. 318 p. double map. bibliog. (p. 311-12). On the activities of Huey Pierce Long, Jr. (1893-1936), his brother Earl, and members of their family in Louisiana and national politics. [5318

H. WAYNE MORGAN. Governor McKinley's misfortune: the Walker-McKinley Fund of 1893. Ohio hist. quar., 69:103-20 (Apr). notes. On the embarrassment of William McKinley, Governor of Ohio, when notes countersigned by him for Robert Walker were presented for payment after Walker's failure in business at Youngstown; the secret collection by 4 of McKinley's friends of funds sufficient to meet the obligation; the lack of evidence that any contributions were made to obtain political favors; and the probably good effect of this misfortune upon his political popularity. [5319

PASCHAL REEVES. Thomas S[taples] Martin [1847-1919]: committee statesman. Va. mag. hist. and biog., 68: 344-64 (Jul). port., views. On his activities and habits during his years as Senator from Virginia, 1895-1919; with some account of his earlier life. [5320

PAUL WILBUR GLAD. The trumpet soundeth: William Jennings Bryan [1860-1925] and his Democracy, 1896-1912. [Lincoln:] Univ. of Nebraska Press, 1960. xii, [2], 242 p. cartoons, facsims., ports., views. bibliog. (p. 219-30), notes (p. 179-217). On his activities in Nebraska and national politics during these years; with some account of his early life in Salem, Ill., and his work as a Nebraska lawyer. [5321

BOYCE HOUSE (1896-1961). Bryan the orator ["probably the greatest the nation has ever seen"]. Ill. State Hist. Soc., Jour., 53:266-82 (autumn). cartoon, port. notes. On political speeches delivered in 1896, 1904, and 1912. [5322

CLAUDE PEPPER (born 1900). Claude Pepper: United States Senator, a personal statement of his philosophy and background. Fla. handbook, 1949-50, p. 133-4. port. On his early life in Alabama, his legal practice in Florida since 1925, and his activities and doctrines as Senator from Florida. [5323

RALPH G. MARTIN & ED PLAUT. Front runner, dark horse. Garden City, N.Y.: Doubleday, 1960. 473 p. Biographies and analyses of John Fitzgerald Kennedy (born 1917) and William Stuart Symington (born 1901) as "contrasting classic political prototypes campaigning for the presidency of the United States." [5324

PAUL ISELIN WELLMAN. Stuart Symington: portrait of a man with a mission. Garden City, N.Y.: Doubleday, 1960. 283 p. On William Stuart Symington (born 1901), his early life and service as an officer in World War I, his studies at Yale, his work as a manufacturer of electrical equipment in New York and as owner of the Emerson Electric Manufacturing Company, St. Louis, and his activities in Missouri and national politics, particularly his services as Senator from Missouri since 1952. [5325

DEXTER PERKINS. "... a statesman of the first order." John Arthur Garraty, ed., The unforgettable Americans (Great Neck, N.Y.: Channel Press [1960]), p. 308-11. On the activities of Charles Evans Hughes in New York and national politics, 1907-41. [5326

STEWART JOHONNOT OLIVER ALSOP. Nixon & Rockefeller: a double portrait. Garden City, N.Y.: Doubleday, 1960. 240 p. On the political activities of Richard Milhous Nixon (born 1913) and Nelson Aldrich Rockefeller (born 1908); with some account of their early lives. [5327

JOE ALEX MORRIS. Nelson [Aldrich] Rockefeller [born 1908]: a biography. N.Y.: Harper [1960. 14], 369 p. ports., views. On his early life and studies, his work as a banker and as manager of Rockefeller Center, New York City, and his activities in New York and national politics. [5328

JAMES POLING. The Rockefeller record: a political self-portrait. N.Y.: Crowell [1960]. xi, 177 p. bibliog. (p. vii-viii). On Nelson Aldrich Rockefeller (born 1908), his early life and studies, his work as a banker and as manager of Rockefeller Center, New York City, and his activities in New York and national politics. [5329

FRANK McNAUGHTON. Mennen Williams of Michigan, fighter for progress. N.Y.: Oceana Publications [1960]. viii, 246, [2] p. On Gerhard Mennen Williams (born 1911), his early life and stidies, and his activities in Michigan and national politics, particularly as Governor of Michigan from 1948 to 1960. [5330

ERNST FRAENKEL. Das deutsche Wilsonbild. Jahrbuch für Amerikastudien, 5:66-120. notes. On the German "image" of Woodrow Wilson since 1912. [5331

WILLIAM COSTELLO. The facts about Nixon: an unauthorized biography. N.Y.: Viking Press, 1960. xiii, 306 p. bibliog. (p. 295-7). On the early life of Richard Milhous Nixon (born 1913), his legal studies, his work as a lawyer in California, his service as a Navy officer in World War II, and his activities in California, and national politics. [5332

CARY TRAVERS GRAYSON (1878-1938). Woodrow Wilson: an intimate memoir. N.Y.: Holt, Rinehart, and Winston [1960]. xi, [3], 143 p. port. Recollections (1924) of the author's daily association with the President as his "personal physician and naval aide," 1913-21. [5333

BELA KORNITZER. The real Nixon: an intimate biography. N.Y.: Rand McNally [1960]. 352 p. facsims., ports., views. On Richard Milhous Nixon (born 1913), his early life, his legal studies and practice of law, his service as a Navy officer in World War II, and his activities in California and national politics. [5334

EARL MAZO. Richard [Milhous] Nixon [born 1913]: a political and personal portrait. N.Y.: Harper [1959]. viii, [2], 309, [1] p. Another edition: Richard Nixon: a political and personal portrait ... specially revised by the author to include new material covering Mr. Nixon's recent activities. N.Y.: Avon Book Division, Hearst Corporation [1960]. 270 p. On his activities in California and national politics since 1945; with some account of his early life in southern California, his studies in Whittier College and Duke University Law School, and his legal practice in Whittier, Calif. [5335

WHY Harvard men go into politics. Harvard alumni bul., 58: 637, 643-6 (19 May 1956). ports. Statements by Leverett Saltonstall ('14), Christian A. Herter ('15), Joseph S. Clark, Jr. ('23), Robert F. Bradford ('23), John F. Kennedy ('40), and Torbert H. Macdonald ('40); with portraits of 11 Harvard men in politics, from John Adams to Franklin D. Roosevelt. [5336

JOSEPH WESTON McCARTHY. The remarkable Kennedys. N.Y.: Dial Press, 1960. 190, [2] p. On John Fitzgerald Kennedy (born 1917); with occasional mention of other children of Joseph P. and Rose (Fitzgerald) Kennedy. [5337

JOACHIM FRANZ JOESTEN. Präsident Kennedy. Stuttgart: Deutsche Verlags-Anstalt [1960]. 233, [3] p. port. On John Fitzgerald Kennedy from his birth in 1917 to his election as President in 1960. [5338

BERNARD BELLUSH. An interpretation of Franklin D. Roosevelt. Donald Sheehan & Harold C. Syrett, eds., Essays in American historiography: papers presented in honor of Allan Nevins (N.Y.: Columbia Univ. Press, 1960), p. 287-309. bibliog., notes. On his career in New York and national politics, 1920-41, and his leadership of "a nation economically destitute, psychologically despondent, and politically discouraged"; with a review of the biographies of Roosevelt and the histories of his administrations. [5339

MADISON KUHN. "... the conscience of the Supreme Court." John Arthur Garraty, ed., The unforgettable Americans (Great Neck, N.Y.: Channel Press [1960]), p. 311-16. On the activities of Frank Murphy in Michigan and national politics, 1920s-1949, particularly his service as an Associate Justice of the U.S. Supreme Court. [5340

EDWARD ALEXANDER ROGGE. The miracle of '48--twenty-six years in forming. South. speech jour., 25:264-72 (summer). notes. On Harry S. Truman as an impromptu political speaker, 1922-48. [5341

VREST ORTON. Calvin Coolidge's unique Vermont inauguration, the facts winnowed from the chaff: the authentic account of the swearing in of Calvin Coolidge as 30th President of the United States by his father at the Coolidge Homestead, Plymouth Notch, Vermont, in 1923. Rutland, Vt.: Tuttle Pub. Co. [1960]. 93, [3] p. facsim., ports., views. bibliog. (p. 87-90), notes. [5342

RICHARD BRILEY III. Death of the Kingfish. Dallas: Triangle Pub. Co. [1960]. 139 p. ports. On the activities of Huey Pierce Long (1893-1935) in Louisiana and national politics, 1928-35, and his assassination by Dr. Carl A. Weiss, Jr. [5343

STAN OPOTOWSKY. The Longs of Louisiana. N.Y.: Dutton, 1960. 271 p. ports. On the activities of Huey Pierce Long (1893-1935), his brother Earl, and his son, Russell L. Long (born 1918), in Louisiana and national politics since 1928. [5344

THOMAS HARRY WILLIAMS. The Gentleman from Louisiana: demagogue or democrat? Jour. South. hist., 26:3-21 (Feb). notes. On the motives and methods of Huey P. Long, Jr., in Louisiana and national politics as viewed by the people of Louisiana, 1928-34; with an effort to define his political ideas in terms of various ideologies. Based largely upon "interviews, many of them tape-recorded, with dozens of Huey P. Long and anti-Long leaders." [5345

GEORGE EDWARD ALLEN. Presidents who have known me. N.Y.: Simon and Schuster [1960]. xi, 290 p. 1st ed.

1950. Facetious recollections and anecdotes of Roosevelt, Truman, and Eisenhower, 1929-60, by a political journalist. [5346

EDWARD O. GUERRANT. Herbert Hoover, Franklin Roosevelt: comparisons and contrasts [in the Presidency, 1929-45]. Cleveland: H. Allen [1960? 12], 114, [2] p. ports. bibliog. (p. 113-14), notes (p. 107-12). (Men and issues in American history.) [5347

ERNEST GORDON BORMANN. This is Huey P. Long talking. Jour. broadcasting, 2:111-22 (spring 1958). notes. On his radio broadcasts, 1931-35, addressed mainly to his Louisiana constituents. [5348

DWIGHT MacDONALD. Henry Wallace: the man and the myth. N.Y.: Vanguard Press [1948]. 187 p. notes (p. 183-7). Critical review of his political career, 1932-47. [5349

JOHN A. WOODS. Roosevelt and modern America. N.Y.: Macmillan [1960, c1959]. 192 p. bibliog. (p. 184-6). (Teach yourself history library.) On Franklin Delano Roosevelt in the Campaign of 1932 and as President, 1932-45, with a chapter on his life before 1932. [5350

DONALD BRUCE JOHNSON. The Republican Party and Wendell [Lewis] Willkie [1892-1944]. Urbana: Univ. of Illinois Press, 1960. ix, [3], 354 p. bibliog. (p. 327-36), notes. Based on thesis--Univ. of Illinois, 1952. Deals mainly with his activities in national politics, 1939-44, particularly in the Campaign of 1940. [5351

JAMES H. JONAS. The third man in Utah politics. Utah Acad. Sciences, Proc., 37:103-25. diagrs., map, tables. bibliog., notes. On the trend of population in Utah since 1940 and its relation to the activities of William A. Dawson in Utah and national politics, 1946-59. [5352

VICTOR LASKY. John F. Kennedy: what's behind the image? Wash.: Free World Press [1960. 8], 300 p. Unfavorable account of his political activities since 1947. [5353

WILLIAM A. REUBEN. The Honorable Mr. Nixon. [N.Y.:] Action Books [1958]. v, [3], 138, [2], 72, [2] p. 1st ed. 1956. On his conduct of the investigation of charges of Communism against Alger Hiss, 1948-50. [5354

KARL M. SCHMIDT. Henry A[gard] Wallace [born 1888]: quixotic crusade, 1948. [Syracuse:] Syracuse Univ. Press, 1960. xii, [4], 362, [1] p. cartoons, ports., tables, views. bibliog. (p. 336-47). (Men and movements series.) On his campaign for the Presidency on the Progressive ticket of 1948. [5355

DOUGLAS PRICE. A note on some recent campaign biographies. Pol. science quar., 75:420-23 (Sep). Commentary on 8 biographies of individuals competing in 1960 for nomination as candidates for the Presidency. [5356

Political Theory

VERNA M. HALL. Christian history of the Constitution of the United States of America: a compilation by Verna M. Hall. Edited by Joseph Allan Montgomery. San Francisco: American Christian Constitution Press [1960. 4], vi, [6], vii-xiv, 481 p. coats of arms, diagrs., facsims., ports., views. bibliog. (p. 430-32). First volume (1607-1782) of a projected 3-volume work consisting of contemporary documents and excerpts from documents indicating that "In proportion as Americans let go of faith in the absolute power of God, they have accepted the belief in an all powerful State" and embodying the result of the compiler's 20-year search "for the fundamental reason why Americans embarked upon a path of socialism, and why Americans continue to travel this ever-increasing and widening road." Contents.--The Christian idea of man and government.--American background in England.--Local self-government. [5357

GILMAN MARSTON OSTRANDER. The rights of man in America, 1606-1861. Columbia: Univ. of Missouri Press [1960]. xiii, 356 p. bibliog. (p. 319-46). In 3 sections: "Liberty," "Equality," and "Brotherhood." [5358

RICHARD L. PERRY, ed. Sources of our liberties: documentary origins of individual liberties in the United States Constitution and Bill of Rights. [N.Y.?] American Bar Foundation [1959]. xxii, [2], 456 p. bibliog. (p. 441-5), notes. Thirty-two English and American documents or groups of documents, from Magna Carta (1215) to the Bill of Rights (1791), including several colonial charters and State constitutions and various other American documents, 1606-1701, 1765-91; with introductions. [5359

MILTON CONOVER. American political thought [1609-1959]. John A. Abbo, Political thought: men and ideas (Westminster, Md.: Newman Press, 1960), p. 385-425. notes [5360

WOLF-DIETER MARSCH. Christlicher Glaube und demokratisches Ethos, dargestellt am Lebenswerk Abraham Lincolns: ein Beitrag aus der Geschichte von America [1620-1865]. Hamburg: Im Furche-Verlag [1958]. 246, [2] p. notes (p. 170-229). On the interrelations of the theological, the historical, and the political, especially in Lincoln's time and as exemplified by his life and activities. [5361

CHARLES MAURICE WILTSE. The Jeffersonian tradition in American democracy. N.Y.: Hill and Wang [1960]. xii, 273, [2] p. notes. (American century series, AC28.) 1st ed. 1935. On the development of "political liberalism" in America, 1634-1935, and the influence of Jefferson upon the American "democratic tradition." [5362

FREDERICK CLIFTON PACKARD, JR., ed. They spoke for democracy: classic statements of the American way. N.Y.: Scribner [1958]. 158 p. ports. Texts or parts of texts of 13 addresses, 1735-1951. [5363

HAROLD W. CURRIE. [Letter to the Editor.] Wm. and Mary quar., 17:433 (Jul). Evidence that political leaders in Massachusetts "were thinking in terms of no taxation without representation as early as January 1764." [5364

RANDOLPH GREENFIELD ADAMS (1892-1951). Political ideas of the American Revolution: Britannic-American contributions to the problem of imperial organization, 1765 to 1775. ... Third edition, with commentary by Merrill Jensen. N.Y.: Barnes & Noble [1958]. vii, 216 p. bibliog. (p. 201-11), notes. Based on thesis--Trinity College, 1919. Includes chapters on "John Adams as a Britannic statesman" and "The legal theories of James Wilson." 1st ed. 1922. Present edition (from 2d, 1939) incorporates "numerous emendations which the late author had prepared or approved," and adds a note and commentary by Jensen (p. 1-31) "in order to bring the discussion up to date in the light of recent historical research." [5365

RICHARD AIKEN & JOHN AIKEN. A footnote to "No taxation without representation" [1765]. Social studies, 51: 224-8 (Nov). Argument that this slogan conceals the "real" reasons for opposition to the Stamp Act. [5366

SAUL KUSSIEL PADOVER, ed. The world of the Founding Fathers: their basic ideas on freedom and self-government. N.Y.: T. Yoseloff [1960]. 648 p. facsims., ports., views. bibliog. (p. 629-38), notes. Reprinted excerpts from writings by 31 "fathers," 1765-96. [5367

CHESTER JAMES ANTIEAU. Natural rights and the Founding Fathers--the Virginians. Wash. and Lee law rev., 17:43-79 (spring). notes. Evidence that "the doctrine was not limited to the select few who directed Virginia's destinies, but was widely held and continually expressed by the popular assemblages throughout the Commonwealth during Revolutionary days," 1766-98, and that it included rights of "conscience and religion," "life, liberty, and the pursuit of happiness," "the right of property," "the right to govern and tax themselves," "freedom of communication," and, debatably, certain other rights. [5368

AMERICAN FOUNDATION FOR CONTINUING EDUCATION. Readings in American democracy. Edited by Gerald Stourzh and Ralph Lerner. N.Y.: Oxford Univ. Press [1959]. ix, 481 p. Contemporary documents and secondary discussions, 1774-1950s, arranged topically. First printed in 1957 as a collection of reproductions from printed and typewritten copy "for use in discussion programs for the education of adults," sponsored by the American Foundation for Political Education. Now reprinted in letterpress by the American Foundation for Continuing Education, with added titles and with substitutions for some of the titles included in the previous printing. [5369

ELISHA P. DOUGLASS. German intellectuals and the American Revolution [1775-83]. Wm. and Mary quar., 17: 200-218 (Apr). notes. Deals particularly with their interest in the political ideas and political issues of the Revolution. [5370

CARL LOTUS BECKER (1873-1945). What is still living in the political philosophy of Thomas Jefferson? Carl L. Becker, Detachment and the writing of history: essays and letters of Carl L. Becker, ed. Phil S. Snyder (Ithaca: Cornell Univ. Press [1958]), p. 214-40. notes. Address (1943). [5371

ROBERT CARTER PITTMAN. Equality versus liberty: the eternal conflict [from the Declaration of Independence to the present]. Am. Bar Assoc. jour., 46:873-80 (Aug). port., views. notes. Printed separately: Equality v. liberty: the eternal conflict. [Richmond: Virginia Commission on Constitutional Government, 1960.] 27 p. notes (p. 25-7). (Statements and papers expounding the role of the States in their relation to the central government, 6.) [5372

JAMES BURNHAM. Congress and the American tradition [1787-1958]. Chicago: Henry Regnery Co., 1959. x, 363 p. notes. A study in political theory, concerned with the checks and balances in American government. [5373

CARL B. CONE. Ideas that made the Constitution. Ky. law jour., 48:5-25 (fall 1959). notes. On "the idea of a higher law which went beyond the common law," the idea of a constitution as distinguished from a legislative act, and the idea that sovereignty resides in the people. [5374

H. B. MAYO. Majority rule and the Constitution in Canada and the United States [1787-1956]. West, pol. quar., 11:49-62 (Mar 1957). notes. [5375

GOTTFRIED DIETZE. The Federalist: a classic on federalism and free government. Baltimore: Johns Hopkins Press [1960]. ix, 378 p. bibliog. (p. 355-8), notes. On this publication (1788) "as a classic on federalism and constitutional democracy ... as a treatise on a broadened concept of federalism, as a classic on free government in peace and security," and its influence in America and abroad. [5376

MAYNARD SMITH. Reason, passion, and political freedom in The Federalist [1788]. Jour, politics, 22:525-44 (Aug). notes. [5377

GERHART D. WIEBE. An historical setting for television journalism. Jour. broadcasting, 1:33-8 (winter 1957). On "the continuing competition and compromise between the ideal of simple democracy and the practical necessity of republican delegation of authority" since 1788, and its bearing on "the question of whether television cameras should have access to legislative, executive and judicial proceedings." [5378

DAVID HERBERT DONALD. An excess of democracy: the American Civil War and the social process. Oxford: Clarendon Press, 1960. 22, [1] p. Inaugural lecture, Oxford University, 2 May 1960. On the war as the "outgrowth of social processes which affected the entire United States during the first half of the nineteenth century." [5379

DONALD ODELL DEWEY. The Sage of Montpelier: James Madison's constitutional and political thought, 1817-1836. Chicago: [Dept. of Photoduplication, Univ. of Chicago Library] 1960. Positive microfilm of typescript. 209 leaves. bibliog. Thesis--Univ. of Chicago. [5380

DAVID BRION DAVIS. Some themes of counter-subversion: an analysis of anti-Masonic, anti-Catholic, and anti-Mormon literature [1820s-50s]. Miss. Valley hist, rev., 47:205-24 (Sep). notes. On the counter-subversives' "image of an evil group conspiring against the nation's welfare," their recommendation of "the most radical means to purge the nation of troublesome groups and to enforce unquestioned loyalty to the state," and the reasons for these beliefs to be found in the psychological make-up of their holders. [5381

FRANK BURT FREIDEL. "... to America ... European ideas." John Arthur Garraty, ed., The unforgettable Americans (Great Neck, N.Y.: Channel Press [1960]), p. 169-73. On Francis Lieber (1800-1872), German emigrant to America in 1827, editor of the Encyclopedia Americana, professor at South Carolina University and Columbia University, political theorist. [5382

SAUL KUSSIEL PADOVER. Ralph Waldo Emerson, the moral voice in politics [1829-62]. Pol. science quar., 74:334-50 (Sep 1959). [5383

OTIS B. WHEELER. Emerson's political quandary. Waldo McNeir & Leo B. Levy, eds., Studies in American literature (Baton Rouge: Louisiana State Univ. Press, 1960 [Louisiana State University studies, Humanities series, 8]), p. 22-32. notes. On his "judgment that the Democrats had the best cause and the Whigs had the best men," and other expressions of his ambivalent attitude toward egalitarianism, 1830s-60s. [5384

FRANCIS F. ADAMS, JR. Robert E. Lee and the concept of democracy [1832-68]. Am. quar., 12:367-73 (fall). notes. [5385

THOMAS COSHOW McCLINTOCK. J[ames] Allen Smith [1860-1926] and the Progressive Movement: a study in intellectual history. Ann Arbor: University Microfilms, 1949 [i. e. 1960]. Positive microfilm of typescript. [601] leaves. Thesis--Univ. of Washington. Abstracted: Dissert. abstracts, 20:4089-90 (Apr). On his 2 books on American government (1907, 1930), his articles, and his service as Professor of Political Economy in the University of Washington (1897-1924); with some account of his early life in Missouri and his study and brief practice of law there. [5386

ALFRED BROOKS ROLLINS, JR. The heart of Lincoln Steffens [1866-1936]. South Atl. quar., 59:239-50 (spring). On Steffens as "a supremely confident dogmatist, busily cramping the changing patterns of life to fit the rigid confines of his chronic presumptions," beginning as a muckraker in 1902 and ending as a Communist. [5387

JOSEPH JAY JONES. Carlyle, Whitman, and the democratic dilemma. Eng. studies in Africa, 3:179-97 (Sep). notes. On the contrast between the "underlying Calvinistic authoritarianism" of Carlyle as shown in his "Shooting Niagara: and after?" (Aug. 1867) and the "transcendentalism" of Whitman in his "Democracy" (Dec. 1867) and "Personalism" (May 1868), and their agreement in envisioning a "leader-class ... as the only possible guide out of chaos." [5388

JAMES KERR POLLOCK. Political science at Michigan: past, present, and future [1881-1960]. University of Michigan, Dept. of Political Science, The status and prospects of political science as a discipline (Ann Arbor [1960]), p. 40-49. [5389

JOHN EDWARD BLEWETT. Democracy as religion: unity in human relations. John Blewett, ed., John Dewey: his thought and influence (N.Y.: Fordham Univ. Press [1960]), p. 33-58. notes. On his "interpretation of democracy" in relation to the development of his "'feeling' of faith, understood as freedom from worry and sense of oneness with nature" during his years in the University of Michigan, 1884-94. [5390

GERALD N. GROB. Origins of the political philosophy of the A. F. of L., 1886-1896. Rev. politics, 22:496-518 (Oct). notes. [5391

VICTOR C. FERKISS. Populist influences on American Fascism [1890s-1940s]. West. pol. quar., 11:350-73 (Jun 1957). notes. [5392

HANS JOACHIM MORGENTHAU. The purpose of American politics. N.Y.: Knopf, 1960. [2], xi, 359, viii, [2] p. notes. On concepts of the "national purpose" of America, 1890-1960; with arguments for the bold exercise of unrestrained power by the President, unhampered by a system of checks and balances and guided by "objective standards" rather than by public opinion. [5393

MYRON Q. HALE. The cosmology of Arthur F. Bentley. Am. pol. science rev., 54:955-61 (Dec). notes. Mainly an examination of his The process of government: a study of social pressures (1908). [5394

WILLIAM S. CHAPMAN. Herbert Croly's The promise of American life [1909]. South Atl. quar., 59:543-55 (autumn). Critical review of the political theory in this volume, of the reasons for its popularity, and of its influence toward "the new nationalism." [5395

JOHN ALANSON PERKINS. Political science instruction as training for participation in public affairs and the public service [University of Michigan, 1910-60]. University of Michigan, Dept. of Political Science, The status and prospects of political science as a discipline (Ann Arbor [1960]), p. 18-31. [5396

LAURENCE W. MARTIN. Necessity and principle: Woodrow Wilson's views [in the realm of political theory, 1912-19]. Rev. politics, 22:96-114 (Jan). notes. [5397

ERWIN A. GAEDE. Reinhold Niebuhr and the relationship of politics and ethics. Ann Arbor: University Microfilms, 1959 [i. e. 1960]. Positive microfilm of typescript. vi, 191 leaves. bibliog. (leaves 181-91). Thesis--Univ. of Notre Dame. Abstracted: Dissert. abstracts, 20:3356 (Feb). On his changing ideas since World War I and his "liberal, Marxist, and pragmatist" periods. [5398

VALDIMER ORLANDO KEY, JR. Issues and problems of political science research [1920-62]. University of Michigan, Dept. of Political Science,

The status and prospects of political science as a discipline (Ann Arbor [1960]), p. 32-9. notes. [5399

VIRGINIA LOUISE RADLEY. Conceptions of American ideals in a program of education. Ann Arbor: University Microfilms, 1958 [i. e. 1960]. Positive microfilm of typescript. [163] leaves. Thesis--Syracuse Univ. Abstracted: Dissert. abstracts, 20:3580 (Mar). On the "thoughts and opinions" of Merle Curti, Henry Steele Commager, Ralph Gabriel, Vernon Louis Parrington, Carl Lotus Becker, and Charles and Mary Beard regarding the ideals of law, individuality, freedom, and equality, 1920-50s, and the implications of the ideas for education. [5400

FLOYD C. WATKINS. William Faulkner, the individual, and the world. Ga. rev., 14:238-47 (fall). On "organizational liberalism," which assumes "that the individual can be important only as a member of a group, never as a free and autonomous citizen," regarded as "the precise antithesis of Faulkner's views," 1920s-50s. [5401

WILLIAM HENRY CHAMBERLIN. The evolution of a conservative. Chicago: Regnery, 1959. vii, 295 p. notes (p. 279-84). On the author's 12 years in Moscow, 1922-34, originally as "a devout fellow-traveler," later disillusioned, and his rejection of both Communism and Fascism; with a comparison of socialism, liberalism, and conservatism. [5402

J. ELDON FIELDS. Book classic: Dewey's "The public and its problems" [1927]. Jour. pub. law, 9:416-27 (fall). notes. [5403

LAWRENCE HAWORTH. The experimental society: Dewey and Jordan. Ethics, 70:27-40 (Oct). notes. On the "notion, that the whole of society might become a laboratory and every activity might be treated as an experiment" as expressed by Dewey in Individualism old and new (1930), The public and its problems (1927), Forms of individuality (1927), and Authority and the individual (1937) and by Elijah Jordan in Theory of legislation (1930) and The good life (1949). [5404

REINHOLD NIEBUHR. Reinhold Niebuhr on politics: his political philosophy and its application to our age as expressed in his writings [1927-59]. Edited by Harry R. Davis and Robert C. Good. N.Y.: Scribner [1960]. xviii, [2], 364 p. notes (p. 343-59). [5405

SYLVESTER CLIFFORD. A study of individualism as shown by analysis of speeches on selected farm relief bills in the United States House of Representatives, 1929-1933. Speech monographs, 27:99-101 (Jun). Abstract of thesis--Univ. of Denver. [5406

DANIEL BELL. The mood of three generations. Daniel Bell, The end of ideology: on the exhaustion of political ideas in the fifties (Glencoe, Ill.: Free Press [1960]), p. 286-99. notes. Reprinted from 4 periodicals, 1955, 1957, 1959. On the changing forms of "radicalism" since the 1930s. [5407

ROBERT C. GOOD. The national interest and political realism: Niebuhr's "debate" with Morgenthau and Kennan. Jour. politics, 22:597-619 (Nov). notes. On doctrines of Reinhold Niebuhr, Hans J. Morgenthau, and George F. Kennan, 1932-59. [5408

JOHN H. BUNZEL. Liberal ideology and the problem of power. West. pol. quar., 13:374-88 (Jun). notes. On fear of power as an American characteristic, and the doctrines of A. A. Berle, Jr., Robert A. Brady, Robert S. Lynd, and others concerning groups, particularly corporations, as the units in which power mainly resides, 1933-57. [5409

JAMES PATRICK SHENTON. Fascism and Father Coughlin. Wis. mag. hist., 44:6-11 (autumn). cartoon, view. notes. Illustrations of the vagueness of the term "Fascism," the political doctrines of the Rev. Charles E. Coughlin (his "social justice"), and "David Riesman's belief that the absence of 'agreement on fundamental values is essential for democratic functioning,'" 1933-41. [5410

ALBERT E. STONE, JR. Seward Collins and the American review: experiment in pro-Fascism, 1933-37. Am. quar., 12:4-20 (spring). notes. On his program of "monarchism" and "an end to parliamentary government," "belief in an elite," "an uncompromising nationalism," "a folk society free of Jews and other dissenters," and "a return to the Middle Ages"; his effort to bring together "the Distributionism of G. K. Chesterton and Hilaire Belloc and the Neo-Scholasticism of Christopher Dawson and Father D'Arcy of Oxford ... the Humanism of Irving Babbitt and Paul Elmer More ... and Southern Agrarianism"; and the resulting disagreements among the contributors. [5411

ANDREW J. RECK. Social, political, and legal philosophy of Paul Weiss. Tulane law rev., 34:69-76 (Dec 1959). notes. On ideas presented in his Reality (1938), Nature and man (1947), Man's freedom (1950), Modes of being (1958), and Our public life (1959). [5412

RALPH E. ELLSWORTH & SARAH M. HARRIS (died 1959). The American right wing: a report to the Fund for the Republic, Inc. [Urbana] 1960. [2], 50 p. bibliog. (p. 33-50). (University of Illinois Library School. Occasional papers, 59.) Review and digest, by joint authors who "have not been either for or against this body of opinion," of the publications of "approximately a thousand voluntary organizations in the United States today which may be called rightist," 1944-58. [5413

STANLEY ROTHMAN. Systematic political theory: observations on the group approach. Am. pol. science rev., 54:15-33 (Mar). notes. Critique of David Truman, The governmental process (1951), and related studies. For comment by Truman see 54:494-5 (Jun). [5414

Public Administration

WILLIAM L. FREDERICK. The history and philosophy of occupational licensing legislation in the United States [1639-1959]. Am. Dental Assoc., Jour., 58(3):18-25 (Mar 1959). [5415

JOHN DAVID MILLER. Government and public administration: the quest for responsible performance [1787-1958, mainly since 1887]. N.Y.: McGraw-Hill, 1959. [2], xii, 484 p. notes. (McGraw-Hill series in political science.) [5416

MILTON MICHAEL CARROW. Sovereign immunity in administrative law [1824-1959]--a new diagnosis. Jour. pub. law, 9:1-23 (spring). notes. [5417

WILLIAM S. WARFORD. Mission unaccomplished--Lincoln and an office-seeker. Ill. State Hist. Soc., Jour., 53:64-9 (spring). port. notes. On the efforts of Cornelius J. Swartwout of Illinois to obtain appointment as surveyor of customs at either Wilmington or Charleston, aided by Orville H. Browning who consulted President Lincoln; with 4 letters from Browning on this subject, 1864-65. [5418

MARVIN LUKE FAIR. Some observations on the theory and performance of the independent regulatory agencies [State and Federal] in regulating the public utility industries [1871-1959]. I. C. C. Practitioners' jour., 27:957-69 (Jun). notes. [5419

HERBERT KAUFMAN. The forest ranger: a study in administrative behavior. Baltimore: Johns Hopkins Press for Resources for the Future [1960]. xviii, 259 p. diagrs., fold. map, fold. table. notes. On public administration in the U.S. Forest Service, 1876-1960. [5420

ARI ARTHUR HOOGENBOOM. An analysis of civil service reformers. Historian, 23:54-78 (Nov). notes. Analysis of the membership of reform associations in New York, Brooklyn, Boston, and California, 1877-85. [5421

GÉRARD CONAC. La fonction publique aux États-Unis: essai sur le régime du civil service fédéral [since 1883]. Paris: Armand Colin, 1958. 251, [9] p. bibliog. (p. 244-52), notes. [5422

U.S. Civil Service Commission. Public Information Office. Biography of an ideal: the diamond anniversary history of the Federal civil service. By Charles [Harris] Cooke. Wash.: U.S. Govt. Print. Off., 1959. x, 170 p. cartoon, facsim., map, ports., tables, views. On the Civil Service Commission, 1883-1958, and the spoils system prevalent in the "ninety-six pre-merit years," 1787-1883. [5423

ROBERT F. MILKEY. Job evaluation after 50 years. Pub. personnel rev., 21:19-23 (Jan). On "a process of analyzing and describing positions, grouping them, and determining their relative value by comparing the duties of different positions in terms of their difficulty, responsibility, and other requirements," 1909-59. [5424

GERALDINE R. KEYES. The right to strike by public employees [1912-52]. Dicta, 31:267-75 (Jul 1954). notes. [5425

TERRY HOY & others. The use of the port authority in the United States [1921-59]; with special reference to the San Francisco Bay area. [Berkeley] 1959. [4], v, 68 p. bibliog. (p. 53-4), notes. (University of California. Bureau of Public Administration. Legislative problems, 1959, no. 2.)

Distinguishes bi-State, Statewide, and local port authorities. [5426

ARCH DOTSON. Fundamental approaches to administrative responsibility. West. pol. rev., 11:701-727 (Sep 1957). notes. Exposition of 5 "basic interpretations" of the problems resulting from "the breakdown of the traditional devices for maintaining the accountability of contemporary government" as expressed in various publications issued between 1932 and 1955. [5427

JOHN W. SWACKHAMER. The right to strike. Mont. Acad. Sciences, Proc., 10 (1951): 113-16. On legislation and litigation regarding the right of employees of governments to strike, 1932-50. [5428

CORNELIUS P. COTTER & J. MALCOLM SMITH. Administrative responsibility: Congressional prescription of interagency relationships. West. pol. quar., 11:765-83 (Dec 1957). diagrs. notes. On "permissive or mandatory solication or receipt of advice of a nonbinding nature," "mandatory performance in accordance with instruction of another agency," and "joint pursuit of policy goals by coordinate agencies," 1933-53, especially as provisions of "economic regulatory legislation." [5429

JOHN MALCOLM SMITH & CORNELIUS P. COTTER. Administrative accountability: reporting to Congress. West. pol. quar., 11:405-15 (Jun 1957). notes. On requirements for annual or other reporting to both houses of Congress or to committees of Congress from agencies exercising "emergency powers" in foreign affairs, military matters, or economic crises, 1933-55. [5430

GERALD L. HUTTON. Public information and rule making provisions of the Administrative Procedure Act of 1946. Temple law quar., 33:58-76 (fall 1959). notes. Includes some account of the Federal Register Act of 1935. [5431

HENRY JACOB FRIENDLY. A look at the Federal administrative agencies [especially since 1938]. Columbia law rev., 60:429-46 (Apr). notes. [5432

ROBERT T. GOLEMBIEWSKI. O & M and the small group. Pub. admin. rev., 20:205-12 (Oct). notes. Case study of a reorganization of procedures and management in the Copy Pulling Section of the Patent Copy Sales Branch of the U.S. Patent Office, 1945-48. [5433

McGEORGE BUNDY. Dean Bundy on national security. Harvard alumni bul., 57:520-22 (9 Apr 1955). On the position of Harvard University in relation to "government security policy" and research contracts, 1946-55. [5434

HENRY S. SAHM. The hearing examiner's role in the Federal administrative process [1946-59]. Fed. Bar jour., 20:74-80 (winter). notes. Mainly on efforts to render completely impossible further "attempts by agencies to impinge upon examiners' independence." [5435

PETER WOLL. The development of shortened procedure in American administrative law [1946-59]. Cornell law quar., 45:56-82 (fall 1959). notes. [5436

PAUL Y. HAMMOND. The National Security Council as a device for interdepartmental coordination: an interpretation and appraisal [1947-60]. Am. pol. science rev., 54:899-910 (Dec). notes. [5437

JASON LEONARD FINKLE. The President makes a decision: a study of Dixon-Yates. Ann Arbor: Institute of Public Administration, Univ. of Michigan, 1960. vii, 204 p. notes. (University of Michigan. Bureau of Government. Michigan governmental studies, 39.) Issued in 1959 in microfilm form as thesis--Univ. of Michigan. On the Dixon-Yates Contract, 1954, involving the issue of private power and the Tennessee Valley Administration and that of conflict of interests, and "the process of presidential decision" resulting in its cancellation. [5438

Public Finance

LAWRENCE SMITH. Money, credit, and public policy. Boston: Houghton Mifflin [1959]. ix, 757 p. diagrs., tables. bibliogs., notes. See Part III, "Monetary experience: past and present," 1620s-1950s, mainly since 1914 (p. 205-354), and historical chapters on "The public regulations of American banking," the Federal Reserve System, and related subjects. [5439

WALTER E. THOMPSON. A manipulation of Robert Morris. Numismatic scrapbook, 26:1256-8 (May). facsims.

On instructions issued by Morris, Superintendent of Finance, for payment of sums due to foreign soldiers who had fought in the Revolution, 1784. [5440

S. STANLEY KATZ. The Federal fiscal year: its origin and prospects. Natl. tax jour., 12:346-62 (Dec 1959). notes. On the "practice of appropriating funds for a given year well after it had already begun," 1789-1959, and the bad consequences that would follow upon a reversion to the January-December fiscal year. [5441

PAUL BARTON TRESCOTT. The United States Government and national income, 1790-1860. Conference on Research in Income and Wealth, Trends in the American economy in the nineteenth century, ed. William N. Parker (Princeton: Princeton Univ. Press, 1960 [Studies in income and wealth, 24]), p. 337-61. tables. notes. On Federal income and expenditures. [5442

LUCIUS WILMERDING, JR. James Monroe and the Furniture Fund. N.-Y. Hist. Soc. quar., 44:132-49 (Apr). plans, port., views. notes. On "an appropriation of $20,000 made by Congress for the purpose of furnishing the President's House, the unorthodox loans from the Fund made by Monroe to himself, the unwise conduct of his agent in intermingling personal financial transactions with those of the White House and the Treasury, the agent's death and investigations by Congress, Monroe's refusal to submit detailed information to Congress about his use of the Fund, his presentation of claims against the Government in 1825, and the failure of Congress to accept Monroe's invitation to make a further study of "this ancient scandal." [5443

IRWIN UNGER. Business men and specie resumption [1865-79]. Pol. science quar., 74:146-50 (Mar 1959). notes. Based on thesis--Columbia Univ., 1958. [5444

RICHARD M. SEGAL. State constitutional limitations on a municipality's power to appropriate funds or extend credit to individuals and associations [1870-1958]. Univ. Pa. law rev., 108:95-115 (Nov 1959). notes. [5445

JOHN MITCHELL FIRESTONE. Federal receipts and expenditures during business cycles, 1879-1958. Princeton: Princeton Univ. Press, 1960. xvi, 176 p. diagrs. (1 fold.), tables (part double). notes. (National Bureau of Economic Research. Studies in business cycles, 9.) "Appendix tables" (p. 87-172). [5446

MARSHALL ALAN ROBINSON. The national debt ceiling: an experiment in fiscal policy [1917-59]. Wash.: Brookings Institution, 1959. vii, 104 p. diagrs., tables. [5447

MORTON S. BARATZ & HELEN T. FARR. Is municipal finance fiscally perverse? Natl. tax jour., 12:276-84 (Sep 1959). tables. notes. On the question whether it "intensifies rather than dampens both upward and downward movements in general business activity," 1920-40, 1948-58. [5448

WARREN C. ROBINSON. The financing of Federal authorities. Am. jour. econ. and sociol., 19:45-63 (Oct 1959). tables. notes. On "guaranteed debt" incurred in the form of securities issued by the Commodity Credit Corporation, the Federal Farm Mortgage Corporation, the Federal Housing Adminostration, the Home Owners Loan Corporation, the Reconstruction Finance Corporation, and the U.S. Housing Authority 1934-41, as "a back-door to increased public debt." [5449

LEONARD PERRY VIDGER. The Federal National Mortgage Association, 1938-1957. Ann Arbor: University Microfilms, 1960. Positive microfilm of typescript. [445] leaves. Thesis (D.B.A.)--Univ. of Washington. Abstracted: Dissert. abstracts, 21: 1413-14 (Dec). [5450

ALEK ARON ROZENTAL. Census of governments--footnotes on a shoehorn. Natl. tax jour., 13:178-83 (Jun). tables. notes. On the difficulties of comparing the 1942 census of governments and the 1957 census of governments; with 5 tables illustrating apparent disparities between these publications with respect to State and local expenditures. [5451

EDGAR CARY BROWN. Federal fiscal policy in the postwar period [1945-58]. Ralph Evans Freeman, ed., Postwar economic trends in the United States (N.Y.: Harper [1960]), p. 139-58. diagrs., double tables. notes. [5452

ROLAND I. ROBINSON. Postwar market for State and local government securities [1946-56]. Princeton: Princeton Univ. Press, 1960. xxiv, 227 p. diagrs., tables. notes. (National Bureau of Economic Research. Studies in capital formation and financing, 5.) Deals particularly with "the erosion of tax exemption as means of supporting state and local government financing." [5453

TAXATION

MAURICE CECIL MACKEY, JR. Ownership and taxation of natural resources [1785-1957]. Dicta, 34:411-21 (Nov-Dec 1957). notes. Deals particularly with mineral depletion allowances, inaugurated in 1918. [5454

RODERICK HAMILTON RILEY. The "bonding period" in Federal taxation of distilled spirits [1791-1958]. Ann Arbor: University Microfilms, 1959 [i. e. 1960]. Positive microfilm of typescript. v, 261 leaves. bibliog. (leaves 255-61). Thesis--Univ. of Wisconsin. Abstracted: Dissert. abstracts, 20:3114-15 (Feb). [5455

EDMUND W. PAVENSTEDT. The United States Court of Claims as a forum for tax cases [1855-1959]. Tax law rev., 15:1-33, 201-28 (Nov 1959, Jan 1960). notes. [5456

SOLOMON ALTMANN. Revenue stamps of the United States, first issue [1862, and second issue, 1867]. Essay proof jour., 13:100-102 (Apr 1956). From the author's Boston revenue book. [5457

CLARENCE WILSON BRAZER (1880-1956). U.S. revenue proofs. Essay proof jour., 12:205-14; 13:35-42 (Oct 1955, Jan 1956). On collections and sales of proofs of U.S. revenue stamps, 1862-75. Apparently left unfinished at the author's death. [5458

GEORGE EIDT LENT. The origin and survival of tax-exempt securities [since 1870]. Natl. tax jour., 12:301-16 (Dec 1959). notes. [5459

ALBERT J. GOULD. The taxpayer's constitutional privilege in income tax investigations. Dicta, 31:325-40 (Sep 1954). notes. On his protection against unlawful search and seizure and against self-incrimination, 1886-1954. [5460

OSCAR H. LENTZ. Mineral economics and the problem of equitable taxation: a study in the legislative rationale of percentage depletion allowances [since 1909]. Golden, Colo., 1960. [8], 111 p. bibliogs., notes. (Colorado School of Mines. Quarterly, v. 5, no. 2.) [5461

JAMES L. POTTS. The relation of the income tax to democracy in the United States [1913-56]. West. pol. quar., 11: 911-25 (Dec 1957). tables. [5462

NORMAN A. SUGARMAN & HARLAN POMEROY. Business income of exempt organizations. Va. law rev., 46:424-38 (Apr). notes. On "the extent to which a tax exempt organization may engage in income producing activities and still maintain its tax exempt status," 1914-59. [5463

CHARLES O. GALVIN. The "ought" and "is" of oil-and-gas taxation [1918-59]. Harv. law rev., 73: 1441-1509 (Jun). notes. [5464

ABDEL MONEM ABDEL HAMID FAWZY. A comparative study of gasoline taxation in the United States [since 1919]. Ann Arbor: University Microfilms, 1953 [i. e. 1960]. Positive microfilm of typescript. [237] leaves. Thesis--Univ. of Kentucky. Abstracted: Dissert. abstracts, 20:4560 (Jun). [5465

ROSWELL FOSTER MAGILL. The exemption of cooperatives from income taxation [1921-59]. Mont. law rev., 21:155-67 (spring). notes. [5466

JACK D. EDWARDS. Executive compensation: the taxation of stock options [1923-59]. Vanderbilt law rev., 13: 475-95 (Mar). notes. [5467

PETER CHARLES BRIANT. The effect of the corporation income tax on stockholders [1925-55]. Ann Arbor: University Microfilms, 1960. Positive microfilm of typescript. [173] leaves. Thesis--Univ. of Michigan. Abstracted: Dissert. abstracts, 21:302-3 (Aug). [5468

LAWRENCE A. MILLER. The doctrine of intergovernmental tax immunity and its effect upon lessees of Federal property [1926-59]. Univ. Pa. law rev., 21:697-709 (Jun). notes. [5469

LAWRENCE R. BLOOMENTHAL. Taxation of damages. Univ. Pittsburgh law rev., 21:25-40 (Oct 1959). notes. On taxability of awards for damages, 1927-59. [5470

DAVID L. MILLER. Treatment of the Federal tax lien in bankruptcy proceedings [1929-58]. Univ. Pa. law rev., 108:77-94 (Nov 1959). notes. [5471

T. R. BEARD. Progressive income taxation, income redistribution, and the consumption function. Natl. tax jour., 13:168-77 (Jun). notes. Review of arguments for progression since the 1930s, and evidence "to support the view that income redistribution via progressive taxation may not stimulate consumption to any appreciable extent (if at all)." [5472

HAMED ABDELLATIF EL-SAYEH. The United States Treasury Department's views on legislation affecting income tax administration since 1932. Ann Arbor: University Microfilms, 1950 [i. e. 1960]. Positive microfilm of typescript. [338] leaves. Thesis--Univ. of Kentucky. Abstracted: Dissert. abstracts, 20:4559-60 (Jun). [5473

B. BERNARD WOLSON. Federal tax liens--a study in confusion and confiscation. Marquette law rev., 43: 180-202 (fall 1959). notes. On the inequity of "the secret and unfiled tax lien" as a means for confiscation of the property of creditors whose claims were registered at a date prior to the creation or assertion of the Federal lien, 1936-59. [5474

JAMES F. NEAL. Deferred compensation plans: qualifying for non-qualified treatment. Vanderbilt law rev., 13: 461-74 (Mar). notes. On the income-tax aspects of such plans, 1938-59. [5475

GEOFFREY J. LANNING. Tax erosion and the "bootstrap sale" of a business [1939-59]. Univ. Pa. law rev., 108: 623-97, 943-84 (Mar, May). notes. [5476

DANIEL MARK HOLLAND. The income-tax burden on stockholders [1940-41, 1944-52]. Princeton: Princeton Univ. Press, 1958. xxv, 241 p. diagrs., views. (National Bureau of Economic Research. Fiscal studies, 5.) [5477

SAMUEL R. SAPIENZA. Regional taxation: an evaluation of the Western Hemisphere Trade Company Act [1942-59]. Inter-Am. econ. affairs, 13(2):47-59 (autumn 1959). tables. notes. On tax reductions available to U.S. corporations that earn at least 95 percent of their income outside the United States but within the Western Hemisphere. [5478

WEYLAND DOUGLAS POE. Local sales taxes in the United States and Canada [since 1945]. Ann Arbor: University Microfilms, 1959 [i. e. 1960]. Positive microfilm of typescript. x, 246, [25] leaves. diagrs., tables. bibliog. (leaves 247-70). Thesis--Indiana Univ. Abstracted: Dissert. abstracts, 20:3988-9 (Apr). [5479

JAMES M. HEIDELL. The purchasing of tax-exempt bonds by individuals in the 1946-1956 decade. [n. p.] c1960. [3], ii, 97, [2] p. (even numbers on recto). tables. notes. Based on thesis--New York Univ. [5480

KENNETH M. KAUFFMAN. Income tax exemption and economic development. Natl. tax jour., 13:141-62, 252-69 (Jun, Sep). tables. notes. On the granting by "underdeveloped countries" of "tax exemptions for what most frequently are called 'pioneer' or 'new and necessary industries'"; and the effects of the policy in Puerto Rico (since 1947), Mexico, and the Philippines. [5481

LEO COHEN. A more recent measurement of the built-in flexibility of the individual income tax [1949-58]. Natl. tax jour., 13:122-6 (Jun). tables. notes. [5482

The Three Branches

F. WILLIAM O'BRIEN. The executive and the separation principle at the Constitutional Convention [1787]. Md. hist. mag., 55:201-20 (Sep). notes. On the motives and purposes of the Founding Fathers in the distribution of powers between the executive and the legislative. [5483

HENRY JULIAN ABRAHAM & EDWARD M. GOLDBERG. A note on the appointment of justices of the Supreme Court of the United States. Am. Bar Assoc. jour., 46:147-50, 219-22 (Feb). ports., tables. On "the elements that affect the confirmation of Justices" by the Senate, 1789-1959. [5484

JACK BELL. The splendid misery: the story of the Presidency and power politics at close range. Garden City, N.Y.: Doubleday, 1960. 474 p. On relations between the President and Congress since 1789, especially since 1901, and the extent of the power and authority of the President to act independently of Congress or to exert force to influence the votes of its members. Includes recollections of the author's participation in several campaigns as a political reporter. [5485

HERMAN FINER. The Presidency [1789-1960]: crisis and regeneration, an essay in possibilities. [Chicago:] Univ. of Chicago Press [1960]. xi, [3], 374 p. notes (p. 347-67). Mainly an argument for "drastic changes" in the Presidency, including the election of

11 vice-presidents (forming a cabinet, none a presiding officer of the Senate), reduction of the powers of the Senate, and 4-year terms for Senators, Representatives, Vice-Presidents, and President, with Vice-Presidents and President sitting in the House of Representatives. [5486

SAMUEL KRISLOV. Jefferson and judicial review: refereeing Cahn, Commager, and Mendelson. Jour. pub. law, 9:374-81 (fall). notes. Effort to determine "the consistency of Jefferson's views" on "the right of the Supreme Court to judge the validity of acts of Congress," 1789-1819, and commentary on references to this subject by Henry Steele Commager, Edmond Cahn, and Wallace Mendelson. [5487

ROBERT J. BERGHEL. Realignment of municipalities--a political question? Wash. and Lee law rev., 17:244-52 (fall). notes. Includes a summary of opinions of the Supreme Court as to the scope of a "political question" (one within the province of the legislative branch, not of the judicial branch), 1796-1958. [5488

WILLIAM A. NORRIS & JULIAN BURKE. Congress and the Supreme Court's appellate jurisdiction. Los Angeles Bar bul., 35:212-15, 229-31 (May). ports. On the absolute or limited power of Congress to restrict the jurisdiction, 1796-1959. [5489

BENJAMIN WHIPPLE PALMER. Judicial review: usurpation or abdication? Am. Bar Assoc. jour., 46: 881-8 (Aug). port. notes. On "the power of courts, particularly the United States Supreme Court, to declare legislative acts unconstitutional," 1798-1959. [5490

GLENDON A. SCHUBERT, JR. The Presidency in the courts. Minneapolis: Univ. of Minnesota Press [1957]. xi, 391 p. notes, table of cases (p. 367-83). On the 38 court "cases holding Presidential decisions unconstitutional," 1799-1956. Organized according to the President's functions as chief administrator, chief of state, commander in chief, and "chief magistrate." [5491

GEORGE L. MONTAGNO. Congressional cakewalk. Wm. and Mary quar., 17:345-9 (Jul). notes. On the opposition of Matthew Lyon, Representative from Vermont, to the custom requiring the members of the House of Representatives to visit as a body the residence of the President and deliver a reply to his opening address to the legislative session--a custom ended by Thomas Jefferson in 1801 by sending a written message to Congress instead of addressing it in person. [5492

RICHARD B. LILLICH. The Chase impeachment. Am. jour. legal hist., 4:49-72 (Jan). notes. On the proceedings of Congress against Associate Justice Samuel Chase, 1805, ending with his acquittal by the Senate; and the good effects of the trial upon the judiciary, the legislative, and the executive branches of the U.S. Government. [5493

ANTON-HERMANN CHROUST. Did President Jackson actually threaten the Supreme Court of the United States with nonenforcement of its injunction against the State of Georgia? Am. jour. legal hist., 4:76-8 (Jan). notes. Evidence, 1831, interpreted by the author as supporting an affirmative answer to this question. [5494

MARY C. LAWTON. The doctrine of primary jurisdiction: a reexamination of its purpose and practicality [1907-59]. Georgetown law jour., 48: 563-76 (spring). notes. On claims "originally cognizable in the courts" but involving "issues which, under a regulatory scheme, have been placed within the special competence of an administrative body," on which action is therefore suspended by the courts to permit referral to administrative agencies "for determination of technical issues." [5495

OSCAR WILLIAM PERLMUTTER. Acheson vs. Congress. Rev. politics, 22:5-44 (Jan). notes. On Congressional criticism of Dean Acheson as an executive officer of the United States, 1933, 1941-53, and his severe criticism of Congress then and later. [5496

RANDALL HYLMAN NELSON. Legislative participation in the treaty and agreement making process [1941-57]. West. pol. quar., 13:154-71 (Mar). notes. [5497

FELIX A. NIGRO. The Pauley case. Southw. social science quar., 40:341-9 (Mar). notes. On the nomination of Edwin Wendell Pauley by President Truman for the post of Assistant Secretary of the Navy, the release by Harold Ickes of information regarding Pauley's activities as a lobbyist for the oil industry, and Truman's withdrawal of the nomination at Pauley's request, 1946. [5498

JOSEPH TANENHAUS. Supreme Court attitudes toward Federal administrative agencies [1947-56]. Jour. politics, 22:502-24 (Aug). tables. notes. [5499

WILLIAM L. FREDERICK. New developments in State governments in the United States [1948-60]. Internal Affairs monthly bul., 28(5):1-8; (6): 12-18 (May, Jun). views. [5500

SAMUEL J. HENRY & THOMAS O. MORRIS, JR. A decade of legislative history in the Supreme Court: 1950-1960. Va. law rev., 46:1408-38 (Nov). notes. On the examination of "legislative journals, committee reports and debates or statements by legislators on the floor of Congress" made during a bill's passage through the legislature as aids to the Court in determining the intent of Congress; and the abuses to which the use of these aids can sometimes lead. [5501

GRANT McCONNELL. The steel seizure of 1952. University, Ala.: Univ. of Alabama Press for the ICP [1960. 2], 53 p. (Inter-University Case Program. ICP case series, 52.) On the events and decisions, Jun. 1950 - Jul. 1952, leading to the seizure of the steel mills by order of the President, the action of the Supreme Court in declaring the seizure illegal, the subsequent strike, and its settlement by collective bargaining. [5502

SEYMOUR SCHER. Congressional committee members as independent agency overseers: a case study. Am. pol. science rev., 54:911-20 (Dec). notes. Study of proceedings of the House Education and Labor Committee "as it reviewed the performance of the National Labor Relations Board in 1953." [5503

THE EXECUTIVE BRANCH

WILFRED ELLSWORTH BINKLEY. The man in the White House: his powers and duties [1787-1958). Baltimore: Johns Hopkins Press [1959, c1958. 14], 310 p. bibliog. (p. 298-304), notes. [5504

HENRY STEELE COMMAGER. The making of a President. Am. rev., 1(1):12-24 (autumn). port. On the processes by which Presidents are nominated and elected, 1787-1960, and the effects of the processes upon the quality of the Presidency. [5505

CLINTON LAWRENCE ROSSITER. The American Presidency [1787-1959. Second edition.] N.Y.: Harcourt, Brace [1960]. 281, [3] p. bibliog. (p. 272-5). (A Harvest book, HB35.) 1st ed. 1956. [5506

DAVID GREGG FARRELLY. The growth of Presidential powers. Am. rev., 1(1):136-44 (autumn). "Bibliographical essay" on publications since The Federalist (1788). [5507

ALBERT ANGUS AUSTEN. The "traditional" Presidential inaugural address. Rudolf Kirk & Charles Fredrick Main, eds., Essays in literary history, presented to J. Milton French (New Brunswick, N.J.: Rutgers Univ. Press [1960]), p. 239-48. notes. On characteristics of the inaugural addresses of American Presidents, 1789-1949. [5508

WILLIAM GRAVES CARLETON. The role of the Presidency. Am. rev., 1(1):25-49 (autumn). On the duties of the President and his means for performing them 1789-1960. [5509

ONA GRIFFIN JEFFRIES. In and out of the White House ... from Washington to the Eisenhowers: an intimate glimpse into the social and domestic aspects of the Presidential life [1789-1960]. N.Y.: W. Funk [1960]. xi, 404 p. cartoons, diagr., facsims., ports., views. A chapter for each President, on the social observances, social and domestic habits, and housekeeping in the White House (and before 1800 in the President's residences in New York City and Philadelphia). [5510

REXFORD GUY TUGWELL. The enlargement of the Presidency. Garden City, N.Y.: Doubleday, 1960. 508 p. tables. notes. On the growth of its duties and its staff since 1789. [5511

H. W. C. FURMAN. Restriction upon use of the Army imposed by the Posse Comitatus Act [of 1956]. Mil. law rev., 7:85-129 (Jan). notes. Based on thesis--Judge Advocate General's School, U.S. Army. On "chief executives' use of army in enforcing laws." 1792-1959. [5512

FREDERIC DELBERT SCHWENGEL. The war powers of President Lincoln. Ralph G. Newman, ed., Lincoln for the ages (Garden City, N.Y.: Doubleday, 1960), p. 273-8. On Lincoln's "firm and wise" use of the powers of the Presidency, 1861-65. [5513

DANIEL JOSEPH BOORSTIN. The direct democracy of public relations: selling the President to the people. Daniel J. Boorstin, America and the image of Europe: reflections on American thought (N.Y.: Meridian Books [1960]), p. 97-117. First printed in 1955. On "certain revolutionary changes in our system of public communications" exemplified in "the rise of the Nationally-Advertised President," Franklin Delano Roosevelt, 1929-45. [5514

WALTER JOHNSON. 1600 Pennsylvania Avenue: Presidents and the people, 1929-1959. Boston: Little, Brown [1960]. x, 390 p. bibliog. (p. 353-73), notes (p. 331-51). [5515

WALTER JOHNSON. The American President and the art of communication: an inaugural lecture delivered before the University of Oxford on 13 May 1958. Oxford: Clarendon Press, 1958. 21, [2] p. On the performances of Roosevelt, Truman, and Eisenhower in press conferences and in radio and television addresses and interviews in relation to the role of "chief of state," "chief legislator," and "party leader," 1932-58. [5516

JOHN MALCOLM SMITH & CORNELIUS P. COTTER. Powers of the President during crises [1933-60]. Wash.: Public Affairs Press [1960]. viii, [2], 184 p. notes (p. 147-75). [5517

THE JUDICIAL BRANCH

CARL WILLIAM UBBELOHDE, JR. The Vice-Admiralty Courts and the American Revolution. Chapel Hill: Univ. of North Carolina Press for the Institute of Early American History and Culture, Williamsburg, Va., 1960. ix, [3], 242, [1] p. bibliog. (p. 215-28), notes. Based on thesis--Univ. of Wisconsin. On the authority, personnel, and procedures of the 11 "salt-water courts" in the British colonies from Newfoundland to Georgia, 1763-76; their extreme unpopularity after they received jurisdiction to collect customs duties, enforce the Stamp Act, and in other ways act "as tribunals for determining crown revenue cases," a function exercised in England by the common-law Court of the Exchequer; and their replacement by State admiralty courts in and after 1776. [5518

W. JOSEPH WAGNER. The history and role of a supreme court in a Federal system [1787-1958]. Mont. law rev., 20:171-91 (spring 1959). notes. [5519

BENJAMIN NATHAN CARDOZO (1880-1938). The nature of the judicial process [since 1789]. New Haven: Yale Univ. Press [1960]. 180 p. notes. (The Storrs lectures, Yale University. A Yale paperbound, Y-21.) 1st ed. 1921. Includes sections on "The method of philosophy," "The methods of history, tradition, and sociology," "The judge as a legislator," "Adherence to precedent," and "The subconscious element in the judicial process." [5520

CHARLES GROVE HAINES (1879-1948). The role of the Supreme Court in American government and politics, 1789-1835. N.Y.: Russell & Russell, 1960. xiii, 679 p. notes. "Table of cases" (p. 663-5). 1st ed. 1944. [5521

ROBERT GREEN McCLOSKEY. The American Supreme Court. [Chicago:] Univ. of Chicago Press [1960]. x, [2], 260 p. bibliog. (p. 236-52). (The Chicago history of American civilization.) A mainly chronological history, 1789-1956, of "the work of the Supreme Court of the United States as a constitutional tribunal, exercising the power of judicial review." [5522

ARTHUR S. MILLER & RONALD F. HOWELL. The myth of neutrality in constitutional adjudication [1789-1959]. Univ. Chicago law rev., 27:661-95 (summer). notes. On "the rewriting of American history" by the Supreme Court, the motivation of its justices by "value preferences" in all 3 periods of its existence (1789-1870, 1870-1937, 1937-), and the inherent inability of courts to judge neutrally. [5523

RULES of decision in nondiversity suits. Yale law jour., 69:1428-52 (Jul). notes. On rules of Federal courts in "suits to which the United States is a party and those which involve interpretation of a federal statute," 1789-1959. [5524

JOHN RICHARD SCHMIDHAUSER. The Supreme Court: its politics, personalities, and procedures [1789-1959]. N.Y.: Holt, Rinehart, and Winston [1960]. viii, [2], 163 p. notes. Deals chiefly with "subtle influences which condition the decision-making process of the Supreme Court," particularly those which may have been related to its diminishing prestige and reputation since 1937. [5525

S. SIDNEY ULMER. Polar classification of Supreme Court justices [1790-1958]. S.C. law jour., 12:407-17 (spring). tables. notes. Statistical interpretation of votes against overruling as a means of classifying justices by degree of "change resistance." [5526

THOMAS CAMPBELL CLARK. The Supreme Court as a protector of liberty under the rule of law [1801-1959]. Marquette law rev., 43:11-19 (summer 1959). notes. [5527

JOHN PAUL FRANK. The historic role of the Supreme Court [1801-1959]. Ky. law jour., 48:26-47 (fall 1959). notes. [5528

JAMES A. GARDNER. The Supreme Court and philosophy of law [1803-1959]. Villanova law rev., 5:181-205 (winter). notes. [5529

JULIUS PAUL. The Supreme Court: mirror of the American conscience [1803-1954]. Am. jour. econ. and sociol., 19:1-15 (Oct 1959). notes. [5530

CLAY PACKER MALICK. The Supreme Court as moral force [1822-1958]. Midwest quar., 1:271-83 (Apr). [5531

FRANK RANSOM STRONG. Trends in Supreme Court interpretation of Constitution and statute [1935-60]. Wayne law rev., 6:285-310 (summer). notes. [5532

WILLIAM SMITH (1762-1840). William Smith declines seat on U.S. Supreme Court. Ala. lawyer, 21:441-3 (Oct). Letter dated Huntsville, 28 Apr. 1837, explaining his action on the ground that he was unwilling to enter into a status in which he could not properly participate in political discussions. [5533

LOUIS H. POLLAK. Racial discrimination and judicial integrity: a reply to Professor Wechsler. Univ. Pa. law rev., 108:1-34 (Oct 1959). notes. Comment on "Toward neutral principles of constitutional law," by Herbert Wechsler, expressing disagreement with Wechsler's criticisms of decisions of the Supreme Court concerning restrictive covenants (1948), segregated public schools (1954), and the white primary (1956); with an examination of related cases under the 14th Amendment. 1873-1958. [5534

JOHN E. REID. Chief Justice Doe and Chief Justice Vanderbilt: a comparison in the techniques of reform. Am. Bar Assoc. jour., 46:278-81, 325-8 (Mar). port. notes. On the methods of Charles Doe, Chief Justice of New Hampshire, 1876-96, and Arthur T. Vanderbilt, Chief Justice of New Jersey, 1948-57. [5535

JOHN ECKLER. Historical review [of "the problem of congested dockets and delay of justice" since 1906]. Am. Acad. Pol. and Social Science, Ann., 328:1-6 (Mar). notes. [5536

SHELDON DOUGLASS ELLIOTT. Improvements in judicial administration, 1906-1956. Arthur L. Harding, ed., The administration of justice in retrospect (Dallas: Southern Methodist Univ., 1957), p. 42-57. [5537

ARTHUR LEON HARDING. Professor Pound makes history. Arthur L. Harding, ed., The administration of justice in retrospect (Dallas: Southern Methodist Univ., 1957), p. 3-23. notes. On Roscoe Pound's address before the American Bar Association, "The causes of popular dissatisfaction with the administration of justice" (1960), and his later contributions to the removal of these causes. [5538

JOSEPH L. CALL. The Constitution v. the Supreme Court. Baylor law rev., 11:383-412 (fall 1959). notes. Review of the history of the Supreme Court, 1787-1958, to demonstrate the falsity of assertions that an interpretation by the Court is "the supreme law of the land" (language of Earl Warren, 1958), that "the Constitution is what the judges say it is" (Charles Evans Hughes, 1908), and that "the only check on our exercise of power is our own sense of self-restraint" (Harlan Fiske Stone, 1936), and to offer evidence that since 1803 the Court has effected "constitutional amendment by judicial prerogative." [5539

The THREE-judge Federal court in constitutional litigation [1908-58]: a procedural anachronism. Univ. Chicago law rev., 27:555-71 (spring). notes. On a requirement that "a federal district court may not grant an injunction restraining the enforcement of a state or federal statute on the ground of unconstitutionality unless the application for the injunction has been heard and determined by three judges." [5540

PAUL ABRAHAM FREUND. The Supreme Court crisis. N.Y. State Bar bul., 31:66-80 (Feb 1959). port. On episodes of severe criticism of the Court, 1917, 1938, 1950s. [5541

ELOISE C. SNYDER. Uncertainty and the Supreme Court's decisions. Am. jour. sociol., 65:241-5 (Nov 1959).

tables. notes. Statistical examination of "the degree to which uncertainty is present in the attempt to resolve major social conflict through court decisions," 1921-53. [5542

HENRY PORTER CHANDLER. The problem of congestion and delay in the Federal courts [since 1922]. Am. Acad. Pol. and Social Science, Ann., 328:144-52 (Mar). notes. [5543

LAWRENCE J. LEE. The emergence and evolution of a constitutional right to a fair trial before a justice of the peace [1927-60]. Fed. Bar jour., 20: 110-24 (spring). notes. Mainly on the fees collected by the justices from convicted defendants as the only compensation received by the justices for their services. [5544

GLENN R. WINTERS. Edson R. Sunderland and judicial administration [1929-57]. Mich. law rev., 58:37-40 (Nov 1959). [5545

EDWARD McWHINNEY. The power value and its public law gradations: a preliminary excursus. Jour. pub. law, 9:43-52 (spring). notes. On constitutional decisions as the product of "the particular interest-conflicts represented in the problem-situations before the courts and the patterns of resolution of such interest-conflicts reflected in the actual decisions of the court," with illustrations from the United States, 1932-58, and elsewhere. [5546

CHARLES EDWARD CLARK. Edson Read Sunderland and the Federal Rules of Civil Procedure [1935-55]. Mich. law rev., 58:6-12 (Nov 1959). notes. [5547

GLENDON A. SCHUBERT, JR. Quantitative analysis of judicial behavior. Glencoe, Ill.: Free Press [1960, c1959]. xxi, 392 p. diagrs. (part fold.), tables. notes, table of cases (p. 364-70). Exposition of a mathematical method for explaining and predicting the acts of decision of judges, and illustrative applications of the method to the U.S. Supreme Court, 1935-57, and the Michigan Supreme Court, 1954-57; with introductory remarks on public law as a province of political science. [5548

WILLIAM ORVILLE DOUGLAS. The Supreme Court and its case load [1938-58]. Cornell law quar., 45:401-14 (spring). tables. notes [5549

JOHN C. McCOID II. Right to jury trial in the Federal courts [1938-60]. Ia. law rev., 45:726-42 (summer). notes. [5550

ROSCOE BERNARD TURNER STEFFEN. The prima facie case in non-jury trials [1940-59]. Univ. Chicago law rev., 27:94-126 (autumn 1959). notes. [5551

THE LEGISLATIVE BRANCH

BYRON ROBERT ABERNETHY. Constitutional limitations on the legislature. Lawrence, 1959. [8], 108 p. notes. (University of Kansas. Governmental Research Center. Governmental research series, 20.) On bills of rights, prohibitions against local and special legislation, restrictions on taxing power and debt, "dedicated revenue," mandates, initiative and referendum, and other limitations imposed by State constitutions upon legislative action, 1776-1959. [5552

JOSEPH F. DOLAN & THOMAS A. GILLIAM. The investigating power of Congress: its scope and limitations [1792-1954]. Dicta, 31:285-319 (Aug 1954). notes. Two articles with the same title, dealing in part with the "inherency" of the power to punish for contempt. [5553

MICHAEL C. SLOTNICK. The Congressional investigating power: ramifications of the Watkins-Barenblatt enigma [1857-1959]. Univ. Miami law rev., 14:381-411 (spring). notes. [5554

MARVIN SUMMERS. The First Amendment as a restraint on the power of Congress to investigate [1857-1959]. Marquette law rev., 43: 459-82 (spring). notes. On "the power of legislatures to compel disclosures" by witnesses. [5555

NORMAN MELLER. Legislative behavior research [1885-1958]. West. pol. quar., 13:131-53 (Mar). notes. [5556

RICHARD LOWITT. The making of an insurgent. Mid-America, 42:105-15 (Apr). notes. On the campaign of George W. Norris, Representative from Nebraska, to curb the powers of Speaker Joseph G. Cannon and to make the House a "representative body instead of a one-man machine," 1903-10. [5557

EUGENE G. PARTAIN. The use of broadcast media in Congressional legislative and quasi-judicial proceedings [1938-58]. Jour. broadcasting, 4:123-39 (spring). notes. [5558

NELSON W. POLSBY. Towards an explanation of McCarthyism [1953-54]. Pol. studies, 8:250-71 (Oct). diagr., tables. notes. Analysis of polls. [5559

SOCIAL HISTORY

JOHN D. HOGAN & FRANCIS A. J. IANNI. American social legislation [1800-1955, mainly in recent years]. N.Y.: Harper [1956]. xvi, 713 p. diagrs., tables. bibliogs., notes. (Harper's social science series.) Sections on "Social thought and social movements," "Family legislation," "The labor movement and labor law," "Social assistance and social insurance," and other subjects, including several historical chapters. [5560

FRANCIS B. DEDMOND. Thoreau as a critic of society [1840s-60s]. Thoreau Soc. bul., 34:[1-3] (Jan 1951). Abstract of thesis (M. A.)--Duke Univ., 1950. [5561

RICHARD HENRY GOLDSTONE. The pariah in modern American and British literature: an illustration of a method for teachers of literature. Ann Arbor: University Microfilms, 1960. Positive microfilm of typescript. [235] leaves. Thesis--Columbia Univ. Abstracted: Dissert. abstracts, 21:893 (Oct). Illustrative study of "the fallen woman and the Negro," 1850s-1930s. [5562

AARON IGNATIUS ABELL. The Catholic factor in the social justice movement [1885-1960]. Thomas Timothy McAvoy, ed., Roman Catholicism and the American way of life ([Notre Dame, Ind.:] Univ. of Notre Dame Press, 1960), p. 70-98. notes. [5563

LUCY KAVALER. The private world of high society. N.Y.: D. McKay Co. [1960]. xiv, 301 p. On the status-conferring activities, affiliations, etc., serving as criteria for listing in the Social register since its establishment in 1887; with a chapter on "Negro high society." [5564

THOMAS COOPER COLEMAN III. The social and moral criticism of F. Scott Fitzgerald [1920 to 1940]. Ann Arbor: University Microfilms, 1959 [i. e. 1960]. Positive microfilm of typescript. [299] leaves. Thesis--Univ. of Southern California. Abstracted: Dissert. abstracts, 20:3289 (Feb). [5565

ERNEST F. DIBBLE. Reinhold Niebuhr's search for social justice [since the 1920s]. Ann Arbor: University Microfilms, 1959 [i. e. 1960]. Positive microfilm of typescript. [230] leaves. Thesis--American Univ. Abstracted: Dissert. abstracts, 20: 2762-3 (Jan). [5566

MURLIN RAY HODGELL. Low-income rural families in an urbanizing society [1934-58]. Ann Arbor: University Microfilms, 1959 [i. e. 1960]. Positive microfilm of typescript. xvii, 429 leaves. maps, tables. bibliog. (leaves 413-29). Thesis--Cornell Univ. Abstracted: Dissert. abstracts, 20:4364 (May). [5567

GEORGE ANTHONY KATEB. Anti-Utopianism. Ann Arbor: University Microfilms, 1960. Positive microfilm of typescript. [318] leaves. Thesis--Columbia Univ. Abstracted: Dissert. abstracts, 21:947 (Oct). Mainly on the "social writings" of Burrhus Frederic Skinner (born 1904), professionally a psychologist, particularly his Walden two (1948). [5568

CLARENCE MERTON BABCOCK. The echo of a whistle. West. folklore, 19: 47-51 (Jan). Compendium of the habits and language of hoboes. [5569

Charities and Welfare

FRANKLIN PARKER, comp. An approach to Peabody's gifts and legacies. Essex Inst. hist. col., 96:291-6 (Oct). Tabulation of gifts and legacies from George Peabody to libraries, hospitals, churches, and other institutions, and for science, education, exploration, art and music, and other charitable purposes in the United States and England, 1837-70. [5570

PERSIA GWENDOLINE CRAWFORD CAMPBELL. Mary Williamson Harriman. N.Y.: [Columbia Univ. Press]

1960. vi, [2], 84 p. ports., view. notes. On Mary Williamson Averell (1851-1932), her early life in New York City and Ogdensburg, N.Y., her marriage to Edward Henry Harriman (died 1909), her inheritance and "successful management" of his whole estate (estimated to be worth 70 million dollars), and her benefactions to promote better government, war work, safety, public health, social welfare, education, and the fine arts. [5571

BENJAMIN JOSEPH KLEBANER. Poor relief and public works during the depression of 1857. Historian, 22: 264-79 (May). notes. [5572

KARL DE SCHWEINITZ. The past as a guide to the function and pattern of social work [in America, 1863-1959, and abroad]. William Wallace Weaver, ed., Frontiers for social work: a colloquium on the fiftieth anniversary of the School of Social Work of the University of Pennsylvania (Phila.: Univ. of Pennsylvania Press [1960]), p. 59-93. notes. [5573

WAYNE VASEY. Government and social welfare: roles of Federal, State, and local governments in administering welfare services [1863-1958, mainly since 1930]. N.Y.: Holt [1958]. vi, 506 p. diagrs., map. bibliogs., notes. [5574

MILDRED HOUGHTON COMFORT. Herbert Hoover [1874-1964], humanitarian: a biographical sketch of the former President of the United States. Minneapolis: T. S. Denison [1960]. 186 p. [5575

JOHN R. FEATHER. The immunity of charitable institutions from tort liability. Baylor law rev., 11:86-107 (winter 1959). On the "doctrine of eleemosynary immunity," 1876-1958, now a "tottering majority position," rejected by 20 States. [5576

Sister MARY JOACHIM. Charitable immunity. Mich. State Bar jour., 38(12):14-24 (Dec 1959). port. notes. On the present status of the doctrine in the States as indicated by court decisions since 1876; with a chronological review of Michigan decisions, 1894-1950. [5577

JOSEPH J. SIMEONE. The doctrine of charitable immunity [1876-1958]. St. Louis Univ. law jour., 5:357-73 (spring 1959). table. notes. [5578

NORMAN S. MARSHALL. The Salvation Army: with heart to God and hand to man (1865-1960). N.Y.: Newcomen Soc. in North America, 1960. 28 p. views. Includes an account of its activities in America since 1880. [5579

VAUGHN DAVIS BORNET. Welfare in America. Norman: Univ. of Oklahoma Press [1960]. xi, 319 p. ports., tables, views. On the work of private charitable organizations, 1881-1960, the welfare activities of government agencies, mainly since 1933, and the "broad issues" in the relation between private and public aid to the poor and the unfortunate. [5580

WILBUR JOSEPH COHEN. Trends and issues in social welfare expenditures and programs [1890-1959]. Am. jour. pub. health, 49:1299-1306 (Oct 1959). notes. [5581

ALLEN FREEMAN DAVIS. Spearheads for reform: the social settlements and the Progressive Movement, 1890-1914. Ann Arbor: University Microfilms, 1959 [i. e. 1960]. Positive microfilm of typescript. v, 398 leaves. bibliog. (leaves 377-98). Thesis--Univ. of Wisconsin. Abstracted: Dissert. abstracts, 20:2768-9 (Jan). [5582

DONALD MEIKLEJOHN. Jane Addams and American democracy [1890s-1930s]. Social service rev., 34:253-64 (Sep). notes. [5583

HENRY BORZO. A chapter in Iowa-Russian relations. Ann. Ia., 34:561-96 (Apr 1959). port. notes. On the Iowa Commission for Russian Famine Relief (organized by Benjamin F. Tillinghast), 1891-92, and the comments in Iowa newspapers concerning its work, the tyranny of the Russian Government, its abuse of the Jews, their tendency to hoard food for sale at an exorbitant profit, and the probability that the famine would stimulate Jewish emigration to America. [5584

HOMER FOLKS. Public health and welfare the citizens' responsibility: selected papers of Homer Folks. Edited by Savel Zimand. N.Y.: Macmillan, 1958. xxxv, 475 p. Forty-nine lectures and papers, 1891-1946, on "child-caring work," juvenile probation, hospitals, insanity, tuberculosis, the aged, public action to promote welfare, etc.; with a biographical sketch of the author, General Agent for the Children's Aid Society of Pennsylvania, 1890-93, head of the State Charities Aid Association of New York, 1893-1947, and official of many other charitable agencies. [5585

RALPH MUNN. Gospel of wealth. Carnegie mag., 34:329-34 (Dec). port., views. On the philanthropies of Andrew Carnegie, 1891-1911. [5586

Sister ANN JOACHIM. Immunity doctrine in the South West. South Tex. law jour., 4:232-48 (summer 1959). notes. On "the tort immunity doctrine" in Arkansas, Kentucky, Missouri, Tennessee, and Texas, with particular reference to the immunity of charitable institutions, 1894-1957, and some account of related decisions in other States. [5587

NEILL H. ALFORD, JR. Voluntary foreign aid and American foreign policy: the element of State control. Va. law rev., 46:477-515 (Apr). notes. On State legal aspects of "private American assistance to persons in foreign countries," 1898-1960, including testamentary charities, with special reference to problems of taxation and administration. [5588

MAURINE McKEANY. The absent father and public policy in the program of aid to dependent children. Berkeley: Univ. of California Press, 1960. [8], 132 p. tables. bibliog. (p. 122-32), notes. (University of California publications in social welfare, 1.) Information collected from State welfare agencies in 1954 and review of publications on the same problem since 1905. [5589

RALPH GREENFIELD. Judicial review and the public assistance programs. Dicta, 31:181-95 (May 1954). notes. On "the claim to public assistance as a legally enforcible right," 1911-53. [5590

MARY G. CARY. Jan Addams knew no "enemy." Am.-German rev., 26(6): 3-5 (Aug-Sep). port., view. On her services under Herbert Hoover in European relief work and in America to collect funds for the work, 1919, and "the attacks on Jane Addams' efforts in behalf of the German child feeding." [5591

ELIAS CLARK. The limitations on political activities: a discordant note in the law of charities [1919-59]. Va. law rev., 46:439-66 (Apr). notes. [5592

BERT S. PRUNTY, JR. Love and the business corporation. Va. law rev., 46:467-76 (Apr). notes. On the legal authority of corporations to contribute funds to charities, 1919-59. [5593

WILLIAM POSNER. Retrospect and prospect in casework with the aged. Jour. Jew. communal service, 36: 121-9 (winter 1959). notes. Includes a review of selected publications since 1926. [5594

EWAN CLAGUE. Economic myth and fact in social work [1930-58]. William Wallace Weaver, ed., Frontiers for social work: a colloquium on the fiftieth anniversary of the School of Social Work of the University of Pennsylvania (Phila.: Univ. of Pennsylvania Press [1960]), p. 17-41. [5595

VICTOR CHRISTGAU. Old-age, survivors, and disability insurance after twenty-five years [1935-60]. Social security bul., 23(8):20-30 (Aug). diagrs., table. [5596

DAVELLA MILLS FOUNDATION, Montclair, N.J. The story of the Davella Mills Foundation, 1935-1955, created for the purpose of benefiting mankind, David Bloss Mills [1857-1944], founder. Montclair, N.J.: Board of Trustees, 1957. [8], 71, [1] p. ports., tables, views. On a fund of more than 10 million dollars, established by a wealthy manufacturer, to be liquidated in 20 years; with a report of its disbursements for educational institutions (39%), health (20%), community chests and welfare activities (15%), and other objects. [5597

KATHRYN D. GOODWIN. Twenty-five years of public assistance [1935-60]. Social security bul., 23(8):31-9 (Aug). [5598

MARICE C. HART. Old-age, survivors, and disability insurance program: history of the benefit formula [since 1935]. Social security bul., 23(9):3-9 (Sep). diagr., tables. [5599

IDA CRAVEN MERRIAM. Social security status of the American people [since 1935]. Social security bul., 23(8):6-19 (Aug). diagrs., tables. [5600

KATHERINE (BROWNELL) OETTINGER. Title V of the Social Security Act [relating to child welfare services]: what it has meant to children [1935-60]. Social security bul., 23(8):39-50 (Aug). diagrs. [5601

U.S. Social Security Administration. Significant events, 1935-60. Social security bul., 23(8):66-70 (Aug). Chronology of events resulting from the Social Security Act of 1935 and its amendments. [5602

EDGAR H. S. CHANDLER. The high tower of refuge: the inspiring story of refugee relief throughout the world [by organizations in America, 1944-60, and abroad]. N.Y.: Praeger [1960]. 264 p. ports., views (1 double). bibliog. (p. 248). (Books that matter.) [5603

CHICAGO, UNIVERSITY OF. School of Social Service Administration. In memoriam. Social service rev., 34:91, 233-4, 345-7 (Mar-Sep). Brief notices about Helen Glenn Tyson (1886-1959), Annie C. Watson (1892-1960), Joanna Carver Colcord (1883-1960), Jacob Ellis Finesinger (1902-59), Margaret Leal (1886-1960), Verval Jane Mueller (1908-60), Jessie Taft (1882-1960), Ida M. Cannon (1877-1960), Edwin E. Witte (1887-1960), and Henrietta Lichtenberg Gordon (1898-1960), social workers. [5604

Communication

RICHARD EARL CHAPIN. Mass communications: a statistical analysis. East Lansing: Michigan State Univ. Press [1957]. viii, 148 p. 76 tables. bibliog. (p. 147-8), notes. Statistical series for the newspaper, book, magazine, radio and television, and motion-picture industries, 1790-1955. [5605

FRANCIS EARLE BARCUS. Communications content: analysis of the research, 1900-1958 (a content analysis of content analysis). Ann Arbor: University Microfilms, 1959 [i. e. 1960]. Positive microfilm of typescript. x, 411 leaves. diagrs., tables. bibliog. (leaves 278-410). Thesis--Univ. of Illinois. Abstracted: Dissert. abstracts, 20:3279 (Feb). Survey and analysis of "more than 1700 studies of the mass media and other means of communication" by books, newspapers, magazines, radio, television, and motion pictures. [5606

ADVERTISING

GERI TROTTA. Forerunners of the fashion photograph. Infinity, 7(10): 32-9 (Dec 1958). ports., views. On fashion engravings, professional photographic portraits, society portraits in newspapers, and photographs in fashion advertising, 1830-1916. [5607

NEWT P. HARRISON. Bleistein--before and after. Miss. law jour., 31: 84-94 (Dec 1959). notes. On advertisements (pictures, labels, text) as "a valid subject of copyright," 1888-1954. [5608

EUGENE M. ELSON. Money-back guarantees in the sale of drugs [and other commodities, 1906-54]. Food drug cosmetic law jour., 14:597-603, 614 (Sep 1959). On the relation of the guarantee to "false or misleading" advertising and labels. [5609

KAY HARRIS. The editorial influence on advertising. Infinity, 7(3):7-11 (Mar 1958). facsims., port., views (1 double). On photography in advertising, 1924-58. [5610

BURNETT (LEO) COMPANY, INC. Reaching for the stars: a book for the silver anniversary. [Chicago, 1960.] 37 p. facsims., col. maps, ports., tables, views (1 fold.). On an advertising agency in Chicago, 1935-60, organizing programs of printed, radio, and television advertising for business firms in the United States and Canada. Includes "Three historic memos by Leo Burnett" (1952, 1958, 1960). [5611

HOWARD L. LYDICK. State control of liquor advertising under the United States Constitution [1936-58]. Baylor law rev., 12:43-59 (winter). notes. [5612

MARCUS ALEXIS. Pathways to the Negro market [1939-59]. Jour. Negro educ., 28:114-27 (spring 1959). tables. notes. Largely on the use of Negro newspapers and radios as media of advertising. [5613

THEODORE R. KUPFERMAN. Copyright protection for commercial prints and labels [i. e., advertisements, 1940-59]. South. Calif. law quar., 33: 163-70 (winter). notes. [5614

FREEDOM OF COMMUNICATION

LEONARD WILLIAMS LEVY. Legacy of suppression: freedom of speech and press in early American history [1620-1812]. Cambridge, Mass.: Belknap Press of Harvard University Press, 1960. xiv, [4], 353 p. bibliog. (p. 321-30), notes. [5615

ROOSEVELT FERGUSON. The right to demonstrate [as a premise of American political philosophy, 18th-20th centuries]. Quar. rev. higher educ. among Negroes, 28:238-49 (Oct). notes. [5616

LLOYD DEAN SPRAGUE. The suppression of dissent during the Civil

War and World War I. Ann Arbor: University Microfilms, 1959 [i.e. 1960]. Positive microfilm of typescript. ix, 787 leaves. bibliog. (leaves 762-86). Thesis--Syracuse Univ. Abstracted: Dissert. abstracts, 20:3359 (Feb). [5617

DAVID FELLMAN. Association with "bad" people. Jour. politics, 22:620-28 (Nov). notes. On efforts "to discourage certain types of association by law," 1873-1960, and the frequent court decision that such laws are unconstitutional. [5618

RICHARD W. LAUGESEN. Freedom of speech and press--anonymous communication. Dicta, 37:384-8 (Nov-Dec). notes. On the freedom to speak, write, and publish anonymously, 1897-1960. [5619

GERALD R. STOCKMAN. Constitutional law--freedom of speech and the corporation. Villanova law rev., 4: 377-95 (spring 1959). notes. On "the proposition that a corporation is not entitled to the right of free speech," 1906-51, and the contrary proposition, with precedents as early as 1894. [5620

IRVING M. MEHLER. Constitutional free speech v. State police power. Dicta, 33:145-66 (May-Jun 1956). port. notes. On attempts to invoke the aid of the Supreme Court against State action in suppressing free speech, 1907-52. [5621

HARRY N. SCHEIBER. The Wilson administration and civil liberties, 1917-1921. Ithaca: Cornell Univ. Press [1960]. ix, 69 p. bibliog. (p. 65-6), notes. (Cornell studies in American history, literature, and folklore, 6.) Revision of thesis (M. A.)--Cornell Univ. On "security measures," censorship by the Post Office Department, prosecutions by Federal attorneys under the Espionage and Sedition Acts, the "Red Scare", and Wilson's "abdication of responsibility" for these abuses. [5622

PHILLIP ALLYN RANNEY. Political free speech for the union man. West. Reserve law rev., 11:661-8 (Sep). notes. On the right of unions to expel members whose expressed political views are opposed to union policy, and to apply members' dues for political purposes, 1921-59. [5623

GABRIEL JACKSON. Reflections on two loyalty purges. Centennial rev. arts & science, 4:223-42 (spring). On analogies between "the purge of Erasmist intellectuals from the Spanish Church and universities in the decade of the 1530's" and the "purge of thousands of civil servants, teachers, actors and writers tainted, however mildly, by Marxist associations," motivated by a "powerful demand for ideological conformity" in America, 1947-55. [5624

ALEXANDER MEIKLEJOHN (1872-1964). Political freedom: the constitutional powers of the people. With a foreword by Malcolm Pitman Sharp. N.Y.: Harper [1960]. xxv, 166 p. notes. Reprint of the author's Free speech and its relation to self-government (1948), and papers, 1948-58, on "The Congress and the people," "The freedom of scholars and teachers," and "Legislative investigation of political beliefs and associations." [5625

Censorship

HOWARD H. FOGEL. Colonial theocracy and a secular press. Journalism quar., 37:525-33 (autumn). notes. Review of control of the press by the church-dominated governments of Massachusetts, 1639-1723, and Pennsylvania, 1685-93. [5626

ROBERT W. HANEY. Comstockery in America: patterns of censorship and control [1650-1959]. Boston: Beacon Press [1960]. xii, 199 p. bibliog. (p. 179-91), notes. [5627

JULIAN PARKS BOYD. Subversive of what? Robert B. Downs, ed., The first freedom: liberty and justice in the world of books and reading (Chicago: American Library Assoc., 1960), p. 224-30. From the Atlantic monthly, Aug. 1948. On the trial of Nicholas Dufief, Philadelphia bookseller, on a charge of "vending subversive if not blasphemous literature" in selling to Thomas Jefferson a copy of Regnault de Bécourt's Sur la création du monde, ou système d'organisation primitive, 1813; with remarks on Jefferson's attitudes toward "subversion and loyalty," 1800-1813. [5628

LEO M. ALPERT. Judicial censorship of obscene literature [in America, 1821-1938, and in England]. Robert B. Downs, ed., The first freedom: liberty and justice in the world of books and reading (Chicago: American Library Assoc., 1960), p. 52-67. From Harvard law review, 1938. The American cases considered are from Massachusetts and New York. [5629

ROBERT E. SHEPHERD, JR. The law of obscenity in Virginia [1847-1958]. Wash. and Lee law rev., 17:322-8 (fall). notes. Deals mainly with the law in other States and in Federal cases, 1821-1958. [5630

HARVEY LYLE ZUCKMAN. Obscenity in the mails. South. Calif. law quar., 33:171-88 (winter). notes. On litigation resulting from the Comstock Act of 1873, with special reference to "the power of the Post Office Department to restrain the mailing of supposedly obscene matter." [5631

BEN RAY REDMAN (1896-1961). Is censorship possible? Robert B. Downs, ed., The first freedom: liberty and justice in the world of books and reading (Chicago: American Library Assoc., 1960), p. 213-15. From Scribner's magazine, May 1930. On the "impracticability" of legal enforcement of censorship, 1908-28. [5632

JOHN E. HARTMANN. The Minnesota gag law and the Fourteenth Amendment. Minn. hist., 37:161-73 (Dec). facsim., ports., view. On the activities of Howard A. Guilford and Jay M. Near as publishers of Minnesota newspapers filled with reports of violence, attacks on minority groups, "grossly exaggerated accounts" of public malfeasance, and private scandals 1913-34, the growing nuisance of other "scandal sheets" and of blackmail by their publishers, a Minnesota statute of 1925 providing for injunction against the issuance of "obscene, lewd, and lascivious" or "malicious, scandalous, and defamatory" newspapers and magazines, and litigation inaugurated by Near, ending when the U.S. Supreme Court decided that the 14th Amendment extended the 1st Amendment to the States and that the Minnesota statute was invalid as a prohibition of freedom of speech. [5633

LEO M. ALPERT. Naughty, naughty! Robert B. Downs, ed., The first freedom: liberty and justice in the world of books and reading (Chicago: American Library Assoc., 1960), p. 4-8. From Colophon, 1939. On prosecutions by the New York Society for the Suppression of Vice and the New England Watch and Ward Society, 1916-36, and the stimulating effects (sometimes delayed) of prosecutions upon sales of the books concerned. [5634

BERNARD AUGUSTINE DE VOTO (1897-1955). The easy chair. Robert B. Downs, ed., The first freedom: liberty and justice in the world of books and reading (Chicago: American Library Assoc., 1960), p. 201-9. From the author's column in Harper's magazine, Aug. 1947 and Apr. 1953. On censorship in America, 1926-47, and the activities of the Select Committee on Pornographic Materials of the U.S. House of Representatives, 1952-53. [5635

HAVELOCK ELLIS (1859-1939). Obscenity and the censor. Robert B. Downs, ed., The first freedom: liberty and justice in the world of books and reading (Chicago: American Library Assoc., 1960), p. 168-71. From the London Saturday review, 17 Nov. 1928. Review of To the pure: a study of obscenity and the censor, by Morris Ernst and William Seagle (N.Y. 1928). [5636

ARTHUR MEIER SCHLESINGER, JR. Notes on a national cultural policy [1934-60]. Daedalus, 89:394-400 (spring). Proposes the establishment by the U.S. Government of "standards in media, like television and radio, which exist by public sufferance." [5637

LOWELL S. THOMAS, JR. Federal Communications Commission: control of "deceptive programming." Univ. Pa. law rev., 108:868-93 (Apr). notes. On authority claimed by the Commission under the Communications Act of 1934 and the question whether the authority can be constitutionally exercised over "television quiz shows ... 'rigged' by the producers and others." [5638

Defamation

PETER J. BELTON. The control of group defamation: a comparative study of law and its limitations [in the United States, 1815-1958, Great Britain, and France]. Tulane law rev., 34:299-342, 468-504 (Feb, Apr). notes. On the very limited success of legal efforts to accomplish such control and the impossibility of their succeeding in any large measure. [5639

JAMES C. BROUGH. Defamation by radio and television. South Tex. law jour., 4:253-76 (summer 1959). notes. On the reading aloud of defamatory words as publication of libel rather than scandal, 1840-1959. [5640

WILLIAM LLOYD PROSSER. Libel per quod. Va. law rev., 46:839-55 (Jun). notes. On damages for "libel whose defamatory imputation is not apparent upon the face of the publication, and arises only by reference to facts known to the reader which are not set forth" (as distinguished from libel per se), 1877-1959; with some account of indications that "the two old torts," libel and slander, are "inching slowly toward some ultimate fusion." [5641

ALFRED H. KNIGHT III. Libel per se and special damages [1887-1959]. Vanderbilt law rev., 13:730-44 (Jun). notes. [5642

EDWARD A. PASTEWKA. Absolute privilege in defamation: the extension by Barr v. Matteo. Univ. Pittsburgh law rev., 21:41-51 (Oct 1959). notes. On the exemption of heads of executive departments from prosecution for defamation, 1895-1959, and the expansion of the privilege to include executive officers of less than cabinet rank. [5643

DENNIS W. SHEEHAN. Broadcasters' immunity from liability for political defamation [1927-59]. Georgetown law jour., 48:544-62 (spring). notes. [5644

Invasion of Privacy

FREDERICK DAVIS. What do we mean by "right to privacy"? S. D. law rev., 4:1-24 (spring 1959). notes. On the "right" since its first recognition as such in 1890, and the desirability of distinguishing it from "infliction of mental suffering" and "expropriation of personality or some property interest therein." [5645

JOE C. MEDINA. Invasion of the right of privacy--status in Colorado. Dicta, 37:107-14 (Mar-Apr). notes. On the right in the United States, 1890-1959, and Colorado, 1913-56. [5646

PRISCILLA L. RIDER. Legal protection of the manifestations of individual personality--the identity--indicia. South. Calif. law rev., 33:31-70 (fall 1959). notes. Thesis (LL. M.)--Univ. of Southern California. On the development of the law of privacy since 1890; with proposals for recognition of a right including both protection of privacy and recognition of a property right in publicity value, with particular reference to "stabilizing the position of the celebrity." [5647

HAROLD R. GORDON. Right of property in name, likeness, personality, and history. Northw. Univ. law rev., 55:553-613 (Nov-Dec). notes. On the right as part of the right of privacy or as a "right to be free from commercial exploitation," 1902-59. [5648

Privileged Communications

GERTRUDE J. BUCK. Confession and the courts. Am. eccles. rev., 142: 77-86 (Feb). notes. On legal recognition of the privileged character of priest-penant communications and the "perpetual and inviolable secrecy" of the penant's confession, 1813-1951. [5649

RALPH SLOVENKO. Psychiatry and a second look at the medical privilege. Wayne law rev., 6:175-203 (spring). notes. On protection of the confidentiality of "the physician-patient relationship" by American law since 1828, first specifically applied to psychiatrists in 1959. [5650

HENRY ROOT STERN, JR. The problem of privilege: historical and juridical sidelights. Am. jour. psychiatry, 115:1071-80 (Jun 1959). notes. On the concept of privileged communications between physician and patient, 1828-1958. [5651

PAUL E. PRESSLEY. The qualified privilege of mercantile agencies as a defense for libelous reports. Mercer law rev., 11:221-8 (fall 1959). notes. On agencies that sell information "about the financial standing and reputation of persons and firms" to buyers who "contemplate doing business" with the persons and firms, 1856-1953. [5652

HERBERT M. ROSENTHAL. The informer privilege in criminal prosecutions [1872-1958]. Hastings law jour., 11:54-63 (Aug 1959). notes. [5653

HERBERT L. MOODY, JR. The priest-penitent privilege in South Carolina--background and development. S.C. law quar., 12:440-53 (spring). notes. On the lack of reference to such a privilege in South Carolina before its establishment by a law of 1959, and its recognition in Federal law as early as 1876 and in the laws of various States. [5654

RAYMOND JAMES HAGAN. Impounding and the subpoena duces tecum. Brooklyn law rev., 26:199-240 (Apr). notes. On the confounding of the 2 powers by district attorneys and grand juries; with a review of "rights in one's papers" in the United States, 1886-1959. [5655

MALACHI L. HARNEY & JOHN C. CROSS. The informer in law enforcement [1895-1959]. Springfield, Ill.: Thomas [1960]. xi, 83 p. [5656

T. D. TAUBENECK & JOHN J. SEXTON. Executive privilege and the court's right to know--discovery against the United States in civil actions in Federal district courts [1932-59]. Georgetown law jour., 48: 486-529 (spring). tables. notes. [5657

JAMES L. STEIMEL. Work product in the Federal discovery procedure. Marquette law rev., 43:329-40 (winter). notes. On the papers, records, and personal knowledge acquired by a lawyer in preparing a case for trial "or at least in anticipation of litigation," and the extent to which this "product" is "privileged," 1940-59. [5658

THOMAS R. HUNT. Corporate law department communications--privilege and discovery. Vanderbilt law rev., 13:287-309 (Dec 1959). notes. Analysis of "traditional notions of the attorney-client privilege, and the newer but even more significant 'work-product' concept, as they relate to house counsel," 1945-59. [5659

GOODLOE E. BYRON. The production and admissibility of Government records in Federal tort claims cases [1946-58]. Md. law rev., 20:117-32 (spring). notes. [5660

JOHN G. PEGG. Hospital records. Ohio State law jour., 21:190-203 (spring). notes. On the extent to which these records are "privileged," 1947-58, with special reference to communications between nurse and patient in hospitals. [5661

Self-Incrimination

JOSEPH P. BROWNE. Some moral implications of the privilege against self-incrimination in the Fifth Amendment to the Constitution of the United States. Wash., 1960. xi, 90 p. bibliog. (p. 81-6), notes. "Dissertatio ad lauream in Facultate S. Theologiae apud Pontificium Athenaeum 'Angelicum' de urbe." On the privilege as "but a statement of the natural law." Includes chapters on "The judicial use of confessions." "The natural right to silence," "Limitations on the right to silence," and "Moral judgment concerning those who invoke the Fifth Amendment." [5662

LEWIS MAYERS. The Federal witness' privilege against self-incrimination: constitutional or common-law? Am. jour. legal hist., 4:107-41 (Apr). notes. On the genesis of the privilege in the Bill of Rights (1791), the commentary and judicial opinions upon it during the next century, the inclusion of similar provisions in the State constitutions, and the legislation since 1857 to compel testimony when immunity from prosecution is offered; with an argument that the constitutional protection applies, and was intended by its framers to apply, only to defendants in criminal cases, and has no application to witnesses. [5663

HARRIS B. STEINBERG. A re-examination of the Fifth Amendment [1791]. N.Y. State Bar bul., 31:230-40 (Jul 1959). port. [5664

JACK KRONER. Self incrimination: the external reach of the privilege. Columbia law rev., 60:816-38 (Jun). notes. On "the scope of the privilege when there is a claim of incrimination under the laws of a jurisdiction other than the one granting the privilege," 1828-1960. [5665

RICHARD JOHN BLOSS. The right of silence and statutory immunity: a study of the privilege against self-incrimination [since 1857], with particular emphasis upon the Immunity Act of 1954. Ann Arbor: University Microfilms, 1960. Positive microfilm of typescript. [264] leaves. Thesis--Univ. of Pennsylvania. Abstracted: Dissert. abstracts, 21:1236 (Nov). Concludes "that only an unrestricted privilege can provide the constitutional protection of the right of silence in the Fifth Amendment" and that the act of 1954 ought to be repealed. [5666

MERLE L. SILVERSTEIN. Federal grand jury testimony and the Fifth Amendment [1917-60]. Wash. Univ. law quar., 1960:215-38 (Jun). notes. [5667

PETER MEGARGEE BROWN. The great wiretapping debate and the crisis in law enforcement [1918-60]. N.Y. law forum, 6:265-82 (Jul). notes. [5668

ROBERT D. GOULD. An analysis of the limited legal value of truth serum [and narcoanalysis, 1926-59]. Syracuse law rev., 11:64-8 (fall 1959). notes. [5669

ROBINSON O. EVERETT. New procedures of scientific investigation and the protection of the accused's rights. Duke law jour., 1959:32-77 (winter 1959). notes. On the legal status of evidence obtained by wiretapping and "electronic eavesdropping," collecting "body fluids and substances" extracted from the defendant without his consent, taking his fingerprints or his photograph, requiring him to provide a sample of his handwriting, and testing him with "truth drugs" or "lie detectors," 1928-58. [5670

DOROTHY KENYON. Wiretapping [as a subject of legislation and litigation, 1928-60]. N.Y. law forum, 6:283-99 (Jul). notes. [5671

ROBERT PRICE. The admissibility of wiretap evidence in the Federal courts [1928-59]. Univ. Miami law rev., 19:57-71 (fall 1959). notes. [5672

ALAN FURMAN WESTIN. Wiretapping: the quiet revolution [since 1928]. Commentary, 29:333-40 (Apr). [5673

ANTHONY P. SAVARESE, JR. Eavesdropping and the law [1934-60]. Am. Bar Assoc. jour., 46:263-6, 332-6 (Mar). port. notes. On litigation as to the legality of wiretapping, 1934-60, especially in New York. [5674

JOHN MICHAEL GARNER. The third degree and coerced confession in State courts [1936-60]. Wash. and Lee law rev., 17:238-44 (fall). notes. [5675

SAMUEL L. HIGHLEYMAN. The deceptive certainty of the "lie detector" [1938-58]. Hastings law jour., 10: 46-64 (Aug 1958). notes. [5676

JOURNALISM

E. R. SMITH. Almanacs. Hobbies, 64(11):124-5 (Jan). On American almanacs printed between 1685 and 1850 as collectibilia. [5677

NEW YORK TIMES. Promotion Dept. The newspaper industry [since 1704]. John G. Glover & Rudolph L. Lagai, eds., The development of American industries: their economic significance, 4th ed. (N.Y.: Simmons-Boardman [1959]), p. 692-705. [5678

WALTER DAVENPORT & JAMES C. DERIEUX. Ladies, gentlemen, and editors. Garden City, N.Y.: Doubleday, 1960. 386 p. facsims., ports. bibliog. (p. 375-80). Chapters on more than 20 general and popular magazines and their publishers and editors, 1741, 1801-1950s, mainly in the second half of the 19th century. [5679

CALDER M. PICKETT. Technology and the New York press in the 19th century. Journalism quar., 37:398-407 (summer). notes. Based on thesis--Univ. of Minnesota. Study of 6 New York City newspapers--their editorial comments on the progress of technology and their use of it in their own operations. [5680

DONALD ODELL DEWEY. A modern technique, but an old idea. Journalism quar., 37:439-40 (summer). notes. On a proposal of James Lyon to James Madison, 2 Jul. 1801, to print a 16-page weekly newspaper in Washington and ship "the printed sheets ... to branch offices throughout the century, where a local entrepreneur was to print a cover consisting of local news and advertising, stitch it to the printed sheets, and sell the finished product for $2.50 a year." [5681

FRANK LUTHER MOTT (1886-1964). "... a consuming desire to ... elevate society." John Arthur Garraty, ed., The unforgettable Americans (Great Neck, N.Y.: Channel Press [1960]), p. 203-7. On Horace Greeley (1811-72), editor of the New York Tribune, ardent participant in movements for social and political reform. [5682

CECIL DE GROTTE EBY, JR. "Porte Crayon": the life of David Hunter Strother [1816-88]. Chapel Hill: Univ. of North Carolina Press [1960]. xi, [3], 258 p. ports., views. bibliog. (p. 239-51), notes. Based on thesis--Univ. of Pennsylvania. On his early life and studies his work as a traveling writer of "descriptive literary sketches" of places and regions (illustrated with his own engravings), his service in the Union Army, his work as editor of the Charles Town, W. Va., Herald, and his service as Consul General in Mexico (1879-85); with lists of his "Published and unpublished writings" (p. 227-31) and his "Journals, correspondence, and sketchbook" (p. 232-8). [5683

HELEN (ROSEN) WOODWARD. The lady persuaders. N.Y.: Ivan Obolensky [1960. 10], 189, [1] p. cartoons, facsims., ports., views. On general magazines for women, 1828-1960, including Godey's lady's book, Ladies' home journal, Delineator, McCall's magazine, Woman's home companion, and Good housekeeping, with special reference to their publishers, editors, editorial policies, and advertising. Based in part upon the author's experience as an editor and an advertising agent. [5684

E. R. SMITH. Tidbits of history from old newspapers. Hobbies, 65(6):109,

113 (Aug). Information and excerpts from The Pennsylvania inquirer (Philadelphia), 1 Jun. 1829, and a "large eight page paper issued by the Rand Avery Co. in 1880, on the occasion of the 250th anniversary of Boston." [5685

LEWIS P. SIMPSON. "Touching 'The stylus'": notes on Poe's vision of literary order. Waldo McNeir & Leo B. Levy, eds., Studies in American literature (Baton Rouge: Louisiana State Univ. Press, 1960 [Louisiana State University studies, Humanities series, 8]), p. 33-48. notes. On his "long-continued, abortive efforts to establish his own literary magazine, which he first called the Penn Magazine and later the Stylus," 1839-49. [5686

THE DIAL: A MAGAZINE FOR LITERATURE, PHILOSOPHY, AND RELIGION. Emerson and Thoreau in the index to The dial. Emerson Soc. quar., 18: leaves 44-9 (1st quar.). Inventory, by George Willis Cooke, to accompany his reprint of The dial, of the titles and authors of all the contributions to the 16 numbers of this periodical, Jul. 1840-Apr. 1844. [5687

JAMES THOMPSON SHEEP. John W[ien] Forney [1817-81]--stormy petrel of American journalism. Ann Arbor: University Microfilms, 1959 [i. e. 1960]. Positive microfilm of typescript. [137] leaves. Thesis--Univ. of Pittsburgh. Abstracted: Dissert. abstracts, 20:3275 (Feb). On his activities as a political journalist in Lancaster, Philadelphia, and Washington, 1844-80. [5688

KENNETH HOLSTON MYERS II. ABC and SRDS: the evolution of two specialized advertising services. Bus. hist. rev., 34:302-26 (autumn). facsims., tables. notes. On the Audit Bureau of Circulations (founded in 1914), the Standard date and rate service (begun in 1919), and earlier agencies and publications concerned with the circulation and advertising rates of newspapers, 1856-1957. [5689

LOUIS MORRIS STARR. Lincoln and the press [1861-65]. Ralph G. Newman, ed., Lincoln for the ages (Garden City, N.Y.: Doubleday, 1960), p. 213-18. [5690

MR. Howe of Beacon Hill. Harvard alumni bul., 55:385-7, 390-91 (7 Feb 1953). ports. On Mark Antony De Wolfe Howe (born 1864), native of Reading, Pa., student at Lehigh University and Harvard, editor of the Youth's companion and the Harvard alumni bulletin, vice-president of the Atlantic monthly corporation, biographer. [5691

ROBERTA CLAY. Literary allusions in selected newspaper editorials. Journalism quar., 37:231-40 (spring). notes. Analysis of selected editorials from the Louisville Courier-journal (1868-1919), the Emporia (Kan.) Gazette (1895-1928), the Atlanta Constitution (1959), and the Little Rock Arkansas gazette (1959). [5692

DOLLENA JOY HUMES. Oswald Garrison Villard [1872-1949], liberal of the 1920's. [Syracuse, N.Y.:] Syracuse Univ. Press, 1960. xiii, [3], 276, [1] p. ports., views. bibliog. (p. 264-8), notes. (Men and movements series.) On his early life and studies, his work as a political journalist, contributor to the Christian century and the Progressive, and editor of the Nation (1918-1932). [5693

WILLIAM RICHARD LINNEMAN. American life as reflected in illustrated humor magazines: 1877-1900. Ann Arbor: University Microfilms, 1960. Positive microfilm of typescript. [362] leaves. Thesis--Univ. of Illinois. Abstracted: Dissert. abstracts, 21:1567-8 (Dec). [5694

GEORGE W. BISHOP, JR. New England journalist: highlights in the newspaper career of Charles H[enry] Dow. Bus. hist. rev., 34:77-93 (spring). view. notes. On his work for The Springfield Republican, 4 Providence papers, and several New York City papers; his founding of Dow, Jones, & Company (1882); and his work as editor and financial analyst of The Wall Street journal. [5695

CHALMERS LOWELL PANCOAST (born 1880). The Chalmers Pancoast story: saga of a roving reporter. By Kathleen Brown, Frankfort, Ind.: G. Y. Fowler's Sons, c1960. [6], xvii, 211, [1] p. facsims., ports., views. On the author's early life in Newark and elsewhere in Ohio, his work as a newspaper reporter, his advertising agencies in New York, his service as "promotion manager" of several New York hotels, his editing of The Grand Encampment review of the Knights Templars, and his life in retirement at Newark. [5696

GEORGE MONTEIRO. A note on the Mark Twain - Whitelaw Reid relationship. Emerson Soc. quar., 19: leaves 20-21 (2d quar.). notes. On the reason why Mark Twain abandoned in 1881 his projected biography of Whitelaw Reid, editor of the New York tribune, whom he regarded as "the polecat of our species." [5697

WILLIAM RICHARD LINNEMAN. Opie Read and The Arkansaw traveler: the trials of a regional humor magazine [Little Rock, 1882-87, and Chicago, 1887-1916]. Midw. folklore, 10:5-10 (spring). notes. On its career till his resignation in 1893. [5698

SCOTT COMPTON OSBORN. Richard Harding Davis [1864-1916]: the development of a journalist. Ann Arbor: University Microfilms, 1953 [i. e. 1960]. Positive microfilm of typescript. ix, 706 leaves. bibliog. (leaves 685-706). Thesis--Univ. of Kentucky. Abstracted: Dissert. abstracts, 20:3474-5 (Mar). On his work as a Philadelphia and New York reporter, a travel writer, and a war correspondent, 1886-1916; with some account of his novels. [5699

DOROTHY STEWARD SAYWARD. Comfort magazine, 1888-1942: a history and critical study. [Orono, Me.] c1960. v, 108, [2] p. facsim. bibliog. (p. 94), notes. (University of Maine studies, 2d ser., no. 75.) On a magazine published in Augusta, Me., founded by William Howard Gannett, containing news, fiction, family advice, editorials, and mail-order advertising. Appended (p. 95-103): "Brief biographies of selected contributors." [5700

LAWRENCE J. GONNER. The C. P. A. has come a long way. Social justice rev., 52:327-9 (Feb). On the Catholic Press Association, founded in 1889. [5701

WILLIAM RICHARD LINNEMAN. Colonel Bill Snort: a Texas Jack Downing. Southw. hist. quar., 64: 185-99 (Oct). views. On Alexander Edwin Sweet (1841-1901), Texas humorist, Democrat, and journalist, and the character created by him as an author of letters from Washington in Sweet's weekly Texas siftings (1889-1890, 1891-1894 or 1895), a satirical observer of the President and his family, his Cabinet, Congress, and the Federal agencies. [5702

LOUIS FILLER. The muckrakers: in flower and in failure [1890s-1916]. Donald Sheehan & Harold C. Syrett, ed., Essays in American historiography: papers presented in honor of Allan Nevins (N.Y.: Columbia Univ. Press, 1960), p. 251-70. notes. [5703

EDWARD ANTHONY (born 1895). This is where I came in: the impromptu confessions of Edward Anthony. Garden City, N.Y.: Doubleday, 1960. 381 p. On the author's early life and Army service, his work as a newspaper reporter, a "free-lance publicity man," a writer, a staff member of Crowell-Collier Publishing Company, and editor of the Woman's home companion and Collier's magazine; with extensive recollections of persons he has known. [5704

ADÈLE LOUISE DE LEEUW. "... a dent on the national consciousness." John Arthur Garraty, ed., The unforgettable Americans (Great Neck, N.Y.: Channel Press [1960]), p. 292-7. On the work of Ida Minerva Tarbell as a muckraking biographer and writer on "political and economic and national problems," 1900-1932. [5705

THOMAS STANLEY MATTHEWS (born 1901). Name and address: an autobiography. N.Y.: Simon and Schuster, 1960. [10], 309 p. On the author's early life and studies, and his work as a book reviewer for the New republic (1925-29) and an editor of Time, the weekly newsmagazine (1929-53); with opinions on liquor, sex, Americanism, and religion. [5706

JUDSON A. GRENIER. Muckraking and the muckrakers: an historical definition [1902-14]. Journalism quar., 37:552-8 (autumn). notes. [5707

KALTY'S fabulous years: the lifetime of a pioneer news analyst. Harvard alumni bul., 53:215-18 (25 Nov 1950). ports. On Hans V. Kaltenborn (born 1878), Harvard 1909, reporter for the Brooklyn Eagle in Washington and Paris, and after 1922 a radio news analyst. [5708

GEORGE AUSTIN TEST. The vital connection: a study of The new republic magazine as a literary journal, 1914-1922. Ann Arbor: University Microfilms, 1960. Positive microfilm of typescript. [288] leaves. Thesis--Univ. of Pennsylvania. Abstracted: Dissert. abstracts, 21:1196-7 (Nov). On the editors, contributors, and contents of the magazine. [5709

HUGH DOWNS (born 1921). Yours truly. N.Y.: Holt, Rinehart, and Winston [1960]. xvi, 201 p. ports. On the author's early life in Lima, Ohio, and his work since 1939 as an announcer and interviewer on radio and television; with his comments on diseases of the television industry. [5710

RICHARD LEE STROUT. Tom Stokes: what he was like. Nieman reports, 13(3):9-10 (Jul 1959). Memories of his habits, characteristics, and ideas during his years in Washington as a reporter, 1921-58. [5711

EDWARD AUGUSTUS WEEKS, JR. Good news and bad. Harvard alumni bul., 52:456-8 (11 Mar 1950). cartoons. On the author's experience in public relations during his Harvard undergraduate years and as editor of the Boston Transcript and the Atlantic monthly, 1921-50. [5712

EDGAR PARKS SNOW. Journey to the beginning. N.Y.: Random House [1958. 10], 434, [1] p. On the author's life and travels abroad since 1928 as a "world correspondent," especially in China and Russia. [5713

KYLE SAMUEL CRICHTON (born 1896). Total recoil. Garden City, N.Y.: Doubleday, 1960. 308 p. On the author's work as an editor of Scribner's magazine and Collier's magazine, 1930 ff.; with a brief account of his early life. Consists largely of undated anecdotes about individuals of his acquaintance. [5714

GABRIEL HEATTER (born 1890). There's good news tonight. Garden City, N.Y.: Doubleday, 1960. 216 p. On the author's work since 1931 as a radio reporter and commentator; with some account of his early life in Brooklyn and his work as a reporter for the New York Sun and editor of The shaft, "a steel magazine." [5715

LOUIS MARTIN LYONS. A glance backward at the press. Nieman reports, 13(1):7-10 (Jan 1959). On changes in the newspaper industry, not all for the better, since 1933. [5716

MARY MARGARET McBRIDE (born 1899). Out of the air. Garden City, N.Y.: Doubleday, 1960. 384 p. ports. On the work of the author as a radio announcer, interviewer, and reporter (under the name "Martha Deane"), in collaboration with Stella Karn, 1934-54. [5717

ABBOTT JOSEPH LIEBLING. Harold Ross--the impresario. Nieman reports, 13(2):14-17 (Apr 1959). Memories of Ross as founder and editor of The New Yorker, 1935-51. [5718

A CASE history of crime. Harvard alumni bul., 55:478-80 (7 Mar 1953). ports. On Alvin M. Josephy (Harvard, 1936), newspaper writer in Mexico, Chief of Special Events in the Office of War Information in Washington during World War II, writer of motion-picture scripts in California, editor of newspapers there, exposer of a "national crime syndicate" in Santa Monica. [5719

WALTER VAN TILBURG CLARK. A timely coming--WR and RW. Contact, 3 (1959): 49-53. facsims., port. On the determination of Ray West, Utah high-school teacher, and several of his friends to establish "an outlet for good writing in their region"; their founding of The intermountain review of English and speech, The intermountain review, and its successor The Rocky Mountain review; the removal of the last as The western review to the University of Kansas and in 1949 to the University of Iowa, and its recent incorporation in Contact. [5720

LEWIS W. GILLENSON. Magazine covers: the editor's story. Infinity, 8(7):12-13 (Sep 1959). views. On the covers of Coronet magazine, their designs and uses, 1937-59. [5721

DAVID SANDERS. Ernest Hemingway's Spanish Civil War experience [1937-39]. Am. quar., 12:133-43 (summer). notes. On the experience as reported in his articles (1938-39) and interpreted in his For whom the bell tolls. Notes that he distinguishes anti-Fascism from Communism. [5722

LOUIS MARTIN LYONS. Twenty years of Nieman Fellowships [1938-58]. Nieman reports, 12(1):7-10 (Jan 1958). [5723

FLY-BLOWN and tattered: the Old Farmer's Almanac, issued by a Harvard man, is the oldest continuous publication in America. Harvard alumni bul., 55:178-9 (8 Nov 1952). port. On the publication of this annual by Robb H. Sagendorph in Dublin, N.H., since 1940. [5724

SCOTT LONG. Writing editorials with a brush: the theory and practice of the political cartoon. Harvard alumni bul., 62:508-11 (2 Apr). cartoons. On the author's work as a cartoonist since ca. 1940. [5725

The GOOD old days. Infinity, 6(5): 20-22, 30 (Christmas 1957). ports. On the American Society of Magazine Photographers, 1944-57. [5726

EDWIN EMERY. The contemporary American daily press [1947-58]. Gazette, 4 (1958): 1-8. [5727

LANGUAGE

ROBERT HARRY LOWIE (1883-1957). Evolution and diffusion in the field of language. Lowie's selected papers in anthropology, ed. Cora Du Bois (Berkeley: Univ. of California Press, 1960), p. 177-86. Manuscript (1955-57?), with references to American Indian languages. [5728

RAVEN IOOR McDAVID, JR. Linguistic geographic and toponymic research. Names, 6:65-73 (Jun 1958). maps. notes. Includes reference to historical elements in place names. [5729

TADEUSZ MILEWSKI. Similarities between the Asiatic and American Indian languages. Internatl. jour Am. linguistics, 26:265-74 (Oct). tables. [5730

GEORGE B. PACE. Linguistic geography and names ending in <i>. Am. speech, 35:175-87 (Oct). maps. notes. Explanation, partly historical, of the present distribution of "-a" and "-y" pronunciations of the final syllable of Cincinnati and Missouri, and shorter consideration of several similarly polysyllabic words spelled with final "-i". [5731

POWELL BURWELL ROGERS. Inland ports. Am. speech, 35:203-5 (Oct). On "towns called ports, harbors, and havens" that "are on the routes of former canals or are on streams that formerly were navigable," most numerous in Pennsylvania and New York (e. g., Williamsport, Pa., and Eagle Harbor, N.Y.). [5732

MORRIS SWADESH. On interhemisphere linguistic connections. Stanley Diamond, ed., Culture in history: essays in honor of Paul Radin (N.Y.: Columbia Univ. Press for Brandeis Univ., 1960), p. 894-924. bibliog. On similarities between Amerindian and Indo-European "linguistic stocks." [5733

HAROLD WENTWORTH & STUART BERG FLEXNER, comps. Dictionary of American slang. N.Y.: Crowell [1960]. xviii, 669 p. diagr. bibliog. (p. 655-69). Includes dated references. Preface (p. vi-xv) and appendix (p. 596-655) are by Flexner, who, according to "Publisher's note," has included, "for the first time in any dictionary, those derogatory and taboo words which play such an important part in American slang." [5734

FREDERIC GOMES CASSIDY. Language on the American frontier. Walker D. Wyman & Clifton B. Kroeber, eds., The frontier in perspective (Madison: Univ. of Wisconsin Press, 1957), p. 185-204. bibliog., notes. On frontier sources of change in the English language brought to America by settlers from England, 17th-19th centuries. [5735

PLINY EARLE GODDARD (1869-1928). The present condition of our knowledge of North American languages. Selected papers from the American anthropologist, 1888-1920, ed. Frederica De Laguna (Evanston, Ill.: Row, Peterson [1960]), p. 385-401. view. bibliog., notes. First printed in 1916. Review of studies of Indian languages, 1632-1914, and bibliography of American and European books and articles. [5736

JOHN C. GREENE. Early scientific interest in the American Indian: comparative linguistics. Am. Philos. Soc., Proc., 104:511-17 (17 Oct). notes. Mainly on Benjamin Smith Barton's New views of the origin of the tribes and nations of America (Philadelphia, 1797); with some account of American references in Peter Simon Pallas, Linguarum totius orbis vocabularia comparativa (St. Petersburg, 1787-89), and in Johann Severin Vater, Mithridates: oder allgemeine Sprachenkunde (Leipzig, 1806-17). [5737

HELEN REEDER CROSS. Noah Webster's best-seller. New-Eng. galaxy, 1(3):20-25 (winter). facsims., port. On his The American spelling book (Boston, 1789), commonly known as "The blue-backed speller," and its moral lessons, its encouragement of spelling bees, and its influence during more than a hundred years in giving America "a unity of speech." [5738

BENJAMIN BOWLES ASHCOM. A note on George Washington and the lexicographers. Am. speech, 35:131-5 (May). notes. On his use of the word "middlings" in letters dated 1792-94, referring only to "the coarser parts of ground wheat as distinguished from flour or bran"; and the erroneous citation of one of the letters by the Oxford English dictionary, the Dictionary of American English, and the Dictionary of Americanisms as evidence that the term applied also to a middle grade of cotton (one of its meanings in the 19th century) and a middle grade of tobacco (a meaning it never had at any time). [5739

ROBERT LAWRENCE COARD. Wide-ranging alliteration. Peabody jour.

educ., 37:29-35 (Jul 1959). On alliterative phrasing in American belles-lettres, oratory, and advertising since the early 19th century. [5740

ARCHER TAYLOR. "Tom, Dick, and Harry." Names, 6:51-4 (Mar 1958). notes. Suggestion that the phrase is "very probably an Americanism," recorded in the United States as early as 1815. [5741

ARCHER TAYLOR & BARTLETT JERE WHITING, comps. A dictionary of American proverbs and proverbial phrases, 1820-1880. Cambridge: Belknap Press of Harvard Univ. Press, 1958. xxii, [2], 418 p. bibliog. (p. xiii-xxii). [5742

GEORGE CONNER. Basil Lanneau Gildersleeve, scholar and humanist, 1831-1924. Ann Arbor: University Microfilms, 1960. Positive microfilm of typescript. [264] leaves. Thesis--Univ. of Wisconsin. Abstracted: Dissert. abstracts, 21:602-3 (Sep). On his studies of Greek and Latin philology and his teaching in the University of Virginia (1856-76) and the Johns Hopkins University. [5743

HIGH flown phraseology. Mo. Hist. Soc., Bul., 16:345-6 (Jul). From the Missouri Republican, St. Louis, 26 Sep. 1834. Current American examples noted by an anonymous contributor. [5744

JULIAN MASON. The etymology of "buckaroo." Am. speech, 35:51-5 (Feb). notes. Argument that it descends from a Gullah word brought from Nigeria (buckra, "white man"), used in altered form (buckeraman) as early as 1835, and in Texas shifted in meaning to "cowboy" through confusion with vaquero. Cites "boccarorra" from Benjamin Franklin without date. [5745

AUDREY R. DUCKERT. Cottage Grove from coast to coast: the genealogy of a place name. Names, 6:180-83 (Sep 1958). On 11 places of this name in various parts of the United States, the earliest probably being the one in Wisconsin so named in 1840. [5746

RALPH T. EUBANKS. The basic derivation of "O. K." Am. speech, 35: 188-92 (Oct). notes. Evidence from 1840 supporting the "Oll Korrect" explanation and weakening the "Old Kinderhook" explanation; with bare mention of "Okeh." [5747

CLARENCE MERTON BABCOCK. Have you got eyes to scoff? Am. speech, 35:310-11 (Dec). notes. On the use of scoff in the meaning "to eat" (from South African usage, from Dutch schoften, "to devour") in America as early as 1850. [5748

MERREL DARE CLUBB, JR. The second personal pronoun in Moby-Dick [1851]. Am. speech, 35:252-60 (Dec). notes. Demonstration of "the necessity of a close analysis of the language of a literary text" and "the practical results ... to be achieved by the application of a linguistic approach to a literary work of art." [5749

HANS SPERBER. Words and phrases in American politics: "grapevine telegraph" [since 1852]. Am. speech, 35: 29-35 (Feb). notes. Evidence that the term (now shortened to grapevine) may have originated as a code name on the Underground Railroad. [5750

HANS GALINSKY. The overseas writer and the literary language of the mother country: American and British English as viewed by American writers from Whitman through Wilder [1855-1954]. Jahrbuch für Amerikastudien, 5:34-65. notes. [5751

ARCHIE GREEN. "Dutchman": an on-the-job etymology. Am. speech, 35:270-74 (Dec). notes. On "a term applied by carpenters to a patch or an insert in woodwork," first recorded in this use in 1859. [5752

ANNE LOHRLI. "Knocked up" in England and the United States. Am. speech, 35:20-28 (Feb). notes. On American use of the expression as early as 1860 in a "low" sense unknown to British usage. [5753

STROTHER BEESON PURDY. The language of Henry James, with emphasis on his diction and vocabulary [1870s-1904]. Ann Arbor: University Microfilms, 1960. Positive microfilm of typescript. [429] leaves. Thesis--Univ. of Illinois. Abstracted: Dissert. abstracts, 21:626 (Sep). [5754

ESTON EVERETT ERICSON. "At the North" ("East," "South"), Am. speech, 35:156-8 (May). notes. Examples of these locutions in fiction dealing with Indiana (1871), Georgia (1955), and Massachusetts (1879). [5755

OLLINGER CRENSHAW & WILLIAM W. PUSEY III. An American classical scholar learns German. Mod. lang. quar., 43:22-5 (Jan 1959). notes. Information from the reminiscences of Milton Wylie Humphreys (manuscript) and his letters to the Lexington gazette (Lexington, Va.) about his experience in learning to speak and understand spoken German in Lexington and during the period of his studies in Germany, 1872-74. [5756

HAROLD CLARK MARTIN. "Gen Ed A" is not English A. Harvard alumni bul., 59:510-13 (6 Apr 1957). cartoons. On "formal instruction in writing in the freshman year" at Harvard, 1884-1957. [5757

JAMES NATHAN TIDWELL. A neglected source of Americanisms. Am. speech, 35:266-9 (Dec). On "a little paper-bound lexicon entitled Two Thousand Words and Their Definitions; not in Webster's Dictionary" (N.Y., 1888; 222 p.), by Anna T. Randall Diehl; with a list of words from this source antedating the earliest citations in the Oxford English dictionary, the Dictionary of American English, and Harold Wentworth's American dialect dictionary, or not occurring in these lexicons. [5758

FRANZ BOAS (1858-1942). On alternating sounds. Selected papers from the American anthropologist, 1888-1920, ed. Frederica De Laguna (Evanston, Ill.: Row, Peterson [1960]), p. 403-9. First printed in 1889. On the varying ways in which different hearers record the same sound or in which a single hearer at different times may do so, and the varying "apperceptions of sounds" by ethnic groups, particularly in the Haida, Kwakiutl, and Eskimo languages. [5759

DONALD CONGER EMERSON. Henry James and the American language. Wis. Acad. Sciences, Trans., 49: 237-47. notes. On his "An animated conversation" (1889), "naming American as the language of the United States and praising its possibilities," and his few later utterances on the same subject, 1892-1907. [5760

HARRY HOIJER. Some problems of American Indian linguistic research [since 1891]. Symposium on American Indian Linguistics, Berkeley, 1951, Papers (Berkeley: Univ. of California Press, 1954 [University of California publications in linguistics, 10]), p. 3-12. notes. [5761

ROBERT HARRY LOWIE (1883-1957). A case of bilingualism. Lowie's selected papers in anthropology, ed. Cora Du Bois (Berkeley: Univ. of California Press, 1960), p. 154-64. notes. From Word, Dec. 1945. Analysis of the author's experience with German and English after his emigration with his family from Austria to America in 1893. [5762

HENRY GRATTAN DOYLE. Jeremiah Denis Matthias Ford [1873-1958]. Mod. lang. jour., 43:59-61 (Feb 1959). On his teaching of the Romance languages at Harvard, 1895-1943, and his publications. [5763

EDWIN BRAY PLACE. Jeremiah Denis Matthias Ford (1873-1958). Hispanic rev., 28:94-6 (Jan). On his teaching of Romance languages at Harvard, 1895-1943, and his bibliographies, textbooks, and editions of Spanish, Italian, and Portuguese literature. [5764

GRIFFITH THOMPSON PUGH. George W. Cable's theory and use of folk speech [1896-98]. South. folklore quar., 24:287-93 (Dec). notes. [5765

ROBERT ANDERSON HALL, JR. Thorstein Veblen and linguistic theory. Am. speech, 35:124-30 (May). notes. Defense of his doctrine (enunciated in his Theory of the leisure class, 1899) that the perpetuation of "'classic' English" and of other "archaic idioms" in other parts of the world "has its roots in a desire to use language as a means of establishing invidious distinctions" between classes of society; that "great purity of speech is presumptive evidence of several successive lives spent in other than vulgarly useful occupations"; and that "the conventional spelling of the English language ... satisfies all the requirements of the canons of reputability under the law of conspicuous waste." [5766

THOMAS ROLLINS FITZGERALD. The language revolution. Cath. educ. rev., 58:361-7 (Sep). notes. On the teaching of foreign languages in America, 1900-1960. [5767

DAVID FRIEND ABERLE. The influence of linguistics on early culture and personality theory [1911-38]. Gertrude E. Dole & Robert L. Carneiro, eds., Essays in the science of culture, in honor of Leslie A. White (N.Y.: Crowell [1960]), p. 1-29. bibliog., notes. Mainly on studies by Ruth Benedict and Edward Sapir. [5768

EDWARD SAPIR (1884-1939). Language and environment. Selected papers from the American anthropologist, 1888-1920, ed. Frederica De Laguna (Evanston, Ill.: Row, Peterson [1960]), p. 434-50. First printed in 1912. [5769

MARY ROSAMOND HAAS. Some genetic affiliations of Algonkin. Stanley Diamond, ed., Culture in history: essays in honor of Paul Radin (N.Y.: Columbia Univ. Press for Brandeis Univ., 1960), p. 977-92. tables. bibliog. notes. On studies and theories, 1913-60, of relations between the Algonkin languages and the Ritwan languages of northern California, the Mosan, the Gulf languages, and Tonkawa, suggesting possible descent from a common source. [5770

FRANZ BOAS (1858-1942). Introduction: International journal of American linguistics [1917]. Margaret Mead & Ruth L. Bunzel, eds., The golden age of American anthropology (N.Y.: George Braziller, 1960), p. 461-9. On the program of a journal "devoted to the study of American aboriginal languages." [5771

THEODORE HUEBENER. Forty years of foreign languages in New York City. Mod. lang. jour., 43:134-5 (Mar 1959). On the teaching of 10 foreign languages in the secondary and elementary schools, 1917-60. [5772

CLARENCE MERTON BABCOCK. Americanisms in the novels of Sinclair Lewis. Am. speech, 35: 110-16 (May). notes. Mainly a list of examples from 3 novels, 1920-25. [5773

EDWARD SAPIR (1884-1939). The grammarian and his language. Margaret Mead & Ruth L. Bunzel, eds., The golden age of American anthropology (N.Y.: George Braziller, 1960), p. 440-49. From the American mercury, 1924. On the "pallid status of linguistics in America." [5774

BENJAMIN LEE WHORF (1897-1941). Language, thought, and reality: selected writings of Benjamin Lee Whorf. Edited and with an introduction by John B. Carroll. [Cambridge:] Technology Press of Massachusetts Institute of Technology [1956]. xi, 278 p. port. bibliog. (p. 271-8), notes. Writings on language, particularly American Indian languages, and its operation as a determinant of thinking, 1927-41; with a biographical sketch and an analysis of his work by the editor (p. 1-34) and a list of his published and manuscript writings. [5775

DONALD DE WITT DURRELL. Research in reading at Boston University [1932-52]. Boston Univ. graduate jour., 1:145-6 (Mar 1953). [5776

WILLIAM GRAVES PERRY, JR. Students' use and misuse of reading skills: a report to a faculty. Harv. educ. rev., 29:193-200 (summer 1959). On an "experiment in reading improvement" at Harvard, 1938-59. [5777

JAMES SEDALIA PETERS II. A study of the Wechsler-Bellevue verbal scores of Negro and white males [1939-52]. Jour. Negro educ., 29: 7-16 (winter). bibliog. Summary of thesis--Illinois Institute of Technology. [5778

HAROLD A. ANDERSON. Teaching the art of listening. National Council of Teachers of English, Perspectives on English: essays to honor W. Wilbur Hatfield (N.Y.: Appleton-Century-Crofts [1960]), p. 89-106. notes. On "listening as a language art" and instruction in the art, 1945-60. [5779

DELL HATHAWAY HYMES. Lexicostatistics so far. Current anthropol., 1:3-42 (Jan). diagrs., tables. bibliog., notes. On glottochronology and lexicostatistics, 1950-59, and earlier studies; with comments by Harold E. Driver, Isidore Dyen, Sarah C. Gudschinsky, and Shirō Hattori. [5780

ROBERT BRAINERD EKVALL. Faithful echo. N.Y.: Twayne Publishers [1960]. 125 p. On the author's work as an oral translator at conferences. Includes some account of his service as a translator from and into Chinese in the Korean negotiations of 1953 at Panmunjom. [5781

POSTAL SERVICE

HARRINGTON ADAMS, comp. Comparative values of ghost towns: the elusive stamps of precanceldom, checked to January 15th, 1960. Winter Park, Fla. [1960]. 14 p. List, alphabetical by States, of "post offices which have been abandoned, those which have been taken over by other offices and are now branches or stations, and post offices which have had their names officially changed by the Post Office Department." [5782

FERGUS R. ELLSWORTH. Postal service development under United States Postmasters General and brief biographical sketch of each [1775-1958. Wauwatosa, Wis., 1960.] 20 p. facsims., ports., tables. bibliog. (p. 20). [5783

ARTHUR E. SUMMERFIELD. U.S. mail: the story of the United States postal service [1775-1960]. By Arthur E. Summerfield as told to Charles Hurd. N.Y.: Holt, Rinehart, and Winston [1960]. 256 p. facsims., map, plan, ports., views. Deals largely with the service during the author's term as Postmaster General, 1953-60, and with current problems of the service. [5784

ARTHUR HECHT, comp. Postal history sources: information contained in registers, lists, tables, guides, and directories of the United States post offices, 1789-1958. Am. philatelist, 73:41-2 (Oct 1959). Guide to types of information. [5785

RUSSELL ALLISON. U.S. and Canadian postal markings. S. P. A. jour., 22:295-6 (Mar). facsims. On the Canadian and U.S. post offices that handled mail crossing the border, 1792-1851. [5786

FRANK I. MORSE. Some famous firsts of the United States Post Office [1792-1929]. S. P. A. jour., 22:217-18 (Jan). [5787

HENRY M. GOODKIND. Montgomery Blair, founder of the U. P. U. Collectors Club philatelist, 39:297-8 (Nov). port. On the action of Blair, Postmaster General, in calling an International Postal Conference that met in Paris and adopted "31 articles of principles for a universal postal union," 1863. [5788

WOLFGANG FRITZSCHE. Catapult airmail. S. P. A. jour., 20:296-9 (Mar 1958). From The German postal specialist (Yeadon, Pa.). On "ship-to-shore airmail," carried from the SS Bremen and the SS Europa in small seaplanes that obtained initial momentum from compressed-air catapults on board, traveling originally only about 69 miles "from ship to USA," eventually an average of 700 miles, 1929-35. [5789

ALBERT A. JACKSON. The billion dollar pork barrel. By Stonewall Jaxson [pseud.]. Boston: Forum Pub. Co. [1960]. 231 p. Observations made by the author as a letter-carrier, later a postal clerk, in New York City, 1930-59, on the inefficiency of the postal service and the prevalence of political patronage in the service; with various proposals for its improvement. [5790

Philately

U.S. Post Office Dept. Office of Special Assistant to the Postmaster General. Postage stamps of the United States: an illustrated description of all United States postage and special service stamps issued by the Post Office Department from July 1, 1847, to December 31, 1959. Wash.: U.S. Govt. Print. Off., 1960. [4], 212 p. facsims., tables. (P.O.D. publication 9 (rev.).) [5791

PHILIP H. WARD, JR. United States early unused blocks, 1847-1869. Am. Philatelic Cong., Congress book, 26: 50-56. facsims. [5792

JULIAN BLANCHARD. History of the vignette on the 1851 eagle carrier stamp. Essay proof jour., 13:173-6 (Jul 1956). facsims. [5793

MORTIMER L. NEINKEN. The United States ten cent stamps of 1855-1859: the plate reconstructions, some postal history, and postal markings of the stamps. [N.Y.: Collectors Club, 1960. 2], 252 p. facsims. Includes sections by Stanley B. Ashbrook (reprinted from his publications) on "Ocean mail to and from California and the Pacific Coast via Panama," "Ship & steamship markings," and "The Great Overland Mail and the Pony Express." [5794

H. S. DICKINSON. Die making and notes on 1863 fourth Nesbitt issue. Am. philatelist, 73:487-8 (Apr). facsim. [5795

H. S. DICKINSON. Die making and notes on fifth and last Nesbitt issue. Am. philatelist, 73:891-4 (Sep). facsims. On "the most controversial issue of all the United States envelopes--the most difficult to distinguish the dies thereof," 1864. [5796

ALFRED J. BARCAN. Official stamps and the just petition. Collectors Club philatelist, 39:117-20 (Mar). facsims., view. On a contract of the Continental Bank Note Company, New York, to print the "general postage stamps" of the U.S. Government, the sudden receipt of orders to print "special stamps" to be used in the correspondence of each of the executive departments, the company's successful petition for compensation of its added expense in filling the order, and the continued use of the dies till 1885, when the stamps were supplanted by penalty envelopes. [5797

J. GARLAND MARKS. Supplementary mail markings on United States postal cards [mailed abroad from the New York City Post Office, 1887, 1879, 1888]. Am. philatelist, 73:421-3 (Mar). facsims. Includes remarks on the rarity of cards thus marked, 1878-98. [5798

THOMAS F. MORRIS. 1894-1898 essays and proofs, Bureau of Engraving & Printing. Essay proof jour., 13:67-75, 205-15 (Apr, Oct 1956). [5799

ALFRED P. H. OVERMENT. U.S. postage meter stamp designs, 1921-1948 (a preliminary type chart). S. P. A. jour., 21:231-3 (Jan 1959). facsims. [5800

HERMAN HERST, JR. Nassau Street: a quarter century of stamp dealing. N.Y.: Duell, Sloan, and Pearce [1960]. ix, 305 p. On the author's life since 1935 as a collector of stamps, a writer about stamps, and a dealer in stamps in New York City. [5801

N. R. HOOVER. History of the Society of Philatelic Americans. S. P. A. jour., 20:320-22, 504-6 (Mar, Jul). These installments: 1944-52. Concludes a series that has been "appearing intermittently" since Jul. 1947. [5802

HAROLD J. FRANKEL. Aboard the world's first atomic submarine. Am. philatelist, 73:53-4 (Oct 1959). facsims. On 4 covers carried aboard the USS Nautilus and autographed there at the author's request by E. P. Wilkinson, commander, and others, 21 Jan. 1954, and later re-mailed for adornment with the signatures of the Secretary of the Navy and of Dwight D. and Mamie (Doud) Eisenhower. [5803

PRINTING, PUBLISHING, AND BOOKSELLING

FRANK LEOPOLD SCHICK. The paperbound book in America: the history of paperbacks and their European background. N.Y.: R. R. Bowker Co., 1958. xviii, 262 p. facsims. bibliog. (p. 245-50), notes. Based on thesis--Univ. of Michigan, 1957. On "American inexpensive books, 1639-1830's," "American paperbounds, 1830-1930," "American paperbacks: the current phase, 1939-1957," and "Publishers of paperbacks." [5804

GEORGE RANKIN ALLEN. Old booksellers of Philadelphia [from Andrew Bradford to A. S. W. Rosenbach, 1720-1940s]. Free Library of Philadelphia, Rare Book Dept., Four talks for bibliophiles ([Phila.] 1958), p. 13-36. [5805

CLARENCE WILLIAM MILLER. Benjamin Franklin's Philadelphia type [1728-66]. Studies in bibliog., 11 (1958): 179-206. facsims. notes. [5806

ROBERT WILSON KIDDER. The contribution of Daniel Fowle to New Hampshire printing, 1756-1787. Ann Arbor: University Microfilms, 1960. Positive microfilm of typescript. [521] leaves. Thesis--Univ. of Illinois. Abstracted: Dissert. abstracts, 20:4666 (Jun). [5807

JANE F. HINDMAN. The Irishman who developed American culture. Am. Cath. Hist. Soc., Rec., 71:23-30 (Mar-Jun). On Mathew Carey (1760-1839), native of Dublin, assistant to Benjamin Franklin in his Passy Press, emigrant to Philadelphia in 1784, publisher of newspapers and magazines there, printer and bookseller, ready participant in controversy, voluminous pamphleteer. [5808

BERTRAM WALLACE KORN. Benjamin Levy [1786-1860]: New Orleans printer and publisher. Bibliog. Soc. Am., Papers, 54:221-64 (4th quar.). facsims., port. notes. On his work in New Orleans as "stationer, bookseller, bookbinder, printer, and commercial publisher," 1811-43 (and possibly in silent association with his son, Alexander Levy, till 1860); with annotated lists (p. 243-64) of the imprints of Benjamin Levy, 1817-41 (310 entries), and Alexander Levy, 1840-6-(22 entries). [5809

WILLIAM C. DABNEY. American Printing House for the Blind, Inc. [Louisville, Ky.] (1858-1960): a century of service to the blind. N.Y.: Newcomen Soc. in North America, 1960. 24 p. views. [5810

JAMES J. SHEA. It's all in the game. By James J. Shea as told to Charles Mercer. N.Y.: Putnam [1960]. 284 p. diagrs., facsims., ports., views. On the Milton Bradley Company, founded in 1860 at Springfield, Mass., by Milton Bradley (1836-1911), publishers and lithographers, makers of lettered blocks, educational games, puzzles, and other devices for kindergarten teaching, publishers of The kindergarten news (begun in 1893), etc.; with some account of Milton Bradley, who settled in Springfield in 1856 as a draftsman and lithographer. [5811

DANIEL HERTZLER. Origin of Mennonite Publishing House. Mennonite hist. bul., 17(4):3-4 (Oct 1956). On a firm established in Chicago by John F. Funk in 1864 to publish the Herald of truth, moved to Elkhart, Ind., in 1867, organized as Mennonite Publishing Company in 1875, and sold to the Mennonite Publishing House in 1908. [5812

IN memoriam: Edwin B[liss] Hill [1866-1949]. Thoreau Soc. bul., 28: [1] (Jul 1949). port. On his life in Michigan, Arizona, and Texas, and his printing of more than a hundred pamphlets and broadsides on a small hand press; with a list of 20 of his imprints by or about Thoreau, 1899-1944. [5813

GORDON HERBERT ROPER. Mark Twain and his Canadian publishers [1870-90]. Am. book collector, 10(10): 13-30 (Jun). cartoon. Includes "Check list of Canadian editions of Mark Twain's work," 1870-189-, 1926. [5814

RAY NASH. The designer's point of view. Dartmouth alumni mag., 52(7): 9-10 (Apr). port. On Daniel Berkeley Updike (1860-1942), book designer for Houghton Mifflin from ca. 1882 to 1894, "the inventor, so to speak, of book designing" as "a distinct calling." [5815

ROGER BURLINGAME. Endless frontiers: the story of McGraw-Hill. N.Y.: McGraw-Hill [1959. 14], 506 p. cartoons, diagrs., facsims., ports., views. notes. On the careers of James Herbert McGraw and John Alexander Hill as publishers of industrial magazines, 1884 ff., the establishment of the McGraw Publishing Company (1899) and the Hill Publishing Company (1902), the joint establishment of the McGraw-Hill Book Company by these 2 companies (1909), and the merger of the 2 companies as the McGraw-Hill Publishing Company (1917). [5816

JOSEPH WILLIAM ROGERS. U.S. national bibliography and the copyright law: an historical study [1790-1960]. N.Y.: Bowker, 1960. xii, 115 p. notes (p. 97-107). Mainly on Catalog of copyright entries, a serial issued by the Copyright Office, 1891-1960. [5817

H. KENNETH DIRLAM. The story of "A message to Garcia." [Mansfield, Ohio, 1960. 24] p. facsim. (in pocket), ports., views. On publishing enterprises of Elbert Hubbard at East Aurora, N.Y., including his parable of 1898, inspired by Lt. Andrew S. Rowan, and The Philistine: a periodical of protest (1895-1915); with an appendix of letters and a facsimile of the Buffalo evening news magazine, 2 Jun. 1945, containing a reminiscent article by Dirlam, "former sales manager of the Roycroft Shops" at East Aurora. [5818

RUDOLPH HJALMAR GJELSNESS. Frank Holme: newspaper artist and designer of books. Lawrence Clark Powell, ed., The Southwest of the bookman ([Los Angeles: Univ. of California Library] 1959), leaves 20-27. notes. First printed 1935. On his Bandarlog Press and its 9 products, 1895-1903, his work as a newspaper artist, and his early death in Arizona from tuberculosis in 1904; with "Bandarlog Press check-list," indicating location of known copies of the publications. [5819

HAL W. TROVILLION. Sharing my note book. Herrin, Ill.: Trovillion Private Press, 1960. [8], 79, [2] p. "Half a century of publishing," on the author's establishment and operation of the Trovillion Private Press at Herrin, 1908-51 (p. 1-3); list of the 51 books published by it in 51 years (p. 81); and 25 essays and anecdotes dealing with literature, natural history, dogs, travel, and other subjects. [5820

WILLIAM J. BARROW & REAVIS C. SPROULL. Permanence in book papers. Science, 129:1075-84 (24 Apr 1959). diagrs., facsims., tables, views. notes. Analysis of the papers of "500 nonfiction books issued by American publishers," 1909-49 (100 books for each decade), to determine the causes of "deterioration of paper in the books of libraries." [5821

SUSAN FOSTER. The Steck Company. Jr. historian (Tex.), 21(2):15-17, 32 (Nov). views. On a printing and publishing firm founded in Austin in 1912. [5822

THOMAS J. WILSON. A publisher speaks out. Harvard alumni bul., 52: 18-22 (24 Sep 1949). ports., view. On the Harvard University Press, 1913-49. [5823

J. E. REYNOLDS (born 1914). The making of a Southwestern bookseller. Lawrence Clark Powell, ed., The Southwest of the bookman ([Los Angeles: Univ. of California Library] 1959), leaves 30-33. On the author's life in Los Angeles County, his sales of books about the American West, and "the rewards of being a bookseller." [5824

NORMAN W. FORGUE. Poorer Richard: an almanac long after Franklin. Foreword by R. Hunter Middleton. Am. book collector, 10(9): 13-22 (May). views. Printed separately in 1944. On the author's career since 1918 as "typesetter, typographer, designer of books, private press printer," collector of "the complete works of The Kelmscott Press," and "a prosperous proprietor of a commercial printing establishment." [5825

MICHAEL JOSEPH WALSH. Adventures in Americana. Free Library of Philadelphia, Rare Book Dept., Four talks for bibliophiles ([Phila.] 1958), p. 81-96. Recollections, by a Boston bookseller, of some of his customers in his "experience of more than forty years," including Frank C. Deering, Matt B. Jones, Edward H. R. Green, and Grenville Kane. [5826

CARL HERTZOG. The printer at the pass. Lawrence Clark Powell, ed., The Southwest of the bookman ([Los Angeles: Univ. of California Library] 1959), leaves 28-9. On the author's life in El Paso as a printer since 1923 and his gradual development of an interest in "the spirit of the old West." [5827

ORION HOWARD CHENEY (1869-1939). Economic survey of the book industry, 1930-1931, as prepared for the National Association of Book Publishers by O. H. Cheney. With 1960 introduction by Robert W. Frase. N.Y.: Bowker [1960]. xxii, 356 p. diagrs., maps, tables. bibliog. (p. 347-8). 1st ed. 1931. [5828

JOSEPH REIDER. The new ornament of Jewish books. Abraham Berger, Lawrence Marwick, & Isidore S. Meyer, eds., The Joshua Bloch memorial volume: studies in booklore and history (N.Y.: New York Public Library, 1960), p. 10-18. notes. On the "revival" in illustration and ornamentation of Jewish books, 1934-60. [5829

NORMAN KENT. The book art of Elfriede Abbe [born 1919]. Am. artist, 24(4):34-9, 58-9 (Apr). facsims., port. On her work since 1944 as a woodcut illustrator of books and a printer of both texts and illustrations on a hand press. [5830

PUBLIC OPINION

EDWARD L. BERNAYS. American public relations: a short history [1865-1955]. Gazette, 2 (1956):69-77. [5831

JOHN M. FENTON. In your opinion ... The managing editor of the Gallup Poll looks at polls, politics, and the people from 1945 to 1960. Boston: Little, Brown [1960]. xv, 220 p. tables. notes. [5832

WENDELL H. DODDS & KENNETH HARWOOD. Governmental issues in U.S. broadcasting, 1946-1955. Jour. broadcasting, 1:161-7 (spring 1957). Based upon Dodd's thesis (M.A.)--Univ. of Southern California, 1957. Report on editorials published by Broadcasting-telecasting magazine expressing attitudes of favor or disfavor; with references to earlier studies. [5833

PUBLIC SPEAKING

GEORGE VROOM BOHMAN. The colonial period [in the history of American public address]. Speech Association of America, A history and criticism of American public address, ed. William Norwood Brigance, 2d ed. (N.Y.: Russell & Russell, 1960), 1: 3-54. bibliog., notes. On the English and other European languages in America, the study and teaching of "rhetoric," and the several "types of speech occasion." [5834

OTA THOMAS. The teaching of rhetoric in the United States during the classical period of education [1643-1800]. Speech Association of America, A history and criticism of American public address, ed. William Norwood Brigance, 2d ed. (N.Y.: Russell & Russell, 1960), 1:193-210. bibliog., notes. On the teaching of elocution in the colleges. [5835

GILES WILKESON GRAY. Thomas Jefferson's interest in parliamentary practice. Speech monographs, 27: 315-22 (Nov). notes. On his Manual of parliamentary practice (1801; 2d ed. 1812), and the reading (begun perhaps as early as 1760) and experience upon which it was based, including his studies of law under George Wythe. [5836

BOWER ALY & GRAFTON P. TANQUARY. The early national period [in the history of American public speaking]: 1788-1860. Speech Association of America, A history and criticism of American public address, ed. William Norwood Brigance, 2d ed. (N.Y.: Russell & Russell, 1960), 1: 55-110. bibliog., notes. [5837

ERNEST J. WRAGE & BARNET BASKERVILLE, eds. American forum: speeches on historic issues, 1788-1900. N.Y.: Harper [1960]. xii, 377, [2] p. bibliog. (p. 369-77), notes. Twenty-six reprinted speeches. [5838

JOHN PILKINGTON, JR. F. Marion Crawford's lecture tour, 1897-1898. Univ. Miss. studies in Eng., 1:66-85. notes. On a "coast-to-coast lecture tour" by the novelist Francis Marion Crawford, speaking on Italian life and art and his adventures in Inda. [5839

WILLARD HAYES YEAGER. Wendell Phillips [1811-84]. Speech Association of America, A history and criticism of American public address, ed. William Norwood Brigance, 2d ed. (N.Y.: Russell & Russell, 1960), 1: 329-62. bibliog., notes. On the oratorical and rhetorical characteristics of his public speaking in promotion of reform movements connected with antislavery, women's rights, labor, temperance, capital punishment, religion, prison management, etc. [5840

RALPH STANLEY POMEROY. Ralph Waldo Emerson as a public speaker. Ann Arbor: University Microfilms, 1960. Positive microfilm of typescript. [342] leaves. Thesis--Stanford Univ. Abstracted: Dissert. abstracts, 20:4461 (May). Study of his preaching, lyceum lecturing, and occasional speaking, 1826-81. [5841

HERBERT AUGUST WICHELNS. Ralph Waldo Emerson [1803-82]. Speech Association of America, A history and criticism of American public address, ed. William Norwood Brigance, 2d ed. (N.Y.: Russell & Russell, 1960), 2:501-25. bibliog., notes. On the oratorical and rhetorical characteristics of his public speaking as a Unitarian minister and "a lecturer on ethical and literary subjects" in the lyceum system, 1826 to ca. 1870. [5842

WILLIAM GRAVES CARLETON. The celebrity cult a century ago. Ga. rev., 14:133-42 (summer). On "the Golden Age of Oratory ... the age of Webster, Clay, and Calhoun," and the oratorical art that "reached its height in the three decades before the Civil War," 1830s-50s. [5843

KENNETH WALTER CAMERON. Notes on the early lectures. Emerson Soc. quar., 20: leaves 25-123 (3d quar.). facsims. Notes elucidating and supplementing The early lectures of Ralph Waldo Emerson, ed. Stephen E. Whicher and Robert E. Spiller, vol. 1 (1833-36), p. 6-424. In the same volume with these notes see also Cameron's review of this publication (leaves 6-8) and his "The challenge of Emerson's early lectures" (leaves 8-10). [5844

ROY CLYDE McCALL. Theodore Parker [1810-60]. Speech Association of America, A history and criticism of American public address, ed. William Norwood Brigance, 2d ed. (N.Y.: Russell & Russell, 1960), 1: 238-64. bibliog., notes. On the oratorical and rhetorical characteristics of his Unitarian sermons and other public speaking, in Boston and elsewhere, 1837-60. [5845

MAUD (MORROW) BROWN. Sarah McGehee Isom [born in "the early 1850's," died 1905]. South. speech jour., 25:27-33 (fall 1959). On her life in Oxford, Miss., her studies in Philadelphia and Boston, her teaching of "oratory" (including speaking and dramatic reading) in the University of Mississippi, and her dramatic readings or recitations in the United States and Europe. [5846

KENNETH WALTER CAMERON. Emerson and Melville lecture in New Haven (1856-1857). Emerson Soc. quar., 19: leaves 85-96 (2d quar.). notes. [5847

KENNETH WALTER CAMERON. Emerson's lecture schedules in Danbury, Connecticut [1856-57, 1859]. Emerson Soc. quar., 19: leaves 81-5 (2d quar.). facsims. notes. [5848

KENNETH GORDON HANCE, HOMER O. HENDRICKSON, & EDWIN W. SCHOENBERGER. The later national period [in the history of American public address]: 1860-1930. Speech Association of America, A history and criticism of American public address, ed. William Norwood Brigance, 2d ed. (N.Y.: Russell & Russell, 1960), 1:111-52. table. bibliog., notes. [5849

NORMAN LEWIS CORWIN. Gettysburg and the few appropriate remarks. Ralph G. Newman, ed., Lincoln for the ages (Garden City, N.Y.: Doubleday, 1960), p. 248-51. On the Gettysburg Address as "an almost perfect small-scale model of Lincoln and his times." [5850

PAUL LEON FATOUT. Mark Twain on the lecture circuit. Bloomington: Indiana Univ. Press, 1960. 321 p. cartoons, facsims., ports. bibliog. (p. 305-10), notes (p. 289-304). On his career as a professional comic lecturer in America and abroad, 1866-1909. [5851

LOUIS MICHAEL EICH. Charles W[illiam] Eliot [1834-1926]. Speech Association of America, A history and criticism of American public address, ed. William Norwood Brigance, 2d ed. (N.Y.: Russell & Russell, 1960), 2: 526-39. bibliog., notes. On the oratorical and rhetorical characteristics of his public speaking on higher education and a wide variety of other subjects, 1869-1923. [5852

CELIA DENUES. Lee Emerson Bassett, 1872-1959. West. speech, 24:110-11 (spring). On his development of the Department of Speech, Stanford University, 1901-38, and his other achievements as "a central figure in the development of speech education in America." [5853

DAYTON DAVID McKEAN. Woodrow Wilson. Speech Association of America, A history and criticism of American public address, ed. William Norwood Brigance, 2d ed. (N.Y.: Russell & Russell, 1960), 2:968-92. bibliog., notes. On the oratorical and rhetorical characteristics of his public speaking, especially on education and politics, 1873-1923. [5854

R. H. BOWERS. Altgeld and Curzon on public speaking. Speech monographs, 27:353-6 (Nov). notes. On John Peter Altgeld's Oratory: its requirements and its rewards (Chicago, 1901), and its inferiority in content and style to Lord Curzon of Kedleston's Modern parliamentary eloquence (1901). [5855

GEORGE WILLIAM DELL. An intensive rhetorical analysis of selected speeches of Robert Maynard Hutchins: 1940-1955. Ann Arbor: University Microfilms, 1960. Positive microfilm of typescript. [592] leaves. Thesis--Univ. of Southern California. Abstracted: Dissert. abstracts, 21: 264-5 (Jul). Study of speeches dealing with war, education, and civil liberties. [5856

SPEECH ASSOCIATION OF AMERICA. [Necrology.] Quar. jour. speech, 46:118, 235-6, 351, 458-9 (Feb-Dec). Memorial sketches, by various contributors, of Louis Michael Eich (1888-1959), Lane Cooper (1875-1959), Lee Emerson Bassett (1872-1959), W. Norwood Brigance (1896-1960), Donald O. Buell (1907-60), Henry Lee Ewbank (1893-1960), and Margaret Cave McClellan (1911-60). [5857

TELECOMMUNICATION

WESTERN UNION TELEGRAPH COMPANY. The telegraph industry [since 1832. By George P. Oslin.] John G. Glover & Rudolph L. Lagai, eds., The development of American industries: their economic significance, 4th ed. (N.Y.: Simmons-Boardman [1959]), p. 706-33. views. [5858

IRVING SETTEL. A pictorial history of radio [1843-1960]. N.Y.: Citadel Press [1960]. 176 p. cartoons, diagrs., facsims., map, ports., views. bibliog. (p. 172). Includes many illustrations of the equipment and operation of "wireless telegraphy" (1899 ff.) and the "wireless telephone" (1920 ff.). [5859

THOMAS BERTRAM COSTAIN. The chord of steel: the story of the invention of the telephone. Garden City, N.Y.: Doubleday, 1960. 238 p. ports., views. Account, semifictional in form, of Alexander Graham Bell (1847-1922) and the Bell family, with special attention to their life in Brantford, Ont., 1870-81. [5860

BERN DIBNER. The Atlantic Cable. Norwalk, Conn.: Burndy Library, 1959. 96 p. diagrs., facsims., fold. col. map, ports., views. bibliog. (p. 94-5), notes. (Burndy Library. Publication 16.) On the work of the New York, Newfoundland, and London Telegraph Company and the Atlantic Telegraph Company in spanning the island of Newfoundland by telegraph and the Atlantic Ocean by cable, 1854-66; with letters from Samuel F. B. Morse and other documents. [5861

ROBERT ALLEN SEDLER. Rights of defrauded quiz show contestants. Wayne law rev., 6:225-51 (spring). notes. Suggests legal concepts (including breach of contract, injury to reputation, fraud, deceit, and prima facie tort, 1854-1959) that might be applied in suits by defeated contestants in contests in which one contestant receives answers in advance without the knowledge of the other or others. [5862

AMERICAN TELEPHONE AND TELEGRAPH COMPANY. The telephone industry [since 1875]. John G. Glover & Rudolph L. Lagai, eds., The development of American industries: their economic significance, 4th ed. (N.Y.: Simmons-Boardman [1959]), p. 734-55. [5863

RADIO CORPORATION OF AMERICA. The radio and television industry [since 1899]. John G. Glover & Rudolph L. Lagai, eds., The development of American industries: their economic significance, 4th ed. (N.Y.: Simmons-Boardman [1959]), p. 768-801. [5864

RONALD HARRY COASE. The Federal Communications Commission [1934-59]. Jour. law & econ., 2:1-40 (Oct 1959). notes. On the development of government regulation of radio broadcasting after 1910 and the lack of competitiveness in the present system of regulation of radio and television. [5865

ROBERT SEARS McMAHON. Harris subcommittee report: 50 years of broadcasting regulation [1910-58]. Jour. broadcasting, 3:56-87 (winter 1959). notes. Excerpts from a study made for a subcommittee of the Committee on Interstate and Foreign Commerce, House of Representatives. [5866

ROGER W. AXFORD. William H[enry] Lighty [1866-1959], radio pioneer. Wis. Acad. Sciences, Trans, 49:283-94. port. notes. On "experimentation with radio" at the University of Wisconsin, 1915 ff., and Lighty's work there in the development of programs for educational broadcasting over the University's Radio Station WHA, ca. 1919 to 1928. [5867

EDGAR E. WILLIS. Sound effects: a look into the past [1921-40]. Jour. broadcasting, 1:327-35 (fall 1957). [5868

CYRIL MONROE JANSKY, JR. The contribution of Herbert Hoover to broadcasting. Jour. broadcasting, 1:241-9 (summer 1957). Participant's recollections and evaluation of the 4 industry-government conferences called by Hoover while Secretary of Commerce "to deal with the problems of radio regulation," 1922-25. [5869

LESLIE J. PAGE, JR. The nature of the broadcast receiver and its market in the United States from 1922 to 1927. Jour. broadcasting, 4:174-82 (spring). notes. [5870

DAVID R. MACKEY. The development of the National Association of Broadcasters [1923-56]. Jour. broadcasting, 1:305-25 (fall 1957). notes. Based on thesis--Northwestern Univ. [5871

The EVOLUTION of television, 1927-1943, as reported in the annual reports of the Federal Radio Commission and the Federal Communications Commission. Jour. broadcasting, 4:198-240 (summer). [5872

ROBERT SEARS McMAHON. Federal regulation of the radio and television broadcast industry in the United States, 1927-1959, with special reference to the establishment and operation of workable administrative standards. Ann Arbor: University Microfilms, 1959 [i.e. 1960]. Positive microfilm of typescript. [366] leaves. Thesis--Ohio State Univ. Abstracted: Dissert. abstracts, 20:3891 (Mar). [5873

WHITNEY NORTH SEYMOUR. Authority of the FCC over broadcast content [1927-60]: memorandum of Special Counsel to National Association of Broadcasters. Jour. broadcasting, 4:18-26 (winter). notes. Presented at hearings in Jan. 1960. Argument that "Those with special views about what the public ought to see, hear or enjoy should first persuade the public to want them rather than to ask the Commission to impose their private notions on the public, which it cannot do." [5874

MILO RYAN. A treasure house of broadcast history. Jour. broadcasting, 1:75-8 (winter 1957). On a collection of transcripts of "important public addresses" made by KIRO in Seattle from broadcasts of CBS, 1939-45, now in possession of the University of Washington, comprising "upwards of 4000 discs, involving around 7500 programs." [5875

RICHARD A. GIVENS. Refusal of radio and television licenses on economic grounds [by the Federal Communications Commission, 1940-60]. Va. law rev., 46:1391-1406 (Nov). notes. [5876

Crime and Punishment

BRADLEY CHAPIN. Colonial and Revolutionary origins of the American law of treason [1676-1782]. Wm. and Mary quar., 17:3-21 (Jan). notes. "Table of cases" (p. 17-21). [5877

JAMES ALLAN CLIFFORD GRANT. Our common law Constitution. Boston: Boston Univ. Press, 1960. [12], 56, [9] p. notes. "Table of cases" (p. 57-61). (The Gaspar G. Bacon lectures on the Constitution of the United States, 1959.) Also printed: Boston Univ. law rev., 40:1-56 (winter). notes. On "procedural guarantees in the field of criminal law," 1701-1958, especially since 1789. [5878

NEIL W. SCHILKE. Right to counsel--an unrecognized right [1701-1959]. Wm. and Mary law rev., 1:318-52. notes. [5879

JOHN P. VUKASIN, JR. Useful or useless? the grand jury. State Bar Calif., Jour., 34:436-47 (Jul-Aug 1959). notes. On the English origin of the grand jury (abolished in England in 1933), its use in America as early as 1734, the growing volume of attacks upon it in recent years, and the value of its powers to investigate, indict, and report. [5880

HENRY LEON SNYDER. Unique aspects of the trials of John Fries. Lehigh Co. Hist. Soc., Proc., 23: 48-59. On resistance by Fries and others to the imposition of a Federal tax "on homes and slaves," their harassment of assessors in eastern Pennsylvania, the 2 trials of Fries "upon the charge of treason" in Philadelphia (1799, 1800), the verdict of guilty in both, and his pardon by President Adams; with an examination of irregularities in the procedures of both trials, particularly the conduct of Judges James Iredell, Richard Peters, and Samuel Chase. [5881

RALPH SLOVENKO. The treatment of the criminal in Louisiana and elsewhere. Tulane law rev., 34:523-70 (Apr). notes. On the death penalty, imprisonment, "impairment of legal personality," executive clemency, parole, and rehabilitation, mainly since 1803. [5882

LESTER BERNHARDT ORFIELD. Arraignment in Federal criminal procedure [1806-1958]. La. law rev., 20:1-31 (Dec 1959). notes. [5883

LESTER BERNHARDT ORFIELD. Pleadings and motions before trial in Federal criminal procedure. Fordham law rev., 29:1-82 (Oct). notes. Includes a history of the drafting of the relevant provisions of the Federal Rules of Criminal Procedure, 1941-44, and of "Federal procedure prior to Rule 12," 1806-1944. [5884

WILLIAM SEAGLE. Acquitted of murder. Chicago: H. Regnery Co., 1958. [8], 257 p. On the murder convictions, and reversals on appeal, of William Hardy (Boston, 1806-7), Edward H. Ruloff (Tompkins County, N.Y., 1857), Mary Theresa (Koehler) Hartfrau (Albany, 1860), Laura D. Fair (San Francisco, 1871-72), William Hall and John Dockery (Murphy, N.C., 1894), William J. Thacker (Fleming Co., Ky., 1901-3), Michael Alex (Queens County, N.Y., 1931-38), Aaron Turner (Philadelphia, 1946-57), and Camilo Weston Leyra, Jr. (New York City, 1950-56); with a concluding chapter analyzing the causes of error in these and other cases in which "the jury has intelligently done its duty and duly convicted the murderer, but some appellate court, while conceding the correctness of the jury's verdict, has nevertheless set him free on some legal technicality wholly unrelated to his guilt or innocence." Notes the particularly leniency of the Court of Appeals for the District of Columbia. [5885

JOHN EVARTS TRACY (1880-1959). Nine famous trials. N.Y.: Vantage Press [1960]. 176 p. Includes accounts of the American trials of Aaron Burr (1807), ---- Holmes, seaman (1841), Andrew Johnson (impeachment, 1868), the Negroes on board the schooner Amistad (1839), and David Neagle, bodyguard of Stephen Dudley Field (1888-89); with a closing chapter on "The so-called technicalities of the law." [5886

LESTER BERNHARDT ORFIELD. Pleas in Federal criminal procedure [1818-1959]. Notre Dame lawyer, 35: 1-47 (Dec 1959). notes. [5887

ALAN K. SIMPSON. Indirect legal consequences of a conviction for felony [1820-1958]. Wyo. law jour., 13:62-7 (fall 1958). notes. [5888

NEGLEY KING TEETERS & DAVID MATZA. The extent of delinquency in the United States [1823-1959]. Jour. Negro educ., 28:200-213 (summer 1959). tables. notes. [5889

JAMES JACKSON KILPATRICK. The man who never laughed. Va. cavalcade, 9(2):4-8 (autumn 1959). facsim., port., views. On Alexander Tardy (1770-1827), native of Saint Domingue, poisoner, pretended doctor in Boston and Charleston, who in collaboration with José Mocando, Felix Barbeido, and José Casares, Cubans, seized the merchant ship Crawford en route from Matanzas to New York, killed several of its officers and crew, and anchored for provisions at Hampton Roads, where suspicions were aroused and an investigation was begun, resulting in the suicide of Tardy to escape capture and the flight of his 3 fellow pirates, who were apprehended by a posse, tried before John Marshall in the Federal Circuit Court at Richmond, and hanged. [5890

DANIEL BELL. The myth of crime waves: the actual decline of crime in the United States [1840s-1958]. Daniel Bell, The end of ideology: on the exhaustion of political ideas in the fifties (Glencoe, Ill.: Free Press [1960]), p. 137-58. [5891

WILLIAM MOSES KUNSTLER. First degree. N.Y.: Oceana Publications, 1960. 239 p. bibliog. (p. 234). A study of 18 murder trials, 1850-1957. [5892

ALAN HYND. Defenders of the damned. N.Y.: A.S. Barnes [1960]. 182 p. From True--the man's magazine, 1952, 1953, 1957. On Clarence Seward Darrow (1857-1938) of Chicago, Earl Rogers (1870-1922) of Los Angeles, and William Joseph Fallon (1886-1927) of New York as attorneys for the defense in criminal cases. [5893

JOHN E. REID. Understanding the New Hampshire doctrine of criminal insanity. Yale law jour., 69:367-420 (Jan). notes. On "the jurisprudential theories and prejudices" of Judge Charles Doe, his development of the New Hampshire doctrine that the alleged insanity of a defendant in a criminal case is entirely for determination by the jury on the basis of all available evidence, including medical testimony, 1865-71, and the relation between this doctrine and the "Durham rule" adopted by the District of Columbia Circuit in 1954. [5894

RICHARD B. LILLICH. The element of materiality in the Federal crime of perjury [1873-1958]. Ind. law jour., 35:1-16 (fall 1959). notes. [5895

BART A. BROWN. The basis of the doctrine of entrapment [1878-1959]. Univ. Kan. law rev., 8:453-61 (Mar). notes. [5896

WILLIAM A. STRUTZ. The doctrine of entrapment [1878-1956]. N. D. law rev., 35:144-51 (Apr 1959). notes. [5897

FRANCIS XAVIER BUSCH. Casebook of the curious and true. Indianapolis: Bobbs-Merrill [1957]. 228 p. Accounts of 8 trials or groups of cases, with fictitious names or other disguises, 1880s-1950s. [5898

FREDERIC SONDERN, JR. Brotherhood of evil: the Mafia. N.Y.: Farrar, Straus, and Cudahy [1959]. xii, 243 p. ports., views. On a secret society of Sicilian and other Italian criminals in the United States, 1880s-1958, which first attracted public attention as a result of incidents in New Orleans in 1890. [5899

RICHARD D. RIVERS. Control of nongovernmental corruption by criminal legislation. Univ. Pa. law rev., 108: 848-67 (Apr). table. notes. On State legislation for the control of "commercial bribery," 1881-1959, and "corruption in athletic contests," 1946-59, and the feasibility of a Federal statute dealing with "corrupt betrayal of trust." [5900

BARBARA BLUMER. Time limitations in criminal prosecution [1884-1956]. Loyola law rev., 10:97-105. notes. [5901

JAMES E. CONWAY. Tainted evidence--an argument for exclusion. Albany law rev., 24:392-403 (Jun). notes. On the admissibility of evidence illegally obtained, 1885-1958. [5902

JUDICIAL limitations on the constitutional protection against cruel and unusual punishment [1885-1959]. Wash. Univ. law quar., 1960:160-70 (Apr). notes. [5903

The MOB'S man, as told to James D[avid] Horan. N.Y.: Crown Publishers [1959]. 256 p. ports., views. Autobiography, fictional in style, of an anonymous criminal, born in 1911, who arrived in New York City in 1929, engaged in "the Harlem numbers syndicate," "the policy racket," the narcotics traffic, and other crime, and was tried for and convicted of, theft from a restaurant in 1931, since which date he has spent most of his life in Sing Sing, Auburn, Riker's Island and Clinton State Prison. [5904

ABRAHAM S. GOLDSTEIN. The state and the accused: balance of advantage in criminal procedure. Yale law jour., 69:1149-99 (Jun). notes. On developments in Federal courts toward "an articulate, albeit clearly operative, rejection of the presumption of innocence in favor of a presumption of guilt," 1915-59. [5905

JEROME NEW FRANK (1889-1957) & BARBARA FRANK. Not guilty.

Garden City, N.Y.: Doubleday, 1957. 261 p. notes (p. 253-61). On American criminal trials resulting in the conviction of innocent persons, 1918-56, and the reasons for the erroneous verdicts. [5906

SOPHIA (MOSES) ROBISON. How effective are current juvenile delinquency preventive programs? Jour. Negro educ., 28:351-65 (summer 1959). notes. Review of programs since the 1920s. [5907

ROBERT L. FLETCHER. Pretrial discovery in State criminal cases [1927-59]. Stanford law rev., 12: 293-322 (Mar). notes. [5908

WILLIAM J. THOMPSON. The judge's responsibility on a plea of guilty [1938-59]. W. Va. law rev., 60:213-22 (Apr). notes. [5909

CURTIS R. REITZ. Federal habeas corpus: postconviction remedy for State prisoners. Univ. Pa. law rev., 108:461-532 (Feb). notes. Study of 35 cases, 1940-59 (summarized in detail in an appendix). [5910

JACK H. FRIEDENTHAL. Government appeals in Federal criminal cases [under the Criminal Appeals Act of 1907 and its amendments of 1942 and 1948]. Stanford law rev., 12:71-102 (Dec 1959). notes. [5911

EDWIN RANDALL TOLLE & FRANK E. HARTUNG. The criminological information contained in professional educational journals. Jour. educ. sociol., 32:328-32 (Mar 1959). notes. Examination of 11 articles, 1951-52, noting that only 3 "would pass a lenient sociological muster." [5912

Education

JAMES A. MULHERN. A history of education: a social interpretation. ... Second edition. N.Y.: Ronald Press Co. [1959]. vii, 754 p. bibliogs., notes. 1st ed. 1946. Includes a chapter on "The development of the American school system," 1606-1957 (p. 569-632). [5913

MARCUS WILSON JERNEGAN (1872-1949). Influences promoting free education [1630-47]. Marcus W. Jernegan, Laboring and dependent classes in colonial America, 1607-1783 (N.Y.: Ungar [1960]), p. 59-68. notes. From School review, May 1915. [5914

WILLIAM MONFORT BARR. American public school finance [1635-1960, mainly in recent years]. N.Y.: American Book Co. [1960]. ix, 406 p. diagr., tables. bibliogs., notes. [5915

EDWARD JOHN POWER. Education for American democracy: an introduction to education. N.Y.: McGraw-Hill Book Co., 1958. xiv, 415 p. diagrs., facsims., tables, views. bibliogs. Includes historical information, 1635-1954. [5916

VIVIAN TROW THAYER. The role of the school in American society [1642-1960]. N.Y.: Dodd, Mead, 1960. xii, [2], 530 p. tables. bibliogs., notes. On "Formative ideas in American education," "Changes in the economic and social status of youth," "Conceptions of learning in their American setting," and "Critical issues in contemporary education." [5917

HERMAN VINCENT YEAGER. The Scottish common-sense philosophy as a factor in American education [ca. 1750 to ca. 1910]. Ann Arbor: University Microfilms, 1959 [i. e. 1960]. Positive microfilm of typescript. [311] leaves. Thesis--Stanford Univ. Abstracted: Dissert. abstracts, 20:3229-30 (Feb). [5918

JOHN ALFRED NIETZ. Evolution of American school textbooks [1762-1900]. Educ. forum, 24:295-305 (Mar). notes. [5919

EDGAR STERN FAMILY FUND. Recognition of excellence: working papers of a project of the Edgar Stern Family Fund. Glencoe, Ill.: Free Press, 1960. xii, 334 p. bibliogs. Includes "The identification, nurturing, and channeling of excellence and potential excellence in young people." 12 chapters, by Adam Yarmolinsky (p. 23-207), containing accounts of the development of tests for the measurement of intelligence (1868-1959) and associated programs for the special education of children with high intelligence quotients; of "the undergraduate origins of men and women who had received doctorates and fellowships" (1924-59); and of "The techniques of major national institutions which now recognize mature excellence" (1768-1959). [5920

WILLIAM HENRY COWLEY. Three curricular conflicts. Liberal educ., 46:467-83 (Dec). notes. On conflicts arising from the "divergent claims of general and special education ... the humanities and the sciences, and ... teaching and research," 1776-1960. [5921

WILLIAM WOLFGANG BRICKMAN. A historical introduction to comparative education [1784-1902]. Comparative educ. rev., 3(3):6-13 (Feb). [5922

DAVID DANIEL ANDERSON. Benjamin Rush, pioneer educational philosopher. College of Educ. quar., 5(3):20-25 (Jul 1959). port. On his writings about education, 1786-98. [5923

LLOYD P. WILLIAMS. Intuitions of a free mind--Emerson's view of the education of his times [1823 ff.]. Peabody jour. educ., 37:365-9 (May). [5924

PHILIP DAVIDSON. "... free, universal, and democratic." John Arthur Garraty, ed., The unforgettable Americans (Great Neck, N.Y.: Channel Press [1960]), p. 165-9. On the service of Horace Mann (1796-1859) as Secretary of the Massachusetts Board of Education and President of Antioch College, 1837-59. [5925

FRANKLIN PARKER. Francis Wayland Parker, 1837-1902. [Austin? Tex., 1960?] 13, 7 leaves. notes. bibliog. (7 leaves). Mainly on his service as a rural teacher in New Hampshire, a high-school teacher in Carrollton, Ill., a school superintendent in Quincy and Boston, Mass., head of the Cook County Norman School, Chicago (1883 ff.), and Director of the Department of Education, University of Chicago. [5926

JOHN S. GOFF. The education of Robert Todd Lincoln [1843-1926]. Ill. State Hist. Soc., Jour., 53:341-60 (winter). ports., view. Information from his manuscript autobiography and other sources about his studies at "Illinois State University" (in the preparatory department of this private school at Springfield), his failure to pass the Harvard entrance examinations, his studies at Phillips Exeter Academy, his 4 years at Harvard College, and his brief attendance at the Harvard Law School. [5927

MORTIMER JEROME ADLER & MILTON SANFORD MAYER. The revolution in education. [Chicago:] Univ. of Chicago Press [1958]. viii, 224 p. bibliog. (p. 201-215). On the impact of "the secularization of society and its 'scientization'" upon education, constituting an "American revolution, 1850-1950," and the educational issues consequently dividing "aristocrat" and "democrat," "realist" and "idealist," and "traditionalist" and "modernist." [5928

JAMES BRYANT CONANT. An old tradition in a new world. Harvard alumni bul., 57:434-5, 438-9 (12 Mar 1955). port. On the "essential differences between the European educational tradition and the American," ca. 1855 to 1955. [5929

ROBERT FREEMAN BUTTS. Centenary of John Dewey [1859-1952]. Teachers College rec., 61:117-20 (Dec 1959). [5930

HAROLD LLOYD RAY. The life and professional contributions of William Gilbert Anderson [1860-1947], M.D. Ann Arbor: University Microfilms, 1959 [i. e. 1960]. Positive microfilm of typescript. [214] leaves. Thesis--Ohio State Univ. Abstracted: Dissert. abstracts, 20:4028-9 (Apr). On his career as "physician, teacher, administrator, lecturer and organizer," founder of "teacher education schools at Adelphi, Yale, and Chautauqua," experimenter in the use of "corrective apparatus" for the physically handicapped, popularizer of music and dancing as part of the physical education curriculum, and founder of the College Physical Education Association and the American Association for Health, Physical Education, and Recreation. [5931

NEVA SEXTON & IRENE ROLOFF. Adelaide Steele Baylor [1860-1935]: leader in homemaking education. Delta Kappa Gamma bul., 24(3):30-37 (spring 1958). port. On her early life in Wabash, Ind., her studies at the University of Chicago and the University of Michigan, her work as a teacher at Wabash and a staff member of the Indiana State Department of Education, and her service as Chief of the Home Economics Education Service, Federal Board for Vocational Education. [5932

ORESTES AUGUSTUS BROWNSON (1803-76). Catholic schools and education. Pierre Albert Duhamel, ed., Essays in the American Catholic tradition (N.Y.: Rinehart [1960]), p. 45-56. From Brownson's quarterly review, Jan. 1862. [5933

ABRAHAM FLEXNER (1866-1959). Abraham Flexner: an autobiography. N.Y.: Simon and Schuster, 1960. xvi, 302 p. port. Revision and extension of the first edition (1940). On the author's early life in Louisville, his studies at Johns Hopkins University, his teaching at the State Normal School, Lexington, Ky., and the Louisville High School, his operation of a college preparatory school in Louisville, his study of psychology in Germany, his service with the Carnegie Foundation for the Advancement of Teaching, the General Education Board, and the Institute for Advanced Study at Princeton, and his studies of medical education in the United States and abroad. [5934

LAWRENCE ARTHUR CREMIN. What happened to progressive education [1870s-1950s]? Teachers College rec., 61:23-9 (Oct. 1959). Includes 4 reasons for the decline and collapse of the movement. [5935

OSCAR HANDLIN. John Dewey's challenge to education: historical perspectives on the cultural context [1884-1916]. N.Y.: Harper [1959]. 59 p. notes (p. 51-9). (The John Dewey Society lectureship series, 2.) [5936

D. BOB GOWIN. Is Dewey's experimentalism compatible with gestalt theory? School rev., 67:195-212 (summer 1959). notes. Based on thesis--Yale Univ. Arguments supporting a negative answer, 1889-1958. [5937

JOHN SEILER BRUBACHER. The misunderstandings of Dewey's educational philosophy [1890s-1950s]. Alfred Stafford Clayton, ed., John Dewey in perspective (Bloomington: Indiana Univ. [1960]), p. 27-42. notes. [5938

CHARLES CLARENCE CHANDLER. Institutionalism and education: an inquiry into the implications of the philosophy of Thorstein Veblen [1890s-1920s]. Ann Arbor: University Microfilms, 1959 [i.e. 1960]. Positive microfilm of typescript. [278] leaves. Thesis--Michigan State Univ. Abstracted: Dissert. abstracts, 20:3661-2 (Mar). [5939

JOHN LAWRENCE CHILDS. John Dewey and American education [1890s-1950s]. Teachers College rec., 61:128-33 (Dec 1959). notes. [5940

JOHN W. DONOHUE. John Dewey: centennial of an educator. Cath. educ. rev., 58:16-27 (Jan). notes. On his theories of education, 1890-1952. [5941

CLARENCE JOSEPH KARIER. The neo-humanist protest in American education, 1890-1930. Ann Arbor: University Microfilms, 1960. Positive microfilm of typescript. [307] leaves. Thesis--Univ. of Wisconsin. Abstracted: Dissert. abstracts, 21:538 (Sep). On ideas of Irving Babbitt and Paul Elmer More concerning education. [5942

MICHIGAN STATE UNIVERSITY OF AGRICULTURE AND APPLIED SCIENCE. College of Education. John Dewey, philosopher of education [1890s-1950s]. College of Educ. quar., 6(3):3-10 (Jul). ports. "Gist of a discussion" with Ernest O. Melby, John F. A. Taylor, and John Barron as participants, broadcast 10 Jan. 1960. [5943

HAROLD ORDWAY RUGG. Dewey and his contemporaries: the frontiers of educational thought in the early 1900's [1890-1940]. Alfred Stafford Clayton, ed., John Dewey in perspective (Bloomington: Division of Research and Field Services, Indiana Univ. [1960]), p. 1-14. [5944

ROBERT I. SPERBER. Federal aid and federal control of education [1890-1959]. Teachers College rec., 61:331-8 (Mar). notes. [5945

LAWRENCE ARTHUR CREMIN. The origins of progressive education [1895-1910]. Educ. forum, 24:133-40 (Jan). [5946

Sister JOSEPH MARY RABY. John Dewey and progressive education [1897-1952]. John Blewett, ed., John Dewey: his thought and influence (N.Y.: Fordham Univ. Press [1960]), p. 85-115. [5947

CARL RAY BARTEL. Origin, development, and work of the American Vocational Association [1906-59]. Ann Arbor: University Microfilms, 1959 [i.e. 1960]. Positive microfilm of typescript. [550] leaves. Thesis (Ed. D.)--Univ. of Missouri. Abstracted: Dissert. abstracts, 20:3615-16 (Mar). [5948

GEORGE WALTER GRILL & WESLEY L. BROWN. ASBO--the first 50 years: the building of the school business management profession. [Evanston? Ill.: Association of School Business Officials of the United States and Canada, 1960.] 84 p. diagr., facsim., ports., tables

(1 double), views (part double, 1 fold.). notes. (Association of School Business Officials of the United States and Canada. Bulletin 20.) Condensation of a detailed history by Grill (more than 400 pages), 1910-55, and continuation by Brown. [5949

ISAAC LEON KANDEL. Revival of American education. Educ. forum, 24:271-8 (Mar). On "causes of the weaknesses of American education," 1912-60. [5950

JAMES A. JORDAN, JR. Interest, choice, and desirability. School rev., 67:174-85 (summer 1959). On Interest and effort in education (1913), by John Dewey. [5951

LAWRENCE ARTHUR CREMIN. John Dewey and the progressive-education movement, 1915-1952. School rev., 67:160-73 (summer 1959). notes. [5952

GEORGE E. BARTON, JR. John Dewey: too soon a period piece? School rev., 67:128-38 (summer 1959). notes. On "ways of developing Dewey's principles to maintain their relevance or to make their relevance apparent," 1916-59. [5953

ROBERT KATZ (born 1917). A movement west. Robert O. Bowen, ed., The new professors (N.Y.: Holt, Rinehart, and Winston [1960]), p. 38-53. On the author's early life and Jewish upbringing in New York, his studies at Brooklyn College, his graduate study of physics at the University of Illinois, his teaching of physics at Kansas State University, and his ideas about teaching as a profession. [5954

COMMISSION FOR THE STUDY OF JEWISH EDUCATION IN THE UNITED STATES. Jewish education in the United States [1918-58]: a summary of the report of the Commission ... By Dr. Alexander M. Dushkin and Dr. Uriah Z. Engelman. Jew. educ., 30(1):4-23, 33 (fall 1959). [5955

LLOYD P. WILLIAMS. Education for quality. Discourse, 3:119-24 (Apr). notes. On controversies regarding this subject, 1918-57. [5956

GLENN LEGGETT. A conservative view. Robert O. Bowen, ed., The new professors (N.Y.: Holt, Rinehart, and Winston [1960]), p. 155-81. On the author's early life in Ohio (ca. 1919 ff.), his studies at Middlebury College and Ohio State University, his teaching of English and history at Massachusetts Institute of Technology, his service as Director of Freshman English at the University of Washington, and his views of teaching as a profession. [5957

EDWARD C. ECHOLS. Say something nasty about Pittsburgh! Robert O. Bowen, ed., The new professors (N.Y.: Holt, Rinehart, and Winston [1960]), p. 202-18. On the author's early life in West Virginia and Charlottesville, Va. (1920s and 1930s), his undergraduate and graduate studies at the University of Virginia, his teaching of Latin and Greek at the University of Alabama and Phillips Exeter Academy, and his satisfaction with teaching as a profession. [5958

HERMAN ESCHENBACHER. Education and social unity in the ante-bellum period [1820-60]. Harv. educ. rev., 30:154-63 (spring). notes. Mainly a criticism of ideas expressed by Horace Mann and Francis Wayland. [5959

HAROLD ORDWAY RUGG (1886-1960). A study in censorship: good concepts and bad words. Robert B. Downs, ed., The first freedom: liberty and justice in the world of books and reading (Chicago: American Library Assoc., 1960), p. 344-9. From Social education, Mar. 1941. On the author's efforts since ca. 1921 "to bring into the schools a full account of modern civilization, an analysis of the psychology of consent as the basis of democratic government, and the ordeal of distinguished Americans who have explored various creative frontiers." Deplores "the ridiculous charges made against teachers and writers in the social studies" and "the present attack on liberalism in education." [5960

ALBERT W. VOGEL. A critical study of the major writings of George S. Counts [on education, 1922-57]. Ann Arbor: University Microfilms, 1960. Positive microfilm of typescript. [194] leaves. Thesis (Ed. D.)--American Univ. Abstracted: Dissert. abstracts, 21:540 (Sep). [5961

EDWARD CLAUDE BOLMEIER. Legal scope of teachers' freedoms [1923-59]. Educ. forum, 24:199-206 (Jan). notes. [5962

SHEPARD A. INSEL. ... The education counselor. Robert O. Bowen, ed., The new professors (N.Y.: Holt, Rinehart, and Winston [1960]), p. 125-54. On the author's early life in New York (ca. 1923 ff.), his work as a skilled laborer in California, his Army service, his studies at Stanford

University, and his teaching of psychology at San Francisco State College; with his views of teaching as a profession. [5963

U.S. Supreme Court. The Supreme Court and education. Edited, with an introduction and notes, by David Fellman. N.Y.: Bureau of Publications, Teachers College, Columbia Univ. [1960]. xiii, [3], 120 p. (Classics in education, 4.) Excerpts from 13 decisions concerning education as related to religion, racial segregation, and academic freedom, 1925-59; with an editorial introduction. [5964

MEIR BEN-HORIN. Major writings in American Jewish education, 1929-1959. Jew. educ., 30(3):4-15 (spring). notes. Bibliographical essay. [5965

ANNIE WEBB BLANTON. Delta Kappa Gamma history, 1929-1944. Delta Kappa Gamma bul., 23(2):38-42 (winter 1957). Account of "a new sorority for women teachers," by its founder. [5966

EUNAH (TEMPLE) JOHNSON HOLDEN. Marking the years to international status [of the Delta Kappa Gamma Society, 1929-56]. Delta Kappa Gamma bul., 23(2):30-37 (winter 1957). [5967

EUNAH (TEMPLE) HOLDEN. Our heritage in the Delta Kappa Gamma Society [1929-60. Austin, Tex., 1960. 16], 325 p. diagrs., facsims., insignia, music, ports. (1 col.), tables (part double), views (part col.). On an organization of "women teachers," formed under the leadership of Annie Webb Blanton, to promote the professional interests of women engaged in teaching; with "Biographies of founders" (p. 17-73). [5968

ROBERT JAMES HAVIGHURST. The impact of population change and working force change on American education [1930-60]. Educ. rec., 41:346-58 (Oct). diagrs., tables. notes. Appended: "Discussion" by Donald R. Brown. [5969

ANTHONY WILLIAM ZAITZ. The history of educational television: 1932-1958. Ann Arbor: University Microfilms, 1960. Positive microfilm of typescript. [373] leaves. Thesis--Univ. of Wisconsin. Abstracted: Dissert. abstracts, 21:271 (Jul). [5970

HARRY ZEITLIN. Efforts to achieve Federal aid to education: developments during the New Deal [1933-44]. Teachers College rec., 61:195-202 (Dec 1959). [5971

JOSEPH JACKSON SCHWAB. The "impossible" role of the teacher in progressive education. School rev., 67:139-59 (summer 1959). Apparently a commentary on Dewey's Experience and education (1939). [5972

STELLA STEWART CENTER. The hazards of semiliteracy [in the United States, 1940-59, and abroad]. National Council of Teachers of English, Perspectives on English: essays to honor W. Wilbur Hatfield, ed. Robert C. Pooley (N.Y.: Appleton-Century-Crofts [1960]), p. 213-35. tables. notes. [5973

PHILIP E. JACOB. Social change and student values [1941-60]. Educ. rec., 41:338-46 (Oct). notes. Appended: "Discussion" by Joshua A. Fishman. [5974

LYLE EDMUND SIVERSON. An analysis of significant books on education as determined by published book reviews in periodicals of general circulation, 1945-1955. Ann Arbor: University Microfilms, 1960. Positive microfilm of typescript. [289] leaves. Thesis (Ed. D.)--Univ. of Southern California. Abstracted: Dissert. abstracts, 21:99-100 (Jul). [5975

RAY O. WERNER. Federal aid to education: some economic aspects of major legislative proposals for support of primary and secondary schools in the United States, 1946-1958. Ann Arbor: University Microfilms, 1960. Positive microfilm of typescript. [308] leaves. Thesis--Univ. of Nebraska. Abstracted: Dissert. abstracts, 21:91 (Jul). [5976

SLOAN RIGDON WAYLAND & EDMUND DE SCHWEINITZ BRUNNER. The educational characteristics of the American people. [N.Y.:] Bureau of Applied Social Research, Columbia Univ., 1958. [2], ii, [2], 258 p. tables. "Analysis ... based on the 1950 U.S. Census." Chapters on elementary, secondary, and collegiate education, "The educational attainment of the American adult," "Education, social indices, and occupations," and "Characteristics of American teachers." [5977

THE EDUCATION OF TEACHERS

LINDLEY JOSEPH STILES & 3 others. Teacher education in the United States [1785-1960]. N.Y.: Ronald Press Co. [1960. 2], viii, 512 p. diagrs.

(1 double), tables. bibliogs., notes. (Douglass series in education.) [5978

CHARLES JOHN BRAUNER. Education as a subject of study [19th and 20th centuries]. Ann Arbor: University Microfilms, 1960. Positive microfilm of typescript. [344] leaves. Thesis--Stanford Univ. Abstracted: Dissert. abstracts, 20:4308 (May). [5979

HARRY GEHMAN GOOD. The rise of the College of Education of the Ohio State University [1817-1960]. Columbus: College of Education, Ohio State University, 1960. viii, 306 p. ports., tables (part double), views. [5980

HANOR A. WEBB. To train a teacher. Peabody jour. educ., 37:132-44 (Nov 1959). notes. On "schools for teachers," 1839-1959. [5981

WILLIAM M. ALEXANDER. Teacher education at George Peabody College for Teachers [Nashville]: past, present, and future [since 1875]. High school jour., 43:231-41 (Feb). [5982

JAY C. WILLIAMS. Dewey and the idea of a science of education [1890s-1950s]. School rev., 67:186-94 (summer 1959). [5983

IDA B. DE PENCIER. The history of the Laboratory Schools, the University of Chicago, 1896-1957. [Chicago:] Univ. of Chicago, ©1960. [2], 204 leaves. bibliog. (leaves 175-204). On an elementary and secondary school organized by John Dewey and headed by him till 1904, augmented by accession of the Chicago Institute, and from its inception regarded as a laboratory of the University of Chicago School of Education. [5984

C. H. ROCHEDIEU. The Fairhope idea in education. Peabody jour. educ., 36:37-8 (Jul 1958). notes. On the Fairhope (Ala.) School of Education, established by Marietta Johnson, based upon the concepts of Rousseau, Pestalozzi, Nathan Oppenheim, and John Dewey, 1907-58. [5985

WILLIAM HOLMAN CARTWRIGHT. Current trends in teacher education [1920-59]. Educ. forum, 24:261-70 (Mar). notes. [5986

FRED WINSTON. A study of the development of teacher training in the skills for the production of audio-visual instructional materials as exemplified by the courses of study in the accredited teacher-training colleges of the Northeastern region of the United States from 1920 to 1952. Ann Arbor: University Microfilms, 1960. Positive microfilm of typescript. [260] leaves. Thesis--New York Univ. Abstracted: Dissert. abstracts, 20:4598 (Jun). [5987

WYLMA R. CURTIN. Requirements for the master's degree with a major in education [1935-59]. Cath. educ. rev., 57:73-96, 145-61 (Feb, Mar 1959). tables (part double). bibliog., notes. [5988

WILLARD PARKER RIDDLES. The doctoral program in education at the University of Colorado, 1941-1956. Ann Arbor: University Microfilms, 1959 [i.e. 1960]. Positive microfilm of typescript. [270] leaves. Thesis (Ed. D.)--Univ. of Colorado. Abstracted: Dissert. abstracts, 20:4044 (Apr). [5989

ELEMENTARY AND SECONDARY EDUCATION

CAWTHON ASBURY BOWEN. Child and church: a history of Methodist church-school curriculum [1785-1960]. N.Y.: Abingdon Press [1960]. 253 p. notes. [5990

SUSAN B. RILEY. Schooling and teaching in the early nineteenth century: Albert Pike's experiences. Peabody jour. educ., 37:77-86 (Sep 1959). notes. On his schooling in a public and a private school in Newburyport and an academy at Framingham (1813-25), his teaching in and near Gloucester and at Newburyport and Fairhaven (1825-31), his removal to Arkansas, and his teaching at Van Buren and Little Piney Creek (1832-33). [5991

JAMES F. ROGERS. Population changes and the high school program [1820-1958]. High school jour., 42:314-22 (May 1959). tables. notes. [5992

PHYLLIS (HYATT) GARDINER. The Hyatt legacy: the saga of a courageous educator and his family in California. N.Y.: Exposition Press [1959]. 301 p. On Edward Hyatt (1858-1919), his early life and studies, and his work as a schoolteacher in San Jacinto, Calif., Superintendent of Schools of Riverside County, and from 1913 to 1919 as California State Superintendent of Public Instruction. Semifictional in form. [5993

RICHARD H. BREINER. Abandonment of school sites in fee simple determinable estates. Mo. law rev.,

25:446-62 (Nov). notes. On cases in Missouri and other States involving "the construction of deeds purporting to convey determinable fees to school districts, the determination of the event that calls for a cessation of the estate in the grantee," and the reversion of the estate to the grantor or his heirs, 1883-1959. [5994

ANNA MARIE KEPPEL. Country schools for country children: backgrounds of the reform movement in rural elementary education, 1890-1914. Ann Arbor: University Microfilms, 1960. Positive microfilm of typescript. [229] leaves. Thesis--Univ. of Wisconsin. Abstracted: Dissert. abstracts, 21:1448-9 (Dec). [5995

NOAH GAYLE SIMMONS. The emerging design for the comprehensive American high school, 1913-1922 (a study of the Commission on the Reorganization of Secondary Education). Ann Arbor: University Microfilms, 1960. Positive microfilm of typescript. [370] leaves. Thesis (Ed. D.)--Washington Univ. Abstracted: Dissert. abstracts, 21:1450-51 (Dec). [5996

EDNA LUE FURNESS. The image of the high school teacher in American literature [1934-59]. Educ. forum, 24:457-64 (May). bibliog. [5997

EUNAH (TEMPLE) JOHNSON HOLDEN. The pioneer figurines. Delta Kappa Gamma bul., 23(3):43-6 (spring 1957). On a collection of "dolls dressed to represent ... pioneer" teachers, presented to Delta Kappa Gamma since 1934 by various State chapters. [5998

MELVILLE JAMES BOYER. The one-room schoolhouse--a social loss. Lehigh Co. Hist. Soc., Proc., 23:91-5. view. On the question: "What have we lost socially when we sold at auction our little red schoolhouses, promoted the school bell to an antique, and voted for consolidation?" [5999

HIGHER EDUCATION

JAMES F. ROGERS. A philosophy for the junior college with implications for curriculum. Jr. college jour., 30:125-31 (Nov 1959). notes. On the "origins and subsequent modifications of the structure of American higher education," 1636-1959. [6000

WILLIAM K. SELDEN. Accreditation: a struggle over standards in higher education [1636-1960]. N.Y.: Harper [1960]. xv, [3], 138 p. bibliog. (p. 110-32), notes (p. 96-109). [6001

GEORGE FRANCIS DONOVAN. The role of fundamental documents in American higher education. Cath. educ. rev., 58:156-73 (Mar). notes. On the "instruments of institutional government in American higher learning," 1650-1959. [6002

NOEL C. STEVENSON. Hereditary scholarships. Am. geneal., 36:96-9, 192 (Apr, Jul). On endowed scholarships available only or preferably to persons eligible on grounds of descent or blood relationship, the earliest established as early as 1687 at Harvard. [6003

ROBERT L. McCAUL. Whitefield's Bethesda College project and other attemp[t]s to found colonial colleges. Ga. hist. quar., 44:263-77, 381-98 (Sep, Dec). notes. On the failure of efforts of the Rev. George Whitefield to found a college in Georgia, 1739-70; with mention of several equally unsuccessful efforts in other colonies, beginning with that of the Rev. George Berkeley for a college in Bermuda (1724-31), and an analysis of the reasons for the failures. [6004

GRAHAM P. CONROY. Berkeley and education in America. Jour. hist. ideas, 21:211-21 (Apr-Jun). notes. On the proposals of George Berkeley to found a college in Bermuda, his decision to transfer the proposed college to Rhode Island, his purchase there (with his personal funds) of a large farm at Whitehall near Newport, his realization that the promised support from the British Government would not be granted, his gift of large collections of books to Harvard and Yale, and his further gift to Yale of his farm to establish a fund for maintaining 2 graduate fellows annually in Latin and Greek studies, 1726-32; with an account of some of the beneficiaries of the Yale fund, of Berkeley's advice to the Rev. Samuel Johnson at the founding of King's College and to the founders of the College of Philadelphia, and of the giving of Berkeley's name to the city in which the University of California was founded. [6005

HORACE MANN BOND. The origin and development of the Negro church related college [1740-1960]. Jour. Negro educ., 29:217-26 (summer). notes. [6006

VIRGINIA WALLER DAVIS. Phi Beta Kappa, December 5, 1776. Va. cavalcade, 9(2):34-41 (autumn 1959). facsim., ports. (1 col.), views (1 col.). On "America's first Greek letter fraternity," founded at Williamsburg in 1776, of whose 50 original members 49 were Virginians. [6007

CHARLES ALBERT QUATTLEBAUM. Federal policies and practices in higher education [1777-1958]. American Assembly, The Federal Government and higher education, ed. Douglas M. Knight (Englewood Cliffs, N.J.: Prentice-Hall, 1960), p. 29-76. table. [6008

JAMES WILLIAM EICHELBERGER. The African Methodist Episcopal Zion Church: the rationale and policies upon which maintenance of its colleges is based [1796-1960]. Jour. Negro educ., 29:323-9 (summer). notes. [6009

WILLIAM K. SELDEN. How long is a college president? Liberal educ., 46:5-15 (Mar). tables. notes. On the "average length of tenure of the chief administrative officer of a college or university," 1804-1959. [6010

SOLOMON WILLIS RUDY. The evolving liberal arts curriculum: a historical review of basic themes [1825-1956. N.Y.:] Bureau of Publications, Teachers College, Columbia Univ., for the Institute of Higher Education [1960]. iv, [4], 135 p. tables. notes. [6011

WILLIAM KAILER DUNNE. The Roman Catholic Church: the rationale and policies underlying the maintenance of higher institutions for Negroes [1829-60]. Jour. Negro educ., 29:307-14 (summer). [6012

FRANCESCO G. MADORMA CORDASCO. Daniel Coit Gilman [1831-1908] and the protean Ph. D.: the shaping of American graduate education. By Francesco Cordasco. Leiden: E.J. Brill, 1960. xii, 160 p. facsim. bibliog. (p. 150-60), notes. On his studies at Yale (1848-52); his service as Professor of Physical Geography in the Sheffield Scientific School, Yale (1855-72), and as President of the University of California (1872-75), Johns Hopkins University (1776-1902), and the Carnegie Institute of Washington (1902-4); and the influence of his methods at Johns Hopkins upon the graduate schools of Harvard and other universities. [6013

SHERMAN LAWRENCE GREENE, JR. The rationale underlying the support of colleges maintained by the African Methodist Episcopal Church [1834-[960]. Jour. Negro educ., 29:319-22 (summer). tables. bibliog. [6014

FREDERICK LESLIE BROWNLEE. Heritage and opportunity: the Negro church-related college, a critical summary [1840s-1960]. Jour. Negro educ., 29:401-7 (summer). notes. [6015

WALTER CROSBY EELLS. Early collegiate degrees for women [1840-1900]. Educ. rec., 40:266-8 (Jul). [6016

MABEL NEWCOMER. A century of higher education for American women [1841-1959]. N.Y.: Harper [1959]. xii, [2], 266 p. bibliog. (p. 257-9). [6017

WESLEY AKIN HOTCHKISS. Congregationalists and Negro education [1846-1960]. Jour. Negro educ., 29:289-98 (summer). table. notes. Mainly on higher education. [6018

BENJAMIN ELIJAH MAYS. The significance of the Negro private and church-related college [1854-1960]. Jour. Negro educ., 29:245-51 (summer). [6019

ROBERT LAWRENCE COARD. In pursuit of the word "professor": an exploration of the uses and associations of the title [1856-1959]. Jour. higher educ., 30:237-45 (May 1959). [6020

PHILLIP WARD PAYTON. Undergraduate specialization or majoring in American colleges and universities [1860s-1920s]. Ann Arbor: University Microfilms, 1959 [i.e. 1960]. Positive microfilm of typescript. vi, 595 leaves. bibliog. (leaves 545-95). Thesis (Ed. D)--Stanford Univ. Abstracted: Dissert. abstracts, 20:3179 (Feb). [6021

WALTER CROSBY EELLS. Geography of the doctorate. Jour. higher educ., 31:46-8 (Jan). tables. notes. On the geographic distribution of "earned doctorates" in the United States, 1861-1957. [6022

BAYARD DODGE. The American University of Beirut [1862-1958]: a brief history of the university and the lands which it serves. Beirut: Khayat's [1958]. vii, 127, [1] p. port., views. [6023

A. H. HALSEY. The changing functions of universities in advanced industrial societies [particularly the United States, 1862-1960]. Harv. educ. rev., 30:118-27 (spring). tables. notes. [6024

RUSSELL I. THACKREY & JAY RICHTER. The land-grant colleges and universities, 1862-1962: an American institution. Higher educ., 16(3):3-8, 20 (Nov 1959). ports., views. [6025

AUGUST MEIER. The racial and educational philosophy of Kelly Miller [1863-1939], 1805-1915. Jour. Negro educ., 29:121-7 (spring). notes. On his early life in South Carolina, his studies at Howard University and Johns Hopkins University, and his service as Dean of Howard University. [6026

TOLLIE L. CAUTION. The Protestant Episcopal Church: policies and rationale upon which support of the Negro colleges is predicated [1865-1960]. Jour. Negro educ., 29:274-83 (summer). [6027

STEPHEN J. WRIGHT. The Negro college in America [1865-1960]. Harv. educ. rev., 30:280-97 (summer). tables. notes. [6028

JAMES S. THOMAS. The rationale underlying support of Negro private colleges by the Methodist Church [1866-1960]. Jour. Negro educ., 29:252-9 (summer). table. notes. [6029

C. D. COLEMAN. The Christian Methodist Episcopal Church: the rationale and policies upon which support of its colleges is predicated [1874-1960]. Jour. Negro educ., 29:315-18 (summer). [6030

L. W. BOTTOMS. The policies and rationale underlying the support of Negro colleges and schools maintained by the Presbyterian Church in the United States [1875-1960]. Jour. Negro educ., 29:264-73 (summer). [6031

EARL JAMES McGRATH. The graduate school and the decline of liberal education [since 1876. N.Y.:] Bureau of Publications, Teachers College, Columbia Univ., for the Institute of Higher Education [1959]. x, [2], 65 p. notes. [6032

CHARLES V. HAMILTON. The constitutional status of the "colored youth" provision in State charters for private Negro colleges [1883-1958]. Jour. Negro educ., 28:467-71 (fall 1959). notes. [6033

LOUIS ROUND WILSON. Harry Woodburn Chase [1883-1955]. Chapel Hill: Univ. of North Carolina Press, 1960. [8], 55 p. notes. On his early life and studies, his service at Clark University as Director of the Clinic for Subnormal Children, and his career as President of the University of North Carolina (1919-30) and the University of Illinois (1930-33) and Chancellor of New York University (1933-51). [6034

JACQUES MARTIN BARZUN. The tyranny of idealism in education. [N.Y., 1960. 2], 14 p. (Woodrow Wilson Foundation. Education in the nation's service: a series of essays on American education today, 6.) 1st ed. 1959. On the conflict between Wilson's ideas and those of John Dewey, and Wilson's unintentional contributions to "the dissociation of the college from intellect," 1890s-1914. [6035

HAROLD WAKELING CRAWFORD. Organizational patterns for industrial education programs in selected land-grant colleges. Ann Arbor: University Microfilms, 1960. Positive microfilm of typescript. [164] leaves. Thesis (Ed. D.)--Wayne State Univ. Abstracted: Dissert. abstracts, 21:1420-21 (Dec). On the 17 land-grant colleges established by the second Morrill Act in 1890, which before 1954 enrolled only Negroes. [6036

NORMAN HONORE HACKETT (born 1874). Come, my boys. [N.Y.:] Hackett Memorial Publication Fund, 1960. xix, 420 p. ports. (1 col.), views. On the author as a member and officer of Theta Delta Chi fraternity since 1894; with some account of his early life in Ontario, his removal to Detroit in 1880, his studies at the University of Michigan, and his career as a professional actor. [6037

[HARVARD and Princeton in American fiction, 1895-1956.] Harvard alumni bul., 58:480-81 (17 Mar 1956). [6038

LOUIS TOMLINSON BENEZET. Once more unto the breach. Liberal educ., 46:21-39 (Mar). On American liberal-arts colleges (1900-1960). [6039

FREDERIC IVES CARPENTER. Fiction and the American college. Am. quar., 12:443-56 (winter). notes. On novels about college, 20th century. [6040

EDMUND J. GLEAZER. Analysis of junior college growth [1900-1959]. Jr. college jour., 30:351-60 (Feb). tables. notes. [6041

W. C. H. PRENTICE. Recent social change and its impact on higher education [1900-1960]. Educ. rec., 41: 329-38 (Oct). notes. Appended: "Discussion" by Nevitt Sanford. [6042

McGEORGE BUNDY. An atmosphere to breathe: Woodrow Wilson and the life of the American university college. [N.Y., 1960. 2], 30 p. notes. (Woodrow Wilson Foundation. Education for the nation's service: a series of essays on American education today, 2.) Critical review of his Presidency of Princeton University, 1902-10, and of his utterances on college education during those years. [6043

FREDERICK D. PATTERSON. Foundation policies in regard to Negro institutions of higher learning [policies of private philanthropic foundations, 1903-59]. Jour. educ. sociol., 32:290-96 (Feb 1959). [6044

FRANCIS PAUL KING. Insurance programs [for staff members] in private colleges and universities [1906-60]. Liberal educ., 46:331-44 (Oct). tables. notes. [6045

JOHN WILLIAM ASHTON. A half-century of change in the State university [1909-59]. Jour. higher educ., 30:187-92 (Apr 1959). [6046

ARCHIBALD MacLEISH. Mr. Wilson and the nation's need. [N.Y., 1960. 2], 12 p. (Woodrow Wilson Foundation. Education in the nation's service: a series of essays on American education today, 1.) On the author's attendance at a speech delivered by Wilson at Harvard, 1 Jul. 1909, on the purpose of American university education. [6047

JOHN MALCUS ELLISON. Policies and rationale underlying the support of colleges maintained by the Baptist denomination [1910-60]. Jour. Negro educ., 29:330-38 (summer). tables. notes. [6048

MARGARET PANNILL. Thirty years of growth for Phi Theta Kappa [and its predecessor, Kappa Phi Omicron, established at Stephens College, Columbia, Mo., in 1910]. Jr. college jour., 30:143-6 (Nov 1959). On "the official honor society for junior colleges in the United States." [6049

RICHARD WAYNE LYKES. A history of the Division of Higher Education, United States Office of Education, from its creation in 1911 until the establishment of the Department of Health, Education, and Welfare in 1953. Ann Arbor: University Microfilms, 1960. Positive microfilm of typescript. [477] leaves. Thesis--American Univ. Abstracted: Dissert. abstracts, 21:608-9 (Sep). [6050

RICHARD E. WELCH, JR. What's the image? Robert O. Bowen, ed., The new professors (N.Y.: Holt, Rinehart, and Winston [1960]), p. 17-37. On the author's early life and studies, his teaching of history at Colgate University, the Virginia Military Institute, and Lafayette College, and his concept of the professorial life and function. [6051

HOMER J. DIETMEIER. The motion picture in higher education [1922-56]. Boston Univ. graduate jour., 4:151-6 (May 1956). bibliog. [6052

GEORGE HENRY WALKER, JR. Analysis of Negro junior college growth [1929-57]. Jr. college jour., 29:268-71 (Jan 1959). tables. [6053

DOUGLAS M. KNIGHT. Purpose and policy in higher education [ca. 1930 to 1960]. American Assembly, The Federal Government and higher education, ed. Douglas M. Knight (Englewood Cliffs, N.J.: Prentice-Hall, 1960), p. 6-28. [6054

JAMES McCORMACK & VINCENT A. FULMER. Federal sponsorship of university research [1930-60]. American Assembly, The Federal Government and higher education, ed. Douglas M. Knight (Englewood Cliffs, N.J.: Prentice-Hall, 1960), p. 76-139. diagrs., tables. notes. [6055

DANIEL CALBERT THOMPSON. Problems of faculty morale [in Negro colleges, 1930-59]. Jour. Negro educ., 29:37-46 (winter). notes. Based on thesis--Columbia Univ. [6056

WALTER EVAN McPHIE. Factors affecting the value of dissertations ["in social studies education"]. Social educ., 24:375-7, 385 (Dec). Based on thesis--Stanford Univ., 1959. On the value of 385 theses, 1934-57, "both to the individuals who wrote them and to the field of knowledge in which they were done." [6057

FRANK A. DE COSTA. The tax-supported college for Negroes [1938-59]. Jour. educ. sociol., 32:260-66 (Feb 1959). notes. [6058

CHARLES HENRY THOMPSON. The prospect of Negro higher education [1938-58]. Jour. educ. sociol., 32: 309-16 (Feb 1959). notes. [6059

MICHAEL VICTOR BELOK. The college professor in the novel, 1940-1957. Ann Arbor: University Microfilms, 1958 [i.e. 1960]. Positive microfilm of typescript. [306] leaves. Thesis--Univ. of Southern California. Abstracted: Dissert. abstracts, 20:4307 (May). Study of 50 American novels. [6060

WILLIAM JOHNSON TRENT, JR. The relative adequacy of sources of income of Negro church-related colleges [1944-59]. Jour. Negro educ., 29:356-67 (summer). tables. notes. [6061

ROBERT ASCHER. When Life (et al.) looks at the junior college. Jr. college jour., 30:136-9 (Nov 1959). notes. Bibliographical essay on articles about junior colleges in popular American magazines, 1945-51. [6062

PAUL ALBERT BRINKER. Our illiberal liberal-arts colleges: the dangers of undergraduate overspecialization [1945-60]. Jour. higher educ., 31: 133-8 (Mar). notes. [6063

MARGARET MEAD. Are marriage and college compatible? Dartmouth alumni mag., 52(6):18-20 (Mar). port. On "a postwar pattern of campus life," 1945-59. [6064

ELBERT WAKEFIELD OCKERMAN. A comparative study of the organization and functions of the commissions and committees of the [six] regional accrediting associations [for colleges and universities, mainly since 1945]. Ann Arbor: University Microfilms, 1950 [i.e. 1960]. Positive microfilm of typescript. 389 leaves. bibliog. (leaves 386-9). Thesis (Ed.D.)--Univ. of Kentucky. Abstracted: Dissert. abstracts, 20:4018 (Apr). [6065

NATHAN MARSH PUSEY. Liberal education and intellectual life. Harvard alumni bul., 55:710-16 (6 Jun 1953). port., views. Excerpts from the semiannual reports of the author during his years as President of Lawrence College, Appleton, Wis., 1945-52, setting forth his "educational philosophy." [6066

PHYSICAL EDUCATION

HAZEL MARIE WACKER. The history of the private single-purpose institutions which prepared teachers of physical education in the United States of America from 1861 to 1958: a study of the founding, progress, current status, and contributions to physical education of twelve single-purpose schools. Ann Arbor: University Microfilms [1960]. Positive microfilm of typescript. xxiii, 542 leaves. diagr., tables. bibliog. (leaves 502-7). Thesis (Ed. D.)--New York Univ. Abstracted: Dissert. abstracts, 20: 3656-7 (Mar). [6067

FORD ALLEN HESS. American objectives of physical education from 1900-1957 assessed in the light of certain historical events. Ann Arbor: University Microfilms, 1959 [i.e. 1960]. Positive microfilm of typescript. [469] leaves. Thesis (Ed. D.)--New York Univ. Abstracted: Dissert. abstracts, 20:3185-6 (Feb). [6068

MADGE MARIE PHILLIPS. Biographies of selected women leaders in physical education in the United States [20th century]. Ann Arbor: University Microfilms, 1960. Positive microfilm of typescript. [440] leaves. Thesis--State Univ. of Iowa. Abstracted: Dissert. abstracts, 20:4581 (Jun). Accounts of Dr. Margaret Bell, Dr. Elizabeth Halsey, Margaret Newell H'Doubler [sic], Mabel Lee, Dr. Gertrude E. Moulton, Dr. J. Anna Norris, Blanche M. Trilling, and Agnes R. Wayman. Based upon recorded interviews with them, supplemented by other information from oral, manuscript, and printed sources. [6069

SPECIAL EDUCATION

RUTH E. BENDER. The conquest of deafness: a history of the long struggle to make possible normal living to those handicapped by lack of normal hearing. Cleveland: Press of Western Reserve Univ. [1960]. 208 p. diagrs., ports., table, views. bibliog. (p. 183-99), notes. On institutions and devices for the education of the deaf in America, 1679-1960, and abroad. [6070

FOREST LEE PENNY. origin and development of industrial education in Kansas [since 1838]. Ann Arbor: University Microfilms, 1960. Positive microfilm of typescript. [322] leaves. Thesis (Ed. D.)--Univ. of Missouri. Abstracted: Dissert. abstracts, 21: 1449 (Dec). [6071

CAROLINE HYMAN BURNES & CATHERINE MARSHALL RAMGER. History of the California School for the Deaf, Berkeley, 1860-1960. Berkeley, 1960. xv, 157 p. diagrs., ports., tables, views. bibliog. (p. 129-30), notes. [6072

DICKSON HARTWELL. Dogs against darkness, revised edition: the story of the Seeing Eye. N.Y.: Dodd, Mead [1960]. vi, 250 p. ports., views. On the establishment of The Seeing Eye, Inc., Morristown, N.J., by Dorothy Eustis, Elliott Humphrey, Willi Ebeling, and Morris Frank as a training school for teaching dogs to lead the blind, and the record of service of the trained dogs, 1929-60. [6073

ROBERT SIDNEY SECKENDORF. The New York State Steering Committee for Industrial Arts: a study of its role in relation to the development of industrial arts education in New York State [1934-59]. Ann Arbor: University Microfilms, 1960. Positive microfilm of typescript. [414] leaves. Thesis (Ed. D.)--New York Univ. Abstracted: Dissert. abstracts, 21: 1120-21 (Nov). [6074

Population

DEMOGRAPHY

FREDERICK HENRY OSBORN. Qualitative aspects of population control: eugenics and euthenics. Law and contemp. problems, 25: 406-25 (summer). tables. notes. Includes references to the population of the United States, 1790-1960. [6075

RUPERT BAYLESS VANCE. The development and status of American demography [since 1790]. Philip M. Hauser & Otis Dudley Duncan, eds., The study of population: an inventory and appraisal ([Chicago:] Univ. of Chicago Press [1959]), p. 286-313. diagrs. bibliog. (p. 308-13). [6076

HSIN-YUAN T'IEN. A demographic aspect of interstate variations in American fertility, 1800-1860. By H. Yuan T'ien. Milbank Memorial Fund quar., 37:49-59 (Jan 1959). diagr., tables. notes. [6077

MELVIN ZELNIK. Estimates of annual births and birth rates for the white population of the United States from 1855 to 1934. Ann Arbor: University Microfilms, 1959 [i.e. 1960]. Positive microfilm of typescript. [141] leaves. Thesis--Princeton Univ. Abstracted: Dissert. abstracts, 20:3882 (Mar). [6078

ALVAN WOODBURY SULLOWAY. The legal and political aspects of population control in the United States. Law and contemp. problems, 25:593-613 (summer). notes. On sterilization, abortion, and contraception as subjects of political debate, legislation, and litigation, 1873-1959. [6079

ROLAND McMILLAN HARPER. Recent trends in age at marrage, with special reference to college students [1890-1950]. Ala. Acad. Science, Proc., 30(4):33-7 (Apr 1959). diagr. notes. [6080

MARY VERONICA DEMPSEY. The death registration States [1900-1933]. Am. rev. tuberculosis, 57:306-7 (Mar 1948). table. [6081

U.S. National Office of Vital Statistics. First things and last: the story of birth and death certificates [1900-1958. [Wash, 1960.] 24 p. diagrs., facsims., map, table. (U.S. Public Health Service. Publication 724.) [6082

CARL L. ERHARDT. Vital statistics--their past and future [1908-58]. Am. jour. pub. health, 49:192-8 (Feb 1959). [6083

WILSON H. GRABILL & PAUL C. GLICK. Demographic and social aspects of childlessness: census data [1910, 1940, 1950-57. Milbank Memorial Fund quar., 37:60-86 (Jan 1959). diagrs., tables. [6084

IWAO MILTON MORIYAMA. Medical certification of infant deaths [1915-59]. Pediatrics, 24:305-10 (Aug 1959). diagr., form. notes. [6085

JAMES DONALD TARVER. Projections of mortality in the United States to 1970. Milbank Memorial Fund quar., 37:132-43 (Apr 1959). tables. notes. Includes data for the years 1930-54. [6086

IWAO MILTON MORIYAMA. Recent changes in infant mortality trend [1933-57] Pub. health reports, 75: 391-405 (May). diagrs., tables. [6087

MARTIN J. BAILEY. Factors associated with variations in maternal death rates [1955]. Human biol., 32:274-87 (Sep). tables. On problems of measurement. [6088

CHARLES ALEXANDER McMAHAN. Demographic aspects of the population of human autopsied cases as reported in the United States, 1955. Human biol., 32:185-96 (May). diagr., maps, tables. bibliog. Indications that persons dying outside the South, dead males, dead non-white persons, and persons dying in States that rank high in wealth, percentage of urban population, and availability of physicians are more likely to be autopsied than dead persons of characteristics opposite to these. [6089

DISTRIBUTION OF POPULATION

City and Country

WILLIAM MANN DOBRINER. The natural history of a reluctant suburb. Yale rev., 49:399-412 (Mar). On "Old Harbor," a village somewhere on the coast of New England, settled as early as 1662, now within the suburban area of a large city; with remarks on the problems arising when each of 168 "great metropolitan centers of the nation is consuming a whole series of villages within its sociological borders." [6090

BENJAMIN BAKER. Municipal autonomy: its relationship to metropolitan government. West. pol. quar., 13:83-98 (Mar). notes. On "the tradition of local independence," "State interference in local affairs," the reassertion of "the right of local self-government" in the form of home rule, its frustration by "rural dominance of State legislatures," and the growing need for governmental units larger than cities, 1790-1959. [6091

JAMES ELMON VANCE, JR. Laborshed, employment field, and dynamic analysis in urban geography. Econ. geog., 36:189-220 (Jul). diagrs., maps, tables. notes. On "the influence of changing circulation within the city region on the functional structure of the area," with special reference to diurnal and long-time "mobility of the urban population" and to "the evolution of transportation within the urban complex," 1832-1958. Includes an analysis of Natick, Mass., in 1951. [6092

GEORGE BURTON PERKINS, JR. The conflict between country and city in the novels of William Dean Howells [1870 to 1890]. Ann Arbor: University Microfilms, 1960. Positive microfilm of typescript. [148] leaves. Thesis--Cornell Univ. Abstracted: Dissert. abstracts, 21:198-9 (Jul). [6093

LEON EDGAR TRUESDELL. Farm population, 1880 to 1950, with special attention to its relation to number of farms and number of agricultural workers. [Wash.] 1960. v, 31 p. diagrs., tables. (U.S. Bureau of the Census. Technical paper 3.) Mainly on standards and methods of enumeration. [6094

RALPH JOCELYN McGINNIS, ed. The good old days: an invitation to memory. Edited and compiled by R. J. McGinnis in cooperation with the staff of the Farm quarterly. N.Y.: Harper [1960]. 256 p. cartoons, diagrs., facsims., views (part col.) Articles by the editor and others dealing reminiscently with country life in the 1890s and somewhat later. Lavishly illustrated. [6095

AMERICAN CONGRESS ON SURVEYING AND MAPPING. The role of the land surveyor (past, present, and future) in urban or city land planning [1898-1960]. Surveying and mapping, 20:305-18 (Sep). port., table. Addresses by W. H. Matheny, W. J. Reese, C. C. Lindsay, Arthur D. Shaw, and C. J. Aggeler. Deals largely with the growing separation between planning and surveying, and the tendency of the planners to exclude the surveyors from the formation of policy. [6096

CLAYTON SUMNER ELLSWORTH. Theodore Roosevelt's Country Life Commission [1908-10]. Agric. hist., 34:155-72 (Oct). notes. Deals particularly with the participation of Gifford Pinchot and Liberty Hyde Bailey in the Commission's program and with the recommendations in its report of 1909. [6097

JEROME D. FELLMANN. Some agricultural consequences of the new urban explosion [1930s-1958]. Land Economics Institute, Univ. of Illinois, 1958, Modern land policy: papers (Urbana: Univ. of Illinois Press, 1960), p. 157-62. On the heavily increased taxation of farm land near expanding cities without increase in farm income, the decline of retail trade in farm towns in such areas, and associated problems. [6098

VINCENT HEATH WHITNEY. Changes in the rural-nonfarm population, 1930-1950. Am. sociol. rev., 25:363-8 (Jun). tables. notes. [6099

EDWARD THOMAS DICKINSON. Desirable commerce, desirable industry, and the desirable community. Jour. educ. sociol., 31:16-20 (Sep 1957). On "suburban expansion" and the efforts to set standards for it, 1933-57. [6100

ASHLEY A. FOARD & HILBERT FEFFERMAN. Federal urban renewal legislation [1941-59]. Law and contemp. problems, 25:635-84 (autumn). tables. notes. [6101

RICHARD H. LEACH. The Federal urban renewal program: a ten-year critique [1949-59]. Law and contemp. problems, 25:777-92 (autumn). notes. [6102

THOMAS OBERSON WILKINSON. Urban structure and industrialization ["circa 1950"]. Am. sociol. rev., 25:356-63 (Jun). tables. notes. [6103

Emigration and Immigration

THEODORE CHRISTIAN BLEGEN. Singing immigrants and pioneers. Joseph J. Kwiat & Mary C. Turpie, eds., Studies in American culture: dominant ideas and images (Minneapolis: Univ. of Minnesota Press [1960]), p. 171-88. On the "songs and ballads of migration" in America. [6104

ERIC L. McKITRICK & STANLEY ELKINS. Institutions in motion. Am. quar., 12:188-97 (summer). notes. On America as "a culture which has been perenially, even chronically, characterized by mass movements of people," and the question "What happens to the institutions and institutional habits which these people carry with them?" [6105

IRVING ROUSE. The entry of man into the West Indies. New Haven: Dept. of Anthropology, Yale Univ., 1960. 26 p. map, views. bibliog. (p. 24-6). (Yale University publications in anthropology, 61. [Part of a volume entitled Papers in Caribbean anthropology, ed. Sidney Wilfred Mintz, containing nos. 57-64 of the series.]) On possible prehistoric migrations into the islands from Florida, Venezuela, and Central America. [6106

MALDWYN ALLEN JONES. American immigration [1607-1959. Chicago:] Univ. of Chicago Press [1960]. vii, [5], 359 p. tables. bibliog. (. 325-41). (The Chicago history of American civilization.) [6107

CARLTON CHESTER QUALEY. Some aspects of European migration to the United States [since 1775]. Donald Sheehan & Harold C. Syrett, eds., Essays in American historiography: papers presented in honor of Allan Nevins (N.Y.: Columbia Univ. Press, 1960), p. 153-68. notes. Bibliographical essay on histories of American immigration published between 1926 and 1957. [6108

GEORGE W. POTTER. To the golden door: the story of the Irish in Ireland and America [1820-61]. Boston: Little, Brown [1960]. viii, 631 p. ports., views. notes. On conditions in Ireland that induced emigration, the ways and means of emigration of the Irish to America, and their life and reputation in America. [6109

INGRID SEMMINGSEN. Norwegian emigration in the nineteenth century. Scandinavian econ. hist. rev., 8: 150-60. notes. Deals largely with emigration to America, 1825-1920, and the return of former emigrants to Norway. [6110

VINCENT P. DE SANTIS. The American historian looks at the Catholic immigrant. Thomas Timonthy McAvoy, ed., Roman Catholicism and the American way of life ([Notre Dame, Ind.:] Univ. of Notre Dame Press, 1960), p. 225-34. notes. On "the attitude of the native American Catholic in relation to the immigrant and the question of immigration," 1830-1924. [6111

EITEL WOLF DOBERT. Deutsche Demokraten in Amerika: die Achtundvierziger und ihre Schriften. Göttingen: Vandenhoeck & Ruprecht [1958]. 233 p. bibliog. (p. 230-33). Chapters in alphabetical order, on 55 German revolutionists who emigrated to America after 1848, and their writings both before and after that date, including writings in English and writings unrelated to Germany or to the Revolution. [6112

PETER PAUL CAHENSLY (1838-1923). Address of Peter Cahensly on the care of emigrants, delivered at the general meeting of the German societies in Trier, Sept. 11, 1865. Social justice rev., 52:22-7, 59-60 (Apr, May 1959). On the lamentable physical and moral conditions in ships transporting German emigrants to America, and the need for expanded Catholic action to provide for their spiritual needs at the ports of embarkation and after their arrival in America. [6113

LARS-OLOV LJUNGMARK. Notes from a travel diary. Swed. pioneer hist. quar., 11:108-15 (Jul 1960). notes. On the journey of Hans Mattson, Commissioner of Emigration of Minnesota and Land Agent of the St. Paul and Pacific Railroad Company, to his native Sweden in 1868, as reported in his memoirs (1890) and illustrated by excerpts from his manuscript diary. [6114

ERNEST ANTHONY REITER. A guide for Catholic German immigrants, 1869. [Translated by John M. Lenhart.] Social justice rev., 52:132-5, 166-9 (Jul-Sep 1959). From the author's Schematismus der katholischen deutschen Geistlichkeit (N.Y., 1869). Advice to immigrants regarding their conduct before leaving Germany, while on board ship, after arriving at port, and after settling in America. [6115

SARA MATILDA SAMUELSON (1848-1937; married Alexander Alexanderson in 1872). An immigrant's letter of 1869. Translated and edited by E. Gustav Johnson. Swed. pioneer hist. quar., 11:21-5 (Jan). Swedish text and English translation of a letter to relatives in Sweden, dated Galesburg, Ill., 13 Jun. 1869, on the author's emigrant voyage from Sweden and travels from New York to Galesburg. [6116

ARTHUR WILLIAM HOGLUND. Finnish immigrants in America, 1880-1920. Madison: Univ. of Wisconsin Press, 1960. vi, [4], 213 p. cartoons, facsims., maps, views. bibliog. (p. 196-203), notes (p. 151-95). Issued in 1957 in microfilm form as thesis (with title: Paradise rebuilt)--Univ. of Wisconsin. On the life and habits of the Finns in America. [6117

ROBERT MERRITT DELL. The representation of the immigrant on the New York stage--1881 to 1910. Ann Arbor: University Microfilms, 1960. Positive microfilm of typescript. [300] leaves. Thesis--New York Univ. Abstracted: Dissert. abstracts, 21:1287 (Nov). [6118

SUREN N. SAROYAN. Our present immigration law and why so few Armenians are admitted [1924-59]. Armenian rev., 12(1):3-12 (Feb). [6119

CHARLES BENJAMIN NAM. Nationality groups and social stratification: a study of the socioeconomic status and mobility of selected European nationality groups in America [1950]. Ann Arbor: University Microfilms, 1959 [i.e. 1960]. Positive microfilm of typescript. [232] leaves. Thesis--Univ. of North Carolina. Abstracted: Dissert. abstracts, 20:2947-8 (Jan). [6120

Internal Migration

MAUD (WADE) EDWARDS. The long trail westward. Pony Express, 26(1): 3-4, 11-12 (Jun 1959). port. On the numerous removals of the author's ancestors--from Wales to Virginia (ca. 1750), Kentucky, Iowa (1830s), Missouri (1841?), and Kansas; and the author's removal with her husband and 5 children to Oakland, Calif., in 1924. [6121

IRA DAVID LANDIS. Westward ho--1884. Mennonite hist. bul., 11(1):1, 3-4 (Jan 1950). notes. On the removal of a number of farm families from eastern Pennsylvania to settle near Abilene, Kan., 1884, with a list of some of the settlers. [6122

PUBLIC HEALTH

JOHN JOSEPH HANLON, FRED B. ROGERS, & GEORGE ROSEN. A bookshelf on the history and philosophy of public health. Am. jour. pub. health, 50:445-58 (Apr). notes. Bibliographical essay. [6123

HENRY ERNEST SIGERIST (1891-1957). American spas in historical perspective [since 1720]. Henry E. Sigerist, Henry E. Sigerist on the history of medicine, ed. Felix Marti-Ibañez (N.Y.: MD Publications [1960]), p. 66-79. notes. Paper read in 1941. Mainly on the reasons for American neglect of balneology, and the low prestige and limited development of mineral-spring health resorts in the United States as compared with Europe; with a "plea for the development of our ... health resorts." [6124

HENRY ERNEST SIGERIST (1891-1957). An outline of the development of the hospital. Henry E. Sigerist, Henry E. Sigerist on the sociology of medicine, ed. Milton I. Roemer (N.Y.: MD Publications [1960]), p. 319-26. First published in 1936. On the hospitals in New York City, 1736-1936, and the national need for further development and greater use of hospitals. [6125

CHARLES ULYSSES LETOURNEAU. A history of hospitals [1751-1959]. Hospital management, 87(3-6): monthly installments (Mar-Jun 1959). maps, plan, ports., views. notes. [6126

LOWELL T. COGGESHALL. The problem of the change [in the relation between the Federal Government and the American medical profession, 1780s-1958]. Jour. med. educ., 34:1-7 (Jan 1959). [6127

BERNHARD JOSEPH STERN. The health of towns and the early public health movement [1830s-1865]. Historical sociology: the selected papers of Bernhard J. Stern (N.Y.: Citadel Press [1960]), p. 386-94. From Ciba symposium, 1948. [6128

CHARLES ULYSSES LETOURNEAU. Hospital sanitation [1835-1959]. Hospital management, 88(1):46-7; (2):51-2, 99 (Jul, Aug 1959). [6129

ANTONIO CIOCCO. On indices for the appraisal of health department activities [1850-1959]. Jour. chronic disease, 11:509-22 (May). notes. [6130

BRUNO GEBHARD. The changing ideology of health museums and health fairs since 1850 [in America and abroad]. Bul. hist. med., 33:160-67 (Mar-Apr 1959). notes. [6131

FREDERICK DODGE MOTT & ROY HUDENBERG. Labor's influence on health care developments [1868-1959]. Hospital management, 88(4-6): monthly installments (Oct-Dec 1959). ports. bibliog. [6132

JAY ARTHUR MYERS. 30,000 per 100,000. Jour. lancet, 76:112-18 (Apr 1956). map. On the mortality rate of tuberculosis in America, 1892-1956. [6133

EDMUND J. LAUBUSCH. Water disinfection practices in the United States [1894-1960]. Am. Water Works Assoc., Jour., 52:1416-26 (Nov). tables. notes. [6134

EDITH CHEN & SIDNEY COBB. Family structure in relation to health and disease: a review of the literature [in America, 1899-1959, and abroad]. Jour. chronic diseases, 12:544-67 (Nov). diagrs., tables (1 double). notes. [6135

ODIN WALDEMAR ANDERSON & MONROE LERNER. Measuring health levels in the United States, 1900-1958. [N.Y.: Health Information Foundation, 1960. 2], 38, [4] p. col. diagrs., tables. notes. (Health Information Foundation. Research series, 11.) [6136

LEROY EDGAR BURNEY. Health and hospitals for an aging population [1900-1958]. College Phys. Phila., Trans. & studies, 26:59-70 (Aug 1958). notes. [6137

CONSTANTINE JOHN FECHER. Health and longevity of today's sisters. Cath. school jour., 59(9):67-9, 82 (Nov 1959). diagrs., port., table. On the health of nuns in relation to their freedom from or exposure to "stress," 1900-1959. [6138

ALBERT P. ISKRANT. Accident mortality data as epidemiological indicators [1900-1960]. Am. jour. public health, 50:161-72 (Feb). diagrs., table. notes. [6139

BERNHARD JOSEPH STERN (1894-1956). Socio-economic aspects of heart diseases [1900-1948]. Historical sociology: the selected papers of Bernhard J. Stern (N.Y.: Citadel Press [1960]), p. 401-11. notes. From Journal of educational sociology, Apr. 1951. [6140

FRANK EDWARD MALONEY. Legal viewpoint. Am. Water Works Assoc., Jour., 52:1180-88 (Sep). notes. On the legal aspects of "drinking water standards," 1904-60. [6141

OMAR C. HOPKINS & OSCAR GULLANS. New USPHS standards. Am. Water Works Assoc., Jour., 52:1161-8 (Sep). tables. On the U.S. Public Health Service Drinking Water Standards, 1914-60. [6142

GENE B. WELSH & JEROME F. THOMAS. Significance of chemical limits in USPHS [U.S. Public Health Service] drinking water standards [1914-60]. Am. Water Works Assoc., Jour., 52:289-300 (Mar). tables. notes. [6143

FREDERICK R. McCRUMB, JR. Immunization. Ann. internal med., 52:1161-9 (May). notes. On procedures against diphtheria, tetanus, pertussis, smallpox, and poliomyelitis, 1915-60. [6144

ELWOOD L. BEAN. Need for professional standard. Am. Water Works Assoc., Jour., 52:1176-80 (Sep). On the development of "water quality standards," 1916-60. [6145

LOUIS M. ORR. Bad politics and good medicine don't mix. N.C. med. jour., 21:264-7 (Jul). On health and medical plans of the Federal Government, 1917-60. [6146

JAMES STEVENS SIMMONS. The medicine of the future. Harvard alumni bul., 53:211-15 (25 Nov 1950). port. Mainly on developments in the prevention of disease since 1917. [6147

JONATHAN E. RHOADS. The increasing value of medical care [1919-60]. College Phys. Phila., Trans. & studies, 27:147-9 (Apr). On its increasing contribution to health and longevity. [6148

HARRY C. SALTZSTEIN. Health insurance and the medical profession [1925-59]. Mich. State Med. Soc., Jour., 59:111-16 (Jan). notes. [6149

LEONARD A. SCHEELE. The state of the nation's health and health problems [1925-58]. Mich. State Med. Soc., Jour., 58:197-204 (Feb 1959). notes. [6150

T. K. CALLISTER. Medicine at the crossroads. Rocky Mt. med. jour., 56(6):41-3 (Jun 1959). On "socio-economic" activities of the American Medical Association, 1929-59. [6151

HENRY ERNEST SIGERIST (1891-1957). Group health plans in the United States. Henry E. Sigerist, Henry E. Sigerist on the sociology of medicine, ed. Milton I. Roemer (N.Y.: MD Publications [1960]), p. 197-208. First published in 1940. On the Farmers' Union Cooperative Hospital Association, Elk City, Okla., and the Ross-Loos Medical Group in Los Angeles, 1929-40. [6152

HENRY ERNEST SIGERIST (1891-1957). Towards a renaissance of the American spa. Henry E. Sigerist, Henry E. Sigerist on the sociology of medicine, ed. Milton I. Roemer (N.Y.: MD Publications [1960]), p. 248-55. First published in 1946. On the developing prestige of balneology since 1929; with arguments for the greater use of health resorts at mineral springs. [6153

LEROY EDGAR BURNEY. Medicine in the U.S. Public Health Service [1930-59]. Mil. med., 125:17-20 (Jan). [6154

E. CUYLER HAMMOND. Trends in cancer death rates and cure rates [1930-56]. Ann. internal med., 50: 300-312 (Feb). diagrs., tables. notes. [6155

HERBERT I. SAUER & PHILIP E. ENTERLINE. Are geographic variations in death rates for the cardiovascular diseases real? Jour. chronic diseases, 10: 513-24 (Dec 1959). tables. notes. On "the extent to which inaccuracies in cause-of-death statements and other factors may limit the usefulness of cardiovascular and coronary heart disease rates for studying geographic variations in death rates in the United States," 1930-52. [6156

WILLIAM HUFFMAN STEWART & MARYLAND Y. PENNELL. Health manpower, 1930-75. Pub. health reports, 75:274-80 (Mar). diagr., tables. notes. On the "supply of physicians, dentists, nurses, and other health personnel." [6157

PAT N. GRONER. Hospital cost statistics [1932-58]: a misleading story. Hospital management, 87(3-5): monthly installments (Mar-May 1959). col. diagrs., tables. notes. [6158

THOMAS FRANCIS, JR. On the doctrine of original antigenic sin. Am. Philos. Soc., Proc., 104:572-8 (15 Dec). diagrs. notes. On American studies of influenza since 1934. [6159

JOSEPH WILLIAM GARBARINO. Health plans and collective bargaining [1935-58]. Berkeley: Univ. of California Press, 1960. xi, 301 p. tables. bibliog. (p. 285-8), notes. (A publication of the Institute of Industrial Relations, University of California.) [6160

PHILIP E. ENTERLINE & WILLIAM H. STEWART. Estimated morbidity in the United States based on monthly labor force report [1938-59]. Pub. health reports, 75:1151-60 (Dec). diagrs., tables. notes. [6161

HENRY ERNEST SIGERIST (1891-1957). Socialized medicine. Henry E. Sigerist, Henry E. Sigerist on the sociology of medicine, ed. Milton I. Roemer (N.Y.: MD Publications [1960]), p. 39-53. From The Yale review, 1938. Definition of the term, consideration of "what it would mean specifically in practice," and argument for adoption of the system. [6162

HENRY ERNEST SIGERIST (1891-1957). The realities of socialized medicine. Henry E. Sigerist, Henry E. Sigerist on the sociology of medicine, ed. Milton I. Roemer (N.Y.: MD Publications [1960]), p. 180-96. From

The Atlantic monthly, 1939. Argument in favor of the system, and severe criticism of the American Medical Association for opposing it. [6163

CLIFTON ORRIN DUMMETT. Dental health problems of the Negro population [1940-60]. Am. Dental Assoc., Jour., 61:308-14 (Sep). notes. [6164

THOMAS P. WEIL. Major medical and "comprehensive" insurance [1940-59]. Hospital management, 87(4-6): monthly installments (Apr-Jun 1959). diagrs. (part col.), tables. notes. [6165

KENNETH BITNER CASTLETON, CHARLES B. PUESTOW, & DEAN SAUER. Is appendicitis decreasing in frequency? Arch. surgery, 78:794-801 (May 1959). diagrs., tables. notes. Evidence of a decrease in both frequency and mortality, 1941-56. [6166

MILDRED GARRETT. The United States-Mexico Border Public Health Association [1943-59]. Nursing outlook, 7:295-7 (May 1959). map, view. bibliog. On a group organized to meet the need "for controlling venereal diseases in areas close to United States military installations" and for other measures promoting health. [6167

ROBERT E. GOSSELIN. Economic poisons in relation to man's health. Jour. chronic diseases, 9:161-9 (Feb 1959). notes. On the effect of "chemicals having toxic properties that are utilized in agriculture, industry, and commerce," 1943-58. [6168

HENRY ERNEST SIGERIST (1891-1957). Medical care for all the people. Henry E. Sigerist, Henry E. Sigerist on the sociology of medicine, ed. Milton I. Roemer (N.Y.: MD Publications [1960]), p. 229-47. First published in 1944. Arguments in favor of compulsory health insurance. [6169

AMERICAN WATER WORKS ASSOCIATION. Status of fluoridation in the United States and Canada, [1945-] 1958. Am. Water Works Assoc., Jour., 52:301-7 (Mar). diagrs., tables. notes. A study by Task Group 2620P (Robert S. Phillips, Chairman). [6170

AMERICAN WATER WORKS ASSOCIATION. Status of fluoridation in the United States and Canada, [1945-] 1959. Am. Water Works Assoc., Jour., 52:1513-20 (Dec). diagrs., tables. notes. Report of Task Group 2620P (F. J. Maier, Chairman). [6171

JOSEPH CHARLES MUHLER. Recent advances in fluoridation [1945-57]. Am. College Dentists, Jour., 27:89-100 (Jun). [6172

BERNHARD JOSEPH STERN (1894-1956). The need for national health legislation. Historical sociology: the selected papers of Bernhard J. Stern (N.Y.: Citadel Press [1960]), p. 412-18. Statement "before the U.S. Senate Committee on Labor and Public Welfare on the Wagner-Murray-Dingell Bill," 23 Apr. 1946, supporting national legislation as a remedy for "the inadequacies in present-day medical practices." [6173

SAMUEL R. WEIBEL. Septic tanks: studies and performance. Agric. engineering, 36:188-91 (Mar 1955). tables. notes. On studies of household septic tank systems, conducted by the U.S. Public Health Service, 1947-54. [6174

LOUIS HARRY SIGLER. The mortality from arteriosclerotic and hypertensive heart diseases in the United States. II. Possible relation to industry [1947-50]. Am. jour. cardiol., 3:605-9 (May 1959). table. [6175

E. ALICE CLARK. Challenge of communicable disease today--venereal disease control [1948-58]. Am. jour. pub. health, 49:865-8 (Jul 1959). notes. [6176

NICHOLAS J. FIUMARA & 3 others. Venereal diseases today. New Eng. jour. med., 261:863-8, 917-24 (23, 30 Apr 1959). diagr. notes. On the continued decline in incidence, 1948-56, and the rising incidence thereafter. [6177

Races and Nationalities

JOHN M. RADZINSKI. The American melting pot: its meaning to us. Am. jour. psychiatry, 115:873-86 (Apr 1959). maps, tables. notes. On the "social ... problem of ethnic mingling and integration" in America and the bad biological effects of "our too liberal immigration laws," 1879-1959. [6178

GEORGE WARD STOCKING, JR. American social scientists and race theory: 1890-1915. Ann Arbor: University Microfilms, 1960. Positive microfilm of typescript. [718] leaves. Thesis--Univ. of Pennsylvania. Abstracted: Dissert. abstracts, 21:1284 (Nov). [6179

JAMES WILBURN BYRD. Stereotypes of white characters in early Negro novels [1900 to ca. 1917] CLA jour., 1:28-35 (Nov 1957). Based on thesis--George Peabody College for Teachers, 1955. On the Benevolent White Father of Mulattoes, the Kind Aristocrat, the Poor-White Villain, the Mean Planter, the Brutal Overseer, and the Northern Champion of the Negro. [6180

INDIANS

ROY G. COFFIN (1878-1960) What we know of Folsom Man. Southw. lore, 26:56-9 (Dec). Paper read in 1958, on the discovery and excavation of the Lindenmeier site (in Larimer County, Colo.) by the author and Claude C. Coffin, the eventual recognition of Folsom points as Archaic artifacts, and the traits of Folsom Man. [6181

JAMES BENNETT GRIFFIN. Some prehistoric connections between Siberia and America. Science, 131: 801-12 (18 Mar). diagrs., tables. notes. [6182

ALFRED IRVING HALLOWELL. The beginnings of anthropology in America. Selected papers from the American anthropologist, 1888-1920, ed. Frederica De Laguna (Evanston, Ill.: Row, Peterson [1960]), p. 1-90. notes. On European theories concerning and studies of the American Indians since 1493, and American theories and studies from 1643 to ca. 1900; with sections on linguistics, ethnology, physical anthropology, and archeology. [6183

ALEŠ HRDLIČKA (1869-1943). Origin of the American aborigines. Margaret Mead & Ruth L. Bunzel, eds., The golden age of American anthropology (N.Y.: George Braziller, 1960), p. 433-8. notes. First printed 1912. [6184

JOINT SESSION OF THE AMERICAN ANTHROPOLOGICAL ASSOCIATION AND SECTION H OF THE AMERICAN ASSOCIATION FOR THE ADVANCEMENT OF SCIENCE, Washington, 27 Dec. 1911. The problems of the unity or plurality and the probable place of origin of the American aborigines. Selected papers from the American anthropologist, 188-1920, ed. Frederica De Laguna (Evanston, Ill.: Row, Peterson [1960]), p. 159-217. notes. First printed in 1912. Articles by J. Walker Tewkes, Aleš Hrdlička, William H. Dall, James W. Gidley, Austin Hobart Clark, William H. Holmes, Walter Hough, Stansbury Hagar, Paul Bartsch, Alexander F. Chamberlain, and Roland B. Dixon. [6185

OLIVER LA FARGE. When the white man came. History, 1:51-62 (Sep 1959). map, port. On the civilization of the American Indians at the beginning of their contact with white men. [6186

IVAN A. LOPATIN. Origin of the native American steam bath. Am. anthropol., 62:977-93 (Dec). map. bibliog., notes. On various types of baths among primitive peoples in various parts of the world, the survival of the steam bath in "the Russian water vapor bath" and the Finnish sauna, and the probability that the American Indian sweat bath was an importation by way of Iceland from northeastern Europe. [6187

CHARLES MILES. Indian relics. Hobbies, 64(11)-65(10): monthly installments (Jan-Dec). Information for collectors of "sandals, moccasins and boots," wooden objects, stone axes, bows and arrows, "fetishes, charms, and 'medicines,'" and other Indian collectibilia. [6188

MACK PARKER. The amazing red man. San Antonio: Naylor Co. [1960]. xi, 66 p. tables. On the American Indians since prehistoric times, and the "Contribution of the American Indian to civilization." [6189

ÉTIENNE BERNARDEAU RENAUD. Classification and description of Indian stone artifacts. [Denver:] Colorado Archaeological Soc., 1960. 36 p. views. bibliog. (p. 35-6). (Southwestern lore, v. 26, no. 1, Jun. 1960.) Manual, first printed in 1941. [6190

ÉTIENNE BERNARDEAU RENAUD. Typology of Yuma, Folsom, and other weapon points. Southw. lore, 26:37-42 (Sep). Defends terminology proposed by the author in 1931 and following years, and deplores the confusion that results from "wholesale renaming" and from "so many new names of little-known places." [6191

THOMAS DALE STEWART. A physical anthropologist's view of the peopling of the New World. Southw. jour. anthropol., 16: 259-73 (autumn). bibliog., notes. Argument, based upon the known "skeletal evidence" and upon recent blood-type studies, that "the existence in eastern Asia in late Pleistocene times of varieties of modern man akin to the later Indians may be accepted as reasonably well established," that "these varieties represent the population from which the first Americans were derived," that the Americas were uninhabited by man before the entry of Asiatics across Bering Strait ca. 20,000 years ago, and that "the resulting population at the time of discovery constituted a major isolate that was homogeneous, both phenotypically and genotypically." [6192

JOHN LEEDS STOUTENBURGH, JR. Dictionary of the American Indian. N.Y.: Philosophical Library [1960. 6], 462 p. A single alphabet without preface, introduction, notes, or bibliography. [6193

ERMINIE (WHEELER) VOEGELIN. History and ethnohistory, and a case in point. International Congress of Anthropological and Ethnological Sciences, 5th, 1956, Men and cultures: selected papers, ed. Anthony F. C. Wallace (Phila.: Univ. of Pennsylvania Press [1960]), p. 364-7. bibliog. On methods of determining "so-called aboriginal occupancy for groups in the eastern and midwestern sections of the United States." [6194

WILLIAM WILMON NEWCOMB, JR. The culture and acculturation of the Delaware Indians. Ann Arbor: Univ. of Michigan, 1956. [6], 141 p. diagrs., map. bibliog. (p. 132-41), notes. (University of Michigan. Museum of Anthropology. Anthropological papers, 10.) Based on thesis--Univ. of Michigan. On the prehistory of the Delawares in New York and New Jersey, the evidence that in the early 17th century they were "a large number of small, dispersed, and essentially autonomous groups" rather than a tribe, their depopulation during the century, their culture, social organization, and ideology, "the alteration of Delaware culture by contact with European and American civilization", their gradual migration westward, ultimately to Indian Territory, and their further acculturation there. [6195

FRED M. KIMMEY. Christianity and Indian lands. Ethnohistory, 7:44-60 (winter). bibliog., notes. On the ethical justification offered by Englishmen for the taking of Indian lands, particularly "the early seventeenth-century English theory that the Indian was receiving fair value for his land since the White man was bringing him the Word of the Lord," 1583-1620. [6196

ALFRED IRVING HALLOWELL. The backwash of the frontier: the impact of the Indian on American culture. Walker D. Wyman & Clifton B. Kroeber, eds., The frontier in perspective (Madison: Univ. of Wisconsin Press, 1957), p. 229-58. Reprinted: Smithsonian Inst., Ann. rep., 1958, p. 447-72. facsims., views. bibliog. On the influence of Indians upon American speech and literature, anthropology, agriculture, medicine, religion, painting, music, and drama, 17th-20th centuries. [6197

RUSSELL McKEE. Brown sugars from red men. Mich. conservation, 28(2):10-15 (Mar-Apr 1959). port., views. On the making of maple sugar by Indians of the Lake States, southeastern Canada, New England, and the Appalachians, 17th-20th centuries, and recent improvements in the process by white men. [6198

PAUL A. W. WALLACE. The John Heckewelder Papers. Pa. hist., 27:248-62 (Jul). port. notes. On the life of Heckewelder (1743-1823) as a Moravian missionary to the Indians in Pennsylvania and Ohio, 1762 ff., and his journals and other writings about Christian and pagan Indians in these areas, New Jersey, and New York. [6199

LAURENCE DAVIS. Criminal jurisdiction over Indian country in Arizona. Ariz. law rev., 1:62-101 (spring 1959). notes. Deals mainly with Federal criminal law relating to Indians as a class, to Indian tribes, to Indian reservations, and to delegation of Federal authority over Indians to the States, 1787-1958. [6200

WILLIAM B. BENGE. Law and order on Indian reservations [as an exclusive responsibility of the U.S. Government and the tribal governments, without participation by the States, 1832-1953]. Fed. Bar jour., 20:223-9 (summer). notes. [6201

SAMUEL J. FLICKINGER. The American Indian. Fed. Bar jour., 20:212-16 (summer). notes. On the legal status of Indians, 1832-1960. [6202

JOHN ALDEN MASON. George G[ustav] Heye, 1874-1957. N.Y., 1958. 31, [1] p. col. mount. port. (Leaflets of the Museum of the American Indian, Heye Foundation, 6.) On his life as a wealthy engineer and banker, his increasing devotion to the collecting of Indian articles, his ethnological and archeological expeditions, the accommodation of his collections in the University Museum of the University of Pennsylvania and in the Museum of the American Indian in New York City, and his tragic domestic life; with a list of his publications, 1906-30. [6203

CHARLES COLEMAN SELLERS. "... there is no better plan." John Arthur Garraty, ed., The unforgettable Americans (Great Neck, N.Y.: Channel Press [1960]), p. 260-63. On the work of Richard Henry Pratt (1840-1924) in establishing a school for Indians at the site of an Army post at Carlisle, Pa., 1879-1904. [6204

GEORGE W. ABBOTT. The American Indian, Federal citizen and State citizen [1886-1960]. Fed. Bar jour., 20:248-54 (summer). notes. [6205

TRIBAL property interests in executive-order reservations: a compensable Indian right. Yale law jour., 69:627-42 (Mar). notes. On the property rights of tribes in the lands of reservations established by executive order between 1871 and 1919 as defined by statutes and litigation, 1887-1959. [6206

ALFRED RUSSEL WALLACE (1823-1913). [The antiquity of man in North America.] Selected papers from the American anthropologist, 1888-1920, ed. Frederica De Laguna (Evanston, Ill.: Row, Peterson [1960]), p. 149. Anonymous summary of Wallace's article of this title in Nineteenth century, Nov. 1887. [6207

MARVIN J. SONOSKY. Oil, gas, and other minerals on Indian reservations [1909-60]. Fed. Bar jour., 20:231-4 (summer). notes. [6208

ROBERT HARRY LOWIE (1883-1957). A new conception of totemism. Lowie's selected papers in anthropology, ed. Cora Du Bois (Berkeley: Univ. of California Press, 1960), p. 293-311. From American anthropologist, Apr.-Jun. 1911. On a recently published study of totemism among the Indians of the northern Plains and British Columbia and the natives of Australia, by A. A. Goldenweiser. [6209

ROBERT HARRY LOWIE (1883-1957). Ceremonialism [among Indian tribes] in North America. Lowie's selected papers in anthropology, ed. Cora Du Bois (Berkeley: Univ. of California Press, 1960), p. 336-64. notes. From American anthropologist, Oct.-Dec. 1914. Also reprinted: Selected papers from the American anthropologist, 1888-1920, ed. Frederica De Laguna (Evanston, Ill.: Row, Peterson [1960]), p. 686-717. bibliog., notes. On "the most important ceremonies in the several cultural provinces"--Eastern Woodland, Southeast, Plains, Southwest, Northwest, and Eskimo. [6210

CLARK WISSLER (1870-1947). Material cultures of the North American Indians. Selected papers from the American anthropologist, 1888-1920, ed. Frederica De Laguna (Evanston, Ill.: Row, Peterson [1960]), p. 801-61. double map. bibliog., notes. First printed in 1914. Sections on "Culture areas," "Culture centers and their problems," "Diffusion of material traits," and other topics. [6211

ALFRED LOUIS KROEBER (1876-1960). [Review of The American Indian: an introduction to the anthropology of the New World (1917), by Clark Wissler.] Selected papers from the American anthropologist, 1888-1920, ed. Frederica De Laguna (Evanston, Ill.: Row, Peterson [1960]), p. 863-9. First printed in 1918. [6212

ARTHUR LAZARUS, JR. Indian rights under the Federal Power Act [1920-60]. Fed. Bar jour., 20:217-22 (summer). notes. [6213

ELMER FRANK BENNETT. Federal responsibility for Indian resources [1934-60]. Fed. Bar jour., 20:255-62 (summer). notes. [6214

FELIX SOLOMON COHEN (1907-53). The Indian's quest for justice. Felix S. Cohen, The legal conscience: selected papers (New Haven: Yale Univ. Press, 1960), p. 211-334. Contents.--Anthropology and the problems of Indian administration [1937].--How long will Indian constitutions last? [1939].--The Spanish origin of Indian rights in the law of the United States [1942].--Indians are citizens! [1944].--Original

Indian title [1947; on land titles].-- Indian self-government [1959].-- Americanizing the white man [1952].-- Indian wardship: the twilight of a myth [1953]. [6215

WESTON LA BARRE. Twenty years of peyote studies [1938-58]. Current anthropol., 1:45-60 (Jan). map. bibliog., notes. Topical digest and critique of publications issued during these years, and incidental references to earlier works. [6216

ROBERT W. BARKER. The Indian Claims Commission--the conscience of the nation in its dealings with the original American [1946-60]. Fed. Bar jour., 20:240-47 (summer). notes. [6217

RALPH A. BARNEY. Some legal problems under the Indian Claims Commission Act [1946-60]. Fed. Bar jour., 20:235-9 (summer). notes. [6218

SOL TAX. Acculturation. International Congress of Anthropological and Ethnological Sciences, 5th, 1956, Men and cultures: selected papers, ed. Anthony F. C. Wallace (Phila.: Univ. of Pennsylvania Press [1960]), p. 192-6. Argument, partly historical, with respect to reservation Indians, "(1) that acculturation is not occurring in North America; (2) that Indian societies lose individuals, but the rate is so slow compared to the vegetative population increase that (3) there are as many or more Indians in communities with Indian culture than there were a generation ago." [6219

JEWS

DANIEL JOSEPH BOORSTIN. A dialogue of two histories: Jewish and American. Daniel J. Boorstin, America and the image of Europe: reflections on American thought (N.Y.: Meridian Books [1960]), p. 165-82. First printed 1949. On differences and similarities between the "American and Jewish historical experiences," with special reference to Jewish "orientation" in America. [6220

IRA ROSENSWAIKE. An estimate and analysis of the Jewish population of the United States in 1790. Am. Jew. Hist. Soc., Pub., 50:23-67 (Sep). tables. notes. [6221

ISAAC M. FEIN. Niles' weekly register on the Jews. Am. Jew. Hist. Soc., Pub., 50:3-22 (Sep). notes. Summary and quotations of references to Jews in this magazine, 1811-49. [6222

MIRIAM KOTTLER FREUND. "Make my eyes look to the future": Henrietta Szold centennial address. Am. Jew. Hist. Soc., Pub., 49:159-72 (Mar). port. On the work of Miss Szold (1860-1945) as a teacher in Baltimore, an editor and promoter of Jewish publications, the founder of Hadassah, and after 1920 an official of various organizations in Palestine. [6223

ALBERT VORSPAN. Giants of justice. N.Y.: Crowell [1960]. xii, 260 p. ports. notes. Biographical sketches of "American Jews who have distinguished themselves as Jews in the field of social justice": Simon Wolf (1836-1923), Louis Brandeis (1856-1941), Louis Marshall (1856-1929), Lillian Wald (1867-1940), Albert Einstein (1879-1955), Stephen Wise (1874-1949), Henry Monsky (1891-1948), Henry Cohen (1863-1950), Henrietta Szold (1860-1945), Edward Israel (1896-1941), David Dubinsky (born 1892), Samuel Mayerberg (born 1892), Abraham Cronbach (born 1882), and Herbert Lehman (born 1879). [6224

GILBERT OSOFSKY. The Hebrew Emigrant Aid Society of the United States (1881-1883). Am. Jew. Hist. Soc., Pub., 49:173-87 (Mar). notes. On an organization "created specifically to give immediate aid to Jewish refugees from the Russian pogroms of 1881-1882." [6225

MIDGE DECTER. The legacy of Henrietta Szold [1860-1945]. Commentary, 30:480-88 (Dec). On her activities as a Zionist in the United States and Palestine, 1893-1945. [6226

MOSES RISCHIN. The early attitude of the American Jewish Committee to Zionism [1906-22]. Am. Jew. Hist. Soc., Pub., 49:188-201 (Mar). notes. [6227

ANITA (LIBMAN) LEBESON. Joshua Bloch [1890-1957] ... an appreciation. Abraham Berger, Lawrence Marwick, & Isidore S. Meyer, eds., The Joshua Bloch memorial volume: studies in booklore and history (N.Y.: New York Public Library, 1960), p. ix-xix. notes. On his emigration from Lithuania in 1907, his education, his teaching of Semitic languages and literatures at New York University, his service as Head of the Jewish Division, New York Public Library, and his publications on Jewish matters. [6228

SAMUEL DENIN. Central agencies for Jewish education: a reevaluation [1910-59]. Jew. educ., 30(3):3-16 (winter). [6229

HERBERT SEBASTIAN AGAR. The saving remnant: an account of Jewish survival. N.Y.: Viking Press, 1960. ix, [3], 269 p. diagrs., maps. bibliog. (p. 257-62), notes. On the activities of the American Jewish Joint Distribution Committee for the relief of Jewish victims of persecution in Europe, 1916-60. [6230

ZALMAN DISKIND. The rationale for Jewish education as expressed in the Jewish education magazine--1929-1955. Jew. educ., 30(3):16-21, 32 (winter). tables. notes. [6231

KARL JAY SHAPIRO. The Jewish writer in America [since ca. 1930]. Karl Shapiro, In defense of ignorance (N.Y.: Random House [1960]), p. 205-17. Includes some account of the author's "consciousness of myself as an American Jew." [6232

ERNEST MAASS. Integration and name changing among Jewish refugees from central Europe in the United States. Names, 6:129-71 (Sep 1958). notes. On changes by Jews "from Germany and Austria who left their native lands" in or after 1933 and by German-speaking Jews who left Czechoslovakia in or after 1938. [6233

ABRAHAM P. GANNES. Jewish juvenile periodicals as aids in teaching about Jewish life [1934-59]. Jew. educ., 30(2):59-62 (winter). Bibliographical essay. [6234

HORACE MAYER KALLEN. American Association for Jewish Education and Jewish education, 1939-1959. Jew. educ., 29(3):21-6 (spring). [6235

PHILIP W. LOWN. A significant anniversary. Jew. educ., 29(3):7-8 (spring). On the American Association for Jewish Education, 1939-59. [6236

JUDAH PILCH. The development of the American Association for Jewish Education and its program [1939-59]. Jew. educ., 29(3):9-20 (spring). notes. [6237

NATIONAL GROUPS

FLORIO SANTINI. Figli d'Italia in America. Lucca: Villaggio del Fanciullo, 1958. 192 p. bibliog. (p. 183-92). On various Italians in America since 1492, and the facilities for the emigration of Italians thither. [6238

JOHN MARY LENHART. Early German settlements in America. Social justice rev., 52:239-41, 274-7, 310-13, 349-52 (Nov 1959 - Feb 1960). On settlements in Arkansas (1720-22), Chicago (1833-36), Louisiana (1721-70), Stallotown (Ohio, ca. 1832), the upper Mississippi (1833-50), and St. Louis (1831-44). [6239

WILLIAM ISAAC THOMAS (1863-1947) & FLORIAN WITOLD ZNANIECKI (1882-1958). The Polish peasant in Europe and America. N.Y.: Dover Publications [1958]. 2 v. xv, [3], 1114, [1]; vi, [2], 1117-2250 p. 1st ed. 1918-20; here reprinted from 2d ed. (1927). Study of the Polish peasant "as a convenient object for the exemplification of a standpoint and method." Contains a voluminous introduction on method; correspondence among European and American members of 50 Polish families, 1901-14; "Organization and reorganization in Poland"; and chapters on emigration from Poland, the Polish-American community, "the super-territorial organization of Polish-American society," demoralization, economic dependency, divorce, murder, delinquency, and sexual immorality with case histories from Chicago court records; and "Life-record of an immigrant," the autobiography of Władek Wiszniewski, Polish immigrant in Chicago, written for money offered by "Dr. Z.". [6240

B. JÄRNSTEDT. Swedish immigration to the United States in the last hundred years and its importance for Swedish American relations [1860-1960]. Swed. pioneer hist. quar., 11:73-81 (Apr). [6241

ANDERS MATTSON MYHRMAN. The Finland-Swedes and their cultural organizations in America. Am. Swed. Hist. Found., Yr. bk., 1957, p. 9-25. notes. On immigrants from Finland "who use Swedish as their family language," their "geographic and economic distribution," their organizations, their newspaper (Finska Amerikanaren, later Norden), and their Americanization. [6242

NEGROES

SAMUEL DU BOIS COOK. A tragic conception of Negro history. Jour. Negro hist., 45:219-40 (Oct). notes. [6243

NATHANIEL WEYL. The Negro in American civilization [1640-1959]. Wash.: Public Affairs Press [1960]. xi, 360 p. notes (p. 322-51). Historical sketch of events "from slavery to segregation," examination of ethnic differences between most Negroes and most Caucasians, and dissection of the results of compulsory desegregation. [6244

RICHARD BARDOLPH. The Negro vanguard. N.Y.: Rinehart [1959. 10], 388 p. bibliog. (p. 343-9), notes (p. 349-69). A topical history of "the most celebrated Negro Americans," 1770-1959. Not a series of biographical sketches. [6245

EARL E. THORPE. Africa in the thought of Negro Americans. Negro hist. bul., 23:5-10, 22 (Oct 1959). notes. On their references to and opinions about Africa, 1772-1956. [6246

JOHN FRASER HART. The changing distribution of the American Negro [1790-1950]. Assoc. Am. Geographers, Ann., 50:242-66 (Sep). diagrs., maps, tables. notes. Evidence that "the American Negro, who was a rural Southerner two generations ago, is rapidly becoming an urban Northerner or Westerner." [6247

LOFTEN MITCHELL. The Negro writer and his materials. Conference of Negro Writers, 1st, 1959, The American Negro writer and his roots (N.Y.: American Soc. of African Culture, 1960), p. 55-60. On portrayals of Negroes in American drama, music, and fiction, 1795-1959. [6248

EARL E. THORPE. Some attitudes of Negroes [since 1865] toward American Presidents [since 1800]. Quar. rev. higher educ. among Negroes, 28: 201-18 (Jul). notes. [6249

HOWARD THURMAN. Deep river: reflections on the religious insight of certain of the Negro spirituals. [Revised and enlarged.] N.Y.: Harper & Brothers [1955]. 93, [3] p. illus. notes. 1st ed. 1945. On "the antebellum Negro preacher," the religious uses of the spirituals, and their expression of the religious beliefs and hopes of slaves; and exposition of the religious message of single spirituals (apparently from the early 19th century). [6250

FREDERICK DOUGLASS (1817?-1895). Narrative of the life of Frederick Douglass, an American slave. Written by himself. Edited by Benjamin Quarles. Cambridge, Mass.: Belknap Press, 1960. xxvi, 163, [2] p. map, port. (The John Harvard library.) 1st ed. 1845. On the early years of the author (real name: Frederick Augustus Washington Bailey) as a slave in Talbot County and Baltimore, Md., his escape to New York in 1838, and his settlement in New Bedford; with a preface by William Lloyd Garrison and an introductory letter by Wendell Phillips. [6251

HELENA M. SMITH. Negro characterization in the American novel: a historical survey of work by white authors [1820s-1950s]. Ann Arbor: University Microfilms, 1959 [i.e. 1960]. Positive microfilm of typescript. [418] leaves. Thesis--Pennsylvania State Univ. Abstracted: Dissert. abstracts, 20:3284-5 (Feb). [6252

EDWARD CLARK. Images of the Negro in the American novel [1851-1955]. Jahrbuch für Amerikastudien, 5:175-84. notes. [6253

HOWARD HOLMAN BELL. The Negro National Council, 1853-1855. Quar. rev. higher educ. among Negroes, 28:258-64 (Oct). notes. [6254

CHARLES U. SMITH. On being a Negro in 1960. Quar. rev. higher educ. among Negroes, 28:250-57 (Oct). notes. Historical review of this state of being since 1857. [6255

ROBERT H. ZOELLNER. Negro colonization: the climate of opinion surrounding Lincoln, 1860-65. Mid-America, 42:131-50 (Jul). notes. [6256

BERNARD EISENBERG. Kelly Miller [1863-1939]: the Negro leader as a marginal man. Jour. Negro hist., 45:182-97 (Jul). notes. On his work as a faculty member at Howard University for 44 years, a regular weekly writer for Negro newspapers, and a lecturer, essayist, and pamphleteer, and his inability to support the programs of Marcus Garvey. [6257

FRANCIS L. BRODERICK. W[illiam] E[dward] B[urghardt] Du Bois [born 1868], Negro leader in a time of crisis. Stanford, Calif.: Stanford Univ. Press, 1959. xiii, [3], 259 p. port. bibliog. (p. 233-6), notes (p. 237-51). On his early life and studies, his teaching of sociology in Wilberforce University and Atlanta University, his publications and articles on Negro subjects, his plans for "the Talented Tenth" of the American Negroes, his criticisms of Booker T. Washington, his editorship of Crisis and later employment by the National Association for the Advancement of Colored People, his novels about Negroes and his severe reviews of other writers' Negro novels, his founding and editorship of Phylon at Atlanta University, his employment by the Council on African Affairs, his work for "peace and socialism," and his admiration for the Soviet Union. [6258

ELLIOTT MORTON RUDWICK. W. E. B. Du Bois: a study in minority group leadership. Phila.: Univ. of Pennsylvania Press [1960]. 382 p. bibliog. (p. 350-68), notes (p. 313-49). On William Edward Burghardt Du Bois (born 1868), his early life and studies, his teaching of sociology at Wilberforce and Atlanta Universities his writings on Negro sociology, his service as an official of the National Association for the Advancement of Colored People, his editorship of its magazine, The crisis, his increasing disagreements with the management and leadership of this organization, and his eventual adherence to Communism. [6259

PATRICK W. RIDDLEBERGER. The Radicals' abandonment of the Negro during Reconstruction [1865-72]. Jour. Negro hist., 45:88-102 (Apr). notes. Mainly on the Liberal Republican movement of 1872 in relation to the status of Negroes. [6260

KARL RICHARDS WALLACE. Booker T. Washington [1856?-1915]. Speech Association of America, A history and criticism of American public address, ed. William Norwood Brigance, 2d ed. (N.Y.: Russell & Russell, 1960), 1:407-33. bibliog., notes. On the oratorical and rhetorical characteristics of his public speaking, mainly in promotion of Negro education and other Negro progress, 1884-1915. [6261

DANIEL WALDEN. The contemporary opposition to the political and educational ideas of Booker T. Washington [1895 to 1915]. Jour. Negro hist., 45:103-15 (Apr). notes. [6262

SAUNDERS REDDING. The Negro writer and his relationship to his roots. Conference of Negro Writers, 1st, 1959, The American Negro writer and his roots: selected papers (N.Y.: American Soc. of African Culture, 1960), p. 1-18. On writing by Negroes since 1902 about Negroes and about the status of Negroes as an influence upon their writing. [6263

ARNA WENDELL BONTEMPS. Ole Sis Goose. Conference of Negro Writers, 1st, 1959, The American Negro writer and his roots (N.Y.: American Soc. of African Culture, 1960), p. 51-5. On obstacles "to the development of Negro writers in the United States," 1905-59, with illustrations from the author's experience. [6264

ELLIOTT MORTON RUDWICK. Booker T. Washington's relations with the National Association for the Advancement of Colored People [1909-15]. Jour. Negro educ., 29:134-44 (spring). notes. [6265

JAMES B. CLARKE. An hour with Harriett Tubman. A. M. E. Zion quar. rev., 60:192-3 (fall 1950). Undated account of an interview with her in a nursing home near Auburn, N.Y., not long before her death in 1913. [6266

ELLIOTT MORTON RUDWICK. Du Bois versus Garvey: race propagandists at war. Jour. Negro educ., 28:421-9 (fall 1959). notes. On conflict between W. E. B. Du Bois and Marcus Garvey "in their separate plans to establish an African state and an international organization of Negroes," 1917-24. [6267

CARL THOMAS ROWAN. The life story of Jackie Robinson ... wait till next year. By Carl T. Rowan with Jackie Robinson. N.Y.: Random House [1960. 8], 339, [2] p. ports. On the early life and studies of John Roosevelt Robinson, his service in World War II as an Army officer, his career from 1946 to 1956 in professional baseball, and his subsequent work for Negro rights. [6268

STUART BURKE JAMES. Race relations in literature and sociology. Ann Arbor: University Microfilms, 1960. Positive microfilm of typescript. [187] leaves. Thesis--Univ. of Washington. Abstracted: Dissert. abstracts, 21:1565 (Dec). On the Negro characters in the works of Eudora Welty, Richard Wright, and William Faulkner, 1930s-50s. [6269

AGNES LOUISE MORELAND. A study of Faulkner's presentation of some problems that relate to Negroes [1930s-40s]. Ann Arbor: University

Microfilms, 1960. Positive microfilm of typescript. [250] leaves. Thesis--Columbia Univ. Abstracted: Dissert. abstracts, 21:1192-3 (Nov). [6270

ORIENTALS

ROSE HUM LEE. The Chinese in the United States of America [1830-1960. Hong Kong:] Hong Kong Univ. Press, 1960. ix, [1], 465 p. fold. maps, tables. bibliog. (p. 441-6), notes. Analysis of a population estimated in 1957 at 135,000 persons. [6271

M. FOSTER FARLEY. John E. Ward [born 1814] and the Chinese coolie trade. Am. Neptune, 20:209-16 (Jul). notes. On his successful efforts, while U.S. Minister to China, to control and reduce the transportation of coolies in American vessels and to end the "kidnapping of coolies under the pretense of shipping as emigrants," 1860. [6272

RACIAL EQUALITY

WILLIAM SUMNER JENKINS. Proslavery thought in the Old South [1660-1860]. Gloucester, Mass.: P. Smith, 1960. xi, [3], 381 p. bibliog. (p. 309-58), notes. 1st ed. 1935. Includes chapters on "The relation of slavery to government," "The moral philosophy of slavery," "The ethnological justification of slavery," and "Theories of slave society," mainly in the period 1790-1860. [6273

JOHN H. WILHARM, JR. Racial intermarriage--a constitutional problem. West. Reserve law rev., 11:93-101 (Dec 1959). notes. On State antimiscegenation laws, 1664-1959. [6274

ROBERT L. GILL. The shaping of race relations by the Federal judiciary in court decisions [1796-1959]. Quar. rev. higher educ. among Negroes, 28:21-7 (Jan). note. [6275

LLOYD C. TAYLOR, JR. Lydia Maria Child and the Indians. Boston Pub. Lib. quar., 12:51-6 (Jan). notes. On her writings about "discrimination against the Indian," 1824-68. [6276

LEONA KING DAVIS. Literary opinions on slavery in American literature from after the American Revolution to the Civil War. Negro hist. bul., 23:99-101, 104, 123-7, 147-50 (Feb-Apr). notes. On the defense of slavery by Cooper in The American democrat (1838) and other writings, and its condemnation by Whittier, Lowell, Whitman, Bryant, and Longfellow. [6277

A. CAMERON GRANT. George Combe [1788-1858] and American slavery. Jour. Negro hist., 45:259-69 (Oct). notes. On the lecture tour of a Scots lawyer in the United States, 1838-40, and the references to Negroes in his manuscript diary. [6278

ALEXANDER LOVELL MURRAY. Canada and the Anglo-American antislavery movement: a study in international philanthropy [1839-61]. Ann Arbor: University Microfilms, 1960. Positive microfilm of typescript. [602] leaves. Thesis--Univ. of Pennsylvania. Abstracted: Dissert. abstracts, 21:865-6 (Oct). [6279

HOWARD HOLMAN BELL. Expressions of Negro militancy in the North, 1840-1860. Jour. Negro hist., 45:11-20 (Jan). notes. [6280

DOUGLAS H. MAYNARD. The World's Anti-Slavery Convention of 1840 [and its American participants]. Miss. Valley hist. rev., 47:452-71 (Dec). notes. [6281

JUSTIN MILLER. Lincoln and the Thirteenth Amendment. Ralph G. Newman, ed., Lincoln for the ages (Garden City, N.Y.: Doubleday, 1960), p. 332-7. On his attitudes toward slavery, 1854-65. [6282

HARVEY WISH, ed. Ante-bellum writings of George Fitzhugh [1806-81] and Hinton Rowan Helper [1829-1909] on slavery. N.Y.: Capricorn Books [1960]. 256 p. facsims. notes. (A Capricorn original, CAP31.) Sociology for the South; or, The failure of free society (1854) and Cannibals all! or, Slaves without masters (1857), by Fitzhugh, and The impending crisis of the South: how to meet it (1857), by Helper; with biographical sketches of Fitzhugh, Virginia proslavery writer, and Helper, North Carolina antislavery writer. [6283

ANTI-JEWISH sentiment in California, 1855. Am. Jew. arch., 12: 15-33 (Apr). views. notes. Long, indignant statements by Rabbis Isaac Leeser (in his Occident) and Isaac M. Wise (in The Israelite) denouncing a proposal by William W. Stow, Speaker of the California House of Representatives, to impose special taxes on Jews in California that would drive them out of the State. [6284

WILLIAM EDWARD FARRISON. Brown's first drama. CLA jour.,

2:104-10 (Dec 1958). On Experience, or how to give a Northern man a backbone, written by William Wells Brown, fugitive slave and "anti-slavery agent," publicly read by him in New England, New York, Pennsylvania, and Ohio in 1856 and 1857, not known to have been published. [6285

GEORGE FITZHUGH (1806-81). Cannibals all! or, Slaves without masters. ... Edited by C. Vann Woodward. Cambridge: Belknap Press of Harvard Univ. Press, 1960. xxxix, 264, [1] p. notes. (The John Harvard library.) 1st ed. 1857. Argument "that the unrestricted exploitation of so-called free society is more oppressive to the laborer than domestic slavery" and that "the White Slave Trade ... is far more cruel than the Black Slave Trade." Expands the arguments of his Sociology for the South; or, The failure of free society (1854). Prefaced by "George Fitzhugh, sui generis," a biographical and critical account by the editor, on Fitzhugh's life and journalistic activities in Virginia. [6286

ROBERT GARDNER. A tenth-hour apology for slavery. Jour. South. hist., 26:352-67 (Aug). notes. On The elements of moral science (New York, 1859, 1860), by John Leadley Dagg (1794-1884), Baptist clergyman in Georgia, participant in the establishment of the Southern Baptist Convention, defender of slavery on political, ethical, ethnological, and religious grounds. [6287

COMER VANN WOODWARD. Equality: the deferred commitment. Comer Vann Woodward, The burden of Southern history (Baton Rouge: Louisiana State Univ. Press [1960]), p. 69-87. On the "curious origins of the commitment to equality during the Civil War and its subsequent abandonment" in the North, 1862-1958. [6288

JOSEPH HENRY TAYLOR. The Fourteenth Amendment, the Negro, and the spirit of the times. Jour. Negro hist., 45:21-37 (Jan). notes. Review of legislation, judicial decisions, and public opinion, 1865-1954. [6289

J. PHILIP WOGAMAN. Methodism's challenge in race relations: a study of strategy [1866-1960]. Boston: Boston Univ. Press, 1960. viii, 76 p. bibliog. (p. 71-6), notes. Based on thesis--Boston Univ. [6290

MARK HUGHLIN HALLER. American eugenics, heredity, and social thought, 1870-1930. Ann Arbor: University Microfilms, 1959 [i.e. 1960]. Positive microfilm of typescript. v, 407 leaves. bibliog. (leaves 398-407), notes. Thesis--Univ. of Wisconsin. Abstracted: Dissert. abstracts, 20:2773 (Jan). On the domination of eugenics by the belief "that social classes reflected innate ability" and the application of "racist, conservative, and anti-democratic ideas" to demography, immigration policy, criminology, education, and politics. [6291

WILSON P. WALCHER. Property rights emancipated: the restrictive covenant cases. Dicta, 26:263-72 (Oct 1949). notes. On "judicial enforcement by state courts of covenants restricting the use or occupancy of real property to persons of the Caucasian race," 1892-1948. [6292

ARTHUR A. NORTH. The Plessy Doctrine: rise and demise. Thought, 35:365-92 (autumn). On the "separate but equal" interpretation of the 14th Amendment in relation to segregated schools and other segregated accommodations, 1896-1956. [6293

ALLEN DAY GRIMSHAW. Urban racial violence in the United States: changing ecological considerations [since 1900]. Am. jour. sociol., 66: 109-19 (Sep). notes. On riots involving Negroes. [6294

JAMES SULLIVAN CLARKSON (1842-1918). J. S. Clarkson letter on civil rights. Edited by Albert Fried. Ann. Ia., 35:216-25 (winter). notes. Excerpts from a letter to James B. Weaver, 16 Jan. 1907, arguing against Weaver's proposals to return the Negroes to Africa as members of a black republic, and defending the right of Negroes to fair treatment and equal opportunity in the United States. [6295

BERNHARD JOSEPH STERN (1894-1956). Human heredity and environment. Historical sociology: the selected papers of Bernhard J. Stern (N.Y.: Citadel Press [1960]), p. 316-27. notes. From Science and society, spring 1950. On doctrines of genetic determinism and their eugenic corollaries, 1911-50. [6296

VIRGIL A. CLIFT. Does the Dewey philosophy have implications for desegregating the schools? Jour. Negro educ., 29:145-54 (spring). notes.

Cites certain writings of Dewey between 1916 and 1940. [6297

ROBERT HARRY LOWIE. Psychology, anthropology, and race. Lowie's selected papers in anthropology, ed. Cora Du Bois (Berkeley: Univ. of California Press, 1960), p. 211-24. notes. From American anthropologist, Jul.-Sep. 1923. On "the farrago of bad logic, bad biology, and bad faith that continues to pervade discussion of racial endowment," with repeated reference to publications of Henry Fairfield Osborn and Madison Grant. [6298

RICHARD FINN TOMASSON. Patterns in Negro-white differential mortality, 1930-1956. Ann Arbor: University Microfilms, 1960. Positive microfilm of typescript. [398] leaves. Thesis--Univ. of Pennsylvania. Abstracted: Dissert. abstracts, 21: 1284-5 (Nov). Condensed by author: Patterns in Negro-white differential mortality, 1930-1957. Milbank Memorial Fund quar., 38:362-86. diagrs., tables. notes. [6299

MERRILL R. GOODALL. Southern politics and school integration. Jour. educ. sociol., 32:62-7 (Oct 1958). notes. On Southern voting records in the House of Representatives, 1933, 1937, 1941, and 1945. [6300

VIVIAN W. HENDERSON. The economic imbalance: an inquiry into the economic status of Negroes in the United States, 1935-1960, with implications for Negro education. Quar. rev. higher educ. among Negroes, 28:84-98 (Apr). tables. notes. [6301

GUY BENTON JOHNSON. Progress in the desegregation of higher education [1935-59]. Jour. educ. sociol., 32: 254-9 (Feb 1959). tables. [6302

MYRON LIEBERMAN. Equality of educational opportunity [for Negro and white students, 1936-59]. Harv. educ. rev., 29:167-83 (summer 1959). notes. [6303

FRANK C. J. McGURK. "Negro vs. white intelligence"--an answer. Harv. educ. rev., 29:54-62 (winter 1959). bibliog. On studies of the comparative intelligence of Negroes and whites, 1937-50, concluding "that the social and economic manipulations of the past 35 years have not changed the psychological test score relationship between Negroes and whites." Defends previous writings of the author on this subject against criticism by W. M. McCord and N.J. Demerath III. [6304

WILLIAM JOHNSON TRENT, JR. Private Negro colleges since the Gaines decision. Jour. educ. sociol., 32:267-74 (Feb 1959). table. On the U.S. Supreme Court decision in the case of Gaines vs. Canada ex rel Missouri, "saying that a sovereign state had the responsibility to provide comparable education within the borders for all of its citizens," and the effect of the decision upon "private colleges for Negro youth," 1938-58. [6305

ARTHUR PAUL DAVIS. Integration and race literature [1941-53]. Conference of Negro Writers, 1st, 1959, The American Negro writer and his roots: selected papers (N.Y.: American Soc. of African Culture, 1960), p. 34-40. [6306

LUIGI LAURENTI. Property values and race: studies in seven cities [San Francisco, Oakland, Philadelphia, Chicago, Kansas City, Detroit, and Portland, Ore., 1947-56]. ... Special research report to the Commission on Race and Housing. Berkeley: Univ. of California Press, 1960. xix, [3], 256 p. diagrs., maps, tables. bibliog. (p. 249-52), notes. [6307

J. HAROLD SAKS & SOL RABKIN. Racial and religious discrimination in housing: a report of legal progress [1947-60]. Ia. law rev., 45:488-524 (spring). notes. On discrimination against Jews, Mexicans, Indians, and Negroes. [6308

Recreation and Sport

HENRY CHAFETZ. Play the devil: a history of gambling in the United States from 1492 to 1955. N.Y.: C.N. Potter [1960. 12], 475 p. bibliog. (p. 455-61). Includes some account of associations between gambling and liquor, narcotics, prostitution, and police corruption; references to lotteries and the stock market; and a section on "The opening of the West." [6309

JOHN SAMUEL EZELL. Fortune's merry wheel: the lottery in America [1682-1894]. Cambridge: Harvard Univ. Press, 1960. viii, [6], 331 p.

facsims., tables. bibliog. (p. 285-98), notes (p. 299-323). Includes some account of lotteries as an "aid to government," to internal improvements, and to churches and schools. [6310

FRANCIS EMMETT WILLIAMS. Lotteries, law, and morals. N.Y.: Vantage Press [1958. 10], 338 p. bibliog. (p. 328-31), table of cases (p. 321-7). On lotteries in the United States since 1748, the "anti-lottery prohibitions" in the constitutions of many States (1821-96), and the gradual relaxation of enforcement of these prohibitions by "arbitrary rulings of the postal officials" and decisions of the courts and by the acceptance of "subterfuges" ("guessing games" offering "prizes"). [6311

ELIZABETH ELIOT. Portrait of a sport: the story of steeplechasing in Great Britain and the United States. Woodstock, Vt.: Countryman Press [1958, c1957]. xii, 141 p. views (part col.). bibliog. (p. 139-41). On "jump racing" in the United States, and its descent from "hurdle races" and "hunt meetings," 1844-1955. [6312

JOSEPH JAMES MATHEWS. The first Harvard-Oxford boat race [on the Thames, 1869]. New Eng. quar., 33:74-82 (Mar). Based mainly upon newspaper reports, attributing the victory of Oxford to English national characteristics. [6313

CHARLES JACOBSEN, comp. A complete chronological history of the National Puzzlers' League, Inc. [1883-1953]. Compiled and presented by Oedipus [pseud.], official anniversary historian, in commemoration of the League's 70th anniversary. [Jackson Heights? N.Y., 1953. 1], 7 leaves. bibliog. (leaf 7). [6314

DONALD V. PEARSON. Laws, lotteries, and business promotion. Univ. Kan. law rev., 8:110-23 (Oct 1959). notes. Review of law relating to "promotional enterprise based upon schemes of chance," 1879-1958. [6315

LAURENCE A. JOHNSON. A Texas game in South Butler. N.Y. folklore quar., 16:266-70 (winter). On "42," a game played with dominoes on a checkerboard, popular in Texas at least as early as ca. 1885 and played also in South Butler, N.Y., in the author's youth. [6316

Mrs. B. A. SINN & KENNETH B. WEBB. A brief history of the American Camping Association [1903-60]. Camping magazine, Light from a thousand campfires, ed. Kenneth B. Webb (N.Y.: Associated Press [1960]), p. 371-5. [6317

WILLIAM G. CARNES. Land resource requirements for a national recreation program [1906-58]. Land Economics Institute, University of Illinois, 1958, Modern land policy: papers (Urbana: Univ. of Illinois Press, 1960), p. 201-13. [6318

EUGENE JAMES LAMB. R-o-d-e-o: back of the chutes. By Gene Lamb. Denver: Bell Press, 1956. [8], 279 p. cartoons, ports. Description of the rodeo industry, by the editor of Rodeo sports news and Rodeo sports news annual; with anecdotes and lore about "live Rodeo Cowboys" since the 1920s and "Glossary of rodeo terms." Presents rodeo as "the last frontier for the individual" and its professionals as "modern Frontiersmen." [6319

CAMPING MAGAZINE. Light from a thousand campfires. Selected from Camping magazine and edited for the American Camping Association, by Kenneth B. Webb. N.Y.: Association Press [1960]. 384 p. views. Collection of 106 articles by 82 authors, mainly directors, counselors, and teachers, on organized summer camping, mainly for the young, including Boy Scouts and Girl Scouts, published 1926-58. [6320

ORGANIZED SPORTS

HAROLD SEYMOUR. Baseball. [Volume I.] The early years [in America, 1762-1900]. N.Y.: Oxford Univ. Press, 1960. x, 373 p. diagrs., facsims., ports., tables, views. bibliog. (p. 359-62), notes. [6321

NINE decades of football [at Princeton University, 1869-1960]. University, 6:21-4 (fall). ports., views. Mainly illustrations of the Princeton football teams. [6322

FREDERICK W. THAYER. Harvard's loss of athletic prestige. Harvard alumni bul., 53:370-71 (10 Feb 1951). From Harvard graduates' magazine, vol. 1 (1892). On the "athletic reverses" of Harvard, 1880-92. [6323

FRANCIS WALLACE. Knute [Kenneth] Rockne [1888-1931]. Garden City, N.Y.: Doubleday, 1960. [2], 286 p. port. On his early life in Chicago, his studies at the University of Notre Dame, and his work there as football coach. [6324

JAMES ALFRED MONTGOMERY. The development of the interscholastic athletics movement in the United States, 1890-1940. Ann Arbor: University Microfilms, 1960. Positive microfilm of typescript. [186] leaves. Thesis (Ed. D.)--George Peabody College for Teachers. Abstracted: Dissert. abstracts, 21:541 (Sep). [6325

ALEXANDER M. WEYAND. The cavalcade of basketball [1891-1960]. N.Y.: Macmillan, 1960. xi, [5], 271 p. ports. [6326

JACK DEMPSEY [real name: William Harrison Dempsey, born 1895]. Dempsey, by the man himself, as told to Bob Considine and Bill Slocum. N.Y.: Simon and Schuster, 1960. [6], 249 p. ports. On his impecunious youth in Colorado and Utah, his career as a boxer (1911-28), his acting in vaudeville and motion pictures, his service in the Coast Guard during World War II, and his restaurant, Jack Dempsey's, in New York City. [6327

FOOTBALL at Harvard sixty years ago: four first-hand appreciations of W. Cameron Forbes, coach and teacher [1896-1911]. Harvard alumni bul., 60:633-4, 638-9 (24 May 1958). facsims. Recollections by Richard C. Harlow, Lothrop Withington, J.W. Farley, and William T. Reid, Jr. [6328

BOB GILLULY. The Grizzly gridiron: football through the years at Montana State University [1897-1959]. Missoula: Montana State Univ. Press [1960]. 168 p. ports., tables, views. [6329

THOMAS MEANY. The Yankee story. N.Y.: Dutton, 1960. 224 p. ports. bibliog. (p. 218-19). On the New York Yankees Baseball Club, 1903-59. [6330

CARROLL F. GETCHELL. Getch remembers. Harvard alumni bul., 62:212-3 (28 Nov 1959). port. On Harvard football and the author's service as business manager of the Department of Athletics, 1904-58. [6331

MAXWELL KEITH. Developments in the application of antitrust laws to professional team sports [1922-58]. Hastings law jour., 10:119-38 (Nov 1958). [6332

BOB QUINCY & JULIAN SCHEER. Choo Choo: the Charlie Justice story. Chapel Hill, N.C.: Bentley Pub. Co., 1958. [10], 132, [1] p. ports., tables, views. On the early life of Charlie Justice (born 1924) in Asheville, N.C., his career as "the most thrilling athlete in the history of the University of North Carolina" (1946-49), and his later work in professional football. [6333

MILTON J. SHAPIRO. The Gil Hodges story. N.Y.: J. Messner [1960]. 192 p. ports., table. On Gilbert Ray Hodges (born 1924), his early life in Princeton, Ind., and his career in professional baseball. [6334

DONALD GREGORY SMITH. New York Giants [1925-59]. N.Y.: Coward-McCann [1960]. 192 p. facsim., ports. (part double), tables, views (part double). (Coward-McCann sports library.) On a football club of the National League. [6335

GENE SCHOOR. Lew Burdette of the Braves. N.Y.: Putnam [1960]. 186 p. On Selva Lewis Burdette, Jr. (born 1926), his early life in Nitro, W. Va., his studies in the University of Richmond, and his career in professional baseball. [6336

JOSEPH ARCHIBALD. The Richie Ashburn story. N.Y.: J. Messner [1960]. 192 p. ports., table. On Don Richard Ashburn (born 1927), his early life in Tilden, Neb., and his work as a professional baseball player since 1948. [6337

ALBERT HIRSHBERG. The Jackie Jensen story. N.Y.: J. Messner [1960]. 192 p. ports., table. On Jackie Jensen (born 1927), his early life in San Francisco, his service in the U.S. Navy, his studies in the University of California and his career in professional baseball. [6338

DONALD GREGORY SMITH. The Frank Gifford story. N.Y.: Putnam, c1960. 192 p. ports., tables. On the early life of Frank Gifford (born 1930) in Santa Monica, Calif., his studies at the University of Southern California, his career in professional football, and his work as a sports writer and broadcaster. [6339

ALBERT HIRSHBERG. The Eddie Mathews story. N.Y.: J. Messner [1960]. 192 p. ports., table. On Edwin Lee Mathews, Jr. (born 1931), his early life in Bonham, Tex., and Santa Barbara, Calif., and his career in professional baseball since 1952. [6340

GENE SCHOOR. Willie Mays, modest champion. N.Y.: Putnam [1960]. 187 p. On William Mays, Jr. (born 1931), his early life in Fairfield, Ala., and his career in professional baseball. [6341

MILTON J. SHAPIRO. The Willie Mays story. N.Y.: J. Messner [1960]. 192 p. ports., table. On William Mays, Jr. (born 1931), his early life in Fairfield, Ala., his career in professional baseball, and his accomplishments as a Negro. [6342

DAN F. McGUIRE. San Francisco 49ers. N.Y.: Coward-McCann [1960]. 189 p. ports., tables, views. (The Coward-McCann sports library.) On a football club of the National League, 1944-60. [6343

Sex and the Family

JOHN GRIFFITHS HUNT & DONALD LINES JACOBUS. Brothers and sisters of the same given names. Am. geneal., 36:158-9 (Jul). Examples. [6344

ROBERT HARRY LOWIE (1883-1957). Exogamy and the classificatory systems of relationship [among Indian tribes]. Lowie's selected papers in anthropology. ed. Cora Du Bois (Berkeley: Univ. of California Press, 1960), p. 48-64. notes. From American anthropoligist, Apr.-Jun. 1915. [6345

BERNHARD JOSEPH STERN (1894-1956). The family and cultural change. Historical sociology: the selected papers of Bernhard J. Stern (N.Y.: Citadel Press [1960]), p. 263-76. notes. From the American sociological review. Apr. 1939. On women as wage earners, 1620-1939, and the effect of their employment upon the family. [6346

LESLIE A. FIEDLER. Love and death in the American novel [1789-1959]. N.Y.: Criterion Books [1960]. xxxiv, 603 p. Includes chapters on Charles Brockden Brown, James Fenimore Cooper, Edgar Allan Poe, The scarlet letter, Moby Dick, and Huckleberry Finn, and numerous other applications of the doctrine that the distinctive characteristic of American fiction is its evasion of "adult life and sexuality" as shown by its "voyeurism," its "independence from women," and its "rejection of fatherhood." [6347

CHARLES EDWIN HOWARD. Romantic love in major American novels, 1789-1860. Ann Arbor: University Microfilms, 1959 [i. e. 1960]. Positive microfilm of typescript. [490] leaves. Thesis--Vanderbilt Univ. Abstracted: Dissert. abstracts, 20:2802-3 (Jan). [6348

NORMA P. JACOB. Parent and child in the courts of the United States [since ca. 1800]. Ann Arbor: University Microfilms, 1959 [i. e. 1960]. Positive microfilm of typescript. [192] leaves. Thesis--Univ. of Pennsylvania. Abstracted: Dissert. abstracts, 20:2877-8 (Jan). [6349

ROBERT SUNLEY. Early nineteenth-century American literature on child rearing [1815-63]. Margaret Mead & Martha Wolfenstein, eds., Childhood in contemporary cultures ([Chicago:] Univ. of Chicago Press [1955]), p. 150-67. bibliog. [6350

RUTH ELAINE (PAINTER) RANDALL. The Lincoln family. Ralph G. Newman, ed., Lincoln for the ages (Garden City, N.Y.: Doubleday, 1960), p. 118-23. Mainly on Lincoln's relations with his 4 boys, 1840s-60s. [6351

FREDERICK RUSSELL EGGAN. Lewis H. Morgan in kinship perspective. Gertrude E. Dole & Robert L. Carneiro, eds., Essays in the science of culture, in honor of Leslie A. White (N.Y.: Crowell [1960]), p. 179-201. bibliog. On his comparison of the kinship systems of the Algonquians and the Iroquoians, 1846-77, recognizing "such relations macroscopically" but neglecting "the detailed structural and functional analysis of individual tribes and communities." [6352

LEWIS HENRY MORGAN (1818-81). General observations upon systems of relationships. Margaret Mead & Ruth L. Bunzel, eds., The golden age of American anthropology (N.Y.: George Braziller, 1960), p. 168-78. First printed 1871. On the origins of the systems "of relationship for the designation and classification of kindred" by the Ojibwa, Iroquois, and Seneca Indians. Based upon observations made by the author, 1846-57. [6353

CLARK GRIFFITH. Sex and death: the significance of Whitman's Calamus themes [1855-60]. Philol. quar., 39:18-38 (Jan). On his concern at this time with heterosexual love as the source of life and homosexual love as sterility. [6354

GERTRUDE EVELYN DOLE. The classification of Yankee nomenclature in the light of evolution in kinship. Gertrude E. Dole & Robert L. Carneiro, eds., Essays in the science of culture, in honor of Leslie A. White (N.Y.: Crowell [1960]), p. 162-78. diagrs., tables. bibliog., notes. On studies of the "kinship nomenclature" of "Yankee" (i. e., "Anglo-American") families, 1868-1957. [6355

MARTIN A. DYER. Parens patriae: basis for compulsory medical care for children. Md. State med. jour., 9:799-807 (Dec). notes. On the authority of courts to require medical and surgical treatment of minors when refused by their parents for religious or other reasons, 1869-1959. [6356

HERBERT FEINSTEIN. Two pair of gloves: Mark Twain and Henry James. Am. imago, 17:349-87 (winter). notes. Psychoanalytic interpretation of "a symbol shared--the use of gloves" by Mark Twain in The innocents abroad (1869) and Henry James in The turn of the screw (1898), arguing "that the gloves symbolize the phallus in both the male and female unconscious mind." [6357

GEORGE WARREN ARMS & WILLIAM WASSERSTROM. That psychological stain and a rejoinder. New Eng. quar., 33:243-5 (Jun). Adverse commentary on an essay by Wasserstrom asserting: "Each of Howells' domestic novels sets out to answer one unformulated question: how can sexual intercourse occur with pure women?"; and reply by Wasserstrom, defending his treatment of Howells's novels, 1870s-90s. [6358

JOHN PETER HINZ. Restless heir: the boy in American fiction [since 1870]. Ann Arbor: University Microfilms, 1959 [i. e. 1960]. Positive microfilm of typescript. vi, 260 leaves. bibliog. (leaves 239-60). Thesis--Columbia Univ. Abstracted: Dissert. abstracts, 20:3727-8 (Mar). [6359

ROBERT HARRY LOWIE (1883-1957). A note on relationship terminologies. Lowie's selected papers in anthropology, ed. Cora Du Bois (Berkeley: Univ. of California Press, 1960), p. 95-9. notes. From American anthropologist, Apr.-Jun. 1928. On confusions in the kinship terminologies of Lewis H. Morgan in his Systems of consanguinity and affinity (1871). [6360

ERNEST R. ARCHAMBEAU, JR. Infancy--shield or sword? Dicta, 36:217-28 (May-Jun 1959). On the privilege of an infant (a person not arrived at voting age) to void his contracts, the "instances where an infant, through a fraudulent misrepresentation of his age, has induced another party to contract with him," and his liability for torts and "criminal delicts," 1880-1958. [6361

BERNHARD JOSEPH STERN (1894-1956). Engels on the family. Historical sociology: the selected papers of Bernhard J. Stern (N.Y.: Citadel Press [1960]), p. 277-303. notes. From Science and society, winter 1948. On Friedrich Engels, Der Ursprung der Familie, des Privateigenthums, und des Staats, im Anschluss an Lewis H. Morgan's Forschungen (1884), treating Morgan's anthropological system as a basis for the Marxian concept of society. [6362

T. RABER TAYLOR. Liability for negligent injury to the unborn [1884-1958]. Dicta, 36:323-8 (Jul-Aug 1959). port. notes. On the question whether "the unborn baby is part of the mother," or "a 'person,'" and "the right of the injured baby to a claim against the tortfeasor." [6363

WILLIAM EDWARD McCURDY. Torts between parent and child [1891-1959]. Villanova law jour., 5:521-60 (summer). notes. [6364

JOSEPH J. NOTARIANNI. The problem of intrafamily torts and their treatment in the field of conflict of laws [1891-1959], Cath. Univ. Am. law rev., 9:52-60 (Jan). notes. [6365

TORTS: narrowing scope of the parental immunity doctrine. Wash. Univ. law quar., 1960:171-81 (Apr). notes. On the immunity of parents in suits brought by their minor child, 1891-1960. [6366

OTIS TUFTON MASON (1838-1908). The carrying of children. Margaret Mead & Ruth L. Bunzel, eds., The golden age of American anthropology

(N.Y.: George Braziller, 1960), p. 180-90. views. notes. First printed in 1894. On methods of transporting "helpless children" by American Indians and other primitive peoples, in cradles, on backboards, etc. [6367

RUTH STOUT. Company coming: six decades of hospitality, do-it-yourself and otherwise. N.Y.: Exposition Press [1958]. 155 p. On the entertainment of guests by the Stout family more than 60 years ago, and in the author's later years; with advice to hosts. [6368

MATTHEW J. BEEMSTERBOER. The juvenile court--benevolence in the star chamber. Jour. crim. law. 50: 464-75 (Jan-Feb). notes. Argument that children appear before such courts deprived of liberty and the protection of other "specifically enumerated constitutional guarantees" without due process of law, 1899-1959. [6369

JOHN M. REGAN. Infants--constitutional rights and the juvenile court--the need for national unity and Federal intervention [1899-1959]. Villanova law rev., 5:107-21 (fall 1959). notes. [6370

D. GRANT COOK. Recovery for prenatal injuries [1900-1959]. Baylor law rev., 12:79-92 (winter). notes. [6371

ROBERT JAMES HAVIGHURST. Adolescence and the postponement of adulthood [1900-1960]. School rev., 68:52-62 (spring). notes. [6372

ROBERT HARRY LOWIE (1883-1960). Nomenclature and social structure. Lowie's selected papers in anthropology, ed. Cora Du Bois (Berkeley: Univ. of California Press, 1960), p. 128-34. table. notes. Manuscript on kinship terminology of various Indian tribes as noted by the author since 1906. [6373

MAURICE R. FRIEND. The historical development of family diagnosis [since 1909]. Social service rev., 34: 2-18 (Mar). bibliog., notes. [6374

IHAB HABIB HASSAN. Love in the modern American novel: expense of spirit and waste of shame [since 1909]. West. humanities rev., 14: 49-61 (spring). [6375

MURIEL G. WAGNER & ICIE MAY HOOBLER. Stepping stones to the golden anniversary White House Conference on Children and Youth [1909-59]. Am. Dietetic Assoc., Jour., 36:13-16 (Jan). On the 5 conferences of this title, 1909, 1919, 1930, 1939, and 1951. [6376

ROBERT HARRY LOWIE (1883-1957). Social organization. Lowie's selected papers in anthropology, ed. Cora Du Bois (Berkeley: Univ. of California Press, 1960), p. 17-47. notes. From American journal of anthropology, Jul. 1914. On kinship systems of Indian tribes; with remarks on scientific method in "the synthetic coördination of ethnological facts." [6377

MARTHA WOLFENSTEIN. Fun morality: an analysis of recent American child-training literature. Margaret Mead & Martha Wolfenstein, eds., Childhood in contemporary cultures ([Chicago:] Univ. of Chicago Press [1955]), p. 168-78. bibliog. Analysis of ideas expressed in Infant care, bulletin of the U.S. Children's Bureau, 1914, 1942, 1945, 1951, showing a changing attitude toward fun as a motive of children. [6378

JOHN E. POWELL. Constitutional safeguards in juvenile courts [1915-59]. Notre Dame lawyer, 35:220-24 (Mar). notes. On safeguards held to be inapplicable because the proceedings in these courts are not criminal but civil, particularly in the District of Columbia. [6379

FRANK GOULDSMITH SPECK (1881-1950). The family hunting band as the basis of Algonkian social organization. Selected papers from the American anthropologist, 1888-1920, ed. Frederica De Laguna (Evanston, Ill.: Row, Peterson [1960]), p. 607-23. notes. First printed in 1915. Based upon the author's observations "among the tribes of the northern and northeastern United States and Canada." [6380

ROBERT HARRY LOWIE (1883-1957). Historical and sociological interpretations of kinship systems [among Indian tribes]. Lowie's selected papers in anthropology, ed. Cora Du Bois (Berkeley: Univ. of California Press, 1960), p. 65-74. notes. First printed in 1916. [6381

ROBERT HARRY LOWIE (1883-1957). Family and sib. Lowie's selected papers in anthropology, ed. Cora Du Bois (Berkeley: Univ. of California Press, 1960), p. 82-94. notes. From American anthropologist, Jan.-Mar. 1919. On similarities and differences between Indian tribes "with the family as the basic unit" and those organized on sib or clan systems. Also printed: Selected papers from the American anthropologist, 1888-1920, ed. Frederica De Laguna (Evanston, Ill.: Row, Peterson [1960]), p. 624-36. [6382

STEPHEN S. STANFORD. Changing ideologies of the American home. Ann Arbor: University Microfilms, 1959 [i. e. 1960]. Positive microfilm of typescript. [155] leaves. Thesis--Univ. of Colorado. Abstracted: Dissert. abstracts, 20:4210 (Apr). Based upon a study of magazine articles, 1919-55. [6383

RUTH (SHONLE) CAVAN. Negro family disorganization and juvenile delinquency [1920-59]. Jour. Negro educ., 28:230-39 (summer 1959). tables. notes. [6384

JOHN CONRAD APPEL. The treatment of childhood years in American biography. Social studies, 51:215-23 (Nov). notes. On problems in the treatment of these years by historians, as illustrated in a number of American biographical works published between 1921 and 1954. [6385

JACK J. RAPPEPORT. Same legal aspects of juvenile court proceedings. Va. law rev., 46:908-25 (Jun). notes. On "the deprivation of civil liberties" that is "inherent" in the functioning of juvenile courts, and the permanent stigma resulting from "an adjudication of delinquency or even the mere appearance of an accused child in juvenile court," and the inhibition of use of juvenile court records in proceedings of other courts, 1921-59. [6386

BERNARD C. FISHER. Juvenile court: purpose, promise, and problems [since 1922]. Social service rev., 34:75-82 (Mar). notes. [6387

ROBERT Y. DRAKE, JR. Frances Newman [1888-1928]: fabulist of decadence. Ga. rev., 14:389-98 (winter). On her life as a librarian in Atlanta and her expression of "the deteriorating relations between the sexes" in The hard-boiled virgin (1926), Dead lovers are faithful lovers (1928), and "her historical-critical collection of short stories, The short story's mutations (1924)." [6388

E. ROY HUNT. Is a college education necessary? Miss. law jour., 31:285-93 (May). notes. On the authority of courts to compel a parent (especially a divorced father) to pay the expenses of a minor child in college, 1926-60. [6389

CYRIL H. WECHT. Medicolegal aspects of blood grouping tests in paternity suits [1931-59]. Univ. Pittsburgh law rev., 21:85-96 (Oct 1959). notes. [6390

W. K. ARCHIBALD. Medical aid for children without parental consent. Wyo. law jour., 13:88-93 (fall 1958). notes. On the power of courts in this contingency, 1933-54, especially when the parents decline on religious grounds to permit surgical or medical treatment. [6391

GEORGE PHILIP RAWICK. The New Deal and youth: the Civilian Conservation Corps, the National Youth Administration, and the American Youth Congress [1933-41]. Ann Arbor: University Microfilms, 1957 [i. e. 1960]. Positive microfilm of typescript. [416] leaves. Thesis--Univ. of Wisconsin. Abstracted: Dissert. abstracts, 20:4645 (Jun). [6392

DALE B. HARRIS. Life problems and interests of adolescents in 1935 and 1957. School rev., 67:335-43 (autumn 1959). tables. [6393

JOHN W. KING. Exclusion of paternity. Ann. internal med., 53:412-19 (Aug). notes. On the use of "blood-grouping tests" in litigation concerning paternity, 1935-57. [6394

KARL MILES WALLACE. Factors hindering mate selection [1940-57]. Sociol. and social research, 44:317-25 (May-Jun). notes. [6395

ROBERT ALAN FRANKLYN. Beauty surgeon. By Robert Alan Franklyn, as told to Alyce Canfield. Long Beach, Calif.: Whitehorn Pub. Co. [1960]. 255 p. ports., views. On the author's work as a cosmetic plastic surgeon for both men and women, Hollywood, Calif., since 1943, and his "pioneering in the field of enlarging women's breasts"; with remarks on the ease and the economic value of "face-lifting," "the fairly recent bosom cult", and illustrations of the happy results of surgery in the lives of several miserable patients. [6396

MARK A. McCLOSKEY. State and municipal youth authorities (or commissions) and their role in juvenile delinquency prevention [1945-59]. Jour. Negro educ., 28:339-50 (summer 1959). bibliog. [6397

ELEANOR HARRIET BERNERT. America's children [1950]. N.Y.: John Wiley & Sons [1958]. xiv, 185 p. diagrs., maps, tables. bibliog. (p. 137-40), notes. (Census monograph series.) Study made for the Social Science Research Council in cooperation with the Bureau of the Census. On the population, support, "living and family arrangements," education, and employment of "children and youth." [6398

WOMEN

CARL HOLLIDAY (1879-1936). Woman's life in colonial days [1620-1783]. N.Y.: F. Ungar Pub. Co. [1960]. xvi, 319 p. bibliog. (p. 313-14), notes. (American classics.) 1st ed. 1922. Chapters on religion, education, the home, dress, social life, marriage, and "the initiative." [6399

ELEANOR FLEXNER. Century of struggle: the woman's rights movement in the United States. Cambridge: Belknap Press of Harvard Univ. Press, 1959. xiv, 384 p. cartoons, ports., views. bibliog. (p. 335-8), notes (p. 339-73). On the efforts of American women, ultimately successful, to obtain the right to vote, 1634-1920. [6400

MARGUERITE VANCE. The lamp lighters: women in the Hall of Fame [New York University]. N.Y.: Dutton, 1960. [2], 254 p. ports. bibliog. (p. 4-6). Biographical sketches of Emma Willard (1787-1870), Mary Lyon (1797-1849), Harriet Beecher Stowe (1811-96), Charlotte Saunders Cushman (1816-89), Susan B. Anthony (1820-1906), Frances Elizabeth Willard (1839-98), and Alice Freeman Palmer (1855-1902). [6401

ROBERT EDGAR RIEGEL. "... women against men." John Arthur Garraty, ed., <u>The unforgettable Americans</u> (Great Neck, N.Y.: Channel Press [1960]), p. 126-30. On the activities of Elizabeth (Cady) Stanton (1815-1902) in the movement for women's rights. [6402

WINIFRED ESTHER WISE. Rebel in petticoats: the life of Elizabeth Cady Stanton [1815-1902]. Phila.: Chilton Co., Book Division [1960]. vii, [3], 204 p. bibliog. (p. 203-4). On her early life and studies, her marriage to Henry Stanton, their life in Boston and in Seneca Falls, N.Y., and her work as a speaker and organizer in behalf of women's rights, particularly the right to vote. [6403

DORIS G. YOAKAM. Women's introduction to the American platform [1828-65]. Speech Association of America, <u>A history and criticism of American public address</u>, ed. William Norwood Brigance, 2d ed. (N.Y.: Russell & Russell, 1960), 1:153-92. bibliog., notes. [6404

CHARLES E. NEU. Olympia Brown [1836-1926] and the woman's suffrage movement. <u>Wis. mag. hist.</u>, 43:277-87 (summer). ports., view. notes. On her entry into the Universalist ministry as "the first woman in America to be ordained to the ministry of a regularly constituted ecclesiastical body" (1863), her activities as a suffragist (beginning in 1866), her life in Racine after 1878, and the many evidences of her "intellectual parochialism." [6405

WALTER HART BLUMENTHAL. Hurdy-gurdies--dollar-a-dance girls: a glance at frontier Terpsichore. <u>Westerners brand book (N.Y.)</u>, 6:73-7, 80-81, 95. On girls and women employed in "dance halls" and saloons as entertainers before the arrival of "the ordinary women homemakers" in areas previously populated almost entirely by men, 1850s-1900; with the conclusion that "men escaped to the West, women pursued them!" [6406

ROBERT LAWRENCE COARD. When women were women with <u>ess</u>. <u>Ga. rev.</u>, 14:385-8 (winter). On the former abundance of "feminine forms used in good faith," as illustrated in writings of William Dean Howells and other Americans, 1850s-90s, and the survival of <u>waitress</u>, <u>actress</u>, <u>hostess</u>, and <u>goddess</u> as forms that do not "elicit a heated protest from women" or "a smirk of amusement from men." [6407

RUSSELL THACHER TRALL (1812-77). Song of the hoops: a vocal exercise taken from <u>The illustrated family gymnasium</u>, by R. T. Trall, M.D. Published in New York in 1857. Mo. Hist. Soc., <u>Bul.</u>, 16:67-8 (Oct 1959). Ridicules the hoop skirts in vogue in 1857, and gives details of their construction. [6408

D. H. ELLETSON. Maryannery: Mary Ann Lincoln and Mary Anne Disraeli. London: J. Murray [1960, c1959; label: Hollywood-by-the-Sea, Fla., Transatlantic Arts]. xii, 164 p. ports., views. bibliog. (p. 156-9). On the "relative position and importance" of Mary Ann (Todd) Lincoln, wife of the President, and Mary Ann (Evans) Lewis Disraeli, Viscountess Beaconsfield, wife of the Prime Minister. [6409

AYLESA FORSEE. Women who reached for tomorrow. Phila.: Macrae Smith Co. [1960]. 203 p. Includes accounts of Christen Audrey Kathleen Hepburn (born 1929; actress), Anne Carroll Moore (born 1871; children's librarian), Althea Gibson (born 1927; tennis player), Wanda Landowska (1879-1959; harpsichordist), Ivy (Baker) Priest (born 1905; leader in Utah and national politics), Florence Rena Sabin (1871-1953; anatomist, medical researcher), Edith Head (fashion designer for motion-picture studios), and Martha Berry (1866-1942; founder of vocational schools in Georgia). [6410

MAUD (WOOD) PARK (1898-1955). Front door lobby. ... Edited by Edna Lamprey Stantial. Boston: Beacon Press [1960. 8], 278 p. ports. bibliog. (p. 278). On the author's work in Washington, D.C., as a "lobbyist" for the National American Woman Suffrage Association, 1916-19. [6411

ETHEL (MICK) SHOTWELL. A history of the founding of the International Order of Job's Daughters [1920-22. Omaha?] c1960. [2], 25, [1] p. facsims., medals. On an organization "to be composed of developing girls, who believe in God and bear a Masonic relationship," founded in Omaha in 1920 at the instance of Ethel Theresa (Wead) Mick and the Omaha Chapter of the Nebraska Order of the Eastern Star. [6412

LUCY FREEMAN, ed. Troubled women. Edited with introduction and notes. Cleveland: World Pub. Co. [1959]. 316, [2] p. bibliogs. Reprinted psychoanalyses of 10 women, by several authors, including the Americans Charles Berg (1948), Harold Greenwald (1958), Helene Deutsch (1945), Robert Lindner (1954), Ruth Mack Brunswick (1929), and Bruno Bettelheim (n. d.). [6413

BETTINA BALLARD. In my fashion. N.Y.: D. McKay Co. [1960]. viii, 312 p. On "people who make fashion important": fashion designers, "women who demand and inspire fashion and whom other women emulate," and "the fashion motivators" (fashion editors and writers, artists, photographers), as observed by the author, a fashion writer and editor with Vogue in Paris, London, Spain, and New York, 1935 to ca. 1955. [6414

ROBERT EMMET JONES. Tennessee Williams' early heroines [1945-47]. Mod. drama, 2:211-19 (Dec 1959). notes. On these characters as "the relics of the moribund tradition of gentility," accepting (but not embodying) "the ideal of the virginal woman." [6415

Social Theory

ANTHROPOLOGY

JOHN MANN GOGGIN. Underwater archaeology: its nature and limitations. Am. antiq., 25:348-54 (Jan). bibliog. On underwater "(1) refuse sites; (2) submerged sites of former human occupation; (3) shrines or places of offerings and interments; and (4) shipwrecks." [6416

ROBERT FLEMING HEIZER. Physical analysis of habitation residues. Robert F. Heizer & Sherburne F. Cook, eds., The application of quantitative methods in archaeology (Chicago: Quadrangle Books, 1960), p. 93-157. bibliog., notes. On the ways in which these archeological materials "have been collected and examined and what inferences about life in the past have been drawn from them." [6417

GEORGE IRVING QUIMBY. Habitat, culture, and archaeology. Gertrude E. Dole & Robert L. Carneiro, eds., Essays in the science of culture, in honor of Leslie A. White (N.Y.: Crowell [1960]), p. 380-89. bibliog. On the author's hypothesis of "the interaction of habitat and culture under certain specified conditions" as a means for reconstructing prehistoric cultures. [6418

ALBERT CLANTON SPAULDING. Statistical description and comparison of artifact assemblages. Robert F. Heizer & Sherburne F. Cook, eds., The application of quantitative methods in archaeology (Chicago: Quadrangle Books, 1960), p. 60-92. tables. notes. "An analysis of the descriptive and comparative operations of archaeological research, together with a discussion of the quantitative aspect of each sort of operation." [6419

L. C. STEEGE. Folsom points. Ann. Wyo., 32:244-6 (Oct). views. [6420

ROBERT C. SUGGS. Historical traditions and archeology in Polynesia. Am. anthropol., 62:764-73 (Aug). bibliog. Deals in part with the inadequate support for the traditions of Hawaii and Samoa in the archeological materials available. [6421

WILSON DALLAM WALLIS. Classical and Indo-Iranian analogues in southeast Asia and Pacific islands. Stanley Diamond, ed., Culture in history: essays in honor of Paul Radin (N.Y.: Columbia Univ. Press for Brandeis Univ., 1960), p. 317-32. notes. Includes some account of similarities between Samoan and Greek customs and between those of Hawaii and those of India. [6422

ROBERT HARRY LOWIE (1883-1957). The development of ethnography as a science [in America, 1724-1953, and abroad]. Lowie's selected papers in anthropology, ed. Cora Du Bois (Berkeley: Univ. of California Press, 1960), p. 480-93. notes. Manuscript (after 1953?). [6423

FRANK CUMMINGS HIBBEN. Digging up America. N.Y.: Hill and Wang [1960]. xii, [2], 239 p. diagrs., views. bibliog. (p. 225-8). On archaeology in the Americas, 1781-1960. [6424

CARL RESEK. Lewis Henry Morgan [1818-81], American scholar. [Chicago:] Univ. of Chicago Press [1960]. xi, 184 p. bibliog. (p. 165-79), notes. On his early life and his work as a lawyer and eventually wealthy businessman, his studies of the Iroquois Indians (beginning as early as 1845), his travels in the West to study other tribes, and his conclusions including a concept of "ethnic stages" in a fixed order, "social evolution according to historical laws," the immutability of these laws, "the unity and Asian origin of the Indian race, and perhaps the unity of mankind," and "faith in a science of society." [6425

BERNHARD JOSEPH STERN (1894-1956). Lewis Henry Morgan [1818-81], American ethnologist. Historical sociology: the selected papers of Bernhard J. Stern (N.Y.: Citadel Press [1960]), p. 163-84. From Social forces, Mar. 1928. On his theories of the evolution of human society, particularly in Ancient society (1877). [6426

BERNHARD JOSEPH STERN (1894-1956). Lewis Henry Morgan [1818-81]: an appraisal of his scientific contributions. Historical sociology: the selected papers of Bernhard J. Stern (N.Y.: Citadel Press [1960]), p. 185-90. From Union worthies, not here dated. On his studies of primitive and early societies. [6427

BERNARD R. BOWRON, LEO MARX, & ARNOLD ROSE. Literature and covert culture. Joseph J. Kwiat & Mary C. Turpie, eds., Studies in American culture: dominant ideas and images (Minneapolis: Univ. of Minnesota Press [1960]), p. 84-95. notes. Illustrations since 1827 of "traits of culture rarely acknowledged" in America, as revealed inadvertently or unconsciously in "written, and particularly literary, evidence." [6428

FREDERICA DE LAGUNA. The development of anthropology. Selected papers from the American anthropologist, 1888-1920, ed. Frederica De Laguna (Evanston, Ill.: Row, Peterson [1960]), p. 91-108. notes. On "anthropology as a scientific discipline in the United States," 1842-1921, with special reference to anthropological organizations. [6429

ROBERT HARRY LOWIE (1883-1957). Lewis H. Morgan in historical perspective. Lowie's selected papers in anthropology, ed. Cora Du Bois (Berkeley: Univ. of California Press, 1960), p. 372-90. notes. First printed in 1936. Critique of Morgan as an ethnologist, 1845 ff. [6430

LEONARD CARMICHAEL. Anthropology and the Smithsonian Institution [1846-1956]. International Congress of Anthropological and Ethnological Sciences, 5th, 1956, Men and cultures: selected papers, ed. Anthony F. C. Wallace (Phila.: Univ. of Pennsylvania Press [1960]), p. 24-8. [6431

ROBERT HARRY LOWIE (1883-1957). Franz Boas, 1858-1942. Lowie's selected papers in anthropology, ed. Cora Du Bois (Berkeley: Univ. of California Press, 1960), p. 425-40. notes. On his work in anthropology as voluminous writer, observer of North American Indians, editor, museum curator, and teacher. [6432

FRED W. VOGET. Man and culture: an essay in changing anthropological interpretation [1860-1960]. Am. anthropol., 62:943-65 (Dec). bibliog. [6433

ALEX DONY KRIEGER. Archaeological typology in theory and practice. International Congress of Amthropological and Ethnological Sciences, 5th, 1956, Men and cultures: selected papers, ed. Anthony F. C. Wallace (Phila.: Univ. of Pennsylvania Press [1960]), p. 141-51. bibliog. On "methods of analyzing material remains recovered by ... New World archaeologists," 1876-1956. [6434

MARVIN KAUFMANN OPLER. Cultural evolution and the psychology of peoples. Gertrude E. Dole & Robert L. Carneiro, eds., Essays in the science of culture, in honor of Leslie A. White (N.Y.: Crowell [1960]), p. 354-79. bibliog. On the failure of American anthropologists after 1877 to "treat psychology of peoples or the results of cultural conditioning and milieu as a causal explanation of particular cultures or cultural traditions," and the indications that now "in American anthropology ... a dynamically oriented, analytic, and generalizing science of culture is on the way." [6435

ROBERT HARRY LOWIE (1883-1957). Contemporary trends in American cultural anthropology [1879-1955]. Lowie's selected papers in anthropology, ed. Cora Du Bois (Berkeley: Univ. of California Press, 1960), p. 461-71. notes. From Sociologus, 1955. [6436

MELVILLE JEAN HERSKOVITS. Acculturation: the study of culture contact. Gloucester, Mass.: P. Smith, 1958. [8], 155 p. bibliog. (p. 131-46). 1st ed. 1938. On the use of the word "acculturation" in the United States as early as 1880, and some of the field studies of acculturation by Americans (since 1896) and others; with "suggestions for future research." [6437

MARGARET MEAD & RUTH LEAH BUNZEL, eds. The golden age of American anthropology. Selected and edited with introduction and notes by Margaret Mead and Ruth L. Bunzel. N.Y.: George Braziller, 1960. x, 630 p. diagrs., maps, views. Includes an introduction by Mead on "the classic period--from 1880 to 1920," regarded as "the period when the young science could still draw on the living memories of Indians and often on their still living practices." [6438

HENRY W. HAMILTON. Jesse Erwin Wrench, 1882-1958. Am. antiq., 25: 106-8 (Jul 1959). port. On his work in America and abroad as an archeologist, his teaching in the University of Missouri (1911-53), and his founding of the Missouri Achaeological Society and service as its president, 1934-58. [6439

CORA ALICE DU BOIS. Paul Radin [1883-1959]: an appreciation. Stanley Diamond, ed., Culture in history: essays in honor of Paul Radin (N.Y.: Columbia Univ. Press for Brandeis Univ., 1960), p. ix-xviii. On his studies in the College of the City of New York and Columbia University and in Munich, and his work as an anthropologist, particularly as a student of Winnebago ethnology and religion. [6440

ROBERT FLEMING HEIZER. Edward Winslow Gifford--1887-1959. Am. antiq., 25:257-9 (Oct 1959). port. On his contributions to "archaeology, mythology, ethnology, kinship, and physical anthropology," and also to conchology and ornithology, his service in the Museum of Anthropology, University of California (1912-55), and his teaching in the University; with a list of his publications on archeology. [6441

AMERICAN ANTHROPOLOGIST. Selected papers from the American anthropologist, 1888-1920. Edited by Frederica De Laguna for the Publications Committee of the American Anthropological Association. Evanston, Ill.: Row, Peterson [1960]. x, 930 p. diagrs., facsims., maps, ports., tables, views. bibliogs., notes. Articles grouped topically.--1. The development of anthropology.--2. American Indian origins.--3. American Indian origins (completed).--4. Physical anthropology.--5. Language.--6. Ethnography.--7. Method and theory of ethnology. Includes detailed introductions to the sections by the editor, containing bibliographical comments. Appended (p. 916-28): "Portraits of contributors to the American anthropologist." [6442

DANIEL GARRISON BRINTON (1837-99). The nomenclature and teaching of anthropology. Selected papers from the American anthropologist, 1888-1920, ed. Frederica De Laguna (Evanston, Ill.: Row, Peterson [1960]), p. 109-17. First printed 1892. "Abstract of an address delivered before the Anthropological Society of

Washington, April 5, 1892"; with appended comments by John Wesley Powell on the "classification and nomenclature of the science of anthropology." [6443

WILLIAM HENRY HOLMES (1846-1933). The World's Fair Congress of Anthropology [Chicago, 1893]. Selected papers from the American anthropologist, 1888-1920, ed. Frederica De Laguna (Evanston, Ill.: Row, Peterson [1960]), p. 119-30. First printed in 1893. Mainly lists and summaries of papers. [6444

RALPH LEON BEALS. Current trends in the development of American ethnology [1894-1954]. International Congress of Anthropological and Ethnological Sciences, 5th, Men and cultures: selected papers, ed. Anthony F. C. Wallace (Phila.: Univ. of Pennsylvania Press [1960]), p. 11-18. tables. notes. Mainly "an analysis of the titles of doctoral dissertations accepted by United States universities in the two decades of 1925 to 1934 [45 titles] and 1945 to 1954 [214 titles]." [6445

FAY-COOPER COLE. Robert Redfield (1897-1958) [cultural anthropologist]. Am. Philos. Soc., Yr. bk., 1959, p. 143-6. [6446

ROBERT HARRY LOWIE (1883-1957). Robert H. Lowie, ethnologist: a personal record. Berkeley: Univ. of California Press, 1959. x, [4], 198 p. ports., views. Reminiscences (1956-57) of the author's studies of anthropology at Columbia University, his service as Assistant and Associate Curator of the American Museum of Natural History and Professor of Anthropology at the University of California, his field studies of the Crow, northern Blackfoot, Assiniboine, Chipewyan, and Hopi Indians, his "success and failure in writing," and his studies of contemporary German society; with a list of his publications, 1898-1957. [6447

RECENT progress in American anthropology: a review of the activities of institutions and individuals from 1902 to 1906, presented to the Fifteenth International Congress of Americanists, Quebec, 1906. Selected papers from the American anthropologist, 1888-1920, ed. Frederica De Laguna (Evanston, Ill.: Row, Peterson [1960]), p. 131-5. notes. First printed in 1906. Anonymous report, the original occupying vol. 8, p. 441-558, of which only p. 441-4 are reprinted here. [6448

GEORGE W. STOCKING, JR. Franz Boas and the founding of the American Anthropological Association [1902]. Am. anthropol., 62:1-17 (Feb). bibliog. On an extreme difference of opinion between Boas and William John McGee as to whether persons other than professional anthropologists should be admitted to the proposed organization, and the disingenuousness of McGee and a few of his supporters in establishing the organization before the dissenters could object. [6449

ROBERT LEONARD CARNEIRO. The culture process. Gertrude E. Dole & Robert L. Carneiro, eds., Essays in the science of culture, in honor of Leslie A. White (N.Y.: Crowell [1960]), p. 145-61. bibliog., notes. On anthropological concepts and definitions of the term "culture process" in America, 1904-56, and abroad. [6450

JOHN REED SWANTON (1873-1958). The social organization of American tribes. Selected papers from the American anthropologist, 1888-1920, ed. Frederica De Laguna (Evanston, Ill.: Row, Peterson [1960]), p. 595-605. notes. First printed in 1905. On the weakness or lack of evidence supporting "the totemic clan theory." [6451

ROBERT HARRY LOWIE (1883-1957). Autobiographical data by Robert H. Lowie. Lowie's selected papers in anthropology, ed. Cora Du Bois (Berkeley: Univ. of California Press, 1960), p. 1-13. notes. Author's review and criticism (1943) of his work as an anthropologist since 1906, particularly his studies of the Crow Indians (1907-16, 1931). [6452

ROBERT HARRY LOWIE (1883-1957). On the principle of convergence in ethnology [as applied by American anthropologists to primitive societies in America and abroad]. Lowie's selected papers in anthropology, ed. Cora Du Bois (Berkeley: Univ. of California Press, 1960), p. 312-35. notes. From Journal of American folk-lore, 1912. [6453

BERNHARD JOSEPH STERN (1894-1956). Franz Boas [1858-1942] as scientist and citizen. Historical sociology: the selected papers of Bernhard J. Stern (N.Y.: Citadel Press [1960]), p. 208-41. notes. From Science and society, fall 1943. On his work in anthropology, 1912-42, and his ideas about society. [6454

RICHARD BENJAMIN WOODBURY. Nels C. Nelson and chronological archaeology. Am. antiq., 25:400-401 (Jan). bibliog. On his establishment of a method of "refined stratigraphic excavations, with comparisons of levels in terms of artifact-type frequencies," 1912-14. [6455

ROLAND BURRAGE DIXON (1875-1934). Some aspects of North American archeology. Selected papers from the American anthropologist, 1888-1920, ed. Frederica De Laguna (Evanston, Ill.: Row, Peterson [1960]), p. 249-77. notes. First printed in 1913. Geographical survey of areas of archeological interest; with comments by George Grant MacCurdy and Berthold Laufer. [6456

ALBERT CARL CAFAGNA. A formal analysis of definitions of "culture." Gertrude E. Dole & Robert L. Carneiro, eds., Essays in the science of culture, in honor of Leslie A. White (N.Y.: Crowell [1960]), p. 111-32. diagrs. bibliog., notes. On uses of the word in anthropology, 1916-55. [6457

FRANZ BOAS (1858-1942). The methods of ethnology. Selected papers from the American anthropologist, 1888-1920, ed. Frederica De Laguna (Evanston, Ill.: Row, Peterson [1960]), p. 877-87. First printed in 1920. [6458

GEORGE McCELLAND FOSTER. Edward Winslow Gifford, 1887-1959. Am. anthropol., 62:327-9 (Apr). port. On his work in "most major anthropological fields--archeology, physical anthropology, social organization, folklore, religion and material culture," and his teaching of anthropology in the University of California, 1920-55. [6459

ALFRED LOUIS KROEBER (1876-1960). [Review of Primitive society (1920), by Robert H. Lowie.] Selected papers from the American anthropologist, 1888-1920, ed. Frederica De Laguna (Evanston, Ill.: Row, Peterson [1960]), p. 871-5. First printed in 1920. Mainly on Lowie's ethnographic method as "descriptive instead of primarily interpretative." [6460

MAURICE ROBERT STEIN. Anthropological perspectives on the modern community. Stanley Diamond, ed., Culture in history: essays in honor of Paul Radin (N.Y.: Columbia Univ. Press for Brandeis Univ., 1960), p. 281-97. notes. On anthropological studies since ca. 1920 of connections between "folk or primitive society ... and urban society." [6461

HARRY ELMER BARNES. My personal friendship for Leslie White. Gertrude E. Dole & Robert L. Carneiro, eds., Essays in the science of culture, in honor of Leslie A. White (N.Y.: Crowell [1960]), p. xi-xlvi. bibliog. On the author's associations with White since 1923; with an analysis of his educational experience, academic career, and "outstanding contributions to anthropology and social science," especially as head of the Department of Anthropology, University of Michigan. [6462

JOHN GREENWAY. The Coffins: discoverers of the Lindenmeier site. Southw. lore, 26:54-5 (Dec). ports. On Claude C. Coffin (1884-1954) and Roy G. Coffin (1878-1960), who in 1924 "picked up on an arroyo bank between Fort Collins and the Wyoming border the first extensive collection of what was later to be identified as Folsom points," and the 11 years of skepticism in the anthropological profession before Folsom Man was "fully established." [6463

BRUCE T. ELLIS. Stanley A. Stubbs, 1906-1959. Am. antiq., 25:587-8 (Apr). port. On his work as a field archeologist, later Curator and Research Associate, of the Laboratory of Anthropology, Santa Fe, 1931-59; with a list of his publications. [6464

WILL CARLETON McKERN. The first quarter century. Am. antiq., 25:449-53 (Apr). On the Society for American Archaeology, organized in 1934, and its organ, American antiquity, begun in 1935. [6465

ROBERT HARRY LOWIE (1883-1957). Cultural anthropology: a science. Lowie's selected papers in anthropology, ed. Cora Du Bois (Berkeley: Univ. of California Press, 1960), p. 391-410. diagr. notes. From American journal of sociology, 1936. On "a science grappling with the phenomena segregated from the remainder of the universe as 'cultural.'" [6466

WALTER ROCHS GOLDSCHMIDT. Culture and human behavior. International Congress of Anthropological and Ethnological Sciences, 5th, 1956, Men and cultures: selected papers, ed. Anthony F. C. Wallace (Phila.: Univ. of Pennsylvania Press [1960]), p. 98-104. bibliog., notes. On the "confusion between culture and behavior" in anthropological studies, 1937-55. [6467

JOSEPH RALSTON CALDWELL. The new American archeology [1940-58]. Science, 129:303-7 (6 Feb 1959): notes. [6468

BETTY JANE MEGGERS. The law of cultural evolution as a practical research tool. Gertrude E. Dole & Robert L. Carneiro, eds., Essays in the science of culture, in honor of Leslie A. White (N.Y.: Crowell [1960]), p. 302-16. notes. On White's "law of energy and cultural evolution," formulated between 1943 and 1949, and its application to "the data of anthropology." [6469

ROBERT HARRY LOWIE (1883-1957). Evolution in cultural anthropology: a reply to Leslie White. Lowie's selected papers in anthropology, ed. Cora Du Bois (Berkeley: Univ. of California Press, 1960), p. 411-24. notes. From American anthropologist, Apr.-Jun. 1946. Largely a defense of the author and of Franz Boas against recent attack by White, advocate and revivalist of the "evolutionism" of Lewis H. Morgan; with Lowie's interpretation of "what constitutes cultural evolution." [6470

IRVING ROUSE. Recent developments in American archeology [1947-56]. International Congress of Anthropological and Ethnological Sciences, 5th, 1956, Men and cultures: selected papers, ed. Anthony F. C. Wallace (Phila.: Univ. of Pennsylvania Press [1960]), p. 64-73. bibliog. [6471

ROBERT HARRY LOWIE (1883-1957). Some problems of geographical distribution. Lowie's selected papers in anthropology, ed. Cora Du Bois (Berkeley: Univ. of California Press, 1960), p. 441-60. notes. First printed in 1951. On causes of similarities in geographically separated cultures. [6472

PSYCHOLOGY AND PSYCHIATRY

GABRIEL DARROW OFIESH. The history, development, present status, and purpose of the first (introductory) course in psychology in American undergraduate education [since ca. 1700.] Ann Arbor: University Microfilms, 1959 [i. e. 1960]. Positive microfilm of typescript. [757] leaves. Thesis (Ed. D.)--Univ. of Denver. Abstracted: Dissert. abstracts, 21: 1249-50 (Nov). [6473

ERIC T. CARLSON & NORMAN DAIN. The psychotherapy that was moral treatment. Am. jour. psychiatry, 117:519-24 (Dec). notes. On the development of nonmedical treatment of patients by their physicians, 1750-1840. [6474

GEORGE ROSEN. Social stress and mental disease from the eighteenth century to the present: some origins of social psychiatry [1774-1957]. Milbank Memorial Fund quar., 37: 5-32 (Jan 1959). notes. On "the social causation of mental disease." [6475

NORMAN DAIN & ERIC T. CARLSON. Social class and psychological medicine in the United States, 1789-1824. Bul. hist. med., 33:454-65 (Sep-Oct). notes. On "class distinctions in psychiatric treatment." [6476

JEROME MORTIMER SCHNECK. A history of psychiatry [in America, ca. 1789 to 1960, and abroad]. Springfield, Ill.: Thomas [1960]. ix, 196 p. ports. notes. [6477

LEANDER L. BOYKIN. Changes in the American way of life in the area of psychology [since ca. 1800]. Quar. rev. higher educ. among Negroes, 28:59-83 (Apr). On possible psychological interpretations of the changes. [6478

EUGENE MEYER. The psychosomatic concept: use and abuse [1805-1959]. Jour. chronic diseases, 9:198-314 (Mar 1959). notes. [6479

ERIC T. CARLSON. Dr. Pliny Earle (1809-1892). Am. jour. psychiatry, 116:557-8 (Dec 1959). On his work as a psychiatrist in several mental institutions and his part in the founding of the American Psychiatric Association. [6480

WILLIAM J. CURRAN. Tort liability of the mentally ill and mentally deficient [1817-1959]. Ohio State law jour., 21:52-74 (winter). notes. [6481

CHARLES ARTHUR CARRIEL. Henry Frost Carriel [1830-1908], M.D., his ancestors and descendants. Pittsburgh: J. T. Carriel, 1960. [6], 161 p. facsim., map, ports., views. Account, by his son, of his early life in New England, his service as Assistant Superintendent of the New Jersey State Lunatic Asylum at Trenton (1857-70) and Superintendent of the Illinois Central Hospital for the Insane at Jacksonville (1870-93), his descent from Nathaniel Carriel (English emigrant to Salem, Mass., ca. 1656), and his descendants. [6482

ERIC T. CARLSON. Charles Poyen [died 1844] brings mesmerism to America. Jour. hist. med., 15:121-32 (Apr). On his stay in America, 1834 to 1838 or 1839, as a lecturer on "animal magnetism" in Boston and elsewhere in New England and as a writer on the same subject. [6483

ERIC T. CARLSON. Addenda to the early history of hypnotic anaesthesia [1836-45]. Jour. hist. med., 15:81-3 (Jan). notes. [6484

SEYMOUR HERSHMAN. Hypnosis in medicine and surgery [1840-1958]. Ark. Med. Soc., Jour., 55:105-8 (Aug 1958). [6485

JAMES LINCOLN McCARTNEY. Medical-legal problems and psychiatry, criminal cases [1843-1960]. N.Y. State jour. med., 60:3621-5 (15 Nov). notes. [6486

WILLIAM F. KNOFF. Modern treatment of the "insane": an historical view of nonrestraint [1844-1960]. N.Y. State jour. med., 60:2236-43 (15 Jul). notes. [6487

WALTER H. OBENAUF. The District Branch of the APA [American Psychiatric Association]: its origin, present status, and future development [1844-1959]. Am. jour. psychiatry, 116:416-22 (Nov 1959). diagr. notes. [6488

LEO KANNER. Child psychiatry: retrospect and prospect [1848-1960]. Am. jour. psychiatry, 117:15-22 (Jul). [6489

IRWIN W. PERR. Epilepsy and the law [1848-1956]. Jour. nervous and mental disease, 128:262-75 (Mar 1959). notes. [6490

NICHOLAS N. KITTRIE. Compulsory mental treatment and the requirements of "due process" [1851-1960]. Ohio State law jour., 21:28-51 (winter). notes. [6491

GEORGE ROSEN. Patterns of discovery and control in mental illness [1851-1960]. Am. jour. pub. health, 50:855-66 (Jun). notes. [6492

BERNIE R. BURRUS & HARRY L. MARKS. Testimonial reliability of drug addicts. N.Y. Univ. law rev., 35: 259-83 (Jan). notes. Study of American cases, 1858-1959, and of medical and psychiatric opinion concerning an association between drugs and mendacity. [6493

CAL BERNSTEIN. Spirit photography. Infinity, 8(7):16-17 (Sep 1959). ports., views. On photographs showing what are alleged to be "spirits" or other psychic entities, and the belief that beings invisible to the unaided eye may be discerned by photographic lenses and films, 1861-1959. [6494

JACK EDWARD WALLACE. The novels of Oliver Wendall Holmes. Chicago: [Dept. of Photoduplication, Univ. of Chicago Library] 1960. Positive microfilm of typescript. 305 leaves. bibliog. Thesis--Univ. of Chicago. On Elsie Venner (1861), The guardian angel (1867), and A mortal antipathy (1885), "medical novels." [6495

CLARENCE B. FARRAR. I remember Stewart Paton [1865-1942]. Am. jour. psychiatry, 117:160-62 (Aug). On his teaching of psychiatry at the Johns Hopkins University and his establishment there of the Henry Phipps Psychiatric Hospital. [6496

WILLIAM JAMES (1842-1910). William James on psychical research. Compiled and edited by Gardner Murphy and Robert O[leson] Ballou. N.Y.: Viking Press, 1960. viii, 338 p. diagr., col. port. notes. Collection of writings first published between 1869 and 1911. [6497

PERCIVAL MALLON SYMONDS (1893-1960). What education has to learn from psychology. VII. Transfer and formal discipline [1869-1959], Teachers College rec., 61:30-45, 86-98, 301-17 (Oct 1959 - Mar 1960). tables. notes. [6498

ROBERT S. HARPER. The laboratory of William James. Harvard alumni bul., 52:169-73 (5 Nov 1949). ports. On the laboratory of experimental psychology established in Lawrence Hall by James, ca. 1875 to 1891, when it was succeeded by the laboratory in Dane Hall in charge of Hugo Munsterberg; with an argument that the James laboratory was "really the world's first psychological laboratory." [6499

ANTON THEOPHILUS BOISEN (born 1876). Out of the depths: an autobiographical study of mental disorder and religious experience. N.Y.: Harper [1960]. 216, [1] p. On the author's early life and studies, his employment by the U.S. Forest Service, his work as a missionary of the Presbyterian Board of Home Missions and during World War I with the Overseas Young Men's Christian

Association, his confinement in 2 Massachusetts mental hospitals (1920-22), his continued theological studies, his employment since 1932 at Elgin (Ill.) State Hospitals as acting chaplain for training programs, and his researches into "the religious factors in schizophrenia"; with a list of his writings, 1910-60. [6500

EUGENE L. BLISS & CHARLES HENRY HARDIN BRANCH. Anorexia nervosa: its history, psychology, and biology. [N.Y.:] Hoeber [1960]. vii, [3], 210 p. tables (part double), views. bibliog. (p. 175-200). (A psychomatic medicine monograph.) On studies of "psychogenic malnutrition" in America (since 1878) and abroad; with an account of 22 cases treated by the authors in Salt Lake City. [6501

ANITA K. BAHN. The development of an effective statistical system in mental illness [1880-1959]. Am. jour. psychiatry, 116:798-800 (Mar). [6502

MORTON LEVITT. Freud and Dewey on the nature of man. N.Y.: Philosophical Library [1960. [12], 180 p. notes. On "areas of reapprochement" in the psychologies of John Dewey and Sigmund Freud, 1890s-1930s, and their "two seemingly opposed but essentially complementary approaches to human nature." [6503

PERCIVAL MALLON SYMONDS (1893-1960). What education has to learn from psychology. IX. Origins of personality. Teachers College rec., 61:301-17 (Mar). notes. Refers to studies since 1890. [6504

IRVIN ROCK. The present status of gestalt psychology [1891-1960]. John G. Peatman & Eugene L. Hartley, eds., Festschrift for Gardner Murphy (N.Y.: Harper [1960]), p. 117-44. bibliog. [6505

FRANCIS JAMES BRACELAND. Francis J. Gerty [born 1892] ... a biographical sketch. Am. jour. psychiatry, 116:11-15 (Jul 1959). port. On his work as a psychiatrist. [6506

JOHN EDWARD WALLACE WALLIN. History of the struggles within the American Psychological Association to attain membership requirements, test standardization, certification of psychological practitioners, and professionalization [1892-1959]. Jour. gen. psychol., 63:287-308 (Oct). notes. [6507

JACK C. WESTMAN. An overview of group psychotherapy [1905-59]. Arch. gen. psychiatry, 2:271-7 (Mar). notes. [6508

EARL DANFORD BOND. Seven years of awakening [in American psychiatry, 1906-13]. Am. jour. psychiatry, 116: 110-13 (Aug 1959). notes. Largely reminiscent. [6509

JOHN CHYNOWETH BURNHAM. Psychiatry, psychology, and the Progressive Movement. Am. quar., 12: 457-65 (winter). notes. On "the elements of Progressivism--optimism, environmentalism, moral fervor and leadership by an enlightened elite" as elements also of "the psychotherapy movement in the psychiatry of that day, and ... the revolt of the behaviorists in contemporaneous psychology," 1907-17, both movements aiming at "the prediction and control of behavior." [6510

J. FRANKLIN ROBINSON. Current status of child psychiatry [1909-59]. Am. jour. psychiatry, 116:712-17 (Feb). [6511

CHARLES JELLEFF CARR. The contributions of medicinal chemistry to psychopharmacology [ca. 1911 to 1959]. Jour. chem. educ., 37:192-5 (Apr). views. [6512

BERTRAM DAVID LEWIN & HELEN ROSS. Psychoanalytic education in the United States [1911-60]. N.Y.: Norton [1960]. xviii, 478 p. diagrs., tables (part double). notes. Mainly a report of a survey of facilities for the teaching of psychoanalysis in the United States (14 institutes and 3 training centers), begun in 1956 for the American Psychoanalytic Association. [6513

ECLECTIC psychiatrist. Harvard alumni bul., 55:360-61 (24 Jan 1953). port. On Wilfred Overholser (Harvard, 1912), student in Boston University Medical School, member of the Army Medical Corps in World War I, Commissioner of Mental Diseases of Massachusetts, and since 1937 Superintendent of St. Elizabeth's Hospital, Washington, D.C. [6514

Y. H. YARBROUGH. A plea for psychopathic wards and hospitals. Med. Assoc. Ga., Jour., 48:287-8 (Jun 1959). From Journal of the Medical Association of Georgia, 1913. [6515

ROBERT HARRY LOWIE (1883-1957). Psychology and sociology. Lowie's selected papers in anthropology, ed. Cora Du Bois (Berkeley: Univ. of California Press, 1960), p. 189-201. notes. From American journal of sociology, Sep. 1915. On the relation between the 2 disciplines; with references to the author's observations of the "odd mode of associating ideas" among the Crow and Hidatsa Indians. [6516

STANLEY COBB. Neuropsychiatry [1917-58]. Arch. internal med., 103: 981-90 (Jun 1959). notes. [6517

LOUIS BENJAMIN FRAIBERG. Psychoanalysis & American literary criticism. Detroit: Wayne State Univ. Press, 1960. x, [2], 263 p. notes (p. 241-58). Four chapters on the teachings of Sigmund Freud, Ernest Jones, Hanns Sachs, and Ernst Kris as expounders of "the classical psychoanalytic views of the psyche and art," and study of the attempted application of "these or related ideas by Van Wyck Brooks (The ordeal of Mark Twain, 1920), Joseph Wood Krutch (Edgar Allen Poe, 1926), Ludwig Lewisohn (Expression in America, 1932), and Kenneth Burke, Edmund Wilson, and Lionel Trilling (in various writings, 1936-56); with the conclusion that only Wilson has closely approached to a correct understanding of psychoanalysis. [6518

ALAN WILLIAM JONES. Age and decade changes in attitudes. Ann Arbor: University Microfilms, 1954 [i. e. 1960]. Positive microfilm of typescript. [140] leaves. Thesis--Ohio State Univ. Abstracted: Dissert. abstracts, 20:3414-17 (Feb). Results of administration of the Pressey X-0 Test ("a simple means of obtaining an individual's reaction to a large number of borderland wrongs, worries, and likes") to students, 1923-43, 1953, and adults, 1953. [6519

JOHN J. BRODERICK. The role of the psychiatrist and psychiatric testimony in civil and criminal trials [1928-60]. Notre Dame lawyer, 35:508-24 (Aug). notes. [6520

BENJAMIN HARRIS BALSER & JAMES F. MASTERSON, JR. Suicide in adolescents [1930-55]. Am. jour. psychiatry, 116:400-404 (Nov 1959). tables. notes. [6521

JOHN GRAY PEATMAN. CCNY's alumni psychologists. John G. Peatman & Eugene L. Hartley, eds., Festschrift for Gardner Murphy (N.Y.: Harper [1960]), p. 12-32. tables. On the "production of graduates who go on to their doctoral degrees in psychology," in the City College of New York, 1930-60. [6522

WALTER JACKSON FREEMAN, FRANKLIN G. EBAUGH, & DAVID A. BOYD, JR. The founding of the American Board of Psychiatry and Neurology, Inc. [1933-34]. Am. jour. psychaitry, 115:769-78 (Mar 1959). port. notes. [6523

LAURETTA BENDER. Children and adolescents who have killed [1935-59]. Am. jour. psychiatry, 116:510-13 (Dec 1959). notes. [6524

JULIAN E. HOCHBERG. Social perception: substance and strategy. John G. Peatman & Eugene L. Hartley, eds., Festschrift for Gardner Murphy (N.Y.: Harper [1960]), p. 145-56. bibliog. On the development of "social-perceptual" psychology in America, 1936-60. [6525

HERBERT S. RIPLEY & JOAN K. JACKSON. Therapeutic factors in Alcoholics Anonymous [1936-59]. Am. jour. psychiatry, 116:44-50 (Jul 1959). notes. [6526

NICHOLAS HENRY PRONKO, RENE SITTERLY, & K. BERG. Twenty years of shock therapy in America, 1937-1956: an annotated bibliography. [Provincetown, Mass.: Journal Press, 1960.] 233-329 p. bibliog. (p. 300-329). (Genetic psychology monographs, v. 62, 2d half, pt. [1].) Connected digest and discussion of the literature, concluding "that the era of shock therapy is fast drawing to its close." [6527

EDWARD SAPIR (1884-1939). The contributions of psychiatry to an understanding of behavior in society. Margaret Mead & Ruth L. Bunzel, eds., The golden age of American anthropology (N.Y.: George Braziller, 1960), p. 610-16. From The American journal of sociology, 1937. [6528

HENRY WECHSLER. The self-help organization in the mental health field: Recovery, Inc., a case study. Jour. nervous and mental diseases, 130:297-314 (Apr). notes. On Recovery, Incorporated: the Association of Nervous and Former Mental Patients, 1937-60, "a lay-run form of self-help," founded by Abraham A. Low, M.D. [6529

ROBERT T. HEWITT. Trends in the care of the mentally ill [1939-59]. Pub. health reports, 75:15-19 (Jan). [6530

GEORGE STUART KLEIN & ROBERT R. HOLT. Problems and issues in current studies of subliminal activation [1939-59]. John G. Peatman & Eugene L. Hartley, eds., Festschrift for Gardner Murphy (N.Y.: Harper [1960]), p. 75-93. bibliog. [6531

ROBERT STRAUS. The comprehensive approach to the problems of alcoholism [1939-59]. Quar. jour. studies alcohol, 20:669-72 (Sep 1959). [6532

EUGENE LEONARD HARTLEY. Profile of a professor. John G. Peatman & Eugene L. Hartley, eds., Festschrift for Gardner Murphy (N.Y.: Harper [1960]), p. 1-11. On Murphy during his years as Professor and Chairman of the Department of Psychology at the City College of New York, 1940-52. [6533

ADELBERT AMES, JR. (1880-1955). The morning notes of Adelbert Ames, Jr., including a correspondence with John Dewey. Edited and with a preface by Hadley Cantril. New Brunswick: Rutgers Univ. Press [1960]. ix, [3], 236 p. diagrs., views. bibliog. (p. 232), notes. "Working memoranda" excerpted from manuscript notes made by Ames at Dartmouth College on physiological optics and the psychology of visual perception, 1941-55; and letters exchanged between Ames and Dewey, 1946-50, on the psychology of perception. [6534

AMERICAN MEDICAL WOMEN'S ASSOCIATION. Programs on alcoholism [1944-60]. Am. Med. Women's Assoc., Jour., 15:592-5 (Jan). [6535

ROBERT T. MORSE. A serious and little-recognized deficit in post-war psychiatric training. Am. jour. psychiatry, 115:899-904 (Apr 1959). On the lack of training of psychiatrists in "communication between the psychiatrist, his medical colleagues, and the patient's family," 1944-58. [6536

ROBERT J. STOLLER & FLOYD M. ESTES. Suicides in medical and surgical wards of general hospitals [1946-55]. Jour. chronic diseases, 12:592-9 (Dec). table. notes. [6537

AMERICAN PSYCHIATRIC ASSOCIATION. [Obituaries.] Am. jour. psychiatry, 115:767-8, 959-60, 1055-56; 116:191, 383-4, 671-2, 863-4, 1055-6; 117:189-90, 479-80, 575-6 (Feb 1959 - Dec 1960). ports. Memorial sketches, by various contributors, of Harry J. Worthing (1888-1958), Edward A. Strecker (1886-1959), Edwin Garvin Zabriskie (1874-1959), Seymour D. Vestermark (1902-59), Jacob E. Finesinger (1902-59), Gregory Zilboorg (1891-1959), Albert Warren Stearns (1885-1959), Richard Sherman Lyman (1891-1959), Flanders Dunbar (1902-59), Peter Jacob Frostig (1896-1959), and Victor Lance Anderson (1878-1960). [6538

SOCIOLOGY

CLEVELAND AMORY. Who killed society? N.Y.: Harper [1960]. viii, 599, [1] p. ports., views. bibliog. (p. 553-5), notes. On "the dominant families" in the several parts of the United States since 1651, "the enmity between Aristocracy and Society," "the matter of birth vs. money," the "firmly antipublicity" habits of old families as distinguished from "publi-ciety," the exclusiveness of clubs, and marriages of American money to foreign titles; with illustrations from the Adams, Astor, Belmont, Biddle, Byrd, Cabot, Du Pont, Field, Gould, Guggenheim, Harriman, Huntington, Lee, Livingston, Lowell, McCormick, Mellon, Randolph, Rockefeller, Roosevelt, Ryan, Vanderbilt, and Whitney families. [6539

G. B. SHARP. Mills and Weber: formalism and the analysis of social structure. Science & soc., 24:113-33 (spring). notes. On a review of W. L. Warner and P. S. Lunt's The social life of a modern community (1942) by C. Wright Mills, citing doctrines of Max Weber but exhibiting at the same time, as do some of Mills's later writings, and "apparent infiltration of Marxist notions." [6540

JURGEN HERBST. From moral philosophy to sociology: Albion Woodbury Small [1854-1926]. Harv. educ. rev., 29:227-44 (summer 1959). notes. On his studies at Colby College and Newton Theological Institution and in Germany, his service as professor of history and president in Colby College and after 1892 as Professor of Social Sciences at the University of Chicago, and his founding of the American journal of sociology. [6541

EMORY STEPHEN BOGARDUS. Some sociological contributions of William Kirk [1880-1959]. Sociol. and social research, 44:269-78 (Mar-Apr). notes. On his 18 articles in Sociology and social research on sociological method and on "preliterate peoples" in New Zealand, northern Australia, Formosa, Japan (the Ainus), Mexico, Guatemala, Paraguay, and South Africa. [6542

DONALD RAMSEY YOUNG. William Fielding Ogburn (1886-1959) [sociologist, statistician, student of social change]. Am. Philos. Soc., Yr. bk., 1959, p. 138-40. [6543

PHILIP MORRIS HAUSER. William Fielding Ogburn, 1888-1959. Am. jour. sociol., 65:74 (Jul 1959). [6544

FERDINAND LUNDBERG. America's 60 families. N.Y.: Citadel Press [1960]. xxiii, 578 p. tables. bibliog. (p. 535-46), notes (p. 547-53). An "unaltered re-publication of the first edition" (1938). Contents.--1. Golden dynasties and their treasures.--2. The sixty families [which own and control "these large fortunes today"].--3-4. The politics of pecuniary aggrandizement, 1896-1920.--5. The politics of finance capital.--6. Intrigue and scandal.--7. The press of the plutocracy.--8. The journalism of pecuniary inhibition.--9. Philanthropy, or non-commercial investment.--10. Education for profit and tax exemption.--11. Danse macabre: extravagance amid poverty.--12. The "New Deal"--and after. Expresses obligation to "the works of Marx and Veblen, which alone provide the basic key to an understanding of the dynamic character of capitalist society." [6545

MILTON MYRON GORDON. Social class in American sociology [since 1899, especially since the 1920s]. Durham, N.C.: Duke Univ. Press, 1958. xiii, [3], 281 p. bibliog. (p. 257-72), notes. (Sociological series.) Based on thesis--Columbia Univ., 1950. [6546

HOWARD Paul Becker, 1899-1960. Am. jour. sociol., 66:289-90 (Nov). Memorial tributes by Harry Elmer Barnes and Frank E. Hartung. [6547

LEONARD REISSMAN. Class in American society. Glencoe, Ill.: Free Press [1960, c1959]. xii, 436 p. notes (p. 405-29). Based in part upon American sociological studies since 1899. [6548

JIRI NEHNEVAJSA. Sociometry: decades of growth [1925-55]. Jacob L. Moreno, ed., The sociometry reader (Glencoe, Ill.: Free Press [1960]), p. 707-53. First printed in 1955. [6549

NORTON E. LONG. The corporation, its satellites, and the local community. Edward Sagendorph Mason, ed., The corporation in modern society (Cambridge: Harvard Univ. Press, 1959), p. 202-17, 318. notes. On the avoidance by absentee-owned industries of involvement in the political and other affairs of the communities in which they are located; "the replacement of robber baron, resident owners, and leading families by a withdrawn managerial elite"; and "the vacuum created in the local social structure by the decline of the old owning families and resident economic dominants." [6550

WILLIAM DAUGHETY AMIS. Social structure and personality: the contribution of Erich Fromm [born 1900] to sociological theory. Ann Arbor: University Microfilms, 1959 [i. e. 1960]. Positive microfilm of typescript. 294 leaves. bibliog. (leaves 283-94). Thesis--Univ. of North Carolina. Abstracted: Dissert. abstracts, 20:2942 (Jan). On the ideology of a disciple of Freud and Marx, 1931-58. [6551

LELAND J. AXELSON. Difference in productivity of doctorates in sociology [1936-56]. Jour. educ. sociol., 33:49-55 (Oct 1959). notes. [6552

LELAND J. AXELSON. Graduate schools and the productivity of their graduates. Am. jour. sociol., 66:171-5 (Sep). tables. Study of the number of publications (appearing in 3 professional sociological journals) of 1,669 individuals who received their doctorates in sociology from 65 schools between 1936 and 1956. For comment by Howard Elinson, and Axelson's reply, see 66:619-21 (May 1961). [6553

CHARLES H. PROCTOR. A summary of findings from community studies reported in Sociometry

[1937-49]. Jacob L. Moreno, ed., The sociometry reader (Glencoe, Ill.: Free Press [1960]), p. 499-505. notes. Bibliographical essay. [6554

ROBERT PELLOUX. Un nouveau Machiavel: James Burnham et ses idées sur la domination du monde [as expressed in his The managerial revolution (1941) and several later works]. Les fondements de la politique extérieur des États-Unis (Paris: Armand Colin, 1949 [Cahiers de la Fondation Nationale des Sciences Politiques, 8]), p. 165-204. [6555

RALPH EUGENE DAKIN. Cultural occasions and group structures: a photographic analysis of American social situations. Am. sociol. rev., 25:66-74 (Feb). tables. notes. Analysis of 1,017 photographs "of social situations" in 24 issues of Life, 1944-45. [6556

AMERICAN SOCIOLOGICAL SOCIETY. [Obituaries of members. By various contributors.] Am. sociol. rev., 25:108-10, 277-8, 417-19, 575-6, 743-6 (Feb-Oct). Brief notices of William Kirk (1880-1959), Robert Horniman Dann (1889-1959), Harry Joseph Walker (1905-59), Samuel Joseph (1881-1959), Gregory Zilboorg (1890-1959), Edward A. Taylor (1902-59), James H. S. Bossard (1888-1960), Louis H. Blumenthal (1893-1959), Jacob Katz (1922-59), Michael Seymour Olmsted (1923-60), Earl Lomon Koos (1905-60), James Lowell Hypes (1885-1960), Howard Becker (1899-1960), Frederick German Detweiler (1881-1960), Curtis Hugh Morrow (1882-1960), Charles Ned Elliott (1907-60), and Florence Greenhoe Robbins (1909-59). [6557

Voluntary Associations

RONALD E. HEATON. Masonic membership of the general officers of the Continental Army. Wash.: Masonic Service Assoc. [1960]. viii, 56 p. facsims., ports. bibliog. (p. iv). Biographical sketches of Revolutionary Masons. [6558

CHARLES NORDHOFF (1830-1901). The communistic societies of the United States: from personal visit and observation [and other sources, 1792-1875]. N.Y.: Hillary House Publishers, 1960. 439 p. facsim., map, ports., tables, views. bibliog. (p. 419-32), notes. Partial contents.--The Amana Society [Iowa].--The Harmonists at Economy [Harmony Society, Economy, Pa.].--The separatists of Zoar [Ohio].--The Shakers.--The Oneida [New York] and Wallingford [Connecticut] Perfectionists.--The Aurora [Oregon] and Bethel [Missouri] communes.--The Icarians [Corning, Ia.].--The Bishop Hill Colony [Illinois].--The Cedar Vale Commune [Kansas].--The Social Freedom Community [Virginia].--Three colonies--not communistic [Anaheim, Calif.; Vineland, N.J.; Silkville Prairie Home, Kan.]. [6559

ROTARY INTERNATIONAL. Adventure in service. Evanston [1960. 6], 116 p. medal, ports. (1 col. mount.), views. On Rotary Clubs in America and abroad, beginning with the Rotary Club of Chicago, organized by Paul P. Harris in 1905. [6560

AMERICAN FRIENDS OF LAFAYETTE. By-laws, historical notes [1932-60], and roster of active members. [Edited by Mrs. Alan MacIntire.] Easton, Pa., 1960. 24 p. col. flags, port. [6561

UNCLASSIFIED AND MISCELLANEOUS HISTORY

CARLISLE H. HUMELSINE. The renaissance of American history. N.J. Hist. Soc., Proc., 78:223-32 (Oct). On Virginians eminent in New Jersey history, and the concern of New Jersey and Virginia in preserving their historic sites and monuments. [6562

ROBIN D. S. HIGHAM, comp. An introduction to maritime, naval, and aeronautical history [since 1500]. Chapel Hill: Univ. of North Carolina Library, 1960. 48 p. (Library study outlines, v. 1, no. 3.) [6563

ALEX W. BEALER III. The smith, a mighty man was he. Emory Univ. quar., 16:85-97 (summer). On American blacksmiths, their work and methods, 19th century. [6564

JARED SPARKS (1789-1866). Jared Sparks helps Abo. [Edited by Marshall W. S. Swan.] Harvard alumni bul., 52: 321 (28 Jan 1950). Letter to "Messrs. Gales & Seaton," publishers of the National intelligencer, Washington, dated London, 10 Jun. 1828, requesting donations of "books, either written in America, or on subjects in some way relating to America," for the University of Åbo, in Finland. [6565

U.S. Congress. House. Presentation of Washington's sword and Franklin's staff, House of Representatives, February 8, 1843. D. A. R. mag., 94: 68-71 (Feb). From the Congressional globe. On relics presented by a grandnephew of George Washington, Samuel T. Washington, including the gold-headed cane which Benjamin Franklin willed to George Washington. [6566

Miscellaneous Biography

LILIAN (THOMPSON) MOWRER. The indomitable John Scott [1632-1704]: citizen of Long Island. N.Y.: Farrar, Straus, and Cudahy [1960]. xviii, 438 p. bibliog. (p. 411-28), notes. On his transportation from England as a convict, his years as an indentured servant of Lawrence Southwick in Salem, Mass., later as a seaman, his settlement in Southampton, Long Island, as a merchant captain and shipowner and a trader and land dealer with the Indians, his leadership of a revolt of the English towns on Long Island against the Duth administration at New York, his definance of the colony of Connecticut in its efforts to annex Long Island, his trial and conviction at Hartford, his escape, his desertion of his wife, and his permanent departure from North America, 1643-65; with some account of his many occupations and adventures after 1665 in the West Indies, England, and Europe. [6567

HISTORICAL SOCIETY OF BERKS COUNTY. Daniel Boone, Berks County's gift to the West. [By Donald R. Shenton.] Hist. rev. Berks Co., 25:20-27 (winter). facsims., ports., views. On the Boone family in Berks County, Pa., and vicinity, 1712-50, the removal of Squire Boone with his son Daniel (born in 1734) and others to the Yadkin Valley in North Carolina, and the well-known later life of Daniel. [6568

ELSWYTH THANE. Washington's lady. N.Y.: Dodd, Mead, 1960. xv, [1], 368 p. col. port. bibliog. (p. 353-6). On Martha (Dandridge) Custis Washington (1731-1802) and her married life with Parke Custis (died 1757) and George Washington (1759 to 1799). [6569

NICHOLAS BIDDLE WAINWRIGHT. George Croghan [died 1782], wilderness diplomat. Chapel Hill: Univ. of North Carolina Press for the Institute of Early American History and Culture, Williamsburg [1959]. viii, [2], 334 p. maps. bibliog. (p. 311-16), notes. On his work in western Pennsylvania and adjacent Virginia, Ohio, and New York as a trader and a negotiator, an administrator of Indian affairs, and a heavy speculator in lands, 1741-82. [6570

GILBERT CHINARD. Thomas Jefferson [1743-1826], the apostle of Americanism. ... Second edition, revised. [Ann Arbor:] Univ. of Michigan Press [1957, c1939. 4], 548 p. (Ann Arbor paperbacks, AA13.) 1st ed. 1929. [6571

ALBERT JAY NOCK (1872/73-1945). Jefferson [1743-1826]. ... Introduction by Merrill D. Peterson. N.Y.: Hill and Wang [1960]. ix, [3], 210, [2] p. bibliog. (p. 203-4). (American century series, AC34.) 1st ed. 1926. [6572

Mrs. ANDREW J. DARBY. Gen. Levi Casey [1749-1807]--pioneer, soldier, and statesman. D. A. R. mag., 94:277-8 (Apr). bibliog. On his service as an officer in the Revolution and his activities in South Carolina and national politics. [6573

WILLIAM GARRARD LEGER. The public life of John Adair [1757-1840]. Ann Arbor: University Microfilms, 1953 [i.e. 1960]. Positive microfilm of typescript. vii, 260 p. bibliog. (leaves 253-60). Thesis--Univ. of Kentucky. Abstracted: Dissert. abstracts, 20:3709 (Mar). On his activities in Kentucky and national politics, 1786-1820s, and his military service in South Carolina during the Revolution and in Canada and New Orleans during the War of 1812. [6574

BERNARD BAILYN. Boyd's Jefferson: notes for a sketch. New Eng. quar., 33:380-400 (Sep). Commentary on Jefferson's activities, thinking, and writings, 1760-89. [6575

CHARLES ORRIN RANSFORD. John Scripps [1785-1865], Methodist preacher--newspaperman. Shelbina, Mo., 1960. xii, 97 p. port. bibliog. (p. 97), notes. On his early life in Morgantown, W. Va., his life in Cape Girardeau County, Mo. (1808 to 1830 or 1831), his service as a Methodist circuit rider in Missouri, Illinois, Indiana, and Arkansas till his superannuation in 1824, his settlement in Rushville, Ill., as a merchant, and his service from 1849 to 1856 as editor of a newspaper in Rushville, The prairie telegraph. Based in part upon notes dictated by him in 1865. [6576

J. H. S. MAYER. Some stayed home. Westerners brand book (N.Y.), 6:89-90. On Archibald Austin (1786?-1854), vacillating and inert relative of Moses and Stephen Austin, resident of Perth Amboy, N.J., his correspondence with Stephen Austin on possible removal to Texas, his short stay in Texas and New Orleans in the early 1840s, and his return to Perth Amboy in 1843 to please his lonesome daughter. [6577

POLAND. Sovereign, 1732-98 (Stanislas II August). The King, the Prince, and Mr. Littlepage. [Edited] by Curtis Carroll Davis. Manuscripts, 12(1):52-3 (winter). facsim. notes. Letter to Prince Potemkin, dated Warsaw, 3 Jun. 1788 (French text and translation), signed: Stanislas Auguste Roy, recommending Lewis Littlepage of Virginia to the good graces of the addressee and mentioning previous services of Littlepage in the interests of Poland. [6578

JAMES CAREY THOMAS FLEXNER. "... the gift for practical things." John Arthur Garraty, ed., The unforgettable Americans (Great Neck, N.Y.: Channel Press [1960]), p. 156-9. On Samuel Finley Breese Morse (1791-1872), painter, founder of the National Academy of Design, inventor of the telegraph and the Morse code. [6579

DUMAS MALONE. "... foe of governmental centralization." John Arthur Garraty, ed., The unforgettable Americans (Great Neck, N.Y.: Channel Press [1960]), p. 98-102. On Thomas Cooper (1759-1839), English emigrant in 1794, lawyer and physician at Northumberland, Pa., President of South Carolina College, writer on political theory. [6580

JOSEPH HARRY DORFMAN & REXFORD GUY TUGWELL. William Beach Lawrence [1800-1881]: American Benthamite. Joseph Dorfman & R. G. Tugwell, Early American policy: six Columbia contributors (N.Y.: Columbia Univ. Press, 1960), p. 205-47. port. notes. From the Columbia University quarterly "in the 1930s." On his early life in New York, his studies at Columbia College, his study of law in the University of Paris, his activities as a lecturer and writer about "economic problems, especially financial ones," and as a land, insurance, and railroad speculator, and his service as U.S. minister to Great Britain; with 2 letters from him to President Buchanan, dated Dresden (23 Sep. 1859) and Venice (15 Jan. 1860). [6581

DAVID LOWENTHAL. The Vermont heritage of George Perkins Marsh [1801-82]: an address before the Woodstock Historical Society. Woodstock, Vt.: Woodstock Historical Soc., 1960. 16 p. facsims. (part double), ports. On the accomplishments of "Woodstock's most eminent native" as "lawyer, editor, farmer, manufacturer, politician, and diplomat," as well as philologist and geographer. [6582

FRED B. ROGERS. William Augustus Newell (1817-1901): physician, governor, Congressman. Med. Soc. N.J., Jour., 56:278-81 (May 1959). port. notes. On his life and medical practice in Allentown, N.J., interrupted by service in Congress (1847-51, 1865-67) and as Governor and "Indian inspector" of Washington Territory (1880-86) and by medical practice in Olympia, Wash. (1886-98). [6583

ROBERT STUART HOLZMAN. "... problems of position." John Arthur Garraty, ed., The unforgettable Americans (Great Neck, N.Y.: Channel Press [1960]), p. 223-7. On Abner Doubleday (1819-93), "inventor" of the game of baseball in 1839, Union officer in the Civil War, organizer of cable-car street railways in San Francisco. [6584

BRUCE CATTON. "... what his country had to have done." John Arthur Garraty, ed., The unforgettable Americans (Great Neck, N.Y.: Channel Press [1960]), p. 217-21. On Ulysses Simpson Grant (1822-85) in war and politics. [6585

ROBERT J. T. JOY. William Walker [1824-60], filibustering physician. New Eng. jour. med., 261:292-4 (6 Aug 1959). port. notes. On his early life in Nashville, Tenn., his medical studies at the University of Pennsylvania and in Europe, his study and practice of law in New Orleans and California, and his activities as a filibuster in Lower California and in Central America. [6586

ROY J. POPKIN. Henry Richard Linderman, M.D. [1825-79]. New Eng. jour. med., 260:31-2 (1 Jan 1959). bibliog. On his studies at the New York College of Physicians and Surgeons, his practice of medicine (1846-53), and his service as Chief Clerk and later as Director of the U.S. Mint at Philadelphia (1853-79). [6587

WILLARD MOSHER WALLACE. Soul of the lion: a biography of General Joshua L[awrence] Chamberlain [1828-1914]. N.Y.: T. Nelson [1960]. 357 p. maps, ports., views. bibliog. (p. 341-5), notes (p. 317-40). On his early life in Maine, his studies at Bowdoin College and Bangor Theological Seminary, his service as professor of logic, rhetoric, and oratory at Bowdoin College (1855-62), his command of the 20th Infantry Regiment, Maine Volunteers, and other officer service in the Civil War, his terms as Governor of Maine (1866-72), his service as President of Bowdoin College and professor there (1871-85), his business activities in Florida and New York, and his employment as Surveyor of the Port of Portland, Me. (1900-1911). [6588

LAWRENCE C. McHENRY, JR. Silas Weir Mitchell [1829-1914]. New Eng. jour. med., 260:712-14 (2 Apr 1959). port. notes. On his concurrent accomplishments as a neurologist and a novelist. [6589

HERMAN AUSUBEL. "... saintly ... dangerous as dynamite." John Arthur Garraty, ed., The unforgettable Americans (Great Neck, N.Y.: Channel Press [1960]), p. 269-73. On the single-tax doctrine and writings of Henry George (1839-97) and his activities in New York politics, 1879-97. [6590

CURTIS CARROLL DAVIS. Wise words from Virginia: the published writings on John S. Wise, of the Eastern Shore and New York City. Bibliog. Soc. Am., Papers, 54:273-85 (4th quar.). notes. On John Sergeant Wise (1846-1913), Virginia and New York lawyer, politician, orator, and sportsman, with particular reference to his substantial accomplishments as an author; with an annotated list of his publications (67 entries), 1875-1919. [6591

CARL FREDERICK WITTKE. "... disillusioned prophet of Utopia." John Arthur Garraty, ed., The unforgettable Americans (Great Neck, N.Y.: Channel Press [1960]), p. 191-4. On Wilhelm Weitling (1808-71), emigrant in 1846, organizer of the Workingmen's League, publisher of Republic of the workers, and founder of Communia, a communal society in Clayton County, Ia. [6592

JAMES P. JONES. John A[lexander] Logan [1826-86]: politician and soldier. Ann Arbor: University Microfilms, 1960. Positive microfilm of typescript. [555] leaves. Thesis--Univ. of Florida. Abstracted: Dissert. abstracts, 20:4641-2 (Jun). On his activities in Illinois and national politics and his service as an officer of the Union Army, 1852-66. [6593

ARTHUR CLARENCE WALWORTH. Woodrow Wilson. I: American prophet. N.Y.: Longmans, Green, 1958. xi, 436 p. port. notes. On his life from 1856 to 1915, particularly as President of Princeton University, Governor of New Jersey, and President of the United States. [6594

THEODORE RAYMOND WILSON. The birth of greatness: a psychological and sociological study of the influences upon Woodrow Wilson during his formative years [1856 to ca. 1882]. Ann Arbor: University Microfilms, 1960. Positive microfilm of typescript. [361] leaves. Thesis--Univ. of Pennsylvania. Abstracted: Dissert. abstracts, 21:733-4 (Oct). [6595

ELSIE (NOBLE) CALDWELL. Last witness for Robert Louis Stevenson. Norman: Univ. of Oklahoma Press [1960]. xiv, 384 p. facsim., double map, ports., views. notes. On his stepdaughter, Isobel (Osbourne) Strong Field (1858-1953), and her parents, Samuel Osbourne and Frances Matilda (Van de Grift) Osbourne Stevenson (1840-1914), their divorce in 1880 as a result of Osbourne's repeated acts of adultery, the marriage of Mrs. Osbourne to Robert Louis Stevenson in the same year, and their life in California, France, England, the Adirondacks, Hawaii, and ultimately in British Samoa, where he died in 1894. [6596

J. RAYMOND CHADWICK. Lincoln and the Harlan family. Ann. Ia., 34:619-23 (Apr 1959). On the friendship between James Harlan, Senator from Iowa, and

Abraham Lincoln, 1860-65, the marriage of Harlan's daughter, Mary, to Robert Todd Lincoln in 1868, the prospective extinction of the Harlan and Lincoln families at the deaths of the 3 grandchildren of Robert Todd Lincoln and Mary (Harlan) Lincoln who were living in 1959, and the bequest made by her in 1926 to Iowa Wesleyan College effective upon the failure of "issue of blood." [6597

IRVING DILLIARD. The centennial year of two great Illinoisans: Jane Addams [1860-1935] and William Jennings Bryan [1860-1926]. Ill. State Hist. Soc., Jour., 53:229-46 (autumn). map, views. [6598

The START of a career. Chicago hist., 5:307-16 (winter). ports. On Edward Payson Weston (1839-1929) and his The pedestrian's adventures, while on his walk from Boston to Washington, in fulfilment of an election wager, performed in ten consecutive days (New York, 1862), on a walk begun 22 Feb. 1861 and finished 4 Mar.; with some account of several of his later "pedestrian feats." [6599

LUCRETIA (GARFIELD) COMER. Strands from the weaving. N.Y.: Vantage Press [1959]. 73 p. ports. On the author's father, Harry Augustus Garfield (1863-1942), his early life at "Lawnfield" (family farm near Mentor, Ohio), his studies at St. Paul's School in New Hampshire and at Williams College, his brief residence in the White House, his life in Cleveland as a lawyer, his year at Princeton as Professor of Government, and his family life until 1914; with excerpts from family letters. [6600

WARREN F. KUEHL. Hamilton Holt [1872-1951]: journalist, internationalist, educator. Gainesville: Univ. of Florida Press, 1960. xi, 303 p. ports., views. bibliog. (p. 289-96), notes (p. 262-88). Based on thesis--Northwestern Univ., 1954. On his early life in Connecticut and New York City, his studies at Yale and at Columbia University, his work as editor of the Independent (1894-1921), his activities in organizations supporting the League of Nations, world peace, and the World-Federation League, and his service as President of Rollins College 1925-49). [6601

ANNA LOUISE CURTIS. Mary S[tone] McDowell [1876-1955], peace crusader. [N.Y.? 1960.] ix, 43 p. port. On her early life in Jersey City, her Quaker upbringing, her studies at Oxford University and Columbia University, her teaching in New York City high schools, and her activities in "peace societies" and other Quaker causes; with a list of her writings. [6602

JOHN GUNTER. Taken at the flood: the story of Albert D[avis] Lasker [1876-1952]. N.Y.: Harper [1960. 14], 368 p. facsims., ports., views. bibliog. (p. 349-56), notes. On his early life in Galveston, Tex., his work as a newspaper publisher there, his establishment of an advertising agency in Chicago (Lord & Thomas), his activities in national politics, his interest in Jewish causes, his many charities, his art collection, and his health and illnesses. [6603

MAURICE STEWARD COLLIS. Nancy Astor: an informal biography. London: Faber and Faber [1960]. 235 p. ports., views. On Nancy Witcher Langhorne (born 1879), Virginian, her marriage to and divorce from Robert Gould Shaw, her marriage to Waldorf, Viscount Astor, and her life after 1906 in England; with accounts of her visits to America in 1922 and 1946. [6604

LOUISE HUNTING (SEAMAN) BECHTEL. The boy with the star lantern: Edwin De Turck Bechtel, 1880-1957, a memoir. N.Y., 1960. [10], 124, [1] p. ports., views. bibliog. (p. 120-22). On his early life in Bechtelsville and Reading, Pa., his studies at Harvard and abroad, his work as a lawyer in New York City, his activities as a rose gardener and a collector of prints, and his writings on law, roses, and prints. [6605

30,000 square feet of hieroglyphs. Harvard alumni bul., 55:275-6 (6 Dec 1952). facsim., port. On Samuel Alfred Browne Mercer (born 1880), Episcopal priest, student at Harvard and Munich, participant in an archeological expedition to Egypt, Professor of Hebrew and Old Testament Literature at Western Theological Seminary, Chicago, and at the University of Toronto, translator of religious texts from the Sakkareh Pyramids in Egypt. [6606

GENE FOWLER (1890-1960). Minutes of the last meeting. N.Y.: Viking Press, 1954. [8], 277 p. cartoons, ports. Reminiscences of Sadakichi Hartmann (1864 or 1867-1944) in the years of the author's interviews with him, 1939-44, when he lived on an Indian reservation near Banning, intermingled with memories of John Barrymore, John Decker, W. C. Fields, and other California associates during these years; and anecdotes of Hartmann, native of Japan, son of a German father and a Japanese mother, art critic, poet, pamphleteer, "vagabond scoffer," King of Bohemia in Greenwich Village, trickster, drinker, interviewer of Walt Whitman (1884-85) and Paul Verlaine, emigrant to the United States in 1882. [6607

WILLIAM MATHIAS LAMERS. Requiescat in pace: Edward A[ugustus] Fitzpatrick [1884-1960], a memorial tribute. Cath. school jour., 60:22-4 (Oct). port. On his early life in New York City, his teaching there, his studies in Columbia University, and his service as a legislative librarian in Wisconsin, Dean of the Graduate School of Marquette University, President of Mount Mary College (Prairie du Chien, Wis.), Army officer in World War II, and editor of the Catholic school journal. [6608

MARQUIS WILLIAM CHILDS. Eisenhower, captive hero: a critical study of the general and the President. N.Y.: Harcourt, Brace [1958. 10], 310 p. cartoons. On the early life of Dwight David Eisenhower (born 1890) in Kansas, and the quality of his activities as an officer in the U.S. Army, President of Columbia University, and President of the United States. [6609

DORIS H. HAMILTON. Some letters of Anna Hempstead Branch [born 1874]. Hobbies, 64(11):110-11, 119 (Jan). facsim. On her letters to an "intimate friend, Edith," during the years of the writer's studies at Adelphi Academy (Brooklyn), Smith College, and the American Academy of Dramatic Art, 1891-1911; with text of a letter dated 18 Aug. 1894 and facsimile of a manuscript poem. [6610

ALFRED BERTRAM GUTHRIE. De Voto--a memoir. Nieman reports, 12(1):3-6 (Jan 1958). Memories of Bernard De Voto (1897-1955) as "journalist, historian, historiographer and fighter for the rights of the Bill of Rights," native of and writer about the West. [6611

ALEX KARMEL. Memorial to my father. Contact, 2 (1958):69-83. On the ideas and habits of an unnamed individual born of Polish emigrant parents in New York City in 1898, student at New York University, mechanical engineer and corporation executive, married in 1928, now dead, particularly his doctrine of "decency" and its centrality in a possible system of ideas. [6612

HYMAN R. SEGAL. They called him Champ: the story of Champ Segal and his fabulous era. N.Y.: Citadel Press [1959]. 480 p. facsims., ports. On the early life of Harry Segal (born 1899) in New York City and his accomplishments as welterweight boxer, restaurant owner, "manager, horse-owner, treasure-hunter and what not." [6613

JOHN G. KALLEEL (born 1925). Mount Lebanon trembled: a true story of one man's pilgrimage and proud return. N.Y.: Greenwhich Book Publishers [1960]. 72 p. Biography of the author's father, George Kalleel (born 1887, apparently living in 1960), emigrant from Lebanon in 1907, unskilled laborer in Warville, Tex., peddler in Elkins, W. Va., proprietor of a poolroom and later of a store in Clarksburg, W. Va., father of 5 children, alcoholic. Semifictional in style. [6614

GEORGE H. SCHWENK (born 1913). The great search. ... Designed and edited by Delmar E. Bordeaux. Monroe, Wis.: Honor System Publishers [1960]. 173 p. On the author's early life in Monroe, Wis., his experience with epilepsy and with corrective brain surgery, his education in St. Louis, and his study of law in Wisconsin. [6615

BARBARA JURGENSEN. Leaping upon the mountains. Minneapolis: Augsburg Pub. House [1960. 4], 100 p. notes. On Hollis Lynn Ofstie (1920-46), his early life in Duluth, Chicago, and Brooklyn, his affliction with spastic paralysis, his work with Good Will Industries in Chicago and Minneapolis and as a newspaper columnist in Minneapolis, and his death by drowning. [6616

COLLECTIVE GENERAL BIOGRAPHY

JOHN ARTHUR GARRATY, ed. The unforgettable Americans. ... Developed as a project of the Society of American Historians, by Allan Nevins. Great Neck, N.Y.: Channel Press [1960]. vii, [7], 338 p. Organized by the Society in cooperation with Broadcast Music, Inc., continuing The American story (1956), edited by Earl Schenck Miers, and making "available to broadcasters an additional group of essays relating to our history in terms not of events but of the lives of significant Americans." Each essay or group of essays is preceded by an editorial note closing with an introduction of the author or authors. [6617

FRANK LAURENCE LUCAS. The art of living: four eighteenth-century minds--Hume, Horace Walpole, Burke, Benjamin Franklin. N.Y.: Macmillan 1959. xv, 285 p. port. "Benjamin Franklin" (p. 203-60). [6618

SAUL KUSSIEL PADOVER. The genius of America: men whose ideas shaped our civilization. N.Y.: McGraw-Hill [1960]. viii, [2], 369, [1] p. bibliog. (p. 343-52). Biographical sketches of George Washington, John Adams, Thomas Jefferson, Alexander Hamilton, James Madison, John Taylor (1753-1824), John Marshall, John C. Calhoun, Abraham Lincoln, Ralph Waldo Emerson, Henry David Thoreau, Walt Whitman, Henry George, William James, Oliver Wendell Holmes, Jr., John Dewey, Theodore Roosvelt, Woodrow Wilson, and Franklin D. Roosevelt, 1732-1945. [6619

SIBLEY'S Harvard graduates, volume XI, 1741-1745: Biographical sketches of those who attended Harvard College in the Classes 1741-1745, with bibliographical and other notes by Clifford K. Shipton. Boston: Massachusetts Historical Soc., 1960. xiv, 649 p. ports. notes. [6620

JOHN DAVID MILLER. Men of "Old Miami." N.Y.: Newcomen Soc. in North America, 1959. 24 p. views. On eminent alumni of Miami University, Oxford, Ohio, founded in 1809. [6621

MAX FORRESTER EASTMAN (born 1883). Great companions: critical memoirs of some famous friends. N.Y.: Farrar, Straus, and Cudahy [1959. 8], 312 p. ports. Recollections of and judgments upon E. W. Scripps, Albert Einstein, Ernest Hemingway, Edna St. Vincent Millay, George Santayana, Pablo Casals, Leon Trotsky, Sigmund Freud, Bertrand Russell, Charlie Chaplin, John Dewey, and the author's mother, the Rev. Annis (Ford) Eastman. [6622

EDGAR NEWTON EISENHOWER (born 1889). Six roads from Abilene: some personal recollections of Edgar Eisenhower. [Reported] by John McCallum. Seattle: Wood & Reber, 1960. [10], 132 p. cartoon, ports., view. On the early life of the author and his younger brothers--Dwight, Milton, Roy, and Earl--in Abilene, Kan., and their close relations and frequent meetings in later years; with some account of the author's studies in the University of Michigan Law School and his practice of law since 1914 in Tacoma, Wash. [6623

DARTMOUTH COLLEGE. CLASS OF 1898. 50 year reunion report and address for the 50 years class ... Both by John R[oland] Spring. [Hanover? 1948]. 72 p. port. Mainly biographical data concerning living and deceased members. [6624

LINNIE SCHLEY. Jefferson County Oxonians. Jefferson Co. Hist. Soc., Mag., 26:10-15. On men from Jefferson County, W. Va., who have studied at Oxford University as Rhodes Fellows or Sparrow Fellows, 1904-38. [6625

HAMILTON COLLEGE, Clinton, N.Y. CLASS OF 1909. Fifty years of Hamilton's Class of 1909. Compiled by William De Loss Love II. [Clinton? N.Y.] 1959. [6], a-b, 173, [2] leaves. ports., seal. [6626

YALE UNIVERSITY. CLASS OF 1910. Yale 1910.: fiftieth year record. Compiled by Richard Dwight Hillis, Class Secretary. [New Haven] 1960. 107, [1] p. (Volume six of the history of the Class of 1910, Yale College.) Biographical and autobiographical sketches, and list of deceased members. [6627

HARVARD UNIVERSITY. CLASS OF 1915. Harvard College Class of 1915: forty-fifth anniversary report. Cambridge: Cosmos Press, 1960. vii, 156 p. Signed: Malcolm J. Logan, Secretary. Biographical and autobiographical sketches. [6628

HELEN (WORDEN) ERSKINE. Out of this world. N.Y.: Putnam [1953]. xiv, 300 p. facsim., ports., views. Accounts of Langley and Homer Collyer, and Mary Elizabeth Wood (of Harlem); Ella Wendel, Mary and William Colgate Colby, Anna and Louise Leary, Sylvia (Green) Wilks (daughter of Hetty Green), Helene and Beatrice Herzog, Acacia Romero and her mother, Mary Bullock Powers, Gertrude Tredwell, Emily Thorn, Sarah Hart and Hetty (Hart) Hawks, and A. Van Horne Stuyvesant (all of New York City); Harriet Coogan [Harriet Gardiner Lynch Coogan] (of Newport); Mrs. Duncan Phyfe, Miss Ann Hubbard, Mrs. James Lee Finney, Mrs. Stoddard Shaw, Rosanna Batchelor (all of New York City); and D. K. Jones, Baby Doe Tabor, and Father Mike O'Neill (all of Colorado); with efforts to explain their hermitism psychologically. [6629

YALE UNIVERSITY. Class of 1927. Twenty-five years out: history of the Class of 1927, Yale University, New Haven, 1953. 590 p. facsims., ports., views. Biographical and autobiographical sketches and list of deceased members; with a digest of letters from Alasdair Macdonald to his mother in Scotland, reporting "his life at Yale in 1927" (p. 13-24), and other introductory materials. [6630

YALE UNIVERSITY. CLASS OF 1929. 25 year record, Yale '29. [New Haven?] 1954. [8], 620 p. cartoons, diagrs., ports., views. Biographical and autobiographical sketches of '29 and '29S members and of deceased members; with "But time and change can naught avail: a note on Yale, 1929-1954," by Alfred Whitney Griswold; "Our quarter century: some freewheeling notes on our times," by Ralph D. Paine, Jr.; and statistics of income, occupation, marital status, etc., compiled by Washington Dodge from an anonymous questionnaire. [6631

YALE UNIVERSITY. CLASS OF 1930. The thirty year book, 1930-1960. [New Haven? 1960? 14], 672 p. ports. Foreword signed: Maurice F. Hanson, Secretary of the Class. Biographical and autobiographical skethces of living members; and lists of deceased members and of "Yale sons of 1930," a review of "The 30 years of 1930" by Maurice F. Hanson, and a summary of statistics compiled from a questionnaire. [6632

DARTMOUTH COLLEGE. CLASS OF 1931. 31-year report, Dartmouth '31. [Hanover? N. H., 1959.] 197, [1] p. cartoons, ports., views. Foreword signed: Dick Holbrook [Richard Greene Holbrook]. Report on the affairs of the Class of 1931 from 1927 to 1958, and biographical and autobiographical sketches. [6633

PRINCETON UNIVERSITY. CLASS OF 1932. Class of 1932: 25 year record. [Princeton? 1957.] xi, 327 p. ports. Biographical and autobiographical sketches. [6634

HARVARD UNIVERSITY. CLASS OF 1935. Harvard Class of 1935: twenty-fifth anniversary report. Cambridge, 1960. xxii, [6], 1549 p. ports. Foreword signed: Frank W. Knowlton, Jr. Biographical and autobiographical sketches of living and deceased members. [6635

YALE UNIVERSITY. CLASS OF 1935. Quarter-century record, Yale Class of 1935. Edited by George D. Vaill. New Haven, 1960. xxix, 400 p. ports. Biographical and autobiographical sketches (including 62 obituary sketches); with an introduction, "Yale today," by Charles Seymour, Jr. [6636

PERSONAL NARRATIVES

JAMES CLYMAN (1792-1881). James Clyman, frontiersman: the adventures of a trapper and covered-wagon emigrant as told in his own reminiscences and diaries. Edited by Charles L[ewis] Camp. Portland, Ore.: Champoeg Press [1960. 6], 352 p. diagr., facsim., maps (part fold.), ports., tables, views. notes. (p. 306-42). 1st ed. 1928. On the author's early life in Fauquier County, Va., his settlement in Ohio, his service in the War of 1812, his work as a surveyor in Indiana and a farmer in Wisconsin, his fur-trading and trapping expeditions to the Rocky Mountains, his service as a guide to wagon trains en route from Missouri to California, and his eventual settlement in Napa, Calif. Appended: biographical sketches of Clyman by Lydia (Clyman) Talman (1879), R. T. Montgomery (1871), and Hiram Beckwith (1879); reminiscences of a wagon-train journey from St. Joseph, Mo., to Napa, 1848, by various members of the party; and list of Clyman documents in the Huntington Library. [6637

JOHN WELD PECK (1819-1902). Recollections by John W. Peck ... of Cynthiana. Edited by [his great-grandson] John W. Peck. Hist. and Philos. Soc. Ohio, Bul., 18:83-104 (Apr). ports. On the author's early life in rural St. Lawrence County, N.Y., his studies in St. Lawrence Academy at Potsdam, his removal to Cynthiana, Ky., in 1840 (with a detailed account of the difficulties of travel in the journey), his teaching near Cynthiana, and his prosperous career in various businesses there till 1891. [6638

GEORGE BANCROFT (1800-1891). A letter from George Bancroft. [Edited by] Andrew Schiller. New Eng. quar., 33:225-37 (Jun). notes. Fragment of a manuscript letter to an unidentified person (Sep. 1823?), enclosing verses; with commentary on Bancroft's interests in poetry and in European culture. [6639

AURELIA (WEEKS) SMITH. Pioneer woman. Vt. Hist. Soc., News and notes, 9:53-7 (Mar 1958). Undated reminiscences of the author's early life in rural Franklin, Vt., and adjacent Canada, her marriage in 1829, and her life on a farm near Andover, Ohio, till 1834. [6640

ANDREW JACKSON SMITH (1832-1928). Andrew Jackson Smith, Pennsylvanian extraordinary: recollections of a century [recorded in 1926. Edited by] David Lindsey. West. Pa. hist. mag., 43:147-55 (Jun). notes. On his early life in Washington, Pa., his removal to Monroe County, Mo., and harassment by Quantrill's Gang there, his service in the Union Army during the Civil War, and his life after 1871 in Wisconsin. [6641

JERRY CRARY (1842-1936). Jerry Crary, 1842-1936: teacher--soldier--industrialist. Warren, Pa.: Newell Press, 1960. [4], 142 p. port. Reminiscences of schooling and schoolteaching in up-State New York, Ohio, and Indiana; diary kept while teaching school in Angola, Ind., 26 Oct. 1860 - 8 Apr. 1861; brief account of the 143d Regiment, New York State Volunteers, 1862-65; diary kept in Company H of this regiment (of which the author was Sergeant), 10 Oct. 1862 - 1 Feb. 1865); and letters to relatives, dated in Virginia, Maryland, Alabama, Tennessee, and Georgia, and in hospitals in Hashville, Jeffersonville (Ind.), and Buffalo (N.Y.), 1862-65; with a biographical sketch by Miner D. Crary and Clare J. Crary, containing some account of the business and political activities of Jerry Crary after the Civil War in Sheffield and Warren, Pa. [6642

LEWIS H. TAYLOR. A letter back home to Jersey from the California Gold Rush of 1849. N.J. genesis, 7: 282, 290 (Jul). Dated San Francisco, 28 Sep. 1849; addressed to Judge Robert Foster at Clinton, N.J. Refers briefly to California; deals mainly with New Jersey business matters. [6643

CHARLES WILLIAM HOLBROOK (born 1828). A Yankee tutor in the Old South. [Edited by] D. D. Hall. New Eng. quar., 33:82-91 (Mar). notes. Excerpts from a diary, 13 Feb. 1850-28 Dec. 1852, kept by Holbrook as a student at Williams College, a resident of Holden, Mass., and a tutor to children of Thomas and Rawley Gallaway in Rockingham County, N.C. Includes entries about the reception of Uncle Tom's cabin there. [6644

THEODORE ROOSEVELT (1858-1919). The autobiography of Theodore Roosevelt. Condensed from the original edition [1913], supplemented by letters, speeches, and other writings, and edited with an introduction by Wayne Andrews. N.Y.: Scribner [1958]. xi, 372 p. bibliog. (p. 359-62). On the author's early life in New York, his interests in natural history, his experiment in North Dakota ranching, and his activities in New York City, New York State, and national politics. [6645

ELISE CHENAULT (BENNETT) SMITH JEFFERSON GAGLIARDINI. From my journal: random thoughts. N.Y., 1958. xii, [4], 107 p. facsim., ports., views. Remarks and reminiscences concerning a variety of subjects, including the author's native Kentucky since the 1870s, some of her ancestors (especially the Clays, the Warfields, the Lewises, and the Chenualts), her 44 voyages to Europe, and "women in religon." [6646

GERTRUDE (CLARK) POWELL (1870-1957). The quiet side of Europe, by Gertrude Clark Powell. With a memoir of the author by her son, Lawrence Clark Powell. Los Angeles, 1959. xxiii, 256, [1] p. Memoir of her life and personality and the affairs of the author and the Powell family during the years in Europe, 1931-34, and after her return to the United States. [6647

RAY LYMAN WILBUR (1875-1949). The memories of Ray Lyman Wilbur, 1875-1949. Edgar Eugene Robinson and Paul Carroll Edwards, editors. Stanford, Calif.: Stanford Univ. Press, 1960. xiv, [2], 687 p. ports. bibliog. (p. 674), notes. Reminiscences (written 1946-49, apparently unfinished) of the author's early life in Iowa, his removal to California in 1887, his studies at Stanford University, his medical studies at Cooper Medical College, San Francisco, and abroad, and his service as Professor of Medicine at Stanford University, Dean of Stanford Medical School (1911-15), President of Stanford University (1916-41), member of the Commission for Relief in Belgium during World War I, and Secretary of the Interior (1929-33). [6648

ALICE TISDALE (NOURSE) HOBART (born 1882). Gusty's child. N.Y.: Longmans, Green, 1959. [8], 343 p. On the author's early life in Chicago, her studies in the University of Chicago, her marriage in 1914 to Earle Tisdale

Hobart, executive of an American oil company in China, their flight from China and ultimate settlement in California, and her novels about China, Mexico, California, and medicine. [6649

FRANK M. LINCKS (born 1882). Memoirs of a Kentucky boy. N.Y.: Vantage Press [1960. 2], 106 p. views. On the early life of the author, a Cherokee, in Kentucky, his early interest in hunting and shooting, his removal to Caspar, Wyo., ca. 1895, his work in the Wyoming oil fields and later as a manager of oil fields in California, Canada, Asia, Africa, Australia, and the East Indies, and his experiences in hunting big game wherever he went. [6650

CHARLES ALEXANDER KEITH (born 1883). Fast balls and college halls: an autobiography. N.Y.: Vantage Press [1960, c1959]. 146 p. On the author's early life near Hot Springs, Ark., his studies at the University of Arkansas, his career in college and professional baseball (1906-10), his teaching in rural schools in Arkansas, his studies at Oxford University, and his service from 1921 to 1953 as Professor of History and Dean of Men at Eastern Kentucky State Teachers' College. [6651

JOSEPHINE (GIBSON) KNOWLTON (born 1885). Butter balls and finger bowls. [Providence?] 1960. xi, 487 p. cartoons, ports., views. Sequel to the author's Longfield. On the author's early life in Flushing, L.I., and Bristol, R.I., her marriage to Daniel W. Knowlton in 1921, their life in Washington, D.C., and the travels and other activities and interests of the author, her husband, her son (Daniel Gibson Knowlton), her brothers (Langdon Gibson, born 1866, and Charles Dana Gibson, illustrator) and 2 sisters and their families, and various other persons. [6652

FRANK BETTGER (born 1889). Benjamin Franklin's secret of success and what it did for me. Englewood Cliffs, N.J.: Prentice-Hall [1960]. xii, [4], 206 p. On the author's early years in professional baseball (particularly with the St. Louis Cardinals), his destitution at age 29 as "a down-and-out ex-ballplayer," his study of the teachings of Dale Carnegie, and his career as an insurance salesman in Philadelphia; with an exposition of "the 13 principles" of success. [6653

PERLE (SKIRVIN) MESTA. Perle--my story. By Perle Mesta with Robert Cahn. N.Y.: McGraw-Hill [1960]. viii, [2], 251 p. ports. On the author's life in and after the 1890s in Oklahoma City as daughter of a wealthy owner of oil wells and a large hotel, her marriage to George Mesta, Pittsburgh industrialist (died 1925), her achievement of renown as a party-giver, and her service as Envoy Extraordinary and Minister Plenipotentiary from the United States to Luxembourg. [6654

NAZARETH SARKIS BARSUMIAN. Stowaway to heaven. [Barrington, Ill.: Armenian Information Bureau, 1960. 4], 264 p. facsims., ports., views. On the author's studies at Central Turkey College in Aintab and at the American University in Beirut, his emigration to America as a stowaway in 1902, his studies at Baltimore Medical College, his establishment of a prosperous Oriental rug and carpet business in Evanston, Ill., his profitable real estate business there, his selling of war bonds during World War II, his patronage of the YMCA and other charities, his service as Director of the Armenian Information Bureau, and his other services to Armenian refugees and other Armenians in the United States. [6655

TYNNE ELEANOR KONGA. I remember. N.Y.: Vantage Press [1955]. 269 p. Apparently fiction with an autobiographical base. Third-person account of "Ellen," born of Finnish parents at Cloquet, Minn., ca. 1904; the removal of the family to Worcester, Mass., and their return in extreme poverty to a Minnesota farm between Moose Lake and Caldwell; her marriage to a drunkard and her divorce at the age of 19 after the birth of 2 children; her work as a nurse; and her second marriage, to a half-indian doctor of medicine. [6656

ABE L. PLOTKIN (born 1889). An immigrant's life as a farmer in Saskatchewan and apartment house builder in Los Angeles: struggle for justice, the autobiography of Abe L. Plotkin. N.Y.: Exposition Press [1960]. 187 p. ports., views. On the author's emigration from Russia in 1904, his work on a farm in Sullivan County, N.Y., his removal to Saskatchewan in 1910, to Manitoba in 1944, and to Los Angeles in 1948, his unhappy relations with his first wife and with his children, and his adherence to Socialism. [6657

EDITH (WARDELL) HILDRETH. Between bay and ocean. N.Y.: Vantage Press [1960]. 92 p. coat of arms, view. On the author's early life in New York City, her marriage in 1906 to E. Raymond Hildreth, medical missionary in Puerto Rico till ca. 1922, and their later years in Jamaica, Suffolk, and Fire Island, L.I. [6658

MAY SARTON (born 1912). I knew a phoenix: sketches for an autobiography. N.Y.: Rinehart [1959]. 222 p. Reminiscences by a daughter of George Sarton (1884-1956) of her early life in Belgium, her removal to the United States in 1915, her schooling in Cambridge, Mass., and the academic community there, her activities from 1929 to 1933 in the Civic Repertoire Theatre, New York City, and her literary acquaintances in London till 1937. [6659

ARCHIE LEE MOORE (born 1916). The Archie Moore story. N.Y.: McGraw-Hill [1960. 12], 240 p. port., tables. On the author's early life in Benoit, Miss., and St. Louis, his stay in the Missouri Training School at Booneville, his service in the Civilian Conservation Corps, and his work as a professional Negro boxer and motion-picture actor. [6660

PAUL MITCHELL. The rape of America. N.Y.: Comet Press Books [1960, ©1959]. xx, [2], 297 p. (A Reflection book.) On the service of the author in the Navy, 1918-34, in Los Angeles as a police officer, and again in the Navy during World War II, and after retirement as a civilian employee in "the Navy station at Rathole" (evidently in California), his detection and attempted exposure of conspiracies between Navy officers and thieves, his experience of several surgical operations demonstrating the incompetence of Navy surgeons, his studies of foreign affairs justifying his condemnation of "forty-one years of ... altogether criminal U.S. foreign policy" and of "'three false prophets,' Wilson, Roosevelt and Truman," his efforts to induce Congress to investigate the iniquities of the Navy and the Department of State, and the disruption of his personal life by his patriotic activities. [6661

JOHN T. BERNHARD. Journey into light. Salt Lake City: Deseret Book Co., 1960. viii, [2], 68 p. On the author's early life in New York City, his college studies in Utah, his employment by the U.S. Indian Service at Fort Apache Indian Reservation (White River, Ariz.), and his service in the U.S. Coast Guard, 1920s-40s; with a long statement of the reasons for his conversion to Mormonism in 1947. [6662

Miscellaneous Collections

LOUIS BROWNLOW (born 1879). The anatomy of the anecdote. [Chicago:] Univ. of Chicago Press [1960]. vi, [2], 154 p. Anecdotes about the Civil War, politics, and other subjects, collected from oral sources and from the author's experience in government. [6663

BENJAMIN FRANKLIN (1706-90). The papers of Benjamin Franklin. Volume I: January 6, 1706, through December 31, 1734 [and Volume II: January 1, 1735, through December 31, 1744]. Leonard W[oods] Labaree, Editor; Whitfield J[enks] Bell, Associate Editor. New Haven: Yale Univ. Press, 1959-60. 2 v. lxxxviii, 400, [1]; xxv, [1], 471 p. coat of arms, diagrs., facsims., geneal charts, fold. map, ports., views. notes. Edition, sponsored by the American Philosophical Society and Yale University, of all identified writings of Franklin and papers addressed to him before 1745; with an introduction on the papers and on the genealogy of the Franklin family. [6664

CHARLES LINCOLN VAN DOREN. Letters to mother: an anthology. Great Neck, N.Y.: Channel Press [1959]. xvi, [2], 350 p. Letters from celebrated men and women, American and foreign, to their mothers, arranged in 10 groups according to occupation of writers, including Americans from Benjamin Franklin (1750?) to Harry S. Truman (1945). [6665

JOHN GRAY BLOUNT (1752-1833). The John Gray Blount Papers. Edited by Alice Barnwell Keith. Volume two. 1790-1795. Raleigh [N.C.]: State Dept. of Archives and History, 1959. xxvi, 689 p. maps (1 fold.), port., views. notes. Vol. 1 published 1952. Selected letters from and to John Gray Blount and John Gray & Thomas Blount, Merchants, Washington, N.C., on "politics, shipping and trade, and land speculation." Blunt's brothers William

(Governor of the Territory of the U.S. South of the Ohio) and Thomas (in Congress in Philadelphia) are among the most frequent writers. [6666

JAMES WELCH PATTON, ed. New England tutors in Granville County, North Carolina, 1845-1850. N.C. hist. rev., 37:544-67 (Oct). notes. Ten letters (9 to Francis Roger Gregory, M.D., Waterloo, N.C., and 1 to Master Herbert Gregory, Waterloo) from Worthington Smith, President of the University of Vermont, and Amos Brickett Little (1821-62) and Charles Nelson Starbird, former tutors of Gregory's children (Little letters dated Newport, N.H., and Washington, D.C.; Starbird letters, Chester, Ill.), on persons known to them who might accept employment as tutors in Waterloo, on affairs in Washington and Illinois, and on politics, slavery, agriculture, etc. [6667

SAMUEL LANGHORNE CLEMENS (1835-1910). Mark Twain's picture of his America. ... Edited by Neal Frank Doubleday. Boston: Heath [1960]. xiv, [2], 174 p. map. notes. (Selected source materials for college research papers.) Excerpts from Roughing it and Life on the Mississippi (p. 25-129) and from novels and reminiscences, several tales, and 6 letters, 1858-1910. [6668

LOUIS A. HASELMAYER. The Doggett-Crane manuscript album. Ann. Ia., 35: 241-76 (spring). facsims., port. notes. On "a somewhat battered black leather, gold stamped, photograph album, containing thirty-two autographs, manuscript letters, patriotic sentiments and hand written poetic extracts ... gathered in 1864 from well-known political personalities, outstanding clergymen, and anti-slavery leaders" (including 7 "prominent American men of letters"), collected by solicitation by Kate Newell Doggett (1827-84) of Chicago and given by her to a "sanitary fair" to be sold for the benefit of men in the armed forces; with a detailed account of its contents. [6669

AMBROSE DUDLEY MANN. "My ever dearest friend": the letters of A. Dudley Mann to Jefferson Davis, 1869-1889. Edited with an introduction by John Preston Moore. Tuscaloosa, Ala.: Confederate Pub. Co., 1960. 114 p. bibliog. (p. 103-7), notes. (Confederate centennial studies, 14.) Excerpts, on war and politics, from 50 letters from a Confederate exile in Paris and Chantilly, France. [6670

GOOD HOUSEKEEPING. The Good housekeeping treasury. Selected from the complete files by Donald Elder and the editors of Good housekeeping. [N.Y.:] Simon and Schuster, 1960. 638 p. cartoons, facsims. (part col.), views (part col.). Articles, editorials, recipes, fiction, poetry, and illustrations, 1885-1959 (mainly from the 1940s and 1950s), in roughly chronological order. [6671

VANITY FAIR. Vanity fair, selections from America's most memorable magazine: a cavalcade of the 1920s and 1930s. Edited by Cleveland Amory and Frederic Bradlee. Picture editor: Katharine Tweed. N.Y.: Viking Press [1960]. 327 p. cartoons (part col.), facsims., ports. (part col.), views (part col., 1 double). Essays, poems, fiction, and illustrations, 1914-36; with an introduction on Conde Nast, publisher of Vanity fair, and Frank Crowninshield, editor. [6672

PAUL ELIOT GREEN. Drama and the weather: some notes and papers on life and the theatre. N.Y.: Samuel French [1958. 10], 220 p. Eighteen undated essays, partly reminiscent, on the author's work as a playwright and a teacher and promoter of drama since 1916, his life in North Carolina, his concept of "the folk," his special interest in Negroes and poor whites as exemplars of the folk, and his views of art, religion, and democracy. [6673

LIFE (Chicago). Great reading from Life: a treasury of the best stories and articles [1938-60]. Chosen by the editors. N.Y.: Harper [1960]. xii, 775, [2] p. illus. In 10 topical sections. [6674

ARTHUR POWELL DAVIES (1902-57). The mind and faith of A. Powell Davies. Edited by William O. Douglas. Garden City, N.Y.: Doubleday & Co., 1959. 334 p. Short excerpts from his books and articles, 1942-57, on counseling, law, literature, and religion; with a biographical and reminiscent introduction on his service as a Methodist, later a Unitarian, minister in Marine, New Jersey, and (from 1944 till his death) Washington, D.C. [6675

THE REPORTER (New York, 1949-). Our times: the best from The reporter. Edited by Max Ascoli. N.Y.: Farrar, Straus, and Cudahy [1960]. x, 502 p. Selections, 1949-60, by various contributors, including articles on the China Lobby, "The wiretappers," "The 'engineering of consent'--a case study," Alger Hiss and Whittaker Chambers, Scott McLeod, Richard M. Nixon, John Foster Dulles, Norman Vincent Peale, Styles Bridges, Claire Boothe Luce, "The Mormon invasion of New York City," and "The most cheerful graveyard in the world" (Forest Lawn Memorial Park, Los Angeles). [6676

AMERICAN HERITAGE. The first year of American heritage: the complete contents of the first six issues of "the magazine of history in book form"--volume VI, numbers 1-6, December 1954--October 1955. N.Y.: American Heritage Pub. Co. [1958]. 1 v. (various pagings). facsims., maps (part col.), ports. (part col.), views (part col.). notes. [6677

AMERICAN HERITAGE. A treasury of American heritage: a selection from the first five years of the magazine of history. [Edited by Oliver Jensen.] N.Y.: Simon & Schuster [1960]. 398, [2] p. cartoons (1 double), diagrs., facsims. (part col.), maps (part col., part double), plans, ports (part col.), views (part col., part double). Forty-three reprinted articles, 1954-59. [6678

Voyages and Travels

THOMAS CHRISTIE. The voyage of the Anne--a daily record. Edited by Robert G. McPherson. Ga. hist. quar., 44: 220-30 (Jun). notes. Record kept by the Recorder of Georgia on a voyage from London to Charleston, 16 Nov. 1732 - 13 Jan. 1733, en route to Georgia. [6679

JOE LESTER NORRIS. Ho! for California. Detroit Hist. Soc., Bul., 15(3): 7-15 (Dec 1958). notes. On the Gold Rush as reported in the Detroit free press and the Detroit daily advertiser, Nov. 1848--Feb. 1849, and recorded in manuscripts in the Burton Historical Collection. [6680

ALICE TAYLOR. Gold rush of '49. Garden City, N.Y.: Doubleday [1960]. 62 p. maps, views (part mount. col.). (The living history program.) On land and sea routes to California and the life in the mining camps there, 1848-49. [6681

WILLIAM S. M'COLLUM (1807/8-1882). California as I saw it: pencillings by the way of its gold and gold diggers, and incidents of travel by land and water. By William M'Collum, M.D., a returned adventurer. ... Edited by Dale L. Morgan. Los Gatos, Calif.: Talisman Press, 1960. 219, [1] p. maps, table, view. notes (p. 193-219). 1st ed. 1850. On the author's voyage from New York City by way of Panama to San Francisco, his experiences in the California mines, and his return voyage to Lockport, N.Y.; with an extensive editorial introduction containing a detailed biographical sketch of the author and a review and evaluation of the earliest narratives of travel to California across Panama. Appended: recollections of San Francisco by Lyman Bradley and Elliott W. Cook (1820?-1877), "Five letters written from the Isthmus in 1849" by W. H. Hecox, and a list of "Arrivals of vessels and passengers at Chagres for California" (27 Dec. 1848 - 30 Apr. 1849). [6682

WILLIAM LEWIS MANLY (born 1820). Death Valley in '49. ... With an introduction by Carl I. Wheat. Los Angeles: Borden Pub. Co. [1949]. xvi, 523, [1] p. fold. map, views. 1st ed. 1894. Reminiscences (ca. 1892-93) of the author's journey from Wisconsin through Wyoming, Utah, and Death Valley to the California gold mines, and his return voyage by way of Panama to New Orleans and St. Louis (1849-51), his second voyage to California by way of Panama (1851), his resumption of work in the mines, and his settlement on a farm near Hillsdale, Calif. (1859); with some account of his earlier life in Vermont, Michigan, and Wisconsin. Appended: Death Valley narratives by M. S. McMahon (p. 396-439), Alexander Combs Erkson (p. 491-7), and Edward Coker (p. 497-501). [6683

JAMES ROGERS (1818-98). Gold Rush letters of the Reverend James Rogers. Edited by Marie Rogers Vail, his grandniece. N.Y. Hist. Soc. quar., 44: 259-95 (Jul). port., views. notes. Letters to members of his family, dated at New York, Havana, Panama, San Francisco, and Sacramento City, 16 Oct. 1849-29 Oct. 1850; with an account by the editor of his life in New York and on the Pacific coast and his work as a Methodist minister and a teacher. [6684

ROGER CONANT (1833-1915). Mercer's belles: the journal of a reporter. ... Edited by Lenna A. Deutsch.

Seattle: Univ. of Washington Press, 1960. xvii, 190 p. facsims., port., views. bibliog. (p. 179-84), notes (p. 169-78). "The cruise of the Continental, or an inside view of life on the ocean wave," a manuscript diary kept by Conant as a reporter for the New York Times on a voyage from New York round South America to San Francisco and Seattle and during a stay in Seattle, 16 Jan. 1866 - 9 Jun. 1867, in company with a party of 100 young unmarried women recruited (mainly in New England) by Asa Shinn Mercer (1839-1917) as emigrants to Washington Territory, of whom 36 left the party at San Francisco and the others proceeded to Seattle, where by June 1867 at least 19 had married; with biographical sketches of the members the party. [6685

HENRY JAMES (1843-1916). The art of travel: scenes and journeys in America, England, France, and Italy from the travel writings of Henry James. Edited and with an introduction by Dauwen Zabel. Garden City, N.Y.: Doubleday & Co., 1958. iv, [2], 567 p. port. bibliog. (p. 563-7). Selected passages dealing almost entirely with cities, including, in America, Saratoga, Newport, Quebec, New York, Boston, Concord and Salem, and Washington, and also Niagara and "New England: an autumn impression," 1870-71, 1904-5. [6686

ALAN COOKE. Stefansson. Dartmouth alumni bul., 52(3):31-3 (Dec 1959). ports. On Vilhjalmur Stefansson (born 1879), his early life in Manitoba and "the Dakota prairies," his studies at Harvard, his anthropological expenditions to the Arctic, and his "great collection of books relating to polar regions," acquired in 1951 by the Dartmouth College Library. [6687

AMERICANS ABROAD

ADOLPH BURNETT BENSON. A pioneer Swedish sealer in the South Atlantic. Am. Swed. Hist. Foundation, Yr. bk., 1960, p. 44-9. facsims. On Elof Benson (or Berndtson) of Stonington, Conn., native of Sweden, probably lost at sea before 1836, his voyages to or near the Antarctic, 1820-21, and his manuscript logbook, "in an incredible phonetic English, bearing many of the Swedish accents and inflections." [6688

JOSEPH L. PARKHURST, JR. Captain Palmer's continent. Pac. discovery, 13(4):20-21 (Jul-Aug). map, port., view. On the discovery of Antarctica by Capt. Nathaniel Brown Palmer (1799-1877) of the sloop Hero, one of a fleet of whaling vessels on a voyage from Stonington, Conn., to the South Shetland Islands, Nov. 1820. [6689

JOHN HOUSTON MIFFLIN (1807-88). The European journals of John Houston Mifflin: 1836-37. [Edited by Richard James Stonesifer.] Lancaster Co. Hist. Soc., Jour., 62:39-57 (Jan 1958). port. notes. Summary of and quotations from 11 letters from a Pennsylvania painter and poet to Charles Gilpin and Charles West Thomson of Philadelphia, evidently intended for publication, constituting "an almost complete journal" of his voyage from New York and his stay in England, France, and Italy and commenting on "the sights and customs of Europe," especially the theater, and the Americans he met there. 6690

DAVID JAFFÉ. The captain who sat for the portrait of Ahab. Boston Univ. studies in Eng., 4:1-22 (spring). notes. Argument that the "prototype for Ahab" was Lt. Charles Wilkes, commander of the U.S. Exploring Expedition round the World, 1838-42, and proof that his Narrative (Philadelphia, 1845) was a "source-book" of Moby-Dick. [6691

FRANKLIN PARKER. George Peabody and the search for Sir John Franklin, 1852-1854. Am. Neptune, 20:104-11 (Apr). notes. On his contribution to the support of an Arctic expedition of Dr. Elisha Kent Kane, the earliest Arctic explorer from the United States to conduct an organized expendition. [6692

ESTUARDO NÚÑEZ. Los viajeros de tierra adentro, 1860-1900. Jour. inter-Am. studies, 2:9-44 (Jan). notes. Includes accounts of the South and Central American travels of John Randolph Tucker, George Augustus Peabody, Alexander Agassiz, Ephraim George Squier, James Orton, and Adolf Bandelier. [6693

JAMES LAWRENCE ORR (1822-73). A letter of James L. Orr, Minister to Russia, 1873. Edited by Joseph O. Baylen. S.C. hist. mag., 61:225-31 (Oct). notes. Letter to the author's brother, John Amaziah Orr, dated St. Petersburg, 19 Mar. 1873, on the author's voyage thither from New York and his impressions of England, France, Germany, and Russia. [6694

MIRIAM UNDERHILL. The Jewell Trail. Appalachia, 33:129-33 (Jun). On the author's mother's cousin, Winfield Scott Jewell (1850-83), one of 18 men who died of starvation in the Lady Franklin Bay Expedition under Lt. Adolphus W. Greely; with a long excerpt from Jewel's diary, dated Fort Conger, Grinnell Land, 12 May 1882, and mention of oral information that "the bodies of those who died were necessarily used to keep the others from starving." [6695

JOHN EDWARD WEEMS. Race for the Pole. ... Preface by Vilhjalmur Stefansson. N.Y.: Holt [1960]. xiv, [2], 240 p. facsims., maps, ports., views. On Arctic explorations of Robert Edwin Peary (1856-1920) and Frederick Albert Cook (1865-1940), 1908-9, and the controversies as to which one should be credited with the discovery of the North Pole; with biographical sketches of the 2 men, and Stefansson's reminiscences of the dispute. Notes that Cook was jailed, 1925-30, after conviction for "using the mails to defraud" for the benefit of an oil firm. [6696

AMERICANS IN AMERICA

CONSTANCE BORDWELL. March of the volunteers: soldiering with Lewis and Clark. Portland, Ore.: Beaver Books [1960. 8], 111 p. map, views. Narrative of the Lewis and Clark Expedition, 1804-6, including selections from its journals. [6697

GENEVIEVE M. DARDEN. 1826 vignette: Yankee in Georgia. Ga. rev. 14: 378-83 (winter). Information from the diary of the author's great-great-aunt, Almira Hathaway Read (born 1797?), of Fairhaven, Mass., "lonely wife of an absent Massachusetts whaling captain," recording her voyage from New York to Savannah, her stay with relatives at Sunbury, Ga., "her constant and Calvinistic battles with her soul," her secular observations in Georgia, and her return voyage, Nov. 1826 - Apr. 1827. [6698

LUCIA SPARHAWK. By road, rail, canal, and lake--from Massachusetts to Michigan in 1836. Inland seas, 16: 224-9 (fall). Letter to "My dear Uncles and Aunts," dated Pontiac, Mich., 13 Apr. 1836, describing the author's travels from Templeton, Mass., to Buffalo, Detroit, and Pontiac, and her impressions of the country she saw. [6699

WILLIAM WOODWARD, JR. A young Yankee in the new West. Soc. Ind. Pioneers, Yr. bk., 1960, p. 5-40. ports. Letters to relatives in Middletown, Conn., 3 Sep. 1847-25 Sep. 1848, reporting the writer's journey from New York to Buffalo, by water to Detroit, "in the cars" to St. Joseph, and by water to Michigan City, Ind., his establishment of a store there, and his health, his social life, and his impressions of Michigan City. [6700

TOM HARRISON. John Brown's shadow. Frontier times, 34(4): 24-5 (fall). map, ports. On the migration of Mary Brown, widow of John Brown, her 3 daughters, her son Salmon, and his family from North Elba, N.Y., across country to Red Bluff, Calif., 1863-64. [6701

RICHARD ELY SELDEN, JR. (1797-1868). A visit to Lake Superior--1866. [Edited] by Ernest H. Rankin. Inland seas, 16:14-24 (spring). Letters to the writer's family in Connecticut, 20 May-18 Jun. 1866, reporting his travels to New York City, by railroad to Albany and Toledo, by boat to Lake Superior and Ontonagon and back to Marquette, and by road to Escanaba. [6702

CHARLES HENRY DOW (1851-1902). Leadville letters. George W. Bishop, Charles H. Dow and the Dow Theory (N.Y.: Appleton-Century-Crofts [1960]), p. 248-354. Nine letters dated 21 May-10 Jul. 1879, reprinted from the Providence journal, May-Jul. 1879, reporting the journey of a party of financiers, geologists, and other interested persons from New York to Denver and South Park by railroad and to Leadville by stage, their inspection of mining properties (especially those of the Little Pittsburg Consolidated Mining Company and of "Colorado's phenomenal city" (Leadville) and its "dance houses and gambling saloons," and their return East; with general remarks on the financial prospects of the mines. [6703

ERIC SLOANE. Return to Taos: a sketchbook of roadside Americana. N.Y.: W. Funk [1960. 8], 120 p. diagrs., maps, views (part col.). On the author's solitary journey in a Model T from Lakewood, N.J., across Pennsylvania and on to Kansas, Colorado, and Taos, N. M., painting signs as he went to pay his expenses, 1925, and his second journey over the same route in 1960; with illustrations by himself, showing landscapes, bridges, advertisements, highway signs, and roadside buildings. [6704

FOREIGNERS IN AMERICA

WASHINGTON IRVING (1783-1859). Voyages and discoveries of the companions of Columbus. N.Y.: Ungar [1960, c1956]. xxvi, 394 p. notes (p. 388-94). Foreword signed: Van Wyck Brooks. 1st ed. 1831. Narrative of explorations of the islands and coasts of the Gulf of Mexico and the Caribbean, 1499-1521, including the stay of Juan Ponce de León in Puerto Rico (as Governor) and his voyages to Florida, 1508-21. [6705

RAYNER UNWIN. The defeat of John Hawkins [1532-95]: a biography of his third slaving voyage [1567-68]. London: Allen & Unwin [1960]. 319 p. maps, ports., views. bibliog. (p. 313-14). Includes brief reference to the supposed travels of David Ingram, a member of the expedition, from Mexico through the present United States to the Atlantic and his return to England. [6706

JAMES JOHN TALMAN. Champlain as an explorer in inland North America [1603-15]. Vt. hist., 28:22-32 (Jan). notes. [6707

RICHARD BRANDON MORRIS. "... a passage to Japan." John Arthur Garraty, ed., The unforgettable Americans (Great Neck, N.Y.: Channel Press [1960]), p. 11-15. On Henry Hudson's explorations of Greenland (1608), the Hudson River and the northern Atlantic coast (1609), and Hudson Bay (1610-11). [6708

THE SCOTS MAGAZINE (Edinburgh, 1739-1826). Pacific voyages: selections from Scots magazine, 1771-1808. Compiled and annotated by James Stirrat Marshall and Carrie Marshall. Portland, Ore.: Binfords & Mort, 1960. [12], 100 p. coat of arms, facsims., col. flag, maps, ports. Facsimile reproductions from the magazine, grouped in chapters (each with an editorial introduction) on Capt. James Cook, "Maritime fur trade," Jean François Galaup de la Perouse, Capt. William Bligh, "The Nootka Sound controversy," and Capt. Simon Metcalfe. [6709

JOSÉ DE ONÍS. Los Estados Unidos vistos por escritores hispanoamericanos. Madrid: Ediciones Cultura Hispánica, 1956. 376, [3] p. bibliog. (p. 343-67), notes. (Colección Hombres e ideas.) Topical study of the United States as described by visitors from Latin America, 1776-1890; and separate chapter on Domingo Faustino Sarmiento, who visited the United States in 1845 and 1865-68. [6710

HELMUT DE TERRA. Motives and consequences of Alexander von Humboldt's visit to the United States (1804). Am. Philos. Soc., Proc., 104:314-16 (15 Jun). notes. [6711

FRANKLIN DANIEL SCOTT & JANE LUNDBLAD. Gosselman on North America in the 1830s. Swed. pioneer hist. quar., 11:99-107 (Jul). On the observations of Carl August Gosselman (1800-1843) in the United States in or soon after 1824 and again in or soon after 1836 as recorded in his Resa i Norra Amerika (1835) and Bref från en vandrande sjöman (1839). [6712

ELIZABETH REZNER DANIEL. Spanish American travelers in the United States before 1900 [mainly after 1830]: a study in inter-American literary relations. Ann Arbor: University Microfilms, 1959 [i. e. 1960]. Positive microfilm of typescript. [402] leaves. Thesis--Univ. of North Carolina. Abstracted: Dissert. abstracts, 20:2796-7 (Jan). [6713

ROBERT KIEFER WEBB. Harriet Martineau [1802-77]: a radical Victorian. London: Heinemann [1960]. xiii, 385 p. facsims, ports., tables, views. bibliog. (p. 368-77), notes. (Kingswood books on social history.) American edition with same title and pagination: N.Y.: Columbia Univ. Press, 1960. Includes a chapter (p. 134-74) on her travels in the United States, 1834-36, her Society in America and Retrospect of western travel, and her continued interest in American affairs. [6714

VERA MARY MAUD WHEATLEY. The life and work of Harriet Martineau [1802-77]. Fair Lawn, N.J.: Essential Books, 1957. 421 p. facsim., ports., views. Includes an account of her travels in the United States, 1834-36 (p. 146-62), her books on America, and her continued interest in it. [6715

FREDERICK MARRYAT (1792-1848). Diary in America. Edited with a foreword by Jules Zanger. Bloomington: Indiana Univ. Press [1960]. 342 p. ports., views. bibliog. (p. 301-5), notes (p. 306-36). 1st ed. 1839 (6 vols.). Record of a voyage from England to New York, Boston, Niagara Falls, Detroit, Sault Ste. Marie, Montreal, Vermont, Philadelphia, Washington, Green Bay and Prairie du Chien, Fort Snelling, St. Louis, Cincinnati and Lexington, "Virginia Springs," and back to England, May 1837 - Nov. 1838. Does not include the chapters on American institutions which occupy all of the original after v. 2, p. 214. [6716

GUSTAF ELIAS MARIUS UNONIUS (1810-1902). A pioneer in northwest America, 1841-1858: the memoirs of Gustaf Unonius. Translated from the Swedish by Jonas Oscar Backlund. Edited by Nils William Olsson. Volume II. Minneapolis: Univ. of Minnesota Press for the Swedish Pioneer Historical Soc. [1960]. vii, 357 p. port., views. notes (p. 327-42). Vol. 1 published in 1950; Swedish original in 1861. On the author's experience as a farmer at Pine Lake, Wis., his studies for the ministry, his missionary labors among Indians and immigrants in Wisconsin, his ministry at Manitowoc and later at Chicago, the relative unpopularity of his faith in competition with other faiths of the Scandinavians, his travels in Illinois and Iowa, his "begging trip" to collect money for building a Swedish-Norwegian church in Chicago, his observation of the "remnants of New Sweden" in the East, and his return to Sweden. The translation omits the "generalized pictures of American political, economic, social, and ecclesiastical conditions" that are included in the Swedish original. [6717

CLARENCE L. HOHL, JR. Lord Acton's visit to America, 1853. Am. Cath. Hist. Soc., Rec., 71:73-84 (Sep-Dec). notes. Information from the diary of John Emerich Edward Dalbert-Acton, 1st Baron Acton, about his travels and observations in New York, New England, and Maryland, and especially his unfavorable impressions of the people in general and of those he met at Harvard in particular. [6718

AXEL REINHOLD AUGUST, BARON ADELSWÄRD (1828-1900). Glimpses from the travel letters of Baron Axel Adelswärd, 1855-1856. [Edited by] Franklin D. Scott. Swed. pioneer hist. quar., 11:145-54 (Oct). port. notes. Summary and quotations from letters to the author's family in Sweden, dated in New York, Philadelphia, Charleston, New Orleans, and Niagara Falls, containing comments on the Americans and on public events. Intended (with a diary lost in America) as the basis for a book on America that was never written. [6719

ROBERT W. RINDEN. The first Japanese embassy. For. Service jour., 37(10):32-3 (Oct). On the reception of a diplomatic party from Japan, visiting Washington to exchange ratifications of a treaty, and their observations on the oddity of American customs, 1860. [6720

DWIGHT W. MORROW, JR. The American impressions of a French botanist, 1873. Agric. hist., 34:71-6 (Apr). notes. On the visit of Jules Émile Planchon (1823-88), by request of the French Ministry of Agriculture and Commerce, "to make a brief survery of the phylloxera-resistant grapevines of the eastern United States"; with translated excerpts from his manuscript "Notes de voyage aux États-Unis," on cities, hotels, meals, etc. [6721

HERBERT R. HISLOP. An English pioneer in Arizona: the letters of Herbert R. Hislop. Kiva, 25(2-4): quarterly installments (Dec 1959-Apr 1960). facsim., port. Letters to relatives in England, dated in New York, Chicago, Los Angeles, Tucson, and Empire Ranch (near Sonoita, Ariz.), 23 May 1876-28 Jun. 1878, on his voyage from England, his railroad journey to San Francisco and voyage to Los Angeles, his travels by stage to Tucson and thence on horseback 52 miles to the ranch (to be headquarters for the Empire Land and Cattle Company), his discovery that "Arizona ... is no place for honest men," his adventures in cooking his own meals, and his preparations for sudden return to England in an unidentified family crisis. [6722

VILHJALMUR STEFANSSON (1879-1962). Sir Hubert Wilkins (1888-1958) [Arctic and Antarctic submarine and aerial explorer]. Am. Philos. Soc., Yr. bk., 1959, p. 146-50. [6723

AMERICA half a century ago: the impressions of an English solicitor. Am. Bar Assoc. jour., 46:863-6 (Aug). Letter from an unnamed Londoner to a friend in Essex, dated Philadelphia, 29 Dec. 1905, on American restaurants, hotels, and city buildings as observed by the writer in Chicago and Philadelphia. [6724

FRED HAGSTOTZ. Fritz' wanderlust, romance, and travels! Boston: meador Pub. Co. [1960]. 154 p. On the author's emigration from Germany to Brooklyn to join relatives there, his work as a bookkeeper in a shoe store, a brakeman on the elevated railroad, and a salesman in a clothing store, his hobo railroad journey to Chicago and back, and his return to Europe, 1905-12; with some account of his travels in Europe, 1912-16. [6725

Regional, State, and Local History

THE NORTHEAST

NEW FRANCE. La Pointe à la Chevelure. Edited by John C. Huden. Translated by Grace B. Huden. Vt. hist., 28:231-4 (Jul). bibliog. Report or abstract of report from the Governor and the Intendant of New France to an unnamed official, 3 Oct. 1741, on the establishment of settlers, granting of lands, and improvement of transportation on Lake Champlain. [6726

RICHARD SANDERS ALLEN. State-line country. Vt. life, 14(3):38-42 (summer). maps. On the boundary between Vermont and New York, 1779-1880. [6727

ROBERT M. LICHTENBERG. One-tenth of a nation: national forces in the economic growth of the New York region [22 counties of New York, New Jersey, and Connecticut, 1780-1960]. Cambridge: Harvard Univ. Press, 1960. xvi, [2], 326 p. diagrs., maps (part col.), tables. notes (p. 301-12). (New York Metropolitan Region study.) On the conditions that attracted manufacturing and commercial enterprises to this area. Includes a chapter on "America's business headquarters." [6728

SIDNEY MARTIN ROBBINS & NESTOR E. TERLECKYI. Money metropolis: a locational study of financial activities in the New York region [22 counties in 3 States, 1784-1956, with projections to 1985]. Cambridge: Harvard Univ. Press, 1960. xviii, [2], 294 p. diagrs., col. maps, tables. notes (p.275-84). (New York Metropolitan Region study [5].) One of a series of studies made by the Graduate School of Business Administration, Harvard University, for the Regional Plan Association. Includes chapers on banking, insurance, and the securities industry. [6729

BENJAMIN CHINITZ. Freight and the metropolis: the impact of America's transport revolutions on the New York Region [22 counties in 3 States, 1800-1957]. Cambridge: Harvard Univ. Press, 1960. xv, 211 p. diagrs., maps (part col.), tables, views. notes (p.199-204). (New York Metropolitan Region study [6].) Study made by the Graduate School of Business Administration, Harvard University, for the Regional Plan Association. [6730

DOROTHY (GODFREY) WAYMAN. Drygoods and cracker barrel. N.Y. folklore quar., 16:104-9 (summer). On "the old 'general store' of the nineteenth century in New England and western New York State." [6731

NELSON MANFRED BLAKE. Eunice against the Shakers. N.Y. hist., 41: 359-78 (Oct). notes. On disharmony between Eunice (Hawley) Chapman and her alcoholic husband, James Chapman, his seizure of their 3 children and entry into a Shaker organization at Watervliet, the granting of a divorce to her by an act of the New York Legislature, the abduction of the children to the Shaker community at Enfield, N.H., and her success in obtaining physical and legal custody of them; with some account of pamphlets and a farce inspired by these events and issues, 1812-19. [6732

R. BARNES. Document. Hist. and Philos. Soc. Ohio, Bul., 18-142-3 (Apr). Letter to the author's father (Jonathan Barnes of Tolland, Conn.), dated Pittsburgh, 16 Nov. 1817, on his journey by steam boat and stagecoach from Hartford to Pittsburgh, en route to Cincinnati. [6733

CHARLES EBEN FISHER. Some old inventories and jacking up locomotive bells. Railway Locomotive Hist. Soc., Bul., 102:43-8 (Apr). table. On "sources of information for the construction of a roster of locomotives for an individual railroad," as illustrated by locomotives of the New York, New Haven, & Hartford Railroad, 1842-57. [6734

ARTHUR MINTON. Names of real-estate developments [in New York City and adjacent parts of New York

State, New Jersey, and Connecticut, 1854-1951]. Names, 7:129-53, 233-55 (Sep, Dec 1959). notes. [6735

R. F. COGGESHALL. The case of Coleman vs. the New Haven Railroad. Railway & Locomotive Hist. Soc., Bul., 103:41-6 (Oct). On a suit brought against the New York, New Haven, & Hartford Railroad by John A. Coleman "for assault and battery in expelling him from a car at Stamford, Conn.," 1870, as shown in the court record and as inflated by legend. [6736

LEUMAN M. WAUGH. Guidance for tomorrow's practice gained from the pioneers of the Northeastern District [of the American Association of Orthodontists, in the New England and Middle Atlantic States and Canada, ca. 1870 to 1958]. Am. jour. orthodontics, 44:612-25 (Aug 1958). port. notes. [6737

HAROLD S. WALKER. The Addison Railroad (Vermont). Railway & Locomotive Hist. Soc., Bul., 102-51-2 (Apr). map, tables, views. On a 15-mile line, the Addison Branch of the Ruthland Railroad, extending from Leicester Junction to Larrabee's Point on Lake Champlain in Addison County, 1871-1960 (and formerly across the lake to Ticonderoga, N.Y., on a wooden trestle, destroyed by a flood in 1927 and never rebuilt). [6738

CHARLES FRANCIS HITCHCOCK ALLEN. Notes on the Ogdensburg and Lake Champlain R. R. Railway & Locomotive Hist. Soc., Bul., 102:49-50 (Apr). facsims., map. Information about its route and schedule between Ogdensburg, N.Y., and Portland, Me., as shown on a timetable dated 17 May 1880. [6739

HOWARD WILLIAM LULL. Forested municipal watersheds [and forest-bounded reservoirs] in the Northeast [1882-1960]. Jour. forestry, 58:83-6 (Feb). table. bibliog. [6740

JOHN M. HEILMAN. Northeast Municipal watersheds. Jour. forestry, 58:305-7 (Apr). Inventory of "forested watersheds" and "forest-protected reservoirs" owned and managed by 10 cities between and including Baltimore and Boston, 1890-1960. [6741

GLADYS KLEINWORT BOWLES, SIEGFRIED HOERMANN, & WAYNE C. ROHRER. Population of the Northeast: growth, composition, and distribution, 1900-1950. [College Park, Md., 1960.] iv, 107 p. diagrs., maps, tables (part double). bibliog. (p. 106-7), notes. On population changes as related to agriculture, metropolitan and nonmetropolitan counties, and urban and rural areas in the New England and Middle Atlantic States, Maryland, and West Virginia. [6742

EDGAR MALONE HOOVER & RAYMOND VERNON. Anatomy of a metropolis: the changing distribution of people and jobs within the New York Metropolitan Region [1900-1956]. Cambridge: Harvard Univ. Press, 1959. xvi, 345 p. diagrs., maps (part col.), tables. notes (p. 311-27). (New York Metropolitan Region study.) [6743

WILLIAM M. FOSTER. Evald B[enjamin] Lawson [born 1904]: a champion for things Swedish. Am. Swed. monthly, 54(2): 11-12 (Feb). port. On his service as President of Upsala College, East Orange, N.J., since 1938; with some account of his early life in Massachusetts, his Swedish emigrant parents, his theological studies, and his service as a Lutheran minister in White Plains, N.Y. [6744

GEORGE HOWE (born 1881). Half a century of property development in Westchester County and southwestern Connecticut [since ca. 1909]: memoirs of a Westchester realtor. N.Y.: Exposition Press [1959]. 134, [1] p. map, views. Profusely illustrated with photographs of wealthy rural estates and suburban apartment houses. [6745

DOROTHY C. MOSES. The Park City. Long Island forum, 23:225, 231 (Oct). view. On "the ferry that used to run between Port Jefferson and Bridgeport during the first half of this century." [6746

MARTIN SEGAL. Wages in the metropolis: their influence on the location of industries in the New York region [1906-55]. Cambridge: Harvard Univ. Press, 1960. xi, 211 p. diagrs., col. maps, tables. notes (p. 183-97). (New York Metropolitan Region study, 4.) Study of an area of 22 counties in 3 States. [6747

HOWARD WILLIAM LULL. Watershed management research in the Northeast. Jour. forestry, 58:285-7 (Apr). On studies "to determine how forest cover, and changes in cover, affect streamflow," 1912, 1932-60. [6748

THOSE live wires at Reading. Flying, 65(6):34-5, 78-9 (Dec 1959). view. On the Reading Air Service, established by Alfred M. Bertolet, R. Harding Breithaupt, and Brooks L. McElroy at Reading, Pa., to deal in commercial planes and operate a commuter service to New York, 1946-59. [6749

New England

RALPH NADING HILL. Yankee Kingdom: Vermont and New Hampshire [1605-1960]. N.Y.: Harper [1960. 12], 338 p. col. maps (1 double). bibliog. (p. 311-24). (Regions of America: a series of books that depict our natural regions, their history, development, and character.) [6750

JAMES LOUIS BLAWIE. Fundamental concepts in considering home rule for New England towns and cities. Ann Arbor: University Microfilms, 1959 [i. e. 1960]. Positive microfilm of typescript. 591 leaves. bibliog. (leaves 566-91). Thesis--Boston Univ. Abstracted: Dissert, abstracts, 20: 2819 (Jan). On "the New England political or social myth-like concept of local independence" since the 1620s, the growth of centralization in the 19th century, and the legislation and constitutional amendments by which the New England courts can be inhibited from restricting or nullifying more recent or current "attempts to secure local independence of action in local affairs." [6751

FESSENDEN SEAVER BLANCHARD. Ghost towns of New England, their ups and downs. N.Y.: Dodd, Mead, 1960. xiv, [2], 205 p. maps, port., views. On Dudleytown, Gay City or Factory Hollow, Mystic, and Mount Riga, Conn.; North River and Dogtown Common, Mass.; Flagstaff, Kingsburg, Willimantic, Amherst, Gotts, and Hurricane, Me.; Roxbury, Lempster, Lyman, and Success, N.H.; and Glastenburg and Somerset, Vt.--communities that have existed at some time since 1623. [6752

MARCUS WILSON JERNEGAN (1872-1949). The development of public poor relief in New England [1629-1768]. Marcus W. Jernegan, Laboring and dependent classes in colonial America, 1607-1783 (N.Y.: Ungar [1960]), p. 189-209. tables. notes. From Social service review, Jun. 1931. [6753

KENNETH M. WILSON. Glass in New England. Sturbridge, Mass.: Old Sturbridge Village [1959]. 34, [2] p. facsim., views (1 double). (Old sturbridge Village booklet series, 9.) On the importation of European window glass and glassware into New England, 1629-1830, and the manufacture of glass and glassware there, 1639, 1752 to ca. 1768, 1780-1888. [6754

ROBERT NELSON LARSON. The governor's council in New England. Ann Arbor: University Microfilms, 1960. Positive microfilm of typescript. [255] leaves. Thesis--Boston Univ. Abstracted: Dissert. abstracts, 21: 947-8 (Oct). On an institution existing as early as the 1630s, provided for in the constitutions adopted after the Declaration of Independence, and still retained in Maine, New Hampshire, and Massachusetts. [6755

NINY ROCCO-BERGERA. La società e i poeti dell' America puritana. [Trieste] 1957. 35 p. bibliog. (p. 35), notes. On the New England poetry of Anne Bradstreet, Michael Wigglesworth, and Edward Taylor, 1630-1720s. [6756

WILLIAM GEORGE WILCOX. The new England convenant theology: its English precursors and early American exponents. Ann Arbor: University Microfilms, 1959 [i. e. 1960]. Positive microfilm of typescript. [372] leaves. Thesis--Duke Univ. Abstracted: Dissert. abstracts, 20:4195 (Apr). On the theology expounded by William Perkins, John Preston, William Ames, John Cotton, Thomas Hooker, and Peter Bulkeley, 1630s-90s, and the close relation required by it between church and state. [6757

MARCUS WILSON JERNEGAN (1872-1949). The beginnings of free public schools [in New England, 1635-47]. Marcus W. Jernegan, Laboring and dependent classes in colonial America, 1607-1783 (N.Y.: Ungar [1960]), p. 69-83. notes. From School review, Jun. 1915. [6758

FRANKLIN PARKER. Ezekiel Cheever [1614/15-1708]: New England colonial teacher. Peabody jour. educ., 37:355-60 (May). bibliog. On his emigration to America in 1637, his teaching in New Haven (1638-50), Ipswich (1650-61), and Charlestown (1661-70), and his service as master of the Boston Latin Grammar School (1670-1708). [6759

EDWARD H. WEST. The story of Jane Hawkins [died 1659]. New Eng. hist. and general. reg., 114:207-11 (Jul). notes. On the banishment of Mrs. Richard Hawkins, follower of Anne Hutchinson, from Boston, 1637 or 1638, and her late life in Portsmouth, R.I. [6760

MARCUS WILSON JERNEGAN (1872-1949). Compulsory and free education for poor children and apprentices [in New England, 1639-1745]. Marcus W. Jernegan, Laboring and dependent classes in colonial America, 1607-1783 (N.Y.: Ungar [1960]), p. 116-28. notes. From Social service review, Sep. 1931. [6761

MARCUS WILSON JERNEGAN (1872-1949). Educational legislation for poor children and apprentices [in New England], 1642-[1776]. Marcus W. Jernegan, Laboring and dependent classes in colonial America, 1607-1783 (N.Y.: Ungar [1960]), p. 84-105. table. notes. From School review, Dec. 1918 and Jan. 1919. [6762

MARIAN (CARD) DONNELLY. New England pyramids, 1651-1705. Soc. Architectural Historians, Jour., 19: 76-7 (Jun). plan, views. On the meaning of "piramides" ("pyramides," etc.) as a designation of some part of New England meetinghouses, presumably pyramidal roofs. [6763

ROLLO GABRIEL SILVER. Financing the publication of early New England sermons [1660s-1797]. Studies in bibliog., 11 (1958): 162-78. table. notes. [6764

J. W. OLMSTED. The voyage of Jean Richer [1630-96] to Acadia in 1670: a study in the relations of science and navigation under Colbert. Am. Philos. Soc., Proc., 104:612-34 (15 Dec). maps. notes. On the vogage of the Saint-Sébastien, a vessel of the French Navy, to test experimental marine chronometers under the auspices of the Académie Royale des Sciences; with evidence that observations were made off the Piscataqua River and in Penobscot Bay and probably not at Port Royal (now Annapolis, N.S.). [6765

The WILLIAM Harris manuscript. R.I. hist., 19:8-9 (Jan). Describes a manuscript account of King Philip's War, dated 12 Aug. 1676, by William Harris (1610-81), recently acquired by the Rhode Island Historical Society. [6766

JESSIE B. TREFETHEN. Trefethen: the family and the landing. Portland, Me.: House of Falmouth [1960. 10], 61 p. views. bibliog. (p. 61). On the descendants of Henry Trethen (Trevethan, Treventhan), who had settled in New Castle, N.H., by 1678; their continuance on the coast and islands of northern New England; the purchase of two ninths of Peaks Island, Me., by Henry Trefethen (1797?-1880) in 1843; and the life of Henery and his descendants on this property, which they called Trefethen's Landing. [6767

ABBOTT LOWELL CUMMINGS. Architecture in early New England. Sturbridge, Mass.: Old Sturbridge Village [1958. 31] p. diagrs. plans, views. (Old Sturbridge village booklet series, 7.) On materials, methods, and styles, ca. 1680 to 1836. [6768

VIOLA FLORENCE BARNES. The Dominion of New England: a study in British colonial policy. N.Y.: F. Ungar Pub. Co. [1960]. viii, [2], 303 p. bibliog. (p. 278-88), notes. (American classics.) 1st ed. 1923. On efforts and experiments of the British Government in "consolidating all the New England colonies under a single head." 1681-91. [6769

COLIN CAMPBELL. Deportations from Scotland in 1685. New Eng. hist. and geneal. reg., 114:150-51 (Apr). On participants in the unsuccessful uprising of Archibald, 9th Earl of Argyll, against James II (1685), who were transported to New England. [6970

CLIFFORD KENYON SHIPTON. Y^e^ mystery of ye ages solved; or, How placing worked at colonial Harvard & Yale. Harvard Alumni bul., 57:258-9, 262-3 (11 Dec 1954). facsims. On the considerations that fixed the order in which the members of a Harvard class or a Yale class recited, helped themselves at table, stood in academic processions, and were listed in the catalogue, 1687-1772. [6771

ADOLPH S. CAVALLO. New England crewel embroideries [18th century]. Conn. Hist. Soc. bul., 24:33-43 (Apr 1959). views. On "embroidery worked with worsteds, or woolen yarns." [6772

WILLIAM LAMSON WARREN. The Pierpont limner and some of his contemporaries. Conn. Hist. Soc. bul., 23:97-113 (Oct 1958). On several New England portraits painted in the years 1710-15 or thereabouts. Appended

(p. 113-28): annotated catalogue, with reproductions, of an exhibition of 27 portraits. [6773

JOHN DYKSTRA EUSDEN. Natural law and covenant theology in New England, 1720-1760. Natural law forum, 5:1-30. notes. [6774

C. C. GOEN. Revivalism and separatism in New England, 1740-1800: strict Congregationalists and Separate Baptists in the Great Awakening. Church hist., 29:480-81 (Dec). Abstract of thesis--Yale Univ. [6775

ROY LEE GALE. A Vermonter's tribute to a Loyalist. Vt. Hist. Soc., News and notes, 7:26-31 (Dec 1955). views. On Justus Sherwood (1747-98), native of Connecticut, who by 1772 had settled in Vermont as one of the Green Mountain Boys, in 1776 joined the British Army, and later settled permanently in Canada. [6776

JACOB BAILEY (1731-1808). [Excerpts from a diary.] Harvard alumni bul., 58:294-5, 315 (14 Jan 1956). Record of the travels of a Harvard undergraduate with William Browne from Cambridge through Connecticut and back, Jul. 1754. [6777

VIRGINIA DOWNS. Indian Joe: Revolutionary scout and friend of the settler. Vt. life, 14(3):11-14 (spring). notes. On a Micmac Indian (1739-1819), native of Canada, who removed with his squaw to the Coos Valley in 1759 and led a roving life in the vicinity of Haverhill and Newbury. [6778

HELEN (HARTNESS) FLANDERS. Folk songs traditional in New England. New-Eng. galaxy, 2(2):2-12 (fall). music, port. Includes texts of "Springfield Mountain" (1761 and later versions), "The Battle of the Frogs of Windham," "The Quebec song," and others selected from the Flanders Ballad Collection at Middlebury College. [6779

CLAUDE MOORE FUESS. The old New England academy. New-Eng. galaxy, 2(1):11-19 (summer). views. On private secondary schools, 1763-1960, most of which were replaced shortly before or after the Civil War by church schools or public high schools. [6780

NINA FLETCHER LITTLE. John Brewster, Jr., 1766-1854: deaf-mute itinerant portrait painter. Antiques, 78:462-3 (Nov). ports. On his life in New England. [6781

CHARLES CURRIER. John Osgood [1770-1840], clockmaker of the Merrimack and Connecticut River Valley. ... As told to Brooks Palmer. Antiques jour., 15(1):15-17, 36 (Jan). views. On his life in North Andover and Haverhill, Mass., and Haverhill, N.H. [6782

GORDON M. DAY. Dartmouth and Saint Francis. Dartmouth alumni mag., 52(2):28-30 (Nov 1959). ports., view. On "the Indian village of Odanak (Saint Francis) in Quebec," the project of Eleazar Wheelock to educate boys from the Saint Francis tribe in his Indian school at Dartmouth College (1772 ff.), the recent moderization of the village, and a recent project of Dartmouth College to photograph the village and its natives, tape-record their speech, and collect "Abenakiana" of all kinds. [6783

ELIZABETH GEORGE SPEARE. Old-time schoolmasters and scholars [in New England, 1778-1836]. New-Eng. galaxy, 1(4):6-15 (spring). facsims., port., view. [6784

RICHARD SANDERS ALLEN. Forty Connecticut crossings. Vt. life, 14(4): 28-9 (summer). view. On highway and railway bridges across the Connecticut River connecting Vermont and New Hampshire since the 1780s. [6785

EDWARD DEMING ANDREWS. The Shakers in New England [since the 1780s]. New-Eng. galaxy, 2(1):2-10 (summer). facsim., views. Deals particularly with their buildings, furniture, and costumes. [6786

SAMUEL PETERS [1735-1826]. A tremenduous [sic] pass in the North. [Edited] by Robert E. Pike. Northeast folklore, 3:52-3 (fall-winter). Excerpt from the author's General history of Connecticut (London, 1781) as reprinted anonymously in The wonderful magazine (London, 1793), about the narrows of the Connecticut River at Bellows Falls. [6787

FRANK WASHBURN GRINNELL. The common law of probation in Massachusetts and, before 1917 and the Federal Probation Act, in the First Federal Circuit: an illustration of the "equitable" growth of the criminal law [1784-1940]. Mass. law quar., 45(3): 70-91 (Oct). notes. From the Journal of criminal law and criminology, May-Jun. 1941. [6788

EDWARD HUGH CAMERON. Samuel Slater [1768-1835], father of American manufactures. [Freeport, Me.:] B.

Wheelwright Co. [1960]. xvi, 206 p. port. bibliog. (p. 201-6), notes. (American saga series.) On his early life and milling experience in England, his emigration to American in 1789, his design and manufacture of cotton-milling machinery, his partnership in a cotton textile mill in Pawtucket, R.I., and his establishment of mills in Rhode Island, Massachusetts, Connecticut, and New Hampshire. [6789

NINA FLETCHER LITTLE. Country art in New England, 1790-1840. Sturbridge, Mass.: Old Sturbridge Village [1960]. 32 p. facsim., ports., views. (Old Sturbridge Village booklet series, 11.) [6790

ANNABELLE (McCONNELL) MELVILLE. Jean Lefebvre de Cheverus, 1768-1836. Milwaukee: Bruce Pub. Co. [1958]. xiv, [2], 527, [1] p. facsim., ports, views. bibliog. (p. 507-14), notes (p. 443-505). On his early life and studies for the priesthood in France, his service from 1797 to 1823 in Maine and Massachusetts as a missionary to the Indians and later as Bishop of Boston, and his closing years in France. [6791

LOUISE (HALL) THARP. Bonnet girls. New-Eng. galaxy, 1(3): 2-10 (winter. facsims., port., views. On Betsey (Metcalf) Baker of Providence (fl. 1797-1859) and later female makers and corporate manufacturers of straw bonnets in New England, 1797-1880. [6792

J. W. FINDLEY. Eliza A[nn] Gardner, mother of the A.M.E. Zion Missionary Society, A.M.E. Zion Church. A.M.E. Zion quar. rev., 66:36-8 (winter 1955). On her services to the Church in New England, her work for abolition and woman suffrage, and her life in Boston, 19th century. [6793

FREDERIC A. SHARF. Fitz Hugh Lane [1804-65]: his life and art. Antiques, 78:452-5 (Nov). views. On his life in Gloucester and his paintings of ships and shore scenes in that area, in Maine, and elsewhere. [6794

C. ERNEST WALKER. Covered bridge ramblings in New England, with 100 reproductions of photos. taken by the author. Contoocook, N.H., 1959. [14], 114 p. diagrs., views. bibliog. (p. 113-14). On covered bridges in New England, built as early as 1804 and as late as 1953; with "List of bridges" (p. 101-12). [6795

AGNES M. DODS. Erastus Salisbury Field [1805-1900]. Hobbies, 65(4):46 (Jun). port. On his work as a portraitist and landscapist in Massachusetts and Connecticut. [6796

LAWRENCE R. DAME. Ophthalmologists: their general and special contributions [in New England, 1817-1960]. New Eng. jour. med., 262:918-20 (5 May). [6797

E. DONALD ASSELIN. Zerubbabel Tuchett (the last of the local drovers). Vt. Hist. Soc., News and notes, 9:31-2 (Dec 1957). Lore transmitted to the author 50 years ago from his great-grandfather about a gigantic Vermonter, an express rider between St. Johnsbury and Boston until railroads destroyed the business (1830s?). [6798

ROBERT C. SENIOR. New England Congregationalism and the Anti-Slavery Movement, 1830-1860. Church hist., 29:481 (Dec). Abstract of thesis--Yale Univ., 1954. [6799

FRANK O. SPINNEY. New England glass in Old Sturbridge Village [made ca. 1830 to ca. 1860]. New-Eng. galaxy, 2(1): 34-7 (summer). views. [6800

THEODORE ROOSEVELT GARRISON. John Greenleaf Whittier: pioneer regionalist and folklorist. Ann Arbor: University Microfilms, 1960. Positive microfilm of typescript. [536] leaves. Thesis--Univ. of Wisconsin. Abstracted: Dissert. abstracts, 21:621-2 (Sep). On his "regional writing" and "his works that are based on New England folklore," particularly that of the Merrimack Valley and Essex County, 1831-47, with later expressions in many of his poems. [6801

CHARLES A. HUGUENIN. The truth about the schooner Hesperus. N.Y. folklore quar., 16:48-53 (spring). notes. On the sinking of this vessel by a gale in Boston Harbor, the great damage done by the gale elsewhere on the New England coast, and the Boston newspaper reports that may have confused Longfellow in his ballad "the wreck of the Hesperus," Dec. 1839. [6802

LANCE EDWIN DAVIS. The New England textile mills and the capital markets: a study of industrial borrowing, 1840-1860. Jour. econ. hist., 20:1-30 (Mar). diagrs., tables. notes. [6803

ALICE MARY KIMBALL. Salute to Ellen Nye [1847-1940]. Vt. Hist. Soc., News and notes, 5:11-14 (Oct 1953). Information from the Nye Papers about her life in North Montpelier as a "musical wonder child," her musical studies and teaching in Boston, and her married life after 1885 in North Montpelier. For a portrait of her at age 14 see 5:37. [6804

KENNETH WOODS PAULI. Evidences of popular support for the land-grant college act of 1862 as revealed in selected speeches in New England, 1850-1860. Ann Arbor: University Microfilms, 1960. Positive microfilm of typescript. [232] leaves. Thesis--Stanford Univ. Abstracted: Dissert. abstracts, 20:4460-61 (May). [6805

JAMES FRANCIS RAGAN. Hawthorne's bulky Puritans. PMLA, 75:420-23 (Sep). notes. Illustrations from his novels, 1850-52, of the fact that "members of past ages ... are given a physical mass in proportion to their lack of refinement"; of his belief that "the great system of human progress ... may be destined gradually to spiritualize us, by refining away our grosser attributes of body"; and his fear that the process of etherealization may go too far. [6806

MADELAINE R. BROWN. The inheritance of progressive muscular atrophy as a dominant trait in two New England families [the Wetherbee family of Massachusetts and the Farr family of Vermont as observed since 1872]. New Eng. jour. med., 262:1280-82 (23 Jun). diagrs., facsims. [6807

FRANCIS CALL WOODMAN. [Reminiscences.] Harvard alumni bul., 52:50, 98, 100 (8-22 Oct 1949). On the author's experiences in the Harvard football team during its games with Yale, 1886-88. [6808

GEORGE EATON. "The schooner Brave." [Contributed by Mrs. Malcom H. Carman.] Northeast folklore, 3: 16-17 (spring). Ballad written by a blind man of Deer Isle, Me., in 1893, about a Maine schooner wrecked in a storm on Newburyport Beach, 4 May 1893, and the "four noble men" on board, all drowned--Capt. Joseph W. Lane, Ed Norton, Fred Thompson, and Sumner Stinson, all from Deer Isle; with advice to their widows and orphans. [6809

STEWART HALL HOLBROOK. That was Columbia Bridge. N.H. profiles, 9(6):22-3, 48-9 (Jun). view. Recollections of the railroad depot in a Coös County village and the railroad bridge across the Connecticut River there, 1893 to ca. 1920. [6810

NEW Englander for New England. Harvard alumni bul., 55:558-9 (4 Apr 1953). port. On Walter Prichard Eaton, Harvard 1900, as a writer for the Boston Journal, dramatic critic for several newspapers, and Chairman of the Department of Drama, Yale University, and his work in promoting conservation in New England. [6811

WILL F. THOMPSON. The shape of New England mountains. Appalachia, 33:145-59 (Dec). views. bibliog., notes. On "geomorphic theories about New England mountains," 1900-1960. Based on thesis--Clark Univ. [6812

CHANNING HARRIS COX. Some reminiscences of Channing H. Cox, '01, "as I remember ...": an interview by Edward Connery Lathem. Dartmouth alumni mag., 52(4):23-7, 36 (Jan). ports. On his studies at Dartmouth College, his activities in Massachusetts politics, and his work as a lawyer and Justice of the Massachusetts Superior Court. [6813

WALTER E. SCOTT. Working on the J. T. Morse. Steamboat bill, 17:36-7 (summer). view. Two letters to Jay Allen, Aug. 1957 and Jun. 1959, on the author's work between "the handles of freight trucks and coal carts" on the steamer J. T. Morse, running between Boston and Maine, in or after 1904. [6814

HELEN (HARTNESS) FLANDERS, ed. Ancient ballads traditionally sung in New England. From the Helen Hartness Flanders Ballad Collection, Middlebury College, Middlebury, Vt. ... Correlated with the numbered Francis James Child Collection. Volume I. Ballads 1-51. Critical analyses by Tristram P. Coffin. Music annotations by Bruno Nettl. Phila.: Univ. of Pennsylvania Press, 1960. 343, [1] p. music, tables. From a collection that contains "close to 9,000 other traditional songs," gathered between 1930 and 1956, mainly from elderly persons who had learned the songs in childhood from elderly persons. Includes 25 "Child ballads," some in more than one version. Each ballad is introduced by an extensive headnote dealing with text and tune. [6815

JOSEPH E. GARLAND. An experiment in medicine: the first twenty years of the Pratt Clinic and the New England Center Hospital of Boston. Cambridge, Mass.: Riverside Press [1960. 2], ix, [5], 107 p. map, view. notes. On the Joseph H. Pratt Diagnostic Hospital and the New England Center Hospital, Boston, and preliminary related activities in Maine, 1931-60. [6816

U.S. Fish and Wildlife Service. Decline of the yellowtail flounder (Limanda ferruginea) off New England [1932-52]. By William F. Royce, Raymond J. Buller, and Ernest D. Prometz. Wash.: U.S. Govt. Print. Off., 1959. iv, 169-267 p. diagrs., maps, tables. notes. (Its Fishery bulletin 146.) [6817

ARTHUR HARRISON COLE. The social significance of New England idiomatic phrases. Am. Antiq. Soc., Proc., 70:21-68 (Apr). notes. On New England characteristics implied by the similes and metaphors in New England speech. Appended (p. 44-68): "A collection of typical New England similes and metaphors" (lacks citations and dates). [6818

FRANK O. SPINNEY. You are closer than you think. New-Eng. galaxy, 1(2): 35-7 (fall). Information from elderly New Englanders received by them in their early youth from grandparents and other elderly persons--"direct-line, firsthand, eyewitness reports of how people lived in New England a century and a quarter ago." [6819

MAINE

SAMUEL ELIOT MORISON. The story of Mount Desert Island, Maine [1525-1960]. Boston: Little, Brown [1960]. viii, [4], 81 p. map, ports., views. bibliog. (p. 67-70), notes. [6820

MAINE WRITERS RESEARCH CLUB. The Maine islands, in story and legend [since ca. 1600]. By Dorothy Simpson. From material compiled by the Maine Writers Research Club. Phila.: Lippincott [1960]. 256 p. maps (1 double), table. bibliog. (p. 226-7). Individual histories of 30 islands or groups of islands, selected from "some two thousand islands along the coast of Maine." Appended (p. 228-43): "The tidewater islands of Maine," a list by Lilliam W. Lewis. The names of the 30 members of the Maine Writers Research Club who contributed to this volume are listed in "Acknowledgments" (p. 223-4). Dorothy Simpson's name is not included. [6821

CHARLES BARTLETT FOBES. Blackstrap Hill. Appalachia, 33:72-5 (Jun). view. bibliog. History of a "low eminence" (503 ft. above sea level) in Falmouth, Me., otherwise known as Mt. Independence, 1616-1959, and the structures on its summit. [6822

GEORGE B. RICHARSON. History of Bustins Island, Casco Bay [Me.], 1660-1960. Bustins Island, ©1960. [11], 84 p. maps, ports., views. [6823

JOSEPH A. PERHAM. The legend of Molly Ockett [1715-1816]. Northeast folklore, 3:1-9 (spring). notes. On a "princess" of the Pequawkett tribe of the Abenaki Indians, known also as Mollylocket, Mollyrocket, and Mollynocket, born probably at the site of Fryeburg, Me., reared in Canada and Maine, mother of a halfbreed daughter and 3 Indian children, resident in her later years of Fryeburg, Bethel, and Andover, "a great traveler," a Christian convert (baptized Mary Agatha), and the subject of many legends. [6824

DANIEL MOULTON. Note abstracted from a notorial record kept by Daniel Moulton of York, Maine, 1746-1784. ... Contributed by L. W. Jenkins. Am. Neptune, 20:43, 67, 103, 111, 117, 145, 190, 216, 236, 249, 269 (Jan-Oct). Selected entries of maritime interest. [6825

B. H. LEFFINGWELL. Ye Olde Stagecoach Homestead, Kennebunk, Maine. Hobbies, 65(4):88-9 (Jun). view. On a "pre-Revolutionary house," originally known as Barnard's Inn, later Towles' Tavern and Frost Tavern, still used as an inn; with an inventory of its contents in 1818. [6826

ALTON ACKLEY NORTON. Moosabec manvelins. [n. p., 1950. 8], 140, [5] p. Anecdotes, family lore, and documents relating to the descendants of Seth Norton, who settled in Maine in 1770, and particularly to the Nortons and their neighbors in and near West Jonesport, Me., and the author's grandfather, Ackley Norton, sea captain, member of George J. Adam's colony at Indian River, Me., who emigrated with the colony to Jaffa, Palestine, in 1866, composed "Sketches of a journey through Syria" in Apr. 1867 (p. 113-30), and wrote poems (several here printed); with some account of the descendants of Ackley Norton in Manistique, Mich., and the author's boyhood memories of fishing and boats in Lake Michigan. [6827

SAMUEL R. WEBBER. Early days in Maine surgery [1775-1865]. New Eng. jour. med., 260-167-9 (22 Jan 1959). notes. [6828

B. H. LEFFINGWELL. Montpelier, the home of General Henry Knox at Thomaston, Me. Hobbies, 65(6):58-9 (Aug). views. On a house built "after the war" and torn down in 1871, the replica of its constructed in 1929-31, and the furnishings of the present house, administered by the Knox Memorial Association. [6829

BURTON W. F. TRAFTON, JR. Hamilton House, South Berwick, Maine [built in 1787 for Col. Jonathan Hamilton]. Antiques, 77:486-9 (May). views. [6830

CLEMENT ELLERY VOSE. The Executive Council of Maine in decline. Brunswick, Me., 1959. 25 p. port. (Bowdoin College. Bureau for Research in Municipal Government. Government research series, 21.) On "an executive council selected by the legislature to check the governor's power," 1820-1959, and its functions as "a confirmation board," "a pardon board," and "an insurance agency." [6831

CONSTANCE CAROLYN MURRAY. Portland, Maine, and the growth of urban responsibility for human welfare, 1830-1860. Ann Arbor: University Microfilms, 1960. Positive microfilm of typescript. [457] leaves. Thesis--Boston Univ. Abstracted: Dissert. abstracts, 21:866-7 (Oct). [6832

FANNIE (HARDY) ECKSTORM (1865-1946). Notes on Thoreau's "Maine woods" [1864]. Thoreau Soc. bul., 51:[1, 3] (spring 1955). Notes in "my old first edition of the 'Maine Woods,'" containing information from her father about persons, places, and events named or alluded to in the book, which is a record of Thoreau's visit to Maine in 1853. [6833

HENRY EDWARD CLEPPER. The Parmachenee Belle. Am. forests, 62(3):12-13, 56-7 (Mar 1956). ports. On fishing in Parmachenee Lake, Me., 1876-1956, and a "trout fly" or "lure" designed by Henry P. Wells ca. 1877-78. [6834

EDWARD D. IVES. The life and work of Larry Gorman: a preliminary report. West. folklore, 19:17-23 (Jan). notes. On Lawrence Gorman (1846-1917), native of Prince Edward Island, emigrant to Maine ca. 1885, lumberjack and "yard hand" in a paper mill, composer of satirical songs, but not "a hard-drinking, two-fisted, golden-voiced bushman." [6835

CHARLES FRANCIS HITCHCOCK ALLEN. Ten-wheelers of the Maine Central [built 1888-1923]. Natl. Railway Hist. Soc., Bul., 25(4):18-23 (4th quar.). views. [6836

E. BOYD LIVESAY. Development of ground-water supplies for the Brunswick and Topsham Water District [Maine, 1903-60]. New Eng. Water Works Assoc., Jour., 74:89-112 (Jun). diagrs., maps, table. [6837

JOHN WILLIAM ASHTON. Marble-playing in Lewiston fifty years ago. Northeast folklore, 3:24-7 (summer). Recollections of "1909 or '10." [6838

PAUL J. FOURNIER. Little planes--big business. Flying, 65(2):46-7, 64-6 (Aug 1959). views. On the use of aircraft in operations of the Maine Woodlands Department of the International Paper Company, 1946-59. [6839

RICHARD G. SMITH. A forest recovers. Am. forests, 66(3):29-30, 53-4 (Mar). views (1 double). On a forest fire on Mount Desert Island, Me., in 1947, and the reforestation of the damaged area. [6840

WALTER RANCO. A Penobscot Indian story of colonial Maine. [Reported] by Nicholas N. Smith. Northeast folklore, 3:10-11 (spring). Tale collected in 1952 from Ranco, a Penobscot, about "an old man that was very hard to get along with" and "a young fellow who had a quick temper," their agreement that the first to lose his temper would have a strip cut off his back wide enough to make a belt," the efforts of each to anger the other, and the collection of the strip by the young man. [6841

GEORGE K. SMITH, JR. A sampling of stories from the area of Machias, Maine. Northeast folklore, 3:39-52 (fall-winter). Twenty-eight anecdotes and legends, presented as "a sample of a much wider gathering made during the fall of 1960 in and around Machias." [6842

NEW HAMPSHIRE

DEBORAH BLOSSOM. Home of the month. N.H. profiles, 9(1-12): monthly installments (Jan-Dec). views. Accounts of restored old houses in various parts of New Hampshire, particularly their interiors and present furnishings. [6843

The SHORT and simple annals of the poor. N.H. profiles, 9(10):28-33 (Oct). views. On old New Hampshire cemeteries and gravestones. [6844

E. HAROLD YOUNG. Suncook Valley [since Indian times]. N.H. profiles, 9(3):28-37 (Mar). views. Includes a section on "The general store." [6845

LOUIS PICHIERRI. Music in New Hampshire, 1623-1800. N.Y.: Columbia Univ. Press, 1960. xv, 297 p. bibliog. (p. 271-81), notes (p. 245-69). Based on thesis--Syracuse Univ. Includes chapters on John Hubbard, Benjamin Dearborn, and Samuel Holyoke, and information on the teaching of music. [6846

The STORY of Exeter Towne. N.H. profiles, 9(1):26-39 (Jan). ports., views. History of Exeter, N.H., "and the sundry Townes which were once Part & Parcel of it," 1638-1960, by Dan Ford; of Phillips Exeter Academy, 1895-1960, by Paul E. Estaver; and of "country correspondents" of Exeter newspapers. [6847

FRANK ALLEN BURT. The story of Mount Washington [1642-1948]. Hanover, N.H.: Dartmouth Publications, 1960. [12], 303 p. diagr., facsims., col. maps, ports., views. notes p. 251-79). On the early settlement of the area, the development of recreational businesses there, and its use in meteorological and aerological studies. [6848

W. P. DUDLEY. History in houses: the Garrison House, Exeter, New Hampshire. Antiques, 78:131-3 (Aug). views. On a house built by Edward Gilman as a "fortified dwelling" of logs ca. 1647, later enclosed and expanded by frame additions, now preserved as a "house museum." [6849

Mrs. NORMA M. CURRIER. New Hampshire women [since 1689]. D. A. R. mag., 94:272-4, 329 (Apr). [6850

HOWARD TREDENNICK OEDEL. Portsmouth, New Hampshire: the role of the provincial capital in the development of the colony (1700-1775). Ann Arbor: University Microfilms, 1960. Positive microfilm of typescript. [1003] leaves. Thesis--Boston Univ. Abstracted: Dissert. abstracts, 21:1169 (Nov). [6851

ALICE POLLARD. The valley of the Connecticut [in New Hampshire]. N.H. profiles, 9(6):16-21 (Jun). map, views. On the history of the area, 1714-1848. 6852

HATTIE WITCOMB TAYLOR. Early history of the town of Bethlehem, N.H. [ca. 1774 to 1917. Bethlehem? N.H.] c1960. 48 p. map, ports., views. [6853

KENNETH SCOTT. Tory associators of Portsmouth. Wm. and Mary quar., 17:507-15 (Oct). table. notes. On a group of 59 Tories organized by John Wentworth, Governor of New Hampshire, and armed by him to protect his person and the royal government, Jan.-Jun. 1775, and their tribulations after his flight. [6854

Mrs. CYE A. DENNIS. A glimpse of East Lebanon as it used to be [1778 ff.]. Lebanon Hist. Soc., Ann. report, 1 (1959), leaves [15-18]. [6855

FRANK O. SPINNEY. A school-house plant on every hill. New-Eng. galaxy, 1(4):34-7 (spring). views. Description, history, and photographs of a small wooden schoolhouse built in Candia, N.H., ca. 1780-90, used continuousy without major structural alteration till 1879 or later, dismantled in 1955, and removed to Old Sturbridge Village. [6856

JEANETTE PROSSER. The Shakers of Canterbury. N.H. profiles, 9(8): 26-30 (Aug). On the present condition of this community (11 members), including buildings erected as early as 1793; with an account of Sister Alice, a member since 1904. [6857

GEORGE HUNTSTON WILLIAMS. The seminary in the wilderness: a representative episode in the cultural history of northern New England. Harv. Lib. bul., 13:369-400; 14:27-58 (autumn 1959, winter 1960). facsims., map, ports., views. notes. On Gilmanton Seminary, a Congregational institution in Gilmanton, N.H., 1835-46; with some account of Gilmanton Academy, 1794 ff. [6858

MARJORIE WHALEN SMITH. "Take notice." N.H. profiles, 9(7):28-9, 39 (Jul). facsims. On advertisements and public notices in New Hampshire newspapers, 1794-1836. [6859

JOHN E. REID. The arena of the giants: Rockingham County, New Hampshire. Am Bar Assoc. jour., 46: 163-6, 214-16 (Feb). ports. Anecdotes of the Rockingham County bar when Jeremiah Smith, Jeremiah Mason, George Sullivan, Ichabod Bartlett, Daniel Webster, and other "strong men" were among its members, 1797-1824. [6860

HELEN COMSTOCK. The Barrett house in New Ipswich, New Hampshire [built for Charles Barrett, Jr., ca. 1800]. Antiques, 77:476-81 (May). views (part col.). On its architecture, its restoration after 1948, and its present furnishings. [6861

CHARLES S. PARSONS. Examples of New Hampshire timepieces [ca. 1800 to ca. 1850]. Natl. Assoc. Watch and Clock Collectors, Bul., 9:362-9 (Oct). diagrs. bibliog. Mainly on mirror or looking-glass clocks. [6862

LOUISE K. ANDERSON. Franklin Pierce and the Pierce mansion. D. A. R. mag., 94:374-5 (May). views. On a house in Hillsboro, N.H., built in 1804, in which the future President was born in the same year. [6863

DANIEL F. FORD. Dan'l Webster's Dartmouth. New-Eng. galaxy, 2(2): 22-7 (fall). port., seal, view. On the schism splitting Dartmouth College from Dartmouth University, the services of Daniel Webster in the Dartmouth College Case, and the death of Dartmouth University, 1814-19. [6864

MAURICE GLEN BAXTER. Should the Dartmouth College Case [1819] have been reargued? New Eng. quar., 33: 19-36 (Mar). notes. On the inadequate consideration of the question whether the College was a private or a public corporation. [6865

STEPHEN T. WHITNEY. Nine covered bridges [in New Hampshire, built 1829-85]. N.H. profiles, 9(8):32-5 (Aug). map, views. [6866

SHIRLEY FRANCES BARKER. The siege of the wolves. N.H. profiles, 9(11):26-7 (Nov). On an invasion of Sandwich, N.H., by wolves, 14 Nov. 1830. [6867

BRADFORD FULLER SWAN. Joseph Seavey Hall [1818-99], White Mountain guide. Appalachia, 33:57-71 (Jun). ports., view. notes. On his services from 1835 to 1861 in the vicinity of Mount Washington and Crawford's Notch as guide, road-builder, hotel-keeper, etc.; with several of his reminiscent letters from Among the clouds. [6868

PHILBROOK PAINE. Alias "Plupy" Shute. N.H. profiles, 9(2):17-18, 44-5 (Feb). ports. On Henry Augustus Shute (1856-1943) of Exeter, Judge of the Exeter Police Court, author of humorous books for boys and farmers, clarinettist, storyteller. [6869

EVELYN (EATON) CONVERSE. The obsolete art of walking. N.H. profiles, 9(5):28-9, 48 (May). view. On the author's father, Daniel E. Eaton (1858?-1951), banker in Meredith, N.H., inveterate walker in the neighborhood of Lake Winnipesaukee, and "the relaxation, the joyous, leisurely quality of life and the peace of mind which he embodied." [6870

LAURENCE FREDERICK WHITTEMORE & HENRY W. MUNRO. JR. Suncook Depot. N.H. profiles, 9(4):22-3 (Apr). view. On the Suncook Valley Railroad, 1869-1952. [6871

CLARENCE N. ROGERS. Boat-train service on Lake Winnipesaukee. Steamboat bill, 17:17-19 (spring). views. On the steamboat Mountain Washington, operated on the lake by the Boston & Maine Railroad, 1872-1930, and by Capt. Leander La Vallee till her destruction by fire in 1939, and her successor, Mount Washington II, operating in 1960 with diesel engines. [6872

DIARY of a death. [Edited] by Beatrice Vaughan. N.H. profiles, 9(2):26-7 (Feb). Anonymous diary kept "up Littleton way," apparently by a young mother of a 3-year-old daughter and wife of "Nathan," recording her gradual loss of strength with the progress of an unnamed disease, Jan.-May 1877. [6873

ARTHUR STANLEY PEASE. Early trailmakers at Randolph and the founding of the R. M. C. Appalachia, 33:187-99 (Dec). Memories of Randolph, N.H., and the "pathmakers" there since the 1880s, and of the Randolph Mountain Club, founded in 1910. [6874

CHARLES DENNIS SMITH. The mountain lover mourns: origins of the movement for a White Mountain National Forest, 1880-1903. New Eng. quar., 33:37-56 (Mar). notes. [6875

C. MIFFLIN FROTHINGHAM. The story of Pasquaney, 1895-1960. [n. p.:] Murphy & Snyder [1960]. x, 188, [2] p. map, ports., views. On a summer camp for boys, on the shore of Newfound Lake near Plymouth, N.H., founded by Edward S. Wilson on land given by his father. Consists largely of letters and reminiscences of boys who have stayed there and of their parents. Includes the author's reminiscences since 1895. [6876

ROBERTS W. FRENCH. Fifty years of the DOC. Dartmouth alumni mag., 52(5):18-24 (Feb). ports., seal, views. On the Dartmouth Outing Club, 1900-1960. [6877

SUMNER KEAN. Father held the reins. N.H. profiles, 9(8):43-7 (Aug). Memories of Peter Roche, New Hampshire horse trainer, "early 1900's." [6878

WALTER SANBORN. Epping album, 1900-1915. N.H. profiles, 9(2):32-5 (Feb). views. Eleven photographs (taken on glass plates) and reminiscent text, by an almost lifelong resident of Epping, N.H. [6879

ANDREW JACKSON SCARLETT. The fifty-year address. Dartmouth alumni mag., 52(10):234 (Jul). port. Reminiscences of Dartmouth College, 1906-10. [6880

KENNETH DUPEE SWAN. Skyline sketch: two summers at Madison Hut. Appalachia, 33:82-6 (Jun). On the author's service as hutmaster of the Madison Spring Hut of the Appalachian Mountain Club, Randolph, N.H., 1909 and 1910. [6881

The BEST of Orne. N.H. profiles, 9(4):10-15 (Apr). port., views. On the work of Harold Orne as a photographer of New Hampshire scenes since 1912. [6882

ALDIS J. CHRISTIE. Forestry at Manchester Water Works--fact or fancy. New Eng. Water Works Assoc., Jour., 74:46-56 (Mar). On the tree-planting, sustained-yield forestry program of the Manchester, N.H., Water Board to protect its water supply in Massabesic Lake, 1913-59. [6883

ELAINE DILL EDWARDS. Before Hollywood: George Mills. N.H. profiles, 9(5):30-31, 39 (May). On the life of Billy B. Van, vaudeville comedian, in Georges Mills and Newport, N.H., from several years before 1915 till his death in 1950; his farm and large dance hall at Georges Mills; and his establishment there of a studio of the Equity Motion Picture Company of New York, ordered by the town to leave when the too scanty costumes of some of the actresses received unfavorable attention. [6884

ALTON HALL BLACKINGTON. The eccentric Dr. Cobb. N.H. profiles, 9(11):16-18 (Nov). port., view. Anecdotes of George E. Rewitzer (died 1948), of Hill's Corner, Blue Job Mountain, North Strafford, N.H., country contributor to the Rochester, N.H., Courier, ca. 1916 till his death. [6885

DANIEL F. FORD. The tradition of family doctoring. N.H. profiles, 9(3): 38-9 (Mar). ports. On the medical practice of Dr. Benjamin Freeman and 4 other physicians in the Suncook Valley since 1918. [6886

PAUL E. ESTAVER. Rum, riches, and revenues. N.H. profiles, 9(7):22-3, 39-43 (Jul). view. On rum-running along the New Hampshire coast, 1919-33. [6887

WINSTON POTE. Old time winter. N.H. profiles, 9(1):10-15 (Jan). views. On winter sports in the snows of New Hampshire, 1920s. [6888

M. ALICE NORMANDIN. Group practice in a small community. Am. Med. Women's Assoc., Jour., 15-1075-7 (Nov). On the author's participation in the Laconia, N.H., Clinic, 1922-60. [6889

PHILBROOK PAINE & PAUL E. ESTAVER. Scattergood Stapleton. N.H. profiles, 9(4):24-5, 41, 43 (Apr). ports., view. Anecdotes of Ed Stapleton as owner of the Suncook Valley Railroad, State representative from Pittsfield, municipal judge of Pittsfield, member of its school board, etc., 1924-60. [6890

WINSTON POTE. The last climb of Old Peppersass. N.H. profiles, 9(8): 16-23 (Aug). views. On a cableless 2-cylinder locomotive designed to operate on the cog railroad on Mt. Washington, 1866-77, retired to a museum, and exhibited for the last time in 1929, when it collapsed in service and "plunged to its destruction"; with the author's recollections of this event, in which a man was killed. [6891

WINSTON POTE. Alpine adventure. N.H. profiles, 9(2):10-16 (Feb). views. On the author's repeated efforts, eventually successful, to photograph skiers in action in the Presidential Range of New Hampshire, 1935-40. [6892

JAMES BURKE FISHER. Students from abroad [in Dartmouth College, 1945-59]. Dartmouth alumni mag., 52(3):258 (Dec 1959). ports. [6893

ROBERT C. HOPKINS. The Cardigan Mountain School: history, 1945 to 1960. [Canaan, N.H.:] Cardigan Mountain School [1960]. 149 p. ports., tables, views. On a private elementary school for boys. [6894

CLARENCE E. FERRY. Water-department planning. New Eng. Water Works Assoc., Jour., 74:35-45 (Mar). diagrs., map. Includes some account of the Manchester, N.H., Water Department, 1948-59. [6895

VERMONT

JOHN H. BAILEY. A ground slate producing site near Vergennes, Vermont. John Charles Huden, ed., Archeology in Vermont (Burlington: Univ. of Vermont, 1960), p. 7-23. notes. From Bulletin of the Champlain Valley Archaeological Society, Jun. 1939. On the artifacts found and the culture of which they are evidences. [6896

HOLMAN FRANCIS DAY (1865-1935). Aunt Shaw's pet jug. Vt. Hist. Soc., News and notes, 6:6-7 (Sep 1954). Verses by a Maine newspaperman, written "many years ago"; with editorial comments on Vermont versions of a tale "about the old fellow who grew tired of the nagging of his wife when he went down cellar with her pet pitcher to draw some cider." [6897

GRANDMOTHER'S goose feather bed. Vt. Hist. Soc., News and notes, 3:77 (Jun 1952). Verses (author unidentified) formerly recited by a graduate of the Normal School at Randolph Center, Vt., as copied by her daughter. [6898

JOHN CHARLES HUDEN, ed. Archaeology in Vermont: some reviews, supplemented by materials from New England and New York. Burlington, 1960. [6], 107 p. views. (University of Vermont. Monograph 3.) Reprinted articles and reviews by various persons about prehistoric archeology in Vermont, 1858-1942. [6899

MURIEL JOY HUGHES, comp. Vermont proverbs and proverbial sayings. Vt. hist., 28:113-42, 200-230 (Apr, Jul). bibliog. [6900

BURGES JOHNSON. Unnatural history notes from Fiddler's Rest. Vt. Hist. Soc., News and notes, 2(9), 3(2, 5), 5(3), 6(6): scattered installments (May 1951 - Feb 1955). On the rubber-neck owl, the riveter-raven, the razoo, the horsehair snake, the uniped, the oomfph and the whappit (with verses about these two), and the whiffet or whiffitt (a flying rabbit), reported as fauna of Vermont. [6901

ROBERT LOUIS PICHER. The Franco-Americans in Vermont [since 1666]. Vt. hist., 28-59-62 (Jan). [6902

LOUISE E. KOIER. Journey to Guilford: Vermont's only independent republic town passes its second century [1754-1954]. Vt. Hist. Soc., News and notes, 5:57-9 (Apr 1954). views. [6903

MARGUERITE MURREY WOLF. The daughter of Dr. Jonas Fay. Vt. Hist. Soc., News and notes, 9:63-5 (Apr 1958). On Susannah (Fay) Fay (1769-1862?), native of Bennington, resident of Burlington after her marriage to her cousin, John Fay, as recorded in papers found in an attic. [6904

CARLO WOLTER. Whitingham [Vt., 1770-1951]. Vt. Hist. Soc., News and notes, 9:1-3 (Sep 1957). [6905

ALLYN R. SCOTT & CHARLES H. SCOTT. The story of Independence stand: a bit of furniture and much history. Vt. Hist. Soc., News and notes, 3:9-11 (Oct 1951). view. On "Resolutions or Declaration of Rights uttered at Chester, Vermont, October 10, 1774," an affirmation of the declaration dated 2 Sep. 1776, the "little stand of wood" on which the affirmation was signed, and the series of owners through whom the stand came into possession of the Vermont Historical Society. [6906

JAMES O'BEIRNE. Some early Irish in Vermont [1776-1840s]. Vt. hist., 28:63-72 (Jan). notes. [6907

TWO men and an anniversary. Vt. Hist. Soc., News and notes, 4:37-8 (Jan 1953). view. On Dr. Jonas Fay (born 1737) of Bennington, clerk of the Vermont conventions of 1776 and 1777, his record of the conventions in an account book which Henry Dawson borrowed in the 19th century and mutilated by cutting out the leaves recording the conventions, the discovery of the stolen leaves in 1903 in the Library of Congress by Senator Redfield Proctor, and their receipt by the Vermont Historical Society. [6908

OUR legislatures: two glimpses--1778 and 1953. Vt. Hist. Soc., News and notes, 4:51-3 (Mar 1953). views. [6909

HOW the wolf saved the spoons. Vt. Hist. Soc., News and notes, 8:51-2 (Apr 1957). On a silver spoon; with verses telling how bounty money from the killing of a wolf was used to pay taxes, which otherwise could have been paid only by selling a set of "six little spoons." [6910

LOUISE E. KOIER. "Some have meat": a glance at bygone Thanksgivings [Vermount, 1784-1840]. Vt. Hist. Soc., News and notes, 5:18-21 (Nov 1953). [6911

ARTHUR WALLACE PEACH. The forgotten Mrs. Allen. New Eng. teacher, 3(5):14-15 (Jun 1956). On the marriages of Frances Buchanan to Ethan Allen at Westminster, Vt., 1784, and, after his death, to Jabez Penniman of Colchester, Vt. [6912

LOUISE E. KOIER. Man overshadowed by a horse: Justin Morgan [1747-98], composer and teacher. Vt. Hist. Soc., News and notes, 6:81-4 (Jul 1955). views. On his life in Randolph Center, Vt., 1788-98, his work as a composer of hymns and a singing-master and as an officeholder, and his ownership of the studhorse Figure, commonly known by his master's name, ancestor of the breed of Morgan horses. [6913

ROYALL TYLER (1757-1826). A Christmas hymn, composed by the Hon. Royall Tyler, Chief Justice of the State of Vermont, and sung at Claremont, N.H., 1793. Vt. Hist. Soc., News & notes, 2(4):1-2 (Dec 1950). facsim., port. Facsimile reproduction of an undated broadside, and reference to "the Royall Tyler collection of manuscripts" in the library of the Vermont Historical Society. [6914

H. F. CROCKER. The Vermont year book. Vt. Hist. Soc., News and notes, 8:68 (Jun 1957). On "the various titles and publishers" of this publication, first issued in 1794 as Vermont almanac & register. [6915

OZIAH D. MATHEWSON. The passing of the pound. Vt. Hist. Soc., News and notes, 8:66-7 (Jun 1957). On pound keepers and pounds in Vermont, 1796-1810. [6916

E. DONALD ASSELIN. Uriah Skinner: Vermont's greatest smuggler. Vt. Hist. Soc., News and notes, 8:75-6 (Jul 1957). Undated lore about the gigantic stature and strength of a resident of Newport, Vt. (early 19th century). [6917

AMOS J. EATON. Memories from the elder years: notes from a letter. Vt. Hist. Soc., News and notes, 3:28-9 (Dec 1951). Family traditions of Barton, Vt., 19th century, mainly about Indians and bears. [6918

PAMELA GEE. The money diggings of Pocock. Vt. hist., 28:302-8 (Oct). bibliog., notes. On excavations for buried treasure in South Mountain, Bristol, Vt., 1800-1860 and ca. 1934. [6919

MADISON CLAIR BATES (1881-1961). Sir Curtis Lampson, Vermont baronet. Vt. hist., 28:3-21 (Jan). notes. On the early life of Curtis Miranda Lampson (1806-85) in New Haven, Vt., from which he removed ca. 1823 to Canada and in 1830 to England, where he became an official of the Hudson's Bay Company. [6920

LLOYD SAVILLE. Patterns in local finance: the case of Orleans County, Vermont [1810-1950]. Natl. tax jour., 12:163-78 (Jun 1959). diagr., tables. notes. Deals particularly with the fiscal history of Irasburg. [6921

REUBEN TOWLE & SARAH TOWLE. Entering the promised land. [Contributed] by Lewis H. Flint. Vt. Hist. Soc., News and notes, 8:73-4 (Jul 1957). Letter dated Huntsburgh [now Franklin], Vt., 23 Mar. 1815, to relatives, from recent settlers who had come from Enfield. [6922

LOUISE E. KOIER. A "tourist" of 1817: President Monroe's visit to Vermont. Vt. Hist. Soc., News and notes, 5:81-4 (Jul 1954). view. [6923

ARTHUR WALLACE PEACH. The white symbols of the Vermonter's faith: the story of a church. Vt. Hist. Soc., News & notes, 2(12);3-5 (Aug 1951). view. On Christ Church, Guilford, the first Episcopal church in Vermont, 1817-1951. [6924

The GENERAL's return and farewell: Lafayette visits Vermont in 1825. Vt. Hist., Soc., News and notes, 31:1-3 (Sep 1951). ports. [6925

STAGECOACH ways and days: Vermont routes 125 years ago. Vt. Hist. Soc., News and notes, 7:33-7 (Jan 1956). views. On the post roads of Vermont ca. 1825. [6926

LYNNE WEBSTER. The history of the Burlington Free press [since 1827]. Vt. hist., 28:143-7 (Apr). bibliog., notes. [6927

ROWLAND E. ROBINSON (1833-1900), Vermont's beloved story-teller: a glimpse of him and his work. Vt. Hist. Soc., News and notes, 3:33-6 (Jan 1952). port. [6928

OLNEY W. HILL. Abraham Brinsmaid [Vermont silversmith]. Vt. Hist. Soc., News and notes, 9:14-15 (Oct

1957). Information about his family and associates, 1834-1955. [6929

LOUISE E. KOIER. Here comes the train! Windsor's great railroad celebration of 1849. Vt. Hist. Soc., News and notes, 6:1-3 (Sep 1954). view. [6930

LEONARD DEMING (1787-1853). Letters of Leonard Deming, 1852. Edited by P. H. Hardacre. Vt. hist., 28:197-9 (Jul). Two questionnaries and a letter for collecting information for a second edition of the author's Catalogue of the principal officers of Vermont (Middlebury, 1851). Apparently the second edition was never published. [6931

LOUISE E. KOIER. The Pied Piper of Pawlet: Mr. Stoddard's steam calliope. Vt. Hist. Soc., News and notes, 4:74-5 (Jun 1953). On Joshua C. Stoddard (born 1814), who invented the steam calliope in 1856; with an account of the Forepaugh Sells Bros. circus as exhibited in Vermont in June 1899. [6932

LOUISE E. KOIER. One hundred years of history at the State House [Montpelier, 1857-1955]. Vt. Hist. Soc., News and notes, 6:41-5 (Feb 1955). views. [6933

LOUISE E. KOIER. Vermont's Father Christmas: the tale of a famous carol. Vt. Hist. Soc., News and notes, 5:25-7 (Dec 1953). port. On John Henry Hopkins, Jr., composer of "We three kings of Orient are" (Christmas of 1857). [6934

"The LORDS of creation." Vt. Hist. Soc., News and notes, 6:20-21 (Nov 1954). music. Folk song recalled by Herbert S. Eaton (born ca. 1861), a native of rural Vermont. [6935

ENNA BATES. A Vermont spring and a cure for cancer. Vt. Hist. Soc., News and notes, 3:49-52 (Mar 1952). facsim., views. On supposedly medicinal springs in Vermont and associated hotels and bottled water, especially the several springs at Sheldon, Vt., 1865 ff. [6936

EDWARD L. TRACY. Burlington water quality and treatment-plant operation [Vermont, 1866-1959]. New Eng. Water Works Assoc., Jour., 74:113-23 (Jun). tables. [6937

GORDON PARKER MANNING. Life in the Colchester Reef Lighhouse. Shelburne, Vt.: Shelburne Museum [1958. 4], 43 p. facsim., map, plans, views. On an installation of the U.S. Lighthouse Service in Lake Champlain a mile off Colchester Point, Vt., built in 1871, decommissioned in 1933, sold in 1952, and dismantled, transported piecemeal, and reassembled as part of the Shelburne Museum. [6938

DOROTHY MAYO HARVEY. The Swedes in Vermont [since 1872]. Vt. hist., 28:39-58 (Jan). tables. notes. Reprinted with revisions and additions: Am. Swed. Hist. Found., Yr. bk., 1960, p. 23-43. bibliog., notes. [6939

JOHN STREETER (1862/64-1942?). The "Vermont panther" won't stay dead. Vt. Hist. Soc., News & notes, 2(2):3-5 (Oct 1950). Recollections (presented before the Windham County Historical Society) of the killing of a panther near West Wardsboro, Vt., in 1875. For further references to panthers killed in Vermont, see 2(5):6-7 (Jan 1951) 3-13-14 (Oct 1951). [6940

PAUL E. ESTAVER. Shiff the Gunman. N.H. profiles, 9(5):20-22, 46 (May). port., view. On Carroll B. Shiffer (1878/79-1951), rural recluse in Woodstock, Vt., mail-order dealer in guns, eccentric; with anecdotes and legends about him as early as 1919. [6941

WALTE R. HARD, SR. Only yesterday: a remembrance of Vermont. Vt. life, 14(3):29-30 (spring). view. Memories of the annual "period known as Mud Time" at the beginning of spring in rural Vermont, 1880s-1930s. [6942

MARI TOMASI. The Italian story in Vermont. Vt. hist., 28:73-87 (Jan). notes. On the Italians in Vermont since 1882. [6943

WALTER R. HARD, JR. & STEPHEN GREENE. The man who wouldn't be bored. Vt. life, 14(2):52-8 (winter). map, port., views. On Clarence A. Adams (1857-1904?), respected citizen of Chester, Vt., who committed 51 burglaries in that area between 1886 and 1902 and was supposed to have died in prison but may have escaped to Canada, leaving in the prison a corpse that was incorrectly identified as his. [6944

DANA WINGATE KELLEY. The Frank Orcutt I knew. Morgan horse mag., 20(10):6, 50 (Nov). port. On Franklin C. Orcutt (died 1960), of West Burke, Vt., breeder of Morgan horses (beginning ca. 1900). [6945

JOAN MARTIN. Forward on skis! Vt. hist., 28:33-8 (Jan). bibliog. On skiing in Vermont since 1907. [6946

GEORGE HENRY PERKINS (1844-1933). History and condition of the State Cabinet Indian relics, 1908-1910. John Charles Huden, ed., Archaeology in Vermont (Burlington: Univ. of Vermont, 1960), p. 44-64. views. On archeological work in Vermont and the information about the Indians which it yielded. [6947

JOHN CHARLES HUDEN, ed. Leslie B. Truax. John Charles Huden, ed., Archaeology in Vermont (Burlington, 1960 [University of Vermont, Monograph 3]), p. 65-77. tables, views. bibliog. "The Indians," by Truax, from the St. Albans, Vt., Messenger, 1914, on relics of Indian habitation in Vermont and Massachusetts; "The Truax Collection," by Horace Eldred, 21 Jan. 1935, on a collection of "Vermont Indian material" gathered by Truax in 60 years of exploring in Franklin and Grand Isle Counties; and list of the collection. [6948

ERNEST FENWICK JOHNSTONE (1867-1938). No Vermonters in Heaven. Vt. Hist. Soc., News and notes, 5:68-9 (May 1954). Poem by a Vermont dentist, "probably ... the most popular poem ever written about Vermont," Composed in 1914. [6949

VERMONT HISTORICAL SOCIETY. Flood headlines of 1927. Vt. Hist. Soc., News and notes, 9:17-24 (Nov 1957). facsim., views. Recollections by Herbert Hoover, Charles B. Adams, Arthur W. Hewitt, Leon S. Gay, and Charles Crane, of disastrous floods in and near the Winooski Valley, Nov. 1927. [6950

SIDNEY CHANDLER HAYWARD. Paul Semple, Vermont artist. Vt. life, 14(2):46-50 (winter). ports., views (part col.). On his work as a painter of Vermont landscapes since 1938. [6951

[HUMAN refrigeration in Vermont. Submitted by James Smith.] Northeast folklore, 3:53-5 (fall-winter). Taken by Smith from "a recent issue of the Rutland Herald," reprinting an undated newspaper clipping about the drugging of 6 persons in January (no year), their freezing and their storage in straw in boxes soon buried in a snow-drift, and their revival in May, four months later. [6952

MASSACHUSETTS

HENRY FORBUSH HOWE. Massachusetts [1003-1960]: there she is--behold her. N.Y.: Harper [1960]. xiv, [2], 290, [1] p. col. maps (part fold.), views. bibliog. (p. 269-77). (Regions of America: a series of books that depict our natural regions, their history, development, and character.) [6953

MILTON A. TRAVERS. The Wampanoag Indian tribute tribes of Martha's Vineyard, the story of the Capowacks of Nope: the Takemmy-Wampanoags, the Nunpaug-Wampanoags, the Aquinnah-Wampanoags of Catachukutcho (Gay Head tribe), the Chappaquiddick-Wampanoags [1602-1960. New Bedford, Mass.? 1960.] 78 p. maps, ports., views. bibliog. (p. 77). Includes some account of Indian descendants now living there. [6954

MELVIN THOMAS COPELAND & ELLIOTT C. ROGERS. The saga of Cape Ann [1605-1959]. Freeport, Me.: Bond Wheelwright Co. [1960]. xiv, [2], 254 p. maps. port., views. notes. Includes an account of Gloucester. [6955

ACUSHNET centennial, Acushnet, Massachusetts, land of the Cushenas, 1860-1960. [Acushnet? 1960.] 52 p. facsim., ports., seal, tables, views. bibliog. (p. 3). Signed: Clement St. Amand, Chairman, Board of Acushnet Selectmen. Includes "an authentic history of Acushnet from the time of the Cuchena Indians to the present." [6956

JOHN JOSEPH BYRNE. Medicine at Plymouth Plantation. New Eng. jour. med., 259:1012-17 (20 Nov 1958). views. bibliog. On the work of Samuel Fuller (1580-1633) and others as physicians in Plymouth colony, 1620-76. [6957

DARRETT BRUCE RUTMAN. The Pilgrims and their harbor. Wm. and Mary quar., 17:164-82 (Apr). notes. Evidence that through Plymouth Harbor had often been visited and mapped during the century before the Pilgrims landed there in 1620, they did not "know of all this earlier activity" and did not "make use of the maps and accounts of prior visits in the selection of Plymouth Harbor as a site for their settlement." [6958

Sir ANTHONY RICHARD WAGNER. The origin of the Mayflower children: Jasper, Richard, and Ellen More [and "a nameless brother"]. New Eng. hist. and geneal. reg., 114:163-8 (Jul). Evidence that Ellen (born 1612), Jasper (1613-20), and Richard (born 1614, living in 1684) were children of Catherine (More) More, adulterous wife of Samuel More of Linley, that their father was Jacob Blakeway, and that Samuel sent them to New England in car of John Carver and Robert Cushman in 1620. [6959

GEORGE FINDLAY WILLISON. "... a civilized man." John Arthur Garraty, ed., The unforgettable Americans (Great Neck, N.Y.: Channel Press [1960]), p. 17-21. On William Brewster (1563?-1643), Mayflower emigrant in 1620, and his life in Plymouth, Mass. [6960

JAMES FREER FAUNCE. The Faunce family. New Eng. hist. and geneal. mag., 114:115-25, 211-17 (Apr, Jul). notes. On John Faunce (born ca. 1602 or ca. 1610, died 1653/54), settler in Plymouth in 1623, his 9 children, and some of his further descendants. [6961

RALPH H. CLOVER. The rule of law in colonial Massachusetts. Univ. Pa. law rev., 108:1001-1037 (May). notes. On "Puritan political thought" of the 1630s, the Body of Liberties (1641), the writings of John Winthrop on government and law, and the "principle of limitation of government by specific legal rules and guarantees" in the Massachusetts Code of 1648. [6962

GEORGE LEE HASKINS. Law and authority in early Massachusetts: a study in tradition and design. N.Y.: Macmillan, 1960. xv, [3], 298 p. notes (p. 232-87). Analysis of legislation and court action in the colony, with special notice of relations between church and state and of "native legal achievements" as distinguished from importation of the common law of England, 1630-50. [6963

MANFRED JONAS. The wills of the early settlers of Essex County, Massachusetts [1630?-1681]. Essex Inst. hist. col., 96:228-35 (Jul). tables. notes. On the "relative economic status" of the makers of the wills. [6964

EDMUND SEARS MORGAN. The Puritan dilemma: the story of John Winthrop [1588-1649]. Boston: Little, Brown [1958]. xii, [2], 224 p. bibliog. (p. 207-15). (The library of American biography.) On his administration of the affairs of Massachusetts, and the ideas by which he was guided, 1630-49. [6965

Mrs. JOHN E. BARCLAY. Jonathan[2] Dunham [1631/32?-1717] of Plymouth and Edgartown, Mass. Am. geneal., 36:243-9 (Oct). Includes some account of his 6 children. [6966

HANOR A. WEBB. The birth of our nation's public schools. Peabody jour. educ., 36:84-92 (Sep 1958). Information from William Gould Vinal. The rise and fall of ye district school in Plimouth Plantation (1800-1900) (1958), dealing with district schools of Plymouth County, Mass., 1636-1882, and commenting on later educational tendencies. [6967

ROBERT GUTMAN. Birth and death registration in Massachusetts. Milbank Memorial Fund quar., 36:58-74, 372-402; 37:297-326, 386-417 (Jan 1958 - Oct 1959). tables. notes. Based on thesis--Columbia Univ., 1956. Organized in 4 periods, 1639-1900. [6968

CHARLES ERNST BOEWE & MURRAY G. MURPHEY. Hester Prynne in history. Am. lit., 32:202-4 (May). notes. On "historical scraps" relating to Salem, 1640s, from which Hawthorne may have "built up" the "composite picture" of a character in The scarlet letter. [6969

NARCISSA G. CHAMBERLAIN. History in houses: the White-Ellery house at Gloucester, Massachusetts. Antiques, 78:570-73 (Dec). views. On a house built possibly in 1640 or possibly in 1703, occupied in 1703 by the Rev. John White and later by Capt. William Ellery and his descendants; with heavily annotated illustrations of some of its furnishings. [6970

RUTH EASTERBROOK THOMAS & ROSS BOOTHE, JR. John Downing [1640?-1694, of Massachusetts and the Island of Nevis]. Am. geneal., 36:68-73 (Apr). Includes a list of his children (born 1669/70-1683) and text of his will (Boston, 1691). [6971

Mrs. JOHN E. BARCLAY. Notes on the Dotey and Churchill families. Am. geneal., 36:1-11 (Jan). On family relationships of Thomas[2] Dotey (1641?-1678) of Plymouth, Mary Churchill (1654-1676/78?), their daughters (Martha, born out of wedlock in 1672, died after 1696, and Hannah, 1675-1764), Eleazer[2] Churchill (1652-1716) of Plymouth, and Joseph Dotey (1651-1732?) of Plymouth. [6972

THEODORE CHASE. John Winthrop and the doctrine of judicial immunity [Massachusetts, 1645]. Am. Bar Assoc. jour., 46:602-8 (Jun), port. notes. [6973

FREDERICK W. WEAD. The family of Nathaniel[2] Kirtland. Am. geneal., 36:88-91 (Apr). On the 10 children of Nathaniel Kirtland, Sr. (died 1686), of

Lynn, Mass., the first born before 1647, the youngest in 1667. [6974

VIRGINIA CROCHERON GILDERSLEEVE. "... the wisdom of one man." John Arthur Garraty, ed., The unforgettable Americans (Great Neck, N.Y.: Channel Press [1960]), p. 22-6. On the emigration of Richard Bourne from England sometime before 1649 and his service as a missionary to the Wampanoag Indians, mainly on Cape Cod. [6975

CLARENCE LESTER VER STEEG. "... eloquent spokesman for representative government." John Arthur Garraty, ed., The unforgettable Americans (Great Neck, N.Y.: Channel Press [1960]), p. 28-31. On John Wise (1652?-1725), his life in Massachusetts, his service as a minister of Chebacco Parish, and his activities in Massachusetts politics. [6976

NINA FLETCHER LITTLE. The house of Tristram Coffin, Jr., Newbury, Massachusetts [probably built in part before 1653, much expanded in the 18th century]. Antiques, 77:482-5 (May). On a house occupied continuously by the Coffin family until 1929, when the house and its original furnishings were conveyed to the Society for the Preservation of New England Antiquities. [6977

WALDO CHAMBERLAIN SPRAGUE. The first wife of John[2] Richmond of Taunton, Mass. Am. geneal., 36:137-8 (Jul). On Susanna Hayward, who married him ca. 1653, bore 4 children, and died ca. 1662. [6978

Mrs. JOHN E. BARCLAY. Elizabeth[2] (Tomson) Swift [1654-1717?] of Middleboro, Mass. Am. geneal., 36:164-70 (Jul). Evidence that her husband was Thomas[3] Swift of the Dorchester Swift family (born 1659, died before 1696), that they married in 1687, and that their only child was Thomas[4] (born 1687); with a list of the 6 children of Thomas[4]. [6979

MONSON HISTORICAL SOCIETY. History of Monson, Massachusetts [1657-1960. Monson] c1960. 171, [1] p. diagr., facsims., insignia, maps, ports., tables, views. bibliog. (p. 169-70). [6980

ELIZABETH (CARLTON) COES. Colonial Quaboag [1660-1798, now Brookfield]. Brookfield, Mass.: Podunk Pedlar Press, 1960. 35 p. diagrs., map. bibliog. (p. 35). [6981

SHIRLEY SILVER. Natick consonants in reference to Proto-Central Algonquian. Internatl. jour. Am. linguistics, 26:112-19, 234-41 (Apr, Jul). notes. Based upon published records of the Natick language of eastern Massachusetts by John Eliot (1661-63), Josiah Cotton (1829), and James Hammond Trumbull (1903). Mainly a list of "cognate sets" (Natick form and starred Proto-Central Algonquian or Proto-Central Eastern Algonquian form). [6982

GEORGE WILLIAM DOLLAR. The life and works of the Reverend Samuel Willard (1640-1707). Ann Arbor: University Microfilms, 1960. Positive microfilm of typescript. [221] leaves. Thesis--Boston Univ. Abstracted: Dissert. abstracts, 21:603 (Sep). On his service as a Congregational minister in Groton, 1662-76, and Boston, 1678-1707. [6983

HELEN PARK. Thomas Dennis [died 1706], Ipswich joiner: a re-examination. Antiques, 78:40-44 (Jul). views. On work attributed to Dennis, ca. 1663 ff., by previous writers, the characteristics of 5 pieces "with an unbroken Dennis family history," and the probability that much of the other work attributed to him was done by his son (Thomas Dennis, Jr.), Joseph Brown, Edward Dear, William Searle, or other Ipswich cabinetmakers. [6984

RACHEL E. BARCLAY. John[3] Rider [1664?-1735?] of Plymouth, Mass. Am. geneal., 36:193-8 (Oct). Includes lists of his 5 children by his first wife, Hannah Barnes (died 1703) and his 8 children by his second wife, Mary ---- (1685?-1766). [6985

HELEN PARK. The seventeenth-century furniture of Essex County and its makers [ca. 1665 to 1700]. Antiques, 78: 350-55 (Oct). views. [6986

RUTH M. RASEY. Salt-box, 1665, Vt. Hist. Soc., News and notes, 8:70-71 (Jun 1957). On family history and household events connected with a box made at Concord, Mass., by the author's ancestor Nathaniel Harwood. [6987

RACHEL E. BARCLAY. Hannah[3] Faunce of Plymouth and Duxbury, Mass. Natl. Geneal. Soc. quar., 48:136-7 (Sep). On a daughter of Joseph[2] Faunce and Judith (Rickard) Faunce, born 1678, who married Ephraim Morton, bore 6 children, married John Cooke of Kingston as her second husband, and died in or possibly before 1760. [6988

DAVID LEVIN, ed. What happened in Salem? ... Second edition. N.Y.: Harcourt, Brace [1960]. xviii, 238 p. bibliog. (p. 237-8). (Harbrace sourcebooks.) 1st ed. 1950. Contemporary documents and comment, 1692, 1711, relating to the witchcraft trials; "Young Goodman Brown" (1835), by Nathaniel Hawthorne; and A mirror for witches (1928), by Esther Forbes. [6989

COTTON MATHER (1663-1728). Selections from Cotton Mather. Edited, with an introduction and notes, by Kenneth B. Murdock. N.Y.: Hafner Pub. Co. [1960]. lxiii, 377 p. bibliog. (p. lxi-lxii), notes. (The Hafner library of classics, 20.) 1st ed. 1926. Biographical introduction (p. ix-lx); excerpts from Magnalia Christi Americana (1702), The Christian philosopher (1721), and Political fables (1692); and "Letter to Dr. Woodward [Secretary of the Royal Society of London] about 'an horrid snow,'" 10 Dec. 1717 (here first printed). [6990

RAYMOND SANGER WILKINS. Harvard and the Supreme Court of Massachusetts [and its predecessor, the Superior Court of Judicature of the Province of Massachusetts Bay]. Harvard alumni bul., 59:513-15 (6 Apr 1957). port. On "the contributions to its personnel which Harvard has made," 1692-1957. [6991

RACHEL E. BARCLAY. John[4] Turner [1693-1778] of Scituate, Mass., his wives and children. Am. geneal., 36:74-9 (Apr). On his marriages to Mercy[4] Bartlett (1694?-1757) and Mary Vinal (died 1794?). [6992

BERNARD BAILYN & LOTTE BAILYN. Massachusetts shipping, 1697-1714: a statistical study. Cambridge: Belknap Press of Harvard Univ. Press, 1959. xi, 148 p. tables. notes. Based upon "a perfectly preserved shipping register for Massachusetts." On the number of ships serving Massachusetts, their makers, their owners, their acquisition, and the investments in them; with tables (p. 78-134) containing all the information in the register as extracted by tabulating machines. [6993

MASSACHUSETTS HISTORICAL SOCIETY, Boston. Portraits of women, 1700-1825. Boston, 1954. [31] p. ports. (A Massachusetts Historical Society picture book.) Foreword signed: Walter Muir Whitehill, Cabinet Keeper. Portraits (from the Society's collections) and biographical sketches of 12 Massachusetts women. [6994

The STORY of the storm. [Edited by] Michael C. J. Putnam. New Eng. quar., 33:489-501 (Dec). notes. Anonymous Latin poem, "Lailapología," dated from internal evidence 1706 or 1707, apparently in the handwriting of Judge Samuel Sewall but probably not composed by him, dedicated to Increase Mather, on "the trouble among the peoples of Europe." [6995

RICHARD H. RANDALL, JR. An eighteenth century partnership. Art quar., 23:153-61 (summer). facsims., views. notes. On the collaboration of Nathan Bowen (1752-1837), Ebenezer Martin, Sr. (1735?-1800), and Ebenezer Martin, Jr. (1773?-1806), Marblehead cabinetmakers. [6996

CHARLES S. PARSONS. An early clock made by Richard Manning of Ipswich, Massachusetts [1741]. Natl. Assoc. Watch and Clock Collectors, Bul., 9:194-9 (Apr). views. [6997

JOHN PHILLIPS MARQUAND (1893-1960). Timothy Dexter [1747-1806] revisited. Boston: Little, Brown [1960. 8], 306, [1] p. views (1 double), notes. On "the extraordinary career of Lord Timothy Dexter," merchant and wealthy eccentric of Newburyport, Mass., author of A pickle for the knowing ones; or, Plain truths in a homespun dress (Salem, 1802); and "the bizarre but often beautiful historical and social climate which permitted such an extraordinary individual to burgeon and to bloom." [6998

ERNEST ALLEN CONNALLY. The Cape Cod house: an introductory study. Soc. Architectural Historians, Jour., 19:47-56 (Jun). map, plans, views. notes. On the varieties of the type of "compact story-and-a-half house" that prevailed on lower Cape Cod (Orleans, Eastham, Wellfleet, Truro, and Provincetown) "approximately 1750-1850." [6999

ROBERT ROOD BUELL. Jacob[2] Kibling (or Kiberlinger) [1752-1839] of Ashburnham, Mass. Am. geneal., 36:58-60 (Jan). [7000

STEPHEN STEGMANN HITEN. The historical background of the election sermon and a rhetorical analysis of five sermons delivered in Massachusetts between 1754 and 1775. Ann Arbor: University Microfilms, 1960. Positive microfilm of typescript. [290] leaves. Thesis--Univ. of Michigan. Abstracted: Dissert. abstracts, 20:4754 (Jun). [7001

MASSACHUSETTS (Colony). General Court. House of Representatives. Journals of the House of Representatives of Massachusetts. [Vol. XXXIII, Part 2.] 1757. [Boston:] Massachusetts Historical Soc., 1960. viii, 231-499 p. Record of the 5th session, 6 Jan.-25 Apr. 1757, reproduced from the original printing; with introduction by Malcolm Freiberg, and index. [7002

TRACY LEWIS SANBORN. Two centuries of Freemasonry: the history of Philanthropic Lodge [Marblehead, Mass., 1760-1960. Marblehead? 1960.] 55 p. facsims., views. [7003

JERALD L. BANNINGA. James Otis on the writs of assistance: a textual investigation. Speech monographs, 27:351-2 (Nov). notes. On 3 texts of a speech delivered by Otis in the Superior Court of Massachusetts, 10 Feb. 1761: (1) the manuscript notes of John Adams, later stolen and not known to exist now; (2) the text in the Massachusetts spy, 29 Apr. 1773, based, according to Adams, upon his stolen notes; (3) the text in William Tudor, The life of James Otis (1823), rephrasing parts of the 1773 copy and omitting parts of it without explanation. [7004

FREDERICK C. WARNER. The identity of Tamsin (Tammy) Read, wife of William Eastman [born 1763] of Granby, Mass. Detroit Soc. Geneal. Research mag., 23:35 (fall 1959). Evidence that Tamsin Read (1770-1808), who married Lt. William Eastman in 1794, was a daughter of Reuben Read (1730-1803) and his wife Tamsin (Meacham) Read, of Warren, Mass. [7005

ELIZABETH MOODY. One if by land. Natl. parks mag., 34(151): 8-9, 17 (Apr). map, views. On the establishment of the Minute Man National Historical Park in the area between Boston and Concord forming "the first battleground of the American Revolution" in April 1775. [7006

ODELL SHEPARD. "... the prompt production of heroes." John Arthur Garraty, ed., The unforgettable Americans (Great Neck, N.Y.: Channel Press [1960]), p. 121-6. On Mary Moody Emerson (born 1775), aunt of Ralph Waldo Emerson, her life in Concord, Mass., her inculcation of some of her ideas in her nephew during his childhood, and her lasting influence upon his thought and literary style. [7007

CHARLES FRANCIS MAHONEY. The case for a popular constitutional convention. Mass. law quar., 44(1):21-8 (Apr 1959). On the constitutional conventions of Massachusetts, 1779-80, 1820-21, 1853, and 1917-19, and the case for another convention. [7008

WILLIAM O'BRIEN. Did the Jennison Case outlaw slavery in Massachusetts? Wm. and Mary quar., 17:219-41 (Apr). notes. On Walker v. Jennison and Jennison v. Caldwell, heard before an Inferior Court of Common Pleas at Worcester and appealed to the Supreme Judicial Court, 1781, the poverty of documentation of the court action in these cases, and the weakness of the evidence that slavery was ruled to be contrary to the constitution of Massachusetts. [7009

DONALD McLEISH MURRAY. Dr. Peter Bryant: preceptor in poetry to William Cullen Bryant. New Eng. quar., 33:513-22 (Dec). notes. Evidence from Bryant family papers that the doctor showed "a zealous and consistent interest in his son's career"; with an account of a manuscript booklet of poems by the father, 1788-91, and of his advice in the publication of The embargo and "Thanatopsis." [7010

RICHARD K. MURDOCH, ed. A case of Salem hospitality. Essex Inst. hist. col., 96:156-67 (Apr). notes. On the stay of the packet boat San Fernando el Rayo in Salem Harbor, and the hospitable treatment of its officers, crew, and passengers by the people of Salem; with a communication from Capt. Francisco Borlasca to Josef de Jaudenes and Josef Ignacio de Viar, Spanish diplomatic agents in Philadelphia (Salem, 18 Oct. 1791), and 2 reports from them to Jośe Moniño, Conde de Floridablanca (25 Oct. and 25 Nov. 1791). [7011

NEAL B. MITCHELL. Study of distribution system in Salem, Massachusetts [1796-1960]. New Eng. Water Works Assoc., Jour., 74:224-35 (Sep). On a system begun with mains made of pine logs. [7012

FRANK O. SPINNEY. Chapman Lee, country cabinet maker. New-Eng. galaxy, 1(3):34-8 (winter). views. Information from the account books kept by him at Charlton, Mass., 1799-1849. [7013

FREDERIC A. SHARF. Fitz Hugh Lane [1804-65] re-considered. Essex Inst. hist. col., 96:75-83 (Jan). view. notes. On the known facts of his life in

Gloucester and Boston, his work as a painter (especially of nautical scenes), and the copies made of some of his paintings by his pupil, Mrs. Mary B. Mellen. [7014

JOHN MORGAN BULLARD. Friends' Academy, 1810-1960: a history of the first one hundred fifty years. New Bedford [Mass.], 1960. 120 p. ports., tables, views. bibliog. (p. 119-20). On an elementary and secondary school for boys and girls, at North Dartmouth, Mass. [7015

JOHN BENEDICT PICKARD. Imagistic and structural unity in "Snow-bound." College Eng., 21:338-43 (Mar). On a reminiscent poem by John Greenleaf Whittier (1866), describing a day and a night of the Whittier family as affected by a heavy snowstorm on their Massachusetts farm about 50 years before the composition of the poem. [7016

RAYMOND WILLIAM ADAMS. Thoreau and his neighbors. Thoreau Soc. bul., 44:[1-4] (summer 1953). Evidence that, with exceptions, he liked children and they liked him but that he disliked and disrespected his Concord neighbors and they disliked and disrespected him. [7017

Mrs. CALEB HENRY WHEELER. Thoreau farm. Thoreau Soc. bul., 42:[2-3] (winter 1953). view. On the house (still standing) near Concord where Thoreau was born in 1817. [7018

Mrs. CALEB HENRY WHEELER. The Thoreau houses. Thoreau Soc. bul., 31:[1-2] (Apr 1950). view. From the Concord journal, 14 May 1942, with revisions by the author. On "all the houses in Concord which have Thoreau associations." [7019

Mrs. CALEB HENRY WHEELER. Thoreau Alcott house. Thoreau Soc. bul., 24:[1] (Jul 1948). view. On a house in Concord built by Josiah Davis sometime between 1819 and 1830, occupied by the Thoreau family from 1849 till after the death of Henry David Thoreau, and later occupied by the Alcott family. [7020

KENNETH WALTER CAMERON. Historical notes on the Concord Academy [1822-42]. Emerson Soc. quar., 19: leaves 46-51 (2d quar.). [7021

JOHN WILSON BLACK. Rufus Choate [1799-1859]. Speech Association of America, A history and criticism of American public address, ed. William Norwood Brigance, 2d ed. (N.Y.: Russell & Russell, 1960), 1:434-58. bibliog., notes. On the oratorical and rhetorical characteristics of his public speaking, especially in connection with his practice of law in Massachusetts, 1823-59. [7022

ROBERT WOODBERRY LOVETT. A nineteenth-century Beverly partnership: the Pickett Coal Company, 1827-1910. Essex Inst. hist. col., 96:85-104, 207-27 (Apr, Jul). On the firm of Richard Pickett & Abraham Edwards, 1827-44; Richard Pickett & John Pickett, 1844-64; John Pickett, 1864-74; John Pickett, Horace Whipple Woodberry, & Jesse G. Trask, 1874-87; Trask & Woodberry, 1887-95; and Woodberry, 1895-1910. [7023

WALTER ROY HARDING. Thoreau and the Concord Lyceum [established in 1829]. Thoreau Soc. bul., 30:[2-3] (Jan 1950). On his membership in the Lyceum (beginning ca. 1831), his service as its secretary and curator, and his experience in lecturing before it. [7024

ELIJAH ADLOW. Lemuel Shaw and municipal corporations [in Massachusetts, 1830-60]. Mass. law quar., 44(2):52-98 (Jul 1959). [7025

ELIJAH ADLOW. Lemuel Shaw and the judicial function [in Massachusetts, 1830-60]. Mass. law quar., 45(3):52-69 (Oct). [7026

THOMAS HENRY O'CONNOR. Massachusetts in the Civil War. Volume I. "The call to arms," 1860-1861. Boston: Massachusetts Civil War Centennial Commission, 1960. 45, [1] p. facsim. On events in Massachusetts and activities of Massachusetts characters leading toward the Civil War, from the founding of William Lloyd Garrison's Liberator to the arrival of the 6th Massachusetts Regiment in Washington, 1831-61. [7027

RICHARD M. ABRAMS. A paradox of Progressivism: Massachusetts on the eve of insurgency. Pol. science quar., 75: 379-99 (Sep). notes. Argument that "before 1900 ... Massachusetts had enjoyed ... all the democratic innovations which Progressives emphasized after 1900," an achievement due "not to any reform movement, but rather to the character of its tradition, rooted in the Puritan-colonial experience," 1836-1900. [7028

DOROTHY LOUISE (BURNETT) PORTER. Anti-slavery movement in Northampton [Mass., 1838 ff.]. Negro hist. bul., 24:33-6 (Nov). notes. [7029

SAMUEL GRAY WARD (1817-1907). Come with me to the feast; or, Transcendentalism in action. [Edited by L. H. Butterfield.] Boston, 1960. 7 p. (M. H. S. miscellany, published occasionally by the Massachusetts Historical Society, 6.) "Samuel Gray Ward's account of a visit from Jones Very in 1839," recording a dialogue with Very which confirmed other indications that he was insane; with an editorial account of his Harvard years and early relations with Ralph Waldo Emerson, and mention of 3 letters by or about Very. [7030

RAYMOND WILLIAM ADAMS. Emerson's house at Walden. Thoreau Soc. bul., 24:[3-7] (Jul 1948). On 14 acres of "woodlot and briarpatch" at Walden Pond, bought by Emerson in 1844 and extended by more than 40 acres in 1845, his plans "to build himself a lodge for study and writing" there, and designs by Thoreau and Amos Bronson Alcott for such a lodge. [7031

WILLIAM HENRY O'CONNELL (1859-1944). Early years in Lowell. Pierre Albert Duhamel, ed., Essays in the American Catholic tradition (N.Y.: Rinehart [1960]), p. 78-85. From the author's Recollections of seventy years (1934). On the emigration of his parents from Ireland to Lowell, and their life and the early years of the author there, ca. 1846 ff. [7032

SPRINGFIELD REPUBLICAN. Marriages and deaths from the Springfield Republican, Springfield, Mass., for the year 1847 (contributed by Mercy Warren Chapter). D. A. R. mag., 94:208, 297, 389-90 (Mar-May). Data for the period from January through 27 Mar. 1847. [7033

RAYMOND WILLIAM ADAMS. The Thoreau library of Alfred W. Hosmer [1851-1903]. Thoreau Soc. bul., 30:[1-2] (Jan 1950). port. On his life in Concord and his "collection of Thoreauviana," consisting of manuscripts, clippings, photographs, botanical checklists, and a herbarium, now in the Concord Free Public Library. See also, by the same author, "Fred Hosmer, the 'lerned clerk,'" 36:[1-2] (Jul. 1951), on Alfred W. Hosmer's life in Concord as a dry-goods clerk, later proprietor of a dry-goods store, botanist and ornithologist, photographer, and collector of materials relating to Thoreau or formerly in his possession. [7034

SAMUEL SHAPIRO. The conservative dilemma: the Massachusetts Constitutional Convention of 1853. New Eng. quar., 33:207-24 (Jun). notes. [7035

RICHARD SANDERS ALLEN. The great bore. Trains. 20(8):18-26 (Jun). diagr., map, views. On the Hoosac Tunnel (between North Adams and Greenfield), dug for the Troy & Greenfield Railroad, begun in 1858, finished in 1875, and in use ever since. [7036

DONALD BARNARD COLE. The collapse of the Pemberton Mill. Essex Inst. hist. col., 96:47-55 (Jan). bibliog. On the sudden fall of a 5-storey cotton mill in Lawrence, Mass., 10 Jan 1860, resulting in the death of 88 persons and in severe injuries to 116 others. [7037

JOHN FRANCIS MITCHELL. Springfield, Massachusetts, and the Civil War. Ann Arbor: University Microfilms, 1960. Positive microfilm of typescript. [253] leaves. Thesis--Boston Univ. Abstracted: Dissert. abstracts, 21:864-5 (Oct). Includes some account of the work of the springfield Armory. [7038

WILLIAM BURTON WEBSTER. George Wendell Adams [1874-1953. Cambridge? Mass., 1960.] 23 p. ports. bibliog. (p. 20). On his early life in Kingston, Mass., his membership in Christian Science churches in Kingston, Plymouth, and Boston, and his service from 1925 to 1953 as a member of the Christian Science Board of Directors; with a list of his published articles. [7039

SPRINGFIELD REPUBLICAN, Springfield, Mass. Sophia A. [i. e. E.] Thoreau [1819-76]. Emerson Soc. quar., 18: leaf 42 (1st quar.). Facsimile reproduction of an obituary in the Boston transcript, 27 Oct. 1876, there reprinted from the Springfield Republican, containing an account of the Thoreau family, descended from John Thoreau (born 1754), emigrant from the island of Jersey, and extinct at the death of his granddaughter Sophia except for "an elderly maiden aunt, the last of the name in America." [7040

RALPH WARREN DEXTER. The Cuvier Natural History Society of Salem [1881-94]. Essex Inst. hist. col., 96:149-55 (Apr). [7041

KENNETH WALTER CAMERON, ed. Emerson, Thoreau, and Concord in early newspapers. Hartford, c1961. 57 leaves. facsims., map, port. (The Emerson Society quarterly, v. 21, 4th quarter 1960.) Facsimile reproductions of The Concord transcript, 19 Sep. 1885, and its supplement ("Old Concord. Celebration of the 250th anniversary"), and parts of several newspapers of 1882 and 1903, referring to Emerson's death and to his centennial. [7042

DOUGLAS J. OLLILA, JR. The Finns on Cape Cod [since 1885]. Am. Swed. Hist. Found., Yr. bk., 1960, p. 86-92. notes. [7043

MARTHA CHURCH. The spatial organization of electric power territories in Massachusetts [since 1891]. Chicago, 1960. xi, 187 p. diagrs., maps, tables. bibliog. (p. 180-87), notes. (University of Chicago, Dept. of Geography. Research paper 69.) Thesis--Univ. of Chicago. Issued also by the University as a microfilm. [7044

BRADFORD ADAMS WHITTEMORE. Davis Goodwin Maraspin [1899-1959]. New Eng. hist. and geneal. reg., 114:1-3 (Jan). port. On his early life in Massachusetts, his work as a lawyer and a naval officer, and his interest in genealogy. [7045

ROBERT W. BOZENHARD, JR. Massachusetts appraisal statute and minority stockholders. Mass. law quar., 45(3):27-41 (Oct). notes. On provisions of "a remedy for dissenting stockholders when there has been the required number of stockholder votes to affect [sic] a material change in the corporation's business," creating for the dissenters "a legal right to receive cash payment for their shares," 1903-59. [7046

CHARLES EBEN FISHER. The New Haven's wooden coaches. Railway & Locomotive Hist. Soc., Bul., 103:57-60 (Oct). views. On coaches of the New Haven Railroad between Boston and Taunton, 1912-18. [7047

EDWARD K. SMITH. Massachusetts personal income tax revision [since 1916]. Natl. tax jour., 12:239-59 (Sep 1959). tables. notes. [7048

NICHOLAS LOUIS ONORATO. The evolution of the budgetary process in Massachusetts [since 1918]. Ann Arbor: University Microfilms, 1959 [i. e. 1960]. Positive microfilm of typescript. [332] leaves. Thesis--Clark Univ. Abstracted: Dissert. abstracts, 20:2634-5 (Jan). [7049

ROBERT HUMPHREY MONTGOMERY. Sacco-Vanzetti: the murder and the myth. N.Y.: Devin-Adair Co., 1960. x, 370 p. On the trials of Nicola Sacco and Bartolomeo Vanzetti, 1920-27. Defends the conduct of the court in the trials and notes apparently intentional deviations from fact in accounts by Felix Frankfurter, Michael Angelo Musmanno, and Arthur M. Schlesinger, Jr. [7050

BARRY C. REED. The Sacco-Vanzetti case: the trial of a century [Massachusetts, 1920-27]. Am. Bar Assoc. jour., 46:867-72 (Aug). ports. [7051

ROBERT PERCY WEEKS, ed. Commonwealth vs. Sacco and Vanzetti. Englewood Cliffs, N.J.: Prentice-Hall, 1958. ix, 287 p. facsims., map, port. bibliog. (p. 274-5). Selections from printed sources, 1920-27. [7052

MICHAEL ANGELO MUSMANNO. The Sacco-Vanzetti jury. Villa-nova law rev., 5:169-80 (winter). notes. Reminiscences by counsel for Nicola Sacco and Bartolomeo Vanzetti, 1921, of the "bitter prejudice" of the trial judge (Webster Thayer), "the wiles and outright dishonesty of the district attorney" (Frederick Katzmann), and the jury as "putty in the hands of two of the most masterful sculptors of deception and hate as [sic] ever molded justice." [7053

R. LOREN GRAHAM. Later years of the Nantasket Beach Steamboat Company. Steamboat bill, 17:41-4, 46 (summer). views. Recollections of its excursion service between Boston and Plymouth and the ships in its fleet, 1924-52. [7054

FRANK WASHBURN GRINNELL. The discussion in 1924: Does the I[nitiative] and R[eferendum] Amendment authorize an "initiative" petition for another constitutional amendment? Mass. law quar., 45(2):10-23 (Jul). From the Massachusetts law quarterly, Jul. 1924. [7055

COMPULSORY automobile insurance: the Massachusetts experience [1927-57]. Insurance law jour., 1959:404-6, 436 (Jul 1959). [7056

T. Z. ELLIOT. Wiggins' wagons. Flying, 67(2):42-3 (Aug). views. On Wiggins Airways, Norwood, Mass., established by Elmer Wiggins ca. 1929. [7057

DANIEL I. CRONIN. Impact of Federal welfare grants on municipal government [in Massachusetts, 1935-59]. Boston Univ. law rev., 40:531-43 (fall). [7058

LORRAINE METCALF. Franklin women ... on call. Delta Kappa Gamma bul., 24(1):5-10 (fall 1957). On a volunteer ambulance unit organized by a group of women in Franklin, Mass., 1941?-1945. [7059

A. DANIEL RUBENSTEIN, HENRY P. MASON, & ELIZABETH L. STASHIO. Hospital use in Massachusetts, 1945-1955. Pub. health reports, 75:51-4 (Jan). diagr., tables. notes. [7060

ROGER CARLETON VAN TASSEL. Conditional grants-in-aid for school construction in Massachusetts [since 1948]. Natl. tax jour., 13:219-31 (Sep). tables. notes. On developments under the Massachusetts School Building Assistance Act. [7061

Boston

MARJORIE DRAKE ROSS. The book of Boston: the colonial period, 1630 to 1775. ... With photographs by Samuel Chamberlain. N.Y.: Hastings House [1960]. 127 p. facsims., maps (part double), ports, table, views (1 double). bibliog. (p. 17-18). Mainly on existing buildings constructed before the Revolution. [7062

EDWIN G. SANFORD. The early years of President John Sanford of Boston, Mass., and Portsmouth, R.I. New Eng. hist. and geneal. reg., 114:83-95 (Apr). notes. On the identity of the John Sanford (a servant of John Winthrop) who arrived in Boston in 1632 and died in Portsmouth ca. 1653, probably aged less than 47. [7063

WALDO CHAMBERLAIN SPRAGUE. Cotton Flack [1577-1658] of Boston, Mass. Am. geneal., 36:22-8 (Oct). On his emigration from England in or before 1633 and his descendants to ca. 1750. [7064

HIC admissionem in collegium jure potest exspectare: the admission policies of Harvard for 300 years [1646-1960]. Harvard alumni bul., 62:688-91 (11 Jun). [7065

CHARLES ALLERTON COLLIGE. How to be a good Fellow. Harvard alumni bul., 58:350-52, 360 (4 Feb 1956). port. On the duties of the members of the Harvard Corporation, 1650-1956. [7066

PAUL MERRICK HOLLISTER. Friends of Eleuthera. Harvard alumni bul., 59:353-4, 358 (2 Feb 1957). port. On "an informal, spontaneous, unofficial, wholly irresponsible company of volunteers concerned only with the perpetuation of freedom, for which eleutheros is the way you say freedom in Greek," commemorating Harvard aid to refugees from the Bahama Islands in 1650 repaid with a cargo of brazilwood from the island of Eleuthera. [7067

R. KEITH KANE & DANA DOTEN. The case for endowment. Harvard alumni bul., 54:211-15 (24 Nov 1951). table, views. On the "history and meaning of the Harvard endowment funds," 1650-1951. [7068

MILTON HALSEY THOMAS. An early American book label. Princeton Univ. Lib. chron., 22:36-7 (autumn). facsims. On a printed book label of John Cotton (1658-1710), 5 Jun. 1675, and other labels known to have been printed for Harvard undergraduates by the Cambridge Press, 1652 ff. [7069

MAX SAVELLE. "... one of the first articulate Americans." John Arthur Garraty, ed., The unforgettable Americans (Great Neck, N.Y.: Channel Press [1960]), p. 32-5. On Cotton Mather (1663-1727), Congregational minister in Boston, as "a typical--and probably the greatest--intellectual leader of his generation." [7070

HOWARD WHITMAN. A New England high school. New Eng. teacher, 1(4):14, 16-17, 24 (Apr 1954). port. On the Boston Latin School, ca. 1670 to 1954. [7071

GERARD J. BRAULT. Pierre Baudouin and the Bowdoin coat of arms. New Eng. hist. and geneal. reg., 114:243-68 (Oct). notes. On the identity and origin of a Huguenot merchant who came to Massachusetts in 1686, his known activities there, his death in Boston probably in 1706, 2 generations of his descendants, and the family seals, tombstone, silver, and bookplates. [7072

PAUL C. CABOT & LEONARD C. LARRABEE. Investing Harvard money [1693-1951]. Harvard alumni bul., 53:628-34 (12 May 1951). diagrs. [7073

HENRY ROUSE VIETS. The problem of the three Isaac Rands. New Eng. jour. med., 260:654-5 (26 Mar 1959). On Isaac Rand, Esq. (1718?-1790), Isaac, Jr. (1743-1822), and Isaac, Tertius (1769-1819), Boston physicians. [7074

TIMOTHY PICKERING (1745-1829). Timothy Pickering's Harvard. Harvard alumni bul., 52:282 (14 Jan 1950). Manuscript (ca. 1825) "describing life at Harvard," 1759-63. [7075

NOAH WEBSTER (1758-1843). Noah Webster's marriage announcement. [Edited by] R. Baird Shuman. Manuscripts, 12(2):32-4 (summer). facsim. notes. Letter to James Greenleaf, dated Boston, 28 Oct. 1789, announcing the writer's marriage to Greenleaf's sister, Rebecca Greenleaf. [7076

HENRY STEELE COMMAGER. Theodore Parker [1810-60]. ... With a new introduction by the author. Boston: Beacon Press [1960]. xi, [1], 339 p. bibliog. (p. 311-31). (Beacon series in liberal religion, LR4.) 1st ed. 1936. On his early life in Lexington, Mass., his studies in the Harvard Divinity School, and his life as a Unitarian minister in Boston; with chapters on "The intellectual gourmand," "The universal reformer," "The socialization of Christianity," "Slavery and the Higher Law," "Fugitive slaves," and "The political leader." [7077

STEPHEN SALISBURY (1798-1884). [Letters.] Harvard alumni bul., 57:380 (26 Feb 1955). Excerpts from letters written to the author's family during his first year at Harvard, 1813. [7078

ERIC T. CARLSON & MAY F. CHALE. Dr. Rufus Wyman [1778-1842] of the McLean Asylum. Am. jour. psychiatry, 116:1034-7 (May). notes. On his service as superintendnent of the McLean Asylum, Boston, 1818-35; with some account of his studies at Harvard and his work as a general practitioner in Chelmsford, Mass. [7079

[The HARVARD term bills of Warren Hobbs, 1818-22.] Harvard alumni bul., 57:3 (25 Sep 1954). facsim. Information about "the expense of a college life at Cambridge" in a file of the "term bills" (quarterly statements of payments due to Harvard College for meals, lodging, instruction, wood, fines, etc.) of a Harvard undergraduate. [7080

HENRY LINCOLN. [Letter.] Harvard alumni bul., 53:290-91 (13 Jan 1951). Letter dated Cambridge, 5 Jun. 1829, to the writer's sister, Mary Ann Lincoln, describing the inauguration of Josiah Quincy as President of Harvard. [7081

KENNETH WALTER CAMERON, ed. Jones Very's academic standing at Harvard. Emerson Soc. quar., 19: leaves 52-60 (2d quar.). facsims. Reproduction of manuscript "Sophomore scales," 1833-34," and of memorial notices from 3 Boston newspapers, 1880. [7082

JAMES BRYANT CONANT. Twenty years. Harvard alumni bul., 55:343-54 (24 Jan 1953). ports., views. On the author's service as President of Harvard University, 1933-53; with appended reminiscences of his work as a professor of chemistry there, an official in Washington during World War I, and a traveler in Germany, 1923. [7083

JAMES WOODBURY BOYDEN. [First days at college.] Harvard alumni bul., 52:6, 30, 50-52 (24 Sep - 8 Oct 1949). Excerpt from the author's diary, kept during his entrance examinations for Harvard College and his "first days" there, 27 Aug.-3 Sep. 1838. [7084

EDWARD SHERMAN HOAR. [Letter to Samuel Hoar, the writer's father, Cambridge, 22 May 1840, on dissensions between Harvard students and the townspeople of Cambridge.] Harvard alumni bul., 52:401-2 (25 Feb 1950). Letter from a Harvard sophomore. Appended: undated account by his brother, Ebenezer Rockwood Hoar, of Edward's removal to San Francisco and work there as a lawyer, his travels in Europe, and his later years as a farmer in Lincoln, Mass. [7085

JAMES LUCE KINGSLEY (1778-1852), supposed author. [Excerpts from an anonymous review of History of Harvard University, by President Josiah Quincy.] Harvard alumni bul., 57:174 (6 Nov 1954). From the American Biblical repository of 1842. [7086

LEVI LINCOLN THAXTER. [Letter to Thomas Wentworth Higginson, dated Cambridge, 22 May 1842.] Harvard alumni bul., 52:442 (11 Mar 1950). On rioting of Harvard students and Cambridge townsmen. [7087

EDWARD EVERETT (1794-1865). [Letter to Charles Greely Lorring, dated Dec. 1847.] Harvard alumni bul., 57:97 (23 Oct 1954). Excerpt containing "a memorandum of the duties performed by the President," who at the time of writing was Everett. [7088

EPHRAIM LITTLEFIELD. How I found Dr. Parkman. Harvard alumni bul., 52:209-15 (19 Nov 1949). ports., views. From Report of the case of John W. Webster (Boston, 1850), by George Bemis. On the discovery by the author, janitor of the Massachusetts Medical College, Harvard University, of part of the remains of Dr. George Parkman in the laboratory of his murderer, John White Webster, Professor of Chemistry and Mineralogy, 1849. [7089

[The CONVERT of Massachusetts.] Harvard alumni bul., 57:498 (9 Apr 1955). On an anonymous novel, "a little, cheap, cloth-covered 'pocket-book,'" published by John Henry and James Parker in London (1850s or 1860s?), dealing with Harvard in the early 18th century and with a hero, Geoffry Morris, who was converted to Episcopalianism. [7090

PAUL DUDLEY WHITE. Charles W. Thiery--1850 to 1958. New Eng. jour. med., 260:77-80 (8 Jan 1959). facsim., port. Medical history of a Cambridge, Mass., silversmith and goldsmith, report of the author's repeated examinations of him, including his autopsy, and effort to account for his longevity. [7091

THE SEPTEM, Cambridge, Mass. The Cambridge Septem. [Edited] by Edward H. Madden. Harvard alumni bul., 57:310-15 (15 Jan 1955). ports. notes. Excerpts from minutes of a "literary and scientific club" formed by 7 members of the Classes of 1851 and 1852, 1856-66. [7092

KIMBALL C. ELKINS. The [Harvard] class album through the years [1852-1950]. Harvard alumni bul., 57:675-6 (4 Jun 1955). views. [7093

EDWARD CONRAD McCLURE (1834-89). [Diary.] Harvard alumni bul., 55:512-14, 573, 593 (21 Mar - 18 Apr 1953). port. Record kept by a South Carolinian during his first year at Harvard, 1 Oct. 1853-18 Apr. 1854. [7094

DAVID THOMAS POTTINGER. Le Baron Russell Briggs [1855-1934]: his centenary. Harvard alumni bul., 58:242, 245 (10 Dec 1855). port. Mainly on his service as Dean of Harvard College and President of Radcliffe College. [7095

REGINALD HENRY PHELPS. Two bushels of wheat: fifty years (and more) of University Extension [1859-1959]. Harvard alumni bul., 62:16-21 (26 Dec 1959). facsim., port., views. [7096

PERRY TOWNSEND RATHBONE. [Maurice] Prendergast [1859-1924] in Boston. Art in Am., 48(3):88-91. views (part col.). On his life as a "lonely citizen of Boston," and the almost complete lack of demand there for his paintings until long after his death. [7097

JAMES RHYNE KILLIAN, JR. Harvard and M. I. T.: a century of coexistence and cooperation [1861-1951]. Harvard alumni bul., 58:589-92 (5 May 1956). [7098

FORTESCUE PERLEY. Harvard voting habits [in Overseer elections, 1865-1949]. Harvard alumni bul., 52:252-5 (3 Dec 1949). diagr., map, tables. [7099

DIANA WHITEHILL LAING. The Cushing-Endicott house: 163 Marlborough Street. Bostonian Soc., Proc., 1960, p. 14-52. plans, views. On a house built for Thomas Forbes Cushing in Back Bay in 1873, bought by William Crowninshield Endicott in 1898, retained by the Endicott family until 1957, now a rooming-house for girls; with excerpts from Endicott family correspondence regarding the house and its occupants. [7100

ALBERT T. MURPHY. "A by-product of my work": Alexander Graham Bell at Boston University [as Professor of Oratory, 1873-79]. Boston Univ. graduate jour., 3:33-5 (Nov 1954). From the Volta review, Jun. 1954. On the interrelatedness of his interests in speech, the teaching of the deaf, and the electrical transmission of sound. [7101

FORTESCUE PERLEY. How good is a Harvard man? Harvard alumni bul., 56:550-55 (17 Apr 1954). diagrs., tables. On the "Harvard loyalties" of graduates of Harvard College, 1878-1952. [7102

"JUST on the other side": coeducation in practice--but not in theory. Harvard alumni bul., 62:65-9 (10 Oct 1959). views. On the relations between Radcliffe College and Harvard College, 1882-1959. [7103

WILLIAM Whiting Nolen [1860-1923], '84--benefactor. Harvard alumni bul., 60:242, 246 (14 Dec 1957). port. On his studies at Harvard College and

Harvard Law School, and his establishment and operation of Manter Hall School to tutor boys who wished to qualify themselves to enter Harvard College. [7104

MARY ELLEN THOMSEN. You've heard of Dr. White. Harvard alumni bul., 58:146-50 (5 Nov 1955). port. On Paul Dudley White (born 1886), his studies at Harvard, his medical service in France and Macedonia during World War I, his career as a specialist in diseases of the heart, and his work as Clinical Professor of Medicine at Harvard Medical School and as chief of the heart service at the Massachusetts General Hospital. [7105

ANTANAS KUČAS. Šv. Petro lietuviu parapija South Bostone. The history of St. Peter's Lithuanian Parish, South Boston [1904-54]. ... Adapted from the Lithuanian text by Albert J. Contons. Boston, 1956. 303 p. facsim., ports., views. bibliog. (p. 299). English text (p. 227-94) apparently abridged. Includes some account of the Lithuanians in Boston since 1889. [7106

ROBERT L. ABRAMS. The story of rapid transit: Boston [1897-1960]. Natl. Railway Hist. Soc., Bul., 25(2):4-17; (3):14-22 (2d, 3d quar.). maps, views. [7107

LOUISE IMOGEN GUINEY (1861-1920). Reminiscences of a fine gentleman. Pierre Albert Duhamel, ed., Essays in the American Catholic tradition (N.Y.: Rinehart [1960]), p. 115-20. From Patrins (1897). Reminiscences of the author's dog, Perseus, a St. Bernard, in Boston. [7108

SAMUEL ELIOT MORISON. Reminiscences of Charles Eliot Norton [1900 to 1908]. New Eng. quar., 33:364-8 (Sep). notes. [7109

VAN WYCK BROOKS. Harvard, 1904-1907. Harvard alumni bul., 56:600-603 (1 May 1954). ports. Recollections. [7110

FORTY years after: the letter "H" still means dependability and steadfast romance. Harvard alumni bul., 53: 546-8 (7 Apr 1951). cartoon. Anonymous reminiscences of the author's years at Harvard, 1904-7. [7111

HENRY ROBINSON SHIPHERD. [Harvard notebooks and reminiscences, 1904-8.] Harvard alumni bul., 56:555, 593; 57:50-52 (17 Apr, 1 May, 9 Oct 1954). On Harvard personalities during the author's student years, particularly Barrett Wendell, William James, and Josiah Royce. [7112

MARIAN (LAWRENCE) PEABODY. Theodore Roosevelt visits Cambridge: reminiscences of his hostess's daughter when the President attended his 25th [class reunion, June 1905]. Harvard alumni bul., 60:596-7, 601 (3 May 1958). view. [7113

JOHN C. POLAND. [Reminiscences.] Harvard alumni bul., 60:400-401 (22 Feb 1958). On "Thursday Evenings," discussions conducted at Stoughton Hall by Charles Miner Stearns, Department of English, ca. 1908 to ca. 1911. [7114

JAMES BRYANT CONANT. Forty years of Harvard College: a portion of the President's report. Harvard alumni bul., 52:336-40 (28 Jan 1950). Excerpt from the author's annual report to the Board of Overseers for 1949, on the "University's progress since 1909." [7115

H. MASON PALMER. Boston Opera Company, first season, 1909-1910. Hobbies, 65(8):30-32 (Oct). ports. [7116

EDWARD STREETER. The Harvard I remember [1911-14]. Harvard alumni bul., 53:506-7 (24 Mar 1951). [7117

WILLIAM GRAVES PERRY, JR., & CHARLES P. WHITLOCK. Of study and the man: on the job training--Harvard's Bureau of Study Counsel [and its predecessors, 1916-58]. Harvard alumni bul., 60:350-54 (8 Feb 1857). facsim., port. [7118

THORNTON NIVEN WILDER. Thoughts for our times. Harvard alumni bul., 53:779-81 (7 Jul 1951). On "attitudes, tacit assumptions, the thought-world of students" as observed by the author during his years as a student and a teacher, 1917-51. [7119

FRANCIS M. WILHOIT (born 1920). Harvard men by Act of Congress: reflections of one of them thirteen years after. Harvard alumni bul., 60:166-7, 173-4 (9 Nov 1957). On the author's early life in rural North Carolina, his service in the Army Air Corps during World War II, and his undergraduate studies from 1945 to 1949 at Harvard; with remarks on "Harvard's response to the challenge posed by the G. I. invaders." [7120

LEONARD WARE. Academe in middle age. Harvard alumni bul., 52:69-72 (8 Oct 1949). On the author's undergraduate studies at Harvard (1921 ff.) and his return for graduate study (1947). [7121

WALTER C. EDMONDS. Who thought of the House Plan? Harvard alumni bul., 61:686-9 (6 Jun 1959). cartoons. On the work of Edward C. Aswell (Harvard, 1926) in establishing the Plan at Harvard, 1925-31. [7122

NATHAN MARSH PUSEY. A fresh look at Harvard. Harvard alumni bul., 56:305-7, 316 (23 Jan 1954). port. "Substantially the full text of the President's Report for the year 1952-53," on changes noted by him "after an absence of 25 years" since the end of his undergraduate studies in 1927-28. [7123

EDWARD K. GRAHAM. How new will the bigger university be? I: Some thoughts on the Graduate School [Boston University, 1929-59]. Boston Univ. graduate jour., 8:3-22 (Oct 1959). [7124

SEYMOUR EDWIN HARRIS. Salaries of full professors at Harvard, 1930 and 1954-55: some comparisons and related issues. Harvard alumni bul., 57:513-14 (9 Apr 1955). tables. Proposal to "require each student to pay the full costs of his education over his lifetime." [7125

ELLIOTT PERKINS. Interim report on the Houses. Harvard alumni bul., 53:260-64 (9 Dec 1950). cartoons, port. On the "strengths and weaknesses of the House system" at Harvard, 1930-50. [7126

HARVARD works for Uncle Sam: the University Office for Research Contracts [1942-54]. Harvard alumni bul., 57:160-63 (6 Nov 1954). ports. [7127

PETER ROBERT EDWIN VIERECK. Babbitt revisited. Harvard alumni bul., 52:715-17 (24 Jun 1950). On the author's observation of a "new-style philistinism" and its "new set of conditioned reflexes" during his years on the faculty at Harvard, 1945-50. [7128

WELDON WOODROW WELFLING & IRVING H. SIEGEL. Patent and other factors in the growth of the electronics industry in the Boston area [1945-55]. Patent, trademark, and copyright jour., 1:119-26, 218-19 (Jun, Dec 1957). notes. [7129

LASHLEY GREY HARVEY. The Institute of Public Service [Graduate School, Boston University, 1947-55]. Boston Univ. graduate jour., 4:31-2 (Oct 1955). [7130

WHERE are they now? A glance at the seven students who came to Harvard as DP's in 1949. Harvard alumni bul., 60:512-14 (5 Apr 1958). ports. Biographical sketches. [7131

RHODE ISLAND

DAVID CORNEL DE JONG. Rhode Island [since the 1630s, and especially as observed by the author since the 1930s]. New-Eng. galaxy, 1(3):11-19 (winter). views. [7132

Mrs. NICHOLAS KELLEY. History and description of Wilbour Woods. Garden Club Am., Bul., 48(6):16-19 (Nov). On an area of land in what is now Little Compton, R.I., purchased from Indians in 1673, acquired by Isaac Wilbour in 1849. [7133

CHARLES W. FARNHAM. The children of Zachariah Rhodes [of Warwick and Smithfield, R. I.] (1676-1761). New Eng. hist. and geneal. reg., 114:282-4 (Oct). [7134

MARTHA R. McPARTLAND. The history of East Greenwich, Rhode Island, 1677-1960; with related genealogy. East Greenwich: East Greenwich Free Library Assoc., 1960. 300 p. fold. map. bibliog. (p. 289-92). Includes "Some old families and their genealogy" (p. 251-70) and an anonymous poem, "An offering to the Greenwich people, or East Greenwich in 1849" (p. 283-8). [7135

ABBOTT LOWELL CUMMINGS. The restoration of the Eleazer Arnold house in Lincoln, Rhode Island. Antiques, 77:490-93 (May). views. On a house built ca. 1687 and recently restored as nearly as possible to "its seventeenth-century appearance." [7136

KENNETH SCOTT. Counterfeiting in colonial Rhode Island [1705-76]. Providence: Rhode Island Historical Soc., 1960. ix, 74 p. facsim., ports., views. notes. [7137

SUSAN BRALEY FRANKLIN. Division Street: a memory and a warning. Newport, R.I., 1948. 40 p. fold. map. (Bulletin of the Newport Historical Society, 104.) History of a Newport residential area since 1707 and of each lot and house in it. [7138

EDWARD H. WEST. Jeremiah Brownell [1749-1835] of Nova Scotia. Am. geneal., 36:65-6 (Apr). On a native of Rhode Island who removed to Nova Scotia ca. 1761 with his widowed mother. [7139

A RHODE Island election broadside, 1767. [Edited by] David S. Lovejoy. Books at Brown, 18:187-93 (Oct). facsim. Reproduction of a printed sheet containing a communication from Elisha Brown and 9 others to Stephen Hopkins, 28 Feb. 1767; letter from Hopkins to Gov. Samuel Ward, 13 Mar., enclosing the preceding; letter to Ward from David Jenckes and 8 others, 13 Mar.; letter from Ward to Hopkins, 25 Mar.; and (enclosed in preceding) letter to Ward from Gideon Wanton and a committee of "Mr. Hopkin's Friends," 25 Mar.; with an introductory statement by Ward, 7 Apr. 1767. [7140

CONSTANCE D. SHERMAN. An account of the scuttling of His Majesty's armed sloop Liberty. Am. Neptune, 20:243-9 (Oct). notes. On a vessel of the Commissioners of Customs, commanded by Capt. William Reid, the scuttling of the vessel and burning of her 2 boats by an angry mob, and the failure to identify any of the persons responsible; with a manuscript ("An account of the destruction of His Majesty's Armed Sloop Libety at Newport, R. I., July 1769") submitted by an unknown person to the editors of the Boston gazette but not published by them. [7141

JOHN J. COLLINS. A history of the Providence Water Works and its treatment methods [Rhode Island, 1870-1959]. New Eng. Water Works Assoc., Jour., 74:12-21 (Mar). tables. [7142

JAMES H. BROWN. The role of fire in altering the species composition of forests in Rhode Island ["in the past 25 to 30 years"]. Ecology, 41:310-16 (Apr). map, tables. bibliog. [7143

RHODE ISLAND, UNIVERSITY OF. From college to university, 1941-58: a summary report. Kingston, R.I., 1960. 60 p. ports., tables, views. Report by the President, Carl Raymond Woodward. Appended (p. 57-60): a list of articles by him, 1942-58. [7144

IRVING A. SPAULDING. Rhode Island population: rural-urban relationships [1950]. Kingston: Univ. of Rhode Island, 1957. 20 p. tables. (Rhode Island. Agricultural Experiment Station, Kingston. Misc. pub. 52.) [7145

CONNECTICUT

BERNARD DENIS. Un état de la Nouvelle-Angleterre: Le Connecticut. Études politiques anglo-saxonnes: Irlande du Nord, Connecticut, New York (Paris: Armand Colin, 1950 [Cahiers de la Fondation Nationale des Sciences Politiques, 13]), p. 87-156. map. bibliog. On the constitutions, colonial and State government, political parties, county governments, and "town" governments of Connecticut since 1635. [7146

ELIZABETH V. H. BANKS. This is Fairfield, 1639-1940: pages from three hundred one years of the town's brilliant history. [Fairfield? Conn., 1960.] 270 p. facsims. (1 fold.), maps, ports., tables, views. bibliog. (p. 256), notes. [7147

KATHLEEN HULSER RYERSON. A brief history of Madison, Conn. [1639-1959]. N.Y.: Pageant Press [1960]. 75 p. tables, views. On an area originally known as East Guilford and detached from Guilford in 1826. [7148

DONALD LINES JACOBUS. Stent family. Am. geneal., 36:191-2 (Jul). On Eleazer Stent (1643?-1706) of Branford, Conn., his wife, Elizabeth Butler (died 1712), and their 10 children (born 1671-91). [7149

HOUGHTON BULKELEY. A discovery on the Connecticut chest. Conn. Hist. Soc. bul., 23:17-19 (Jan 1958). view. Evidence that Peter Blin (1639/40?-1725), of Wethersfield, may have made the 65 or 70 exemplars of "the Connecticut or Sunflower Chest" that are known to have survived. [7150

NORMAN LITCHFIELD & SABINA CONNOLLY HOYT. History of the town of Oxford, Connecticut [1675-1960. n. p., c1960.] xii, 328 p. diagrs., ports., tables, views. bibliog. (p. 293-4). [7151

FRÉDÉRIC PALMER & LILLIAN BLANKLEY COGAN. The Hempstead house. Antiques, 77:179-85 (Feb). plan. views (part col.). On a house built by Joshua Hempstead I in New London, 1678, recently restored, its former and present furniture, and the information about house and furnishings in the diary kept by Joshua Hempstead II from 1711 to 1758. [7152

ERNEST JOSEPH CAULFIELD. Connecticut gravestones. VI. Conn. Hist. Soc. bul., 23:33-9 (Apr 1958). facsims. On the work of a Joseph Johnson, Middletown stonecutter, probably born in New Haven in 1698 and still living in 1770. [7153

NEW CANAAN HISTORICAL SOCIETY, New Canaan, Conn. What's in a name?--how New Canaan named its roads. New Canaan Hist. Soc. ann., 5(2):103-41 (Oct). view. Historical data relating to 261 roads, most of which "were built in the past twenty-five years," the earliest perhaps named in 1709. [7154

LORA M. (FREER) WACHENHEIM. Trumbull churches and people [1718-1960]. ... Volume I, Edition I. Trumbull, Conn.: [Brewer-Borg Corp.] c1960. viii, 149 p. ports., views. notes. [7155

MORSE ALLEN. Place-names in Salisbury, Connecticut [settled in 1719]. Names, 6:97-111 (Jun 1958). notes. [7156

WILLIAM LAMSON WARREN. Were the Guilford painted chests made in Saybrook? Conn. Hist. Soc. bul., 23:1-10, 50-60 (Jan, Apr 1958). views. On the evidence that Charles Gillam (died 1727), Saybrook cabinetmaker, may have been the decorator of several painted chests; with detailed descriptions of 13 chests. [7157

E. H. ADAMS. Higley's coppers--"Granby coinage." Selections from The numismatist: United States paper money, tokens, medals, and miscellaneous (Racine, Wis.: Whitman Pub. Co., 1960), p. 25-7. coins. First printed Aug. 1908. On copper coins struck by John Highley, blacksmith, of Granby, Conn., 1737-39. [7158

CHARLES SPENCER BISSELL. Treasure in pewter brought to light. Conn. Hist. Soc. bul., 24:44-6 (Apr 1959). view. On a pewter tankard used as a communion cup by the Second Congregational Church of Suffield, 1746 to ca. 1793, probably made in New England ca. 1680. [7159

ERNEST JOSEPH CAULFIELD. A rare broadside. Conn. Hist. Soc. bul., 23:78-80 (Jul 1958). On the contents of A lamentation on occasion of the sickness and mortality in East-Guilford, Anno Domini 1751, a poem by J. H., on the ravages of an unnamed disease, probably dysentery; with a list of all the persons who died in East Guilford (now Madison) between 26 Dec. 1750 and 24 Nov. 1751 (totaling 45). [7160

LOOMIS HAVEMEYER. "Go to your room": a story of undergraduate societies and fraternities at Yale [1753-1960. New Haven? 1960. 8], 107, [24] p. views. notes. [7161

SILVIO A. BEDINI. Aaron Willard and Son. Hobbies, 65(3): 41-2 (May). On Aaron Willard (1757-1844) and his sons Henry (born 1802) and Aaron, Jr. (1783-1864), Connecticut clock-makers from ca. 1780 to 1850. [7162

KENNETH SCOTT. A "dust" at Yale and a "blessing" for President Clap. Conn. Hist. Soc. bul., 23:46-9 (Apr 1958). On disorderly conduct of Simon Woodruff and other Yale students, who broke windows and window frames and pulled down gates at the house of President Thomas Clap, 30 Jul. 1765. [7163

SAMUEL PETERS (1735-1826). The Hebron frog. Conn. Hist. Soc. bul., 23:27-9 (Apr 1958). Letter to Augustus B. Woodward of Detroit, dated Washington, 22 Mar. 1806, describing a rock near Hebron, Conn., reported to have been "growing higher for 150 years whereby it had become a nuisance to Carriages and Travelers," and blasted to pieces in the author's presence in 1770, disclosing in a cavity a living frog. [7164

HOUGHTON BULKELEY. Amos Denison Allen [1774-1855, of Windham], cabinetmaker. Conn. Hist. Soc. bul., 24:60-64 (Apr 1959). facsims., views. [7165

WILLIAM LAMSON WARREN. Connecticut pastels, 1775-1820. Conn. Hist. Soc. bul., 24:97-128 (Oct 1959). ports. Catalogue of pastel portraits in an exhibition at the Connecticut Historical Society, containing descriptions and reproductions of 31 portraits and accounts of the painters. [7166

EARLE D. SHERWOOD. The Connecticut cent (auctori Connec) [1785-88]. Numismatic scrapbook, 26:2146-50 (Jul). coins, table. [7167

FRÉDÉRIC PALMER. East Haddam Congregational Church [built 1794]: its preservation and restoration. Conn. Hist. Soc. bul., 24:47-59 (Apr 1959). views. [7168

L. W. SLAUGHTER. "The magic of Terry." Hobbies, 64(10):46-7, 53; (11):44-5, 47 (Dec 1959, Jan 1960). views. On clocks made by Eli Terry

(1772-1852) and members of his family, 1795-1884, mainly at Plymouth, Conn. [7169

NEWTON CASE BRAINARD. Chapin secretary. Conn. Hist. Soc. bul., 23:44-5 (Apr 1958). On a cherry secretary made by Aaron Chapin ca. 1800. [7170

SHIRLEY SPAULDING DEVOE. Great-grandmother's tea tray. Antiques jour., 15(2):24-5, 37 (Feb). views. On trays made by craftsmen in the Hartford area, sold mainly in rural areas and known as "country tin," 1815 ff.; and the better quality and much greater number of the trays imported from England. [7171

CONSTANCE D. SHERMAN. A French naturalist visits Connecticut. Conn. Hist. Soc. bul., 23:40-43 (Apr 1958). Information from Jacques Gérard Milbert, Itinéraire pittoresque du Fleuve Hudson et des parties latérales de l'Amérique du Nord (Paris, 1829-29), concerning his observations in Connecticut in or soon after 1815. [7172

JOHN COTTON SMITH (1765-1845). John Cotton Smith Papers: Papers of John Cotton Smith while Lieutenant Governor, Acting Governor, and Governor of the State of Connecticut. Volume V, February 4, 1815-June 8, 1816. Hartford, 1957. xiii, 277 p. (Collections of the Connecticut Historical Society, 29.) [7173

BROOKS PALMER. Side column clocks [shelf clocks made by several clockmakers in Connecticut, 1818 to ca. 1880]. Antiques jour., 15(17):15-17 (Jul). views. [7174

T. PAUL TREMONT. The status of riparian rights in Connecticut [1828-1959]. Conn. Bar jour., 33:430-39 (Dec 1959). notes. Deals particularly with such rights in "the land between the high and low-water mark," which is owned by the State. [7175

WILLIAM Henry Brown, 1808-1883. Conn. Hist. Soc. bul., 23:90-94 (Jul 1958). ports., views. On a "famous silhouette artist" and his visits to Hartford in 1831 and 1843. [7176

ELAM KENDALL & G. & H. FRANCIS. Contract of master and apprentice. Ann. Ia., 35:391-2 (summer). Indenture, 15 Oct. 1834, by which Albert Kendall (born 1815), son of Elam Kendall of Grundy, Conn., is apprenticed to the Francises of Hartford to learn "the art, trade or mystery of the wood work of carriage making." [7177

MINETTE SCHEMEL RIEGER (1819?-1843). Diary of Minette Schemel Rieger. Am.-German rev., 26(6):23-5 (Aug-Sep). Entries made apparently in Hartford, 14-18 Sep. 1840, on her journey from New York as a missionary and her observations in Hartford, particularly its religious and charitable institutions. [7178

SHIRLEY SPAULDING DEVOE. The Litchfield Manufacturing Company, makers of japanned papier mâché [1850-54]. Antiques, 78:150-53 (Aug). facsim., views. On clocks, boxes, tabletops, and other articles made of this material. [7179

PHYLLIS KIHN. Colt in Hartford. Conn. Hist. Soc. bul., 24:74-7 (Jul 1959). views. On the dealings of Samuel Colt and Colt's Patent Fire-Arms Manufacturing Company with the Common Council of Hartford with regard to land, roads, taxes, etc., 1853-62, the destruction of a 500-foot factory by fire in 1864, and the stimulating influence of the fire upon the insurance industry. [7180

The NORWALK disaster of 1853. New Eng. jour. med., 259; 405-6 (21 Aug 1958). On a train wreck at Norwalk, Conn., which killed 7 physicians (from New England and New York) returning from an annual meeting of the American Medical Association, 6 May 1853. [7181

BRIDGEPORT, UNIVERSITY OF. SOCIOLOGY COLLOQUIUM. The Polish-Americans of Bridgeport [1872-1900]. Bridgeport, Conn.: The Sociology Colloquium in cooperation with the Dept. of Sociology, Univ. of Bridgeport, 1960. 47, [1] p. table. bibliog. (p. 46-7), notes. Papers by 16 students in a class in sociological method under the general supervision of Dr. J. M. Van der Kroef. [7182

DAVID MARS. Connecticut public defenders [1872-1959]. Conn. Bar jour., 33:297-314 (Sep 1959). notes. [7183

EDGAR MARVIN HAWKINS (born 1874). Life in Tolland, Connecticut, during the 1880's. [Hingham? Mass.] c1960. 25, 16 leaves. Reminiscences. [7184

THEODORE W. BENEDICT. Before the turn of the century--Main and Elm Street [New Canaan, Conn.]. New Canaan Hist. Soc. ann., 5:86-95 (Oct). views. Reminiscent effort "to locate and briefly describe the various stores and to identify the proprietors who occupied them" during approximately the years 1885-1900. [7185

ELIZABETH CHOATE SPYKMAN. Westover. Middlebury, Conn., 1959. 141, [1] p. ports., views. History of Westover School, Middlebury, 1909-59. [7186

MARY LOUISE KING. New Canaan no longer is provincial: the paving of Main Street [New Canaan, Conn., 1916]. New Canaan Hist. Soc. ann., 5:96-101 (Oct). views. [7187

HENRY W. LITTLEFIELD. The role of the private community colleges of Connecticut [1928-58]. Jr. college jour., 29:81-8 (Oct 1958). tables. [7188

CONNECTICUT. AGRICULTURAL EXPERIMENT STATION, Storrs. Measures of social change, Connecticut counties and towns, 1940-1958. [By] Robert G. Burnight. Storrs, 1960. 95 p. tables. (Its Bulletin 347). Statistics for estimated population, births and deaths, schools, physicians, dentists, local taxation, and dairy farms, 1940, 1950, 1955-58. [7189

GUNAR N. BOHAN. New Haven's court clinic: a casefinding source [1942-59]. Pub. health reports, 75:997-9 (Nov). table. On a court-connected service established in obedience to a Connecticut law requiring "every individual arrested for an alleged morals offense, to be examined for veneral disease." [7190

The Middle Atlantic States

FREDERICK W. BOGERT. Founder of the earliest Bergen County Bogert family line. Geneal. mag. N.J., 35: 97-100 (Sep). On Cornelis Jansen Bongaert, recorded in New Amsterdam 1651 ff. and in Bergen County, N.J., 1676-77, died in 1681. [7191

JOHN WILSON TAYLOR. Scandal monger in New Amsterdam. N.Y. geneal. and biog. rec., 91:194-7 (Oct). On Geertje Jacobs, adultress and circulator of rumors of adultery by others, 1656-67. [7192

MARY MAPLES. A cause to plead: the political thought and career of William Penn from 1660 to 1701. Ann Arbor: University Microfilms, 1959 [i.e. 1960]. Positive microfilm of typescript. [263] leaves. Thesis--Bryn Mawr. Abstracted: Dissert. abstracts, 20:3710. Deals in large part with his work for religious toleration and his development of the colonies of Pennsylvania and Delaware, 1682-1701. [7193

MILTON RUBINCAM. Baron Isak Banér (1662-1713), of Sweden and New Jersey. Natl. Geneal. Soc. quar., 48: 211-12 (Dec). bibliog. On his life in Philadelphia and Penn's Neck, N.J., ca. 1700 to 1713; his marriage to Maria Jaquet; the sending of his 4 children to Sweden after his death; and his widow's later years in New Jersey. [7194

JOHN W. HARPER & MARTHA B. HARPER. The Palatine migration--1723: from Schoharie [N.Y.] to Tulpehocken [Pa.]. Hist. rev. Berks Co., 25:80-82 (summer). Includes a map showing the route, mainly along the upper Susquehanna and the Delaware. [7195

R. T. HOOBER. Colonial paper currencies of Pennsylvania and New Jersey [1758-78]. Selections from The numismatist: United States paper money, tokens, medals, and miscellaneous (Racine, Wis.: Whitman Pub. Co., 1960), p. 13-41. facsims. First printed Dec. 1944. [7196

MUNCY & MONROE TURNPIKE ROAD COMPANY. Report of the President and Managers, to the stockholders of the Muncy & Munroe Turnpike Road Company. Now and then, 12:139-44 (Jan 1959). Undated report, signed by E. J. Eldred, President, of a corporation chartered in 1832, dealing mainly with 4 proposed routes between Northumberland, Pa., and Geneva, N.Y., including one by way of Williamsport. [7197

JOHN MARY LENHART. Father Anthony Van Riel [1850-1924], a stabilized pioneer. Social justice rev., 52:97-8 (Jun 1959). On his service as a Catholic priest at Pittsburgh (1877-83) and Egg Harbor City, N.J. (1883-1921). [7198

PALISADES INTERSTATE PARK COMMISSION (New York and New Jersey). Palisades Interstate Park, 1900-1960. Bear Mountain, N.Y. [1960]. 106 p. diagr., facsims., maps, tables, views. Cover title: 60 years of park cooperation: N.Y. - N.J.

Palidades Interstate Park Commission, a history, 1900-1960. Reprint of 2 previous pamphlets with same title, covering the years 1900-1929 and 1929-47, with an added account of the period 1947-60. [7199

JOHN EHLE. Shepherd of the streets: the story of the Reverend James A[lfred] Gusweller [born 1923] and his crusade on the New York West Side. N.Y.: Sloane, 1960. xi, [3], 239 p. port. On his early life in Glen Ridge, N.J., his Army service in World War II, his studies in Carleton College and in the General Seminary, and his service as a minister in Keyport, N.J., and since 1956 at the Church of St. Matthew and St. Timothy, New York City, the latter situated in "an expanding Puerto Rican ghetto," where the minister encouraged parents to marry and took action against landlords of deteriorating rental properties. [7200

U.S. Geological Survey. Floods of July 18, 1942, in north-central Pennsylvania [in the Susquehanna, Allegheny, and Genesee River Drainage Basins of Pennsylvania and southern New York]. By W. S. Eisenlohr, Jr. ... With a section on Descriptive details of the storm and floods, by J. E. Stewart. Wash.: U.S. Govt. Print. Off., 1952. vii, 59-158 p. diagrs., maps (1 fold.), tables, views. bibliog. (p. 155-6). (Its Water-supply paper 1134-B.) [7201

NEW YORK

ALFRED KIDDER GUTHE. The cultural background of the Iroquois. Gertrude E. Dole & Robert L. Carneiro, eds., Essays in the science of culture, in honor of Leslie A. White (N.Y.: Crowell [1960]), p. 202-15. bibliog. [7202

EDMUND WILSON. Apologies to the Iroquois. N.Y.: Farrar, Straus, and Cudahy [1960]. vi, [4], 310 p. facsims., views. Reprinted from The New Yorker with revisions. Interviews and observations by the author, 1957-58, among the Onondaga, Mohawk, Tuscarora, and Seneca Indians on their reservations in New York, noting particularly the beliefs and ceremonies surviving in their white environment and their traditions of earlier times. [7203

IRENAEUS JOSEPH HERSCHER. The Franciscans and New York's year of history. Am. Cath. Hist. Soc., Rec., 71:14-22 (Mar-Jun). Summary of the history of the Franciscans in New York State, 1524-25, 1626-1959. [7204

CHARLES ALBERT SLEICHER. The Adirondacks: American playground. N.Y.: Exposition Press [1960]. 287 p. map, ports., views. bibliog. (p. 277-8), notes. History, description, and lore of the Adirondack Mountains, 1570-1960. [7205

HENRY NOBLE MacCRACKEN. Our creative river. Dutchess Co. Hist. Soc., Yr. bk., 44 (1959): 54-62. On the Hudson River and Valley since 1609. [7206

NEW YORK. Legislature. Joint Legislative Committee on Preservation and Restoration of Historic Sites. Report ... 1958-59. [Albany, 1959.] 80 p. views (1 col.). (Legislative document (1959) no. 82.) Appended: "Forts of the Champlain-Lake George area" (8 forts); "A valley of forts--a tribute to its history" (Lake George and Lake Champlain, 1609-1815); and "Chronology of New York in the Revolution." [7207

WILLIAM A. OWENS. Pocantico Hills, 1609-1959. Tarrytown, N.Y.: Sleepy Hollow Restorations [1960. 6], 53, [4] p. map, views (part double). bibliog. (p. 55-6). On Tarrytown and Sleepy Hollow. [7208

ADRIAAN JACOB BARNOUW. The Netherlands, background of New Netherland [since 1624]. Dutchess Co. Hist. Soc., Yr. bk., 43 (1958): 23-34. [7209

NEW YORK. Dept. of Social Welfare. Bureau of Research and Statistics. Milestones in public welfare in New York State: a chronology of significant landmarks in 330 years of public welfare history in New York State [1626-1954]. Albany, 1960. 6 leaves. [7210

WALDRON PHOENIX BELKNAP, JR. (1899-1949). Notes on the Schuyler family. Waldron Phoenix Belknap, Jr., American colonial painting: materials for a history, ed. Charles Coleman Sellers (Cambridge: Belknap Press of Harvard Univ. Press, 1959), p. 149-74. On Philip Pieterse Schuyler of Albany (1628-1683/1711), his 10 children (born 1652-72), and some of their New York descendants in the 17th and 18th centuries. [7211

H. WARD JACKSON. The seventeenth century mission to the Iroquois. P. E. Church, Hist. mag., 29:240-55

(Sep). notes. On Jesuit, Dutch Reformed and Church of England relations with the Five Nations, 1628-1712. [7212

WALDRON PHOENIX BELKNAP, JR. (1899-1949), & CHARLES KNOWLES BOLTON (1867-1950). Portraits in the Dutch background. Waldron Phoenix Belknap, Jr., American colonial painting: materials for a history, ed. Charles Coleman Sellers (Cambridge: Belknap Press of Harvard Univ. Press, 1959), p. 37-46. ports. Correspondence between the two, 1941-42, concerning 4 portraits, painted in the Netherlands and brought to America, of members of the De Peyster family born 1629/39 who died 1646/1710. [7213

MICHIGAN STATE LIBRARY. Couwenhoven-Jans-Van Vleck-Van der Boogh-Wilsie-Beeckmans-De Loney-Kip Bible records. Mich. heritage, 1:134-50; 2:18-21 (summer, autumn). notes. Description and texts of records entered in a Bible published in 1647 and of records, 1637-1804, kept in New York City and on Long Island, the whole photostated for George L. Hammel in 1934. [7214

WALDRON PHOENIX BELKNAP, JR. (1899-1949). Notes on the Duyckinck family. Waldron Phoenix Belknap, Jr., American colonial painting: materials for a history, ed. Charles Coleman Sellers (Cambridge: Belknap Press of Harvard Univ. Press, 1959), p. 63-147. coats of arms. On Evert Duyckinck I (1620/21-1700/1703), Dutch emigrant to New Amsterdam ca. 1638, maker of coats of arms for windows; his 9 children (born 1647-60); and some of their New York descendants before 1800. [7215

EDMUND SNOW CARPENTER. Alcohol in the Iroquois dream quest. Am. jour. psychiatry, 116:148-51 (Aug 1959). bibliog., notes. On the use by Iroquois Indians of "alcohol to stimulate their mystical faculties," 1642-1800. [7216

ROY W. MOGER. Our town Roslyn [1643-1960]: a brief history of the Roslyn area to serve the staff in guiding their students on trips around Roslyn. Roslyn, N.Y.: Roslyn Public Schools, ©1960. vii, 31, [5] leaves. maps (1 double), views. notes (leaves 35-6). [7217

WALDRON PHOENIX BELKNAP, JR. (1899-1949). Notes on four painters. Waldron Phoenix Belknap, Jr., American colonial paintings: materials for a history, ed. Charles Coleman Sellers (Cambridge: Belknap Press of Harvard Univ. Press, 1959), p. 191-206. Biographical and genealogical data concerning Raphael Goelet (1696-1747/48), Nehemiah Partridge (born 1684, died before 1737), Jacob Gerritsen Strycker (emigrant in 1651, died 1687), and Pieter Vanderlyn (1687-1778). [7218

JOHN DARDESS. A medical history of Columbia County [N.Y., 1654-1959]. N.Y. State jour. med., 59:2769-76 (15 Jul 1959). bibliog. [7219

HAROLD MINOT PITMAN. Fockens--Heermans. Am. geneal., 36:215-19 (Oct). On Focke Jansz, Dutch immigrant to New Amsterdam in 1660, his 7 children (born ca. 1641-ca. 1660), and some of their descendants; with evidence that the eldest son, Jan Focken, and the youngest, Egbert Fockenszen, took the surname Hermans (Heromans, Heermans) and passed it on to their children. [7220

PAUL MAHLON HAMLIN. New York's first bar association. N.Y. law forum, 5:348-67 (Oct 1959). notes. On a group of New York lawyers formed in defense against legislation to regulate attorneys' fees, 1709-10; with some account of such fees in earlier years since 1665. [7221

ELLIS KELLERT. Chester Averill [1804-36] and the chlorination of drinking water. N.Y. State jour. med., 59:2947-51 (1 Aug). facsim. notes. On a pamphlet by Averill, Professor of Chemistry and Ancient Languages at Union College, on the disinfecting powers of chlorine; with an account of the public water supply of Schenectady, 1670-1892. [7222

PATRICIA JOAN GORDON. The Livingstons of New York, 1675-1860: kinship and class. Ann Arbor: University Microfilms, 1959 [i.e. 1960]. Positive microfilm of typescript. vii, 338 leaves. geneal. tables. bibliog. (leaves 328-38). Thesis--Columbia Univ. Abstracted: Dissert. abstracts, 20:3877 (Mar). [7223

LAWRENCE H. LEDER. Robert Livingston (1654-1728): a biographical study of politics in early New York. Ann Arbor: University Microfilms, 1960. Positive microfilm of typescript. [677] leaves. Thesis--New York Univ. Abstracted: Dissert. abstracts, 21:180 (Jul). On his various activities in New York, 1675-1728. [7224

WALDRON PHOENIX BELKNAP, JR. (1899-1949). Notes on the Beekman family. Waldron Phoenix Belknap, Jr., American colonial painting: materials for a history, ed. Charles Coleman Sellers (Cambridge: Belknap Press of Harvard Univ. Press, 1959), p. 175-82. On Col. Gerardus Beekman (died 1722/23), his 11 children (born 1679-1704), and some of their descendants in the 18th century. [7225

ST. MATTHEW'S CHURCH, Bedford, N.Y. A sesquicentennial history of St. Matthew's Protestant Episcopal Church, Bedford, New York [1810-1960]. By members of the parish family.]Bedford, 1960.] 70, [1] p. facsim., map, ports., views (1 col. mount.). Foreword signed: H. Bartow Farr. Includes an account of the Anglican Church in Bedford, 1680-1818. [7226

NEW YORK (Colony). Supreme Court of Judicature. Supreme Court of Judicature of the Province of New York, 1691-1704. [Volume III.] Biographical dictionary, glossary, sources, indexes. [Compiled by] Paul M[ahlon] Hamlin ... and Charles E[dwin] Baker. N.Y., 1959. [6], 562 p. port. bibliog. (p. 235-49). (Collections of the New-York Historical Society for the year 1947: the John Watts De Peyster Publication Fund Series, 80.) "Biographical dictionary of the bench and bar" (p. 3-220), "Index of cases by plaintiffs," "Cross-index from defendants to plaintiffs," "Index of persons and places," "Subject index," and other information. Completes a series of 3 volumes, 1952-59. [7227

RUTH E. BARLOW. The South Amenia neighborhood [since 1694]. Dutchess Co. Hist. Soc., Yr. bk., 45:31-8. [7228

JOHN MEREDITH GRAHAM II. History in houses: Van Cortlandt Manor [built for Stephanus Van Cortlandt, Croton, N.Y., ca. 1697]. Antiques, 78:472-7 (Nov). views (1 col.). On the efforts of its present owner, John D. Rockefeller, Jr., to reassemble its furnishings as they may have been while Pieere Van Cortlandt I lived there from 1749 to 1814. [7229

CHARLES A. HUGUENIN. Condemned to the noose. N.Y. folklore quar., 16: 187-96 (autumn). notes. Lore about Ralph Sutherland (real name William Salisbury) of Leeds, in the Catskills, reputed to have murdered his slave girl Nattee and to have been sentenced to wear a halter round his neck and, if living at age 99, to be hanged; with an account of printed references to him, 1841-1959, particularly a novel by Miriam Coles Harris, The Sutherlands (1871). [7230

ELIZABETH SHARTS. Land o' Goshen, then and now. ... Edited by Mildred Parker Seese. Goshen, N.Y.: The Bookmill, 1960. xi, [1], 147 p. facsims., ports., seal, tables, views. On Goshen, N.Y., 1703-1960. [7231

U.S. National Park Service. Vanderbilt Mansion, national historic site, New York. By Charles W. Snell. Wash., 1960. [4], 52 p. maps (1 double), ports., views. bibliog. (p. 52). (Its Historical handbook series, 32.) On "a magnificent example of the palatial estates developed by financiers and industrialists in the period between the Civil War and World War I," the mansion built for Frederick William Vanderbilt, occupied by him from 1895 to 1938, and given by his heir to the United States in 1940; with some account of the area (211 acres) since 1705. [7232

JOHN JACOB VROOMAN. Conrad Weiser [1696-1760] and the New York Colony. Hist. rev. Berks Co., 25:76-9, 97, 99 (summer). port., views. On his turbulent life in the German settlements on the Hudson and the Schoharie, 1709-29. [7233

CHARLES K. WINNE, JR., ed. Two old wills, with notes on the allied families of Quackenbush, De Forest, Fonda (Fondey), and others. Dutch Settlers Soc. Albany, Yr. bk., 34-35: 11-25. geneal. tables. notes. Wills of Wouter Quackenbos, Jr (28 Aug. 1711), and Jesse De Foreest (9 Oct. 1750), with information about the persons named in them. [7234

ELIZABETH BUCKLEY. The story of Amenia Union. Dutchess Co. Hist. Soc., Yr. bk., 45:27-30. On an area in Oblong Valley, Dutchess County, formerly called Hitchcock Corners, 1714-1960. [7235

ROSCOE COLEMAN MARTIN. Water for New York: a study in State administration of water resources [1724-1958. Syracuse, N.Y.:] Syracuse Univ. Press [1960]. viii, 264 p. maps. notes. Includes chapters on the Cannonsville Reservoir, the Black River War, the Buffalo River case, and the allocation of St. Lawrence power. [7236

U.S. District Court. New York (Southern District). Gift of silver oar to United States District Court for the Southern District of New York. Univ. Chicago law rev., 27:75-8 (autumn 1959). Proceedings, 14 Feb. 1941, at the presentation to the Court of "the Silver Oar," the mace of the Vice-Admiralty Court of the Province of New York, made by Charles Le Roux (1689-1745), New York silversmith, ca. 1725, and retained in the family of Thomas Ludlow, Jr., marshal of the court, from its dissolution in 1775 till ca. 1939. [7237

DUTCH REFORMED CHURCH, Claverack, N.Y. Marriages of the Dutch Reformed Church of Claverack, Columbia County, New York [1727-1829]. N.Y. geneal. and biog. rec., 88:49-52, 85-90, 174-9; 89:27-34, 90-96; 90:42-8, 83-91, 166-70, 197-203; 91:152 (Jan 1957 - Jul 1960). [7238

FUSCO ADVERTISING AGENCY, INC., Utica, N.Y. A city reborn. [Utica, 1960?] 53, [19] p. facsims., maps, ports., views. 22 x 28 cm. On Utica since 1734. Deals mainly with the closing of the 6 textile mills in or near this "one-industry community," 1951-59, and its rapid transformation into "a multi-industry area." [7239

ELSEA (THORN) HAIGHT (1775-1844) & ISAAC HAIGHT, JR. Elsea Haight's book. Dutchess Co. Hist. Soc., Yr. bk., 43 (1958):52-8. Rearranged contents of a typed copy of a manuscript volume containing lists of births and deaths of members of the Haight and Thorn families of Dutchess County, 1734-1886. [7240

WALKER LEWIS. The right to complain: the trial of John Peter Zenger [New York, 1734-35]. Am. Bar Assoc. jour., 46:27-30, 108-11 (Jan). [7241

VINCENT BURANELLI, ed. The trial of Peter Zenger, edited and with an introduction and notes by Vincent Buranelli. [N.Y.:] New York Univ. Press, 1957. viii, 152 p. facsim. bibliog. (p. 147-50), notes (p. 144-7). Documents relating to the trial in the Supreme Court of Judicature of the Province of New York in 1735 for the offense of printing and publishing a libel against the government. Includes most of the text of A brief narrative of the case and tryal of John Peter Zenger, printer of the New York weekly journal (1736), written anonymously by James Alexander (p. 77-134). [7242

LEONARD WILLIAMS LEVY. Did the Zenger Case really matter? freedom of the press in colonial New York [1735]. Wm. and Mary quar., 17:35-50 (Jan). notes. Evidence, 1735-70 supporting a negative answer and indicating that "the common law of seditious libel: remained in full effect. [7243

DUTCH REFORMED CHURCH OF COXSACKIE, Greene County, N.Y. Baptisms of the Dutch Reformed Church of Coxsackie, Greene County, New York. N.Y. geneal. and biog. rec., 88:105-15, 154-60, 211-18; 89:15-24, 69-78, 220-28; 90:137-46; 91:142-52 (Apr 1957 - Jul 1960). Records from 1738 through 1800. [7244

RAYMOND POLIN. Theories of limited government in the Province of New York, 1750-1769, with special emphasis on the press of New York City. Ann Arbor: University Microfilms, 1959 [i.e. 1960]. Positive microfilm of typescript. xv, 327 leaves. bibliog. (leaves 297-315). Thesis--New York Univ. Abstracted: Dissert. abstracts, 20:3274 (Feb). [7245

WILLIAM NELSON FENTON. The Hiawatha wampum belt of the Iroquois League for Peace: a symbol for the International Congress of Anthropological and Ethnological Sciences, 5th, 1956, Men and cultures: selected papers (Phila.: Univ. of Pennsylvania Press [1960]), p. 3-7. view. bibliog. On a wampum belt probably made between 1755 and 1774, intended as a "mnemonic device for remembering the founding of the original League for Peace in the Stone Age of America" and presented to the New York State Museum in 1898. [7246

MILTON MARTIN KLEIN. Prelude to revolution in New York: jury trials and judicial tenure [1760-67]. Wm. and Mary quar., 17:439-62 (Oct). notes. Mainly on the efforts of Cadwallader Colden, Lieutenant Governor, to reduce the power of the lawyers in the colonial government. [7247

NEIL B. REYNOLDS. The Butlers of Wyoming and Cherry Valley. Am. geneal., 36:201-3 (Oct). On Lt. Walter Butler of New London, who removed to the Mohawk Valley ca. 1728 and died ca. 1760, and some of his descendants. [7248

ALBANY COUNTY, N.Y. The freeholders of the City and County of Albany, 1763. [Edited] by Kenneth Scott. Natl. Geneal. Soc. quar., 48: 171-82 (Dec). notes. Manuscript signed: H[armanus] Schuyler, Shireff, listing persons eligible to serve as jurors. [7249

BENJAMIN GINSBURG. The furniture of Alban's Cherry Hill. Antiques, 77: 562-6 (Jun). views. On a house built in 1768 for Philip Van Rensselaer and still occupied by his descendants; with a description of 13 pieces of furniture from it in the "Albany style," 18th century (some probably much older than the house). [7250

WILLIAM ADAMS (fl. 1771-73). A doctor's bill of early days. [Edited by Charles K. Winne, Jr.] Dutch Settlers Soc. Albany, Yr. bk., 34-35:28-32. Bill rendered to Maj. Jellis Fonda by an Albany physician for visits and medicines between 17 Jul. 1771 and 6 Jan. 1773, with notes identifying the medicines. [7251

GERALD GUNTHER. Governmental power and New York Indian lands [1777-1958]--reassessment of a particular problem of Federal-State relations. Buffalo law rev., 8:1-26 (fall 1958). notes. [7252

NEW YORK, UNIVERSITY OF THE STATE OF. The regents of the University of the State of New York, 1784-1959. ... Compiled and edited by Albert B[ickmore] Corey, Hugh M. Flick, [and] Frederick A. Morse. Albany, 1959. 48 p. ports., tables. Biographical sketches and other information. [7253

ROBERT WARREN SILSBY. Mortgage credit in the Phelps-Gorham Purchase [Ontario and Steuben Counties, N.Y., 1790-1820]. N.Y. hist., 41:3-34 (Jan). tables. notes. [7254

AMY PEARCE VER NOOY. John Forbus [1758-1827] and his family. Dutchess Co. Hist. Soc., Yr. bk., 44 (1959): 63-73. bibliog. On his life and descendants in Poughkeepsie, 1793-1877. [7255

HENRY SACKETT MANLEY. Indian reservation ownership in New York. N.Y. State Bar bul., 32:134-8 notes. On the question whether land on any of the 6 reservations in the State can be owned by an individual, 1794-1960. [7256

PITT PETRI. The postal history of western New York: its post offices, its postmasters [1795-1960. Buffalo? N.Y., c1960. 6], 272 p. maps, tables. On postal service in 8 counties--Erie, Niagara, Orleans, Genesee, Wyoming, Chautauqua, Cattaraugus, and Allegany. [7257

ADELAIDE EDDY SUNDERLIN. Starkey Township of bonnie Dundee: honey recipes and illustrated tales of Starkey, past and present [1796-1960. n. p., 1960. 50] p. views. On an area in Yates County, N.Y., on the west side of Seneca Lake. Appended (p. [15-48]): "Honey recipes." [7258

PITT PETRI. The early postal history of the Niagara frontier [beginning on the Canadian side in 1789, on the American in 1797, here traced to 1820]. Am. Philatelic Cong., Congress book, 26:63-75. facsims., map, view. [7259

PITT PETRI. U.S. - Canada mails: the early Niagara post offices and their markings. Collectors Club philatelist, 39:25-9 (Jan). facsims., map, view. On the British post office at present Niagara-on-the-Lake, the U.S. post office opened with the name Niagara at Fort Niagara, and the confusion between their postal markings, 1797-1813. [7260

BALTUS B. VAN KLEECK. Speed laws and the sanitary code in 1866. Dutchess Co. Hist. Soc., Yr. bk., 43 (1958): 44-8. Quotes and comments upon the charter and laws of Poughkeepsie as published by the Common Council of the City of Poughkeepsie in "a small volume printed in 1866," and refers to earlier regulations since the incorporation of Poughkeepsie as a village in 1799. [7261

ROBERT ROOD BUELL, comp. Pound Cemetery burials, Neversink, N.Y. [1802-1913]. Am. geneal., 36: 19-20 (Jan). [7262

HARRY EMMETT BOLTON, comp. Otsego County, New York, inscriptions. New Eng. hist. and geneal. mag., 114:305-8 (Oct). Inscriptions from Gledhill Cemetery near Garrattsville, N.Y., 1804-1911. [7263

CHARLES MALCOLM NICHOLS. The early post offices of Chautauqua County, New York [1805-1956]. Jamestown, N.Y., 1960. 152 p. facsims., map, tables, views. [7264

JULIAN URSYN NIEMCEWICZ (1758-1841). Journey to Niagara, 1805, from the diary of Julian Ursyn Niemcewicz. Translated from the original manuscript [in French] with an introduction and notes by Metchie J. E. Budka. N.-Y. Hist. Soc. quar., 44:72-113 (Jan). double map, ports., views. notes. Record of the travels of a "Polish poet and patriot" from

New York City to Albany, Utica, Buffalo, and Niagara-on-the-Lake, 5-26 Oct. 1805. [7265

DONALD C. RINGWALD. The beginning of Hudson River steamboating. Am. Neptune, 20:220-22 (Jul). notes. Evidence that the vessel of Robert Fulton that navigated the Hudson, 1807-14, enrolled throughout this period as North River Steam Boat, was referred to informally as early as 1810 as the Clermont, and was not known as "the Katharine of Clermont." [7266

ELIZABETH L. CROCKER. Yesterdays ... in and around Pomfret [N.Y., 1808-45]. Fredonia, N.Y., 1960. [4], 69 p. [7267

Sister MARIE DE LOURDES WALSH. The Sisters of Charity [of St. Vincent de Paul] of New York, 1809-1959. N.Y.: Fordham Univ. Press [1960]. 3 v. xviii, 364; ix, 339; x, 355 p. ports., maps, views. bibliog. (3: 305-18), notes. [7268

WILLIAM COOPER (1754-1809). A guide to the wilderness; or, The history of the first settlements in the western counties of New York, with useful instructions to future settlers. In a series of letters addressed by Judge Cooper, of Coopers-Town, to William Sampson, barrister, of New York. Dublin: Printed by Gilbert and Hodges ... 1810. Jahrbuch für Amerikastudien, 5:308-39. note. Letter of inquiry from Sampson containing 7 questions concerning the natural resources of western New York, the best methods of settling there, the kinds of men who are best fitted to settle, and the prospects of the country; and Cooper's reply, containing information and advice for settlers. [7269

KATHERINE WILCOX THOMPSON. Penfield's past, 1810-1960. ... Published in observance of its 150th anniversary by the town of Penfield, New York. [Penfield] 1960. vii, 213 p. facsims., maps, ports., tables, views. bibliog. (p. 197-8). [7270

THE WESTERN NEW YORK BAPTIST MAGAZINE, Morrisville, N.Y. Death notices from The western New York Baptist magazine, Volume I (1814-1816). [Abstracted by Elizabeth Hayward.] Natl. Geneal. Soc. quar., 48: 154-6 (Sep). [7271

NATHAN MILLER. "... through the Appalachian barrier." John Arthur Garraty, ed., The unforgettable Americans (Great Neck, N.Y.: Channel Press [1960]), p. 115-19. On the activities of De Witt Clinton in the construction of the Erie Canal, 1815-25. [7272

FRED T. STILES. Pioneer doctor of upstate New York. N.Y. folklore quar., 16:279-86 (winter). On the author's ancestor, Dr. Nathaniel Rhoades of Pike Brook, Washington County, where he practiced medicine from 1816 till his death in 1858 or 1859, at which time he was reported to be 107 years old. [7273

WHITNEY NORTH SEYMOUR, JR. Circumstantial evidence in the courts of Schoharie County. N.Y. State Bar bul., 32:310-12 (Oct). view. On the trial, conviction, and execution of John Van Anstyne for the murder of Deputy Sheriff William Huddleston, 1818-19. [7274

CHARLES ATWELL & MARVIN A. RAPP. Ned Foster, hunter. N.Y. folklore quar., 16:174-9 (autumn). Lore about an Adirondack hunter and his "fabulous reputation" in the 1820s. [7275

EDITH MALCOLM WHITE. Looking backward. Intelligencer, 18:[8-10]. Recollections and family traditions concerning Ossining since ca. 1820. [7276

GARRET K. LAWRENCE (died 1837). An unpublished letter from G. K. Lawrence to C[onstantine] S[amuel] Rafinesque, October 8, 1828. [Edited by] Alex Berman. Bul. hist. med., 34: 461-70 (Sep-Oct). facsim. notes. Letter from a Shaker physician and medical botanist of New Lebanon, N.Y., describing the author's "experience with eleven plant medicinals used by the Shakers" and presenting a bill for 33 pounds of "plant drugs"; with excerpts from a printed herbal by Rafinesque, showing his use of some of the information from Lawrence. [7277

MONROE COUNTY, N.Y. A western New York farm inventory--1829. [Edited by] James M. Edmunds. N.Y. folklore quar., 16:57-63 (spring). Inventory (by Elisha Mau and Russell Thayer, appraisers), 2 Jan. 1829, of the property of Chester White (died 1828), farmer near Brockport; with editorial comment on the items and their valuation. [7278

HAROLD KLORFEIN. Public policy and the rule against perpetuities [in New York, 1830-1958]. N.Y. law forum, 51:169-78 (Apr 1959). notes. [7279

THE JAMESTOWN SUN, Jamestown, N.Y. The A. M. E. Zion Church and slavery. A. M. E. Zion quar. rev., 64:140-42 (summer 1953). On Catherine Harris (1809-1907), Jamestown resident from 1831 to 1907, remembered as a Negro nurse and midwife and especially as a friend of runaway slaves en route to Canada. [7280

ERICA R. DAVIES. Daybook for two. N.Y. folklore quar., 16:197-202 (autumn). Information from an account book kept by John Livingston Snedecker, wheelwright and farmer "in what was then Snedekers' [sic] Landing, later Walberg, and now Congers, in Clarkstown, New York," 1835 to 1841 or later, and by Martha Smith, 1888-96. [7281

J. ELET MILTON. Oneida Lake and River: some recollections [since 1882] and the story of the first steamboat on the lake [the Oswego, 1835]. Steamboat bill, 17:99-102, 108 (winter). views. [7282

FLORIAN SCHWENNINGER (died 1868). Documents. [Translated and edited by Gunther R. Rolfson.] Am. Benedictine rev., 11:107-35, 245-65; 12:154-78 (Mar 1959-Jun 1960). notes. Memorial from a Benedictine missionary to his brethren in Fiecht, Austria, dated Weaverville, Calif., 10 Jan. 1854, on his reasons for becoming a missionary, his travels in Europe and voyage to New York, the various forms of misconduct of Catholic priests in New York and elsewhere, the threats of the Nativists, and his service as pastor of Utica, 1844; with notes on the individuals named by him. A second part of the manuscript is lost. [7283

PIERRE DE NIO. A Delaware River raftsman. N.Y. folklore quar., 16: 287-94 (winter). On George Quillen (1845-1918), of Fish's Eddy, on the East Branch of the Delaware, lumberman and rafter, trickster, clown, singer, poet, "a jester and a roving minstrel." [7284

MULFORD QUICKERT SIBLEY. Oneida's challenge to American culture. Joseph J. Kwiat & Mary C. Turpie, eds., Studies in American culture: dominant ideas and images (Minneapolis: Univ. of Minnesota Press [1960]), p. 41-62. notes. On the "communitarian communist society" at Oneida, N.Y., and its system of "Complex Marriage" and "stirpiculture," forming a combination of "economic communism and communism in love," 1848-81. [7285

HARLEY J. McKEE. Greek Revival weighlock, Syracuse, 1849-1850. Soc. Architectural Historians, Jour., 19: 172-3 (Dec). views. notes. On a building overhanging the Erie Canal to enclose a lock in which canal boats and their cargoes were weighed and containing space for the weigh master and toll collector, offices, and sleeping quarters, constructed 1849-50, occupied after the canal was filled in by offices of the State Department of Public Works till 1957, now to be preserved as the Weighlock Canal Museum. [7286

LEWIS HENRY MORGAN (1818-81). League of the Iroquois. Margaret Mead & Ruth L. Bunzel, eds., The golden age of American anthropology (N.Y.: George Braziller, 1960), p. 129-38. From the author's League of the Ho-de-no-sau-nee or Iroquois (1851). On the "civil and domestic institutions, and ... capabilities for further elevation," of the "present Iroquois" Indians. [7287

DORRIS M. BERNING, comp. Cemetery records from Brewerton, Onondaga Co., N.Y. [1853-1947]. Detroit Soc. Geneal. Research mag., 23:81 (winter 1959). [7288

RAY FERRISS. The Great Rifle Match. Gun digest, 15:83-5. port., view. notes. On Nelson Lewis (1811-88), Troy hunter and gunmaker, and Morgan James (1814?-1878), Utica gunmaker, and the test of muzzle-loading rifles made by them in a match at Fort Plain, 12 Jun. 1854, ending with victory for James. [7289

MARYLIN KLOSTY & HOWARD J. WEISS. Illegitimacy. Brooklyn law rev., 26:45-91 (Dec 1959). notes. On the legal status of illegitimate children in New York, 1855-1959. [7290

ISABELLE KEATING SAVELL. The Executive Mansion in Albany: an informal history, 1856-1960. [Albany, 1960.] 47, [1] p. ports., views (part col.). On a structure built for Thomas Olcott in 1856, later occupied by Robert L. Johnson, rented to Governor-Elect Samuel J. Tilden in 1874, and sold to the State of New York in 1877; with brief accounts of "Governors who have occupied the Executive Mansion." [7291

KATHERINE (KURZ) BURTON. Cry jubilee! Allegany, N.Y. [1960]. ix, [3], 227 p. ports., tables, views. On the Sisters of the Third Order Regular of St. Francis of Allegany, New York, 1859-1959. [7292

ABNER H. THOMAS (born 1841). Notes from the diary of Abner H. Thomas, town of Ulysses, Tompkins Co., New York, 1863-1864-1865. Transcribed by his daughter, Eva A. Thomas, 1948. Ithaca, N.Y.: Published for De Witt Historical Soc. of Tompkins County, 1960. 46 p. Record, 1 Jan. 1863-31 Dec. 1865, of farm work, purchases, prices, funerals and other neighborhood events, etc. [7293

ELIZABETH B. POTWINE. Faithfully yours, Eliza Kellas [1864-1943]. Troy, N.Y.: Emma Willard School [1960]. 132 p. ports., views. On her early life and studies, her teaching at the Plattsburgh Normal School, her further studies at Radcliffe College, and her service as head of the Emma Willard School and of Russell Sage College, Troy. [7294

WALTER B. PATTERSON. The last of her kind: a Victorian lady in this modern age--Miss Ellen C[rosby] Roosevelt [1868-1954]. Dutchess Co. Hist. Soc., Yr. bk., 43 (1958): 35-42. Anecdotes and recollections of her life at "Rosedale." Appended (p. 43): "The Columbia crew: verses by Ellen C. Roosevelt, written June 1895," celebrating each member of a rowing crew. [7295

EDWIN ZACHARIAH CARPENTER (1835-1917). The supernatural in Scotia. [Edited by] Neil B. Reynolds. N.Y. folklore quar., 16:298-300 (winter). notes. Excerpts from "a mass of historical material, including reports of conversations with his older neighbors," collected by Carpenter between 1870 and 1890. [7296

JEAN MURRAY LYON, MARION LYNCH QUELLMALZ, & PRUDENCE WAGONER ROBINSON. Hail, Saint Agnes! Ninety years of Saint Agnes School history. Albany, 1960. 159 p. facsims., ports., tables, views. bibliog. (p. 11). On Saint Agnes School of the Order of the Holy Child Jesus, a secondary school for girls in the Catholic Diocese of Albany, 1870-1960, moved to Loudonville, N.Y., in 1932. Includes reminiscenses by Huybertie Lansing Pruyn Hamlin, '91, Marion C. Morkill Guthrie, '10, and other alumnae. [7297

JULIA HULL WINNER. The money diggers of Niagara County. N.Y. folklore quar., 16:221-5 (autumn). Lore about witchcraft, superstition, and buried treasure in the German settlement at Wolcottsville, ca. 1870. [7298

CLARA WISHNER. Americana--the story of Gowanda. Chicago Jew. forum, 18:43-8 (fall 1959). On the Jews in this community, 30 miles south of Buffalo, since 1870. [7299

LOUIS CLARK JONES. Jared Van Wagenen, Jr., 1871-1960. N.Y. hist., 41:245-6 (Apr). On his contributions to "education, history and agriculture," particularly in New York State. [7300

JUDITH SANBORN. The Mud House. ... As told by Evelyn Squire Culp. Intelligencer, 18:[3-5]. On a cement house in Ossining built in 1873 for an unnamed "wealthy American," used as a residence and later as a medical office, a hospital, a restaurant, and a school. [7301

HELEN E. (RUTLEDGE) ALLYN. Life & ancestry of William Noah Allyn [born 1874]. Skaneateles, N.Y.: Lakeside Print. Co. [1960. 8], 53 p. coat of arms, facsims., geneal. tables (1 fold.), map, ports., tables, views. bibliog. (p. 51-2). Account, by his wife, of his life in up-State New York, his founding and operation of Welch Allyn, Inc., Skaneateles, maker of diagnostic medical instruments, and his descent from Matthew Allyn (1605-70), English emigrant in 1632, settler in Windsor, Conn. [7302

TIMOTHY McGUIRE. The indeterminate sentence in New York [1877-1959]. Brooklyn law rev., 26:92-104 (Jan 1959). notes. [7303

BALTUS B. VAN KLEECK. The Poughkeepsie Tennis Club: its first fifty years [1891-1940]. Dutchess Co. Hist. Soc., Yr. bk., 44 (1959): 27-53. Includes some account of "organized tennis in Poughkeepsie" since 1879. [7304

JEREMY POLLARD FELT. The regulation of child labor in New York State, 1886-1942, with emphasis upon the work of the New York Child Labor Committee. Ann Arbor: University Microfilms, 1959 [i.e. 1960]. Positive microfilm of typescript. [315] leaves. Thesis--Syracuse Univ. Abstracted: Dissert. abstracts, 20:2771-2 (Jan). [7305

ROBERT HANSON WOODWARD. Harold Frederic and New York folklore. N.Y. folklore quar., 16:83-9 (summer). notes. On folklore in his novels and tales about the Mohawk Valley, 1887-98. [7306

LUCY (REISSIG) SCHENCK. Seven, eight, shut the gate! The heartwarming story of an American family. N.Y.: Greenwich Book Publishers [1958. 2], 86 p. On the early life of the author and her 7 brothers and sisters, children of an unnamed Lutheran minister (from Germany) and his wife, Dorothea, in "East Potter," "West Henrietta," and "Farmington," N.Y., ca. 1889 ff. [7307

FRED MERZ. Going--going--gone. Natl. Railway Hist. Soc., Bul., 25(3): 4-11 (3d quar.). facsim., views. On the Rome, Watertown, and Ogdensburg Railroad, extending from Rochester to Ogdensburg, acquired (in 1891) by the New York Central as its Ontario Division; with the author's memories of trains going through Charlotte (now part of Rochester) between 1908 and 1935, and a reproduction of a timetable of 26 June 1892. [7308

EUGENE HOTCHKISS 3rd. Jacob Gould Schurman and the Cornell tradition: a study of Jacob Gould Schurman, scholar and educator, and his administration of Cornell University, 1892-1920. Ann Arbor: University Microfilms, 1960. Positive microfilm of typescript. [374] leaves. Thesis--Cornell Univ. Abstracted: Dissert. abstracts, 21:106 (Jul). [7309

NORTHERN CENTRAL NEW YORK VOLUNTEER FIREMEN'S ASSOCIATION. The history of Northern Central New York Volunteer Firemen's Association, Inc. By Samuel J. Pitcher [Secretary]. Rochester, N.Y., c1960. [18], 15, [1], 14 [1], 48, [8], 5, 4, [1] leaves. On an organization of firemen in Cayuga, Monroe, Onondaga, and Wayne Counties, 1896-1960. [7310

EMIL L. COHEN & JACOB D. HYMAN. Scope of city home rule in New York: revising ward boundaries for election of supervisors serving on county board [1898-1959]. Buffalo law rev., 9:1-25 (fall 1959). notes. [7311

ROY WHIPPLE. So you want to go back. Antique automobile, 24:196-8 (Jun). view. On the author's adventures in driving and selling automobiles in and near Binghamton, N.Y., 1898-1902. [7312

H. L. IVES. The scheme of H. L. Ives. [Edited by] Earl R. Hutchinson. N.Y. folklore quar., 16:64-7 (spring). Letter to the editor of the Potsdam Courier and freeman, 2 Jun. 1909, proposing establishment of a park, which actually came into being (sometime after 1931) as Ives Park. [7313

ERICH FRED BORDNE. Water resources of a western New York region: a case study of water resources and use in the Genesee Valley and western Lake Ontario Basin [1912-52. Syracuse:] Syracuse Univ. Press, 1960. xix, 149 p. diagrs., maps, tables. bibliog. (p. 129-49), notes. Study of the Genesee Valley and the coastal plain from Rochester to the Niagara River, forming all or parts of 8 counties in New York and 1 in Pennsylvania. [7314

ALF EVERS. The time Old Bella lost her cud. N.Y. folklore quar., 16: 271-9 (winter). On folk remedies applied to a sick cow in Ulster County by Charley Wood in 1915. [7315

JAMES L. MAGAVERN. County home rule: freedom from legislative interference [in New York, 1915-58]. Buffalo law, 8:252-67 (winter 1959). notes. [7316

CHARLES GORDON HEYD, ADA CHREE REID, & J. MILLER WALKER. Physicians' Home: forty years, 1919 to 1959. N.Y. State jour. med., 59: 3837-40 (15 Oct). table. On an organization in New York established by physicians to aid indigent members of their profession. [7317

JOHN H. BROWE. The Bureau of Nutrition of the New York State Department of Health [since the early 1920s]. N.Y. State jour. med., 60: 2735-8 (1 Sep). [7318

JEWEL (LUBIN) BELLUSH. Roosevelt's good right arm: Lieut. Governor Herbert H. Lehman. N.Y. hist., 41:423-43 (Oct). notes. On his service as Lieutenant Governor of New York, 1928-32. [7319

DONALD RALPH VOSBURGH. Gloversville, New York: a community study of industrial transition and social change [1930, 1950-58]. Ann Arbor: University Microfilms, 1958 [i.e. 1960]. Positive microfilm of typescript. [294] leaves. Thesis (D.S.S.)--Syracuse Univ. Abstracted: Dissert. abstracts, 20:3881-2 (Mar). On "the center of the American glove industry," a city in Fulton County, N.Y. [7320

LESTER FOX. Pleasure and profit. Am. forests, 66(6):17-19 (Jun). port., table, view. On the conservation practices of Henry U. Webster on his farm in Cayuga County, N.Y., 1932-57. [7321

FRITZ H. WIESSNER. Early rock climbing in the Shawangunks. Appalachia, 33:18-25 (Jun). views. Recollections of climbing in a range of mountains extending "from the three-state corner of New Jersey, New York and Pennsylvania for 35 miles in north-northeasterly direction" to a point about 12 miles south of Kingston, 1935-46. [7322

HELEN HALL JENNINGS. Leadership and sociometric choice. Jacob L. Moreno, ed., The sociometry reader (Glencoe, Ill.: Free Press [1960]), p. 437-54. bibliog., notes. On a study of the inmates of the New York Training School for Girls, 1937, as reported in the author's Leadership and isolation (1943, 1950). [7323

LEONA BAUMGARTNER, HAROLD JACOBZINER, & JEAN PAKTER. A critical survey of the New York program for the care of premature infants [1938-59]. Jour. pediatrics, 54: 725-40 (Jun 1959). tables. notes. [7324

LOUIS CLARK JONES. Things that go bump in the night. N.Y.: Hill and Wang [1959. 2], xii, 208 p. illus. bibliog. (p. 185-97). Ghost tales and beliefs collected from relatives and neighbors by students in the author's folklore course in the New York State College for Teachers at Albany, 1940-46, selected from the Archive of New York Folklore (now at Cooperstown). Includes chapters on "Why they return," "Haunted houses," "Violence and sudden death," "Haunted history," and "The ghostly hitchhiker." [7325

CHARLES VERT WILLIE. Age status and residential stratification [Syracuse, N.Y., 1940, 1950] Am. sociol. rev., 25:260-64 (Apr). tables. notes. Based on thesis--Syracuse Univ. [7326

CHARLES HENRY HOLMES. The transfer student in the College of Liberal Arts (a ten-year comparative study of 1,553 four-year institution and 385 junior college transfer students in the College of Liberal Arts at Syracuse University: 1946-1955). Ann Arbor: University Microfilms, 1960. Positive microfilm of typescript. Thesis (D.S.S.)--Syracuse Univ. Abstracted: Dissert. abstracts, 21:304 (Aug). [7327

NORMAN CAZDEN, ed. Catskill lockup songs. N.Y. folklore quar., 16: 90-103 (summer). music. notes. Six texts (with tunes) "from the manuscript 'Music from the Catskills' sponsored by Camp Woodland, Inc., of Phoenicia, New York" (not described or dated), sung by George Edwards, Charles Hinckley, and Elwyn Davis, about experiences in jail. [7328

MARY ETHEL KINDLE, ed. Authors of Rockland County: a directory. Nyack, N.Y.: Public Schools, c1960. [4], 52 leaves. Biographical sketches of 109 writers living in the County. [7329

New York City

JOHN REED. The Hudson River Valley [1524-1960]. N.Y.: C. N. Potter [1960]. 239 p. maps, views (part double). Introduction (p. 7-33), photographs taken for this volume (p. 34-207), text (p. 209-35), and chronology (p. 236-8). [7330

MICHEL GUILLAUME. La Cité de New York: étude politique et administrative [1624-1949]. Études politiques anglo-saxonnes: Irlande du Nord, Connecticut, New York (Paris: Armand Colin, 1950 [Cahiers de la Fondation Nationale des Sciences Politiques, 13]), p. 157-223. map, tables. bibliog. [7331

THEODORE ROSENTHAL. Venereal disease control in New York City: a backward glance [1638-1957]. N.Y. State jour. med., 59:445-52 (1 Feb 1959). tables. notes. [7332

GEORGE J. FLUHR. The historical geography of the West Bronx [N.Y., 1646-1960]. N.Y.: Aidan Press, c1960. [2], 14, [5] leaves. maps. bibliog. (leaves 12-14). [7333

CAMERON ALLEN. The paternity of Aert Theunissen Middagh: a suggestion. The ancestry of Theunis Gysbertszen Bogaert: a caveat. Am. geneal., 36:129-36 (Jul). Suggests that Bogaert (arrived in New Amsterdam ca. 1652) may have been the father of Middagh (in New Amsterdam by 1654). [7334

RAY T. KELLY. The Spuyten Duyvil enigma. N.Y. folklore quar., 16: 255-65 (winter). notes. On the origin of the name (in use as early as 1653 in the form "Spuyt den Duyvel") of "that bluff of the mainland, just across the Harlem River from Manhattan's northwestern tip," and of a creek adjacent to the bluff. [7335

KENNETH SCOTT. The French refugee Pierre Legrand of New York City [recorded there 1684-1707]. N.Y. geneal. and biog. rec., 91:1-4 (Jan). [7336

WILLIAM GARLAND ROGERS & MILDRED WESTON. Carnival crossroads: the story of Times Square [since 1713]. Garden City, N.Y.: Doubleday, 1960. 183 p. cartoons (1 double). bibliog. (p. 181-3). [7337

RICHARD SHARPE PATTERSON. The Department's new home--175 years ago. For. Service jour., 37(1):33-4 (Jan). view. On Fraunces Tavern, New York City, erected in 1719 as a residence of Stephen De Lancey, acquired by Samuel Fraunces in 1762 for use as a tavern, occupied by the U.S. Department of Foreign Affairs from Jan. 1785 to May 1788, now preserved by the Sons of the Revolution. [7338

PERRY E. BORCHERS. Saint Paul's Chapel recorded. Soc. Architectural Historians, Jour., 19:32-4 (Mar). plans. On the measurements of the church of Trinity Parish, New York City, built 1764-66 (spire and portico 1794-96). [7339

HAROLD LESLIE PETERSON. Some notes on James Potter and his sabers. Mil. collector & historian, 12:107-8 (winter). views. On his work in New York City as a swordsmith during the Revolution. [7340

RITA SUSSWEIN GOTTESMAN, ed. The arts and crafts in New York, 1777-1799: advertisements and news items from New York City newspapers. N.Y., 1954. [2], xix, 484 p. facsims. (Collections of the New-York Historical Society for the year 1948: the John Watts De Peyster Publication Fund Series, 81.) Texts of advertisements of painting and engraving, silver and jewelry, china, earthenware, and glass, pewter, furniture, clocks and watches, builders and buildings, ships and boats, metal workers and iron works, paper manufacturers, printers, and bookbinders, fabrics and needlework, costume, painting and glazing, coach makers and coaches, music and musical instruments, etc.; with "Illustrative woodcuts and engravings: a representative list from New York newspapers, 1777-1799," and a detailed index. Continues a volume collected by the same editor covering the years 1726-76, published in 1938. [7341

VIVIAN CONSTANCE HOPKINS. The most famous student in Columbia's first class--De Witt Clinton. Columbia Lib. columns, 9(3):9-13 (May). port. On his studies at Columbia College and his continued interest in it, 1784-1825. [7342

EGAL FELDMAN. Fit for men: a study of New York's clothing trade [1786-1861]. Wash.: Public Affairs Press [1960]. vii, [3], 138 p. notes (p. 126-35). On "the production and sale of coats, vests, and trousers, and such furnishings as shirts, collars, and cuffs" in New York City; with chapters on trade with the South and the West, "Outfitting the Forty-Niners," and "The country merchant in the big town." [7343

WALDRON PHOENIX BELKNAP, JR. (1899-1949). A discussion of a group of portraits by Charles Willson Peale. Waldron Phoenix Belknap, Jr., American colonial painting: materials for a history, ed. Charles Coleman Sellers (Cambridge: Belknap Press of Harvard Univ. Press, 1959), p. 47-58. ports. On several portraits of members of the De Peyster family, painted in New York City in 1792 and 1798, as documented by Peale's diary. [7344

LILLIAN MOORE. New York's first ballet season [1792]. N.Y. Pub. Lib., Bul, 64:478-90 (Sep). ports. notes. Appended: "Ballets and pantomimes produced at the John St Theatre, New York, by Alexandre Placide and his company of French dancers, with members of the Old American company of actors," 15 Jan.-14 May 1792. [7345

NEW YORK CITY. Common Council. Of historical note. A. M. E. Zion quar. rev., 64:210-14 (fall 1953). Information from the Minutes of the Common Council of the City of New York, 1784-1831, about the African Methodist Episcopal Zion Church there, 1798-1826. [7346

TRINITY CHURCH, New York. Records of Trinity Church Parish, New York City. N.Y. geneal. and biog. rec., 79: 148-52; 81:18-23, 96-100, 218-24; 82:98-102, 156-60; 83:42-52; 84:32-8, 108-11; 85:35-40; 86:28-34, 232-8; 87: 231-7; 88:235-42; 89:109-15, 146-50 (Jul 1948 - Jul 1958). These installments: marriages, Apr. 1802-Dec. 1861. [7347

J. FRASER MUIRHEAD. Thomas Addis Emmet [1764-1827], William James MacNeven [1763-1841]. New Eng. jour. med., 262:460-61 (3 Mar). bibliog. On the activities of Emmet as a lawyer in New York City and of MacNeven as a physician there after their emigration from Ireland, Emmet in 1804 and MacNeven in 1805. [7348

LORRAINE W. PEARCE. The work of Charles-Honoré Lannuier [1779-1819], French cabinetmaker in New York [from 1804 till his death]. Md. hist. mag., 55:14-29 (Mar). views. notes. Detailed analysis of his designs, materials, and methods. [7349

FIFTH AVENUE PRESBYTERIAN CHURCH, New York. A noble landmark of New York: the Fifth Avenue Presbyterian Church, 1808-1958. N.Y., 1960. xiii, [3], 174 p. plan, ports., tables, views. Includes "Historical account of the Fifth Avenue Presbyterian Church," by George T. Peck (p. 1-110), and "A history of our church's music," by Robert S. Baker (p. 111-19). [7350

HUMANE SOCIETY OF NEW YORK CITY. The Humane Society of New York City in 1811. Presbyt. Hist. Soc., Jour., 38:248-52 (Dec). Letter from J. [or I.?] Van den Heiwel [spelling doubtful], Secretary of the Society, to the Rev. John Brodhead Romeyn, mainly on the Society's distribution of soup to persons jailed for debts and its legal services to procure the release of such persons. [7351

HERMAN DAVID BLOCH. The New York City Negro and occupational eviction, 1860-1910. Internatl. rev. soc. hist., 5:26-38. notes. Includes a section on "The establishment of a Negro job ceiling, 1820-1860." [7352

EMMA COHN. Ezekiel J. Connell, 1822-1896. N.Y. Pub. Lib., Bul., 64: 647-51 (Dec). port. On his prosperous career in New York City as a cotton dealer, the ideas expressed in his 7 books and pamphlets (published 1872-89), and his bequest of about a million dollars for the erection of a fireproof library building. [7353

JAMES L. CROUTHAMEL. James Watson Webb [1802-84]: mercantile editor. N.Y. hist., 41:400-422 (Oct). notes. Based on thesis--Univ. of Rochester. On his editorship of the Morning courier and New York enquirer, "a mercantile newspaper," 1827-61, and his related business and political activities, editorial policies, and ideas and doctrines. [7354

EGAL FELDMAN. Jews in the early growth of New York City's men's clothing trade [1830-60]. Am. Jew. arch., 12:5-14 (Apr). notes. Evidence that in these years Jews were not numerous or influential in the trade in New York City. [7355

CHARLES E. ROSENBERG. The cholera epidemic of 1832 in New York City. Bul. hist. med., 33:37-49 (Jan-Feb 1959). notes. Based on thesis (M. A.)--Columbia Univ., 1957. [7356

JULIAN BLANCHARD. Bank note origin of Greig's City Despatch Post stamp. Essay proof jour., 13:3-13 (Jan 1956). facsims. On the stamp used by Alexander M. Greig "for his private local post in New York City in 1842 ... the first adhesive postage stamp issued in the United States--or in the Western Hemisphere," and the uncertainty as to "the origin of the vignette used, its engraver, and the producer of the stamp." [7357

DOROTHY G. BECKER. The visitor to the New York City poor, 1843-1920: the role and contributions of volunteer visitors of the New York Association for the Improvement of the Condition of the Poor, State Charities Aid Association, and New York Charity Organization Society. Ann Arbor: University Microfilms, 1960. Positive microfilm of typescript. [535] leaves. Thesis (D.S.W.)--Columbia Univ. Abstracted: Dissert. abstracts, 21: 697 (Sep). [7358

ROBERT HUNTER MORRIS (1802-55). Postmaster Robert Morris of N.Y.: being letters for the period June 11, 1847, to February 28, 1848. Extracted with a commentary by Winthrop S[millie] Boggs. N.Y.: Collectors Club, 1960. 206 p. facsims., ports., views. Texts of 226 official letters (selected from a letterbook containing copies of 979 letters), illustrating the administration and procedures of the New York Post Office. [7359

FRIEDRICH HECKER (1811-81). A Hecker letter. Am.-German rev., 26(4):18-19 (Apr-May). Letter to the author's wife, dated New York, 7 Oct. 1848, on his voyage from England, his observations in New York City, and his success there in collecting funds to promote revolution in Germany. [7360

E. W. PROBASCO. [Letter to Benjamin F. Honness, dated New York, 24 Mar. 1851.] N.J. genesis, 8:303 (Oct). On the author's commercial occupations since his recent arrival in New York, and his opinions of the city. [7361

MELVIN FULD & GEORGE FULD. The token collector's page. Numismatist, 73:1642-4 (Nov). coins. On tokens issued by John K. Curtis, New York City jeweler, watchmaker, and dealer in "autographs, portraits, curiosities & antiques," 1859-61, probably engraved by G. H. Lovett. [7362

ALFRED BLALOCK. A boyhood portrait of William Stewart Halsted (1852-1922). Bul. hist. med., 34: 195-8 (May-Jun). ports. (1 col.). On a portrait showing Mary Louisa (Haines) Halsted of New York City and 3 of her children, including William Stewart Halsted, ca. 1860. [7363

KARL F. HOFFMANN. The history of the Rudolf Virchow Medical Society in the City of New York, 1860 to 1960. Joseph Berberich, Henry Lax, & Rudolf Stern, eds., Jubilee volume, 100th anniversary, Festschrift ... Rudolf Virchow Medical Society in the City of New York, N.Y. (Basel, N.Y.: S. Karger, 1960), p. 12-14. facsims., maps, ports. bibliog., notes. On an organization founded as Deutscher Medizinischer Leseverein von New York, later named Medizinisch-chirurgischer Verein deutscher Ärzte von New York und Umgegend. [7364

TRAVIS EDWARD TRITTSCHUH. The ballad-seller and his kind. Jour. Am. folklore, 72:54-6 (Jan-Mar). notes. On street vendors of sheet music in New York City, 1867-1900. [7365

ADA CHREE REID. Elise Strang L'Esperance [1879-1959]. Am. Med. Women's Assoc., Jour., 14:432-3 (May 1959). port., view. On her studies at the Women's Medical College of the New York Infirmary, her service as a pathologist, and her establishment of the Kate Depew Strang Tumor Clinic of the New York Infirmary. [7366

IRVING WERSTEIN. The blizzard of '88 [New York City, 11-13 Mar. 1888]. N.Y.: Crowell [1960]. xi, [5], 157 p. table, views (part double). [7367

GEORGE W. ALGER. Lillian D. Wald [1867-1940]. Am. jour. nursing, 60: 354-7 (Mar). ports. On her service as founder and head of the Visiting Nurse Service of New York, ca. 1890 to 1937. [7368

RICHARD SCHICKEL. The world of Carnegie Hall [New York City, 1891-1960]. N.Y.: Messner [1960. 10], 438 p. cartoons, music ports., view. "A history of the most important concert hall in America." [7369

SOPHIE (GUGGENHEIMER) UNTERMEYER & ALIX WILLIAMSON. mother is Minnie. Garden City, N.Y.: Doubleday, 1960. 213 p. ports. On Minnie (Schafer) Guggenheimer (born 1892), her life in New York City, her marriage to Charles S. Guggenheimer, her establishment of free band concerts in New York City and eventually of the "Stadium Concerts" at Lewisohn Stadium, and "her full-time unsalaried job as impresaria of the world's largest-scale musical project." [7370

CORNELIA GOLDSMITH. Child day care, a public health responsibility [New York City, 1895-1959]. Am. jour. pub. health, 49:1069-73 (Aug 1959). [7371

JACOB RALPH SCHWARTZ (born 1890). Orchard Street. N.Y.: Comet Press Books, 1960. [10], 309 p. (A Carlton reflection book.) On the author's life on Orchard Street, his Jewish upbringing, his work in his father's butcher shop and as a painter of signs and show-cards, his studies in the New York University School of Dentistry, and his entry into dental practice under his original Russian name as J. R. Charney, D.D.S., 1899-1914. [7372

ZEVI H. HARRIS. A study of trends in Jewish education for girls in New York City [since 1900]. Ann Arbor: University Microfilms, 1959 [i.e. 1960]. Positive microfilm of typescript. 10, vii, 300 leaves. tables. bibliog. (leaves 280-85). Thesis--Yeshiva Univ. Abstracted: Dissert. abstracts, 20:3617-18 (Mar). [7373

STEVEN C. SWETT. The test of a reformer: a study of Seth Low, New York City mayor, 1902-1903. N.-Y. Hist. Soc. quar., 44:4-41 (Jan). port. notes. [7374

NEWMAN LEVY. The Nan Patterson case. N.Y.: Simon and Schuster, 1959. viii, 245, [2] p. On Anna Eliza Patterson (born 1882/83), chorus girl and actress in New York City; her "notorious affair" with Francis Thomas Young; the murder of Young in 1904; and the indictment and acquittal of Nan Patterson on a charge of murder. Based in part upon information from the author's father, Abe Levy, counsel for the defense in this case. [7375

PHILIP HENRY CORNICK. The property tax and housing. Am. jour. econ. and sociol., 19:17-25 (Oct 1959). On the reasons why a "land value tax" should be substituted for the "real property tax," as illustrated in the experience of New York City since 1906. [7376

ROSA LEE NEMIR & 3 others. History of the Women's Medical Association of New York City (Branch Fourteen): 1909-1959. Am. Med. Women's Assoc., Jour., 15:781-3 (Aug). ports. [7377

BYRON POLK STOOKEY. "What is past is prologue." Arch. neurol., 1:467-74 (Nov 1959). bibliog. On the Neurological Institute, Columbia-Presbyterian Medical Center, 1909-59. [7378

FREDERIC ALEXANDER BIRMINGHAM (born 1911). It was fun while it lasted. Phila.: Lippincott [1960]. 224 p. On the author's early life in Harlem, then "a prosperous residential heaven of Manhattan, content to be just as it had always been since the Dutch settled there," and his family vacations on the Delaware and the Hudson and in New England. [7379

JOHN FRANCIS KIERAN. A natural history of New York City: a personal report after fifty years of study & enjoyment of wildlife within the boundaries of Greater New York. Boston: Houghton Mifflin, 1959. xi, [5], 428 p. views. On the author's observations of weather, water and land, rocks, wild plants, and wild animals in and near New York City since 1914. [7380

CHARLES KALISH. A vignette ... George Bergleightner [1885-1954], watchmaker. Natl. Assoc. Watch and Clock Collectors, Bul., 9:327-8 (Aug). port., views. On his life in New York City as "a watchmaker's watchmaker," 1915-54, and his earlier years in Austria. [7381

HANS ZEISEL, HARRY KALVEN, JR., BERNARD BUCHHOLZ. Delay in the court. Boston: Little, Brown, 1959. xxvii, 312 p. diagrs., tables. bibliog. (p. 297-303), notes. (A University of Chicago Law School study in judicial administration.) Quantitative analysis of records of the Supreme Court of New York County, 1915-57, to determine causes of delay and to suggest remedies. [7382

JAMES FELT. Modern zoning for New York City [1916-60]. Municipal Engineers jour., 46:52-9 (2d quar.). [7383

ALLAN D. VESTAL. A study in perfidy. Ind. law jour., 35:17-44 (fall 1959). notes. On Martin T. Manton (1880-1946), New York City lawyer, Judge of the Federal District Court for the Southern District of New York (1916-18) and of the Court of Appeals for the Second Circuit (1918-39), indicted and convicted in 1939 of having accepted bribes totaling $435,000 while in office, and sentenced to confinement in a penitentiary. [7384

AMERICAN FEDERATION OF ARTS. Jacob Lawrence [born 1917]. By Aline B[ernstein] Saarinen.]N.Y., 1960.] 19 p. port., views (part col.). bibliog. (p. 12-14). On his life in New York City as a Negro, his teaching of art, and his work as a painter and magazine illustrator, mainly showing Negroes at work or play; with a catalogue of a retrospective exhibition. [7385

ROBERT NELSON BURROWS. The image of urban life as it is reflected in the New York City novel, 1920-1930. Ann Arbor: University Microfilms, 1959 [i.e. 1960]. Positive microfilm of typescript. [466] leaves. Thesis--Univ. of Pennsylvania. Abstracted: Dissert. abstracts, 20:2796 (Jan). [7386

ASSOCIATION OF THE BAR OF THE CITY OF NEW YORK. Library. The Presidents of this Association, 1927-1945. Assoc. Bar City N.Y., Rec., 15: 200-209 (Apr). Tabulated biographical data and lists of writings by and about the 9 Presidents. [7387

DANNY BARKER. Jelly Roll Morton in New York. Jazz rev., 2(4):12-14 (May 1959). port. Memories of jazz sessions at the Rhythm Club, 1930 ff. [7388

RALPH SCHOENSTEIN (born 1933). The block. N.Y.: Random House [1960. 10], 137, [2] p. On the author's life in the 200 block of West 78th Street on "Manhattan's West Side" till his family moved away in 1955, and the almost complete change in the racial composition and other sociological characteristics of the neighborhood before the end of this period. [7389

WILLIAM PAUL BROWN. The political and administrative leadership of Fiorello H. Laguardia [i.e. La Guardia] as Mayor of the City of New York, 1934-1941. Ann Arbor: University Microfilms, 1960. Positive microfilm of typescript. [365] leaves. Thesis--New York Univ. Abstracted: Dissert. abstracts, 21:1243-4 (Nov). [7390

KAREL B. ABSOLON (1878-1960). Dr. Bernhard Aschner: surgeon, scientist, and scholar (1883 to 1960). Surgery, 48:979-83 (Nov). facsim., port., views. On his emigration to America (1938) and his work as director of the arthritis clinics of the Stuyvesant and Lebanon Hospitals, New York City; with some account of his earlier years in Austria and Germany. [7391

MORRIS EAGLE. The Puerto Ricans in New York City [1939-57]. Nathan Glazer & Davis McEntire, eds., Studies in housing & minority groups ... special research report to the Commission on Race and Housing (Berkeley: Univ. of California Press, 1960), p. 144-77. maps, tables. notes. [7392

MORRIS AARON HOROWITZ. The New York [City] hotel industry [1939-57]: a labor relations study. Cambridge: Harvard Univ. Press, 1960. xx, 265 p. diagrs., ports., tables (1 double), views. notes (p. 247-62). (Wertheim publications in industrial relations.) [7393

ERNESTINE KOPP & ROSALIND SNYDER. In-service improvement program for new instructors [at the Fashion Institute of Technology, an agency of the New York City Board of Education, 1944-59]. Jr. college jour., 30:90-94 (Oct 1959). [7394

MARGARET GILBERT BENZ. A study of faculty and administrative staff who have retired from New York University, 1945-1956. Jour. educ. sociol., 31:282-93 (Apr 1958). tables. [7395

MOUNT SINAI HOSPITAL, New York. In memoriam. Mt. Sinai Hospital, Jour., 26:417-23; 27:277-9, 379-81, 485-7, 569-71 (Sep-Oct 1959, May-Dec 1960). ports. Memorial sketches, by various contributors, of Bernard Sutro Oppenheimer (1876-1958), Reuben Ottenberg (1882-1959), Samuel Silbert (1894-1959), David Adlersberg (1897-1960), Ernst Peter Pick (1872-1960), and Sol Wiener Ginsburg (1899-1960). [7396

[Brooklyn and Queens]

WILLIAM C. MATTISON. Brooklyn's court houses--a history. N.Y. State Bar jour., 31:203-13 (Jun 1959). port. views. Account of 10 buildings erected between 1668 and 1959. [7397

WALT WHITMAN (1819-92). An uncollected Whitman article. [Edited] by Arthur Golden. N.Y. Pub. Lib., Bul., 64:353-60 (Jul). notes. "An old landmark gone: an interesting reminiscence of old times in Brooklyn," unsigned, from the Brooklyn Daily eagle, 9 Oct. 1862, containing the author's recollections of an undated interview with Andrew Demarest (1779?-1862) about the demolition of the First Dutch Church of Brooklyn in 1807 and the discovery in it of the body of a British officer "in remarkable preservation," killed during the Battle of Brooklyn in 1776 and exhumed in the presence of Demarest and of a lady who as a child had witnessed the burial. [7398

JACOB JUDD. The history of Brooklyn, 1834-1855: political and administrative aspects. Ann Arbor: University Microfilms, 1959 [i.e. 1960]. Positive microfilm of typescript. [296] leaves. Thesis--New York Univ. Abstracted: Dissert. abstracts, 20:3271 (Feb). [7399

ALONZO GIBBS. New Year's calling. N.Y. folklore quar., 16:295-7 (winter). On a New Year's custom in Brooklyn in "the late nineteenth and early twentieth centuries." [7400

ARTHUR T. ANTONY. The legacy of the past. Am. jour. obstet. and gynecol., 78:1341-6 (Dec 1959). On the Brooklyn [N.Y.] Gynecological Society, 1890-1958. [7401

WILLIAM D. SLADE. Brooklyn Elevated had its ups & downs. Long Island forum, 23:250-51, 254 (Nov). On ramps used by streetcars and elevated cars, 1895-1919. [7402

HENRY C. JORALEMON. Brooklyn Heights boyhood. Long Island forum, 23:5-6 (Jan). view. Undated reminiscences (ca. 1900?). [7403

HAROLD MALES (born 1932). More Jewish dialect stories. [Edited by Richard M. Dorson.] Midw. folklore, 10:133-46 (fall). Sixteen anecdotes and tales recalled by Males from his youth in Brooklyn. [7404

[Staten Island]

GEORGE ENGLERT McCRACKEN. The date of the Staten Island census [probably 1708 or 1709]. Am. geneal., 36:67-8 (Apr). [7405

Long Island

DOUGLAS TUOMEY. What's in a name? Long Island forum, 23:29-30, 109 (Feb, May). views. On the origins of a number of Long Island place names. [7406

HILDA M. TURNER. Ancient Long Island. Long Island forum, 23:123-4, 137, 149-50, 165-6, 177, 182-3, 188-9 (Jun-Aug). views. On the archeology of the island, believed to have been inhabited by Indians as early as 5,000 B.C. [7407

OSBORN SHAW. Historic storms and gales [on Long Island, 1635-1938]. Long Island forum, 23:31-2, 44-5, 61-3, 85-7, 91, 96 (Feb-Apr). views. Published as a pamphlet in 1939. Includes some account of changes in the beaches. [7408

PETER LUYSTER VAN SANTVOORD. Long Island's first white settlers. Long Island forum, 23:245-6, 260-62 (Nov). facsim., views. On several individuals who settled in 1636 and 1637. [7409

HARRIET G. VALENTINE, ANDRUS T. VALENTINE, & ESTELLE V. NEWMAN. Main Street, Cold Spring Harbor [1653-1960]. Long Island, N.Y.: Huntington Historical Soc., 1960. [4], 28 p. double map, views. Annotated inventory of 76 buildings on the street. [7410

PETER LUYSTER VAN SANTVOORD. The Wrights and the starch works. Long Island forum, 23:175-6, 190 (Aug). views. On the Wright family of Oyster Bay since 1653, and the Duryea Starch Works, Glen Cove, N.Y., founded in 1855 and moved West soon after 1900. [7411

GERALD J. SCHLAEGER. Mitchell Field ... a history and heritage. Flying, 67(6):54-5, 93-4 (Dec). ports., views (1 double). On "the only natural prairie east of the Allegheny Mountains," purchased from the Indians in 1657, used as a British supply base in the Revolution, as a training base for soldiers in 4 19th-century wars, and as an aeronautical center since 1909, acquired by the U.S. Government in 1917, and now the site of Mitchell Air Force Base. [7412

JOHN WALLACE. Treasure trove in Lattingtown. Long Island forum, 23:27, 45-6 (Feb). view. On papers of the Latting family at "Rose Cottage," with references to or quotations from papers dated 1667-1850. [7413

KATE WHEELER STRONG. Madame Martha's recipes. Long Island forum, 23:33-4, 54 (Feb, Mar). On "a great book" purchased by Col. William Smith of Tangier in 1675 and a "second pigskin book," containing culinary and medical recipes entered by his wife, Martha (Tunstall) Smith; with texts of 9 of the recipes. [7414

MACLEAN W. McLEAN. Wills of two **Benjamin Haines [sic]** of Southampton, New York. Am. geneal., 36:92-4 (Apr). Information from the wills of Benjamin Haines, Sr. (1643-87), and his son Benjamin (1666?-1714). [7415

DOUGLAS TUOMEY. Jonathan Four-Fingers. Long Island forum, 23:195-6, 200, 203-4 (Sep). view. Traditions about a thievish Massapequa Indian, active in Suffolk County, L. I., apparently before 1700. [7416

THOMAS R. BAYLES. The South Haven [Presbyterian] Church [1740-1960]. Long Island forum, 23:101-2, 109 (May). view. Mainly on the years before 1867. [7417

CHESTER GORHAM OSBORNE. Benjamin Havens [fl. 1749-90] of Moriches. Long Island forum, 23: 157-8 (Jul). On his many occupations there as "a censustaker, a fish-carter, an innkeeper, a stage-coach manager, and the operator of a Saw Mill" and perhaps "also a spy." [7418

JOHN REYNOLDS. Long Island behind the British lines during the Revolution [1776-83]. Setauket, L.I.: Soc. for the Preservation of Long Island Antiquities, 1960. 40 p. map, ports. (1 mount.), view. bibliog. (p. 37), notes (p. 38-40). Includes references to Loyalists. [7419

AMY O. BASSFORD. John Lyon Gardiner [1770-1816]. Long Island forum, 23:125-6, 140, 162-3 (Jun, Jul). port., view. On the farming and stockraising activities of the 7th proprietor of Gardiner's Island as recorded in a manuscript book of accounts, notes, and correspondence, 1797-1801. [7420

LINDA E. BRANER. The mailman cometh to Jericho. Long Island forum, 23:129-32, 140-42 (Jun). Excerpts from a booklet of the same title, on postal service in Jericho, L.I., since 1802. [7421

DOUGLAS TUOMEY. The exploit of Henry Green. Long Island forum, 23:147, 164-5 (Jul). On an unidentified "Money-Ship" abandoned by its crew off Southampton, L.I., the murder of the crew by wreckers as they came ashore, the discovery of "a torrent of silver dollars" in the ship by Henry Green, the breaking up of the ship in a storm, and the frequent finding, ever since 1816, of silver coins along the beach where floating timbers of the vessel had come to rest. [7422

BENJAMIN TUTTLE, JR., BENJAMIN TUTTLE, SR., & ENOCH MILLER. Apprentice of 1828. Long Island forum, 23:199-200 (Sep). view. Indenture obligating Benjamin Jr. of Southampton, with the consent of his father, to serve Miller, of Brookfield, with the purpose of learning "the Art, Trade and Mystery of Boot and Shoe Makeing," and binding Miller to feed, lodge, and educate him and to pay him wages, signed 9 Jan. 1828. [7423

PETER LUYSTER VAN SANTVOORD. St. Paul's Parish [Episcopal], Glen Cove [since 1833]. Long Island forum, 23:55-6, 66-7 (Mar). view. [7424

FELIX E. REIFSCHNEIDER. Island pioneered transportation. Long Island forum, 23:7-8, 12 (Jan). view. On railroads on Long Island, 1834-1947. [7425

ROY E. LOTT. Early Huntington church music [1836?-1868]. Long Island forum, 23:51-2 (Mar). view. [7426

WILLIAM D. SLADE. R.R. at Woodhaven. Long Island forum, 23:115, 118 (May). On "some of the railroad facilities" in this area since 1836. [7427

C. H. MacLACHLAN. Walt Whitman as a country editor [at Huntington, L.I., 1838-39, as editor of The Long-Islander]. Long Island forum, 23:75-6, 80 (Apr). port. [7428

VERNE DYSON. A century of Brentwood. Brentwood, L. I.: Brentwood Village Press, 1950-53. 2 v. [6], v, [3], 301, iii; [4], 161 p. ports., views. bibliog. (2:143-9). History, 1841-1950, including some account of American Utopian communities. [7429

NORVAL DWYER. Elihu Miller [1848-1940]--Wading River botanist. Long Island forum, 23:171-2, 180 (Aug). port. On his work as a botanist, a collector of wild plants on Long Island, and a horticulturist. [7430

PETER LUYSTER VAN SANTVOORD. Dr. Wright, political leader. Long Island forum, 23:103-4, 117 (May). On Frederick Augustus Wright (1848-1910), M.D., of Glen Cove, general practitioner, Republican leader. [7431

DOUGLAS TUOMEY. The death of Margaret Fuller. Long Island forum 23:277-8, 285 (Dec). port. On the wreck of the 3-masted bark Elizabeth off Point o' Woods, L.I., 19 Jul. 1850, with a loss of 10 lives, including Margaret (Fuller) Ossoli, her husband (Count Giovanni Ossoli), their infant son (Angelo), and an Italian maid of the Ossolis, all of whom, apparently, might have escaped to shore if the Countess Ossoli had not refused to leave the ship. [7432

SAMUEL F. THOMAS. Nassau County (L. I.]: its governments and their expenditure and revenue patterns [1853-1956]. N.Y.: City College Press, 1960. xiv, [2], 117 p. diagrs., map, tables. notes. (City College of New York. Institute of New York Area Studies. Monograph 4.) 1st ed. 1958. [7433

DOUGLAS TUOMEY. Fire Island relief huts. Long Island forum, 23:79 (Apr). view. On huts furnished with stoves, wood, fresh water, biscuits, and tea for the relief of victims of shipwreck, erected ca. 1855 and used until the U.S. Life Saving stations were established on Fire Island. [7434

IRIS GIBBS & ALONZO GIBBS. Swingletree days. Long Island forum, 23:173-4, 178 (Aug). Recollections of Ambrose Whaley (1857?-1953?), "blacksmith and local preacher" in Plainedge, L.I. [7435

FELIX E. REIFSCHNEIDER. The Hempstead and Rockaway Railroad [1869-79]. Long Island forum, 23: 205-7, 214 (Sep). view. [7436

JULIAN DENTON SMITH. Long Island cedars. Long Island forum, 23:78, 82-4 (Apr). On junipers and white cedars on Long Island, the abundance of white cedars as late as 1870, the location of surviving stands of these trees, and some Long Island place names referring to them. [7437

WILBUR A. CORWIN. Wreck of the schooner Avlona [on the beach a mile east of the Bellport Life Saving Station, 1885]. Long Island forum, 23:28, 34-5 (Feb). Information from the author's father (Wilbur R. Corwin) and from his own recollections. [7438

D. N. RAYNOR. Memories of Huntington [since 1885]. Long Island forum, 23:135, 138, 140 (Jun). view. [7439

ROY E. LOTT. The light that failed. Long Island forum, 23:223, 237 (Oct). port. On the unsuccessful efforts of the Rev. Francis C. Hill to establish an electric lighting system in Huntington, 1893. [7440

KATE WHEELER STRONG. Old time sports and pleasures [among the author's neighbors and relatives in

Port Jefferson, L.I., early 20th century]. Long Island forum, 23:81-2, 134-5, 210-11 (Apr, Jun, Sep). views. [7441

HERBERT S. HALE. Summer capitol at Oyster Bay. Long Island forum, 23: 271-2 (Dec). view. On the building in Oyster Bay where "national and international press headquarters were set up" during the years when Theodore Roosevelt was President, 1901-9. [7442

MYRTLE W. REEVE. Old Landing Recreation Club [Roanoke, L.I., 1905-60]. Long Island forum, 23:197-8 (Sep). views. [7443

FELIX E. REIFSCHNEIDER. Wreck Lead. Long Island forum, 23:274-6 (Dec). On the stations along the Long Beach branch of the Long Island Railroad, 1908-15, as recalled by the author. [7444

LOUIS PINE PEARSALL. Wreck of the "Arlington" [3-masted schooner, off the Long Beach Life Saving Station, L.I., 17 Aug. 1909]. Long Island forum, 23:86-7 (Apr). view. [7445

CHESTER GORHAM OSBORNE. The bridge to Paradise. Long Island forum, 23:9-11 (Jan). view. On the bridge and causeway connecting Smith's Point and Great South Beach, built by the Tangier Manor Corporation, 1910-24. See also added information recalled by Capt. Wilbur A. Corwin (p. 98, 108, May). [7446

LOUIS PINE PEARSALL. Old time grocery story. By Lou Pearsall. Long Island forum, 23:161, 164 (Jul). On the store of the author's uncle, Pine L. Pearsall, in East Rockaway, ca. 1910. [7447

PAUL BAILEY. Rogers, Stone, and Bailey. Long Island forum, 23:99-100, 116-17 (May). views. Memories of the author's Long Island sun, which he founded at Amityville in 1911, and of his horse-riding neighbors, Fred Stone and Will Rogers, cowboy actors and acrobats. [7448

HENRY C. JORALEMON. Chris Morley and the L.I. R.R. Long Island forum, 23:127-9 (Jun). port. On references by Christopher Morley to steam and electric railroads between New York City and Roslyn, L.I., 1920 ff. [7449

W. FRED WELSCH. Conservation [of water] in Nassau County [N.Y., 1925-60]. Am. Water Works Assoc., jour., 52:1494-8 (Dec). [7450

Rochester

BLAKE FAUS McKELVEY. An historic site tour of old and new landmarks [in Rochester]. Rochester: Rochester Public Library, 1960. 19, [1] p. map. (Rochester history, v. 22, no. 1, Jan. 1960.) Revision of a guide published in 1950. [7451

BLAKE FAUS McKELVEY. Civic medals awarded posthumously. Rochester: Rochester Public Library, 1960. 24 p. (Rochester history, v. 22, no. 2, Apr. 1960.) Biographical sketches of 41 citizens of Rochester born between 1766 and 1886 who have "merited local civic recognition," not including any of the 63 "former Rochesterians of national distinction" listed in a former issue of Rochester history. [7452

BLAKE FAUS McKELVEY. The men's clothing industry in Rochester's history [since 1812]. Rochester: Rochester Public Library, 1960. 32 p. bibliog. (Rochester history, v. 22, no. 3, Jul. 1960.) [7453

SKETCH of Frederick Douglass' life in Rochester, New York [1847-72]. A. M. E. Zion quar. rev., 63:193-6 (fall 1952). On his work in Rochester as a Negro newspaper editor, a campaigner against racial discrimination, and a collaborator in the program of the Underground Railroad. [7454

BLAKE FAUS McKELVEY. The Italians of Rochester: an historical review [since 1860]. Rochester: Rochester Public Library, 1960. 24 p. bibliog. (Rochester history, v. 22, no. 4, Oct. 1960.) [7455

Buffalo

SELIG ADLER & THOMAS EDMUND CONNOLLY. From Ararat to suburbia: the history of the Jewish community of Buffalo [1814-1954]. Phila.: Jewish Publication Soc. of America, 1960. xvi, 498, [1] p. facsims., views. bibliog. (p. 467-79), notes (p. 413-62). (The Jacob R. Schiff library of Jewish contributions to American democracy, 12.) [7456

LEON F. SILBERGER. Streambank stabilization. Agric. engineering, 40: 214-17 (Apr 1959). diagrs., views. On the Buffalo Creek Watershed, Buffalo, N.Y., 1938-58. [7457

NEW JERSEY

FORGOTTEN cemeteries of N.J. N.J. genesis, 5:162-3; 7:265, 267, 279-80 (Jan 1958, Jan, Apr 1960). Inscriptions from the Richards-French Cemetery of Springfield, the Henry Woods Burying Ground at East Camden, the Trinity Church Burying Ground at Newark, the White Oak Ridge Cemetery at Millburn, and the Presbyterian Cemetery at Springfield. [7458

ROBERT QUILLMAN ROGERS. From Slooterdam to Fair Lawn: a history of the Fair Lawn area, Bergen County, New Jersey [1609-1960]. Fair Lawn: Thomas Jefferson Junior High School, 1960. iv, [3] leaves, 129 p. facsims., views. bibliog. (p. 127-9). [7459

JAMES BYRON KENYON. Industrial localization and metropolitan growth: the Paterson-Passaic district. Chicago, 1960. xvii, 224 p. diagrs., maps, tables, views. bibliog. (p. 214-24), notes. (University of Chicago. Dept. of Geography. Research paper 67.) Sections on "Early industrial history of the district: 1630-1840" and "A century of silk: 1840-1940," study of the later silk and rayon industry, account of "Selected industrial sections" within the district, and sections on plant location. [7460

RICHARD JOSEPH PURCELL (1887-1950). Irish settlers in early New Jersey: colony and State [as early as 1667]. N.J. genesis, 6:222, 224-7, 236-9, 248-50 (Apr-Oct 1959). bibliog. Reproduced from The recorder, published by the American Irish Historical Society, "a little less than a decade ago." [7461

NEW JERSEY. State Highway Dept. Bureau of Public Information. Development of the State highway system [1673-1959. Trenton, 1959.] 15 p. [7462

JOHN SELLER & WILLIAM FISHER. A map of New Jersey in America. ... London, 1677. [Providence] 1958. facsim. (col. map 44 x 92 cm.) and "A note on the facsimile" ([4] p.). Reproduced in collotype by the Meriden Gravure Company from original in the John Carter Brown Library. At foot: "The description of the Province of West-Jersey in America. As also, Proposals to such as desire to have any propriety therein." Inset: "New York" (view). [7463

The PROPRIETORS of the Eastern Division of New Jersey. N.J. genesis, 8:301, 304 (Oct). On the General Board of Proprietors of the Eastern Division of New Jersey, a corporation founded in 1681; with some account of its records and the genealogical information to be found in them. [7464

HAZEL B. SIMPSON. Old Gloucester County [N.J., since 1682]. N.J. genesis, 7:272-5 (Apr). Deals particularly with sources of genealogical information. [7465

LEWIS D. COOK. Fenwick, Adams, Hedge, and Champneys, of Salem, N.J. Geneal. mag. N.J., 35:108-20 (Sep). On John Fenwick (died 1683), the "Founder of Salem, N.J.," his 3 children, and their descendants till ca. 1750; with a copy of his will (1683). [7466

JOHN GRIFFITHS HUNT. The Kingsland family of Barbados and New Jersey: the Shotwell-Burton alliance, Barbados, New Jersey. Am. geneal., 36:106-7 (Apr). Evidence of family relationship in the will of Nathaniel Kingsland of Barbados, 14 Mar. 1685, leaving to his "nephew" Isaac Kingsland, his sons John and Nathaniel, and his 4 daughters his plantation in New Jersey. [7467

ELMER GARFIELD VAN NAME. Members of the House of Assembly of "1686" of County of Gloucester. N.J. genesis, 5:159 (Oct 1957). Evidence that the county was formed by act of the West Jersey General Assembly, 15 May 1686. [7468

HARRY BISCHOFF WEISS & GRACE M. WEISS. Early sports and pastimes in New Jersey [1686-1860]. Trenton: Past Times Press, 1960. vii, 148 p. facsims., tables, views. notes. [7469

HENRY HAROLD BISBEE. West Jersey Propriet[ar]y: soil and government. N.J. genesis, 7:282-5 (Jul). On the Council of Proprietors of West Jersey, a corporation formed in 1688 and still in existence. [7470

BAYARD RANDOLPH KRAFT (1894-1956). Under Barnegat's beam: light on happenings along the Jersey Shore. N.Y., 1960. viii, [4], 120 p. map, ports., views. bibliog. (p. 117). On Long Beach, N.J., 1690s-1960, a narrow island some 20 miles long, and its lighthouse, lifeboat stations, and hotels. [7471

MARGARET E. WHITE. Further notes on early furniture of New Jersey [1690-1870]. Antiques, 78:136-9 (Aug). views. [7472

WALTER LEE SHEPPARD, JR. Dayton and Ireland of South Jersey. Am. geneal., 36:171-4 (Jul). On the identity of Dayton Ireland (recorded 1779) and of the first wife of Ephraim Dayton (probably Bethiah Curtiss, fl. 1709-16). [7473

WILLIAM CORNELIUS COPE. Abraham Lincoln's New Jersey ancestors. N.J. genesis, 5:186, 188-90; 6:208 (Jul 1958, Oct 1959). map (p. 192). On descendants of Mordecai Lincoln II and his brother Abraham, who arrived in New Jersey probably in 1710 or 1712 and settled at Clarksburg in Monmouth County, and of Mordecai's wife, Hannah Salter; and sites associated with them. [7474

HUBERT GLASGOW SCHMIDT, comp. The Germans in colonial New Jersey. N.J. genesis, 4:104-9, 117-21, 127-33, 139-43; 5:151-5, 164-9, 175-9 (Oct 1956-Apr 1958). bibliog. Annotated list of the German families and individuals known to have lived in New Jersey before 1801, most of whom had arrived there after 1714. [7475

DONALD LINES JACOBUS. Certain Halsey-Pool groups, Morris County, New Jersey. Am. geneal., 36:21-8 (Jan). On descendants of Samuel[4] Halsey (born 1715/18), Benjamin Halsey (1721-88), and Ezra Halsey (1727?-1775), brothers, and their sister, Jerusha (1728?-1803; married Jonathan Wood), and their complicated connections with the Pool family. [7476

FRED B. ROGERS. Hezekiah Stites (1726-1796): "regular practitioner." Med. Soc. N.J., Jour., 56:630-32 (Oct 1959). view. notes. On his practice of medicine in Cranbury, N.J., and his service as an official of the Medical Society of New Jersey. [7477

JACOB JANEWAY. The Janeway account books, 1735-1746. [Abstracted] by Kenn Stryker-Rodda. Geneal. mag. N.J., 33:1-10, 73-81; 34:41-8, 73-84; 35:40-47, 91-6 (Jan 1958-May1960). Annotated list of names in the journals and ledgers of the proprietor of a store at Bound Brook, near New Brunswick. [7478

BEAVERS, Bevers, Bieber-Beaver, Beavours, Beavoirs, Bevier, etc. N.J. genesis, 5:184-5 (Apr 1958). On families of these names in New Jersey as early as 1743. [7479

BENJAMIN R. PITTENGER. First Presbyterian church at Hazen, N.J. [1744-1800]. N.J. genesis, 5:182 (Apr 1958). [7480

BARBARA HOSKINS & others. Washington Valley: an informal history, Morris County, New Jersey [1749-1960. Morristown? N.J.] 1960. [2], xii, 329 p. facsims., maps (part double), ports., tables, views. bibliog. (p. 327-9). On a formerly rural area 3 miles west of Morristown. [7481

WILLIAM HOGG. British aid to education in America: a letter of William Hogg to Aaron Burr [dated Edinburgh, 28 Aug. 1755]. Presbyt. Hist. Soc., Jour., 38:244-7 (Dec). notes. Report to the President of the College of New Jersey on funds collected in Scotland for the support of the college. [7482

ARTHUR DUDLEY PIERCE. Smugglers' Woods: jaunts and journeys in colonial and Revolutionary New Jersey. New Brunswick, N.J.: Rutgers Univ. Press [1960]. xiii, 322 p. facsims., ports., views. bibliog. (p. 305-13), notes (p. 291-304). On "New Jersey during the American Revolution and the cold war that preceded it," 1763-83. [7483

LORIN WEISENFELD. Death of a city. N.J. Hist. Soc., Proc., 78:149-60 (Jul). notes. On Batsto (Batstowe, Batstoo, etc.), at the forks of the Mullican River in Burlington and Gloucester Counties, the Batsto Iron Works, processor of bog iron ore, and the Batsto Glass Works, maker of window glass, 1764-1876. [7484

HARRY BISCHOFF WEISS & GRACE M. WEISS. Forgotten mills of early New Jersey: oil, plaster, bark, indigo, fanning, tilt, rolling, and slitting mills, nail and screw making [1770-1882]. Trenton: New Jersey Agricultural Soc., 1960. 94 p. diagrs., tables, views. bibliog. (p. 90-91), notes. [7485

GEORGE OLIN ZABRISKIE. Two Jacob Zabriskies. Geneal. mag. N.J., 35:70-72 (May). On Jacob C. Zabriskie (1774-1846), married to Elizabeth Terhune, and Jacob A. Zabriskie (1772-1815), married to Elizabeth Hopper, both of Paramus, N.J., and their children. [7486

IRWIN F. CORTELYOU. Micah Williams [1782?-1837], pastel-list. Antiques, 78:459-61 (Nov). ports. New biographical information about him, his family, and his life in New Brunswick, N.J., and account of several paintings by "this primitive artist." [7487

GEORGE OLIN ZABRISKIE. Annotations for the North Schraalenburgh Church death records of 1783-1824. Geneal. mag. N.J., 34:19-24, 86-91; 35:25-33 (Jul 1959-Jan 1960). [7488

NELSON ROLLIN BURR. The critical period of the Episcopal Church in New Jersey [1784-90]. P. E. Church, Hist. mag., 29:139-44 (Jun). notes. [7489

OLD papers discovered in the "Burnett Homestead" in Union (Connecticut Farms), N.J. N.J. genesis, 5:210, 212-14 (Jan 1959). On recently discovered papers of Col. Daniel Burnett (1788-1854) and of some of his ancestors and descendants, including "deeds, mortgages, tax bills, receipts for school instruction, family bills, military records, insurance policies, surveys, letters, bills for breeding of horses, household bills, farm equipment," etc.; with some account of the family. [7490

DAVID ENGLISH. A brief description of Joseph Priestley in a letter of David English to Charles D. Green. Presbyt. Hist. Soc., Jour., 38:124-7 (Jun). Letter dated Princeton, 20 Jun. 1794, from a tutor and librarian of the College of New Jersey to a college friend, giving college and personal news, opinions on "publick affairs," and a hasty impression of the appearance and manners of Dr. Priestley, recently arrived from England. [7491

ARCHEOLOGICAL SOCIETY OF NEW JERSEY. The Green Sergeant's covered bridge. Archeol. Soc. N.J., News letter, 52:5-6 (Mar). On the only covered bridge surviving in New Jersey, a structure in Hunterdon County, "little changed since the early 1800's," now in "grave danger" of destruction. [7492

PRESENT day names of streets on old map. N.J. genesis, 5:183-4 (Apr 1958). map. "1800-1810 map of 'South Mountain' area of what is now sections of Maplewood and Millburn once comprising part of 'Springfield Township,'" by "a Mr Vanderveer"; with commentary by the editor. [7493

WALTER HERBERT STOWE. The Christian Knowledge Society and the revival of the Episcopal Church in New Jersey. [Austin, Tex.: Church Historical Soc., 1960.] 40 p. facsims., port., tables. notes. (Church Historical Society. Publication 49.) From the Historical magazine of the Protestant Episcopal Church, 29:11-47 (Mar. 1960). On the Episcopal Society of New Jersey for the Promotion of Christian Knowledge and Piety, 1810-32 (with an outline of its history to 1959); with a copy of its constitution, a report of its Board of Directors (20 Aug. 1818), and biographical sketches of Bp. John Croes (1762-1832), John Churchill Rudd (1779-1848), and James Chapman (1785-1857). [7494

GERRISH THURBER. The Lawrenceville School, 1810-1960. N.J. Hist. Soc., Proc., 78:233-56 (Oct). views. On a boys' school founded under Presbyterian auspices by the Rev. Isaac Van Arsdale Brown as the Academy of Maidenhead, renamed Lawrenceville Academy after 1816. [7495

TAM D. CONOVER & JUDIDA H. PETTIE, comps. Ocean County gravestones: Zion Methodist Cemetery, near New Egypt. Geneal. mag. N.J., 35:1-6, 73-5 (Jan). List of inscriptions, 1811-1945 (copied in 1946 and checked in 1947). [7496

GEORGE SWETNAM. A possible new technique for retrieving lost or fragmentary folk hymns. Keystone folklore quar., 5(3):9-19 (autumn). Texts of 21 verse inscriptions from the Christian Church Cemetary, Johnsonburg, N.J., appearing "to belong to the period from 1825 to 1875," and analysis of their relation to hymns. [7497

WILLIAM H. GERDTS. Henry Inman [1801-46] in New Jersey. N.J. Hist. Soc., Proc., 78:178-87 (Jul). ports. On his visits to and residence in New Jersey, 1828, 1832-34, and his paintings of New Jersey people and landscapes. [7498

HELEN P. ALLEMAN & FRED ALLEMAN, comps. Atlantic County gravestones: St. Mary of the Assumption Catholic Cemetery, Mullica Township. Geneal. mag. N.J., 35:101-7 (Sep). List of inscriptions, 1834-98. [7499

BRAY HAMMOND. The Princeton Bank's 125th anniversary. N.J. Hist. Soc., Proc., 78:12-21 (Jan). On the Princeton Bank, Princeton, N.J., 1834-1959. [7500

BOOKS you should consult on genealogy in New Jersey. N.J. genesis, 5:157, 160; 7:277-8. On Genealogy of early settlers in Trenton and Ewing of old Hunterdon County, by Hannah L. Cooley (Trenton, 1883), and Family records, or, Genealogies of the first settlers of Passaic Valley and vicinity, above Chatham, by John Littell (1852). [7501

JOSEPH ALTMAN. Music by the beautiful sea. Music jour., 18(3):9 (Mar.) port., view. On conventions of musical organizations in Atlantic City, N.J., since 1854. [7502

STORMING of Stevens Castle. Hist. preservation, 11 (1959): 140-43. views. On a Victorian mansion built by Robert Livingston Stevens in 1854 and destroyed by order of the Board of Trustees of Stevens Institute of Technology, Hoboken, N.J., in 1959 in spite of requests for its preservation. [7503

WILLIAM PIERSON, JR. (1830-1900). "To repeal all medical laws ..." [Edited by] Fred B. Rogers. Med. Soc. N.J., Jour., 56:745-6 (Dec 1959). Letter to Dr. J. Henry Clark, dated Orange, 15 Feb. 1858, on "problems of professional education, medical licensure and legal right of The Medical Society of New Jersey." [7504

MIRIAM F. BRUNNER. Guide map and story of historical Ocean Grove today. Hatfield, Pa.: E. F. Brunner Co. [1960. 4], 32 p. fold. map, views. On Ocean Grove, N.J., 1869-1960. [7505

CHARLES A. PARKER. A study of the preaching at the Ocean Grove, New Jersey, Camp Meeting, 1870-1900. Ann Arbor: University Microfilms, 1959 [i. e. 1960]. Positive microfilm of typescript. [308] leaves. Thesis--Louisiana State Univ. Abstracted: Dissert. abstracts, 20:2961 (Jan). [7506

B. F. WHEELER. The New Jersey Conference [of the African Methodist Episcopal Zion Church, 1874-1949]. A. M. E. Zion quar. rev., 59:86-8 (spring 1949). [7507

ARTHUR BARNARD PRICE (born 1877). Artie's Newark: memories of the 1880's. Political torchlight parades. N.J. Hist. Soc., Proc., 78:276-8 (Oct). A chapter of the author's "book-length reminiscences." [7508

LABOR arbitration in New Jersey [1886-1959]. Rutgers law rev., 14: 143-84 (fall 1959). notes. [7509

ANOTHER glimpse of "post Civil War North Newark," the "First River" area. N.J. genesis, 7:278-9 (Apr). Anonymous recollections of the 1890s. [7510

HARDIN CRAIG. Woodrow Wilson at Princeton. Norman: Univ. of Oklahoma Press [1960]. xii, 175, [1] p. port. Appraisal of his activities as Professor of Political Science and later as President of Princeton University, 1890-1910. Includes reminiscences of the author's graduate studies there in 1898. [7511

GLIMPSES of 19th century Newark, N.J.: the old "horse cars." N.J. genesis, 6:210, 214-15 (Jan 1959). Anonymous reminiscences of the 1890s. [7512

LIST of burials in Newark's (N.J.) second oldest cemetery, that of the old First Presbyterian Church on Broad Street, recently abandoned and replaced by a parking lot. N.J. genesis, 6:242-4, 252-4, 260-63 (Jul 1959-Jan 1960). List of 1,294 burials, compiled from manuscript lists of 1891 and 1904. On efforts to save the cemetery see 5:186-7 and 6:222-3, with the editor's remarks on the spreading practice of desecreating cemeteries for commercial profit and the declining literalness of the phrase "Christian burial." [7513

THOMAS J. REYNOLDS. Factory employment in New Jersey, 1899-1956: growth and structural change. Ann Arbor: University Microfilms, 1960. Positive microfilm of typescript. [246] leaves. Thesis--Columbia Univ. Abstracted: Dissert. abstracts, 20: 4550-51 (Jun). [7514

PAUL JOHNSTON STRAYER. New Jersey's financial problem [1900-1960]. New Brunswick, N.J.: Rutgers Univ. Press [1960]. 96 p. tables. notes. [7515

HOWARD E. JOHNSTON. The New Jersey short line railroads [1906-50, mainly in the 1930s]: photo album. [Plainfield, N.J., 1959.] 20 p. facsims., views. [7516

SAMUEL BERG. The Essex County Pathologic and Anatomic Society: the first fifty years [1907-57]. Med Soc. N.J., Jour., 56:81-4 (Feb 1959). notes. [7517

MONROE BERKOWITZ. Workmen's compensation: the New Jersey experience [1911-57]. New Brunswick, N.J.: Rutgers Univ. Press, 1960. xiii, [3], 298 p. diagrs., tables. bibliog. (p. 280-94), notes. [7518

WALTER HERBERT STOWE. Profile of Paul Matthews (1866-1954), Fifth Bishop of New Jersey, 1915-1937. P. E. Church, Hist. mag., 29:185-91 (Sep). notes. [7519

HAROLD STEIN. Note for the good of the order: safeguards for academic freedom at Princeton [1918-59]. Am. pol. science rev., 54:981-3 (Dec). [7520

EDWARD R. WHITE. A unified dental service for county institutions [of Hudson County, N.J., ca. 1920 to 1960]. Am. Dental Assoc., Jour., 60:35-8 (Jan). [7521

LESLIE HERBERT WILLIS. Guidance services in Bloomfield, New Jersey, public schools, 1925 through 1958. Ann Arbor: University Microfilms, 1959 [i. e. 1960]. Positive microfilm of typescript. [424] leaves. Thesis (Ed. D.)--Rutgers Univ. Abstracted: Dissert. abstracts, 20:3641 (Mar). [7522

ROGER A. CUNNINGHAM. Control of land use in New Jersey by means of zoning [1930-59]. Rutgers law rev., 14:37-100 (fall 1959). notes. [7523

CHARLES V. MATHIS. "Shear" hard work. Am. forests, 65(5):6-7, 50 (May 1959). views. On the work of Gus Yearicks as a topiary gardener at Wildwood-by-the-Sea, N.J., engaged in "bush-barbering" or trimming hedges into geometrical, animal, and other forms, 1932-59. [7524

LOUIS LOHR MARTZ. The unicorn in Paterson: William Carlos Williams. Thought, 35:537-54 (autumn). On his poem Paterson (1946-51). [7525

FRANK G. SCHLOSSER. Dry revolution: diary of a Constitutional Convention. Newton, N.J.: Onnabrite Press, 1960. 303 p. Day-by-day record, by a delegate, of the New Jersey Constitutional Convention held at New Brunswick, 12 Jun.-4 Nov. 1947, including the author's commentary on the proceedings. [7526

PENNSYLVANIA

ROBERT H. JOHNSTON. The aborigines of Cawichnowane [the Great Island in the Susquehanna near Lock Haven]. Lock Haven bul., 2:27-33. notes. Evidence that this area "was visited and possibly inhabited by aborigines between 8,000 and 9,000 years ago," and that many tribes passed through it in the 18th century. [7527

LEHIGH COUNTY HISTORICAL SOCIETY. In memoriam. Lehigh Co. Hist. Soc., Proc., 23:108-19. Brief obituary sketches of eminent citizens of Lehigh County. [7528

ELMER LEWIS SMITH, ed. The almanac of Pennsylvania Dutch folklore. Akron, Pa.: Applied Arts, 1960. 39 p. cartoons, diagr., views. Collection of home remedies, epitaphs, weather lore and signs, superstitions, tall tales, "Holiday lore and beliefs," "Dumb Dutch stories," "Amish stories," "Proverbs and sayings," "Ferhuddled English," etc. Apparently from oral sources. [7529

JOHN JOSEPH STOUDT. The cultural contributions of the Pennsylvania Germans. Hist. rev. Berks Co., 25: 40-45, 62-5 (spring). facsim., views. Deals particularly with "German cultural values which were translated into American idiom and perspective" as distinguished from the "basically Teutonic cultural value tone" of "the Pennsylvania German culture island in eastern Pennsylvania." [7530

SOPHIE LEWIS (HUTCHINSON) DRINKER. Pennsylvania's honoured mistress: unanswered questions in the life of Hannah Callowhill Penn [1671-1726]. Old York Road Hist. Soc. bul., 21:3-12 (Mar). On problems left unsolved by the author in her edition of the letters of the wife of William Penn. [7531

WILLIAM F. HARTMAN. Tall clocks. Lancaster Co. Hist. Soc., Jour., 63: 1-11 (Jan 1959). views. On the manufacture of "grandfather" clocks in Pennsylvania, 1680s-1830s, especially in Lancaster County. [7532

ROY WATSON CURRY. William Penn, mankind's true friend. Carnegie mag., 34:199-202 (Jun). port., view. On his founding of Pennsylvania, 1681-82. [7533

WILLIAM HENRY BLISS. English influence on common law development in colonial Pennsylvania [1682-1776]. Ann Arbor: University Microfilms, 1959 [i. e. 1960]. Positive microfilm of typescript. [194] leaves. Thesis--Univ. of Pittsburgh. Abstracted: Dissert. abstracts, 20:3266-7 (Feb). [7534

A. H. CARSTENS. Pennsylvania's best: the story of Pennsylvania's contributions to life, liberty, and the pursuit of happiness, for students of history, libraries, armchair travelers, and everyone who is proud to be associated in any way with Pennsylvania [1682-1960]. Clearfield, Pa.: Kurtz Bros. [1960]. x, 318 p. ports., views. notes. [7535

JEFFERSON BARNES FORDHAM & CARROLL C. MORELAND. Pennsylvania's statutory imbroglio: the need of statute law revision. Univ. Pa. law rev., 108:1093-1123 (Jun). notes. On the accumulation of statutes since

1682, the "unofficial compilations," and the need for "general statute revision." [7536

SCHMIDT (C.) & SONS, INC. Taverns of yesteryear [in Pennsylvania, 1682-1850]: good food, good drink, good cheer. Published to commemorate the one hundredth anniversary of Schmidt's of Philadelphia. [Phila., 1960.] 55 p. music, ports., tables. "... a story of old Pennsylvania Inns and Taverns, of early eating and drinking customs, of old-time recipes, spiced with a sprinkling of all but forgotten songs." [7537

S. LAURENCE SHAIMAN. The history of imprisonment for debt and insolvency laws in Pennsylvania as they evolved from the common law [1682-1913]. Am. jour. legal hist., 4:205-25 (Jul). notes. [7538

NEGLEY KING TEETERS. Public executions in Pennsylvania: 1682-1834. [Lancaster, Pa.:] Lancaster County Historical Soc., 1960. 85-164 p. facsims., views. bibliog. (p. 129-30, notes (p. 120-29). (Journal of the Lancaster County Historical Society, v. 64, no. 2, spring 1960.) Includes alphabetical and chronological lists of the 252 persons executed. [7539

J. HERBERT WALKER. Pennsylvania's war on wolves. Pa. game news, 21(1): 16-21 (Jan). On the bounty on wolves from 1682 till 1892, when the wolves were approaching extermination; with some account of wolf-hunters, the varieties, traits, and habits of Pennsylvania wolves, and particularly the descriptions of their howls. [7540

J. HERBERT WALKER. Pioneers and panthers. Pa. game news, 21(2):26-31 (Feb). views. On "the Pennsylvania Lion, cougar, panther, painter" (Felis cougar), known also as bender, abundant in Pennsylvania in 1682, very rare by 1900, seen possibly as late as 1940 or 1941. [7541

MARY SULLIVAN PATTERSON. John Barnes [died 1710]--the man who owned Jenkintown. Old York Road Hist. Soc. bul., 21:13-29 (Mar). facsims., views. On his removal from England to Philadelphia in 1683, his extensive purchases and sales of land, his work as a tailor, and his 2 marriages. [7542

MARIAN WALLACE RENINGER. Ann Letort [emigrated from France in 1686, died ca. 1728]. Lancaster Co. Hist. Soc., Jour., 64:49-52 (winter). On her life with her husband, James Letort, keeper of Indian trading posts on the Schuylkill and the Susquehanna. [7543

ANDRES BRINER. Conrad Beissel and Thomas Mann. Am.-German rev., 26(2):24-5, 38 (Dec 1959-Jan 1960). On Johann Conrad Beissel (1690-1768) of Ephrata, Pa., musician and mystic, as a character in Mann's novel Dr. Faustus (1947). [7544

JOHN LOCHER. A history of mining in Lancaster County: 1700-1900. Lancaster Co. Hist. Soc., Jour., 64:1-16 (winter). map. notes. [7545

ALFRED LEWIS SHOEMAKER. Eastertide in Pennsylvania: a folk cultural study. Kutztown: Pennsylvania Folklore Soc., 1960. 96 p. facsims., ports., views. On "Pennsylvania folklore from Shrove Tuesday through Whitmonday," 18th-20th centuries, including the symbolism of Easter rabbits, Easter eggs and egg trees, and the Moravian Easter service; with numerous citations from 19th-century newspapers. [7546

J. CLAYTON SHANK. Panoramic pageantry of Shank family names. Lancaster Co. Hist. Soc., Jour., 62:169-74 (Jul 1958). On names borne by members of the Schenk (Shenk, Shank, etc.) family in Lancaster Township since ca. 1708, the variant spellings of the names of individuals and of close relatives, and the assignment of forenames. [7547

CHARLES DEWEY SPOTTS. The Gault Graveyard. Lancaster Co. Hist. Soc., Jour., 64:34-48 (winter). view. On some of the descendants of Robert Galt, "Scotch-Irish Pioneer immigrant" who settled in Lancaster County ca. 1709, particularly those buried in the graveyard on his property in Salisbury Township and named Galt or Gault. [7548

CARLTON O. WHITTLINGER. Early manufacturing in Lancaster County, Pennsylvania: 1710-1840. Lancaster Co. Hist. Soc., Jour., 58:149-92; 59: 149-80; 61:83-120; 62:1-20 (1954-55, 1957-58). facsims., views. notes. Based on thesis--Univ. of Pennsylvania. [7549

JAMES Y. HECKLER (1829-1901). History of Franconia Township [Montgomery County, Pa., 1714-1900. Edited by Roy C. Kulp. Harleysville, Pa.: C. D. Hendricks] 1960. 112 p. map, ports., views. From the Harleysville news, 27 Nov. 1901. [7550

HISTORICAL SOCIETY OF BERKS COUNTY. First in iron: Berks County's iron industry, 1716 to 1815. [By Edna M. Handwork.] Hist. rev. Berks Co., 25:120-27 (fall). diagr., views. bibliog. [7551

AMBROSE BARCROFT (1681-1724). Life in Bucks County in 1722/23. Edited by Harold B. Hancock. Pa. hist., 27:397-402 (Oct). notes. Letter from a farmer in Solebury, Bucks County, to his father in England, 1 Mar. 1723, on lands, crops, prices, labor, weather, etc., as observed by the writer since he left England in 1720. [7552

A. WAYNE MORRIS. The Octorara family of churches. Honey Brook, Pa.: Herald Pub. Co. [1960. 47] p. diagr., views. 21 x 24 cm. On the Church of Upper Octorara, founded in 1720, and the Presbyterian churches descended from it in Chester and Lancaster Counties, 1724-1953. [7553

MARION WALLACE RENINGER. Via Mulberry Street and Lime. ... Sketches by Florence Starr Taylor. Lancaster, Pa., 1960. [8], 56 p. map, views. bibliog. (p. 55-6). On the streets of Lancaster, Pa., 1720-1960. [7554

AMOS K. STAUFFER. The ministers and deacons at Lampeter (Mellinger) Meetinghouse [Lampeter Township, Lancaster County, Pa., 1722-1915]. Mennonite hist. bul., 10(4):1-3 (Oct 1949). Includes 24 biographical sketches. [7555

DONALD FLOYD DURNBAUGH, ed. Two early letters from Germantown. Pa. mag. hist. and biog., 84:219-33 (Apr). notes. Letter of John George Käsebier to Casimir, Count of Sayn-Wittgengestein-Berleburg, dated Roxborough, 7 Nov. 1724, describing the writer's voyage from Rotterdam to Philadelphia and the farming, employments, etc., in the vicinity (with a note by his widow reporting his death in December 1724); and letter from John Christopher Sauer to friends in Germany, dated Germantown, 1 Aug. 1725, giving a very favorable account of the Philadelphia area and its people and offering advice to prospective immigrants thither. [7556

FRIEDRICH KREBS. Annotations to Strassburger and Hinke's Pennsylvania German pioneers. Pa. geneal. mag., 21:235-48. Translated from articles contributed by the author to several German genealogical periodicals, 1954-58. Lists of emigration permits issued to Germans going to America from Heidelberg (1726-27, 1741-49, 1737, 1738, 1751, 1754), Wurttemberg (1749-50), Oppenheim (1742-49), and "the region now a part of the Palatinate and that of Nahe and Hunsrueck"; and information from other records in Germany. [7557

MARION WALLACE RENINGER. Susanna Wright [1697?-1784]. Lancaster Co. Hist. Soc., Jour., 63:173-90 (Oct 1959). notes. On her life in Lancaster County as housekeeper and business manager for her father, John Wright, and her brother James, and as an experimenter in agriculture, a scrivener, a prothonotary, a writer of Quaker poetry, etc., 1726-84; with texts of some of her correspondence with Benjamin and Deborah Franklin. [7558

NORMAN W. BAUMAN. A history of the Manheim Bishop District, the Rapho Mennonite Meetinghouse, also known as the Lehman but now Hernley Meetinghouse [Lancaster County, Pa., 1727-1957]. Mennonite hist. bul., 19(4):1-2, 4-6 (Oct 1958). port., table. notes. [7559

ARTHUR W. OSBORN. Riegelsville people, places, and events (Pennsylvania) [1727-1959]. Riegelsville [1960. 8], 291 p. map, tables. bibliog. (p. 95). History of a community in Bucks County. Appended (p. 97-291): "Genealogical (thumbnail) sketches." [7560

ALLEN M. FRETZ. The Meyer or Moyer family. Mennonite hist. bul., 17(1):5-7 (Jan 1956). From The Pennsylvania-German, Oct. 1905. On descendants (named Meyer, Meyers, Myers, Moyer, etc.) of Christian Meyer (of Montgomery County, Pa.) and Hans Meyer who purchased land there in 1729. [7561

M. MARTINA HAMMILL. The expansion of the Catholic Church in Pennsylvania: a brief sketch of the organization and expansion of the Church from the colonial period to the present [1729-1960. Pittsburgh? 1960. 10], 205 p. bibliog. (p. 188-92), notes (p. 181-7). Chapters on the Dioceses of Philadelphia, Pittsburgh, Erie, Harrisburg, Scranton, Altoona-Johnstown, and Greensburg. [7562

FREDERICK SHEELY WEISER. Conrad Weiser [1696-1760], peacemaker of colonial Pennsylvania. Hist. rev. Berks Co., 25:83-97 (summer). facsims., views. On his life in Berks County, his work as an interpreter and negotiator for the province in dealings with Indians, and his services as a justice of the peace and a Lutheran layman, 1729-60. [7563

PENNSYLVANIA. Historical and Museum Commission. Ephrata Cloister, Ephrata, Pa. [settlement of Seventh-Day German Baptists congregated round Conrad Beissel ca. 1730, disbanded soon after 1796]. D. A. R. mag., 94:620-24 (Nov). view. [7564

MARY MARGARET GREER. From trail dust to star dust ... the story of Johnstown, Pennsylvania, a city resulting from its environment [1731-1889, with a few references to later events. Johnstown: W. M. Greer] 1960. 120, [7] p. facsims., fold. map, ports., tables, views. bibliog. (p. 119-20), notes. Left unfinished at the author's death in the 1950s. [7565

ADELAIDE BROOKS HALL. Ann Wood Henry, 1732-1798. Lancaster Co. Hist. Soc., Jour., 64:223-6 (autumn). notes. On Ann Wood, who married William Henry (born 1729), Lancaster gunsmith, in 1756. [7566

LANCASTER COUNTY, Pa. Early legal records of Jews of Lancaster County, Pennsylvania. [By] Irwin S. Rhodes. Am. Jew. arch., 12:96-108 (Apr). Abstracts of 145 deeds, wills, etc., 1732-1914 (mainly 1740s and 1750s). [7567

PRESTON ALBERT BARBA. They came to Emmaus, a history [1736-1959. Emmaus, Pa.: Borough of Emmaus, 1960.] xiii, [3], 378 p. facsims., fold. maps, ports., tables, views. notes. "Centenary edition." Includes excerpts from the diary of the Emmaus Moravian Church. [7568

JAMES C. MASSEY. The Bertolet-Herbein cabin. Am.-German rev., 26(3):12-14 (Feb-Mar). views. On a log cabin in the Oley Valley east of Reading, built by Elizabeth Bertolet, and sold, with a farm, to Jonathan Harbein in 1745. [7569

DONALD RAY BELCHER. The Board of Trustees of the University of Pennsylvania [1740-1960]. Phila.: Univ. of Pennsylvania Press [1960]. 112 p. tables. bibliog. (p. 111-12), notes (p. 109-10). (Reports of the Educational Survey.) [7570

G. CLYMER BROOKE. Birdsboro: company with a past, built to last. N.Y.: Newcomen Soc. in North America, 1959. 24 p. views. On the Birdsboro Steel Foundry and Machine Company, traced by the author to the New Pine Forge founded by William Bird on the Schuylkill in 1740 and the Hopewell Furnace constructed by his son Mark in 1770 and to the consolidation of all the iron works in the area by the author's ancestor, Matthew Brooke, in 1809. [7571

WILLIAM F. HARTMAN. Clockmakers of Lancaster Co. [Pa., 1740s-1860s]. Lancaster Co. Hist. Soc., Jour., 63: 12-16 (Jan 1959). bibliog. List. [7572

JOHN POIST KEFFER. The Keffers of the Conewago Valley. Trenton: McCrellish & Quigley, printers, 1960. 187 p. coat of arms, facsims., map, ports., views. bibliog. (p. 185-7). Narrative family history (not a genealogy), centered in McSherrystown, Pa., of the descendants of Matthias Keffer (Matheis Kaffer, Mathia Kafer), born 1706/7, emigrant from Holland to Philadelphia in 1740; with the author's recollections (p. 119-44) of the Conewago Valley "during the first quarter of the present century." [7573

DIETMAR ROTHERMUND. The German problem of colonial Pennsylvania. Pa. mag. hist. and biog., 84:3-21 (Jan). notes. On political, educational, and religious problems resulting from the presence of a growing German minority, 1740s-60s. [7574

SCHUYLER C. BROSSMAN. A historical booklet of Altalaha Evangelical Lutheran Church, Rehrersburg, Berks County, Pennsylvania [1746-1957]. ... George C. Myers, Jr., editor. [Rehrersburg? 1957.] 44 p. ports., tables, views. [7575

FREDERIC SHRIVER KLEIN. Robert Coleman [1748-1825], millionaire ironmaster. Lancaster Co. Hist. Soc., Jour., 64:17-33 (winter). views. notes. On his career in the iron industry in Pennsylvania, 1766-1825, his associations with Henry William Stiegel and John Dickinson, and his activities in "transportation, banking, politics, and leadership in community projects." [7576

GOTTLIEB MITTELBERGER. Journey to Pennsylvania. ... Edited and translated by Oscar Handlin and John Clive. Cambridge: Belknap Press of Harvard University Press, 1960. xix, [3], 102 p. maps, notes. (The John Harvard library.) Translation of an anti-emigration pamphlet (German original, 1756), recording the author's voyage from Germany, his work in New Providence, Pa., as schoolmaster and church organist, and his return to

Germany, 1750-54, containing a "Description of the Province of Pennsylvania" (p. 33-95) and "a detailed account of the sad and unfortunate circumstances of most of the Germans who have moved to that country or are about to do so," designed to counteract the fraudulent representations circulated in Germany by emigrant agents (paid by the head) and warning the reader of the miseries and high mortality of Germans on emigrant ships; with an introduction on the German migration to America in this period and the inadequacies of a previous translation by Charles Theodore Eben. [7577

BURL NEFF OSBURN. Mysteries of Martic. Lancaster Co. Hist. Soc., Jour., 63:163-82 (Oct 1959). diagr., facsims., map, views. notes. On Martic Furnace and Martic Forge, an industry in Lancaster County, "built in mid or late 1750s" by Thomas & William Smith, seized by the sheriff in 1769 as security for debts, and apparently not operated thereafter; with a history of the debts and the lands till 1872. [7578

MILTON EMBICK FLOWER. Carpenter's companies and Carlisle architecture. Carlisle, Pa.: Hamilton Library and Historical Association of Cumberland County, 1955. 28 p. diagrs., views. Papers read in 1946 and 1953. On buildings and builders in Carlisle, 1751-1861. [7579

GEORGE L. HEIGES. Benjamin Franklin in Lancaster County. Lancaster Co. Hist. Soc., Jour., 61:1-26 (Jan 1957). facsims., port. notes. On his "successful efforts ... to procure horses and wagons for Braddock's army" in Lancaster County, his sponsorship of the first printing press there, his pamphlet on the massacre of the Conestoga Indians, his appointment of a mail carrier, and his correspondence with Susanna and James Wright of Wright's Ferry and with Peter Miller of Ephrata, 1751-87; with texts of several letters, a broadside, and other documents. [7580

JOHN W. MAXSON, JR. Nathan Sellers [1751-1830], America's first large-scale maker of paper moulds. Paper maker, 29(1):1-16 (Feb). facsims. (part col.), port. notes. On his life in Darby, Pa., and his work as a manufacturer of wire paper moulds. [7581

ANTHRACITE INSTITUTE. The Pennsylvania anthracite industry [since 1755]. John G. Glover & Rudolph L. Lagai, eds., The development of American industries: their economic significance, 4th ed. (N.Y.: Simmons-Boardman [1759]), p. 205-12. [7582

ALLEN family portraits in a descendant's home. Lehigh Co. Hist. Soc., Proc., 23:9-31. On descendants of William Allen (1704-80), Chief Justice of Pennsylvania, founder of "Allen's Town" in 1762; with reproductions of portraits in possession of a descendant in England. [7583

GENE COLEMAN. Susquehanna treasure: legend or fact? Pa. game news, 21(5):34-7 (May). views. Lore about silver, gold, and lead mines in the north branch of the Susquehanna Valley, 1763-1960, which have left no historical evidence of their existence and are incompatible with the geology of the area. [7584

ERIC DE JONGE. An illuminated fractur. Antiques, 78:480-81 (Nov). facsims. On a manuscript prayer book (title dated 1766) in the possession of Francois Xavier Schwebel, Pennsylvanian in the Army in Mexico, from 1833 to 1848 or later, ornamented with floral frontispiece, illuminated initials, decorative borders, and floral vignettes--possibly brought to America from Alsatia. [7585

ROBERT C. BATCHELDER. A Lancaster footnote in American history. Lancaster Co. Hist. Soc., Jour., 64: 226-33 (autumn). view. notes. On the stay of William Johnson (born ca. 1750), half-Mohawk son of Sir William Johnson, in Lancaster to "study and live in the house of the Rev. Thomas Barton," 1767-68, and his failure there, as previously in the Rev. Eleazer Wheelock's school in Lebanon, Conn., to conduct himself peacably and apply himself to his studies. Includes 3 letters from Barton to the senior Johnson. [7586

ROBERT D. CROMPTON. James Thackara [1767-1848], engraver, of Philadelphia and Lancaster, Pa. Lancaster Co. Hist. Soc., Jour., 62:64-95 (Apr 1958). facsim., map, ports., view. notes. On his partnership with John Vallance (Thackara & Vallance, 1790-1796/97) and with his son William Wood Thackara (J. Thackara & Son, 1815 to ca. 1825) and his independent work as an engraver, his service as Clerk of the Pennsylvania House of Representatives (1807-10) and a member of it (1818-20), commissioner for the building of Eastern State Penitentiary (1821-33), curator of the Pennsylvania Academy of the Fine Arts (1816-28), bookseller, etc.; with a detailed account of his family. [7587

SOME Muncy lawyers. Now and then, 12:204-11, 264-6 (Oct 1959, Apr 1960). Biographical sketches of George Frederick Beal (1811-56), George Guise Dykins (born 1871), Henry Drinker Ellis (1803?- 1851), William Cox Ellis (1786?-1871), William H. Foucar (1885-1952), William Ellis Haines (1872-1926), Charles Hall (1767-1821), Chester E. Hall (1872-1950), Robert Hawley (1827-1905?), and Henry Johnson (1819-95). [7588

DON NEAL. Freedom outpost. Pa. game news, 21(7):6-10 (Jul). views. On the settlement of the Fair Play Men in the "Tiadaughton Strip" along the west branch of the Susquehanna on land claimed by the Seneca Indians, 1768; their "declaration of independence," 4 Jul. 1776; and the acquisition of the land from the Senecas by the State of Pennsylvania, which respected the squatter rights of the settlers, 1784. [7589

WILLIS WOLF EISENHART. A brief history of Saint John Evangelical Lutheran Church of Abbottstown, Pa. [1770-1960. Abbottstown?] 1960. v, 61 p. ports., tables, views. [7590

MAURICE ALLISON MOOK. An early Amish colony in Chester County, Pennsylvania. Mennonite hist. bul., 16(3):1-3 (Jul 1955). views. On a group of Amish families near Malvern, ca. 1770 to ca. 1834, and their cemetery and stone meetinghouse. [7591

ELEANOR COLDREN. Portion of a deposition made by Eleanor Coldren, widow of Abraham Dewitt, in the matter of disputed title to certain lands opposite the Great Island, involving the Fair Play Men, and dated at Sunbury, June 7, 1797. Now and then, 12: 220-22 (Oct 1959). On the deponent's knowledge of a piece of land in Lycoming County since 1774. [7592

ROSALIND LORRAINE BRANNING. Pennsylvania constitutional development [1776-1960. Pittsburgh:] Univ. of Pittsburgh Press [1960. 8], 166 p. bibliog. (p. 157-60), notes. Data treated as evidence supporting a call for a new constitutional convention. [7593

FRANK T. KOCHER, JR. West Branch and other Cawleys. Now and then, 12; 166-8 (Apr 1959). On Thomas Cawley (died 1806) and his brother James (died 1813), recorded in Northampton County, Pa., as early as 1776, and their grandfather, John Cawley, English immigrant ca. 1729, who died in Bucks County in 1766; with some account of the descendants of the brothers. [7594

THOMAS RICHARD MEEHAN. The Pennsylvania Supreme Court in the law and politics of the Commonwealth, 1776-1790. Ann Arbor: University Microfilms, 1960. Positive microfilm of typescript. [628] leaves. Thesis--Univ. of Wisconsin. Abstracted: Dissert. abstracts, 21:1546 (Dec). [7595

WILLIAM ELLERY (1727-77). Revolutionary War travel in Berks. [Edited and paraphrased] by J. Bennett Nolan. Hist. rev. Berks Co., 25:59-61 (spring). port. Excerpts from the diary of a Massachusetts member of the Continental Congress, en route to York, Pa., 11-15 Nov. 1777. [7596

FRANCES LICHTEN. A masterpiece of Pennsylvania-German furniture. Antiques, 77:176-8 (Feb). views. On a schrank or wardrobe of walnut made for Georg Huber, probably in Lancaster County, 1779. [7597

DON NEAL. Haunted hunting grounds ... Long's rambling rifle. Pa. game news, 21(2):32-7 (Feb). views. Lore about Bill Long as a hunter of panthers and wolves in northwestern Pennsylvania, 1780s-1830s. [7598

LESTER G. SHANNON. History of the Lutheran Church in and around the borders of Lycoming County [1785-1954]. Now and then, 12:77-86 (Jul 1958). bibliog. The writer is apparently Lester D. Shannon. [7599

CHARLES SCOTT WILLIAMS. Early Methodism in north central Pennsylvania [1787 to ca. 1850]. Now and then, 12:177-85 (Jul 1959). view. bibliog. [7600

A BRIEF history of Warrier Run Presbyterian Church [near Watsontown, Pa., 1789-1930]. Now and then, 12:97-113 (Oct 1958). view. Includes a list of inscriptions in Warrior Run Presbyterian Churchyard, 1789-1919. [7601

NATHAN KESSLER. Common law offenses and penalties in Pennsylvania [1790-1955]. Temple law quar., 33: 419-30 (summer). notes. Includes an alphabetical list of "Specific common law offenses in Pennsylvania" and cites judicial recognition of each offense. [7602

WILLIAM MOWRY. The development of school plants and building procedures in Pennsylvania [since 1790]. Ann Arbor: University Microfilms, 1960. Positive microfilm of typescript. [280] leaves. Thesis (Ed. D.)--Pennsylvania State Univ. Abstracted: Dissert. abstracts, 21:109-10 (Jul). [7603

DON NEAL. Starring Dave Lewis. Pa. game news, 21(8):16-20 (Aug). On the "Widow Lewis" who made "rot-gut whiskey" and sold it to travelers at Chinkclacamoose in western Pennsylvania (late 1700s and early 1800s), and her son, Dave Lewis, highway robber, captured and mortally wounded by a posse somewhere in the vicinity of Bellefonte and Milesburg. [7604

HISTORY of the "German Lutheran Congregation of Muncy," later known as Immanuel's Lutheran Church [1791-1957]. Now and then, 12:1-21 (Oct 1957). view. Includes an alphabetical list of burials in Immanuel Churchyard, Muncy Creek Township, 1792-1949. [7605

GEORGE GERSHON KORSON. Black rock: mining folklore of the Pennsylvania Dutch. Baltimore: Johns Hopkins Press [1960]. xi, 453 p. music. notes (p. 403-36). Lore collected by the author, mainly in 1957, from former miners; with some account of coal mining in Northampton County and adjacent areas since 1791 and of "the contours of the Pennsylvania Dutch penetration" of this region. Includes songs and ballads, legends, superstitions, "religious lore," samples of folk speech, and information about folk medicine, courtship and marriage customs, and other Pennsylvania Dutch usages and beliefs current in the West End of Schuylkill County. [7606

JOHN ADLUM (1759-1836). John Adlum on the Allegheny: memoirs for the year 1794. [Edited by Donald H. Kent and Merle H. Deardorff.] Pa. mag. hist. and biog., 84:265-324, 435-80 (Jul, Oct). map, port. notes. Recollections of surveying and reserving lands in north-western Pennsylvania for James Wilson, the Holland Land Company, and others, and of dealing with the Seneca Indians in order to avert war. Heavily annotated by the editors. [7607

LEHIGH COUNTY HISTORICAL SOCIETY. Dedication of "Springwood," memorial to General Harry Clay Trexler, April 18, 1954. Lehigh Co. Hist. Soc., Proc., 23:75-86. port., views. Includes an address by Gen. Charles C. Curtis on Trexler's life in Lehigh County as an industrialist, an agriculturist, an officer of the Pennsylvania National Guard, and a philanthropist; an account of the reconstruction of a log cabin which stood on Springwood Plantation in 1794; and "Text of the original Springwood Plantation deed" (11 Mar. 1794). [7608

LAWRENCE A. MILLER. The Sunday-closing law: a violation of religious liberty [Pennsylvania, 1794-1959]. Univ. Pittsburgh law rev., 21:123-32 (Oct 1959). notes. [7609

JOHN PEARSON (1740-1829). John Pearson's description of Lancaster and Columbia in 1801. [Edited by James H. Mast.] Lancaster Co. Hist. Soc., Jour., 61:49-61 (Apr 1957). view. notes. Detailed account of streets, buildings, and some of the inhabitants of the 2 towns. Heavily annotated. [7610

JOHN ANDREW HOSTETLER. The Amish in Center County, Pennsylvania [1804-40, 1949-50]. Mennonite hist. bul., 12(2):2-3 (Apr 1951). [7611

MELVIN HORST. Covered bridges of Pennsylvania Dutchland [1805-1960]. Photography by Mel Horst; text by Elmer L[ewis] Smith. Akron, Pa.: Applied Arts [1960]. 42 p. views (part col.). Includes photographs of "nearly half of the existing covered bridges" in 9 counties. [7612

S. R. SLAYMAKER II. White Chimneys, 1807-1957: a brief history of the home and those who lived there. Lancaster County Hist. Soc., Jour., 61:27-38 (Jan 1957). ports., views. On "the dwelling place of eight successive generations of the Slaymaker family of Lancaster County," on land received by Mathias Slaymaker from the Penns in or soon after 1710. [7613

ERNEST T. SCHULEEN. The story of Safe Harbor. Lancaster Co. Hist. Soc., Jour., 63:79-110 (Apr 1959). maps, views. notes. On a town at the confluence of Conestoga Creek and the Susquehanna River, 1811-1958. [7614

S. R. SLAYMAKER II. A Lancaster County businessman and the War of 1812. Lancaster Co. Hist. Soc., Jour., 63:57-78 (Apr 1959). ports., views. On the business activities of Amos Slaymaker (1755-1837) of Salisbury Township, 1812-15; with excerpts from his family correspondence dealing with war, politics, and business. [7615

SILVER SPRING PRESBYTERIAN CHURCH, Cumberland County, Pa. Silver Spring Presbyterian Church, Cumberland County, Pa., church and cemetery records. Compiled by Helen I. Harman for Cumberland County Chapter. D. A. R. mag., 94:505-6 (Aug-Sep). This installment: marriages by the Rev. Henry R. Wilson, 1814-24. [7616

BOB McCAFFERY. Lehigh County map found in garage. Lehigh Co. Hist. Soc., Proc., 23:96-100. On "A draft of the original surveys in the County of Lehigh from the drafts and notes of James Scull, formerly Dept. Sur., by Isaac A. Chapman," a manuscript map dated 1816; with German text and translation of a newspaper advertisement by Chapman, 11 Dec. 1817, soliciting subscriptions to a proposed map of Northampton and Lehigh Counties. [7617

NORMAN DAIN & ERIC T. CARLSON. Milieu therapy in the nineteenth century: patient care at the Friends' Asylum, Frankford, Pennsylvania, 1817-1861. Jour. nervous and mental diseases, 131:277-90 (Oct). notes. [7618

ELMER LEWIS SMITH. Christmas among the Amish [in Pennsylvania.] Hist. rev. Berks Co., 25:10-15 (winter). views. On traditional observances, none here dated earlier than 1817. [7619

DAVID G. WILLIAMS. A roof was built. Lehigh Co. Hist. Soc., Proc., 23:68-74. diagrs., views. Detailed description and illustrations of the "hand finished oak timber structure" supporting the roof of a farmhouse near Mechanicsville, Pa., built probably "somewhere around 1820-1830." [7620

BARBARA SNOW. Living with antiques: the home of Mr. and Mrs. J. Stanley Lee, Newtown, Pennsylvania. Antiques, 78:239-43 (Sep). views (1 col.). On a house built by Edward Hicks, Quaker painter, in 1821, and the Hicks paintings and other memorabilia now preserved in it. [7621

ROBERT BERGER. The story of Baptist beginnings in Lycoming County [1822 to ca. 1850]. Now and then, 12:274-80 (Jul). view. [7622

WILLARD RAYMOND RHOADS. The Pennsylvania Canal. West. Pa. hist. mag., 43:203-38 (Sep). diagrs., map. table, views. bibliog., notes. On a system of canals constructed by the State of Pennsylvania between 1826 and 1858, intended to connect Philadelphia with Pittsburgh and Erie, of which 718 miles were finished and 240 left unfinished; with an account of the structures composing it, its operation by the State till 1901, and the sale of its segments in installments between 1858 and 1901. [7623

ROBERT B. WENGER. A history of Metzlers Mennonite Congregation [Lancaster County, Pa., 1827-1944]. Mennonite hist. bul., 18(3):1-4 (Jul 1957). view. bibliog., notes. [7624

THOMAS A. FORBES. Archery specialities. By Tom Forbes. Pa. game news, 21(1):57-60; (2):62-4 (Jan, Feb). port., views. On archers as hunters of wild game in Pennsylvania, 1828-1960. [7625

C. DANIEL LITTLE. Major Samuel Bryan [1831-92] of Bryantown. Now and then, 12:37-41 (Jan 1958). bibliog. On his life in Bryantown, where he inherited his father's woolen mills, and his service as an officer in a Pennsylvania regiment during the Civil War (with excerpts from 2 letters by him). [7626

HISTORICAL SOCIETY OF BERKS COUNTY. Early railroads in Berks, 1833-1893. [By Edwin B. Yeich.] Hist. rev. Berks Co., 25:48-53 (spring). map, views. [7627

ELIZABETH YARNALL. The other branch. Anna (Cox) Brinton, ed., Then and now: Quaker essays, historical and contemporary, by friends of Henry Joel Cadbury (Phila.: Univ. of Pennsylvania Press [1960]), p. 180-87. On Addison Hutton (1834-1916), Pennsylvania Quaker and architect. [7628

THADDEUS STEVENS (1793-1868). Three speeches of Thaddeus Stevens. Lancaster Co. Hist. Soc., Jour., 62: 179-204 (Oct 1958). "Speech opposing debilitation of the Public School Act" (1835), "Speech advocating State endowment of colleges and academies" (1838), and "Plea for religious liberty in Pennsylvania, before the Pennsylvania Supreme Court" (1848), the last dealing with a man prosecuted for working on Sunday. [7629

HUBERTIS MAURICE CUMMINGS. John Augustus Roebling and the public works of Pennsylvania. Internal Affairs monthly bul., 28(5-9): monthly installments (May-Sep). On his work "as a civil engineer on such important State public works projects as canals, railroads, suspension bridges, and aqueducts," 1836-48, and his special interest in the development and uses of wire rope. [7630

THOMAS W. LEIDY & ROSANNE D. LEIDY. Stouchsburg Academy [Stouchsburg, Pa., 1839-78]. Hist. rev. Berks Co., 25:29-30 (winter). view. [7631

MARSHALL REID ANSPACH. A history of the Lycoming Fire Insurance Company (1840-1885): the story of its rise and fall. Now and then, 12: 288-93 (Jul). view. [7632

ALBERT G. BREHM. History, St. Marys Church. [St. Marys, Pa.:] Lenze Associated Enterprises [1960]. 89 p. facsims., ports., tables, views. notes. On the German Catholic settlement founded in Elk County, Pa., as Marienstadt in 1842, and its church till 1954. [7633

JOHN WARD WILSON LOOSE. Harrison Township retraced. Lancaster Co. Hist. Soc., Jour., 63:128-31 (Jul 1959). map. On a township in Lancaster County established in 1845 by division of East Donegal, Rapho, and Mount Joy Townships, and abolished by court action in 1846. [7634

WILLIAM KENNETH SCHUSLER. The railroad comes to Pittsburgh. West. Pa. hist. mag., 43:251-66 (Sep). maps. notes. Based on thesis--Univ. of Pittsburgh. On lines constructed in western Pennsylvania and serving Pittsburgh, 1848-84. [7635

GILBERT ABRAMSON. Grounds for divorce [in Pennsylvania, 1849-1958]. Temple law quar., 33:219-30 (winter 1959). notes. [7636

JOHN WARD WILLSON LOOSE, ed. Cholera in Lancaster and Columbia in 1854. Lancaster Co. Hist. Soc., Jour., 62:109-46 (Apr 1958). map, port., tables. notes. Reports of John Light Atlee (1799-1883), M.D., and T. Heber Jackson, M.D., both dated 1855; "Modern knowledge of cholera," by John L. Atlee, Jr., and William A. Atlee; remarks by J. Franklin Reigert, "engineer and civic leader" (from a 15-page pamphlet by him, 1855), Ebenezer Erskine, Presbyterian minister (from his published sermon on the cholera as a visitation from God, 1 Oct. 1854), and Stephen Greene (editorials in The Columbia spy, 25 Sep. 1854); and excerpts from the report of a Sanitation Committee in Columbia. [7637

Mrs. ELLIS BLOCKSON. St. Matthew's Church, Sewickley, Pa. [1857-1957]. A. M. E. Zion quar. rev., 68:41-5 (winter 1956). [7638

MUNCY LUMINARY, Muncy, Pa. Marriages and deaths from the Muncy luminary. Now and then, 12:26, 68-9, 71-2, 93-4, 145, 147-9, 169, 172-4, 217-19, 366-70 (Oct 1957-Apr 1960). These installments: Jan. 1857-Jan. 1860. [7639

THOMAS J. DEMPSEY. Evidence of prices in Pennsylvania eminent domain proceedings [1858-1958]. Dickinson law rev., 63:5-44 (Oct 1958). notes. [7640

PAUL HENRY GIDDENS. The significance of the Drake well [Titusville, Pa., 1858-64]. Centennial Seminar on the History of the Petroleum Industry, Harvard University, 1959, Oil's first century: papers ([Boston:] Harvard Graduate School of Business Administration [1960]), p. 21-5. view. notes. [7641

SAUL SACK. The first junior college. Jr. college jour., 30:13-15 (Sep 1959). notes. On Susquehanna University (originally the Missionary Institute of the Evangelical Lutheran Church), Selinsgrove, Snyder County, Pa., 1858-94. [7642

EUGENE WILLARD MILLER. Population and functional changes of villages in western Pennsylvania [Armstrong, Butler, Venango, Clarion, Jefferson, and Forest Counties, in "the dissected Allegheny Plateau," 1859-1955]. West. Pa. hist. mag., 43:59-75 (Mar). maps. notes. [7643

MARGARET TSCHAN RILEY. Evan Pugh of Pennsylvania State University [then the Agricultural College of Pennsylvania] and the Morrill Land-Grant Act [1859-64]. West. Pa. hist. mag., 27:338-60 (Oct). ports., views. notes. [7644

RUSSELL J. BORDEN. Hospitalizing the mentally ill in Pennsylvania [1860-1958]. Temple law quar., 33: 165-208 (winter 1959). notes. Mainly on the Pennsylvania Mental Health Act of 1951. [7645

ETHEL R. MILLEN. History of two Lebanon streets [Elm Street and Kimball Street since 1860]. Lebanon Hist. Soc., Ann. rep., 2, leaves [10-15]. [7646

EDWIN W. TOMPKINS. Cameron County centennial: "a pageant of progress," 1860-1960. Internal Affairs monthly bul., 28(3-4):20-25 (Mar-Apr). views. [7647

U.S. Dept. of Commerce. Office of Area Development. A community attack on chronic unemployment: Hazleton, Pennsylvania, a case study. By John R. Fernstrom. [Wash.] 1960. v, [1], 56 p. diagr., maps (1 double), tables, views. bibliog. (p. 49-50), notes. (Its Community development series, 1.) On the decline of anthracite coal mining in Hazleton, the resulting unemployment, and recent measures to develop other industry there, 1860-1960. [7648

DAVID M. LUDLUM. The weather at Gettysburg. Weatherwise, 13:101-5, 130 (Jun). map, port., views. On observations of temperature, pressure, wind, and clouds made by Michael Jacobs (1808-71), Professor of Mathematics and Science, Gettysburg College, during July 1863. [7649

WILLIAM J. McKENNA. The income tax in Pennsylvania [1864-1959]. Pa. hist., 27:291-310 (Jul). notes. [7650

HARRY CURTIS KEMP (born 1868/69). Kemp's life story. N.Y.: Carlton Press, 1960. [4], 100 p. (A Comet reflection book.) Chronology of the author's life near Nelson and later near Wellsboro, Tioga County, Pa., as a farmer, a carpenter, a maker of maple syrup, and a Presbyterian layman. [7651

ALFRED JOHN PARSONS (1842-90). Alfred Parsons' diary--a boating holiday. Edited by Charles Morse Stotz. West. Pa. hist. mag., 43:349-65 (Dec). map, views. Record of a voyage with friends in "the Eight oared racing Barge of the Xanthe Club," from Pittsburgh by river and canal to the Beaver River, French Creek, the Allegheny River, and back to Pittsburgh, 18-29 Aug. 1869; with remarks on the scenery and the healthful effects of the exercise. [7652

PENNSYLVANIA. Topographic and Geologic Survey. History, present status, and future possibilities of secondary recovery operations in Pennsylvania [1869-1960]. By William S. Lytle. [Harrisburg:] Dept. of Internal Affairs, 1960. 28-42 p. diagrs., maps. bibliog. (p. 41-2). (Its Bulletin M41.) From Interstate Oil Compact Commission Committee bulletin, Dec. 1959. [7653

I. HERMAN STERN. Judicial enforcement of labor contracts and employment rights under Pennsylvania law [1869-1959]. Villanova law rev., 5:32-58, 561-89 (fall 1959, summer 1960). notes. [7654

M. LUTHER HEISEY. Along the streets of old Lancaster. Lancaster Co. Hist. Soc., Jour., 61:62-73 (Apr 1957). cartoon, views. notes. On "customs, manners and mode of living" in Lancaster, 1870s-90s. [7655

JOHN ANDREW HOSTETLER. Joseph W[arren] Yoder (1872-1956). Mennonite hist. bul., 18(1):1-2 (Jan 1957). port. On his life in Pennsylvania, his work as a teacher of music, his books about the Amish, and his collection (recorded from oral sources) of Amische Lieder (1942). [7656

C. DANIEL LITTLE. A journey through Sullivan County in 1874 (based upon notes prepared by John F. Meginness and A. R. Sprout as a prospectus for a railroad to Binghamton, N.Y.). Now and then, 12:281-7 (Jul). map. [7657

HENRY EDWARD CLEPPER. Pennsylvania's forestry heritage [1875-1959]. Am. forests, 65(10):15, 78-82 (Oct 1959). ports. [7658

THOMAS T. TABER III. Logging railroads and logging locomotives in eastern Pennsylvania [1875-1932]. Now and then, 12:225-36 (Jan). double map, views. [7659

DAVID A. MILLER. Macungie, former hub for telegraph. Lehigh Co. Hist. Soc., Proc., 23:41-7. On the Macungie and East Texas Telegraph Co., soon renamed the Lehigh Telegraph Co., chartered in or before 1876 and merged with larger companies ca. 1891; with the writer's recollections of his employment by the company. [7660

MILTON EMBICK FLOWER. Aaron Mountz [1873-1949], primitive woodcarver. Antiques, 77:586-7 (Jun). notes. On carvings done by him on the Mountz farm near Carlisle, Pa., in the 1880s and 1890s. [7661

KARL B. REICHARD. The great Milton [Pa.] fire of 1880. Now and then, 12:114-26 (Oct 1958). views. bibliog., notes. [7662

THOMAS KENNETH WOOD (1877-1958). Cherry. Now and then, 12:136-9 (Jan 1959). port. Memories of the author's father's farm at the edge of Muncy, Pa., 1880s. [7663

MAE (TOWNSEND) PEASE (born 1881). Reminiscences from lamplight to satellite. Phila.: Dorrance [1960. 10]. 136 p. ports., views. On the author's early life in Philadelphia as a banker's daughter, her marriage to Henry H. Pease, business executive, and their life in Wilkes-Barre and Philadelphia. [7664

CLAUDE ALVIN VILLEE. Short history of Lancaster Fire Department since 1882. Lancaster Co. Hist. Soc., Jour., 63:137-48 (Jul 1959). port., views. Includes "Chronology of major fires in Lancaster City since 1882." [7665

EMILY EDNA FARNHAM. Charles Demuth [1883-1935]: his life, psychology, and works. Ann Arbor: University Microfilms, 1959 [i.e. 1960]. Positive microfilm of typescript. [1084] leaves. Thesis--Ohio State Univ. Abstracted: Dissert. abstracts, 20:4069 (Apr). On his life in Lancaster, Pa., and his work as a painter; with a catalogue of his works. [7666

MUNCY Traction Engine Company [incorporated 1886, apparently still in business in 1892]. Now and then, 12: 201-4 (Oct 1959). facsim. [7667

HERBERT H. HARMAN. The North Washington Street Gang in the late eighteen eighties. Now and then, 12: 186-9 (Jul 1959). Recollections (1940s) of Muncy, Pa. [7668

WAYNE E. HOMAN. The Great Blizzard of 1888 [in Reading]. Hist. rev. Berks Co., 25:6-9, 34-5 (winter). views. [7669

MARIETTA JOHNSTON. House of the Good Shepherd: the stranger within our gates. Hist. rev. Berks Co., 25: 16-19 (winter). views. On the Convent of the Good Shepherd, a community of nuns of the Order of the Good Shepherd, administering Marymount, a community of delinquent girls committed to them for rehabilitation, 1889-1959. [7670

IRA DAVID LANDIS. The largest ordination class in Pennsylvania Mennonite history [4 miles north of Lititz, 5 Sep. 1889]. Mennonite hist. bul., 9(4):1-3 (Oct 1948). port. Includes biographical sketches of the 22 individuals then ordained. [7671

HELEN THEODOSIA (IVES) LYON. The little red schoolhouse. N.Y. folklore quar., 16:179-86 (autumn). Memories of teaching in 3 country schools near Wellsboro, Pa., 1890 ff. [7672

HELEN CHAMBERLIN POTTS. Hughesville in the nineties. Now and then, 12:242-6 (Jan). Recollections. [7673

GEORGE L. HEIGES. The Lancaster General Hospital: first twenty-five years [1893-1918]. Lancaster Co. Hist. Soc., Jour., 62:147-68 (Jul 1958). ports., views. notes. [7674

MAURICE E. SHERMAN. When deer were few. Pa. game news, 21(4):26-30 (Apr). On the extreme scarcity of deer in Pennsylvania as early as 1897 and especially during the years of the author's service as a State trooper and a game protector in Cameron, Elk, and McLean Counties, 1915-19. [7675

M. LUTHER HEISEY. Games and amusements in olden days. Lancaster Co. Hist. Soc., Jour., 63:132-5 (Jul 1959). Recollections of Lancaster County, ca. 1898. [7676

RALPH C. WIBLE. Re-building Penn's Woods. Am. forests, 65(10):22-3, 69-73 (Oct 1959). views (1 double). On State forests in Pennsylvania, 1898-1959. [7677

JAN HAROLD BRUNVAND. The cars that went in the river--a Pennsylvania railroaders' legend in Indiana. Keystone folklore quar., 5(1-2):3-6 (spring-summer). On versions of an incident supposed to have occurred at Scranton in 1902. [7678

ROBERT J. CORNELL. The anthracite coal strike of 1902. Wash.: Catholic Univ. of America Press, 1957. xii, 279 p. map. bibliog. (p. 260-70), notes. Thesis--Catholic Univ. of America. On disorders centered in Pennsylvania. [7679

IN my merry Oldsmobile. Now and then, 12:261-2 (Apr). facsims. On the 131 automobiles registered in the prothonotary's office, Williamsport, Pa., as then required by law, 11 May 1903-18 Nov. 1905, recording name of owner, type of automobile, and residence of owner. [7680

LAUN C. SMITH. I saw a Pennsylvania panther. Pa. game news, 21(9):12-15 (Sep). views. On a panther seen by the author during a hunting trip in Clearfield County in 1906. [7681

JOHN H. VINYARD. Infant mortality in Pennsylvania, 1954-58. Pub. health reports, 75:407-12 (May). tables. notes. Includes data for 1906 and following years. [7682

JESSE ROFFE WIKE II. The Pennsylvania Manufacturers' Association [1909-60]. Phila.: Univ. of Pennsylvania Press [1960]. 356 p. tables. bibliog. (p. 339-47), notes. Based on thesis--Univ. of Pennsylvania. [7683

H. M. CRANMER, ed. Two early Pennsylvania ballads. Keystone folklore quar., 5(4):13-18 (winter). "The saga of Billy French," apparently by French himself, "a farmer and wagoner of Northern Pennsylvania," and "Amanda," about a girl captured by Indians and rescued from burning by the intervention of a chief--both ballads learned by Cranmer from his father in Clinton County "fifty years or more ago." [7684

MARIE KATHERN NUSCHKE. The dam that could not break. Camp Hill, Pa.: Plank's Suburban Press, ©1960. [8], 40 p. views. notes. Eyewitness account of the flood that destroyed Austin and Costello, lumber towns in a narrow valley in Potter County, Pa., 30 Sep. 1911; with a list of 78 persons known to have been drowned, and some account of the towns since 1827. [7685

JOHN M. McLAUGHLIN. The compensability of heart injuries under the Pennsylvania Workmen's Compensation Act. Univ. Pittsburgh law rev., 21:445-92 (Mar). notes. Review of court decisions, 1912-56. [7686

MABEL McGINNIS (born 1916). Life with George: ups and downs on the farm. N.Y.: Exposition Press [1959]. 170 p. ports., views. On her years as a town girl in Eau Claire, Butler County, Pa., her eagerness to marry a farmer and live on a farm, her marriage to George McGinnis (ca. 1936?), and details of their life on 3 farms in Butler County for about 10 years thereafter. [7687

WILLIAM THOMAS TSIOURIS. Admission of a defendant's convictions in a first-degree murder trial as information for a jury in Pennsylvania [1925-57]--an undue concession to expediency. Temple law quar., 33: 89-98 (fall 1959). notes. [7688

DON NEAL. The deer hunter's loss. Pa. game news, 31(12):4-7 (Dec). views. Memories of "the fun and fellowship" of a party of deer hunters in camp between Clearfield and Du Bois, Pa., in 1926, in a time when deer-hunting "was a group operation in which every member was only part of a team." [7689

NICHOLAS BIDDLE. Bow hunting in Pennsylvania [1929-60]. Pa. game news, 21(10):50-53 (Oct). views. [7690

MAURICE ALLISON MOOK. Crawford County No. 3. Mennonite hist. bul., 14(3):6-8 (Jul 1953). On an Old Order Amish community near Bear Lake, northwestern Warren County, Pa., 1933-34. [7691

NATHANIEL KRUM. The man from Hawk Mountain. Am. forests, 65(10): 32-5, 64-6, 68-9 (Oct 1959). port., views. On the Hawk Mountain Sanctuary, near Drehersville, Pa., established by Mrs. Charles Noel Edge and managed by Maurice Broun, as a sanctuary for hawks, ferns, and other wildlife, 1934-59. [7692

JOHN J. POSERINA, JR. Appointed attorney general's power to supersede an elected district attorney [in Pennsylvania, 1936-59]. Temple law quar., 33:78-88 (fall 1959). notes. Includes some account of the history of the Pennsylvania offices of attorney general and district attorney. [7693

NICHOLAS UNKOVIC. Mass picketing law in Pennsylvania [1937-58]. Dickinson law rev., 63:111-19 (Jan). notes. [7694

ROBERT CHAUNCEY ANGUS. Changes in efficiency of marketing milk in Philadelphia and Pittsburgh, 1940 to 1957. Ann Arbor: University Microfilms, 1960. Positive microfilm of typescript. [250] leaves. Thesis--Pennsylvania State Univ. Abstracted: Dissert. abstracts, 21:78 (Jul). [7695

CHARLES H. DORNBUSCH. Pennsylvania German barns. ... With introduction and descriptive text by John K. Heyl. [Allentown, Pa., 1958.] xxiv, 312 p. diagrs., views. (Pennsylvania German Folklore Society. [Yearbook], 21.) Compiled by Heyl from notes and photographs collected by Dornbusch in an architectural study, 1940-47. [7696

KENNETH WHALEY MASTERS. Population changes in Pennsylvania for 18 year period, 1940 to 1958. Internal Affairs monthly bul., 28(3-4):6-11, 16; (5):26-9 (Mar-Apr, May). tables. notes. [7697

ARCHIBALD RUTLEDGE. Cumberland Valley memories. Pa. game news, 21(9):36-8 (Sep). views. On the author's experiences in hunting and fishing in the vicinity of Mercersburg, Pa., since 1940. [7698

PENNSYLVANIA. General Assembly. Joint State Government Commission. Structure and growth of Pennsylvania's economy: an outline of trends, 1946-1956. Harrisburg, 1959. vi, 46 p. diagrs. (part fold.), maps (part fold.), tables. [7699

JACOB JOSEPH KAUFMAN & HELMUT J. GOLATZ. Chronic unemployment in Pennsylvania [1947-57]. University Park: Bureau of Business Research, College of Business Administration, Pennsylvania State Univ., 1960. [4], 115 p. tables. notes. Summary of an unpublished study made in 1959 for the Bureau of Employment Security, Department of Labor and Industry, Commonwealth of Pennsylvania. [7700

MAURICE ALLISON MOOK. Nicknames among the Amish [in Lancaster and Mifflin Counties, Pa.]. Keystone folklore quar., 5(4):3-12 (winter). [7701

COLLIER RHOADS. Pennsylvania German groundhog lodges. Keystone folklore quar., 5(1-2):7-9 (spring-summer). On annual "Groundhog lodge suppers," usually in late January or early February, characterized by "good food and good songs" and "good fellowship," intended "to preserve the Pennsylvania German language and customs." [7702

Philadelphia

EDWARD PINKOWSKI. Philadelphia street cries. Keystone folklore quar., 5(1-2):10-12 (spring-summer). On cries of retailers hawking their wares in the streets of Philadelphia since "William Penn's time." [7703

LIONEL DARCY WYLD. Civilization's meeting places. Keystone folklore quar., 5(1-2):15-29 (spring-summer). notes. On inns, taverns, and coffeehouses in Philadelphia, 1691-1800. [7704

RUTH L. SPRINGER & LOUISE WALLMAN, eds. Two Swedish pastors describe Philadelphia, 1700 and 1702. Pa. mag. hist. and biog., 84:194-218 (Apr). notes. Letters to Sweden from Andreas Rudman, "Pastor at Wicaco in Pennsylvania," undated (evidently 1700), and his successor, Andreas Sandel (17 Jun. 1702), on the Lutheran church and its Swedish congregation, the other churches, the Indians, the American weather, prices, etc. [7705

HORACE HOWARD FURNESS JAYNE. A silver can by Francis Richardson, Jr. Phila. Mus. bul., 55:10-13 (autumn 1959-winter 1960). views. On Francis Richardson II (1681?-1729) and his sons Francis III, called Francis Jr., and Joseph, and Joseph's sons Joseph Jr. and Nathaniel, Philadelphia silversmiths active from 1701 till after 1800. [7706

JOHN MEREDITH GRAHAM II. An early Philadelphia desk. Antiques, 77:100-101 (Jan). facsim., views. On a "secretary-desk" signed by Edward Evans, 1707. [7707

GEORGE HENRY ECKHARDT. Edward Duffield [1720-1801], Benjamin Franklin's clockmaker. Antiques, 77: 284-6 (Mar). views. On his work as a clockmaker in Philadelphia, with illustrations of 7 clocks that he made. [7708

HANNAH BENNER ROACH. Benjamin Franklin slept here. Pa. mag. hist. and biog., 84:127-74 (Apr). map. notes. On the houses in Philadelphia occupied by Franklin and his family, 1723-90. [7709

FREDERICK BARNES TOLLES. Quietism versus enthusiasm: the Philadelphia Quakers and the Great Awakening [1739-41]. Frederick B. Tolles, Quakers and the Atlantic culture (N.Y.: Macmillan, 1960), p. 91-113. notes. From the Pennsylvania magazine of history and biography, 1945. [7710

NEDA M. WESTLAKE. William Smith [1727-1803], first provost of the University. Lib. chron., 26:30-34 (winter). facsim. On a printed recommendation that he be granted the degree of Doctor of Divinity by Oxford (1759), and 4 manuscript notebooks of lectures delivered by him at the College of Philadelphia (1767-69); with some account of his policies as Provost of the College, 1754 ff. [7711

PAUL GINSBURG SIFTON. Pierre Eugène Du Simitière: illustrator of nascent America. Antiques, 78:576-8 (Dec). facsims., map, views. On 6 illustrations engraved by him for the Pennsylvania magazine, 1774-76; with reproductions. [7712

DAVID SELLIN. A Benbridge conversation piece. Phila. Mus. bul., 55: 3-9 (autumn 1959 - winter 1960). facsim., ports. notes. Reprinted, with same title: Antiques, 78:236-8 (Sep). ports. On a group portrait of Dr. Enoch Edwards, his bride, Frances (Gordon) Edwards, a Miss Edwards, and the painter, Henry Benbridge (1743-1812), done by Benbridge in Philadelphia, probably in 1779; with some account of his career as a painter. [7713

RICHARD HARRISON SHRYOCK. The College of Physicians of Philadelphia in historical perspective [1787-1960]. College Phys. Phila., Trans. & studies, 27:150-57 (Apr). notes. [7714

WALTER E. THOMPSON. Frank Stewart and the first mint building. Numismatic scrapbook, 26:2838-40 (Oct). views. On the "original building constructed by Director of the Mint David Rittenhouse for use of the Mint in 1792" in Philadelphia, and a picture of it painted for Stewart, its owner in 1914, as "an artists's conception" of its original appearance. [7715

JAMES HARDIE (1760?-1826). Grub Street in Philadelphia, 1794-1795: more about James Hardie. [Edited] by Rollo G. Silver. N.Y. Pub. Lib., Bul., 64:130-42 (Mar). notes. Letters to Mathew Carey, Philadelphia publisher, dated at Philadelphia and Princeton, on Hardie's work as proofreader and indexer, explaining unavoidable delays in submitting copy, giving details of his extreme poverty, requesting prepayment for some of his services, and making emergency requests for loans. [7716

RANSOM R. PATRICK. The early life of John Neagle [1799?-1865], Philadelphia portrait painter. Ann Arbor: University Microfilms, 1959 [i.e. 1960]. Positive microfilm of typescript. [222] leaves. Thesis--Princeton Univ. Abstracted: Dissert. abstracts, 20:3685 (Mar). [7717

CHESTER RAPKIN & WILLIAM G. GRIGSBY. The demand for housing in racially mixed areas: a study of the nature of neighborhood change. Berkeley: Univ. of California Press, 1960. xx, 177 p. diagrs., form, maps, tables. notes. "Special research report to the Commission on Race and Housing and the Philadelphia Redevelopment Authority," based mainly upon a survey made in 1955. Includes a historical review of Negro housing in Philadelphia, 1810-1956. [7718

GEORGE EGON HATVARY. Horace Binney Wallace [1817-52]: a critical biography. Ann Arbor: University Microfilms, 1957 [i.e. 1960]. Positive microfilm of typescript. [377] leaves. Thesis--New York Univ. Abstracted: Dissert. abstracts, 20:3293-4 (Feb). On his life in Philadelphia as a lawyer, a novelist and essayist, and a literary and political commentator, his "passion for anonymity," his travels in Europe and the essays they inspired, and his suicide in Paris. [7719

NEGLEY KING TEETERS. The early days of the Philadelphia House of Refuge. Pa. hist., 27:165-87 (Apr). views. notes. On a penal institution "for Juvenile Offenders," 1823-31. [7720

THE EVENING BULLETIN, Philadelphia. Lafayette's visit to Philadelphia in 1824. Picket post, 68:8-12 (May). views. From the issue of 30 Sep. 1924. [7721

ANNA PIRSCENOK. William Gunn Malin (1801-1887). Jour. hist. med., 15:147-53 (Apr). port. bibliog. On his service as clerk, librarian, Steward of the Department of the Insane, and Steward of the Department of the Sick and Injured, Pennsylvania Hospital, 1824-83, and his reports and other writings. [7722

TWO Tucker beakers. Phila. Mus. bul., 54:67-70 (spring 1959). views. On 2 porcelain vases made by William Ellis Tucker in 1827, decorated with views of the Woodlands and the Solitude, country houses within the present limits of Philadelphia, both delineated by Tucker from engravings in Thomas Birch's Country seats. [7723

MARION BALL WILSON. Ludwig Greiner [1804?-1874], doll head maker. Am.-German rev., 26(2): 29-31, 33 (Dec 1959-Jan 1960). port., views. On his emigration from Germany to Philadelphia in "the early 1830's" and the characteristics of the dolls manufactured by him between 1840 and 1883. [7724

LEWIS CASS SCHEFFEY. Albert Holmes Smith [1835-85]: a study in courage. Am. jour. obstet. and gynecol., 78:929-38 (Nov). On his life in Philadelphia and his work as a physician, particularly his obstetrical practice. [7725

HENRY McALLISTER. John G. Johnson [1841-1917], lawyer. Dicta. 26:149-53 (Jun 1949). On his life in Philadelphia and his eminence as "the unquestioned leader of the American bar." [7726

FRED B. ROGERS. William Pepper, 1843-1898: physician, educator, philanthropist. Jour. med. educ., 34: 885-9 (Sep 1959). facsim., port., view. bibliog. On his life in Philadelphia, his studies at the University of Pennsylvania Medical School, his medical practice and teaching of medicine, his service as Provost of the University of Pennsylvania, and his establishment of the Pepper Laboratory of Clinical Medicine. [7727

JOHN WILLIAM ALEXANDER, JR. Eleven times ten: a history of the Eta Chapter of Delta Phi at the University of Pennsylvania, 1849-1960. Phila.: St. Elmo Club, 1960. [6], 98 p. port., views. bibliog. (p. 98). [7728

JOSEPH SAMUEL HEPBURN. Fredrika Bremer and Philadelphia. Am. Swed. Hist. Found., Yr. bk., 1960, p. 1-22. facsim. notes. On the visits of a Swedish traveler to Philadelphia, Jun. 1850 and Jul. 1851, "the institutions and places" that she noted, and "the Philadelphians whom she met." [7729

WILLIAM SCHACK. Art and Argyrol: the life and career of Dr. Albert C[oombs] Barnes [1872-1951]. N.Y.: T. Yoseloff [1960]. 412 p. port. On his early life and medical studies and his study of chemistry in Germany, his preparation of Argyrol (a patent remedy) and establishment of the pharmaceutical firm of Barnes & Hille, Philadelphia, his activities as a collector of paintings and sculpture, his founding of the Barnes Foundation to administer the collection in a museum, and his involvement in acrimonious controversies as a result of the limitations that he placed upon access to the museum. [7730

ARTHUR H. LEWIS. The worlds of Chippy Patterson. N.Y.: Harcourt, Brace [1960. 6], 311 p. On Christopher Stuart Patterson, Jr. (1875-1933), and his career from 1902 till 1932 as a shabbily dressed Philadelphia criminal lawyer. [7731

WILLIAM STANDLEY STOKES, JR. A legend of service to children. N.Y.: Newcomen Soc. in North America, 1960. 24 p. views. On St. Christopher's Hospital for Children, Philadelphia, 1875-1960, affiliated with Temple University. [7732

JAMES C. MASSEY. The Provident Trust buildings, 1879-1897. Soc. Architectural Historians, Jour., 19: 79-81 (Jun). views. notes. On 5 buildings (or additions to buildings) designed by Frank Furness for the Provident Life and Trust Company, Philadelphia, of which 4 were demolished in 1936 or 1937 and the last in 1960. [7733

SILVIO A. BEDINI. The Five O'Clock Club. Hobbies, 64(12):42-4 (Feb). view. On an organization founded by M. Richards Muckle of Philadelpha for "the promotion of good fellowship," 1883-1937, and a souvenir spoon manufactured for its 20th anniversary. [7734

DONALD E. WILLARD, JR. W. W. Keen's "first modern brain case." College Phys. Phila., Trans. & studies, 26:146-50 (Feb 1959). notes. On his treatment, with medication and surgery, of a brain tumor of a patient at St. Mary's Hospital, Philadelphia, 1887, and the survival of the patient till 1918. [7735

EDWARD S. GIFFORD, JR. The evil eye in Pennsylvania medical history. Keystone folklore quar., 5(3):3-8 (autumn). From American journal of ophthalmology, Aug. 1957. Instances of "prenatal influence" and other phenomena supposed to result from exposure to the evil eye in Philadelphia, 1892-1957. [7736

ROBERT THOMPSON McCRACKEN. Fifty years at the bar. Pa. Bar Assoc. quar., 30:13-20 (Oct 1958). Reminiscences of legal practice and the habits of lawyers in Philadelphia, 1908-58. [7737

ABRAHAM P. GANNES. The Philadelphia Council on Jewish Education [and predecessor organizations, 1909-60]. Jew. educ., 30(2):17-34 (winter). notes. [7738

DONALD W. DISBROW. Reform in Philadelphia under Mayor [Rudolph] Blankenburg, 1912-1916. Pa. hist., 27:379-96 (Oct). views. notes. Based on thesis--Univ. of Rochester. [7739

A. J. MacDOWELL. Women can shoot. Pa. game news, 21(6):21-5 (Jun). ports., view. On the Women's Trap Shooting League, Philadelphia, 1920-59. [7740

FRED D. BALDWIN. Smedley D. Butler and prohibition enforcement in Philadelphia, 1924-1925. Pa. mag. hist. and biog., 84:352-68 (Jul). notes. [7741

HENRY CLARENCE PITZ. Francis Speight: painter of the Schuylkill Valley [since ca. 1925]. Am. artist, 24(4):28-33, 68-9 (Apr). port., views (1 col.). On his paintings of scenes in Manayunk and Roxborough; with remarks on "the Schuylkill Valley painters" as "not a 'school,' ... just individual talents drawn to a challenging strip of paintable country near Philadelphia." [7742

PAUL EDWARD LOTH. A study of certain Christian elementary day schools situated in metropolitan Philadelphia [1947-59]. Ann Arbor: University Microfilms, 1960. Positive microfilm of typescript. [121] leaves. Thesis (Ed. D.)--Temple Univ. Abstracted: Dissert. abstracts, 21: 1468-9 (Dec). [7743

DONALD RICHARD CAMPION. Patterns of suicide in Philadelphia: 1948-1952. Ann Arbor: University Microfilms, 1960. Positive microfilm of typescript. [337] leaves. Thesis--Univ. of Pennsylvania. Abstracted: Dissert. abstracts, 21:1279-80 (Nov). [7744

Pittsburgh

MARGARET PEARSON BOTHWELL. Edward Ward [died 1793], trail blazing pioneer. West. Pa. hist. mag., 43: 99-127 (Jun). notes. On his military and civilian activities in Pittsburgh, 1754-93; with "A list of some of the more interesting real estate conveyances in which Edward Ward was either grantor or grantee." [7745

REGISTER of Fort Duquesne, 1754-1756. [Translated and edited by] A[ndrew] A[rnold] Lambing. Memorial edition. [Pittsburgh: Catholic Historical Soc. of Western Pennsylvania] 1954. [6], 97 p. plan, view. notes. Reprint of The baptismal register of Fort Duquesne, translated and edited by Lambing (Pittsburgh, 1885), consisting of an essay on "The French in western Pennsylvania," by the editor, "The first mass at the shrine of Mary, on 'the Beautiful River,' " 17 Apr. 1754, Registres des baptesmes et sepultures qui se sont faits au Fort Duquesne, pendant les anneés 1753, 1754, 1755, & 1756 (N.Y.: Cramoisy Press of John Gilmary Shea, 1859), with French and English on facing pages, and notes by Lambing on Shea's text. The register proper consists of 4 entries by Father Gabriel Anheuser and 53 by Father Denys Baron, Recollect priests, including 2 entries made at Presque Isle and 6 at the fort on French Creek. [7746

WILLIAM GRANT SWAIN. Making up for 200-year loss in Pittsburgh. Landscape architecture, 50:76-80 (winter). diagr., map, views. notes. On the Pittsburgh landscape since 1754, and the growing interest of landscape architects in it since 1910, when Frederick Law Olmsted studied the area for the Pittsburgh Civic Commission. [7747

IRA R. PARKAS. Sources of early western Pennsylvania culture [centered in Pittsburgh, 1758-1834]. West. Pa. hist. mag., 43:47-57 (Mar). notes. [7748

MARGARET PEARSON BOTHWELL. "Allegany Town." West. Pa. hist. mag., 43:394-6 (Dec). facsim. notes. On the "Reserve Tract of Land Opposite Pittsburgh," ordered by the General Assembly of Pennsylvania in 1787 to be laid out in lots to be sold at public auction, incorporated as a borough in 1828 and as a city in 1840 and merged with the City of Pittsburgh in 1907. [7749

EBENEZER DENNY (1761-1822). Papers relating to the mercantile pursuits of Ebenezer Denny [of Pittsburgh]. West. Pa. hist. mag., 43:93-8 (Mar). Invoices from Philadelphia firms, 5 May-6 Oct. 1792, and undated list of Denny's customers. [7750

ELLA CHALFANT. Religion and education in early Pittsburgh. Carnegie mag., 34:63-7 (Feb). views. On bequests in early Pittsburgh wills, 1793 to ca. 1800, for religious and educational purposes. [7751

C. STANTON BELFOUR. Charles Avery [1784-1858], early Pittsburgh philanthropist. West. Pa. hist. mag., 43:19-22 (Mar). On his life in Pittsburgh, 1812-58, as a prosperous businessman, a lay preacher of the Methodist Episcopal and later the Methodist Protestant Church, an antislavery worker, and a generous giver to charitable causes. [7752

ANNE HARRIET BOWES, ed. Old manuscripts reveal public interest in early Pittsburgh markets, 1831-1836. West. Pa. hist. mag., 43:185-7 (Jun). view. notes. Committee reports, an ordinance, and several petitions. [7753

DAVID LEECH. [Petition to the Board of Council for the City of Pittsburgh, 25 Jun. 1832, and attached documents.] West. Pa. hist. mag., 43:303-6 (Sep). Request from the operator of a canal packet service for permission to excavate a basin beside the canal to accommodate a warehouse; with approval by the Board of Canal Commissioners, 18 May 1832, and by the Board of Council. [7754

WALTER SCOTT NETTROUR. Albert G. Walter [1811-76], nineteenth century pioneer in the surgery of trauma. Am. jour. surgery, 97:624-6 (May 1959). On his early life and medical education in Germany, his emigration to Pittsburgh in 1837, and his practice of surgery there; with a list of his publications, 1857-77. [7755

LABERTA DYSART. Chatham College: the first ninety years [1869-1959. Pittsburgh:] Chatham College, 1959 [c1960. 4], v, [5], 283, [1] p. facsims., ports., col. mount. seal, views. notes (p. 239-55). On a Pittsburgh institution founded under Presbyterian auspices as Pennsylvania Female College, later named the Pennsylvania College for Women (1890-1955), renamed Chatham College in 1955. [7756

JOSEPH A. KATARINCIC. The Allegheny County Bar Association, 1870-1960. West. Pa. hist. mag., 43:307-49 (Dec). notes. [7757

GRACE H. CRANE. The luxurious homes on Ridge Avenue. Carnegie mag., 34:131-7 (Apr). views. On the Pittsburgh mansions of J. Frederic Byers, Henry W. Oliver, B. F. Jones, William P. Snyder, and Maitland Alexander, built between 1879 and 1908. [7758

JAMES D. VAN TRUMP. Lions in the streets. Carnegie mag., 34:41-4, 52 (Feb). views. On sculptured lions in Pittsburgh, 1884-1960. [7759

JAMES D. VAN TRUMP. Of footbridges and preservation. West. Pa. hist. mag., 43:135-46 (Jun). view. On the Bridge of Sighs, connecting the Allegheny County Court House and the Jail (built in the middle 1880s), the bridge connecting the 2 sections of the Diamond Market House (built in 1915), and current proposals to demolish all these structures. [7760

JOHN LOFTON. The revival of Unitarianism in Pittsburgh [and western Pennsylvania, 1889-1900]. West. Pa. hist. mag., 43:367-80 (Dec). notes. Mainly on the religious and civic activities of the Rev. Charles E. St. John in Pittsburgh, 1891-1900. [7761

ST. JOHN CHRYSOSTOM GREEK CATHOLIC CHURCH, Pittsburgh. Golden anniversary and solemn rededication of newly decorated St. John Chrysostom Greek Catholic Church. [Pittsburgh, 1960? 92] p. facsims., ports., tables, views. Includes a brief historical sketch of the church, 1910-60, founded by immigrants from the Carpathian Mountains. [7762

THEODORE L. HAZLETT, JR. Pittsburgh authorities--key to renaissance. Internal Affairs monthly bul., 28(1-2): 1-6 (Jan-Feb). view. On the Urban Redevelopment Authority of Pittsburgh, the Housing Authority of the City of Pittsburgh, the Public Auditorium Authority of Pittsburgh and Allegheny County, the Public Parking Authority of Pittsburgh, and the County Sanitary Authority, 1937-59. [7763

MARY ELLEN PATNO. Mortality and economic level in an urban area [Pittsburgh, Pa., 1940-50]. Pub. health reports, 75:841-51 (Sep). tables. notes. [7764

ALLEGHENY CONFERENCE ON COMMUNITY DEVELOPMENT. Pittsburgh and Allegheny County planning to reality: an era of progress and accomplishment. [Pittsburgh, 1956?] 36 p. maps, views (part col.). 29 x 36 cm. On the "renaissance" of Pittsburgh, industrial, architectural, and cultural, since the establishment of the Conference in 1943. [7765

PENNSYLVANIA ECONOMY LEAGUE, INC. Pittsburgh redevelopment brings tax revenue spurt. Internal Affairs monthly bul., 28(10):16-19; (11):18-22 (Oct, Nov). From the League's News letter for western Pennsylvania, May-Jun. 1960. On "the fiscal gains of the Pittsburgh 'Renaissance' to date," 1948-60. [7766

DELAWARE

CHARLES G. DORMAN. Delaware cabinetmakers and allied artisans, 1655-1855. Wilmington: Historical Soc. of Delaware, 1960. [6], 111-217 p. facsims., port., views. notes. (Delaware history, v. 9, no. 2, Oct. 1960.) Mainly "Biographies of cabinetmakers and allied artisans, alphabetically arranged." [7767

LAWRENCE HENRY GIPSON. An anomalous American colony. Pa. hist.,

27:144-64 (Apr). notes. On Delaware, known before the Revolution as the Three Lower Counties on the Delaware, 1682-1770. [7768

J. BENNETT HILL. The Simon Kollocks of Sussex in the eighteenth century. Del. hist., 9:51-65 (Mar). geneal. chart. notes. On Simon Kollock (born ca. 1688, probably dead before 1758), son of Jacob Kollock; his nephew Simon (1737-1817); and his grandson Simon (born 1744)--respectively distinguished by father's name: Simon of Jacob, Simon of Cornelius, and Simon of Shephard. Mentions the possibility that there was also a Simon, son of Simon of Jacob. [7769

PETER C. WELSH. Brandywine: an early flour-milling center. Smithsonian Inst., Ann. rep., 1959, p. 677-86. diagrs., facsims., ports., views. notes (p. 684-6). On "the flour mills of Wilmington, generally referred to as the 'Brandywine Mills,'" situated on Brandywine Creek, 1742-1926. [7770

HAROLD BELL HANCOCK & NORMAN B. WILKINSON. Thomas and Joshua Gilpin, papermakers. Paper maker, 27(2):1-11 (Sep 1958). facsims., ports., view. bibliog. On paper mills established by Joshua Gilpin on Brandywine Creek, Del., 1787-1837. [7771

U.S. Census Office. 2d Census, 1800. 1800 census of New Castle County, Delaware. Transcribed and edited by Ellen Stanley Rogers and Louise E. Easter. Bladensburg, Md.: Genealogical Recorders, 1960. [4] leaves, 112 p. map. [7772

CHARLES A. SILLIMAN. The story of Christ Church Hundred [Episcopalian unit in New Castle County, Del.] and its people [1815-1951]. Wilmington, Del., 1960. x, [2], 211 p. facsim., maps, ports., seal, views. bibliog. (p. 187), notes (p. 189-201). [7773

JOHN C. PIERSON. James Guie Spackman, M.D. [1889-1959]. Del. State med. jour., 32:138-41 (Apr). port. On his work as a surgeon in Wilmington, 1915-59. [7774

THE SOUTH

THOMAS PERKINS ABERNETHY. The Southern frontier, an interpretation. Walker D. Wyman & Clifton B. Kroeber, eds., The frontier in perspective (Madison: Univ. of Wisconsin Press, 1957), p. 129-42. bibliog. [7775

JAMES BENNETT GRIFFIN. Relationships between the Caddoan area and the Mississippi Valley. Tex. Archeol. Soc., Bul., 31:27-51. bibliogs. Includes discussion by Philip Phillips, Stephen Williams, and Alex D. Krieger. [7776

HARNETT THOMAS KANE. Gone are the days: an illustrated history of the Old South [1513-1865]. N.Y.: Dutton, 1960. viii, 344 p. facsims., ports., views. bibliog. (p. 334-5). "Picture credits" (p. 334). [7777

BABETTE MAY LEVY. Early Puritanism in the Southern and island colonies. Am. Antiq. Soc., Proc., 70: 69-348 (Apr). bibliog. (p. 326-48), notes. On Puritanism as the common element in Congregationalism, Presbyterianism, and Quakerism, and the development of these faiths in Virginia, Maryland, the Carolinas, and the British West Indies, 1606 to ca. 1700; with a closing chapter on Southern Puritanism and its successor, Methodism." [7778

MARCUS WILSON JERNEGAN (1872-1949). Influences affecting education in the South [1607-1724]. Marcus W. Jernegan, Laboring and dependent classes in colonial America, 1607-1783 (N.Y.: Ungar [1960]), p. 131-40. notes. From School review, May 1919. [7779

CLARENCE HUGH HOLMAN. The Southerner as American writer [1621-1960]. Charles Grier Sellers, Jr., ed., The Southerner as American (Chapel Hill: Univ. of North Carolina Press [1960]), p. 180-99. notes. [7780

MARCUS WILSON JERNEGAN (1872-1949). Slavery and the beginnings of industrialism. Marcus W. Jernegan, Laboring and dependent classes in colonial America, 1607-1783 (N.Y.: Ungar [1960]), p. 3-23. notes. From American historical review, Jan. 1920. On the "employment of slaves in industries, other than those purely agricultural, in the South," 1649-1776. [7781

ULRICH BONNELL PHILLIPS (1877-1934), ed. Plantation and frontier, 1649-1863. Selected, collated, and edited with introduction by Ulrich B. Phillips. [N.Y.: Russell & Russell, 1958.] 2 v. [6], ix, 7-375; 379 p. facsims. (1 fold.), tables. bibliog. (1:105-7). (A documentary history of American industrial society, 1-2.) 1st ed. 1909. Documents from manuscript and printed primary sources (particularly newspapers) of Southern history, grouped in 22 topical sections dealing with plantation routine, products, and labor, slavery, Negroes, immigration and internal migration, manufacturing, "town labor," and "frontier society." Includes "Introduction" (1:69-104) on the economic history of the Old South, and a new preface by Louis Filler on the main publications concerning the pre-1863 history of the South issued since 1909. [7782

CAROLYN (THOMAS) FOREMAN. The Yuchi: children of the sun. Chron. Okla., 37:480-96 (winter). ports. notes. On a small group of Indians in the Southeastern United States, speaking an independent language, 1656 ff., their removal with members of the Creek Confederacy to the Indian Territory in the early 19th century, and their most recent chiefs, Samuel W. Brown, Sr. (1843-1935), and Samuel William Brown, Jr. (1879-1957). [7783

THOMAS CHALMERS McCORVEY (1851-1932). The masses and the classes in Southern politics. T. C. McCorvey, Alabama historical sketches, ed. George Burke Johnston (Charlottesville: Univ. of Virginia Press, 1960), p. 208-22. From The South in the building of the nation, v. 4 (1909). On the conflict between the loose constructionists and the strict constructionists, 1707-1908. [7784

KENNETH SCHUYLER LYNN. Mark Twain and Southwestern humor. Boston: Little, Brown [1960, c1959. 14], 300 p. cartoons, ports., views. notes. On "the Southwestern tradition" from William Byrd II through Mark Twain, 1730s-1890s. [7785

JAMES MANFORD CARSELOWEY. Cherokee notes. Fayetteville, Ark.: Washington County Historical Soc., 1960. 73 p. port. Biographical, genealogical, and anecdotal account, by a Cherokee, of the Cherokee Nation in Arkansas (from a time "as early as 1735," when a few members of the tribe lived there, till 1828/29) and Oklahoma (since 1829); with references to the previous life of the Cherokees in the southern Appalachians. [7786

Mrs. HARRY TODD MILES. Old churches in the Shenandoah--their descendants in Kentucky: both people and churches. Filson Club hist. quar., 34:323-34 (Oct). notes. On Presbyterian churches established in the Shenandoah Valley between 1737 and 1771, and in Kentucky between 1783 and 1819. [7787

MABEL VAN DYKE BAER. The ancestry of Edward West of Lexington, Kentucky, 1757-1827. Ky. Hist. Soc., Reg., 58:354-63 (Oct). notes. Evidence that Edward West, Jr., silversmith and steamboat inventor, father of 12 children, was a son of Edward West, Sr. (died 1792), of Woodford County, Ky., previously of Fredericksburg, Va., gunsmith, son of John West (died 1744/45) of Stafford County, Va. [7788

EDWARD WALTER RAIL WAUGH & ELIZABETH WAUGH. The South builds: new architecture in the Old South. Chapel Hill: Univ. of North Carolina Press [1960. 10], 173 p. maps, plans, views. Mainly on recent buildings in the South, but with references to structures existing as early as 1758. [7789

FERNANDO DE ARMAS MEDINA. Luisiana y Florida en el reinado de Carlos III [1763-85]. Estudios am., 19:67-85 (Jan). fold. map. notes. Mainly on transfers of territory between Spain and Great Britain, and the administrative dependency of Louisiana and Florida upon the Capitanía General de Cuba. [7790

WILLIAM PRESCOTT OGILVIE. Sequoya. Am. forests, 65(5):31, 46-8 (May 1959). port. On Sequoya (born George Guess, 1773?-1843), Cherokee half-Indian, his life in Tennessee, Georgia, Arkansas, and Oklahoma, and the Cherokee alphabet that he devised between ca. 1809 and 1821, which became the medium of publications in the Cherokee language. [7791

CHARLES GRIER SELLERS, JR. The travail of slavery. Charles Grier Sellers, Jr., ed., The Southerner as American (Chapel Hill: Univ. of North Carolina Press [1960]), p. 40-71. notes. On the "paradox of the slaveholding South's devotion to 'liberty'" as the "key to the tragedy of southern history," 1774-1866. [7792

PATON YODER. Private hospitality in the South, 1775-1850. Miss. Valley hist. rev., 47:419-33 (Dec). notes. [7793

THOMAS PAYNE GOVAN. Americans below the Potomac. Charles Grier Sellers, Jr., ed., The Southerner as American (Chapel Hill: Univ. of North Carolina Press [1960]), p. 19-39. notes. On the effect of the defense of slavery and the "concern with maintenance of white supremacy" in differentiating the South from the North, 1787-1865. [7794

MARY WILLIS SHUEY. When the quarter horse first moved West. Quarter horse jour., 12(5):91, 94-5, 132-4 (Feb). facsims., view. On the migration of quarter horses and their owners from Virginia and North Carolina to "Kentucke," especially Lexington, 1787-1804; with excerpts from contemporary documents. [7795

RICHARD W. GRIFFIN. Poor white laborers in Southern cotton factories, 1789-1865. S.C. hist. mag., 61:26-40 (Jan). notes. [7796

GEORGE RUBLE WOOLFOLK. Taxes and slavery in the ante bellum South. Jour. South. hist., 26:180-200 (May). notes. On the taxation of slaves as property, 1789-1861. [7797

ROBERT C. HUNT. John Hunt. Ala. hist. quar., 22:88-93 (spring-summer). notes. On John Hunt, Sr., recorded in Tennessee as early as 1790 and in Madison County, Ala., between 1804/5 and 1809, and his sons David, George, William, and John, Jr., of whom David and William remained in Alabama. [7798

AMY CHAMBLISS. Edmund Ruffin of Virginia [1794-1865]. Ga. rev., 14: 417-32 (winter). On his life in Virginia, his experiments in "soil chemistry," his introduction of the use of marl to improve the productivity of "acid" soils, his founding and editorship of the Farmers' register (1833-42), his other publications on scientific agriculture, his profitable plantations, his active promotion of secession after John Brown's raid at Harper's Ferry, his "firing the first shot for independence" in 1861, his participation as an elderly civilian in Confederate military operations, and his suicide. [7799

WAYNE GARD. Racing on the frontier. Quarter horse jour., 7(7):62-6 (Apr 1955). On horse racing in Kentucky, Tennessee, and Texas since 1798; with an account of horses owned by Sam Bass of Denton, Tex., particularly the Denton Mare, foaled in 1870, sold by Bass in 1876, mother of distinguished colts. [7800

PAUL TABOR. The Cherokee rose. Ga. rev., 14:231-6 (fall). On "an evergreen rose from China" very similar to the MaCartney rose (introduced from China "a few years" after 1798 and not commonly distinguished from the Cherokee rose), the adoption of the Cherokee rose as the State flower of Georgia in 1916, and the complete falsity of the belief that it is indigenous to the Cherokee country of northern Georgia. [7801

EUGENE D. GENOVESE. The limits of agrarian reform in the slave South. Ann Arbor: University Microfilms, 1959 [i.e. 1960]. Positive microfilm of typescript. [247] leaves. Thesis--Columbia Univ. Abstracted: Dissert. abstracts, 20:4088 (Apr). On the evil effects of slavery as a limitation upon the progress and improvement of agriculture, 1800-1860. [7802

HENRY SAVAGE, JR. Seeds of time: the background of Southern thinking. N.Y.: Holt [1959]. viii, [2], 312 p. On ideas in and about the South, 19th and 20th centuries. [7803

ROBERT SAMUEL RODDENBERY, JR. Ancestors and descendants of Cader Atkins Parker, 1810-1886. By his great grandson. Adel, Ga.: Press of the Patten Publishers [1959]. 140 p. diagr., ports. On his early life in North Carolina, settlement in Georgia, Alabama, and Texas, work as a Primitive Baptist preacher, and marriage to Louisa (Candler) Beard (1804-89); with his autobiography, biographical sketches of his 9 children, and an appendix (p. 107-34) of family letters, obituaries, and other documents, including the autobiography of Daniel Hall Parker (1845-1926) and reminiscent verses by him on the Battle of Chickamauga. [7804

MARTIN GILLETTE (born 1787). Martin Gillette's letters about the War of 1812. [Edited] by Joseph S. Van Why. Conn. Hist. Soc. bul., 23:81-4 (Jul 1958). Letters to the writer's father, Joseph Gillette of Lyme, Conn., dated Baltimore, 5 and 24 Sep. 1814, on their business interests and on military activities in Washington and Baltimore. [7805

ARTHUR H. DE ROSIER, JR. Negotiations for the removal of the Choctaw [from Mississippi to the Indian Territory]: U.S. policies of 1820 and 1830. Chron. Okla., 38:85-100 (spring). notes. [7806

NELLIE COFFMAN. A short biography of Samuel Coffman [1822-94]. Mennonite hist. bul., 19(1):1, 4, 6, 8 (Jan 1958). port. On his early life near the site of Lewisburg, W. Va., his later years in the Shenandoah Valley, and his work as a Mennonite bishop. [7807

JOHN RUSHING WELSH. William Gilmore Simms, critic of the South [1825 to 1870]. Jour. South. hist., 26: 201-14 (May). notes. Evidence of the falsity of the allegations that he "ruined his art through blind devotion to Southern imperialistic dreams and the plantation-gentleman ideal," that he was "the pathetic victim of attachment to his native state which refused him the honors his literary powers merited," and that he saw "no shortcomings in a society he warmly admired." [7808

THOMAS DIONYSIUS CLARK. Humor in the stream of Southern history [1830s-1930s]. Miss. quar., 13:176-88 (fall). [7809

STILES BAILEY LINES. Slaves and churchmen: the work of the Episcopal Church among Southern Negroes, 1830-1860. Ann Arbor: University Microfilms, 1960. Positive microfilm of typescript. [323] leaves. Thesis--Columbia Univ. Abstracted: Dissert. abstracts, 21:976-7 (Oct). [7810

MAURICE SEYMOUR NICHOLS. A study of the decisions of the highest State court in Maryland, Virginia, and West Virginia relating to public education [ca. 1830 to 1957]. Ann Arbor: University Microfilms, 1959 [i.e. 1960]. Positive microfilm of typescript. [446] leaves. Thesis (Ed. D.)--Univ. of Maryland. Abstracted: Dissert. abstracts, 20:3159 (Feb). [7811

EDD WINFIELD PARKS. The intent of the ante-bellum Southern humorists [1830-61]. Miss. quar., 13:163-8 (fall). [7812

GILMER B. RANDOLPH & CARL M. GUELZO. Freight rates in Southern Freight Association Territory [1830-1960]. Scranton: International Correspondence Schools, ©1960. [2], 89, 2 p. diagrs., maps, port., tables. [7813

WILLARD THORP. Suggs and Sut in modern dress: the latest chapter in Southern humor. Miss. quar., 13: 169-75 (fall). notes. On "the parallels between the older Southern humor and the new," 1830s-1950s. [7814

LA MAR C. BERRETT. history of the Southern States Mission [of the Church of Jesus Christ of Latter-Day Saints], 1831-1861. [Riverton, Utah, 1960.] ii leaves, iii-x, 306, 4 p. maps, tables. bibliog. (p. 301-6), notes. Thesis (M.S.)--Brigham Young Univ. Includes extensive excerpts from journals, reports, and other documents. [7815

EUGENE D. GENOVESE. The medical and insurance costs of slaveholding in the Cotton Belt [1832-60]. Jour. Negro hist., 45:141-55 (Jul). notes. [7816

EARLY locomotives in the South [1833-69]: additional material relating to Bulletin no. 101. Railway and Locomotive Hist. Soc., Bul., 103:68-76 (Oct). map, tables. [7817

GEORGE H. GIBSON. Opinion in North Carolina regarding the acquisition of Texas and Cuba, 1835-1855. N.C. hist. rev., 37:1-21, 185-201 (Jan, Apr). notes. Concludes that "North Carolina was not fundamentally interested in the acquisition of Texas and Cuba because North Carolina was provincial, sectional, and conservative and had less to gain by the continuation of the plantation-slavery system than any other slaveholding State." [7818

ANTHONY HILLBRUNER. Inequality, the great chain of being, and ante-bellum Southern oratory. South. speech jour., 25:172-89 (spring). notes. On John Caldwell Calhoun, Alexander H. Stephens, and William Andrew Smith as Southern orators who condemned "the equalitarian ideal" and "upheld the caste system of the 'Great Chain of Being,'" i.e., "the hierarchical society with its 'peculiar institution,'" bringing "to American soil the outmoded doctrine of the Greek democracy," 1836-54. [7819

CLYDE HULL CANTRELL. The reading habits of ante-bellum Southerners. Ann Arbor: University Microfilms, 1960. Positive microfilm of typescript. [419] leaves. Thesis--Univ. of Illinois. Abstracted: Dissert. abstracts, 21:1573 (Dec). Detailed study of the reading of 13 persons from 6 Southern States, totaling 1,157 titles (undated, 1840s-50s?). [7820

CLEMENT EATON. Slave-hiring in the upper South [1840s-50s]: a step toward freedom. Miss. Valley hist. rev., 46:663-78 (Mar). notes. [7821

ROBERT ROYAL RUSSEL. Economic aspects of Southern sectionalism, 1840-1861. N.Y.: Russell & Russell, 1960. 325 p. tables. bibliog. (p. 299-313), notes. Reproduction of the 1st ed., 1924. [7822

EDWARD STONE. Usher, Poquelin, and Miss Emily: the progress of Southern Gothic. Ga. rev., 14:433-43 (winter). Commentary on resemblances between Poe's "The Fall of the House of Usher," George Washington Cable's "Jean-ah-Poquelin," and Faulkner's "A rose for Emily," 1840s-1930s, in each of which the main character, "fortifying himself in an anachronistic, essentially horrible, and yet majestic stronghold, ignores or defies the insistent encroachments of time and progress." [7823

FRANK WINKLER RYAN, JR. The opinions of editor William Gilmore Simms of the Southern quarterly review, 1849-1854. S.C. Hist. Assoc., Proc., 1959, p. 25-35. notes. Based on thesis--Univ. of North Carolina, 1956. [7824

DARRETT BRUCE RUTMAN. Philip Alexander Bruce [1856-1933]: a divided mind of the South. Va. mag. hist. and biog., 68:387-407 (Oct). port. notes. On his "sadness for the Old South that had gone" and his "enthusiasm ... for the New South ... and concern for the problem it faced," as exhibited in his historical and other writings. [7825

ROBERT C. BLACK III. Thoughts on the Confederacy. Donald Sheehan & Harold C. Syrett, eds., Essays in American historiography: papers presented in honor of Allan Nevins (N.Y.: Columia Univ. Press, 1960), p. 20-36. notes. On causes for the failure of the Confederacy and the survival of its "essential substance." [7826

W. HARRISON DANIEL. The Southern Baptists in the Confederacy [1860-65]. Civil War hist., 6:389-401 (Dec). notes. [7827

C. J. AFFLECK & BENJAMIN M. DOUGLAS. Confederate bonds and certificates [1861-65]: a listing with a description of the Confederate States of America bonds and certificates, showing the degree of rarity and price. [Winchester? Va., 1960. 4], 38 p. facsims., tables. [7828

WILLIAM WEST BRADBEER. Southern State currency [1861-65]. Selections from The numismatist: United States paper money, tokens, medals, and miscellaneous (Racine, Wis.: Whitman Pub. Co., 1960), p. 199-201. facsims. First printed Feb. 1913. [7829

PETER ALEXANDER BRANNON. The organization of the Confederate Postoffice Department at Montgomery, and a story of the Thomas Welsh provisional stamped envelope. Together with the activities of the Montgomery Postoffice in the Confederate period [1861-65]. Montgomery, Ala., 1960. xi, 164, [2] p. facsims., ports., views. bibliog. (p. 163-4), notes. Includes letters from Lt. Abner N. Steele (died 1852) to relatives, 22 Jun. 1861 - 22 Jul. 1862 (p. 98-103). [7830

DAVID HERBERT DONALD. Died of democracy. David Herbert Donald, ed., Why the North won the Civil War ([Baton Rouge:] Louisiana State Univ. Press [1960]), p. 77-90. On the "democratic tendencies of the Confederacy" as its "real weakness," 1861-65. [7831

VIRGINIA LEE JONES. The Confederate Great Seal and its replicas. Spinning wheel, 16(9):24 (Sep). seals. On the Great Seal of the Confederate States of America, designed by Judah Benjamin, and the 1,000 replicas made by John J. Pickett in 1873. [7832

LAURENCE MASSILLON KEITT (1824-64). Laurence M. Keitt's letters from the Provisional Congress of the Confederacy, 1861. Edited by Elmer Don Herd, Jr. S.C. hist. mag., 61: 19-25 (Jan). notes. Letters to Gen. James H. Hammond and Susan Sparks Keitt, dated Montgomery, 13 Feb.-15 May 1861, and Richmond, 20 Aug. 1861. [7833

GEORGE N. MALPASS. Unusual dates on Confederate covers. S. P. A. jour., 21:323-5 (Mar 1959). facsims. On mail stamped on "historic days" (e.g.. 12 Apr. 1861, "the day the 'shooting war' began"). [7834

DAVID H. OVERY, JR. The Wisconsin carpetbagger: a group portrait. Wis. mag. hist., 44:15-49 (autumn). cartoon, ports., views. notes. Based on thesis (M.A.)--Univ. of Wisconsin. On Wisconsin men who settled in the South during and after the Civil War (including Harrison Reed, William H. Gleason, Lewis J. Higby, John Lockwood, John S. Harris, Edward Daniels, John B. Callis, and George W. Honey, "promoters and adventurers"), 1861-1870s; with some account of the reputation of the South in Wisconsin before the War and the impressions of it formed by Wisconsin soldiers. [7835

LEWIS MILES RAISIG. The Confederate $20 Diana note [1861]. Numismatic scrapbook, 26:1249-55 (May). facsim., view. bibliog. [7836

LAWRENCE DUNBAR REDDICK. The Negro as Southerner and American [1861-1960]. Charles Grier Sellers, Jr., ed., The Southerner as American (Chapel Hill: Univ. of North Carolina Press [1960]), p. 130-47. notes. [7837

HARVEY E. SHEPPARD. The Confederate Postmasters' provisionals in the [Thomas K.] Tapling Collection [bequeathed to the British Museum]. Am. Philatelic Cong., Congress book, 26:111-29. facsims. [7838

WILLIAM WILSON (1807-86). The William Wilson records, being the personal and business papers of William Wilson (1807-1886), Prairie Grove, Arkansas. Edited by W[alter] J. Lemke. Fayetteville: Washington County Historical Soc., 1960. 138 p. port., tables, views. Tax and other receipts, deeds, business and legal correspondence, bills, and other papers, 1824-86, recording Wilson's activities as an Arkansas planter and landowner, and letters addressed to him by relatives and friends in Texas and at Colquitt, La., 1861-84. [7839

JOHN CAYLOR, ed. A path of light. Atlanta: Home Mission Board, Southern Baptist Convention [1959]. 118 p. Biographical sketches, by the editor and 7 other contributors, of 8 Southern Baptist missionaries: Lucien C. Smith, General Lee Phelps, Nancy Kathryn Sewell, Mary Prosser Jayne, Emma Leachman, Christine Garnett, Joseph Franklin Plainfield, and Mrs. H. R. Moseley. [7840

CONFEDERATE STATES OF AMERICA. 2d Congress. Proceedings of the Second Confederate Congress ... Edited by Frank E. Vandiver. Richmond, Va.: Virginia Historical Soc., 1958-59. 2 v. xi, 475; xx, 800 p. (Southern Historical Society papers, 51-52. New series, 13-14.) "Debates" in the Senate and the House of Representatives, 2 May - 14 Jun. 1864, 7 Nov. 1864 - 18 Mar. 1865, "copied mainly from the Richmond Examiner." To be distinguished from the journals of the 2 houses. Concludes with v. 52 the series of publications of the Southern Historical Society, founded in 1869 and dissolved by its last surviving member, Douglas Southall Freeman, in 1953. Includes a tribute to Freeman by the editor. [7841

JOHN W. DONOHUE. Biracial public school education in the South [1865-1954]. Thought, 35:393-420 (autumn). notes. [7842

WALTER LYNWOOD FLEMING (1874-1932), ed. Documentary history of Reconstruction: political, military, social, religious, educational, & industrial, 1865 to the present time. Gloucester, Mass.: P. Smith, 1960 [c1935]. 2 v. [2], xviii, 493; xiv, 480 p. facsims. notes. (Micro-offset books.) 1st ed. 1906. Four pages of original text reproduced on each page of reprint. Collection of "laws, state and federal, official reports, and political platforms; accounts of Northern men and foreigners living or traveling in the South; accounts of Southerners, white and black, ex-Confederates and Unionists, Conservatives and Radicals," 1865-77, and a few pages on the years after 1877. [7843

THEODORE L. GROSS. Albion W[inegar] Tourgèe [1838-1905]: reporter of the Reconstruction. Ann Arbor: University Microfilms, 1960. Positive microfilm of typescript. [277] leaves. Thesis--Columbia Univ. Abstracted: Dissert. abstracts, 21:894 (Oct). On his experience as a Republican Northerner active in North Caroline politics during Reconstruction, and his expression of the experience in 6 novels about the South after the Civil War. [7844

WILLIAM HORD NICHOLLS. Southern tradition and regional economic progress. South. econ. jour., 26:187-98 (Jan). port. notes. On 24 Southern traditions that since 1865 have acted as barriers to economic progress, grouped in categories as "(1) the dominance of agrarian values, (2) the rigidity of the social structure, (3) the undemocratic political structure, (4) the weakness of social responsibility and (5) conformity of thought and behavior." [7845

THEODORE SALOUTOS. Farmer movements in the South, 1865-1933. Berkeley: Univ. of California Press, 1960. ix, [3], 354 p. bibliog. (p. 333-41), notes (p. 289-329). (University of California publications in history, 64.) [7846

HARVEY MAGEE WATTERSON (1811-91). A Southerner views the South, 1865: letters of Harvey M. Watterson. Edited by Martin Abbott. Va. mag. hist. and biog., 68:478-89 (Oct). notes. Reports to Andrew Johnson, dated in Richmond, New

Bern, Raleigh, and Wilmington, 7 Jun.-8 Jul. 1865, on the condition of the South [7847

RAY M. ATCHISON. The land we love: a Southern post-bellum magazine of agriculture, literature, and military history [edited and published by Gen. Daniel Harvey Hill, ex-Confederate officer, Charlotte, 36 issues, 1866-69]. N.C. hist. rev., 37:506-15 (Oct). notes. [7848

LEWIS M. KILLIAN. The ambivalent position of the Negro in the South, 1867-1900. Negro hist. bul., 23:81-6 (Jan). ports. notes. [7849

THOMAS CHALMERS McCORVEY (1851-1932). The invisible empire. T. C. McCorvey, Alabama historical sketches, ed. George Burke Johnston (Charlottesville: Univ. of Virginia Press, 1960), p. 157-76. notes. Unpublished lecture, 18 Jun. 1910. On the Ku Klux Klan and the Knights of the White Camellia in the South, 1867-68. [7850

FRANKLIN PARKER. Robert E. Lee, George Peabody, and sectional reunion. Peabody jour. educ., 37:195-202 (Jan). notes. On a meeting of Southerners at White Sulphur Springs to honor Peabody's establishment of a fund to promote education in the South, 27 Jul. 1869; and Peabody's endowment of Washington College (under the presidency of his friend Robert E. Lee) in Aug. 1869. [7851

JOHN MILLER MACLACHLAN (1905-60). Southern humor as a vehicle of social evaluation [1870s-1950s]. Miss. quar., 13:157-62 (fall). [7852

GEORGE BROWN TINDALL. The central theme revisited. Charles Grier Sellers, Jr., ed., The Southerner as American (Chapel Hill: Univ. of North Carolina Press [1960]), p. 104-29. notes. On Southern "preoccupation with the issue of race, its mythology and its symbolism," and with "the ideological defense of white supremacy," 1872-1960. [7853

COMER VANN WOODWARD. A Southern critique for the Gilded Age: Melville, Adams, and James. Comer Vann Woodward, The burden of Southern history (Baton Rouge: Louisiana State Univ. Press [1960]), p. 109-40. On "the running critique of Yankee morals" by the South, and its acknowledgment in the "critique of American society" offered by Herman Melville in Clarel (1876), Henry Adams in Democracy (1880), and Henry James in The Bostonians (1886), each of whom presents as a character "a veteran of the Confederate Army ... in a sympathetic role." [7854

NOREEN (DUNN) TATUM. A crown of service: a story of woman's work in the Methodist Episcopal Church, South, from 1878-1940. Nashville: Parthenon Press [1960]. 418 p. ports., views. Deals particularly with the Woman's Missionary Council and other organizations of Methodist Episcopal women. [7855

COMER VANN WOODWARD. The search for Southern identity [since 1880]. Comer Vann Woodward, The burden of Southern history (Baton Rouge: Louisiana State Univ. Press [1960]), p. 3-25. From The Virginia quarterly review, 1958. [7856

COMER VANN WOODWARD. The strange career of Jim Crow. New and revised edition. N.Y.: Oxford Univ. Press, 1957. xix, 183 p. bibliog. (p. 181-3). (A Galaxy book, GB6.) 1st ed. 1955. Evidence that as late as the 1880s segregation of Negroes and whites had not been established in the South and that Jim Crow legislation, including disfranchisement, began ca. 1890 and was not entirely dissolved in 1954; and comparison in this respect of "the First Reconstruction" (1865-77) and "the Second Reconstruction" (1954-57). [7857

RUTHERFORD BIRCHARD HAYES (1822-93). Teach the freedman: the correspondence of Rutherford B. Hayes and the Slater Fund for Negro Education, 1881-1887 [and 1888-1893]. Edited by Louis D[ecimus] Rubin. [Baton Rouge:] Louisiana State Univ. Press [1959]. 2 v. lv, 236; [6], 302 p. notes. Letters from and to Hayes, President of the Board of Trustees of the John F. Slater Fund for the Education of Freedmen; with an extensive introduction. [7858

CHARLES DENNIS SMITH. The Appalachian National Park movement, 1885-1901. N.C. hist. rev., 37:38-65 (Jan). views. notes. On the establishment of "a Southern Appalachian national forest reserve" in response "to the cry of the scenery lover, fisherman, and hunter" and later also "that of the practical forester and lumberman." [7859

MARVIN G. BAUER. Henry W. Grady [1850-89]. Speech Association of America, A history and criticism of American public address, ed. William

Norwood Brigance, 2d ed. (N.Y.: Russell & Russell, 1960), 1:387-406. bibliog., notes. Based on thesis--Univ. of Wisconsin, 1936. Mainly on his address, "The New South," 1886, and later speeches promoting "the idea of the oneness of the American people." [7860

JACOB E. COOKE. The New South. Donald Sheehan & Harold C. Syrett, eds., Essays in American historiography: papers presented in honor of Allan Nevins (N.Y.: Columbia Univ. Press, 1960), p. 50-80. notes. On histories, 1886-1957, of the "integration of the post-Reconstruction South into the economy and politics of the nation." [7861

DEWEY WESLEY GRANTHAM, JR. An American politics for the South [1890-1960]. Charles Grier Sellers, Jr., ed., The Southerner as American (Chapel Hill: Univ. of North Carolina Press [1960]), p. 148-79. notes. [7862

IGNATZ JAMES PIKL, JR. Southern forest-products and forestry: developments and prospects [1890s-1960]. Jour. farm econ., 42:268-81 (May). tables. notes. [7863

LOUISE (SHILLINGBURG) COWAN. The communal world of Southern literature. Ga. rev., 14:248-57 (fall). On the Southern "vision of shared human life" in contrast to the "insistent theme of loneliness which has so noticeably marked the twentieth-century arts." [7864

TOM DEARMORE. The enigma of W[illiam] J[oseph] Cash [1901-41]. Nieman reports, 14(2):30-32 (Apr). On his life and thinking as a Southerner and his The mind of the South (1941). [7865

THOMAS HODGIN MARSH, ed. Letters to a bishop. South. speech jour., 25: 205-16 (spring). notes. On the papers of Bishop Edwin Du Bose Mouzon (1869-1937), nearly 19,000 pieces, relating mainly to affairs of the Methodist Church in the South; with excerpts from letters from and to him, all undated, presumably written in or after 1910, the date of his ordination. [7866

E. CHARLES CHATFIELD. The Southern Sociological Congress [1912-20]: organization of uplift. Tenn. hist. quar., 19:328-47 (Dec). notes. On an association of Southerners to promote public health, human equality, "the conservation of human life and happiness," and "organized social evangelism to make democracy a reality in America." [7867

RICHARD EDWIN McARDLE. What the South is doing today to drive wildfire out of the woods. Am. forests, 62(5): 24-5, 83-6 (May 1956). ports. On the gradual abandonment of the belief, prevalent in the South as recently as 1916, "that fire was really a good thing for the woods," and the growing problem of suppressing the incendiary activities of Southerners who continue in this belief. See also a panel discussion by participants in the Southern Forest Fire Prevention Conference, 62(5): 26-35. [7868

GEORGE PICKETT WILSON. Josiah H. Combs and folk speech. Ky. folklore rec., 6:104-7. notes. On his contributions to the study of Southern dialect, 1916-31. [7869

JOHN R. CARREKER. Correlation of machinery and conservation practices [in the South, 1920-52]. Agric. engineering, 33:623-4, 643 (Oct 1952). diagr., views. notes. [7870

ALLEN TATE. A Southern mode of the imagination. Joseph J. Kwiat & Mary C. Turpie, eds., Studies in American culture: dominant ideas and images (Minneapolis: Univ. of Minnesota Press [1960]), p. 96-108. On the causes of the "modern literary renaissance" in the South since ca. 1920. [7871

HENRY LARKIN TERRIE, JR. The poetry of history: William Faulkner's image of the South [1920s-1960]. Dartmouth alumni mag., 52(8):43-5 (May). [7872

JOSIAH HENRY COMBS (1886-1960). The highlander's music. [Edited by D. K. Wilgus.] Ky. folklore rec., 6:108-22. notes. On the "folk-music" of "the Southern highlands in the United States." [7873

PAUL OLIVER. Special agents: an introduction to the recording of folk blues in the twenties [especially in the South]. Jazz rev., 2(2):20-25 (Feb 1959). facsims. Includes an account of "a touring recording unit" of the Columbia Company in Georgia, Louisiana, and Texas, 1926-30. [7874

DOROTHY B. SCHLEGEL. James Branch Cabell and Southern romanticism [1926-47]. Longwood College, Institute of Southern Culture, The

South in perspective, ed. Francis B. Simkins (Farmville, Va., 1959), p. 31-48. notes. [7875

GEORGE F. GANT. Factors influencing the growth of research in Southern universities [1930-54]. Va. jour. science, 5:1-11 (Jan 1954). [7876

RUPERT BAYLESS VANCE. The sociological implications of Southern regionalism [especially since the 1930s]. Jour. South. hist., 26:44-56 (Feb). notes. [7877

SOUTHERN REGIONAL EDUCATION BOARD. Physicians for the South. By Winfred L. Godwin. [Atlanta] 1960. vii, 79 p. diagrs., tables. notes. On "trends in the supply and distribution of physicians" in the South, and the need for more physicians and more or larger medical schools, 1931-59. [7878

KENNETH BROWNRIDGE POMEROY. Time to "pull a new streak." Am. forests, 66(12):2, 45-6 (Dec). view. On the production of "gum naval stores" from Southern pine, 1934-60. [7879

JESSIE PARKHURST GUZMAN. Twenty years of court decisions affecting higher education in the South, 1938-1958. [Tuskegee Institute, Ala.] 1960. [2], 36 p. notes. Digest of 26 cases or groups of cases involving segregation of Negro and white students. Summarized: Jour. educ. sociol., 32:247-53 (Feb 1959). notes. [7880

KENNETH BROWNRIDGE POMEROY. Pinpointing the fire problem. Am. forests, 62(10):50-52, 54 (Oct 1956). port. On the studies of Dr. John P. Shea to "find out why people set forest fires and effect a cure," 1938-39, and the progress of control over "man-made fires" in 9 Southern States. [7881

HORACE P. TAYLOR, JR. The heart is a lonely hunter [by Carson McCullers, 1940]: a Southern waste land. Waldo McNeir & Leo B. Levy, eds., Studies in American literature (Baton Rouge: Louisiana State Univ. Press, 1960 [Louisiana State University studies, Humanities series, 8]), p. 154-60. notes. [7882

HAVILAH BABCOCK (1898-1964). My health is better in November: thirty-five stories of hunting and fishing in the South. N.Y.: Holt, Rinehart, and Winston [1960. 4], 284 p. views. 1st ed. 1947; there reprinted from Field and stream, Outdoor life, and 3 other sport magazines. Several of the sketches deal with South Carolina. [7883

REDDING S. SUGG, JR., & GEORGE HILTON JONES. The Southern Regional Education Board: ten years of regional cooperation in higher education [1948-58]. Baton Rouge: Louisiana State Univ. Press [1960]. xv, 179 p. facsims., ports., tables (1 double), view. notes. Includes a list of the Board's publications (p. 170-74). [7884

GORDON REID WOOD. Heard in the South: the progress of a word geography. Tenn. Folklore Soc. bul., 26: 1-7 (Mar). maps. On work toward a linguistic geography of the United States, with illustrations of the distribution of snake doctor, mosquito hawk, and redworm. [7885

The Southern Atlantic States

RICHARD MORGAN. Love & Life near the Chesapeake: true tales of romances, pirates, ghosts, & famous persons who give glamour to the Chesapeake Bay area, as depicted in over 50 chapters & 40 photographs. N.Y.: Washington Book Co. [1953. 2], 124, [2] p., [4] leaves, 5-22 p., [2] leaves, [2] p. (One or more leaves lacking after p. 124.) [7886

JOFFRE LANNING COE. Prehistoric cultural change and stability in the Carolina Piedmond area [beginning ca. 7000 B.C.]. Ann Arbor: University Microfilms, 1960. Positive microfilm of typescript. [403] leaves. Thesis--Univ. of Michigan. Abstracted: Dissert. abstracts, 20:4486-7 (Jun). [7887

GILBERT VALLIANT BYRON. Early explorations of the Chesapeake Bay [1524-1634]. Baltimore: Maryland Historical Soc., 1960. vii, 23, [1] p. maps (1 double), port., views. bibliog. (p. 23). [7888

RICHARD PARES (1902-58). Merchants and planters. Cambridge [Eng.]: Published for the Economic history review at the University Press, 1960. [8], 91 p. notes (p. 56-91). (The economic history review. Supplements, 4.) Study of "three examples of plantation enterprise--the British tobacco colonies, the British and the French sugar colonies of the seventeenth and eighteenth centuries". [7889

FRANK TYRER. Richard Blundell [1677-1704] in Virginia and Maryland. Va. mag. hist. and biog., 68:429-47 (Oct). port., view. notes. On his activities in America as "an agent or factor" of a Mr. Houghton, Liverpool merchant, 1702-4, as recorded in the diary and letters of his brother, Nicholas Blundell; with copies of letters from Nicholas to Richard. [7890

CHARLES EDGAR RANDALL. New park at Great Falls of the Potomac. Am. forests, 66(5):26-7, 39-41 (May). views. On the area of Great Falls and Difficult Run since 1749, acquired by the National Park Service in 1960. [7891

RICHARD MOTT GUMMERE. Jonathan Boucher [1738-1804]. Toryissimus. Md. hist. mag., 55:138-45 (Jun). notes. On his life in Virginia and Maryland as "classical educator" and "pugnacious politically-minded churchman," 1759-75; with a summary of his View of the causes and consequences of the American Revolution. [7892

HUGH COLEMAN BAILEY. The upcountry academies of Moses Waddel [1770-1840]. S.C. Hist. Assoc., Proc., 1959, p. 36-43. notes. On private secondary schools conducted by him near Appling, Ga., and Vienna and Willington, S.C., 1794-1819. [7893

LIFE on the C. & O. Canal: 1859. Edited by Ella E. Clark. Md. hist. mag., 55:82-122 (Jun). views. notes. Recollections (1889?) by an anonymous New Englander who worked as a boatman on a voyage from Cumberland to Alexandria and back, 1859, including details of his observations in Cumberland, Williamsport, and Georgetown. [7894

ESRON McGRUDER FARIS, JR. Exemption of insurance and other property [of debtors] in the Virginias [sic] and Carolinas [1868-1958]. Wash. and Lee law rev., 17:19-42 (Spring). notes. [7895

"FROG" SMITH. Outside the rulebook. Railroad mag., 71(5):38-43 (Aug). view. Recollections and anecdotes of short-line railroading in Florida and southern Georgia, 1903-44. [7896

MARYLAND

MARYLAND HISTORICAL SOCIETY. Maryland history notes: quarterly news bulletin of the Maryland Historical Society. [Vols. 14-16.] Baltimore, May 1956-Feb. 1959. 3 v. (12 issues). 16; 16; 16 p. ports., views. Includes somewhat detailed accounts of accessions, particularly manuscripts and paintings. [7897

JAMES WILLIAM FOSTER. George Calvert [born ca. 1580]: his Yorkshire boyhood. Md. hist. mag., 55:261-74 (Dec). notes. On the situation of Leonard Calvert and his wife and sons George and Christopher as Catholics under pressure to profess Anglicanism, 1580-1602. [7898

ALICE LECZINSKA (LOWE) FERGUSON (died 1951) & HENRY GARDINER FERGUSON. The Piscataway Indians of southern Maryland [1608-1793]. Accokeek, Md.: Alice Ferguson Foundation, 1960. ii, 46 p. maps (1 col.), table, views. bibliog. (p. 44-6), notes. On a group of Indians who occupied Conoy Island from 1699 to ca. 1711 and removed to the Susquehanna "soon after 1711." [7899

JAMES HIGH. A facet of sovereignty: the proprietary government and the Maryland charter [1632-1776]. Md. hist. mag., 55:67-81 (Jun). notes. On the diminishing rights and authority of the Proprietors of Maryland and the increasing authority of the Assembly of Maryland. [7900

EDNA WARREN. Forests and parks in the Old Line State. Am. forests, 62(10):13-26, 56-8, 62-72 (Oct 1956). col. insignia, ports., views. On forests in Maryland since 1633 and the growth of a State forestry program since 1906. [7901

EDWIN WARFIELD BEITZELL. The Jesuit missions of St. Mary's County, Maryland [1634-1959. Abell? Md.] 1959 [c1960. 12], 320 p. map, tables. notes (p. 238-67). [7902

MARTHA SPRIGG POOLE. Mount Air: the story of an early Maryland estate [Charles County, 1641-1960]. Md. hist. mag., 55:123-37 (Jun). views. notes. [7903

HISTORIC ANNAPOLIS. Historic Annapolis [1650-1959. Compiled by St. C. Wright, Vice President, with the assistance of Joy Gary, Vice President for Publications. Annapolis, 1960, c1959. 20] p. facsims., map, views (1 double). Account, mainly pictorial, of some of the historic buildings saved by the efforts of Historic Annapolis, "a non-profit educational organization dedicated to the preservation of colonial landmarks." [7904

MARYLAND. Hall of Records Commission. The county courthouses and records of Maryland. Part one: The courthouses. By Morris L[eon] Radoff. Annapolis, 1960. xvi, 175 p. facsims., plans, views. notes. (Its Publication 12.) Histories and illustrations of the courthouses, arranged by name of county, 1654-1960. [7905

CHARLES FRANCIS STEIN. A history of Calvert County, Maryland [1654-1954. Baltimore] 1960. xv, 404 p. maps, tables, views. bibliog. (p. 382-4). Includes "Genealogy of families" (p. 233-339), "The Calvert County tax assessment list of 1782" (p. 339-74), and "Various lists of taxables of 1733" (p. 375-81). [7906

J. REANEY KELLY. Old Quaker burying ground: West River Quaker Burial Ground, Anne Arundel County, Maryland [laid out before 1671]. Md. hist. mag., 55:334-45 (Dec). notes. A history of the land and the Quaker community in West River since 1656; with an explanation of the almost complete disappearance of the Quakers from the county. [7907

ADVENTURES in graciousness. Am. forests, 62(10):36-7, 90-91 (Oct 1956). port., views. Historical sketches of houses in Port Tobacco and vicinity, Charles County, Md., 1658-1956. [7908

WILLIAM S. DEWEY. The coinage of Lord Baltimore. Selections from The numismatist: United States paper money, tokens, medals, and miscellaneous (Racine, Wis.: Whitman Pub. Co., 1960), p. 29-31. First printed Mar. 1941. On the minting of coins in Maryland, 1659-62. [7909

MICHAEL G. KAMMEN. The causes of the Maryland revolution of 1689. Md. hist. mag., 55:293-333 (Dec). notes. On disharmony between "the Proprietary Party and the Party of Resistance," 1660-89, the former of which "rooted its claims in the charter" while the latter "stressed the precedents set by the House of Commons and the rights of seventeenth century Englishmen." [7910

DORCHESTER COUNTY, Md. Abstracts from the land records of Dorchester County, Maryland. Volume 1 (Libers Old No. 1 - Old No. 2). Compiled by James A. McAllister, Jr. [Cambridge? Md.:] James A. McAllister, Jr., c1960. [3], 75, xxvii leaves. Chronologically arranged abstracts of No. 1 (1669-83) and No. 2 (1719-23). No statement is made concerning the gap between the volumes. [7911

CHARLES H. BOHNER. "As much history as ... invention": John P. Kennedy's Rob of the Bowl [1838]. Wm. and Mary quar., 17:329-40 (Jul). notes. On events and personalities in Maryland, 1681, treated by Kennedy in his "historical romance." [7912

NELSON WAITE RIGHTMYER. Parishes of the Diocese of Maryland [Protestant Episcopal, 1692-1960]. Reiserstown, Md.: Educational Research Associates, 1960. 47 p. maps (part fold.; in pocket). [7913

PETER WALNE. The Great Seal Deputed of Maryland [1692-1715]. Md. hist. mag., 55:30-37 (Mar). seal. notes. [7914

JOHN FREDERICK DORMAN. Maynard family of Frederick County, Maryland. Natl. Geneal. Soc. quar., 48:187-95 (Dec). notes. On Henry Maynard (recorded in Maryland 1702-12), his 3 children (Thomas, Henry, and Mary), and their descendants till ca. 1850. [7915

NOTES on the Indians of Maryland, 1705-1706. [Edited by D. I. Bushnell, Jr.] Selected papers from the American anthropologist, 1888-1920, ed. Frederica De Laguna (Evanston, Ill.: Row, Peterson [1960]), p. 517-18. notes. Printed in 1913. Excerpt from an anonymous manuscript by a British traveler. [7916

WILBUR HARVEY HUNTER, JR. Home at last. Art in Am., 48(4):91. port. On a portrait of Charles Calvert, 5th Lord Baltimore (1699-1751), attributed to Herman van der Myn, ca. 1730, probably brought from England to Maryland by Baltimore in 1732, evidently hung in the "council room" at Annapolis, admired by the youthful Charles Willson Peale in the 1760s, acquired by him in 1823 for his museum in Philadelphia, and presented to the Peale Museum in Baltimore in 1957. [7917

CUMBERLAND, Md. Fort Cumberland Bicentennial Committee. Fort Cumberland bicentennial, 1755-1955: souvenir program, August 14-20. [Cumberland, 1955.] 64, [4] p. maps, ports., views. By various contributors. [7918

WILLIAM H. McCLAIN. The Julius K. Hofmann Memorial Fund in Baltimore. Am.German rev., 26(1):7-9 (Oct-Nov 1959). facsim., medal. On the Germans in Baltimore since 1755, and the fund established in 1930 "for the purpose of encouraging the study of the

German language in the schools of Baltimore City and/or the State of Maryland." [7919

ROSAMOND RANDALL BEIRNE & ELEANOR PINKERTON STEWART. John Shaw [1745-1829], cabinetmaker. Antiques, 78:554-8 (Dec). facsim., views. On his life in Annapolis, 1763-1829, and his work as a cabinetmaker, State armorer, supervisor of State buildings, funeral director, vestryman, etc. [7920

ASSOCIATED STAMP CLUBS OF THE CHESAPEAKE AREA. Postal markings of Maryland, 1766-1855. Edited by Roger T. Powers. [Towson? Md.] 1960. [4], iv, 100 p. facsims., tables. Includes a list of "all of the post offices known to have existed in Maryland under the Constitution down to January 1, 1856" (p. 71-87). [7921

ROSAMOND RANDALL BEIRNE. Two anomalous Annapolis architects: Joseph Horatio Anderson [died in or before 1781] and Robert Key. Md. hist. mag., 55:183-200 (Sep). notes. Collection of the ascertainable facts about the stay in Annapolis of Anderson, 1770-74, and Key, 1768?-1806? [7922

EDWARD JOHN LONG. Crabtown on the Severn. Am. forests, 62(10):28-31, 84-5 (Oct 1956). views. On Annapolis and its historic sites, buildings, and exhibits, 1772-1956. [7923

JANET AUSTIN CURTIS, comp. Trappe Church cemetery inscriptions, Harford County, Maryland [1788-1889]. South. genealogist's exchange quar., 2(13):7 (spring). Copied in 1954, at which time the cemetery was "overgrown, abandoned." [7924

THEKLA FUNDENBERG WEEKS. The first State road, 1789-1959--a contrast. Glades star, 2:557-9 (Mar). views. On the Garrett County segment of the Virginia-Maryland road from Winchester to Morgantown and Clarksburg. [7925

KENNETH L. CARROLL. The court inquires about a ghost. Md. hist. mag., 55:38-43 (Mar). notes. Information from Authentic account of the appearance of a ghost in Queen Ann's County, Maryland (Baltimore, 1807), by William Briggs, reporting supposed appearances of the ghost of Thomas Harris (died 1791) to express the wish that Harris's brother James should administer Harris's property till the youngest of his 4 illegitimate children reached the age of 7 years; and litigation instituted by James Harris's estate after the discovery that the property of Thomas Harris was entailed and therefore could not be sold and could not descend to illegitimate offspring. [7926

FRANKLIN PARKER. George Peabody [1795-1869] and Maryland. Peabody jour. educ., 37:150-57 (Nov 1959). notes. On his early life in South Danvers (now Peabody), Mass., his life in Maryland from 1814 to 1837 as a merchant, his later years as a banker in London, and his Maryland philanthropies, particularly to the Maryland Historical Society and the Peabody Institute of Baltimore. [7927

JOHN A. WAGNER. Nineteenth century pathologists and the development of pathology in Maryland [1807 ff.]. Md. State med. jour., 9:58-9 (Feb). [7928

ERNEST JEROME YANCY. Maryland in our history. [n. p., 1957.] 27 p. On the State of Maryland in Liberia, founded by the Maryland State Colonization Society, 1833-34, and annexed at its own request in 1857 to form Maryland County, Republic of Liberia. [7929

ROSS COMPTON DURST. The old log school house. Glades star, 2:561-3 (Mar). view. On the log building known as the Compton School, standing on a lot acquired by the School Commissioners of Allegany County, Md., in 1863 and sold by the Board of Education of Garrett County in 1940. [7930

EDWARD A. COLBURN (born 1830). A Baltimore rebel, 1861. Md. hist. mag., 55:243 (Sep). Letter from the rector of Holy Trinity Church, Churchville, Md., to his father, Harvey Colburn of Baltimore, dated "Rectory, Dec. 5th/64," requesting him to intercede for the relief of Jacob Enfield, a member of the congregation, found guilty of disloyalty in displaying a rebel flag and sentenced to hard labor. [7931

DANIEL W. MOYLAN. Inheritance by and from illegitimates under Maryland intestacy law [1868-1959]. Md. law rev., 20:276-82 (summer). notes. [7932

W. W. PRICE. Richter's hand made leather. Glades star, 2:563-6 (Mar). ports. On the tannery established at Accident, Md., by John L. Richter and continued by his son, Adam John Richter, 1872-1928, as described by the latter in an interview. [7933

LEONARD E. COHEN. The Maryland law of strikes, boycotts, and picketing [1893-1959]. Md. law rev., 20:230-63 (summer). notes. [7934

ARTHUR W. MACHEN, JR. The apportionment of stock distributions in trust accounting practice [in Maryland, 1894-1959]. Md. law rev., 20:89-116 (spring). notes. [7935

POLLY (POBST) ROSS. Unto the least of these. Easton, Md.: Easton Pub. Co. [1960]. 181 p. port., views. On the life of the author and her sister at the Children's Home of the Eastern Shore of Maryland, Easton, from ca. 1924 to 1933. [7936

C. P. MERRICK. Maryland's public drainage program [1935-53]. Agric. engineering, 35:106, 108 (Feb 1954). [7937

ALBERT D. DARLEY, JR. He made legal history. Am. forests, 62(10):27, 87-90 (Oct 1956). port. On litigation concerning the validity of the Maryland Forest Conservancy Districts Act (enacted in 1943), and a ruling by Chief Judge George Henderson of the Fourth Judicial Circuit of Maryland affirming its constitutionality, 1947. [7938

Baltimore

JOHNSON, JOHONNOT, AND COMPANY, Baltimore. The conduct of business in Baltimore, 1783-1785, as seen in the letterbook of Johnson, Johonnot, and Co. By Rhoda M. Dorsey. Md. hist. mag., 55:230-42 (Sep). facsim. notes. Summary of and quotations from a letterbook recording the outgoing correspondence of Henry Johnson, Nov. 1783-May 1784, and his successor, George Johonnot, May 1784-Feb. 1785, in charge of the Baltimore branch of the Boston firm of Johnson and Francis and George Johonnot, commission merchants and distillers. Includes their comments on Baltimore and the Baltimoreans. [7939

VERNON SEBASTIAN VAVRINA. The history of public education in the City of Baltimore, 1829-1956. Cath. educ. rev., 57:338 (May 1959). Abstract of thesis--Catholic Univ. of America. [7940

ARTHUR HOWES. An interesting new organ in an unusual church. Organ Inst. quar., 8(3):23-6; (4):21-6 (autumn, winter). Includes a historical sketch of Mount Calvary Episcopal Church, Baltimore, 1846-1960. [7941

MELVIN FULD & GEORGE FULD. Some Baltimore Civil War tokens. Numismatist, 73:725-6 (Jun). coins. bibliog. [7942

ANNE (SCARBOROUGH) PHILBIN. The past and the promised: a history of the Alumnae Association, College of Notre Dame of Maryland, Baltimore, Maryland. Baltimore, 1959. xvi, 297 p. ports., views. On the Institute of Notre Dame, founded by the School Sisters of Notre Dame in 1863, the Collegiate Institute and Preparatory School for Young Ladies founded under its auspices in 1873, and the chartering of the Institute as a college in 1896. [7943

FRANKLIN PARKER. Influences on the founders of the Johns Hopkins University and the Johns Hopkins Hospital. Bul. hist. med., 34:148-53 (Mar-Apr). notes. On George Peabody of London, Dr. Joseph Parrish of Philadelphia, and Dr. Patrick Macaulay of Baltimore as persons who advised or may have advised Johns Hopkins to apply his wealth to the formation of a university and a hospital, 1866-73. [7944

HUGH HAWKINS. Pioneer: a history of the Johns Hopkins University, 1874-1889. Ithaca, N.Y.: Cornell Univ. Press [1960]. xiv, 368 p. port. bibliog. (p. 336-44), notes. On the University under the administration of Daniel Coit Gilman as "a strictly graduate university." [7945

STEPHEN D. MAGUIRE. Trolley line in cemetery. Railroad mag., 71(4):22-3 (Jun). views. On a 2-car line operated inside Loudon Park, a large cemetery in West Baltimore, Md., by the cemetery company through arrangement with the United Electric Railway, 1905-31. [7946

RUSSELL ROBBINS LORD. Forester apprentices. Am. forests, 66(1):26-7, 59-63; (2):30-32, 58-60 (Jan, Feb). port., views (1 double). On the author's life in Baltimore County, Md., and his studies at the Agricultural High School of Baltimore County at Sparks, Md., 1909-13, with memories of the teaching of Bertram Hanford Crocheron there and the program of woods and forestry camping instruction organized by him in Baltimore County. [7947

DAVID C. ELLIOTT. The Federal Reserve System, 1914-29. Herbert V. Prochnow, ed., The Federal Reserve System (N.Y.: Harper [1960]), p. 295-316. table. bibliog., notes. [7948

SIDNEY HOLLANDER FOUNDATION, Baltimore. Toward equality, Baltimore's progress report: a chronicle of progress since World War II toward the achievement of equal rights and opportunities for Negroes in Maryland [1946-60. Baltimore, 1960.] 92 p. cartoon, facsims., maps, ports., views. [7949

THE DISTRICT OF COLUMBIA

JACK R. McMILLEN. The trees of Arlington National Cemetery. Arlington hist. mag., 1(4):3-13. views. On the trees in this "relatively undisturbed" area since 1608, and its almost unchanged ecology. [7950

LOUIS DOW SCISCO (1868-1956). A site for the "Federal City": the original proprietors and their negotiations with Washington [1783-92. Edited by Oliver W. Holmes.] Columbia Hist. Soc., Rec., 57-59:123-47. notes. Mainly on the dealings of George Washington with owners of lands within the future District of Columbia. [7951

L. L. HUNTER. Vision and work: the Supervising Architect's contribution to magnificent Washington. Columbia Hist. Soc., Rec., 57-59:69-81. On the Office of the Supervising Architect, established by the Secretary of the Treasury in 1853; the previous service of the Secretary of the Treasury as "his own Supervising Architect virtually from the beginning of our Government until at least 1836 and perhaps 1853"; and some of the works constructed by these officials in the District of Columbia. [7952

JOHN ERVIN HUSS. I felt God's presence in the Nation's Capital. Grand Rapids, Mich.: Zondervan Pub. House [1960]. 133 p. views. Sermons on the Library of Congress, the National Gallery of Art, the Federal Bureau of Investigation, the Washington Monument, the Supreme Court, the Tomb of the Unknown Soldier, and the White House, by a Baptist minister from Florida who "felt God's presence" in each of these structures; with incidental historical references since 1790. [7953

U.S. Library of Congress. Legislative Reference Service. The Capitol in story and pictures. [Wash.: U.S. Govt. Print. Off., 1956.] 80 p. facsim., map, ports., views (part col.). On the Capitol building since 1790, the activities centered in it, and some of the other Federal buildings and activities in Washington. [7954

JANE (TOMPKINS) McCONNELL & BURT MORTON McCONNELL. The White House: a history with pictures. N.Y.: Studio Publications in association with Crowell [1954]. 80 p. flag., ports., views (part col.). bibliog. (p. 77-8). On the designing, building, and alterations of the executive mansion in Washington, 1791-1954, and the furnishings provided by its successive occupants; with a chapter on "The White House china." [7955

JOHN V. HINKEL. St. Patrick's: mother church of Washington. Columbia Hist. Soc., Rec., 57-59:33-43. view. On St. Patrick's Parish (Catholic), "organized about 1792," originally with a mainly Irish congregation. [7956

J. BANTON. ... View of the General Post Office in the City of Washington ... taken 22d May 1818 by J. Banton ... Columbia Hist. Soc., Rec., 57-59: double view following p. 122 (with descriptive text on back by Josephine Cobb). Black-and-white reproduction of a watercolor drawing, showing Blodgett's Hotel (built in 1793, acquired by the U.S. Government in 1810, and burned in 1836) and several adjacent buildings. [7957

HILLEL MARANS. Jews in Greater Washington: a panoramic history of Washington Jewry for the years 1795-1960. [Wash.?] c1960. 13 leaves. Apparently an outline of a proposed work. [7958

HENRY HODGMAN SAYLOR. The Octagon [1796-1959]. A. I. A. jour., 32(4):50-54 (Oct 1959). plans, views. [7959

DOROTHY (CLARK) WINCHCOLE. The First Baptist Church in Washington, D.C. [1801-1959]. Columbia Hist. Soc., Rec., 57-59:44-57. port., view. [7960

WILLIAM YOWELL, JR. Historical highlights of Washington's oldest bank. Columbia Hist. Soc., Rec., 57-59: 58-68. On the National Bank of Washington, 1809-1959. [7961

FRANCIS SCOTT KEY (1779-1843). A forgotten letter of Francis Scott Key. Edited by Franklin R. Mullaly. Md. hist. mag., 55:359-60 (Dec). notes. Letter to his mother, dated "Geo Town," 2 Sep. 1814, mainly on the British in that vicinity. [7962

ELIZABETH ORLAN CULLEN. The coming of the railroads to Washington, D.C. [1827-36]. Columbia Hist. Soc., Rec., 57-59:26-32. [7963

NATIONAL INTELLIGENGER, Washington, D.C. Vital statistics from the National intelligencer, 1829. Copied by George A. Martin. Natl. Geneal. Soc. quar., 48:21-30, 81-9, 142-50, 196-207 (Mar-Dec). Abstracts of marriage and death notices, in alphabetical order. [7964

LLOYD ALLEN DUNLAP. White House routine under Lincoln. Ralph G. Newman, ed., Lincoln for the ages (Garden City, N.Y.: Doubleday, 1960), p. 263-7. [7965

MARGARET ALICE FLINT. The Lincolns in the Executive Mansion. Ralph G. Newman, ed., Lincoln for the ages (Garden City, N.Y.: Doubleday, 1960), p. 208-12. On social activities in the White House, 1861-65. [7965a

HERBERT MITGANG. Washington in Lincoln's time [1861-65]. Ralph G. Newman, ed., Lincoln for the ages (Garden City, N.Y.: Doubleday, 1960), p. 187-90. [7966

U.S. Congress. Senate. Committee on Public Works. Extension of the United States Capitol Building. Wash.: U.S. Govt. Print. Off., 1958. iii, 80 p. Hearings on S. 2883, a bill to amend the legislative appropriation act, 1956, to eliminate the requirement that the extension, reconstruction, and replacement of the central portion of the United States Capitol be in substantial accord with Scheme B of the architectural plan of March 3, 1905. On proposals since 1863 for "the extension of the central portion of the Capitol eastward, to complete the effect intended when the wings and dome were built." Includes a report to the Committee from J. George Stewart, Architect of the Capitol (p. 7-22). [7967

U.S. Congress. House. Documentary history of the construction and development of the United States Capitol Building and Grounds. Wash.: U.S. Govt. Print. Off., 1960. ii, 26 p. (86th Cong., 1st sess. House. Document 234.) Selected official documents, 1864-1959. [7968

JAMES M. NABRIT, JR. Howard University looks to the future. Jour. Negro educ., 29:412-20 (fall). Includes some account of the University since 1867. [7969

ROLAND M. BRENNAN. Brigadier General Richard L. Hoxie [1844-1930], United States Army, 1861-1930. Columbia Hist. Soc., Rec., 57-59: 87-95. port. On his service, while an Army lieutenant, as engineer officer of the Temporary Board of Commissioners of the District of Columbia, 1874-78, and assistant to the Engineer Commissioner of the District, 1878-84; with a biographical sketch. [7970

FRANK GEORGE CARPENTER (1855-1924). Carp's Washington. ... Arranged and edited by Frances Carpenter. N.Y.: McGraw-Hill [1960]. xv, 314, [1] p. Columns reprinted from the Cleveland leader, 1882-88, on "The Clevelands in the White House," "The burning question of civil service," "The high cost of Washington's works of art," the Washington Monument, the death of U.S. Grant, "The woman's rights movement," "Our colored citizens," "Ben Harrison's era," scandals in high society, "Fashions and fads," "the Capitol and Congress ... horsecars and herdic cabs ... salons and saloons ... the boardinghouse life so common in the days before the coming of the apartment house," and a wide variety of other Washington subjects. [7971

ULYSSES SIMPSON GRANT III. The national capital: reminiscences of sixty-five years [since 1894]. Columbia Hist. Soc., Rec., 57-59:1-15. port. [7972

JACOB A. STEIN. Doctrine of attractive nuisance. Bar Assoc. Dist. Col., Jour., 27:239-42 (May). Summary of "the decided appellate cases in the District of Columbia," 1894-1943. [7973

CHARLES A. R. DUNN. The origins of the District of Columbia flag [1917-38]. Columbia Hist. Soc., Rec., 57-59:82-6. flags. Recollections. [7974

ERWIN KNOLL. The truth about desegregation in the Washington, D.C., public schools [1946-58]. Jour. Negro educ., 28:92-113 (spring 1959). [7975

GORDON GOUVERNEUR BARNEWALL. Factors affecting the optimum location and layout of planned suburban industrial districts [Washington, D.C., and vicinity, 1948]. Ann Arbor: University Microfilms, 1953 [i. e. 1960]. Positive microfilm of typescript. [439] leaves. Thesis--Ohio State Univ. Abstracted: Dissert. abstracts, 20:2598-2601 (Jan). [7976

VIRGINIA

ARTHUR KYLE DAVIS, JR., ed. More traditional ballads of Virginia. Collected with the cooperation of members of the Virginia Folklore Society.

Edited ... with the editorial assistance of Matthew Joseph Bruccoli, George Walton Williams, [and] Paul Clayton Worthington. Chapel Hill: Univ. of North Carolina Press [1960]. xxvii, 371 p. music. bibliog. (p. 361-6). Supplement to the editor's Traditional ballads of Virginia (1929). Contains texts and tunes of 46 "older traditional ballads ('Child' ballads)," with extensive editorial comments, an introduction on methods, and references to large collections that are still unpublished. [7977

JOHN FREDERICK DORMAN. A guide to the counties of Virginia. Va. geneal., 3:38-42, 86-90, 126-31, 171-4; 4:38-40, 79-86, 127-31, 171-5 (Jan 1959-Dec 1960). "Information about each county in Virginia and West Virginia, listing extant court records, other genealogical materials, and data which may be of use in research." These installments: Accomac-Bedford. [7978

THOMAS CHALMERS McCORVEY (1851-1932). The original Pocahontas. T. C. McCorvey, Alabama historical sketches, ed. George Burke Johnston (Charlottesville: Univ. of Virginia Press, 1960), p. 90-94. From Gulf States historical magazine, 1904. On the capture and threatened execution of Juan Ortiz, a member of Hernando de Soto's expedition, by Indians in Alabama, who spared him by request of the daughter of Chief Ucita, 1540, as reported in a Portugese narrative of the expedition; the translation of the narrative as part of Richard Hakluyt's Virginia richly valued (1609); and the probability that this example of an "Indian 'princess' who interposed to save the life of a white captive from the vengeance of an enraged father" inspired Capt. John Smith in his narrative of rescue by Pocahontas, daughter of Chief Powhatan. [7979

DONALD RANSONE TAYLOR. Out of the past--the future: a history of Hampton, Virginia [1570-1960]. Hampton: Prestige Press [for the Council of the City of Hampton], 1960. 44 p. facsims., maps (1 double), ports., views (1 double, part col.). notes. [7980

CHARLES EDGAR GILLIAM. Ajacan, the Algonkian name for Hampton Roads, Virginia. Names, 6:57-9 (Mar 1958). Evidence, 1571-87, that the name meant "a crossing over water." [7981

FRANCIS BUTLER SIMKINS, SPOTSWOOD HUNNICUTT, & SIDMAN P. POOLE. Virginia: history, government, geography [since 1584]. ix, 599, xi-lxxii p. facsims., maps (1 col.), ports., views (part col.). Textbook "written and published under the supervision" of the Virginia History and Government Textbook Commission, an agency of the Commonwealth of Virginia. [7982

GARY S. DUNBAR. Some curious analogies in explorers' preconceptions of Virginia. Va. jour. science, 9:323-6 (Jul 1958). bibliog. On "the views they held concerning this land before they arrived," 1585-1670. [7983

DARRETT BRUCE RUTMAN. The historian and the marshal: a note on the background of Sir Thomas Dale [died 1619]. Va. mag. hist. and biog., 68:284-94 (Jul). notes. On the documented facts of his life from ca. 1588 till his landing in Virginia in 1611 as "deputy governor and marshal of Virginia"; with correction of errors in the accounts of him by Alexander Brown and other historians. [7984

PHILIP L. BARBOUR. Captain John Smith's observations on life in Tartary. Va. mag. hist. and biog., 68:271-83 (Jul). view. On the veracity and the English style of his account of captivity in Tartary in 1602 in The true travels, adventures, and observations of Captain John Smith (1630), and the value of his experience as a preparation for his later work in Virginia. [7985

W. R. MORRIS. Folk lore of Blueridge Mountain, their first Sunday school and founders, other places of interest. Court records dating back to 1605. [Fancy Gap? Va.] c1953-60. 3 v. [2], 55, [3]; [2], ix, 57-166, [1]; [2], 167-279 p. col. coat of arms, ports., views. Miscellany of history and lore of Carroll County, Va., various Morris families in Virginia and the South, land titles, the Methodists in Virginia, and other subjects; with family letters (including several from Shadrick Morris, Jr., in St. Clair County, Ala., 1838-72) and other documents, and "The lost soldier boy," a poem by Judge D. W. Bolen (1895). [7986

MARSHALL WILLIAM FISHWICK. Jamestown revisited. Longwood College, Institute of Southern Culture, The South in perspective, ed. Francis B. Simkins (Farmville, Va.: Longwood College, 1959), p. 7-17. [7987

CHARLES FRANCIS COCKE. Parish lines, Diocese of Southwestern Virginia [of the Protestant Episcopal Church]. Richmond, 1960. 196 p.

diagrs., col. maps, tables. bibliog. (p. 179-80), notes. (Virginia State Library. Publications, 14.) On the origins and divisions of the parishes in 32 counties, 1607-1958. [7988

CHILES T. LARSON. A Jamestown portfolio. Va. cavalcade, 9(4):23-9 (spring). views (1 double col.). Nine photographs and a painting, apparently reproducing scenes from a pageant or exhibit showing Jamestown events, 1607-12. [7989

JOHN SMITH (1580-1631). The capture and release of Captain John Smith, including his rescue from death by Pocahontas, in his own words. [Ann Arbor:] Reprinted for the Clements Library Associates, 1960. 19, [1] p. mount. facsim., views (part col.). Excerpt (modernized text) from his The generall historie of Virginia (1624), reporting events of Dec. 1607 near Jamestown; with an introduction by Howard Henry Peckham on the veracity of the narrative. [7990

MORRIS TALPALAR. The sociology of colonial Virginia [1607-1776]. N.Y.: Philosophical Library [1960]. xi, 371 p. notes. Contents.--The background of Virginia's launching.--The rise of colonial Virginia's aristocracy.--The mind of colonial Virginia's aristocracy.--Colonial Virginia's labor base. [7991

U.S. Southeastern Forest Experiment Station, Asheville, N.C. Virginia forest resources and industries [since 1607. By] Ronald Craig, Forest Economist. Wash.: U.S. Govt. Print. Off., 1949. iv, 64 p. diagrs., maps (1 col. fold.), 33 tables, views. bibliog. (p. 55). (U.S. Dept. of Agriculture. Miscellaneous publication 681.) Mainly a report of a survey made in 1940. [7992

TERENCE HENRY O'BRIEN. The London livery companies and the Virginia Company. Va. mag. hist. and biog., 68:137-55 (Apr). views. notes. Information from records of "eleven of the twelve Great Companies" of London merchants, stockholders in the Virginia Company, 1609-24. [7993

WILLIAM H. LITTLETON. Alexander Whitaker (1585-1617). "the Apostle of Virginia." P. E. Church, Hist. mag., 29:325-48 (Dec). notes. On his service as "first minister of Henrico Parish," 1611-17. [7994

ULRICH TROUBETZKOY. Bowls and skittles. Va. cavalcade, 9(4):11-16 (spring). port., views (1 col.). On bowling in Virginia since 1611 or earlier and "ninepins, or skittles," since the 1630s. [7995

ULRICH TROUBETZKOY. Welcome to Shirley. Va. cavalcade, 9(2):9-17 (autumn 1959). views (part col., 1 double). On an estate on the north bank of the James River 1613-1959, the families associated with it, and the remarkably good preservation of its buildings and their contents and of its agricultural productivity. [7996

ROBERT C. JOHNSON, ed. The "running lotteries" of the Virginia Company [1616-21]. Va. mag. hist. and biog., 68:156-65 (Apr). notes. Four documents from municipal records of Norwich, 1617, and 3 from municipal records of Leicester, 1618; with an introduction. [7997

PARKE SHEPHERD ROUSE, JR. Smithfield: town of quiet self-sufficiency [since 1619]. Commonwealth (Va.), 27(12): 23-7, 36, 41 (Dec). ports., views. [7998

MARCUS WILSON JERNEGAN (1872-1949). Education for poor children in Virginia through the apprenticeship system [1642-1779]. Marcus W. Jernegan, Laboring and dependent classes in colonial America, 1607-1783 (N.Y.: Ungar [1960], p. 157-71. tables. notes. From School review, Feb. 1920. [7999

MARCUS WILSON JERNEGAN (1872-1949). The development of public poor relief in Virginia [1646-1785]. Marcus W. Jernegan, Laboring and dependent classes in colonial America, 1607-1783 (N.Y.: Ungar [1960]), p. 175-88. table. notes. From Social service review, Mar. 1929. [8000

ISABEL GOUGH. Wicomico's colonial church. Commonwealth (Va.), 27(12):10, 12 (Dec). On the church of Wicomico Parish (Episcopal), Northumberland County, Va., founded as early as 1648, and particularly the church building ordered to be erected in 1763 and in ruins when sold in 1840. [8001

JEANNE JOHNSON RUST. A history of the town of Fairfax [1649-1960. Fairfax? Va.] 1960. 67, [1] p. facsims., maps, views. bibliog. (p. 68). [8002

LOUIS OTTENBERG. The Northampton Protest, 1652: the first American protest against taxation without representation. Bar Assoc. D.C., Jour., 27:245-58, 281-8 (May, Jun). notes. On a document signed by 6 men, professing to represent grievances of "the Inhabitants of Northampton

Countie in Virginia" and making "statements of fact which at least several of the signers must have known to be untrue." [8003

HENRY FILMER (died 1871). "Henry Filmer of Mulberry Island, Gentleman": a collection of letters from Virginia, 1653-1671. Edited by Peter Walne. Va. mag. hist. and biog., 68: 408-28 (Oct). notes. Correspondence between Filmer, in Virginia, and his nephew, Sir Robert Filmer, London lawyer, on Henry Filmer's estate in England and his orders of goods and services from England; with 2 letters from Francis Berkeley. [8004

MARCUS WILSON JERNEGAN (1872-1949). Virginia's educational legislation for poor children [1656-1776]. Marcus W. Jernegan, Laboring and dependent classes in colonial America, 1607-1783 (N.Y.: Ungar [1960]), p. 141-56. table. notes. [8005

A. H. ELDRIDGE. Warren County, Virginia [since 1669]: its people, past and present. Natl. Geneal. Soc. quar., 48:12-18 (Mar). [8006

LOUIS BOOKER WRIGHT. "... a Virginia planter of the upper class." John Arthur Garraty, ed., The unforgettable Americans (Great Neck, N.Y.: Channel Press [1960]), p. 37-40. On William Byrd II (1674-1744), Virginia planter and author. [8007

ULRICH TROUBETZKOY. F. F. V. of Old Dominion gardens. Va. calvalcade, 9(4):42-8 (spring). views (1 col.). On the growing of daffodils in Virginia, perhaps as early as 1684, and the commercial development of a daffodil industry in Gloucester and Mathews Counties in the 20th century by Charles Heath and his son George. [8008

DEUEL PEAD. A sermon preached at James City in Virginia, the 23d of April 1686, before the Loyal Society of Citizens born in and about London and inhabiting in Virginia. By Deuel Pead, Minister of Middlesex County in Virginia. Edited, with an introduction, by Richard Beale Davis. Wm. and Mary quar., 17:371-94 (Jul). Sermon on the first anniversary of the coronation of James II, equating "loyalty to Church ... unequivocally with loyalty to Crown" and standing "foursquare for the inseparable union of king, Church, high morals, and peace." [8009

JOHN LYMAN. The Belfield family: a record of the descendants of Dr. Joseph Belfield [born 1685/86], immigrant to Virginia about 1700. Wash., 1960. 20 p. On the family in Virginia. [8010

EDD WINFIELD PARKS. William Byrd as man of letters. Ga. rev., 14:172-6 (summer). Commentary on his personal habits as recorded in 3 shorthand diaries, recently published, 1709-12, 1717-21, 1739-41. [8011

SAINT PAUL'S PARISH, King George County, Va. The register of Saint Paul's Parish, 1715-1798: Stafford County, Virginia, 1715-1776; King George County, Virginia, 1777-1798. Arranged alphabetically by surnames in chronological order by George Harrison Sanford King. Fredericksburg, Va., 1960. xxxiii, 157 p. view. [8012

MARCUS WHIFFEN. The eighteenth-century houses of Williamsburg: a study of architecture and building in the colonial capital of Virginia. Williamsburg, Va.: Colonial Williamsburg; distributed by Holt, Rinehart, and Winston, N.Y. [1960]. xx, 223 p. diagrs., facsim., map, plans, views. notes (p. 201-16). (Williamsburg architectural studies, 2.) Histories and descriptions of 32 houses, built between 1716 and ca. 1830; with chapters on building materials, the building crafts and craftsmen, the craftsmen's tools and books, and design, construction, and detail. [8013

D. M. M. SHORBOCKS. Transportation of felons from Sandwich [in Kent] to Virginia, 1721-1773. Va. mag. hist. and biog., 68:295-300 (Jul). table. notes. [8014

IDA R. SHOWALTER. History of the expansion of the Mennonite Church in Northern District of Virginia Conference [1727-1951]. Mennonite hist. bul., 12(3):1-3; (4):2-4 (Jul, Oct 1951). view. notes. [8015

PRINCE GEORGE COUNTY, Va. Some records from burned counties. Va. geneal., 4:65-6 (Apr-Jun). Four items, 1728, 1734, 1741, 1765, in possession of the Western Reserve Historical Society, Cleveland. [8016

JAMES G. SCOTT & EDWARD AVERY WYATT IV. Peterburg's story: a history [1730-1960]. Petersburg, Va., 1960. xiii, 390, [1] p. facsims., flag, maps (1 double), tables, ports., views. bibliog. (p. 353-71). [8017

GOOCHLAND COUNTY, Va. Marriages of Goochland County, Virginia, 1733-1815. Compiled and published by

Kathleen Booth Williams. [Alexandria, Va., 1960. 4], 148 p. diagr. "Copied from the Marriage Register in the Virginia State Library, which Register was compiled from original records by the Virginia State Library Staff." [8018

WILLIAM MONTGOMERY CLEMENS (1860-1931), comp. Virginia wills before 1799 [filed 1734-1803]: a complete abstract register of all names mentioned in over six hundred recorded wills, arranged alphabetically from Adams to Wright. Copied from the Court House records of Amherst, Bedford, Campbell, Loudon, Prince William, and Rockbridge Counties. Baltimore: Southern Book Co., 1958. 107 p. 1st ed. 1924. [8019

JOHN MERCER (1705-68). Notes from the journal of John Mercer, Esquire ... of Marlborough, Stafford County, Virginia. [Edited] by George Harrison Sanford King. Va. geneal., 4:99-110, 153-62 (Jul, Dec). notes. Excerpts and abstracts, 1740-68, from the diary of a lawyer, containing record of births, marriages, deaths, visits, etc., of named persons. [8020

ERNEST V. WOODALL. Benjamin West [born 1740/50, living in 1796] of Louisa County, Virginia. Va. geneal., 4:30-32 (Jan-Mar). notes. On Benjamin, his 4 sons, and his 33 or more grandchildren. [8021

WILLIAM EVERETT BROCKMAN. Orange County, Virginia, families. Volume II [and III. Minneapolis?] c1956[-59]. 2 v. [1], viii, [1] leaves, 147 p.; [2], iv, 163 p. facsim., map, ports., view. Vol. 1 published in 1949. "Orange County, Virginia, marriage records," 1747, 1756-57, 1761, 1770-1824 (1:1-50), other lists, and accounts of the Collins, Brockman, Gayden, Rhodes, Woolfolk, Simms, Ellis, Catterton, Chapman, Terrett, and other families. Includes information from "Private collections of J. W. Browning, County Clerk from 1901 to 1936, copied from bonds, guardianships, administrations, Revolutionary War claims, and other records. [8022

GEORGE G. GRATTAN IV. Revocation of wills by subsequent instrument [Virginia, 1748-1958]. Va. law rev., 46: 373-89 (Mar). notes. [8023

RALEIGH TRAVERS GREEN. Genealogical and historical notes on Culpeper County, Virginia. Embracing a revised and enlarged edition of Philip Slaughter's History of St. Mark's Parish [1877]. Baltimore: Southern Book Co., 1958. [12], viii, 120, 160, xxvi p. facsim. 1st ed. 1909. "A history of St. Mark's Parish, Culpeper County, Virginia, with notes of old churches and old families and illustrations of the manners and customs of the olden time," by Slaughter; and Green's "Culpeper County history" [2], 160, xxvi p.), a discursive account of the county, formed in 1748, with lists of Culpeper men enlisted in Confederate forces, names mentioned in wills and marriage records, etc., family histories by various contributors, "Culpeper as a battle ground in the War between the States" by Daniel Amon Grimsley, "The Baptists of Culpeper," by E. W. Winfrey and H. C. Burrows, and other special sections. [8024

DAVID ALAN WILLIAMS. The phantom governorship of John Robinson, Sr., 1749. Va. mag. hist. and biog., 68: 104-6 (Jan). notes. Evidence that John Robinson (1683-1749), formerly supposed to have functioned briefly as acting Governor of Virginia after the departure of Governor William Gooch, could have done so only in the middle part of August, and that "the adverse wind which held Gooch in the York River until after Robinson's death" probably prevented Robinson from serving at all. [8025

JAMES H. SOLTOW. Scottish traders in Virginia, 1750-1775. Econ. hist. rev., 12:83-98 (Aug 1959). notes. [8026

HELEN MICHAELIS. The sons of Janus. Quarter horse jour., 3(7):23, 88-99 (Apr 1951). views. On the desendants of Janus (1746-82), "a horse of Barb, Arabian and Galloway blood," believed to be the "most potent progenitor of the American Quarter Running Horse," imported from England ca. 1752 and owned by John Goode of Mecklenburg County, Va. [8027

NEW JERSEY ZINC COMPANY. Bertha Mineral Division. 200th anniversary of Austinville mine. [By W. L. Albers.] Mineral industries jour., 3(3):5-6 (Sep 1956). views. On a lead-zinc mine in Wythe County, Va., 1756-1956. [8028

EDWIN T. WILLIAMS. Goronwy Owen [1722-69]: a Welsh bard in Virginia. Va. cavalcade. 9(2):42-7 (autumn 1959). facsims., port., views. On his early life, linguistic studies, and service as a clergyman in Wales and England; his employment as master of the grammar school at the College of William and Mary (1758-61) and as Rector of St. Andrews Parish (1761-69); and the publication of the many writings by him (mainly in Welsh) and about him. [8029

FRANCES LONG HARROLD. Thomas Jefferson and the Commonwealth of Virginia [1760s-80s]: a study in constitutional thought. Ann Arbor: University Microfilms, 1960. Positive microfilm of typescript. [368] leaves. Thesis--Bryn Mawr. Abstracted: Dissert. abstracts, 21:1541-2 (Dec). [8030

AMHERST COUNTY, Va. An abstract of all items in Deed Book A, 1761-1765, Amherst County, Virginia. Compiled by Bailey Fulton Davis. [Amherst? Va., 1960.] ix, 50 p. (Amherst County, Virginia, courthouse miniatures.) [8031

TERRANCE LEON MAHAN. Virginia reaction to British policy, 1763-1776. Ann Arbor: University Microfilms, 1960. Positive microfilm of typescript. [426] leaves. Thesis--Univ. of Wisconsin. Abstracted: Dissert. abstracts, 21:1544-5 (Dec). [8032

ROBERT WORMELEY CARTER (1734-97). The daybook of Robert Wormeley Carter of Sabine Hall [in Richmond County, Va.], 1766. Edited by Louis Morton. Va. mag. hist. and biog., 68: 301-16 (Jul). notes. Includes details of plantation management. [8033

Mrs. C. D. PERKINS. Jefferson's Monticello. Garden Club Am., Bul., 48(2):30-32 (Feb). On his gardens there, 1768-1826, and their survival or restoration. [8034

SURRY COUNTY, Va. Marriage bonds and ministers' returns of Surry County, Virginia, 1768-1825. Compiled and published by Catherine Lindsay Knorr. [Pine Bluff, Ark.] 1960. [10], 112 p. map, port. [8035

FARRAN ZERBE. Virginia colony notes on "James River Bank" blanks. Selections from The numismatist: United States paper money, tokens, medals, and miscellaneous (Racine, Wis.: Whitman Pub. Co., 1960), p. 142-4. First printed Aug. 1918. On "Virginia Colony notes produced and issued on blanks printed for Virginia James River Bank." 1773-75. [8036

ROBERT COLIN McLEAN. George Tucker [1775-1861]: moral philosopher and man of letters. Ann Arbor: University Microfilms, 1960. Positive microfilm of typescript. [391] leaves. Thesis--Washington Univ. Abstracted: Dissert. abstracts, 20:4398-9 (May). On his life in Virginia as a lawyer and legislator, his service as Professor of Moral Philosophy at the University of Virginia, his imaginative writings, and his ideas concerning aesthetics and literary criticism, philosophy, domestic slavery, and progress. [8037

GEORGE BROWN OLIVER. A constitutional history of Virginia, 1776-1860. Ann Arbor: University Microfilms, 1959 [i. e. 1960]. Positive microfilm of typescript. [457] leaves. Thesis--Duke Univ. Abstracted: Dissert. abstracts, 20:3712 (Mar). [8038

NORTON (JOHN) & SONS, Winchester, Va. Amherst County magistrates, 1779-1798. Contributed by Aubrey H. Starke. Va. geneal., 4:125-6 (Jul-Sep). Chronological list. [8039

ROBERT McCOLLEY. Slavery in Jefferson's Virginia [1780s-1803]. Cent. Miss. Valley Am. Studies Assoc., Jour., 1(1):23-31 (spring). notes. [8040

ALFRED PERCY. Origin of the Lynch law, 1780. Madison Heights, Va.: Percy Press, 1959. [8], 75 p. facsims., fold. map, views. bibliog. (p. 51-65). On its origin in Virginia in connection with the names of Charles Lynch and William Lynch. [8041

CULPEPER COUNTY, Va. Marriages of Culpeper County, Virginia, 1781-1815. Compiled and published by Catherine Lindsay Knorr. [Pine Bluff, Ark.: Perdue Co.] 1954. [8], 127 p. diagr. Abstracts. [8042

PERCY C. SMITH. Ball's Cross Roads. Arlington hist. mag., 1(4):54-8. On an area in Arlington County, 1798-1890s. [8043

ALEXANDRIA, Va. Alexandria, Virginia, Second Ward 1799 census. Va. geneal., 4:117-24, 163-70 (Jul-Dec). [8044

ALEXANDRIA, Va. Alexandria, Virginia, 1800 tax list. Va. geneal., 4: 17-26 (Jan-Mar). List prepared by William Lamphier. Includes "List of licenses granted to merchants." [8045

ALEXANDRIA, Va. Alexandria, Virginia, Fourth Ward 1800 census. Va. geneal., 4:51-9 (Apr-Jun). "Not a part of the United States Census of 1800." [8046

JACQUES GÉRARD MILBERT (1766-1840). A French artist portrays the Natural Bridge. By Constance D. Sherman. Va. mag. hist. and biog., 68:155-70 (Apr). view. notes. Translated excerpt from his Itinéraire pittoresque du Fleuve Hudson et des parties latérales de l'Amérique du Nord (1828-29), on his visit to Virginia at some time between 1815 and 1823. [8047

MARGARET (BURKHOLDER) BLOSSER (1804-95). Statement concerning a division in the Mennonite Church of Virginia in the year 1825. Mennonite hist. bul., 10(3):2-3 (Jul 1948). On disagreement in Rockingham and Augusta Counties on the issue of association with the revivalistic United Brethren, 1825-30. [8048

WILLIAM BAINTER O'NEAL. Primitive into painter: life and letters of John Toole [or O'Toole, 1815-60]. Charlottesville: Univ. of Virginia Press, 1960. [14], 113, [2] p. ports., views. bibliog. (p. 104-5), notes. On his early life in Ireland, his emigration in 1827, and his work as an itinerant painter in Virginia, with headquarters at Charlottesville. Consists mainly of excerpts from his letters to his wife, Mary Jane (Suddarth) Toole (1817-1902), and other persons, and from her letters to him. Appended: list of 306 paintings by him, 1838-57 and undated, and list of 115 letters, 1838-56, with abstracts. [8049

HAROLD L. LUNGER. Alexander Campbell's political activities and views. Perry Epler Gresham, ed., The sage of Bethany: a pioneer in broadcloth (St. Louis: Bethany Press [1960]), p. 147-63. notes. Mainly on his participation in the Virginia Constitutional Convention at Richmond, 1829-30. [8050

CHARLES H. BOHNER. Swallow Barn [1832]: John P. Kennedy's chronicle of Virginia society. Va. mag. hist. and biog., 68:317-30 (Jul). notes. [8051

MENNONITE CHURCH. Conferences. Virginia. The 1835 meeting of Virginia Mennonite Conference. [Edited and translated] by Ernest G. Gehman. Mennonite hist. bul., 20(1):1-2, 4 (Jan 1959). Report dated Rockingham County, Va., 10 Apr. 1835. [8052

C. E. SEARS, JR. Manganese deposits of the Appalachian area of Virginia [1838-1957]. Mineral industries jour., 4(1):1-4 (Mar 1957). map, tables, views. bibliog. [8053

ULYSSES WALSH. Polk Miller [1844-1913] and his "Old South" Quartet. By Jim Walsh. Hobbies, 64(11):34-7 (Jan). port. On his life in Virginia, his Confederate Army service, his work as a druggist in Richmond, and his Edison recordings in 1910 as a singer, banjoist, and guitarist with his 4 Negro friends. Includes correspondence with his daughter, Mrs. Garland C. Chewning, and a biographical sketch by his son, Withers Miller. [8054

E. LEWIS KNOWLES. The Stonewall Brigade Band of Staunton. Commonwealth (Va.), 27(7):11-12, 48 (Jul). ports., views. On a band organized in 1855, now composed of about 40 persons. [8055

HERBERT CLARENCE BRADSHAW. Murder at Hampden-Sydney. Va. cavalcade, 9(4):30-34 (spring). facsim., port., views. On the fatal stabbing of Charles T. Edie, student at Hampden-Sydney College, by Edward A. Langhorne, fellow student, after Edie declined to withdraw an insulting remark made the night before and repeatedly assaulted and cursed Langhorne, 27 Jan. 1857, the trial of Langhorne at Prince Edward Courthouse on a charge of murder, the reliance of the defense on "the code of honor," the verdict of "not guilty," and the protests of several Presbyterian ministers against the code. [8056

JANE STUBBS. Virginians run the sea blockade [1861-65]. Va. cavalcade, 9(4):17-22 (spring). ports., views. [8057

JAMES CITY COUNTY, Va. Abstracts of wills, Will Book I [probated or inventoried Dec. 1865 - Apr. 1871]. Submitted by Mrs. Janet A. Curtis. South. genealogist's exchange quar., 2(13):2-4 (spring). [8058

CECIL DE GROTTE EBY, JR. "Porte Crayon's" quarrel with Virginia. W. Va. hist., 21:65-75 (Jan). On uncomplimentary references to Virginia and Virginians by David Hunter Strother of Berkeley Springs, 1866; with remarks on the snobbery of Virginians and on their distortion of history so far as it concerns Strother. [8059

BYRON NELSON COOPER. Manganese in Virginia [1867-1950]. Mineral industries jour., 1(2):1-5 (Jun 1954). port., tables, bibliog., notes. [8060

VIRGINIA POLYTECHNIC INSTITUTE, Blacksburg. Some facts about Virginia Tech. Blacksburg, 1960. 14, [1] p. map, tables, views. (Its Bulletin, v. 53, no. 12.) First published in 1941 under title: Some V. P. I. facts. On an institution founded in 1872 as the Virginia Agricultural and Mechanical College. [8061

ROBERT SIDNEY SMITH. Mill on the Dan: a history of Dan River Mills, 1882-1950. Durham, N.C.: Duke Univ. Press, 1960. [2], xi, 579 p. tables. notes. On an enterprise originally named Riverside Cotton Mills, Danville (1882-1909), later Riverside & Dan River Cotton Mills (1909-45), and its expansion by absorption of the Dan River Power & Manufacturing Company and other firms in the Danville area. [8062

EDWARD J. MARCIN. The tin mines of Irish Creek, Virginia. Rocks and minerals, 35:336-8 (Jul-Aug). maps. On "test pits, trenches, shafts and tunnels," and dumps marking the sites of mines operated in Rockbridge County ca. 1883. [8063

GEORGE FREEMAN POLLOCK (1869-1947). Skyland: the heart of the Shenandoah National Park. ... Edited by Stuart E. Brown, Jr. [n. p., 1960.] xv, [1], 283 p. ports., views. notes (p. 270-83). On the author's summer resort at Stony Man Mountain, 1894-1937, and his part in the establishment of the Shenandoah National Park. [8064

VIRGINIA POLYTECHNIC INSTITUTE, Blacksburg. School of Agriculture. Virginia agriculture, 1900-1958: handbook of information. Compiled by the agricultural faculty. [Blacksburg:] Virginia Agricultural Experiment Station and the Virginia Agricultural Extension Service, U.S.D.A. [1960]. viii, 139 p. map, tables. (Its Miscellaneous publication 1.) [8065

JOHN LAMBERT COTTER. Archeological excavations at Jamestown, Virginia [between 1901 and 1958]. Ann Arbor: University Microfilms, 1959 [i. e. 1960]. Positive microfilm of typescript. [339] leaves. Thesis--Univ. of Pennsylvania. Abstracted: Dissert. abstracts, 20:4239-40 (May). Deals particularly with "the major and culminating excavations of 1953-57, conducted by the writer," resulting in the uncovering of 142 "structures of all types" and the discovery of "the earliest glass factory, brick kiln, ice storage device, pottery kilns, forge and iron smelting pits in English America." [8066

JAMES HOWARD BREWER. The war against Jim Crow in the land of Goshen. Negro hist. bul., 24:53-7 (Dec). notes. On an order of the Virginia Passenger and Power Company requiring separation of Negroes and whites on streetcars in Richmond, the boycott organized by the Negroes under John Mitchell, Jr., the bankruptcy of the Company, and the adoption of legislation requiring separation of the races, 1904-6. [8067

WILLIAM A. WRAY. "The defendant is insured." Wm. and Mary law rev., 2:475-84. On "admission of insurance coverage" in tort actions as reversible error in Virginia courts, 1907-58. [8068

LOUISA VENABLE KYLE. The good old summertime in Virginia 50 years ago. Commonwealth (Va.), 27(6):58-61 (Jun). views. On the popularity of "seashore or mountain vacations," health resorts, beach cottages, excursions, etc. [8069

GEORGE WESLEY McKINNEY, JR. The Federal Reserve discount window: administration in the Fifth District. New Brunswick, N.J.: Rutgers Univ. Press [1960]. xi, 157 p. diagrs., forms, tables. bibliog. (p. 151-7), notes (p. 144-50). (Rutgers banking series.) On "the factors taken into consideration" by the Federal Reserve Bank of Richmond "in extending credit to member banks," and the differing policies of the member banks with respect to availing themselves of the opportunity to borrow, 1913-57. [8070

PAT PERKINSON. Crusader against tuberculosis. Commonwealth (Va.), 27(1):13-14 (Jan). ports. On the work of Nora Spencer Hamner as Executive Director of the Virginia Tuberculosis Association, Richmond, since 1919. [8071

W. TAYLOE MURPHY, JR. Damages for loss of consortium [in Virginia law, 1932-59]. Va. law rev., 46:184-93 (Jan). notes. [8072

DOXEY ALPHONSO WILKERSON. The Negro school movement in Virginia from "equalization" to "integration" [1934-57]. Jour. Negro educ., 29:17-29 (winter). tables. notes. [8073

ROBERT W. JEFFREY. The 25th birthday of James Lees' plant at Glasgow. Commonwealth (Va.), 27(7):20-21 (Jul). ports., views. On the rug factory established by James Lees & Sons (of Pennsylvania) at Glasgow, Va., in 1935. [8074

CARL McFARLAND & T. MUNFORD BOYD. The Virginia Administrative Agencies Act [1944]: a major problem in statutory construction. Va. law rev., 46:808-35 (May). notes. [8075

Richmond

SHOCKOE HILL CEMETERY, Richmond, Va. Shockoe Hill Cemetery, Richmond, Virginia: register of interments, April 10, 1822-December 31, 1950. Compiled and edited by A[lice] Böhmer Rudd. [Volume I.] Wash. [1960]. x, [4], 98, [3]; [8], 274, [2] p. facsim. Abstract of a record "kept by the city official in charge of the cemetery," in chronological order, with an index. [8076

WILLIAM JOSEPH KIMBALL, ed. Richmond in time of war. Boston: Houghton Mifflin [1960]. x, 166 p. table. bibliog. (p. iv). (Houghton Mifflin research series, 5.) Excerpts from newspapers, diaries, reminiscences, and other contemporary writings on Richmond during the Civil War. [8077

REMBERT WALLACE PATRICK. The fall of Richmond. Baton Rouge: Louisiana State Univ. Press [1960]. ix, 144, [1] p. map, ports., views. bibliog. (p. 137-8), notes. (The Walter Lynwood Fleming lectures in Southern history.) On military events and civilian behavior in the capital of the Confederacy, 2-4 Apr. 1865. [8078

JOSEPH CHRISTIAN (1828-1905). The Capitol disaster, April 27, 1870: a letter of Joseph Christian to his wife [Maria Augusta Healy Christian]. Edited by William M. E. Rachal. Va. mag. hist. and biog., 68:193-7 (Apr). Eyewitness account, Richmond, 27 Apr. 1870, of the collapse of a crowded gallery and upper floor of the Capitol, with heavy casualties. [8079

HELEN COVEY MILIUS. Robins--the house that integrity built. Commonwealth (Va.), 27(3):11-16 (Mar). port., views. On A. H. Robins Company, Richmond, Va., manufacturer of drugs for physicians only, founded by Albert Hartley Robins in 1878 and continued by his son, his daughter-in-law, and his grandson, E. Claiborne Robins. [8080

WEBSTER S. RHOADS, JR. Miller & Rhoads: seventy-five years of growth. N.Y.: Newcomen Soc. in North America, 1960. 36 p. views. On a department store in Richmond, 1885-1960. [8081

JENNIE HUGHES. All Saints Episcopal Church, Richmond, Virginia, 1888-1958. Richmond, 1960. xiii, 69 p. ports., views. [8082

NORTH CAROLINA

CHARLOTTE IVEY HASTINGS, ed. Our North Carolina heritage. [Revised edition. Charlotte, N.C.: School Print. Service] 1960. 212 p. facsims., ports., views. "Collection of stories and legends on North Carolina history written or collected by the children" of North Carolina and, with few exceptions, unsigned. [8083

BILL SHARPE. A new geography of North Carolina. [Volumes I and II.] Raleigh: Sharpe Pub. Co., 1954-58. 2 v. [8], 533; [8], 535-1114 p. maps, ports., views. Description, lore, and history of each of 46 counties. Part of a series to be completed in 4 volumes. Includes reference to events as early as 1584. [8084

CLARENCE E. LOWREY. The Lumbee Indians of North Carolina. Lumberton, N.C., 1960. 64 p. ports., tables, views. On their supposed origin by interbreeding between the English settlers of Roanoke Island and the Croatan Indians after 1587, their supposed settlement on the Lumbee River in present Robeson County, N.C., ca. 1650, and the growth of the Indian population of the county from 1,459 in 1860 to 5,895 in 1960; with an account of James Lowrey, who removed to Robeson County in 1791, the marriages of some of his descendants to Lumbee Indians, the illegal execution of a Lowrey by the Home Guard of Robeson County in 1864, the activities of his son, Henry Berry Lowrey (born ca. 1847), in organizing a group of avengers to kill the 30 participants in the execution, their success with respect to 29 of the 30, the extracurricular activities of the "Lowrey Gang" as thieves and robbers, the break-up of the Gang, and the permanent disappearance of Henry Berry Lowrey. [8085

LACY W. MAYNOR. The Lumbee Indian of Robeson County, North Carolina. New Eng. teacher, 5(5):12-13 (Jun 1958). Account, by a member of the "tribe," of supposed descendants of North Carolina colonists who disappeared ca. 1587 and interbred with

Indians ("White's Lost Colony"), now numbering more than 30,000 persons, with a "capital" at Pembroke. [8086

HAZEL GRIFFIN. Foods in early North Carolina [1657 ff.]. N.C. folklore, 8(2):45-6 (Dec). bibliog. [8087

CORNELIUS M. D. THOMAS. James Forte, Azalea edition: a 17th century settlement, possibly pre-1625. ... An enigma presented in booklet form. [Wilmington? N.C., 1959.] xi, 56 p. facsims., 2 fold. maps, views. bibliog. (p. 55). (Clarendon imprint 3.) Reproduces "the earliest known map of the Cape Fear River, the John Locke pen and pencil sketch of the [Nicholas] Shapley map of the Cape Fear River, 1662," the map of the Cape Fear River by James Lancaster (1679), and A relation of a discovery lately made on the coast of Florida (1664), by James Hilton. Another printing, with same title: Wilmington, N.C.: J. E. Hicks for the Charles Towne Preservation Trust, 1959. xi, 59 p. facsims., 3 maps (2 fold.) views. (Clarendon imprint 3.) Adds "Appendix" (p. 57-9) and part of a map by Edward Moseley (1733?). [8088

HUGH F. RANKIN. The pirates of colonial North Carolina [1685-1720]. Raleigh: State Dept. of Archives and History, 1960. viii, 72 p. ports., views. bibliog. (p. 72). Includes chapters on Stede Bonnet and Blackbeard, and "A who's who of North Carolina's colonial pirates." [8089

JOHN GULICK. Cherokees at the crossroads. Chapel Hill, 1960. xv, [3], 202 p. diagrs., maps, tables. bibliog. (p. 187-93). (University of North Carolina. Institute for Research in Social Science. Monographs.) Historical references to the Cherokees in North Carolina since ca. 1700, and study, based upon recent field research by anthropologists, of their "present-day ways of life" on a reservation in western North Carolina. [8090

JOSEPH PARSONS BROWN. The Commonwealth of Onslow: a history. New Bern, N.C.: O. G. Dunn [1960]. v, [3], 434 p. coat of arms, maps, ports., views. bibliog. On Onslow County, N.C., 1706-1960. Includes "Roster of settlers who took up land by grant in Onslow County, 1706-1800" (p. 377-86), and rosters of Onslow County military units, 1754, 1777, 1812, 1861-65 (p. 387-417). [8091

GARY SEAMANS DUNBAR. The Hatteras Indians of North Carolina. Ethnohistory, 7:410-18 (winter). bibliog., notes. Review of documentary references, 1709-88, indicating the lack of evidence that these Indians were identical with the Croatan Indians as recorded in 1587. [8092

ARTHUR PALMER HUDSON. Animal lore in Lawson's and Brickell's histories of North Carolina. Miss. quar., 13:189-207 (fall). facsims., views. notes. On descriptions and illustrations of animals in the History of North Carolina (London, 1709) by John Lawson, and The natural history of North Carolina (Dublin, 1737) by John Brickell. Also printed: N.C. folklore, 8(2):1-15 (Dec). facsims., views. notes. [8093

CRAVEN COUNTY, N.C. Records of Craven County, North Carolina. Volume one. By Elizabeth Moore [Deputy Clerk of the Superior Court of Craven County]. Bladensburg, Md.: Genealogical Recorders, ©1960. [4]. iii, 229, [2] p. bibliog. (p. 231). Texts and abstracts of wills and inventories, deeds, land transfers, depositions, petitions, etc., dated mainly between 1735 and 1850 (some as early as 1712); "Newspaper notices," 1818-54; and various lists. [8094

ANSON COUNTY, N.C. Anson County, North Carolina, abstracts of early records [1749-1828. Compiled by May Wilson McBee. Greenwood? Miss., 1950.] vii, 180 p. Land grants and surveys, deeds, county-court minutes, probate reports, wills, petitions, and certain records of Montgomery and Richmond Counties, detached from Anson County in 1779. [8095

LENOIR RAY. Flat Rock, N.C., Charleston of the mountains [1790-1959]. D. A. R. mag., 94:29, 60 (Jan). On "the first summer resort town in western North Carolina." [8096

CLAIR ALAN BROWN. Vegetation of the outer banks of North Carolina. Baton Rouge: Louisiana State Univ. Press [1959]. x, 179 p. diagrs., maps, views. bibliog. (p. 116-19). (Louisiana State University studies. Coastal studies series, 4.) Reproduction of a report prepared by the Coastal Studies Institute, Louisiana State University, under contract with the U.S. Office of Naval Research, 1957. Includes a review of botanical observations in this area since 1795 and an account (p. 55-61) of "A century of change at Cape Hatteras." [8097

EDWARD W. PHIFER. Money, banking, and Burke County in the antebellum era [1795-1874]. N.C. hist. rev., 37: 22-37 (Jan). facsims. notes. Deals particularly with the State Bank of North Carolina at Morganton (1826-33), the Bank of the State of North Carolina at Morganton (1833-60), and the Bank of North Carolina at Morganton (1860-74). [8098

GEORGE NEWTON. Shining figures on Chimney Rock. N.C. folklore, 8(1): 27-8 (Jun). "Extraordinary phenomenon," reprinted from The Raleigh register and North Carolina State gazette, 15 Sep. 1806, about the mysterious apparition of a crowd of "beings resembling the human species ... all clad with brilliant white raiment," flying about the Chimney Mountain in Rutherford County, 31 Jul. 1806. [8099

BEN F. WILLIAMS. Jacob Marling [1773?-1833], early Raleigh painter. N.C. Mus. Art bul., 1(3):21-9 (autumn 1957). ports., views. notes. On his life in Raleigh as a painter from "some time before 1813" till his death, and the teaching of drawing and painting in the Raleigh Academy by his wife, Louisa. [8100

CHARLES CROSSFIELD WARE. Hookerton history. [New Bern? N.C.] 1960. 74, [6] p. facsims., tables. Historical sketches of churches of the Hookerton Union of North Carolina Christian Churches (Disciples of Christ) and predecessor churches, 1828-1960. Includes several letters and other documents. [8101

JO ANN CARRIGAN. Early nineteenth century folk remedies. La. folklore misc., 1(4):43-64 (Jan). notes. Based on thesis (M. A.)--Louisiana State Univ. Deals particularly with "a handwritten compilation of remedies" by an unnamed North Carolina planter, prepared in the 1830's partly from oral and partly from printed sources. [8102

WILLIAM GORDON KORNEGAY. A historical study of teachers' associations in North Carolina, 1830-1883. Ann Arbor: University Microfilms, 1959 [i. e. 1960]. Positive microfilm of typescript. [201] leaves. Thesis--Univ. of North Carolina. Abstracted: Dissert. abstracts, 20:2669 (Jan). [8103

The STORY of the Bechtler gold coinage. Selections from The numismatist: United States paper money, tokens, medals, and miscellaneous (Racine, Wis.: Whitman Pub. Co., 1960), p. 32-41. First printed Sep. 1929. On the minting of gold coins by Christopher Bechtler and his sons in Rutherfordton, N.C., 1831-47. [8104

DONALD J. BALLAS. Notes on the population, settlement, and ecology of the Eastern Cherokee Indians [Swain and Jackson Counties, N.C., 1838-1956]. Jour. geog., 59:258-67 (Sep). views. notes. [8105

NORTH CAROLINA. State Dept. of Archives and History. Hall of History Railroad. Written and illustrated by Ann Beal. Raleigh, 1960. [12] p. facsims., map, views. 1st ed. 1953. On a collection of model railroads which "tell the story of railroading in North Carolina," 1840-1950. [8106

JOHN ELLIOTT WOOD. Yankee schoolmaster in the South. Harvard alumni bul., 54:146, 148, 150 (10 Nov 1951). On Ezekiel Gilman, from Newburyport, Mass., Harvard graduate in 1839, master of an academy in Shiloh, N.C., from 1840 till ca. 1900. [8107

JOHN CALHOUN ELLEN, JR. Newspaper finance in North Carolina's Piedmont and Mountain sections during the 1850's. N.C. hist. rev., 37: 488-50 (Oct). notes. [8108

PASCHAL REEVES. The "deaf mute" confidence-man: Melville's imposter in action. Mod. lang. notes, 75:18-20 (Jan). notes. On "the imposter who had passed himself off as a deaf and dumb Hermann Melville," during his visit to the home of Samuel W. Tillinghast, merchant in Fayetteville, N.C., Apr. 1850; and the certainty that the real Herman Melville must have had this individual in mind in The confidence-man (1857). [8109

GEORGE HIGBY THROOP (1818-96). Nag's Head and Bertie: two novels by George Higby Throop. With an introduction by Richard Walser. Charlotte [N.C.]: Heritage House, 1958. xxi, [3] p., facsim. ([2], 180 p.), [2] p., facsim. ([2], 242 p.). Nag's Head: or, Two months among "The Bankers": a story of sea-shore life and manners (Philadelphia, 1850) and Bertie; or, Life in the old field: a humorous novel (Philadelphia, 1851); with a biographical sketch of the author. [8110

DAVID HYDE PRINCE. A history of the State Department of Public Instruction in North Carolina, 1852-1956. Ann Arbor: University Microfilms, 1959 [i. e. 1960]. Positive microfilm of typescript. [491] leaves. Thesis--Univ. of North Carolina. Abstracted: Dissert. abstracts, 20:2670 (Jan). [8111

Miss B. L. BROWN. Tribute to Joseph Charles Price [1854-93]. A. M. E. Zion quar. rev., 60:37-40 (winter 1950). On his life in North Carolina, his college studies, his services to the African Methodist Episcopal Zion Church, his initiative in founding Zion Wesley Institute (renamed Livingstone College), and his service as its first president. [8112

J. W. FINDLEY. Biographical sketch of Joseph Charles Price [1854-93]. A. M. E. Zion quar. rev., 64:144-53 (summer 1953). On his life in North Carolina and his work as a minister of the African Methodist Episcopal Zion Church and founder and president of Livingstone College. [8113

CHARLES NAPOLEON BONAPARTE EVANS. A letter from the Fool Killer. Edited by Daniel Wilkins Paterson. N.C. folklore, 8(2):22-5 (Dec). cartoon. notes. From the Milton chronicle, 12 Feb 1857. Letter dated High Rock, N.C., Feb. 1857, signed: Jesse Holmes the Fool Killer. Ridicules some of the follies noted by him in North Carolina. [8114

NORMAN C. DELANEY. Charles Henry Foster [1830-82] and the Unionists of eastern North Carolina. N.C. hist. rev., 37:348-66 (Jul). notes. On his political and military activities, centered in the Outer Banks, 1861-65. [8115

GEORGE E. Davis [1862-1959]. Jour. Negro hist., 45:62-4 (Jan). On his life in North Carolina, his studies at Biddle University (now Johnson C. Smith University), his teaching of natural science there from the 1880s till 1920, and his later work as an agent of the Rosenwald Foundation. [8116

CHARLES LEWIS PRICE. Railroads and Reconstruction in North Carolina, 1865-1871. Ann Arbor: University Microfilms, 1959 [i. e. 1960]. Positive microfilm of typescript. [630] leaves. Thesis--Univ. of North Carolina. Abstracted: Dissert. abstracts, 20:2777 (Jan). [8117

DANIEL JAY WHITENER. The Republican Party and public education in North Carolina, 1867-1900. N.C. hist. rev., 37:382-96 (Jul). notes. [8118

WILLARD BADGETTE GATEWOOD, JR. Eugene Clyde Brooks [1871-1947]: educator and public servant. Durham, N.C.: Duke Univ. Press, 1960. ix, [5], 279 p. cartoon, port., tables. notes. On his early life and studies, his editorial experience, and his work as a teacher and administrator in North Carolina schools, Professor of Education in Trinity College, editor of North Carolina education, State Superintendent of Public Instruction, and President of North Carolina State College of Agriculture and Engineering. [8119

MARY ELEANOR CRAIG. Recent history of the North Carolina furniture manufacturing industry [since 1888], with special attention to locational factors. Ann Arbor: University Microfilms, 1959 [i. e. 1960]. Positive microfilm of typescript. [286] leaves. Thesis--Duke Univ. Abstracted: Dissert. abstracts, 20:3562-3 (Mar). [8120

LITTLE Will and Big Will. [Edited by Elaine Penninger.] Jour. Am. folklore, 72:57-8 (Jan-Mar). Tale collected from the author's grandmother, Mrs. B. W. Young, heard by her as a child in Yancey County, N.C. [8121

JEAN WOOD WALSTON, ed. Hunting and fishing tales. N.C. folklore, 8(1): 7-11 (Jan). Tales collected in North Carolina from oral sources, 1959-60, and from newspapers as early as 1890. [8122

BLUM'S ALMANAC, Winston-Salem, N.C. Anatomical superstitions in Blum's almanac. By Addison Barker. N.C. folklore, 8(2):47-8 (Dec). Based on Barker's thesis (M. A.)--Univ. of North Carolina, 1950. Selected single-sentence superstitions about anatomical traits (e. g., shape and color of finger nails), 1891-1950. [8123

HEATH THOMAS. Alec Whitley: the man and the ballad. N.C. folklore, 8(2):16-21 (Dec). music. On a "man of dark and evil reputation" in Stanly County, N.C., thief, barn-burner, murderer of Bert Tucker, apprehended in Stanly County by a posse after the murder and lynched at Albemarle in 1892; and a ballad inspired by these events. [8124

WILTON MASON. The music of the Waldensians in Valdese, North Carolina [settled in 1893 by emigrants from "the Cottian Alps of Italy"]. N.C. folklore, 8(1):1-6 (Jun). music. notes. Includes 3 texts (1 in Italian, 2 in French). [8125

ROBERT BURTON HOUSE. [Charles Brantley] Aycock and universal education [in North Carolina, 1898-1905]. N.C. hist. rev., 37:211-16 (Apr). [8126

WILLIAM H. KAMPSCHMIDT. Why the Evangelical Lutheran Church established and maintains a college for Negroes. Jour. Negro educ., 29: 299-306 (summer). On Immanuel Luthern College, Concord, N.C., 1903-60. [8127

BENJAMIN EARLE WASHBURN. Rutherford County and its hospital. Spindale, N.C.: Spindale Press, 1960. 96 p. map, ports., views. On the Rutherford Hospital, Rutherfordton, N.C., 1906-60. [8128

BENJAMIN EARLE WASHBURN. As I recall ... the hookworm campaigns initiated by the Rockefeller Sanitary Commission and the Rockefeller Foundation, in the Southern United States and tropical America [1909-14]. N.Y.: Rockefeller Foundation [1960]. viii, 183 p. facsim., port., views. Mainly on the Commission's work in North Carolina, particularly in Nash and Wilson Counties. [8129

ELIZABETH CONARD CORKEY. Chronic disease program in the Charlotte-Mecklenburg Health Department [1919-60]. N.C. med. jour., 21: 465-9 (Oct). table. [8130

INA B. FORBUS. Orange County home cures. N.C. folklore, 8(1):12-16 (Jun). Information from oral sources about remedies that "seem barbarous, but twenty or twenty-five years ago ... were common practice." [8131

J. W. R. NORTON, JAMES F. DONNELLY, & ANNE LAMB. Twenty-one years' experience with a public health contraceptive service [in North Carolina, 1937-58]. Am. jour. pub. health, 49:993-1000 (Aug 1959). diagrs., tables. notes. [8132

JOHN W. JOHNSON. Journey to enlightenment. D. A. R. mag., 94:427-8 (Jun-Jul). On the author's intermittent studies at a school at Tamassee, in the mountains of western North Carolina, 1939-47, and his return to teach there in 1959 with a degree of B. S. in Education. [8133

IDA (BROOKS) KELLAM & LESLIE HUBERT BROWN, JR., comps. Duplin County, North Carolina, gravestone records ... collected in November 1960. Wilmington, N.C., 1960. [4], 147 p. maps, views. Full texts of inscriptions from 34 cemeteries, including 26 family cemeteries, forming "only a small part of the cemeteries in Duplin county"; with maps locating the cemeteries, and drawings of some of the stones. [8134

TUCKER R. LITTLETON. Ghosts and haunted houses of eastern North Carolina. N.C. folklore, 8(1):19-26 (Jun). Twenty-two tales and anecdotes collected from residents of Beaufort, Swansboro, and other communities in "the central coastal region." [8135

JOHN A. PARRIS. My mountains, my people. Asheville, N.C.: Citizen-Times Pub. Co. [1957. 12], 259 p. A continuation of the author's Roaming the mountains (1955). Dedicated to his grandfather, William Riley Tallent, "the Old Man of a thousand tales that chronicle the life and times of my mountains and my people." [8136

JOHN A. PARRIS. Roaming the mountains with John Parris. Asheville, N.C.: Citizen-Times Pub. Co., 1955. [10], 246 p. Sketches reprinted from the author's column in The Asheville citizen-times, 1954-55, describing western North Carolina and its inhabitants. Includes information from the author's grandfather, aged 96. [8137

W. TODD REECE. Mores of mountain music. N.C. folklore, 8(2):32-7 (Dec). On traditional and recent tunes, instruments, and musicians in "the southwestern tip" of North Carolina as observed by the author. [8138

RICHARD GAITHER WALSER. Picturebook of Tar Heel authors. Second edition enlarged. Raleigh, N.C.: State Dept. of Archives and History, 1960. 46 p. ports. 1st ed. 1957. Biographical sketches of 46 writers, living and dead. [8139

SOUTH CAROLINA

JOHN HENRY LOGAN (1822-85). A history of the upper country of South Carolina, from the earliest periods to the close of the War of Independence. ... Vol. I. Charleston: S. G. Courtenay, 1859. [Spartanburg, S.C.: Reprint Co., 1960. 10], 521 p. (South Carolina heritage series, 5.) Running title: Ancient territory of the Cherokees. On the natural history and related lore of South Carolina and the Indians, their trade and wars with white men from 1700 to 1758. Closes with a reference to a second volume, which was never published. [8140

KATHARINE M. JONES, ed. Port Royal under six flags. Indianapolis: Bobbs-Merrill [1960]. 368 p. double map, ports., views. bibliog. (p. 361-8), notes. Reprinted contemporary accounts of the Sea Islands of South Carolina from Edisto Island to Hilton Head Island, 1520-1958, with particular attention to Port Royal Island and the City of Beaufort. [8141

WILLIAM FRANCIS GUESS. South Carolina: annals of pride and protest [1670-1960]. N.Y.: Harper [1960]. vii, [3], 337 p. col. maps (1 double), col. views. bibliog. (p. 325-9). (A Regions of America book.) [8142

CAROLINE T. MOORE & AGATHA ALMAR SIMMONS, comps. Abstracts of the wills of the State of South Carolina, 1670-1740. Volume 1. [Columbia, S.C.: R. L. Bryan Co., 1960.] xiii, 346 p. Arranged in roughly chronological order, with an index. [8143

DAVID RAMSAY (1749-1815). Ramsay's history of South Carolina, from its first settlement in 1670 to the year 1808. ... Newberry, S.C.: W. J. Duffie, 1858. Spartanburg, S.C.: The Reprint Co., 1959. 2 v. [4], viii, 274; 307 p. maps. notes. (South Carolina heritage series, 3-4.) Facsimile reproduction, Narrative history, most detailed for the years 1776-82; and chapters on ecclesiastical, medical, legal and constitutional, fiscal, agricultural, commercial history, and etc., and "Civil history"; with "Biographical sketches of literary men and other distinguished characters" (2:251-77), "A statistical account of Edisto Island" and shorter accounts of 8 other areas. [8144

ARCHIBALD HAMILTON RUTLEDGE (born 1883). The world around Hampton. N.Y.: Bobbs-Merrill [1960]. 192 p. views. On a plantation "in the wilderness, fifty miles north of Charleston, South Carolina," owned by the author's family since 1686, and "the wild life around Hampton"; with anecdotes of hunting rattlesnakes, deer, and wild boars in the marshes and islands. [8145

FRANK JOSEPH KLINGBERG, ed. Early attempts at Indian education in South Carolina: a documentary. S.C. hist. mag., 61: 1-10 (Jan). notes. Letters or parts of letters to various persons from Thomas Nairne, John Norris, James De Gignillat, Robert Maule, and Benjamin Dennis, 20 Aug. 1705-2 Aug. 1711. [8146

LOUISE M. WATSON. Old Ninety Six, Star Fort, and Cambridge: historical sketch of a focal point of importance and interest in the early development of the South Carolina back country [in Greenwood County, 1715-1960]. Greenwood, S.C.: Greenwood County Historical Soc., 1960. 51 p. maps, port. bibliog. (p. 48-51). [8147

RAY BAKER HARRIS. Eleven gentlemen of Charleston, founders of the Supreme Council, mother council of the world, Ancient and Accepted Scottish Rite of Freemasonry. Wash., 1959. 70 p. facsims., ports., views. Biographical sketches of founders of the Supreme Council for the Southern Jurisdiction, born between ca. 1741 and 1770, died between 1805 and 1845. [8148

OLGA MARY (ROLATER) WHITLEY. Colonel Joseph Howe [1743-99], York County, South Carolina: his decendants and his brothers. [Commerce? Tex.] c1960. [4], vii, 97 leaves. tables. notes. On his settlement in Bethel, S.C., as early as 1771, his service as an Army officer in the Revolution, his activities in South Carolina and national politics, and his decendants mainly in the South. [8149

WILLIAM TENNENT III (1740-77). Writings of the Reverend William Tennent, 1740-1777. Edited by Newton B. Jones. S.C. mag. hist., 61:129-45, 189-209 (Jul, Oct). notes. Writings of a Presbyterian minister and leader of anti-British agitation in Charleston, consisting of a letter dated Freehold, N.J., 25 Jan. 1763 (to Susan Vergereau of New York City, proposing marriage), 3 anonymous letters to Charleston newspapers (2-23 Aug. 1774). "Historic remarks on the session of Assembly began to be holden Tuesday, September 17th, 1776 [and continued to 21 Oct.]" (manuscript), and "Petition of the Dissenters" (manuscript) and "Mr. Tennent's speech on the Dissenting petition, delivered in the House of Assembly," Charleston, 11 Jan. 1777 (printed in 1777), arguing for religious liberty in South Carolina and proposing disestablishment of the Church of England. [8150

SOUTH CAROLINA (Colony). Provincial Congress. Extracts from the journals of the Provincial Congresses of South Carolina, 1775-1776. William Edwin Hemphill, editor; Wylma Anne Wates, assistant editor. Columbia: South Carolina Archives Dept., 1960.

xxxiv, 299, [1] p. facsim., tables. notes. (South Carolina. Archives Dept. The State records of South Carolina.) Contains "all of the available journals of the conventions that led South Carolina into independence from Great Britain"--the First Provincial Congress, 11-17 Jan. and 1-22 Jun. 1775, and the Second Provincial Congress, 1-29 Nov. 1775, 1 Feb.-26 Mar. 1776; with list of "State officials elected March 26-28, 1776." Reprinted from the Extracts published in 1775 and 1776. [8151

HENRY MIOT COX, comp. Notes on the Boyce family of Laurens and Newberry. S.C. hist. mag., 61:82-5 (Apr). notes. Bible and cemetery records of John Boyce (1779?-1843) of Laurens County (son of John Boyce of Newberry County, died 1806), the 3 wives of John Boyce of Laurens County, and some of their descendants. [8152

JOHN BELTON O'NEAL LANDRUM. History of Spartanburg County: embracing an account of many important events, and biographical sketches of statesmen, divines, and other public men [1785-1900]. Atlanta: Franklin Prtg. and Pub. Co., 1900. [Spartanburg, S.C.: Reprint Co., 1960.] 543 p. ports., views. (South Carolina heritage series, 2.) Includes chapters on many individuals and families; a list of heads of families in the 1790 census (p. 488-95); and a list of Confederate soldiers from Spartanburg County (p. 495-539). [8153

FENELON DE VERE SMITH. The economic development of the textile industry in the Columbia, South Carolina, area from 1790 through 1916. Ann Arbor: University Microfilms, 1952 [i. e. 1960]. Positive microfilm of typescript. ix, 342 leaves. tables. bibliog. (leaves 333-9). Thesis--Univ. of Kentucky. Abstracted: Dissert. abstracts, 20:3563-4 (Mar). [8154

NATHALIA WRIGHT. Francis Kinloch [1798-1840]: a South Carolina artist. S.C. hist. mag., 61:99-100 (Apr). notes. On his life in Paris and Florence, 1831-40, and the apparent failure of any of his works to survive. [8155

ALFRED S. REID, ed. The arts in Greenville, 1800-1960. Greenville, S.C.: Furman Univ., 1960. 158 p. views. bibliog. (p. 145-9), notes. From Furman studies, Nov. 1960. Contents.--A social history, by Laura Smith Ebaugh.--Music, by Lennie Lusby.--Architecture, by Lila Easley Earle.--Painting, by Evelyn Pack Daniel.--Theater arts, by Dorothy Richey.--Greenville and the Southern tradition, by Albert N. Sanders. [8156

GEORGETOWN METHODIST CHURCH, Georgetown, S.C. Records of the Georgetown Methodist Church, 1811-1897. Contributed by Anne A. White and Frances H. Leonard. S.C. hist. mag., 61:41-50, 101-13 (Jan, Apr). notes. Marriages and baptisms, 1811-42, and deaths, 1816-97. [8157

CHRISTOPHER HAPPOLDT (1823-78). The Christopher Happoldt journal: his European tour with the Rev. John Bachman (June-December 1838). Edited with preface and biographies by Claude Henry Neuffer. Charleston, S.C., 1960. 214, [14] p. facsim., ports., view. notes. (Contributions from the Charleston Museum, 13.) Text of the journal (p. 119-214), recording the observations of a 14-year-old boy in England, Germany, and France and the scientific and religious interests of Bachman; and biographical sketches of Happoldt, (p. 17-28), and of Bachman (p. 29-118). [8158

EUGENE PAUL WILLGING & HERTA HATZFIELD. Catholic serials of the nineteenth century in South Carolina [Charleston, 1822-61, 1869-73]. Am. Cath. Hist. Soc., Rec., 71:40-58 (Mar-Jun). notes. Detailed histories of the 5 serials. [8159

SARAH LEVERETTE. The Carolina law journal of 1830. S.C. law quar., 12:193-201 (winter). On the contents of a serial published by Abram Blanding and D. J. McCord at Columbia, S.C., 1830-31, discontinued with its fourth issue. [8160

GERMAN COLONIZATION SOCIETY, Charleston, S.C. German colony protocol. Translated by B. E. Schaeffer. [Walhalla, S.C., 1960. 143] p. 3 fold. maps (in pocket), tables. "Sponsored by Oconee County Library." Translated text of a manuscript volume (212 p.), "The Minute Book of the German Colonization Society of Charleston, S.C., founders of the Town of Walhalla," 1848-89. [8161

THOMAS A. ROONEY. A note on "Sweet Jane." By Jim Lee. South. folklore quar., 24:284-6 (Dec). "A true song" from the author's anonymous American rhymes, all original, by a Southern Poet (Knoxville, Tenn., 1855), about a South Carolina youth who bade farewell to "his own sweet Jane," sailed to Australia, dug gold industriously for 3 years, returned home, and married Jane; with editorial information about the oral currency of the poem in 5 States. [8162

PAUL QUATTLEBAUM. The Kingston Presbyterian Church, Pee Dee Presbytery, Conway, South Carolina, 1858-1958. Conway: Kingston Presbyterian Church [1958]. x, 126 p. ports., views. [8163

JAMES DAVIDSON. The post-bellum poor-white as seen by J[ohn] W[illiam] De Forest. South. folklore quar., 24: 101-8 (Jun). notes. On observations made by an officer of the Bureau of Refugees, Freedmen, and Abandoned Lands, in charge of a 3-county area centered in Greenville, S.C., reported in his A Union officer in the Reconstruction (1948) as dialogues between himself and applicants for assistance, attempting to reproduce the dialect of "the low-downers." [8164

ERNEST McPHERSON LANDER, JR. A history of South Carolina, 1865-1960. Chapel Hill: Univ. of North Carolina Press, 1960. viii, [4]. 260 p. maps, tables. bibliog. (p. 246-8), notes. Survey "of South Carolina's political, economic, educational and religious development" during this period. [8165

HOWARD H. QUINT. Profile in black and white: a frank portrait of South Carolina. Wash.: Public Affairs Press [1958]. vii, [3], 214 p. notes (p. 187-209). On the status of Negroes in South Carolina, 1889-1957, particularly since 1954. [8166

JAMES McBRIDE DABBS (born 1896). The road home. Phila.: Christian Education Press [1960]. 245 p. bibliog. (p. 243-5). On the author's early life and studies, his Army service in World War I, his teaching of literature at the University of South Carolina, his life as a farmer in Sumter County, his family affairs, his reading and reflections on a variety of subjects, and particularly his mystical religious experiences. [8167

THOMAS STEPHEN BUIE. From pines to pines. Am. forests, 62(6):2-23, 54-5 (Jun 1956). port., views (1 double). On woodland salvage and reforestation in the Sand Hills of South Carolina, 1905-56; with the author's memories of part of Chesterfield County, stripped of timber between 1899 and 1904, farmed till in the 1930s the soil was nearly exhausted, and later replanted to pine. [8168

AMBROSE GILES FLEMING. The bicentennial history of Wesley Memorial Methodist Church, formerly Waverly Methodist Episcopal Church, South, Columbia, South Carolina [1910-60. Columbia, 1960. 16], 45, [3] p. map, ports., tables, views (1 double). [8169

J. KENNETH CASS. Music is the heart of a city. Music jour., 18(6):5, 65 (Sep). port. On music in Greenville, S.C., since 1937. [8170

Charleston

SAMUEL GAILLARD STONEY. This is Charleston: a survey of the architectural heritage of a unique American city [since ca. 1700. Second edition, revised.] Charleston, S.C.: Carolina Art Assoc. [1960]. x, [2], 137 p. maps, views. 1st ed. 1944. Photographic inventory of early, "valuable," "notable," or "nationally important" buildings. [8171

MARGARET (BRETT) KENNETT. An account of Charles Town in 1725. Contributed by Brian J. Enright. S.C. hist. mag., 61:13-18 (Jan). notes. Letter from a recently arrived emigrant to her mother (or stepmother) in England, dated "Charles Town," S.C., 20 Jan. 1725, on the city, the country, and the badness of the people. [8172

EVERETT MENDELSOHN. John Lining [1708-60] and his contribution to early American science. Isis, 51:278-92 (Sep). notes. On his emigration from Scotland to Charleston, S.C., in 1730, his medical practice there, his studies of yellow fever, his daily record of Charleston weather (1737-53), his measurements of his own bodily responses to weather, and his experiments in electricity; with a list of his publications. [8173

NELSON VAN DE LUYSTER. The German Friendly Society of Charleston [1766-1960]. Am.-German rev., 26(4): 20-23, 36 (Apr-May). port. [8174

ERNEST McPHERSON LANDER, JR. Charleston: manufacturing center of the Old South [1768-1860]. Jour. South. hist., 26:330-51 (Aug). notes. [8175

ANNIE ROULHAC COFFIN. Maria Martin (1796-1863). Art quar., 23:281-300 (autumn). views. notes. On her life in Charleston, her paintings of flowers, birds, insects, and reptiles, and her assistance to John James Audubon in adding the plant backgrounds to some of his bird pictures and in making drawings for his use; with excerpts from his correspondence mentioning his indebtedness to her, and some account of her unpublished sketchbooks and portfolios. [8176

CHARLES FRASER (1782-1860). A Charleston sketchbook, 1796-1806: forty watercolor drawings of the city and the surrounding country, including plantations and parish churches. ... With an introduction and notes by Alice R. Huger Smith. Rutland, Vt.: C. E. Tuttle Co. for the Carolina Art Assoc. [1959]. xv p., 40, [1] leaves, xvii-xix p. col. views. 1st ed. 1940. Colored drawings of town houses, country "seats" and their rural surroundings, and a few landscapes, with related text by the editor and a biographical introduction. [8177

ALBERT PIKE (1809-91). A historical inquiry in regard to the Grand constitutions of 1786. With a foreword by Luther A. Smith. Wash.: Supreme Council 33°, Ancient and Accepted Scottish Rite, 1958. [2], 66 p. port. notes. Previously printed. Includes some account of Freemasons in Charleston, 1797-1808; with "Memoir by Jacob E. Levy, Esquire," aged 84, written in or after 1871, containing recollections of early Freemasons in Charleston. [8178

NITA KATHARINE PYBURN. The public school system of Charleston before 1860 [i. e. 1811-60]. S.C. hist. mag., 61:86-98 (Apr). notes. [8179

Sister MARY MARCIAN LOWMAN. James Andrew Corcoran: editor. theologian, scholar (1820-1889). Am. Cath. Hist. Soc., Rec., 69:67-97; 70: 32-57 (Sep 1958, Jun 1959). bibliog., notes. Thesis--St. Louis Univ. On his life in Charleston, his studies in Rome (1833-43), and his service in Charleston as a priest and as editor of The miscellany. [8180

CHARLES KAUFMAN ROGERS (1839-96). Beleaguered Charleston: letters from the city, 1860-1864. Edited by Martin Abbott ... and Elmer L. Puryear. S.C. hist. mag., 61:61-74, 164-75, 210-17 (Apr-Oct). notes. Letters to the author's sister, Emeline (Rogers) Divver reporting all kinds of personal and public news from Charleston. [8181

KATHARINE (WARING) WHIPPLE. Childhood in Charleston in the not-so-gay nineties [1890-98. Charleston? S.C.] c1960. [3], 93 leaves. Reminiscences. [8182

ALBERT SIMONS. Forty years of preservation. A. I. A. jour., 34(6):26-9 (Dec). views. On the work of the Society for the Preservation of Old Dwellings (now the Preservation Society of Charleston, Inc.,), 1910-60. [8183

GEORGIA

HENRY VAN DER SCHALIE & PAUL W. PARMALEE. Animal remains [mollusks and vertebrates] from the Etowah site, Mound C, Bartow County, Georgia [occupied by man ca. 160 to ca. 1700]. Fla. anthropol., 13:37-54 (Sep). tables, views. bibliogs. [8184

ELLIS MERTON COULTER. Georgia: a short history [1512-1959]. ... Revised and enlarged edition. Chapel Hill: Univ. of North Carolina Press [1960]. xxii, 537 p. facsims., map, ports., views. bibliog. (p. 479-98), notes. 1st ed. 1933. [8185

IVAN EARNEST ALLEN. The Cherokee Nation: Fort Mountain, Vann House, Chester Inns, New Echota. Atlanta: I. Allen Co. [1958?]. 59 p. facsim., maps, ports., views. History and lore of the Cherokee Indians in the northeast corner of Georgia, and account of some Cherokee landmarks, ca. 1540 to 1838. [8186

LEWIS H. LARSON, JR. A Mississippian headdress from Etowah, Georgia. Am. antiq., 25:109-12 (Jul 1959). views. bibliog. On "types of embossed sheet-copper badges," with indications from early observers in the Southeast (16th-18th centuries) that "at least some of the headdresses were made with feathers attached to the framework." [8187

FOLKS HUXFORD. Pioneers of Wiregrass Georgia, Volume II [-IV]: a biographical account of some of the early settlers of that portion of Wiregrass Georgia embraced in the original counties of Irwin, Appling, Wayne, Camden, and Glynn. [Homerville? Ga., 1954-60.] 3 v. xxi, 369, [1]; vi, 476; viii, 454 p. facsims., ports. Vol. 1 published in 1951. Biographical dictionary (one alphabet in each volume) of persons born between 1723 and 1839 and residing in the area now forming 25 counties of southern Georgia; with an account of cemeteries, additions and corrections to the dictionary, and indexes. Completes a series of volumes containing "nearly 2000 sketches or records of pioneers in this section of South Georgia," but notes the need for several added volumes "to resonably cover the territory." [8188

ERNEST FREEMAN LEVERETT. Higher standards for the bar in Georgia [1732-1958]. Ga. Bar jour., 21:371-81, 514-26 (Feb, May 1959). notes. [8189

PATRICK TAILFER, HUGH ANDERSON, & DAVID DOUGLAS. A true and historical narrative of the Colony of Georgia. ... With comments by the Earl of Egmont. Edited with an introduction by Clarence L. Ver Steeg. Athens: Univ. of Georgia Press [1960]. xxxiv, 169 p. facsims., port. notes. (Wormslow Foundation publications, 4.) 1st ed. 1741. Critical and satirical review, by 3 former settlers in Georgia, of the plans and policies of the Trustees of Georgia and of their agent, Gen. James Edward Oglethorpe, and other Georgia officials; with voluminous marginal notes and comments made by John Perceval, 1st Earl of Egmont, one of the Trustees, in his copy of the printed original, and a detailed editorial introduction on the 3 authors, the causes of discontent in Georgia since its founding in 1732 and settlement in 1733, and the 3 editions of the book issued in 1741. [8190

SHERWIN HARRY COOPER. The rural settlement of the lower Savannah River Basin in Georgia [since 1733]. Ann Arbor: University Microfilms, 1960. Positive microfilm of typescript. [248] leaves. Thesis--Univ. of Michigan. Abstracted: Dissert. abstracts, 21:330-31 (Aug). [8191

HENRY THOMPSON MALONE. The Episcopal Church in Georgia, 1733-1957. Atlanta: Protestant Episcopal Church in the Diocese of Atlanta [1960]. xiv, 334 p. maps, ports., tables, views. [8192

FREDERICK DOVETON NICHOLS. The early architecture of Georgia. ... With a pictorial survey by Frances Benjamin Johnston. Chapel Hill: Univ. of North Carolina Press, 1957. xvi, 292 p. maps, plans, views. notes. 34 cm. Chapters on cities and towns, domestic architecture of coastal Georgia and of the Piedmont, and "civil architecture," 1733-1861 [8193

GROVES HARRISON CARTLEDGE (1820-99). Historical sketches of Presbyterianism in Georgia [1755/56-1835, especially before 1800]. Groves Harrison Cartledge, Historical sketches: Presbyterian churches and early settlers in northeast Georgia, ed. Jessie Julia Mize & Virginia Louise Newton (Athens, Ga., 1960), p. 107-48. Printed from clippings, believed to have been cut from the Christian messenger (date unknown). [8194

A PAIR of odes commemorating the departure of the Royal Governour of the Colony of Georgia for England and the welcoming of his successor, February the sixteenth of the year 1757. By an unknown hand. Darien, Ga.: Ashantilly Press, 1960. [8] p. (Ashantilly leaflets. Ser. 2: Regional history, 1.) Facsimile reproductions and printed texts of 2 manuscripts by "Americanus," "On Governour Reynolds departure for England, ode," and "On Governour Ellis's arrival in Georgia, ode," the former expressing the extreme unpopularity of Capt. John Reynolds, R. N., and the second expressing the happiness of the colony at the arrival of Ellis. [8195

E. R. R. GREEN. Queensborough Township [on the Great Ogeechee River]: Scotch-Irish emigration and the expansion of Georgia, 1763-1776. Wm. and Mary quar., 17:183-99 (Apr). notes. [8196

GEORGIA. Old letters. Selected by Sylvia Head. Ga. rev., 14:3-8 (spring). Letter from James Wright, Royal Governor of Georgia, on board HMS Scarborough at Cockspur, 13 Feb. 1776, to James Mackay and His Majesty's Council; 3 petitions (Mar, May, Aug 1781); and report from Anthony Wayne to John Martin, Governor of the State of Georgia, dated Sharon, 2 Jul. 1782. [8197

EARL LEASTON BELL & KENNETH CHARLES CRABBE. The Augusta chronicle, indomitable voice of Dixie, 1785-1960. Athens: Univ. of Georgia Press [1960]. xii, 273 p. facsims., ports., views. bibliog. (p. 259-62), notes. History of "the South's Oldest Newspaper" and, to some extent, of Augusta, Ga. Appended (p. 240-48): "Augusta chronology," 1540-1958. [8198

GROVES HARRISON CARTLEDGE (1820-99). Sketches of the early history of Madison County [Ga., 1786-1863]. Groves Harrison Cartledge, Historical sketches: Presbyterian churches and early settlers in northeast Georgia, ed. Jessie Julia Mize & Virginia Louise Newton (Athens, Ga., 1960), p. 47-78. Written ca. 1885-86; here printed from the Danielsville Monitor, Danielsville, Ga., 1916. [8199

GROVES HARRIS CARTLEDGE (1820-99). Historical sketches of New Hope Church. Groves Harrison Cartledge, Historical sketches: Presbyterian churches and early settlers in northeast Georgia, ed. Jessie Julia Mize & Virginia Louise Newton (Athens, Ga., 1960), p. 20-46. From The Southern Presbyterian (Columbia, S.C.), 1875. On a church established by Scotch-Irish Presbyterians from Pennsylvania soon after their arrival in 1787 in Madison County, Ga. [8200

GROVES HARRISON CARTLEDGE (1820-99). Biographical sketches. Groves Harrison Cartledge, Historical sketches: Presbyterian churches and early settlers in northeast Georgia, ed. Jessie Julia Mize & Virginia Louise Newton (Athens, Ga., 1960), p. 149-56. Manuscript memorials (undated) of Henry Safford (1790/95-1870), John C. Humphrey (1829-59), Francis Power (died early in 19th century), and Charles Tuggle (died ca. 1836/37), residents of Georgia, of whom Safford and Humphrey were Presbyterian ministers. [8201

GROVES HARRISON CARTLEDGE (1820-99). Historical sketches of Hebron Church [Banks County, Ga., 1796-1875]. Groves Harrison Cartledge, Historical sketches: Presbyterian churches and early settlers in northeast Georgia, ed. Jessie Julia Mize & Virginia Louise Newton (Athens, Ga., 1960), p. 79-106. facsim. From The Southern Presbyterian (Columbia, S.C.), 1876. [8202

LINCOLN COUNTY, Ga. Estrays, Lincoln County, Ga., 1797-1807. [Edited] by William H. Dumont. Natl. Geneal. Soc. quar., 48:72-4 (Jun). notes. Records naming the finders and the 2 appraisers of stray animals and the justices of the peace who reported the finding. [8203

LINCOLN COUNTY, Ga. Lincoln County, Ga., tavern licenses, 1802-1820. [Edited] by William H. Dumont. Natl. Geneal. Soc. quar., 48:185-6 (Dec). List of applicants. [8204

OLD CAPITAL HISTORICAL SOCIETY, Milledgeville, Ga. Sesquicentennial of Milledgeville and Baldwin County, Georgia, 1803-1953, May 2-29, 1953; souvenir program. [Milledgeville, 1953. 44] p. facsims., maps, ports., views. [8205

J. LANETTE (O'NEAL) FAULK & BILLY WALKER JONES. History of Twiggs County, Georgia [1809-1959. Volume I.] Jeffersonville, Ga.,: Major General John Twiggs Chapter, Daughters of the American Revolution [1960]. vi, 479 p. facsims., geneal charts, map, ports., tables, views. Includes abstracts of tax records, 1818, 1826, 1853 (p. 194-230), and deeds, 1809-1900 (p. 231-53), and "Genealogical appendix (biographies)" (p. 359-463). [8206

GROVES HARRISON CARTLEDGE (1820-99). Autobiography of Rev. Groves H. Cartledge. Edited by his sons, Rev. Thomas D. Cartledge and Rev. Samuel J. Cartledge. Groves Harrison Cartledge, Historical sketches: Presbyterian churches and early settlers in northeast Georgia, ed. Jessie Julia Mize & Virginia Louise Newton (Athens, Ga., 1960), p. 1-19. Published in 1903; written ca. 1893. On the author's early life in rural Georgia, his studies in Oglethorpe University, and his service as pastor of Hebron and Homer churches (Presbyterian); with some account of the Cartledge and Groves families in Georgia. In the same volume are a memorial sketch by the Rev. R. E. Telford; a memorial of Anna Maria (Lane) Cartledge, by the Rev. H. F. Hoyt; letters exchanged between husband and wife, 1846-47; and a genealogy of his descendants, by the editors. [8207

JANE (McINTOSH) HAWKINS. [Letter to Col. Duncan G. Campbell and Maj. James Meriwether, Indian Commissioners, dated Fayette County, Ga., 3 May 1825.] Ga. rev., 14:128-9 (summer). On the execution of the author's husband, Col. Samuel Hawkins, and her father, Chief William McIntosh, by Creek Indians determined "to kill all who had any hand in selling the Land" of the Indians. [8208

PEGGY McINTOSH & SUSANNAH McINTOSH. [Letter to Col. Duncan G. Campbell and Maj. James Meriwether, Indian Commissioners, dated Line Creek, Fayette County, Ga., 3 May 1825. Edited] by Sylvia Head. Ga. rev., 14:126-7 (summer). Letter from 2 wives of Chief William McIntosh, on his execution by Creek Indians "in revenge for his signing away of the Creek lands at the Indian Springs Treaty," and the burning and plundering of his property. [8209

JOHN ROGERS VINTON (1801-47). Journal of a mission to Georgia in 1827. [Edited] by James C. Bonner.

Ga. hist. quar., 44:74-85 (Mar). notes. Excerpts from the travel record of a lieutenant of the U.S. Army, 8 Feb.-28 Mar. 1827, containing expressions of his dislike of Milledgeville, the Methodists, the Georgia roads and taverns, etc. [8210

THOMAS CONN BRYAN, ed. Letters concerning Georgia gold mines, 1830-1834. Ga. hist. quar., 44:338-46 (Sep). Letters from James Gwyn, William L. Gwyn, and C. P. Gordon to Col. Hamilton Brown (of the Wilkesboro Mining Company, Wilkesboro, N.C.), reporting the goldmining activities of the writers in the northwest corner of Georgia. [8211

WILLIAM BAILEY WILLIFORD. Americus through the years: the first one hundred and twenty-five years of a Georgia town and its people, 1831-1956. Atlanta, 1960. [10], 207, [1] p. ports., tables, views. bibliog. (p. 203-4), notes (p. 190-202). [8212

JOHN A. COBB. [Letter to the writer's son, Howell Cobb, student at the University of Georgia, dated Savannah, 24 Apr. 1832. Edited] by Sylvia Head. Ga. rev., 14:227-8 (fall). Refers briefly to the son's "late misguided conduct" (not identified) and urges him to keep up "with your class in their studies" and to avoid "idleness & the society of empty headed associates." [8213

JOHN BASIL LAMAR. [Letter to the writer's sister, Mary Ann Lamar (aged 16), undated (probably 1833). Edited] by Sylvia Head. Ga. rev., 14: 228-30 (fall). Offers detailed advice to the future wife of Howell Cobb about her conversation, reading, confidants, etc. [8214

JOHN ERWIN TALMADGE. Rebecca Latimer Felton [1835-1930]: nine stormy decades. Athens: Univ. of Georgia Press [1960]. xi, 187 p. cartoon, ports. bibliog. (p. 178-82), notes (p. 161-77). On her early life near Decatur, Ga., her studies at Madison Female College, her Confederate activities, her marriage to William Harrell Felton, her activities in Georgia politics, her work as a newspaper columnist, her agitation in behalf of temperance and women's rights, and her distinction as the "First Woman Member of the Senate of the United States." [8215

JOHN DONALD WADE. Georgia scenes [1835], by A[ugustus] B[aldwin] Longstreet. Ga. rev., 14:444-7 (winter). [8216

ELBERT COUNTY, Ga. Georgia slave trials, 1837-1849. [Edited] by Robert G. McPherson. Am. jour. legal hist., 4:257-84, 364-77 (Jul, Oct). notes. Texts of records of the Inferior Court for Elbert County, 1837, 1839, 1847, 1849. [8217

MARGARET DAVIS CATE. Mistakes in Fanny Kemble's Georgia journal. Ga. hist. quar., 44:1-17 (Mar). map, port., views. notes. On the stay of Frances Anne Kemble (Mrs. Pierce Butler) on her husband's 3 coastal plantations in Georgia, Dec. 1838-Apr. 1839, the unavailability of the manuscript journal that she evidently kept while there, and the "errors of fact and ... fictitious account of events" in the journal as published by her in 1863, much rewritten by her to "add drama to the story" and to arouse "public indignation against the slaveholding people of the South." [8218

MEDICAL ASSOCIATION OF GEORGIA. Report of MAG Milledgeville Study Committee. W. Bruce Schaefer, chairman. Med. Assoc. Ga., Jour., 48:275-85 (Jun 1959). notes. On the Milledgeville State Hospital, 1843-1959, particularly the weaknesses and scandals in its recent administration and the reforms needed to effect their correction. [8219

JOHN ERWIN TALMADGE. Joseph E. Brown's missing correspondence. Ga. hist. quar., 44:411-18 (Dec). notes. On the inadequate documentation of his political and business activities in Georgia, 1857-94; with evidence that most of his Civil War papers were burned by his wife to prevent their falling into Federal hands, and that his later papers may have been destroyed in large part by Brown himself to conceal "his devious activities in leasing convicts, winning elections, and changing political parties." [8220

CHARLES NICHOLAS FEATHERSTON (1839-1909). A student's letters from ante-bellum Emory. Emory Univ. quar., 16:26-31 (spring). notes. Four letters to the author's sister, Zerlina Catherine Featherston, and her future husband, George Washington Peddy, dated "Emory College," 1858-59. [8221

FLORENCE FLEMING CORLEY. Confederate City: Augusta, Georgia, 1860-1865. Columbia: Univ. of South Carolina Press, 1960. xiv, 130 p.

facsims., col. flag, map, music, ports., views. notes (p. 101-26). [8222

ELIZA FRANCES ANDREWS (1840-1931). The war-time journal of a Georgia girl, 1864-1865. Edited by Spencer Bidwell King, Jr. Macon [Ga.]: Ardivan Press, 1960. xvii, [3], 396 p. col. maps, port. notes. 1st ed. 1908. Diary of a journey from her home at Washington, Ga., to Albany, Ga., her stay at Pine Bluff Plantation, her visit to Cuthbert, and her return to Washington, Dec. 1864 - Apr. 1865, and her activities at home to 29 August 1865. Prepared for publication by the author in 1908, omitting "matters strictly personal to the writer." Includes a biographical sketch by the present editor. [8223

ELEANOR S. NORTH. Martha [McChesney] Berry [1866-1942] ... pioneer in "different" education. Delta Kappa Gamma bul., 24(1):12-19 (fall 1957). On her early life in Georgia, and her establishment of the Berry Schools and College near Rome, Ga., as "Christian self-help schools." [8224

GEORGIA. General Assembly. House of Representatives. Negroes in the Georgia Legislature: the case of F. H. Fyall of Macon County. Edited by Willard E. Wight. Ga. hist. quar., 44: 85-97 (Mar). notes. Records of the House relating to the disqualification of Fyall, elected as a Representative from Macon County, on the ground that he was not a resident of the county and that he was of partly Negro blood, 1868. [8225

DERRELL CLAYTON ROBERTS. Joseph E. Brown and the convict lease system [1874-91]. Ga. hist. quar., 44:399-410 (Dec). notes. On his treatment of convicts leased to the Dade Coal Company, Dade County Ga., for $11 a year per convict besides food, clothing, and lodging. [8226

EDWARD T. BRENNAN. Justice Logan E. Bleckley [born 1827]. Ga. Bar jour., 22:514-23 (May). notes. Mainly excerpts from and commentaries on his opinions written during his years in the Supreme Court of Georgia, 1875-79, 1887-94. [8227

HUGH WILLIAM DIVINE. Interpreting the Georgia Constitution [of 1877] today. Mercer law rev., 10:219-25 (spring 1959). notes. [8228

CAROLINE LEWIS GORDON. Plantation life with General John B. Gordon [the author's father]. Ga. rev., 14: 17-34 (spring). Excerpts from an unpublished book, De Gin'ral and Miss Fanny, about his estates of Sutherland and Beechwood, Christmas gifts to the Negroes and other festivities at Beechwood, and a visit of Grover Cleveland to the Executive Mansion in 1884 (when Gordon was Governor of Georgia). [8229

Mrs. HAZARD H. STAY. America's first garden club. Garden Club Am., Bul., 48(6):22-5 (Nov). views. On the Ladies Garden Club, Athens, Ga., 1891-1960. [8230

JOHN R. CARREKER & W. J. LIDDELL. Results of irrigation research in Georgia. Agric. engineering, 29:243-4, 250, 301-2, 304 (Jun, Jul 1948). diagrs., tables, views. notes. Includes a summary of "drought frequency by months" and "drought periods" by years at Athens, Ga., 1920-44. [8231

G. J. LOVE & W. W. SMITH. Murine typhus investigations in southwestern Georgia [1926-57]. Pub. health reports, 75:429-40 (May). diagrs., maps, tables, view. notes. [8232

J. J. McDONOUGH. Georgia: a State in transition. Ga. rev., 14:9-16 (spring). On industrial development in Georgia, 1929-59, and the contributions of the Georgia Power Company to the development. [8233

GEORGE ANDERSON. Economics of site preparation and land regeneration in the South: example of an industry concept. Jour. forestry, 56:754-6 (Oct 1958). diagrs., views. On forest management by the Brunswick Pulp and Paper Company, Brunswick, Ga., 1940-57. [8234

LESTER M. PETRIE. To each his own: a State occupational health program. Am. jour. pub. health, 49: 1658-63 (Dec 1959). view. notes. On the Industrial Hygiene Program of Georgia, 1941-59. [8235

WEIMAR JONES. My affair with a weekly. Winston-Salem [N.C.]: J. F. Blair, 1960. viii, [2], 116 p. On the author's work as editor and publisher of The Franklin press and the Highlands Maconian, Franklin, Macon County, Ga., 1945-60. [8236

JOHN THOMAS HARRIS. An analysis of capital use on owner-operated farms in the lower piedmont area of Georgia [1950. Athens, Ga.:] College of Agriculture, Univ. of Georgia, 1960. 91 p. diagrs., map, tables.

(Georgia. Experiment Stations. Bulletin, n. s., 74.) Issued in 1958 in microfilm form as thesis--Univ. of Illinois. [8237

Atlanta

FRANK HENRY NEELY. Rich's, a Southern institution since 1867. N.Y.: Newcomen Soc. in North America, 1960. 24 p. views. On a department store in Atlanta founded by Morris, Dan, and Emanuel Rich. [8238

AUGUST MEIER. History of the Negro upper class in Atlanta, Georgia, 1890-1958. Jour. Negro educ., 28:128-39 (spring 1959). notes. [8239

FRANCIS WRIGHT BRADLEY. Little Mary Fagan. South. folklore quar., 24: 144-6 (Jun). On the murder of Mary Phagan, aged 14, in an Atlanta pencil factory, the trial and conviction of Leo M. Frank as her murderer, and his lynching by a mob, 1913-15; with 2 undated oral versions of a ballad, collected in South Carolina, reciting these events. [8240

FLORIDA

BERTHA ERNESTINE BLOODWORTH. Florida place-names. Ann Arbor: University Microfilms, 1959 [i. e. 1960]. Positive microfilm of typescript. [264] leaves. Thesis--Univ. of Florida. Abstracted: Dissert. abstracts, 20:2790-91 (Jan). Study of a sample consisting of some 2,400 names. [8241

JOHN MANN GOGGIN. The first Floridians. Fla. handbook, 1951-52, p. 343-8. On the Indians of Florida since prehistoric times, particularly the Seminoles, who began to move into the peninsula ca. 1750. Repeated in later biennial editions. [8242

The INNER glory: why we are proud of our State. Fla. handbook, 1951-52, p. 1-30. maps, ports., seals, view. Miscellany of description and history, including accounts of the Battle of Marianna and the Battle of Olustee (1864), the Dade Massacre (1835), and the Suwanee River. Reprinted in part in later biennial editions. [8243

WILLIAM C. LAZARUS. Human figurines from the coast of northwest Florida. Fla. anthropol., 13:61-70 (Sep). map, tables, views. bibliog. On a whole figurine and 4 fragments, found on sites at Choctawhatchee Bay and St. Andrews Bay. [8244

WILLIAM HULSE SEARS. The Bayshore Homes site, St. Petersburg, Florida. Gainesville: Univ. of Florida, 1960. [8], 35, [3] p. diagrs., maps, plans, tables, views. bibliog. (p. 34-5). (Contributions of the Florida State Museum: social sciences, 6.) On recent investigations of an Indian mound and the culture in which it originated. [8245

JOHN MANN GOGGIN. The Spanish olive jar: an introductory study. New Haven: Dept. of Anthropology, Yale Univ., 1960. 40 p. diagrs., tables, views. bibliog. (p. 35-7). (Yale University publications in anthropology, 62. [Part of a volume entitled: Papers in Caribbean anthropology, ed. Sidney Wilfred Mintz, containing nos. 57-64 of the series.]) On the styles and varieties of clay jars made in Spain "primarily ... for the shipping of liquid, semisolid, and perhaps solid materials," 1490s?-early 1800s; with a list of sites in Florida, Cuba, the Bahamas, etc., where shards of these jars have been found. [8246

DOROTHY MORRIS & ALLEN MORRIS. Florida's names: the traces of the years. Fla. handbook, 1955-56, p. 1-41. bibliog. Alphabetical encyclopedia of Florida place-name origins and histories since 1513. Repeated in later biennial editions. [8247

REMBERT WALLACE PATRICK. Florida under five flags [1513-1960. Third edition.] Gainesville: Univ. of Florida Press, 1960. xii, 158 p. facsims., maps, ports., tables, views. bibliog. (p. 148-51). 1st ed. 1945. [8248

JAMES LEITCH WRIGHT, JR. Sixteenth century English-Spanish rivalry in La Florida [1513-1600]. Fla. hist. quar., 38:265-79 (Apr). notes. [8249

TONY JOSEPH CUNHA. Florida: birthplace of nation's beef industry. Fla. handbook, 1953-54, p. 170-75. view. On Florida as the landing-place of the first cattle "introduced to the American mainland," 1520, the Seminoles as "the first cattlemen of Florida," the poor quality of Florida cattle in the next 3 centuries, and the recent great improvements in quality and expansion of production of beef cattle in the State. [8250

LEO ARTHUR GOLDBLATT. Don Dorotheo Theodoro, first chemical technologist of the New World. Jour. chem. educ., 36:519-20 (Oct 1959). notes. On his participation in a

Spanish expedition under Pánfilo de Narváez to Florida, and his supervision of the pitching of boats with resin near Apalachicola Bay, Fla., 1527-28. [8251

CLEVELAND VAN DRESSER. Multiple use wildlife refuge. Am. forests, 65(3):20-21, 46-8 (Mar 1959). views. On St. Marks National Wildlife Refuge, "107,000 acres of land and water lying on the Gulf Coast some twenty miles south of Tallahassee," in an area explored as early as 1527. [8252

JUNIUS ELMORE DOVELL. Transportation: the magic key. Fla. handbook, 1953-54, p. 23-35. views. On boats and ships, roads and highways, and railroads in Florida, 1560s-1950s. Repeated in later biennial editions. [8253

A FRENCH document relating to the destruction of the French colony in Florida at the hands of the Spanish. Translated and edited by A. E. Hammond. Fla. hist. quar., 39:55-61 (Jul). notes. Translation of anonymous letter, of which the text was printed as early as 1591; with editorial remarks on the indifference of the French Government, dominated by Catholics, toward pressing for reparations for atrocities of which almost all the victims were Protestants. [8254

CHARLES W. ARNADE. The failure of Spanish Florida [1565-1763]. Americas, 16:271-81 (Jan). notes. On the causes of "failure." [8255

ARTHUR FORREST CAMP. Citrus growing in Florida [since 1579]. Fla. handbook, 1951-52, p. 50-51. On the growing of oranges, grapefruit, and lemons, and their shipment to distant markets. See also "Citrus processing," by L. G. MacDowell (same volume, p. 52-4), on the preparation of citrus fruit juices and frozen orange concentrate since the early 1920s. [8256

JAMES LEITCH WRIGHT, JR. Andrew Ranson [born ca. 1650]: seventeenth century pirate? Fla. hist. quar., 39: 135-44 (Oct). notes. On his privateering or piratical activities off Florida, his capture in 1684, his trial as a pirate in St. Augustine, the breaking of the rope at his intended execution, his rescue by Franciscan friars, his stay in St. Augustine as a prisoner working as a carpenter and engineer, and his release in 1702 as a reward for services in the defense of St. Augustine against an attack from South Carolina. [8257

ETHEL CUTLER FREEMAN. Culture stability and change among the Seminoles of Florida [1700-1956]. International Congress of Anthropological and Ethnological Sciences, 5th, 1956, Men and cultures: selected papers, ed. Anthony F. C. Wallace (Phila.: Univ. of Pennsylvania Press [1960]), p. 249-54. [8258

JOHN JAY TE PASKE. The governorship of Spanish Florida, 1700-1763. Ann Arbor: University Microfilms, 1959 [i. e. 1960]. Positive microfilm of typescript. [569] leaves. Thesis--Duke Univ. Abstracted: Dissert, abstracts, 20:3702 (Mar). [8259

THEODORE THOMAS WENTWORTH, JR. Pensacola memorabilia. Fla. hist. quar., 39:46-51 (Jul). Remarks on Andrew Jackson in Florida (1821) and St. Michael's Cemetery (first used in 1781). [8260

EDWIN DART LAMBRIGHT. Gasparilla, last of the buccaneers. Fla. handbook, 1953-54, p. 21-3. Based upon the author's book of the same title (1936). On José Gaspar (born ca. 1756), originally an officer of the Spanish Navy, who turned pirate in 1783, established headquarters at Charlotte Harbor, Fla., "captained a crew of marauders", and in 1821 committed suicide to avoid capture by the USS Enterprise; with mention of buried treasure. [8261

HELEN HORNBECK TANNER. The 1789 Saint Augustine celebration. Fla. hist. quar., 38:280-93 (Apr). notes. On observances organized by Gov. Vicente Manuel de Zéspedes in honor of the ascension of Charles IV to the Spanish throne. [8262

WILLIAM THOMAS CASH (1878-1951). Andrew Jackson in Florida [1814, 1818, 1821]. Fla. handbook, 1949-50, p. 157-60. port. Repeated in later biennial editions. [8263

VIRGINIA K. JONES, ed. The Bowie letters, 1819 and 1821. Ala. hist. quar., 22:231-43 (winter). notes. George Bowie to his brother John (Abbeville, S.C., 24 Aug. and 29 Sep. 1819), on the writer's plans to remove to Pensacola; Louisa Bowie (daughter of George) to a cousin in Abbeville (Pensacola, 18 Jun. 1821), describing Pensacola and the recent settlement of the George Bowie family there; and parts of 2 letters from Mrs. Andrew Jackson to friends in Nashville (Pensacola, 21 Jun. and 23 Jul. 1821). [8264

JANE KELLY SHEARER. Furniture and household textiles of residents of middle Florida, 1820-1865. Ann Arbor: University Microfilms, 1960. Positive microfilm of typescript. [221] leaves. Thesis--Florida State Univ. Abstracted: Dissert. abstracts, 20:4390 (May). [8265

ORIGIN of county names [in Florida since 1821]. Fla. handbook, 1949-50, p 171-6. view. [8266

The GOVERNORS of Florida [1822-1959]. Fla. handbook, 1949-50, p. 8-14. Biographical sketches in chronological order. Repeated in later biennial editions, with added sketches. [8267

LAURA BELLINGER JONES, comp. South Carolineans [sic] who removed to Florida: miscellaneous notes. South. genealogist's exchange quar., 2(7):10-12; (14):4-6 (fall 1958, summer 1960). Information mainly from the Southern Christian advocate, the Southern Baptist, and the Southern intelligencer, about persons who married or died in Florida, 1822, 1853-64. [8268

DOROTHY DODD. Tallahassee: out of the wilderness [1823-1949]. Fla. handbook, 1951-52, p. 25-9. map. Repeated in later biennial editions. [8269

KENNETH WIGGINS PORTER. Thlonoto-Sassa: a note on an obscure Seminole village of the early 1820s. Fla. anthropol., 13:115-19 (Dec). notes. On a name meaning "plenty of flints," variously applied to "a chain of ponds," a "hammock," and probably a village, all near Tampa Bay, between 1823 and 1838. [8270

U.S. Dept. of State. The Territorial papers of the United States. Compiled and edited by Clarence Edwin Carter. Volume XXIV [and XXV]. The Territory of Florida, 1824-1834 [and 1834-1839]. Wash.: National Archives, 1959[-60]. 2 v. [8], 1143; [8], 790 p. maps. notes. Papers relating to the administrations of Governors William P. Du Val, John H. Eaton, and Richard K. Call. [8271

H. MARSHALL TAYLOR. He first made ice. Fla. handbook, 1849-50, p. 144-8. port. On Dr. John Gorrie (1803-55), who practiced medicine at Apalachicola, Fla., from 1833 till his death, experimented with "controlling temperature as a therapeutic measure in treating fevers," invented an ice-making machine patented in 1851, but failed to obtain financial support for manufacturing it. [8272

RUPERT JAMES LONGSTREET. The story of Mount Dora, Florida [1836-1960. Mount Dora:] Mount Dora Historical Soc., 1960. xiii, [3], 246 p. maps, ports., tables, views. bibliog. (p. xiii), notes. On "a Florida town almost entirely settled by northern people"; with a section on "The early families" (p. 175-213). [8273

THOMAS W. HAGAN. The long battle for Statehood [Florida, 1837-45]. Fla. handbook, 1953-54, p. 87-95. double map. Repeated in later biennial editions. [8274

U.S. Census Office. 6th Census, 1840. 6th Census of Florida, 1840, U.S. South. genealogist's exchange quar., 1(1-3, 5-8), 2(9-10): quarterly installments (spring 1957 - summer 1959). [8275

A. G. MATTHEWS. Water: friend and foe. Fla. handbook, 1949-50, p. 280-96. view. On "water problems in Florida," 1847-1947, beginning with a report by Buckingham Smith recommending Federal assistance in the drainage and development of the Everglades. [8276

KARL AUGUST BICKEL. General Lee surveys the coast. Fla. handbook, 1951-52, p. 21-4. On visits of Robert E. Lee to Florida, 1848, 1861, 1862, 1870. [8277

FRANK EDWARD MOLONEY & SHELDON J. PLAGER. Florida's lakes: problems in a water paradise. Univ. Fla. law rev., 13:1-82 (spring). table. notes. On rights of riparian owners, the public, and commercial users to use of the shores and waters of navigable lakes, and "rights attributable to non-navigable lakes," 1856-1959; with a list of "Meandered Florida lakes." [8278

Mrs. C. E. FIELDS, comp. Oak Hill Cemetery, Bartow, Polk County, Florida. South. genealogist's exchange quar., 2(16):5-11 (winter). Inscriptions, 1859-1959. [8279

HELEN (STEERE) HAINES & ROBERT THOBURN. 75 years of dentistry. Gainesville: Univ. of Florida Press, 1960. xv, 418 p. facsims., map, ports., tables, views. notes. On the Florida State Dental Society, 1884-1959. Includes chapters on "The pioneer dentists of Florida" (1860s-80s), the Florida State Board of Dental

Examiners (founded 1887), and the Journal of the Florida State Dental Society (begun in 1922). [8280

JOHN EDWIN JOHNS. Florida in the Confederacy. Ann Arbor: University Microfilms, 1959 [i. e. 1960]. Positive microfilm of typescript. 460 leaves. bibliog. (leaves 435-60). Thesis--Univ. of North Carolina. Abstracted: Dissert. abstracts, 20:3270 (Feb). [8281

JOSEPH D. CUSHMAN, JR. The Episcopal Church in Florida during the Civil War. Fla. hist. quar., 38: 294-301 (Apr). notes. [8282

DOROTHY DODD. Florida in the War, 1861-1865. Fla. handbook, 1959-60, p. 1-90. facsims., maps, ports., views. notes. [8283

FLORIDA on the eve of the Civil War as seen by a Southern reporter. Edited by William Warren Rogers. Fla. hist. quar., 39:145-58 (Oct). notes. From the Charleston Daily courier, 1-8 Apr. 1861. Six letters from "Batchelor," 27 Mar.-5 Apr. 1861, on "the landscape and various forms of plant and animal life ... the towns he visited and the activities he found within them." [8284

JOE M. RICHARDSON. The Freedmen's Bureau and Negro labor in Florida. Fla. hist. quar., 39:167-74 (Oct). notes. On the activities of the Bureau in supervising labor contracts between Negroes and planters and in enforcing fulfillment of the contracts by both parties, 1866-67. [8285

ALEXANDER LOVELL MURRAY. Harriet Beecher Stowe on racial segregation in the schools. Am. quar., 12:518-19 (winter). notes. Quotations from her correspondence about a school established by her at Mandarin, Fla., for "both white and black children," to meet in a single large room, "divided by folding doors, one [section] for the whites and one for the blacks," 1869. [8286

JEANNE BELLAMY. The Everglades National Park. Fla. handbook, 1955-56, p. 43-50. port., views. Repeated in later biennial editions. On the flora and fauna of the area; with an account of the traffic in "egret scalps--skins with the feathers on" as ornaments on women's hats, ca. 1870 to ca. 1910. [8287

HAROLD MEHLING. The most of everything: the story of Miami Beach [1870-1960]. N.Y.: Harcourt, Brace [1960. 8], 182 p. bibliog. (p. 181-2). deals largely with the now declining hotel industry of this community. [8288

JAMES RUFUS TRYON (born 1837). The yellow fever epidemic of 1874 at Pensacola, Florida: the report of Surgeon J. R. Tryon, U.S. Navy. Edited by Eugene F. Kramer. Mil. med., 125:351-5 (May). notes. Report dated U.S. Naval Hospital, Pensacola, addressed to Surgeon General Joseph Beale, 26 Nov. 1874, on the "causes and course of the epidemic together with recommendations to prevent another outbreak." [8289

EDWARD C. WILLIAMSON. George F[ranklin] Drew [died 1900]: Florida's Redemption governor [1877-80]. Fla. hist. quar., 38:206-15 (Jan). notes. [8290

CARL D. BROREIN. Telephone communications [in Florida, since 1880]. Fla. handbook, 1951-52, p. 42-5. Repeated in later biennial editions. [8291

ULYSSES SIMPSON GRANT (1822-85). Grant forecasts the future of Florida. Edited by James P. Jones. Fla. hist. quar., 39:52-4 (Jul). notes. Letter to Elihu B. Washburne, 18 Jan. 1880, applauding the climate, natural resources, and business prospects of Florida. [8292

CARLTON JONATHAN CORLISS. Henry M. Flagler--railroad builder. Fla. hist. quar., 38:195-205 (Jan). On his contributions to the hotel and railroad industries of Florida, 1883-1913, his founding and development of Miami, and particularly his construction of the Key West Extension, a railroad begun in 1904, finished in 1914, and sold to the State (except the section north of Florida City) as the foundation for an oversea highway after 1935. [8293

ROBERT BARNWELL FULLER. The phosphate industry [in Florida, since 1883]. Fla. handbook, 1951-52, p. 36-8. [8294

McGREGOR SMITH. Electric power [in Florida, since 1883]. Fla. handbook, 1951-52, p. 40-42. Repeated in later biennial editions. [8295

U.S. Weather Bureau. Hurricane facts. By Richard W. Gray. Revised by Grady Norton. Fla. handbook, 1949-50, p. 236-40. tables. "Abridged slightly from a Weather Bureau document available in its entirety for five cents from the Government Printing Office." On the 78 "tropical cyclones of all intensities" that have visited Florida between 1886 and 1948, of which "50 have been known to be of hurricane intensity," and their associations with tornadoes and tides. Repeated in later biennial editions. [8296

ELEANOR HOWARD (DEAN) PEARSE. Florida's vanishing era. From the journals of a young girl and her father [Charles A. Dean], 1887 to 1910. [Second edition. Winnetka? Ill., 1949. 18], 72, [1], 73-75, [6] p. map, ports., views. 1st ed. 1947. On boating and fishing, weather, hotels, etc., as observed by the Dean family from Boston, winter boarders in Punta Gorda and the Charlotte Harbor area and travelers as far as Miami, Key West, and the Caloosahatchee River. Lavishly illustrated with photographs taken by the author and her father. Appended: letters from Henry F. Libby, 7-28 Dec. 1918, on his search for "The Great White Crane" and his participation in a turkey hunt, and "Alligators I have met," by Charles A. Dean, 10 Feb. 1907, on his encounters with these reptiles since his first visit to Florida in 1862. [8297

WILLIAM C. STURTEVANT. A Seminole medicine maker. Joseph B. Casagrande, ed., In the company of man: twenty portraits by anthropologists (N.Y.: Harper [1960]), p. 505-32. ports. On Josie Billie (born ca. 1887), Seminole of Big Cypress Reservation, Fla., medicine man, later a convert to Christianity, interviewed by the author between 1951 and 1953. [8298

WILLIAM J. SCHELLINGS. Florida and the Cuban Revolution, 1895-1898. Fla. hist. quar., 39:175-86 (Oct). notes. Survey of newspaper opinion, emphasizing the fear prevalent in Florida that war with Cuba would be followed by annexation, which would bring "Cuban competition in the areas of citrus fruit growing, truck farming, and sugar cane," and also in cigar-manufacturing and the tourist trade. [8299

EMRYS C. HARRIS. Gateway of the Americas. Harvard alumni bul., 58: 353-5, 361 (4 Feb 1956). views. On Miami, Fla., 1896-1956. [8300

FLORIDA. Geological Survey. Exploration for oil and gas in Florida (20th century). By Dr. Herman Gunter. Fla. handbook, 1949-50, p. 297-9. "A digest of Information Circular No. 1 (revised), Florida Geological Survey, with data added for 1949 to September 1, 1949." Repeated with revisions in later biennial editions. [8301

PAUL D. TROXLER. Water control progress in the Everglades [1901-60]. Am. Water Works Assoc., Jour., 52:742-8 (Jun). maps, view. [8302

WILLIAM C. LAZARUS. Wings over Florida. Fla. handbook, 1949-50, p. 165-8. Chronology of aviation in Florida, 1908-49. [8303

JAMES T. HOPKINS. Fifty years of citrus: the Florida Citrus Exchange, 1909-1959. Gainesville: Univ. of Florida Press, 1960. ix, [1], 279 p. ports., views. On an organization formed by the Florida Orange Growers Convention as a marketing outlet, and its efforts in recent years to protect the fresh-fruit trade against processed fruit and against concentration of buying power in chain or "volume buyers." [8304

SAMUEL PROCTOR. William Jennings Bryan and the University of Florida. Fla. hist. quar., 39:1-15 (Jul). notes. On his speeches at the University on the infallibility of Scripture, the wickedness of all evolutionary doctrines, the sinfulness of drinking alcoholic beverages, and need of college young men and women for constant moral surveillance and guidance from college authorities, 1916-25, and his service in campaigns to collect money and promote legislation in support of these causes. [8305

JOSEPH F. McDERMOTT. Statutory rape: previous chaste character in Florida [1918-59]. Univ. Fla. law rev., 13:201-14 (summer). notes. [8306

FRANKLIN L. JONES. The pulp industry. Fla. handbook, 1951-52, p. 45-7. view. On the Kraft or Sulphate process for making pulp from Southern pine in Florida since 1931. Repeated in later biennial editions. [8307

A SLEEPLESS revolution. Fla. handbook, 1951-52, p. 63-4. On the success of markets operated by the Florida Agricultural Marketing Board, 1935-51, established as the result of efforts of Nathan Mayo, Florida Commissioner of Agriculture, to improve the quality and profits of the marketing of Florida agricultural products. [8308

ELIZABETH L. VIRRICK. New housing for Negroes in Dade County, Florida [1937-56]. Nathan Glazer & Davis McEntire, eds., Studies in housing & minority groups (Berkeley: Univ. of California Press, 1960), p. 135-43. table. notes. [8309

ELSIE MAY (LANDIS) YODER. Bay Shore Mennonite Church [Sarasota, Fla., 1937-53]. Mennonite hist. bul., 15(1):1-3 (Jan 1954). view. [8310

BENJAMIN F. ROGERS. Florida in World War II: tourists and citrus [1941-45]. Fla. hist. quar., 39:34-41 (Jul). notes. [8311

CLAUDE F. WERTZ. Miami lime recovery plant [1941-59]. Am. Water Works Assoc., Jour., 52:326-32 (Mar). tables. [8312

CLEMENT HAROLD DONOVAN. Florida's State and local tax structure [1942-59]. Univ. Fla. law rev., 13: 518-30 (winter). tables. [8313

FRANKIE WARNER. Sand, surf, and quarter horses. West. horseman, 25(1):32, 76-7, 82 (Jan). port., views. On the Florida Quarter Horse Association, 1945-59. [8314

CLEVELAND VAN DRESSER. Elbow room for sportsmen. Am. forests, 62(6):18-19 (Jun 1956). port., views. On the Steinhatchee Wildlife Management Area, a hunting and fishing area on the Gulf coast of Florida, established by the Florida State Game and Fresh Water Fish Commission, 1948-56. [8315

JOHN MELVIN DE GROVE. The Florida Flood Control District. University, Ala.: Univ. of Alabama Press for the ICP [1960]. 24 p. maps. notes. (Inter-University Case Program. ICP case series, 58.) On conflict between W. Turner Wallis, executive officer of the Central and Southern Florida Flood Control District, and members of its governing board, appointed by the successive Governors of Florida, 1949-56. [8316

U.S. Congress. Senate. Committee on Interior and Insular Affairs. Castillo de San Marcos National Monument. Wash.: U.S. Govt. Print. Off., 1960. iii, 42 p. Hearings, 7 Jun. 1960, before the Subcommittee on Public Lands, on H. R. 8266, an act to add certain lands to Castillo de San Marcos National Monument in the State of Florida, proposing to demolish a number of old houses in St. Augustine to provide parking space for tourists visiting the Castillo de San Marcos. [8317

The Southeast

THOMAS McDOWELL NELSON LEWIS & MADELINE KNEBERG. The Archaic culture in the middle South. Am. antiq., 25:161-83 (Oct 1959). chron. chart, tables, views. bibliog. Study of "data from 22 Archaic sites in four ecologically similar regions in Kentucky, Tennessee, Alabama, and Georgia," ca. 6000 B.C. to the early Christian era. [8318

EDWARD V. McMICHAEL & JAMES H. KELLAR. Archaeological salvage in the Oliver Basin. Athens: Univ. of Georgia, 1960. [6], iii, 221, [2] p. diagrs., maps (1 fold.), plans, tables, views. bibliog. (p. 220-21). (University of Georgia. Laboratory of Archaeology. Report 2.) Report of recent investigations on the Alabama and Georgia sides of the Chattahoochee River above Columbus, Ga., in an area to be flooded by the Oliver Dam, revealing 51 prehistoric sites and indications of 13 historic sites, occupied from ca. 8000 B.C. to A.D. 1836. [8319

EDWARD V. McMICHAEL. Towards the estimation of prehistoric population. Ind. Acad. Science, Proc., 69: 78-82. diagrs. bibliog. Exposition of a method applied to prehistoric materials in the Oliver Basin of the Chattahoochee Valley in Alabama and Georgia. [8320

WILLIAM C. STURTEVANT. The significance of ethnological similarities between Southeastern North America and the Antilles. New Haven: Dept. of Anthropology, Yale Univ., 1960. 58 p. bibliog. (p. 45-58). (Yale University publications in anthropology, 64. Part of a volume edited by Sidney Wilfred Mintz containing nos. 57-64 of the series, with title: Papers in Caribbean anthropology.) Demonstration "that the ethnological evidence thought by various writers to point to Antillean influences throughout the Southeast does not in fact run counter to the archeological indications that such influence did not take place," and that if there was "a cultural relationship between south Florida and western Cuba," it was "more likely to have been an influence of the Southeast on the West Indies than the reverse." [8321

GREGORY JOSEPH KEEGAN & LEANDRO TORMO SANZ. Experiencia misionera en la Florida (siglos XVI y XVII). Madrid: Consejo Superior de Investigaciones Científicas, 1957. 404, [1] p. fold. maps. bibliog. (p. 27-46), notes. (Instituto Santo Toribio de Mogrovejo. Biblioteca "Missionalia Hispanica," serie B, vol. VII.) On efforts to establish missions in Florida and adjacent areas as early as 1526, the failures and martyrdoms of various Jesuit and Franciscan missionaries, the establishment of missions in northern Florida and on the coasts of Georgia and of South Carolina, and the condition of the Franciscan missions in 1655 and 1675; with preliminary chapters on the geography, Indians, and discovery and exploration of Florida. [8322

JAMES HENRI HOWARD. The Yamasee: a supposedly extinct Southeastern tribe rediscovered. Am. anthropol., 62:681-3 (Aug). On the recorded career of this tribe in Georgia, the Carolinas, and Florida, 1540-1778; with indications that the "Altamaha Cherokee" now living about 10 miles south of Augusta, Ga., are actually a remnant of the Yamasees, though they "have lost their native speech." [8323

EMMA LILA FUNDABURK, comp. Southeastern Indians, life portraits: a catalogue of pictures, 1564-1860. Luverne, Ala., 1958. 135, [1] p. maps, ports., views. Reproductions of 343 paintings and prints showing Indians in the area from Virginia to the Mississippi and the Gulf of Mexico (p. 6-95); and "Notes on the illustrations" (p. 96-133), including excerpts from works on the Indians, with bibliographical citations. [8324

ERHARD ROSTLUND. The geographic range of the historic bison in the Southeast. Assoc. Am Geographers, Ann., 50:395-407 (Dec). map. notes. Review of historic evidence (1565-1779), archeological evidence, and place names, indicating that "In 1500 A.D. the buffalo (Bison bison) had not yet entered the Southeast," that a migration began after 1650 and reached its widest extent by ca. 1700. Relates the incursions of the buffalo to a great decline in the Indian population, reducing the number of hunters and leaving "old fields" in grass. [8325

JAMES ADAIR (died 1783). The Cheerake Nation. Margaret Mead & Ruth L. Bunzel, eds., The golden age of American anthropology (N.Y.: George Braziller, 1960), p. 106-11. From the author's History of the American Indians (London, 1775). On the wars, games, and government of the Cherokees in western North Carolina and adjoining parts of Georgia and Tennessee as observed by the author, a trader, since the 1730s. [8326

KNOX MELLON, JR. Christian Priber and the Jesuit myth. S.C. hist. mag., 61:75-81 (Apr). notes. Evidence that this individual, who lived among the Cherokees for some years after 1736, was not a Jesuit and that his full name was Christian Gottlieb Priber, born in Zittau, Saxony, in 1697, author of a Latin dissertation (Erfurt, 1722), lawyer in Zittau, with a wife and children there. [8327

JAMES EDWARD OGLETHORPE (1696-1785). Oglethorpe's statement on Christian Pryber. Edited by Katharine De Baillou. Ga. hist. quar., 44:100-101 (Mar). notes. Enclosure in a letter to the Duke of Newcastle, 22 Apr. 1743, on the capture of Pryber by Indians and the seizure of his journals and other papers, indicating that he intended to establish among the Cherokee Indians a community of "debtors, Transport Felons, Servants, & Negroe Slaves" escaping from the Carolinas and Virginia, and to incite the Indians to kill the English traders among them. [8328

EAST FLORIDA (British colony). English gifts to the Indians: 1765-1766. [Edited] by James Covington. Fla. anthropol., 13:71-5 (Sep). bibliog. "Account of presents delivered to the Indians at the Congress of Picolata," 15 Nov. 1765, by Alex Skinner, "Keeper of Indian Presents and Clerk of the Public Accounts"; "State of presents wanting to compleat an assortment for meeting proposed to be held with Indians in 1766," by James Grant, Governor; and "Glossary of terms." [8329

DANIEL MALLOY SMITH. James Seagrove and the mission to Tuckaubatchee, 1793. Ga. hist. quar., 44: 41-55 (Mar). notes. On his success, as an agent of the U.S. Government, in crossing the Georgia boundary "into the turbulent Creek nation," and preventing a major war between the Creeks and the United States. [8330

MARTIN MARSHALL (1782-1865). Herbs, hoecakes, and husbandry: the daybook of a planter of the old South. Edited by Weymouth T[yree] Jordan. Tallahassee: Florida State Univ. Press, 1960. 137 p. bibliog. (p. 131-2), notes. (Florida State University studies, 34.) "Martin Marshall's book," a volume kept by Marshall and his family at Columbia, S.C., on a small plantation near Columbia, and later on his plantation near Fort Claiborne, Ala., from 1802 till the 1860s, containing clippings and manuscript information on housekeeping, cooking, herbs and their medicinal uses, home remedies, veterinary practices, farming methods, etc. [8331

HUNT FAMILY. [Letters.] Ala. hist. quar., 22:94-100 (spring-summer). Letters from John Hunt (26 Jul. 1826), David and Elizabeth Hunt (Nov. 1830), and William B. Hunt (28 Jul. 1835 - 17 Nov. 1839), to various members of the Hunt family. Williams letters from Florida relate to his service as a captain in the Alabama Volunteers during the Seminole War. [8332

DAVID JONES. Clifford Anderson Lanier [1844-1908]. Ga. rev., 14: 205-14 (summer). On Sidney Lanier's younger brother, Georgian, Confederate soldier, businessman in Montgomery, Ala., poet, novelist; with an examination of his writings. [8333

ROBERT A. THOMPSON, HYLAN LEWIS, & DAVIS McENTIRE. Atlanta and Birmingham: a comparative study in Negro housing [1880-1955]. Nathan Glazer & Davis McEntire, eds., Studies in housing & minority groups (Berkeley: Univ. of California Press, 1960), p. 13-83. maps, tables. notes. [8334

MARY TUTWILER ANDERSON. Mountain people. Tenn. Folklore Soc. bul., 26:87-91 (Dec). Recollections of 74 years at the foot of, or on, Lookout Mountain, at the intersection of Alabama, Georgia, and Tennessee. [8335

WILLARD BADGETTE GATEWOOD, JR. North Carolina's role in the establishment of the Great Smoky Mountains National Park [1899-1940]. N.C. hist. rev., 37:165-84 (Apr). views. notes. On activities of North Carolina in conjunction with Tennessee and the U.S. Government [8336

CARLOS CLINTON CAMPBELL. Birth of a national park in the Great Smoky Mountains: an unprecedented crusade which created, as gift of the people, the nation's most popular park. [Knoxville: Univ. of Tennessee Press, 1960.] xii, 155 p. facsims., maps (1 double), ports., tables, views. notes. On the work of the Great Smoky Mountains Conservation Association (founded in 1923), the establishment of the Great Smoky Mountains National Park in North Carolina and Tennessee in 1934, and its development and expansion to 1960. [8337

ARTHUR STUPKA. Great Smoky Mountains National Park, North Carolina and Tennessee [1923-60]. Wash., 1960. [4], 75 p. fold. map, views (1 double). bibliog. (p. 68-70). (U.S. National Park Service. Natural history handbook series, 5.) Deals mainly with the natural history of the area. [8338

MELTON FISHER WRIGHT. Fortress of faith: the story of Bob Jones University. Grand Rapids: Eerdmans [1960]. 300 p. ports., views. On Bob Jones College, an interdenominational college at New Panama City, Fla., 1926-33, and Cleveland, Tenn., 1933-46, continued at Greenville, S.C., as Bob Jones University since 1947; with an account of its founder, Robert Reynolds Jones (born 1883), his early life in Dale County, Ala., his studies at Southern University in Greensboro, Ala., and his work as a minister and evangelist of an unnamed denomination. [8339

T. MADISON BYAR. The student population in the institutions of higher education in the southern Appalachian region, 1933-1958. Ann Arbor: University Microfilms, 1959 [i. e. 1960]. Positive microfilm of typescript. [228] leaves. Thesis (Ed. D.)--Univ. of Tennessee. Abstracted: Dissert. abstracts, 20:3177-8 (Feb). [8340

GEORGE B. NUTT. Mechanization of Southeast agriculture [in 8 States, 1935-49]. Agric. engineering, 31: 443-4 (Sep 1950). table. [8341

JOSEPH SARGENT HALL. Smoky Mountain folks and their lore. [Asheville? N.C.:] Published in cooperation with Great Smoky Mountains Natural History Assoc. [1960]. 68, [4] p. ports., views. Lore about the "old ways of life ... memorable events of the past ... folk tales ... tall tales ... proverbial sayings," anecdotes of hunting and murder, "Mountain beliefs and remedies," and "Smokies dialect," collected by the author from "interviews and conversations" with residents, mainly elderly, of areas later condemned or purchased for the Great Smoky Mountains National Park in Tennessee and North Carolina, 1937-57. [8342

ARCHIE REECE DYKES. A study of public school finance in the southern Appalachian region [1939-58]. Ann Arbor: University Microfilms, 1959 [i. e. 1960]. Positive microfilm of typescript. [285] leaves. Thesis (Ed. D.)--Univ. of Tennessee. Abstracted: Dissert. abstracts, 20: 4318-19 (May). [8343

U.S. Geological Survey. Floods of August 1940 in the Southeastern States [Virginia, the Carolinas, Georgia, West Virginia, and Tennessee]. Prepared by Water Resources Branch. Wash.: U.S. Govt. Print. Off., 1949. xi, 554 p. diagrs., fold. maps, tables, views. (Its Water-supply paper 1066.) [8344

E. V. SMITH. Agricultural engineering challenges in the Southeast [1943-48]. Agric. engineering, 29:162 (Apr 1948). [8345

ALTO LUTHER GARNER. Migration of notables to and from the Southeast. Ann Arbor: University Microfilms, 1954 [i. e. 1960]. Positive microfilm of typescript. xx, 530 leaves. map, tables. bibliog. (leaves 529-30). Thesis (Ed. D.)--Univ. of Kentucky. Abstracted: Dissert. abstracts, 20: 4310-11 (May). Based upon Who's who in America, 1952-53. [8346

JOHN EDMUND BREWTON. Folk rimes of Southern children. Tenn. Folklore Soc. bul., 26:92-9 (Dec). notes. Texts collected in Tennessee and in Marion County, Ga. [8347

BEVERLY LAZARUS LEVENSON & MYRON H. LEVENSON. Some Southern folk remedies and related beliefs. N.C. folklore, 9(2):26-31 (Dec). notes. Lore from 5 unnamed towns in the Carolinas and Alabama. [8348

The Gulf States

WILLIAM HULSE SEARS. The Gulf coastal plain in North American prehistory. International Congress of Anthropological and Ethnological Sciences, 5th, 1956, Men and cultures: selected papers, ed. Anthony F. C. Wallace (Phila.: Univ. of Pennsylvania Press [1960]), p. 632-8. diagrs. On the archeology of the area from eastern Texas and southeastern Oklahoma to the northwest coast of Florida. [8349

DANIEL A. JACOBSON. The origin of the Koasati community of Louisiana. Ethnohistory, 7:97-120 (spring). map. bibliog., notes. On the Koasati Indians as "subsistence farmers, hunters, and fishermen" with a "so-called mother town" near the junction of the Coosa and Tallapoosa Rivers in 1540, who were removing to the Red River in Louisiana in 1795, living in 2 villages on the Trinity River in Texas in 1820, settling on the Calcasieu River near Kinder, La., by 1850, and removing in and after 1884 to their present settlement on Bayou Blue, in Allen Parish, La., where since ca. 1910 they have been mainly employed as wage-earners on rice plantations. [8350

MARION ELIAS LAZENBY (1885-1957). History of Methodism in Alabama and West Florida [1808-1955. Edited by Franklin Shackelford Moseley. Nashville? 1960.] 1256 p. ports., tables, views. bibliog. (p. 13-14). [8351

THOMAS W. BELL (1815-71). Thomas W. Bell letters. Edited by Llerena Friend. Southw. hist. quar., 63:99-109, 299-310, 457-68, 589-99 (Jul 1959 - Apr 1960). Letters to the author's father (William Adam Bell of Gibson County, Tenn.) and other relatives, 10 Oct. 1836 - 18 Oct. 1853, on his farming at Grenada, Miss., his removal to Texas in 1839, his life as a carpenter in Austin, his teaching in Rutersville and studies in Rutersville College, his service in the Mier Expedition and imprisonment by the Mexicans, and his return to Gibson County, Tenn. [8352

ALAN LOMAX, ed. The rainbow sign: a Southern documentary. N.Y.: Duell, Sloan, and Pearce [1959. 6], 209 p. Edited from tape recordings of the reminiscences of "Nora;" of reminiscences and folk tales by the Rev. ---- Renfrew; and of "a country revival in northern Mississippi" in 1942. [8353

RICHARD WALTER MASSEY, JR. A history of the lumber industry in Alabama and West Florida, 1880-1914. Ann Arbor: University Microfilms, 1960. Positive microfilm of typescript. [233] leaves. Thesis--Vanderbilt Univ. Abstracted: Dissert. abstracts, 20:4385-6 (May). [8354

HAROLD COURLANDER, collector. Negro songs from Alabama. ... Music transcribed by John Benson Brooks. N.Y.: Published with the assistance of the Wenner-Gren Foundation for Anthropological Research, c1960. [4], 76 p. music. Words and music of 75 songs recorded in Alabama and Mississippi in 1950. Refers for fuller information to Negro folk music of Alabama (6 12-in. long-play records, 1950-56, and an accompaning 43-page pamphlet). [8355

ALABAMA

LOU ELLEN BALLARD, recorder. Some tales of local color from southeast Alabama. South. folklore quar., 24:147-56 (Jun). notes. Collected from "old folks" in Crenshaw, Butler, and Covington Counties. [8356

T. W. DANIEL, JR., & EARL L. HASTINGS. A preliminary geological and archaeological survey of the Weiss Dam Reservoir [in the Coosa Valley of Cherokee County, Ala.]. Ala. Acad. Science, Jour., 30(3):16-20 (Jan). bibliog. Includes some account of historic sites that will be flooded. [8357

CARL ELLIOTT, ed. Annals of northwest Alabama. [Volume II.] Tuscaloosa, Ala.: Priv. print., 1959. 288 p. Thirty-six contributions by various authors. Includes reminiscences by William Jesse Bonds, Florence Sizemore, and Margaret Jane Massey Byram; biographical sketches of John Williams Rogers, Hezekiah Massey, Allen Talmadge Owen, and Dr. Alvin Steele Davidson; accounts of the Wakefield and Lucas-Dodson families and of Old Jasper Academy (1859-92), the Hamilton Agricultural School (1895-1933), and other institutions; "Some Franklin County, Alabama, gravestone records"; a list of post offices; 1830 U.S. Census of Walker County; "Sketch of early Cullman County, Alabama," by Marc Miller; "Early days of Franklin County," by William H. Key, Jr.; "Glimpses of early Fayette County, Alabama," by James A. Windle and Margaret D. Sizemore; etc. [8358

VIRGINIA ODEN FOSCUE. Sumter County place-names: a selection. Ala. rev., 13:52-67 (Jan). bibliog. Names of communities and settlements, selected from the author's thesis (M. A.)--Univ. of Alabama, 1959. [8359

DAVID LLOYD DE JARNETTE & ASAEL T. HANSEN. The archeology of the Childersburg site, Alabama. Tallahassee, 1960. vi, 65 p. diagrs., maps, tables, views. bibliog. (p. 64-5), notes. (Florida State University. Dept. of Anthropology. Notes in anthropology, 4.) Based on De Jarnette's thesis (M. A.)--Univ. of Alabama. On a site in Talladega County, Ala., believed to have been the site of Coosa, an Upper Creek town visited by the De Soto expedition in 1540, but shown by archeological evidence to have been occupied only from ca. 1700 to ca. 1825; with a detailed review of the historical and the archeological evidence. [8360

THOMAS CHALMERS McCORVEY (1851-1932). Tuscaloosa [1540-1925]: the second State capital of Alabama. T. C. McCorvey, Alabama historical sketches, ed. George Burke Johnston (Charlottesville: Univ. of Virginia Press, 1960), p. 95-116. notes. Printed as a "Tuscaloosa Rotary Club pamphlet, 1925." [8361

FLORENCE (DOLIVE) SCOTT. Montrose as it was recorded, told about, and lived [1768-1959. Montrose? Ala.] 1959 [c1960. 8], 168 p. coats of arms, maps, ports., views. Largely biographical. [8362

ALABAMA HALL OF FAME, Montgomery. Alabama Hall of Fame: its origin and thumbnail sketches of the Alabamians elected to membership. Montgomery, 1960. [28] p. 18 x 22 cm. col. coat of arms, facsim. Biographical sketches of 20 deceased "citizens of Alabama who have rendered exceptional service to the State and nation," born 1772-1874. [8363

J. M. STAUFFER. The timber resource of "the southwest Alabama forest empire" [1773-1956]. Ala. Acad. Science, Jour., 30(3):52-67 (Jan 1959). tables. bibliog. [8364

THOMAS CHALMERS McCORVEY (1851-1932). The Highland Scotch element in the early settlement of Alabama [1780s-1901]. T. C. McCorvey, Alabama historical sketches, ed. George Burke Johnston (Charlottesville: Univ. of Virginia Press, 1960), p. 65-76. bibliog. From the Alabama historical quarterly, 1930. Mainly on North Carolina Scots who removed to Alabama after 1814. [8365

RICHARD WORDEN GRIFFIN III. The manufacturing interests of Alabama planters, 1810-1830. Ala. Acad. Science, Jour., 30(2):63-71 (Oct 1958). notes. On efforts to promote the manufacture of coarse cotton goods (bagging, canvas, rope, etc.). [8366

JAMES FREDERICK SULZBY, JR. Historic Alabama hotels and resorts. [University:] Univ. of Alabama Press, 1960. [10], 294 p. views. bibliog. (p. 269-78). Detailed histories and descriptions of 56 "old watering places, taverns, country hotels and camp meeting places" established between 1815 and 1908, a few of which are still in operation. [8367

THOMAS CHALMERS McCORVEY (1851-1932). The vine and olive: a sketch of the colony of French imperialists that settled in Marengo County, Alabama, in 1818. T. C. McCorvey, Alabama historical sketches, ed. George Burke Johnston (Charlottesville: Univ. of Virginia Press, 1960), p. 77-89. bibliog. From the New Orleans Times-Democrat, 22 Feb. 1885. On the settlements of Demopolis and Eagleville, established by followers of Napoleon I, and their efforts to establish the culture of vines and olives, 1818-28. [8368

MARY GRANTHAM MARSHALL, comp. Greene County, Alabama, records. Compiled by Mrs. S. M. Marshall. Edited by Elizabeth Wood Thomas. Tuscaloosa, Ala.: Willo Pub. Co. [1960]. 139 p. Cemetery records, "Newspaper death notices" (1830-32, 1859, 1872-74), "Land patents" (1818-32), and "1830 census schedule." [8369

HERBERT MOSES NEWELL, JR., & JEANIE (PATTERSON) NEWELL. History of Fayette County, Alabama [1819-1959]. Fayette, Ala.: Newell Offset Print., c1960. [2], iii, 460, [1] p. maps, table. bibliog. (p. 426). "Family genealogies" (p. 196-425). [8370

JAY EMMETT THOMASON. The development of the administrative organization of the public school system of Alabama [1819-1935]. Ann Arbor: University Microfilms, 1959 [i. e. 1960]. Positive microfilm of typescript. [358] leaves. Thesis (Ed. D.)--Univ. of Alabama. Abstracted: Dissert. abstracts, 20:3618 (Mar). [8371

SIMON J. SMITH (born 1894). Toadvine in its heyday [ca. 1823 to 1960. Toadvine? Ala., 1960?] vii, [1], 184 p. geneal. charts, ports., tables, views. Includes "Genealogy" (p. 100-157) and the author's reminiscences (p. 90-99). [8372

WALTER BROWNLOW POSEY. Alabama in the 1830's. Emory Univ. quar., 16:129-38 (fall). bibliog. On impressions of Alabama formed by 6 British travelers: Tyrone Power, James Stuart, Thomas Hamilton, Harriet Martineau, James Silk Buckingham, and George W. Featherstonhaugh. [8373

GEORGE C. WHATLEY III. The Alabama Presbyterian and his slave, 1830-1864. Ala. rev., 13:40-51 (Jan). notes. [8374

NELLA JEAN CHAMBERS (died 1959). Early days in east Alabama. Ala. rev., 13:177-84 (Jul). notes. On Chambers County, Ala., 1813-43. [8375

THOMAS CHALMERS McCORVEY (1851-1932). Henry Tutwiler [1807-84] and the influence of the University of Virginia on education in Alabama. T. C. McCorvey, Alabama historical sketches, ed. George Burke Johnston (Charlottesville: Univ. of Virginia Press, 1960), p. 3-32. notes. From Transactions of the Alabama Historical Society, 1905. On his studies in the University of Virginia (1825-31); his service as the "first professor of ancient languages in the University of Alabama"; his later teaching at the Alabama Institute of Literature and Industry and at La Grange College (1837-47); and his work as founder and head of the Greene Springs School for Boys (1847-84). [8376

THOMAS CHALMERS McCORVEY (1851-1932). The mission of Francis Scott Key to Alabama in 1833. T. C. McCorvey, Alabama historical sketches, ed. George Burke Johnston (Charlottesville: Univ. of Virginia Press, 1960), p. 33-64. notes. From Transactions of the Alabama Historical Society, 1904. On his assignment to represent the U.S. Government in a conflict between State and Federal authority in an area within the boundaries of Alabama ceded to the United States by the Creek Indians in 1832; with some account of earlier Creek treaties since 1814. [8377

ANDREW GLAZE. Birmingham [Ala., 1834-1953]--or what has happened to Pink Worthington's frog pond. Harvard alumni bul., 55:505-7, 512 (21 Mar 1953). views. [8378

HENRY COUNTY, Ala. Transcripts [of] Henry County legal documents. Contributed by Mrs. Ethel Teague Jones. Ala. hist. quar., 22:273-5 (winter). Indenture for the sale of land on the Chattahoochee River by George Jones to Isaac D. Morgan, 28 Feb. 1835; and indenture conveying Chattahoochee lands from David H. Newton to George Jones, same date. [8379

HOROLD I. APOLINSKY. The development of riparian law in Alabama [since 1838]. Ala. law rev., 12:155-73 (fall 1959). notes. [8380

EMMA (PAYNE) FLOWERS. Ozark High School's march of time. Montgomery, Ala.: Brown Print. Co. [1960. 2], 52 p. facsims., ports., views. On the Ozark High School, Ozark, Ala., the Dale County High School, and their predecessors, 1841-1960. [8381

JOHN EDWARD THORNTON. Parol evidence for the construction of deeds and wills in Alabama [1841-1959]. Ala. law rev., 12:1-65 (fall 1959). notes. [8382

DAVID HENRY BRADLEY, SR. History of Big Zion Church, Mobile, Ala. [1842-1948]. A. M. E. Zion quar. rev., 68 (1957): 153-5. [8383

JAMES A. PATE. The development of the instructional program at Howard College, 1842-1957. Ann Arbor: University Microfilms, 1959 [i. e. 1960]. Positive microfilm of typescript. [608] leaves. Thesis (Ed. D.)--Univ. of Alabama. Abstracted: Dissert. abstracts, 20:3178-9 (Feb). Study of an institution founded by the Alabama Baptist State Convention. [8384

OSCAR LEALON TOMPKINS. Impeachment and removal of three circuit judges. Ala. lawyer, 21:211-21 (Apr). bibliog. On proceedings proposed or carried out against John P. Booth (1842), John B. Tally (1894), and "one Griffith" (1934). [8385

JAMES FLEETWOOD FOSTER (died 1912). Ante-bellum floating palaces of the Alabama River and the "good old times in Dixie" [1850-76]. ... Edited and annotated by Bert Neville. Selma, Ala., 1960. [4], 66 p. facsims., maps, views. notes. Nineteen reminiscent articles from The Wilcox banner, Camden, Ala., 1904. [8386

NANCY C. ROBERSON. Social mobility in ante-bellum Alabama. Ala. rev., 13: 135-45 (Apr). diagr., table. notes. On "the extent to which white people with differing economic backgrounds intermarried, as determined by an analysis of unpublished census data and marriage records" of Bibb, Clarke, Lawrence, Madison, and St. Clair Counties, 1851-55. [8387

BISHOP John Wesley Alstork [1852-1920]: a biographical sketch for release. A. M. E. Zion quar. rev., 64:103-4 (spring 1953). On his life in Alabama as a minister of the African Methodist Episcopal Church. [8388

THOMAS CHALMERS McCORVEY (1851-1932). Samuel Minturn Peck [born 1854]. T. C. McCorvey, Alabama historical sketches, ed. George Burke Johnston (Charlottesville: Univ. of Virginia Press, 1960), p. 246-54. First printed in 1909. On his life in Tuscaloosa, his studies at the University of Alabama and his medical education in New York City, his frequent travels in Europe, and his poems, prose sketches, and short stories. [8389

HARRY M. ROLLER, JR. The pulp and paper industry in the southwest Alabama forest empire [1856-1959]. Ala. Acad. Science, Jour., 30(3):67-72 (Jan 1959). bibliog. [8390

JAMES MONROE TORBERT. James M. Torbert's journal for 1857-1874. Ala. hist. quar., 22:1-76. Record of plantation and family affairs, health, and weather near Fort Bainbridge in Macon County, consisting of daily entries for 1857 and the first 4 months of 1859 and annual entries for 1858, 1859, and the following years; with various appended entries, including a list of 59 Negroes owned by the author with their dates of birth and death and the prices paid for them. Entries for 1856 were printed in this periodical in 1956. [8391

SUSAN MYRICK. Editress Lizzie Lynn; or, Who started all this? Ga. rev., 14:292-5 (fall). On the "articles about child-raising" in the Ladies' Department (edited by Lizzie Lynn) of The American cotton planter and the soil of the South (Montgomery, Ala.), 1860. [8392

ROBERT LOVE PARTIN. Dr. Jerome Cochran [1831-96], yellow fever fighter [in Alabama, 1865-89]. Ala. rev., 13:21-39 (Jan). notes. [8393

WILLIAM WARREN ROGERS. Agrarianism in Alabama, 1865-1896. Ann Arbor: University Microfilms, 1959 [i. e. 1960]. Positive microfilm of typescript. [580] leaves. Thesis--Univ. of North Carolina. Abstracted: Dissert. abstracts, 20:2764-5 (Jan).

On the efforts of Alabama farmers to better their lot through agricultural organizations and later through political action. [8394

GLENN N. SISK. The poor in provincial Alabama [in the 10-county Black Belt, 1865-1918]. Ala. hist. quar., 22: 101-2 (spring-summer). notes. [8395

WILLIAM WARREN ROGERS. The establishment of Alabama's land grant college [Agricultural and Mechanical College of Alabama, Auburn, 1871-73]. Ala. rev., 13:5-20 (Jan). notes. [8396

THOMAS D. RUSSELL. Russell of Alabama. N.Y.: Newcomen Soc. in North America, 1960. 32 p. port., views. On Benjamin Russell (1876-1941), the author's father, founder of the Russell Manufacturing Company, Alexander City, Ala., maker of cotton yarn and cotton cloth, cotton underwear and athletic apparel, and owner and operator of cotton plantations, tree farms, sawmills, and iron foundries. [8397

RALPH KENNAMER. A case of arson. Ala. lawyer, 21:333-5 (Jul). On the trial, conviction, and execution of George Smith and George and Asbury Hughes and the sentence of John Grayson to life imprisonment for the burning of the house of Henry Porter in Jackson County, Ala., 1883-84. [8398

EDWARD PALMER (1831-1911). Alabama notes made in 1883-1884: description of towns, Indian mounds, forts, Tuscaloosa, mounds near Blakely, Montgomery, etc. Ala. hist. quar., 22:244-72 (winter). Jottings made in Alabama by an investigator for the Bureau of American Ethnology. Includes information about hotels, meals, caves, and a variety of other subjects. [8399

EVANS C. JOHNSON. Oscar W. Underwood: a fledgling politician [in Alabama, 1884-94]. Ala. rev., 13: 109-26 (Apr). notes. [8400

ALABAMA BUSINESS RESEARCH COUNCIL. Water and economic growth: a study of Alabama and the Southeast. [University, Ala.:] School of Commerce and Business Administration, Univ. of Alabama, 1960. ix, 45 p. diagrs., form, maps, tables. notes. On "the supply side" and "the demand side" of "the water resources balance sheet" since 1885, with projections to 1975. [8401

WILLIAM WARREN ROGERS. The Negro Alliance in Alabama [1887-92]. Jour. Negro hist., 45:38-44 (Jan). notes. On local Negro farmers' organizations, working more or less in harmony with corresponding white organizations to further their agricultural interests, but gradually transformed into political groups. [8402

JOHN WILL GAY, SR. The judges of Jackson County [1889-1959]. North Ala. Hist. Assoc., Bul., 5:21-3. [8403

WILLIAM WARREN ROGERS. Alabama's reform press: militant spokesman for agrarian revolt [1889-96]. Agric. hist., 34:62-70 (Apr). notes. [8404

OUR schools and colleges. A. M. E. Zion quar., 60:216-17 (fall 1950). On Lomax-Hannon College, Greenville, Ala., the only school of the African Methodist Episcopal Zion Church in the Deep South, 1893-1950. [8405

F. L. PETERSON. Why the Seventh-Day Adventist Church established and maintains a Negro college (and schools for Negroes below college grade). Jour. Negro educ., 29:284-8 (summer). notes. Mainly on Oakwood College, near Huntsville, Ala., 1895-1960. [8406

HERBERT ELLSWORTH STEELE. Compensating injured State employees in Alabama [1900-1956]. Ala. lawyer, 21:30-53 (Jan). notes. [8407

J. P. LAMB, JR., & THOMAS LAWSON, JR. How are you fixed for Shays? Trains, 20(6):38-41 (Apr). map, views. On a 16-mile line (originally the Warrior Southern Railway, built 1901-4) now serving the Twin Seams Mining Company, operator of strip coal mines near Kellerman, Ala. [8408

C. M. STANLEY. Some personal recollections of Oscar W. Underwood [in Alabama, 1901-29]. Ala. law rev., 21:198-208 (Apr). [8409

GUSSIE (ALEXANDER) BALLARD. Remember our yesterdays? New Orleans: Pelican Pub. Co. [1960. 10], 84 p. ports., views. On the life of the author and her husband, Carl M. Ballard, in Grand Bay, Ala., since 1916, their various occupations there and in Pascagoula and Mobile, and their many illnesses; with some account of their earlier years in Grand Rapids, Mich. [8410

THEODORE SALOUTOS. The Alabama Farm Bureau Federation: early beginnings [1921-37]. Ala. rev., 13: 185-98 (Jul). notes. [8411

JAMES ALLEN TOWER. Southwest Alabama: geographic view. Ala. Acad. Science, Jour., 30(3):44-51 (Jan 1959). maps. notes. On population changes and amount and sources of income in 12 counties, 1929-57. [8412

JAMES RUFUS AGEE (1909-55) & WALKER EVANS. Let us now praise famous men: three tenant families. Boston: Houghton Mifflin [1960]. xxii, 471 p. ports., views. 1st ed. 1941. Photographs and text illustrating Agee's daily living with "three representative white tenant families" in Alabama, Jul.-Aug. 1936, in order to collect materials for "an article on cotton tenantry in the United States" (never published). "Actually, the effort is to recognize the stature of a portion of unimagined existence, and to contrive techniques proper to its recording, communication, analysis, and defense." [8413

CLARENCE W. ALLGOOD. Operation of the wage earners' plan [of the Bankruptcy Act of 1938] in the Northern District of Alabama. Rutgers law rev., 14:578-85 (spring). notes. On deductions made by employers from wages of bankrupt employees and transmitted to a trustee in bankruptcy. [8414

RALPH H. ALLEN, JR. Wildlife resources in the southwest Alabama empire [1940-57]. Ala. Acad. Science, Jour., 30(3):78-81 (Jan 1959). [8415

T. E. CORLEY & 3 others. Preparing land for mechanization in the Southeast. Agric. engineering, 38:730-32 (Oct 1957). diagrs., views. notes. On an experimental study by the Alabama Agricultural Experiment Station in preparing rolling land for the use of tractors and other machinery, 1949-56. [8416

MISSISSIPPI

JOHN KNOX BETTERSWORTH. Mississippi: a history [1539-1958]. Austin: Steck Co. [1959]. xi, 595, 32 p. facsims., maps, ports., views. bibliog. (p. 569-71). [8417

ALBERT EUGENE CASEY, comp. Amite County, Mississippi, 1699-1865. Volume II. The churches: minutes from the original books of the Baptist and Presbyterian churches; diaries and autobiographies of Methodist ministers; association records for the Baptist, Methodist, and Presbyterian churches, and other data from various sources, indexed. Birmingham, Ala.: Amite County Historical Fund, 1950. viii, 696 p. Includes autobiography of Learner Blackman, 1804-8; autobiography, diary, and letter book of William Winans, 1788-1857; autobiography of Jacob Young, 1807-8; and autobiography of Lorenzo Dow, 1803-16. [8418

ALBERT EUGENE CASEY, comp. Amite County, Mississippi, 1699-1890. Volume III. The environs. Birmingham, Ala.: Amite County Historical Fund, 1957. v, 750 p. maps. Includes lists of marriages in St. Helena Parish, La. (1813-75) and East Feliciana Parish, La. (1834-70), and in Wilkinson County (1802-1924), Franklin County (1817-68), Pike County (1816-76), Adams County (1799-1821), and Amite County (1820-38, 1867-90), Miss.; lists of Revolutionary, Mexican War, and Confederate soldiers in Amite County; "Index of estate papers, Amite Co., Miss.," 1809-66 (p. 279-413); various other lists and records; and genealogies. [8419

MORTON BRANDON KING, JR., HARALD A. PEDERSEN, & JOHN N. BURRUS. Mississippi's people, 1950. University, Miss., 1955. vi, 95, [2] p. maps, tables. notes. (University of Mississippi. Bureau of Public Administration. Sociological study series, 5.) Includes some account of Mississippi population since 1716. Deals with fertility, mortality, migration, and composition of population. [8420

ROBERT V. HAYNES. Law enforcement in frontier Mississippi [1795-1817]. Jour. Miss. hist., 22:27-42 (Jan). notes. [8421

JOHN FRANCIS HAMTRAMCK CLAIBORNE (1809-84). Claiborne's "Journalism in Mississippi": a fragment from the unpublished second volume of his history of Mississippi [burned in 1884]. Edited by John Hebron Moore. Jour. Miss. hist., 22: 87-100 (Jan). notes. From the Jackson Clarion, 5 Mar. 1885. Paper read by Claiborne in 1882 on journalism in Mississippi since 1797 or 1798; with his recollections of many of the journalists. [8422

THOMAS LUTHER ROBERTSON, JR. The unfolding magnolia: a literary history of Mississippi [from ca. 1800] until 1876. Ann Arbor: University Microfilms, 1960. Positive microfilm of typescript. [326] leaves. Thesis--Vanderbilt Univ. Abstracted: Dissert. abstracts, 21:628-9 (Sep). [8423

RICHARD WORDEN GRIFFIN III. Manufacturing interests of Mississippi planters, 1810-1832. Jour. Miss. hist., 22:110-22 (Apr). notes. On efforts to promote the manufacture of coarse cotton goods (bagging, canvas, rope, etc.). [8424

EDWARD HENRY HOBBS, ed. Yesterday's constitution today: an analysis of the Mississippi Constitution of 1890. [With conclusions and recommendations.] ... University, 1960. xiv, 151 p. notes. (University of Mississippi. Bureau of Public Administration. State administration series, 19.) Contents.--1. Mississippi's constitutional history [1817-90], by Huey Blair Howerton.--2. The Bill of Rights, by Charles N. Fortenberry.--3. The legislature, by William F. Winter.--4. The executive, by Donald S. Vaughan.--5. The judiciary, by W. Joel Blass.--6. Corporations, by George W. Rogers.--7. Suffrage and elections, by Russell H. Barrett.--8. Legislative apportionment, by Edward H. Hobbs.--9. Constitutional change and other important subjects, by Frederick H. Gareau. [8425

JOHN HEBRON MOORE. Economic conditions in Mississippi on the eve of the Civil War [1850-61]. Jour. Miss. hist., 22:167-78 (Jul). notes. [8426

JACK WINTON GUNN. Mississippi in 1860 as reflected in the activities of the Governor's office. Jour. Miss. hist., 22:179-91 (Jul). notes. On "the non-secession activities in the Mississippi of 1860" of concern to Gov. John Jones Pettus, Nov. 1859-Nov. 1860. [8427

WILLIAM DAVID McCAIN. Education in Mississippi in 1860. Jour. Miss. hist., 22:153-66 (Jul). Includes remarks on the reasons why "Education generally has always been poorly supported in Mississippi." [8428

MARGARET DES CHAMPS MOORE. Religion in Mississippi in 1860. Jour. Miss. hist., 22:223-38 (Oct). notes. [8429

PETER FRANKLIN WALKER. Vicksburg: a people at war, 1860-1865. Chapel Hill: Univ. of North Carolina Press [1960]. xvi, 235 p. map, views (1 double). bibliog. (p. 255-30), notes. Based on thesis--Vanderbilt Univ., 1958. [8430

MISSISSIPPI. Commission on the War between the States. Mississippi in the War between the States: a booklet of facts for the information of Mississippians in connection with the observance of the Civil War Centennial, 1961-1965. [Jackson, 1960.] 36 p. bibliog. (p. 32-3). Includes a chronology of "Battles, skirmishes, and events in Mississippi, 1861-1865," compiled by Edwin C. Bearss (p. 16-24), and a list of historical markers. [8431

WILLIAM HENRY ELDER (1819-1904). Civil War diary (1862-1865) of Bishop William Henry Elder, [Catholic] Bishop of Natchez. [Natchez? Miss.:] R. O. Gerow, Bishop of Natchez-Jackson [1960? 4], 125 p. [8432

LUCIUS OSMOND CROSBY, JR. Crosby, a story of men and trees. N.Y.: Newcomen Soc. in North America, 1960. 32 p. views. On the life of Lucius Olen Crosby, Sr. (1869-1948), in Mississippi as a farmer, a wholesale lumber dealer, organizer of the Goodyear Yellow Pine Company at Picayune in 1916, and his success in rehabilitating the dwindling forests of Pearl River County and in developing a dairy industry and a tung-tree industry there; his partnership with his 3 sons, dissolved in 1944; and the division of its activities among his sons, Howell Crosby, Hollis Crosby, and Lucius Osmond Crosby. [8433

WILLIAM ELBERT MIDDLETON. The history and development of public school pupil transportation in Mississippi [1910-58]. Ann Arbor: University Microfilms, 1959 [i. e. 1960]. Positive microfilm of typescript. [268] leaves. Thesis (Ed. D.)--Univ. of Mississippi. Abstracted: Dissert. abstracts, 20:2669-70 (Jan). [8434

GEORGE COLEMAN OSBORN. Pass Christian, the winter White House, Christmas 1913. Jour. Miss. hist., 22:1-26 (Jan). notes. On Woodrow Wilson's vacation there to recuperate from influenza, Dec. 1913-Jan. 1914. [8435

P. D. EAST. The magnolia jungle: the life, times, and education of a Southern editor. N.Y.: Simon and Schuster, 1960. xi, 243 p. On the author's early life in Mississippi (ca. 1921 to ca. 1941), his experiences as a Negro, his Army service in World War II, and his establishment of a weekly newspaper (The Petal paper, Petal, Miss.) in 1953, of which the main circulation was outside Mississippi. [8436

VICTOR B. MacNAUGHTON. For land's sake! Am. forests, 66(1):34-5, 46-8 (Jan). double view. On flood and erosion control in Lafayette County, Miss., 1946-59. [8437

LOUISIANA

DAUGHTERS OF THE AMERICAN REVOLUTION. Louisiana. Louisiana tombstone inscriptions. [Shreveport?] 1954-60. 11 v. Copied by the chapters of the Louisiana Society, Daughters of the American Revolution, and arranged by parishes. [8438

JAMES HOWELL STREET (1903-54). Louisiana [its traditions and characteristics]. Holiday, American panorama west of the Mississippi: a Holiday magazine book (Garden City, N.Y.: Doubleday [1960]), p. 276-99. [8439

JOSEPH LE SAGE TISCH. French in Louisiana: a study of the historical development of the French language of Louisiana. New Orleans: A. F. Laborde [1959. 4], 68 p. bibliog. (p. 66-8), notes. Thesis (M. A.)--Notre Dame Seminary, New Orleans. On the characteristics of the French spoken by the Acadians in Acadia, 1604-1750s, and by Acadian emigrants and other Frenchmen in Louisiana, 1690s-1950s. [8440

FRED BOWERMAN KNIFFEN. The outdoor oven in Louisiana. La. hist., 1:25-35 (winter). map, views. notes. On the use, distribution, and foreign analogues of the "country oven (four de campagne)" as "one element in the material complex that characterizes parts of rural south Louisiana," introduced from France ca. 1700 and now apparently "doomed to early extinction." [8441

CHAN LEE. A culture history of rice, with special reference to Louisiana [since ca. 1700]. Ann Arbor: University Microfilms, 1960. Positive microfilm of typescript. [254] leaves. Thesis--Louisiana State Univ. Abstracted: Dissert. abstracts, 21: 586-7 (Sep). [8442

Mother MARIE TRANCHEPAIN DE ST. AUGUSTIN (died 1733). An adventurous voyage to French colonial Louisiana: the narrative of Mother Tranchepain, 1727. [Edited and translated] by Marion Ware. La. hist., 1: 212-29 (summer). views. notes. Translation of her Relation du voyage des premiéres Ursulines á la Nouvelle Orleans et de leur établissement en cette ville (New York, 1859), a narrative of the voyage of 12 Ursuline nuns from France to New Orleans, 22 Feb.-7 Aug. 1727, with descriptive details of the Mississippi below New Orleans and of the town itself. [8443

JOSEPH PATRICK ROPPOLO. Folklore in Louisiana drama: a challenge. La. folklore misc., 1(4):65-81 (Jan). notes. On several plays, beginning with Le pére Indien, written or produced in or dealing with Louisiana, 1753-1950. [8444

OPELOUSAS POST, La. Marriage contracts of the Opelousas Post, 1766-1803. Translated and abstracted by Jacqueline O. Vidrine and Winston De Ville. With ... a brief history of the Opelousas Post by Edwin A. Davis. [Ville Platte? La.] 1960. [5], ix, 84 leaves. map. Contracts recorded by the captain or colonel "commandant civil et militaire des Opelousas" or "des Attakapas et Opeloussas," a district then comprising all of southwestern Louisiana. Lists names of bride and groom and of their parents, names of witnesses, and property of bride and groom. [8445

HENRY GEORGE McMAHON. The background, structure, and composition of the Louisiana Code of Civil Procedure [1769-1960]. La. Bar jour., 7:246-55 (Feb). [8446

EDWARD BANE ROBERT. Highlights of progress in public education in Louisiana [1771-1960]. Louisiana State University, College of Education, The progress of education in Louisiana ([Baton Rouge:] Bureau of Educational Materials and Research, College of Education [1960]), p. 1-27. table. bibliog., notes. [8447

HARRY OSTER & REVON REED. County Mardi Gras in Louisiana. La. folklore misc., 1(4):1-17 (Jan). notes. On rural celebrations of this annual festival since the 1780s; with texts (in French and English) of several traditional songs. [8448

GLEN LEE GREENE. A history of the Baptists of Oak Ridge, Louisiana, 1797-1960. Nashville, Tenn.: Parthenon Press, 1960. 183 p. maps, ports., views. bibliog. (p. 175-7), notes. [8449

LUTHER E. CHANDLER. A study of parish government in Louisiana [1804-1959]. Hammond, La., 1960. 27 p. notes. (Southeastern Louisiana College. College bulletin, v. 17, no. 2.) Includes reference to the 12 counties established in 1804 and replaced in 1806 by 19 parishes. [8450

SIDNEY ALBERT MARCHAND. Across the years. Donaldsonville, La., ©1949. [6], 198 p. ports., views. History and anecdotes of Donaldsonville, 1806-1949; with excerpts from The Donaldsonville chief, founded in 1871 (most of its early files destroyed by fire in 1911). [8451

CLARENCE J. MORROW. Matrimonial property law in Louisiana [1808-1959]. Tulane law rev., 34:3-50 (Dec 1959). notes. From Matrimonial property law, ed. W. Friedman (1955), with added references of later date. Includes an introduction on French and Spanish elements in Louisiana law. [8452

MARK E. BORTON & HAROLD H. ELLIS. Some legal aspects of water use in Louisiana [1812-1958. Baton Rouge:] Louisiana State Univ. and Agricultural and Mechanical College, 1960. 114 p. maps, views. notes. (Louisiana. Agricultural Experiment Station, Baton Rouge. Bulletin 537.) [8453

KATHLEEN GRAHAM. Some old families of the parish. Mary Frances Fletcher, ed., Historical studies of Lincoln Parish (Ruston, La.: Louisiana Polytechnic Institute [1960?]), p. 8-14. bibliog., notes. On the descendants of the May, Kidd, Calhoun, and Delony families in Ruston, La., since ca. 1812. [8454

LEON DAYRIES HUBERT, JR. History of jurisdiction and venue in criminal cases in Louisiana [1812-1959]. Tulane law rev., 34:255-68 (Feb). notes. [8455

JERRY A. BROWN. Supervisory powers of the Supreme Court of Louisiana over inferior courts [1813-1959]. Tulane law rev., 34:165-78 (Dec 1959). notes. [8456

JAMES E. WESNER. Attorney's fees as an element of damages in Louisiana [1817-1959]. Tulane law rev., 34: 146-64 (Dec 1959). notes. [8457

KATHLEEN GRAHAM. Landmarks of Lincoln Parish. Mary Frances Fletcher, ed., Historical studies of Lincoln Parish (Ruston, La.: Louisiana Polytechnic Institute [1960]), p. 15-19. notes. On James M. Roane (born 1824, died after 1904), planter in Ruston, La.; with texts of an order to him (as Captain, 1st Company, 2d Battalion, 29th Regiment, Louisiana Militia) from Col. Thomas B. Rutland, undated (1846), and a notice by Roane (Jackson Parish, La., 11 Aug. 1846), including a list of the officers and privates of the Company. [8458

LOUISIANA STATE UNIVERSITY AND AGRICULTURAL AND MECHANICAL COLLEGE. Library. Louisiana paintings of the nineteenth century, lent by Mr. and Mrs. W[illiam] E. Groves, New Orleans: an exhibition. [Catalogue by Corinne McNeir.] Baton Rouge [1959. 20] p. port., views. List of 50 undated paintings by 27 painters (including 6 "unknown artists"); biographical sketches of 21 of the painters, active in Louisiana between 1828 and 1888; and accounts of some of their subjects. [8459

JOHN CHRISTIAN LUDWIG ANDREASSEN. Frances Benjamin Johnston [1864-1952] and her views of Uncle Sam. La. hist., 1:130-36 (spring). views. notes. On the several buildings of Uncle Sam Plantation, on the Mississippi near Convent, La., built in the 1840s, photographed by Miss Johnston in 1938, and demolished in 1940; with a biographical sketch of Miss Johnston, journalist and photographer. [8460

JOHN QUINCY ANDERSON. Folkways in writing about northeast Louisiana before 1865. La folklore misc., 1(4):18-32 (Jan). notes. Information mainly from local newspapers and Madison Parish court records, 1841-61. [8461

GORDON EARL GILLSON. The Louisiana State Board of Health: the formative years [1855-79]. Ann Arbor: University Microfilms, 1960. Positive microfilm of typescript. [444] leaves. Thesis--Louisiana State Univ. Abstracted: Dissert. abstracts, 21:598-9 (Sep). [8462

HETTIE CARY HALE, ed. Excerpts from old letters. Mary Frances Fletcher, ed., Historical studies of Lincoln Parish (Ruston, La.: Louisiana Polytechnic Institute [1960]), p. 20-25. bibliog. Letters or parts of letters from A. C. Davis (Camp Moore, La., 10 Jul. 1861), Lt. J. G. Huey (Camp Magruder, 1 Aug. 1861), John T. Sawyer (Trenton, La., 11 Aug. 1883; Ruston, La., 1 Nov. 1886), Eliza Mitchell (Vienna, La., 16 Jul. 1886),

Mrs. S. P. Colvin (1898 or 1899?), Capt. William C. C. Claiborne, Jr. (Camp near Shreveport, 11 Jul. 1864), and others, 1855-75. [8463

NOEL DILLARD SMITH. 100 years for Louisiana State Board of Health [1855-1955]. Southw. water works jour., 37(2):18, 20 (May 1955). [8464

BILL PARSONS. The debut of Adah Isaacs Menken [1835-68]. Quar. jour. speech, 46:8-13 (Feb). notes. Summary, from Louisiana newspapers, of references to "Mrs. Ada B. Menken" and her husband, Alexander Isaac Menken, as actors in the company of James S. Charles on tour from New Orleans to Houma, Opelousas, probably Alexandria and Natchitoches, and Shreveport, 3 Sep. 1856 - 13 Jun. 1857. [8465

EMMA (LAY) LANE. A letter from a Yankee bride in ante-bellum Louisiana. Edited by John Q. Anderson. La. hist., 1:245-50 (summer). notes. Letter to a Mrs. Rogers in New England from Mrs. James Tyson Lane, dated Weston Place, Clinton, La., 6 Oct. 1857, describing her father-in-law's plantation and the ways of life there. [8466

RALPH SLOVENKO. Control over the jury verdict [by the judge] in Louisiana criminal law [1857-1959]. La. law rev., 20:657-702 (Jun). notes. [8467

LOUISIANA. Governor, 1856-60 (Robert Charles Wickliffe). Annual message of Robert C. Wickliffe, Governor of the State of Louisiana, to the General Assembly. Baton Rouge: J. M. Taylor, State Printer. 1860. La. hist., 1:165-79 (fall). Photoreproduction. [8468

LOUISIANA. Governor, 1860-64 (Thomas Overton Moore). Inaugral address of Governor Thomas O. Moore, delivered January 23, 1860, to the Legislature of the State of Louisiana. Baton Rouge: J. M. Taylor, State Printer. 1860. La. hist., 1:380-85 (fall). Photoreproduction. [8469

LOUISIANA. Governor, 1860-64 (Thomas Overton Moore). Special message of Thomas O. Moore, Governor of the State of Louisiana, to the General Assembly. December 1860. Baton Rouge: J. M. Taylor, State Printer. 1860. La. hist., 1:387-94 (fall). Photoreproduction. Document dated 10 Dec. 1860. [8470

SARAH IDA FOWLER MORGAN (1842-1909; married Francis Warrington Dawson in 1874). A Confederate girl's diary. ... Introduction by Warrington Dawson. Edited with a foreword and notes by James I. Robertson, Jr. Bloomington: Indiana Univ. Press [1960]. xxxvi, [2], 473 p. double facsim., ports., views. notes (p. 443-73). (Civil War centennial series.) 1st ed. 1913. Diary kept in and near Baton Rouge and New Orleans, 9 Mar. 1862 - 2 May 1865; with a detailed biographical sketch. [8471

V. C. CLARKE & JAMES EARL BRADLEY. Pay the preacher! two letters from Louisiana, 1864. Edited by Willard E[ugene] Wright. La. hist., 1:251-9 (summer). notes. Letter from Clarke, dated "Plaquemine Brulee," 12 Jul. 1864, to the Rev. James Earl Bradley, applauding his recent sermon on the duty of charitable giving to Methodist ministers and to soldiers and enclosing "this 7.30 note"; and acknowledgment from Bradley, dated 8 Aug. 1864, concurring in denunciation of the "miserable misers, who count it all gain to stint their preachers and defraud him of his just earnings, and then go to church to sing psalmody." [8472

JOSEPH CHARLES MELE. A description and analysis of the speaking in the Louisiana anti-lottery movement. Ann Arbor: University Microfilms, 1959 [i. e. 1960]. Positive microfilm of typescript. viii, 180 leaves. ports. bibliog. (leaves 173-9). Thesis--Louisiana State Univ. Abstracted: Dissert. abstracts, 20:2960-61 (Jan). On the Louisiana State Lottery Company, a "giant gambling monopoly" that "all but controlled the state economically and politically," and the victorious campaign of the Anti-Lottery League for its abolition, 1869-92. [8473

GEORGE M. SNELLINGS III. Louisiana law on the nullity of marriage [1870-1959]. La. law rev., 20:563-83 (Apr). notes. [8474

WINNIE D. EVANS. Early doctors of Lincoln Parish [1873 or earlier to 1918]. Mary Frances Fletcher, ed., Historical studies of Lincoln Parish (Ruston, La.: Louisiana Polytechnic Institute [1960]), p. 26-40. bibliog., notes. Based mainly upon interviews in 1949 with descendants of the physicians. [8475

JOHN P. GRAHAM. Were you there when ...? Mary Frances Fletcher, ed., Historical studies of Lincoln Parish (Ruston, La.: Louisiana Polytechnic Institute [1960]), p. 41-7. bibliog., notes. On the early settlers of Ruston, founded in 1884. [8476

MARGARET TOWERS MONROE. Pierian Club to celebrate sixtieth anniversary. Mary Frances Fletcher, ed., Historical studies of Lincoln Parish (Ruston, La.: Louisiana Polytechnic Institute [1960]), p. 48-60. bibliog., notes. On the "oldest woman's club" in Ruston, 1889-1959; with a list of its members in the years 1889-1919. [8477

RICHARD K. MAZEAU. Legislative waiver of governmental immunity [in Louisiana, 1897-1959]. Loyola law rev, 10:105-12. On the continued immunity from tort liability even when immunity from suit is waived. [8478

IRWIN L. SAVESON. Drainage of sugar-cane land [in Louisiana, 1899-1949]. Agric. engineering, 31:451-4 (Sep 1950). diagrs., views. [8479

LOUISIANA. AGRICULTURAL EXPERIMENT STATION, Baton Rouge. Louisiana farm products prices, 1910-1959. By J[oseph] P. Montgomery, [Baton Rouge:] Louisiana State Univ. and Agricultural and Mechanical College, 1960. 72 p. diagrs., tables. bibliog. (p. 8), notes. (Its Bulletin 530.) [8480

HENRY GEORGE McMAHON & BEN R. MILLER, JR. The Crain myth--a criticism of the Duree and Stephens cases. La. law rev., 20:449-85 (Apr). tables. notes. On legislative "authorizations for suits in tort by state employees, or legislative waiver of the state's immunity from liability for the wrongful acts of its employees," especially in cases of wrongful death, physical injury, or property damage, Louisiana, 1921-59. [8481

LILLIAN JONES HALL. A historical study of programming techniques and practices of Radio Station KWKH, Shreveport, Louisiana: 1922-1950. Ann Arbor: University Microfilms, 1959 [i.e. 1960]. Positive microfilm of typescript. [233] leaves. Thesis--Louisiana State Univ. Abstracted: Dissert. abstracts, 20:2953-4 (Jan). [8482

WEX S. MALONE. Total disability evaluation under the Louisiana Compensation Act [1932-59]. La. law rev., 20:486-521 (Apr). notes. [8483

LOUISIANA. Legislative Council. A brief biography of the members of the [1960] Louisiana Legislature. Baton Rouge, 1960. iii, 19 leaves. tables. 22x36 cm. Tabulation of selected items of information, including prior service (one member having served continuously since 1934). [8484

FRANK J. COOGAN. Waste control in a Southern paper mill [Springhill Mill, International Paper Company, Bodcau, La., 40 miles northwest of Shreveport, 1938-59]. Water Pollution Control Fed., Jour., 32:853-7 (Aug). [8485

VERNON FREDERICK GALLIANO. AN occupational study of the College of Agriculture graduates of Southwestern Louisiana Institute, 1938-1958. Ann Arbor: University Microfilms, 1960. Positive microfilm of typescript. [224] leaves. Thesis--Louisiana State Univ. Abstracted: Dissert. abstracts, 20:4594-5 (Jun). [8486

IRÉNE THÈRÉSE WHITFIELD. Acadian folk songs. Baton Rouge: Louisiana State Univ. Press [1955. 6], 58 p. music. notes. Chapter from the author's Louisiana French folk songs (1939). On the forms, tunes, and ideas of Cajun songs in Louisiana, their probably indigenous origin in Louisiana, and their expression of "the character of the Louisiana Cajuns"; with texts collected by the author from oral sources, printed mainly in standard French with interlined phonetic transcription in dialect. [8487

IRWIN L. SAVESON. Machinery aspects of land drainage [in Louisiana, 1944-52]. Agric. engineering, 34:303-6 (May 1953). diagr., views. [8488

SHELBY MARION JACKSON. Public education in Louisiana today [1947-60]. Louisiana State University, College of Education, The progress of public education in Louisiana during the past one hundred years ([Baton Rouge:] Bureau of Educational Materials and Research, College of Education [1960]), p. 28-35. [8489

LESLIE J. SCHIFF. The doctor-patient privilege in civil cases in Louisiana [1949-58]. La. law rev., 20:418-25 (Feb). notes. [8490

New Orleans

AMERICAN INSTITUTE OF ARCHITECTS. New Orleans Chapter. Guide Book Committee. A guide to architecture of New Orleans--1699-1959. By Samuel Wilson, Jr. [Chairman]. N.Y.: Reinhold Pub. Corp. [1959]. 80 p. maps, views. [8491

TULANE UNIVERSITY. Urban Life Research Institute. The eighth generation: cultures and personalities of New

Orleans Negroes. Editors: John H[arrison] Rohrer [and] Munro S. Edmonson. Co-authors: Harold Lief, Daniel Thompson, [and] William Thompson. N.Y.: Harper [1960]. xi, [3], 346 p. diagrs., facsims., tables. notes. Follow-up study, 1953-56, of 47 of the 277 individuals interviewed by Allison Davis and John Dollard as reported in their Children of bondage (1940); with a chapter on the Negroes in New Orleans since 1719. Applies psychiatric, psychological, and sociological analysis to the data collected. [8492

SAMUEL WILSON, JR. The architecture of historic New Orleans [1721 to ca. 1850]. A. I. A. jour., 32(2):32-5 (Aug 1959). plans, views. [8493

JACK DAVID LAZARUS HOLMES. The two series of the Moniteur de la Louisiane. N.Y. Pub. Lib., Bul., 64: 323-8 (Jun). notes. On "the first newspaper published in Louisiana, along the Gulf Coast, or even in the lower Mississippi Valley," New Orleans, 3 Mar. 1794 - 2 Jul. 1814 (suspended "some time in 1795 or 1796" and resumed 13 Nov. 1797). [8494

LAWRENCE VAUGHAN HOWARD & ROBERT S. FRIEDMAN. Government in metropolitan New Orleans. New Orleans: Tulane Univ., 1959 [c1960]. 227 p. diagrs., fold. map (inserted), tables. notes. (Tulane studies in political science, 6.) On the forms and functions of the municipal government of New Orleans and the governments of adjoining areas, 1805-1958. [8495

E. HARPER CHARLTON. New Orleans & Carrollton Railroad. Railway & Locomotive Hist. Soc., Bul., 103:77-8 (Oct). On a street railway in New Orleans, 1833-1935. [8496

MARTHA ANN PETERS. The St. Charles Hotel: New Orleans social center, 1837-1860. La. hist., 1:191-211 (summer). notes. [8497

JOHN DUFFY. Erasmus Darwin Fenner (1807-1866): journalist, educator, and sanitarian. Jour. med. educ., 35:819-31 (Sep). facsim., port., view. notes. On his medical practice in New Orleans, 1841-66, his editing and publication of 3 medical periodicals there, his initiative in establishing the New Orleans School of Medicine, and his other contributions to the progress of medicine. [8498

HENRI HERZ (1803 or 1806 - 1888). A French traveler's view of ante-bellum New Orleans. [Edited and translated] by Henry Bertram Hill and Larry Gara. La. hist., 1:335-41 (fall). notes. Translated excerpt from the author's Mes voyages en Amérique (Paris, 1866), recalling his visit to New Orleans as a concert pianist in 1846. [8499

NELSON McCLANAHAN. [Letter to John R. MacClanahan of Jackson, Tenn., dated New Orleans, 19 Jun. 1847.] Password, 5:114-15 (Jul). On the "world of wonders" seen by the author in New Orleans, including the gigantic Col. Alexander William Doniphan and his Regiment of Missouri Volunteers. [8500

HENRY ERNEST SIGERIST (1891-1957). The cost of illness to the City of New Orleans in 1850. Henry E. Sigerist, Henry E. Sigerist on the sociology of medicine, ed. Milton I. Roemer (N.Y.: MD Publications (1960]), p. 169-79. tables. notes. First published in 1944. [8501

ISIDORE COHN. Rudolph Matas [1860-1957]: a biography of one of the great pioneers in surgery. Garden City, N.Y.: Doubleday, 1960. 431 p. ports. notes. On his early life, his medical education in Louisiana, his practice of medicine and surgery in New Orleans, his service as a member of the Yellow Fever Commission in Havana, as Professor of Surgery at Tulane University, and as President of the New Orleans Medical and Surgical Society, his collectanea and writings on the history of medicine in Louisiana, his friendships with George Washington Cable and Lafcadio Hearn, and his habits and traits as observed by the author in "fifty-four years of personal contact." [8502

JAMES O. LANG. Gloom envelops New Orleans: April 24 to May 2, 1862. La. hist., 1:281-99 (fall). map, views. notes. On the evacuation of the city by Confederate naval and land forces, its surrender to Adm. David G. Farragut, its occupation by the forces under Gen. Benjamin F. Butler, and the behavior of angry civilians during this period. [8503

THOMAS CHALMERS McCORVEY (1851-1932). A dramatic incident of the Reconstruction era. T. C. McCorvey, Alabama historical sketches, ed. George Burke Johnston (Charlottesville: Univ. of Virginia Press, 1960),

p. 177-84. From the Montgomery, Ala., Advertiser, 11 Sep. 1910. On armed conflicts between members of the White League and the metropolitan police in New Orleans, 1874-75, and the proposal of Gen. Philip H. Sheridan to declare the leaders of the White League "banditti" so that "they could be tried by military commission." [8504

EDWARD JOSEPH DOHERTY. A nun with a gun, Sister Stanislaus: a biography. By Eddie Doherty. Milwaukee: Bruce Pub. Co. [1960]. viii, [2], 194 p. On her work as director of nursing education at Charity Hospital, New Orleans, 1884-1949; with some account of her early life near Marysville, Calif., her removal to Virginia City, Nev., and her education as a Sister of Charity at Mount Hope, Baltimore. [8505

EUGENE G. LAFORET. Edmond Souchon II [born 1897]. New Eng. jour. med., 260:280-81 (5 Feb 1959). notes. On his life in New Orleans, his studies at Tulane University and at Loyola University (Chicago), his work as a surgeon, and his concurrent activities as a jazz guitarist. [8506

FORREST EMMANUEL LA VIOLETTE. The Negro in New Orleans [1910-58]. Nathan Glazer & Davis McEntire, eds., Studies in housing & minority groups ... special research report to the Commission on Race and Housing (Berkeley: Univ. of California Press, 1960), p. 110-34. [8507

G. THOMAS FAIRCLOUGH. "New light" on "Old Zion": a study of the names of white and Negro Baptist churches in New Orleans [1941, 1959]. Names, 8:75-85 (Jun). notes. [8508

TEXAS

SEÁN O'FAOLÁIN. Texas [its traditions and characteristics]. Holiday, American panorama west of the Mississippi: a Holiday magazine book (Garden City, N.Y.: Doubleday [1960]), p. 230-43. [8509

E. RAYMOND RING, JR. An evaluation of radiocarbon dates from the Galena site, southeastern Texas. Tex. Archeol. Soc., Bul., 31:317-25. bibliog. On a shell midden in Galena Park, some 10 miles east of the central business district of Houston, in which 2 samples of Rangia shell found in direct contact with potsherds produced radiocarbon dates of 1900 ± 105 years and 3350 ± 115 years B. P. respectively--dates which, if correct, require drastic revision of previous chronologies in this area. [8510

Mrs. ARTHUR SCHUSTER. Texas souvenir spoons. Hobbies, 65(7):52-3 (Sep). views. [8511

TEXAS ARCHEOLOGICAL SOCIETY. New radiocarbon dates from Texas. Tex. Archeol. Soc., Bul., 31:327-30. bibliog. Short contributions from Frank H. Watt, E. Raymond Ring, Jr., Thomas C. Kelly, and Charles B. Fleming, reporting dates from Bell County (more than 10,000 years ago), McLennan County (A. D. 1277 ± 150), Harris County (A. D. 59 ± 105, 1391 ± 115 B. C.), Travis County (1315 ± 125 B. C.), and Austin County (2569 ± 80 B. C.). [8512

U.S. National Park Service. An archeological survey of Blackburn Crossing Reservoir on the upper Neches River. [By] Le Roy Johnson, Jr. Tex. Archeol. Soc., Bul., 31:213-72. map, tables, views. bibliog. On a survey of areas to be flooded in Anderson, Cherokee, Henderson, and Smith Counties, Tex. [8513

FRED WENDORF & ALEX D. KRIEGER. New light on the Midland discovery. Am. antiq., 25:66-78 (Jul 1959). chron. chart, map, view. bibliog. On the dating of human remains found at Midland, Tex. [8514

JOHN EDWIN CONNER, JACK EDWARD CONNER, & ROBBIE C. HARPER. Your Texas and mine. Oklahoma City: Harlow Pub. Corp. [1960]. vii, [5], 573 p. facsims., maps, ports., views. A history, 1519-1960. [8515

HERBERT PICKENS GAMBRELL & VIRGINIA GAMBRELL. A pictorial history of Texas [1519-1959]. N.Y.: Dutton [1960. 6], 217 p. brands, cartoons, facsims., flags, maps, music, ports., seals, views. "Sources of illustrations" (p. 212-15). [8516

HERBERT C. TAYLOR, JR. Archeological notes on the route of Cabeza de Vaca. Tex. Archeol. Soc., Bul., 31: 273-90. bibliog., notes. Brief consideration of 4 routes proposed by previous students, all of which indicate that the route of Alvar Nunez Cabeza de Vaca included Texas, 1528-36. [8517

ERNEST WALLACE, ed. Documents of Texas history. Volume I (1528-1846). Edited ... with the assistance of David M. Vigness. Lubbock, Tex.: Library, Texas Technological College [1960. 10], 152 p. Seventy contemporary documents from manuscript and printed sources, including translations from Spanish and French. [8518

DONALD SLOAN. Padre Island [1553-1958]. Jr. historian (Tex.), 19(5):5-6, 12 (Mar 1959). Deals largely with wrecks and buried treasure. [8519

HORACE BAILEY CARROLL, comp. Missions in Texas along the Rio Grande and in adjacent areas [founded 1659-1789]. Southw. hist. quar., 63:606-7 (Apr). List, and request for added information. [8520

DONALD CHARLES McLEAISH. The laws of the State of Texas affecting church property [1659-1957]. Wash.: Catholic Univ. of America Press, 1960. xii, 205, [4] p. bibliog. (p. 195-9), table of cases (p. 200-202). (Catholic University of America. Canon law studies, 405.) Thesis (Doctor of Canon Law)--Catholic Univ. of America. [8521

PAUL CARL BOETHEL. History of Lavaca County [1685-1932]. Revised edition. Austin, Tex.: Von Boeckmann-Jones [1959. 10], 172 p. 1st ed. 1936. [8522

MICHAEL J. VAUGHN. The history of Cayuga [Anderson County, Tex., 1685-1960. Cayuga?] ©1960. [2], 2-52 leaves. Includes an account of Wildcat Ferry on the Trinity and the adjoining community of Judson, both established in 1846. [8523

JAMES DOUGLAS RHOTON. Roans Prairie's first citizens. Jr. historian (Tex.), 20(1):12-14, 27 (Sep 1959). On the Bidai Indians of Grimes County, 1776-1854. [8524

JAMES M. DAY. A preliminary guide to the study of buffalo trails in Texas. West Tex. Hist. Assoc. yr. bk., 36: 137-55. map. notes. Deals particularly with records of the range and routes of migration of the bison in "the prairies and grassy plains of the state," 1787-1870s. [8525

STUART ALEXANDER MacCORKLE & DICK SMITH. Texas government [1787-1959]. ... Fourth edition. N.Y.: McGraw-Hill, 1960. ix, 518 p. diagrs., maps, tables, views. bibliogs., notes. 1st ed. 1949. [8526

BENNETT CLAYTON LAY. The lives of Ellis P[eter] Bean [1783-1846]. Austin: Univ. of Texas Press [1960]. x, [4], 227 p. facsim., maps (part double), plan, port., views. notes (p. 177-201). On his early life in Tennessee, his filibustering activities with Philip Nolan in Mexico (1800-1801) and long imprisonment in Acapulco, his service with the rebels in the Mexican War of Independence, his appointment as Mexican agent to the Cherokees in Texas, his service in the Mexican Army in the Texas War of Independence, his life as a rancher near Nacogdoches, Tex., his removal to Mexico, and the complications resulting from his having a wife in Texas and a wife in Mexico. [8527

BETTY PAGE. Texas tarrabees. Jr. historian (Tex.), 19(3):22, 32 (Dec 1958). view. On a wooden implement (Spanish tarabilla) used in spinning horsehair, mohair, and Spanish moss, 19th century. [8528

NETTIE LEE BENSON. Texas failure to send a deputy to the Spanish Cortes, 1810-1812. Southw. hist. quar., 64: 14-35 (Jul). notes. [8529

MARY LOUISE (CHILTON) BRYAN. Texas! One and indivisible. [Houston: Chilton Bryan, 1960? 6], 183, [1] p. port. Twenty essays on the Austin family and various other topics in the history of Texas, 1820s-1930s. [8530

DAVID BARR HARDWICK. Vanished Velasco. Jr. historian (Tex.), 21(2): 21-2 (Nov). view. On a town at the mouth of the Brazos River, founded in 1821, consolidated with Freeport in 1950 under the name of the latter. [8531

EVELYN JACOBY. A brief history of Navasota [since 1822]. Jr. historian (Tex.), 20(2):29-32 (Nov 1959). [8532

WALTER PRESCOTT WEBB (1888-1963). The story of the Texas Rangers [1823-1934]. N.Y.: Grosset & Dunlap [1957]. vi, [2], 152 p. views. (Illustrated true books.) [8533

T. R. HAVINS. Livestock and Texas law [1827-1929]. West Tex. Hist. Assoc. yr. bk., 36:18-32. notes. [8534

HORACE BAILEY CARROLL. Masonic influences on education in the Republic of Texas [1828-95]. Waco: Texas Lodge of Research, A. F. & A. M., 1960. 30 p. port. notes. [8535

JOYCE GAYE HOKE. The city that became a town. Jr. historian (Tex.), 21(2):6-9, 31 (Nov). maps, port., view. On Huntsville, Tex., 1830s-1950, and the mystery of its failure to grow in the 20th century. [8536

MALCOLM D. McLEAN. Horse racing in Texas in the early days [1830-35]. Quarter horse, 3(8):25; (9):20 (Nov, Dec 1948). table. notes. [8537

FORREST E. WARD. Pre-Revoluntionary activity in Brazoria County [1830-36]. Southw. hist. quar., 64: 212-31 (Oct). notes. [8538

STEPHEN FULLER AUSTIN (1793-1836) & CHARLES G. SAYRE. Stephen F. Austin - Charles G. Sayre correspondence. Contributed by Walter E. Grover. Southw. hist. quar., 63: 454-6 (Jan). port. Austin to Sayre, dated Harrisburg, Tex., 6 Feb. 1832, and Sayre's reply, Brazoria, 7 Feb., on relations between Texas colonists and the Mexican Government. [8539

A LIST of names compiled from the papers of Ancil McDonald Jackson, early settler in Bexar, Kerr, Gonzales, and Guadalupe Counties and one of the first settlers in Wilson County, Texas (1832-1904). Contributed by the descendants of Laura Jackson Hassell. Our heritage, 1:13-14, 41-3, 77-9 (Oct 1959-Apr 1960). [8540

TEXAS TECHNOLOGICAL COLLEGE, Lubbock. Southwest Collection. Builders of the Southwest. Edited by Seymour V[aughan] Connor. Lubbock, 1959. xiii, 321 p. ports. 1st ed. 1957. Biographical sketches of 67 West Texas men and women born between 1833 and the early 20th century "who have made a positive contribution to the social, cultural, or economic development of their communities," and histories of 6 West Texas firms. [8541

ZANE MASON. Some experiences of Baptists on the Texas frontier [1834-86]. West Tex. Hist. Assoc. yr. bk., 36:51-62. notes. [8542

JOSEPH GUSTAVE ROUNTREE II (born 1879). History of Bee County, Texas [1834-1960. Beeville? 1960.] 143, 56 p. map, tables. Includes lists of early settlers with dates of birth and death and of landowners in 1959, reminiscences by the author, a "Texas ranchman," his "My trip through Old Mexico, 1955," and reminiscences by his uncle, W. T. Henderson of Tornillo, Tex. [8543

WILLIAM ALBERT PHILPOTT, JR. Texas currency inflation. Numismatist, 73:1657-63 (Nov). facsims. From The Texas bankers record, Feb. 1960. On the "practically worthless" currency issued by the Republic of Texas, 1835-45. [8544

VIRGIL E. BAUGH. Rendezvous at the Alamo: highlights in the lives of Bowie, Crockett, and Travis. N.Y.: Pageant Press [1960]. 251 p. coat of arms, facsims., ports., views. notes (p. 227-46). On James Bowie (1796-1836) of Kentucky, Georgia, Tennessee, and Louisiana, slave-smuggler and land speculator in Texas, supposed inventor of the Bowie knife, professional gambler; David Crockett (1798-1836) of Tennessee, Indian fighter, political leader; William Barret Travis (1809-36) of South Carolina, lawyer and political leader in Texas; their participation in the Texas Revolution and their death at the fall of the Alamo; and the "myths, legends, and hoaxes that have sprung up around the Alamo, the siege, and the men who died there." [8545

NICK BOONE. The steer on the church seal. Jr. historian (Tex.), 19(3):2-6 (Dec 1958). seal, views. On the early years of the Protestant Episcopal Church in Texas, 1836-74, and the bishops of the Diocese of Texas since 1849. [8546

ORA E. ROBBINS JINKS, comp. Independents Cemetery inscriptions, Washington County, Texas [1836-1950]. South. genealogist's exchange quar., 2(13):5-6 (spring). Evidently a cemetery of Independence (name appearing on many of the markers). Complete listing was impossible because of "the brush, weeds and tall grass." [8547

JOSEPH WEBB McKNIGHT. The Spanish influence on the Texas law of civil procedure. Tex. law rev., 38: 24-54 (Nov 1959). notes. On decisions of Texas courts which were probably influenced, or may have been influenced, by Spanish procedure, 1836-57. [8548

JANE PATTIE. Profile of a trail blazer, Charles Goodnight [1836-1929]. Quarter horse jour., 12(12):18-20, 42, 44, 142-3 (Sep). ports., views (1 double). bibliog. On his life in Texas, his service in the Texas Rangers, his work in delivering Texas cattle to market in distant places, and his long career as a cattle rancher in Palo Duro Canyon and at Goodnight, Tex. [8549

ROBERT LEWIS PETERSON. State regulation of railroads in Texas, 1836-1920. Ann Arbor: University Microfilms, 1960. Positive microfilm of typescript. [513] leaves. Thesis--Univ. of Texas. Abstracted: Dissert. abstracts, 20:4643 (Jun). [8550

JOSEPH WILLIAM SCHMITZ. Texas culture, 1836-1846: in the days of the Republic. San Antonio: Naylor Co. [1960]. vii, [1], 152 p. views. bibliog. (p. 139-48), notes. Previously published in part as Thus they lived (1935). On "the daily life of the ordinary Texans ... their daily struggle for existence, their problems and how they solved them, their distractions and amusements." [8551

A. O. THOMAS. Money of the Republic of Texas [1836 ff.]. Selections from The numismatist: United States paper money, tokens, medals, and miscellaneous (Racine, Wis.: Whitman Pub. Co., 1960), p. 156-62. facsims., tables. First printed Sep. 1944. [8552

M'LISS MORCK. A historical tour of Seguin. Jr. historian (Tex.), 19(3):31-2 (Dec 1958). On surviving landmarks there, the oldest constructed in 1838. [8553

CHARLES H. DILLON. The arrival of the telegraph in Texas [1839-77]. Southw. hist. quar., 64:200-211 (Oct). [8554

DORMAN H. WINFREY. The archive wars in Texas. Am. archivist, 23:431-7 (Oct). views. notes. On disputes as to the location of the capital and the public records, 1839-42, 1951-57. [8555

WALKER A. BRENTS, JR. Tax assessors' deeds. Baylor law rev., 12: 312-29 (summer). notes. On the legal effect of deeds executed by county and city tax collectors in Texas declaring that the land conveyed thereby is sold for taxes, 1840-1960. [8556

MARLIN, Tex. HIGH SCHOOL. EX-STUDENTS ASSOCIATION. Marlin's public schools from the 1840's to 1960, of Marlin Independent School District, Marlin Texas. [Edited by Roy Eddins. Marlin] 1960. [8], 133, [5] p. ports., tables, views. [8557

DONALD A. TYREE. The small-loan industry in Texas [1840-1958]. Austin, 1960. ix, 147 p. tables. bibliog. (p. 139-47), notes. (University of Texas. Bureau of Business Research. Research monograph 19.) [8558

PATSY WALKER. The history of Texas sugar. Jr. historian (Tex.), 20(3):27-8 (Dec 1959). On the Imperial Sugar Company and its predecessors, Sugar Land, Tex., 1840-1959. [8559

JIMMY BROWNING. Stephens County [since 1841]--100 years old. Jr. historian (Tex.), 19(3):12-16 (Dec 1958). view. [8560

JOHN D. OSBURN. McKenzie College. Southw. hist. quar., 63:533-53 (Apr). facsim., views. notes. On John Witherspoon Pettigrew McKenzie (1806-81), Methodist minister, and the school founded by him near Clarksville, Tex., in 1841, operated under the title of "Itinerant Retreat" in his home till 1854, chartered as McKenzie Institute in that year, rechartered as McKenzie Male and Female College in 1860, and closed in 1868; with an account of its curriculum and student life. [8561

MOSES ALBERT LEVY. Surgeon Moses Albert Levy: letters of a Texas patriot. [Supplement. Edited] by Saul Viener. Am. Jew. Hist. Soc., Pub., 49:202-7 (Mar). notes. Letters to Rachel C. Levy, 7 Oct. 1842, and to Richard Sanxay, 29 Jan. 1848, both dated at Matagorda, Tex., added to Levy's letters published in 1956. [8562

MATTHEW CLAY LINDSEY (died 1955). The trail of years in Dawson County, Texas [1842-1960. Completed by Mrs. M. C. Lindsey. Forth Worth? Tex., 1960?] 266 p. ports., tables, views. Includes an account of the city of Lamesa, founded in 1903 with the author as one of the founders. "Early families" (p. 211-66). [8563

JAMES R. NORVELL. Lewis v. Ames [Texas, 1872-75]--an ancient cause revisited. Southw. law jour., 13:301-19 (summer 1959). notes. On a case involving the scandalous conduct of Robert Potter (killed in 1842) in North Carolina and Texas, Mrs. Harriet A. Page, "married by bond" to Potter while Page was living and undivorced and married after Potter's death to Charles Ames, Potter's bequest of his property to Mrs. Sophia Ann Mayfield (died 1852), and the belated efforts of Mrs. Mayfield's heirs to enforce their claim to land occupied by Mrs. Ames and her Potter offspring continuously since her cohabitation with Potter. Based largely upon a manuscript by Mrs. Ames. [8564

DORMAN H. WINFREY. The Texan Archive War of 1842. Southw. hist. quar., 64:171-84 (Oct). facsim., map, views. notes. On the illegal and fruitless efforts of President Sam Houston to remove the public records of Texas from Austin to Houston and later to

Washington-on-the-Brazos; with illustrative documents. [8565

WAYNE GRAD. Hoofbeats of old Steel Dust. Quarter horse jour, 7(3):40-44 (Dec 1954). On the "fog of conflicting legends" about a quarter-horse racer and studhorse, foaled in 1843, brought to Texas by his owners (Middleton Perry and Jones Greene) in 1844, still living in 1864, and supposed to have "lived into" the 1870s, the strong demand for "Steel Dust colts," and the high prestige of "Steel Dust blood." [8566

TEXAS (Republic). Texas Indian papers, 1844-1845. Edited from the original manuscript copies in the Texas State Archives by Dorman H. Winfrey. Austin: Texas State Library, 1960. [8], 453 p. map, views. Texts of 401 letters, reports, accounts, and other documents relating to the administration of Indian affairs in Texas, mainly or entirely records of the Superintendent of Indian Affairs of the Republic of Texas, Thomas G. Western, including reports to him from Indian agents and traders and instructions from him to them. Continues a volume of earlier documents, 1825-43 (1959). [8567

BRUCE KOWERT. E[ngelbert] Krauskopf [1820-81], pioneer extraordinary. Jr. historian (Tex.), 19(5):1-4 (Mar 1959). On his emigration from Germany in 1845 and his life in Fredericksburg as a gunsmith and the discoverer of a previously unrecorded variety of yucca. [8568

DELIA ANN DAVIDSON. Memories of Meusebach, the father of Fredericksburg. Jr. historian (Tex.), 19(2):23-5 (Nov 1958). port. On John O. Meusebach (1812-97), Commissioner General of the Society for the Protection of German Immigrants in Texas, himself a German settler there, founder of Fredericksburg in 1846, later a resident of Loyal Valley. [8569

GILLESPIE COUNTY HISTORICAL SOCIETY. Pioneers in God's hills: a history of Fredericksburg and Gillespie County people and events [since 1846]. Austin, Tex.: Von Boeckmann-Jones [1960]. xxi, [3], 305 p. maps, ports., tables, views. bibliog. (p. 287-90). "Biographies" (p. 1-238). Includes a copy of the 1850 U.S. Census of Gillespie County (p. 267-86), indicating a mainly German population. [8570

BRUCE KOWERT. They buried our dead. Jr. historian (Tex.), 20(2):1-4, 32 (Nov 1959). port., view. On the cemeteries and the burial practices of Fredericksburg since 1846, and the Schaetter Funeral Home, founded by Heinrich Schaetter in 1882. [8571

MARY JOHNSON POSEY. Hand made town. Frontier times, 34(4): 16-17, 58 (fall). views. On early buildings and other evidences of the ingenuity and careful workmanship of the German founders of Fredericksburg, Tex., settled in 1846. [8572

TEXAS. Texas Indian papers, 1846-1859. Edited from the original manuscript copies in the Texas States Archives by Dorman H. Winfrey. Austin: Texas State Library, 1960. [6], 373 p. maps (1 double), views. Texts of 234 letters, reports, accounts, and other documents "from almost all governmental departments that dealt with Indian matters" in Texas. Includes long descriptions and discussions of the Indians of Texas by Maj. Robert S. Neighbors, Indian Agent, transmitted to Henry R. Schoolcraft, 29 Sep. 1847, and undated, and a similar communication to Schoolcraft from William B. Parker, 14 Mar. 1855, and field notes of a survey of limits for an Indian reservation by Capt. R.B. Marcy, Jan. 1855. Continues 2 volumes of documents of the Republic of Texas (published 1959-60). [8573

GINGER JONES. The lost city of Padre Island. Jr. historian (Tex.), 203(3): 11-14, 16 (Dec 1959). map. On buildings of the ranch of John and Johanna Shaw Singer, occupied by them from 1847 to 1861 and later by others until the site was covered with sand during a hurricane in 1880. [8574

NICK BOONE. Texas shells--past and present. Jr. historian (Tex.), 20(6): 1-6, 21 (May). ports., views. Includes an account of Joseph Daniel Mitchell (1848-1922), Texas conchologist. [8575

JOE G. RESWEBER & FELIX SALAZAR, JR. The Texas Mental Health Code [1958]. South Tex. law jour., 4:209-31 (summer 1959). notes. Includes some account of earlier Texas statutes "dealing with persons afflicted with mental aberrations," 1848-1957. [8576

WAYNE GARD. 100 years of Shiloh. Quarter horse jour., 8(3):24-7 (Dec 1955). On a quarter horse stallion (foaled ca. 1844, died 1874), brought by his owner, Jack Batchler, from Tennessee to Ellis County, Tex., in

1849, and some of the Texas descendants of Shiloh. [8577

CASPAR REAL. A tradition lives on. Jr. historian (Tex.), 19(6):1-4 (May 1959). views. On "my great-great-grandfather, the first Caspar Real" (1824-93), German emigrant to Texas in 1849, sheep rancher in Kerr County. [8578

WILBUR STANLEY SHEPPERSON. Some plans for British immigration to Texas in 1849 and 1850. Southw. hist. quar., 63:439-49 (Jan). notes. On projects of the North Texas Colonization Company of London and the Universal Emigration and Colonization Company. [8579

JEANNETTE STROUD. Live Oak Presbyterian Church [De Witt County, Tex., 1849-93]. Jr. historian (Tex.), 19(3):17-18 (Dec 1958). [8580

SARAH McCLELLAN. From the diary of Sarah McClellan ... Contributed by Mrs. Sam Woolford. Our heritage, 1:72-4 (Apr). Record of a voyage from New Orleans to Galveston and Indianola and up the Guadalupe River to Victoria and by land toward Seguin, 8-25 Apr. (1850?), with ecstatic comments on Texas scenery. [8581

R. W. SUNDSTROM. Ground-water resources in Texas [1850-1954]. Southw. water works jour., 37(9):8-18 (Dec 1955). diagrs. (1 col.), maps. On the problems resulting from the "mining" of ground water, particularly in the areas surrounding Houston, San Antonio, and El Paso and in the High Plains. [8582

J. W. TOLBERT. The proud Texan. Jr. historian (Tex.), 20(4):21-3, 30 (Jan). port. On Andrew J. Mather (1851-1929), a Texas Ranger in 1874; with anecdotes about his life in Georgetown, Tex., and information about his "madstone." [8583

ANNALEE (WENTWORTH) BURNS. Gone are the days. San Antonio: Naylor Co. [1860]. xiv, 95 p. On Utopia, Uvalde County, settled in 1852; with chapters on "Summer kin," threshing, "Play and pastimes," "Oldtime religion," "Remedies and cures," Christmas, folklore, and other subjects as observed by the author during her youth there in the 1920s. [8584

DICK GOSS. The Millie King Stagecoach Inn. Jr. historian (Tex.), 20(6): 16-17, 21 (May). view. On a structure near Belmont, Tex., built in 1852, now in almost ruinous condition. [8585

KATHLYN OTTMERS. Gottfried Ottmers [died 1895], pioneer. Jr. historian (Tex.), 19(4):1-4 (Jan 1959). views. On his emigration from Germany in 1852 and his life in and near Fredericksburg. [8586

ADELAIDE HALL PIERCE, comp. Deming's Bridge Cemetery, Trespalacios Baptist Church, 1852-1898, and Hawley Cemetery, 1898-1960, Matagorda County, Texas. Palacios, Tex.: Palacios Beacon, 1960. 75, [5] p. facsim., ports. Text of the original "Minute Book" of the Church, recording "Services, Conferences, Protracted Meetings, deaths of Members or their Dismissions, or Exclusions from the Church," 1852-92 (p. 14-71), and list of inscriptions in a cemetery near Blessing, 1852-1960. [8587

BRADLEY FARMER. The history of the Gonzales Inquirer [1853-1968]. Jr. historian (Tex.), 19(4):23-5 (Jan 1959). [8588

JANE PATTIE. Shanghai Pierce: Webster on cattle. Quarter horse jour., 12(9):16, 104-5 (Jun). On Able Head Pierce (1834-1900), New England emigrant to Texas in 1853, cattle rustler, Confederate soldier, later a cattle rancher. [8589

BETTY JO WIEST. Adverse possession in Texas [1853-1958]. Tex. law rev., 38:320-29 (Feb). notes. [8590

EMMA MURCK ALTGELT (1834-1912). Emma Altgelt's sketches of life in Texas. [Translated and edited by] Henry B. Dielman. Southw. hist. quar., 63:363-84 (Jan). views. Translation of her "Schilderungen aus dem texicanischen Leben," published in the New Braunfels Zeitung in 1930 but written in 1887. Memories of her voyage from Germany and her travels from Indianola to San Antonio, her visits to New Braunfels and other German settlements, and her life with her husband, Ernst Hermann Altgelt, at Comfort, 1854 to ca. 1865, with various references to later years. [8591

JOHN DAVID SAVAGE. John Chisum, cattle king and "trail blazer." Jr. historian (Tex.), 20(2):17-19, 28 (Nov 1959). map, view. On John Simpson Chisum (1824-84), Texas cattleman from 1854 till his death. [8592

DEANNA DIMMITT. The Seminole-Negroes of Texas: a forgotten people. Jr. historian (Tex.), 20(5):8-10, 30 (Mar). ports., view. On a group of Negroes and Seminole Indians who fled from the Indian Territory across Texas into Mexico after 1855, some of whom later lettled in Texas at Fort Clark. [8593

OVIE CLARK FISHER. The life and times of King Fisher [1855-84]. Southw. hist. quar., 64:232-47 (Oct). port. On his life in Texas and his activities as "the most colorful and notorious outlaw who ever operated on the Texas border," later deputy sheriff of Medina County, killed in San Antonio. [8594

Mrs. C. N. FRY, comp. Inscriptions from the cemetery at Indianola, Texas. Our heritage, 1:140-41 (Jul). Twenty inscriptions, 1855, 1867-77, 1886. [8595

SARAH T. HUGHES. Handling of juvenile delinquents in Texas [1856-1959]. Tex. law rev., 38:290-302 (Feb). notes. [8596

KERR COUNTY, Tex. Kerr County marriages--Book A. Contributed by Mrs. M. C. Pearce. Our heritage, 1:87-9, 135-8 (Apr, Jul). List of names in chronological order, 1856-66. [8597

THOMAS L. MILLER. The Texas Court of Claims, 1856-1861. Agric. hist., 34:35-40 (Jan). notes. On the office of the Commissioner of Claims, established "to protect the State of Texas from fraudulent land and money claims of all sorts." [8598

LINDA REAL. The kindred cycle. Jr. historian (Tex.), 21(1):7-10 (Sep). ports., view. On Hermann Stieler (born 1849), German emigrant to Texas in 1856, early resident of Comfort, rancher. [8599

FRANK MacD. SPINDLER. The history of Hempstead and the formation of Waller County, Texas [1856-73]. Southw. hist. quar., 63:404-27 (Jan). notes. [8600

PAGE DOUGLAS. Frederick Sovereign Wade [1836-1926], a Texan by choice. Jr. historian (Tex.), 19(5): 13-15, 18 (Mar 1959). On the author's great-grandfather, settler in Texas in 1857, schoolteacher, officer in the C.S. Army, farmer, Democratic leader. [8601

FRANCES PRESTON. The Whites come to Texas. Jr. historian (Tex.), 21(1):1-4, 32 (Sep). map, port. On John Preston White (1832-1905), who settled at Seguin with his family in 1857 and served as lawyer, judge, and court reporter, eventually at Austin. [8602

HAMILTON HERALD-NEWS. Parade of progress, Hamilton County, 1858-1958. Centennial edition. [Hamilton, Tex., 1958? 72] p. ports., views. 45 cm. Signed historical articles by P. M. Rice, Mrs. Bessie Brown, Cecil B. James, C. Applegate, Joy Kauitsch, Charles Patterson, and others; reminiscences by several early settlers; "Short sketches of early settlers: authentic biographies up to 1896"; and antiquarian advertisements of local businesses. [8603

FRANK MacD. SPINDLER. Saint Bartholomew's Church [Episcopal], Hempstead, Texas [1858-1959, mainly before 1890]. P. E. Church, Hist. mag., 29:56-90 (Mar). notes. [8604

GEORGE WILKINS KENDALL (1809-67). Letters from a Texas sheep ranch, written in the years 1860 and 1867, by George Wilkins Kendall to Henry Stephens Randall. Edited by Harry James Brown. Urbana: Univ. of Illinois Press, 1959. vi, [2], 156 p. facsims., map, ports. notes. Long letters on sheep, politics, Texas weather, etc., dated "Rancho near New Braunfels," 1 Jan.-4 Dec. 1860, and Boerne, Kendall County, 7 Apr.-24 Jun. 1867. [8605

HORTENSE (WARNER) WARD. A century of missionary effort: the Church of the Good Shepherd, 1860-1960. [Austin? Tex., 1960.] xi, [3], 211 p. ports., tables, views (1 col.). notes (p. 192-203). On a Protestant Episcopal church in Corpus Christi. [8606

FLOYD F. EWING, JR. Suggestions for the observance in West Texas of the Civil War centennial. West Tex. Hist. Assoc. yr. bk., 36:33-40. notes. Includes a "brief summary of the effects of the Civil War on West Texas" and "the informality of the role of West Texas in the Civil War." [8607

JEAN MARIE ODIN (1801-70). A letter of the Bishop of Galveston, 1861. Translated and edited by Willard E. Wight. Southw. hist. quar., 63:450-53 (Jan). notes. Letter to the President and the Members of the Council of the Propagation of the Faith, Lyons, dated Galveston, 26 Jan. 1861, on the state of the Catholic Church in Texas. [8608

HAROLD PREECE. Lone Star man: Ira Aten [1862-1953], last of the old Texas Rangers. N.Y.: Hastings House [1960]. 256 p. map, ports. (1 double), views. bibliog. (p. 249). On his early life near Austin and his Ranger service. [8609

Mrs. A. D. ROOKE & others, comps. Inscriptions from the cemetery at Sutherland Springs, Texas [1862-1960]. Our heritage, 1:91-8 (Apr). [8610

ETHEL FROMÉN. John Peter Sjolander, 1851-1939, "the Sage of Cedar Bayou." Am. Swed. Hist. Foundation, Yr. bk., 1960, p. 63-8. On a native of Sweden who emigrated to America sometime after 1870, and his life in Texas as a writer of stories and poems. [8611

LEE JORDEN. The Salt Grass Trail. Jr. historian (Tex.), 20(4):5-8, 28 (Jan). views. On cattle drives to the Texas coast, where the cattle wintered in salt marshes, 1870s-1902. [8612

RAY JACK ROBERTS. Educational objectives and curriculum legislation in Texas, 1870-1957. Ann Arbor: University Microfilms, 1960. Positive microfilm of typescript. [384] leaves. Thesis--Univ. of Texas. Abstracted: Dissert. abstracts, 21:1449-50 (Dec). [8613

MIKE LEVY. The Mercer logs. Jr. historian (Tex.), 19(4): 12-14 (Jan 1959). map. On diaries kept by Robert A. Mercer (born 1799) and his sons John G. and Edward T., " pioneer pilots on the Port Aransas coast" during a period that included the years 1871-1919. [8614

L. MANDELBAUM. Texas merchants after the Civil War, 1871. Am. Jew. arch., 12:71-4 (Apr). Excerpts from a diary, 2-3 Feb. 1871, describing retail clothing stores operated by Asher Mandelbaum at Bremond and Philip Mandelbaum at Kosse. [8615

SANDRA L. MYRES. S[amuel] D[ale] Myres [born 1871] and the Myres Saddle Company of Sweetwater. West Tex. Hist. Assoc. yr. bk., 36:116-36. notes. On his life in Texas, his founding and management of the S. D. Myres Saddle Company in Sweetwater and his services as "community builder" and "fighting mayor" there, 1897-1920, and his removal to El Paso. [8616

THOMAS O'DWYER. $180,000--ninety feet down. Frontier times, 34(3):28-9, 48-50 (summer). map. On the supposed theft of a strongbox containing U.S. gold coins by Edward Young and other members of the crew of the British freighter South Wind at Port O'Connor, Tex., the supposed concealment of the box at the bottom of Matagorda Bay, and the efforts of John Clay Jermain, Manhattan ex-convict, and others to find the lost treasure, 1871. [8617

EDNA (TURLEY) CARPENTER (born 1872). Tales from the Manchaca hills: the unvarnished memoirs of a Texas gentlewoman ... as edited and recorded by Jand and Bill Hogan [Jane (Carpenter) Hogan and William Ransom Hogan]. New Orleans: Hauser Press [1960]. x, [6], 221 p. cartoon, facsim., map, ports. On the author's early life on a ranch near Onion Creek, Tex., her studies in Sam Houston State Normal School, her marriage to Tommie Carpenter, and their life in Manchaca and Taft, Tex. [8618

SETH THOMAS BAILEY & RALPH J. WEAVER. The nine lives of Captain Frank Jones [1856-93]. Frontier times, 34(2):6-9, 36-40 (spring). port. On his career in the Texas Rangers, 1873-93, and his several escapes from violent death in the Mason County War on the Mexican border. [8619

RALPH WOOD JONES. A history of Southwestern University [Georgetown, Tex.], 1873-1949. Ann Arbor: University Microfilms, 1960. Positive microfilm of typescript. [676] leaves. Thesis--Univ. of Texas. Abstracted: Dissert. abstracts, 20:4576 (Jun). [8620

JAMES LEWELLYN ALLHANDS. Railroads to the Rio. Salado, Tex.: Anson Jones Press, 1960. 213 p. facsims., maps, ports., views. bibliog. (p. 213), notes. On the organization and construction of railroads in the area between San Antonio, Corpus Christi, Brownsville, and Laredo, 1874-1927, and the author's participation in the business as early as 1903. Includes chapters on the St. Louis, Brownsville, & Mexico Railway Company and its Hidalgo Branch, the San Antonio, Chapin, & Rio Grande Valley Railway Company, and the Southern Pacific Railroad; the railroad-building activities of Uriah Lott, Sam A. Robertson, Lon C. Hill, John Clossner, and Presley M. and Benjamin F. Johnston; and "Townsites carved out of the wilderness." [8621

HARRY H. CAMPBELL. The early history of Motley County [1874-1958, mainly before 1900]. San Antonio: Naylor Co. [1958]. 74 p. ports., views. Includes the author's reminiscences of the county since 1892 and of the Matador Ranch (established by his father, Henry H. Campbell, manager of the

Matador Land and Cattle Company from 1879 to 1891); the speech of Henry H. Campbell at the time of his resignation in 1891; and text of an interview with Frank Collinson, settler in the county in 1874. [8622

FRANKLIN REYNOLDS. Outlaw's horses. Quarter horse jour., 4(1): 10-11, 39 (Oct 1951). On "a light sorrel with flaxey mane and tail," of uncertain origin, from Tennessee, in possession of John Wesley Hardin, Texas gambler and killer, in 1874, sold by him to Crawford Sikes, and known as "Old Rondo" in distinction from "Sike's (or Syke's) Rondo," foaled ca. 1887, died ca. 1907. [8623

MICHAEL BONINE. Buffalo Gap, the living ghost town [Taylor County, Tex., 1875-1959]. Jr. historian (Tex.), 20(1):1-5, 30 (Sep 1959). map, port., views. [8624

JAMES EVETTS HALEY. F[rank] Reaugh [1860-1945]: man and artist. El Paso, Tex.: C. Hertzog, 1960. [16] p. ports., views (part col., 1 double). On his removal from Illinois to Texas in 1876, his life near Terrell, and his paintings, "largely of the great prairies of Texas and the longhorned cattle of fifty years ago." [8625

RONALD LAMB. The railroad comes to Seguin. Jr. historian (Tex.), 19(2): 6-7 (Nov 1958). On the Galveston, Harrisburg, and San Antonio Railway, 1876. [8626

JOHN M. SANDERS. The deed of an insane grantor [in Texas law, 1876-1955]. Baylor law rev., 11:436-50; 12:62-78 (fall 1959, winter 1960). notes. [8627

NANCY BROWN. Harpersville--where something is. Jr. historian (Tex.), 19(6):17-20, 25 (May 1959). views. History of "a small community in Stephens County." 1877-1959. [8628

JUNE WILLIAMS. Muleshoe Ranch. Jr. historian (Tex.), 20(5):27-8, 32 (Mar). On a ranch set up by William Henry Harrison Black (1839-1906) near Breckenridge, Tex., in 1877, and the discovery of oil on the ranch in 1922. [8629

ARTHUR HECHT. Postal history in the Texas Panhandle. Canyon, Tex.: Panhandle-Plains Historical Soc., 1960. 58, [6] p. List of the 532 post offices in the 44 counties, with location, dates of founding and discontinuance, and names of postmasters, 1878-1959. [8630

BERNARD BUIE. The open range of sixty-five northwest Texas counties. Southw. hist. quar., 64: fold. col. map following p. 156. Shows "a number of the outstanding landmarks, trails, and ranches of the 1880's," and includes text printed on the back concerning "the open range history" of this area. Indicates each ranch in the area by its brand but does not name the brands. [8631

RICHARD GRAHAM. The investment boom in British-Texan cattle companies, 1880-1885. Bus. hist. rev., 34:421-45 (winter). tables, view. notes. [8632

LEWIS A. NORDYKE. Traveler country. Quarter horse jour., 7(3): 16-17, 30-31 (Dec 1954). views. Based upon an article by Ed Bateman in The quarter horse, Jul. 1946. "Legend and lore" about a quarter-horse stallion brought to Texas as a work horse, discovered to have brilliant potentialities as a racer, and in great demand as s studhorse, early 1880s. [8633

WILLARD H. PORTER. It takes tough horses. Quarter horse jour., 7(10): 6-7, 17-18 (Jul 1955). views (1 double). On "cowboy 'tournaments'" in Texas, begun in "the 1880s," later a feature at "livestock picnics" and county fairs ("fairgrounding"), consisting of "running after and jerking down steers," an operation known as "steer busting or steer jerking" and performed by "steer roping teams--men and horses." [8634

DOLLIE WILLIAMS. Hunters of the Big Thicket [parts of Chambers, Hardin, Tyler, and Polk Counties in eastern Texas, 1880s to early 1900s]. Jr. historian (Tex.), 19(2):8-10, 32 (Nov 1958). view. [8635

JOHN D. McCALL. Legal problems related to issuance of time warrants. Baylor law rev., 11:347-62 (fall 1959). Table of cases. notes. On a form of interest-bearing securities issued in lieu of cash payment by Texas counties and cities, 1881-1936. [8636

ULYSSES WALSH. Vernon Dalhart [real name: Marion Try Slaughter, 1883-1948]. By Jim Walsh. Hobbies, 65(3-10): monthly installments (May-Dec). facsims., ports. On his early life in Texas, his work as a singer of popular songs and "concert ballards," his phonograph recordings (1915-39), and his supposed authorship of "The prisoner's song." [8637

C. M. ROBERTS. P. M. Kelly & Sons. West. horseman, 25(5):78-9, 160-61 (May). ports., views. On the manufacture of bits and spurs by P. M. Kelly (born 1886) in Texas, eventually in El Paso, 1903-60. [8638

RALPH TAYLOR WOOTTON. Oscar Henry Cooper [1852-1932], master builder in Texas education. Ann Arbor: University Microfilms [1960]. Positive microfilm of typescript. viii, 309 leaves. ports. bibliog. (leaves 299-309). Thesis (Ed. D.)--Univ. of Texas. Abstracted: Dissert. abstracts, 20:3608 (Mar). On his service as State Superintendent of Public Instruction, Superintendent of Schools at Galveston, President of Baylor University, and President of Simmons College, 1886-1909. [8639

HAZEL GANDRE. Monthalia Methodist Church [12 miles from Gonzales, Tex., 1887-1953]. Jr. historian (Tex.), 19(4):15-16, 30 (Jan 1959). [8640

BENNY GALLAWAY. Rock Creek coal mines, Parker County. Jr. historian (Tex.), 20(5):29-30 (Mar). view. On the town of Rock Creek, founded in 1890, abandoned in 1909. [8641

BEVERLY KIEL. A history of Texas Lutheran College [at Brenham, later at Seguin, 1891-1959]. Jr. historian (Tex.), 20(1):16-17 (Sep 1959). view. [8642

RONALD DE WAYNE GODARD. The Odessa Meteor Crater. Jr. historian (Tex.), 21(3):14-16 (Dec). On "the third-largest crater in the United States," near Odessa, Tex., discovered in 1892, first recognized as a meteoric crater in 1922. [8643

REBECCA MURRAY. Rabke Methodist Church. Jr. historian (Tex.), 19(6): 26-7 (May 1959). view. On a small wooden church built in southwestern De Witt County in 1894 in the now extinct community of Rabke but still in use. [8644

JOHN BROUSSARD. Arthur Stilwell's dream city [Port Arthur, Tex., 1895-99]. Jr. historian (Tex.), 21(3):3-8, 16 (Dec). port., views. [8645

CLAUDE W. BRYANT. Lumbering along in Texas. San Antonio: Naylor Co. [1960]. ix, 201 p. facsims., ports., views. On the author's early life in Kosse, Tex., his studies at Baylor University, and his activities since 1897 in the lumber business in Texas. [8646

MERLE MEARS DUNCAN. The death of Senator Coke. Southw. hist. quar., 63:385-403 (Jan). ports., views. notes. Information from Texas newspapers about the death of Richard Coke (1829-97) on his plantation near Waco, his funeral and burial, the extraordinary electrical storm during the funeral service, and the monument erected in his memory in the cemetery. [8647

ORA E. ROBBINS JINKS, comp. Styles Cemetery inscriptions, Hwy. 17, Old Styles Ranch, Williamson County, Texas [1897-1944]. South. genealogist's exchange quar., 2(14):7 (summer). [8648

ELVIN E. TACKETT. Remedy for unjust and unfair ad valorem tax assessment [in Texas, 1897-1959]. Baylor law rev., 11:363-82 (fall 1959). notes. [8649

J. LEE MURRAY. Fifty years with my horses. Quarter horse, 3(1):18-19 (Apr 1948). Reminiscences of the author's life on Texas ranches, his work as a racer of quarter horses, and his part in founding the National Quarter Horse Breeders Association. [8650

EDWARD MUEGGE SCHIWETZ (born 1898). Buck Schiwetz' Texas: drawings and paintings by E. M. Schiwetz. Introduction by Walter Prescott Webb. Austin: Univ. of Texas Press [1960]. 134 p. views (part col.). 23x30 cm. Black-and-white reproductions and colored reproductions of paintings of Texas landscapes, town scenes, and old buildings, and "The artist's comments on his pictures; with a biographical sketch by Webb, on Schiwetz's early life in Cuero and his work as a commercial artist. [8651

JOE R. THOMPSON. Steaming in the rain. Trains, 20(10):26-7 (Aug). map, views. On the Moscow, Camden, & San Augustine Railroad, connecting Moscow and Camden, Tex., and serving the W. T. Carter Lumber Company at Camden, 1898-1960. [8652

LAURA VERNON HAMNER. Cow carols and windmill music. Cattleman, 46(10):42-3, 62 (Mar). ports., views. On Florence (Fenley) Wilson, brought up on a ranch near Sanderson, Tex., educated at Texas State College for Women, twice widowed, member of the Texas House of Representatives, operator of a goat ranch near Uvalde, writer of newspaper articles expressing "her overpowering love of cattle and ranch life." [8653

MARYNELL HOLLE. David H[enry] Dunn [1869-1916], Panhandle missionary. Jr. historian (Tex.), 21(1):21-4 (Sep). On his service as a Catholic priest in Texas, 1900-1916, eventually with headquarters at Amarillo. [8654

C. C. JEFFRIES. Life at Winkler. Southw. hist. quar., 64:36-41 (Jul). Reminiscences of a town in central Texas (ca. 1900?). [8655

ROBERT LESLIE MARTIN. The city moves west: economic and industrial growth of the southern Llano Estacado [in west Texas, 1900-1958]. Ann Arbor: University Microfilms, 1959 [i.e. 1960]. Positive microfilm of typescript. [262] leaves. Thesis--Univ. of Oklahoma. Abstracted: Dissert. abstracts, 20:4385 (May). [8656

AUGUST PLATE. Tales of Terlingua. Jr. historian (Tex.), 21(1):16-17, 29 (Sep). view. On a town in the Big Bend country, connected with "the second largest group of quick-silver mines in the world," 1900-1946, now abandoned. [8657

FRANCES PRESTON. Yellow magic of the Texas Gulf coast. Jr. historian (Tex.), 20(5):1-4, 26 (Mar). map, views. On the sulphur industry in Texas since 1900. [8658

A. M. HARTUNG. Memories of Billy Anson. Quarter horse jour., 4(7):24-5, 102-4 (Apr 1952). port. On William Anson, Englishman, son of an earl, breeder and trainer of quarter horses in Coleman County, Tex., from 1901 till ca. 1911 or later, and his eventual return to England. [8659

TOMMY KING. Sheriff F. M. Fly and the mob at the Gonzales County Jail. Jr. historian (Tex.), 20(2):25-6 (Nov 1959). port. Information from Fly on his repulse of a mob trying to get possession of Gregorio Cortez, murderer of a sheriff and of a member of his posse, 1901. [8660

LEWIS A. NORDYKE. Nubbin Ridge. Garden City, N.Y.: Doubleday, 1960. 264 p. On the author's early life on a farm on Green Briar Creek in Callahan County, 17 miles south-southeast of Baird, Tex., from some time after 1901 till 1919. [8661

J. L. SWANSON. At Port Arthur, Texas: history of water supply [ca. 1905 to 1955]. Southw. water works jour., 37(9):34-5 (Dec 1955). [8662

ROBERT E. LEE MILLER. The Bellevue tornado of April 26, 1906. [Reported by] Catherine Young Clack. Southw. hist. quar., 63:584-8 (Apr). Oral recollections of "the awful windstorm that blew away the town of Bellevue" and killed 17 persons. [8663

BILLY GREEN. The acropolis of San Angelo. Jr. historian (Tex.), 21(2): 1-5, 32 (Nov). views. On the San Angelo Collegiate Institute, 1907-12. [8664

AMERICAN FEDERATION OF ARTS. Everett Spruce [born 1908]. By John Palmer Leeper. N.Y. [1959]. 28 p. port., views (part col.). bibliog. (p. 21-3). On his life in Texas as an art student, a painter, and a teacher of art; with a catalogue of a retrospective exhibition. [8665

LAWRENCE LESTER GRAVES. Lubbock, an epitome of urbanization [since 1908]. West Tex. Hist. Assoc. yr. bk., 36:3-17. notes. [8666

A. M. HARTUNG. Long live the buckskin color. Quarter horse jour., 4(1): 12, 43 (Oct 1951). port., view. On Texas quarter horses bred by Tom Waggoner (W. T. Waggoner) "around 1910" and later, exhibiting "yellow and golden ... dun and grulla colors," some with black manes and tails and zebra stripes above knees and hocks. [8667

The STORY of Sam King. Quarter horse jour., 5(7):70-71 (Apr 1953). From The quarter horse, Sep. 1946. On a quarter-horse racer, polo horse, and studhorse, foaled in Texas in 1910 (or 1914), "founder of a family of Quarter Horses that rate with the all-time greats ... without doubt the most famous horse this country has ever produced." [8668

---- ANGLIN. The return of Cap Anglin's leggins [sic] ... as told to Bill Leftwich by Cap Anglin. Cattleman, 46(8):33 (Jan). port., view. Recollections, by the City Marshal of McAllen, Tex., of the apprehension of Mexican bandits engaged in buying or stealing horses, guns, etc., for use in carrying out the Plan of San Diego ("to take, by force, the land that lies between the Nueces River and the Rio Grande and give it to the Mexicans and Negroes"), 1912. [8669

BRUNETTIE BURROW. Angels in white. San Antonio: Naylor Co. [1959]. ix, 132 p. port. On the author's training in a nurses' school, 1912-14, and her work as a registered nurse in Texas, 1914 to ca. 1939. [8670

MAYNETT COX. The little railroad that went to war. Jr. historian (Tex.), 19(3):19-21, 28 (Dec 1958). views. On the San Antonio, Fredericksburg, and Northern Railway (later the Fredericksburg and Northern Railway Company), 1912-44. [8671

BOB KIESLING. Partial revocation of a will by excision, obliteration, cancellation, or insertion [in Texas cases, 1912-59]. Baylor law rev., 12:194-201 (spring). notes. [8672

DURWOOD DOUGLAS CRAWFORD. Legal rights of married women in Texas [1913-58]. Southw. law jour., 13:84-212 (winter 1959). notes. [8673

WILLARD H. PORTER. Wizard with a rope. Quarter horse jour., 3(5):4-5, 27 (Feb 1951). ports. On Toots Mansfield (born 1914), rancher in Texas, rodeo performer. [8674

JOSIE BIRCK. Alfred "Smokey" Klaerner [born 1877], law of Gillespie County. Jr. historian (Tex.), 20(5):5-7 (Mar). ports. On his service as sheriff of the county, 1918-42. [8675

JOHN R. BROWN. Hail to the chief: Hutcheson the judge. Tex. law rev., 38:140-46 (Dec 1959). port. notes. On Joseph C. Hutcheson, Jr. (born 1879), as a U.S. district judge and later a U.S. circuit judge in Texas, 1918-59. [8676

ELIZABETH JEAN GIBSON. The Welfare League of Coleman County [1919-59]. West Tex. Hist. Assoc. yr. bk., 36:187-99. notes. [8677

NELSON CORAL NYE. A foundation for speed. Quarter horse jour., 4(2): 16-17, 70 (Nov 1951). port., views. On "probably the greatest speed line in modern Quarter stock," progeny of Joe Reed (1920-47), owned by John Wesley House of Cameron, Tex. [8678

WILLARD H. PORTER. Roping is his trade. Quarter horse jour., 6(8):8-9 (May 1954). port. On John D. Holleyman (born 1920), his early life in Texas and his work since 1940 as a professional steer-roper in rodeos. [8679

R. A. TOLER. 30 years of water works progress at Giddings, Texas [1925-55]. Southw. water works jour., 38(3):10-14 (Jun 1956). views. [8680

ROBERT S. READING. Arrows over Texas. San Antonio: Naylor Co. [1960]. xv, 269 p. views. bibliog. (p. 260-61). On the author's activities since ca. 1930 in collecting more than 44,000 Indian artifacts from various parts of Texas, displayed in the Museum of Texas Western College, El Paso. [8681

EVERETT SPRUCE (born 1908). A portfolio of eight paintings. [With an introduction by Jerry Bywaters.] Austin: Univ. of Texas Press, 1958. [8] p. 8 col. views. 48 cm. (Blaffer series of Southwestern art, 1.) Colored reproductions of oil paintings of Texas landscapes, undated; with some account of the painter's youth in Arkansas, his studies in the Dallas Art Institute, and his work in Texas since 1930 as a museum curator, a teacher of art, and a painter. [8682

ROY C. DAVIS. King P-234. Quarter horse jour., 4(7):22-3, 76, 78-83 (Apr 1952). views. On a South Texas quarter-horse racer, rodeo horse, and studhorse (foaled 1931). [8683

WARNER E. MILLS, JR. Martial law in east Texas. University, Ala.: Univ. of Alabama Press for the ICP [1960. 4], 41, [3] p. (Inter-University Case Program. ICP case series, 53.) On the proclamation of martial law by Ross Shaw Sterling, Governor of Texas, to prevent "physical waste of oil and gas" in a newly exploited oil field as the result of unrestrained competitive drilling there and to maintain law and order till the Railroad Commission of Texas could hold hearings, and the resulting litigation and legislation, 1931-32. [8684

JERRY ARMSTRONG. Jim Bob Altizer [born 1932]--champion calf roper. West. horseman, 25(7):34, 88-90 (Jul). On his early life on a ranch near Del Rio, his career as a rodeo performer, and his return to ranching at Del Rio. [8685

HORACE L. LEITHEAD. Runoff in relation to range condition in the Big Bend - Davis Mountain section of Texas [1932-51]. Jour. range management, 12:83-7 (Mar 1959). diagrs., map, tables, view. [8686

BRAD BUTLER. Big Bend National Park. Jr. historian (Tex.), 20(1):8-11 (Sep 1959). views. On Texas Canyons State Park, established in 1933, renamed Big Bend State Park in 1934, and transferred to the National Park Service in 1944. [8687

NAYLOR'S EPIC-CENTURY: THE MAGAZINE OF TEXAS AND THE GREAT SOUTHWEST. The new Texas reader. Edited by C[linton] Stanley Banks and Grace Taylor McMillan. San Antonio: Naylor Co. [1960]. xix, 280, 280a-280d, 281-291 p. col. map, ports., views (part col.). notes. Reprint of The Texas reader (1947) with an added article (p. 280a-280d). Very short stories and articles from "a quarterly whose pages have been penned by some of the best-loved writers of Texas," 1935-47, with additions by its staff writers and editors. Includes series by Chris Emmett, Jack C. Butterfield, and Doris Killingsworth and Single contributions by J. Frank Dobie, Clarence R. Wharton, James T. De Shields, Joseph William Schmitz, Jacob F. Wolters, Ettie M. Doughty, Florence Johnson Scott, Howard W. Peak III, and others. [8688

T. M. DIAMOND. New tools for the Carpenter case. Baylor law rev., 11:1-18 (winter 1959). diagrs., notes. On standards of compensation to owners of Texas lands taken by eminent domain, 1936-54. [8689

JOSEPH G. ROLLINS, JR. The controlled access highway--conflicting rights of highway users and abutting commercial enterprises [in Texas, 1936-58]. Baylor law rev., 11:148-67 (spring 1959). diagrs. notes. [8690

TEXAS, UNIVERSITY OF. Institute of Public Affairs. Public employee retirement in Texas [1937-53. By] John E. Swanson [and] Francis A. Miskell. Austin, 1955. xi, 147 p. tables. notes. (Its Public affairs series, 21.) [8691

BURKE MUSGROVE. Snakes alive! Jr. historian (Tex.), 19(5):16-18 (Mar 1959). port., view. On P. C. Walker as a hunter and exhibitor of rattlesnakes, organizer of the Irish Snake Hunters' Association in Stephens County, Tex., ca. 1938. [8692

WALTER PRESCOTT WEBB (1888-1963). Flat Top: a story of modern ranching. Cattleman, 46(7-11): monthly installments (Dec 1959-Apr 1960). ports., views. On a tract of 17,000 acres damaged by "overgrazing and erosion," in Bosque County, Tex., acquired by Charles Pettit in 1938, his development of herds of Hereford cattle and Yorkshire hogs, and his encouragement of deer, turkeys, water birds, and other wildlife by promoting the growth of woods and making 75 lakes; with some account of his earlier life in Texas as teacher, merchant, and wealthy oilman. [8693

CHARLES ROSSON. Cal Farley's Boy's Ranch. Quarter horse jour., 12(7):102-6, 134-5 (Apr). ports., views (1 double). On a foster home for boys at the ghost town of Tascosa, 40 miles west of Amarillo, founded in 1939 by Cal Farley; his "policy of mixing about 50 per cent good boys with an equal amount who have been in trouble"; and his "97 per cent success record in raising youngsters to become useful and responsible citizens." [8694

R. C. UTLEY. The city of Big Spring [Tex.] met the water supply challenge [1939-56]. Southw. water works jour., 38(7):58-62 (Oct 1956). map, views. notes. [8695

JACK E. DODSON. Minority group housing in two Texas cities [San Antonio and Houston, 1940-56]. Nathan Glazer & Davis McEntire, eds., Studies in housing & minority groups ... special research report to the Commission on Race and Housing (Berkeley: Univ. of California Press, 1960, p. 84-109. map, tables. [8696

U.S. Geological Survey. Texas floods of 1940. By Seth D. Breeding. Wash.: U.S. Govt. Print. Off., 1948. iv, 91 p. diagrs., fold. maps, tables, views. (Its Water-supply paper 1046.) On the flood (rainfall and runoff) in the San Jacinto River Basin, Jun.-Jul. 1940. [8697

ROBERT MOORMAN DENHARDT. Squaw H--she had it! By Bob Denhardt. Quarter horse jour., 7(1):5, 34-5 (Oct 1954). views. On a quarter-horse racing mare (foaled 1941), trained by Blaine Speers of Rocksprings, Tex.; with an account of her by Speers, who describes her as "by far and away the most perfect individual I have ever seen." [8698

J. W. SORENSON. Mechanization of peanut production in Texas [1941-51]. Agric. engineering, 33:561-2 (Sep 1952). views. notes. [8699

TEXAS, UNIVERSITY OF. Institute of Public Affairs. Financing State government in Texas [1941-49]. By Lynn F[oster] Anderson [and] T.E. McMillan, Jr. Austin, 1953. x, 196, [2] p. diagrs., tables. notes. (Its Public affairs series, 13.) [8700

WILLIAM GARDNER WINTERS, JR. The shoreline for Spanish and Mexican grants in Texas. Tex. law rev., 38: 523-37 (May). notes. On litigation involving "the location of the shoreline" and "the ownership of accretion," 1944-56. [8701

MARILYN B. DAVIS. Local approach to the Sweatt case. Negro hist. bul., 23:133-7 (Mar). bibliog., notes. On the litigation by which Heman Marion Sweatt, Negro, forced the State of Texas to admit him to the University of Texas Law School, 1946-50, and his withdrawal from the school in 1952 "because of failing grades," leaving several other Negroes as students continuing their studies there. [8702

DE WITT CARTER REDDICK. Fisher of men. Presbyt. survey, 47(11):24-6 (Nov 1957). On Swanson Yarbrough (1893?-1956) and his Presbyterian activities in Tyler, Tex., 1947-56. [8703

ED KAHN. Texas folktale version of "Get up and bar the door" (Child 275). West folklore, 19:169-71 (Jul). notes. Includes a prose version recited in 1958 by Clark Taylor of Waco, Tex., learned by him long ago from Curtis Thomason, also of Waco. [8704

JOHN GRAVES. Goodbye to a river: a narrative. N.Y.: Knopf, 1960. [10], 306, [2] p. double map. bibliog. (p. 303-6). Account of the author's solitary canoe voyage down the Brazos from Fling Bend, in Palo Pinto, Parker, Hood, and Somervell Counties, intermingled with description, history, and lore concerning this area, soon to be flooded behind a dam. [8705

JOHN NATHAN CRAVENS. Anniversary celebrations. West Tex. Hist. Assoc. yr. bk., 36:201-4. On celebrations during 1960 by counties and towns in western Texas upon attaining their 25th, 50th, or 75th anniversary. [8706

Austin

JOHN GILLESPIE. Government in metropolitan Austin. Austin, 1956. [6], 82 p. map, tables. notes. (University of Texas. Institute of Public Affairs. Public affairs series. 26.) Based on thesis--Univ. of Texas, 1954. On the 36 local governments within Travis County, Tex., 1840-1955, mainly since 1940. [8707

TIPPY NEWTON. St. David's Church [Episcopalian, in Austin, 1853-1959]. Jr. historian (Tex.), 20(3):4-8 (Dec 1959). port., views. [8708

EVELYN M. CARRINGTON. A fresh and inquiring mind. Delta Kappa Gamma bul., 23(1):11-15 (fall 1956). On Lilian Carrington (1864-1956), her early life near Austin, her studies in the University of Texas, and her work as the owner and principal of the University Preparatory and Grammar School (later the Carrington School), Austin. [8709

WALTER E. LONG. The longhorn crossing. [Austin? Tex., 1960. 2], 34, [1] p. double map, ports., views (1 col.). bibliog. (p. 34), notes. On a cattle crossing of the Colorado River in Austin, Tex., which "led to the railhead at Abilene, Kansas," 1867-1880s, the early mills using the site for water power, and the more recent plans for construction of a dam there. [8710

The TEXAS Capitol [Austin, 1875-1960]: How it was built. Cattleman, 46(10):40-41, 68-70, 74-80 (Mar). views (1 col.). From The Humble way. Detailed description of the building and its exhibits. [8711

BILL PETMECKY. Millett and Hancock opera houses [in Austin]. Jr. historian (Tex.), 19(4):31-2 (Jan 1959). On the Millett Opera House, built in 1878, and the Hancock Opera House, 1896. [8712

FRANCES PRESTON. The era of Peregrinus and Alexander Frederic Claire. Jr. historian (Tex.), 19(5): 25-8, 32 (Mar 1959). port., views. On horseplay and mascots of students of the Law School and the College of Engineering, University of Texas, 1880s-1958. [8713

TOMMY SMITH. O. Henry's Austin days. Jr. historian (Tex.), 19(5):8-12 (Mar 1959). ports., view. On the life of William Sydney Porter in Austin as a bookkeeper, a draftsman in the General Land Office, a bank teller, an author, and an editor, 1884-98. [8714

STEVE SIMON. The death of Austin's indestructible dam. Jr. historian (Tex.), 19(4):5-8 (Jan 1959). views. On a dam built in 1890-93 and destroyed by a flood of the Colorado River in 1900. [8715

AUGUST WATKINS HARRIS. Cass Gilbert's Old Library Building: the Eugene C. Barker Texas History Center [University of Texas], 1910-1960. Southw. hist. quar., 64:1-13 (Jul). port., views (1 col.). notes. [8716

Dallas and Fort Worth

JOHN WILLIAM ROGERS. The lusty Texans of Dallas. ... New enlarged edition. N.Y.: Dutton, 1960. 416 p. col. maps, port. bibliog. (p. 397-8), notes. (Society in America series.) 1st ed. 1951. Anecdotal treatment of arts, music, crime, churches, schools, land speculation, entertainments, oil, and other components of the history of Dallas, settled in 1844. [8717

JAMES FARBER. Fort Worth in the Civil War. Belton, Tex.: Peter Hansbrough Bell Press, 1960, 1960. 58, [1] p. ports., views. From the Fort Worth star-telegram. [8718

BETTY J. MARTIN. Diary of a Black Belt farmer--1889. Jr. historian (Tex.), 20(3):25-6 (Dec 1959). Information from a record kept by George Washington James on a 165-acre farm in Dallas County (near the now extinct town of Breckenridge). [8719

H. A. MAGNUSSEN. Horseman merchant. West. horseman, 25(5):60, 122 (May). ports., view. On Don Ryon, Jr., rancher, rodeo performer, founder and operator of Don Windy Ryon's Saddle & Ranch Supply Company, Fort Worth, 1944-60. [8720

El Paso

HELEN ORNDORFF. The development of agriculture in the El Paso Valley--the Spanish period [1659-1821]. Password, 5:138-47 (Oct). views. notes. [8721

CLYDE WISE, JR. The effects of the railroads upon El Paso [1881-85]. Password, 5:91-100 (Jul). port., view. notes. Mainly on the activities of the town government and the rise of new businesses. [8722

ESTELLE GOODMAN LEVY. The Myra Opera House and other theaters in old El Paso. Password, 5:65-73 (Apr). view. notes. Recollections of the building of the opera house by Henry M. Myra and its destruction by fire, 1884-87, and later theatrical structures in El Paso. [8723

CUQUI CONTRERAS. The song of time. N.Y.: Carlton Press, 1960. [12], 63 p. (A Reflection book.) On the author's life in El Paso with her husband, Primo Contreras, and the infancy and childhood of their 10 children and many grandchildren. Written in the form of letters to members of the family, none containing a date, but evidently of the 20th century. [8724

Galveston and Houston

KAREY PATTERSON. The bayou that built a city. Jr. historian (Tex.), 20(3):17-21 (Dec 1959). views. On Buffalo Bayou, Houston, 1820s-1959, once "a 6-foot creek," now "a 37-foot world port." [8725

CAROLINE BROUGHTON. Houston theaters, past and present [1836-1944]. Jr. historian (Tex.), 19(3):23-6 (Dec 1958). facsim, view. [8726

RICHARD JOHLE. The Kellum-Noble house. Jr. historian (Tex.), 20(1):18-21, 25 (Sep 1959). views. On a house in Houston, begun by Nathaniel Kellum in 1847 or 1848, completed by others, and restored by the Harris County Heritage Society in 1956. [8727

LYNETTE M. ROBINSON. The first Jewish congregation in Texas [Congregation Beth Israel, Houston, 1854-1959]. Jr. historian (Tex.), 20(2):5-8, 16 (Nov 1959). port., view. [8728

ANDREW FOREST MUIR. Railroads come to Houston, 1857-1861. Southw. hist. quar., 64:42-63 (Jul). notes. [8729

SHERYL WEDDELL. "Buttermilk Station": the history of La Marque, Texas [Galveston County, 1867-1959]. Jr. historian (Tex.), 20(5):11-14 (Mar). [8730

ANNE A. BRINDLEY. [Walter E. Grover, 1869-1960, Galveston native, businessman, naturalist, and historian.] Southw. hist. quar., 64:148-9 (Jul). [8731

MIMI CHRISTENSEN. The start of a new government in Galveston. Jr. historian (Tex.), 20(2):9-11 (Nov 1959). diagr., view. On the commission government established in 1901 with a mayor-president and 4 commissioners. [8732

PIERCE SHANNON. Cruse Aviation center. Flying, 66(6):36-7, 108-9 (Jun). port., views. On Cruse Aviation, Inc., established by King Cruse, Houston, Tex., in 1944 to distribute Cessna airplanes. [8733

TRUMAN GRAVES BLOCKER, JR., & 3 others. Follow-up medical survey of the Texas City disaster [1947-56]. Am. jour. surgery, 97:604-23 (May 1959). diagrs., tables. notes. [8734

San Antonio

JUAN AGUSTIN DE MORFI (died 1783). Excerpt from Viaje de Indios y diario del Nuevo Mexico. ... Translation by Robert E. McDonald. ... Contributed by Mrs. Walter J. Achning. Our heritage, 1:121-9 (Jul). Record kept by the Franciscan chaplain of an expedition of Teodoro de Croix, in and near San Antonio, 31 Dec. 1777-13 Jan. 1778, on the scenery along the San Antonio River, the garrison, and the 5 missions in the vicinity. [8735

FRITZ ARNOLD TOEPPERWEIN. Footnotes of the Buckhorn, a Lone Star State landmark: items of interest, old and new. Boerne, Tex.: Highland Press [1960]. 63, [1] p. facsims., ports., views. On the Buckhorn Saloon, San Antonio, founded in 1881, surviving today as the Buckhorn Bar of the Lone Star Brewing Company, and the attached Buckhorn Hall of Horns, exhibiting horns of animals from many parts of the world and also rattlesnake skins and rattles, murals and dioramas, and other attractions. [8736

SAM WOOLFORD. Carry Nation in Texas. Southw. hist. quar., 63:554-66 (Apr). On her visit to San Antonio, 9-10 Jan. 1908, and her efforts to discourage the use of tobacco and alcohol and the decoration of saloon walls with "high art," as reported in 3 San Antonio newspapers; with remarks on "personal journalism" in Texas. [8737

ELLIS SHAPIRO. The San Antonio water system [1925-55]. Southw. water works jour., 37(7):34-6 (Oct 1955). view. [8738

SUSAN SELBY. The San Antonio River beautification project [1929-41]. Jr. historian (Tex.), 20(5):21-2, 32 (Mar). map, view. [8739

W. N. WELLS. San Antonio sewage treatment plant [1930-55]. Southw. water works jour., 37(7):37, 40 (Oct 1955). port., view. [8740

The Border States

FREEMAN HANSFORD HART. [... a series of articles on Virginians who led in establishing the colony's frontier.] Commonwealth (Va.), 27(9), 10, 12): irregular installments (Sep, Oct, Dec). facsim., ports., views. On activities of James Patton (settled in Virginia ca. 1740, killed by Indians in 1755), Dr. Thomas Walker (1715-94), and Col. William Preston (1729-83, settled in Virginia ca. 1740) in present West Virginia and Kentucky, 1740s-70s. [8741

HARRIETTE LOUISA (SIMPSON) ARNOW. The pioneer farmer and his corps in the Cumberland region. Tenn. hist. quar., 19:291-327 (Dec). notes. On crops, livestock, tools, tillage and other work, buildings and fences, marketing, timber and wood, game, and farm management in the Cumberland Valley of Tennessee and Kentucky, 1779-1818. [8742

INA GABLER. Lovely's Purchase and Lovely County. Ark. hist. quar., 19:31-9 (spring). maps. notes. On an area in present northwest Arkansas and northeast Oklahoma, 1816-28, now occupied by 7 counties or parts of counties of Oklahoma and 3 of Arkansas. [8743

ROY CLEO WOODS. Effect of educational opportunities on the Hatfield-McCoy feud in West Virginia and Kentucky [1870-1950]. W. Va. Acad. Science, Proc., 31:97-101. notes. On "the importance of education in the decline of feud." [8744

DOROTHY E. HOLZBAUER. Hung by his boots! True West, 7(3):35-6 (Jan-Feb). ports. On the trial and conviction of Charles Evans on a charge of murder before Judge Isaac Charles Parker, and his execution on 6 Sep. 1875, the first of 88 men sentenced to the gallows by Parker as Judge of the Federal Court for the Western District of Arkansas and the Indian Territory. [8745

FANNIE BROWNLEE MISCH. Redmond Selecman Cole [1881-1959]. Chron. Okla., 38:242-4 (autumn). port. On his early life in Missouri, his removal to Oklahoma, his legal practice and judicial service there, and his genealogical activities. [8746

DEWEY WESLEY GRANTHAM, JR. Black Patch War: the story of the Kentucky and Tennessee night riders, 1905-1909. South Atl. quar., 59:215-25 (spring). On collective action by tobacco farmers to raise the prices received by them for tobacco, and their campaign of arson and violence against farmers who would not join them. [8747

OTTO ERNEST RAYBURN. Some fabulous monsters and other folk beliefs from the Ozarks. Midw. folklore, 10:27-32 (spring). A selection from lore collected by the author in the past 40 years. [8748

HAROLD BROWN CLARK. The role of farmers' cooperative associations in the marketing of dark tobacco in Kentucky-Tennessee from 1931 to 1950. Ann Arbor: University Microfilms, 1950 [i. e. 1960]. Positive microfilm of typescript. 271 leaves. diagrs., maps, tables. bibliog. (leaves 221-4). Thesis--Univ. of Kentucky. Abstracted: Dissert. abstracts, 20:3978-9 (Apr). [8749

WEST VIRGINIA

JEFFERSON COUNTY [W. VA.] HISTORICAL SOCIETY. Tombstone inscriptions. Jefferson Co. Hist. Soc., Mag., 26:26-43. Inscriptions copied in Jefferson County by Mrs. J. M. Miller and Carrie B. Wilson in and before 1934, with later additions from graveyards that they did not visit. [8750

FRANK MARYL SETZLER. Welcome Mound and the effigy pipes of the Adena people. [Wash.: U.S. Govt. Print. Off., 1960.] 451-458 p. maps, views. bibliog. (p. 458). (U.S. National Museum. Proceedings, v. 12, no. 3441.) On a mound excavated by the author in 1957 near New Martinsville, W. Va., and the styles and designs of the stone tobacco pipes he found there. [8751

WEST VIRGINIA. State Dept. of History and Archives. State history as featured by the press. W. Va. hist., 21:130-34, 207-10 (Jan, Apr). Abstracts of articles relating to West Virginia history in recent magazines and West Virginia newspapers. [8752

ROBERT KELVIN HOLLIDAY. A portrait of Fayette County [W. Va., 1671-1960]. Oak Hill, W. Va.: Fayette Tribune, 1960. [8], 6, 311, [13] p. facsims. (part double), map, ports., views. [8753

ROBERT LEE BATES & HARRY HOWARD BATES. The story of Smithfield (Middleway), Jefferson County, West Virginia. Endicott, N.Y., 1958. 2 v. in 1. [4], v, 236; [2], iv, 249 p. facsims., maps, ports., views. History of the community, 1729-1958, and account of the Smith, Grantham, Shirley, Bates, and Fry families living there. [8754

MANLY WADE WELLMAN. Harpers Ferry, prize of war [1743-1870. Charlotte, N.C.:] McNally of Charlotte, 1960. vi, [2], 183 p. views. bibliog. (p. 175-7), notes (p. 161-74). [8755

WILL BARKER. Historic Harper's Ferry [1747-1956]. Am. forests, 62(10):32-5 (Oct 1956). views. [8756

ELIZABETH K. ROGERS. The Hite v Fairfax suit. Jefferson Co. Hist. Soc., Mag., 25 (1959): 15-27. bibliog. On litigation relating to the title to 140,000 acres of land in northern Virginia, 1749-87, with particular accounts of the parts of this land that lie in present Jefferson County, W. Va. [8757

BARBARA RUTH KIDD. The history of Sweet Springs, Monroe County, West Virginia [1751-1941]. W. Va. hist., 21: 233-68 (Jul). port., view. notes. On the mineral springs there, the changing ownership of the land, and the resorts. [8758

NANCY SUE SMITH. An early history of Mingo County, West Virginia [1755-1960. Williamson? W. Va.:] Williamson Print. Co., c1960. [4], 24 p. [8759

EARL LEMLEY CORE. Chronicles of Core [W. Va.], second (bicentennial) edition, 1760-1960. Core, W. Va., 1960. [8], 369 p. map, ports., tables, views. notes. Includes some account of events since publication of the first edition in 1937. [8760

BERKELEY COUNTY, Va. (now W. Va.). Berkeley County, West Virginia, guardians' bonds, 1776-1796. Va. geneal., 4:3-7, 60-63 (Jan, Jun). Abstracts. [8761

LAWRENCE SHERWOOD. Bishop Francis Asbury in West Virginia [34 visits, 1776-1815, to "at least twenty-two of the present counties of West Virginia"]. W. Va. hist., 21:76-83 (Jan). On his journal as "an almost inexhaustible mine of material for biographical and historical research" concerning places and persons in West Virginia. [8762

ROSS B. JOHNSON, comp. West Virginia estate settlements. W. Va. hist., 21:123-9, 200-206 (Jan, Apr). This installment: abstracts of records of Breenbrier County, 1781-1849. [8763

BRUCE ROBERTS. Harper's Ferry in pictures. [Text by W. J. McNally.] Charlotte [N. C.]: McNally, 1960. [48] p. facsims., map, ports., views (part double). On Harpers Ferry, W. Va., since 1794, mainly as it appears now. [8764

The SHEPHERDSTOWN Manse and John Kearsley. Jefferson Co. Hist. Soc., Mag., 25 (1959): 9-14. view. On the brick dwelling in Sheperdstown, W. Va., acquired in 1902 by the Presbyterian Church as a manse, probably built in or before 1796 and expanded by John Kearsley (1756-1819) soon after 1814; with an account of him and his descendants. [8765

PHILIP MALLORY CONLEY. History of the West Virginia coal industry [1797-1960]. Charleston, W. Va.: Education Foundation, 1960. [16], 311 p. tables, views. bibliog. (p. 297-308), notes (p. 291-6). [8766

WILLARD D. LORENSEN. Aggravated assaults in West Virginia [1819-1959]. W. Va. law rev., 60:319-38 (Jun). notes. [8767

EARL LEMLEY CORE. Morgantown Disciples: a history of the First Christian Church of Morgantown, West Virginia [1835-1959]. Parsons, W. Va.: McClain Print. Co., 1960. [8], 229 p. ports., views. notes. [8768

PAUL HOLLAND PRICE. Archeology in West Virginia [1838-1960]. W. Va. Acad. Science, Proc., 32:168-73. table. bibliog. [8769

FRANK E. SHAFFER. The West End story. Trains, 20(10):28-39; (11):38-43 (Aug, Sep). map, views. On the West End of the Cumberland Division of the Baltimore & Ohio Railroad between Keyser and Grafton, W. Va., its problems of snow and steep grades, and its equipment, 1850s-1960. [8770

KYLE McCORMICK. West Virginia's capitol buildings [1851-1933]. D. A. R. mag., 94:600 (Oct). [8771

HARPER'S Ferry, 1859. Va. cavalcade, 9(2):23-33 (autumn 1959). cartoon, facsims., ports., views (1 col.). Reproductions of contemporary engravings. [8772

BARBARA LOUISE EMMERTH. Slavery in present West Virginia in 1860. W. Va. hist., 21:275-7 (Jul). notes. [8773

BERNARD GAINER. Early oil development in West Virginia [1860-63, 1889-1900]. W. Va. hist., 21:84-7 (Jan). views. [8774

CLAUDE J. DAVIS, EUGENE R. ELKINS, & PAUL E. KIDD. The justice of the peace in West Virginia [1862-1958]. Morgantown, 1958. vii, 38, [2] p. tables. notes. (West Virginia University. Bureau for Government Research. Publication 23.) [8775

NATHANIEL HAWTHORNE (1804-64). Hawthorne at Harpers Ferry. [Communicated by Cecil Eby.] Jefferson Co. Hist. Soc., Mag., 25 (1959); 28-31. From the Atlantic monthly, Jul. 1863. Part of an account of a visit in March or April 1862, describing "this God-forsaken town" and expressing the opinion that John Brown had been justly hanged. [8776

JOHN G. MORGAN. West Virgina Governors. Charleston, W. Va.: Newspaper Agency Corp., 1960. 103 p. cartoons, ports. bibliog. (p. 103). Text in 5 columns. From the Sunday gazette-mail, Charleston, W. Va. Biographical sketches of "the 25 Governors of West Virginia," 1863-1960. [8777

LARRICK BRUCE STAPLETON. Equality and uniformity in property taxes [in West Virginia, 1863-1959]. W. Va. law rev., 60:70-83 (Dec 1959). notes. [8778

ELIZABETH COMETTI. Swiss immigration to West Virginia, 1864-1884: a case study. Miss. Valley hist. rev. 47:66-87 (Jun). notes. On the efforts of Joseph H. Diss Debar, Commissioner of Emigration of West Virginia, to attract Swiss emigrants to the State, the fraudulent activities of Carl Emmanuel Lutz as an organizer of Swiss settlements there, and the concurrent efforts of authorities in Switzerland to curb the fraudulent activities of emigrant agents. [8779

GEORGE WILLIAM BAGBY (1828-83). Charlestown [sic] and Shepherdstown. Jefferson Co. Hist. Soc., Mag., 26: 22-5. Description by a visitor, 28 Mar. 1881, apparently reprinted from a Richmond newspaper of that year. [8780

KYLE McCORMICK. Charleston's railroad. W. Va. hist., 21:197-9 (Apr). On the entry of the Ohio Central Railway into Charleston, 29 Nov. 1883, after resistance from Charleston property owners had caused Collis P. Huntington to run his Chesapeake & Ohio Railroad along the south side of the Kanawha River and to build the city of Huntington as its terminus on the Ohio. [8781

CHARLES T. HOLLAND. Research and education can improve personnel safety in coal mining. Mineral industries jour., 1(4):3-4 (Dec 1954). tables. notes. On coal-mining accidents in West Virginia, 1885-1954. [8782

SIRUS ORESTES BOND (1877-1959). The light of the hills: a history of Salem College, Salem, West Virginia [1890-1960]. Charleston, W. Va.: Education Foundation, 1960. [12], 434 p. ports., tables, views. History of an institution founded under Baptist auspices; with biographical sketches of the Presidents of the Board of Directors, the Presidents of the College, and the Deans of the College (p. 34-258), including the author's third-person autobiography (p. 145-205). [8733

ADA MAE ELKINS. Thirty-eight years in the parsonage: the fruitful career of the Reverend Opie Kldridge Elkins [1894-1958] in the Methodist ministry of rural and urban West Virginia--perceptively recounted by his wife and fellow worker. N.Y.: William-Frederick Press, 1960. [10], 101 p. On his service in many small rural churches (unnamed); with excerpts from his diary, one of his poems, and 2 undated sermons. [8784

SABRA SMITH TATE, ed. Gilmer County issue. [Fairmont, W. Va.: West Virginia Folklore Soc., 1960.] 53-68 p. (West Virginia folklore, v. 10, no. 4, summer 1960.) Two tales, 3 religious songs, and 2 collections of "superstitions and remedies," written, recited, or collected by various persons in Gilmer County, W. Va., including a song sung in 1898 and other lore current as much as 40 years ago. [8785

RUTH ANN MUSICK, ed. The trickster story in West Virginia. Midw. folklore, 10:125-32 (fall). Three texts from oral sources, originally brought to West Virginia by European miners "in the early 1900's." [8786

EVELYN L. K. HARRIS & FRANK J. KREBS. From humble beginnings: West Virginia State Federation of Labor, 1903-1957. [Charleston:] West Virginia Labor History Pub. Fund [1960]. xxv, 553 p. facsims., ports., tables. notes (p. 495-518). [8787

ROCCO PANTALONE. The tales of Rocco Pantalone. [Fairmont, W. Va.: West Virginia Folklore Soc., 1960.] 16 p. (West Virginia folklore, v. 11, no. 1, fall 1960.) Seven tales, of Italian origin, told by an Italian who arrived in West Virginia in 1906 and worked in the mines till 1952. [8788

WILLIAM DEAN DE LA MATER. A brief survey of the West Virginia law of compensability [1913-59]. W. Va. law rev., 60:303-18 (Jun). notes. [8789

WEST VIRGINIA FOLKLORE SOCIETY. More stories of the mine. [Fairmont, W. Va., 1960.] 17-36 p. (West Virginia folklore, v. 10, no. 2, winter 1960.) Twelve accounts of coal-mine accidents, fires, ghosts, etc. (11 in West Virginia, 1 in Pennsylvania), collected from oral sources by Frank Martino, John Tilko, James S. Salina, and Frank J. Puskas, sons of miners, referring to incidents some of which occurred as much as 40 years ago. [8790

GEORGE P. SCHRADER. Joint industry and city waste treatment: combined approach as viewed by industry. Water Pollution Control Fed., Jour., 32: 157-63 (Feb). maps, table. notes. On cooperative efforts by the City of South Charleston, W. Va., and the South Charleston Plant of Union Carbide Chemicals Company to reduce pollution of the Kanawha River, 1923-59. [8791

HARRY W. YAWNEY & G. R. TRIMBLE, JR. West Virginia's unusual pine plantation. Jour. forestry, 56: 849-51 (Nov 1958). tables, views. On the plantation at Clover Run, Monongahela National Forest, 1932-57. [8792

U.S. Geological Survey. Flood of August 4-5, 1943, in central West Virginia [in the Little Kanawha River Basin]. By H. M. Erskine. Wash.: U.S. Govt. Print. Off., 1951. iv, 57 p. diagrs., maps (1 fold.), tables, views. bibliog. (p. 49). (Its Water-supply paper 1134-A.) [8793

RUTH ANN MUSICK, ed. Ballads, folk songs, & folk tales from West Virginia. Morgantown: West Virginia Univ. Library, 1960. v, 71 p. music. Selections from the editor's "collection of manuscripts and tape recordings," gathered by her and by her students (at Fairmont State College). Contents.--Ballads and folksongs from W. Va.--West Virginia ghost stories.--European folktales.--Omens and tokens.--Rhymes, riddles, and stories for children.--Tales of the coal miners.--Fortune telling. [8794

WEST VIRGINIA FOLKLORE SOCIETY. Superstitions, remedies, weather lore, tales, etc.--mostly about spring. [Fairmont, W. Va., 1960.] 37-52 p. (West Virginia folklore, v. 10, no. 3, spring 1960.) Lore collected from oral sources in West Virginia. [8795

KENTUCKY

MARY SUE BRYSON, comp. Emison, Dinelli, and Compton Bible records. Ky. geneal., 1:83-91 (Jul-Sep 1959). Lists of names, mainly of Kentuckians. [8796

DAUGHTERS OF THE AMERICAN REVOLUTION. Kentucky. Kentucky Records Research Committee. Kentucky cemetery records. Volume I. Compiled, edited, and indexed by the Kentucky Records Research Committee. [Lexington?] Kentucky Soc., Daughters of the American Revolution, 1960. [14], 471 p. "Acknowledgments" signed: Emma Jane Walker, Chairman. Inscriptions copied by chapters of the Kentucky Society during the past 50 years, arranged by counties; with a name index (p. 383-471). [8797

TOMBSTONE inscriptions [from small Kentucky family cemeteries]. Ky. geneal., 1:32-4, 104-7; 2:32-5, 64-7, 144-7 (Apr 1959-Dec 1960). Lists, by several contributors, of inscriptions in Muhlenberg, Boone, Kenton, Nelson, and Nicholas Counties. [8798

ROBERT LEE SPRAU. History of Kentucky dentistry: 1636-1910. [Louisville? 1960. 8], 168 p. ports., tables, views. bibliog. (p. [5]). Appended (p. 125-34): "Dentisty in Kentucky, period 1911-1960," by Edward B. Gernert. [8799

MELLIE SCOTT HORTIN. A history of the Scotch-Irish and their influence in Kentucky [since 1769]. Filson Club hist. quar., 34:248-55 (Jul). notes. Deals largely with eminent Kentuckians whose ancestors came from Ulster. [8800

EVELYN CRADY ADAMS. Wilford Lee (1774-1849), gentleman: son of John Lee [174-?-1788], Kentucky pioneer. Filson Club hist. quar., 34:115-35 (Apr). notes. On his life in Nelson and Bullitt Counties as a planter, his 12 children, his brothers and sisters, and some of his ancestors. [8801

JOHN WINSTON COLEMAN, JR. John Bradford [1749-1830] and the Kentucky gazette. Filson Club hist. quar., 34:24-34 (Jan). notes. On his life in Lexington, 1779/80-1830, his work as a printer, his founding and editing of the first newspaper in Kentucky (1787-1827), and his other publications, including almanacs. [8802

SAMUEL HAYCRAFT (1795-1878). A history of Elizabethtown, Kentucky, and its surroundings [1779-1869. Elizabethtown?] Hardin County Historical Soc., 1960. 264 p. port. 1st ed. 1921; written in 1869. Includes the recollections of the author, a native of the town, and biographical sketches of some of its early settlers. [8803

CHARLES GANO TALBERT. The life and times of Benjamin Logan [1743-1802]. Ann Arbor: University Microfilms, 1952 [i. e. 1960]. Positive microfilm of typescript. ix, 531 leaves. bibliog. (leaves 510-31). Thesis--Univ. of Kentucky. Abstracted: Dissert. abstracts, 20:4092 (Apr). On his military and political activities in Kentucky, 1779-1802, and his earlier life and military experience in Pennsylvania and southwestern Virginia. [8804

EVELYN CRADY ADAMS. Phillips' Fort (1780), Nolin Station, earliest settlement in Larue County, Kentucky. Ky. Hist. Soc., Reg., 58:308-21 (Oct). notes. On a log structure built by Capt. Philip Phillips to protect his settlement at Nolin Station (near the site of Hodgenville); the affairs of the settlement till his removal to Davidson County, Tenn., in 1795 (where he died in 1797); and some of his descendants. [8805

EDSEL T. GODBEY. The Governors of Kentucky and education, 1780-1852. Lexington, 1960. 122 p. ports. bibliog. (p. 118-22), notes. (University of Kentucky. Bureau of School Service. Bulletin, v. 32, no. 4.) [8806

MARGARET MORRIS BRIDWELL. Three early Kentucky silversmiths. Antiques, 78:579-81 (Dec). port. On David Humphreys (recorded at Lexington 1789-1815), Edward West 1757-1827, settled in Kentucky in 1783), and Samuel Ayres (1767-1824, arrived in Kentucky after 1784), all of whom had sons who were also silversmiths. [8807

ARTHUR BRUCE MOSES. Francis Asbury's powder horn. A. M. E. Zion quar. rev., 64:4-7 (winter 1953). On the travels of Asbury and party from the Holston River to Lexington, Ky., where he convened the first Methodist conference in Kentucky, Apr.-May

1790, and the precautions taken by the travelers against attack by Indians. [8808

JOHN JACOB WEISERT. Beginnings of the Kentucky theatre circuit [1790-1818]. Filson Club hist. quar., 34: 264-85 (Jul). notes. [8809

ROBERT LEE COLLIER (1933-60). Education, religion, and the Kentucky Court of Appeals. Lexington, 1960. 149 p. map, port. bibliog. (p. 147-9), notes. (University of Kentucky. Bureau of School Service. Bulletin, v. 33, no. 2.) On "the legal relationship of religion to public education in Kentucky," 1792-1960, and the pertinent decisions of the Kentucky Court of Appeals, 1891-1956. [8810

SHELBY COUNTY, Ky. Marriage bonds for the years 1792-1793-1794 of Shelbyville, Shelby Co., Ky. (compiled by Mrs. Gertrude Hardeman ...). D. A. R. mag., 94:27 (Jan). [8811

LOWELL HAYES HARRISON. John Breckinridge [died 1806] of Kentucky: planter, speculator, and businessman. Filson Club hist. quar., 34:205-27 (Jul). notes. On his management of his plantation, Cabell's Dale, near Lexington, 1793-1806, his large purchases of land, and his investment in an iron-mining company. [8812

AMHERST COUNTY, Va. Some Amherst County, Virginia, deeds pertaining to Kentucky [1803-11]. Abstracted by the Rev. Baily Fulton Davis. Ky. geneal., 1:123-7 (Jul-Sep 1959). [8813

PRENTISS PRICE. Thomas Hart Clay Bible. Ky. geneal., 1:32-6 (Jan-Mar 1959). Lists of the brothers, sisters, and some of the descendants of Clay (1803-71), a son of Henry Clay (1777-1852); with added information about the family from other sources. [8814

HOPKINS COUNTY, Ky. Part I. Hopkins County, Kentucky, tax list, 1807 [prepared by William Davis, Commissioner]. Copied from a Hopkins County newspaper published in 1933. Original records were destroyed by water in 1937. Part II. Hopkins County, Kentucky marriages, 1807-1869. Copied from Marriage record book no. 1, Hopkins County Court Clerk's Office by Mrs. Evelyn M. Cox, and prepared for distribution by Mrs. Cox and Mrs. Lalla F. McCulley. [Madisonville, Ky., 1960. 4], 129 p. [8815

LUCIEN BECKNER. Kentucky's oil claim. Filson Club hist. quar., 34:193 (Apr). From The Louisville times, 18 Sep. 1959. Evidence, 1811-54, that "the first oil and the first gas wells in America" were in Kentucky. [8816

LAWRENCE A. CASSIDY. Kentucky fairs, 1816-1959: a brief history with related data and commentary. [Lyndon? Ky.] c1960. [3], 52, vi leaves. tables. 30 cm. [8817

JOHN WINSTON COLEMAN, JR. Steamboats on the Kentucky River [1816-1920]. Lexington, Ky.: Winburn Press, 1960. 41 p. views. notes (p. 39-41). [8818

HERMAN CLYDE REEVES & LAWRENCE A. CASSIDY. Fairs in Kentucky [1816-1959]. Filson Club hist. quar., 34:335-57 (Oct). Includes an account of the Kentucky State Fair, inaugurated in 1902. [8819

JAMES L. MILLER, JR. Transylvania University as the nation saw it: 1818-1828. Filson Club hist. quar., 34:305-18 (Oct). notes. On "the national attention which Transylvania received" during the presidency of Horace Holley as expressed in 6 national magazines. [8820

DAVIESS COUNTY, Ky. Daviess County, Kentucky, Justice of Peace Court civil docket, 1819-1832. Contributed by M. J. Edgeworth. Ky. geneal., 2:123-7 (Oct-Dec). Abstracts of entries by Amos Riley, J. P. (1819-24), and Samuel Hawes, J. P. (1825-32). [8821

WILLIAM BRYAN GATES. William Gilmore Simms and The Kentucky tragedy. Am. lit., 32:958-66 (May). notes. On his Beauchampe; or, The Kentucky tragedy (1842), of which the first part was reprinted as Charlemont; or, The pride of the village (1856) and the second part, without change of title, was reprinted in the same year as the sequel to Charlemont; with an examination of the known facts of seduction and murder involving Ann Cook, Solomon P. Sharp, and Jereboam O. Beauchamp, 1819-26, and Simms's wide departure from the facts in his novel. [8822

EDWARD H. HILLIARD. When Kentucky had two courts of appeals. Filson Club hist. quar., 34:228-36 (Jul). On action of the Kentucky legislature to force creditors to accept depreciated paper currency at face value in payment of debts, 1820-26, the refusal of the Court of Appeals to confirm this impairment of contract, the abolition of the Court in 1824 and the establishment of a new court, the refusal of the Old Court to recognize this legislation, the judicial chaos and threat of civil war during the period of 2 courts

(December 1824 to December 1826), and the repeal of the legislation. [8823

U.S. Census Office. 4th Census, 1820. Knox County, Kentucky, 1820 census. Ky. geneal., 1(1):37-9, 109-16 (Jan-Sep 1959). [8824

WALTER HERBERT RANKINS. Money for minerals but not one cent for athletics at Augusta College. Filson Club hist. quar., 34:136-9 (Apr). On Augusta College, Augusta, Ky., the Rev. John P. Durbin (1800-1876), professor of languages there, and his purchase for the college of a large collection of minerals in the possession of a Mr. Cloud in Philadelphia in 1826. [8825

LORINE LETCHER BUTLER. History [of the] First Christian Church, Paris, Kentucky [1827-1959. Lexington? Ky.] 1960. 141 p. ports., views. bibliog. (p. 114). [8826

ELMER GRIFFITH SULZER. A Kentucky thoroughbred, a workhorse, and two old sires, being an account of four segments of the Louisville & Nashville. Railway & Locomotive Hist. Soc., Bul., 102:6-26 (Apr). facsims., tables, views. On the Lexington & Frankfort Railroad, 1834-48; the Lexington & Ohio Railroad, 1838-55; the Maysville and Lexington Railroad, through the bluegrass horse country, 1850 ff.; and the Bloomfield Branch of the last-mentioned; with details of their many changes of name and ownership. [8827

JAMES W. GIBBS. The Meek chronometer. Natl. Assoc. Watch and Clock Collectors, Bul., 9:132-4 (Feb). views. On Benjamin F. Meek (1816?-1901), jeweler and maker of fishing reels in Frankfort and Louisville, Ky., 1835-98, and a chronometer signed by him at Frankfort, 1852. [8828

DAVIESS COUNTY, Mo. Marriage records of Daviess County, Missouri, 1836-1855. Compiled by Elizabeth Prather Ellsberry. Chillicothe, Mo. [196-? 1], 53 leaves. Abstracts. [8829

WALLACE BLYTHE TURNER. Kentucky in a decade of change, 1850-1860. Ann Arbor: University Microfilms, 1954 [i. e. 1960]. Positive microfilm of typescript. vi, 316 leaves. bibliog. (leaves 305-16). Thesis--Univ. of Kentucky. Abstracted: Dissert, abstracts, 20:3721 (Mar). On "politics, slavery, antislavery, education, agriculture, transportation, commerce and industry, social and intellectual life." [8830

WALLACE BLYTHE TURNER. Kentucky slavery in the last ante bellum decade [1850-60]. Ky. Hist. Soc., Reg., 58:291-307 (Oct). notes. [8831

FAYETTE COUNTY, Ky. Some Fayette County, Kentucky, marriages filed in 1853. Contributed by John Frederick Dorman. Ky. geneal., 2:93-100 (Jul-Sep). [8832

KENTUCKY. Kentucky vital statistics. Ky. Hist. Soc., Reg., 58:49-74, 247-62 (Jan, Jul). Lists of deaths in Logan County, 1853-54, 1856-59, 1861, and Lyon County, 1853-59, 1861, 1893, 1903, and 1908. [8833

GARRETT GLENN CLIFT. The Kentucky General Assemblies of 1860 and 1960. Ky. Hist. Soc., Reg., 58:29-48 (Jan). Mainly lists of members. [8834

BEATRICE POWELL. The old-fashioned association. Ky. folklore rec., 6:77-85. notes. Information from the author's parents and grandparents about Baptist associations ("meetings of the Baptist churches within given districts, each composed of three or four counties"), in Russell County, Ky., "fifty to one hundred years ago." [8835

ROBERT GUNN CRAWFORD. A history of the Kentucky penitentiary system, 1865-1937. Ann Arbor: University Microfilms, 1955 [i. e. 1960]. Positive microfilm of typescript. v, 376 leaves. bibliog. (leaves 370-76). Thesis--Univ. of Kentucky. Abstracted: Dissert. abstracts, 20:3705 (Mar). [8836

PAULINE (STEPHENS) HAZELIP. Tales of Glasgow Junction. Ky. folklore rec., 6:1-8. On some of the tales and anecdotes heard by the author in the town "in which I grew up," originally called Three Forks, renamed Glasgow Junction in 1871, now Park City, in Barren County, Ky. [8837

ARCH and Gordon. [Edited] by D. K. Wilgus. Ky. folklore rec., 6:51-60. music. Two texts of a ballad sung in 1956 by Mrs. Will Cline about the killing of Archibald Dixon Brown, son of the Governor of Kentucky, and Nellie Bush Gordon by Fulton Gordon, the latter's husband, when he found them in bed together in a "Disreputable resort" in Louisville, 1895. [8838

HELEN B. DANIEL. The haunts of Piney Woods. Ky. folklore rec., 6: 87-9. Lore from Mona Shelton and others about ghosts observed "a good many years ago" in this area of Clinton County and adjacent counties. [8839

"JOHN Ferguson." Ky. folklore rec., 6:15-17. Ballad contributed by Cora Boggs, current sometime before 1937, about the murder of Ferguson by ---- Williams on Caines Creek, Lawrence County, Ky., in 1901. [8840

Mrs. WARREN SIGHTS. The Land between the Rivers. Garden Club Am., Bul., 48(1):30-32 (Jan). On the Kentucky Woodland Wildlife National Refuge, on the ridge separating the lower courses of the Tennessee and the Cumberland, 1920-60. [8841

BILLY C. CLARK. A long row to hoe. N.Y.: Crowell [1960. 6], 233 p. On the author's early life in Catlettsburg, Ky., as a member of a very poor family among very poor neighbors, his early employments on the river front of the Big Sandy and the Ohio, and the dawn of his literary abilities in high school, 1928 to ca. 1946. [8842

"The DEATH of Sammie Adams." Ky. folklore rec., 6:123-4. Song attributed to Grover Frazier, 1931, about the murder of Adams in Johnson County, Ky., by Joe Schuster and 3 accomplices. [8843

MARY LOUISE WASHINGTON. The folklore of the Cumberlands as reflected in the writings of Jesse Stuart. Ann Arbor: University Microfilms, 1960. Positive microfilm of typescript. [518] leaves. Thesis--Univ. of Pennsylvania. Abstracted: Dissert. abstracts, 21:844-5 (Oct). On his writings about the "northeastern Kentucky hill people and their way of life," 1934-59. [8844

KENTUCKY, UNIVERSITY OF. Bureau of Business Research. Some economic effects of the Lexington Northern Belt Line [1945-57]. Lexington: Univ. of Kentucky, 1960. vii leaves, 143 p. maps, tables, views. notes. On "a 6.2 mile bypass" built between 1949 and 1953, planned in 1947 as "the first link" in a limited-access circumferential highway but, after construction, operated without limitation of access. [8845

GORDON F. LEWIS. A comparison of some aspects of the backgrounds and careers of small businessmen and American business leaders [Lexington, Ky., 1950]. Am. jour. sociol., 65: 348-55 (Jan). tables. notes. [8846

Louisville

MELVILLE O. BRINEY. Some glimpses of early Louisville [1810-20]. Filson Club hist. quar., 34:105-14 (Apr). [8847

THEODORE M. BROWN. Introduction to Louisville architecture [1832-1960]. Louisville, Ky.: Louisville Free Public Library [1960]. 38 p. views (part double). [8848

TENNESSEE

PAUL FLOWERS. Place names in Tennessee. West Tenn. Hist. Soc. papers, 14:113-23. [8849

ELERY ARNOLD LAY. An industrial and commercial history of the Tri-Cities in Tennessee. Ann Arbor: University Microfilms, 1960. Positive microfilm of typescript. [301] leaves. Thesis (Ed. D.)--George Peabody College for Teachers. Abstracted: Dissert. abstracts, 21:600 (Sep). On the area of Bristol, Johnson City, and Kingsport since prehistoric times. [8850

FRED DECATUR MATTHEWS. History of Sevier County [Tenn., 1780-1960. Knoxville] ©1950, revised 1960. 55 p. port. [8851

TED N. WEISSBUCH. The mysterious State of Franklin Mint. Numismatic scrapbook, 26:1266-8 (May). notes. Indications that this short-lived government (1784-86) had a mint and that "coinage did take place." [8852

E. KATHERINE CREWS. Early musical activities in Knoxville, Tennessee, 1791-1861. East Tenn. Hist. Soc. pub., 32:2-17. music. notes. [8853

JOHN B. CLARK, JR. Andrew Jackson: fire fighter. Tenn. hist. quar., 19:162-5 (Jun). notes. On 2 versions of his unsolicited leadership of efforts to put out a fire in a stable in Jonesboro, Tenn., 1798 or more probably 1803. [8854

HAWKINS COUNTY, Tenn. Early East Tennessee taxpayers. Compiled by Pollyanna Creekmore. VIII. Hawkins County, 1809-1812. East Tenn. Hist. Soc. pub., 32:117-31. notes. Lists prepared for the county court of a county including all or parts of present Knox, Grainger, Claiborne, Hancock, and Hamblen Counties. [8855

WALTER WOMACK. McMinnville at a milestone, 1810-1960: a memento of the sesquicentennial year of McMinnville, Tennessee, 1960, and Warren County, Tennessee, 1958. McMinnville: Standard Pub. Co., 1960. [8], 327 p. facsims., double maps, double plan, ports., tables, views. bibliog. (p. 327). [8856

WILLIAM H. PEASE & JANE HANNA PEASE. A new view of Nashoba. Tenn. hist. quar., 19:99-109 (Jun). notes. On "a cooperative community" established by Frances Wright in Tennessee "to purchase Negro slaves, to establish an organized and regulated community in which to train them for freedom, and then to provide for their colonization outside the United States," the Negro to pay for his freedom, the cost of his maintenance, and the expenses of his settlement abroad by his labor in the community (near Memphis), 1825-30. [8857

JOHN H. PEAY. Punitive damages in Tennessee [1840-1960]. Tenn. law rev., 27:381-9 (spring). notes. [8858

JOHN H. ELLIS. Henry Morton Woodson [1845-1917]: Confederate veteran, historian, Memphian. West Tenn. Hist. Soc. papers, 14:74-90. notes. On his service in the C.S. Army as a private (with information from his unpublished diary), his various employments, his history of the Woodson family, and his life in Tennessee. [8859

THEODORE ALLYN SMEDLEY. Wrongful death actions in Tennessee [1851-1960]. Tenn. law rev., 27:447-500 (summer). notes. [8860

M. THOMAS INGE. Sut Lovingood: an examination of the nature of a "nat'ral born durn'd fool." Tenn. hist. quar., 19:231-51 (Sep). notes. On the "representative of the East Tennessee mountaineers" in a series of sketches by George Washington Harris, 1858-68, "as unique and singular a fictional comic character as has ever been spawned by the pen of any writer"; with remarks on previous criticism of this character. [8861

JOHN COFFEE WILLIAMSON (1833-98). The education of a Southern mind: extracts from the diary of John Coffee Williamson, 1860-1861. East Tenn. Hist. Soc. pub., 32:94-105. notes. Excerpts from a diary kept in Old Fort and Cleveland, Tenn., 6 Nov. 1860-30 Jan. 1861, referring to the author's schoolteaching, his reading of law, and local and national events. [8862

JOSEPH J. PITTS. A Methodist circuit rider between the lines: the private journal of Joseph J. Pitts, 1862-1864. Tenn. hist. quar., 19:252-9 (Sep). Record of the writer's activities on Smith's Fork Circuit of the Tennessee Conference, about 50 miles east of Nashville, 1 Dec. 1862-31 Dec. 1864, and the added difficulties of his work resulting from the presence of both Union and Confederate troops. [8863

HALL BARRETT. History of the First Presbyterian Church, Cookeville, Tennessee [1867-1959. Cookeville?] 1960. 11, [1] p. ports., table, views. [8864

FIRST METHODIST CHURCH, Martin, Tenn. A history of First Methodist Church, Martin, Tennessee, 1874-1960. [Prepared by the History Committee. O. J. Hoffman, Chairman.] Martin, ©1960. 86 p. ports., tables, views. [8865

ANTOINETTE ELIZABETH TAYLOR. The woman suffrage movement in Tennessee [1876-1920]. N.Y.: Bookman Associates [1957]. 150 p. bibliog. (p. 143-5), notes (p. 127-42). [8866

PHILIP P. DURAND. Delegation of power to administrative agencies in Tennessee [1899-1960]. Tenn. law rev., 27:569-86 (summer). notes. [8867

ELMER B. INMAN. A history of the development of the University of Tennessee, Martin Branch [founded in 1900 by the Beulah Baptist Association as Hall-Moody Institute]. Ann Arbor: University Microfilms, 1960. Positive microfilm of typescript. [250] leaves. Thesis (Ed. D.)--Univ. of Tennessee. Abstracted: Dissert. abstracts, 21:311 (Aug). [8868

RUSSELL L. STOCKARD. The election and second administration of Governor Ben W. Hooper of Tennessee as reflected in the State press [1912-14]. East Tenn. Hist. Soc. pub., 32: 51-71. notes. Based on thesis (M. A.)--Tennessee State Univ., Nashville. [8869

RAYMOND S. GINGER. Six days or forever? Tennessee v. John Thomas Scopes. Boston: Beacon Press [1958. 10], 258 p. 4 bibliog. (p. 242-9), notes. Examination of the trial (Dayton, Tenn., 1925) from the point of view of political theory and judicial procedure. [8870

SHELDON NORMAN GREBSTEIN, ed. Monkey trial: the State of Tennessee vs. John Thomas Scopes. Boston: Houghton Mifflin [1960]. xiii, 221 p. cartoon. bibliog. (p. 210-19). (Houghton Mifflin research series, 4.) Contemporary documents relating to the trial by the Circuit Court of Rhea County, Jul. 1925, and on appeal by the Supreme Court of Tennessee, Jan. 1926. [8871

The SCOPES case: a 1960 view. Univ. Chicago law rev., 27:505-34 (spring). notes. On Scopes v. State of Tennessee, tried at Dayton, Tenn., in 1925, reviewed by the Tennessee Supreme Court in 1927, and nolle prossed by the Attorney General of Tennessee. Contents.--A commemorative case note, Scopes v. State, by Harry Kalven, Jr.--The Scopes case in modern dress, by Thomas I. Emerson & David Haber.--Science, religion, and the Scopes case, by Malcolm P. Sharp [mainly on current freedom of schools to control their curricula]. [8872

EDGELL MIDGETT HEARN. Public educational changes through legislation in Tennessee, 1935-1959. Ann Arbor: University Microfilms, 1959 [i. e. 1960]. Positive microfilm of typescript. [394] leaves. Thesis (Ed. D.)--Univ. of Tennessee. Abstracted: Dissert. abstracts, 20:4329 (May). [8873

JEAN LIBERTY PENNOCK & ELISABETH LACEY SPEER. Changes in rural family income and spending in Tennessee, 1943-1944. [Wash.:] U.S. Dept. of Agriculture, 1949. vi, 106 p. diagr., forms, 36 tables. (U.S. Dept. of Agriculture. Miscellaneous publication 666.) "Study ... made by the Bureau of Human Nutrition and Home Economics of the United States Department of Agriculture and the College of Home Economics, University of Tennessee, cooperatively." Survey of 380 white farm families and 129 white rural nonfarm families. [8874

TENNESSEE FOLKLORE SOCIETY. Anecdotes illustrating the folk idiom in the American South. Tenn. Folklore Soc. bul., 26:8-19 (Mar). From several contributors living in Tennessee or quoting persons living there. [8875

Nashville

ALFRED LELAND CRABB. Nashville: personalty of a city [1779-1960]. Indianapolis: Bobbs-Merrill [1960]. 288 p. bibliog. (p. 273-5). [8876

LEE NATHANIEL NEWCOMER, ed. Two New England teachers in Nashville, 1818. Tenn. hist. quar., 19:74-9 (Mar). notes. Letters to the Rev. William Bentley from S. Berry and Daniel Berry, M.D., Nashville, 6 Jun. and 5 Aug. 1818, on their teaching in the Nashville Female Academy and their impressions of Nashville and Tennessee. [8877

VIRGINIA (HALEY) DENIS. The Old City Cemetery, Nashville, Tenn. [opened in 1822 and still in use]. D. A. R. mag., 94:7-8, 34 (Jan). views. [8878

JOHN F. WOOLVERTON. Philip Lindsley and the cause of education in the Old Southwest. Tenn. hist. quar., 19:3-22 (Mar). notes. On his presidency of Cumberland College, Nashville, 1824-50, his low opinion of Tennessee, and his ideas concerning Christianity, education, morals, agriculture and commerce, the poor, and a variety of other subjects. [8879

KENIMER HOUZE MORGAN. The University of Nashville, 1825-1850. Ann Arbor: University Microfilms, 1960. Positive microfilm of typescript. [883] leaves. Thesis--George Peabody College for Teachers. Abstracted: Dissert. abstracts, 21:539-40 (Sep). [8880

Memphis

CHARLES H. NASH. The human continuum of Shelby County, Tennessee. West Tenn. Hist. Soc. papers, 14:5-31. maps. notes. Examination of archeological evidence in reverse chronological order from 1795 to 1541 and thence at least as early as 6000 B.C. in this area. [8881

ASHBEL SMITH (1805-86). On the practicability and advantages of a first-class university in Memphis: a letter from Dr. Ashbel Smith in 1849. Edited by Jack D. L. Holmes. Tenn. hist. quar., 19:64-73 (Mar). notes. Letter to a committee of the Trustees of the University, 25 Jan. 1849, replying to a request from them (also printed, dated 13 Jan.). On Memphis as "preeminently the most eligible place" for a university "adequate to the wants of the great Southern Missisippi valley"; with consideration of the financial support, enrollment, buildings, and curriculum of such an institution. [8882

EARLE LIGON WHITTINGTON. Centennial history, St. John's Methodist Church, 1859-1959. Memphis [1960].

95 p. facsims., ports., tables (part double), views. [8883

EUGENE KERR BRISTOW. Charley Broom, variety manager in Memphis, Tennessee, 1866-1872. South. speech jour., 25:11-20 (fall 1959). notes. A study of his business methods and of "low varieties," an entertainment industry combining vaudeville, song-and-dance girls, and "pretty waitresses serving drinks and cigars to all-male audiences"--requiring a manager possessing the qualifications of house manager, saloonkeeper, and theater manager. [8884

ENOCH L. MITCHELL. A dentist looks at Memphis, 1897. West Tenn. Hist. Soc. papers, 14:91-102. Information from a diary (365 entries) kept throughout 1897 by Dr. James F. Gwinner, age 20, dentist, "recording the most minute details of his practice and his observations of Memphis in that year." [8885

BOYCE HOUSE (1896-1961). Memphis memories of 50 years ago [1909-11]. West Tenn. Hist. Soc. papers, 14: 103-12. [8886

MISSOURI

STATE HISTORICAL SOCIETY OF MISSOURI. Missouri history not found in textbooks. Mo. hist. rev., 54: 219-21, 319-26, 408-15 (Jan-Jul). Excerpts from early and recent newspapers, and lists of articles on Missouri history in magazines. [8887

PHILIP DUFFIELD STONG (1899-1957). Missouri [its traditions and characteristics]. Holiday, American panorama west of the Mississippi: a Holiday magazine book (Garden City, N.Y.: Doubleday [1960]), p. 385-405. [8888

VIRGIL J. VOGEL. The origin and meaning of "Missouri." Mo. Hist. Soc., Bul., 16:213-22 (Apr). notes. [8889

DANIEL McKINLEY. A chronology and bibliography of wildlife in Missouri [1700-1936]. Columbia: Univ. of Missouri Library [1960]. 128 p. (The University of Missouri bulletin, v. 61, no. 13. Library series, 26.) "A contribution of the Missouri Cooperative Wildlife Research Unit. Based on thesis (M.A.)--Univ. of Missouri, 1957. "Alphabetical list of periodicals" (p. 55-60). [8890

DANIEL McKINLEY. A history of the passenger pigeon in Missouri [1700-1902]. Auk, 77:399-420 (Oct). bibliog. Based on thesis--Univ. of Missouri, 1957. [8891

FLOYD CALVIN SHOEMAKER. Osceola [and St. Clair County]: land of Osage River lore [1719-1959]. Mo. hist. rev., 54:327-34 (Jul). ports. view. [8892

CHARLES VAN RAVENSWAAY. Observations on the weather [of St. Louis and Missouri, 1792-1959]. Mo. Hist. Soc., Bul., 16:273-5 (Apr). [8893

DANIEL McKINLEY. The American elk in pioneer Missouri [1802-41, with doubtful reports of later date till 1886]. Mo. hist. rev., 54:356-65 (Jul). view. notes. [8894

MISSOURI, UNIVERSITY OF. Engineering Experiment Station. The wood charcoal industry in the State of Missouri [since 1815/16]. By J. Pitts Jarvis, Jr. [Columbia: Univ. of Missouri, 1960.] 31 p. plans, tables, maps, views. bibliog. (p. 30-31). (Its Engineering series bulletin 48.) [8895

WILLIAM RICHARD GENTRY, JR. Ann Hawkins Gentry [1791-1870]. Mo. Hist. Soc., Bul., 17:61-5 (Oct). On her removal with her husband, Richard Gentry, from Kentucky to Missouri in 1816, and her life as a widow in Columbia, innkeeper and postmaster till 1868. [8896

FRANCES ETHEL GLEASON. The first hundred years. Lebanon, Mo.: Laclede County Centennial, 1949. [8], 130 p. ports., views. History of Lebanon and Laclede County, Mo., 1817-1949. [8897

FRANCES (LEA) McCURDY. Invective in frontier Missouri. Quar. jour. speech, 46:54-8 (Feb). notes. Examples from contemporary sources, 1817-50. [8898

J. C. LUDLOW. News from the Chariton, 1818. Mo. hist. rev., 54: 413 (Jul). From the Franklin County record, Union, Mo., 30 Nov. 1876. Letter to "Dear Will," dated Boonslick Settlement, Mo., 20 Nov. 1818, referring briefly to St. Louis and several settlements on and near the Missouri River in Missouri. [8899

HUGH PRITCHARD WILLIAMSON. Abiel Leonard [1797-1863], lawyer and judge. Mo. Bar, Jour., 15:267-73 (Jun 1959). port. notes. On his life in Missouri, 1818-63, and his service as a justice of the Missouri Supreme Court, 1855-57; with excerpts from his opinions. [8900

HUGH PRITCHARD WILLIAMSON. Hamilton Rowan Gamble [1798-1864]: lawyer, jurist, statesman. Mo. Bar, Jour., 15:531-8 (Dec 1959). port. notes. On his life in Missouri, 1818-64, his legal practice in St. Louis, his service as a justice of the Missouri Supreme Court (1851-54), and his terms as Governor of Missouri (1861-64). [8901

COOPER COUNTY, Mo. Early marriage records (1819-1850) and will records (1820-1870) of Cooper County, Missouri. ... Compiled and published by Elizabeth Prather Ellsberry. Chillicothe, Mo. [196-? 2], iii, 146 leaves. Abstracts. [8902

FRANK C. TUCKER. Old McKendree Chapel. Cape Girardeau, Mo.: Missourian Litho and Printing Co. [1959]. 54 p. views. On "the oldest Methodist Church west of the Mississippi," built in 1819 and used till 1888, and partly restored in the 20th century. [8903

CHARITON COUNTY, Mo. Marriage records of Chariton County, Missouri [1821-52]. Compiled by Elizabeth Prather Ellsberry. Chillicothe, Mo. [196-? 1], 72 leaves. Abstracts. [8904

LAFAYETTE COUNTY, Mo. Lafayette County, Missouri, marriage records, 1821-1850. Compiled by Elizabeth Prather Ellsberry. Chillicothe, Mo. [196-? 1], ii, 78 leaves. Abstracts. [8905

SALINE COUNTY, Mo. Will records of Saline County, Missouri, 1821-1863. Compiled by Elizabeth Prather Ellsberry. Chillicothe, Mo. [196-? 1], ii, 42 leaves. Abstracts. [8906

MABEL (MANES) MOTTAZ. Lest we forget: a history of Pulaski County, Missouri [since ca. 1826], and Fort Leonard Wood [since 1940]: a compilation of newspaper and magazine articles and radio talks. [Springfield? Mo.] 1960. xvi, 81 p. map, ports., views. Includes an account of Waynesville. [8907

RANDOLPH COUNTY, Mo. Early marriage records of Randolph County, Missouri, 1829-1859. Compiled by Elizabeth Prather Ellsberry. Chillicothe, Mo. [196-? 1], iii, 60 leaves. Abstracts. [8908

ALVIN R. DYER. The refiner's fire: historical highlights of Missouri. Salt Lake City: Deseret Book Co. [1960]. xiii, [5], 141 p. map, views (part col.). notes. On the Church of Jesus Christ of Latter-Day Saints in Missouri, 1831-39, the persecution and expulsion of its members there, and the present condition of the properties it acquired and the sites, buildings, and monuments associated with it. [8909

MONROE COUNTY, Mo. Monroe County, Missouri, 1832-1852: letters, wills, administrations. Copied from the original records from the courthouse in Paris, Mo. Compiled by Elizabeth Prather Ellsberry. Chillicothe, Mo. [196-? 1], iii, 37 leaves. Abstracts. [8910

HUGH PRITCHARD WILLIAMSON. William B. Napton [1808-83]: man of two worlds. Mo. Bar, Jour., 16:208-12 (May). port. notes. On his life in Missouri, 1832-83, his legal practice there, and his service as a justice of the Missouri Supreme Court, 1839-51, 1857-61, 1873-80. [8911

RICHARD L. BUSHMAN. Mormon persecutions in Missouri, 1833. Brigham Young Univ. studies, 3:11-20 (autumn). notes. [8912

CARROLL COUNTY, Mo. Carroll County, Missouri, wills and administrations, 1834-1879. Compiled by Elizabeth Prather Ellsberry. [Chillicothe? Mo., 1960? 1], iv, 52 leaves. Abstracts. [8913

BETTY H. PRITCHETT. C[arr] W[aller] Pritchett [1823-1919], early Missouri teacher. Mo. Hist. Soc., Bul., 16:223-9 (Apr). On his work in Missouri as a Methodist circuit rider, head of Central College (Fayette), Pritchett School Institute (Glasgow), and the Morrison Observatory (Glasgow). [8914

ELIZABETH (PRATHER) ELLSBERRY, comp. Cemetery records with biography excerpts of 1882 of central Linn County, Missouri. ... Volume II. Chillicothe, Mo., 1958. [70] leaves. Inscriptions, 1837-1954. [8915

LINN COUNTY, Mo. Linn County, Missouri: list of settlers of 1837-1840, deed book A-1837-1844, list of landowners in county in 1876: nativity, land locations, year of settlement. Compiled by Elizabeth Prather Ellsberry. Chillicothe, Mo. [196-? 1], ii, [1], 79 leaves. [8916

LIVINGSTON COUNTY, Mo. Will and administration records of Livingston County, Missouri, 1837-1870. Compiled by Elizabeth Prather Ellsberry.

Chillicothe, Mo., [196-? 1], 30 leaves. Abstracts. [8917

GRUNDY COUNTY, Mo. Marriage records, 1841-1844, of Grundy County, Mo. (contributed by Gen. John Sullivan Chapter). D.A.R. mag., 94:711-12 (Dec). [8918

MARY LILLIANA OWENS. Growth of the Lorettines in Missouri, 1841-1874. Part II. Am. Cath. Hist. Soc., Rec., 71:93-111 (Sep-Dec). notes. On the Sisters of Loretto at the Foot of the Cross and their Loretto Academy at Florissant, near St. Louis; with some account of their other schools and foundations in Missouri till 1959. [8919

AUDREY CHANEY. A history of Sikeston [Mo., 1844-1900]. Cape Girardeau, Mo.: Rampfre Press [1960. 10], 134 p. ports., views. [8920

CALDWELL COUNTY, Mo. Marriage records of Caldwell County, Missouri, 1845-1871. Compiled by Elizabeth Prather Ellsberry. Chillicothe, Mo. [196-? 1], ii, 51 leaves. Abstracts. [8921

WILLIAM FERRELL BROADHEAD (1836-1915). Travel by stage on the Boonslick Road. Mo. hist. rev., 54: 335-40 (Jul). views. notes. Letters to Rebecca Heald McCleur, dated Clayton, Mo., 27 Jun. 1913, containing recollections of "the stage stations between St. Louis and Fulton" when the stage service was operated by J. Frink & Company, 1848-56. [8922

SULLIVAN COUNTY, Mo. Will records of Sullivan County, Missouri, 1849-1880. Copied in 1958 from the original will records from the court house in Milan, Missouri. Compiled by Elizabeth Prather Ellsberry. Chillicothe, Mo. [196-? 1], 21, [1], 6, [1] leaves. Abstracts. [8923

ELIZABETH (PRATHER) ELLSBERRY, comp. Early will records of north central counties of Missouri. [Chillicothe? Mo., 1960? 1], 7, [4], 75 leaves. "Excerpts of earliest wills on record" in Caldwell County (1850-80), Daviess County (1890-94), Grundy County (1876-85), and Mercer County (1853-96). [8924

SAMUEL FARRINGTON (1833/34?-1862). School days in Hermann. [Edited] by Frances Hurd Stadler. Mo. Hist. Soc., Bul., 16:322-8 (Jul). notes. Letters from a St. Louis boy attending the school of Christoph Moller at Hermann, to his friend Edward P. Wade, dated 18 Feb. 1850-26 Jan. 1851, on his life and observations in Hermann. [8925

HENRY F. LUEPKE, JR. Comments on the evidence in Missouri. St. Louis Univ. law jour., 5:424-45 (spring 1959). notes. On Missouri legislation of 1855, still in effect, inhibiting judges from commenting on the evidence as distinguished from the law. [8926

DONALD ASHTON. Meeting the Pony Express, April 3, 1860. Pony Express, 26(6):3-5 (Nov 1959). view. On the run of a train of the Hannibal & St. Joseph Railroad from Hannibal to St. Joseph, with Addison Clark as engineer, 206 miles in a few minutes more than 4 hours, with mail immediately turned over to John Frey, the first express rider of the Pony Express going west. [8927

OLAF T. HAGEN. The Pony Express starts from St. Joseph [Apr. 1860]. Mo. hist. rev., 54:231-6 (Apr). view. notes. Information from Missouri newspapers. [8928

CHARITON COUNTY, Mo. Chariton County, Missouri, wills and administrations, 1861-1875. Compiled by Elizabeth Prather Ellsberry. Chillicothe, Mo. [196-? 1], iii, 35 leaves. Abstracts. [8929

EDWARD FREDRICK BRUNNER. The development of differentiated teaching certificates in the State of Missouri [1865-1958]. Ann Arbor: University Microfilms, 1960. Positive microfilm of typescript. [185] leaves. Thesis (Ed. D.)--Univ. of Missouri. Abstracted: Dissert. abstracts, 21:1448 (Dec). [8930

WILLIAM THOMAS DOHERTY, JR. Louis Houck [1840-1925]: Missouri historian and entrepreneur. Columbia: Univ. of Missouri Press [1960]. xi, 158 p. map, tables. bibliog. (p. 127-39), notes. (University of Missouri studies, 33.) Based on thesis--Univ. of Missouri. On his life in Missouri, 1868-1925, as a lawyer, a newspaper columnist, a resident of Cape Girardeau, an organizer and builder of railroads, a promoter of other enterprises in the swamps of southeastern Missouri ("the Missouri Bootheel"), and a historian of Missouri;

with some account of his early years in Illinois, his studies at the University of Wisconsin, and his practice of law in Illinois. [8931

MARJORIE LEE WEBB. The right to counsel in criminal cases in Missouri [1882-1958]. Univ. Kan. City law rev., 28:160-69 (summer). notes. [8932

HISTORY of the Bethel Church, Cass County, Missouri [1886-1935]. Mennonite hist. bul., 13(2):3-4 (Apr 1952). notes. [8933

ERNEST JESSE PALMER. The lead mines of southwest Missouri. Mo. hist. rev., 54:323-4 (Apr). Letter dated Webb City, Mo., 15 Aug. 1959, from a resident of that community since 1891, on the characteristics that have made southwest Missouri "distinctly different from other mining regions." [8934

M. RANDALL VANET. Judicial notice of foreign law as developed in Missouri tort law [1910-60]. Mo. law rev., 25: 176-87 (Apr). notes. [8935

OLD Mrs. Tucker. [Edited by Tristram P. Coffin.] Jour. Am. folklore, 72:156 (Apr-Jun). Text collected in northwest Missouri ca. 1920, referring to Mrs. Dan Tucker. [8936

DWIGHT DAVID SMITH. A 20-year appraisal of engineering practices in soil and water conservation [near Bethany, Mo., 1930-51]. Agric. engineering, 33:553-6 (Sep 1952). diagrs., views. [8937

JESSE COTHER GRADY, JR. The vegetable industry of Missouri [1935-54]. Ann Arbor: University Microfilms, 1959 [i. e. 1960]. Positive microfilm of typescript. [146] leaves. Thesis--Univ. of Missouri. Abstracted: Dissert. abstracts, 20: 2459-60 (Jan). [8938

LUCILE H. BLUFORD. The Lloyd Gaines story. Jour. educ. sociol., 32:242-6 (Feb 1959). On the early life and studies of Lloyd Gaines (born 1912), his rejection for admission to the University of Missouri Law School on the ground that he was a Negro, litigation in his behalf by the N.A.A.C.P., the decision by the U.S. Supreme Court ordering his admission, the legal efforts of the State of Missouri to avoid compliance with the order, and the permanent disappearance of Gaines in April 1939. [8939

HARRY GERSHENSON. Experience in Missouri with judicial selection under the non-partisan plan [1940-60]. Am. Bar Assoc. jour., 46:287-9 (Mar). port. [8940

DOROTHY J. CALDWELL. Missouri's heritage to be perpetuated in Historic Sites Survey records. Mo. hist. rev., 54:341-7 (Jul). view. notes. On the Missouri Historic Sites Survey of the State Historical Society of Missouri, established in 1957 to make "an inventory of the nature, location, and condition of historic sites in each Missouri county." [8941

St. Louis

ERNEST KIRSCHTEN. Catfish and crystal. Garden City, N.Y.: Doubleday, 1960. 482 p. tables. On St. Louis, Mo., 1764-1960. [8942

CHARLES VAN RAVENSWAAY. Gateway to the West: an historical guide to St. Louis [1764-1952]. Harvard alumni bul., 54:548-50, 554 (5 Apr 1952). view. [8943

LEO MAX KAISER. Flood of silver, flood of gold: oratory in St. Louis. Mo. Hist. Soc., Bul., 16:302-21 (Jul). notes. On famous speeches delivered in St. Louis, 1804-65; with long excerpts from the speeches. [8944

S. M. ARNOLD. The earliest known postmark from St. Louis [21 Apr. 1805]. S.P.A. jour., 22:449-50 (Jun). facsims. [8945

MARVIN E. HOLDERNESS. Curtain time in Forest Park: a narrative of the St. Louis Municipal Opera, 1919-1958. [St. Louis: St. Louis Municipal Theatre Assoc., 1960?] xi, 143, [1] p. ports., tables, views. On an outdoor theater in Forest Park, producing "operas, operettas and musical comedies"; with some account of opera and theater in St. Louis in the preceding century, 1819-1919. [8946

JOHN WHITEHILL (1794-1871?). John Whitehill, carpenter. [Edited] by Charles Van Ravenswaay. Mo. Hist. Soc., Bul., 16:342-4 (Jul). On the author's life in St. Louis, 1819-66, as a carpenter and operator of lumber yards; with some account of his early years in the East. [8947

JOHN FRANCIS McDERMOTT. Dr. Brown's St. Louis. Mo. hist. rev., 54: 245-53 (Apr). views. notes. On the life of Dr. Benjamin B. Brown as a dentist and surgeon in St. Louis, 1833-48; with an account, compiled from contemporary sources, of "the St. Louis in which he lived and worked." [8948

Mrs. MAX W. MYER. Sarah [Walworth] Beaumont [1822-1913]: her life and loves. Mo. Hist. Soc., Bul., 17:16-44 (Oct). On her early years in various Army posts as the daughter of William Beaumont, Army surgeon, the settlement of the Beaumonts in St. Louis in 1835, her marriages to Lt. Douglass Sims Irwin and to Isaac Keim, and her friendship with Capt. Ethan Allen Hitchcock. [8949

WALTER BROOKFIELD HENDRICKSON. The Western Academy of Natural Sciences of St. Louis [1838-43]. Mo. Hist. Soc., Bul., 16:114-29 (Jan). notes. Includes a biographical sketch of Dr. George Engelmann and some account of the other members of this scientific society. [8950

WILLIAM B. JEFFERIES. The Montesquiou murder case: a possible source for some incidents in Pudd'nhead Wilson [1894]. Am. lit., 31:488-90 (Jan). notes. On the murder of 2 men by Gonzalve, Comte de Montesquiou, in St. Louis, 1849, and the reports of the murders and the trial in the Missouri courier, Hannibal, where Samuel L. Clemens was an apprentice printer. [8951

LEO MAX KAISER, ed. German verse in American cemeteries. Am.-German rev., 26(4):25-8 (Apr-May). views. Rimed inscriptions, 1851-1913, copied in 1959 in the Catholic Cemetery of SS. Peter and Paul and the Evangelical Cemetery of St. Marcus, St. Louis, Mo. [8952

FRANCES HURD STADLER, ed. Letters from Minoma. Mo. Hist. Soc., Bul., 16:237-59 (Apr). notes. Letters received by William Hancock Clark, from his uncle Jefferson Kearny Clark and his father, Meriwether Lewis Clark (1809-81), son of William Clark, dated in St. Louis and "Minoma," the suburban estate of Jefferson K. Clark, 8 May - 18 Dec. 1860, on family matters, heath, local news, etc. [8953

CLARENCE E. MILLER. William Marion Reedy [1862-1920]: a patchwork portrait. Mo. Hist. Soc., Bul., 17:45-56 (Oct). on his life in St. Louis, his work as a journalist, his editing of the St. Louis Mirror (1894-1920), his involvements in alcholic and matrimonial confusion, and his picturesque personal habits; with the author's recollections of him as early as 1898, and a partial list of his publications. [8954

SAINT Louis in the 1870's, then as now a city of diversified industry. Mo. Hist. Soc., Bul., 16: [4] leaves following p. 160 (Jan). Nineteen views, reproduced from contemporary prints and photographs, with captions by the editor. [8955

ST. LOUIS REVIEW COMPANY. St. Louis business and industry, 1877. Selected from a series of articles prepared by the St. Louis Review Company and published in the St. Louis Republican, May to June 1877. Mo. Hist. Soc., Bul., 16:151-72 (Jan). notes. [8956

ROY ARTHUR KLAGES. An analysis and interpretation of the factors influencing the decentralization of the downtown department stores in St. Louis [1948-54]. Ann Arbor: University Microfilms, 1959 [i. e. 1960]. Positive microfilm of typescript. iv, 210 leaves. bibliog. (leaves 200-209). Thesis--St. Louis Univ. Abstracted: Dissert. abstracts, 20:3552 (Mar). [8957

Kansas City

LLEWELLYN WHITE (1899-1959). Kansas City ... Twelfth Street. The reporter, Our times: the best from The reporter, ed. Max Ascoli (N.Y.: Farrar, Straus, and Cudahy [1960]), p. 254-63. First printed in 1958. On "Twelfth, or Sin, Street in Kansas City, Missouri," center for liquor gambling, prostitution, and the political activities of Jim and Tom Pendergast, 1880-1949. [8958

ED LEWIS. Kansas City brass: Ed Lewis' story as told to Frank Driggs. Jazz rev., 2(4):16-18 (May 1959). ports. On the author's life in Kansas City since 1912 and his work as a jazz musician since 1924, including 6 years in Bennie Moten's Orchestra. [8959

ARKANSAS

CLYDE BRION DAVIS. Arkansas [its traditions and characteristics]. Holiday, American panorama west of the Mississippi: a Holiday magazine book

(Garden City, N.Y.: Doubleday [1960]), p. 261-75. [8960

CHARLES ALBERT STUCK. The story of Craighead County: a narrative of people and events in northeast Arkansas. [Jonesboro, Ark., 1960.] 335 p. maps (1 double), ports., tables, views (part double). bibliog. (p. 11). On the county since prehistoric times, its first settlers (in or shortly before 1839), and its county seat, Jonesboro; with a section on "Folklore" (p. 281-329). [8961

MARK RAYMOND HARRINGTON. The Ozark bluff-dwellers. N.Y.: Museum of the American Indian, Heye Foundation, 1960. xiii, 185 p. maps, plans, views. bibliog. (p. 183-5), notes. (Indian notes and monographs, 12.) Report of an expedition to rock shelters on the White River in Benton and Carroll Counties, 1922-23, occupied probably during part of the period from 400 to 600. [8962

JOHN CASPER BRANNER (1850-1922). Some old French place names in the State of Arkansas. Ark. hist. quar., 19:191-206 (autumn). notes. From Modern language notes, Feb. 1899. Annotated list, compiled from early records of the Arkansas Geological Survey and other early sources in English, mainly between 1774 and 1853. [8963

WALTER J. LEMKE. Some notes on the Washburns--father and son: Cephas Washburn [1793-1860], founder of Dwight Mission, 1820, and Edward Payson Washburn [died 1860], painter of "The Arkansas Traveler." Also two accounts of how the painting originated, 1) by Mrs. Zella Hargrove Gaither of Little Rock [1919 or before], 2) by Col. James P. Neal of Prairie Grove [undated manuscript]. Fayetteville, Ark., 1955. 20 leaves. ports., views. (Washington County Historical Society, Fayetteville, Ark. Bulletin series, 11.) [8964

FARRAR NEWBERRY. Jacob Barkman [1784-1852]. Ark. hist. quar., 19: 314-24 (winter). notes. On his removal from Kentucky to Arkansas in 1811, his large purchases of land between Blakelytown and the Caddo River, his store and large brick house on the Caddo, his river trade with New Orleans, his use of the house as an inn, his other business ventures, and his activities in Arkansas politics. [8965

ROBERT R. LOGAN. Notes on the first land surveys in Arkansas [1815-16]. Ark. hist. quar., 19:260-70 (autumn). map, view. notes. [8966

LONNIE J. WHITE. James Miller [1776-1851], Arkansas' first Territorial governor [1819-24]. Ark. hist. quar., 19:12-30 (spring). notes. Deals in part with his retarded arrival in the Territory, 10 months after his appointment, his dislike of the country, his absence from it between June 1823 and his resignation in December 1824, and his several shorter absences on account of bad health. [8967

BOYD W. JOHNSON. Benjamin Desha [1790?-1835]. Ark. hist. quar., 19: 348-60 (winter). notes. On his activities in Arkansas politics, 1824-31. [8968

GEORGE IZARD (1777-1828). The will of Governor George Izard and the records pertaining to it. Edited by J. H. Atkinson. Ark. hist. quar., 19:169-73 (summer). Will of the Governor of Arkansas (Philadelphia, 2 Apr. 1827), and letters of administration. [8969

LONNIE J. WHITE. The Election of 1827 and the Conway-Crittenden duel. Ark. hist. quar., 19:293-313 (winter). notes. On the Territorial Election of 1827 in Arkansas, involving Henry W. Conway, seeking reelection as delegate to Congress, his opponent Robert C. Oden, Secretary Robert Crittenden, and others, and charges of illegal use of public funds by either Crittenden or Conway; the victory of Conway; the publication by him of a libel against Crittenden; the duel between the two, resulting in Conway's death; and further charges of falsehood on both sides. [8970

CORLISS C. CURRY. Early timber operations in southeast Arkansas. Ark. hist. quar., 19:111-18 (summer). notes. On lumbering in the present counties of Ashley, Bradley, and Drew, 1830s-1890. [8971

JOHN HALLUM (1833-1906). A letter from John Hallum to Tom W. Campbell. Edited by J. H. Atkinson. Ark. hist. quar., 19:371-3 (winter). Dated Sweet Home, Ark., 15 Oct. 1901. Anecdotes of Albert Pike and Alfred W. Arrington as Arkansas characters, 1830s-50s. [8972

BESS GALLOWAY. Our town: the story of Delight [1837-1960]. Delight, Ark. [1960]. 60 p. double view. [8973

U.S. Census Office. 7th Census, 1850. Arkansas travelers. [Wash.: Inez Raney Waldenmaier, 1958-60.] 45 p. map. Issued in consecutively paged installments with Genealogical newsletter, summer 1958, summer and fall 1958, spring-fall 1960. Contains "a listing of every man from every county in Arkansas who was 60 years or older in 1850," giving age, place of birth, name of wife, township, and county. [8974

JAMES MADISON HUDSON (1842-1925). Edited by Walter C. Hudson. Ark. hist. quar., 19:271-9 (autumn). Written by request of the author's son (Charles Edward Hudson), recalling his experiences near Pine Bluff, Ark., as a planter in "the Arkansas bottoms," a hunter of outlaws, and a member of the Ku Klux Klan, 1865-70. [8975

CLARA B. KENNAN. Educational journals in Arkansas. Ark. hist. quar., 19:325-47 (winter). On the 6 journals of education published in Arkansas since 1870. [8976

JAMES A. WALDEN (1843-95). The journals of James A. Walden. Vol. II--Methodist minister. W[alter] J. Lemke, editor. Fayetteville, Ark., 1954. [110] p. port. (Washington County Historical Society, Fayetteville, Ark. Bulletin series, 5.) Diary kept by Walden as a minister in northwestern Arkansas, 7 Jul. 1870-15 Apr. 1890. [8977

D. C. SANDERS. Echoes of the farm. San Antonio: Naylor Co. [1960, c1959. 8], 54 p. cartoons. Reminiscences by an author born "just before the turn of the century," of his early years near Philadelphia, Ark., and in Magnolia; with rural anecdotes and folklore. [8978

BOYCE HOUSE (1896-1961). In a little town, long ago. Ark. hist. quar., 19:151-68 (summer). Memories of Brinkley, Ark., "about 1903-05." [8979

DANIEL BOONE LACKEY. Cutting and floating red cedar logs in north Arkansas. Ark. hist. quar., 19:361-70 (winter). port. Recollections of Newton County and the Buffalo River, 1905. [8980

GENE DUNNUCK, MILES McPEEK, & HILLARD JACKSON. Prices and price indexes for Arkansas farm products, 1910-1959. Fayetteville, 1960. 59, [1] p. tables. notes. (Arkansas. Agricultural Experiment Station, Fayetteville. Bulletin 627.) A publication of the Experiment Station in cooperation with the Agricultural Marketing Service, U.S. Dept of Agriculture, at Little Rock. [8981

O. A. ROGERS, JR. The Elaine race riots of 1919 [in Phillips County, Ark.]. Ark. hist. quar., 19:142-50 (summer). notes. [8982

M. S. VENKATARAMANI. Norman Thomas, Arkansas sharecroppers, and the Roosevelt agricultural policies, 1933-1937. Miss. Valley hist. rev., 47: 225-46 (Sep). notes. On his efforts to induce Federal action to relieve the distressed sharecroppers as well as the distressed landowners. [8983

CHARLES PRICE LOOMIS. Informal social systems and decision-making. Jacob L. Moreno, ed., The sociometry reader (Glencoe, Ill.: Free Press [1960]), p. 494-8. diagr., map. notes. On a study of a "New Deal resettlement" community, Dyess Colony, Ark., established by the Federal Emergency Relief Administration, 1936-38. [8984

Fayetteville and Washington County

CUMBERLAND PRESBYTERIAN CHURCH, Cane Hill, Ark. Session minutes of the Cumberland Presbyterian Church, Cane Hill, Arkansas, 1828-1843. [Edited by Walter J. Lemke.] Fayetteville, Ark., 1955. [23] leaves. (Washington County Historical Society, Fayetteville, Ark. Bulletin series, 12.) [8985

WALTER J. LEMKE. Early colleges and academies of Washington County, Arkansas. Fayetteville, 1954. 96 p. facsim., map, view. bibliog. (p. 95-6). (Washington County Historical Society, Fayetteville, Ark. Bulletin series, 6.) On 6 schools for boys, 5 for girls, and 1 for both, 1835-1890s, of which only Cane Hill College (1850-87) and Elm Springs Male and Female Academy (1849-1890s) existed after the Civil War. [8986

ROBERT W. MECKLIN (1795-1871). The Mecklin letters, written in 1863-64 at Mt. Comfort. By Robert W. Mecklin, the founder of Ozark Institute. ... W[alter] J. Lemke, editor. Fayetteville, Ark., 1955. 45 p. (Washington County Historical Society. Bulletin series, 10.) Letters from a retired schoolteacher, living close to Fayetteville, addressed to his wife's sister, Katherine (Anderson) Dinsmore, a refugee in Texas, 9 Aug. 1863-4 Feb. 1864, on family affairs, the author's health, the weather, his "attending to such matters as are to be done on a small farm during the winter," the activities of Federal forces in foraging for food, burning houses, and insulting, abusing, and murdering civilians, the retaliatory activities of the "bushwhackers," and the almost daily threats to the author and his wife and family. [8987

Little Rock

BEVERLY E. RYAN. Little Rock municipal water works' plans for the future. Southwest water works jour., 38(7):34-40 (Oct 1956). views. Includes the history of the works, 1878-1956. [8988

OKLAHOMA

DON C. AHSHAPANEK & ROBERT D. BURNS. Mammals associated with prehistoric people of Oklahoma. Okla. Acad. Science, Proc., 40:16-19. table. bibliog. On animal remains found in association with remains of human occupancy in the course of excavations in Garvin County, 1937. [8989

DEBS MYERS. Oklahoma [its traditions and characteristics]. Holiday, American panorama west of the Mississippi: a Holiday magazine book (Garden City, N.Y.: Doubleday [1960]), p. 244-60. [8990

OKLAHOMA. Geological Survey. Geological report on the Heavener "rune stone." Chron. Okla., 37:506-7 (winter). Signed: William E. Ham, Associate Director. Report of examination of an inscribed stone found in Le Flore County, concluding from geological evidence that "it is not impossible that the cutting was done a thousand years ago." [8991

ARTHUR H. DOERR & JOHN W. MORRIS. The Oklahoma Panhandle--a cross section of the southern High Plains. Econ. geog., 36:70-88 (Jan). diagrs., maps, views. notes. Study of Beaver, Cimarron, and Texas Counties, 1541-1959. [8992

STEVE WILSON. Mines, mining, and minerals in the Wichita Mountains [Oklahoma, 1650-1960]. Okla. Junior Acad. Science, Trans., 3:12-19. bibliog. [8993

DORIS H. HAMILTON. An Indian agent in Indiana Territory. Hobbies, 65(7): 110-11 (Sep). On a manuscript notebook kept by John Johnston while "agent for Indian affairs," 1801-11; with excerpts. [8994

OKLAHOMA HISTORICAL SOCIETY. Preliminary report of survey of inscriptions along Santa Fe Trail in Oklahoma [dated 15 Aug. 1960]. Chron. Okla., 38:311-22 (autumn). views. notes. Report of a committee "under the joint sponsorship of the Oklahoma Historical Society and the Oklahoma Science and Arts Foundation" (William G. Fisher, Chairman). List of the still legible names and initials cut in sandstone rocks along the course of the trail crossing the Oklahoma Panhandle in Cimarron County, some of which are dated between 1844 and 1926. [8995

ALTHA LEAH (BIERBOWER) BASS. The story of Tullahassee. Oklahoma City: Semco Color Press [1960. 10], 271 p. facsims., maps, plans, ports., views. notes. On William Schenck Robertson (1820-81), his wife, Ann Eliza (Worcester) Robertson (1826-1905), and the Presbyterian mission and school established by them for the Creek Indians near Tullahassee, Okla., in 1849; with extensive quotations from family papers. [8996

OKLAHOMA HISTORICAL SOCIETY. Rock Mary report. Chron. Okla., 38: 130-53 (summer). maps, views. notes. Report of a committee (Robert H. Dott, Chairman), 1 May 1960, on the location and identity of several "natural mounds" or sandstone buttes near Hinton in northern Caddo County, first described by Lt. James H. Simpson, Topographical Engineers, in 1849. [8997

JAMES HERVEY SIMPSON (1813-83). Lieutenant Simpson's California road across Oklahoma. [Edited] by Robert H. Dott. Chron. Okla., 38:154-79 (summer). fold. map, table. notes. Excerpts from a report (Santa Fe, 13 Aug. 1849) and a letter (camp on south side of Canadian River, 15 May 1849, to the commanding officer of the Corps of Topographical Engineers), arranged in geographical order from the entry of an Army surveying expedition at the Arkansas line to its exit at the Texas line, 11 Apr.-31 May 1849, identifying his route and describing the country. [8998

JAMES DAVIDSON MORRISON. Note on abolitionism in the Choctaw Nation. Chron. Okla., 38:78-84 (spring). notes. On a controversy between the Northern standard, Clarksville, Tex., and the Choctaw intelligencer, Doaksville, Okla., over the charge by the former that missionaries in the Choctaw Nation were encouraging the Choctaws to harbor runaway slaves, 1850, the lack of evidence for the truth of the charge, the conclusion of the American Board of Commissioners for Foreign Missions that its Choctaw Mission "appeared to condone slavery," and the separation of the Mission, by its own request, from the Board in 1859. [8999

GEORGE JONES GOODMAN. Camp Arbuckle, a century later. Asa Gray bul., 3:63-4 (spring 1955). Includes an excerpt from an article by Dr. J. M. Bigelow in "Pac. R. R. Rept. 4: p. 2" (1857), describing the flora of the area of Camp Arbuckle, Okla., in 1853. [9000

OKLAHOMA HISTORICAL SOCIETY. [No Man's Land.] Southw. hist. quar., 64:261-3 (Oct). Text or part of the text of "a recent brochure." On the Oklahoma Panhandle, 34 miles wide, 168 miles long, 1854-90. [9001

GASPARE SIGNORELLI. Fort Sill, Indian Terr., & Oklahoma. S. P. A. jour., 20:485-7 (Jul 1958). facsims. On the post office there and its postal markings since 1869. [9002

ELSTON G. BRADFIELD. Osage Indian medals. Numismatics, 73: 1795-9 (Dec). coins, table. On 14 medals, designed by Ferdinand Rebechini, struck in 1,000 copies in 1958 and 1959, commemorating leaders of the Osage Indians since 1870. [9003

ORPHA B. RUSSELL. Notes on Samuel William Brown, Jr. [1879-1957], Yuchi chief. Chron. Okla., 37:497-501 (winter). On his life in Oklahoma. [9004

ROBERT EARL CUNNINGHAM. I preserve the past. Infinity, 9(8): 12-15 (Oct). views. On the author's collecting of "old glass photographic plates" showing Oklahoma scenes, 1880s and later, particularly those made by William S. Prettyman, itinerant photographer. See also "Out of the West," by C. Arrowsmith, 9(2):20-21 (Feb.), reproducing 12 portraits and a view taken by an unidentified photographer, now recognized by Cunningham as work by Prettyman. [9005

FRANK ALLEN BALYEAT. Arthur Grant Evans [1858-1928]. Chron. Okla., 38:245-52 (autumn). port. notes. On his work in Oklahoma as a teacher in schools of the Cherokee Nation and a Presbyterian minister, 1884 ff., and as President of the University of Oklahoma, 1908-11; with some account of his earlier life in India and England and his later years in California. [9006

BERNICE NORMAN CROCKETT. The story of Rock Cut. Chron. Okla., 38:253-64 (autumn). fold. map, views. notes. On a track of the Santa Fe Railroad blasted along the course of the Washita River and through the Arbuckle Mountains between Davis and Ardmore, 1884-87, partly relocated between 1909 and 1912 as a result of floods; with anecdotes of the vicinity. [9007

FRANK F. FINNEY, SR. Maria Tallchief, in history: Oklahoma's own ballerina. Chron. Okla., 38:8-11 (spring). port. Undated references to Mrs. Henry D. Paschen, Jr., of Chicago, dancer, native of Oklahoma, and account of some of her Osage ancestors since 1884. [9008

MESHACH H. COUCH. Meshach H. Couch letter, 1885. Chron. Okla., 37: 502, 505-6 (winter). Letter to Harden Holbrook (in North Carolina), dated Douglas, Butler County, Ky., 8 Feb. 1885, on the author's claim in Oklahoma, the intention of the author and 5,000 or 10,000 others to enter Oklahoma and take possession of lands without permission from the U.S. Government, and the good quality of Oklahoma land. [9009

FIRST PRESBYTERIAN CHURCH, Tulsa, Okla. A history of the First Presbyterian Church of Tulsa, Oklahoma, 1885-1960. [Tulsa, 1960. 8], 60 p. ports., tables, views. [9010

WILLIAM PACKER BLAKE. [Letter to Grant Foreman, dated Hyattsville,

Md., 3 Mar. 1937.] Chron. Okla., 38:270-73 (autumn). facsim. On the author's work as a Baptist missionary to the Seminoles in Oklahoma, superintendent of their Seminole Academy for girls (at Sasakwa) and of Emahaka Academy for girls, 1887-1906. [9011

HARRIET (PATRICK) GILSTRAP. Memoirs of a pioneer teacher. Chron. Okla., 38:20-34 (spring). ports., view. notes. On the author's life at the Sac and Fox Agency, in present Lincoln County, Okla., 1888 ff., her teaching in Indian schools, her marriage to Harry B. Gilstrap in 1899, and her subsequent life in Oklahoma; with appended editorial accounts of her former pupils Earnest Spybuck (died 1949), Shawnee painter of Indian scenes, and Jim Thorpe (James Francis Thorpe, 1888-1953), "the World's greatest athlete." [9012

BERLIN BASIL CHAPMAN. Oklahoma City, from public land to private property. Chron. Okla., 37:211-37, 330-53, 440-79 (summer 1959-winter 1960). facsims., map, plans, seal, table, view. notes. Reprinted separately, with same title: [Oklahoma City?] 1960. vi, 96 p. illus. On controversies over the appropriation by individuals of land in Oklahoma City belonging to the United States, and the authority of a de facto government there to grant such land or to grant privileges in its use, 1889-90. [9013

CLARENCE C. CULLIMORE. Perry's first doctor. Chron. Okla., 38:191-5 (summer). port., view. notes. On the author's father, Dr. Thomas McIntyre Cullimore (1849-99), who removed from Jacksonville, Ill., to Perry, Okla., in 1889, and after 3 years left Oklahoma in a further search for a climate favorable to his failing health. [9014

ROBERT EARL CUNNINGHAM. Oklahoma's missing link. Chron. Okla., 38:185-90 (summer). ports., views. On the "several thousand superb pictures" of events in Oklahoma from 1889 to 1893, including those made by William S. Prettyman and A. A. Forbes. [9015

WILLIAM CX HANCOCK. I knew Quanah Parker. ... By Wm. Cx Hancock as told by Wylie W. Bennett. Frontier times, 34(2):26-7, 49-50 (spring). ports. Oklahoma recollections, 1889-1905. [9016

MARY E. NEWBERN. Fred L. Wenner [1865-1956]: reporter. Chron. Okla., 38:43-9 (spring). port., view. On his life as a newspaperman in Guthrie, 1889-1956. [9017

ARRELL MORGAN GIBSON. Joe Kagey [1890-1959]: Indian educator. Chron. Okla., 38:12-19 (spring). port., view. notes. On his teaching in Goodland School and Orphanage, near Hugo, and Jones Academy, near Hartshorne, both serving the Choctaw Nation, 1913-28, and his service as Principal of the Seneca Indian School, near Wyandotte, Okla., 1928-56. [9018

FRED E. HOLDREDGE. Kid on the run! True West, 7(3):26-7, 51-2 (Jan-Feb). views. Memories of participation in the Oklahoma land rush (Cherokee Strip), Sep. 1893. [9019

IRVIN HURST. Robbingest robber. Frontier times, 34(2):16-17, 52, 54 (spring). ports., view. On the career of Henry Starr (1873?-1921) as a murderer and a bank robber, especially in Oklahoma, 1893-1921 (including 6 years in penitentiaries). [9020

ROBERT E. TREVATHAN. School days at Emahaka Academy. Chron. Okla., 38:265-70 (autumn). port. On a Seminole Indian girls' secondary school near Wewoka, built 1892-93, as recalled by Byron S. Blake (born 1888), who by special arrangement attended it from 1894 to 1897. [9021

THOMAS A. HIGGINS. Stories relating to Oklahoma Territorial courts and law. [Contributed by L. Wayne Johnston.] Chron. Okla., 38:101-6 (spring). Anecdotes collected by Higgins as Court Reporter of the U.S. District Court at Guthrie, 1900 to ca. 1912. [9022

VELMA NIEBERDING. The Very Reverend Urban de Hasque, S.T.D., L.L.D., pioneer priest of Indian Territory. Chron. Okla., 38:35-42 (spring). ports. notes. On Urban Alphonse de Hasque (1875-1954), native of Belgium, ordained a priest in 1900, and his service as a Catholic priest in Oklahoma, 1900-1954. [9023

BESS ROGERS. Big Jake's Crossing. Chron. Okla., 38:50-54 (spring). Memories of the ferry across the Washita River, kept by the author's father with a small store patronized by Indians, 1900-1901. [9024

GEORGE H. SHIRK. Judge Edgar S[ullins] Vaught [1873-1959]. Chron. Okla., 37:394-403 (winter). facsim., port., views. On his life in Oklahoma City, 1901-59, his service there as superintendent of the school system till 1906, his practice of law, his service as U.S. District Judge for the Western District of Oklahoma (1928-56), and his many civic interests. [9025

STARR OTTO DOYEL. Y. W. C. A., national--local: Central State College, Edmond, Oklahoma, 1902-1960. [Edmond? 1960. 2], iii, [1], 83 leaves. facsims., ports., tables, views. bibliog. (leaves 78-81). [9026

NAT M. TAYLOR. The name "Lookeba" in Caddo County. Chron. Okla., 38:324-5 (autumn). On the "coined" name of a town settled in 1902. [9027

ALICE CUNNINGHAM FLETCHER (1838-1923). The Hako: a Pawnee ceremony. Margaret Mead & Ruth L. Bunzel, eds., The golden age of American anthropology (N.Y.: George Braziller, 1960), p. 239-45. First printed in 1904. On a ceremony intended to insure "that the tribe may increase; and also that the people may have long life, enjoy plenty, and be happy and at peace"; with accompanying songs. [9028

Mrs. WALTER WOOD. Charles Page [1860-1926]: a man--a dream--an opportunity. Chron. Okla., 38:196-201 (summer). port., views. On his early years in rural Wisconsin, his prosperity in business, his charitable interests in Oklahoma after his settlement there in 1905, and his establishment of the Sand Springs Home in 1912 to administer a home for children and a colony for widows. [9029

HOMER CROY. America's greatest prison removal. Westerners brand book (N.Y.), 5:83. On the keeping of Oklahoma prisoners in Kansas prisons by contract with the State of Kansas, the act of the Oklahoma Legislature to establish a penitentiary in Oklahoma, and the transportation of 620 convicts in a specially constructed train from Lansing, Kan., to McAlester, where they arrived in a blizzard and were housed in sheds surrounded by an electrified fence and were required to clear the 2,000 acres and construct the prison "that was going to be their home," 1907-9. [9030

W. R. WITHINGTON. Checotah-Eufala court-house riot. Chron. Okla., 38:323-4 (autumn). Recollections of a violent competition between the 2 towns for choice as county seat of McIntosh County, 1908. [9031

ELMER L. LUCAS. The fiftieth anniversary of the Oklahoma Academy of Science [1909-59]. Okla. Acad. Science, Proc., 40:[10-13]. [9032

CHARLES S. BRANT. Indian-white cultural relations in southwestern Oklahoma. Chron. Okla., 37:433-9 (winter). notes. On "the reactions to the Ghost Dance by white people" in this area, 1910-18, the decision of the Commissioner of Indian Affairs that the dance "is a pernicious custom," the effort to eliminate it by withholding annuity payments from participants, and the resulting "period of spying by Government authorities, treachery by individual Indians and general increase of tension in the Indian community." [9033

EARL F. KEYES. The removal of the Great Seal of the State from Guthrie to Oklahoma City, 1901. Chron. Okla., 38:203-5 (summer). Recollections (1952) in a letter by an eyewitness. [9034

EDGAR SULLINS VAUGHT (1873-1959). A new chapter in an old story. Chron. Okla., 37:405-10 (winter). view. notes. Reminiscent address, 1945, on "the location and construction of the State Capitol of Oklahoma," 1910-14. [9035

MAURICE HITCHCOCK MERRILL. The implied covenant of further exploration in Oklahoma. Okla. law rev., 13:249-66 (Aug). notes. On the implied agreement of the lessee of gas and oil rights to continue exploration under certain conditions, 1919-58. [9036

DON HENDERSON. Pawhuska's little horse. Quarter horse jour., 4(11):16, 18 (Aug 1952). On the author's work as a trainer of polo ponies for E. W. Marland (of the Marland Oil Company) at Ponca, Okla., from ca. 1921 "until the bottom fell out of oil toward the end of the 1920s." [9037

FRANCIS LA FLESCHE (1857-1932). Rite of the chiefs: prayer for painting the body. Margaret Mead & Ruth L. Bunzel, eds., The golden age of

American anthropology (N.Y.: George Braziller, 1960), p. 237-8. First printed in 1921. Text of an Osage prayer as recorded by the author, an Omaha Indian. [9038

LESLIE A. McRILL. Music in Oklahoma by the Billy McGinty Cowboy Band. Chron. Okla., 38:66-74 (spring). port. On a group formed at Ripley, Okla., as early as 1921, originally called the Old Time Fiddlers, composed of "local musicians who liked to play old time tunes," and the beginning of its wider celebrity with its appearance on a radio program from Bristow, Okla., in 1925. [9039

FRANK TURLEY. The present-day Oklahoma fancy war dance. Midw. folklore, 10:213-16 (winter). On an Indian men's dance "first ... introduced approximately thirty-five years ago," now part of the public powwows of several tribes. [9040

ARTHUR F. HALLORAN & CLAUD A. SHRADER. Longhorn cattle management on Wichita Mountains Wildlife Refuge [Comanche County, Okla., 1927-59]. Jour. wildlife management, 24:191-6 (Apr). table, view. bibliog. [9041

BERTHOLD BRENNER. On suicide rate differentials in Tulsa [1937-56]. Am. sociol. rev., 25:265-6 (Apr). tables. notes. For comment by Jack P. Gibbs and Walter T. Martin, and Brenner's reply, see 25:733-4. [9042

ED FRANKLIN CRIM, JR. The effect of regional public expenditures on the level of regional income as illustrated by the State of Oklahoma [1940-41, 1946-55]. Ann Arbor: University Microfilms, 1960. Positive microfilm of typescript. [146] leaves. Thesis--Univ. of Illinois. Abstracted: Dissert. abstracts, 20:4548 (Jun). [9043

WILLIAM E. BITTLE. The desegregated all-white institution ... the University of Oklahoma [1946-59]. Jour. educ. sociol., 32:275-82 (Feb 1959). notes. [9044

THE MIDDLE WEST

GEORGE IRVING QUIMBY. Indian life in the Upper Great Lakes, 11,000 B.C. to A.D. 1800. [Chicago:] Univ. of Chicago Press [1960]. xv, 182 p. diagrs., maps, tables, views. bibliog. (p. 165-76). [9045

HOLM WOLFRAM NEUMANN. Diagnostic morphological traits for the Walcolid variety of American Indians. Ind. Acad. Science, Proc., 69:69-72. tables. Study of 98 skulls found in Indiana, Illinois, and Nebraska, of persons probably living sometime between 1200 and 1500. [9046

WILLIAM JOHN PETERSEN. The Winnebago Indians. Iowa City, 1960. 325-356 p. col. ports., views (1 col.). (The palimpsest, v. 41, no. 7.) On the first visit to these Indians of the Green Bay area by a white person (Jean Nicolet, 1634), their beliefs and customs, their removal from Wisconsin, their stay in the "Neutral Ground" of Iowa from 1839 to 1848, and their later career in Minnesota and Nebraska. [9047

PAUL WALLACE GATES. Frontier estate builders and farm laborers. Walker D. Wyman & Clifton B. Kroeber, eds., The frontier in perspective (Madison: Univ. of Wisconsin Press, 1957), p. 143-63. bibliog., notes. On the multiplication of hired laborers, tenant farmers, and "capitalist estate builders" in the rural Middle West, conventionally supposed to be a country of small farmers owning their farms, 19th century. [9048

MATE GRAYE HUNT. The last march of the Potawatomi. Mich. heritage, 1:129-34 (summer). views. On the various stages in the forcible removal of these Indians from their lands in Michigan, Indiana, and Wisconsin, 1825-40. [9049

ARTHUR HECHT. Postal history in newspapers. Am. philatelist, 73:903-5 (Sep). Examples of information found by the author in "approximately 2,400 newspapers published in Wisconsin, Indiana, Missouri, Illinois, and mainly in Iowa for the years 1833-50." [9050

WILLIAM JOHN PETERSEN. Railroads come to Iowa. Iowa City, 1960.

177-260, [2] p. facsims., maps, views (part col. fold.). (The palimpsest, v. 41, no. 4.) On the construction of several lines westward across Illinois to the Mississippi (Chicago & Rock Island Railway Line, 1847-54; Galena & Chicago Union Railroad and the Chicago & North Western Railway Company, 1836-64; Illinois Central Railroad Company, 1851-55; Chicago, Burlington, & Quincy Railroad Company, 1852-55) and of a line through Wisconsin (Milwaukee & Mississippi Railroad Company, 1847-57); with a list of their branches in Iowa in 1860 and references to numerous predecessor and subsidiary companies. [9051

ALLAN G. BOGUE. Social theory and the pioneer. Agric. hist., 34:21-34 (Jan). notes. Study of "a number of characteristics of the population and environment which have held true in most new communities in that part of the Middle West stretching from the central prairies of Illinois westward through Iowa and on into Kansas and Nebraska, a region settled for the most part between 1840 and 1900"; with a long introduction on theories of the relations between the "pioneer" and the "frontier" in various parts of the United States. [9052

CARL STAMM MEYER. Lutheran immigrant churches face the problems of the frontier. Church hist., 29:440-62 (Dec). notes. Deals particularly with Lutheranism among German and Scandinavian immigrants in the Middle West, 1840s-80s. [9053

WILLIAM JOHN PETERSEN, ed. Moving the Winnebago into Iowa. Ia. jour. hist., 58:357-76 (Oct). notes. "Speech of Governor Henry Dodge," of Iowa, Apr. 1840, delivered to the Winnebago Indians, and secretary's minutes of "Council held with the Winnebagoes on the 1st May 1840 at Prairie du Chien," in which Gen. Henry Atkinson was spokesman for the U.S. Government, seeking compliance by the Indians with orders to remove from Wisconsin to the "Neutral Ground" reserved for them in Iowa. [9054

ROSINA (MOSSER) GERBER (born 1842). Personal memoirs: the pioneer home. Mennonite hist. bul., 16(2):4-5 (Apr 1955). Memories (1914) of the author's rural childhood and Mennonite upbringing near Orrville, Wayne County, Ohio, and in Adams County, Ind., and her married life on a farm in Hickory County, Mo. [9055

BERNARD G. CORBIN & WILLIAM KERKA. Steam locomotives of the Burlington route [Chicago, Burlington, and Quincy Railroad Company, 1849-1959. Red Oak? Ia., 1960.] 304 p. diagrs., facsims. (1 col.) maps, ports., tables, views (1 col.). bibliog. (p. 20, 165). Heavily illustrated. [9056

IVAN D. WOOD. Irrigation in the Middle West [1950-57]. Agric. engineering, 38:418-21 (Jun 1957). tables, views. [9057

ALBERT H. PRATT. Search for fortune along the Mississippi: Pratt letters, 1860-1861. [Edited by Dorothy J. Ernst.] Mid-America, 42:44-52 (Jan). notes. Letters to Daniel Wells, Jr. (1808-1902), Milwaukee businessman, 22 Jun. 1860(?)-22 Dec. 1861, on the various reasons why Pratt does not pay a debt owed to Wells, his brief partnership in a St. Louis news agency, his search for other employment, and his acceptance of work as a Chicago bookkeeper at $400 a year. [9058

JACOB B. MENSCH (1835-1912). The travel notes of Jacob B. Mensch. Mennonite hist. bul., 15(2):3-4; (3):2-5 (Apr, Jul 1954). Record of a missionary railroad journey from Pennsylvania to visit Mennonites in Kansas, Nebraska, South Dakota, Illinois, Indiana, Ohio, and western Pennsylvania, 9 Sep.-6 Nov. 1889 (39 meetings), and a journey to Ohio and Ontario, Sep.-Oct. 1897 (14 meetings). [9059

ABRAM B. KOLB. A Western trip. Mennonite hist. bul., 13(3):7-8 (Jul 1952). Letter to C. Z. Yoder, dated Elkhart, Ind., 12 Nov. 1891, presenting "an outline of the trip mapped out for Bro. Isaac Miller" from Ohio through Missouri to Kansas and Nebraska and back through Iowa, with information about number of Mennonites available on the route for visitation and names of individuals to whom he should write for further information. [9060

JAY ARTHUR MYERS. "It is not best to swap horses while crossing the river." Jour. lancet, 80:140-47 (Apr). On hospitals specializing in the treatment of tuberculosis, especially in Wisconsin and Minnesota, 1893-1959, and the foolishness of prematurely closing them and dispersing their staffs. [9061

WAYNE DINSMORE. The racing record of Peter McCue. Quarter horse jour., 4(2):33, 75 (Nov 1951). tables. On a horse (perhaps not "a true Quarter Horse") foaled in 1895, trained and raced by Charles Watkins of Petersburg, Ill., in the Middle West and Canada, 1897-99, retired to service as a studhorse, and still living in 1907. [9062

WALTER J. PELTON & RUTH DEE BOTHWELL. The dental profession in the Great Lakes region. Am. College Dentists, Jour., 26:3-27 (Mar 1959). diagrs., map, tables. notes. On "persons-per-dentist ratios," age of dentists, distribution, and prospects of future supply, 1930-58. [9063

MEREDITH K. ESSIG. Middle West quarter racing [1943-51]. Quarter horse jour., 4(2):24, 72 (Nov 1951), views. Mainly on races of Indiana and Illinois horses on the track at Albany, Ind. [9064

The QUARTER horse in the Midwest [1944-49]. Quarter horse, 5(4):15-17 (Jul 1949). views. [9065

HARRY ROBERT STEVENS. Recent writings on Midwestern economic history [published 1944-59]. Ohio hist. quar., 69:1-31 (Jan). notes. Critical commentary. [9066

The East North Central States

THE MILWAUKEE SENTINEL. Cities of Wisconsin and Upper Michigan: up to date facts on their business, industry, farming, education, civic progress, and recreational facilities. Reprinted from the Milwaukee sentinel. [Milwaukee, 1955, ©1954.] 56 p. maps, ports., views. 36 cm. Historical and other information about 55 cities, including 8 in the western part of the Upper Peninsula of Michigan. [9067

WALTER EDWIN HAVIGHURST, ed. Land of the long horizons. N.Y.: Coward-McCann [1960]. 437 p. cartoon, facsims., ports., views (part double). bibliog. (p. 6). Collection of reprinted primary and early secondary sources, mainly records of "personal experiences," relating to "the old Northwest Territory, consisting of Ohio, Indiana, Illinois, Michigan, Wisconsin, and part of Minnesota." 1634-1946. [9068

HAROLD HICKERSON. The feast of the dead among the seventeenth century Algonkians of the upper Great Lakes. Am. anthropol., 62:81-107 (Feb). map. bibliog., notes. On a custom of the Saulteur Indians ("the lineal ancestors of the modern Chippewa"), first described in 1641, probably derived by the Saulteurs from the Hurons, and nearly extinct by 1695, and its relation to the "atomism" of the Chippewa Indians. [9069

JOSEPH A. PARSONS, JR. Civilizing the Indians of the Old Northwest, 1800-1810. Ind. mag. hist., 56:195-216 (Sep). notes. On the failure of the U.S. Government in whatever it may have planned to do: "whether to cheat the Indian of his lands or to civilize him and make him one with the American people." [9070

ALEXIS A. PRAUS. Enoch Harris [1785?-1870]--Negro pioneer. Mich. heritage, 2:60-66 (winter). port. notes. On Harris (a Negro) and his wife Deborah (1793-1881, mulatto) in Pennsylvania, Ohio, and Oshtemo Township, Kalamazoo County, Mich., and their daughter Louisa (born 1815), who married John Henry Powers (in 1837?); with Bible records of the Powers family. [9071

RALPH WILLARD HIDY & MURIEL E. HIDY. Anglo-American merchant bankers and the railroads of the Old Northwest, 1848-1860. Bus. hist. rev., 34:150-69 (summer). view. notes. Deals particularly with George Peabody & Company, London. [9072

ROBERT MARK WARNER. Chase Salmon Osborn, 1860-1949. Ann Arbor: Univ. of Michigan [1960]. 30, [1] p. ports. bibliog. (p. 31). (Michigan Historical Collections. Bulletin 10.) On his early life near Wabash, Ind., his work as a newspaperman in Chicago, Milwaukee, and Florence, Wis., and as owner and editor of the Sault Ste Marie News, and his service as Governor of Michigan. Based mainly upon his papers in the Michigan Historical Collections. [9073

JOSEPH SWASTEK. Michigan's foremost Polish priest, Reverend Joseph

Dabrowski [1842-1903], the father of the Polish school system in America. Poles in Michigan Associated, Poles in Michigan (Detroit, 1953 [i.e. 1955]), 1:26-36. port. On his emigration in 1869, his service in the Sacred Heart Parish, Polonia, Wis. (1869-82), and in Detroit (1882-1903), his part in bringing the Felician Sisters to America, his writing and printing of several Polish textbooks, his founding of Polish parochial schools and of the Polish Seminary, and his other services to Polish Catholicism in America. [9074

MARY ELOISE THOMAS. A study of the causes and consequences of the economic status of migratory farm workers in Illinois, Indiana, Michigan, and Wisconsin, 1940-1958. Ann Arbor: University Microfilms, 1960. Positive microfilm of typescript. [456] leaves. Thesis--Univ. of Notre Dame. Abstracted: Dissert. abstracts, 21:481 (Sep). [9075

PAUL A. WHISLER & GEORGE V. FRUSHOUR. Engineers advance art of making grass silage. Agric. engineering, 34:315-18 (May 1953). views. Report of experiments of the Allis-Chalmers Manufacturing Company in Wisconsin, in Ohio, and particularly in La Porte County, Ind., 1942-52. [9076

JIM SCRIBBINS. Milwaukee Road's Milwaukee Division: story and photographs by Jim Scribbins. Natl. Railway Hist. Soc., Bul., 25(1):22-5 (1st quar.). views. Record of observations made in 1953 in a railway district extending from Chicago to Iron Mountain and Ontonagon. [9077

OHIO

CALEB ATWATER (1778-1867). Conjectures, respecting the origin and history of the authors of the ancient works in Ohio, etc. Margaret Mead & Ruth L. Bunzel, eds., The golden age of American anthropology (N.Y.: George Braziller, 1960), p. 102-5. notes. Speculations (printed 1820) on the Mound Builders of Ohio. [9078

OHIO. Division of Elementary and Secondary Education. The musical heritage of Ohio. [n. p., 195-? 2] leaves, 53 p. col. flag, maps (1 col.), seal, col. views. bibliog. (p. 49-53). On music in Ohio since Indian times; with lists of music and of films. [9079

DAVID DANIEL ANDERSON. Small boys and French explorers in Lorain County. Ohioana, 3:10-12 (spring). cartoon. On a report in the Lorain Republican (7 Jun. 1843) of 2 inscribed stones, dated 1533 and 1553, the second carved with the words "Louis Vagard" and "La France," and the obliteration of the inscriptions by boys who cracked hickory nuts on the stones (1838); and the discovery by small boys of a rusted and pitted anchor in the bank of the Black River in 1904, inscribed with fleurs-de-lis and probably French lettering, which they sold to a junk dealer. [9080

GEORGE C. CROUT. Middletown, U.S.A., All-America city [1796-1960]. Middletown, Ohio: Perry Print. Co., 1960. 160 p. ports., views. bibliog. (p. 144). [9081

MANASSEH CUTLER (1742-1823). A frontier mission. Margaret Mead & Ruth L. Bunzel, eds., The golden age of American anthropology (N.Y.: George Braziller, 1960), p. 95-7. First printed in 1888. Charge delivered in Hamilton, Mass., 15 Aug. 1798, at the ordination of the Rev. Mr. Story, pastor of the Congregational Church in Marietta, Ohio, called by Cutler "the first regularly ordained and settled minister of the Congregational denomination in that extensive country westward of the Alleghany Mountains"; with some account of Cutler's observations on the natural history of Ohio during his stay there, including "A note on the antiquity of the Ohio mounds as shown by the count of tree rings." [9082

MARGARET A. RODEE. Pewter making in early Ohio [1798-1860]. Ohioana, 3:3-6, 14 (spring). views [9083

HAZEL SPENCER PHILLIPS. Banking in Warren County [Ohio, 1805-1960. Oxford, Ohio, 1960. 8], 69 p. facsims., port., views. [9084

STARK COUNTY HISTORICAL SOCIETY. The Stark County story. [By Edward Thornton Heald, Historian of the Stark County Historical Society.] Canton: Stark County Historical Soc., 1949-59. 4 v. in 6. xvi, 688; xvi, 706; xvi, 822; xvi, 856; xvi, 850; xvi, 1065 p. maps, ports., views. bibliogs., notes. A history of Stark County, "being Scripts [1]-463 as broadcast over WHBC-WHBC-FM, rearranged and edited as a county history with bibliography, references, and index; a contribution to the Stark County (Ohio) Sesquicentennial, 1809-1959." [9085

FIRST EVANGELICAL AND REFORMED CHURCH, Canton, Ohio. History of the First Evangelical and Reformed Church (United Church of Christ) [1810-1960]. Canton [1960?] 116 p. facsims., port., tables, views (1 col.). Prepared by a History Committee (Chairman: Paul G. Schneider). On a congregation which in its early years was of mainly German membership. [9086

Mrs. OTIS O. FLEMING. Records from Chenoweth Cemetery, Franklin Co., Ohio [1815-1903]. Detroit Soc. Geneal. Research mag., 23:173-4 (summer). Inscriptions from a rural cemetery about a mile north of Harrisburg, abandoned and "in very bad condition" when the inscriptions were copied in 1935. [9087

HARRY N. SCHEIBER. The Ohio canal movement, 1820-1825. Ohio hist. quar., 69:231-56 (Jul). notes. [9088

WILLARD S. KRABILL. A brief sketch of the origins and growth of the Beech Mennonite Church [Louisville, Ohio, 1823-1949]. Mennonite hist. bul., 11(4):1-3 (Oct 1950). view. On a congregation originally formed by Alsatian Amish emigrants. [9089

PETER FOX SMITH. A Granville cooper's experience with barter in the 1820's. Ohio hist. quar., 69:58-68 (Jan). notes. Information from a ledger kept by Asa Shepardson, cooper and shinglemaker in Granville, 1827 to ca. 1842. [9090

EDMUND LOUIS BINSFELD. Francisca Bauer [1775?-1859], the Sister of the Woods. Ohio hist. quar., 69: 353-66 (Oct). notes. On a native of Alsace, who came to Norwalk, Ohio, with relatives in 1828 and lived alone in a small log house on her land near Norwalk; her part in procuring the establishment of a Catholic church there and in bringing to the settlement the Redemptorists, the Fathers of the Precious Blood, and the Sisters of the Precious Blood; and her many other services to the Catholic community, including schoolteaching and gifts of land. [9091

LEONARD ERNEST ERICKSON. The color line in Ohio public schools, 1829-1890. Ann Arbor: University Microfilms, 1959 [1960]. Positive microfilm of typescript. vi, 468 leaves. maps, tables. bibliog. (leaves 451-67). Thesis--Ohio State Univ. Abstracted: Dissert. abstracts, 20:3617 (Mar). On the extent of segregation of Negro and white children in schools. [9092

HELEN ARNOLD CAMERON. Taxation of insurance companies in Ohio [since 1830]. Ann Arbor: University Microfilms, 1960. Positive microfilm of typescript. [346] leaves. Thesis--Ohio State Univ. Abstracted: Dissert. abstracts, 21:1095 (Nov). [9093

DELBERT GRÄTZ. Swiss Mennonites come to Putnam County, Ohio [since 1833]. Mennonite life, 15:165-7 (Oct). ports, view. [9094

JOHN LEECH STOVER. The changing regionalization of sheep husbandry in Ohio [since 1840]. Ann Arbor: University Microfilms, 1960. Positive microfilm of typescript. [297] leaves. Thesis--Univ. of Wisconsin. Abstracted: Dissert. abstracts, 21:589 (Sep). [9095

CLARENCE BASINGER. An Ohio Mennonite pioneer. Mennonite hist. bul., 15(3):8 (Jul 1954). On Clarence Z. Yoder (1845-1939), resident of Wayne County, Ohio, and from 1865 to 1939 a member, eventually deacon and minister, of the Oak Grove congregation. [9096

MINNIE (HITE) MOODY. Ohio's most notable eccentric, "the immortal J. N." Ohioana, 3:74-5 (fall). cartoon. Anecdotes about Jacob Newman Free, born in Pennsylvania, who practised law for a time in Cincinnati, became deranged before the Civil War, tried to negotiate a meeting between Abraham Lincoln and Jefferson Davis, traveled incessantly on Ohio railroads, entertained the guests of hotels with his "stories and conversation," lectured, etc., and died in 1906 in the Toledo State Hospital for the Insane. [9097

FRANK C. VAN CLEEF. The rise and decline of the cheese industry in Lorain County [1850-1913]. Ohio hist. quar., 69:32-57 (Jan). notes. [9098

JOHN J. DUFFEY. Non-charter municipalities: local self-government [in Ohio, 1851-1960]. Ohio State law jour., 21:304-30 (spring). notes [9099

JOHN HOWARD LAMNECK. The country squire: the romance of a law-abiding citizen. Boston: Christopher Pub. House [1960]. 289 p. ports. On the author's father, Philip Lamneck (1845-1934/35), emigrant from Germany to Port Washington, Ohio, in 1856, justice of the peace there nearly 50 years, farmer, officeholder, local orator, builder, unprofitable investor; with some account of his brief settlement 30 miles from Great Falls, Mont., 1889-90, and his return to Port Washington. [9100

SHERMAN BISBEE BARNES. Learning and piety in Ohio colleges, 1865-1900. Ohio hist. quar., 69:327-52 (Oct). notes. On the influence of religion upon, and its place in, their curricula. [9101

MENNONITE CHURCH. Conferences. Ohio. The 1868 meeting of Ohio Mennonite Conference. Mennonite hist. bul., 20(3):1-2 (Jul 1959). From "an undated but recent reprint published by the Wisler Mennonites of Ohio." English text of report of proceedings. [9102

KENNETH S. P. MORSE. Ohio trolleys [1885-1949]. Baltimore: Sutherland Press [1960. 4], 67, [1] p. facsims., maps, tables, views. notes (p. 10-12). On the lines in Cleveland, Toledo, Youngstown, Ashtabula, and Salem, some of the interurban lines in northeastern Ohio, and a few lines in Wheeling, W. Va., Johnstown, Pa., Muskegon, Mich., and Hamilton, Ont. [9103

ROSCOE L. BARROW. Robert S. Marx, 1889-1960. Univ. Cincinnati law rev., 29:401-5 (fall). On his work in Ohio as a lawyer, a judge, and a teacher of law. [9104

RALPH WARREN DEXTER. The summer field meetings of the Ohio Academy of Science (1892-1905). Ohio jour. science, 60:262-5 (Sep). [9105

JAMES HAROLD MALOON. The Ohio death taxes [since 1893]. Ann Arbor: University Microfilms, 1960. Positive microfilm of typescript. [439] leaves. Thesis--Indiana Univ. Abstracted: Dissert. abstracts, 21:794-5 (Oct). [9106

ROBERT MOFFETT REESER. Land use in Ohio: trends, prospects, and evaluation [1900-1955]. Ann Arbor: University Microfilms, 1960. Positive microfilm of typescript. [234] leaves. Thesis--Ohio State Univ. Abstracted: Dissert. abstracts, 21:1090-91 (Nov). [9107

JAMES W. FARRELL, JR. Municipal public utility powers [in Ohio, 1902-60]. Ohio State law jour., 21:390-410 (winter). notes. [9108

PHILLIP RAYMOND SHRIVER. The years of youth: Kent State University, 1910-1960. Kent, Ohio: Kent State Univ. Press, 1960. viii, 266 [1] p. facsims., ports., tables, views. bibliog. (p. 245-7), notes. On an institution earlier known as Kent State Normal School (1911-12) and Kent State Normal College (1912-35). [9109

NORMAL BLUME. Municipal home rule in Ohio: the new look [1913-59]. West. Reserve law rev., 11:538-60 (Sep). notes. [9110

JAMES L. FULLIN & PAUL E. WEILAND. The Public Utilities Commission of Ohio [1913-60]. Ohio engineer, 28(12):6-7 (Nov). diagr., port. [9111

WILLIAM W. TELZROW. Ohio insurance: a study in legal adroitness. West. Reserve law rev., 11:290-98 (Mar). notes. On a distinction in Ohio law between accidental death or injury and death or injury from accidental means, 1914-53. [9112

MURRAY DANFORTH LINCOLN (born 1892). Vice president in charge of revolution. By Murray D. Lincoln, as told to David Karp. N.Y.: McGraw-Hill [1960. 10], 342 p. port. On the author's work as agricultural representative of the Cleveland Society for Savings, 1917-20, and Executive Secretary of the Ohio Farm Bureau Federation; with some account of his early life in Raynham, Mass., his studies at the Massachusetts Agricultural College, and his work on farm matters for the Plymouth County Trust Company, Brockton. [9113

CHARLES EMORY GLANDER. Analysis and critique of State pre-emption of municipal excise and income taxes under Ohio home rule [1919-60]. Ohio State law jour., 21:343-63 (spring). notes. [9114

JAMES A. YOUNG. Contributory negligence--the dwindling defense. West.

Reserve law rev., 11:109-23 (Dec 1959). notes. On Ohio law regarding negligence of automobile driver and passenger in collisions at railroad crossings, 1921-57. [9115

DANIEL B. CLOSE. Joint bank accounts in Ohio [1926-56]. West. Reserve law rev., 11:511-37 (Sep). notes. [9116

LLOYD A. CHACEY. The panorama in Ohio. Ohio engineer, 18(3):16-17 (Mar). port., view. On the Ohio Society of Professional Engineers, 1933-60. [9117

EDMUND PHILIP LEARNED. A case study of pricing patterns [of petroleum products in Ohio, 1937-57]. Centennial Seminar on the History of the Petroleum Industry, Harvard University, 1959, Oil's first century: papers ([Cambridge:] Harvard Graduate School of Business Administration [1960]), p. 85-92. views. [9118

DONALD L. BRAKENSIEK & C. R. AMERMAN. Evaluating effect of land use on stream flow. Agric. engineering, 41:158-61, 167 (Mar). diagrs., map, tables. notes. Analysis of rainfall and runoff records from 4 watersheds near Coshocton, Ohio, 1938-57. [9119

PAUL GENE CRAIG. A study of the long range cost of unemployment compensation and the variables that control costs in Ohio [1939-53]. Ann Arbor: University Microfilms, 1953 [i. e. 1960]. Positive microfilm of typescript. [427] leaves. Thesis--Ohio State Univ. Abstracted: Dissert. abstracts, 20:2604-7 (Jan). [9120

ROBERT EDWIN LAUBIS. An analysis of the financial structure of agricultural cooperative business organizations in Ohio [1940-57], and suggestions for improvement. Ann Arbor: University Microfilms, 1959 [i.e. 1960]. Positive microfilm of typescript. [319] leaves. Thesis--Ohio State Univ. Abstracted: Dissert. abstracts, 20:3979-80 (Apr). [9121

RICHARD FICKES HEIGES. The Ohio Administrative Procedure Act, 1943-1959: an analysis and evaluation of its effect. Ann Arbor: University Microfilms, 1959 [i. e. 1960]. Positive microfilm of typescript. [415] leaves. Thesis--Ohio State Univ. Abstracted: Dissert. abstracts, 20:4152 (Apr). [9122

LLOYD L. HARROLD. Use of soil porosity for water conservation [Coshocton, Ohio, 1945-51]. Agric. engineering, 33:287-9, 292 (May 1952). diagrs., tables. notes. [9123

STANLEY RAY SCHULTZ. An economic analysis of manufacturing milk production in Ohio. Ann Arbor: University Microfilms, 1960. Positive microfilm of typescript. [119] leaves. Thesis--Ohio State Univ. Abstracted: Dissert. abstracts, 21:83 (Jul). On "the decline in the number of farmers producing milk for manufacturing purposes" since 1945. [9124

CHARLES V. RILEY. The ecology of water areas associated with coal strip-mined lands in Ohio. Ohio jour. science, 59:106-21 (Mar). map, tables. bibliog. Study of the topography, soil, water, flora, and fauna of such lands in 15 counties of southeastern Ohio, 1946-57. [9125

Cincinnati

GEORGE P. STIMSON. Cincinnati in bronze. [With photographs by William R. Randall. Cincinnati: W. R. Randall, 1959. 3], 30, [2] p. facsims., maps, ports., views. 15 x 22 cm. Photographs of markers commemorating historical events in Cincinnati since 1786, with accompanying illustrations and text. [9126

MERRILL WEED. Ohio engineering: "Cincinnativity." Ohio engineer, 18(3):6-7, 47-9 (Mar). views. On Cincinnati since 1790, with particular notice of engineering works there. [9127

MARIA PAULA DICKORÉ, comp. Census for Cincinnati, Ohio, 1817; and Hamilton County, Ohio, voters' lists, 1798 and 1799. Cincinnati, 1960. vii, 98 p. [9128

MILLCREEK TOWNSHIP, Hamilton County, Ohio. Millcreek Township, Hamilton County, Ohio. [Edited] by Marie Dickoré. Hist. and Philos. Soc. Ohio, Bul., 18:152-7, 219-21 (Apr, Jul). facsim. Tax lists for 1811 (taken by Peter Hathaway Kemper, Clerk) and 1812 (by William Cary, Clerk), with identification (by the editor) of some of the persons named in the lists. [9129

CLYDE WILLIAM PARK. Reunion in Cincinnati. Hist. and Philos. Soc. Ohio, Bul., 18:278-9 (Oct). Anecdote of Lafayette's visit to Cincinnati (1824?). [9130

CELIA JACKSON OTTO. Cincinnati hog-back sofa. Hist. and Philos. Soc. Ohio, Bul., 18:19-23 (Jan). diagrs., view. On a "sofa made in Cincinnati circa 1840 of mahogany and back horsehair with hog-back and scrolls"; with information from the Book of prices of the United Society of the Journeyman Cabinet Makers of Cincinnati, for the manufacture of cabinet ware (1836). [9131

BRUCE W. BROWN. Glendale College capers. Hist. and Philos. Soc. Ohio, Bul., 18:253-9 (Oct). views. On Glendale Female College, Glendale, Ohio, near Cincinnati, opened in 1854 and closed in 1930. [9132

HISTORICAL AND PHILOSOPHICAL SOCIETY OF OHIO. 100 years ago in Cincinnati ... (As recorded by newspapers and directories in the Society's collection.) Hist. and Philos. Soc. Ohio, Bul., 18:78-80, 158-9, 222-4, 296-9 (Jan-Oct). On events in Cincinnati during January, April, July, and October 1860. [9133

IPHIGENE BETTMAN. Elmhurst. Hist. and Philos. Soc. Ohio, Bul., 18:201-17 (Jul). facsims., port., views. On Elmhurst Place, a suburb of Cincinnati, acquired as 25 acres of woodland on the Ohio River by William Slocum Groesbeck in 1870; with an account of his house ("Elmhurst") and Levi Addison Ault's "Milles Roches" (built 1904), both now dismantled. [9134

CHALMERS HADLEY (1872-1958). "Dear Julia": letter from Cincinnati, written in 1870. Hist. and Philos. Soc. Ohio, Bul., 18:105-15 (Apr). views. Letter to Mrs. Alexander J. Dexter, Philadelphia ("My dearest Julia"), dated Cincinnati, 1 Nov. 1870, from "Fanny," reporting events and personalities in Cincinnati, with attention to costumes, menus, and other matters. On the authorship see p. 279, presenting evidence that the author was Hadley, formerly Cincinnati Public Librarian, who had presented the letter as a paper before the Cincinnati Literary Club "more than twenty years ago" without suspicion that it would be mistakenly regarded as authentic. [9135

JOHN H. WHITE. The College Hill narrow gauge. Hist. and Philos. Soc. Ohio, Bul. 18:226-39 (Oct). diagr., facsim., map, table, view. notes. On the College Hill Railroad, connecting Cincinnati and Mt. Pleasant, 1873-84, and its successor, the Cincinnati Northwestern Railway, 1884-1901, converted to an electric interurban, abandoned in 1938. [9136

NANCY R. FitzPATRICK. Cincinnati's amateur china painting ... prelude to Rookwood. Spinning wheel, 16(4):14, 16 (Apr). port., views. On Cincinnati's "burst of feminine talent in the art of china and pottery painting that was to make it the artistic center of the mid-West," 1874-80, with particular note of the work of Mary Louise McLaughlin (born 1847), self-taught, later the author of 6 books on the art. [9137

ROBERT KOCH. Rookwood pottery. Antiques, 77:288-9 (Mar). views. On the Rookwood Pottery, Cincinnati, founded in 1880, still in existence in 1960. [9138

DANIEL R. BEAVER. Herbert Seely Bigelow: reformer and politician 1870-1951. Hist. and Philos. Soc. Ohio, Bul., 18:3-12 (Jan). port., view. On his service as a Congregational minister in Cincinnati, 1895-1951, and his agitation for the single-tax doctrine of Henry George, municipal ownership of public utilities, the initiative and referendum, old-age pensions, "the Social Gospel," pacifism, etc. [9139

ROBERT TAFT, JR. Epilogue for a lady: the passing of the Times-star. Hist. and Philos. Soc. Ohio, Bul., 18:260-77 (Oct). On the decline and death of a Cincinnati newspaper, 1930-58. [9140

Cleveland

DALLAS M. YOUNG. Twentieth-century experience in urban transit: a study of the Cleveland system and its development [1875-1960]. Cleveland: Press of Western Reserve Univ. [1960. 2], 26 p. tables, notes. [9141

CLEVELAND'S mystery writer. Ohioana, 3:15, 20 (spring). On an anonymous novel about Cleveland politics, Among the rascals (Cleveland, 1897). [9142

DALLAS M. YOUNG. Fifty years of labor arbitration in Cleveland transit [1910-60]. Monthly labor rev., 83: 464-71 (May). notes. [9143

ROBERT C. BENSING & OLIVER SCHROEDER, JR. Homicide in an urban community. ... With an introductory section by Perry B. Jackson. Springfield, Ill.: Thomas [1960]. xii, 193 p. diagrs., maps, tables, views. notes. On legal and social aspects of 662 homicides in "Cuyahoga County (Greater Cleveland), Ohio," 1947-53. [9144

Columbus

HENRY LOUIS HUNKER. Columbus, Ohio: the industrial evolution of a commercial center [1812-1953]. Ann Arbor: University Microfilms, 1953 [i.e. 1960]. Positive microfilm of typescript. [290] leaves. Thesis--Ohio State Univ. Abstracted: Dissert. abstracts, 20:2749-51 (Jan). [9145

SILAS STUART ANDERSON. Development and administration of some important student personnel services at Ohio University during the nineteenth century [after 1837]. Ann Arbor: University Microfilms, 1960. Positive microfilm of typescript. [513] leaves. Thesis--Ohio State Univ. Abstracted: Dissert. abstracts, 21:120-21 (Jul). [9146

CLARK GUERNSEY (fl. 1837). A visit to the Ohio State Prison in 1837. Ohio hist. quar., 69:69-72 (Jan). Excerpt from the manuscript diary of a visitor to Columbus, 7 Mar. 1837. [9147

KATHRYN ELIZABETH UTZ. Columbus, Ohio, theatre, seasons 1840-41 to 1860-61. Ann Arbor: University Microfilms, 1952 [i.e. 1960]. Positive microfilm of typescript. [901] leaves. Thesis--Ohio State Univ. Abstracted: Dissert. abstracts, 20:2811-13 (Jan). [9148

FRED J. BUNYAN. Columbus prepared for progress. Flying, 64(1):50, 84 (Jan 1959). views. On the airport of Columbus, Ohio, 1929-58. [9149

Toledo

JOHN QUINCY REED. Artemus Ward's first lecture. Am. lit., 32: 317-19 (Nov). notes. Evidence that Ward lectured in Toledo 20 Oct. 1860 and 1 Feb. 1861. [9150

INDIANA

CHARLES H. FAULKNER. A possible Early Woodland cache discovery in northern Indiana. Ind. Acad. Science, Proc., 69:92-8. diagrs. bibliog. On a cache of 463 stone blades discovered in Green Township, Marshall County, Ind., 1947. [9151

OLIN DEE MORRISON. Indiana, "Hoosier State": new historical atlas of Indiana. Athens, Ohio: E. M. Morrison, ©1958. ix leaves, 296 maps (often more than 1 on a leaf), 297-308 leaves. 30 cm. (His Indiana series, 2.) Maps showing Indiana at various times between 1679 and 1952. [9152

BENJAMIN F. RICHASON, JR. The nature, extent, and drainage of the wet lands of northern Indiana with special reference to Cass County [since 1799]. Ann Arbor: University Microfilms, 1960. Positive microfilm of typescript. [453] leaves. Thesis--Univ. of Nebraska. Abstracted: Dissert. abstracts, 21:1519-20 (Dec). [9153

JOHN FRASER HART. Changing census concepts of rural population in Indiana [1800-1950]. Ind. Acad. Science, Proc., 69:249-53. table. notes. [9154

JOHN S. LONG. Planning Hoosierdom--a historical sketch [1807-1956]. Indiana Academy of the Social Sciences, Problems of planning Indiana's future, ed. Schuyler F. Otteson (Indianapolis: Indiana Economic Council, 1957 [Indiana Academy of the Social Sciences, Proceedings, 1956]), p. 1-3. notes. Evidence that "planning has certainly played an important part in the development" of Indiana. [9155

NORMAN C. EVANS. Spring Mill (Hidden Valley Village): the story of southern Indiana's pioneer village. Mitchell, Ind.: Mill Lake Press, ©1958. 175 p. ports., views. 1st ed. 1953. On a mill and surrounding village in Lawrence County, 1814-93, the establishment of the area as an Indiana park in 1927, and some of the buildings and exhibits there; with anecdotes and lore about early settlers. [9156

HOWARD DEVON HAMILTON, JOSEPH E. BEARDSLEY, & CARLETON C. COATS. Legislative reapportionment in Indiana [1816-1960]: some observations and a suggestion. Notre Dame lawyer, 35:368-404 (May). maps, tables. notes. [9157

PHILIP VAN DOREN STERN. The Indiana years of Abraham Lincoln

[1816 to 1830]. Ralph G. Newman, ed., Lincoln for the ages (Garden City, N.Y.: Doubleday, 1960), p. 53-7. [9158

CAROLINE DUNN. With the notes of the robin and bluebird. Soc. Ind. Pioneers, Yr. bk., 1960, p. 41-4. port. On Sara T. Bolton (1820-93) as a resident of Madison, 1823-31, and thereafter of Indianapolis, and her many poems. [9159

CLAY COUNTY, Ind. Marriage affidavits, Clay County, Indiana, to 1852. Compiled and edited by Carolynne Wendel. Ind. mag. hist., 56:243-8 (Sep). Record prepared in 1852 after the original marriage records were lost in a courthouse fire, authenticating marriages between 1826 and 1851. [9160

U.S. Census Office. 5th Census, 1830. Heads of families in Clay County, Indiana, 1830. Compiled and edited by Dorothy Riker. Ind. mag. hist., 56: 239-42 (Sep). [9161

CLARK COUNTY, Ind. The medical inventory of a pioneer doctor. Edited by Gerald O. Haffner. Ind. mag. hist., 56:37-63 (Mar). facsim. notes. "An inventory and appraisment of the personal estate of Doct Andrew Rodgers decesd," by Andrew P. Hay and John Work, signed 31 Aug. 1833, presumably in Charlestown, Ind., where Rodgers had practiced medicine as early as 1827; with full editorial identifications of the medical instruments, medical books, and medicines named in the inventory. [9162

FIRST METHODIST CHURCH, Michigan City, Ind. One hundred twenty-fifth anniversary, First Methodist Church, Michigan City, Indiana, 1835-1960. [Michigan City, 1960.] 57 p. ports., tables, views. [9163

WILLIAM DE PREZ INLOW. The Indiana physician as geologist and naturalist [1837 to ca. 1900]. Ind. mag. hist., 56:1-35 (Mar). ports. notes. [9164

MILLARD S. MARKLE. The influence of Quakers on science in Indiana. Ind. Acad. Science, Proc., 69:243-6. On scientific studies at Earlham College, Richmond, 1847-1959. [9165

ANDERSON, Ind. Minutes and ordinances of the Town of Anderson, Indiana, 1849-1850. Edited by Donald F. Carmony. Ind. mag. hist., 56:227-38 (Sep). notes. Record kept by the Trustees of Anderson, 28 May 1849-8 Jan. 1850. [9166

LLOYD V. CONRAD. A centennial history of the Holdeman Mennonite Church [Wakarusa, Ind., 1851-1951]. Mennonite hist. bul., 13(1):1-4 (Jan 1952). Reprinted (with notes omitted) from 100th anniversary, 1851-1951, Holdeman Mennonite Church. [9167

GEORGE JOSEPH HUYS. The legal aspects of school district reorganization in Indiana [since 1851]. Ann Arbor: University Microfilms, 1959 [i.e. 1960]. Positive microfilm of typescript. [295] leaves. Thesis (Ed. D.)--Indiana Univ. Abstracted: Dissert. abstracts, 20:3596-7 (Mar). [9168

DEAN H. MITCHELL. Northern Indiana Public Service Company: serving today--building for the future in the workshop of America. N.Y.: Newcomen Soc. in North America, 1960. 32 p. facsims., views. On a corporation formed by the consolidation of numerous local gas and electric companies, the oldest of which was the Fort Wayne Gas Company (founded in 1853). [9169

LOIS SMELTZER. History of the Olive Mennonite Church [near Elkhart, 1855-1945]. Mennonite hist. bul., 9(2):4 (Apr 1948). [9170

FRANK I. MORSE. First balloon airpost. S. P. A. jour., 21:297 (Feb 1959). On the transportation of mail from Lafayette to Crawfordsville, Ind., in Prof. John Wise's balloon Jupiter, 17 Aug. 1859. [9171

CURT PROSKAUER. Two dental advertisements on mock-bills. Jour. hist. med., 15:408-16 (Oct). facsims. notes. On advertisements in the form of 100-dollar bills, with table of fees on back, distributed by Dr. N. B. Slayton, dentist in Madison, Ind., issued sometime between 1859 and 1864, and "mock-bills" issued by Antoine-Malagou Désirabode, Paris dentist, in 1823. [9172

CARL WILLIAM BREIHAN. America's first train robberies. Frontier times, 34(3):20-21, 55-7 (summer). views. On train robberies by the Reno brothers and their confederates at and near Seymour, Ind., and the lynching of Volney Elliott, Charles Rosenbaum,

Lefty Clinton, Charles Anderson, and Frank, William, and Simeon Reno by vigilantes, 1866-68. [9173

CATHARINE ANN BRENNEMAN-MITSCHELEN (1865-1945). Cures by "powwowing" from my grandmother's notebook. Submitted by Mrs. Jennie Catherine Huntzinger. Midw. folklore, 10:55-6 (Mar). Examples from a Swiss-German neighborhood in the vicinity of Wakarusa, Ind., 1868 ff. [9174

CLEON H. FOUST. The use of criminal law as a standard of civil responsibility in Indiana. Ind. law rev., 35:45-68 (fall 1959). notes. On "the statutory negligence formula" in Indiana, 1871-1951. [9175

JOHN CHRISTIAN WENGER, ed. Documents on the Daniel Brenneman division. Mennonite quar. rev., 34:48-56 (Jan). notes. "Daniel Brenneman's account of the schism occurring in the Mennonite Church in Elkhart County, Indiana," on the events leading to and resulting from his expulsion from the church in 1874; "The expulsion of Daniel Brenneman," proceedings of a conference held 25 Apr. 1874 on his defiance of the Mennonite Church in his defense of and participation in revivalistic meetings; and "List of Daniel Brenneman's adherents in 1874 and shortly thereafter," compiled by his son, T. H. Brenneman. [9176

ORA TROYER. A history of the Conservative Mennonite Churches in northern Indiana [1876-1960]. Mennonite hist. bul., 20:1-2, 4, 6, 7 (Apr 1959). tables. Deals particularly with Amish organizations in Elkhart and Lagrange Counties. [9177

DALE B. RANDALL, JR. Dialect in the verse of "The Hoosier Poet" [James Whitcomb Riley]. Am. speech, 35:35-50 (Feb). notes. Includes excerpts from his correspondence on this subject, 1880-97, and a table of dialectal forms from 5 poems, 1879-91; with comments on the authenticity of his dialect and the appropriateness of his use of it. [9178

JERRY MARLETTE. Electric railroads of Indiana. Indianapolis: Council for Local History, 1959. [4], 158 p. facsims., fold. map, plans, tables, views. bibliog. (p. 134-6). On lines having less than half of their tracks within municipal limits (i.e. interurbans), 1898-1953, and intramunicipal lines as early as 1888; with histories of the companies (p. 48-119) and reproductions of timetables (p. 137-58). [9179

J. HAROLD KIRACOFE. The Chicago and Wabash Valley Railroad. Railway & Locomotive Hist. Soc., Bul., 102:53-8 (Apr). On a 36-mile line in Jasper and Lake Counties, Ind., 1891-1914. [9180

VINCENT H. GADDIS & JASPER ABRAHAM HUFFMAN. The story of Winona Lake, a memory and a vision: the remarkable story of one of the world's largest Bible conferences--its environing institutions, its present personalities, and its future [1895-1960]. Winona Lake, Ind.: Winona Lake Christian Assembly [1960]. 156, [8] p. ports., views. bibliog. (p. 156. 1st ed. (by Gaddis), 1949. On the seat of the Winona Lake Bible Conference, the School of Theology, the Rodeheaver School of Sacred Music, the School of Missions (Jewish), the American Association for Jewish Evangelism, the residence of Billy Sunday, and associated recreational and commercial facilities. [9181

JOHN SYLVANUS UMBLE. Organization of the Goshen College Mennonite Church [1903-53]. Mennonite hist. bul., 15(1):7-8 (Jan 1954). On an organization that was at first both Mennonite and Amish. [9182

MADISON STATE HOSPITAL, North Madison, Ind. Madison State Hospital [1905-60]: the first half century. Edited and partly written by George A[nderson] Zirkle, consultant in psychology. Madison, 1960. ix, [3], 108, [1] p. maps, ports., table, views. bibliog. (p. 109). On an institution founded as Southeastern Hospital for the Insane. [9183

CHARLES A. HYMAN. Artifacting in northwest Indiana. Ohio archaeol., 10:67-70 (Apr). port., views. On collections made by the author in the dunes and swamps of Lake and Porter Counties, 1907 to ca. 1942. [9184

GERALD EDWARD ACKERMAN. Changes in productivity of farm resources in a central Indiana area. Ann Arbor: University Microfilms, 1960. Positive microfilm of typescript. [121] leaves. Thesis--Purdue Univ. Abstracted: Dissert. abstracts, 21: 77-8 (Jul). Study in Forest and

Johnson Townships of an unnamed county, 1910-55. [9185

JACK J. DETZLER. South Bend, 1910-1920: a decade dedicated to reform. [South Bend, Ind.: Northern Indiana Historical Soc., 1960.] 120 p. bibliog. (p. 115-16), notes. [9186

BENJAMIN F. RICHASON, JR. Wetland transformation in the Wisconsin drift area of Indiana [1920-50]. Ind. Acad. Science, Proc., 69:290-99. maps. notes. On improvements made by drainage in approximately the northern half of the State. [9187

WILLIAM D. SHILLINGER & GEORGE G. FASSNACHT. Cross-connection hazards and controls [in Indiana water systems, 1924-59]. Am. Water Works Assoc., Jour., 52:36-40 (Jan). On efforts to prevent the contamination of public water supplies by water from other sources (including backflow of water used by industrial plants). [9188

LEE GUERNSEY. Land use changes caused by a quarter century of strip coal mining in Indiana [1934-59]. Ind. Acad. Science, Proc., 69:200-209. maps, table. notes. [9189

ELEANOR NOBLE NISHIURA. Internal migration in Indiana [1935-40, 1949-50]. Ann Arbor: University Microfilms, 1959 [i.e. 1960]. Positive microfilm of typescript. [293] leaves. Thesis--Purdue Univ. Abstracted: Dissert. abstracts, 20:2948 (Jan). [9190

JOHN L. O'DONNELL. Trends in external financing in Indiana, 1935-55. Indiana Academy of the Social Sciences, Problems of planning Indiana's future, ed. Schuyler F. Otteson (Indianapolis: Indiana Economic Council, 1957 [Indiana Academy of the Social Sciences, Proceedings, 1956]), p. 35-43. tables. notes. On "the role played by Indiana investment bankers in providing new capital for local businesses, and the flotation of municipal bonds." [9191

DAVID GOLDBERG. Another look at the Indianapolis fertility data. Milbank Memorial Fund quar., 38:23-36 (Jan). tables. notes. Interpretation of data collected by C. Kiser and P. Whelpton in Indianapolis in 1941, suggesting "that the inverse relationship between socioeconomic variables and fertility was confounded by a third variable, urban-rural background." [9192

ROBERT H. STIFFNEY. Lightning Dude Ranch. West. horseman, 25(5):42, 161-2 (May). ports., views. On a ranch operated near Knox, Ind., by Ced White, where children are "schooled in basic horsemanship," 1945-60. [9193

INDIANA. Employment Security Division. Indiana labor force, employment, and unemployment [1947-59]. Indianapolis, 1960. [24] leaves. diagrs., tables. 22x28 cm. Mainly tabular. [9194

WILLIAM SAMUEL FULLER. Space allocation, pupil capacity, and unit costs of 20 selected public secondary school buildings constructed in Indiana during 1948 to 1958. Ann Arbor: University Microfilms, 1960. Positive microfilm of typescript. [208] leaves. Thesis (Ed. D.)--Indiana Univ. Abstracted: Dissert. abstracts, 21:517 (Sep). [9195

ILLINOIS

JOHN DRURY. This is Macon County, Illinois: an up-to-date histori[c]al narrative with county map and many unique aerial photographs of cities, towns, villages, and farmsteads. Chicago: Loree Co., c1954. x, 366 p. map, views. (The American aerial county history series, 1.) Photographic atlas with minimal historical information about places and none about settlers. [9196

MERTON LYNN DILLION. Abolitionism comes to Illinois [1816-42]. Ill. State Hist. Soc., Jour., 53:389-403 (winter). notes. [9197

MARGARET BEATTIE BOGUE. Patterns from the sod: land use and tenure in the Grand Prairie, 1850-1900. Springfield, 1959. 327 p. diagrs., maps, tables. bibliog. (p. 307-23), notes (p. 267-306). (Collections of the Illinois State Historical Library, v. 34. and series, v. 1.) Issued also in microfilm form as thesis--Cornell Univ. Study of 8 counties in east central Illinois--Champaign, Ford, Iroquois, Kankakee, Livingston, McLean, Piatt, and Vermilion, 1822-1900. [9198

ROBERT S. McGINNIS, JR. Shawneetown's oldest church: a history of the First Presbyterian Church (the United Presbyterian Church in the U.S.A.), Shawneetown, Illinois, established

A. D. 1826. Shawneetown: Davis Print. Shop, 1960. 36 p. map, ports., tables, views. notes (p. 36). [9199

WILLIAM ELDON BARINGER. Lincoln enters politics [Illinois, 1830-41]. Ralph G. Newman, ed., Lincoln for the ages (Garden City, N.Y.: Doubleday, 1960), p. 69-73. [9200

JAMES WELCH PATTON, ed. Letters from North Carolina emigrants in the Old Northwest, 1830-1834. Miss. Valley hist. rev., 47:263-77 (Sep). notes. Six letters from Joseph and Elisabeth Cress and Daniel F. and George E. Ludewick, farmers in Montgomery County, Ill., to relatives in North Carolina, on the country and the land, sickness, weather, and family matters. Includes a letter from George E. Ludewick (23 Jun. 1832) on his service in the Black Hawk War. [9201

PAUL McCLELLAND ANGLE. Lincoln in New Salem. Ralph G. Newman, ed., Lincoln for the ages (Garden City, N.Y.: Doubleday, 1960), p. 59-62. On his service in the Black Hawk War and his activities in Illinois law and politics, 1831-37. [9202

OLIVE CARRUTHERS. Abraham Lincoln's first loves. Ralph G. Newman, ed., Lincoln for the ages (Garden City, N.Y.: Doubleday, 1960), p. 63-8. On his courtship of Ann Rutledge and Mary Owens in New Salem, 1831-36. [9203

LEO ALFRED LERNER. Lincoln emerges as a [political] leader [in Illinois, 1832]. Ralph G. Newman, ed., Lincoln for the ages (Garden City, N.Y.: Doubleday, 1960), p. 85-9. [9204

ROBERT MIZE SUTTON. Lincoln and the railroads of Illinois [1832-60]. O. Fritiof Ander, ed., Lincoln images: Augustana College centennial essays (Rock Island, Ill.: Augustana College Library, 1960), p. 41-60. [9205

C. R. McLAGAN. Nostalgia and glee in Sycamore, Illinois [1834-1960]. Sycamore, Ill.: D. C. Lithographers, c1960. [20], 344, [1] p. ports., tables, views (1 col.). [9206

RUTH EWERS HABERKORN. Nehemiah Matson [1816-83]--historian of northern Illinois. Ill. State Hist. Soc., Jour., 53:149-62 (summer). port., view. On his life in Bureau County, 1836-83, as a surveyor and as an author or compiler of 8 books (published 1867-82). [9207

JOHN J. DUFF (1902-61). A. Lincoln: prairie lawyer. N.Y.: Rinehart [1960]. viii, [2], 433 p. facsims., maps, ports., views. bibliog. (p. 403-13), notes (p. 371-98). On his practice of law in Illinois, 1837-60. [9208

GEORGE F. REMM. The history of the Catholic Church in Peoria County, Illinois, from 1837 to 1877. Saint Paul, 1959 [c1960]. ix, 144 leaves. tables. bibliog. (leaves 138-44), notes. Thesis (M. A.)--Saint Paul Seminary. [9209

ROBERT M. LILLIBRIDGE. Architectural currents on the Mississippi River frontier: Nauvoo, Illinois. Soc. Architectural Historians, Jour., 19: 109-14 (Sep). map, views. notes. On Mormon houses and religious buildings constructed there between 1839 and 1846. [9210

MARION DOLORES PRATT. Abraham Lincoln takes a wife. Ralph G. Newman, ed., Lincoln for the ages (Garden City, N.Y.: Doubleday, 1960), p. 79-84. On his courtship of and marriage to Mary Todd, 1839-42. [9211

WILLARD LEROY KING. Lincoln the lawyer [in Illinois, 1840-60]. Ralph G. Newman, ed., Lincoln for the ages (Garden City, N.Y.: Doubleday, 1960), p. 90-95. [9212

GEORGE THOMAS TANSELLE. Herman Melville's visit to Galena in 1840. Ill. State Hist. Soc., Jour., 53: 376-88 (winter). ports., view. notes. On events and conditions in Galena in 1840 at the time of Melville's visit to his uncle, Maj. Thomas Melvill [sic] (1776-1845), a resident since 1837, and the latter's family. [9213

HARRY L. ROGERS, ed. Letters to my grandfather--Wesley Rogers [born 1818]. Now and then, 12:132-5 (Jan 1959). Description of and excerpts from 30 letters to Wesley Rogers in Muncy, Pa., from his father, James Rogers (born 1786), and other members of the family, dated in Dixon, Ill., 1843-65, on their journey to Illinois, farming, prices, etc.; with complete text of a letter to Wesley Rogers from his friend E. Bockenoogen, dated Rockford, Ill., 25 Jul. 1849, on his travels from Pennsylvania through western New

York, to Rockford, Illinois and on the excellence of the prairie lands and the ease and profitability of farming there. [9214

ELIZABETH E. EGGLESTON. Spoon River homestead. N.Y.: Vantage Press [1960. 2], 281 p. On the author's mother, Mary (Winthrop) Tazewell (born 1858), of Stark County, Ill., her marriage in 1874 to William Tazewell, and their life on a farm in the Spoon River Valley. Semifictional in form. [9215

CONRAD JOHN IMMANUEL BERGENDOFF. On the occasion of the centennial of Augustana College [1860-1960]. Swed. pioneer hist. quar., 11:35-44 (Apr). Deals particularly with the changing relation of the College to Sweden, the Swedish language, and the Swedish traditions brought to America by immigrants. [9216

CLARENCE NELSON ROBERTS. North Central College: a century of liberal education, 1861-1961. Naperville, Ill.: North Central College, 1960. x, [2], 318 p. facsims., ports., tables, views. notes. On an institution founded as the Plainfield College of the Evangelical Association of North America (1861-64) and later named North-Western College (1864-1926), moved from Plainfield to Naperville in 1870, and renamed North Central College in 1926. [9217

HAROLD WINFORD HANNAH. History and scope of Illinois drainage law [1869-1959]. Univ. Ill. law forum, 1960:189-97 (summer). notes. [9218

HERBERT GEORGE GUTMAN. The Braidwood lockout of 1874. Ill. State Hist. Soc., Jour., 53:5-28 (spring). notes. On labor-management relations in the coal industry of Will County, Ill., centered at Braidwood, 1872-77. [9219

CHICAGO BAR ASSOCIATION. Committee on Antitrust Law. A study of the laws of Illinois relating to competition. Chicago [1960. 1], ix, 285 leaves. Compiled by a Special Subcommittee on Illinois Antitrust Laws, Robert W. Bergstrom, Chairman. Review of statutes and court decisions, 1874-1960. [9220

JAMES A. RHODES & DEAN JAUCHIUS. The trial of Mary Todd Lincoln. Indianapolis: Bobbs-Merrill Co. [1959]. 200 p. bibliog. (p. 191-5). On hearings in Chicago, May 1875, at which she was adjudged a "lunatic" and committed to a mental institution, and in Springfield, Jun. 1876, at which she was adjudged sane and was released; with passages of fiction inserted to indicate how she might have been successfully defended at the first hearing, and an argument that the first trial was the result of a conspiracy of political enemies of President Grant to deceive Robert Todd Lincoln and bring him into discredit for sending his mother to a lunatic asylum. [9221

ALBERT BRITT. Revolution on the farm. Yale rev., 50:234-46 (winter). On the rural world in Warren County, Ill., the farm work and the country schools there, as seen by the author in the 1880s and 1890s, and the national meaning of the changes noted by him when he returned after an absence of 25 years. [9222

GILBERT YALE STEINER & SAMUEL KIMBALL GOVE. Legislative politics in Illinois [1902-58]. Urbana: Univ. of Illinois Press, 1960. x, [2], 208 p. double diagr., tables (part double). notes. On activities of the Illinois General Assembly, especially in the 1950s, concerning redistricting, the reorganization of "the state fiscal machinery," and a proposed "judicial reorganization." [9223

STANLEY ALCIDE CHANGNON, JR. Summary of weather conditions at Champaign-Urbana, Illinois [1904-57. Urbana, 1959.] 95 p. diagrs., map, views. bibliog. (p. 95). 22x28 cm. (Illinois. Water Survey. Bulletin 47.) [9224

WALTER H. CHEELY. The madstone, a medical curio. Ill. State Hist. Soc., Jour., 53:409-12 (winter). On a stone in the author's possession, formerly the property of his great-grandfather, Dr. James Squire (1843-1929) of Carrollton, Ill.; with testimonials to its curative powers by John Rice and Charles Vigus, both of Carrollton, 1904. [9225

DEANE G. CARTER. Some concepts of farm building management [1919-48]. Agric. engineering, 30:65-6, 70 (Feb 1958). view. Based on thesis--Univ. of Illinois. Conclusions from a study of structures on 13 farms owned by the University of Illinois. [9226

JAMES WELDON GALLAGHER. Drought in southern Illinois [1925-55]. Ann Arbor: University Microfilms, 1959 [i. e. 1960]. Positive microfilm of typescript. [212] leaves. Thesis--Univ. of Illinois. Abstracted: Dissert. abstracts, 20:3260 (Feb). [9227

GEORGE RAGLAND, JR. Edson R. Sunderland's contributions to the reform of civil procedure in Illinois [1929-33]. Mich. law rev., 58:27-36 (Nov 1959). notes. [9228

ELMER LOUIS SAUER. Economics of soil conservation [Illinois, 1936-47]. Agric. engineering, 30:226-8 (May 1949). diagrs., tables, views. [9229

ILLINOIS. Commission on Human Relations. Human relations progress in Illinois: the role of the Illinois Commission on Human Relations, 1943-1960. Chicago, 1960. [1], 14, [2] leaves. bibliog. (leaf 15). [9230

Chicago

CHARLES BYRON JOHNSON. Growth of Cook County. Vol. I ... A history of the large lake-shore county that includes Chicago [1673-1958. Chicago: Board of Commissioners of Cook County, Ill., 1960.] xii, 321 p. map, ports., tables, views. notes. Deals in part with hospitals. [9231

OTTO McFEELY. Oak Park's bit of the forest primeval. Ill. State Hist. Soc., Jour., 53:412-14 (winter). On 4 acres of land in "Austin Garden" formerly owned by Henry Warren Austin, settler in 1850, given to the park district of Oak Park by his son, Henry Warren Austin II, in 1947. [9232

CHAMBER OF COMMERCE, Park Ridge, Ill. Park Ridge [1852-1960. Park Ridge, 1960.] 42, [2] p. maps (1 double), tables, views. [9233

ISHBEL ROSS. Silhouette in diamonds: the life of Mrs. Potter Palmer. N.Y.: Harper [1960]. xi, 276 p. facsims., ports., views. bibliog. (p. 263-7), notes (p. 255-62). On Bertha Mathilde (Honoré) Palmer (1849-1918), resident of Chicago from 1855 till her death, wife of Potter Palmer, hostess, woman suffragist, art collector, a promoter and manager of the Columbian Exposition (1893), developer of businesses in Sarasota, Fla. [9234

JAY FERRIS LUDWIG. James H. McVicker and his theatre. Quar. jour. speech, 46:14-25 (Feb). notes. On McVicker's Theatre, Chicago, 1857-96. [9235

POTTER Palmer's Chicago. Chicago hist., 5:289-300 (winter). views. On an album of 79 photographs of buildings owned by Palmer in the Palmer Block "about the year 1868"; with other information about his real-estate holdings in Chicago. [9236

ERICH ROSENTHAL. This was North Lawndale: the transplantation of a Jewish community. Jew. social studies, 22:67-82 (Apr). views. notes. On a western residential suburb of Chicago, founded in 1870, initially largely Irish and German, by 1915 mainly a Jewish community of large apartment buildings, and by 1955 "a solid Negro community"; with a study of its Jewish institutions. [9237

HELEN E. HAYES. The Great Chicago Fire [1871]. Detroit Soc. Geneal. Research mag., 24:1-4 (fall). Information from the author's grandfather, Dr. Justin Hayes (died 1892), who saved all the inmates of his sanitarium. [9238

SIDNEY I. ROBERTS. Businessmen in revolt: Chicago, 1874-1900. Ann Arbor: University Microfilms, 1960. Positive microfilm of typescript. [285] leaves. Thesis--Northwestern Univ. Abstracted: Dissert. abstracts, 21:1180 (Nov). [9239

CHICAGO TRIBUNE. Warriors who fought Custer visited Chicago in 1877. [Edited by Harry Anderson.] Westerners brand book (Chicago), 16:50-51 (Sep 1959). From the issue of 22 Sep. 1877. On the passage through Chicago of 22 Sioux chiefs en route to Washington, and the great public attention that they attracted. [9240

CHICAGO HISTORICAL SOCIETY. Number, please. Chicago hist., 6:1-6 (fall). On "a microfilm copy of all Chicago telephone directories, classified as well as alphabetical," 1878-1960, and other materials concerning telephones in Chicago. [9241

HARROLD C. SCHIFFLER. The Chicago church-theater controversy of 1881-1882. Ill. State Hist. Soc., Jour., 53:361-75 (winter). ports., view. notes. Deals particularly with attacks upon James H. McVicker and his theater by Dr. Herrick Johnson

(Presbyterian) and with McVicker's defense, and the failure of the Presbytery to endorse the attack. [9242

ROBERT EUGENE TOSTBERG. Educational ferment in Chicago, 1883-1904. Ann Arbor: University Microfilms, 1960. Positive microfilm of typescript. [284] leaves. Thesis--Univ. of Wisconsin. Abstracted: Dissert. abstracts, 21:1451 (Dec). Deals in large part with the ideas and practices of Col. Francis W. Parker, John Dewey, and Ella Flagg Young. [9243

ALLEN FREEMAN DAVIS. Jane Addams vs. the ward boss. Ill. State Hist. soc., Jour., 53:247-65 (autumn). port. notes. On her unsuccessful campaign to procure the defeat of Johnny Powers as alderman of the Nineteenth Ward, 1889-96; and the lessons she learned from her experience. [9244

ROBERT L. McCAUL. Dewey's Chicago. School rev., 67:258-80 (summer 1959). notes. On his service as head of the Department of Philosophy (including pedagogy), University of Chicago, and of an experimental school in the University, his relations with educators and educational affairs there (particularly Col. Francis W. Parker and his school), and his interests in "Chicago life," 1894-1904. [9245

THOMAS G. MANNING, ed. The Chicago Strike of 1894: industrial labor in the late nineteenth century. N.Y.: Holt [1960]. xiii, 65 p. notes (p. 65). (Select problems in historical interpretation, 4.) Reprinted documents, connected by headnotes. [9246

SIDNEY I. ROBERTS. The Municipal Voters' League and Chicago's boodlers [1895-96]. Ill. State Hist. Soc., Jour., 53:117-48 (summer). cartoon, ports. notes. [9247

TOMAZ J. TURLEY. On the minerals of the Chicago area [1902-59]. Rocks and minerals, 34:393-5 (Sep-Oct 1959). notes. [9248

MILBURN P. AKERS. Chicago's newspaper concentration: "an ex parte view." Nieman reports, 13(3):20-22 (Jul 1959). On "the inexorable workings of economic laws" upon Chicago newspapers since 1910. [9249

FELICIAN SISTERS OF THE ORDER OF ST. FRANCIS. Province of Chicago. Fifty years: a memoir on the fiftieth anniversary of the Mother of Good Counsel Province of the Congregation of the Sisters of St. Felix (Felician Sisters), 1910-October 1960. [Compiled and edited by Sister Mary Feliciana. Chicago] 1960. xxxiv, 140 p. diagrs., maps, ports., tables, views. bibliog. (p. 130-31). [9250

JOHN R. BAYLIS. Operator's viewpoint. Am. Water Works Assoc., Jour., 52:1169-76 (Sep). On the author's operation of a public filtration plant in Chicago, 1914-60. [9251

FREDERIC MILTON THRASHER (1892-1962). The gang: a study of 1,313 gangs in Chicago. ... Second revised edition [new impression]. Chicago: Univ. of Chicago Press [1960. 18], 605 p. fold. map, tables, views. bibliog. (p. 554-80), notes. 1st ed. 1927. Based upon court records (1914-24), interviews, and the author's observations. [9252

JOAN HESS MICHEL. Richard Florsheim [born 1916]: painter of city lights. Am. artist, 24(7):50-55, 74-6 (Sep). port., views (1 col.). On his life in Chicago and his paintings of Chicago scenes, mainly nocturnal. [9253

CHADWICK CLARKE HANSEN. Social influences on jazz style: Chicago, 1920-30. Am quar., 12:493-507 (winter). notes. Based on thesis--Univ. of Minnesota. Mainly on the improved situation of Negro musicians from New Orleans and on the objections made to their performing "popular or classical music" as distinguished from "music of Negro origin." [9254

JOHN H. LYLE. The dry and lawless years. Englewood Cliffs, N.J.: Prentice-Hall [1960]. 311 p. cartoons, facsims., map, ports., views. On liquor, gambling, prostitution, bribery, theft, robbery, hired murder, extortion, blackmail, and corruption of the police in Chicago during the years of Prohibition, 1920-33, and to some extent before and after these years. Based upon the author's observations as a Chicago lawyer since 1910, a member of the Chicago City Council, and from 1924 to 1936 a judge of the Municipal Court of Chicago. Includes details of his dealings with Al Capone, Johnny Torrio, Dion O'Banion, and other "mobsters." [9255

COOK COUNTY, Ill. Criminal Court. The amazing crime and trial of Leopold and Loeb. [Edited] by Maureen McKernan. With an introduction by Clarence Darrow and Walter Bachrach. [N.Y.:] New American Library [1957]. 300, [4] p. ports., views. bibliog. (p. 300). (A Signet book, D1469.) Record of the trial of Nathan Freudenthal Leopold (born 1904/5) and Richard A. Loeb (1905/6-1936) for the murder of Robert Franks (1909/10-1924), and for kidnaping for ransom. [9256

ART HODES. Play the blues. Jazz rev., 2(5):9-11 (Jun 1959). ports. A pianist's memories of Chicago jazz, "late 20's" to 1938. [9257

ERICH ROSENTHAL. Acculturation without assimilation? the Jewish community of Chicago, Illinois [1928-59]. Am. jour. sociol., 66:275-88 (Nov.). notes. [9258

SIEGFRIED SCHMITZ. Die Sozialkritik in der Romantrilogie "Studs Lonigan" [1932-35] von James T. Farrell. Mainz, 1956. [3], vi, 210 p. bibliog. (p. 205-9), notes. Inaugural-Dissertation--Mainz. [9259

MARTIN W. REINEMANN. The pattern and distribution of manufacturing in the Chicago area [the Chicago Standard Metropolitan Area, 5 counties in Illinois and 1 in Indiana, 1939-54]. Econ. geog., 36:139-44 (Apr). maps, tables. notes. Based on thesis--Northwestern Univ. [9260

BEVERLY DUNCAN & PHILIP MORRIS HAUSER. Housing a metropolis--Chicago [1940-56]. Glencoe, Ill.: Free Press [1960]. xxii, [2], 278 p. diagrs., tables (part double). bibliog. (p. 266-70). [9261

EZRA SOLOMON & ZARKO G. BILBIJA. Metropolitan Chicago: an economic analysis. Glencoe, Ill.: Free Press [1960, c1959]. xix, [3], 208 p. diagrs., tables. notes. (University of Wisconsin. Graduate School of Business. Studies in business.) Study of Cook, Du Page, Kane, Lake, and Will Counties, Ill., and Lake County, Ind., mainly in the years 1940 and 1946-58. [9262

EDWIN NEAL THOMAS. Areal associations between population growth and selected factors in the Chicago Urbanized Area [1940-50]. Econ. geog., 36:158-70 (Apr). diagrs., maps, tables. notes. Based on thesis--Northwestern Univ. [9263

JAMES ROY BLAYNEY. A report on thirteen years of water floridation in Evanston, Ill. [1947-60]. Am. Dental Assoc., Jour., 61:76-9 (Jul). tables. [9264

SULTAN S. HASHMI. A socio-economic explanation of variations in fertility among the census tracts of Chicago: 1950. Chicago: [Dept. of Photoduplication, Univ. of Chicago Library] 1960. Positive microfilm of typescript. 82 leaves. bibliog. Thesis--Univ. of Chicago. [9265

Springfield

WILLIAM GRANT STRATTON. Lincoln in Springfield [1837-61]. Ralph G. Newman, ed., Lincoln for the ages (Garden City, N.Y.: Doubleday, 1960), p. 113-17. [9266

FRANCES JANE (TODD) WALLACE (1817-99). Mrs. Frances Jane (Todd) Wallace describes Lincoln's wedding. Edited by Wayne C. Temple. ... Harrogate, Tenn.: Lincoln Memorial Univ. Press for the members of the National Lincoln - Civil War Council, 1960. [2], 12 p. notes (p. 11-12). From the Chicago Sunday times-herald, 25 Aug. 1895. Interview with a sister of Mary (Todd) Lincoln, recalling the latter's marriage to Abraham Lincoln, Springfield, 1842. [9267

ALBERT ALEXANDER WOLDMAN. Lincoln and Herndon. Ralph G. Newman, ed., Lincoln for the ages (Garden City, N.Y.: Doubleday, 1960), p. 101-6. On the law partnership of Lincoln and William Herndon, Springfield, Ill., 1844-61. [9268

JAMES T. HICKEY. Lincoln the real estate agent. Ill. State Hist. Soc., Jour., 53:70-78 (spring). facsim. Documents recording his efforts to sell land within the limits of Springfield belong to Mrs. Lincoln's aunt, Maria L. Todd Bullock of Kentucky, 1855-61. [9269

EARL SCHENCK MIERS. Lincoln's last days in Illinois. Ralph G. Newman, ed., Lincoln for the ages (Garden City, N.Y.: Doubleday, 1960), p. 155-9. On his visit to Springfield, Feb. 1864. [9270

CARL G. HODGES. The kidnaped cornerstone. Ill. State Hist. Soc., Jour., 53:29-36 (spring). views. On the 2-ton cornerstone of the Illinois State Capital, Springfield, laid 5 Oct. 1868, removed and buried about 10 feet away when cracks developed in 1870, and dug up, cleaned, and repaired in 1944; and the legend that it had been removed by Masons because the name of the infidel Robert G. Ingersoll appeared on it. [9271

JAMES L. CROUTHAMEL. The Springfield [Ill.] race riot of 1908. Jour. Negro hist., 45:164-81 (Jul). notes. On disorders during preparations for celebrating the centennial of Lincoln's birth, and the influence of the riots upon the establishment of the National Association for the Advancement of Colored People in 1910. [9272

MICHIGAN

LOUISE COLLINS. Post cards of Michigan. Hobbies, 64(10):116-19; (11):116-19 (Dec 1959, Jan 1960). facsims. [9273

RACHEL M. HILBERT, ed. Michigan authors. Ann Arbor: Michigan Assoc. of School Librarians, 1960. [8], 68 p. ports. bibliogs. Biographical sketches of 76 writers, living and dead. [9274

EDWIN WALLACE McMULLEN. More information on Michigan prairie names. Names, 8:53-6 (Mar). Suggestions and information received from Virgil J. Vogel for addition to the author's article, "Prairie generics in Michigan" (in Names, Sep. 1959), referring particularly to Indian names of Michigan prairies. [9275

HELEN MANDEVILLE MARTIN. Michigan story. Mich. conservation, 19(2):5-8 (Mar-Apr 1950). view. On the natural resources of Michigan and their use and conservation, 1564-1949. [9276

CHARLES F. FOEHLER. Fort Wilkins, symbol of an era. Mich. conservation, 23(4):18-21 (Jul-Aug 1954). map, views. On explorations for copper in the Keweenaw Peninsula since 1612, the establishment of Fort Wilkins at Copper Harbor in 1844, and the preservation of its site as Fort Wilkins State Park. [9277

ERNEST J. LAJEUNESSE, ed. The Windsor border region, Canada's southernmost frontier: a collection of documents. Toronto: Champlain Soc., 1960. cxxix, 374 p. maps (2 fold.), plans, ports., tables, views. bibliog. (p. 361-4), notes. (The publications of the Champlain Society. Ontario series, 4.) Collection of 202 documents in English, French, or Latin (with translations of those in French or Latin), 1640/41-1800, relating to the "20-by-30-mile rectangular peninsula" bounded on 3 sides by Lake St. Clair, the Detroit River, and Lake Erie, comprising the whole area of present Essex County, Ont., and including the settlements of Sandwich, and Amherstburg; with an extensive introduction, "Abstracts from the Detroit notarial records," 1765-95 (p. 312-34), "Genealogies" (p. 335-42), other lists of names, and many references to Michigan and the Great Lakes. [9278

CLIFFORD R. HUMPHREYS. Treasure by the ton. Mich. conservation, 22(3): 2-6 (May-Jun 1953). view. Based on thesis--Michigan State Univ. On evidences of former mining of copper by Indians working with stone tools in Ontonagon County, noted as early as 1665, the industry of mining "virgin" copper there from 1845 to 1921, and present plans to process copper ore. [9279

PHILIP PARKER MASON. Michigan's first outdoorsmen. Mich. conservation, 29(2):40-45; (3):26-9 (Mar, Jun). views. On the "hunting, fishing, and agriculture of Michigan's various Indian tribes," 1670 ff. [9280

HANS L. PETERSEN. River of Sands. Mich. conservation, 26(4):24-6 (Jul-Aug 1957). views. On the Au Sable River, 1670-1957. [9281

ELSKET BARSTOW CHANEY. The story of Portage. [Onekama, Mich., 1960.] 75, [1] p. facsims., maps., ports., views. bibliog. (p. 73-5). On Manistee County, Mich., and particularly Portage Lake, 1675-1960. [9282

ERNEST V. BLOHM. Pontiac Lake State Recreation Area. Mich. conservation, 24(3):22-5 (May-Jun 1955). views. Historical sketch of the area of Pontiac Lake, Oakland County, 1760-1955. [9283

KENYON BOYER. Should we bring the Great Seal and Flag of Michigan up to date? Mich. heritage, 1:89-92 (spring). Traces the seal to that of the Northwest Territory, 1792, and follows its evolutions to the adoption of the present seal in 1911. [9284

WILLIAM WIRT BLUME. Probate and administration on the American frontier: a study of the probate records of Wayne County--Northwest Territory, 1796-1803; Indiana Territory, 1803-1805; Michigan Territory, 1805-1816. Mich. law rev., 58:209-46 (Dec 1959). notes. Information from records of Wayne County, which until 1817 embraced all of Michigan except Indian lands. [9285

Mrs. GEORGE O. ROSS, comp. Luick Farm Cemetery, Washtenaw County, Michigan [6.5 miles west of Ann Arbor]. Detroit Soc. Geneal. Research mag., 24:29-32 (fall). List of inscriptions, 1805-1958. [9286

STEPHEN WLOSZCZEWSKI. The trail of the Polish emigrants in Michigan [1808-1870s]. Poles in Michigan Associated, Poles in Michigan (Detroit, 1953 [i. e. 1955]), 1:25-9. bibliog. [9287

DEAN DE LA MATER. Retracement survey. Mich. conservation, 21(1):9-12 (Jan-Feb 1952). ports., views. On early methods of marking boundaries and section corners in Michigan by means of posts and of "bearings" carved on blazed trees, 1815-1951. [9288

CHARLES CHRISTOPHER TROWBRIDGE (1800-1883). Indian tales of C. C. Trowbridge: The red head. [Edited by] C. E. Schorer. Midw. folklore, 10:86-95 (summer). notes. Manuscript of a tale written in Detroit "during the third decade of the nineteenth century," dealing with "a loathsome woman's conquest of a beautiful but evasive man," both transformed into birds. [9289

FREDERICK A. COLER & RICHARD A. SINNOT, JR. Washtenaw County Medical Society: a brief account of its origin and growth [1827-1959]. Mich. State Med. Soc., Jour., 58:363-72 (Mar 1959). bibliog. [9290

ANN McCOLLUM (1816-1908). A pioneer comes to Tecumseh. ... Contributed by Mrs. W. Dale Perkins. Detroit Soc. Geneal. Research mag., 23:93-4 (spring). Undated recollections of the voyage of the McCollum family from Buffalo to Detroit and their travels with teams to their new farm in the woods near Tecumseh, Lenawee County, Mich., 1828, and details of their discomforts and inconveniences there. [9291

ERNEST V. BLOHM. Albert E. Sleeper State Park. Mich. conservation, 23 (5):27-9 (Sep-Oct 1953). On lumbering in the area of Caseville, 1830-1953, and the establishment of a State park at the tip of the Thumb. [9292

HAROLD B. FIELDS. Free Negroes in Cass County before the Civil War [1830-60]. Mich. hist., 44:375-83 (Dec). notes. [9293

GEORGE L. HAMMELL (1887-1952). Pioneer Ingham County families. Mich. heritage, 1:58-61, 104-10, 168-72; 2:32-4 (winter 1959 - autumn 1960). bibliogs. On descedants of Phineas P. Fox (1790-1872), Israel G. Atkins (died 1858), Robert Grovenor Hayward (1800-1866), Petrus Longyear (1784-1845), Henry William Longyear (1818-49), Parley Parker Moore (1809-58), Enos Northrup (1813-98), and William Webb (1779-1859), who settled in Ingham County in the 1830s and 1840s. [9294

HELEN MANDEVILLE MARTIN. Dawn of iron. Mich. conservation, 27(4):23-6 (Jul-Aug 1958). facsim., views. On the discovery and mining of iron ore in Michigan, 1830-1958. [9295

J. K. ALTLAND. Rural community health [in Mich. State Med. Soc., Jour., 59:243-6 (Feb). views. [9296

LILLIAN McCORMACK, comp. St. Paul's Catholic Cemetery, Grosse Pointe Farms, Mich. Detroit Soc. Geneal. Research mag., 24:67-73 (winter). Inscriptions, 1831-1950. [9297

DOMINIC P. PARIS. The Newburgh Cemetery. Mich. hist., 44:67-74 (Mar). notes. Information from the ledger of a burial society in Livonia, containing a plot of the cemetery and minutes of all meetings, 1832-1923. [9298

EMERY T. CARLSON. Gypsum. Mich. conservation, 26(5):21-3 (Sep-Oct 1957). views. On its production in Michigan, 1834-1957. [9299

ERNEST V. BLOHM & E. A. BOTTKE. Pinckney Recreation Area. Mich. conservation, 22(3):21-3 (May-Jun 1953). views. On Pinckney, Washtenaw

County, Mich., settled in 1835, and the recreation area established there in 1944. [9300

ANN HOLLINSHEAD. Albion College celebrates its 125th anniversary [1835-1960]. Mich. hist., 44:241-6 (Jun). [9301

MARY S. KIRBY. The Upjohn family. Mich. heritage, 1:81-8, 160-66 (spring, summer). On descendants of William Upjohn (1770-1853, emigrant to America in 1826), particularly his sons William (1807-87, father of 2 daughters) and Uriah (1808-96, father of 12 children), physicians, who arrived in Kalamazoo County, Mich., in 1835. [9302

CARL VAN WEELDEN. Yankee Springs, past and present. Mich. conservation, 21(4):3-4, 22-3 (Jul-Aug 1952). port., view. On a place in Barry County, site of a stagecoach station established by William Lewis in 1836 and of a village, the abandonment of the area by settlers after exhaustion of the soil, and its eventual acquisition by the State as the Yankee Springs Recreation Area. [9303

ERNEST V. BLOHM. Waterloo Recreation Area. Mich. conservation, 22(4): 3-6 (Jul-Aug 1953). view. On Waterloo, Mich., settled in 1836, and the recreation area established in adjacent parts of Washtenaw and Jackson Counties in 1933. [9304

ARTHUR BOOTH, comp. Otisville Cemetery inscriptions, Wayne County, Mich. [2 miles south of Belleville]. Detroit Soc. Geneal, Research mag., 24:74-6 (winter). Inscriptions, 1836-1957. [9305

LOUISE E. KOIER. A new kind of sugar story: Vermont syrup-making goes West. Vt. Hist. Soc., News and notes, 6:57-61 (Apr 1955). facsim., views. On Vermontville, Mich., settled in 1836 by Vermonters; with information from a letter from Mrs. Sylvester Cochrane, 1838. [9306

MARY (COBB) LANGLEY. History of Caseville: biographies and legends. Pigeon, Mich.: Thumb Publications, c1960. 104 p. Account of a town on the east shore of Saginaw Bay, 1836-1959. [9307

ALLEGAN COUNTY, Mich. 47 marriages in Allegan County, Michigan, 1837-1873. Contributed by Mrs. C. A. Monteith. Detroit Soc. Geneal. Research mag., 23:38-9 (fall 1959). [9308

KALAMAZOO VALLEY GENEALOGICAL SOCIETY. [Fairbanks family.] Mich. heritage, 2:38-42, 113 (autumn, winter). Bible records (in a volume published in 1857), contributed by Grace Keeler; cemetery records copied by Elizabeth Schuyler Hamilton Chapter, D. A. R., Holland, Mich.; and "Additional Fairbanks datum," by Ruth Monteith, on members of the family in Allegan and Kalamazoo Counties since 1837. [9309

MICHIGAN. Dept. of State. Michigan State census of Kalamazoo County--1837. Pavilion Township. Compiled from original by Mrs. Chalmers A. (Ruth) Monteith. Annotated by Ethel W. Williams. Mich. heritage, 1:70-71, 123-4, 154-8 (winter 1959-summer 1960). Includes notes offering added identification of the individuals named. [9310

JOHN PATRICK WHITE. Michigan political history and demography [1837-1936]. Institute in Practical Partisan Politics, University of Michigan, 1959, Selected papers, ed. Sybil L. Stokes & Lynn W. Eley (Ann Arbor, 1960 [University of Michigan, Institute of Public Administration, Papers in public administration, 38]), leaves 35-45. [9311

DAVID A. ARNOLD. About wolves [in Michigan, 1838-1950]. Mich. conservation, 21(1):23-5 (Jan-Feb 1952). [9312

OAKLAND COUNTY, Mich. Probate Court records of Oakland County, Michigan. Abstracted & contributed by Alice D. Serrell. Detroit Soc. Geneal. Research mag., 23:29-34, 75-80, 115-20, 166-71 (fall 1959-summer 1960). Records of wills, administrations, and guardianships, Jan. 1839-Dec. 1849. [9313

KENYON BOYER. People of iron. Mich. conservation, 27(2):11-15 (Mar-Apr 1958). views. On the "nationality pattern of the settling of mining communities in the Upper Peninsula" since 1840. [9314

PAUL DAYTON KILBURN. Effects of logging and fire on xerophytic forests in northern Michigan [in Cheboygan County, 1840-1960]. Torrey Bot. Club, Bul., 87:402-5 (Nov-Dec). diagrs., table. bibliog. [9315

JOHN EDGAR KEPHART. A voice for freedom: the Signal of liberty. Ann Arbor: University Microfilms, 1960. Positive microfilm of typescript. [241] leaves. Thesis--Univ. of Michigan. Abstracted: Dissert. abstracts, 21:347 (Aug). On "the official newspaper of the Michigan State Anti-Slavery Society and of the Michigan Liberty Party," edited by Theodore Foster aided by the Rev. Guy Beckley, 1841-48. [9316

BESSIE JANE REED. Lucinda Hinsdale Stone [1814-1900]: a Michigan pioneer in education for women. Mich. heritage, 2:1-8 (autumn). port. bibliog. On her life in Kalamazoo, 1843-1900, where she taught till 1863 in a school that developed into Kalamazoo College, founded and conducted the Kalamazoo Young Ladies Seminary (1863-66), and later promoted the Ladies Library Association of Kalamazoo and other women's clubs, the admission of women into institutions of higher learning, and the Michigan Women's Press Association; with some account of her early life in Vermont and her schoolteaching there and in Mississippi. [9317

ALEXANDER J. SHELDON (1823-76). The Kalamazoo Mound: a letter from Alexander J. Sheldon. Edited by Alexis A. Praus. Mich. hist., 44: 384-400 (Dec). notes. Parts of a letter to Levi Bishop, President of the Detroit Historical Society, Feb. 1874, on the author's observations in Kalamazoo during his residence there from 1843 to ca. 1853, his studies of the Bronson Park Mount at that time, his conviction that "there has never been anything deposited in or under this Mound, prior to 1850", and his theory as to the origin of the mound; with excerpts from articles by Henry Little on the same subject (in the Kalamazoo Daily telegraph, 1874). [9318

H. J. HARDENBERG. 800,000,000 tons. Mich. conservation, 27(1):12-15 (Jan-Feb 1958). map, views. On iron-ore production in Michigan, 1844-1957. [9319

KNOX JAMISON. The Kaug. Mich. conservation, 22(4):27-9 (Jul-Aug 1953). port., view. On the Porcupine Mountains, "the highest mountain range in the Middle West," 1844-1953, and the copper mining, logging, hunting, fishing, and tourist industry there. [9320

MARK OLIVER KISTLER. The German language press in Michigan: a survey and bibliography. Mich. hist., 44: 303-23 (Sep). notes. On German newspapers and magazines published in Michigan, 1844-1926; with a list of those that have been identified. [9321

KNOX JAMISON. Mountain logging [in the Porcupine Mountains, 1845-1950]. Mich. conservation, 19(2):31-2 (Mar-Apr 1950). [9322

PAUL DAYTON KILBURN. Effect of settlement on the vegetation of the University of Michigan Biological Station. Mich. Acad. Science, Papers, 45:77-81. table. bibliog. On "the fire and logging history" of an area in Cheboygan County, 1845-1956. [9323

ALBERT HYMA. Early Dutch settlements in Michigan. Mich. heritage, 2:101-4 (winter). On the founding of Holland, Mich., by emigrants from the Netherlands organized by the Rev. Albertus C. Van Raalte, 1847, and the multiplication of the Dutch and their descendants "in the vicinity between the Grand and Kalamazoo Rivers," in which "some fifty Dutch towns and villages can be found." [9324

BENJAMIN SILSBE. Benjamin Silsbe's account books, Clinton County, Mich. Contributed by Mrs. George L. McCutchan. Detroit Soc. Geneal. Research mag., 23:82-4 (winter 1959). Record of a general store in Wacousta, 1847-54, and a sawmill in De Witt, 1855. [9325

JOSEPH SZAREK. The oldest Polish village in Michigan: Parisville--the glory of its pioneers. Poles in Michigan Associated, Poles in Michigan (Detroit, 1953 [i. e. 1955]), 1:64-9. On the first settlement of Poles in Huron County, formed sometime between 1848 and 1851. [9326

ELIZABETH K. WATHEN. Muskegon's Old Indian Cemetery. Mich. heritage, 2:92-4 (winter). On an area in downtown Muskegon used as a cemetery from 1848 till 1854, given to the city in 1926 with a fund for its perpetual maintenance, and recent litigation to defeat the City's effort to "abandon the entire Indian Cemetery permanently and remove any remains to other locations." [9327

DEATHS IN Branch County, Michigan, during year ending 1 June 1850. Mich. heritage, 1:92, 103, 110, 115, 122, 140, 148 (spring, summer). Tabulation, including information about age, sex, State of birth, date of death, occupation, and residence. [9328

DEATHS in Ottawa County, Michigan, during year ending 1 June 1850. Mich. heritage, 1:148, 159; 2:17, 31, 37 (summer, autumn). Includes tabulated information about age, sex, State of birth, date of death, occupation, and residence. [9329

PAULUS DEN BLEYKER (1804-72). Paulus Den Bleyker: type and prototype. [Edited] by Timothy Rey. Mich. heritage, 2:11-17 (autumn). Editorial account of his prosperous early years in the Netherlands, his organization of a party of 27 emigrants who settled in Kalamazoo in 1850, and his great prosperity in business there; and "A letter from Paulus Den Bleyker," undated, addressed apparently to promoters of the enterprise in Holland, on the voyage of the party to America and the handling of funds made available for this purpose; with an appended "Passenger list of ship 'Catherine'" (10 Aug. 1850) and references to other documents. [9330

JOHN H. JACKSON. Eminent domain--procedure--relation of judge and jury in Michigan condemnation proceedings [1850-1958]. Mich. law rev., 58:248-73 (Dec 1959). notes. [9331

G. S. McINTIRE. 100 years of Michigan forests [1850-1957. By] G. S. McIntire, as told to Russell McKee. Mich. conservation, 26(2):2-8 (Mar-Apr 1957). maps, views (1 double). [9332

DAVID HALL JENKINS. Hunting, 1852 style. Mich. conservation, 20(6):2-4, 19-21 (Nov-Dec 1951). col. map. Information from a diary of O. H. Perry, recording his travels by steamer from Cleveland to Lexington, Mich., his "elk and deer hunting expedition" in the Thumb, and his journey by wagon from Saginaw to Detroit, Sep.-Oct. 1852. [9333

RUTH B. BORDIN. A Michigan lumbering family. Bus. hist. rev., 34: 64-76 (spring). views. notes. On the activities of Gideon Olin Whittemore, his sons James, Charles, and William, and his son-in-law A. B. Mathews, all of Pontiac, in the white-pine lumber industry in the vicinity of Tawas City, 1853-66. [9334

FORD KELLUM. Return to Deward. Mich. conservation, 28(3):25-9 (May-Jun 1959), views (part double). On a logging community on the Manistee River near present Frederic, Mich., in white-pine country, founded, in 1854 and virtually abandoned in 1912, now included in the Au Sable State Forest. [9335

VICTOR F. LEMMER. The impact of the Civil War on iron ore mining in Michigan. [Ironwood? Mich.] c1960. [4], 13 leaves. table. On mining in the Marquette, Menominee, and Gogebic Ranges, 1854-74. [9336

EDWARD GROESBECK VOSS. Charles W[esley] Fallass (1854-1942): a pioneer Michigan botanist. Asa Gray bul., 3:77-96 (spring 1955). facsims., ports. bibliog., notes. On his life as a merchant and a farmer in various parts of Michigan, his studies at Albion College, his work as an amateur botanist and collector in Emmet County, and his herbarium, housed in his home in Petoskey. [9337

M. J. DE BOER. Sunken log salvage. Mich. conservation, 19(4):23-6 (Jul-Aug 1950). view. On logs sunk in Michigan rivers, and litigation about their ownership, 1855-1950. [9338

FRANCES WOOD. Steam travel bids Grand Rapids farewell. Mich. hist., 44:75-81 (Mar). On the first passenger train to enter Grand Rapids, 4 Jul. 1858, and the last, 18 Oct. 1958. [9339

WILLIS FREDERICK DUNBAR. Flora Temple and her times. Mich. heritage, 1:48-51, 116-22 (winter 1959, spring 1960). On events in Michigan during 1859; with prefatory mention of Flora Temple, a "very famous" and "very fast" trotting horse, who "set the world's record here in Kalamazoo," 15 Oct. 1859. [9340

EUGENE THOR PETERSEN. Wildlife conservation in Michigan [since 1859]. Mich. hist., 44:129-46 (Jun). [9341

DARRELL HENRY POLLARD. The development of Michigan's oil industry, 1860-1935. Ann Arbor: University Microfilms, 1959 [i. e. 1960]. Positive microfilm of typescript. [350] leaves. Thesis--Univ. of Michigan. Abstracted: Dissert. abstracts, 20:4386 (May). [9342

HERBERT BRINKS. The effect of the Civil War in 1861 on Michigan lumbering and mining industries. Mich. hist., 44:101-7 (Mar). notes. [9343

RICHARD H. SEWELL. Michigan farmers and the Civil War. Mich. hist., 44:353-74 (Dec). notes. On agriculture in Michigan, 1861-65. [9344

A. B. GLASPIE. ... But all gone now. Mich. conservation, 29(3):30-32 (May-Jun). view. From The Michigan sportsman, May 1918. On passenger pigeons in Michigan, 1864-1918. [9345

W. HARRIS COATES. The fight for clean water [in Michigan, 1865-1958]. Mich. conservation, 27(5):18-21 (Sep-Oct 1958). views. [9346

ELMER B. HESS. The Kalamazoo Valley paper industry. Ind. Acad. Science, Proc., 69:224-35. maps. On the "dominant industry in the Kalamazoo River Valley" and the reasons why the paper industry is located there, 1866-1959. [9347

A. B. COOK. Trout for the fisherman [in Michigan, 1870s-1960]. Mich. conservation, 29(2):2-6 (Mar-Apr). facsim., views. [9348

M. J. DE BOER. Nature's masterpiece ... the brook trout. Mich. conservation, 26(3):2-5 (May-Jun 1957). views. On its introduction from the Upper Peninsula into the Lower in the 1870s, its multiplication till in the 1890s it was the most abundant and widespread of Michigan game fishes, and the reasons for its increasing rarity since 1900. [9349

MICHIGAN, UNIVERSITY OF. Program for Research in Population and Human Ecology. Estimates of population change in Michigan, 1950-1960. By David Goldberg ... Allen Feldt ... [and] J. William Smith. Ann Arbor, 1960. [4], 49, [1], 4 leaves. tables. bibliog. (leaves 48-9), notes. (Its Michigan population studies, 1.) Includes comparative data for the years 1870-1950. [9350

STEPHEN WLOSZOZEWSKI. Posen: the history of an old Polish settlement in northern Michigan [in Presque Isle County, settled "even before 1870" but not recorded before 1874]. Poles in Michigan Associated, Poles in Michigan (Detroit, 1953 [i. e. 1955]), 1:37-40. [9351

M. M. BERGMAN. Forest fire control under Clarke-McNary Act [1924-48]. Mich. conservation, 18(4):18-20 (Jul-Aug 1949). Includes mention of forest fires in Michigan between 1871 and 1911. [9352

M. M. BERGMAN. Lest we forget. Mich. conservation, 29(5):49-51 (Sep-Oct). views. On forest fires in Michigan, 1871-1960. [9353

WILLIS FREDERICK DUNBAR. The high school on trial: the Kalamazoo Case. Mich. Acad. Science, Papers, 45:187-200. notes. On litigation concerning the authority of the Village of Kalamazoo to levy taxes for a high school in Kalamazoo, 1873-74. [9354

FISH and the license dollar. Mich. conservation, 28(1):18-21 (Jan-Feb 1959). views. From the Grand Rapids herald. On "fish management in Michigan" by the State government, 1873-1958. [9355

JOHN MUNRO LONGYEAR (1850-1922). From the reminiscences [1912] of John Munro Longyear: landlooker in the Upper Peninsula of Michigan. [Marquette:] Marquette County Historical Soc. of Michigan, 1960. [8], 80 p. facsims., maps (part col.), ports. (1 col.), views. On the author's work as a surveyor of State mineral lands on Isle Royale, the Keweenaw Peninsula, and the Ontonagon and Menominee Rivers, 1873-78; with "Glossary of place names" (p. 72-7). [9356

ARCHIE P. NEVINS. The Kalamazoo Case. Mich. hist., 44:91-100 (Mar). notes. On litigation initiated in Kalamazoo and ending in the Supreme Court, 1873-74, challenging the authority of a school board to expend public funds for the support of a secondary school, and the decision of the Court that such action in a community, when voted by its citizens, was not a violation of the constitution or laws of Michigan. [9357

JOHN EDWARD WILLIAMS. Northern pike management. Mich. conservation, 21(2):5-7, 33 (Mar-Apr 1952). views. On the breeding and fishing of pike in Michigan, 1875-1950. [9358

HUDSON KEENAN. America's first successful logging railroad. Mich. hist., 44:292-302 (Sep). notes. On the Lake George and Muskegon River

Railroad, some 8 miles long (eventually extended to 19.8 miles), running from the Muskegon River into pine forest in Clare County, 1876-87. [9359

LACEY D. STEPHAN. A family and a river. [By] Lacey D. Stephan, Au Sable River guide, as told to Russell McKee. Mich. conservation, 25(3):12-15 (May-Jun 1956). ports., views. On the author's grandfather, Peter W. Stephan, French emigrant who settled on a farm 7 miles east of Grayling in 1876, and the author's life as a fisherman and guide. [9360

LAWRENCE E. BLADES. Historical and theoretical foundation for the use of cy pres in Michigan [since 1879]. Mich. State Bar jour., 39(10):13-18 (Oct). port. [9361

CLARK L. BRODY (born 1879). In the service of the farmer: my life in the Michigan Farm Bureau. [East Lansing:] Michigan State Univ. Press, 1959. xi, 140 p. port. On the author's early life in St. Joseph County, his studies in Michigan Agricultural College, his work as a farmer in his native county, and his service as an agricultural agent in St. Clair County, 1915-21, and as Secretary-Manager, Executive Secretary-Treasurer and General Manager, and Executive Vice President of the Michigan State Farm Bureau, 1921-59. [9362

The EDUCATIONAL work of the Felician Sisters in Michigan [since 1879]. Poles in Michigan Associated, Poles in Michigan (Detroit, 1953 [i. e. 1955]), 1:70-76. tables. [9363

VIRGIL STEWART PRATT. Southern Michigan trout streams. Mich. conservation, 19(3):10-12 (May-Jun 1950). view. On the stocking of Michigan streams with trout from State hatcheries, 1879-1950. [9364

MICHIGAN FUNERAL DIRECTORS ASSOCIATION. A history of the Michigan Funeral Directors Association [1880-1960. Lansing, Mich., 1960.] 103, [5] p. ports., views. notes. [9365

EUGENE THOR PETERSEN & ROBIN A DREWS. In days of old ... carp was king. Mich. conservation, 26(3):10-12 (May-Jun 1957). views. On a game fish introduced into Michigan in 1880 and soon found to be a pest. [9366

DONALD THOMAS SHANOWER. A comparative and descriptive study of three opera houses in southern Michigan, 1880-1900. Ann Arbor: University Microfilms, 1960. Positive microfilm of typescript. [258] leaves. Thesis--Univ. of Michigan. Abstracted: Dissert. abstracts, 20: 4757 (Jun). Study of "Opera House activity in Adrian, Marshall, and Mason, Michigan." [9367

DALE J. HAGENAH. The new Michigan flora, an opportunity for local botanists. Asa Gray bul., 1:353-7 (Oct 1952). Comment on published statewide and local floras of Michigan, with a catalogue of such publications, 1881-1952, and suggestions for further work in "botanically unexplored" parts of the State. [9368

EDWIN LAVERN COOPER. Every trout a trophy. Mich. conservation, 20(2):14-18 (Mar-Apr 1951). port., view. On trout fishing in the North Branch of the Au Sable River, 1885-1950. See also, by the same author, "The North Branch story," 21(2):8-11 (Mar-Apr 1952). [9369

REX P. GRANT. Michigan oil: its past, present, and future [1886-1955]. Mich. conservation, 24(4):25-8 (Jul-Aug). map, view. [9370

LOUISE B. CLANCY & FLORENCE DAVIES. The believer: the life story of Mrs. Henry Ford. N.Y.: Coward-McCann [1960. 2], 215 p. facsims., ports., views. Account, semifictional in form, of the domestic life of Henry Ford from his marriage to Clara J. Bryant in 1888 till his death on 1947. Not a biography of Mrs. Ford. [9371

LOIS ELAINE COULSON. Evolution of the recreational occupance of Berrien County, Michigan [since 1890], with emphasis on the present recreational landscape. Ann Arbor: University Microfilms, 1959 [i. e. 1960]. Positive microfilm of typescript. [137] leaves. Thesis--Univ. of Illinois. Abstracted: Dissert. abstracts, 20:3259 (Feb). [9372

WILLIAM R. GANNON. History repeats at old Winchester. Mich. conservation, 24(2):27-9 (Mar-Apr 1955). views. On a dam built in 1890 by the Mecosta Lumber Company on a branch of the Chippewa River at Winchester, raising the water level in 14 lakes and the adjoining marshes and providing good cover for wildlife, neglected after 1900 until the construction of a new dam in 1954, forming Lake Winchester. [9373

BERNARD McTIVER. Con Culhane, real-life Paul Bunyan. Mich. conservation, 23(1):11-14 (Jan-Feb 1954). port., view. Lore collected from men who worked under him, about his career as a lumberman in Luce and Chippewa Counties from "somewhere around 1890" till his death "about 1906." [9374

EARL J. SENNINGER, JR. The chicory industry of Michigan [1890-1954]. Mich. Acad. Science, Papers, 45: 145-53. maps, tables. notes. On an industry now extinct in Michigan, formerly localized in the Saginaw Valley and the Thumb. [9375

WILLIAM H. COLBURN. 7 million acres and all yours. Mich. conservation, 25(1):19-23 (Jan 1956). views. On State and Federal lands in Michigan, 1893-1955. [9376

LAURA (JACKSON) CRANK. Laura Jackson Crank: an autobiography. In collaboration with Rose Askew Stevens. Mich. heritage, 2:83-5. On her years of study and teaching in rural schools in Montmorency County, Mich., 1894-1928. [9377

ELIZABETH SUTHERLAND TROW. Botanical Gardens of the University of Michigan [1897-1957] and the new Director, Dr. A. Geoffrey Norman. Asa Gray bul., 3:273-6 (spring 1957). port. [9378

WINIFRED NELSON BEECHY. History of the White Cloud Mennonite Church at White Cloud, Michigan [1898-1952]. Mennonite hist. bul., 13(3):1-4 (Jul 1952). view. notes. [9379

JOHN McNICKLE BALL. Changes in sugar beet production in Michigan, 1899-1958. Mich. Acad. Science, Papers, 45:137-44. diagr., maps. notes. [9380

FRED A. WESTERMAN. Warm-water fishes [i. e., "almost all sport fish except trout," in Michigan, 1899-1949]. Mich. conservation, 18(3):3-6 (May-Jun 1949). views. [9381

KATHERINE S. GROOMES. Memories--Ann Arbor near the turn of the century. Washtenaw impressions, 14(3):21-4 (Jun). [9382

ALBERT SIDNEY HAZZARD. The rainbow problem. Mich. conservation, 19(2):12-14, 33-4 (Mar-Apr 1950). view. On rainbow trout as "a problem to conservation administrators" in Michigan since 1900. [9383

LEE MORTON JAMES. Property taxes and alternatives for Michigan. Jour. forestry, 58:86-92 (Feb). notes. On the taxation of forest lands in Michigan, 1900-1960. [9384

CLARENCE M. TAUBE. Riverine lakes. Mich. conservation, 21(3):18-20 (May-Jun 1952). view. On "impoundments" in Michigan, 1900-1951. [9385

G. S. McINTIRE. A history of State forest management [in Michigan, 1903-58]. Mich. conservation, 27(2): 22-6 (Mar-Apr 1958). table, views. [9386

NORMAN FOSTER SMITH. Plantation harvest. Mich. conservation, 23(2): 31-2 (Mar-Apr 1954). On the planting of trees in forest plantations by the Forestry Division of the Michigan Department of Conservation, 1904-54. [9387

HELEN LAURA FOSTER. Today's forests--he helped them grow. Mich. conservation, 18(3):9-11 (May-Jun 1949). port., view. On Marcus Schaaf as State Forester of Michigan, 1910-49; with some account of his studies at the Biltmore Forestry School in North Carolina and his work as forester for the Cleveland-Cliffs Iron Company at Negaunee, Mich., 1906-10. [9388

ROBERT N. STONE. Preliminary report on the survey of forest plantations in northern Lower Michigan. Mich. Acad. Science, Papers, 45: 93-102. diagrs., map. On "areas of forest planting," public and private, mainly of pine, 1906-56. [9389

EUGENE THOR PETERSEN. Fly fishing only in the good old days. Mich. conservation, 25(3):8-11 (May-Jun 1956). On a "fly-fishing-only law for the North Branch of the Au Sable," enacted 1907, repealed 1913; with some account of fishing there as early as 1875. [9390

NORMAN FOSTER SMITH. Forestry ahead. Mich. conservation, 28(3):2-7 (May-Jun 1959). facsim., views. On "public forest management" in Michigan, 1909-59. [9391

RAY VOSS. It's your land. Mich. conservation, 21(2):12-16 (Mar-Apr 1952). views. From the Grand Rapids herald. On recreation areas in Michigan owned by the State or by the U.S. Government, 1909-52. [9392

ILO H. BARTLETT. Deer hunting, 1950-1951. Mich. conservation, 20(6):5-7, 21-3 (Nov-Dec 1951). col. diagrs., col. maps. Comparative figures for 1910, 1920, 1930, 1940, and 1950 in Michigan. [9393

ALGER BUELL CRANDELL. Belleville the happy town. [Belleville, Mich.: Belleville Committee of 1912, 1960. 12], 190 p. ports., views (1 double). On the author's life and schooling in Sumpter Township, southwestern Wayne County, 1911-13. [9394

JASON L. HONIGMAN. Edson R. Sunderland's role in Michigan procedure [1915-31]. Mich. law rev., 58:13-18 (Nov 1959). notes. [9395

OTTO FAILING. Pigeon River elk. Mich. conservation, 20(5):4-6, 23 (Sep-Oct 1951). views. On a herd descended from 24 animals imported from Wyoming by the Michigan Public Domain Commission in 1916. [9396

C. HOWARD ROSS. Geriatrics unlimited. Am. Geriatrics Soc., Jour., 7:880-88 (Nov 1959). bibliog. Mainly on the author's observations of the way of living of retired persons in Michigan, 1916-59, and the related medical problems. [9397

CHARLES F. BOEHLER. The pines of Interlochen. Mich. conservation, 23(5):23-5 (Sep-Oct 1954). views. On 200 acres of "original pine forest" in Grand Traverse County that "somehow escaped the lumberman," purchased by the State in 1917 and established as Interlochen State Park. [9398

RALPH I. BLOUCH. Introductions all around. Mich. conservation, 23(3):6-9 (May-Jun 1954). views. On the introduction of non-native wildlife by the Michigan Department of Conservation, 1917-54. [9399

ROBERT GEORGE SCIGLIANO. The Michigan one-man jury and the courts: an appraisal [1917-57]. Univ. Detroit law jour., 37:432-9 (Feb). notes. [9400

RALPH I. BLOUCH. Pheasant anniversary. Mich. conservation, 19(5): 11-12, 26 (Sep-Oct 1950). On the introduction of the ringneck pheasant into Michigan by the Michigan Department of Conservation in 1918 and the open seasons for hunting it, 1925-50. [9401

DONALD W. DOUGLASS. Turn of the tide, 1949. Mich. conservation, 18(5): 3-6 (Sep-Oct 1949). view. On fluctuations or cycles, not entirely understood, in the supply of wild game in Michigan, and the uncertain effects of closed seasons and bounties in controlling wildlife populations, 1918-49. [9402

STANLEY C. HOLLANDER & GARY A. MARPLE. Henry Ford: inventor of the supermarket? East Lansing, 1960. [4], 54, [2] p. tables. notes (p. 42-50). (Michigan State Univ. Bureau of Business and Economic Research. Marketing and transportation paper 9.) On the establishment and operation of retail stores by the Ford Motor Company for the use of its employees, 1919-28. [9403

SOLOMON JACOB AXELROD & W. R. MILLS. Medical manpower in Michigan. Mich. State Med. Soc., Jour., 59:252-7, 779-84, 792 (Feb, May). diagrs., maps, tables. notes. Contents.--The distribution of physicians [1930-57].--Supply of physicians and type of practice [1920-57]. [9404

ARTHUR C. ELMER. Parks and recreation areas [in Michigan, 1920-49], present and future. Mich. conservation, 18(4):3-6 (May-Jun). views. [9405

JOHN FRASER HART. A rural retreat for Northern Negroes. Geog. rev., 50:147-68 (Apr). maps, views. notes. On Negroes in Lake County, Mich., numbering 13 in 1920 and 1,300 in 1950, concentrated near Baldwin and in the "Negro resort and retirement community" at Lake Idlewild, including a high proportion of elderly persons with small incomes, and the effects of their presence upon the economy and government of the county. [9406

RAYMOND DARWIN BURROUGHS. Conservation is big business. Mich. conservation, 20(2):6-8, 22-3 (Mar-Apr 1951). port., view. On the Michigan Department of Conservation, 1921-51. [9407

GERALD ERNEST EDDY. Who foots the bill? Mich. conservation, 29(5):2-6 (Sep-Oct). facsims., views. On the various activities of the Michigan Department of Conservation, 1921-60. [9408

JAMES C. HODGES. 15 million dollars for conservation. Mich. conservation, 25(2):7-9 (Mar-Apr 1956). diagrs. On the use of Federal and State funds for conservation in Michigan, 1921-56. [9409

NICHOLAS V. OLDS. Legal progress to control pollution: Michigan leads the way. Mich. conservation, 21(1):6-8 (Jan-Feb 1952). On the legal control of "pollution of lakes, rivers and streams caused by waste disposal of municipalities, industries and individuals" by the Michigan Stream Control Commission, 1921-51. [9410

WILLIAM E. LAYCOCK. No place for reindeer! Mich. conservation, 29(2): 12-16 (Mar-Apr). views. On an attempt to raise reindeer in Michigan, 1922-27. [9411

WARREN W. SHAPTON. Bear tracks and hound music. Mich. conservation, 19(1):7-10 (Jan-Feb 1950). view. On the regulation of bear-hunting in Michigan, 1925-48. [9412

NICHOLAS V. OLDS. Fishing--a public trust. Mich. conservation, 19(3):33-4 (May-Jun 1950). On litigation about the right to fish in the streams of Michigan, 1926 and 1943. [9413

M. M. BERGMAN. Science, skill, and forest fire. Mich. conservation, 25(3):22-6 (May-Jun 1956). views. On the Forest Fire Experiment Station of the Michigan Department of Conservation, at Roscommon, 1928-56. [9414

MICHIGAN, UNIVERSITY OF. Institute of Public Administration. State supervision of Michigan local governments: the water pollution problem [1929-59]. By Ernest F. Ross. Ann Arbor, 1960. vii p., 64 leaves. notes. On the work of the Stream Control Commission, the Water Resources Commission, and the Department of Health. [9415

G. I. STEWART. Of fires and machines. Mich. conservation, 24(1):15-18 (Jan-Feb 1955). port., views. On the "modern machine shops" at the Forest Fire Experiment Station of the Michigan Department of Conservation, Roscommon, 1929-54. [9416

MARILYN CASTOR. Timber! Mich. conservation, 21(3):11-14 (May-Jun 1952). views. On the Edith E. Pettee Forest, Roscommon County, established in 1930 with money contributed by the students of Eastern High School, Detroit. [9417

M. R. KINDE. W. K. Kellogg Foundation [Battle Creek, Mich., 1930-59]. Jour. med. educ., 34:848-51 (Aug 1959). [9418

RUSSELL McKEE. 25 busy years in conservation. Mich. conservation, 26(1):2-7 (Jan-Feb 1957). views. On the activities of the Michigan Department of Conservation, 1931-56. [9419

W. C. RYDER. Farms and game. Mich. conservation, 18(5):27-9 (Sep-Oct 1949). On "food and cover management for the improvement of small game on privately-owned lands in Michigan," 1932-48. [9420

UNIVERSITY OF MICHIGAN PRESS CLUB. Michigan's tax crisis: addresses delivered to the University of Michigan Press Club, 41st annual meeting, October 10, 11, 1958, Ann Arbor. Edited by Harvey E[lliot] Brazer. Ann Arbor, 1958. [4], 53 leaves. (University of Michigan. Institute of Public Administration. Papers in public administration, 29.) Five lectures, including "Why Michigan has a tax crisis," by Robert S. Ford (leaves 1-9), on tax crises in Michigan since 1932. [9421

T. E. DAW. Remember the CCC? Time stamps approval. ... As told to Russell McKee. Mich. conservation, 24(4):12-14 (Jul-Aug). views. On the Civilian Conservation Corps in Michigan, 1933 ff. [9422

REGARDING Polish commerce and Polish merchants in the State of Michigan. Poles in Michigan Associated, Poles in Michigan (Detroit, 1953 [i. e. 1955]), 1:88-91. On the Federation of Polish Merchants in the State of Michigan, formed in 1933, now the First Division of the National Federation of Polish Merchants. [9423

DURWARD ROBSON. Conservation on the wing. Mich. conservation. 25(4): 8-11 (Jul-Aug 1956). ports., views (1 double). On the use of airplanes by the Michigan Department of Conservation, 1933-56. [9424

SHIRLEY BREHM. What about the women? Mich. conservation,21(1):13-14 (Jan-Feb 1952). On conferences sponsored by women's clubs in Michigan and held at the Conservation Training School, Higgins Lake, 1934-51. [9425

HENRY L. WOOLFENDEN. History of the State Bar of Michigan [1935-59]. Mich. State Bar jour., 38(4):21-56 (Apr 1959). ports., views (part col.). See also "25 years of progress" (addresses by Roscoe O. Bonisteel and George E. Brand), 39(11):20-24 (Nov.). [9426

ILO H. BARTLETT. Those Michigan bow hunters. Mich. conservation, 19(5):15, 29-30 (Sep-Oct 1950). On deer-hunting in Michigan by archers, 1937-49. [9427

STICKS and strings. Mich. conservation, 24(5):15-18 (Sep-Oct 1955). views. On Michigan archers as hunters of wild game, 1937-55. [9428

WARREN W. SHAPTON. P-R report. Mich. conservation, 20(1-5): bimonthly installments (Jan-Oct 1951). On the use of funds provided by the Pittman-Robertson Act for wildlife restoration, land acquisition, and "scientific research into all types of game problems" in Michigan, 1938-51. [9429

O. H. CLARK. Habitat improvement--to provide more fish. Mich. conservation. 18(3):15-20 (May-Jun 1949). views. On Michigan legislation for "lake and stream improvement," 1939-49. [9430

HOWARD T. KNOBLOCH. "Fern was a doctor's doctor, parent's doctor, patient's doctor." Mich. State Med. Soc., Jour., 59:455-9 (Mar). ports. On the pediatric practice of Louis Fernald Foster (died 1959) in Bay City, Mich., during the years of the author's association with him, 1939 ff. [9431

JAMES T. MORGAN & M. B. DICKERMAN. Return of the forest. Mich. conservation, 29(1):18-21 (Jan-Feb). views. On the restoration of "northern Lower Peninsula forests" in Michigan since ca. 1939. [9432

KENNETH CHIEN ING CHENG. Economic development and geographical disparities in farm wage rates in Michigan, 1940-1957. Ann Arbor: University Microfilms, 1959. Positive microfilm of typescript. [241] leaves. Thesis--Michigan State Univ. Abstracted: Dissert. abstracts, 20:4552 (Jun). [9433

RAYMOND DARWIN BURROUGHS. Michigan's training center for conservation. Mich. conservation, 26(1): 15-18 (Jan-Feb 1957). views. On the Michigan Department of Conservation Training School, Higgins Lake, 1941-57. [9434

DAWNE HULETT. Michigan calf ropers [1941-51]. Quarter horse jour., 3(9):8-9, 28 (Jun 1951). views. [9435

PAUL WOODARD THOMPSON. The Michigan Botanical Club [1941-53]. Asa Gray bul., 2:196-8 (spring 1953). [9436

CASH HENRY WONSER. Southern Michigan deer hunting. Mich. conservation, 18(6):21-3 (Nov-Dec 1949). col. map. On open seasons, 1941-48, to control deer populations that had multiplied excessively in the years before 1941, when the killing of deer was illegal in the southern counties. [9437

CECIL M. BIRCH. Local revenue and taxing powers [in Michigan, 1942-57]. Mich. Acad. Science, Papers, 45: 169-77. tables. [9438

EARL GOLZ. The Michigan quarter horse industry [in Berrien County, 1945-59]. Quarter horse jour., 12(3): 144, 176 (Dec 1959). port., views. [9439

RALPH JOSSMAN. The Forty Year Marketable Title Act [Michigan, effective beginning in 1948]: a reappraisal. Univ. Detroit law jour., 37:422-31 (Feb). notes. On an act for the control of land-title litigation. [9440

E. H. KIDDER & J. R. DAVIS. Supplemental irrigation on sandy soils in Michigan [1948-53]. Agric. engineering, 34:761-5, 768 (Nov 1953). diagrs., maps, tables. notes. [9441

SIDNEY SONENBLUM. Regional economic analysis and social accounts: an interindustry application [Kalamazoo County, Mich., 1954]. Ann Arbor: University Microfilms, 1959 [i. e. 1960]. Positive microfilm of typescript. iv, 275 leaves. tables. bibliog. (leaves 270-75). Thesis--Columbia Univ. Abstracted: Dissert. abstracts, 20:3545-6 (Mar). [9442

BRUCE CATTON. The real Michigan. Detroit Hist. Soc., Bul., 15(7):4-8 (Apr 1959). port. (on cover), view. Excerpts reprinted from Holiday, 1957, on the characteristics of Michigan; with reminiscences of the author's early life in Benzonia. [9443

Detroit

DANIEL B. REIBEL. But who owned the land? Detroit Hist. Soc., Bul., 16(6):6-11 (Mar). maps (1 double), views. notes. On the titles to the lands in and around Detroit, 1700-1829, with special reference to feudal titles and Indian titles. [9444

NEIL CAROTHERS. Deming and Jones families in early Detroit [1818-97]. Detroit Soc. Geneal. Research mag., 23:141-6 (summer). On De Garmo Jones (1787-1846), John Jay Deming (1792-1864), John Palmer (born 1796), and some of their descendants in Detroit (none recorded since 1897). [9445

PHILEMON D. SABBE & LEON BUYSE. Belgians in America. Tielt: Lannoo [1960]. 317 p. ports., views. notes. On Belgians (especially Flemings) in Detroit since 1832. [9446

LUDWIK GOZDAWA. First Polish settlers in Detroit [1837-70]. Poles in Michigan Associated, Poles in Michigan (Detroit, 1953 [i. e. 1955]), 1:41-4. [9447

HARRY N. SCHEIBER. George Bancroft and the Bank of Michigan, 1837-41. Mich. hist., 44:82-90 (Mar). notes. On the relations between this Detroit bank and the U.S. Government, and the work of Bancroft as the bank's "agent and lobbyist." [9448

Mrs. ROY HATHAWAY. Country schools of yesterday in and near present day Highland Park [1840s to ca. 1900]. Detroit Hist. Soc., Bul., 16(2):4-9 (Nov 1959). map. views. [9449

CENTRAL METHODIST CHURCH, Detroit. Central Methodist Church records, Detroit, Michigan. Copied from the original records by Mrs. W. Dale Perkins and Mrs. Raymond H. Millbrook. Detroit Soc. Geneal. Research mag., 23:23-8, 69-74, 121-6, 161-4 (fall 1959-summer 1960). Membership list (1841-55), baptisms (1841-70), and marriages (1856-70). [9450

ST. STEPHEN'S EPISCOPAL CHURCH OF WYANDOTTE, MICHIGAN. St. Stephen's Episcopal Church of Wyandotte, Michigan: a centennial record, 1860-1960. Wyandotte: St. Stephen's Episcopal Parish [1960. 16], 96 p. facsims., ports., tables, views. bibliog. (p. [9]). Prepared by the "Book Project," Mrs. Joseph C. De Windt, Chairman. [9451

The ORIGIN and growth of the first Polish parish in Detroit [St. Albertus Parish, 1871-75]. Poles in Michigan Associated, Poles in Michigan (Detroit, 1953 [i. e. 1955]), 1:45-9. [9452

R. JARZABKOWSKA. History of the Polish press in Detroit [1874-1900]. Poles in Michigan Associated, Poles in Michigan (Detroit, 1953 [i. e. 1955]), 1:77-81. [9453

GEORGE WASHINGTON STARK. Time and the old City Hall. Detroit Hist. Soc., Bul., 16(3):4-9 (Dec 1959). views. Memories of City Hall and the adjoining areas of Detroit since the 1880s. [9454

BENJAMIN STANCZYK. The rise and growth of the Polish National Alliance in Detroit. Poles in Michigan Associated, Poles in Michigan (Detroit, 1953 [i. e. 1955]), 1:50-53. On the Detroit members and units of the Alliance, 1885-1931. [9455

JOY REESE SHAW. Gustave Albin Carlson [born 1877]. Am. Swed. Hist. Found., Yr. bk., 1960, p. 55-62. On his early life in Sweden, his emigration to America in 1891, his work as engineer and inventor in various factories in Detroit, and his founding of the Detroit Stamping Company, makers of mantles and dies. [9456

GEORGE WASHINGTON STARK. Sixty cycles of song. Detroit Hist. Soc., Bul., 16(8):4-9 (May). ports., view. On the Orpheus Club of Detroit, "Detroit's greatest singing unit," 1900-1960; with some account of "male choral singing" in Detroit as early as 1879. [9457

CYNTHIA BOYES YOUNG. WWJ--pioneer in broadcasting. Mich. hist., 44:411-33 (Dec). notes. On the Detroit News radio station, 1920-28, and the interest of James E. Scripps, founder of the News, in Detroit radio as early as 1901. [9458

GEORGE WASHINGTON STARK. The Players. Detroit Hist. Soc., Bul., 17(2):4-10 (Nov). On a Detroit Thespian organization, 1910-60, and the Players' Playhouse, built in 1925. [9459

CLARA SWIECZKOWSKI. Central Citizen's Committee. Poles in Michigan Associated, Poles in Michigan (Detroit, 1953 [i. e. 1955]), 1:82-7. Recollections of a committee representing Polish parochial and fraternal organizations in Detroit, formed to send aid to Poland after a flood in 1914 and continued as an organization for war relief and the recruitment of soldiers for the Polish Army in World Wars I and II and for the promotion of Polish interests in the United States. [9460

ALBERT J. MAYER. Russel Woods, change without conflict: a case study of neighborhood racial transition in Detroit [1919-56]. Nathan Glazer & Davis McEntire, eds., Studies in housing & minority groups (Berkeley: Univ. of California Press, 1960), p. 198-220. [9461

KUPPY SCOTT. Streets of Hamtramck. [Edited by Archie Green.] West. folklore, 19:58-60 (Jan). Parody of "The cowboy's lament," written by Miss Scott "for a specific strike situation--the Dodge Pension Strike of 1949." [9462

WISCONSIN

ROBERT LEONARD HALL. The Carcajou site (Je2) and Oneota development in Wisconsin. Ann Arbor: University Microfilms, 1960. Positive microfilm of typescript. [448] leaves. Thesis--Univ. of Wisconsin. Abstracted: Dissert. abstracts, 21:424 (Sep). On a site in Jefferson County, Wis., occupied by a Winnebago village in the years 1828-32 but yielding charcoal samples dated by radiocarbon analysis 998, 1028, and 1528 ± 250 years. [9463

HAMILTON NELSON ROSS. La Pointe [Wis.]--village outpost [1362-1957]. St. Paul: North Central Pub. Co., 1960. xix, 200 p. diagrs., maps (part double), plans, ports., tables, views. bibliog. (p. 185-9), notes. [9464

NANCY (OESTREICH) LURIE. Winnebago protohistory. Stanley Diamond, ed., Culture in history: essays in honor of Paul Radin (N.Y.: Columbia Univ. Press for Brandeis Univ., 1960), p. 790-808. notes. Evidence, 1623-74, that the historic Winnebago Indians of Wisconsin are not descended from the prehistoric Winnebagoes. [9465

LOIS BARLAND. Sawdust City. [Stevens Point, Wis.: Worzalla Pub. Co., 1960. 8], 139, [1] p. diagrs., maps, ports., tables, views. bibliog. (p. 139). History of Eau Claire, Wis., 1767-1910. [9466

PETER T. HARSTAD. Sickness and disease on the Wisconsin frontier. Wis. mag. hist., 43:83-96, 203-20, 253-63 (winter-summer). facsim., map, ports., views. Based on thesis (M. A.)--Univ. of Wisconsin. Contents.--Malaria, 1820-1850.--Cholera [1832-55].--Smallpox and other diseases [1770-1852]. [9467

MILWAUKEE ADVERTISING CLUB. Ten major Wisconsin industries [1827-1960. Reprinted from Torch, the publication of the Milwaukee Advertising Club. Madison:] Governor's Office, Division of Industrial and Port Development [1960?]. 50 p. facsim., ports., views. Ten sections, each by a different contributor, on "paper, food, machinery, electrical machinery, printing industry, transportation industry, fabricated metals, primary metals, chemical industry, [and] banking and insurance." [9468

GRAHAM PARKER HAWKS. Increase A[llen] Lapham [1811-75], Wisconsin's first scientist. Ann Arbor: University Microfilms, 1960. Positive microfilm of typescript. [314] leaves. Thesis--Univ. of Wisconsin. Abstracted: Dissert. abstracts, 21:1542 (Dec). On his studies of the natural history and the archeology of Wisconsin, and his business and civic activities there, 1836-75. [9469

GEORGE J. KUEHNL. The Wisconsin business corporation [1836-75]. Madison: Univ. of Wisconsin Press, 1959. x, [2], 284 p. tables. notes. (p. 225-69). Deals particularly with Wisconsin law governing corporations. [9470

SANDRA LINE. A doctor in retrospect. Wis. med. jour., 59:166-8 (Feb). view. On Christian Linde (1814-87), Danish emigrant, physician in Oshkosh from 1842 till his death. [9471

NASHOTAH HOUSE, Nashotah, Wis. Nashotah liturgy. With introduction by Edward S. White. P. E. Church, Hist. mag., 29:197-301 (Dec). facsims.

notes. "Office of devotion of the united brethren of the religious house established at Nashotah, W. T.," a manuscript for use by "a brotherhood of celibate clergy," 1842, perhaps prepared by the Rev. James Lloyd Breck. [9472

ANGELIA KUMLIEN MAIN (1883-1952). Thure Kumlien [1819-88], Swedish-American naturalist. Am. Swed. Hist. Found., Yr. bk., 1960, p. 69-76. notes. On his emigration from Sweden in 1843, his settlement at Lake Koshkonong, his work as a collector of birds, their nests and eggs for Eastern purchasers, his teaching of natural history and service as Conservator to the Public Museum in Milwaukee, his correspondence with scholars in the East and in Europe, and his writings on natural history. [9473

RICHARD W. E. PERRIN. An architectural remnant of Old Muskego: John Bergen's log house. Wis. mag. hist., 44:12-14 (autumn). views. notes. On a house built probably by Østen Gullickson Moland, probably ca. 1843, still standing, and the Norwegian elements in its design and carpentry. [9474

RICHARD W. E. PERRIN. A Fachwerk church in Wisconsin. Wis. mag. hist., 43:239-44 (summer). facsim., plan, views. notes. Information from a manuscript "Chronica" kept by the Rev. L. F. E. Krause, concerning the architecture of Trinity Evangelical Lutheran Church, Friestadt, Ozaukee County, Wis., a half-timber structure built for a congregation of some 20 German families, 1844-45, dismantled in 1870. [9475

FRANCIS J. DEMET. Massive resistance and Negro rights in Wisconsin [1847-66]. Wis. mag. hist., 43:288-9 (summer). [9476

JOHN OWEN. "The natives are grasping": a Welshman's letter from Wisconsin. Edited by Wilbur S. Shepperson. Wis. mag. hist., 43:129-32 (winter). notes. Translated letter to Griffith Owen in Wales, dated Baraboo, near Fort Winnebago, Wis., 27 May 1847, on the "exceptionally good" land in Wisconsin, the good prospects of the author and other Welsh farmers recently settled there, and the need for Welsh Methodist missionaries. [9477

WILLIAM F. HOEFS & 3 others. Wisconsin law relating to protection of the family on death of the property owner. Wis. law rev., 1960:110-26 (Jan). notes. On inheritance rights of surviving spouses and descendants, 1849-1957. [9478

SAM J. RECHT. Venue in civil actions in Wisconsin [1849-1960]. Wis. law rev., 1960:663-82 (Jul). notes. [9479

JOSEPH BARTHOLOMEW CASAGRANDE. John Mink [1850?-1943], Ojibwa informant. Joseph B. Casagrande, ed., In the company of men: twenty portraits by anthropologists (N.Y.: Harper [1960]), p. 467-88. port. On the "spiritual leader of a small company of 'pagans'" in Lac Court Oreilles Indian Reservation in northwestern Wisconsin; with Ojibwa lore and traditions collected from him by Casagrande between 1941 and 1943. [9480

R. CHARLES WATHEN. Warranty and deceit--remedy for misrepresentation in contract negotiations [in Wisconsin, 1853-1949]. Marquette law rev., 43:244-51 (fall 1959). notes. [9481

FRANK S. BECK. Christian communists in America: a history of the Colony of Saint Nazianz, Wisconsin, during the pastorate of its founder, Father Ambrose Oschwald, 1854-1873. St. Paul, 1959. [2], vii p., viii-ix leaves, 181 p. bibliog. (p. 178-81), notes. Thesis (M. A.)--Saint Paul Seminary, St. Paul, Minn. On a settlement of German emigrants from the Grand Duchy of Baden, in Manitowoc County, Wis.; with a biographical sketch of Father Oschwald (1801-73). [9482

PAXTON HART. The making of Menominee County. Wis. mag. hist., 43:181-9 (spring). map, views. notes. On the Menominee Indian Reservation, 1854-1958, the proposed transfer of the tribal assets to Menominee Enterprises, Inc., and the proposed formation of Menominee County in 1959. [9483

MAURICE M. VANCE. Charles Richard Van Hise [1857-1918]: scientist progressive. Madison: State Historical Soc. of Wisconsin, 1960. [8], 246 p. music, ports. bibliog. (p. 223-7), notes (p. 189-222). On his life in Wisconsin, his studies at the University of Wisconsin, his service as Geologist in Charge, Lake Superior Division, U.S. Geological Survey (1888-1903), and as President of the University of

Wisconsin (1903-18), his teaching of geology and his publications in that field, and his many other activities and interests. [9484

BERNARD P. BERRY. The survival of a jurisprudential anomaly: the dead man's rule in Wisconsin. Marquette law rev., 43:73-88 (summer 1959). notes. On the rule as "the last relic of the disqualification by interest rule," abolished by many States since 1843 and by Wisconsin in 1858, at which time Wisconsin enacted "the first dead man's statute." [9485

WAUKESHA DAILY FREEMAN. Waukesha daily freeman, 1859-1959: a century of community service to Greater Waukesha. [Waukesha: Freeman Print. Co., 1959. 296] p. 58 cm. maps, ports., views. Weekly supplements to this newspaper, 28 Mar.-20 Jun. 1959, on early settlers, "Our country neighbors," communications, organizations, government, recreation, education, industry, transportation, culture, science, business, and the future. [9486

ROBERT SIDNEY MAXWELL. Emmanuel L[orenz] Philipp [1861-1925], Wisconsin stalwart. Madison: State Historical Soc. of Wisconsin, 1959. xvi, 272 p. ports., views. bibliog. (p. 260-64), notes (p. 223-59). On his early years as a farm boy in Sauk County, his several business enterprises, his opposition to "the progressive machine" of the Lafollette organization, his victory in a libel suit against McClure's magazine for printing falsehoods about rebates, his success in establishing "the nucleus of a conservative Republican organization in Wisconsin," and his service as Governor of Wisconsin from 1914 to 1920. [9487

Mrs. R. E. BANNEN. Most doctors per square mile. Wis. med. jour., 59:685-6 (Oct). On 11 physicians born in Scott Township, Crawford County, Wis., between 1863 and 1925. [9488

STATE HISTORICAL SOCIETY OF WISCONSIN. The way it was, [by] Raymond S. Sivesind: a report by the Chief of the Society's Sites and Markers Division. Wis. mag. hist., 43: 273-6 (summer). maps, views. On the restoration of the house of Nelson Dewey at Stonefield (built 1868) and several other early buildings. [9489

THEDA RADFORD. A 1900 doctor: Dr. Burton Clark [born 1869]. Wis. med. jour., 59:386-8 (Jun). port. From Badger history, Jan. 1960. On his early life in rural Waushara County, Wis., his studies at the University of Wisconsin and Rush Medical College (Chicago), and his practice of medicine in Oshkosh. [9490

ROLLA U. CAIRNS. Pierce County. Wis. med. jour., 59:585-6 (Sep). On the physicians of Pierce County, Wis., 1870-1926. [9491

LUTIE EUGENIA STEARNS (1866-1943). My seventy-five years. [Edited by Beryl E. Whitney.] Wis. mag. hist., 42:211-18, 282-7; 43:97-105 (spring 1959-winter 1960). ports., view. Reminiscences of the author's life in Milwaukee, 1871-1942, her work as a teacher, her organization of Wisconsin libraries, her lectures and books on librarianship and other subjects, her support of woman suffrage, prohibition, and world peace, her weekly column in the Milwaukee journal, and her associations with Jane Addams, Ellen Clara Sabin, Myrtle Reed, Zona Gale, Frank A. Hutchins, and others. [9492

MARTIN JAMES GILLEN (1872-1943). Martin J. Gillen's boyhood reminiscences [1926]. Edited by George S. May. Wis. mag. hist., 43:121-8 (winter). On the author's life in Racine as the son of a prosperous "marine contractor," his Catholic upbringing, his studies in parochial and public schools in Racine, and his attendance at the University of Wisconsin, 1892-96. [9493

ELMER EDWARD NOYES. The window glass industry of Omro, Wisconsin. Wis. mag. hist., 43:108-18 (winter). views. notes. On the Omro Glass Company, 1876-78. [9494

RUDOLPH J. VECOLI. Sterilization: a Progressive measure? Wis. mag. hist., 43:190-202 (spring). notes. On the "tendency to see paupers, criminals, the insane, and the feebleminded as products of evil heredity," "the racist and elitist implications of the eugenic doctrines," the development of these theories in Wisconsin after 1877, "the restriction of procreation among the unfit" by segregation, restrictive marriage laws, and sterilization, the strong Progressive support of the Wisconsin sterilization law enacted in 1913, and its congruity with "the Progressive mentality ... in a reform movement basically middle class in leadership and outlook." [9495

LEE M. MODJESKA. Psychology and law: an examination of the concept of insane delusions. Wis. law rev., 1960: 54-73 (Jan). notes. On "the doctrine of insane delusions in relation to testamentary capacity" in Wisconsin, 1878-1957. [9496

PAULA BORCHERS. Charles [W.] Oviatt [1853-1912], miracle doctor. Wis. med. jour., 59:340-42 (May). port. From Badger history, Feb. 1960. On his practice of medicine in Oshkosh, 1888-1912, and his eminence as a surgeon; with some account of his early life in Cleveland and his studies at Oberlin College and Jefferson Medical College, Philadelphia. [9497

DENIS ROOKSBY. The Sandley story. San Francisco: Hesperian House [1960]. 72, [6] p. diagr., facsim., plan, ports., views (1 col.). On the Sandley Light Railway Equipment Works at Janesville, Wis., maker of miniature locomotives and cars, and the Riverside and Great Northern Railway at Wisconsin Dells, a 15-inch gage line to accommodate tourists, 1950-60, established by Elmer M. Sandley (born 1891), for many years a Chicago railroad mechanic, and his son Norman Kenneth Sandley (born 1926); with some account of their earlier lives in Wisconsin and Chicago. [9498

STAR Prairie will long remember its beloved Doctor Perrin. Wis. med. jour., 59:771-2 (Dec). port. On Henry E. Perrin (1869-1952), his studies at Northwestern University Medical School, and his service from ca. 1894 to 1952 as a physician in St. Croix County, Wis. [9499

JAMES BENNETT GRIFFIN. A hypothesis for the prehistory of the Winnebago. Stanley Diamond, ed., Culture in history: essays in honor of Paul Radin (N.Y.: Columbia Univ. Press for Brandeis Univ., 1960), p. 809-65. diagrs., maps, table, views. bibliog. Conclusions from archeological investigations of prehistoric Winnebago sites in Wisconsin, 1900-1957. [9500

CHARLES Q. KAMPS. Interference with contractual relations: a survey of the Wisconsin law [1901-56]. Marquette law rev., 43:231-43 (fall 1959). notes. On "the tort of inducing a breach of contract ... extended so as to impose liability for acts rendering performance of a contract impossible." [9501

GEORGE CLARKE SELLERY. Some ferments at Wisconsin, 1901-1947: memories and reflections. Madison: Univ. of Wisconsin Press for the Univ. of Wisconsin Library, 1960. vii, 124 p. port. On "controversies" in the University of Wisconsin during the period of the author's service as Dean of the College of Letters and Science, particularly those centered in intercollegiate athletics, the administrative policies of Presidents C. R. Van Hise and Glenn Frank, and the Experimental College (1927-32) under Alexander Meiklejohn. [9502

JOHN COBB. Kemah Arabians. West. horseman, 25(12):18, 72-3 (Nov). ports., view. On the breeding and raising of Arabian horses by Albert W. Harris, "the 'dean' of the Arabian horse breeders in America," and his son, Norman Harris (Chicago banker), at Kemah, Wis., 1907-60. [9503

HERBERT LAWRENCE GAEDE. The development of the water power of the Wisconsin River [1907-57]. Ann Arbor: University Microfilms, 1959 [i. e. 1960]. Positive microfilm of typescript. x, 308 leaves. diagrs., maps. bibliog. (leaves 305-8). Thesis--Northwestern Univ. Abstracted: Dissert. abstracts, 20:3688 (Mar). [9504

WALTER C. ANDREWS, WILLIAM A. FISCHER, & ROBERT M. MOORE. Raymond G[regory] Arveson, M.D., 1883-1960. Jour. lancet, 80:523-5 (Nov). port. On his practice of medicine in Frederic, Wis., 1909-60. [9505

CLAUDE LEVI-STRAUSS. Four Winnebago myths: a structural sketch. Stanley Diamond, ed., Culture in history: essays in honor of Paul Radin (N.Y.: Columbia Univ. Press for Brandeis Univ., 1960), p. 352-62. diagr. notes. Comparison (with respect to theme and structure) of 4 myths collected by Radin between 1909 and 1912. [9506

SAMUEL TRASK DANA. Half century of progress. Am. forests, 66(7):32-5, 90 (Jul). ports., views. On the Forest Products Laboratory of the U.S. Forest Service at Madison, Wis., 1910-60. [9507

SAM BLOWSNAKE. The autobiography of a Winnebago Indian. [Edited by] Paul Radin. Margaret Mead & Ruth L. Bunzel, eds., The golden age of American anthropology (N.Y.: George Braziller, 1960), p. 602-9. From Crashing Thunder: the autobiography of a Winnebago Indian (1926), edited by Radin. The first printing of this narrative, The autobiography of a Winnebago Indian (1920), designates the Indian as Sam Blowsnake. In the 1926 reprint his family is "named Blow Snake" and the narrator is apparently designated as "Crashing Thunder, the younger brother of the family"; no reference is made to the name "Sam." Neither text indicates the date of birth of the Indian or specifies whether the narrative was written by him or dictated to Radin or another recorder. [9508

JOHN HIEH RIEW. Forty years of property values in Wisconsin [1920s-50s]. Ann Arbor: University Microfilms, 1960. Positive microfilm of typescript. [212] leaves. Thesis--Univ. of Wisconsin. Abstracted: Dissert, abstracts, 20:4305-6 (May). Information from rural and urban real-estate tax records. [9509

R. FRANKLIN SMITH. "Oldest station in the nation"? Jour. broadcasting, 4:40-57 (winter). notes. Examination of the claim of WHA (University of Wisconsin) to this distinction, 1920-59. [9510

RICHARD C. NINNEMAN & DAVID L. WALTHER. Abolition of breach of promise [to marry] in Wisconsin--scope and constitutionality [1925-60]. Marquette law rev., 43:341-64 (winter). notes. [9511

MARY ELIZABETH THOMPSON. The Wisconsin Idea in the Wisconsin High School Forensic Association [founded as the Wisconsin Lyceum Association in 1895]. Ann Arbor: University Microfilms, 1960. Positive microfilm of typescript. [161] leaves. Thesis--Northwestern Univ. Abstracted: Dissert. abstracts, 21:1293 (Nov). On the sponsorship of the Association since 1925 by the Extension Division of the University of Wisconsin. [9512

HERBERT DUBACKER. Airborne penmanship. Flying, 65(5):40, 78-9 (Nov 1959). ports., view. On the use of airplanes by the Parker Pen Company, Janesville, Wis., to move its executives and dealers and their families and to rush shipments of its product, 1928-59. [9513

RICHARD GLEN GREENWOOD. Assumption of risk in automobile cases [in Wisconsin, 1930-59]. Marquette law rev., 43:203-16 (fall 1959). notes. On "acquiescence or a willingness to proceed in the face of danger" by a guest rider who has "knowledge and appreciation" of the danger and does not use his opportunity to protest against it. [9514

RICHARD G. GUILFORD. The impact of Federal grants-in-aid for "child welfare services" on the development of the local public child welfare program in the State of Wisconsin, 1936-1952. Chicago: [Dept. of Photoduplication, Univ. of Chicago Library] 1960. Positive microfilm of typescript. vi, 136 leaves. tables. bibliog. (leaves 134-6). Thesis--Univ. of Chicago. [9515

FRANK ALLAN HANNA, JOSEPH A. PECHMAN, & SIDNEY M. LERNER. Analysis of Wisconsin income. N.Y.: National Bureau of Economic Research [1948]. xviii, 261, [5] p. diagrs., tables. notes. (Conference on Research in Income and Wealth. Studies in income and wealth, 9.) Statistical examination of income received in Wisconsin, 1936. [9516

JOHN F. COOK. The battle against blight. Marquette law rev., 43:444-58 (spring). notes. On Wisconsin legislation and decisions concerning "slum and blighted areas" in cities, 1945-60. [9517

ALAN D. WADE. The Youth Authority proposal [of the American Law Institute] in Wisconsin: a history of the Youth Service Program, 1947 to 1949. Social service rev., 34:354 (Sep). Abstract of thesis--Univ. of Chicago. [9518

Milwaukee

HERBERT PAUL BRUMDER. The life story of George and Henriette Brumder. [Milwaukee:] Printed by the North American Press [1960]. xii, 148 p. facsims., maps, ports., tables, geneal. tables, views. On the author's grandparents, George Brumder (1839-1910) and Henriette (Brandhorst) Brumder (1841-1924), German emigrants in 1853, his work in Milwaukee as a bookseller, a printer, and a publisher of German-language books and periodicals, their 11 children, and some of their further descendants. [9519

ADOLF GERD KORMAN. A social history of industrial growth and immigrants: a study with particular reference to Milwaukee, 1890-1920. Ann Arbor: University Microfilms, 1959 [i. e. 1960]. Positive microfilm of typescript. vi, 485 leaves. maps, tables. bibliog. (leaves 460-85). Thesis--Univ. of Wisconsin. Abstracted: Dissert. abstracts, 20:2776-7 (Jan). [9520

The West North Central States

JACK WARNER SCHAEFER. Dakota [its traditions and characteristics]. Holiday, American panorama west of the Mississippi: a Holiday magazine book (Garden City, N.Y.: Doubleday [1960]), p. 301-19. On the former Dakota Territory, its geographic unity, and its political division into 2 States. [9521

JAMES HENRI HOWARD, ed. Two Teton Dakota winter count texts. N. D. hist., 27:67-79 (Apr). view. bibliog., notes. "Calendrical records," the first by John No-Ear (died 1918), covering the years 1759-1918, the second perhaps by Edward Roan-Bear (born ca. 1860, living in 1952), covering the years 1850-1906--each in Dakota text and English translation. [9522

JOHN INSLEY BLAIR (1802-99). Surveying the first railroad across Iowa: the journal of John I. Blair. Edited by Anthony L. Cassen. Ann. Ia., 35:321-62 (summer). map, port. notes. Record by a Pennsylvania capitalist of his travels in a party of 10 to examine a route for the Cedar Rapids & Missouri River Railroad from Boonsboro, Ia., to Columbus, Neb., and back to the railroad at Marshalltown, 15-29 Jun. 1863, and his return by rail to Blairstown, Pa., where he arrived 3 Jul. 1863. [9523

JAY ARTHUR MYERS. The first ninety years. Jour. lancet, 80:191-3 (May). On the Northwestern medical and surgical journal (1870-72), the Northwestern lancet (1881-1911), and the Journal lancet to 1960, serving the medical profession particularly in Minnesota and the Dakotas. [9524

JOHN FRETZ FUNK (1835-1930). John F. Funk's trip to Manitoba in 1873. Edited by Melvin Gingerich. Mennonite quar. rev., 34:147-50 (Apr). Letter to the author's wife, dated on the steamer Dakota on the Red River of the North, 27-29 Jun. 1873, about his travels with a Mennonite land-inspection party from Fargo, N. D., to Fort Garry and back to Grand Forks, including an excursion 30 miles west from Pembina. [9525

MELVIN GINGERICH. Russian Mennonites react to their new environment. Mennonite life, 15:175-81 (Oct). views. bibliog. On their experiences in Kansas, Nebraska, Minnesota, and the Dakotas, 1873-79. [9526

MELVIN GINGERICH. The reactions of the Russian Mennonite immigrants of the 1870's to the American frontier. Mennonite quar. rev., 34:137-46 (Apr). notes. Based upon letters from Mennonites in Iowa, Minnesota, Kansas, Nebraska, and the Dakotas, 1874-79. [9527

HARRY A. DIENER. Kansas-Nebraska Mennonite Conference (1879-1920). Mennonite hist. bul., 15(2):2-3 (Apr 1954). [9528

CATHERINE CORSON WEST. Olga Sophie Hansen [born 1890], M. D. [Mrs. J. C. Litzenberg]. Jour. lancet, 80:401-4 (Aug). port. On her early life in South Dakota and her medical practice since 1916 in Minneapolis. [9529

JOHN G. ARNEBERG. From mountains to prairies: a Norwegian-American saga. Minneapolis, 1958. x, 215 p. ports. On the author's emigration from Norway in 1892, his life as "a farm worker, teacher, and book agent" in the Red River Valley of Minnesota and North Dakota, his medical studies in the University of Minnesota (1901-5) and abroad, and his practice of medicine in Leeds, N. D. (1905-7) and in Grand Forks; with full accounts of his several later visits to Europe, and homilies on politics and international affairs. [9530

SIMON GINGERICH. A history of the Iowa-Nebraska Conference [1920-49]. Mennonite hist. bul., 13(3):5-7 (Jul 1952). notes. Omits appendixes to be found in the manuscript (deposited in the Goshen College Historical Library). [9531

HAROLD BYRON ALLEN. Distribution patterns of place-name pronunciations. Names, 6:74-9 (Jun 1958). maps. Study of field records of the Linguistic Atlas of the Upper Midwest; with maps showing distribution of pronunciations of Des Moines, Omaha, Chicago, Illinois, Missouri, and Iowa in 5 West North Central States, and references to changes from "the historical pronunciation." [9532

MINNESOTA

THEODORE CHRISTIAN BLEGEN & THEODORE L. NYDAHL. Minnesota history: a guide to reading and study.

Minneapolis: Univ. of Minnesota Press [1960. 10], 223 p. maps. bibliogs. 1st ed. 1937. An outline or syllabus, with references for further study. [9533

THEODORE CHRISTIAN BLEGEN. What's past is prologue. Lawrence Martin Brings, ed., Minnesota heritage (Minneapolis: T. S. Denison [1960]), p. 2-9. port. On the relation between the American past and the American present, with illustrations from Minnesota. [9534

GRACE FLANDRAU. Minnesota [its traditions and characteristics]. Holiday, American panorama west of the Mississippi: a Holiday magazine book (Garden City, N.Y.: Doubleday [1960]), p. 355-70. [9535

RUSSELL W. FRIDLEY. Preserving and interpreting Minnesota's historic sites. Minn. hist., 37:58-70 (Jun). views. [9536

J. MERLE HARRIS. Minnesota heritage in the making. Lawrence Martin Brings, ed., Minnesota heritage (Minneapolis: T. S. Denison [1960]), p. 10-39. diagrs., maps, tables, views. bibliog. On the geology and natural resources of Minnesota in relation to its history. [9537

WARREN KLIEWER, ed. More Low German children's rhymes. Mennonite life, 15:173-4, 180 (Oct). Ten texts collected in and near Mountain Lake, Minn., "spoken by children to children," with translations. [9538

WILLIAM MADISON (Indian name: May-zhuc-ke-ge-shig or Clearing Sky) & WINIFRED JOURDAIN. Our Ojibway or Chippeway neighbors [in Minnesota and adjacent Canada since prehistoric times]. Lawrence Martin Brings, ed., Minnesota heritage (Minneapolis: T. S. Denison [1960]), p. 82-8. ports., views. [9539

LLOYD ALDEN WILFORD. The first Minnesotans. Lawrence Martin Brings, ed., Minnesota heritage (Minneapolis: T. S. Denison [1960]), p. 40-79. diagrs., map, ports., views. On the Indians of Minnesota since prehistoric times. [9540

GRACE LEE NUTE. By Minnesota waters. Lawrence Martin Brings, ed., Minnesota heritage (Minneapolis: T. S. Denison [1960]), p. 89-119. facsims., maps (1 double), music, ports., views. On "waterways ... in Minnesota history," ca. 1618 to ca. 1850. Includes some account of the voyageurs, the exploration of the headwaters of the Mississippi, and the missions among the Indians in the canoe country of northern Minnesota. [9541

DANIEL J. HAFREY. The church [Catholic and Protestant] in Minnesota [1630s-1960]. Lawrence Martin Brings, ed., Minnesota heritage (Minneapolis: T. S. Denison [1960]), p. 139-47. port., views. [9542

JAY ARTHUR MYERS. Invited and conquered: historical sketch of tuberculosis in Minnesota [1659-1948. St. Paul: Minnesota Public Health Assoc., 1949.] xvii, 738 p. diagrs., facsims., ports., tables, views. On incidence, treatment, hospitals and sanatoria, health officers and boards of health, organizations and associations, surveys, specialists, etc. Acknowledges the joint authorship of Theodore L. Streukens, Jr. (1913-40), a victim of tuberculosis, for the section dealing with the period before 1900. [9543

ANNA AUGUSTA (VON HELMHOLTZ) PHELAN. Writers and poets of Minnesota [since 1680]. Lawrence Martin Brings, ed., Minnesota heritage (Minneapolis: T. S. Denison [1960]), p. 400-405. Mainly quotations from an article by John K. Sherman (1949). Appended: "Poets of Minnesota," 1935-58, by Margarette Ball Dickson. [9544

JULIUS ANTHONY COLLER II. The Shakopee story. [Shakopee, Minn.: North Star Pictures, 1960.] xvi, 772 p. facsims., map, ports., tables, views. notes (p. 734-45). On a community settled in 1851; with some account of the area since 1681. [9545

DEWEY ALBINSON & 10 others. Art in Minnesota: painting, sculpture, and architecture [early 1800s to 1960]. Lawrence Martin Brings, ed., Minnesota heritage (Minneapolis: T. S. Denison [1960]), p. 390-99. views. [9546

WILLIAM ANDERSON. Intergovernmental relations in review. Minneapolis: Univ. of Minnesota Press [1960]. xix, 178, [1] p. tables. notes (p. 167-71). (Intergovernmental relations in the United States (as observed in Minnesota): a series of monographs edited by William Anderson and Edward W. Weidner, 10.) On the relations between and among the Federal, State, and local governments in Minnesota, 1805-1959, and their "competitive-cooperative situation" as an example of the workings of federalism. Completes a series of 10 monographs on this subject, published 1946-60. Includes a preface reviewing the author's experience as a student of government since 1909 and of the work of himself and others in the U.S. Commission on Intergovernmental Relations and other agencies and organizations concerned with intergovernmental relations. [9547

THEODORE HERMAN FENSKE. From furs to farming. Lawrence Martin Brings, ed., Minnesota heritage (Minneapolis: T. S. Denison [1960]), p. 148-75. table, views. On agriculture in Minnesota, 1805-1960. [9548

WILLOUGHBY MAYNARD BABCOCK. Smoke signals to telephone. Lawrence Martin Brings, ed., Minnesota heritage (Minneapolis: T. S. Denison [1960]), p. 294-312. facsim., maps, ports., views. On the development of communications in Minnesota by river travel, railroads, newspapers, the telegraph, and the telephone, 1812-78. [9549

J. W. CLARK. Minnesota business and industry [1820-1960]. Lawrence Martin Brings, ed., Minnesota heritage (Minneapolis: T. S. Denison [1960]), p. 250-93. views. [9550

ANNA AUGUSTA (VON HELMHOLTZ) PHELAN & JOHN K. SHERMAN. The theatre in Minnesota [1821-1960]. Lawrence Martin Brings, ed., Minnesota's heritage (Minneapolis: T. S. Denison [1960]), p. 372-84. views. [9551

ESTHER CHAPMAN ROBB. The "Swede-Indian." Am. Swed. Hist. Found., Yr. bk., 1960, p. 50-54. On Jacob Fahlström, "the First Swede in Minnesota," who arrived there in 1827 from Hudson Bay with his Chippewa wife and died there in 1859. [9552

P. W. MANSON & C. O. ROST. Farm drainage--an important conservation practice [in Minnesota, 1830-1950]. Agric. engineering, 32:325-7 (Jun 1951). diagrs., map. notes. [9553

GRACE ORR ARMSTRONG & BERNICE DAINARD GESTIE. Education in Minnesota [1832-1957]. Lawrence Martin Brings, ed., Minnesota heritage (Minneapolis: T. S. Denison [1960]), p. 176-86. ports., views. [9554

VAL BJORNSON. Minnesota melting pot. Lawrence Martin Brings, ed., Minnesota heritage (Minneapolis: T. S. Denison [1960]), p. 120-27. views. On immigration to Minnesota, 1840-1957. [9555

RUTH ELIZABETH ECKERT & R. EDITH STEDMAN. Public higher education in Minnesota. Lawrence Martin Brings, ed., Minnesota heritage (Minneapolis: T. S. Denison [1960]), p. 218-40. map, view. On the University of Minnesota, the 5 State colleges (formerly normal schools or teachers' colleges), and the 9 public junior colleges, 1849-1960. [9556

EDWIN EMERY. The mass media mature: newspapers, magazines, graphic arts, radio, and television [Minnesota, 1849-1960]. Lawrence Martin Brings, ed., Minnesota heritage (Minneapolis: T. S. Denison [1960]), p. 313-28. facsims., ports., views. [9557

VICTOR GILBERTSEN. Early postal history of Winona County, Minnesota [1851-1960. n. p.: Winona County Historical Soc., 1960. 4], 19, [1] p. ports., tables, views. bibliog. (p. 19). [9558

JAMES TAYLOR DUNN. The Minnesota State Prison during the Stillwater era, 1853-1914. Minn. hist., 37:137-51 (Dec). views. notes. [9559

OSWALD EARL DOLVEN. Famous firsts in Minnesota Lutheranism. [Horace, N. D., 1960.] 47, [1] p. port., tables, views. bibliog. (p. 45-7). Thesis (Th. D.)--Burton College and Seminary. On "the oldest church in each of the seventeen Lutheran Synods [founded 1854-1916] as they exist today in the State of Minnesota." [9560

LEAL AUBREY HEADLEY. Private liberal arts colleges [in Minnesota, 1854-1960]. Lawrence Martin Brings, ed., Minnesota heritage (Minneapolis: T. S. Dension [1960]), p. 187-217. map, ports., seals, views. Historical sketches of 14 colleges. [9561

JOHANNES RIEDEL Music in Minnesota [1854-1960]. Lawrence Martin Brings, ed., Minnesota heritage (Minneapolis: T. S. Denison [1960]), p. 406-21. cartoon, music, ports., views. [9562

CECIL HAROLD MEYERS. Financing a frontier city: the pioneer banks of Duluth [1857-93]. Minn. hist., 37: 119-25 (Sep). views. notes. [9563

G. THEODORE MITAU. Constitutional change by amendment: recommendations of the Minnesota Constitutional Commission in ten years' perspective.

Minn. law rev., 44:461-81 (Jan). notes. On the recommendations of an interim commission established by a Minnesota statute of 1947 to study the Constitution of 1857 and its amendments and to propose desirable revisions to the legislature. [9564

SAMUEL TRASK DANA. Forest ownership in Minnesota--problems and prospects [1858-1960]. Am. forests, 66(10):32-8, 48-60 (Oct). diagrs. (part col.), maps (part col.), views. [9565

JAMES RUSSELL ECKMAN. The ghost journals of Minnesota. I. The Minnesota homeopath [published by Dr. George T. Hadfield, St. Paul, 1858-59]. Jour. lancet, 80:257-8 (May). facsim., port. notes. [9566

PAUL W. KLAMMER. Collecting log cabins a photographer's hobby. Minn. hist., 37:71-7 (Jun). views. On the author's photographic survey of log buildings in the area between Chaska and New Ulm, built between "the late 1850s" and "about 1890", with details of their log construction. [9567

KARL THURN & HELEN THURN, eds. Round robin of Kandiyohi County, centennial year, 1858-1958. Willmar, Minn. [1958. 6], 253, [5] p. col. views. Sections by numerous contributors, arranged alphabetically by title from "Agriculture" to "Willmar." [9568

THOREAU in Minnesota. Thoreau Soc. bul., 57:[1-4] (fall 1956). Reproduction of "A week on the frontier," by W. A. C., in the Minneapolis State atlas, 3 July. 1861, reporting the itinerary of "an excursion party of about 200 Minnesotians" (including "Henry D. Thoreau, Esq. the celebrated abolitionist") from Minneapolis up the Minnesota River by steamboat to Red Wood, where the Governor of Minnesota held a meeting with the Sioux Indians, who presented their complaints and staged a dance, Jun. 1861. [9569

CLAUDE AUGUST CROMMELIN (1840-74). A Dutch investor in Minnesota, 1866: the diary of Claude August Crommelin. Translated by A. Hermina Poatgieter. Edited by Muriel E. Hidy. Minn. hist., 37:152-60 (Dec). map, port., views. Excerpts, 9-20 Jun. 1866, recording his voyage from La Crosse to St. Paul and Monticello and back to La Crosse, and his observations on the country and its economic future, especially that of the railroads. [9570

JOHN LEWIS HARNSBERGER. Land, lobbies, railroads, and the origins of Duluth [1868-73]. Minn. hist., 37: 89-100 (Sep). map, views. notes. [9571

WALTER F. BECKER. An old inspection engine on the Milwaukee & St. Paul Railway ... the "Messenger." Railway & Locomotive Hist. Soc., Bul., 103:66-7 (Oct). On a locomotive used to inspect a track between St. Paul and Mendota, Minn., 1869. [9572

RAYMOND SCALLEN. The law of medical practice requirements in Minnesota: some historic observations [1869-1960]. Jour. lancet, 80:234-41 (May). table. [9573

JOHN TOWNSEND TROWBRIDGE (1827-1916). Railroad route from St. Paul to Duluth in 1869. ... Edited by Rhode R. Gilman. Minn. hist., 37: 101-18 (Sep). map, views. Excerpts from letters to The Atlantic monthly describing the movements of an excursion party by railroad, wagon, and steamboat from St. Paul to Duluth, and their inspection of Duluth, 12-22 Aug. 1869. [9574

FREDRICK ARTHUR WILLIUS. Henry Stanley Plummer [1874-1936]--a diversified genius. Springfield, Ill.: Thomas [1960]. viii, 71 p. map, ports., views. On his early life in Hamilton, Minn., his studies at the University of Minnesota and the Medical School of Northwestern University, his practice of medicine at Racine, Minn., and his partnership with the Mayo Brothers in Rochester, Minn. [9575

EMEROY JOHNSON. God gave the growth: the story of the Lutheran Minnesota Conference, 1876-1958. Minneapolis: T. S. Denison [1958]. ix, 266 p. facsim., ports., views. notes. [9576

JAMES P. SHANNON. Archbishop Ireland colonizes. Lawrence Martin Brings, ed., Minnesota heritage (Minneapolis: T. S. Denison [1960]), p. 128-38. facsims., map, views. On the establishment of "Catholic colonies" in Minnesota by John Ireland, Coadjutor Bishop of St. Paul, 1876-81. [9577

MURRAY FIFE BUELL & VERA FACEY. Forest-prairie transition west of Itasca Park, Minnesota. Torrey Bot. Club, Bul., 87:46-58 (Jan). diagr., tables. bibliog. On the soils and vegetation of this region as reported in publications since 1884, recalled by early settlers who came to the area then or somewhat later, and observed recently by the authors. [9578

CARL B. DRAKE. The Minnesota Academy of Medicine: an historical account [1887-1958]. Minn. med., 43: 244-50 (Apr). notes. [9579

WILSON W. SAWYER. Mallards for the market. Ann. Ia., 35:454-63 (fall). Memories of hunting in southern Minnesota, 1887. [9580

S. MARX WHITE. Frank F. Wesbrook [1868-1918], M.D.: action in medical education and public health in Minnesota. Jour. lancet, 80:259-64 (May). port. On his service as Professor of Bacteriology and Pathology at the University of Minnesota and as bacteriologist of the Minnesota State Board of Health, 1895-1913; with some account of his early life and medical education in Canada and his service as President of the University of British Columbia. [9581

THOMAS A. PEPPARD. Henry L. Ulrich, M.D. [born 1876]. Jour. lancet, 80:86-8 (Feb). port. On his medical teaching and practice in Minnesota since 1901. [9582

LEMEN J. WELLS & C. A. McKINLAY. Hal Downey, Ph. D., 1877-1959. Jour. lancet, 80:445-9 (Sep). ports. On his teaching of zoology and anatomy in the University of Minnesota, 1903-46, and his work in hematology; with a list of his publications, 1909-59. [9583

MINNESOTA STATE MEDICAL ASSOCIATION. Minnesota laws on practice of medicine [1905-58]. Minn. med., 43:145-6 (Feb). [9584

JAY ARTHUR MYERS. William Wallace Will, M.D. [born 1879]. Jour. lancet, 80:494-6 (Oct). port. On his medical practice in Bertha, Minn., 1906-60. [9585

C. L. McNELLY. The county agent story: the impact of extension work on farming and country life, Minnesota [1907-60]. Berryville, Ark.: Braswell Print. Co. [1960]. 191 p. ports., tables, views. bibliog. (p. 191). [9586

M. M. WILLIAMS. Minnesota State Sanatorium at the half-century mark [Ah-gwah-ching, Minn., 1907-60]. Jour. lancet, 80:153-7 (Apr). [9587

LEMEN W. WELLS. Elexious Thompson Bell, M.D. [born 1880]. Jour. lancet, 80:41-4 (Jan). ports. On his teaching of medicine at the University of Minnesota and his other medical activities in Minnesota, 1911-59; with a list of his publications. [9588

JOHN THEODORE FLANAGAN. The Minnesota backgrounds of Sinclair Lewis' fiction [1915-51]. Minn. hist., 37:1-13 (Mar). ports., views. notes. [9589

JOHN HARVEY. The dance in Minnesota [1917-60]. Lawrence Martin Brings, ed., Minnesota heritage (Minneapolis: T. S. Denison [1960]), p. 385-7. ports., view. [9590

WALTER HENRY JUDD. Charles Edward Proshek [1893-1957], M.D. Jour. lancet, 80:308-9 (Jun). port. On his medical practice in Minnesota, 1917, 1928-46, 1948-57. [9591

JOHN C. KIDNEIGH. In the interests of humanity. Lawrence Martin Brings, ed., Minnesota heritage (Minneapolis: T. S. Denison [1960]), p. 344-71. views. On public and private welfare and social-work organizations in Minnesota, 1917-60. [9592

JAY ARTHUR MYERS. John Silas Lundy, M.D. [born 1894]. Jour. lancet, 80:134-5 (Mar). port. On his work as an anesthesiologist in Minnesota since 1924. [9593

HERMAN ERTRESVAAG HILLEBOE. Edwin J. Simons [1896-1958], M.D. Jour. lancet, 80:184-9 (Apr). port. On his medical practice and experiments in Swanville, Minn., 1925-50, and his service as executive director of Minnesota Medical Services, Inc.; with a list of his publications. [9594

RALPH FREIMUTH BERDIE & MARTIN L. SNOKE. A continuing experiment in high school - college relations [Minnesota, 1928-58]. Jour. higher educ., 30:46-9 (Jan 1959). [9595

JOHN R. BORCHERT. A quarter-century of change in the Finland community of northeastern Minnesota. [Duluth?] 1960. [16] p. maps, view. bibliog. (p. [16]). (Publication of the Social Sciences Research Trust Fund at the University of Minnesota, 2.) On Finland, Minn., since 1934. Continues an article by Darrel H. Davis published in that year, on the community since 1895. [9596

OLOF I. SOHLBERG. Blue Shield--past and present. Minn. med., 42: 100-104 (Feb 1959). On medical insurance plans in Minnesota since 1942. [9597

PAUL HELLMUTH HOEPNER. An economic analysis of risk and uncertainty in dairy and hog production [southeastern Minnesota, 1945-54]. Ann Arbor: University Microfilms, 1960. Positive microfilm of typescript. [245] leaves. Thesis--Univ. of Minnesota. Abstracted: Dissert. abstracts, 21:785 (Oct). [9598

Minneapolis and St. Paul

JOHN C. MASSMANN. Friedrich Orthwein [born 1824]: Minnesota's first German editor. Am.-German rev., 26(4):16-17, 38 (Apr-May). On his publication of the Minnesota deutsche Zeitung and the Minnesota National Demokrat, Minneapolis and St. Paul, 1855-59, and his later years there and in Wisconsin and Chicago till his disappearance from record in 1869. [9599

EDWARD A. CHMIELEWSKI. A history of Holy Cross Parish, Minneapolis, Minnesota, 1886-1914: a Polish-American community. Saint Paul, 1960. xii, 104 leaves. bibliog. (leaf 102), notes. Thesis (M. A.)--Saint Paul Seminary. [9600

DONALD HOUGH (1895-1965). The streetcar house. N.Y.: Duell, Sloan, and Pearce [1960. 8], 180 p. On the habits and ideas of the author's father, an official of the Tri-State Telephone Company, St. Paul, who built a house at Wildwood, on White Bear Lake, from 10 discarded streetcars; with the author's memories of his childhood there, 1905-11. [9601

HENRY L. ULRICH. Thomas A[lbert] Peppard, M.D. [born 1887]. Jour. lancet, 80:356-7 (Jul). port. On his medical studies, practice, and teaching in Minneapolis since 1906. [9602

GARETH D. HIEBERT. Saint Paul is my beat. By Oliver Towne (Gareth Hiebert). [St. Paul: North Central Pub. Co., 1958. 6], 154 p. fold. map, port., views. "A collection of stories published since 1954 in the 'Oliver Towne' column in the St. Paul Dispatch," dealing with "the moods, charms, history, neighborhoods and neighbors you meet on the streets of our city." [9603

Rochester

WALTMAN WALTERS. A surgeon's progress. Minn. med., 43:385-9 (Jun). Reminiscences of surgical practice at the Mayo Clinic, 1920-60. [9604

IOWA

GEORGE ALLEN AGOGINO & W. D. FRANKFORTER. A paleo-Indian bison-kill in northwestern Iowa. Am. antiq., 25:414-15 (Jan). view. On a deposit of bison bones associated with artifacts near Quimby, Cherokee County, with a radiocarbon date of 6471 B. C. ± 520 years. [9605

HENRY LEE DEAN. A stone fish trap in eastern Iowa [in the Iowa River near Homestead]. Ohio archaeol., 10:79-81 (Jul). view. On a V-shaped arrangement of stones in the river, with a narrow opening at the apex, where Indians speared or trapped fish. [9606

PAUL HAMILTON ENGLE. Iowa [its traditions and characteristics]. Holiday, American panorama west of the Mississippi: a Holiday magazine book (Garden City, N.Y.: Doubleday [1960]), p. 371-84. [9607

WILLIAM JOHN PETERSEN. Some historic sites in Iowa. Iowa City, 1960. 293-324 p. views (part col.). (The palimpsest, v. 41, no. 6.) Reproductions of 64 photographs and prints; with a list of references on inside of back cover. [9608

STATE HISTORICAL SOCIETY OF IOWA. The Ioway Indians. Iowa City, 1960. 261-292 p. facsim., double col. map, col. ports., col. views. (The palimpsest, v. 41, no. 5, May 1960.) Contributions by William J. Petersen, F. R. Aumann, Ruth A. Gallaher, and Alanson Skinner. On these Indians in Iowa from the earliest record of them in 1676 till their removal to Kansas in 1838; with accounts of their chief Mahaska or White Cloud (1784?-1834) and his wife Rantchewaime and of "An Ioway village" on the Riviere des Moines. [9609

WILLIAM JOHN PETERSEN. Wolves in Iowa. Iowa City, 1960. 517-564, 16 p. (The palimpsest, v. 41, no. 12.) On the gray wolf or timber wolf and the coyote or prairie wolf since 1804, the enmity between them and the pioneers, "circular wolf hunts," and the payment of bounties on wolf scalps (still necessary in 1960). [9610

WILLIAM JOHN PETERSEN. The pioneer log cabin. Iowa City, 1960. 485-516 p. facsims., map, views (part col.). (The palimpsest, v. 41, no. 11.) On log buildings in Iowa, 1820-1870s, including houses, schools, churches, stores, courthouses, and forts; with details of their construction and furnishings. [9611

KENNETH E. COLTON. The stagecoach comes to Iowa [1836-45]. Ann. Ia., 35:161-86 (winter). map. Based on thesis (M.A.)--State Univ. of Iowa, 1942. [9612

ARTHUR HECHT, comp. Iowa list of letters. Natl. Geneal. Soc. quar., 48: 133-5 (Sep). List of 226 lists of unclaimed letters in 12 Iowa newspapers, 1836-50; with an introduction on Federal procedures for advertising such letters. [9613

A. LLOYD SWARTZENDRUBER. Samuel D. Guengerich [1836-1929]. Mennonite hist. bul., 11(4):1, 3 (Oct 1950). On the life in rural Iowa as an Amish layman, editor of religious periodicals, and teacher of Sunday schools. [9614

LEWIS K. FERGUSON, FRED R. MARCKHOFF, & WALTER ROSENE, JR., comps. Currency and banking in early Iowa. Numismatist, 73:17-25, 143-6, 299-303, 441-6, 861-7, 1343-53 (Jan-Apr, Jul-Aug). facsims. bibliog. Annotated list of paper currency issued by or for Iowa institutions, 1837-65. [9615

H. E. O'NEAL & VADA YULE KLITH. 120 years of the medical profession in Cedar County, Iowa [1838-1959]. Ia. State Med. Soc., Jour., 50:581-6, 645-50, 687-94, 761-9 (Sep-Dec). ports., view. [9616

RUSSELL MARION ROSS. The government and administration of Iowa [1838-1957]. N.Y.: Crowell [1957]. xiv, [2], 382 p. diagrs., maps, tables. bibliog. (p. 365-72), notes. (American commonwealths series, 13.) [9617

MELVIN GINGERICH. A Mennonite pioneer in Iowa: John Carl Krehbiel (1811-1886). Mennonite life, 15:57-9 (Apr). On his early life in Germany, his emigration in 1833, his various occupations in Ohio and Indiana, his settlement in Lee County, Ia., in 1839, his ordination there in 1851 as a Mennonite minister, and his ministerial service at West Point till his death. [9618

MELVIN GINGERICH. Mennonites in [and near] Lee and Davis Counties, Iowa [1839-1905]. Mennonite life, 15: 51-2, 56 (Apr). map. [9619

JOHN CARL KREHBIEL (1811-86). The founding of the General Conference Mennonite Church: early years at West Point, Iowa. ... Translated by John Umble. Mennonite life, 15:53-6 (Apr). facsims., map, views. Excerpt translated from the manuscript "Stammbuch der evangelischen Menoniten-Gemeinde in Wespoint, Lee County, Iowa," 1839-64. [9620

PIONEERS celebrate the Fourth of July [in Iowa City, Fort Madison, and Bedford, 1839]. Ann. Ia., 35:67-9 (Jul 1959). [9621

IOWA law firm in business 120 years. Ann. Ia., 35:226-9 (winter). On the firm of O'Connor, Thomas, McDermott, & Wright, Dubuque, founded in 1840 as Davis and Crawford. [9622

EARLY Des Moines document. Ann. Ia., 35:464-7 (fall). "Proceedings of a claim meeting held at John B. Scott's trading house near Fort Des Moines, Raccoon Fort, Iowa Territory," 14 Oct. 1845, signed "by almost all the known founders of the capital city of Iowa." [9623

STATE HISTORICAL SOCIETY OF IOWA. The Harlan-Lincoln home. Iowa City, 1960. 145-176 p. plan, ports., views. (The palimpsest, v. 41, no. 3.) Contributions by William J. Petersen and J. Raymond Chadwick. On James Harlan (1820-99), resident of Iowa from 1846 till his death, active in Iowa law, politics, and higher education and in national politics, friend of Lincoln; his house at Mt. Pleasant, Ia.; the marriage of his daughter Mary to Robert Todd Lincoln in 1868; and the prospective receipt by Iowa Wesleyan College of a trust fund established by her after her husband's death, expected to be worth at least $1,000,000. [9624

KENNETH E. COLTON. John Frink & Company, 1846-1854. Ann. Ia., 35: 401-88 (fall). port. notes. Based on thesis (M. A.)--State Univ. of Iowa, 1942. On an Illinois stagecoach line that entered Iowa in 1847 and was sold to the Western State Company in 1854. [9625

FRANCIS MARION DRAKE (1830-1903). Attorneys in Iowa in 1847. Ann. Ia., 34:533-8 (Jan 1959). Reminiscent address, 1896, containing a list of the lawyers practising in Iowa in 1847 and information about the later careers of some of them. [9626

JAMES BAIRD WEAVER (1833-1912). A pioneer Iowa wedding [May 1848]. Ann. Ia., 34:539-43 (Jan 1959). Eyewitness account of the rescue of Emmeline, 18-year-old daughter of a Mormon farmer about to take her against her will to Utah, by a volunteer force organized by a Mexican War ex-captain; her marriage on the spot to her fiancé, John Paris, aged 21; and their settlement in Davis County on his "splendid claim" of 160 acres of prairie and timber. [9627

WILLIAM L. BOWERS. Crawford Township, 1850-1870: a population study of a pioneer community [in Washington County, Ia.]. Ia. jour. hist., 58:1-30 (Jan). tables. notes. Includes "conclusions ... as to the correctness of earlier frontier assumptions, and comparison ... of the findings of this study with those of other studies made of other parts of the frontier." [9628

LEONARD FLOYD RALSTON. Railroads and the government of Iowa, 1850-1872. Ann Arbor: University Microfilms, 1960. Positive microfilm of typescript. [524] leaves. Thesis--State Univ. of Iowa. Abstracted: Dissert. abstracts, 20:4643-4 (Jun). [9629

HOWARD DANIEL RAID. Farm succession at Donnellson, Iowa. Mennonite life, 15:60-61 (Apr). view. On the inheritance or other transfer of farms from Mennonites to their children since 1851. [9630

THOMAS PETER CHRISTENSEN. Homer Horatio Seerley [1848-1932]. Ann. Ia., 35:363-85 (summer). port. bibliog. On his life in Iowa, 1854-1932, as a farm boy, a rural schoolteacher, superintendent of schools at Oskaloosa, and Principal and later President of the Iowa State Normal School from 1886 to 1928 (renamed Iowa State Teachers College in 1909). [9631

JAMES M. TROSKY & EMMETT POLDER. Some mammal remains from a Jackson County cave. Ia. Acad. Science, Proc., 67:607-9. On the discovery of bone fragments in an Iowa cave, believed to be "representative of some species that were close to extinction soon after settlement of the state by white men," ca. 1854. [9632

BARBARA (SCHNEIDER) YAMBURA (born 1917). A change and a parting: my story of Amana. Ames: Iowa State Univ. Press [1960]. 361 p. On the Society of Free Inspiration, otherwise known as the Amana Society, Amana, Ia., 1855-1960, a communal organization till 1932; with the author's reminiscences of her life there till that year. [9633

MILDRED THRONE (1902-60), ed. Iowa farm letters, 1856-1865. Ia. jour. hist., 58:37-88 (Jan). notes. Letters from Ephraim Gard Fairchild, tenant farmer in Jones County, Ia., to his parents in New Jersey, 1857-58, and from John Kenyon, tenant farmer in Delaware County, his wife, Sarah, and her sister, Mary Ellis, to relatives in Rhode Island, 1856-65. [9634

W. M. WALLIKER & RALPH F. LUSE. The Clinton County Medical Society [1857-1959]. Ia. State Med. Soc., Jour., 49:781-2 (Dec 1959). [9635

LEONARD FLOYD RALSTON. Governor Ralph P. Lowe and State aid to railroads: Iowa politics in 1859. Ia. jour. hist., 58:207-18 (Jul). notes. [9636

CARL A. ANDERSON. The saga of Swedesburg. Ann. Ia., 35:187-205 (winter). History of an almost entirely Swedish community in Henry County and of its Augustana Lutheran church, 1864-1960. [9637

CURTIS L. JOHNSON. E[ugene] S[tafford] Ellsworth [1848-1907]: Iowa land baron. Ann. Ia., 35:1-35 (Jul 1959). port., views. notes. Based on thesis (M.A.)--State Univ. of Iowa. On his life in Iowa Falls, 1864-1907, as a livery-stable boy, a dealer in lands and farm mortgages in Iowa, Minnesota, the Dakotas, Nebraska, and Kansas, an owner of various businesses, and a large contributor to many local charities. [9638

OLIVE G. WYSE. A brief history of the Sebastian Gerig family. Mennonite hist. bul., 15(1):5-6 (Jan 1954). On Sebastian Gerig (1838-1924), Alsatian emigrant, Amish minister, settler in rural Iowa in 1864, and his 12 children. [9639

MYRTLE T. BEINHAUER. Development of the Grange in Iowa, 1868-1930. Ann. Ia., 34:561-96 (Apr 1959). [9640

U.S. Bureau of Statistics (Treasury Dept.). Book for immigrants. Ann. Ia., 34:546-8 (Jan 1959). Excerpts relating to Iowa from Report of the Chief of Bureau of Statistics on immigration (1871), compiled by Edward Young, containing information on "the prices and rentals of land, the staple products, facilities of access to market, cost of farm stock, kind of labor in demand," etc. [9641

LOUIS A. HASELMAYER. Das Deutsche Kollegium: Wesleyan's Teutonic past. Ann. Ia., 35:206-15 (winter). bibliog. From The purple and white, Iowa Wesleyan alumni quarterly. On an institution "known officially as Das Deutsche Kollegium and popularly as the German College," founded "for the theological training of German Methodist ministers to serve German speaking churches" by the Southwest German Conference of the Methodist Church and located at Mt. Pleasant, Ia., in affiliation with Iowa Wesleyan College, 1873-1909. [9642

JAMES C. OLSON. Ned C[ulbertson] Abbott [1874-1960]. Neb. hist., 41: 79-81 (Jun). port. On his life in Iowa, his many civic responsibilities there, his historical writings, and the deposit of his papers in the Nebraska State Historical Society. [9643

M. M. MORRIS. Hotel Colfax. Ann. Ia., 34:544-5 (Jan 1959). On a resort hotel constructed near Colfax, Ia., to take advantage of healing mineral waters there, later used as a veterans' hospital, the headquarters of the National Purebred Livestock Exchange, a hospital for alcoholics, and now as a school of the Catholic Society of the Divine Savior, 1877-1958. [9644

RESTORATION of capital punishment [Iowa, 1878]. Ann. Ia., 35:69-72 (Jul 1959). [9645

HOWARD DANIEL RAID. The migration from a rural community: Donnellson migrations analyzed. Mennonite life, 15:62-3, 91 (Apr). On migration of Mennonites from Donnellson, Ia., 1890-1950. [9646

G. F. HARKNESS. Times have changed. Ia. State Med. Soc., Jour., 49:59-62 (Jan 1959). On the author's studies at the College of Medicine, University of Iowa, his medical practice in Iowa, and the changes in the medical profession since ca. 1900. [9647

AL MOORE (1852?-1916). The record of Engine No. 216. Ann. Ia., 35:386-90 (summer). From the author's Cab. coach, caboose (Des Moines, 1902), there apparently reprinted from an unnamed and undated newspaper. On the ride of the author in this locomotive from Clinton to Ames with its engineer, Herm Mells, who ran a mile in 39.5 seconds. [9648

JAY NORWOOD DARLING (1876-1962). Midwest farming as portrayed by a selection from Ding's cartoons [1907-48]. Des Moines: Pioneer Hi-bred Corn Co., 1960. 103 p. cartoons, facsim. 31 cm. Cartoons contributed to the Des Moines register, 1907-48, showing not only the daily activities of Iowa farmers but their political and other opinions. [9649

FELIX A. HENNESSY. Some reminiscences of a northeast Iowa doctor. Ia. State Med. Soc., Jour., 50:54-8 (Jan). port. notes. On the author's practice of medicine in Calmar since 1907. [9650

PAUL HAMILTON ENGLE. Old fashioned Christmas. [Des Moines: Register and Tribune Syndicate, 1960.] 48 p. port., views. "... a complete reprint of the series of articles published in newspapers under the same title." Mainly memories of Christmases during the author's childhood in Cedar Rapids, Ia., 1908 ff.; with some account of Christmas customs elsewhere in America and abroad. [9651

PAUL HAMILTON ENGLE. Prairie Christmas. N.Y.: Longmans, Green, 1960. [10], 51 p. Apparently another printing of the author's Old fashioned Christmas, with changes. [9652

PIONEER LAWMAKERS OF IOWA ASSOCIATION. Recollections of pioneer lawmakers of Iowa. By David A. Dancer, Secretary. Ann. Ia., 35:36-66 (Jul 1959). Proceedings of the 35th biennial session. Includes reminiscent speeches by Karl M. Le Compte (1911 ff.) and others. [9653

VIRGINIA M. LUCKEY. The first rural public hospital. Ia. State Med. Soc., Jour., 50:165-6 (Mar). notes. On the Washington County (Iowa) Hospital, 1912-60. [9654

LEE McNEELY (1876-1960). The Judicial District of Northern Iowa. Ann. Ia., 35:277-87 (spring). Recollections of the author's service as Clerk of the U.S. District Court for the Northern District of Iowa, 1912-57. [9655

LOUIS R. HOWSON. Revenues, rates, and advance planning [by the Des Moines, Ia., Water Board, 1919-59]. Am. Water Works Assoc., Jour., 52: 153-61 (Feb). diagrs. notes. [9656

JACOB ARMSTRONG SWISHER. Kiwanis in Iowa [since 1919]. Iowa City, 1960. 437-484 p. ports., view. (The palimpsest, v. 41, no. 10, Oct. 1960.) On the Iowa clubs of the Illinois - Eastern Iowa District and the Nebraska-Iowa District of Kiwanis International; with verses by the author. [9657

WENDELL L. DOWNING. Then and now. Ia. State Med. Soc., Jour., 49:181-4 (Mar 1959). port. Reminiscences of the author's practice of medicine in Iowa since 1920. [9658

GEORGE B. MATHER. A preliminary report of an analysis of the effects of the use of voting machines in voting on special questions [submitted to referendum] in Iowa--1920 to 1956. Iowa City: Institute of Public Affairs, State Univ. of Iowa, 1960. 47 p. diagr., tables (1 double). notes. Concludes "that substantially fewer votes are cast on special questions when voting machines are used." [9659

OTTO W. KNAUTH. The winter of 1935-36. Ann. Ia., 35:288-93 (spring). On the unprecedented severity of the weather in Iowa, 16 Jan.-26 Feb. 1936. [9660

GEORGE A. PAVELIS & JOHN F. TIMMONS. Programming small watersheds. Jour. farm econ., 42: 225-40 (May). diagrs., tables. notes. On the development of the Nepper Watershed of the Little Sioux River drainage area of Iowa, 1939-60. [9661

EDWIN FREYBURGER. Flood control in the Little Sioux Watershed in Iowa [1944-50]. Agric. engineering, 32: 152-4 (Mar 1951). views. notes. [9662

DONALD THOMAS BUTLER. Factors affecting trade union organizing of manufacturing firms in Iowa, 1946 to 1957. Ann Arbor: University Microfilms, 1959 [i. e. 1960]. Positive microfilm of typescript. v, 156 leaves. map. bibliog. (leaf 156). Thesis--Univ. of Wisconsin. Abstracted: Dissert. abstracts, 20: 2635 (Jan). [9663

COUNTY zoning in Iowa [1947-60]. Ia. law rev., 45:743-66 (summer). notes. [9664

STEVEN POLGAR. Biculturation of Mesquakie teenage boys. Am. anthropol., 62:217-35 (Apr). bibliog. Field study in a settlement near Tama, Ia., 1952-53, on the ways by which the Indian boys there "were socialized into Indian and White culture concurrently." [9665

IOWA. State Dept. of History and Archives. Iowa's notable dead. Ann. Ia., 34:551-60, 624-32; 35:74-80, 151-60, 232-40, 311-20, 395-400, 471-80 (Jan 1959-winter 1960). Memorial sketches of eminent Iowans recently deceased. [9666

IOWA ACADEMY OF SCIENCE. In memoriam. Ia. Acad. Science, Proc., 67:39-46. ports. Brief sketches of Frank E. Brown (1882-1959), Charles Harvey Brown (1875-1960), Samuel Wheeler Edgecombe (1908-59), Bruce F. Stiles (1897-1959), John A. Schulz (1894-1959), Lester Yoder (1882-1959), and Thomas W. Zbornik (1913-59). [9667

NORTH DAKOTA

OMER CALL STEWART. Cart-using Indians of the American plains. International Congress of Anthropological and Ethnological Sciences, 5th, 1956, Men and cultures: selected papers, ed. Anthony F. C. Wallace (Phila.: Univ. of Pennsylvania Press [1960]), p. 350-55. view. notes. On the use of horse-drawn 2-wheeled carts for spring and fall buffalo hunts by the Plains Ojibwa Indians of North Dakota and Manitoba, 1815-65. [9668

ALAN R. WOOLWORTH & W. RAYMOND WOOD. The archeology of a small trading post (Kipp's Post, 32MN1) in the Garrison Reservoir, North Dakota. U.S., Bureau of American Ethnology, River Basin Surveys, River Basin Surveys papers, nos. 15-20, ed. Frank H. H. Roberts, Jr. (Wash.: U.S. Govt. Print. Off., 1960 [U.S., National Museum, Bulletin 176]), p. 239-305. maps (1 fold.), plan, fold. table, views. bibliog. (p. 292-3). On a site in Mountrail County occupied by a Columbia Fur Company trading post from 1826 to 1829 or 1830; with an inventory of building remains and artifacts excavated there in 1951 and 1954. [9669

GEORGE CATLIN (1796-1872). A Mandan village on the upper Missouri. Margaret Mead & Ruth L. Bunzel, eds., The golden age of American anthropology (N.Y.: George Braziller, 1960), p. 115-28. views. From

Catlin's Letters and notes on the manners, customs, and conditions of the North American Indians (1st ed. 1841, 2d 1842). On the way of life of the Mandan Indians, visited by Catlin in or about 1832 and illustrated by his paintings. [9670

BUTTERFLY, Mandan Indian. Butterfly's Mandan winter count: 1833-1876. [Edited by] James H. Howard. Ethnohistory, 7: 28-43 (winter). bibliog., notes. Chronology dictated by Butterfly, "the keeper of the winter count," to Edward Goodbird, intended to be used with pictographs on a tanned buffalo hide, which apparently has not been preserved; with explanatory comments by the editor. [9671

JAMES B. CONNOLLY. Father [Pierre Jean] De Smet in North Dakota. N.D. hist., 27:5-24 (Jan). port. bibliog., notes. On his voyages up and/or down the Missouri through what is now North Dakota, 1840-68; with extensive quotations from his letters describing the country and the Indians. [9672

CHESTER J. FRANCIS. Drainage in the Red River Valley of North Dakota [1861-1951]. Agric. engineering, 33:787-90 (Dec 1952). table. [9673

JOHANNES PALMER KVAM (born 1897). Memories of the prairies. [Everett? Wash.] c1960. [3], xi, 75 leaves. geneal. table. On the author's early life on homesteaded farms in Ransom County and near Balfour in Sheridan County, N.D., 1897-1923; with some account of his father, Johannes Jens Kvam (1857-1943), emigrant from Norway to Minnesota in 1864, homesteader in Ransom and Sheridan Counties, N.D., and all of his descendants. [9674

OLIVER HOLMES KNIGHT, JR. Mark Kellogg telegraphed for Custer's rescue. N.D. hist., 27:95-8 (spring). notes. Evidence that Kellogg, may have been "the man who telegraphed for rescue when General and Mrs. Custer, along with a good many other persons, were stranded on a train imbedded in a massive snow drift in the spring of 1876," and that the freight cars in the train were "loaded with merchandise for Bismarck merchants hoping to profit from the Black Hills," where gold had been found. [9675

WILL H. NORTHROP (born 1869). The true story of Northrop pioneering in North Dakota. [Fargo? 1960.] vii, 92 p. ports., views. On the author's life in North Dakota since 1882, his studies, and his work as a rural schoolteacher and a farmer, a businessman in Fargo, a leader in North Dakota politics, and as a Presbyterian layman. [9676

MELVIN E. KOONS, JR., & HANS C. WALKER, JR. Jurisdiction over Indian country in North Dakota [1883-1959]. N.D. law rev., 36:51-62 (Jan). notes. [9677

STEVEN S. SCHWARZSCHILD. The Marquis de Mores: the story of a failure (1858-1896). Jew. social studies, 22:3-26 (Jan). notes. Biographical sketch of Antoine-Amédée-Marie-Vincent Manca de Vallombrosa, Marquis de Morès et de Montemaggiore, dealing with his various activities in France, India, Indochina, and Africa, and from 1883 to 1887 in America, where he made plans for a national consumers' league and planned and in part established in the Bad Lands of North Dakota an enterprise for growing, slaughtering, and marketing livestock and for financing his operations with his own bank. Deals mainly with his antisemitism. [9678

RAY H. MATTISON. Roosevelt's Elkhorn Ranch [in the Bad Lands of western North Dakota, acquired by him in 1884, sold in 1897]. N.D. hist., 27:51-65 (spring). notes. Mainly on the buildings (completely dismantled by 1901) and their contents. [9679

WILLIAM WINGATE SEWALL (1845-1930) & MARY SEWALL. Life at Roosevelt's Elkhorn Ranch ... [Edited] by Ray H. Mattison. N.D. hist., 27: 106-41 (summer-fall). port., view. Letters from husband and wife to relatives in Maine, 17 Aug. 1884-7 Aug. 1886, on Sewall's management of Roosevelt's ranch in the Bad Lands 35 miles north of Medora, the care of the horses and cattle, the lack of profit in the cattle business, the quality of the land and water, the climate, and the Indians and wild game in the vicinity. [9680

AMISH in North Dakota [since 1893]. Mennonite hist. bul., 14(1):4-5 (Jan 1953). On a church that by 1953 had dwindled to 8 members. Attributed incorrectly to Floyd E. Kauffman; see 14(2):4. [9681

EDWARD L. KAUFFMAN. A history of the Spring Valley Congregation, Kenmare, North Dakota [1901-41]. Mennonite hist. bul., 13(2):1-2 (Apr

1952). notes. On a congregation completely dispersed by the removal of its members, leaving only a cemetery. [9682

J. H. NEWTON. The North Dakota Bar Board [1905-58]. N.D. law rev., 35: 220-23 (Jul 1959). [9683

A. C. SUMMERFIELD. The way back. By A. C. Summerfield as told to T. J. Kerttula. True West, 7(3):30-31, 46-7 (Jan-Feb). port., views. Memories of a blizzard near Mandan, N.D., 3 Oct. 1906. [9684

NORTH DAKOTA. AGRICULTURAL EXPERIMENT STATION, Fargo. The North Dakota economy: factors related to economic development [1920-58. By] Thor A. Hertsgaard, Fred R. Taylor, [and] Alvah R. Tetrault. Fargo, 1960. 32 p. tables. notes. (Its Bulletin 428.) [9685

T. P. McELROY. North Dakota's anticorporate farming act [1932-59]. N.D. law rev., 36:96-103 (Apr). notes. [9686

LOIS (PHILLIPS) HUDSON. The cold wave: a reminiscence of childhood in North Dakota [61° below zero, 1935]. The reporter, Our times: the best from The reporter, ed. Max Ascoli (N.Y.: Farrar, Straus, and Cudahy [1960]), p. 210-18. First published in 1958. [9687

THORDUR WALDIMAR THORDARSON. Supervised correspondence study in North Dakota [in high schools, 1935-60]. Discourse, 3:251-8 (Oct). [9688

MELVIN E. KOONS, JR. A history of the Grand Forks County Bar Association, 1937-1959. N.D. law rev., 36: 225-35 (Jul). [9689

ROBERT EDWIN SULLIVAN. Conservation of oil and gas in North Dakota: a legal history, 1948-1958. Grand Forks, 1960. 12 p. notes (p. 9-12). (North Dakota. Geological Survey. Bulletin 33.) Excerpt from American Bar Association, Section of Mineral and Natural Resources Law, Conservation of oil & gas: a legal history, 1958, ed. Robert E. Sullivan (Chicago, 1960). [9690

SOUTH DAKOTA

HUGH CARSON CUTLER & GEORGE A. AGOGINO. Analysis of maize from the Four Bear site [in Dewey County] and two other Arikara locations in South Dakota [La Roche site, Stanley County, and unnamed site in Gregory County]. Southw. jour. anthropol., 16:312-16 (autumn). diagr. bibliog., notes. [9691

SHIRLEY E. JOHNSON. Charles Mix County in retrospect [since its prehistoric occupance by the Arikara Indians]. S.D. report and hist. col., 30:349-64. bibliog., notes. [9692

MARTHA GROVES McKELVIE. The hills of yesterday. Phila.: Dorrance [1960]. vii, [3], 117, [1] p. col. flag, col. ports., col. views. History and lore of the Black Hills and the Sioux Indians of South Dakota. [9693

DIANA LEE. All ded but me. S.D. report and hist. col., 30:369-72. bibliog. On a stone found by Louis and Ivan Thoen in the Black Hills in 1887, inscribed by Ezra Kind with the message that he and 6 others had found gold there and that Indians had killed the 6 others, 1833-34; with an account of efforts to establish the authenticity of the inscription. [9694

JOHN S. GRAY. Brave Bear meets the hangman. Westerners brand book (Chicago), 17:49-51, 56 (Sep). bibliog. On a Sioux Indian born ca. 1840, repeatedly arrested on suspicion of robbery or murder in Dakota Territory, who repeatedly escaped from jail but was hanged at last in 1882 at Yankton. [9695

MILDRED FIELDER. Lawrence County, South Dakota [1857-1960]. Mildred Fielder, ed., Lawrence County ([Lead? S.D., 1960]), p. 12-19. map. [9696

MILDRED FIELDER. Transportation [in Lawrence County, 1870s-1960]. Mildred Fielder, ed., Lawrence County ([Lead? S.D., 1960]), p. 134-43. views. [9697

J. A. BOESE. The story of the Mennonites at Avon, South Dakota [1874-1960]. Mennonite life, 15:39-45 (Jan). facsim., ports., views. Appended: passenger list of the steamship Colina, which arrived in New York 2 Sep. 1874, with information added by the editor concerning the marriages and places of settlement of the Mennonite passengers. [9698

CLARENCE N. KRAVIG. Mining in Lawrence County, S.D., 1874-1960. Mildred Fielder, ed., Lawrence County ([Lead? S.D., 1960]), p. 87-102. ports., table, views. bibliog. On mining in the Black Hills. [9699

FOSTER BUNDAY. Boom town--ghost town [Le Beau, Walworth Co., S.D., 1875-1925]. S.D. report and hist. col., 30:365-8. bibliog., notes. [9700

CLARENCE P. COOPER. Churches [in Lawrence County, S.D., 1876-1960]. Mildred Fielder, ed., Lawrence County ([Lead? S.D., 1960]), p. 157-65. views. [9701

DORETTE DARLING. Education: historical background, schools, and libraries [in Lawrence County, S.D., 1876-1960]. Mildred Fielder, ed., Lawrence County ([Lead? S.D., 1960]), p. 144-52. tables, view. bibliog. [9702

DEATH of Wild Bill. Westerners brand book (Chicago), 16:71-2 (Nov 1959). From the Chicago inter-ocean, 17 Aug. 1876. Submitted by "Doc," special correspondent, Deadwood, 3 Aug. 1876, on the killing of J. B. Hickok by John McCall, the trial of McCall, ending in a verdict of "not guilty," and the funeral. [9703

MILDRED FIELDER. Wong family of Deadwood. Wi-iyohi, 13(11):1-2 (Feb). On the family "headed by Fee Lee Wong, better known as Wing Tsue, a merchant and dealer in luxury items imported from China," Deadwood, ca. 1876 to some date after 1890; with some account of the Chinese in the Black Hills. [9704

HENRY FRAWLEY & ANNE FRAWLEY. Agriculture, dairying, ranching [in Lawrence County, S.D., 1876-1959]. Mildred Fielder, ed., Lawrence County ([Lead? S.D., 1960]), p. 103-14. ports., table. [9705

JOHN J. GERING. Deadwood [1876-1960]. Mildred Fielder, ed., Lawrence County ([Lead? S.D., 1960]), p. 20-30. port., views (1 double). [9706

BERNADINE HANSEN & MARGARET E. FUROIS. Saint Onge [S.D., 1876-1960]. Mildred Fielder, ed., Lawrence County ([Lead? S.D., 1960]), p. 77-86. views. [9707

DONALD P. HOWE. Lead [S.D., 1876-1960]. Mildred Fielder, ed., Lawrence County ([Lead? S.D., 1960]), p. 31-47. views (1 double). [9708

JAMES D. JELBERT. Spearfish [S.D., 1876-1960]. Mildred Felder, ed., Lawrence County ([Lead? S.D., 1960]), p. 59-68. views (1 double). [9709

C. A. POLLEY. Lumber and timber [in Lawrence County, S.D., 1876-1960]. Mildred Fielder, ed., Lawrence County ([Lead? S.D., 1960]), p. 115-23. views. On the lumber industry of the Black Hills. [9710

CARLTON O. GORDER. Sports [in Lawrence County, S.D., 1877-1960]. Margaret Fielder, ed., Lawrence County ([Lead? S.D., 1960]), p. 166-86. ports., views. [9711

SAMUEL GOODALE PRICE. Central City [1877-1960]. Mildred Fielder, ed., Lawrence County ([Lead? S.D., 1960]), p. 48-58. views. [9712

MILDRED FIELDER. Railroads of the Black Hills [1881-1960]. S.D. report and hist. col., 30:35-316. fold. maps, ports., views. bibliog. (p. 314-15). On the Black Hills and Fort Pierre Railroad (1881-1901), the Deadwood Central (1888-1930), the Burlington Lines in the Black Hills (1891-1960), the Fremont, Elkhorn, and Missouri Valley Railroad Company (1886-1903), the Chicago and North Western Railway (1903-28), the Rapid Canyon Line (1890?-1947), and the Black Hills Central (1957-60); with rosters of their employees, some account of their locomotives, and reminiscences by many of the employees. [9713

CHARLES CHRUTCHETT. Grand View, Douglas County's ghost town [1882-95]. S.D. report and hist. col., 30:373-435. maps, views. notes. [9714

ROBERT EDWARD DRISCOLL, SR. Diary of a country banker. N.Y.: Vantage Press [1960]. 140 p. On the removal of Robert Henry Driscoll (1856?-1932), the author's father, from Salem, Mass., to Lead, S.D., and his activities there as a banker, a lawyer, and a manager of mining concerns, 1883-1932; with the author's "interpretation and conception of the entries" in his father's diary and long quotations from it, and some account of the author's association with him in the banking business in the Black Hills. [9715

HELEN F. MORGANTI. The Badger Clark story. [n. p.] c1960. [4], 89 p. ports., views. bibliog. (p. 87-8). On Charles Badger Clark (1883-1957), his early life in South Dakota, his studies at Dakota Wesleyan University, his work on a plantation in Cuba, his recovery from tuberculosis in Arizona, his later years in "the Badger Hole" at Hot Springs, S.D., and his career as a poet, eventually Poet Laureate of South Dakota. [9716

SOD houses. Wi-iyohi, 14(1):1-6 (Apr). views. Photographs and descriptions of 15 sod houses in South Dakota, built between 1883 and 1927. [9717

OEHLRICHS, not a ghost town. [Pierre: South Dakota Historical Soc., 1960.] 15, [1] p. map, port., views. notes. (The wi-iyohi, v. 13, no. 10, Jan. 1960.) On a town developed on a ranch in Fall River County, S.D., owned by Harry Oelrichs, cattleman; with reminiscences by Blanche Myrtle (Thompson) Horton (born 1881) and a tax list for 1889. [9718

ROYAL G. SWEELEY. Wakonda community history, 1885 to 1960: diamond jubilee, 75 years of progress. [n. p.] 1960. 79, [1] p. map, ports., tables, views. On a town and its vicinity in Clay County, S.D. Includes reminiscent letters from early settlers. [9719

MARGARET E. FUROIS & CATHERINE A. GRANT. Whitewood [S.D., 1887-1960]. Mildred Fielder, ed., Lawrence County ([Lead? S.D., 1960]), p. 69-76. views (1 double). [9720

CARL B. HOY (born 1893). According to Hoy: memoirs of a university coach. Vermillion: State Univ. of South Dakota, 1960. 104 p. port. On the author's early life in South Dakota, his studies at Vermillion, his teaching in Gregory and Platte, and his work at Vermillion since 1927 as coach of athletics. [9721

LEO D. HECK. Brief history of the Bar of South Dakota. S.D. Bar jour., 27(3):33-6 (Jan 1959). On the Bar of the State of South Dakota, 1897-1931, and the State Bar of South Dakota, 1931-58. [9722

ALLEN FRANCIS AGNEW. Oil tests in Black Hills fringe, South Dakota [1910-59]. S.D. Acad. Science, Proc., 38 (1959): 60-65. maps, tables. Evidence that only 3 percent of 175 test wells were drilled deep enough to test "all of the potentially productive sands of the Black Hills area." [9723

A. L. HAINES. The first third of a century of the South Dakota Academy of Science [1915-48]. S.D. Acad. Science, Proc., 27 (1948): 20-25. [9724

WALTER WILLIAM LUDEMAN. The Indian student in college. Jour. educ. sociol., 33:333-5 (Mar). table. On American Indian students at Southern State Teachers College, Springfield, S.D., 1925-58. [9725

NEBRASKA

MARI SUSETTE SANDOZ. Nebraska [its traditions and characteristics]. Holiday, American panorama west of the Mississippi: a Holiday magazine book (Garden City, N.Y.: Doubleday [1960]), p. 320-38. [9726

DONALD DEAN JACKSON. Lewis and Clark among the Oto. Neb. hist., 4:237-48 (Sep). view. notes. On a meeting of Meriwether Lewis and William Clark with the Oto Indians on the Platte River in Nebraska, Aug. 1804. Includes a previously unpublished text of the message addressed by Lewis and Clark to the Little Thief, principal chief of the Oto, 4 Aug. 1804. [9727

WILDCAT banks and currency [Nebraska, 1855-57]. Selections from The numismatist: United States paper money, tokens, medals, and miscellaneous (Racine, Wis.: Whitman Pub. Co., 1960], p. 188-9. facsim. First printed in May 1936. [9728

HENRY JAMES HUDSON (born 1822). Henry James Hudson and the Genoa settlement. Edited by Marguerette R. Burke. Neb. hist., 41:201-35 (Sep). port., view. notes. Dairy, letter to The Mormon, and speech, recording the journey of Mormon colonists from St. Louis to Nebraska, their establishment of Genoa City, and their departure from it after its enclosure in an Indian reservation and its destruction by a fire set by the Indian agent there or by his trader, 1857-59. [9729

WALLACE BROWN. George L. Miller and the struggle over Nebraska Statehood. Neb. hist., 41:299-318 (Dec). port. notes. On his campaign for office and for the promotion of Omaha through his editorship of the Omaha herald, 1864-67, and his opposition to Statehood. [9730

WILLIAM HAMILTON (1811-91). Mission work among the Omaha Indians. Presbyt. Hist. Soc., Jour., 38:182-90 (Sep). notes. Letter to the Rev. John C. Lowrie, dated Omaha Mission, 1 Feb. 1868, on the Omaha and other Indians there, the farm, the school, and religious instruction. [9731

E. PHILLIP CLEMENS. Origin and early history of the Mennonite Church in Nebraska [since the early 1870s]. Mennonite hist. bul., 17(1):1-3, 7 (Jan 1956). port. notes. [9732

MYRON PLESKAC. History of the Catholic Church among the Czechs of Brainard, Dwight, and Loma, Nebraska [1875-1960]. St. Paul, 1960. [1], iv, 91 leaves. tables. bibliog. (leaves 89-91), notes. Thesis (M. A.)--Saint Paul Seminary. [9733

JOHN ANDREW HOSTETLER. The Amish in Gosper County, Nebraska [1880-1904]. Mennonite hist. bul., 10(4):1-2 (Oct 1949). [9734

JAMES IVERNE DOWIE. Luther Academy [Wahoo, Neb.], 1883 to 1903: a facet of Swedish pioneer life in Nebraska. Ann Arbor: University Microfilms, 1957 [i. e. 1960]. Positive microfilm of typescript. 367, lii leaves. col. maps, table, view. bibliog. (leaves 343-67). Thesis--Univ. of Minnesota. Abstracted: Dissert. abstracts, 20: 4382-3 (May). On an institution of the Augustana Synod. [9735

AMOS EDWIN DONNELL (1859-1921). The letters of Ed Donnell, Nebraska pioneer. Edited by Charles J. Wilkerson. Neb. hist., 41:123-51 (Jun). ports., view. notes. Letters to the author's parents and other relatives in Missouri, 13 Apr. 1884-28 Apr. 1888, on his farming on homesteaded land in Sherman County, Neb. [9736

CHARLES DE WITT O'KIEFFE (born 1879). Western story: the recollections of Charley O'Kieffe, 1884-1898. With an introduction by A. B. Guthrie, Jr. [Lincoln:] Univ. of Nebraska Press, 1960. xvi, 224 p. facsim., map. bibliog. (p. 205-6), notes (p. 206-22). (The pioneer heritage series, 2.) On his early life in Johnson County, Neb., his removal with his parents and 8 brothers and sisters to homesteaded land in Sheridan County, his work on the ranch, as a laborer at Pine Ridge, S.D., and as a store clerk in Rushville, Neb., his removal to Omaha in 1898, and the activities of the other members of the O'Kieffe family during these years. [9737

AMMON E. STOLTZFUS. History of Wood River Congregation [Nebraska, since 1905]. Mennonite hist. bul., 17(1):4-5 (Jun 1956). [9738

A. J. STENNER. Ball of fire! Frontier times, 34(4):30-31, 60 (fall). Recollections of a prairie fire in the sand hills of Nebraska, started by the intentional carelessness of "Bill Springfield," who in retribution was burned alive in his shack, 1910-11. [9739

G. THOMAS FAIRCLOUGH, ed. Nebraska place-names [1925], by Lilian L[inder] Fitzpatrick [died 1935], including selections from The origin of place names in Nebraska [1933], by John Thomas Link [1873-1936]. Edited, with an introduction, by G. Thomas Fairclough. [Lincoln:] Univ. of Nebraska Press, 1960. xi, 227 p. bibliog. (p. 148-52). (A Bison book, BB107.) [9740

ELWIN RANNEY. Rodeo at the University of Nebraska [1938-60]. West. horseman, 25(12):34-5, 86-7 (Dec). cartoons, views. On an enterprise of the University of Nebraska Rodeo Club and its predecessor, the Farmers Fair Board, not supported by the University as a college sport. [9741

ANN YOKLEY. Bill Coffee and the Hat Creek spread. Quarter horse jour., 12(8):18-21, 80 (May). ports., views (part double). On William B. Coffee, breeder and raiser of quarter horses at Hat Creek Ranch, near Harrison, Neb., since 1942. [9742

KANSAS

KANSAS STATE HISTORICAL SOCIETY. Bypaths of Kansas history. Kan. hist. quar., 26:103, 228, 340, 456 (spring-winter). Excerpts from early Kansas newspapers. [9743

DEBS MYERS. Kansas [its traditions and characteristics]. Holiday, American panorama west of the Mississippi: a Holiday magazine book (Garden City, N.Y.: Doubleday [1960]), p. 339-54. [9744

RALPH RALPH DYKSTRA. Veterinary medicine in Kansas. [n. p.: Kansas Veterinary Medical Assoc.] 1952 [c1953]. 110 p. On the veterinary profession in Kansas since the establishment of Fort Leavenworth in 1827; with a chapter on "Some veterinary pioneers in Kansas," a list of veterinary publications of the Kansas Agricultural Experiment Station (p. 84-97), and an account of the School of Veterinary Medicine, Kansas State College. [9745

ROSCOE WILMETH. Kansa village locations in the light of McCoy's 1828 journal. Kan. hist. quar., 26:152-7 (summer). map. notes. Information from a diary of Isaac McCoy in eastern Kansas (published in 1936). [9746

GEORGE PIERSON MOREHOUSE. Along the Kaw trail. Everett Rich, ed., The heritage of Kansas (Lawrence: Univ. of Kansas Press, 1960), p. 20-28. First printed in 1904. History and lore of the Kaw or Kansas Indians in Morris County and adjacent areas, 1840s-1873; with the author's recollections of them, 1871-73. [9747

CARL LOTUS BECKER (1873-1945). Kansas. Everett Rich, ed., The heritage of Kansas: selected commentaries on past times (Lawrence: Univ. of Kansas Press, 1960), p. 340-59. First published 1910. On "the Kansas spirit" and the quality of civilization in Kansas, ca. 1850 to 1910. [9748

JOHN P. HARRIS. Beautiful Katie. Everett Rich, ed., The heritage of Kansas (Lawrence: Univ. of Kansas Press, 1960), p. 213-23. From the Kansas magazine, 1936. On Kate Bender (born 1851) and her father, keepers of "a grocery and a travelers' rest" in Labette County between Osage Mission and Cherryvale, their sudden and permanent disappearance, and the discovery in their cellar of the bodies of 8 missing travelers for whom a search had been organized. [9749

FRY WILLIAM GILES (1819-98). Thirty years in Topeka: a historical sketch ... With a foreword by Zula Bennington Greene. A summary of events in the capital city of Kansas during the period beginning 1854. [Kansas centennial edition. Topeka: Stauffer Publications] 1960. 167 p. maps (1 col. fold., 1 double), ports., views. 1st ed. 1886. Includes the author's reminiscences of Topeka, 1854-86. [9750

EVERETT RICH, ed. The heritage of Kansas: selected commentaries on past times. Lawrence: Univ. of Kansas Press, 1960. [8], 359 p. Mainly contemporary or reminiscent articles, tales, and selections from books, chosen to "give a panoramic view of Kansas life," 1854-1900. [9751

EMILY L. HARTMAN. The F. B. and Rena G. Ross Natural History Reservation. Emporia: Graduate Division, Kansas State Teachers College, 1960. 40 p. diagrs., maps (1 double), views. bibliog. (p. 36-7). (The Emporia State research studies, v. 8, no. 4.) On the history and natural history of a tract of 1,040 acres of hills and prairies in Lyon and Chase Counties, 14 miles north of Emporia, 1856-1960, given to the College in 1958. [9752

HARRY SINCLAIR DRAGO. Wild, woolly, & wicked: the history of the Kansas cow towns and the Texas cattle trade [1865-86]. N.Y.: C. N. Potter [1960]. viii, [2], 354 p. bibliog. (p. 351-4), notes (p. 343-9). On Abilene, Ellsworth, Newton, Wichita, Caldwell, and Dodge City as points where cattle driven from Texas were loaded into railroad cars for shipment and where facilities were established for the reception and entertainment of the drivers. [9753

CHARLES R. WETZEL. Monument Station, Gove County. Kan. hist. quar., 26:250-54 (autumn). notes. On a stage station and temporary military post on the Smoky Hill River, 1865-68. [9754

MARY SMITH of Sheffield, Ohio. Miss Smith crosses the Plains in 1866. Edited by Dorothy Gardiner. Westerners brand book (N.Y.), 5 (1959): 77-81, 90-91. Diary sent in installments as letters to the writer's sister, recording her journey with a wagon train from an unnamed point (Kansas City?) to Ft. Larned, Kan., and thence by stagecoach to Ft. Lyon, Kan., 18 Jun.-26 Jul. 1866; with an introduction by the editor on conditions of travel across Kansas to Colorado. [9755

ROBERT R. DYKSTRA. The last days of "Texan" Abilene: a study in community conflict on the farmer's frontier. Agric. hist., 34:107-19 (Jul). notes. On Abilene in 1867 and in 1871 and the reasons why "herd laws" were adopted in 1872 which virtually expelled the cattle trade from Dickinson County and ended the prosperity of Abilene. [9756

EUGENE FITCH WARE (1841-1911). History of Sun-Gold Section. Everett Rich, ed., The heritage of Kansas (Lawrence: Univ. of Kansas Press, 1960), p. 82-95. From the Kansas historical quarterly, Aug. 1937. On the author's removal from Iowa through Missouri to the "Sun-Gold Section" near Fort Scott, Kan., and his establishment of a homestead there, 1868-70. [9757

ROBERT SCHRAG. A frontier town on the Chisholm Trail: Newton, Kansas [1870-84]. Mennonite life, 15:26-9 (Jan). view. On Newton as briefly "the principal shipping point for Texas cattle" and later a place of settlement for Mennonite immigrants. [9758

WAYNE LELAND WHEELER. An analysis of social change in a Swedish-immigrant community: the case of Lindsborg, Kansas [since the 1870s?]. Ann Arbor: University Microfilms, 1959 [i. e. 1960]. Positive microfilm of typescript. [387] leaves. Thesis--Univ. of Missouri. Abstracted: Dissert. abstracts, 20:2950 (Jan). [9759

ANN JACOBS FAILING & MAURICE E. ROBINSON. Shoo Fly City. [Oxford, Kan.: Oxford Register] c1960. 109 p. facsim., ports., views. History of South Haven, Kan., 1871-1901, which went under the name of Shoo Fly City till 1884. [9760

CHARLES M. HAWKES. Business and agricultural conditions in Kansas, 1871-1888, as reported by a New England mortgage broker. [Edited and abstracted by] Glenn H. Miller, Jr. Kan. hist. quar., 26:67-73 (spring). notes. Based on the editor's thesis (M. A.)--Univ. of Kansas, 1954. Quotations from and summaries of letters from a dealer in Kansas mortgages and real estate, on Kansas crops and finance. [9761

ANNE E. BINGHAM. The grasshopper plague. Everett Rich, ed., The heritage of Kansas (Lawrence: Univ. of Kansas Press, 1960), p. 149-50. From Collections of the Kansas Historical Society, 1919-22. On an invasion of Geary County by grasshoppers as seen by the author in 1874. [9762

LEONARD E. MUIR. Elam Bartholomew [1852-1934], farmer extraordinary. Agric. hist., 34:189-93 (Oct). port. notes. On his life as a farmer in Rooks County, Kan., 1874-1929, his diary (1871-1934), his weather records, his work as a self-taught mycologist, and his large-scale agricultural experiments. [9763

PHYLLIS A. DINKEL. Old marriage customs in Herzog (Victoria), Kansas ["prevalent in the late 1800's and in the early 1900's" among the "Russian-Germans" there]. West. folklore, 19: 99-105 (Apr). notes. Information mainly from oral sources, 1957-58. [9764

EARL B. SHURTZ. Some thoughts on ground water development in Kansas [1877-1957]. Rocky Mt. law rev., 32: 515-26 (Jun). notes. [9765

HENRY KING (1842-1915). At Kawsmouth Station. Everett Rich, ed., The heritage of Kansas (Lawrence: Univ. of Kansas Press, 1960), p. 103-11. From the Atlantic monthly, Aug. 1879. Anecdote of a loquacious promoter of Kansas, lecturing in a railroad station, about "the land of ozone and wheat,--the verdurous, agueless slopes and the odors that Homer sang," etc. [9766

GLEN SCHWENDEMANN. Wyandotte and the first "Exodusters" of 1879. Kan. hist. quar., 26:233-49 (autumn). notes. On the inconvenience and confusion resulting from the unexpected migration of thousands of Negroes up the Mississippi and the Missouri to Kansas, particularly Wyandotte, and the efforts of Wyandotte and other local authorities and of the State of Kansas to provide for their accommodation, Apr.-Jun. 1879. [9767

WILLIAM R. SMITH. The wonderful mirage. [Reported by T. A. McNeal.] Everett Rich, ed., The heritage of Kansas (Lawrence: Univ. of Kansas Press, 1960), p. 20-28. From the Topeka Capital, undated. On the author's observations while traveling on horseback between Sheridan Lake and Water Valley, Colo., near the Kansas border, spring 1879, when he witnessed a collision between a "cyclone" and a mirage. [9768

VAL J. HEADINGS, JR. A history of the Old Order Amish Mennonite Sunday School at East Center Congregation, Hutchinson, Kansas [1883-1947]. Mennonite hist. bul., 20(2):7 (Apr 1959). Previously printed as "an 8-page pamphlet without date or place of publication." [9769

RAY M. BEAUCHAMP. The town that died laughing. Frontier times, 34(3): 30-31, 50-52 (summer). Recollections of Frisco, Morton County, Kan., and the gunfighters, outlaws, and "alcoholic show-offs" who repeatedly disturbed the peace there, 1885-87. [9770

CHARLES BENEDICT DRISCOLL (1885-1951). Notes for an autobiography. Everett Rich, ed., The heritage of Kansas (Lawrence: Univ. of Kansas Press, 1960), p. 247-59. From the Kansas magazine, 1941. On the author's early life in Wichita, 1885-1903, particularly his reading, and the strong prejudice in his family against reading novels. [9771

PAUL ERB. Tillman M. Erb, 1865-1929. Mennonite hist. bul., 10(3):1, 4 (Jul 1949). port. On his life in Kansas as a dairy farmer and a Mennonite minister near Newton from ca. 1885 till his death. [9772

ROBERT SCHRAG. A center of Mennonite businesses: Newton, Kansas [1885-1956]. Mennonite life, 15:64-7 (Apr). port., table, views. Includes an account of "Mennonite publication work" there since 1897. [9773

O. P. BYERS. The blizzard of 1886. Everett Rich, ed., The heritage of Kansas (Lawrence: Univ. of Kansas Press, 1960), p. 151-5. From Collections of the Kansas State Historical Society, 1911-12. Reminiscences of western Kansas in January 1886. [9774

BAR ASSOCIATION OF THE STATE OF KANSAS. Services in honor of Arthur J. Mellott [1888-1957]. Bar Assoc. State Kan., Jour., 27:137-44 (Nov 1958). port. On his life in Kansas and his work as a lawyer and a judge. [9775

MORRIS McNEIL MUSSELMAN. Wheels in his head. Everett Rich, ed., The heritage of Kansas (Lawrence: Univ. of Kansas Press, 1960), p. 172-82. From the Atlantic monthly, Aug. 1945. Anecdotes about the author's father, A[lvah?] J. Musselman, inventor, who as a boy and a young man in Kansas was repeatedly in trouble as a result of his inventions. [9776

CARLETON BEALS. Kansas at the World's Fair. Everett Rich, ed., The heritage of Kansas (Lawrence: Univ. of Kansas Press, 1960), p. 291-300. From the Kansas magazine, 1942. On the Kansas exhibit at the Chicago World's Fair, 1893. [9777

CATHARINE (WIGGINS) PORTER (1873-1952). College days at Cooper Memorial, 1895-1898. Edited by Kenneth Wiggins Porter. Kan. hist. quar., 26:383-409 (winter). notes. Recollections (1938/45) of attendance at a college (now Sterling College) in Sterling, Kan. Heavily annotated. [9778

The heritage of Kansas (Lawrence: Univ. of Kansas Press, 1960), p. 317-30. From Outlook, 31 Jul. 1929. On the saloon-closing activities of Carry Nation in Medicine Lodge and Kiowa, Kan., 1899. [9779

ELLSWORTH E. KELLEY. The little boy and his pa. Everett Rich, ed., The heritage of Kansas (Lawrence: Univ. of Kansas Press, 1960), p. 226-33. From McClure's magazine, Jun. 1900. Tale of a 10-year-old boy and his father in rural Kansas. [9780

RUSSELL L. CULP. History and present status of chlorination practice in Kansas [1908-60]. Am. Water Works Assoc., Jour., 52:888-96 (Jul). diagrs. notes. [9781

RALPH TENNAL. The rise and fall of Barber. Everett Rich, ed., The heritage of Kansas (Lawrence: Univ. of Kansas Press, 1960), p. 300-306. From the Kansas magazine, Apr. 1909. Tale of Populism, slot machines, and the Anti-Saloon and Purity League in "Grass City," Kan. [9782

KENNETH E. MERRILL. Kansas rural electric cooperatives--twenty years with the REA. [Lawrence:] Center for Research in Business, Univ. of Kansas [1960. 12], 214 p. diagrs., maps, table. bibliog. (p. 211-14), notes. Individual histories of all the Kansas rural electric cooperatives established by the U.S. Rural Electrification Administration, 1937-58 (p. 82-210), and account of earlier electric lines in rural Kansas, 1910 ff. [9783

FRANK TENNEY STOCKTON. A history of fire schools in Kansas. Lawrence: Univ. of Kansas, 1955. 28 p. notes. (University of Kansas. University Extension research report.) On conferences and schools in Kansas for instruction in professional fire-fighting, 1917-54. [9784

FRED W. RAUSCH, JR. Extradition in Kansas [1937-59]. Univ. Kan. City law rev., 28:150-59 (summer). notes. [9785

MALCOLM EDWIN JEWELL. Party and primary competition in Kentucky State legislative races [1947-57]. Ky. law jour., 48:517-35 (summer). maps, tables. notes. [9786

THE FAR WEST

STEPHEN C. CAPPANNARI. The concept of property among Shoshoneans. Gertrude E. Dole & Robert L. Carneiro, eds., Essays in the science of culture, in honor of Leslie A. White (N.Y.: Crowell [1960]), p. 133-44. bibliog. Based on thesis--Univ. of California. On property concepts of the Kawaiisu, Tubatulabal, Ute, Gosiute, Paiute, Shoshoni, and Hopi Indians in the Far West, mainly in the Great Basin or near it. [9787

HARRY HOIJER. Athapaskan languages of the Pacific coast. Stanley Diamond, ed., Culture in history: essays in honor of Paul Radin (N.Y.: Columbia Univ. Press for Brandeis Univ., 1960), p. 960-76. tables. bibliog. On the relation between a group of languages spoken by Indians of southern Oregon and northern California and those spoken by the Navajo and Apache Indians. [9788

WILLIAM THOMAS HAMILTON (1822-1908). My sixty years on the plains, trapping, trading, and Indian fighting. ... From the original edition by E. T. Sieber, with an introduction by Donald J. Berthrong. Norman: Univ. of Oklahoma Press [1960]. xxiii, 184 p. port., views. (The Western frontier library.) 1st ed. 1905. Recollections by an early resident of St. Louis, trapper and trader in the Rocky Mountains, gold miner in California, participant in Indian wars in California, Nevada, Oregon, and Washington, Indian trader and Army scout in Oregon, Washington, and Montana--a narrative ending with 1874. [9789

DAVID E. MILLER. Peter Skene Ogden's trek into Utah, 1828-29. Pac. Northw. quar., 51:16-25 (Jan). map, port., view. notes. On the route of an expedition made by order of the Hudson's Bay Company; with details of movement from the Humboldt River (which Ogden discovered) across the northwest corner of Utah into southeast Idaho as far as the Bear River, and back, Dec. 1828-Apr. 1829. [9790

DOYCE BLACKMAN NUNIS, JR. The Sublettes of Kentucky and the Far West, 1830-1857. Ky. Hist. Soc., Reg., 58:129-44 (Apr). notes. On the activities of William Sublette and his brothers Milton, and Solomon Perry as fur traders, guides, businessmen, farmers, etc., originally with St. Louis as their base of operations. Notes that the family name became extinct in 1857. [9791

ROBERT V. HINE. The Kern brothers and the image of the West. Utah hist. quar., 28:350-61 (Oct). ports., views. On Benjamin J. Kern (1819-49), Richard H. Kern (1821-53), and Edward Meyer Kern (1823-63) as artists and observers in topographic expeditions in the Far West, 1845-53, the lack of exaggeration and of idealization in their drawings and sketches, and the addition of these Romantic qualities when "the lithographers ... superimposed their own ideas upon the work of the artist" (with illustrations showing 2 cases of this process). [9792

DANIEL WEBSTER JONES (1830-1915). Forty years among the Indians: a true yet thrilling narrative of the author's experiences among the natives. Los Angeles: Westernlore Press, 1960. 378, [3] p. (Great West and Indian series, 19.) 1st ed. 1890. On the author's Army service in the Mexican War, his activities as an Indian trader in Utah, his conversion to Mormonism, his service as an official of the Church of Jesus Christ of Latter-Day Saints, and his establishment of a Mormon colony in Mexico, 1847-86. [9793

LEWIS CASS GRANGER (1819-90). Letters: report of the journey from Salt Lake to Los Angeles in 1849, and of conditions in southern California in the early fifties. Introduction and notes by Le Roy R. Hafen. Los Angeles: G. Dawson, 1959. 50 p. facsims. (1 fold.), port. (Early California travels series, 47.) Letter to the author's father, Los Angeles, 8 Apr. 1850, describing southern California and his route across it from Nevada; letters to Abel Stearns, Antonio Coronel, and ---- Risser (Los Angeles, 1851, 1854), and to the author's wife (Oroville, 16 Mar. 1857); letters to him from Abel Stearns (San Jose, 11 Feb. 1851) and Amasa Lyman (San Bernardino, 22 Sep. 1852); and facsimile reproduction of a mutilated copy of a printed "address relating to territorial government for southern California," signed by Agustin Olivera, Granger, and 5 others, Los Angeles, 15 Sep. 1851. [9794

A. JAY HERTZ. The Shoe-String Express: a study of the little-known Western expresses. Am. Philatelic

Cong., Congress book, 26:15-27. facsims. Examples of express-line postal markings from the Far West, 1850-70, and study of the means by which some of the expresses can be identified and dated. [9795

HOWARD A. JOHNSON. Law in the mining camps. Westerners brand book (Chicago), 17:25-6 (Jun). On the laws adopted and enforced by associated miners in their camps in California and other parts of the Far West, 1850 ff. [9796

JACK J. RAPPEPORT. The husband's management of community real property [in Arizona, Idaho, Nevada, New Mexico, and Washington, 1865-1958]. Ariz. law rev., 1:13-61 (spring 1959). Deals largely with the Spanish origins of the concept of community property. [9797

ISABELLA LUCY BIRD (1831-1904). A lady's life in the Rocky Mountains. ... With an introduction by Daniel J. Boorstin. Norman: Univ. of Oklahoma Press [1960]. xxiii, 252, [2] p. views. notes. (The Western frontier library, [14].) 1st ed. 1879. "Originally written" as letters to the author's sister in England, 2 Sep-12 Dec. 1873, reporting the author's travels from San Francisco to Cheyenne by railroad. Consists mainly of an account of observations of Lake Tahoe and vicinity and her travels from Greeley, Colo., to Estes Park and adjoining parts of the Rocky Mountains, which she visited on horseback in company of a guide. [9798

JOHN F. DUGAN. The Anaconda Company and Montana [1875-1959]. Westerners brand book (Chicago), 16:33-5, 38-40 (Jul 1959). On "Butte, its copper mines, and miners," the mining of copper, zinc, and manganese by the Company in Montana, and the expansion of its interests to phosphate in Idaho, aluminum in Montana, copper in Chile, Mexico, and Nevada, iron in Ontario, and uranium ores in New Mexico. [9799

FRED A. RIECKER (born 1878). Horatio Algebra and Chief One and One. Tucson, Ariz.: Pima Print. Co., c1960. [4], 67 p. facsims. Facetious reminiscenses of the author's early life in Tucson, his studies at the University of Arizona, his work as a railroad laborer in several Rocky Mountain States, and his later work as a surveyor and topographical engineer for a division of the Union Pacific, the Southern Pacific Railroad, and the Chicago, Milwaukee, and St. Paul Railroad. [9800

BYRON A. ASHLEY. Boss of the treasure box. True West, 7(3): 32-4 (Jan-Feb). port. On the successful resistance of Aaron Ross, gigantic guard employed by Wells, Fargo, and Company, to efforts to rob a Central Pacific Train somewhere Toano, Nev., and Tecoma (Utah?), Jan. 1882. [9801

WILFRED P. SCHOENBERG. Father Dave: David Plante McAstocker [1884-1958], S.J. Milwaukee: Bruce Pub. Co. [1960]. xv, 123 p. port. On his early life in Ontario, his education and training for the priesthood, his service as a priest at Havre (Mont.), Tacoma, Riverside (Calif.), and San Diego, and his death from tuberculosis. [9802

HARRY FRENCH BLANEY & MARTIN R. HUBERTY. Irrigation in the Far West [in 9 States, 1889-1950]. Agric. engineering, 38:414-17, 421 (Jun 1957). tables, views. [9803

DOYLE L. GREEN. Howard William Hunter [born 1907]: apostle from California. Improvement era, 63:18-21, 36-8 (Jan). ports. On his early life in Boise, Idaho, his settlement in Los Angeles, his work in banking, his legal studies in Southwestern University, Los Angeles, his practice of law there, and his selection in 1959 as a member of the Council of the Twelve Apostles of the Church of Jesus Christ of Latter-Day Saints. [9804

G. F. HORNE. Watershed management in the Department of the Interior: three case studies in cooperation. Jour. forestry, 58:302-4 (Apr). On the 15-Mile Creek watershed near Worland, Wyo., the Oregon City watershed near Portland, and the Hill Creek watershed, northeastern Utah, 1916-60. [9805

LAURENCE ILSLEY HEWES (1876-1950). Western forest highways come of age. Am. forests, 66(2):42-4, 55-7; (3):34-40 (Feb, Mar). views (1 double). Reminiscent article written "several years" before 1950, about the effects of the Forest Highway Act (1921) in the Far West. [9806

WILLIAM GILLIAM HILL. Federal grants to the States for community mental health services with special reference to some Western States [Arizona, California, Nevada, Oregon, Washington, 1946-56]. Ann Arbor: University Microfilms, 1960. Positive microfilm of typescript. [339] leaves. Thesis (D.S.W.)--Univ. of Southern California. Abstracted: Dissert. abstracts, 20:4455-6 (May). [9807

The Rocky Mountain States

CARLING ISAAC MALOUF. Tipi rings. Southw. lore, 25(4):3-5 (Mar). On prehistoric stone circles found along the route of a gas line between Green River, Wyo., and Denver. [9808

ROBERT FRANCIS MURPHY & YOLANDA MURPHY. Shoshone-Bannock subsistence and society. [Berkeley: Univ. of California Press, 1960.] v, 293-388 p. map. bibliog. (p. 335-8). (Anthropological records, v. 16, no. 7.) On the eastern Shoshone Indians of southwestern Wyoming and northeastern Utah and the Shoshone and Bannock Indians of southeastern Idaho, 1700-1875. [9809

FRANCIS HAINES. Nez Perce horses: how they changed the Indian way of life. Idaho yesterdays, 4(1):8-11 (spring). views. On a tribe first seen by white men in 1805, owning herds of thousands of horses, their selective breeding of the horses, their exchange of horses for guns and ammunition from traders, their cultural borrowings from the Plains Indians, and their increasing transformation from sedentary fishermen to nomadic buffalo hunters. [9810

NEWELL C. REMINGTON. A history of the gilsonite industry. Salt Lake City: R. L. Jensen [1959. 2], ix, [1], 338 p. diagrs., tables. bibliog. (p. 310-38), notes. Thesis (M.S.)--Univ. of Utah. On the discovery of gilsonite (i.e. uintaite) deposits in the Uinta Basin of Colorado and Utah as early as 1865 and their commercial exploitation since 1888; with some account of the Basin since 1776. [9811

EDITH E. KEARNEY. The Thoroughbred and the Maxwell Land Grant. West. horseman, 25(2):24-5, 60 (Feb). map, views. bibliog. On an area of northeast New Mexico and adjacent Colorado, settled in 1841, later acquired by Lucien B. Maxwell, and found to be a suitable environment for raising Thoroughbreds. [9812

STEVE LOWELL. Maxwell's living monument. N. M., 38(5):16-23, 35-7, 39 (May). map, port., views (part col., 1 double). On the area of 1,714,765 acres New Mexico and Colorado obtained by Lucien Bonaparte Maxwell (1818?-1875) in and after 1841 and sold by him in 1870, and the great development of its resources since his time. [9813

LAUREN C. BRAY. Hiram Vasquez [real name: Hiram Ashcraft, 1843-1939], frontiersman. Colo. mag., 37:61-71 (Jan). port., views. notes. On his early life in Missouri and at Fort Bridger, Wyo., his removal to New Mexico in 1863, his various occupations in northern New Mexico and southern Colorado, and his later years at La Veta, Colo. [9814

UTAH (Territory). The year of the census. Utah hist. quar., 28:191-2 (Apr). Order from Brigham Young, Governor of Utah Territory, to Thomas Bullock to take a census of the Territory, 28 Mar. 1851; and Bullock's report, 26 Jun. 1851. [9815

JOHN WESLEY POWELL (1834-1902). Stone art in America. Selected papers from the American anthropologist, 1888-1920, ed. Frederica De Laguna (Evanston: Row, Peterson [1960]), p. 151-7. views. First printed in 1895. On the making and use of stone artifacts as observed by the author in his explorations of Wyoming, Colorado, Utah, and Arizona, 1867-73, and by earlier travelers among the Indians in the Far West. [9816

GEORGE ANDERSON WEAR (born 1885). Reminiscences of George A. Wear. As told to J. N. Neal. Recorded by Mrs. Ethel Starbuck. Colo. mag., 31:133-7 (Apr). port. On the life of the author in northwestern Colorado and southwestern Wyoming as a cowboy, later a rancher. [9817

FRANK R. HOLLENBACK. The Laramie Plains Line, Laramie, Wyoming, to Coalmont, Colorado [1901-60]. Denver: Sage Books [1960]. 94 p. facsims., maps (part fold.), port., tables, views. bibliog. (p. 94), notes (p. 86-92). On an 111-mile railroad organized by Isaac Van Horn as the Laramie, Hahns Park, and Pacific Railway Company (1901-14), the

Colorado, Wyoming, and Eastern Railroad Company (1914-24), the Northern Colorado and Eastern Railroad Company (1924), and the Laramie, North Park, & Western Railroad Company (1924-51), acquired by the Union Pacific in 1935 and reorganized as the Coalmont Branch of the Union Pacific Railroad in 1951. [9818

RAPHAEL MOSES. Irrigation corporations [in the Rocky Mountain States, 1901-59, particularly Colorado]. Rocky Mt. law rev., 32:527-33 (Jun). notes. [9819

LUCIAN C. SPRAGUE. Narrow-gage memories. Railroad mag., 71(4);16-20 (Jun). viens. On the Uintah Railway Company connecting Mack, Colo., and Watson, Utah, and used for transporting gilsonite; the author's service as superintendent and general manager, 1923-32; and his replacement of the Shay locomotives by specially constructed Baldwin locomotives. [9820

ROBERT R. ALEXANDER. Thinning lodgepole pine in the central Rocky Mountains [Colorado and Wyoming, 1924-55]. Jour. forestry, 58:99-104 (Feb). diagr., tables, view. notes. [9821

OTTO KUHLER. Tracking ghost trains through the Rockies. Natl. Railway Hist. Soc., Bul., 25(2):22-30 (2d quar.). views. On the "research that lies behind" the author's "world famous railway paintings"; with black-and-white reproductions of 10 undated paintings. [9822

MONTANA

ALFRED BERTRAM GUTHRIE, JR. Montana [its traditions and characteristics]. Holiday, American panorama west of the Mississippi: a Holiday magazine book (Garden City, N.Y.: Doubleday [1960]), p. 117-31. [9823

CRAIG A. HOPPERSTAD. Some aspects of the changing Crow kin terminological system. Mont. Acad. Sciences, Proc., 20:56-7. [9824

JOSEPH KINSEY HOWARD (1906-51). Montana: high, wide, and handsome. ... Preface by A. B. Guthrie, Jr. ... New illustrated edition. New Haven: Yale Univ. Press, 1959. xiv, 347 p. views. bibliog. (p. 330-29). 1st ed. 1943. Chronological chapters treating Montana as "a subject colony" and "an object lesson in American domestic imperialism." [9825

THOMAS F. KEHOE & ALICE B. KEHOE. Observations on the butchering technique at a prehistoric bison-kill in Montana [on the Blackfoot Indian Reservation]. Am. antiq., 25: 420-23 (Jan). tables. bibliog. [9826

MAYNARD O. BOWERS. Through the years in Glacier National Park (established in 1910]: an administrative history. [West Glacier, Mont.:] Glacier Natural History Assoc., 1960. [1], v, 111, [9] leaves. map, ports., views. bibliog. (leaves 114-18), notes (leaves 112-13). Based in part upon materials assembled by Donald H. Robinson. Includes some account of the history of the area since the first visit by a white man, perhaps as early as 1792. [9827

LEO H. HANNA. Botanical exploration of western Montana antedating the year 1850 [1804-49]. Mont. Acad. Sciences, Proc., 13 (1953): 35-8. bibliog. [9828

ROBERT HENRY FLETCHER. Free grass to fences: the Montana cattle range story [1805-1959]. ... Illustrations by Charles M. Russell [and others]. N.Y.: University Publishers for the Historical Soc. of Montana [1960]. xii, [8], 233, [3] p. facsims., double map, ports., views (part col). notes. Includes an account of the Montana Stockgrowers Association, 1885-1960. [9829

HELEN B. WEST. Blackfoot country. Montana, 10(4):34-45 (Oct). double map, ports., views. notes. "Blackfoot Country: a historical map by Helen B. West," showing the country between Glacier National Park and the present Highway U.S. 91, in Glacier, Toole, and Pondera Counties; with historical accounts of 41 numbered places, 1806-1910. [9830

ALLEN SPITZER & MARY L. SPITZER. Religious reorganization among the Montana Blackfeet. Rev. religious research, 2:19-35 (summer). On their religion when they were first visited by Catholic missionaries in the 1830s, and their present fusion "of Catholic and Indian religious ideas." [9831

WILFRED P. SCHOENBERG. Jesuits in Montana, 1840-1960. [Portland: Oregon-Jesuit, 1960.] 120 p. facsims., map, ports., views. [9832

LEO A. HANNA. A chapter in the natural history exploration of southeastern Montana and environs [1853-82]. Mont. Acad. Sciences, Proc., 15 (1955): 9-11. notes. [9833

PETER JOHN POWELL. Issiwun: scared buffalo hat of the Northern Cheyenne. Montana, 10(1):24-40 (Jan). ports. notes. History and lore of a Cheyenne sacred property, recorded as early as 1853 and recently examined by the Keeper of the Sacred Hat in the author's presence. [9834

LESLIE WATSON RANDALL. The toughest man in Montana Territory. By Gay Randall. Frontier times, 34(3);22-4, 46-8 (summer). port. Anecdotes and recollections of Horn Miller (1825?-1913), native of St. Louis, undefeated fighter with bare knuckles, trapper, Army scout, prospector, who settled in Montana (in the 1860s?) and lived on the author's father's ranch near Gardiner, Mont., in the early 1900s. [9835

ROBERT G. ATHEARN. Civil War days in Montana. Pac. hist. rev., 29: 19-33 (Feb). notes. Mainly on political activities there. [9836

C. BURT EVANS. Another Montana pioneer. [Pasadena?] c1960. 139 p. On the life of Charles A. Evans (1848-1932), in Montana as a trapper, a cattleman, and a worker in various other rural occupations, 1867-1932; with some account of his early years in Michigan and his service in the Union Army, and references to the author's life with his father in the Judith Basin till 1924. [9837

GENEVA HIGHLAND. Big Dry country. Billings, Mont.: Billings Print. Co., c1960. [5], viii, 176 p. col. fold. map, ports., tables, views. bibliog. (p. i-vii). Even Roman numbers on recto. On the area in Garfield County, Mont., drained by or close to Big Dry Creek and its tributaries, 1867-1960. [9838

MICHAEL HARRISON. Chief Charlot's battle with bureaucracy. Montana, 10(4):27-33 (Oct). ports., view. On "the removal of the Flathead tribe of Indians from the Bitterroot Valley to the Jocko Reservation in Montana Territory," 1872 ff., and the evidence that their First Chief, Charlot, never signed the agreement published with his signature and that the agreement was tainted with fraud. [9839

JEAN M. MOORE. Buried treasure on the Little Big Horn. True West, 7(6): 26-7, 59 (Jul-Aug). views. On the possible existence and location of a cache of money, watches, rings, and other personal belongings removed from the bodies of men killed in Custer's battle there, 25 Jun. 1876. [9840

JOHN S. GRAY. The short-lived death of Liver-Eating Johnson. Westerners brand book (Chicago), 16:79-80 (Dec). On a false report of the death of John Johnston or Johnson (1822?-1900) in 1877. Includes an interview with Brig. Gen. Samuel D. Sturgis on the service of "the hepatophagous scout" in the Seventh Cavalry (from the Bismarck Tribune, 7 Feb. 1878), and other newspaper notices. [9841

The ART of C. M. Russell. Montana, 10(3):78-9 (Jul). Letters to the editor from 11 readers, agreeing with or dissenting from "the so-called 'overplay' given C. M. Russell [1864-1926] and his art in your magazine." [9842

KATHERINE CRUMB. Montana's first bounty collector. Montana, 10(2):44-5 (Apr). port., view. On Ryland R. Crumb, "commonly known as Roy Crumb," who shot a bear in the Whitetail Basin in May 1883. [9843

LESLIE WATSON RANDALL. "If you want to see me, Teddy--you know where I live!" By Gay Randall. Frontier times, 34(1):12-13, 47 (winter). views. On Yankee Jim George (fl. 1883-1903), owner of a toll road and a 5-room log hotel on the Yellowstone in Yankee Jim Canyon north of Yellowstone Park, "probably one of the most fabulous old liars of all the West," known to Rudyard Kipling and Theodore Roosevelt and to the author. [9844

LESLIE WATSON RANDALL. The man who put the dude in dude ranching. Montana, 10(3):29-41 (Jul). ports., views. On the author's father, James Norris Randall (1867-1957), cowboy, trapper and hunter, stage-driver, and "guide to big-game hunters" in Montana, 1884 ff., and his headquarters at the OTO Ranch in the Cedar Creek Valley, where from 1910 till 1934 he provided and advertised log cabins and other accommodations for wealthy hunters from the East. [9845

BOB HUDSON & ISABELLE JOHNSON. The Indians' last trip to Nye. Mont. Inst. Arts quar., 10(4):15-16 (summer 1958). Recollections of the misbehavior of some Crow Indians in 1886. [9846

MARTY KELLY. Yogo! True West, 7(3):22-3, 54 (Jan-Feb). views. On blue-sapphire mines in Yogo Canyon in the Little Belt Mountains of Montana, near the former Hoover City, and their development by British and American capital, 1886-1949. [9847

R. A. DIGHTMAN & M. E. BEATTY. Recent Montana glacier and climate trends [1887-1951]. Mont. Acad. Sciences, Proc., 12 (1952): 127-39. diagr., tables. notes. From the Monthly weather review, May 1952. [9848

REGINA FLANNERY. Individual variation in culture. International Congress of Anthropological and Ethnological Sciences, 5th, 1956, Men and cultures: selected papers, ed. Anthony F. C. Wallace (Phila.: Univ. of Pennsylvania Press [1960]), p. 87-92. notes. On attitudes of Gros Ventre women in Montana and the deviations of one of the women, Coming Daylight, from the "dominant trend" of their culture. [9849

BESS (SNOW) McCOLLUM. Old Granite remembered. Montana, 10(1):61 (Jan). On Granite, Mont., during the years of the author's residence there, 1889 to ca. 1895. [9850

MICHAEL STEPHEN KENNEDY. O[laf] C[arl] Seltzer [1877-1957?]: meticulous master of Western art. Montana, 10(3):2-21 (Jul). port., views. notes. On his emigration from Denmark to Great Falls in 1892, his work there as a machinist, his lessons in painting from C. M. Russell, and after 1921 his work as a painter in watercolors and oils, especially of Montana scenes and frontier characters; with reproductions of 40 of his paintings. [9851

EDWARD L. KIMBALL. Defamation: the Montana law [since 1895]. Mont. law rev., 20:1-39 (fall 1958). notes. [9852

JACOBA (BAKKER) BOOTHMAN BRAD (born 1879). Homestead on the Kootenai. Caldwell, Idaho: Caxton Printers, 1960. 180 p. ports., view. On the life of the author and her husband, Harry Boothman, on a ranch near Libby, Mont., 1898-1917. [9853

CLARK WISSLER (1870-1947). The social life of the Blackfoot Indians. Margaret Mead & Ruth L. Bunzel, eds., The golden age of American anthropology (N.Y.: George Braziller, 1960), p. 344-61. diagrs., tables, views. notes. First printed 1911-12. Based upon observations by the author in 1903. [9854

ROBERT HARRY LOWIE (1883-1957), ed. Crow texts. Berkeley: Univ. of California Press, 1960. xiii, 550 p. notes. Preface signed: Luella Cole Lowie. Texts collected by the editor at the Crow Reservation, Montana, 1906-16, 1931, with his interlinear translation. Contents.--1. Accounts dealing with actual events or customs.--2. Mythological tales and other fictional stories.--3. Tales from the Coyote cycle.--4. Myths concerning the Creation.--5. Stories of Crow heroes.--6. Historical and semi-historical accounts.--7. Songs, prayers, and sayings.--8. Miscellaneous short stories and fragments. [9855

ROBERT HARRY LOWIE (1883-1957), comp. Crow word lists: Crow-English and English-Crow vocabularies. [Edited by Luella Cole Lowie.] Berkeley: Univ. of California Press, 1960. x, [2], 411 p. "Designed to accompany [the compiler's] Crow texts." [9856

RICHARD T. RUETTEN. Anaconda journalism: the end of an era. Journalism quar., 37:3-12, 104 (winter). notes. On the secret ownership of Montana newspapers by the Anaconda Copper Mining Company as early as 1906, totaling 8 papers in the years 1929-59, all of which were sold in 1959 to the Lee Syndicate; with an analysis of the Company's editorial policies and those of the many "anti-company papers." [9857

ROBERT HARRY LOWIE (1883-1957). Observations on the literary style of the Crow Indians. Lowie's selected papers in anthropology, ed. Cora Du Bois (Berkeley: Univ. of California Press, 1960), p. 165-76. notes. From Festschrift Professor Dr. Richard Thurnwald zu seinem achtzigsten Geburtstag gewidmet (Berlin, 1950). Includes translations of 2 oral versions (1907, 1931) of an account of the same event. [9858

KENNETH M. BOE. Periodicity of cone crops for five Montana counties [1908-53]. Mont. Acad. Sciences, Proc., 14 (1954): 5-9. tables. bibliog. [9859

FAY KUHLMAN. The way of an artist. Mont. Inst. Arts quar., 10(4); 13-14 (summer 1958). port. On Earl Snook (died 1951) and Eleonora (Schroeder) Snook, proprietors of the Snook Art Company, dealing in "paints and decorating supplies ... good china, prints, pictures, and objets d'art" in Billings, Mont., as early as 1908, and their encouragement and support of Montana artists. [9860

PAUL BUSCH. Montana's only interurban. Railroad mag., 71(1):29-30 (Dec 1959). view. On the Gallatin Valley Electric Railway, connecting Bozeman and Three Forks, 1909-30, as recalled by the author, "the last survivor of its original employees." [9861

GORDON A. HUTTON. Timber mortality [from fire, insects, and disease]--a loss to Montana's economy [1910-52]. Mont. Acad. Sciences, Proc., 13 (1953): 79-82. [9862

ROBERT HARRY LOWIE (1883-1957). My Crow interpreter. Joseph B. Casagrande, ed., In the company of men: twenty portraits by anthropologists (N.Y.: Harper [1960]), p. 427-37. port. On James Carpenter (died 1937), Lowie's interpreter, guide, teacher, and informant in his visits to the Crow Indian Reservation in southern Montana, 1910-37; with several letters from Carpenter on matters of Crow grammar, customs, etc. [9863

JESSIE (STAINES) LINCOLN MITCHELL C[harles] M[arion] Russell--the White Indian. Montana, 10(1):2-13 (Jan). ports., views. Recollections and anecdotes of Russell as a neighbor and fellow artist in Great Falls, 1912-26. [9864

WILLIAM WILDSCHUT (died 1955). Crow Indian medicine bundles. ... Edited by John C. Ewers. N.Y., 1960. ix, 178 p. port., views (part col.). bibliog. (p. 174-78). (Contributions from the Museum of the American Indian, Heye Foundation, 17.) Manuscript written for the Museum in 1927 by a Billings, Mont., businessman who since 1918 had collected more than 260 medicine bundles in the Crow Reservation. Consists of a chapter on each of 10 classes of these bundles and the beliefs associated with them, and a "Historical and comparative survey," by the editor, of the prehistoric and historic Crow Indians and the use of medicine bundles by them and "other upper Missouri tribes." [9865

JIM LOGAN. Branson G. Stevenson: artist in many fields. Mont. Inst. Arts quar., 11(3):3-6 (spring 1959). ports., view. On his avocations in painting, engraving, ceramics, and sculpture since his settlement in Great Falls ca. 1922. [9866

LESLIE B. DAVIS. Folktale research among the Upper Pend'Oreille [sic] Indians of Montana [1923-59]. Mont. Acad. Sciences, Proc., 20:58-62. [9867

L. S. MATTHEW. Christmas trees ... profitable woodland crops. Am. forests, 62(12):14-16, 63 (Dec 1956). views. On the raising of Douglas firs for Christmas trees in Montana, 1927-56. [9868

GORDON BROWDER. Redistribution of Montana population [1930-50]. Mont. Acad. Sciences, Proc., 13 (1953): 77-8. [9869

A. R. STAGE. Growth of thinned ponderosa pine in western Montana [1933-58]. Jour. forestry, 56:757-60 (Oct 1958). diagrs., tables. [9870

ROBERT HARRY LOWIE (1883-1957). The Crow Indians. Margaret Mead & Ruth L. Bunzel, eds., The golden age of American anthropology (N.Y.: George Braziller, 1960), p. 362-76. From the author's book of the same title (1935). [9871

MONTANA STATE UNIVERSITY. Bureau of Business and Economic Research. Personal income estimates for Montana counties, selected years, 1939-1956. Edward J. Chambers, Director. Missoula, 1960. iv, 56 leaves. diagr., maps, tables. bibliog. (leaves 50-56), notes. (Its Regional study 13.) [9872

ARMAND PETER RUDERMAN. Unity and diversity in Montana's economic life [1939-51]. Mont. Acad. Sciences, Proc., 10 (1951):105-11. [9873

JESSE LEE McWILLIAMS & PHILIP E. VAN CLEAVE. A comparison of crested wheatgrass and native grass mixtures seeded on rangeland in eastern Montana [1940-57]. Jour. range management, 13:91-4 (Mar). table, views. [9874

GORDON BROWDER & VERNA M. MILLER. Crime in a Montana community. Mont. Acad. Sciences, Proc., 19 (1959): 26-8. On "crime rates, as indicated by arrests," in Missoula, 1947-56. [9875

MURLYN BENNETT DICKERMAN & S. BLAIR HUTCHISON. Montana's timber base for industrial growth [1947-51]. Mont. Acad. Sciences, Proc., 11 (1952): 43-6. [9876

IDAHO

ALFRED BERTRAM GUTHRIE, JR. Idaho [its traditions and characteristics]. Holiday, American panorama west of the Mississippi: a Holiday magazine book (Garden City, N.Y.: Doubleday [1960]), p. 101-16. [9877

LEEDICE KISSANE. Footprints into footnotes. [Pocatello? Idaho, 1960. 1], 18 leaves. (At head of title: Idaho State College, faculty seminar, April 12, 1960.) Examples of the "usability of Idaho resources in American studies programs," indicating information in Idaho records, historical manuscripts, and newspapers about Cariboo (ghost town), the settlement of New Sweden, Ellen (Rolfe) Veblen (Mrs. Thorstein Veblen), Bigfoot (Snake Indian, died 1868), and the murder of ex-Gov. Frank Steunenburg by Harry Orchard. [9878

SVEN LILJEBLAD. The Indians of Idaho. Idaho yesterdays, 4(3):22-8 (fall). [9879

WILLARD B. ROBINSON. Frontier architecture: Father [Anthony] Ravalli and the design of the Coeur d'Alene Mission of the Sacred Heart. Idaho yesterdays, 3(4):2-6 (winter). diagrs., view. notes. On the construction and the modified Greek Revival style of the Cataldo Mission, built before 1853. [9880

THE LAWYER, Nez Perce chief. Grievances of the Nez Perce. Idaho yesterdays, 4(3):6-7 (fall). From the Golden Age, Lewiston, Idaho, 27 Aug. 1864. Translated address of the Chief of the Nez Perce Indians to Caleb Lyon, Governor of Idaho, 21 Aug. 1864, complaining that the treaty made in 1855 between the United States and the tribe had not been fulfilled by the United States. [9881

ELIAS DAVIDSON PIERCE (1824-97). Orofino gold! E. D. Pierce's own story. Edited by Dr. Ralph Burcham. Idaho yesterdays, 4(3):2-5, 8-9 (fall). ports. Part of manuscript recollections of prospecting by the author and his associates near the Nez Perce country on the Clearwater but outside their reservation, and the discovery of gold there, Feb.-Oct. 1860. [9882

MERRILL D. BEAL. Cache Valley pioneers: the founding of Franklin in 1860. Idaho yesterdays, 4(1):2-7 (spring). facsims. Includes a diary kept by William Woodward, 6 Apr.-21 Oct. 1861, and refers briefly to later events in this Mormon community till 1879. [9883

IDAHO HISTORICAL SOCIETY. Clearwater gold rush [as reported in contemporary newspapers, 1861]. Idaho yesterdays, 4(1):12-15, 18-26 (spring). views. notes. Includes accounts by M. J. Noyes, C. H. Armstrong, A. J. Thibodo, J. C. Franklin, W. F. Bassett, J. H. Fairchild, Charles Getzler, David C. Hatch, and Israel Mitchell. [9884

IDAHO HISTORICAL SOCIETY. News from the Nez Perce mines. Idaho yesterdays, 3(4):19-29 (winter). facsims., map, port. notes. Accounts of the discovery of gold on Orofino Creek and the founding of Pierce as reported in contemporary newspapers, Feb.-Apr. 1861. Includes reports from S. F. Ledyard, William Cox, M. J. Noyes, John R. Bernfeil, and A. B. Power, and a long narrative by C. L. Goodrich of his travels from Walla Walla to the mines. [9885

ORO FINO MINING DISTRICT, Idaho. Mining laws of the Oro Fino District. Idaho yesterdays, 3(4):18 (winter). Text of laws "adopted at a mass meeting of the miners of said District," 5 Jan. 1861, including revisions up to Mar. 1861. [9886

DORINE GOERTZEN. Boise Basin brocade. Boise, Idaho: Capitol Lithograph and Print, ©1960. [24] p. maps (on cover). Legends and history, 1862-65, concerning "the fabulous Boise Basin, scene of America's greatest gold rush," centered in Idaho City. [9887

MILDRETTA (HAMILTON) ADAMS. Historic Silver City: the story of the Owyhees. Homedale, Idaho: Owyhee Chronicle, ©1960. 60 p. facsims., map, ports., table, views. bibliog. (p. 60). On Owyhee County and Silver City, Idaho, 1863-1904. [9888

SALLY JEAN LAIDLAW. Federal Indian land policy and the Fort Hall Indians. Pocatello, Idaho, 1960. [2], ii-iii, 61 p. bibliog. (p. 58-61). (Occasional papers of the Idaho State College Museum, 3.) On the "injustice and stupidity" of "Federal policy on Indian affairs" as illustrated by the Fort Hall Indian Reservation, Idaho, established in 1868 for the Shoshone and Bannock Indians. [9889

KETCHUM Keystone. Univ. Idaho, Bookmark, 12: leaves 78-83 (Mar). History of a newspaper, 1881-98. [9890

A. McKAY RICH. The two Montpeliers. Idaho yesterdays, 3(4):8-14 (winter). views. notes. On the rapid growth of this Bear Lake settlement after the arrival of the Union Pacific Railroad in 1882, the division and hostility between the original Mormon town and the "downtown" formed round the railroad station, the jailing of polygamists by the town authorities and the Mormon condemnation of liquor, tobacco, dancing, and the "opera house," and the gradual disappearance of hostility after 1896. [9891

JASPER RAND. [Letter to Probate Judge John C. Harkness of Shoshone County, 20 Sep. 1885.] Idaho yesterdays, 3(4):7 (winter). News about the apprehension of 8 murderers of D. M. Fraser, merchant, and the execution of 5 of them at Pierce City. Appended: account of the murder of Fraser and the lynching of 5 Chinese by "Indians," from the Spokane review of 26 Sep. 1885. [9892

CHARLES RATHBONE STARK, JR. The Hercules and the Day family. Pac. Northwesterner, 4:1-7 (winter). On the discovery of a low-grade silver-and-lead quartz vein somewhere near Milo (later Wardner), Idaho, by "Harry" Day (Henry Loren Day II) in 1889, the organization of the Hercules Mining Company, Burke, Idaho, in 1898 and the "vast empire of other mines" acquired by the Day family and organized in 1947 as Day Mines, Inc. [9893

FRANK P. ROWLAND. Founding of McCall, Idaho. Boise, Idaho, 1960. 24 p. port., views. Mainly eyewitness recollections, 1891-1960. [9894

THOSE were the days ... when a house like this was called a "cottage." Idaho yesterdays, 3(4):16-17 (winter). views. On an "ornate Victorian house" designed by J. E. Tourtellotte for Walter E. Pierce (Mayor of Boise in 1896, builder of an interurban railroad), later occupied by Senator Borah and family. [9895

HENRY D. BECKER. History of the Mennonites in Idaho [since 1899]. Mennonite hist. bul., 11(1):1-3 (Jan 1950). [9896

IDAHO STATE TRIBUNE, Wallace, Idaho. Disaster on the Northern Pacific--a contemporary report of the north Idaho snow slide of 1903. Idaho yesterdays, 4(1):32 (spring). views. From the issue of 11 Feb. 1903. On the plunge of a car and a locomotive of the Northern Pacific 80 feet into a gorge from a collapsed trestle, without injury to crew or passengers. [9897

LEEDICE KISSANE. The Haywood trial: Steve Adams, the speechless witness. Idaho yesterdays, 4(3):18-21 (fall). port., view. On the criminal activities to which he confessed, his expected use as a witness in proceedings against William D. Haywood and others, and his repudiation of the confession. [9898

ABE CARL RAVITZ & JAMES NEAL PRIMM, eds. The Haywood case: materials for analysis. San Francisco: Chandler Pub. Co. [1960]. viii, [2], 244 p. Contemporary documents relating to the extradition of William Dudley Haywood from Colorado to Idaho and his trial and acquittal at Boise on charges of participation in the murder of Frank Steunenberg, former Governor of Idaho, 1907. Includes addresses by William E. Borah, Prosecutor, and Clarence Darrow, defense counsel. [9899

STEPHEN SCHEINBERG. The Haywood trial: Theodore Roosevelt's "undesirable citizens." Idaho yesterdays, 4(3):10-15 (fall). port., view. On the trial of William D. Haywood and 2 other members of the Western Federation of Miners on charges of being accessories to the murder of former Gov. Frank Steunenberg of Idaho, Roosevelt's published comments hostile to the defendants, and his characterization of their acquittal as "a gross miscarriage of justice," 1907. [9900

JERRY ARMSTRONG. Harry Charters [born 1925], champion bulldogger. West. horseman, 25(12):10, 70-71 (Dec). ports. On his early life in Melba, Idaho, and his career as a rodeo performer. [9901

IRVEN O. BUSS & RICHARD D. DAUGHERTY. The effects of hunting by the Nez Perce Indians on big-game populations in northern Idaho [1934-55]. State College Wash., Research studies, 26:119-57 (Sep 1958). map, tables, views. bibliog., notes. [9902

ANN GERMO. A contrast of mining communities. Delta Kappa Gamma bul., 23(3):52-5 (spring 1957). On the author's work as a teacher in Kellogg, Idaho, since ca. 1935. [9903

WADE H. ANDREWS. Idaho hand book of population, agricultural, and business data, 1940-1950-1954, with 1960 estimates of population. Moscow: Highway Economics Research, Bureau of Business and Economic Research, College of Business Administration, Univ. of Idaho [1960]. ii, 63 p. tables. [9904

DONALD S. DOUGLAS, A. L. HAFENRICHTER, & K. H. KLAGES. Cultural methods and their relation to establishment of native and exotic grasses in range seedings [Aberdeen, Idaho, 1947-59]. Jour. range management, 13:53-7 (Mar). tables. [9905

WYOMING

HAMILTON BASSO (1904-64). Wyoming [its traditions and characteristics]. Holiday, American panorama west of the Mississippi: a Holiday magazine book (Garden City, N.Y.: Doubleday [1960]), p. 132-52. [9906

ÅKE HULTKRANTZ. Religious aspects of the Wind River [Wyo.] Shoshoni folk literature. Stanley Diamond, ed., Culture in history: essays in honor of Paul Radin (N.Y.: Columbia Univ. Press for Brandeis Univ., 1960), p. 552-69. notes. [9907

WILLIAM THOMAS MULLOY. The James Allen site, near Laramie, Wyoming. Am. antiq., 25:112-16 (Jul 1959). views. bibliog. On "a bison-kill site in Wyoming with a radiocarbon age of about 8000 years," yielding "numerous points of a type formerly termed 'Oblique Yuman,'" which the author proposes to call "Allen points"; with some account of their characteristics and their distribution in the West. [9908

WELDON FAIRBANKS HEALD. The Yellowstone story [1807-72]: genesis of the national park idea. Utah hist. quar., 28:98-110 (Apr). ports., views. [9909

MICHAEL FROME. Let's go trail riding. Am. forests, 66(1):20-23, 42-4 (Jan). ports., views. Includes a historical sketch of the area of Bridger National Forest, Wyo., 1823-1959. [9910

PHILLIP ROCHLIN. Frémont for the philatelist: the centennial of John Charles Frémont's campaign for the Presidency. Essay proof jour., 13:177-84 (Jul. 1956). facsims., views. notes. Deals particularly with his ascent of what he described as "the highest peak of the Rocky Mountains", the various engravings since 1849 that represent the ascent, and the commemorative 5-cent stamp issued in 1898. [9911

DALE LOWELL MORGAN. The ferries of the Forty-Niners. Ann. Wyo., 31:4-31, 145-89; 32:51-69, 167-203 (Apr 1959-Oct 1960). views. notes. Exhaustive collection of information from the known diaries, letters, and reminiscences, including many in manuscript, kept during 1849 by Gold Rush travelers crossing the North Platte, the Green River, and other Wyoming rivers. [9912

JAMES CHISHOLM (1838-1903). South Pass, 1868: James Chisholm's journal of the Wyoming gold rush. Introduced and edited by Lola M. Homsher. [Lincoln:] Univ. of Nebraska Press, 1960. vi, 244, [1] p. cartoons, facsims., maps, views. bibliog. (p. 232-9), notes. (The pioneer heritage series, 3.) Diary from 8 Sep. 1868 to some date after 18 Sep., unfinished, recording his travels from Green River to South Pass City and his visits to mines, with notes for articles and illustrative drawings; newspaper letters by him dated Cheyenne, 21, 22, and 27 Mar. 1868, manuscript letter to a Mrs. Garrison (27 Mar. 1868), and 2 undated letters to his daughter, embedded in introduction and notes; and biographical information and some account of the confusing and enigmatic documents printed in this volume. [9913

JAMES B. DALY & 4 others. The minor courts of Wyoming [justice-of-the-peace courts and police courts, 1868-1959]. Wyo. law jour., 15:22-47 (fall). notes. Deals largely with proposals for reorganization. [9914

WALTER HALL WHEELER. The uintatheres and the Cope-Marsh War. Science, 131:1171-6 (22 Apr). ports., views. notes. On a controversy between Edward Drinker Cope and Othniel Charles Marsh about large fossils discovered by them in Wyoming, 1868-90. [9915

MABEL BASS. What's in a name? Ann. Wyo., 32:164-6 (Oct). view. On Jim Moore (died ca. 1875), former Pony Express rider, cattleman in present Goshen County, who fashioned his JM brand ca. 1869, and the use of the name for the Jay Em Ranch, Jay

Em Creek, the post office of Jay Em (established 1899), and the village of Jay Em. [9916

WELDON FAIRBANKS HEALD. Lost for 37 days in Yellowstone. Frontier times, 34(2):20-21, 43-5 (spring). ports., views. On an experience of Truman C. Everts, a member of the Washburn-Doane Expedition to the Yellowstone country, 1870. [9917

JAMES W. BROWN. The administration of law in Yellowstone National Park [1872-1959]. Wyo. law jour., 14:9-16 (fall 1959). notes. On the exclusive jurisdiction of the U.S. Government over the administration of justice there. [9918

RICHARD TRIMBLE (1857-1924). Harvard man out West: the letters of Richard Trimble, 1882-1887. Edited by Gene M. Gressley. Montana, 10(1): 14-23 (Jan). ports., views. notes. Letters to his family in New York, dated in Wyoming and elsewhere, 27 Aug. 1882-1 May 1887, on his partnership with Hubert E. Teschemacher and Frederic De Billier in the Wyoming cattle business. [9919

U.S. Bureau of Mines. Petroleum and natural gas fields in Wyoming (1884-1960). By Paul Biggs and Ralph H[omeward] Espach. Wash.: U.S. Govt. Print. Off., 1960. ix, 538 p. diagrs. (part fold.), facsims., maps (part fold.), tables (part double). bibliog. (p. 531-8), notes. (Its Bulletin 582.) [9920

THELMA GATCHELL CONDIT. The Hole-in-the-Wall. ... Part VI. Ono--early post office. Ann. Wyo., 32:70-101 (Apr). map, ports. On a community about 30 miles south of Buffalo, Wyo., close to the Big Horn Mountains in Johnson County, 1888-96, and some of the dogs, horses, and early settlers there. [9921

THELMA GATCHELL CONDIT. The Hole-in-the-Wall. Part VII--Section I--Early day dances. Ann. Wyo., 32: 205-17 (Oct). ports., views. Anecdotes about dances, picnics, barbecues, and other recreations of the early settlers in southern Johnson County, Wyo., and adjacent areas, 1894-1907, especially on the Hat Ranch of Lou Webb and Janet (Mercer) Webb. [9922

SILAS DISHNO (born 1858). Dishno of the Big Hole Valley. [Reported] by Grace Roffey Pratt. Montana, 10(2): 32-41 (Apr). ports., views. notes. Recollections by a centenarian who lived in the Big Hole Basin near Jackson, Wyo., as a rancher from 1895 to ca. 1930. [9923

ROBERT F. STRAIT. The old McShane tie camp and the Rockwood fire. As told to C. C. Rawlings by Robert F. Strait. Ann. Wyo., 32:144-63 (Oct). ports., views. On the author's work for the McShane Tie Company on the Tongue River in the Big Horn Mountains, 1898-99; with an account of its flumes, mills, and other properties, its crews, its headquarters at Rockwood, and the forest fire that almost destroyed it. [9924

DELMER WOOD BERRY. Geology and ground-water resources of the Rawlins area, Carbon County, Wyoming [1900-1955]. Wash.: U.S. Govt. Print. Off., 1960. iv, 74 p. diagrs., maps, tables (part double). bibliog. (p. 71), notes. (U.S. Geological Survey. Water-supply paper 1458.) [9925

FRANK J. TRELEASE. Severance of water rights from Wyoming lands [1909-59]: a report to the Wyoming Legislative Research Committee. [Cheyenne, 1960. 3], 54 leaves. (Wyoming Legislative Research Committee. Research report 2.) [9926

CHARLES CARROLL NIEHUIS. I tackled a grizzly with a .22 hi-power [Wyoming, Feb. 1921]. True West, 7(4):32-3, 47-8 (Mar-Apr). Recollections by a professional hunter for the U.S. Biological Survey. [9927

CHARLES E. HAMILTON. De novo judicial review of Wyoming administrative findings [1937-58]. Wyo. law jour., 15:67-72 (fall). notes. [9928

WYOMING PIONEER ASSOCIATION. Emigrant Trail Trek No. 10. ... Compiled by Maurine Carley, Trek Historian. Ann. Wyo., 32:102-23, 219-38 (Apr, Oct). maps, views. Report of an annual antiquarian expedition along the emigrant trail on the north side of the Platte River from the Nebraska line to Sage Creek, 166 miles, including the sites of Fort Laramie and Fort Fetterman, 3-5 Jul. 1959; with historical addresses about these and other landmarks along the trail, by Bruce McKinstry (presenting excerpts, 1850, from the diary of his ancestor, Byron N. McKinstry) and several other participants. [9929

COLORADO

ROBERT B. McCOY. People of the Mesa Verde. Natl. parks mag., 34(158): 8-10 (Nov). views. On the prehistoric inhabitants of the Mesa Verde in Colorado, occupied from ca. 1 to ca. 1300, abandoned by degrees as the result of a great drought that began in 1276. [9930

JACK CLIFFORD MOOMAW. The "Ring Makers." Southw. lore, 25(4): 5-9 (Mar). On prehistoric stone circles found in "the eastern foothills of northern Colorado." [9931

DEBS MYERS. Colorado [its traditions and characteristics]. Holiday, American panorama west of the Mississippi: a Holiday magazine book (Garden City, N.Y.: Doubleday [1960]), p. 183-99. [9932

STATE HISTORICAL SOCIETY OF COLORADO. Historical map of early Colorado and highlights of Colorado history. Denver, 1958 [c1949]. col. map. In pocket with: Colorado. State Planning Commission. Colorado, 1956-1958: year book of the State of Colorado. [n. p., n. d.] Map embellished "with portraits of distinguished leaders and portrayals of historic events, frontier forts, and pioneer trails." On back: chronology from "20,000 years ago" to 1945. [9933

LOUIS BERNHARDT SPORLEDER, SR. (1857-1943). The romance of the Spanish Peaks. [n. p.:] O'Brien Print & Stationery Co., 1960. 31, [2] p. ports., views. History and legends of the Huajatolla Mountains and the upper Cucharas Valley, Huerfano County, Colo., probably first seen by white men in 1706 and unsettled by whites till ca. 1845, and the author's life there during more than 50 years. [9934

ROBERT B. McCOY. The Black Canyon--place of "high rocks and much water." Natl. parks mag., 35(155):4-7 (Aug). facsim., views. On explorations and surveys of the Black Canyon of the Gunnison River, Colorado, since 1761, and the establishment of the Black Canyon National Monument in 1933. [9935

CHARLES WESLEY HURD. Bents' Stockade hidden in the hills. [Las Animas? Colo., 1960. 4], 88, [4] p. ports., tables, views. bibliog. (p. 89). On the activities of William Bent (1809-69) and his brother Charles as trappers and Indian traders on the Arkansas River in Colorado, their partnership with Ceran St. Vrain (1822-69), and their headquarters at Bent's Stockade and Bent's Fort; with numerous documents copied from manuscript. [9936

EDNA SIROIS RYAN. Narrative history of Buffalo Creek and Buffalo Park, Jefferson County, Colorado [1844-1960. Denver? 1960.] 34, [1] p. views. [9937

A. M. HARTUNG. White Head, the horse thief. Quarter horse jour., 7(3):84-5 (Dec 1954). On a wild horse caught by Cheyenne Indians in Colorado and trained by them to round up and drive herds of tame horses "to help them on their horse-stealing expeditions," 1848-49. [9938

DONALD CAMPBELL KEMP. Story of the Grand Island Mining District of Boulder County, Colorado: silver, gold, and black iron [1858-1960]. Denver: Sage Books [1960]. 230 p. facsim., maps (1 fold.), port., tables, views. bibliog. (p. 221-5). Includes chapters on Caribou, Nederland, and Happy Valley; and 56 plates, with a detailed description of each. [9939

HAROLD E. POPHAM. Early mining in Colorado [1858 to ca. 1900]. Dicta, 36:163-8 (Mar-Apr 1859). port. Includes reference to earlier mining in Colorado. [9940

ALLEN DU PONT BRECK. The centennial history of the Jews of Colorado, 1859-1959. Denver: Hirschfeld Press, 1960. xv, 360 p. ports., tables, views. bibliog. (p. 334-43), notes. (The West in American history, 1.) [9941

F. M. BROWN. Two early entomological collectors in Colorado. Entomol. news, 68:41-7 (Feb 1957). bibliog. On the visits of Winslow J. Howard (fl. 1860-66), 1860-65, and of William S. Wood, Jr. (fl. 1858-84), 1859: with the scanty biographical data available. [9942

ROBERT G. DUNBAR. The significance of the Colorado agricultural frontier. Agric. hist., 34:119-25 (Jul). notes. On "problems of land, credit, and markets" faced by the farmers settled "in the valleys of the South Platte and its tributaries," and particularly their establishment of the Doctrine of Prior Appropriation of water and their rejection of the Doctrine of Riparian Rights, 1859-80. [9943

GOLDING FAIRFIELD. The original "rush to the Rockies." Dicta, 36:131-8 (Mar-Apr 1959). port. On law and government in Colorado, 1859-72. [9944

ALBERT T. FRANTZ. Colorado appellate courts--the first hundred years [1859-1959]. Dicta, 36:103-10 (Mar-Apr 1959). port. notes. [9945

JESSE WILLIAM GERN. Colorado mountain theatre: history of theatre at Central City, 1859-1885. Ann Arbor: University Microfilms, 1960. Positive microfilm of typescript. [638] leaves. Thesis--Ohio State Univ. Abstracted: Dissert. abstracts, 21:1289 (Nov). [9946

CLYDE THOMAS HANKEY. A Colorado word geography. Ann Arbor: University Microfilms, 1960. Positive microfilm of typescript. [154] leaves. Thesis--Univ. of Michigan. Abstracted: Dissert. abstracts, 21:339-40 (Aug). Printed: A Colorado word geography. University: Univ. of Alabama Press for the Society, 1960. ix, 82 p. maps, tables. bibliog. (p. 75-6), notes. (American Dialect Society. Publication 34.) On the sources and distribution of dialects in English speech in Colorado since 1859. Based upon materials collected for the Linguistic Atlas of the Rocky Mountains. [9947

JULIA F. LIPSEY. Governor Hunt of Colorado Territory: his life and his family. Colorado Springs: Priv. print. by J. J. Lipsey, Western Books, 1960. 24 p. ports., views. On the activities of Alexander Cameron Hunt (1825?-1894) in Colorado business and politics, 1859-83. [9948

WILLIAM HEDGES ROBINSON, JR. The Supreme Court of the Territory of Jefferson [Oct. 1959-Jun. 1861]. Dicta, 36:155-62 (Mar-Apr 1959). port. [9949

JAMES GRAFTON ROGERS. The beginnings of law in Colorado [1859-61]. Dicta, 36:111-20 (Mar-Apr 1959). port. On mining districts, "claim clubs," and "people's courts." [9950

VALERIE WHYMAN. Benjamin Woodbury [1831-1910]. Colo. mag., 37:13-17 (Jan). ports. bibliog. On the author's great-grandfather, who removed from Maine to Colorado in 1859, mined gold, and established the firm of Woodbury & Norton, millwrights and contractors, at Black Hawk. [9951

JOHN EVANS. From stagecoach to space age: 100 years of banking in the Rocky Mountain West (1860-1960). N.Y.: Newcomen Soc. in North America, 1960. 24 p. views. On the First National Bank of Denver. [9952

The PIONEER Men and Women of Colorado celebrate their centennial. Colo. mag., 37:241-4 (Oct). view. On the Ladies Union Aid Society (1860-72), renamed the Pioneer Ladies Aid Society (1872-1934), the Society of Colorado Pioneers (1872-1943), the Pioneer Women of Colorado, and the merger of the last 2 as the Pioneer Men and Women of Colorado. [9953

PONY Express centennial. Colo. mag., 37:219-24 (Jul). facsims., views. On the stations and riders of the Pony Express in Colorado, 1860-61. [9954

GEORGE CHARLES ROCHE III. Mt. Princeton Hot Springs: a brief history [since "the early 1860's"]. Colo. mag., 37:18-27 (Jan). views. notes. On the Heywood Hot Springs House, the silver-mining boom and its collapse, and the "magnificent" Princeton Hot Springs Hotel (completed in 1884 and razed in 1950). [9955

ROBERT M. JOHNSON. Municipal home-rule in Colorado: self-determination v. State supremacy [1861-1960]. Dicta, 37:240-58 (Jul-Aug). notes. [9956

EVERETT BAIR. Bloody trail of the Espinosas. True West, 7(4):12-13, 51-3 (Mar-Apr). ports., view. On Felipe Nerio Espinosa and a younger relative, their career of "wanton, demoniacal murder" in southern Colorado, and their apprehension by Tom Tobin, who shot them, cut off their heads, and collected bounty, 1863. [9957

RODMAN WILSON PAUL. Colorado as a pioneer of science in the mining West. Miss. Valley hist. rev., 47:34-50 (Jun). notes. On the heavy losses of the early mining industry in Colorado through ignorance, its increasingly "heavy reliance on scientific advice" in the years between 1868 and 1894, and its movement in this respect away from its "California prototype." [9958

ELIZABETH VIRGINIA (STEELE) WALLACE. Gunnison country. By Betty Wallace. Denver: Sage Books [1960]. 208 p. facsim., maps, ports., views. bibliog. (p. 205-8), notes. On the area bounded by the crest of the Continental Divide, the San Juans, the Uncompahgre River, and the Elk Mountains, 1868-1960. [9959

M. HAZEL HOWE. The story of Silver Plume. [Colorado Springs? 1960. 4], 38 p. views. bibliog. (p. 38). On a "silver camp" in the mountains 45 miles west of Denver, settled in 1870. [9960

BEN GRAY LUMPKIN. Colorado folk songs. West. folklore, 19:77-97 (Apr). music. notes. Examples, 1870s-1950s, all in English; with mention of Spanish, Welsh, and Cornish songs current in Colorado. [9961

CHARLES SPALDING THOMAS (1849-1934). The heritage of the Colorado Bar. Dicta, 25:7-16 (Jan 1948). Reminiscent address, 1925, containing memories and anecdotes of lawyers and judges in Denver and Leadville, 1871-80. [9962

ROBERT TAFT (1894-1955). Asa Gray's ascent of Gray's Rock [in Colorado, 1872]. Asa Gray bul., 1:103-6 (Apr 1952). port. From Transactions of the Kansas Academy of Science, Mar. 1951. [9963

YALE HUFFMAN. Human steaks and a whiskey chaser. Dicta, 36:179-85 (Mar-Apr 1959). port. On the imprisonment at Saguache of Alfred Packer suspected of having robbed, killed, and eaten 5 men in 1873, his escape, his apprehension in 1883, his trial and conviction to be hanged, his retrial on a charge of manslaughter, his pardon by the Governor after 14 years in the Colorado Penetentiary, and his death in 1907; with the speech supposed to have been made by the trial judge, mentioning among "the sickening details of your crime" the fact that "you have eaten up the Democratic majority of Hinsdale County." [9964

VASCO G. SEAVY, JR. Involuntary confessions--fourth stage in Colorado [1873-1950]. Dicta, 31:133-42 (Apr 1954). notes. [9965

MORRIS FRADIN. Pre-historic "Shangri-la." Am. forests, 66(5): 24-5, 55-9 (May). views. On Mesa Verde National Park, Colo., established in 1906 to make accessible and to protect ruins of a prehistoric time discovered in 1874. [9966

ERNEST R. ARCHAMBEAU, JR. Municipal tort liability in Colorado [1875-1960]. Dicta, 37:133-63 (May-Jun). notes. [9967

LOIS BORLAND. Ouray remembered. Colo. mag., 37:188-92 (Jul). On a town settled ca. 1875 as a mining camp. [9968

HAROLD HATHAWAY DUNHAM. Colorado's Constitution of 1876. Dicta, 36:121-30 (Mar-Apr 1959). port. notes. [9969

ROBERT G. ATHEARN. Captivity of the Denver and Rio Grande. Colo. mag., 37:39-58 (Jan). port., views. notes. On the leasing of the Denver and Rio Grande Railroad to the Atchison, Topeka, & Santa Fe, the litigation instituted by the former on charges that the latter had violated the terms of the lease, ending with the cancellation of the lease, and an accommodation between the competing lines, Dec. 1878-Mar. 1880. [9970

A MICHIGAN correspondent in Colorado, 1878. Edited by Sidney Glazer. Colo. mag., 37:207-18 (Jul). views. notes. Five letters from "T.," reprinted from The Michigan Christian herald, Oct. and Nov. 1878, describing Colorado as seen in railroad travels from Denver to the Pike's Peak area and Alamosa and from Denver to Golden and Central City. [9971

THEODORE E. BEYER. The Gold Rush--its cost in health and life. Rocky Mt. med. jour., 56(5):59-61 (May 1959). facsims. On the "health hazards" of the "gold mining community" of Central City and Gilpin County, Colo., 1879-80. [9972

CHARLES McCLUNG LEONARD (1860-1951). Forty years in Colorado mining camps. Colo. mag., 37:161-84 (Jul). views. On the author's life from 1879 to 1918 in Leadville and "most of the [other] mining camps then active in Colorado." [9973

NOLA G. (KIRKPATRICK) KASTEN. Early days in southeastern Colorado. Colo. mag., 37:122-7 (Apr). ports. notes. On the author's life on several ranches in the area within 75 miles of West Las Animas, 1880-86, and in La Junta, 1886-1920. [9974

SAMUEL WALLACE JOHNSON (born 1872). Autobiography of Samuel Wallace Johnson: lawyer, politician, district attorney for six years [1909-16], judge of the district court of First Judicial District of Colorado for twenty-four years. Denver: Big Mountain Press [1960]. 232 p. port. On the author's life in Denver since 1881 and his legal, judicial, and political activities there; with his recollections of many persons eminent in Colorado politics and business. [9975

LESLIE R. KEHL. Enforceability of interest on interest in Colorado [1881-1942]. Dicta, 31:167-72 (May 1954). notes. [9976

OTIS MARSTON. River runners: fast water navigation. Utah hist. quar., 28:290-308 (Jul). ports., views. On "river-running navigation of the Colorado River" in the upper canyons (above the Grand Canyon), 1882-1956. [9977

FRANK R. HOLLENBACK. The Gilpin Tram. Denver: Sage Books [1958]. 64 p. diagrs., facsims., maps (1 fold.), views. On the Gilpin Tramway Company, an ore-hauling line in Gilpin County, Colo., 1886-1917. [9978

JOSIE MOORE CRUM. Three little lines: Silverton Railroad, Silverton, Gladstone, & Northerly, Silverton Northern [San Juan County, Colo., 1887-1942. Durango, Colo.: Durango Herald-News, 1960.] vii, 71 p. facsims., maps (1 fold.), medal, tables, views. bibliog. (p. 71). First printed in 1948; reprinted with "additional information and pictures." [9979

JOHN C. BANKS. Annexation in Colorado. Dicta, 37:259-64 (Jul-Aug). notes. On annexation by municipalities, 1888-1959. [9980

DONALD S. MOLEN. A history of the Denver and Colorado bar associations. Dicta, 36:169-78 (Mar-Apr 1959). port. On the Denver Bar Association (organized in 1891), the Colorado Bar Association (organized in 1897), and their joint activities since 1948. [9981

WILLIAM W. WARDELL. Cripple Creek memories. Colo. mag., 37:28-38 (Jan). views. Reminiscences, 1895-1900. [9982

NELSON ROCKWELL. The case of the bungling bank robbers. Frontier times, 34(4):20-21, 56, 58 (fall). ports., view. On the robbery of the Bank of Meeker, at Meeker, Colo., by Jim Shirley, George Law, and "The Kid", all 3 killed by townsmen, 1896. [9983

ARTHUR HAWTHORNE CARHART. The first ranger. Am. forests, 62(2): 26-7, 55-6 (Feb 1956). ports. On the service of William R. Kreutzer (born 1877) as a U.S. forest ranger in Colorado, 1898-1939. [9984

HOMER E. ROOT. Tangled Roots. N.Y.: Greenwich Book Publishers [1960. 2], 137 p. On the author's undated search for Basketmaker ruins and artifacts in south western Colorado (La Plata and Montezuma Counties); with religious meditations inspired by his findings and by the natural history of the area. [9985

THOMAS A. LEAR. The mudhens of the Denver & Rio Grande. Natl. Railway Hist. Soc., Bul., 25(1):11-14 (1st quar.). views. On 15 "outside frame 2-8-2's" of "the 125 class," serving the Denver & Rio Grande and the Rio Grande Southern, 1903-58. [9986

CARROLL H. COBERLY. Ashcroft. Colo. mag., 37:81-104 (Apr). views. notes. Memories of a lead- and silver-mining town (14 miles from Aspen) during the author's stay from 1906 to ca. 1914. [9987

DWIGHT L. HAMILTON. John Otto [died 1952], trailbuilder. Natl. parks mag., 34(150):13 (Mar). port., views. On his part in the establishment of Colorado National Monument, near Grand Junction, and his service as Honorary Custodian, 1906-52. [9988

WALTER S. LOVELACE. Journalism at the University of Colorado. Colo. mag., 37:265-84 (Oct). notes. Reminiscences and anecdotes, 1909-15. [9989

TERRITORIAL Daughters [of Colorado] celebrate fifty years of accomplishments. Colo. mag., 37:105-7 (Apr). On an organization formed in 1910; with an account of its history and activities by Mrs. Norris Miles, President. [9990

MELVIN ARNOLD COFFEE. Colorado interest law. Dicta, 34:398-410 (Nov-Dec 1957). port. notes. On "small-loan regulation" in Colorado, 1913-56. [9991

WILLIAM E. MEYERS. Twenty-six years under the Colorado Declaratory Judgments Act [1923-49]. Dicta., 27: 177-81 (May 1950). notes. [9992

BOB LLOYD. Good hand for horses. West. horseman, 25(2):42-3, 75-6 (Feb). ports. On Robert Hankla (born 1926), rancher, horse-trainer, and rodeo performer near Pueblo, Colo., and the ingenuity with which he has continued his work since losing his left hand and crippling his right in an accident in 1946. [9993

LAWRENCE DUDLEY LOVE & B. C. GOODELL. Watershed research on the Fraser Experimental Forest [Colorado, 1929-59]. Jour. forestry, 58:272-5 (Apr). table, view. notes. On studies of snow accumulation and "streamflow" in relation to patterns of timber harvesting. [9994

MELVIN ARNOLD COFFEE. Twenty years of Colorado Supreme Court decisions without law. Dicta, 34:61-4 (Jan-Feb 1957). diagr., table. note. On the bad results of "the trend in the Colorado supreme court to affirm district and county court rulings without written opinions, without stating reasons and without citing authority to sustain affirmance," Jan. 1936-Jan. 1956. [9995

HELEN McCARTHY CRENNELL. History of the Colorado Public Health Association, 1938-1958. [Denver?] Reproduced and distributed by the History Committee, Colorado Public Health Assoc. [1959. 5], 52, [2] leaves. bibliog. (leaves 38-40), notes. Reproduction of thesis (M.A.)--Univ. of Colorado. [9996

BOB LLOYD. The Likes of rodeo. West. horseman, 25(9):28, 98-101 (Sep). ports. On Jim Like of Walsenburg, Colo., as a rodeo performer, 1938-55, crippled by poliomyelitis in 1955, subsequently an official of the Rodeo Cowboys Association. [9997

PHILIP HORNBEIN, JR. Labor injunctions under the Colorado Labor Peace Act [1943-48]. Dicta, 26:63-72 (Mar 1949). notes. [9998

BYRON CHURCH. A case history of housing. Appraisal jour., 28:209-12 (Apr). On "the interplay of various government agencies, trade organizations, and the finance and housing industries" in and near Colorado Springs, 1949-59. [9999

Denver

ARTHUR LEON CAMPA. Spanish folksongs in metropolitan Denver. South. folklore quar., 24:179-92 (Sep). notes. On types and origins of songs of Colorado descendants of New Mexico colonials of Mexican ancestry, and of Colorado Sephardic Jews from the Levant or of Levantine ancestry; with several short texts. [10000

G. H. KING. The Clark Gruber & Co. private coinage [Denver, 1860-62]. Selections from The numismatist: United States paper money, tokens, medals, and miscellaneous (Racine, Wis.: Whitman Pub. Co., 1960), p. 53-4. First printed Apr. 1920. [10001

CHARLES B. ROTH. C. T., sage of the Rockies. Denver: Sage Books [1960]. 85 p. ports. On Chauncey Thomas (1872-1941), Denver writer and eccentric; with excerpts from his letters and recollections of his conversation, organized topically. [10002

CHARLOTTE A. BARBOUR. Vanished neighborhood on Capitol Hill, Denver. Colo. mag., 37:254-64 (Oct). views. On 7 "big, family homes of prominent pioneers," built between 1879 and 1895 and torn down in recent years. [10003

FLOYD F. MILES. Fabularis qui advocato. Dicta, 30:344-6 (Sep 1953). Lore about John A. Deweese, Denver lawyer, 1882-1920s. [10004

WILLIAM L. MYATT. Cotillion Hall, Denver. Colo. mag., 37:193-7 (Jul). ports. On a dance hall and dancing academy purchased by William Warren in 1894 and operated by him and later his widow till 1922. [10005

LEIGHTON L. BAKER. How Peterson barrels were made. Am. rifleman, 108(8):26-9 (Aug). ports., views. On the manufacture of rifle barrels by Axel W. Peterson in Denver, 1904-46. [10006

NOLIE MUMEY. The Pioneer Monument: the greatest in the West, the first of its kind to be built in the State. Denver: Denver Board of Realtors, 1955. [6], 27 p. ports., views. notes. On a "fountain-monument" in Denver, designed by Frederick MacMonnies, dedicated in 1910, and unveiled in 1911. [10007

GEORGE T. EVANS. Has the doctrine of stare decisis been abandoned in Colorado? Dicta, 25:91-5 (Apr 1958). notes. On a series of cases involving the authority of the City and County of Denver to regulate the liquor traffic, 1913-43. [10008

BOETTCHER mansion becomes new executive residence. Colo. mag., 37: 198-206 (Jul). views. On a Denver mansion planned and built by the widow and the daughter of Walter Scott Cheesman, acquired by Claude Kedzie Boettcher and Edna (Case) Boettcher in 1926, and presented to the State of

Colorado by Charles Boettcher II in 1960 "as a residence for present and future Governors." [10009

UTAH

AUSTIN E. FIFE. Folk elements in the formation of the Mormon personality [in Utah]. Brigham Young Univ. studies, 2:1-17 (autumn-winter 1959-60). [10010

JESSE DAVID JENNINGS. Early man in Utah. Utah hist. quar., 28:2-27 (Jan). maps, views. On "human occupancy of Utah," which "goes back 10,000 years," and its Desert, Pueblo, and historic periods till the 1870s. [10011

SAMUEL WOOLLEY TAYLOR. Utah [its traditions and characteristics]. Holiday, American panorama west of the Mississippi: a Holiday magazine book (Garden City, N.Y.: Doubleday [1960]), p. 167-82. [10012

JAMES H. GUNNERSON. The Fremont Culture: internal dimensions and external relationships. Am. antiq., 25:373-80 (Jan). bibliog. On "Pueblo and Pueblo-like complexes in Utah north of the Colorado River," ca. 950 to ca. 1200, and their relation to Anasazi culture. [10013

ROBERT HILL LISTER. The Coombs site. [Salt Lake City: Univ. of Utah Press] 1959. xii, 114, [3] p. maps, plans, views. bibliog. (University of Utah. Dept. of Anthropology. Anthropological papers, 41. Glen Canyon series, 8.) On a site at Boulder, Garfield County, Utah, exhibiting evidence of a culture "predominantly Anasazi" and occupied probably between 1075 and 1275. Includes a chapter on pottery by Florence Cline Lister. [10014

MILTON REED HUNTER. Utah Indian stories. [Fourth edition, revised, enlarged, and illustrated.] Salt Lake City: Deseret Book Co., 1960. vi, 128 p. ports., views. 1st ed. 1946. Twenty-two narratives in simple language, mainly from printed sources, about the Indians in and near Utah, 1806-66. [10015

NORMAN F. FURNISS. The Mormon conflict, 1850-1859. New Haven: Yale Univ. Press, 1960. viii, [4], 311 p. map, ports., views. bibliog. (p. 235-49), notes (p. 250-302). (Yale historical publications. Miscellany, 72.) On the relations between the Utah Mormons and the U.S. Government, 1847-61, the intervention of Army forces under Col. Albert Sidney Johnson, the delaying tactics of the Mormons, the unavowed withdrawal by Buchanan and his advisers from "their intention of using force in Utah," and the resulting ambiguities in policy, confusing both to the Army and to Congress but averting armed hostilities in Utah. [10016

THERON H. LUKE. Utah's 40 years of historical amnesia. Westerners brand book (Chicago), 16:9-11, 16 (Apr 1959). On the Mormons in Utah, 1847-96, and the great harm done to the memory of Brigham Young and his followers by polygamy; with particular notice of "the number of things which Mormons today accept as facts and which are little more than legends." [10017

LELAND HANS MONSON. Shakespeare in early Utah. Improvement era, 63: 718-21, 763-4 (Oct). views. On "Shakespearean performances in the Salt Lake Theater and in cities in other parts of the state," 1847-1900. [10018

HARVEY L. HANSEN. Bishop's money of Utah. Selections from The numismatist: United States paper money, tokens, medals, and miscellaneous (Racine, Wis.: Whitman Pub. Co., 1960). p. 162-6. facsims. First printed Sep. 1933. On scrip issued by the Church of Jesus Christ of Latter-Day Saints, 1848-1908. [10019

PAUL C. ROHLOFF. The State of Deseret. S. P. A. jour., 22:95-100 (Nov 1959). On its postal markings and those of the newly established Utah Territory, 1849-51. [10020

RALPH VARY CHAMBERLAIN. The University of Utah: a history of its first hundred years, 1850 to 1950. ... Harold W. Bentley, editor. Salt Lake City: Univ. of Utah Press, 1960. xix, 616 p. facsims., plans, ports., tables, views. notes. On the University of the State of Deseret, 1850-52, 1867-92, also called the University of Deseret, and the University of Utah, 1892-1950; with "Biographical notes" (p. 577-93) on its regents and faculty members. [10021

WILLIAM BLAKE BEATTY. Early papermaking in Utah [1853-93]. Paper maker, 28(1):9-20 (Feb 1959). facsims., maps, ports., views. bibliog. [10022

AMY L. VAN COTT & ALLEN W. LEIGH. Generations of Websters. Cedar City, Utah: Thomas Webster

Family Organization, 1960. x, 282 p. diagr. bibliog. (p. 274-5). On Francis Webster (1830-1906), English Mormon, who settled in Cedar City, Utah, in 1856 after mining gold in Australia and California; his brother William (1836-1922), who arrived in Cedar City in 1892; and 2 generations of their Utah descendants. Consists mainly of biographical and autobiographical sketches. [10023

KATE B. CARTER. Utah and the Pony Express [1960-61. Salt Lake City?] Utah Pony Express Centennial Commission [1960. 2], 88, [2] p. facsims., double map, ports., tables. Includes biographical and autobiographical sketches of agents, freighters, and riders from Utah who were employed by the Express. [10024

WILLIAM FREDERICK FISHER (1839?-1918). Pony Express lore. [Edited by] Raymond W. Settle. Romance on the trail. Am. philatelist, 73:729-30 (Jul). port., seal. Letter from a Pony Express rider to his financée, Millenium Andrus Van Etten, dated Ruby Valley, 17 Jun. 1860, expressing his love, reporting that "The Indians are raising the devil out here now," and enclosing 3 stanzas of verse "To one I love." [10025

DONALD D. McKAY. The founding of Huntsville [1860-1960]: its people and projects. Huntsville, Utah, c1960. [4], 64, [1] p. ports., table, views. Includes the author's reminiscences. [10026

JOHN CLIFTON MOFFITT. A century of service, 1860-1960: a history of the Utah Education Association. [Salt Lake City:] Utah Education Assoc. [1960]. ix, [3], 680 p. diagrs., tables, views. notes. [10027

WILLIAM FRANK LYE. Edward Wheelock Tullidge [1829-94], the Mormons' rebel historian. Utah hist. quar., 28:56-75 (Jan). facsims., ports. notes. On his life in Utah, 1861 ff., as a member of the Church Historian's Office, later a heretic denying the divine authorization of the temporal power of the Church, publisher of Peep o' day (1864), the Utah magazine (1868-69), and other Utah serials, author of plays, fiction and nonfiction; with an annotated chronological list of his works, 1864-89. [10028

C. MERRILL HOUGH. Two school systems in conflict: 1867-1890. Utah hist. quar., 28:112-28 (Apr). views. notes. On the mission schools established by the Protestant Episcopal Church in Utah, the mild opposition between them and the schools of the Mormons, and the successful campaign to establish a system of free public schools. [10029

LAWRENCE BACON LEE. Homesteading in Zion. Utah hist. quar., 28:28-38 (Jan). facsim., port., view. notes. On "Mormon utilization of the Homestead Act," 1867-1904. [10030

BILL DURHAM. Rocky Mountain mariners. Steamboat bill, 17:105-7 (winter). map, view. On the schooners and steamers that navigated the Great Salt Lake, 1868-75. [10031

WILLIAM MILLER McPHEE. Vignettes of Park City [since 1872]. Utah hist. quar., 28:136-53 (Apr). views. For a correction by Sam Raddon see p. 423. [10032

SAMUEL WOOLLEY TAYLOR. Impossible journey. True West, 7(5): 6-10, 38-41 (May-Jun). ports., views. On the journey of Mormon settlers with wagons from Escalante to the San Juan River by way of Hole-in-the-Rock, Nov.-Dec. 1879. [10033

RONALD J. OCKEY & ARTHUR L. BEELEY. The death penalty in Utah, together with some reflections on execution [1889-1960]. Utah Acad. Sciences, Proc., 37:127-33. tables. notes. [10034

Mrs. W. G. KING. Our Ute Indians. Colo. mag., 37:128-32 (Apr). port. On the author's acquaintance with many of these indians during her stay at Dragon, Utah, near the Uinta-Ouray Reservation, as a nurse in the Indian Service, 1912 to 1916 or later. [10035

GEORGE WASHINGTON CRADDOCK. Floods controlled on Davis County watersheds [Utah, 1923-58]. Jour. forestry, 58:291-3 (Apr). view. bibliog. On prevention of floods by controlling fire, removing livestock, cutting "contour trenches," and seeding perennial grasses. [10036

FRANK R. LEMON. Health problems of the Navajos in Monument Valley, Utah [1927-58]. Pub. health reports, 75:1055-61 (Nov). diagr., tables. notes. [10037

MILDRED L. THOREN. A Rainbow Bridge adventure. Natl. parks mag., 34(149):4-6 (Feb). views. On the author's camping trip in the area of Rainbow Bridge, Utah, 1935. [10038

CHARLES H. HOLMES. Factors affecting development of the steel industry in intermountain America. Jour. geog., 59:20-31 (Jan). maps, view. On geographic elements in the location of the Geneva Works of the U.S. Steel Corporation near Provo, Utah, 1943-59. [10039

Salt Lake City

LESTER F. HEWLETT. "Thunder in their throats." Music jour., 18(3): 80-81 (Mar). ports. On Mormon singing since 1847, and the development of the Salt Lake Tabernacle Choir, beginning when the first Tabernacle organ was brought from Australia in 1857 by its maker, Joseph Ridges. [10040

J. BRACKEN LEE. Music is the heart of a city. Music jour., 18(7):7, 80-81 (Oct). port., views. On musical organizations and programs in Salt Lake City since 1847. [10041

PAUL LEON FATOUT. Artemus Ward among the Mormons. West. humanities rev., 14:193-9 (spring). notes. On his scurrilous remarks about the Mormons in a sketch published in 1861, his kind reception in Salt Lake City in Jan. 1864, and the "not ... overwhelming success" of his comic lecture there on 8 Feb. as reported in the newspapers. [10042

HERBERT S. HAMLIN. Salt Lake City's Emmerson School. Pony Express, 26(5):7-9 (Oct 1959). ports. Memories of an elementary school, 1894-1901, and of some of the boys and girls attending in those years. [10043

JOHN DANIEL WILLIAMS. The defeat of home rule in Salt Lake City [1955-59. N.Y.?] Holt, Rinehart, and Winston [1960]. 16 p. maps. (Case studies in practical politics.) Account by "a participant-observer"; with information about home rule as "a possibility in Utah" since 1932. [10044

NEW MEXICO

GEORGE ALLEN AGOGINO. The Santa Ana pre-ceramic sites: an Archaic seed-gathering culture in Sandoval County, New Mexico. Southw. lore, 25(4):17-21 (Mar). notes. [10045

GEORGE ALLEN AGOGINO. The San Jose sites: a Cochise-like manifestation in the middle Rio Grande [near Grants, N.M.]. Southw. lore, 26:43-8 (Sep). notes. [10046

ELAINE ANN BLUHM. Mogollon settlement patterns in Pine Lawn Valley, New Mexico [200 B.C.-A.D. 1250]. Am. antiq., 25:538-46 (Apr). maps, table. bibliog. Study and review of studies of an area west of Reserve, N. M. [10047

FRANK HAMILTON CUSHING (1857-1900). Primitive copper working: an experimental study. Selected papers from the American anthropologist, 1888-1920, ed. Frederica De Laguna (Evanston, Ill.: Row, Peterson, 1960), p. 533-58. diagrs., views. notes. First printed in Jan. 1894. On copper working by prehistoric Indians, particularly the Zuñi, and the author's experiments demonstrating the possibility of firing copper ore, extracting copper from it, forming the copper into thin sheets, and working the sheets into designs and artifacts without the use of any means other than wood, bone, and stone. [10048

ALFRED EDWARD DITTERT, JR. Culture change in the Cebolleta Mesa region, central western New Mexico. Ann Arbor, Mich.: University Microfilms [1959]. Positive microfilm of typescript. xix, 610 leaves. map, plans, tables. bibliog. (leaves 596-610). Thesis--Univ. of Arizona. Abstracted: Dissert. abstracts, 20: 645-6 (Aug 1959). Report of excavations in the "Acoma Culture Province," 1947-52, and study of cultural changes in the pueblos from Paleo-Indian times to the present. [10049

EDWARD P. DOZIER. A comparison of Eastern Keresan and Tewa kinship systems [among Pueblo Indians in New Mexico]. International Congress of Anthropological and Ethnological Sciences, 5th, 1956, Men and cultures: selected papers, ed. Anthony F. C. Wallace (Phila.: Univ. of Pennsylvania Press [1960]), p. 430-36. bibliog. [10050

OLIVER LA FARGE. New Mexico [its traditions and characteristics]. Holiday, American panorama west of the Mississippi: a Holiday magazine book (Garden City, N.Y.: Doubleday [1960]), p. 216-29. [10051

NIELS CHRISTIAN NELSON. Chronology of the Tano ruins, New Mexico. Selected papers from the American anthropologist, 1888-1920, ed. Frederica De Laguna (Evanston, Ill.: Row, Peterson [1960]), p. 279-302. diagrs., tables, views. notes. First printed in 1916. Effort to define the types of pottery found in the ruins in 1912 and to arrange them as a chronological succession. [10052

THOMAS MATTHEWS PEARCE. The New Mexico place name dictionary: a polyglot in six language [Tanoan, Keresan, Athapascan, Zuñi, Spanish, English]. Names, 6:217-25 (Dec 1958). notes. Account of a work in progress. [10053

TED RAYNOR. Old timers talk in southwestern New Mexico. El Paso: Texas Western Press, 1960. xiii, [3], 86, [2] p. views. notes. Mainly reprinted from the author's column, "Folklore corner," appearing in various New Mexico newspapers and magazines. History and lore about "New Mexico's past and her people," collected from "long-time residents of Southwestern New Mexico". [10054

MANECK S. WADIA. Some aspects of Pueblo religion. Ind. Acad. Science, Proc., 69:83-5. On the continued strength of the native religion at Tesuque, N. M., including particularly "secret ceremonies and dances." [10055

MARJORIE BUTLER WHITE. What's in a name ? N. M., 38(7):10-11, 40-42 (Jul). On the origins of the names of some New Mexico places. [10056

LESLIE A. WHITE. The world of the Keresan Pueblo Indians. Stanley Diamond, ed., Culture in history: essays in honor of Paul Radin (N.Y.: Columbia Univ. Press for Brandeis Univ., 1960), p. 52-64. map. bibliog., notes. History and lore of the Keresan Pueblo Indians since 1540, particularly their "origin myths." Based largely upon observations of the pueblos of Acoma, Laguna, Santo Domingo, San Felipe, Santa Ana, Sia, and Cochiti. [10057

BRYANT BANNISTER. Tree-ring dating of archaeological sites in the Chaco Canyon region, New Mexico. Ann Arbor: University Microfilms, 1960. Positive microfilm of typescript. [390] leaves. Thesis--Univ. of Arizona. Abstracted: Dissert. abstracts, 20:3702-3 (Mar). Study of 828 tree-ring dates "from the late 600's to the present day," representing 46 sites. [10058

REX E. GERALD. The Mimbres Indians. Password, 5:119-25 (Oct). bibliog. On the archeological remains of a people who lived in southwestern New Mexico in the Mimbres Valley for a time after ca. 1000 or 1050. [10059

CHARLES H. LANGE. Cochití: a New Mexico pueblo, past and present [1540-1953]. Austin: Univ. of Texas Press [1960, ©1959]. xxiv, 618 p. diagrs. (1 fold.), maps (1 fold. in pocket), ports., plans, tables (part double, views. bibliog. (p. 575-85), notes. Based on thesis--Univ. of New Mexico, 1950. On the "social anthropology" of an Indian community. Includes information from Franciscan records at Pẽna Blanca (maintained since 1870) and from observations made by the author in visits between 1946 and 1953. [10060

CHARLES H. LANGE. Forces of change and tradition at Cochití Pueblo, New Mexico. Tex. quar., 3(3):63-72 (autumn). 16 views. Based upon "empirical observation" by the author since 1946 and historical documents beginning in 1540. [10061

EDWARD A. MARINSEK. The effect of cultural difference in the education of Apache Indians. [Albuquerque: College of Education, Univ. of New Mexico, 1960.] iii, 78 leaves. maps. bibliog. (leaves 77-8), notes. (The University of New Mexico Research Study: the adjustment of Indian and non-Indian children in the public schools of New Mexico.) On "the cultural heritage of the Apache" of New Mexico as observed since 1540--their religion, medical practices, social organization, marriage, "sex mores," economy, and education--and the necessity of knowledge of their cultural differences from "Anglo" children as a basis for devising suitable methods of teaching them. [10062

JOSÉ EDMUNDO ESPINOSA. Saints in the valleys: Christian sacred images in the history, life, and folk art of Spanish New Mexico [1598-1960]. Albuquerque: Univ. of New Mexico Press, 1960. xiii, 122 p. map, views. bibliog. (p. 101-7), notes. On wooden statuary and paintings representing Christ, the Virgin, and the saints; with discussion of 12 painters and several carvers, and comment on the lack of encouragement of these arts by "the Spanish, Mexican, New Mexican and American clergy." [10063

ELIZABETH BOYD (WHITE) HALL. Popular arts of colonial New Mexico. By E. Boyd [pseud.]. Santa Fe: Museum of International Folk Art [1959].

51, [1] p. views (part col.). bibliog. On houses, furniture, utensils, textiles, and religious paintings and statuary, 1598-1846, and tinware of later date. [10064

WICK R. MILLER. Spanish loanwords in Acoma [acquired presumably since 1598]. Internatl. jour. Am. linguistics, 25:147-53; 26:41-9 (Jul 1959, Jan 1960). notes. [10065

HORACIO ULIBARRI. The effect of cultural differences in the education of Spanish Americans. [Albuquerque: College of Education, Univ. of New Mexico, 1958.] xi, 104 leaves. diagrs., map, tables. bibliog. (leaves 102-4), notes. (The University of New Mexico Research Study: the adjustment of Indian and non-Indian children in the public schools of New Mexico.) On the religion, family organization, education, economics, health, politics, and recreations of New Mexicans of Spanish descent since 1598, the cultural conflict between them and the "Anglos" since 1846, and the necessity of understanding of the cultural differences between the 2 groups before the Spanish-American children can be properly taught by "Anglo" teachers. [10066

CHARLES BASIL MARTIN. The survivals of medieval religious drama in New Mexico. Ann Arbor: University Microfilms, 1959 [i. e. 1960]. Positive microfilm of typescript. [193] leaves. Thesis--Univ. of Missouri. Abstracted: Dissert. abstracts, 20:3298-9 (Feb). Study of "the ten extant plays in New Mexico today" (current there perhaps since the 17th century), all of which deal with Biblical themes and have retained their "religious and devotional spirit." [10067

INA SIZER CASSIDY. 350 years of art in Santa Fe [1610-1960]. N.M., 38(6): 35, 39 (Jun). Mainly on "the permanent settlement of artists here" since the late 1880s. [10068

WILLIAM THETFORD LEVINESS. A salute to Santa Fe's 350th anniversary [1610-1960]. N. M., 38(6):15-28, 39 (Jun). map, views (part col., 1 double). [10069

WAYNE WINTERS. We found the Spanish Queen. Frontier times, 34(1): 26-7, 41-2 (winter). views. On evidence that before the uprising of 1680 the Indians of the Jemez Mission in New Mexico were forced to work in mines in the Jemez Mountains, that after the expulsion of the Spaniards the Indians caved in the entrances to the mines, and that a small mine found by the author in Jemez Canyon may have been one of the copper mines. [10070

FREMONT KUTNEWSKY. From conquistador to metropolis. N.M., 38(10): 16-23, 39-40 (Oct). views (part col., 1 double). On Albuquerque since 1706. [10071

ELEANOR BURNHAM ADAMS. Viva el Rey! N.M. hist. rev., 35:284-92 (Oct). notes. On the ceremonies and celebrations in Santa Fe, 24 Jan. 1748, at the proclamation of the accession of Ferdinand VI to the throne of Spain. [10072

FRANK DRIVER REEVE. Navaho-Spanish diplomacy, 1770-1790. N.M. hist. rev., 35:200-235 (Jul). notes. On the fairly successful efforts of the Spanish authorities in New Mexico to substitute negotiation for war. [10073

ROBERT EMMET CLARK. The Pueblo rights doctrine in New Mexico. N.M. hist. rev., 35:265-83 (Oct). notes. On problems of New Mexico water law since 1789 as reviewed in recent litigation. [10074

JACKSON EDMUND TOWNE. Printing in New Mexico beyond Santa Fe and Taos, 1848-1875. N.M. hist. rev., 35: 109-17 (Apr). notes. Includes "Notes from manuscript by Douglas C. McMurtrie." [10075

WILLIAM JACKSON PARISH. The German Jew and the commercial revolution in Territorial New Mexico, 1850-1900. N.M. hist. rev., 35:1-29, 129-50 (Jan, Apr). map, tables. notes. Reprinted from the New Mexico quarterly, autumn 1959, with revisions. Appended (p. 143-50): correspondence of the author with George A. Spiegelberg, L. E. Freudenthal, and Arthur Bibo, on errors in the first printing. [10076

MONK LOFTON. Wagon Tire Canyon. True West, 7(5):11, 34 (May-Jun). view. On the disappearance of a party consisting of a man, a woman, and several children while traversing this canyon, near Carlsbad Caverns, leaving no trace except the iron tires of their burned wagon, 1855. [10077

CHARLES LELAND SONNICHSEN. Tularosa, last of the frontier West. N.Y.: Devin-Adair Co., 1960. [10], 336 p. map, ports., views. bibliog. (p. 293-9), notes (p. 300-324). On the Tularosa Valley and the White Sands, southeastern New Mexico, 1862-1960, with biographical sketches of its prominent early settlers, particularly cattle thieves, robbers, and murderers. [10078

GEORGE MICHAEL FITZPATRICK. The real Elfego Baca [born 1865]. N.M., 38(4):2-6, 40; (5):12-15, 39 (Apr, May). ports. On his life in New Mexico as a merchant, a peace officer, a lawyer, an agent in New Mexico for Francisco Villa and other Mexicans, an editor, etc.; with the author's memories of association with him in his later years. [10079

STANLEY J. BRASHER. Cradle of violence. True West, 7(5):16-17 50-51 (May-Jun). On robbery, murder, and lynching in Elizabethtown or E Town, Colfax County, N.M. 1869-71. [10080

MARY FRANCES BERKHOLZ. Minerals of Bayard area, New Mexico [1870-1960]. Mineralogist, 28:154-8 (Sep-Oct). map. bibliog. [10081

E. W. NORTHNAGEL. Kelly's ghost. N.M., 38(2):3-7 (Feb). map, views. On a silver-mining town near Magdalena, N.M., founded in 1870, abandoned ca. 1931. [10082

TOM TAKETO SASAKI. Fruitland, New Mexico: a Navaho community in transition [1876-1956]. Ithaca: Cornell Univ. Press [1960]. xvii, [3], 217 p. diagrs., map, tables. notes. (Cornell studies in anthropology.) Sociological study, based in part upon the author's residence and interviews in the community, 1948-56. [10083

ROBERT NORVILLE MULLIN. Lincoln, New Mexico, July 19, 1878. Showing principal locations involved in the "Three Day Battle." [n. p.] c1956. map 26x91 cm. [10084

ROBERT NORVILLE MULLIN. Lincoln, New Mexico: Lincoln County War period. [Toledo] c1950. map 26x91 cm., and key ([4] leaves). Revision of a map "first undertaken in Lincoln in 1816," attempting "to reconcile the sometimes divergent opinions ... and the often contradictory evidence of many who have written concerning the Lincoln of Lincoln County War days," 1878-81. [10085

PATRICK DONAN. Billy the Kid. Westerners brand book (Chicago), 16:66-7, 71 (Nov 1959). Communication from "Corr. St. Louis Globe-Democrat," here reprinted from the Chicago tribune, 7 Aug. 1881. Dispatch dated Lamy, N.M., "Judy [sic] 29, 1881," based upon interviews, reviewing a career of crime in New Mexico since 1879. [10086

H. GLENN CARSON. Deserted village. N.M., 38(1):28-9, 39-40 (Jan). views. On Guadalupe, about 15 miles northwest of Fort Sumner, N.M., settled in the 1880s, abandoned by its last family in 1955. [10087

NELL MURBARGER. He guards the ghosts. True West, 7(4):14-15, 48-50 (Mar-Apr). port., views. On the abandoned town of White Oaks, N.M., with information about it since 1880 from Dave Jackson, aged 97 in 1957, a continuous resident of White Oaks since 1897. [10088

FRANK MASON. Hanging Bill Coons was such fun! Frontier times, 34(2): 24-5, 54 (spring). On the lynching of a participant in the Lincoln County War on his 43d birthday, 1881. [10089

SUSAN E. (TAYLOR) LEE. These also served: brief histories of pioneers ... short stories and pictures relative to Catron, Grant, Sierra, Socorro, and Valencia Counties of New Mexico [1882-1960]. Los Lunas, N.M., 1960. xiv, [2], 208 p. map, ports., views. Includes chapters on Winston, Silver City, Magdalena, Luna, and the Mogollon country. [10090

FRANK HAMILTON CUSHING (1857-1900). The preparation of the cornfield. Margaret Mead & Ruth L. Bunzel, eds., The golden age of American anthropology (N.Y.: George Braziller, 1960), p. 207-11. plan. From The millstone, Minneapolis, 1887-88. Account of a Zuñi ceremonial. [10091

ALLEN WOODROW JONES, ed. [Correspondence of E. Ben George.] N.M. hist. rev., 35:327-35 (Oct). Letters from G. W. Campbell to George (1889) on the scenery and people of Sonora, and from George, at Hilton, N.M., to his nephew M. A. George, Jr., at Williams Mill, Ala. (1890-91), on his travels in Sonora and on the scenery, Indian traditions, and economic resources of the New Mexico mountains. [10092

LEE PRIESTLEY. Ghosts in search of a grave. Frontier times, 34(4):8-9 (fall). views. On the murder of Col. Albert J. Fountain, New Mexico lawyer active as a prosecutor of cattle thieves, and his young son, en route from Lincoln County to Las Cruces, by persons unknown, and the unsuccessful search for their bodies in the white gypsum dunes called the White Sands, 1896. [10093

NEW MEXICO. Dept. of Game and Fish. Deer of New Mexico [since 1897]. By E[dward] M[aguire] Lang, Wildlife Biologist. Santa Fe, 1957. [6], 41, [1] p. diagrs., maps, tables, views. bibliog. (p. 39). (Its Bulletin 5.) [10094

NEW MEXICO. Dept. of Game and Fish. New Mexico beaver management. By William S. Huey, Wildlife Biologist. Santa Fe, 1956. [4], 49 p. diagrs., tables, views. bibliog. (p. 49). (Its Bulletin 4.) On the control of the beaver population by the State since 1897. [10095

BEULAH MEEKS. Village of Corona, New Mexico [since 1899]. N.M., 38(11):20-21, 36, 38 (Nov). views. [10096

WAYNE WINTERS. I saw a town die. Frontier times, 34(3):18-19, 55 (summer). views. On the decline and decay of Cabezon, N.M., 1902-57. [10097

MATILDA COXE (EVANS) STEVENSON (1850-1915). Zuñi origin myth: the origin of corn. Margaret Mead & Ruth L. Bunzel, eds., The golden age of American anthropology (N.Y.: George Braziller, 1960), p. 212-14. notes. First printed in 1905. [10098

Mrs. LOUIS A. KIRK. Hoss woman. [Edited] by Amelia Downing. Quarter horse jour., 8(3):76-7 (Dec 1955). ports., view. On the breeding and racing of quarter horses by the author and her husband in New Mexico, 1906-55. [10099

TROY KEMPER. Wall of water! True West, 7(3):21, 52 (Jan-Feb). facsim., port. On a flood at Folsom, N.M., causing large property damage and loss of life, 27 Aug. 1908. [10100

C. BURTON DUSTIN. Peyotism and New Mexico [since 1910]. Farmington, N. M., c1960. 51 p. ports., views. bibliog. (p. 51). On the Native American Church and its peyote ritual, and the legality of a resolution (1940) of the Navajo Tribal Council prohibiting the use, possession, or sale of peyote within the Navajo Reservation. [10101

BEULAH MEEKS. 1910-1960: Powder Can church. N.M., 38(2):16-17, 40 (Feb). views. On a church building made of metal cans, in service from 1910 to ca. 1913, for miners and their families at a limestone quarry near Vaughn, N.M. [10102

C. E. HELLBUSCH. Horses and cattle. Quarter horse jour., 8(3):16, 60 (Dec 1955). port. On the breeding of quarter horses by W. I. Driggers and his son, Buster Driggers, forming with other members of the family the Driggers Cattle Company, Santa Rosa, N.M., 1911-55. [10103

ELSIE WORTHINGTON CLEWS PARSONS (1875-1941). The Zuñi a'Doshlě and suukě. Selected papers from the American anthropologist, 1888-1920, ed. Frederica De Laguna (Evanston, Ill.: Row, Peterson [1960]), p. 638-47. notes. First printed in 1916. On the use of "masks whose special function is that of terrifying the young children" as a disciplinary measure among the Zuñi Indians as observed by the author. [10104

C. E. HELLBUSCH. At home with the Heplers. Quarter horse jour., 3(10): 6-7, 30 (Jul 1951). port., views. On the breeding and raising of quarter horses by Roy, Charlie, and Elmer Hepler of Carlsbad, N.M., 1918-51. [10105

ELSIE WORTHINGTON CLEWS PARSONS (1875-1941). Nativity myth at Laguna and Zuni. Margaret Mead & Ruth L. Bunzel, eds., The golden age of American anthropology (N.Y.: George Braziller, 1960), p. 551-9. notes. First printed in 1918. Based upon observations of the author in New Mexico. [10106

JOHN ADAIR. A Pueblo G. I. Joseph B. Casagrande, ed., In the company of man: twenty portraits by anthropologists (N.Y.: Harper [1960]), p. 489-503. On the personality and social relations of Marcus Tafoya (born ca. 1920?), resident of an unnamed reservation, enlisted man in World War II. [10107

BERNARD J. SIEGEL & ALAN R. BEALS. Pervasive factionalism. Am. anthropol., 62:394-417 (Jun). bibliog., notes. Includes an account of internal division in Taos Pueblo since ca. 1920 on the issue of peyote rituals, and its relation to various traits of the Taos "theocracy." [10108

WILLIAM HENRY MAULDIN (born 1921). The year of the cowboy. N.M., 38(5):24-9 (May). cartoons, ports. Reminiscences of some of the author's interests and pranks as a boy in La

Luz, N.M., and the "Mountain Park-Cloudcroft area." [10109

PEGGY (POND) CHURCH. The house at Otowi Bridge: the story of Edith Warner [1891/92-1951] and Los Alamos. Albuquerque: Univ. of New Mexico Press [1960. 10], 149 p. On her removal from Pennsylvania to New Mexico in 1922, her personality, and her fraternization with Indians of San Ildefonso Pueblo and personnel from Los Alamos Project; with long excerpts from her letters and diary and slight mention of her teaching in an Indian school. [10110

CHARLES D. HARRIS. New Mexico's role in the development of the law of underground water [1927-51]. Dicta, 31:41-50 (Feb 1954). [10111

JACK WILKINSON. Background for culture. N.M., 38(10):14-15, 38 (Oct). port., view. On the development of Albuquerque organizations to promote music and the theater since the late 1920s. [10112

ARTHUR NEWTON PACK. The Ghost Ranch story. Phila.: Board of Christian Education, United Presbyterian Church in the U.S.A. [1960]. 63, [1] p. History and lore of Rio Arriba County, N.M., the resort or dude ranch established there by the author in 1933, and its use since 1955 as "the National Conference Center of the United Presbyterian Church U.S.A." [10113

C. E. HELLBUSCH. The Landon K. Moore ranch. Quarter horse jour., 4(8):8, 35 (May 1952). port. On the breeding of palomino and quarter horses by Kelley Moore, Raton, N.M.; with an account of 2 stallions, Smokey Moore and Brush Mount, both foaled in 1937. [10114

MAURICE TRIMMER. Ernie Pyle called Albuquerque "home." N.M., 38(10):4-5, 34 (Oct). port., view. On the settlement of "the skinny, little World War II journalist" and his wife, Jerry, in Albuquerque in 1940, and his few short visits there in intervals of his work as a military correspondent. [10115

ARIZONA

JESSE WALTER FEWKES (1850-1930). The prehistoric culture of Tusayan, Selected papers from the American anthropologist, 1888-1920, ed. Frederica De Laguna (Evanston, Ill.: Row, Peterson [1960]), p. 223-45. notes. First printed in 1896. On the culture of the Indians of an area in northeastern Arizona as indicated by excavations of the ruins of Sikyatki and by accounts of explorers and missionaries. [10116

EMIL WALTER HAURY. Association of fossil fauna and artifacts of the Sulphur Spring stage, Cochise culture. Am. antiq., 25:609-10 (Apr). bibliog. Argument that the association, first noted in Cochise County, Ariz., in 1926, is not fortuitous. [10117

EMIL WALTER HAURY, E. B. SAYLES, & WILLIAM W. WASLEY. The Lehner mammoth site, southeastern Arizona. Am. antiq., 25:2-42 (Jul 1959). diagrs., maps, tables, views. bibliog. On a site near Hereford, Ariz. where projectiles and butchering tools were found among the remains of "nine immature mammoths and elements of horse, bison, and tapir," associated with "charcoal from two fires," with radiocarbon dates of "11,000 to 12,000 B. P." and an estimated "geological age of 13,000 or more years." Appended: "Geological age of the Lehner mammoth site," by Ernst Antevs (p. 31-4), and "Faunal remains from the Lehner mammoth site," by John F. Lance (p. 35-9). [10118

PAUL SIDNEY MARTIN & JAMES SCHOENWETTER. Arizona's oldest cornfield. Science, 132:33-4 (1 Jul). notes. Evidence that corn was raised at the Cienega site in Graham County, Ariz., perhaps as early as ca. 4,200 years B. P. [10119

DEBS MYERS. Arizona [its traditions and characteristics]. Holiday, American panorama west of the Mississippi: a Holiday magazine book (Garden City, N.Y.: Doubleday [1960]), p. 201-15. [10120

STUART D. SCOTT. Pottery figurines from central Arizona. Kiva, 26(2): 11-26 (Dec). map, views. bibliog. Analysis of "403 pieces of modelled clay," collected south of Prescott. [10121

CLARA LEE TANNER. Crafts of Arizona Indians [since prehistoric times]. Ariz. highways, 36(7):8-35 (Jul). views (part col.). Notes that some of the crafts have developed within the past century or less, and that some of the indigenous crafts have made increasing use of commercial dyes, clays, and other materials. [10122

HAROLD SELLERS COLTON. Black sand: prehistory in northern Arizona. Albuquerque: Univ. of New Mexico Press [1960]. viii, 132 p. diagrs., maps, plans, views. bibliog. (p. 121-6). On an area of about 800 square miles northeast of Flagstaff, covered with black volcanic ash from an eruption of Sunset Crater, ca. 1065, the archeological studies of the author and others in the area since 1916, and their conclusions regarding its inhabitants between 500 and 1300. [10123

RICHARD E. KLINCK. Casa Grande. Ariz. highways, 36(1):1-3 (Jan). views (1 col.). On an area 12 miles west of Florence, Ariz., now protected as Casa Grande National Monument, occupied from ca. 700 to ca. 1400 by Hohokam and Salado Indians, and the 3-storey "castle" built by the Salados perhaps a hundred years before they abandoned the site. [10124

CHARLES FRANKLIN PARKER & JEANNE S. HUMBURG. Yavapai County: the mother of counties and land of enchantment [700-1960]. Ariz. highways, 36(5):7-31 (May). map, views (part col.). [10125

NATT NOYES DODGE. Land of the Black Shadow. Natl. parks mag., 34(159):7-9 (Dec). views. On an Arizona mountain that originated suddenly in a volcanic eruption on flat land in A.D. 1066, the ruins of pre-eruption settlement there, the attraction of new settlement by the increased fertility resulting from a layer of volcanic ash, the abandonment of the area during droughts between 1215 and 1300, and the establishment of the Sunset Crater National Monument at the site. [10126

RICHARD GERALD SNYDER. Hyperodontia in prehistoric Southwest Indians. Southw. jour. anthropol., 16:492-502 (winter). tables. bibliog., notes. Study of "some 658 deciduous teeth and 3019 permanent teeth from ... 350 individuals" living in Arizona between 1150 and 1450. [10127

JEAN C. CONGER. Arizona's calenday. Ariz. highways, 36(7):2-7 (Jul). diagrs. bibliog. On calendar sticks and other chronological records of Arizona Indian tribes, and their names for months and seasons, ca. 1300 to 1960. [10128

WILLIAM CROFT BARNES (1858-1936). William C. Barnes' Arizona place names [1540-1960]. Revised and enlarged by Byrd H. Granger. Tucson: Univ. of Arizona Press, 1960. xix, [3], 519, [2] p. maps (p. 409-26), table, views. bibliog. (p. 403-7), "Map bibliography" (p. 397-401). 1st ed. 1935. Alphabetical entries arranged by county and thereunder by name of place, showing origin of name, location of place, pronunciation, dates of post offices, and references to sources. Substantially a new work, incorporating the information collected by Barnes for a new edition and adding data from interviews, microfilms, maps, manuscripts, and other sources. [10129

RONALD LORING IVES. The last journey of Melchior Diaz [died 1541]. Jour. geog., 59:61-6 (Feb). maps, view. On his expedition, by order of Coronado, from the Sonora River through northwestern Sonora and the southwestern corner of Arizona to the Gila and the Colorado at the site of Yuma, down the Colorado nearly to its mouth, back to Yuma, and thence to "the mud volcano field at Volcano Lake," Lower Calif., in the delta of the Colorado, 1540. [10130

RONALD LORENZ IVES. Navigation methods of Eusebio Francisco Kino, S. J. Ariz. and the West, 2:213-43 (autumn). diagrs., map. notes. On the surprising accuracy of his astronomical observations in Sonora, 1685-1711, and of a map drawn by him in 1701; with speculations as to the instruments he may have used and the sources from which he may have acquired his competency in determining geographic positions. [10131

HERBERT EUGENE BOLTON (1870-1953). Rim of Christendom: a biography of Eusebio Francisco Kino [1644-1711], Pacific coast pioneer. N.Y.: Russell & Russell, 1960 [c1936]. xiv, 644 p. facsims., fold. maps, views. bibliog. (p. 597-627), notes. On his early life in Italy, his assignment to Mexico as a Jesuit missionary in 1681, his efforts to establish missions in Lower California and his success in establishing several in Sonora (beginning in 1687 with headquarters at Mission Dolores), his explorations into present Arizona as far as the Gila and the Colorado, his special charge of the Pima Indians, and his accomplishments as "ranchman, Indian diplomat, cartographer, and historian." [10132

HENRY F. DOBYNS & 3 others. What were Nixoras? Southw. jour. anthropol., 16:230-58 (summer). bibliog., notes.

On a name current in northern Sonora and southern Arizona, 1716-1847, believed by some to designate a tribe, by others to designate captives or slaves sold by Arizona Indians to the Spaniards; with evidence that the latter interpretation is the correct one. Appended: documents, 1781-1847. [10133

J. AUGUSTINE DONOHUE. The unlucky Jesuit mission of Bac, 1732-1767. Ariz. and the West, 2:127-39 (summer). notes. [10134

EDWARD HADDUCK PEPLOW, JR., & CHARLES H. DUNNING. Miracle of the mines. Ariz. highways, 36(11):12-27 (Nov). ports., views (part col.). On mining in Arizona since 1736. [10135

HAROLD O. WEIGHT. Lost mines of old Arizona. Twentynine Palms, Calif.: Calico Press [1959]. 76 p. double map, views. (Southwest panorama, 4.) Accounts of 9 mines, "lost" at various dates since 1780. [10136

TUCSON'S treasure. Ariz. architect, 4(1):11, 13, 27 (Sep). views. On Mission San Xavier del Bac, built 1785-98, restored in 1906, "America's most beautiful mission in active use to-day." [10137

EDNA PEARL (HOFFMAN) EVANS. Arizona cattle brands [as early as 1812]. Ariz. highways, 36(11):2-11 (Nov). brands, views (part col.). [10138

JAMES M. MURPHY. The Arizona Bar--from individualism to integration. Ariz. law rev., 2:37-77 (summer). notes. On the laws, courts, lawyers, and judges of Arizona since 1821, the Bar Association of Arizona (1895-1905), the Arizona Bar Association (1906-31), and the State Bar of Arizona (1933-60). [10139

ELLIOTT ARNOLD. "... personally responsible for his people." John Arthur Garraty, ed., The unforgettable Americans (Great Neck, N.Y.: Channel Press [1960]), p. 252-60. On Cochise as leader of the Chiricahua Apache Indians, Arizona, mid-1830s to 1874. [10140

FENTON W. TAYLOR. The West's bloodiest pass! True West, 7(4):6-10, 38-41 (Mar-Apr). views. On Apache Pass, in the Chiricahua Mountains of Arizona, the scene of numerous robberies and killings, 1853 ff., and the establishment of Fort Bowie in the vicinity, founded in 1862, abandoned in 1896. [10141

NELL MURBARGER. Ghost towns of Arizona. Ariz. highways, 36(8):14-31 (Aug). map, port., views (part col.). On 36 towns mainly mining camps settled after 1858 and abandoned after exhaustion of their mines; with some account of the author's methods of collecting information about them. [10142

THOMAS E. WAY. Frontier Arizona. N.Y.: Carlton Press, 1960. xvi, 279 p. (A Milestone book.) "Incidents and stories," 1858-1901, "depicting the sometimes callous, the often humorous indifference of the average person for the value of human life in Territorial Arizona, the last frontier." [10143

BOB HUNT. They bought a ghost town. Ariz. highways, 36(5):36-9 (May). views. On Bumble Bee, settled in the 1860s, almost abandoned soon after 1900, now restored by Charles A. and Helen Penn. [10144

WILLIAM ESENWEIN. Yarnell [1863-1960]. Ariz. highways, 36(5):32-5 (May). views. [10145

HARWOOD P. HINTON, JR. Frontier speculation: a study of the Walker mining districts. Pac. hist. rev., 29: 245-55 (Aug). notes. On districts organized by Joseph Reddeford Walker and his associates on the Ookilsipava River and Lynx Creek, Ariz., 1863-65; with some account of the methods and motives in the organization and conduct of mining districts. [10146

NAT McKELVEY. Arizona giant. Frontier times, 34(1):14-15, 42-4 (winter). port. On Albert Franklin Banta (1843-1924), native of Indiana, settler in Arizona in 1863, "customs inspector, justice of the peace, deputy sheriff, probate judge, deputy assessor and tax collector, constable, notary public, census taker and business man," etc. [10147

PAULINE HENSON. Why Prescott? Ariz. highways, 36(5):2-7 (May). On Prescott, Ariz., 1864-1960, and its rapid growth and progress in recent years. [10148

DOUGLAS DE VENY MARTIN. The lamp in the desert: the story of the University of Arizona [1885-1960]. Tucson: Univ. of Arizona Press, 1960. xiii, 304 p. tables (1 double), ports., views. bibliog. (p. 295-6). Includes some account of education in Arizona in the years from 1864 to 1885. [10149

EDWARD BRIDGE DANSON, JR. Last of the frontier merchants. Natl. parks mag., 34(152):7-9 (May). views. On the Hubbell Trading Post, Ganado, Ariz., in the Navajo Reservation, founded in 1875, bought by John Lorenzo Hubbell (born 1853) in 1876, in constant operation since that time, now to be included in the national park system. [10150

COLUMBUS R. FREEMAN (born 1872). Pioneers of the trail: reminiscences of the Old West. [Recorded] by Artie Elizabeth Freeman. N.Y.: Greenwich Book Publishers [1960, c1959]. 27 p. On Freeman's early life in Kanosh, Utah, his removal with his parents to Arizona in 1879, and his work there as a cowboy, later as a cattle rancher at Conella till his retirement in 1942. [10151

LLOYD HAMILL & ROSE HAMILL. Hamill's Tombstone picture gallery: photographs and drawings plus elegant and moving prose about Tombstone, Cochise County, A. T. [1879-1960]. [Glendale, Calif.: Western Americana Press of Glendale, 1960.] 23, [1] p. facsims., ports., views. Guide for tourists. [10152

ANDREW WALLACE. To the memory of Will Croft Barnes, 1858-1936. Ariz. and the West, 2:203-4 (autumn). port. On his life in Arizona as a soldier, a cattleman, a forester, an authority on Arizona place-names, and a writer, 1879-1936. [10153

EVE BALL. The greatest medicine man. True West, 7(4):30-31, 54-6 (Mar-Apr). ports. On the "special God-given Power" which the Apaches in the 1880s believed was possessed by Geronimo, as recalled by Asa Daklugie and other Apaches interviewed by the author. [10154

PAUL JOSEPH SCHEIPS. Will Croft Barnes [1858-1936]: soldier and citizen of Arizona. Ariz. and the West, 2:205-12 (autumn). notes. On his work in Arizona as a telegrapher in the Signal Corps, 1880-83. Appended: "A chronological list of the works of Will C. Barnes," 1885-1941, compiled by Andrew Wallace. [10155

JO JEFFERS. Commodore Perry Owens [1852-1919]. Ariz. highways, 36(10):2-7 (Oct). ports., view. On his life in Arizona as a guard, a deputy sheriff, a sheriff, and later a saloonkeeper, ca. 1881 to 1919. [10156

DON BUFKIN. Tombstone, 1882, Territory of Arizona. Tucson [1957]. col. map (incl. 2 inset views). [10157

ROBERT NORVILLE MULLIN. Business section, Tombstone, A. T., May 1882. Toledo, c1950. map 39x59 cm. Prepared "from a sketch made in 1916 based on information secured from Tombstone residents ... revised and extended by reference to files of the Tombstone Nugget, the Epitaph and the Commercial Advertiser" and other sources. On back: key to 213 numbered locations. [10158

DONALD M. POWELL. The Peralta Grant: James Addison Reavis [1843-1914] and the Barony of Arizona. Norman: Univ. of Oklahoma Press [1960]. xiii, 186 p. coat of arms, facsims., maps, ports. bibliog. (p. 178-82), notes. On his assertion in 1882, as Baron of Arizona, of a claim to ownership of the "whole Salt River Valley in central Arizona" and his efforts to collect money from landowners to confirm their titles; the assembling of evidence by the U.S. Government that he had inserted forged documents into the records; the trial and conviction of Reavis and his wife in 1896 as "fraudulent and fictitious claimants for said property"; and his imprisonment, 1896-98; with some account of his early life in Missouri, his Confederate Army service, and his real-estate activities in St. Louis. [10159

A. D. LE BARON. Bisbee's five black ghosts. True West, 7(6):12-14, 56-7 (Jul-Aug). view. On robbery and murder committed in Bisbee by masked men, their apprehension and trial, and their hanging at Tombstone, 1883. [10160

ERNEST JEROME HOPKINS & ALFRED THOMAS, JR. The Arizona State University story. Phoenix, Ariz.: Southwest Pub. Co., 1960. x, 305 p. cartoon, facsim., plan, ports., tables, views. On an institution at Tempe founded as the Territorial Normal School in 1885 and eventually becoming Arizona State University. [10161

KENNETH I. LANGE. The jaguar in Arizona [1885-1959]. Kan. Acad. Science, Trans., 63:96-101 (summer). map. bibliog. [10162

EDWARD HADDOCK PEPLOW, JR. 75 years of higher education in a frontier State [Arizona, 1885-1960].

Ariz. highways, 36(10):16-29 (Oct). views (part col.). Deals mainly with the University of Arizona. [10163

C. OTTO LINDH. The Aztec case: a story of two centuries. Am. forests, 65(12):24-7, 48-9 (Dec 1959). views (1 double). On litigation between the Santa Fe Pacific Railroad Company and the Aztec Land and Cattle Company concerning ownership of railroad land-grant lands in Arizona, and the eventual acquisition of part of the lands by the U.S. Forest Service, 1886-1959. [10164

MURIEL THAYER PAINTER. Easter at Pascua Village. [Second edition, revised and enlarged.] Tucson: Univ. of Arizona Press, 1960. 35 p. diagrs., map, plans. 1st ed. 1950. On the Yaqui Indians near Tucson and the annual passion-play performed by them at Easter since 1909. [10165

JOHNIE FAIN & LEARAH COOPER MORGAN. The cowboy and the rodeo [at Prescott, Ariz., since 1888]. Ariz. highways, 36(2):30-33 (Feb). views. [10166

JESSE WALTER FEWKES (1850-1930). Hopi snake washing. Margaret Mead & Ruth L. Bunzel, eds., The golden age of American anthropology (N.Y.: George Braziller, 1960), p. 215-19. notes. First printed in 1898. On a Hopi ceremonial as observed by the author in Arizona, 1891-97. [10167

PAUL ERNEST KLOPSTEG. Four "little Pimas" and how they happened. Kiva, 26(1):10-15 (Oct). views. On 4 "ironwood carvings of Pima Indians," made in the 1940s and 1950s by Aaron J. Cosner. Appended (p. 16-18): "A Salado spinning stick," by Cosner. [10168

HENRY P. EWING. The Pai tribes. ... Robert C. Euler and Henry F. Dobyns, eds. Ethnohistory, 7:61-80 (winter). bibliog., notes. Manuscript (1903) by the former agent of the Indian Service in the Walapai Indian Reservation, northwestern Arizona, where he had taken charge in 1895, on "the Walapai, Havasupai and Apache Yuma or Yavapai tribes." [10169

MELISSA GATEWOOD JONES. Teaching in Arizona Territory: a personal recollection. Ariz. and the West, 2: 371-5 (winter). Memories of teaching and of life in Safford, Ariz., ca. 1895 to ca. 1899. [10170

WALTER HOUGH (1859-1935). A revival of the ancient Hopi pottery art. Selected papers from the American anthropologist, 1888-1920, ed. Frederica De Laguna (Evanston, Ill.: Row, Peterson [1960]), p. 246-7. First printed in 1917. On the revival of the Hopi pottery art by a Hopi Indian woman, Nampeo, of Hano, Ariz., who admired the shards found by Dr. J. Walter Fewkes in the ruins of Sikyatki and learned to duplicate their materials, forms, colors, and designs in or before 1896, at a time when "the decay of the Hopi potter's art was seen to be almost complete." [10171

PAUL J. LINDAMAN. The forgotten men. True West, 7(5):20-21, 34 (May-Jun). port. Memories of prospectors in southeastern Arizona since 1907. [10172

WILLARD H. PORTER. The fabulous Figueroas. Quarter horse jour., 8(7):10-12 (Apr 1956). ports. On Francisco Figueroa, Mexican emigrant to Rosemont, Ariz., ca. 1910, and the activities of his sons as breeders and trainers of quarter horses on a ranch near Tucson. [10173

HELEN (HUMPHREYS) SEARGEANT (born 1878). House by the Buckeye Road. San Antonio: Naylor Co. [1960]. xv, 210 p. ports., views. On the author's life as the wife of Jonathan William Seargeant, farmer 12 miles west of Phoenix; with some account of her earlier life in Arizona and New Mexico and her education in California. Deals mainly with her early years on the Seargeant farm, her neighbors, and the early settlers in the neighborhood. [10174

MARK HERRA. Those were the days!! Quarter horse jour., 8(7):49, 52 (Apr 1956). Recollections of horse-racing in Arizona, 1912-56, particularly of racing by quarter horses. [10175

EDGAR ELLINGER, JR. Goldroad and Oatman. Ariz. highways, 36(4): 36-9 (Apr). port., views. On 2 abandoned mining towns between Kingman and Topock, dating from a gold rush of ca. 1915. [10176

DEAN E. MANN. Law and politics of groundwater [sic] in Arizona [1919-60]. Ariz. law rev., 2:241-67 (winter). notes. [10177

ROSS SANTEE. Old time cow show Ariz. highways, 36(2):1-4 (Feb). views. Recollections of a rodeo at

Globe, Ariz., "some forty years ago," with illustrations by the author. [10178

MOYCA MANOIL. The Phoenix Little Theater [1921-60]. Ariz. highways, 36(1):22-3, 32-5 (Jan). ports., views. [10179

EDGAR ELLINGER, JR. He breeds for speed. West. horseman, 25(6): 12, 72-3 (Jun). port. On the breeding of Thoroughbreds and quarter horses by Melville H. Haskell of Tucson, 1924-60. [10180

JOHN FREDERICK PRINCE. A biography of E. W. Montgomery [born 1882] during his superintendency of the Phoenix Union High School and Phoenix College District, 1925-1953. Ann Arbor: University Microfilms, 1960. Positive microfilm of typescript. [221] leaves. Thesis--Univ. of Arizona. Abstracted: Dissert. abstracts, 21:117-18 (Jul). [10181

C. K. SPAULDING. The Heber trick tank--a cistern for stock water [Sitgreaves National Forest, Ariz., 1935-58]. Jour. forestry, 56:429-30 (Jun 1958). diagrs., views. [10182

JOCELYN McALPINE. Rodeo ... university style. Ariz. highways, 36(2): 12-15 (Feb). ports., views. On the University of Arizona Rodeo Club, 1938-60, and the competitions of its members with other schools and in other States. [10183

EDGAR ELLINGER, JR. The Finley ranches. Quarter horse jour., 12(6): 31-2, 50 (Mar). ports., view. On the breeding of quarter horses by Jim Finley and his sons, Tom and Jack, near Gilbert, Ariz., 1941-60. [10184

WILLARD H. PORTER. Arizona's sprinting straightaways. Quarter horse jour., 7(7):16-17, 46 (Apr 1955). port., views (1 double). On the race tracks of Arizona, subsidized by the State from funds for county and State fairs, 1943-55, and Tucson as "the Quarter Horse racing capital of the world." [10185

THE PACIFIC STATES

RALPH WARREN ANDREWS. Indian primitive. Seattle: Superior Pub. Co. [1960]. 175 p. ports., views (part double). bibliog. (p. 172). Pictorial history of the 26 "Indian tribes living in the coastal area between Trinidad Bay in Northwestern California and Alaska's Yakutat Bay ... before 'white men' began to interfere with their singular lives." [10186

ALAN LYLE BRYAN & DONALD R. TUOHY. A basalt quarry in northeastern Oregon. Am. Philos. Soc., Proc., 104:485-510 (17 Oct). map, views. bibliog. On 115 chipped tools of "fine-grained glassy basalt," probably prehistoric, found at a site in Union County; with an extensive discussion of the early use of basalt artifacts elsewhere in "the American Plateau" of the Far West. [10187

CHESTER S. CHARD. Northwest coast - northeast Asiatic similarities: a new hypothesis. International Congress of Anthropological and Ethnological Sciences, 5th, 1956, Men and cultures: selected papers, ed. Anthony F. C. Wallace (Phila.: Univ. of Pennsylvania Press [1960]), p. 235-40 bibliog. On an assumed "ancient arc of related culture and population around the entire rim of the North Pacific from Kamchatka to Puget Sound ... a belt of sedentary maritime peoples ... leading a roughly similar type of life based on fishing and varying degrees of sea-mammal hunting," and the "cultural, linguistic, and racial" indications of its later submergence by "inland Palaeo-Asiatic tribes." [10188

LUTHER SHEELEIGH CRESSMAN. Cultural sequences at The Dalles, Oregon: a contribution to Pacific Northwest prehistory. Phila.: American Philosophical Soc., 1960. 108 p. diagrs., maps (3 fold. in pocket), profiles, tables, views. bibliog. (p. 79-80). (Transactions of the American Philosophical Society, new ser., v. 50, pt. 10.) [10189

BILL DURHAM. Canoes and kayaks of Western America. Seattle: Copper Canoe Press, 1960. [2], 103, [1] p. diagrs., views (1 double). bibliog. (p. 104). On all the kinds of boats and other floating equipment used by the prehistoric and historic Indians in the area between Alaska and "the Northern interior" and south to the Gulf of California. [10190

ALBERT B. ELSASSER. The archaeology of the Sierra Nevada in California and Nevada. [Berkeley, 1960. 2], ii, 93 p. chron. chart, maps, tables, views. bibliog. (p. 81-91). (University of California Archaeological Survey. Report 51.) Effort "to review all known data pertaining to prehistoric culture chronology and distribution in the Sierra Nevada," first occupied by man perhaps "about 2,500 years ago." [10191

MELVILLE JACOBS. The areal spread of sound features in the languages north of California. Symposium on American Indian Linguistics, Berkeley, 1951, Papers (Berkeley, 1954: Univ. of California Press [University of California publications in linguistics, 10]), p. 46-56. notes. [10192

OREGON ARCHAEOLOGICAL SOCIETY. Wakemap Mound and nearby sites on the Long Narrows of the Columbia River. Portland: Oregon Museum of Science and Industry, 1959 [i. e. 1960. 3], 38, [3] p. (even numbers on recto). maps, plan, views. (Its Publication 1.) On the archeology of an area about 4 miles long (now submerged behind a dam), first occupied by man "over 10,000 years ago"; with an effort to reconstruct the culture indicated by artificts, and historical references since 1805. [10193

PAUL SCHUMACHER. Observations made in the ruins of the villages of the original inhabitants of the Pacific coast of North America [in California and Oregon]. Univ. Calif. Archaeol. Survey, Rep., 50:19-23. notes. (Papers on California archaeology, 82.) Translated from Mittheilunger der Anthropologischen Gesellschaft in Wien, v. 7 (1876). [10194

JOHN REED SWANTON (1873-1958). The development of the clan system and of secret societies among the Northwestern tribes [from California to Alaska]. Selected papers from the American anthropologist, 1888-1920, ed. Frederica De Laguna (Evanston, Ill.: Row, Peterson [1960]) p. 583-93. First printed in 1904. [10195

BENJAMIN POFF DRAPER. Canoes, campfires, and Carbon 14. Pac. discovery, 13(3):14-20 (May-Jun). double map, ports., views. On recently determined radiocarbon dates for earliest known human occupancy of various Pacific areas, including Hawaii (A.D. 124), Samoa (A.D. 9), Yap (A.D. 178), and Saipan (1527 B.C.). [10196

BERN ANDERSON. Surveyor of the sea: the life and voyages of Captain George Vancouver [1757-98]. Seattle: Univ. of Washington Press [1960]. xii, 274 p. maps (1 double), port., views. bibliog. (p. 259-66), notes (p. 241-58). Based on thesis--Harvard Univ. On his command of a Pacific hydrographic survey of the Royal Navy, including inspections of Puget Sound, the Columbia River, and California (1792), the Hawaiian Islands (1792, 1793, 1794), and Alaska (1794); with some account of his life in England and his other services as a naval officer. [10197

LLOYD CUSTER MAYHEW HARE. Salted tories: the story of the whaling fleets of San Francisco [1822-1923]. Mystic, Conn., 1960. ix, 114 p. views. (Marine Historical Association, Mystic, Conn. [Publication] 37.) [10198

ALEXANDER GABRIOLOVICH ROTCHEV (1813?-1873). Letters of A. Rotchev, last commandant at Fort Ross [1829-41], and the résumé of the report of the Russian-American Company for the year 1850-51. Translated from the German, with an introduction, by Frederick C. Cordes. Calif Hist. Soc. quar., 39:97-115 (Jun). views. notes. Translated from the German translation in Archiv für wissenschaftliche Kunde von Russland, from the Russian original in Sievernaia pchela, 1852. Seven letters (St. Thomas, Panamá, and California, 23 Aug. 1851-23 Feb. 1852, probably to the Russian-American Company) on the author's voyage from England to San Francisco, his examination of mines in California, the possibility of collecting the debt of John Augustus Sutter, the profits of hunting on the Alaska coasts and trading with Hawaii and California, and the desirability of establishing a well-capitalized company for lucrative operations in California and a Russian-Finnish Whaling Company to operate in the northern Pacific. [10199

THOMAS DALE STEWART. The Chinook sign of freedom: a study of the skull of the famous Chief Comcomly [1765-1830]. Smithsonian Inst., Ann. rep., 1959, p. 563-76. diagrs., tables, view. notes. On a skull in the possession of the Clatsop County Historical Society, Astoria, Ore., exhibiting "a distinctive culture trait, namely, head flattening"; with an analysis of its measurements and a study of other flattened Chinook skulls from the area of the lower Columbia River. [10200

GORDON R. NEWELL & JOE WILLIAMSON. Pacific lumber ships [1843-1953]. Seattle: Superior Pub. Co. [1960]. 192 p. facsims., views (part double). Account, mainly pictorial, of wooden sailing ships transporting lumber from Washington and Oregon. [10201

MODESTE (sloop of the Royal Navy). HMS Modeste on the Pacific coast, 1845-47: log and letters. [Edited by Priscilla Knuth.] Ore. hist. quar., 61:408-36 (Dec). notes. Record of movements from South America to California, the Columbia, Victoria, Hawaii, and Tahiti; with an introduction on the mission of the sloop's commander "to visit and report on British settlements on the Northwest Coast." [10202

EUGENE EDWARD CAMPBELL. The Mormon gold mining mission of 1849. Brigham Young Univ. studies, 2:19-31 (autumn-winter 1959-60). notes. On the failure of efforts to mine gold profitably in California and the success of efforts to convert the natives of the Hawaiian Islands, 1849-50. [10203

HENRY W. CLARK. Buck Choquette [1829-98], stampeder. [Wash.? 1960. 2] 3, 152 p. port. bibliog. (p. 1-3) On Alexandre Choquette, native of Quebec, miner in California, Oregon Territory, and British Columbia from 1849 to 1859, trader with the Tlingit Indians in southeastern Alaska, prospector and miner in Alaska and Yukon Territory. [10204

JOHN QUINCY REED. Mark Twain: west coast journalist. Midwest quar., 1:141-61 (Jan). bibliog. On his work as a writer in Virginia City, Nev., and San Francisco, 1861-66. [10205

PATRICK M. RYAN, JR. Mark Twain: frontier theatre critic [in Nevada and California, 1863-66]. Ariz. quar., 16: 197-209 (summer). notes. [10206

SETH THOMAS BAILEY. The man who won and lost an empire. By Tom Bailey. True West, 76(6):6-10, 43-6 (Jul-Aug). ports., views. On the financial operations, partly fraudulent, of William C. Ralston and his associate, William Sharon, in California and Nevada mining, banking, and other enterprises, 1864-75. [10207

PATRICK MANOGUE (1831-95). Some letters of Patrick Manogue, gold miner and Bishop of Nevada and California. [Edited] by John Berhard McGloin, S. J. Am. Cath. Hist. Soc., Rec., 71: 3-13 (Mar-Jun). Reports to the Société pour la Propagation de la Foi dated in Virginia City, Nev., Grass Valley, Calif., and Baltimore, 1868, 1873, 1876, 1881-84, on the author's service as Pastor of St. Mary's in the Mountains (Virginia City) and Coadjutor Bishop, later Bishop, of Grass Valley. [10208

OLIVER ROBERTS (full name: Oliver Robert de La Fontaine, 1857-1919). The Death Valley Kid. (Edited and introduction by H[erbert S.] Hamlin.) Pony Express, 17(4)-25(9): scattered installments (Sep 1950-Apr 1959). facsims., maps, ports., views. Reminiscences of the author's early life in Woonsocket, R. I., his journey to Nevada in 1873, and his work at a variety of occupations in Bodie, Darwin, and Lookout, Calif., and Carson City, Nev., 1873 to ca. 1880; with brief mention of his later work as a prospector and a mining engineer and assayer in Nevada and California. Fictional in style. An earlier version appeared as The great understander: true life story of the last of the Wells Fargo shotgun express messengers, compiled by William W. Walter (Aurora, Ill. [1931]). [10209

RALPH WARREN ANDREWS & A. K. LARSSEN. Fish and ships. Seattle: Superior Pub. Co. [1959]. 173 p. ports., views. On the ocean fisheries of Oregon, Washington, British Columbia, and Alaska, 1880s-1920s, particularly the salmon, halibut, cod, seal, and whale fisheries, the ships and their owners and crews, and the canneries. Includes recollections, anecdotes, and numerous photographs (many dated). [10210

HARRY LAWTON. Willie Boy, a desert manhunt. [Balboa Island, Calif.:] Paisano Press [1960]. xii, [2], 224, [1] p. facsims., maps, ports., views. bibliog. (p. 221-4). On a Paiute Indian known as Willie Boy or Billy Boy (1880/81-1909), his life as a cowboy in Nevada and California, his murder of "Old Mike Boniface," a Chemehuevi Indian, his elopement with Boniface's daughter Lolita, his murder of Lolita, his flight for more than 500 miles to elude a posse from Banning, Calif., and his suicide on Ruby Mountain; with some account of the reporting of the chase by Randolph W. Madison and the national newspaper publicity that it received. Fictional in form. [10211

JACOB ADLER. The Oceanic Steamship Company [1881-1905]: a link in Claus Spreckels' Hawaiian sugar empire. Pac. hist. rev., 29:257-69

(Aug). notes. Based on thesis--Columbia Univ., 1959. A study in competition and monopoly. [10212

LUCILE (SAUNDERS) McDONALD. Letter to the editor. Ore. hist. quar., 61:64-7 (Mar). views. On Herman Wittenberg (1860?-1912), organizer of the Portland Cracker Company and associated firms manufacturing crackers, biscuits, and cookies in Portland, Tacoma, Seattle, and Spokane, later also in California, 1883-1912. [10213

FRANZ BOAS (1858-1942). Physical characteristics of the Indians of the north Pacific coast. Selected papers from the American anthropologist, 1888-1920, ed. Frederica De Laguna (Evanston, Ill.: Row, Peterson [1960]), p. 358-66. diagrs., tables. notes. First printed in 1891. Report of 15 measurements made by the author on each of 263 Indians, male and female, aged 20-50, of various tribes in Oregon, Washington, and British Columbia, grouped by sex and geographic location, 1890. [10214

STANLEY A. FREED. Changing Washo kinship. [Berkeley: Univ. of California Press, 1960. 4], 349-418 p. diagrs., tables. bibliog. (p. 417-18). (Anthropological records, v. 14, no. 6.) On "Washo social organization ... and ... the changes which have occurred within it since the end of the aboriginal period." Based upon observations made by the author in 4 Washo settlements in Nevada and California, 1952-57, and studies by previous visitors, 1907-53. [10215

HALL S. LUSK. James Alger Fee, 1888-1959. Ore. law rev., 39:91-4 (Dec 1959). On his work as U.S. Judge for the District of Oregon, 1931-54, and as a judge of the U.S. Court of Appeals for the Ninth Circuit, San Francisco, 1954-59. [10216

DONALD SIMS. SP&S. Trains, 20(5): 34-41; (6):26-34 (Mar, Apr). map, views. On the Oregon Electric and Oregon Trunk segments of the Spokane, Portland, & Seattle Railway, connecting Portland and Spokane, since 1933; with some account of their earlier histories as independent lines. [10217

MARSHALL DAVID SAHLINS. Political power and the economy in primitive society. Gertrude E. Dole & Robert L. Carneiro, eds., Essays in the science of culture, in honor of Leslie A. White (N.Y.: Crowell [1960]), p. 390-415. bibliog. Comparative analyses of the "Tolowa-Tutuni Athapascan food gatherers of northern California and the Oregon coast," 1936-37, and the primitive societies of Siberia and Oceania. [10218

LEON I. TWAROG. Soviet historical novelists look at America. Am. Slavic and East European rev., 19:561-76 (Dec). notes. On Ivan Kratt's Ostrov Baranova (1945) and Koloni ja Ross (1950) and Vladimir Grigor'ev's Grigorij Shelikov (1952), dealing with the Russians in Alaska and California, the necessary reliance of these works upon Hubert Howe Bancroft's histories of Alaska and California, and their expressions of current Communist ideology in their treatment of the Americans and the British. [10219

CALIFORNIA

RALPH L. BEALS & JOSEPH A. HESTER, JR. A new ecological typology of the California Indians. International Congress of Anthropological and Ethnological Sciences, 5th, Men and cultures: selected papers, ed. Anthony F. C. Wallace (Phila.: Univ. of Pennsylvania Press [1960]), p. 411-19. tables. bibliog. Groups the Indians as coastal, riverine, lake, valley or plains, foothill, and desert Indians. [10220

WILLIAM OLIVER BRIGHT. Some Northern Hokan relationships: a preliminary report. Papers from the Symposium on American Indian Linguistics held at Berkeley, July 7, 1951 (Berkeley: Univ of California Press, 1954 [University of California publications in linguistics, 10]), p. 63-7. notes. On the relations between and among 5 languages of the Indians of northern California. [10221

CALIFORNIA, UNIVERSITY OF. Archaeological Survey. Papers on California archaeology: 76-88. Berkeley: Dept. of Anthropology, Univ. of California, 1960. [2], 51 p. diagrs., maps, plans, views. bibliogs., notes. (Its Reports, 50.) Partial contents.--76. A San Nicolas Island twined basketry water bottle, by Robert F. Heizer.--77. Some prehistoric wooden objects from San Nicolas Island, by Robert F. Heizer.--78. Some prehistoric bullroarers from California caves, by Robert F. Heizer.--87. Six chert knives from Tulare County, California, by J. C. Von Werlhof. [10222

ROBERT W. DURRENBERGER. The geography of California in essays [by Durrenberger] and readings [reprinted from works by others]. Los Angeles: Brewster Publications [1959. 2], iv, 196, [2] p. maps, tables. notes. Includes passages relating to the historical and prehistoric geography of California. [10223

ROBERT W. DURRENBERGER. Patterns on the land: geographical, historical, and political maps of California. [Second edition.] Northridge, Calif.: Roberts Pub. Co. [1960. 4], 68 p. diagrs. (part col.), maps (part col.), views. Includes accompanying text on the geography, history, resources, and commerce and industry of the State. 1st ed. 1957. [10224

ALICE HUNT. Archeology of the Death Valley salt pan, California [occupied by man perhaps as early as 7000 B.C. Salt Lake City: Univ. of Utah Press] 1960. xvi, 313, [5] p. maps, views. bibliog. (p. 293-305). (University of Utah. Dept. of Anthropology. Anthropological papers, 47.) [10225

HARRY CLEBOURNE JAMES. The Cahuilla Indians: the men called master. [Los Angeles:] Westernlore Press [1960]. 185, [4] p. maps, ports., views. bibliog. (p. 181-4). (Great West and Indian series, 18.) On a group otherwise known as the Kawia Indians, in the area between Banning and the Salton Sea, since prehistoric times. [10226

KENNETH A. R. KENNEDY. The dentition of Indian crania of the early and late archaeological horizons in central California. Univ. Calif. Archaeol. Survey, Rep., 50:41-50. tables. bibliog. (Papers on California archaeology, 88.) Study of 100 crania in 2 series, 2500-1500 B.C., and A.D. 300-1700. [10227

DOWNEY D. RAIBOURN. Two forms of Iroquois cousin terminology and their functions [among 2 dialectically related Wintun societies in central California]. Ind. Acad. Science, Proc., 69:86-91. table. bibliog. On "Iroquois type" terminology among Indians who are not Iroquois. [10228

FRANCIS A. RIDDELL. The archaeology of the Karlo site (LAS-7), California. [Berkeley: Dept. of Anthropology, Univ. of California, 1960. 2], ii, 110 p. diagrs., map, tables, views. bibliog. (p. 100-104). (Reports of the University of California Archaeological Survey, 53.) On a Great Basin site in Lassen County north of Honey Lake, containing remains of human occupancy with a radiocarbon date of 2350 ± 150 years before present; with discussion of "prehistoric cultural and temporal relationships between California proper and the Great Basin, and an appended "Description of human skeletal remains from the Karlo site," by Grover Krantz (p. 93-9). [10229

JAMES G. RONEY, JR. Palaeopathology of a California archaeological site. Bul. hist. med., 33:97-109 (Mar-Apr 1959). tables. bibliog. On evidences of disease in skeletons excavated in a midden on Bodega Head (a peninsula about 45 miles north of the Golden Gate), probably occupied "between two and three thousand years ago." [10230

PAUL SCHUMACHER. The manufacture of shell fish-hooks by the early inhabitants of the Santa Barbara Channel Islands. Univ. Calif. Archaeol. Survey, Rep., 50:23-4. (Papers on California archaeology, 83.) Translated from Archiv für Anthropologie, v. 8 (1875). [10231

IRVING STONE. California [its traditions and characteristics]. Holiday, American panorama west of the Mississippi: a Holiday magazine book (Garden City, N.Y.: Doubleday [1960]), p. 35-57. [10232

B. K. SWARTZ, JR. Blade manufacture in southern California. Am. antiq., 25:405-7 (Jan) diagrs., views. bibliog. On "the striking of long, slender, parallel-sided flakes, or blades, from prepared cores ... in the Late Horizon in both mainland and island Canaliño sites in that part of the Santa Barbara Channel region ... which was ethnographically occupied by the Chumash." [10233

B. K. SWARTZ, JR. Evidence for the Indian occupation of Santa Barbara Island. Kiva, 26(1):7-9 (Oct). view. bibliog. Recently noted indications that the island "was inhabited, but only temporarily or by periodic visits, perhaps for quarrying materials." [10234

KARL V. TEETER. Notes on Humboldt County, California, place names of Indian origin. Names, 6:55-6 (Mar 1958). [10235

JAMES DAVID HART. American images of Spanish California. Berkeley: Friends of the Bancroft Library, Univ.

of California [1960]. vi, 39 p. ports., views. bibliog. (p. 35-9). On "the texts that helped to shape American consciousness of the character of California," published 1510-1935; with an effort "to show how the written word, literary and sub-literary, established and then altered a popular conception of California," particularly for the years "from about 1830 to 1846." [10236

ARNOLD R. ROJAS (born 1899). Last of the vaqueros. Fresno, Calif.: Academy Library Guild, 1960. [8], 165 p. ports., views. On the author's "life as a vaquero" in the San Joaquin Valley during a period of "some fifty odd years" and his recollections of mainly Spanish-speaking cowboys there; with history and lore about horses and horsemen in California since 1535. [10237

CYNTHIA (HOBART) LINDSAY. The climate of lunacy: an unnatural history of Southern California. London: H. Hamilton [1960]. vii, [3], 174 p. Satirical examination of customs and ways of life in this region, particularly in and near Los Angeles; with occasional references to events as early as 1542. [10238

EDWARD P. VON DER PORTEN. Our first New England. U.S.N. Inst. proc., 86(12):62-6 (Dec). map. port., views. On the visit of Sir Francis Drake to California in the Golden Hind, 1579, and the discovery of the site of his landfall in Drake's Bay in 1952. [10239

CALIFORNIA. Dept. of Natural Resources. Division of Beaches and Parks. California historical landmarks [722 items, 1769-1960. Sacramento, 1960. 2], 94 p. 16x23 cm. [10240

PETER THOMAS CONMY. Miguel José Serra, Padre Junípero, O.F.M. [commonly known as Junípero Serra, 1713-84]. San Francisco: Grand Parlor, Native Sons of the Golden West, 1960. 39 p. ports. bibliog. (p. 37-9), notes. On his missionary service in Mexico and Baja California, 1749-69, and in Alta California, 1769-84; with some account of his early years in Majorca and Spain. [10241

MAYNARD JOSEPH GEIGER. The Sierra Trail in picture and story. [Santa Barbara? Calif.: Franciscan Fathers of California, 1960.] viii, 222, [2] p. port. Reproductions of engravings and photographs of scenes and buildings associated with the life and missionary activities of Junipero Serra, O.F.M. (1713-84), in Majorca, Spain, Mexico, Lower California, and (1769-84) Upper California; with descriptive text. [10242

HAROLD KIRKER. California's architectural frontier: style and tradition in the nineteenth century [1769-1915]. San Marino, Calif.: Huntington Library, 1960. xiv, [2], 224 p. plans, views. bibliog. (p. 197-216), notes. "A social history of California architecture," undertaken "to explain the colonial nature of California's frontier society in terms of its architecture." Appended (p. 203-16): "Biographical sources, California architects in the nineteenth century." [10243

HENRY A. TURNER & JOHN ALBERT VIEG. The government and politics of California [1769-1960]. N.Y.: McGraw-Hill, 1960. xi, 275 p. cartoons, diagrs., facsims., tables, views. bibliog., notes. (McGraw-Hill series in political science.) [10244

SHERBURNE FRIEND COOK. The aboriginal population of Alameda and Contra Costa Counties, California. [Berkeley: Univ. of California Press, 1957.] iii, 131-154 p. maps. bibliog. (p. 150-51). (Anthropological records, v. 16, no. 4.) Backward projection from historical records, 1772-1811, indicating that the population in 1770 was 2,248 and that there was no general tribal designation for the inhabitants of the area. [10245

SHERBURNE FRIEND COOK. The aboriginal population of the San Joaquin Valley, California. [Berkeley: Univ. of California Press, 1955.] iii, 31-78 p. maps (1 fold.), tables. bibliog. (p. 72-4). (Anthropological records, v. 16, no. 2.) Data from historical records for the period 1770-1850, indicating a total population of 83,820 (ca. 1770?) for "the territory of the Plains and Sierra Miwok, the Yokuts, the Western Mono, the Tulutulabal, and the Kawaiisu," and a decline to 19,000 in 1850. [10246

SIDNEY TWICHELL HARDING. Water in California [1770-1960]. Palo Alto, Calif.: N-P Publications [1960. 2], xiii, [1], 231 p. maps (1 fold.), tables, views. Chapters on water conditions in 1848, "Water rights and water laws," "Use of water in mining," navigation, irrigation, "Municipal water supply," hydroelectric power, reclamation, flood control, "Recreation and related uses of water," and plans and projects. [10247

ROBERT FLEMING HEIZER. California population densities, 1770 and 1950. Univ. Calif. Archaeol. Survey, Rep., 50:9-12. bibliog. (Papers on California archaeology, 79.) [10248

MICHAEL CROWLEY. California--wineland of America. Westerners brand book (Chicago), 16:73-5, 79-80 (Dec 1959). On the vineyards and wineries of California since 1771. [10249

ANNIE ROSALIND MITCHELL. Land of the tules. ... With original pen and ink drawings by Adele Bradley. Visalia, Calif., 1949. [6], 92, [4] p. maps, ports., views. A history of Tulare County, Calif., 1772-1949, an area formerly including all the counties bounding the present Tulare County. Written "for elementary school children." [10250

ROCCO LOUIS GENTILCORE. Ontario, California, and the agricultural boom of the 1880s. Agric. hist., 34:77-87 (Apr). maps. notes. On a city east of Los Angeles, established by George and William Chaffey in 1883, the changing landscape of the area between 1776 and 1904, its conversion from livestock ranches to irrigated orange groves, and its engineering devices for control of its water supply. [10251

DONALD C. CUTTER. Malaspina in California. [San Francisco:] J. Howell, 1960. [6], viii, 96 p. diagrs., map, tables (part fold.), views (part col.). bibliog. (p. 84-7), notes. On a scientific expedition of the Spanish Government to Monterey, 1791, led by Alessandro Malaspina (1754-1809), the survey of the port, the observations made, the plants, animals, and Indian artifacts collected, and the failure of the Government to publish any report of the expedition and its findings; with reproductions of its map of the Bay of Monterey and of 10 paintings or drawings made at the time by José Cardero and others. Based mainly upon records in the Museo Naval, Madrid. [10252

ROBERT FLEMING HEIZER. Two early representations of California Indians. Univ. Calif. Archaeol. Survey, Rep., 50:12-13. views. bibliog. (Papers on California archaeology, 80.) Reproduces a drawing by ---- Cardero, showing a Costanoan woman at Monterey (1791) and a drawing of a group of Indians from the "Upper Sacramento Valley," by H. D. Brown (1852). [10253

SHERBURNE FRIEND COOK. The aboriginal population of the north coast of California. [Berkeley: Univ. of California Press, 1956.] iii, 81-129 p. tables. bibliog. (p. 128-9). (Antropological records, v. 16, no. 3.) Backward projection from historical records, indicating a total population of 70,440 (ca. 1800?) for the Yurok, Wiyot, Karok, Hupa, Tolowa, Yuki, Pomo, Coast and Lake Miwok, Wappo, Wintun, and 8 groups of Athapascans. [10254

SHERBURNE FRIEND COOK, ed. Colonial expeditions to the interior of California Central Valley, 1800-1820. [Berkeley: Univ. of California Press, 1960.] iii, 239-292 p. bibliog. (p. 291-2), notes (p. 282-90). (Anthropological records, v. 16, no. 6.) Translations and abstracts of letters, reports, and diaries, 1785, 1795-1821, 1878, comprising "all the pertinent documents I can find dealing with the Central Valley of California in the period from 1800 to 1820." Includes diaries, etc., of Fray Juan Martín (1815), Fray José de Zalvidea (1806), Fray Pedro Muñoz (1806), José Palomares (1808), Fray José Viader (1810), Gervasio Argüello (1811, 1813), Juan Ortega (1815), José Dolores Pico (1815), Fr. Luís Antonio Martínez (1816), Fr. Juan Cabot (1816), and others. [10255

ROBERT MATHESON NORRIS. Desert San Nicolas and the last Nicoleño. Pac. discovery, 13(3):10-13 (May-Jun). views. On a barren island 60 miles offshore from Ventura County, probably discovered in 1543, whose male Indian inhabitants were butchered by Aleut otter-hunters in 1811; the removal of the surviving female inhabitants (except one) to the mainland in 1835; the rescue of the lone inhabitant of the island in 1853; her death in Santa Barbara the same year, aged about 45, the last living Nicoleño; and the later history and natural history of the island. [10256

GEORGE VAN DUERS. The Russians logged the redwoods first. Am. forests, 65(1):29-31, 61-2 (Jan 1959). map, views. On the Russian Fort Ross and adjacent houses, constructed of hewn redwood, on the coast about 18 miles north of Bodega Bay, 1812-42, a trading post of the Russian American Company. [10257

ROBERT W. DURRENBERGER. Freezes and their effect upon the California citrus industry [1821-1949]. Weatherwise, 13:200-202 (Oct). diagrs. [10258

WOODROW JAMES HANSEN. The search for authority in California. Oakland, Calif.: Biobooks, 1960. [10], 192, [3] p. fold. col. map, table. bibliog. (p. 190-92), notes (p. 180-89). (California heritage, 47.) Based on thesis--Brown Univ. On efforts to establish a system of government adequate to the needs and wishes of the Mexican and American inhabitants, 1822-50, with special attention to the Constitutional Convention at the end of the period. [10259

JOSÉ MARÍA GUZMÁN. Breve noticia que da al Supremo Gobierno del actual estado del territorio de la Alta California, y medios que propone para la ilustración y comercio en aquel país, el Guardián del Colegio Apostólico de San Fernando de México, año de 1833. México: Vargas Rea, 1956. 28 p. (Biblioteca aportación histórica.) 1st ed. 1833. Addressed to the Vice-President of the United States of the Mexican Republic, 29 Apr. 1833. Compiled mainly from manuscript reports by Franciscan missionaries. [10260

EDWARD GEOFFREY VAN DYKE BANGS. Portals West: a folio of late nineteenth century architecture in California [1834-1960]. Preface by Robert Gordon Sproul. [San Francisco, 1960.] 86, [1] p. 36 views. 32 cm. (California Historical Society. Special publication 35.) Views of buildings erected in northern California, mainly in "smaller communities and rural areas," between 1834 and 1878, some of which no longer exist; with descriptive text. [10261

WALKER A. TOMPKINS. Santa Barbara's Royal Rancho: the fabulous history of Los Dos Pueblos. Berkeley, Calif.: Howell-North, 1960. viii, [2], 282 p. facsims., maps, ports., views. bibliog. (p. 276-7). On Los Dos Pueblos Rancho, north of Santa Barbara with a 10-mile frontage on the Pacific, now increasingly occupied by real-estate developments; with an account of its founder, Nicholas Augustus Henry Den (1812-62), who arrived in southern California in 1836, and of some of his descendants and later owners of the ranch. [10262

MICHAEL MATHES. Judicial transformation in California--1837-1851. Los Angeles Bar bul., 35:359-64 (Sep). port. bibliog., notes. On the transition from the Mexican to the American system. [10263

KENNETH W. THOMPSON. Historic flooding in the Sacramento Valley. Pac. hist. rev., 29:349-60 (Nov). notes. On the geography and hydrology of the Sacramento River Basin, and the floods known to have occurred there between 1837 and 1852, aggravated after 1848 by the deposition of debris from hydraulic mining. [10264

JUAN FRANCISCO DANA (1838-1936). The blond ranchero: memories of Juan Francisco Dana as told to Rocky Dana and Marie Harrington. Los Angeles: Dawson's Book Shop [1960]. 133, [2] p. facsim., ports., views. On the author's life on Nipomo Ranch, San Luis Obispo County, Calif.; with some account of the Dana family in California. [10265

CALIFORNIA. Dept. of Natural Resources. Division of Beaches and Parks. Old Sacramento: a report on its signifiance to the city, State, and nation, with recommendations for the preservation and use of its principal historical structures and sites. [By Carroll Douglas Hall, Hero Eugene Rensch, Jack R. Dyson, & Norman L. Wilson.] Sacramento, 1958-60. 3 v. [2], 17 leaves; vi, 83 p.; [2], 16 leaves. facsims., maps, tables, views. On "architecture worth saving" in Sacramento, 1839-1960. [10266

C. RAYMOND CLAR. John Sutter, lumberman. Jour. forestry, 56:259-65 (Apr 1958). map. bibliog. On Johann August Sutter (1803-80), emigrant to California in 1839, settler at Sonoma. [10267

AUSTIN DRAKE. Big Bear Valley: it's history, legends, & tales. Big Bear Lake, Calif.: Grizzly Little Press in the Pines [1949]. 79 p. map, ports., views. On an area in the San Bernardino Mountains, 1841-1948, including the town of Pine Knot (renamed Big Bear Lake in 1938). [10268

ALBERT SHUMATE. Rancho San Luis Gonzaga (San Joaquin Valley's oldest house). Pony Express, 27(5):3-5 (Oct). port., view. On a 48,000-acre ranch in San Bonito and Merced Counties, the only California ranch that remains undivided, soon to be flooded behind a dam, and an adobe building constructed there soon after 1843. [10269

GEORGE RIPPEY STEWART. Donner Pass and those who crossed it: the story of the country made notable by the Stevens Party, the Donner Party, the gold-hunters, and the railroad builders [1844-1960]. With old and new illustrations showing the pass in summer and winter. San Francisco: California Historical Soc. [1960]. 96 p. facsim., maps, ports., views. On a pass northwest of Lake Tahoe, close to the present highway between Reno and Sacramento. [10270

THOMAS COAKLEY. Early California law: vignettes on the Mother Lode. State Bar Calif., Jour., 35:516-29 (Sep-Oct). Anecdotes and personalities, 1846 to ca. 1860. [10271

LÉON RENÉ YANKWICH. Social attitudes as reflected in early California law [1846-1958]. Hastings law jour., 10:250-70 (Feb 1959). notes. [10272

JAMES M. JENSEN. Cattle drives from the ranchos [in southern California] to the gold fields of California [1847-70]. Ariz. and the West, 2: 341-52 (winter). notes. [10273

THOMAS OLIVER LARKIN (1802-58). The Larkin Papers: personal, business, and official correspondence of Thomas Oliver Larkin, merchant and United States Consul in California. Edited by George P. Hammond ... Volume VII, 1847-1848. Berkeley and Los Angeles: Univ. of California Press for the Bancroft Library, 1960. xxviii, [2], 369, [1] p. port. notes. Letters and other documents written by or addressed to Larkin, 1 Oct. 1847 - 4 Oct. 1848. [10274

JOSEPH ARMSTRONG BAIRD, JR. Architectural legacy of Sacramento: a study of 19th century style [1848-1914]. Calif. Hist. Soc. quar., 39: 193-207 (Sep). map, views. notes. [10275

RUSSELL EUGENE BIDLACK, ed. Letters home: the story of Ann Arbor's Forty-Niners. Ann Arbor: Ann Arbor Publishers, 1960. [10], 56 p. facsims., views. notes (p. 53-6). Letters reprinted from Ann Arbor newspapers, from George Corselius, David T. McCollum, Dr. Caleb N. Ormsby, Dr. Thomas Blackwood, and De Witt C. Downer, 30 Jan. 1849-3 Aug. 1850; with other California information from the same newspapers, 1848-50. [10276

HOWARD F. GREGOR. Push to the desert. Science, 129:1329-39 (15 May 1959). diagrs., maps, views. notes. On "irrigation developments in California," 1848-1959. [10277

EDWARD MELVIN LEE. Background of California private gold coins [1848-50]. Selections from The numismatist: United States paper money, tokens, medals, and miscellaneous (Racine, Wis.: Whitman Pub. Co., 1960), p. 44-6. First printed Jun. 1931. [10278

JOHN ALFRED SWAN (1817-96). A trip to the gold mines of California in 1848. ... Edited, with introduction and notes, by John A. Hussey. San Francisco: Book Club of California, 1960. xxxv, 51, [2] p. port. notes (p. 37-51). Manuscript reminiscences (1870) of a journey from Monterey to Placerville and of mining gold on Dry Creek, 1848; with an introductory biographical sketch by the editor. [10279

GEORGE FRANCIS WRIGHT, ed. Reproduction of Thompson and West's History of Sacramento County, California, with illustrations. With introduction by Allan R. Ottley. Berkeley, Calif.: Howell-North, 1960. [8] p., facsim. (294 p.). col. maps (1 fold.), ports., tables, views (part double). 28x36 cm. Text in triple columns. 1st ed. 1880 (Oakland: Thompson & West). Narrative and topical history, mainly for the years from 1848 to 1880. Includes a section of "Biographical and statistical matter of our patrons" (p. 243-94); and more than 200 lithographs from original sketches. The introduction contains biographical sketches of the contributors and of the publishers, Thomas Hinckley Thompson (1841-1915) and Albert Augustus West (1841-1918), and a list of their 17 publications (atlases, a State history, and county histories, 1876-92). [10280

CALIFORNIA. Dept. of Finance. California's State capitol. [Sacramento, 1960.] 95, [1] p. facsims., views. bibliog. (p. 94-5). On structures erected at Monterey, San Jose, Vallejo, Benicia, and Sacramento at various times between 1849 and 1874, including the present building, begun in 1860. [10281

A. JAY HERTZ. James M. Hutchings, California illustrator [from 1849 to 1886]. Am. philatelist, 73:807-14 (Aug). facsims., views. On his engravings and descriptions of California scenes in his Illustrated California magazine (1856-61) and several books and broadsides, including engraved sheets of writing paper and engraved covers; with facsimile and reprinted text of his The miner's ten commandments. [10282

WILLIAM TURRENTINE JACKSON. Lewis Richard Price [1817-82], British mining entrepreneur and traveler in California. Pac. hist. rev., 29:331-48 (Nov). notes. On his mercantile activities in Mexico, 1833-65, his visits to California mines in 1849 and 1871, and his involvement in the affairs of the North Star Gold Mining Company, the Sierra Buttes Gold Mining Company, and the London and California Mining Company, 1869-82. [10283

HOWARD BRETT MELENDY. Who was John McDougal? Pac. hist. rev., 29:231-43 (Aug). notes. Biographical sketch of John McDougal (1818-66), dealing mainly with his activities in California politics, 1849-56, his addiction to drink, and the confusion of historians who have identified him with his contemporary James A. McDougall (died 1867). [10284

LEWIS RICHARD PRICE. Mazatlán to the Estanislao: the narrative of Lewis Richard Price's journey to California in 1849. With introduction and notes by W. Turrentine Jackson. Calif. Hist. Soc. quar., 39:35-51 (Mar). views. notes. Record by an English merchant in Mexico of his voyage from Mazatlán to San Francisco, his examination of mines in the Tuolumne area, and his return voyage to Mazatlán, 8 Sep.-10 Nov. 1849. [10285

ISABEL G. SCHRADER. Souvenir spoons of California. Hobbies, 65(1): 51-3 (Mar). view. On the author's collection, showing California scenes and characters since 1849. [10286

EDWARD B. SCOTT. Squaw Valley [Calif. ... a photographic historical of the squaw Valley-Sierra Nevada region [1849-1960. Lake Tahoe, Nev.: Sierra-Tahoe Pub. Co., 1960.] 88 p. facsims., maps, ports., views. notes (p. 87-8). On an area inhabited by Washoe Indians as late as 1849, the mining, ranching, and logging industries there, and more recently the development of skiing. [10287

HORACE GORDON THOMASSON, JR., FRANKLIN HOWARD OLMSTED, & EDMUND F. LE ROUX. Geology, water resources, and usable groundwater storage capacity of part of Solano County, California [1849-1952]. Wash.: U.S. Govt. Print. Off., 1960. x, 693 p. diagrs. (part fold.), maps (part col., part fold.), tables (part double), views. notes. (U.S. Geological Survey. Water-supply paper 1464.) Prepared by the Geological Survey in cooperation with the U.S. Bureau of Reclamation. [10288

EDWIN W. YOUNG. The adoption of the common law in California [1849-50]. Am. jour. legal hist., 4:355-63 (Oct). notes. [10289

CLIFFORD HERSHEY BISSEL. The French language press in California. Calif. Hist. Soc. quar., 39:1-17, 141-71, 219-62, 311-53 (Mar-Dec). cartoons, ports., view. notes. Chronological history of French-language newspapers and magazines in northern California, 1850-1959, and southern California, 1857-1959; with "Alphabetical list of journals and locations of copies." [10290

PING CHIU. Chinese labor in California, 1850-1880: an economic study. Ann Arbor: University Microfilms, 1960. Positive microfilm of typescript. [299] leaves. Thesis--Univ. of Wisconsin. Abstracted: Dissert. abstracts, 20:4086-7 (Apr). [10291

GERALD D. NASH. Problems and projects in the history of nineteenth-century California land policy. Ariz. and the West, 2:327-40 (winter). notes. On the geographic and climatic, entrepreneurial, and institutional conditions since the 1850s that have promoted "the great concentration of land ownership in twentieth-century California." [10292

KERMIT RAYBORN. Ramrod justice. True West, 7(4):34-6 (Mar-Apr). Anecdotes of California justices of the peace in mining towns, 1850 ff. [10293

GEORGIA WILLIS READ. Bruff's route in eastern California. Calif. Hist. Soc. quar., 39:263-6 (Sep). map, view. On a search in present Lassen County by Joseph Goldsbrough Bruff and Peter Lassen for a probably mythical Gold Lake, 1850. [10294

The WADES and Wade Hamptons of Virginia. Pony Express, 26(3):6-10 (Aug 1959). map, ports., views. On descendants of Dawson Wade and of Wade Hampton who settled in California, beginning with Joseph Hampton who arrived in 1850. [10295

RUBY LINDBERG. August Wetterman [1828-1923]--California pioneer. Am. Swed. Hist. Found., Yr. bk., 1959, p. 14-32. On his voyage from Sweden to San Francisco in 1851, his brief experience in the mines, his career as a bandmaster and orchestral conductor in Sacramento, his activities in Scandinavian groups, and his later years in a home for the aged that he had helped to found. [10296

WENDELL ROBIE. World's finest horses on 100 mile ride. Pony Express, 26(2):4-5 (Jul 1959). port. On Capt. Ben Taylor, who brought a herd of stallions and mares to California in 1851, from which "the fine horses on the ranges of Nevada County and the Sacramento Region of California, grew and multiplied." [10297

BOOK CLUB OF CALIFORNIA, San Francisco. California sheet music covers. [San Francisco] 1959. 12 fold. leaves issued in a case. (Its Keepsake series.) Facsimile reproductions of the covers of 12 songs (2 colored), each with an account (by a different editor) of scene or occasion, composer, lithographer, and publisher, and some with reprinted texts or parts of texts. Contains: The California pioneers, The Exhibition Fair, Pull away cheerily! the gold digger's song, The wines of Los Angeles County, The San Francisco quadrilles, arranged from the most favourite Negro melodies for the piano forte, El eco del Pacifico, New express galop, "I do not want to be drowned": a song respectfully dedicated to the survivors of the wreck of the Golden-Gate, Independent City Guards: quick step, California flood mazurka, Bay-View-Park galup, Hank Monk schottische. [10298

WALTER G. COLLINS. Steam schooners of the redwood coast. Am. forests, 62(8):20-21, 46-8 (Aug 1956). views. On shipment of redwood lumber by steamer from the northern coast of California, 1852-1912. [10299

ERNEST CLEVELAND STUMP, JR. History of the organization and development of public education in Shasta County, California [since 1853]. Ann Arbor: University Microfilms, 1959 [i.e. 1960]. Positive microfilm of typescript. [325] leaves. Thesis (Ed. D.)--Univ. of Southern California. Abstracted: Dissert. abstracts, 20:4022 (Apr). [10300

ROBERT H. POWER. Pioneer skiing in California [1854-1960]. Vacaville, Calif.: Nut Tree, 1960. x, 26 p. facsims., map, ports., views. notes (p. 21-6). [10301

KELD J. REYNOLDS. A pioneer California surgeon and medical educator: Elias Samuel Cooper [1822-62]. Jour. med. educ., 34:631-43 (Jul 1959). facsim., port. bibliog., notes. On his early life in Butler County, Ohio, his medical studies in Cincinnati, his service as a physician and surgeon in Danville and Peoria, Ill., and after 1854 in San Francisco, his part in the founding of the Medico-Chirurgical Society of San Francisco, the California State Medical Society, and the San Francisco medical press, and his establishment of the medical department of the University of the Pacific at Santa Clara (now the School of Medicine of Stanford University). [10302

LOUIS CLARK JONES. Ever hear of F. R. Bennet? Art in Am., 48(1):12; (3):86. view. Query as to the date of a painting with caption "Dance on a sequoia stump"; and discovery of a passage in Harper's weekly, 5 Jul. 1858, reporting that the tree (15 miles from Murphy's Diggings, Calif.) had been cut down in 1855, leaving a stump 96 feet in circumference, on which "theatrical performances were given ... in May, 1855," and which offered "ample space for 32 persons to dance." [10303

ARVO VAN ALSTYNE. Claims against public entities: chaos in California law. U.C.L.A. law rev., 6:205-68 (Mar 1959). tables. notes. On the tort liability or immunity of the State, counties, cities, and districts of California, 1855-1958. [10304

JAMES WILLIAM ALBERT WRIGHT (1834-94). The Cement hunters: lost gold mine of the High Sierra. [Edited by Richard E. Lingenfelter.] Los Angeles: G. Dawson, 1960. [2], xi, [1], 52 p. mount. port. notes (p. 49-52). From the San Francisco Daily evening post, 8 Nov.-13 Dec. 1879. On the "Lost Cement," a mine "somewhere along the rugged eastern slope of the Sierra about the headwaters of the Owens River," and efforts to find it, 1857-79. [10305

LESLIE J. FREEMAN. Murphy's Diggings. Pony Express, 25(8):3-4 (Jan 1959). port. On Murphy's Hotel, opened in 1856, and other surviving structures of the gold-mining town. [10306

HOWARD BRETT MELENDY. Orleans Bar. Calif. Hist. Soc. quar., 39:53-9 (Mar). notes. On a town selected as the county seat of Klamath County in 1856 and still in existence in 1899; with an account of the dissolution of the county in 1874. [10307

JOHN AUGUSTUS SUTTER (1803-80). Part of the correspondence between J. A. Sutter and Col. T. T. Henley, Superintendent of Indian Affairs, San Francisco, 1856, Univ. Calif. Archaeol. Survey, Rep., 50:27-31. (Papers on California archaeology, 85.) Two letters, dated Hock Farm, 9 Feb. and 1 Dec. 1856, on the conflict of interests between the Indians and the squatters in that area and the question whether the Indians should be removed to a reservation. [10308

JULIAN O. VON KALINOWSKI & JOHN J. HANSON. The California antitrust laws [1856-1958]: a comparison with the Federal antitrust laws. U.C.L.A. law rev., 6:533-59 (Jul 1959). notes. [10309

NELL MURBARGER. Hell-hole of the San Bernardinos. True West, 7(6): 18-19, 46-8 (Jul-Aug). views. On Dobie and other short-lived mining towns in Holcomb Valley, Calif., where gold was discovered in 1860. [10310

NELL MURBARGER. The lost Van Duzen Mine [1860s-1940s]. Frontier times, 34(4):13, 55 (fall). view. On a mine supposed to have been found by ---- Van Duzen in Van Duzen Canyon in the San Bernardino Mountains sometime before 1868, the murder of Van Duzen, and the continued searches for the mine as late as 1945. [10311

WALTER WALLACE WEIR. Land drainage in California: a century of history-making drainage-engineering development [1860-1953]. Agric. engineering, 35:482-5 (Jul 1954). views. [10312

GORDON C. ROADARMEL, comp. Some California dates of 1861. Calif. Hist. Soc. quar., 39:289-308 (Dec). port., view. Chronology. [10313

FERGUS L. FAIRBANKS. Thomas R[obert] Bard [1841-1915]. Ventura Co. Hist. Soc. quar., 5(2):2-8 (Feb). ports., view. On his management of oil properties and his other business, agricultural, and civic enterprises centered in Hueneme, 1865-1915. [10314

STANFORD RESEARCH INSTITUTE. Southern California Laboratories, South Pasadena. The savings and loan industry in California [1865-1958]. By C. Joseph Clawson, Frank W. Barsalou, and others. South Pasadena, 1960. [430] p. diagrs., tables. notes. (SRI project I-3065.) Prepared for the Savings and Loan Commissioner, State of California, Los Angeles. [10315

ROBERT L. OSWALT. Gualala. Names, 8:57-8 (Mar). On the name of "A small coastal town in Mendocino County, California and ... the river at whose mouth the town lies"; with indications that before 1867 the name was spelled Walala and that it was borrowed from the Pomo Indians. [10316

DOUG DEMAREST. Son of the Sierra Nevada. Am. forests, 64(4):32-4, 61-3 (Apr 1958). facsim., port., double view. On John Muir (1838-1914) as a naturalist and conservationist in the Sierra Nevada Mountains, California, 1869-1914. [10317

JOSEPH LE CONTE (1823-1901). A journal of ramblings through the High Sierra of California by the University Excursion Party. San Francisco: Sierra Club [1960]. xii, [4], 148, [2] p. ports., views. bibliog. (p. 149-50). 1st ed. 1875. Record of a camping trip of 9 students from the University of California, accompanied by the author, Professor of Natural Sciences there, on horseback to the Yosemite Valley, Mono Lake, and Lake Tahoe, 21 Jul.-26 Aug. 1870; with observations on the geology of the Sierra Nevada. [10318

JOSEPH E. BROWN. Duel at dusk. Frontier times, 34(4):18-19, 52-4 (fall). On the efficiency of Harry N. Morse, Sheriff of Alameda County, in tracking and capturing outlaws, alive or dead, particularly his finding and killing of Juan Soto in 1871. [10319

HELEN MICHAELIS. Great racers of old California [1871-96]. Quarter horse jour., 6(2):27 (Nov 1953). [10320

CORINNE LATHROP GILB. [The State Bar of California and predecessor organizations.] State Bar Calif., Jour., 34:38-43, 356-61, 866-72 (Jan-Feb, May-Jun, Sep-Oct 1959). port. notes. Based on thesis--Radcliffe College, 1956. On local voluntary bar associations in California as early as 1872, the California Bar Association (1909-27), and the State Bar of California (1927-59). [10321

JANE (HOWELL) WATTERS (born 1875). Forest Hill's Lower Town that produced its wealth. By Mrs. Jane Howell Watters, veteran daughter of California's early pioneers, and resident for many years of Forest Hill. As told to H. Hamlin. Pony Express, 27(3):3-8 (Aug). ports., view. Recollections by a native. [10322

JESSE L. CARR. The coroner and the common law [in California, 1876-1960]. Calif. med., 92:323-5, 426-9; 93:32-4, 99-101, 157-9 (May-Sep). [10323

JOHN W. ARMSTRONG. Judicial murder: the opinion of Judge John W. Armstrong in the case of F. A. Sprague, convicted of first degree murder for the killing of T[homas] W[allace] More in March 1877. Ventura Co. Hist. Soc. quar., 5(4): 18-20 (Aug). Letter addressed to and requested by George Stoneman, Governor of California, dated Sacramento, 9 Nov. 1883. [10324

ALBERT B. ELSASSER. The history of culture classification in California. Univ. Calif. Archaeol. Survey, Rep., 49:1-10. bibliog. (Papers on California archaeology, 74.) On classifications of California Indian cultures by observation of surviving Indians and by archeological analysis, 1877-1958. [10325

HENRY CHAPMAN FORD. Notes on excavations made in Indian burial places in Carpinteria [12 miles from Santa Barbara, 1877]. Univ. Calif. Archaeol. Survey, Rep., 50:14-19. (Papers on California archaeology, 81.) From Report of proceedings of the Santa Barbara Society of Natural History, Mar. 1887. [10326

J. EDWARD JOHNSON. [Justices of the Supreme Court of California.] State Bar Calif., Jour., 34:873-7; 35:92-6, 486-90 (Sep-Oct 1959, Jan-Feb, Jul-Aug 1960). ports. notes. Contents of these installments.--Erskine Mayo Ross [1845-1928, served 1880-86].--John Randolph Sharpstein [1823-92, served 1880-92].--Samuel Bell McKee [1822-90, served 1879-86]. [10327

WILLIAM STEIN. Recollections of a pioneer oil driller [in Santa Clara County, Ventura County, and elsewhere in California, 1880-89]. Ventura Co. Hist. Soc. quar., 5(3):2-20 (May). ports. bibliog. Unfinished manuscript (1936). [10328

WILLIAM DAVID PATTISON. Harold W. Fairbanks [1860-1952], California geographer. Jour. geog., 59:351-7 (Nov). port., view. notes. On his activities in California, 1882 ff., as a geologist, a geological consultant and promoter of mining claims, "the most important geographic photographer on the West Coast" (ca. 1895 to ca. 1907), and an author of textbooks of California and world geography (1899-1929). [10329

JOHN J. McLEAN. Shell-heaps near Cape Mendocino, Humboldt County, California. Univ. Calif. Archaeol. Survey, Rep., 50:25-7. (Papers on California archaeology, 84.) From Smithsonian contributions to knowledge, v. 25 (1885). Description communicated in 1883. [10330

HENRY WETHERBEE HENSHAW (1850-1930). The Mission Indian vocabularies of H. W. Henshaw. Edited, with ethnographic notes, by R[obert] F[leming] Heizer. [Berkeley: Univ. of California Press, 1955. 4], 85-202 p. facsim. bibliog. (p. 201-2), notes. (Anthropological records, v. 15, no. 2.) Six Chumash vocabularies; 4 Costanoan vocabularies; 3 lists of Chumash villages (p. 194-200); and 2 letters from Juan Esteban Pico to Henshaw (San Buenaventura, 21 Apr. 1891, and undated, the second containing English text of a newspaper editorial, 4 Jul. 1890, Spanish translation, and Chumash translation); with a biographical introduction on Henshaw. [10331

EDITH RONALD MIRRIELEES. Stanford: the story of a university. N.Y.: Putnam [1960, ©1959]. 255 p. facsim., ports., table, views. On Stanford University, 1887-1959. [10332

FREDERICK G. BOHME. Bishop Nichols of California: a disputed election and a delayed telegram. P. E. Church, Hist. mag., 29:145-52 (Jun). notes. On the controversy in the Diocese of California concerning the election of William Ford Nichols as Bishop Coadjutor of California and the proposed separation of the Southern Convocation to form the Diocese of Los Angeles, 1889. [10333

ESTHER McCOY & RANDELL L. MAKINSON. Five California architects [active in California as early as 1889]. N.Y.: Reinhold Pub. Corp.

[1960]. vii, [1], 200 p. plans, ports., views. Biographical sketches of Bernard R. Maybeck (1862-1957), Irving John Gill (1870-1936), R. M. Schindler (1887-1953), Charles Sumner Greene (1868-1957), and Henry Mather Greene (1870-1954). [10334

CHARLES F. OUTLAND. Historic water diversion proposals [in Ventura County, 1893-1926]. Ventura Co. Hist. Soc. quar., 5(4):2-17 (Aug). port., views. [10335

PAUL B. HUBBARD. Garlock memories: a tribute to east Kern County's pioneer citizens. [n. p., 1960.] 44 p. maps (1 doubler), ports., views. On a gold-mining town founded in 1895 or 1896, abandoned by 1903. [10336

U. S. Farmer Cooperative Service. Sunkist Growers, Inc.: a California adventure in agricultural cooperation. By Irwin W[alter] Rust and Kelsey B[eeler] Gardner. [Wash., 1960.] iv, 120 p. diagrs., facsims., map, tables, views. bibliog. (p. 89-90), notes. (Its FCS circular 27.) On a "nonprofit cooperative marketing association" for the sale of oranges, grapefruit, and lemons, known as the Southern California Fruit Exchange (1895-1904), the California Fruit Growers Exchange (1904-52), and Sunkist Growers, Inc. (1952-60). [10337

SAN JUAN RECORD. Fair Oaks and San Juan area memories [1896-1959] as compiled and printed by the San Juan record during its silver anniversary year, 1958, and the following year. ... Edited by Selden Menefee, Patricia Fitzgerald, and Geraldine Fitzgerald. Fair Oaks, Calif.: San Juan Record Press, 1960. 103 p. ports., views. Text in 4 columns. Recollections by Grant Vail Wallace, John E. Holst, and 92 other early residents of Fair Oaks, a community on the American River east of Sacramento. [10338

THEODORE G. WURM & ALVIN C. GRAVES. The crookedest railroad in the world: a history of the Mt. Tamalpais and Muir Woods Railroad of California [1896-1930. Second revised edition.] Berkeley, Calif.: Howell-North, 1960. 123 p. facsims., maps, plans, ports., table, views. bibliog. (p. 115-17). 1st ed. 1954. On a line in Marin County named originally the Mill Valley and Mt. Tamalpais Scenic Railway, patronized mainly by sight-seers. [10339

MARTIN A. BAUMHOFF. California Athabascan groups. [Berkeley: Univ. of California Press, 1958.] v, 157-237 p. maps, views. bibliog. (p. 230-31). (Anthropological records, v. 16, no. 5.) On the culture of the Hupa, Whilkut, Nongatl, Bear River, Mattole, Lelangkok, Sinkyone, Kato, Wailaki (3 groups), and Lassik Indians (total population estimated at 6,000 in 1925 and 17,447 in 1956). Based in large part upon data collected by Pliny Earle Goddard, 1897-1900, and C. Hart Merriam, 1910-42. [10340

HENRY R. THOMAS, JR. The unavoidable-accident instruction [in California trial courts, 1897-1958]. South. Calif. law rev., 33:72-81 (fall 1959). notes. [10341

JANE FORD ADAMS, comp. [Buttons worn by uniformed employees of California railroad lines, 20th century.] Natl. button bul., 18:126-30, 227-30 (May, Sep 1959). views. Annotated lists of Los Angeles area interurban lines, northern California electric lines, and steam railroads, with descriptions of their uniform buttons. [10342

ALFRED LOUIS KROEBER (1876-1960) & SAMUEL ALFRED BARRETT. Fishing among the Indians of northwestern California. [Berkeley: Univ. of California Press, 1960.] vi, 210 p. maps, tables, views. bibliog. (p. 135-41). (Anthropological records, v. 21, no. 1.) On fishing methods and equipment of the Yurok, Hupa, Karok, Wiyot, Chilula, Whilkut, and Tolowa tribes and several adjacent groups. Based upon notes of Kroeber, E. W. Gifford, and G. W. Hewes and upon printed sources. [10343

ALFRED LOUIS KROEBER (1876-1960) & GEORGE WILLIAM GRACE, eds. The Sparkman grammar of Luiseño. Berkeley: Univ. of California Press, 1960. ix, 257 p. port. bibliog. (p. 255-7). (University of California publications in linguistics, 16.) Manuscript of a Luiseño grammar and lexicon compiled by Philip Stedman Sparkman and revised in 1909 by Kroeber and Feliz Calac (p. 5-174); grammar and dictionary fragment by Pablo Tac; texts recorded by Sparkman and transcribed by Feliz Calac in 1909; letter from Calac to Kroeber, 1909; and texts recorded by Grace in 1951 from Willy Calac, Johnny McDowell, and 2 other Luiseños. [10344

ALFRED LOUIS KROEBER (1876-1960). Yurok speech usages. Stanley Diamond, ed., Culture in history: essays in honor of Paul Radin (N.Y.: Columbia Univ. Press for Brandeis Univ., 1960), p. 993-9. bibliog. Based largely upon observations made by Kroeber in the very early 20th century in northwestern California. [10345

CLINTON HART MERRIAM (1855-1942). Data pertaining to various Indian ceremonial houses in northern California. Univ. Calif. Archaeol. Survey, Rep., 50:31-7. (Papers on California archaeology, 86.) Undated field notes (early 20th century?) "referring to four historic ceremonial houses representing Miwok, Nisenan, and Pit River Achomawi" Indians. [10346

PAGES OF HISTORY, Sausalito, Calif. Jade in California [1936-60]. Sausalito, Calif. [1960]. 23, [1] p. maps, tables, views. bibliog. (p. 21-4). Includes a suggestion that jade may have been surreptitiously collected by the Chinese from abandoned mining dumps before 1900. [10347

PHILIP MILLS JONES (1870-1916). Archaeological investigations on Santa Rosa Island in 1901. Edited by R. F. Heizer and A. B. Elsasser. [Berkeley: Univ. of California Press, 1956. 4], 201-280 p. map, views on 45 plates. bibliog. (p. 222). (Anthropological records, v. 17, no. 2.) Jones's journal, his notebook recording excavations, and plates with accompanying descriptions. [10348

ALFRED LOUIS KROEBER. Reproduction of cylinder recordings at the Museum of Anthropology at the University of California at Berkeley. Folklore and folk music archivist, 3(1): [2] (spring). On recordings made in and after 1902, mainly of Indian languages, including some that are now extinct. [10349

U.S. Geological Survey. Geology, water resources, and usable ground-water storage capacity of Solano County, California [1904-51]. By H[orace] G[ordon] Thomasson, Jr., F. H. Olmsted, and E. F. Le Roux. Wash.: U.S. Govt. Print. Off., 1960. x, 692 p. diagrs. (part in portfolio, part fold.), maps (part in portfolio, part col., part fold.), tables, views. bibliog. (p. 376-9), notes. (Its Water-supply paper 1464.) [10350

JEAN PUFFER & W. MAX CHAPMAN. Local public health laboratory service in California [1905-59]. Am. jour. pub. health, 49: 22-7 (Jan 1959). notes. [10351

ROLLAND BURRAGE DIXON (1875-1934) & ALFRED LOUIS KROEBER. Numeral systems of the languages of California. Selected papers from the American anthropologist, 1888-1920, ed. Frederica De Laguna (Evanston, Ill.: Row, Peterson [1960]), p. 423-32. maps. First printed in Dec. 1907. On methods of counting among the Indians of California. [10352

JAMES WILLIAM HAMILTON. Surf, sand, tide, and title. Los Angeles Bar bul., 35:389-95, 408-11 (Oct). port. On "the effect in title, as between the State and a private upland owner, of accretion and erosion to the beach," resulting from currents along the California coastline, 1907-60. [10353

CALIFORNIA CROP AND LIVESTOCK REPORTING SERVICE. California prices received by farmers for farm commodities, monthly and season average prices, 1908-1960. [Prepared by Harley M. Brewer, Statistician.] Sacramento [1960. 4], 55 p. tables. notes. [10354

EPHRAIM B. MARGOLIN. Duties and rights of California unions [1908-58]. Hastings law jour., 11:23-53 (Aug 1959). notes. [10355

EDWARD H. GOFF. Lost bullion of Cerro Gordo. Pony Express, 25(11): 3-6 (Apr 1959). Memories of Owens Lake and the towns of Olancha and Keeler, 1909 and anecdotes of Webb Walker of Olancha. [10356

GORDON B. GREB. The golden anniversary of broadcasting [1909-59]. Jour. broadcasting, 3:3-13 (winter 1959). notes. On Herrold's Station of the Garden City Bank Building, San Jose, Calif., founded by Charles David Herrold, later designated as KQW, finally as KCBS, "World's First Regular Broadcasting Station." [10357

NINA (PAUL) SHUMWAY. Your desert and mine. ... With an introduction by Harold O. Weight. Los Angeles: Westernlore Press, 1960. xv, [3], 322, [1] p. ports., views. On the author's removal in 1909 from Oregon to the Coachella Valley, with her father, William L. Paul, and other members of the family, her marriage to Steve Shumway, eventually manager of the Paul properties, her writings to encourage the sale and consumption of dates, the decreasing profits of the family date industry, the sale of the ranch by the family in 1947, and its conversion to a real-estate development, "Palm Desert." [10358

THOR BRANDT-ERICHSEN. From the Danish Quarter of Solvang. Solvang, Calif.: Santa Ynez Valley News [1960]. 64, [1] p. flag., ports., views. On the Danes in a community in Santa Barbara County, 1911-60. [10359

EDWARD WINSLOW GIFFORD. Central Miwok ceremonies. [Berkeley: Univ. of California Press, 1955. 4], 261-318 p. views. bibliog. (p. 318). (Anthropological records, v. 14, no. 4.) Data concerning religious dances, collected from informants in Stanislaus, Tuolumne, and Calaveras Counties, particularly from Molestu or Tom Williams, chief of a village near Jamestown, then an octogenarian. [10360

EUGENE C. LEE. The politics of nonpartisanship: a study of California city elections [1911-60]. Berkeley: Univ. of California Press, 1960. xiii, 232 p. map, tables. bibliog. (p. 205-24), notes. [10361

RICHARD WILLARD ARMOUR (born 1906). Drug store days: my youth among the pills & potions. N.Y.: McGraw-Hill [1959. 6], 184, [2] p. views. Facetious recollections of Pomona, Calif., the life of the Armour family there, and "the family drug store" (Armour's Drug Store), 1912 to ca. 1924. [10362

NORRIS C. HUNDLEY, JR. Katherine Philips Edson [1870-1933] and the fight for the California minimum wage, 1912-1923. Pac. hist. rev., 29:271-85 (Aug). notes. On her successful campaign "for the protection of women and children in the state" and for the elimination of "sweatshop conditions." [10363

CORINNE LATHROP GILB. Justice Jesse W[ashington] Carter [1888-1959], an American individualist. Pac. hist. rev., 29:145-57 (May). notes. On his legal practice in northern California and his service as a district attorney in Shasta County, State senator, and Justice of the California Supreme Court, 1913-59. [10364

FRED GUNSKY. Trouble on the Tuolumne. Natl. parks mag., 35(155): 8-10 (Aug). map, views. On the Hetch Hetchy Dam, on the Tuolumne River, built by authority of Congress to supply water and electric power to San Francisco, 1913-60, and the present demand of San Francisco for further concessions to destroy scenic values in order to increase the yield of power. [10365

DANIEL S. CARLTON & LEON GREEN. In memoriam--Jesse W. Carter [1888-1959]. Hastings law jour., 10: 353-69 (May 1959). port. On his work in California as a lawyer and a judge, 1914-59. [10366

LARY BURTON. No prison riots here. Am. forests, 62(9):28-9, 44-7 (Sep 1956). double view. On prison honor camps in California as an "answer to inmate idleness" and "a remarkably successful" means of "rehabilitating prisoners," 1915-56. [10367

STEPHEN B. REICHERT, JR. The end of the four-year junior college in California [1915-59]. Jr. college jour., 29:307-12, 439-43 (Feb, Apr 1959). notes. Based on thesis (Ed. D.)--Univ. of California at Los Angeles. On the "college" in the 6-4-4 plan. [10368

WILLIAM E. BUCKNER. Eminent domain powers exercisable over California property by oil and gas corporations [for pipelines and underground storage, 1917-58]. U.C.L.A. law rev., 7:327-44 (Mar). notes. [10369

WELDON FAIRBANKS HEALD. Wanderer of the wild palms. Pac. discovery, 13(6):14-16 (Nov-Dec). port., views. On Randall Henderson's studies of fan palms (Washingtonia filifera) in California and his searches for them in the austere and rugged canyons of the great California Desert," 1920-60. [10370

ELIZABETH HARDWICK. The life and death of Caryl [Whittier] Chessman [1921-60]. Partisan re 27:503-13 (summer). Commentary on his life and writings. [10371

WILLIAM OLIVER BRIGHT. Karok names. Names, 6:172-9 (Sep 1958). notes. On "naming patterns" of a tribe of Indians along the Klamath River in northwestern California as recorded since 1925. [10372

J. R. TAVERNETTI & B. B. EWING. Cotton mechanization studies in California [1928-50]. Agric. engineering, 32:489-92 (Sep 1951). diagrs., table, views. notes. [10373

JOHN JOHNSON. The wreck of the Harvard. Steamboat bill, 17:107-9 (winter). view. Undated report, by the salvage expert of Merritt, Chapman, & Scott, on the stranding of this steamer on Point Arguello, 53 miles south of Santa Barbara, and the limited success of efforts to salvage fittings and cargo, May-Jun. 1931. [10374

HARRY BRUCE WALKER. A resume of sixteen years of research in sugarbeet mechanization [at the California Agricultural Experiment Station, 1931-47]. Agric. engineering, 29: 425-30 (Oct 1948). views. notes. [10375

FRANK WILBUR YOUNG. Adaptation and pattern integration of a California sect. Rev. religious research, 1:137-50 (winter). On "Pentecostal-type" churches in "North Segura," Calif., with a study of the "Highland Church" in this area and the beliefs and practices of its members, 1932 to 1954 or later. [10376

BEN H. READ. How legislation affects dentistry. Am. jour. orthodontics, 46:433-9 (Jun). On the Public Health League of California, 1933-60. [10377

J. D. SINCLAIR. Watershed management research in southern California's brush covered mountains. Jour. forestry, 58:266-8 (Apr). views. On the San Dimas Experimental Forest of the U.S. Forest Service in the San Gabriel Mountains about 30 miles northeast of Los Angeles, 1933-59. [10378

WILSON RECORD. Racial diversity in California public schools [1940-58]. Jour. Negro educ., 28:15-25 (winter 1959). [10379

JUSTIN J. STEIN. The number and distribution of physicians in California [1940-58]. Calif. med., 92:189-93 (Mar). tables. notes. [10380

U.S. Geological Survey. Water resources of southern California with special reference to the drought of 1944-51. By Harold C[oble] Troxell. Wash.: U.S. Govt. Print. Off., 1957. vi, 139 p. diagrs., maps, tables. (Its Water-supply paper 1366.) [10381

GEORGE WADA & JAMES C. DAVIES. Riots and rioters. West pol. quar., 11:864-74 (Dec 1957). tables. notes. On a riot in "Manzanar," a California relocation center for persons of Japanese birth or ancestry, in Dec. 1942, as recalled by participants or eyewitnesses interviewed in 1954-55; with particular notice of psychological and other differences between the rioters and the non-rioters. [10382

F. LELAND ELAM. C. S. H. A., a "doing" organization. West. horseman, 25(8):40-42 (Aug). ports., views. On the California State Horsemen's Association, 1945-60. [10383

PERSIS RUTH EMMETT. The development and location of shopping centers; and common location characteristics in selected areas in California [since World War II]. Ann Arbor: University Microfilms, 1960. Positive microfilm of typescript. [337] leaves. Thesis--Stanford Univ. Abstracted: Dissert. abstracts, 21:86-7 (Jul). [10384

FRANK R. MARTINEZ. The California Junior College Student Government Association [1945-59]. Jr. college jour., 30:29-34 (Sep 1959). [10385

DWIGHT MONTGOMERY BISSELL & ROBERT S. McINNES. Accident control: a local health department's experience in development and evaluation of a home accident program [San Jose, Calif., 1946-57]. Am. jour. pub. health, 49:1646-52 (Dec 1959). diagr., tables. [10386

DANIEL BLAIN. A program for mental hygiene in California [1946-60]. Calif. med., 93:263-8 (Nov). notes. [10387

CALIFORNIA. AGRICULTURAL EXPERIMENT STATION, Berkeley. Timber marketing and land ownership in the Central Sierra Nevada region [1946-58. By] Dennis Teeguarden, Paul Casamajor, [and] John Zivnuska. [Berkeley:] Division of Agricultural Sciences, Univ. of California [1960]. 71, [1] p. diagrs., map, tables, views. bibliog. (p. 72), notes. (Its Bulletin 774.) [10388

GEORGE S. ROSS. An eagle with one wing. Flying, 67(6):52-3, 87-90 (Dec). views. On the work of Michael Ross Jose as a flyer of crop-dusting airplanes in California since the loss of an arm in 1946. [10389

RON TAYLOR. Night dusting. Flying, 64(6):37, 102-4 (Jun 1959). port., view. On insecticidal dusting of crop lands from the air in the San Joaquin Valley by George Willet, 1946-59. [10390

VIVIAN KIRK. Quarter tracks in California [1947-55]. Quarter horse jour., 7(7):18-19 (Apr 1955). views (1 double). [10391

The CARYL Chessman case: a legal analysis [California, 1948-60]. Minn. law rev., 44:941-97 (Apr). notes. [10392

RALPH N. KLEPS. Certiorarified mandamus reviewed: the courts and California administrative decisions--1949-1959. Stanford law rev., 12: 554-84 (May). notes. Continues a review for the years 1939-49, by the same author, in Stanford law review, 1950. On "the use of the writ of mandamus to review quasi-judicial administrative action" as "a California invention which has now reached maturity." [10393

San Diego

JAMES ROBERT MILLS. San Diego--where California began [San Diego:] San Diego Historical Soc., c1960. 37 p. table, views. Printed also, with same title, as vol. 6, no. 1, of the San Diego Historical Society quarterly (Jan. 1960). 37, [1] p. "A brief history of the events of four centuries," 1542-1960. Appended: "San Diego area histories" (list). [10394

RICHARD F. POURADE. The history of San Diego. Volume one of a planned series on the historic birthplace of California. The explorers [1542-1774. San Diego:] Union-Tribune Pub. Co. [1960]. xx, 203, [1] p. facsims., maps (part col.), ports. (1 col.), views (part col.). bibliog. (p. 189-95). [10395

ANTOINETTE LE MARQUIS. San Diego medical practice: a historical sketch [1769-1890]. Am. Med. Women's Assoc., Jour., 14:513-15 (Jun 1959). notes. [10396

ROBERT W. BRACKETT. This history of San Diego County ranchos: the Spanish, Mexican, and American occupation of San Diego County and the story of the ownership of land grants therein [1823-1960. Fifth edition.] San Diego, Calif.: Union Title Insurance Co. [1960. 6], 70 p. col. double maps. bibliog. (p. 65). 1st ed. 1939. Information from the records of the Union Title Insurance Company regarding 20 tracts of land granted between 1823 and 1846. [10397

JUNE A. STRUDWICK. The Whaley house. [San Diego] 1960. [39]-76 p. facsims., port., views. (San Diego Historical Society quarterly, v. 6, no. 2, Apr. 1960.) On Thomas Whaley (1823-90), "pioneer merchant and civic leader," emigrant to California in 1849, settler in San Francisco and in 1851 in San Diego, builder in 1855-57 of "the oldest brick structure in southern California"; with an account of the brief use of the building as a courthouse, its long deterioration, and its recent restoration. [10398

IRENE (LADD) PHILLIPS. Development of the mission olive industry, and other South Bay stories. [National City, Calif.: South Bay Press, 1960.] 100 p. tables, views (1 double). (Her Story of El Rancho de la Nacion, 4.) Mainly on Frank Kimball (born 1832), who settled in San Diego County in 1869, developed olive culture there, and organized the Otay Watch Company, Otay, Calif. [10399

ROLLIN PEIRCE. "Little red schoolhouse" days in Ramona [1880s-1930s]. San Diego Hist. Soc. quar., 6:85-7 (Jul). views. [10400

HAROLD PETER SIMONSON. Francis Grierson in San Diego: an episode in charlatanry. Am. quar., 12:198-204 (summer). notes. On the activities of Benjamin Henry Jesse Francis Shepard, alias Francis Grierson, in San Diego, 1887-89, as a "piano improvisator," a holder of Spiritualist seances, builder of the Villa Montezuma, and defrauder of his creditors. [10401

DICK BARTHELMESS. The clubhouse on Steamship Wharf. San Diego Hist. Soc. quar., 6:94-7 (Oct). view. On the San Diego Rowing Club, otherwise known as the Excelsior Rowing and Swimming Club, 1888-1919. [10402

CHARLES ROSENBERG. Horology and real estate. Natl. Assoc. Watch and Clock Collectors, Bul., 9:406-7 (Oct). On the Otay Watch Company, National City, Calif., 1889-90. [10403

WINIFRED DAVIDSON. Old town talk (historical gossip of and in pioneer San Diego). San Diego Hist. Soc. quar., 4:1-4; 5:57-60 (Jan 1958, Oct 1959). On the author's visits to Mrs. Lucy Brown Wentworth and her housemate, Miss Lily Whaley, their efforts to instruct the author in the pronunciation of Spanish and the niceties of costume and etiquette, and their memories of earlier times in San Diego. [10404

NORMA ENGEL. Ballast Point Lighthouse [San Diego Bay, 1890-1960]. San Diego Hist. Soc. quar., 6:91-3 (Oct). view. Includes the author's memories of her father's life there, 1914-31. [10405

HELEN WALLACE. The Zlac Rowing Club. San Diego Hist. Soc. quar., 6:97-100 (Oct). view. On a women's rowing club founded in 1891, still active. [10406

LAURENCE MONROE KLAUBER. A store at Campo in 1899. San Diego Hist. Soc. quar., 6:77-80 (Jul). view. Memories of a small store owned by Klauber Wangenheim Company and of its stock of goods, retail methods, and customers. [10407

JERRY MacMULLEN. Inchcliffe Castle, Melbourne for Los Angeles. Am. Neptune, 20:270-71 (Oct). On the discovery by the waterfront reporter for the San Diego union that nautical information was being copied from his paper by the San Diego sun, and his proof of the theft by inserting news of nonexistent vessels in the Union, faithfully copied by the Sun. [10408

MANUEL MADRUGA. Fourth of July on the Bay. San Diego Hist. Soc. quar., 6:87-9 (Jul). view. On "fishermen's races" at San Diego (ca. 1900?). [10409

BILL VIRDEN. Farewell to Colonel Cody. San Diego Hist. Soc. quar., 6:81-4 (Jul). facsim., view. On the exhibition of Buffalo Bill's Wild West and Rough Riders of the World, San Diego, 25 Sep. 1902; with a reproduction of a newspaper advertisement of its program. [10410

BILL VIRDEN. Minor maritime disaster. San Diego Hist. Soc. quar., 6:101-2 (Oct). view. On the grounding of the wooden steamer Noyo, with a cargo of railroad ties, in San Diego Bay, 1915. [10411

MARGARET SIEMS & ELIZABETH CONFORTH. "Firsts" at the San Diego Zoo Hospital [1928-59]. Am. Med. Women's Assoc., Jour., 14:519-20 (Jun 1959). [10412

Los Angeles

ADAN EDUARDO TREGANZA & AGNES BIERMAN. The Topanga Culture: final report on excavations, 1948. [Berkeley: Univ. of California Press, 1958.] iv, 45-86 p. diagrs., maps, tables, views. bibliog. (p. 76). (Anthropological records, v. 20, no. 2.) On the culture indicated by archeological remains in Topanga Canyon, Los Angeles County, with an estimated duration from 8000/4000 to 5000/2500 B.C. [10413

JOHN ALBERT WILSON. Reproduction of Thompson and West's History of Los Angeles County, California, with illustrations. With introduction by W. W. Robinson. Berkeley, Calif.: Howell-North, 1959. [4] p., reprint (192 p.). col. map, tables, views (1 double). bibliog. (p. 12). 28x36 cm. Text in 4 columns. 1st ed. (Oakland: Thompson & West, 1880) has title: History of Los Angeles County, California. With illustrations descriptive of its scenery, residences, fine blocks and manufactories, from original sketches by artists of the highest ability. Topical and chronological history of the area of present Los Angeles and Orange Counties, 1769-1880, including a chapter on each of 16 townships, a chapter on Santa Catalina and San Clemente Islands, and "Biographical sketches of prominent citizens of Los Angeles County" (p. 175-84); with "88 pages devoted to lithographic plates of homes, ranches, business buildings, churches, and schools" (artists unnamed). [10414

REMI A. NADEAU. Los Angeles: from mission to modern city. N.Y.: Longmans, Green, 1960. xvi, [2], 302 p. ports., views. bibliog. (p. viii-xi). "... the story of how an American community, dedicated to growth for its own sake, became a victim of its own success," 1771-1960. [10415

RICHARD BIGGER. Flood control in metropolitan Los Angeles. Berkeley: Univ. of California Press, 1959. [8], 194 p. fold. diagr., fold. col. map, tables. bibliog. (p. 183-90), notes (p. 161-79). (University of California publications in political science, 6.) On the 21 floods in Los Angeles between 1811 and 1954 and the public agencies established since 1914 to control floods, particularly the Los Angeles County Flood Control District. [10416

E. S. TAYLOR. Restoring the house of the "Scotch paisano." Pac. discovery, 13(1):22-5 (Mar-Apr). facsim., views. On the restoration of an adobe building constructed in 1840 by Hugh Reid (Don Perfecto), emigrant from Scotland, on his wheat and cattle ranch, in what is now part of the Los Angeles State and County Arboretum, Arcadia. [10417

WILLIAM WESLEY SNIDER. A historical study of school district organization in Los Angeles County [since the 1850s?]. Ann Arbor: University Microfilms, 1959 [i.e. 1960]. Positive microfilm of typescript.

[295] leaves. Thesis (Ed. D.)--Univ. of Southern California. Abstracted: Dissert. abstracts, 20:4575-6 (Jun). [10418

JACKSON ALPHEUS GRAVES (1852-1933). Reminiscences of the early bar of Los Angeles [1876-1904]. Los Angeles Bar bul., 34:131-3, 150-60, 171-6, 190-92, 241-5 (Mar, Apr, Jun 1959). Address delivered before the Los Angeles Bar Association, 1909. [10419

KENNETH HOWARD SHANKS. An historical and critical study of the preaching career of Aimee Semple McPherson [1890-1944]. Ann Arbor: University Microfilms, 1960. Positive microfilm of typescript. [193] leaves. Thesis--Univ. of Southern California. Abstracted: Dissert. abstracts, 21: 1666-7 (Dec). [10420

WILLIAM WEBB CLARY. Louis W. Myers, 1872-1960. Los Angeles Bar bul., 35:191-3 (Apr). On his work as a lawyer and judge in Los Angeles, ca. 1895 to 1960. [10421

JERRY GIESLER [real name: Harold Lee Giesler, born 1886]. The Jerry Giesler story. By Jerry Giesler as told to Pete Martin [i. e. Thornton Martin]. N.Y.: Simon and Schuster, 1960. vii, [3], 341, [1] p. ports. On the author's life in Los Angeles since 1907 as a lawyer, mainly "a defense lawyer," counsel for Errol Flynn, Charlie Chaplin, Norman Selby, Benjamin Siegel, and other eminent individuals; with some account of his early years in Iowa and his inspiration by the example of Clarence Darrow. [10422

CLAY LANCASTER. Some sources of Greene and Greene. A. I. A. jour., 34(2):39-46 (Aug). plans, views. Examination of 2 houses designed by Charles Sumner Greene and Henry Mather Greene in Pasadena, 1907 and 1909, indicating that they "derived suggestions for architectural styling from the Japanese, and forms and plans from traditional and contemporary buildings in the United States." [10423

FREDERICK E. CASE. Los Angeles real estate: a study of investment experience [1911-54]. Los Angeles: Real Estate Research Program, Division of Research, Graduate School of Business Administration, Univ. of California [1960]. xi, 103 p. diagrs., map, tables (1 double). bibliog. (p. 103), notes. [10424

EDWARD F. STANIFORD. Business decentralization in metropolitan Los Angeles. [Los Angeles:] Bureau of Governmental Research [Univ. of California], 1960. iv leaves, 57 p. On the development of branch stores, banks, and offices and of suburban commercial centers in Los Angeles, Orange, Ventura, and San Bernardino Counties, 1912-60. [10425

ADELA ROGERS ST. JOHNS. First step up toward heaven: Hubert Eaton and Forest Lawn. Englewood Cliffs, N.J.: Prentice-Hall [1959]. xxi, 293, [3] p. ports., views. On Forest Lawn Memorial-Park, Glendale, Calif., founded in 1917 by Hubert Lewright Eaton, who "revolutionized cemetery development" by the use of architecture, sculpture, painting, and stained glass; with some account of his early life in Liberty, Mo., his studies at William Jewell College, and his work in Montana, Colorado, and Nevada as a mining chemist and mining engineer. [10426

JAMES CLIFFORD FINDLEY. The economic boom of the 'twenties in Los Angeles. Ann Arbor: University Microfilms, 1958 [i. e. 1960]. Positive microfilm of typescript. [462] leaves. Thesis--Claremont Graduate School. Abstracted: Dissert. abstracts, 20:2772 (Jan). [10427

LOU JACOBS, JR. The architectural photographer. Infinity, 9(7):12, 14 (Sep). views. On the work of Julius Shulman of Los Angeles as an architectural photographer, 1936-60. [10428

HAROLD J. JACOBS. Marineland diver. By Jake Jacobs, chief diver, Marineland of the Pacific, as told to Sylvia Jacobs. N.Y.: Dodd, Mead, 1960. xii, 178 p. ports., views. On the author's work as a professional deep-sea diver in California since ca. 1941, more recently at Marineland of the Pacific, Palos Verdes Estates, Los Angeles County. [10429

LOIS C. PHILMUS. Business flying co-operative. Flying, 66(1):26-7, 58, 60 (Jan). port., views (1 double). On Sky Roamers Air Travel, Inc., Lockheed Air Terminal, Los Angeles, a cooperative organization established by southern California businessmen for the transportation of the members, 1946-59. [10430

SAMUEL G. ARMISTEAD & JOSEPH H. SILVERMAN. Hispanic balladry among the Sephardic Jews of the West Coast. West. folklore, 19:229-44 (Oct).

Report of work in progress among some 4,000 Sephardic Jews in Los Angeles; with several texts, and remarks on the Judeo-Spanish dialect. [10431

San Francisco

JAMES THOMAS DAVIS. The archaeology of the Fernandez site, a San Francisco Bay region shellmound. Univ. Calif. Archaeol. Survey, Rep., 49:11-52. diagr., map, fold. table, views. bibliog. (Papers on California archaeology, 75.) On excavations and collections at this site, 1935-59, and its virtual destruction in 1958; with an analysis of artifacts and human remains found there, indicating human occupancy from ca. 3000 B.C. to A.D. 1850. [10432

HAROLD THOMPSON GILLIAM. The face of San Francisco. Garden City, N.Y.: Doubleday, 1960. 256 p. maps, views (part double). Heavily illustrated account of the streets and hills of San Francisco, its buildings, its institutions, and the plans for its future. [10433

WILLIAM D. HOHENTHAL & SHEILAGH THOMPSON BROOKS. An archaeological scaphocephal from California. Am. jour. phys. anthropol., 18:59-64 (Mar). tables, views. notes. On an excessively narrow and (anteroposteriorly) long skull, showing no indication of artificial deformation, probably more than 1,200 years old, found in a mound at the Newark site near Alvarado on the southeast shore of San Francisco Bay. [10434

WILLIAM JAMES WALLACE & DONALD W. LATHRAP. Ceremonial bird burials in San Francisco Bay shellmounds. Am. antiq., 25:262-4 (Oct 1959). Evidence of "the persistence of the practice of ceremonially burying large raptorial birds from at least 2000 B.C. into recent times." [10435

LUCIUS MORRIS BEEBE & CHARLES M. CLEGG. San Francisco's golden era: a picture story of San Francisco before the fire [1579-1906]. Berkeley, Calif.: Howell-North, 1960. 255 p. cartoons, facsims., ports. (1 double), views (part col., part double). Mainly reproductions of prints and photographs. [10436

ALFRED MARTINEZ. Heavenly place in the Bay. Am. forests, 66(2):26-8, 65 (Feb). views (1 double). On Angel Island, in San Francisco Bay, discovered in 1775, used and abandoned by the U.S. Army, declared surplus by the U.S. Government in 1947, now the site of a State park. [10437

ALAN K. BROWN. Salt for the scraping: origin of the San Francisco Bay salt industry [1795-1871]. Calif. Hist. Soc. quar., 39:117-20 (Jun). notes. [10438

RICHARD H. DILLON. Embarcadero. N.Y.: Coward-McCann [1959. 2], 313 p. ports., views. On the central waterfront of San Francisco and "some of the history-making maritime adventure which emanated from it" throughout the Pacific, 1846-1913. Includes chapters on Bernard Gilboy, William Henry Hayes, the USS Saginaw and William Halford, Robert H. Waterman, Benjamin Boyd, Asbury Harpending, Edgar Wakeman, Sam Brennan, "Clipper skippers," Japanese castaways, "Wells Fargo's gold boat" (the Antelope), shipwrecks, and "Shanghai days in San Francisco". [10439

SAN FRANCISCO CHRONICLE. Hills of San Francisco. Foreword by Herb[ert Eugene] Caen. [San Francisco, 1959. 4], 87 p. cartoons, maps, ports., view. (A San Francisco classic chronicle.) Compiled from a series of newspaper articles describing 42 hills or groups of hills as occupied since 1848. [10440

ROBERT EDWARD LEE KNIGHT. Industrial relations in the San Francisco Bay area, 1900-1918. Berkeley: Univ. of California Press, 1960. x, [2], 463 p. map. bibliog. (p. 437-45), notes (p. 395-436). (Publications of the Institute of Industrial Relations, University of California.) Includes an introductory chapter on labor-management relations in the area from 1849 to 1900. [10441

DAVID DE CAMP. The pronunciation of English in San Francisco. Orbis, 7 (1958): 372-91; 8 (1959): 54-77. notes. map, tables. notes. Based on thesis--Univ. of California. Data from a linguistic survey made in 1952; with a historical explanation, 1850-1940. [10442

JOHN MARSHALL WOODBRIDGE & SALLY BYRNE WOODBRIDGE. Buildings of the Bay Area: a guide to the architecture of the San Francisco Bay region [1860-1960]. N.Y.: Grove Press [1960. 160] p. maps, views. [10443

HAROLD KIRKER. The Lick House, San Francisco, 1861-1862. Soc. Architectural Historians, Jour., 19:77-9

(Jun). view. notes. On "the grandest and largest hotel on the Pacific Coast," designed for James Lick by Henry Kenitzer and David Farquharson, destroyed by fire in 1906. [10444

LAWRANCE ROGER THOMPSON. The California boyhood of Robert Frost [in San Francisco, 1876-85]. University, 2:16-20 (fall 1959). port. [10445

ELEANOR (MEANS) HULL. Suddenly the sun: a biography of Shizuko Takahashi. N.Y.: Friendship Press [1957]. ix, [3], 130 p. On Shizu (Higuchi) Takahashi (1876?-1945/46), native of Japan, her studies in a Quaker school in Tokyo, her conversion to Christianity, her marriage in 1901 to Chiyokichi Takahashi, tailor, their life in Oakland and Berkeley, their 12 children, their internment during World War II, her embodiment of Christian principles, and her hospitality to ministers and missionaries. Fictional in form. [10446

ROBERT LUTHER DUFFUS. The tower of jewels: memories of San Francisco. N.Y.: W. W. Norton [1960]. 250 p. facsims., ports., views. On the author's work as a reporter for the San Francisco bulletin, 1911-18, and his memories of its editor, Fremont Older (1856-1935). [10447

HARRY H. L. KITANO. Housing of Japanese-Americans in the San Francisco Bay area [1920-56]. Nathan Glazer & Davis McEntire, eds., Studies in housing & minority groups ... special research report to the Commission on Race and Housing (Berkeley: Univ. of California Press, 1960), p. 178-97. map, tables. notes. [10448

HERBERT EUGENE CAEN. Only in San Francisco. By Herb Caen. Garden City, N.Y.: Doubleday, 1960. 286 p. Observations made by the author "in twenty-two years of writing a column about the city," with an assignment "to write about San Francisco and San Franciscans. [10449

NEVADA

MYRON ANGEL (1827-1911), ed. Reproduction of Thompson and West's History of Nevada, 1881. With illustrations and biographical sketches of its prominent men and pioneers. With introduction by David F. Myrick. Berkeley, Calif.: Howell-North, 1958. [3], D-J, xiv, 680 p. diagrs., facsims., map, ports., tables, views (1 double). Account of the area from prehistoric times to 1880 and of each of its counties, with numerous lithographs by unnamed artists. Includes contributions by William Wright ("Dan De Quille," on early journalism in Virginia City), Henry G. Shaw, D. R. Sessions, and C. N. Harris. [10450

LUCIUS MORRIS BEEBE. Nevada [its traditions and characteristics]. Holiday, American panorama west of the Mississippi: a Holiday magazine book (Garden City, N.Y.: Doubleday [1960]), p. 153-66. [10451

HELEN SWISHER CARLSON. Nevada place names: origin and meaning. Ann Arbor: University Microfilms, 1959 [i. e. 1960]. Positive microfilm of typescript. [437] leaves. Thesis--Univ. of New Mexico. Abstracted: Dissert. abstracts, 20:2791 (Jan). Survey of "some 3,000 names, representing perhaps a tenth of the name body of Nevada," entered in alphabetical order. [10452

T. G. GRIEDER, JR. Beowawe: a Nevada place name. West. folklore, 19:53-4 (Jan). notes. Definitive evidence that the name of a place in Eureka County, Nev., is a Paiute phrase, Beo-wa-we, meaning "great posterior," probably suggested by the exuberant development of the gluteal area of a particular Caucasian. [10453

GORDON L. GROSSCUP. The culture history of Lovelock Cave, Nevada [first occupied by man ca. 2000 B.C. Berkeley, 1960. 4], ii, 72 p. diagrs., maps, views. bibliog. (p. 67-71). (University of California. California Archaeological Survey, Reports, 52.) [10454

ROBERT FLEMING HEIZER & MARTIN A. BAUMHOFF. Great Basin petroglyphs and prehistoric game trails [in northern and central Nevada]. Science, 129:904-5 (3 Apr 1959). [10455

GLORIA GRIFFEN CLINE. Peter Skene Ogden's Nevada explorations [1825, 1826, 1828, 1829]. Back number, 3(3):3-11 (Jul-Sep). notes. Based on thesis--Univ. of California. [10456

NAVADA. Secretary of State. Political history of Nevada [1851-1960]. (Fourth edition.) Carson City: State Print. Off., 1960. 123 p. flag, maps, ports., seal, tables. "Compiled in the office of the Nevada Legislative Counsel

Bureau." Inside back cover: "The lure of the sagebrush," verses by Sam P. Davis. [10457

Sir RICHARD BURTON (1821-90). City of the Saints. Back number, 3(2):5-35 (Apr-Jun). port., views. Excerpt from the author's book of the same title (1860), describing his travels from Willow Springs, Utah, to Genoa, Nev., 13 miles south of Carson City, 1-19 Oct. 1860; with modern photographs of the ruins of several "stations." [10458

VINCENT PAUL GIANELLA. Site of Williams Station, Nevada. Back number, 3(4):5-12 (Oct-Dec). maps, views. notes. On "a station, or trading post," kept by "two men known as the Williams boys" and later by Honey Lake Smith, on the Carson River (northeast of the present village of Silver Springs), 1860 ff., evidently abandoned by 1868. [10459

SAMUEL LANGHORNE CLEMENS (1835-1910). Mark Twain's source for "The latest sensation" hoax? [Edited by] William C. Miller. Am. lit., 32: 75-8 (Mar). notes. Report in the Virginia City, Nev., Territorial enterprise (here reprinted from the Sacramento Daily union), 22 Jul. 1863, of a man named Cornell, who severely wounded 8 men in Austin, Nev., with an ax and was found later "with his throat cut from ear to ear." [10460

Sir CHARLES WENTWORTH DILKE (1843-1911). Sir Charles Wentworth Dilke, a Republican baronet in Nevada. Contributed by Wilbur S. Shepperson. Back number, 3(4):13-29 (Oct-Dec). view. Excerpt from his Greater Britain: a record of travel in English-speaking countries (1868), narrating his stagecoach journey from the Great Salt Lake to Austin, Virginia City, Carson City, and Lake Tahoe, 1866. [10461

JOHN MILLIAN. Life and confession of John Millian. Reno: Nevada Historical Soc., 1960. [4] p., facsim. ([2], 16 p.), [4] p. ("The back number ...": the quarterly of the Nevada Historical Society, v. 3, no. 1, Jan.-Mar. 1960.) Original title page: Life and confession of John Millian, (properly, Jean Marie A. Villain,) convicted as the murderer of Julia Bulette, as given by him to his attorney. Virginia: Lammon, Gregory & Palmer. 1868. Account by the publishers of the murder and robbery, 20 Jan. 1867, of "a woman of the town," aged 35, native of London, "an honorary member of Virginia Engine Company No. 1"; and narrative by Attorney Charles E. De Long, dated Virginia, 23 Apr. 1868, containing Millian's declaration that the murder was committed by "two men, one named Douglass and one named Dillon". [10462

DON ASHBAUGH. Bonanza buffoonery. True West, 7(5):22-4, 41-4 (May-Jun). facsim., views. Anecdotes of W. J. Forbes (died 1873) as an editor of newspapers in Nevada mining towns. [10463

ELSA BARKER. Grandmother wore velvet. N.M., 38(2):12-15 (Feb). views. On old dresses, mainly wedding gowns of the 1880s and 1890s, sought out by the Pilot Club of Las Vegas, N.M., with information about them from descendants of their wearers. [10464

FRANK P. TONDEL. As I remember Goldfield. Back number, 3(3):13-19 (Jul-Sep). On "the greatest gold camp on earth," which "sprang up" in 1902 and "was on the downgrade" by 1908, as observed by the author while working in the bank there, 1906-8. [10465

JOHN D. WILLIAMS. Goldfield--and the Wyatt Earp I knew. By Jack Williams as told to Lea Franklin McCarty. Frontier times, 34(1):16-17, 51 (winter). ports., views. Recollections of Goldfield, Nev., when Tex Rickard and Wyatt Earp lived there, 1906. [10466

JOHN HOFFMAN. Hassayamper Hayes--burro man. Frontier times, 34(1):24-5, 44-6 (winter). port., views. Recollections of Victor, Nev., 1907, and of a prospector in that area who exemplified the now extinct type called "burro men." [10467

ROBERT HARRY LOWIE (1883-1957). Economic factors and culture. Lowie's selected papers in anthropology, ed. Cora Du Bois (Berkeley: Univ. of California Press, 1960), p. 240-46. notes. Manuscript (1939 or 1940?). Includes an account of economic aspects of celebrations by Shoshonean Indians in Nevada. [10468

ANDY NORRID. The busy blacksmith. West. horseman, 25(5):8-9 (May). ports., views. On the mobile blacksmith shop of Erni Cassinelli of Reno, Nev., 1946-60. [10469

JACK STODELLE. A case of suicide. Trains, 20(4):26-8 (Feb). views. On the last run of Locomotive 26 (built 1907) of the Virginia & Truckee Railroad, Reno to Minden and back to Reno, 1 May 1950, and her destruction in the burning of the roundhouse at Reno on the evening of the same day. [10470

OREGON

H. L. DAVIS. Oregon [its traditions and characteristics]. Holiday, American panorama west of the Mississippi: a Holiday magazine book (Garden City, N.Y.: Doubleday [1960]), p. 58-80. [10471

MALCOLM H. CLARK, JR. "Oregon" revisited. Ore. hist. quar., 61:211-19 (Jun). Review of previous efforts to find the origin of the name, of which the first known use was by Robert Rogers in 1766. [10472

HARRIOTT D. MUNNICK. "Dupatti" (Jean Baptiste Desportes McKay). Marion Co. hist., 6:26-32. On an individual known also as Dupaty, Duparty, Desportes, Deshortz, McKoy, McRoy, McAy, etc. (1793?-1853), half-Indian native of Canada, employee of John Jacob Astor in the Oregon Country "sometime in 1810 or 1811," trapper for the Hudson's Bay Company in Oregon and California, settler at Champoeg in the Williamette Valley, farmer, guide to travelers, friend of Methodist missionaries, Catholic, common-law husband of 3 Indian women. [10473

JOHN CLARK HUNT. Story of a mountain. Am. forests, 66(9):34-9 (Sep). views (1 double). On explorations and settlements in the area of Steens Mountain, southeastern Oregon, 1826 ff., and its eventual ownership and management by the U.S. Bureau of Land Management. [10474

INEZ LONG FORTT. The Oregon legend. Old Oregon, 38(12):3, 27-8 (Apr-May 1959). On immigration to and life in Oregon, 1829-59. [10475

THEODORE STERN. A Umatilla prophet cult: an episode in culture change. International Congress of Anthropological and Ethnological Sciences, 5th, 1956, Men and cultures: selected papers (Phila.: Univ. of Pennsylvania Press [1960]), p. 346-50. notes. On a messianic movement among the Umatilla Indians of Oregon, 1830-1956. [10476

CLIFFORD LLEWELLYN CONSTANCE. Chronology of Oregon schools, 1834-1958. Eugene: Univ of Oregon Books, 1960. ix, 80 p. (University of Oregon monographs. Studies in education, 2.) Brief accounts of all the schools in Oregon. [10477

JERRY ALEXANDER O'CALLAGHAN. The disposition of the public domain in Oregon [1840-1949, mainly before 1910]. Wash.: U.S. Govt. Print. Off., 1960. xii, 113 p. tables. bibliog. (p. 109-13), notes. Revision of thesis--Stanford Univ., 1950. [10478

ALMIRA (DAVID) RAYMOND (born 1813) & WILLIAM W. RAYMOND. Westward to Oregon: diary and letters of Almira David Raymond and W. W. Raymond, Oregon pioneers with Rev. Jason Lee. Introduction, commentary, and family notes by Leon Thomas David. Los Angeles, 1959. [3], 49, [4] leaves. notes. Excerpts from her diary and letters to relatives dated on the ship Lausanne and at Honolulu (1840), at "Wallamette" (1840-45), at or near Astoria (1852, 1853, 1862?), and at Clatsop Plains (1880), on farming, sickness, the Raymond children, Methodist affairs, and the Indians; with an appendix on the David family. [10479

ROY V. OHMART. Fabritus Smith. Marion Co. hist., 6:25-7. port. On Fabritus Reynolds Smith (1819-98), native of Rochester, N.Y., settler in Salem in 1846, farmer and State Representative. [10480

JOHN C. BROUGHER. Scotts Mills, Marion County, Oregon [1847-1959]. Marion Co. hist., 6:32-42. views. notes. [10481

ELLIS LUCIA. Sequoia Johnny and his nuggets. Am. forests, 66(6):34-5, 55-6 (Jun). views (1 double). On the planting of sequoia cones from California by John Porter in the Tualatin Valley, west of Portland, Ore., sometime soon after 1847. [10482

DAUGHTERS OF THE AMERICAN REVOLUTION. Oregon. Tualatin Chapter. Early marriage records, Clackamas County, Wasco County, Oregon [1848-65. Abstracted by Mrs. Emmett Stoddard (Clackamas County) and Mrs. Wayne E. Gurley (Wasco County).] Oswego, Ore., 1960. 65 leaves. Marriages recorded 1853-64 (Clackamas County), 1856-65 (Wasco County). [10483

G. A. PIPES. The story of the beaver coins of Oregon. Selections from The numismatist: United States paper money, tokens, medals, and miscellaneous (Racine, Wis.: Whitman Pub. Co., 1960), p. 41-4. coins. First printed Feb. 1925. On the minting of gold coins in Oregon City, Oregon Territory, 1849. [10484

LEE H. NELSON. A century of Oregon covered bridges. Ore. hist. quar., 61: 101-209 (Jun). plans, ports., views. notes. On "problems that caused the covered bridge to be introduced, developed, and finally snuffed out as a valid solution for spanning the stream-crossed valleys of Oregon," 1851-1924; with views and histories of 43 bridges. [10485

LOIS ATHEL (DEVINE) WILLIS. The family of Silas and Jane Ann (Blair) Brown, Oregon pioneers. Gaston, Ore., c1960. [1], 18, vi leaves. On Silas Brown (1820-96), his wife, Jane Ann (Blair) Hyatt (1813-96), their 6 children, the removal of the family to Oregon in 1851, and its multiplication there; with some account of Benjamin Brown (1797?-1853), probably born in Kentucky, settled in Franklin County, Mo., by 1812, father of Silas. [10486

ADELAIDE TOBIE ORANGE & ARETA JONES HARPER. History of Pioneer School, District 13, a centennial school, 1852-1959. Marion Co. hist., 6:42-6. view. On an elementary school near Gervais, Ore. [10487

FREDERIC A. YERKE, JR. The law of nuisance in Oregon [1864-1959]. Willamette law jour., 1:289-313 (fall). notes. [10488

FLORENCE DONNELLY. Oregon's pioneer paper mill, first in the Northwest. Paper maker, 27(1):12-22 (Feb 1958). facsim., col. map, ports., views. On W. W. Buck and Associates, established by Wentworth William Buck at Oregon City, 1866-67. [10489

FLORENCE DONNELLY. Oregon's second venture in papermaking: the Clackamas Mill. Paper maker, 27(2): 21-8 (Sep 1958). ports., view. On the establishment of a paper mill at Clackamas, Ore., by Wentworth William Buck, his son Heman S. Buck, and Henry L. Pittock, owner of the Daily Oregonian and the Weekly Oregonian, and the operation of the mill by William Lewthwaite, 1867-92. [10490

JOSEPHINE EVANS HARPHAM. Walton House, Eugene. Ore. hist. quar., 61:459-61 (Dec). view. On a house built by J. J. Walton, Jr. (born 1838), in 1867. [10491

SETH THOMAS BAILEY. The Lost Grizzly Mine. By Tom Bailey. True West, 7(4):16-17, 41-4 (Mar-Apr). On a mine found by Louis J. Ormond (Jake Ormond) near the Applegate River in southern Oregon, Nov. 1871, left unclaimed after he died from the effects of being clawed by a bear, and its rediscovery in 1908 by the author and his father, who found gold in it worth only $647. [10492

ROBERT MOULTON GATKE. Building the new courthouse [in Salem], 1872-1873. Marion Co. hist., 6:3-20. notes. [10493

W. L. THOMPSON. A university and its friends. Old Oregon, 37(5):10-11; (6):12-13 (Apr-Jul 1957). ports., views. On financial endowments of the University of Oregon since 1872. [10494

INEZ LONG FORTT. Pioneer pranksters. Old Oregon, 39(1):8-9 (Aug-Sep 1959). cartoon. On practical jokes at the University of Oregon, 1876-1923. [10495

INEZ LONG FORTT. Old-time commencements [at the University of Oregon, 1878-97]. Old Oregon, 38(13):6, 30 (Jun-Jul 1959). facsims., views. [10496

INEZ LONG FORTT. Theirs was the simple life. Old Oregon, 38(11):9-10 (Feb-Mar 1959). On "Rules for the government of the students of the Oregon State University," 11 Nov. 1882. [10497

INEZ LONG FORTT. Football comes to Oregon [late 1880s to ca. 1900]. Old Oregon, 38(9):7-8 (Dec 1958-Jan 1959). cartoons. [10498

BEN MAXWELL. Salem's first streetcar line. Marion Co. hist., 6:20-25. views. On the Salem Street Railway Company (a horsecar line), 1888-97, and the Capital City Railway Company, 1889-1927, and the completion of the "switch-over from streetcars to busses" in 1927. [10499

ROBERT C. WOODWARD. William S. U'Ren [born 1859]: a Progressive Era personality. Idaho yesterdays, 4(2): 4-10 (summer). cartoon, port. notes. On his activities in Oregon as an advocate of the single tax, the initiative and referendum, the direct primary, the short ballot, the direct election of U.S. senators, the abolition of the State senate, minimum-wage legislation, and other changes, 1889-1914. Includes comment by Thomas J. Pressly. [10500

THOMAS B. BRAND. Rylands v. Fletcher [England, 1865] in Oregon. Willamette law rev., 1:344-55 (fall). notes. On Oregon cases of damage to lands by waters, rocks, offensive or noxious gases, or other substances escaping from adjoining or neighboring lands as a result of action by the owners or occupants of those lands, 1893-1958. [10501

MARGARET KIRK. Walter Wilmeth's quarter horses. Quarter horse jour., 3(12):10, 36-7 (Sep 1951). port., view. On his life in Oklahoma since 1894 and his work as a breeder of quarter horses. [10502

MARIE HOLST POTTSMITH. Pioneering years in Hamlet, Oregon, a Finnish community. Ore. hist. quar., 61:4-45 (Mar). views. notes. On a named place that "was not a village, but a valley of homestead farmers" and of fishermen, in Clatsop County, 1896-1957, where the author taught school in 1908. Includes reminiscences by Alma Sarpole Freerksen. [10503

PAUL LINTON PATTERSON [1901-55]--statesman and benefactor. Old Oregon, 36(24):6-7, 28 (Jan-Feb 1956). ports. On his studies at the University of Oregon and its School of Law, and his activities in Oregon politics. [10504

THOMAS O'DWYER. The unfinished letter. Frontier times, 34(1):11, 46-7 (winter). port. On an unfinished letter by Joe Crossen, aged about 70, addressed to "Dear Doe Eyes," written in anticipation of death and found with his dead body in his tent near Wolf Creek, Ore., Sep. 1902, telling her the location of a bucket of nuggets hidden in a tree, promising to disclose where he had picked them up, and expressing his intention to leave all his property to her; her identification as his niece, Eleanor Crossen, of Eau Claire, Wis.; the publication of the letter in the Milwaukee Sentinel; and the many unsuccessful searches for the source of the nuggets. [10505

CHUCK CUSTER. Hectic history of the "O." Old Oregon, 40(2):9-10 (Oct-Nov). On a concrete letter "O" on Skinner's Butte, close to the University of Oregon, 1908-60. [10506

EVERETT CUTTER. Half century at Oregon. Old Oregon, 39(2):7-8 (Oct-Nov 1959). port. On Karl William Onthank as a student at the University of Oregon, a teacher in Oregon public schools, and director of graduate placement and employment at the University, 1909-59. [10507

ROBERT C. WOODWARD. W[illiam] S[imon] U'Ren and the single tax in Oregon [1909-17]. Ore. hist. quar., 61:46-63 (Mar). notes. Based on thesis (M. A.)--Univ. of Oregon, 1956. [10508

PHILIP A. LEVIN. The Oregon Employers' Liability Law: a study in judicial legislation [1910-58]. Willamette law jour., 1:1-16 (autumn 1959). notes. [10509

WILLIAM T. SCHANTZ. The Oregon Employers' Liability Law [1910] and the Federal overlap. Willamette law jour., 1:77-94 (autumn 1959). notes. On protection of various classes of injured workmen by several Federal statutes, 1908 ff., that apply in part to injured workmen eligible for relief under the Oregon law. [10510

ROBERT W. CHANDLER. Robert W. Sawyer: "He thought in terms of forever." Am. forests, 65(12):16-17, 44, 46-9 (Dec 1959). ports. On his work as editor of the Bend, Ore., Bulletin, 1913-53, as historian, as political leader, and particularly as conservationist. [10511

VICTORIA HOWARD (died 1930). Clackamas Chinook texts. [Edited] by Melville Jacobs. [Bloomington, Ind., 1958-59.] 2 v. [6], 293; viii, 295-663 p. (Indiana University. Research Center in Anthropology, Folk-Lore, and Linguistics. Publication[s] 8, 11.) Texts of 148 "myths," "stories of transitional times," "stories of pre-white times," and "ethnographic texts," dictated to the editor by Mrs. Howard at West Linn, Ore., 1929-30; with English translations and abstracts. [10512

MELVILLE JACOBS. Humor and social structure in an oral literature. Stanley Diamond, ed., Culture in history: essays in honor of Paul Radin (N.Y.: Columbia Univ. Press for Brandeis Univ., 1960), p. 180-89. On the author's recording of "humor situations ... in one of the Chinook languages, that of the Clackamas group which once lived in the vicinity of Portland, Oregon," extinct since the 1930s. [10513

MELVILLE JACOBS. The people are coming soon: analyses of Clackamas Chinook myths and tales. Seattle: Univ. of Washington Press, 1960. xii, 359 p. ports. notes (p. 359). Abstracts of and commentaries on the narratives in the Clackamas Chinook texts dictated by Victoria Howard, 1929-30, and published by Jacobs, 1958-59; with Freudian interpretations imposed by Jacobs. [10514

BOB LLOYD. Bobby ... the educated steer. West. horseman, 25(11):44, 46 (Nov). port., views. On "the first trained cow brute," a Longhorn-Brahma steer owned and trained by Monte Reger of Woodward, Okla., "used in rodeos as an outlaw bucking steer," 1933 to ca. 1943. [10515

JOHN BERNARD GRANTHAM. The Oregon Forest Products Research Center [1941-58]. Jour. forestry, 56: 574-7 (Aug 1958). views. On an organization known before 1957 as the Oregon Forest Products Laboratory, Corvallis. [10516

HERB KARNER. The Moores, Jeanne and Bill, of Broken Arrow. Quarter horse jour., 6(6):5, 36 (Mar 1954). port., view. On the racing of quarter horses by Bill and Jeanne Moore of Broken Arrow, Okla., 1942-54. [10517

LAWRENCE C. MERRIAM, JR. An application of recreational forestry. Jour. forestry, 58:810, 813-15 (Oct). views. notes. On the Henry B. Van Duzer Forest Corridor, Tillamook and Polk Counties, Ore., 1946-60. [10518

BILL SANDERSON. Oregon's quarter horse capital. West. horseman, 25(4): 44-5, 94-5 (Apr). port., views. On the breeding and raising of quarter horses by Lloyd Claver of Coquille, Ore., 1946-60. [10519

Portland

Mother MARY CYPRIAN. The Catholic sentinel [Portland, 1870-1960], pioneer Catholic newspaper of Oregon. Am. Cath. Hist. Soc., Rec., 71:85-92 (Sep-Dec). notes. Deals almost entirely with newspapers other than the one named in the title (especially the Catholic telegraph, Cincinnati) and with the general history of Portland and Oregon. [10520

SETH THOMAS BAILEY. The duck that laid golden eggs. By Tom Bailey. Frontier times, 34(1):18-19, 36-9 (winter). On Joseph Kelly (1838-1934), native of England, resident of Portland, Ore., from 1879 to 1881, described by the police as "Joseph (Bunco) Kelly who procures seamen for ship duty by inducing, swindling or coercing them", later jailed 13 years for murder, author of a book on his adventures. [10521

WASHINGTON

ROY L. CARLSON. Chronology and culture change in the San Juan Islands [since "the first millennium B. C."]. Am. antiq., 25:562-86 (Apr). diagrs., maps, tables, views. bibliog. Based on thesis (M.A.)--Univ. of Washington, 1954. [10522

MAYNARD BENEDICT JONES. Washington [its traditions and characteristics]. By Nard Jones. Holiday, American panorama west of the Mississippi: a Holiday magazine book (Garden City, N.Y.: Doubleday [1960]), p. 81-99. [10523

THOMAS HAZARD. Rank or class on the Northwest Coast [among the Coast Salish Indians, 1780-1955]? Mont. Acad. Sciences, Proc., 20:63-6. [10524

CARL LANDERHOLM. Vancouver area chronology, 1784-1958. Vancouver, Wash., 1960. [43], 395 leaves. List of events in or affecting Clark County and Vancouver, Wash., 3,225 entries, with source or authority for each, and subject index. [10525

ERNA GUNTHER. Vancouver and the Indians of Puget Sound. Pac. Northw. quar., 51:1-12 (Jan). views. notes. On Indian artifacts (now in the British Museum) collected by George Goodman Hewitt, surgeon's first mate on the Discovery in the expedition of Capt. George Vancouver, 1790-95. [10526

TOM BURRIER. The park misnamed Deception. Am. forests, 66(6):36-7 43-4 (Jun). views. On Deception Pass, between Whidbey Island and Fidalgo Island, Puget Sound, 1792-1960, and Deception Pass State Park. [10527

DELMAR H. CARYL. With angels to the rear: an informal portrait of early Meadowdale. Edmonds, Wash.: Dilemma Press [1960]. 159 p. maps, views. bibliog. (p. 153-4). On an area in Snohomish County on Puget Sound between Seattle and Everett, probably first seen by white men in 1792, surveyed in 1859, and settled in 1871. [10528

OPAL (SWEAZEA) ALLEN. Narcissa Whitman: an historical biography. Portland, Ore.: Binfords & Mort [1959. 6], 325 p. ports., views. bibliog. (p. 314-16). Account, "fictionized in form," of Narcissa (Prentiss) Whitman (1808-47) and her husband, the Rev. Marcus Whitman (1802-47), missionaries who crossed the continent from New York to Washington in 1836 and labored there till killed by Indians. [10529

HUDSON'S BAY COMPANY. The Fort Nisqually census of 1838-1839. [Edited by] Herbert C. Taylor, Jr. Ethnohistory, 7:399-409 (winter). tables. bibliog., notes. Includes a very detailed analysis of the census information (for 15 tribes of Puget Sound, totaling 5,563 individuals). [10530

ERIK BROMBERG. Frontier humor: plain and fancy. Ore. hist. quar., 61:261-342 (Sep). A "somewhat shorter version of the manuscript compiled by the author, which was originally turned out as a column for seventy weekly newspapers in Washington." Anecdotes, mainly 1840s-90s, from printed and oral sources. [10531

VERNE FREDERICK RAY. The Columbia Indian Confederacy, a league of Central Plateau tribes. Stanley Diamond, ed., Culture in history: essays in honor of Paul Radin (N.Y.: Columbia Univ. Press for Brandeis Univ., 1960), p. 771-89. notes. On a league of 4 Salish-speaking tribes of central Washington (Columbia, Wenatchee, Entiat, and Chelan), of "pre-white origin", ended in 1884; and its last leader, Chief Moses (died ca. 1900). [10532

ELWOOD R. MAUNDER. Building on sawdust. Pac. Northw. quar., 51:57-62 (Apr). views. notes. On forest industries as an element in the growth of Seattle and Washington, 1851-1959. [10533

JUDITH M. JOHNSON. Source materials for Pacific Northwest history: Washington Mill Company papers. Pac. Northw. quar., 57:136-8 (Jul). notes. On a lumber company at Seabeck on the Hood Canal, 1857-86, and the information to be found in its records. [10534

HELEN GOVE (McREAVY) ANDERSEN (born 1882). How, when, and where, on Hood Canal. [Everett, Wash.:] Puget Press, 1960. 83 p. ports., views. Autobiography of a lifelong resident of Union, Wash., where she served as Postmaster from 1915 to 1952; biography of her father, John McReavy (1840-1918), native of Maine, emigrant by way of Panama to Puget Sound in 1861, proprietor of a logging business in Union City, promoter and builder of a canal for the Hood Canal Land & Improvement Company; reminiscences (ca. 1924) by her mother, Fannie Dow (Gove) McReavy (p. 16-20), and other family papers; and account of Skokomish, settled ca. 1858, later known as Union City and since 1895 as Union. [10535

WILLIAM B. STOEBUCK. The law of adverse possession in Washington [1881-1957]. Wash. law rev., 35:53-87 (spring). notes. [10536

FLORENCE DONNELLY. Camas paper mill, first in Washington. Paper maker, 29(2):14-28 (Sep). port., views (1 fold.). On the Columbia River Paper Company, established by W. Lewthwaite, R. L. Pittock, and J. K. Gill, now the Camas Division of the Crown Zellerbach Corporation, 1884-1960. [10537

JOHN M. O'BRIEN, JR. The story of old Ruby. Pac. Northwesterner, 4:27-32 (spring). On a mining town in Okanogan County, Wash., settled in 1886 and deserted by 1899. [10538

SONYA LOFTNESS EVANS. Pacific Lutheran College [Tacoma, Wash., 1890-1960]. Am.Scandinavian rev., 48:277-82 (Sep). views. [10539

DANIEL COWAN JACKLING (1869-1956). Col. Jackling's 110-mile ride sixty years ago. Pony Express, 27(2):7-9 (Jul). port. Letter to Herb S. Hamlin, dated San Francisco, 25 May 1955, on the author's one-day ride of 110 miles on horseback from Republic, Wash., to Grand Forks, B.C., and Kettle Falls, Wash., and part way back, on a half-Appaloosa, half-thoroughbred horse, 1900. [10540

CALVIN FISHER SCHMID & VINCENT A. MILLER. Population trends and educational change in the State of Washington [1900-1960]. Seattle: Washington State Census Board, 1960. vii, 150 p. diagrs., maps, tables. notes. [10541

P. BRUCE WILSON. The Bulk Sales Law in Washington [1901-59]. Wash. law rev., 35:453-64 (autumn). notes. [10542

TORGER BIRKELAND. Echoes of Puget Sound: fifty years of logging and steamboating. ... With a foreword by Joshua Green. Caldwell, Idaho: Caxton Printers, 1960. 251 p. col. fold. map, ports., views (1 col.). On his emigration from Norway in 1903 and his work in Washington logging camps and on Puget Sound steamboats, ultimately as senior master of a ferry-boat, the Washington State motorship Evergreen State. [10543

STAN KISTLER. Loggers and lokeys. Trains, 20(6):44-52 (Apr). map, table, views. On Rayonier, Inc., producer of "chemical cellulose and fine papers," and its logging railroads in the areas of Grays Harbor and Clallam, northwest Washington, built between 1903 and 1906 for earlier owners. [10544

PHILIP A. TRAUTMAN. Forum non conveniens in Washington [1904-59]--a dead issue? Wash. law rev., 35:88-104 (spring). notes. On the authority of Washington courts to dismiss an action when another forum is available. [10545

EDWARD SAPIR (1884-1939). Preliminary report on the language and mythology of the upper Chinook. Selected papers from the American anthropologist, 1888-1920, ed. Frederica De Laguna (Evanston, Ill.: Row, Peterson [1960]), p. 411-22. tables. notes. First printed in 1907. Based upon observations made by the author on the Yakima Reservation in Washington, 1905. [10546

HARRY CHARLES BAUER. Requiem for an anthem. Pac. Northw. quar., 51:80-85 (Apr). cartoon, ports. On Washington, beloved, a song adopted by the Washington legislature as "the state anthem of Washington" in 1909, presumably superseded in 1959 by Washington, my home. [10547

BINA G. LUITEN. Harness maker. West. horseman, 25(9):42-3 (Sep). ports. On E. Joe King (born 1882) as an apprentice harnessmaker in Wisconsin, his practice of his profession in Spokane since 1910, and his founding and operation of the Indiana Harness and Saddlery, Spokane, 1940-57. [10548

RALPH W. JOHNSON. Riparian and public rights to lakes and streams [in Washington, 1917-60]. Wash. law rev., 35:580-616 (winter). notes. [10549

HERMAN KARL HAEBERLIN (1891-1918). SBeTeTDA'Q, a shamanistic performance of the coast Salish. Selected papers from the American anthropologist, 1888-1920, ed. Frederica De Laguna (Evanston, Ill.: Row, Peterson [1960]), p. 735-43. diagrs. First printed in 1918. On sbEtEtda'q (so printed in text), a ceremony "formerly performed by all or most of the Salish tribes on Puget Sound," intended "to regain the guardian-spirit of some person from the land of the dead," the person being alive. [10550

ROY JOSEPH DEFERRARI. Reminiscences of the early years of the Catholic Sisters College [Catholic University of America]. Cath. educ. rev., 58:233-9 (Apr). On administrative difficulties during the period of the author's service as Professor of Latin and Greek, 1919-20. [10551

ROBERT J. MOSER. ... and then there was one ... Am. forests, 65(12):21, 43-4 (Dec 1959). views. On the "last ... fast water ... flume" in America, "the longest ever built," owned by the Broughten Lumber Company near Underwood, Wash., 1923-59. [10552

ALFRED McKENZIE PHILIPS. Relationships between enrollments and fees in public school adult education classes in the State of Washington [1924-56]. Jr. college jour., 30:464-8 (Apr). tables. Based on thesis--State College of Washington. [10553

PAUL BECKETT & CELESTE SUNDERLAND. Washington State's lawmakers: some personnel factors in the Washington legislature [1925-35, 1941-51]. West. pol. quar., 11:180-202 (Mar 1957). tables. notes. [10554

ARVAL A. MORRIS. Toward effective municipal zoning [in Washington, 1926-60]. Wash. law rev., 35:534-79 (winter). notes. [10555

WILLIAM L. CARTER. The scope of Washington's business and occupation tax [1933-59]. Wash. law rev., 35:121-42 (spring). notes. [10556

PAT THOMSON. Omak suicide race. West. horseman, 25(7):10-11, 65 (Jul). ports., view. On the Omak Stampede, an annual rodeo held at Omak, Wash., since 1933. [10557

THAD BYRNE. I've seen them come, I've seen them go. North. junket, 7(1):2-5 (May). On the Merrymakers Club, "one of the oldest of Spokane's square dance clubs," 1941-60. [10558

IRVING PETITE. Science and mythology manage a forest. Am. forests, 62(9):30-31, 54-6 (Sep 1956). map, port. On the Yakima Indian Forest in the Yakima Reservation in southeastern Washington, 1941-56. [10559

HORACE L. LEITHEAD. Grass management pays big dividends. Jour. range management, 13:206-10 (Jul). diagr., tables. On a grass-management program on a ranch owned by Howard Sachs in Douglas County, Wash., 1946-57. [10560

Seattle

SEATTLE, Wash. CLEVELAND HIGH SCHOOL. The Duwamish diary, 1849-1949: information and data compiled by the laboratory writing classes of Cleveland High School. Seattle: Seattle Public Schools [1949]. xii, 119 p. maps (1 fold.), ports., views. notes (p. 117-19). A first-person history of Seattle, with the Duwamish River as narrator. [10561

ANNEMARIE MARGARET SAUERLANDER. Henry L[eiter] Yesler [1810-92] in early Seattle. Am.-German rev., 26(3):7-12 (Feb-Mar). map, port., views. On his life in Seattle as a landowner, operator of a steam sawmill, builder of stores and warehouses for new businesses, trustee of the Seattle and Walla Walla Railroad, and Mayor of Seattle, 1852-92; with some account of his early life in Maryland and Ohio. [10562

GORDON S. CLINTON. Music is the heart of a city. Music jour., 18(1): 14-15 (Jan). ports. On music in Seattle since 1861. [10563

WASHINGTON, UNIVERSITY OF. The vision on the knoll, 1861-1961: the first hundred years of the University of Washington. [Seattle, 1958.] 31 p. ports., views. [10564

HOMER G. BENTON. Seattle Coal & Transportation Company. Railway & Locomotive Hist. Soc., Bul., 103:47-56 (Oct). map, views. bibliog. On a railroad and steamship service established by the Company to move coal from Elliott Bay to Lake Washington, soon absorbed by the Seattle & Walla Walla Railroad, later the Columbia & Puget Sound Railroad, 1871-80; with lists of its locomotives, steamers, and barges. [10565

ALLEN BEACH. Bainbridge landings. [Bainbridge Island, Wash.:] Driftwood Press [1960. 44] p. double map, tables, views. notes. On the steamers and the landing facilities of the steamboat lines providing daily service between Bainbridge Island and Seattle, 8 miles, 1872-1938, and the surviving ruins of the docks and wharves. [10566

THERESA McMAHON. Communications. Pac. Northw. quar., 51: 47-8 (Jan). On the quality of the service of Dr. T. F. Kane as President of the University of Washington, 1902-14. [10567

ALLEN EMMETT THOMPSON. Timber and water--twin harvest on Seattle's Cedar River Watershed [source of the city's water supply, 1905-60]. Jour. forestry, 58:299-302 (Apr). [10568

JAMES F. O'GORMAN. The Hoo Hoo House, Alaska-Yukon-Pacific Exposition, Seattle, 1909. Soc. Architectural Historians, Jour., 19:123-5 (Sep). plan, views. notes. On a clubhouse designed by Ellsworth Prime Storey (1879-1960) for the Hoo Hoo, "a national lumberman's fraternity," erected in 1909, demolished in 1959. [10569

CALVIN FISHER SCHMID. Urban crime areas. Am. sociol. rev., 25: 527-42, 655-78 (Aug, Oct). diagrs., maps, tables. On crime rates in Seattle in relation to social and demographic variables, 1949-51. [10570

ALASKA

THE ALASKA SPORTSMAN. From Ketchikan to Barrow ... items of current or historic interest about Alaska or Alaskans. Alaska sportsman, 26(1-12):monthly installments (Jan-Dec). ports., views. [10571

JAMES WARNER BELLAH. Alaska [its traditions and characteristics]. Holiday, American panorama west of the Mississippi: a Holiday magazine book (Garden City, N.Y.: Doubleday [1960]), p. 1-18. [10572

JOHN MARTIN CAMPBELL. The Kayuk complex of Arctic Alaska. Am. antiq., 25:94-105 (Jul 1959). bibliog.

views. On prehistoric remains found on the banks of Kayuk Creek, in the Brooks Range of northwest Alaska. [10573

JAMES LOUIS GIDDINGS, JR. First traces of man in the Arctic. Natural hist., 69(9):10-19 (Nov). col. chron. chart, col. map, views. Approach to the chronology of artifacts on the coasts of the Seward Peninsula and Kotzebue Sound by analysis of "ocean beach ridges," indicating continuous human occupance beginning as early as 2500 B.C. [10574

JAMES LOUIS GIDDINGS. The archeology of Bering Strait, Current anthropol., 1:128-38 (Mar). map, table. bibliog., notes. Study of sites in the Chukchi Peninsula and the adjoining parts of Alaska and on St. Lawrence Island, and suggested chronology of human occupance; with comments by Chester S. Chard (p. 130-36) and others. [10575

ANDREI LOBANOV-ROSTOVSKY. Russian expansion in the Far East in the light of the Turner hypothesis. Walker D. Wyman & Clifton B. Kroeber, eds., The frontier in perspective (Madison: Univ. of Wisconsin Press, 1957), p. 79-110. bibliog. On the expansion of Russia eastward to Bering Strait and Alaska, and the differences between this frontier and the westward-moving frontier in the United States. [10576

PAULINE TEKESKY, comp. Seward's folly: the story of Alaska. Chapel Hill, N.C., 1960. 32 p. (University of North Carolina Library. Library study outlines, v. 1, no. 4.) Annotated topical list of 49 books. [10577

ROBERT WIKSTROM. Alaska oddities: a collection of true and fascinating facts about Alaska, the 49th star in our flag. Compiled and drawn in cartoon style by Robert Wikstrom. Seattle: R. D. Seal [1958. 76] p. cartoons. [10578

THEODORE P. BANK II. Experiences of scientific exploration in the Aleutian Islands [1741-1949]. Asa Gray bul., 1:77-86 (Jan 1952). cartoon, map, view. [10579

MARGARET ELIZABETH BELL. Touched with fire: Alaska's George William Steller [1709-46]. N.Y.: Morrow, 1960. 189 p. maps (part double). On his early life and scientific education in Germany, his work as physician, botanist, and zoologist in Russia and Siberia, and his participation in the Bering expedition from Kamchatka to southeastern Alaska in 1741. [10580

ANDREW JACKSON DADISMAN. Aborigines of Alaska [1741-1958]. W. Va. Acad. Science, Proc., 32: 217-20. bibliog. [10581

GEORGE WILLIAM ROGERS. Alaska in transition: the southeast region. Baltimore: Johns Hopkins Press for Resources of the Future [1960]. xiii, [1], 384 p. diagrs., fold. maps, tables, views. notes. A study in economic and social policy, especially since 1869; with chapters on "The aboriginal heritage and economic attitudes" (1741-1950) and "The Federal bureaucracy and the Indian". [10582

GEORGE THORNTON EMMONS. Native account of the meeting between La Perouse and the Tlingit. Selected papers from the American anthropologist, 1888-1920, ed. Frederica De Laguna (Evanston, Ill.: Row, Peterson [1960]), p. 761-4. views. First printed in 1911. On the shipwreck of the expedition under Jean François de Galamp, Comte de Lapérouse, on the coast of southeastern Alaska near the Fairweather Mountains, 1786, and the oral account of the wreck and the stay of the French party on shore communicated to Emmons in 1886 by Cowee, "the principal chief of the Auk quan of the Tlingit people," at Sintaka-heenee, Gastineaux Channel. [10583

ELLIOTT B. ROBERTS. The day the Bay ran over. U.S.N. Inst. proc., 86(5):62-6 (May). map, views. On the perilous navigation of Lituya Bay, Alaska, 1786-1958, the "cataclysmic" waves formed by its configuration during storms and volcanic disturbances, and the strength of the evidence that a wave in 1958 reached "a height of more than 1,600 feet." [10584

ROBERT FLEMING HEIZER. Archaeology of the Uyak site, Kodiak Island, Alaska. [Berkeley: Univ. of California Press, 1956.] vi, 199 p. maps, tables, views. bibliog. (p. 98-102). (Anthropological records, v. 17, no. 1.) On collections and excavations made by Aleš Hrdlička and the author, 1931-36, of an Eskimo site probably abandoned ca. 1800. [10585

LOUIS CHORIS (1795-1828). An early nineteenth-century artist in Alaska: Louis Chroris and the first Kotzebue expedition. [Edited] by James W. Van

Stone. Pac. Northw. quar., 51:145-58 (Oct). views. notes. Translated excerpt from his Voyage pittoresque autour du monde (Paris, 1822), recording his voyage on the Rurik under Lit. Otto von Kotzebue from Kamchatka to St. Lawrence Island, the north coast of Seward Peninsula, Kotzebue Sound, Unalaska, and the west coast of Bering Strait, 5 Jun.-6 Aug. 1816. [10586

CLARA GALBRAITH KNOLL. The Kuskokwim. Alaska sportsman, 26(11):30-31, 49-50 (Nov). port., views. On an Alaskan river since its discovery in 1829. [10587

J. SONNENFELD. Changes in an Eskimo hunting technology: an introduction to implement geography. Assoc. Am. Geographers, Ann., 50:172-86 (Jun). diagr. notes. On "the efficacy of implement introductions and replacements among the Barrow Eskimo, a maritime hunting people occupying the northernmost zone of settlement in Alaska," 1848-1954. [10588

DOROTHY JEAN RAY. The Eskimo dwelling [since ca. 1850]. Alaska sportsman, 26(8):13-15, 61-2 (Aug). view. On the various forms and materials of Eskimo dwellings in the area from Greenland to Siberia, the extreme rarity of snow and ice houses, and the common use of logs, boards, sod, stone, bone, and sheet iron, often in combination, in these structures. [10589

Father ILLARION (born 1818). Eskimos and Indians of western Alaska, 1861-1868: extracts from the diary of Father Illarion. Wendell H. Oswalt, editor. Univ. Alaska, Anthropol. papers, 8:100-118 (May). map. bibliog. notes. Information recorded by a "Russian Orthodox Greek Catholic priest" about the natives of the Kuskokwim and lower Yukon Valleys. [10590

MARGARET LANTIS, ed. Eskimo childhood and interpersonal relationships: Nunivak biographies and genealogies. Seattle: Univ. of Washington Press, 1960. xv, 215, [4] p. map, geneal. tables, tables, views. bibliog. (p. 215). Biographical and autobiographical sketches of 18 Eskimos (the oldest born in 1861) of Nunivak Island, Alaska, collected by the author in 1939-40, 1946, and 1955-56; with her interpretations of Rorschach tests administered to these individuals. [10591

ARCHIE M. BYERS. The timber industry and industrial forestry in Alaska [1867-1960]. Jour. forestry, 58:474-7 (Jun). [10592

FREDERICK A. SEATON. Alaska's struggle for Statehood [1867-1960]. Neb. law rev., 39:253-64 (Mar). On Alaska as "a land without law (1867-1884)," "the District of Alaska" (1884-1912), the Territory of Alaska (1912-59), and the State of Alaska (1959-). [10593

HAROLD JOHN LUTZ. Aboriginal man and white man as historical causes of fires in the boreal forest, with particular reference to Alaska [mainly in the years 1868-1915]. New Haven: Yale Univ., 1959. [6], 49 p. bibliog. (p. 43-9). (Yale Univ. School of Forestry. Bulletin 65.) [10594

H. C. FASSETT. The Aleut sea otter hunt in the late nineteenth century. [Edited by Robert Fleming Heizer.] Univ. Alaska, Anthropol. papers, 8:131-5 (May). From the San Francisco chronicle, 28 Dec. 1890. [10595

J. ARTHUR LAZELL. Alaskan apostle: the life story of Sheldon Jackson [1834-1909]. N.Y.: Harper [1960]. 218 p. maps (part col., 1 double), ports., views. On his service as a Presbyterian missionary and as U.S. General Agent, his concurrent speechmaking and collecting of funds for Alaskan missions and schools, and his project to bring reindeer from Lapland to Alaska, 1877-1906; with some account of his early life and studies, and his service as a Presbyterian missionary in Oklahoma and Minnesota and as superintendent of Presbyterian missions in Iowa, Nebraska, the Dakotas, Wyoming, Montana, Idaho, and Utah. [10596

U.S. Bureau of Commercial Fisheries. Statistics of the Alaska herring fishery, 1878-1956. By Bernard E[inar] Skud, Henry M. Sakuda, and Gerald M. Reid. Wash., 1960. iv, 21 p. maps, tables. (U.S. Fish and Wildlife Service. Statistical digest 48.) [10597

ROBERT N. DE ARMOND. And a town grew. By Bob De Armond. Alaska sportsman, 26(8):34-46 (Aug). port., views. On Juneau (originally Harrisburg, later Rockwell), 1880-1960. Heavily illustrated. [10598

DONALD EUGENE BRUYERE. The sequent occupance of Skagway, Alaska [1884-1952]. Mich. Acad.

Science, Papers, 45:155-68. diagr., maps. notes. Based on thesis--Univ. of Michigan. [10599

U.S. Fish and Wildlife Service. Factors causing decline in sockeye salmon [Oncorhynchus nerka] of Karluk River, Alaska [Kodiak Island, 1887-1951]. By George A. Rounsefell. Wash.: U.S. Govt. Print. Off., 1958. iii, 83-169 p. diagrs., map, tables. bibliog. (p. 150-52). (Its Fishery bulletin 130.) [10600

PAULINE W. INMAN. The Knapp paintings of Alaska. Antiques, 77:576-7 (Jun). views. On paintings done by Martha Severance Knapp (1837-1928), wife of Gov. Lyman E. Knapp, during her residence in Sitka, 1889-93. [10601

MASON B. BRUCE. National forests in Alaska [1892-1960]. Jour. forestry, 58:437-42 (Jun). map, views. [10602

AUGUST BUSCHMANN. I grew up with the North. Alaska sportsman, 26(10):10-13, 59 (Oct). port., views. On the author's work as a deck hand and a cook on his father's fishing schooner in the Alaskan seas, in his father's salmon canneries in Alaska, and his later service as an executive of the Northwestern Fisheries Company of Seattle, 1893 ff. [10603

S. G. HAYMAN. Alaska Steamship story. Alaska sportsman, 26(12):10-15, 60-61 (Dec). views. On the Alaska Steamship Company and its service between Seattle and Alaska, 1895-1960; with some account of its fleet. [10604

ELSA PEDERSEN. Homer. Alaska sportsman, 26(1):14-17, 38-41 (Jan). views. On an unincorporated town on the Kenai Peninsula, 1896-1959, now having nearly 1,300 inhabitants. [10605

HULETT M. WELLS (born 1878). Back door to the Klondike. Alaska sportsman, 26(4-9): monthly installments (Apr-Sep). maps, ports., views. On the author's travels from Seattle to Glenora and Atlin Lake, his discovery that mining claims were restricted to British citizens, his school teaching at Atlin, his travels to Skagway, and his return by boat to Seattle, 1897-99. [10606

RICHARD C. ANZER. Klondike gold rush [as recalled by a participant]. By Richard C. (Dixie) Anzer. N.Y.: Pageant Press [1959]. 236 p. Memories of Skagway, Dawson, White Horse, Bennett, Log Cabin, etc., 1898. [10607

ANDREW BAIRD. Days of the big rush. Alaska sportsman, 26(9):40-41, 53-4; (10):30-31, 50-54 (Sep-Oct). views. On the author's travels from Australia to Skagway and Dawson and his experience in prospecting for gold and mining it, 1898-99. [10608

LAWRENCE E. NIELSEN. The Valdez and Klutina Glaciers, Alaska. Appalachia, 33:31-6 (Jun). map, view. On the 25-mile journeys of "thousands of men on their way to the interior of Alaska" from Valdez to the end of Klutina Glacier, 1898-1900, a route unused after a pack trail was blasted through Keystone Canyon; with a report on the author's visit to this area in 1959, the relics of 1898 that he found there, and 7 place names dating from that time. [10609

JED JORDAN. Fool's gold: an unrefined account of Alaska in 1899. By Jed Jordan as told to M. M[arion] Marberry. N.Y.: J. Day Co. [1960]. 255 p. On the author's voyage from San Francisco to Nome and his operation of the Ophir Saloon and Gambling Hall in Nome, 1899-1901. [10610

MAURICE W. KELLY. The wolf--and the coyote [in Alaska]. Alaska sportsman, 26(10):36-8 (Oct). views. On the varieties, habitats, and diets of the wolf, a native of Alaska, and the coyote, which first appeared in Alaska ca. 1900 and exhibited a "phenomenal increase" in numbers; and the bounty on wolves since 1917 and on coyotes since 1927. [10611

VICTOR A. KALLSTROM. A winter at Nome. Alaska sportsman, 26(2):19, 36-7 (Feb). views. On the experience of the author and his partner, Otto Fosback, as campers and prospectors at Osborn Creek, near Nome, in the winter and spring of 1901-2. [10612

RAYMOND THOMPSON. Racing sled dogs. Alaska sportsman, 26(2):6, 43-4, 46 (Feb). view. On the sport of sled-dog racing in Alaska, 1908-59. [10613

DOROTHY JEAN RAY. The mystery of the billiken. Alaska sportsman, 26(9):36-7, 56 (Sep). views. On ivory statuettes and toy banks made by Eskimo craftsmen, copies of toys invented and patented by Florence Pretz of Kansas City and manufactured under the trade name "billikens" by the American Doll and Toy Company, 1909-10, forgotten in the United States but perennially popular in Alaska. [10614

LOIS McGARVEY (1885-1959). Along Alaska trails. N.Y.: Vantage Press [1960. 2], 200 p. ports., views. On the author's early life in Michigan; her removal to Alaska in 1911; her marriage to Frank McGarvey, in 1913; her varied occupations including work as a seamstress, a fur trapper and buyer, a prospector for gold, a boarding-house keeper, a real-estate dealer; her winters in Los Angeles with her husband; and her disablement by paralysis in 1952; with a chapter on "Bush pilots I have known" (p. 116-37). [10615

GEORGE K. SHAFFER. 38 years in the black gold rush. Old Oregon, 38(7):27-8 (Aug-Sep 1958). ports., views. On Carroll M. Wagner, student in the University of Oregon, 1911-15, petroleum explorer and executive in Mexico and Alaska. [10616

HUGH HAMMOND BENNETT (1881-1960). Exploring Alaska. Am. forests, 65(7):12-13, 56-60 (Jul 1959). port. On travels of the author on business of the Department of the Interior, 1914. [10617

R. R. ROBINSON. Forest and range fire control in Alaska [late 1920s to 1960]. Jour. forestry, 58:448-53 (Jun). views. [10618

DONNIS STARK THOMPSON. Thirteen years in Unga. Alaska sportsman, 26(10):32-5, 49-50 (Oct). ports., views (1 double). On the service of Allan Petersen as Deputy U.S. Marshal at Unga, responsible for a maritime territory about 270 miles long as served by boat, 1934 ff. [10619

F. M. SCHMIDT. The Mantanuska [sic] Valley colony and its tokens. Selections from the numismatist: United States paper money, tokens, medals, and miscellaneous (Racine, Wis.: Whitman Pub. Co., 1960), p. 107-8. coins. First printed Nov. 1937. On a colony established by the U.S. Government in the Matanuska Valley in Alaska to rehabilitate "201 farmers and their families from drought-stricken lands in the Middle West," and the tokens issued by the Alaska Rural Rehabilitation Corporation, 1935-37. [10620

E. L. BARTLETT. Alaska's transport panorama--sleds to superjets [1939-59]. Karl M. Muppenthal, Revolution in transportation (Stanford, Calif.: Graduate School of Business, Stanford Univ. [1960]), p. 138-47. [10621

OLIVE BARBER. Meet me in Juneau. Portland, Ore.: Binfords & Mort, 1960. [8], 175 p. ports., views. On the author's summers in southeastern Alaska with her husband, a commercial fisherman, and her travels by air to various parts of the State, during a period of 12 years. [10622

CHARLES CAMPBELL HUGHES. An Eskimo village in the modern world. Ithaca, N.Y.: Cornell Univ. Press [1960]. xiv, [2], 419 p. maps, tables, views. bibliog. (p. 399-410), notes. (Cornell studies in anthropology.) Based on thesis--Cornell Univ. Information from field notes gathered in the village of Gambell (Eskimo name Sivokak), St. Lawrence Island, by Alexander H. Leighton in 1940 and from observations by the author there in 1954-55, concerning changes in the "system of belief" of the natives; with historical references as early as 1648. [10623

SIMON PANEAK. We hunt to live. Alaska sportsman, 26(3):12-13, 55 (Mar). port., views. Details of the life of the author and his neighbors, nomadic followers of the caribou herds above the Arctic Circle in the interior about half way between Fairbanks and Point Barrow, 1940-60, written and published without editing of the idioms of its "Eskimo English." [10624

DOROTHY JEAN RAY. Skins against the weather. Alaska sportsman, 26(1):26-7, 36-8 (Jan). views. On the manufacture of Eskimo clothing by the Nome Skin Sewers Cooperative Organization, 1940-59; with some account of "making clothes for others" by Eskimo seamstresses since the 1830s. [10625

JOHN JOSEPH RYAN (born 1922). The Maggie Murphy. N.Y.: Norton [1951]. 224 p. On an undated voyage by the author and Ed Braddock, Tacoma schoolboys, from Tacoma to Ketchikan and the islands between Ketchikan and Juneau in a small vessel, their profitable summer of fishing among the islands from this vessel, their encounters with fishermen, saloon-keepers, prostitutes, and other waterfront dwellers, and the return of Ryan to Tacoma, leaving Braddock to continue the fishery. Reprinted in The Alaska sportsman, 1958. [10626

GEORGE H. ATWOOD. Along the Alcan. N.Y.: Pageant Press [1960]. ix, [3], 212 p. maps. On the author's work along the Alaska or Alcan Highway between Dawson Creek, B.C., and Fairbanks, Alaska, as an engineer constructing airports, hangars, line camps, and pumping stations, 1942-44. [10627

ALBERT HEINRICH. Structural features of northwestern Alaskan Eskimo kinship. Southw. jour. anthropol., 16:110-26 (spring). notes. Based upon oral information collected from speakers of the Inupiaq language, 1944-55. [10628

NORMAN A. CHANCE. Culture change and integration: an Eskimo example. Am. anthropol., 62:1028-44 (Dec). bibliog., notes. On the rapid changes among the Eskimos of Kaktovik, on the Arctic coast, 1945-60. [10629

SALLY CARRIGHAR. Wild voice of the North. Garden City, N.Y.: Doubleday, 1959. 191 p. views. On the author's studies of lemmings in Alaska of the habits and mental characteristics of Arctic dogs, especially "wolf dogs" (huskies), during a period of more than 7 years before and including 1953. [10630

ELSA PEDERSEN. Soldatna. Alaska sportsman, 26(9):10-12, 62 (Sep). views. On oil and gas production in the vicinity of a town on the Kenai Peninsula, 1947-60. [10631

HELEN RHODE. The big rack. Alaska sportsman, 26(1):25, 38 (Jan). ports. On Dyton Gilliand as a guide for hunters in Alaska, and "the all-time world record for Alaska-Yukon moose" set by a moose killed by him in 1947 as determined by careful measurement of its horns. [10632

AUSTIN EDWARD HELMERS. Alaska forestry--a research frontier [1948-60]. Jour. forestry, 58:465-71 (Jun). views. notes. [10633

FREDERICA DE LAGUNA. The story of a Tlingit community: a problem in the relationship between archaeological, ethnological, and historical methods. Wash.: U.S. Govt. Print. Off., 1960. x, 254 p. diagrs., maps, views. bibliog. (p. 207-9), notes. (U.S. Bureau of American Ethnology. Bulletin 172.) Report of a field study at Angoon, on Admiralty Island, 1949-50; and "History of Angoon" since 1804 (p. 128-206). [10634

LOIS CRISLER. Arctic wild. N.Y.: Harper [1958]. xv, [3], 301 p. ports., views. On a visit by the author and her husband to the Brooks Range in northern Alaska, to photograph wild animals and study their habits, especially those of wolves and caribou, 1953. [10635

HAWAII

CHARLES ALEXANDER BORDEN. Hawaii ... fiftieth State. Phila.: Macrae Smith Co. [1960]. 188 p. maps, ports., tables, views. On the Hawaiian Islands since prehistoric times. [10636

IRVING GOLDMAN. The evolution of Polynesian societies [including that of Hawaii]. Stanley Diamond, ed., Culture in history: essays in honor of Paul Radin (N.Y.: Columbia Univ. Press for Brandeis Univ., 1960), p. 687-712. table. bibliog. [10637

LORAINE E. KUCK. Story of the lei: customs, varieties, care, use [since prehistoric times. Honolulu: Tongg Pub. Co., 1960.] 48 p. ports., views (1 col.). 1st ed. 1956. [10638

FRANK J. TAYLOR. Hawaii [its traditions and characteristics]. Holiday, American panorama west of the Mississippi: a Holiday magazine book (Garden City, N.Y.: Doubleday [1960]), p. 19-33. [10639

EDWARD JOESTING. The first Hawaiians: Polynesian pioneers. Natural hist., 69(5):36-47 (May). port., views (part double). On the artifacts and way of life of the earliest inhabitants of Hawaii, settled there, as indicated by radiocarbon dates, as early as A.D. 500, and supposed to have come thither from Tahiti. [10640

DOROTHY BROWN ASPINWALL. Languages in Hawaii. PMLA, 75(4, pt. 2):7-13 (Sep). tables. On the 6 or more languages (English, Japanese, Cantonese, Korean, Portuguese, Ilocano) spoken there in addition to Hawaiian and pidgin, 1778-1960, the current teaching of the languages as well as French, Spanish, German, Russian, and Latin, and the recent work of the Committee for the Preservation of Hawaiian Language and Culture. [10641

NEAL S. BLAISDELL. Music is the heart of a city. Music jour., 18(4):8, 66-7 (Apr-May). ports. On music in Honolulu since the 1770s. [10642

NORMAN K. CARLSON. Honaunau Forest [Hawaii, 1778-1960]. Am. forests, 66(4):16-18, 53, 55-8 (Apr). views. [10643

KATHARINE LUOMALA. The native dog in the Polynesian system of values. Stanley Diamond, ed., Culture in history: essays in honor of Paul Radin (N.Y.: Columbia Univ. for Brandeis Univ., 1960), p. 190-240. bibliog. Includes some account of dogs as part of the primitive society of the Hawaiian Islands, 1778 ff. [10644

KATHARINE LUOMALA. A history of the binomial classification of the Polynesian native dog. Pac. science, 14:193-223 (Jul). views. bibliog. On the names, traits, and uses of dogs in the Polynesian communities on the Pacific islands (including the Hawaiian Islands and Samoa) as indicated by archeological remains and the observations and drawings made since 1779 by travelers and others. [10645

E. J. BRITTEN. Volcano ranching: problems and opportunities in management of Hawaiian range land [1793-1959]. Jour. range management, 12:303-6 (Nov 1959). diagr., views. bibliog. [10646

HARRY LOREN ARNOLD, JR. American medicine in Hawaii, 1820-1859. New Eng. jour. med., 261:694-9 (1 Oct 1959). notes. [10647

CHARLES K. L. DAVIS. The music of Hawaii [especially since the 1820s]. Music jour., 18(4):18, 31 (Apr-May). port. [10648

WAYNE DEHONEY. Our fiftieth State, Hawaii: Paradise lost? Paradise regained? Quar. rev. (Bapt.), 20(1):48-53 (Jan-Mar). On Christianity in Hawaii since 1820 and Southern Baptist work there since 1940. [10649

JERRY PAUL EATON & K. J. MURATA. How volcanoes grow. Science, 132:925-38 (7 Oct). diagrs., maps, tables, views. notes. On studies of volcanic activity in the Hawaiian Islands, 1823-1960. [10650

RICHARD E. WARNER. A forest dies on Mauna Kea. Pac. discovery, 13(2): 6-14 (Mar-Apr). diagr., map, views. On the flora of a volcanic peak in Hawaii, gradually destroyed by wild descendants of sheep introduced in 1834 when overbrowsing promoted the erosion of the light volcanic-ash soil, and the great acceleration of the damage by government policies since 1950. [10651

A. KOSOFF. Money of Hawaii [paper and coins, 1835-1935]. Numismatist, 73:547-56 (May). coins, facsims. [10652

ALPHAEUS HOMER ALBERT. Uniform buttons of Hawaii [1836-1959]. Natl. button bul., 19:55-7 (Mar). views. [10653

EDITH GAINES. Titian Peale's paintings of Hawaii. Antiques, 78:140-41 (Aug). port., views. Reproduces 4 oil paintings done by Titian Ramsay Peale (1799-1885) while an artist for the U.S. Exploring Expedition under Lt. Charles Wilkes, 1840. [10654

ROBERT W. PARKINSON. Fiftieth star. Steamboat bill, 16: 104-7; 17: 20-22 (winter 1959, spring 1960). views. On some of the steamships that have visited Hawaii since 1846; with references to further information about them. [10655

J. P. G. ARNDT. The coins of Hawaii [1848-93]. Selections from the numismatist: United States paper money, tokens, medals, and miscellaneous (Racine, Wis.: Whitman Pub. Co., 1960), p. 145-8. coins. First printed Mar. 1918. [10656

OTTO DEGENER. Wilhelm Hillebrand, 1821-1886. Asa Gray bul., 3:193-8 (spring 1957). ports. From the Hawaii weekly, 18 Nov. 1951. On his medical practice and botanical studies in Hawaii, 1851-71, and his Flora of the Hawaiian Islands (1888). [10657

ALFONS L. KORN. The Victorian visitors: an account of the Hawaiian Kingdom, 1861-1866. Honolulu: Univ. of Hawaii Press, ©1958. [10], 351, [2] p. facsim., map. notes (p. 309-37). Account of the Hawaiian Islands as seen by Lady Jane Griffin Franklin and her companion, Sophia Cracroft, consisting mainly of long letters from Miss Cracroft to friends and relatives in England, dated in the "Sandwich Islands," 22 Apr.-25 Jun. 1861; brief references to the journal of Lady Franklin and to a second visit of the 2 women to the islands, Dec. 1861; correspondence of Robert Crichton Wyllie and others, 1862-64; account of the travels of Queen Emma of

Hawaii (1836-85), known as Kaleleonalani, in England, France, and Italy, 1865-66; and appendix of biographical sketches of persons named in the text. [10658

MERZE TATE. British opposition to the cession of Pearl Harbor [to the United States, 1873-88]. Pac. hist. rev., 29:381-94 (Nov). notes. [10659

EDGAR C. KNOWLTON, JR. Portuguese in Hawaii [since "the middle 1870's"]. Ky. for. lang. quar., 7: 212-18 (4th quar.). notes. On the characteristics of the Hawaiian dialect of Portuguese, the publications in it, the teaching of the language, and its present obsolescence. [10660

HENRY ALBERT MEYER. The registry rates and markings of Hawaii [1875-99]. Am. Philatelic Cong., Congress book, 26:29-40. facsims. [10661

JACOB ADLER. Water rights and cabinet shuffles: how Claus Spreckels' Hawaiian career began [1878]. Bus. hist. rev., 34:50-63 (spring). facsim., map, ports., view. notes. Based on thesis--Columbia Univ., 1959. On his lease from King David Kalakaua of water rights on the island of Maui sufficient to irrigate his sugar lands there and his coincidental loan of $40,000 and gift of $10,000 to the King after his abrupt dismissal of a cabinet that opposed this concession. [10662

CHUNG KUN AI (born 1865). My seventy nine years in Hawaii. [Hong Kong: Cosmorama Pictorial Publisher, 1960. 12], 430, [2], 128, [2] p. maps, ports., tables, views. On the early life of the author in China, his family there, his removal to Hawaii in 1879, his studies at Iolani College, his establishment and operation of a rice mill (City Mill Company, Ltd., Honolulu, 1899-1957) and his other business ventures, his religious interests, and his charities and philanthropies, centered in the Chung Kun Ai Foundation. [10663

ROBERT A. RAMSAY. The Kahului Railroad. Railway & Locomotive Hist. Soc., Bul., 102:27-34 (Apr). tables, views. On the operations of the Kahului & Wailuku Railroad, on the sugar-producing island of Maui between Kahului and Haiku, 1879-1960, and the discontinuance of its passenger service in 1937. [10664

MERZE TATE. Hawaii's program of primacy in Polynesia. Ore. hist. quar., 61:377-407 (Dec). notes. On the plans of King Kalakaua and the head of his cabinet, Walter Murray Gibson, to assume "a protectorate over unprotected South Sea islanders," 1880-87, and the objections of the United States, Great Britain, and Germany to the plans, particularly those involving Samoa. [10665

SHERWOOD GREENWELL. The changing picture in Hawaiian range management. Jour. range management, 12:99-103 (May 1959). port., views. On changes in water supply, forage, and other particulars as illustrated by the operation of a cattle ranch by the author, his father, and his grandfather, on the Island of Hawaii, 1881-1959. [10666

JACOB ADLER. Coinage of the Hawaiian Kingdom: King Kalakaua's coins [1883-1904]. Numismatist, 73:131-8, 259-66 (Feb, Mar). coins, ports., views. notes. Based on thesis--Columbia Univ., 1959. [10667

SILVIO A. BEDINI. The horological collection of the Bernice P. Bishop Museum. Natl. Assoc. Watch and Clock Collectors, Bul., 9:200-205 (Apr). port., views. Includes a history of the museum, founded in 1889 at Honolulu, and an account of a collection recently donated to it by Dr. William Barclay Stephens. [10668

SILVIO A. BEDINI. The Lilioukalani clock. Hobbies, 65(1):42, 53 (Mar). views. On a large wall clock presented by Queen Lilioukalani to the Waialua church in 1892, probably made at her order by Welch, Spring, & Company, Forestville, Conn. [10669

JANE FORD ADAMS & PAULINE R. BENNETT. Non-military buttons of Hawaii [since 1893 or earlier]. Natl. button bul., 19:218-20 (Sep). views. [10670

CATHERINE CUNNINGHAM. Hawaii doctor, fighter of disease. Am. Swed. monthly, 54(10):10-12 (Oct). port. On Dr. Nils Paul Larson (born 1890), Swedish emigrant to New York in 1893, his practice of medicine in Honolulu since 1922, and his many other activities in Hawaii. [10671

HARRY VERNON BALL, JR. Social structure and rent-control violations

[Honolulu, 1941-52]. Am. jour. sociol., 65:598-604 (May). tables. notes. Based on thesis--Univ. of Minnesota, 1956. [10672

HAWAII. Governor's Advisory Committee on Financing. The State of Hawaii's finances: a description and analysis of Hawaii's economy, her government, and her public debt [1947-60. Honolulu, 1960.] 55 p. col. diagrs., col. map, port., tables, views (1 double). 31x34 cm. "Appendix" ([44] p.) in pocket. [10673

TERRITORIES AND DEPENDENCIES OF THE UNITED STATES

Pacific Territories

THE PHILIPPINES, 1898-1946

A. V. H. HARTENDROP. History of industry and trade of the Philippines [mainly since 1898, especially since 1941]. Manila: American Chamber of Commerce of the Philippines, 1958. 2 v. xx, [4], 743; xi, 532 p. Based upon articles in the American Chamber of Commerce journal, Manila, Aug. 1952 - Jun. 1953, Sep. 1955-Sep. 1957, and upon the author's Short history of industry and trade of the Philippines (1953). [10674

REED J. IRVINE. American trade with the Philippines [1898-1957, particularly since 1945]. Conference on American Trade with Asia and the Far East, Marquett University, 1958, American trade with Asia and the Far East, ed. Robert J. Barr (Milwaukee: Marquette Univ. Press, 1959), p. 173-83. [10675

MORTON NORTON COHEN. Mark Twain and the Philippines: containing an unpublished letter. Cent. Miss. Valley Am. Studies Assoc., Jour., 1(2):25-31 (fall). facsims. notes. On his bitter opposition to "American imperialism" in the Philippines; with a letter to him from Abner Goodell, 30 Dec. 1900, applauding his views, and Mark Twain's reply, 31 Dec. [10676

ELEANOR G. RISS. Forty years--preparation for freedom. Delta Kappa Gamma bul., 24(2):5-12 (winter 1958). On free school established by the U.S. Government in the Philippines, 1901-46. [10677

AVELINA N. ABELLA. The role of vocational education in the economic development of La Union Province. Centro Escolar Univ., Graduate and faculty studies, 10:49-59. table. notes. Mainly on the La Union School of Arts and Trades, 1907-58. [10678

MIGUEL CANIZARES. The tuberculosis problem in the Philippines [1910-47]. Am. rev. tuberculosis, 57: 149-54 (Feb 1948). table. [10679

ROY MANNING STUBBS. Philippine radicalism: the central Luzon uprisings, 1925-1935. U.S., Dept. of State, Office of Intelligence Research, Abstracts of completed doctoral dissertations, 1950-51 ([Wash.] 1952), p. 371. Abstract of thesis--Univ. of California. [10680

OTHER PACIFIC TERRITORIES

JOHN ALEXANDER CLINTON GRAY. Amerika Samoa: a history of American Samoa [since prehistoric times] and its United States Naval Administration [since 1900]. Annapolis: United States Naval Institute [1960]. xx, 295, [2] p. maps (part col.), port., views. bibliog. (p. 270-82). [10681

EDWARD WINSLOW GIFFORD & DELILA S. GIFFORD. Archaeological excavations in Yap. [Berkeley: Univ. of California Press, 1960. 4], 149-224 p. map, plans, tables, views. bibliog. (p. 201). (Anthropological records, v. 18, no. 2.) Report of investigations in 1956, uncovering evidences of human occupancy with radiocarbon dates as early as 176. [10682

JOHN ALEXANDER CLINTON GRAY. The Apia [Samoa] hurricane of 1889. U.S.N. Inst. proc., 86(6):34-9 (Jun). map, views. On the damage suffered by naval and merchant shipping in the harbor there, and the loss of nearly 150 lives. For an addition by Rear Adm. A. M. Charlton see 86(11):105. [10683

ROBERT R. SOLENBERGER. Contrasting patterns of Carolinian population distribution in the Marianas. International Congress of Anthropological and Ethnological Sciences, 5th, 1956, Men and cultures: selected papers, ed. Anthony F. C. Wallace

(Phila.: Univ. of Pennsylvania Press [1960]), p. 513-18. On the "spatial location of Caroline Islanders entering the Marianas" since the Americans occupied Guam in 1898. [10684

ELMER YALE DAWSON. Changes in Palmyra Atoll and its vegetation through the activities of man, 1913-1958. Solvang, Calif.: Beaudette Foundation for Biological Research, 1959. 51 p. diagrs., maps, views. bibliog. (p. 50- 51), notes. (Pacific naturalist, v. 1, no. 2, 4 Feb. 1959.) Deals particularly with the effects of a military air station established on this previously uninhabited island during World War II. [10685

RONALD WILLIAM TAYLOR. Polynesian paradise. Mountain View, Calif.: Pacific Press Pub. Assoc. [1960. 8], 136 p. ports.views. On Seventh-Day Adventist missions in Samoa since 1930, and the author's service as a missionary there. [10686

ALICE M. HETZEL. Health survey of the Trust Territory of the Pacific Islands [by a medical staff on the USS Whidby, 1948-50]. U.S. Armed Forces med. jour., 10:1199-1222 (Oct 1959). [10687

Caribbean Territories

PUERTO RICO

MONICA FLAHERTY FRASSETTO. A preliminary report on petroglyphs in Puerto Rico. Am. antiq., 25:381-91 (Jan). map, views. bibliog. Study of 60 "surface prints" made by the author at 13 sites, probably occupied between 350 and 1584; with an exposition of her method of recording or copying petroglyphs. [10688

ISMAEL D'ALZINA. Graphic history of Puerto Rico. First era [1493-1811]. Drawings and text by Ismael d'Alzina. English version by Justo Pastor Lozada. [San Juan, P. R.: Ediciones Limitadas Cemi, 1957. Text ([32] p. in a brochure) and 81 plates (ports. and views) in a portfolio. Artist's conceptions of events and personages, with explanatory text. [10689

RALPH LOWELL HANCOCK. Puerto Rico: a success story [1493-1960]. Princeton, N.J.: Van Nostrand [1960]. ix, 187 p. notes. Mainly on economic and social policies since 1940. [10690

OTTO OLIVERA. Breve historia de la literatura antillana. Mexico, 1957. 222, [1] p. bibliog. (p. 197-204), notes. (Manuales studium, 7.) On "el desarrollo literario de las Antillas españolas (Cuba, la República Domicana y Puerto Rico) con énfasis especial en la llamada creación imaginativa," 16th-20th centuries. [10691

PETROAMÉRICA PAGÁN DE COLÓN. Puerto Rican society in transition [1508-1959]. University of Florida, School of Interamerican Studies, The Caribbean: British, Dutch, French, United States, ed. A. Curtis Wilgus (Gainesville: Univ. of Florida Press, 1958), p. 180-89. bibliog. [19692

FRANCISCO M. ZENO VÁZQUEZ. Historia de la capital de Puerto Rico (monumentos, reliquias, e insignias históricas [since 1514]). Tomo II. [San Juan, P. R.:] Gobierno de la Capital [1959]. xiv, [2], 240 [1] p. ports., views. notes. Tomo I published in 1948 with title: La capital de Puerto Rico (bosquejo histórico). [10693

YVETTE DE LOURDES CABRERA F. La décima popular en Puerto Rico: historia, verisificación, temática. México, 1960. 281, [3] p. bibliog. (p. 275-81), notes (p. 265-71). Tesis (Doctor en Letras)--Univ. Nacional Autónoma de México. On 10-line poems or stanzas, with some account of the Spanish sources of the form and its distribution in Spanish America. Refers to an example before 1700 and a dated example of 1747. [10694

MARTIN SEBASTIAN SORIA (1911-61). Painters in Puerto Rico: Paret and Campeche. Art quar., 23:229-30 (autumn). port., views. On Luis Paret y Alcázar (1746-99), Spanish court painter who lived in Puerto Rico in the years 1775-78, and José Campeche (1752-1809), a native painter influenced by him; with an account of Campeche's portrait of José Màs Ferrer, painted ca. 1790-92. [10695

ADAM SZÁSZDI. La Municipalidad de San Germán en Puerto Rico (1798-1808). Jour. inter-Am. studies, 1: 489-513 (Oct 1959). Based entirely on "el libro inédito de actas capitulares de San Germán para la década 1798-1808." [10696

EDWARD BLISS EMERSON (1805-34) & CHARLES CHAUNCY EMERSON (1808-36). Puerto Rico through New England eyes, 1831-1834. Edited by Frank Otto Gatell. Jour. inter-Am. studies, 1:281-92 (Jul 1959). Excerpts from letters to each other, to their elder brother Ralph Waldo Emerson, and to other members of the family, 30 Oct. 1831-29 Jun. 1834, on the scenery and people of the island; and parts of a lecture, "One of the West Indies islands," delivered by Charles Chauncy Emerson before the Concord Lyceum, 9 Jan. 1833. [10697

TERRENCE LESLIE HANSEN. The types of the folktale in Cuba, Puerto Rico, the Dominican Republic, and Spanish South America. Berkeley: Univ. of California Press, 1957. xvi, 202 p. bibliog. (p. xi-xiii). (University of California publications. Folklore studies, 8.) Arranged under classifications 1-2199, grouped as animal tales, magic tales, religious tales, romantic tales, tales of the stupid ogre, jokes and anecdotes, and formula tales; with a detailed subject index. Based upon printed sources, 1883-1952. [10698

DANIEL JOSEPH BOORSTIN. Paths to national self-discovery: U.S.A. and Puerto Rico [1898-1956]. Daniel J. Boorstin, America and the image of Europe: reflections on American thought (N.Y.: Meridian Books [1960]), p. 139-63. First printed in 1956. On the efforts of Puerto Rico to analyze itself and to impute to itself a distinctive culture. [10699

DEAN KENNETH FUHRIMAN & R. M. SMITH. Irrigation practices in Puerto Rico [1898-1950]. Agric. engineering, 32:46, 48, 50 (Jan 1951). map, table, views. [10700

ARTURO MORALES CARRIÓN. The historical roots and political significance of Puerto Rico [since 1898]. University of Florida, School of Inter-American Studies, The Caribbean: British, Dutch, French, United States, ed. A. Curtis Wilgus (Gainesville: Univ. of Florida Press, 1958), p. 139-69. notes. [10701

EUSTAQUIO ZAYAS ALVARADO (born 1908). Worker in the cane: a Puerto Rican life history. By Sidney W[ilfred] Mintz. New Haven: Yale Univ. Press, 1960. ix, [5], 288 p. facsim., maps, ports., views. (Caribbean series, 2.) Case study, by Mintz, in the cultural anthropology of rural Puerto Rico, consisting of Zayas Alvarado's written reminiscences of his life in Barrio Jauca, his labor on sugar plantations, and his activities in local and union politics, and wire recordings of interviews in 1953 and 1956 with him and his wife, Elisabeth; with a search for the patterns and tendencies in the recent society of Puerto Rico as exhibited and exemplified by them. [10702

FRANK OTTO GATELL. The art of the possible: Luis Muñoz Rivera and the Puerto Rican Jones Bill. Americas, 17:1-20 (Jul). notes. On his efforts, as leader of the Unionist Party and Resident Commissioner for Puerto Rico (in Washington), to obtain as much autonomy as possible for Pureto Rico, 1911-16, and the probable effect of his death in 1916 upon the passage of the Jones Bill in 1917. [10703

The CASE of [Pedro] Albizu y Campos [Harvard, 1916], Puerto Rican revolutionist. Harvard alumni bul., 53:170-71 (11 Nov 1950). port. On his studies at Harvard and the Harvard Law School, his practice of law in Puerto Rico, his activities in the Nationalist Party of Puerto Rico, his imprisonment in the Federal Penitentiary at Atlanta for conspiracy to overthrow the government by force, and his participation in the attempt to assassinate President Truman. [10704

RAFAEL V. URRUTIA. Puerto Rico Aqueduct and Sewer Authority [1941-59]. Am. Water Works Assoc., Jour., 52:6-12 (Jan). diagrs., map. [10705

JOHN S. DE BEERS. A study of Puerto Rico's banking system [1942-59]. Prepared ... for the Finance Council of Puerto Rico. [San Juan, P. R.: Finance Council] 1960. 160, [1] p. tables. notes. [10706

MOHINDER S. BHATIA. Tax exemption in a developing economy: a case study of Puerto Rico [1948-60]. Natl. tax jour., 13:341-9 (Dec). notes. [10707

AMOR GOSFIELD. Input-output analysis of the Puerto Rican economy [1949]. Conference on Research in Income and Wealth, Input-output analysis: an appraisal (Princeton: Princeton Univ. Press, 1955 [Studies in income and wealth, 18]), p. 321-67. [10708

THE VIRGIN ISLANDS

ISIDOR PAIEWONSKY. Jewish historical development in the Virgin Islands, 1665-1959. Saint Thomas [V. I.] 1959 [stamped: c1960. 23] p. view. notes. [10709

ROBERT W. NOBLES. Forestry in the U.S. Virgin Islands [1930-60]. Jour. forestry, 58:524-7 (Jul). views. [10710

THE CANAL ZONE

W. H. CHALONER. The birth of the Panama Canal, 1869-1914. History today, 9:482-92 (Jul 1959). ports., views. [10711

ALTERNATIVE REGIONAL CONCEPTS

The East

WILLIAM AUGUSTUS RITCHIE & DON W. DRAGOO. The Eastern dispersal of Adena. Am. antiq., 25:43-50 (Jul 1959). bibliog. On the occurrence of Adena remains in Maryland, New Jersey, New York, and New England; with indications that "the arrival of Hopewell groups from the Illinois area into the Adena heartland in the central Ohio Valley" led to eastward migration of some of the Adena people, in progress at the beginning of the Christian era. [10712

JOHN WITTHOFT. Notes on the Archaic of the Appalachian region. Am. antiq., 25:79-85 (Jul 1959). views. bibliog. [10713

WALTER WILLIAM RISTOW. Augustine Herrman's map of Virginia and Maryland. Lib. Cong. quar. jour., 17: 221-6 (Aug). fold. map. notes. Printed map entitled Virginia and Maryland as it is planted and inhabited this present year 1670 surveyed and exactly drawn by the only labor & endeavour of Herrman Bohemiensis (1673), engraved by W. Faithorne, showing southern New Jersey, the lowermost parts of the Delaware and the Susquehanna, all of the Delmarva Peninsula and Chesapeake Bay, and the courses or lower courses of its western tributary rivers, and including blocks of descriptive and historical text; with a biographical sketch of Herrman, alias Augustus Heermanns (born 1605), native of Bohemia, settler of Bohemia Manor, Md., in 1661 or 1662. [10714

ANDREW BURNABY (1734?-1812). Travels through the middle settlements in North-America, in the years 1759 and 1760; with observations upon the state of the colonies. [Reprinted from] the second edition [1775]. Ithaca, N.Y.: Great Seal Books [1960]. x, [2], 154, [2] p. facsims. notes (p. 155-6). Diary of a voyage from England to Virginia, travels by land as far as New Hampshire, and the return voyage to England, 27 Apr. 1759 - 21 Nov. 1760; with introductory remarks on the threatened revolt of the colonies in 1775. [10715

RALPH D. GRAY. The early history of the Chesapeake and Delaware Canal. Del. hist., 8:207-63, 354-97 (Mar, Sep 1959). facsims., maps, tables, view. On various surveys and plans for a canal across the neck of the Delaware Peninsula, 1769 ff., the chartering of the Chesapeake and Delaware Canal Company by Maryland, Delaware, and Pennsylvania (1799, 1801), the years of "delay, debate, and relocation" till 1824, the completion of the canal in 1827, and its sale to the U.S. Government in 1919. [10716

RALPH D. GRAY. Philadelphia and the Chesapeake and Delaware Canal, 1769-1823. Pa. mag. hist. and biog., 84:401-23 (Oct). notes. [10717

EARL J. HEYDINGER. Commercial fishing in the Susquehanna River [1772-1910]. Lancaster Co. Hist. Soc., Jour., 64:194-7 (summer). [10718

JANE N. GARRETT. Philadelphia and Baltimore, 1790-1840: a study of intra-regional unity. Md. hist. mag., 55:1-13 (Mar). notes. On their "direct contacts, cultural interchange and ... urban-rural relationships with an overlapping hinterland" as evidence that "a Middle Atlantic orientation must be acknowledged for Baltimore and for a large portion of Maryland." Based on honors thesis--Univ. of Delaware. [10719

ESTHER FELT BENTLEY, ed. An error of judgment and not of the heart. Princeton Univ. Lib. chron., 22:1-20 (autumn). notes. Analysis and texts of correspondence of Osborn Sprigg, Samuel L. Southard, his daughter Virginia E. Southard, and Margaret G. Mead, 21 Oct. 1836 to some date after 13 Feb. 1838, concerning the courtship of Miss Southard by Mr. Sprigg and the flirtatious duplicity of Miss Southard ending with her marriage to another man. Includes the editor's comments on the proper way of conducting a courtship. [10720

MARYLAND. AGRICULTURAL EXPERIMENT STATION, College Park. Population change and urbanization in the Northeast [West Virginia, Maryland, Delaware, Pennsylvania, New Jersey, New York, and the New England States, 1870-1950]. By Wayne C. Rohrer and Robert K. Hirzel. [College Park] 1959. [2], 45 leaves. maps, tables. notes. (Its Contribution 3024.) [10721

HOWARD A. HANLON. The ballhooter: from the forests they felled--cities grew. Prospect, N.Y.: Prospect Books, 1960. xvi, 368 p. maps, ports., views. notes (p. 365-8). On "the workmen who harvested the forest crop during the period from 1881 until 1921 on the watersheds of the Susquehanna and the upper Allegheny Rivers in Pennsylvania, and the upper reaches of the Greenbrier and the Cheat Rivers in West Virginia." Includes information from interviews with former lumber workers and from the author's recollections since 1905. [10722

CECIL NUCKOLS SMITH. Some recent trends in the Appalachian apple industry [1909-51. Blacksburg:] Virginia Polytechnic Institute [1953]. 61 p. diagrs., maps, tables. notes. (Virginia. Agricultural Experiment Station, Blacksburg. Bulletin 462.) Prepared with cooperation of the Agricultural Experiment Stations of Maryland, Pennsylvania, and West Virginia and the U.S. Bureau of Agricultural Economics. [10723

The Interior: Overlap of East and West

CLARENCE WALWORTH ALVORD (1868-1928). The Mississippi Valley and experiments in imperialism culminating in the American Revolution. N.Y.: Russell & Russell, 1959. 2 v. 358; 396 p. maps. bibliog. (p. 265-320), notes. 1st ed. 1916. On "the various attempts made by the successive British ministeries to solve the problem of the West," 1759-76. Includes in the West the Great Lakes and West Florida as well as the Mississippi Valley. Appended (2: 253-64): "Special bibliography: the pamphlet warfare, 1759-1763," listing all known pamphlets (totaling 65) that deal with "the cessions in America to be demanded from France at the close of the Seven Years' War," with special reference to Guadeloupe, Canada, and Louisiana. [10724

THE GREAT LAKES

ALFRED IRVING HALLOWELL. Ojibwa ontology, behavior, and world view. Stanley Diamond, ed., Culture in history: essays in honor of Paul Radin (N.Y.: Columbia Univ. Press for Brandeis Univ., 1960), p. 19-52. bibliog., notes. [10725

ALIDA SIMS MALKUS. Blue-water boundary: epic highway of the Great Lakes and the Saint Lawrence. N.Y.: Hastings House [1960]. x, [2], 308 p. ports., views, col. maps. bibliog. (p. 292-4). On the lakes and the river since prehistoric times, and their service as a border between the United States and Canada. [10726

HELEN MANDEVILLE MARTIN. How people came to Mackinac. Mich. hist., 44:401-4 (Dec). Indian myth about the origin of the island and the creation of man there, and brief reference to the settlement of white men. [10727

FRANK A. MYERS. Historic sites marked in Manitoulin Island region. Inland seas, 16:196-202 (fall). Includes reference to routes of voyageurs and other Great Lakes travelers, 1618-1845. [10728

WILLIAM RATIGAN. Great Lakes shipwrecks & survivals [1679-1959]. Grand Rapids: Eerdmans [1960]. 298, [2] p. views. (His Great Lakes panorama.) [10729

CLIFF SPIELER & TOM HEWITT. Niagara power, from Joncaire to Moses. Lewiston, N.Y.: Niagara Power Publishers, ©1959. 80 p. maps, ports., views. On projects and apparatuses for the utilization of the water power of the Niagara River, 1751-1959, particularly the Niagara River hydroelectric project of the New York State Power Authority undertaken in 1958. -- [Second edition, revised.] Lewiston, N.Y.: Niagara Power Publishers, c1960. 44 p. col. diagr., maps, ports., table, views. [10730

ERIK HEYL, comp. Steamboats enrolled at Buffaloe [sic] Creek District during the first twenty-five years of steam navigation on the Great Lakes, 1818-1843. Steamboat bill, 17: 16-17 (spring). List prepared from records of the Buffalo office of the U.S. Customs Service. [10731

PAMELA WILSON REEVES. Navigation on Lake Erie, 1825-1860. Inland seas, 14:256-63; 15:55-60, 97-105, 191-9, 306-11; 16:25-31, 100-110 (winter 1958 - summer 1960). notes. Thesis (M. A.)--Western Reserve Univ. 10732

NILES' NATIONAL REGISTER. The Great Lakes in Niles' national register. ... Selected by Gordon W. Thayer. Inland seas, 12:58-9, 128-9, 296-7; 13:54-5, 151-2, 313-14; 14:56-7, 163-4, 227-8, 314-15; 15:61-2, 152-3, 238-9, 312-13; 16:63-4, 148-51, 230-31, 313-14 (spring 1956-winter 1960). Excerpts relating to the Great Lakes. These installments: 1826-39. [10733

EBENEZER P. DORR. Captain Dorr's story. [Edited] by William A. McDonald. Inland seas, 16:115-18 (summer). view. Reminiscences (1873) of the almost miraculous good fortune of the "round-sterned vessel" Erie under the author's command in a gale on Lake Erie, Nov. 1839. [10734

T. E. LAUER. District control of water resources. Univ. Detroit law jour., 37:28-75 (Oct 1959). notes. On the types and functions of water districts in the 8 Great Lakes States as defined in their statutes, 1839-1959. [10735

H. A. MUSHAM. Early Great Lakes steamboats: hard times and the Erie disaster, 1840-1841. Am. Neptune, 20:79-103 (Apr). views. notes. Part of a work in progress on the maritime history of the Great Lakes. Includes an account of the burning of the steamship Erie 38 miles from Buffalo, with a loss of about 130 lives, 9 Aug. 1841. [10736

H. A. MUSHAM. Early Great Lakes steamboats: the last years of the hard times, 1842-1843. Am. Neptune, 20: 250-69 (Oct). bibliog., notes. [10737

THOMAS DAVID ODLE. Great Lakes history and the St. Clair Flats. Detroit Hist. Soc., Bul., 15(5):7-15 (Feb 1959). double map. notes. On "the shallow channel through the St. Clair River delta," the efforts of Whigs and Republicans to obtain Federal aid for dredging the channel and for improving the navigation of the Detroit Reiver, the opposition of the Democrats to the expenditure of Federal funds for this internal improvement, 1842-60, and the effect of the resulting indignation in the Great Lakes area in promoting the defeat of the Democrats in 1860. [10738

W. R. WILLIAMS. Colonel McKnight's Lake Superior Line [1847-60]. Inland seas, 16:138-44 (summer). view. On Sheldon McKnight (1810-60), who established a portage road and later "a mile-long strap railroad" at Sault Ste. Marie and built up a fleet of several ore-carrying boats for service on Lake Superior and thence to Buffalo; with some account of the earlier and later careers of the vessels composing the fleet. [10739

A REPORT on the loss of the G. P. Griffith. [Edited] by Sidney Glazer. Inland seas, 16:232-3 (fall). Letter from an anonymous Clevelander to the Michigan Christian herald, 4 Jul. 1850, on the burning of this vessel in harbor at Cleveland with heavy loss of life, 28 Apr. 1850, a misfortune ascribed to the fact that the vessel had sailed from Buffalo on the Lord's Day. [10740

OLIVER SCHROEDER, JR. Crime and the Seaway. West. Reserve law rev., 11:54-79 (Dec 1959). notes. On the "admiralty and maritime jurisdiction" of the Federal Government throughout the Great Lakes, 1851-1959, including jurisdiction over crimes committed on American vessels in Canadian waters of the Great Lakes; and the extent of the jurisdiction of Ohio over crimes committed on Lake Erie. [10741

JOHN LINDSAY MAHAR. One hundredth anniversary of the Lady Elgin. Inland seas, 16:4-13 (spring). view. On "the most tragic collision in the history of maritime enterprise on the Great Lakes," when the schooner Auguste rammed and sank the steamer Lady Elgin off Winnetka, Ill., with a loss of about 350 lives, 8 Sep. 1860. [10742

NEIL F. MORRISON. Navigation news of 1860. Inland seas, 16:283-8 (winter).

Representative excerpts from newspapers of that year concerning navigation on the Great Lakes. [10743

ERIK HEYL. The side-wheeler Troy. Inland seas, 16:145-7 (summer). view. On a vessel built at Maumee City, Ohio, employed on the Great Lakes, and scrapped in 1861. [10744

ANNA G. YOUNG. Sounding: three long and two short. Inland seas, 16:111-14 (summer). On Capt. Robert Foote and several of his brothers and nephews as navigators on the Great Lakes, 1864-1958. [10745

NEIL F. MORRISON. The life and times of Captain James Donaldson Morrison [1870-1936]. Inland seas, 16:180-89 (fall). views. Revision of an article in Western Ontario historical notes, Mar. 1951. On his many maritime occupations in Ontario and Michigan, 1887-1933. [10746

ALEXANDER CLARK. How Captain Clark was burnt out at the Chicago Fire. [Edited] by William A. McDonald. Inland seas, 16:36-8 (spring). views. On the burning of Clark's steamer, the Navarino, "down to the water" in the Chicago River, 1871. [10747

JUSTIN W. LEONARD. Our stake in the Great Lakes. Mich. conservation, 26(5):9-13 (Sep-Oct 1957). map, views. Deals especially with the concern of the Michigan Department of Conservation and its predecessors in the waters, fisheries, and beaches of the lakes since 1873. [10748

MERLIN DEWEY WOLCOTT. Heroism at Marblehead. Inland seas, 16:269-74 (winter). medal, port. On the work of Capt. Lucien M. Clemons, the author's greatuncle, as a lifesaving officer on Marblehead Peninsula, on the Ohio shore of Lake Erie, 1875-97. [10749

JULIUS FREDERIC WOLFF, JR. Some noted shipwrecks on the Michigan coast of Lake Superior [1885-1901]. Inland seas, 16:172-9 (fall). views. notes. [10750

SEABOARD. Excursion boats at Buffalo. Steamboat bill, 17:80-81 (fall). view. News from the issue of 12 May 1892. [10751

JAMES R. WARD. Harbor disaster. Inland seas, 16:95-9 (summer). view. On a whaleback excursion ship, the Christopher Columbus, built in 1893, disabled in the Milwaukee River when she struck a water tower and was hit by the falling water tank (with a loss of 16 lives), 30 Jun. 1917, repaired, continued in service till 1930, and scrapped in 1936. [10752

JOHN GRAY. A man, a boat, an era. Mich. conservation, 28(4):22-6 (Jul-Aug 1959). ports., views. On Kal Johannas Allers (born 1894), his early life on Beaver Island, his work as a merchant seaman on the Great Lakes, and his service as Master of Patrol Boats of the Michigan Conservation Commission. [10753

TEDDY REMICK. The wreck of the Idaho. Inland seas, 16:65-6 (summer). view. On a steamer built at Cleveland in 1863, which foundered off Long Point, Ont., 5 Nov. 1897, with a loss of 19 lives. [10754

A. T. ZILLMER. The Lake Erie Excursion Company [1899-1924]. Inland seas, 16:275-82 (winter). view. Includes some account of the purchase of the Company in 1924 by the Buffalo & Crystal Beach Company, bankrupt and reorganized in 1934 as the Crystal Beach Transit Company, which was sold in 1959 to the Toledo Excursion Lines. [10755

MARVIN H. GLUNTZ. Harry Defoe [1875?-1957], shipbuilder extraordinary. Inland seas, 16:88-94 (summer). On the Defoe Boat and Motor Works, Saginaw, 1905-57 (renamed the Defoe Shipbuilding Company before 1941). [10756

SPENCER M. BOWER. First fish of spring. Mich. conservation, 23(2):2-4 (Mar-Apr 1954). views. On the first planting of smelt in the Great Lakes in 1906 and the commercial smelt fishery there since 1931. [10757

FRED LANDON. Shipwreck on Isle Royale. Inland seas, 16:60-62 (summer). views. On the wreck of the Canadian passenger steamer Monarch (commissioned in 1890), 6 Dec. 1906, with a loss of only 1 life. [10758

PAUL LINCOLN ADAMS. Diversion of Lake Michigan waters [by the City of Chicago and the State of Illinois, 1913-59]. Univ. Detroit law jour., 37:149-56 (Oct 1959). notes. On the resulting damage to the interests of all the other Great Lakes States (except Minnesota) and to Ontario. [10759

FRANK BARCUS. Freshwater fury: yarns and reminiscences of the greatest storm in inland navigation.

Detroit: Wayne State Univ. Press, 1960. xvii, 166, [1] p. map, port., tables, views. On "the greatest disaster in the history of the Great Lakes," a storm in which 251 sailors drowned, Nov. 1913, as reported in "the direct accounts of the men who survived the Great Storm" and in contemporary newspapers. [10760

JACK J. BILLOW. The tragedy of the Eastland. Inland seas, 16:190-95 (fall). views. Eyewitness account of the capsizing and sinking of an excursion ship in the Chicago River, 24 Jul. 1915, with an officially reported loss of 812 lives, unofficially stated to be a loss of 1,100 lives. [10761

SPENCER M. BOWER. Great Lakes fisheries [1920-47]. Mich. conservation, 19(5):7-10, 25-6 (Sep-Oct 1950). views. [10762

PAUL LINCOLN ADAMS. The Chicago water diversion controversy. Mich. conservation, 28(5):18-21 (Sep-Oct 1959). views. On litigation by Michigan, Ohio, Pennsylvania, New York, Wisconsin, and Minnesota to protect their interest in the waters of the Great Lakes from impairment by Chicago and Illinois, 1922-58. [10763

MILTON P. ADAMS. Water pollution control in the Great Lakes region. Univ. Detroit law jour., 37:96-120 (Oct 1959). notes. Includes an account of the work of State agencies concerned with water pollution in each of the 8 Great Lakes States, 1927-59. [10764

W. F. CARBINE. One answer for a fishery. Mich. conservation, 29(4): 25-7 (Jul-Aug). views. On trawling in the Great Lakes, 1930-60. [10765

THE MISSISSIPPI VALLEY

GEORGE K. NEUMANN. Origins of the Indians of the middle Mississippi area. Ind. Acad. Science, Proc., 69: 66-8. [10766

SIDNEY SNOOK. Echoes on the river. Midw. folklore, 10:70-78 (summer). On the names of the steamboats "which once traveled America's western rivers," and the tall tales and other lore associated with the boats. [10767

VIRGINIA SPENCER COWLES. The great swindle: the story of the South Sea bubble. N.Y.: Harper [1960]. 191 p. ports. Includes slight reference to plans of the Mississippi Company (in association with the South Sea Company) for heavy investment in the development of trade and colonies in the Mississippi Valley, 1717-20. [10768

OTTO HAGERMAN. Tales from geode land. Mineralogist, 28:51-3 (Apr-May). Lore and anecdotes about the finding of geodes along the Fox River in Missouri and the Des Moines in Iowa since ca. 1800. [10769

CECIL C. HUMPHREYS. The formation of Reelfoot Lake and consequent land and social problems. West Tenn. Hist. Soc. papers, 14:32-73. On the New Madrid earthquake of 1811, which changed the course of the Mississippi and formed the lake and surrounding swamps, the hunting and fishing there after white settlement began in 1819, the frustrated efforts of James C. Harris to get possession of the lake and drain it, the monopoly of control established by the West Tennessee Land Company, the secret campaign of intimidation and murder against it by the Night Riders, the acquisition or reacquisition of the area by the State through purchase and condemnation in 1914, and its administration by the Tennessee Division of Game and Fish. [10770

LEONARD VICTOR HUBER, comp. Advertisements of lower Mississippi River steamboats, 1812-1920: a scrapbook, with introduction and index of vessels and lines. With a foreword by Frederick Way, Jr. West Barrington, R.I.: Steamship Historical Soc. of America, 1959. xii, 100 p. (Steamship Historical Society of America. Publication 8.) Reproductions of newspaper and other advertisements in alphabetical order by name of boat; and reproductions of a few receipts and other documents. [10771

FRANCES (MILTON) TROLLOPE (1780-1863). Mrs. Trollope's valentine to Cincinnati. Edited by Martha Weber Fligor. Hist. and Philos. Soc. Ohio, Bul., 18:13-18 (Jan). cartoon, port. Letter to Charles Wilkes of New York, dated Cincinnati, 14 Feb. 1828, on the author's prompt disillusionment about Frances Wright's colony of Nashoba (near Memphis) and her decision to settle in Cincinnati with her children, to be joined there by her husband when he could leave England. [10772

WILLIAM JOHN PETERSEN. Rafting on the Mississippi: prologue to prosperity [1833-70]. Ia. jour. hist., 58:289-320 (Oct). facsim., views. notes. Deals particularly with the Iowa lumber trade and with the Mississippi River lumber traffic as observed from Iowa ports. [10773

DWIGHT P. GREEN, SR. Down the Mississippi with Currier & Ives. Westerners brand book (Chicago), 16: 17-19, 22-4 (May 1959). On the colored prints published by N. Currier, 1835-57, and Currier & Ives, 1857-1907; with descriptions of several of their Mississippi River prints in the author's collection. [10774

FRANKLIN JULIUS MEINE. The Mississippi: highway of humor. Westerners brand book (Chicago), 17:17-19, 24 (May). On "frontier fun to be found in newspapers, journals, and almanacs of the days of Mark Twain," 1840s-70s; with examples. [10775

GAIL BORDEN (1801-74). Trips up the River: 1855 and 1857. Edited by Joe B. Frantz. La. hist., 1:147-52 (spring). notes. Excerpts from 3 letters to John P. Cole, describing the author's journeys by steamer from New Orleans to Cairo. [10776

GEORGE WESLEY SIEBER. Sawmilling on the Mississippi: the W. J. Young Lumber Company, 1858-1900. Ann Arbor: University Microfilms, 1960. Positive microfilm of typescript. [636] leaves. Thesis--State Univ. of Iowa. Abstracted: Dissert. abstracts, 20:4645-6 (Jun). On an enterprise with headquarters at Clinton, Ia., and after 1871 a connection with the Mississippi River Logging Company. [10777

ROBERT CHASE TOOLE. Behind the lines: La Crosse Packet Company during the Civil War [operating between Rock Island and St. Paul, 1861-66]. Bus. hist. rev., 34:170-93 (summer). map, tables, views. notes. [10778

JULIAN LEE RAYFORD. The Mississippi River leadline chant. Am. book collector, 10(10):6-8 (Jun). Recollections of hearing the chant on the Mississippi in 1946 and of receiving instruction as to its meaning from professional masters and pilots. [10779

The Ohio Valley

HARRIETTE LOUISA (SIMPSON) ARNOW. Seedtime on the Cumberland. N.Y.: Macmillan, 1960. xviii, [2], 449 p. maps (part double). bibliog. (p. xv-xviii), notes. Effort, by a native of Wayne County, Ky., "to re-create a few of the more important aspects of pioneer life as it was lived on the Cumberland by ordinary men and women"; with some account of the geology and geography and of the prehistoric Indians of the Cumberland Valley of Kentucky and Tennessee. Includes chapters on the first explorers and settlers, the historic Indians, "the Shirttail Men," the travelers, the woodsmen, "the bare essentials," "Silk handkerchiefs and feather beds," and "Around the family hearth." [10780

EDWIN WILLIAM HYDE. Mid-Ohio Valley paleo-Indian and suggested sequence of the fluted point cultures. [Moundsville?] West Virginia Archeological Soc., 1960. [6], 48 p. diagrs., maps, tables, views. (West Virginia Archeological Society, Publication series, 5.) On archeological discoveries in the area of Parkersburg, Marietta, and Blennerhassett Island. [10781

JAMES H. KELLAR. The C. L. Lewis Stone Mound and the stone mound problem. Indianapolis: Indiana Historical Soc., 1960. [4], 357-481 p. diagrs., map, plan, tables (1 double), views. bibliog. (p. 465-74). (Indiana Historical Society. Prehistory research series, v. 3, no. 4.) Based on thesis--Indiana Univ., 1956. On "the low slab burial mounds that formerly were frequent on the hilltops in southeastern Indiana," the author's study of a mound in Shelby County (1951-52) consisting of layers separated and lined with slabs of stone and containing calcined or partly calcined skeletal remains, and the puzzling mortuary customs implied by the structure and contents of this and other "stone mounds" in the eastern United States, particularly the central Ohio Valley. [10782

WILLIAM SNYDER WEBB. Archaic people of the shell middens [in the Ohio Valley from "some 6000 B.C." to ca. 1500 B.C.]. Ohio archaeol., 10: 77-8 (Jul). port. [10783

AUGUST CARL MAHR. Shawnee names and migrations in Kentucky and West Virginia. Ohio jour. science, 60: 155-64 (May). double map. bibliog. Deduction from scanty linguistic evidence that in the early 17th century the Eastern Shawnees were on the Savannah River and the Western Shawnees on the Cumberland in Kentucky and Tennessee; that between

1720 and 1749 the Western Shawnees moved east as far as the Beaver River and the Great Kanawha River, reversing a migration they had made ca. 1600; and that in the process they met and mingled with the Eastern Shawnees, who had begun to migrate to Pennsylvania as early as 1707. [10784

LLOYD ARNOLD BROWN. Early map makers of the Ohio Valley [mainly in the 18th century]. West. Pa. hist. mag., 43:239-50 (Sep). [10785

IRWIN S. RHODES. John Marshall [1755-1835] and the Western country, early days. Hist. and Philos. Soc. Ohio, Bul., 18:116-36 (Apr). facsim., port., views. notes. On his holdings of land in Kentucky, his relatives there, and the Kentucky and Ohio cases that came before him as a judge. [10786

JACOB PARKHURST (born 1772). Sketches of the life and adventures of Jacob Parkhurst. Written with his own hand when about three score and ten years of age ... Adding a few facts to the many accorded instances of the sufferings of the early pioneers along the Ohio River. [Third edition. Sherman Oaks, Calif., 1957. 4], 109, [2] leaves. maps, port., geneal. tables, views. 1st ed. 1842. On his early life in Washington County, Pa., his removal to Trumble (i.e., Trumbull) County, Ohio, in 1802, and his later years in Fayette and Henry Counties, Ind. Contains little information about his activities after 1793 other than his religious experiences. [10787

RAY H. SANDEFUR. Logan's oration--how authentic? Quar. jour. speech, 46:289-96 (Oct). notes. On a speech supposed to have been made by "the Mingo Indian Chief John Logan" in Ohio near the Ohio River, 1774, published in 2 newspaper versions in 1775 and in a third version in Jefferson's Notes on the State of Virginia (1784). [10788

CHAUNCEY DEPEW LEAKE. Daniel Drake (1785-1852), persevering idealist. Jour. med. educ., 34:561-70 (Jun 1959). port. bibliog. On his early life in Kentucky, his medical studies at the University of Pennsylvania, his medical practice in Cincinnati, his teaching of medicine at the Medical College of Ohio, the Louisville Medical College, and the Transylvania Medical School, and his medical writings. [10789

ROBERT ALEXANDER HARPER. River junction communities of the lower Ohio Valley--a study of functional change. Jour. geog., 59:364-70 (Nov). map, table. Study of Mt. Vernon, Ind., Uniontown, Smithland, and Paducah, Ky., and Cairo, Ill., 1800-1960. [10790

JOHN STOUGH (1762-1845). The diaries of John Stough, 1806-1807. [Translated and edited] by Theodore G. Tappert. Luth. quar., 12:44-50 (Feb). "Extracts from my diaries as traveling preacher," 18 Jun. 1806 - 17 Mar. 1807, signed: Johannes Stauch, recording 5 journeys from Washington, Pa., to congregations of German families in western Pennsylvania, West Virginia, and eastern Ohio. [10791

STERLING NORTH. Lincoln's boyhood [in Kentucky and Indiana, 1809-19]. Ralph G. Newman, ed., Lincoln for the ages (Garden City, N.Y.: Doubleday, 1960), p. 48-52. [10792

ROBERT GERALD McMURTRY. The world of Tom and Nancy Lincoln. Ralph G. Newman, ed., Lincoln for the ages (Garden City, N.Y.: Doubleday, 1960), p. 43-7. On the marriage of Thomas Lincoln (1778-1851) and Nancy Hanks (1784-1818), and their life in Kentucky and Indiana, 1816-18. [10793

JAMES A. TAGUE. William D[avis] Gallagher [1808-94], champion of Western literary periodicals. Ohio hist. quar., 69:257-71 (Jul). notes. On his work as an editor of newspapers and magazines, 1826-50, particularly the Cincinnati mirror (1831-36), the Western literary journal and monthly review (Cincinnati, 1836), the Western monthly magazine and literary journal (Louisville, 1837), and the Hesperian (Columbus and Cincinnati, 1838-39).

Mrs. ROBERT RUNYAN. If this boulder could talk: legends of Presidents. By Mrs. Robert Runyan as related by James Wade Emison. Filson Club hist. quar., 34:319-22 (Oct). On the courtship of Sarah Knox Taylor, daughter of Zachary Taylor, by Jefferson Davis, their secret meetings in Louisville and Vincennes, and their marriage in 1835; with mention of a granite boulder near Vincennes, "used originally as a step to mount horses" and probably used for this purpose by Miss Taylor. [10795

JESSIE JANE (HUSSEY) CHILDERS CASKEY (born 1875). Journalizing Jane: the autobiography of Jessie Jane Caskey. N.Y.: Exposition Press [1960]. 143 p. On the author's early life in Cincinnati and elsewhere, her marriage to Hugh Childers, her life with him in Georgetown and Lebanon, Ky., their divorce, her marriage to Charles Caskey, and their life in Kentucky; with details in their lives of dozens of her relatives. [10796

SIDNEY SNOOK. River songs bring memories. Music jour., 18(1):38, 74-5 (Jan). On riverboat songs of the Ohio, collected by Mary Guthrie Wheeler (born 1892) of Paducah, Ky. [10797

THOMAS FRANK BARTON. The sewer or waste disposal use of the Ohio River. Jour. geog., 49:326-36 (Oct). notes. On La Belle Rivière, which in the 18th century was "one of the most beautiful rivers in North America" and since 1900 has become so polluted by human, industrial, and mining wastes that it has lost most of its "ability for self-purification"; and the efforts of the Ohio River Valley Water Sanitation Commission, established by a compact of 8 States in 1948, to solve the resulting problems. [10798

JEAN B. HESS. Twenty-five years ago. Steamboat bill, 17:7-10 (spring). views. Memories of an excursion on the steamboat Gordon C. Greene from Pittsburgh to Cincinnati and back to Pittsburgh, with included sightseeing in both cities, Jul. 1935. [10799

The Tennessee Valley

WILLIAM HORD NICHOLLS. Factors affecting gross farm income per worker, upper east Tennessee Valley, 1899-1954. Jour. farm econ., 42: 356-62 (May). table. notes. [10800

RICHARD KILBOURNE. Watershed improvement in the Tennessee Valley [1934-60]. Jour. forestry, 58:294-6 (Apr). [10801

H. A. SMITH. The Chestuee project. Am. forests, 62(6):24-6, 48-9 (Jun 1956). col. map, views. On the Chestuee Creek Watershed of the Tennessee Valley Authority, in Monroe, McMinn, and Polk Counties, Tenn., ca. 1940 to 1956, and the treatment of the area to prevent further erosion and flooding and to restore part of it to forest. [10802

The Missouri Valley

ROBERT G. ATHEARN. High country empire: the High Plains and Rockies [1732-1957]. N.Y.: McGraw-Hill [1960]. viii, [2], 358 p. maps, ports., views (part double). bibliog. (p. 335-52), notes. On the upper part of "the great Missouri River drainage," comprising all or part of Kansas, Nebraska, the Dakotas, Colorado, Wyoming, and Montana, as an area subject to "exploitation and experimentation carried on by remote control from the more settled parts of the country" through the agency of "the mountain men ... the miner, the cattleman, the land speculator, the timber baron, and the oil wildcatter." [10803

JOHN EDWIN MILLS. Historic sites archeology in the Fort Randall Reservoir, South Dakota. U.S., Bureau of American Ethnology, River Basin Surveys, River Basin Surveys papers, nos. 15-20, ed. Frank H. H. Roberts, Jr. (Wash.: U.S. Govt. Print. Off., 1960 [U.S., Bureau of American Ethnology, Bulletin 176]), p. 25.48). map, plans, views. bibliog. (p. 47-8), notes. Written in 1953. Report on work at Fort Randall (occupied by the Army 1856-92), Whetstone Indian Agency and Army Post (1858-72), Lower Brulé Indian Agency (1868-92), Fort Lower Brulé (1870 ff.), Fort Lookout Military and Trading Pots, Fort Hale, and Fort Recovery. [10804

EXPLORER Clark's field notes presented to Yale Library. Manscripts, 12(1):55-8 (winter). On notes kept by William Clark on the Lewis and Clark Expedition, 1803-4, recording the movement of the expedition up the Missouri to Fort Mandan, N.D., discovered in private possession in 1952, claimed by the U.S. Government as Federal property, determined in court action to be private property, and acquired by Yale University. [10805

G. HUBERT SMITH. Fort Pierre II (39ST217), a historic trading post in the Oahe Dam area, South Dakota. U.S., Bureau of American Ethnology, River Basin Surveys, River Basin Surveys papers, nos. 15-20, ed. Frank H. H. Roberts, Jr. (Wash.: U.S. Govt. Print. Off., 1960 [U.S., Bureau of American Ethnology, Bulletin 176]), p. 83-158. fold. maps, views. bibliog. (p. 155-8). On a post "constructed after 1855" by P. Chouteau, Jr., and Company and abandoned perhaps in 1866, and the building remains and artifacts found at its site; with some account of other posts in the vicinity, occupied between ca. 1817 and ca. 1866. [10806

CARL F. MILLER. The excavation and investigation of Fort Lookout Trading Post II (39LM57) in the Fort Randall Reservoir, South Dakota. U.S., Bureau of American Ethnology, River Basin Surveys, River Basin Surveys papers, nos. 15-20, ed. Frank H. H. Roberts, Jr. (Wash.: U.S. Govt. Print. Off., 1960 [U.S., Bureau of American Ethnology, Bulletin 176]), p. 49-82. diagrs., map, plans, views. bibliog. (p. 81-2). Written in 1953. On building remains, beads, pipes, china and earthenware, glass, buttons, pins, and metal articles excavated at a site "probably established in 1831 by the French Fur Trading Co. and subsequently occupied, 1840-51, by the trader La Barge." [10807

LOUIS GEORGE JOHNSON. Floods and flood control in the Missouri River Basin [since 1832]. Ann Arbor: University Microfilms, 1959 [i.e. 1960]. Positive microfilm of typescript. [366] leaves. Thesis--Univ. of Missouri. Abstracted: Dissert. abstracts, 20:3701 (Mar). [10808

JOHN E. PARSONS. Steamboats in the "Idaho" gold rush. Montana, 10(1): 51-61 (Jan). facsims., map, ports., views. notes. On the steamers of the Idaho Steam Packet Company and 3 other lines navigating the Missouri River as far upstream as Fort Benton, bringing miners and supplies, 1864-68. [10809

RALPH CHESTER HENRY. The gold ship. By Eric Thane [pseud.] Frontier times, 34(3):15, 58 (summer). facsim., view. On the voyage of the Luella, with gold worth $1,250,000 on board, from Fort Benton, Mont., to St. Louis, "sailing through more sand, more Indians, more buffalo and less water than any other Missouri steamer before or since," Sep.-Oct. 1866. [10810

MERRILL J. MATTES. Historic sites archeology on the Upper Missouri. U.S., Bureau of American Ethnology, River Basin Surveys, River Basin Surveys papers, nos. 15-20, ed. Frank H. H. Roberts (Wash.: U.S. Govt. Print. Off., 1960 [U.S., Bureau of American Ethnology, Bulletin 176]), p. 1-23. bibliog. (p. 20-23). Written in 1954. On the program of the Smithsonian Institution and the National Park Service to survey and salvage historic sites on the Missouri River "threatened or doomed by the prospect of inundation," especially in the Dakotas, and the work accomplished between 1950 and 1954. [10811

THE GREAT PLAINS

MORRIS E. GARNSEY. The Great Plains as a region. West. humanities rev., 14:61-8 (winter). [10812

ALICE B. KEHOE. Ceramic affiliations in the northwestern Plains ["roughly, the High Plains north of the 45th parallel and west of the 101st meridian"]. Am. antiq., 25:237-46 (Oct 1959). maps. bibliog. [10813

WILLIAM J. MAYER-OAKES. The Plains Archaic concept. International Congress of Anthropological and Ethnological Sciences, 5th, 1956, Men and cultures: selected papers, ed. Anthony F. C. Wallace (Phila.: Univ. of Pennsylvania Press [1960]), p. 580-87. bibliog. On a preceramic "basic hunting-gathering economy" as a "cultural unit of historical continuity over a period of perhaps 4-5000 years within the Plains and Prairies geographic areas ... near the close of the Pleistocene." [10814

WILLIAM THOMAS MULLOY. Late prehistoric stone circles [especially in Wyoming and Montana]. Southw. lore, 25(4):1-3 (Mar). [10815

ELIAS HOWARD SELLARDS & GLEN L. EVANS. The Paleo-Indian culture succession in the central high plains of Texas and New Mexico. International Congress of Anthropological and Ethnological Sciences, 5th, 1956, Men and cultures: selected papers, ed. Anthony F. C. Wallace (Phila.: Univ. of Pennsylvania Press [1960]), p. 639-47. diagr., map, views. bibliog., notes. [10816

L. C. STEEGE. Clovis points. Ann. Wyo., 32:124-6 (Apr). views. On stone arrows of the Great Plains from New Mexico to Canada, sometimes found in association with bones of mammoths, tapirs, and an extinct species of horse, in use ca. 11,000 years ago, and evidently earlier than the "Folsom" points. [10817

BERTEN WENDELL ALLRED. Historical highlights of grazing in the central and southern Great Plains [1540-1960]. Jour. range management, 13:135-8 (May). table. [10818

JAMES HENRI HOWARD. The cultural position of the Dakota: a reassessment. Gertrude E. Dole & Robert L. Carneiro, eds., Essays in the science of culture, in honor of Leslie A. White (N.Y.: Crowell [1960]), p. 249-68. bibliog., notes. On the Santee (Eastern Dakota), Wičiyela (Middle Dakota), and Teton (Western Dakota) "subcultures of ... the Dakota or Sioux" Indians in Minnesota, Iowa, Nebraska, the Dakotas, Colorado, Wyoming, Montana, and Canada, 17th-20th centuries. [10819

JAMES FRANK DOBIE. Comanches and their horses [1774-1867]. Frontier times, 34(2):32-3, 45-6 (spring). [10820

DONALD EMMET WORCESTER. Wild horses West: fact and fancy. Ariz. and the West, 2:140-46 (summer). On "the many layers of myth and legend which surround" the "famous mustang of the Great Plains," properly regarded as "an ordinary horse of unusual hardiness," 1798-1830s. [10821

GEORGE BIRD GRINNELL (1849-1938). The Cheyenne Indians. Margaret Mead & Ruth L. Bunzel, eds., The golden age of American anthropology (N.Y.: George Braziller, 1960), p. 139-50. From the author's book of the same title (1923), on the Plains Indians, particularly the Cheyennes, in the 19th century and later; with an appendix (p. 148-50), "The disappearance of the buffalo," from his Blackfoot lodge tales: the story of a prairie people (1903). [10822

HENRY WEBER CASPER. History of the Catholic Church in Nebraska: the Church on the Northern Plains, 1838-1874. Milwaukee: Catholic Life Publications, 1960. xx, 344 p. facsim., ports., views. Deals with "the origins of the Catholic Church not only in Nebraska but in the northern plains states which were comprised in the original Vicariate of Nebraska." To be continued in later volumes. [10823

EDWARD ADAMSON HOEBEL. The Cheyennes: Indians of the Great Plains [1840-1936]. N.Y.: Holt [1960]. vii, 103 p. map, ports., views. bibliog. (p. 100-103). (Case studies in cultural anthropology.) Based in part upon field studies by the author among the Northern Cheyennes, 1935-36. On their ceremonies, social organizations, subsistence, warfare, "World view and religion," and "Personality and culture." [10824

FRANK MARION KING. Correcting the record. Westerners brand book (N.Y.), 5 (1959): 73, 75-6. port. Communication to an unnamed person, "early 1930s," referring to the writer's experience as a cowboy (beginning in 1877) and correcting published misstatements about the Chisholm Trail and particularly about his mother's uncle, Jess Chisholm (who drove his first herd in Texas in 1843), and the latter's cousin, John S. Chisum (died 1844), Texas and New Mexico cattleman. [10825

ELLA M. ROBINSON. The Daugherty Ranch, Creek Nation. Chron. Okla., 38:75-7 (spring). On James Monroe Daugherty (born 1850 in Texas) and his cattle ranches in Oklahoma (1885-1906) and Texas (1866 till 1937 or later). [10826

TONY SLAUGHTER. The Waggoner 3-D brand. Quarter horse jour., 6(7): 10-11, 36 (Apr 1954). ports., views. On a ranch of "something like 750,000 acres" in several counties of Texas, New Mexico, and Oklahoma, acquired since "the late 1850's" by Dan Waggoner and his descendants, consisting of "vast pastures ... not only saturated with cattle and horses but with oil." Deals particularly with the raising of quarter horses and Hereford cattle by Tom Waggoner and his sons. [10827

GEORGE BLUESTONE. The changing cowboy: from dime novel to dollar film [1860-1960]. West. humanities rev., 14:331-7 (summer). [10828

WILLIAM MINER RICHARDS. Hitherto unknown Pony Express riders. Am. philatelist, 73:901-2 (Sep). Letter to Pony Express Celebration Committee, San Francisco, dated Susanville, Calif., 1 Sep. 1923, on the author's short experience as a Pony Express rider in 1860, the route followed between St. Joseph and Cheyenne, and some of the riders on this part of the route. [10829

WESLEY ROBERT HURT, JR. The Yankton Dakota Church: a nationalistic movement of Northern Plains Indians [1955-60]. Gertrude E. Dole & Robert L. Carneiro, eds., Essays in the science of culture, in honor of Leslie A. White (N.Y.: Crowell [1960]), p. 269-87. bibliog. Includes accounts of "other nationalistic Northern Plains churches" since 1862 and of other "recent Pan-Indian movements." [10830

J. T. BOND (1866-1947). Tom Bond: bronc-buster, cow-poke, and trail driver. [Edited] by Josie Baird. Sweetwater, Tex.: Watson-Focht Co. [1960]. x, 135 p. ports. Reminiscences reprinted from the Jayton chronicle (Jayton, Tex.) and supplemented by information from the editor's interviews, concerning the author's early life in Williamson and Burnett Counties, Tex., his work as a cowboy in Texas, New Mexico, and Oklahoma, and his settlement as a rancher near Ninnekah, Okla., and in 1905 near Jayton, Tex. [10831

CHARLES MOREAU HARGER (born 1863). Cattle-trails of the prairies. Everett Rich, ed., The heritage of Kansas (Lawrence: Univ. of Kansas Press, 1960), p. 183-96. From Scribner's magazine, Jun. 1892. On cattle drives from Texas to Kansas, 1866-91. [10832

ERNEST MORE FLETCHER (1867-1941). The wayward horseman. ... Edited by Forbes Parkhill. Denver: Sage Books [1958]. 217 p. ports., views. On the author's early life; his wanderings as a cowboy in Texas, Colorado, Kansas, and Nebraska; his theft of horses and cattle; his 5-year imprisonment in the penitentiary at Canon City, Colo.; his life as a homesteader in Yuma County, Colo.; his 2 marriages; and his removal from his farm to the town of Yuma, Colo. Includes ballads about Sam Bass and "Crossing the Plains", and long accounts of his stay in the penitentiary and the capricious conduct of his first wife, Lillian E. Bagbee. [10833

JOE SANDERS. The Abilene promoter. Cattleman, 46(9):19, 30, 33 (Feb). On the purchase of Abilene, Kan. (15 buildings and adjacent land), by Joseph Geating McCoy, his establishment of facilities for shipping cattle by railroad to Eastern markets, his marking of a trail for cattle from Corpus Christi to Kansas, and his victory over many difficulties in the marketing of Texas cattle by way of Kansas, 1867-68. [10834

JAMES SANKS BRISBIN (1837-92). The beef bonanza; or, How to get rich on the Plains, being a description of cattle-growing, sheep-farming, horse-raising, and dairying in the West. ... With a foreword by Gilbert C. Fite. [New edition.] Norman: Univ. of Oklahoma Press [1959]. xvii, 208 p. views. (The Western frontier library, 13.) 1st ed. 1881. Based upon observations made by the author, an officer of the Second Cavalry, since 1868. On livestock industries of the Great Plains, and the high profits to be expected in Montana and Colorado. Includes lists of ranchers, and several letters from cattlemen and others. [10835

FRED GROVE. Plains Indian humor [1870s ff.]. Cattleman, 46(9):21, 34 (Feb). [10836

"SODDIES." Hist. preservation, 12: 140-41. views. On the sod houses of the Great Plains, most of which were built in the 1870s and 1880s, of which probably only 11 survive. [10837

ROBERT F. SCOTT. The red buffalo. Frontier times, 34(4):14-15, 46 (fall). On prairie fires of the Great Plains, 1872-94. [10838

HARRY H. ANDERSON. Cheyennes at the Little Big Horn--a study of statistics. N.D. hist., 27:81-93 (spring). notes. Effort to estimate "the total population of the Northern Cheyenne tribe" in the years 1874-77. [10839

JOSEPH A. DACUS. The Comanches: an ethnological sketch. Mo. Hist. Soc., Bul., 16:333-41 (Jul). From Ware's Valley monthly (St. Louis), May 1875. On the customs and traditions of these Indians at the time of writing. [10840

KANSAS PACIFIC RAILWAY COMPANY. Guide map of the best and shortest cattle trail to the Kansas Pacific Railway; with a concise and accurate description of the route, showing distances, streams, crossings, camping grounds, wood and water, supply stores, etc., from the Red River Crossing to Ellis, Russell, Ellsworth, Brookville, Salina, Solomon, and Abilene. [Kansas City, Mo., 1875.] Pecos, Tex.: Bill Leftwich, c1958. 21 p. fold. col. map. Shows routes of cattle trails originating on the Texas coast or at various points in central and southwestern Texas, converging at Red River Station; the "Ellsworth Cattle Trail" from that point through Indian Territory to the railroad in Kansas; and a trail from Fort Sumner, N. M., to the railroad at Las Animas, Colo. [10841

JOHN JOHNSON (born 1864). The Southwest's greatest tracker. [Recorded] by Florence Fenley. Frontier times, 34(2):18-19, 50-52 (spring). port. Recollections by a former slave of his experience as a cattle-driver between Texas and Nebraska, 1877-85, and as a hunter of wild cattle in Texas. [10842

FLOYD C. BARD (born 1879). Horse wrangler: sixty years in the saddle in Wyoming and Montana. By Floyd C. Bard as told to Agnes Wright Srping. Norman: Univ. of Oklahoma Press [1960]. xi, 296 p. diagrs., map, ports., views. Reminiscences of the author's early life on ranches near Cheyenne and Buffalo, Wyo., his work as a cowboy in Wyoming, Montana, and Canada, his ranch at Mead Creek, Wyo., his work as a horse dealer in Nebraska, and his employment as foreman of a ranch near Sheridan, Wyo., 1879-1918. [10843

MARY EINSEL. Some notes on the Comanche Cattle Pool. Kan. hist. quar., 26:59-66 (spring). ports. notes. On an organization of cattlemen in Barber and Comanche Counties, Kan., and the Cherokee Strip, 1880-86. [10844

JAMES ELMER ROWAN. Agricultural land utilization in the Llano Estacado of eastern New Mexico and western Texas [since 1885]. Ann Arbor: University Microfilms, 1960. Positive microfilm of typescript. [303] leaves. Thesis--Univ. of Nebraska. Abstracted: Dissert. abstracts, 20:4365 (May). [10845

JOHN A. BROWN. In re Charles A. Siringo. Westerners brand book (Chicago), 16:89-91 (Feb). On his employment as an agent of the Pinkerton National Detective Agency, 1886-1908, under written contract not to disclose "any information secured by him as a part of his employment" without permission of the agency, and the action of Brown, as attorney for the agency, in obtaining injunctions against publication of the original versions of Siringo's A cowboy detective (1912) and Riata and spurs (1927), which contained information violating the contract. [10846

J. J. BALLARD. I rode the cattle trails. Frontier times, 34(1):28-9, 34 (winter). views. Recollections of cattle drives between Texas and North Dakota, 1891. [10847

FANNIE L. (GOPFERT) EISELE (born 1884). We came to live in Oklahoma Territory. Chron. Okla., 38:55-65 (spring). ports., views. notes. On the life of the author in Beattie, Kan., 1891-94, and in Garfield County, Okla., 1894-1959 (with intervals on homesteaded land in the Panhandle), and her marriage to Ernest John Eisele in 1909. [10848

HENRY C. HARDING. Trail trouble. ... As told to Guy Harding Goodman and Wilda Warren. Cattleman, 46(8):29, 58, 60, 62, 64, 66 (Jan). From the author's Tales of the range. Recollections of driving a herd of 2,000 or 3,000 cattle, with the help of "eight hands," from Eddy County, N.M., to summer pasturage in Indian Territory near Minco, Mar.-Jun. 1891, and the complications introduced by Indians, sandstorms, and floods. [10849

JAMES MOONEY (1861-1921). The ghost-dance religion [and the Sioux outbreak of 1890]. Margaret Mead & Ruth L. Bunzel, eds., The golden age of anthropology (N.Y.: George Braziller, 1960), p. 257-74. First printed in 1896. Based upon observations made by the author in 1891. [10850

WILFRED H. PINE. Land problems of the Great Plains [1898-1957]. Land Economics Institute, University of Illinois, 1958, Modern land policy: papers (Urbana: Univ. of Illinois Press, 1960), p. 359-66. notes. [10851

GEORGE BIRD GRINNELL (1849-1938). Coup and scalp among the Plains Indians. Selected papers from the American anthropologist, 1888-1920, ed. Frederica De Laguna (Evanston, Ill.: Row, Peterson [1960]), p. 650-64. First printed in 1910. On the customs of scalping, "counting coup," and dancing to celebrate these accomplishments among the Cheyenne, Omaha, Sioux, Arapaho, Comanche, Apache, Kiowa, and Blackfeet Indians. Based largely upon observations by the author. [10852

ROBERT HARRY LOWIE (1883-1957). Some cases of repeated reproduction. Lowie's selected papers in anthropology, ed. Cora Du Bois (Berkeley: Univ. of California Press, 1960), p. 143-53. notes. First printed in 1942. On variations in North American Indian tales when a single teller tells a tale 2 or more times; with particular accounts of Crow and Hidatsa tales collected by the author from oral sources, 1910-31. [10853

ROBERT HARRY LOWIE (1883-1957). The kinship systems of the Crow and Hidatsa [in Montana and North Dakota]. Lowie's selected papers in anthropology, ed. Cora Du Bois (Berkeley: Univ. of California Press, 1960),

p. 75-81. notes. From the Proceedings (1917) of the 19th International Congress of Americanists, 1915. [10854

ROBERT HARRY LOWIE (1883-1957). A note on aesthetics. Lowie's selected papers in anthropology, ed. Cora Du Bois (Berkeley: Univ. of California Press, 1960), p. 137-42. tables. notes. From American anthropologist, Apr.-Jun. 1921. Comparison of the decorations on Crow and Shoshoni parfleches (rawhide bags). [10855

LESLIE SPIER (1893-1961). The sun dance of the Plains Indians: comparison with the tribal ceremonial system. Margaret Mead & Ruth L. Bunzel, eds., The golden age of American anthropology (N.Y.: George Braziller, 1960), p. 392-7. notes. First printed in 1921. On the sun dances of the Blackfoot, Crow, and Arapaho Indians. [10856

ROBERT HARRY LOWIE (1883-1957). Incorporeal property in primitive society. Lowie's selected papers in anthropology, ed. Cora Du Bois (Berkeley: Univ. of California Press, 1960), p. 225-39. notes. From Yale law journal, Mar. 1928. Includes some account of the "reality of incorporeal ownership" among the Omaha, Pawnee, Blackfoot, and Crow Indians of the Great Plains. [10857

ROBERT HARRY LOWIE (1883-1957). The Omaha and Crow kinship terminologies. Lowie's selected papers in anthropology, ed. Cora Du Bois (Berkeley: Univ. of California Press, 1960), p. 100-110. From the Verhandlungen (1934) of the 24th International Congress of Americanists, 1930. [10858

EDWARD EVERETT DALE. The cow country in transition. Everett Rich, ed., The heritage of Kansas: selected commentaries on past times (Lawrence: Univ. of Kansas Press, 1960), p. 196-212. First printed 1937. On the change in the Great Plains from a cattle-raising to a crop-raising economy, from a society of cowboys to a society of farmers. [10859

The West

SETH THOMAS BAILEY. Looking for a lost mine? By Tom Bailey. True West, 7(3):12-14, 48-50 (Jan-Feb). cartoon. Effort to describe "all the best-known" lost mines and to determine "which ones actually were lost and which ones are pure legend." [10860

ROBERT E. BELL. Relationships between the Caddoan area and the Plains. Tex. Archeol. Soc., Bul., 31:53-64. bibliogs. Includes discussion by David A. Baerreis, Marvin F. Kivett, and Robert L. Stephenson. [10861

WILLIAM ARTHUR BERG. Mysterious horses of western North America [since prehistoric times]. N.Y.: Pageant Press [1960]. 298 p. col. maps. Mainly on Appaloosa and Pinto horses. Includes lore about Sacajawea, Captain Bonneville, and other Western characters. [10862

CHARLES DEAN MILLER. The ghost town directory, by Karl von Muller [pseud.]: a comprehensive guide and directory to abandoned and deserted settlements, old townsites of historical significance, and old cow, lumber, and mining camps in the twenty-two States of the United States west of the Mississippi River. Beverly Hills, Calif.: Associated Geographers of America [1959. 4], 65 p. [10863

JOHN MYERS MYERS. For an enlarged Western pantheon. Westerners brand book (N.Y.), 7:10-11. On Jack Swilling, Ned McGowan, and Charles D. Poston as examples of "distinguished exiles from common knowledge" who ought to be even better known than such characters as Sam Bass. [10864

ELIAS HOWARD SELLARDS. Some early stone artifact developments in North America. Southw. jour. anthropol., 16:160-73 (summer). views. bibliog., notes. Study of 7 sites in Texas, Nevada, southern California, and Mexico. [10865

LAURENCE R. VEYSEY. Myth and reality in approaching American regionalism. Am. quar., 12:31-43 (spring). notes. Mainly on the treatment of the West by Henry Nash Smith and of southern California by Franklin Walker and Carey McWilliams. [10866

WALTER PRESCOTT WEBB (1888-1963). Geographical-historical concepts in American history. Assoc. Am. Geographers, Ann., 50:85-97 (Jun).

maps. On the 17 States properly to be considered the West, definable by "the concept of the great desert, with the plains on the right flank and the Pacific Coast on its left flank." Concludes: "It is the desert that makes the West what it is and keeps it that way." Appended: comments by Lorrin Kennamer, D. W. Meinig, and David H. K. Amiran. [10867

WALTER PRESCOTT WEBB (1888-1963). Three geographical and historical concepts essential to an understanding of the American West. Westerners brand book (Chicago), 16:81-3 (Jan). On the 98th meridian as a border between "the humid woodland and the semi-arid plains," the determination of "the character of the American West ... by the desert at its heart", and the "north-south axis" of "the seventeen western states"; with an argument that the West South Central States and the West North Central States are not part of the West and that the South Central States and the North Central States should not be divided into eastern and western groups. [10868

EARL SPENCER POMEROY. Rediscovering the West. Am. quar., 12: 20-30 (spring). On misconceptions about the motives of the discoverers, settlers, and modern visitors of the West, 16th-20th centuries. [10869

WALTER BROWNLOW POSEY. The challenge of the heroic. Filson Club hist. quar., 34:140-55 (Apr). notes. On the efforts of the churches, especially Presbyterian, Baptist, and Methodist, to equip "the rapidly rising civilization of the West with Christian institutions and ideals ... to smooth rough edges from western civilization and to fit it into softer forms and more refined molds," 1760s-1850s. [10870

WILLIAM C. RATHKE. Chief Waubonsie and the Pottawattamie Indians. Ann. Ia., 35:81-100 (fall 1959). map, port. On the history of these Indians in the area between Ohio at the east and Kansas and Oklahoma at the west since 1763, with particular notice of their stay in Iowa, 1836-46, and their chief Waubonsie. [10871

PHILLIP O. FOSS. Politics and grass: the administration of grazing on the public domain [since 1780]. Seattle: Univ. of Washington Press, 1960. ix, 236 p. tables. bibliog. (p. 227-32), notes (p. 209-25). Deals particularly with the Taylor Grazing Act and its applications (1934-46). [10872

RUSH WELTER. The frontier West as image of American society: conservative attitudes before the Civil War. Miss. Valley hist. rev., 46:593-614 (Mar). notes. Evidence, 1790s-1850s, that "Within two generations after the founding of the Republic ... eastern conservatives were apparently ready to embrace a West they had begun by rejecting," and that they "identified themselves with their emigrant countrymen's achievements in the West." [10873

CARL EDWARD SKEEN. Jefferson and the West [particularly the Ohio Valley], 1798-1808. Columbus: Ohio State Museum, 1960. [3], 54 leaves. bibliog. (leaves 52-4), notes. (Ohio. Anthony Wayne Parkway Board. Papers on the War of 1812 in the Northwest, 7.) Thesis (M. A.)--Ohio State Univ. [10874

DOYCE BLACKMAN NUNIS, JR. Tarascon's dream of an American commercial empire in the West. Mid-America, 42:170-84 (Jul). notes. On the plans of Louis Anastasius Tarascon (born 1759), French emigrant, Philadelphia merchant, to send "fully rigged ships, built in Pittsburgh," down the Ohio and the Mississippi and to foreign ports and thence to Philadelphia, 1799-1806; his removal to Shippingport as a more suitable location for building larger ships; his An address on trade with the Western country (1806), written in collaboration with James Berthoud; his bankruptcy; and his later advocacy of Federal wagon roads west to the Pacific (especially in pamphlets published in 1836 and 1837); with excerpts from his publications. [10875

MYRA COOLEY. Meet me on the green: the saga of beads and buckskin--historical incidents of the early West [19th century]. N.Y.: William-Frederick Press, 1960. [6], 240 p. Miscellany. [10876

WILLIAM H. GOETZMANN. The West and the American age of exploration. Ariz. and the West, 2:265-78 (autumn). notes. On "the history of exploration in the American West as part of the general history of American and European culture between the years 1800 and 1860" and, thus regarded, as an antidote to the "the old Turnerean tyranny." [10877

MERIWETHER LEWIS (1774-1809) & WILLIAM CLARK (1770-1838). The Lewis and Clark Expedition [1804-6]. Margaret Mead & Ruth L. Bunzel, eds., The golden age of American anthropology (N.Y.: George Braziller, 1960), p. 35-43. Selections relating to the Shoshone, Chinook, and Columbia River Indians, Indian canoes, and the position of women and old people among the Indians. [10878

CARL PARCHER RUSSELL. The guns of the Lewis and Clark Expedition [1804-6]. N. D. hist., 27:25-34 (Jan). views. bibliog., notes. [10879

WENDELL GEORGE SWANK. Progress report on a native animal. Natural hist., 69(7):40-45 (Aug-Sep). views (1 double). On the reduction of the population of pronghorn antelopes from 20 or 40 million in 1806 to ca. 17,000 in 1907, and subsequent measures for protection of the survivors, especially in Arizona. [10880

DOYCE BLACKMAN NUNIS, JR. Andrew [Whitley] Sublette, Rocky Mountain prince, 1808-1853. Los Angeles: Dawson's Book Shop, 1960. [14], 123, [1] p. port., view. notes. On his early life in Kentucky, his work as a trapper and trader in the Rocky Mountains, his service in the Mexican War and later as an Army guide in the West, his work as a guide of wagon trains from Missouri to California, his experience as a miner and a peace officer, and his death in a conflict with a bear. [10881

EDWIN RALPH BINGHAM, ed. The fur trade in the West, 1815-1856: selected source materials for college research papers. Boston: Heath [1960. 12], 116 p. double map. bibliog. (p. 114-16), notes. Excerpts from 11 printed primary sources. [10882

STEPHEN FULLER AUSTIN (1793-1836). Stephen F. Austin's oration of July 4, 1818: early commentary on the American frontier. Edited by Leo M. Kaiser. Southw. hist. quar., 64:71-9 (Jul). notes. From the only known copy of the Missouri gazette and public advertiser, St. Louis, for 24 Jul. 1818, from which the concluding part of the text has been cut out. Speech delivered at Potosi, Mo., on "the probable rise and improvement of that vast tract of country" from the Great Lakes to the Pacific, the peculiar appropriateness of the American spirit to effect "this herculian work," and the prospect of liberating "the enslaved colonies of Spain" and awakening their inhabitants "from the stupor of slaves to the energy of freemen, from the degradation of vassals to the dignity of sovereigns." [10883

HAROLD McCRACKEN. Our Western documentarians. Am. artist, 24(3): 22-7, 64-7 (Mar). ports., views. On "documentary artists" in "the northern plains and the adjoining Rocky Mountain area," attempting "a pictorial record" of Western scenes and characters, 1819-1920s, and the full representation of their work in the Whitney Gallery of Western Art, Cody, Wyo. (opened in 1959). [10884

LE ROY REUBEN HAFEN & ANN (WOODBURY) HAFEN, eds. Handcarts to Zion: the story of a unique Western migration, 1856-1860, with contemporary journals, accounts, reports, and rosters of members of the ten handcart companies. Glendale, Calif.: A. H. Clark Co., 1960. 328 p. map, ports., views. notes. (The Far West and the Rockies historical series, 1820-1875, v. 14.) Account of organized movements of Mormon settlers on foot from Iowa City to Salt Lake City. Appended (p. 199-276): reports and accounts by Daniel D. McArthur, Franklin D. Richards, Daniel Spencer, George D. Grant, Joseph Young, Harvey Cluff, and Millen Atwood; addresses by Brigham Young and Heber C. Kimball; and several "handcart songs." [10885

RAY ALLEN BILLINGTON. "... touched by the wand of savagery." John Arthur Garraty, ed., The unforgettable Americans (Great Neck, N.Y.: Channel Press [1960]), p. 150-54. On "Old Bill" Williams (1787-1849), his early life in North Carolina and Missouri and his work as a trapper in the Rocky Mountains. [10886

RICHARD HOUSEWORTH & WILLIAM ELMORE. "Ride and Kill! Kill! Kill!" Frontier times, 34(2):10-13, 41-3 (spring). ports., views. On the Indian paintings and journals of George Catlin (1796-1872). [10887

HYRUM LESLIE ANDRUS. Joseph Smith and the West. Brigham Young Univ. studies, 2:129-47 (spring-summer). notes. On the "Mormon view of colonizing the West," 1830-49. [10888

RAYMOND W. SETTLE & MARY ANNA (LUND) SETTLE. The early careers of William Bradford Waddell [1807-72] and William Hepburn Russell [1812-72], frontier capitalists.

Kan. hist. quar., 26:355-82 (winter). notes. On their ancestry, their early life in the East, their settlement in Lexington, Mo., their prosperous mercantile enterprises and their business and social relations, their formation of the freighting firm of Waddell, Russell, & Co., Dec. 28, 1854), and the eventual failure of all their enterprises, including the Pony Express. [10889

JANET (SHAW) LECOMPTE. Old Maurice. Westerners brand book (N.Y.), 5:85-7, 91 (1959). On the wandering life of Maurice Le Duc, Jr. (died 1880?), French-Canadian, as a trapper on the upper Missouri and as far west as Nevada, 1832 to ca. 1840, and later as a threatening, quarrelsome, thievish, alcoholic inhabitant of southeast Colorado and New Mexico, the subject of many anecdotes. [10890

LAWRENCE WILLSON. The Transcendentalist view of the West. West. humanities rev., 14:183-91 (spring). notes. On Thoreau's views and ideas concerning the real and the symbolical West, 1838-62. [10891

MATTHEW C. FIELD (1812-44). Matt Field on the Santa Fe Trail. Collected by Clyde and Mae Reed Porter. Edited and with an introduction and notes by John E[dward] Sunder. Norman: Univ. of Oklahoma Press [1960]. xxix, 322 p. map, ports., views (1 col.). notes. (The American exploration and travel series, [29].) Manuscript diary, partly in verse, of a journey with a wagon train from Cotton Grove, Kan., to Bent's Fort, Colo., and Santa Fe and back to Independence, Mo., 15 Jul. - 30 Oct. 1839 (p. 3-59); and 85 articles forming a series, "Sketches of the mountains and the prairies," reprinted from the New Orleans Picayune, 10 Dec. 1839-4 Oct. 1841. Heavily annotated. [10892

WILLIAM JAY POWELL. The sign said: "Road to Oregon." Pac. Northwesterner, 4:33-40 (summer). On the overland migration from Missouri to the Willamette Valley, 1839-43; with a detailed account of the travels of the wagon train under Jesse Applegate in 1843 as described in his memoirs. [10893

EDWIN RALPH BINGHAM. Literary landmarks along the Oregon Trail. Old Oregon, 38(6):9, 27 (Jun-Jul 1958). port. On 3 novels and 5 historical works concerned with the Trail and with Oregon. [10894

O. J. PRUITT. John Y. Nelson: plainsman. Ann. Ia., 35:294-303 (spring). Anecdotes of an alcoholic "expert bull whacker, rifleman and guide" in Miller's Hollow (now Council Bluffs), settled there before the coming of the Mormons, guide of Brigham Young's wagon train to Utah, trapper in Nebraska, stagecoach driver in "the first Buffalo Bill wild west show to play in Council Bluffs many years ago." [10895

DONALD BERT RUSSELL. The lives and legends of Buffalo Bill. Norman: Univ. of Oklahoma Press [1960]. x, 514, [2] p. cartoon, facsim., map, ports., tables, views. bibliog. (p. 482-93), notes. On William Frederick Cody (1846-1917), his early life in Iowa, his employment as a Pony Express rider, his service in the Union Army during the Civil War and as an Army scout in Indian wars, his work as a buffalo hunter and as a guide to hunters, his roles in stage plays about the West, his Wild West Show, his later appearance in circuses, and the publicity obtained for him in the fiction of Ned Buntline (Edward Zane Carroll Judson). Appended: list of dime novels by Buffalo Bill and about him, 1872-1912 (p. 494-503). [10896

GEORGE RIPPEY STEWART. Ordeal by hunger: the story of the Donner Party. ... New edition, with a supplement and three accounts by survivors. Boston: Houghton Mifflin, 1960. xii, [2], 394 p. facsim., maps, views. bibliog. (p. 371-50, notes (p. 377-87). 1st ed. 1936. On the misfortunes of a party of settlers led by George Donner from Illinois to California, 1846-47. Appended: diaries of Patrick Breen (Nov. 1846 - Mar. 1847) and James F. Reed (Feb.-Mar. 1847) and letter from Virginia Reed (16 May 1847). [10897

RICHARD IRVING DODGE (1827-95). Our wild Indians: thirty-three years' personal experience among the Red Men of the great West. N.Y.: Archer House [1960, c1959. 2], xxxix, [29]-657 p. facsim., ports., views. 1st ed. 1882. "A popular account of their social life, religion, habits, traits, customs, exploits, etc., with thrilling adventures and experiences on the Great Plains and in the mountains of our wide frontier," as noted by the author, a colonel in the Army, during his service in the West between 1848 and 1882. [10898

LE ROY REUBEN HAFEN & ANN (WOODBURY) HAFEN, eds. Fremont's fourth expedition: a documentary account of the disaster of 1848-1849, with diaries, letters, and reports by participants in the tragedy. Glendale, Calif.: A. H. Clark Co., 1960. 319 p. facsims., maps (1 fold.), ports., views. notes. (The Far West and the Rockies historical series, 1820-1875, v. 11.) Account of the expedition of John Charles Frémont and a party of 33 men from the site of Kansas City to the Arkansas River, the Sangre de Cristo Mountains, the South Fork of the Rio Grande, a spur of the San Juan Mountains, and down the Rio Grande and to Taos, 8 Oct. 1848-11 Feb. 1849--an expedition intended to explore a central route for a Pacific railroad, supported entirely by private funds, and ending in failure after the loss of 10 men by freezing or starvation. Includes a speech and reminiscences by Senator Thomas Hart Benton; diaries of J. H. Simpson and of Benjamin, Richard, and Edward M. Kern; letters of Frémont, Edward M. and Benjamin Kern, Thomas A. Hereford, Antoine Leroux, Thomas Fitzpatrick, and Lancaster P. Lupton; and reminiscences by Thomas S. Martin, Micajah McGehee, Thomas E. Breckenridge, Alexis Godey, Jessie (Benton) Frémont, and Charles Taplin. [10899

JOSEPH WARING BERRIEN. Overland from St. Louis to the California gold field in 1849: the diary of Joseph Waring Berrien. Edited by Ted and Caryl Hinckley. Ind. mag. hist., 56: 272-352 (Dec). map. notes. Detailed daily record, by a young man from Belleville, Ill., of a journey from St. Louis to Kansas by water and overland to Sacramento with a wagon train, 31 Mar.-15 Aug. 1849. [10900

BENJAMIN BUTLER HARRIS (1824-97). The Gila trail: the Texas Argonauts and the California Gold Rush. ... Edited and annotated by Richard H. Dillon. Norman: Univ. of Oklahoma Press [1960]. xv, 175 p. double map, port., views. bibliog. (p. 164-7), notes. (The American exploration and travel series, [31].) Manuscript reminiscences (ca. 1890) of the author's travels in a gold-seeking party led by Capt. Isaac H. Duval from Panola County, Tex., through New Mexico, northern Mexico, and Arizona to Sonora, Calif., and his experiences in the California mines, 25 Mar. 1849 to sometime in 1850; with a biographical sketch of Harris. [10901

REUBEN KNOX (1801-51). Reuben Knox letters, 1849-1851. Edited by Charles W. Turner. N.C. hist. rev., 37:66-93, 248-70, 397-418 (Jan-Jul). facsim., map, ports. notes. Letters from a St. Louis physician to his son Joseph A. Knox and his wife, Eliza Heritage 16 Jul. 1849, 14 Jan. 1850 - 27 May 1851, on his plans for a journey to California with his sons Joseph and Henry, his nephew Reuben F. Knox, and his stepson Franklin Grist, his travels from St. Louis by way of the Platte River and Salt Lake City to Sacramento, and his activities in California as a miner, renter of "Novato Ranch," and owner of a store in San Francisco; with letters from Joseph A. Knox (25 Sep. 1850, 17 May 1856) and Reuben F. Knox (Novato Ranch, 24 Feb. 1852). [10902

HARLOW BURGESS MILLS. Grandfather Burgess was a Forty-Niner. Ill. State Hist. Soc., Jour., 53:404-9 (winter). Information and excerpts from the few surviving papers of Joseph H. Burgess (1826-98), Illinois farmer, on his journey to, stay in, and return from California, 1849 to 1852 or later. [10903

ED ELLSWORTH BARTHOLOMEW. Western hard-cases; or, Gunfighters named Smith. Ruidoso, N.M.: Frontier Book Co., 1960. 191 p. Biographical sketches of "Men named Smith, who were connected with Western law and order" (including those who violated both), ca. 1850 to ca. 1900. [10904

THOMAS G. BREDLOW. Stagecoach! Frontier times, 34(3):16-17, 52 (summer). diagrs., port., view. On modifications of "the Concord Coach" to adapt it to the rugged climate and topography and the bad roads of the West, the schedules and drivers of these vehicles, and the precautions taken against Indians and other robbers, 1850s-90s. [10905

JOHN S. GRAY. Frank Grouard [1850-1905]: Kanaka scout or mulatto renegade? Westerners brand book (Chicago), 16:57-9, 62-4 (Oct 1959). On truth and falsehood in his memoirs as edited by Joseph De Barthe and published in 1894. Includes a letter from George Boyd to an unnamed person, dated Fort Peck, Montana Territory, 10 Oct. 1876, denouncing Grouard as a "renegade and horse thief." [10906

LEA FRANKLIN McCARTY. The gunfighters. Paintings and text by Lea F. McCarty. [Berkeley, Calif., 1959.] 44 p. ports. Paintings and biographical sketches of 20 Western outlaws and law officers, 1850s-90s. [10907

BYRON NATHAN McKINSTRY (born 1818). A grandfather's journal of the Oregon Trail. [Summarized and quoted by his grandson, Bruce McKinstry." Westerners brand book (Chicago), 16:1-3, 7-8 (Mar 1959). Record of the author's journey "from Smith's Corners, Illinois, to Hangtown, California," by way of Wyoming, Utah, and Nevada, 18 Mar.-17 Sep. 1850. [10908

JAMES W. MILGRAM. Estill & Co. Express. Am. philatelist, 73:47-9 (Oct 1959). facsim., map. bibliog. On a projected "company organized for carrying the mail and passengers from Independence, Missouri, to San Francisco," promoted by Col. I. M. Estill of Missouri, 1850. Includes a letter from Albert S. Holmes to his wife, Sarah A. Holmes (at Hoosick, Wis.), dated 24 Jun. 1850, on the movements of his wagon train from Fort Laramie, Wyo., to a point probably more than 180 miles farther west. [10909

MARK F. WILCOX. On restless wing. Phila.: Dorrance [1960]. 164 p. Account of the early life of the author's father, William Cullen Wilcox (1850-1928), based upon his manuscript autobiography and recast in fictional form, recalling his youth on a farm in Ohio, his running away from home, his life in Montana as a cowboy and later a clerk in a store at Deer Lodge, and his return home, and briefly referring to his later years as a missionary in Natal. [10910

FRANK M. STAHL (1841-1937). One-way ticket to Kansas: the autobiography of Frank M. Stahl as told by Margaret Whittemore. Lawrence: Univ. of Kansas Press, 1959 [i.e. 1960. 10], 146 p. facsim., ports., views. Reminiscences by a native of Dade County, Ohio, emigrant to Kansas in 1856, antislavery worker, gold miner in Colorado, soldier in the 2d Kansas Cavalry during the Civil War, cowboy in drives from New Mexico to Kansas, Indian fighter, Kansas cattle rancher, and participant in Kansas politics. [10911

PHOCION R. WAY (1827-98). Overland via "Jackass Mail" in 1858: the diary of Phocion R. Way. Edited and annotated by William A. Duffen. Ariz. and the West, 2:35-53, 147-64, 279-92, 353-70 (spring-winter). facsims., views. notes. Remarkably detailed daily record of the author's travels by water from Cairo, Ill., to New Orleans and Indianola, Tex., by coach to San Antonio, thence by the San Antonio - San Diego Mail Line to El Paso and Tucson, and on horseback to Tubac, 11 May-17 Jun. 1858, and of his activities in the Tubac area as an agent of the Santa Rita Mining Company till 3 Jul. 1858. Illustrated with reproductions of pencil sketches by the diarist. Heavily annotated. [10912

LUCIAN JOHNSTON EASTIN (1814-76). Emigrants' guide to Pike's Peak. Leavenworth City, K. T.: L. J. Eastin [1859. 8] p. map. 50 cm. (1859 Pike's Peak guidebooks, 15.) Reproduction, in a portfolio, with "Eastin 1859 Pike's Peak guide," by Nolie Mumey (1 leaf), mounted on inside cover. Evidently a special issue of the Kansas herald, 1 Mar. 1859. Text in 5 columns. Includes "Map of the gold mines and three prominent routes leading thereto" and detailed description of the routes; "Leavenworth City; its past, present and future; its advantages as an outfitting and starting point for Pike's Peak and the Gold Mines"; "The Gold Fields of Kansas"; gold-rush letters from D.C. Collier, G. W. Smith, J. C. Hemingray and F. Hawn, A. J. Davis, J. L. Scudder, and others; news from the mines; and advertisements of Leavenworth establishments and services. [10913

WILL PRICE. A pair of dried ears. True West, 7(4):18-19, 44-6 (Mar-Apr). port., views. On Joseph Alfred Slade, known as Jack Slade, native of Indiana, agent of the Overland Stage Company in Nebraska, killer of 26 men in the course of his employment, later an alcoholic trouble-maker in Virginia City, Mont., hanged there by vigilantes, 1859-64. [10914

EDWARD DUNSHA STEELE (1829-65). Edward Dunsha Steele, 1829-1865, pioneer, schoolteacher, cabinetmaker, and musician: a diary of his journey from Lodi, Wisconsin, across the plains to Boulder, Colorado, in the year 1859. Edited by Nolie Mumey. Boulder, Colo.: Johnson Pub. Co.,

1960. 90 p. mount. fold. facsims., fold. map (in pocket), mount. port., tables. notes. Daily record of his journey across Iowa and Nebraska with a wagon train of goldseekers, 17 May-31 Aug. 1859; with a biographical sketch by the editor, and reproductions of 6 Boulder newspapers (The Boulder County pioneer, v. 1, no. 1, 10 Feb. 1869; Rocky Mountain eagle, v. 2, no. 21, 4 Feb. 1875; Daily news, v. 1, no. 1, 8 Jun. 1880; The daily Colorado banner, v. 1, no. 1, 17 Apr. 1880; The Boulder County news, v. 1, no. 1, 12 Oct. 1869; and The Boulder herald, v. 1, no. 1, 17 Apr. 1880). [10915

ROBERT WEST HOWARD. Hoofbeats of destiny: the story of the Pony Express' critical role in holding the West "for the Union" during the intrigues of "secesh" and the Confederacy's campaign to steal all of the United States of America west of the Mississippi River [1860-61]. N.Y.: New American Library [1960]. 191, [1] p. facsims., map, ports., views. bibliog. (p. 186-9). (Signet books, D1814.) [10916

ILENE KINGSBURY. Salute to the Pony Express [1860-61]. Utah hist. quar., 28:130-34 (Apr). view. [10917

MERRILL J. MATTES & PAUL HENDERSON. The Pony Express: across Nebraska from St. Joseph to Fort Laramie. Neb. hist., 41:83-122 (Jun). fold. map, port., table, views. bibliog. (p. 88-92). On the 1 Missouri station, the 11 Kansas stations, the 37 Nebraska stations, and the 3 Wyoming stations between and including these points (a run of 641 miles), and the pony riders, 1860-61. [10918

FRANK LEE MOFFETT (born 1860). [Autobiography.] Southw. hist. quar., 63:469-71 (Jan). Sketch by the author's son, George Moffett, giving in the third person the reminiscences of Frank Lee Moffett, native of Texas, formerly a buffalo-hunter, miner, and rancher in Texas, Colorado, Wyoming, Montana, and Alaska, and since 1889 a landowner in Hardeman County; with added information in his own handwriting. [10919

NOLIE MUMEY. Hoofs to wings, the Pony Express: dramatic story of a mail service from East to West which existed one hundred years ago [Apr. 1860 - Nov. 1861]. Boulder, Colo.: Johnson Pub. Co., 1960. [14], 116 p. facsims., fold. col. map, ports., seals (1 mount.), tables, views (1 col.). notes. [10920

LEWIS A. NORDYKE. "John B": the hat of the West. Quarter horse jour., 3(12):8-9, 34 (Sep 1951). views. On a hat improvised by John B. Stetson (1830-1906) in the 1860s, his venture in making the hat commercially as "The Boss of the Plains," his advertisements to promote its sale, its almost immediate popularity with cattlemen, the continuing industry based upon it, and its interest as "the only piece of wearing apparel that is distinctively American." [10921

JAMES R. PIERSON. The Pony Express trail, 1860-1861. St. Joseph, Mo.: Pony Express Productions [1960. 4], 27 p. facsims., col. fold. map, views. [10922

RAYMOND W. SETTLE & MARY ANNA (LUND) SETTLE. Origin of the Pony Express [1860]: a centennial commemoration. Mo. Hist. Soc., Bul., 16:199-212 (Apr). notes. [10923

MARJORIE VANDERVELDE. The Pony Express [1860-61]. West. horseman, 25(4):30-31 (Apr). port., seal, view. [10924

DON DE VERE WALKER. Reading on the range: the literary habits of the American cowboy. Ariz. and the West, 2:307-18 (winter). notes. On the extent and subject matter of the publications read by cowboys, 1860s-90s. [10925

DONALD HUGH WELSH. The Pony Express in retrospect [1860-61]. Mo. hist. rev., 54:237-44 (Apr). ports., views. notes. [10926

THE WESTERNERS. Chicago Corral. Centennial of the Pony Express [1860-61]. Westerners brand book (Chicago), 17:9-11, 13-16 (Apr). Remarks by Bob Howard, Richard McP. Cabeen, Don Russell, and John S. Gray. [10927

GEORGE B. ABDILL. Rails West. Seattle: Superior Pub. Co. [1960]. 191 p. facsim., views (part double). Account, largely pictorial, of railroads in the trans-Mississippi West, 1861 to ca. 1900. [10928

CHARLES MONROE CHASE (1829-1902). An editor looks at early-day Kansas: the letters of Charles Monroe Chase. Edited by Lela Barnes. Kan. hist. quar., 26:113-51, 267-301 (summer, autumn). From the True

Republican and sentinel (Sycamore, Ill.), Aug. 1863, and the Vermont union (Lyndon, Vt.), 1873. [10929

HARRIET AMELIA SMITH (1840-1923; married Wesley Nickle in 1881). To Pike's Peak by ox-wagon: the Harriet A. Smith day-book. Edited by Fleming Fraker, Jr. Ann. Ia., 35:112-48 (fall 1959). map. notes. Diary of the movements of the wagon train of the writer's uncle, Porter T. Hinman, from Des Moines to Omaha, the Platte River, and Boulder, 21 Ju.-30 Sep. 1863. [10930

JAMES KNOX POLK MILLER (1845-91). The road to Virginia City: the diary of James Knox Polk Miller. Edited by Andrew F. Rolle. Norman: Univ. of Oklahoma Press [1960]. xxiii, 143, [1] p. facsim., map, ports., views. notes. (The American exploration and travel series, 30.) Manuscript record of the author's travels by railroad from Chicago to St. Joseph, Mo., and by wagon to Deadwood and Salt Lake City where he kept a saloon and restaurant, his journey to Virginia City, Mont. and as a bookkeeper and clerk, his association with vigilantes, his journey to Fort Benton, Mont., and down the Missouri to St. Joseph, and his railroad journey to Washington, D.C., 10 Aug. 1864-21 Jun. 1867. An unprinted continuation of the diary records his travels in Europe. [10931

STACY W. OSGOOD. "Wildest of the wild bunch." Westerners brand book (Chicago), 17:33-5, 37-40 (Jul). On Harvey Logan (1868?-1904), known by the name of Kid Curry and many other aliases, and his career as a cattle thief, bank robber, and train robber in the area "from Canada to the Mexican line and from Nevada to eastern Tennessee," ca. 1880 till his violent death; with remarks on the inconsistencies in the various accounts of him and his crimes. [10932

ALVIRA PACKINGHAM (SULLIVAN) EARP (1847-1947). The story of Mrs. Virgil Earp: the Earp brothers of Tombstone. [Recollected by Mrs. Earp in Los Angeles in 1936. Edited and expanded] by Frank [Joseph] Waters. N.Y.: C. N. Potter [1960. 8], 247 p. col. maps. bibliog. (p. 235-7), notes (p. 239-47). On the activities of the 5 Earp brothers in New Mexico and Arizona, 1879-82, and particularly the bad character of Wyatt Earp; with some account of the Earps in Dodge City, Kan. (1869-79), the activities of Wyatt Earp in California, and the author's early life in Florence, Neb., and Council Bluffs, Ia. Implies that Wyatt Earp's first wife, Mattie, killed herself after his bigamous second marriage and that threats from his widow prevented the publication of this book in the 1930s. [10933

ELEANOR H. GOSS. Experiences of a pioneer Pueblo family. Colo. mag., 37:138-9 (Apr). On the journey of Calvin William Goss and his family from Kansas to Pueblo in 1869 and their settlement at Rye. [10934

ROGER VICTOR CLEMENTS. British investment in the Trans-Mississippi West, 1870-1914, its encouragement, and the metal mining interests. Pac. hist. rev., 29:35-50 (Feb). notes. [10935

ROGER NORMAN CONGER. The emigration of the N. H. Conger family from Oneida, Illinois, to Waco, Texas, in 1870. Southw. hist. quar., 64:80-91 (Jul). port. On the journey of the author's grandfather, Norman Hurd Conger (1828?-1876), his family, and 2 other families, a caravan of 22 persons; with a newspaper clipping (probably from Knoxville, Ill.) about the Congers in Illinois, recollections in a letter from Charles Conger (7 Jan. 1931), and excerpts from the diary kept during the whole journey, 1 Sep.-9 Oct. 1870, by Clara Conger (1853?-1879). [10936

LINCOLN ELLISON. Influence of grazing on plant succession of rangelands. Botanical rev., 26:1-78 (Jan-Mar). table. bibliog. On the effect of grazing upon the composition of range vegetation and upon erosion in the West, 1870-1959. [10937

FRANKLIN REYNOLDS. Seventy years with horses. Quarter horse jour., 3(11):8, 32-3; (12):12, 38 (Aug, Sep 1951). port. On George Hampton (born 1872), trainer of race horses in Kentucky and Texas. [10938

HENRY NASH SMITH. Mark Twain as an interpreter of the Far West: the structure of Roughing it [1872]. Walker D. Wyman & Clifton B. Kroeber, eds., The frontier in perspective (Madison: Univ. of Wisconsin Press, 1957), p. 205-28. bibliog. [10939

DAVID HUNTER STROTHER (1816-88). "Porte Crayon" in the Rocky Mountains. Edited by Dr. Cecil D. Eby, Jr. Colo. mag., 37:108-21 (Apr). notes. Diary of the journey of "a distinguished company of Eastern naturalists and editors" on an excursion from Charles Town, W. Va., by railroad to St. Louis, Dallas, Kansas City, Denver, Colorado Springs, Boulder, Georgetown, Cheyenne, Salt Lake City, Ogden, Omaha, Chicago, and Pittsburgh, 15 Jul.-22 Aug. 1873. [10940

ZOE AGNES (STRATTON) TILGHMAN. Spotlight: Bat Masterson and Wyatt Earp as U.S. deputy marshals. San Antonio: Naylor Co. [1960. 6], 21 p. Review of the known activities of William Barclay Masterson and Wyatt Berry Stapp Earp in Kansas and Arizona between 1874 and 1882, indicating that Masterson was not a U.S. deputy marshal in either State, that Earp was not a deputy marshal in Kansas, but that one of the Earp brothers was a deputy marshal at Tombstone, Ariz. [10941

WALLACE TUFFORD. The wire that tamed the West. Montana, 10(1):62-7 (Jan). facsim., ports., views. On barbed-wire fencing, 1874-83. [10942

JERRY BRYAN. An Illinois gold hunter in the Black Hills: the diary of Jerry Bryan, March 13 to August 20, 1876. With an introduction and notes by Clyde C. Walton, Illinois State Historian. Springfield: Illinois State Historical Soc., 1960. 40 p. maps, views. notes. (Illinois State Historical Society. Pamphlet series, 2.) Record of a journey from Cordova, Ill., to Deadwood, of digging for gold near Deadwood, and of the return journey. [10943

JESSIE DONALDSON SCHULTZ. Adventuresome, amazing Apikuni. Montana, 10(4):2-26 (Oct). ports., views. Reflections on the life and work of James Willard Schultz as seen by his widow, on his life among the Blackfeet and other Indians, 1877-1903, and his novels and other books about them, 1907-40. Appended: "An appreciation of James Willard Schultz," by Verne Dusenberry, on his success "in capturing and recording the inner quality of the Indian"; and "Apikuni's ageless audience," by Harry C. James, on the great popularity of his more than 30 books for boys" (1912 ff.). [10944

DAISY (BROWN) ACKLEY (born 1872). Wagon wheels a'rollin': an autobiography. [n. p.] 1960. [4], 57 leaves. port. On the author's early life in rural Nebraska, Kansas, and Missouri; her journey with her family, in a wagon train of several families, from Nebraska to Olympia, 1880-81; and their settlement at Tumwater, Wash., near Olympia. [10945

KATIE MAUDE (DAYTON) ASA (born 1880). My life's story. Los Angeles, 1960. 125 p. ports., views. On the author's early years on a farm near McCool, York County, Neb., her marriage in 1900 to Orsemus Asa (1879-1918), their life on farms near McCool and Morrill, her removal with her 5 children to Orange County, Calif., in 1920, her support of the family by dressmaking and other employments, and the settlement of the family in Los Angeles in 1933. [10946

STACY W. OSGOOD. Harry Tracy [1870?-1902]--meanest man, alive or dead. Westerners brand book (Chicago), 16:41-3, 46-8, 78-9 (Aug, Dec). bibliog. On his career of theft, robbery, and murder in several Western States, 1880s-1902; with a list of his 23 "Known ... and Claimed Murders." [10947

OLGA (WISNER) SOLIE. Deep roots: the story of Hans and Olga Solie. Compiled and published for their living children so that their descendants may enjoy in the printed word incidents and events they have experienced at first hand. [Everett? Wash.] 1958. [10], 143 p. cartoons, ports., views. On Hans Solie and Olga Wisner, their marriage in Stanley, Wis., in 1902, their removal in 1903 to Everett, Wash., where he worked as a carpenter and builder, their life from 1914 to 1923 on a farm on the Snohomish River, their return to Everett, their children and grandchildren, and their travels to Norway, Alaska, and Mexico. [10948

LLOYD TEVIS. Growth of California and the West. Pony Express, 26(2):6-9 (Jul 1959). facsim., table, view. Part of an address by the President of Wells, Fargo, & Company, delivered before the American Bankers Association, 10 Aug. 1881. [10949

NEW YORK HERALD. Rapacious land grabbers. Westerners brand book (N.Y.), 6:82-5. Dispatch from "Our Special Correspondent" in Washington, 12 Aug. 1885, headed: "Four millions of government acres illegally appropriated. The outrageous barbed wire fence formidable obstruction to the settlement of the country. Crowding out small farmers." Contains complaints from J. Judevine, "Special Agent Hobbs," John Willits and Sons,

J. McFarland, Peter W. Hey, Jacob Paden, B. A. Arnold, and William A. Hall, 1883-84, on the illegal fencing of public lands by cattlemen in Nebraska, Kansas, Colorado, and Idaho. [10950

BILL LEFTWICH. The saddler of Big Bend. Quarter horse jour., 12(6):60, 167-8 (Mar). port., view. On C. H. Werner (born 1890) as a harness-maker and saddler in Iowa, Illinois, North Dakota, and Montana, 1905-25, and since 1925 in Alpine, Tex. [10951

ISABELLE JOHNSON. Of Will James [1892-1942]. Mont. Inst. Arts quar., 10(4):8-12 (summer 1958). port. On his early years as a rodeo rider, his 20 books of Western or juvenile fiction, his many articles and lectures about horses and other subjects, and his oil paintings and magazine illustrations (especially of Montana scenes). [10952

RAY ALLEN BILLINGTON. The West of Frederick Jackson Turner. Neb. hist., 41:261-79 (Dec). notes. On the continued applicability of his frontier thesis, with particular reference to Nebraska. Includes citations from his papers, 1900-1931, indicating his own understanding of what he had written in 1893. [10953

C. H. McKENNON. Case of the missing miners. Frontier times, 34(1):30 (winter). port. On 12 men who set out from Coalgate, Indian Territory, for the Alaska gold mines, and were never heard of after they went aboard the Helen W. Almy, which foundered at sea; with a photograph of the 12 men at the railroad station at Coalgate, 1 Mar. 1898, each identified by name. [10954

FAY E. WARD. The cowboy at work: all about his job and how he does it, with 600 detail drawings by the author. N.Y.: Hastings House [1958]. xviii, 289 p. drawings on 80 plates. Intended as "an authoritative reference work for all those interested in the cowhand as he functioned in his job during the period when there was still plenty of open range for him to circulate in." Written and illustrated after the author had "worked as a horse wrangler, cowhand, bronc breaker and roughstring rider for cow outfits in Canada, and for outfits extending from there to the border of Mexico, for a period of over forty years." Deals particularly with practices in Texas, California, and Mexico. [10955

GEORGE FRANKLIN ALLEE. Beyond prison walls: the story of Frank Novak [born 1884], once a desperate criminal and convict, now national prison chaplain no. 1 by the grace of God. Kansas City, Mo.: Beacon Hill Press [1960]. 96 p. On his emigration from Czechoslovakia in 1901, his work as a laborer in Chicago, his criminal activities in the Middle West, his confinement in the Washington State Prison (Walla Walla) and in an honor camp at Kalama, Wash., his recovery from tuberculosis, his religious conversion, his chaplain service in Washington prisons, his lectures in prisons in various parts of the United States, and his success in converting criminals in jail; with some account of his life in Seattle since ca. 1917. [10956

DORYS CROW GROVER. Pick-up man. West. horseman, 25(2):16, 59, 62 (Feb). ports. On Bryce Baker (born 1902) of Texas and New Mexico, later a cowboy in Oregon, a "pick-up man" in rodeos, and a rancher in Ellensburg, Wash. [10957

W. I. ROBERTSON (born 1902). Robertson replies. Montana, 10(1):79 (Jan). On the author's early experience in the cattle industry in southern California, his "acquaintanceship with cowmen and their riders from one end of the West to the other," and his conviction that the "cowboys" of the present have no "relationship to old-time cowmen." [10958

BETTY ROSENBERG. "A complete life mode." Lawrence Clark Powell, ed., The Southwest of the bookman ([Los Angeles: Univ. of California Library] 1959), leaves 46-55. On "the western novel" since 1902. [10959

VIVIAN A. PALADIN. He painted characters of the Old West as they really were. Montana, 10(3):53-8 (Jul). ports. On Lea Franklin McCarty (1905-60), painter of Western portraits; with reproductions of his paintings of 20 gunmen, "frontiersmen," "lawmen," etc., and a biographical sketch of each individual portrayed. [10960

CHARLES WAYLAND TOWNE. Buffaloed bulls. True West, 7(6):16-17, 49-51 (Jul-Aug). On the railroad journey of 2 buffalo bulls from South Dakota to Juárez, and their defeat of all the "Spanish" bulls entered against them in the bull ring there, Jan. 1907. [10961

JAMES A. McRAE (born 1889). Call me tomorrow. Toronto: Ryerson Press [1960. 8], 240 p. Mainly reminiscences of the author's early and later life in Canada and his wanderings there as a lumberjack and a miner before 1925. Includes some account of his work in lumbering and railroad construction in Washington and Montana and his return across the United States to his home near Sarnia, Ont., 1908. [10962

RUSSELL D. JACOBSON. The rear-end collision doctrine as a theory of negligence in Kansas [and Missouri, 1917-59]. Univ. Kan. City law rev., 28:41-72 (winter). notes. On a "theory, doctrine, rule, presumption, or whatever it may be called ... which may be employed where one motor vehicle has trespassed the hind quarters of another vehicle in a violent and forceful manner." [10963

ROBERT ANDERSON. Reduction of variants as a measure of cultural integration. Gertrude E. Dole & Robert L. Carneiro, eds., Essays in the science of culture, in honor of Leslie A. White (N.Y.: Crowell [1960]), p. 50-62. bibliog., notes. On studies of the variations in the sun dance of the northern Cheyenne and northern Ute Indians as compared with the sun dance of the Comanche Indians, 1919-55. [10964

ROBERT EMMET CLARK. New water law problems and old public law principles. Rocky Mt. law rev., 32: 437-51 (Jun). notes. On "the Western trend in ground water legislation since 1927" toward recognition of the imperative requirement that in "the arid and semi-arid regions of the West ... all available water be utilized beneficially and without waste." [10965

ROBERT NEWELL (1807-69). Memoranda: travles [sic] in the teritory of Missourie; travle to the Kayuse War; together with a report on the Indians south of the Columbia River. Edited, with notes and introduction, by Dorothy O. Johansen. [Portland, Ore.:] Champoeg Press, 1959. [6], 159 p. maps (1 fold.), tables, views. notes. Entries in a notebook, 7 Mar. 1828 to the end of 1842, on the author's hunting and trapping between St. Louis and the Snake River and his settlement in 1841 as a farmer on the Willamette River (p. 31-40); accounts, 1836-41, by Newell; report of his travels from Oregon City to Walla Walla and back as a member of a peace commission to treat with the Indians, 29 Jan.-25 Mar. 1848 (p. 105-14); documents relating to the Peace Commissioners, 1848, from the Oregon spectator, 6 Apr. 1848; and "A report on the Indians of sub-agency first district south of the Columbia," 10 Aug. 1849, incomplete manuscript, evidently by Newell (p. 144-59); with an extensive introduction by the editor, and voluminous notes. [10966

WILLIAM ROSS HALLIDAY. Adventure is underground: the story of the great caves of the West and the men who explore them. N.Y.: Harper [1959]. xviii, 206 p. maps, views. Undertakes "a detailed compilation of the discovery and exploration of the great caves of the West," in the Black Hills and the Far West, mainly since the 1930s. [10967

PHILLIP O. FOSS. The grazing fee dilemma. University, Ala.: Univ. of Alabama Press for the ICP [1960. 2], 10 p. notes. (Inter-University Case Program. ICP case series, 57.) On the Grazing Service of the Department of the Interior, established by the Taylor Grazing Act in 1934 to collect fees for grazing on public lands and abolished in 1946. [10968

ELI SETH JENKINS. H[arold] L[enoir] Davis [1896-1960]: a critical study. Ann Arbor: University Microfilms, 1960. Positive microfilm of typescript. [198] leaves. Thesis--Univ. of Southern California. Abstracted: Dissert. abstracts, 21:197-8 (Jul). On his novels (1935-57), short stories, essays, and poems, dealing mainly with the West, particularly his native Oregon. [10969

JOSEPH DAVID ARONSON. BCG vaccination among American Indians [in Arizona, Wyoming, the Dakotas, and Alaska, 1936-41, 1946-47]. Am. rev. tuberculosis, 57:96-9 (Jan 1948). tables. [10970

JODY KINCAID. A top jocky. Quarter horse jour., 7(7):50 (Apr 1955). port. On the career of Dale Centers as a quarter-horse jockey in the West since 1936, professionally since 1953. [10971

U.S. Bureau of Mines. Control of fires in inactive coal deposits in Western United States, including Alaska, 1948-58. By T. R. Jolley and H. W. Russell. [Wash.] 1959. [2], ii, 22 p. diagr., tables, views. (Its Information circular 7932.) [10972

THE PACIFIC NORTHWEST

B. ROBERT BUTLER & DOUGLAS OSBORNE. Archaeological evidence for the use of atlatl weights in the Northwest [Columbia and Fraser Valleys]. Am. antiq., 25:215-24 (Oct 1959). table, views. bibliog. [10973

HENRY AXEL PERSON. Bottomless lakes of the Pacific Northwest. West. folklore, 19:278-80 (Oct). Current lore, including mention of a sea serpent in Payette Lake, Idaho, and of lakes having underground connections with one another and with Puget Sound. [10974

RUTH MURRAY UNDERHILL. Indians of the Pacific Northwest. Wash.: Branch of Education, Bureau of Indian Affairs, U.S. Dept. of the Interior [1960]. 232 p. diagrs., maps, views. bibliog. (p. 226-32). 1st ed. 1945. On their diet, housing, clothing, home life, government, and religion, and the changes since the coming of the white man. [10975

CLIFFORD MERRILL DRURY. I, the Lawyer, head chief of the Nez Perce. Westerners brand book (N.Y.), 7:1-3, 14-21. ports. notes. On the Lawyer (born probably ca. 1794, died 1876), Chief of the Nez Perce Indians from 1848 to 1871, friend of Army officers and missionaries in Washington and Idaho as early as the 1830s, in his later years an elder of the Presbyterian Church in Kamiah, Idaho, interpreter and language teacher, "by far the most influential Indian of the Pacific Northwest during the 19th century." [10976

THOMAS EDWIN JESSETT. Chief Spokan Garry, 1811-1892: Christian, statesman, and friend of the white man. Minneapolis: T. S. Denison [1960]. 232 p. facsims., maps, ports., views. bibliog. (p. 219-23), notes. On his life in Washington as a Spokan Indian, his education at the Red River School, his assistance to missionaries in the Pacific Northwest, and his service as a chief of the Spokan Indians. [10977

RICHARD T. CONN. The Iroquois in the West. Pac. Northwesterner, 4:59-63 (fall). On the employment of Iroquois Indians as boatmen and hunters for fur companies in the Pacific Northwest, as early as ca. 1820 and as late as 1846, and the return of most of them "to their homes in Ontario." [10978

ROY J. POPKIN. Dr. John McLoughlin [1784-1857]. New Eng. jour. med., 263:1132-3 (1 Dec). coin. bibliog. On his training and work as a physician for the Hudson's Bay Company in Canada and his service after 1824 as Chief Factor and Superintendent of the Columbia Department of the Company, with headquarters at Fort Vancouver. [10979

HERMAN JULIUS DEUTSCH. The evolution of Territorial and State boundaries in the Inland Empire of the Pacific Northwest [1825-86]. Pac. Northw. quar., 51:115-51 (Jul). maps, port., views. [10980

MAYNARD BENEDICT JONES. The great command: the story of Marcus and Narcissa Whitman and the Oregon country pioneers. By Nard Jones. Boston: Little, Brown [1959]. xiv, [2], 398 p. ports., views. notes (p. 375-90). A general history of Oregon, 1835-47, semifictional in form, giving particular attention to the missionary activities of Marcus Whitman, M.D., and Narcissa (Prentiss) Whitman, Henry Harmon Spalding and Eliza (Hart) Spalding (at Lapwai, Idaho), and various Methodist, Episcopalian, and Catholic missionaries in Oregon and Washington, the growing conflict of interests between a rapidly increasing population of white settlers and the Indians, and the tendency of some of the missionaries to neglect their duties to the Indians and transfer their efforts to the settlers. [10981

MARY HOTCHKISS HOAG. Eliza Hart Spalding [1808-51], runner-up. D.A.R. mag., 94:625-8 (Nov). view. On her service with her husband, the Rev. Henry Harmon Spalding, as a Presbyterian missionary among the Nez Perce Indians at Lapwai, Idaho, 1836-47, and at a school at Brownsville, Ore., 1847-51; with excerpts from her diary kept while crossing the Plains in 1836, and reasons why she is less well known than Narcissa Whitman. [10982

U.S. Geological Survey. Irrigation and streamflow depletion in Columbia River Basin above The Dalles, Oregon. By W[ilbur] D[ouglas] Simons. ... An evaluation of the consumptive use of water based on the amount of irrigation [1836-1946]. Wash.: U.S. Govt. Print. Off., 1953. iv, 126 p. fold. map, tables. bibliog. (p. 123). (Its Water-supply paper 1220.) Concludes that the depletion attributable to irrigation by diversion of waters from the

Columbia and its tributaries "is relatively small in comparison to the fluctuations caused by the vagaries in climatic conditions." [10983

ELLA ELIZABETH CLARK. Indian thanksgiving in the Pacific Northwest. Ore. hist. quar., 61:437-56 (Dec). notes. On Indian myths connected with ceremonies of gratitude as recorded since the 1840s. [10984

EDWARD R. GEARY. Historical narrative of the Presbytery of Oregon. Presbyt. Hist. Soc., Jour., 38:103-9, 166-81 (Jun, Sep). From the Presbyterian home missionary, Jul.-Sep. 1885. On an organization embracing Oregon, Washington, and Idaho, 1846-76. [10985

WARREN JUDSON BRIER. How Washington Territory got its name [1853]. Pac. Northw. quar., 51:13-15 (Jan). ports. notes. [10986

HARVEY ERICKSON. Northwest Indian treaties [1853-71]. Pac. Northwesterner, 4:41-8 (summer). [10987

WILLIS A. KATZ. Public printers of Washington Territory, 1853-1862 [and 1863-89]. Pac. Northw. quar., 51:103-14, 171-81 (Jul, Oct). facsims., port. notes. [10988

ISAAC VAN DORSEY MOSSMAN (1830-1912). Oregon's famous Pony Express rider. [Edited] by H[erbert S.] Hamlin. Pony Express, 25(12):3-9 (May 1959). facsims., port. Reminiscences (1890s?) of the author's work in Oregon, Washington, and Idaho as a miner, a mail carrier, a volunteer Indian fighter, and operator of Mossman's Express to the Idaho mines, 1853-63. [10989

H. D. FORD. Nightmare in the Bitterroots. Frontier times, 34(2): 14-15, 54-6 (spring). facsim., port., views. On the robbery and murder of Lloyd Magruder and 3 of his employees between Virginia City, Mont., and Lewiston, Idaho, by Doc Howard, D. C. Lowry, and Jim Romaine, their apprehension by the private efforts of Hill Beachy, and the trial and execution of the murderers, 1862-64. [10990

YOUNG CAMERON MANSFIELD (1859-1929). Fifty years among the dumb animals. [Edited] by Robert M. Showacre. Pac. Northwesterner, 4:8-16 (winter). Excerpts from 10 articles in the Twice-a-week spokesman-review, May-Oct. 1928, recalling the author's railroad journey from Omaha to San Francisco in 1878 and his experience as a farm laborer in Oregon and Washington and a rancher and horse trader in Whitman County, Wash.; with remarks on the apprehension of livestock thieves, the care of farm animals, and the improvement of the soil. [10991

JAMES NEVILLE TATTERSALL. The economic development of the Pacific Northwest to 1920 [mainly after 1880]. Ann Arbor: University Microfilms, 1960. Positive microfilm of typescript. [314] leaves. Thesis--Univ. of Washington. Abstracted: Dissert. abstracts, 21:414-15 (Dec). [10992

LEVI ANKENY. Murder on the Snake. Frontier times, 34(2):30-31, 64 (spring). view. On the robbery and murder of E. H. Cummings, agent of the Oregon-Washington River Navigation Company at Dayton, Wash., by Canada Owenby, J. H. McPherson, and Ezra Snodderly, and the apprehension and death of the murderers, 1882-84. [10993

JOHN R. FAHEY. Spokane Falls and Northern. Pac. Northwesterner, 4:17-26 (spring). On the stay of Daniel Chase Corbin in the Pacific Northwest to organize the Coeur d'Alene Railway & Navigation Company, the Spokane Falls & Idaho branch of the Northern Pacific, and the Spokane Falls and Northern Railway, 1886-89; with some account of his earlier business enterprises in Nebraska, Colorado, and Montata (1852-76) and in New York City (1876-86). [10994

LAWRENCE RAKESTRAW. Before McNary: the Northwestern conservationist, 1889-1913. Pac. Northw. quar., 51:49-56 (Apr). ports. notes. On the "forest conservation movement" in the Pacific Northwest during these years, and its "local leaders." [10995

DALE NELSON. Steamboat through Hell's Canyon. True West, 7(6):22-3, 40, 42-3 (Jul-Aug). map, port., view. On the navigation of the Snake River (the Idaho-Oregon boundary) by Capt. William P. Gray on the Norma, from Huntington to Lewiston, May 1895. [10996

HENRY JAMES KINGSBURY. Bucking the tide. [Seattle? 1949.] 192 p. On the author's life as a printer in Chicago, Perrine City, Idaho, and Uburna, Ore.; with some account of his early life in England, the life of his father-in-law, the history and condition of Perrine City, and the church affairs of Uburna, and a review (p. 134-92) of recent British politics. [10997

JESSE BENJAMIN MANIFOLD (born 1881). My first seventy-five years: memoirs of a very common man. [Ann Arbor? 1957.] iii, 73 p. facsims., ports., views. On the author's early life and studies, his settlement in 1909 on homesteaded land near Harrison, Idaho, his removal in 1945 to the Spokane Valley, his work there in real estate and construction, and his genealogical travels; with an account of his Manifold, Cowgill, and Payne ancestry, and facetious verses on various subjects. [10998

JOE B. HALM. Gallant Joe Halm tells his dramatic experience. Montana, 10(4):55-8 (Oct). Recollections of the great Montana-Idaho fire, 18-20 Aug. 1910, by a forester then stationed at Wallace, Idaho. [10999

GARRETT B. HOLLOWAY. Golden anniversary of fiery horror occasions thoughtful reappraisal. Montana, 10(4): 49-54 (Oct). views. On "the terrible conflagration of 1910 ... in Western Montana and Northern Idaho," covering "some three million acres." [11000

RUBY EL HULT. Northwest disaster: avalanche and fire. Portland, Ore.: Binfords & Mort, 1960. [10], 228 p. maps, ports., views. bibliog. (p. 209-20). On an avalanche in the Cascade Mountains at Wellington, Wash., Feb. 1910, and a forest fire in the Bitter Root Mountains of Idaho and Montana, Aug. 1910, as recorded in newspapers and public records and recalled by survivors. [11001

GEORGE W. REYNOLDS. Nature sets the stage as defeated men pray for quenching rains. Montana, 10(4):46-9 (Oct). views. On the weather preceding and during the devastating forest fire in Montana and Idaho in 1910. [11002

CLAUDE W. NICHOLS, JR. Brotherhood in the woods: the Loyal Legion of Loggers and Lumbermen, a twenty year attempt at "industrial cooperation" [Pacific Northwest, 1917-36]. Ann Arbor: University Microfilms, 1959 [i. e. 1960]. Positive microfilm of typescript. [193] leaves. Thesis--Univ. of Oregon. Abstracted: Dissert. abstracts, 20:3267 (Feb). [11003

ROBERT L. TYLER. The United States Government as union organizer: the Loyal Legion of Loggers and Lumbermen. Miss. Valley hist. rev., 47:434-51 (Dec). notes. On an organization established to counteract a strike of the Industrial Workers of the World against the lumber operators in Washington and Idaho during World War I, 1917-18, continued under Col. Brice P. Disque for the War Department, and disbanded in 1935 after the adoption of the Wagner Act. [11004

WILLIS BUNGAY MERRIAM. A history of the Northwest Scientific Association [Spokane, 1923-60. Pullman, Wash.] 1960. [2], 62 p. table. [11005

L. J. SMITH. The development of rural electrification in the Pacific Northwest [1923-48]. Agric. engineering, 29: 444-52 (Oct 1958). view. [11006

CARL H. FRITZE. The time lag factor in ratemaking. I.C.C. Practitioners' jour., 27:709-13 (Apr). notes. On rates for transportation of bulk petroleum in the Pacific Northwest, 1930-57. [11007

L. M. NAFFZIGER & G. M. HORNER. Effect of cropping and tillage practices on runoff and erosion in the Palouse area of Washington and Idaho [1930-58]. Am. Soc. Agric. Engineers, Trans., 1 (1958): 34-5. tables. notes. [11008

PAUL W. LIGHT. Water transportation on the Columbia River system [1938-59]. Karl M. Ruppenthal, ed., Revolution in transportation (Stanford, Calif.: Graduate School of Business, Stanford Univ. [1960]), p. 51-4. [11009

THE SOUTHWEST

JOSEPH BARTHOLOMEW CASAGRANDE. The Southwest Project in Comparative Psycholinguistics: a preliminary report. International Congress of Anthropological and Ethnological Sciences, 5th, 1956, Men and cultures: selected papers, ed. Anthony F. C. Wallace (Phila.: Univ. of Pennsylvania Press [1960]), p. 777-82. notes. On linguistic and psychological studies of "six Southwestern groups partaking of a variety of cultural traditions and speaking diverse languages"--Navajo, Hopi, Zuñi, Spanish-American, and "Hopi-Tewa and the related Tewa-speaking people of Santa Clara Pueblo." [11010

CONFERENCE ON CADDOAN ARCHEOLOGY, 5th. Proceedings of the fifth Conference on Caddoan Archeology [Norman, Okla., 1958]. Edited by

E. Mott Davis. Tex. Archeol. Soc., Bul., 31:73-143. diagrs., maps. bibliog. Transcripts of discussions. Partial contents.--Distinguishing the Caddoan area.--Archaic and early ceramic complexes ancestral, or related, to the Gibson Aspect.--Correlation of Lower Red River and Caddoan sequences.--The historical development from Archaic to Gibson Aspect.--Historic sites in the Caddoan area.--Gibson Aspect chronology. [11011

E. MOTT DAVIS. The Caddoan area: an introduction to the Symposium. Tex. Archeol. Soc., Bul., 31:3-10. map. Remarks on Caddoan archeology, prefatory to the text of proceedings of a symposium on "Relationships between the Caddoan area and neighboring areas," at the 23d annual meeting of the Society for American Archaeology, 2 May 1958. According to the map, the area comprises southwestern Arkansas, southeastern Oklahoma, northwestern Louisiana, and a considerable part of eastern Texas. [11012

JAMES THOMAS DAVIS. An appraisal of certain speculations on prehistoric Puebloan subsistence. Southw. jour. anthropol., 16:15-21 (spring). bibliog., notes. On the belief, that "agriculture supplanted, to almost near exclusion, a reliance upon animal foods in the native diet." [11013

ODD S. HALSETH. Adobe in architecture [in the Southwest]. Ariz. architect, 3(7):13-17 (Mar). port., views. [11014

EDWARD B. JELKS. Relationships between the Caddoan area and Texas. Tex. Archeol. Soc., Bul., 31:65-73. Includes discussion by T. N. Campbell. [11015

J. CHARLES KELLEY. North Mexico and the correlation of Mesoamerican and Southwestern cultural sequences. International Congress of Anthropological and Ethnological Sciences, 5th, 1956, Men and cultures: selected papers, ed. Anthony F. C. Wallace (Phila.: Univ. of Pennsylvania Press [1960]), p. 566-73. chron. chart. notes. [11016

ALFRED VINCENT KIDDER. Southwestern archaelogy: conclusions. Margaret Mead & Ruth L. Bunzel, eds., The golden age of American anthropology (N.Y.: George Braziller, 1960), p. 280-95. maps. From the author's An introduction to the study of Southwestern archaeology (1924). On prehistoric, particularly pre-Pueblo, peoples of Utah, Colorado, Arizona, and New Mexico. [11017

HARRY PERCIVAL MERA (1875-1951). Indian silverwork of the Southwest. ... [Second edition.] Volume one. Globe, Ariz.: Dale Stuart King, 1960. vi, 122 p. port., views. On a collection of Navajo and Zuñi silver work in the Laboratory of Anthropology, Santa Fe. [11018

CLARENCE H. WEBB. Relationships between the Caddoan and central Louisiana culture sequences. Tex. Archeol. Soc., Bul., 31:11-25. bibliog. Includes discussion by Alex D. Krieger and James A. Ford. [11019

EDWARD A. MARINSEK. The effect of cultural difference in the education of Pueblo Indians. [Albuquerque: College of Education, Univ. of New Mexico, 1958. 1], 96 leaves. diagr., map, table. notes. (The University of New Mexico Research Study: the adjustment of Indian and non-Indian children in the public schools of New Mexico.) On the history, language, government, economy, family organization, religion, "world view, morals and ethics," and personality of these Indians, settled in communities in the Rio Grande and Pecos valleys since ca. 1276, and the impossibility of effective teaching of their children without full knowledge of their cultural differences from "Anglo" children. [11020

BERT SALWEN. The introduction of leather footgear in the Pueblo area. Ethnohistory, 7:206-38 (summer). bibliog., notes. Review of historical evidence, 1540-1601, and archeological evidence, concluding that the change from yucca-fiber sandals to leather footgear "must ... have taken place between AD 1300-1375 and AD 1540" and that the later form of footgear may have been an "independent invention." [11021

LYNN IRWIN PERRIGO. Our Spanish Southwest. Dallas: B. Upshaw [1960. 14], 498 p. double maps, tables. bibliog. (p. 403-72). Narrative history, 1528 to ca. 1900, of a region including most of Texas, all of New Mexico and Arizona, and part of California; with several topical chapters on this area in the 20th century. Text in double columns. [11022

RAYMOND BRANDES. Archaeological awareness of the Southwest as illustrated in literature [from 1539] to

1890. Ariz. and the West, 2:6-25 (spring). notes. [11023

JACK DOUGLAS FORBES. Apache, Navaho, and Spaniard. Norman: Univ. of Oklahoma Press [1960]. xxvi, 304, [1] p. maps, views. bibliog. (p. 286-93), notes. On the southern Athapascan Indians in New Mexico, Colorado, and the adjacent parts of bordering States, "and their relations with other Indians and with the Spanish Empire," 1540-1698. [11024

DONALD CULROSS PEATTIE (1898-1964). America's Don Quixote. Everett Rich, ed., The heritage of Kansas (Lawrence: Univ. of Kansas Press, 1960), p. 1-6. From the New York times magazine, 2 Jun. 1940. On the exploration of the Southwest by the expedition of Francisco Vásquez de Coronado, 1540. [11025

CLARA LEE TANNER. The influence of the white man on Southwest Indian art [since 1540]. Ethnohistory, 7: 137-50 (spring). On the replacement of native by manufactured materials in sculpture, painting, and the decorative arts, the limited mechanization of methods, the still more limited standardization of designs, and the development of new Indian arts applied to commercial materials, particularly silver and turquoise. [11026

ALFRED POKORN. Apatschen-Indianer: Geschichte, Ansiedlung, Sprache, Sitte, und Verwaltung der Mescaleros. München: R. Oldenbourg [1960]. 72, [2] p. maps, music, port., tables, views. (Orion-Bücher, 136.) On the Apache Indians of Arizona, New Mexico, and Texas since 1541; with observations made by the author during a visit to the Mescalero Indian Reservation, N. M., in 1953. [11027

CECIL ROBINSON. Mexico and the Hispanic Southwest in American literature. Ann Arbor: University Microfilms, 1960. Positive microfilm of typescript. [520] leaves. Thesis--Columbia Univ. Abstracted: Dissert. abstracts, 20:4662 (Jun). On Mexico and the Southwest as a theme of and an influence upon American literature since ca. 1600. [11028

LE ROY CONDIE. The effect of cultural difference in the education of Navajo Indians. [Albuquerque: College of Education, Univ. of New Mexico, 1958.] iii, [1], 119 leaves. map. notes. (The University of New Mexico Research Study: the adjustment of Indian and non-Indian children in the public schools of New Mexico.) On the history of the Navajo Indians of New Mexico and Arizona since 1540, their relations with other Indians and with the Spaniards and "Anglos," their institutions, religion, education, and health, and the necessity of knowledge of their cultural differences from "Anglo" children as a basis for devising suitable methods of teaching them. [11029

LUIS NAVARRO GARCIA. El norte de Nueva España como problema político en el siglo XVIII. Estudios am., 20:15-31 (Jul-Aug). On international complications accompanying the expansion of New Spain toward and into Louisiana, Texas, New Mexico, Arizona, and Upper California, and the effort to strengthen the frontier by forming it into a single comandancia general. [11030

ROBERT MacLEAN QUINN. Baroque architecture. Ariz. architect, 3(10): 6-15; 4(1):20-27 (Jun, Sep). port., views. On the Italian, Spanish, and Mexican origins of the style, and its introduction into the present Southwest in the 18th century. [11031

JOSEPH ANTONIO VILLA-SEÑOR Y SÁNCHEZ. Theatro americano: descripción general de los reynos, y provincias, de la Nueva-España, y sus jurisdicciones. México: En la Imprenta de la Viuda de D. Joseph Bernardo de Hogal, 1746-48. [México: Editora Nacional, 1952.] 2 v. [2] p., facsim. ([2] p.), [10] p., facsim. ([16], 382, [10] p.); [2] p., facsim. ([14], 428, [10] p.). Reproduction of the original, with a biographical introduction by Francisco Golzález de Cossío. Survey of the Viceroyalty of New Spain, compiled by the author from official reports submitted to the Viceroy from all jurisdictions of New Spain. Includes accounts of California, Nuevo León, Coahuila, Texas, Sonora, and New Mexico. [11032

JACK LANE. Federal-Quapaw relations, 1800-1833. Ark. hist. quar., 19:61-74 (spring). notes. On the removal of the Quapaw Indians from their ancestral lands in the vicinity of Arkansas Post to join the Caddo Indians on the Red River and thence, in 1833, to a reservation in present Oklahoma. [11033

LONNIE J. WHITE. Disturbances on the Arkansas-Texas border, 1827-1831. Ark. hist. quar., 19:95-110 (summer). notes. On the unsettled ownership of the land to the southwest of the Red River, claimed by both the United States and Mexico, and complicated by the uncertain allegiance of settlers, the depredations of Indians, and the plans of Benjamin R. Milam of Texas to colonize part of the area. [11034

MARGUERITE RIORDAN. The Comancheros. Cattleman, 46(12):29, 62, 67-70 (May). views. notes. On traders who met with the Comanche Indians to exchange trade goods for their loot from raided wagon trains, a trade well established by 1832, at its height in the 1860s, and ended by military action ca. 1870; with an account of some of their bartering places in the Texas Panhandle. [11035

MATTHEW CALDWELL. Matthew Caldwell and the Texan Santa Fe Expedition. [Edited by] George Nielsen. Southw. hist. quar., 63: 580-83 (Apr). Letter to the author's wife, dated in a hospital, Guanajuato, Mex., 10 Feb. 1842, on the miscarriage of the expedition and the imprisonment of its survivors. [11036

REBECCA (HUMPHREYS) TURNER (1842-1929). My story. By Rebecca Humphreys Turner, pioneer. [Pasadena?] Typecraft, 1960. [6], 177 p. ports., views. On the author's early life in Arkansas; her travels with her family and other families in a wagon train across Texas, Chihuahua, Sonora, and Arizona to Los Angeles in 1861; her marriage to William Francis Turner, miller and storekeeper; their life at El Monte; and their removal to Los Angeles in 1877. [11037

EDWARD DREWRY JERVEY. The history of Methodism in Southern California and Arizona [1846-1960]. Nashville: Parthenon Press for the Historical Soc. of the Southern California - Arizona Conference [1960]. 247 p. ports., views. bibliog. (p. 233-42), notes (p. 211-31). Issued in 1958 in microfilm form as thesis--Boston Univ. [11038

THEODORE BOREK. Some significant factors affecting the growth and development of the arid region of the Southwestern United States [from 1850] to 1950. Ann Arbor: University Microfilms, 1959 [i. e. 1960]. Positive microfilm of typescript. [212] leaves. Thesis--Univ. of Pittsburgh. Abstracted: Dissert. abstracts, 20:3103-4 (Feb). On "the Arid Region" formed by Arizona, Nevada, Utah, 5 counties of southeastern California, and "the metropolitan areas of Albuquerque, New Mexico, and El Paso, Texas." [11039

CLARA LEE TANNER. Contemporary Southwest Indian silver. Kiva, 25(3): 1-22 (Feb). mount. view. bibliog. On a silvermaking craft developed among the Navajo and Zuñi Indians, beginning perhaps as early as 1853 or as late as 1868, to which work in native and imported turquoise was added ca. 1878; with mention of the slight activity of the other New Mexico and Arizona Indians in the craft. [11040

FLOYD S. FIERMAN. Jewish pioneering in the Southwest: a record of the Freudenthal-Lesinsky-Solomon families. Ariz. and the West, 2:54-72 (spring). notes. On Julius Freudenthal, his nephew Henry Lesinski, and their mercantile partnership in Las Cruces; Henry's development of the Longfellow Copper Mining Company, Clifton, Ariz.; Isador Elkan Solomon who settled in Arizona at Pueblo Viejo and expanded from merchant to banker; and other members of the families. [11041

RAMON FREDERICK ADAMS. A fitting death for Billy the Kid. Norman: Univ. of Oklahoma Press [1960]. ix, 310 p. ports., views. On Henry McCarty, alias William H. Bonney (1859-81), and his criminal activities after 1873 in New Mexico and Arizona, ended when he was killed by Patrick Floyd Garrett, Sheriff of Lincoln County, N. M. Mainly a critical analysis of earlier publications and an attempt to correct them. [11042

KENNETH FRANKLIN NEIGHBOURS. Indian exodus out of Texas in 1859. West Tex. Hist. Assoc. yr. bk., 36: 80-97. notes. On the removal of the Indians of Texas (1,420 individuals) from their reservations to land in the Washita Valley near present Anadarko, Okla., under supervision of Maj. Robert S. Neighbors, U.S. Superintendent of Indian Affairs for Texas, 1859. [11043

HETTYE (WALLACE) BRANCH. The story of "80 John" ... a biography of one of the most respected Negro ranchmen in the Old West. N.Y.: Greenwich Book Publishers [1960]. 59 p. On the author's father, Daniel Webster Wallace (1860-1939), born a slave in Texas, his work as a cowboy in Texas, New Mexico, and Mexico, and his ranches in Navarro and Mitchell Counties, Tex. [11044

RICHARD O'CONNOR. Pat Garrett: a biography of the famous marshal and the killer of Billy the Kid. Garden City, N.Y.: Doubleday, 1960. 286 p. bibliog. (p. 283-6). On Patrick Floyd Garrett (1850-1908), his early life in Alabama and Louisiana, his removal to Texas in 1869, his many employments as he alternated between western Texas and eastern New Mexico, his celebrated feat of killing Billy the Kid, and the mysterious circumstances of his violent death. [11045

GARY UNDERWOOD. General James J. Byrne: a Yankee in orbit. Jr. historian (Tex.), 20(4):1-4, 30 (Jan). view. On his service as chief of the surveying corps of the Texas and Pacific Railway Company, 1872-79, his later work as "Land Locator and Surveyor," and his murder by Indians in Texas or New Mexico in 1880. [11046

LELIA JEANETTE WADE. "Our community" (organization and development of Nolan County): heritage of the great Southwest [1873-1960. n. p.] 1960. x, 87 p. cartoon, diagrs., maps, ports., views. notes. Includes the history of Sweetwater, and "Tales of the Old West" (lore and anecdotes, p. 80-87). [11047

FRANK G. ANDERSON. Intertribal relations in the Pueblo kachina cult. International Congress of Anthropological and Ethnological Sciences, 5th, Men and cultures, ed. Anthony F. C. Wallace (Phila.: Univ. of Pennsylvania Press [1960]), p. 377-83. bibliog. On Zuñi, Hopi, Keresan, Acoma, Tewa, and Tiwa influences on the growth of the kachina cult in New Mexico and eastern Arizona, ca. 1880 to 1956. [11048

JOSEPH SAUL STOCKER. Arizona's fabulous baron. Ariz. highways, 36(8):32-7 (Aug). facsims., map, ports. On the fraudulent claim of James Addison Reeves to some 11 million acres in Arizona and New Mexico, composing the fictitious "Peralta Grant," 1880s-90s. [11049

WELLS ALECK HUTCHINS. Pueblo water rights in the West. Tex. law rev., 38:748-62 (Jun). notes. On decisions in California, 1881-1943, and New Mexico, 1914-59; with reasons for believing that the decisions rest upon undocumented assumptions regarding Spanish and Mexican law and have the effect of authorizing growing cities to appropriate water without compensation to its owners. [11050

GARFORD WILKINSON. Jim Harkey [born 1881]; he bred Dodger. Quarter horse jour., 12(6):16-17, 39-40, 95-6 (Mar). ports. (1 double), views. On his life as a Texas cowboy and as a breeder of quarter horses in Texas and New Mexico. [11051

HERBERT HERRICK FLETCHER. The quest of the earth's fullness: the saga of James Walker Cain. Salado, Tex.: Anson Jones Press, 1960. 70, [5] p. map, mount. port., views. bibliog. (p. 73). On the discovery of salt in 1916 and of sulphur in 1924 in the process of drilling for oil in the Palangana Dome in Duval County, the formation of the Duval Texas Sulphur Company by James Walker Cain and Alfred H. Smith in 1926 to mine sulphur at the Palangana Dome, the operations of the company there and later in Fort Bend County, Tex., and the expansion of its activities to mine potassium chloride in Carlsbad, N. M. (1952), and copper in Esperanza, Ariz. (1959); with some account of James Walker Cain (born 1882), native of Texas, originally a "petroleum engineer," and a brief history of salt-mining in Texas and the laws applying to it. [11052

FRANK H. GRUBBS. Frank Bond: gentleman sheepherder of northern New Mexico, 1883-1915. N. M. hist. rev., 35:169-99, 293-308 (Jul, Oct). port., view. notes. On G. W. Bond & Bro., a partnership of George Washington Bond and Franklin Bond, merchants and wool buyers, with stores at Espanola, N. M., and Trinidad, Colo., 1890-1911; and the later separate business of Franklin Bond in wool, hides and pelts, lumber, and general merchandise, transacted in several stores in northern New Mexico and southern Colorado. [11053

MARGARET SCHEVILL LINK. From the desk of Washington Matthews [11842-1905]. Jour. Am. folklore, 72:317-25 (Oct-Dec). Data concerning his work as "the most important of the early observers of Navajo life and ritual"; with a list of his publications on "Navajo subjects" (1883-1902) and text of "The female beauty chant" as recited to him by Old Torlino (28 Oct. 1893). [11054

CLYDE KAY MABEN KLUCKHOHN (1905-60). A Navaho politician. Joseph B. Casagrande, ed., In the company of man: twenty portraits by anthropologists (N.Y.: Harper [1960]), p. 439-65. port., view. notes. On Bill Begay, alias Little Schoolboy (born ca. 1892 or 1893), Navajo Indian, delegate to the Navajo Council, interpreter, informant of the author; with data from interviews with him, 1936-58, and from his autobiography, exhibiting the author's effort to analyze his psyche. [11055

ALEXANDER MacGREGOR STEPHEN (died 1894). The Navajo. Selected papers from the American anthropologist, 1888-1920, ed. Frederica De Laguna (Evanston, Ill.: Row, Peterson [1960]), p. 457-74. diagr. First printed in Oct. 1893. On their habitat, ways of life, and beliefs, and "their steady advance toward civilization." [11056

HARRY SMITH. The way of horse-racing and senoritas. [Edited] by James P. Welsh. Quarter horse jour., 7(3):53-5 (Dec 1954). On the author's travels with his grandfather, Corky Bill Watkins, from Missouri to Texas and Mexico to race their quarter horses, 1896, and their entertainment by the wealthy and lavish "Juan Hernandez," on his ranch "just across the line in Chihuahua," whose prize mare was defeated in a race by Watkins's Log Cabin. [11057

DOUGHBELLY PRICE (born 1897). Short stirrups: the saga of Doughbelly Price. Los Angeles: Westernlore Press, 1960. 205 p. On the author's early life on a ranch near Fort Worth, his career as a professional "bronk rider" in rodeos (1912-28), and his activities as a bootlegger, a restaurant proprietor, a real-estate operator, etc., mainly in the Southwest. [11058

FLORENCE (CRANNELL) MEANS. Sunlight on the Hopi mesas: the story of Abigail E[lizabeth] Johnson [1872-1958]. Phila.: Judson Press [1960]. 171 p. On her service as a missionary at the Watonga Agency, Indian Territory, 1898-1901, and the Hopi village of Polacca (First Mesa), N. M., 1901-37; with some account of her early life and studies, and her life in retirement in California, and of the Hopi mission since 1937. [11059

WASHINGTON MATTHEWS (1843-1905). The night chant: a Navaho ceremony. Margaret Mead & Ruth L. Bunzel, eds., The golden age of American anthropology (N.Y.: George Braziller, 1960), p. 220-26. diagrs. First printed in 1902. [11060

NEIL MERTON JUDD. Reminiscences in Southwest archaeology. Kiva, 26(1):1-6 (Oct). On the author's excavations in southeastern Utah, southern Colorado, and northwestern New Mexico, summers of 1907, 1908, and 1909. [11061

ALFRED VINCENT KIDDER. Reminiscences in Southwestern archaeology. Kiva, 25(4):1-32 (Apr). port. On the author's earliest field work, in southwestern Colorado, southeastern Utah, and northern New Mexico, summer of 1907. [11062

BEEFMASTERS. Cattleman, 46(12):31, 46-50 (May). views. On Beefmaster cattle, developed by interbreeding Brahmans, shorthorns, and Herefords, 1908-60, raised by Edward C. Lasater of Falfurrias, Tex., and his son, Tom Lasater of Matheson, Colo. [11063

ROY ROTH. Missionary endeavors in the South. Mennonite hist. bul., 9:1-3 (Jan 1948). view. On Mennonite missions at Culp, Ark., Adair, Okla., and Allemands, La., and in the Ozarks, 1908-42. [11064

RICHARD G. SCHAUS. Dave Parker's boys. Quarter horse jour., 5(7):24, 101 (Apr 1953). ports. On the cattle-ranching and horse-racing activities of Dave Parker of Hachita, N. M., and of his sons, Bud Parker, O. P. Parker (Ope), and W. D. Parker (Dink), in Arizona, 1911-53. [11065

MARK HERRA. Gene Rambo [born 1920]. Quarter horse jour., 3(3):9, 29 (Dec 1950). ports. On his early life in San Miguel, Calif., and his career since 1938 as a rodeo performer in the Southwest. [11066

VIVIAN KIRK. Ace jockey ... Milo Trevino [born 1925]. Quarter horse jour., 3(2):15 (Nov 1950). ports. On his early life in Gonzales, Tex., and his career since 1936 as a jockey in Texas, New Mexico, Arizona, and California. [11067

GARFORD WILKINSON. Hugh Bennett, all-round cowboy-rancher. Quarter horse jour., 12(1):10-11, 28, 30, 107-8, 126-7 (Oct 1959). facsim., ports., views. On his early life in Knox County, Tex., his studies at Abilene Christian College, his travels as a rodeo performer from 1925 to ca.

1950, his ranches in Arizona and Texas, and his breeding and training of quarter horses. [11068

ALICE FINCH. After graduation--what? Delta Kappa Gamma bul., 24(3):5-14 (summer 1958). On the author's service as a teacher among the Navajo, Ute, and Paiute Indians, 1931-44. [11069

LEONORA SCOTT MUSE CURTIN. Reminiscences in Southwest archaeology. Kiva, 26(2):1-10 (Dec). On the author's travels in the Navajo country of New Mexico and Arizona and adjacent parts of Utah and Colorado in the summer of 1932. [11070

MORRIS EDWARD OPLER. Myth and practice in Jicarilla Apache eschatology. Jour. Am. folklore, 72:133-53 (Apr-Jun). notes. Based upon field studies made in 1934-35. [11071

RICHARD G. SCHAUS. A cowboy's rope horse. Quarter horse jour., 4(3):6-7, 29 (Dec 1951). ports. On Shorty, a quarter-horse gelding foaled in 1942, owned by Clifford Whatley, used as a rodeo horse in Texas and a working horse in Arizona. [11072

VIVIAN KIRK. Top quarter running sires [in the Southwest, 1943-52]. Quarter horse jour., 4(7):33, 95 (Apr 1952). view. [11073

L. S. TERBUSH. The small-dam program in flood control [in the Washita River Watershed, Oklahoma and Texas, 1944-51]. Agric. engineering, 34:716 (Nov 1952). [11074

EVON ZARTMAN VOGT. The automobile in contemporary Navaho culture [Arizona and New Mexico, 1945-56]. International Congress of Anthropological and Ethnological Sciences, 5th, 1956, Men and cultures: selected papers, ed. Anthony F. C. Wallace (Phila.: Univ. of Pennsylvania Press [1960]), p. 359-63. bibliog., notes. [11075

PAUL D. BUTT. Branch banking and economic growth in Arizona and New Mexico [1947-60]. Albuquerque [1960]. ix, 39 p. maps, tables. bibliog. (p. 37-9), notes. (University of New Mexico, Bureau of Business Research. New Mexico studies in business and economics, 7.) Based on thesis (M.B.A.)--Univ. of New Mexico. [11076

GEORGE C. McLEOD. He trains quarter racers. Quarter horse jour., 7(7):14-15, 43-4 (Apr 1955). ports., double view. On John Hazlewood (born 1893) as a trainer of quarter horses in Oklahoma, Colorado, and Arizona, his methods, and some of the prize-winners he has trained, especially since 1947. [11077

IRVING K. FOX & ISABEL PICKEN. The upstream-downstream controversy in the Arkansas-White-Red Basins Survey ... a case study in resources administration supported by a grant from Resources for the Future, Inc. University, Ala.: Univ. of Alabama Press for the ICP [1960. 6], 53, [1] p. diagr., maps, view. bibliog. (p. 54). (Inter-University Case Program. ICP case series, 55.) On the efforts of an interagency committee to accomplish "the integration of the flood management plans of the Corps of Engineers and the Department of Agriculture" in this region, containing Oklahoma and parts of Louisiana, Texas, New Mexico, Colorado, Kansas, Missouri, and Arkansas, 1950-54, and the failure of the committee, as indicated in its final report in 1955, to reduce the differences of opinion regarding flood-control programs. [11078

The Rio Grande Valley

CHARLES HARRISON McNUTT. Excavation and interpretation of early Puebloan occupations at Tesuque By-Pass site and in the upper Rio Grande Valley [750-1300]. Ann Arbor: University Microfilms, 1960. Positive microfilm of typescript. [274] leaves. Thesis--Univ. of Michigan. Abstracted: Dissert. abstracts, 21:285 (Aug). [11079

CHARLES L. GHOLZ. El Paso's shifting sands. Jr. historian (Tex.), 19(4):26-30 (Jan 1959). col. map, views. On transfers of land between Juárez and El Paso as a result of changes of course of the Rio Grande, 1852-1911. [11080

GILBERT DEMENTIS. Resource allocation in the lower Rio Grande River Valley, 1940-1956. Chicago: [Dept. of Photoduplication, Univ. of Chicago Library] 1960. Positive microfilm of typescript. 99 leaves. bibliog. Thesis--Univ. of Chicago. [11081

WALTER WILLARD TAYLOR & FRANCISCO GONZÁLEZ RUL. An archeological reconnaissance behind the Diablo Dam, Coahuila, Mexico. Tex. Archeol. Soc., Bul., 31:153-65. maps, tables. bibliog. Based in part upon González Rul's thesis--Escuela Nacional de Antropologia e Historia. Report of a survey undertaken in 1958 by Mexican and U.S. agencies in the area on the Rio Grande and its tributaries in Coahuila and Texas to be flooded by the Friendship International Dam. [11082

The Colorado Valley

C. GREGORY CRAMPTON. Historical sites in Glen Canyon, mouth of San Juan River to Lee's Ferry [1776-1910. Salt Lake City: Univ. of Utah Press] 1960. xvi, 130, [4] p. maps, views. bibliog. (p. 105-9), notes. (University of Utah. Dept. of Anthropology. Anthropological papers, 46. Glen Canyon series, 12.) Records all obtainable facts from documentary sources and from inspection of 58 sites, including the point where Fathers Francisco Atanasio Domínguez and Silvestre Vélez de Escalante crossed the river in 1776, various Navajo sites, camps of the Powell Survey (1869-73), mining sites of the gold rush of 1883-92, Lee's Ferry, and Rainbow Bridge. [11083

JESSE DAVID JENNINGS. The aboriginal peoples [of the Upper Colorado River and Valley]. Utah hist. quar., 28:210-21 (Jul). maps, views. [11084

UTAH, UNIVERSITY OF. Dept. of Anthropology. The Glen Canyon Archaeological Survey. [Salt Lake City: Univ. of Utah Press] 1959. 2 v. in 3. xiv, 316; [6], 319-707, [4]; vii, 98, [3] p. diagrs., forms, maps (part fold.), tables, views. (Its Anthropological papers, 39. Glen Canyon series, 6.) Prepared by agreement between the National Park Service and the University of Utah as part of the Upper Colorado River Basin Salvage Program, in preparation for flooding of a large area of the Colorado Valley in southern Utah and a small area in northern Arizona. Partial contents.--Findings.--The Glen Canyon right bank survey, by Robert H. Lister.--Extended survey of the right bank of the Glen Canyon, by Dee Ann Suhm.--The Waterpocket Fold, by Robert H. Lister.--Archeological survey of the Kaiparowits Plateau, by James H. Gunnerson.--Glen Canyon main stem survey, by Don D. Fowler.--San Juan Triangle survey, by Ted Weller.--[Report on work in 1959], by Don D. Fowler. [11085

PAGES OF HISTORY, Sausalito, Calif. The Mojave of the Colorado: the story of the Mojave Indians of the Colorado River and their meetings with the explorers of the Southwest [1540-1860]. Sausalito, Calif., ©1960. 23, [1] p. maps, ports., views. bibliog. (p. 24). [11086

C. GREGORY CRAMPTON. Historic Glen Canyon [Utah and Arizona, 1776-1960]. Utah hist. quar., 28: 274-89 (Jul). maps, ports., views. [11087

WILLIAM M. PURDY. Green River: main stem of the Colorado [1776-1954]. Utah hist. quar., 28:250-61 (Jul). views. [11088

WILLIAM M. PURDY. An outline of the history of the Flaming Gorge area. [Salt Lake City: Univ. of Utah Press] 1959. vii, 45 p. maps, port., views. bibliog. (p. 40-42). (University of Utah. Dept. of Anthropology. Anthropological papers, 37. Upper Colorado series, 1.) On the history, since 1825, of an area along the course of the Green River in Utah and Wyoming, to be flooded behind the Flaming Gorge Dam. [11089

WILLIAM CULP DARRAH. Powell of the Colorado. Utah hist. quar., 28:222-31 (Jul). port., views. On explorations of the Colorado River under the direction of John Wesley Powell, 1868-77, and his later proposals for surveying the lands and conserving the waters, soils, and forests of the Colorado Valley by action of the U.S. Government. [11090

DWIGHT LA VERN SMITH. The engineer and the Canyon. Utah hist. quar., 28:262-73 (Jul). ports., view. notes. On a survey directed by Robert Brewster Stanton "to determine the feasibility and worth of a railroad along the river from Grand Junction, Colorado, to the Gulf of California," 25 May 1889 - 26 Apr. 1890. [11091

ALFRED LOUIS KROEBER (1876-1960). Preliminary sketch of the Mohave Indians. Selected papers from the American anthropologist, 1888-1920, ed. Frederica De Laguna (Evanston, Ill.: Row, Peterson [1960]), p. 506-15. First printed in 1904. Based upon observations made by the author in California, Arizona, and Nevada, 1900 and 1902. [11092

JAY R. BINGHAM. Reclamation and the Colorado. Utah hist. quar., 28: 232-49 (Jul). maps, ports., views. On plans for controlling and conserving the river waters and for dividing them equitably among the States of the Colorado River Basin and between the United States and Mexico, 1902-56. [11093

ALFRED LOUIS KROEBER & MICHAEL J. HARNER. Mohave pottery. [Berkeley: Univ. of California Press, 1955.] v, 30 p. diagrs., views. bibliog. (p. 20). (Anthropological records, v. 16, no. 1.) Illustrations and descriptions of pieces collected by Kroeber "in Mohave Valley, on both sides of the Colorado River," 1902-4. [11094

EDWARD W. CLYDE. Present conflicts on the Colorado River. Rocky Mt. law rev., 32:534-65 (Jun). notes. On the Colorado River Compact, which became operative in 1929, the Upper Colorado River Basin Compact, signed in 1948, related legislation and litigation, and resulting conflicts between the States of the Upper Basin and those of the Lower Basin, among the States within each basin, and within individual States. [11095

Serials Cited

A. I. A. jour. A. I. A. journal. [Formerly Journal of the American Institute of Architects.] Wash.

A. M. E. Zion quar. rev. The A. M. E. Zion quarterly review. Bedford, Pa.: Publishing Board, A. M. E. Zion Church.

Abstracts of Eng. studies. Abstracts of English studies: an official publication of the National Council of Teachers of English. [Boulder, Colo.]

Agric. engineering. Agricultural engineering: the journal of the American Society of Agricultural Engineers. [St. Joseph, Mich.]

Agric. hist. Agricultural history: a publication of the Agricultural History Society. [Champaign, Ill.: Garrard Press.]

Air Univ. quar. rev. Air University quarterly review. [Published by Air University as the professional journal of the United States Air Force.] Maxwell Air Force Base, Ala.: Air Univ.

Ala. Acad. Science, Jour. The journal of the Alabama Academy of Science. Birmingham.

Ala. hist. quar. The Alabama historical quarterly. [n. p.:] State Dept. of Archives and History.

Ala. law rev. Alabama law review. University: School of Law, Univ. of Alabama.

Ala. lawyer. The Alabama lawyer: official organ, State Bar of Alabama. Montgomery.

Ala. rev. The Alabama review: a quarterly journal of Alabama history. University: Univ. of Alabama Press in cooperation with the Alabama Historical Assoc.

Alaska sportsman. Alaska sportsman. Juneau: Alaska-Northwest Pub. Co.

Albany law rev. Albany law review. Albany: Law Review Board of Albany Law School.

Am. Acad. Pol. and Social Science, Ann. The annals of the American Academy of Political and Social Science. Phila.

Am. anthropol. American anthropologist. Menasha, Wis.: American Anthropological Assoc.

Am. antiq. American antiquity: a quarterly review of American archaeology. Salt Lake City: Univ. of Utah Press for the Soc. for American Archaeology.

Am. Antiq. Soc., Proc. Proceedings of the American Antiquarian Society. Worcester.

Am. archivist. The American archivist. [Cedar Rapids, Ia.:] Soc. of American Archivists.

Am. artist. American artist. N.Y.: Watson-Guptill Publications, Inc.

Am. Assoc. Health, Phys. Educ., and Recr., Research quar. The research quarterly of the American Association of Health, Physical Education, and Recreation. Wash.

Am. Bar Assoc. jour. American Bar Association journal. [Chicago.]

Am. Benedictine rev. The American Benedictine review. Newark, N.J.: American Benedictine Academy.

Am. book collector. The American book collector: a scholarly journal of bibliography. [Chicago: W. B. Thorsen.]

Am. Cath. Hist. Soc., Rec. Records of the American Catholic Historical Society of Philadelphia: a quarterly publication devoted exclusively to the study of the history of the Catholic Church in America. Phila.

Am. College Dentists, Jour. Journal of the American College of Dentists. Fulton, Mo.: Ovid Bell Press.

Am. Dental Assoc., Jour. The journal of the American Dental Association. Chicago.

Am. Dietetic Assoc., Jour. Journal of the American Dietetic Association. Baltimore.

Am. eccles. rev. The American ecclesiastical review: a monthly publication for the clergy. [Wash.:] Catholic Univ. of America Press.

Am. econ. rev. The American economic review. [Menasha, Wis.: American Economic Assoc.]

Am. forests. American forests. Wash.: American Forestry Assoc.

Am. geneal. The American genealogist. New Haven: Donald Lines Jacobus.

Am. Geophysical Union, Trans. Transactions of the American Geophysical

Union: a bimonthly journal devoted to the broad field of geophysics. Wash.: American Geophysical Union, National Academy of Sciences, National Research Council.

Am. Geriatrics Soc., Jour. Journal of the American Geriatrics Society. Baltimore: Williams & Wilkins Co.

Am.-German rev. The American-German review. Phila.: Carl Schurz Memorial Foundation.

Am. hist. rev. The American historical review. Richmond, Va.: Macmillan Co. for the American Historical Assoc., Wash.

Am. imago. The American imago ... a psychoanalytic journal for the arts and sciences. Boston: American Imago.

Am. Jew. arch. American Jewish archives: devoted to the preservation and study of American Jewish historical records. Cincinnati: Hebrew Union College - Jewish Institute of Religion.

Am. Jew. Hist. Soc., Pub. Publication of the American Jewish Historical Society. [Phila.]

Am. Jew. yr. bk. American Jewish year book. N.Y.: American Jewish Committee, and Jewish Publication Soc. of America, Phila.

Am. jour. cardiol. The American journal of cardiology: official journal of the American College of Cardiology. N.Y.

Am. jour. diseases of children. American journal of diseases of children. Chicago: American Medical Assoc.

Am. jour. econ. and sociol. The American journal of economics and sociology. Published quarterly under grant from the Robert Schalkenbach Foundation in the interest of constructive synthesis in the social sciences. Lancaster, Pa.

Am. jour. legal hist. The American journal of legal history ... official publication of the American Society of Legal History. Phila.: Temple Univ. School of Law.

Am. jour. nursing. The American journal of nursing: official organ of the American Nurses' Association. N.Y.: American Journal of Nursing Co.

Am. jour. obstetrics and gynecol. American journal of obstetrics and gynecology. St. Louis: C. V. Mosby Co.

Am. jour. optometry. American journal of optometry and archives of American Academy of Optometry. Minneapolis: American Journal of Optometry Pub. Assoc.

Am. jour. orthodontics. American journal of orthodontics: official publication of the American Association of Orthodontists, its component societies, and the American Board of Orthodontists. St. Louis: C. V. Mosby Co.

Am. jour. pharmaceutical educ. The American journal of pharmaceutical education. Pullman, Wash.: Washington State Univ. Press for the American Assoc. of Colleges of Pharmacy.

Am. jour. phys. anthropol. American journal of physical anthropology. Phila.: Wistar Institute of Anatomy and Biology.

Am. jour. psychiatry. The American journal of psychiatry. Hanover, N.H.: American Psychiatric Assoc.

Am. jour. pub. health. American journal of public health and The nation's health. [N.Y.: American Public Health Assoc.]

Am. jour. sociol. The American journal of sociology. Chicago: Univ. of Chicago Press.

Am. jour. surgery. The American journal of surgery. N.Y.: American Journal of Surgery, Inc.

Am. jour. tuberculosis and pulm. dis. The American journal of tuberculosis and pulmonary diseases: official journal of American Trudeau Society medical section of National Tuberculosis Association. Baltimore: National Tuberculosis Assoc. [Formerly The American review of tuberculosis: a journal of pulmonary diseases. Title changed with v. 80, no. 1, Jul. 1959, to The American review of respiratory diseases.]

Am. lit. American literature: a journal of literary history, criticism, and bibliography. [Durham, N.C.:] Duke Univ. Press with the cooperation of the American Literature Group of the Modern Language Assoc. of America.

Am. Med. Women's Assoc., Jour. Journal of the American Medical Women's Association. Nashville, Tenn.

Am. Micros. Soc., Trans. Transactions of the American Microscopical Society. Columbus, Ohio.

Am. Musicol. Soc., Jour. Journal of the American Musicological Society. Richmond, Va.: William Byrd Press.

Am. Neptune. The American Neptune: a quarterly journal of maritime history. Salem, Mass.: American Neptune, Inc.

Am. Philatelic Cong., Congress book. The Congress book. [n. p.:] American Philatelic Congress.

Am. philatelist. The American philatelist. State College, Pa.: American Philatelic Soc.

Am. Philos. Soc., Proc. Proceedings of the American Philosophical Society Held at Philadelphia for Promoting Useful Knowledge. Phila.

Am. Philos. Soc., Yr. bk. Year book. Phila.: American Philosophical Soc.

Am. pol. science rev. The American political science review. Wash.: American Political Science Assoc.

Am. quar. American quarterly. Phila.: Univ. of Pennsylvania in cooperation with the American Studies Assoc.

Am. record guide. The American record guide. N.Y.

Am. rev. The American review. [Bologna: European Center of the Johns Hopkins Univ. Bologna Center.]

Am. rev. resp. dis. The American review of respiratory diseases: official journal of the American Trudeau Society, medical section of the National Tuberculosis Association. Baltimore: National Tuberculosis Assoc.

Am. rev. tuberculosis. The American review of tuberculosis: a journal of pulmonary diseases. Baltimore: American Trudeau Soc., Medical Section of the National Tuberculosis Assoc.

Am. rifleman. The American rifleman. Wash.: National Rifle Assoc. of America.

Am.-Scandinavian rev. The American-Scandinavian review. N.Y.: American-Scandinavian Foundation.

Am. scientist. American scientist, published in the interest of scientific research. Easton, Pa.: Soc. of the Sigma Chi.

Am. Slavic and East European rev. The American Slavic and East European review. [N.Y.:] Columbia Univ. Press for the American Assoc. for the Advancement of Slavic Studies, Inc.

Am. Soc. Agric. Engineers, Trans. Transactions of the ASAE: selected contributions in the field of agricultural engineering. [St. Joseph, Mich.]

Am. sociol. rev. American sociological review: official journal of the American Sociological Society. Albany, N.Y.

Am. speech. American speech: a quarterly of linguistic usage. [N.Y.:] Columbia Univ. Press.

Am. Statistical Assoc., Jour. Journal of the American Statistical Association. Menasha, Wis.

Am. Swed. Hist. Foundation, Yr. bk. Year book. Phila.: American Swedish Historical Foundation.

Am. Swed. monthly. the American Swedish monthly. N.Y.: Swedish Chamber of Commerce of the United States of America.

Am. Univ. law rev. The American University law review. [Wash.:] Washington College of Law.

Am. Water Works Assoc., Jour. Journal. N.Y.: American Water Works Assoc.

Americas. The Americas: a quarterly review of inter-American cultural history. Wash.: Academy of American Franciscan History.

Analyst. The analyst. [Evanston, Ill.:] Dept of English, Northwestern Univ.

Ann. dentistry. Annals of dentistry: official publication of the New York Academy of Dentistry. N.Y.

Ann. Ia. Annals of Iowa: a magazine of history. Des Moines: Iowa State Dept. of History and Archives.

Ann. internal med. Annals of internal medicine, published monthly by the American College of Physicians. [Lancaster, Pa.]

Ann. surgery. Annals of surgery: a monthly review of surgical science and practice. Also the official publication of the American Surgical Association, the Southern Surgical Association, Philadelphia Academy of Surgery, [and] New York Surgical Society. Phila.: J. B. Lippincott.

Ann. Wyo. Annals of Wyoming ... official publication of the Wyoming State Historical Society. Cheyenne: Wyoming State Archives and Historical Dept.

Antique automobile. The antique automobile ... official publication of Antique Automobile Club of America, Inc. [Stonington, Conn.]

Antiques. Antiques, N.Y.: Straight Enterprises, Inc.

Antiques jour. The antiques journal. Westfield, N.Y.: Guide Pub. Co.

Anuario estudios am. Anuario de estudios americanos. Sevilla: [Escuela de Estudios Hispano-Americanos de Sevilla.].

Appalachia. Appalachia. Boston: Appalachian Mountain Club.

Appraisal jour. The appraisal journal. Chicago: American Institute of Real Estate Appraisers of the National Association of Real Estate Boards.

Arch. dermatol. A. M. A. archives of dermatology. Chicago: American Medical Assoc.

Arch. gen. psychiatry. A. M. A. archives of general psychiatry. Chicago: American Medical Assoc.
Arch. internal med. Archives of internal medicine. [Chicago:] American Medical Assoc.
Arch. neurol. A. M. A. archives of neurology. Chicago: American Medical Assoc.
Arch. neurol. and psychiatry. Archives of neurology and psychiatry. Chicago: American Medical Assoc.
Arch. surgery. Archives of surgery: official publication for the Central Surgical Association and the Western Surgical Association. Chicago: American Medical Assoc.
Archeol. Soc. N.J., News letter. Archeological Society of New Jersey. News letter. [Trenton.]
Ariz. and the West. Arizona and the West: a quarterly journal of history. [Tucson:] Univ. of Arizona.
Ariz. architect. Arizona architect: official publication of the Arizona Society of Architects. Phoenix.
Ariz. highways. Arizona highways. Phoenix: Arizona Highway Dept.
Ariz. law rev. Arizona law review. Tucson: College of Law of the Univ. of Arizona.
Ariz. quar. The Arizona quarterly. [Tucson:] Univ. of Arizona.
Ark. hist. quar. The Arizona historical quarterly. Van Buren: Arkansas Historical Assoc.
Ark. Med. Soc., Jour. The journal of the Arkansas Medical Society. Fort Smith, Ark.
Arlington hist. mag. The Arlington historical magazine. Arlington, Va.: Arlington Historical Soc.
Armenian rev. The Armenian review. Boston: hairenik Assoc., Inc.
Art bul. The art bulletin: a quarterly published by the College Art Association of America. [N.Y.]
Art in Am. Art in America. N.Y.: Art in America Co.
Art quar. The art quarterly. [Detroit: Detroit Institute of Arts.]
Asa Gray bul. The Asa Gray bulletin. Ann Arbor: Gray Memorial Botanical Assoc. and the Botanical Gardens Assoc. of the Univ. of Michigan.
Assoc. Am. Geographers, Ann. Annals of the Association of American Geographers. Lancaster, Pa.
Assoc. Am. Physicians, Trans. Transactions of the Association of American Physicians. [n. p.]
Assoc. Bar City N.Y., Rec. The record of the Association of the Bar of the City of New York. N.Y.
Audubon mag. Audubon magazine ... a bimonthly devoted to the conservation of wildlife, plants, soil, and water. N.Y.: National Audubon Soc.
Auk. The auk: a quarterly journal of ornithology. [Lancaster, Pa.:] American Ornithologists' Union.
Back number. "The back number ...": the quarterly of the Nevada Historical Society. Reno.
Bacteriol. rev. Bacteriological reviews: a publication of the Society of American Bacteriologists. Baltimore: Williams & Wilkins Co.
Bar Assoc. Dist. Col., Jour. The journal of the Bar Association of the District of Columbia.
Bar Assoc. State Kan., Jour. The journal of the Bar Association of the State of Kansas. Topeka.
Baylor law rev. Baylor law review. Waco, Tex.: Law Students of Baylor Univ.
Bibliog. Soc. Am., Papers. The papers of the Bibliographical Society of America. N.Y.
Books at Brown. Books at Brown. Providence: Friends of the Library of Brown Univ.
Boston Pub. Lib. quar. The Boston Public Library quarterly. Boston: The Trustees [of the Public Library of the City of Boston].
Boston Univ. graduate jour. Boston University graduate journal: a review of current graduate and research activities. Boston: Graduate School, Boston Univ.
Boston Univ. law rev. Boston University law review. Boston: Boston Univ. Law School.
Boston Univ. studies in Eng. Boston University studies in English. Boston: Dept. of English, Graduate School.
Bostonian Soc., Proc. Proceedings of the Bostonian Society. Boston.
Botanical rev. The botanical review, interpreting botanical progress. N.Y.: New York Botanical Garden.
Brigham Young Univ. studies. Brigham Young University studies. [Provo, Utah: Brigham Young Univ.]
Brit. Assoc. Am. Studies, Bul. Bulletin. [n. p.:] British Assoc. for American Studies.
Brooklyn law rev. Brooklyn law review. Brooklyn: Students of Brooklyn Law School.
Bucknell rev. Bucknell review: a scholarly journal of letters, arts, and science. Lewisburg, Pa.: Bucknell Univ. Press.
Buffalo law rev. Buffalo law review. Buffalo, N.Y.: [Univ. of Buffalo School of Law].
Bul. bibliog. Bulletin of bibliography. Boston: F. W. Faxon Co.

Bul. hist. med. Bulletin of the history of medicine: organ of the American Association for the History of Medicine and of the Johns Hopkins Institute of the History of Medicine. Baltimore: Johns Hopkins Press.

Bus. hist. rev. The business history review. Boston: Graduate School of Business Administration, Harvard Univ.

CLA jour. CLA journal: official publication of the College Language Association. Baltimore

Calif. Hist. Soc. quar. California Historical Society quarterly. San Francisco.

Calif. jour. educ. research. California journal of educational research. San Francisco: California Teachers Assoc. for the California Advisory Council on Educational Research.

Calif. med. California medicine: official journal of the California Medical Association. [San Francisco.]

Can. hist. rev. The Canadian historical review. [Toronto:] Univ. of Toronto Press.

Carnegie mag. Carnegie magazine. [Pittsburgh: Carnegie Institute. Carnegie Library, and Carnegie Institute of Technology.]

Cath. educ. rev. The Catholic educational review. Wash.: Catholic Education Press under the direction of the Dept. of Education, Catholic Univ. of America.

Cath. hist. rev. The Catholic historical review: official organ of the American Catholic Historical Association. Wash.: Catholic Univ. of America Press.

Cath. school jour. The Catholic school journal. Milwaukee: Bruce Pub. Co.

Cath. Univ. Am. law rev. The Catholic University of America law review. Wash.: Catholic Univ. of America Press.

Cattleman. The cattleman. Fort Worth: Texas and Southwestern Cattle Raisers Assoc.

Cent. Miss. Valley Am. Studies Assoc., Jour. Journal of the Central Mississippi Valley American Studies Association. Lawrence: Univ. of Kansas.

Centennial rev. arts & science. The centennial review of arts & science. [East Lansing, Mich.: College of Science and Arts, Michigan State Univ.]

Centro Escolar Univ., Graduate and faculty studies. Graduate and faculty studies. [Manila: Graduate School, Centro Escolar Univ.]

Chicago hist. Chicago history. [Chicago:] Chicago Historical Soc.

Chicago Jew. forum. The Chicago Jewish forum: a national quarterly. Chicago: Benjamin Weintroub.

Chron. Okla. The chronicles of Oklahoma. Oklahoma City: Oklahoma Historical Soc.

Church hist. Church history. [Berne, Ind.: American Soc. of Church History.]

Civil War hist. Civil War history. [Iowa City:] State Univ. of Iowa.

Classical jour. The classical journal. [Boulder, Colo.:] Classical Assoc. of the Middle West and South [etc.].

Collectors Club philatelist. The Collectors Club philatelist: a magazine devoted to philatelic study & research. N.Y.: Collectors Club.

College and research lib. College and research libraries. Fulton, Mo.: Assoc. of College and Research Libraries, American Library Assoc.

College art jour. College art journal. N.Y.: College Art Assoc. of America.

College Educ. quar. College of Education quarterly. [East Lansing, Mich.: College of Education, Michigan State Univ.]

College Eng. College English, an official organ of the National Council of Teachers of English. [Champaign, Ill.]

College Phys. Phila., Trans. & studies. Transactions & studies of the College of Physicians of Philadelphia. Baltimore: Waverly Press.

Colo. mag. The Colorado magazine. Denver: State Historical Soc. of Colorado.

Colo. quar. The Colorado quarterly. Boulder: Univ. of Colorado.

Columbia Hist. Soc., Rec. Records of the Columbia historical Society of Washington, D.C. Wash.

Columbia law rev. Columbia law review. N.Y.: [Directors of Columbia Law Review Assoc., Inc.].

Columbia Lib. columns. Columbia Library columns. N.Y.: Friends of the Columbia Libraries.

Commentary. Commentary. N.Y.: [American Jewish Committee].

Commonwealth (Va.). The commonwealth: the magazine of Virginia. Richmond: Virginia State Chamber of Commerce.

Comparative educ. rev. Comparative education review: official organ of the Comparative Education Society. N.Y.

Conn. Bar jour. Connecticut Bar journal. Hartford: State Bar Assoc. of Connecticut.

Conn. Hist. Soc. bul. The Connecticut Historical Society bulletin. [Hartford.]

Construction rev. Construction review. [Wash.:] Business and Defense Services Admin.

Contact. Contact: the San Francisco journal of new writing, art, and ideas. Sausalito, Calif.: Angel Island Publications.

Copeia. Copeia. [Phila.:] American Soc. of Ichthyologists and Herpetologists.

Cornell law quar. Cornell law quarterly. Ithaca: [Cornell Univ.].

Criticism. Criticism: a quarterly for literature and the arts. Detroit: Wayne State Univ. Press.

Cross & cockade jour. Cross & cockade journal. [Santa Ana, Calif.:] Soc. of World War I Aero Historians.

Current anthropol. Current anthropology: a world journal of the sciences of man. [Chicago: Univ. of Chicago for] Wenner-Gren Foundation for Anthropological Research.

D. A. R. mag. The Daughters of the American Revolution magazine. Wash.: National Society, Daughters of the American Revolution.

D.C. lib. D.C. libraries. Wash.: District of Columbia Library Assoc.

Daedalus. Daedalus: journal of the American Academy of Arts and Sciences. Middletown, Conn.: Published jointly by the American Academy of Arts and Sciences and the Wesleyan Univ. Press.

Dalhousie rev. The Dalhousie review. Halifax, N.S.: Review Pub. Co., Ltd.

Dartmouth alumni mag. Dartmouth alumni magazine. Brattleboro, Vt.: Dartmouth Secretaries Assoc.

Del. hist. Delaware history. [Wilmington:] Historical Soc. of Delaware.

Del. State med. jour. Delaware State medical journal. Wilmington: Medical Soc. of Delaware.

Delta Kappa Gamma bul. The Delta Kappa Gamma bulletin. Austin, Tex.: Delta Kappa Gamma Soc., International.

De Paul law rev. De Paul law review. [Chicago: De Paul Univ. College of Law.]

Detroit Hist. Soc., Bul. Bulletin of the Detroit Historical Society. Detroit.

Detroit Soc. Geneal. Research mag. The Detroit Society for Genealogical Research magazine. Detroit.

Dickinson law rev. Dickinson law review. Carlisle, Pa.: Dickinson School of Law.

Dicta. Dicta. Denver: Denver Bar Assoc., Colorado Bar Assoc., and Univ. of Denver College of Law.

Discourse. Discourse: a review of the liberal arts. [Moorhead, Minn.:] Concordia College.

Dissert. abstracts. Dissertation abstracts (formerly Microfilm abstracts): a guide to dissertations and monographs available in microform. Ann Arbor, Mich.: University Microfilms.

Duke bar jour. Duke bar journal. Durham, N.C.: School of Law, Duke Univ.

Duke law jour. Duke law journal. Durham, N.C.: Duke Univ. School of Law.

Dutch Settlers Soc. Albany, Yr. bk. Yearbook. Albany: Dutch Settlers Soc. of Albany.

Dutchess Co. Hist. Soc., Yr. bk. Year book. [Poughkeepsie, N.Y.:] Dutchess County Historical Soc.

ELH. ELH. Baltimore: Johns Hopkins Press [for the Tudor and Stuart Club of the Johns Hopkins Univ.].

East Tenn. Hist. Soc. pub. The East Tennessee Historical Society's publications. Knoxville.

Ecology. Ecology: all forms of life in relation to environment. Official publication of the Ecological Society of America, continuing the Plant world. Durham, N.C.: Ecological Soc. of America and the Duke Univ. Press.

Econ. botany. Economic botany, devoted to applied botany and plant utilization. N.Y.: New York Botanical Garden.

Econ. geog. Economic geography. Worcester: Clark Univ.

Econ. hist. rev. The economic history review. Utrecht: N. V. A. Oosthoek's Uitgevers Mij for the Economic History Soc.

Educ. forum. The educational forum. [Menasha, Wis.: George Banta Pub. Co. for] Kappa Delta Pi, an honor society in education.

Educ. rec. The educational record. [Wash.:] American Council on Education.

Educ. theatre jour. Educational theatre journal. Columbia, Mo.: Artcraft Press for the American Educational Theatre Assoc.

Element. school jour. The elementary school journal. Chicago: Univ. of Chicago Press for the Dept. of Education, Univ. of Chicago.

Emerson Soc. quar. The Emerson Society quarterly. Hartford.

Emory Univ. quar. The Emory University quarterly. Atlanta: Emory Univ.

Eng. studies. English studies: a journal of English letters and philology. Amsterdam: Swets & Zeitlinger.

Eng. studies in Africa. English studies in Africa. Johannesburg: Witwatersrand Univ. Press.

Engineering and science. Engineering and science. Pasadena, Calif.: California Institute of Technology.

Entomological news. Entomological news. Phila.: American Entomological Soc., Academy of Natural Sciences of Philadelphia.

Essay-proof jour. The essay-proof journal: devoted to the historical background of stamps and paper money. [N.Y.:] Essay-Proof Soc.

Essex Inst. hist. col. Essex Institute historical collections. Salem, Mass.: Essex Institute.

Estudios am. Estudios americanos: revista de síntesis e interpretación. [Sevilla: Escuela de Estudios Hispano Americanos.]

Ethics. Ethics: an international journal of social, political, and legal philosophy. Chicago: Univ. of Chicago Press.

Ethnohist. Ethnohistory. [Sponsored by the American Indian Ethnohistoric Conference. Bloomington: Indiana Univ.]

Ethnomusicol. Ethnomusicology: journal of the Society for Ethnomusicology. Middletown, Conn.: Wesleyan Univ. Press.

Fed. Bar jour. The Federal Bar journal: the official publication of the Federal Bar Association. Wash.

Filson Club hist. quar. The Filson Club history quarterly. Louisville, Ky.: Filson Club.

Fla. anthropol. The Florida anthropologist. Tallahassee: Dept. of Anthropology, Univ. of Florida, for the Florida Anthropological Soc.

Fla. handbook. The Florida handbook ... Compiled by Allen Morris. Tallahassee: Peninsular Pub. Co.

Fla. hist. quar. The Florida historical quarterly. [Jacksonville:] Florida Historical Soc.

Flying. Flying. N.Y.: Ziff-Davis Pub. Co.

Folklore and folk music archivist. The folklore and folk music archivist ... a joint publication of the Folklore Archive and the Archives of Folk and Primitive Music, divisions of the Research Center in Anthropology, Folklore, and Linguistics, Indiana University. Bloomington.

Food drug cosmetic law jour. Food drug cosmetic law journal. [Chicago:] Commerce Clearing House, Inc. [in association with the Food Law Institute].

For. affairs. Foreign affairs: an American quarterly review. N.Y.: Council on Foreign Relations.

For. Service jour. Foreign Service journal. Wash.: American Foreign Service Assoc.

Fordham law rev. Fordham law review. [N.Y.:] Fordham Univ. Press.

Forest hist. Forest history. St. Paul: Forest History Foundation.

Forest science. Forest science: a quarterly journal of research and technical progress. [Wash.: Soc. of American Foresters.]

Franklin Inst., Jour. Journal of the Franklin Institute, devoted to science and the mechanic arts. Phila.: Franklin Institute of the State of Pennsylvania.

Frontier times. Frontier times. Austin, Tex.: Western Publications.

Ga. Bar jour. Georgia Bar journal. Macon: Georgia Bar Assoc.

Ga. hist. quar. The Georgia historical quarterly. Athens: Edited and published at the Univ. of Georgia by the Georgia Historical Soc., Savannah.

Ga. rev. The Georgia review. Athens: Univ. of Georgia Press for the Univ. of Georgia.

Garden Club Am., Bul. Bulletin of the Garden Club of America. Baltimore.

Gazette. Gazette: international journal for mass communications studies. [Leiden: H. E. Steinert Kroese.]

Geneal. mag. N.J. The genealogical magazine of New Jersey. Newark: Genealogical Soc. of New Jersey.

Geneal. newsletter. Genealogical newsletter: news, reviews, and listings of current family and county histories. [Wash.: Inez Raney Waldenmaier.]

Geo. Wash. law rev. The George Washington law review, devoted exclusively to public law. Wash.: George Washington Univ.

Geog. rev. The geographical review. N.Y.: American Geographical Soc.

Geol. Soc. Am., Bul. Bulletin of the Geological Society of America. N.Y.

Georgetown law jour. The Georgetown law journal. Wash.: Georgetown Univ. Law Center.

Glades star. The Glades star. Oakland, Md.: Garrett Co. Hist. Soc.

Gun digest. Gun digest. Edited by John T. Amber. Chicago: Gun Digest Co.

Gun rep. The gun report ... "dedicated to the interests of gun enthusiasts everywhere." Aledo, Ill.: World-Wide Gun Report, Inc.

Harv. alumni bul. Harvard alumni bulletin. Cambridge, Mass.: Harvard Alumni Assoc.

Harv. educ. rev. Harvard educational review. Cambridge: Graduate School of Education, Harvard Univ.

Harv. law rev. Harvard law review. Cambridge: Harvard Law Review Assoc.

Harv. Lib. bul. Harvard Library bulletin. Cambridge: Harvard Univ. Library.

Hastings law jour. The Hastings law journal. San Francisco: Hastings College of Law.

High school jour. The high school journal. Chapel Hill: Univ. of North Carolina Press for the School of Education, Univ. of North Carolina.

Higher educ. Higher education, reporting Federal educational activities at college and university levels. Wash.: U.S. Dept. of Health, Education, and Welfare.

Hisp. Am. hist. rev. The Hispanic American historical review. Durham, N.C.: Duke Univ. Press.

Hispanic rev. Hispanic review: a quarterly journal devoted to research in the Hispanic languages & literatures. [Phila.:] Univ. of Pennsylvania Press.

Hist. and Philos. Soc. Ohio, Bul. Bulletin of the Historical and Philosophical Society of Ohio. Cincinnati.

Hist. mexicana. Historia mexicana. [México:] Colegio de México.

Hist. preservation. Historic preservation: quarterly of the National Trust for Historic Preservation. [Wash.]

Hist. rev. Berks Co. Historical review of Berks County. Reading, Pa.: Historical Soc. of Berks County.

Historian. The historian: a journal of history. [Allentown, Pa."] Phi Alpha Theta.

History today. History today. London.

Hobbies. Hobbies: the magazine for collectors. [Chicago: Lightner Pub. Corp.]

Hospital management. Hospital management: the journal for administrators and department heads. Chicago: Hospital Management, Inc.

Howard law jour. Howard law journal. [Wash.: Howard Univ. School of Law.]

Human biol. Human biology: a record of research. Detroit: Wayne Univ. Press.

Huntington Lib. quar. The Huntington Library quarterly: a journal for the history and interpretation of English and American civilization. San Marino, Calif.: Huntington Library.

I. C. C. Practitioners' jour. I. C. C. Practitioners' journal. [Wash.:] Assoc. of Interstate Commerce Commission Practitioners.

Ia. Acad. Science, Proc. Proceedings of the Iowa Academy of Science. Des Moines: State of Iowa.

Ia. jour. hist. Iowa journal of history. Iowa City: State Historical Soc. of Iowa.

Ia. law rev. Iowa law review. Iowa City: College of Law, State Univ. of Iowa.

Ia. State Med. Soc., Jour. Journal of the Iowa State Medical Society. Des Moines.

Idaho yesterdays. Idaho yesterdays: the quarterly journal of the Idaho Historical Society. Boise.

Ill. State Hist. Soc., Jour. Journal of the Illinois State Historical Society. [Springfield: Illinois State Historical Library.]

Improvement era. The improvement era: official monthly organ of the priesthood quorums ... and other agencies of the Church of Jesus Christ of Latter-Day Saints. Salt Lake City: The General Boards of the Mutual Improvement Associations.

Ind. Acad. Science, Proc. Proceedings of the Indiana Academy of Science. Indianapolis.

Ind. law jour. Indiana law journal. Bloomington: Indiana Univ. School of Law.

Ind. mag. hist. Indiana magazine of history. Bloomington: Dept. of history, Indiana Univ., in cooperation with the Indiana Historical Soc.

Ind. State med. Assoc., Jour. The journal of the Indiana State Medical Association. Indianapolis.

Indus. and labor rel. rev. Industrial and labor relations review. Ithaca: New York State School of Industrial and Labor Relations at Cornell Univ.

Infinity. Infinity. N.Y.: American Soc. of Magazine Photographers.

Inland seas. Inland seas: quarterly journal of the Great Lakes Historical Society. Cleveland.

Insurance law jour. The insurance law journal. Chicago: Commerce Clearing House.

Intelligencer. The intelligencer. Ossining, N.Y.: Ossining Historical Soc.

Inter-Am. econ. affairs. Inter-American economic affairs. Wash.

Internal Affairs monthly bul. Internal Affairs monthly bulletin.

[Harrisburg:] Dept. of Internal Affairs, Commonwealth of Pennsylvania.

Internatl. abstracts surgery. International abstracts of surgery. Chicago: Franklin H. Martin Foundation.

Internatl. jour. Am. linguistics. International journal of American linguistics. Baltimore: Waverly Press for Indiana Univ. under the auspices of the Joint Committee on American Native Languages of the American Council of Learned Societies, the American Anthropological Association, and the Linguistic Society of America.

Internatl. rev. social hist. International review of social history. Assen: Royal Vangorcum for Internationaal Instituut voor Sociale Geschiedenis, Amsterdam.

Irish sword. The Irish sword: the journal of the Military History Society of Ireland. Dublin.

Isis. Isis: an international review devoted to the history of science and its cultural influences. [Seattle: Univ. of Washington for the History of Science Soc.]

Jahrbuch für Amerikastudien. Jahrbuch für Amerikastudien im Auftrage der Deutschen Gesellschaft für Amerikastudien. Heidelberg: Carl Winter, Universitätsverlag.

Jazz. Jazz: a quarterly of American music. Berkeley: Jazz Publications.

Jazz rev. The jazz review. N.Y.

Jefferson Co. Hist. Soc., Mag. Magazine of the Jefferson County Historical Society. [Charles Town, W. Va.]

Jesuit educ. quar. Jesuit educational quarterly. N.Y.: Jesuit Educational Assoc.

Jew. educ. Jewish education. [N.Y.:] National Council for Jewish Education with the assistance of the American Assoc. for Jewish Education.

Jew. social studies. Jewish social studies: a quarterly journal devoted to contemporary and historical aspects of Jewish life. N.Y.: Conference on Jewish Social Studies.

Johns Hopkins Hospital, Bul. Bulletin of the Johns Hopkins Hospital: the publication of the medical School and Hospital. Baltimore: Johns Hopkins Press.

Jour. air law and commerce. The journal of air law and commerce. Evanston: Transportation Center, Northwestern Univ., for the School of Law and School of Commerce.

Jour. Am. folklore. Journal of American Folklore. Phila.: American Folklore Soc.

Jour. astronautical sciences. The journal of the astronautical sciences. [N.Y.: American Astronautical Soc.]

Jour. broadcasting. Journal of broadcasting. Los Angeles: Assoc. for Professional Broadcasting Education.

Jour. chem. educ. Journal of chemical education. Easton, Pa.: Division of Chemical Education, American Chemical Soc.

Jour. chronic diseases. Journal of chronic diseases: a journal devoted to the problems and management of chronic illness in all age groups. St. Louis: C. V. Mosby.

Jour. crim. law. The journal of criminal law, criminology, and police science. Baltimore: Williams & Wilkins Co. for Northwestern Univ. School of Law, Chicago.

Jour. econ. hist. The journal of economic history. N.Y.: New York Univ. Press for the Economic History Assoc.

Jour. educ. research. Journal of educational research. Madison: Dembar Publications.

Jour. educ. sociol. The journal of educational sociology: a magazine of theory and practice. [N.Y.: Payne Educational Sociology Foundation of Rho Chapter, Phi Delta Kappa, at New York Univ.]

Jour. Eng. and Germanic philol. The journal of English and Germanic philology. [Urbana:] Univ. of Illinois Press.

Jour. farm econ. Journal of farm economics. Menasha, Wis.: American Farm Economic Assoc.

Jour. forestry. Journal of forestry. Wash.: Soc. of American Foresters.

Jour. gen. psychol. The journal of general psychology: experimental, theoretical, clinical, and historical psychology. Provincetown, Mass.: Journal Press.

Jour. geog. Journal of geography. For teachers of elementary, high school, and college geography. [Chicago:] A. J. Nystrom & Co. for the National Council for Geographic Education.

Jour. geol. educ. Journal of geological education. [Lawrence, Kan.: National Assoc. of Geology Teachers.]

Jour. higher educ. The journal of higher education. Columbus: Ohio State Univ. Press.

Jour. hist. ideas. Journal of the history of ideas: a quarterly devoted to cultural and intellectual history. Lancaster, Pa., and New York:

Journal of the History of Ideas, Inc., City College, N.Y.

Jour. hist. med. Journal of the history of medicine and allied sciences. New Haven: Dept. of the History of Medicine, Yale Univ.

Jour. home econ. Journal of home economics: official organ of the American Home Economics Association. Wash.

Jour. inter-Am. studies. Journal of inter-American studies. Gainesville: School of Inter-American Studies, Univ. of Florida.

Jour. Jew. communal service. Journal of Jewish communal service ... a quarterly of professional trends and developments. N.Y.: National Conference of Jewish Communal Service.

Jour. lancet. The journal lancet, serving the medical profession of Minnesota, North Dakota, South Dakota, and Montana. Minneapolis: Lancet Publications.

Jour. law & econ. The journal of law & economics. [Chicago:] Univ. of Chicago Law School.

Jour. legal educ. Journal of legal education. [Durham, N.C.: Faculty of Law, Duke Univ., for] the Assoc. of American Law Schools.

Jour. med. educ. The journal of medical education: official publication of the Association of American Medical Colleges. Chicago: Univ. of Chicago Press.

Jour. Miss. hist. The journal of Mississippi history. Jackson: Mississippi Historical Soc. in co-operation with the Mississippi Dept. of Archives and History.

Jour. mod. hist. The journal of modern history. Published in co-operation with the Modern European History Section of the American Historical Association. Chicago: Univ. of Chicago Press.

Jour. Negro educ. The journal of Negro education: a quarterly review of problems incident to the education of Negroes. Wash.: Howard Univ. Press for the Bureau of Educational Research, Howard Univ.

Jour. Negro hist. The journal of Negro history. Wash.: Assoc. for the Study of Negro Life and History, Inc.

Jour. nervous and mental disease. The journal of nervous and mental disease: an educational journal of neuropsychiatry. Baltimore: Williams & Wilkins Co.

Jour. pediatrics. The journal of pediatrics. St. Louis: C. V. Mosby Co.

Jour. philos. The journal of philosophy. Lancaster, Pa.: Journal of Philosophy, Inc.

Jour. politics. The journal of politics. [Gainesville:] Southern Political Science Assoc. and the Univ. of Florida.

Jour. prosthetic dentistry. The journal of prosthetic dentistry. St. Louis: C. V. Mosby Co.

Jour. pub. law. Journal of public law. Emory University Ga.: Emory Univ. Law School.

Jour. range management. Journal of range management. [Portland, Ore.:] American Soc. of Range Management.

Jour. South. hist. The journal of Southern history. [Houston, Tex."] Southern Historical Assoc.

Jour. urol. The journal of urology: official organ of the American Urological Association. Baltimore: Williams & Wilkins Co.

Jour. wildlife management. The journal of wildlife management. Lawrence Kan.: Wildlife Soc.

Journalism quar. Journalism quarterly, devoted to research in journalism and mass communications. Minneapolis: Assoc. for Education in Journalism.

Jr. college jour. Junior college journal: official organ of American Association of Junior Colleges. Wash.

Jr. historian (Tex.). The junior historian of the Texas State Historical Association. Austin.

Kan. Acad. Science, Trans. Transactions of the Kansas Academy of Science. [Lawrence.]

Kan. hist. quar. The Kansas historical quarterly. Topeka: Kansas State Historical Soc.

Keystone folklore quar. Williamsport, Pa.: Lycoming College and the Pennsylvania Folklore Soc.

Kiva. The kiva: a journal of the Arizona Archaeological and Historical Society, an affiliate of the Arizona State Museum, University of Arizona. Tucson.

Ky. folklore rec. Kentucky folklore record. Bowling Green, Ky.: Kentucky Folklore Soc.

Ky. for. lang. quar. Kentucky foreign language quarterly. Lexington: Dept. of Modern Foreign Languages, Univ. of Kentucky.

Ky. geneal. The Kentucky genealogist. [Wash.: Martha Porter Miller.]

Ky. Hist. Soc., Reg. The register of the Kentucky Historical Society. [Frankfort.]

<u>Ky. law jour.</u> Kentucky law journal. Lexington: College of Law, Univ. of Kentucky.

<u>La. Bar jour.</u> Louisiana Bar journal, published quarterly by the Louisiana State Bar Association. New Orleans.

<u>La. folklore misc.</u> Louisiana folklore miscellany. Baton Rouge: Louisiana Folklore Soc.

<u>La. hist.</u> Louisiana history. [Baton Rouge:] Louisiana Historical Assoc. in cooperation with Louisiana State univ.

<u>La. law rev.</u> Louisiana law review. Baton Rouge: Louisiana Law Review [Louisiana State Univ. Law School].

<u>Labor hist.</u> Labor history. [N.Y.: Tamiment Institute.]

<u>Labor law jour.</u> Labor law journal. Chicago: Commerce Clearing House.

Lancaster Co. Hist. Soc. <u>Jour.</u> Journal of the Lancaster County Historical Society. Lancaster, Pa.

<u>Landscape architecture.</u> Landscape architecture. Boston: American Soc. of Landscape Architects.

<u>Law and contemp. problems.</u> Law and contemporary problems. [Durham, N.C.:] School of Law, Duke Univ.

<u>Law lib. jour.</u> Law library journal. [n. p.:] American Assoc. of Law Libraries.

Lebanon Hist. Soc., <u>Ann. rep.</u> Annual report. [Lebanon, N.Y.:] Lebanon Historial Soc.

Lehigh Co. Hist. Soc., <u>Proc.</u> Proceedings of the Lehigh County Historical Society. Allentown, Pa.: [Press of H. Ray Haas & Co.].

<u>Lib. chron.</u> The Library chronicle. Phila.: Friends of the Library, Univ. of Pennsylvania.

<u>Lib. Cong. quar. jour.</u> The Library of Congress quarterly journal of current acquisitions. Published as a supplement to the Annual report of the Librarian of Congress. [Wash.]

<u>Lib. quar.</u> The library quarterly: a journal of investigation and discussion in the field of library science. Chicago: [Univ. of Chicago Press.]

<u>Liberal educ.</u> Liberal education: the bulletin of the Association of American Colleges. Wash.

<u>Lock Haven bul.</u> The Lock Haven bulletin. Lock Haven, Pa.: State Teachers College.

<u>Log Mystic Seaport.</u> The log of Mystic Seaport. Mystic, Conn.: Marine Historical Assoc., Inc.

<u>Long Island forum.</u> The Long Island forum. Westhampton Beach, N.Y.

<u>Los Angeles Bar bul.</u> Los Angeles Bar bulletin. Los Angeles: Los Angeles Bar Assoc.

<u>Loyola law rev.</u> Loyola law review. New Orleans: School of Law, Loyola Univ.

<u>Luth. quar.</u> The Lutheran quarterly. Gettysburg, Pa.; Editorial Council of Lutheran Theological Seminaries.

<u>M. H. S. misc.</u> M. H. S. miscellany. Published occasionally by the Massachusetts Historical Society. Boston.

<u>Manuscripts.</u> Manuscripts. N.Y.: Manuscript Soc.

<u>Marion Co. hist.</u> Marion County history. Salem, Ore.: Marion County Historical Soc.

<u>Marquette law rev.</u> Marquette law rev. Milwaukee: Students and faculty of the Marquette Univ. School of Law.

<u>Mass. law quar.</u> Massachusetts law quarterly. Boston: Massachusetts Bar. Assoc.

<u>Mass. rev.</u> The Massachusetts review ... a quarterly of literature, the arts, and public affairs. [Amherst, Mass.: Univ. of Massachusetts.]

<u>Md. hist. mag.</u> Maryland historical magazine. Baltimore: Maryland Historical Soc.

<u>Md. hist. notes.</u> Maryland history notes: quarterly news bulletin of the Maryland Historical Society. Baltimore.

<u>Md. law rev.</u> Maryland law review. Baltimore: Univ. of Maryland School of Law.

<u>Md. State med. jour.</u> Maryland State medical journal ... official publication of the Medical and Chirurgical Faculty of the State of Maryland. Baltimore.

<u>Mech. engineering.</u> Mechanical engineering. N.Y.: American Soc. of Mechanical Engineers.

<u>Med. ann. Dist. Col.</u> Medical annals of the District of Columbia: a monthly publication of the Medical Society of the District of Columbia. Wash.

Med. Assoc. Ga., <u>Jour.</u> Journal of the Medical Association [of] Georgia. Atlanta.

Med. Lib. Assoc., <u>Bul.</u> Bulletin of the Library Association. [Baltimore: Waverly Press.]

Med. Soc. N.J., <u>Jour.</u> The journal of the Medical Society of New Jersey. Trenton.

<u>Mennonite hist. bul.</u> Mennonite historical bulletin. Scottdale, Pa.: Historical Committee of Mennonite General Conference.

<u>Mennonite life.</u> Mennonite life: an illustrated quarterly. North Newton, Kan.: Bethel College.

<u>Mennonite quar. rev.</u> The Mennonite quarterly review. Goshen, Ind.:

Mennonite Historical Soc., Goshen College.

Mercer law rev. Mercer law review. [Macon, Ga.: Walter F. George School of Law, Mercer Univ.]

Mich. Acad. Science, Papers. Papers of the Michigan Academy of Science, Arts, and Letters. Ann Arbor: Univ. of Michigan Press.

Mich. conservation. Michigan conservation. Lansing: Michigan Dept. of Conservation.

Mich. heritage. Michigan heritage. [Kalamazoo, Mich.:] Kalamazoo Valley Genealogical Soc.

Mich. hist. Michigan history. Lansing: Michigan Historical Commission.

Mich. law rev. Michigan law reveiw. Ann Arbor: Univ. of Michigan Law School.

Mich. State Bar jour. Michigan State Bar journal. Lansing: State Bar of Michigan.

Mich. State Med. Soc., Jour. The journal of the Michigan State Medical Society. St. Paul, Minn.

Mid-America. Mid-America: an historical quarterly. Chicago: Institute of Jesuit History, Loyola Univ.

Midw. folklore. Midwest folklore. Bloomington, Ind.: Indiana Univ.

Midw. quar. The Midwest quarterly: a journal of contemporary thought. Pittsburg: Kansas State College of Pittsburg.

Mil. affairs. Military affairs. ... Devoted to American military (including naval and air) history. Wash.: American Military Institute.

Mil. collector & historian. Military collector & historian. Wash.: Company of Military Collectors & Historians.

Mil. law rev. Military law review. [Wash.:] Dept. of the Army.

Mil. med. Military medicine: journal of the Association of Military Surgeons of the United States. Wash.

Mil. rev. Military review. Fort Leavenworth, Kan.: U.S. Command and General Staff College.

Milbank Memorial Fund quar. The Milbank Memorial Fund quarterly. N.Y.

Mineral industries jour. Mineral industries journal. Blacksburg, Va.: Mineral Industries Depts., School of Engineering and Architecture, Virgina Polytechnic Institute.

Mineralogist. The mineralogist ... a national semi-technical magazine devoted to mineralogy, gem cutting, and the collector. [Portland, Ore.: Mineralogist Pub. Co.]

Minn. hist. Minnesota history. [St. Paul: Minnesota Historical Soc.]

Minn. law rev. Minnesota law review: journal of the State Bar Association. Minneapolis: Law School, Univ. of Minnesota.

Minn. med. Minnesota medicine. St. Paul: Minnesota State Medical Assoc.

Miss. Acad. Sciences, Jour. Journal of the Mississippi Academy of Sciences, Inc. [Ann Arbor, Mich.]

Miss. law jour. Mississippi law journal. University, Miss.: Mississippi State Bar and the Univ. of Mississippi School of Law.

Miss. quar. The Mississippi quarterly. State College, Miss.: Liberal Arts Division [Mississippi State Univ.].

Miss. Valley hist. rev. The Mississippi Valley historical review: a journal of American history. Cedar Rapids, Ia.: Mississippi Valley Historical Assoc.

Mo. Bar, Jour. Journal of the Missouri Bar. Jefferson City.

Mo. hist. rev. Missouri historical review. Columbia: State Historical Soc. of Missouri.

Mo. Hist. Soc., Bul. Bulletin of the Missouri Historical Society. St. Louis.

Mo. law rev. Missouri law review. Columbia: School of Law, Univ. of Missouri.

Mod. drama. Modern drama. Lawrence, Kan.: A.C. Edwards.

Mod. lang. jour. The modern language journal. [Menasha, Wis.:] National Federation of Modern Language Teachers Associations.

Mod. lang. notes. Modern language notes. Baltimore: Johns Hopkins Press.

Mod. lang. quar. Modern language quarterly. Seattle: Univ. of Washington.

Mont. Acad. Sciences, Proc. Proceedings of the Montana Academy of Sciences. Billings.

Mont. Inst. Arts quar. The Montana Institute of the Arts quarterly. [n. p.]

Mont. law rev. Montana law review. Missoula: Students of the School of Law, Montana State Univ.

Montana. Montana: the magazine of Western history. Helena: Historical Soc. of Montana.

Monthly labor rev. Monthly labor review. [Wash.:] Bureau of Labor Statistics, U.S. Dept. of Labor.

Monthly rev. Monthly review: an independent Socialist magazine, [N.Y.: Monthly Review, Inc.]

Morgan horse mag. The Morgan horse magazine. N.Y.: Morgan Horse Club.
Mt. Sinai Hospital, Jour. Journal of the Mount Sinai Hospital, New York. Baltimore: Committee on Medical Education and Publications, Mount Sinai Hospital, New York.
Municipal Engineers jour. The Municipal Engineers journal. N.Y.: The Municipal Engineers of the City of New York.
Museum. The Museum. Newark, N.J.: Newark Museum Assoc.
Music jour. Music journal. East Stroudsburg, Pa.: Music Journal, Inc.
N.C. folklore. North Carolina folklore. Chapel Hill: North Carolina Folklore Soc. and the Univ. of North Carolina Folklore Council.
N.C. hist. rev. The North Carolina historical review. Raleigh: State Dept. of Archives and History.
N.C. law rev. The North Carolina law review. Chapel Hill: Univ. of North Carolina Press for the Univ. of North Carolina School of Law.
N.C. med. jour. North Carolina medical journal: official organ of the Medical Society of North Carolina. Winston-Salem.
N.C. Mus. Art bul. The North Carolina Museum of Art bulletin. [Raleigh.]
N.D. hist. North Dakota history. Bismarck: State Historical Soc. of North Dakota.
N.D. law rev. North Dakota law review: journal of the State Bar Association. [Grand Forks:] State Bar Assoc. of North Dakota in co-operation with the Univ. of North Dakota School of Law.
N.H. profiles. New Hampshire profiles. Portsmouth: New Hampshire Profiles Corps.
N.J. genesis. The New Jersey genesis: genealogical and historical data of early New Jersey. Springfield, N.J.: Harold A. Sonn.
N.J. Hist. Soc., Proc. Proceedings of the New Jersey Historical Society: a magazine of New Jersey history. [Newark.]
N.M. New Mexico: land of enchantment. [Albuquerque: Bureau of Publications, State of New Mexico.]
N.M. hist. rev. New Mexico historical review. [Santa Fe: Historical Soc. of New Mexico and the Univ. of New Mexico.]
N.Y. Acad. Sciences, Trans. Transactions of the New York Academy of Sciences. N.Y.
N.Y. folklore quar. New York folklore quarterly. Cooperstown: New York Folklore Soc.
N.Y. geneal. and biog. rec. The New York genealogical and biographical record. N.Y.: New York Genealogical and Biographical Soc.
N.Y. hist. New York history. Cooperstown: New York State Historical Assoc.
N.-Y. Hist. Soc. quar. The New-York historical Society quarterly. N.Y.
N.Y. law forum. New York law forum. N.Y.: New York Law School.
N.Y. Pub. Lib., Bul. Bulletin of the New York Public Library, Astor, Lenox, and Tilden Foundations, N.Y.
N.Y. State Bar bul. New York State Bar bulletin. Albany: New York State Bar Assoc.
N.Y. State jour. med. New York State journal of medicine. N.Y.: Medical Soc. of the State of New York.
N.Y. Univ. law rev. New York University law review. [N.Y.:] New York Univ. School of Law.
Names. Names: journal of the American Name Society. Berkeley.
Natl. Acad. Sciences, Biog. memoirs. Biographical memoirs. N.Y.: Columbia Univ. Press for the National Academy of Sciences.
Natl. Assoc. Referees in Bankruptcy, Jour. Journal of the National Association of Referees in Bankruptcy. [n. p.]
Natl. Assoc. Watch and Clock Collectors, Bul. Bulletin of the National Association of Watch and Clock Collectors. Columbia, Pa.
Natl. button bul. The national button bulletin. [n. p.:] National Button Soc. of America.
Natl. Geneal. Soc. quar. National Genealogical Society quarterly. Wash.
Natl. Music Council bul. National Music Council bulletin. N.Y.
Natl. parks mag. National parks magazine. Wash.: National Parks Assoc.
Natl. Railway Hist. Soc., Bul. The bulletin. [n. p.:] National Railway Historical Soc.
Natl. tax jour. National tax journal, published quarterly by the National Tax Association. Phila.
Natural hist. Natural history: the magazine of the American Museum of Natural History. N.Y.
Natural law forum. Natural law forum. [Notre Dame, Ind.:] Notre Dame Law School. Univ. of Notre Dame.
Neb. Acad. Sciences, Proc. Proceedings of the Nebraska Academy of Sciences. Lincoln: Univ. of Nebraska.
Neb. hist. Nebraska history: a quarterly magazine. Lincoln: Nebraska State Historical Soc.

Neb. law rev. Nebraska law review. Published by the Nebraska State Bar Association and the College of Law of the University of Nebraska. Lincoln.

Negro hist. bul. The Negro history bulletin. Wash.: Assoc. for the Study of Negro Life and History.

New Canaan Hist. Soc. ann. The New Cannan Historical Society annual. New Canaan, Conn.

New-Eng. galaxy. The New-England galaxy. Sturbridge, Mass.: Old Sturbridge, Inc. [for the Friends of Old Sturbridge Village].

New Eng. hist. and geneal. reg. The New England historical and genealogical Soc.

New Eng. jour. med. The New England journal of medicine: official organ of the Massachusetts Medical Society. Boston.

New Eng. quar. The New England quarterly: a historical review of New England life and letters. [Burnswick, Me.:] New England Quarterly, Inc.

New Eng. teacher. The New England teacher. Boston: New England Teacher Pub. Co.

New Eng. Water Works Assoc., Jour. Journal of the New England Water Works Association. Boston

Newberry Lib. bul. The Newberry Library bulletin. Chicago.

Newport Hist. Soc., Bul. Bulletin by Newport Historical Society. Newport.

Nieman reports. Nieman reports. Cambridge: Nieman Alumni Council.

Nineteenth-cent. fiction. Nineteenth-century fiction. Berkeley and Los Angeles: Univ. of California Press.

North Ala. Hist. Assoc. Bul. Bulletin of the North Alabama Historical Association. Florence, Ala.: North Alabama Historical Assoc. in cooperation with Florence State College.

North. junket. Northern junket. [Keene N.H.: Ralph Page.]

Northeast folklore. Northeast folklore. Published quarterly by the Northeast Folklore Society, under the auspices of the Department of English, University of Maine. Orono, Me.

Northw. Univ. law rev. Northwestern University law review. [Chicago:] Northwestern Univ. School of Law.

Notes in anthropol. Notes in anthropology. Tallahassee: Dept. of Anthropology and Archaeology, Florida State Univ.

Notre Dame lawyer. Notre Dame lawyer: a quarterly law review. [Notre Dame, Ind.: The Students of Law, Notre Dame Law School.]

Now and then. Now and then, established in 1868: a quarterly magazine of history, biography, & genealogy. [Muncy, Pa.: Muncy Historical Soc. and Museum of History.]

Numismatic lit. Numismatic literature. N.Y.: American Numismatic Soc.

Numismatic scrapbook. Numismatic scrapbook magazine: a monthly magazine for the collector of coins, tokens, medals, and paper money. [Chicago: Hewitt Bros.]

Numismatist. The numismatist, for collectors of coins, medals, and paper money. Wichita, Kan.: American Numismatic Assoc.

Nursing outlook. Nursing outlook: official organ of the National League for Nursing. N.Y.: American Journal of Nursing Co.

Ohio archaeol. [n. p.:] Archaeological Soc. of Ohio.

Ohio engineer. The Ohio engineer. Columbus: Ohio Soc. of Professional Engineers.

Ohio hist. quar. The Ohio historical quarterly. Columbus: Ohio Historical Soc.

Ohio jour. science. The Ohio journal of science. Columbus: Ohio State Univ. and the Ohio Academy of Science.

Ohio State law jour. Ohio State law journal. Columbus: College of Law, Ohio State Univ.

Ohioana. Ohioana: of Ohio and Ohioans. Columbus: Martha Kinney Cooper Ohioana Library Assoc.

Ohio Univ. rev. The Ohio University review: contributions in the humanities. Athens: Ohio Univ.

Okla. Acad. Science, Proc. Proceedings of the Oklahoma Academy of Science. [n. p.]

Okla. Junior Acad. Science Trans. Transactions of the Oklahoma Junior Academy of Science. Stillwater: Arts & Sciences Extension, Oklahoma State Univ.

Okla, law rev. Oklahoma law review. Edited by the School of Law, the University of Oklahoma. Norman: Univ. of Oklahoma Press.

Old Oregon. Old Oregon. [Eugene, Ore.: Univ. of Oregon Alumni Assoc.]

Old Print Shop portfolio. The Old Print Shop portfolio. [N.Y.: Harry Shaw Newman.]

Old York Road Hist. Soc. bul. Old York Road Historical Society bulletin. [Jenkintown, Pa.]

Orbis. Orbis: bulletin international de documentation linguistique. Louvain:

Centre International de Dialectologie Générale [près l'Université Catholique de Louvain].

Ore. hist. quar. Oregon historical quarterly. [Portland:] Oregon Historical Soc.

Ore. law rev. Oregon law review. Eugene: Univ. of Oregon.

Organ Inst. quar. Organ Institute quarterly. Andover, Mass.

Our heritage. Our heritage: amor patriae. San Antonio: San Antonio Genealogical and Historical Soc.

P. E. Church, Hist. mag. Historical magazine of the Protestant Episcopal Church. New Burnswick, N.J.: Joint Commission of the General Convention.

PMLA. PMLA: Publications of the Modern Language Association of America. Menasha, Wis.: George Banta Co.

Pa. Bar Assoc. quar. Pennsylvania Bar Association quarterly. [Harrisburg:] Publications Committee of the Pennsylvania Bar Assoc.

Pa. game news. Pennsylvania game news. Harrisburg: Pennsylvania Game Commission.

Pa. geneal. mag. The Pennsylvania genealogical magazine. Phila.: Genealogical Soc. of Pennsylvania.

Pa. hist. Pennsylvania history: quarterly journal of the Pennsylvania Historical Association. [Gettysburg.]

Pa. mag. hist. and giog. The Pennsylvania magazine of history and biography. Phila.: Historical Soc. of Pennsylvania.

Pac. discovery. Pacific discovery. Berkeley: California Academy of Sciences.

Pac. hist. rev. Pacific historical review. Issued quarterly by the Pacific Coast Branch of the American Historical Association. Berkeley and Los Angles: Univ. of California Press.

Pac. naturalist. Pacific naturalist: contributions from the Beaudette Foundation for Biological Research. Solvang, Calif.

Pac. Northw. quar. Pacific Northwest quarterly. Seattle: Univ. of Washington Press for the Univ. of Washington cooperating with the Washington State Historical Soc.

Pac. Northwesterner. The Pacific Northwesterner. [Spokane: The Westerners, Spokane Corral.]

Pac. science. Pacific science: a quarterly devoted to the biological and physical sciences of the Pacific region. Honolulu: Univ. of Hawaii.

Pac. sociol. rev. The Pacific sociological Society. [Eugene, Ore.]

Palimpsest. The palimpsest. Iowa City: State Historical Soc. of Iowa.

Paper maker. The paper maker. Wilmington, Del.: Paper Makers Chemical Dept., Hercules Powder Co.

Partisan rev. Partisan review. N.Y.: American Committee for Cultural Freedom.

Password. Password of the El Paso Historical Society. [El Paso.]

Patent, trademark, and copyright jour. The patent, trademark, and copyright journal of research and education. [Wash.:] Patent, Trademark, and Copyright Foundation, George Washington Univ.

Peabody jour. educ. Peabody journal of education. Nashville, Tenn.: Peabody Press, George Peabody College for Teachers.

Pediatrics. Pediatrics: official publication of the American Academy of Pediatrics, Inc. Springfield, Ill.: Charles C. Thomas.

Phi Chi quar. Phi Chi quarterly ... official publication of the Phi Chi Medical Fraternity, Incorporated, International. Springfield, Ill.

Phila. Mus. bul. The Philadelphia Museum bulletin. Phila.: Philadelphia Museum of Art.

Philol. quar. Philological quarterly: a journal devoted to scholarly investigation of the classical and modern languages and literatures. Iowa City: State Univ. of Iowa.

Philos. of science. Philosophy of science: organ of the Philosophy of Science Association. Bruges, Belgium: St. Catherine Press.

Picket post. The picket post: a record of patriotism. Valley Forge Pa.: Valley Forge Historical Soc.

Pol. science quar. Political science quarterly. Edited for the Academy of Political Science by the Faculty of Political Science of Columbia University. N.Y.

Pol. studies. Political studies: the journal of the Political Studies Association of the United Kingdom. Oxford: Claredon Press.

Poles in Mich. Poles in Michigan. Detroit: Poles in Michigan Associated.

Pony Express. The Pony Express: stories of pioneers and old trails. [Sonora, Calif.: Herb S. Hamlin.]

Portfolio. Portfolio. [N.Y.:] Art Foundation Press.

Postgraduate med. Postgraduate medicine: official journal of the

Interstate Postgraduate Medical Association. Minneapolis: IPMA Pub. Co.

Pound newsletter. The Pound newsletter. [Berkeley, Calif.]

Prairie schooner. Prairie schooner. [Lincoln:] Univ. of Nebraska Press.

Presbyt. Hist. Soc., Jour. Journal of the Presbyterian Historical Society. Lancaster and Phila.: Dept. of History of the United Presbyterian Church in the U.S.A.

Presbyt. survey. Presbyterian survey: official magazine of the Presbyterian Church in the United States. Richmond: Board of the Presbyterian Survey for the General Assembly of the Presbyterian Church in the United States.

Princeton Univ. Lib. chron. The Princeton University Library chronicle. Princeton: Princeton Univ. Library [for the Friends of the Princeton Library].

Pub. admin. rev. Public administration review: the journal of the American Society for Public Administration. Chicago.

Pub. health reports. Public health reports. [Wash.:] Public Health Service, U.S. Dept. of Health, Education, and Welfare.

Pub. personnel rev. Public personnel review: the journal of the Public Personnel Association. Chicago.

Quar. jour. speech. The quarterly journal of speech. Columbia, Mo.: Speech Assoc. of America.

Quar. jour. studies alcohol. Quarterly journal of studies on alcohol. New Haven: Laboratory of Applied Biodynamics, Yale Univ.

Quar. rev. (Bapt.). The quarterly review ... a survey of Southern Baptist progress. [Nashville, Tenn.: Sunday School Board of the Southern Baptist Convention.]

Quar. rev. higher educ. among Negroes. The quarterly review of higher education among Negroes. Charolette, N.C.: Johnson C. Smith Univ.

Quarter horse. The quarter horse. Knox City, Tex.: National Quarter Horse Breeders Assoc.

Quarter horse jour. The quarter horse journal. Amarillo, Tex.: American Quarter Horse Assoc.

R.I. hist. Rhode Island history. [Providence: Rhode Island Historical Soc.]

Railroad mag. Railroad magazine: the magazine of adventurous railroading. Canton, Ohio: Popular Publications, Inc.

Railway & Locomotive Hist. Soc., Bul. Bulletin. Boston: Railway & Locomotive Historical Soc., Inc., Baker Library, Harvard Business School.

Record research. Record research: magazine of record statistics and information. [Brooklyn, N.Y.]

Religion in life. Religion in life: a Christian quarterly of opinion and discussion. [Nashville, Tenn."] Abingdon Press.

Rev. and expositor. Review and expositor: a Baptist teheological quarterly. Louisville, Ky.: Faculty Club of the Southern Baptist Theological Seminary.

Rev. econ. and statistics. The review of economics and statistic. Cambridge, Mass.: Harvard Univ. Press [for the Dept. of Economics. Harvard Univ.].

Rev. hist. Am. Revista de historia de América. México: [Comisión de Historia, Instituto Panamericano de Geografía e Historia].

Rev. hist. Am. franciase. Revue d'histoire de l'Amérique française. Montréal: Institut d'Histoire de l'Amérique Française.

Rev. hist. dipl. Revue d'histoire diplomatique. Publiée par la Société d'Histoire Générale et d'Histoire Diplomatique. Paris: Éditions A. Pedone.

Rev. lit. comparée. Revue de littérature comparée. Paris: Librairie Marcel Didier.

Rev. politics. The review of politics. Notre Dame, Ind.: Univ. of Notre Dame.

Rev. religious research. Review of religious research: official journal of the Religious Research Association. [N.Y.]

Rev. social econ. Review of social economy. [Milwaukee:] Maquette Univ. Press for the Catholic Economic Assoc.

Rochester hist. Rochester history. Rochester, N.Y.: Rochester Public Library.

Rocks and minerals. Rocks and minerals. [Peekskill: Peder Zodac.]

Rocky Mt. law rev. The Rocky Mountain law review. Boulder: Univ. of Colorado School of Law.

Rocky Mt. med. jour. Rocky Mountain medical journal. Denver: Colorado State Medical Soc.

Rutgers law rev. Rutgers law review. New Brunswick, N.Y.: Rutgers Univ. Press.

Rutgers Univ. Lib., Jour. The journal of the Rutgers University Library, the State University of New Jersey.

New Brunswick: Associated Friends of the Library of Rutgers Univ.

S.C. Hist. Assoc., Proc. The proceedings of the South Carolina Historical Association. Columbia.

S.C. hist. mag. South Carolina historical magazine. Charleston: South Carolina Historical Soc.

S.C. law quar. The South Carolina law quarterly. Columbia: [South Carolina Bar Association and the Faculty and Students of the Univ. of South Carolina School of Law].

S.D. Acad. Science, Proc. Proceedings of the South Dakota Academy of Science. Vermillion: Univ. of South Dakota.

S.D. Bar jour. South Dakota Bar journal: official organ, the State Bar of South Dakota. [Pierre, S.D.]

S.D. law rev. South Dakota law review. [Vermillion: School of Law of South Dakota Univ.]

S.D. report and hist. col. South Dakota Department of History report and historical collections. Pierre: South Dakota Historical Soc., administering the Dept. of History, State of South Dakota.

S. P. A. jour. The S. P. A. journal: official organ of the Society of Philatelic Americans, the organization for the average collector. Ord, Neb.: Quiz Industries.

San Diego Hist. Soc. quar. San Diego Historical Society quarterly. [San Diego, Calif.]

Savannah State College, Faculty research edition. Faculty research edition of the Savannah State College bulletin. Savannah.

Scandinavian econ. hist. rev. The Scandinavian economic history review. [København? Scandinavian Soc. for Economic and Social History and Historical Geography.]

School rev. The school review: a journal of secondary education. Chicago: Univ. of Chicago Press and the Dept. of Education, Univ. of Chicago.

Science. Science. Wash.: American Assoc. for the Advancement of Science.

Science & soc. Science & society. N.Y.: Science and Society, Inc.

Science educ. Science education: the official organ of the National Association for Research in Science Teaching, the National Council on Elementary Science, [and] the Association of Science Teachers of the Middle States. Albany, N.Y.

Smithsonian Inst., Ann. rep. Annual report of the Board of Regents of the Smithsonian Instituion. Wash.: U.S. Govt. Print. Off.

Soc. Architectural Historians, Jour. Journal of the Society of Architectural Historians. [n. p.]

Soc. Ind. Pioneers, Yr. bk. Year book of the Society of Indiana Pioneers. [n. p.]

Social educ. Social education. [Wash.:] National Council for the Social Studies in collaboration with the American Historical Assoc.

Social justice rev. Social justice review: pioneer American journal of Catholic social action. [St. Louis: Catholic Central Union (Verein) of America.]

Social research. Social research: an international quarterly of political and social science. N.Y.: New School for Social Research.

Social security bul. Social security bulletin. Wash.: Social Security Administration.

Social service rev. The social service review: a quarterly devoted to the scientific and professional interests of social work. Chicago: Univ. of Chicago Press [for the Faculty of the School of Social Service Administration, Univ. of Chicago].

Social studies. The social studies: a periodical for teachers and administrators. [Phila.: McKinley Pub. Co.]

Sociol. and social research. Sociology and social research: an international journal. Los Angeles: Univ. of Southern California Press.

South Atl. quar. The South Atlantic quarterly. Durham, N.C.: Duke Univ. Press.

South Tex. law jour. South Texas law journal. Houston: South Texas Law Journal, Inc., of South Texas College of Law.

South. Calif. law rev. Southern California law review. Los Angeles: School of Law, Univ. of Southern California.

South. econ. jour. The Southern economic journal: a joint publication of the Southern Economic Association and the University of North Carolina. Chapel Hill.

South. folklore quar. Southern folklore quarterly: a publication devoted to the historical and descriptive study of folklore and to the discussion of folk material as a living tradition. Gainesville: Univ. of Florida in cooperation with the South Atlantic Modern Language Assoc.

South. genealogist's exchange quar. The Southern genealogist's exchange quarterly. [Jacksonville, Fla.: Aurora C. Shaw.]

South. speech jour. The Southern speech journal. [Jacksonville, Fla.:] Southern Speech Assoc.

South. Univ. bul., creative and research issue. Creative and research issue, the Southern University bulletin. Baton Rouge, La.: Southern Univ. and Agricultural and Mechanical College.

Southw. hist. quar. The Southwestern historical quarterly. Austin: Texas State Historical Assoc.

Southw. jour. anthropol. Southwestern journal of anthropology. Published by the University of New Mexico and the Laboratory of Anthropology Santa Fé, in the interest of general anthropology. Albuquerque; univ. of New Mexico.

Southw. law jour. Southwestern law journal ... a joint publication of Southern Methodist University School of Law and the Southwestern Legal Foundation. [Dallas: Southern Methodist Univ.]

Southw. lore. Southwestern lore. Boulder: Colorado Archaeological Soc.

Southw. rev. Southwest review. [Dallas: Southern Methodist Univ. Press.]

Southw. social science quar. The Southwestern social science quarterly. Austin, Tex.: Southwestern Social Science Assoc.

Southw. water works jour. Southwest water works journal. Temple, Tex.: Southwest Section, American Water Works Assoc.

Spectrum. Spectrum. Goleta, Calif.: Associated Students of the Univ. of California, Santa Barbara.

Speech monographs. Speech monographs. Baton Rouge, La.: Speech Assoc. of America.

Spinning wheel. Spinning wheel: a national magazine about antiques. [Taneytown, Md.: The Spinning Wheel Publishers, Inc.]

St. John's law rev. St. John's law review. [Brooklyn: St. John's Univ. School of Law.]

St. Louis Univ. law jour. Saint Louis University law journal. [St. Louis: St. Louis Univ. School of Law.]

Stanford law rev. Stanford law review. [n. p.: Board of Trustees of the Leland Stanford Junior Univ.]

Stanford med. bul. Stanford medical bulletin. Stanford, Calif.: Stanford Medical Alumni Assoc.

State Bar Calif., Jour. Journal of the State Bar of California. [San Francisco.]

State College Wash., Research studies. Research studies: a quarterly publication of Washington State University. Pullman, Wash.

Steamboat bill. Steamboat bill ... journal of the Steamship Historical Society of America. West Barrington, R.I.

Studi americani. Studi americani: rivista annual dedicata alle lettere e alle arti negli Stati Uniti d' America. [Roma: Edizioni di Storia e Letteratura.]

Studies in bibliog. Studies in bibliography: papers of the Bibliographical Society of the University of Virginia. Charlottesville.

Studies in philol. Studies in philology. Chapel Hill: Univ. of North Carolina Press.

Surgery. Surgery: a monthly journal devoted to the art and science of surgery [official publication, Society of University Surgeons, Society for Vascular Surgery]. St. Louis: C. V. Mosby Co.

Surgery, gynecol., & obstet. Surgery, gynecology, & obstetrics, with international abstracts of surgery: official journal of the American College of Surgery. Chicago: Franklin H. Martin Memorial Foundation.

Surveying and mapping. Surveying and mapping ... a quarterly journal devoted to advancement of the sciences of surveying and mapping. Wash.: American Congress on Surveying and Mapping.

Swed. pioneer hist. quar. The Swedish pioneer historical quarterly. Rock Island, Ill.: Swedish Pioneer Historical Soc.

Syracuse law rev. Syracuse law review. Syracuse: College of Law, Syracuse Univ.

Tax law rev. Tax law review. N.Y.: New York Univ. School of Law.

Teachers College rec. Teachers College record. N.Y.: Teachers College, Columbia Univ.

Technol. and culture. Technology and culture: the international quarterly of the Society for the History of Technology. [Detroit:] Wayne State Univ. Press.

Temple law quar. Temple law quarterly. Phila.: Temple Univ. School of Law.

Tenn. Folklore Soc. bul. Tennessee Folklore Society bulletin. Nashville.

Tenn. hist. quar. Tennessee historical quarterly. Nashville: Tennessee Historical Soc. and the Tennessee Historical Commission.

Tenn. law rev. Tennessee law review. Edited by the Students and Faculty of the University of Tennessee College of Law. Official publication of the Bar Association of Tennessee. [Knoxville: Tennessee Law Review Assoc., Inc.]

Tenn. studies in lit. Tennessee studies in literature. Knoxville: Univ. of Tennessee Press.

Tex. Archeol. Soc., Bul. Bulletin of the Texas Archeological Society. Austin.

Tex. law rev. Texas law review. Austin: Texas Law Review at the Univ. of Texas School of Law.

Tex. quar. The Texas quarterly. [Austin:] Univ. of Texas Press.

Tex. studies in lit. and lang. Texas studies in literature and language: a journal of the humanities. [Austin:] Univ. of Texas Press.

Theatre annual. The theatre annual ... a publication of information and research in the arts and history of the theatre. N.Y.: Theatre Library Assoc.

Thoreau Soc. bul. The Thoreau Society bulletin. [Genesee, N.Y.]

Thought. Thought: Fordham University quarterly. N.Y.: Fordham Univ. Press.

Torrey Bot. Club, Bul. Bulletin of the Torrey Botanical Club. Lancaster, Pa.: Business Press.

Trains. Trains: the magazine of railroading. [Milwaukee: Kalmbach Pub. Co.]

True, Automobile yearbook. True's automobile yearbook. Greenwhich, Conn.: Fawcett Publications.

True West. True West: all true--all fact--stories of the real West. Austin Tex.: Western Publications.

Tulane drama rev. The Tulane drama review. New Orleans: Tulane Univ.

Tulane law rev. Tulane law review. New Orleans: Tulane Law Review Assoc., Tulane Univ.

Tulane studies in Eng. Tulane studies in English. New Orleans: Tulane Univ.

Twentieth cent. lit. Twentieth century literature: a scholarly and critical journal. [Denver: Alan Swallow.]

U. C. L. A. law rev. U. C. L. A. law review. Los Angeles: School of Law, Univ. of California, Los Angeles.

U.S. Armed Forces med. jour. United States Armed Forces medical journal. Published monthly by the Armed Forces Medical Publication Agency, Department of Defense, Wash.: U.S. Govt. Print. Off.

U.S.N. Inst. proc. United States Naval Institute proceedings, for the advancement of professional, literary, and scientific knowledge in the Navy. Annapolis: United States Naval Institute.

Univ. Alaska, Anthropol. papers. Anthropological papers of the University of Alaska. College, Alaska.

Univ. Calif. Archaeol. Survey, Rep. Reports of the University of California Archaeological Survey. Berkeley: Dept. of Anthropology Univ. of California.

Univ. Chicago law rev. The University of Chicago law review. [Chicago:] Univ. of Chicago Press [for the University of Chicago Law School].

Univ. Cincinnati law rev. University of Cincinnati law review. Cincinnati: Univ. of Cincinnati College of Law.

Univ. Detroit law jour. University of Detroit law journal. [Detroit:] Univ. of Detroit School of Law.

Univ. Fla. law rev. University of Florida law review. Gainesville: Univ. of Florida College of Law.

Univ. Idaho, Bookmark. The bookmark. Moscow: Library, Univ. of Idaho.

Univ. Ill. law forum. The University of Illinois law forum. [n. p.:] College of Law, Univ. of Illinois.

Univ. Kan. City law rev. The University of Kansas City law review. Kansas City [Mo.].

Univ. Kan. City rev. The University of Kansas City review. Kansas City, Mo.: Univ. of Kansas City.

Univ. Kan. law rev. University of Kansas law review. Lawrence, Kan.: Kansas Law Review, Inc.

Univ. Miami law rev. University of Miami law review. Coral Gables, Fla.: Univ. of Miami School of Law.

Univ. Miss., Studies in Eng. Studies in English. University, Miss.: Dept. of English, Univ. of Mississippi.

Univ. Pa. law rev. University of Pennsylvania law review. Phila.: Univ. of Pennsylvania Law School.

Univ. Pittsburgh law rev. University of Pittsburgh law review. Pittsburgh.

University. University: a Princeton magazine. [Princeton: Princeton Univ.]

Utah Acad. Sciences, Proc. Proceedings of the Utah Academy of Sciences, Arts, and Letters. [n. p.]

Utah hist. quar. Utah historical quarterly. Salt Lake City: Utah State Historical Soc.

Va. cavalcade. Virginia cavalcade. Richmond: History Division, Virginia State Library.

Va. geneal. The Virginia genealogist. Wash.: John Frederick Dorman.

Va. jour. science. The Virginia journal of science. [Farmville, Va: Virginia Academy of Science.]

Va. law rev. Virginia law review. Charlottesville: Virginia Law Review Assoc.

Va. mag. hist. and biog. The Virginia magazine of history and biography. Richmond: Virginia Historical Soc.

Vanderbilt law rev. Vanderbilt law review. Nashville, Tenn.: Vanderbilt Univ. School of Law.

Ventura Co. Hist. Soc. quar. The Ventura County Historical Society quarterly [Ventura, Calif.]

Victorian studies. Victorian studies: a quarterly journal of the humanities, arts, and sciences. [Bloomington:] Indiana Univ.

Villanova law rev. Villanova law review. Villanova Pa.: Villanova School of Law.

Vita humana. Vita humana. Internationale Zeitschrift für Lebensaltersforschung. International journal of human development. Journal international de développement humain. Basel, New York: S. Karger.

Vt. hist. Vermont history.]Montpelier, Vt.: Vermont Historical Soc.]

Vt. Hist. Soc., News & notes. News & notes: a monthly newsletter for all members of the Society. Montpelier, Vt.: Vermont Historical Soc. [Title changed to News and notes and subtitle deleted beginning with v. 3, Sept. 1951.]

Vt. Hist. Soc., News and notes. Montpelier, Vt.: Vermont Historical Soc.

Vt. life. Vermont life: official publication of the State of Vermont. Montpelier: Vermont Development Commission.

W. Va. Acad. Science, Proc. Proceedings of the West Virginia Academy of Science. Morgantown: West Virginia Univ.

W. Va. folklore. West Virginia folklore. [Fairmont, W. Va.: West Virginia Folklore Soc.]

W. Va. Hist. West Virginia history: a quarterly magazine. Charleston, W. Va.: State Dept. of Archives and History.

W. Va. law rev. West Virginia law review. Morgantown: [College of Law of West Virginia Univ.].

Wash. and Lee law rev. Washington and Lee law review. Lexington, Va.: School of Law, Washington and Lee Univ.

Wash. law rev. Washington law review and State Bar journal. Seattle: Washington Law Review Assoc., School of Law, Univ. of Washington.

Wash. Univ. law quar. Washington University law quarterly. St. Louis.

Washtenaw impressions. Washtenaw impressions. Published occasionally by the Washtenaw Historical Society. Ann Arbor.

Water Pollution Control Fed., Jour. Journal of the Water Pollution Control Federation. Wash. [Formerly Sewage and industrial wastes.]

Wayne law rev. Wayne law review. Detroit: Wayne Univ. Law School.

Weatherwise. Weatherwise: the magazine about weather. Boston: American Meteorological Soc.

West Tenn. Hist. Soc. papers. The West Tennessee Historical Society papers. Memphis.

West Tex. Hist. Assoc. yr. bk. The West Texas Historical Association year book. Abilene.

West. folklore. Western folklore, Berkeley and Los Angeles: Univ. of California Press for the California Folklore Soc.

West. horseman. The Western horseman. Colorado Springs: Western Horseman Inc.

West. humanities rev. Western humanities review. [Salt Lake City: Center for Intercultural Studies, Univ. of Utah.]

West. Pa. hist. mag. The western Pennsylvania historical magazine. [Pittsburgh:] Historical Soc. of Western Pennsylvania.

West. pol. quar. The Western political quarterly ... official journal of Western Political Science Association, Pacific Northwest Political Science Association, [and] Southern California Political Science Association. Salt Lake City: Institute of Government, Univ. of Utah.

West. Reserve law rev. Western Reserve law review. [Cleveland:] School of Law of Western Reserve Univ.

West. speech. Western speech: the official journal of the Western Speech Association. South San Francisco, Calif.: Paragon Publications.

Westerners brand book (Chicago). The Westerners brand book. Winnetka, Ill.: Chicago Corral of Westerners.

Westerners brand book (N.Y.). The Westerners New York Posse brand book. N.Y.: The Westerners, New York Posse.

Wi-iyohi. The wi-iyohi: monthly bulletin of the South Dakota Historical Society. [Pierre.]

Willamette law jour. The Willamette law journal. Salem, Ore.: Willamette Univ. College of Law.

Wilson lib. bul. Wilson library bulletin. N.Y.: H. W. Wilson Co.

Wis. Acad. Sciences, Trans. Transactions of the Wisconsin Academy of Sciences, Arts, and Letters. Madison.

Wis. law rev. Wisconsin law review. Madison: Univ. of Wisconsin Law School.

Wis. mag. hist. Wisconsin magazine of history. Madison: State Historical Soc. of Wisconsin.

Wis. med. jour. The Wisconsin medical journal: official publication of the State Medical Society of Wisconsin. Madison.

Wm. and Mary law rev. William and Mary law review. Published by law students of the Marshall-Wythe School of Law. [Williamsburg, Va.: College of William and Mary.]

Wm. and Mary quar. The William and Mary quarterly: a magazine of early American history. Williamsburg: Institute of Early American History and Culture.

World politics. World politics: a quarterly journal of international relations. [Princeton:] Princeton Univ. Press for the Center of International Studies, Princeton Univ.

Wyo. law jour. Wyoming law journal. ... Published under the joint auspices of the University of Wyoming College of Law and the Wyoming State Bar. [n. p.]

Yale jour. biol. and med. The Yale journal of biology and medicine. New Haven.

Yale law jour. The Yale law journal. New Haven: Yale Law Journal Co.

Yale rev. The Yale review: a national quarterly. [New Haven:] Yale Univ. Press.

Yale Univ. Lib. gaz. The Yale University Library gazette. [New Haven.]

Zeitschrift für Anglistik. Zeitschrift für Anglistik und Amerikanistik. Berlin: VEB Deutscher Verlag der Wissenschaften.

Index

This is a name and place index only. Indexed are the names of all authors, editors, and compilers, both personal and corporate. These are signified by an asterisk placed before the item number. Also indexed are the names of all persons and corporate bodies indicated as subjects so far as can be determined by the language of the entries. Place entries are limited to names of foreign countries, regions, States, geographical features, and a few outstanding cities; normally cities, towns, and counties in the United States have not been indexed, it being assumed that the entries for States are a sufficient guide. The reader is referred to the Table of Contents for common-noun subjects in so far as they have been brought together.

Numbers refer to items, not to pages.

A

C

D

E

H

I

K

L

O

Q

R

T

U

UNITED STATES GOVERNMENT

END OF GOVERNMENT ENTRIES

V

Y

☆U.S. GOVERNMENT PRINTING OFFICE : 1972 O - 454-157